THE
NAUTICAL ALMANAC

FOR THE YEAR
1981

SUN

OCT.—MAR. App. Alt.	Lower Limb	Upper Limb	APR.—SEPT. App. Alt.	Lower Limb	Upper Limb
9 34	+10·8	−21·5	9 39	+10·6	−21·2
9 45	+10·9	−21·4	9 51	+10·7	−21·1
9 56	+11·0	−21·3	10 03	+10·8	−21·0
10 08	+11·1	−21·2	10 15	+10·9	−20·9
10 21	+11·2	−21·1	10 27	+11·0	−20·8
10 34	+11·3	−21·0	10 40	+11·1	−20·7
10 47	+11·4	−20·9	10 54	+11·2	−20·6
11 01	+11·5	−20·8	11 08	+11·3	−20·5
11 15	+11·6	−20·7	11 23	+11·4	−20·4
11 30	+11·7	−20·6	11 38	+11·5	−20·3
11 46	+11·8	−20·5	11 54	+11·6	−20·2
12 02	+11·9	−20·4	12 10	+11·7	−20·1
12 19	+12·0	−20·3	12 28	+11·8	−20·0
12 37	+12·1	−20·2	12 46	+11·9	−19·9
12 55	+12·2	−20·1	13 05	+12·0	−19·8
13 14	+12·3	−20·0	13 24	+12·1	−19·7
13 35	+12·4	−19·9	13 45	+12·2	−19·6
13 56	+12·5	−19·8	14 07	+12·3	−19·5
14 18	+12·6	−19·7	14 30	+12·4	−19·4
14 42	+12·7	−19·6	14 54	+12·5	−19·3
15 06	+12·8	−19·5	15 19	+12·6	−19·2
15 32	+12·9	−19·4	15 46	+12·7	−19·1
15 59	+13·0	−19·3	16 14	+12·8	−19·0
16 28	+13·1	−19·2	16 44	+12·9	−18·9
16 59	+13·2	−19·1	17 15	+13·0	−18·8
17 32	+13·3	−19·0	17 48	+13·1	−18·7
18 06	+13·4	−18·9	18 24	+13·2	−18·6
18 42	+13·5	−18·8	19 01	+13·3	−18·5
19 21	+13·6	−18·7	19 42	+13·4	−18·4
20 03	+13·7	−18·6	20 25	+13·5	−18·3
20 48	+13·8	−18·5	21 11	+13·6	−18·2
21 35	+13·9	−18·4	22 00	+13·7	−18·1
22 26	+14·0	−18·3	22 54	+13·8	−18·0
23 22	+14·1	−18·2	23 51	+13·9	−17·9
24 21	+14·2	−18·1	24 53	+14·0	−17·8
25 26	+14·3	−18·0	26 00	+14·1	−17·7
26 36	+14·4	−17·9	27 13	+14·2	−17·6
27 52	+14·5	−17·8	28 33	+14·3	−17·5
29 15	+14·6	−17·7	30 00	+14·4	−17·4
30 46	+14·7	−17·6	31 35	+14·5	−17·3
32 26	+14·8	−17·5	33 20	+14·6	−17·2
34 17	+14·9	−17·4	35 17	+14·7	−17·1
36 20	+15·0	−17·3	37 26	+14·8	−17·0
38 36	+15·1	−17·2	39 50	+14·9	−16·9
41 08	+15·2	−17·1	42 31	+15·0	−16·8
43 59	+15·3	−17·0	45 31	+15·1	−16·7
47 10	+15·4	−16·9	48 55	+15·2	−16·6
50 46	+15·5	−16·8	52 44	+15·3	−16·5
54 49	+15·6	−16·7	57 02	+15·4	−16·4
59 23	+15·7	−16·6	61 51	+15·5	−16·3
64 30	+15·8	−16·5	67 17	+15·6	−16·2
70 12	+15·9	−16·4	73 16	+15·7	−16·1
76 26	+16·0	−16·3	79 43	+15·8	−16·0
83 05	+16·1	−16·2	86 32	+15·9	−15·9
90 00			90 00		

STARS AND PLANETS

App. Alt.	Corrⁿ
9 56	−5·3
10 08	−5·2
10 20	−5·1
10 33	−5·0
10 46	−4·9
11 00	−4·8
11 14	−4·7
11 29	−4·6
11 45	−4·5
12 01	−4·4
12 18	−4·3
12 35	−4·2
12 54	−4·1
13 13	−4·0
13 33	−3·9
13 54	−3·8
14 16	−3·7
14 40	−3·6
15 04	−3·5
15 30	−3·4
15 57	−3·3
16 26	−3·2
16 56	−3·1
17 28	−3·0
18 02	−2·9
18 38	−2·8
19 17	−2·7
19 58	−2·6
20 42	−2·5
21 28	−2·4
22 19	−2·3
23 13	−2·2
24 11	−2·1
25 14	−2·0
26 22	−1·9
27 36	−1·8
28 56	−1·7
30 24	−1·6
32 00	−1·5
33 45	−1·4
35 40	−1·3
37 48	−1·2
40 08	−1·1
42 44	−1·0
45 36	−0·9
48 47	−0·8
52 18	−0·7
56 11	−0·6
60 28	−0·5
65 08	−0·4
70 11	−0·3
75 34	−0·2
81 13	−0·1
87 03	0·0
90 00	

App. Alt.	Additional Corrⁿ
	1981
	VENUS
	Jan. 1–Sept. 27
42°	+ 0·1
	Sept. 28–Nov. 13
47°	+ 0·2
	Nov. 14–Dec. 10
46°	+ 0·3
	Dec. 11–Dec. 26
11°	+ 0·4
41°	+ 0·5
	Dec. 27–Dec. 31
6°	+ 0·5
20°	+ 0·6
31°	+ 0·7
	MARS
	Jan. 1–Dec. 31
60°	+ 0·1

DIP

Ht. of Eye (m)	Corrⁿ	Ht. of Eye (ft.)	Ht. of Eye (m)	Corrⁿ
2·4	−2·8	8·0	1·0	−1·8
2·6	−2·9	8·6	1·5	−2·2
2·8	−3·0	9·2	2·0	−2·5
3·0	−3·1	9·8	2·5	−2·8
3·2	−3·2	10·5	3·0	−3·0
3·4	−3·3	11·2	See table ←	
3·6	−3·4	11·9		
3·8	−3·5	12·6	m	
4·0	−3·6	13·3	20	−7·9
4·3	−3·7	14·1	22	−8·3
4·5	−3·8	14·9	24	−8·6
4·7	−3·9	15·7	26	−9·0
5·0	−4·0	16·5	28	−9·3
5·2	−4·1	17·4		
5·5	−4·2	18·3	30	−9·6
5·8	−4·3	19·1	32	−10·0
6·1	−4·4	20·1	34	−10·3
6·3	−4·5	21·0	36	−10·6
6·6	−4·6	22·0	38	−10·8
6·9	−4·7	22·9		
7·2	−4·8	23·9	40	−11·1
7·5	−4·9	24·9	42	−11·4
7·9	−5·0	26·0	44	−11·7
8·2	−5·1	27·1	46	−11·9
8·5	−5·2	28·1	48	−12·2
8·8	−5·3	29·2	ft.	
9·2	−5·4	30·4	2	−1·4
9·5	−5·5	31·5	4	−1·9
9·9	−5·6	32·7	6	−2·4
10·3	−5·7	33·9	8	−2·7
10·6	−5·8	35·1	10	−3·1
11·0	−5·9	36·3	See table ←	
11·4	−6·0	37·6		
11·8	−6·1	38·9	ft.	
12·2	−6·2	40·1		
12·6	−6·3	41·5	70	−8·1
13·0	−6·4	42·8	75	−8·4
13·4	−6·5	44·2	80	−8·7
13·8	−6·6	45·5	85	−8·9
14·2	−6·7	46·9	90	−9·2
14·7	−6·8	48·4	95	−9·5
15·1	−6·9	49·8		
15·5	−7·0	51·3	100	−9·7
16·0	−7·1	52·8	105	−9·9
16·5	−7·2	54·3	110	−10·2
16·9	−7·3	55·8	115	−10·4
17·4	−7·4	57·4	120	−10·6
17·9	−7·5	58·9	125	−10·8
18·4	−7·6	60·5		
18·8	−7·7	62·1	130	−11·1
19·3	−7·8	63·8	135	−11·3
19·8	−7·9	65·4	140	−11·5
20·4	−8·0	67·1	145	−11·7
20·9	−8·1	68·8	150	−11·9
21·4		70·5	155	−12·1

App. Alt. = Apparent altitude = Sextant altitude corrected for index error and dip.
For daylight observations of Venus, see page 260.

App. Alt.	OCT.–MAR. SUN		APR.–SEPT.		STARS PLANETS
	Lower Limb	Upper Limb	Lower Limb	Upper Limb	
0 00	−18·2	−50·5	−18·4	−50·2	−34·5
03	17·5	49·8	17·8	49·6	33·8
06	16·9	49·2	17·1	48·9	33·2
09	16·3	48·6	16·5	48·3	32·6
12	15·7	48·0	15·9	47·7	32·0
15	15·1	47·4	15·3	47·1	31·4
0 18	−14·5	−46·8	−14·8	−46·6	−30·8
21	14·0	46·3	14·2	46·0	30·3
24	13·5	45·8	13·7	45·5	29·8
27	12·9	45·2	13·2	45·0	29·2
30	12·4	44·7	12·7	44·5	28·7
33	11·9	44·2	12·2	44·0	28·2
0 36	−11·5	−43·8	−11·7	−43·5	−27·8
39	11·0	43·3	11·2	43·0	27·3
42	10·5	42·8	10·8	42·6	26·8
45	10·1	42·4	10·3	42·1	26·4
48	9·6	41·9	9·9	41·7	25·9
51	9·2	41·5	9·5	41·3	25·5
0 54	−8·8	−41·1	−9·1	−40·9	−25·1
0 57	8·4	40·7	8·7	40·5	24·7
1 00	8·0	40·3	8·3	40·1	24·3
03	7·7	40·0	7·9	39·7	24·0
06	7·3	39·6	7·5	39·3	23·6
09	6·9	39·2	7·2	39·0	23·2
1 12	−6·6	−38·9	−6·8	−38·6	−22·9
15	6·2	38·5	6·5	38·3	22·5
18	5·9	38·2	6·2	38·0	22·2
21	5·6	37·9	5·8	37·6	21·9
24	5·3	37·6	5·5	37·3	21·6
27	4·9	37·2	5·2	37·0	21·2
1 30	−4·6	−36·9	−4·9	−36·7	−20·9
35	4·2	36·5	4·4	36·2	20·5
40	3·7	36·0	4·0	35·8	20·0
45	3·2	35·5	3·5	35·3	19·5
50	2·8	35·1	3·1	34·9	19·1
1 55	2·4	34·7	2·6	34·4	18·7
2 00	−2·0	−34·3	−2·2	−34·0	−18·3
05	1·6	33·9	1·8	33·6	17·9
10	1·2	33·5	1·5	33·3	17·5
15	0·9	33·2	1·1	32·9	17·2
20	0·5	32·8	0·8	32·6	16·8
25	−0·2	32·5	0·4	32·2	16·5
2 30	+0·2	−32·1	−0·1	−31·9	−16·1
35	0·5	31·8	+0·2	31·6	15·8
40	0·8	31·5	0·5	31·3	15·5
45	1·1	31·2	0·8	31·0	15·2
50	1·4	30·9	1·1	30·7	14·9
2 55	1·6	30·7	1·4	30·4	14·7
3 00	+1·9	−30·4	+1·7	−30·1	−14·4
05	2·2	30·1	1·9	29·9	14·1
10	2·4	29·9	2·1	29·7	13·9
15	2·6	29·7	2·4	29·4	13·7
20	2·9	29·4	2·6	29·2	13·4
25	3·1	29·2	2·9	28·9	13·2
3 30	+3·3	−29·0	+3·1	−28·7	−13·0

App. Alt.	OCT.–MAR. SUN		APR.–SEPT.		STARS PLANETS
	Lower Limb	Upper Limb	Lower Limb	Upper Limb	
3 30	+3·3	−29·0	+3·1	−28·7	−13·0
35	3·6	28·7	3·3	28·5	12·7
40	3·8	28·5	3·5	28·3	12·5
45	4·0	28·3	3·7	28·1	12·3
50	4·2	28·1	3·9	27·9	12·1
3 55	4·4	27·9	4·1	27·7	11·9
4 00	+4·5	−27·8	+4·3	−27·5	−11·8
05	4·7	27·6	4·5	27·3	11·6
10	4·9	27·4	4·6	27·2	11·4
15	5·1	27·2	4·8	27·0	11·2
20	5·2	27·1	5·0	26·8	11·1
25	5·4	26·9	5·1	26·7	10·9
4 30	+5·6	−26·7	+5·3	−26·5	−10·7
35	5·7	26·6	5·5	26·3	10·6
40	5·9	26·4	5·6	26·2	10·4
45	6·0	26·3	5·8	26·0	10·3
50	6·2	26·1	5·9	25·9	10·1
4 55	6·3	26·0	6·0	25·8	10·0
5 00	+6·4	−25·9	+6·2	−25·6	−9·9
05	6·6	25·7	6·3	25·5	9·7
10	6·7	25·6	6·4	25·4	9·6
15	6·8	25·5	6·6	25·2	9·5
20	6·9	25·4	6·7	25·1	9·4
25	7·1	25·2	6·8	25·0	9·2
5 30	+7·2	−25·1	+6·9	−24·9	−9·1
35	7·3	25·0	7·0	24·8	9·0
40	7·4	24·9	7·2	24·6	8·9
45	7·5	24·8	7·3	24·5	8·8
50	7·6	24·7	7·4	24·4	8·7
5 55	7·7	24·6	7·5	24·3	8·6
6 00	+7·8	−24·5	+7·6	−24·2	−8·5
10	8·0	24·3	7·8	24·0	8·3
20	8·2	24·1	8·0	23·8	8·1
30	8·4	23·9	8·1	23·7	7·9
40	8·6	23·7	8·3	23·5	7·7
6 50	8·7	23·6	8·5	23·3	7·6
7 00	+8·9	−23·4	+8·6	−23·2	−7·4
10	9·1	23·2	8·8	23·0	7·2
20	9·2	23·1	9·0	22·8	7·1
30	9·3	23·0	9·1	22·7	7·0
40	9·5	22·8	9·2	22·6	6·8
7 50	9·6	22·7	9·4	22·4	6·7
8 00	+9·7	−22·6	+9·5	−22·3	−6·6
10	9·9	22·4	9·6	22·2	6·4
20	10·0	22·3	9·7	22·1	6·3
30	10·1	22·2	9·8	22·0	6·2
40	10·2	22·1	10·0	21·8	6·1
8 50	10·3	22·0	10·1	21·7	6·0
9 00	+10·4	−21·9	+10·2	−21·6	−5·9
10	10·5	21·8	10·3	21·5	5·8
20	10·6	21·7	10·4	21·4	5·7
30	10·7	21·6	10·5	21·3	5·6
40	10·8	21·5	10·6	21·2	5·5
9 50	10·9	21·4	10·6	21·2	5·4
10 00	+11·0	−21·3	+10·7	−21·1	−5·3

Additional corrections for temperature and pressure are given on the following page.

For bubble sextant observations ignore dip and use the star corrections for Sun, planets, and stars.

ADDITIONAL REFRACTION CORRECTIONS FOR NON-STANDARD CONDITIONS

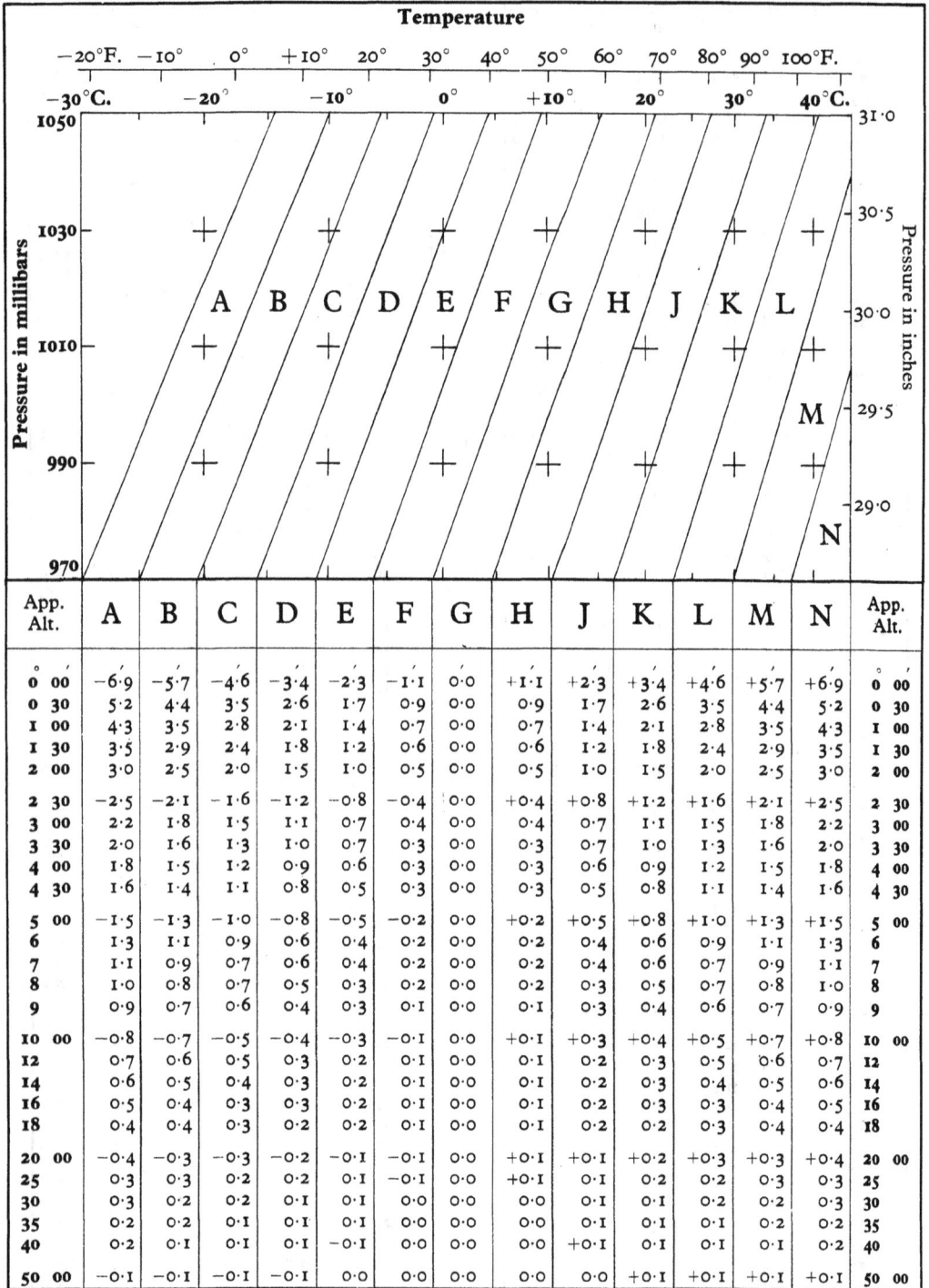

App. Alt.	A	B	C	D	E	F	G	H	J	K	L	M	N	App. Alt.
0 00	−6.9	−5.7	−4.6	−3.4	−2.3	−1.1	0.0	+1.1	+2.3	+3.4	+4.6	+5.7	+6.9	0 00
0 30	5.2	4.4	3.5	2.6	1.7	0.9	0.0	0.9	1.7	2.6	3.5	4.4	5.2	0 30
1 00	4.3	3.5	2.8	2.1	1.4	0.7	0.0	0.7	1.4	2.1	2.8	3.5	4.3	1 00
1 30	3.5	2.9	2.4	1.8	1.2	0.6	0.0	0.6	1.2	1.8	2.4	2.9	3.5	1 30
2 00	3.0	2.5	2.0	1.5	1.0	0.5	0.0	0.5	1.0	1.5	2.0	2.5	3.0	2 00
2 30	−2.5	−2.1	−1.6	−1.2	−0.8	−0.4	0.0	+0.4	+0.8	+1.2	+1.6	+2.1	+2.5	2 30
3 00	2.2	1.8	1.5	1.1	0.7	0.4	0.0	0.4	0.7	1.1	1.5	1.8	2.2	3 00
3 30	2.0	1.6	1.3	1.0	0.7	0.3	0.0	0.3	0.7	1.0	1.3	1.6	2.0	3 30
4 00	1.8	1.5	1.2	0.9	0.6	0.3	0.0	0.3	0.6	0.9	1.2	1.5	1.8	4 00
4 30	1.6	1.4	1.1	0.8	0.5	0.3	0.0	0.3	0.5	0.8	1.1	1.4	1.6	4 30
5 00	−1.5	−1.3	−1.0	−0.8	−0.5	−0.2	0.0	+0.2	+0.5	+0.8	+1.0	+1.3	+1.5	5 00
6	1.3	1.1	0.9	0.6	0.4	0.2	0.0	0.2	0.4	0.6	0.9	1.1	1.3	6
7	1.1	0.9	0.7	0.6	0.4	0.2	0.0	0.2	0.4	0.6	0.7	0.9	1.1	7
8	1.0	0.8	0.7	0.5	0.3	0.2	0.0	0.2	0.3	0.5	0.7	0.8	1.0	8
9	0.9	0.7	0.6	0.4	0.3	0.1	0.0	0.1	0.3	0.4	0.6	0.7	0.9	9
10 00	−0.8	−0.7	−0.5	−0.4	−0.3	−0.1	0.0	+0.1	+0.3	+0.4	+0.5	+0.7	+0.8	10 00
12	0.7	0.6	0.5	0.3	0.2	0.1	0.0	0.1	0.2	0.3	0.5	0.6	0.7	12
14	0.6	0.5	0.4	0.3	0.2	0.1	0.0	0.1	0.2	0.3	0.4	0.5	0.6	14
16	0.5	0.4	0.3	0.3	0.2	0.1	0.0	0.1	0.2	0.3	0.3	0.4	0.5	16
18	0.4	0.4	0.3	0.2	0.2	0.1	0.0	0.1	0.2	0.2	0.3	0.4	0.4	18
20 00	−0.4	−0.3	−0.3	−0.2	−0.1	−0.1	0.0	+0.1	+0.1	+0.2	+0.3	+0.3	+0.4	20 00
25	0.3	0.3	0.2	0.2	0.1	−0.1	0.0	+0.1	0.1	0.2	0.2	0.3	0.3	25
30	0.3	0.2	0.2	0.1	0.1	0.0	0.0	0.0	0.1	0.1	0.2	0.2	0.3	30
35	0.2	0.2	0.1	0.1	0.1	0.0	0.0	0.0	0.1	0.1	0.1	0.2	0.2	35
40	0.2	0.1	0.1	0.1	−0.1	0.0	0.0	0.0	+0.1	0.1	0.1	0.1	0.2	40
50 00	−0.1	−0.1	−0.1	−0.1	0.0	0.0	0.0	0.0	0.0	+0.1	+0.1	+0.1	+0.1	50 00

The graph is entered with arguments temperature and pressure to find a zone letter; using as arguments this zone letter and apparent altitude (sextant altitude corrected for dip), a correction is taken from the table. This correction is to be applied to the sextant altitude in addition to the corrections for standard conditions (for the Sun, stars and planets from page A2 and for the Moon from pages xxxiv and xxxv).

PREFACE

The British and American editions of *The Nautical Almanac*, which are identical in content, are produced jointly by H. M. Nautical Almanac Office, Royal Greenwich Observatory, under the supervision of the Superintendent, and by the Nautical Almanac Office, United States Naval Observatory, under the supervision of P. K. Seidelmann and P. M. Janiczek, to the general requirements of the Royal Navy and of the United States Navy. The Almanac is printed separately in the United Kingdom and in the United States of America.

The data in this Almanac can be made available, in a form suitable for direct photographic reproduction, to the appropriate almanac-producing agency in any country; language changes in the headings of the ephemeral pages can be introduced, if desired, during reproduction. Under this arrangement, this Almanac, with minor modifications and changes of language, has been adopted for the Brazilian, Danish, Greek, Indian, Indonesian, Italian, Korean, Mexican, Norwegian, Peruvian and Swedish almanacs.

F. GRAHAM SMITH,
Director,
Royal Greenwich Observatory,
Herstmonceux Castle, East Sussex,
BN27 1RP, England

JOSEPH C. SMITH,
Captain, U.S. Navy,
Superintendent, U.S. Naval Observatory,
Washington, D.C. 20390,
U.S.A.

April 1979

RELIGIOUS CALENDARS

Epiphany ... ... Jan. 6	Low Sunday ... ... Apr. 26
Septuagesima Sunday ... ... Feb. 15	Rogation Sunday ... ... May 24
Quinquagesima Sunday ... ... Mar. 1	Ascension Day—Holy Thursday ... May 28
Ash Wednesday... ... ... Mar. 4	Whit Sunday—Pentecost ... ... June 7
Quadragesima Sunday ... ... Mar. 8	Trinity Sunday ... ... June 14
Palm Sunday ... ... Apr. 12	Corpus Christi ... ... June 18
Good Friday ... ... Apr. 17	First Sunday in Advent ... ... Nov. 29
Easter Day ... ... Apr. 19	Christmas Day ... ... Dec. 25

Passover, First day of (Pesach)... ... Apr. 19   Day of Atonement (Yom Kippur) ... Oct. 8
Feast of Weeks (Shebuoth) ... ... June 8   Tabernacles, First day of (Succoth) ... Oct. 13
Jewish New Year 5742 (Rosh Hashanah) Sept. 29

Islamic New Year (1402) ... ... Oct. 30   Ramadân, First day of (tabular) ... July 3

CIVIL CALENDAR—UNITED KINGDOM

Accession of Queen Elizabeth II ... Feb. 6   Birthday of Prince Philip, Duke of
St. David (Wales) ... ... Mar. 1   Edinburgh ... ... June 10
Commonwealth Day ... ... Mar. 9   The Queen's Official Birthday... ... June 13
St. Patrick (Ireland) ... ... Mar. 17   Remembrance Sunday ... ... Nov. 8
Birthday of Queen Elizabeth II ... Apr. 21   Birthday of the Prince of Wales ... Nov. 14
St. George (England) ... ... Apr. 23   St. Andrew (Scotland) ... ... Nov. 30
Coronation Day... ... ... June 2

Bank Holidays in England and Wales—Jan. 1, Apr. 20, May 4, May 25, Aug. 31, Dec. 26
Northern Ireland—Jan. 1, Mar. 17, Apr. 20, May 4, May 25, July 13, Aug. 31, Dec. 26
Scotland—Jan. 1, Jan. 2, Apr. 17, May 4, May 25, Aug. 3, Dec. 25, Dec. 26

CIVIL CALENDAR—UNITED STATES OF AMERICA

New Year's Day ... ... Jan. 1   Labor Day ... ... Sept. 7
Lincoln's Birthday ... ... Feb. 12   Columbus Day ... ... Oct. 12
Washington's Birthday ... ... Feb. 16   Election Day (in certain States) ... Nov. 3
Memorial Day ... ... May 25   Veterans Day ... ... Nov. 11
Independence Day ... ... July 4   Thanksgiving Day ... ... Nov. 26

PHASES OF THE MOON

New Moon	First Quarter	Full Moon	Last Quarter
d h m	d h m	d h m	d h m
Jan. 6 07 24	Jan. 13 10 10	Jan. 20 07 39	Jan. 28 04 19
Feb. 4 22 14	Feb. 11 17 49	Feb. 18 22 58	Feb. 27 01 14
Mar. 6 10 31	Mar. 13 01 50	Mar. 20 15 22	Mar. 28 19 34
Apr. 4 20 19	Apr. 11 11 11	Apr. 19 07 59	Apr. 27 10 14
May 4 04 19	May 10 22 22	May 19 00 04	May 26 21 00
June 2 11 32	June 9 11 33	June 17 15 04	June 25 04 25
July 1 19 03	July 9 02 39	July 17 04 39	July 24 09 40
July 31 03 52	Aug. 7 19 26	Aug. 15 16 37	Aug. 22 14 16
Aug. 29 14 43	Sept. 6 13 26	Sept. 14 03 09	Sept. 20 19 47
Sept. 28 04 07	Oct. 6 07 45	Oct. 13 12 49	Oct. 20 03 40
Oct. 27 20 13	Nov. 5 01 09	Nov. 11 22 26	Nov. 18 14 54
Nov. 26 14 38	Dec. 4 16 22	Dec. 11 08 41	Dec. 18 05 47
Dec. 26 10 10			

DAYS OF THE WEEK AND DAYS OF THE YEAR

Day of Month	JAN. Week	JAN. Year	FEB. Week	FEB. Year	MAR. Week	MAR. Year	APR. Week	APR. Year	MAY Week	MAY Year	JUNE Week	JUNE Year	JULY Week	JULY Year	AUG. Week	AUG. Year	SEPT. Week	SEPT. Year	OCT. Week	OCT. Year	NOV. Week	NOV. Year	DEC. Week	DEC. Year
1	Th.	1	Su.	32	Su.	60	W.	91	F.	121	M.	152	W.	182	S.	213	Tu.	244	Th.	274	Su.	305	Tu.	335
2	F.	2	M.	33	M.	61	Th.	92	S.	122	Tu.	153	Th.	183	Su.	214	W.	245	F.	275	M.	306	W.	336
3	S.	3	Tu.	34	Tu.	62	F.	93	Su.	123	W.	154	F.	184	M.	215	Th.	246	S.	276	Tu.	307	Th.	337
4	Su.	4	W.	35	W.	63	S.	94	M.	124	Th.	155	S.	185	Tu.	216	F.	247	Su.	277	W.	308	F.	338
5	M.	5	Th.	36	Th.	64	Su.	95	Tu.	125	F.	156	Su.	186	W.	217	S.	248	M.	278	Th.	309	S.	339
6	Tu.	6	F.	37	F.	65	M.	96	W.	126	S.	157	M.	187	Th.	218	Su.	249	Tu.	279	F.	310	Su.	340
7	W.	7	S.	38	S.	66	Tu.	97	Th.	127	Su.	158	Tu.	188	F.	219	M.	250	W.	280	S.	311	M.	341
8	Th.	8	Su.	39	Su.	67	W.	98	F.	128	M.	159	W.	189	S.	220	Tu.	251	Th.	281	Su.	312	Tu.	342
9	F.	9	M.	40	M.	68	Th.	99	S.	129	Tu.	160	Th.	190	Su.	221	W.	252	F.	282	M.	313	W.	343
10	S.	10	Tu.	41	Tu.	69	F.	100	Su.	130	W.	161	F.	191	M.	222	Th.	253	S.	283	Tu.	314	Th.	344
11	Su.	11	W.	42	W.	70	S.	101	M.	131	Th.	162	S.	192	Tu.	223	F.	254	Su.	284	W.	315	F.	345
12	M.	12	Th.	43	Th.	71	Su.	102	Tu.	132	F.	163	Su.	193	W.	224	S.	255	M.	285	Th.	316	S.	346
13	Tu.	13	F.	44	F.	72	M.	103	W.	133	S.	164	M.	194	Th.	225	Su.	256	Tu.	286	F.	317	Su.	347
14	W.	14	S.	45	S.	73	Tu.	104	Th.	134	Su.	165	Tu.	195	F.	226	M.	257	W.	287	S.	318	M.	348
15	Th.	15	Su.	46	Su.	74	W.	105	F.	135	M.	166	W.	196	S.	227	Tu.	258	Th.	288	Su.	319	Tu.	349
16	F.	16	M.	47	M.	75	Th.	106	S.	136	Tu.	167	Th.	197	Su.	228	W.	259	F.	289	M.	320	W.	350
17	S.	17	Tu.	48	Tu.	76	F.	107	Su.	137	W.	168	F.	198	M.	229	Th.	260	S.	290	Tu.	321	Th.	351
18	Su.	18	W.	49	W.	77	S.	108	M.	138	Th.	169	S.	199	Tu.	230	F.	261	Su.	291	W.	322	F.	352
19	M.	19	Th.	50	Th.	78	Su.	109	Tu.	139	F.	170	Su.	200	W.	231	S.	262	M.	292	Th.	323	S.	353
20	Tu.	20	F.	51	F.	79	M.	110	W.	140	S.	171	M.	201	Th.	232	Su.	263	Tu.	293	F.	324	Su.	354
21	W.	21	S.	52	S.	80	Tu.	111	Th.	141	Su.	172	Tu.	202	F.	233	M.	264	W.	294	S.	325	M.	355
22	Th.	22	Su.	53	Su.	81	W.	112	F.	142	M.	173	W.	203	S.	234	Tu.	265	Th.	295	Su.	326	Tu.	356
23	F.	23	M.	54	M.	82	Th.	113	S.	143	Tu.	174	Th.	204	Su.	235	W.	266	F.	296	M.	327	W.	357
24	S.	24	Tu.	55	Tu.	83	F.	114	Su.	144	W.	175	F.	205	M.	236	Th.	267	S.	297	Tu.	328	Th.	358
25	Su.	25	W.	56	W.	84	S.	115	M.	145	Th.	176	S.	206	Tu.	237	F.	268	Su.	298	W.	329	F.	359
26	M.	26	Th.	57	Th.	85	Su.	116	Tu.	146	F.	177	Su.	207	W.	238	S.	269	M.	299	Th.	330	S.	360
27	Tu.	27	F.	58	F.	86	M.	117	W.	147	S.	178	M.	208	Th.	239	Su.	270	Tu.	300	F.	331	Su.	361
28	W.	28	S.	59	S.	87	Tu.	118	Th.	148	Su.	179	Tu.	209	F.	240	M.	271	W.	301	S.	332	M.	362
29	Th.	29			Su.	88	W.	119	F.	149	M.	180	W.	210	S.	241	Tu.	272	Th.	302	Su.	333	Tu.	363
30	F.	30			M.	89	Th.	120	S.	150	Tu.	181	Th.	211	Su.	242	W.	273	F.	303	M.	334	W.	364
31	S.	31			Tu.	90			Su.	151			F.	212	M.	243			S.	304			Th.	365

ECLIPSES

There are three eclipses, two of the Sun and one of the Moon.

1. *An Annular Eclipse of the Sun*, February 4-5. See map on page 6. The eclipse begins at 4d 19h 28m and ends at 5d 00h 49m; the annular phase begins at 4d 20h 33m and ends at 4d 23h 44m. The maximum duration of the annular phase is 1m 11s.

2. *A Partial Eclipse of the Moon*, July 17. The eclipse begins at 03h 25m and ends at 06h 09m. It is visible from Africa except the north-eastern part, south-western Europe, the Atlantic Ocean, Antarctica, South America, North America except the north-western part, the eastern Pacific Ocean and New Zealand. At the time of maximum eclipse 0·55 of the Moon's diameter is obscured.

3. *A Total Eclipse of the Sun*, July 31. See map on page 7. The eclipse begins at 01h 11m and ends at 06h 20m; the total phase begins at 02h 18m and ends at 05h 14m. The maximum duration of the total phase is 2m 02s.

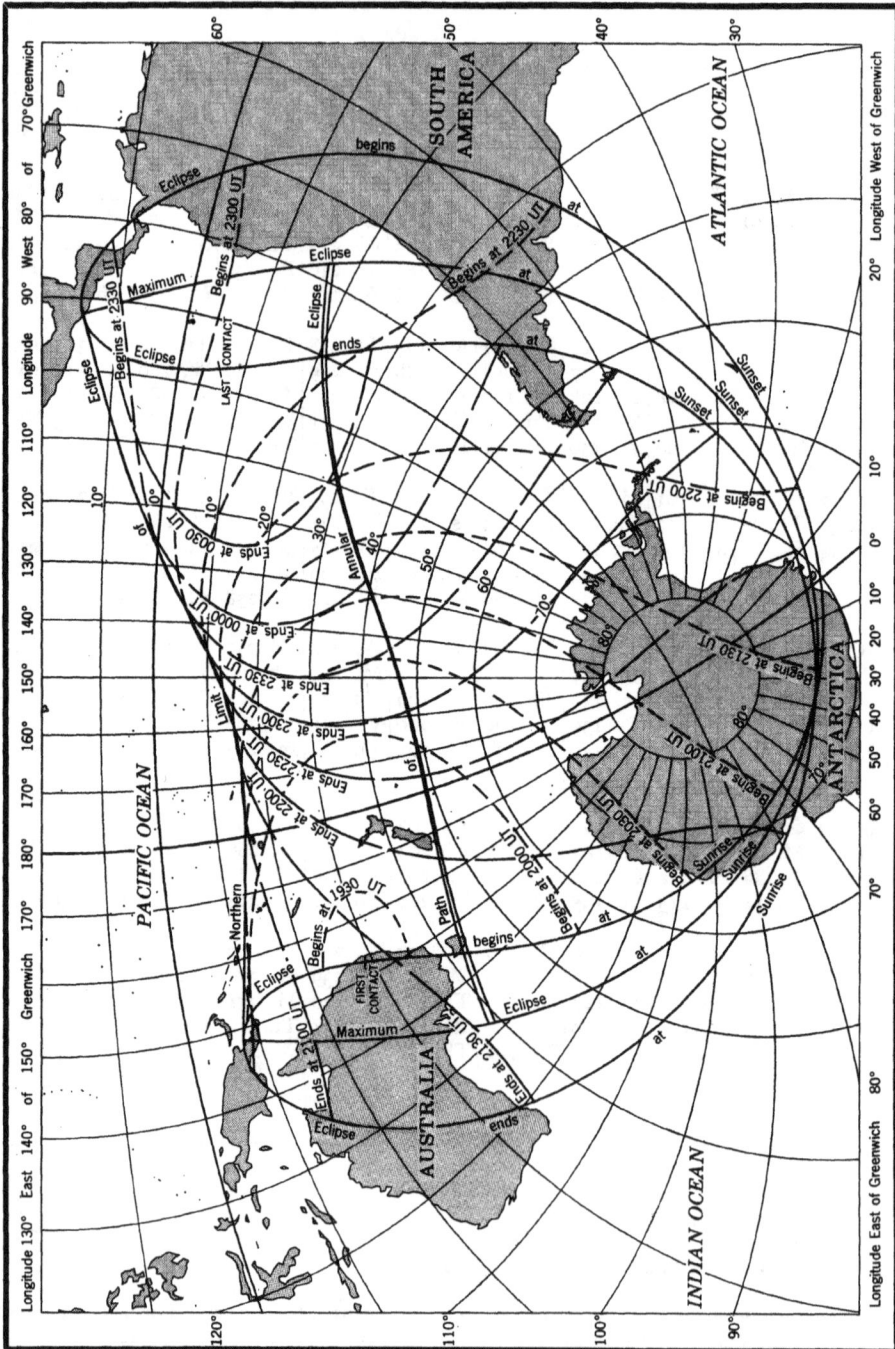

SOLAR ECLIPSE DIAGRAMS

The principal features shown on the above diagrams are: the paths of total and annular eclipses; the northern and southern limits of partial eclipse; the sunrise and sunset curves ; and contour lines showing the time of middle of eclipse and the semi-duration of partial eclipse. The times of beginning and end of partial eclipse at any place can be found by applying the semi-duration to the time of middle of the eclipse, both being interpolated for that place from the contour lines.

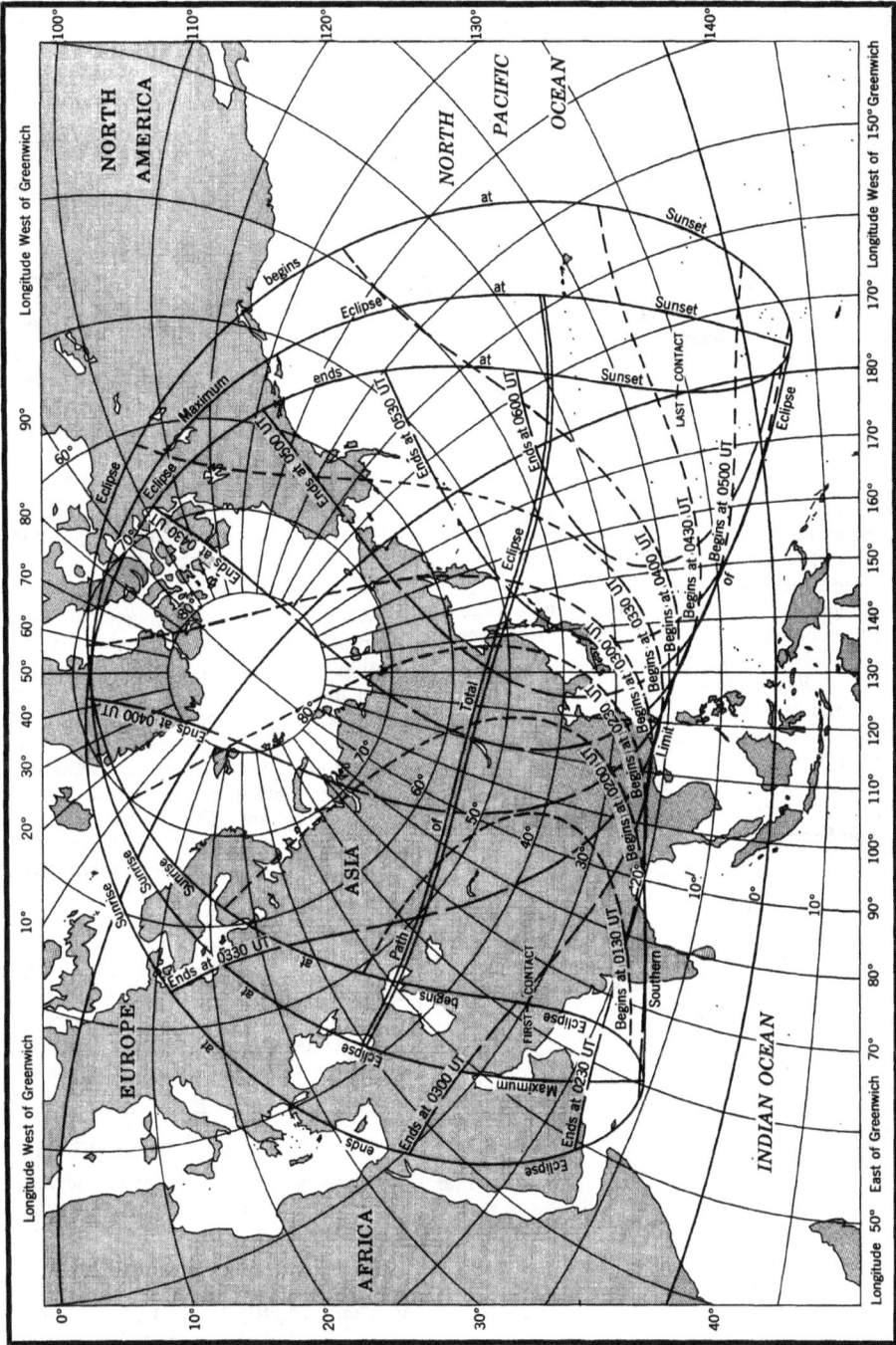

SOLAR ECLIPSE DIAGRAMS

For total and annular eclipses the mid-times of the total and annular phases are generally within 5 minutes of those given for the middle of eclipse ; but semi-durations, which depend on the precise position relative to the path, are not given. Further details of the paths and times of central eclipse are given in the *Astronomical Almanac*.

VISIBILITY OF PLANETS

VENUS is a brilliant object in the morning sky from the beginning of the year until mid-February (when it becomes too close to the Sun for observation), and in the evening sky from late May until the end of the year. Venus is in conjunction with Mercury on June 9, with Saturn on August 25 and Jupiter on August 28.

MARS is visible as a reddish object in Capricornus shortly after sunset in January; it then becomes too close to the Sun for observation until early in June, when it can be seen in Taurus. The western elongation gradually increases while it moves through Taurus (passing 6° N. of *Aldebaran* on June 19), Gemini (passing 6° S. of *Pollux* on August 23), Cancer, Leo (passing 1°·1 N. of *Regulus* on October 19), and into Virgo in early December. Mars is in conjunction with Mercury on January 23 and February 10.

JUPITER and SATURN both rise at about midnight at the beginning of the year and are at opposition on March 26 and March 27 respectively, when they can both be seen throughout the night. From late June until late September they are visible only in the evening sky, and then become too close to the Sun for observation. They can be seen only in the morning sky from late October until the end of the year. Both planets remain in Virgo throughout the year, and are in conjunction with each other on January 14, February 19 and July 30. Jupiter is in conjunction with Venus on August 28, and Mercury on September 13 and November 6, while Saturn is in conjunction with Venus on August 25 and Mercury on September 10.

MERCURY can only be seen low in the east before sunrise, or low in the west after sunset (about the time of beginning or end of civil twilight). It is visible in the mornings between the following approximate dates: February 23 (+1·9) to April 20 (−1·1), June 30 (+2·2) to August 2 (−1·4), October 25 (+1·1) to November 24 (−0·7); the planet is brighter at the end of each period. It is visible in the evenings between the following approximate dates: January 15 (−0·9) to February 12 (+1·5), May 5 (−1·4) to June 14 (+2·3), August 19 (−0·9) to October 13 (+1·7), December 26 (−0·7) to December 31 (−0·7); the planet is brighter at the beginning of each period. The figures in parentheses are the magnitudes.

PLANET DIAGRAM

General Description. The diagram on the opposite page shows, in graphical form for any date during the year, the local mean time of meridian passage of the Sun, of the five planets Mercury, Venus, Mars, Jupiter, and Saturn, and of each 30° of S.H.A.; intermediate lines, corresponding to particular stars, may be drawn in by the user if he so desires. It is intended to provide a general picture of the availability of planets and stars for observation.

On each side of the line marking the time of meridian passage of the Sun a band, 45^m wide, is shaded to indicate that planets and most stars crossing the meridian within 45^m of the Sun are too close to the Sun for observation.

Method of use and interpretation. For any date the diagram provides immediately the local mean times of meridian passage of the Sun, planets and stars, and thus the following information:

(a) whether a planet or star is too close to the Sun for observation;

(b) some indication of its position in the sky, especially during twilight;

(c) the proximity of other planets.

When the meridian passage of an outer planet occurs at midnight the body is in opposition to the Sun and is visible all night; a planet may then be observable during both morning and evening twilights. As the time of meridian passage decreases, the body eventually ceases to be observable in the morning, but its altitude above the eastern horizon at sunset gradually increases; this continues until the body is on the meridian during evening twilight. From then onwards the body is observable above the western horizon and its altitude at sunset gradually decreases; eventually the body becomes too close to the Sun for observation. When the body again becomes visible it is seen low in the east during morning twilight; its altitude at sunrise increases until meridian passage occurs during morning twilight. Then, as the time of meridian passage decreases to 0^h, the body is observable in the west during morning twilight with a gradually decreasing altitude, until it once again reaches opposition.

DO NOT CONFUSE

Jupiter with Saturn from the beginning of the year until mid-September; Jupiter is always the brighter object.

Mercury with Mars in late January when Mercury is the brighter object, and again in early February when it is only slightly brighter. The reddish tint of Mars should assist in its identification.

Venus with Mercury in early June, and with Saturn and Jupiter in late August; on all occasions Venus is the brighter object.

Mercury with Saturn in early September when Mercury is the brighter object, and with Jupiter in mid-September and early November; on both occasions Mercury is fainter than Jupiter.

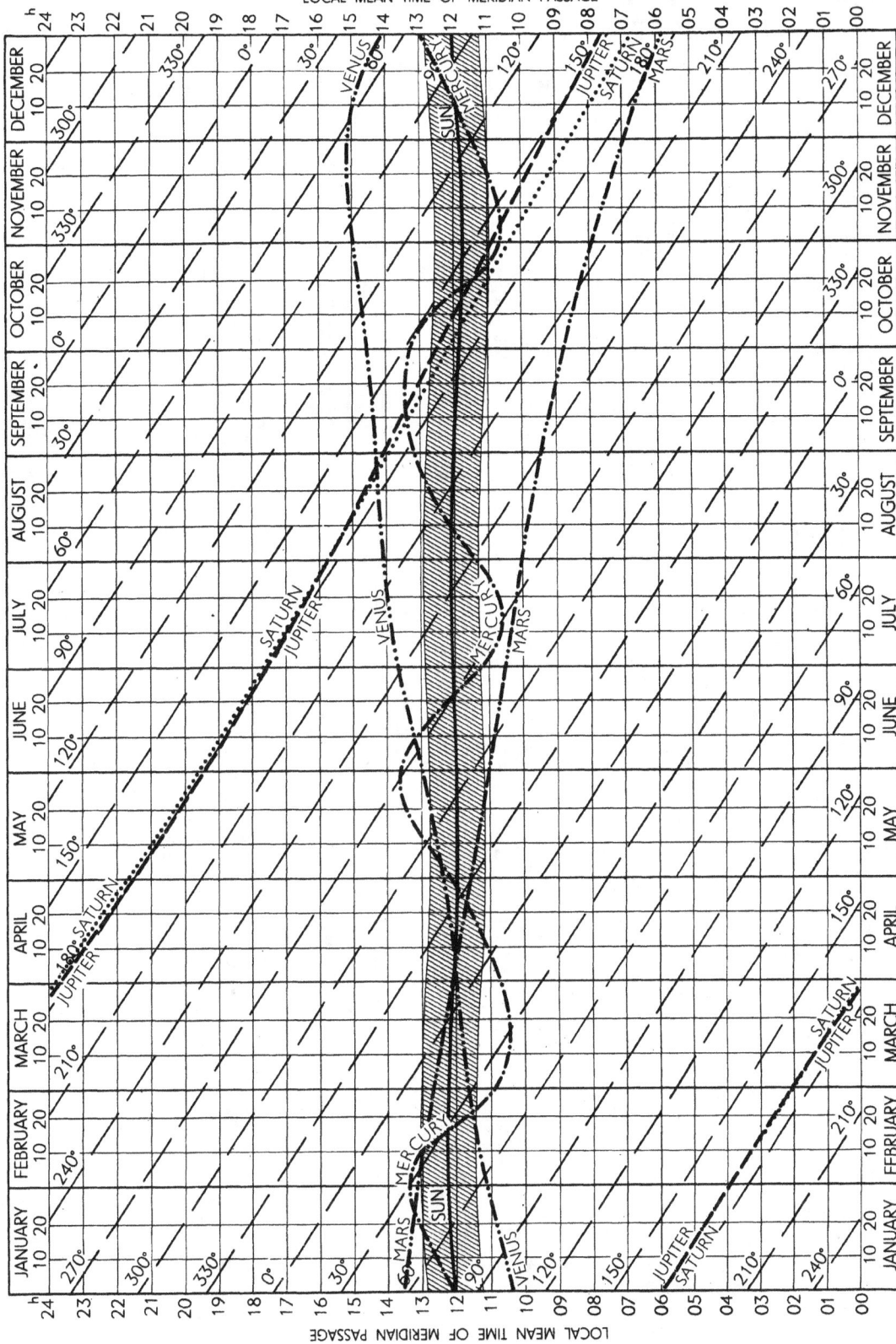

LOCAL MEAN TIME OF MERIDIAN PASSAGE

1981 JANUARY 1, 2, 3 (THURS., FRI., SAT.)

G.M.T.	ARIES G.H.A.	VENUS −3.4 G.H.A.	Dec.	MARS +1.4 G.H.A.	Dec.	JUPITER −1.6 G.H.A.	Dec.	SATURN +1.0 G.H.A.	Dec.	STARS Name	S.H.A.	Dec.
1 00	100 33.4	204 26.5	S21 57.7	157 14.8	S21 04.5	271 18.5	S 2 33.9	270 54.0	S 1 36.0	Acamar	315 36.9	S40 23.2
01	115 35.9	219 25.6	58.1	172 15.2	04.1	286 20.8	34.0	285 56.4	36.1	Achernar	335 45.0	S57 20.4
02	130 38.4	234 24.7	58.5	187 15.6	03.6	301 23.1	34.1	300 58.8	36.1	Acrux	173 36.9	S62 59.3
03	145 40.8	249 23.9 ··	58.9	202 16.1 ··	03.2	316 25.4 ··	34.1	316 01.2 ··	36.1	Adhara	255 31.6	S28 56.8
04	160 43.3	264 23.0	59.3	217 16.5	02.8	331 27.7	34.2	331 03.6	36.1	Aldebaran	291 17.5	N16 28.2
05	175 45.8	279 22.1	21 59.7	232 16.9	02.3	346 30.0	34.2	346 06.0	36.1			
06	190 48.2	294 21.2	S22 00.1	247 17.3	S21 01.9	1 32.3	S 2 34.3	1 08.4	S 1 36.2	Alioth	166 42.4	N56 03.6
07	205 50.7	309 20.3	00.5	262 17.7	01.5	16 34.6	34.4	16 10.8	36.2	Alkaid	153 18.5	N49 24.3
T 08	220 53.1	324 19.5	00.9	277 18.1	01.0	31 36.9	34.4	31 13.1	36.2	Al Na'ir	28 15.0	S47 03.4
H 09	235 55.6	339 18.6 ··	01.2	292 18.5 ··	00.6	46 39.2 ··	34.5	46 15.5 ··	36.2	Alnilam	276 11.1	S 1 12.9
U 10	250 58.1	354 17.7	01.6	307 19.0	21 00.2	61 41.5	34.5	61 17.9	36.2	Alphard	218 20.1	S 8 34.5
R 11	266 00.5	9 16.8	02.0	322 19.4	20 59.7	76 43.7	34.6	76 20.3	36.3			
S 12	281 03.0	24 15.9	S22 02.4	337 19.8	S20 59.3	91 46.0	S 2 34.7	91 22.7	S 1 36.3	Alphecca	126 32.2	N26 46.7
D 13	296 05.5	39 15.1	02.8	352 20.2	58.9	106 48.3	34.7	106 25.1	36.3	Alpheratz	358 09.2	N28 59.2
A 14	311 07.9	54 14.2	03.2	7 20.6	58.4	121 50.6	34.8	121 27.5	36.3	Altair	62 32.7	N 8 49.1
Y 15	326 10.4	69 13.3 ··	03.6	22 21.0 ··	58.0	136 52.9 ··	34.8	136 29.9 ··	36.3	Ankaa	353 40.1	S42 24.9
16	341 12.9	84 12.4	03.9	37 21.4	57.6	151 55.2	34.9	151 32.3	36.4	Antares	112 56.9	S26 23.3
17	356 15.3	99 11.5	04.3	52 21.9	57.1	166 57.5	35.0	166 34.6	36.4			
18	11 17.8	114 10.6	S22 04.7	67 22.3	S20 56.7	181 59.8	S 2 35.0	181 37.0	S 1 36.4	Arcturus	146 18.4	N19 16.9
19	26 20.3	129 09.8	05.1	82 22.7	56.3	197 02.1	35.1	196 39.4	36.4	Atria	108 21.5	S68 59.4
20	41 22.7	144 08.9	05.5	97 23.1	55.8	212 04.4	35.1	211 41.8	36.4	Avior	234 27.5	S59 26.8
21	56 25.2	159 08.0 ··	05.8	112 23.5 ··	55.4	227 06.7 ··	35.2	226 44.2 ··	36.4	Bellatrix	278 58.2	N 6 19.9
22	71 27.6	174 07.1	06.2	127 23.9	54.9	242 09.0	35.3	241 46.6	36.5	Betelgeuse	271 27.7	N 7 24.1
23	86 30.1	189 06.2	06.6	142 24.4	54.5	257 11.3	35.3	256 49.0	36.5			
2 00	101 32.6	204 05.3	S22 07.0	157 24.8	S20 54.1	272 13.6	S 2 35.4	271 51.4	S 1 36.5	Canopus	264 06.6	S52 41.2
01	116 35.0	219 04.4	07.3	172 25.2	53.6	287 15.9	35.4	286 53.8	36.5	Capella	281 10.6	N45 58.8
02	131 37.5	234 03.5	07.7	187 25.6	53.2	302 18.2	35.5	301 56.2	36.5	Deneb	49 48.7	N45 12.9
03	146 40.0	249 02.7 ··	08.1	202 26.0 ··	52.7	317 20.5 ··	35.6	316 58.5 ··	36.6	Denebola	182 58.8	N14 40.7
04	161 42.4	264 01.8	08.4	217 26.4	52.3	332 22.8	35.6	332 00.9	36.6	Diphda	349 20.7	S18 05.7
05	176 44.9	279 00.9	08.8	232 26.9	51.9	347 25.1	35.7	347 03.3	36.6			
06	191 47.4	294 00.0	S22 09.2	247 27.3	S20 51.4	2 27.4	S 2 35.7	2 05.7	S 1 36.6	Dubhe	194 21.6	N61 51.0
07	206 49.8	308 59.1	09.5	262 27.7	51.0	17 29.7	35.8	17 08.1	36.6	Elnath	278 43.5	N28 35.5
08	221 52.3	323 58.2	09.9	277 28.1	50.5	32 32.0	35.8	32 10.5	36.6	Eltanin	90 58.2	N51 29.5
F 09	236 54.7	338 57.3 ··	10.3	292 28.5 ··	50.1	47 34.3 ··	35.9	47 12.9 ··	36.7	Enif	34 11.6	N 9 47.3
R 10	251 57.2	353 56.4	10.6	307 29.0	49.6	62 36.6	36.0	62 15.3	36.7	Fomalhaut	15 51.4	S29 43.6
I 11	266 59.7	8 55.6	11.0	322 29.4	49.2	77 38.9	36.0	77 17.7	36.7			
D 12	282 02.1	23 54.7	S22 11.3	337 29.8	S20 48.8	92 41.2	S 2 36.1	92 20.1	S 1 36.7	Gacrux	172 28.4	S57 00.0
A 13	297 04.6	38 53.8	11.7	352 30.2	48.3	107 43.5	36.1	107 22.5	36.7	Gienah	176 17.7	S17 26.0
Y 14	312 07.1	53 52.9	12.1	7 30.6	47.9	122 45.8	36.2	122 24.9	36.8	Hadar	149 23.3	S60 16.5
15	327 09.5	68 52.0 ··	12.4	22 31.1 ··	47.4	137 48.1 ··	36.2	137 27.3 ··	36.8	Hamal	328 28.6	N23 22.4
16	342 12.0	83 51.1	12.8	37 31.5	47.0	152 50.4	36.3	152 29.6	36.8	Kaus Aust.	84 17.0	S34 23.6
17	357 14.5	98 50.2	13.1	52 31.9	46.5	167 52.7	36.4	167 32.0	36.8			
18	12 16.9	113 49.3	S22 13.5	67 32.3	S20 46.1	182 55.0	S 2 36.4	182 34.4	S 1 36.8	Kochab	137 19.8	N74 13.8
19	27 19.4	128 48.4	13.8	82 32.7	45.6	197 57.3	36.5	197 36.8	36.8	Markab	14 03.1	N15 06.2
20	42 21.9	143 47.5	14.2	97 33.1	45.2	212 59.6	36.5	212 39.2	36.9	Menkar	314 40.7	N 4 00.8
21	57 24.3	158 46.6 ··	14.5	112 33.6 ··	44.7	228 01.9 ··	36.6	227 41.6 ··	36.9	Menkent	148 36.9	S36 16.3
22	72 26.8	173 45.7	14.9	127 34.0	44.3	243 04.3	36.6	242 44.0	36.9	Miaplacidus	221 44.1	S69 38.2
23	87 29.2	188 44.9	15.2	142 34.4	43.9	258 06.6	36.7	257 46.4	36.9			
3 00	102 31.7	203 44.0	S22 15.6	157 34.8	S20 43.4	273 08.9	S 2 36.8	272 48.8	S 1 36.9	Mirfak	309 15.5	N49 47.7
01	117 34.2	218 43.1	15.9	172 35.3	43.0	288 11.2	36.8	287 51.2	36.9	Nunki	76 29.3	S26 19.2
02	132 36.6	233 42.2	16.2	187 35.7	42.5	303 13.5	36.9	302 53.6	37.0	Peacock	53 58.7	S56 47.9
03	147 39.1	248 41.3 ··	16.6	202 36.1 ··	42.1	318 15.8 ··	36.9	317 56.0 ··	37.0	Pollux	243 57.6	N28 04.3
04	162 41.6	263 40.4	16.9	217 36.5	41.6	333 18.1	37.0	332 58.4	37.0	Procyon	245 25.3	N 5 16.4
05	177 44.0	278 39.5	17.3	232 36.9	41.2	348 20.4	37.0	348 00.8	37.0			
06	192 46.5	293 38.6	S22 17.6	247 37.4	S20 40.7	3 22.7	S 2 37.1	3 03.2	S 1 37.0	Rasalhague	96 29.7	N12 34.5
07	207 49.0	308 37.7	17.9	262 37.8	40.3	18 25.0	37.1	18 05.6	37.0	Regulus	208 09.6	N12 03.6
S 08	222 51.4	323 36.8	18.3	277 38.2	39.8	33 27.3	37.2	33 08.0	37.1	Rigel	281 35.5	S 8 13.5
A 09	237 53.9	338 35.9 ··	18.6	292 38.6 ··	39.3	48 29.6 ··	37.2	48 10.4 ··	37.1	Rigil Kent.	140 25.9	S60 45.0
T 10	252 56.4	353 35.0	18.9	307 39.0	38.9	63 31.9	37.3	63 12.8	37.1	Sabik	102 41.2	S15 42.0
U 11	267 58.8	8 34.1	19.3	322 39.5	38.4	78 34.2	37.4	78 15.2	37.1			
R 12	283 01.3	23 33.2	S22 19.6	337 39.9	S20 38.0	93 36.6	S 2 37.4	93 17.5	S 1 37.1	Schedar	350 08.8	N56 26.2
D 13	298 03.7	38 32.3	19.9	352 40.3	37.5	108 38.9	37.5	108 19.9	37.1	Shaula	96 55.9	S37 05.3
A 14	313 06.2	53 31.4	20.3	7 40.7	37.1	123 41.2	37.5	123 22.3	37.2	Sirius	258 55.2	S16 41.5
Y 15	328 08.7	68 30.5 ··	20.6	22 41.2 ··	36.6	138 43.5 ··	37.6	138 24.7 ··	37.2	Spica	158 57.4	S11 03.6
16	343 11.1	83 29.6	20.9	37 41.6	36.2	153 45.8	37.6	153 27.1	37.2	Suhail	223 10.2	S43 21.2
17	358 13.6	98 28.7	21.3	52 42.0	35.7	168 48.1	37.7	168 29.5	37.2			
18	13 16.1	113 27.8	S22 21.6	67 42.4	S20 35.3	183 50.4	S 2 37.7	183 31.9	S 1 37.2	Vega	80 56.1	N38 46.C
19	28 18.5	128 26.9	21.9	82 42.9	34.8	198 52.7	37.8	198 34.3	37.2	Zuben'ubi	137 33.0	S15 57.6
20	43 21.0	143 26.0	22.2	97 43.3	34.3	213 55.0	37.8	213 36.7	37.2		S.H.A.	Mer. Pass.
21	58 23.5	158 25.1 ··	22.5	112 43.7 ··	33.9	228 57.3 ··	37.9	228 39.1 ··	37.3			
22	73 25.9	173 24.2	22.9	127 44.1	33.4	243 59.7	37.9	243 41.5	37.3	Venus	102 32.8	10 24
23	88 28.4	188 23.3	23.2	142 44.5	33.0	259 02.0	38.0	258 43.9	37.3	Mars	55 52.2	13 30
Mer. Pass.	17 11.0	v −0.9	d 0.4	v 0.4	d 0.4	v 2.3	d 0.1	v 2.4	d 0.0	Jupiter	170 41.0	5 50
										Saturn	170 18.8	5 52

G.M.T.	SUN G.H.A.	SUN Dec.	MOON G.H.A.	v	Dec.	d	H.P.
1 00	179 08.9	S23 01.5	241 12.2	14.7	S 9 54.2	9.1	54.3
01	194 08.6	01.3	255 45.9	14.8	10 03.3	9.0	54.3
02	209 08.3	01.1	270 19.7	14.7	10 12.3	9.0	54.3
03	224 08.0	·· 00.9	284 53.4	14.6	10 21.3	9.0	54.3
04	239 07.7	00.7	299 27.0	14.6	10 30.3	8.9	54.3
05	254 07.4	00.5	314 00.6	14.6	10 39.2	8.9	54.3
06	269 07.1	S23 00.3	328 34.2	14.6	S10 48.1	8.9	54.3
07	284 06.8	23 00.1	343 07.8	14.5	10 57.0	8.8	54.3
T 08	299 06.5	22 59.9	357 41.3	14.4	11 05.8	8.8	54.3
H 09	314 06.2	·· 59.7	12 14.7	14.4	11 14.6	8.7	54.3
U 10	329 05.9	59.5	26 48.1	14.4	11 23.3	8.7	54.3
R 11	344 05.6	59.3	41 21.5	14.4	11 32.0	8.6	54.4
S 12	359 05.3	S22 59.1	55 54.9	14.2	S11 40.6	8.6	54.4
D 13	14 05.0	58.8	70 28.1	14.3	11 49.2	8.6	54.4
A 14	29 04.7	58.6	85 01.4	14.2	11 57.8	8.5	54.4
Y 15	44 04.4	·· 58.4	99 34.6	14.1	12 06.3	8.4	54.4
16	59 04.1	58.2	114 07.7	14.1	12 14.7	8.5	54.4
17	74 03.8	58.0	128 40.8	14.1	12 23.2	8.3	54.4
18	89 03.5	S22 57.8	143 13.9	14.0	S12 31.5	8.3	54.4
19	104 03.2	57.6	157 46.9	14.0	12 39.8	8.3	54.4
20	119 02.9	57.3	172 19.9	13.9	12 48.1	8.2	54.5
21	134 02.7	·· 57.1	186 52.8	13.9	12 56.3	8.2	54.5
22	149 02.4	56.9	201 25.7	13.8	13 04.5	8.1	54.5
23	164 02.1	56.7	215 58.5	13.8	13 12.6	8.0	54.5
2 00	179 01.8	S22 56.5	230 31.3	13.7	S13 20.6	8.0	54.5
01	194 01.5	56.3	245 04.0	13.7	13 28.6	8.0	54.5
02	209 01.2	56.0	259 36.7	13.6	13 36.6	7.9	54.5
03	224 00.9	·· 55.8	274 09.3	13.6	13 44.5	7.8	54.5
04	239 00.6	55.6	288 41.9	13.5	13 52.3	7.8	54.6
05	254 00.3	55.4	303 14.4	13.5	14 00.1	7.7	54.6
06	269 00.0	S22 55.1	317 46.9	13.4	S14 07.8	7.7	54.6
07	283 59.7	54.9	332 19.3	13.4	14 15.5	7.6	54.6
08	298 59.4	54.7	346 51.7	13.3	14 23.1	7.6	54.6
F 09	313 59.1	·· 54.5	1 24.0	13.2	14 30.7	7.5	54.6
R 10	328 58.8	54.2	15 56.2	13.2	14 38.2	7.4	54.6
I 11	343 58.6	54.0	30 28.4	13.3	14 45.6	7.4	54.7
D 12	358 58.3	S22 53.8	45 00.6	13.1	S14 53.0	7.3	54.7
A 13	13 58.0	53.6	59 32.7	13.0	15 00.3	7.2	54.7
Y 14	28 57.7	53.3	74 04.7	13.0	15 07.5	7.2	54.7
15	43 57.4	·· 53.1	88 36.7	12.9	15 14.7	7.2	54.7
16	58 57.1	52.9	103 08.6	12.9	15 21.9	7.0	54.7
17	73 56.8	52.6	117 40.5	12.8	15 28.9	7.0	54.8
18	88 56.5	S22 52.4	132 12.3	12.8	S15 35.9	6.9	54.8
19	103 56.2	52.2	146 44.1	12.7	15 42.8	6.9	54.8
20	118 55.9	51.9	161 15.8	12.7	15 49.7	6.8	54.8
21	133 55.6	·· 51.7	175 47.5	12.6	15 56.5	6.7	54.8
22	148 55.4	51.4	190 19.1	12.5	16 03.2	6.7	54.8
23	163 55.1	51.2	204 50.6	12.5	16 09.9	6.6	54.9
3 00	178 54.8	S22 51.0	219 22.1	12.4	S16 16.5	6.5	54.9
01	193 54.5	50.7	233 53.5	12.4	16 23.0	6.4	54.9
02	208 54.2	50.5	248 24.9	12.3	16 29.4	6.4	54.9
03	223 53.9	·· 50.3	262 56.2	12.2	16 35.8	6.3	54.9
04	238 53.6	50.0	277 27.4	12.2	16 42.1	6.3	54.9
05	253 53.3	49.8	291 58.6	12.2	16 48.4	6.1	54.9
06	268 53.0	S22 49.5	306 29.8	12.0	S16 54.5	6.1	55.0
07	283 52.7	49.3	321 00.8	12.1	17 00.6	6.0	55.0
S 08	298 52.5	49.0	335 31.9	11.9	17 06.6	5.9	55.0
A 09	313 52.2	·· 48.8	350 02.8	11.9	17 12.5	5.9	55.0
T 10	328 51.9	48.6	4 33.7	11.9	17 18.4	5.8	55.1
U 11	343 51.6	48.3	19 04.6	11.8	17 24.2	5.7	55.1
R 12	358 51.3	S22 48.1	33 35.4	11.7	S17 29.9	5.6	55.1
D 13	13 51.0	47.8	48 06.1	11.7	17 35.5	5.5	55.1
A 14	28 50.7	47.6	62 36.8	11.6	17 41.0	5.5	55.1
Y 15	43 50.4	·· 47.3	77 07.4	11.6	17 46.5	5.3	55.2
16	58 50.2	47.1	91 38.0	11.5	17 51.8	5.3	55.2
17	73 49.9	46.8	106 08.5	11.4	17 57.1	5.3	55.2
18	88 49.6	S22 46.6	120 38.9	11.4	S18 02.4	5.1	55.2
19	103 49.3	46.3	135 09.3	11.3	18 07.5	5.0	55.2
20	118 49.0	46.0	149 39.6	11.3	18 12.5	5.0	55.3
21	133 48.7	·· 45.8	164 09.9	11.2	18 17.5	4.9	55.3
22	148 48.4	45.5	178 40.1	11.2	18 22.4	4.7	55.3
23	163 48.1	45.3	193 10.3	11.1	18 27.1	4.7	55.3
S.D. 16.3	d 0.2		S.D. 14.8		14.9		15.0

Lat.	Twilight Naut.	Twilight Civil	Sunrise	Moonrise 1	2	3	4
N 72	08 23	10 40	■	04 25	06 15	08 31	■
N 70	08 04	09 48	■	04 06	05 45	07 29	09 25
68	07 49	09 16	■	03 52	05 22	06 54	08 25
66	07 37	08 52	10 26	03 41	05 05	06 29	07 51
64	07 26	08 34	09 49	03 31	04 51	06 10	07 26
62	07 17	08 18	09 22	03 23	04 39	05 54	07 07
60	07 09	08 05	09 02	03 16	04 29	05 41	06 51
N 58	07 02	07 54	08 45	03 10	04 20	05 30	06 37
56	06 56	07 44	08 31	03 04	04 12	05 20	06 26
54	06 50	07 36	08 19	02 59	04 06	05 12	06 16
52	06 44	07 28	08 08	02 55	04 00	05 04	06 07
50	06 39	07 20	07 59	02 51	03 54	04 57	05 59
45	06 28	07 05	07 38	02 42	03 42	04 42	05 42
N 40	06 18	06 52	07 22	02 35	03 33	04 30	05 28
35	06 09	06 40	07 08	02 29	03 24	04 20	05 16
30	06 00	06 30	06 56	02 24	03 17	04 11	05 06
20	05 44	06 12	06 36	02 15	03 04	03 56	04 48
N 10	05 28	05 55	06 17	02 07	02 53	03 42	04 33
0	05 12	05 38	06 00	01 59	02 43	03 30	04 18
S 10	04 53	05 20	05 43	01 52	02 33	03 17	04 04
20	04 31	05 00	05 25	01 44	02 22	03 04	03 49
30	04 03	04 36	05 03	01 35	02 10	02 49	03 32
35	03 44	04 21	04 50	01 30	02 03	02 40	03 21
40	03 22	04 03	04 36	01 24	01 55	02 30	03 10
45	02 52	03 41	04 18	01 17	01 46	02 19	02 56
S 50	02 09	03 12	03 56	01 09	01 35	02 04	02 40
52	01 43	02 58	03 46	01 05	01 29	01 58	02 32
54	01 03	02 41	03 34	01 01	01 24	01 51	02 24
56	////	02 19	03 20	00 57	01 17	01 43	02 14
58	////	01 52	03 04	00 52	01 10	01 34	02 03
S 60	////	01 09	02 45	00 46	01 03	01 23	01 51

Lat.	Sunset	Twilight Civil	Twilight Naut.	Moonset 1	2	3	4
N 72	■	13 29	15 46	11 37	11 19	10 40	■
N 70	■	14 21	16 04	11 57	11 51	11 43	11 30
68	■	14 53	16 19	12 12	12 14	12 19	12 30
66	13 42	15 16	16 32	12 25	12 32	12 44	13 05
64	14 20	15 35	16 42	12 35	12 47	13 04	13 30
62	14 46	15 50	16 51	12 44	13 00	13 20	13 49
60	15 07	16 03	16 59	12 52	13 10	13 34	14 06
N 58	15 23	16 14	17 06	12 59	13 20	13 46	14 19
56	15 37	16 24	17 13	13 05	13 28	13 56	14 31
54	15 50	16 33	17 19	13 11	13 35	14 05	14 41
52	16 00	16 41	17 24	13 16	13 42	14 13	14 51
50	16 10	16 48	17 29	13 20	13 48	14 20	14 59
45	16 30	17 04	17 41	13 30	14 00	14 35	15 16
N 40	16 46	17 17	17 51	13 38	14 11	14 48	15 31
35	17 00	17 28	18 00	13 45	14 20	14 59	15 43
30	17 12	17 38	18 08	13 51	14 28	15 09	15 54
20	17 33	17 57	18 24	14 02	14 42	15 25	16 12
N 10	17 51	18 14	18 40	14 11	14 54	15 39	16 28
0	18 08	18 30	18 56	14 20	15 05	15 53	16 43
S 10	18 25	18 48	19 15	14 29	15 17	16 06	16 58
20	18 43	19 08	19 37	14 38	15 29	16 21	17 14
30	19 05	19 32	20 05	14 49	15 43	16 37	17 32
35	19 18	19 47	20 23	14 56	15 51	16 47	17 43
40	19 32	20 05	20 46	15 03	16 00	16 58	17 55
45	19 50	20 27	21 15	15 11	16 11	17 11	18 09
S 50	20 12	20 55	21 59	15 21	16 24	17 27	18 27
52	20 22	21 10	22 24	15 26	16 30	17 34	18 35
54	20 34	21 27	23 03	15 31	16 37	17 42	18 45
56	20 47	21 48	////	15 37	16 45	17 52	18 55
58	21 03	22 17	////	15 43	16 53	18 02	19 07
S 60	21 23	22 57	////	15 51	17 03	18 14	19 21

Day	SUN Eqn. of Time 00h	12h	Mer. Pass.	MOON Mer. Pass. Upper	Lower	Age	Phase
	m s	m s	h m	h m	h m	d	
1	03 24	03 38	12 04	08 10	20 32	25	
2	03 52	04 06	12 04	08 54	21 17	26	◐
3	04 20	04 34	12 05	09 41	22 06	27	

G.M.T.	ARIES G.H.A.	VENUS −3.4 G.H.A.	Dec.	MARS +1.4 G.H.A.	Dec.	JUPITER −1.6 G.H.A.	Dec.	SATURN +1.0 G.H.A.	Dec.	STARS Name	S.H.A.	Dec.
4 00	103 30.8	203 22.4 S22	23.5	157 45.0 S20	32.5	274 04.3 S 2	38.1	273 46.3 S 1	37.3	Acamar	315 36.9	S40 23.2
01	118 33.3	218 21.5 ··	23.8	172 45.4 ··	32.1	289 06.6 ··	38.1	288 48.7 ··	37.3	Achernar	335 45.0	S57 20.4
02	133 35.8	233 20.6	24.1	187 45.8	31.6	304 08.9	38.2	303 51.1	37.3	Acrux	173 36.8	S62 59.3
03	148 38.2	248 19.7 ··	24.4	202 46.2 ··	31.1	319 11.2 ··	38.2	318 53.5 ··	37.4	Adhara	255 31.6	S28 56.8
04	163 40.7	263 18.8	24.8	217 46.7	30.7	334 13.5	38.3	333 55.9	37.4	Aldebaran	291 17.5	N16 28.2
05	178 43.2	278 17.9	25.1	232 47.1	30.2	349 15.8	38.3	348 58.3	37.4			
06	193 45.6	293 17.0 S22	25.4	247 47.5 S20	29.8	4 18.2 S 2	38.4	4 00.7 S 1	37.4	Alioth	166 42.4	N56 03.6
07	208 48.1	308 16.1	25.7	262 47.9	29.3	19 20.5	38.4	19 03.1	37.4	Alkaid	153 18.5	N49 24.3
08	223 50.6	323 15.2	26.0	277 48.4	28.8	34 22.8	38.5	34 05.5	37.4	Al Na'ir	28 15.0	S47 03.4
S 09	238 53.0	338 14.3 ··	26.3	292 48.8 ··	28.4	49 25.1 ··	38.5	49 07.9 ··	37.4	Alnilam	276 11.1	S 1 12.9
U 10	253 55.5	353 13.4	26.6	307 49.2	27.9	64 27.4	38.6	64 10.3	37.5	Alphard	218 20.1	S 8 34.6
N 11	268 58.0	8 12.5	26.9	322 49.7	27.4	79 29.7	38.6	79 12.7	37.5			
D 12	284 00.4	23 11.6 S22	27.2	337 50.1 S20	27.0	94 32.0 S 2	38.7	94 15.1 S 1	37.5	Alphecca	126 32.2	N26 46.7
A 13	299 02.9	38 10.7	27.5	352 50.5	26.5	109 34.4	38.7	109 17.5	37.5	Alpheratz	358 09.2	N28 59.2
Y 14	314 05.3	53 09.8	27.8	7 50.9	26.1	124 36.7	38.8	124 19.9	37.5	Altair	62 32.7	N 8 49.1
15	329 07.8	68 08.9 ··	28.1	22 51.4 ··	25.6	139 39.0 ··	38.8	139 22.3 ··	37.5	Ankaa	353 40.1	S42 24.9
16	344 10.3	83 08.0	28.4	37 51.8	25.1	154 41.3	38.9	154 24.7	37.5	Antares	112 56.9	S26 23.3
17	359 12.7	98 07.1	28.7	52 52.2	24.7	169 43.6	38.9	169 27.1	37.6			
18	14 15.2	113 06.2 S22	29.0	67 52.6 S20	24.2	184 45.9 S 2	39.0	184 29.5 S 1	37.6	Arcturus	146 18.4	N19 16.8
19	29 17.7	128 05.3	29.3	82 53.1	23.7	199 48.3	39.0	199 31.9	37.6	Atria	108 21.5	S68 59.4
20	44 20.1	143 04.3	29.6	97 53.5	23.3	214 50.6	39.1	214 34.3	37.6	Avior	234 27.5	S59 26.8
21	59 22.6	158 03.4 ··	29.9	112 53.9 ··	22.8	229 52.9 ··	39.1	229 36.7 ··	37.6	Bellatrix	278 58.2	N 6 19.9
22	74 25.1	173 02.5	30.2	127 54.3	22.3	244 55.2	39.2	244 39.1	37.6	Betelgeuse	271 27.7	N 7 24.1
23	89 27.5	188 01.6	30.5	142 54.8	21.9	259 57.5	39.2	259 41.5	37.6			
5 00	104 30.0	203 00.7 S22	30.8	157 55.2 S20	21.4	274 59.9 S 2	39.3	274 43.9 S 1	37.6	Canopus	264 06.6	S52 41.3
01	119 32.5	217 59.8	31.1	172 55.6	20.9	290 02.2	39.3	289 46.3	37.7	Capella	281 10.5	N45 58.8
02	134 34.9	232 58.9	31.4	187 56.1	20.5	305 04.5	39.4	304 48.7	37.7	Deneb	49 48.7	N45 12.8
03	149 37.4	247 58.0 ··	31.6	202 56.5 ··	20.0	320 06.8 ··	39.4	319 51.1 ··	37.7	Denebola	182 58.8	N14 40.7
04	164 39.8	262 57.1	31.9	217 56.9	19.5	335 09.1	39.5	334 53.6	37.7	Diphda	349 20.7	S18 05.7
05	179 42.3	277 56.2	32.2	232 57.3	19.1	350 11.4	39.5	349 56.0	37.7			
06	194 44.8	292 55.3 S22	32.5	247 57.8 S20	18.6	5 13.8 S 2	39.6	4 58.4 S 1	37.7	Dubhe	194 21.6	N61 51.0
07	209 47.2	307 54.4	32.8	262 58.2	18.1	20 16.1	39.6	20 00.8	37.7	Elnath	278 43.5	N28 35.5
08	224 49.7	322 53.5	33.1	277 58.6	17.6	35 18.4	39.7	35 03.2	37.8	Eltanin	90 58.2	N51 29.5
M 09	239 52.2	337 52.5 ··	33.3	292 59.1 ··	17.2	50 20.7 ··	39.7	50 05.6 ··	37.8	Enif	34 11.6	N 9 47.2
O 10	254 54.6	352 51.6	33.6	307 59.5	16.7	65 23.1	39.8	65 08.0	37.8	Fomalhaut	15 51.4	S29 43.6
N 11	269 57.1	7 50.7	33.9	322 59.9	16.2	80 25.4	39.8	80 10.4	37.8			
D 12	284 59.6	22 49.8 S22	34.2	338 00.4 S20	15.8	95 27.7 S 2	39.9	95 12.8 S 1	37.8	Gacrux	172 28.4	S57 00.1
A 13	300 02.0	37 48.9	34.4	353 00.8	15.3	110 30.0	39.9	110 15.2	37.8	Gienah	176 17.7	S17 26.0
Y 14	315 04.5	52 48.0	34.7	8 01.2	14.8	125 32.3	40.0	125 17.6	37.8	Hadar	149 23.2	S60 16.5
15	330 07.0	67 47.1 ··	35.0	23 01.6 ··	14.3	140 34.7 ··	40.0	140 20.0 ··	37.8	Hamal	328 28.6	N23 22.4
16	345 09.4	82 46.2	35.3	38 02.1	13.9	155 37.0	40.1	155 22.4	37.9	Kaus Aust.	84 17.0	S34 23.6
17	0 11.9	97 45.3	35.5	53 02.5	13.4	170 39.3	40.1	170 24.8	37.9			
18	15 14.3	112 44.4 S22	35.8	68 02.9 S20	12.9	185 41.6 S 2	40.2	185 27.2 S 1	37.9	Kochab	137 19.7	N74 13.8
19	30 16.8	127 43.4	36.1	83 03.4	12.4	200 44.0	40.2	200 29.6	37.9	Markab	14 03.1	N15 06.2
20	45 19.3	142 42.5	36.3	98 03.8	12.0	215 46.3	40.3	215 32.0	37.9	Menkar	314 40.9	N 4 00.8
21	60 21.7	157 41.6 ··	36.6	113 04.2 ··	11.5	230 48.6 ··	40.3	230 34.4 ··	37.9	Menkent	148 36.9	S36 16.3
22	75 24.2	172 40.7	36.9	128 04.7	11.0	245 50.9	40.4	245 36.8	37.9	Miaplacidus	221 44.0	S69 38.2
23	90 26.7	187 39.8	37.1	143 05.1	10.5	260 53.3	40.4	260 39.2	37.9			
6 00	105 29.1	202 38.9 S22	37.4	158 05.5 S20	10.1	275 55.6 S 2	40.5	275 41.7 S 1	37.9	Mirfak	309 15.5	N49 47.7
01	120 31.6	217 38.0	37.6	173 06.0	09.6	290 57.9	40.5	290 44.1	38.0	Nunki	76 29.3	S26 19.2
02	135 34.1	232 37.1	37.9	188 06.4	09.1	306 00.2	40.5	305 46.5	38.0	Peacock	53 58.7	S56 47.9
03	150 36.5	247 36.1 ··	38.2	203 06.8 ··	08.6	321 02.6 ··	40.6	320 48.9 ··	38.0	Pollux	243 57.6	N28 04.3
04	165 39.0	262 35.2	38.4	218 07.3	08.1	336 04.9	40.6	335 51.3	38.0	Procyon	245 25.2	N 5 16.4
05	180 41.4	277 34.3	38.7	233 07.7	07.7	351 07.2	40.7	350 53.7	38.0			
06	195 43.9	292 33.4 S22	38.9	248 08.1 S20	07.2	6 09.5 S 2	40.7	5 56.1 S 1	38.0	Rasalhague	96 29.7	N12 34.4
07	210 46.4	307 32.5	39.2	263 08.6	06.7	21 11.9	40.8	20 58.5	38.0	Regulus	208 09.6	N12 03.6
08	225 48.8	322 31.6	39.4	278 09.0	06.2	36 14.2	40.8	36 00.9	38.0	Rigel	281 35.5	S 8 13.5
T 09	240 51.3	337 30.7 ··	39.7	293 09.4 ··	05.7	51 16.5 ··	40.9	51 03.3 ··	38.0	Rigil Kent.	140 25.8	S60 45.0
U 10	255 53.8	352 29.7	39.9	308 09.9	05.3	66 18.9	40.9	66 05.7	38.1	Sabik	102 41.2	S15 42.0
E 11	270 56.2	7 28.8	40.2	323 10.3	04.8	81 21.2	41.0	81 08.1	38.1			
S D 12	285 58.7	22 27.9 S22	40.4	338 10.7 S20	04.3	96 23.5 S 2	41.0	96 10.6 S 1	38.1	Schedar	350 08.8	N56 26.2
A 13	301 01.2	37 27.0	40.7	353 11.2	03.8	111 25.8	41.1	111 13.0	38.1	Shaula	96 55.9	S37 05.3
Y 14	316 03.6	52 26.1	40.9	8 11.6	03.3	126 28.2	41.1	126 15.4	38.1	Sirius	258 55.2	S16 41.5
15	331 06.1	67 25.2 ··	41.2	23 12.0 ··	02.8	141 30.5 ··	41.1	141 17.8 ··	38.1	Spica	158 57.4	S11 03.8
16	346 08.6	82 24.2	41.4	38 12.5	02.4	156 32.8	41.2	156 20.2	38.1	Suhail	223 10.2	S43 21.2
17	1 11.0	97 23.3	41.6	53 12.9	01.9	171 35.2	41.2	171 22.6	38.1			
18	16 13.5	112 22.4 S22	41.9	68 13.3 S20	01.4	186 37.5 S 2	41.3	186 25.0 S 1	38.1	Vega	80 56.1	N38 46.0
19	31 15.9	127 21.5	42.1	83 13.8	00.9	201 39.8	41.3	201 27.4	38.2	Zuben'ubi	137 33.0	S15 57.6
20	46 18.4	142 20.6	42.4	98 14.2	20 00.4	216 42.2	41.4	216 29.8	38.2			
21	61 20.9	157 19.7 ··	42.6	113 14.6	19 59.9	231 44.5 ··	41.4	231 32.2 ··	38.2		S.H.A.	Mer. Pass.
22	76 23.3	172 18.7	42.8	128 15.1	59.5	246 46.8	41.5	246 34.7	38.2	Venus	98 30.7	10 29
23	91 25.8	187 17.8	43.1	143 15.5	59.0	261 49.1	41.5	261 37.1	38.2	Mars	53 25.2	13 28
Mer. Pass.	16 59.2	v −0.9 d 0.3		v 0.4 d 0.5		v 2.3 d 0.0		v 2.4 d 0.0		Jupiter	170 29.9	5 39
										Saturn	170 14.0	5 40

SUN and MOON

G.M.T.	SUN G.H.A.	SUN Dec.	MOON G.H.A.	v	MOON Dec.	d	H.P.
4 00	178 47.9	S22 45.0	207 40.4	11.0	S18 31.8	4.7	55.3
01	193 47.6	44.8	222 10.4	11.0	18 36.5	4.5	55.4
02	208 47.3	44.5	236 40.4	10.9	18 41.0	4.4	55.4
03	223 47.0	.. 44.2	251 10.3	10.9	18 45.4	4.3	55.4
04	238 46.7	44.0	265 40.2	10.8	18 49.7	4.3	55.4
05	253 46.4	43.7	280 10.0	10.8	18 54.0	4.2	55.4
06	268 46.2	S22 43.5	294 39.8	10.7	S18 58.2	4.0	55.5
07	283 45.9	43.2	309 09.5	10.7	19 02.2	4.0	55.5
08	298 45.6	42.9	323 39.2	10.6	19 06.2	3.9	55.5
S 09	313 45.3	.. 42.7	338 08.8	10.5	19 10.1	3.8	55.5
U 10	328 45.0	42.4	352 38.3	10.5	19 13.9	3.7	55.6
N 11	343 44.7	42.1	7 07.8	10.5	19 17.6	3.6	55.6
D 12	358 44.4	S22 41.9	21 37.3	10.3	S19 21.2	3.5	55.6
A 13	13 44.2	41.6	36 06.6	10.4	19 24.7	3.4	55.6
Y 14	28 43.9	41.3	50 36.0	10.3	19 28.1	3.3	55.6
15	43 43.6	.. 41.1	65 05.3	10.2	19 31.4	3.2	55.7
16	58 43.3	40.8	79 34.5	10.2	19 34.6	3.1	55.7
17	73 43.0	40.5	94 03.7	10.1	19 37.7	3.0	55.7
18	88 42.7	S22 40.3	108 32.8	10.1	S19 40.7	2.9	55.7
19	103 42.5	40.0	123 01.9	10.1	19 43.6	2.8	55.8
20	118 42.2	39.7	137 31.0	10.0	19 46.4	2.8	55.8
21	133 41.9	.. 39.4	152 00.0	9.9	19 49.2	2.6	55.8
22	148 41.6	39.2	166 28.9	9.9	19 51.8	2.5	55.8
23	163 41.3	38.9	180 57.8	9.9	19 54.3	2.4	55.8
5 00	178 41.1	S22 38.6	195 26.7	9.8	S19 56.7	2.3	55.9
01	193 40.8	38.3	209 55.5	9.7	19 59.0	2.2	55.9
02	208 40.5	38.1	224 24.2	9.8	20 01.2	2.1	55.9
03	223 40.2	.. 37.8	238 53.0	9.6	20 03.3	2.0	55.9
04	238 39.9	37.5	253 21.6	9.7	20 05.3	1.8	56.0
05	253 39.6	37.2	267 50.3	9.5	20 07.1	1.8	56.0
06	268 39.4	S22 37.0	282 18.8	9.6	S20 08.9	1.7	56.0
07	283 39.1	36.7	296 47.4	9.5	20 10.6	1.6	56.0
08	298 38.8	36.4	311 15.9	9.5	20 12.2	1.4	56.1
M 09	313 38.5	.. 36.1	325 44.4	9.4	20 13.6	1.4	56.1
O 10	328 38.2	35.8	340 12.8	9.4	20 15.0	1.2	56.1
N 11	343 38.0	35.5	354 41.2	9.3	20 16.2	1.1	56.1
D 12	358 37.7	S22 35.3	9 09.5	9.3	S20 17.3	1.1	56.2
A 13	13 37.4	35.0	23 37.8	9.3	20 18.4	0.9	56.2
Y 14	28 37.1	34.7	38 06.1	9.3	20 19.3	0.8	56.2
15	43 36.9	.. 34.4	52 34.4	9.2	20 20.1	0.7	56.2
16	58 36.6	34.1	67 02.6	9.1	20 20.8	0.5	56.3
17	73 36.3	33.8	81 30.7	9.2	20 21.3	0.5	56.3
18	88 36.0	S22 33.5	95 58.9	9.1	S20 21.8	0.4	56.3
19	103 35.7	33.2	110 27.0	9.1	20 22.2	0.2	56.3
20	118 35.5	32.9	124 55.1	9.0	20 22.4	0.2	56.3
21	133 35.2	.. 32.7	139 23.1	9.0	20 22.6	0.0	56.4
22	148 34.9	32.4	153 51.1	9.0	20 22.6	0.1	56.4
23	163 34.6	32.1	168 19.1	9.0	20 22.5	0.2	56.4
6 00	178 34.4	S22 31.8	182 47.1	8.9	S20 22.3	0.3	56.4
01	193 34.1	31.5	197 15.0	8.9	20 22.0	0.4	56.4
02	208 33.8	31.2	211 42.9	8.9	20 21.6	0.6	56.5
03	223 33.5	.. 30.9	226 10.8	8.8	20 21.0	0.6	56.5
04	238 33.2	30.6	240 38.6	8.9	20 20.4	0.8	56.5
05	253 33.0	30.3	255 06.5	8.8	20 19.6	0.9	56.5
06	268 32.7	S22 30.0	269 34.3	8.8	S20 18.7	1.0	56.6
07	283 32.4	29.7	284 02.1	8.7	20 17.7	1.1	56.6
08	298 32.1	29.4	298 29.8	8.8	20 16.6	1.2	56.6
T 09	313 31.9	.. 29.1	312 57.6	8.7	20 15.4	1.4	56.6
U 10	328 31.6	28.8	327 25.3	8.7	20 14.0	1.4	56.7
E 11	343 31.3	28.5	341 53.0	8.7	20 12.6	1.6	56.7
S 12	358 31.0	S22 28.2	356 20.7	8.7	S20 11.0	1.7	56.7
D 13	13 30.8	27.9	10 48.4	8.7	20 09.3	1.8	56.7
A 14	28 30.5	27.6	25 16.1	8.6	20 07.5	1.9	56.7
Y 15	43 30.2	.. 27.3	39 43.7	8.7	20 05.6	2.0	56.8
16	58 30.0	27.0	54 11.4	8.6	20 03.6	2.2	56.8
17	73 29.7	26.6	68 39.0	8.6	20 01.4	2.2	56.8
18	88 29.4	S22 26.3	83 06.6	8.6	S19 59.2	2.4	56.8
19	103 29.1	26.0	97 34.2	8.6	19 56.8	2.5	56.9
20	118 28.9	25.7	112 01.8	8.6	19 54.3	2.6	56.9
21	133 28.6	.. 25.4	126 29.4	8.6	19 51.7	2.7	56.9
22	148 28.3	25.1	140 57.0	8.6	19 49.0	2.9	56.9
23	163 28.0	24.8	155 24.6	8.6	19 46.1	2.9	57.0
	S.D. 16.3	d 0.3	S.D. 15.1		15.3		15.4

Twilight and Moonrise

Lat.	Twilight Naut.	Twilight Civil	Sunrise	Moonrise 4	5	6	7
N 72	08 20	10 30	■	■	■	■	■
N 70	08 02	09 43	■	09 25	■	■	11 55
68	07 47	09 12	11 30	08 25	09 45	10 38	11 02
66	07 35	08 50	10 20	07 51	09 03	09 56	10 29
64	07 25	08 32	09 45	07 26	08 34	09 27	10 05
62	07 16	08 17	09 20	07 07	08 12	09 06	09 46
60	07 08	08 04	09 00	06 51	07 54	08 48	09 30
N 58	07 01	07 53	08 44	06 37	07 40	08 33	09 17
56	06 55	07 43	08 30	06 26	07 27	08 21	09 06
54	06 49	07 35	08 18	06 16	07 16	08 10	08 55
52	06 43	07 27	08 07	06 07	07 06	08 00	08 46
50	06 39	07 20	07 58	05 59	06 57	07 51	08 38
45	06 28	07 05	07 38	05 42	06 39	07 33	08 21
N 40	06 18	06 52	07 22	05 28	06 24	07 17	08 07
35	06 09	06 41	07 09	05 16	06 11	07 05	07 55
30	06 01	06 31	06 57	05 06	06 00	06 54	07 44
20	05 45	06 13	06 36	04 48	05 41	06 34	07 26
N 10	05 30	05 56	06 19	04 33	05 25	06 18	07 11
0	05 13	05 39	06 02	04 18	05 09	06 02	06 56
S 10	04 55	05 22	05 45	04 04	04 54	05 47	06 41
20	04 33	05 02	05 27	03 49	04 38	05 30	06 26
30	04 05	04 38	05 05	03 32	04 19	05 11	06 08
35	03 47	04 23	04 53	03 21	04 08	05 00	05 57
40	03 25	04 06	04 38	03 10	03 56	04 47	05 45
45	02 56	03 44	04 21	02 56	03 41	04 32	05 31
S 50	02 14	03 16	04 00	02 40	03 23	04 14	05 13
52	01 49	03 02	03 49	02 32	03 14	04 05	05 05
54	01 13	02 45	03 38	02 24	03 05	03 56	04 56
56	////	02 25	03 24	02 14	02 54	03 45	04 46
58	////	01 58	03 09	02 03	02 42	03 32	04 34
S 60	////	01 19	02 50	01 51	02 28	03 17	04 20

Sunset, Twilight and Moonset

Lat.	Sunset	Twilight Civil	Twilight Naut.	Moonset 4	5	6	7
N 72	■	13 42	15 52	■	■	■	14 30
N 70	■	14 29	16 10	11 30	■	■	14 30
68	12 42	14 59	16 24	12 30	12 57	13 55	15 23
66	13 51	15 22	16 36	13 05	13 40	14 37	15 55
64	14 27	15 40	16 46	13 30	14 09	15 05	16 19
62	14 52	15 55	16 55	13 49	14 31	15 27	16 38
60	15 11	16 07	17 03	14 06	14 48	15 44	16 53
N 58	15 28	16 18	17 10	14 19	15 03	15 59	17 06
56	15 43	16 28	17 16	14 31	15 16	16 11	17 17
54	15 53	16 36	17 22	14 41	15 27	16 22	17 27
52	16 04	16 44	17 27	14 51	15 37	16 32	17 36
50	16 13	16 51	17 32	14 59	15 46	16 41	17 44
45	16 33	17 06	17 43	15 16	16 04	16 59	18 00
N 40	16 49	17 19	17 53	15 31	16 19	17 14	18 14
35	17 03	17 30	18 02	15 43	16 32	17 27	18 26
30	17 14	17 41	18 10	15 54	16 43	17 38	18 36
20	17 35	17 59	18 26	16 12	17 02	17 56	18 53
N 10	17 52	18 15	18 41	16 28	17 19	18 13	19 08
0	18 09	18 32	18 58	16 43	17 35	18 28	19 22
S 10	18 26	18 49	19 16	16 58	17 50	18 43	19 36
20	18 44	19 09	19 38	17 14	18 07	18 59	19 51
30	19 05	19 33	20 06	17 32	18 26	19 18	20 07
35	19 18	19 47	20 23	17 43	18 37	19 29	20 17
40	19 32	20 05	20 45	17 55	18 50	19 41	20 28
45	19 49	20 26	21 14	18 09	19 05	19 56	20 42
S 50	20 11	20 54	21 56	18 27	19 23	20 14	20 57
52	20 21	21 08	22 21	18 35	19 32	20 22	21 05
54	20 33	21 25	22 56	18 45	19 42	20 31	21 13
56	20 46	21 45	////	18 55	19 53	20 42	21 22
58	21 01	22 11	////	19 07	20 05	20 54	21 33
S 60	21 20	22 49	////	19 21	20 20	21 08	21 45

SUN and MOON

Day	SUN Eqn. of Time 00h	12h	Mer. Pass.	MOON Mer. Pass. Upper	Lower	Age	Phase
4	04 48	05 02	12 05	10 30	22 56	28	
5	05 09	05 29	12 05	11 22	23 48	29	●
6	05 42	05 55	12 06	12 15	24 42	00	

G.M.T.	ARIES G.H.A.	VENUS −3.4 G.H.A.	Dec.	MARS +1.4 G.H.A.	Dec.	JUPITER −1.7 G.H.A.	Dec.	SATURN +1.0 G.H.A.	Dec.	STARS Name	S.H.A.	Dec.
7 d h												
00	106 28.3	202 16.9	S22 43.3	158 16.0	S19 58.5	276 51.5	S 2 41.5	276 39.5	S 1 38.2	Acamar	315 36.9	S40 23.2
01	121 30.7	217 16.0	43.5	173 16.4	58.0	291 53.8 ..	41.6	291 41.9	38.2	Achernar	335 45.1	S57 20.4
02	136 33.2	232 15.1	43.8	188 16.8	57.5	306 56.1	41.6	306 44.3	38.2	Acrux	173 36.8	S62 59.3
03	151 35.7	247 14.2 ..	44.0	203 17.3 ..	57.0	321 58.5 ..	41.7	321 46.7 ..	38.2	Adhara	255 31.6	S28 56.9
04	166 38.1	262 13.2	44.2	218 17.7	56.5	337 00.8	41.7	336 49.1	38.2	Aldebaran	291 17.5	N16 28.2
05	181 40.6	277 12.3	44.4	233 18.1	56.0	352 03.1	41.8	351 51.5	38.2			
06	196 43.1	292 11.4	S22 44.7	248 18.6	S19 55.6	7 05.5	S 2 41.8	6 53.9	S 1 38.3	Alioth	166 42.3	N56 03.6
W 07	211 45.5	307 10.5	44.9	263 19.0	55.1	22 07.8	41.9	21 56.4	38.3	Alkaid	153 18.5	N49 24.3
E 08	226 48.0	322 09.6	45.1	278 19.4	54.6	37 10.1	41.9	36 58.8	38.3	Al Na'ir	28 15.1	S47 03.4
D 09	241 50.4	337 08.6 ..	45.3	293 19.9 ..	54.1	52 12.5 ..	41.9	52 01.2 ..	38.3	Alnilam	276 11.1	S 1 13.0
N 10	256 52.9	352 07.7	45.6	308 20.3	53.6	67 14.8	42.0	67 03.6	38.3	Alphard	218 20.1	S 8 34.6
E 11	271 55.4	7 06.8	45.8	323 20.8	53.1	82 17.2	42.0	82 06.0	38.3			
S 12	286 57.8	22 05.9	S22 46.0	338 21.2	S19 52.6	97 19.5	S 2 42.1	97 08.4	S 1 38.3	Alphecca	126 32.2	N26 46.7
D 13	302 00.3	37 05.0	46.2	353 21.6	52.1	112 21.8	42.1	112 10.8	38.3	Alpheratz	358 09.2	N28 59.2
A 14	317 02.8	52 04.0	46.4	8 22.1	51.6	127 24.2	42.1	127 13.2	38.3	Altair	62 32.7	N 8 49.1
Y 15	332 05.2	67 03.1 ..	46.7	23 22.5 ..	51.1	142 26.5 ..	42.2	142 15.7 ..	38.3	Ankaa	353 40.1	S42 24.9
16	347 07.7	82 02.2	46.9	38 23.0	50.7	157 28.8	42.2	157 18.1	38.3	Antares	112 56.9	S26 23.3
17	2 10.2	97 01.3	47.1	53 23.4	50.2	172 31.2	42.3	172 20.5	38.4			
18	17 12.6	112 00.4	S22 47.3	68 23.8	S19 49.7	187 33.5	S 2 42.3	187 22.9	S 1 38.4	Arcturus	146 18.4	N19 16.8
19	32 15.1	126 59.4	47.5	83 24.3	49.2	202 35.8	42.4	202 25.3	38.4	Atria	108 21.4	S68 59.4
20	47 17.5	141 58.5	47.7	98 24.7	48.7	217 38.2	42.4	217 27.7	38.4	Avior	234 27.4	S59 26.9
21	62 20.0	156 57.6 ..	47.9	113 25.2 ..	48.2	232 40.5 ..	42.4	232 30.1 ..	38.4	Bellatrix	278 58.2	N 6 19.9
22	77 22.5	171 56.7	48.1	128 25.6	47.7	247 42.9	42.5	247 32.6	38.4	Betelgeuse	271 27.7	N 7 24.1
23	92 24.9	186 55.7	48.3	143 26.0	47.2	262 45.2	42.5	262 35.0	38.4			
8 00	107 27.4	201 54.8	S22 48.5	158 26.5	S19 46.7	277 47.5	S 2 42.6	277 37.4	S 1 38.4	Canopus	264 06.6	S52 41.3
01	122 29.9	216 53.9	48.7	173 26.9	46.2	292 49.9	42.6	292 39.8	38.4	Capella	281 10.5	N45 58.8
02	137 32.3	231 53.0	48.9	188 27.4	45.7	307 52.2	42.6	307 42.2	38.4	Deneb	49 48.7	N45 12.8
03	152 34.8	246 52.0 ..	49.1	203 27.8 ..	45.2	322 54.6 ..	42.7	322 44.6 ..	38.4	Denebola	182 58.7	N14 40.6
04	167 37.3	261 51.1	49.3	218 28.2	44.7	337 56.9	42.7	337 47.0	38.4	Diphda	349 20.7	S18 05.7
05	182 39.7	276 50.2	49.5	233 28.7	44.2	352 59.2	42.8	352 49.5	38.4			
06	197 42.2	291 49.3	S22 49.7	248 29.1	S19 43.7	8 01.6	S 2 42.8	7 51.9	S 1 38.5	Dubhe	194 21.6	N61 51.0
07	212 44.7	306 48.4	49.9	263 29.6	43.2	23 03.9	42.9	22 54.3	38.5	Elnath	278 43.5	N28 35.5
T 08	227 47.1	321 47.4	50.1	278 30.0	42.7	38 06.3	42.9	37 56.7	38.5	Eltanin	90 58.2	N51 29.4
H 09	242 49.6	336 46.5 ..	50.3	293 30.4 ..	42.2	53 08.6 ..	42.9	52 59.1 ..	38.5	Enif	34 11.6	N 9 47.2
U 10	257 52.0	351 45.6	50.5	308 30.9	41.7	68 10.9	43.0	68 01.5	38.5	Fomalhaut	15 51.4	S29 43.6
R 11	272 54.5	6 44.7	50.7	323 31.3	41.2	83 13.3	43.0	83 04.0	38.5			
S 12	287 57.0	21 43.7	S22 50.9	338 31.8	S19 40.7	98 15.6	S 2 43.1	98 06.4	S 1 38.5	Gacrux	172 28.4	S57 00.1
D 13	302 59.4	36 42.8	51.1	353 32.2	40.2	113 18.0	43.1	113 08.8	38.5	Gienah	176 17.7	S17 26.1
A 14	318 01.9	51 41.9	51.3	8 32.7	39.7	128 20.3	43.1	128 11.2	38.5	Hadar	149 23.2	S60 16.5
Y 15	333 04.4	66 41.0 ..	51.5	23 33.1 ..	39.2	143 22.7 ..	43.2	143 13.6 ..	38.5	Hamal	328 28.6	N23 22.4
16	348 06.8	81 40.0	51.6	38 33.5	38.7	158 25.0	43.2	158 16.0	38.5	Kaus Aust.	84 17.0	S34 23.6
17	3 09.3	96 39.1	51.8	53 34.0	38.2	173 27.3	43.2	173 18.5	38.5			
18	18 11.8	111 38.2	S22 52.0	68 34.4	S19 37.7	188 29.7	S 2 43.3	188 20.9	S 1 38.5	Kochab	137 19.6	N74 13.8
19	33 14.2	126 37.3	52.2	83 34.9	37.2	203 32.0	43.3	203 23.3	38.5	Markab	14 03.1	N15 06.2
20	48 16.7	141 36.3	52.4	98 35.3	36.7	218 34.4	43.4	218 25.7	38.6	Menkar	314 40.7	N 4 00.8
21	63 19.2	156 35.4 ..	52.6	113 35.8 ..	36.2	233 36.7 ..	43.4	233 28.1 ..	38.6	Menkent	148 36.9	S36 16.3
22	78 21.6	171 34.5	52.7	128 36.2	35.7	248 39.1	43.4	248 30.6	38.6	Miaplacidus	221 44.0	S69 38.2
23	93 24.1	186 33.5	52.9	143 36.6	35.2	263 41.4	43.5	263 33.0	38.6			
9 00	108 26.5	201 32.6	S22 53.1	158 37.1	S19 34.7	278 43.8	S 2 43.5	278 35.4	S 1 38.6	Mirfak	309 15.5	N49 47.7
01	123 29.0	216 31.7	53.3	173 37.5	34.2	293 46.1	43.6	293 37.8	38.6	Nunki	76 29.3	S26 19.2
02	138 31.5	231 30.8	53.4	188 38.0	33.7	308 48.5	43.6	308 40.2	38.6	Peacock	53 58.7	S56 47.9
03	153 33.9	246 29.8 ..	53.6	203 38.4 ..	33.2	323 50.8 ..	43.6	323 42.7 ..	38.6	Pollux	243 57.5	N28 04.3
04	168 36.4	261 28.9	53.8	218 38.9	32.7	338 53.2	43.7	338 45.1	38.6	Procyon	245 25.2	N 5 16.4
05	183 38.9	276 28.0	53.9	233 39.3	32.2	353 55.5	43.7	353 47.5	38.6			
06	198 41.3	291 27.1	S22 54.1	248 39.8	S19 31.7	8 57.8	S 2 43.7	8 49.9	S 1 38.6	Rasalhague	96 29.7	N12 34.4
07	213 43.8	306 26.1	54.3	263 40.2	31.1	24 00.2	43.8	23 52.3	38.6	Regulus	208 09.5	N12 03.6
08	228 46.3	321 25.2	54.4	278 40.7	30.6	39 02.5	43.8	38 54.8	38.6	Rigel	281 35.5	S 8 13.6
F 09	243 48.7	336 24.3 ..	54.6	293 41.1 ..	30.1	54 04.9 ..	43.9	53 57.2 ..	38.6	Rigil Kent.	140 25.8	S60 45.0
R 10	258 51.2	351 23.3	54.8	308 41.5	29.6	69 07.2	43.9	68 59.6	38.6	Sabik	102 41.2	S15 42.0
I 11	273 53.6	6 22.4	54.9	323 42.0	29.1	84 09.6	43.9	84 02.0	38.6			
D 12	288 56.1	21 21.5	S22 55.1	338 42.4	S19 28.6	99 11.9	S 2 44.0	99 04.4	S 1 38.6	Schedar	350 08.8	N56 26.2
A 13	303 58.6	36 20.6	55.3	353 42.9	28.1	114 14.3	44.0	114 06.9	38.7	Shaula	96 55.9	S37 05.3
Y 14	319 01.0	51 19.6	55.4	8 43.3	27.6	129 16.6	44.0	129 09.3	38.7	Sirius	258 55.2	S16 41.5
15	334 03.5	66 18.7 ..	55.6	23 43.8 ..	27.1	144 19.0 ..	44.1	144 11.7 ..	38.7	Spica	158 57.3	S11 03.6
16	349 06.0	81 17.8	55.7	38 44.2	26.6	159 21.3	44.1	159 14.1	38.7	Suhail	223 10.2	S43 21.3
17	4 08.4	96 16.8	55.9	53 44.7	26.1	174 23.7	44.1	174 16.5	38.7			
18	19 10.9	111 15.9	S22 56.0	68 45.1	S19 25.5	189 26.0	S 2 44.2	189 19.0	S 1 38.7	Vega	80 56.1	N38 46.0
19	34 13.4	126 15.0	56.2	83 45.6	25.0	204 28.4	44.2	204 21.4	38.7	Zuben'ubi	137 33.0	S15 57.6
20	49 15.8	141 14.1	56.3	98 46.0	24.5	219 30.7	44.3	219 23.8	38.7		S.H.A.	Mer. Pass.
21	64 18.3	156 13.1 ..	56.5	113 46.5 ..	24.0	234 33.1 ..	44.3	234 26.2 ..	38.7		° '	h m
22	79 20.8	171 12.2	56.6	128 46.9	23.5	249 35.5	44.3	249 28.7	38.7	Venus	94 27.4	10 33
23	94 23.2	186 11.3	56.8	143 47.4	23.0	264 37.8	44.4	264 31.1	38.7	Mars	50 59.1	13 26
	h m									Jupiter	170 20.1	5 28
Mer. Pass.	16 47.4	v −0.9	d 0.2	v 0.4	d 0.5	v 2.3	d 0.0	v 2.4	d 0.0	Saturn	170 10.0	5 29

G.M.T.	SUN G.H.A.	SUN Dec.	MOON G.H.A.	MOON v	MOON Dec.	MOON d	MOON H.P.
d h	° '	° '	° '	'	° '	'	'
7 00	178 27.8	S22 24.5	169 52.2	8.5	S19 43.2	3.1	57.0
01	193 27.5	24.2	184 19.7	8.6	19 40.1	3.2	57.0
02	208 27.2	23.8	198 47.3	8.5	19 36.9	3.3	57.0
03	223 26.9 ··	23.5	213 14.8	8.6	19 33.6	3.4	57.0
04	238 26.7	23.2	227 42.4	8.6	19 30.2	3.5	57.1
05	253 26.4	22.9	242 10.0	8.5	19 26.7	3.6	57.1
06	268 26.1	S22 22.6	256 37.5	8.6	S19 23.1	3.8	57.1
W 07	283 25.9	22.3	271 05.1	8.5	19 19.3	3.8	57.1
E 08	298 25.6	21.9	285 32.6	8.6	19 15.5	4.0	57.1
D 09	313 25.3 ··	21.6	300 00.2	8.6	19 11.5	4.1	57.2
N 10	328 25.1	21.3	314 27.8	8.5	19 07.4	4.2	57.2
E 11	343 24.8	21.0	328 55.3	8.6	19 03.2	4.3	57.2
S 12	358 24.5	S22 20.7	343 22.9	8.6	S18 58.9	4.4	57.2
D 13	13 24.2	20.3	357 50.5	8.6	18 54.5	4.6	57.3
A 14	28 24.0	20.0	12 18.1	8.6	18 49.9	4.6	57.3
Y 15	43 23.7 ··	19.7	26 45.7	8.6	18 45.3	4.8	57.3
16	58 23.4	19.4	41 13.3	8.6	18 40.5	4.9	57.3
17	73 23.2	19.0	55 40.9	8.6	18 35.6	4.9	57.3
18	88 22.9	S22 18.7	70 08.5	8.6	S18 30.7	5.1	57.4
19	103 22.6	18.4	84 36.1	8.7	18 25.6	5.2	57.4
20	118 22.4	18.1	99 03.8	8.6	18 20.4	5.3	57.4
21	133 22.1 ··	17.7	113 31.4	8.7	18 15.1	5.4	57.4
22	148 21.8	17.4	127 59.1	8.7	18 09.7	5.6	57.4
23	163 21.6	17.1	142 26.8	8.7	18 04.1	5.6	57.5
8 00	178 21.3	S22 16.7	156 54.5	8.7	S17 58.5	5.7	57.5
01	193 21.0	16.4	171 22.2	8.7	17 52.8	5.9	57.5
02	208 20.8	16.1	185 49.9	8.8	17 46.9	5.9	57.5
03	223 20.5 ··	15.7	200 17.7	8.7	17 41.0	6.1	57.6
04	238 20.2	15.4	214 45.4	8.8	17 34.9	6.1	57.6
05	253 20.0	15.1	229 13.2	8.8	17 28.8	6.3	57.6
06	268 19.7	S22 14.7	243 41.0	8.8	S17 22.5	6.3	57.6
T 07	283 19.4	14.4	258 08.8	8.8	17 16.2	6.5	57.7
H 08	298 19.2	14.1	272 36.6	8.9	17 09.7	6.6	57.7
U 09	313 18.9 ··	13.7	287 04.5	8.8	17 03.1	6.6	57.7
R 10	328 18.6	13.4	301 32.3	8.9	16 56.5	6.8	57.7
S 11	343 18.4	13.0	316 00.2	8.9	16 49.7	6.9	57.7
D 12	358 18.1	S22 12.7	330 28.1	9.0	S16 42.8	7.0	57.7
A 13	13 17.9	12.4	344 56.1	8.9	16 35.8	7.0	57.7
Y 14	28 17.6	12.0	359 24.0	9.0	16 28.8	7.2	57.8
15	43 17.3 ··	11.7	13 52.0	9.0	16 21.6	7.3	57.8
16	58 17.1	11.3	28 20.0	9.0	16 14.3	7.3	57.8
17	73 16.8	11.0	42 48.0	9.0	16 07.0	7.5	57.8
18	88 16.5	S22 10.6	57 16.0	9.1	S15 59.5	7.5	57.9
19	103 16.3	10.3	71 44.1	9.1	15 52.0	7.7	57.9
20	118 16.0	10.0	86 12.2	9.1	15 44.3	7.7	57.9
21	133 15.8 ··	09.6	100 40.3	9.2	15 36.6	7.9	57.9
22	148 15.5	09.3	115 08.5	9.1	15 28.7	7.9	57.9
23	163 15.2	08.9	129 36.6	9.2	15 20.8	8.0	57.9
9 00	178 15.0	S22 08.6	144 04.8	9.2	S15 12.8	8.1	57.9
01	193 14.7	08.2	158 33.0	9.3	15 04.7	8.3	58.0
02	208 14.4	07.9	173 01.3	9.2	14 56.5	8.3	58.0
03	223 14.2 ··	07.5	187 29.5	9.3	14 48.2	8.4	58.0
04	238 13.9	07.2	201 57.8	9.3	14 39.8	8.4	58.0
05	253 13.7	06.8	216 26.1	9.4	14 31.4	8.6	58.0
06	268 13.4	S22 06.4	230 54.5	9.3	S14 22.8	8.6	58.0
07	283 13.1	06.1	245 22.8	9.4	14 14.2	8.8	58.1
08	298 12.9	05.7	259 51.2	9.4	14 05.4	8.8	58.1
F 09	313 12.6 ··	05.4	274 19.6	9.5	13 56.6	8.8	58.1
R 10	328 12.4	05.0	288 48.1	9.5	13 47.8	9.0	58.1
I 11	343 12.1	04.7	303 16.6	9.5	13 38.8	9.1	58.1
D 12	358 11.9	S22 04.3	317 45.1	9.5	S13 29.7	9.1	58.2
A 13	13 11.6	03.9	332 13.6	9.6	13 20.6	9.2	58.2
Y 14	28 11.3	03.6	346 42.2	9.5	13 11.4	9.3	58.2
15	43 11.1 ··	03.2	1 10.7	9.6	13 02.1	9.4	58.2
16	58 10.8	02.9	15 39.3	9.7	12 52.7	9.4	58.2
17	73 10.6	02.5	30 08.0	9.6	12 43.3	9.5	58.2
18	88 10.3	S22 02.1	44 36.6	9.7	S12 33.8	9.6	58.2
19	103 10.1	01.8	59 05.3	9.7	12 24.2	9.7	58.3
20	118 09.8	01.4	73 34.0	9.8	12 14.5	9.7	58.3
21	133 09.5 ··	01.0	88 02.8	9.7	12 04.8	9.8	58.3
22	148 09.3	00.7	102 31.5	9.8	11 55.0	9.9	58.3
23	163 09.0	00.3	117 00.3	9.8	11 45.1	10.0	58.3
	S.D. 16.3	d 0.3	S.D. 15.6		15.7		15.8

Lat.	Twilight Naut.	Twilight Civil	Sunrise	Moonrise 7	Moonrise 8	Moonrise 9	Moonrise 10
°	h m	h m	h m	h m	h m	h m	h m
N 72	08 15	10 19	■■■	■■■	12 32	12 02	11 45
N 70	07 58	09 36	■■■	11 55	11 43	11 36	11 31
68	07 44	09 08	11 10	11 02	11 12	11 17	11 19
66	07 33	08 46	10 13	10 29	10 49	11 01	11 09
64	07 23	08 29	09 40	10 05	10 30	10 48	11 00
62	07 14	08 14	09 16	09 46	10 15	10 37	10 53
60	07 07	08 02	08 57	09 30	10 03	10 27	10 47
N 58	07 00	07 51	08 41	09 17	09 52	10 19	10 41
56	06 54	07 42	08 28	09 06	09 42	10 11	10 36
54	06 48	07 34	08 16	08 55	09 33	10 05	10 32
52	06 43	07 26	08 06	08 46	09 26	09 59	10 28
50	06 38	07 19	07 57	08 38	09 19	09 54	10 24
45	06 28	07 04	07 38	08 21	09 04	09 42	10 16
N 40	06 18	06 52	07 22	08 07	08 52	09 32	10 09
35	06 09	06 41	07 09	07 55	08 41	09 24	10 04
30	06 01	06 31	06 57	07 44	08 32	09 17	09 58
20	05 46	06 13	06 37	07 26	08 17	09 04	09 50
N 10	05 31	05 57	06 20	07 11	08 03	08 53	09 42
0	05 15	05 41	06 03	06 56	07 50	08 43	09 34
S 10	04 57	05 24	05 46	06 41	07 37	08 32	09 27
20	04 35	05 04	05 29	06 26	07 23	08 21	09 19
30	04 08	04 41	05 08	06 08	07 07	08 08	09 10
35	03 50	04 26	04 55	05 57	06 58	08 01	09 05
40	03 28	04 09	04 41	05 45	06 47	07 52	08 59
45	03 00	03 48	04 24	05 31	06 35	07 42	08 52
S 50	02 19	03 20	04 03	05 13	06 20	07 30	08 44
52	01 56	03 07	03 53	05 05	06 12	07 25	08 40
54	01 22	02 50	03 42	04 56	06 04	07 19	08 36
56	////	02 31	03 29	04 46	05 56	07 12	08 31
58	////	02 06	03 14	04 34	05 46	07 04	08 26
S 60	////	01 30	02 56	04 20	05 34	06 55	08 20

Lat.	Sunset	Twilight Civil	Twilight Naut.	Moonset 7	Moonset 8	Moonset 9	Moonset 10
°	h m	h m	h m	h m	h m	h m	h m
N 72	■■■	13 55	15 59	■■■	15 46	18 06	20 11
N 70	■■■	14 38	16 16	14 30	16 34	18 31	20 24
68	13 05	15 06	16 30	15 23	17 04	18 49	20 34
66	14 01	15 28	16 42	15 55	17 27	19 04	20 42
64	14 34	15 45	16 51	16 19	17 44	19 16	20 50
62	14 58	16 00	17 00	16 38	17 59	19 26	20 56
60	15 17	16 12	17 07	16 53	18 11	19 35	21 01
N 58	15 33	16 23	17 14	17 06	18 22	19 42	21 05
56	15 46	16 32	17 20	17 17	18 31	19 49	21 10
54	15 58	16 40	17 26	17 27	18 39	19 55	21 13
52	16 08	16 48	17 31	17 36	18 46	20 00	21 17
50	16 17	16 55	17 35	17 44	18 53	20 05	21 20
45	16 36	17 09	17 46	18 00	19 06	20 16	21 26
N 40	16 52	17 22	17 56	18 14	19 18	20 24	21 31
35	17 05	17 33	18 04	18 26	19 28	20 31	21 36
30	17 17	17 43	18 12	18 36	19 36	20 38	21 40
20	17 37	18 00	18 28	18 53	19 51	20 49	21 47
N 10	17 54	18 17	18 43	19 08	20 03	20 59	21 53
0	18 10	18 33	18 59	19 22	20 15	21 08	21 59
S 10	18 27	18 50	19 17	19 36	20 27	21 16	22 04
20	18 45	19 09	19 38	19 51	20 39	21 26	22 10
30	19 06	19 33	20 05	20 07	20 54	21 37	22 17
35	19 18	19 47	20 23	20 17	21 02	21 43	22 21
40	19 32	20 04	20 45	20 28	21 11	21 50	22 25
45	19 49	20 25	21 13	20 42	21 22	21 58	22 30
S 50	20 10	20 52	21 53	20 57	21 35	22 07	22 36
52	20 20	21 06	22 16	21 05	21 41	22 12	22 39
54	20 31	21 22	22 49	21 13	21 48	22 17	22 42
56	20 44	21 42	////	21 22	21 55	22 22	22 45
58	20 59	22 06	////	21 33	22 04	22 28	22 49
S 60	21 17	22 41	////	21 45	22 13	22 35	22 53

Day	SUN Eqn. of Time 00h	SUN Eqn. of Time 12h	SUN Mer. Pass.	MOON Mer. Pass. Upper	MOON Mer. Pass. Lower	Age	Phase
	m s	m s	h m	h m	h m	d	
7	06 08	06 21	12 06	13 09	00 42	01	
8	06 34	06 47	12 07	14 02	01 36	02	
9	07 00	07 12	12 07	14 55	02 29	03	●

G.M.T.	ARIES G.H.A.	VENUS −3.3 G.H.A.	Dec.	MARS +1.4 G.H.A.	Dec.	JUPITER −1.7 G.H.A.	Dec.	SATURN +1.0 G.H.A.	Dec.	STARS Name	S.H.A.	Dec.
10 00	109 25.7	201 10.3	S22 56.9	158 47.8	S19 22.5	279 40.2	S 2 44.4	279 33.5	S 1 38.7	Acamar	315 36.9	S40 23.2
01	124 28.1	216 09.4	57.1	173 48.3	22.0	294 42.5	44.4	294 35.9	38.7	Achernar	335 45.1	S57 20.4
02	139 30.6	231 08.5	57.2	188 48.7	21.4	309 44.9	44.5	309 38.4	38.7	Acrux	173 36.8	S62 59.3
03	154 33.1	246 07.5	·· 57.4	203 49.2	·· 20.9	324 47.2	·· 44.5	324 40.8	·· 38.7	Adhara	255 31.6	S28 56.9
04	169 35.5	261 06.6	57.5	218 49.6	20.4	339 49.6	44.5	339 43.2	38.7	Aldebaran	291 17.5	N16 28.2
05	184 38.0	276 05.7	57.7	233 50.1	19.9	354 51.9	44.6	354 45.6	38.7			
06	199 40.5	291 04.8	S22 57.8	248 50.5	S19 19.4	9 54.3	S 2 44.6	9 48.1	S 1 38.7	Alioth	166 42.3	N56 03.6
07	214 42.9	306 03.8	57.9	263 51.0	18.9	24 56.6	44.6	24 50.5	38.7	Alkaid	153 18.4	N49 24.3
S 08	229 45.4	321 02.9	58.1	278 51.4	18.3	39 59.0	44.7	39 52.9	38.7	Al Na'ir	28 15.1	S47 03.4
A 09	244 47.9	336 02.0	·· 58.2	293 51.9	·· 17.8	55 01.3	·· 44.7	54 55.3	·· 38.7	Alnilam	276 11.1	S 1 13.0
T 10	259 50.3	351 01.0	58.3	308 52.3	17.3	70 03.7	44.7	69 57.8	38.7	Alphard	218 20.1	S 8 34.6
U 11	274 52.8	6 00.1	58.5	323 52.8	16.8	85 06.1	44.8	85 00.2	38.7			
R 12	289 55.3	20 59.2	S22 58.6	338 53.2	S19 16.3	100 08.4	S 2 44.8	100 02.6	S 1 38.8	Alphecca	126 32.2	N26 46.6
D 13	304 57.7	35 58.2	58.7	353 53.7	15.8	115 10.8	44.8	115 05.0	38.8	Alpheratz	358 09.2	N28 59.2
A 14	320 00.2	50 57.3	58.9	8 54.1	15.2	130 13.1	44.9	130 07.5	38.8	Altair	62 32.7	N 8 49.1
Y 15	335 02.6	65 56.4	·· 59.0	23 54.6	·· 14.7	145 15.5	·· 44.9	145 09.9	·· 38.8	Ankaa	353 40.2	S42 24.9
16	350 05.1	80 55.4	59.1	38 55.0	14.2	160 17.8	44.9	160 12.3	38.8	Antares	112 56.9	S26 23.3
17	5 07.6	95 54.5	59.2	53 55.5	13.7	175 20.2	45.0	175 14.7	38.8			
18	20 10.0	110 53.6	S22 59.4	68 55.9	S19 13.2	190 22.6	S 2 45.0	190 17.2	S 1 38.8	Arcturus	146 18.4	N19 16.8
19	35 12.5	125 52.6	59.5	83 56.4	12.6	205 24.9	45.0	205 19.6	38.8	Atria	108 21.4	S68 59.4
20	50 15.0	140 51.7	59.6	98 56.8	12.1	220 27.3	45.1	220 22.0	38.8	Avior	234 27.4	S59 26.9
21	65 17.4	155 50.8	·· 59.7	113 57.3	·· 11.6	235 29.6	·· 45.1	235 24.4	·· 38.8	Bellatrix	278 58.2	N 6 19.9
22	80 19.9	170 49.8	22 59.9	128 57.7	11.1	250 32.0	45.1	250 26.9	38.8	Betelgeuse	271 27.7	N 7 24.1
23	95 22.4	185 48.9	23 00.0	143 58.2	10.6	265 34.4	45.2	265 29.3	38.8			
11 00	110 24.8	200 48.0	S23 00.1	158 58.6	S19 10.0	280 36.7	S 2 45.2	280 31.7	S 1 38.8	Canopus	264 06.6	S52 41.3
01	125 27.3	215 47.0	00.2	173 59.1	09.5	295 39.1	45.2	295 34.1	38.8	Capella	281 10.6	N45 58.8
02	140 29.7	230 46.1	00.3	188 59.5	09.0	310 41.4	45.3	310 36.6	38.8	Deneb	49 48.7	N45 12.8
03	155 32.2	245 45.2	·· 00.4	204 00.0	·· 08.5	325 43.8	·· 45.3	325 39.0	·· 38.8	Denebola	182 58.7	N14 40.6
04	170 34.7	260 44.2	00.5	219 00.4	07.9	340 46.2	45.3	340 41.4	38.8	Diphda	349 20.7	S18 05.7
05	185 37.1	275 43.3	00.7	234 00.9	07.4	355 48.5	45.4	355 43.9	38.8			
06	200 39.6	290 42.4	S23 00.8	249 01.4	S19 06.9	10 50.9	S 2 45.4	10 46.3	S 1 38.8	Dubhe	194 21.5	N61 51.0
07	215 42.1	305 41.4	00.9	264 01.8	06.4	25 53.2	45.4	25 48.7	38.8	Elnath	278 43.5	N28 35.5
08	230 44.5	320 40.5	01.0	279 02.3	05.8	40 55.6	45.5	40 51.1	38.8	Eltanin	90 58.1	N51 29.4
S 09	245 47.0	335 39.6	·· 01.1	294 02.7	·· 05.3	55 58.0	·· 45.5	55 53.6	·· 38.8	Enif	34 11.6	N 9 47.2
U 10	260 49.5	350 38.6	01.2	309 03.2	04.8	71 00.3	45.5	70 56.0	38.8	Fomalhaut	15 51.4	S29 43.6
N 11	275 51.9	5 37.7	01.3	324 03.6	04.3	86 02.7	45.5	85 58.4	38.8			
D 12	290 54.4	20 36.8	S23 01.4	339 04.1	S19 03.7	101 05.1	S 2 45.6	101 00.9	S 1 38.8	Gacrux	172 28.3	S57 00.1
A 13	305 56.9	35 35.8	01.5	354 04.5	03.2	116 07.4	45.6	116 03.3	38.8	Gienah	176 17.6	S17 26.1
Y 14	320 59.3	50 34.9	01.6	9 05.0	02.7	131 09.8	45.6	131 05.7	38.8	Hadar	149 23.1	S60 16.5
15	336 01.8	65 34.0	·· 01.7	24 05.4	·· 02.2	146 12.1	·· 45.7	146 08.2	·· 38.8	Hamal	328 28.6	N23 22.4
16	351 04.2	80 33.0	01.8	39 05.9	01.6	161 14.5	45.7	161 10.6	38.8	Kaus Aust.	84 17.0	S34 23.6
17	6 06.7	95 32.1	01.9	54 06.4	01.1	176 16.9	45.7	176 13.0	38.8			
18	21 09.2	110 31.2	S23 02.0	69 06.8	S19 00.6	191 19.2	S 2 45.8	191 15.4	S 1 38.8	Kochab	137 19.6	N74 13.8
19	36 11.6	125 30.2	02.1	84 07.3	19 00.0	206 21.6	45.8	206 17.9	38.8	Markab	14 03.1	N15 06.2
20	51 14.1	140 29.3	02.2	99 07.7	18 59.5	221 24.0	45.8	221 20.3	38.8	Menkar	314 40.8	N 4 00.8
21	66 16.6	155 28.4	·· 02.3	114 08.2	·· 59.0	236 26.3	·· 45.8	236 22.7	·· 38.8	Menkent	148 36.8	S36 16.4
22	81 19.0	170 27.4	02.4	129 08.6	58.5	251 28.7	45.9	251 25.2	38.8	Miaplacidus	221 44.0	S69 38.2
23	96 21.5	185 26.5	02.5	144 09.1	57.9	266 31.1	45.9	266 27.6	38.8			
12 00	111 24.0	200 25.6	S23 02.5	159 09.6	S18 57.4	281 33.4	S 2 45.9	281 30.1	S 1 38.8	Mirfak	309 15.5	N49 47.7
01	126 26.4	215 24.6	02.6	174 10.0	56.9	296 35.8	46.0	296 32.5	38.8	Nunki	76 29.3	S26 19.2
02	141 28.9	230 23.7	02.7	189 10.5	56.3	311 38.2	46.0	311 34.9	38.8	Peacock	53 58.7	S56 47.9
03	156 31.4	245 22.7	·· 02.8	204 10.9	·· 55.8	326 40.5	·· 46.0	326 37.3	·· 38.8	Pollux	243 57.5	N28 04.3
04	171 33.8	260 21.8	02.9	219 11.4	55.3	341 42.9	46.1	341 39.8	38.8	Procyon	245 25.2	N 5 16.4
05	186 36.3	275 20.9	03.0	234 11.8	54.7	356 45.3	46.1	356 42.2	38.8			
06	201 38.7	290 19.9	S23 03.1	249 12.3	S18 54.2	11 47.6	S 2 46.1	11 44.6	S 1 38.8	Rasalhague	96 29.7	N12 34.4
07	216 41.2	305 19.0	03.1	264 12.8	53.7	26 50.0	46.1	26 47.1	38.8	Regulus	208 09.5	N12 03.5
08	231 43.7	320 18.1	03.2	279 13.2	53.1	41 52.4	46.2	41 49.5	38.8	Rigel	281 35.5	S 8 13.6
M 09	246 46.1	335 17.1	·· 03.3	294 13.7	·· 52.6	56 54.8	·· 46.2	56 51.9	·· 38.8	Rigil Kent.	140 25.7	S60 45.0
O 10	261 48.6	350 16.2	03.4	309 14.1	52.1	71 57.1	46.2	71 54.4	38.8	Sabik	102 41.2	S15 42.0
N 11	276 51.1	5 15.3	03.4	324 14.6	51.5	86 59.5	46.2	86 56.8	38.8			
D 12	291 53.5	20 14.3	S23 03.5	339 15.1	S18 51.0	102 01.9	S 2 46.3	101 59.2	S 1 38.8	Schedar	350 08.8	N56 26.2
A 13	306 56.0	35 13.4	03.6	354 15.5	50.5	117 04.2	46.3	117 01.7	38.8	Shaula	96 55.8	S37 05.3
Y 14	321 58.5	50 12.5	03.7	9 16.0	49.9	132 06.6	46.3	132 04.1	38.8	Sirius	258 55.2	S16 41.5
15	337 00.9	65 11.5	·· 03.7	24 16.4	·· 49.4	147 09.0	·· 46.4	147 06.5	·· 38.8	Spica	158 57.3	S11 03.6
16	352 03.4	80 10.6	03.8	39 16.9	48.8	162 11.4	46.4	162 09.0	38.8	Suhail	223 10.2	S43 21.3
17	7 05.8	95 09.6	03.9	54 17.4	48.3	177 13.7	46.4	177 11.4	38.8			
18	22 08.3	110 08.7	S23 03.9	69 17.8	S18 47.8	192 16.1	S 2 46.4	192 13.8	S 1 38.8	Vega	80 56.1	N38 45.9
19	37 10.8	125 07.8	04.0	84 18.3	47.2	207 18.5	46.5	207 16.3	38.8	Zuben'ubi	137 32.9	S15 57.6
20	52 13.2	140 06.8	04.1	99 18.7	46.7	222 20.8	46.5	222 18.7	38.8		S.H.A.	Mer. Pass.
21	67 15.7	155 05.9	·· 04.1	114 19.2	·· 46.2	237 23.2	·· 46.5	237 21.1	·· 38.8			h m
22	82 18.2	170 05.0	04.2	129 19.7	45.6	252 25.6	46.5	252 23.6	38.8	Venus	90 23.2	10 37
23	97 20.6	185 04.0	04.2	144 20.1	45.1	267 28.0	46.6	267 26.0	38.8	Mars	48 33.8	13 24
	h m									Jupiter	170 11.9	5 17
Mer. Pass.	16 35.6	v −0.9	d 0.1	v 0.5	d 0.5	v 2.4	d 0.0	v 2.4	d 0.0	Saturn	170 06.9	5 17

G.M.T.		SUN G.H.A.	Dec.	MOON G.H.A.	v	Dec.	d	H.P.
10	00	178 08.8	S21 59.9	131 29.1	9.9	S11 35.1	10.0	58.3
	01	193 08.5	59.6	145 58.0	9.8	11 25.1	10.1	58.3
	02	208 08.3	59.2	160 26.8	9.9	11 15.0	10.2	58.4
	03	223 08.0	·· 58.8	174 55.7	10.0	11 04.8	10.2	58.4
	04	238 07.8	58.5	189 24.7	9.9	10 54.6	10.3	58.4
	05	253 07.5	58.1	203 53.6	10.0	10 44.3	10.3	58.4
	06	268 07.2	S21 57.7	218 22.6	9.9	S10 34.0	10.4	58.4
	07	283 07.0	57.4	232 51.5	10.1	10 23.6	10.5	58.4
S	08	298 06.7	57.0	247 20.6	10.1	10 13.1	10.6	58.5
A	09	313 06.5	·· 56.6	261 49.6	10.1	10 02.5	10.6	58.5
T	10	328 06.2	56.2	276 18.7	10.0	9 51.9	10.6	58.5
U	11	343 06.0	55.9	290 47.7	10.1	9 41.3	10.7	58.5
R	12	358 05.7	S21 55.5	305 16.8	10.2	S 9 30.6	10.8	58.5
D	13	13 05.5	55.1	319 46.0	10.1	9 19.8	10.8	58.5
A	14	28 05.2	54.7	334 15.1	10.2	9 09.0	10.9	58.5
Y	15	43 05.0	·· 54.4	348 44.3	10.2	8 58.1	10.9	58.5
	16	58 04.7	54.0	3 13.5	10.2	8 47.2	11.0	58.6
	17	73 04.5	53.6	17 42.7	10.2	8 36.2	11.1	58.6
	18	88 04.2	S21 53.2	32 11.9	10.3	S 8 25.1	11.1	58.6
	19	103 04.0	52.8	46 41.2	10.2	8 14.0	11.1	58.6
	20	118 03.7	52.4	61 10.4	10.3	8 02.9	11.2	58.6
	21	133 03.5	·· 52.1	75 39.7	10.3	7 51.7	11.2	58.6
	22	148 03.2	51.7	90 09.0	10.3	7 40.5	11.3	58.6
	23	163 03.0	51.3	104 38.3	10.4	7 29.2	11.3	58.6
11	00	178 02.7	S21 50.9	119 07.7	10.3	S 7 17.9	11.4	58.7
	01	193 02.5	50.5	133 37.0	10.4	7 06.5	11.4	58.7
	02	208 02.2	50.1	148 06.4	10.4	6 55.1	11.5	58.7
	03	223 02.0	·· 49.8	162 35.8	10.4	6 43.6	11.5	58.7
	04	238 01.7	49.4	177 05.2	10.4	6 32.1	11.5	58.7
	05	253 01.5	49.0	191 34.6	10.4	6 20.6	11.6	58.7
	06	268 01.2	S21 48.6	206 04.0	10.5	S 6 09.0	11.6	58.7
	07	283 01.0	48.2	220 33.5	10.4	5 57.4	11.6	58.7
S	08	298 00.7	47.8	235 02.9	10.5	5 45.8	11.7	58.8
U	09	313 00.5	·· 47.4	249 32.4	10.5	5 34.1	11.7	58.8
N	10	328 00.2	47.0	264 01.9	10.5	5 22.4	11.8	58.8
	11	343 00.0	46.6	278 31.4	10.5	5 10.6	11.8	58.8
D	12	357 59.8	S21 46.2	293 00.9	10.5	S 4 58.8	11.8	58.8
A	13	12 59.5	45.8	307 30.4	10.5	4 47.0	11.8	58.8
Y	14	27 59.3	45.4	321 59.9	10.5	4 35.2	11.9	58.8
	15	42 59.0	·· 45.0	336 29.4	10.5	4 23.3	11.9	58.8
	16	57 58.8	44.6	350 58.9	10.6	4 11.4	11.9	58.8
	17	72 58.5	44.3	5 28.5	10.5	3 59.5	12.0	58.9
	18	87 58.3	S21 43.9	19 58.0	10.6	S 3 47.5	12.0	58.9
	19	102 58.0	43.5	34 27.6	10.5	3 35.5	12.0	58.9
	20	117 57.8	43.1	48 57.1	10.6	3 23.5	12.0	58.9
	21	132 57.6	·· 42.7	63 26.7	10.5	3 11.5	12.0	58.9
	22	147 57.3	42.3	77 56.2	10.6	2 59.5	12.1	58.9
	23	162 57.1	41.8	92 25.8	10.6	2 47.4	12.1	58.9
12	00	177 56.8	S21 41.4	106 55.4	10.5	S 2 35.3	12.1	58.9
	01	192 56.6	41.0	121 24.9	10.6	2 23.2	12.1	58.9
	02	207 56.3	40.6	135 54.5	10.6	2 11.1	12.1	58.9
	03	222 56.1	·· 40.2	150 24.1	10.5	1 59.0	12.2	58.9
	04	237 55.9	39.8	164 53.6	10.6	1 46.8	12.1	59.0
	05	252 55.6	39.4	179 23.2	10.6	1 34.7	12.2	59.0
	06	267 55.4	S21 39.0	193 52.8	10.5	S 1 22.5	12.2	59.0
	07	282 55.1	38.6	208 22.3	10.6	1 10.3	12.2	59.0
	08	297 54.9	38.2	222 51.9	10.6	0 58.1	12.2	59.0
M	09	312 54.6	·· 37.8	237 21.4	10.6	0 45.9	12.2	59.0
O	10	327 54.4	37.4	251 51.0	10.5	0 33.7	12.2	59.0
N	11	342 54.2	37.0	266 20.5	10.6	0 21.5	12.2	59.0
D	12	357 53.9	S21 36.6	280 50.1	10.5	S 0 09.3	12.2	59.0
A	13	12 53.7	36.1	295 19.6	10.5	N 0 02.9	12.3	59.0
Y	14	27 53.5	35.7	309 49.1	10.5	0 15.2	12.2	59.1
	15	42 53.2	·· 35.3	324 18.6	10.5	0 27.4	12.2	59.1
	16	57 53.0	34.9	338 48.1	10.5	0 39.6	12.2	59.1
	17	72 52.7	34.5	353 17.6	10.5	0 51.8	12.3	59.1
	18	87 52.5	S21 34.1	7 47.1	10.4	N 1 04.1	12.2	59.1
	19	102 52.3	33.7	22 16.5	10.5	1 16.3	12.2	59.1
	20	117 52.0	33.2	36 46.0	10.4	1 28.5	12.2	59.1
	21	132 51.8	·· 32.8	51 15.4	10.4	1 40.7	12.2	59.1
	22	147 51.6	32.4	65 44.8	10.4	1 52.9	12.0	59.1
	23	162 51.3	32.0	80 14.2	10.4	2 05.1	12.2	59.1
		S.D. 16.3	d 0.4	S.D. 15.9		16.0		16.1

Lat.	Twilight Naut.	Civil	Sunrise	Moonrise 10	11	12	13
N 72	08 10	10 08	■	11 45	11 32	11 21	11 09
N 70	07 53	09 29	■	11 31	11 25	11 20	11 15
68	07 40	09 02	10 53	11 19	11 19	11 20	11 20
66	07 29	08 42	10 05	11 09	11 14	11 19	11 24
64	07 20	08 25	09 34	11 00	11 10	11 19	11 28
62	07 12	08 11	09 12	10 53	11 06	11 19	11 31
60	07 05	07 59	08 54	10 47	11 03	11 18	11 34
N 58	06 58	07 49	08 38	10 41	11 00	11 18	11 36
56	06 52	07 40	08 26	10 36	10 58	11 18	11 38
54	06 47	07 32	08 14	10 32	10 56	11 18	11 40
52	06 42	07 25	08 04	10 28	10 53	11 18	11 42
50	06 37	07 18	07 55	10 24	10 51	11 18	11 44
45	06 27	07 04	07 37	10 16	10 47	11 17	11 47
N 40	06 18	06 51	07 21	10 09	10 44	11 17	11 50
35	06 09	06 41	07 08	10 04	10 41	11 17	11 53
30	06 02	06 31	06 57	09 58	10 38	11 17	11 55
20	05 47	06 14	06 38	09 50	10 33	11 16	11 59
N 10	05 32	05 58	06 20	09 42	10 29	11 16	12 03
0	05 16	05 42	06 04	09 34	10 25	11 16	12 07
S 10	04 59	05 25	05 48	09 27	10 21	11 16	12 10
20	04 38	05 06	05 31	09 19	10 17	11 15	12 14
30	04 11	04 43	05 10	09 10	10 13	11 15	12 18
35	03 53	04 29	04 58	09 05	10 10	11 15	12 21
40	03 32	04 12	04 44	08 59	10 07	11 15	12 23
45	03 05	03 52	04 28	08 52	10 03	11 15	12 27
S 50	02 25	03 25	04 07	08 44	09 59	11 15	12 31
52	02 03	03 12	03 58	08 40	09 57	11 15	12 33
54	01 32	02 56	03 47	08 36	09 55	11 14	12 35
56	00 31	02 37	03 34	08 31	09 52	11 14	12 37
58	////	02 13	03 19	08 26	09 50	11 14	12 39
S 60	////	01 41	03 02	08 20	09 47	11 14	12 42

Lat.	Sunset	Twilight Civil	Naut.	Moonset 10	11	12	13
N 72	■	14 09	16 07	20 11	22 10	24 08	00 08
N 70	■	14 48	16 23	20 24	22 15	24 05	00 05
68	13 24	15 14	16 36	20 34	22 18	24 02	00 02
66	14 12	15 35	16 47	20 42	22 21	24 00	00 00
64	14 42	15 52	16 57	20 50	22 24	23 58	25 34
62	15 05	16 05	17 05	20 56	22 26	23 57	25 28
60	15 23	16 17	17 12	21 01	22 28	23 55	25 24
N 58	15 38	16 27	17 18	21 05	22 30	23 54	25 20
56	15 51	16 36	17 24	21 10	22 31	23 53	25 16
54	16 02	16 44	17 29	21 13	22 32	23 52	25 13
52	16 12	16 52	17 34	21 17	22 34	23 51	25 10
50	16 21	16 58	17 39	21 20	22 35	23 51	25 07
45	16 40	17 13	17 49	21 26	22 37	23 49	25 01
N 40	16 55	17 25	17 58	21 31	22 39	23 47	24 56
35	17 08	17 36	18 07	21 36	22 41	23 46	24 52
30	17 19	17 45	18 15	21 40	22 42	23 45	24 48
20	17 39	18 02	18 29	21 47	22 45	23 43	24 42
N 10	17 56	18 18	18 44	21 53	22 47	23 41	24 36
0	18 12	18 34	19 00	21 59	22 49	23 40	24 31
S 10	18 28	18 51	19 17	22 04	22 51	23 38	24 26
20	18 45	19 10	19 39	22 10	22 54	23 36	24 20
30	19 06	19 33	20 05	22 17	22 56	23 34	24 14
35	19 17	19 47	20 22	22 21	22 57	23 33	24 10
40	19 31	20 03	20 43	22 25	22 59	23 32	24 06
45	19 48	20 24	21 11	22 30	23 01	23 30	24 01
S 50	20 08	20 50	21 50	22 36	23 03	23 29	23 55
52	20 18	21 03	22 11	22 39	23 04	23 28	23 53
54	20 28	21 19	22 42	22 42	23 05	23 27	23 50
56	20 41	21 37	23 36	22 45	23 06	23 26	23 47
58	20 55	22 01	////	22 49	23 07	23 25	23 43
S 60	21 13	22 33	////	22 53	23 09	23 24	23 39

Day	SUN Eqn. of Time 00h	12h	Mer. Pass.	MOON Mer. Pass. Upper	Lower	Age	Phase
	m s	m s	h m	h m	h m	d	
10	07 24	07 37	12 08	15 47	03 21	04	
11	07 49	08 01	12 08	16 37	04 12	05	◗
12	08 12	08 24	12 08	17 28	05 03	06	

G.M.T.	ARIES G.H.A.	VENUS −3.3 G.H.A.	Dec.	MARS +1.4 G.H.A.	Dec.	JUPITER −1.7 G.H.A.	Dec.	SATURN +1.0 G.H.A.	Dec.	STARS Name	S.H.A.	Dec.
13 00	112 23.1	200 03.1	S23 04.3	159 20.6	S18 44.5	282 30.3	S 2 46.6	282 28.4	S 1 38.8	Acamar	315 36.9	S40 23.2
01	127 25.6	215 02.1	04.4	174 21.1	44.0	297 32.7	46.6	297 30.9	38.8	Achernar	335 45.1	S57 20.4
02	142 28.0	230 01.2	04.4	189 21.5	43.5	312 35.1	46.6	312 33.3	38.8	Acrux	173 36.7	S62 59.3
03	157 30.5	245 00.3 ··	04.5	204 22.0 ··	42.9	327 37.5 ··	46.7	327 35.7 ··	38.8	Adhara	255 31.6	S28 56.9
04	172 33.0	259 59.3	04.5	219 22.4	42.4	342 39.8	46.7	342 38.2	38.8	Aldebaran	291 17.5	N16 28.2
05	187 35.4	274 58.4	04.6	234 22.9	41.8	357 42.2	46.7	357 40.6	38.8			
06	202 37.9	289 57.5	S23 04.6	249 23.4	S18 41.3	12 44.6	S 2 46.7	12 43.1	S 1 38.8	Alioth	166 42.3	N56 03.5
07	217 40.3	304 56.5	04.7	264 23.8	40.8	27 47.0	46.8	27 45.5	38.8	Alkaid	153 18.4	N49 24.3
T 08	232 42.8	319 55.6	04.7	279 24.3	40.2	42 49.3	46.8	42 47.9	38.8	Al Na'ir	28 15.1	S47 03.4
U 09	247 45.3	334 54.6 ··	04.8	294 24.8 ··	39.7	57 51.7 ··	46.8	57 50.4 ··	38.8	Alnilam	276 11.1	S 1 13.0
E 10	262 47.7	349 53.7	04.8	309 25.2	39.1	72 54.1	46.8	72 52.8	38.8	Alphard	218 20.0	S 8 34.6
S 11	277 50.2	4 52.8	04.9	324 25.7	38.6	87 56.5	46.9	87 55.2	38.8			
D 12	292 52.7	19 51.8	S23 04.9	339 26.1	S18 38.0	102 58.8	S 2 46.9	102 57.7	S 1 38.8	Alphecca	126 32.1	N26 46.6
A 13	307 55.1	34 50.9	05.0	354 26.6	37.5	118 01.2	46.9	118 00.1	38.8	Alpheratz	358 09.2	N28 59.2
Y 14	322 57.6	49 50.0	05.0	9 27.1	37.0	133 03.6	46.9	133 02.6	38.8	Altair	62 32.7	N 8 49.1
15	338 00.1	64 49.0 ··	05.0	24 27.5 ··	36.4	148 06.0 ··	47.0	148 05.0 ··	38.8	Ankaa	353 40.2	S42 24.9
16	353 02.5	79 48.1	05.1	39 28.0	35.9	163 08.4	47.0	163 07.4	38.8	Antares	112 56.8	S26 23.3
17	8 05.0	94 47.1	05.1	54 28.5	35.3	178 10.7	47.0	178 09.9	38.8			
18	23 07.5	109 46.2	S23 05.1	69 28.9	S18 34.8	193 13.1	S 2 47.0	193 12.3	S 1 38.8	Arcturus	146 18.3	N19 16.8
19	38 09.9	124 45.3	05.2	84 29.4	34.2	208 15.5	47.1	208 14.8	38.8	Atria	108 21.3	S68 59.4
20	53 12.4	139 44.3	05.2	99 29.9	33.7	223 17.9	47.1	223 17.2	38.8	Avior	234 27.4	S59 26.9
21	68 14.8	154 43.4 ··	05.3	114 30.3 ··	33.1	238 20.3 ··	47.1	238 19.6 ··	38.8	Bellatrix	278 58.2	N 6 19.9
22	83 17.3	169 42.5	05.3	129 30.8	32.6	253 22.6	47.1	253 22.1	38.8	Betelgeuse	271 27.7	N 7 24.1
23	98 19.8	184 41.5	05.3	144 31.3	32.0	268 25.0	47.2	268 24.5	38.8			
14 00	113 22.2	199 40.6	S23 05.3	159 31.7	S18 31.5	283 27.4	S 2 47.2	283 26.9	S 1 38.8	Canopus	264 06.6	S52 41.3
01	128 24.7	214 39.6	05.4	174 32.2	30.9	298 29.8	47.2	298 29.4	38.8	Capella	281 10.6	N45 58.8
02	143 27.2	229 38.7	05.4	189 32.7	30.4	313 32.2	47.2	313 31.8	38.8	Deneb	49 48.8	N45 12.8
03	158 29.6	244 37.8 ··	05.4	204 33.1 ··	29.8	328 34.5 ··	47.3	328 34.3 ··	38.8	Denebola	182 58.7	N14 40.6
04	173 32.1	259 36.8	05.4	219 33.6	29.3	343 36.9	47.3	343 36.7	38.8	Diphda	349 20.7	S18 05.7
05	188 34.6	274 35.9	05.5	234 34.1	28.7	358 39.3	47.3	358 39.2	38.8			
06	203 37.0	289 35.0	S23 05.5	249 34.5	S18 28.2	13 41.7	S 2 47.3	13 41.6	S 1 38.8	Dubhe	194 21.5	N61 51.0
07	218 39.5	304 34.0	05.5	264 35.0	27.6	28 44.1	47.3	28 44.0	38.8	Elnath	278 43.5	N28 35.5
W 08	233 42.0	319 33.1	05.5	279 35.5	27.1	43 46.5	47.4	43 46.5	38.8	Eltanin	90 58.1	N51 29.4
E 09	248 44.4	334 32.1 ··	05.6	294 35.9 ··	26.5	58 48.8 ··	47.4	58 48.9 ··	38.8	Enif	34 11.6	N 9 47.2
D 10	263 46.9	349 31.2	05.6	309 36.4	26.0	73 51.2	47.4	73 51.4	38.8	Fomalhaut	15 51.4	S29 43.6
N 11	278 49.3	4 30.3	05.6	324 36.9	25.4	88 53.6	47.4	88 53.8	38.7			
E 12	293 51.8	19 29.3	S23 05.6	339 37.3	S18 24.9	103 56.0	S 2 47.4	103 56.2	S 1 38.7	Gacrux	172 28.3	S57 00.1
S 13	308 54.3	34 28.4	05.6	354 37.8	24.3	118 58.4	47.5	118 58.7	38.7	Gienah	176 17.6	S17 26.1
D 14	323 56.7	49 27.4	05.6	9 38.3	23.8	134 00.8	47.5	134 01.1	38.7	Hadar	149 23.1	S60 16.5
A 15	338 59.2	64 26.5 ··	05.6	24 38.7 ··	23.2	149 03.2 ··	47.5	149 03.6 ··	38.7	Hamal	328 28.6	N23 22.4
Y 16	354 01.7	79 25.6	05.6	39 39.2	22.7	164 05.5	47.5	164 06.0	38.7	Kaus Aust.	84 16.9	S34 23.6
17	9 04.1	94 24.6	05.7	54 39.7	22.1	179 07.9	47.6	179 08.5	38.7			
18	24 06.6	109 23.7	S23 05.7	69 40.2	S18 21.6	194 10.3	S 2 47.6	194 10.9	S 1 38.7	Kochab	137 19.5	N74 13.8
19	39 09.1	124 22.8	05.7	84 40.6	21.0	209 12.7	47.6	209 13.3	38.7	Markab	14 03.1	N15 06.1
20	54 11.5	139 21.8	05.7	99 41.1	20.5	224 15.1	47.6	224 15.8	38.7	Menkar	314 40.8	N 4 00.8
21	69 14.0	154 20.9 ··	05.7	114 41.6 ··	19.9	239 17.5 ··	47.6	239 18.2 ··	38.7	Menkent	148 36.8	S36 16.4
22	84 16.4	169 19.9	05.7	129 42.0	19.3	254 19.9	47.7	254 20.7	38.7	Miaplacidus	221 44.0	S69 38.2
23	99 18.9	184 19.0	05.7	144 42.5	18.8	269 22.2	47.7	269 23.1	38.7			
15 00	114 21.4	199 18.1	S23 05.7	159 43.0	S18 18.2	284 24.6	S 2 47.7	284 25.6	S 1 38.7	Mirfak	309 15.5	N49 47.7
01	129 23.8	214 17.1	05.7	174 43.4	17.7	299 27.0	47.7	299 28.0	38.7	Nunki	76 29.3	S26 19.2
02	144 26.3	229 16.2	05.7	189 43.9	17.1	314 29.4	47.7	314 30.4	38.7	Peacock	53 58.7	S56 47.9
03	159 28.8	244 15.2 ··	05.7	204 44.4 ··	16.6	329 31.8 ··	47.8	329 32.9 ··	38.7	Pollux	243 57.5	N28 04.3
04	174 31.2	259 14.3	05.7	219 44.9	16.0	344 34.2	47.8	344 35.3	38.7	Procyon	245 25.2	N 5 16.3
05	189 33.7	274 13.4	05.7	234 45.3	15.4	359 36.6	47.8	359 37.8	38.7			
06	204 36.2	289 12.4	S23 05.7	249 45.8	S18 14.9	14 39.0	S 2 47.8	14 40.2	S 1 38.7	Rasalhague	96 29.7	N12 34.4
07	219 38.6	304 11.5	05.6	264 46.3	14.3	29 41.4	47.8	29 42.7	38.7	Regulus	208 09.5	N12 03.5
T 08	234 41.1	319 10.6	05.6	279 46.7	·13.8	44 43.8	47.9	44 45.1	38.7	Rigel	281 35.5	S 8 13.6
H 09	249 43.6	334 09.6 ··	05.6	294 47.2 ··	13.2	59 46.1 ··	47.9	59 47.6 ··	38.7	Rigil Kent.	140 25.7	S60 45.0
U 10	264 46.0	349 08.7	05.6	309 47.7	12.7	74 48.5	47.9	74 50.0	38.6	Sabik	102 41.2	S15 42.0
R 11	279 48.5	4 07.7	05.6	324 48.2	12.1	89 50.9	47.9	89 52.5	38.6			
S 12	294 50.9	19 06.8	S23 05.6	339 48.6	S18 11.5	104 53.3	S 2 47.9	104 54.9	S 1 38.6	Schedar	350 08.8	N56 26.2
D 13	309 53.4	34 05.9	05.6	354 49.1	11.0	119 55.7	47.9	119 57.3	38.6	Shaula	96 55.8	S37 05.3
A 14	324 55.9	49 04.9	05.6	9 49.6	10.4	134 58.1	48.0	134 59.8	38.6	Sirius	258 55.2	S16 41.6
Y 15	339 58.3	64 04.0 ··	05.5	24 50.1 ··	09.9	150 00.5 ··	48.0	150 02.2 ··	38.6	Spica	158 57.3	S11 03.6
16	355 00.8	79 03.0	05.5	39 50.5	09.3	165 02.9	48.0	165 04.7	38.6	Suhail	223 10.2	S43 21.3
17	10 03.3	94 02.1	05.5	54 51.0	08.7	180 05.3	48.0	180 07.1	38.6			
18	25 05.7	109 01.2	S23 05.5	69 51.5	S18 08.2	195 07.7	S 2 48.0	195 09.6	S 1 38.6	Vega	80 56.1	N38 45.9
19	40 08.2	124 00.2	05.5	84 52.0	07.6	210 10.1	48.1	210 12.0	38.6	Zuben'ubi	137 32.9	S15 57.7
20	55 10.7	138 59.3	05.4	99 52.4	07.0	225 12.5	48.1	225 14.5	38.6			
21	70 13.1	153 58.4 ··	05.4	114 52.9 ··	06.5	240 14.9 ··	48.1	240 16.9 ··	38.6			
22	85 15.6	168 57.4	05.4	129 53.4	05.9	255 17.3	48.1	255 19.4	38.6			
23	100 18.1	183 56.5	05.3	144 53.8	05.3	270 19.6	48.1	270 21.8	38.6			
Mer. Pass. 16 23.8		*v* −0.9 *d* 0.0		*v* 0.5 *d* 0.6		*v* 2.4 *d* 0.0		*v* 2.4 *d* 0.0				

Name	S.H.A.	Mer. Pass.
Venus	86 18.3	10 42
Mars	46 09.5	13 21
Jupiter	170 05.2	5 05
Saturn	170 04.7	5 05

G.M.T.	SUN G.H.A.	SUN Dec.	MOON G.H.A.	v	Dec.	d	H.P.
13 00	177 51.1	S21 31.6	94 43.6	10.4	N 2 17.3	12.2	59.1
01	192 50.8	31.1	109 13.0	10.4	2 29.5	12.1	59.1
02	207 50.6	30.7	123 42.4	10.3	2 41.6	12.2	59.1
03	222 50.4	·· 30.3	138 11.7	10.3	2 53.8	12.1	59.1
04	237 50.1	29.9	152 41.0	10.3	3 05.9	12.2	59.2
05	252 49.9	29.5	167 10.3	10.3	3 18.1	12.1	59.2
06	267 49.7	S21 29.0	181 39.6	10.2	N 3 30.2	12.1	59.2
07	282 49.4	28.6	196 08.8	10.3	3 42.3	12.0	59.2
08	297 49.2	28.2	210 38.1	10.2	3 54.3	12.1	59.2
T 09	312 49.0	·· 27.7	225 07.3	10.2	4 06.4	12.0	59.2
U 10	327 48.7	27.3	239 36.5	10.1	4 18.4	12.1	59.2
E 11	342 48.5	26.9	254 05.6	10.2	4 30.5	11.9	59.2
S 12	357 48.3	S21 26.5	268 34.8	10.1	N 4 42.4	12.0	59.2
D 13	12 48.0	26.0	283 03.9	10.1	4 54.4	12.0	59.2
A 14	27 47.8	25.6	297 33.0	10.0	5 06.4	11.9	59.2
Y 15	42 47.6	·· 25.2	312 02.0	10.1	5 18.3	11.9	59.2
16	57 47.3	24.7	326 31.1	10.0	5 30.2	11.8	59.2
17	72 47.1	24.3	341 00.1	10.0	5 42.0	11.8	59.2
18	87 46.9	S21 23.9	355 29.1	9.9	N 5 53.8	11.8	59.2
19	102 46.6	23.4	9 58.0	9.9	6 05.6	11.8	59.2
20	117 46.4	23.0	24 26.9	9.9	6 17.4	11.7	59.2
21	132 46.2	·· 22.6	38 55.8	9.9	6 29.1	11.7	59.2
22	147 46.0	22.1	53 24.7	9.8	6 40.8	11.7	59.3
23	162 45.7	21.7	67 53.5	9.8	6 52.5	11.6	59.3
14 00	177 45.5	S21 21.3	82 22.3	9.7	N 7 04.1	11.6	59.3
01	192 45.3	20.8	96 51.0	9.7	7 15.7	11.5	59.3
02	207 45.0	20.4	111 19.7	9.7	7 27.2	11.5	59.3
03	222 44.8	·· 19.9	125 48.4	9.7	7 38.7	11.5	59.3
04	237 44.6	19.5	140 17.1	9.6	7 50.2	11.4	59.3
05	252 44.4	19.1	154 45.7	9.6	8 01.6	11.4	59.3
06	267 44.1	S21 18.6	169 14.3	9.5	N 8 13.0	11.3	59.3
W 07	282 43.9	18.2	183 42.8	9.5	8 24.3	11.3	59.3
E 08	297 43.7	17.7	198 11.3	9.5	8 35.6	11.3	59.3
D 09	312 43.4	·· 17.3	212 39.8	9.4	8 46.8	11.2	59.3
N 10	327 43.2	16.8	227 08.2	9.4	8 58.0	11.2	59.3
E 11	342 43.0	16.4	241 36.6	9.3	9 09.2	11.0	59.3
S 12	357 42.8	S21 16.0	256 04.9	9.3	N 9 20.2	11.1	59.3
D 13	12 42.5	15.5	270 33.2	9.3	9 31.3	10.9	59.3
A 14	27 42.3	15.1	285 01.5	9.2	9 42.2	11.0	59.3
Y 15	42 42.1	·· 14.6	299 29.7	9.2	9 53.2	10.8	59.3
16	57 41.9	14.2	313 57.9	9.2	10 04.0	10.8	59.3
17	72 41.6	13.7	328 26.1	9.1	10 14.8	10.8	59.3
18	87 41.4	S21 13.3	342 54.2	9.0	N10 25.6	10.7	59.3
19	102 41.2	12.8	357 22.2	9.0	10 36.3	10.6	59.3
20	117 41.0	12.4	11 50.2	9.0	10 46.9	10.6	59.3
21	132 40.7	·· 11.9	26 18.2	8.9	10 57.5	10.4	59.3
22	147 40.5	11.5	40 46.1	8.9	11 07.9	10.5	59.3
23	162 40.3	11.0	55 14.0	8.9	11 18.4	10.4	59.3
15 00	177 40.1	S21 10.5	69 41.9	8.7	N11 28.8	10.3	59.3
01	192 39.9	10.1	84 09.6	8.8	11 39.1	10.2	59.3
02	207 39.6	09.6	98 37.4	8.7	11 49.3	10.1	59.3
03	222 39.4	·· 09.2	113 05.1	8.7	11 59.4	10.1	59.3
04	237 39.2	08.7	127 32.8	8.6	12 09.5	10.1	59.3
05	252 39.0	08.3	142 00.4	8.5	12 19.6	9.9	59.3
06	267 38.8	S21 07.8	156 27.9	8.5	N12 29.5	9.9	59.3
07	282 38.5	07.3	170 55.4	8.5	12 39.4	9.8	59.3
T 08	297 38.3	06.9	185 22.9	8.4	12 49.2	9.7	59.3
H 09	312 38.1	·· 06.4	199 50.3	8.4	12 58.9	9.6	59.3
U 10	327 37.9	06.0	214 17.7	8.4	13 08.5	9.6	59.3
R 11	342 37.7	05.5	228 45.1	8.2	13 18.1	9.5	59.3
S 12	357 37.4	S21 05.0	243 12.3	8.3	N13 27.6	9.4	59.3
D 13	12 37.2	04.6	257 39.6	8.2	13 37.0	9.3	59.3
A 14	27 37.0	04.1	272 06.8	8.1	13 46.3	9.2	59.3
Y 15	42 36.8	·· 03.6	286 33.9	8.1	13 55.5	9.2	59.3
16	57 36.6	03.2	301 01.0	8.1	14 04.7	9.0	59.3
17	72 36.3	02.7	315 28.1	8.0	14 13.7	9.0	59.3
18	87 36.1	S21 02.2	329 55.1	7.9	N14 22.7	8.9	59.3
19	102 35.9	01.8	344 22.0	8.0	14 31.6	8.8	59.3
20	117 35.7	01.3	358 49.0	7.8	14 40.4	8.7	59.3
21	132 35.5	·· 00.8	13 15.8	7.8	14 49.1	8.6	59.3
22	147 35.3	21 00.4	27 42.6	7.8	14 57.7	8.5	59.3
23	162 35.1	20 59.9	42 09.4	7.7	15 06.2	8.5	59.3
	S.D. 16.3 d 0.4		S.D. 16.1		16.2		16.2

Lat.	Twilight Naut.	Twilight Civil	Sunrise	Moonrise 13	14	15	16
N 72	08 03	09 56	■	11 09	10 57	10 41	10 16
N 70	07 48	09 21	■	11 15	11 10	11 05	11 00
68	07 36	08 56	10 38	11 20	11 21	11 24	11 29
66	07 25	08 36	09 56	11 24	11 30	11 39	11 52
64	07 17	08 21	09 28	11 28	11 38	11 51	12 09
62	07 09	08 08	09 07	11 31	11 45	12 02	12 24
60	07 02	07 56	08 49	11 34	11 51	12 11	12 37
N 58	06 56	07 46	08 35	11 36	11 56	12 19	12 47
56	06 50	07 38	08 23	11 38	12 00	12 26	12 57
54	06 45	07 30	08 12	11 40	12 05	12 32	13 05
52	06 40	07 23	08 02	11 42	12 08	12 38	13 12
50	06 36	07 17	07 54	11 44	12 12	12 43	13 19
45	06 26	07 03	07 35	11 47	12 19	12 54	13 34
N 40	06 17	06 51	07 21	11 50	12 25	13 03	13 46
35	06 09	06 40	07 08	11 53	12 31	13 11	13 56
30	06 02	06 31	06 57	11 55	12 36	13 18	14 05
20	05 47	06 14	06 38	11 59	12 44	13 31	14 21
N 10	05 33	05 59	06 21	12 03	12 51	13 42	14 34
0	05 17	05 43	06 05	12 07	12 58	13 52	14 47
S 10	05 00	05 27	05 50	12 10	13 05	14 02	15 00
20	04 40	05 08	05 33	12 14	13 13	14 13	15 14
30	04 13	04 46	05 13	12 18	13 22	14 26	15 30
35	03 57	04 32	05 01	12 21	13 27	14 33	15 40
40	03 36	04 16	04 48	12 23	13 32	14 42	15 50
45	03 09	03 56	04 32	12 27	13 39	14 52	16 03
S 50	02 32	03 30	04 12	12 31	13 47	15 04	16 18
52	02 11	03 17	04 02	12 33	13 51	15 09	16 26
54	01 43	03 02	03 52	12 35	13 55	15 16	16 34
56	00 56	02 44	03 40	12 37	14 00	15 22	16 43
58	////	02 22	03 26	12 39	14 05	15 30	16 53
S 60	////	01 52	03 09	12 42	14 11	15 39	17 05

Lat.	Sunset	Twilight Civil	Twilight Naut.	Moonset 13	14	15	16
N 72	■	14 23	16 16	00 08	02 08	04 14	06 35
N 70	■	14 58	16 31	00 05	01 57	03 52	05 52
68	13 41	15 23	16 43	00 02	01 48	03 35	05 24
66	14 23	15 43	16 54	00 00	01 40	03 21	05 02
64	14 51	15 58	17 02	25 34	01 34	03 10	04 45
62	15 12	16 11	17 10	25 28	01 28	03 00	04 31
60	15 29	16 23	17 17	25 24	01 24	02 52	04 19
N 58	15 44	16 32	17 23	25 20	01 20	02 45	04 09
56	15 56	16 41	17 28	25 16	01 16	02 39	04 00
54	16 07	16 49	17 34	25 13	01 13	02 33	03 53
52	16 17	16 56	17 38	25 10	01 10	02 28	03 46
50	16 25	17 02	17 43	25 07	01 07	02 23	03 39
45	16 43	17 16	17 53	25 01	01 01	02 14	03 26
N 40	16 58	17 28	18 01	24 56	00 56	02 05	03 14
35	17 11	17 38	18 09	24 52	00 52	01 58	03 05
30	17 22	17 47	18 17	24 48	00 48	01 52	02 57
20	17 41	18 04	18 31	24 42	00 42	01 42	02 42
N 10	17 57	18 20	18 46	24 36	00 36	01 32	02 30
0	18 13	18 35	19 01	24 31	00 31	01 24	02 18
S 10	18 29	18 51	19 18	24 26	00 26	01 15	02 06
20	18 46	19 10	19 38	24 20	00 20	01 06	01 54
30	19 05	19 32	20 04	24 14	00 14	00 55	01 40
35	19 17	19 46	20 21	24 10	00 10	00 49	01 32
40	19 30	20 02	20 42	24 06	00 06	00 42	01 22
45	19 46	20 22	21 08	24 01	00 01	00 34	01 11
S 50	20 06	20 47	21 45	23 55	24 25	00 25	00 58
52	20 15	21 00	22 06	23 53	24 20	00 20	00 52
54	20 26	21 15	22 33	23 50	24 15	00 15	00 45
56	20 38	21 33	23 16	23 47	24 10	00 10	00 38
58	20 51	21 55	////	23 43	24 04	00 04	00 29
S 60	21 08	22 24	////	23 39	23 57	24 20	00 20

Day	SUN Eqn. of Time 00h	12h	Mer. Pass.	MOON Mer. Pass. Upper	Lower	Age	Phase
	m s	m s	h m	h m	h m	d	
13	08 35	08 46	12 09	18 19	05 53	07	
14	08 58	09 08	12 09	19 11	06 45	08	◑
15	09 19	09 30	12 09	20 05	07 38	09	

G.M.T.	ARIES G.H.A.	VENUS −3.3 G.H.A. Dec.	MARS +1.4 G.H.A. Dec.	JUPITER −1.7 G.H.A. Dec.	SATURN +0.9 G.H.A. Dec.	STARS Name	S.H.A.	Dec.
16 00	115 20.5	198 55.5 S23 05.3	159 54.3 S18 04.8	285 22.0 S 2 48.1	285 24.3 S 1 38.6	Acamar	315 36.9	S40 23.2
01	130 23.0	213 54.6 05.3	174 54.8 04.2	300 24.4 48.2	300 26.7 38.6	Achernar	335 45.1	S57 20.4
02	145 25.4	228 53.7 05.3	189 55.3 03.7	315 26.8 48.2	315 29.2 38.6	Acrux	173 36.7	S62 59.3
03	160 27.9	243 52.7 ·· 05.2	204 55.8 ·· 03.1	330 29.2 ·· 48.2	330 31.6 ·· 38.5	Adhara	255 31.5	S28 56.9
04	175 30.4	258 51.8 05.2	219 56.2 02.5	345 31.6 48.2	345 34.1 38.5	Aldebaran	291 17.5	N16 28.2
05	190 32.8	273 50.8 05.1	234 56.7 02.0	0 34.0 48.2	0 36.5 38.5			
06	205 35.3	288 49.9 S23 05.1	249 57.2 S18 01.4	15 36.4 S 2 48.2	15 39.0 S 1 38.5	Alioth	166 42.2	N56 03.5
07	220 37.8	303 49.0 05.1	264 57.7 00.8	30 38.8 48.3	30 41.4 38.5	Alkaid	153 18.4	N49 24.3
08	235 40.2	318 48.0 05.0	279 58.1 18 00.3	45 41.2 48.3	45 43.9 38.5	Al Na'ir	28 15.1	S47 03.4
F 09	250 42.7	333 47.1 ·· 05.0	294 58.6 17 59.7	60 43.6 ·· 48.3	60 46.3 ·· 38.5	Alnilam	276 11.1	S 1 13.0
R 10	265 45.2	348 46.2 05.0	309 59.1 59.1	75 46.0 48.3	75 48.8 38.5	Alphard	218 20.0	S 8 34.6
I 11	280 47.6	3 45.2 04.9	324 59.6 58.6	90 48.4 48.3	90 51.2 38.5			
D 12	295 50.1	18 44.3 S23 04.9	340 00.0 S17 58.0	105 50.8 S 2 48.3	105 53.7 S 1 38.5	Alphecca	126 32.1	N26 46.6
A 13	310 52.5	33 43.3 04.8	355 00.5 57.4	120 53.2 48.3	120 56.1 38.5	Alpheratz	358 09.2	N28 59.2
Y 14	325 55.0	48 42.4 04.8	10 01.0 56.8	135 55.6 48.4	135 58.6 38.5	Altair	62 32.6	N 8 49.0
15	340 57.5	63 41.5 ·· 04.7	25 01.5 ·· 56.3	150 58.0 ·· 48.4	151 01.0 ·· 38.5	Ankaa	353 40.2	S42 24.9
16	355 59.9	78 40.5 04.7	40 02.0 55.7	166 00.4 48.4	166 03.5 38.5	Antares	112 56.8	S26 23.3
17	11 02.4	93 39.6 04.6	55 02.4 55.1	181 02.8 48.4	181 05.9 38.4			
18	26 04.9	108 38.7 S23 04.6	70 02.9 S17 54.6	196 05.2 S 2 48.4	196 08.4 S 1 38.4	Arcturus	146 18.3	N19 16.8
19	41 07.3	123 37.7 04.5	85 03.4 54.0	211 07.6 48.4	211 10.8 38.4	Atria	108 21.3	S68 59.4
20	56 09.8	138 36.8 04.5	100 03.9 53.4	226 10.0 48.4	226 13.3 38.4	Avior	234 27.4	S59 26.9
21	71 12.3	153 35.8 ·· 04.4	115 04.3 ·· 52.9	241 12.4 ·· 48.5	241 15.7 ·· 38.4	Bellatrix	278 58.2	N 6 19.8
22	86 14.7	168 34.9 04.4	130 04.8 52.3	256 14.8 48.5	256 18.2 38.4	Betelgeuse	271 27.7	N 7 24.1
23	101 17.2	183 34.0 04.3	145 05.3 51.7	271 17.2 48.5	271 20.6 38.4			
17 00	116 19.7	198 33.0 S23 04.2	160 05.8 S17 51.1	286 19.6 S 2 48.5	286 23.1 S 1 38.4	Canopus	264 06.6	S52 41.3
01	131 22.1	213 32.1 04.2	175 06.3 50.6	301 22.0 48.5	301 25.5 38.4	Capella	281 10.6	N45 58.8
02	146 24.6	228 31.2 04.1	190 06.7 50.0	316 24.4 48.5	316 28.0 38.4	Deneb	49 48.8	N45 12.8
03	161 27.0	243 30.2 ·· 04.1	205 07.2 ·· 49.4	331 26.8 ·· 48.5	331 30.4 ·· 38.4	Denebola	182 58.7	N14 40.6
04	176 29.5	258 29.3 04.0	220 07.7 48.8	346 29.2 48.6	346 32.9 38.4	Diphda	349 20.7	S18 05.7
05	191 32.0	273 28.3 03.9	235 08.2 48.3	1 31.6 48.6	1 35.3 38.4			
06	206 34.4	288 27.4 S23 03.9	250 08.7 S17 47.7	16 34.0 S 2 48.6	16 37.8 S 1 38.3	Dubhe	194 21.4	N61 51.0
07	221 36.9	303 26.5 03.8	265 09.2 47.1	31 36.5 48.6	31 40.3 38.3	Elnath	278 43.5	N28 35.5
S 08	236 39.4	318 25.5 03.7	280 09.6 46.5	46 38.9 48.6	46 42.7 38.3	Eltanin	90 58.1	N51 29.4
A 09	251 41.8	333 24.6 ·· 03.7	295 10.1 ·· 46.0	61 41.3 ·· 48.6	61 45.2 ·· 38.3	Enif	34 11.6	N 9 47.2
T 10	266 44.3	348 23.7 03.6	310 10.6 45.4	76 43.7 48.6	76 47.6 38.3	Fomalhaut	15 51.4	S29 43.6
U 11	281 46.8	3 22.7 03.5	325 11.1 44.8	91 46.1 48.6	91 50.1 38.3			
R 12	296 49.2	18 21.8 S23 03.4	340 11.6 S17 44.2	106 48.5 S 2 48.7	106 52.5 S 1 38.3	Gacrux	172 28.3	S57 00.1
D 13	311 51.7	33 20.8 03.4	355 12.0 43.7	121 50.9 48.7	121 55.0 38.3	Gienah	176 17.6	S17 26.1
A 14	326 54.2	48 19.9 03.3	10 12.5 43.1	136 53.3 48.7	136 57.4 38.3	Hadar	149 23.0	S60 16.5
Y 15	341 56.6	63 19.0 ·· 03.2	25 13.0 ·· 42.5	151 55.7 ·· 48.7	151 59.9 ·· 38.3	Hamal	328 28.6	N23 22.4
16	356 59.1	78 18.0 03.1	40 13.5 41.9	166 58.1 48.7	167 02.3 38.3	Kaus Aust.	84 16.9	S34 23.6
17	12 01.5	93 17.1 03.0	55 14.0 41.4	182 00.5 48.7	182 04.8 38.2			
18	27 04.0	108 16.2 S23 03.0	70 14.5 S17 40.8	197 02.9 S 2 48.7	197 07.3 S 1 38.2	Kochab	137 19.5	N74 13.8
19	42 06.5	123 15.2 02.9	85 14.9 40.2	212 05.3 48.7	212 09.7 38.2	Markab	14 03.2	N15 06.1
20	57 08.9	138 14.3 02.8	100 15.4 39.6	227 07.7 48.8	227 12.2 38.2	Menkar	314 40.8	N 4 00.8
21	72 11.4	153 13.4 ·· 02.7	115 15.9 ·· 39.0	242 10.1 ·· 48.8	242 14.6 ·· 38.2	Menkent	148 36.8	S36 16.4
22	87 13.9	168 12.4 02.6	130 16.4 38.5	257 12.6 48.8	257 17.1 38.2	Miaplacidus	221 43.9	S69 38.3
23	102 16.3	183 11.5 02.5	145 16.9 37.9	272 15.0 48.8	272 19.5 38.2			
18 00	117 18.8	198 10.5 S23 02.5	160 17.4 S17 37.3	287 17.4 S 2 48.8	287 22.0 S 1 38.2	Mirfak	309 15.5	N49 47.7
01	132 21.3	213 09.6 02.4	175 17.8 36.7	302 19.8 48.8	302 24.4 38.2	Nunki	76 29.3	S26 19.2
02	147 23.7	228 08.7 02.3	190 18.3 36.1	317 22.2 48.8	317 26.9 38.2	Peacock	53 58.7	S56 47.9
03	162 26.2	243 07.7 ·· 02.2	205 18.8 ·· 35.6	332 24.6 ·· 48.8	332 29.4 ·· 38.1	Pollux	243 57.5	N28 04.3
04	177 28.7	258 06.8 02.1	220 19.3 35.0	347 27.0 48.8	347 31.8 38.1	Procyon	245 25.2	N 5 16.3
05	192 31.1	273 05.9 02.0	235 19.8 34.4	2 29.4 48.8	2 34.3 38.1			
06	207 33.6	288 04.9 S23 01.9	250 20.3 S17 33.8	17 31.8 S 2 48.9	17 36.7 S 1 38.1	Rasalhague	96 29.7	N12 34.4
07	222 36.0	303 04.0 01.8	265 20.8 33.2	32 34.3 48.9	32 39.2 38.1	Regulus	208 09.5	N12 03.5
08	237 38.5	318 03.1 01.7	280 21.2 32.7	47 36.7 48.9	47 41.6 38.1	Rigel	281 35.5	S 8 13.6
S 09	252 41.0	333 02.1 ·· 01.6	295 21.7 ·· 32.1	62 39.1 ·· 48.9	62 44.1 ·· 38.1	Rigil Kent.	140 25.7	S60 45.0
U 10	267 43.4	348 01.2 01.5	310 22.2 31.5	77 41.5 48.9	77 46.6 38.1	Sabik	102 41.1	S15 42.0
N 11	282 45.9	3 00.3 01.4	325 22.7 30.9	92 43.9 48.9	92 49.0 38.1			
D 12	297 48.4	17 59.3 S23 01.3	340 23.2 S17 30.3	107 46.3 S 2 48.9	107 51.5 S 1 38.1	Schedar	350 08.9	N56 26.2
A 13	312 50.8	32 58.4 01.2	355 23.7 29.7	122 48.7 48.9	122 53.9 38.0	Shaula	96 55.8	S37 05.3
Y 14	327 53.3	47 57.4 01.1	10 24.2 29.1	137 51.1 48.9	137 56.4 38.0	Sirius	258 55.2	S16 41.6
15	342 55.8	62 56.5 ·· 01.0	25 24.6 ·· 28.6	152 53.6 ·· 48.9	152 58.9 ·· 38.0	Spica	158 57.3	S11 03.6
16	357 58.2	77 55.6 00.9	40 25.1 28.0	167 56.0 49.0	168 01.3 38.0	Suhail	223 10.2	S43 21.3
17	13 00.7	92 54.6 00.8	55 25.6 27.4	182 58.4 49.0	183 03.8 38.0			
18	28 03.1	107 53.7 S23 00.7	70 26.1 S17 26.8	198 00.8 S 2 49.0	198 06.2 S 1 38.0	Vega	80 56.1	N38 45.9
19	43 05.6	122 52.8 00.5	85 26.6 26.2	213 03.2 49.0	213 08.7 38.0	Zuben'ubi	137 32.9	S15 57.7
20	58 08.1	137 51.8 00.4	100 27.1 25.6	228 05.6 49.0	228 11.2 38.0			
21	73 10.5	152 50.9 ·· 00.3	115 27.6 ·· 25.0	243 08.1 ·· 49.0	243 13.6 ·· 38.0		S.H.A.	Mer. Pass.
22	88 13.0	167 50.0 00.2	130 28.1 24.5	258 10.5 49.0	258 16.1 37.9	Venus	82 13.4	10 46
23	103 15.5	182 49.0 00.1	145 28.5 23.9	273 12.9 49.0	273 18.5 37.9	Mars	43 46.1	13 19
						Jupiter	170 00.0	4 54
Mer. Pass. 16 12.0	v −0.9 d 0.1	v 0.5 d 0.6	v 2.4 d 0.0	v 2.5 d 0.0	Saturn	170 03.4	4 54

G.M.T.	SUN G.H.A.	SUN Dec.	MOON G.H.A.	v	MOON Dec.	d	H.P.
	° ′	° ′	° ′	′	° ′	′	′
16 00	177 34.8	S20 59.4	56 36.1	7.7	N15 14.7	8.3	59.3
01	192 34.6	59.0	71 02.8	7.7	15 23.0	8.3	59.3
02	207 34.4	58.5	85 29.5	7.6	15 31.3	8.1	59.3
03	222 34.2	·· 58.0	99 56.1	7.5	15 39.4	8.0	59.3
04	237 34.0	57.5	114 22.6	7.5	15 47.4	8.0	59.3
05	252 33.8	57.1	128 49.1	7.5	15 55.4	7.8	59.3
06	267 33.6	S20 56.6	143 15.6	7.4	N16 03.2	7.8	59.3
07	282 33.3	56.1	157 42.0	7.3	16 11.0	7.6	59.3
08	297 33.1	55.6	172 08.3	7.4	16 18.6	7.6	59.2
F 09	312 32.9	·· 55.2	186 34.7	7.3	16 26.2	7.4	59.2
R 10	327 32.7	54.7	201 01.0	7.2	16 33.6	7.3	59.2
I 11	342 32.5	54.2	215 27.2	7.2	16 40.9	7.3	59.2
D 12	357 32.3	S20 53.7	229 53.4	7.2	N16 48.2	7.1	59.2
A 13	12 32.1	53.2	244 19.6	7.1	16 55.3	7.0	59.2
Y 14	27 31.9	52.8	258 45.7	7.1	17 02.3	6.9	59.2
15	42 31.6	·· 52.3	273 11.8	7.0	17 09.2	6.8	59.2
16	57 31.4	51.8	287 37.8	7.0	17 16.0	6.7	59.2
17	72 31.2	51.3	302 03.8	7.0	17 22.7	6.5	59.2
18	87 31.0	S20 50.8	316 29.8	6.9	N17 29.2	6.5	59.2
19	102 30.8	50.3	330 55.7	6.9	17 35.7	6.3	59.2
20	117 30.6	49.9	345 21.6	6.8	17 42.0	6.3	59.2
21	132 30.4	·· 49.4	359 47.4	6.9	17 48.3	6.1	59.2
22	147 30.2	·48.9	14 13.3	6.7	17 54.4	6.0	59.2
23	162 30.0	48.4	28 39.0	6.8	18 00.4	5.9	59.1
17 00	177 29.8	S20 47.9	43 04.8	6.7	N18 06.3	5.8	59.1
01	192 29.6	47.4	57 30.5	6.7	18 12.1	5.6	59.1
02	207 29.4	46.9	71 56.2	6.7	18 17.7	5.5	59.1
03	222 29.1	·· 46.4	86 21.9	6.6	18 23.2	5.5	59.1
04	237 28.9	46.0	100 47.5	6.6	18 28.7	5.2	59.1
05	252 28.7	45.5	115 13.1	6.5	18 33.9	5.2	59.1
06	267 28.5	S20 45.0	129 38.6	6.6	N18 39.1	5.1	59.1
07	282 28.3	44.5	144 04.2	6.5	18 44.2	4.9	59.1
S 08	297 28.1	44.0	158 29.7	6.5	18 49.1	4.8	59.1
A 09	312 27.9	·· 43.5	172 55.2	6.4	18 53.9	4.7	59.1
T 10	327 27.7	43.0	187 20.6	6.5	18 58.6	4.5	59.0
U 11	342 27.5	42.5	201 46.1	6.4	19 03.1	4.5	59.0
R 12	357 27.3	S20 42.0	216 11.5	6.4	N19 07.6	4.3	59.0
D 13	12 27.1	41.5	230 36.9	6.4	19 11.9	4.2	59.0
A 14	27 26.9	41.0	245 02.3	6.3	19 16.1	4.0	59.0
Y 15	42 26.7	·· 40.5	259 27.6	6.4	19 20.1	4.0	59.0
16	57 26.5	40.0	273 53.0	6.3	19 24.1	3.8	59.0
17	72 26.3	39.5	288 18.3	6.3	19 27.9	3.7	59.0
18	87 26.1	S20 39.0	302 43.6	6.3	N19 31.6	3.5	58.9
19	102 25.9	38.5	317 08.9	6.3	19 35.1	3.4	58.9
20	117 25.7	38.0	331 34.2	6.2	19 38.5	3.3	58.9
21	132 25.5	·· 37.5	345 59.4	6.3	19 41.8	3.2	58.9
22	147 25.3	37.0	0 24.7	6.3	19 45.0	3.0	58.9
23	162 25.1	36.5	14 50.0	6.2	19 48.0	2.9	58.9
18 00	177 24.9	S20 36.0	29 15.2	6.2	N19 50.9	2.8	58.9
01	192 24.7	35.5	43 40.4	6.3	19 53.7	2.6	58.9
02	207 24.5	35.0	58 05.7	6.2	19 56.3	2.6	58.8
03	222 24.3	·· 34.5	72 30.9	6.2	19 58.9	2.3	58.8
04	237 24.1	34.0	86 56.1	6.2	20 01.2	2.3	58.8
05	252 23.9	33.5	101 21.3	6.2	20 03.5	2.1	58.8
06	267 23.7	S20 33.0	115 46.5	6.2	N20 05.6	2.0	58.8
07	282 23.5	32.4	130 11.7	6.3	20 07.6	1.9	58.8
08	297 23.3	31.9	144 37.0	6.2	20 09.5	1.7	58.7
S 09	312 23.1	·· 31.4	159 02.2	6.2	20 11.2	1.6	58.7
U 10	327 22.9	30.9	173 27.4	6.3	20 12.8	1.5	58.7
N 11	342 22.7	30.4	187 52.7	6.2	20 14.3	1.3	58.7
D 12	357 22.5	S20 29.9	202 17.9	6.2	N20 15.6	1.2	58.7
A 13	12 22.3	29.4	216 43.1	6.3	20 16.8	1.1	58.7
Y 14	27 22.1	28.9	231 08.4	6.3	20 17.9	0.9	58.6
15	42 21.9	·· 28.4	245 33.7	6.3	20 18.8	0.8	58.6
16	57 21.7	27.8	259 59.0	6.3	20 19.6	0.7	58.6
17	72 21.5	27.3	274 24.3	6.3	20 20.3	0.6	58.6
18	87 21.3	S20 26.8	288 49.6	6.3	N20 20.9	0.4	58.6
19	102 21.1	26.3	303 14.9	6.4	20 21.3	0.3	58.6
20	117 20.9	25.8	317 40.3	6.3	20 21.6	0.1	58.5
21	132 20.8	·· 25.3	332 05.6	6.4	20 21.7	0.1	58.5
22	147 20.6	24.7	346 31.0	6.4	20 21.8	0.2	58.5
23	162 20.4	24.2	0 56.4	6.5	20 21.6	0.2	58.5
	S.D. 16.3	d 0.5	S.D. 16.1		16.1		16.0

Twilight / Sunrise / Moonrise

Lat.	Naut.	Civil	Sunrise	Moonrise 16	17	18	19
°	h m	h m	h m	h m	h m	h m	h m
N 72	07 56	09 44	■	10 16	□	□	□
N 70	07 42	09 12	11 43	11 00	10 52	□	□
68	07 31	08 49	10 24	11 29	11 42	12 11	13 13
66	07 21	08 31	09 47	11 52	12 13	12 51	13 52
64	07 13	08 16	09 21	12 09	12 37	13 19	14 19
62	07 05	08 03	09 01	12 24	12 56	13 40	14 40
60	06 59	07 53	08 45	12 37	13 11	13 58	14 58
N 58	06 53	07 43	08 31	12 47	13 24	14 12	15 12
56	06 48	07 35	08 19	12 57	13 36	14 25	15 24
54	06 43	07 27	08 09	13 05	13 46	14 36	15 35
52	06 39	07 21	07 59	13 12	13 55	14 45	15 44
50	06 34	07 15	07 51	13 19	14 03	14 54	15 53
45	06 25	07 01	07 34	13 34	14 20	15 12	16 11
N 40	06 16	06 50	07 19	13 46	14 34	15 27	16 26
35	06 09	06 40	07 07	13 56	14 46	15 40	16 38
30	06 01	06 31	06 56	14 05	14 56	15 51	16 49
20	05 47	06 14	06 38	14 21	15 14	16 10	17 08
N 10	05 34	05 59	06 22	14 34	15 30	16 27	17 24
0	05 19	05 44	06 07	14 47	15 45	16 42	17 39
S 10	05 02	05 29	05 51	15 00	15 59	16 58	17 55
20	04 42	05 11	05 35	15 14	16 15	17 15	18 11
30	04 16	04 49	05 15	15 30	16 34	17 34	18 30
35	04 00	04 35	05 04	15 40	16 44	17 45	18 41
40	03 40	04 19	04 51	15 50	16 56	17 58	18 53
45	03 14	04 00	04 35	16 03	17 11	18 13	19 08
S 50	02 38	03 35	04 16	16 18	17 29	18 32	19 26
52	02 19	03 23	04 07	16 26	17 37	18 41	19 34
54	01 53	03 08	03 57	16 34	17 47	18 51	19 44
56	01 15	02 51	03 45	16 43	17 57	19 02	19 55
58	////	02 30	03 32	16 53	18 09	19 15	20 07
S 60	////	02 03	03 16	17 05	18 23	19 30	20 21

Sunset / Twilight / Moonset

Lat.	Sunset	Civil	Naut.	Moonset 16	17	18	19
°	h m	h m	h m	h m	h m	h m	h m
N 72	■	14 38	16 25	06 35	□	□	□
N 70	12 38	15 09	16 39	05 52	07 59	□	□
68	13 57	15 32	16 51	05 24	07 10	08 41	09 40
66	14 34	15 50	17 00	05 02	06 39	08 01	09 00
64	15 00	16 05	17 09	04 45	06 15	07 33	08 32
62	15 20	16 18	17 16	04 31	05 57	07 12	08 11
60	15 36	16 28	17 22	04 19	05 42	06 55	07 54
N 58	15 50	16 38	17 28	04 09	05 29	06 41	07 40
56	16 02	16 46	17 33	04 00	05 18	06 28	07 27
54	16 12	16 53	17 38	03 53	05 08	06 17	07 16
52	16 21	17 00	17 42	03 46	05 00	06 08	07 07
50	16 30	17 06	17 46	03 39	04 52	05 59	06 58
45	16 47	17 20	17 56	03 26	04 36	05 41	06 40
N 40	17 01	17 31	18 04	03 14	04 22	05 26	06 25
35	17 14	17 41	18 12	03 05	04 11	05 14	06 12
30	17 24	17 50	18 19	02 57	04 01	05 03	06 01
20	17 43	18 06	18 33	02 42	03 43	04 44	05 42
N 10	17 59	18 21	18 47	02 30	03 28	04 27	05 25
0	18 14	18 36	19 02	02 18	03 14	04 12	05 10
S 10	18 29	18 52	19 18	02 06	03 00	03 57	04 54
20	18 46	19 10	19 38	01 54	02 46	03 40	04 38
30	19 05	19 31	20 03	01 40	02 28	03 22	04 18
35	19 16	19 45	20 20	01 32	02 19	03 11	04 07
40	19 29	20 00	20 39	01 22	02 07	02 58	03 54
45	19 44	20 20	21 05	01 11	01 54	02 43	03 39
S 50	20 03	20 44	21 41	00 58	01 38	02 25	03 20
52	20 12	20 56	22 00	00 52	01 30	02 16	03 12
54	20 22	21 11	22 25	00 45	01 22	02 07	03 02
56	20 34	21 27	23 01	00 38	01 12	01 56	02 50
58	20 47	21 48	////	00 29	01 02	01 44	02 38
S 60	21 03	22 14	////	00 20	00 49	01 29	02 23

Day	SUN Eqn. of Time 00h	SUN Eqn. of Time 12h	Mer. Pass.	MOON Mer. Pass. Upper	MOON Mer. Pass. Lower	Age	Phase
	m s	m s	h m	h m	h m	d	
16	09 40	09 50	12 10	21 01	08 33	10	
17	10 01	10 10	12 10	21 58	09 29	11	◖
18	10 20	10 30	12 10	22 56	10 27	12	

G.M.T.	ARIES G.H.A.	VENUS −3.3 G.H.A.	VENUS Dec.	MARS +1.4 G.H.A.	MARS Dec.	JUPITER −1.7 G.H.A.	JUPITER Dec.	SATURN +0.9 G.H.A.	SATURN Dec.	STARS Name	S.H.A.	Dec.
19 00	118 17.9	197 48.1	S23 00.0	160 29.0	S17 23.3	288 15.3	S 2 49.0	288 21.0	S 1 37.9	Acamar	315 36.9	S40 23.2
01	133 20.4	212 47.2	22 59.8	175 29.5	22.7	303 17.7	49.0	303 23.5	37.9	Achernar	335 45.2	S57 20.4
02	148 22.9	227 46.2	59.7	190 30.0	22.1	318 20.1	49.0	318 25.9	37.9	Acrux	173 36.6	S62 59.3
03	163 25.3	242 45.3	·· 59.6	205 30.5	·· 21.5	333 22.6	·· 49.0	333 28.4	·· 37.9	Adhara	255 31.5	S28 56.9
04	178 27.8	257 44.4	59.5	220 31.0	20.9	348 25.0	49.0	348 30.8	37.9	Aldebaran	291 17.5	N16 28.2
05	193 30.3	272 43.4	59.4	235 31.5	20.3	3 27.4	49.1	3 33.3	37.9			
06	208 32.7	287 42.5	S22 59.2	250 32.0	S17 19.7	18 29.8	S 2 49.1	18 35.8	S 1 37.9	Alioth	166 42.2	N56 03.5
07	223 35.2	302 41.6	59.1	265 32.5	19.2	33 32.2	49.1	33 38.2	37.8	Alkaid	153 18.3	N49 24.3
08	238 37.6	317 40.6	59.0	280 33.0	18.6	48 34.7	49.1	48 40.7	37.8	Al Na'ir	28 15.1	S47 03.4
M 09	253 40.1	332 39.7	·· 58.8	295 33.4	·· 18.0	63 37.1	·· 49.1	63 43.2	·· 37.8	Alnilam	276 11.1	S 1 13.0
O 10	268 42.6	347 38.8	58.7	310 33.9	17.4	78 39.5	49.1	78 45.6	37.8	Alphard	218 20.0	S 8 34.6
N 11	283 45.0	2 37.8	58.6	325 34.4	16.8	93 41.9	49.1	93 48.1	37.8			
D 12	298 47.5	17 36.9	S22 58.5	340 34.9	S17 16.2	108 44.3	S 2 49.1	108 50.5	S 1 37.8	Alphecca	126 32.1	N26 46.6
A 13	313 50.0	32 36.0	58.3	355 35.4	15.6	123 46.8	49.1	123 53.0	37.8	Alpheratz	358 09.2	N28 59.2
Y 14	328 52.4	47 35.0	58.2	10 35.9	15.0	138 49.2	49.1	138 55.5	37.8	Altair	62 32.6	N 8 49.0
15	343 54.9	62 34.1	·· 58.0	25 36.4	·· 14.4	153 51.6	·· 49.1	153 57.9	·· 37.7	Ankaa	353 40.2	S42 24.9
16	358 57.4	77 33.2	57.9	40 36.9	13.8	168 54.0	49.1	169 00.4	37.7	Antares	112 56.8	S26 23.3
17	13 59.8	92 32.2	57.8	55 37.4	13.2	183 56.4	49.1	184 02.9	37.7			
18	29 02.3	107 31.3	S22 57.6	70 37.9	S17 12.6	198 58.9	S 2 49.1	199 05.3	S 1 37.7	Arcturus	146 18.3	N19 16.8
19	44 04.8	122 30.4	57.5	85 38.4	12.1	214 01.3	49.1	214 07.8	37.7	Atria	108 21.2	S68 59.4
20	59 07.2	137 29.4	57.3	100 38.9	11.5	229 03.7	49.1	229 10.2	37.7	Avior	234 27.4	S59 26.9
21	74 09.7	152 28.5	·· 57.2	115 39.3	·· 10.9	244 06.1	·· 49.1	244 12.7	·· 37.7	Bellatrix	278 58.2	N 6 19.8
22	89 12.1	167 27.6	57.1	130 39.8	10.3	259 08.6	49.2	259 15.2	37.7	Betelgeuse	271 27.7	N 7 24.1
23	104 14.6	182 26.6	56.9	145 40.3	09.7	274 11.0	49.2	274 17.6	37.6			
20 00	119 17.1	197 25.7	S22 56.8	160 40.8	S17 09.1	289 13.4	S 2 49.2	289 20.1	S 1 37.6	Canopus	264 06.6	S52 41.3
01	134 19.5	212 24.8	56.6	175 41.3	08.5	304 15.8	49.2	304 22.6	37.6	Capella	281 10.6	N45 58.8
02	149 22.0	227 23.8	56.5	190 41.8	07.9	319 18.3	49.2	319 25.0	37.6	Deneb	49 48.7	N45 12.8
03	164 24.5	242 22.9	·· 56.3	205 42.3	·· 07.3	334 20.7	·· 49.2	334 27.5	·· 37.6	Denebola	182 58.6	N14 40.6
04	179 26.9	257 22.0	56.2	220 42.8	06.7	349 23.1	49.2	349 30.0	37.6	Diphda	349 20.7	S18 05.7
05	194 29.4	272 21.1	56.0	235 43.3	06.1	4 25.5	49.2	4 32.4	37.6			
06	209 31.9	287 20.1	S22 55.9	250 43.8	S17 05.5	19 28.0	S 2 49.2	19 34.9	S 1 37.5	Dubhe	194 21.4	N61 51.0
07	224 34.3	302 19.2	55.7	265 44.3	04.9	34 30.4	49.2	34 37.4	37.5	Elnath	278 43.5	N28 35.5
08	239 36.8	317 18.3	55.5	280 44.8	04.3	49 32.8	49.2	49 39.8	37.5	Eltanin	90 58.1	N51 29.4
T 09	254 39.2	332 17.3	·· 55.4	295 45.3	·· 03.7	64 35.2	·· 49.2	64 42.3	·· 37.5	Enif	34 11.6	N 9 47.2
U 10	269 41.7	347 16.4	55.2	310 45.8	03.1	79 37.7	49.2	79 44.8	37.5	Fomalhaut	15 51.4	S29 43.6
E 11	284 44.2	2 15.5	55.1	325 46.3	02.5	94 40.1	49.2	94 47.2	37.5			
S 12	299 46.6	17 14.5	S22 54.9	340 46.8	S17 01.9	109 42.5	S 2 49.2	109 49.7	S 1 37.5	Gacrux	172 28.2	S57 00.1
D 13	314 49.1	32 13.6	54.7	355 47.3	01.3	124 45.0	49.2	124 52.2	37.4	Gienah	176 17.6	S17 26.1
A 14	329 51.6	47 12.7	54.6	10 47.8	00.7	139 47.4	49.2	139 54.6	37.4	Hadar	149 23.0	S60 16.6
Y 15	344 54.0	62 11.8	·· 54.4	25 48.3	17 00.1	154 49.8	·· 49.2	154 57.1	·· 37.4	Hamal	328 28.6	N23 22.4
16	359 56.5	77 10.8	54.2	40 48.7	16 59.5	169 52.2	49.2	169 59.6	37.4	Kaus Aust.	84 16.9	S34 23.6
17	14 59.0	92 09.9	54.1	55 49.2	58.9	184 54.7	49.2	185 02.0	37.4			
18	30 01.4	107 09.0	S22 53.9	70 49.7	S16 58.3	199 57.1	S 2 49.2	200 04.5	S 1 37.4	Kochab	137 19.4	N74 13.8
19	45 03.9	122 08.0	53.7	85 50.2	57.7	214 59.5	49.2	215 07.0	37.4	Markab	14 03.2	N15 06.1
20	60 06.4	137 07.1	53.6	100 50.7	57.1	230 02.0	49.2	230 09.4	37.3	Menkar	314 40.8	N 4 00.8
21	75 08.8	152 06.2	·· 53.4	115 51.2	·· 56.5	245 04.4	·· 49.2	245 11.9	·· 37.3	Menkent	148 36.7	S36 16.4
22	90 11.3	167 05.3	53.2	130 51.7	55.9	260 06.8	49.2	260 14.4	37.3	Miaplacidus	221 43.9	S69 38.3
23	105 13.7	182 04.3	53.0	145 52.2	55.3	275 09.3	49.2	275 16.8	37.3			
21 00	120 16.2	197 03.4	S22 52.9	160 52.7	S16 54.7	290 11.7	S 2 49.2	290 19.3	S 1 37.3	Mirfak	309 15.5	N49 47.8
01	135 18.7	212 02.5	52.7	175 53.2	54.1	305 14.1	49.2	305 21.8	37.3	Nunki	76 29.2	S26 19.2
02	150 21.1	227 01.5	52.5	190 53.7	53.5	320 16.6	49.2	320 24.3	37.3	Peacock	53 58.6	S56 47.9
03	165 23.6	242 00.6	·· 52.3	205 54.2	·· 52.9	335 19.0	·· 49.2	335 26.7	·· 37.2	Pollux	243 57.5	N28 04.3
04	180 26.1	256 59.7	52.1	220 54.7	52.3	350 21.4	49.2	350 29.2	37.2	Procyon	245 25.2	N 5 16.3
05	195 28.5	271 58.8	52.0	235 55.2	51.7	5 23.9	49.2	5 31.7	37.2			
06	210 31.0	286 57.8	S22 51.8	250 55.7	S16 51.1	20 26.3	S 2 49.2	20 34.1	S 1 37.2	Rasalhague	96 29.6	N12 34.4
W 07	225 33.5	301 56.9	51.6	265 56.2	50.5	35 28.7	49.2	35 36.6	37.2	Regulus	208 09.5	N12 03.5
E 08	240 35.9	316 56.0	51.4	280 56.7	49.9	50 31.2	49.2	50 39.1	37.2	Rigel	281 35.5	S 8 13.6
D 09	255 38.4	331 55.0	·· 51.2	295 57.2	·· 49.2	65 33.6	·· 49.2	65 41.5	·· 37.1	Rigil Kent.	140 25.6	S60 45.0
N 10	270 40.9	346 54.1	51.0	310 57.7	48.6	80 36.0	49.2	80 44.0	37.1	Sabik	102 41.1	S15 42.0
E 11	285 43.3	1 53.2	50.8	325 58.2	48.0	95 38.5	49.2	95 46.5	37.1			
S 12	300 45.8	16 52.3	S22 50.6	340 58.7	S16 47.4	110 40.9	S 2 49.2	110 49.0	S 1 37.1	Schedar	350 08.9	N56 26.2
D 13	315 48.2	31 51.3	50.5	355 59.2	46.8	125 43.3	49.2	125 51.4	37.1	Shaula	96 55.8	S37 05.3
A 14	330 50.7	46 50.4	50.3	10 59.7	46.2	140 45.8	49.2	140 53.9	37.1	Sirius	258 55.2	S16 41.6
Y 15	345 53.2	61 49.5	·· 50.1	26 00.2	·· 45.6	155 48.2	·· 49.2	155 56.4	·· 37.0	Spica	158 57.2	S11 03.7
16	0 55.6	76 48.6	49.9	41 00.7	45.0	170 50.6	49.2	170 58.8	37.0	Suhail	223 10.2	S43 21.3
17	15 58.1	91 47.6	49.7	56 01.2	44.4	185 53.1	49.2	186 01.3	37.0			
18	31 00.6	106 46.7	S22 49.5	71 01.7	S16 43.8	200 55.5	S 2 49.2	201 03.8	S 1 37.0	Vega	80 56.1	N38 45.9
19	46 03.0	121 45.8	49.3	86 02.2	43.2	215 57.9	49.2	216 06.3	37.0	Zuben'ubi	137 32.9	S15 57.7
20	61 05.5	136 44.9	49.1	101 02.7	42.6	231 00.4	49.2	231 08.7	37.0			
21	76 08.0	151 43.9	·· 48.9	116 03.2	·· 42.0	246 02.8	·· 49.2	246 11.2	·· 37.0		S.H.A.	Mer. Pass.
22	91 10.4	166 43.0	48.7	131 03.7	41.3	261 05.3	49.2	261 13.7	36.9	Venus	78 08.6	10 51
23	106 12.9	181 42.1	48.5	146 04.2	40.7	276 07.7	49.2	276 16.2	36.9	Mars	41 32.8	13 17
Mer. Pass. 16 00.2		v −0.9	d 0.2	v 0.5	d 0.6	v 2.4	d 0.0	v 2.5	d 0.0	Jupiter	169 56.3	4 42
										Saturn	170 03.0	4 42

G.M.T.	SUN G.H.A.	SUN Dec.	MOON G.H.A.	v	MOON Dec.	d	H.P.
19 00	177 20.2	S20 23.7	15 21.9	6.4	N20 21.4	0.4	58.5
01	192 20.0	23.2	29 47.3	6.5	20 21.0	0.4	58.4
02	207 19.8	22.7	44 12.8	6.6	20 20.6	0.7	58.4
03	222 19.6 ··	22.1	58 38.4	6.5	20 19.9	0.7	58.4
04	237 19.4	21.6	73 03.9	6.6	20 19.2	0.9	58.4
05	252 19.2	21.1	87 29.5	6.6	20 18.3	1.0	58.4
06	267 19.0	S20 20.6	101 55.1	6.6	N20 17.3	1.1	58.3
07	282 18.8	20.0	116 20.7	6.7	20 16.2	1.3	58.3
M 08	297 18.6	19.5	130 46.4	6.7	20 14.9	1.4	58.3
O 09	312 18.5 ··	19.0	145 12.1	6.8	20 13.5	1.5	58.3
N 10	327 18.3	18.5	159 37.9	6.8	20 12.0	1.7	58.3
D 11	342 18.1	17.9	174 03.7	6.8	20 10.3	1.7	58.2
A 12	357 17.9	S20 17.4	188 29.5	6.8	N20 08.6	1.9	58.2
Y 13	12 17.7	16.9	202 55.3	7.0	20 06.7	2.0	58.2
14	27 17.5	16.3	217 21.3	6.9	20 04.7	2.2	58.2
15	42 17.3 ··	15.8	231 47.2	7.0	20 02.5	2.2	58.2
16	57 17.1	15.3	246 13.2	7.0	20 00.3	2.4	58.1
17	72 16.9	14.7	260 39.2	7.1	19 57.9	2.5	58.1
18	87 16.8	S20 14.2	275 05.3	7.2	N19 55.4	2.6	58.1
19	102 16.6	13.7	289 31.5	7.1	19 52.8	2.8	58.1
20	117 16.4	13.1	303 57.6	7.3	19 50.0	2.9	58.0
21	132 16.2 ··	12.6	318 23.9	7.3	19 47.1	3.0	58.0
22	147 16.0	12.1	332 50.2	7.3	19 44.1	3.1	58.0
23	162 15.8	11.5	347 16.5	7.4	19 41.0	3.2	58.0
20 00	177 15.6	S20 11.0	1 42.9	7.4	N19 37.8	3.3	57.9
01	192 15.5	10.5	16 09.3	7.5	19 34.5	3.5	57.9
02	207 15.3	09.9	30 35.8	7.6	19 31.0	3.5	57.9
03	222 15.1 ··	09.4	45 02.4	7.6	19 27.5	3.7	57.9
04	237 14.9	08.9	59 29.0	7.6	19 23.8	3.8	57.9
05	252 14.7	08.3	73 55.6	7.7	19 20.0	3.9	57.8
06	267 14.5	S20 07.8	88 22.3	7.8	N19 16.1	4.1	57.8
07	282 14.4	07.2	102 49.1	7.9	19 12.0	4.1	57.8
T 08	297 14.2	06.7	117 16.0	7.9	19 07.9	4.3	57.8
U 09	312 14.0 ··	06.1	131 42.9	7.9	19 03.6	4.3	57.7
E 10	327 13.8	05.6	146 09.8	8.0	18 59.3	4.5	57.7
S 11	342 13.6	05.1	160 36.8	8.1	18 54.8	4.5	57.7
D 12	357 13.5	S20 04.5	175 03.9	8.2	N18 50.3	4.7	57.7
A 13	12 13.3	04.0	189 31.1	8.2	18 45.6	4.8	57.6
Y 14	27 13.1	03.4	203 58.3	8.3	18 40.8	4.9	57.6
15	42 12.9 ··	02.9	218 25.6	8.3	18 35.9	5.0	57.6
16	57 12.7	02.3	232 52.9	8.4	18 30.9	5.1	57.6
17	72 12.6	01.8	247 20.3	8.5	18 25.8	5.2	57.5
18	87 12.4	S20 01.2	261 47.8	8.6	N18 20.6	5.3	57.5
19	102 12.2	00.7	276 15.4	8.6	18 15.3	5.4	57.5
20	117 12.0	20 00.1	290 43.0	8.7	18 09.9	5.5	57.4
21	132 11.8	19 59.6	305 10.7	8.7	18 04.4	5.6	57.4
22	147 11.7	59.0	319 38.4	8.8	17 58.8	5.7	57.4
23	162 11.5	58.5	334 06.2	8.9	17 53.1	5.8	57.4
21 00	177 11.3	S19 57.9	348 34.1	9.0	N17 47.3	5.9	57.3
01	192 11.1	57.4	3 02.1	9.0	17 41.4	5.9	57.3
02	207 11.0	56.8	17 30.1	9.1	17 35.5	6.1	57.3
03	222 10.8 ··	56.3	31 58.2	9.2	17 29.4	6.2	57.3
04	237 10.6	55.7	46 26.4	9.3	17 23.2	6.2	57.2
05	252 10.4	55.2	60 54.7	9.3	17 17.0	6.4	57.2
06	267 10.3	S19 54.6	75 23.0	9.4	N17 10.6	6.4	57.2
07	282 10.1	54.1	89 51.4	9.4	17 04.2	6.6	57.2
W 08	297 09.9	53.5	104 19.8	9.6	16 57.6	6.6	57.1
E 09	312 09.7 ··	52.9	118 48.4	9.6	16 51.0	6.7	57.1
D 10	327 09.6	52.4	133 17.0	9.7	16 44.3	6.8	57.1
N 11	342 09.4	51.8	147 45.7	9.7	16 37.5	6.8	57.0
E 12	357 09.2	S19 51.3	162 14.4	9.9	N16 30.7	7.0	57.0
S 13	12 09.0	50.7	176 43.3	9.9	16 23.7	7.0	57.0
D 14	27 08.9	50.1	191 12.2	9.9	16 16.7	7.1	57.0
A 15	42 08.7 ··	49.6	205 41.1	10.1	16 09.6	7.2	56.9
Y 16	57 08.5	49.0	220 10.2	10.1	16 02.4	7.3	56.9
17	72 08.4	48.5	234 39.3	10.2	15 55.1	7.3	56.9
18	87 08.2	S19 47.9	249 08.5	10.3	N15 47.8	7.5	56.9
19	102 08.0	47.3	263 37.8	10.4	15 40.3	7.5	56.8
20	117 07.8	46.8	278 07.2	10.4	15 32.8	7.5	56.8
21	132 07.7 ··	46.2	292 36.6	10.5	15 25.3	7.7	56.8
22	147 07.5	45.6	307 06.1	10.6	15 17.6	7.7	56.7
23	162 07.3	45.1	321 35.7	10.6	15 09.9	7.8	56.7
	S.D. 16.3	d 0.5	S.D. 15.9		15.7		15.5

Lat.	Twilight Naut.	Twilight Civil	Sunrise	Moonrise 19	20	21	22
N 72	07 48	09 31	■	□	□	15 09	17 18
N 70	07 35	09 02	11 05	□	13 55	15 53	17 41
68	07 25	08 41	10 10	13 13	14 42	16 21	17 59
66	07 16	08 24	09 37	13 52	15 13	16 43	18 14
64	07 08	08 10	09 14	14 19	15 35	17 00	18 26
62	07 01	07 58	08 55	14 40	15 53	17 14	18 36
60	06 55	07 48	08 39	14 58	16 08	17 25	18 44
N 58	06 50	07 39	08 26	15 12	16 21	17 36	18 52
56	06 45	07 32	08 15	15 24	16 32	17 44	18 58
54	06 40	07 24	08 05	15 35	16 42	17 52	19 04
52	06 36	07 18	07 56	15 44	16 50	17 59	19 09
50	06 32	07 12	07 48	15 53	16 58	18 06	19 14
45	06 23	06 59	07 32	16 11	17 14	18 19	19 24
N 40	06 15	06 48	07 18	16 26	17 28	18 30	19 33
35	06 08	06 39	07 06	16 38	17 39	18 40	19 40
30	06 01	06 30	06 56	16 49	17 49	18 48	19 46
20	05 48	06 14	06 38	17 08	18 06	19 03	19 57
N 10	05 34	06 00	06 22	17 24	18 21	19 15	20 07
0	05 20	05 45	06 07	17 39	18 35	19 27	20 16
S 10	05 04	05 30	05 53	17 55	18 48	19 39	20 25
20	04 44	05 13	05 37	18 11	19 03	19 51	20 35
30	04 20	04 51	05 18	18 30	19 20	20 05	20 46
35	04 04	04 39	05 07	18 41	19 30	20 13	20 52
40	03 44	04 24	04 54	18 53	19 41	20 23	20 59
45	03 20	04 05	04 40	19 08	19 54	20 34	21 07
S 50	02 45	03 40	04 21	19 26	20 10	20 47	21 17
52	02 27	03 29	04 12	19 34	20 18	20 53	21 22
54	02 03	03 15	04 03	19 44	20 26	21 00	21 27
56	01 30	02 59	03 52	19 55	20 36	21 07	21 32
58	////	02 39	03 39	20 07	20 46	21 16	21 38
S 60	////	02 14	03 24	20 21	20 58	21 25	21 45

Lat.	Sunset	Twilight Civil	Naut.	Moonset 19	20	21	22
N 72	■	14 52	16 35	□	□	11 31	11 06
N 70	13 18	15 21	16 48	□	10 54	10 47	10 41
68	14 13	15 42	16 59	09 40	10 06	10 17	10 22
66	14 45	15 59	17 07	09 00	09 35	09 55	10 07
64	15 09	16 13	17 15	08 32	09 12	09 37	09 54
62	15 28	16 24	17 22	08 11	08 54	09 23	09 43
60	15 43	16 35	17 28	07 54	08 38	09 10	09 34
N 58	15 56	16 43	17 33	07 40	08 25	09 00	09 26
56	16 08	16 51	17 38	07 27	08 14	08 50	09 19
54	16 18	16 58	17 42	07 16	08 04	08 42	09 12
52	16 26	17 05	17 47	07 07	07 55	08 34	09 06
50	16 34	17 11	17 51	06 58	07 47	08 28	09 01
45	16 51	17 23	17 59	06 40	07 30	08 13	08 50
N 40	17 05	17 34	18 07	06 25	07 16	08 01	08 40
35	17 16	17 44	18 15	06 12	07 05	07 51	08 32
30	17 27	17 52	18 22	06 01	06 54	07 42	08 25
20	17 44	18 08	18 35	05 42	06 36	07 27	08 12
N 10	18 00	18 22	18 48	05 25	06 21	07 13	08 01
0	18 15	18 37	19 02	05 10	06 06	07 00	07 51
S 10	18 30	18 52	19 18	04 54	05 51	06 47	07 40
20	18 45	19 09	19 38	04 38	05 36	06 33	07 29
30	19 04	19 30	20 02	04 18	05 18	06 17	07 16
35	19 15	19 43	20 18	04 07	05 07	06 08	07 09
40	19 27	19 58	20 37	03 54	04 55	05 58	07 00
45	19 42	20 17	21 02	03 39	04 40	05 45	06 50
S 50	20 00	20 41	21 35	03 20	04 23	05 30	06 38
52	20 09	20 52	21 53	03 12	04 15	05 23	06 33
54	20 18	21 06	22 16	03 02	04 05	05 15	06 26
56	20 29	21 22	22 48	02 50	03 55	05 06	06 19
58	20 42	21 41	////	02 38	03 43	04 56	06 11
S 60	20 57	22 05	////	02 23	03 29	04 44	06 02

Day	SUN Eqn. of Time 00h	12h	Mer. Pass.	MOON Mer. Pass. Upper	Lower	Age	Phase
	m s	m s	h m	h m	h m	d	
19	10 39	10 48	12 11	23 53	11 25	13	
20	10 57	11 06	12 11	24 47	12 20	14	○
21	11 14	11 23	12 11	00 47	13 14	15	

G.M.T.	ARIES G.H.A.	VENUS −3.3 G.H.A.	Dec.	MARS +1.4 G.H.A.	Dec.	JUPITER −1.8 G.H.A.	Dec.	SATURN +0.9 G.H.A.	Dec.	STARS Name	S.H.A.	Dec.
22 00	121 15.3	196 41.2	S22 48.3	161 04.7	S16 40.1	291 10.1	S 2 49.2	291 18.6	S 1 36.9	Acamar	315 37.0	S40 23.2
01	136 17.8	211 40.2	48.1	176 05.2	39.5	306 12.6	49.2	306 21.1	36.9	Achernar	335 45.2	S57 20.4
02	151 20.3	226 39.3	47.8	191 05.7	38.9	321 15.0	49.2	321 23.6	36.9	Acrux	173 36.6	S62 59.3
03	166 22.7	241 38.4 ··	47.6	206 06.2 ··	38.3	336 17.5 ··	49.2	336 26.0 ··	36.9	Adhara	255 31.5	S28 56.9
04	181 25.2	256 37.5	47.4	221 06.7	37.7	351 19.9	49.2	351 28.5	36.8	Aldebaran	291 17.5	N16 28.2
05	196 27.7	271 36.5	47.2	236 07.2	37.1	6 22.3	49.2	6 31.0	36.8			
06	211 30.1	286 35.6	S22 47.0	251 07.8	S16 36.5	21 24.8	S 2 49.2	21 33.5	S 1 36.8	Alioth	166 42.1	N56 03.5
07	226 32.6	301 34.7	46.8	266 08.3	35.8	36 27.2	49.2	36 35.9	36.8	Alkaid	153 18.3	N49 24.3
T 08	241 35.1	316 33.8	46.6	281 08.8	35.2	51 29.7	49.2	51 38.4	36.8	Al Na'ir	28 15.1	S47 03.4
H 09	256 37.5	331 32.8 ··	46.4	296 09.3 ··	34.6	66 32.1 ··	49.2	66 40.9 ··	36.7	Alnilam	276 11.1	S 1 13.0
U 10	271 40.0	346 31.9	46.1	311 09.8	34.0	81 34.5	49.2	81 43.4	36.7	Alphard	218 20.0	S 8 34.6
R 11	286 42.5	1 31.0	45.9	326 10.3	33.4	96 37.0	49.2	96 45.8	36.7			
S 12	301 44.9	16 30.1	S22 45.7	341 10.8	S16 32.8	111 39.4	S 2 49.2	111 48.3	S 1 36.7	Alphecca	126 32.1	N26 46.6
D 13	316 47.4	31 29.2	45.5	356 11.3	32.2	126 41.9	49.2	126 50.8	36.7	Alpheratz	358 09.2	N28 59.2
A 14	331 49.8	46 28.2	45.3	11 11.8	31.5	141 44.3	49.2	141 53.3	36.7	Altair	62 32.6	N 8 49.0
Y 15	346 52.3	61 27.3 ··	45.0	26 12.3 ··	30.9	156 46.8 ··	49.2	156 55.7 ··	36.6	Ankaa	353 40.2	S42 24.9
16	1 54.8	76 26.4	44.8	41 12.8	30.3	171 49.2	49.2	171 58.2	36.6	Antares	112 56.8	S26 23.3
17	16 57.2	91 25.5	44.6	56 13.3	29.7	186 51.7	49.2	187 00.7	36.6			
18	31 59.7	106 24.5	S22 44.3	71 13.8	S16 29.1	201 54.1	S 2 49.2	202 03.2	S 1 36.6	Arcturus	146 18.3	N19 16.8
19	47 02.2	121 23.6	44.1	86 14.3	28.5	216 56.5	49.2	217 05.6	36.6	Atria	108 21.2	S68 59.4
20	62 04.6	136 22.7	43.9	101 14.8	27.9	231 59.0	49.2	232 08.1	36.6	Avior	234 27.4	S59 26.9
21	77 07.1	151 21.8 ··	43.7	116 15.3 ··	27.2	247 01.4 ··	49.2	247 10.6 ··	36.5	Bellatrix	278 58.2	N 6 19.8
22	92 09.6	166 20.9	43.4	131 15.8	26.6	262 03.9	49.2	262 13.1	36.5	Betelgeuse	271 27.7	N 7 24.1
23	107 12.0	181 19.9	43.2	146 16.3	26.0	277 06.3	49.2	277 15.6	36.5			
23 00	122 14.5	196 19.0	S22 43.0	161 16.9	S16 25.4	292 08.8	S 2 49.1	292 18.0	S 1 36.5	Canopus	264 06.6	S52 41.3
01	137 17.0	211 18.1	42.7	176 17.4	24.8	307 11.2	49.1	307 20.5	36.5	Capella	281 10.6	N45 58.8
02	152 19.4	226 17.2	42.5	191 17.9	24.1	322 13.7	49.1	322 23.0	36.4	Deneb	49 48.7	N45 12.7
03	167 21.9	241 16.3 ··	42.2	206 18.4 ··	23.5	337 16.1 ··	49.1	337 25.5 ··	36.4	Denebola	182 58.6	N14 40.6
04	182 24.3	256 15.3	42.0	221 18.9	22.9	352 18.6	49.1	352 27.9	36.4	Diphda	349 20.8	S18 05.7
05	197 26.8	271 14.4	41.8	236 19.4	22.3	7 21.0	49.1	7 30.4	36.4			
06	212 29.3	286 13.5	S22 41.5	251 19.9	S16 21.7	22 23.5	S 2 49.1	22 32.9	S 1 36.4	Dubhe	194 21.4	N61 51.0
07	227 31.7	301 12.6	41.3	266 20.4	21.1	37 25.9	49.1	37 35.4	36.3	Elnath	278 43.5	N28 35.5
08	242 34.2	316 11.7	41.0	281 20.9	20.4	52 28.4	49.1	52 37.9	36.3	Eltanin	90 58.1	N51 29.4
F 09	257 36.7	331 10.7 ··	40.8	296 21.4 ··	19.8	67 30.8 ··	49.1	67 40.3 ··	36.3	Enif	34 11.6	N 9 47.2
R 10	272 39.1	346 09.8	40.5	311 21.9	19.2	82 33.3	49.1	82 42.8	36.3	Fomalhaut	15 51.4	S29 43.6
I 11	287 41.6	1 08.9	40.3	326 22.4	18.6	97 35.7	49.1	97 45.3	36.3			
D 12	302 44.1	16 08.0	S22 40.0	341 23.0	S16 17.9	112 38.2	S 2 49.1	112 47.8	S 1 36.3	Gacrux	172 28.2	S57 00.1
A 13	317 46.5	31 07.1	39.8	356 23.5	17.3	127 40.6	49.1	127 50.3	36.2	Gienah	176 17.5	S17 26.1
Y 14	332 49.0	46 06.2	39.5	11 24.0	16.7	142 43.1	49.1	142 52.7	36.2	Hadar	149 23.0	S60 16.6
15	347 51.4	61 05.2 ··	39.3	26 24.5 ··	16.1	157 45.5 ··	49.1	157 55.2 ··	36.2	Hamal	328 28.6	N23 22.4
16	2 53.9	76 04.3	39.0	41 25.0	15.5	172 48.0	49.1	172 57.7	36.2	Kaus Aust.	84 16.9	S34 23.6
17	17 56.4	91 03.4	38.8	56 25.5	14.8	187 50.4	49.0	188 00.2	36.2			
18	32 58.8	106 02.5	S22 38.5	71 26.0	S16 14.2	202 52.9	S 2 49.0	203 02.7	S 1 36.1	Kochab	137 19.3	N74 13.8
19	48 01.3	121 01.6	38.3	86 26.5	13.6	217 55.3	49.0	218 05.1	36.1	Markab	14 03.2	N15 06.1
20	63 03.8	136 00.7	38.0	101 27.0	13.0	232 57.8	49.0	233 07.6	36.1	Menkar	314 40.8	N 4 00.8
21	78 06.2	150 59.7 ··	37.7	116 27.5 ··	12.3	248 00.2 ··	49.0	248 10.1 ··	36.1	Menkent	148 36.7	S36 16.4
22	93 08.7	165 58.8	37.5	131 28.1	11.7	263 02.7	49.0	263 12.6	36.1	Miaplacidus	221 43.9	S69 38.3
23	108 11.2	180 57.9	37.2	146 28.6	11.1	278 05.1	49.0	278 15.1	36.0			
24 00	123 13.6	195 57.0	S22 37.0	161 29.1	S16 10.5	293 07.6	S 2 49.0	293 17.5	S 1 36.0	Mirfak	309 15.6	N49 47.8
01	138 16.1	210 56.1	36.7	176 29.6	09.8	308 10.0	49.0	308 20.0	36.0	Nunki	76 29.2	S26 19.2
02	153 18.6	225 55.2	36.4	191 30.1	09.2	323 12.5	49.0	323 22.5	36.0	Peacock	53 58.6	S56 47.8
03	168 21.0	240 54.2 ··	36.2	206 30.6 ··	08.6	338 14.9 ··	49.0	338 25.0 ··	36.0	Pollux	243 57.5	N28 04.3
04	183 23.5	255 53.3	35.9	221 31.1	08.0	353 17.4	49.0	353 27.5	35.9	Procyon	245 25.2	N 5 16.3
05	198 25.9	270 52.4	35.6	236 31.6	07.3	8 19.9	49.0	8 29.9	35.9			
06	213 28.4	285 51.5	S22 35.4	251 32.2	S16 06.7	23 22.3	S 2 48.9	23 32.4	S 1 35.9	Rasalhague	96 29.6	N12 34.4
07	228 30.9	300 50.6	35.1	266 32.7	06.1	38 24.8	48.9	38 34.9	35.9	Regulus	208 09.5	N12 03.5
S 08	243 33.3	315 49.7	34.8	281 33.2	05.5	53 27.2	48.9	53 37.4	35.8	Rigel	281 35.5	S 8 13.6
A 09	258 35.8	330 48.8 ··	34.5	296 33.7 ··	04.8	68 29.7 ··	48.9	68 39.9 ··	35.8	Rigil Kent.	140 25.6	S60 45.0
T 10	273 38.3	345 47.8	34.3	311 34.2	04.2	83 32.1	48.9	83 42.4	35.8	Sabik	102 41.1	S15 42.0
U 11	288 40.7	0 46.9	34.0	326 34.7	03.6	98 34.6	48.9	98 44.8	35.8			
R 12	303 43.2	15 46.0	S22 33.7	341 35.2	S16 03.0	113 37.0	S 2 48.9	113 47.3	S 1 35.8	Schedar	350 08.9	N56 26.1
D 13	318 45.7	30 45.1	33.4	356 35.7	02.3	128 39.5	48.9	128 49.8	35.7	Shaula	96 55.8	S37 05.3
A 14	333 48.1	45 44.2	33.1	11 36.3	01.7	143 42.0	48.9	143 52.3	35.7	Sirius	258 55.2	S16 41.6
Y 15	348 50.6	60 43.3 ··	32.9	26 36.8 ··	01.1	158 44.4 ··	48.9	158 54.8 ··	35.7	Spica	158 57.2	S11 03.7
16	3 53.1	75 42.4	32.6	41 37.3	16 00.4	173 46.9	48.8	173 57.3	35.7	Suhail	223 10.1	S43 21.3
17	18 55.5	90 41.5	32.3	56 37.8	15 59.8	188 49.3	48.8	188 59.8	35.7			
18	33 58.0	105 40.6	S22 32.0	71 38.3	S15 59.2	203 51.8	S 2 48.8	204 02.2	S 1 35.6	Vega	80 56.1	N38 45.9
19	49 00.4	120 39.6	31.7	86 38.8	58.5	218 54.3	48.8	219 04.7	35.6	Zuben'ubi	137 32.8	S15 57.7
20	64 02.9	135 38.7	31.4	101 39.4	57.9	233 56.7	48.8	234 07.2	35.6		S.H.A.	Mer. Pass.
21	79 05.4	150 37.8 ··	31.1	116 39.9 ··	57.3	248 59.2 ··	48.8	249 09.7 ··	35.6		° ′	h m
22	94 07.8	165 36.9	30.9	131 40.4	56.7	264 01.6	48.8	264 12.2	35.6	Venus	74 04.5	10 55
23	109 10.3	180 36.0	30.6	146 40.9	56.0	279 04.1	48.8	279 14.7	35.5	Mars	39 02.4	13 14
Mer. Pass. 15 48.4		v −0.9	d 0.2	v 0.5	d 0.6	v 2.5	d 0.0	v 2.5	d 0.0	Jupiter	169 54.3	4 31
										Saturn	170 03.5	4 30

G.M.T.	SUN G.H.A.	Dec.	MOON G.H.A.	v	Dec.	d	H.P.	Lat.	Twilight Naut.	Civil	Sunrise	Moonrise 22	23	24	25
	° '	° '	° '	'	° '	'	'	°	h m	h m	h m	h m	h m	h m	h m
								N 72	07 39	09 18	■	17 18	19 10	20 54	22 34
22 00	177 07.2	S19 44.5	336 05.3	10.7	N15 02.1	7.9	56.7	N 70	07 28	08 52	10 41	17 41	19 23	21 00	22 33
01	192 07.0	43.9	350 35.0	10.8	14 54.2	7.9	56.7	68	07 18	08 33	09 57	17 59	19 34	21 05	22 33
02	207 06.8	43.4	5 04.8	10.9	14 46.3	8.0	56.6	66	07 10	08 17	09 28	18 14	19 43	21 09	22 32
03	222 06.7	·· 42.8	19 34.7	10.9	14 38.3	8.1	56.6	64	07 03	08 04	09 06	18 26	19 50	21 12	22 32
04	237 06.5	42.2	34 04.6	11.1	14 30.2	8.1	56.6	62	06 57	07 53	08 48	18 36	19 56	21 15	22 32
05	252 06.3	41.6	48 34.7	11.0	14 22.1	8.2	56.5	60	06 51	07 44	08 34	18 44	20 02	21 18	22 32
06	267 06.2	S19 41.1	63 04.7	11.2	N14 13.9	8.3	56.5	N 58	06 46	07 35	08 21	18 52	20 07	21 20	22 31
07	282 06.0	40.5	77 34.9	11.2	14 05.6	8.3	56.5	56	06 42	07 28	08 11	18 58	20 11	21 22	22 31
T 08	297 05.8	39.9	92 05.1	11.3	13 57.3	8.4	56.5	54	06 37	07 21	08 01	19 04	20 15	21 24	22 31
H 09	312 05.7	·· 39.4	106 35.4	11.4	13 48.9	8.4	56.4	52	06 33	07 15	07 53	19 09	20 18	21 25	22 31
U 10	327 05.5	38.8	121 05.8	11.5	13 40.5	8.5	56.4	50	06 30	07 09	07 45	19 14	20 21	21 27	22 31
R 11	342 05.3	38.2	135 36.3	11.5	13 32.0	8.6	56.4	45	06 21	06 57	07 29	19 24	20 28	21 30	22 31
S 12	357 05.2	S19 37.6	150 06.8	11.6	N13 23.4	8.6	56.4	N 40	06 14	06 47	07 16	19 33	20 34	21 33	22 30
D 13	12 05.0	37.1	164 37.4	11.7	13 14.8	8.7	56.3	35	06 07	06 38	07 05	19 40	20 38	21 35	22 30
A 14	27 04.8	36.5	179 08.1	11.7	13 06.1	8.7	56.3	30	06 00	06 29	06 55	19 46	20 43	21 37	22 30
Y 15	42 04.7	·· 35.9	193 38.8	11.8	12 57.4	8.8	56.3	20	05 47	06 14	06 38	19 57	20 50	21 40	22 30
16	57 04.5	35.3	208 09.6	11.9	12 48.6	8.9	56.2	N 10	05 35	06 00	06 23	20 07	20 56	21 44	22 29
17	72 04.3	34.8	222 40.5	11.9	12 39.7	8.9	56.2	0	05 21	05 46	06 08	20 16	21 02	21 47	22 29
18	87 04.2	S19 34.2	237 11.4	12.0	N12 30.8	8.9	56.2	S 10	05 05	05 32	05 54	20 25	21 08	21 49	22 29
19	102 04.0	33.6	251 42.4	12.1	12 21.9	9.0	56.2	20	04 47	05 15	05 38	20 35	21 15	21 53	22 29
20	117 03.8	33.0	266 13.5	12.2	12 12.9	9.1	56.1	30	04 23	04 54	05 21	20 46	21 22	21 56	22 29
21	132 03.7	·· 32.4	280 44.7	12.2	12 03.8	9.0	56.1	35	04 07	04 42	05 10	20 52	21 26	21 58	22 28
22	147 03.5	31.9	295 15.9	12.3	11 54.8	9.2	56.1	40	03 49	04 27	04 58	20 59	21 31	22 00	22 28
23	162 03.4	31.3	309 47.2	12.3	11 45.6	9.2	56.1	45	03 25	04 09	04 44	21 07	21 37	22 03	22 28
23 00	177 03.2	S19 30.7	324 18.5	12.4	N11 36.4	9.2	56.0	S 50	02 52	03 46	04 26	21 17	21 43	22 06	22 28
01	192 03.0	30.1	338 49.9	12.5	11 27.2	9.3	56.0	52	02 35	03 35	04 18	21 22	21 46	22 08	22 28
02	207 02.9	29.5	353 21.4	12.5	11 17.9	9.3	56.0	54	02 13	03 22	04 08	21 27	21 49	22 09	22 28
03	222 02.7	·· 28.9	7 53.0	12.6	11 08.6	9.4	56.0	56	01 45	03 07	03 58	21 32	21 53	22 11	22 28
04	237 02.6	28.3	22 24.6	12.6	10 59.2	9.4	55.9	58	00 54	02 48	03 46	21 38	21 57	22 13	22 28
05	252 02.4	27.8	36 56.2	12.8	10 49.8	9.5	55.9	S 60	////	02 25	03 32	21 45	22 02	22 15	22 28

G.M.T.	SUN G.H.A.	Dec.	MOON G.H.A.	v	Dec.	d	H.P.	Lat.	Sunset	Twilight Civil	Naut.	Moonset 22	23	24	25
06	267 02.2	S19 27.2	51 28.0	12.8	N10 40.3	9.5	55.9								
07	282 02.1	26.6	65 59.8	12.9	10 30.8	9.5	55.8	Lat.	Sunset	Civil	Naut.	22	23	24	25
08	297 01.9	26.0	80 31.7	12.9	10 21.3	9.6	55.8								
F 09	312 01.8	·· 25.4	95 03.6	13.0	10 11.7	9.6	55.8	°	h m	h m	h m	h m	h m	h m	h m
R 10	327 01.6	24.8	109 35.6	13.0	10 02.1	9.6	55.8	N 72	■	15 07	16 46	11 06	10 51	10 40	10 29
I 11	342 01.5	24.2	124 07.6	13.1	9 52.5	9.7	55.7	N 70	13 43	15 32	16 57	10 41	10 36	10 32	10 27
D 12	357 01.3	S19 23.6	138 39.7	13.2	N 9 42.8	9.7	55.7	68	14 28	15 52	17 07	10 22	10 24	10 25	10 25
A 13	12 01.1	23.1	153 11.9	13.2	9 33.1	9.8	55.7	66	14 57	16 08	17 15	10 07	10 14	10 19	10 23
Y 14	27 01.0	22.5	167 44.1	13.3	9 23.3	9.7	55.7	64	15 19	16 21	17 22	09 54	10 06	10 15	10 22
15	42 00.8	·· 21.9	182 16.4	13.4	9 13.6	9.9	55.6	62	15 36	16 31	17 28	09 43	09 58	10 10	10 21
16	57 00.7	21.3	196 48.8	13.4	9 03.7	9.8	55.6	60	15 51	16 41	17 33	09 34	09 52	10 07	10 20
17	72 00.5	20.7	211 21.2	13.4	8 53.9	9.9	55.6	N 58	16 03	16 49	17 38	09 26	09 46	10 04	10 19
18	87 00.4	S19 20.1	225 53.6	13.5	N 8 44.0	9.9	55.6	56	16 14	16 57	17 43	09 19	09 41	10 01	10 18
19	102 00.2	19.5	240 26.1	13.6	8 34.1	9.9	55.5	54	16 23	17 03	17 47	09 12	09 37	09 58	10 17
20	117 00.1	18.9	254 58.7	13.6	8 24.2	10.0	55.5	52	16 31	17 09	17 51	09 06	09 33	09 56	10 17
21	131 59.9	·· 18.3	269 31.3	13.7	8 14.2	10.0	55.5	50	16 39	17 15	17 55	09 01	09 29	09 54	10 16
22	146 59.7	17.7	284 04.0	13.7	8 04.2	10.0	55.5	45	16 55	17 27	18 03	08 50	09 21	09 49	10 15
23	161 59.6	17.1	298 36.7	13.8	7 54.2	10.0	55.5								
24 00	176 59.4	S19 16.5	313 09.5	13.8	N 7 44.2	10.1	55.4	N 40	17 08	17 37	18 10	08 40	09 14	09 45	10 13
01	191 59.3	15.9	327 42.3	13.9	7 34.1	10.1	55.4	35	17 19	17 47	18 17	08 32	09 08	09 41	10 12
02	206 59.1	15.3	342 15.2	14.0	7 24.0	10.1	55.4	30	17 29	17 55	18 24	08 25	09 03	09 38	10 12
03	221 59.0	·· 14.7	356 48.2	13.9	7 13.9	10.1	55.4	20	17 46	18 10	18 37	08 12	08 54	09 33	10 10
04	236 58.8	14.1	11 21.1	14.1	7 03.8	10.2	55.3	N 10	18 01	18 24	18 49	08 01	08 46	09 28	10 09
05	251 58.7	13.5	25 54.2	14.1	6 53.6	10.2	55.3	0	18 16	18 37	19 03	07 51	08 39	09 24	10 07
06	266 58.5	S19 12.9	40 27.3	14.1	N 6 43.4	10.1	55.3	S 10	18 30	18 52	19 18	07 40	08 31	09 19	10 06
07	281 58.4	12.3	55 00.4	14.2	6 33.3	10.3	55.3	20	18 45	19 09	19 37	07 29	08 23	09 15	10 04
S 08	296 58.2	11.7	69 33.6	14.2	6 23.0	10.2	55.2	30	19 03	19 29	20 01	07 16	08 14	09 09	10 03
A 09	311 58.1	·· 11.1	84 06.8	14.2	6 12.8	10.2	55.2	35	19 13	19 41	20 16	07 09	08 08	09 06	10 02
T 10	326 57.9	10.5	98 40.0	14.3	6 02.6	10.3	55.2	40	19 25	19 56	20 34	07 00	08 02	09 02	10 01
U 11	341 57.8	09.9	113 13.3	14.4	5 52.3	10.3	55.2	45	19 39	20 14	20 58	06 50	07 55	08 58	09 59
R 12	356 57.6	S19 09.3	127 46.7	14.4	N 5 42.0	10.3	55.2	S 50	19 57	20 37	21 30	06 38	07 46	08 53	09 58
D 13	11 57.5	08.7	142 20.1	14.4	5 31.7	10.3	55.1	52	20 05	20 48	21 47	06 33	07 42	08 50	09 57
A 14	26 57.3	08.1	156 53.5	14.5	5 21.4	10.3	55.1	54	20 14	21 00	22 08	06 26	07 38	08 48	09 56
Y 15	41 57.2	·· 07.5	171 27.0	14.5	5 11.1	10.4	55.1	56	20 25	21 15	22 36	06 19	07 33	08 45	09 55
16	56 57.0	06.9	186 00.5	14.6	5 00.7	10.3	55.1	58	20 37	21 33	23 21	06 11	07 27	08 42	09 54
17	71 56.9	06.3	200 34.1	14.6	4 50.4	10.5	55.0	S 60	20 50	21 56	////	06 02	07 21	08 38	09 53
18	86 56.7	S19 05.7	215 07.7	14.6	N 4 40.0	10.4	55.0								
19	101 56.6	05.0	229 41.3	14.7	4 29.6	10.4	55.0			SUN			MOON		
20	116 56.4	04.4	244 15.0	14.7	4 19.2	10.4	55.0	Day	Eqn. of Time 00ʰ	12ʰ	Mer. Pass.	Mer. Pass. Upper	Lower	Age	Phase
21	131 56.3	·· 03.8	258 48.7	14.7	4 08.8	10.5	55.0								
22	146 56.2	03.2	273 22.4	14.8	3 58.4	10.4	54.9		m s	m s	h m	h m	h m	d	
23	161 56.0	02.6	287 56.2	14.8	3 48.0	10.4	54.9	22	11 31	11 39	12 12	01 39	14 04	16	
								23	11 47	11 55	12 12	02 27	14 51	17	
	S.D. 16.3	d 0.6	S.D. 15.4		15.2		15.0	24	12 02	12 09	12 12	03 13	15 35	18	◗

G.M.T.	ARIES G.H.A.	VENUS −3.3 G.H.A.	Dec.	MARS +1.4 G.H.A.	Dec.	JUPITER −1.8 G.H.A.	Dec.	SATURN +0.9 G.H.A.	Dec.	STARS Name	S.H.A.	Dec.
25 00	124 12.8	195 35.1	S22 30.3	161 41.4	S15 55.4	294 06.6	S 2 48.8	294 17.1	S 1 35.5	Acamar	315 37.0	S40 23.2
01	139 15.2	210 34.2	30.0	176 41.9	54.8	309 09.0	48.8	309 19.6	35.5	Achernar	335 45.2	S57 20.4
02	154 17.7	225 33.3	29.7	191 42.5	54.1	324 11.5	48.7	324 22.1	35.5	Acrux	173 36.6	S62 59.3
03	169 20.2	240 32.4	·· 29.4	206 43.0	·· 53.5	339 13.9	·· 48.7	339 24.6	·· 35.5	Adhara	255 31.6	S28 56.9
04	184 22.6	255 31.5	29.1	221 43.5	52.9	354 16.4	48.7	354 27.1	35.4	Aldebaran	291 17.5	N16 28.2
05	199 25.1	270 30.5	28.8	236 44.0	52.2	9 18.9	48.7	9 29.6	35.4			
06	214 27.5	285 29.6	S22 28.5	251 44.5	S15 51.6	24 21.3	S 2 48.7	24 32.1	S 1 35.4	Alioth	166 42.1	N56 03.5
07	229 30.0	300 28.7	28.2	266 45.0	51.0	39 23.8	48.7	39 34.5	35.4	Alkaid	153 18.3	N49 24.3
08	244 32.5	315 27.8	27.9	281 45.6	50.3	54 26.3	48.7	54 37.0	35.3	Al Na'ir	28 15.1	S47 03.4
S 09	259 34.9	330 26.9	·· 27.6	296 46.1	·· 49.7	69 28.7	·· 48.7	69 39.5	·· 35.3	Alnilam	276 11.2	S 1 13.0
U 10	274 37.4	345 26.0	27.3	311 46.6	49.1	84 31.2	48.6	84 42.0	35.3	Alphard	218 20.0	S 8 34.6
N 11	289 39.9	0 25.1	27.0	326 47.1	48.4	99 33.7	48.6	99 44.5	35.3			
D 12	304 42.3	15 24.2	S22 26.7	341 47.6	S15 47.8	114 36.1	S 2 48.6	114 47.0	S 1 35.2	Alphecca	126 32.0	N26 46.6
A 13	319 44.8	30 23.3	26.4	356 48.1	47.2	129 38.6	48.6	129 49.5	35.2	Alpheratz	358 09.2	N28 59.1
Y 14	334 47.3	45 22.4	26.1	11 48.7	46.5	144 41.0	48.6	144 52.0	35.2	Altair	62 32.6	N 8 49.0
15	349 49.7	60 21.5	·· 25.7	26 49.2	·· 45.9	159 43.5	·· 48.6	159 54.4	·· 35.2	Ankaa	353 40.2	S42 24.9
16	4 52.2	75 20.6	25.4	41 49.7	45.2	174 46.0	48.6	174 56.9	35.1	Antares	112 56.8	S26 23.3
17	19 54.7	90 19.7	25.1	56 50.2	44.6	189 48.4	48.6	189 59.4	35.1			
18	34 57.1	105 18.7	S22 24.8	71 50.7	S15 44.0	204 50.9	S 2 48.5	205 01.9	S 1 35.1	Arcturus	146 18.2	N19 16.8
19	49 59.6	120 17.8	24.5	86 51.3	43.3	219 53.4	48.5	220 04.4	35.1	Atria	108 21.1	S68 59.3
20	65 02.0	135 16.9	24.2	101 51.8	42.7	234 55.8	48.5	235 06.9	35.1	Avior	234 27.4	S59 27.0
21	80 04.5	150 16.0	·· 23.9	116 52.3	·· 42.1	249 58.3	·· 48.5	250 09.4	·· 35.0	Bellatrix	278 58.2	N 6 19.8
22	95 07.0	165 15.1	23.5	131 52.8	41.4	265 00.8	48.5	265 11.9	35.0	Betelgeuse	271 27.7	N 7 24.1
23	110 09.4	180 14.2	23.2	146 53.3	40.8	280 03.3	48.5	280 14.4	35.0			
26 00	125 11.9	195 13.3	S22 22.9	161 53.9	S15 40.1	295 05.7	S 2 48.5	295 16.9	S 1 35.0	Canopus	264 06.6	S52 41.4
01	140 14.4	210 12.4	22.6	176 54.4	39.5	310 08.2	48.4	310 19.3	34.9	Capella	281 10.6	N45 58.8
02	155 16.8	225 11.5	22.3	191 54.9	38.9	325 10.7	48.4	325 21.8	34.9	Deneb	49 48.7	N45 12.7
03	170 19.3	240 10.6	·· 21.9	206 55.4	·· 38.2	340 13.1	·· 48.4	340 24.3	·· 34.9	Denebola	182 58.6	N14 40.6
04	185 21.8	255 09.7	21.6	221 55.9	37.6	355 15.6	48.4	355 26.8	34.9	Diphda	349 20.8	S18 05.7
05	200 24.2	270 08.8	21.3	236 56.5	37.0	10 18.1	48.4	10 29.3	34.8			
06	215 26.7	285 07.9	S22 20.9	251 57.0	S15 36.3	25 20.5	S 2 48.4	25 31.8	S 1 34.8	Dubhe	194 21.3	N61 51.0
07	230 29.2	300 07.0	20.6	266 57.5	35.7	40 23.0	48.4	40 34.3	34.8	Elnath	278 43.5	N28 35.5
08	245 31.6	315 06.1	20.3	281 58.0	35.0	55 25.5	48.3	55 36.8	34.8	Eltanin	90 58.1	N51 29.3
M 09	260 34.1	330 05.2	·· 20.0	296 58.6	·· 34.4	70 28.0	·· 48.3	70 39.3	·· 34.7	Enif	34 11.6	N 9 47.2
O 10	275 36.5	345 04.3	19.6	311 59.1	33.8	85 30.4	48.3	85 41.8	34.7	Fomalhaut	15 51.4	S29 43.6
N 11	290 39.0	0 03.4	19.3	326 59.6	33.1	100 32.9	48.3	100 44.2	34.7			
D 12	305 41.5	15 02.5	S22 19.0	342 00.1	S15 32.5	115 35.4	S 2 48.3	115 46.7	S 1 34.7	Gacrux	172 28.2	S57 00.1
A 13	320 43.9	30 01.6	18.6	357 00.7	31.8	130 37.8	48.3	130 49.2	34.6	Gienah	176 17.5	S17 26.1
Y 14	335 46.4	45 00.7	18.3	12 01.2	31.2	145 40.3	48.3	145 51.7	34.6	Hadar	149 22.9	S60 16.6
15	350 48.9	59 59.8	·· 17.9	27 01.7	·· 30.5	160 42.8	·· 48.2	160 54.2	·· 34.6	Hamal	328 28.6	N23 22.3
16	5 51.3	74 58.9	17.6	42 02.2	29.9	175 45.3	48.2	175 56.7	34.6	Kaus Aust.	84 16.9	S34 23.6
17	20 53.8	89 58.0	17.3	57 02.7	29.3	190 47.7	48.2	190 59.2	34.6			
18	35 56.3	104 57.1	S22 16.9	72 03.3	S15 28.6	205 50.2	S 2 48.2	206 01.7	S 1 34.5	Kochab	137 19.3	N74 13.8
19	50 58.7	119 56.2	16.6	87 03.8	28.0	220 52.7	48.2	221 04.2	34.5	Markab	14 03.2	N15 06.1
20	66 01.2	134 55.3	16.2	102 04.3	27.3	235 55.2	48.2	236 06.7	34.5	Menkar	314 40.8	N 4 00.8
21	81 03.7	149 54.4	·· 15.9	117 04.8	·· 26.7	250 57.6	·· 48.1	251 09.2	·· 34.5	Menkent	148 36.7	S36 16.4
22	96 06.1	164 53.5	15.5	132 05.4	26.0	266 00.1	48.1	266 11.7	34.4	Miaplacidus	221 43.9	S69 38.3
23	111 08.6	179 52.6	15.2	147 05.9	25.4	281 02.6	48.1	281 14.2	34.4			
27 00	126 11.0	194 51.7	S22 14.8	162 06.4	S15 24.7	296 05.1	S 2 48.1	296 16.7	S 1 34.4	Mirfak	309 15.6	N49 47.8
01	141 13.5	209 50.8	14.5	177 06.9	24.1	311 07.5	48.1	311 19.1	34.3	Nunki	76 29.2	S26 19.2
02	156 16.0	224 49.9	14.1	192 07.5	23.5	326 10.0	48.0	326 21.6	34.3	Peacock	53 58.6	S56 47.8
03	171 18.4	239 49.0	·· 13.8	207 08.0	·· 22.8	341 12.5	·· 48.0	341 24.1	·· 34.3	Pollux	243 57.5	N28 04.3
04	186 20.9	254 48.1	13.4	222 08.5	22.2	356 15.0	48.0	356 26.6	34.3	Procyon	245 25.2	N 5 16.3
05	201 23.4	269 47.2	13.1	237 09.0	21.5	11 17.4	48.0	11 29.1	34.2			
06	216 25.8	284 46.3	S22 12.7	252 09.6	S15 20.9	26 19.9	S 2 48.0	26 31.6	S 1 34.2	Rasalhague	96 29.6	N12 34.4
07	231 28.3	299 45.4	12.4	267 10.1	20.2	41 22.4	48.0	41 34.1	34.2	Regulus	208 09.4	N12 03.5
T 08	246 30.8	314 44.5	12.0	282 10.6	19.6	56 24.9	47.9	56 36.6	34.2	Rigel	281 35.5	S 8 13.6
U 09	261 33.2	329 43.6	·· 11.6	297 11.2	·· 18.9	71 27.4	·· 47.9	71 39.1	·· 34.1	Rigil Kent.	140 25.5	S60 45.0
E 10	276 35.7	344 42.7	11.3	312 11.7	18.3	86 29.8	47.9	86 41.6	34.1	Sabik	102 41.1	S15 42.0
S 11	291 38.1	359 41.8	10.9	327 12.2	17.6	101 32.3	47.9	101 44.1	34.1			
D 12	306 40.6	14 41.0	S22 10.6	342 12.7	S15 17.0	116 34.8	S 2 47.9	116 46.6	S 1 34.0	Schedar	350 08.9	N56 26.1
A 13	321 43.1	29 40.1	10.2	357 13.3	16.3	131 37.3	47.8	131 49.1	34.0	Shaula	96 55.7	S37 05.3
Y 14	336 45.5	44 39.2	09.8	12 13.8	15.7	146 39.8	47.8	146 51.6	34.0	Sirius	258 55.2	S16 41.6
15	351 48.0	59 38.3	·· 09.5	27 14.3	·· 15.0	161 42.2	·· 47.8	161 54.1	·· 34.0	Spica	158 57.2	S11 03.7
16	6 50.5	74 37.4	09.1	42 14.9	14.4	176 44.7	47.8	176 56.6	34.0	Suhail	223 10.1	S43 21.4
17	21 52.9	89 36.5	08.7	57 15.4	13.7	191 47.2	47.8	191 59.1	33.9			
18	36 55.4	104 35.6	S22 08.3	72 15.9	S15 13.1	206 49.7	S 2 47.8	207 01.6	S 1 33.9	Vega	80 56.0	N38 45.9
19	51 57.9	119 34.7	08.0	87 16.4	12.4	221 52.2	47.7	222 04.1	33.9	Zuben'ubi	137 32.8	S15 57.7
20	67 00.3	134 33.8	07.6	102 17.0	11.8	236 54.6	47.7	237 06.6	33.9			
21	82 02.8	149 32.9	·· 07.2	117 17.5	·· 11.1	251 57.1	·· 47.7	252 09.1	·· 33.8		S.H.A.	Mer. Pass.
22	97 05.3	164 32.0	06.9	132 18.0	10.5	266 59.6	47.7	267 11.6	33.8	Venus	70 01.4	11 00
23	112 07.7	179 31.1	06.5	147 18.6	09.8	282 02.1	47.7	282 14.1	33.8	Mars	36 42.0	13 12
										Jupiter	169 53.8	4 19
Mer. Pass. 15 36.6		v −0.9	d 0.3	v 0.5	d 0.6	v 2.5	d 0.0	v 2.5	d 0.0	Saturn	170 04.9	4 18

G.M.T.	SUN G.H.A.	SUN Dec.	MOON G.H.A.	v	Dec.	d	H.P.
	° ′	° ′	° ′	′	° ′	′	′
25 00	176 55.9	S19 02.0	302 30.0	14.9	N 3 37.6	10.4	54.9
01	191 55.7	01.4	317 03.9	14.9	3 27.2	10.5	54.9
02	206 55.6	00.8	331 37.8	14.9	3 16.7	10.4	54.9
03	221 55.4	19 00.2	346 11.7	14.9	3 06.3	10.4	54.9
04	236 55.3	18 59.5	0 45.6	15.0	2 55.9	10.5	54.8
05	251 55.1	58.9	15 19.6	15.0	2 45.4	10.4	54.8
06	266 55.0	S18 58.3	29 53.6	15.0	N 2 35.0	10.5	54.8
07	281 54.9	57.7	44 27.6	15.1	2 24.5	10.4	54.8
08	296 54.7	57.1	59 01.7	15.1	2 14.1	10.5	54.8
S 09	311 54.6 ··	56.5	73 35.8	15.1	2 03.6	10.5	54.7
U 10	326 54.4	55.8	88 09.9	15.1	1 53.1	10.4	54.7
N 11	341 54.3	55.2	102 44.0	15.2	1 42.7	10.5	54.7
D 12	356 54.2	S18 54.6	117 18.2	15.1	N 1 32.2	10.4	54.7
A 13	11 54.0	54.0	131 52.3	15.3	1 21.8	10.5	54.7
Y 14	26 53.9	53.4	146 26.6	15.2	1 11.3	10.5	54.7
15	41 53.7 ··	52.7	161 00.8	15.2	1 00.8	10.4	54.6
16	56 53.6	52.1	175 35.0	15.3	0 50.4	10.5	54.6
17	71 53.5	51.5	190 09.3	15.3	0 39.9	10.4	54.6
18	86 53.3	S18 50.9	204 43.6	15.3	N 0 29.5	10.5	54.6
19	101 53.2	50.2	219 17.9	15.3	0 19.0	10.4	54.6
20	116 53.0	49.6	233 52.2	15.4	N 0 08.6	10.4	54.6
21	131 52.9 ··	49.0	248 26.6	15.3	S 0 01.8	10.4	54.6
22	146 52.8	48.4	263 00.9	15.4	0 12.2	10.5	54.5
23	161 52.6	47.7	277 35.3	15.4	0 22.7	10.4	54.5
26 00	176 52.5	S18 47.1	292 09.7	15.4	S 0 33.1	10.4	54.5
01	191 52.3	46.5	306 44.1	15.4	0 43.5	10.4	54.5
02	206 52.2	45.9	321 18.5	15.4	0 53.9	10.4	54.5
03	221 52.1 ··	45.2	335 52.9	15.5	1 04.3	10.3	54.5
04	236 51.9	44.6	350 27.4	15.4	1 14.6	10.4	54.5
05	251 51.8	44.0	5 01.8	15.5	1 25.0	10.4	54.5
06	266 51.7	S18 43.3	19 36.3	15.5	S 1 35.4	10.3	54.4
07	281 51.5	42.7	34 10.8	15.4	1 45.7	10.3	54.4
08	296 51.4	42.1	48 45.2	15.5	1 56.0	10.3	54.4
M 09	311 51.3 ··	41.5	63 19.7	15.5	2 06.3	10.4	54.4
O 10	326 51.1	40.8	77 54.2	15.5	2 16.7	10.2	54.4
N 11	341 51.0	40.2	92 28.7	15.5	2 26.9	10.3	54.4
D 12	356 50.9	S18 39.6	107 03.2	15.5	S 2 37.2	10.3	54.4
A 13	11 50.7	38.9	121 37.7	15.5	2 47.5	10.2	54.4
Y 14	26 50.6	38.3	136 12.2	15.5	2 57.7	10.3	54.4
15	41 50.5 ··	37.6	150 46.7	15.5	3 08.0	10.2	54.4
16	56 50.3	37.0	165 21.2	15.6	3 18.2	10.2	54.3
17	71 50.2	36.4	179 55.8	15.5	3 28.4	10.2	54.3
18	86 50.1	S18 35.7	194 30.3	15.5	S 3 38.6	10.1	54.3
19	101 50.0	35.1	209 04.8	15.5	3 48.7	10.2	54.3
20	116 49.8	34.5	223 39.3	15.5	3 58.9	10.1	54.3
21	131 49.7 ··	33.8	238 13.8	15.5	4 09.0	10.1	54.3
22	146 49.6	33.2	252 48.3	15.5	4 19.1	10.1	54.3
23	161 49.4	32.5	267 22.8	15.5	4 29.2	10.1	54.3
27 00	176 49.3	S18 31.9	281 57.3	15.5	S 4 39.3	10.0	54.3
01	191 49.2	31.3	296 31.8	15.5	4 49.3	10.0	54.3
02	206 49.0	30.6	311 06.3	15.4	4 59.3	10.0	54.3
03	221 48.9 ··	30.0	325 40.7	15.5	5 09.3	10.0	54.3
04	236 48.8	29.3	340 15.2	15.5	5 19.3	10.0	54.3
05	251 48.7	28.7	354 49.7	15.4	5 29.3	9.9	54.3
06	266 48.5	S18 28.0	9 24.1	15.4	S 5 39.2	9.9	54.3
07	281 48.4	27.4	23 58.5	15.5	5 49.1	9.9	54.2
08	296 48.3	26.8	38 33.0	15.4	5 59.0	9.9	54.2
T 09	311 48.2 ··	26.1	53 07.4	15.4	6 08.9	9.8	54.2
U 10	326 48.0	25.5	67 41.8	15.4	6 18.7	9.8	54.2
E 11	341 47.9	24.8	82 16.2	15.3	6 28.5	9.7	54.2
S 12	356 47.8	S18 24.2	96 50.5	15.4	S 6 38.3	9.7	54.2
D 13	11 47.7	23.5	111 24.9	15.3	6 48.0	9.7	54.2
A 14	26 47.5	22.9	125 59.2	15.4	6 57.7	9.7	54.2
Y 15	41 47.4 ··	22.2	140 33.6	15.3	7 07.4	9.7	54.2
16	56 47.3	21.6	155 07.9	15.3	7 17.1	9.6	54.2
17	71 47.2	20.9	169 42.2	15.2	7 26.7	9.6	54.2
18	86 47.0	S18 20.3	184 16.4	15.3	S 7 36.3	9.6	54.2
19	101 46.9	19.6	198 50.7	15.2	7 45.9	9.5	54.2
20	116 46.8	19.0	213 24.9	15.2	7 55.5	9.5	54.2
21	131 46.7 ··	18.3	227 59.1	15.2	8 05.0	9.4	54.2
22	146 46.6	17.7	242 33.3	15.2	8 14.4	9.5	54.2
23	161 46.4	17.0	257 07.5	15.1	8 23.9	9.4	54.2
	S.D. 16.3	d 0.6	S.D. 14.9		14.8		14.8

Lat.	Twilight Naut.	Twilight Civil	Sunrise	Moonrise 25	26	27	28
°	h m	h m	h m	h m	h m	h m	h m
N 72	07 30	09 05	11 40	22 34	24 12	00 12	01 52
N 70	07 20	08 42	10 21	22 33	24 05	00 05	01 38
68	07 11	08 24	09 44	22 33	24 00	00 00	01 27
66	07 04	08 10	09 17	22 32	23 55	25 17	01 17
64	06 57	07 58	08 57	22 32	23 51	25 10	01 10
62	06 52	07 47	08 41	22 32	23 48	25 03	01 03
60	06 47	07 38	08 28	22 32	23 45	24 57	00 57
N 58	06 42	07 31	08 16	22 31	23 42	24 52	00 52
56	06 38	07 24	08 06	22 31	23 40	24 48	00 48
54	06 34	07 17	07 57	22 31	23 38	24 44	00 44
52	06 30	07 11	07 49	22 31	23 36	24 40	00 40
50	06 27	07 06	07 42	22 31	23 34	24 37	00 37
45	06 19	06 55	07 26	22 31	23 30	24 30	00 30
N 40	06 12	06 45	07 14	22 30	23 27	24 24	00 24
35	06 06	06 36	07 03	22 30	23 24	24 19	00 19
30	05 59	06 28	06 54	22 30	23 22	24 14	00 14
20	05 47	06 14	06 37	22 30	23 18	24 06	00 06
N 10	05 35	06 01	06 23	22 29	23 14	24 00	00 00
0	05 22	05 47	06 09	22 29	23 11	23 53	24 37
S 10	05 07	05 33	05 55	22 29	23 08	23 47	24 28
20	04 49	05 17	05 40	22 29	23 04	23 41	24 18
30	04 26	04 57	05 23	22 29	23 01	23 33	24 07
35	04 11	04 45	05 13	22 28	22 58	23 29	24 01
40	03 53	04 31	05 02	22 28	22 56	23 24	23 54
45	03 30	04 14	04 48	22 28	22 53	23 18	23 46
S 50	02 59	03 52	04 31	22 28	22 49	23 12	23 36
52	02 43	03 41	04 23	22 28	22 48	23 09	23 32
54	02 24	03 29	04 14	22 28	22 46	23 05	23 27
56	01 58	03 15	04 04	22 28	22 44	23 02	23 21
58	01 19	02 58	03 53	22 28	22 42	22 58	23 15
S 60	////	02 37	03 40	22 28	22 40	22 53	23 08

Lat.	Sunset	Twilight Civil	Twilight Naut.	Moonset 25	26	27	28
°	h m	h m	h m	h m	h m	h m	h m
N 72	12 46	15 21	16 56	10 29	10 19	10 08	09 56
N 70	14 05	15 44	17 07	10 27	10 22	10 17	10 12
68	14 43	16 02	17 15	10 25	10 25	10 25	10 25
66	15 09	16 17	17 23	10 23	10 27	10 31	10 35
64	15 29	16 29	17 29	10 22	10 29	10 36	10 44
62	15 45	16 39	17 35	10 21	10 31	10 41	10 52
60	15 58	16 48	17 40	10 20	10 32	10 45	10 59
N 58	16 10	16 55	17 44	10 19	10 33	10 48	11 04
56	16 20	17 02	17 48	10 18	10 35	10 51	11 10
54	16 29	17 09	17 52	10 17	10 36	10 54	11 14
52	16 37	17 14	17 56	10 17	10 37	10 57	11 18
50	16 44	17 20	17 59	10 16	10 37	10 59	11 22
45	16 59	17 31	18 07	10 15	10 39	11 04	11 31
N 40	17 12	17 41	18 14	10 13	10 41	11 09	11 38
35	17 23	17 49	18 20	10 12	10 42	11 13	11 44
30	17 32	17 57	18 26	10 12	10 44	11 16	11 49
20	17 48	18 11	18 38	10 10	10 46	11 22	11 58
N 10	18 03	18 25	18 50	10 09	10 48	11 27	12 06
0	18 16	18 38	19 03	10 07	10 49	11 31	12 14
S 10	18 30	18 52	19 18	10 06	10 51	11 36	12 22
20	18 45	19 08	19 36	10 04	10 53	11 41	12 30
30	19 02	19 28	19 59	10 03	10 55	11 47	12 39
35	19 12	19 40	20 13	10 02	10 56	11 51	12 45
40	19 24	19 54	20 31	10 01	10 58	11 54	12 51
45	19 37	20 11	20 54	09 59	10 59	11 59	12 58
S 50	19 53	20 32	21 24	09 58	11 01	12 04	13 07
52	20 01	20 43	21 40	09 57	11 02	12 07	13 11
54	20 10	20 55	21 59	09 56	11 03	12 09	13 15
56	20 19	21 09	22 24	09 55	11 04	12 12	13 20
58	20 31	21 25	23 00	09 54	11 05	12 16	13 26
S 60	20 44	21 46	////	09 53	11 07	12 19	13 32

	SUN			MOON			
Day	Eqn. of Time 00ʰ	12ʰ	Mer. Pass.	Mer. Pass. Upper	Lower	Age	Phase
	m s	m s	h m	h m	h m	d	
25	12 16	12 23	12 12	03 57	16 18	19	
26	12 30	12 36	12 13	04 39	17 00	20	
27	12 43	12 49	12 13	05 21	17 42	21	

G.M.T.	ARIES G.H.A.	VENUS −3.3 G.H.A.	Dec.	MARS +1.4 G.H.A.	Dec.	JUPITER −1.8 G.H.A.	Dec.	SATURN +0.9 G.H.A.	Dec.	STARS Name	S.H.A.	Dec.
28 00	127 10.2	194 30.3	S22 06.1	162 19.1	S15 09.2	297 04.6	S 2 47.6	297 16.6	S 1 33.7	Acamar	315 37.0	S40 23.2
01	142 12.6	209 29.4	05.7	177 19.6	08.5	312 07.1	47.6	312 19.1	33.7	Achernar	335 45.2	S57 20.4
02	157 15.1	224 28.5	05.3	192 20.1	07.9	327 09.5	47.6	327 21.5	33.7	Acrux	173 36.5	S62 59.4
03	172 17.6	239 27.6 ··	05.0	207 20.7 ··	07.2	342 12.0 ··	47.6	342 24.0 ··	33.7	Adhara	255 31.6	S28 57.0
04	187 20.0	254 26.7	04.6	222 21.2	06.6	357 14.5	47.6	357 26.5	33.6	Aldebaran	291 17.5	N16 28.2
05	202 22.5	269 25.8	04.2	237 21.7	05.9	12 17.0	47.5	12 29.0	33.6			
06	217 25.0	284 24.9	S22 03.8	252 22.3	S15 05.3	27 19.5	S 2 47.5	27 31.5	S 1 33.6	Alioth	166 42.1	N56 03.5
W 07	232 27.4	299 24.0	03.4	267 22.8	04.6	42 22.0	47.5	42 34.0	33.6	Alkaid	153 18.2	N49 24.3
E 08	247 29.9	314 23.1	03.0	282 23.3	04.0	57 24.4	47.5	57 36.5	33.5	Al Na'ir	28 15.1	S47 03.4
D 09	262 32.4	329 22.2 ··	02.7	297 23.9 ··	03.3	72 26.9 ··	47.4	72 39.0 ··	33.5	Alnilam	276 11.2	S 1 13.0
N 10	277 34.8	344 21.4	02.3	312 24.4	02.7	87 29.4	47.4	87 41.5	33.5	Alphard	218 20.0	S 8 34.6
E 11	292 37.3	359 20.5	01.9	327 24.9	02.0	102 31.9	47.4	102 44.0	33.4			
S 12	307 39.8	14 19.6	S22 01.5	342 25.5	S15 01.3	117 34.4	S 2 47.4	117 46.5	S 1 33.4	Alphecca	126 32.0	N26 46.6
D 13	322 42.2	29 18.7	01.1	357 26.0	00.7	132 36.9	47.4	132 49.0	33.4	Alpheratz	358 09.3	N28 59.1
A 14	337 44.7	44 17.8	00.7	12 26.5	15 00.0	147 39.4	47.3	147 51.5	33.4	Altair	62 32.6	N 8 49.0
Y 15	352 47.1	59 16.9	22 00.3	27 27.1	14 59.4	162 41.9 ··	47.3	162 54.0 ··	33.3	Ankaa	353 40.2	S42 24.9
16	7 49.6	74 16.0	21 59.9	42 27.6	58.7	177 44.3	47.3	177 56.5	33.3	Antares	112 56.7	S26 23.3
17	22 52.1	89 15.2	59.5	57 28.1	58.1	192 46.8	47.3	192 59.0	33.3			
18	37 54.5	104 14.3	S21 59.1	72 28.7	S14 57.4	207 49.3	S 2 47.2	208 01.5	S 1 33.3	Arcturus	146 18.2	N19 16.8
19	52 57.0	119 13.4	58.7	87 29.2	56.8	222 51.8	47.2	223 04.0	33.2	Atria	108 21.1	S68 59.3
20	67 59.5	134 12.5	58.3	102 29.7	56.1	237 54.3	47.2	238 06.5	33.2	Avior	234 27.4	S59 27.0
21	83 01.9	149 11.6 ··	57.9	117 30.3 ··	55.4	252 56.8 ··	47.2	253 09.0 ··	33.2	Bellatrix	278 58.2	N 6 19.8
22	98 04.4	164 10.7	57.5	132 30.8	54.8	267 59.3	47.2	268 11.5	33.1	Betelgeuse	271 27.7	N 7 24.1
23	113 06.9	179 09.9	57.1	147 31.3	54.1	283 01.8	47.1	283 14.0	33.1			
29 00	128 09.3	194 09.0	S21 56.7	162 31.9	S14 53.5	298 04.3	S 2 47.1	298 16.6	S 1 33.1	Canopus	264 06.6	S52 41.4
01	143 11.8	209 08.1	56.3	177 32.4	52.8	313 06.8	47.1	313 19.1	33.1	Capella	281 10.6	N45 58.8
02	158 14.2	224 07.2	55.9	192 32.9	52.2	328 09.2	47.1	328 21.6	33.0	Deneb	49 48.7	N45 12.7
03	173 16.7	239 06.3 ··	55.5	207 33.5 ··	51.5	343 11.7 ··	47.0	343 24.1 ··	33.0	Denebola	182 58.6	N14 40.6
04	188 19.2	254 05.4	55.1	222 34.0	50.8	358 14.2	47.0	358 26.6	33.0	Diphda	349 20.8	S18 05.7
05	203 21.6	269 04.6	54.7	237 34.5	50.2	13 16.7	47.0	13 29.1	32.9			
06	218 24.1	284 03.7	S21 54.2	252 35.1	S14 49.5	28 19.2	S 2 47.0	28 31.6	S 1 32.9	Dubhe	194 21.3	N61 51.0
07	233 26.6	299 02.8	53.8	267 35.6	48.9	43 21.7	46.9	43 34.1	32.9	Elnath	278 43.5	N28 35.5
T 08	248 29.0	314 01.9	53.4	282 36.1	48.2	58 24.2	46.9	58 36.6	32.8	Eltanin	90 58.0	N51 29.3
H 09	263 31.5	329 01.0 ··	53.0	297 36.7 ··	47.5	73 26.7 ··	46.9	73 39.1 ··	32.8	Enif	34 11.6	N 9 47.2
U 10	278 34.0	344 00.2	52.6	312 37.2	46.9	88 29.2	46.9	88 41.6	32.8	Fomalhaut	15 51.4	S29 43.6
R 11	293 36.4	358 59.3	52.2	327 37.7	46.2	103 31.7	46.8	103 44.1	32.8			
S 12	308 38.9	13 58.4	S21 51.7	342 38.3	S14 45.6	118 34.2	S 2 46.8	118 46.6	S 1 32.7	Gacrux	172 28.1	S57 00.2
D 13	323 41.4	28 57.5	51.3	357 38.8	44.9	133 36.7	46.8	133 49.1	32.7	Gienah	176 17.5	S17 26.1
A 14	338 43.8	43 56.6	50.9	12 39.4	44.2	148 39.2	46.8	148 51.6	32.7	Hadar	149 22.9	S60 16.6
Y 15	353 46.3	58 55.8 ··	50.5	27 39.9 ··	43.6	163 41.7 ··	46.7	163 54.1 ··	32.6	Hamal	328 28.7	N23 22.3
16	8 48.7	73 54.9	50.1	42 40.4	42.9	178 44.2	46.7	178 56.6	32.6	Kaus Aust.	84 16.9	S34 23.6
17	23 51.2	88 54.0	49.6	57 41.0	42.2	193 46.6	46.7	193 59.1	32.6			
18	38 53.7	103 53.1	S21 49.2	72 41.5	S14 41.6	208 49.1	S 2 46.7	209 01.6	S 1 32.6	Kochab	137 19.2	N74 13.8
19	53 56.1	118 52.3	48.8	87 42.0	40.9	223 51.6	46.6	224 04.1	32.5	Markab	14 03.2	N15 06.1
20	68 58.6	133 51.4	48.3	102 42.6	40.3	238 54.1	46.6	239 06.6	32.5	Menkar	314 40.8	N 4 00.8
21	84 01.1	148 50.5 ··	47.9	117 43.1 ··	39.6	253 56.6 ··	46.6	254 09.1 ··	32.5	Menkent	148 36.7	S36 16.4
22	99 03.5	163 49.6	47.5	132 43.7	38.9	268 59.1	46.6	269 11.6	32.4	Miaplacidus	221 43.9	S69 38.3
23	114 06.0	178 48.8	47.1	147 44.2	38.3	284 01.6	46.5	284 14.1	32.4			
30 00	129 08.5	193 47.9	S21 46.6	162 44.7	S14 37.6	299 04.1	S 2 46.5	299 16.6	S 1 32.4	Mirfak	309 15.6	N49 47.8
01	144 10.9	208 47.0	46.2	177 45.3	36.9	314 06.6	46.5	314 19.2	32.3	Nunki	76 29.2	S26 19.2
02	159 13.4	223 46.1	45.8	192 45.8	36.3	329 09.1	46.5	329 21.7	32.3	Peacock	53 58.6	S56 47.8
03	174 15.9	238 45.3 ··	45.3	207 46.4 ··	35.6	344 11.6 ··	46.4	344 24.2 ··	32.3	Pollux	243 57.5	N28 04.3
04	189 18.3	253 44.4	44.9	222 46.9	34.9	359 14.1	46.4	359 26.7	32.3	Procyon	245 25.2	N 5 16.3
05	204 20.8	268 43.5	44.4	237 47.4	34.3	14 16.6	46.4	14 29.2	32.2			
06	219 23.2	283 42.6	S21 44.0	252 48.0	S14 33.6	29 19.1	S 2 46.3	29 31.7	S 1 32.2	Rasalhague	96 29.6	N12 34.4
07	234 25.7	298 41.8	43.6	267 48.5	32.9	44 21.6	46.3	44 34.2	32.2	Regulus	208 09.4	N12 03.5
08	249 28.2	313 40.9	43.1	282 49.1	32.3	59 24.1	46.3	59 36.7	32.1	Rigel	281 35.6	S 8 13.6
F 09	264 30.6	328 40.0 ··	42.7	297 49.6 ··	31.6	74 26.6 ··	46.3	74 39.2 ··	32.1	Rigil Kent.	140 25.5	S60 45.0
R 10	279 33.1	343 39.1	42.2	312 50.1	30.9	89 29.1	46.2	89 41.7	32.1	Sabik	102 41.1	S15 42.0
I 11	294 35.6	358 38.3	41.8	327 50.7	30.3	104 31.6	46.2	104 44.2	32.0			
D 12	309 38.0	13 37.4	S21 41.3	342 51.2	S14 29.6	119 34.1	S 2 46.2	119 46.7	S 1 32.0	Schedar	350 09.0	N56 26.1
A 13	324 40.5	28 36.5	40.9	357 51.8	28.9	134 36.6	46.2	134 49.2	32.0	Shaula	96 55.7	S37 05.3
Y 14	339 43.0	43 35.7	40.4	12 52.3	28.3	149 39.1	46.1	149 51.7	31.9	Sirius	258 55.2	S16 41.6
15	354 45.4	58 34.8 ··	40.0	27 52.8 ··	27.6	164 41.6 ··	46.1	164 54.3 ··	31.9	Spica	158 57.2	S11 03.7
16	9 47.9	73 33.9	39.5	42 53.4	26.9	179 44.1	46.1	179 56.8	31.9	Suhail	223 10.1	S43 21.4
17	24 50.3	88 33.1	39.1	57 53.9	26.3	194 46.6	46.0	194 59.3	31.9			
18	39 52.8	103 32.2	S21 38.6	72 54.5	S14 25.6	209 49.1	S 2 46.0	210 01.8	S 1 31.8	Vega	80 56.0	N38 45.8
19	54 55.3	118 31.3	38.2	87 55.0	24.9	224 51.6	46.0	225 04.3	31.8	Zuben'ubi	137 32.8	S15 57.7
20	69 57.7	133 30.4	37.7	102 55.5	24.3	239 54.2	46.0	240 06.8	31.8		S.H.A.	Mer. Pass.
21	85 00.2	148 29.6 ··	37.3	117 56.1 ··	23.6	254 56.7 ··	45.9	255 09.3 ··	31.7		° '	h m
22	100 02.7	163 28.7	36.8	132 56.6	22.9	269 59.2	45.9	270 11.8	31.7	Venus	65 59.7	11 04
23	115 05.1	178 27.8	36.4	147 57.2	22.3	285 01.7	45.9	285 14.3	31.7	Mars	34 22.5	13 09
	h m									Jupiter	169 54.9	4 07
Mer. Pass. 15 24.8	v −0.9	d 0.4	v 0.5	d 0.7	v 2.5	d 0.0	v 2.5	d 0.0	Saturn	170 07.2	4 06

SUN / MOON

G.M.T.	SUN G.H.A.	SUN Dec.	MOON G.H.A.	v	Dec.	d	H.P.
28 00	176 46.3	S18 16.4	271 41.6	15.1	S 8 33.3	9.4	54.2
01	191 46.2	15.7	286 15.7	15.1	8 42.7	9.3	54.2
02	206 46.1	15.0	300 49.8	15.1	8 52.0	9.3	54.2
03	221 46.0	·· 14.4	315 23.9	15.0	9 01.3	9.3	54.2
04	236 45.8	13.7	329 57.9	15.0	9 10.6	9.2	54.2
05	251 45.7	13.1	344 31.9	15.0	9 19.8	9.2	54.2
06	266 45.6	S18 12.4	359 05.9	15.0	S 9 29.0	9.2	54.2
W 07	281 45.5	11.8	13 39.9	14.9	9 38.2	9.1	54.2
E 08	296 45.4	11.1	28 13.8	14.9	9 47.3	9.1	54.2
D 09	311 45.3	·· 10.4	42 47.7	14.9	9 56.4	9.1	54.2
N 10	326 45.1	09.8	57 21.6	14.8	10 05.5	9.0	54.2
E 11	341 45.0	09.1	71 55.4	14.8	10 14.5	8.9	54.3
S 12	356 44.9	S18 08.5	86 29.2	14.8	S10 23.4	9.0	54.3
D 13	11 44.8	07.8	101 03.0	14.7	10 32.4	8.8	54.3
A 14	26 44.7	07.1	115 36.7	14.7	10 41.2	8.9	54.3
Y 15	41 44.6	·· 06.5	130 10.4	14.7	10 50.1	8.8	54.3
16	56 44.4	05.8	144 44.1	14.6	10 58.9	8.7	54.3
17	71 44.3	05.1	159 17.7	14.6	11 07.6	8.8	54.3
18	86 44.2	S18 04.5	173 51.3	14.6	S11 16.4	8.6	54.3
19	101 44.1	03.8	188 24.9	14.5	11 25.0	8.6	54.3
20	116 44.0	03.1	202 58.4	14.5	11 33.6	8.6	54.3
21	131 43.9	·· 02.5	217 31.9	14.4	11 42.2	8.6	54.3
22	146 43.8	01.8	232 05.3	14.4	11 50.8	8.4	54.3
23	161 43.6	01.1	246 38.7	14.4	11 59.2	8.5	54.3
29 00	176 43.5	S18 00.5	261 12.1	14.3	S12 07.7	8.4	54.3
01	191 43.4	17 59.8	275 45.4	14.3	12 16.1	8.3	54.3
02	206 43.3	59.1	290 18.7	14.2	12 24.4	8.3	54.4
03	221 43.2	·· 58.5	304 51.9	14.2	12 32.7	8.3	54.4
04	236 43.1	57.8	319 25.1	14.2	12 41.0	8.1	54.4
05	251 43.0	57.1	333 58.3	14.1	12 49.1	8.2	54.4
06	266 42.9	S17 56.4	348 31.4	14.1	S12 57.3	8.1	54.4
07	281 42.8	55.8	3 04.5	14.0	13 05.4	8.0	54.4
T 08	296 42.7	55.1	17 37.5	14.0	13 13.4	8.0	54.4
H 09	311 42.5	·· 54.4	32 10.5	13.9	13 21.4	7.9	54.4
U 10	326 42.4	53.8	46 43.4	13.9	13 29.3	7.9	54.4
R 11	341 42.3	53.1	61 16.3	13.8	13 37.2	7.8	54.4
S 12	356 42.2	S17 52.4	75 49.1	13.8	S13 45.0	7.8	54.5
D 13	11 42.1	51.7	90 21.9	13.8	13 52.8	7.7	54.5
A 14	26 42.0	51.1	104 54.7	13.7	14 00.5	7.7	54.5
Y 15	41 41.9	·· 50.4	119 27.4	13.6	14 08.2	7.6	54.5
16	56 41.8	49.7	134 00.0	13.6	14 15.8	7.5	54.5
17	71 41.7	49.0	148 32.6	13.6	14 23.3	7.5	54.5
18	86 41.6	S17 48.3	163 05.2	13.5	S14 30.8	7.4	54.5
19	101 41.5	47.7	177 37.7	13.4	14 38.2	7.4	54.6
20	116 41.4	47.0	192 10.1	13.4	14 45.6	7.3	54.6
21	131 41.3	·· 46.3	206 42.5	13.3	14 52.9	7.3	54.6
22	146 41.2	45.6	221 14.8	13.3	15 00.2	7.1	54.6
23	161 41.1	44.9	235 47.1	13.3	15 07.3	7.2	54.6
30 00	176 40.9	S17 44.3	250 19.4	13.2	S15 14.5	7.0	54.6
01	191 40.8	43.6	264 51.6	13.1	15 21.5	7.0	54.6
02	206 40.7	42.9	279 23.7	13.1	15 28.5	6.9	54.7
03	221 40.6	·· 42.2	293 55.8	13.0	15 35.4	6.9	54.7
04	236 40.5	41.5	308 27.8	13.0	15 42.3	6.7	54.7
05	251 40.4	40.9	322 59.8	12.9	15 49.1	6.7	54.7
06	266 40.3	S17 40.2	337 31.7	12.9	S15 55.8	6.7	54.7
07	281 40.2	39.5	352 03.6	12.8	16 02.5	6.6	54.7
08	296 40.1	38.8	6 35.4	12.7	16 09.1	6.5	54.8
F 09	311 40.0	·· 38.1	21 07.1	12.7	16 15.6	6.5	54.8
R 10	326 39.9	37.4	35 38.8	12.7	16 22.1	6.4	54.8
I 11	341 39.8	36.7	50 10.5	12.5	16 28.5	6.3	54.8
D 12	356 39.7	S17 36.0	64 42.0	12.6	S16 34.8	6.2	54.8
A 13	11 39.6	35.4	79 13.6	12.4	16 41.0	6.2	54.8
Y 14	26 39.5	34.7	93 45.0	12.4	16 47.2	6.1	54.9
15	41 39.4	·· 34.0	108 16.4	12.4	16 53.3	6.0	54.9
16	56 39.3	33.3	122 47.8	12.3	16 59.3	6.0	54.9
17	71 39.2	32.6	137 19.1	12.2	17 05.3	5.9	54.9
18	86 39.1	S17 31.9	151 50.3	12.2	S17 11.2	5.8	54.9
19	101 39.0	31.2	166 21.5	12.1	17 17.0	5.7	54.9
20	116 38.9	30.5	180 52.6	12.1	17 22.7	5.6	55.0
21	131 38.8	·· 29.8	195 23.7	12.0	17 28.3	5.6	55.0
22	146 38.8	29.1	209 54.7	12.0	17 33.9	5.5	55.0
23	161 38.7	28.4	224 25.7	11.8	17 39.4	5.4	55.1
S.D. 16.3	d 0.7		S.D. 14.8		14.8		14.9

Twilight / Sunrise / Moonrise

Lat.	Naut.	Civil	Sunrise	Moonrise 28	29	30	31
N 72	07 20	08 52	10 56	01 52	03 38	05 37	■■
N 70	07 11	08 31	10 03	01 38	03 14	04 54	06 42
68	07 03	08 15	09 31	01 27	02 55	04 26	05 57
66	06 57	08 02	09 07	01 17	02 40	04 04	05 27
64	06 51	07 51	08 49	01 10	02 28	03 47	05 05
62	06 46	07 41	08 34	01 03	02 18	03 34	04 47
60	06 42	07 33	08 21	00 57	02 10	03 22	04 32
N 58	06 37	07 25	08 10	00 52	02 02	03 12	04 20
56	06 34	07 19	08 01	00 48	01 55	03 03	04 09
54	06 30	07 13	07 52	00 44	01 49	02 55	04 00
52	06 27	07 08	07 45	00 40	01 44	02 48	03 51
50	06 24	07 03	07 38	00 37	01 39	02 42	03 44
45	06 17	06 52	07 23	00 30	01 29	02 28	03 28
N 40	06 10	06 43	07 11	00 24	01 20	02 17	03 15
35	06 04	06 34	07 01	00 19	01 13	02 08	03 03
30	05 58	06 27	06 52	00 14	01 06	02 00	02 54
20	05 47	06 13	06 36	00 06	00 55	01 45	02 37
N 10	05 35	06 01	06 23	00 00	00 46	01 33	02 22
0	05 23	05 48	06 10	24 37	00 37	01 22	02 09
S 10	05 08	05 34	05 56	24 28	00 28	01 10	01 55
20	04 51	05 19	05 42	24 18	00 18	00 58	01 41
30	04 29	05 00	05 26	24 07	00 07	00 44	01 25
35	04 15	04 48	05 16	24 01	00 01	00 36	01 15
40	03 58	04 35	05 06	23 54	24 27	00 27	01 04
45	03 36	04 19	04 52	23 46	24 16	00 16	00 52
S 50	03 07	03 58	04 36	23 36	24 04	00 04	00 36
52	02 52	03 47	04 29	23 32	23 58	24 29	00 29
54	02 33	03 36	04 20	23 27	23 51	24 21	00 21
56	02 10	03 23	04 11	23 21	23 44	24 12	00 12
58	01 38	03 07	04 00	23 15	23 36	24 02	00 02
S 60	////	02 47	03 48	23 08	23 26	23 50	24 23

Sunset / Twilight / Moonset

Lat.	Sunset	Civil	Naut.	Moonset 28	29	30	31
N 72	13 32	15 36	17 08	09 56	09 41	09 17	■■
N 70	14 25	15 56	17 17	10 12	10 07	10 00	09 51
68	14 57	16 12	17 24	10 25	10 26	10 29	10 37
66	15 20	16 26	17 31	10 35	10 42	10 51	11 07
64	15 39	16 37	17 36	10 44	10 55	11 09	11 30
62	15 54	16 46	17 41	10 52	11 06	11 23	11 48
60	16 06	16 54	17 46	10 59	11 15	11 36	12 03
N 58	16 17	17 02	17 50	11 04	11 23	11 46	12 16
56	16 26	17 08	17 54	11 10	11 30	11 56	12 27
54	16 35	17 14	17 57	11 14	11 37	12 04	12 37
52	16 42	17 19	18 00	11 18	11 43	12 11	12 45
50	16 49	17 24	18 03	11 22	11 48	12 18	12 53
45	17 03	17 35	18 10	11 31	11 59	12 32	13 10
N 40	17 15	17 44	18 17	11 38	12 09	12 44	13 24
35	17 26	17 52	18 23	11 44	12 17	12 54	13 35
30	17 35	18 00	18 29	11 49	12 24	13 03	13 45
20	17 50	18 13	18 40	11 58	12 37	13 18	14 03
N 10	18 04	18 26	18 51	12 06	12 48	13 32	14 18
0	18 17	18 38	19 04	12 14	12 58	13 44	14 32
S 10	18 30	18 52	19 18	12 22	13 08	13 57	14 47
20	18 44	19 07	19 35	12 30	13 19	14 10	15 02
30	19 00	19 26	19 57	12 39	13 32	14 26	15 20
35	19 10	19 37	20 11	12 45	13 39	14 35	15 30
40	19 20	19 51	20 28	12 51	13 48	14 45	15 42
45	19 33	20 07	20 49	12 58	13 57	14 57	15 56
S 50	19 49	20 28	21 18	13 07	14 09	15 12	16 12
52	19 56	20 37	21 33	13 11	14 15	15 18	16 20
54	20 05	20 49	21 51	13 15	14 21	15 26	16 29
56	20 14	21 02	22 13	13 20	14 28	15 35	16 39
58	20 25	21 17	22 44	13 26	14 35	15 44	16 51
S 60	20 37	21 36	23 42	13 32	14 44	15 55	17 04

SUN / MOON

Day	SUN Eqn. of Time 00h	12h	Mer. Pass.	MOON Mer. Pass. Upper	Lower	Age	Phase
28	12 54	13 00	12 13	06 04	18 25	22	
29	13 06	13 11	12 13	06 47	19 10	23	
30	13 16	13 21	12 13	07 33	19 56	24	◖

G.M.T.	ARIES G.H.A.	VENUS −3.3 G.H.A.	Dec.	MARS +1.4 G.H.A.	Dec.	JUPITER −1.8 G.H.A.	Dec.	SATURN +0.9 G.H.A.	Dec.	STARS Name	S.H.A.	Dec.
31 00	130 07.6	193 27.0	S21 35.9	162 57.7	S14 21.6	300 04.2	S 2 45.8	300 16.8	S 1 31.6	Acamar	315 37.0	S40 23.2
01	145 10.1	208 26.1	·· 35.4	177 58.3	20.9	315 06.7	45.8	315 19.3	31.6	Achernar	335 45.3	S57 20.4
02	160 12.5	223 25.2	35.0	192 58.8	20.2	330 09.2	45.8	330 21.9	31.6	Acrux	173 36.5	S62 59.4
03	175 15.0	238 24.4	·· 34.5	207 59.4	·· 19.6	345 11.7	·· 45.7	345 24.4	·· 31.5	Adhara	255 31.6	S28 57.0
04	190 17.5	253 23.5	34.0	222 59.9	18.9	0 14.2	45.7	0 26.9	31.5	Aldebaran	291 17.5	N16 28.2
05	205 19.9	268 22.7	33.6	238 00.4	18.2	15 16.7	45.7	15 29.4	31.5			
06	220 22.4	283 21.8	S21 33.1	253 01.0	S14 17.6	30 19.2	S 2 45.7	30 31.9	S 1 31.4	Alioth	166 42.0	N56 03.5
07	235 24.8	298 20.9	32.6	268 01.5	16.9	45 21.7	45.6	45 34.4	31.4	Alkaid	153 18.2	N49 24.3
S 08	250 27.3	313 20.1	32.2	283 02.1	16.2	60 24.2	45.6	60 36.9	31.4	Al Na'ir	28 15.1	S47 03.4
A 09	265 29.8	328 19.2	·· 31.7	298 02.6	·· 15.5	75 26.7	·· 45.6	75 39.4	·· 31.3	Alnilam	276 11.2	S 1 13.0
T 10	280 32.2	343 18.3	31.2	313 03.2	14.9	90 29.2	45.5	90 41.9	31.3	Alphard	218 20.0	S 8 34.6
U 11	295 34.7	358 17.5	30.8	328 03.7	14.2	105 31.7	45.5	105 44.5	31.3			
R 12	310 37.2	13 16.6	S21 30.3	343 04.3	S14 13.5	120 34.3	S 2 45.5	120 47.0	S 1 31.2	Alphecca	126 32.0	N26 46.6
D 13	325 39.6	28 15.7	29.8	358 04.8	12.9	135 36.8	45.4	135 49.5	31.2	Alpheratz	358 09.3	N28 59.1
A 14	340 42.1	43 14.9	29.3	13 05.3	12.2	150 39.3	45.4	150 52.0	31.2	Altair	62 32.6	N 8 49.0
Y 15	355 44.6	58 14.0	·· 28.9	28 05.9	·· 11.5	165 41.8	·· 45.4	165 54.5	·· 31.1	Ankaa	353 40.2	S42 24.9
16	10 47.0	73 13.2	28.4	43 06.4	10.8	180 44.3	45.3	180 57.0	31.1	Antares	112 56.7	S26 23.3
17	25 49.5	88 12.3	27.9	58 07.0	10.2	195 46.8	45.3	195 59.5	31.1			
18	40 52.0	103 11.4	S21 27.4	73 07.5	S14 09.5	210 49.3	S 2 45.3	211 02.0	S 1 31.0	Arcturus	146 18.2	N19 16.8
19	55 54.4	118 10.6	26.9	88 08.1	08.8	225 51.8	45.3	226 04.6	31.0	Atria	108 21.0	S68 59.3
20	70 56.9	133 09.7	26.5	103 08.6	08.1	240 54.3	45.2	241 07.1	31.0	Avior	234 27.4	S59 27.0
21	85 59.3	148 08.9	·· 26.0	118 09.2	·· 07.5	255 56.9	·· 45.2	256 09.6	·· 30.9	Bellatrix	278 58.2	N 6 19.8
22	101 01.8	163 08.0	25.5	133 09.7	06.8	270 59.4	45.2	271 12.1	30.9	Betelgeuse	271 27.7	N 7 24.1
23	116 04.3	178 07.1	25.0	148 10.3	06.1	286 01.9	45.1	286 14.6	30.9			
1 00	131 06.7	193 06.3	S21 24.5	163 10.8	S14 05.4	301 04.4	S 2 45.1	301 17.1	S 1 30.8	Canopus	264 06.6	S52 41.4
01	146 09.2	208 05.4	24.0	178 11.4	04.8	316 06.9	45.1	316 19.6	30.8	Capella	281 10.6	N45 58.8
02	161 11.7	223 04.6	23.5	193 11.9	04.1	331 09.4	45.0	331 22.2	30.8	Deneb	49 48.7	N45 12.7
03	176 14.1	238 03.7	·· 23.0	208 12.5	·· 03.4	346 11.9	·· 45.0	346 24.7	·· 30.7	Denebola	182 58.6	N14 40.6
04	191 16.6	253 02.9	22.6	223 13.0	02.7	1 14.4	45.0	1 27.2	30.7	Diphda	349 20.8	S18 05.7
05	206 19.1	268 02.0	22.1	238 13.6	02.1	16 17.0	44.9	16 29.7	30.7			
06	221 21.5	283 01.2	S21 21.6	253 14.1	S14 01.4	31 19.5	S 2 44.9	31 32.2	S 1 30.6	Dubhe	194 21.3	N61 51.0
07	236 24.0	298 00.3	21.1	268 14.7	00.7	46 22.0	44.9	46 34.7	30.6	Elnath	278 43.6	N28 35.5
08	251 26.4	312 59.4	20.6	283 15.2	14 00.0	61 24.5	44.8	61 37.2	30.6	Eltanin	90 58.0	N51 29.3
S 09	266 28.9	327 58.6	·· 20.1	298 15.8	13 59.3	76 27.0	·· 44.8	76 39.8	·· 30.5	Enif	34 11.6	N 9 47.2
U 10	281 31.4	342 57.7	19.6	313 16.3	58.7	91 29.5	44.8	91 42.3	30.5	Fomalhaut	15 51.4	S29 43.6
N 11	296 33.8	357 56.9	19.1	328 16.8	58.0	106 32.0	44.7	106 44.8	30.5			
D 12	311 36.3	12 56.0	S21 18.6	343 17.4	S13 57.3	121 34.6	S 2 44.7	121 47.3	S 1 30.4	Gacrux	172 28.1	S57 00.2
A 13	326 38.8	27 55.2	18.1	358 17.9	56.6	136 37.1	44.7	136 49.8	30.4	Gienah	176 17.5	S17 26.1
Y 14	341 41.2	42 54.3	17.6	13 18.5	55.9	151 39.6	44.6	151 52.3	30.4	Hadar	149 22.8	S60 16.6
15	356 43.7	57 53.5	·· 17.1	28 19.0	·· 55.3	166 42.1	·· 44.6	166 54.9	·· 30.3	Hamal	328 28.7	N23 22.3
16	11 46.2	72 52.6	16.6	43 19.6	54.6	181 44.6	44.6	181 57.4	30.3	Kaus Aust.	84 16.8	S34 23.6
17	26 48.6	87 51.8	16.1	58 20.2	53.9	196 47.1	44.5	196 59.9	30.3			
18	41 51.1	102 50.9	S21 15.6	73 20.7	S13 53.2	211 49.7	S 2 44.5	212 02.4	S 1 30.2	Kochab	137 19.1	N74 13.8
19	56 53.6	117 50.1	15.1	88 21.3	52.5	226 52.2	44.4	227 04.9	30.2	Markab	14 03.2	N15 06.1
20	71 56.0	132 49.2	14.5	103 21.8	51.9	241 54.7	44.4	242 07.4	30.2	Menkar	314 40.8	N 4 00.8
21	86 58.5	147 48.4	·· 14.0	118 22.4	·· 51.2	256 57.2	·· 44.4	257 10.0	·· 30.1	Menkent	148 36.6	S36 16.4
22	102 00.9	162 47.5	13.5	133 22.9	50.5	271 59.7	44.3	272 12.5	30.1	Miaplacidus	221 43.9	S69 38.3
23	117 03.4	177 46.7	13.0	148 23.5	49.8	287 02.3	44.3	287 15.0	30.1			
2 00	132 05.9	192 45.8	S21 12.5	163 24.0	S13 49.1	302 04.8	S 2 44.3	302 17.5	S 1 30.0	Mirfak	309 15.6	N49 47.8
01	147 08.3	207 45.0	12.0	178 24.6	48.5	317 07.3	44.2	317 20.0	30.0	Nunki	76 29.2	S26 19.2
02	162 10.8	222 44.1	11.5	193 25.1	47.8	332 09.8	44.2	332 22.5	30.0	Peacock	53 58.6	S56 47.8
03	177 13.3	237 43.3	·· 10.9	208 25.7	·· 47.1	347 12.3	·· 44.2	347 25.1	·· 29.9	Pollux	243 57.5	N28 04.3
04	192 15.7	252 42.4	10.4	223 26.2	46.4	2 14.9	44.1	2 27.6	29.9	Procyon	245 25.2	N 5 16.3
05	207 18.2	267 41.6	09.9	238 26.8	45.7	17 17.4	44.1	17 30.1	29.8			
06	222 20.7	282 40.7	S21 09.4	253 27.3	S13 45.0	32 19.9	S 2 44.1	32 32.6	S 1 29.8	Rasalhague	96 29.6	N12 34.3
07	237 23.1	297 39.9	08.9	268 27.9	44.4	47 22.4	44.0	47 35.1	29.8	Regulus	208 09.4	N12 03.5
08	252 25.6	312 39.0	08.3	283 28.4	43.7	62 25.0	44.0	62 37.7	29.7	Rigel	281 35.6	S 8 13.6
M 09	267 28.1	327 38.2	·· 07.8	298 29.0	·· 43.0	77 27.5	·· 43.9	77 40.2	·· 29.7	Rigil Kent.	140 25.4	S60 45.0
O 10	282 30.5	342 37.4	07.3	313 29.5	42.3	92 30.0	43.9	92 42.7	29.7	Sabik	102 41.0	S15 42.1
N 11	297 33.0	357 36.5	06.8	328 30.1	41.6	107 32.5	43.9	107 45.2	29.6			
D 12	312 35.4	12 35.7	S21 06.2	343 30.7	S13 40.9	122 35.0	S 2 43.8	122 47.7	S 1 29.6	Schedar	350 09.0	N56 26.1
A 13	327 37.9	27 34.8	05.7	358 31.2	40.3	137 37.6	43.8	137 50.3	29.6	Shaula	96 55.7	S37 05.3
Y 14	342 40.4	42 34.0	05.2	13 31.8	39.6	152 40.1	43.8	152 52.8	29.5	Sirius	258 55.2	S16 41.6
15	357 42.8	57 33.1	·· 04.7	28 32.3	·· 38.9	167 42.6	·· 43.7	167 55.3	·· 29.5	Spica	158 57.2	S11 03.7
16	12 45.3	72 32.3	04.1	43 32.9	38.2	182 45.1	43.7	182 57.8	29.5	Suhail	223 10.1	S43 21.4
17	27 47.8	87 31.5	03.6	58 33.4	37.5	197 47.7	43.6	198 00.3	29.4			
18	42 50.2	102 30.6	S21 03.1	73 34.0	S13 36.8	212 50.2	S 2 43.6	213 02.9	S 1 29.4	Vega	80 56.0	N38 45.8
19	57 52.7	117 29.8	02.5	88 34.5	36.1	227 52.7	43.6	228 05.4	29.3	Zuben'ubi	137 32.8	S15 57.7
20	72 55.2	132 28.9	02.0	103 35.1	35.5	242 55.2	43.5	243 07.9	29.3		S.H.A.	Mer. Pass.
21	87 57.6	147 28.1	·· 01.5	118 35.6	·· 34.8	257 57.8	·· 43.5	258 10.4	·· 29.3			
22	103 00.1	162 27.3	00.9	133 36.2	34.1	273 00.3	43.5	273 12.9	29.2	Venus	61 59.6	11 08
23	118 02.5	177 26.4	00.4	148 36.8	33.4	288 02.8	43.4	288 15.5	29.2	Mars	32 04.1	13 07
Mer. Pass.	15 13.1	v −0.9	d 0.5	v 0.5	d 0.7	v 2.5	d 0.0	v 2.5	d 0.0	Jupiter	169 57.7	3 55
										Saturn	170 10.4	3 54

G.M.T.	SUN G.H.A.	SUN Dec.	MOON G.H.A.	v	Dec.	d	H.P.
31 00	176 38.6	S17 27.7	238 56.5	11.9	S17 44.8	5.4	55.1
01	191 38.5	27.1	253 27.4	11.7	17 50.2	5.2	55.1
02	206 38.4	26.4	267 58.1	11.7	17 55.4	5.2	55.1
03	221 38.3	·· 25.7	282 28.8	11.7	18 00.6	5.1	55.1
04	236 38.2	25.0	296 59.5	11.6	18 05.7	5.0	55.2
05	251 38.1	24.3	311 30.1	11.5	18 10.7	4.9	55.2
06	266 38.0	S17 23.6	326 00.6	11.5	S18 15.6	4.9	55.2
07	281 37.9	22.9	340 31.1	11.4	18 20.5	4.7	55.2
S 08	296 37.8	22.2	355 01.5	11.4	18 25.2	4.7	55.3
A 09	311 37.7	·· 21.5	9 31.9	11.3	18 29.9	4.6	55.3
T 10	326 37.6	20.8	24 02.2	11.2	18 34.5	4.5	55.3
U 11	341 37.5	20.1	38 32.4	11.2	18 39.0	4.4	55.3
R 12	356 37.4	S17 19.4	53 02.6	11.1	S18 43.4	4.3	55.3
D 13	11 37.4	18.7	67 32.7	11.1	18 47.7	4.2	55.4
A 14	26 37.3	18.0	82 02.8	11.0	18 51.9	4.2	55.4
Y 15	41 37.2	·· 17.3	96 32.8	10.9	18 56.1	4.1	55.4
16	56 37.1	16.6	111 02.7	10.9	19 00.2	3.9	55.4
17	71 37.0	15.9	125 32.6	10.8	19 04.1	3.9	55.5
18	86 36.9	S17 15.2	140 02.4	10.8	S19 08.0	3.8	55.5
19	101 36.8	14.4	154 32.2	10.7	19 11.8	3.7	55.5
20	116 36.7	13.7	169 01.9	10.7	19 15.5	3.6	55.5
21	131 36.6	·· 13.0	183 31.6	10.6	19 19.1	3.5	55.6
22	146 36.6	12.3	198 01.2	10.5	19 22.6	3.4	55.6
23	161 36.5	11.6	212 30.7	10.5	19 26.0	3.3	55.6
1 00	176 36.4	S17 10.9	227 00.2	10.4	S19 29.3	3.2	55.6
01	191 36.3	10.2	241 29.6	10.4	19 32.5	3.1	55.7
02	206 36.2	09.5	255 59.0	10.3	19 35.6	3.0	55.7
03	221 36.1	·· 08.8	270 28.3	10.3	19 38.6	2.9	55.7
04	236 36.0	08.1	284 57.6	10.2	19 41.5	2.9	55.8
05	251 35.9	07.4	299 26.8	10.2	19 44.4	2.7	55.8
06	266 35.9	S17 06.7	313 56.0	10.1	S19 47.1	2.6	55.8
07	281 35.8	06.0	328 25.1	10.0	19 49.7	2.5	55.8
S 08	296 35.7	05.2	342 54.1	10.0	19 52.2	2.4	55.9
U 09	311 35.6	·· 04.5	357 23.1	9.9	19 54.6	2.4	55.9
N 10	326 35.5	03.8	11 52.0	9.9	19 57.0	2.2	55.9
11	341 35.4	03.1	26 20.9	9.9	19 59.2	2.1	55.9
D 12	356 35.4	S17 02.4	40 49.8	9.7	S20 01.3	2.0	56.0
A 13	11 35.3	01.7	55 18.5	9.8	20 03.3	1.9	56.0
Y 14	26 35.2	01.0	69 47.3	9.7	20 05.2	1.8	56.0
15	41 35.1	17 00.2	84 16.0	9.6	20 07.0	1.7	56.1
16	56 35.0	16 59.5	98 44.6	9.6	20 08.7	1.6	56.1
17	71 35.0	58.8	113 13.2	9.5	20 10.3	1.5	56.1
18	86 34.9	S16 58.1	127 41.7	9.5	S20 11.8	1.3	56.1
19	101 34.8	57.4	142 10.2	9.5	20 13.1	1.3	56.2
20	116 34.7	56.7	156 38.7	9.4	20 14.4	1.2	56.2
21	131 34.6	·· 55.9	171 07.1	9.3	20 15.6	1.0	56.2
22	146 34.6	55.2	185 35.4	9.3	20 16.6	0.9	56.3
23	161 34.5	54.5	200 03.7	9.3	20 17.5	0.9	56.3
2 00	176 34.4	S16 53.8	214 32.0	9.2	S20 18.4	0.7	56.3
01	191 34.3	53.1	229 00.2	9.2	20 19.1	0.6	56.3
02	206 34.2	52.3	243 28.4	9.1	20 19.7	0.5	56.4
03	221 34.2	·· 51.6	257 56.5	9.1	20 20.2	0.4	56.4
04	236 34.1	50.9	272 24.6	9.0	20 20.6	0.3	56.4
05	251 34.0	50.2	286 52.6	9.0	20 20.9	0.1	56.5
06	266 33.9	S16 49.5	301 20.6	9.0	S20 21.0	0.1	56.5
07	281 33.9	48.7	315 48.6	8.9	20 21.1	0.1	56.5
08	296 33.8	48.0	330 16.5	8.9	20 21.0	0.2	56.6
M 09	311 33.7	·· 47.3	344 44.4	8.9	20 20.8	0.2	56.6
O 10	326 33.6	46.6	359 12.3	8.8	20 20.6	0.4	56.6
N 11	341 33.6	45.8	13 40.1	8.8	20 20.2	0.6	56.6
D 12	356 33.5	S16 45.1	28 07.9	8.7	S20 19.6	0.6	56.7
A 13	11 33.4	44.4	42 35.6	8.7	20 19.0	0.7	56.7
Y 14	26 33.3	43.7	57 03.3	8.7	20 18.3	0.9	56.7
15	41 33.3	·· 42.9	71 31.0	8.6	20 17.4	1.0	56.8
16	56 33.2	42.2	85 58.6	8.7	20 16.4	1.1	56.8
17	71 33.1	41.5	100 26.3	8.5	20 15.3	1.2	56.8
18	86 33.0	S16 40.7	114 53.8	8.6	S20 14.1	1.3	56.9
19	101 33.0	40.0	129 21.4	8.5	20 12.8	1.5	56.9
20	116 32.9	39.3	143 48.9	8.5	20 11.3	1.5	56.9
21	131 32.8	·· 38.5	158 16.4	8.5	20 09.8	1.7	56.9
22	146 32.8	37.8	172 43.9	8.4	20 08.1	1.8	57.0
23	161 32.7	37.1	187 11.3	8.5	20 06.3	1.9	57.0
	S.D. 16.3	d 0.7	S.D. 15.1		15.3		15.4

Lat.	Twilight Naut.	Twilight Civil	Sunrise	Moonrise 31	1	2	3
N 72	07 10	08 39	10 28	■	■	■	
N 70	07 02	08 20	09 46	06 42	■	■	10 19
68	06 55	08 05	09 18	05 57	07 23	08 30	09 06
66	06 50	07 53	08 57	05 27	06 44	07 46	08 29
64	06 45	07 43	08 40	05 05	06 17	07 17	08 02
62	06 40	07 34	08 26	04 47	05 56	06 55	07 42
60	06 36	07 27	08 14	04 32	05 39	06 37	07 25
N 58	06 32	07 20	08 04	04 20	05 24	06 22	07 11
56	06 29	07 14	07 55	04 09	05 12	06 09	06 59
54	06 26	07 09	07 47	04 00	05 02	05 58	06 48
52	06 23	07 04	07 40	03 51	04 52	05 49	06 39
50	06 20	06 59	07 34	03 44	04 44	05 40	06 30
45	06 14	06 49	07 20	03 28	04 26	05 21	06 12
N 40	06 08	06 40	07 09	03 15	04 11	05 06	05 58
35	06 02	06 32	06 59	03 03	03 59	04 53	05 45
30	05 57	06 25	06 50	02 54	03 48	04 42	05 34
20	05 46	06 13	06 36	02 37	03 30	04 23	05 16
N 10	05 35	06 01	06 23	02 22	03 13	04 06	04 59
0	05 23	05 48	06 10	02 09	02 59	03 51	04 44
S 10	05 10	05 36	05 58	01 55	02 44	03 35	04 29
20	04 53	05 21	05 44	01 41	02 28	03 18	04 13
30	04 32	05 03	05 29	01 25	02 09	02 59	03 54
35	04 18	04 52	05 19	01 15	01 59	02 48	03 43
40	04 02	04 39	05 09	01 04	01 47	02 36	03 31
45	03 41	04 23	04 57	00 52	01 33	02 21	03 16
S 50	03 14	04 04	04 42	00 36	01 15	02 02	02 58
52	03 00	03 54	04 34	00 29	01 07	01 54	02 50
54	02 43	03 43	04 27	00 21	00 58	01 44	02 40
56	02 22	03 31	04 18	00 12	00 48	01 33	02 29
58	01 54	03 18	04 08	00 02	00 36	01 20	02 17
S 60	01 10	02 58	03 56	24 23	00 23	01 06	02 03

Lat.	Sunset	Twilight Civil	Twilight Naut.	Moonset 31	1	2	3
N 72	14 01	15 50	17 19	■	■	■	
N 70	14 43	16 08	17 27	09 51	■	■	11 41
68	15 11	16 23	17 33	10 37	10 55	11 37	12 54
66	15 32	16 35	17 39	11 07	11 34	12 21	13 31
64	15 48	16 45	17 44	11 30	12 02	12 50	13 57
62	16 02	16 54	17 48	11 48	12 23	13 12	14 17
60	16 14	17 01	17 52	12 03	12 40	13 30	14 34
N 58	16 24	17 08	17 56	12 16	12 55	13 45	14 47
56	16 33	17 14	17 59	12 27	13 07	13 58	14 59
54	16 41	17 19	18 02	12 37	13 18	14 09	15 10
52	16 48	17 24	18 05	12 45	13 27	14 18	15 19
50	16 54	17 29	18 08	12 53	13 36	14 27	15 27
45	17 08	17 39	18 14	13 10	13 54	14 46	15 45
N 40	17 19	17 48	18 20	13 24	14 09	15 01	15 59
35	17 29	17 55	18 26	13 35	14 22	15 14	16 11
30	17 37	18 02	18 31	13 45	14 33	15 25	16 22
20	17 52	18 15	18 41	14 03	14 51	15 44	16 40
N 10	18 05	18 27	18 52	14 18	15 08	16 01	16 56
0	18 17	18 39	19 04	14 32	15 23	16 16	17 10
S 10	18 30	18 52	19 17	14 47	15 39	16 32	17 25
20	18 43	19 06	19 34	15 02	15 55	16 48	17 41
30	18 58	19 24	19 55	15 20	16 14	17 07	17 58
35	19 07	19 35	20 08	15 30	16 25	17 18	18 09
40	19 18	19 48	20 24	15 42	16 37	17 31	18 20
45	19 30	20 03	20 45	15 56	16 52	17 46	18 34
S 50	19 45	20 23	21 12	16 12	17 11	18 04	18 51
52	19 52	20 32	21 25	16 20	17 19	18 12	18 59
54	19 59	20 43	21 42	16 29	17 29	18 22	19 08
56	20 08	20 55	22 02	16 39	17 40	18 33	19 18
58	20 18	21 09	22 29	16 51	17 52	18 45	19 29
S 60	20 29	21 21	23 10	17 04	18 07	19 00	19 42

Day	SUN Eqn. of Time 00h	SUN Eqn. of Time 12h	SUN Mer. Pass.	MOON Mer. Pass. Upper	MOON Mer. Pass. Lower	Age	Phase
	m s	m s	h m	h m	h m	d	
31	13 26	13 30	12 14	08 21	20 45	25	
1	13 34	13 38	12 14	09 11	21 37	26	◑
2	13 42	13 46	12 14	10 03	22 30	27	

G.M.T.	ARIES G.H.A.	VENUS −3.3 G.H.A.	Dec.	MARS +1.4 G.H.A.	Dec.	JUPITER −1.8 G.H.A.	Dec.	SATURN +0.9 G.H.A.	Dec.	STARS Name	S.H.A.	Dec.
3 00	133 05.0	192 25.6	S20 59.8	163 37.3	S13 32.7	303 05.4	S 2 43.4	303 18.0	S 1 29.2	Acamar	315 37.0	S40 23.2
01	148 07.5	207 24.7	59.3	178 37.9	32.0	318 07.9	43.3	318 20.5	29.1	Achernar	335 45.3	S57 20.4
02	163 09.9	222 23.9	58.8	193 38.4	31.3	333 10.4	43.3	333 23.0	29.1	Acrux	173 36.5	S62 59.4
03	178 12.4	237 23.1	·· 58.2	208 39.0	·· 30.6	348 12.9	·· 43.3	348 25.5	·· 29.1	Adhara	255 31.6	S28 57.0
04	193 14.9	252 22.2	57.7	223 39.5	30.0	3 15.5	43.2	3 28.1	29.0	Aldebaran	291 17.5	N16 28.2
05	208 17.3	267 21.4	57.1	238 40.1	29.3	18 18.0	43.2	18 30.6	29.0			
06	223 19.8	282 20.6	S20 56.6	253 40.7	S13 28.6	33 20.5	S 2 43.1	33 33.1	S 1 28.9	Alioth	166 42.0	N56 03.5
07	238 22.3	297 19.7	56.0	268 41.2	27.9	48 23.1	43.1	48 35.6	28.9	Alkaid	153 18.2	N49 24.2
T 08	253 24.7	312 18.9	55.5	283 41.8	27.2	63 25.6	43.1	63 38.2	28.9	Al Na'ir	28 15.1	S47 03.4
U 09	268 27.2	327 18.0	·· 54.9	298 42.3	·· 26.5	78 28.1	·· 43.0	78 40.7	·· 28.8	Alnilam	276 11.2	S 1 13.0
E 10	283 29.7	342 17.2	54.4	313 42.9	25.8	93 30.6	43.0	93 43.2	28.8	Alphard	218 20.0	S 8 34.7
S 11	298 32.1	357 16.4	53.8	328 43.4	25.1	108 33.2	42.9	108 45.7	28.8			
D 12	313 34.6	12 15.5	S20 53.3	343 44.0	S13 24.4	123 35.7	S 2 42.9	123 48.3	S 1 28.7	Alphecca	126 32.0	N26 46.6
A 13	328 37.0	27 14.7	52.7	358 44.6	23.7	138 38.2	42.9	138 50.8	28.7	Alpheratz	358 09.3	N28 59.1
Y 14	343 39.5	42 13.9	52.2	13 45.1	23.1	153 40.8	42.8	153 53.3	28.6	Altair	62 32.6	N 8 49.0
15	358 42.0	57 13.0	·· 51.6	28 45.7	·· 22.4	168 43.3	·· 42.8	168 55.8	·· 28.6	Ankaa	353 40.3	S42 24.9
16	13 44.4	72 12.2	51.0	43 46.2	21.7	183 45.8	42.7	183 58.4	28.6	Antares	112 56.7	S26 23.3
17	28 46.9	87 11.4	50.5	58 46.8	21.0	198 48.4	42.7	199 00.9	28.5			
18	43 49.4	102 10.5	S20 49.9	73 47.4	S13 20.3	213 50.9	S 2 42.7	214 03.4	S 1 28.5	Arcturus	146 18.2	N19 16.7
19	58 51.8	117 09.7	49.4	88 47.9	19.6	228 53.4	42.6	229 05.9	28.5	Atria	108 20.9	S68 59.3
20	73 54.3	132 08.9	48.8	103 48.5	18.9	243 56.0	42.6	244 08.5	28.4	Avior	234 27.4	S59 27.0
21	88 56.8	147 08.1	·· 48.2	118 49.0	·· 18.2	258 58.5	·· 42.5	259 11.0	·· 28.4	Bellatrix	278 58.3	N 6 19.8
22	103 59.2	162 07.2	47.7	133 49.6	17.5	274 01.0	42.5	274 13.5	28.3	Betelgeuse	271 27.7	N 7 24.1
23	119 01.7	177 06.4	47.1	148 50.2	16.8	289 03.6	42.5	289 16.0	28.3			
4 00	134 04.2	192 05.6	S20 46.5	163 50.7	S13 16.1	304 06.1	S 2 42.4	304 18.6	S 1 28.3	Canopus	264 06.6	S52 41.4
01	149 06.6	207 04.7	46.0	178 51.3	15.4	319 08.6	42.4	319 21.1	28.2	Capella	281 10.6	N45 58.8
02	164 09.1	222 03.9	45.4	193 51.8	14.8	334 11.2	42.3	334 23.6	28.2	Deneb	49 48.7	N45 12.7
03	179 11.5	237 03.1	·· 44.8	208 52.4	·· 14.1	349 13.7	·· 42.3	349 26.1	·· 28.1	Denebola	182 58.5	N14 40.6
04	194 14.0	252 02.3	44.3	223 53.0	13.4	4 16.2	42.2	4 28.7	28.1	Diphda	349 20.8	S18 05.7
05	209 16.5	267 01.4	43.7	238 53.5	12.7	19 18.8	42.2	19 31.2	28.1			
06	224 18.9	282 00.6	S20 43.1	253 54.1	S13 12.0	34 21.3	S 2 42.2	34 33.7	S 1 28.0	Dubhe	194 21.2	N61 51.0
W 07	239 21.4	296 59.8	42.6	268 54.7	11.3	49 23.8	42.1	49 36.2	28.0	Elnath	278 43.6	N28 35.5
E 08	254 23.9	311 59.0	42.0	283 55.2	10.6	64 26.4	42.1	64 38.8	28.0	Eltanin	90 58.0	N51 29.3
D 09	269 26.3	326 58.1	·· 41.4	298 55.8	·· 09.9	79 28.9	·· 42.0	79 41.3	·· 27.9	Enif	34 11.6	N 9 47.2
N 10	284 28.8	341 57.3	40.8	313 56.3	09.2	94 31.5	42.0	94 43.8	27.9	Fomalhaut	15 51.4	S29 43.6
E 11	299 31.3	356 56.5	40.3	328 56.9	08.5	109 34.0	41.9	109 46.3	27.8			
S 12	314 33.7	11 55.7	S20 39.7	343 57.5	S13 07.8	124 36.5	S 2 41.9	124 48.9	S 1 27.8	Gacrux	172 28.1	S57 00.2
D 13	329 36.2	26 54.8	39.1	358 58.0	07.1	139 39.1	41.9	139 51.4	27.8	Gienah	176 17.5	S17 26.2
A 14	344 38.6	41 54.0	38.5	13 58.6	06.4	154 41.6	41.8	154 53.9	27.7	Hadar	149 22.8	S60 16.6
Y 15	359 41.1	56 53.2	·· 37.9	28 59.2	·· 05.7	169 44.1	·· 41.8	169 56.5	·· 27.7	Hamal	328 28.7	N23 22.3
16	14 43.6	71 52.4	37.3	43 59.7	05.0	184 46.7	41.7	184 59.0	27.6	Kaus Aust.	84 16.8	S34 23.6
17	29 46.0	86 51.5	36.8	59 00.3	04.3	199 49.2	41.7	200 01.5	27.6			
18	44 48.5	101 50.7	S20 36.2	74 00.9	S13 03.6	214 51.8	S 2 41.6	215 04.0	S 1 27.6	Kochab	137 19.1	N74 13.7
19	59 51.0	116 49.9	35.6	89 01.4	02.9	229 54.3	41.6	230 06.6	27.5	Markab	14 03.2	N15 06.1
20	74 53.4	131 49.1	35.0	104 02.0	02.2	244 56.8	41.6	245 09.1	27.5	Menkar	314 40.8	N 4 00.8
21	89 55.9	146 48.3	·· 34.4	119 02.5	·· 01.5	259 59.4	·· 41.5	260 11.6	·· 27.4	Menkent	148 36.6	S36 16.4
22	104 58.4	161 47.4	33.8	134 03.1	00.8	275 01.9	41.5	275 14.2	27.4	Miaplacidus	221 43.9	S69 38.4
23	120 00.8	176 46.6	33.2	149 03.7	13 00.1	290 04.5	41.4	290 16.7	27.4			
5 00	135 03.3	191 45.8	S20 32.6	164 04.2	S12 59.4	305 07.0	S 2 41.4	305 19.2	S 1 27.3	Mirfak	309 15.6	N49 47.8
01	150 05.8	206 45.0	32.1	179 04.8	58.7	320 09.6	41.3	320 21.7	27.3	Nunki	76 29.2	S26 19.2
02	165 08.2	221 44.2	31.5	194 05.4	58.0	335 12.1	41.3	335 24.3	27.2	Peacock	53 58.6	S56 47.8
03	180 10.7	236 43.4	·· 30.9	209 05.9	·· 57.3	350 14.6	·· 41.2	350 26.8	·· 27.2	Pollux	243 57.5	N28 04.3
04	195 13.1	251 42.5	30.3	224 06.5	56.6	5 17.2	41.2	5 29.3	27.2	Procyon	245 25.2	N 5 16.3
05	210 15.6	266 41.7	29.7	239 07.1	55.9	20 19.7	41.2	20 31.9	27.1			
06	225 18.1	281 40.9	S20 29.1	254 07.6	S12 55.2	35 22.3	S 2 41.1	35 34.4	S 1 27.1	Rasalhague	96 29.6	N12 34.3
07	240 20.5	296 40.1	28.5	269 08.2	54.5	50 24.8	41.1	50 36.9	27.0	Regulus	208 09.4	N12 03.5
T 08	255 23.0	311 39.3	27.9	284 08.8	53.8	65 27.4	41.0	65 39.5	27.0	Rigel	281 35.6	S 8 13.6
H 09	270 25.5	326 38.5	·· 27.3	299 09.3	·· 53.1	80 29.9	·· 41.0	80 42.0	·· 27.0	Rigil Kent.	140 25.4	S60 45.1
U 10	285 27.9	341 37.6	26.7	314 09.9	52.4	95 32.4	40.9	95 44.5	26.9	Sabik	102 41.0	S15 42.1
R 11	300 30.4	356 36.8	26.1	329 10.5	51.7	110 35.0	40.9	110 47.1	26.9			
S 12	315 32.8	11 36.0	S20 25.5	344 11.0	S12 51.0	125 37.5	S 2 40.8	125 49.6	S 1 26.8	Schedar	350 09.0	N56 26.1
D 13	330 35.3	26 35.2	24.9	359 11.6	50.3	140 40.1	40.8	140 52.1	26.8	Shaula	96 55.7	S37 05.3
A 14	345 37.8	41 34.4	24.3	14 12.2	49.6	155 42.6	40.7	155 54.6	26.8	Sirius	258 55.2	S16 41.6
Y 15	0 40.3	56 33.6	·· 23.6	29 12.7	·· 48.9	170 45.2	·· 40.7	170 57.2	·· 26.7	Spica	158 57.1	S11 03.7
16	15 42.7	71 32.8	23.0	44 13.3	48.2	185 47.7	40.6	185 59.7	26.7	Suhail	223 10.1	S43 21.4
17	30 45.2	86 32.0	22.4	59 13.9	47.5	200 50.3	40.6	201 02.2	26.6			
18	45 47.6	101 31.2	S20 21.8	74 14.4	S12 46.8	215 52.8	S 2 40.6	216 04.8	S 1 26.6	Vega	80 56.0	N38 45.8
19	60 50.1	116 30.3	21.2	89 15.0	46.1	230 55.4	40.5	231 07.3	26.6	Zuben'ubi	137 32.7	S15 57.7
20	75 52.6	131 29.5	20.6	104 15.6	45.4	245 57.9	40.5	246 09.8	26.5			
21	90 55.0	146 28.7	·· 20.0	119 16.1	·· 44.7	261 00.5	·· 40.4	261 12.4	·· 26.5		S.H.A.	Mer. Pass.
22	105 57.5	161 27.9	19.4	134 16.7	44.0	276 03.0	40.4	276 14.9	26.4	Venus	58 01.4	11 12
23	121 00.0	176 27.1	18.8	149 17.3	43.3	291 05.5	40.3	291 17.4	26.4	Mars	29 46.6	13 04
Mer. Pass. 15 01.3		v −0.8 d 0.6		v 0.6 d 0.7		v 2.5 d 0.0		v 2.5 d 0.0		Jupiter	170 01.9	3 43
										Saturn	170 14.4	3 42

G.M.T.	SUN G.H.A.	Dec.	MOON G.H.A.	v	Dec.	d	H.P.	Lat.	Twilight Naut.	Civil	Sunrise	Moonrise 3	4	5	6
d h	° ′	° ′	° ′	′	° ′	′	′	°	h m	h m	h m	h m	h m	h m	h m
3 00	176 32.6	S16 36.4	201 38.8	8.4	S20 04.4	2.0	57.0	N 72	06 59	08 25	10 04	■	11 18	10 24	10 04
01	191 32.5	35.6	216 06.2	8.3	20 02.4	2.2	57.1	N 70	06 52	08 09	09 30	10 19	10 00	09 52	09 45
02	206 32.5	34.9	230 33.5	8.4	20 00.2	2.2	57.1	68	06 47	07 56	09 05	09 06	09 21	09 28	09 31
03	221 32.4 ··	34.2	245 00.9	8.3	19 58.0	2.4	57.1	66	06 42	07 45	08 46	08 29	08 54	09 09	09 19
04	236 32.3	33.4	259 28.2	8.3	19 55.6	2.5	57.2	64	06 38	07 35	08 31	08 02	08 33	08 54	09 08
05	251 32.3	32.7	273 55.5	8.3	19 53.1	2.7	57.2	62	06 34	07 27	08 18	07 42	08 16	08 41	09 00
06	266 32.2	S16 32.0	288 22.8	8.3	S19 50.4	2.7	57.2	60	06 30	07 20	08 07	07 25	08 02	08 30	08 52
07	281 32.1	31.2	302 50.1	8.2	19 47.7	2.8	57.2	N 58	06 27	07 14	07 58	07 11	07 50	08 21	08 46
08	296 32.1	30.5	317 17.3	8.3	19 44.9	3.0	57.3	56	06 24	07 09	07 49	06 59	07 39	08 12	08 40
09	311 32.0 ··	29.7	331 44.6	8.2	19 41.9	3.1	57.3	54	06 21	07 04	07 42	06 48	07 30	08 05	08 34
T 10	326 31.9	29.0	346 11.8	8.2	19 38.8	3.2	57.3	52	06 19	06 59	07 35	06 39	07 22	07 58	08 30
U 11	341 31.9	28.3	0 39.0	8.2	19 35.6	3.3	57.4	50	06 16	06 55	07 29	06 30	07 14	07 52	08 25
E 12	356 31.8	S16 27.5	15 06.2	8.1	S19 32.3	3.5	57.4	45	06 10	06 45	07 16	06 12	06 58	07 39	08 16
S 13	11 31.7	26.8	29 33.3	8.2	19 28.8	3.5	57.4	N 40	06 05	06 37	07 06	05 58	06 45	07 29	08 08
D 14	26 31.7	26.1	44 00.5	8.2	19 25.3	3.7	57.4	35	06 00	06 30	06 57	05 45	06 34	07 19	08 01
A 15	41 31.6 ··	25.3	58 27.7	8.1	19 21.6	3.8	57.5	30	05 55	06 24	06 49	05 34	06 24	07 11	07 55
Y 16	56 31.5	24.6	72 54.8	8.1	19 17.8	3.9	57.5	20	05 45	06 12	06 35	05 16	06 07	06 57	07 45
17	71 31.5	23.8	87 21.9	8.2	19 13.9	4.1	57.5	N 10	05 35	06 00	06 22	04 59	05 53	06 45	07 36
18	86 31.4	S16 23.1	101 49.1	8.1	S19 09.8	4.1	57.6	0	05 24	05 49	06 10	04 44	05 39	06 33	07 27
19	101 31.3	22.4	116 16.2	8.1	19 05.7	4.3	57.6	S 10	05 11	05 37	05 59	04 29	05 25	06 22	07 18
20	116 31.3	21.6	130 43.3	8.1	19 01.4	4.4	57.6	20	04 55	05 23	05 46	04 13	05 10	06 09	07 09
21	131 31.2 ··	20.9	145 10.4	8.1	18 57.0	4.4	57.6	30	04 35	05 06	05 31	03 54	04 53	05 55	06 59
22	146 31.2	20.1	159 37.5	8.1	18 52.6	4.7	57.7	35	04 22	04 54	05 23	03 43	04 43	05 47	06 53
23	161 31.1	19.4	174 04.6	8.1	18 47.9	4.7	57.7	40	04 07	04 43	05 13	03 31	04 32	05 38	06 46
4 00	176 31.0	S16 18.6	188 31.7	8.1	S18 43.2	4.8	57.7	45	03 47	04 28	05 01	03 16	04 19	05 27	06 38
01	191 31.0	17.9	202 58.8	8.0	18 38.4	5.0	57.8	S 50	03 21	04 09	04 47	02 58	04 02	05 13	06 28
02	206 30.9	17.2	217 25.8	8.1	18 33.4	5.1	57.8	52	03 08	04 00	04 40	02 50	03 55	05 07	06 23
03	221 30.8 ··	16.4	231 52.9	8.1	18 28.3	5.2	57.8	54	02 52	03 50	04 33	02 40	03 46	05 00	06 18
04	236 30.8	15.7	246 20.0	8.1	18 23.1	5.3	57.8	56	02 33	03 39	04 25	02 29	03 37	04 52	06 13
05	251 30.7	14.9	260 47.1	8.1	18 17.8	5.4	57.9	58	02 09	03 25	04 15	02 17	03 26	04 43	06 07
06	266 30.7	S16 14.2	275 14.2	8.1	S18 12.4	5.5	57.9	S 60	01 34	03 09	04 04	02 03	03 13	04 33	06 00

G.M.T.	SUN G.H.A.	Dec.	MOON G.H.A.	v	Dec.	d	H.P.	Lat.	Sunset	Twilight Civil	Naut.	Moonset 3	4	5	6
W 07	281 30.6	13.4	289 41.3	8.1	18 06.9	5.7	57.9	°	h m	h m	h m	h m	h m	h m	h m
E 08	296 30.5	12.7	304 08.4	8.1	18 01.2	5.7	58.0	N 72	14 25	16 04	17 31	■	12 37	15 25	17 37
D 09	311 30.5 ··	11.9	318 35.5	8.1	17 55.5	5.9	58.0	N 70	15 00	16 20	17 37	11 41	13 55	15 56	17 54
N 10	326 30.4	11.2	333 02.6	8.1	17 49.6	6.0	58.0	68	15 24	16 34	17 43	12 54	14 33	16 19	18 07
E 11	341 30.4	10.4	347 29.7	8.1	17 43.6	6.1	58.0	66	15 43	16 44	17 47	13 31	14 59	16 37	18 18
S 12	356 30.3	S16 09.7	1 56.8	8.1	S17 37.5	6.2	58.1	64	15 58	16 54	17 52	13 57	15 19	16 51	18 27
D 13	11 30.3	08.9	16 23.9	8.2	17 31.3	6.3	58.1	62	16 11	17 02	17 55	14 17	15 36	17 03	18 34
A 14	26 30.2	08.2	30 51.1	8.1	17 25.0	6.4	58.1	60	16 22	17 08	17 59	14 34	15 49	17 13	18 41
Y 15	41 30.1 ··	07.4	45 18.2	8.2	17 18.6	6.5	58.1	N 58	16 31	17 15	18 02	14 47	16 01	17 22	18 47
16	56 30.1	06.7	59 45.4	8.1	17 12.1	6.7	58.2	56	16 39	17 20	18 05	14 59	16 11	17 30	18 52
17	71 30.0	05.9	74 12.5	8.2	17 05.4	6.7	58.2	54	16 47	17 25	18 07	15 10	16 20	17 36	18 56
18	86 30.0	S16 05.2	An Annular Eclipse of					52	16 53	17 30	18 10	15 19	16 28	17 43	19 00
19	101 29.9	04.4	the Sun occurs on this					45	17 12	17 43	18 18	15 45	16 50	18 00	19 12
20	116 29.9	03.7	date. See page 5.					N 40	17 23	17 51	18 23	15 59	17 03	18 10	19 19
21	131 29.8 ··	02.9						35	17 32	17 58	18 28	16 11	17 13	18 18	19 24
22	146 29.8	02.2						30	17 40	18 05	18 33	16 22	17 23	18 25	19 29
23	161 29.7	01.4						20	17 54	18 18	18 43	16 40	17 38	18 38	19 38
5 00	176 29.7	S16 00.6	175 23.0	8.2	S16 16.0	7.5	58.4	N 10	18 06	18 28	18 53	16 56	17 52	18 49	19 45
01	191 29.6	15 59.9	189 50.2	8.3	16 08.5	7.6	58.4	0	18 17	18 39	19 04	17 10	18 05	18 59	19 52
02	206 29.5	59.1	204 17.5	8.3	16 00.9	7.7	58.4	S 10	18 29	18 51	19 17	17 25	18 18	19 09	19 59
03	221 29.5 ··	58.4	218 44.8	8.3	15 53.2	7.8	58.4	20	18 42	19 05	19 32	17 41	18 31	19 20	20 07
04	236 29.4	57.6	233 12.1	8.3	15 45.4	7.9	58.5	30	18 56	19 22	19 52	17 58	18 47	19 32	20 15
05	251 29.4	56.9	247 39.4	8.4	15 37.5	7.9	58.5	35	19 05	19 32	20 05	18 09	18 56	19 39	20 19
06	266 29.3	S15 56.1	262 06.8	8.4	S15 29.6	8.1	58.5	40	19 15	19 44	20 20	18 20	19 06	19 47	20 25
07	281 29.3	55.3	276 34.2	8.3	15 21.5	8.2	58.5	45	19 26	19 59	20 40	18 34	19 18	19 56	20 31
T 08	296 29.2	54.6	291 01.5	8.4	15 13.3	8.3	58.6	S 50	19 40	20 17	21 05	18 51	19 32	20 07	20 38
H 09	311 29.2 ··	53.8	305 28.9	8.5	15 05.0	8.4	58.6	52	19 47	20 26	21 18	18 59	19 39	20 12	20 42
U 10	326 29.1	53.1	319 56.4	8.4	14 56.6	8.4	58.6	54	19 54	20 36	21 33	19 08	19 46	20 18	20 45
R 11	341 29.1	52.3	334 23.8	8.5	14 48.2	8.6	58.6	56	20 02	20 48	21 52	19 18	19 54	20 24	20 49
S 12	356 29.0	S15 51.5	348 51.3	8.4	S14 39.6	8.7	58.7	58	20 11	21 01	22 15	19 29	20 04	20 31	20 54
D 13	11 29.0	50.8	3 18.7	8.5	14 30.9	8.7	58.7	S 60	20 22	21 17	22 48	19 42	20 14	20 39	20 59
A 14	26 28.9	50.0	17 46.2	8.6	14 22.2	8.9	58.7								
Y 15	41 28.9 ··	49.3	32 13.8	8.5	14 13.3	8.9	58.7								
16	56 28.8	48.5	46 41.3	8.6	14 04.4	9.0	58.7								
17	71 28.8	47.7	61 08.9	8.6	13 55.4	9.2	58.8								

Day	SUN Eqn. of Time 00ʰ	12ʰ	Mer. Pass.	MOON Mer. Pass. Upper	Lower	Age	Phase
	m s	m s	h m	h m	h m	d	
3	13 49	13 53	12 14	10 57	23 25	28	
4	13 56	13 59	12 14	11 52	24 19	29	
5	14 01	14 04	12 14	12 46	00 19	01	●

18	86 28.8	S15 47.0	75 36.5	8.6	S13 46.2	9.2	58.8
19	101 28.7	46.2	90 04.1	8.6	13 37.0	9.2	58.8
20	116 28.7	45.4	104 31.7	8.7	13 27.8	9.4	58.9
21	131 28.6 ··	44.7	118 59.4	8.6	13 18.4	9.5	58.8
22	146 28.6	43.9	133 27.0	8.7	13 08.9	9.5	58.9
23	161 28.5	43.1	147 54.7	8.8	12 59.4	9.7	58.9

| S.D. 16.2 | d 0.7 | S.D. 15.6 | 15.8 | 16.0 |

G.M.T.	ARIES G.H.A.	VENUS −3.4 G.H.A.	Dec.	MARS +1.4 G.H.A.	Dec.	JUPITER −1.9 G.H.A.	Dec.	SATURN +0.8 G.H.A.	Dec.	STARS Name	S.H.A.	Dec.
6 00	136 02.4	191 26.3	S20 18.1	164 17.9	S12 42.6	306 08.1	S 2 40.3	306 20.0	S 1 26.4	Acamar	315 37.0	S40 23.2
01	151 04.9	206 25.5	17.5	179 18.4	41.9	321 10.6	40.2	321 22.5	26.3	Achernar	335 45.3	S57 20.4
02	166 07.4	221 24.7	16.9	194 19.0	41.2	336 13.2	40.2	336 25.0	26.3	Acrux	173 36.4	S62 59.4
03	181 09.8	236 23.9	·· 16.3	209 19.6	·· 40.5	351 15.7	·· 40.1	351 27.6	·· 26.2	Adhara	255 31.6	S28 57.0
04	196 12.3	251 23.1	15.7	224 20.1	39.8	6 18.3	40.1	6 30.1	26.2	Aldebaran	291 17.6	N16 28.2
05	211 14.8	266 22.3	15.0	239 20.7	39.1	21 20.8	40.0	21 32.6	26.1			
06	226 17.2	281 21.5	S20 14.4	254 21.3	S12 38.4	36 23.4	S 2 40.0	36 35.2	S 1 26.1	Alioth	166 42.0	N56 03.5
07	241 19.7	296 20.7	13.8	269 21.8	37.7	51 25.9	39.9	51 37.7	26.1	Alkaid	153 18.1	N49 24.2
08	256 22.1	311 19.9	13.2	284 22.4	37.0	66 28.5	39.9	66 40.2	26.0	Al Na'ir	28 15.1	S47 03.3
F 09	271 24.6	326 19.1	·· 12.5	299 23.0	·· 36.3	81 31.1	·· 39.8	81 42.8	·· 26.0	Alnilam	276 11.2	S 1 13.0
R 10	286 27.1	341 18.2	11.9	314 23.6	35.6	96 33.6	39.8	96 45.3	25.9	Alphard	218 20.0	S 8 34.7
I 11	301 29.5	356 17.4	11.3	329 24.1	34.9	111 36.2	39.7	111 47.8	25.9			
D 12	316 32.0	11 16.6	S20 10.7	344 24.7	S12 34.2	126 38.7	S 2 39.7	126 50.4	S 1 25.9	Alphecca	126 31.9	N26 46.5
A 13	331 34.5	26 15.8	10.0	359 25.3	33.5	141 41.3	39.6	141 52.9	25.8	Alpheratz	358 09.3	N28 59.1
Y 14	346 36.9	41 15.0	09.4	14 25.8	32.8	156 43.8	39.6	156 55.5	25.8	Altair	62 32.6	N 8 49.0
15	1 39.4	56 14.2	·· 08.8	29 26.4	·· 32.0	171 46.4	·· 39.5	171 58.0	·· 25.7	Ankaa	353 40.3	S42 24.8
16	16 41.9	71 13.4	08.1	44 27.0	31.3	186 48.9	39.5	187 00.5	25.7	Antares	112 56.6	S26 23.3
17	31 44.3	86 12.6	07.5	59 27.6	30.6	201 51.5	39.4	202 03.1	25.6			
18	46 46.8	101 11.8	S20 06.9	74 28.1	S12 29.9	216 54.0	S 2 39.4	217 05.6	S 1 25.6	Arcturus	146 18.2	N19 16.7
19	61 49.2	116 11.0	06.2	89 28.7	29.2	231 56.6	39.3	232 08.1	25.6	Atria	108 20.9	S68 59.3
20	76 51.7	131 10.2	05.6	104 29.3	28.5	246 59.1	39.3	247 10.7	25.5	Avior	234 27.4	S59 27.0
21	91 54.2	146 09.4	·· 04.9	119 29.9	·· 27.8	262 01.7	·· 39.2	262 13.2	·· 25.5	Bellatrix	278 58.3	N 6 19.8
22	106 56.6	161 08.6	04.3	134 30.4	27.1	277 04.2	39.2	277 15.7	25.4	Betelgeuse	271 27.8	N 7 24.1
23	121 59.1	176 07.8	03.7	149 31.0	26.4	292 06.8	39.1	292 18.3	25.4			
7 00	137 01.6	191 07.1	S20 03.0	164 31.6	S12 25.7	307 09.4	S 2 39.1	307 20.8	S 1 25.3	Canopus	264 06.7	S52 41.4
01	152 04.0	206 06.3	02.4	179 32.2	25.0	322 11.9	39.0	322 23.4	25.3	Capella	281 10.6	N45 58.8
02	167 06.5	221 05.5	01.7	194 32.7	24.3	337 14.5	39.0	337 25.9	25.3	Deneb	49 48.7	N45 12.7
03	182 09.0	236 04.7	·· 01.1	209 33.3	·· 23.6	352 17.0	·· 38.9	352 28.4	·· 25.2	Denebola	182 58.5	N14 40.6
04	197 11.4	251 03.9	20 00.4	224 33.9	22.8	7 19.6	38.9	7 31.0	25.2	Diphda	349 20.8	S18 05.7
05	212 13.9	266 03.1	19 59.8	239 34.4	22.1	22 22.1	38.8	22 33.5	25.1			
06	227 16.4	281 02.3	S19 59.2	254 35.0	S12 21.4	37 24.7	S 2 38.8	37 36.0	S 1 25.1	Dubhe	194 21.2	N61 51.1
07	242 18.8	296 01.5	58.5	269 35.6	20.7	52 27.3	38.7	52 38.6	25.0	Elnath	278 43.6	N28 35.5
S 08	257 21.3	311 00.7	57.9	284 36.2	20.0	67 29.8	38.7	67 41.1	25.0	Eltanin	90 58.0	N51 29.3
A 09	272 23.7	325 59.9	·· 57.2	299 36.7	·· 19.3	82 32.4	·· 38.6	82 43.7	·· 25.0	Enif	34 11.6	N 9 47.2
T 10	287 26.2	340 59.1	56.6	314 37.3	18.6	97 34.9	38.6	97 46.2	24.9	Fomalhaut	15 51.4	S29 43.6
U 11	302 28.7	355 58.3	55.9	329 37.9	17.9	112 37.5	38.5	112 48.7	24.9			
R 12	317 31.1	10 57.5	S19 55.2	344 38.5	S12 17.2	127 40.1	S 2 38.5	127 51.3	S 1 24.8	Gacrux	172 28.0	S57 00.2
D 13	332 33.6	25 56.7	54.6	359 39.1	16.4	142 42.6	38.4	142 53.8	24.8	Gienah	176 17.5	S17 26.2
A 14	347 36.1	40 55.9	53.9	14 39.6	15.7	157 45.2	38.4	157 56.4	24.7	Hadar	149 22.8	S60 16.6
Y 15	2 38.5	55 55.2	·· 53.3	29 40.2	·· 15.0	172 47.7	·· 38.3	172 58.9	·· 24.7	Hamal	328 28.7	N23 22.3
16	17 41.0	70 54.4	52.6	44 40.8	14.3	187 50.3	38.3	188 01.4	24.7	Kaus Aust.	84 16.8	S34 23.6
17	32 43.5	85 53.6	52.0	59 41.4	13.6	202 52.9	38.2	203 04.0	24.6			
18	47 45.9	100 52.8	S19 51.3	74 41.9	S12 12.9	217 55.4	S 2 38.2	218 06.5	S 1 24.6	Kochab	137 19.0	N74 13.7
19	62 48.4	115 52.0	50.6	89 42.5	12.2	232 58.0	38.1	233 09.1	24.5	Markab	14 03.2	N15 06.1
20	77 50.9	130 51.2	50.0	104 43.1	11.5	248 00.5	38.1	248 11.6	24.5	Menkar	314 40.8	N 4 00.8
21	92 53.3	145 50.4	·· 49.3	119 43.7	·· 10.8	263 03.1	·· 38.0	263 14.1	·· 24.4	Menkent	148 36.6	S36 16.4
22	107 55.8	160 49.6	48.7	134 44.2	10.0	278 05.7	38.0	278 16.7	24.4	Miaplacidus	221 43.9	S69 38.4
23	122 58.2	175 48.9	48.0	149 44.8	09.3	293 08.2	37.9	293 19.2	24.3			
8 00	138 00.7	190 48.1	S19 47.3	164 45.4	S12 08.6	308 10.8	S 2 37.8	308 21.8	S 1 24.3	Mirfak	309 15.6	N49 47.8
01	153 03.2	205 47.3	46.7	179 46.0	07.9	323 13.4	37.8	323 24.3	24.3	Nunki	76 29.1	S26 19.2
02	168 05.6	220 46.5	46.0	194 46.6	07.2	338 15.9	37.7	338 26.8	24.2	Peacock	53 58.6	S56 47.8
03	183 08.1	235 45.7	·· 45.3	209 47.1	·· 06.5	353 18.5	·· 37.7	353 29.4	·· 24.2	Pollux	243 57.5	N28 04.3
04	198 10.6	250 44.9	44.6	224 47.7	05.8	8 21.0	37.6	8 31.9	24.1	Procyon	245 25.2	N 5 16.3
05	213 13.0	265 44.2	44.0	239 48.3	05.0	23 23.6	37.6	23 34.5	24.1			
06	228 15.5	280 43.4	S19 43.3	254 48.9	S12 04.3	38 26.2	S 2 37.5	38 37.0	S 1 24.0	Rasalhague	96 29.5	N12 34.3
07	243 18.0	295 42.6	42.6	269 49.5	03.6	53 28.7	37.5	53 39.5	24.0	Regulus	208 09.4	N12 03.5
08	258 20.4	310 41.8	42.0	284 50.0	02.9	68 31.3	37.4	68 42.1	23.9	Rigel	281 35.6	S 8 13.6
S 09	273 22.9	325 41.0	·· 41.3	299 50.6	·· 02.2	83 33.9	·· 37.4	83 44.6	·· 23.9	Rigil Kent.	140 25.4	S60 45.1
U 10	288 25.3	340 40.2	40.6	314 51.2	01.5	98 36.4	37.3	98 47.2	23.9	Sabik	102 41.0	S15 42.1
N 11	303 27.8	355 39.5	39.9	329 51.8	00.8	113 39.0	37.2	113 49.7	23.8			
D 12	318 30.3	10 38.7	S19 39.3	344 52.3	S12 00.0	128 41.6	S 2 37.2	128 52.3	S 1 23.8	Schedar	350 09.0	N56 26.1
A 13	333 32.7	25 37.9	38.6	359 52.9	11 59.3	143 44.1	37.1	143 54.8	23.7	Shaula	96 55.6	S37 05.3
Y 14	348 35.2	40 37.1	37.9	14 53.5	58.6	158 46.7	37.1	158 57.3	23.7	Sirius	258 55.2	S16 41.6
15	3 37.7	55 36.3	·· 37.2	29 54.1	·· 57.9	173 49.3	·· 37.0	173 59.9	·· 23.6	Spica	158 57.1	S11 03.7
16	18 40.1	70 35.6	36.5	44 54.7	57.2	188 51.8	37.0	189 02.4	23.6	Suhail	223 10.1	S43 21.4
17	33 42.6	85 34.8	35.8	59 55.3	56.4	203 54.4	36.9	204 05.0	23.5			
18	48 45.1	100 34.0	S19 35.2	74 55.8	S11 55.7	218 57.0	S 2 36.9	219 07.5	S 1 23.5	Vega	80 56.0	N38 45.8
19	63 47.5	115 33.2	34.5	89 56.4	55.0	233 59.5	36.8	234 10.1	23.4	Zuben'ubi	137 32.7	S15 57.7
20	78 50.0	130 32.5	33.8	104 57.0	54.3	249 02.1	36.8	249 12.6	23.4		S.H.A.	Mer. Pass.
21	93 52.5	145 31.7	·· 33.1	119 57.6	·· 53.6	264 04.7	·· 36.7	264 15.2	·· 23.4			
22	108 54.9	160 30.9	32.4	134 58.2	52.9	279 07.2	36.6	279 17.7	23.3	Venus	54 05.5	11 16
23	123 57.4	175 30.1	31.7	149 58.7	52.2	294 09.8	36.6	294 20.2	23.3	Mars	27 30.0	13 01
Mer. Pass.	14 49.5	v −0.8	d 0.7	v 0.6	d 0.7	v 2.6	d 0.1	v 2.5	d 0.0	Jupiter	170 07.8	3 31
										Saturn	170 19.3	3 30

SUN / MOON

G.M.T.	SUN G.H.A.	SUN Dec.	MOON G.H.A.	v	Dec.	d	H.P.
6 00	176 28.5	S15 42.4	162 22.5	8.7	S12 49.7	9.7	58.9
01	191 28.4	41.6	176 50.2	8.8	12 40.0	9.8	58.9
02	206 28.4	40.8	191 18.0	8.8	12 30.2	9.8	58.9
03	221 28.3	·· 40.1	205 45.8	8.8	12 20.4	10.0	59.0
04	236 28.3	39.3	220 13.6	8.8	12 10.4	10.0	59.0
05	251 28.3	38.5	234 41.4	8.9	12 00.4	10.1	59.0
06	266 28.2	S15 37.8	249 09.3	8.9	S11 50.3	10.2	59.0
07	281 28.2	37.0	263 37.2	8.9	11 40.1	10.2	59.0
08	296 28.1	36.2	278 05.1	9.0	11 29.9	10.4	59.0
F 09	311 28.1	·· 35.4	292 33.1	8.9	11 19.5	10.4	59.1
R 10	326 28.0	34.7	307 01.0	9.0	11 09.1	10.4	59.1
I 11	341 28.0	33.9	321 29.0	9.0	10 58.7	10.6	59.1
D 12	356 28.0	S15 33.1	335 57.0	9.1	S10 48.1	10.6	59.1
A 13	11 27.9	32.4	350 25.1	9.0	10 37.5	10.7	59.1
Y 14	26 27.9	31.6	4 53.1	9.1	10 26.8	10.7	59.1
15	41 27.8	·· 30.8	19 21.2	9.1	10 16.1	10.8	59.2
16	56 27.8	30.0	33 49.3	9.1	10 05.3	10.9	59.2
17	71 27.8	29.3	48 17.4	9.2	9 54.4	10.9	59.2
18	86 27.7	S15 28.5	62 45.6	9.2	S 9 43.5	11.0	59.2
19	101 27.7	27.7	77 13.8	9.2	9 32.5	11.1	59.2
20	116 27.7	26.9	91 42.0	9.2	9 21.4	11.1	59.2
21	131 27.6	·· 26.2	106 10.2	9.2	9 10.3	11.1	59.2
22	146 27.6	25.4	120 38.4	9.3	8 59.2	11.3	59.2
23	161 27.5	24.6	135 06.7	9.3	8 47.9	11.3	59.3
7 00	176 27.5	S15 23.8	149 35.0	9.3	S 8 36.6	11.3	59.3
01	191 27.5	23.0	164 03.3	9.3	8 25.3	11.4	59.3
02	206 27.4	22.3	178 31.6	9.4	8 13.9	11.4	59.3
03	221 27.4	·· 21.5	193 00.0	9.4	8 02.5	11.5	59.3
04	236 27.4	20.7	207 28.4	9.4	7 51.0	11.6	59.3
05	251 27.3	19.9	221 56.8	9.4	7 39.4	11.6	59.3
06	266 27.3	S15 19.1	236 25.2	9.4	S 7 27.8	11.6	59.3
07	281 27.3	18.4	250 53.6	9.5	7 16.2	11.7	59.4
S 08	296 27.2	17.6	265 22.1	9.4	7 04.5	11.7	59.4
A 09	311 27.2	·· 16.8	279 50.5	9.5	6 52.8	11.8	59.4
T 10	326 27.2	16.0	294 19.0	9.5	6 41.0	11.8	59.4
U 11	341 27.1	15.2	308 47.5	9.6	6 29.2	11.9	59.4
R 12	356 27.1	S15 14.5	323 16.1	9.5	S 6 17.3	11.9	59.4
D 13	11 27.1	13.7	337 44.6	9.6	6 05.4	11.9	59.4
A 14	26 27.0	12.9	352 13.2	9.6	5 53.5	12.0	59.4
Y 15	41 27.0	·· 12.1	6 41.8	9.6	5 41.5	12.0	59.4
16	56 27.0	11.3	21 10.4	9.6	5 29.5	12.0	59.5
17	71 26.9	10.5	35 39.0	9.6	5 17.5	12.1	59.4
18	86 26.9	S15 09.7	50 07.6	9.7	S 5 05.4	12.1	59.5
19	101 26.9	09.0	64 36.3	9.6	4 53.3	12.1	59.5
20	116 26.8	08.2	79 04.9	9.7	4 41.2	12.2	59.5
21	131 26.8	·· 07.4	93 33.6	9.7	4 29.0	12.2	59.5
22	146 26.8	06.6	108 02.3	9.7	4 16.8	12.2	59.5
23	161 26.8	05.8	122 31.0	9.7	4 04.6	12.2	59.5
8 00	176 26.7	S15 05.0	136 59.7	9.8	S 3 52.4	12.3	59.5
01	191 26.7	04.2	151 28.5	9.7	3 40.1	12.3	59.5
02	206 26.7	03.4	165 57.2	9.8	3 27.8	12.3	59.5
03	221 26.7	·· 02.7	180 26.0	9.7	3 15.5	12.3	59.5
04	236 26.6	01.9	194 54.7	9.8	3 03.2	12.3	59.5
05	251 26.6	01.1	209 23.5	9.8	2 50.9	12.4	59.5
06	266 26.6	S15 00.3	223 52.3	9.8	S 2 38.5	12.4	59.5
07	281 26.5	14 59.5	238 21.1	9.8	2 26.1	12.4	59.5
08	296 26.5	58.7	252 49.9	9.8	2 13.7	12.4	59.5
S 09	311 26.5	·· 57.9	267 18.7	9.8	2 01.3	12.4	59.5
U 10	326 26.5	57.1	281 47.5	9.9	1 48.9	12.5	59.5
N 11	341 26.4	56.3	296 16.3	9.9	1 36.4	12.5	59.5
D 12	356 26.4	S14 55.5	310 45.2	9.8	S 1 24.0	12.4	59.5
A 13	11 26.4	54.7	325 14.0	9.8	1 11.6	12.5	59.5
Y 14	26 26.4	53.9	339 42.8	9.9	0 59.1	12.5	59.5
15	41 26.4	·· 53.1	354 11.7	9.8	0 46.6	12.4	59.5
16	56 26.3	52.3	8 40.5	9.9	0 34.2	12.5	59.5
17	71 26.3	51.5	23 09.4	9.8	0 21.7	12.5	59.6
18	86 26.3	S14 50.8	37 38.2	9.9	S 0 09.2	12.5	59.6
19	101 26.3	50.0	52 07.1	9.8	N 0 03.2	12.5	59.6
20	116 26.2	49.2	66 35.9	9.9	0 15.7	12.5	59.6
21	131 26.2	·· 48.4	81 04.8	9.9	0 28.2	12.4	59.6
22	146 26.2	47.6	95 33.7	9.8	0 40.6	12.5	59.6
23	161 26.2	46.8	110 02.5	9.9	0 53.1	12.5	59.6
S.D.	16.2	d 0.8	S.D. 16.1		16.2		16.2

Twilight / Sunrise / Moonrise

Lat.	Twilight Naut.	Twilight Civil	Sunrise	Moonrise 6	7	8	9
N 72	06 48	08 12	09 43	10 04	09 50	09 37	09 26
N 70	06 42	07 57	09 14	09 45	09 40	09 35	09 30
68	06 38	07 45	08 52	09 31	09 32	09 32	09 33
66	06 34	07 36	08 35	09 19	09 25	09 31	09 36
64	06 30	07 27	08 21	09 08	09 20	09 29	09 38
62	06 27	07 20	08 09	09 00	09 15	09 28	09 40
60	06 24	07 14	07 59	08 52	09 10	09 26	09 42
N 58	06 21	07 08	07 51	08 46	09 06	09 25	09 43
56	06 19	07 03	07 43	08 40	09 03	09 24	09 45
54	06 17	06 59	07 36	08 34	09 00	09 23	09 46
52	06 14	06 54	07 30	08 30	08 57	09 23	09 47
50	06 12	06 50	07 25	08 25	08 55	09 22	09 48
45	06 07	06 42	07 13	08 16	08 49	09 20	09 51
N 40	06 02	06 34	07 03	08 08	08 44	09 19	09 53
35	05 58	06 28	06 54	08 01	08 40	09 18	09 54
30	05 53	06 22	06 47	07 55	08 37	09 17	09 56
20	05 44	06 11	06 33	07 45	08 30	09 15	09 59
N 10	05 35	06 00	06 22	07 36	08 25	09 13	10 01
0	05 24	05 49	06 11	07 27	08 20	09 12	10 03
S 10	05 12	05 38	06 00	07 18	08 15	09 10	10 06
20	04 57	05 24	05 48	07 09	08 09	09 09	10 08
30	04 38	05 08	05 34	06 59	08 03	09 07	10 11
35	04 26	04 58	05 26	06 53	07 59	09 06	10 13
40	04 11	04 47	05 16	06 46	07 55	09 05	10 15
45	03 53	04 33	05 05	06 38	07 50	09 04	10 17
S 50	03 28	04 15	04 52	06 28	07 45	09 02	10 20
52	03 16	04 07	04 46	06 23	07 42	09 01	10 21
54	03 02	03 57	04 39	06 18	07 39	09 01	10 22
56	02 44	03 46	04 31	06 13	07 36	09 00	10 24
58	02 23	03 34	04 23	06 07	07 32	08 59	10 26
S 60	01 54	03 19	04 13	06 00	07 28	08 58	10 27

Sunset / Twilight / Moonset

Lat.	Sunset	Twilight Civil	Twilight Naut.	Moonset 6	7	8	9
N 72	14 46	16 18	17 43	17 37	19 42	21 43	23 44
N 70	15 16	16 33	17 48	17 54	19 49	21 42	23 35
68	15 37	16 44	17 52	18 07	19 55	21 42	23 28
66	15 54	16 54	17 56	18 18	20 00	21 41	23 22
64	16 08	17 02	17 59	18 27	20 04	21 41	23 17
62	16 20	17 09	18 03	18 34	20 07	21 40	23 13
60	16 30	17 16	18 05	18 41	20 10	21 40	23 10
N 58	16 38	17 21	18 08	18 47	20 13	21 40	23 06
56	16 46	17 26	18 10	18 52	20 15	21 40	23 03
54	16 53	17 31	18 13	18 56	20 18	21 39	23 01
52	16 59	17 35	18 15	19 00	20 20	21 39	22 59
50	17 04	17 39	18 17	19 04	20 21	21 39	22 56
45	17 16	17 47	18 22	19 12	20 25	21 39	22 52
N 40	17 26	17 54	18 27	19 19	20 28	21 38	22 48
35	17 35	18 01	18 31	19 24	20 31	21 38	22 45
30	17 42	18 07	18 35	19 29	20 34	21 38	22 42
20	17 55	18 18	18 44	19 38	20 38	21 37	22 37
N 10	18 07	18 28	18 54	19 45	20 41	21 37	22 32
0	18 18	18 39	19 04	19 52	20 45	21 36	22 28
S 10	18 29	18 51	19 16	19 59	20 48	21 36	22 24
20	18 41	19 04	19 31	20 07	20 51	21 35	22 19
30	18 54	19 20	19 50	20 15	20 55	21 35	22 14
35	19 02	19 29	20 02	20 19	20 58	21 34	22 11
40	19 11	19 41	20 16	20 25	21 00	21 34	22 08
45	19 22	19 54	20 35	20 31	21 03	21 34	22 04
S 50	19 35	20 12	20 59	20 38	21 06	21 33	22 00
52	19 41	20 20	21 11	20 42	21 08	21 33	21 58
54	19 48	20 29	21 25	20 45	21 10	21 33	21 56
56	19 56	20 40	21 41	20 49	21 12	21 32	21 53
58	20 04	20 52	22 02	20 54	21 14	21 32	21 50
S 60	20 14	21 07	22 30	20 59	21 16	21 32	21 47

SUN / MOON

Day	SUN Eqn. of Time 00h	12h	SUN Mer. Pass.	MOON Mer. Pass. Upper	Lower	Age	Phase
6	14 06	14 08	12 14	13 40	01 13	02	
7	14 10	14 12	12 14	14 32	02 06	03	
8	14 13	14 14	12 14	15 24	02 58	04	◑

G.M.T.	ARIES G.H.A.	VENUS −3.4 G.H.A.	Dec.	MARS +1.4 G.H.A.	Dec.	JUPITER −1.9 G.H.A.	Dec.	SATURN +0.8 G.H.A.	Dec.	Name	S.H.A.	Dec.
9 00	138 59.8	190 29.4	S19 31.0	164 59.3	S11 51.4	309 12.4	S 2 36.5	309 22.8	S 1 23.2	Acamar	315 37.1	S40 23.2
01	154 02.3	205 28.6	30.3	179 59.9	50.7	324 15.0	36.5	324 25.3	23.2	Achernar	335 45.3	S57 20.4
02	169 04.8	220 27.8	29.7	195 00.5	50.0	339 17.5	36.4	339 27.9	23.1	Acrux	173 36.4	S62 59.4
03	184 07.2	235 27.0	·· 29.0	210 01.1	·· 49.3	354 20.1	·· 36.4	354 30.4	·· 23.1	Adhara	255 31.6	S28 57.0
04	199 09.7	250 26.3	28.3	225 01.7	48.6	9 22.7	36.3	9 33.0	23.0	Aldebaran	291 17.6	N16 28.2
05	214 12.2	265 25.5	27.6	240 02.2	47.8	24 25.2	36.2	24 35.5	23.0			
06	229 14.6	280 24.7	S19 26.9	255 02.8	S11 47.1	39 27.8	S 2 36.2	39 38.1	S 1 22.9	Alioth	166 41.9	N56 03.6
07	244 17.1	295 24.0	26.2	270 03.4	46.4	54 30.4	36.1	54 40.6	22.9	Alkaid	153 18.1	N49 24.3
08	259 19.6	310 23.2	25.5	285 04.0	45.7	69 33.0	36.1	69 43.1	22.9	Al Na'ir	28 15.1	S47 03.3
M 09	274 22.0	325 22.4	·· 24.8	300 04.6	·· 45.0	84 35.5	·· 36.0	84 45.7	·· 22.8	Alnilam	276 11.2	S 1 13.0
O 10	289 24.5	340 21.7	24.1	315 05.2	44.2	99 38.1	36.0	99 48.2	22.8	Alphard	218 20.0	S 8 34.7
N 11	304 27.0	355 20.9	23.4	330 05.7	43.5	114 40.7	35.9	114 50.8	22.7			
D 12	319 29.4	10 20.1	S19 22.7	345 06.3	S11 42.8	129 43.3	S 2 35.8	129 53.3	S 1 22.7	Alphecca	126 31.9	N26 46.5
A 13	334 31.9	25 19.3	22.0	0 06.9	42.1	144 45.8	35.8	144 55.9	22.6	Alpheratz	358 09.3	N28 59.1
Y 14	349 34.3	40 18.6	21.3	15 07.5	41.4	159 48.4	35.7	159 58.4	22.6	Altair	62 32.6	N 8 49.0
15	4 36.8	55 17.8	·· 20.6	30 08.1	·· 40.6	174 51.0	·· 35.7	175 01.0	·· 22.5	Ankaa	353 40.3	S42 24.8
16	19 39.3	70 17.0	19.9	45 08.7	39.9	189 53.5	35.6	190 03.5	22.5	Antares	112 56.6	S26 23.3
17	34 41.7	85 16.3	19.2	60 09.2	39.2	204 56.1	35.6	205 06.1	22.4			
18	49 44.2	100 15.5	S19 18.5	75 09.8	S11 38.5	219 58.7	S 2 35.5	220 08.6	S 1 22.4	Arcturus	146 18.1	N19 16.7
19	64 46.7	115 14.8	17.7	90 10.4	37.8	235 01.3	35.4	235 11.2	22.3	Atria	108 20.8	S68 59.3
20	79 49.1	130 14.0	17.0	105 11.0	37.0	250 03.9	35.4	250 13.7	22.3	Avior	234 27.4	S59 27.1
21	94 51.6	145 13.2	·· 16.3	120 11.6	·· 36.3	265 06.4	·· 35.3	265 16.3	·· 22.2	Bellatrix	278 58.3	N 6 19.8
22	109 54.1	160 12.5	15.6	135 12.2	35.6	280 09.0	35.3	280 18.8	22.2	Betelgeuse	271 27.8	N 7 24.1
23	124 56.5	175 11.7	14.9	150 12.8	34.9	295 11.6	35.2	295 21.4	22.2			
10 00	139 59.0	190 10.9	S19 14.2	165 13.3	S11 34.1	310 14.2	S 2 35.1	310 23.9	S 1 22.1	Canopus	264 06.7	S52 41.4
01	155 01.4	205 10.2	13.5	180 13.9	33.4	325 16.7	35.1	325 26.5	22.1	Capella	281 10.7	N45 58.8
02	170 03.9	220 09.4	12.8	195 14.5	32.7	340 19.3	35.0	340 29.0	22.0	Deneb	49 48.7	N45 12.7
03	185 06.4	235 08.7	·· 12.0	210 15.1	·· 32.0	355 21.9	·· 35.0	355 31.5	·· 22.0	Denebola	182 58.5	N14 40.6
04	200 08.8	250 07.9	11.3	225 15.7	31.3	10 24.5	34.9	10 34.1	21.9	Diphda	349 20.8	S18 05.7
05	215 11.3	265 07.1	10.6	240 16.3	30.5	25 27.0	34.8	25 36.6	21.9			
06	230 13.8	280 06.4	S19 09.9	255 16.9	S11 29.8	40 29.6	S 2 34.8	40 39.2	S 1 21.8	Dubhe	194 21.2	N61 51.1
07	245 16.2	295 05.6	09.2	270 17.5	29.1	55 32.2	34.7	55 41.7	21.8	Elnath	278 43.6	N28 35.5
08	260 18.7	310 04.9	08.4	285 18.0	28.4	70 34.8	34.7	70 44.3	21.7	Eltanin	90 57.9	N51 29.3
T 09	275 21.2	325 04.1	·· 07.7	300 18.6	·· 27.6	85 37.4	·· 34.6	85 46.8	·· 21.7	Enif	34 11.6	N 9 47.2
U 10	290 23.6	340 03.3	07.0	315 19.2	26.9	100 39.9	34.5	100 49.4	21.6	Fomalhaut	15 51.5	S29 43.6
E 11	305 26.1	355 02.6	06.3	330 19.8	26.2	115 42.5	34.5	115 51.9	21.6			
S 12	320 28.6	10 01.8	S19 05.6	345 20.4	S11 25.5	130 45.1	S 2 34.4	130 54.5	S 1 21.5	Gacrux	172 28.0	S57 00.2
D 13	335 31.0	25 01.1	04.8	0 21.0	24.7	145 47.7	34.4	145 57.0	21.5	Gienah	176 17.4	S17 26.2
A 14	350 33.5	40 00.3	04.1	15 21.6	24.0	160 50.3	34.3	160 59.6	21.4	Hadar	149 22.7	S60 16.6
Y 15	5 35.9	54 59.6	·· 03.4	30 22.2	·· 23.3	175 52.8	·· 34.2	176 02.1	·· 21.4	Hamal	328 28.7	N23 22.3
16	20 38.4	69 58.9	02.6	45 22.8	22.6	190 55.4	34.2	191 04.7	21.3	Kaus Aust.	84 16.8	S34 23.6
17	35 40.9	84 58.1	01.9	60 23.3	21.8	205 58.0	34.1	206 07.2	21.3			
18	50 43.3	99 57.3	S19 01.2	75 23.9	S11 21.1	221 00.6	S 2 34.1	221 09.8	S 1 21.2	Kochab	137 18.9	N74 13.7
19	65 45.8	114 56.5	19 00.5	90 24.5	20.4	236 03.2	34.0	236 12.3	21.2	Markab	14 03.2	N15 06.1
20	80 48.3	129 55.8	18 59.7	105 25.1	19.7	251 05.8	33.9	251 14.9	21.1	Menkar	314 40.9	N 4 00.8
21	95 50.7	144 55.0	·· 59.0	120 25.7	·· 18.9	266 08.3	·· 33.9	266 17.5	·· 21.1	Menkent	148 36.6	S36 16.4
22	110 53.2	159 54.3	58.3	135 26.3	18.2	281 10.9	33.8	281 20.0	21.1	Miaplacidus	221 43.9	S69 38.4
23	125 55.7	174 53.5	57.5	150 26.9	17.5	296 13.5	33.7	296 22.6	21.0			
11 00	140 58.1	189 52.8	S18 56.8	165 27.5	S11 16.7	311 16.1	S 2 33.7	311 25.1	S 1 21.0	Mirfak	309 15.7	N49 47.8
01	156 00.6	204 52.0	56.0	180 28.1	16.0	326 18.7	33.6	326 27.7	20.9	Nunki	76 29.1	S26 19.2
02	171 03.1	219 51.3	55.3	195 28.6	15.3	341 21.3	33.6	341 30.2	20.9	Peacock	53 58.5	S56 47.8
03	186 05.5	234 50.5	·· 54.6	210 29.2	·· 14.6	356 23.8	·· 33.5	356 32.8	·· 20.8	Pollux	243 57.5	N28 04.3
04	201 08.0	249 49.8	53.8	225 29.8	13.8	11 26.4	33.4	11 35.3	20.8	Procyon	245 25.2	N 5 16.3
05	216 10.4	264 49.0	53.1	240 30.4	13.1	26 29.0	33.4	26 37.9	20.7			
06	231 12.9	279 48.3	S18 52.3	255 31.0	S11 12.4	41 31.6	S 2 33.3	41 40.4	S 1 20.7	Rasalhague	96 29.5	N12 34.3
07	246 15.4	294 47.6	51.6	270 31.6	11.7	56 34.2	33.2	56 43.0	20.6	Regulus	208 09.4	N12 03.5
W 08	261 17.8	309 46.8	50.9	285 32.2	10.9	71 36.8	33.2	71 45.5	20.6	Rigel	281 35.6	S 8 13.6
E 09	276 20.3	324 46.1	·· 50.1	300 32.8	·· 10.2	86 39.4	·· 33.1	86 48.1	·· 20.5	Rigil Kent.	140 25.3	S60 45.1
D 10	291 22.8	339 45.3	49.4	315 33.4	09.5	101 41.9	33.1	101 50.6	20.5	Sabik	102 41.0	S15 42.1
N 11	306 25.2	354 44.6	48.6	330 34.0	08.7	116 44.5	33.0	116 53.2	20.4			
E 12	321 27.7	9 43.8	S18 47.9	345 34.6	S11 08.0	131 47.1	S 2 32.9	131 55.7	S 1 20.4	Schedar	350 09.0	N56 26.1
S 13	336 30.2	24 43.1	47.1	0 35.2	07.3	146 49.7	32.9	146 58.3	20.3	Shaula	96 55.6	S37 05.3
D 14	351 32.6	39 42.3	46.4	15 35.8	06.5	161 52.3	32.8	162 00.8	20.3	Sirius	258 55.2	S16 41.6
A 15	6 35.1	54 41.6	·· 45.6	30 36.3	·· 05.8	176 54.9	·· 32.7	177 03.4	·· 20.2	Spica	158 57.1	S11 03.7
Y 16	21 37.6	69 40.9	44.9	45 36.9	05.1	191 57.5	32.7	192 06.0	20.2	Suhail	223 10.1	S43 21.4
17	36 40.0	84 40.1	44.1	60 37.5	04.4	207 00.1	32.6	207 08.5	20.1			
18	51 42.5	99 39.4	S18 43.4	75 38.1	S11 03.6	222 02.7	S 2 32.5	222 11.1	S 1 20.1	Vega	80 56.0	N38 45.8
19	66 44.9	114 38.6	42.6	90 38.7	02.9	237 05.2	32.5	237 13.6	20.0	Zuben'ubi	137 32.7	S15 57.7
20	81 47.4	129 37.9	41.9	105 39.3	02.2	252 07.8	32.4	252 16.2	20.0		S.H.A.	Mer. Pass.
21	96 49.9	144 37.2	·· 41.1	120 39.9	·· 01.4	267 10.4	·· 32.4	267 18.7	·· 19.9		° ′	h m
22	111 52.3	159 36.4	40.3	135 40.5	00.7	282 13.0	32.3	282 21.3	19.9	Venus	50 12.0	11 20
23	126 54.8	174 35.7	39.6	150 41.1	00.0	297 15.6	32.2	297 23.8	19.8	Mars	25 14.4	12 59
Mer. Pass.	h m 14 37.7	v −0.8	d 0.7	v 0.6	d 0.7	v 2.6	d 0.1	v 2.6	d 0.0	Jupiter Saturn	170 15.2 170 24.9	3 18 3 18

SUN and MOON

G.M.T.	SUN G.H.A.	Dec.	MOON G.H.A.	v	Dec.	d	H.P.
9 00	176 26.2	S14 46.0	124 31.4	9.8	N 1 05.6	12.4	59.6
01	191 26.1	45.2	139 00.2	9.9	1 18.0	12.4	59.6
02	206 26.1	44.4	153 29.1	9.8	1 30.4	12.5	59.6
03	221 26.1	·· 43.6	167 57.9	9.9	1 42.9	12.4	59.6
04	236 26.1	42.8	182 26.8	9.8	1 55.3	12.4	59.6
05	251 26.1	42.0	196 55.6	9.9	2 07.7	12.4	59.5
06	266 26.1	S14 41.2	211 24.5	9.8	N 2 20.1	12.4	59.5
07	281 26.0	40.4	225 53.3	9.8	2 32.5	12.3	59.5
M 08	296 26.0	39.6	240 22.1	9.8	2 44.8	12.4	59.5
O 09	311 26.0	·· 38.8	254 50.9	9.9	2 57.2	12.3	59.5
N 10	326 26.0	37.9	269 19.8	9.8	3 09.5	12.3	59.5
11	341 26.0	37.1	283 48.6	9.8	3 21.8	12.3	59.5
D 12	356 26.0	S14 36.3	298 17.4	9.7	N 3 34.1	12.2	59.5
A 13	11 25.9	35.5	312 46.1	9.8	3 46.3	12.3	59.5
Y 14	26 25.9	34.7	327 14.9	9.8	3 58.6	12.2	59.5
15	41 25.9	·· 33.9	341 43.7	9.7	4 10.8	12.2	59.5
16	56 25.9	33.1	356 12.4	9.8	4 23.0	12.1	59.5
17	71 25.9	32.3	10 41.2	9.7	4 35.1	12.2	59.5
18	86 25.9	S14 31.5	25 09.9	9.7	N 4 47.3	12.1	59.5
19	101 25.9	30.7	39 38.6	9.7	4 59.4	12.0	59.5
20	116 25.8	29.9	54 07.3	9.7	5 11.4	12.1	59.5
21	131 25.8	·· 29.1	68 36.0	9.7	5 23.5	12.0	59.5
22	146 25.8	28.3	83 04.7	9.6	5 35.5	11.9	59.5
23	161 25.8	27.5	97 33.3	9.7	5 47.4	12.0	59.5
10 00	176 25.8	S14 26.7	112 02.0	9.6	N 5 59.4	11.8	59.5
01	191 25.8	25.8	126 30.6	9.6	6 11.2	11.9	59.5
02	206 25.8	25.0	140 59.2	9.6	6 23.1	11.8	59.5
03	221 25.8	·· 24.2	155 27.8	9.6	6 34.9	11.8	59.5
04	236 25.8	23.4	169 56.4	9.5	6 46.7	11.7	59.5
05	251 25.7	22.6	184 24.9	9.6	6 58.4	11.7	59.5
06	266 25.7	S14 21.8	198 53.5	9.5	N 7 10.1	11.7	59.4
07	281 25.7	21.0	213 22.0	9.5	7 21.8	11.6	59.4
T 08	296 25.7	20.2	227 50.5	9.4	7 33.4	11.5	59.4
U 09	311 25.7	·· 19.4	242 18.9	9.5	7 44.9	11.5	59.4
E 10	326 25.7	18.5	256 47.4	9.4	7 56.4	11.5	59.4
S 11	341 25.7	17.7	271 15.8	9.4	8 07.9	11.4	59.4
D 12	356 25.7	S14 16.9	285 44.2	9.4	N 8 19.3	11.3	59.4
A 13	11 25.7	16.1	300 12.6	9.4	8 30.6	11.3	59.4
Y 14	26 25.7	15.3	314 41.0	9.3	8 41.9	11.3	59.4
15	41 25.7	·· 14.5	329 09.3	9.3	8 53.2	11.2	59.4
16	56 25.7	13.7	343 37.6	9.3	9 04.4	11.1	59.4
17	71 25.7	12.8	358 05.9	9.3	9 15.5	11.1	59.4
18	86 25.7	S14 12.0	12 34.2	9.2	N 9 26.6	11.0	59.4
19	101 25.6	11.2	27 02.4	9.2	9 37.6	10.9	59.4
20	116 25.6	10.4	41 30.6	9.2	9 48.5	10.9	59.4
21	131 25.6	·· 09.6	55 58.8	9.1	9 59.4	10.9	59.3
22	146 25.6	08.7	70 26.9	9.2	10 10.3	10.7	59.3
23	161 25.6	07.9	84 55.1	9.1	10 21.0	10.8	59.3
11 00	176 25.6	S14 07.1	99 23.2	9.0	N10 31.8	10.6	59.3
01	191 25.6	06.3	113 51.2	9.1	10 42.4	10.6	59.3
02	206 25.6	05.5	128 19.3	9.0	10 53.0	10.5	59.3
03	221 25.6	·· 04.6	142 47.3	9.0	11 03.5	10.4	59.3
04	236 25.6	03.8	157 15.3	8.9	11 13.9	10.4	59.3
05	251 25.6	03.0	171 43.2	9.0	11 24.3	10.3	59.3
06	266 25.6	S14 02.2	186 11.2	8.8	N11 34.6	10.2	59.2
07	281 25.6	01.4	200 39.0	8.9	11 44.8	10.2	59.2
W 08	296 25.6	14 00.5	215 06.9	8.8	11 55.0	10.1	59.2
E 09	311 25.6	13 59.7	229 34.7	8.9	12 05.1	10.0	59.2
D 10	326 25.6	58.9	244 02.6	8.7	12 15.1	9.9	59.2
N 11	341 25.6	58.1	258 30.3	8.8	12 25.0	9.8	59.2
E 12	356 25.6	S13 57.2	272 58.1	8.7	N12 34.8	9.8	59.2
S 13	11 25.6	56.4	287 25.8	8.7	12 44.6	9.7	59.2
D 14	26 25.6	55.6	301 53.5	8.6	12 54.3	9.6	59.2
A 15	41 25.6	·· 54.8	316 21.1	8.6	13 03.9	9.6	59.2
Y 16	56 25.6	53.9	330 48.7	8.6	13 13.5	9.4	59.1
17	71 25.6	53.1	345 16.3	8.6	13 22.9	9.4	59.1
18	86 25.6	S13 52.3	359 43.9	8.5	N13 32.3	9.3	59.1
19	101 25.6	51.5	14 11.4	8.5	13 41.6	9.2	59.1
20	116 25.6	50.6	28 38.9	8.4	13 50.8	9.1	59.1
21	131 25.6	·· 49.8	43 06.3	8.4	13 59.9	9.0	59.1
22	146 25.6	49.0	57 33.7	8.4	14 08.9	8.9	59.1
23	161 25.6	48.2	72 01.1	8.4	14 17.8	8.9	59.1
	S.D. 16.2	d 0.8	S.D. 16.2		16.2		16.1

Twilight, Sunrise and Moonrise

Lat.	Naut.	Civil	Sunrise	Moonrise 9	10	11	12
N 72	06 36	07 58	09 24	09 26	09 14	08 59	08 39
N 70	06 32	07 45	08 59	09 30	09 25	09 20	09 14
68	06 28	07 35	08 40	09 33	09 34	09 36	09 40
66	06 25	07 26	08 24	09 36	09 41	09 49	10 00
64	06 22	07 19	08 12	09 38	09 48	10 00	10 16
62	06 20	07 12	08 01	09 40	09 53	10 09	10 29
60	06 18	07 07	07 52	09 42	09 58	10 17	10 40
N 58	06 15	07 02	07 44	09 43	10 02	10 24	10 50
56	06 13	06 57	07 37	09 45	10 06	10 30	10 59
54	06 11	06 53	07 30	09 46	10 10	10 36	11 07
52	06 09	06 49	07 25	09 47	10 13	10 41	11 14
50	06 08	06 46	07 20	09 48	10 16	10 46	11 20
45	06 03	06 38	07 09	09 51	10 22	10 56	11 34
N 40	05 59	06 31	06 59	09 53	10 27	11 04	11 45
35	05 55	06 25	06 51	09 54	10 32	11 12	11 54
30	05 51	06 20	06 44	09 56	10 36	11 18	12 03
20	05 43	06 09	06 32	09 59	10 43	11 29	12 18
N 10	05 34	06 00	06 21	10 01	10 49	11 39	12 30
0	05 25	05 50	06 11	10 03	10 55	11 48	12 43
S 10	05 13	05 39	06 00	10 06	11 01	11 58	12 55
20	04 59	05 26	05 49	10 08	11 08	12 08	13 08
30	04 41	05 11	05 36	10 11	11 15	12 19	13 23
35	04 29	05 02	05 29	10 13	11 20	12 26	13 32
40	04 15	04 51	05 20	10 15	11 24	12 34	13 42
45	03 58	04 38	05 10	10 17	11 30	12 43	13 54
S 50	03 35	04 21	04 57	10 20	11 37	12 53	14 08
52	03 24	04 13	04 52	10 21	11 40	12 59	14 15
54	03 11	04 04	04 45	10 22	11 44	13 04	14 22
56	02 55	03 54	04 38	10 24	11 48	13 10	14 31
58	02 35	03 43	04 30	10 26	11 52	13 17	14 40
S 60	02 10	03 29	04 21	10 27	11 57	13 25	14 51

Sunset, Twilight and Moonset

Lat.	Sunset	Civil	Naut.	Moonset 9	10	11	12
N 72	15 06	16 32	17 55	23 44	25 48	01 48	04 02
N 70	15 31	16 45	17 59	23 35	25 30	01 30	03 28
68	15 50	16 55	18 02	23 28	25 15	01 15	03 03
66	16 06	17 04	18 05	23 22	25 04	01 04	02 44
64	16 18	17 11	18 08	23 17	24 54	00 54	02 29
62	16 29	17 17	18 10	23 13	24 46	00 46	02 16
60	16 38	17 23	18 12	23 10	24 38	00 38	02 06
N 58	16 46	17 28	18 14	23 06	24 32	00 32	01 57
56	16 53	17 32	18 16	23 03	24 27	00 27	01 48
54	16 59	17 36	18 18	23 01	24 22	00 22	01 41
52	17 05	17 40	18 20	22 59	24 17	00 17	01 35
50	17 10	17 44	18 22	22 56	24 13	00 13	01 29
45	17 21	17 51	18 26	22 52	24 05	00 05	01 17
N 40	17 30	17 58	18 34	22 48	23 57	25 06	01 06
35	17 38	18 04	18 34	22 45	23 51	24 57	00 57
30	17 45	18 09	18 38	22 42	23 46	24 50	00 50
20	17 57	18 19	18 54	22 37	23 36	24 36	00 36
N 10	18 08	18 29	18 54	22 32	23 28	24 25	00 25
0	18 18	18 39	19 04	22 28	23 20	24 14	00 14
S 10	18 28	18 50	19 15	22 24	23 13	24 03	00 03
20	18 39	19 02	19 29	22 19	23 05	23 52	24 41
30	18 52	19 17	19 47	22 14	22 55	23 39	24 25
35	18 59	19 26	19 58	22 11	22 50	23 31	24 16
40	19 08	19 37	20 12	22 08	22 44	23 22	24 05
45	19 18	19 50	20 29	22 04	22 37	23 12	23 52
S 50	19 30	20 06	20 52	22 00	22 28	23 00	23 37
52	19 36	20 14	21 03	21 58	22 25	22 55	23 30
54	19 42	20 23	21 16	21 56	22 20	22 48	23 22
56	19 49	20 32	21 31	21 53	22 16	22 42	23 13
58	19 57	20 44	21 50	21 50	22 10	22 34	23 03
S 60	20 06	20 57	22 14	21 47	22 05	22 25	22 52

SUN and MOON

Day	SUN Eqn. of Time 00h	12h	Mer. Pass.	MOON Mer. Pass. Upper	Lower	Age	Phase
9	14 15	14 16	12 14	16 16	03 50	05	
10	14 17	14 17	12 14	17 08	04 42	06	
11	14 17	14 18	12 14	18 01	05 34	07	◑

G.M.T.	ARIES G.H.A.	VENUS −3.4 G.H.A.	Dec.	MARS +1.4 G.H.A.	Dec.	JUPITER −1.9 G.H.A.	Dec.	SATURN +0.8 G.H.A.	Dec.	STARS Name	S.H.A.	Dec.
12 00	141 57.3	189 34.9	S18 38.8	165 41.7	S10 59.2	312 18.2	S 2 32.2	312 26.4	S 1 19.8	Acamar	315 37.1	S40 23.2
01	156 59.7	204 34.2	38.1	180 42.3	58.5	327 20.8	32.1	327 29.0	19.7	Achernar	335 45.4	S57 20.4
02	172 02.2	219 33.5	37.3	195 42.9	57.8	342 23.4	32.0	342 31.5	19.7	Acrux	173 36.4	S62 59.4
03	187 04.7	234 32.7	·· 36.5	210 43.5	·· 57.0	357 26.0	·· 32.0	357 34.1	·· 19.6	Adhara	255 31.6	S28 57.0
04	202 07.1	249 32.0	35.8	225 44.1	56.3	12 28.6	31.9	12 36.6	19.6	Aldebaran	291 17.6	N16 28.2
05	217 09.6	264 31.2	35.0	240 44.7	55.6	27 31.1	31.8	27 39.2	19.5			
06	232 12.0	279 30.5	S18 34.2	255 45.3	S10 54.9	42 33.7	S 2 31.8	42 41.7	S 1 19.5	Alioth	166 41.9	N56 03.6
07	247 14.5	294 29.8	33.5	270 45.9	54.1	57 36.3	31.7	57 44.3	19.4	Alkaid	153 18.1	N49 24.3
T 08	262 17.0	309 29.0	32.7	285 46.5	53.4	72 38.9	31.6	72 46.8	19.4	Al Na'ir	28 15.1	S47 03.3
H 09	277 19.4	324 28.3	·· 31.9	300 47.0	·· 52.7	87 41.5	·· 31.6	87 49.4	·· 19.3	Alnilam	276 11.2	S 1 13.0
U 10	292 21.9	339 27.6	31.2	315 47.6	51.9	102 44.1	31.5	102 52.0	19.3	Alphard	218 20.0	S 8 34.7
R 11	307 24.4	354 26.8	30.4	330 48.2	51.2	117 46.7	31.4	117 54.5	19.2			
S 12	322 26.8	9 26.1	S18 29.6	345 48.8	S10 50.5	132 49.3	S 2 31.4	132 57.1	S 1 19.2	Alphecca	126 31.9	N26 46.5
D 13	337 29.3	24 25.4	28.9	0 49.4	49.7	147 51.9	31.3	147 59.6	19.1	Alpheratz	358 09.3	N28 59.1
A 14	352 31.8	39 24.6	28.1	15 50.0	49.0	162 54.5	31.2	163 02.2	19.1	Altair	62 32.5	N 8 49.0
Y 15	7 34.2	54 23.9	·· 27.3	30 50.6	·· 48.3	177 57.1	·· 31.2	178 04.7	·· 19.0	Ankaa	353 40.3	S42 24.8
16	22 36.7	69 23.2	26.5	45 51.2	47.5	192 59.7	31.1	193 07.3	19.0	Antares	112 56.6	S26 23.3
17	37 39.2	84 22.5	25.8	60 51.8	46.8	208 02.3	31.0	208 09.9	18.9			
18	52 41.6	99 21.7	S18 25.0	75 52.4	S10 46.0	223 04.9	S 2 31.0	223 12.4	S 1 18.9	Arcturus	146 18.1	N19 16.7
19	67 44.1	114 21.0	24.2	90 53.0	45.3	238 07.5	30.9	238 15.0	18.8	Atria	108 20.8	S68 59.3
20	82 46.5	129 20.3	23.4	105 53.6	44.6	253 10.1	30.8	253 17.5	18.8	Avior	234 27.5	S59 27.1
21	97 49.0	144 19.5	·· 22.7	120 54.2	·· 43.8	268 12.7	·· 30.8	268 20.1	·· 18.7	Bellatrix	278 58.3	N 6 19.8
22	112 51.5	159 18.8	21.9	135 54.8	43.1	283 15.3	30.7	283 22.7	18.7	Betelgeuse	271 27.8	N 7 24.1
23	127 53.9	174 18.1	21.1	150 55.4	42.4	298 17.9	30.6	298 25.2	18.6			
13 00	142 56.4	189 17.4	S18 20.3	165 56.0	S10 41.6	313 20.5	S 2 30.6	313 27.8	S 1 18.6	Canopus	264 06.7	S52 41.4
01	157 58.9	204 16.6	19.5	180 56.6	40.9	328 23.1	30.5	328 30.3	18.5	Capella	281 10.7	N45 58.8
02	173 01.3	219 15.9	18.8	195 57.2	40.2	343 25.6	30.4	343 32.9	18.5	Deneb	49 48.7	N45 12.6
03	188 03.8	234 15.2	·· 18.0	210 57.8	·· 39.4	358 28.2	·· 30.4	358 35.5	·· 18.4	Denebola	182 58.5	N14 40.6
04	203 06.3	249 14.5	17.2	225 58.4	38.7	13 30.8	30.3	13 38.0	18.4	Diphda	349 20.8	S18 05.7
05	218 08.7	264 13.7	16.4	240 59.0	38.0	28 33.4	30.2	28 40.6	18.3			
06	233 11.2	279 13.0	S18 15.6	255 59.6	S10 37.2	43 36.0	S 2 30.2	43 43.1	S 1 18.2	Dubhe	194 21.2	N61 51.1
07	248 13.7	294 12.3	14.8	271 00.2	36.5	58 38.6	30.1	58 45.7	18.2	Elnath	278 43.6	N28 35.5
08	263 16.1	309 11.6	14.0	286 00.8	35.7	73 41.2	30.0	73 48.3	18.1	Eltanin	90 57.9	N51 29.3
F 09	278 18.6	324 10.9	·· 13.3	301 01.4	·· 35.0	88 43.8	·· 30.0	88 50.8	·· 18.1	Enif	34 11.6	N 9 47.2
R 10	293 21.0	339 10.1	12.5	316 02.0	34.3	103 46.4	29.9	103 53.4	18.0	Fomalhaut	15 51.5	S29 43.6
I 11	308 23.5	354 09.4	11.7	331 02.6	33.5	118 49.0	29.8	118 55.9	18.0			
D 12	323 26.0	9 08.7	S18 10.9	346 03.2	S10 32.8	133 51.6	S 2 29.7	133 58.5	S 1 17.9	Gacrux	172 28.0	S57 00.2
A 13	338 28.4	24 08.0	10.1	1 03.8	32.1	148 54.2	29.7	149 01.1	17.9	Gienah	176 17.4	S17 26.2
Y 14	353 30.9	39 07.2	09.3	16 04.4	31.3	163 56.8	29.6	164 03.6	17.8	Hadar	149 22.7	S60 16.6
15	8 33.4	54 06.5	·· 08.5	31 05.0	·· 30.6	178 59.5	·· 29.5	179 06.2	·· 17.8	Hamal	328 28.7	N23 22.3
16	23 35.8	69 05.8	07.7	46 05.6	29.8	194 02.1	29.5	194 08.7	17.7	Kaus Aust.	84 16.7	S34 23.6
17	38 38.3	84 05.1	06.9	61 06.2	29.1	209 04.7	29.4	209 11.3	17.7			
18	53 40.8	99 04.4	S18 06.1	76 06.8	S10 28.4	224 07.3	S 2 29.3	224 13.9	S 1 17.6	Kochab	137 18.9	N74 13.7
19	68 43.2	114 03.7	05.3	91 07.4	27.6	239 09.9	29.3	239 16.4	17.6	Markab	14 03.2	N15 06.1
20	83 45.7	129 02.9	04.5	106 08.0	26.9	254 12.5	29.2	254 19.0	17.5	Menkar	314 40.9	N 4 00.8
21	98 48.1	144 02.2	·· 03.7	121 08.6	·· 26.2	269 15.1	·· 29.1	269 21.6	·· 17.5	Menkent	148 36.5	S36 16.5
22	113 50.6	159 01.5	02.9	136 09.2	25.4	284 17.7	29.1	284 24.1	17.4	Miaplacidus	221 43.9	S69 38.4
23	128 53.1	174 00.8	02.1	151 09.8	24.7	299 20.3	29.0	299 26.7	17.4			
14 00	143 55.5	189 00.1	S18 01.3	166 10.4	S10 23.9	314 22.9	S 2 28.9	314 29.2	S 1 17.3	Mirfak	309 15.7	N49 47.8
01	158 58.0	203 59.4	18 00.5	181 11.0	23.2	329 25.5	28.8	329 31.8	17.3	Nunki	76 29.1	S26 19.2
02	174 00.5	218 58.7	17 59.7	196 11.6	22.5	344 28.1	28.8	344 34.4	17.2	Peacock	53 58.5	S56 47.8
03	189 02.9	233 57.9	·· 58.9	211 12.2	·· 21.7	359 30.7	·· 28.7	359 36.9	·· 17.1	Pollux	243 57.5	N28 04.3
04	204 05.4	248 57.2	58.1	226 12.8	21.0	14 33.3	28.6	14 39.5	17.1	Procyon	245 25.2	N 5 16.3
05	219 07.9	263 56.5	57.3	241 13.4	20.2	29 35.9	28.6	29 42.1	17.0			
06	234 10.3	278 55.8	S17 56.5	256 14.0	S10 19.5	44 38.5	S 2 28.5	44 44.6	S 1 17.0	Rasalhague	96 29.5	N12 34.3
07	249 12.8	293 55.1	55.7	271 14.6	18.8	59 41.1	28.4	59 47.2	16.9	Regulus	208 09.4	N12 03.5
S 08	264 15.3	308 54.4	54.8	286 15.2	18.0	74 43.7	28.3	74 49.7	16.9	Rigel	281 35.6	S 8 13.6
A 09	279 17.7	323 53.7	·· 54.0	301 15.8	·· 17.3	89 46.3	·· 28.3	89 52.3	·· 16.8	Rigil Kent.	140 25.3	S60 45.1
T 10	294 20.2	338 53.0	53.2	316 16.5	16.5	104 48.9	28.2	104 54.9	16.8	Sabik	102 41.0	S15 42.1
U 11	309 22.6	353 52.3	52.4	331 17.1	15.8	119 51.5	28.1	119 57.4	16.7			
R 12	324 25.1	8 51.6	S17 51.6	346 17.7	S10 15.0	134 54.2	S 2 28.1	135 00.0	S 1 16.7	Schedar	350 09.1	N56 26.1
D 13	339 27.6	23 50.9	50.8	1 18.3	14.3	149 56.8	28.0	150 02.6	16.6	Shaula	96 55.6	S37 05.3
A 14	354 30.0	38 50.1	50.0	16 18.9	13.6	164 59.4	27.9	165 05.1	16.6	Sirius	258 55.2	S16 41.6
Y 15	9 32.5	53 49.4	·· 49.1	31 19.5	·· 12.8	180 02.0	·· 27.8	180 07.7	·· 16.5	Spica	158 57.1	S11 03.7
16	24 35.0	68 48.7	48.3	46 20.1	12.1	195 04.6	27.8	195 10.3	16.5	Suhail	223 10.1	S43 21.5
17	39 37.4	83 48.0	47.5	61 20.7	11.3	210 07.2	27.7	210 12.8	16.4			
18	54 39.9	98 47.3	S17 46.7	76 21.3	S10 10.6	225 09.8	S 2 27.6	225 15.4	S 1 16.3	Vega	80 55.9	N38 45.8
19	69 42.4	113 46.6	45.9	91 21.9	09.9	240 12.4	27.6	240 18.0	16.3	Zuben'ubi	137 32.7	S15 57.7
20	84 44.8	128 45.9	45.1	106 22.5	09.1	255 15.0	27.5	255 20.5	16.2		S.H.A.	Mer. Pass.
21	99 47.3	143 45.2	·· 44.2	121 23.1	·· 08.4	270 17.6	·· 27.4	270 23.1	·· 16.2		° '	h m
22	114 49.8	158 44.5	43.4	136 23.7	07.6	285 20.2	27.3	285 25.7	16.1	Venus	46 21.0	11 23
23	129 52.2	173 43.8	42.6	151 24.3	06.9	300 22.9	27.3	300 28.2	16.1	Mars	22 59.6	12 56
										Jupiter	170 24.1	3 06
Mer. Pass. 14 25.9	v −0.7 d 0.8			v 0.6 d 0.7		v 2.6 d 0.1		v 2.6 d 0.1		Saturn	170 31.4	3 06

G.M.T.	SUN G.H.A.	SUN Dec.	MOON G.H.A.	v	Dec.	d	H.P.
12 00	176 25.7	S13 47.3	86 28.5	8.3	N14 26.7	8.7	59.0
01	191 25.7	46.5	100 55.8	8.3	14 35.4	8.7	59.0
02	206 25.7	45.7	115 23.1	8.3	14 44.1	8.6	59.0
03	221 25.7	.. 44.8	129 50.4	8.2	14 52.7	8.4	59.0
04	236 25.7	44.0	144 17.6	8.2	15 01.1	8.4	59.0
05	251 25.7	43.2	158 44.8	8.2	15 09.5	8.3	59.0
06	266 25.7	S13 42.3	173 12.0	8.1	N15 17.8	8.2	59.0
07	281 25.7	41.5	187 39.1	8.1	15 26.0	8.1	59.0
T 08	296 25.7	40.7	202 06.2	8.1	15 34.1	8.0	59.0
H 09	311 25.7	.. 39.9	216 33.3	8.0	15 42.1	7.9	58.9
U 10	326 25.7	39.0	231 00.3	8.0	15 50.0	7.8	58.9
R 11	341 25.7	38.2	245 27.3	8.0	15 57.8	7.7	58.9
S 12	356 25.7	S13 37.4	259 54.3	7.9	N16 05.5	7.6	58.9
D 13	11 25.7	36.5	274 21.2	7.9	16 13.1	7.5	58.9
A 14	26 25.8	35.7	288 48.1	7.9	16 20.6	7.4	58.9
Y 15	41 25.8	.. 34.9	303 15.0	7.9	16 28.0	7.3	58.9
16	56 25.8	34.0	317 41.9	7.8	16 35.3	7.2	58.8
17	71 25.8	33.2	332 08.7	7.8	16 42.5	7.1	58.8
18	86 25.8	S13 32.3	346 35.5	7.8	N16 49.6	7.0	58.8
19	101 25.8	31.5	1 02.3	7.7	16 56.6	6.9	58.8
20	116 25.8	30.7	15 29.0	7.7	17 03.5	6.7	58.8
21	131 25.8	.. 29.8	29 55.7	7.7	17 10.2	6.7	58.8
22	146 25.8	29.0	44 22.4	7.7	17 16.9	6.5	58.8
23	161 25.9	28.2	58 49.1	7.6	17 23.4	6.5	58.7
13 00	176 25.9	S13 27.3	73 15.7	7.6	N17 29.9	6.3	58.7
01	191 25.9	26.5	87 42.3	7.6	17 36.2	6.2	58.7
02	206 25.9	25.6	102 08.9	7.5	17 42.4	6.1	58.7
03	221 25.9	.. 24.8	116 35.4	7.5	17 48.5	6.0	58.7
04	236 25.9	24.0	131 01.9	7.5	17 54.5	5.9	58.7
05	251 25.9	23.1	145 28.4	7.5	18 00.4	5.8	58.7
06	266 26.0	S13 22.3	159 54.9	7.5	N18 06.2	5.7	58.6
07	281 26.0	21.4	174 21.4	7.4	18 11.9	5.5	58.6
08	296 26.0	20.6	188 47.8	7.4	18 17.4	5.4	58.6
F 09	311 26.0	19.8	203 14.2	7.4	18 22.8	5.3	58.6
R 10	326 26.0	18.9	217 40.6	7.4	18 28.1	5.2	58.6
I 11	341 26.0	18.1	232 07.0	7.3	18 33.3	5.1	58.6
D 12	356 26.1	S13 17.2	246 33.3	7.4	N18 38.4	5.0	58.6
A 13	11 26.1	16.4	260 59.7	7.3	18 43.4	4.8	58.5
Y 14	26 26.1	15.5	275 26.0	7.3	18 48.2	4.7	58.5
15	41 26.1	.. 14.7	289 52.3	7.3	18 52.9	4.6	58.5
16	56 26.1	13.9	304 18.6	7.2	18 57.5	4.5	58.5
17	71 26.1	13.0	318 44.8	7.3	19 02.0	4.4	58.5
18	86 26.2	S13 12.2	333 11.1	7.2	N19 06.4	4.2	58.5
19	101 26.2	11.3	347 37.3	7.2	19 10.6	4.2	58.5
20	116 26.2	10.5	2 03.5	7.2	19 14.8	4.0	58.4
21	131 26.2	.. 09.6	16 29.7	7.2	19 18.8	3.9	58.4
22	146 26.2	08.8	30 55.9	7.2	19 22.7	3.7	58.4
23	161 26.3	07.9	45 22.1	7.2	19 26.4	3.7	58.4
14 00	176 26.3	S13 07.1	59 48.3	7.1	N19 30.1	3.5	58.4
01	191 26.3	06.2	74 14.4	7.2	19 33.6	3.4	58.4
02	206 26.3	05.4	88 40.6	7.1	19 37.0	3.3	58.3
03	221 26.4	.. 04.6	103 06.7	7.2	19 40.3	3.1	58.3
04	236 26.4	03.7	117 32.9	7.1	19 43.4	3.0	58.3
05	251 26.4	02.9	131 59.0	7.1	19 46.4	2.9	58.3
06	266 26.4	S13 02.0	146 25.1	7.2	N19 49.3	2.8	58.3
07	281 26.4	01.2	160 51.3	7.1	19 52.1	2.7	58.3
S 08	296 26.5	13 00.3	175 17.4	7.1	19 54.8	2.5	58.2
A 09	311 26.5	12 59.5	189 43.5	7.1	19 57.3	2.4	58.2
T 10	326 26.5	58.6	204 09.6	7.1	19 59.7	2.3	58.2
U 11	341 26.5	57.8	218 35.7	7.2	20 02.0	2.1	58.2
R 12	356 26.6	S12 56.9	233 01.9	7.1	N20 04.1	2.1	58.2
D 13	11 26.6	56.1	247 28.0	7.1	20 06.2	1.9	58.2
A 14	26 26.6	55.2	261 54.1	7.1	20 08.1	1.8	58.1
Y 15	41 26.6	.. 54.3	276 20.2	7.2	20 09.9	1.6	58.1
16	56 26.7	53.5	290 46.4	7.1	20 11.5	1.5	58.1
17	71 26.7	52.6	305 12.5	7.2	20 13.0	1.5	58.1
18	86 26.7	S12 51.8	319 38.7	7.1	N20 14.5	1.2	58.1
19	101 26.7	50.9	334 04.8	7.2	20 15.7	1.2	58.1
20	116 26.8	50.1	348 31.0	7.2	20 16.9	1.0	58.0
21	131 26.8	.. 49.2	2 57.2	7.1	20 17.9	0.9	58.0
22	146 26.8	48.4	17 23.3	7.2	20 18.8	0.8	58.0
23	161 26.9	47.5	31 49.5	7.3	20 19.6	0.7	58.0
	S.D. 16.2	d 0.8	S.D. 16.0		16.0		15.9

Lat.	Naut.	Civil	Sunrise	Moonrise 12	13	14	15
N 72	06 23	07 44	09 06	08 39	▢	▢	▢
N 70	06 21	07 33	08 44	09 14	09 08	08 54	▢
68	06 18	07 24	08 27	09 40	09 49	10 10	10 58
66	06 16	07 17	08 13	10 00	10 17	10 48	11 39
64	06 14	07 10	08 02	10 16	10 39	11 15	12 07
62	06 12	07 05	07 52	10 29	10 57	11 35	12 28
60	06 11	07 00	07 44	10 40	11 11	11 52	12 46
N 58	06 09	06 55	07 37	10 50	11 24	12 06	13 00
56	06 07	06 51	07 30	10 59	11 34	12 19	13 13
54	06 06	06 47	07 24	11 07	11 44	12 29	13 24
52	06 04	06 44	07 19	11 14	11 52	12 39	13 34
50	06 03	06 41	07 14	11 20	12 00	12 47	13 42
45	05 59	06 34	07 04	11 34	12 16	13 05	14 01
N 40	05 56	06 28	06 56	11 45	12 30	13 20	14 16
35	05 53	06 22	06 48	11 54	12 41	13 33	14 28
30	05 49	06 17	06 42	12 03	12 51	13 44	14 39
20	05 42	06 08	06 30	12 18	13 09	14 02	14 58
N 10	05 34	05 59	06 20	12 30	13 24	14 19	15 15
0	05 25	05 50	06 11	12 43	13 38	14 34	15 30
S 10	05 14	05 40	06 01	12 55	13 52	14 50	15 46
20	05 01	05 28	05 51	13 08	14 08	15 06	16 02
30	04 44	05 14	05 39	13 23	14 25	15 25	16 21
35	04 33	05 05	05 32	13 32	14 36	15 36	16 33
40	04 20	04 55	05 24	13 42	14 48	15 49	16 45
45	04 03	04 42	05 14	13 54	15 01	16 04	17 00
S 50	03 42	04 27	05 03	14 08	15 19	16 23	17 19
52	03 31	04 20	04 57	14 15	15 27	16 32	17 27
54	03 19	04 11	04 52	14 22	15 36	16 41	17 37
56	03 05	04 02	04 45	14 31	15 46	16 52	17 48
58	02 47	03 51	04 38	14 40	15 57	17 05	18 01
S 60	02 25	03 39	04 29	14 51	16 11	17 20	18 15

Lat.	Sunset	Civil	Naut.	Moonset 12	13	14	15
N 72	15 24	16 46	18 07	04 02	▢	▢	▢
N 70	15 46	16 57	18 10	03 28	05 30	07 41	▢
68	16 03	17 06	18 12	03 03	04 49	06 25	07 35
66	16 17	17 13	18 14	02 44	04 21	05 47	06 54
64	16 28	17 20	18 16	02 29	04 00	05 21	06 26
62	16 37	17 25	18 17	02 16	03 43	05 01	06 04
60	16 46	17 30	18 19	02 06	03 29	04 44	05 46
N 58	16 53	17 34	18 21	01 57	03 17	04 30	05 32
56	16 59	17 38	18 22	01 48	03 06	04 18	05 19
54	17 05	17 42	18 24	01 41	02 57	04 07	05 08
52	17 10	17 45	18 25	01 35	02 49	03 58	04 59
50	17 15	17 48	18 26	01 29	02 42	03 50	04 50
45	17 25	17 55	18 30	01 17	02 26	03 32	04 31
N 40	17 33	18 01	18 33	01 06	02 13	03 17	04 16
35	17 41	18 07	18 36	00 57	02 02	03 05	04 04
30	17 47	18 12	18 40	00 50	01 53	02 54	03 52
20	17 58	18 21	18 47	00 36	01 37	02 36	03 33
N 10	18 08	18 30	18 55	00 25	01 22	02 20	03 17
0	18 18	18 39	19 04	00 14	01 09	02 05	03 01
S 10	18 27	18 49	19 14	00 03	00 56	01 50	02 46
20	18 37	19 00	19 27	24 41	00 41	01 34	02 29
30	18 49	19 14	19 44	24 25	00 25	01 16	02 10
35	18 56	19 23	19 55	24 16	00 16	01 05	01 58
40	19 04	19 33	20 08	24 05	00 05	00 53	01 46
45	19 13	19 45	20 24	23 52	24 38	00 38	01 30
S 50	19 25	20 00	20 45	23 37	24 21	00 21	01 12
52	19 30	20 07	20 55	23 30	24 12	00 12	01 03
54	19 36	20 16	21 07	23 22	24 03	00 03	00 53
56	19 42	20 25	21 21	23 13	23 53	24 42	00 42
58	19 49	20 35	21 38	23 03	23 41	24 29	00 29
S 60	19 57	20 47	21 59	22 52	23 27	24 14	00 14

	SUN Eqn. of Time 00ʰ	SUN Eqn. of Time 12ʰ	SUN Mer. Pass.	MOON Mer. Pass. Upper	MOON Mer. Pass. Lower	Age	Phase
Day	m s	m s	h m	h m	h m	d	
12	14 17	14 17	12 14	18 56	06 28	08	
13	14 17	14 16	12 14	19 51	07 23	09	◖
14	14 15	14 14	12 14	20 48	08 20	10	

G.M.T.	ARIES G.H.A.	VENUS −3.4 G.H.A.	Dec.	MARS +1.4 G.H.A.	Dec.	JUPITER −1.9 G.H.A.	Dec.	SATURN +0.8 G.H.A.	Dec.	STARS Name	S.H.A.	Dec.
15 00	144 54.7	188 43.1	S17 41.8	166 24.9	S10 06.1	315 25.5	S 2 27.2	315 30.8	S 1 16.0	Acamar	315 37.1	S40 23.2
01	159 57.1	203 42.4	40.9	181 25.5	05.4	330 28.1	27.1	330 33.3	16.0	Achernar	335 45.4	S57 20.3
02	174 59.6	218 41.7	40.1	196 26.1	04.7	345 30.7	27.0	345 35.9	15.9	Acrux	173 36.3	S62 59.5
03	190 02.1	233 41.0	·· 39.3	211 26.7	·· 03.9	0 33.3	·· 27.0	0 38.5	·· 15.9	Adhara	255 31.6	S28 57.0
04	205 04.5	248 40.3	38.5	226 27.4	03.2	15 35.9	26.9	15 41.0	15.8	Aldebaran	291 17.6	N16 28.2
05	220 07.0	263 39.6	37.6	241 28.0	02.4	30 38.5	26.8	30 43.6	15.8			
06	235 09.5	278 38.9	S17 36.8	256 28.6	S10 01.7	45 41.1	S 2 26.7	45 46.2	S 1 15.7	Alioth	166 41.9	N56 03.6
07	250 11.9	293 38.2	36.0	271 29.2	00.9	60 43.7	26.7	60 48.7	15.6	Alkaid	153 18.0	N49 24.3
08	265 14.4	308 37.5	35.1	286 29.8	10 00.2	75 46.4	26.6	75 51.3	15.6	Al Na'ir	28 15.1	S47 03.3
S 09	280 16.9	323 36.8	·· 34.3	301 30.4	9 59.4	90 49.0	·· 26.5	90 53.9	·· 15.5	Alnilam	276 11.2	S 1 13.0
U 10	295 19.3	338 36.1	33.5	316 31.0	58.7	105 51.6	26.5	105 56.5	15.5	Alphard	218 20.0	S 8 34.7
N 11	310 21.8	353 35.4	32.6	331 31.6	58.0	120 54.2	26.4	120 59.0	15.4			
D 12	325 24.2	8 34.7	S17 31.8	346 32.2	S 9 57.2	135 56.8	S 2 26.3	136 01.6	S 1 15.4	Alphecca	126 31.9	N26 46.5
A 13	340 26.7	23 34.0	31.0	1 32.8	56.5	150 59.4	26.2	151 04.2	15.3	Alpheratz	358 09.3	N28 59.1
Y 14	355 29.2	38 33.3	30.1	16 33.4	55.7	166 02.0	26.2	166 06.7	15.3	Altair	62 32.5	N 8 49.0
15	10 31.6	53 32.6	·· 29.3	31 34.0	·· 55.0	181 04.7	·· 26.1	181 09.3	·· 15.2	Ankaa	353 40.3	S42 24.8
16	25 34.1	68 31.9	28.5	46 34.7	54.2	196 07.3	26.0	196 11.9	15.2	Antares	112 56.6	S26 23.3
17	40 36.6	83 31.3	27.6	61 35.3	53.5	211 09.9	25.9	211 14.4	15.1			
18	55 39.0	98 30.6	S17 26.8	76 35.9	S 9 52.7	226 12.5	S 2 25.9	226 17.0	S 1 15.0	Arcturus	146 18.1	N19 16.7
19	70 41.5	113 29.9	25.9	91 36.5	52.0	241 15.1	25.8	241 19.6	15.0	Atria	108 20.7	S68 59.3
20	85 44.0	128 29.2	25.1	106 37.1	51.2	256 17.7	25.7	256 22.1	14.9	Avior	234 27.5	S59 27.1
21	100 46.4	143 28.5	·· 24.3	121 37.7	·· 50.5	271 20.4	·· 25.6	271 24.7	·· 14.9	Bellatrix	278 58.3	N 6 19.8
22	115 48.9	158 27.8	23.4	136 38.3	49.7	286 23.0	25.6	286 27.3	14.8	Betelgeuse	271 27.8	N 7 24.1
23	130 51.4	173 27.1	22.6	151 38.9	49.0	301 25.6	25.5	301 29.8	14.8			
16 00	145 53.8	188 26.4	S17 21.7	166 39.5	S 9 48.3	316 28.2	S 2 25.4	316 32.4	S 1 14.7	Canopus	264 06.7	S52 41.4
01	160 56.3	203 25.7	20.9	181 40.1	47.5	331 30.8	25.3	331 35.0	14.7	Capella	281 10.7	N45 58.8
02	175 58.7	218 25.0	20.0	196 40.7	46.8	346 33.4	25.2	346 37.5	14.6	Deneb	49 48.7	N45 12.6
03	191 01.2	233 24.4	·· 19.2	211 41.4	·· 46.0	1 36.1	·· 25.2	1 40.1	·· 14.5	Denebola	182 58.5	N14 40.6
04	206 03.7	248 23.7	18.3	226 42.0	45.3	16 38.7	25.1	16 42.7	14.5	Diphda	349 20.8	S18 05.7
05	221 06.1	263 23.0	17.5	241 42.6	44.5	31 41.3	25.0	31 45.3	14.4			
06	236 08.6	278 22.3	S17 16.6	256 43.2	S 9 43.8	46 43.9	S 2 24.9	46 47.8	S 1 14.4	Dubhe	194 21.2	N61 51.1
07	251 11.1	293 21.6	15.8	271 43.8	43.0	61 46.5	24.9	61 50.4	14.3	Elnath	278 43.6	N28 35.5
08	266 13.5	308 20.9	14.9	286 44.4	42.3	76 49.2	24.8	76 53.0	14.3	Eltanin	90 57.9	N51 29.3
M 09	281 16.0	323 20.2	·· 14.1	301 45.0	·· 41.5	91 51.8	·· 24.7	91 55.5	·· 14.2	Enif	34 11.6	N 9 47.2
O 10	296 18.5	338 19.6	13.2	316 45.6	40.8	106 54.4	24.6	106 58.1	14.2	Fomalhaut	15 51.4	S29 43.6
N 11	311 20.9	353 18.9	12.4	331 46.2	40.0	121 57.0	24.6	122 00.7	14.1			
D 12	326 23.4	8 18.2	S17 11.5	346 46.9	S 9 39.3	136 59.6	S 2 24.5	137 03.3	S 1 14.0	Gacrux	172 28.0	S57 00.2
A 13	341 25.9	23 17.5	10.7	1 47.5	38.5	152 02.3	24.4	152 05.8	14.0	Gienah	176 17.4	S17 26.2
Y 14	356 28.3	38 16.8	09.8	16 48.1	37.8	167 04.9	24.3	167 08.4	13.9	Hadar	149 22.6	S60 16.6
15	11 30.8	53 16.1	·· 08.9	31 48.7	·· 37.0	182 07.5	·· 24.3	182 11.0	·· 13.9	Hamal	328 28.7	N23 22.3
16	26 33.2	68 15.5	08.1	46 49.3	36.3	197 10.1	24.2	197 13.5	13.8	Kaus Aust.	84 16.7	S34 23.6
17	41 35.7	83 14.8	07.2	61 49.9	35.5	212 12.7	24.1	212 16.1	13.8			
18	56 38.2	98 14.1	S17 06.4	76 50.5	S 9 34.8	227 15.4	S 2 24.0	227 18.7	S 1 13.7	Kochab	137 18.8	N74 13.7
19	71 40.6	113 13.4	05.5	91 51.2	34.0	242 18.0	23.9	242 21.3	13.7	Markab	14 03.2	N15 06.1
20	86 43.1	128 12.7	04.6	106 51.8	33.3	257 20.6	23.9	257 23.8	13.6	Menkar	314 40.9	N 4 00.8
21	101 45.6	143 12.1	·· 03.8	121 52.4	·· 32.5	272 23.2	·· 23.8	272 26.4	·· 13.5	Menkent	148 36.5	S36 16.5
22	116 48.0	158 11.4	02.9	136 53.0	31.8	287 25.9	23.7	287 29.0	13.5	Miaplacidus	221 43.9	S69 38.4
23	131 50.5	173 10.7	02.1	151 53.6	31.0	302 28.5	23.6	302 31.5	13.4			
17 00	146 53.0	188 10.0	S17 01.2	166 54.2	S 9 30.3	317 31.1	S 2 23.6	317 34.1	S 1 13.4	Mirfak	309 15.7	N49 47.8
01	161 55.4	203 09.3	17 00.3	181 54.8	29.5	332 33.7	23.5	332 36.7	13.3	Nunki	76 29.1	S26 19.2
02	176 57.9	218 08.7	16 59.5	196 55.4	28.8	347 36.4	23.4	347 39.3	13.3	Peacock	53 58.5	S56 47.7
03	192 00.3	233 08.0	·· 58.6	211 56.1	·· 28.0	2 39.0	·· 23.3	2 41.8	·· 13.2	Pollux	243 57.5	N28 04.3
04	207 02.8	248 07.3	57.7	226 56.7	27.3	17 41.6	23.2	17 44.4	13.1	Procyon	245 25.2	N 5 16.3
05	222 05.3	263 06.6	56.9	241 57.3	26.5	32 44.2	23.2	32 47.0	13.1			
06	237 07.7	278 06.0	S16 56.0	256 57.9	S 9 25.8	47 46.9	S 2 23.1	47 49.6	S 1 13.0	Rasalhague	96 29.5	N12 34.3
07	252 10.2	293 05.3	55.1	271 58.5	25.0	62 49.5	23.0	62 52.1	13.0	Regulus	208 09.4	N12 03.5
08	267 12.7	308 04.6	54.2	286 59.1	24.3	77 52.1	22.9	77 54.7	12.9	Rigel	281 35.6	S 8 13.6
T 09	282 15.1	323 04.0	·· 53.4	301 59.8	·· 23.5	92 54.7	·· 22.8	92 57.3	·· 12.9	Rigil Kent.	140 25.2	S60 45.1
U 10	297 17.6	338 03.3	52.5	317 00.4	22.8	107 57.4	22.8	107 59.9	12.8	Sabik	102 40.9	S15 42.1
E 11	312 20.1	353 02.6	51.6	332 01.0	22.0	123 00.0	22.7	123 02.4	12.7			
S 12	327 22.5	8 01.9	S16 50.7	347 01.6	S 9 21.3	138 02.6	S 2 22.6	138 05.0	S 1 12.7	Schedar	350 09.1	N56 26.1
D 13	342 25.0	23 01.3	49.9	2 02.2	20.5	153 05.2	22.5	153 07.6	12.6	Shaula	96 55.5	S37 05.3
A 14	357 27.5	38 00.6	49.0	17 02.8	19.8	168 07.9	22.4	168 10.2	12.6	Sirius	258 55.2	S16 41.7
Y 15	12 29.9	52 59.9	·· 48.1	32 03.4	·· 19.0	183 10.5	·· 22.4	183 12.7	·· 12.5	Spica	158 57.0	S11 03.7
16	27 32.4	67 59.3	47.2	47 04.1	18.2	198 13.1	22.3	198 15.3	12.5	Suhail	223 10.1	S43 21.5
17	42 34.8	82 58.6	46.4	62 04.7	17.5	213 15.8	22.2	213 17.9	12.4			
18	57 37.3	97 57.9	S16 45.5	77 05.3	S 9 16.7	228 18.4	S 2 22.1	228 20.5	S 1 12.3	Vega	80 55.9	N38 45.8
19	72 39.8	112 57.3	44.6	92 05.9	16.0	243 21.0	22.0	243 23.0	12.3	Zuben'ubi	137 32.6	S15 57.7
20	87 42.2	127 56.6	43.7	107 06.5	15.2	258 23.6	22.0	258 25.6	12.2			
21	102 44.7	142 55.9	·· 42.8	122 07.1	·· 14.5	273 26.3	·· 21.9	273 28.2	·· 12.2		S.H.A.	Mer. Pass.
22	117 47.2	157 55.3	41.9	137 07.8	13.7	288 28.9	21.8	288 30.8	12.1	Venus	42 32.6	11 27
23	132 49.6	172 54.6	41.1	152 08.4	13.0	303 31.5	21.7	303 33.3	12.1	Mars	20 45.7	12 53
	h m									Jupiter	170 34.4	2 54
Mer. Pass. 14 14.1		v −0.7	d 0.9	v 0.6	d 0.7	v 2.6	d 0.1	v 2.6	d 0.1	Saturn	170 38.6	2 53

SUN / MOON

G.M.T.	SUN G.H.A.	SUN Dec.	MOON G.H.A.	v	MOON Dec.	d	H.P.
d h	° ′	° ′	° ′	′	° ′	′	′
15 00	176 26.9	S12 46.7	46 15.8	7.2	N20 20.3	0.5	58.0
01	191 26.9	45.8	60 42.0	7.2	20 20.8	0.4	58.0
02	206 26.9	44.9	75 08.2	7.3	20 21.2	0.3	57.9
03	221 27.0 ··	44.1	89 34.5	7.3	20 21.5	0.1	57.9
04	236 27.0	43.2	104 00.8	7.2	20 21.6	0.1	57.9
05	251 27.0	42.4	118 27.0	7.4	20 21.7	0.1	57.9
06	266 27.1	S12 41.5	132 53.4	7.3	N20 21.6	0.3	57.9
07	281 27.1	40.7	147 19.7	7.3	20 21.3	0.3	57.8
08	296 27.1	39.8	161 46.0	7.4	20 21.0	0.5	57.8
S 09	311 27.2 ··	38.9	176 12.4	7.4	20 20.5	0.6	57.8
U 10	326 27.2	38.1	190 38.8	7.5	20 19.9	0.7	57.8
N 11	341 27.2	37.2	205 05.3	7.4	20 19.2	0.8	57.8
D 12	356 27.3	S12 36.4	219 31.7	7.5	N20 18.4	1.0	57.8
A 13	11 27.3	35.5	233 58.2	7.5	20 17.4	1.0	57.7
Y 14	26 27.3	34.6	248 24.7	7.5	20 16.4	1.2	57.7
15	41 27.4 ··	33.8	262 51.2	7.6	20 15.2	1.3	57.7
16	56 27.4	32.9	277 17.8	7.6	20 13.9	1.5	57.7
17	71 27.4	32.1	291 44.4	7.6	20 12.4	1.6	57.7
18	86 27.5	S12 31.2	306 11.0	7.7	N20 10.8	1.6	57.6
19	101 27.5	30.3	320 37.7	7.7	20 09.2	1.8	57.6
20	116 27.5	29.5	335 04.4	7.7	20 07.4	2.0	57.6
21	131 27.6 ··	28.6	349 31.1	7.8	20 05.4	2.0	57.6
22	146 27.6	27.7	3 57.9	7.8	20 03.4	2.2	57.6
23	161 27.6	26.9	18 24.7	7.8	20 01.2	2.2	57.6
16 00	176 27.7	S12 26.0	32 51.5	7.9	N19 59.0	2.4	57.5
01	191 27.7	25.1	47 18.4	7.9	19 56.6	2.5	57.5
02	206 27.8	24.3	61 45.3	8.0	19 54.1	2.7	57.5
03	221 27.8 ··	23.4	76 12.3	8.0	19 51.4	2.7	57.5
04	236 27.8	22.5	90 39.3	8.0	19 48.7	2.8	57.5
05	251 27.9	21.7	105 06.3	8.1	19 45.9	3.0	57.4
06	266 27.9	S12 20.8	119 33.4	8.1	N19 42.9	3.1	57.4
07	281 27.9	20.0	134 00.5	8.2	19 39.8	3.2	57.4
08	296 28.0	19.1	148 27.7	8.2	19 36.6	3.3	57.4
M 09	311 28.0 ··	18.2	162 54.9	8.3	19 33.3	3.4	57.4
O 10	326 28.1	17.3	177 22.2	8.3	19 29.9	3.6	57.3
N 11	341 28.1	16.5	191 49.5	8.3	19 26.3	3.6	57.3
D 12	356 28.1	S12 15.6	206 16.8	8.4	N19 22.7	3.8	57.3
A 13	11 28.2	14.7	220 44.2	8.5	19 18.9	3.8	57.3
Y 14	26 28.2	13.9	235 11.7	8.5	19 15.1	4.0	57.3
15	41 28.3 ··	13.0	249 39.2	8.5	19 11.1	4.1	57.2
16	56 28.3	12.1	264 06.7	8.6	19 07.0	4.2	57.2
17	71 28.3	11.3	278 34.3	8.7	19 02.8	4.2	57.2
18	86 28.4	S12 10.4	293 02.0	8.7	N18 58.6	4.4	57.2
19	101 28.4	09.5	307 29.7	8.8	18 54.2	4.6	57.2
20	116 28.5	08.7	321 57.5	8.8	18 49.6	4.6	57.1
21	131 28.5 ··	07.8	336 25.3	8.8	18 45.0	4.7	57.1
22	146 28.6	06.9	350 53.1	9.0	18 40.3	4.8	57.1
23	161 28.6	06.0	5 21.1	8.9	18 35.5	4.9	57.1
17 00	176 28.6	S12 05.2	19 49.0	9.1	N18 30.6	5.0	57.1
01	191 28.7	04.3	34 17.1	9.1	18 25.6	5.1	57.0
02	206 28.7	03.4	48 45.2	9.1	18 20.5	5.2	57.0
03	221 28.8 ··	02.5	63 13.3	9.2	18 15.3	5.4	57.0
04	236 28.8	01.7	77 41.5	9.3	18 09.9	5.4	57.0
05	251 28.9	12 00.8	92 09.8	9.3	18 04.5	5.5	57.0
06	266 28.9	S11 59.9	106 38.1	9.4	N17 59.0	5.6	56.9
07	281 29.0	59.0	121 06.5	9.4	17 53.4	5.7	56.9
08	296 29.0	58.2	135 34.9	9.5	17 47.7	5.8	56.9
T 09	311 29.1 ··	57.3	150 03.4	9.6	17 41.9	5.8	56.9
U 10	326 29.1	56.4	164 32.0	9.6	17 36.1	6.0	56.9
E 11	341 29.2	55.5	179 00.6	9.7	17 30.1	6.1	56.8
S 12	356 29.2	S11 54.7	193 29.3	9.7	N17 24.0	6.2	56.8
D 13	11 29.3	53.8	207 58.0	9.8	17 17.8	6.2	56.8
A 14	26 29.3	52.9	222 26.8	9.9	17 11.6	6.3	56.8
Y 15	41 29.3 ··	52.0	236 55.7	9.9	17 05.3	6.5	56.8
16	56 29.4	51.2	251 24.6	10.0	16 58.8	6.5	56.7
17	71 29.4	50.3	265 53.6	10.0	16 52.3	6.6	56.7
18	86 29.5	S11 49.4	280 22.6	10.1	N16 45.7	6.7	56.7
19	101 29.5	48.5	294 51.7	10.2	16 39.0	6.7	56.7
20	116 29.6	47.6	309 20.9	10.3	16 32.3	6.9	56.6
21	131 29.6 ··	46.8	323 50.2	10.3	16 25.4	6.9	56.6
22	146 29.7	45.9	338 19.5	10.3	16 18.5	7.0	56.6
23	161 29.7	45.0	352 48.8	10.4	16 11.5	7.1	56.6
	S.D. 16.2	d 0.9	S.D. 15.7		15.6		15.5

Twilight / Sunrise / Moonrise

Lat.	Naut.	Civil	Sunrise	Moonrise 15	16	17	18
°	h m	h m	h m	h m	h m	h m	h m
N 72	06 11	07 30	08 48	□	□	12 15	14 38
N 70	06 09	07 21	08 29	□	11 17	13 17	15 08
68	06 08	07 13	08 14	10 58	12 17	13 52	15 30
66	06 07	07 07	08 02	11 39	12 51	14 17	15 47
64	06 06	07 01	07 52	12 07	13 16	14 36	16 01
62	06 05	06 56	07 43	12 28	13 35	14 52	16 13
60	06 03	06 52	07 36	12 46	13 51	15 05	16 23
N 58	06 02	06 48	07 29	13 00	14 05	15 16	16 31
56	06 01	06 45	07 23	13 13	14 16	15 26	16 39
54	06 00	06 41	07 18	13 24	14 27	15 35	16 45
52	05 59	06 39	07 13	13 34	14 36	15 42	16 51
50	05 58	06 36	07 09	13 42	14 44	15 49	16 57
45	05 55	06 30	07 00	14 01	15 01	16 04	17 09
N 40	05 53	06 24	06 52	14 16	15 15	16 16	17 18
35	05 50	06 19	06 45	14 28	15 27	16 27	17 27
30	05 47	06 15	06 39	14 39	15 37	16 36	17 34
20	05 40	06 06	06 29	14 58	15 55	16 51	17 46
N 10	05 33	05 58	06 20	15 15	16 10	17 05	17 57
0	05 25	05 50	06 11	15 30	16 25	17 18	18 07
S 10	05 15	05 40	06 02	15 46	16 40	17 30	18 18
20	05 03	05 29	05 52	16 02	16 55	17 44	18 28
30	04 47	05 16	05 41	16 21	17 13	17 59	18 41
35	04 36	05 08	05 35	16 33	17 23	18 08	18 48
40	04 24	04 59	05 27	16 45	17 35	18 18	18 56
45	04 09	04 47	05 19	17 00	17 49	18 30	19 05
S 50	03 49	04 33	05 08	17 19	18 06	18 45	19 17
52	03 39	04 26	05 03	17 27	18 14	18 51	19 22
54	03 28	04 18	04 58	17 37	18 23	18 59	19 28
56	03 14	04 10	04 52	17 48	18 32	19 07	19 34
58	02 59	04 00	04 45	18 01	18 44	19 16	19 41
S 60	02 39	03 48	04 37	18 15	18 57	19 27	19 49

Twilight / Sunset / Moonset

Lat.	Sunset	Civil	Naut.	Moonset 15	16	17	18
°	h m	h m	h m	h m	h m	h m	h m
N 72	15 42	17 00	18 20	□	□	10 04	09 27
N 70	16 00	17 09	18 21	□	09 11	09 02	08 56
68	16 15	17 16	18 22	07 35	08 11	08 26	08 33
66	16 27	17 23	18 23	06 54	07 36	08 00	08 15
64	16 38	17 28	18 24	06 26	07 11	07 40	08 00
62	16 46	17 33	18 25	06 04	06 51	07 24	07 47
60	16 54	17 37	18 26	05 46	06 35	07 11	07 37
N 58	17 00	17 41	18 27	05 32	06 21	06 59	07 28
56	17 06	17 45	18 28	05 19	06 09	06 49	07 19
54	17 11	17 48	18 29	05 08	05 59	06 40	07 12
52	17 16	17 51	18 30	04 59	05 50	06 32	07 06
50	17 20	17 53	18 31	04 50	05 41	06 24	07 00
45	17 29	17 59	18 34	04 31	05 24	06 09	06 47
N 40	17 37	18 05	18 36	04 16	05 09	05 56	06 36
35	17 44	18 09	18 39	04 04	04 57	05 45	06 27
30	17 49	18 14	18 42	03 52	04 46	05 35	06 19
20	18 00	18 22	18 48	03 33	04 28	05 19	06 05
N 10	18 09	18 30	18 55	03 17	04 12	05 04	05 53
0	18 18	18 39	19 04	03 01	03 57	04 50	05 42
S 10	18 26	18 48	19 13	02 46	03 42	04 37	05 30
20	18 36	18 58	19 25	02 29	03 25	04 22	05 18
30	18 47	19 12	19 41	02 10	03 07	04 05	05 04
35	18 53	19 19	19 51	01 58	02 56	03 55	04 55
40	19 00	19 29	20 03	01 46	02 43	03 44	04 46
45	19 09	19 40	20 18	01 30	02 28	03 31	04 35
S 50	19 19	19 54	20 38	01 12	02 10	03 14	04 21
52	19 24	20 01	20 48	01 03	02 02	03 07	04 15
54	19 29	20 08	20 59	00 53	01 52	02 58	04 08
56	19 35	20 17	21 11	00 42	01 41	02 48	04 00
58	19 42	20 26	21 27	00 29	01 29	02 37	03 51
S 60	19 49	20 38	21 46	00 14	01 14	02 25	03 41

SUN / MOON

Day	Eqn. of Time 00h	12h	Mer. Pass.	Mer. Pass. Upper	Lower	Age	Phase
	m s	m s	h m	h m	h m	d	
15	14 13	14 11	12 14	21 44	09 16	11	
16	14 09	14 08	12 14	22 38	10 11	12	○
17	14 05	14 03	12 14	23 30	11 04	13	

G.M.T.	ARIES G.H.A.	VENUS −3.4 G.H.A.	Dec.	MARS +1.4 G.H.A.	Dec.	JUPITER −1.9 G.H.A.	Dec.	SATURN +0.8 G.H.A.	Dec.	STARS Name	S.H.A.	Dec.
18 00	147 52.1	187 53.9	S16 40.2	167 09.0	S 9 12.2	318 34.2	S 2 21.6	318 35.9	S 1 12.0	Acamar	315 37.1	S40 23.2
01	162 54.6	202 53.3	39.3	182 09.6	11.5	333 36.8	21.6	333 38.5	11.9	Achernar	335 45.4	S57 20.3
02	177 57.0	217 52.6	38.4	197 10.2	10.7	348 39.4	21.5	348 41.1	11.9	Acrux	173 36.3	S62 59.5
03	192 59.5	232 51.9	·· 37.5	212 10.9	·· 10.0	3 42.1	·· 21.4	3 43.6	·· 11.8	Adhara	255 31.6	S28 57.0
04	208 02.0	247 51.3	36.6	227 11.5	09.2	18 44.7	21.3	18 46.2	11.8	Aldebaran	291 17.6	N16 28.2
05	223 04.4	262 50.6	35.7	242 12.1	08.4	33 47.3	21.2	33 48.8	11.7			
06	238 06.9	277 50.0	S16 34.9	257 12.7	S 9 07.7	48 49.9	S 2 21.2	48 51.4	S 1 11.6	Alioth	166 41.9	N56 03.6
W 07	253 09.3	292 49.3	34.0	272 13.3	06.9	63 52.6	21.1	63 53.9	11.6	Alkaid	153 18.0	N49 24.3
E 08	268 11.8	307 48.6	33.1	287 13.9	06.2	78 55.2	21.0	78 56.5	11.5	Al Na'ir	28 15.0	S47 03.3
D 09	283 14.3	322 48.0	·· 32.2	302 14.6	·· 05.4	93 57.8	·· 20.9	93 59.1	·· 11.5	Alnilam	276 11.2	S 1 13.0
N 10	298 16.7	337 47.3	31.3	317 15.2	04.7	109 00.5	20.8	109 01.7	11.4	Alphard	218 20.0	S 8 34.7
E 11	313 19.2	352 46.6	30.4	332 15.8	03.9	124 03.1	20.7	124 04.3	11.4			
S 12	328 21.7	7 46.0	S16 29.5	347 16.4	S 9 03.2	139 05.7	S 2 20.7	139 06.8	S 1 11.3	Alphecca	126 31.8	N26 46.5
D 13	343 24.1	22 45.3	28.6	2 17.0	02.4	154 08.4	20.6	154 09.4	11.2	Alpheratz	358 09.3	N28 59.1
A 14	358 26.6	37 44.7	27.7	17 17.7	01.6	169 11.0	20.5	169 12.0	11.2	Altair	62 32.5	N 8 49.0
Y 15	13 29.1	52 44.0	·· 26.8	32 18.3	·· 00.9	184 13.6	·· 20.4	184 14.6	·· 11.1	Ankaa	353 40.3	S42 24.8
16	28 31.5	67 43.4	25.9	47 18.9	9 00.1	199 16.3	20.3	199 17.1	11.1	Antares	112 56.5	S26 23.3
17	43 34.0	82 42.7	25.0	62 19.5	8 59.4	214 18.9	20.2	214 19.7	11.0			
18	58 36.4	97 42.0	S16 24.1	77 20.1	S 8 58.6	229 21.6	S 2 20.2	229 22.3	S 1 10.9	Arcturus	146 18.1	N19 16.7
19	73 38.9	112 41.4	23.2	92 20.8	57.9	244 24.2	20.1	244 24.9	10.9	Atria	108 20.7	S68 59.3
20	88 41.4	127 40.7	22.3	107 21.4	57.1	259 26.8	20.0	259 27.5	10.8	Avior	234 27.5	S59 27.1
21	103 43.8	142 40.1	·· 21.4	122 22.0	·· 56.4	274 29.5	·· 19.9	274 30.0	·· 10.8	Bellatrix	278 58.3	N 6 19.8
22	118 46.3	157 39.4	20.5	137 22.6	55.6	289 32.1	19.8	289 32.6	10.7	Betelgeuse	271 27.8	N 7 24.1
23	133 48.8	172 38.8	19.6	152 23.2	54.8	304 34.7	19.7	304 35.2	10.7			
19 00	148 51.2	187 38.1	S16 18.7	167 23.9	S 8 54.1	319 37.4	S 2 19.7	319 37.8	S 1 10.6	Canopus	264 06.7	S52 41.5
01	163 53.7	202 37.5	17.8	182 24.5	53.3	334 40.0	19.6	334 40.4	10.5	Capella	281 10.7	N45 58.8
02	178 56.2	217 36.8	16.9	197 25.1	52.6	349 42.6	19.5	349 42.9	10.5	Deneb	49 48.7	N45 12.6
03	193 58.6	232 36.2	·· 16.0	212 25.7	·· 51.8	4 45.3	·· 19.4	4 45.5	·· 10.4	Denebola	182 58.5	N14 40.6
04	209 01.1	247 35.5	15.1	227 26.4	51.0	19 47.9	19.3	19 48.1	10.4	Diphda	349 20.8	S18 05.7
05	224 03.6	262 34.9	14.2	242 27.0	50.3	34 50.6	19.2	34 50.7	10.3			
06	239 06.0	277 34.2	S16 13.3	257 27.6	S 8 49.5	49 53.2	S 2 19.2	49 53.2	S 1 10.2	Dubhe	194 21.1	N61 51.1
07	254 08.5	292 33.6	12.3	272 28.2	48.8	64 55.8	19.1	64 55.8	10.2	Elnath	278 43.6	N28 35.5
T 08	269 10.9	307 32.9	11.4	287 28.8	48.0	79 58.5	19.0	79 58.4	10.1	Eltanin	90 57.9	N51 29.2
H 09	284 13.4	322 32.3	·· 10.5	302 29.5	·· 47.3	95 01.1	·· 18.9	95 01.0	·· 10.0	Enif	34 11.6	N 9 47.1
U 10	299 15.9	337 31.6	09.6	317 30.1	46.5	110 03.7	18.8	110 03.6	10.0	Fomalhaut	15 51.4	S29 43.5
R 11	314 18.3	352 31.0	08.7	332 30.7	45.7	125 06.4	18.7	125 06.2	09.9			
S 12	329 20.8	7 30.3	S16 07.8	347 31.3	S 8 45.0	140 09.0	S 2 18.7	140 08.7	S 1 09.9	Gacrux	172 27.9	S57 00.3
D 13	344 23.3	22 29.7	06.9	2 32.0	44.2	155 11.7	18.6	155 11.3	09.8	Gienah	176 17.4	S17 26.2
A 14	359 25.7	37 29.0	06.0	17 32.6	43.5	170 14.3	18.5	170 13.9	09.8	Hadar	149 22.6	S60 16.7
Y 15	14 28.2	52 28.4	·· 05.0	32 33.2	·· 42.7	185 16.9	·· 18.4	185 16.5	·· 09.7	Hamal	328 28.7	N23 22.3
16	29 30.7	67 27.8	04.1	47 33.8	41.9	200 19.6	18.3	200 19.1	09.6	Kaus Aust.	84 16.7	S34 23.6
17	44 33.1	82 27.1	03.2	62 34.5	41.2	215 22.2	18.2	215 21.6	09.6			
18	59 35.6	97 26.5	S16 02.3	77 35.1	S 8 40.4	230 24.9	S 2 18.1	230 24.2	S 1 09.5	Kochab	137 18.7	N74 13.7
19	74 38.1	112 25.8	01.4	92 35.7	39.7	245 27.5	18.1	245 26.8	09.5	Markab	14 03.2	N15 06.1
20	89 40.5	127 25.2	16 00.4	107 36.3	38.9	260 30.2	18.0	260 29.4	09.4	Menkar	314 40.9	N 4 00.8
21	104 43.0	142 24.5	15 59.5	122 36.9	·· 38.1	275 32.8	·· 17.9	275 32.0	·· 09.3	Menkent	148 36.5	S36 16.5
22	119 45.4	157 23.9	58.6	137 37.6	37.4	290 35.4	17.8	290 34.5	09.3	Miaplacidus	221 43.9	S69 38.5
23	134 47.9	172 23.3	57.7	152 38.2	36.6	305 38.1	17.7	305 37.1	09.2			
20 00	149 50.4	187 22.6	S15 56.8	167 38.8	S 8 35.9	320 40.7	S 2 17.6	320 39.7	S 1 09.2	Mirfak	309 15.7	N49 47.8
01	164 52.8	202 22.0	55.8	182 39.4	35.1	335 43.4	17.5	335 42.3	09.1	Nunki	76 29.1	S26 19.2
02	179 55.3	217 21.3	54.9	197 40.1	34.3	350 46.0	17.5	350 44.9	09.0	Peacock	53 58.5	S56 47.7
03	194 57.8	232 20.7	·· 54.0	212 40.7	·· 33.6	5 48.7	·· 17.4	5 47.5	·· 09.0	Pollux	243 57.5	N28 04.3
04	210 00.2	247 20.1	53.1	227 41.3	32.8	20 51.3	17.3	20 50.0	08.9	Procyon	245 25.2	N 5 16.3
05	225 02.7	262 19.4	52.1	242 41.9	32.1	35 53.9	17.2	35 52.6	08.9			
06	240 05.2	277 18.8	S15 51.2	257 42.6	S 8 31.3	50 56.6	S 2 17.1	50 55.2	S 1 08.8	Rasalhague	96 29.5	N12 34.3
07	255 07.6	292 18.1	50.3	272 43.2	30.5	65 59.2	17.0	65 57.8	08.7	Regulus	208 09.4	N12 03.5
08	270 10.1	307 17.5	49.3	287 43.8	29.8	81 01.9	16.9	81 00.4	08.7	Rigel	281 35.6	S 8 13.6
F 09	285 12.5	322 16.9	·· 48.4	302 44.5	·· 29.0	96 04.5	·· 16.9	96 03.0	·· 08.6	Rigil Kent.	140 25.2	S60 45.1
R 10	300 15.0	337 16.2	47.5	317 45.1	28.3	111 07.2	16.8	111 05.5	08.6	Sabik	102 40.9	S15 42.1
I 11	315 17.5	352 15.6	46.6	332 45.7	27.5	126 09.8	16.7	126 08.1	08.5			
D 12	330 19.9	7 15.0	S15 45.6	347 46.3	S 8 26.7	141 12.5	S 2 16.6	141 10.7	S 1 08.4	Schedar	350 09.1	N56 26.1
A 13	345 22.4	22 14.3	44.7	2 47.0	26.0	156 15.1	16.5	156 13.3	08.4	Shaula	96 55.5	S37 05.3
Y 14	0 24.9	37 13.7	43.8	17 47.6	25.2	171 17.7	16.4	171 15.9	08.3	Sirius	258 55.2	S16 41.7
15	15 27.3	52 13.1	·· 42.8	32 48.2	·· 24.4	186 20.4	·· 16.3	186 18.5	·· 08.3	Spica	158 57.0	S11 03.8
16	30 29.8	67 12.4	41.9	47 48.8	23.7	201 23.0	16.2	201 21.1	08.2	Suhail	223 10.1	S43 21.5
17	45 32.3	82 11.8	41.0	62 49.5	22.9	216 25.7	16.2	216 23.6	08.1			
18	60 34.7	97 11.2	S15 40.0	77 50.1	S 8 22.2	231 28.3	S 2 16.1	231 26.2	S 1 08.1	Vega	80 55.9	N38 45.8
19	75 37.2	112 10.5	39.1	92 50.7	21.4	246 31.0	16.0	246 28.8	08.0	Zuben'ubi	137 32.6	S15 57.8
20	90 39.7	127 09.9	38.1	107 51.3	20.6	261 33.6	15.9	261 31.4	07.9		S.H.A.	Mer. Pass.
21	105 42.1	142 09.3	·· 37.2	122 52.0	·· 19.9	276 36.3	·· 15.8	276 34.0	·· 07.9	Venus	38 46.9	11 30
22	120 44.6	157 08.7	36.3	137 52.6	19.1	291 38.9	15.7	291 36.6	07.8	Mars	18 32.6	12 50
23	135 47.0	172 08.0	35.3	152 53.2	18.3	306 41.6	15.6	306 39.1	07.8	Jupiter	170 46.1	2 41
Mer. Pass. 14 02.3		v −0.6	d 0.9	v 0.6	d 0.8	v 2.6	d 0.1	v 2.6	d 0.1	Saturn	170 46.5	2 41

SUN and MOON

G.M.T.	SUN G.H.A.	SUN Dec.	MOON G.H.A.	v	MOON Dec.	d	H.P.
18 00	176 29.8	S11 44.1	7 18.2	10.5	N16 04.4	7.2	56.6
01	191 29.8	43.2	21 47.7	10.6	15 57.2	7.2	56.5
02	206 29.9	42.4	36 17.3	10.6	15 50.0	7.4	56.5
03	221 30.0 ··	41.5	50 46.9	10.7	15 42.6	7.4	56.5
04	236 30.0	40.6	65 16.6	10.7	15 35.2	7.5	56.5
05	251 30.1	39.7	79 46.3	10.8	15 27.7	7.5	56.5
06	266 30.1	S11 38.8	94 16.1	10.9	N15 20.2	7.6	56.4
07	281 30.2	38.0	108 46.0	10.9	15 12.6	7.7	56.4
W 08	296 30.2	37.1	123 15.9	11.0	15 04.9	7.8	56.4
E 09	311 30.3 ··	36.2	137 45.9	11.1	14 57.1	7.9	56.4
D 10	326 30.3	35.3	152 16.0	11.1	14 49.2	7.9	56.3
N 11	341 30.4	34.4	166 46.1	11.2	14 41.3	8.0	56.3
E 12	356 30.4	S11 33.5	181 16.3	11.2	N14 33.3	8.0	56.3
S 13	11 30.5	32.7	195 46.5	11.3	14 25.3	8.1	56.3
D 14	26 30.5	31.8	210 16.8	11.4	14 17.2	8.2	56.3
A 15	41 30.6 ··	30.9	224 47.2	11.4	14 09.0	8.3	56.2
Y 16	56 30.7	30.0	239 17.6	11.5	14 00.7	8.3	56.2
17	71 30.7	29.1	253 48.1	11.6	13 52.4	8.3	56.2
18	86 30.8	S11 28.2	268 18.7	11.6	N13 44.1	8.5	56.2
19	101 30.8	27.3	282 49.3	11.7	13 35.6	8.5	56.2
20	116 30.9	26.5	297 20.0	11.7	13 27.1	8.5	56.1
21	131 30.9 ··	25.6	311 50.7	11.9	13 18.6	8.7	56.1
22	146 31.0	24.7	326 21.6	11.8	13 09.9	8.6	56.1
23	161 31.1	23.8	340 52.4	11.9	13 01.3	8.8	56.1
19 00	176 31.1	S11 22.9	355 23.3	12.0	N12 52.5	8.8	56.1
01	191 31.2	22.0	9 54.3	12.1	12 43.7	8.8	56.0
02	206 31.2	21.1	24 25.4	12.1	12 34.9	8.9	56.0
03	221 31.3 ··	20.2	38 56.5	12.2	12 26.0	8.9	56.0
04	236 31.4	19.4	53 27.7	12.2	12 17.1	9.1	56.0
05	251 31.4	18.5	67 58.9	12.3	12 08.0	9.0	55.9
06	266 31.5	S11 17.6	82 30.2	12.3	N11 59.0	9.1	55.9
07	281 31.5	16.7	97 01.5	12.5	11 49.9	9.2	55.9
T 08	296 31.6	15.8	111 33.0	12.4	11 40.7	9.2	55.9
H 09	311 31.7 ··	14.9	126 04.4	12.5	11 31.5	9.2	55.9
U 10	326 31.7	14.0	140 35.9	12.6	11 22.3	9.3	55.8
R 11	341 31.8	13.1	155 07.5	12.7	11 13.0	9.4	55.8
S 12	356 31.8	S11 12.2	169 39.2	12.7	N11 03.6	9.4	55.8
D 13	11 31.9	11.3	184 10.9	12.7	10 54.2	9.4	55.8
A 14	26 32.0	10.4	198 42.6	12.8	10 44.8	9.5	55.8
Y 15	41 32.0 ··	09.6	213 14.4	12.9	10 35.3	9.5	55.7
16	56 32.1	08.7	227 46.3	12.9	10 25.8	9.5	55.7
17	71 32.2	07.8	242 18.2	13.0	10 16.3	9.6	55.7
18	86 32.2	S11 06.9	256 50.2	13.0	N10 06.7	9.7	55.7
19	101 32.3	06.0	271 22.2	13.1	9 57.0	9.7	55.7
20	116 32.4	05.1	285 54.3	13.1	9 47.3	9.7	55.6
21	131 32.4 ··	04.2	300 26.4	13.2	9 37.6	9.7	55.6
22	146 32.5	03.3	314 58.6	13.2	9 27.9	9.8	55.6
23	161 32.5	02.4	329 30.8	13.3	9 18.1	9.8	55.6
20 00	176 32.6	S11 01.5	344 03.1	13.3	N 9 08.3	9.9	55.5
01	191 32.7	11 00.6	358 35.4	13.4	8 58.4	9.9	55.5
02	206 32.7	10 59.7	13 07.8	13.5	8 48.5	9.9	55.5
03	221 32.8 ··	58.8	27 40.3	13.5	8 38.6	10.0	55.5
04	236 32.9	57.9	42 12.8	13.6	8 28.6	9.9	55.5
05	251 32.9	57.0	56 45.3	13.6	8 18.7	10.1	55.4
06	266 33.0	S10 56.1	71 17.9	13.6	N 8 08.6	10.1	55.4
07	281 33.1	55.2	85 50.5	13.7	7 58.6	10.1	55.4
08	296 33.1	54.3	100 23.2	13.7	7 48.5	10.1	55.4
F 09	311 33.2 ··	53.4	114 55.9	13.8	7 38.4	10.1	55.4
R 10	326 33.3	52.5	129 28.7	13.8	7 28.3	10.1	55.3
I 11	341 33.4	51.6	144 01.5	13.9	7 18.2	10.2	55.3
D 12	356 33.4	S10 50.7	158 34.4	13.9	N 7 08.0	10.2	55.3
A 13	11 33.5	49.8	173 07.3	13.9	6 57.8	10.2	55.3
Y 14	26 33.6	48.9	187 40.2	14.0	6 47.6	10.3	55.3
15	41 33.6 ··	48.0	202 13.2	14.1	6 37.3	10.2	55.2
16	56 33.7	47.1	216 46.3	14.1	6 27.1	10.3	55.2
17	71 33.8	46.2	231 19.4	14.1	6 16.8	10.3	55.2
18	86 33.8	S10 45.3	245 52.5	14.1	N 6 06.5	10.4	55.2
19	101 33.9	44.4	260 25.6	14.3	5 56.1	10.3	55.2
20	116 34.0	43.5	274 58.9	14.2	5 45.8	10.4	55.2
21	131 34.1 ··	42.6	289 32.1	14.3	5 35.4	10.3	55.1
22	146 34.1	41.7	304 05.4	14.3	5 25.1	10.4	55.1
23	161 34.2	40.8	318 38.7	14.3	5 14.7	10.4	55.1
S.D.	16.2	d 0.9	S.D. 15.3		15.2		15.1

Twilight, Sunrise, Moonrise

Lat.	Naut.	Civil	Sunrise	Moonrise 18	19	20	21
N 72	05 58	07 16	08 31	14 38	16 35	18 23	20 04
N 70	05 58	07 09	08 15	15 08	16 52	18 31	20 07
68	05 57	07 02	08 02	15 30	17 06	18 39	20 08
66	05 57	06 57	07 51	15 47	17 17	18 44	20 10
64	05 57	06 52	07 42	16 01	17 26	18 49	20 11
62	05 56	06 48	07 34	16 13	17 34	18 54	20 12
60	05 56	06 44	07 27	16 23	17 41	18 58	20 13
N 58	05 55	06 41	07 22	16 31	17 47	19 01	20 14
56	05 55	06 38	07 16	16 39	17 52	19 04	20 14
54	05 54	06 35	07 12	16 45	17 56	19 06	20 15
52	05 54	06 33	07 07	16 51	18 01	19 09	20 16
50	05 53	06 30	07 03	16 57	18 04	19 11	20 16
45	05 51	06 25	06 55	17 09	18 13	19 16	20 17
N 40	05 49	06 20	06 48	17 18	18 20	19 20	20 18
35	05 47	06 16	06 42	17 27	18 26	19 23	20 19
30	05 44	06 12	06 36	17 34	18 31	19 26	20 20
20	05 39	06 05	06 27	17 46	18 40	19 31	20 21
N 10	05 32	05 57	06 19	17 57	18 47	19 36	20 22
0	05 25	05 49	06 11	18 07	18 55	19 40	20 23
S 10	05 16	05 41	06 02	18 18	19 02	19 44	20 24
20	05 04	05 31	05 54	18 28	19 10	19 49	20 26
30	04 49	05 19	05 43	18 41	19 19	19 54	20 27
35	04 40	05 11	05 38	18 48	19 24	19 57	20 28
40	04 28	05 02	05 31	18 56	19 30	20 00	20 29
45	04 14	04 52	05 23	19 05	19 36	20 04	20 30
S 50	03 55	04 39	05 13	19 17	19 44	20 08	20 31
52	03 46	04 32	05 09	19 22	19 48	20 11	20 31
54	03 36	04 25	05 04	19 28	19 52	20 13	20 32
56	03 24	04 17	04 59	19 34	19 56	20 15	20 33
58	03 09	04 08	04 52	19 41	20 01	20 18	20 33
S 60	02 52	03 58	04 46	19 49	20 07	20 21	20 34

Sunset, Twilight, Moonset

Lat.	Sunset	Civil	Naut.	Moonset 18	19	20	21
N 72	15 58	17 13	18 33	09 27	09 09	08 56	08 45
N 70	16 14	17 21	18 32	08 56	08 50	08 46	08 41
68	16 27	17 27	18 32	08 33	08 36	08 37	08 37
66	16 38	17 32	18 32	08 15	08 23	08 29	08 34
64	16 47	17 37	18 32	08 00	08 13	08 23	08 31
62	16 55	17 41	18 33	07 47	08 04	08 17	08 28
60	17 01	17 45	18 33	07 37	07 57	08 13	08 26
N 58	17 07	17 48	18 34	07 28	07 50	08 08	08 24
56	17 12	17 51	18 34	07 19	07 44	08 05	08 23
54	17 17	17 53	18 35	07 12	07 39	08 01	08 21
52	17 21	17 56	18 35	07 06	07 34	07 58	08 20
50	17 25	17 58	18 36	07 00	07 30	07 55	08 19
45	17 33	18 03	18 38	06 47	07 20	07 49	08 16
N 40	17 40	18 08	18 40	06 36	07 12	07 44	08 13
35	17 46	18 12	18 42	06 27	07 05	07 40	08 11
30	17 52	18 16	18 44	06 19	06 59	07 36	08 10
20	18 01	18 23	18 49	06 05	06 49	07 29	08 06
N 10	18 09	18 31	18 55	05 53	06 39	07 23	08 04
0	18 17	18 38	19 03	05 42	06 31	07 17	08 01
S 10	18 25	18 47	19 12	05 30	06 22	07 11	07 58
20	18 34	18 56	19 23	05 18	06 12	07 05	07 55
30	18 44	19 09	19 38	05 04	06 01	06 57	07 52
35	18 50	19 16	19 47	04 55	05 55	06 53	07 50
40	18 56	19 25	19 59	04 46	05 48	06 49	07 48
45	19 04	19 35	20 13	04 35	05 39	06 43	07 45
S 50	19 13	19 48	20 31	04 21	05 29	06 36	07 42
52	19 18	19 54	20 40	04 15	05 25	06 33	07 41
54	19 23	20 01	20 50	04 08	05 19	06 30	07 39
56	19 28	20 09	21 02	04 00	05 14	06 26	07 38
58	19 34	20 16	21 16	03 51	05 07	06 22	07 36
S 60	19 40	20 28	21 33	03 41	05 00	06 17	07 34

SUN / MOON

Day	Eqn. of Time 00h	Eqn. of Time 12h	Mer. Pass.	Mer. Pass. Upper	Mer. Pass. Lower	Age	Phase
	m s	m s	h m	h m	h m	d	
18	14 01	13 58	12 14	24 19	11 55	14	
19	13 56	13 53	12 14	00 19	12 43	15	
20	13 50	13 46	12 14	01 06	13 28	16	○

G.M.T.	ARIES G.H.A.	VENUS −3.4 G.H.A.	Dec.	MARS +1.4 G.H.A.	Dec.	JUPITER −1.9 G.H.A.	Dec.	SATURN +0.8 G.H.A.	Dec.	STARS Name	S.H.A.	Dec.
21 00	150 49.5	187 07.4	S15 34.4	167 53.9	S 8 17.6	321 44.2	S 2 15.5	321 41.7	S 1 07.7	Acamar	315 37.1	S40 23.2
01	165 52.0	202 06.8	33.4	182 54.5	16.8	336 46.9	15.4	336 44.3	07.6	Achernar	335 45.4	S57 20.3
02	180 54.4	217 06.1	32.5	197 55.1	16.0	351 49.5	15.4	351 46.9	07.6	Acrux	173 36.3	S62 59.5
03	195 56.9	232 05.5 ··	31.6	212 55.7 ··	15.3	6 52.2 ··	15.3	6 49.5 ··	07.5	Adhara	255 31.6	S28 57.0
04	210 59.4	247 04.9	30.6	227 56.4	14.5	21 54.8	15.2	21 52.1	07.5	Aldebaran	291 17.6	N16 28.2
05	226 01.8	262 04.3	29.7	242 57.0	13.8	36 57.5	15.1	36 54.7	07.4			
06	241 04.3	277 03.6	S15 28.7	257 57.6	S 8 13.0	52 00.1	S 2 15.0	51 57.2	S 1 07.3	Alioth	166 41.8	N56 03.6
07	256 06.8	292 03.0	27.8	272 58.3	12.2	67 02.8	14.9	66 59.8	07.3	Alkaid	153 18.0	N49 24.3
S 08	271 09.2	307 02.4	26.8	287 58.9	11.5	82 05.4	14.8	82 02.4	07.2	Al Na'ir	28 15.0	S47 03.3
A 09	286 11.7	322 01.8 ··	25.9	302 59.5 ··	10.7	97 08.1 ··	14.7	97 05.0 ··	07.1	Alnilam	276 11.2	S 1 13.0
T 10	301 14.2	337 01.1	24.9	318 00.8	09.9	112 10.7	14.6	112 07.6	07.1	Alphard	218 20.0	S 8 34.7
U 11	316 16.6	352 00.5	24.0	333 00.8	09.2	127 13.4	14.6	127 10.2	07.0			
R 12	331 19.1	6 59.9	S15 23.0	348 01.4	S 8 08.4	142 16.0	S 2 14.5	142 12.8	S 1 07.0	Alphecca	126 31.8	N26 46.5
D 13	346 21.5	21 59.3	22.1	3 02.0	07.6	157 18.7	14.4	157 15.4	06.9	Alpheratz	358 09.3	N28 59.1
A 14	1 24.0	36 58.7	21.1	18 02.7	06.9	172 21.3	14.3	172 17.9	06.8	Altair	62 32.5	N 8 49.0
Y 15	16 26.5	51 58.0 ··	20.2	33 03.3 ··	06.1	187 24.0 ··	14.2	187 20.5 ··	06.8	Ankaa	353 40.3	S42 24.8
16	31 28.9	66 57.4	19.2	48 03.9	05.3	202 26.6	14.1	202 23.1	06.7	Antares	112 56.5	S26 23.3
17	46 31.4	81 56.8	18.3	63 04.6	04.6	217 29.3	14.0	217 25.7	06.7			
18	61 33.9	96 56.2	S15 17.3	78 05.2	S 8 03.8	232 31.9	S 2 13.9	232 28.3	S 1 06.6	Arcturus	146 18.0	N19 16.7
19	76 36.3	111 55.6	16.4	93 05.8	03.0	247 34.6	13.8	247 30.9	06.5	Atria	108 20.6	S68 59.3
20	91 38.8	126 54.9	15.4	108 06.5	02.3	262 37.3	13.7	262 33.5	06.5	Avior	234 27.5	S59 27.1
21	106 41.3	141 54.3 ··	14.4	123 07.1 ··	01.5	277 39.9 ··	13.7	277 36.1 ··	06.4	Bellatrix	278 58.3	N 6 19.8
22	121 43.7	156 53.7	13.5	138 07.7	00.7	292 42.6	13.6	292 38.6	06.3	Betelgeuse	271 27.8	N 7 24.1
23	136 46.2	171 53.1	12.5	153 08.3	8 00.0	307 45.2	13.5	307 41.2	06.3			
22 00	151 48.6	186 52.5	S15 11.6	168 09.0	S 7 59.2	322 47.9	S 2 13.4	322 43.8	S 1 06.2	Canopus	264 06.8	S52 41.5
01	166 51.1	201 51.8	10.6	183 09.6	58.4	337 50.5	13.3	337 46.4	06.2	Capella	281 10.7	N45 58.8
02	181 53.6	216 51.2	09.6	198 10.2	57.7	352 53.2	13.2	352 49.0	06.1	Deneb	49 48.7	N45 12.6
03	196 56.0	231 50.6 ··	08.7	213 10.9 ··	56.9	7 55.8 ··	13.1	7 51.6 ··	06.0	Denebola	182 58.4	N14 40.6
04	211 58.5	246 50.0	07.7	228 11.5	56.1	22 58.5	13.0	22 54.2	06.0	Diphda	349 20.8	S18 05.7
05	227 01.0	261 49.4	06.8	243 12.1	55.4	38 01.1	12.9	37 56.8	05.9			
06	242 03.4	276 48.8	S15 05.8	258 12.8	S 7 54.6	53 03.8	S 2 12.8	52 59.4	S 1 05.8	Dubhe	194 21.1	N61 51.1
07	257 05.9	291 48.2	04.8	273 13.4	53.8	68 06.5	12.7	68 01.9	05.8	Elnath	278 43.6	N28 35.5
08	272 08.4	306 47.6	03.9	288 14.0	53.1	83 09.1	12.7	83 04.5	05.7	Eltanin	90 57.8	N51 29.2
S 09	287 10.8	321 46.9 ··	02.9	303 14.7 ··	52.3	98 11.8 ··	12.6	98 07.1 ··	05.7	Enif	34 11.6	N 9 47.1
U 10	302 13.3	336 46.3	01.9	318 15.3	51.5	113 14.4	12.5	113 09.7	05.6	Fomalhaut	15 51.4	S29 43.5
N 11	317 15.8	351 45.7	01.0	333 15.9	50.8	128 17.1	12.4	128 12.3	05.5			
D 12	332 18.2	6 45.1	S15 00.0	348 16.6	S 7 50.0	143 19.7	S 2 12.3	143 14.9	S 1 05.5	Gacrux	172 27.9	S57 00.3
A 13	347 20.7	21 44.5	14 59.0	3 17.2	49.2	158 22.4	12.2	158 17.5	05.4	Gienah	176 17.4	S17 26.2
Y 14	2 23.1	36 43.9	58.1	18 17.8	48.5	173 25.1	12.1	173 20.1	05.3	Hadar	149 22.6	S60 16.7
15	17 25.6	51 43.3 ··	57.1	33 18.5 ··	47.7	188 27.7 ··	12.0	188 22.7 ··	05.3	Hamal	328 28.8	N23 22.3
16	32 28.1	66 42.7	56.1	48 19.1	46.9	203 30.4	11.9	203 25.3	05.2	Kaus Aust.	84 16.7	S34 23.6
17	47 30.5	81 42.1	55.2	63 19.7	46.2	218 33.0	11.8	218 27.9	05.1			
18	62 33.0	96 41.5	S14 54.2	78 20.4	S 7 45.4	233 35.7	S 2 11.7	233 30.4	S 1 05.1	Kochab	137 18.7	N74 13.8
19	77 35.5	111 40.8	53.2	93 21.0	44.6	248 38.4	11.6	248 33.0	05.0	Markab	14 03.2	N15 06.1
20	92 37.9	126 40.2	52.2	108 21.6	43.9	263 41.0	11.5	263 35.6	05.0	Menkar	314 40.9	N 4 00.8
21	107 40.4	141 39.6 ··	51.3	123 22.3 ··	43.1	278 43.7 ··	11.5	278 38.2 ··	04.9	Menkent	148 36.5	S36 16.5
22	122 42.9	156 39.0	50.3	138 22.9	42.3	293 46.3	11.4	293 40.8	04.8	Miaplacidus	221 44.0	S69 38.5
23	137 45.3	171 38.4	49.3	153 23.5	41.6	308 49.0	11.3	308 43.4	04.8			
23 00	152 47.8	186 37.8	S14 48.3	168 24.2	S 7 40.8	323 51.7	S 2 11.2	323 46.0	S 1 04.7	Mirfak	309 15.8	N49 47.7
01	167 50.3	201 37.2	47.4	183 24.8	40.0	338 54.3	11.1	338 48.6	04.6	Nunki	76 29.0	S26 19.2
02	182 52.7	216 36.6	46.4	198 25.5	39.3	353 57.0	11.0	353 51.2	04.6	Peacock	53 58.5	S56 47.7
03	197 55.2	231 36.0 ··	45.4	213 26.1 ··	38.5	8 59.6 ··	10.9	8 53.8 ··	04.5	Pollux	243 57.5	N28 04.3
04	212 57.6	246 35.4	44.4	228 26.7	37.7	24 02.3	10.8	23 56.4	04.4	Procyon	245 25.2	N 5 16.3
05	228 00.1	261 34.8	43.4	243 27.4	36.9	39 05.0	10.7	38 58.9	04.4			
06	243 02.6	276 34.2	S14 42.4	258 28.0	S 7 36.2	54 07.6	S 2 10.6	54 01.5	S 1 04.3	Rasalhague	96 29.4	N12 34.3
07	258 05.0	291 33.6	41.5	273 28.6	35.4	69 10.3	10.5	69 04.1	04.3	Regulus	208 09.4	N12 03.5
08	273 07.5	306 33.0	40.5	288 29.3	34.6	84 13.0	10.4	84 06.7	04.2	Rigel	281 35.6	S 8 13.6
M 09	288 10.0	321 32.4 ··	39.5	303 29.9 ··	33.9	99 15.6 ··	10.3	99 09.3 ··	04.1	Rigil Kent.	140 25.2	S60 45.1
O 10	303 12.4	336 31.8	38.5	318 30.5	33.1	114 18.3	10.2	114 11.9	04.1	Sabik	102 40.9	S15 42.1
N 11	318 14.9	351 31.2	37.6	333 31.2	32.3	129 20.9	10.1	129 14.5	04.0			
D 12	333 17.4	6 30.6	S14 36.6	348 31.8	S 7 31.6	144 23.6	S 2 10.1	144 17.1	S 1 03.9	Schedar	350 09.1	N56 26.1
A 13	348 19.8	21 30.0	35.6	3 32.4	30.8	159 26.3	10.0	159 19.7	03.9	Shaula	96 55.5	S37 05.3
Y 14	3 22.3	36 29.4	34.6	18 33.1	30.0	174 28.9	09.9	174 22.3	03.8	Sirius	258 55.2	S16 41.7
15	18 24.8	51 28.8 ··	33.6	33 33.7 ··	29.2	189 31.6 ··	09.8	189 24.9 ··	03.7	Spica	158 57.0	S11 03.8
16	33 27.2	66 28.2	32.6	48 34.4	28.5	204 34.3	09.7	204 27.5	03.7	Suhail	223 10.1	S43 21.5
17	48 29.7	81 27.6	31.6	63 35.0	27.7	219 36.9	09.6	219 30.1	03.6			
18	63 32.1	96 27.0	S14 30.6	78 35.6	S 7 26.9	234 39.6	S 2 09.5	234 32.7	S 1 03.5	Vega	80 55.9	N38 45.7
19	78 34.6	111 26.4	29.7	93 36.3	26.2	249 42.3	09.4	249 35.3	03.5	Zuben'ubi	137 32.6	S15 57.8
20	93 37.1	126 25.8	28.7	108 36.9	25.4	264 44.9	09.3	264 37.8	03.4		S.H.A.	Mer. Pass.
21	108 39.5	141 25.2 ··	27.7	123 37.5 ··	24.6	279 47.6 ··	09.2	279 40.4 ··	03.4	Venus	35 03.8	11 33
22	123 42.0	156 24.6	26.7	138 38.2	23.8	294 50.3	09.1	294 43.0	03.3	Mars	16 20.3	12 47
23	138 44.5	171 24.0	25.7	153 38.8	23.1	309 52.9	09.0	309 45.6	03.2	Jupiter	170 59.2	2 28
Mer. Pass.	13 50.5	v −0.6	d 1.0	v 0.6	d 0.8	v 2.7	d 0.1	v 2.6	d 0.1	Saturn	170 55.2	2 29

SUN / MOON

G.M.T.	SUN G.H.A.	Dec.	MOON G.H.A.	v	Dec.	d	H.P.
21 00	176 34.3	S10 39.9	333 12.0	14.4	N 5 04.3	10.5	55.1
01	191 34.3	39.0	347 45.4	14.5	4 53.8	10.4	55.1
02	206 34.4	38.1	2 18.9	14.4	4 43.4	10.4	55.0
03	221 34.5	·· 37.2	16 52.3	14.5	4 33.0	10.5	55.0
04	236 34.6	36.3	31 25.8	14.6	4 22.5	10.5	55.0
05	251 34.6	35.4	45 59.4	14.5	4 12.0	10.5	55.0
06	266 34.7	S10 34.5	60 32.9	14.6	N 4 01.5	10.4	55.0
07	281 34.8	33.6	75 06.5	14.7	3 51.1	10.5	55.0
S 08	296 34.9	32.7	89 40.2	14.6	3 40.6	10.6	54.9
A 09	311 34.9	·· 31.8	104 13.8	14.7	3 30.0	10.5	54.9
T 10	326 35.0	30.9	118 47.5	14.8	3 19.5	10.5	54.9
U 11	341 35.1	30.0	133 21.3	14.7	3 09.0	10.5	54.9
R 12	356 35.2	S10 29.1	147 55.0	14.8	N 2 58.5	10.5	54.9
D 13	11 35.2	28.2	162 28.8	14.8	2 48.0	10.6	54.9
A 14	26 35.3	27.3	177 02.6	14.8	2 37.4	10.5	54.8
Y 15	41 35.4	·· 26.4	191 36.4	14.9	2 26.9	10.6	54.8
16	56 35.5	25.5	206 10.3	14.9	2 16.3	10.5	54.8
17	71 35.5	24.6	220 44.2	14.9	2 05.8	10.6	54.8
18	86 35.6	S10 23.6	235 18.1	15.0	N 1 55.2	10.5	54.8
19	101 35.7	22.7	249 52.1	14.9	1 44.7	10.6	54.8
20	116 35.8	21.8	264 26.0	15.0	1 34.1	10.5	54.7
21	131 35.9	·· 20.9	279 00.0	15.0	1 23.6	10.6	54.7
22	146 35.9	20.0	293 34.0	15.1	1 13.0	10.5	54.7
23	161 36.0	19.1	308 08.1	15.0	1 02.5	10.6	54.7
22 00	176 36.1	S10 18.2	322 42.1	15.1	N 0 51.9	10.5	54.7
01	191 36.2	17.3	337 16.2	15.1	0 41.4	10.5	54.7
02	206 36.2	16.4	351 50.3	15.1	0 30.8	10.5	54.7
03	221 36.3	·· 15.5	6 24.4	15.1	0 20.3	10.5	54.6
04	236 36.4	14.6	20 58.5	15.2	N 0 09.8	10.5	54.6
05	251 36.5	13.6	35 32.7	15.2	S 0 00.7	10.6	54.6
06	266 36.6	S10 12.7	50 06.9	15.2	S 0 11.3	10.5	54.6
07	281 36.6	11.8	64 41.1	15.2	0 21.8	10.5	54.6
08	296 36.7	10.9	79 15.3	15.2	0 32.3	10.5	54.6
S 09	311 36.8	·· 10.0	93 49.5	15.2	0 42.8	10.5	54.6
U 10	326 36.9	09.1	108 23.7	15.2	0 53.3	10.4	54.5
N 11	341 37.0	08.2	122 57.9	15.3	1 03.7	10.5	54.5
D 12	356 37.1	S10 07.3	137 32.2	15.3	S 1 14.2	10.5	54.5
A 13	11 37.1	06.4	152 06.5	15.2	1 24.7	10.4	54.5
Y 14	26 37.2	05.4	166 40.7	15.3	1 35.1	10.4	54.5
15	41 37.3	·· 04.5	181 15.0	15.3	1 45.5	10.4	54.5
16	56 37.4	03.6	195 49.3	15.3	1 56.0	10.4	54.5
17	71 37.5	02.7	210 23.6	15.4	2 06.4	10.4	54.5
18	86 37.6	S10 01.8	224 58.0	15.3	S 2 16.8	10.4	54.4
19	101 37.6	00.9	239 32.3	15.3	2 27.2	10.3	54.4
20	116 37.7	10 00.0	254 06.6	15.3	2 37.5	10.4	54.4
21	131 37.8	9 59.0	268 40.9	15.4	2 47.9	10.3	54.4
22	146 37.9	58.1	283 15.3	15.3	2 58.2	10.3	54.4
23	161 38.0	57.2	297 49.6	15.4	3 08.5	10.3	54.4
23 00	176 38.1	S 9 56.3	312 24.0	15.3	S 3 18.8	10.3	54.4
01	191 38.1	55.4	326 58.3	15.4	3 29.1	10.3	54.4
02	206 38.2	54.5	341 32.7	15.4	3 39.4	10.2	54.4
03	221 38.3	·· 53.6	356 07.1	15.3	3 49.6	10.2	54.3
04	236 38.4	52.6	10 41.4	15.4	3 59.8	10.2	54.3
05	251 38.5	51.7	25 15.8	15.3	4 10.0	10.2	54.3
06	266 38.6	S 9 50.8	39 50.1	15.4	S 4 20.2	10.2	54.3
07	281 38.7	49.9	54 24.5	15.4	4 30.4	10.1	54.3
08	296 38.8	49.0	68 58.9	15.4	4 40.5	10.1	54.3
M 09	311 38.8	·· 48.1	83 33.2	15.4	4 50.6	10.1	54.3
O 10	326 38.9	47.1	98 07.6	15.3	5 00.7	10.1	54.3
N 11	341 39.0	46.2	112 41.9	15.4	5 10.8	10.0	54.3
D 12	356 39.1	S 9 45.3	127 16.3	15.3	S 5 20.8	10.1	54.3
A 13	11 39.2	44.4	141 50.6	15.4	5 30.9	10.0	54.3
Y 14	26 39.3	43.5	156 25.0	15.3	5 40.9	9.9	54.3
15	41 39.4	·· 42.5	170 59.3	15.3	5 50.8	10.0	54.3
16	56 39.5	41.6	185 33.6	15.3	6 00.8	9.9	54.2
17	71 39.6	40.7	200 07.9	15.3	6 10.7	9.9	54.2
18	86 39.6	S 9 39.8	214 42.2	15.3	S 6 20.6	9.8	54.2
19	101 39.7	38.9	229 16.5	15.3	6 30.4	9.9	54.2
20	116 39.8	37.9	243 50.8	15.3	6 40.3	9.8	54.2
21	131 39.9	·· 37.0	258 25.1	15.3	6 50.1	9.7	54.2
22	146 40.0	36.1	272 59.4	15.2	6 59.8	9.8	54.2
23	161 40.1	35.2	287 33.6	15.2	7 09.6	9.7	54.2
	S.D. 16.2	d 0.9	S.D. 15.0		14.9		14.8

Moonrise

Lat.	Twilight Naut.	Civil	Sunrise	21	22	23	24
N 72	05 44	07 02	08 15	20 04	21 44	23 24	25 06
N 70	05 45	06 56	08 01	20 07	21 40	23 12	24 47
68	05 46	06 51	07 49	20 08	21 36	23 03	24 31
66	05 47	06 46	07 40	20 10	21 33	22 56	24 19
64	05 48	06 43	07 32	20 11	21 31	22 50	24 09
62	05 48	06 39	07 25	20 12	21 29	22 44	24 00
60	05 48	06 36	07 19	20 13	21 27	22 40	23 52
N 58	05 48	06 34	07 14	20 14	21 25	22 36	23 46
56	05 48	06 31	07 09	20 14	21 24	22 32	23 40
54	05 48	06 29	07 05	20 15	21 22	22 29	23 35
52	05 48	06 27	07 01	20 16	21 21	22 26	23 30
50	05 47	06 25	06 58	20 16	21 20	22 23	23 26
45	05 46	06 20	06 50	20 17	21 18	22 17	23 17
N 40	05 45	06 16	06 44	20 18	21 16	22 13	23 09
35	05 43	06 13	06 38	20 19	21 14	22 09	23 03
30	05 41	06 09	06 33	20 20	21 13	22 05	22 57
20	05 37	06 03	06 25	20 21	21 10	21 59	22 47
N 10	05 31	05 56	06 17	20 22	21 08	21 53	22 39
0	05 25	05 49	06 10	20 23	21 06	21 48	22 31
S 10	05 17	05 41	06 03	20 24	21 04	21 43	22 23
20	05 06	05 32	05 55	20 26	21 02	21 38	22 15
30	04 52	05 21	05 46	20 27	20 59	21 32	22 05
35	04 43	05 14	05 40	20 28	20 58	21 28	21 59
40	04 32	05 06	05 34	20 29	20 56	21 24	21 53
45	04 19	04 56	05 27	20 30	20 55	21 20	21 46
S 50	04 02	04 44	05 19	20 31	20 52	21 14	21 38
52	03 53	04 38	05 15	20 31	20 51	21 12	21 34
54	03 44	04 32	05 10	20 32	20 50	21 09	21 29
56	03 33	04 25	05 05	20 33	20 49	21 06	21 24
58	03 20	04 16	05 00	20 33	20 48	21 03	21 19
S 60	03 04	04 07	04 54	20 34	20 46	20 59	21 13

Moonset

Lat.	Sunset	Twilight Civil	Naut.	21	22	23	24
N 72	16 14	17 27	18 46	08 45	08 35	08 24	08 13
N 70	16 28	17 33	18 44	08 41	08 36	08 31	08 26
68	16 39	17 38	18 43	08 37	08 37	08 36	08 36
66	16 49	17 42	18 42	08 34	08 37	08 41	08 45
64	16 57	17 46	18 41	08 31	08 38	08 45	08 52
62	17 03	17 49	18 41	08 28	08 38	08 48	08 59
60	17 09	17 52	18 40	08 26	08 39	08 51	09 04
N 58	17 14	17 55	18 40	08 24	08 39	08 54	09 09
56	17 19	17 57	18 40	08 23	08 40	08 56	09 14
54	17 23	17 59	18 40	08 21	08 40	08 58	09 18
52	17 27	18 01	18 40	08 20	08 40	09 00	09 21
50	17 30	18 03	18 41	08 19	08 40	09 02	09 24
45	17 38	18 07	18 41	08 16	08 41	09 06	09 32
N 40	17 44	18 11	18 43	08 13	08 41	09 09	09 38
35	17 49	18 15	18 44	08 11	08 42	09 12	09 43
30	17 54	18 18	18 46	08 10	08 42	09 14	09 47
20	18 02	18 25	18 50	08 06	08 43	09 19	09 55
N 10	18 10	18 31	18 56	08 04	08 43	09 23	10 02
0	18 17	18 38	19 02	08 01	08 44	09 26	10 09
S 10	18 24	18 45	19 10	07 58	08 44	09 30	10 15
20	18 32	18 54	19 21	07 55	08 45	09 34	10 22
30	18 41	19 05	19 34	07 52	08 45	09 38	10 30
35	18 46	19 12	19 43	07 50	08 46	09 40	10 35
40	18 52	19 20	19 54	07 48	08 46	09 43	10 40
45	18 59	19 30	20 07	07 45	08 46	09 47	10 46
S 50	19 07	19 42	20 24	07 42	08 47	09 51	10 53
52	19 11	19 47	20 32	07 41	08 47	09 52	10 57
54	19 16	19 54	20 41	07 39	08 47	09 54	11 01
56	19 20	20 01	20 52	07 38	08 48	09 57	11 05
58	19 26	20 09	21 05	07 36	08 48	09 59	11 09
S 60	19 32	20 18	21 20	07 34	08 48	10 02	11 15

SUN / MOON

Day	Eqn. of Time 00h	12h	Mer. Pass.	Mer. Pass. Upper	Lower	Age	Phase
21	13 43	13 40	12 14	01 50	14 12	17	
22	13 36	13 32	12 14	02 34	14 55	18	◖
23	13 28	13 24	12 13	03 16	15 37	19	

G.M.T.	ARIES G.H.A.	VENUS −3.4 G.H.A.	Dec.	MARS +1.4 G.H.A.	Dec.	JUPITER −1.9 G.H.A.	Dec.	SATURN +0.8 G.H.A.	Dec.	STARS Name	S.H.A.	Dec.
24 00	153 46.9	186 23.5	S14 24.7	168 39.5	S 7 22.3	324 55.6	S 2 08.9	324 48.2	S 1 03.2	Acamar	315 37.2	S40 23.2
01	168 49.4	201 22.9	23.7	183 40.1	21.5	339 58.3	08.8	339 50.8	03.1	Achernar	335 45.4	S57 20.3
02	183 51.9	216 22.3	22.7	198 40.7	20.8	355 00.9	08.7	354 53.4	03.0	Acrux	173 36.3	S62 59.5
03	198 54.3	231 21.7 ··	21.7	213 41.4 ··	20.0	10 03.6 ··	08.6	9 56.0 ··	03.0	Adhara	255 31.6	S28 57.0
04	213 56.8	246 21.1	20.7	228 42.0	19.2	25 06.3	08.5	24 58.6	02.9	Aldebaran	291 17.6	N16 28.2
05	228 59.2	261 20.5	19.7	243 42.7	18.4	40 08.9	08.4	40 01.2	02.8			
06	244 01.7	276 19.9	S14 18.7	258 43.3	S 7 17.7	55 11.6	S 2 08.3	55 03.8	S 1 02.8	Alioth	166 41.8	N56 03.6
07	259 04.2	291 19.3	17.7	273 43.9	16.9	70 14.3	08.2	70 06.4	02.7	Alkaid	153 18.0	N49 24.3
08	274 06.6	306 18.7	16.7	288 44.6	16.1	85 16.9	08.1	85 09.0	02.6	Al Na'ir	28 15.0	S47 03.3
T 09	289 09.1	321 18.1 ··	15.7	303 45.2 ··	15.4	100 19.6 ··	08.1	100 11.6 ··	02.6	Alnilam	276 11.3	S 1 13.0
U 10	304 11.6	336 17.5	14.7	318 45.8	14.6	115 22.3	08.0	115 14.2	02.5	Alphard	218 20.0	S 8 34.7
E 11	319 14.0	351 17.0	13.7	333 46.5	13.8	130 24.9	07.9	130 16.8	02.4			
S 12	334 16.5	6 16.4	S14 12.7	348 47.1	S 7 13.0	145 27.6	S 2 07.8	145 19.4	S 1 02.4	Alphecca	126 31.8	N26 46.5
D 13	349 19.0	21 15.8	11.7	3 47.8	12.3	160 30.3	07.7	160 22.0	02.3	Alpheratz	358 09.3	N28 59.1
A 14	4 21.4	36 15.2	10.7	18 48.4	11.5	175 32.9	07.6	175 24.6	02.3	Altair	62 32.5	N 8 49.0
Y 15	19 23.9	51 14.6 ··	09.7	33 49.0 ··	10.7	190 35.6 ··	07.5	190 27.2 ··	02.2	Ankaa	353 40.3	S42 24.8
16	34 26.4	66 14.0	08.7	48 49.7	09.9	205 38.3	07.4	205 29.8	02.1	Antares	112 56.5	S26 23.3
17	49 28.8	81 13.4	07.7	63 50.3	09.2	220 40.9	07.4	220 32.3	02.1			
18	64 31.3	96 12.9	S14 06.7	78 51.0	S 7 08.4	235 43.6	S 2 07.2	235 34.9	S 1 02.0	Arcturus	146 18.0	N19 16.7
19	79 33.7	111 12.3	05.7	93 51.6	07.6	250 46.3	07.1	250 37.5	01.9	Atria	108 20.6	S68 59.3
20	94 36.2	126 11.7	04.7	108 52.2	06.9	265 49.0	07.0	265 40.1	01.9	Avior	234 27.5	S59 27.1
21	109 38.7	141 11.1 ··	03.7	123 52.9 ··	06.1	280 51.6 ··	06.9	280 42.7 ··	01.8	Bellatrix	278 58.3	N 6 19.8
22	124 41.1	156 10.5	02.7	138 53.5	05.3	295 54.3	06.8	295 45.3	01.7	Betelgeuse	271 27.8	N 7 24.1
23	139 43.6	171 09.9	01.7	153 54.2	04.5	310 57.0	06.7	310 47.9	01.7			
25 00	154 46.1	186 09.4	S14 00.7	168 54.8	S 7 03.8	325 59.6	S 2 06.6	325 50.5	S 1 01.6	Canopus	264 06.8	S52 41.5
01	169 48.5	201 08.8	13 59.7	183 55.5	03.0	341 02.3	06.5	340 53.1	01.5	Capella	281 10.7	N45 58.8
02	184 51.0	216 08.2	58.6	198 56.1	02.2	356 05.0	06.4	355 55.7	01.5	Deneb	49 48.7	N45 12.6
03	199 53.5	231 07.6 ··	57.6	213 56.7 ··	01.4	11 07.7 ··	06.3	10 58.3 ··	01.4	Denebola	182 58.4	N14 40.6
04	214 55.9	246 07.0	56.6	228 57.4	7 00.7	26 10.3	06.2	26 00.9	01.3	Diphda	349 20.8	S18 05.7
05	229 58.4	261 06.5	55.6	243 58.0	6 59.9	41 13.0	06.1	41 03.5	01.3			
06	245 00.9	276 05.9	S13 54.6	258 58.7	S 6 59.1	56 15.7	S 2 06.0	56 06.1	S 1 01.2	Dubhe	194 21.1	N61 51.1
07	260 03.3	291 05.3	53.6	273 59.3	58.3	71 18.4	05.9	71 08.7	01.1	Elnath	278 43.7	N28 35.5
W 08	275 05.8	306 04.7	52.6	288 59.9	57.6	86 21.0	05.8	86 11.3	01.1	Eltanin	90 57.8	N51 29.2
E 09	290 08.2	321 04.1 ··	51.5	304 00.6 ··	56.8	101 23.7 ··	05.7	101 13.9 ··	01.0	Enif	34 11.6	N 9 47.1
D 10	305 10.7	336 03.6	50.5	319 01.2	56.0	116 26.4	05.6	116 16.5	00.9	Fomalhaut	15 51.4	S29 43.5
N 11	320 13.2	351 03.0	49.5	334 01.9	55.2	131 29.1	05.5	131 19.1	00.9			
E 12	335 15.6	6 02.4	S13 48.5	349 02.5	S 6 54.5	146 31.7	S 2 05.4	146 21.7	S 1 00.8	Gacrux	172 27.9	S57 00.3
S 13	350 18.1	21 01.8	47.5	4 03.2	53.7	161 34.4	05.3	161 24.3	00.7	Gienah	176 17.4	S17 26.2
D 14	5 20.6	36 01.3	46.5	19 03.8	52.9	176 37.1	05.2	176 26.9	00.7	Hadar	149 22.5	S60 16.7
A 15	20 23.0	51 00.7 ··	45.4	34 04.4 ··	52.1	191 39.8 ··	05.1	191 29.5 ··	00.6	Hamal	328 28.8	N23 22.3
Y 16	35 25.5	66 00.1	44.4	49 05.1	51.4	206 42.4	05.0	206 32.1	00.5	Kaus Aust.	84 16.6	S34 23.6
17	50 28.0	80 59.5	43.4	64 05.7	50.6	221 45.1	04.9	221 34.7	00.5			
18	65 30.4	95 59.0	S13 42.4	79 06.4	S 6 49.8	236 47.8	S 2 04.8	236 37.3	S 1 00.4	Kochab	137 18.6	N74 13.8
19	80 32.9	110 58.4	41.4	94 07.0	49.0	251 50.5	04.7	251 39.9	00.3	Markab	14 03.2	N15 06.1
20	95 35.3	125 57.8	40.3	109 07.7	48.3	266 53.1	04.6	266 42.5	00.3	Menkar	314 40.9	N 4 00.8
21	110 37.8	140 57.3 ··	39.3	124 08.3 ··	47.5	281 55.8 ··	04.5	281 45.1 ··	00.2	Menkent	148 36.4	S36 16.5
22	125 40.3	155 56.7	38.3	139 09.0	46.7	296 58.5	04.4	296 47.7	00.1	Miaplacidus	221 44.0	S69 38.5
23	140 42.7	170 56.1	37.3	154 09.6	45.9	312 01.2	04.3	311 50.3	00.1			
26 00	155 45.2	185 55.5	S13 36.2	169 10.2	S 6 45.2	327 03.8	S 2 04.2	326 52.9	S 1 00.0	Mirfak	309 15.8	N49 47.7
01	170 47.7	200 55.0	35.2	184 10.9	44.4	342 06.5	04.1	341 55.5	0 59.9	Nunki	76 29.0	S26 19.2
02	185 50.1	215 54.4	34.2	199 11.5	43.6	357 09.2	04.0	356 58.1	59.9	Peacock	53 58.4	S56 47.7
03	200 52.6	230 53.8 ··	33.2	214 12.2 ··	42.8	12 11.9 ··	03.9	12 00.7 ··	59.8	Pollux	243 57.5	N28 04.3
04	215 55.1	245 53.3	32.1	229 12.8	42.0	27 14.6	03.8	27 03.3	59.7	Procyon	245 25.2	N 5 16.3
05	230 57.5	260 52.7	31.1	244 13.5	41.3	42 17.2	03.7	42 05.9	59.7			
06	246 00.0	275 52.1	S13 30.1	259 14.1	S 6 40.5	57 19.9	S 2 03.6	57 08.5	S 0 59.6	Rasalhague	96 29.4	N12 34.3
07	261 02.5	290 51.6	29.1	274 14.8	39.7	72 22.6	03.5	72 11.1	59.5	Regulus	208 09.4	N12 03.5
T 08	276 04.9	305 51.0	28.0	289 15.4	38.9	87 25.3	03.4	87 13.7	59.5	Rigel	281 35.7	S 8 13.6
H 09	291 07.4	320 50.4 ··	27.0	304 16.0 ··	38.2	102 28.0 ··	03.3	102 16.3 ··	59.4	Rigil Kent.	140 25.1	S60 45.1
U 10	306 09.8	335 49.9	26.0	319 16.7	37.4	117 30.6	03.2	117 18.9	59.3	Sabik	102 40.9	S15 42.1
R 11	321 12.3	350 49.3	24.9	334 17.3	36.6	132 33.3	03.1	132 21.5	59.3			
S 12	336 14.8	5 48.7	S13 23.9	349 18.0	S 6 35.8	147 36.0	S 2 03.0	147 24.1	S 0 59.2	Schedar	350 09.1	N56 26.0
D 13	351 17.2	20 48.2	22.9	4 18.6	35.1	162 38.7	02.9	162 26.7	59.1	Shaula	96 55.5	S37 05.3
A 14	6 19.7	35 47.6	21.8	19 19.3	34.3	177 41.4	02.8	177 29.3	59.1	Sirius	258 55.2	S16 41.7
Y 15	21 22.2	50 47.0 ··	20.8	34 19.9 ··	33.5	192 44.0 ··	02.7	192 31.9 ··	59.0	Spica	158 57.0	S11 03.8
16	36 24.6	65 46.5	19.8	49 20.6	32.7	207 46.7	02.6	207 34.5	58.9	Suhail	223 10.1	S43 21.5
17	51 27.1	80 45.9	18.7	64 21.2	31.9	222 49.4	02.5	222 37.1	58.9			
18	66 29.6	95 45.4	S13 17.7	79 21.9	S 6 31.2	237 52.1	S 2 02.4	237 39.7	S 0 58.8	Vega	80 55.9	N38 45.7
19	81 32.0	110 44.8	16.7	94 22.5	30.4	252 54.8	02.3	252 42.3	58.7	Zuben'ubi	137 32.6	S15 57.8
20	96 34.5	125 44.2	15.6	109 23.1	29.6	267 57.4	02.2	267 44.9	58.7			
21	111 37.0	140 43.7 ··	14.6	124 23.8 ··	28.8	283 00.1 ··	02.1	282 47.5 ··	58.6		S.H.A.	Mer. Pass.
22	126 39.4	155 43.1	13.5	139 24.4	28.1	298 02.8	02.0	297 50.1	58.5	Venus	31 23.3	11 36
23	141 41.9	170 42.6	12.5	154 25.1	27.3	313 05.5	01.9	312 52.7	58.5	Mars	14 08.7	12 44
										Jupiter	171 13.6	2 16
Mer. Pass. 13 38.7		v −0.6 d 1.0		v 0.6 d 0.8		v 2.7 d 0.1		v 2.6 d 0.1		Saturn	171 04.5	2 16

G.M.T.	SUN G.H.A.	Dec.	MOON G.H.A.	v	Dec.	d	H.P.
24 00	176 40.2	S 9 34.3	302 07.8	15.3	S 7 19.3	9.7	54.2
01	191 40.3	33.3	316 42.1	15.2	7 29.0	9.6	54.2
02	206 40.4	32.4	331 16.3	15.2	7 38.6	9.6	54.2
03	221 40.5	·· 31.5	345 50.5	15.2	7 48.2	9.6	54.2
04	236 40.6	30.6	0 24.7	15.1	7 57.8	9.6	54.2
05	251 40.6	29.6	14 58.8	15.2	8 07.4	9.5	54.2
06	266 40.7	S 9 28.7	29 33.0	15.1	S 8 16.9	9.5	54.2
07	281 40.8	27.8	44 07.1	15.1	8 26.4	9.4	54.2
T 08	296 40.9	26.9	58 41.2	15.1	8 35.8	9.4	54.2
U 09	311 41.0	·· 26.0	73 15.3	15.1	8 45.2	9.4	54.2
E 10	326 41.1	25.0	87 49.4	15.1	8 54.6	9.3	54.2
S 11	341 41.2	24.1	102 23.5	15.0	9 03.9	9.3	54.2
D 12	356 41.3	S 9 23.2	116 57.5	15.0	S 9 13.2	9.3	54.2
A 13	11 41.4	22.3	131 31.5	15.0	9 22.5	9.2	54.2
Y 14	26 41.5	21.3	146 05.5	15.0	9 31.7	9.1	54.2
15	41 41.6	·· 20.4	160 39.5	14.9	9 40.8	9.2	54.2
16	56 41.7	19.5	175 13.4	14.9	9 50.0	9.1	54.2
17	71 41.8	18.6	189 47.3	14.9	9 59.1	9.0	54.2
18	86 41.9	S 9 17.6	204 21.2	14.9	S10 08.1	9.1	54.2
19	101 42.0	16.7	218 55.1	14.9	10 17.2	8.9	54.2
20	116 42.1	15.8	233 29.0	14.8	10 26.1	9.0	54.2
21	131 42.2	·· 14.8	248 02.8	14.8	10 35.1	8.8	54.2
22	146 42.3	13.9	262 36.6	14.7	10 43.9	8.9	54.2
23	161 42.4	13.0	277 10.3	14.8	10 52.8	8.8	54.2
25 00	176 42.5	S 9 12.1	291 44.1	14.7	S11 01.6	8.7	54.2
01	191 42.6	11.1	306 17.8	14.7	11 10.3	8.7	54.2
02	206 42.7	10.2	320 51.5	14.6	11 19.0	8.7	54.2
03	221 42.7	·· 09.3	335 25.1	14.6	11 27.7	8.6	54.2
04	236 42.8	08.4	349 58.7	14.6	11 36.3	8.6	54.2
05	251 42.9	07.4	4 32.3	14.6	11 44.9	8.5	54.2
06	266 43.0	S 9 06.5	19 05.9	14.5	S11 53.4	8.5	54.2
W 07	281 43.1	05.6	33 39.4	14.5	12 01.9	8.4	54.2
E 08	296 43.2	04.6	48 12.9	14.4	12 10.3	8.4	54.2
D 09	311 43.3	·· 03.7	62 46.3	14.5	12 18.7	8.3	54.2
N 10	326 43.4	02.8	77 19.8	14.3	12 27.0	8.3	54.2
E 11	341 43.5	01.8	91 53.1	14.4	12 35.3	8.2	54.2
S 12	356 43.6	S 9 00.9	106 26.5	14.3	S12 43.5	8.2	54.2
D 13	11 43.7	9 00.0	120 59.8	14.3	12 51.7	8.1	54.2
A 14	26 43.8	8 59.1	135 33.1	14.2	12 59.8	8.0	54.2
Y 15	41 43.9	·· 58.1	150 06.3	14.2	13 07.8	8.1	54.2
16	56 44.0	57.2	164 39.5	14.2	13 15.9	7.9	54.2
17	71 44.1	56.3	179 12.7	14.1	13 23.8	7.9	54.2
18	86 44.3	S 8 55.3	193 45.8	14.1	S13 31.7	7.9	54.3
19	101 44.4	54.4	208 18.9	14.1	13 39.6	7.8	54.3
20	116 44.5	53.5	222 52.0	14.0	13 47.4	7.7	54.3
21	131 44.6	·· 52.5	237 25.0	14.0	13 55.1	7.7	54.3
22	146 44.7	51.6	251 58.0	13.9	14 02.8	7.6	54.3
23	161 44.8	50.7	266 30.9	13.9	14 10.4	7.6	54.3
26 00	176 44.9	S 8 49.7	281 03.8	13.8	S14 18.0	7.5	54.3
01	191 45.0	48.8	295 36.6	13.8	14 25.5	7.4	54.3
02	206 45.1	47.9	310 09.4	13.8	14 32.9	7.4	54.3
03	221 45.2	·· 46.9	324 42.2	13.7	14 40.3	7.3	54.3
04	236 45.3	46.0	339 14.9	13.7	14 47.6	7.3	54.3
05	251 45.4	45.1	353 47.6	13.6	14 54.9	7.2	54.4
06	266 45.5	S 8 44.1	8 20.2	13.6	S15 02.1	7.1	54.4
07	281 45.6	43.2	22 52.8	13.5	15 09.2	7.1	54.4
T 08	296 45.7	42.3	37 25.3	13.5	15 16.3	7.0	54.4
H 09	311 45.8	·· 41.3	51 57.8	13.5	15 23.3	7.0	54.4
U 10	326 45.9	40.4	66 30.3	13.4	15 30.3	6.8	54.4
R 11	341 46.0	39.5	81 02.7	13.3	15 37.1	6.9	54.4
S 12	356 46.1	S 8 38.5	95 35.0	13.4	S15 44.0	6.7	54.4
D 13	11 46.2	37.6	110 07.4	13.2	15 50.7	6.7	54.4
A 14	26 46.3	36.6	124 39.6	13.2	15 57.4	6.6	54.5
Y 15	41 46.4	·· 35.7	139 11.8	13.2	16 04.0	6.6	54.5
16	56 46.5	34.8	153 44.0	13.1	16 10.6	6.5	54.5
17	71 46.7	33.9	168 16.1	13.1	16 17.1	6.4	54.5
18	86 46.8	S 8 32.9	182 48.2	13.0	S16 23.5	6.3	54.5
19	101 46.9	32.0	197 20.2	13.0	16 29.8	6.3	54.5
20	116 47.0	31.0	211 52.2	12.9	16 36.1	6.2	54.5
21	131 47.1	·· 30.1	226 24.1	12.9	16 42.3	6.1	54.6
22	146 47.2	29.1	240 56.0	12.8	16 48.4	6.1	54.6
23	161 47.3	28.2	255 27.8	12.8	16 54.5	6.0	54.6
	S.D. 16.2	d 0.9	S.D. 14.8		14.8		14.8

Lat.	Twilight Naut.	Civil	Sunrise	Moonrise 24	25	26	27
N 72	05 30	06 48	07 59	25 06	01 06	02 58	05 21
N 70	05 33	06 43	07 46	24 47	00 47	02 24	04 08
68	05 35	06 39	07 37	24 31	00 31	02 01	03 31
66	05 37	06 36	07 28	24 19	00 19	01 42	03 05
64	05 38	06 33	07 22	24 09	00 09	01 27	02 45
62	05 39	06 31	07 16	24 00	00 00	01 15	02 29
60	05 40	06 28	07 10	23 52	25 04	01 04	02 15
N 58	05 41	06 26	07 06	23 46	24 55	00 55	02 04
56	05 41	06 24	07 02	23 40	24 47	00 47	01 54
54	05 42	06 22	06 58	23 35	24 40	00 40	01 45
52	05 42	06 21	06 55	23 30	24 34	00 34	01 37
50	05 42	06 19	06 52	23 26	24 28	00 28	01 30
45	05 42	06 16	06 45	23 17	24 16	00 16	01 15
N 40	05 41	06 12	06 40	23 09	24 06	00 06	01 02
35	05 40	06 09	06 35	23 03	23 57	24 52	00 52
30	05 39	06 06	06 30	22 57	23 50	24 43	00 43
20	05 35	06 01	06 23	22 47	23 37	24 27	00 27
N 10	05 30	05 55	06 16	22 39	23 25	24 13	00 13
0	05 25	05 49	06 10	22 31	23 15	24 00	00 00
S 10	05 17	05 42	06 03	22 23	23 04	23 48	24 34
20	05 07	05 34	05 56	22 15	22 53	23 34	24 18
30	04 55	05 23	05 48	22 05	22 40	23 19	24 01
35	04 46	05 17	05 43	21 59	22 33	23 10	23 51
40	04 36	05 10	05 38	21 53	22 25	23 00	23 39
45	04 24	05 01	05 31	21 46	22 15	22 48	23 25
S 50	04 08	04 50	05 24	21 38	22 03	22 33	23 09
52	04 00	04 44	05 20	21 34	21 58	22 27	23 01
54	03 51	04 39	05 16	21 29	21 52	22 19	22 52
56	03 41	04 32	05 12	21 24	21 46	22 11	22 42
58	03 29	04 24	05 07	21 19	21 38	22 02	22 31
S 60	03 15	04 16	05 01	21 13	21 30	21 51	22 19

Lat.	Sunset	Twilight Civil	Naut.	Moonset 24	25	26	27
N 72	16 29	17 41	18 59	08 13	07 59	07 40	06 52
N 70	16 41	17 45	18 56	08 26	08 20	08 14	08 06
68	16 51	17 49	18 53	08 36	08 37	08 39	08 44
66	16 59	17 52	18 51	08 45	08 50	08 58	09 10
64	17 06	17 55	18 50	08 52	09 02	09 14	09 31
62	17 12	17 57	18 48	08 59	09 11	09 27	09 48
60	17 17	17 59	18 47	09 04	09 19	09 38	10 02
N 58	17 21	18 01	18 47	09 09	09 27	09 48	10 14
56	17 25	18 03	18 46	09 14	09 33	09 56	10 24
54	17 29	18 05	18 46	09 18	09 39	10 04	10 33
52	17 32	18 06	18 46	09 21	09 44	10 10	10 41
50	17 35	18 08	18 45	09 24	09 49	10 16	10 49
45	17 42	18 11	18 45	09 32	09 59	10 30	11 05
N 40	17 47	18 15	18 46	09 38	10 08	10 41	11 17
35	17 52	18 17	18 47	09 43	10 15	10 50	11 29
30	17 56	18 20	18 48	09 47	10 21	10 58	11 38
20	18 04	18 26	18 51	09 55	10 33	11 12	11 55
N 10	18 10	18 31	18 56	10 02	10 43	11 25	12 10
0	18 16	18 37	19 02	10 09	10 52	11 37	12 23
S 10	18 23	18 44	19 09	10 15	11 01	11 48	12 37
20	18 30	18 52	19 18	10 22	11 11	12 01	12 52
30	18 38	19 02	19 31	10 30	11 22	12 15	13 08
35	18 42	19 08	19 39	10 35	11 29	12 24	13 18
40	18 48	19 14	19 49	10 40	11 37	12 33	13 29
45	18 54	19 24	20 01	10 46	11 45	12 44	13 43
S 50	19 01	19 35	20 17	10 53	11 56	12 58	13 59
52	19 05	19 40	20 24	10 57	12 01	13 04	14 06
54	19 09	19 46	20 33	11 01	12 06	13 11	14 15
56	19 13	19 53	20 43	11 05	12 12	13 19	14 24
58	19 18	20 00	20 54	11 09	12 19	13 28	14 35
S 60	19 23	20 08	21 08	11 15	12 27	13 38	14 47

Day	SUN Eqn. of Time 00ʰ	12ʰ	Mer. Pass.	MOON Mer. Pass. Upper	Lower	Age	Phase
	m s	m s	h m	h m	h m	d	
24	13 19	13 15	12 13	03 58	16 20	20	
25	13 10	13 06	12 13	04 41	17 03	21	◑
26	13 01	12 56	12 13	05 26	17 48	22	

G.M.T.	ARIES G.H.A.	VENUS −3.4 G.H.A.	Dec.	MARS +1.4 G.H.A.	Dec.	JUPITER −2.0 G.H.A.	Dec.	SATURN +0.7 G.H.A.	Dec.	STARS Name	S.H.A.	Dec.
d h	° ′	° ′	° ′	° ′	° ′	° ′	° ′	° ′	° ′		° ′	° ′
27 00	156 44.3	185 42.0	S13 11.5	169 25.7	S 6 26.5	328 08.2	S 2 01.8	327 55.3	S 0 58.4	Acamar	315 37.2	S40 23.2
01	171 46.8	200 41.4	10.4	184 26.4	25.7	343 10.9	01.7	342 57.9	58.3	Achernar	335 45.5	S57 20.3
02	186 49.3	215 40.9	09.4	199 27.0	24.9	358 13.5	01.6	358 00.5	58.3	Acrux	173 36.2	S62 59.5
03	201 51.7	230 40.3	·· 08.3	214 27.7	·· 24.2	13 16.2	·· 01.5	13 03.1	·· 58.2	Adhara	255 31.7	S28 57.0
04	216 54.2	245 39.8	07.3	229 28.3	23.4	28 18.9	01.4	28 05.8	58.1	Aldebaran	291 17.6	N16 28.2
05	231 56.7	260 39.2	06.2	244 29.0	22.6	43 21.6	01.3	43 08.4	58.1			
06	246 59.1	275 38.6	S13 05.2	259 29.6	S 6 21.8	58 24.3	S 2 01.2	58 11.0	S 0 58.0	Alioth	166 41.8	N56 03.6
07	262 01.6	290 38.1	04.2	274 30.3	21.0	73 27.0	01.1	73 13.6	57.9	Alkaid	153 17.9	N49 24.3
08	277 04.1	305 37.5	03.1	289 30.9	20.3	88 29.6	01.0	88 16.2	57.9	Al Na'ir	28 15.0	S47 03.3
F 09	292 06.5	320 37.0	·· 02.1	304 31.6	·· 19.5	103 32.3	·· 00.9	103 18.8	·· 57.8	Alnilam	276 11.3	S 1 13.0
R 10	307 09.0	335 36.4	01.0	319 32.2	18.7	118 35.0	00.8	118 21.4	57.7	Alphard	218 20.0	S 8 34.7
I 11	322 11.4	350 35.9	13 00.0	334 32.9	17.9	133 37.7	00.7	133 24.0	57.6			
D 12	337 13.9	5 35.3	S12 58.9	349 33.5	S 6 17.2	148 40.4	S 2 00.6	148 26.6	S 0 57.6	Alphecca	126 31.8	N26 46.5
A 13	352 16.4	20 34.8	57.9	4 34.2	16.4	163 43.1	00.5	163 29.2	57.5	Alpheratz	358 09.3	N28 59.1
Y 14	7 18.8	35 34.2	56.8	19 34.8	15.6	178 45.7	00.4	178 31.8	57.4	Altair	62 32.5	N 8 49.0
15	22 21.3	50 33.7	·· 55.8	34 35.5	·· 14.8	193 48.4	·· 00.3	193 34.4	·· 57.4	Ankaa	353 40.3	S42 24.8
16	37 23.8	65 33.1	54.7	49 36.1	14.0	208 51.1	00.2	208 37.0	57.3	Antares	112 56.5	S26 23.3
17	52 26.2	80 32.6	53.7	64 36.8	13.3	223 53.8	00.1	223 39.6	57.2			
18	67 28.7	95 32.0	S12 52.6	79 37.4	S 6 12.5	238 56.5	S 2 00.0	238 42.2	S 0 57.2	Arcturus	146 18.0	N19 16.7
19	82 31.2	110 31.5	51.6	94 38.1	11.7	253 59.2	1 59.9	253 44.8	57.1	Atria	108 20.5	S68 59.3
20	97 33.6	125 30.9	50.5	109 38.7	10.9	269 01.9	59.7	268 47.4	57.0	Avior	234 27.5	S59 27.1
21	112 36.1	140 30.4	·· 49.5	124 39.4	·· 10.1	284 04.6	·· 59.6	283 50.0	·· 57.0	Bellatrix	278 58.3	N 6 19.8
22	127 38.6	155 29.8	48.4	139 40.0	09.4	299 07.2	59.5	298 52.6	56.9	Betelgeuse	271 27.8	N 7 24.1
23	142 41.0	170 29.3	47.4	154 40.7	08.6	314 09.9	59.4	313 55.2	56.8			
28 00	157 43.5	185 28.7	S12 46.3	169 41.3	S 6 07.8	329 12.6	S 1 59.3	328 57.8	S 0 56.8	Canopus	264 06.8	S52 41.5
01	172 45.9	200 28.2	45.3	184 42.0	07.0	344 15.3	59.2	344 00.4	56.7	Capella	281 10.8	N45 58.8
02	187 48.4	215 27.6	44.2	199 42.6	06.2	359 18.0	59.1	359 03.0	56.6	Deneb	49 48.6	N45 12.6
03	202 50.9	230 27.1	·· 43.1	214 43.3	·· 05.5	14 20.7	·· 59.0	14 05.7	·· 56.6	Denebola	182 58.4	N14 40.6
04	217 53.3	245 26.5	42.1	229 43.9	04.7	29 23.4	58.9	29 08.3	56.5	Diphda	349 20.8	S18 05.7
05	232 55.8	260 26.0	41.0	244 44.6	03.9	44 26.1	58.8	44 10.9	56.4			
06	247 58.3	275 25.4	S12 40.0	259 45.2	S 6 03.1	59 28.8	S 1 58.7	59 13.5	S 0 56.3	Dubhe	194 21.1	N61 51.1
07	263 00.7	290 24.9	38.9	274 45.9	02.3	74 31.4	58.6	74 16.1	56.3	Elnath	278 43.7	N28 35.5
S 08	278 03.2	305 24.3	37.9	289 46.5	01.5	89 34.1	58.5	89 18.7	56.2	Eltanin	90 57.8	N51 29.2
A 09	293 05.7	320 23.8	·· 36.8	304 47.2	·· 00.8	104 36.8	·· 58.4	104 21.3	·· 56.1	Enif	34 11.6	N 9 47.1
T 10	308 08.1	335 23.2	35.7	319 47.8	6 00.0	119 39.5	58.3	119 23.9	56.1	Fomalhaut	15 51.4	S29 43.5
U 11	323 10.6	350 22.7	34.7	334 48.5	5 59.2	134 42.2	58.2	134 26.5	56.0			
R 12	338 13.1	5 22.2	S12 33.6	349 49.1	S 5 58.4	149 44.9	S 1 58.1	149 29.1	S 0 55.9	Gacrux	172 27.9	S57 00.3
D 13	353 15.5	20 21.6	32.5	4 49.8	57.6	164 47.6	58.0	164 31.7	55.9	Gienah	176 17.4	S17 26.2
A 14	8 18.0	35 21.1	31.5	19 50.4	56.9	179 50.3	57.9	179 34.3	55.8	Hadar	149 22.5	S60 16.7
Y 15	23 20.4	50 20.5	·· 30.4	34 51.1	·· 56.1	194 53.0	·· 57.8	194 36.9	·· 55.7	Hamal	328 28.8	N23 22.3
16	38 22.9	65 20.0	29.4	49 51.7	55.3	209 55.7	57.7	209 39.5	55.7	Kaus Aust.	84 16.6	S34 23.6
17	53 25.4	80 19.4	28.3	64 52.4	54.5	224 58.3	·57.6	224 42.1	55.6			
18	68 27.8	95 18.9	S12 27.2	79 53.0	S 5 53.7	240 01.0	S 1 57.4	239 44.8	S 0 55.5	Kochab	137 18.5	N74 13.8
19	83 30.3	110 18.4	26.2	94 53.7	53.0	255 03.7	57.3	254 47.4	55.4	Markab	14 03.2	N15 06.0
20	98 32.8	125 17.8	25.1	109 54.3	52.2	270 06.4	57.2	269 50.0	55.4	Menkar	314 40.9	N 4 00.8
21	113 35.2	140 17.3	·· 24.0	124 55.0	·· 51.4	285 09.1	·· 57.1	284 52.6	·· 55.3	Menkent	148 36.4	S36 16.5
22	128 37.7	155 16.8	23.0	139 55.6	50.6	300 11.8	57.0	299 55.2	55.2	Miaplacidus	221 44.0	S69 38.5
23	143 40.2	170 16.2	21.9	154 56.3	49.8	315 14.5	56.9	314 57.8	55.2			
1 00	158 42.6	185 15.7	S12 20.8	169 56.9	S 5 49.0	330 17.2	S 1 56.8	330 00.4	S 0 55.1	Mirfak	309 15.8	N49 47.7
01	173 45.1	200 15.1	19.7	184 57.6	48.3	345 19.9	56.7	345 03.0	55.0	Nunki	76 29.0	S26 19.2
02	188 47.5	215 14.6	18.7	199 58.2	47.5	0 22.6	56.6	0 05.6	55.0	Peacock	53 58.4	S56 47.7
03	203 50.0	230 14.1	·· 17.6	214 58.9	·· 46.7	15 25.3	·· 56.5	15 08.2	·· 54.9	Pollux	243 57.5	N28 04.3
04	218 52.5	245 13.5	16.5	229 59.6	45.9	30 28.0	56.4	30 10.8	54.8	Procyon	245 25.2	N 5 16.3
05	233 54.9	260 13.0	15.5	245 00.2	45.1	45 30.7	56.3	45 13.4	54.8			
06	248 57.4	275 12.5	S12 14.4	260 00.9	S 5 44.4	60 33.4	S 1 56.2	60 16.1	S 0 54.7	Rasalhague	96 29.4	N12 34.3
07	263 59.9	290 11.9	13.3	275 01.5	43.6	75 36.1	56.1	75 18.7	54.6	Regulus	208 09.4	N12 03.5
08	279 02.3	305 11.4	12.2	290 02.2	42.8	90 38.7	56.0	90 21.3	54.5	Rigel	281 35.7	S 8 13.6
S 09	294 04.8	320 10.9	·· 11.2	305 02.8	·· 42.0	105 41.4	·· 55.9	105 23.9	·· 54.5	Rigil Kent.	140 25.1	S60 45.1
U 10	309 07.3	335 10.3	10.1	320 03.5	41.2	120 44.1	55.8	120 26.5	54.4	Sabik	102 40.8	S15 42.1
N 11	324 09.7	350 09.8	09.0	335 04.1	40.4	135 46.8	55.6	135 29.1	54.3			
D 12	339 12.2	5 09.3	S12 07.9	350 04.8	S 5 39.7	150 49.5	S 1 55.5	150 31.7	S 0 54.3	Schedar	350 09.1	N56 26.0
A 13	354 14.7	20 08.7	06.9	5 05.4	38.9	165 52.2	55.4	165 34.3	54.2	Shaula	96 55.4	S37 05.3
Y 14	9 17.1	35 08.2	05.8	20 06.1	38.1	180 54.9	55.3	180 36.9	54.1	Sirius	258 55.3	S16 41.7
15	24 19.6	50 07.7	·· 04.7	35 06.7	·· 37.3	195 57.6	·· 55.2	195 39.5	·· 54.1	Spica	158 57.0	S11 03.8
16	39 22.0	65 07.1	03.6	50 07.4	36.5	211 00.3	55.1	210 42.1	54.0	Suhail	223 10.1	S43 21.5
17	54 24.5	80 06.6	02.6	65 08.1	35.7	226 03.0	55.0	225 44.8	53.9			
18	69 27.0	95 06.1	S12 01.5	80 08.7	S 5 35.0	241 05.7	S 1 54.9	240 47.4	S 0 53.8	Vega	80 55.8	N38 45.7
19	84 29.4	110 05.5	12 00.4	95 09.4	34.2	256 08.4	54.8	255 50.0	53.8	Zuben'ubi	137 32.6	S15 57.8
20	99 31.9	125 05.0	11 59.3	110 10.0	33.4	271 11.1	54.7	270 52.6	53.7		S.H.A.	Mer. Pass.
21	114 34.4	140 04.5	·· 58.2	125 10.7	·· 32.6	286 13.8	·· 54.6	285 55.2	·· 53.6		° ′	h m
22	129 36.8	155 04.0	57.2	140 11.3	31.8	301 16.5	54.5	300 57.8	53.6	Venus	27 45.2	11 39
23	144 39.3	170 03.4	56.1	155 12.0	31.0	316 19.2	54.4	316 00.4	53.5	Mars	11 57.8	12 41
Mer. Pass.	h m 13 26.9	v −0.5	d 1.1	v 0.7	d 0.8	v 2.7	d 0.1	v 2.6	d 0.1	Jupiter	171 29.1	2 03
										Saturn	171 14.4	2 04

G.M.T.	SUN G.H.A.	Dec.	MOON G.H.A.	v	Dec.	d	H.P.
27 00	176 47.4	S 8 27.3	269 59.6	12.7	S17 00.5	5.9	54.6
01	191 47.5	26.3	284 31.3	12.6	17 06.4	5.8	54.6
02	206 47.6	25.4	299 02.9	12.7	17 12.2	5.8	54.6
03	221 47.7	.. 24.5	313 34.6	12.5	17 18.0	5.7	54.7
04	236 47.9	23.5	328 06.1	12.5	17 23.7	5.6	54.7
05	251 48.0	22.6	342 37.6	12.5	17 29.3	5.6	54.7
06	266 48.1	S 8 21.6	357 09.1	12.4	S17 34.9	5.4	54.7
07	281 48.2	20.7	11 40.5	12.4	17 40.3	5.4	54.7
08	296 48.3	19.8	26 11.9	12.3	17 45.7	5.3	54.7
F 09	311 48.4	.. 18.8	40 43.2	12.2	17 51.0	5.2	54.8
R 10	326 48.5	17.9	55 14.4	12.2	17 56.2	5.2	54.8
I 11	341 48.6	16.9	69 45.6	12.2	18 01.4	5.1	54.8
D 12	356 48.7	S 8 16.0	84 16.8	12.0	S18 06.5	4.9	54.8
A 13	11 48.8	15.1	98 47.8	12.1	18 11.4	5.0	54.8
Y 14	26 49.0	14.1	113 18.9	12.0	18 16.4	4.8	54.9
15	41 49.1	.. 13.2	127 49.9	11.9	18 21.2	4.7	54.9
16	56 49.2	12.2	142 20.8	11.9	18 25.9	4.7	54.9
17	71 49.3	11.3	156 51.7	11.8	18 30.6	4.6	54.9
18	86 49.4	S 8 10.3	171 22.5	11.8	S18 35.2	4.4	54.9
19	101 49.5	09.4	185 53.3	11.7	18 39.6	4.5	55.0
20	116 49.6	08.5	200 24.0	11.7	18 44.1	4.3	55.0
21	131 49.8	.. 07.5	214 54.7	11.6	18 48.4	4.2	55.0
22	146 49.9	06.6	229 25.3	11.5	18 52.6	4.2	55.0
23	161 50.0	05.6	243 55.8	11.5	18 56.8	4.0	55.1
28 00	176 50.1	S 8 04.7	258 26.3	11.5	S19 00.8	4.0	55.1
01	191 50.2	03.7	272 56.8	11.4	19 04.8	3.9	55.1
02	206 50.3	02.8	287 27.2	11.3	19 08.7	3.8	55.1
03	221 50.4	.. 01.9	301 57.5	11.3	19 12.5	3.7	55.2
04	236 50.6	00.9	316 27.8	11.2	19 16.2	3.6	55.2
05	251 50.7	8 00.0	330 58.0	11.2	19 19.8	3.5	55.2
06	266 50.8	S 7 59.0	345 28.2	11.1	S19 23.3	3.4	55.2
07	281 50.9	58.1	359 58.3	11.1	19 26.7	3.4	55.3
S 08	296 51.0	57.1	14 28.4	11.0	19 30.1	3.2	55.3
A 09	311 51.1	.. 56.2	28 58.4	11.0	19 33.3	3.1	55.3
T 10	326 51.2	55.2	43 28.4	10.9	19 36.4	3.1	55.3
U 11	341 51.4	54.3	57 58.3	10.9	19 39.5	3.0	55.4
R 12	356 51.5	S 7 53.3	72 28.2	10.8	S19 42.5	2.8	55.4
D 13	11 51.6	52.4	86 58.0	10.7	19 45.3	2.8	55.4
A 14	26 51.7	51.5	101 27.7	10.7	19 48.1	2.7	55.4
Y 15	41 51.8	.. 50.5	115 57.4	10.7	19 50.8	2.5	55.5
16	56 51.9	49.6	130 27.1	10.6	19 53.3	2.5	55.5
17	71 52.1	48.6	144 56.7	10.5	19 55.8	2.4	55.5
18	86 52.2	S 7 47.7	159 26.2	10.5	S19 58.2	2.3	55.5
19	101 52.3	46.7	173 55.7	10.5	20 00.5	2.2	55.6
20	116 52.4	45.8	188 25.2	10.4	20 02.7	2.0	55.6
21	131 52.5	.. 44.8	202 54.6	10.3	20 04.7	2.0	55.6
22	146 52.7	43.9	217 23.9	10.3	20 06.7	1.9	55.7
23	161 52.8	42.9	231 53.2	10.3	20 08.6	1.8	55.7
1 00	176 52.9	S 7 42.0	246 22.5	10.2	S20 10.4	1.6	55.7
01	191 53.0	41.0	260 51.7	10.1	20 12.0	1.6	55.7
02	206 53.1	40.1	275 20.8	10.1	20 13.6	1.5	55.8
03	221 53.3	.. 39.1	289 49.9	10.1	20 15.1	1.5	55.8
04	236 53.4	38.2	304 19.0	10.0	20 16.4	1.3	55.8
05	251 53.5	37.2	318 48.0	10.0	20 17.7	1.2	55.9
06	266 53.6	S 7 36.3	333 17.0	9.9	S20 18.9	1.0	55.9
07	281 53.7	35.3	347 45.9	9.8	20 19.9	1.0	55.9
08	296 53.9	34.4	2 14.7	9.9	20 20.9	0.8	56.0
S 09	311 54.0	.. 33.4	16 43.6	9.7	20 21.7	0.7	56.0
U 10	326 54.1	32.5	31 12.3	9.8	20 22.4	0.7	56.0
N 11	341 54.2	31.5	45 41.1	9.6	20 23.1	0.5	56.1
D 12	356 54.3	S 7 30.6	60 09.7	9.7	S20 23.6	0.4	56.1
A 13	11 54.5	29.6	74 38.4	9.6	20 24.0	0.3	56.1
Y 14	26 54.6	28.7	89 07.0	9.5	20 24.3	0.2	56.1
15	41 54.7	.. 27.7	103 35.5	9.5	20 24.5	0.0	56.2
16	56 54.8	26.8	118 04.0	9.5	20 24.5	0.0	56.2
17	71 55.0	25.8	132 32.5	9.4	20 24.5	0.1	56.2
18	86 55.1	S 7 24.9	147 00.9	9.4	S20 24.4	0.3	56.2
19	101 55.2	23.9	161 29.3	9.4	20 24.1	0.3	56.3
20	116 55.3	23.0	175 57.7	9.3	20 23.8	0.5	56.3
21	131 55.5	.. 22.0	190 26.0	9.3	20 23.3	0.6	56.3
22	146 55.6	21.1	204 54.3	9.2	20 22.7	0.7	56.4
23	161 55.7	20.1	219 22.5	9.2	20 22.0	0.8	56.4
	S.D. 16.2	d 0.9	S.D. 14.9		15.1		15.3

Moonrise

Lat.	Twilight Naut.	Civil	Sunrise	27	28	1	2
N 72	05 15	06 33	07 43	05 21	■	■	■
N 70	05 20	06 30	07 32	04 08	06 05	■	■
68	05 23	06 28	07 24	03 31	04 59	06 16	07 06
66	05 26	06 25	07 17	03 05	04 24	05 33	06 24
64	05 29	06 23	07 11	02 45	03 59	05 04	05 55
62	05 30	06 22	07 06	02 29	03 39	04 42	05 34
60	05 32	06 20	07 02	02 15	03 23	04 24	05 16
N 58	05 33	06 18	06 58	02 04	03 09	04 09	05 01
56	05 34	06 17	06 54	01 54	02 57	03 56	04 49
54	05 35	06 16	06 51	01 45	02 47	03 45	04 38
52	05 35	06 14	06 48	01 37	02 38	03 36	04 28
50	05 36	06 13	06 46	01 30	02 30	03 27	04 19
45	05 37	06 11	06 40	01 15	02 13	03 08	04 01
N 40	05 37	06 08	06 35	01 02	01 58	02 53	03 46
35	05 36	06 06	06 31	00 52	01 47	02 40	03 33
30	05 35	06 03	06 27	00 43	01 36	02 29	03 22
20	05 33	05 59	06 21	00 27	01 18	02 10	03 03
N 10	05 29	05 54	06 15	00 13	01 03	01 54	02 46
0	05 24	05 48	06 09	00 00	00 48	01 38	02 30
S 10	05 18	05 42	06 04	24 34	00 34	01 23	02 15
20	05 09	05 35	05 57	24 18	00 18	01 06	01 58
30	04 57	05 26	05 50	24 01	00 01	00 48	01 39
35	04 50	05 20	05 46	23 51	24 37	00 37	01 28
40	04 40	05 13	05 41	23 39	24 24	00 24	01 16
45	04 29	05 05	05 36	23 25	24 09	00 09	01 01
S 50	04 14	04 55	05 29	23 09	23 51	24 42	00 42
52	04 07	04 50	05 26	23 01	23 43	24 33	00 33
54	03 59	04 45	05 22	22 52	23 33	24 24	00 24
56	03 50	04 39	05 18	22 42	23 22	24 13	00 13
58	03 39	04 32	05 14	22 31	23 10	24 00	00 00
S 60	03 26	04 24	05 09	22 19	22 56	23 45	24 49

Moonset

Lat.	Sunset	Twilight Civil	Naut.	27	28	1	2
N 72	16 44	17 54	19 13	06 52	■	■	■
N 70	16 54	17 57	19 08	08 06	07 50	■	■
68	17 03	17 59	19 04	08 44	08 55	09 24	10 24
66	17 09	18 02	19 01	09 10	09 31	10 07	11 05
64	17 15	18 03	18 58	09 31	09 57	10 36	11 34
62	17 20	18 05	18 56	09 48	10 17	10 58	11 55
60	17 25	18 07	18 55	10 02	10 33	11 16	12 13
N 58	17 28	18 08	18 53	10 14	10 47	11 31	12 27
56	17 32	18 09	18 52	10 24	10 59	11 44	12 40
54	17 35	18 10	18 51	10 33	11 10	11 55	12 51
52	17 38	18 12	18 51	10 41	11 19	12 05	13 00
50	17 40	18 13	18 50	10 49	11 27	12 14	13 09
45	17 46	18 15	18 49	11 05	11 45	12 32	13 27
N 40	17 51	18 18	18 49	11 17	12 00	12 48	13 42
35	17 55	18 20	18 49	11 29	12 12	13 00	13 55
30	17 58	18 22	18 50	11 38	12 23	13 12	14 06
20	18 05	18 27	18 53	11 55	12 41	13 31	14 24
N 10	18 10	18 32	18 56	12 10	12 57	13 48	14 41
0	18 16	18 37	19 01	12 23	13 12	14 03	14 56
S 10	18 21	18 43	19 07	12 37	13 27	14 19	15 11
20	18 28	18 50	19 16	12 52	13 43	14 35	15 27
30	18 35	18 59	19 27	13 08	14 02	14 54	15 46
35	18 39	19 04	19 35	13 18	14 12	15 06	15 57
40	18 43	19 11	19 44	13 29	14 25	15 18	16 09
45	18 49	19 19	19 55	13 43	14 39	15 33	16 24
S 50	18 55	19 29	20 10	13 59	14 57	15 52	16 41
52	18 58	19 33	20 17	14 06	15 06	16 01	16 50
54	19 02	19 39	20 24	14 15	15 15	16 10	16 59
56	19 05	19 45	20 33	14 24	15 26	16 21	17 09
58	19 10	19 51	20 44	14 35	15 38	16 34	17 21
S 60	19 14	19 59	20 56	14 47	15 52	16 49	17 35

Day	SUN Eqn. of Time 00h	12h	Mer. Pass.	MOON Mer. Pass. Upper	Lower	Age	Phase
27	12 51	12 45	12 13	06 12	18 36	23	
28	12 40	12 34	12 13	07 00	19 25	24	
1	12 29	12 23	12 12	07 51	20 17	25	◑

G.M.T.	ARIES G.H.A.	VENUS −3.4 G.H.A.	Dec.	MARS +1.4 G.H.A.	Dec.	JUPITER −2.0 G.H.A.	Dec.	SATURN +0.7 G.H.A.	Dec.
2 00	159 41.8	185 02.9	S11 55.0	170 12.6	S 5 30.3	331 21.9	S 1 54.2	331 03.0	S 0 53.4
01	174 44.2	200 02.4	53.9	185 13.3	29.5	346 24.6	54.1	346 05.6	53.4
02	189 46.7	215 01.8	52.8	200 13.9	28.7	1 27.3	54.0	1 08.2	53.3
03	204 49.2	230 01.3 ..	51.7	215 14.6 ..	27.9	16 30.0 ..	53.9	16 10.9 ..	53.2
04	219 51.6	245 00.8	50.7	230 15.3	27.1	31 32.7	53.8	31 13.5	53.1
05	234 54.1	260 00.3	49.6	245 15.9	26.3	46 35.4	53.7	46 16.1	53.1
06	249 56.5	274 59.7	S11 48.5	260 16.6	S 5 25.5	61 38.1	S 1 53.6	61 18.7	S 0 53.0
07	264 59.0	289 59.2	47.4	275 17.2	24.8	76 40.8	53.5	76 21.3	52.9
08	280 01.5	304 58.7	46.3	290 17.9	24.0	91 43.5	53.4	91 23.9	52.9
M 09	295 03.9	319 58.2 ..	45.2	305 18.5 ..	23.2	106 46.2 ..	53.3	106 26.5 ..	52.8
O 10	310 06.4	334 57.6	44.1	320 19.2	22.4	121 48.9	53.2	121 29.1	52.7
N 11	325 08.9	349 57.1	43.0	335 19.9	21.6	136 51.6	53.1	136 31.7	52.6
D 12	340 11.3	4 56.6	S11 42.0	350 20.5	S 5 20.8	151 54.3	S 1 52.9	151 34.4	S 0 52.6
A 13	355 13.8	19 56.1	40.9	5 21.2	20.1	166 57.0	52.8	166 37.0	52.5
Y 14	10 16.3	34 55.6	39.8	20 21.8	19.3	181 59.7	52.7	181 39.6	52.4
15	25 18.7	49 55.0 ..	38.7	35 22.5 ..	18.5	197 02.4 ..	52.6	196 42.2 ..	52.4
16	40 21.2	64 54.5	37.6	50 23.1	17.7	212 05.1	52.5	211 44.8	52.3
17	55 23.6	79 54.0	36.5	65 23.8	16.9	227 07.8	52.4	226 47.4	52.2
18	70 26.1	94 53.5	S11 35.4	80 24.5	S 5 16.1	242 10.5	S 1 52.3	241 50.0	S 0 52.2
19	85 28.6	109 53.0	34.3	95 25.1	15.3	257 13.2	52.2	256 52.6	52.1
20	100 31.0	124 52.4	33.2	110 25.8	14.6	272 15.9	52.1	271 55.3	52.0
21	115 33.5	139 51.9 ..	32.1	125 26.4 ..	13.8	287 18.6 ..	52.0	286 57.9 ..	51.9
22	130 36.0	154 51.4	31.0	140 27.1	13.0	302 21.3	51.9	302 00.5	51.9
23	145 38.4	169 50.9	29.9	155 27.7	12.2	317 24.0	51.7	317 03.1	51.8
3 00	160 40.9	184 50.4	S11 28.8	170 28.4	S 5 11.4	332 26.7	S 1 51.6	332 05.7	S 0 51.7
01	175 43.4	199 49.8	27.7	185 29.1	10.6	347 29.4	51.5	347 08.3	51.7
02	190 45.8	214 49.3	26.7	200 29.7	09.8	2 32.1	51.4	2 10.9	51.6
03	205 48.3	229 48.8 ..	25.6	215 30.4 ..	09.1	17 34.8 ..	51.3	17 13.5 ..	51.5
04	220 50.8	244 48.3	24.5	230 31.0	08.3	32 37.5	51.2	32 16.2	51.4
05	235 53.2	259 47.8	23.4	245 31.7	07.5	47 40.2	51.1	47 18.8	51.4
06	250 55.7	274 47.3	S11 22.3	260 32.3	S 5 06.7	62 42.9	S 1 51.0	62 21.4	S 0 51.3
07	265 58.1	289 46.7	21.2	275 33.0	05.9	77 45.6	50.9	77 24.0	51.2
08	281 00.6	304 46.2	20.1	290 33.7	05.1	92 48.3	50.8	92 26.6	51.2
T 09	296 03.1	319 45.7 ..	19.0	305 34.3 ..	04.3	107 51.0 ..	50.6	107 29.2 ..	51.1
U 10	311 05.5	334 45.2	17.9	320 35.0	03.6	122 53.7	50.5	122 31.8	51.0
E 11	326 08.0	349 44.7	16.8	335 35.6	02.8	137 56.4	50.4	137 34.5	50.9
S 12	341 10.5	4 44.2	S11 15.7	350 36.3	S 5 02.0	152 59.1	S 1 50.3	152 37.1	S 0 50.9
D 13	356 12.9	19 43.7	14.6	5 37.0	01.2	168 01.9	50.2	167 39.7	50.8
A 14	11 15.4	34 43.2	13.4	20 37.6	5 00.4	183 04.6	50.1	182 42.3	50.7
Y 15	26 17.9	49 42.6 ..	12.3	35 38.3	4 59.6	198 07.3 ..	50.0	197 44.9 ..	50.7
16	41 20.3	64 42.1	11.2	50 38.9	58.8	213 10.0	49.9	212 47.5	50.6
17	56 22.8	79 41.6	10.1	65 39.6	58.1	228 12.7	49.8	227 50.1	50.5
18	71 25.3	94 41.1	S11 09.0	80 40.3	S 4 57.3	243 15.4	S 1 49.7	242 52.8	S 0 50.4
19	86 27.7	109 40.6	07.9	95 40.9	56.5	258 18.1	49.5	257 55.4	50.4
20	101 30.2	124 40.1	06.8	110 41.6	55.7	273 20.8	49.4	272 58.0	50.3
21	116 32.6	139 39.6 ..	05.7	125 42.2 ..	54.9	288 23.5 ..	49.3	288 00.6 ..	50.2
22	131 35.1	154 39.1	04.6	140 42.9	54.1	303 26.2	49.2	303 03.2	50.2
23	146 37.6	169 38.6	03.5	155 43.6	53.3	318 28.9	49.1	318 05.8	50.1
4 00	161 40.0	184 38.1	S11 02.4	170 44.2	S 4 52.6	333 31.6	S 1 49.0	333 08.4	S 0 50.0
01	176 42.5	199 37.6	01.3	185 44.9	51.8	348 34.3	48.9	348 11.1	49.9
02	191 45.0	214 37.1	11 00.2	200 45.5	51.0	3 37.0	48.8	3 13.7	49.9
03	206 47.4	229 36.5	10 59.1	215 46.2 ..	50.2	18 39.7 ..	48.7	18 16.3 ..	49.8
04	221 49.9	244 36.0	58.0	230 46.9	49.4	33 42.5	48.5	33 18.9	49.7
05	236 52.4	259 35.5	56.8	245 47.5	48.6	48 45.2	48.4	48 21.5	49.6
06	251 54.8	274 35.0	S10 55.7	260 48.2	S 4 47.8	63 47.9	S 1 48.3	63 24.1	S 0 49.6
07	266 57.3	289 34.5	54.6	275 48.8	47.0	78 50.6	48.2	78 26.8	49.5
W 08	281 59.7	304 34.0	53.5	290 49.5	46.3	93 53.3	48.1	93 29.4	49.4
E 09	297 02.2	319 33.5 ..	52.4	305 50.2 ..	45.5	108 56.0 ..	48.0	108 32.0 ..	49.4
D 10	312 04.7	334 33.0	51.3	320 50.8	44.7	123 58.7	47.9	123 34.6	49.3
N 11	327 07.1	349 32.5	50.2	335 51.5	43.9	139 01.4	47.8	138 37.2	49.2
E 12	342 09.6	4 32.0	S10 49.0	350 52.2	S 4 43.1	154 04.1	S 1 47.6	153 39.8	S 0 49.1
S 13	357 12.1	19 31.5	47.9	5 52.8	42.3	169 06.8	47.5	168 42.5	49.1
D 14	12 14.5	34 31.0	46.8	20 53.5	41.5	184 09.5	47.4	183 45.1	49.0
A 15	27 17.0	49 30.5 ..	45.7	35 54.1 ..	40.7	199 12.2 ..	47.3	198 47.7 ..	48.9
Y 16	42 19.5	64 30.0	44.6	50 54.8	40.0	214 15.0	47.2	213 50.3	48.9
17	57 21.9	79 29.5	43.5	65 55.5	39.2	229 17.7	47.1	228 52.9	48.8
18	72 24.4	94 29.0	S10 42.4	80 56.1	S 4 38.4	244 20.4	S 1 47.0	243 55.5	S 0 48.7
19	87 26.9	109 28.5	41.2	95 56.8	37.6	259 23.1	46.9	258 58.2	48.6
20	102 29.3	124 28.0	40.1	110 57.5	36.8	274 25.8	46.7	274 00.8	48.6
21	117 31.8	139 27.5 ..	39.0	125 58.1 ..	36.0	289 28.5 ..	46.6	289 03.4 ..	48.5
22	132 34.2	154 27.0	37.9	140 58.8	35.2	304 31.2	46.5	304 06.0	48.4
23	147 36.7	169 26.5	36.8	155 59.4	34.4	319 33.9	46.4	319 08.6	48.3
Mer. Pass.	13 15.1	v −0.5	d 1.1	v 0.7	d 0.8	v 2.7	d 0.1	v 2.6	d 0.1

STARS

Name	S.H.A.	Dec.
Acamar	315 37.2	S40 23.2
Achernar	335 45.5	S57 20.3
Acrux	173 36.2	S62 59.5
Adhara	255 31.7	S28 57.1
Aldebaran	291 17.7	N16 28.2
Alioth	166 41.8	N56 03.6
Alkaid	153 17.9	N49 24.3
Al Na'ir	28 15.0	S47 03.2
Alnilam	276 11.3	S 1 13.0
Alphard	218 20.0	S 8 34.7
Alphecca	126 31.7	N26 46.5
Alpheratz	358 09.3	N28 59.0
Altair	62 32.5	N 8 48.9
Ankaa	353 40.3	S42 24.8
Antares	112 56.4	S26 23.3
Arcturus	146 18.0	N19 16.7
Atria	108 20.4	S68 59.3
Avior	234 27.6	S59 27.2
Bellatrix	278 58.4	N 6 19.8
Betelgeuse	271 27.8	N 7 24.1
Canopus	264 06.8	S52 41.5
Capella	281 10.8	N45 58.8
Deneb	49 48.6	N45 12.6
Denebola	182 58.4	N14 40.6
Diphda	349 20.8	S18 05.7
Dubhe	194 21.1	N61 51.1
Elnath	278 43.7	N28 35.5
Eltanin	90 57.7	N51 29.2
Enif	34 11.6	N 9 47.1
Fomalhaut	15 51.4	S29 43.5
Gacrux	172 27.9	S57 00.3
Gienah	176 17.3	S17 26.2
Hadar	149 22.5	S60 16.7
Hamal	328 28.8	N23 22.3
Kaus Aust.	84 16.6	S34 23.6
Kochab	137 18.5	N74 13.8
Markab	14 03.2	N15 06.0
Menkar	314 40.9	N 4 00.8
Menkent	148 36.4	S36 16.5
Miaplacidus	221 44.0	S69 38.5
Mirfak	309 15.8	N49 47.7
Nunki	76 29.0	S26 19.2
Peacock	53 58.4	S56 47.7
Pollux	243 57.5	N28 04.3
Procyon	245 25.2	N 5 16.3
Rasalhague	96 29.4	N12 34.3
Regulus	208 09.4	N12 03.5
Rigel	281 35.7	S 8 13.6
Rigil Kent.	140 25.1	S60 45.1
Sabik	102 40.8	S15 42.1
Schedar	350 09.1	N56 26.0
Shaula	96 55.4	S37 05.3
Sirius	258 55.3	S16 41.7
Spica	158 57.0	S11 03.8
Suhail	223 10.1	S43 21.5
Vega	80 55.8	N38 45.7
Zuben'ubi	137 32.5	S15 57.8

	S.H.A.	Mer. Pass.
Venus	24 09.5	11 41
Mars	9 47.5	12 38
Jupiter	171 45.8	1 50
Saturn	171 24.8	1 51

G.M.T.	SUN G.H.A.	SUN Dec.	MOON G.H.A.	v	Dec.	d	H.P.
d h	° ′	° ′	° ′	′	° ′	′	′
2 00	176 55.8	S 7 19.2	233 50.7	9.1	S20 21.2	0.9	56.5
01	191 56.0	18.2	248 18.8	9.2	20 20.3	1.0	56.5
02	206 56.1	17.3	262 47.0	9.0	20 19.3	1.2	56.5
03	221 56.2	·· 16.3	277 15.0	9.1	20 18.1	1.2	56.6
04	236 56.3	15.4	291 43.1	9.0	20 16.9	1.4	56.6
05	251 56.5	14.4	306 11.1	9.0	20 15.5	1.5	56.6
06	266 56.6	S 7 13.4	320 39.1	8.9	S20 14.0	1.6	56.7
07	281 56.7	12.5	335 07.0	8.9	20 12.4	1.7	56.7
M 08	296 56.8	11.5	349 34.9	8.9	20 10.7	1.9	56.8
O 09	311 57.0	·· 10.6	4 02.8	8.9	20 08.8	1.9	56.8
N 10	326 57.1	09.6	18 30.7	8.8	20 06.9	2.1	56.8
D 11	341 57.2	08.7	32 58.5	8.8	20 04.8	2.2	56.9
A 12	356 57.3	S 7 07.7	47 26.3	8.7	S20 02.6	2.3	56.9
Y 13	11 57.5	06.8	61 54.0	8.8	20 00.3	2.4	56.9
14	26 57.6	05.8	76 21.8	8.7	19 57.9	2.5	57.0
15	41 57.7	·· 04.9	90 49.5	8.6	19 55.4	2.6	57.0
16	56 57.8	03.9	105 17.1	8.7	19 52.8	2.8	57.0
17	71 58.0	02.9	119 44.8	8.6	19 50.0	2.9	57.1
18	86 58.1	S 7 02.0	134 12.4	8.9	S19 47.1	3.0	57.1
19	101 58.2	01.0	148 40.0	8.6	19 44.1	3.1	57.1
20	116 58.4	7 00.1	163 07.6	8.5	19 41.0	3.2	57.2
21	131 58.5	6 59.1	177 35.1	8.5	19 37.8	3.4	57.2
22	146 58.6	58.2	192 02.6	8.5	19 34.4	3.4	57.2
23	161 58.7	57.2	206 30.1	8.5	19 31.0	3.6	57.3
3 00	176 58.9	S 6 56.2	220 57.6	8.5	S19 27.4	3.7	57.3
01	191 59.0	55.3	235 25.1	8.4	19 23.7	3.8	57.4
02	206 59.1	54.3	249 52.5	8.5	19 19.9	3.9	57.4
03	221 59.3	·· 53.4	264 20.0	8.4	19 16.0	4.1	57.4
04	236 59.4	52.4	278 47.4	8.4	19 11.9	4.1	57.5
05	251 59.5	51.5	293 14.8	8.3	19 07.8	4.3	57.5
06	266 59.7	S 6 50.5	307 42.1	8.4	S19 03.5	4.4	57.5
07	281 59.8	49.5	322 09.5	8.3	18 59.1	4.5	57.6
08	296 59.9	48.6	336 36.8	8.3	18 54.6	4.6	57.6
T 09	312 00.1	·· 47.6	351 04.1	8.3	18 50.0	4.8	57.6
U 10	327 00.2	46.7	5 31.4	8.3	18 45.2	4.9	57.7
E 11	342 00.3	45.7	19 58.7	8.3	18 40.3	4.9	57.7
S 12	357 00.4	S 6 44.7	34 26.0	8.3	S18 35.4	5.1	57.8
D 13	12 00.6	43.8	48 53.3	8.2	18 30.3	5.2	57.8
A 14	27 00.7	42.8	63 20.5	8.3	18 25.1	5.4	57.8
Y 15	42 00.8	·· 41.9	77 47.8	8.2	18 19.7	5.4	57.9
16	57 01.0	40.9	92 15.0	8.3	18 14.3	5.5	57.9
17	72 01.1	39.9	106 42.3	8.2	18 08.8	5.7	57.9
18	87 01.2	S 6 39.0	121 09.5	8.2	S18 03.1	5.8	58.0
19	102 01.4	38.0	135 36.7	8.2	17 57.3	5.9	58.0
20	117 01.5	37.1	150 03.9	8.2	17 51.4	6.0	58.0
21	132 01.6	·· 36.1	164 31.1	8.2	17 45.4	6.1	58.1
22	147 01.8	35.1	178 58.3	8.2	17 39.3	6.3	58.1
23	162 01.9	34.2	193 25.5	8.2	17 33.0	6.3	58.1
4 00	177 02.0	S 6 33.2	207 52.7	8.1	S17 26.7	6.5	58.2
01	192 02.2	32.3	222 19.8	8.2	17 20.2	6.5	58.2
02	207 02.3	31.3	236 47.0	8.2	17 13.7	6.7	58.3
03	222 02.4	·· 30.3	251 14.2	8.1	17 07.0	6.8	58.3
04	237 02.6	29.4	265 41.3	8.2	17 00.2	6.9	58.3
05	252 02.7	28.4	280 08.5	8.2	16 53.3	7.0	58.4
06	267 02.9	S 6 27.5	294 35.7	8.1	S16 46.3	7.2	58.4
07	282 03.0	26.5	309 02.8	8.2	16 39.1	7.2	58.4
W 08	297 03.1	25.5	323 30.0	8.2	16 31.9	7.3	58.5
E 09	312 03.3	·· 24.6	337 57.2	8.1	16 24.6	7.5	58.5
D 10	327 03.4	23.6	352 24.3	8.2	16 17.1	7.5	58.5
N 11	342 03.5	22.6	6 51.5	8.2	16 09.6	7.7	58.6
E 12	357 03.7	S 6 21.7	21 18.7	8.1	S16 01.9	7.8	58.6
S 13	12 03.8	20.7	35 45.8	8.2	15 54.1	7.8	58.6
D 14	27 03.9	19.8	50 13.0	8.2	15 46.3	8.0	58.7
A 15	42 04.1	·· 18.8	64 40.2	8.1	15 38.3	8.1	58.7
Y 16	57 04.2	17.8	79 07.4	8.2	15 30.2	8.2	58.7
17	72 04.4	16.9	93 34.6	8.2	15 22.0	8.3	58.8
18	87 04.5	S 6 15.9	108 01.8	8.1	S15 13.7	8.3	58.8
19	102 04.6	14.9	122 28.9	8.2	15 05.4	8.5	58.8
20	117 04.8	14.0	136 56.1	8.3	14 56.9	8.6	58.9
21	132 04.9	·· 13.0	151 23.4	8.2	14 48.3	8.7	58.9
22	147 05.0	12.0	165 50.6	8.2	14 39.6	8.8	58.9
23	162 05.2	11.1	180 17.8	8.2	14 30.8	8.9	59.0
	S.D. 16.2 d 1.0		S.D. 15.5		15.7		16.0

Lat.	Twilight Naut.	Twilight Civil	Sunrise	Moonrise 2	3	4	5
°	h m	h m	h m	h m	h m	h m	h m
N 72	05 00	06 19	07 27	■	■	08 53	08 24
N 70	05 07	06 17	07 18	■	08 19	08 08	08 00
68	05 11	06 16	07 12	07 06	07 28	07 37	07 41
66	05 15	06 14	07 06	06 24	06 56	07 15	07 26
64	05 19	06 13	07 01	05 55	06 32	06 57	07 14
62	05 21	06 12	06 57	05 34	06 13	06 42	07 03
60	05 23	06 11	06 53	05 16	05 58	06 29	06 54
N 58	05 25	06 10	06 50	05 01	05 44	06 19	06 46
56	05 27	06 10	06 47	04 49	05 33	06 09	06 39
54	05 28	06 09	06 44	04 38	05 23	06 01	06 33
52	05 29	06 08	06 42	04 28	05 14	05 53	06 27
50	05 30	06 07	06 40	04 19	05 06	05 46	06 22
45	05 31	06 05	06 35	04 01	04 49	05 32	06 11
N 40	05 32	06 04	06 31	03 46	04 35	05 20	06 01
35	05 33	06 02	06 27	03 33	04 23	05 10	05 53
30	05 32	06 00	06 24	03 22	04 12	05 01	05 46
20	05 31	05 56	06 18	03 03	03 54	04 45	05 34
N 10	05 28	05 52	06 13	02 46	03 39	04 31	05 23
0	05 24	05 48	06 09	02 30	03 24	04 19	05 13
S 10	05 18	05 43	06 04	02 15	03 09	04 06	05 03
20	05 10	05 36	05 58	01 58	02 54	03 52	04 52
30	04 59	05 28	05 52	01 39	02 36	03 36	04 40
35	04 53	05 23	05 49	01 28	02 25	03 27	04 32
40	04 44	05 17	05 44	01 16	02 13	03 17	04 24
45	04 34	05 10	05 40	01 01	01 59	03 04	04 15
S 50	04 20	05 00	05 34	00 42	01 42	02 49	04 03
52	04 14	04 56	05 31	00 33	01 34	02 42	03 58
54	04 06	04 51	05 28	00 24	01 25	02 35	03 52
56	03 58	04 46	05 25	00 13	01 14	02 26	03 45
58	03 48	04 40	05 21	00 00	01 03	02 16	03 37
S 60	03 36	04 33	05 17	24 49	00 49	02 05	03 29

Lat.	Sunset	Twilight Civil	Twilight Naut.	Moonset 2	3	4	5
°	h m	h m	h m	h m	h m	h m	h m
N 72	16 59	18 08	19 27	■	■	12 24	14 47
N 70	17 07	18 09	19 20	■	11 03	13 09	15 10
68	17 14	18 10	19 15	10 24	11 54	13 38	15 27
66	17 20	18 11	19 11	11 05	12 25	14 00	15 41
64	17 24	18 12	19 07	11 34	12 49	14 17	15 52
62	17 28	18 13	19 04	11 55	13 07	14 31	16 02
60	17 32	18 14	19 02	12 13	13 22	14 43	16 10
N 58	17 35	18 15	19 00	12 27	13 35	14 53	16 18
56	17 38	18 15	18 59	12 40	13 46	15 02	16 24
54	17 41	18 16	18 57	12 51	13 56	15 10	16 30
52	17 43	18 17	18 56	13 00	14 05	15 17	16 35
50	17 45	18 18	18 55	13 09	14 13	15 24	16 39
45	17 50	18 19	18 53	13 27	14 29	15 37	16 49
N 40	17 54	18 21	18 52	13 42	14 43	15 48	16 57
35	17 57	18 23	18 52	13 55	14 54	15 58	17 04
30	18 00	18 24	18 52	14 06	15 04	16 06	17 11
20	18 06	18 28	18 53	14 24	15 21	16 21	17 21
N 10	18 11	18 32	18 56	14 41	15 36	16 33	17 30
0	18 15	18 36	19 00	14 56	15 50	16 45	17 39
S 10	18 20	18 41	19 06	15 11	16 04	16 56	17 47
20	18 25	18 47	19 13	15 27	16 19	17 08	17 56
30	18 31	18 55	19 24	15 46	16 35	17 22	18 07
35	18 35	19 00	19 31	15 57	16 45	17 30	18 12
40	18 39	19 06	19 39	16 09	16 56	17 39	18 19
45	18 43	19 13	19 49	16 24	17 09	17 50	18 27
S 50	18 49	19 22	20 02	16 41	17 25	18 03	18 36
52	18 52	19 26	20 09	16 50	17 32	18 09	18 40
54	18 55	19 31	20 16	16 59	17 40	18 15	18 45
56	18 58	19 36	20 24	17 09	17 50	18 22	18 50
58	19 01	19 42	20 34	17 21	18 00	18 30	18 55
S 60	19 05	19 48	20 45	17 35	18 12	18 40	19 02

Day	SUN Eqn. of Time 00h	SUN Eqn. of Time 12h	SUN Mer. Pass.	MOON Mer. Pass. Upper	MOON Mer. Pass. Lower	Age	Phase
	m s	m s	h m	h m	h m	d	
2	12 17	12 11	12 12	08 43	21 10	26	
3	12 05	11 58	12 12	09 37	22 04	27	
4	11 52	11 46	12 12	10 32	22 59	28	◗

G.M.T.	ARIES G.H.A.	VENUS −3.4 G.H.A.	Dec.	MARS +1.4 G.H.A.	Dec.	JUPITER −2.0 G.H.A.	Dec.	SATURN +0.7 G.H.A.	Dec.	STARS Name	S.H.A.	Dec.
5 00	162 39.2	184 26.0 S10	35.6	171 00.1 S 4	33.7	334 36.6 S 1	46.3	334 11.2 S 0	48.3	Acamar	315 37.2	S40 23.2
01	177 41.6	199 25.5	34.5	186 00.8	32.9	349 39.4	46.2	349 13.9	48.2	Achernar	335 45.5	S57 20.3
02	192 44.1	214 25.0	33.4	201 01.4	32.1	4 42.1	46.1	4 16.5	48.1	Acrux	173 36.2	S62 59.6
03	207 46.6	229 24.5 ··	32.3	216 02.1 ··	31.3	19 44.8 ··	46.0	19 19.1 ··	48.1	Adhara	255 31.7	S28 57.1
04	222 49.0	244 24.0	31.2	231 02.8	30.5	34 47.5	45.8	34 21.7	48.0	Aldebaran	291 17.7	N16 28.2
05	237 51.5	259 23.5	30.0	246 03.4	29.7	49 50.2	45.7	49 24.3	47.9			
06	252 54.0	274 23.0 S10	28.9	261 04.1 S 4	28.9	64 52.9 S 1	45.6	64 26.9 S 0	47.8	Alioth	166 41.7	N56 03.6
07	267 56.4	289 22.5	27.8	276 04.7	28.1	79 55.6	45.5	79 29.6	47.8	Alkaid	153 17.9	N49 24.3
T 08	282 58.9	304 22.0	26.7	291 05.4	27.3	94 58.3	45.4	94 32.2	47.7	Al Na'ir	28 15.0	S47 03.2
H 09	298 01.4	319 21.5 ··	25.5	306 06.1 ··	26.6	110 01.1 ··	45.3	109 34.8 ··	47.6	Alnilam	276 11.3	S 1 13.0
U 10	313 03.8	334 21.0	24.4	321 06.7	25.8	125 03.8	45.2	124 37.4	47.5	Alphard	218 20.0	S 8 34.7
R 11	328 06.3	349 20.6	23.3	336 07.4	25.0	140 06.5	45.0	139 40.0	47.5			
S 12	343 08.7	4 20.1 S10	22.2	351 08.1 S 4	24.2	155 09.2 S 1	44.9	154 42.7 S 0	47.4	Alphecca	126 31.7	N26 46.5
D 13	358 11.2	19 19.6	21.0	6 08.7	23.4	170 11.9	44.8	169 45.3	47.3	Alpheratz	358 09.3	N28 59.0
A 14	13 13.7	34 19.1	19.9	21 09.4	22.6	185 14.6	44.7	184 47.9	47.2	Altair	62 32.4	N 8 48.9
Y 15	28 16.1	49 18.6 ··	18.8	36 10.1 ··	21.8	200 17.3 ··	44.6	199 50.5 ··	47.2	Ankaa	353 40.3	S42 24.8
16	43 18.6	64 18.1	17.6	51 10.7	21.0	215 20.1	44.5	214 53.1	47.1	Antares	112 56.4	S26 23.3
17	58 21.1	79 17.6	16.5	66 11.4	20.2	230 22.8	44.4	229 55.7	47.0			
18	73 23.5	94 17.1 S10	15.4	81 12.1 S 4	19.5	245 25.5 S 1	44.2	244 58.4 S 0	47.0	Arcturus	146 18.0	N19 16.7
19	88 26.0	109 16.6	14.3	96 12.7	18.7	260 28.2	44.1	260 01.0	46.9	Atria	108 20.4	S68 59.3
20	103 28.5	124 16.1	13.1	111 13.4	17.9	275 30.9	44.0	275 03.6	46.8	Avior	234 27.6	S59 27.2
21	118 30.9	139 15.6 ··	12.0	126 14.0 ··	17.1	290 33.6 ··	43.9	290 06.2 ··	46.7	Bellatrix	278 58.4	N 6 19.8
22	133 33.4	154 15.1	10.9	141 14.7	16.3	305 36.4	43.8	305 08.8	46.7	Betelgeuse	271 27.9	N 7 24.1
23	148 35.9	169 14.7	09.7	156 15.4	15.5	320 39.1	43.7	320 11.5	46.6			
6 00	163 38.3	184 14.2 S10	08.6	171 16.0 S 4	14.7	335 41.8 S 1	43.6	335 14.1 S 0	46.5	Canopus	264 06.9	S52 41.5
01	178 40.8	199 13.7	07.5	186 16.7	13.9	350 44.5	43.4	350 16.7	46.4	Capella	281 10.8	N45 58.8
02	193 43.2	214 13.2	06.3	201 17.4	13.1	5 47.2	43.3	5 19.3	46.4	Deneb	49 48.6	N45 12.6
03	208 45.7	229 12.7 ··	05.2	216 18.0 ··	12.4	20 49.9 ··	43.2	20 21.9 ··	46.3	Denebola	182 58.4	N14 40.6
04	223 48.2	244 12.2	04.1	231 18.7	11.6	35 52.6	43.1	35 24.6	46.2	Diphda	349 20.9	S18 05.7
05	238 50.6	259 11.7	02.9	246 19.4	10.8	50 55.4	43.0	50 27.2	46.1			
06	253 53.1	274 11.2 S10	01.8	261 20.0 S 4	10.0	65 58.1 S 1	42.9	65 29.8 S 0	46.1	Dubhe	194 21.1	N61 51.2
07	268 55.6	289 10.8 10	00.7	276 20.7	09.2	81 00.8	42.8	80 32.4	46.0	Elnath	278 43.7	N28 35.5
08	283 58.0	304 10.3 9	59.5	291 21.4	08.4	96 03.5	42.6	95 35.0	45.9	Eltanin	90 57.7	N51 29.2
F 09	299 00.5	319 09.8 ··	58.4	306 22.0 ··	07.6	111 06.2 ··	42.5	110 37.7 ··	45.9	Enif	34 11.6	N 9 47.1
R 10	314 03.0	334 09.3	57.3	321 22.7	06.8	126 09.0	42.4	125 40.3	45.8	Fomalhaut	15 51.4	S29 43.5
I 11	329 05.4	349 08.8	56.1	336 23.4	06.0	141 11.7	42.3	140 42.9	45.7			
D 12	344 07.9	4 08.3 S 9	55.0	351 24.0 S 4	05.2	156 14.4 S 1	42.2	155 45.5 S 0	45.6	Gacrux	172 27.8	S57 00.3
A 13	359 10.3	19 07.9	53.8	6 24.7	04.5	171 17.1	42.1	170 48.1	45.6	Gienah	176 17.3	S17 26.3
Y 14	14 12.8	34 07.4	52.7	21 25.4	03.7	186 19.8	41.9	185 50.8	45.5	Hadar	149 22.4	S60 16.7
15	29 15.3	49 06.9 ··	51.6	36 26.0 ··	02.9	201 22.5 ··	41.8	200 53.4 ··	45.4	Hamal	328 28.8	N23 22.3
16	44 17.7	64 06.4	50.4	51 26.7	02.1	216 25.3	41.7	215 56.0	45.3	Kaus Aust.	84 16.6	S34 23.6
17	59 20.2	79 05.9	49.3	66 27.4	01.3	231 28.0	41.6	230 58.6	45.3			
18	74 22.7	94 05.4 S 9	48.1	81 28.0 S 4	00.5	246 30.7 S 1	41.5	246 01.2 S 0	45.2	Kochab	137 18.4	N74 13.8
19	89 25.1	109 05.0	47.0	96 28.7 3	59.7	261 33.4	41.4	261 03.9	45.1	Markab	14 03.2	N15 06.0
20	104 27.6	124 04.5	45.9	111 29.4	58.9	276 36.1	41.3	276 06.5	45.0	Menkar	314 41.0	N 4 00.8
21	119 30.1	139 04.0 ··	44.7	126 30.0 ··	58.1	291 38.9 ··	41.1	291 09.1 ··	45.0	Menkent	148 36.4	S36 16.5
22	134 32.5	154 03.5	43.6	141 30.7	57.3	306 41.6	41.0	306 11.7	44.9	Miaplacidus	221 44.0	S69 38.5
23	149 35.0	169 03.0	42.4	156 31.4	56.6	321 44.3	40.9	321 14.4	44.8			
7 00	164 37.5	184 02.6 S 9	41.3	171 32.0 S 3	55.8	336 47.0 S 1	40.8	336 17.0 S 0	44.7	Mirfak	309 15.8	N49 47.7
01	179 39.9	199 02.1	40.2	186 32.7	55.0	351 49.7	40.7	351 19.6	44.7	Nunki	76 29.0	S26 19.2
02	194 42.4	214 01.6	39.0	201 33.4	54.2	6 52.5	40.6	6 22.2	44.6	Peacock	53 58.3	S56 47.7
03	209 44.8	229 01.1 ··	37.9	216 34.0 ··	53.4	21 55.2 ··	40.4	21 24.8 ··	44.5	Pollux	243 57.5	N28 04.3
04	224 47.3	244 00.6	36.7	231 34.7	52.6	36 57.9	40.3	36 27.5	44.4	Procyon	245 25.3	N 5 16.3
05	239 49.8	259 00.2	35.6	246 35.4	51.8	52 00.6	40.2	51 30.1	44.4			
06	254 52.2	273 59.7 S 9	34.4	261 36.0 S 3	51.0	67 03.3 S 1	40.1	66 32.7 S 0	44.3	Rasalhague	96 29.3	N12 34.3
07	269 54.7	288 59.2	33.3	276 36.7	50.2	82 06.1	40.0	81 35.3	44.2	Regulus	208 09.4	N12 03.5
S 08	284 57.2	303 58.7	32.1	291 37.4	49.4	97 08.8	39.9	96 37.9	44.2	Rigel	281 35.7	S 8 13.6
A 09	299 59.6	318 58.3 ··	31.0	306 38.1 ··	48.7	112 11.5 ··	39.7	111 40.6 ··	44.1	Rigil Kent.	140 25.0	S60 45.2
T 10	315 02.1	333 57.8	29.8	321 38.7	47.9	127 14.2	39.6	126 43.2	44.0	Sabik	102 40.8	S15 42.1
U 11	330 04.6	348 57.3	28.7	336 39.4	47.1	142 16.9	39.5	141 45.8	43.9			
R 12	345 07.0	3 56.8 S 9	27.5	351 40.1 S 3	46.3	157 19.7 S 1	39.4	156 48.4 S 0	43.9	Schedar	350 09.1	N56 26.0
D 13	0 09.5	18 56.4	26.4	6 40.7	45.5	172 22.4	39.3	171 51.1	43.8	Shaula	96 55.4	S37 05.3
A 14	15 12.0	33 55.9	25.2	21 41.4	44.7	187 25.1	39.2	186 53.7	43.7	Sirius	258 55.3	S16 41.7
Y 15	30 14.4	48 55.4 ··	24.1	36 42.1 ··	43.9	202 27.8 ··	39.0	201 56.3 ··	43.6	Spica	158 56.9	S11 03.8
16	45 16.9	63 54.9	22.9	51 42.7	43.1	217 30.6	38.9	216 58.9	43.6	Suhail	223 10.2	S43 21.6
17	60 19.3	78 54.5	21.8	66 43.4	42.3	232 33.3	38.8	232 01.6	43.5			
18	75 21.8	93 54.0 S 9	20.6	81 44.1 S 3	41.5	247 36.0 S 1	38.7	247 04.2 S 0	43.4	Vega	80 55.8	N38 45.7
19	90 24.3	108 53.5	19.5	96 44.7	40.7	262 38.7	38.6	262 06.8	43.3	Zuben'ubi	137 32.5	S15 57.8
20	105 26.7	123 53.0	18.3	111 45.4	40.0	277 41.4	38.5	277 09.4	43.3		S.H.A.	Mer. Pass.
21	120 29.2	138 52.6 ··	17.2	126 46.1 ··	39.2	292 44.2 ··	38.3	292 12.0 ··	43.2	Venus	20 35.9	11 43
22	135 31.7	153 52.1	16.0	141 46.8	38.4	307 46.9	38.2	307 14.7	43.1	Mars	7 37.7	12 34
23	150 34.1	168 51.6	14.9	156 47.4	37.6	322 49.6	38.1	322 17.3	43.0	Jupiter	172 03.5	1 37
Mer. Pass. 13 03.3		v −0.5 d 1.1		v 0.7 d 0.8		v 2.7 d 0.1		v 2.6 d 0.1		Saturn	171 35.8	1 39

G.M.T. (d h)	SUN G.H.A.	SUN Dec.	MOON G.H.A.	v	Dec.	d	H.P.
5 00	177 05.3	S 6 10.1	194 45.0	8.2	S14 21.9	9.0	59.0
01	192 05.5	09.1	209 12.2	8.3	14 12.9	9.0	59.0
02	207 05.6	08.2	223 39.5	8.2	14 03.9	9.2	59.1
03	222 05.7	·· 07.2	238 06.7	8.3	13 54.7	9.3	59.1
04	237 05.9	06.3	252 34.0	8.3	13 45.4	9.4	59.1
05	252 06.0	05.3	267 01.3	8.2	13 36.0	9.4	59.2
06	267 06.2	S 6 04.3	281 28.5	8.3	S13 26.6	9.6	59.2
07	282 06.3	03.4	295 55.8	8.3	13 17.0	9.6	59.2
T 08	297 06.4	02.4	310 23.1	8.3	13 07.4	9.7	59.2
H 09	312 06.6	·· 01.4	324 50.4	8.3	12 57.7	9.8	59.3
U 10	327 06.7	6 00.5	339 17.7	8.4	12 47.9	9.9	59.3
R 11	342 06.9	5 59.5	353 45.1	8.3	12 38.0	10.0	59.3
S 12	357 07.0	S 5 58.5	8 12.4	8.3	S12 28.0	10.1	59.4
D 13	12 07.1	57.6	22 39.7	8.4	12 17.9	10.2	59.4
A 14	27 07.3	56.6	37 07.1	8.4	12 07.7	10.2	59.4
Y 15	42 07.4	·· 55.6	51 34.5	8.3	11 57.5	10.3	59.4
16	57 07.6	54.7	66 01.8	8.4	11 47.2	10.5	59.5
17	72 07.7	53.7	80 29.2	8.4	11 36.7	10.4	59.5
18	87 07.9	S 5 52.7	94 56.6	8.4	S11 26.3	10.6	59.5
19	102 08.0	51.8	109 24.0	8.5	11 15.7	10.7	59.6
20	117 08.1	50.8	123 51.5	8.4	11 05.0	10.7	59.6
21	132 08.3	·· 49.8	138 18.9	8.4	10 54.3	10.8	59.6
22	147 08.4	48.8	152 46.3	8.5	10 43.5	10.9	59.6
23	162 08.6	47.9	167 13.8	8.4	10 32.6	10.9	59.7
6 00	177 08.7	S 5 46.9	181 41.2	8.5	S10 21.7	11.0	59.7
01	192 08.9	45.9	196 08.7	8.5	10 10.7	11.1	59.7
02	207 09.0	45.0	210 36.2	8.5	9 59.6	11.2	59.7
03	222 09.1	·· 44.0	225 03.7	8.5	9 48.4	11.2	59.8
04	237 09.3	43.0	239 31.2	8.5	9 37.2	11.3	59.8
05	252 09.4	42.1	253 58.7	8.6	9 25.9	11.4	59.8
06	267 09.6	S 5 41.1	268 26.3	8.5	S 9 14.5	11.4	59.8
07	282 09.7	40.1	282 53.8	8.6	9 03.1	11.5	59.8
08	297 09.9	39.2	297 21.4	8.5	8 51.6	11.6	59.9
F 09	312 10.0	·· 38.2	311 48.9	8.6	8 40.0	11.6	59.9
R 10	327 10.2	37.2	326 16.5	8.6	8 28.4	11.7	59.9
I 11	342 10.3	36.3	340 44.1	8.6	8 16.7	11.7	59.9
D 12	357 10.4	S 5 35.3	355 11.7	8.6	S 8 05.0	11.8	60.0
A 13	12 10.6	34.3	9 39.3	8.6	7 53.2	11.9	60.0
Y 14	27 10.7	33.3	24 06.9	8.6	7 41.3	11.9	60.0
15	42 10.9	·· 32.4	38 34.5	8.7	7 29.4	12.0	60.0
16	57 11.0	31.4	53 02.2	8.6	7 17.4	12.0	60.0
17	72 11.2	30.4	67 29.8	8.7	7 05.4	12.1	60.1
18	87 11.3	S 5 29.5	81 57.5	8.6	S 6 53.3	12.1	60.1
19	102 11.5	28.5	96 25.1	8.7	6 41.2	12.1	60.1
20	117 11.6	27.5	110 52.8	8.7	6 29.1	12.2	60.1
21	132 11.8	·· 26.5	125 20.5	8.7	6 16.9	12.3	60.1
22	147 11.9	25.6	139 48.2	8.7	6 04.6	12.3	60.1
23	162 12.1	24.6	154 15.9	8.7	5 52.3	12.3	60.2
7 00	177 12.2	S 5 23.6	168 43.6	8.7	S 5 40.0	12.4	60.2
01	192 12.3	22.7	183 11.3	8.7	5 27.6	12.4	60.2
02	207 12.5	21.7	197 39.0	8.8	5 15.2	12.5	60.2
03	222 12.6	·· 20.7	212 06.8	8.7	5 02.7	12.5	60.2
04	237 12.8	19.7	226 34.5	8.7	4 50.2	12.5	60.2
05	252 12.9	18.8	241 02.2	8.8	4 37.7	12.6	60.2
06	267 13.1	S 5 17.8	255 30.0	8.7	S 4 25.1	12.6	60.3
07	282 13.2	16.8	269 57.7	8.8	4 12.5	12.6	60.3
S 08	297 13.4	15.9	284 25.5	8.7	3 59.9	12.7	60.3
A 09	312 13.5	·· 14.9	298 53.2	8.8	3 47.2	12.7	60.3
T 10	327 13.7	13.9	313 21.0	8.7	3 34.5	12.7	60.3
U 11	342 13.8	12.9	327 48.8	8.7	3 21.8	12.7	60.3
R 12	357 14.0	S 5 12.0	342 16.5	8.8	S 3 09.1	12.8	60.3
D 13	12 14.1	11.0	356 44.3	8.8	2 56.3	12.8	60.3
A 14	27 14.3	10.0	11 12.1	8.7	2 43.5	12.8	60.4
Y 15	42 14.4	·· 09.0	25 39.9	8.8	2 30.7	12.8	60.4
16	57 14.6	08.1	40 07.7	8.8	2 17.9	12.8	60.4
17	72 14.7	07.1	54 35.5	8.8	2 05.1	12.9	60.4
18	87 14.9	S 5 06.1	69 03.3	8.7	S 1 52.2	12.9	60.4
19	102 15.0	05.2	83 31.0	8.8	1 39.3	12.8	60.4
20	117 15.2	04.2	97 58.8	8.8	1 26.5	12.9	60.4
21	132 15.3	·· 03.2	112 26.6	8.8	1 13.6	12.9	60.4
22	147 15.5	02.2	126 54.4	8.8	1 00.7	13.0	60.4
23	162 15.6	01.3	141 22.2	8.8	0 47.7	12.9	60.4
	S.D. 16.1　d 1.0		S.D. 16.2		16.3		16.4

Lat.	Naut.	Civil	Sunrise	Moonrise 5	6	7	8
N 72	04 45	06 04	07 11	08 24	08 08	07 54	07 42
N 70	04 53	06 04	07 05	08 00	07 54	07 49	07 43
68	04 59	06 04	06 59	07 41	07 43	07 44	07 44
66	05 04	06 03	06 54	07 26	07 34	07 40	07 45
64	05 08	06 03	06 51	07 14	07 26	07 37	07 46
62	05 12	06 03	06 47	07 03	07 20	07 34	07 47
60	05 15	06 03	06 44	06 54	07 14	07 31	07 47
N 58	05 17	06 02	06 42	06 46	07 09	07 29	07 48
56	05 19	06 02	06 39	06 39	07 04	07 27	07 48
54	05 21	06 02	06 37	06 33	07 00	07 25	07 49
52	05 22	06 01	06 35	06 27	06 56	07 23	07 49
50	05 24	06 01	06 33	06 22	06 53	07 22	07 49
45	05 26	06 00	06 29	06 11	06 46	07 18	07 50
N 40	05 28	05 59	06 26	06 01	06 39	07 16	07 51
35	05 29	05 58	06 23	05 53	06 34	07 13	07 51
30	05 29	05 57	06 21	05 46	06 29	07 11	07 52
20	05 28	05 54	06 16	05 34	06 21	07 07	07 53
N 10	05 26	05 51	06 12	05 23	06 14	07 04	07 54
0	05 23	05 47	06 08	05 13	06 07	07 01	07 54
S 10	05 18	05 43	06 04	05 03	06 00	06 58	07 55
20	05 11	05 37	05 59	04 52	05 53	06 54	07 56
30	05 02	05 30	05 54	04 40	05 45	06 51	07 57
35	04 56	05 26	05 51	04 32	05 40	06 49	07 58
40	04 48	05 20	05 48	04 24	05 35	06 46	07 58
45	04 38	05 14	05 44	04 15	05 28	06 43	07 59
S 50	04 26	05 06	05 39	04 03	05 20	06 40	08 00
52	04 20	05 02	05 37	03 58	05 17	06 38	08 01
54	04 13	04 58	05 34	03 52	05 13	06 37	08 01
56	04 06	04 53	05 31	03 45	05 09	06 35	08 02
58	03 57	04 47	05 28	03 37	05 04	06 33	08 03
S 60	03 46	04 41	05 25	03 29	04 58	06 30	08 03

Lat.	Sunset	Civil	Naut.	Moonset 5	6	7	8
N 72	17 14	18 21	19 41	14 47	16 57	19 04	21 09
N 70	17 20	18 21	19 33	15 10	17 09	19 06	21 04
68	17 25	18 21	19 26	15 27	17 18	19 08	20 59
66	17 30	18 21	19 21	15 41	17 25	19 10	20 55
64	17 33	18 21	19 16	15 52	17 31	19 12	20 52
62	17 37	18 21	19 13	16 02	17 37	19 13	20 49
60	17 40	18 21	19 10	16 10	17 41	19 14	20 47
N 58	17 42	18 21	19 07	16 18	17 45	19 15	20 45
56	17 44	18 22	19 05	16 24	17 49	19 16	20 43
54	17 47	18 22	19 03	16 30	17 52	19 17	20 41
52	17 48	18 22	19 01	16 35	17 55	19 17	20 40
50	17 50	18 22	19 00	16 39	17 58	19 18	20 38
45	17 54	18 23	18 57	16 49	18 04	19 19	20 35
N 40	17 57	18 24	18 56	16 57	18 08	19 20	20 33
35	18 00	18 25	18 55	17 04	18 13	19 21	20 31
30	18 02	18 26	18 54	17 11	18 16	19 22	20 29
20	18 07	18 29	18 54	17 21	18 22	19 24	20 25
N 10	18 11	18 32	18 56	17 30	18 28	19 25	20 22
0	18 15	18 35	18 59	17 39	18 33	19 26	20 20
S 10	18 19	18 40	19 04	17 47	18 38	19 27	20 17
20	18 23	18 45	19 11	17 56	18 43	19 29	20 14
30	18 28	18 52	19 20	18 07	18 49	19 30	20 11
35	18 31	18 56	19 26	18 12	18 52	19 31	20 09
40	18 34	19 01	19 34	18 19	18 56	19 31	20 06
45	18 38	19 08	19 43	18 27	19 00	19 32	20 04
S 50	18 43	19 16	19 55	18 36	19 06	19 33	20 01
52	18 45	19 19	20 01	18 40	19 08	19 34	20 00
54	18 47	19 24	20 08	18 45	19 11	19 34	19 58
56	18 50	19 28	20 15	18 50	19 13	19 35	19 56
58	18 53	19 33	20 24	18 55	19 17	19 36	19 55
S 60	18 56	19 40	20 34	19 02	19 20	19 36	19 52

Day	SUN Eqn. of Time 00h	12h	Mer. Pass.	MOON Mer. Pass. Upper	Lower	Age	Phase
	m s	m s	h m	h m	h m	d	
5	11 39	11 32	12 12	11 26	23 53	29	●
6	11 25	11 19	12 11	12 20	24 47	00	
7	11 11	11 04	12 11	13 14	00 47	01	

G.M.T.	ARIES G.H.A.	VENUS −3.4 G.H.A.	Dec.	MARS +1.4 G.H.A.	Dec.	JUPITER −2.0 G.H.A.	Dec.	SATURN +0.7 G.H.A.	Dec.	STARS Name	S.H.A.	Dec.
8 00	165 36.6	183 51.2	S 9 13.7	171 48.1	S 3 36.8	337 52.3	S 1 38.0	337 19.9	S 0 43.0	Acamar	315 37.2	S40 23.2
01	180 39.1	198 50.7	12.6	186 48.8	36.0	352 55.1	37.9	352 22.5	42.9	Achernar	335 45.5	S57 20.3
02	195 41.5	213 50.2	11.4	201 49.4	35.2	7 57.8	37.7	7 25.2	42.8	Acrux	173 36.2	S62 59.6
03	210 44.0	228 49.7	·· 10.3	216 50.1	·· 34.4	23 00.5	·· 37.6	22 27.8	·· 42.7	Adhara	255 31.7	S28 57.1
04	225 46.4	243 49.3	09.1	231 50.8	33.6	38 03.2	37.5	37 30.4	42.7	Aldebaran	291 17.7	N16 28.2
05	240 48.9	258 48.8	08.0	246 51.4	32.8	53 06.0	37.4	52 33.0	42.6			
06	255 51.4	273 48.3	S 9 06.8	261 52.1	S 3 32.0	68 08.7	S 1 37.3	67 35.7	S 0 42.5	Alioth	166 41.7	N56 03.6
07	270 53.8	288 47.9	05.6	276 52.8	31.3	83 11.4	37.2	82 38.3	42.4	Alkaid	153 17.9	N49 24.3
08	285 56.3	303 47.4	04.5	291 53.5	30.5	98 14.1	37.0	97 40.9	42.4	Al Na'ir	28 15.0	S47 03.2
S 09	300 58.8	318 46.9	·· 03.3	306 54.1	·· 29.7	113 16.9	·· 36.9	112 43.5	·· 42.3	Alnilam	276 11.3	S 1 13.0
U 10	316 01.2	333 46.5	02.2	321 54.8	28.9	128 19.6	36.8	127 46.2	42.2	Alphard	218 20.0	S 8 34.7
N 11	331 03.7	348 46.0	9 01.0	336 55.5	28.1	143 22.3	36.7	142 48.8	42.1			
D 12	346 06.2	3 45.5	S 8 59.9	351 56.1	S 3 27.3	158 25.0	S 1 36.6	157 51.4	S 0 42.1	Alphecca	126 31.7	N26 46.5
A 13	1 08.6	18 45.1	58.7	6 56.8	26.5	173 27.8	36.4	172 54.0	42.0	Alpheratz	358 09.3	N28 59.0
Y 14	16 11.1	33 44.6	57.5	21 57.5	25.7	188 30.5	36.3	187 56.6	41.9	Altair	62 32.4	N 8 48.9
15	31 13.6	48 44.1	·· 56.4	36 58.1	·· 24.9	203 33.2	·· 36.2	202 59.3	·· 41.8	Ankaa	353 40.3	S42 24.8
16	46 16.0	63 43.7	55.2	51 58.8	24.1	218 35.9	36.1	218 01.9	41.8	Antares	112 56.4	S26 23.3
17	61 18.5	78 43.2	54.1	66 59.5	23.3	233 38.7	36.0	233 04.5	41.7			
18	76 20.9	93 42.7	S 8 52.9	82 00.2	S 3 22.5	248 41.4	S 1 35.9	248 07.1	S 0 41.6	Arcturus	146 18.0	N19 16.7
19	91 23.4	108 42.3	51.7	97 00.8	21.8	263 44.1	35.7	263 09.8	41.5	Atria	108 20.3	S68 59.3
20	106 25.9	123 41.8	50.6	112 01.5	21.0	278 46.9	35.6	278 12.4	41.5	Avior	234 27.6	S59 27.2
21	121 28.3	138 41.4	·· 49.4	127 02.2	·· 20.2	293 49.6	·· 35.5	293 15.0	·· 41.4	Bellatrix	278 58.4	N 6 19.8
22	136 30.8	153 40.9	48.2	142 02.8	19.4	308 52.3	35.4	308 17.6	41.3	Betelgeuse	271 27.9	N 7 24.1
23	151 33.3	168 40.4	47.1	157 03.5	18.6	323 55.0	35.3	323 20.3	41.2			
9 00	166 35.7	183 40.0	S 8 45.9	172 04.2	S 3 17.8	338 57.8	S 1 35.1	338 22.9	S 0 41.2	Canopus	264 06.9	S52 41.5
01	181 38.2	198 39.5	44.8	187 04.9	17.0	354 00.5	35.0	353 25.5	41.1	Capella	281 10.8	N45 58.8
02	196 40.7	213 39.0	43.6	202 05.5	16.2	9 03.2	34.9	8 28.2	41.0	Deneb	49 48.6	N45 12.5
03	211 43.1	228 38.6	·· 42.4	217 06.2	·· 15.4	24 05.9	·· 34.8	23 30.8	·· 40.9	Denebola	182 58.4	N14 40.6
04	226 45.6	243 38.1	41.3	232 06.9	14.6	39 08.7	34.7	38 33.4	40.9	Diphda	349 20.9	S18 05.6
05	241 48.1	258 37.7	40.1	247 07.6	13.8	54 11.4	34.5	53 36.0	40.8			
06	256 50.5	273 37.2	S 8 38.9	262 08.2	S 3 13.0	69 14.1	S 1 34.4	68 38.7	S 0 40.7	Dubhe	194 21.1	N61 51.2
07	271 53.0	288 36.7	37.8	277 08.9	12.3	84 16.9	34.3	83 41.3	40.6	Elnath	278 43.7	N28 35.5
08	286 55.4	303 36.3	36.6	292 09.6	11.5	99 19.6	34.2	98 43.9	40.6	Eltanin	90 57.7	N51 29.2
M 09	301 57.9	318 35.8	·· 35.4	307 10.2	·· 10.7	114 22.3	·· 34.1	113 46.5	·· 40.5	Enif	34 11.6	N 9 47.1
O 10	317 00.4	333 35.4	34.3	322 10.9	09.9	129 25.0	34.0	128 49.2	40.4	Fomalhaut	15 51.4	S29 43.5
N 11	332 02.8	348 34.9	33.1	337 11.6	09.1	144 27.8	33.8	143 51.8	40.3			
D 12	347 05.3	3 34.4	S 8 31.9	352 12.3	S 3 08.3	159 30.5	S 1 33.7	158 54.4	S 0 40.3	Gacrux	172 27.8	S57 00.4
A 13	2 07.8	18 34.0	30.8	7 12.9	07.5	174 33.2	33.6	173 57.0	40.2	Gienah	176 17.3	S17 26.3
Y 14	17 10.2	33 33.5	29.6	22 13.6	06.7	189 36.0	33.5	188 59.7	40.1	Hadar	149 22.4	S60 16.7
15	32 12.7	48 33.1	·· 28.4	37 14.3	·· 05.9	204 38.7	·· 33.4	204 02.3	·· 40.0	Hamal	328 28.8	N23 22.3
16	47 15.2	63 32.6	27.2	52 15.0	05.1	219 41.4	33.2	219 04.9	40.0	Kaus Aust.	84 16.5	S34 23.6
17	62 17.6	78 32.2	26.1	67 15.6	04.3	234 44.2	33.1	234 07.5	39.9			
18	77 20.1	93 31.7	S 8 24.9	82 16.3	S 3 03.5	249 46.9	S 1 33.0	249 10.2	S 0 39.8	Kochab	137 18.4	N74 13.8
19	92 22.5	108 31.2	23.7	97 17.0	02.7	264 49.6	32.9	264 12.8	39.7	Markab	14 03.2	N15 06.0
20	107 25.0	123 30.8	22.6	112 17.7	02.0	279 52.3	32.8	279 15.4	39.6	Menkar	314 41.0	N 4 00.8
21	122 27.5	138 30.3	·· 21.4	127 18.3	·· 01.2	294 55.1	·· 32.6	294 18.0	·· 39.6	Menkent	148 36.4	S36 16.5
22	137 29.9	153 29.9	20.2	142 19.0	3 00.4	309 57.8	32.5	309 20.7	39.5	Miaplacidus	221 44.1	S69 38.6
23	152 32.4	168 29.4	19.0	157 19.7	2 59.6	325 00.5	32.4	324 23.3	39.4			
10 00	167 34.9	183 29.0	S 8 17.9	172 20.3	S 2 58.8	340 03.3	S 1 32.3	339 25.9	S 0 39.3	Mirfak	309 15.9	N49 47.7
01	182 37.3	198 28.5	16.7	187 21.0	58.0	355 06.0	32.2	354 28.6	39.3	Nunki	76 28.9	S26 19.2
02	197 39.8	213 28.1	15.5	202 21.7	57.2	10 08.7	32.0	9 31.2	39.2	Peacock	53 58.3	S56 47.7
03	212 42.3	228 27.6	·· 14.3	217 22.4	·· 56.4	25 11.5	·· 31.9	24 33.8	·· 39.1	Pollux	243 57.6	N28 04.3
04	227 44.7	243 27.2	13.2	232 23.0	55.6	40 14.2	31.8	39 36.4	39.0	Procyon	245 25.3	N 5 16.3
05	242 47.2	258 26.7	12.0	247 23.7	54.8	55 16.9	31.7	54 39.1	39.0			
06	257 49.7	273 26.3	S 8 10.8	262 24.4	S 2 54.0	70 19.7	S 1 31.6	69 41.7	S 0 38.9	Rasalhague	96 29.3	N12 34.3
07	272 52.1	288 25.8	09.6	277 25.1	53.2	85 22.4	31.4	84 44.3	38.8	Regulus	208 09.4	N12 03.5
08	287 54.6	303 25.3	08.5	292 25.7	52.4	100 25.1	31.3	99 46.9	38.7	Rigel	281 35.7	S 8 13.6
T 09	302 57.0	318 24.9	·· 07.3	307 26.4	·· 51.7	115 27.9	·· 31.2	114 49.6	·· 38.7	Rigil Kent.	140 25.0	S60 45.2
U 10	317 59.5	333 24.4	06.1	322 27.1	50.9	130 30.6	31.1	129 52.2	38.6	Sabik	102 40.8	S15 42.1
E 11	333 02.0	348 24.0	04.9	337 27.8	50.1	145 33.3	30.9	144 54.8	38.5			
S D 12	348 04.4	3 23.5	S 8 03.8	352 28.4	S 2 49.3	160 36.1	S 1 30.8	159 57.5	S 0 38.4	Schedar	350 09.2	N56 26.0
A 13	3 06.9	18 23.1	02.6	7 29.1	48.5	175 38.8	30.7	175 00.1	38.4	Shaula	96 55.4	S37 05.3
Y 14	18 09.4	33 22.6	01.4	22 29.8	47.7	190 41.5	30.6	190 02.7	38.3	Sirius	258 55.3	S16 41.7
15	33 11.8	48 22.2	8 00.2	37 30.5	·· 46.9	205 44.3	·· 30.5	205 05.3	·· 38.2	Spica	158 56.9	S11 03.8
16	48 14.3	63 21.7	7 59.0	52 31.1	46.1	220 47.0	30.3	220 08.0	38.1	Suhail	223 10.2	S43 21.6
17	63 16.8	78 21.3	57.9	67 31.8	45.3	235 49.7	30.2	235 10.6	38.1			
18	78 19.2	93 20.9	S 7 56.7	82 32.5	S 2 44.5	250 52.5	S 1 30.1	250 13.2	S 0 38.0	Vega	80 55.8	N38 45.7
19	93 21.7	108 20.4	55.5	97 33.2	43.7	265 55.2	30.0	265 15.9	37.9	Zuben'ubi	137 32.5	S15 57.8
20	108 24.2	123 20.0	54.3	112 33.8	42.9	280 57.9	29.9	280 18.5	37.8			
21	123 26.6	138 19.5	·· 53.1	127 34.5	·· 42.1	296 00.7	·· 29.7	295 21.1	·· 37.7		S.H.A.	Mer. Pass.
22	138 29.1	153 19.1	52.0	142 35.2	41.3	311 03.4	29.6	310 23.7	37.7	Venus	17 04.2	11 46
23	153 31.5	168 18.6	50.8	157 35.9	40.6	326 06.1	29.5	325 26.4	37.6	Mars	5 28.5	12 31
										Jupiter	172 22.0	1 24
Mer. Pass. 12 51.5		v −0.5	d 1.2	v 0.7	d 0.8	v 2.7	d 0.1	v 2.6	d 0.1	Saturn	171 47.2	1 26

G.M.T.	SUN G.H.A.	SUN Dec.	MOON G.H.A.	v	Dec.	d	H.P.
8 00	177 15.8	S 5 00.3	155 50.0	8.8	S 0 34.8	12.9	60.4
01	192 15.9	4 59.3	170 17.8	8.8	0 21.9	12.9	60.4
02	207 16.1	58.3	184 45.6	8.7	S 0 09.0	13.0	60.4
03	222 16.2	·· 57.4	199 13.3	8.8	N 0 04.0	12.9	60.4
04	237 16.4	56.4	213 41.1	8.8	0 16.9	12.9	60.4
05	252 16.6	55.4	228 08.9	8.8	0 29.8	13.0	60.4
06	267 16.7	S 4 54.4	242 36.7	8.7	N 0 42.8	12.9	60.4
07	282 16.9	53.5	257 04.4	8.8	0 55.7	12.9	60.4
08	297 17.0	52.5	271 32.2	8.8	1 08.6	12.9	60.5
S 09	312 17.2	·· 51.5	286 00.0	8.7	1 21.5	12.9	60.5
U 10	327 17.3	50.5	300 27.7	8.8	1 34.4	12.9	60.5
N 11	342 17.5	49.6	314 55.5	8.7	1 47.3	12.9	60.5
D 12	357 17.6	S 4 48.6	329 23.2	8.7	N 2 00.2	12.9	60.5
A 13	12 17.8	47.6	343 50.9	8.8	2 13.1	12.8	60.5
Y 14	27 17.9	46.6	358 18.7	8.7	2 25.9	12.9	60.5
15	42 18.1	·· 45.7	12 46.4	8.7	2 38.8	12.8	60.5
16	57 18.2	44.7	27 14.1	8.7	2 51.6	12.8	60.5
17	72 18.4	43.7	41 41.8	8.7	3 04.4	12.8	60.5
18	87 18.6	S 4 42.7	56 09.5	8.7	N 3 17.2	12.8	60.4
19	102 18.7	41.8	70 37.2	8.6	3 30.0	12.7	60.4
20	117 18.9	40.8	85 04.8	8.7	3 42.7	12.7	60.4
21	132 19.0	·· 39.8	99 32.5	8.6	3 55.4	12.7	60.4
22	147 19.2	38.8	114 00.1	8.7	4 08.1	12.7	60.4
23	162 19.3	37.8	128 27.8	8.6	4 20.8	12.6	60.4
9 00	177 19.5	S 4 36.9	142 55.4	8.6	N 4 33.4	12.6	60.4
01	192 19.6	35.9	157 23.0	8.6	4 46.0	12.6	60.4
02	207 19.8	34.9	171 50.6	8.6	4 58.6	12.5	60.4
03	222 20.0	·· 33.9	186 18.2	8.6	5 11.1	12.5	60.4
04	237 20.1	33.0	200 45.8	8.5	5 23.6	12.5	60.4
05	252 20.3	32.0	215 13.3	8.6	5 36.1	12.4	60.4
06	267 20.4	S 4 31.0	229 40.9	8.5	N 5 48.5	12.4	60.4
07	282 20.6	30.0	244 08.4	8.5	6 00.9	12.3	60.4
08	297 20.7	29.1	258 35.9	8.5	6 13.2	12.3	60.4
M 09	312 20.9	·· 28.1	273 03.4	8.5	6 25.5	12.3	60.4
O 10	327 21.1	27.1	287 30.9	8.5	6 37.8	12.2	60.4
N 11	342 21.2	26.1	301 58.4	8.5	6 50.0	12.2	60.4
D 12	357 21.4	S 4 25.1	316 25.9	8.4	N 7 02.2	12.1	60.3
A 13	12 21.5	24.2	330 53.3	8.4	7 14.3	12.1	60.3
Y 14	27 21.7	23.2	345 20.7	8.4	7 26.4	12.0	60.3
15	42 21.8	·· 22.2	359 48.1	8.4	7 38.4	12.0	60.3
16	57 22.0	21.2	14 15.5	8.4	7 50.4	11.9	60.3
17	72 22.2	20.2	28 42.9	8.3	8 02.3	11.9	60.3
18	87 22.3	S 4 19.3	43 10.2	8.3	N 8 14.2	11.8	60.3
19	102 22.5	18.3	57 37.5	8.3	8 26.0	11.7	60.3
20	117 22.6	17.3	72 04.8	8.3	8 37.7	11.7	60.3
21	132 22.8	·· 16.3	86 32.1	8.3	8 49.4	11.6	60.2
22	147 23.0	15.4	100 59.4	8.3	9 01.0	11.6	60.2
23	162 23.1	14.4	115 26.7	8.2	9 12.6	11.5	60.2
10 00	177 23.3	S 4 13.4	129 53.9	8.2	N 9 24.1	11.4	60.2
01	192 23.4	12.4	144 21.1	8.2	9 35.5	11.4	60.2
02	207 23.6	11.4	158 48.3	8.2	9 46.9	11.3	60.2
03	222 23.7	·· 10.5	173 15.5	8.1	9 58.2	11.3	60.2
04	237 23.9	09.5	187 42.6	8.1	10 09.5	11.1	60.1
05	252 24.1	08.5	202 09.7	8.1	10 20.6	11.1	60.1
06	267 24.2	S 4 07.5	216 36.8	8.1	N10 31.7	11.1	60.1
07	282 24.4	06.5	231 03.9	8.1	10 42.8	10.9	60.1
08	297 24.6	05.6	245 31.0	8.0	10 53.7	10.9	60.1
T 09	312 24.7	·· 04.6	259 58.0	8.0	11 04.6	10.8	60.1
U 10	327 24.9	03.6	274 25.0	8.0	11 15.4	10.7	60.1
E 11	342 25.0	02.6	288 52.0	8.0	11 26.1	10.7	60.0
S 12	357 25.2	S 4 01.6	303 19.0	7.9	N11 36.8	10.6	60.0
D 13	12 25.4	4 00.7	317 45.9	8.0	11 47.4	10.5	60.0
A 14	27 25.5	3 59.7	332 12.9	7.9	11 57.9	10.4	60.0
Y 15	42 25.7	·· 58.7	346 39.8	7.9	12 08.3	10.3	60.0
16	57 25.8	57.7	1 06.7	7.8	12 18.6	10.3	59.9
17	72 26.0	56.7	15 33.5	7.9	12 28.9	10.1	59.9
18	87 26.2	S 3 55.8	30 00.4	7.8	N12 39.0	10.1	59.9
19	102 26.3	54.8	44 27.2	7.8	12 49.1	10.0	59.9
20	117 26.5	53.8	58 54.0	7.7	12 59.1	9.9	59.9
21	132 26.7	·· 52.8	73 20.7	7.8	13 09.0	9.8	59.9
22	147 26.8	51.8	87 47.5	7.7	13 18.8	9.7	59.8
23	162 27.0	50.8	102 14.2	7.7	13 28.5	9.7	59.8
	S.D. 16.1	d 1.0	S.D. 16.5		16.4		16.4

Lat.	Twilight Naut.	Civil	Sunrise	Moonrise 8	9	10	11
N 72	04 29	05 49	06 56	07 42	07 30	07 16	06 57
N 70	04 38	05 50	06 51	07 43	07 38	07 33	07 27
68	04 46	05 51	06 47	07 44	07 45	07 46	07 49
66	04 52	05 52	06 43	07 45	07 51	07 57	08 07
64	04 58	05 53	06 40	07 46	07 55	08 07	08 21
62	05 02	05 54	06 38	07 47	08 00	08 15	08 33
60	05 06	05 54	06 35	07 47	08 03	08 22	08 44
N 58	05 09	05 54	06 33	07 48	08 07	08 28	08 53
56	05 11	05 55	06 31	07 48	08 10	08 33	09 01
54	05 14	05 55	06 30	07 49	08 12	08 38	09 08
52	05 16	05 55	06 28	07 49	08 15	08 43	09 14
50	05 17	05 55	06 27	07 49	08 17	08 47	09 20
45	05 21	05 55	06 24	07 50	08 22	08 56	09 33
N 40	05 23	05 54	06 21	07 51	08 26	09 03	09 43
35	05 25	05 54	06 19	07 51	08 30	09 10	09 52
30	05 26	05 53	06 17	07 52	08 33	09 15	10 00
20	05 26	05 52	06 14	07 53	08 38	09 25	10 14
N 10	05 25	05 49	06 10	07 54	08 43	09 34	10 26
0	05 22	05 47	06 07	07 54	08 48	09 42	10 38
S 10	05 18	05 43	06 04	07 55	08 53	09 51	10 49
20	05 13	05 38	06 00	07 56	08 58	10 00	11 01
30	05 04	05 32	05 56	07 57	09 04	10 10	11 16
35	04 58	05 28	05 54	07 58	09 07	10 16	11 24
40	04 51	05 24	05 51	07 58	09 11	10 23	11 33
45	04 43	05 18	05 48	07 59	09 15	10 31	11 44
S 50	04 32	05 11	05 44	08 00	09 21	10 40	11 58
52	04 26	05 08	05 42	08 01	09 23	10 45	12 04
54	04 20	05 04	05 40	08 01	09 26	10 50	12 11
56	04 13	05 00	05 38	08 02	09 29	10 55	12 19
58	04 05	04 55	05 35	08 03	09 32	11 01	12 28
S 60	03 56	04 49	05 32	08 03	09 36	11 08	12 38

Lat.	Sunset	Twilight Civil	Naut.	Moonset 8	9	10	11
N 72	17 28	18 35	19 56	21 09	23 17	25 31	01 31
N 70	17 32	18 33	19 46	21 04	23 02	25 03	01 03
68	17 36	18 32	19 38	20 59	22 50	24 42	00 42
66	17 40	18 31	19 31	20 55	22 41	24 25	00 25
64	17 43	18 30	19 26	20 52	22 33	24 12	00 12
62	17 45	18 29	19 21	20 49	22 26	24 00	00 00
60	17 47	18 29	19 17	20 47	22 20	23 51	25 18
N 58	17 49	18 28	19 14	20 45	22 14	23 42	25 06
56	17 51	18 28	19 11	20 43	22 10	23 35	24 56
54	17 52	18 28	19 09	20 41	22 06	23 28	24 48
52	17 54	18 27	19 07	20 40	22 02	23 23	24 40
50	17 55	18 27	19 05	20 38	21 59	23 17	24 33
45	17 58	18 27	19 01	20 35	21 51	23 06	24 18
N 40	18 00	18 27	18 59	20 33	21 45	22 56	24 06
35	18 02	18 28	18 57	20 31	21 40	22 48	23 55
30	18 04	18 28	18 56	20 29	21 35	22 41	23 45
20	18 08	18 30	18 55	20 25	21 27	22 29	23 31
N 10	18 11	18 32	18 56	20 22	21 20	22 18	23 17
0	18 14	18 35	18 59	20 20	21 14	22 08	23 04
S 10	18 17	18 38	19 03	20 17	21 07	21 59	22 52
20	18 20	18 42	19 08	20 14	21 00	21 49	22 38
30	18 24	18 48	19 17	20 11	20 52	21 36	22 22
35	18 27	18 52	19 22	20 09	20 48	21 29	22 13
40	18 29	18 57	19 29	20 06	20 43	21 21	22 03
45	18 33	19 02	19 37	20 04	20 37	21 12	21 51
S 50	18 36	19 09	19 48	20 01	20 30	21 01	21 37
52	18 38	19 12	19 54	20 00	20 26	20 56	21 30
54	18 40	19 16	20 00	19 58	20 23	20 50	21 22
56	18 42	19 20	20 06	19 56	20 19	20 44	21 14
58	18 45	19 25	20 14	19 55	20 14	20 37	21 05
S 60	18 47	19 30	20 23	19 52	20 09	20 29	20 54

Day	SUN Eqn. of Time 00h	12h	Mer. Pass.	MOON Mer. Pass. Upper	Lower	Age	Phase
	m s	m s	h m	h m	h m	d	
8	10 57	10 50	12 11	14 07	01 40	02	
9	10 42	10 35	12 11	15 01	02 34	03	◑
10	10 27	10 20	12 10	15 55	03 28	04	

G.M.T.	ARIES G.H.A.	VENUS −3.4 G.H.A.	VENUS Dec.	MARS +1.3 G.H.A.	MARS Dec.	JUPITER −2.0 G.H.A.	JUPITER Dec.	SATURN +0.7 G.H.A.	SATURN Dec.
11 00	168 34.0	183 18.2	S 7 49.6	172 36.6	S 2 39.8	341 08.9	S 1 29.4	340 29.0	S 0 37.5
01	183 36.5	198 17.7	48.4	187 37.2	39.0	356 11.6	29.3	355 31.6	37.4
02	198 38.9	213 17.3	47.2	202 37.9	38.2	11 14.3	29.1	10 34.3	37.4
03	213 41.4	228 16.8	·· 46.1	217 38.6	·· 37.4	26 17.1	·· 29.0	25 36.9	·· 37.3
04	228 43.9	243 16.4	44.9	232 39.3	36.6	41 19.8	28.9	40 39.5	37.2
05	243 46.3	258 15.9	43.7	247 39.9	35.8	56 22.5	28.8	55 42.1	37.1
06	258 48.8	273 15.5	S 7 42.5	262 40.6	S 2 35.0	71 25.3	S 1 28.6	70 44.8	S 0 37.1
W 07	273 51.3	288 15.1	41.3	277 41.3	34.2	86 28.0	28.5	85 47.4	37.0
E 08	288 53.7	303 14.6	40.1	292 42.0	33.4	101 30.7	28.4	100 50.0	36.9
D 09	303 56.2	318 14.2	·· 38.9	307 42.6	·· 32.6	116 33.5	·· 28.3	115 52.7	·· 36.8
N 10	318 58.6	333 13.7	37.8	322 43.3	31.8	131 36.2	28.2	130 55.3	36.8
E 11	334 01.1	348 13.3	36.6	337 44.0	31.0	146 38.9	28.0	145 57.9	36.7
S 12	349 03.6	3 12.8	S 7 35.4	352 44.7	S 2 30.2	161 41.7	S 1 27.9	161 00.5	S 0 36.6
D 13	4 06.0	18 12.4	34.2	7 45.4	29.4	176 44.4	27.8	176 03.2	36.5
A 14	19 08.5	33 12.0	33.0	22 46.0	28.7	191 47.2	27.7	191 05.8	36.4
Y 15	34 11.0	48 11.5	·· 31.8	37 46.7	·· 27.9	206 49.9	·· 27.5	206 08.4	·· 36.4
16	49 13.4	63 11.1	30.6	52 47.4	27.1	221 52.6	27.4	221 11.1	36.3
17	64 15.9	78 10.6	29.5	67 48.1	26.3	236 55.4	27.3	236 13.7	36.2
18	79 18.4	93 10.2	S 7 28.3	82 48.7	S 2 25.5	251 58.1	S 1 27.2	251 16.3	S 0 36.1
19	94 20.8	108 09.8	27.1	97 49.4	24.7	267 00.8	27.1	266 19.0	36.1
20	109 23.3	123 09.3	25.9	112 50.1	23.9	282 03.6	26.9	281 21.6	36.0
21	124 25.8	138 08.9	·· 24.7	127 50.8	·· 23.1	297 06.3	·· 26.8	296 24.2	·· 35.9
22	139 28.2	153 08.4	23.5	142 51.5	22.3	312 09.0	26.7	311 26.8	35.8
23	154 30.7	168 08.0	22.3	157 52.1	21.5	327 11.8	26.6	326 29.5	35.8
12 00	169 33.1	183 07.6	S 7 21.1	172 52.8	S 2 20.7	342 14.5	S 1 26.4	341 32.1	S 0 35.7
01	184 35.6	198 07.1	19.9	187 53.5	19.9	357 17.3	26.3	356 34.7	35.6
02	199 38.1	213 06.7	18.7	202 54.2	19.1	12 20.0	26.2	11 37.4	35.5
03	214 40.5	228 06.2	·· 17.6	217 54.8	·· 18.3	27 22.7	·· 26.1	26 40.0	·· 35.4
04	229 43.0	243 05.8	16.4	232 55.5	17.6	42 25.5	26.0	41 42.6	35.4
05	244 45.5	258 05.4	15.2	247 56.2	16.8	57 28.2	25.8	56 45.3	35.3
06	259 47.9	273 04.9	S 7 14.0	262 56.9	S 2 16.0	72 31.0	S 1 25.7	71 47.9	S 0 35.2
07	274 50.4	288 04.5	12.8	277 57.6	15.2	87 33.7	25.6	86 50.5	35.1
T 08	289 52.9	303 04.1	11.6	292 58.2	14.4	102 36.4	25.5	101 53.2	35.1
H 09	304 55.3	318 03.6	·· 10.4	307 58.9	·· 13.6	117 39.2	·· 25.3	116 55.8	·· 35.0
U 10	319 57.8	333 03.2	09.2	322 59.6	12.8	132 41.9	25.2	131 58.4	34.9
R 11	335 00.3	348 02.7	08.0	338 00.3	12.0	147 44.6	25.1	147 01.0	34.8
S 12	350 02.7	3 02.3	S 7 06.8	353 01.0	S 2 11.2	162 47.4	S 1 25.0	162 03.7	S 0 34.8
D 13	5 05.2	18 01.9	05.6	8 01.6	10.4	177 50.1	24.9	177 06.3	34.7
A 14	20 07.6	33 01.4	04.4	23 02.3	09.6	192 52.9	24.7	192 08.9	34.6
Y 15	35 10.1	48 01.0	·· 03.2	38 03.0	·· 08.8	207 55.6	·· 24.6	207 11.6	·· 34.5
16	50 12.6	63 00.6	02.0	53 03.7	08.0	222 58.3	24.5	222 14.2	34.4
17	65 15.0	78 00.1	7 00.8	68 04.3	07.2	238 01.1	24.4	237 16.8	34.4
18	80 17.5	92 59.7	S 6 59.6	83 05.0	S 2 06.4	253 03.8	S 1 24.2	252 19.5	S 0 34.3
19	95 20.0	107 59.3	58.4	98 05.7	05.6	268 06.6	24.1	267 22.1	34.2
20	110 22.4	122 58.8	57.2	113 06.4	04.9	283 09.3	24.0	282 24.7	34.1
21	125 24.9	137 58.4	·· 56.1	128 07.1	·· 04.1	298 12.0	·· 23.9	297 27.4	·· 34.1
22	140 27.4	152 58.0	54.9	143 07.7	03.3	313 14.8	23.7	312 30.0	34.0
23	155 29.8	167 57.5	53.7	158 08.4	02.5	328 17.5	23.6	327 32.6	33.9
13 00	170 32.3	182 57.1	S 6 52.5	173 09.1	S 2 01.7	343 20.3	S 1 23.5	342 35.3	S 0 33.8
01	185 34.7	197 56.7	51.3	188 09.8	00.9	358 23.0	23.4	357 37.9	33.8
02	200 37.2	212 56.3	50.1	203 10.5	2 00.1	13 25.7	23.3	12 40.5	33.7
03	215 39.7	227 55.8	·· 48.9	218 11.1	1 59.3	28 28.5	·· 23.1	27 43.1	·· 33.6
04	230 42.1	242 55.4	47.7	233 11.8	58.5	43 31.2	23.0	42 45.8	33.5
05	245 44.6	257 55.0	46.5	248 12.5	57.7	58 34.0	22.9	57 48.4	33.4
06	260 47.1	272 54.5	S 6 45.3	263 13.2	S 1 56.9	73 36.7	S 1 22.8	72 51.0	S 0 33.4
07	275 49.5	287 54.1	44.1	278 13.9	56.1	88 39.4	22.6	87 53.7	33.3
08	290 52.0	302 53.7	42.9	293 14.6	55.3	103 42.2	22.5	102 56.3	33.2
F 09	305 54.5	317 53.2	·· 41.7	308 15.2	·· 54.5	118 44.9	·· 22.4	117 58.9	·· 33.1
R 10	320 56.9	332 52.8	40.5	323 15.9	53.7	133 47.7	22.3	133 01.6	33.1
I 11	335 59.4	347 52.4	39.3	338 16.6	53.0	148 50.4	22.1	148 04.2	33.0
D 12	351 01.9	2 52.0	S 6 38.1	353 17.3	S 1 52.2	163 53.2	S 1 22.0	163 06.8	S 0 32.9
A 13	6 04.3	17 51.5	36.9	8 18.0	51.4	178 55.9	21.9	178 09.5	32.8
Y 14	21 06.8	32 51.1	35.7	23 18.6	50.6	193 58.6	21.8	193 12.1	32.7
15	36 09.2	47 50.7	·· 34.4	38 19.3	·· 49.8	209 01.4	·· 21.6	208 14.7	·· 32.7
16	51 11.7	62 50.2	33.2	53 20.0	49.0	224 04.1	21.5	223 17.4	32.6
17	66 14.2	77 49.8	32.0	68 20.7	48.2	239 06.9	21.4	238 20.0	32.5
18	81 16.6	92 49.4	S 6 30.8	83 21.4	S 1 47.4	254 09.6	S 1 21.3	253 22.5	S 0 32.4
19	96 19.1	107 49.0	29.6	98 22.0	46.6	269 12.4	21.1	268 25.3	32.4
20	111 21.6	122 48.5	28.4	113 22.7	45.8	284 15.1	21.0	283 27.9	32.3
21	126 24.0	137 48.1	·· 27.2	128 23.4	·· 45.0	299 17.8	·· 20.9	298 30.5	·· 32.2
22	141 26.5	152 47.7	26.0	143 24.1	44.2	314 20.6	20.8	313 33.2	32.1
23	156 29.0	167 47.3	24.8	158 24.8	43.4	329 23.3	20.7	328 35.8	32.0
Mer. Pass.	12 39.7	v −0.4	d 1.2	v 0.7	d 0.8	v 2.7	d 0.1	v 2.6	d 0.1

STARS

Name	S.H.A.	Dec.
Acamar	315 37.2	S40 23.2
Achernar	335 45.5	S57 20.3
Acrux	173 36.2	S62 59.6
Adhara	255 31.7	S28 57.1
Aldebaran	291 17.7	N16 28.2
Alioth	166 41.7	N56 03.6
Alkaid	153 17.9	N49 24.3
Al Na'ir	28 15.0	S47 03.2
Alnilam	276 11.3	S 1 13.0
Alphard	218 20.0	S 8 34.7
Alphecca	126 31.7	N26 46.5
Alpheratz	358 09.3	N28 59.0
Altair	62 32.4	N 8 48.9
Ankaa	353 40.3	S42 24.7
Antares	112 56.4	S26 23.3
Arcturus	146 17.9	N19 16.7
Atria	108 20.3	S68 59.3
Avior	234 27.6	S59 27.2
Bellatrix	278 58.4	N 6 19.8
Betelgeuse	271 27.9	N 7 24.1
Canopus	264 06.9	S52 41.5
Capella	281 10.8	N45 58.8
Deneb	49 48.6	N45 12.5
Denebola	182 58.4	N14 40.6
Diphda	349 20.9	S18 05.6
Dubhe	194 21.1	N61 51.2
Elnath	278 43.7	N28 35.5
Eltanin	90 57.7	N51 29.2
Enif	34 11.6	N 9 47.1
Fomalhaut	15 51.4	S29 43.5
Gacrux	172 27.8	S57 00.4
Gienah	176 17.3	S17 26.3
Hadar	149 22.4	S60 16.7
Hamal	328 28.8	N23 22.3
Kaus Aust.	84 16.5	S34 23.5
Kochab	137 18.3	N74 13.8
Markab	14 03.2	N15 06.0
Menkar	314 41.0	N 4 00.8
Menkent	148 36.3	S36 16.5
Miaplacidus	221 44.1	S69 38.6
Mirfak	309 15.9	N49 47.7
Nunki	76 28.9	S26 19.2
Peacock	53 58.3	S56 47.7
Pollux	243 57.6	N28 04.3
Procyon	245 25.3	N 5 16.3
Rasalhague	96 29.3	N12 34.3
Regulus	208 09.4	N12 03.5
Rigel	281 35.7	S 8 13.6
Rigil Kent.	140 25.0	S60 45.2
Sabik	102 40.7	S15 42.1
Schedar	350 09.2	N56 26.0
Shaula	96 55.3	S37 05.3
Sirius	258 55.3	S16 41.7
Spica	158 56.9	S11 03.8
Suhail	223 10.2	S43 21.6
Vega	80 55.7	N38 45.7
Zuben'ubi	137 32.5	S15 57.8

	S.H.A.	Mer. Pass.
Venus	13 34.4	11 48
Mars	3 19.7	12 28
Jupiter	172 41.4	1 11
Saturn	171 59.0	1 14

G.M.T.	SUN G.H.A.	Dec.	MOON G.H.A.	v	Dec.	d	H.P.
11 00	177 27.1	S 3 49.9	116 40.9	7.7	N13 38.2	9.5	59.8
01	192 27.3	48.9	131 07.6	7.6	13 47.7	9.4	59.8
02	207 27.5	47.9	145 34.2	7.7	13 57.1	9.4	59.8
03	222 27.6 ··	46.9	160 00.9	7.6	14 06.5	9.3	59.7
04	237 27.8	45.9	174 27.5	7.6	14 15.8	9.1	59.7
05	252 28.0	45.0	188 54.1	7.5	14 24.9	9.1	59.7
06	267 28.1	S 3 44.0	203 20.6	7.6	N14 34.0	9.0	59.7
W 07	282 28.3	43.0	217 47.2	7.5	14 43.0	8.8	59.7
E 08	297 28.5	42.0	232 13.7	7.5	14 51.8	8.8	59.6
D 09	312 28.6 ··	41.0	246 40.2	7.5	15 00.6	8.7	59.6
N 10	327 28.8	40.0	261 06.7	7.5	15 09.3	8.5	59.6
E 11	342 28.9	39.1	275 33.2	7.4	15 17.8	8.5	59.6
S 12	357 29.1	S 3 38.1	289 59.6	7.4	N15 26.3	8.3	59.5
D 13	12 29.3	37.1	304 26.0	7.5	15 34.6	8.3	59.5
A 14	27 29.4	36.1	318 52.5	7.3	15 42.9	8.1	59.5
Y 15	42 29.6 ··	35.1	333 18.8	7.4	15 51.0	8.1	59.5
16	57 29.8	34.2	347 45.2	7.4	15 59.1	7.9	59.5
17	72 29.9	33.2	2 11.6	7.3	16 07.0	7.8	59.4
18	87 30.1	S 3 32.2	16 37.9	7.3	N16 14.8	7.8	59.4
19	102 30.3	31.2	31 04.2	7.3	16 22.6	7.6	59.4
20	117 30.4	30.2	45 30.5	7.3	16 30.2	7.5	59.4
21	132 30.6 ··	29.2	59 56.8	7.2	16 37.7	7.4	59.3
22	147 30.8	28.3	74 23.0	7.3	16 45.1	7.3	59.3
23	162 30.9	27.3	88 49.3	7.2	16 52.4	7.1	59.3
12 00	177 31.1	S 3 26.3	103 15.5	7.2	N16 59.5	7.1	59.3
01	192 31.3	25.3	117 41.7	7.2	17 06.6	6.9	59.2
02	207 31.4	24.3	132 07.9	7.2	17 13.5	6.8	59.2
03	222 31.6 ··	23.3	146 34.1	7.2	17 20.3	6.8	59.2
04	237 31.8	22.4	161 00.3	7.1	17 27.1	6.6	59.2
05	252 31.9	21.4	175 26.4	7.1	17 33.7	6.4	59.1
06	267 32.1	S 3 20.4	189 52.6	7.1	N17 40.1	6.4	59.1
07	282 32.3	19.4	204 18.7	7.1	17 46.5	6.3	59.1
T 08	297 32.4	18.4	218 44.8	7.1	17 52.8	6.1	59.1
H 09	312 32.6 ··	17.4	233 10.9	7.1	17 58.9	6.0	59.0
U 10	327 32.8	16.5	247 37.0	7.1	18 04.9	5.9	59.0
R 11	342 32.9	15.5	262 03.1	7.1	18 10.8	5.8	59.0
S 12	357 33.1	S 3 14.5	276 29.2	7.1	N18 16.6	5.6	59.0
D 13	12 33.3	13.5	290 55.3	7.0	18 22.2	5.6	58.9
A 14	27 33.4	12.5	305 21.3	7.1	18 27.8	5.4	58.9
Y 15	42 33.6 ··	11.5	319 47.4	7.0	18 33.2	5.3	58.9
16	57 33.8	10.6	334 13.4	7.1	18 38.5	5.1	58.9
17	72 34.0	09.6	348 39.5	7.0	18 43.6	5.1	58.8
18	87 34.1	S 3 08.6	3 05.5	7.0	N18 48.7	4.9	58.8
19	102 34.3	07.6	17 31.5	7.1	18 53.6	4.8	58.8
20	117 34.5	06.6	31 57.6	7.0	18 58.4	4.7	58.8
21	132 34.6 ··	05.6	46 23.6	7.0	19 03.1	4.6	58.7
22	147 34.8	04.6	60 49.6	7.1	19 07.7	4.4	58.7
23	162 35.0	03.7	75 15.7	7.0	19 12.1	4.3	58.7
13 00	177 35.1	S 3 02.7	89 41.7	7.0	N19 16.4	4.2	58.7
01	192 35.3	01.7	104 07.7	7.0	19 20.6	4.1	58.6
02	207 35.5	3 00.7	118 33.7	7.1	19 24.7	3.9	58.6
03	222 35.6	2 59.7	132 59.8	7.0	19 28.6	3.8	58.6
04	237 35.8	58.7	147 25.8	7.0	19 32.4	3.7	58.6
05	252 36.0	57.8	161 51.8	7.1	19 36.1	3.6	58.5
06	267 36.2	S 2 56.8	176 17.9	7.0	N19 39.7	3.4	58.5
07	282 36.3	55.8	190 43.9	7.1	19 43.1	3.3	58.5
08	297 36.5	54.8	205 10.0	7.0	19 46.4	3.2	58.5
F 09	312 36.7 ··	53.8	219 36.0	7.1	19 49.6	3.1	58.4
R 10	327 36.8	52.8	234 02.1	7.1	19 52.7	2.9	58.4
I 11	342 37.0	51.8	248 28.2	7.0	19 55.6	2.8	58.4
D 12	357 37.2	S 2 50.9	262 54.2	7.1	N19 58.4	2.7	58.4
A 13	12 37.4	49.9	277 20.3	7.1	20 01.1	2.6	58.3
Y 14	27 37.5	48.9	291 46.4	7.2	20 03.7	2.4	58.3
15	42 37.7 ··	47.9	306 12.6	7.1	20 06.1	2.3	58.3
16	57 37.9	46.9	320 38.7	7.1	20 08.4	2.2	58.3
17	72 38.0	45.9	335 04.8	7.2	20 10.6	2.0	58.2
18	87 38.2	S 2 44.9	349 31.0	7.2	N20 12.6	2.0	58.2
19	102 38.4	44.0	3 57.2	7.2	20 14.6	1.8	58.2
20	117 38.6	43.0	18 23.4	7.2	20 16.4	1.6	58.2
21	132 38.7 ··	42.0	32 49.6	7.2	20 18.0	1.6	58.1
22	147 38.9	41.0	47 15.8	7.3	20 19.6	1.4	58.1
23	162 39.1	40.0	61 42.1	7.2	20 21.0	1.3	58.1
	S.D. 16.1	d 1.0	S.D. 16.2		16.1		15.9

Lat.	Twilight Naut.	Civil	Sunrise	Moonrise 11	12	13	14
°	h m	h m	h m	h m	h m	h m	h m
N 72	04 12	05 33	06 40	06 57	06 14	□	□
N 70	04 24	05 36	06 37	07 27	07 20	07 06	□
68	04 33	05 39	06 34	07 49	07 56	08 12	08 49
66	04 41	05 41	06 32	08 07	08 22	08 48	09 31
64	04 47	05 43	06 30	08 21	08 42	09 13	10 00
62	04 52	05 44	06 28	08 33	08 58	09 33	10 22
60	04 56	05 45	06 26	08 44	09 12	09 50	10 40
N 58	05 00	05 46	06 25	08 53	09 24	10 04	10 54
56	05 04	05 47	06 24	09 01	09 34	10 16	11 07
54	05 06	05 47	06 23	09 08	09 43	10 27	11 18
52	05 09	05 48	06 22	09 14	09 52	10 36	11 28
50	05 11	05 48	06 21	09 20	09 59	10 44	11 37
45	05 15	05 49	06 18	09 33	10 15	11 02	11 55
N 40	05 18	05 50	06 17	09 43	10 28	11 17	12 10
35	05 21	05 50	06 15	09 52	10 39	11 29	12 23
30	05 22	05 50	06 14	10 00	10 48	11 40	12 34
20	05 24	05 49	06 11	10 14	11 05	11 59	12 54
N 10	05 23	05 48	06 09	10 26	11 20	12 15	13 10
0	05 22	05 46	06 07	10 38	11 34	12 30	13 26
S 10	05 19	05 43	06 04	10 49	11 48	12 45	13 42
20	05 14	05 39	06 01	11 01	12 02	13 02	13 59
30	05 06	05 34	05 58	11 16	12 20	13 21	14 18
35	05 01	05 31	05 56	11 24	12 30	13 32	14 29
40	04 55	05 27	05 54	11 33	12 41	13 44	14 42
45	04 47	05 22	05 52	11 44	12 55	13 59	14 57
S 50	04 37	05 16	05 49	11 58	13 11	14 18	15 16
52	04 32	05 13	05 47	12 04	13 19	14 27	15 25
54	04 27	05 10	05 46	12 11	13 28	14 36	15 35
56	04 20	05 06	05 44	12 19	13 37	14 47	15 46
58	04 13	05 02	05 42	12 28	13 49	15 00	15 59
S 60	04 05	04 57	05 40	12 38	14 02	15 15	16 14

Lat.	Sunset	Twilight Civil	Naut.	Moonset 11	12	13	14
°	h m	h m	h m	h m	h m	h m	h m
N 72	17 42	18 49	20 11	01 31	04 11	□	□
N 70	17 45	18 46	19 59	01 03	03 07	05 19	□
68	17 47	18 43	19 49	00 42	02 32	04 14	05 34
66	17 50	18 41	19 41	00 25	02 06	03 38	04 51
64	17 52	18 39	19 35	00 12	01 47	03 13	04 23
62	17 53	18 37	19 29	00 00	01 31	02 53	04 01
60	17 55	18 36	19 25	25 18	01 18	02 36	03 43
N 58	17 56	18 35	19 21	25 06	01 06	02 23	03 28
56	17 57	18 34	19 18	24 56	00 56	02 11	03 16
54	17 58	18 33	19 15	24 48	00 48	02 01	03 05
52	17 59	18 33	19 12	24 40	00 40	01 51	02 55
50	18 00	18 32	19 10	24 33	00 33	01 43	02 46
45	18 02	18 31	19 05	24 18	00 18	01 26	02 27
N 40	18 04	18 31	19 02	24 06	00 06	01 12	02 12
35	18 05	18 30	19 00	23 55	25 00	01 00	02 00
30	18 06	18 30	18 58	23 46	24 49	00 49	01 48
20	18 09	18 31	18 56	23 31	24 31	00 31	01 29
N 10	18 11	18 32	18 56	23 17	24 15	00 15	01 13
0	18 13	18 34	18 58	23 04	24 01	00 01	00 57
S 10	18 15	18 36	19 01	22 52	23 46	24 41	00 41
20	18 18	18 40	19 06	22 38	23 30	24 25	00 25
30	18 21	18 45	19 13	22 22	23 12	24 05	00 05
35	18 23	18 48	19 18	22 13	23 02	23 54	24 50
40	18 25	18 52	19 24	22 03	22 50	23 41	24 37
45	18 27	18 56	19 31	21 51	22 36	23 26	24 22
S 50	18 30	19 02	19 41	21 37	22 19	23 08	24 04
52	18 31	19 04	19 46	21 30	22 10	22 59	23 55
54	18 33	19 08	19 51	21 22	22 01	22 49	23 45
56	18 34	19 12	19 57	21 14	21 51	22 38	23 34
58	18 36	19 16	20 04	21 05	21 40	22 25	23 21
S 60	18 38	19 20	20 12	20 54	21 27	22 10	23 06

Day	SUN Eqn. of Time 00h	12h	Mer. Pass.	MOON Mer. Pass. Upper	Lower	Age	Phase
	m s	m s	h m	h m	h m	d	
11	10 12	10 04	12 10	16 51	04 23	05	
12	09 56	09 48	12 10	17 47	05 19	06	
13	09 40	09 32	12 10	18 44	06 15	07	◗

1981 MARCH 14, 15, 16 (SAT., SUN., MON.)

G.M.T.	ARIES G.H.A.	VENUS −3.4 G.H.A.	VENUS Dec.	MARS +1.3 G.H.A.	MARS Dec.	JUPITER −2.0 G.H.A.	JUPITER Dec.	SATURN +0.7 G.H.A.	SATURN Dec.	STARS Name	S.H.A.	Dec.
d h	° ′	° ′	° ′	° ′	° ′	° ′	° ′	° ′	° ′		° ′	° ′
14 00	171 31.4	182 46.8 S 6 23.6		173 25.5 S 1 42.6		344 26.1 S 1 20.5		343 38.4 S 0 32.0		Acamar	315 37.3	S40 23.2
01	186 33.9	197 46.4	22.4	188 26.1	41.8	359 28.8	20.4	358 41.1	31.9	Achernar	335 45.5	S57 20.2
02	201 36.4	212 46.0	21.2	203 26.8	41.1	14 31.6	20.3	13 43.7	31.8	Acrux	173 36.2	S62 59.6
03	216 38.8	227 45.6 ··	20.0	218 27.5 ··	40.3	29 34.3 ··	20.2	28 46.3 ··	31.7	Adhara	255 31.7	S28 57.1
04	231 41.3	242 45.1	18.8	233 28.2	39.5	44 37.0	20.0	43 49.0	31.7	Aldebaran	291 17.7	N16 28.2
05	246 43.7	257 44.7	17.6	248 28.9	38.7	59 39.8	19.9	58 51.6	31.6			
06	261 46.2	272 44.3 S 6 16.4		263 29.5 S 1 37.9		74 42.5 S 1 19.8		73 54.2 S 0 31.5		Alioth	166 41.7	N56 03.6
07	276 48.7	287 43.9	15.2	278 30.2	37.1	89 45.3	19.7	88 56.9	31.4	Alkaid	153 17.8	N49 24.3
S 08	291 51.1	302 43.4	14.0	293 30.9	36.3	104 48.0	19.5	103 59.5	31.3	Al Na'ir	28 15.0	S47 03.2
A 09	306 53.6	317 43.0 ··	12.7	308 31.6 ··	35.5	119 50.8 ··	19.4	119 02.1 ··	31.3	Alnilam	276 11.3	S 1 13.0
T 10	321 56.1	332 42.6	11.5	323 32.3	34.7	134 53.5	19.3	134 04.8	31.2	Alphard	218 20.0	S 8 34.7
U 11	336 58.5	347 42.2	10.3	338 33.0	33.9	149 56.2	19.2	149 07.4	31.1			
R 12	352 01.0	2 41.8 S 6 09.1		353 33.6 S 1 33.1		164 59.0 S 1 19.0		164 10.0 S 0 31.0		Alphecca	126 31.7	N26 46.5
D 13	7 03.5	17 41.3	07.9	8 34.3	32.3	180 01.7	18.9	179 12.7	31.0	Alpheratz	358 09.3	N28 59.0
A 14	22 05.9	32 40.9	06.7	23 35.0	31.5	195 04.5	18.8	194 15.3	30.9	Altair	62 32.4	N 8 48.9
Y 15	37 08.4	47 40.5 ··	05.5	38 35.7 ··	30.7	210 07.2 ··	18.7	209 17.9 ··	30.8	Ankaa	353 40.3	S42 24.7
16	52 10.9	62 40.1	04.3	53 36.4	29.9	225 10.0	18.5	224 20.6	30.7	Antares	112 56.3	S26 23.4
17	67 13.3	77 39.7	03.1	68 37.1	29.1	240 12.7	18.4	239 23.2	30.6			
18	82 15.8	92 39.2 S 6 01.9		83 37.7 S 1 28.4		255 15.5 S 1 18.3		254 25.8 S 0 30.6		Arcturus	146 17.9	N19 16.7
19	97 18.2	107 38.8 6 00.7		98 38.4	27.6	270 18.2	18.2	269 28.5	30.5	Atria	108 20.2	S68 59.4
20	112 20.7	122 38.4 5 59.4		113 39.1	26.8	285 20.9	18.0	284 31.1	30.4	Avior	234 27.6	S59 27.2
21	127 23.2	137 38.0 ··	58.2	128 39.8 ··	26.0	300 23.7 ··	17.9	299 33.7 ··	30.3	Bellatrix	278 58.4	N 6 19.8
22	142 25.6	152 37.6	57.0	143 40.5	25.2	315 26.4	17.8	314 36.4	30.3	Betelgeuse	271 27.9	N 7 24.1
23	157 28.1	167 37.1	55.8	158 41.2	24.4	330 29.2	17.7	329 39.0	30.2			
15 00	172 30.6	182 36.7 S 5 54.6		173 41.8 S 1 23.6		345 31.9 S 1 17.5		344 41.6 S 0 30.1		Canopus	264 07.0	S52 41.5
01	187 33.0	197 36.3	53.4	188 42.5	22.8	0 34.7	17.4	359 44.3	30.0	Capella	281 10.8	N45 58.8
02	202 35.5	212 35.9	52.2	203 43.2	22.0	15 37.4	17.3	14 46.9	29.9	Deneb	49 48.6	N45 12.5
03	217 38.0	227 35.5 ··	51.0	218 43.9 ··	21.2	30 40.2 ··	17.2	29 49.5 ··	29.9	Denebola	182 58.4	N14 40.6
04	232 40.4	242 35.0	49.7	233 44.6	20.4	45 42.9	17.0	44 52.2	29.8	Diphda	349 20.9	S18 05.6
05	247 42.9	257 34.6	48.5	248 45.3	19.6	60 45.7	16.9	59 54.8	29.7			
06	262 45.3	272 34.2 S 5 47.3		263 45.9 S 1 18.8		75 48.4 S 1 16.8		74 57.4 S 0 29.6		Dubhe	194 21.1	N61 51.2
07	277 47.8	287 33.8	46.1	278 46.6	18.0	90 51.2	16.7	90 00.1	29.6	Elnath	278 43.7	N28 35.5
08	292 50.3	302 33.4	44.9	293 47.3	17.2	105 53.9	16.5	105 02.7	29.5	Eltanin	90 57.6	N51 29.2
S 09	307 52.7	317 33.0 ··	43.7	308 48.0 ··	16.5	120 56.6 ··	16.4	120 05.3 ··	29.4	Enif	34 11.5	N 9 47.1
U 10	322 55.2	332 32.5	42.5	323 48.7	15.7	135 59.4	16.3	135 08.0	29.3	Fomalhaut	15 51.4	S29 43.5
N 11	337 57.7	347 32.1	41.2	338 49.4	14.9	151 02.1	16.2	150 10.6	29.2			
D 12	353 00.1	2 31.7 S 5 40.0		353 50.1 S 1 14.1		166 04.9 S 1 16.0		165 13.3 S 0 29.2		Gacrux	172 27.8	S57 00.4
A 13	8 02.6	17 31.3	38.8	8 50.7	13.3	181 07.6	15.9	180 15.9	29.1	Gienah	176 17.3	S17 26.3
Y 14	23 05.1	32 30.9	37.6	23 51.4	12.5	196 10.4	15.8	195 18.5	29.0	Hadar	149 22.4	S60 16.8
15	38 07.5	47 30.5 ··	36.4	38 52.1 ··	11.7	211 13.1 ··	15.7	210 21.2 ··	28.9	Hamal	328 28.8	N23 22.3
16	53 10.0	62 30.0	35.2	53 52.8	10.9	226 15.9	15.5	225 23.8	28.9	Kaus Aust.	84 16.5	S34 23.5
17	68 12.5	77 29.6	33.9	68 53.5	10.1	241 18.6	15.4	240 26.4	28.8			
18	83 14.9	92 29.2 S 5 32.7		83 54.2 S 1 09.3		256 21.4 S 1 15.3		255 29.1 S 0 28.7		Kochab	137 18.3	N74 13.8
19	98 17.4	107 28.8	31.5	98 54.9	08.5	271 24.1	15.2	270 31.7	28.6	Markab	14 03.2	N15 06.0
20	113 19.8	122 28.4	30.3	113 55.5	07.7	286 26.9	15.0	285 34.3	28.5	Menkar	314 41.0	N 4 00.8
21	128 22.3	137 28.0 ··	29.1	128 56.2 ··	06.9	301 29.6 ··	14.9	300 37.0 ··	28.5	Menkent	148 36.3	S36 16.6
22	143 24.8	152 27.6	27.9	143 56.9	06.1	316 32.4	14.8	315 39.6	28.4	Miaplacidus	221 44.1	S69 38.6
23	158 27.2	167 27.1	26.6	158 57.6	05.3	331 35.1	14.7	330 42.2	28.3			
16 00	173 29.7	182 26.7 S 5 25.4		173 58.3 S 1 04.6		346 37.9 S 1 14.5		345 44.9 S 0 28.2		Mirfak	309 15.9	N49 47.7
01	188 32.2	197 26.3	24.2	188 59.0	03.8	1 40.6	14.4	0 47.5	28.2	Nunki	76 28.9	S26 19.2
02	203 34.6	212 25.9	23.0	203 59.6	03.0	16 43.4	14.3	15 50.1	28.1	Peacock	53 58.3	S56 47.6
03	218 37.1	227 25.5 ··	21.8	219 00.3 ··	02.2	31 46.1 ··	14.2	30 52.8 ··	28.0	Pollux	243 57.6	N28 04.3
04	233 39.6	242 25.1	20.5	234 01.0	01.4	46 48.8	14.0	45 55.4	27.9	Procyon	245 25.3	N 5 16.3
05	248 42.0	257 24.7	19.3	249 01.7	1 00.6	61 51.6	13.9	60 58.0	27.8			
06	263 44.5	272 24.3 S 5 18.1		264 02.4 S 0 59.8		76 54.3 S 1 13.8		76 00.7 S 0 27.8		Rasalhague	96 29.3	N12 34.3
07	278 47.0	287 23.8	16.9	279 03.1	59.0	91 57.1	13.6	91 03.3	27.7	Regulus	208 09.4	N12 03.5
08	293 49.4	302 23.4	15.7	294 03.8	58.2	106 59.8	13.5	106 06.0	27.6	Rigel	281 35.7	S 8 13.6
M 09	308 51.9	317 23.0 ··	14.4	309 04.4 ··	57.4	122 02.6 ··	13.4	121 08.6 ··	27.5	Rigil Kent.	140 24.9	S60 45.2
O 10	323 54.3	332 22.6	13.2	324 05.1	56.6	137 05.3	13.3	136 11.2	27.4	Sabik	102 40.7	S15 42.1
N 11	338 56.8	347 22.2	12.0	339 05.8	55.8	152 08.1	13.1	151 13.9	27.4			
D 12	353 59.3	2 21.8 S 5 10.8		354 06.5 S 0 55.0		167 10.8 S 1 13.0		166 16.5 S 0 27.3		Schedar	350 09.2	N56 26.0
A 13	9 01.7	17 21.4	09.6	9 07.2	54.2	182 13.6	12.9	181 19.1	27.2	Shaula	96 55.3	S37 05.3
Y 14	24 04.2	32 21.0	08.3	24 07.9	53.4	197 16.3	12.8	196 21.8	27.1	Sirius	258 55.3	S16 41.7
15	39 06.7	47 20.6 ··	07.1	39 08.6 ··	52.7	212 19.1 ··	12.6	211 24.4 ··	27.1	Spica	158 56.9	S11 03.8
16	54 09.1	62 20.1	05.9	54 09.3	51.9	227 21.8	12.5	226 27.0	27.0	Suhail	223 10.2	S43 21.6
17	69 11.6	77 19.7	04.7	69 09.9	51.1	242 24.6	12.4	241 29.7	26.9			
18	84 14.1	92 19.3 S 5 03.5		84 10.6 S 0 50.3		257 27.3 S 1 12.3		256 32.3 S 0 26.8		Vega	80 55.7	N38 45.7
19	99 16.5	107 18.9	02.2	99 11.3	49.5	272 30.1	12.1	271 35.0	26.7	Zuben'ubi	137 32.5	S15 57.8
20	114 19.0	122 18.5 5 01.0		114 12.0	48.7	287 32.8	12.0	286 37.6	26.7			
21	129 21.4	137 18.1 4 59.8		129 12.7 ··	47.9	302 35.6 ··	11.9	301 40.2 ··	26.6		S.H.A.	Mer. Pass.
22	144 23.9	152 17.7	58.6	144 13.4	47.1	317 38.3	11.8	316 42.9	26.5		° ′	h m
23	159 26.4	167 17.3	57.3	159 14.1	46.3	332 41.1	11.6	331 45.5	26.4	Venus	10 06.2	11 50
										Mars	1 11.3	12 25
Mer. Pass. 12 27.9		v −0.4 d 1.2		v 0.7 d 0.8		v 2.7 d 0.1		v 2.6 d 0.1		Jupiter	173 01.4	0 58
										Saturn	172 11.1	1 01

G.M.T.	SUN G.H.A.	Dec.	MOON G.H.A.	v	Dec.	d	H.P.
	° ′	° ′	° ′	′	° ′	′	′
14 00	177 39.2	S 2 39.0	76 08.3	7.3	N20 22.3	1.2	58.0
01	192 39.4	38.0	90 34.6	7.3	20 23.5	1.0	58.0
02	207 39.6	37.1	105 00.9	7.4	20 24.5	1.0	58.0
03	222 39.8	·· 36.1	119 27.3	7.3	20 25.5	0.8	58.0
04	237 39.9	35.1	133 53.6	7.4	20 26.3	0.6	57.9
05	252 40.1	34.1	148 20.0	7.4	20 26.9	0.6	57.9
06	267 40.3	S 2 33.1	162 46.4	7.5	N20 27.5	0.4	57.9
07	282 40.5	32.1	177 12.9	7.4	20 27.9	0.3	57.9
S 08	297 40.6	31.1	191 39.3	7.5	20 28.2	0.2	57.8
A 09	312 40.8	·· 30.2	206 05.8	7.5	20 28.4	0.1	57.8
T 10	327 41.0	29.2	220 32.3	7.6	20 28.5	0.1	57.8
U 11	342 41.2	28.2	234 58.9	7.6	20 28.4	0.2	57.8
R 12	357 41.3	S 2 27.2	249 25.5	7.6	N20 28.2	0.3	57.7
D 13	12 41.5	26.2	263 52.1	7.6	20 27.9	0.5	57.7
A 14	27 41.7	25.2	278 18.7	7.7	20 27.4	0.5	57.7
Y 15	42 41.9	·· 24.2	292 45.4	7.7	20 26.9	0.7	57.7
16	57 42.0	23.3	307 12.1	7.8	20 26.2	0.8	57.6
17	72 42.2	22.3	321 38.9	7.8	20 25.4	0.9	57.6
18	87 42.4	S 2 21.3	336 05.7	7.8	N20 24.5	1.1	57.6
19	102 42.6	20.3	350 32.5	7.8	20 23.4	1.1	57.6
20	117 42.7	19.3	4 59.3	7.9	20 22.3	1.3	57.5
21	132 42.9	·· 18.3	19 26.2	8.0	20 21.0	1.4	57.5
22	147 43.1	17.3	33 53.2	8.0	20 19.6	1.5	57.5
23	162 43.3	16.3	48 20.2	8.0	20 18.1	1.6	57.5
15 00	177 43.4	S 2 15.4	62 47.2	8.0	N20 16.5	1.8	57.4
01	192 43.6	14.4	77 14.2	8.1	20 14.7	1.9	57.4
02	207 43.8	13.4	91 41.3	8.2	20 12.8	2.0	57.4
03	222 44.0	·· 12.4	106 08.5	8.2	20 10.8	2.1	57.4
04	237 44.1	11.4	120 35.7	8.2	20 08.7	2.2	57.3
05	252 44.3	10.4	135 02.9	8.3	20 06.5	2.3	57.3
06	267 44.5	S 2 09.4	149 30.2	8.3	N20 04.2	2.5	57.3
07	282 44.7	08.4	163 57.5	8.4	20 01.7	2.5	57.3
08	297 44.8	07.5	178 24.9	8.4	19 59.2	2.7	57.2
S 09	312 45.0	·· 06.5	192 52.3	8.4	19 56.5	2.8	57.2
U 10	327 45.2	05.5	207 19.7	8.5	19 53.7	2.9	57.2
N 11	342 45.4	04.5	221 47.2	8.6	19 50.8	3.0	57.2
D 12	357 45.5	S 2 03.5	236 14.8	8.6	N19 47.8	3.1	57.2
A 13	12 45.7	02.5	250 42.4	8.7	19 44.7	3.2	57.1
Y 14	27 45.9	01.5	265 10.1	8.7	19 41.5	3.4	57.1
15	42 46.1	2 00.6	279 37.8	8.7	19 38.1	3.4	57.1
16	57 46.3	1 59.6	294 05.5	8.8	19 34.7	3.6	57.1
17	72 46.4	58.6	308 33.3	8.9	19 31.1	3.6	57.0
18	87 46.6	S 1 57.6	323 01.2	8.9	N19 27.5	3.8	57.0
19	102 46.8	56.6	337 29.1	9.0	19 23.7	3.9	57.0
20	117 47.0	55.6	351 57.1	9.0	19 19.8	4.0	57.0
21	132 47.1	·· 54.6	6 25.1	9.1	19 15.8	4.0	56.9
22	147 47.3	53.6	20 53.2	9.1	19 11.8	4.2	56.9
23	162 47.5	52.7	35 21.3	9.2	19 07.6	4.3	56.9
16 00	177 47.7	S 1 51.7	49 49.5	9.2	N19 03.3	4.4	56.9
01	192 47.9	50.7	64 17.7	9.3	18 58.9	4.5	56.8
02	207 48.0	49.7	78 46.0	9.4	18 54.4	4.6	56.8
03	222 48.2	·· 48.7	93 14.4	9.4	18 49.8	4.7	56.8
04	237 48.4	47.7	107 42.8	9.4	18 45.1	4.8	56.8
05	252 48.6	46.7	122 11.2	9.6	18 40.3	4.9	56.8
06	267 48.7	S 1 45.7	136 39.8	9.5	N18 35.4	5.0	56.7
07	282 48.9	44.8	151 08.3	9.7	18 30.4	5.1	56.7
08	297 49.1	43.8	165 37.0	9.7	18 25.3	5.2	56.7
M 09	312 49.3	·· 42.8	180 05.7	9.7	18 20.1	5.2	56.7
O 10	327 49.5	41.8	194 34.4	9.8	18 14.9	5.4	56.6
N 11	342 49.6	40.8	209 03.2	9.9	18 09.5	5.5	56.6
D 12	357 49.8	S 1 39.8	223 32.1	9.9	N18 04.0	5.5	56.6
A 13	12 50.0	38.8	238 01.0	10.0	17 58.5	5.7	56.6
Y 14	27 50.2	37.8	252 30.0	10.1	17 52.8	5.7	56.5
15	42 50.4	·· 36.9	266 59.1	10.1	17 47.1	5.9	56.5
16	57 50.5	35.9	281 28.2	10.1	17 41.2	5.9	56.5
17	72 50.7	34.9	295 57.3	10.2	17 35.3	6.0	56.5
18	87 50.9	S 1 33.9	310 26.5	10.3	N17 29.3	6.1	56.5
19	102 51.1	32.9	324 55.8	10.4	17 23.2	6.2	56.4
20	117 51.3	31.9	339 25.2	10.4	17 17.0	6.3	56.4
21	132 51.4	·· 30.9	353 54.6	10.4	17 10.7	6.4	56.4
22	147 51.6	29.9	8 24.0	10.6	17 04.3	6.4	56.4
23	162 51.8	29.0	22 53.6	10.6	16 57.9	6.5	56.4
	S.D. 16.1	d 1.0	S.D. 15.7		15.6		15.4

Twilight / Moonrise

Lat.	Naut.	Civil	Sunrise	Moonrise 14	15	16	17
°	h m	h m	h m	h m	h m	h m	h m
N 72	03 54	05 18	06 25	▢	▢	▢	12 05
N 70	04 08	05 22	06 23	▢	08 39	10 49	12 42
68	04 19	05 26	06 21	08 49	09 59	11 31	13 08
66	04 28	05 29	06 20	09 31	10 37	11 59	13 28
64	04 36	05 32	06 19	10 00	11 04	12 21	13 43
62	04 42	05 34	06 18	10 22	11 25	12 38	13 57
60	04 47	05 36	06 17	10 40	11 41	12 52	14 08
N 58	04 52	05 38	06 17	10 54	11 55	13 04	14 17
56	04 55	05 39	06 16	11 07	12 07	13 15	14 26
54	04 59	05 40	06 15	11 18	12 18	13 24	14 33
52	05 02	05 41	06 15	11 28	12 27	13 32	14 40
50	05 04	05 42	06 14	11 37	12 36	13 40	14 46
45	05 10	05 44	06 13	11 55	12 54	13 55	14 59
N 40	05 14	05 45	06 12	12 10	13 08	14 08	15 09
35	05 16	05 46	06 11	12 23	13 20	14 19	15 18
30	05 19	05 46	06 10	12 34	13 31	14 29	15 26
20	05 21	05 47	06 09	12 54	13 50	14 45	15 40
N 10	05 22	05 46	06 07	13 10	14 06	15 00	15 52
0	05 21	05 45	06 06	13 26	14 21	15 13	16 03
S 10	05 19	05 43	06 04	13 42	14 36	15 26	16 14
20	05 15	05 40	06 02	13 59	14 52	15 41	16 26
30	05 08	05 36	06 00	14 18	15 10	15 57	16 39
35	05 04	05 34	05 59	14 29	15 21	16 07	16 47
40	04 58	05 30	05 57	14 42	15 33	16 17	16 56
45	04 51	05 26	05 56	14 57	15 47	16 30	17 06
S 50	04 42	05 21	05 54	15 16	16 05	16 45	17 19
52	04 38	05 19	05 53	15 25	16 13	16 53	17 25
54	04 33	05 16	05 51	15 35	16 23	17 01	17 31
56	04 28	05 13	05 50	15 46	16 33	17 10	17 38
58	04 21	05 09	05 49	15 59	16 45	17 20	17 46
S 60	04 14	05 05	05 47	16 14	16 59	17 31	17 55

Twilight / Moonset

Lat.	Sunset	Civil	Naut.	Moonset 14	15	16	17
°	h m	h m	h m	h m	h m	h m	h m
N 72	17 56	19 03	20 28	▢	▢	▢	07 50
N 70	17 57	18 58	20 13	▢	07 39	07 19	07 11
68	17 58	18 54	20 02	05 34	06 18	06 37	06 44
66	17 59	18 51	19 52	04 51	05 40	06 08	06 24
64	18 00	18 48	19 45	04 23	05 13	05 46	06 07
62	18 01	18 45	19 38	04 01	04 52	05 28	05 53
60	18 02	18 43	19 33	03 43	04 35	05 14	05 42
N 58	18 03	18 42	19 28	03 28	04 21	05 01	05 32
56	18 03	18 40	19 24	03 15	04 09	04 50	05 23
54	18 04	18 39	19 20	03 05	03 58	04 41	05 15
52	18 04	18 38	19 17	02 55	03 48	04 32	05 08
50	18 05	18 37	19 15	02 46	03 40	04 24	05 01
45	18 06	18 35	19 09	02 27	03 22	04 08	04 47
N 40	18 07	18 34	19 05	02 12	03 07	03 54	04 36
35	18 07	18 33	19 02	02 00	02 54	03 43	04 26
30	18 08	18 32	19 00	01 48	02 43	03 33	04 18
20	18 10	18 32	18 57	01 28	02 24	03 16	04 03
N 10	18 11	18 32	18 56	01 13	02 08	03 00	03 50
0	18 12	18 33	18 57	00 57	01 52	02 46	03 37
S 10	18 14	18 35	18 59	00 41	01 37	02 32	03 25
20	18 15	18 37	19 03	00 25	01 20	02 16	03 12
30	18 17	18 41	19 09	00 05	01 01	01 59	02 56
35	18 18	18 44	19 13	24 50	00 50	01 48	02 47
40	18 19	18 47	19 19	24 37	00 37	01 36	02 37
45	18 21	18 51	19 25	24 22	00 22	01 22	02 25
S 50	18 23	18 56	19 34	24 04	00 04	01 05	02 11
52	18 24	18 58	19 38	23 55	24 57	00 57	02 04
54	18 25	19 01	19 43	23 45	24 48	00 48	01 56
56	18 26	19 04	19 49	23 34	24 38	00 38	01 48
58	18 28	19 07	19 55	23 21	24 27	00 27	01 38
S 60	18 29	19 11	20 02	23 06	24 13	00 13	01 27

Day	SUN Eqn. of Time 00ʰ	12ʰ	Mer. Pass.	MOON Mer. Pass. Upper	Lower	Age	Phase
	m s	m s	h m	h m	h m	d	
14	09 23	09 15	12 09	19 39	07 12	08	
15	09 07	08 58	12 09	20 33	08 07	09	
16	08 50	08 41	12 09	21 25	09 00	10	◐

G.M.T.	ARIES G.H.A.	VENUS −3.4 G.H.A.	Dec.	MARS +1.3 G.H.A.	Dec.	JUPITER −2.0 G.H.A.	Dec.	SATURN +0.7 G.H.A.	Dec.	STARS Name	S.H.A.	Dec.
17 00	174 28.8	182 16.9 S 4 56.1		174 14.8 S 0 45.5		347 43.8 S 1 11.5		346 48.2 S 0 26.3		Acamar	315 37.3	S40 23.1
01	189 31.3	197 16.5	54.9	189 15.4	44.7	2 46.6	11.4	1 50.8	26.3	Achernar	335 45.5	S57 20.2
02	204 33.8	212 16.1	53.6	204 16.1	43.9	17 49.3	11.2	16 53.4	26.2	Acrux	173 36.2	S62 59.6
03	219 36.2	227 15.7 ··	52.4	219 16.8 ··	43.1	32 52.1 ··	11.1	31 56.1 ··	26.1	Adhara	255 31.7	S28 57.1
04	234 38.7	242 15.3	51.2	234 17.5	42.4	47 54.8	11.0	46 58.7	26.0	Aldebaran	291 17.7	N16 28.2
05	249 41.2	257 14.8	50.0	249 18.2	41.6	62 57.6	10.9	62 01.3	26.0			
06	264 43.6	272 14.4 S 4 48.7		264 18.9 S 0 40.8		78 00.3 S 1 10.7		77 04.0 S 0 25.9		Alioth	166 41.7	N56 03.7
07	279 46.1	287 14.0	47.5	279 19.6	40.0	93 03.1	10.6	92 06.6	25.8	Alkaid	153 17.8	N49 24.3
08	294 48.6	302 13.6	46.3	294 20.2	39.2	108 05.8	10.5	107 09.2	25.7	Al Na'ir	28 14.9	S47 03.2
T 09	309 51.0	317 13.2 ··	45.1	309 20.9 ··	38.4	123 08.6 ··	10.3	122 11.9 ··	25.6	Alnilam	276 11.3	S 1 13.0
U 10	324 53.5	332 12.8	43.8	324 21.6	37.6	138 11.3	10.2	137 14.5	25.6	Alphard	218 20.0	S 8 34.7
E 11	339 55.9	347 12.4	42.6	339 22.3	36.8	153 14.1	10.1	152 17.2	25.5			
S 12	354 58.4	2 12.0 S 4 41.4		354 23.0 S 0 36.0		168 16.8 S 1 10.0		167 19.8 S 0 25.4		Alphecca	126 31.6	N26 46.5
D 13	10 00.9	17 11.6	40.2	9 23.7	35.2	183 19.6	09.8	182 22.4	25.3	Alpheratz	358 09.3	N28 59.0
A 14	25 03.3	32 11.2	38.9	24 24.4	34.4	198 22.3	09.7	197 25.1	25.3	Altair	62 32.4	N 8 48.9
Y 15	40 05.8	47 10.8 ··	37.7	39 25.1 ··	33.6	213 25.1 ··	09.6	212 27.7 ··	25.2	Ankaa	353 40.3	S42 24.7
16	55 08.3	62 10.4	36.5	54 25.7	32.8	228 27.8	09.5	227 30.3	25.1	Antares	112 56.3	S26 23.4
17	70 10.7	77 10.0	35.2	69 26.4	32.1	243 30.6	09.3	242 33.0	25.0			
18	85 13.2	92 09.6 S 4 34.0		84 27.1 S 0 31.3		258 33.4 S 1 09.2		257 35.6 S 0 24.9		Arcturus	146 17.9	N19 16.7
19	100 15.7	107 09.2	32.8	99 27.8	30.5	273 36.1	09.1	272 38.3	24.9	Atria	108 20.2	S68 59.4
20	115 18.1	122 08.8	31.6	114 28.5	29.7	288 38.9	09.0	287 40.9	24.8	Avior	234 27.7	S59 27.2
21	130 20.6	137 08.4 ··	30.3	129 29.2 ··	28.9	303 41.6 ··	08.8	302 43.5 ··	24.7	Bellatrix	278 58.4	N 6 19.8
22	145 23.1	152 08.0	29.1	144 29.9	28.1	318 44.4	08.7	317 46.2	24.6	Betelgeuse	271 27.9	N 7 24.1
23	160 25.5	167 07.6	27.9	159 30.6	27.3	333 47.1	08.6	332 48.8	24.5			
18 00	175 28.0	182 07.2 S 4 26.6		174 31.2 S 0 26.5		348 49.9 S 1 08.4		347 51.4 S 0 24.5		Canopus	264 07.0	S52 41.5
01	190 30.4	197 06.8	25.4	189 31.9	25.7	3 52.6	08.3	2 54.1	24.4	Capella	281 10.9	N45 58.8
02	205 32.9	212 06.4	24.2	204 32.6	24.9	18 55.4	08.2	17 56.7	24.3	Deneb	49 48.5	N45 12.5
03	220 35.4	227 06.0 ··	23.0	219 33.3 ··	24.1	33 58.1 ··	08.1	32 59.4 ··	24.2	Denebola	182 58.4	N14 40.6
04	235 37.8	242 05.6	21.7	234 34.0	23.3	49 00.9	07.9	48 02.0	24.2	Diphda	349 20.9	S18 05.6
05	250 40.3	257 05.2	20.5	249 34.7	22.5	64 03.6	07.8	63 04.6	24.1			
06	265 42.8	272 04.8 S 4 19.3		264 35.4 S 0 21.8		79 06.4 S 1 07.7		78 07.3 S 0 24.0		Dubhe	194 21.1	N61 51.2
07	280 45.2	287 04.4	18.0	279 36.1	21.0	94 09.1	07.6	93 09.9	23.9	Elnath	278 43.7	N28 35.5
W 08	295 47.7	302 04.0	16.8	294 36.7	20.2	109 11.9	07.4	108 12.5	23.8	Eltanin	90 57.6	N51 29.2
E 09	310 50.2	317 03.6 ··	15.6	309 37.4 ··	19.4	124 14.6 ··	07.3	123 15.2 ··	23.8	Enif	34 11.5	N 9 47.1
D 10	325 52.6	332 03.2	14.3	324 38.1	18.6	139 17.4	07.2	138 17.8	23.7	Fomalhaut	15 51.4	S29 43.5
N 11	340 55.1	347 02.7	13.1	339 38.8	17.8	154 20.1	07.0	153 20.5	23.6			
E 12	355 57.5	2 02.3 S 4 11.9		354 39.5 S 0 17.0		169 22.9 S 1 06.9		168 23.1 S 0 23.5		Gacrux	172 27.8	S57 00.4
S 13	11 00.0	17 02.0	10.6	9 40.2	16.2	184 25.6	06.8	183 25.7	23.5	Gienah	176 17.3	S17 26.3
D 14	26 02.5	32 01.5	09.4	24 40.9	15.4	199 28.4	06.7	198 28.4	23.4	Hadar	149 22.3	S60 16.8
A 15	41 04.9	47 01.2 ··	08.2	39 41.6 ··	14.6	214 31.1 ··	06.5	213 31.0 ··	23.3	Hamal	328 28.8	N23 22.3
Y 16	56 07.4	62 00.8	06.9	54 42.3	13.8	229 33.9	06.4	228 33.7	23.2	Kaus Aust.	84 16.5	S34 23.5
17	71 09.9	77 00.4	05.7	69 42.9	13.0	244 36.7	06.3	243 36.3	23.1			
18	86 12.3	92 00.0 S 4 04.5		84 43.6 S 0 12.3		259 39.4 S 1 06.2		258 38.9 S 0 23.1		Kochab	137 18.2	N74 13.8
19	101 14.8	106 59.6	03.2	99 44.3	11.5	274 42.2	06.0	273 41.6	23.0	Markab	14 03.1	N15 06.0
20	116 17.3	121 59.2	02.0	114 45.0	10.7	289 44.9	05.9	288 44.2	22.9	Menkar	314 41.0	N 4 00.8
21	131 19.7	136 58.8	4 00.8	129 45.7 ··	09.9	304 47.7 ··	05.8	303 46.8 ··	22.8	Menkent	148 36.3	S36 16.6
22	146 22.2	151 58.4	3 59.5	144 46.4	09.1	319 50.4	05.6	318 49.5	22.7	Miaplacidus	221 44.2	S69 38.6
23	161 24.7	166 58.0	58.3	159 47.1	08.3	334 53.2	05.5	333 52.1	22.7			
19 00	176 27.1	181 57.6 S 3 57.1		174 47.8 S 0 07.5		349 55.9 S 1 05.4		348 54.8 S 0 22.6		Mirfak	309 15.9	N49 47.7
01	191 29.6	196 57.2	55.8	189 48.5	06.7	4 58.7	05.3	3 57.4	22.5	Nunki	76 28.9	S26 19.2
02	206 32.0	211 56.8	54.6	204 49.2	05.9	20 01.4	05.1	19 00.0	22.4	Peacock	53 58.2	S56 47.6
03	221 34.5	226 56.4 ··	53.4	219 49.8 ··	05.1	35 04.2 ··	05.0	34 02.7 ··	22.4	Pollux	243 57.6	N28 04.3
04	236 37.0	241 56.0	52.1	234 50.5	04.3	50 06.9	04.9	49 05.3	22.3	Procyon	245 25.3	N 5 16.3
05	251 39.4	256 55.6	50.9	249 51.2	03.5	65 09.7	04.8	64 08.0	22.2			
06	266 41.9	271 55.2 S 3 49.7		264 51.9 S 0 02.8		80 12.5 S 1 04.6		79 10.6 S 0 22.1		Rasalhague	96 29.3	N12 34.3
07	281 44.4	286 54.8	48.4	279 52.6	02.0	95 15.2	04.5	94 13.2	22.0	Regulus	208 09.4	N12 03.5
T 08	296 46.8	301 54.4	47.2	294 53.3	01.2	110 18.0	04.4	109 15.9	22.0	Rigel	281 35.7	S 8 13.6
H 09	311 49.3	316 54.0 ··	45.9	309 54.0 S 0 00.4		125 20.7 ··	04.2	124 18.5 ··	21.9	Rigil Kent.	140 24.9	S60 45.2
U 10	326 51.8	331 53.6	44.7	324 54.7 N 0 00.4		140 23.5	04.1	139 21.2	21.8	Sabik	102 40.7	S15 42.1
R 11	341 54.2	346 53.2	43.5	339 55.4	01.2	155 26.2	04.0	154 23.8	21.7			
S 12	356 56.7	1 52.8 S 3 42.2		354 56.1 N 0 02.0		170 29.0 S 1 03.9		169 26.4 S 0 21.6		Schedar	350 09.2	N56 26.0
D 13	11 59.2	16 52.4	41.0	9 56.7	02.8	185 31.7	03.7	184 29.1	21.6	Shaula	96 55.3	S37 05.3
A 14	27 01.6	31 52.0	39.8	24 57.4	03.6	200 34.5	03.6	199 31.7	21.5	Sirius	258 55.3	S16 41.7
Y 15	42 04.1	46 51.6 ··	38.5	39 58.1 ··	04.4	215 37.2 ··	03.5	214 34.3 ··	21.4	Spica	158 56.9	S11 03.8
16	57 06.5	61 51.2	37.3	54 58.8	05.2	230 40.0	03.3	229 37.0	21.3	Suhail	223 10.2	S43 21.6
17	72 09.0	76 50.8	36.1	69 59.5	05.9	245 42.8	03.2	244 39.6	21.3			
18	87 11.5	91 50.4 S 3 34.8		85 00.2 N 0 06.7		260 45.5 S 1 03.1		259 42.3 S 0 21.2		Vega	80 55.7	N38 45.7
19	102 13.9	106 50.0	33.6	100 00.9	07.5	275 48.3	03.0	274 44.9	21.1	Zuben'ubi	137 32.4	S15 57.8
20	117 16.4	121 49.6	32.3	115 01.6	08.3	290 51.0	02.8	289 47.5	21.0			
21	132 18.9	136 49.2 ··	31.1	130 02.3 ··	09.1	305 53.8 ··	02.7	304 50.2 ··	20.9		S.H.A.	Mer. Pass.
22	147 21.3	151 48.8	29.9	145 03.0	09.9	320 56.5	02.6	319 52.8	20.9	Venus	6 39.2	11 52
23	162 23.8	166 48.5	28.6	160 03.7	10.7	335 59.3	02.5	334 55.5	20.8	Mars	359 00.3	12 21
										Jupiter	173 21.9	0 45
Mer. Pass. 12 16.1		v −0.4　d 1.2		v 0.7　d 0.8		v 2.8　d 0.1		v 2.6　d 0.1		Saturn	172 23.5	0 48

G.M.T.	SUN G.H.A.	SUN Dec.	MOON G.H.A.	v	Dec.	d	H.P.
17 00	177 52.0	S 1 28.0	37 23.2	10.6	N16 51.4	6.6	56.3
01	192 52.2	27.0	51 52.8	10.7	16 44.8	6.7	56.3
02	207 52.3	26.0	66 22.5	10.8	16 38.1	6.8	56.3
03	222 52.5	·· 25.0	80 52.3	10.8	16 31.3	6.9	56.3
04	237 52.7	24.0	95 22.1	10.9	16 24.4	6.9	56.2
05	252 52.9	23.0	109 52.0	10.9	16 17.5	7.0	56.2
06	267 53.1	S 1 22.0	124 21.9	11.1	N16 10.5	7.1	56.2
07	282 53.2	21.1	138 52.0	11.0	16 03.4	7.2	56.2
08	297 53.4	20.1	153 22.0	11.2	15 56.2	7.2	56.2
09	312 53.6	·· 19.1	167 52.2	11.1	15 49.0	7.3	56.1
10	327 53.8	18.1	182 22.3	11.3	15 41.7	7.4	56.1
11	342 54.0	17.1	196 52.6	11.3	15 34.3	7.5	56.1
12	357 54.2	S 1 16.1	211 22.9	11.4	N15 26.8	7.5	56.1
13	12 54.3	15.1	225 53.3	11.4	15 19.3	7.7	56.1
14	27 54.5	14.1	240 23.7	11.5	15 11.6	7.6	56.0
15	42 54.7	·· 13.1	254 54.2	11.5	15 04.0	7.8	56.0
16	57 54.9	12.2	269 24.7	11.6	14 56.2	7.8	56.0
17	72 55.1	11.2	283 55.3	11.7	14 48.4	7.9	56.0
18	87 55.2	S 1 10.2	298 26.0	11.7	N14 40.5	7.9	56.0
19	102 55.4	09.2	312 56.7	11.8	14 32.6	8.1	55.9
20	117 55.6	08.2	327 27.5	11.9	14 24.5	8.1	55.9
21	132 55.8	·· 07.2	341 58.4	11.9	14 16.4	8.1	55.9
22	147 56.0	06.2	356 29.3	11.9	14 08.3	8.2	55.9
23	162 56.2	05.2	11 00.2	12.0	14 00.1	8.3	55.9
18 00	177 56.3	S 1 04.2	25 31.2	12.1	N13 51.8	8.3	55.8
01	192 56.5	03.3	40 02.3	12.1	13 43.5	8.4	55.8
02	207 56.7	02.3	54 33.4	12.2	13 35.1	8.5	55.8
03	222 56.9	·· 01.3	69 04.6	12.3	13 26.6	8.5	55.8
04	237 57.1	1 00.3	83 35.9	12.3	13 18.1	8.6	55.8
05	252 57.3	0 59.3	98 07.2	12.3	13 09.5	8.6	55.7
06	267 57.4	S 0 58.3	112 38.5	12.4	N13 00.9	8.7	55.7
07	282 57.6	57.3	127 09.9	12.5	12 52.2	8.8	55.7
08	297 57.8	56.3	141 41.4	12.5	12 43.4	8.8	55.7
09	312 58.0	·· 55.4	156 12.9	12.6	12 34.6	8.8	55.7
10	327 58.2	54.4	170 44.5	12.6	12 25.8	8.9	55.6
11	342 58.4	53.4	185 16.1	12.7	12 16.9	9.0	55.6
12	357 58.5	S 0 52.4	199 47.8	12.8	N12 07.9	9.0	55.6
13	12 58.7	51.4	214 19.6	12.7	11 58.9	9.1	55.6
14	27 58.9	50.4	228 51.3	12.9	11 49.8	9.1	55.6
15	42 59.1	·· 49.4	243 23.2	12.9	11 40.7	9.2	55.6
16	57 59.3	48.4	257 55.1	12.9	11 31.5	9.2	55.5
17	72 59.5	47.4	272 27.0	13.0	11 22.3	9.2	55.5
18	87 59.6	S 0 46.5	286 59.0	13.1	N11 13.1	9.3	55.5
19	102 59.8	45.5	301 31.1	13.1	11 03.8	9.4	55.5
20	118 00.0	44.5	316 03.2	13.1	10 54.4	9.4	55.5
21	133 00.2	·· 43.5	330 35.3	13.2	10 45.0	9.4	55.4
22	148 00.4	42.5	345 07.5	13.3	10 35.6	9.5	55.4
23	163 00.6	41.5	359 39.8	13.3	10 26.1	9.5	55.4
19 00	178 00.7	S 0 40.5	14 12.1	13.3	N10 16.6	9.6	55.4
01	193 00.9	39.5	28 44.4	13.4	10 07.0	9.6	55.4
02	208 01.1	38.6	43 16.8	13.4	9 57.4	9.6	55.3
03	223 01.3	·· 37.6	57 49.2	13.5	9 47.8	9.7	55.3
04	238 01.5	36.6	72 21.7	13.6	9 38.1	9.7	55.3
05	253 01.7	35.6	86 54.3	13.5	9 28.4	9.8	55.3
06	268 01.8	S 0 34.6	101 26.8	13.7	N 9 18.6	9.8	55.3
07	283 02.0	33.6	115 59.5	13.6	9 08.8	9.8	55.3
08	298 02.2	32.6	130 32.1	13.8	8 59.0	9.9	55.2
09	313 02.4	·· 31.6	145 04.9	13.7	8 49.1	9.9	55.2
10	328 02.6	30.7	159 37.6	13.8	8 39.2	9.9	55.2
11	343 02.8	29.7	174 10.4	13.9	8 29.3	9.9	55.2
12	358 03.0	S 0 28.7	188 43.3	13.8	N 8 19.4	10.0	55.2
13	13 03.1	27.7	203 16.1	14.0	8 09.4	10.1	55.2
14	28 03.3	26.7	217 49.1	13.9	7 59.3	10.1	55.1
15	43 03.5	·· 25.7	232 22.0	14.0	7 49.3	10.1	55.1
16	58 03.7	24.7	246 55.0	14.1	7 39.2	10.1	55.1
17	73 03.9	23.7	261 28.1	14.1	7 29.1	10.1	55.1
18	88 04.1	S 0 22.8	276 01.2	14.1	N 7 19.0	10.2	55.1
19	103 04.3	21.8	290 34.3	14.2	7 08.8	10.2	55.1
20	118 04.4	20.8	305 07.5	14.2	6 58.6	10.2	55.0
21	133 04.6	·· 19.8	319 40.7	14.2	6 48.4	10.2	55.0
22	148 04.8	18.8	334 13.9	14.3	6 38.2	10.3	55.0
23	163 05.0	17.8	348 47.2	14.3	6 27.9	10.3	55.0
	S.D. 16.1	d 1.0	S.D. 15.3		15.2		15.0

(TUESDAY = day 17, WEDNESDAY = day 18, THURSDAY = day 19)

Twilight / Sunrise / Moonrise

Lat.	Naut.	Civil	Sunrise	17	18	19	20
N 72	03 35	05 02	06 09	12 05	14 06	15 56	17 39
N 70	03 52	05 08	06 09	12 42	14 27	16 07	17 44
68	04 05	05 13	06 09	13 08	14 44	16 17	17 47
66	04 16	05 18	06 09	13 28	14 57	16 25	17 50
64	04 25	05 21	06 09	13 43	15 08	16 31	17 53
62	04 31	05 24	06 08	13 57	15 17	16 37	17 55
60	04 37	05 27	06 08	14 08	15 25	16 41	17 57
N 58	04 43	05 29	06 08	14 17	15 32	16 46	17 59
56	04 47	05 31	06 08	14 26	15 38	16 49	18 00
54	04 51	05 33	06 08	14 33	15 43	16 53	18 02
52	04 55	05 34	06 08	14 40	15 48	16 56	18 03
50	04 58	05 35	06 08	14 46	15 52	16 59	18 04
45	05 04	05 38	06 07	14 59	16 02	17 05	18 06
N 40	05 09	05 40	06 07	15 09	16 10	17 10	18 09
35	05 12	05 42	06 07	15 18	16 17	17 14	18 10
30	05 15	05 43	06 07	15 26	16 23	17 18	18 12
20	05 19	05 44	06 06	15 40	16 33	17 24	18 15
N 10	05 20	05 44	06 05	15 52	16 42	17 30	18 17
0	05 20	05 44	06 05	16 03	16 50	17 36	18 19
S 10	05 19	05 43	06 04	16 14	16 59	17 41	18 22
20	05 16	05 41	06 03	16 26	17 08	17 47	18 24
30	05 10	05 38	06 02	16 39	17 18	17 53	18 27
35	05 07	05 36	06 01	16 47	17 24	17 57	18 28
40	05 02	05 33	06 01	16 56	17 30	18 01	18 30
45	04 56	05 30	06 00	17 06	17 38	18 06	18 32
S 50	04 48	05 26	05 58	17 19	17 47	18 12	18 35
52	04 44	05 24	05 58	17 25	17 51	18 15	18 36
54	04 39	05 22	05 57	17 31	17 56	18 18	18 37
56	04 34	05 19	05 56	17 38	18 01	18 21	18 38
58	04 29	05 16	05 56	17 46	18 07	18 24	18 40
S 60	04 22	05 13	05 55	17 55	18 14	18 28	18 41

Twilight / Moonset

Lat.	Sunset	Civil	Naut.	17	18	19	20
N 72	18 09	19 17	20 45	07 50	07 28	07 13	07 01
N 70	18 09	19 11	20 28	07 11	07 05	07 00	06 54
68	18 09	19 05	20 14	06 44	06 48	06 49	06 49
66	18 09	19 01	20 03	06 24	06 33	06 40	06 44
64	18 09	18 57	19 54	06 07	06 22	06 32	06 40
62	18 09	18 54	19 47	05 53	06 12	06 25	06 37
60	18 09	18 51	19 41	05 42	06 03	06 20	06 33
N 58	18 09	18 49	19 35	05 32	05 55	06 14	06 31
56	18 09	18 47	19 31	05 23	05 49	06 10	06 28
54	18 09	18 45	19 26	05 15	05 43	06 06	06 26
52	18 09	18 43	19 23	05 08	05 37	06 02	06 24
50	18 10	18 41	19 20	05 01	05 32	05 59	06 22
45	18 10	18 39	19 13	04 47	05 21	05 51	06 18
N 40	18 10	18 37	19 08	04 36	05 12	05 45	06 15
35	18 10	18 35	19 05	04 26	05 05	05 40	06 12
30	18 10	18 34	19 02	04 18	04 58	05 35	06 09
20	18 10	18 32	18 58	04 03	04 46	05 27	06 05
N 10	18 11	18 32	18 56	03 50	04 36	05 19	06 01
0	18 11	18 32	18 56	03 37	04 26	05 12	05 57
S 10	18 12	18 33	18 57	03 25	04 16	05 05	05 53
20	18 13	18 35	19 00	03 12	04 06	04 58	05 49
30	18 14	18 38	19 05	02 56	03 53	04 49	05 44
35	18 14	18 40	19 09	02 47	03 46	04 44	05 41
40	18 15	18 42	19 14	02 37	03 38	04 39	05 38
45	18 16	18 45	19 20	02 25	03 29	04 32	05 35
S 50	18 17	18 49	19 27	02 11	03 18	04 24	05 30
52	18 17	18 51	19 31	02 04	03 12	04 21	05 28
54	18 18	18 53	19 35	01 56	03 06	04 17	05 26
56	18 19	18 56	19 40	01 48	03 00	04 12	05 23
58	18 19	18 58	19 46	01 38	02 52	04 07	05 21
S 60	18 20	19 02	19 52	01 27	02 44	04 01	05 18

SUN / MOON

Day	Eqn. of Time 00h	12h	Mer. Pass.	Mer. Pass. Upper	Lower	Age	Phase
	m s	m s	h m	h m	h m	d	
17	08 32	08 24	12 08	22 15	09 50	11	
18	08 15	08 06	12 08	23 01	10 38	12	◯
19	07 57	07 49	12 08	23 46	11 24	13	

G.M.T.	ARIES G.H.A.	VENUS −3.4 G.H.A.	Dec.	MARS +1.3 G.H.A.	Dec.	JUPITER −2.0 G.H.A.	Dec.	SATURN +0.7 G.H.A.	Dec.	Star Name	S.H.A.	Dec.
20 00	177 26.3	181 48.1 S 3	27.4	175 04.3 N 0	11.5	351 02.0 S 1	02.3	349 58.1 S 0	20.7	Acamar	315 37.3	S40 23.1
01	192 28.7	196 47.7	26.1	190 05.0	12.3	6 04.8	02.2	5 00.7	20.6	Achernar	335 45.5	S57 20.2
02	207 31.2	211 47.3	24.9	205 05.7	13.1	21 07.5	02.1	20 03.4	20.5	Acrux	173 36.2	S62 59.6
03	222 33.6	226 46.9 ··	23.7	220 06.4 ··	13.9	36 10.3 ··	01.9	35 06.0 ··	20.5	Adhara	255 31.8	S28 57.1
04	237 36.1	241 46.5	22.4	235 07.1	14.6	51 13.1	01.8	50 08.7	20.4	Aldebaran	291 17.7	N16 28.2
05	252 38.6	256 46.1	21.2	250 07.8	15.4	66 15.8	01.7	65 11.3	20.3			
06	267 41.0	271 45.7 S 3	19.9	265 08.5 N 0	16.2	81 18.6 S 1	01.6	80 13.9 S 0	20.2	Alioth	166 41.7	N56 03.7
07	282 43.5	286 45.3	18.7	280 09.2	17.0	96 21.3	01.4	95 16.6	20.2	Alkaid	153 17.8	N49 24.3
08	297 46.0	301 44.9	17.5	295 09.9	17.8	111 24.1	01.3	110 19.2	20.1	Al Na'ir	28 14.9	S47 03.2
F 09	312 48.4	316 44.5 ··	16.2	310 10.6 ··	18.6	126 26.8 ··	01.2	125 21.9 ··	20.0	Alnilam	276 11.4	S 1 13.0
R 10	327 50.9	331 44.1	15.0	325 11.3	19.4	141 29.6	01.0	140 24.5	19.9	Alphard	218 20.0	S 8 34.7
I 11	342 53.4	346 43.7	13.7	340 12.0	20.2	156 32.3	00.9	155 27.1	19.8			
D 12	357 55.8	1 43.3 S 3	12.5	355 12.6 N 0	21.0	171 35.1 S 1	00.8	170 29.8 S 0	19.8	Alphecca	126 31.6	N26 46.5'
A 13	12 58.3	16 43.0	11.3	10 13.3	21.8	186 37.9	00.7	185 32.4	19.7	Alpheratz	358 09.3	N28 59.0
Y 14	28 00.8	31 42.6	10.0	25 14.0	22.6	201 40.6	00.5	200 35.1	19.6	Altair	62 32.3	N 8 48.9
15	43 03.2	46 42.2 ··	08.8	40 14.7 ··	23.3	216 43.4 ··	00.4	215 37.7 ··	19.5	Ankaa	353 40.3	S42 24.7
16	58 05.7	61 41.8	07.5	55 15.4	24.1	231 46.1	00.3	230 40.3	19.4	Antares	112 56.3	S26 23.4
17	73 08.1	76 41.4	06.3	70 16.1	24.9	246 48.9	00.1	245 43.0	19.4			
18	88 10.6	91 41.0 S 3	05.1	85 16.8 N 0	25.7	261 51.6 S 1	00.0	260 45.6 S 0	19.3	Arcturus	146 17.9	N19 16.7
19	103 13.1	106 40.6	03.8	100 17.5	26.5	276 54.4 0	59.9	275 48.3	19.2	Atria	108 20.1	S68 59.4
20	118 15.5	121 40.2	02.6	115 18.2	27.3	291 57.2	59.8	290 50.9	19.1	Avior	234 27.7	S59 27.2
21	133 18.0	136 39.8 ··	01.3	130 18.9 ··	28.1	306 59.9 ··	59.6	305 53.5 ··	19.0	Bellatrix	278 58.4	N 6 19.8
22	148 20.5	151 39.4 3	00.1	145 19.6	28.9	322 02.7	59.5	320 56.2	19.0	Betelgeuse	271 27.9	N 7 24.1
23	163 22.9	166 39.0 2	58.8	160 20.3	29.7	337 05.4	59.4	335 58.8	18.9			
21 00	178 25.4	181 38.7 S 2	57.6	175 21.0 N 0	30.5	352 08.2 S 0	59.2	351 01.5 S 0	18.8	Canopus	264 07.0	S52 41.5
01	193 27.9	196 38.3	56.4	190 21.6	31.2	7 10.9	59.1	6 04.1	18.7	Capella	281 10.9	N45 58.8
02	208 30.3	211 37.9	55.1	205 22.3	32.0	22 13.7	59.0	21 06.7	18.7	Deneb	49 48.5	N45 12.5
03	223 32.8	226 37.5 ··	53.9	220 23.0 ··	32.8	37 16.5 ··	58.9	36 09.4 ··	18.6	Denebola	182 58.4	N14 40.6
04	238 35.3	241 37.1	52.6	235 23.7	33.6	52 19.2	58.7	51 12.0	18.5	Diphda	349 20.9	S18 05.6
05	253 37.7	256 36.7	51.4	250 24.4	34.4	67 22.0	58.6	66 14.7	18.4			
06	268 40.2	271 36.3 S 2	50.1	265 25.1 N 0	35.2	82 24.7 S 0	58.5	81 17.3 S 0	18.3	Dubhe	194 21.1	N61 51.2
07	283 42.6	286 35.9	48.9	280 25.8	36.0	97 27.5	58.3	96 19.9	18.3	Elnath	278 43.8	N28 35.5
S 08	298 45.1	301 35.5	47.6	295 26.5	36.8	112 30.2	58.2	111 22.6	18.2	Eltanin	90 57.6	N51 29.2
A 09	313 47.6	316 35.1 ··	46.4	310 27.2 ··	37.6	127 33.0 ··	58.1	126 25.2 ··	18.1	Enif	34 11.5	N 9 47.1
T 10	328 50.0	331 34.8	45.2	325 27.9	38.4	142 35.8	58.0	141 27.9	18.0	Fomalhaut	15 51.4	S29 43.5
U 11	343 52.5	346 34.4	43.9	340 28.6	39.1	157 38.5	57.8	156 30.5	17.9			
R 12	358 55.0	1 34.0 S 2	42.7	355 29.3 N 0	39.9	172 41.3 S 0	57.7	171 33.2 S 0	17.9	Gacrux	172 27.8	S57 00.4
D 13	13 57.4	16 33.6	41.4	10 30.0	40.7	187 44.0	57.6	186 35.8	17.8	Gienah	176 17.3	S17 26.3
A 14	28 59.9	31 33.2	40.2	25 30.7	41.5	202 46.8	57.5	201 38.4	17.7	Hadar	149 22.3	S60 16.8
Y 15	44 02.4	46 32.8 ··	38.9	40 31.3 ··	42.3	217 49.5 ··	57.3	216 41.1 ··	17.6	Hamal	328 28.8	N23 22.3
16	59 04.8	61 32.4	37.7	55 32.0	43.1	232 52.3	57.2	231 43.7	17.6	Kaus Aust.	84 16.4	S34 23.5
17	74 07.3	76 32.0	36.4	70 32.7	43.9	247 55.1	57.1	246 46.4	17.5			
18	89 09.7	91 31.7 S 2	35.2	85 33.4 N 0	44.7	262 57.8 S 0	56.9	261 49.0 S 0	17.4	Kochab	137 18.2	N74 13.8
19	104 12.2	106 31.3	34.0	100 34.1	45.5	278 00.6	56.8	276 51.6	17.3	Markab	14 03.1	N15 06.0
20	119 14.7	121 30.9	32.7	115 34.8	46.2	293 03.3	56.7	291 54.3	17.2	Menkar	314 41.0	N 4 00.8
21	134 17.1	136 30.5 ··	31.5	130 35.5 ··	47.0	308 06.1 ··	56.6	306 56.9 ··	17.2	Menkent	148 36.3	S36 16.6
22	149 19.6	151 30.1	30.2	145 36.2	47.8	323 08.8	56.4	321 59.6	17.1	Miaplacidus	221 44.2	S69 38.6
23	164 22.1	166 29.7	29.0	160 36.9	48.6	338 11.6	56.3	337 02.2	17.0			
22 00	179 24.5	181 29.3 S 2	27.7	175 37.6 N 0	49.4	353 14.4 S 0	56.2	352 04.8 S 0	16.9	Mirfak	309 15.9	N49 47.7
01	194 27.0	196 28.9	26.5	190 38.3	50.2	8 17.1	56.0	7 07.5	16.8	Nunki	76 28.8	S26 19.2
02	209 29.5	211 28.6	25.2	205 39.0	51.0	23 19.9	55.9	22 10.1	16.8	Peacock	53 58.2	S56 47.6
03	224 31.9	226 28.2 ··	24.0	220 39.7 ··	51.8	38 22.6 ··	55.8	37 12.8 ··	16.7	Pollux	243 57.6	N28 04.3
04	239 34.4	241 27.8	22.7	235 40.4	52.6	53 25.4	55.7	52 15.4	16.6	Procyon	245 25.3	N 5 16.3
05	254 36.9	256 27.4	21.5	250 41.1	53.3	68 28.1	55.5	67 18.0	16.5			
06	269 39.3	271 27.0 S 2	20.2	265 41.7 N 0	54.1	83 30.9 S 0	55.4	82 20.7 S 0	16.4	Rasalhague	96 29.2	N12 34.3
07	284 41.8	286 26.6	19.0	280 42.4	54.9	98 33.7	55.3	97 23.3	16.4	Regulus	208 09.4	N12 03.5
08	299 44.2	301 26.2	17.7	295 43.1	55.7	113 36.4	55.1	112 26.0	16.3	Rigel	281 35.8	S 8 13.6
S 09	314 46.7	316 25.8 ··	16.5	310 43.8 ··	56.5	128 39.2 ··	55.0	127 28.6 ··	16.2	Rigil Kent.	140 24.9	S60 45.2
U 10	329 49.2	331 25.5	15.3	325 44.5	57.3	143 41.9	54.9	142 31.3	16.1	Sabik	102 40.7	S15 42.1
N 11	344 51.6	346 25.1	14.0	340 45.2	58.1	158 44.7	54.7	157 33.9	16.1			
D 12	359 54.1	1 24.7 S 2	12.8	355 45.9 N 0	58.9	173 47.5 S 0	54.6	172 36.5 S 0	16.0	Schedar	350 09.2	N56 25.9
A 13	14 56.6	16 24.3	11.5	10 46.6 0	59.7	188 50.2	54.5	187 39.2	15.9	Shaula	96 55.3	S37 05.3
Y 14	29 59.0	31 23.9	10.3	25 47.3 1	00.4	203 53.0	54.4	202 41.8	15.8	Sirius	258 55.3	S16 41.7
15	45 01.5	46 23.5 ··	09.0	40 48.0 ··	01.2	218 55.7 ··	54.2	217 44.5 ··	15.7	Spica	158 56.9	S11 03.8
16	60 04.0	61 23.2	07.8	55 48.7	02.0	233 58.5	54.1	232 47.1	15.7	Suhail	223 10.2	S43 21.6
17	75 06.4	76 22.8	06.5	70 49.4	02.8	249 01.3	54.0	247 49.7	15.6			
18	90 08.9	91 22.4 S 2	05.3	85 50.1 N 1	03.6	264 04.0 S 0	53.8	262 52.4 S 0	15.5	Vega	80 55.7	N38 45.7
19	105 11.4	106 22.0	04.0	100 50.8	04.4	279 06.8	53.7	277 55.0	15.4	Zuben'ubi	137 32.4	S15 57.8
20	120 13.8	121 21.6	02.8	115 51.5	05.2	294 09.5	53.6	292 57.7	15.3			
21	135 16.3	136 21.2 ··	01.5	130 52.2 ··	06.0	309 12.3 ··	53.5	308 00.3 ··	15.3		S.H.A.	Mer. Pass.
22	150 18.7	151 20.8 2	00.3	145 52.9	06.7	324 15.0	53.3	323 03.0	15.2	Venus	3 13.3	11 54
23	165 21.2	166 20.5 1	59.0	160 53.5	07.5	339 17.8	53.2	338 05.6	15.1	Mars	356 55.6	12 18
Mer. Pass. 12 04.3		v −0.4	d 1.2	v 0.7	d 0.8	v 2.8	d 0.1	v 2.6	d 0.1	Jupiter	173 42.8	0 31
										Saturn	172 36.1	0 36

G.M.T.	SUN G.H.A.	Dec.	MOON G.H.A.	v	Dec.	d	H.P.
	° ′	° ′	° ′	′	° ′	′	′
20 00	178 05.2 S 0 16.8		3 20.5 14.4 N 6 17.6			10.3	55.0
01	193 05.4	15.8	17 53.9 14.3	6 07.3		10.3	55.0
02	208 05.6	14.8	32 27.2 14.5	5 57.0		10.3	55.0
03	223 05.7 ··	13.9	47 00.7 14.4	5 46.7		10.4	54.9
04	238 05.9	12.9	61 34.1 14.5	5 36.3		10.4	54.9
05	253 06.1	11.9	76 07.6 14.5	5 25.9		10.4	54.9
06	268 06.3 S 0 10.9		90 41.1 14.5 N 5 15.5			10.4	54.9
07	283 06.5	09.9	105 14.6 14.6	5 05.1		10.4	54.9
08	298 06.7	08.9	119 48.2 14.6	4 54.7		10.5	54.9
F 09	313 06.9 ··	07.9	134 21.8 14.7	4 44.2		10.4	54.8
R 10	328 07.0	06.9	148 55.5 14.6	4 33.8		10.5	54.8
I 11	343 07.2	06.0	163 29.1 14.7	4 23.3		10.5	54.8
D 12	358 07.4 S 0 05.0		178 02.8 14.8 N 4 12.8			10.5	54.8
A 13	13 07.6	04.0	192 36.6 14.7	4 02.3		10.5	54.8
Y 14	28 07.8	03.0	207 10.3 14.8	3 51.8		10.5	54.8
15	43 08.0 ··	02.0	221 44.1 14.8	3 41.3		10.6	54.8
16	58 08.2 S 0 01.0		236 17.9 14.8	3 30.7		10.5	54.7
17	73 08.4 0 00.0		250 51.7 14.9	3 20.2		10.6	54.7
18	88 08.5 N 0 00.9		265 25.6 14.9 N 3 09.6			10.5	54.7
19	103 08.7	01.9	279 59.5 14.9	2 59.1		10.6	54.7
20	118 08.9	02.9	294 33.4 14.9	2 48.5		10.6	54.7
21	133 09.1 ··	03.9	309 07.3 15.0	2 37.9		10.5	54.7
22	148 09.3	04.9	323 41.3 14.9	2 27.4		10.6	54.7
23	163 09.5	05.9	338 15.2 15.0	2 16.8		10.6	54.7
21 00	178 09.7 N 0 06.9		352 49.2 15.0 N 2 06.2			10.6	54.6
01	193 09.8	07.9	7 23.2 15.1	1 55.6		10.6	54.6
02	208 10.0	08.8	21 57.3 15.0	1 45.0		10.6	54.6
03	223 10.2 ··	09.8	36 31.3 15.1	1 34.4		10.6	54.6
04	238 10.4	10.8	51 05.4 15.1	1 23.8		10.6	54.6
05	253 10.6	11.8	65 39.5 15.1	1 13.2		10.6	54.6
06	268 10.8 N 0 12.8		80 13.6 15.1 N 1 02.6			10.6	54.6
07	283 11.0	13.8	94 47.7 15.2	0 52.0		10.6	54.5
S 08	298 11.2	14.8	109 21.9 15.1	0 41.4		10.6	54.5
A 09	313 11.3 ··	15.8	123 56.0 15.2	0 30.8		10.6	54.5
T 10	328 11.5	16.7	138 30.2 15.2	0 20.2		10.6	54.5
U 11	343 11.7	17.7	153 04.4 15.2 N 0 09.6			10.6	54.5
R 12	358 11.9 N 0 18.7		167 38.6 15.2 S 0 01.0			10.6	54.5
D 13	13 12.1	19.7	182 12.8 15.2	0 11.6		10.5	54.5
A 14	28 12.3	20.7	196 47.0 15.3	0 22.2		10.5	54.5
Y 15	43 12.5 ··	21.7	211 21.3 15.2	0 32.7		10.6	54.5
16	58 12.7	22.7	225 55.5 15.3	0 43.3		10.6	54.4
17	73 12.9	23.6	240 29.8 15.2	0 53.9		10.5	54.4
18	88 13.0 N 0 24.6		255 04.0 15.3 S 1 04.4			10.5	54.4
19	103 13.2	25.6	269 38.3 15.3	1 14.9		10.6	54.4
20	118 13.4	26.6	284 12.6 15.3	1 25.5		10.5	54.4
21	133 13.6 ··	27.6	298 46.9 15.3	1 36.0		10.6	54.4
22	148 13.8	28.6	313 21.2 15.3	1 46.5		10.5	54.4
23	163 14.0	29.6	327 55.5 15.3	1 57.0		10.5	54.4
22 00	178 14.2 N 0 30.6		342 29.8 15.4 S 2 07.5			10.5	54.4
01	193 14.4	31.5	357 04.2 15.3	2 18.0		10.4	54.3
02	208 14.5	32.5	11 38.5 15.3	2 28.4		10.5	54.3
03	223 14.7 ··	33.5	26 12.8 15.4	2 38.9		10.4	54.3
04	238 14.9	34.5	40 47.2 15.3	2 49.3		10.4	54.3
05	253 15.1	35.5	55 21.5 15.3	2 59.7		10.4	54.3
06	268 15.3 N 0 36.5		69 55.8 15.3 S 3 10.1			10.4	54.3
07	283 15.5	37.5	84 30.2 15.3	3 20.5		10.4	54.3
08	298 15.7	38.4	99 04.5 15.4	3 30.9		10.4	54.3
S 09	313 15.9 ··	39.4	113 38.9 15.3	3 41.3		10.3	54.3
U 10	328 16.1	40.4	128 13.2 15.4	3 51.6		10.3	54.3
N 11	343 16.2	41.4	142 47.6 15.3	4 01.9		10.3	54.3
D 12	358 16.4 N 0 42.4		157 21.9 15.3 S 4 12.2			10.3	54.2
A 13	13 16.6	43.4	171 56.2 15.4	4 22.5		10.2	54.2
Y 14	28 16.8 ··	44.4	186 30.6 15.3	4 32.7		10.2	54.2
15	43 17.0 ··	45.3	201 04.9 15.4	4 43.0		10.2	54.2
16	58 17.2	46.3	215 39.2 15.4	4 53.2		10.2	54.2
17	73 17.4	47.3	230 13.6 15.3	5 03.4		10.1	54.2
18	88 17.6 N 0 48.3		244 47.9 15.3 S 5 13.5			10.2	54.2
19	103 17.8	49.3	259 22.2 15.3	5 23.7		10.1	54.2
20	118 17.9	50.3	273 56.5 15.3	5 33.8		10.1	54.2
21	133 18.1 ··	51.3	288 30.8 15.3	5 43.9		10.0	54.2
22	148 18.3	52.2	303 05.1 15.3	5 53.9		10.1	54.2
23	163 18.5	53.2	317 39.4 15.3	6 04.0		10.0	54.2
	S.D. 16.1 d 1.0		S.D. 14.9		14.8		14.8

Lat.	Twilight Naut.	Civil	Sunrise	Moonrise 20	21	22	23
°	h m	h m	h m	h m	h m	h m	h m
N 72	03 15	04 46	05 54	17 39	19 19	20 59	22 41
N 70	03 35	04 54	05 55	17 44	19 17	20 50	22 25
68	03 50	05 00	05 56	17 47	19 16	20 44	22 12
66	04 02	05 06	05 57	17 50	19 14	20 38	22 01
64	04 12	05 10	05 58	17 53	19 13	20 33	21 52
62	04 21	05 14	05 59	17 55	19 12	20 29	21 45
60	04 28	05 18	05 59	17 57	19 11	20 25	21 38
N 58	04 34	05 20	06 00	17 59	19 11	20 22	21 32
56	04 39	05 23	06 00	18 00	19 10	20 19	21 27
54	04 43	05 25	06 00	18 02	19 09	20 16	21 23
52	04 47	05 27	06 01	18 03	19 09	20 14	21 19
50	04 51	05 29	06 01	18 04	19 08	20 12	21 15
45	04 58	05 32	06 02	18 06	19 07	20 07	21 07
N 40	05 04	05 35	06 02	18 09	19 06	20 04	21 00
35	05 08	05 37	06 03	18 10	19 06	20 00	20 55
30	05 11	05 39	06 03	18 12	19 05	19 57	20 50
20	05 16	05 41	06 03	18 15	19 04	19 53	20 41
N 10	05 18	05 43	06 04	18 17	19 03	19 48	20 34
0	05 19	05 43	06 04	18 19	19 02	19 44	20 27
S 10	05 19	05 43	06 04	18 22	19 01	19 40	20 20
20	05 16	05 42	06 04	18 24	19 00	19 36	20 12
30	05 12	05 40	06 04	18 27	18 59	19 31	20 04
35	05 09	05 39	06 04	18 28	18 58	19 28	19 59
40	05 05	05 37	06 04	18 30	18 58	19 25	19 54
45	05 00	05 34	06 03	18 32	18 57	19 22	19 47
S 50	04 53	05 31	06 03	18 35	18 56	19 17	19 40
52	04 49	05 29	06 03	18 36	18 56	19 16	19 37
54	04 46	05 27	06 03	18 37	18 55	19 13	19 33
56	04 41	05 25	06 03	18 38	18 55	19 11	19 29
58	04 36	05 23	06 02	18 40	18 54	19 09	19 24
S 60	04 30	05 20	06 02	18 41	18 53	19 06	19 19

Lat.	Sunset	Twilight Civil	Naut.	Moonset 20	21	22	23
°	h m	h m	h m	h m	h m	h m	h m
N 72	18 23	19 32	21 04	07 01	06 50	06 40	06 28
N 70	18 21	19 23	20 43	06 54	06 49	06 44	06 39
68	18 20	19 16	20 27	06 49	06 48	06 48	06 47
66	18 19	19 11	20 15	06 44	06 48	06 51	06 54
64	18 18	19 06	20 06	06 40	06 47	06 54	07 01
62	18 17	19 02	19 56	06 37	06 46	06 56	07 06
60	18 17	18 58	19 49	06 33	06 46	06 58	07 11
N 58	18 16	18 55	19 43	06 31	06 46	07 00	07 15
56	18 16	18 53	19 37	06 28	06 45	07 01	07 18
54	18 15	18 50	19 33	06 26	06 45	07 03	07 22
52	18 15	18 48	19 28	06 24	06 44	07 04	07 25
50	18 14	18 47	19 25	06 22	06 44	07 06	07 27
45	18 14	18 43	19 17	06 18	06 43	07 08	07 33
N 40	18 13	18 40	19 12	06 15	06 43	07 10	07 38
35	18 12	18 38	19 07	06 12	06 42	07 12	07 43
30	18 12	18 36	19 04	06 09	06 42	07 14	07 47
20	18 11	18 33	18 59	06 05	06 41	07 17	07 53
N 10	18 11	18 32	18 56	06 01	06 41	07 20	07 59
0	18 10	18 31	18 55	05 57	06 40	07 22	08 05
S 10	18 10	18 31	18 56	05 53	06 39	07 25	08 10
20	18 10	18 32	18 58	05 49	06 38	07 27	08 16
30	18 10	18 34	19 02	05 44	06 38	07 30	08 23
35	18 10	18 35	19 05	05 41	06 37	07 32	08 27
40	18 10	18 37	19 09	05 38	06 37	07 34	08 31
45	18 10	18 39	19 14	05 35	06 36	07 36	08 36
S 50	18 10	18 43	19 20	05 30	06 35	07 39	08 42
52	18 10	18 44	19 24	05 28	06 35	07 40	08 45
54	18 11	18 46	19 27	05 26	06 34	07 42	08 48
56	18 11	18 48	19 32	05 23	06 34	07 43	08 52
58	18 11	18 50	19 36	05 21	06 33	07 45	08 56
S 60	18 11	18 52	19 42	05 18	06 33	07 47	09 00

Day	SUN Eqn. of Time 00ʰ	12ʰ	Mer. Pass.	MOON Mer. Pass. Upper	Lower	Age	Phase
	m s	m s	h m	h m	h m	d	
20	07 40	07 31	12 08	24 30	12 08	14	
21	07 22	07 13	12 07	00 30	12 51	15	
22	07 04	06 55	12 07	01 12	13 33	16	◯

G.M.T.	ARIES G.H.A.	VENUS −3.4 G.H.A.	VENUS Dec.	MARS +1.3 G.H.A.	MARS Dec.	JUPITER −2.0 G.H.A.	JUPITER Dec.	SATURN +0.7 G.H.A.	SATURN Dec.	STARS Name	S.H.A.	Dec.
23 00	180 23.7	181 20.1	S 1 57.8	175 54.2	N 1 08.3	354 20.6	S 0 53.1	353 08.2	S 0 15.0	Acamar	315 37.3	S40 23.1
01	195 26.1	196 19.7	56.5	190 54.9	09.1	9 23.3	52.9	8 10.9	14.9	Achernar	335 45.6	S57 20.2
02	210 28.6	211 19.3	55.3	205 55.6	09.9	24 26.1	52.8	23 13.5	14.9	Acrux	173 36.2	S62 59.7
03	225 31.1	226 18.9	·· 54.0	220 56.3	·· 10.7	39 28.8	·· 52.7	38 16.2	·· 14.8	Adhara	255 31.8	S28 57.1
04	240 33.5	241 18.5	52.8	235 57.0	11.5	54 31.6	52.6	53 18.8	14.7	Aldebaran	291 17.8	N16 28.2
05	255 36.0	256 18.2	51.5	250 57.7	12.3	69 34.4	52.4	68 21.4	14.6			
06	270 38.5	271 17.8	S 1 50.3	265 58.4	N 1 13.1	84 37.1	S 0 52.3	83 24.1	S 0 14.6	Alioth	166 41.7	N56 03.7
07	285 40.9	286 17.4	49.0	280 59.1	13.8	99 39.9	52.2	98 26.7	14.5	Alkaid	153 17.8	N49 24.3
08	300 43.4	301 17.0	47.8	295 59.8	14.6	114 42.6	52.0	113 29.4	14.4	Al Na'ir	28 14.9	S47 03.2
M 09	315 45.8	316 16.6	·· 46.5	311 00.5	·· 15.4	129 45.4	·· 51.9	128 32.0	·· 14.3	Alnilam	276 11.4	S 1 13.0
O 10	330 48.3	331 16.2	45.3	326 01.2	16.2	144 48.2	51.8	143 34.7	14.2	Alphard	218 20.0	S 8 34.7
N 11	345 50.8	346 15.9	44.0	341 01.9	17.0	159 50.9	51.7	158 37.3	14.2			
D 12	0 53.2	1 15.5	S 1 42.8	356 02.6	N 1 17.8	174 53.7	S 0 51.5	173 39.9	S 0 14.1	Alphecca	126 31.6	N26 46.5
A 13	15 55.7	16 15.1	41.5	11 03.3	18.6	189 56.4	51.4	188 42.6	14.0	Alpheratz	358 09.3	N28 59.0
Y 14	30 58.2	31 14.7	40.3	26 04.0	19.4	204 59.2	51.3	203 45.2	13.9	Altair	62 32.3	N 8 48.9
15	46 00.6	46 14.3	·· 39.0	41 04.7	·· 20.1	220 01.9	·· 51.1	218 47.9	·· 13.8	Ankaa	353 40.3	S42 24.7
16	61 03.1	61 13.9	37.8	56 05.4	20.9	235 04.7	51.0	233 50.5	13.8	Antares	112 56.3	S26 23.4
17	76 05.6	76 13.6	36.5	71 06.1	21.7	250 07.5	50.9	248 53.1	13.7			
18	91 08.0	91 13.2	S 1 35.3	86 06.7	N 1 22.5	265 10.2	S 0 50.8	263 55.8	S 0 13.6	Arcturus	146 17.9	N19 16.7
19	106 10.5	106 12.8	34.0	101 07.4	23.3	280 13.0	50.6	278 58.4	13.5	Atria	108 20.1	S68 59.4
20	121 13.0	121 12.4	32.8	116 08.1	24.1	295 15.7	50.5	294 01.1	13.4	Avior	234 27.7	S59 27.2
21	136 15.4	136 12.0	·· 31.5	131 08.8	·· 24.9	310 18.5	·· 50.4	309 03.7	·· 13.4	Bellatrix	278 58.5	N 6 19.8
22	151 17.9	151 11.7	30.3	146 09.5	25.6	325 21.3	50.2	324 06.4	13.3	Betelgeuse	271 27.9	N 7 24.1
23	166 20.3	166 11.3	29.0	161 10.2	26.4	340 24.0	50.1	339 09.0	13.2			
24 00	181 22.8	181 10.9	S 1 27.8	176 10.9	N 1 27.2	355 26.8	S 0 50.0	354 11.6	S 0 13.1	Canopus	264 07.0	S52 41.5
01	196 25.3	196 10.5	26.5	191 11.6	28.0	10 29.5	49.9	9 14.3	13.1	Capella	281 10.9	N45 58.8
02	211 27.7	211 10.1	25.3	206 12.3	28.8	25 32.3	49.7	24 16.9	13.0	Deneb	49 48.5	N45 12.5
03	226 30.2	226 09.7	·· 24.0	221 13.0	·· 29.6	40 35.1	·· 49.6	39 19.6	·· 12.9	Denebola	182 58.4	N14 40.6
04	241 32.7	241 09.4	22.8	236 13.7	30.4	55 37.8	49.5	54 22.2	12.8	Diphda	349 20.9	S18 05.6
05	256 35.1	256 09.0	21.5	251 14.4	31.2	70 40.6	49.3	69 24.9	12.7			
06	271 37.6	271 08.6	S 1 20.3	266 15.1	N 1 31.9	85 43.3	S 0 49.2	84 27.5	S 0 12.7	Dubhe	194 21.1	N61 51.2
07	286 40.1	286 08.2	19.0	281 15.8	32.7	100 46.1	49.1	99 30.1	12.6	Elnath	278 43.8	N28 35.5
08	301 42.5	301 07.8	17.7	296 16.5	33.5	115 48.9	49.0	114 32.8	12.5	Eltanin	90 57.5	N51 29.2
T 09	316 45.0	316 07.5	·· 16.5	311 17.2	·· 34.3	130 51.6	·· 48.8	129 35.4	·· 12.4	Enif	34 11.5	N 9 47.1
U 10	331 47.5	331 07.1	15.2	326 17.9	35.1	145 54.4	48.7	144 38.1	12.3	Fomalhaut	15 51.4	S29 43.5
E 11	346 49.9	346 06.7	14.0	341 18.6	35.9	160 57.1	48.6	159 40.7	12.3			
S 12	1 52.4	1 06.3	S 1 12.7	356 19.3	N 1 36.7	175 59.9	S 0 48.4	174 43.3	S 0 12.2	Gacrux	172 27.8	S57 00.4
D 13	16 54.8	16 05.9	11.5	11 20.0	37.4	191 02.7	48.3	189 46.0	12.1	Gienah	176 17.3	S17 26.3
A 14	31 57.3	31 05.6	10.2	26 20.7	38.2	206 05.4	48.2	204 48.6	12.0	Hadar	149 22.3	S60 16.8
Y 15	46 59.8	46 05.2	·· 09.0	41 21.3	·· 39.0	221 08.2	·· 48.1	219 51.3	·· 11.9	Hamal	328 28.8	N23 22.3
16	62 02.2	61 04.8	07.7	56 22.0	39.8	236 10.9	47.9	234 53.9	11.9	Kaus Aust.	84 16.4	S34 23.5
17	77 04.7	76 04.4	06.5	71 22.7	40.6	251 13.7	47.8	249 56.6	11.8			
18	92 07.2	91 04.0	S 1 05.2	86 23.4	N 1 41.4	266 16.5	S 0 47.7	264 59.2	S 0 11.7	Kochab	137 18.1	N74 13.8
19	107 09.6	106 03.7	04.0	101 24.1	42.2	281 19.2	47.5	280 01.8	11.6	Markab	14 03.1	N15 06.0
20	122 12.1	121 03.3	02.7	116 24.8	42.9	296 22.0	47.4	295 04.5	11.6	Menkar	314 41.0	N 4 00.8
21	137 14.6	136 02.9	·· 01.5	131 25.5	·· 43.7	311 24.7	·· 47.3	310 07.1	·· 11.5	Menkent	148 36.3	S36 16.6
22	152 17.0	151 02.5	1 00.2	146 26.2	44.5	326 27.5	47.1	325 09.8	11.4	Miaplacidus	221 44.2	S69 38.6
23	167 19.5	166 02.1	0 59.0	161 26.9	45.3	341 30.3	47.0	340 12.4	11.3			
25 00	182 21.9	181 01.8	S 0 57.7	176 27.6	N 1 46.1	356 33.0	S 0 46.9	355 15.1	S 0 11.2	Mirfak	309 15.9	N49 47.7
01	197 24.4	196 01.4	56.4	191 28.3	46.9	11 35.8	46.8	10 17.7	11.2	Nunki	76 28.8	S26 19.2
02	212 26.9	211 01.0	55.2	206 29.0	47.7	26 38.5	46.6	25 20.3	11.1	Peacock	53 58.2	S56 47.6
03	227 29.3	226 00.6	·· 53.9	221 29.7	·· 48.4	41 41.3	·· 46.5	40 23.0	·· 11.0	Pollux	243 57.6	N28 04.3
04	242 31.8	241 00.2	52.7	236 30.4	49.2	56 44.1	46.4	55 25.6	10.9	Procyon	245 25.3	N 5 16.3
05	257 34.3	255 59.9	51.4	251 31.1	50.0	71 46.8	46.2	70 28.3	10.8			
06	272 36.7	270 59.5	S 0 50.2	266 31.8	N 1 50.8	86 49.6	S 0 46.1	85 30.9	S 0 10.8	Rasalhague	96 29.2	N12 34.3
07	287 39.2	285 59.1	48.9	281 32.5	51.6	101 52.3	46.0	100 33.6	10.7	Regulus	208 09.4	N12 03.5
W 08	302 41.7	300 58.7	47.7	296 33.2	52.4	116 55.1	45.9	115 36.2	10.6	Rigel	281 35.8	S 8 13.6
E 09	317 44.1	315 58.3	·· 46.4	311 33.9	·· 53.1	131 57.9	·· 45.7	130 38.8	·· 10.5	Rigil Kent.	140 24.9	S60 45.2
D 10	332 46.6	330 58.0	45.2	326 34.6	53.9	147 00.6	45.6	145 41.5	10.4	Sabik	102 40.7	S15 42.1
N 11	347 49.1	345 57.6	43.9	341 35.3	54.7	162 03.4	45.5	160 44.1	10.4			
E 12	2 51.5	0 57.2	S 0 42.7	356 36.0	N 1 55.5	177 06.1	S 0 45.3	175 46.8	S 0 10.3	Schedar	350 09.2	N56 25.9
S 13	17 54.0	15 56.8	41.4	11 36.7	56.3	192 08.9	45.2	190 49.4	10.2	Shaula	96 55.2	S37 05.3
D 14	32 56.4	30 56.4	40.1	26 37.4	57.1	207 11.7	45.1	205 52.1	10.1	Sirius	258 55.4	S16 41.7
A 15	47 58.9	45 56.1	·· 38.9	41 38.0	·· 57.9	222 14.4	·· 45.0	220 54.7	·· 10.1	Spica	158 56.9	S11 03.8
Y 16	63 01.4	60 55.7	37.6	56 38.7	58.6	237 17.2	44.8	235 57.3	10.0	Suhail	223 10.2	S43 21.6
17	78 03.8	75 55.3	36.4	71 39.4	1 59.4	252 19.9	44.7	251 00.0	09.9			
18	93 06.3	90 54.9	S 0 35.1	86 40.1	N 2 00.2	267 22.7	S 0 44.6	266 02.6	S 0 09.8	Vega	80 55.6	N38 45.7
19	108 08.8	105 54.6	33.9	101 40.8	01.0	282 25.5	44.4	281 05.3	09.7	Zuben'ubi	137 32.4	S15 57.8
20	123 11.2	120 54.2	32.6	116 41.5	01.8	297 28.2	44.3	296 07.9	09.7			
21	138 13.7	135 53.8	·· 31.4	131 42.2	·· 02.6	312 31.0	·· 44.2	311 10.6	·· 09.6			
22	153 16.2	150 53.4	30.1	146 42.9	03.3	327 33.8	44.1	326 13.2	09.5			
23	168 18.6	165 53.0	28.9	161 43.6	04.1	342 36.5	43.9	341 15.8	09.4			
Mer. Pass.	h m 11 52.5	v −0.4	d 1.3	v 0.7	d 0.8	v 2.8	d 0.1	v 2.6	d 0.1			

	S.H.A.	Mer. Pass.
	° ′	h m
Venus	359 48.1	11 56
Mars	354 48.1	12 15
Jupiter	174 04.0	0 18
Saturn	172 48.8	0 23

G.M.T.	SUN G.H.A.	SUN Dec.	MOON G.H.A.	v	MOON Dec.	d	H.P.
	° '	° '	° '	'	° '		
23 00	178 18.7	N 0 54.2	332 13.7	15.3	S 6 14.0	10.0	54.2
01	193 18.9	55.2	346 48.0	15.2	6 24.0	9.9	54.1
02	208 19.1	56.2	1 22.2	15.3	6 33.9	9.9	54.1
03	223 19.3	.. 57.2	15 56.5	15.2	6 43.8	9.9	54.1
04	238 19.5	58.2	30 30.7	15.2	6 53.7	9.9	54.1
05	253 19.7	0 59.1	45 04.9	15.2	7 03.6	9.8	54.1
06	268 19.8	N 1 00.1	59 39.1	15.3	S 7 13.4	9.8	54.1
07	283 20.0	01.1	74 13.4	15.1	7 23.2	9.8	54.1
M 08	298 20.2	02.1	88 47.5	15.2	7 33.0	9.8	54.1
O 09	313 20.4	.. 03.1	103 21.7	15.2	7 42.8	9.7	54.1
N 10	328 20.6	04.1	117 55.9	15.1	7 52.5	9.6	54.1
11	343 20.8	05.1	132 30.0	15.2	8 02.1	9.7	54.1
D 12	358 21.0	N 1 06.0	147 04.2	15.1	S 8 11.8	9.6	54.1
A 13	13 21.2	07.0	161 38.3	15.1	8 21.4	9.5	54.1
Y 14	28 21.4	08.0	176 12.4	15.1	8 30.9	9.6	54.1
15	43 21.5	.. 09.0	190 46.5	15.0	8 40.5	9.5	54.1
16	58 21.7	10.0	205 20.5	15.1	8 50.0	9.4	54.1
17	73 21.9	11.0	219 54.6	15.0	8 59.4	9.4	54.1
18	88 22.1	N 1 11.9	234 28.6	15.0	S 9 08.8	9.4	54.1
19	103 22.3	12.9	249 02.6	15.0	9 18.2	9.4	54.1
20	118 22.5	13.9	263 36.6	15.0	9 27.6	9.3	54.1
21	133 22.7	.. 14.9	278 10.6	14.9	9 36.9	9.2	54.1
22	148 22.9	15.9	292 44.5	14.9	9 46.1	9.3	54.1
23	163 23.1	16.9	307 18.4	14.9	9 55.4	9.1	54.1
24 00	178 23.3	N 1 17.8	321 52.3	14.9	S10 04.5	9.2	54.1
01	193 23.4	18.8	336 26.2	14.9	10 13.7	9.1	54.1
02	208 23.6	19.8	351 00.1	14.8	10 22.8	9.0	54.1
03	223 23.8	.. 20.8	5 33.9	14.8	10 31.8	9.0	54.1
04	238 24.0	21.8	20 07.7	14.8	10 40.8	9.0	54.0
05	253 24.2	22.8	34 41.5	14.8	10 49.8	8.9	54.0
06	268 24.4	N 1 23.8	49 15.3	14.7	S10 58.7	8.9	54.0
07	283 24.6	24.7	63 49.0	14.7	11 07.6	8.8	54.0
T 08	298 24.8	25.7	78 22.7	14.7	11 16.4	8.8	54.0
U 09	313 25.0	.. 26.7	92 56.4	14.7	11 25.2	8.7	54.0
E 10	328 25.2	27.7	107 30.1	14.6	11 33.9	8.7	54.0
S 11	343 25.3	28.7	122 03.7	14.6	11 42.6	8.6	54.0
D 12	358 25.5	N 1 29.7	136 37.3	14.6	S11 51.2	8.6	54.0
A 13	13 25.7	30.6	151 10.9	14.5	11 59.8	8.6	54.0
Y 14	28 25.9	31.6	165 44.4	14.5	12 08.4	8.5	54.0
15	43 26.1	.. 32.6	180 17.9	14.5	12 16.9	8.4	54.1
16	58 26.3	33.6	194 51.4	14.4	12 25.3	8.4	54.1
17	73 26.5	34.6	209 24.8	14.5	12 33.7	8.3	54.1
18	88 26.7	N 1 35.6	223 58.3	14.4	S12 42.0	8.3	54.1
19	103 26.9	36.5	238 31.7	14.3	12 50.3	8.2	54.1
20	118 27.1	37.5	253 05.0	14.3	12 58.5	8.2	54.1
21	133 27.2	.. 38.5	267 38.3	14.3	13 06.7	8.1	54.1
22	148 27.4	39.5	282 11.6	14.3	13 14.8	8.1	54.1
23	163 27.6	40.5	296 44.9	14.2	13 22.9	8.0	54.1
25 00	178 27.8	N 1 41.5	311 18.1	14.2	S13 30.9	7.9	54.1
01	193 28.0	42.4	325 51.3	14.2	13 38.8	7.9	54.1
02	208 28.2	43.4	340 24.5	14.1	13 46.7	7.9	54.1
03	223 28.4	.. 44.4	354 57.6	14.1	13 54.6	7.8	54.1
04	238 28.6	45.4	9 30.7	14.1	14 02.4	7.7	54.1
05	253 28.8	46.4	24 03.8	14.0	14 10.1	7.7	54.1
06	268 29.0	N 1 47.3	38 36.8	14.0	S14 17.8	7.6	54.1
07	283 29.1	48.3	53 09.8	13.9	14 25.4	7.5	54.1
W 08	298 29.3	49.3	67 42.7	13.9	14 32.9	7.5	54.1
E 09	313 29.5	.. 50.3	82 15.6	13.9	14 40.4	7.4	54.1
D 10	328 29.7	51.3	96 48.5	13.8	14 47.8	7.4	54.1
N 11	343 29.9	52.3	111 21.3	13.8	14 55.2	7.3	54.1
E 12	358 30.1	N 1 53.2	125 54.1	13.8	S15 02.5	7.2	54.1
S 13	13 30.3	54.2	140 26.9	13.7	15 09.7	7.2	54.1
D 14	28 30.5	55.2	154 59.6	13.7	15 16.9	7.1	54.1
A 15	43 30.7	.. 56.2	169 32.3	13.7	15 24.0	7.0	54.1
Y 16	58 30.9	57.2	184 05.0	13.6	15 31.0	7.0	54.2
17	73 31.1	58.2	198 37.6	13.5	15 38.0	6.9	54.2
18	88 31.2	N 1 59.1	213 10.1	13.5	S15 44.9	6.9	54.2
19	103 31.4	2 00.1	227 42.6	13.5	15 51.8	6.8	54.2
20	118 31.6	01.1	242 15.1	13.5	15 58.6	6.7	54.2
21	133 31.8	.. 02.1	256 47.6	13.4	16 05.3	6.6	54.2
22	148 32.0	03.1	271 20.0	13.3	16 11.9	6.6	54.2
23	163 32.2	04.0	285 52.3	13.4	16 18.5	6.5	54.2
S.D.	16.1	d 1.0	S.D. 14.7		14.7		14.7

Lat.	Twilight Naut.	Twilight Civil	Sunrise	Moonrise 23	24	25	26
°	h m	h m	h m	h m	h m	h m	h m
N 72	02 54	04 29	05 38	22 41	24 30	00 30	02 36
N 70	03 17	04 39	05 41	22 25	24 02	00 02	01 43
68	03 35	04 47	05 44	22 12	23 41	25 11	01 11
66	03 49	04 54	05 46	22 01	23 25	24 48	00 48
64	04 00	04 59	05 47	21 52	23 11	24 30	00 30
62	04 10	05 04	05 49	21 45	23 00	24 15	00 15
60	04 18	05 08	05 50	21 38	22 51	24 02	00 02
N 58	04 24	05 12	05 51	21 32	22 42	23 51	24 58
56	04 30	05 15	05 52	21 27	22 35	23 42	24 46
54	04 35	05 18	05 53	21 23	22 29	23 34	24 36
52	04 40	05 20	05 54	21 19	22 23	23 26	24 28
50	04 44	05 22	05 55	21 15	22 18	23 20	24 28
45	04 52	05 27	05 56	21 07	22 06	23 05	24 03
N 40	04 59	05 30	05 57	21 00	21 57	22 54	23 49
35	05 04	05 33	05 58	20 55	21 49	22 44	23 38
30	05 08	05 35	05 59	20 50	21 42	22 35	23 28
20	05 13	05 39	06 01	20 41	21 30	22 20	23 10
N 10	05 17	05 41	06 02	20 34	21 19	22 07	22 55
0	05 18	05 42	06 03	20 27	21 10	21 55	22 41
S 10	05 19	05 43	06 04	20 20	21 00	21 43	22 27
20	05 17	05 43	06 05	20 12	20 50	21 30	22 13
30	05 14	05 42	06 06	20 04	20 38	21 15	21 55
35	05 12	05 41	06 06	19 59	20 32	21 07	21 46
40	05 08	05 40	06 07	19 54	20 24	20 57	21 34
45	05 04	05 38	06 07	19 47	20 15	20 46	21 21
S 50	04 58	05 36	06 08	19 40	20 05	20 32	21 05
52	04 55	05 34	06 08	19 37	20 00	20 26	20 58
54	04 52	05 33	06 08	19 33	19 54	20 19	20 49
56	04 48	05 32	06 09	19 29	19 48	20 11	20 40
58	04 43	05 30	06 09	19 24	19 42	20 03	20 29
S 60	04 38	05 28	06 09	19 19	19 34	19 53	20 17

Lat.	Sunset	Twilight Civil	Twilight Naut.	Moonset 23	24	25	26
°	h m	h m	h m	h m	h m	h m	h m
N 72	18 37	19 47	21 25	06 28	06 15	05 57	05 24
N 70	18 34	19 36	21 00	06 39	06 33	06 26	06 18
68	18 31	19 28	20 41	06 47	06 47	06 48	06 51
66	18 29	19 21	20 27	06 54	06 59	07 05	07 15
64	18 27	19 15	20 15	07 01	07 09	07 19	07 34
62	18 25	19 10	20 05	07 06	07 17	07 31	07 49
60	18 24	19 06	19 57	07 11	07 25	07 41	08 02
N 58	18 23	19 02	19 50	07 15	07 31	07 50	08 14
56	18 22	18 59	19 44	07 18	07 37	07 58	08 23
54	18 21	18 56	19 39	07 22	07 42	08 05	08 32
52	18 20	18 54	19 34	07 25	07 47	08 11	08 40
50	18 19	18 51	19 30	07 27	07 51	08 17	08 47
45	18 17	18 47	19 21	07 33	08 00	08 29	09 02
N 40	18 16	18 43	19 15	07 38	08 08	08 39	09 14
35	18 15	18 40	19 10	07 43	08 14	08 48	09 25
30	18 14	18 38	19 06	07 47	08 20	08 56	09 34
20	18 12	18 34	19 00	07 53	08 30	09 09	09 50
N 10	18 11	18 32	18 56	07 59	08 39	09 21	10 04
0	18 10	18 30	18 54	08 05	08 48	09 32	10 17
S 10	18 08	18 29	18 54	08 10	08 56	09 43	10 30
20	18 07	18 29	18 55	08 16	09 05	09 54	10 44
30	18 06	18 30	18 58	08 23	09 15	10 08	11 00
35	18 06	18 31	19 00	08 27	09 21	10 16	11 10
40	18 05	18 32	19 04	08 31	09 28	10 24	11 21
45	18 05	18 34	19 08	08 36	09 36	10 35	11 33
S 50	18 04	18 36	19 14	08 42	09 45	10 48	11 49
52	18 03	18 37	19 16	08 45	09 50	10 53	11 56
54	18 03	18 38	19 20	08 48	09 55	11 00	12 04
56	18 03	18 40	19 23	08 52	10 00	11 07	12 13
58	18 02	18 41	19 28	08 56	10 06	11 15	12 23
S 60	18 02	18 43	19 32	09 00	10 15	11 25	12 35

Day	SUN Eqn. of Time 00h	SUN Eqn. of Time 12h	SUN Mer. Pass.	MOON Mer. Pass. Upper	MOON Mer. Pass. Lower	Age	Phase
	m s	m s	h m	h m	h m	d	
23	06 46	06 36	12 07	01 54	14 16	17	
24	06 27	06 18	12 06	02 37	14 59	18	◐
25	06 09	06 00	12 06	03 21	15 43	19	

G.M.T.	ARIES G.H.A.	VENUS −3.5 G.H.A.	Dec.	MARS +1.3 G.H.A.	Dec.	JUPITER −2.0 G.H.A.	Dec.	SATURN +0.6 G.H.A.	Dec.	STARS Name	S.H.A.	Dec.
26 00	183 21.1	180 52.7 S 0 27.6		176 44.3 N 2 04.9		357 39.3 S 0 43.8		356 18.5 S 0 09.3		Acamar	315 37.3	S40 23.1
01	198 23.6	195 52.3	26.3	191 45.0	05.7	12 42.0	43.7	11 21.1	09.3	Achernar	335 45.6	S57 20.2
02	213 26.0	210 51.9	25.1	206 45.7	06.5	27 44.8	43.5	26 23.8	09.2	Acrux	173 36.1	S62 59.7
03	228 28.5	225 51.5 ··	23.8	221 46.4 ··	07.3	42 47.6 ··	43.4	41 26.4 ··	09.1	Adhara	255 31.8	S28 57.1
04	243 30.9	240 51.1	22.6	236 47.1	08.0	57 50.3	43.3	56 29.1	09.0	Aldebaran	291 17.8	N16 28.2
05	258 33.4	255 50.8	21.3	251 47.8	08.8	72 53.1	43.2	71 31.7	09.0			
06	273 35.9	270 50.4 S 0 20.1		266 48.5 N 2 09.6		87 55.8 S 0 43.0		86 34.3 S 0 08.9		Alioth	166 41.7	N56 03.7
07	288 38.3	285 50.0	18.8	281 49.2	10.4	102 58.6	42.9	101 37.0	08.8	Alkaid	153 17.8	N49 24.4
T 08	303 40.8	300 49.6	17.6	296 49.9	11.2	118 01.4	42.8	116 39.6	08.7	Al Na'ir	28 14.9	S47 03.1
H 09	318 43.3	315 49.3 ··	16.3	311 50.6 ··	12.0	133 04.1 ··	42.6	131 42.3 ··	08.6	Alnilam	276 11.4	S 1 13.0
U 10	333 45.7	330 48.9	15.1	326 51.3	12.7	148 06.9	42.5	146 44.9	08.6	Alphard	218 20.0	S 8 34.8
R 11	348 48.2	345 48.5	13.8	341 52.0	13.5	163 09.6	42.4	161 47.5	08.5			
S 12	3 50.7	0 48.1 S 0 12.5		356 52.7 N 2 14.3		178 12.4 S 0 42.3		176 50.2 S 0 08.4		Alphecca	126 31.6	N26 46.5
D 13	18 53.1	15 47.7	11.3	11 53.4	15.1	193 15.2	42.1	191 52.8	08.3	Alpheratz	358 09.3	N28 59.0
A 14	33 55.6	30 47.4	10.0	26 54.1	15.9	208 17.9	42.0	206 55.5	08.2	Altair	62 32.3	N 8 48.9
Y 15	48 58.0	45 47.0 ··	08.8	41 54.8 ··	16.7	223 20.7 ··	41.9	221 58.1 ··	08.2	Ankaa	353 40.3	S42 24.7
16	64 00.5	60 46.6	07.5	56 55.5	17.4	238 23.4	41.7	237 00.8	08.1	Antares	112 56.3	S26 23.4
17	79 03.0	75 46.2	06.3	71 56.2	18.2	253 26.2	41.6	252 03.4	08.0			
18	94 05.4	90 45.9 S 0 05.0		86 56.8 N 2 19.0		268 29.0 S 0 41.5		267 06.1 S 0 07.9		Arcturus	146 17.9	N19 16.7
19	109 07.9	105 45.5	03.8	101 57.5	19.8	283 31.7	41.4	282 08.7	07.9	Atria	108 20.0	S68 59.4
20	124 10.4	120 45.1	02.5	116 58.2	20.6	298 34.5	41.2	297 11.3	07.8	Avior	234 27.8	S59 27.2
21	139 12.8	135 44.7 S 0 01.2		131 58.9 ··	21.4	313 37.2 ··	41.1	312 14.0 ··	07.7	Bellatrix	278 58.5	N 6 19.8
22	154 15.3	150 44.4 0 00.0		146 59.6	22.1	328 40.0	41.0	327 16.6	07.6	Betelgeuse	271 28.0	N 7 24.1
23	169 17.8	165 44.0 N 0 01.3		162 00.3	22.9	343 42.8	40.8	342 19.3	07.5			
27 00	184 20.2	180 43.6 N 0 02.5		177 01.0 N 2 23.7		358 45.5 S 0 40.7		357 21.9 S 0 07.5		Canopus	264 07.1	S52 41.5
01	199 22.7	195 43.2	03.8	192 01.7	24.5	13 48.3	40.6	12 24.6	07.4	Capella	281 10.9	N45 58.8
02	214 25.2	210 42.8	05.0	207 02.4	25.3	28 51.0	40.5	27 27.2	07.3	Deneb	49 48.5	N45 12.5
03	229 27.6	225 42.5 ··	06.3	222 03.1 ··	26.1	43 53.8 ··	40.3	42 29.8 ··	07.2	Denebola	182 58.4	N14 40.6
04	244 30.1	240 42.1	07.5	237 03.8	26.8	58 56.6	40.2	57 32.5	07.1	Diphda	349 20.9	S18 05.6
05	259 32.5	255 41.7	08.8	252 04.5	27.6	73 59.3	40.1	72 35.1	07.1			
06	274 35.0	270 41.3 N 0 10.1		267 05.2 N 2 28.4		89 02.1 S 0 39.9		87 37.8 S 0 07.0		Dubhe	194 21.1	N61 51.3
07	289 37.5	285 41.0	11.3	282 05.9	29.2	104 04.9	39.8	102 40.4	06.9	Elnath	278 43.8	N28 35.5
08	304 39.9	300 40.6	12.6	297 06.6	30.0	119 07.6	39.7	117 43.1	06.8	Eltanin	90 57.5	N51 29.2
F 09	319 42.4	315 40.2 ··	13.8	312 07.3 ··	30.7	134 10.4 ··	39.6	132 45.7 ··	06.8	Enif	34 11.5	N 9 47.1
R 10	334 44.9	330 39.8	15.1	327 08.0	31.5	149 13.1	39.4	147 48.3	06.7	Fomalhaut	15 51.4	S29 43.4
I 11	349 47.3	345 39.4	16.3	342 08.7	32.3	164 15.9	39.3	162 51.0	06.6			
D 12	4 49.8	0 39.1 N 0 17.6		357 09.4 N 2 33.1		179 18.7 S 0 39.2		177 53.6 S 0 06.5		Gacrux	172 27.8	S57 00.5
A 13	19 52.3	15 38.7	18.9	12 10.1	33.9	194 21.4	39.0	192 56.3	06.4	Gienah	176 17.3	S17 26.3
Y 14	34 54.7	30 38.3	20.1	27 10.8	34.7	209 24.2	38.9	207 58.9	06.4	Hadar	149 22.3	S60 16.8
15	49 57.2	45 37.9 ··	21.4	42 11.5 ··	35.4	224 26.9 ··	38.8	223 01.6 ··	06.3	Hamal	328 28.8	N23 22.3
16	64 59.7	60 37.6	22.6	57 12.2	36.2	239 29.7	38.7	238 04.2	06.2	Kaus Aust.	84 16.4	S34 23.5
17	80 02.1	75 37.2	23.9	72 12.9	37.0	254 32.5	38.5	253 06.8	06.1			
18	95 04.6	90 36.8 N 0 25.1		87 13.6 N 2 37.8		269 35.2 S 0 38.4		268 09.5 S 0 06.0		Kochab	137 18.1	N74 13.8
19	110 07.0	105 36.4	26.4	102 14.3	38.6	284 38.0	38.3	283 12.1	06.0	Markab	14 03.1	N15 06.0
20	125 09.5	120 36.1	27.6	117 15.0	39.3	299 40.7	38.2	298 14.8	05.9	Menkar	314 41.0	N 4 00.8
21	140 12.0	135 35.7 ··	28.9	132 15.7 ··	40.1	314 43.5 ··	38.0	313 17.4 ··	05.8	Menkent	148 36.3	S36 16.6
22	155 14.4	150 35.3	30.2	147 16.4	40.9	329 46.3	37.9	328 20.1	05.7	Miaplacidus	221 44.3	S69 38.6
23	170 16.9	165 34.9	31.4	162 17.1	41.7	344 49.0	37.8	343 22.7	05.7			
28 00	185 19.4	180 34.5 N 0 32.7		177 17.8 N 2 42.5		359 51.8 S 0 37.6		358 25.3 S 0 05.6		Mirfak	309 16.0	N49 47.7
01	200 21.8	195 34.2	33.9	192 18.5	43.2	14 54.5	37.5	13 28.0	05.5	Nunki	76 28.8	S26 19.2
02	215 24.3	210 33.8	35.2	207 19.1	44.0	29 57.3	37.4	28 30.6	05.4	Peacock	53 58.1	S56 47.6
03	230 26.8	225 33.4 ··	36.4	222 19.8 ··	44.8	45 00.1 ··	37.3	43 33.3 ··	05.3	Pollux	243 57.6	N28 04.3
04	245 29.2	240 33.0	37.7	237 20.5	45.6	60 02.8	37.1	58 35.9	05.3	Procyon	245 25.3	N 5 16.3
05	260 31.7	255 32.7	38.9	252 21.2	46.4	75 05.6	37.0	73 38.6	05.2			
06	275 34.2	270 32.3 N 0 40.2		267 21.9 N 2 47.1		90 08.3 S 0 36.9		88 41.2 S 0 05.1		Rasalhague	96 29.2	N12 34.3
07	290 36.6	285 31.9	41.5	282 22.6	47.9	105 11.1	36.7	103 43.8	05.0	Regulus	208 09.4	N12 03.5
S 08	305 39.1	300 31.5	42.7	297 23.3	48.7	120 13.9	36.6	118 46.5	04.9	Rigel	281 35.8	S 8 13.6
A 09	320 41.5	315 31.2 ··	44.0	312 24.0 ··	49.5	135 16.6 ··	36.5	133 49.1 ··	04.9	Rigil Kent.	140 24.8	S60 45.2
T 10	335 44.0	330 30.8	45.2	327 24.7	50.3	150 19.4	36.4	148 51.8	04.8	Sabik	102 40.6	S15 42.1
U 11	350 46.5	345 30.4	46.5	342 25.4	51.0	165 22.1	36.2	163 54.4	04.7			
R 12	5 48.9	0 30.0 N 0 47.7		357 26.1 N 2 51.8		180 24.9 S 0 36.1		178 57.1 S 0 04.6		Schedar	350 09.2	N56 25.9
D 13	20 51.4	15 29.7	49.0	12 26.8	52.6	195 27.7	36.0	193 59.7	04.6	Shaula	96 55.2	S37 05.3
A 14	35 53.9	30 29.3	50.3	27 27.5	53.4	210 30.4	35.8	209 02.3	04.5	Sirius	258 55.4	S16 41.7
Y 15	50 56.3	45 28.9 ··	51.5	42 28.2 ··	54.2	225 33.2 ··	35.7	224 05.0 ··	04.4	Spica	158 56.9	S11 03.8
16	65 58.8	60 28.5	52.8	57 28.9	54.9	240 35.9	35.6	239 07.6	04.3	Suhail	223 10.3	S43 21.6
17	81 01.3	75 28.1	54.0	72 29.6	55.7	255 38.7	35.5	254 10.3	04.2			
18	96 03.7	90 27.8 N 0 55.3		87 30.3 N 2 56.5		270 41.5 S 0 35.3		269 12.9 S 0 04.2		Vega	80 55.6	N38 45.7
19	111 06.2	105 27.4	56.5	102 31.0	57.3	285 44.2	35.2	284 15.6	04.1	Zuben'ubi	137 32.4	S15 57.8
20	126 08.6	120 27.0	57.8	117 31.7	58.1	300 47.0	35.1	299 18.2	04.0			
21	141 11.1	135 26.6 0 59.0		132 32.4 ··	58.8	315 49.7 ··	35.0	314 20.8 ··	03.9		S.H.A.	Mer. Pass.
22	156 13.6	150 26.3 1 00.3		147 33.1 2 59.6		330 52.5	34.8	329 23.5	03.9	Venus	356 23.4	11 57
23	171 16.0	165 25.9 01.6		162 33.8 3 00.4		345 55.3	34.7	344 26.1	03.8	Mars	352 40.8	12 11
										Jupiter	174 25.3	0 05
Mer. Pass. 11 40.7		v −0.4 d 1.3		v 0.7 d 0.8		v 2.8 d 0.1		v 2.6 d 0.1		Saturn	173 01.7	0 11

SUN / MOON

G.M.T.	SUN G.H.A.	SUN Dec.	MOON G.H.A.	v	Dec.	d	H.P.
d h	° '	° '	° '	'	° '	'	'
26 00	178 32.4	N 2 05.0	300 24.7	13.2	S16 25.0	6.4	54.2
01	193 32.6	06.0	314 56.9	13.3	16 31.4	6.4	54.2
02	208 32.8	07.0	329 29.2	13.2	16 37.8	6.3	54.2
03	223 33.0	·· 08.0	344 01.4	13.1	16 44.1	6.2	54.3
04	238 33.1	08.9	358 33.5	13.1	16 50.3	6.2	54.3
05	253 33.3	09.9	13 05.6	13.1	16 56.5	6.1	54.3
06	268 33.5	N 2 10.9	27 37.7	13.0	S17 02.6	6.0	54.3
07	283 33.7	11.9	42 09.7	13.0	17 08.6	5.9	54.3
T 08	298 33.9	12.9	56 41.7	13.0	17 14.5	5.9	54.3
H 09	313 34.1	·· 13.8	71 13.7	12.8	17 20.4	5.7	54.3
U 10	328 34.3	14.8	85 45.5	12.9	17 26.1	5.7	54.3
R 11	343 34.5	15.8	100 17.4	12.8	17 31.8	5.7	54.3
S 12	358 34.7	N 2 16.8	114 49.2	12.8	S17 37.5	5.5	54.4
D 13	13 34.9	17.8	129 21.0	12.7	17 43.0	5.5	54.4
A 14	28 35.0	18.7	143 52.7	12.7	17 48.5	5.4	54.4
Y 15	43 35.2	·· 19.7	158 24.4	12.6	17 53.9	5.3	54.4
16	58 35.4	20.7	172 56.0	12.6	17 59.2	5.3	54.4
17	73 35.6	21.7	187 27.6	12.5	18 04.5	5.1	54.4
18	88 35.8	N 2 22.7	201 59.1	12.5	S18 09.6	5.1	54.4
19	103 36.0	23.6	216 30.6	12.5	18 14.7	5.0	54.5
20	118 36.2	24.6	231 02.1	12.4	18 19.7	5.0	54.5
21	133 36.4	·· 25.6	245 33.5	12.3	18 24.7	4.8	54.5
22	148 36.6	26.6	260 04.8	12.4	18 29.5	4.8	54.5
23	163 36.8	27.6	274 36.2	12.2	18 34.3	4.6	54.5
27 00	178 37.0	N 2 28.5	289 07.4	12.3	S18 38.9	4.6	54.5
01	193 37.1	29.5	303 38.7	12.2	18 43.5	4.5	54.5
02	208 37.3	30.5	318 09.9	12.1	18 48.0	4.5	54.6
03	223 37.5	·· 31.5	332 41.0	12.1	18 52.5	4.3	54.6
04	238 37.7	32.5	347 12.1	12.0	18 56.8	4.2	54.6
05	253 37.9	33.4	1 43.1	12.0	19 01.0	4.2	54.6
06	268 38.1	N 2 34.4	16 14.1	12.0	S19 05.2	4.1	54.6
07	283 38.3	35.4	30 45.1	11.9	19 09.3	4.0	54.7
08	298 38.5	36.4	45 16.0	11.9	19 13.3	3.9	54.7
F 09	313 38.7	·· 37.4	59 46.9	11.8	19 17.2	3.8	54.7
R 10	328 38.9	38.3	74 17.7	11.8	19 21.0	3.7	54.7
I 11	343 39.0	39.3	88 48.5	11.7	19 24.7	3.7	54.7
D 12	358 39.2	N 2 40.3	103 19.2	11.7	S19 28.4	3.5	54.7
A 13	13 39.4	41.3	117 49.9	11.6	19 31.9	3.5	54.8
Y 14	28 39.6	42.2	132 20.5	11.6	19 35.4	3.4	54.8
15	43 39.8	·· 43.2	146 51.1	11.6	19 38.8	3.3	54.8
16	58 40.0	44.2	161 21.7	11.5	19 42.1	3.1	54.8
17	73 40.2	45.2	175 52.2	11.5	19 45.2	3.1	54.8
18	88 40.4	N 2 46.2	190 22.7	11.4	S19 48.3	3.0	54.9
19	103 40.6	47.1	204 53.1	11.4	19 51.3	2.9	54.9
20	118 40.8	48.1	219 23.5	11.3	19 54.2	2.9	54.9
21	133 40.9	·· 49.1	233 53.8	11.3	19 57.1	2.7	54.9
22	148 41.1	50.1	248 24.1	11.3	19 59.8	2.6	55.0
23	163 41.3	51.0	262 54.4	11.2	20 02.4	2.5	55.0
28 00	178 41.5	N 2 52.0	277 24.6	11.1	S20 04.9	2.5	55.0
01	193 41.7	53.0	291 54.7	11.2	20 07.4	2.3	55.0
02	208 41.9	54.0	306 24.9	11.0	20 09.7	2.3	55.0
03	223 42.1	·· 55.0	320 54.9	11.1	20 12.0	2.1	55.1
04	238 42.3	55.9	335 25.0	11.0	20 14.1	2.1	55.1
05	253 42.5	56.9	349 55.0	10.9	20 16.2	1.9	55.1
06	268 42.7	N 2 57.9	4 24.9	10.9	S20 18.1	1.9	55.1
07	283 42.8	58.9	18 54.8	10.9	20 20.0	1.7	55.2
S 08	298 43.0	2 59.8	33 24.7	10.8	20 21.7	1.7	55.2
A 09	313 43.2	3 00.8	47 54.5	10.8	20 23.4	1.5	55.2
T 10	328 43.4	01.8	62 24.3	10.8	20 24.9	1.5	55.2
U 11	343 43.6	02.8	76 54.1	10.7	20 26.4	1.3	55.3
R 12	358 43.8	N 3 03.7	91 23.8	10.6	S20 27.7	1.3	55.3
D 13	13 44.0	04.7	105 53.4	10.7	20 29.0	1.1	55.3
A 14	28 44.2	05.7	120 23.1	10.6	20 30.1	1.1	55.3
Y 15	43 44.4	·· 06.7	134 52.7	10.5	20 31.2	0.9	55.4
16	58 44.5	07.6	149 22.2	10.5	20 32.1	0.9	55.4
17	73 44.7	08.6	163 51.7	10.5	20 33.0	0.7	55.4
18	88 44.9	N 3 09.6	178 21.2	10.4	S20 33.7	0.6	55.5
19	103 45.1	10.6	192 50.6	10.4	20 34.3	0.6	55.5
20	118 45.3	11.5	207 20.0	10.4	20 34.9	0.4	55.5
21	133 45.5	·· 12.5	221 49.4	10.3	20 35.3	0.3	55.5
22	148 45.7	13.5	236 18.7	10.3	20 35.6	0.2	55.6
23	163 45.9	14.5	250 48.0	10.2	20 35.8	0.2	55.6
	S.D. 16.1	d 1.0	S.D. 14.8		14.9		15.1

Twilight / Sunrise / Moonrise

Lat.	Naut.	Civil	Sunrise	Moonrise 26	27	28	29
°	h m	h m	h m	h m	h m	h m	h m
N 72	02 30	04 12	05 23	02 36	■	■	■
N 70	02 58	04 24	05 27	01 43	03 35	■	■
68	03 19	04 34	05 31	01 11	02 41	04 05	05 06
66	03 35	04 42	05 34	00 48	02 09	03 22	04 20
64	03 48	04 48	05 37	00 30	01 45	02 53	03 50
62	03 58	04 54	05 39	00 15	01 26	02 32	03 27
60	04 07	04 59	05 41	00 02	01 11	02 14	03 09
N 58	04 15	05 03	05 43	24 58	00 58	01 59	02 54
56	04 22	05 07	05 44	24 46	00 46	01 47	02 41
54	04 27	05 10	05 46	24 36	00 36	01 36	02 29
52	04 32	05 13	05 47	24 28	00 28	01 26	02 19
50	04 37	05 16	05 48	24 20	00 20	01 17	02 11
45	04 46	05 21	05 50	24 03	00 03	00 59	01 52
N 40	04 53	05 25	05 52	23 49	24 44	00 44	01 36
35	04 59	05 29	05 54	23 38	24 31	00 31	01 23
30	05 04	05 32	05 56	23 28	24 20	00 20	01 12
20	05 10	05 36	05 58	23 10	24 01	00 01	00 53
N 10	05 15	05 39	06 00	22 55	23 45	24 36	00 36
0	05 17	05 41	06 02	22 41	23 30	24 20	00 20
S 10	05 19	05 43	06 04	22 27	23 15	24 04	00 04
20	05 18	05 44	06 06	22 13	22 58	23 47	24 40
30	05 16	05 44	06 08	21 55	22 40	23 28	24 21
35	05 14	05 43	06 09	21 46	22 29	23 17	24 10
40	05 11	05 43	06 10	21 34	22 16	23 04	23 58
45	05 08	05 42	06 11	21 21	22 02	22 49	23 43
S 50	05 03	05 40	06 13	21 05	21 44	22 30	23 25
52	05 00	05 40	06 13	20 58	21 35	22 21	23 16
54	04 57	05 39	06 14	20 49	21 26	22 11	23 07
56	04 54	05 38	06 15	20 40	21 15	22 00	22 56
58	04 51	05 37	06 16	20 29	21 03	21 48	22 43
S 60	04 46	05 35	06 17	20 17	20 49	21 33	22 29

Sunset / Twilight / Moonset

Lat.	Sunset	Civil	Naut.	Moonset 26	27	28	29
°	h m	h m	h m	h m	h m	h m	h m
N 72	18 51	20 02	21 48	05 24	■	■	■
N 70	18 46	19 50	21 18	06 18	06 03	■	■
68	18 42	19 40	20 56	06 51	06 58	07 16	07 59
66	18 39	19 31	20 39	07 15	07 31	07 58	08 46
64	18 36	19 24	20 26	07 34	07 55	08 27	09 16
62	18 33	19 19	20 15	07 49	08 14	08 49	09 38
60	18 31	19 14	20 06	08 02	08 30	09 07	09 56
N 58	18 29	19 09	19 58	08 14	08 43	09 22	10 12
56	18 28	19 05	19 51	08 23	08 55	09 35	10 25
54	18 26	19 02	19 45	08 32	09 05	09 46	10 36
52	18 25	18 59	19 40	08 40	09 14	09 56	10 46
50	18 24	18 56	19 35	08 47	09 22	10 04	10 55
45	18 21	18 51	19 26	09 02	09 39	10 23	11 13
N 40	18 19	18 46	19 18	09 14	09 54	10 38	11 29
35	18 17	18 43	19 12	09 25	10 06	10 51	11 42
30	18 16	18 40	19 08	09 34	10 16	11 02	11 53
20	18 13	18 35	19 01	09 50	10 34	11 21	12 12
N 10	18 11	18 32	18 56	10 04	10 50	11 38	12 29
0	18 09	18 29	18 53	10 17	11 05	11 54	12 45
S 10	18 07	18 28	18 52	10 30	11 19	12 09	13 00
20	18 05	18 27	18 52	10 44	11 35	12 26	13 17
30	18 03	18 27	18 54	11 00	11 53	12 45	13 36
35	18 02	18 27	18 56	11 10	12 04	12 56	13 47
40	18 01	18 27	18 58	11 21	12 16	13 09	14 00
45	17 59	18 28	19 02	11 33	12 30	13 24	14 15
S 50	17 57	18 29	19 07	11 49	12 48	13 43	14 33
52	17 57	18 30	19 09	11 56	12 56	13 52	14 42
54	17 56	18 31	19 11	12 04	13 05	14 02	14 52
56	17 55	18 32	19 15	12 13	13 15	14 13	15 03
58	17 54	18 33	19 19	12 23	13 27	14 25	15 15
S 60	17 53	18 34	19 23	12 35	13 41	14 40	15 30

SUN / MOON

Day	SUN Eqn. of Time 00ʰ	12ʰ	Mer. Pass.	MOON Mer. Pass. Upper	Lower	Age	Phase
	m s	m s	h m	h m	h m	d	
26	05 51	05 42	12 06	04 06	16 29	20	
27	05 33	05 23	12 05	04 53	17 17	21	◐
28	05 14	05 05	12 05	05 42	18 07	22	

1981 MARCH 29, 30, 31 (SUN., MON., TUES.)

G.M.T.	ARIES G.H.A.	VENUS −3.5 G.H.A.	Dec.	MARS +1.4 G.H.A.	Dec.	JUPITER −2.0 G.H.A.	Dec.	SATURN +0.7 G.H.A.	Dec.	STARS Name	S.H.A.	Dec.
29 00	186 18.5	180 25.5 N 1	02.8	177 34.5 N 3	01.2	0 58.0 S 0	34.6	359 28.8 S 0	03.7	Acamar	315 37.3	S40 23.1
01	201 21.0	195 25.1	04.1	192 35.2	01.9	16 00.8	34.4	14 31.4	03.6	Achernar	335 45.6	S57 20.2
02	216 23.4	210 24.8	05.3	207 35.9	02.7	31 03.5	34.3	29 34.1	03.5	Acrux	173 36.1	S62 59.7
03	231 25.9	225 24.4 ··	06.6	222 36.6 ··	03.5	46 06.3 ··	34.2	44 36.7 ··	03.5	Adhara	255 31.8	S28 57.1
04	246 28.4	240 24.0	07.8	237 37.3	04.3	61 09.1	34.1	59 39.3	03.4	Aldebaran	291 17.8	N16 28.2
05	261 30.8	255 23.6	09.1	252 38.0	05.1	76 11.8	33.9	74 42.0	03.3			
06	276 33.3	270 23.3 N 1	10.3	267 38.7 N 3	05.8	91 14.6 S 0	33.8	89 44.6 S 0	03.2	Alioth	166 41.6	N56 03.7
07	291 35.8	285 22.9	11.6	282 39.4	06.6	106 17.3	33.7	104 47.3	03.1	Alkaid	153 17.8	N49 24.4
08	306 38.2	300 22.5	12.9	297 40.1	07.4	121 20.1	33.5	119 49.9	03.1	Al Na'ir	28 14.9	S47 03.1
S 09	321 40.7	315 22.1	14.1	312 40.8 ··	08.2	136 22.9 ··	33.4	134 52.6 ··	03.0	Alnilam	276 11.4	S 1 13.0
U 10	336 43.1	330 21.7	15.4	327 41.5	09.0	151 25.6	33.3	149 55.2	02.9	Alphard	218 20.0	S 8 34.8
N 11	351 45.6	345 21.4	16.6	342 42.2	09.7	166 28.4	33.2	164 57.8	02.8			
D 12	6 48.1	0 21.0 N 1	17.9	357 42.9 N 3	10.5	181 31.1 S 0	33.0	180 00.5 S 0	02.8	Alphecca	126 31.6	N26 46.5
A 13	21 50.5	15 20.6	19.1	12 43.6	11.3	196 33.9	32.9	195 03.1	02.7	Alpheratz	358 09.3	N28 59.0
Y 14	36 53.0	30 20.2	20.4	27 44.3	12.1	211 36.7	32.8	210 05.8	02.6	Altair	62 32.3	N 8 48.9
15	51 55.5	45 19.9 ··	21.6	42 45.0 ··	12.8	226 39.4 ··	32.7	225 08.4 ··	02.5	Ankaa	353 40.3	S42 24.7
16	66 57.9	60 19.5	22.9	57 45.7	13.6	241 42.2	32.5	240 11.1	02.4	Antares	112 56.2	S26 23.4
17	82 00.4	75 19.1	24.2	72 46.4	14.4	256 44.9	32.4	255 13.7	02.4			
18	97 02.9	90 18.7 N 1	25.4	87 47.0 N 3	15.2	271 47.7 S 0	32.3	270 16.3 S 0	02.3	Arcturus	146 17.9	N19 16.7
19	112 05.3	105 18.4	26.7	102 47.7	15.9	286 50.5	32.1	285 19.0	02.2	Atria	108 19.9	S68 59.4
20	127 07.8	120 18.0	27.9	117 48.4	16.7	301 53.2	32.0	300 21.6	02.1	Avior	234 27.8	S59 27.3
21	142 10.3	135 17.6 ··	29.2	132 49.1 ··	17.5	316 56.0 ··	31.9	315 24.3 ··	02.1	Bellatrix	278 58.5	N 6 19.8
22	157 12.7	150 17.2	30.4	147 49.8	18.3	331 58.7	31.8	330 26.9	02.0	Betelgeuse	271 28.0	N 7 24.1
23	172 15.2	165 16.8	31.7	162 50.5	19.1	347 01.5	31.6	345 29.6	01.9			
30 00	187 17.6	180 16.5 N 1	32.9	177 51.2 N 3	19.8	2 04.3 S 0	31.5	0 32.2 S 0	01.8	Canopus	264 07.1	S52 41.5
01	202 20.1	195 16.1	34.2	192 51.9	20.6	17 07.0	31.4	15 34.8	01.7	Capella	281 10.9	N45 58.8
02	217 22.6	210 15.7	35.5	207 52.6	21.4	32 09.8	31.3	30 37.5	01.7	Deneb	49 48.4	N45 12.5
03	232 25.0	225 15.3 ··	36.7	222 53.3 ··	22.2	47 12.5 ··	31.1	45 40.1 ··	01.6	Denebola	182 58.4	N14 40.6
04	247 27.5	240 15.0	38.0	237 54.0	22.9	62 15.3	31.0	60 42.8	01.5	Diphda	349 20.9	S18 05.6
05	262 30.0	255 14.6	39.2	252 54.7	23.7	77 18.1	30.9	75 45.4	01.4			
06	277 32.4	270 14.2 N 1	40.5	267 55.4 N 3	24.5	92 20.8 S 0	30.7	90 48.1 S 0	01.4	Dubhe	194 21.1	N61 51.3
07	292 34.9	285 13.8	41.7	282 56.1	25.3	107 23.6	30.6	105 50.7	01.3	Elnath	278 43.8	N28 35.5
08	307 37.4	300 13.5	43.0	297 56.8	26.0	122 26.3	30.5	120 53.3	01.2	Eltanin	90 57.5	N51 29.2
M 09	322 39.8	315 13.1 ··	44.2	312 57.5 ··	26.8	137 29.1 ··	30.4	135 56.0 ··	01.1	Enif	34 11.5	N 9 47.1
O 10	337 42.3	330 12.7	45.5	327 58.2	27.6	152 31.9	30.2	150 58.6	01.0	Fomalhaut	15 51.4	S29 43.4
N 11	352 44.7	345 12.3	46.7	342 58.9	28.4	167 34.6	30.1	166 01.3	01.0			
D 12	7 47.2	0 11.9 N 1	48.0	357 59.6 N 3	29.1	182 37.4 S 0	30.0	181 03.9 S 0	00.9	Gacrux	172 27.8	S57 00.5
A 13	22 49.7	15 11.6	49.3	13 00.3	29.9	197 40.1	29.9	196 06.6	00.8	Gienah	176 17.3	S17 26.3
14	37 52.1	30 11.2	50.5	28 01.0	30.7	212 42.9	29.7	211 09.2	00.7	Hadar	149 22.3	S60 16.8
15	52 54.6	45 10.8 ··	51.8	43 01.7 ··	31.5	227 45.7 ··	29.6	226 11.8 ··	00.7	Hamal	328 28.8	N23 22.3
16	67 57.1	60 10.4	53.0	58 02.4	32.2	242 48.4	29.5	241 14.5	00.6	Kaus Aust.	84 16.4	S34 2 5
17	82 59.5	75 10.1	54.3	73 03.1	33.0	257 51.2	29.4	256 17.1	00.5			
18	98 02.0	90 09.7 N 1	55.5	88 03.8 N 3	33.8	272 53.9 S 0	29.2	271 19.8 S 0	00.4	Kochab	137 18.1	N74 13.9
19	113 04.5	105 09.3	56.8	103 04.5	34.6	287 56.7	29.1	286 22.4	00.3	Markab	14 03.1	N15 06.0
20	128 06.9	120 08.9	58.0	118 05.2	35.3	302 59.4	29.0	301 25.1	00.3	Menkar	314 41.0	N 4 00.8
21	143 09.4	135 08.6 1	59.3	133 05.9 ··	36.1	318 02.1 ··	28.8	316 27.7 ··	00.2	Menkent	148 36.2	S36 16.6
22	158 11.9	150 08.2 2	00.5	148 06.6	36.9	333 05.0	28.7	331 30.3 S 0	00.1	Miaplacidus	221 44.3	S69 38.7
23	173 14.3	165 07.8	01.8	163 07.3	37.7	348 07.7	28.6	346 33.0 0	00.0			
31 00	188 16.8	180 07.4 N 2	03.1	178 08.0 N 3	38.4	3 10.5 S 0	28.5	1 35.6	00.0	Mirfak	309 16.0	N49 47.7
01	203 19.2	195 07.0	04.3	193 08.7	39.2	18 13.2	28.3	16 38.3 N 0	00.1	Nunki	76 28.8	S26 19.2
02	218 21.7	210 06.7	05.6	208 09.4	40.0	33 16.0	28.2	31 40.9	00.2	Peacock	53 58.1	S56 47.6
03	233 24.2	225 06.3 ··	06.8	223 10.1 ··	40.8	48 18.8 ··	28.1	46 43.6 ··	00.3	Pollux	243 57.6	N28 04.3
04	248 26.6	240 05.9	08.1	238 10.8	41.5	63 21.5	28.0	61 46.2	00.3	Procyon	245 25.3	N 5 16.3
05	263 29.1	255 05.5	09.3	253 11.5	42.3	78 24.3	27.8	76 48.8	00.4			
06	278 31.6	270 05.2 N 2	10.6	268 12.2 N 3	43.1	93 27.0 S 0	27.7	91 51.5 N 0	00.5	Rasalhague	96 29.2	N12 34.3
07	293 34.0	285 04.8	11.8	283 12.9	43.9	108 29.8	27.6	106 54.1	00.6	Regulus	208 09.4	N12 03.5
08	308 36.5	300 04.4	13.1	298 13.6	44.6	123 32.6	27.5	121 56.8	00.7	Rigel	281 35.8	S 8 13.6
T 09	323 39.0	315 04.0 ··	14.3	313 14.3 ··	45.4	138 35.3 ··	27.3	136 59.4 ··	00.7	Rigil Kent.	140 24.8	S60 45.3
U 10	338 41.4	330 03.6	15.6	328 15.0	46.2	153 38.1	27.2	152 02.1	00.8	Sabik	102 40.6	S15 42.1
E S 11	353 43.9	345 03.3	16.8	343 15.7	47.0	168 40.8	27.1	167 04.7	00.9			
D 12	8 46.4	0 02.9 N 2	18.1	358 16.4 N 3	47.7	183 43.6 S 0	27.0	182 07.3 N 0	01.0	Schedar	350 09.2	N56 25.9
A 13	23 48.8	15 02.5	19.4	13 17.1	48.5	198 46.3	26.8	197 10.0	01.0	Shaula	96 55.2	S37 05.3
Y 14	38 51.3	30 02.1	20.6	28 17.8	49.3	213 49.1	26.7	212 12.6	01.1	Sirius	258 55.4	S16 41.7
15	53 53.7	45 01.7 ··	21.9	43 18.5 ··	50.1	228 51.9 ··	26.6	227 15.3 ··	01.2	Spica	158 56.9	S11 03.8
16	68 56.2	60 01.4	23.1	58 19.2	50.8	243 54.6	26.4	242 17.9	01.3	Suhail	223 10.3	S43 21.6
17	83 58.7	75 01.0	24.4	73 19.9	51.6	258 57.4	26.3	257 20.5	01.4			
18	99 01.1	90 00.6 N 2	25.6	88 20.6 N 3	52.4	274 00.1 S 0	26.2	272 23.2 N 0	01.5	Vega	80 55.6	N38 45.7
19	114 03.6	105 00.2	26.9	103 21.3	53.1	289 02.9	26.1	287 25.8	01.5	Zuben'ubi	137 32.4	S15 57.8
20	129 06.1	119 59.9	28.1	118 21.9	53.9	304 05.7	25.9	302 28.5	01.6			
21	144 08.5	134 59.5 ··	29.4	133 22.6 ··	54.7	319 08.4 ··	25.8	317 31.1 ··	01.7		S.H.A.	Mer. Pass.
22	159 11.0	149 59.1	30.6	148 23.3	55.5	334 11.2	25.7	332 33.8	01.7	Venus	352 58.8	11 59
23	174 13.5	164 58.7	31.9	163 24.0	56.2	349 13.9	25.6	347 36.4	01.8	Mars	350 33.6	12 08
Mer. Pass. 11 28.9		v −0.4	d 1.3	v 0.7	d 0.8	v 2.8	d 0.1	v 2.6	d 0.1	Jupiter	174 46.6	23 47
										Saturn	173 14.6	23 5?

SUN and MOON

G.M.T.	SUN G.H.A.	SUN Dec.	MOON G.H.A.	v	MOON Dec.	d	H.P.
29 00	178 46.1	N 3 15.4	265 17.2	10.3	S20 36.0	0.0	55.6
01	193 46.3	16.4	279 46.5	10.1	20 36.0	0.1	55.7
02	208 46.4	17.4	294 15.6	10.2	20 35.9	0.2	55.7
03	223 46.6	·· 18.4	308 44.8	10.1	20 35.7	0.4	55.7
04	238 46.8	19.3	323 13.9	10.1	20 35.3	0.4	55.7
05	253 47.0	20.3	337 43.0	10.0	20 34.9	0.5	55.8
06	268 47.2	N 3 21.3	352 12.0	10.0	S20 34.4	0.6	55.8
07	283 47.4	22.3	6 41.0	10.0	20 33.8	0.8	55.8
08	298 47.6	23.2	21 10.0	10.0	20 33.0	0.8	55.9
S 09	313 47.8	·· 24.2	35 39.0	9.9	20 32.2	1.0	55.9
U 10	328 48.0	25.2	50 07.9	9.9	20 31.2	1.1	55.9
N 11	343 48.1	26.2	64 36.8	9.8	20 30.1	1.1	56.0
D 12	358 48.3	N 3 27.1	79 05.6	9.8	S20 29.0	1.3	56.0
A 13	13 48.5	28.1	93 34.4	9.8	20 27.7	1.4	56.0
Y 14	28 48.7	29.1	108 03.2	9.8	20 26.3	1.5	56.1
15	43 48.9	·· 30.1	122 32.0	9.7	20 24.8	1.6	56.1
16	58 49.1	31.0	137 00.7	9.7	20 23.2	1.8	56.1
17	73 49.3	32.0	151 29.4	9.7	20 21.4	1.8	56.2
18	88 49.5	N 3 33.0	165 58.1	9.7	S20 19.6	1.9	56.2
19	103 49.7	33.9	180 26.8	9.6	20 17.7	2.1	56.2
20	118 49.8	34.9	194 55.4	9.6	20 15.6	2.2	56.3
21	133 50.0	·· 35.9	209 24.0	9.5	20 13.4	2.3	56.3
22	148 50.2	36.9	223 52.5	9.6	20 11.1	2.3	56.3
23	163 50.4	37.8	238 21.1	9.5	20 08.8	2.5	56.4
30 00	178 50.6	N 3 38.8	252 49.6	9.5	S20 06.3	2.7	56.4
01	193 50.8	39.8	267 18.1	9.5	20 03.6	2.7	56.4
02	208 51.0	40.7	281 46.6	9.4	20 00.9	2.8	56.5
03	223 51.2	·· 41.7	296 15.0	9.4	19 58.1	3.0	56.5
04	238 51.3	42.7	310 43.4	9.5	19 55.1	3.0	56.5
05	253 51.5	43.7	325 11.9	9.3	19 52.1	3.2	56.6
06	268 51.7	N 3 44.6	339 40.2	9.4	S19 48.9	3.3	56.6
07	283 51.9	45.6	354 08.6	9.3	19 45.6	3.4	56.6
08	298 52.1	46.6	8 36.9	9.3	19 42.2	3.5	56.7
M 09	313 52.3	·· 47.5	23 05.2	9.3	19 38.7	3.6	56.7
O 10	328 52.5	48.5	37 33.5	9.3	19 35.1	3.8	56.8
N 11	343 52.7	49.5	52 01.8	9.3	19 31.3	3.8	56.8
D 12	358 52.9	N 3 50.5	66 30.1	9.2	S19 27.5	4.0	56.8
A 13	13 53.0	51.4	80 58.3	9.2	19 23.5	4.0	56.9
Y 14	28 53.2	52.4	95 26.5	9.2	19 19.5	4.2	56.9
15	43 53.4	·· 53.4	109 54.7	9.2	19 15.3	4.3	56.9
16	58 53.6	54.3	124 22.9	9.2	19 11.0	4.4	57.0
17	73 53.8	55.3	138 51.1	9.1	19 06.6	4.6	57.0
18	88 54.0	N 3 56.3	153 19.2	9.2	S19 02.0	4.6	57.1
19	103 54.2	57.3	167 47.4	9.1	18 57.4	4.7	57.1
20	118 54.4	58.2	182 15.5	9.1	18 52.7	4.9	57.1
21	133 54.5	3 59.2	196 43.6	9.1	18 47.8	5.0	57.2
22	148 54.7	4 00.2	211 11.7	9.1	18 42.8	5.0	57.2
23	163 54.9	01.1	225 39.8	9.0	18 37.8	5.2	57.2
31 00	178 55.1	N 4 02.1	240 07.8	9.1	S18 32.6	5.3	57.3
01	193 55.3	03.1	254 35.9	9.0	18 27.3	5.5	57.3
02	208 55.5	04.0	269 03.9	9.0	18 21.8	5.5	57.4
03	223 55.7	·· 05.0	283 31.9	9.0	18 16.3	5.6	57.4
04	238 55.9	06.0	297 59.9	9.0	18 10.7	5.8	57.4
05	253 56.0	06.9	312 27.9	9.0	18 04.9	5.8	57.5
06	268 56.2	N 4 07.9	326 55.9	9.0	S17 59.1	6.0	57.5
07	283 56.4	08.9	341 23.9	9.0	17 53.1	6.1	57.6
08	298 56.6	09.8	355 51.9	8.9	17 47.0	6.2	57.6
T 09	313 56.8	·· 10.8	10 19.8	9.0	17 40.8	6.3	57.6
U 10	328 57.0	11.8	24 47.8	8.9	17 34.5	6.4	57.7
E 11	343 57.2	12.8	39 15.7	8.9	17 28.1	6.5	57.7
S 12	358 57.4	N 4 13.7	53 43.6	9.0	S17 21.6	6.6	57.8
D 13	13 57.5	14.7	68 11.6	8.9	17 15.0	6.7	57.8
A 14	28 57.7	15.7	82 39.5	8.9	17 08.3	6.9	57.8
Y 15	43 57.9	·· 16.6	97 07.4	8.9	17 01.4	6.9	57.9
16	58 58.1	17.6	111 35.3	8.9	16 54.5	7.1	57.9
17	73 58.3	18.6	126 03.2	8.9	16 47.4	7.1	57.9
18	88 58.5	N 4 19.5	140 31.1	8.8	S16 40.3	7.3	58.0
19	103 58.7	20.5	154 58.9	8.9	16 33.0	7.4	58.0
20	118 58.8	21.5	169 26.8	8.9	16 25.6	7.5	58.1
21	133 59.0	·· 22.4	183 54.7	8.8	16 18.1	7.6	58.1
22	148 59.2	23.4	198 22.5	8.9	16 10.5	7.6	58.1
23	163 59.4	24.4	212 50.4	8.8	16 02.9	7.8	58.2
	S.D. 16.0	d 1.0	S.D. 15.3		15.5		15.7

Twilight, Sunrise, Moonrise

Lat.	Twilight Naut.	Twilight Civil	Sunrise	Moonrise 29	30	31	1
N 72	02 02	03 54	05 07	■	■	07 55	06 51
N 70	02 37	04 09	05 13	■	06 58	06 28	06 18
68	03 02	04 20	05 18	05 06	05 36	05 49	05 53
66	03 20	04 29	05 23	04 20	04 58	05 21	05 35
64	03 35	04 37	05 26	03 50	04 32	05 00	05 19
62	03 47	04 44	05 29	03 27	04 11	04 43	05 06
60	03 57	04 49	05 32	03 09	03 54	04 29	04 55
N 58	04 05	04 54	05 34	02 54	03 39	04 16	04 46
56	04 13	04 59	05 36	02 41	03 27	04 06	04 38
54	04 19	05 02	05 38	02 29	03 16	03 56	04 30
52	04 25	05 06	05 40	02 19	03 07	03 48	04 23
50	04 30	05 09	05 41	02 11	02 58	03 41	04 17
45	04 40	05 15	05 45	01 52	02 40	03 25	04 04
N 40	04 48	05 20	05 48	01 36	02 26	03 11	03 53
35	04 55	05 25	05 50	01 23	02 13	03 00	03 44
30	05 00	05 28	05 52	01 12	02 02	02 50	03 36
20	05 08	05 33	05 56	00 53	01 43	02 33	03 22
N 10	05 13	05 37	05 59	00 36	01 27	02 18	03 09
0	05 16	05 41	06 01	00 20	01 12	02 04	02 58
S 10	05 18	05 43	06 04	00 04	00 56	01 51	02 46
20	05 19	05 44	06 06	24 40	00 40	01 36	02 34
30	05 18	05 45	06 09	24 21	00 21	01 19	02 19
35	05 16	05 46	06 11	24 10	00 10	01 09	02 11
40	05 14	05 46	06 13	23 58	24 57	00 57	02 02
45	05 12	05 46	06 15	23 43	24 44	00 44	01 50
S 50	05 07	05 45	06 17	23 25	24 27	00 27	01 37
52	05 05	05 45	06 18	23 16	24 20	00 20	01 31
54	05 03	05 44	06 20	23 07	24 11	00 11	01 24
56	05 00	05 44	06 21	22 56	24 01	00 01	01 16
58	04 57	05 43	06 22	22 43	23 50	25 07	01 07
S 60	04 54	05 42	06 24	22 29	23 38	24 57	00 57

Sunset, Twilight, Moonset

Lat.	Sunset	Twilight Civil	Twilight Naut.	Moonset 29	30	31	1
N 72	19 05	20 19	22 16	■	■	08 51	11 47
N 70	18 58	20 04	21 37	■	07 57	10 17	12 19
68	18 53	19 52	21 12	07 59	09 17	10 56	12 42
66	18 48	19 42	20 52	08 46	09 55	11 22	13 00
64	18 45	19 34	20 37	09 16	10 22	11 43	13 14
62	18 41	19 27	20 25	09 38	10 42	12 00	13 26
60	18 39	19 21	20 14	09 56	10 59	12 13	13 36
N 58	18 36	19 16	20 06	10 12	11 13	12 25	13 45
56	18 34	19 12	19 58	10 25	11 25	12 35	13 53
54	18 32	19 08	19 51	10 36	11 36	12 44	14 00
52	18 30	19 04	19 46	10 46	11 45	12 52	14 06
50	18 28	19 01	19 40	10 55	11 53	12 59	14 12
45	18 25	18 55	19 30	11 13	12 11	13 15	14 24
N 40	18 22	18 49	19 22	11 29	12 25	13 27	14 34
35	18 20	18 45	19 15	11 42	12 38	13 38	14 42
30	18 17	18 41	19 10	11 53	12 48	13 47	14 49
20	18 14	18 36	19 02	12 12	13 06	14 03	15 02
N 10	18 11	18 32	18 56	12 29	13 22	14 17	15 13
0	18 08	18 28	18 53	12 45	13 37	14 30	15 23
S 10	18 05	18 26	18 50	13 00	13 52	14 43	15 33
20	18 02	18 24	18 50	13 17	14 07	14 56	15 44
30	17 59	18 23	18 51	13 36	14 25	15 12	15 56
35	17 57	18 23	18 52	13 47	14 36	15 21	16 04
40	17 56	18 23	18 54	14 00	14 47	15 31	16 11
45	17 53	18 24	18 57	14 15	15 01	15 43	16 21
S 50	17 51	18 23	19 00	14 33	15 18	15 58	16 32
52	17 50	18 23	19 02	14 42	15 26	16 04	16 37
54	17 48	18 24	19 04	14 52	15 35	16 12	16 43
56	17 47	18 24	19 07	15 03	15 45	16 20	16 49
58	17 45	18 24	19 10	15 15	15 57	16 29	16 56
S 60	17 44	18 25	19 13	15 30	16 10	16 40	17 04

SUN / MOON

Day	SUN Eqn. of Time 00h	12h	Mer. Pass.	MOON Mer. Pass. Upper	Lower	Age	Phase
	m s	m s	h m	h m	h m	d	
29	04 56	04 47	12 05	06 32	18 58	23	
30	04 38	04 29	12 04	07 24	19 51	24	
31	04 20	04 11	12 04	08 17	20 44	25	

1981 APRIL 1, 2, 3 (WED., THURS., FRI.)

G.M.T.	ARIES G.H.A.	VENUS −3.5 G.H.A.	Dec.	MARS +1.4 G.H.A.	Dec.	JUPITER −2.0 G.H.A.	Dec.	SATURN +0.7 G.H.A.	Dec.	STARS Name	S.H.A.	Dec.
1 00	189 15.9	179 58.3	N 2 33.1	178 24.7	N 3 57.0	4 16.7	S 0 25.4	2 39.0	N 0 01.9	Acamar	315 37.3	S40 23.1
01	204 18.4	194 58.0	34.4	193 25.4	57.8	19 19.4	25.3	17 41.7	02.0	Achernar	335 45.6	S57 20.1
02	219 20.8	209 57.6	35.6	208 26.1	58.6	34 22.2	25.2	32 44.3	02.0	Acrux	173 36.1	S62 59.7
03	234 23.3	224 57.2 ··	36.9	223 26.8	3 59.3	49 25.0 ··	25.1	47 47.0 ··	02.1	Adhara	255 31.8	S28 57.1
04	249 25.8	239 56.8	38.1	238 27.5	4 00.1	64 27.7	24.9	62 49.6	02.2	Aldebaran	291 17.8	N16 28.2
05	264 28.2	254 56.4	39.4	253 28.2	00.9	79 30.5	24.8	77 52.3	02.3			
06	279 30.7	269 56.1	N 2 40.6	268 28.9	N 4 01.6	94 33.2	S 0 24.7	92 54.9	N 0 02.4	Alioth	166 41.6	N56 03.7
W 07	294 33.2	284 55.7	41.9	283 29.6	02.4	109 36.0	24.6	107 57.5	02.4	Alkaid	153 17.8	N49 24.4
E 08	309 35.6	299 55.3	43.2	298 30.3	03.2	124 38.7	24.4	123 00.2	02.5	Al Na'ir	28 14.8	S47 03.1
D 09	324 38.1	314 54.9 ··	44.4	313 31.0 ··	04.0	139 41.5 ··	24.3	138 02.8 ··	02.6	Alnilam	276 11.4	S 1 13.0
N 10	339 40.6	329 54.6	45.7	328 31.7	04.7	154 44.3	24.2	153 05.5	02.7	Alphard	218 20.0	S 8 34.8
E 11	354 43.0	344 54.2	46.9	343 32.4	05.5	169 47.0	24.1	168 08.1	02.7			
S 12	9 45.5	359 53.8	N 2 48.2	358 33.1	N 4 06.3	184 49.8	S 0 23.9	183 10.8	N 0 02.8	Alphecca	126 31.5	N26 46.5
D 13	24 48.0	14 53.4	49.4	13 33.8	07.0	199 52.5	23.8	198 13.4	02.9	Alpheratz	358 09.3	N28 59.0
A 14	39 50.4	29 53.0	50.7	28 34.5	07.8	214 55.3	23.7	213 16.0	03.0	Altair	62 32.3	N 8 48.9
Y 15	54 52.9	44 52.7 ··	51.9	43 35.2 ··	08.6	229 58.0 ··	23.6	228 18.7 ··	03.0	Ankaa	353 40.3	S42 24.6
16	69 55.3	59 52.3	53.2	58 35.9	09.4	245 00.8	23.4	243 21.3	03.1	Antares	112 56.2	S26 23.4
17	84 57.8	74 51.9	54.4	73 36.6	10.1	260 03.6	23.3	258 24.0	03.2			
18	100 00.3	89 51.5	N 2 55.7	88 37.3	N 4 10.9	275 06.3	S 0 23.2	273 26.6	N 0 03.3	Arcturus	146 17.8	N19 16.7
19	115 02.7	104 51.1	56.9	103 38.0	11.7	290 09.1	23.1	288 29.2	03.4	Atria	108 19.9	S68 59.4
20	130 05.2	119 50.8	58.2	118 38.7	12.4	305 11.8	22.9	303 31.9	03.4	Avior	234 27.8	S59 27.3
21	145 07.7	134 50.4	2 59.4	133 39.4 ··	13.2	320 14.6 ··	22.8	318 34.5 ··	03.5	Bellatrix	278 58.5	N 6 19.8
22	160 10.1	149 50.0	3 00.7	148 40.1	14.0	335 17.3	22.7	333 37.2	03.6	Betelgeuse	271 28.0	N 7 24.1
23	175 12.6	164 49.6	01.9	163 40.8	14.7	350 20.1	22.6	348 39.8	03.7			
2 00	190 15.1	179 49.2	N 3 03.2	178 41.5	N 4 15.5	5 22.9	S 0 22.4	3 42.5	N 0 03.7	Canopus	264 07.1	S52 41.5
01	205 17.5	194 48.9	04.4	193 42.2	16.3	20 25.6	22.3	18 45.1	03.8	Capella	281 11.0	N45 58.8
02	220 20.0	209 48.5	05.7	208 42.9	17.1	35 28.4	22.2	33 47.7	03.9	Deneb	49 48.4	N45 12.5
03	235 22.5	224 48.1 ··	06.9	223 43.6 ··	17.8	50 31.1 ··	22.1	48 50.4 ··	04.0	Denebola	182 58.4	N14 40.6
04	250 24.9	239 47.7	08.2	238 44.3	18.6	65 33.9	21.9	63 53.0	04.0	Diphda	349 20.8	S18 05.6
05	265 27.4	254 47.3	09.4	253 45.0	19.4	80 36.6	21.8	78 55.7	04.1			
06	280 29.8	269 46.9	N 3 10.7	268 45.7	N 4 20.1	95 39.4	S 0 21.7	93 58.3	N 0 04.2	Dubhe	194 21.1	N61 51.3
07	295 32.3	284 46.6	11.9	283 46.4	20.9	110 42.2	21.6	109 01.0	04.3	Elnath	278 43.8	N28 35.5
T 08	310 34.8	299 46.2	13.2	298 47.1	21.7	125 44.9	21.4	124 03.6	04.3	Eltanin	90 57.4	N51 29.2
H 09	325 37.2	314 45.8 ··	14.4	313 47.8 ··	22.4	140 47.7 ··	21.3	139 06.2 ··	04.4	Enif	34 11.5	N 9 47.1
U 10	340 39.7	329 45.4	15.7	328 48.5	23.2	155 50.4	21.2	154 08.9	04.5	Fomalhaut	15 51.3	S29 43.4
R 11	355 42.2	344 45.0	16.9	343 49.2	24.0	170 53.2	21.1	169 11.5	04.6			
S 12	10 44.6	359 44.7	N 3 18.2	358 49.9	N 4 24.7	185 55.9	S 0 20.9	184 14.2	N 0 04.7	Gacrux	172 27.8	S57 00.5
D 13	25 47.1	14 44.3	19.4	13 50.6	25.5	200 58.7	20.8	199 16.8	04.7	Gienah	176 17.3	S17 26.3
A 14	40 49.6	29 43.9	20.7	28 51.3	26.3	216 01.4	20.7	214 19.4	04.8	Hadar	149 22.2	S60 16.9
Y 15	55 52.0	44 43.5 ··	21.9	43 52.0 ··	27.1	231 04.2 ··	20.6	229 22.1 ··	04.9	Hamal	328 28.8	N23 22.3
16	70 54.5	59 43.1	23.2	58 52.7	27.8	246 07.0	20.4	244 24.7	05.0	Kaus Aust.	84 16.3	S34 23.5
17	85 56.9	74 42.8	24.4	73 53.4	28.6	261 09.7	20.3	259 27.4	05.0			
18	100 59.4	89 42.4	N 3 25.7	88 54.1	N 4 29.4	276 12.5	S 0 20.2	274 30.0	N 0 05.1	Kochab	137 18.0	N74 13.9
19	116 01.9	104 42.0	26.9	103 54.8	30.1	291 15.2	20.1	289 32.6	05.2	Markab	14 03.1	N15 06.0
20	131 04.3	119 41.6	28.1	118 55.5	30.9	306 18.0	19.9	304 35.3	05.3	Menkar	314 41.0	N 4 00.8
21	146 06.8	134 41.2 ··	29.4	133 56.2 ··	31.7	321 20.7 ··	19.8	319 37.9 ··	05.3	Menkent	148 36.2	S36 16.6
22	161 09.3	149 40.8	30.6	148 56.9	32.4	336 23.5	19.7	334 40.6	05.4	Miaplacidus	221 44.3	S69 38.7
23	176 11.7	164 40.5	31.9	163 57.6	33.2	351 26.2	19.6	349 43.2	05.5			
3 00	191 14.2	179 40.1	N 3 33.1	178 58.3	N 4 34.0	6 29.0	S 0 19.4	4 45.9	N 0 05.6	Mirfak	309 16.0	N49 47.7
01	206 16.7	194 39.7	34.4	193 59.0	34.7	21 31.8	19.3	19 48.5	05.6	Nunki	76 28.7	S26 19.2
02	221 19.1	209 39.3	35.6	208 59.7	35.5	36 34.5	19.2	34 51.1	05.7	Peacock	53 58.1	S56 47.6
03	236 21.6	224 38.9 ··	36.9	224 00.4 ··	36.3	51 37.3 ··	19.1	49 53.8 ··	05.8	Pollux	243 57.7	N28 04.3
04	251 24.1	239 38.6	38.1	239 01.1	37.0	66 40.0	18.9	64 56.4	05.9	Procyon	245 25.4	N 5 16.3
05	266 26.5	254 38.2	39.4	254 01.8	37.8	81 42.8	18.8	79 59.1	06.0			
06	281 29.0	269 37.8	N 3 40.6	269 02.5	N 4 38.6	96 45.5	S 0 18.7	95 01.7	N 0 06.0	Rasalhague	96 29.2	N12 34.3
07	296 31.4	284 37.4	41.9	284 03.2	39.3	111 48.3	18.6	110 04.3	06.1	Regulus	208 09.4	N12 03.5
F 08	311 33.9	299 37.0	43.1	299 03.9	40.1	126 51.0	18.4	125 07.0	06.2	Rigel	281 35.8	S 8 13.6
R 09	326 36.4	314 36.6 ··	44.4	314 04.6 ··	40.9	141 53.8 ··	18.3	140 09.6 ··	06.3	Rigil Kent.	140 24.8	S60 45.3
I 10	341 38.8	329 36.3	45.6	329 05.3	41.6	156 56.6	18.2	155 12.3	06.3	Sabik	102 40.6	S15 42.1
D 11	356 41.3	344 35.9	46.9	344 05.9	42.4	171 59.3	18.1	170 14.9	06.4			
A 12	11 43.8	359 35.5	N 3 48.1	359 06.6	N 4 43.2	187 02.1	S 0 17.9	185 17.6	N 0 06.5	Schedar	350 09.2	N56 25.9
Y 13	26 46.2	14 35.1	49.3	14 07.3	43.9	202 04.8	17.8	200 20.2	06.6	Shaula	96 55.1	S37 05.3
14	41 48.7	29 34.7	50.6	29 08.0	44.7	217 07.6	17.7	215 22.8	06.6	Sirius	258 55.4	S16 41.7
15	56 51.2	44 34.3 ··	51.8	44 08.7 ··	45.5	232 10.3 ··	17.6	230 25.5 ··	06.7	Spica	158 56.9	S11 03.8
16	71 53.6	59 34.0	53.1	59 09.4	46.2	247 13.1	17.5	245 28.1	06.8	Suhail	223 10.3	S43 21.6
17	86 56.1	74 33.6	54.3	74 10.1	47.0	262 15.8	17.3	260 30.8	06.9			
18	101 58.6	89 33.2	N 3 55.6	89 10.8	N 4 47.8	277 18.6	S 0 17.2	275 33.4	N 0 06.9	Vega	80 55.6	N38 45.7
19	117 01.0	104 32.8	56.8	104 11.5	48.5	292 21.3	17.1	290 36.0	07.0	Zuben'ubi	137 32.4	S15 57.8
20	132 03.5	119 32.4	58.1	119 12.2	49.3	307 24.1	17.0	305 38.7	07.1		S.H.A.	Mer. Pass.
21	147 05.9	134 32.0	3 59.3	134 12.9 ··	50.1	322 26.8 ··	16.8	320 41.3 ··	07.2		° '	h m
22	162 08.4	149 31.6	4 00.6	149 13.6	50.8	337 29.6	16.7	335 44.0	07.2	Venus	349 34.2	12 01
23	177 10.9	164 31.3	01.8	164 14.3	51.6	352 32.4	16.6	350 46.6	07.3	Mars	348 26.4	12 05
Mer. Pass. 11 17.1		v −0.4	d 1.2	v 0.7	d 0.8	v 2.8	d 0.1	v 2.6	d 0.1	Jupiter	175 07.8	23 34
										Saturn	173 27.4	23 41

G.M.T.	SUN G.H.A.	SUN Dec.	MOON G.H.A.	v	MOON Dec.	d	H.P.
1 00	178 59.6	N 4 25.3	227 18.2	8.9	S15 55.1	7.9	58.2
01	193 59.8	26.3	241 46.1	8.8	15 47.2	8.0	58.3
02	209 00.0	27.3	256 13.9	8.9	15 39.2	8.1	58.3
03	224 00.1	.. 28.2	270 41.8	8.8	15 31.1	8.2	58.3
04	239 00.3	29.2	285 09.6	8.8	15 22.9	8.3	58.4
05	254 00.5	30.1	299 37.4	8.8	15 14.6	8.4	58.4
06	269 00.7	N 4 31.1	314 05.2	8.9	S15 06.2	8.6	58.5
W 07	284 00.9	32.1	328 33.1	8.8	14 57.6	8.6	58.5
E 08	299 01.1	33.0	343 00.9	8.8	14 49.0	8.7	58.5
D 09	314 01.3	.. 34.0	357 28.7	8.8	14 40.3	8.8	58.6
N 10	329 01.4	35.0	11 56.5	8.8	14 31.5	8.9	58.6
E 11	344 01.6	35.9	26 24.3	8.8	14 22.6	9.0	58.7
S 12	359 01.8	N 4 36.9	40 52.1	8.8	S14 13.6	9.1	58.7
D 13	14 02.0	37.9	55 19.9	8.8	14 04.5	9.1	58.7
A 14	29 02.2	38.8	69 47.7	8.8	13 55.4	9.3	58.8
Y 15	44 02.4	.. 39.8	84 15.5	8.8	13 46.1	9.4	58.8
16	59 02.6	40.8	98 43.3	8.8	13 36.7	9.5	58.9
17	74 02.7	41.7	113 11.1	8.8	13 27.2	9.6	58.9
18	89 02.9	N 4 42.7	127 38.9	8.8	S13 17.6	9.6	58.9
19	104 03.1	43.6	142 06.7	8.7	13 08.0	9.8	59.0
20	119 03.3	44.6	156 34.4	8.8	12 58.2	9.8	59.0
21	134 03.5	.. 45.6	171 02.2	8.8	12 48.4	9.9	59.1
22	149 03.7	46.5	185 30.0	8.8	12 38.5	10.0	59.1
23	164 03.9	47.5	199 57.8	8.8	12 28.5	10.1	59.1
2 00	179 04.0	N 4 48.5	214 25.6	8.7	S12 18.4	10.2	59.2
01	194 04.2	49.4	228 53.3	8.8	12 08.2	10.3	59.2
02	209 04.4	50.4	243 21.1	8.8	11 57.9	10.4	59.2
03	224 04.6	.. 51.3	257 48.9	8.7	11 47.5	10.4	59.3
04	239 04.8	52.3	272 16.6	8.8	11 37.1	10.6	59.3
05	254 05.0	53.3	286 44.4	8.8	11 26.5	10.6	59.4
06	269 05.2	N 4 54.2	301 12.2	8.7	S11 15.9	10.7	59.4
07	284 05.3	55.2	315 39.9	8.8	11 05.2	10.7	59.5
T 08	299 05.5	56.2	330 07.7	8.7	10 54.5	10.9	59.5
H 09	314 05.7	.. 57.1	344 35.4	8.8	10 43.6	10.9	59.5
U 10	329 05.9	58.1	359 03.2	8.7	10 32.7	11.0	59.5
R 11	344 06.1	4 59.0	13 30.9	8.8	10 21.7	11.1	59.6
S 12	359 06.3	N 5 00.0	27 58.7	8.7	S10 10.6	11.2	59.6
D 13	14 06.4	01.0	42 26.4	8.8	9 59.4	11.2	59.6
A 14	29 06.6	01.9	56 54.2	8.7	9 48.2	11.3	59.7
Y 15	44 06.8	.. 02.9	71 21.9	8.7	9 36.9	11.4	59.7
16	59 07.0	03.8	85 49.6	8.8	9 25.5	11.4	59.7
17	74 07.2	04.8	100 17.4	8.7	9 14.1	11.6	59.8
18	89 07.4	N 5 05.8	114 45.1	8.7	S 9 02.5	11.6	59.8
19	104 07.6	06.7	129 12.8	8.7	8 50.9	11.6	59.9
20	119 07.7	07.7	143 40.5	8.7	8 39.3	11.7	59.9
21	134 07.9	.. 08.6	158 08.2	8.7	8 27.6	11.8	59.9
22	149 08.1	09.6	172 35.9	8.7	8 15.8	11.9	59.9
23	164 08.3	10.6	187 03.6	8.7	8 03.9	11.9	60.0
3 00	179 08.5	N 5 11.5	201 31.3	8.7	S 7 52.0	12.0	60.0
01	194 08.7	12.5	215 59.0	8.7	7 40.0	12.0	60.0
02	209 08.8	13.4	230 26.7	8.7	7 28.0	12.1	60.1
03	224 09.0	.. 14.4	244 54.4	8.7	7 15.9	12.2	60.1
04	239 09.2	15.3	259 22.1	8.6	7 03.7	12.2	60.1
05	254 09.4	16.3	273 49.7	8.7	6 51.5	12.2	60.2
06	269 09.6	N 5 17.3	288 17.4	8.7	S 6 39.3	12.3	60.2
07	284 09.8	18.2	302 45.1	8.6	6 27.0	12.4	60.2
08	299 09.9	19.2	317 12.7	8.6	6 14.6	12.4	60.3
F 09	314 10.1	.. 20.1	331 40.3	8.7	6 02.2	12.5	60.3
R 10	329 10.3	21.1	346 08.0	8.6	5 49.7	12.5	60.3
I 11	344 10.5	22.1	0 35.6	8.6	5 37.2	12.6	60.3
D 12	359 10.7	N 5 23.0	15 03.2	8.6	S 5 24.6	12.6	60.4
A 13	14 10.9	24.0	29 30.8	8.6	5 12.0	12.7	60.4
Y 14	29 11.0	24.9	43 58.4	8.6	4 59.3	12.7	60.4
15	44 11.2	.. 25.9	58 26.0	8.6	4 46.6	12.7	60.5
16	59 11.4	26.8	72 53.6	8.5	4 33.9	12.8	60.5
17	74 11.6	27.8	87 21.1	8.6	4 21.1	12.8	60.5
18	89 11.8	N 5 28.7	101 48.7	8.5	S 4 08.3	12.9	60.5
19	104 11.9	29.7	116 16.2	8.5	3 55.4	12.9	60.6
20	119 12.1	30.7	130 43.7	8.6	3 42.5	12.9	60.6
21	134 12.3	.. 31.6	145 11.3	8.5	3 29.6	12.9	60.6
22	149 12.5	32.6	159 38.8	8.5	3 16.7	13.0	60.6
23	164 12.7	33.5	174 06.3	8.4	3 03.7	13.0	60.7
	S.D. 16.0	d 1.0	S.D. 16.0		16.2		16.4

Lat.	Twilight Naut.	Twilight Civil	Sunrise	Moonrise 1	2	3	4
N 72	01 27	03 36	04 51	06 51	06 29	06 13	06 00
N 70	02 14	03 53	04 59	06 18	06 10	06 04	05 58
68	02 43	04 06	05 06	05 53	05 55	05 56	05 56
66	03 05	04 17	05 11	05 35	05 43	05 49	05 54
64	03 21	04 26	05 15	05 19	05 33	05 44	05 53
62	03 35	04 33	05 19	05 06	05 24	05 39	05 52
60	03 46	04 40	05 23	04 55	05 17	05 35	05 51
N 58	03 56	04 45	05 26	04 46	05 10	05 31	05 50
56	04 04	04 50	05 28	04 38	05 04	05 27	05 49
54	04 11	04 55	05 31	04 30	04 59	05 24	05 48
52	04 17	04 59	05 33	04 23	04 54	05 22	05 48
50	04 23	05 02	05 35	04 17	04 50	05 19	05 47
45	04 34	05 10	05 39	04 04	04 40	05 14	05 46
N 40	04 43	05 15	05 43	03 53	04 32	05 09	05 44
35	04 50	05 20	05 46	03 44	04 25	05 05	05 43
30	04 56	05 24	05 48	03 36	04 19	05 01	05 43
20	05 05	05 31	05 53	03 22	04 09	04 55	05 41
N 10	05 11	05 36	05 57	03 09	04 00	04 50	05 40
0	05 15	05 40	06 00	02 58	03 51	04 45	05 39
S 10	05 18	05 43	06 04	02 46	03 43	04 40	05 38
20	05 20	05 45	06 07	02 34	03 33	04 34	05 36
30	05 20	05 47	06 11	02 19	03 23	04 28	05 35
35	05 19	05 48	06 13	02 11	03 17	04 25	05 34
40	05 17	05 49	06 16	02 02	03 10	04 20	05 33
45	05 15	05 49	06 19	01 50	03 02	04 16	05 32
S 50	05 12	05 50	06 22	01 37	02 52	04 10	05 31
52	05 11	05 50	06 23	01 31	02 47	04 08	05 30
54	05 09	05 50	06 25	01 24	02 42	04 05	05 30
56	05 07	05 50	06 27	01 16	02 37	04 01	05 29
58	05 04	05 50	06 29	01 07	02 30	03 58	05 28
S 60	05 01	05 50	06 31	00 57	02 23	03 54	05 28

Lat.	Sunset	Twilight Civil	Twilight Naut.	Moonset 1	2	3	4
N 72	19 19	20 36	22 54	11 47	14 02	16 10	18 18
N 70	19 11	20 18	22 00	12 19	14 18	16 17	18 16
68	19 04	20 04	21 29	12 42	14 31	16 23	18 15
66	18 58	19 53	21 06	13 00	14 42	16 27	18 14
64	18 54	19 44	20 49	13 14	14 51	16 31	18 13
62	18 49	19 36	20 35	13 26	14 59	16 35	18 13
60	18 46	19 29	20 23	13 36	15 05	16 38	18 12
N 58	18 43	19 23	20 14	13 45	15 11	16 40	18 11
56	18 40	19 18	20 05	13 53	15 16	16 42	18 11
54	18 38	19 14	19 58	14 00	15 21	16 45	18 11
52	18 35	19 10	19 51	14 06	15 25	16 46	18 10
50	18 33	19 06	19 46	14 12	15 28	16 48	18 10
45	18 29	18 59	19 34	14 24	15 36	16 52	18 09
N 40	18 25	18 52	19 25	14 34	15 43	16 55	18 08
35	18 22	18 47	19 18	14 42	15 49	16 57	18 08
30	18 19	18 43	19 12	14 49	15 54	17 00	18 07
20	18 15	18 37	19 03	15 02	16 02	17 04	18 06
N 10	18 11	18 32	18 56	15 13	16 10	17 07	18 05
0	18 07	18 28	18 52	15 23	16 17	17 10	18 04
S 10	18 03	18 24	18 49	15 33	16 24	17 13	18 04
20	18 00	18 22	18 47	15 44	16 31	17 17	18 03
30	17 56	18 19	18 47	15 56	16 39	17 20	18 02
35	17 53	18 19	18 48	16 04	16 44	17 23	18 01
40	17 51	18 18	18 49	16 11	16 49	17 25	18 00
45	17 48	18 17	18 51	16 21	16 55	17 28	17 59
S 50	17 44	18 17	18 54	16 32	17 03	17 31	17 59
52	17 43	18 16	18 55	16 37	17 06	17 32	17 58
54	17 41	18 16	18 57	16 43	17 10	17 34	17 58
56	17 39	18 16	18 59	16 49	17 14	17 36	17 57
58	17 37	18 16	19 02	16 56	17 18	17 38	17 56
S 60	17 35	18 16	19 04	17 04	17 23	17 40	17 56

Day	SUN Eqn. of Time 00h	12h	Mer. Pass.	MOON Mer. Pass. Upper	Lower	Age	Phase
	m s	m s	h m	h m	h m	d	
1	04 02	03 53	12 04	09 10	21 37	26	
2	03 44	03 35	12 04	10 04	22 31	27	◑
3	03 26	03 18	12 03	10 58	23 24	28	

G.M.T.	ARIES G.H.A.	VENUS −3.5 G.H.A.	Dec.	MARS +1.4 G.H.A.	Dec.	JUPITER −2.0 G.H.A.	Dec.	SATURN +0.7 G.H.A.	Dec.	STARS Name	S.H.A.	Dec.
4 00	192 13.3	179 30.9 N 4 03.0		179 15.0 N 4 52.4		7 35.1 S 0 16.5		5 49.2 N 0 07.4		Acamar	315 37.3	S40 23.1
01	207 15.8	194 30.5	04.3	194 15.7	53.1	22 37.9	16.3	20 51.9	07.5	Achernar	335 45.6	S57 20.1
02	222 18.3	209 30.1	05.5	209 16.4	53.9	37 40.6	16.2	35 54.5	07.5	Acrux	173 36.1	S62 59.7
03	237 20.7	224 29.7 ··	06.8	224 17.1 ··	54.6	52 43.4 ··	16.1	50 57.2 ··	07.6	Adhara	255 31.8	S28 57.1
04	252 23.2	239 29.3	08.0	239 17.8	55.4	67 46.1	16.0	65 59.8	07.7	Aldebaran	291 17.8	N16 28.2
05	267 25.7	254 29.0	09.3	254 18.5	56.2	82 48.9	15.9	81 02.4	07.8			
06	282 28.1	269 28.6 N 4 10.5		269 19.2 N 4 56.9		97 51.6 S 0 15.7		96 05.1 N 0 07.8		Alioth	166 41.6	N56 03.7
07	297 30.6	284 28.2	11.7	284 19.9	57.7	112 54.4	15.6	111 07.7	07.9	Alkaid	153 17.8	N49 24.4
S 08	312 33.0	299 27.8	13.0	299 20.6	58.5	127 57.1	15.5	126 10.4	08.0	Al Na'ir	28 14.8	S47 03.1
A 09	327 35.5	314 27.4 ··	14.2	314 21.3 4 59.2		142 59.9 ··	15.4	141 13.0 ··	08.1	Alnilam	276 11.4	S 1 13.0
T 10	342 38.0	329 27.0	15.5	329 22.0 5 00.0		158 02.6	15.2	156 15.6	08.1	Alphard	218 20.0	S 8 34.8
U 11	357 40.4	344 26.6	16.7	344 22.7	00.8	173 05.4	15.1	171 18.3	08.2			
R 12	12 42.9	359 26.3 N 4 18.0		359 23.4 N 5 01.5		188 08.1 S 0 15.0		186 20.9 N 0 08.3		Alphecca	126 31.5	N26 46.5
D 13	27 45.4	14 25.9	19.2	14 24.1	02.3	203 10.9	14.9	201 23.6	08.4	Alpheratz	358 09.3	N28 59.0
A 14	42 47.8	29 25.5	20.4	29 24.8	03.1	218 13.7	14.7	216 26.2	08.4	Altair	62 32.2	N 8 48.9
Y 15	57 50.3	44 25.1 ··	21.7	44 25.5 ··	03.8	233 16.4 ··	14.6	231 28.8 ··	08.5	Ankaa	353 40.3	S42 24.6
16	72 52.8	59 24.7	22.9	59 26.2	04.6	248 19.2	14.5	246 31.5	08.6	Antares	112 56.2	S26 23.4
17	87 55.2	74 24.3	24.2	74 26.9	05.3	263 21.9	14.4	261 34.1	08.7			
18	102 57.7	89 23.9 N 4 25.4		89 27.6 N 5 06.1		278 24.7 S 0 14.3		276 36.8 N 0 08.8		Arcturus	146 17.8	N19 16.7
19	118 00.2	104 23.5	26.7	104 28.3	06.9	293 27.4	14.1	291 39.4	08.8	Atria	108 19.8	S68 59.4
20	133 02.6	119 23.2	27.9	119 29.0	07.6	308 30.2	14.0	306 42.1	08.9	Avior	234 27.9	S59 27.3
21	148 05.1	134 22.8 ··	29.1	134 29.7 ··	08.4	323 32.9 ··	13.9	321 44.7 ··	09.0	Bellatrix	278 58.5	N 6 19.8
22	163 07.5	149 22.4	30.4	149 30.4	09.2	338 35.7	13.8	336 47.3	09.1	Betelgeuse	271 28.0	N 7 24.1
23	178 10.0	164 22.0	31.6	164 31.1	09.9	353 38.4	13.6	351 50.0	09.1			
5 00	193 12.5	179 21.6 N 4 32.9		179 31.8 N 5 10.7		8 41.2 S 0 13.5		6 52.6 N 0 09.2		Canopus	264 07.1	S52 41.5
01	208 14.9	194 21.2	34.1	194 32.5	11.4	23 43.9	13.4	21 55.3	09.3	Capella	281 11.0	N45 58.8
02	223 17.4	209 20.8	35.3	209 33.2	12.2	38 46.7	13.3	36 57.9	09.4	Deneb	49 48.4	N45 12.5
03	238 19.9	224 20.4 ··	36.6	224 33.9 ··	13.0	53 49.4 ··	13.2	52 00.5 ··	09.4	Denebola	182 58.4	N14 40.6
04	253 22.3	239 20.1	37.8	239 34.6	13.7	68 52.2	13.0	67 03.2	09.5	Diphda	349 20.8	S18 05.6
05	268 24.8	254 19.7	39.1	254 35.3	14.5	83 54.9	12.9	82 05.8	09.6			
06	283 27.3	269 19.3 N 4 40.3		269 36.0 N 5 15.3		98 57.7 S 0 12.8		97 08.5 N 0 09.7		Dubhe	194 21.1	N61 51.3
07	298 29.7	284 18.9	41.5	284 36.7	16.0	114 00.4	12.7	112 11.1	09.7	Elnath	278 43.8	N28 35.5
08	313 32.2	299 18.5	42.8	299 37.4	16.8	129 03.2	12.5	127 13.7	09.8	Eltanin	90 57.4	N51 29.2
S 09	328 34.7	314 18.1 ··	44.0	314 38.1 ··	17.5	144 05.9 ··	12.4	142 16.4 ··	09.9	Enif	34 11.4	N 9 47.1
U 10	343 37.1	329 17.7	45.3	329 38.8	18.3	159 08.7	12.3	157 19.0	10.0	Fomalhaut	15 51.3	S29 43.4
N 11	358 39.6	344 17.3	46.5	344 39.5	19.1	174 11.4	12.2	172 21.6	10.0			
D 12	13 42.0	359 17.0 N 4 47.7		359 40.2 N 5 19.8		189 14.2 S 0 12.1		187 24.3 N 0 10.1		Gacrux	172 27.8	S57 00.5
A 13	28 44.5	14 16.6	49.0	14 40.9	20.6	204 16.9	11.9	202 26.9	10.2	Gienah	176 17.3	S17 26.3
Y 14	43 47.0	29 16.2	50.2	29 41.6	21.3	219 19.7	11.8	217 29.6	10.3	Hadar	149 22.2	S60 16.9
15	58 49.4	44 15.8 ··	51.5	44 42.3 ··	22.1	234 22.4 ··	11.7	232 32.2 ··	10.3	Hamal	328 28.9	N23 22.2
16	73 51.9	59 15.4	52.7	59 43.0	22.9	249 25.2	11.6	247 34.8	10.4	Kaus Aust.	84 16.3	S34 23.5
17	88 54.4	74 15.0	53.9	74 43.7	23.6	264 27.9	11.5	262 37.5	10.5			
18	103 56.8	89 14.6 N 4 55.2		89 44.4 N 5 24.4		279 30.7 S 0 11.3		277 40.1 N 0 10.5		Kochab	137 18.0	N74 13.9
19	118 59.3	104 14.2	56.4	104 45.1	25.1	294 33.4	11.2	292 42.8	10.6	Markab	14 03.1	N15 06.0
20	134 01.8	119 13.8	57.6	119 45.8	25.9	309 36.2	11.1	307 45.4	10.7	Menkar	314 41.0	N 4 00.8
21	149 04.2	134 13.4 4 58.9		134 46.5 ··	26.7	324 38.9 ··	11.0	322 48.0 ··	10.8	Menkent	148 36.2	S36 16.6
22	164 06.7	149 13.1 5 00.1		149 47.2	27.4	339 41.7	10.8	337 50.7	10.8	Miaplacidus	221 44.4	S69 38.7
23	179 09.1	164 12.7	01.4	164 47.9	28.2	354 44.4	10.7	352 53.3	10.9			
6 00	194 11.6	179 12.3 N 5 02.6		179 48.6 N 5 28.9		9 47.2 S 0 10.6		7 56.0 N 0 11.0		Mirfak	309 16.0	N49 47.7
01	209 14.1	194 11.9	03.8	194 49.3	29.7	24 49.9	10.5	22 58.6	11.1	Nunki	76 28.7	S26 19.2
02	224 16.5	209 11.5	05.1	209 50.0	30.5	39 52.7	10.4	38 01.2	11.1	Peacock	53 58.0	S56 47.6
03	239 19.0	224 11.1 ··	06.3	224 50.7 ··	31.2	54 55.4 ··	10.2	53 03.9 ··	11.2	Pollux	243 57.7	N28 04.3
04	254 21.5	239 10.7	07.5	239 51.4	32.0	69 58.2	10.1	68 06.5	11.3	Procyon	245 25.4	N 5 16.3
05	269 23.9	254 10.3	08.8	254 52.1	32.7	85 00.9	10.0	83 09.2	11.4			
06	284 26.4	269 09.9 N 5 10.0		269 52.8 N 5 33.5		100 03.7 S 0 09.9		98 11.8 N 0 11.4		Rasalhague	96 29.1	N12 34.3
07	299 28.9	284 09.5	11.2	284 53.4	34.3	115 06.4	09.8	113 14.4	11.5	Regulus	208 09.4	N12 03.5
08	314 31.3	299 09.1	12.5	299 54.1	35.0	130 09.2	09.6	128 17.1	11.6	Rigel	281 35.8	S 8 13.6
M 09	329 33.8	314 08.8 ··	13.7	314 54.8 ··	35.8	145 11.9 ··	09.5	143 19.7 ··	11.7	Rigil Kent.	140 24.8	S60 45.3
O 10	344 36.3	329 08.4	14.9	329 55.5	36.5	160 14.7	09.4	158 22.4	11.7	Sabik	102 40.6	S15 42.1
N 11	359 38.7	344 08.0	16.2	344 56.2	37.3	175 17.4	09.3	173 25.0	11.8			
D 12	14 41.2	359 07.6 N 5 17.4		359 56.9 N 5 38.0		190 20.2 S 0 09.2		188 27.6 N 0 11.9		Schedar	350 09.2	N56 25.9
A 13	29 43.6	14 07.2	18.6	14 57.6	38.8	205 22.9	09.0	203 30.3	12.0	Shaula	96 55.1	S37 05.3
Y 14	44 46.1	29 06.8	19.9	29 58.3	39.6	220 25.7	08.9	218 32.9	12.0	Sirius	258 55.4	S16 41.7
15	59 48.6	44 06.4 ··	21.1	44 59.0 ··	40.3	235 28.4 ··	08.8	233 35.5 ··	12.1	Spica	158 56.9	S11 03.8
16	74 51.0	59 06.0	22.3	59 59.7	41.1	250 31.2	08.7	248 38.2	12.2	Suhail	223 10.3	S43 21.7
17	89 53.5	74 05.6	23.6	75 00.4	41.8	265 33.9	08.6	263 40.8	12.3			
18	104 56.0	89 05.2 N 5 24.8		90 01.1 N 5 42.6		280 36.7 S 0 08.4		278 43.5 N 0 12.3		Vega	80 55.5	N38 45.7
19	119 58.4	104 04.8	26.0	105 01.8	43.3	295 39.4	08.3	293 46.1	12.4	Zuben'ubi	137 32.4	S15 57.8
20	135 00.9	119 04.4	27.3	120 02.5	44.1	310 42.2	08.2	308 48.7	12.5		S.H.A.	Mer. Pass.
21	150 03.4	134 04.0 ··	28.5	135 03.2 ··	44.9	325 44.9 ··	08.1	323 51.4 ··	12.6			
22	165 05.8	149 03.6	29.7	150 03.9	45.6	340 47.7	08.0	338 54.0	12.6	Venus	346 09.1	12 03
23	180 08.3	164 03.2	31.0	165 04.6	46.4	355 50.4	07.8	353 56.7	12.7	Mars	346 19.3	12 01
	h m									Jupiter	175 28.7	23 21
Mer. Pass. 11 05.3	v −0.4 d 1.2	v 0.7 d 0.8		v 2.8 d 0.1		v 2.6 d 0.1				Saturn	173 40.1	23 28

SUN and MOON

G.M.T.	SUN G.H.A.	SUN Dec.	MOON G.H.A.	v	MOON Dec.	d	H.P.
4 00	179 12.9	N 5 34.5	188 33.7	8.5	S 2 50.7	13.1	60.7
01	194 13.0	35.4	203 01.2	8.5	2 37.6	13.1	60.7
02	209 13.2	36.4	217 28.7	8.4	2 24.5	13.1	60.7
03	224 13.4	.. 37.3	231 56.1	8.4	2 11.4	13.1	60.7
04	239 13.6	38.3	246 23.5	8.4	1 58.3	13.1	60.8
05	254 13.8	39.3	260 50.9	8.4	1 45.2	13.2	60.8
06	269 13.9	N 5 40.2	275 18.3	8.4	S 1 32.0	13.2	60.8
07	284 14.1	41.2	289 45.7	8.4	1 18.8	13.2	60.8
S 08	299 14.3	42.1	304 13.1	8.3	1 05.6	13.2	60.8
A 09	314 14.5	.. 43.1	318 40.4	8.3	0 52.4	13.2	60.9
T 10	329 14.7	44.0	333 07.7	8.3	0 39.2	13.0	60.9
U 11	344 14.9	45.0	347 35.0	8.3	0 25.9	13.2	60.9
R 12	359 15.0	N 5 45.9	2 02.3	8.3	S 0 12.7	13.3	60.9
D 13	14 15.2	46.9	16 29.6	8.3	N 0 00.6	13.2	60.9
A 14	29 15.4	47.8	30 56.9	8.2	0 13.8	13.3	60.9
Y 15	44 15.6	.. 48.8	45 24.1	8.2	0 27.1	13.3	61.0
16	59 15.8	49.7	59 51.3	8.2	0 40.4	13.3	61.0
17	74 15.9	50.7	74 18.5	8.2	0 53.7	13.3	61.0
18	89 16.1	N 5 51.6	88 45.7	8.1	N 1 07.0	13.2	61.0
19	104 16.3	52.6	103 12.8	8.2	1 20.2	13.3	61.0
20	119 16.5	53.5	117 40.0	8.1	1 33.5	13.0	61.0
21	134 16.7	.. 54.5	132 07.1	8.1	1 46.8	13.3	61.0
22	149 16.8	55.4	146 34.2	8.0	2 00.1	13.2	61.0
23	164 17.0	56.4	161 01.2	8.1	2 13.3	13.3	61.1
5 00	179 17.2	N 5 57.3	175 28.3	8.0	N 2 26.6	13.2	61.1
01	194 17.4	58.3	189 55.3	8.0	2 39.8	13.3	61.1
02	209 17.6	5 59.2	204 22.3	8.0	2 53.1	13.2	61.1
03	224 17.7	6 00.2	218 49.3	7.9	3 06.3	13.2	61.1
04	239 17.9	01.1	233 16.2	7.9	3 19.5	13.2	61.1
05	254 18.1	02.1	247 43.1	7.9	3 32.7	13.1	61.1
06	269 18.3	N 6 03.0	262 10.0	7.9	N 3 45.8	13.2	61.1
07	284 18.5	04.0	276 36.9	7.8	3 59.0	13.1	61.1
08	299 18.6	04.9	291 03.7	7.9	4 12.1	13.1	61.1
S 09	314 18.8	.. 05.9	305 30.6	7.7	4 25.2	13.0	61.1
U 10	329 19.0	06.8	319 57.4	7.7	4 38.2	13.1	61.1
N 11	344 19.2	07.8	334 24.1	7.8	4 51.3	13.0	61.1
D 12	359 19.4	N 6 08.7	348 50.9	7.7	N 5 04.3	13.0	61.2
A 13	14 19.5	09.7	3 17.6	7.7	5 17.3	12.9	61.2
Y 14	29 19.7	10.6	17 44.3	7.6	5 30.2	12.9	61.2
15	44 19.9	.. 11.6	32 10.9	7.7	5 43.1	12.9	61.2
16	59 20.1	12.5	46 37.6	7.6	5 56.0	12.9	61.2
17	74 20.3	13.5	61 04.2	7.5	6 08.9	12.8	61.2
18	89 20.4	N 6 14.4	75 30.7	7.6	N 6 21.7	12.7	61.2
19	104 20.6	15.4	89 57.3	7.5	6 34.4	12.7	61.2
20	119 20.8	16.3	104 23.8	7.5	6 47.1	12.7	61.2
21	134 21.0	.. 17.3	118 50.3	7.4	6 59.8	12.6	61.2
22	149 21.2	18.2	133 16.7	7.5	7 12.4	12.6	61.2
23	164 21.3	19.2	147 43.2	7.4	7 25.0	12.5	61.2
6 00	179 21.5	N 6 20.1	162 09.6	7.3	N 7 37.5	12.5	61.2
01	194 21.7	21.1	176 35.9	7.4	7 50.0	12.5	61.2
02	209 21.9	22.0	191 02.3	7.3	8 02.5	12.3	61.2
03	224 22.0	.. 22.9	205 28.6	7.2	8 14.8	12.3	61.1
04	239 22.2	23.9	219 54.8	7.3	8 27.1	12.3	61.1
05	254 22.4	24.8	234 21.1	7.2	8 39.4	12.2	61.1
06	269 22.6	N 6 25.8	248 47.3	7.2	N 8 51.6	12.1	61.1
07	284 22.8	26.7	263 13.5	7.1	9 03.7	12.1	61.1
08	299 22.9	27.7	277 39.6	7.1	9 15.8	12.0	61.1
M 09	314 23.1	.. 28.6	292 05.7	7.1	9 27.8	12.0	61.1
O 10	329 23.3	29.6	306 31.8	7.1	9 39.8	11.8	61.1
N 11	344 23.5	30.5	320 57.9	7.0	9 51.6	11.8	61.1
D 12	359 23.6	N 6 31.4	335 23.9	7.0	N10 03.4	11.8	61.1
A 13	14 23.8	32.4	349 49.9	7.0	10 15.2	11.7	61.1
Y 14	29 24.0	33.3	4 15.9	6.9	10 26.9	11.5	61.1
15	44 24.2	.. 34.3	18 41.8	6.9	10 38.4	11.6	61.1
16	59 24.4	35.2	33 07.7	6.9	10 50.0	11.4	61.0
17	74 24.5	36.2	47 33.6	6.8	11 01.4	11.4	61.0
18	89 24.7	N 6 37.1	61 59.4	6.8	N11 12.8	11.3	61.0
19	104 24.9	38.0	76 25.2	6.8	11 24.1	11.2	61.0
20	119 25.1	39.0	90 51.0	6.8	11 35.3	11.1	61.0
21	134 25.2	.. 39.9	105 16.8	6.7	11 46.4	11.0	61.0
22	149 25.4	40.9	119 42.5	6.7	11 57.4	11.0	61.0
23	164 25.6	41.8	134 08.2	6.6	12 08.4	10.8	61.0
	S.D. 16.0	d 0.9	S.D. 16.6		16.7		16.6

Twilight, Sunrise and Moonrise

Lat.	Naut.	Civil	Sunrise	Moonrise 4	5	6	7
N 72	00 18	03 16	04 35	06 00	05 47	05 33	05 15
N 70	01 47	03 36	04 45	05 58	05 52	05 46	05 39
68	02 23	03 52	04 53	05 56	05 56	05 56	05 58
66	02 48	04 04	04 59	05 54	05 59	06 05	06 13
64	03 07	04 14	05 05	05 53	06 02	06 12	06 25
62	03 23	04 23	05 10	05 52	06 04	06 18	06 35
60	03 35	04 30	05 14	05 51	06 07	06 24	06 44
N 58	03 46	04 37	05 17	05 50	06 09	06 29	06 52
56	03 55	04 42	05 21	05 49	06 10	06 33	06 59
54	04 03	04 47	05 24	05 48	06 12	06 37	07 06
52	04 09	04 52	05 26	05 48	06 13	06 41	07 11
50	04 16	04 55	05 29	05 47	06 15	06 44	07 17
45	04 28	05 04	05 34	05 46	06 18	06 51	07 28
N 40	04 38	05 11	05 38	05 44	06 20	06 57	07 37
35	04 46	05 16	05 42	05 43	06 22	07 02	07 45
30	04 52	05 21	05 45	05 43	06 24	07 07	07 52
20	05 02	05 28	05 50	05 41	06 27	07 15	08 05
N 10	05 09	05 34	05 55	05 40	06 30	07 22	08 16
0	05 15	05 39	05 59	05 39	06 33	07 29	08 26
S 10	05 18	05 43	06 04	05 38	06 36	07 36	08 36
20	05 20	05 46	06 08	05 36	06 39	07 43	08 47
30	05 21	05 49	06 13	05 35	06 43	07 51	09 00
35	05 21	05 50	06 16	05 34	06 45	07 56	09 08
40	05 20	05 52	06 19	05 33	06 47	08 02	09 16
45	05 19	05 53	06 22	05 32	06 50	08 08	09 26
S 50	05 17	05 54	06 27	05 31	06 53	08 16	09 38
52	05 16	05 55	06 29	05 30	06 55	08 20	09 44
54	05 14	05 55	06 31	05 30	06 57	08 24	09 50
56	05 13	05 56	06 33	05 29	06 58	08 28	09 57
58	05 11	05 56	06 36	05 28	07 00	08 33	10 05
S 60	05 08	05 57	06 38	05 28	07 03	08 39	10 14

Twilight, Sunset and Moonset

Lat.	Sunset	Civil	Naut.	Moonset 4	5	6	7
N 72	19 33	20 54	////	18 18	20 28	22 45	25 18
N 70	19 23	20 33	22 28	18 16	20 18	22 23	24 32
68	19 15	20 17	21 48	18 15	20 10	22 06	24 02
66	19 08	20 04	21 21	18 14	20 03	21 52	23 40
64	19 02	19 54	21 01	18 13	19 57	21 41	23 23
62	18 58	19 45	20 46	18 13	19 52	21 32	23 09
60	18 53	19 37	20 33	18 12	19 48	21 23	22 57
N 58	18 49	19 31	20 22	18 11	19 44	21 16	22 46
56	18 46	19 25	20 13	18 11	19 41	21 10	22 37
54	18 43	19 20	20 05	18 11	19 38	21 05	22 29
52	18 40	19 15	19 57	18 10	19 35	21 00	22 22
50	18 38	19 11	19 51	18 10	19 32	20 55	22 16
45	18 33	19 03	19 38	18 09	19 27	20 45	22 02
N 40	18 28	18 56	19 28	18 08	19 23	20 37	21 50
35	18 24	18 50	19 20	18 08	19 19	20 30	21 41
30	18 21	18 45	19 14	18 07	19 15	20 24	21 32
20	18 15	18 38	19 04	18 06	19 09	20 14	21 18
N 10	18 10	18 32	18 56	18 05	19 04	20 04	21 05
0	18 06	18 27	18 51	18 04	18 59	19 56	20 53
S 10	18 02	18 23	18 47	18 04	18 55	19 47	20 41
20	17 57	18 19	18 45	18 03	18 49	19 38	20 29
30	17 52	18 16	18 44	18 02	18 44	19 28	20 14
35	17 49	18 15	18 44	18 01	18 40	19 22	20 06
40	17 46	18 13	18 44	18 00	18 36	19 15	19 57
45	17 42	18 12	18 46	17 59	18 32	19 07	19 46
S 50	17 38	18 10	18 48	17 59	18 27	18 58	19 32
52	17 36	18 10	18 49	17 58	18 24	18 53	19 26
54	17 34	18 09	18 50	17 58	18 22	18 48	19 19
56	17 31	18 09	18 51	17 57	18 19	18 43	19 12
58	17 29	18 08	18 53	17 56	18 16	18 37	19 03
S 60	17 26	18 07	18 55	17 56	18 12	18 31	18 53

Day	SUN Eqn. of Time 00h	12h	Mer. Pass.	MOON Mer. Pass. Upper	Lower	Age	Phase
4	03 09	03 00	12 03	11 52	24 19	29	●
5	02 52	02 43	12 03	12 46	00 19	01	
6	02 34	02 26	12 02	13 42	01 14	02	

G.M.T.	ARIES G.H.A.	VENUS −3.5 G.H.A.	Dec.	MARS +1.4 G.H.A.	Dec.	JUPITER −2.0 G.H.A.	Dec.	SATURN +0.7 G.H.A.	Dec.	STARS Name	S.H.A.	Dec.
7 00	195 10.8	179 02.9 N 5	32.2	180 05.3 N 5	47.1	10 53.2 S 0	07.7	8 59.3 N 0	12.8	Acamar	315 37.3	S40 23.1
01	210 13.2	194 02.5	33.4	195 06.0	47.9	25 55.9	07.6	24 01.9	12.9	Achernar	335 45.6	S57 20.1
02	225 15.7	209 02.1	34.7	210 06.7	48.6	40 58.7	07.5	39 04.6	12.9	Acrux	173 36.1	S62 59.7
03	240 18.1	224 01.7 ··	35.9	225 07.4 ··	49.4	56 01.4 ··	07.4	54 07.2 ··	13.0	Adhara	255 31.9	S28 57.1
04	255 20.6	239 01.3	37.1	240 08.1	50.2	71 04.2	07.2	69 09.8	13.1	Aldebaran	291 17.8	N16 28.2
05	270 23.1	254 00.9	38.4	255 08.8	50.9	86 06.9	07.1	84 12.5	13.1			
06	285 25.5	269 00.5 N 5	39.6	270 09.5 N 5	51.7	101 09.7 S 0	07.0	99 15.1 N 0	13.2	Alioth	166 41.6	N56 03.7
07	300 28.0	284 00.1	40.8	285 10.2	52.4	116 12.4	06.9	114 17.8	13.3	Alkaid	153 17.7	N49 24.4
T 08	315 30.5	298 59.7	42.1	300 10.9	53.2	131 15.1	06.8	129 20.4	13.4	Al Na'ir	28 14.8	S47 03.1
U 09	330 32.9	313 59.3 ··	43.3	315 11.6 ··	53.9	146 17.9 ··	06.6	144 23.0 ··	13.4	Alnilam	276 11.4	S 1 13.0
E 10	345 35.4	328 58.9	44.5	330 12.3	54.7	161 20.6	06.5	159 25.7	13.5	Alphard	218 20.0	S 8 34.8
S 11	0 37.9	343 58.5	45.7	345 13.0	55.4	176 23.4	06.4	174 28.3	13.6			
D 12	15 40.3	358 58.1 N 5	47.0	0 13.7 N 5	56.2	191 26.1 S 0	06.3	189 30.9 N 0	13.7	Alphecca	126 31.5	N26 46.6
A 13	30 42.8	13 57.7	48.2	15 14.4	57.0	206 28.9	06.2	204 33.6	13.7	Alpheratz	358 09.3	N28 59.0
Y 14	45 45.2	28 57.3	49.4	30 15.1	57.7	221 31.6	06.0	219 36.2	13.8	Altair	62 32.2	N 8 48.9
15	60 47.7	43 56.9 ··	50.7	45 15.8 ··	58.5	236 34.4 ··	05.9	234 38.9 ··	13.9	Ankaa	353 40.3	S42 24.6
16	75 50.2	58 56.5	51.9	60 16.5 5	59.2	251 37.1	05.8	249 41.5	14.0	Antares	112 56.2	S26 23.4
17	90 52.6	73 56.1	53.1	75 17.2 6	00.0	266 39.9	05.7	264 44.1	14.0			
18	105 55.1	88 55.7 N 5	54.3	90 17.9 N 6	00.7	281 42.6 S 0	05.6	279 46.8 N 0	14.1	Arcturus	146 17.8	N19 16.7
19	120 57.6	103 55.3	55.6	105 18.6	01.5	296 45.4	05.5	294 49.4	14.2	Atria	108 19.8	S68 59.4
20	136 00.0	118 54.9	56.8	120 19.3	02.2	311 48.1	05.3	309 52.1	14.2	Avior	234 27.9	S59 27.3
21	151 02.5	133 54.5 ··	58.0	135 20.0 ··	03.0	326 50.8 ··	05.2	324 54.7 ··	14.3	Bellatrix	278 58.5	N 6 19.8
22	166 05.0	148 54.1 5	59.3	150 20.7	03.7	341 53.6	05.1	339 57.3	14.4	Betelgeuse	271 28.0	N 7 24.1
23	181 07.4	163 53.7 6	00.5	165 21.4	04.5	356 56.3	05.0	355 00.0	14.5			
8 00	196 09.9	178 53.3 N 6	01.7	180 22.1 N 6	05.2	11 59.1 S 0	04.9	10 02.6 N 0	14.5	Canopus	264 07.2	S52 41.5
01	211 12.4	193 52.9	02.9	195 22.8	06.0	27 01.8	04.7	25 05.2	14.6	Capella	281 11.0	N45 58.8
02	226 14.8	208 52.5	04.2	210 23.5	06.8	42 04.6	04.6	40 07.9	14.7	Deneb	49 48.4	N45 12.5
03	241 17.3	223 52.2 ··	05.4	225 24.2 ··	07.5	57 07.3 ··	04.5	55 10.5 ··	14.8	Denebola	182 58.4	N14 40.6
04	256 19.7	238 51.8	06.6	240 24.9	08.3	72 10.1	04.4	70 13.1	14.8	Diphda	349 20.8	S18 05.6
05	271 22.2	253 51.4	07.8	255 25.6	09.0	87 12.8	04.3	85 15.8	14.9			
06	286 24.7	268 51.0 N 6	09.1	270 26.3 N 6	09.8	102 15.6 S 0	04.1	100 18.4 N 0	15.0	Dubhe	194 21.1	N61 51.3
W 07	301 27.1	283 50.6	10.3	285 27.0	10.5	117 18.3	04.0	115 21.1	15.1	Elnath	278 43.9	N28 35.5
E 08	316 29.6	298 50.2	11.5	300 27.7	11.3	132 21.0	03.9	130 23.7	15.1	Eltanin	90 57.4	N51 29.2
D 09	331 32.1	313 49.8 ··	12.7	315 28.4 ··	12.0	147 23.8 ··	03.8	145 26.3 ··	15.2	Enif	34 11.4	N 9 47.1
N 10	346 34.5	328 49.4	14.0	330 29.1	12.8	162 26.5	03.7	160 29.0	15.3	Fomalhaut	15 51.3	S29 43.4
E 11	1 37.0	343 49.0	15.2	345 29.8	13.5	177 29.3	03.6	175 31.6	15.3			
S 12	16 39.5	358 48.6 N 6	16.4	0 30.5 N 6	14.3	192 32.0 S 0	03.4	190 34.2 N 0	15.4	Gacrux	172 27.8	S57 00.5
D 13	31 41.9	13 48.2	17.6	15 31.2	15.0	207 34.8	03.3	205 36.9	15.5	Gienah	176 17.3	S17 26.3
A 14	46 44.4	28 47.8	18.9	30 31.8	15.8	222 37.5	03.2	220 39.5	15.6	Hadar	149 22.2	S60 16.9
Y 15	61 46.9	43 47.4 ··	20.1	45 32.5 ··	16.5	237 40.3 ··	03.1	235 42.2 ··	15.6	Hamal	328 28.9	N23 22.2
16	76 49.3	58 47.0	21.3	60 33.2	17.3	252 43.0	03.0	250 44.8	15.7	Kaus Aust.	84 16.3	S34 23.5
17	91 51.8	73 46.6	22.5	75 33.9	18.0	267 45.7	02.9	265 47.4	15.8			
18	106 54.2	88 46.2 N 6	23.7	90 34.6 N 6	18.8	282 48.5 S 0	02.7	280 50.1 N 0	15.9	Kochab	137 18.0	N74 13.9
19	121 56.7	103 45.7	25.0	105 35.3	19.5	297 51.2	02.6	295 52.7	15.9	Markab	14 03.1	N15 06.0
20	136 59.2	118 45.3	26.2	120 36.0	20.3	312 54.0	02.5	310 55.3	16.0	Menkar	314 41.0	N 4 00.8
21	152 01.6	133 44.9 ··	27.4	135 36.7 ··	21.0	327 56.7 ··	02.4	325 58.0 ··	16.1	Menkent	148 36.2	S36 16.6
22	167 04.1	148 44.5	28.6	150 37.4	21.8	342 59.5	02.3	341 00.6	16.1	Miaplacidus	221 44.4	S69 38.7
23	182 06.6	163 44.1	29.9	165 38.1	22.5	358 02.2	02.1	356 03.2	16.2			
9 00	197 09.0	178 43.7 N 6	31.1	180 38.8 N 6	23.3	13 04.9 S 0	02.0	11 05.9 N 0	16.3	Mirfak	309 16.0	N49 47.6
01	212 11.5	193 43.3	32.3	195 39.5	24.0	28 07.7	01.9	26 08.5	16.4	Nunki	76 28.7	S26 19.2
02	227 14.0	208 42.9	33.5	210 40.2	24.8	43 10.4	01.8	41 11.2	16.4	Peacock	53 58.0	S56 47.6
03	242 16.4	223 42.5 ··	34.7	225 40.9 ··	25.5	58 13.2 ··	01.7	56 13.8 ··	16.5	Pollux	243 57.7	N28 04.3
04	257 18.9	238 42.1	36.0	240 41.6	26.3	73 15.9	01.6	71 16.4	16.6	Procyon	245 25.4	N 5 16.3
05	272 21.3	253 41.7	37.2	255 42.3	27.0	88 18.7	01.4	86 19.1	16.6			
06	287 23.8	268 41.3 N 6	38.4	270 43.0 N 6	27.8	103 21.4 S 0	01.3	101 21.7 N 0	16.7	Rasalhague	96 29.1	N12 34.3
07	302 26.3	283 40.9	39.6	285 43.7	28.5	118 24.1	01.2	116 24.3	16.8	Regulus	208 09.4	N12 03.5
T 08	317 28.7	298 40.5	40.8	300 44.4	29.3	133 26.9	01.1	131 27.0	16.9	Rigel	281 35.8	S 8 13.6
H 09	332 31.2	313 40.1 ··	42.1	315 45.1 ··	30.0	148 29.6 ··	01.0	146 29.6 ··	16.9	Rigil Kent.	140 24.7	S60 45.3
U 10	347 33.7	328 39.7	43.3	330 45.8	30.8	163 32.4	00.9	161 32.2	17.0	Sabik	102 40.5	S15 42.1
R 11	2 36.1	343 39.3	44.5	345 46.5	31.5	178 35.1	00.7	176 34.9	17.1			
S 12	17 38.6	358 38.9 N 6	45.7	0 47.2 N 6	32.3	193 37.8 S 0	00.6	191 37.5 N 0	17.2	Schedar	350 09.2	N56 25.9
D 13	32 41.1	13 38.5	46.9	15 47.9	33.0	208 40.6	00.5	206 40.2	17.2	Shaula	96 55.1	S37 05.3
A 14	47 43.5	28 38.1	48.1	30 48.6	33.8	223 43.3	00.4	221 42.8	17.3	Sirius	258 55.4	S16 41.7
Y 15	62 46.0	43 37.7 ··	49.4	45 49.3 ··	34.5	238 46.1 ··	00.3	236 45.4 ··	17.4	Spica	158 56.8	S11 03.8
16	77 48.5	58 37.3	50.6	60 50.0	35.3	253 48.8 S 0	00.2	251 48.1	17.4	Suhail	223 10.3	S43 21.7
17	92 50.9	73 36.9	51.8	75 50.7	36.0	268 51.5 0	00.0	266 50.7	17.5			
18	107 53.4	88 36.5 N 6	53.0	90 51.4 N 6	36.8	283 54.3 N 0	00.1	281 53.3 N 0	17.6	Vega	80 55.5	N38 45.7
19	122 55.8	103 36.1	54.2	105 52.1	37.5	298 57.0	00.2	296 56.0	17.7	Zuben'ubi	137 32.3	S15 57.8
20	137 58.3	118 35.6	55.4	120 52.8	38.3	313 59.8	00.3	311 58.6	17.7			
21	153 00.8	133 35.2 ··	56.7	135 53.5 ··	39.0	329 02.5 ··	00.4	327 01.2 ··	17.8		S.H.A.	Mer. Pass.
22	168 03.2	148 34.8	57.9	150 54.2	39.8	344 05.3	00.5	342 03.9	17.9	Venus	342 43.5	12 05
23	183 05.7	163 34.4	59.1	165 54.9	40.5	359 08.0	00.6	357 06.5	17.9	Mars	344 12.2	11 58
Mer. Pass. 10 53.6		v −0.4 d 1.2		v 0.7 d 0.8		v 2.7 d 0.1		v 2.6 d 0.1		Jupiter	175 49.2	23 08
										Saturn	173 52.7	23 16

SUN and MOON

G.M.T.	SUN G.H.A.	SUN Dec.	MOON G.H.A.	v	MOON Dec.	d	H.P.
7 00	179 25.8	N 6 42.8	148 33.8	6.7	N12 19.2	10.8	60.9
01	194 25.9	43.7	162 59.5	6.5	12 30.0	10.7	60.9
02	209 26.1	44.6	177 25.0	6.6	12 40.7	10.6	60.9
03	224 26.3	·· 45.6	191 50.6	6.6	12 51.3	10.5	60.9
04	239 26.5	46.5	206 16.2	6.5	13 01.8	10.4	60.9
05	254 26.6	47.5	220 41.7	6.4	13 12.2	10.3	60.9
06	269 26.8	N 6 48.4	235 07.1	6.5	N13 22.5	10.3	60.8
07	284 27.0	49.3	249 32.6	6.4	13 32.8	10.1	60.8
08	299 27.2	50.3	263 58.0	6.4	13 42.9	10.0	60.8
09	314 27.4	·· 51.2	278 23.4	6.4	13 52.9	9.9	60.8
10	329 27.5	52.2	292 48.8	6.3	14 02.8	9.9	60.8
11	344 27.7	53.1	307 14.1	6.4	14 12.7	9.7	60.7
12	359 27.9	N 6 54.0	321 39.5	6.3	N14 22.4	9.6	60.7
13	14 28.1	55.0	336 04.8	6.2	14 32.0	9.5	60.7
14	29 28.2	55.9	350 30.0	6.3	14 41.5	9.4	60.7
15	44 28.4	·· 56.9	4 55.3	6.2	14 50.9	9.3	60.7
16	59 28.6	57.8	19 20.5	6.2	15 00.2	9.2	60.6
17	74 28.8	58.7	33 45.7	6.1	15 09.4	9.1	60.6
18	89 28.9	N 6 59.7	48 10.8	6.2	N15 18.5	9.0	60.6
19	104 29.1	7 00.6	62 36.0	6.1	15 27.5	8.9	60.6
20	119 29.3	01.5	77 01.1	6.1	15 36.4	8.7	60.5
21	134 29.5	·· 02.5	91 26.2	6.1	15 45.1	8.7	60.5
22	149 29.6	03.4	105 51.3	6.1	15 53.8	8.5	60.5
23	164 29.8	04.4	120 16.4	6.0	16 02.3	8.4	60.5
8 00	179 30.0	N 7 05.3	134 41.4	6.0	N16 10.7	8.3	60.4
01	194 30.2	06.2	149 06.4	6.0	16 19.0	8.2	60.4
02	209 30.3	07.2	163 31.4	6.0	16 27.2	8.0	60.4
03	224 30.5	·· 08.1	177 56.4	6.0	16 35.2	8.0	60.4
04	239 30.7	09.0	192 21.4	5.9	16 43.2	7.8	60.3
05	254 30.8	10.0	206 46.3	6.0	16 51.0	7.7	60.3
06	269 31.0	N 7 10.9	221 11.3	5.9	N16 58.7	7.5	60.3
07	284 31.2	11.8	235 36.2	5.9	17 06.2	7.5	60.3
08	299 31.4	12.8	250 01.1	5.9	17 13.7	7.3	60.2
09	314 31.5	·· 13.7	264 26.0	5.9	17 21.0	7.2	60.2
10	329 31.7	14.7	278 50.9	5.9	17 28.2	7.1	60.2
11	344 31.9	15.6	293 15.8	5.8	17 35.3	7.0	60.2
12	359 32.1	N 7 16.5	307 40.6	5.9	N17 42.3	6.8	60.1
13	14 32.2	17.5	322 05.5	5.8	17 49.1	6.7	60.1
14	29 32.4	18.4	336 30.3	5.9	17 55.8	6.6	60.1
15	44 32.6	·· 19.3	350 55.2	5.8	18 02.4	6.4	60.0
16	59 32.8	20.3	5 20.0	5.8	18 08.8	6.4	60.0
17	74 32.9	21.2	19 44.8	5.8	18 15.2	6.2	60.0
18	89 33.1	N 7 22.1	34 09.6	5.9	N18 21.4	6.0	59.9
19	104 33.3	23.1	48 34.5	5.8	18 27.4	5.9	59.9
20	119 33.4	24.0	62 59.3	5.8	18 33.3	5.8	59.9
21	134 33.6	·· 24.9	77 24.1	5.8	18 39.1	5.7	59.9
22	149 33.8	25.8	91 48.9	5.8	18 44.8	5.6	59.8
23	164 34.0	26.8	106 13.7	5.8	18 50.4	5.4	59.8
9 00	179 34.1	N 7 27.7	120 38.5	5.8	N18 55.8	5.2	59.8
01	194 34.3	28.6	135 03.3	5.8	19 01.0	5.2	59.7
02	209 34.5	29.6	149 28.1	5.9	19 06.2	5.0	59.7
03	224 34.6	·· 30.5	163 53.0	5.8	19 11.2	4.9	59.7
04	239 34.8	31.4	178 17.8	5.8	19 16.1	4.7	59.6
05	254 35.0	32.4	192 42.6	5.8	19 20.8	4.6	59.6
06	269 35.2	N 7 33.3	207 07.4	5.9	N19 25.4	4.5	59.6
07	284 35.3	34.2	221 32.3	5.8	19 29.9	4.3	59.5
08	299 35.5	35.2	235 57.1	5.9	19 34.2	4.2	59.5
09	314 35.7	·· 36.1	250 22.0	5.9	19 38.4	4.1	59.5
10	329 35.8	37.0	264 46.9	5.9	19 42.5	3.9	59.4
11	344 36.0	37.9	279 11.8	5.9	19 46.4	3.9	59.4
12	359 36.2	N 7 38.9	293 36.7	5.9	N19 50.3	3.6	59.4
13	14 36.4	39.8	308 01.6	5.9	19 53.9	3.5	59.3
14	29 36.5	40.7	322 26.5	6.0	19 57.4	3.4	59.3
15	44 36.7	·· 41.7	336 51.5	6.0	20 00.8	3.3	59.3
16	59 36.9	42.6	351 16.5	5.9	20 04.1	3.1	59.2
17	74 37.0	43.5	5 41.4	6.1	20 07.2	3.0	59.2
18	89 37.2	N 7 44.4	20 06.5	6.0	N20 10.2	2.9	59.2
19	104 37.4	45.4	34 31.5	6.0	20 13.1	2.7	59.1
20	119 37.5	46.3	48 56.5	6.1	20 15.8	2.6	59.1
21	134 37.7	·· 47.2	63 21.6	6.1	20 18.4	2.4	59.1
22	149 37.9	48.1	77 46.7	6.1	20 20.8	2.3	59.0
23	164 38.1	49.1	92 11.8	6.2	20 23.1	2.2	59.0
	S.D. 16.0	d 0.9	S.D. 16.5		16.4		16.2

Twilight, Sunrise and Moonrise

Lat.	Naut.	Civil	Sunrise	Moonrise 7	8	9	10
N 72	////	02 56	04 19	05 15	04 44	▭	▭
N 70	01 11	03 19	04 31	05 39	05 31	05 17	▭
68	02 01	03 37	04 40	05 58	06 02	06 12	06 39
66	02 31	03 51	04 48	06 13	06 25	06 45	07 23
64	02 53	04 03	04 54	06 25	06 43	07 10	07 52
62	03 10	04 12	05 00	06 35	06 58	07 29	08 14
60	03 24	04 21	05 05	06 44	07 11	07 45	08 32
N 58	03 36	04 28	05 09	06 52	07 22	07 59	08 47
56	03 46	04 34	05 13	06 59	07 31	08 11	09 00
54	03 54	04 39	05 16	07 06	07 40	08 21	09 11
52	04 02	04 44	05 19	07 11	07 47	08 30	09 21
50	04 08	04 49	05 22	07 17	07 54	08 38	09 30
45	04 22	04 58	05 28	07 28	08 09	08 56	09 49
N 40	04 33	05 06	05 33	07 37	08 21	09 10	10 04
35	04 42	05 12	05 38	07 45	08 32	09 22	10 17
30	04 49	05 17	05 41	07 52	08 41	09 33	10 28
20	05 00	05 26	05 48	08 05	08 57	09 51	10 48
N 10	05 08	05 32	05 53	08 16	09 11	10 07	11 04
0	05 14	05 38	05 59	08 26	09 24	10 22	11 20
S 10	05 18	05 42	06 04	08 36	09 37	10 38	11 36
20	05 21	05 47	06 09	08 47	09 51	10 54	11 53
30	05 23	05 51	06 15	09 00	10 08	11 12	12 13
35	05 23	05 53	06 18	09 08	10 17	11 23	12 24
40	05 23	05 55	06 22	09 16	10 28	11 36	12 37
45	05 23	05 57	06 26	09 26	10 41	11 51	12 53
S 50	05 21	05 59	06 31	09 38	10 57	12 09	13 12
52	05 21	06 00	06 34	09 44	11 04	12 18	13 21
54	05 20	06 01	06 36	09 50	11 12	12 27	13 31
56	05 19	06 02	06 39	09 57	11 22	12 38	13 43
58	05 17	06 03	06 42	10 05	11 32	12 51	13 56
S 60	05 16	06 04	06 46	10 14	11 44	13 05	14 11

Sunset, Twilight and Moonset

Lat.	Sunset	Civil	Naut.	Moonset 7	8	9	10
N 72	19 48	21 13	////	25 18	01 18	▭	▭
N 70	19 36	20 49	23 08	24 32	00 32	02 49	▭
68	19 26	20 30	22 10	24 02	00 02	01 54	03 29
66	19 18	20 16	21 37	23 40	25 21	01 21	02 46
64	19 11	20 04	21 14	23 23	24 57	00 57	02 17
62	19 06	19 54	20 57	23 09	24 38	00 38	01 55
60	19 01	19 45	20 42	22 57	24 23	00 23	01 37
N 58	18 56	19 38	20 30	22 46	24 10	00 10	01 22
56	18 52	19 31	20 20	22 37	23 58	25 09	01 09
54	18 49	19 26	20 11	22 29	23 48	24 58	00 58
52	18 46	19 21	20 04	22 22	23 39	24 48	00 48
50	18 43	19 16	19 57	22 16	23 31	24 39	00 39
45	18 36	19 07	19 43	22 02	23 15	24 21	00 21
N 40	18 31	18 59	19 32	21 50	23 01	24 06	00 06
35	18 27	18 52	19 23	21 41	22 49	23 53	24 51
30	18 23	18 47	19 16	21 32	22 39	23 42	24 40
20	18 16	18 38	19 05	21 18	22 21	23 23	24 20
N 10	18 10	18 32	18 56	21 05	22 06	23 06	24 03
0	18 05	18 26	18 50	20 53	21 52	22 50	23 47
S 10	18 00	18 21	18 46	20 41	21 37	22 35	23 32
20	17 55	18 17	18 42	20 29	21 22	22 18	23 15
30	17 49	18 13	18 40	20 14	21 05	21 59	22 55
35	17 45	18 11	18 40	20 06	20 55	21 47	22 44
40	17 41	18 08	18 40	19 57	20 43	21 35	22 31
45	17 37	18 06	18 40	19 46	20 30	21 19	22 15
S 50	17 32	18 04	18 41	19 32	20 13	21 01	21 56
52	17 29	18 03	18 42	19 26	20 05	20 52	21 47
54	17 27	18 02	18 43	19 19	19 57	20 42	21 37
56	17 24	18 01	18 44	19 12	19 47	20 31	21 25
58	17 21	18 00	18 45	19 03	19 36	20 18	21 12
S 60	17 17	17 59	18 47	18 53	19 23	20 04	20 57

SUN and MOON data

Day	Eqn. of Time 00ʰ	Eqn. of Time 12ʰ	Mer. Pass.	Mer. Pass. Upper	Mer. Pass. Lower	Age	Phase
7	02 17	02 09	12 02	14 40	02 11	03	
8	02 00	01 52	12 02	15 38	03 09	04	
9	01 44	01 36	12 02	16 36	04 07	05	◑

G.M.T.	ARIES G.H.A.	VENUS −3.5 G.H.A.	Dec.	MARS +1.4 G.H.A.	Dec.	JUPITER −2.0 G.H.A.	Dec.	SATURN +0.7 G.H.A.	Dec.	STARS Name	S.H.A.	Dec.
10 00	198 08.2	178 34.0 N 7	00.3	180 55.6 N 6	41.3	14 10.7 N 0	00.8	12 09.1 N 0	18.0	Acamar	315 37.3	S40 23.1
01	213 10.6	193 33.6	01.5	195 56.3	42.0	29 13.5	00.9	27 11.8	18.1	Achernar	335 45.6	S57 20.1
02	228 13.1	208 33.2	02.7	210 57.0	42.7	44 16.2	01.0	42 14.4	18.2	Acrux	173 36.1	S62 59.8
03	243 15.6	223 32.8 ··	03.9	225 57.7 ··	43.5	59 19.0 ··	01.1	57 17.0 ··	18.2	Adhara	255 31.9	S28 57.1
04	258 18.0	238 32.4	05.2	240 58.4	44.2	74 21.7	01.2	72 19.7	18.3	Aldebaran	291 17.8	N16 28.2
05	273 20.5	253 32.0	06.4	255 59.1	45.0	89 24.4	01.3	87 22.3	18.4			
06	288 23.0	268 31.6 N 7	07.6	270 59.8 N 6	45.7	104 27.2 N 0	01.5	102 24.9 N 0	18.4	Alioth	166 41.6	N56 03.8
07	303 25.4	283 31.2	08.8	286 00.5	46.5	119 29.9	01.6	117 27.6	18.5	Alkaid	153 17.7	N49 24.4
08	318 27.9	298 30.8	10.0	301 01.1	47.2	134 32.6	01.7	132 30.2	18.6	Al Na'ir	28 14.8	S47 03.1
F 09	333 30.3	313 30.3 ··	11.2	316 01.8 ··	48.0	149 35.4 ··	01.8	147 32.9 ··	18.7	Alnilam	276 11.4	S 1 13.0
R 10	348 32.8	328 29.9	12.4	331 02.5	48.7	164 38.1	01.9	162 35.5	18.7	Alphard	218 20.1	S 8 34.8
I 11	3 35.3	343 29.5	13.6	346 03.2	49.5	179 40.9	02.0	177 38.1	18.8			
D 12	18 37.7	358 29.1 N 7	14.9	1 03.9 N 6	50.2	194 43.6 N 0	02.1	192 40.8 N 0	18.9	Alphecca	126 31.5	N26 46.6
A 13	33 40.2	13 28.7	16.1	16 04.6	51.0	209 46.3	02.3	207 43.4	18.9	Alpheratz	358 09.3	N28 59.0
Y 14	48 42.7	28 28.3	17.3	31 05.3	51.7	224 49.1	02.4	222 46.0	19.0	Altair	62 32.2	N 8 48.9
15	63 45.1	43 27.9 ··	18.5	46 06.0 ··	52.4	239 51.8 ··	02.5	237 48.7 ··	19.1	Ankaa	353 40.3	S42 24.6
16	78 47.6	58 27.5	19.7	61 06.7	53.2	254 54.6	02.6	252 51.3	19.2	Antares	112 56.2	S26 23.4
17	93 50.1	73 27.1	20.9	76 07.4	53.9	269 57.3	02.7	267 53.9	19.2			
18	108 52.5	88 26.7 N 7	22.1	91 08.1 N 6	54.7	285 00.0 N 0	02.8	282 56.6 N 0	19.3	Arcturus	146 17.8	N19 16.8
19	123 55.0	103 26.2	23.3	106 08.8	55.4	300 02.8	02.9	297 59.2	19.4	Atria	108 19.7	S68 59.4
20	138 57.4	118 25.8	24.5	121 09.5	56.2	315 05.5	03.1	313 01.8	19.4	Avior	234 27.9	S59 27.3
21	153 59.9	133 25.4 ··	25.7	136 10.2 ··	56.9	330 08.2 ··	03.2	328 04.5 ··	19.5	Bellatrix	278 58.5	N 6 19.8
22	169 02.4	148 25.0	27.0	151 10.9	57.7	345 11.0	03.3	343 07.1	19.6	Betelgeuse	271 28.0	N 7 24.1
23	184 04.8	163 24.6	28.2	166 11.6	58.4	0 13.7	03.4	358 09.7	19.7			
11 00	199 07.3	178 24.2 N 7	29.4	181 12.3 N 6	59.1	15 16.5 N 0	03.5	13 12.4 N 0	19.7	Canopus	264 07.2	S52 41.5
01	214 09.8	193 23.8	30.6	196 13.0 6	59.9	30 19.2	03.6	28 15.0	19.8	Capella	281 11.0	N45 58.8
02	229 12.2	208 23.4	31.8	211 13.7 7	00.6	45 21.9	03.7	43 17.6	19.9	Deneb	49 48.3	N45 12.5
03	244 14.7	223 22.9 ··	33.0	226 14.4 ··	01.4	60 24.7 ··	03.9	58 20.3 ··	19.9	Denebola	182 58.4	N14 40.6
04	259 17.2	238 22.5	34.2	241 15.1	02.1	75 27.4	04.0	73 22.9	20.0	Diphda	349 20.8	S18 05.6
05	274 19.6	253 22.1	35.4	256 15.8	02.9	90 30.1	04.1	88 25.5	20.1			
06	289 22.1	268 21.7 N 7	36.6	271 16.5 N 7	03.6	105 32.9 N 0	04.2	103 28.2 N 0	20.2	Dubhe	194 21.2	N61 51.3
07	304 24.6	283 21.3	37.8	286 17.2	04.3	120 35.6	04.3	118 30.8	20.2	Elnath	278 43.9	N28 35.5
S 08	319 27.0	298 20.9	39.0	301 17.9	05.1	135 38.3	04.4	133 33.4	20.3	Eltanin	90 57.4	N51 29.2
A 09	334 29.5	313 20.5 ··	40.2	316 18.6 ··	05.8	150 41.1 ··	04.5	148 36.1 ··	20.4	Enif	34 11.4	N 9 47.1
T 10	349 31.9	328 20.0	41.4	331 19.3	06.6	165 43.8	04.7	163 38.7	20.4	Fomalhaut	15 51.3	S29 43.4
U 11	4 34.4	343 19.6	42.6	346 20.0	07.3	180 46.6	04.8	178 41.3	20.5			
R 12	19 36.9	358 19.2 N 7	43.8	1 20.7 N 7	08.0	195 49.3 N 0	04.9	193 44.0 N 0	20.6	Gacrux	172 27.8	S57 00.5
D 13	34 39.3	13 18.8	45.0	16 21.4	08.8	210 52.0	05.0	208 46.6	20.6	Gienah	176 17.3	S17 26.3
A 14	49 41.8	28 18.4	46.3	31 22.1	09.5	225 54.8	05.1	223 49.2	20.7	Hadar	149 22.2	S60 16.9
Y 15	64 44.3	43 18.0 ··	47.5	46 22.8 ··	10.3	240 57.5 ··	05.2	238 51.9 ··	20.8	Hamal	328 28.8	N23 22.2
16	79 46.7	58 17.6	48.7	61 23.5	11.0	256 00.2	05.3	253 54.5	20.9	Kaus Aust.	84 16.2	S34 23.5
17	94 49.2	73 17.1	49.9	76 24.1	11.8	271 03.0	05.4	268 57.1	20.9			
18	109 51.7	88 16.7 N 7	51.1	91 24.8 N 7	12.5	286 05.7 N 0	05.5	283 59.8 N 0	21.0	Kochab	137 17.9	N74 13.9
19	124 54.1	103 16.3	52.3	106 25.5	13.2	301 08.4	05.7	299 02.4	21.1	Markab	14 03.1	N15 06.0
20	139 56.6	118 15.9	53.5	121 26.2	14.0	316 11.2	05.8	314 05.0	21.1	Menkar	314 41.0	N 4 00.8
21	154 59.1	133 15.5 ··	54.7	136 26.9 ··	14.7	331 13.9 ··	05.9	329 07.7 ··	21.2	Menkent	148 36.2	S36 16.7
22	170 01.5	148 15.1	55.9	151 27.6	15.5	346 16.6	06.0	344 10.3	21.3	Miaplacidus	221 44.5	S69 38.7
23	185 04.0	163 14.6	57.1	166 28.3	16.2	1 19.4	06.1	359 12.9	21.3			
12 00	200 06.4	178 14.2 N 7	58.3	181 29.0 N 7	16.9	16 22.1 N 0	06.2	14 15.6 N 0	21.4	Mirfak	309 16.0	N49 47.6
01	215 08.9	193 13.8 7	59.5	196 29.7	17.7	31 24.8	06.3	29 18.2	21.5	Nunki	76 28.7	S26 19.2
02	230 11.4	208 13.4 8	00.7	211 30.4	18.4	46 27.6	06.5	44 20.8	21.6	Peacock	53 57.5	S56 47.6
03	245 13.8	223 13.0 ··	01.9	226 31.1 ··	19.2	61 30.3 ··	06.6	59 23.5 ··	21.6	Pollux	243 57.7	N28 04.3
04	260 16.3	238 12.5	03.1	241 31.8	19.9	76 33.0	06.7	74 26.1	21.7	Procyon	245 25.4	N 5 16.3
05	275 18.8	253 12.1	04.3	256 32.5	20.6	91 35.8	06.8	89 28.7	21.8			
06	290 21.2	268 11.7 N 8	05.5	271 33.2 N 7	21.4	106 38.5 N 0	06.9	104 31.4 N 0	21.8	Rasalhague	96 29.1	N12 34.3
07	305 23.7	283 11.3	06.7	286 33.9	22.1	121 41.2	07.0	119 34.0	21.9	Regulus	208 09.4	N12 03.5
08	320 26.2	298 10.9	07.9	301 34.6	22.9	136 44.0	07.1	134 36.6	22.0	Rigel	281 35.8	S 8 13.6
S 09	335 28.6	313 10.4 ··	09.1	316 35.3 ··	23.6	151 46.7 ··	07.2	149 39.2 ··	22.0	Rigil Kent.	140 24.7	S60 45.3
U 10	350 31.1	328 10.0	10.3	331 36.0	24.3	166 49.4	07.4	164 41.9	22.1	Sabik	102 40.5	S15 42.1
N 11	5 33.5	343 09.6	11.5	346 36.7	25.1	181 52.2	07.5	179 44.5	22.2			
D 12	20 36.0	358 09.2 N 8	12.7	1 37.4 N 7	25.8	196 54.9 N 0	07.6	194 47.1 N 0	22.3	Schedar	350 09.1	N56 25.9
A 13	35 38.5	13 08.8	13.9	16 38.1	26.5	211 57.6	07.7	209 49.8	22.3	Shaula	96 55.1	S37 05.3
Y 14	50 40.9	28 08.3	15.1	31 38.8	27.3	227 00.4	07.8	224 52.4	22.4	Sirius	258 55.5	S16 41.7
15	65 43.4	43 07.9 ··	16.2	46 39.5 ··	28.0	242 03.1 ··	07.9	239 55.0 ··	22.5	Spica	158 56.8	S11 03.8
16	80 45.9	58 07.5	17.4	61 40.2	28.8	257 05.8	08.0	254 57.7	22.5	Suhail	223 10.3	S43 21.7
17	95 48.3	73 07.1	18.6	76 40.9	29.5	272 08.6	08.1	270 00.3	22.6			
18	110 50.8	88 06.7 N 8	19.8	91 41.6 N 7	30.2	287 11.3 N 0	08.2	285 02.9 N 0	22.7	Vega	80 55.5	N38 45.7
19	125 53.3	103 06.2	21.0	106 42.3	31.0	302 14.0	08.4	300 05.6	22.7	Zuben'ubi	137 32.3	S15 57.8
20	140 55.7	118 05.8	22.2	121 42.9	31.7	317 16.8	08.5	315 08.2	22.8		S.H.A.	Mer. Pass.
21	155 58.2	133 05.4 ··	23.4	136 43.6 ··	32.4	332 19.5 ··	08.6	330 10.8 ··	22.9	Venus	339 16.9	12 07
22	171 00.7	148 05.0	24.6	151 44.3	33.2	347 22.2	08.7	345 13.5	23.0	Mars	342 05.0	11 55
23	186 03.3	163 04.5	25.8	166 45.0	33.9	2 25.0	08.8	0 16.1	23.0	Jupiter	176 09.1	22 55
Mer. Pass. 10 41.8		v −0.4 d 1.2		v 0.7 d 0.7		v 2.7 d 0.1		v 2.6 d 0.1		Saturn	174 05.1	23 03

G.M.T.	SUN G.H.A.	SUN Dec.	MOON G.H.A.	v	MOON Dec.	d	H.P.
d h	° ′	° ′	° ′	′	° ′	′	′
10 00	179 38.2	N 7 50.0	106 37.0	6.2	N20 25.3	2.1	59.0
01	194 38.4	50.9	121 02.2	6.2	20 27.4	1.9	58.9
02	209 38.6	51.9	135 27.4	6.2	20 29.3	1.7	58.9
03	224 38.7 ··	52.8	149 52.6	6.3	20 31.0	1.7	58.9
04	239 38.9	53.7	164 17.9	6.3	20 32.7	1.5	58.8
05	254 39.1	54.6	178 43.2	6.4	20 34.2	1.4	58.8
06	269 39.2	N 7 55.6	193 08.6	6.3	N20 35.6	1.2	58.8
07	284 39.4	56.5	207 33.9	6.4	20 36.8	1.1	58.7
08	299 39.6	57.4	221 59.3	6.5	20 37.9	1.0	58.7
F 09	314 39.7 ··	58.3	236 24.8	6.5	20 38.9	0.8	58.7
R 10	329 39.9	7 59.2	250 50.3	6.5	20 39.7	0.7	58.6
I 11	344 40.1	8 00.2	265 15.8	6.6	20 40.4	0.6	58.6
D 12	359 40.3	N 8 01.1	279 41.4	6.6	N20 41.0	0.4	58.6
A 13	14 40.4	02.0	294 07.0	6.6	20 41.4	0.4	58.5
Y 14	29 40.6	02.9	308 32.6	6.7	20 41.8	0.1	58.5
15	44 40.8 ··	03.9	322 58.3	6.7	20 41.9	0.1	58.4
16	59 40.9	04.8	337 24.0	6.8	20 42.0	0.1	58.4
17	74 41.1	05.7	351 49.8	6.8	20 41.9	0.2	58.4
18	89 41.3	N 8 06.6	6 15.6	6.9	N20 41.7	0.3	58.3
19	104 41.4	07.5	20 41.5	6.9	20 41.4	0.5	58.3
20	119 41.6	08.5	35 07.4	7.0	20 40.9	0.6	58.3
21	134 41.8 ··	09.4	49 33.4	7.0	20 40.3	0.7	58.2
22	149 41.9	10.3	63 59.4	7.1	20 39.6	0.8	58.2
23	164 42.1	11.2	78 25.5	7.1	20 38.8	1.0	58.2
11 00	179 42.3	N 8 12.2	92 51.6	7.1	N20 37.8	1.1	58.1
01	194 42.4	13.1	107 17.7	7.3	20 36.7	1.2	58.1
02	209 42.6	14.0	121 44.0	7.2	20 35.5	1.3	58.1
03	224 42.8 ··	14.9	136 10.2	7.4	20 34.2	1.5	58.0
04	239 42.9	15.8	150 36.6	7.4	20 32.7	1.6	58.0
05	254 43.1	16.8	165 03.0	7.4	20 31.1	1.7	58.0
06	269 43.3	N 8 17.7	179 29.4	7.5	N20 29.4	1.8	57.9
07	284 43.4	18.6	193 55.9	7.5	20 27.6	2.0	57.9
S 08	299 43.6	19.5	208 22.4	7.7	20 25.6	2.0	57.9
A 09	314 43.8 ··	20.4	222 49.1	7.6	20 23.6	2.2	57.8
T 10	329 43.9	21.3	237 15.7	7.8	20 21.4	2.3	57.8
U 11	344 44.1	22.3	251 42.5	7.7	20 19.1	2.5	57.8
R 12	359 44.3	N 8 23.2	266 09.2	7.9	N20 16.6	2.5	57.7
D 13	14 44.4	24.1	280 36.1	7.9	20 14.1	2.7	57.7
A 14	29 44.6	25.0	295 03.0	8.0	20 11.4	2.8	57.7
Y 15	44 44.7 ··	25.9	309 30.0	8.0	20 08.6	2.8	57.6
16	59 44.9	26.8	323 57.0	8.1	20 05.8	3.0	57.6
17	74 45.1	27.8	338 24.1	8.2	20 02.8	3.2	57.6
18	89 45.2	N 8 28.7	352 51.3	8.2	N19 59.6	3.2	57.5
19	104 45.4	29.6	7 18.5	8.3	19 56.4	3.3	57.5
20	119 45.6	30.5	21 45.8	8.3	19 53.1	3.5	57.5
21	134 45.7 ··	31.4	36 13.1	8.5	19 49.6	3.6	57.4
22	149 45.9	32.3	50 40.6	8.5	19 46.0	3.6	57.4
23	164 46.1	33.3	65 08.1	8.5	19 42.4	3.8	57.4
12 00	179 46.2	N 8 34.2	79 35.6	8.6	N19 38.6	3.9	57.3
01	194 46.4	35.1	94 03.2	8.7	19 34.7	4.0	57.3
02	209 46.6	36.0	108 30.9	8.8	19 30.7	4.1	57.3
03	224 46.7 ··	36.9	122 58.7	8.8	19 26.6	4.2	57.2
04	239 46.9	37.8	137 26.5	8.9	19 22.4	4.3	57.2
05	254 47.0	38.7	151 54.4	8.9	19 18.1	4.5	57.2
06	269 47.2	N 8 39.7	166 22.3	9.1	N19 13.6	4.5	57.1
07	284 47.4	40.6	180 50.4	9.1	19 09.1	4.6	57.1
08	299 47.5	41.5	195 18.5	9.1	19 04.5	4.7	57.1
S 09	314 47.7 ··	42.4	209 46.6	9.3	18 59.8	4.9	57.0
U 10	329 47.9	43.3	224 14.9	9.3	18 54.9	4.9	57.0
N 11	344 48.0	44.2	238 43.2	9.3	18 50.0	5.0	57.0
D 12	359 48.2	N 8 45.1	253 11.5	9.5	N18 45.0	5.1	56.9
A 13	14 48.3	46.0	267 40.0	9.5	18 39.9	5.2	56.9
Y 14	29 48.5	46.9	282 08.5	9.6	18 34.7	5.3	56.9
15	44 48.7 ··	47.9	296 37.1	9.6	18 29.4	5.4	56.9
16	59 48.8	48.8	311 05.7	9.8	18 24.0	5.5	56.8
17	74 49.0	49.7	325 34.5	9.8	18 18.5	5.6	56.8
18	89 49.2	N 8 50.6	340 03.3	9.8	N18 12.9	5.7	56.8
19	104 49.3	51.5	354 32.1	10.0	18 07.2	5.8	56.7
20	119 49.5	52.4	9 01.1	10.0	18 01.4	5.9	56.7
21	134 49.6 ··	53.3	23 30.1	10.0	17 55.5	5.9	56.7
22	149 49.8	54.2	37 59.1	10.2	17 49.6	6.1	56.6
23	164 50.0	55.1	52 28.3	10.2	17 43.5	6.1	56.6
	S.D. 16.0	d 0.9	S.D. 16.0		15.7		15.5

Lat.	Twilight Naut.	Twilight Civil	Sunrise	Moonrise 10	11	12	13
°	h m	h m	h m	h m	h m	h m	h m
N 72	////	02 33	04 03	□	□	□	09 30
N 70	////	03 01	04 16	□		08 18	10 18
68	01 34	03 22	04 27	06 39	07 41	09 10	10 48
66	02 12	03 38	04 36	07 23	08 23	09 43	11 11
64	02 37	03 51	04 44	07 52	08 52	10 06	11 29
62	02 57	04 02	04 50	08 14	09 14	10 25	11 43
60	03 12	04 11	04 56	08 32	09 31	10 41	11 56
N 58	03 25	04 19	05 01	08 47	09 46	10 54	12 06
56	03 36	04 26	05 05	09 00	09 59	11 05	12 15
54	03 46	04 32	05 09	09 11	10 10	11 15	12 24
52	03 54	04 37	05 13	09 21	10 19	11 24	12 31
50	04 01	04 42	05 16	09 30	10 28	11 31	12 37
45	04 16	04 53	05 23	09 49	10 47	11 48	12 51
N 40	04 28	05 01	05 29	10 04	11 02	12 02	13 03
35	04 37	05 08	05 34	10 17	11 14	12 13	13 13
30	04 45	05 14	05 38	10 28	11 25	12 24	13 21
20	04 57	05 23	05 45	10 48	11 44	12 41	13 36
N 10	05 06	05 31	05 52	11 04	12 01	12 56	13 49
0	05 13	05 37	05 58	11 20	12 17	13 10	14 01
S 10	05 18	05 42	06 04	11 36	12 32	13 24	14 13
20	05 22	05 48	06 10	11 53	12 49	13 39	14 26
30	05 25	05 52	06 17	12 13	13 08	13 57	14 40
35	05 26	05 55	06 20	12 24	13 19	14 07	14 49
40	05 26	05 58	06 25	12 37	13 32	14 18	14 58
45	05 26	06 00	06 30	12 53	13 47	14 32	15 10
S 50	05 26	06 03	06 36	13 12	14 05	14 48	15 23
52	05 25	06 05	06 39	13 21	14 14	14 56	15 30
54	05 25	06 06	06 42	13 31	14 23	15 04	15 36
56	05 24	06 07	06 45	13 43	14 34	15 14	15 44
58	05 24	06 09	06 49	13 56	14 47	15 25	15 53
S 60	05 22	06 11	06 53	14 11	15 01	15 37	16 03

Lat.	Sunset	Twilight Civil	Twilight Naut.	Moonset 10	11	12	13
°	h m	h m	h m	h m	h m	h m	h m
N 72	20 03	21 35	////	□	□	□	06 19
N 70	19 49	21 05	////	□	□	05 43	05 30
68	19 38	20 44	22 37	03 29	04 26	04 50	04 59
66	19 28	20 27	21 56	02 46	03 44	04 17	04 35
64	19 20	20 14	21 29	02 17	03 15	03 53	04 17
62	19 14	20 03	21 08	01 55	02 53	03 34	04 01
60	19 08	19 53	20 52	01 37	02 35	03 18	03 49
N 58	19 03	19 45	20 39	01 22	02 20	03 05	03 38
56	18 58	19 38	20 28	01 09	02 07	02 53	03 28
54	18 54	19 32	20 18	00 58	01 56	02 43	03 19
52	18 51	19 26	20 10	00 48	01 46	02 34	03 12
50	18 47	19 21	20 02	00 39	01 38	02 26	03 05
45	18 40	19 11	19 47	00 21	01 19	02 08	02 50
N 40	18 34	19 02	19 35	00 06	01 04	01 54	02 38
35	18 29	18 55	19 26	24 51	00 51	01 42	02 27
30	18 25	18 49	19 18	24 40	00 40	01 32	02 18
20	18 17	18 39	19 06	24 20	00 20	01 13	02 02
N 10	18 10	18 32	18 56	24 03	00 03	00 58	01 48
0	18 04	18 25	18 50	23 47	24 43	00 43	01 35
S 10	17 58	18 20	18 44	23 32	24 28	00 28	01 22
20	17 52	18 14	18 40	23 15	24 12	00 12	01 08
30	17 45	18 09	18 37	22 55	23 53	24 51	00 51
35	17 41	18 07	18 36	22 44	23 42	24 42	00 42
40	17 37	18 04	18 35	22 31	23 30	24 31	00 31
45	17 32	18 01	18 35	22 15	23 15	24 18	00 18
S 50	17 25	17 58	18 35	21 56	22 57	24 02	00 02
52	17 23	17 57	18 36	21 47	22 49	23 55	25 03
54	17 20	17 55	18 36	21 37	22 39	23 47	24 57
56	17 16	17 54	18 37	21 25	22 29	23 38	24 49
58	17 12	17 52	18 37	21 12	22 16	23 27	24 41
S 60	17 08	17 50	18 38	20 57	22 02	23 15	24 32

Day	SUN Eqn. of Time 00h	SUN Eqn. of Time 12h	SUN Mer. Pass.	MOON Mer. Pass. Upper	MOON Mer. Pass. Lower	Age	Phase
	m s	m s	h m	h m	h m	d	
10	01 27	01 19	12 01	17 34	05 05	06	
11	01 11	01 03	12 01	18 30	06 02	07	
12	00 55	00 48	12 01	19 23	06 57	08	◑

G.M.T.	ARIES	VENUS −3.5		MARS +1.4		JUPITER −2.0		SATURN +0.8		STARS		
	G.H.A.	G.H.A.	Dec.	G.H.A.	Dec.	G.H.A.	Dec.	G.H.A.	Dec.	Name	S.H.A.	Dec.
d h	° ′	° ′	° ′	° ′	° ′	° ′	° ′	° ′	° ′		° ′	° ′
13 00	201 05.6	178 04.1 N 8 27.0		181 45.7 N 7 34.7		17 27.7 N 0 08.9		15 18.7 N 0 23.1		Acamar	315 37.4	S40 23.0
01	216 08.0	193 03.7	28.2	196 46.4	35.4	32 30.4	09.0	30 21.4	23.2	Achernar	335 45.6	S57 20.1
02	231 10.5	208 03.3	29.4	211 47.1	36.1	47 33.1	09.1	45 24.0	23.2	Acrux	173 36.1	S62 59.8
03	246 13.0	223 02.8 ··	30.6	226 47.8 ··	36.9	62 35.9 ··	09.2	60 26.6 ··	23.3	Adhara	255 31.9	S28 57.1
04	261 15.4	238 02.4	31.8	241 48.5	37.6	77 38.6	09.4	75 29.2	23.4	Aldebaran	291 17.8	N16 28.2
05	276 17.9	253 02.0	33.0	256 49.2	38.3	92 41.3	09.5	90 31.9	23.4			
06	291 20.4	268 01.6 N 8 34.1		271 49.9 N 7 39.1		107 44.1 N 0 09.6		105 34.5 N 0 23.5		Alioth	166 41.6	N56 03.8
07	306 22.8	283 01.1	35.3	286 50.6	39.8	122 46.8	09.7	120 37.1	23.6	Alkaid	153 17.7	N49 24.4
08	321 25.3	298 00.7	36.5	301 51.3	40.5	137 49.5	09.8	135 39.8	23.6	Al Na'ir	28 14.7	S47 03.1
M 09	336 27.8	313 00.3 ··	37.7	316 52.0 ··	41.3	152 52.3 ··	09.9	150 42.4 ··	23.7	Alnilam	276 11.5	S 1 13.0
O 10	351 30.2	327 59.9	38.9	331 52.7	42.0	167 55.0	10.0	165 45.0	23.8	Alphard	218 20.1	S 8 34.8
N 11	6 32.7	342 59.4	40.1	346 53.4	42.7	182 57.7	10.1	180 47.7	23.8			
D 12	21 35.2	357 59.0 N 8 41.3		1 54.1 N 7 43.5		198 00.4 N 0 10.2		195 50.3 N 0 23.9		Alphecca	126 31.5	N26 46.6
A 13	36 37.6	12 58.6	42.5	16 54.8	44.2	213 03.2	10.3	210 52.9	24.0	Alpheratz	358 09.3	N28 59.0
Y 14	51 40.1	27 58.1	43.7	31 55.5	44.9	228 05.9	10.5	225 55.5	24.1	Altair	62 32.2	N 8 48.9
15	66 42.5	42 57.7 ··	44.9	46 56.2 ··	45.7	243 08.6 ··	10.6	240 58.2 ··	24.1	Ankaa	353 40.3	S42 24.6
16	81 45.0	57 57.3	46.0	61 56.9	46.4	258 11.4	10.7	256 00.8	24.2	Antares	112 56.1	S26 23.4
17	96 47.5	72 56.9	47.2	76 57.6	47.1	273 14.1	10.8	271 03.4	24.3			
18	111 49.9	87 56.4 N 8 48.4		91 58.2 N 7 47.9		288 16.8 N 0 10.9		286 06.1 N 0 24.3		Arcturus	146 17.8	N19 16.8
19	126 52.4	102 56.0	49.6	106 58.9	48.6	303 19.5	11.0	301 08.7	24.4	Atria	108 19.7	S68 59.4
20	141 54.9	117 55.6	50.8	121 59.6	49.3	318 22.3	11.1	316 11.3	24.5	Avior	234 27.9	S59 27.3
21	156 57.3	132 55.2 ··	52.0	137 00.3 ··	50.1	333 25.0 ··	11.2	331 14.0 ··	24.5	Bellatrix	278 58.5	N 6 19.8
22	171 59.8	147 54.7	53.2	152 01.0	50.8	348 27.7	11.3	346 16.6	24.6	Betelgeuse	271 28.0	N 7 24.1
23	187 02.3	162 54.3	54.3	167 01.7	51.5	3 30.4	11.4	1 19.2	24.7			
14 00	202 04.7	177 53.9 N 8 55.5		182 02.4 N 7 52.3		18 33.2 N 0 11.6		16 21.8 N 0 24.7		Canopus	264 07.2	S52 41.5
01	217 07.2	192 53.4	56.7	197 03.1	53.0	33 35.9	11.7	31 24.5	24.8	Capella	281 11.0	N45 58.8
02	232 09.7	207 53.0	57.9	212 03.8	53.7	48 38.6	11.8	46 27.1	24.9	Deneb	49 48.3	N45 12.5
03	247 12.1	222 52.6	8 59.1	227 04.5 ··	54.5	63 41.4 ··	11.9	61 29.7 ··	24.9	Denebola	182 58.4	N14 40.6
04	262 14.6	237 52.1	9 00.3	242 05.2	55.2	78 44.1	12.0	76 32.4	25.0	Diphda	349 20.8	S18 05.6
05	277 17.0	252 51.7	01.4	257 05.9	55.9	93 46.8	12.1	91 35.0	25.1			
06	292 19.5	267 51.3 N 9 02.6		272 06.6 N 7 56.7		108 49.5 N 0 12.2		106 37.6 N 0 25.1		Dubhe	194 21.2	N61 51.3
07	307 22.0	282 50.8	03.8	287 07.3	57.4	123 52.3	12.3	121 40.3	25.2	Elnath	278 43.9	N28 35.5
08	322 24.4	297 50.4	05.0	302 08.0	58.1	138 55.0	12.4	136 42.9	25.3	Eltanin	90 57.3	N51 29.2
T 09	337 26.9	312 50.0 ··	06.2	317 08.7 ··	58.9	153 57.7 ··	12.5	151 45.5 ··	25.4	Enif	34 11.4	N 9 47.1
U 10	352 29.4	327 49.5	07.4	332 09.4	7 59.6	169 00.4	12.6	166 48.1	25.4	Fomalhaut	15 51.3	S29 43.4
E 11	7 31.8	342 49.1	08.5	347 10.1	8 00.3	184 03.2	12.7	181 50.8	25.5			
S 12	22 34.3	357 48.7 N 9 09.7		2 10.8 N 8 01.1		199 05.9 N 0 12.9		196 53.4 N 0 25.6		Gacrux	172 27.8	S57 00.6
D 13	37 36.8	12 48.2	10.9	17 11.5	01.8	214 08.6	13.0	211 56.0	25.6	Gienah	176 17.3	S17 26.3
A 14	52 39.2	27 47.8	12.1	32 12.1	02.5	229 11.3	13.1	226 58.7	25.7	Hadar	149 22.2	S60 16.9
Y 15	67 41.7	42 47.4 ··	13.3	47 12.8 ··	03.3	244 14.1 ··	13.2	242 01.3 ··	25.8	Hamal	328 28.8	N23 22.2
16	82 44.1	57 46.9	14.4	62 13.5	04.0	259 16.8	13.3	257 03.9	25.8	Kaus Aust.	84 16.2	S34 23.5
17	97 46.6	72 46.5	15.6	77 14.2	04.7	274 19.5	13.4	272 06.5	25.9			
18	112 49.1	87 46.1 N 9 16.8		92 14.9 N 8 05.4		289 22.2 N 0 13.5		287 09.2 N 0 26.0		Kochab	137 17.9	N74 13.9
19	127 51.5	102 45.6	18.0	107 15.6	06.2	304 25.0	13.6	302 11.8	26.0	Markab	14 03.0	N15 06.0
20	142 54.0	117 45.2	19.2	122 16.3	06.9	319 27.7	13.7	317 14.4	26.1	Menkar	314 41.0	N 4 00.8
21	157 56.5	132 44.8 ··	20.3	137 17.0 ··	07.6	334 30.4 ··	13.8	332 17.1 ··	26.2	Menkent	148 36.2	S36 16.7
22	172 58.9	147 44.3	21.5	152 17.7	08.4	349 33.1	13.9	347 19.7	26.2	Miaplacidus	221 44.5	S69 38.7
23	188 01.4	162 43.9	22.7	167 18.4	09.1	4 35.9	14.0	2 22.3	26.3			
15 00	203 03.9	177 43.5 N 9 23.9		182 19.1 N 8 09.8		19 38.6 N 0 14.1		17 24.9 N 0 26.4		Mirfak	309 16.0	N49 47.6
01	218 06.3	192 43.0	25.0	197 19.8	10.5	34 41.3	14.3	32 27.6	26.4	Nunki	76 28.6	S26 19.2
02	233 08.8	207 42.6	26.2	212 20.5	11.3	49 44.0	14.4	47 30.2	26.5	Peacock	53 57.9	S56 47.6
03	248 11.3	222 42.1 ··	27.4	227 21.2 ··	12.0	64 46.8 ··	14.5	62 32.8 ··	26.6	Pollux	243 57.7	N28 04.3
04	263 13.7	237 41.7	28.6	242 21.9	12.7	79 49.5	14.6	77 35.4	26.6	Procyon	245 25.4	N 5 16.3
05	278 16.2	252 41.3	29.7	257 22.6	13.5	94 52.2	14.7	92 38.1	26.7			
06	293 18.6	267 40.8 N 9 30.9		272 23.3 N 8 14.2		109 54.9 N 0 14.8		107 40.7 N 0 26.8		Rasalhague	96 29.1	N12 34.3
W 07	308 21.1	282 40.4	32.1	287 24.0	14.9	124 57.6	14.9	122 43.3	26.8	Regulus	208 09.4	N12 03.5
E 08	323 23.6	297 39.9	33.3	302 24.6	15.6	140 00.4	15.0	137 46.0	26.9	Rigel	281 35.9	S 8 13.6
D 09	338 26.0	312 39.5 ··	34.4	317 25.3 ··	16.4	155 03.1 ··	15.1	152 48.6 ··	27.0	Rigil Kent.	140 24.7	S60 45.3
N 10	353 28.5	327 39.1	35.6	332 26.0	17.1	170 05.8	15.2	167 51.2	27.0	Sabik	102 40.5	S15 42.1
E 11	8 31.0	342 38.6	36.8	347 26.7	17.8	185 08.5	15.3	182 53.8	27.1			
S 12	23 33.4	357 38.2 N 9 37.9		2 27.4 N 8 18.6		200 11.3 N 0 15.4		197 56.5 N 0 27.2		Schedar	350 09.1	N56 25.8
D 13	38 35.9	12 37.7	39.1	17 28.1	19.3	215 14.0	15.5	212 59.1	27.2	Shaula	96 55.0	S37 05.3
A 14	53 38.4	27 37.3	40.3	32 28.8	20.0	230 16.7	15.6	228 01.7	27.3	Sirius	258 55.5	S16 41.7
Y 15	68 40.8	42 36.9 ··	41.5	47 29.5 ··	20.7	245 19.4 ··	15.7	243 04.3 ··	27.4	Spica	158 56.8	S11 03.8
16	83 43.3	57 36.4	42.6	62 30.2	21.5	260 22.1	15.9	258 07.0	27.4	Suhail	223 10.4	S43 21.7
17	98 45.8	72 36.0	43.8	77 30.9	22.2	275 24.9	16.0	273 09.6	27.5			
18	113 48.2	87 35.5 N 9 45.0		92 31.6 N 8 22.9		290 27.6 N 0 16.1		288 12.2 N 0 27.6		Vega	80 55.5	N38 45.7
19	128 50.7	102 35.1	46.1	107 32.3	23.6	305 30.3	16.2	303 14.9	27.6	Zuben'ubi	137 32.3	S15 57.8
20	143 53.1	117 34.7	47.3	122 33.0	24.4	320 33.0	16.3	318 17.5	27.7			S.H.A.	Mer. Pass.
21	158 55.6	132 34.2 ··	48.5	137 33.7 ··	25.1	335 35.7 ··	16.4	333 20.1 ··	27.8			° ′	h m
22	173 58.1	147 33.8	49.6	152 34.4	25.8	350 38.5	16.5	348 22.7	27.8	Venus	335 49.1	12 09
23	189 00.5	162 33.3	50.8	167 35.1	26.5	5 41.2	16.6	3 25.4	27.9	Mars	339 57.7	11 51
	h m									Jupiter	176 28.5	22 42
Mer. Pass. 10 30.0		v −0.4	d 1.2	v 0.7	d 0.7	v 2.7	d 0.1	v 2.6	d 0.1	Saturn	174 17.1	22 51

G.M.T.	SUN G.H.A.	Dec.	MOON G.H.A.	v	Dec.	d	H.P.
	° ′	° ′	° ′	′	° ′	′	′
13 00	179 50.1	N 8 56.0	66 57.5	10.3	N17 37.4	6.2	56.6
01	194 50.3	57.0	81 26.8	10.4	17 31.2	6.3	56.6
02	209 50.4	57.9	95 56.2	10.4	17 24.9	6.4	56.5
03	224 50.6	·· 58.8	110 25.6	10.5	17 18.5	6.5	56.5
04	239 50.8	8 59.7	124 55.1	10.6	17 12.0	6.5	56.5
05	254 50.9	9 00.6	139 24.7	10.6	17 05.5	6.7	56.4
06	269 51.1	N 9 01.5	153 54.3	10.7	N16 58.8	6.7	56.4
07	284 51.2	02.4	168 24.0	10.8	16 52.1	6.8	56.4
08	299 51.4	03.3	182 53.8	10.9	16 45.3	6.9	56.4
M 09	314 51.6	·· 04.2	197 23.7	10.9	16 38.4	6.9	56.3
O 10	329 51.7	05.1	211 53.6	11.0	16 31.5	7.1	56.3
N 11	344 51.9	06.0	226 23.6	11.0	16 24.4	7.1	56.3
D 12	359 52.0	N 9 06.9	240 53.6	11.1	N16 17.3	7.2	56.2
A 13	14 52.2	07.8	255 23.7	11.2	16 10.1	7.2	56.2
Y 14	29 52.4	08.7	269 53.9	11.3	16 02.9	7.4	56.2
15	44 52.5	·· 09.6	284 24.2	11.3	15 55.5	7.4	56.2
16	59 52.7	10.5	298 54.5	11.4	15 48.1	7.4	56.1
17	74 52.8	11.4	313 24.9	11.5	15 40.7	7.6	56.1
18	89 53.0	N 9 12.4	327 55.4	11.5	N15 33.1	7.6	56.1
19	104 53.2	13.3	342 25.9	11.6	15 25.5	7.7	56.1
20	119 53.3	14.2	356 56.5	11.7	15 17.8	7.8	56.0
21	134 53.5	·· 15.1	11 27.2	11.7	15 10.0	7.8	56.0
22	149 53.6	16.0	25 57.9	11.8	15 02.2	7.9	56.0
23	164 53.8	16.9	40 28.7	11.9	14 54.3	8.0	56.0
14 00	179 53.9	N 9 17.8	54 59.6	11.9	N14 46.3	8.0	55.9
01	194 54.1	18.7	69 30.5	12.0	14 38.3	8.1	55.9
02	209 54.3	19.6	84 01.5	12.1	14 30.2	8.1	55.9
03	224 54.4	·· 20.5	98 32.6	12.1	14 22.1	8.2	55.9
04	239 54.6	21.4	113 03.7	12.2	14 13.9	8.3	55.8
05	254 54.7	22.3	127 34.9	12.2	14 05.6	8.4	55.8
06	269 54.9	N 9 23.2	142 06.1	12.3	N13 57.2	8.4	55.8
07	284 55.0	24.1	156 37.4	12.4	13 48.8	8.4	55.8
08	299 55.2	25.0	171 08.8	12.4	13 40.4	8.5	55.7
T 09	314 55.4	·· 25.9	185 40.2	12.5	13 31.9	8.6	55.7
U 10	329 55.5	26.8	200 11.7	12.6	13 23.3	8.6	55.7
E 11	344 55.7	27.7	214 43.3	12.6	13 14.7	8.7	55.7
S 12	359 55.8	N 9 28.6	229 14.9	12.7	N13 06.0	8.8	55.6
D 13	14 56.0	29.5	243 46.6	12.7	12 57.2	8.9	55.6
A 14	29 56.1	30.4	258 18.3	12.8	12 48.5	8.9	55.6
Y 15	44 56.3	·· 31.3	272 50.1	12.9	12 39.6	8.9	55.6
16	59 56.4	32.2	287 22.0	12.9	12 30.7	8.9	55.6
17	74 56.6	33.1	301 53.9	12.9	12 21.8	9.0	55.5
18	89 56.8	N 9 34.0	316 25.8	13.1	N12 12.8	9.1	55.5
19	104 56.9	34.9	330 57.9	13.0	12 03.7	9.1	55.5
20	119 57.1	35.8	345 29.9	13.2	11 54.6	9.1	55.5
21	134 57.2	·· 36.6	0 02.1	13.2	11 45.5	9.2	55.4
22	149 57.4	37.5	14 34.3	13.2	11 36.3	9.3	55.4
23	164 57.5	38.4	29 06.5	13.3	11 27.0	9.3	55.4
15 00	179 57.7	N 9 39.3	43 38.8	13.3	N11 17.7	9.3	55.4
01	194 57.8	40.2	58 11.1	13.4	11 08.4	9.4	55.4
02	209 58.0	41.1	72 43.5	13.5	10 59.0	9.4	55.3
03	224 58.2	·· 42.0	87 16.0	13.5	10 49.6	9.4	55.3
04	239 58.3	42.9	101 48.5	13.6	10 40.2	9.5	55.3
05	254 58.5	43.8	116 21.1	13.6	10 30.7	9.6	55.3
06	269 58.6	N 9 44.7	130 53.7	13.6	N10 21.1	9.6	55.3
07	284 58.8	45.6	145 26.3	13.7	10 11.5	9.6	55.2
W 08	299 58.9	46.5	159 59.0	13.8	10 01.9	9.7	55.2
E 09	314 59.1	·· 47.4	174 31.8	13.8	9 52.3	9.7	55.2
D 10	329 59.2	48.3	189 04.6	13.8	9 42.6	9.8	55.2
N 11	344 59.4	49.2	203 37.4	13.9	9 32.8	9.7	55.2
E 12	359 59.5	N 9 50.1	218 10.3	13.9	N 9 23.1	9.8	55.1
S 13	14 59.7	51.0	232 43.2	14.0	9 13.3	9.9	55.1
D 14	29 59.8	51.9	247 16.2	14.1	9 03.4	9.9	55.1
A 15	45 00.0	·· 52.7	261 49.3	14.0	8 53.5	9.9	55.1
Y 16	60 00.1	53.6	276 22.3	14.2	8 43.6	9.9	55.1
17	75 00.3	54.5	290 55.5	14.1	8 33.7	10.0	55.0
18	90 00.4	N 9 55.4	305 28.6	14.2	N 8 23.7	10.0	55.0
19	105 00.6	56.3	320 01.8	14.3	8 13.7	10.0	55.0
20	120 00.7	57.2	334 35.1	14.2	8 03.7	10.1	55.0
21	135 00.9	·· 58.1	349 08.3	14.4	7 53.6	10.1	55.0
22	150 01.0	59.0	3 41.7	14.3	7 43.5	10.1	55.0
23	165 01.2	59.9	18 15.0	14.4	7 33.4	10.1	54.9
	S.D. 16.0	d 0.9	S.D. 15.3		15.2		15.0

Lat.	Twilight Naut.	Civil	Sunrise	Moonrise 13	14	15	16
°	h m	h m	h m	h m	h m	h m	h m
N 72	////	02 08	03 46	09 30	11 41	13 33	15 18
N 70	////	02 42	04 01	10 18	12 06	13 48	15 24
68	00 58	03 06	04 14	10 48	12 25	13 59	15 30
66	01 51	03 24	04 24	11 11	12 41	14 09	15 34
64	02 21	03 39	04 33	11 29	12 53	14 17	15 38
62	02 43	03 51	04 40	11 43	13 04	14 23	15 42
60	03 01	04 01	04 47	11 56	13 13	14 29	15 45
N 58	03 15	04 10	04 52	12 06	13 20	14 34	15 47
56	03 27	04 18	04 57	12 15	13 27	14 39	15 49
54	03 37	04 24	05 02	12 24	13 33	14 43	15 51
52	03 46	04 30	05 06	12 31	13 39	14 47	15 53
50	03 54	04 36	05 10	12 37	13 44	14 50	15 55
45	04 10	04 47	05 17	12 51	13 55	14 57	15 59
N 40	04 23	04 56	05 24	13 03	14 04	15 03	16 02
35	04 33	05 04	05 30	13 13	14 11	15 08	16 04
30	04 41	05 10	05 35	13 21	14 18	15 13	16 07
20	04 54	05 21	05 43	13 36	14 29	15 21	16 11
N 10	05 04	05 29	05 50	13 49	14 39	15 28	16 14
0	05 12	05 36	05 57	14 01	14 49	15 34	16 18
S 10	05 18	05 42	06 04	14 13	14 58	15 41	16 21
20	05 23	05 48	06 11	14 26	15 08	15 47	16 25
30	05 26	05 54	06 18	14 40	15 19	15 55	16 29
35	05 28	05 57	06 23	14 49	15 26	16 00	16 31
40	05 29	06 00	06 28	14 58	15 33	16 05	16 34
45	05 30	06 04	06 34	15 10	15 42	16 11	16 37
S 50	05 30	06 08	06 40	15 23	15 52	16 18	16 40
52	05 30	06 09	06 44	15 30	15 57	16 21	16 42
54	05 30	06 11	06 47	15 36	16 02	16 24	16 44
56	05 30	06 13	06 51	15 44	16 08	16 28	16 46
58	05 30	06 15	06 55	15 53	16 15	16 33	16 48
S 60	05 29	06 17	07 00	16 03	16 22	16 37	16 50

Lat.	Sunset	Twilight Civil	Naut.	Moonset 13	14	15	16
°	h m	h m	h m	h m	h m	h m	h m
N 72	20 19	22 00	////	06 19	05 49	05 32	05 19
N 70	20 02	21 24	////	05 30	05 22	05 16	05 10
68	19 49	20 59	23 19	04 59	05 02	05 03	05 02
66	19 38	20 40	22 17	04 35	04 46	04 52	04 56
64	19 30	20 24	21 44	04 17	04 32	04 43	04 51
62	19 22	20 12	21 21	04 01	04 21	04 35	04 46
60	19 15	20 01	21 03	03 49	04 11	04 28	04 42
N 58	19 10	19 52	20 48	03 38	04 03	04 22	04 39
56	19 04	19 45	20 36	03 28	03 55	04 17	04 36
54	18 59	19 38	20 25	03 19	03 48	04 12	04 33
52	18 56	19 32	20 16	03 12	03 42	04 08	04 30
50	18 52	19 26	20 08	03 05	03 37	04 04	04 28
45	18 44	19 15	19 52	02 50	03 25	03 56	04 23
N 40	18 37	19 05	19 39	02 38	03 15	03 48	04 18
35	18 32	18 58	19 28	02 27	03 07	03 42	04 15
30	18 26	18 51	19 20	02 18	02 59	03 37	04 11
20	18 18	18 40	19 07	02 02	02 46	03 27	04 05
N 10	18 10	18 32	18 57	01 48	02 35	03 19	04 00
0	18 04	18 25	18 49	01 35	02 24	03 11	03 55
S 10	17 57	18 18	18 43	01 22	02 13	03 03	03 50
20	17 50	18 12	18 38	01 04	02 02	02 54	03 45
30	17 42	18 06	18 34	00 51	01 49	02 45	03 39
35	17 37	18 03	18 32	00 42	01 41	02 39	03 36
40	17 32	18 00	18 31	00 31	01 32	02 32	03 32
45	17 26	17 56	18 30	00 18	01 22	02 25	03 27
S 50	17 19	17 52	18 29	00 02	01 09	02 16	03 21
52	17 16	17 50	18 29	25 03	01 03	02 11	03 19
54	17 13	17 48	18 29	24 57	00 57	02 07	03 16
56	17 09	17 46	18 29	24 49	00 49	02 01	03 13
58	17 04	17 44	18 30	24 41	00 41	01 56	03 09
S 60	16 59	17 42	18 30	24 32	00 32	01 49	03 05

Day	SUN Eqn. of Time 00ʰ	12ʰ	Mer. Pass.	MOON Mer. Pass. Upper	Lower	Age	Phase
	m s	m s	h m	h m	h m	d	
13	00 40	00 32	12 01	20 13	07 48	09	
14	00 25	00 17	12 00	21 00	08 37	10	
15	00 10	00 02	12 00	21 45	09 23	11	◖

G.M.T.	ARIES G.H.A.	VENUS −3.5 G.H.A.	Dec.	MARS +1.4 G.H.A.	Dec.	JUPITER −2.0 G.H.A.	Dec.	SATURN +0.8 G.H.A.	Dec.	STARS Name	S.H.A.	Dec.
16 00	204 03.0	177 32.9 N 9 52.0		182 35.7 N 8 27.3		20 43.9 N 0 16.7		18 28.0 N 0 28.0		Acamar	315 37.4	S40 23.0
01	219 05.5	192 32.4	53.1	197 36.4	28.0	35 46.6	16.8	33 30.6	28.0	Achernar	335 45.6	S57 20.1
02	234 07.9	207 32.0	54.3	212 37.1	28.7	50 49.3	16.9	48 33.2	28.1	Acrux	173 36.2	S62 59.8
03	249 10.4	222 31.5 ··	55.5	227 37.8 ··	29.4	65 52.1 ··	17.0	63 35.9 ··	28.2	Adhara	255 31.9	S28 57.1
04	264 12.9	237 31.1	56.6	242 38.5	30.2	80 54.8	17.1	78 38.5	28.2	Aldebaran	291 17.8	N16 28.2
05	279 15.3	252 30.7	57.8	257 39.2	30.9	95 57.5	17.2	93 41.1	28.3			
06	294 17.8	267 30.2 N 9 59.0		272 39.9 N 8 31.6		111 00.2 N 0 17.3		108 43.7 N 0 28.4		Alioth	166 41.6	N56 03.8
07	309 20.2	282 29.8 10 00.1		287 40.6	32.3	126 02.9	17.4	123 46.4	28.4	Alkaid	153 17.7	N49 24.4
T 08	324 22.7	297 29.3	01.3	302 41.3	33.1	141 05.7	17.5	138 49.0	28.5	Al Na'ir	28 14.7	S47 03.1
H 09	339 25.2	312 28.9 ··	02.5	317 42.0 ··	33.8	156 08.4 ··	17.6	153 51.6 ··	28.6	Alnilam	276 11.5	S 1 13.0
U 10	354 27.6	327 28.4	03.6	332 42.7	34.5	171 11.1	17.7	168 54.2	28.6	Alphard	218 20.1	S 8 34.8
R 11	9 30.1	342 28.0	04.8	347 43.4	35.2	186 13.8	17.8	183 56.9	28.7			
S 12	24 32.6	357 27.5 N10 05.9		2 44.1 N 8 35.9		201 16.5 N 0 18.0		198 59.5 N 0 28.8		Alphecca	126 31.5	N26 46.6
D 13	39 35.0	12 27.1	07.1	17 44.8	36.7	216 19.2	18.1	214 02.1	28.8	Alpheratz	358 09.3	N28 59.0
A 14	54 37.5	27 26.6	08.3	32 45.4	37.4	231 22.0	18.2	229 04.7	28.9	Altair	62 32.2	N 8 48.9
Y 15	69 40.0	42 26.2 ··	09.4	47 46.1 ··	38.1	246 24.7 ··	18.3	244 07.4 ··	29.0	Ankaa	353 40.3	S42 24.6
16	84 42.4	57 25.7	10.6	62 46.8	38.8	261 27.4	18.4	259 10.0	29.0	Antares	112 56.1	S26 23.4
17	99 44.9	72 25.3	11.7	77 47.5	39.6	276 30.1	18.5	274 12.6	29.1			
18	114 47.4	87 24.8 N10 12.9		92 48.2 N 8 40.3		291 32.8 N 0 18.6		289 15.2 N 0 29.2		Arcturus	146 17.8	N19 16.8
19	129 49.8	102 24.4	14.1	107 48.9	41.0	306 35.5	18.7	304 17.9	29.2	Atria	108 19.7	S68 59.4
20	144 52.3	117 23.9	15.2	122 49.6	41.7	321 38.3	18.8	319 20.5	29.3	Avior	234 28.0	S59 27.3
21	159 54.7	132 23.5 ··	16.4	137 50.3 ··	42.4	336 41.0 ··	18.9	334 23.1 ··	29.4	Bellatrix	278 58.5	N 6 19.8
22	174 57.2	147 23.0	17.5	152 51.0	43.2	351 43.7	19.0	349 25.7	29.4	Betelgeuse	271 28.0	N 7 24.1
23	189 59.7	162 22.6	18.7	167 51.7	43.9	6 46.4	19.1	4 28.4	29.5			
17 00	205 02.1	177 22.1 N10 19.9		182 52.4 N 8 44.6		21 49.1 N 0 19.2		19 31.0 N 0 29.6		Canopus	264 07.2	S52 41.5
01	220 04.6	192 21.7	21.0	197 53.1	45.3	36 51.8	19.3	34 33.6	29.6	Capella	281 11.0	N45 58.8
02	235 07.1	207 21.2	22.2	212 53.8	46.0	51 54.6	19.4	49 36.2	29.7	Deneb	49 48.3	N45 12.5
03	250 09.5	222 20.8 ··	23.3	227 54.5 ··	46.8	66 57.3 ··	19.5	64 38.9 ··	29.8	Denebola	182 58.4	N14 40.6
04	265 12.0	237 20.3	24.5	242 55.1	47.5	82 00.0	19.6	79 41.5	29.8	Diphda	349 20.8	S18 05.5
05	280 14.5	252 19.9	25.6	257 55.8	48.2	97 02.7	19.7	94 44.1	29.9			
06	295 16.9	267 19.4 N10 26.8		272 56.5 N 8 48.9		112 05.4 N 0 19.8		109 46.7 N 0 29.9		Dubhe	194 21.2	N61 51.3
07	310 19.4	282 19.0	27.9	287 57.2	49.6	127 08.1	19.9	124 49.4	30.0	Elnath	278 43.9	N28 35.5
08	325 21.9	297 18.5	29.1	302 57.9	50.4	142 10.8	20.0	139 52.0	30.1	Eltanin	90 57.3	N51 29.2
F 09	340 24.3	312 18.1 ··	30.2	317 58.6 ··	51.1	157 13.6 ··	20.1	154 54.6 ··	30.1	Enif	34 11.4	N 9 47.1
R 10	355 26.8	327 17.6	31.4	332 59.3	51.8	172 16.3	20.2	169 57.2	30.2	Fomalhaut	15 51.3	S29 43.4
I 11	10 29.2	342 17.1	32.6	348 00.0	52.5	187 19.0	20.3	184 59.9	30.3			
D 12	25 31.7	357 16.7 N10 33.7		3 00.7 N 8 53.2		202 21.7 N 0 20.4		200 02.5 N 0 30.3		Gacrux	172 27.8	S57 00.6
A 13	40 34.2	12 16.2	34.9	18 01.4	54.0	217 24.4	20.5	215 05.1	30.4	Gienah	176 17.3	S17 26.3
Y 14	55 36.6	27 15.8	36.0	33 02.1	54.7	232 27.1	20.6	230 07.7	30.5	Hadar	149 22.2	S60 16.9
15	70 39.1	42 15.3 ··	37.2	48 02.8 ··	55.4	247 29.8 ··	20.7	245 10.3 ··	30.5	Hamal	328 28.8	N23 22.2
16	85 41.6	57 14.9	38.3	63 03.5	56.1	262 32.6	20.8	260 13.0	30.6	Kaus Aust.	84 16.2	S34 23.5
17	100 44.0	72 14.4	39.5	78 04.1	56.8	277 35.3	20.9	275 15.6	30.7			
18	115 46.5	87 13.9 N10 40.6		93 04.8 N 8 57.5		292 38.0 N 0 21.0		290 18.2 N 0 30.7		Kochab	137 17.9	N74 13.9
19	130 49.0	102 13.5	41.8	108 05.5	58.3	307 40.7	21.1	305 20.8	30.8	Markab	14 03.0	N15 06.0
20	145 51.4	117 13.0	42.9	123 06.2	59.0	322 43.4	21.2	320 23.5	30.9	Menkar	314 41.0	N 4 00.8
21	160 53.9	132 12.6 ··	44.1	138 06.9	8 59.7	337 46.1 ··	21.3	335 26.1 ··	30.9	Menkent	148 36.2	S36 16.7
22	175 56.3	147 12.1	45.2	153 07.6	9 00.4	352 48.8	21.5	350 28.7	31.0	Miaplacidus	221 44.6	S69 38.7
23	190 58.8	162 11.7	46.3	168 08.3	01.1	7 51.5	21.6	5 31.3	31.0			
18 00	206 01.3	177 11.2 N10 47.5		183 09.0 N 9 01.9		22 54.2 N 0 21.7		20 34.0 N 0 31.1		Mirfak	309 16.0	N49 47.6
01	221 03.7	192 10.7	48.6	198 09.7	02.6	37 57.0	21.8	35 36.6	31.2	Nunki	76 28.6	S26 19.2
02	236 06.2	207 10.3	49.8	213 10.4	03.3	52 59.7	21.9	50 39.2	31.2	Peacock	53 57.9	S56 47.6
03	251 08.7	222 09.8 ··	50.9	228 11.1 ··	04.0	68 02.4 ··	22.0	65 41.8 ··	31.3	Pollux	243 57.7	N28 04.4
04	266 11.1	237 09.4	52.1	243 11.8	04.7	83 05.1	22.1	80 44.4	31.4	Procyon	245 25.4	N 5 16.3
05	281 13.6	252 08.9	53.2	258 12.4	05.4	98 07.8	22.2	95 47.1	31.4			
06	296 16.1	267 08.4 N10 54.4		273 13.1 N 9 06.1		113 10.5 N 0 22.3		110 49.7 N 0 31.5		Rasalhague	96 29.1	N12 34.3
07	311 18.5	282 08.0	55.5	288 13.8	06.9	128 13.2	22.4	125 52.3	31.6	Regulus	208 09.4	N12 03.5
S 08	326 21.0	297 07.5	56.7	303 14.5	07.6	143 15.9	22.5	140 54.9	31.6	Rigel	281 35.9	S 8 13.6
A 09	341 23.5	312 07.0 ··	57.8	318 15.2 ··	08.3	158 18.6 ··	22.6	155 57.6 ··	31.7	Rigil Kent.	140 24.7	S60 45.3
T 10	356 25.9	327 06.6 10 58.9		333 15.9	09.0	173 21.4	22.7	171 00.2	31.8	Sabik	102 40.5	S15 42.1
U 11	11 28.4	342 06.1 11 00.1		348 16.6	09.7	188 24.1	22.8	186 02.8	31.8			
R 12	26 30.8	357 05.7 N11 01.2		3 17.3 N 9 10.4		203 26.8 N 0 22.9		201 05.4 N 0 31.9		Schedar	350 09.1	N56 25.8
D 13	41 33.3	12 05.2	02.4	18 18.0	11.2	218 29.5	23.0	216 08.0	31.9	Shaula	96 55.0	S37 05.3
A 14	56 35.8	27 04.7	03.5	33 18.7	11.9	233 32.2	23.1	231 10.7	32.0	Sirius	258 55.5	S16 41.7
Y 15	71 38.2	42 04.3 ··	04.6	48 19.4 ··	12.6	248 34.9 ··	23.2	246 13.3 ··	32.1	Spica	158 56.8	S11 03.8
16	86 40.7	57 03.8	05.8	63 20.0	13.3	263 37.6	23.3	261 15.9	32.1	Suhail	223 10.4	S43 21.7
17	101 43.2	72 03.3	06.9	78 20.7	14.0	278 40.3	23.4	276 18.5	32.2			
18	116 45.6	87 02.9 N11 08.1		93 21.4 N 9 14.7		293 43.0 N 0 23.5		291 21.1 N 0 32.3		Vega	80 55.4	N38 45.7
19	131 48.1	102 02.4	09.2	108 22.1	15.4	308 45.7	23.6	306 23.8	32.3	Zuben'ubi	137 32.3	S15 57.9
20	146 50.6	117 01.9	10.3	123 22.8	16.1	323 48.4	23.7	321 26.4	32.4			
21	161 53.0	132 01.5 ··	11.5	138 23.5 ··	16.9	338 51.2 ··	23.8	336 29.0 ··	32.5		S.H.A.	Mer. Pass.
22	176 55.5	147 01.0	12.6	153 24.2	17.6	353 53.9	23.9	351 31.6	32.5	Venus	332 20.0	12 11
23	191 58.0	162 00.5	13.7	168 24.9	18.3	8 56.6	24.0	6 34.2	32.6	Mars	337 50.2	11 48
Mer. Pass.	10 18.2	v −0.5 d 1.2		v 0.7 d 0.7		v 2.7 d 0.1		v 2.6 d 0.1		Jupiter	176 47.0	22 29
										Saturn	174 28.9	22 38

G.M.T.	SUN G.H.A.	SUN Dec.	MOON G.H.A.	v	Dec.	d	H.P.
16 00	180 01.3	N10 00.7	32 48.4	14.5	N 7 23.3	10.2	54.9
01	195 01.5	01.6	47 21.9	14.4	7 13.1	10.2	54.9
02	210 01.6	02.5	61 55.3	14.5	7 02.9	10.2	54.9
03	225 01.8	·· 03.4	76 28.8	14.6	6 52.7	10.2	54.9
04	240 01.9	04.3	91 02.4	14.6	6 42.5	10.3	54.9
05	255 02.1	05.2	105 36.0	14.6	6 32.2	10.3	54.8
06	270 02.2	N10 06.1	120 09.6	14.7	N 6 21.9	10.3	54.8
07	285 02.4	07.0	134 43.3	14.6	6 11.6	10.3	54.8
T 08	300 02.5	07.8	149 16.9	14.8	6 01.3	10.4	54.8
H 09	315 02.7	·· 08.7	163 50.7	14.7	5 50.9	10.4	54.8
U 10	330 02.8	09.6	178 24.4	14.8	5 40.6	10.4	54.8
R 11	345 03.0	10.5	192 58.2	14.8	5 30.2	10.4	54.7
S 12	0 03.1	N10 11.4	207 32.0	14.9	N 5 19.8	10.5	54.7
D 13	15 03.3	12.3	222 05.9	14.8	5 09.3	10.4	54.7
A 14	30 03.4	13.2	236 39.7	14.9	4 58.9	10.5	54.7
Y 15	45 03.6	·· 14.0	251 13.6	15.0	4 48.4	10.4	54.7
16	60 03.7	14.9	265 47.6	14.9	4 38.0	10.5	54.7
17	75 03.9	15.8	280 21.5	15.0	4 27.5	10.5	54.7
18	90 04.0	N10 16.7	294 55.5	15.0	N 4 17.0	10.5	54.6
19	105 04.2	17.6	309 29.5	15.0	4 06.5	10.4	54.6
20	120 04.3	18.5	324 03.5	15.1	3 55.9	10.5	54.6
21	135 04.5	·· 19.3	338 37.6	15.1	3 45.4	10.6	54.6
22	150 04.6	20.2	353 11.7	15.1	3 34.8	10.5	54.6
23	165 04.8	21.1	7 45.8	15.1	3 24.3	10.6	54.6
17 00	180 04.9	N10 22.0	22 19.9	15.2	N 3 13.7	10.6	54.6
01	195 05.1	22.9	36 54.1	15.1	3 03.1	10.6	54.5
02	210 05.2	23.7	51 28.2	15.2	2 52.5	10.6	54.5
03	225 05.4	·· 24.6	66 02.4	15.2	2 41.9	10.6	54.5
04	240 05.5	25.5	80 36.6	15.3	2 31.3	10.6	54.5
05	255 05.6	26.4	95 10.9	15.2	2 20.7	10.6	54.5
06	270 05.8	N10 27.3	109 45.1	15.3	N 2 10.1	10.6	54.5
07	285 05.9	28.1	124 19.4	15.3	1 59.5	10.6	54.5
08	300 06.1	29.0	138 53.7	15.3	1 48.9	10.7	54.5
F 09	315 06.2	·· 29.9	153 28.0	15.3	1 38.2	10.6	54.4
R 10	330 06.4	30.8	168 02.3	15.3	1 27.6	10.6	54.4
I 11	345 06.5	31.7	182 36.6	15.4	1 17.0	10.7	54.4
D 12	0 06.7	N10 32.5	197 11.0	15.3	N 1 06.3	10.6	54.4
A 13	15 06.8	33.4	211 45.3	15.4	0 55.7	10.6	54.4
Y 14	30 07.0	34.3	226 19.7	15.4	0 45.1	10.7	54.4
15	45 07.1	·· 35.2	240 54.1	15.4	0 34.4	10.6	54.4
16	60 07.2	36.1	255 28.5	15.4	0 23.8	10.6	54.4
17	75 07.4	36.9	270 02.9	15.4	0 13.2	10.7	54.4
18	90 07.5	N10 37.8	284 37.3	15.4	N 0 02.5	10.6	54.3
19	105 07.7	38.7	299 11.7	15.5	S 0 08.1	10.6	54.3
20	120 07.8	39.6	313 46.2	15.4	0 18.7	10.6	54.3
21	135 08.0	·· 40.4	328 20.6	15.5	0 29.3	10.6	54.3
22	150 08.1	41.3	342 55.1	15.4	0 39.9	10.7	54.3
23	165 08.2	42.2	357 29.5	15.5	0 50.6	10.6	54.3
18 00	180 08.4	N10 43.1	12 04.0	15.5	S 1 01.2	10.6	54.3
01	195 08.5	43.9	26 38.5	15.5	1 11.8	10.5	54.3
02	210 08.7	44.8	41 13.0	15.4	1 22.3	10.6	54.3
03	225 08.8	·· 45.7	55 47.4	15.5	1 32.9	10.6	54.3
04	240 09.0	46.5	70 21.9	15.5	1 43.5	10.6	54.2
05	255 09.1	47.4	84 56.4	15.5	1 54.1	10.5	54.2
06	270 09.2	N10 48.3	99 30.9	15.5	S 2 04.6	10.5	54.2
07	285 09.4	49.2	114 05.4	15.5	2 15.1	10.6	54.2
S 08	300 09.5	50.0	128 39.9	15.5	2 25.7	10.5	54.2
A 09	315 09.7	·· 50.9	143 14.4	15.5	2 36.2	10.5	54.2
T 10	330 09.8	51.8	157 48.9	15.5	2 46.7	10.5	54.2
U 11	345 10.0	52.7	172 23.4	15.5	2 57.2	10.5	54.2
R 12	0 10.1	N10 53.5	186 57.9	15.5	S 3 07.7	10.4	54.2
D 13	15 10.2	54.4	201 32.4	15.5	3 18.1	10.5	54.2
A 14	30 10.4	55.3	216 06.9	15.5	3 28.6	10.4	54.2
Y 15	45 10.5	·· 56.1	230 41.4	15.5	3 39.0	10.4	54.2
16	60 10.7	57.0	245 15.9	15.4	3 49.4	10.4	54.1
17	75 10.8	57.9	259 50.3	15.5	3 59.8	10.4	54.1
18	90 10.9	N10 58.7	274 24.8	15.5	S 4 10.2	10.3	54.1
19	105 11.1	10 59.6	288 59.3	15.4	4 20.5	10.4	54.1
20	120 11.2	11 00.5	303 33.7	15.5	4 30.9	10.3	54.1
21	135 11.4	·· 01.3	318 08.2	15.4	4 41.2	10.3	54.1
22	150 11.5	02.2	332 42.7	15.4	4 51.5	10.3	54.1
23	165 11.6	03.1	347 17.1	15.4	5 01.8	10.2	54.1
	S.D. 16.0	d 0.9	S.D. 14.9		14.8		14.8

Lat.	Naut.	Civil	Sunrise	Moonrise 16	17	18	19
N 72	////	01 39	03 28	15 18	16 58	18 38	20 19
N 70	////	02 21	03 47	15 24	16 58	18 32	20 06
68	////	02 49	04 01	15 30	16 59	18 26	19 55
66	01 25	03 10	04 13	15 34	16 59	18 22	19 46
64	02 03	03 27	04 23	15 38	16 59	18 19	19 38
62	02 29	03 40	04 31	15 42	16 59	18 15	19 32
60	02 48	03 51	04 38	15 45	16 59	18 13	19 26
N 58	03 04	04 01	04 44	15 47	16 59	18 10	19 21
56	03 17	04 09	04 50	15 49	16 59	18 08	19 17
54	03 29	04 17	04 55	15 51	16 59	18 06	19 13
52	03 38	04 23	04 59	15 53	16 59	18 05	19 09
50	03 47	04 29	05 03	15 55	16 59	18 03	19 06
45	04 04	04 41	05 12	15 59	16 59	18 00	18 59
N 40	04 18	04 51	05 20	16 02	17 00	17 57	18 54
35	04 29	05 00	05 26	16 04	17 00	17 54	18 49
30	04 38	05 07	05 31	16 07	17 00	17 52	18 44
20	04 52	05 18	05 41	16 11	17 00	17 48	18 37
N 10	05 02	05 27	05 49	16 14	17 00	17 45	18 31
0	05 11	05 35	05 56	16 18	17 00	17 42	18 24
S 10	05 18	05 42	06 04	16 21	17 00	17 39	18 18
20	05 23	05 49	06 11	16 25	17 01	17 36	18 12
30	05 28	05 56	06 20	16 29	17 01	17 33	18 05
35	05 30	05 59	06 25	16 31	17 01	17 30	18 01
40	05 32	06 03	06 31	16 34	17 01	17 28	17 56
45	05 33	06 07	06 37	16 37	17 01	17 26	17 51
S 50	05 35	06 12	06 45	16 40	17 01	17 22	17 44
52	05 35	06 14	06 49	16 42	17 02	17 21	17 41
54	05 35	06 16	06 53	16 44	17 02	17 19	17 38
56	05 36	06 19	06 57	16 46	17 02	17 18	17 34
58	05 36	06 21	07 02	16 48	17 02	17 16	17 30
S 60	05 36	06 24	07 07	16 50	17 02	17 14	17 26

Lat.	Sunset	Civil	Naut.	Moonset 16	17	18	19
N 72	20 35	22 30	////	05 19	05 07	04 56	04 44
N 70	20 16	21 44	////	05 10	05 04	04 58	04 52
68	20 01	21 14	////	05 02	05 02	05 00	04 59
66	19 49	20 52	22 43	04 56	04 59	05 02	05 05
64	19 39	20 35	22 01	04 51	04 58	05 04	05 10
62	19 30	20 21	21 34	04 46	04 56	05 05	05 14
60	19 23	20 10	21 14	04 42	04 55	05 06	05 18
N 58	19 16	20 00	20 57	04 39	04 54	05 07	05 22
56	19 11	19 51	20 44	04 36	04 52	05 08	05 25
54	19 05	19 44	20 33	04 33	04 51	05 09	05 27
52	19 01	19 37	20 23	04 30	04 51	05 10	05 30
50	18 57	19 31	20 14	04 28	04 50	05 11	05 32
45	18 48	19 19	19 56	04 23	04 48	05 12	05 37
N 40	18 40	19 09	19 42	04 18	04 46	05 14	05 41
35	18 34	19 00	19 31	04 15	04 45	05 15	05 45
30	18 28	18 53	19 22	04 11	04 44	05 16	05 48
20	18 19	18 41	19 08	04 05	04 42	05 18	05 53
N 10	18 11	18 32	18 57	04 00	04 40	05 19	05 58
0	18 03	18 24	18 48	03 55	04 38	05 20	06 03
S 10	17 55	18 17	18 41	03 50	04 37	05 22	06 07
20	17 47	18 10	18 36	03 45	04 35	05 23	06 12
30	17 39	18 03	18 31	03 39	04 32	05 25	06 17
35	17 33	17 59	18 29	03 36	04 31	05 26	06 21
40	17 28	17 55	18 27	03 32	04 30	05 27	06 24
45	17 21	17 51	18 25	03 27	04 28	05 28	06 28
S 50	17 13	17 46	18 24	03 21	04 26	05 30	06 33
52	17 10	17 44	18 23	03 19	04 25	05 31	06 36
54	17 06	17 42	18 23	03 16	04 24	05 31	06 38
56	17 01	17 39	18 22	03 13	04 23	05 32	06 41
58	16 56	17 37	18 22	03 09	04 22	05 33	06 44
S 60	16 51	17 34	18 22	03 05	04 20	05 34	06 48

Day	SUN Eqn. of Time 00h	12h	Mer. Pass.	MOON Mer. Pass. Upper	Lower	Age	Phase
16	00 05	00 12	12 00	22 28	10 07	12	
17	00 19	00 26	12 00	23 10	10 49	13	○
18	00 33	00 40	11 59	23 52	11 31	14	

G.M.T.	ARIES G.H.A.	VENUS −3.5 G.H.A.	Dec.	MARS +1.4 G.H.A.	Dec.	JUPITER −2.0 G.H.A.	Dec.	SATURN +0.8 G.H.A.	Dec.	Name	S.H.A.	Dec.
19 00	207 00.4	177 00.1 N11 14.9		183 25.6 N 9 19.0		23 59.3 N 0 24.1		21 36.9 N 0 32.6		Acamar	315 37.4	S40 23.0
01	222 02.9	191 59.6	16.0	198 26.3	19.7	39 02.0	24.2	36 39.5	32.7	Achernar	335 45.6	S57 20.0
02	237 05.3	206 59.1	17.2	213 27.0	20.4	54 04.7	24.3	51 42.1	32.8	Acrux	173 36.2	S62 59.8
03	252 07.8	221 58.7 ··	18.3	228 27.6 ··	21.1	69 07.4 ··	24.4	66 44.7 ··	32.8	Adhara	255 31.9	S28 57.1
04	267 10.3	236 58.2	19.4	243 28.3	21.8	84 10.1	24.5	81 47.3	32.9	Aldebaran	291 17.8	N16 28.2
05	282 12.7	251 57.7	20.6	258 29.0	22.6	99 12.8	24.6	96 50.0	33.0			
06	297 15.2	266 57.3 N11 21.7		273 29.7 N 9 23.3		114 15.5 N 0 24.7		111 52.6 N 0 33.0		Alioth	166 41.6	N56 03.8
07	312 17.7	281 56.8	22.8	288 30.4	24.0	129 18.2	24.8	126 55.2	33.1	Alkaid	153 17.7	N49 24.5
08	327 20.1	296 56.3	24.0	303 31.1	24.7	144 20.9	24.9	141 57.8	33.1	Al Na'ir	28 14.7	S47 03.1
S 09	342 22.6	311 55.8 ··	25.1	318 31.8 ··	25.4	159 23.6 ··	24.9	157 00.4 ··	33.2	Alnilam	276 11.5	S 1 13.0
U 10	357 25.1	326 55.4	26.2	333 32.5	26.1	174 26.3	25.0	172 03.1	33.3	Alphard	218 20.1	S 8 34.8
N 11	12 27.5	341 54.9	27.4	348 33.2	26.8	189 29.0	25.1	187 05.7	33.3			
D 12	27 30.0	356 54.4 N11 28.5		3 33.9 N 9 27.5		204 31.7 N 0 25.2		202 08.3 N 0 33.4		Alphecca	126 31.5	N26 46.6
A 13	42 32.4	11 54.0	29.6	18 34.5	28.2	219 34.5	25.3	217 10.9	33.5	Alpheratz	358 09.2	N28 59.0
Y 14	57 34.9	26 53.5	30.7	33 35.2	29.0	234 37.2	25.4	232 13.5	33.5	Altair	62 32.1	N 8 49.0
15	72 37.4	41 53.0 ··	31.9	48 35.9 ··	29.7	249 39.9 ··	25.5	247 16.2 ··	33.6	Ankaa	353 40.3	S42 24.6
16	87 39.8	56 52.5	33.0	63 36.6	30.4	264 42.6	25.6	262 18.8	33.7	Antares	112 56.1	S26 23.4
17	102 42.3	71 52.1	34.1	78 37.3	31.1	279 45.3	25.7	277 21.4	33.7			
18	117 44.8	86 51.6 N11 35.3		93 38.0 N 9 31.8		294 48.0 N 0 25.8		292 24.0 N 0 33.8		Arcturus	146 17.8	N19 16.8
19	132 47.2	101 51.1	36.4	108 38.7	32.5	309 50.7	25.9	307 26.6	33.8	Atria	108 19.6	S68 59.4
20	147 49.7	116 50.6	37.5	123 39.4	33.2	324 53.4	26.0	322 29.3	33.9	Avior	234 28.0	S59 27.3
21	162 52.2	131 50.2 ··	38.6	138 40.1 ··	33.9	339 56.1 ··	26.1	337 31.9 ··	34.0	Bellatrix	278 58.6	N 6 19.8
22	177 54.6	146 49.7	39.8	153 40.7	34.6	354 58.8	26.2	352 34.5	34.0	Betelgeuse	271 28.1	N 7 24.1
23	192 57.1	161 49.2	40.9	168 41.4	35.3	10 01.5	26.3	7 37.1	34.1			
20 00	207 59.6	176 48.7 N11 42.0		183 42.1 N 9 36.0		25 04.2 N 0 26.4		22 39.7 N 0 34.2		Canopus	264 07.3	S52 41.5
01	223 02.0	191 48.3	43.1	198 42.8	36.7	40 06.9	26.5	37 42.4	34.2	Capella	281 11.1	N45 58.8
02	238 04.5	206 47.8	44.3	213 43.5	37.5	55 09.6	26.6	52 45.0	34.3	Deneb	49 48.3	N45 12.5
03	253 06.9	221 47.3 ··	45.4	228 44.2 ··	38.2	70 12.3 ··	26.7	67 47.6 ··	34.3	Denebola	182 58.4	N14 40.6
04	268 09.4	236 46.8	46.5	243 44.9	38.9	85 15.0	26.8	82 50.2	34.4	Diphda	349 20.8	S18 05.5
05	283 11.9	251 46.4	47.6	258 45.6	39.6	100 17.7	26.9	97 52.8	34.5			
06	298 14.3	266 45.9 N11 48.7		273 46.3 N 9 40.3		115 20.4 N 0 27.0		112 55.4 N 0 34.5		Dubhe	194 21.2	N61 51.4
07	313 16.8	281 45.4	49.9	288 47.0	41.0	130 23.1	27.1	127 58.1	34.6	Elnath	278 43.9	N28 35.5
08	328 19.3	296 44.9	51.0	303 47.6	41.7	145 25.8	27.2	143 00.7	34.6	Eltanin	90 57.3	N51 29.2
M 09	343 21.7	311 44.4 ··	52.1	318 48.3 ··	42.4	160 28.5 ··	27.3	158 03.3 ··	34.7	Enif	34 11.3	N 9 47.1
O 10	358 24.2	326 44.0	53.2	333 49.0	43.1	175 31.2	27.4	173 05.9	34.8	Fomalhaut	15 51.2	S29 43.4
N 11	13 26.7	341 43.5	54.3	348 49.7	43.8	190 33.9	27.5	188 08.5	34.8			
D 12	28 29.1	356 43.0 N11 55.5		3 50.4 N 9 44.5		205 36.6 N 0 27.6		203 11.2 N 0 34.9		Gacrux	172 27.8	S57 00.6
A 13	43 31.6	11 42.5	56.6	18 51.1	45.2	220 39.3	27.7	218 13.8	35.0	Gienah	176 17.3	S17 26.3
Y 14	58 34.1	26 42.0	57.7	33 51.8	45.9	235 42.0	27.8	233 16.4	35.0	Hadar	149 22.2	S60 16.9
15	73 36.5	41 41.6 ··	58.8	48 52.5 ··	46.6	250 44.7 ··	27.9	248 19.0 ··	35.1	Hamal	328 28.8	N23 22.2
16	88 39.0	56 41.1 11 59.9		63 53.2	47.3	265 47.4	28.0	263 21.6	35.1	Kaus Aust.	84 16.2	S34 23.5
17	103 41.4	71 40.6 12 01.1		78 53.8	48.0	280 50.1	28.1	278 24.2	35.2			
18	118 43.9	86 40.1 N12 02.2		93 54.5 N 9 48.7		295 52.8 N 0 28.1		293 26.9 N 0 35.3		Kochab	137 17.9	N74 14.0
19	133 46.4	101 39.6	03.3	108 55.2	49.5	310 55.5	28.2	308 29.5	35.3	Markab	14 03.0	N15 06.0
20	148 48.8	116 39.1	04.4	123 55.9	50.2	325 58.2	28.3	323 32.1	35.4	Menkar	314 41.1	N 4 00.8
21	163 51.3	131 38.7 ··	05.5	138 56.6 ··	50.9	341 00.9 ··	28.4	338 34.7 ··	35.4	Menkent	148 36.2	S36 16.7
22	178 53.8	146 38.2	06.6	153 57.3	51.6	356 03.6	28.5	353 37.3	35.5	Miaplacidus	221 44.6	S69 38.7
23	193 56.2	161 37.7	07.7	168 58.0	52.3	11 06.3	28.6	8 39.9	35.6			
21 00	208 58.7	176 37.2 N12 08.9		183 58.7 N 9 53.0		26 09.0 N 0 28.7		23 42.6 N 0 35.6		Mirfak	309 16.0	N49 47.6
01	224 01.2	191 36.7	10.0	198 59.3	53.7	41 11.7	28.8	38 45.2	35.7	Nunki	76 28.6	S26 19.2
02	239 03.6	206 36.2	11.1	214 00.0	54.4	56 14.4	28.9	53 47.8	35.8	Peacock	53 57.8	S56 47.6
03	254 06.1	221 35.8 ··	12.2	229 00.7 ··	55.1	71 17.1 ··	29.0	68 50.4 ··	35.8	Pollux	243 57.8	N28 04.4
04	269 08.5	236 35.3	13.3	244 01.4	55.8	86 19.8	29.1	83 53.0	35.9	Procyon	245 25.4	N 5 16.3
05	284 11.0	251 34.8	14.4	259 02.1	56.5	101 22.5	29.2	98 55.6	35.9			
06	299 13.5	266 34.3 N12 15.5		274 02.8 N 9 57.2		116 25.2 N 0 29.3		113 58.3 N 0 36.0		Rasalhague	96 29.0	N12 34.3
07	314 15.9	281 33.8	16.6	289 03.5	57.9	131 27.9	29.4	129 00.9	36.1	Regulus	208 09.4	N12 03.5
08	329 18.4	296 33.3	17.7	304 04.2	58.6	146 30.6	29.5	144 03.5	36.1	Rigel	281 35.9	S 8 13.6
T 09	344 20.9	311 32.8 ··	18.8	319 04.8 9 59.3		161 33.3 ··	29.6	159 06.1 ··	36.2	Rigil Kent.	140 24.7	S60 45.4
U 10	359 23.3	326 32.3	20.0	334 05.5 10 00.0		176 36.0	29.7	174 08.7	36.2	Sabik	102 40.5	S15 42.1
E 11	14 25.8	341 31.8	21.1	349 06.2	00.7	191 38.7	29.8	189 11.3	36.3			
S 12	29 28.3	356 31.4 N12 22.2		4 06.9 N10 01.4		206 41.4 N 0 29.8		204 13.9 N 0 36.4		Schedar	350 09.1	N56 25.8
D 13	44 30.7	11 30.9	23.3	19 07.6	02.1	221 44.1	29.9	219 16.6	36.4	Shaula	96 55.0	S37 05.3
A 14	59 33.2	26 30.4	24.4	34 08.3	02.8	236 46.8	30.0	234 19.2	36.5	Sirius	258 55.5	S16 41.7
Y 15	74 35.7	41 29.9 ··	25.5	49 09.0 ··	03.5	251 49.5 ··	30.1	249 21.8 ··	36.5	Spica	158 56.8	S11 03.8
16	89 38.1	56 29.4	26.6	64 09.7	04.2	266 52.2	30.2	264 24.4	36.6	Suhail	223 10.4	S43 21.7
17	104 40.6	71 28.9	27.7	79 10.3	04.9	281 54.8	30.3	279 27.0	36.7			
18	119 43.0	86 28.4 N12 28.8		94 11.0 N10 05.6		296 57.5 N 0 30.4		294 29.6 N 0 36.7		Vega	80 55.4	N38 45.7
19	134 45.5	101 27.9	29.9	109 11.7	06.3	312 00.2	30.5	309 32.3	36.8	Zuben'ubi	137 32.3	S15 57.9
20	149 48.0	116 27.4	31.0	124 12.4	07.0	327 02.9	30.6	324 34.9	36.8		S.H.A.	Mer. Pass.
21	164 50.5	131 26.9 ··	32.1	139 13.1 ··	07.7	342 05.6 ··	30.7	339 37.5 ··	36.9	Venus	328 49.2	12 13
22	179 52.9	146 26.4	33.2	154 13.8	08.4	357 08.3	30.8	354 40.1	37.0	Mars	335 42.6	11 45
23	194 55.4	161 25.9	34.3	169 14.5	09.1	12 11.0	30.9	9 42.7	37.0	Jupiter	177 04.6	22 16
Mer. Pass. 10 06.4		v −0.5 d 1.1		v 0.7 d 0.7		v 2.7 d 0.1		v 2.6 d 0.1		Saturn	174 40.2	22 25

SUN and MOON

G.M.T.	SUN G.H.A.	SUN Dec.	MOON G.H.A.	v	Dec.	d	H.P.
19 00	180 11.8	N11 03.9	1 51.5	15.5	S 5 12.0	10.3	54.1
01	195 11.9	04.8	16 26.0	15.4	5 22.3	10.2	54.1
02	210 12.0	05.7	31 00.4	15.4	5 32.5	10.2	54.1
03	225 12.2	·· 06.5	45 34.8	15.4	5 42.7	10.1	54.1
04	240 12.3	07.4	60 09.2	15.4	5 52.8	10.2	54.1
05	255 12.5	08.3	74 43.6	15.3	6 03.0	10.1	54.1
06	270 12.6	N11 09.1	89 17.9	15.4	S 6 13.1	10.1	54.1
07	285 12.7	10.0	103 52.3	15.3	6 23.2	10.1	54.1
08	300 12.9	10.9	118 26.6	15.4	6 33.2	10.0	54.0
S 09	315 13.0	·· 11.7	133 01.0	15.3	6 43.2	10.0	54.0
U 10	330 13.2	12.6	147 35.3	15.3	6 53.2	10.0	54.0
N 11	345 13.3	13.5	162 09.6	15.3	7 03.2	10.0	54.0
D 12	0 13.4	N11 14.3	176 43.9	15.3	S 7 13.2	9.9	54.0
A 13	15 13.6	15.2	191 18.2	15.2	7 23.1	9.9	54.0
Y 14	30 13.7	16.0	205 52.4	15.3	7 33.0	9.8	54.0
15	45 13.8	·· 16.9	220 26.7	15.2	7 42.8	9.8	54.0
16	60 14.0	17.8	235 00.9	15.2	7 52.6	9.8	54.0
17	75 14.1	18.6	249 35.1	15.2	8 02.4	9.8	54.0
18	90 14.2	N11 19.5	264 09.3	15.2	S 8 12.2	9.7	54.0
19	105 14.4	20.4	278 43.5	15.1	8 21.9	9.7	54.0
20	120 14.5	21.2	293 17.6	15.1	8 31.6	9.6	54.0
21	135 14.6	·· 22.1	307 51.7	15.2	8 41.2	9.7	54.0
22	150 14.8	22.9	322 25.9	15.0	8 50.9	9.5	54.0
23	165 14.9	23.8	336 59.9	15.1	9 00.4	9.6	54.0
20 00	180 15.0	N11 24.7	351 34.0	15.1	S 9 10.0	9.5	54.0
01	195 15.2	25.5	6 08.1	15.0	9 19.5	9.4	54.0
02	210 15.3	26.4	20 42.1	15.0	9 28.9	9.5	54.0
03	225 15.5	·· 27.2	35 16.1	15.0	9 38.4	9.4	54.0
04	240 15.6	28.1	49 50.1	14.9	9 47.8	9.3	54.0
05	255 15.7	28.9	64 24.0	14.9	9 57.1	9.3	54.0
06	270 15.9	N11 29.8	78 57.9	14.9	S10 06.4	9.3	54.0
07	285 16.0	30.7	93 31.8	14.9	10 15.7	9.2	54.0
08	300 16.1	31.5	108 05.7	14.9	10 24.9	9.2	54.0
M 09	315 16.3	·· 32.4	122 39.6	14.8	10 34.1	9.1	54.0
O 10	330 16.4	33.2	137 13.4	14.8	10 43.2	9.1	54.0
N 11	345 16.5	34.1	151 47.2	14.8	10 52.3	9.1	54.0
D 12	0 16.6	N11 34.9	166 21.0	14.7	S11 01.4	9.0	54.0
A 13	15 16.8	35.8	180 54.7	14.7	11 10.4	8.9	54.0
Y 14	30 16.9	36.7	195 28.4	14.7	11 19.3	8.9	54.0
15	45 17.0	·· 37.5	210 02.1	14.7	11 28.2	8.9	54.0
16	60 17.2	38.4	224 35.8	14.6	11 37.1	8.8	54.0
17	75 17.3	39.2	239 09.4	14.6	11 45.9	8.8	54.0
18	90 17.4	N11 40.1	253 43.0	14.6	S11 54.7	8.7	54.0
19	105 17.6	40.9	268 16.6	14.5	12 03.4	8.7	54.0
20	120 17.7	41.8	282 50.1	14.6	12 12.1	8.6	54.0
21	135 17.8	·· 42.6	297 23.7	14.4	12 20.7	8.6	54.0
22	150 18.0	43.5	311 57.1	14.5	12 29.3	8.5	54.0
23	165 18.1	44.3	326 30.6	14.4	12 37.8	8.5	54.0
21 00	180 18.2	N11 45.2	341 04.0	14.4	S12 46.3	8.4	54.0
01	195 18.4	46.0	355 37.4	14.3	12 54.7	8.3	54.0
02	210 18.5	46.9	10 10.7	14.4	13 03.0	8.3	54.0
03	225 18.6	·· 47.7	24 44.1	14.3	13 11.3	8.3	54.0
04	240 18.7	48.6	39 17.4	14.2	13 19.6	8.2	54.0
05	255 18.9	49.4	53 50.6	14.2	13 27.8	8.1	54.0
06	270 19.0	N11 50.3	68 23.8	14.2	S13 35.9	8.1	54.0
07	285 19.1	51.1	82 57.0	14.2	13 44.0	8.0	54.0
08	300 19.3	52.0	97 30.2	14.1	13 52.0	8.0	54.0
T 09	315 19.4	·· 52.8	112 03.3	14.1	14 00.0	7.9	54.0
U 10	330 19.5	53.7	126 36.4	14.0	14 07.9	7.9	54.0
E 11	345 19.6	54.5	141 09.4	14.0	14 15.8	7.8	54.0
S 12	0 19.8	N11 55.4	155 42.4	14.0	S14 23.6	7.7	54.0
D 13	15 19.9	56.2	170 15.4	13.9	14 31.3	7.7	54.0
A 14	30 20.0	57.1	184 48.3	13.9	14 39.0	7.6	54.0
Y 15	45 20.1	·· 57.9	199 21.2	13.9	14 46.6	7.6	54.0
16	60 20.3	58.8	213 54.1	13.8	14 54.2	7.4	54.0
17	75 20.4	11 59.6	228 26.9	13.8	15 01.6	7.5	54.0
18	90 20.5	N12 00.4	242 59.7	13.8	S15 09.1	7.3	54.0
19	105 20.7	01.3	257 32.5	13.7	15 16.4	7.3	54.0
20	120 20.8	02.1	272 05.2	13.7	15 23.7	7.3	54.0
21	135 20.9	·· 03.0	286 37.9	13.6	15 31.0	7.1	54.0
22	150 21.0	03.8	301 10.5	13.6	15 38.1	7.1	54.0
23	165 21.2	04.7	315 43.1	13.6	15 45.2	7.1	54.0
	S.D. 15.9	d 0.9	S.D. 14.7		14.7		14.7

Twilight, Sunrise, Moonrise

Lat.	Naut.	Civil	Sunrise	Moonrise 19	20	21	22
N 72	////	00 58	03 10	20 19	22 06	24 06	00 06
N 70	////	01 58	03 31	20 06	21 42	23 24	25 14
68	////	02 32	03 48	19 55	21 24	22 55	24 27
66	00 50	02 56	04 01	19 46	21 10	22 34	23 57
64	01 43	03 14	04 12	19 38	20 58	22 17	23 35
62	02 14	03 29	04 21	19 32	20 48	22 03	23 17
60	02 36	03 41	04 29	19 26	20 39	21 52	23 02
N 58	02 53	03 52	04 36	19 21	20 32	21 42	22 49
56	03 08	04 01	04 42	19 17	20 25	21 33	22 39
54	03 20	04 09	04 48	19 13	20 19	21 25	22 29
52	03 30	04 16	04 53	19 09	20 14	21 18	22 21
50	03 39	04 23	04 57	19 06	20 09	21 12	22 13
45	03 58	04 36	05 07	18 59	19 59	20 58	21 57
N 40	04 13	04 47	05 15	18 54	19 51	20 47	21 44
35	04 24	04 56	05 22	18 49	19 43	20 38	21 32
30	04 34	05 03	05 28	18 44	19 37	20 30	21 23
20	04 49	05 16	05 38	18 37	19 26	20 16	21 06
N 10	05 01	05 26	05 47	18 31	19 16	20 03	20 51
0	05 10	05 34	05 56	18 24	19 07	19 52	20 38
S 10	05 18	05 42	06 04	18 18	18 59	19 40	20 24
20	05 24	05 50	06 12	18 12	18 49	19 28	20 10
30	05 30	05 58	06 22	18 05	18 38	19 14	19 53
35	05 32	06 02	06 28	18 01	18 32	19 06	19 44
40	05 35	06 06	06 34	17 56	18 25	18 57	19 33
45	05 37	06 11	06 41	17 51	18 17	18 47	19 20
S 50	05 39	06 17	06 50	17 44	18 08	18 34	19 05
52	05 40	06 19	06 54	17 41	18 03	18 28	18 57
54	05 40	06 22	06 58	17 38	17 58	18 22	18 49
56	05 41	06 24	07 03	17 34	17 53	18 14	18 40
58	05 42	06 28	07 08	17 30	17 47	18 06	18 30
S 60	05 42	06 31	07 14	17 26	17 40	17 57	18 19

Twilight, Sunset, Moonset

Lat.	Sunset	Civil	Naut.	Moonset 19	20	21	22
N 72	20 52	23 19	////	04 44	04 31	04 14	03 46
N 70	20 30	22 07	////	04 52	04 46	04 39	04 30
68	20 13	21 31	////	04 59	04 58	04 58	04 59
66	19 59	21 06	23 25	05 05	05 09	05 14	05 21
64	19 48	20 47	22 21	05 10	05 17	05 26	05 39
62	19 38	20 31	21 48	05 14	05 25	05 37	05 53
60	19 30	20 18	21 25	05 18	05 31	05 46	06 05
N 58	19 23	20 08	21 07	05 22	05 37	05 54	06 16
56	19 17	19 58	20 52	05 25	05 42	06 01	06 25
54	19 11	19 50	20 40	05 27	05 47	06 08	06 33
52	19 06	19 43	20 29	05 30	05 51	06 14	06 41
50	19 01	19 36	20 20	05 32	05 54	06 19	06 47
45	18 51	19 23	20 01	05 37	06 03	06 30	07 02
N 40	18 43	19 12	19 46	05 41	06 09	06 40	07 13
35	18 36	19 03	19 34	05 45	06 15	06 48	07 24
30	18 30	18 55	19 24	05 48	06 21	06 55	07 32
20	18 20	18 42	19 09	05 53	06 30	07 08	07 48
N 10	18 11	18 32	18 57	05 58	06 38	07 18	08 01
0	18 02	18 23	18 48	06 03	06 45	07 29	08 14
S 10	17 54	18 15	18 40	06 07	06 53	07 39	08 26
20	17 45	18 08	18 34	06 12	07 01	07 50	08 40
30	17 35	18 00	18 28	06 17	07 10	08 02	08 55
35	17 30	17 56	18 25	06 21	07 15	08 10	09 04
40	17 23	17 51	18 23	06 24	07 21	08 18	09 15
45	17 16	17 46	18 20	06 28	07 28	08 28	09 27
S 50	17 07	17 41	18 18	06 33	07 37	08 39	09 41
52	17 03	17 38	18 17	06 36	07 41	08 45	09 48
54	16 59	17 35	18 16	06 38	07 45	08 51	09 56
56	16 54	17 32	18 16	06 41	07 50	08 58	10 04
58	16 49	17 29	18 15	06 44	07 55	09 05	10 14
S 60	16 42	17 26	18 14	06 48	08 01	09 14	10 25

SUN / MOON

Day	SUN Eqn. of Time 00h	12h	Mer. Pass.	MOON Mer. Pass. Upper	Lower	Age	Phase
	m s	m s	h m	h m	h m	d	
19	00 47	00 53	11 59	24 35	12 13	15	
20	01 00	01 06	11 59	00 35	12 56	16	○
21	01 13	01 19	11 59	01 18	13 40	17	

G.M.T.	ARIES G.H.A.	VENUS −3.4 G.H.A.	Dec.	MARS +1.4 G.H.A.	Dec.	JUPITER −1.9 G.H.A.	Dec.	SATURN +0.8 G.H.A.	Dec.	STARS Name	S.H.A.	Dec.
22 00	209 57.8	176 25.5	N12 35.4	184 15.2	N10 09.8	27 13.7	N 0 31.0	24 45.3	N 0 37.1	Acamar	315 37.4	S40 23.0
01	225 00.3	191 25.0	36.5	199 15.8	10.5	42 16.4	31.1	39 47.9	37.1	Achernar	335 45.6	S57 20.0
02	240 02.8	206 24.5	37.6	214 16.5	11.2	57 19.1	31.2	54 50.6	37.2	Acrux	173 36.2	S62 59.8
03	255 05.2	221 24.0 ··	38.7	229 17.2 ··	11.9	72 21.8 ··	31.2	69 53.2 ··	37.3	Adhara	255 31.9	S28 57.1
04	270 07.7	236 23.5	39.8	244 17.9	12.6	87 24.5	31.3	84 55.8	37.3	Aldebaran	291 17.8	N16 28.2
05	285 10.2	251 23.0	40.9	259 18.6	13.3	102 27.2	31.4	99 58.4	37.4			
06	300 12.6	266 22.5	N12 42.0	274 19.3	N10 14.0	117 29.9	N 0 31.5	115 01.0	N 0 37.4	Alioth	166 41.7	N56 03.8
W 07	315 15.1	281 22.0	43.1	289 20.0	14.7	132 32.6	31.6	130 03.6	37.5	Alkaid	153 17.7	N49 24.5
E 08	330 17.5	296 21.5	44.2	304 20.7	15.4	147 35.2	31.7	145 06.2	37.6	Al Na'ir	28 14.7	S47 03.0
D 09	345 20.0	311 21.0 ··	45.3	319 21.3 ··	16.1	162 37.9 ··	31.8	160 08.8 ··	37.6	Alnilam	276 11.5	S 1 13.0
N 10	0 22.5	326 20.5	46.4	334 22.0	16.8	177 40.6	31.9	175 11.5	37.7	Alphard	218 20.1	S 8 34.8
E 11	15 24.9	341 20.0	47.5	349 22.7	17.5	192 43.3	32.0	190 14.1	37.7			
S 12	30 27.4	356 19.5	N12 48.6	4 23.4	N10 18.2	207 46.0	N 0 32.1	205 16.7	N 0 37.8	Alphecca	126 31.5	N26 46.6
D 13	45 29.9	11 19.0	49.7	19 24.1	18.9	222 48.7	32.2	220 19.3	37.9	Alpheratz	358 09.2	N28 59.0
A 14	60 32.3	26 18.5	50.8	34 24.8	19.6	237 51.4	32.3	235 21.9	37.9	Altair	62 32.1	N 8 49.0
Y 15	75 34.8	41 18.0 ··	51.9	49 25.5 ··	20.3	252 54.1 ··	32.3	250 24.5 ··	38.0	Ankaa	353 40.2	S42 24.5
16	90 37.3	56 17.5	52.9	64 26.1	21.0	267 56.8	32.4	265 27.1	38.0	Antares	112 56.1	S26 23.4
17	105 39.7	71 17.0	54.0	79 26.8	21.6	282 59.5	32.5	280 29.8	38.1			
18	120 42.2	86 16.5	N12 55.1	94 27.5	N10 22.3	298 02.2	N 0 32.6	295 32.4	N 0 38.2	Arcturus	146 17.8	N19 16.8
19	135 44.6	101 16.0	56.2	109 28.2	23.0	313 04.8	32.7	310 35.0	38.2	Atria	108 19.6	S68 59.5
20	150 47.1	116 15.5	57.3	124 28.9	23.7	328 07.5	32.8	325 37.6	38.3	Avior	234 28.0	S59 27.3
21	165 49.6	131 15.0 ··	58.4	139 29.6 ··	24.4	343 10.2 ··	32.9	340 40.2 ··	38.3	Bellatrix	278 58.6	N 6 19.8
22	180 52.0	146 14.5	12 59.5	154 30.3	25.1	358 12.9	33.0	355 42.8	38.4	Betelgeuse	271 28.1	N 7 24.1
23	195 54.5	161 14.0	13 00.6	169 30.9	25.8	13 15.6	33.1	10 45.4	38.4			
23 00	210 57.0	176 13.5	N13 01.7	184 31.6	N10 26.5	28 18.3	N 0 33.2	25 48.0	N 0 38.5	Canopus	264 07.3	S52 41.5
01	225 59.4	191 13.0	02.8	199 32.3	27.2	43 21.0	33.2	40 50.7	38.6	Capella	281 11.1	N45 58.8
02	241 01.9	206 12.5	03.8	214 33.0	27.9	58 23.7	33.3	55 53.3	38.6	Deneb	49 48.2	N45 12.5
03	256 04.4	221 12.0 ··	04.9	229 33.7 ··	28.6	73 26.4 ··	33.4	70 55.9 ··	38.7	Denebola	182 58.4	N14 40.6
04	271 06.8	236 11.5	06.0	244 34.4	29.3	88 29.0	33.5	85 58.5	38.7	Diphda	349 20.8	S18 05.5
05	286 09.3	251 11.0	07.1	259 35.1	30.0	103 31.7	33.6	101 01.1	38.8			
06	301 11.8	266 10.4	N13 08.2	274 35.7	N10 30.7	118 34.4	N 0 33.7	116 03.7	N 0 38.9	Dubhe	194 21.2	N61 51.4
07	316 14.2	281 09.9	09.3	289 36.4	31.4	133 37.1	33.8	131 06.3	38.9	Elnath	278 43.9	N28 35.5
T 08	331 16.7	296 09.4	10.3	304 37.1	32.1	148 39.8	33.9	146 08.9	39.0	Eltanin	90 57.3	N51 29.3
H 09	346 19.1	311 08.9 ··	11.4	319 37.8 ··	32.7	163 42.5 ··	34.0	161 11.5 ··	39.0	Enif	34 11.3	N 9 47.1
U 10	1 21.6	326 08.4	12.5	334 38.5	33.4	178 45.2	34.1	176 14.2	39.1	Fomalhaut	15 51.2	S29 43.3
R 11	16 24.1	341 07.9	13.6	349 39.2	34.1	193 47.9	34.1	191 16.8	39.2			
S 12	31 26.5	356 07.4	N13 14.7	4 39.9	N10 34.8	208 50.5	N 0 34.2	206 19.4	N 0 39.2	Gacrux	172 27.8	S57 00.6
D 13	46 29.0	11 06.9	15.8	19 40.5	35.5	223 53.2	34.3	221 22.0	39.3	Gienah	176 17.3	S17 26.3
A 14	61 31.5	26 06.4	16.8	34 41.2	36.2	238 55.9	34.4	236 24.6	39.3	Hadar	149 22.2	S60 17.0
Y 15	76 33.9	41 05.9 ··	17.9	49 41.9 ··	36.9	253 58.6 ··	34.5	251 27.2 ··	39.4	Hamal	328 28.8	N23 22.2
16	91 36.4	56 05.4	19.0	64 42.6	37.6	269 01.3	34.6	266 29.8	39.4	Kaus Aust.	84 16.2	S34 23.5
17	106 38.9	71 04.9	20.1	79 43.3	38.3	284 04.0	34.7	281 32.4	39.5			
18	121 41.3	86 04.3	N13 21.1	94 44.0	N10 39.0	299 06.7	N 0 34.8	296 35.0	N 0 39.6	Kochab	137 17.9	N74 14.0
19	136 43.8	101 03.8	22.2	109 44.6	39.7	314 09.3	34.9	311 37.7	39.6	Markab	14 03.0	N15 06.0
20	151 46.3	116 03.3	23.3	124 45.3	40.4	329 12.0	34.9	326 40.3	39.7	Menkar	314 41.1	N 4 00.8
21	166 48.7	131 02.8 ··	24.4	139 46.0 ··	41.0	344 14.7 ··	35.0	341 42.9 ··	39.7	Menkent	148 36.2	S36 16.7
22	181 51.2	146 02.3	25.5	154 46.7	41.7	359 17.4	35.1	356 45.5	39.8	Miaplacidus	221 44.6	S69 38.7
23	196 53.6	161 01.8	26.5	169 47.4	42.4	14 20.1	35.2	11 48.1	39.8			
24 00	211 56.1	176 01.3	N13 27.6	184 48.1	N10 43.1	29 22.8	N 0 35.3	26 50.7	N 0 39.9	Mirfak	309 16.0	N49 47.6
01	226 58.6	191 00.8	28.7	199 48.8	43.8	44 25.4	35.4	41 53.3	40.0	Nunki	76 28.6	S26 19.2
02	242 01.0	206 00.2	29.7	214 49.4	44.5	59 28.1	35.5	56 55.9	40.0	Peacock	53 57.8	S56 47.6
03	257 03.5	220 59.7 ··	30.8	229 50.1 ··	45.2	74 30.8 ··	35.6	71 58.5 ··	40.1	Pollux	243 57.8	N28 04.4
04	272 06.0	235 59.2	31.9	244 50.8	45.9	89 33.5	35.6	87 01.1	40.1	Procyon	245 25.5	N 5 16.3
05	287 08.4	250 58.7	33.0	259 51.5	46.6	104 36.2	35.7	102 03.7	40.2			
06	302 10.9	265 58.2	N13 34.0	274 52.2	N10 47.2	119 38.9	N 0 35.8	117 06.4	N 0 40.2	Rasalhague	96 29.0	N12 34.3
07	317 13.4	280 57.7	35.1	289 52.9	47.9	134 41.5	35.9	132 09.0	40.3	Regulus	208 09.5	N12 03.5
08	332 15.8	295 57.1	36.2	304 53.5	48.6	149 44.2	36.0	147 11.6	40.4	Rigel	281 35.9	S 8 13.6
F 09	347 18.3	310 56.6 ··	37.3	319 54.2 ··	49.3	164 46.9 ··	36.1	162 14.2 ··	40.4	Rigil Kent.	140 24.7	S60 45.4
R 10	2 20.8	325 56.1	38.3	334 54.9	50.0	179 49.6	36.2	177 16.8	40.5	Sabik	102 40.5	S15 42.1
I 11	17 23.2	340 55.6	39.4	349 55.6	50.7	194 52.3	36.3	192 19.4	40.5			
D 12	32 25.7	355 55.1	N13 40.4	4 56.3	N10 51.4	209 54.9	N 0 36.3	207 22.0	N 0 40.6	Schedar	350 09.1	N56 25.8
A 13	47 28.1	10 54.6	41.5	19 57.0	52.1	224 57.6	36.4	222 24.6	40.6	Shaula	96 55.0	S37 05.3
Y 14	62 30.6	25 54.0	42.6	34 57.6	52.7	240 00.3	36.5	237 27.2	40.7	Sirius	258 55.5	S16 41.7
15	77 33.1	40 53.5 ··	43.6	49 58.3 ··	53.4	255 03.0 ··	36.6	252 29.8 ··	40.8	Spica	158 56.8	S11 03.8
16	92 35.5	55 53.0	44.7	64 59.0	54.1	270 05.7	36.7	267 32.4	40.8	Suhail	223 10.4	S43 21.7
17	107 38.0	70 52.5	45.8	79 59.7	54.8	285 08.3	36.8	282 35.0	40.9			
18	122 40.5	85 52.0	N13 46.8	95 00.4	N10 55.5	300 11.0	N 0 36.9	297 37.7	N 0 40.9	Vega	80 55.4	N38 45.7
19	137 42.9	100 51.4	47.9	110 01.1	56.2	315 13.7	36.9	312 40.3	41.0	Zuben'ubi	137 32.3	S15 57.9
20	152 45.4	115 50.9	49.0	125 01.7	56.9	330 16.4	37.0	327 42.9	41.0		S.H.A.	Mer. Pass.
21	167 47.9	130 50.4 ··	50.0	140 02.4 ··	57.5	345 19.1 ··	37.1	342 45.5 ··	41.1		° '	h m
22	182 50.3	145 49.9	51.1	155 03.1	58.2	0 21.7	37.2	357 48.1	41.2	Venus	325 16.5	12 16
23	197 52.8	160 49.3	52.2	170 03.8	58.9	15 24.4	37.3	12 50.7	41.2	Mars	333 34.7	11 41
Mer. Pass.	h m 9 54.6	v −0.5	d 1.1	v 0.7	d 0.7	v 2.7	d 0.1	v 2.6	d 0.1	Jupiter	177 21.3	22 03
										Saturn	174 51.1	22 13

G.M.T.	SUN G.H.A.	Dec.	MOON G.H.A.	v	Dec.	d	H.P.
22 00	180 21.3	N12 05.5	330 15.7	13.5	S15 52.3	6.9	54.0
01	195 21.4	06.4	344 48.2	13.5	15 59.2	6.9	54.1
02	210 21.5	07.2	359 20.7	13.5	16 06.1	6.9	54.1
03	225 21.7	·· 08.0	13 53.2	13.4	16 13.0	6.7	54.1
04	240 21.8	08.9	28 25.6	13.4	16 19.7	6.7	54.1
05	255 21.9	09.7	42 58.0	13.3	16 26.4	6.6	54.1
W 06	270 22.0	N12 10.6	57 30.3	13.3	S16 33.0	6.6	54.1
E 07	285 22.2	11.4	72 02.6	13.2	16 39.6	6.5	54.1
D 08	300 22.3	12.2	86 34.8	13.3	16 46.1	6.4	54.1
N 09	315 22.4	·· 13.1	101 07.1	13.1	16 52.5	6.3	54.1
E 10	330 22.5	13.9	115 39.2	13.2	16 58.8	6.3	54.1
S 11	345 22.6	14.8	130 11.4	13.1	17 05.1	6.2	54.1
D 12	0 22.8	N12 15.6	144 43.5	13.0	S17 11.3	6.1	54.1
A 13	15 22.9	16.4	159 15.5	13.0	17 17.4	6.0	54.1
Y 14	30 23.0	17.3	173 47.5	13.0	17 23.4	6.0	54.1
15	45 23.1	·· 18.1	188 19.5	13.0	17 29.4	5.9	54.2
16	60 23.3	19.0	202 51.5	12.9	17 35.3	5.8	54.2
17	75 23.4	19.8	217 23.4	12.8	17 41.1	5.7	54.2
18	90 23.5	N12 20.6	231 55.2	12.8	S17 46.8	5.7	54.2
19	105 23.6	21.5	246 27.0	12.8	17 52.5	5.6	54.2
20	120 23.7	22.3	260 58.8	12.7	17 58.1	5.5	54.2
21	135 23.9	·· 23.1	275 30.5	12.7	18 03.6	5.4	54.2
22	150 24.0	24.0	290 02.2	12.7	18 09.0	5.3	54.2
23	165 24.1	24.8	304 33.9	12.6	18 14.3	5.3	54.2
23 00	180 24.2	N12 25.6	319 05.5	12.6	S18 19.6	5.2	54.2
01	195 24.3	26.5	333 37.1	12.5	18 24.8	5.1	54.2
02	210 24.5	27.3	348 08.6	12.5	18 29.9	5.0	54.3
03	225 24.6	·· 28.1	2 40.1	12.5	18 34.9	4.9	54.3
04	240 24.7	29.0	17 11.6	12.4	18 39.8	4.9	54.3
05	255 24.8	29.8	31 43.0	12.4	18 44.7	4.8	54.3
06	270 24.9	N12 30.6	46 14.4	12.3	S18 49.5	4.7	54.3
07	285 25.1	31.5	60 45.7	12.3	18 54.2	4.6	54.3
T 08	300 25.2	32.3	75 17.0	12.2	18 58.8	4.5	54.3
H 09	315 25.3	·· 33.1	89 48.2	12.3	19 03.3	4.4	54.3
U 10	330 25.4	34.0	104 19.5	12.1	19 07.7	4.3	54.4
R 11	345 25.5	34.8	118 50.6	12.2	19 12.0	4.3	54.4
S 12	0 25.7	N12 35.6	133 21.8	12.1	S19 16.3	4.2	54.4
D 13	15 25.8	36.5	147 52.9	12.0	19 20.5	4.1	54.4
A 14	30 25.9	37.3	162 23.9	12.1	19 24.6	4.0	54.4
Y 15	45 26.0	·· 38.1	176 55.0	12.0	19 28.6	3.9	54.4
16	60 26.1	38.9	191 26.0	11.9	19 32.5	3.8	54.4
17	75 26.2	39.8	205 56.9	11.9	19 36.3	3.7	54.4
18	90 26.4	N12 40.6	220 27.8	11.9	S19 40.0	3.6	54.5
19	105 26.5	41.4	234 58.7	11.8	19 43.6	3.5	54.5
20	120 26.6	42.3	249 29.5	11.8	19 47.2	3.4	54.5
21	135 26.7	·· 43.1	264 00.3	11.8	19 50.6	3.4	54.5
22	150 26.8	43.9	278 31.1	11.7	19 54.0	3.3	54.5
23	165 26.9	44.7	293 01.8	11.7	19 57.3	3.2	54.5
24 00	180 27.1	N12 45.6	307 32.5	11.6	S20 00.5	3.1	54.5
01	195 27.2	46.4	322 03.1	11.6	20 03.6	2.9	54.6
02	210 27.3	47.2	336 33.7	11.6	20 06.5	2.9	54.6
03	225 27.4	·· 48.0	351 04.3	11.5	20 09.4	2.9	54.6
04	240 27.5	48.9	5 34.8	11.5	20 12.3	2.7	54.6
05	255 27.6	49.7	20 05.3	11.5	20 15.0	2.6	54.6
06	270 27.7	N12 50.5	34 35.8	11.5	S20 17.6	2.5	54.6
07	285 27.9	51.3	49 06.3	11.3	20 20.1	2.4	54.7
08	300 28.0	52.2	63 36.6	11.4	20 22.5	2.4	54.7
F 09	315 28.1	·· 53.0	78 07.0	11.3	20 24.9	2.2	54.7
R 10	330 28.2	53.8	92 37.3	11.3	20 27.1	2.1	54.7
I 11	345 28.3	54.6	107 07.6	11.3	20 29.2	2.1	54.7
D 12	0 28.4	N12 55.5	121 37.9	11.2	S20 31.3	1.9	54.7
A 13	15 28.5	56.3	136 08.1	11.2	20 33.2	1.9	54.8
Y 14	30 28.7	57.1	150 38.3	11.2	20 35.1	1.7	54.8
15	45 28.8	·· 57.9	165 08.5	11.1	20 36.8	1.7	54.8
16	60 28.9	58.7	179 38.6	11.1	20 38.5	1.5	54.8
17	75 29.0	12 59.6	194 08.7	11.0	20 40.0	1.5	54.8
18	90 29.1	N13 00.4	208 38.8	11.1	S20 41.5	1.3	54.9
19	105 29.2	01.2	223 08.9	11.0	20 42.8	1.2	54.9
20	120 29.3	02.0	237 38.9	10.9	20 44.0	1.2	54.9
21	135 29.4	·· 02.8	252 08.8	11.0	20 45.2	1.0	54.9
22	150 29.5	03.7	266 38.8	10.9	20 46.2	1.0	54.9
23	165 29.7	04.5	281 08.7	10.9	20 47.2	0.8	55.0
	S.D. 15.9	*d* 0.8	S.D. 14.7		14.8		14.9

Lat.	Twilight Naut.	Civil	Sunrise	Moonrise 22	23	24	25
°	h m	h m	h m	h m	h m	h m	h m
N 72	////	////	02 51	00 06	■	■	■
N 70	////	01 31	03 16	25 14	01 14	■	■
68	////	02 13	03 34	24 27	00 27	01 56	03 09
66	////	02 41	03 49	23 57	25 15	01 15	02 19
64	01 19	03 01	04 02	23 35	24 46	00 46	01 48
62	01 57	03 18	04 12	23 17	24 25	00 25	01 24
60	02 23	03 32	04 21	23 02	24 08	00 08	01 05
N 58	02 42	03 43	04 28	22 49	23 53	24 50	00 50
56	02 58	03 53	04 35	22 39	23 41	24 37	00 37
54	03 11	04 02	04 41	22 29	23 30	24 25	00 25
52	03 22	04 10	04 47	22 21	23 20	24 15	00 15
50	03 32	04 16	04 52	22 13	23 12	24 06	00 06
45	03 52	04 31	05 02	21 57	22 53	23 47	24 36
N 40	04 08	04 42	05 11	21 44	22 39	23 31	24 21
35	04 20	04 52	05 18	21 32	22 26	23 18	24 08
30	04 31	05 00	05 25	21 23	22 15	23 07	23 57
20	04 47	05 13	05 36	21 06	21 57	22 47	23 37
N 10	04 59	05 24	05 46	20 51	21 40	22 30	23 20
0	05 09	05 34	05 55	20 38	21 25	22 14	23 05
S 10	05 18	05 42	06 04	20 24	21 10	21 58	22 49
20	05 25	05 51	06 13	20 10	20 54	21 42	22 32
30	05 31	05 59	06 24	19 53	20 36	21 22	22 13
35	05 34	06 04	06 30	19 44	20 25	21 11	22 01
40	05 37	06 09	06 37	19 33	20 13	20 58	21 48
45	05 40	06 15	06 45	19 20	19 58	20 42	21 33
S 50	05 43	06 21	06 54	19 05	19 41	20 24	21 14
52	05 44	06 24	06 59	18 57	19 32	20 15	21 05
54	05 45	06 27	07 03	18 49	19 23	20 05	20 55
56	05 46	06 30	07 09	18 40	19 13	19 54	20 44
58	05 48	06 34	07 15	18 30	19 01	19 41	20 31
S 60	05 49	06 38	07 22	18 19	18 47	19 26	20 16

Lat.	Sunset	Twilight Civil	Naut.	Moonset 22	23	24	25
°	h m	h m	h m	h m	h m	h m	h m
N 72	21 10	////	////	03 46	■	■	■
N 70	20 44	22 35	////	04 30	04 15	■	■
68	20 25	21 49	////	04 59	05 03	05 13	05 43
66	20 10	21 20	////	05 21	05 33	05 55	06 33
64	19 57	20 58	22 45	05 39	05 56	06 23	07 05
62	19 47	20 41	22 04	05 53	06 15	06 45	07 28
60	19 38	20 27	21 38	06 05	06 30	07 03	07 47
N 58	19 30	20 15	21 17	06 16	06 43	07 18	08 02
56	19 23	20 05	21 01	06 25	06 54	07 30	08 16
54	19 17	19 56	20 47	06 33	07 04	07 41	08 27
52	19 11	19 48	20 36	06 41	07 13	07 51	08 37
50	19 06	19 41	20 26	06 47	07 20	08 00	08 46
45	18 55	19 27	20 05	07 02	07 37	08 18	09 06
N 40	18 46	19 15	19 50	07 13	07 51	08 33	09 21
35	18 39	19 05	19 37	07 24	08 03	08 46	09 34
30	18 32	18 57	19 27	07 32	08 13	08 57	09 46
20	18 21	18 43	19 10	07 48	08 31	09 16	10 05
N 10	18 11	18 32	18 58	08 01	08 46	09 33	10 23
0	18 02	18 23	18 47	08 14	09 00	09 49	10 38
S 10	17 53	18 14	18 39	08 26	09 15	10 04	10 54
20	17 43	18 06	18 32	08 40	09 30	10 21	11 11
30	17 32	17 57	18 25	08 55	09 48	10 40	11 31
35	17 26	17 52	18 22	09 04	09 58	10 51	11 42
40	17 19	17 47	18 19	09 15	10 10	11 04	11 55
45	17 11	17 41	18 16	09 27	10 24	11 19	12 11
S 50	17 02	17 35	18 13	09 41	10 41	11 38	12 30
52	16 57	17 32	18 12	09 48	10 49	11 47	12 39
54	16 52	17 29	18 10	09 56	10 58	11 57	12 49
56	16 47	17 26	18 09	10 04	11 08	12 08	13 00
58	16 41	17 22	18 08	10 14	11 20	12 20	13 13
S 60	16 34	17 18	18 07	10 25	11 33	12 35	13 28

Day	SUN Eqn. of Time 00h	12h	Mer. Pass.	MOON Mer. Pass. Upper	Lower	Age	Phase
	m s	m s	h m	h m	h m	d	
22	01 25	01 31	11 58	02 03	14 26	18	
23	01 37	01 42	11 58	02 49	15 13	19	
24	01 48	01 53	11 58	03 37	16 01	20	

G.M.T.	ARIES G.H.A.	VENUS −3.4 G.H.A.	Dec.	MARS +1.5 G.H.A.	Dec.	JUPITER −1.9 G.H.A.	Dec.	SATURN +0.8 G.H.A.	Dec.	STARS Name	S.H.A.	Dec.
25 00	212 55.2	175 48.8	N13 53.2	185 04.5	N10 59.6	30 27.1	N 0 37.4	27 53.3	N 0 41.3	Acamar	315 37.4	S40 23.0
01	227 57.7	190 48.3	54.3	200 05.2	11 00.3	45 29.8	37.5	42 55.9	41.3	Achernar	335 45.6	S57 20.0
02	243 00.2	205 47.8	55.3	215 05.8	01.0	60 32.5	37.5	57 58.5	41.4	Acrux	173 36.2	S62 59.8
03	258 02.6	220 47.2 ··	56.4	230 06.5 ··	01.6	75 35.1 ··	37.6	73 01.1 ··	41.4	Adhara	255 32.0	S28 57.1
04	273 05.1	235 46.7	57.4	245 07.2	02.3	90 37.8	37.7	88 03.7	41.5	Aldebaran	291 17.8	N16 28.2
05	288 07.6	250 46.2	58.5	260 07.9	03.0	105 40.5	37.8	103 06.3	41.5			
06	303 10.0	265 45.7	N13 59.6	275 08.6	N11 03.7	120 43.2	N 0 37.9	118 08.9	N 0 41.6	Alioth	166 41.7	N56 03.8
07	318 12.5	280 45.1	14 00.6	290 09.2	04.4	135 45.8	38.0	133 11.6	41.7	Alkaid	153 17.7	N49 24.5
S 08	333 15.0	295 44.6	01.7	305 09.9	05.1	150 48.5	38.1	148 14.2	41.7	Al Na'ir	28 14.6	S47 03.0
A 09	348 17.4	310 44.1 ··	02.7	320 10.6 ··	05.7	165 51.2 ··	38.1	163 16.8 ··	41.8	Alnilam	276 11.5	S 1 13.0
T 10	3 19.9	325 43.6	03.8	335 11.3	06.4	180 53.9	38.2	178 19.4	41.8	Alphard	218 20.1	S 8 34.8
U 11	18 22.4	340 43.0	04.8	350 12.0	07.1	195 56.6	38.3	193 22.0	41.9			
R 12	33 24.8	355 42.5	N14 05.9	5 12.7	N11 07.8	210 59.2	N 0 38.4	208 24.6	N 0 41.9	Alphecca	126 31.4	N26 46.6
D 13	48 27.3	10 42.0	06.9	20 13.3	08.5	226 01.9	38.5	223 27.2	42.0	Alpheratz	358 09.2	N28 59.0
A 14	63 29.7	25 41.4	08.0	35 14.0	09.2	241 04.6	38.6	238 29.8	42.1	Altair	62 32.1	N 8 49.0
Y 15	78 32.2	40 40.9 ··	09.0	50 14.7 ··	09.8	256 07.3 ··	38.6	253 32.4 ··	42.1	Ankaa	353 40.2	S42 24.5
16	93 34.7	55 40.4	10.1	65 15.4	10.5	271 09.9	38.7	268 35.0	42.2	Antares	112 56.1	S26 23.4
17	108 37.1	70 39.9	11.1	80 16.1	11.2	286 12.6	38.8	283 37.6	42.2			
18	123 39.6	85 39.3	N14 12.2	95 16.8	N11 11.9	301 15.3	N 0 38.9	298 40.2	N 0 42.3	Arcturus	146 17.8	N19 16.8
19	138 42.1	100 38.8	13.2	110 17.4	12.6	316 18.0	39.0	313 42.8	42.3	Atria	108 19.5	S68 59.5
20	153 44.5	115 38.3	14.3	125 18.1	13.2	331 20.6	39.1	328 45.4	42.4	Avior	234 28.1	S59 27.3
21	168 47.0	130 37.7 ··	15.3	140 18.8 ··	13.9	346 23.3 ··	39.1	343 48.0 ··	42.4	Bellatrix	278 58.6	N 6 19.8
22	183 49.5	145 37.2	16.4	155 19.5	14.6	1 26.0	39.2	358 50.6	42.5	Betelgeuse	271 28.1	N 7 24.1
23	198 51.9	160 36.7	17.4	170 20.2	15.3	16 28.6	39.3	13 53.2	42.6			
26 00	213 54.4	175 36.1	N14 18.5	185 20.8	N11 16.0	31 31.3	N 0 39.4	28 55.8	N 0 42.6	Canopus	264 07.3	S52 41.5
01	228 56.9	190 35.6	19.5	200 21.5	16.6	46 34.0	39.5	43 58.5	42.7	Capella	281 11.1	N45 58.8
02	243 59.3	205 35.1	20.6	215 22.2	17.3	61 36.7	39.5	59 01.1	42.7	Deneb	49 48.2	N45 12.5
03	259 01.8	220 34.5 ··	21.6	230 22.9 ··	18.0	76 39.3 ··	39.6	74 03.7 ··	42.8	Denebola	182 58.4	N14 40.6
04	274 04.2	235 34.0	22.7	245 23.6	18.7	91 42.0	39.7	89 06.3	42.8	Diphda	349 20.8	S18 05.5
05	289 06.7	250 33.5	23.7	260 24.2	19.3	106 44.7	39.8	104 08.9	42.9			
06	304 09.2	265 32.9	N14 24.7	275 24.9	N11 20.0	121 47.4	N 0 39.9	119 11.5	N 0 42.9	Dubhe	194 21.3	N61 51.4
07	319 11.6	280 32.4	25.8	290 25.6	20.7	136 50.0	40.0	134 14.1	43.0	Elnath	278 43.9	N28 35.5
08	334 14.1	295 31.8	26.8	305 26.3	21.4	151 52.7	40.1	149 16.7	43.0	Eltanin	90 57.2	N51 29.3
S 09	349 16.6	310 31.3 ··	27.9	320 27.0 ··	22.1	166 55.4 ··	40.1	164 19.3 ··	43.1	Enif	34 11.3	N 9 47.1
U 10	4 19.0	325 30.8	28.9	335 27.7	22.7	181 58.0	40.2	179 21.9	43.2	Fomalhaut	15 51.2	S29 43.3
N 11	19 21.5	340 30.2	30.0	350 28.3	23.4	197 00.7	40.3	194 24.5	43.2			
D 12	34 24.0	355 29.7	N14 31.0	5 29.0	N11 24.1	212 03.4	N 0 40.4	209 27.1	N 0 43.3	Gacrux	172 27.8	S57 00.6
A 13	49 26.4	10 29.2	32.0	20 29.7	24.8	227 06.1	40.5	224 29.7	43.3	Gienah	176 17.3	S17 26.3
Y 14	64 28.9	25 28.6	33.1	35 30.4	25.4	242 08.7	40.5	239 32.3	43.4	Hadar	149 22.1	S60 17.0
15	79 31.3	40 28.1 ··	34.1	50 31.1 ··	26.1	257 11.4 ··	40.6	254 34.9 ··	43.4	Hamal	328 28.8	N23 22.2
16	94 33.8	55 27.5	35.1	65 31.7	26.8	272 14.1	40.7	269 37.5	43.5	Kaus Aust.	84 16.1	S34 23.5
17	109 36.3	70 27.0	36.2	80 32.4	27.5	287 16.7	40.8	284 40.1	43.5			
18	124 38.7	85 26.4	N14 37.2	95 33.1	N11 28.1	302 19.4	N 0 40.9	299 42.7	N 0 43.6	Kochab	137 17.9	N74 14.0
19	139 41.2	100 25.9	38.2	110 33.8	28.8	317 22.1	41.0	314 45.3	43.6	Markab	14 03.0	N15 06.0
20	154 43.7	115 25.4	39.3	125 34.5	29.5	332 24.7	41.0	329 47.9	43.7	Menkar	314 41.0	N 4 00.8
21	169 46.1	130 24.8 ··	40.3	140 35.1 ··	30.2	347 27.4 ··	41.1	344 50.5 ··	43.7	Menkent	148 36.2	S36 16.7
22	184 48.6	145 24.3	41.3	155 35.8	30.8	2 30.1	41.2	359 53.1	43.8	Miaplacidus	221 44.7	S69 38.7
23	199 51.1	160 23.7	42.4	170 36.5	31.5	17 32.7	41.3	14 55.7	43.9			
27 00	214 53.5	175 23.2	N14 43.4	185 37.2	N11 32.2	32 35.4	N 0 41.4	29 58.3	N 0 43.9	Mirfak	309 16.0	N49 47.6
01	229 56.0	190 22.6	44.4	200 37.9	32.9	47 38.1	41.4	45 00.9	44.0	Nunki	76 28.5	S26 19.2
02	244 58.5	205 22.1	45.5	215 38.5	33.5	62 40.8	41.5	60 03.5	44.0	Peacock	53 57.8	S56 47.5
03	260 00.9	220 21.6 ··	46.5	230 39.2 ··	34.2	77 43.4 ··	41.6	75 06.1 ··	44.1	Pollux	243 57.8	N28 04.4
04	275 03.4	235 21.0	47.5	245 39.9	34.9	92 46.1	41.7	90 08.7	44.1	Procyon	245 25.5	N 5 16.3
05	290 05.8	250 20.5	48.5	260 40.6	35.6	107 48.8	41.8	105 11.3	44.2			
06	305 08.3	265 19.9	N14 49.6	275 41.3	N11 36.2	122 51.4	N 0 41.8	120 13.9	N 0 44.2	Rasalhague	96 29.0	N12 34.3
07	320 10.8	280 19.4	50.6	290 41.9	36.9	137 54.1	41.9	135 16.5	44.3	Regulus	208 09.5	N12 03.5
08	335 13.2	295 18.8	51.6	305 42.6	37.6	152 56.8	42.0	150 19.1	44.3	Rigel	281 35.9	S 8 13.6
M 09	350 15.7	310 18.3 ··	52.7	320 43.3 ··	38.3	167 59.4 ··	42.1	165 21.7 ··	44.4	Rigil Kent.	140 24.6	S60 45.4
O 10	5 18.2	325 17.7	53.7	335 44.0	38.9	183 02.1	42.2	180 24.4	44.4	Sabik	102 40.4	S15 42.1
N 11	20 20.6	340 17.2	54.7	350 44.7	39.6	198 04.7	42.2	195 27.0	44.5			
D 12	35 23.1	355 16.6	N14 55.7	5 45.3	N11 40.3	213 07.4	N 0 42.3	210 29.6	N 0 44.6	Schedar	350 09.1	N56 25.8
A 13	50 25.6	10 16.1	56.7	20 46.0	40.9	228 10.1	42.4	225 32.2	44.6	Shaula	96 54.9	S37 05.3
Y 14	65 28.0	25 15.5	57.8	35 46.7	41.6	243 12.7	42.5	240 34.8	44.7	Sirius	258 55.5	S16 41.7
15	80 30.5	40 15.0 ··	58.8	50 47.4 ··	42.3	258 15.4 ··	42.6	255 37.4 ··	44.7	Spica	158 56.8	S11 03.9
16	95 33.0	55 14.4	14 59.8	65 48.0	43.0	273 18.1	42.6	270 40.0	44.8	Suhail	223 10.4	S43 21.7
17	110 35.4	70 13.9	15 00.8	80 48.7	43.6	288 20.7	42.7	285 42.6	44.8			
18	125 37.9	85 13.3	N15 01.9	95 49.4	N11 44.3	303 23.4	N 0 42.8	300 45.2	N 0 44.9	Vega	80 55.4	N38 45.7
19	140 40.3	100 12.8	02.9	110 50.1	45.0	318 26.1	42.9	315 47.8	44.9	Zuben'ubi	137 32.3	S15 57.9
20	155 42.8	115 12.2	03.9	125 50.8	45.6	333 28.7	42.9	330 50.4	45.0			
21	170 45.3	130 11.7 ··	04.9	140 51.4 ··	46.3	348 31.4 ··	43.0	345 53.0 ··	45.0		S.H.A.	Mer. Pass.
22	185 47.7	145 11.1	05.9	155 52.1	47.0	3 34.1	43.1	0 55.6	45.1	Venus	321 41.7	12 18
23	200 50.2	160 10.5	06.9	170 52.8	47.6	18 36.7	43.2	15 58.2	45.1	Mars	331 26.5	11 38
Mer. Pass.	h m 9 42.8	v −0.5	d 1.0	v 0.7	d 0.7	v 2.7	d 0.1	v 2.6	d 0.1	Jupiter	177 36.9	21 50
										Saturn	175 01.5	22 00

SUN / MOON

G.M.T.	SUN G.H.A.	SUN Dec.	MOON G.H.A.	v	MOON Dec.	d	H.P.
25 00	180 29.8	N13 05.3	295 38.6	10.9	S20 48.0	0.8	55.0
01	195 29.9	06.1	310 08.5	10.8	20 48.8	0.6	55.0
02	210 30.0	06.9	324 38.3	10.8	20 49.4	0.6	55.1
03	225 30.1	.. 07.7	339 08.1	10.8	20 50.0	0.4	55.1
04	240 30.2	08.6	353 37.9	10.7	20 50.4	0.3	55.1
05	255 30.3	09.4	8 07.6	10.8	20 50.7	0.2	55.1
06	270 30.4	N13 10.2	22 37.4	10.7	S20 50.9	0.2	55.1
07	285 30.5	11.0	37 07.1	10.6	20 51.1	0.0	55.1
S 08	300 30.6	11.8	51 36.7	10.7	20 51.1	0.1	55.2
A 09	315 30.8	.. 12.6	66 06.4	10.6	20 51.0	0.1	55.2
T 10	330 30.9	13.4	80 36.0	10.6	20 50.8	0.3	55.2
U 11	345 31.0	14.3	95 05.6	10.6	20 50.5	0.4	55.2
R 12	0 31.1	N13 15.1	109 35.2	10.6	S20 50.1	0.5	55.3
D 13	15 31.2	15.9	124 04.8	10.5	20 49.6	0.6	55.3
A 14	30 31.3	16.7	138 34.3	10.5	20 49.0	0.7	55.3
Y 15	45 31.4	.. 17.5	153 03.8	10.5	20 48.3	0.8	55.3
16	60 31.5	18.3	167 33.3	10.4	20 47.5	0.9	55.4
17	75 31.6	19.1	182 02.7	10.5	20 46.6	1.0	55.4
18	90 31.7	N13 19.9	196 32.2	10.4	S20 45.6	1.2	55.4
19	105 31.8	20.7	211 01.6	10.4	20 44.4	1.2	55.4
20	120 31.9	21.6	225 31.0	10.4	20 43.2	1.4	55.5
21	135 32.0	.. 22.4	240 00.4	10.4	20 41.8	1.4	55.5
22	150 32.1	23.2	254 29.8	10.3	20 40.4	1.6	55.5
23	165 32.2	24.0	268 59.1	10.3	20 38.8	1.6	55.5
26 00	180 32.4	N13 24.8	283 28.4	10.3	S20 37.2	1.8	55.6
01	195 32.5	25.6	297 57.7	10.3	20 35.4	1.9	55.6
02	210 32.6	26.4	312 27.0	10.3	20 33.5	2.0	55.6
03	225 32.7	.. 27.2	326 56.3	10.2	20 31.5	2.1	55.6
04	240 32.8	28.0	341 25.5	10.3	20 29.4	2.2	55.7
05	255 32.9	28.8	355 54.8	10.2	20 27.2	2.3	55.7
06	270 33.0	N13 29.6	10 24.0	10.2	S20 24.9	2.4	55.7
07	285 33.1	30.4	24 53.2	10.2	20 22.5	2.5	55.8
S 08	300 33.2	31.2	39 22.4	10.2	20 20.0	2.6	55.8
U 09	315 33.3	.. 32.0	53 51.6	10.1	20 17.4	2.8	55.8
N 10	330 33.4	32.9	68 20.7	10.2	20 14.6	2.8	55.8
D 11	345 33.5	33.7	82 49.9	10.1	20 11.8	3.0	55.9
A 12	0 33.6	N13 34.5	97 19.0	10.1	S20 08.8	3.0	55.9
Y 13	15 33.7	35.3	111 48.1	10.2	20 05.8	3.2	55.9
14	30 33.8	36.1	126 17.3	10.1	20 02.6	3.3	56.0
15	45 33.9	.. 36.9	140 46.4	10.0	19 59.3	3.4	56.0
16	60 34.0	37.7	155 15.4	10.1	19 55.9	3.4	56.0
17	75 34.1	38.5	169 44.5	10.1	19 52.5	3.6	56.1
18	90 34.2	N13 39.3	184 13.6	10.0	S19 48.9	3.7	56.1
19	105 34.3	40.1	198 42.6	10.1	19 45.2	3.9	56.1
20	120 34.4	40.9	213 11.7	10.0	19 41.3	3.9	56.1
21	135 34.5	.. 41.7	227 40.7	10.0	19 37.4	4.0	56.2
22	150 34.6	42.5	242 09.7	10.0	19 33.4	4.1	56.2
23	165 34.7	43.3	256 38.7	10.0	19 29.3	4.3	56.2
27 00	180 34.8	N13 44.1	271 07.7	10.0	S19 25.0	4.3	56.3
01	195 34.9	44.9	285 36.7	10.0	19 20.7	4.5	56.3
02	210 35.0	45.7	300 05.7	10.0	19 16.2	4.5	56.3
03	225 35.1	.. 46.5	314 34.7	10.0	19 11.7	4.7	56.4
04	240 35.2	47.3	329 03.7	9.9	19 07.0	4.8	56.4
05	255 35.3	48.1	343 32.6	10.0	19 02.2	4.9	56.4
06	270 35.4	N13 48.9	358 01.6	10.0	S18 57.3	5.0	56.5
07	285 35.5	49.7	12 30.6	9.9	18 52.3	5.0	56.5
08	300 35.6	50.5	26 59.5	9.9	18 47.3	5.2	56.5
M 09	315 35.7	.. 51.3	41 28.4	10.0	18 42.1	5.4	56.6
O 10	330 35.8	52.0	55 57.4	9.9	18 36.7	5.4	56.6
N 11	345 35.9	52.8	70 26.3	9.9	18 31.3	5.5	56.6
D 12	0 36.0	N13 53.6	84 55.2	10.0	S18 25.8	5.6	56.7
A 13	15 36.1	54.4	99 24.2	9.9	18 20.2	5.7	56.7
Y 14	30 36.2	55.2	113 53.1	9.9	18 14.5	5.9	56.7
15	45 36.3	.. 56.0	128 22.0	9.9	18 08.6	5.9	56.8
16	60 36.4	56.8	142 50.9	9.9	18 02.7	6.0	56.8
17	75 36.5	57.6	157 19.8	9.9	17 56.7	6.2	56.9
18	90 36.6	N13 58.4	171 48.7	9.9	S17 50.5	6.2	56.9
19	105 36.7	13 59.2	186 17.6	9.9	17 44.3	6.4	56.9
20	120 36.8	14 00.0	200 46.5	9.9	17 37.9	6.4	57.0
21	135 36.9	.. 00.8	215 15.4	9.8	17 31.5	6.6	57.0
22	150 36.9	01.6	229 44.2	9.9	17 24.9	6.6	57.0
23	165 37.0	02.3	244 13.1	9.9	17 18.3	6.8	57.1
	S.D. 15.9	d 0.8	S.D. 15.1		15.2		15.4

Twilight / Sunrise / Moonrise

Lat.	Naut.	Civil	Sunrise	Moonrise 25	26	27	28
N 72	////	////	02 31	■	■	---	05 25
N 70	////	00 54	03 00	■	■	04 56	04 39
68	////	01 52	03 21	03 09	03 48	04 03	04 08
66	////	02 25	03 38	02 19	03 03	03 30	03 45
64	00 47	02 48	03 51	01 48	02 34	03 06	03 27
62	01 39	03 07	04 02	01 24	02 11	02 46	03 12
60	02 09	03 22	04 12	01 05	01 53	02 31	02 59
N 58	02 31	03 34	04 21	00 50	01 38	02 17	02 48
56	02 48	03 45	04 28	00 37	01 25	02 06	02 39
54	03 02	03 55	04 35	00 25	01 14	01 56	02 30
52	03 15	04 03	04 40	00 15	01 04	01 46	02 23
50	03 25	04 10	04 46	00 06	00 55	01 38	02 16
45	03 47	04 26	04 57	24 36	00 36	01 21	02 01
N 40	04 03	04 38	05 07	24 21	00 21	01 07	01 49
35	04 16	04 48	05 15	24 08	00 08	00 55	01 39
30	04 27	04 57	05 22	23 57	24 44	00 44	01 30
20	04 44	05 11	05 34	23 37	24 26	00 26	01 14
N 10	04 58	05 23	05 45	23 20	24 11	00 11	01 00
0	05 08	05 33	05 54	23 05	23 56	24 47	00 47
S 10	05 18	05 42	06 04	22 49	23 41	24 34	00 34
20	05 26	05 52	06 14	22 32	23 25	24 21	00 21
30	05 33	06 01	06 26	22 13	23 07	24 05	00 05
35	05 36	06 06	06 32	22 01	22 57	23 56	24 58
40	05 40	06 12	06 40	21 48	22 44	23 45	24 50
45	05 43	06 18	06 48	21 33	22 30	23 33	24 40
S 50	05 47	06 25	06 59	21 14	22 13	23 18	24 28
52	05 49	06 28	07 04	21 05	22 04	23 11	24 23
54	05 50	06 32	07 09	20 55	21 55	23 03	24 17
56	05 52	06 35	07 15	20 44	21 45	22 54	24 10
58	05 53	06 40	07 21	20 31	21 33	22 44	24 02
S 60	05 55	06 44	07 29	20 16	21 19	22 32	23 54

Sunset / Twilight / Moonset

Lat.	Sunset	Civil	Naut.	Moonset 25	26	27	28
N 72	21 30	////	////	■	■	■	08 48
N 70	21 00	23 19	////	■	■	07 28	09 34
68	20 38	22 10	////	05 43	06 49	08 22	10 04
66	20 21	21 35	////	06 33	07 34	08 54	10 26
64	20 07	21 10	23 24	07 05	08 03	09 18	10 43
62	19 55	20 51	22 22	07 28	08 25	09 36	10 57
60	19 45	20 36	21 51	07 47	08 43	09 52	11 10
N 58	19 36	20 23	21 28	08 02	08 58	10 05	11 20
56	19 29	20 12	21 10	08 16	09 11	10 16	11 29
54	19 22	20 03	20 55	08 27	09 22	10 26	11 37
52	19 16	19 54	20 43	08 37	09 32	10 35	11 44
50	19 11	19 47	20 32	08 46	09 41	10 42	11 50
45	18 59	19 31	20 10	09 06	09 59	10 59	12 04
N 40	18 49	19 18	19 53	09 21	10 14	11 13	12 15
35	18 41	19 08	19 40	09 34	10 27	11 24	12 25
30	18 34	18 59	19 29	09 46	10 38	11 34	12 33
20	18 22	18 45	19 11	10 05	10 57	11 52	12 48
N 10	18 11	18 33	18 58	10 23	11 14	12 07	13 00
0	18 01	18 22	18 47	10 38	11 29	12 21	13 12
S 10	17 51	18 13	18 38	10 54	11 45	12 34	13 24
20	17 41	18 04	18 30	11 11	12 01	12 49	13 36
30	17 29	17 54	18 22	11 31	12 20	13 06	13 50
35	17 23	17 49	18 19	11 42	12 31	13 15	13 58
40	17 15	17 43	18 15	11 55	12 43	13 27	14 07
45	17 07	17 37	18 11	12 11	12 58	13 40	14 18
S 50	16 56	17 30	18 08	12 30	13 16	13 56	14 31
52	16 51	17 26	18 06	12 39	13 24	14 03	14 37
54	16 46	17 23	18 05	12 49	13 34	14 12	14 43
56	16 40	17 19	18 03	13 00	13 44	14 21	14 51
58	16 33	17 15	18 01	13 13	13 57	14 31	14 59
S 60	16 26	17 10	17 59	13 28	14 11	14 43	15 08

SUN / MOON

Day	SUN Eqn. of Time 00h	12h	Mer. Pass.	MOON Mer. Pass. Upper	Lower	Age	Phase
	m s	m s	h m	h m	h m	d	
25	01 59	02 04	11 58	04 26	16 52	21	
26	02 09	02 14	11 58	05 17	17 42	22	◐
27	02 19	02 24	11 58	06 08	18 34	23	

G.M.T.	ARIES G.H.A.	VENUS −3.4 G.H.A.	Dec.	MARS +1.5 G.H.A.	Dec.	JUPITER −1.9 G.H.A.	Dec.	SATURN +0.9 G.H.A.	Dec.	STARS Name	S.H.A.	Dec.
28 00	215 52.7	175 10.0	N15 08.0	185 53.5	N11 48.3	33 39.4	N 0 43.3	31 00.8	N 0 45.2	Acamar	315 37.4	S40 23.0
01	230 55.1	190 09.4	09.0	200 54.2	49.0	48 42.0	43.3	46 03.4	45.2	Achernar	335 45.6	S57 20.0
02	245 57.6	205 08.9	10.0	215 54.8	49.7	63 44.7	43.4	61 06.0	45.3	Acrux	173 36.2	S62 59.9
03	261 00.1	220 08.3	·· 11.0	230 55.5	·· 50.3	78 47.4	·· 43.5	76 08.6	·· 45.3	Adhara	255 32.0	S28 57.0
04	276 02.5	235 07.8	12.0	245 56.2	51.0	93 50.0	43.6	91 11.2	45.4	Aldebaran	291 17.8	N16 28.2
05	291 05.0	250 07.2	13.0	260 56.9	51.7	108 52.7	43.6	106 13.8	45.4			
06	306 07.4	265 06.7	N15 14.0	275 57.5	N11 52.3	123 55.3	N 0 43.7	121 16.4	N 0 45.5	Alioth	166 41.7	N56 03.8
07	321 09.9	280 06.1	15.0	290 58.2	53.0	138 58.0	43.8	136 19.0	45.6	Alkaid	153 17.7	N49 24.5
08	336 12.4	295 05.5	16.1	305 58.9	53.7	154 00.7	43.9	151 21.5	45.6	Al Na'ir	28 14.6	S47 03.0
09	351 14.8	310 05.0	·· 17.1	320 59.6	·· 54.3	169 03.3	·· 44.0	166 24.1	·· 45.7	Alnilam	276 11.5	S 1 13.0
10	6 17.3	325 04.4	18.1	336 00.3	55.0	184 06.0	44.0	181 26.7	45.7	Alphard	218 20.1	S 8 34.8
11	21 19.8	340 03.9	19.1	351 00.9	55.7	199 08.6	44.1	196 29.3	45.8			
12	36 22.2	355 03.3	N15 20.1	6 01.6	N11 56.3	214 11.3	N 0 44.2	211 31.9	N 0 45.8	Alphecca	126 31.4	N26 46.6
13	51 24.7	10 02.7	21.1	21 02.3	57.0	229 14.0	44.3	226 34.5	45.9	Alpheratz	358 09.2	N28 58.9
14	66 27.2	25 02.2	22.1	36 03.0	57.7	244 16.6	44.3	241 37.1	45.9	Altair	62 32.1	N 8 49.0
15	81 29.6	40 01.6	·· 23.1	51 03.6	·· 58.3	259 19.3	·· 44.4	256 39.7	·· 46.0	Ankaa	353 40.2	S42 24.5
16	96 32.1	55 01.0	24.1	66 04.3	59.0	274 21.9	44.5	271 42.3	46.0	Antares	112 56.0	S26 23.4
17	111 34.6	70 00.5	25.1	81 05.0	11 59.7	289 24.6	44.6	286 44.9	46.1			
18	126 37.0	84 59.9	N15 26.1	96 05.7	N12 00.3	304 27.3	N 0 44.6	301 47.5	N 0 46.1	Arcturus	146 17.8	N19 16.8
19	141 39.5	99 59.4	27.1	111 06.4	01.0	319 29.9	44.7	316 50.1	46.2	Atria	108 19.5	S68 59.5
20	156 41.9	114 58.8	28.1	126 07.0	01.6	334 32.6	44.8	331 52.7	46.2	Avior	234 28.1	S59 27.3
21	171 44.4	129 58.2	·· 29.1	141 07.7	·· 02.3	349 35.2	·· 44.9	346 55.3	·· 46.3	Bellatrix	278 58.6	N 6 19.8
22	186 46.9	144 57.7	30.1	156 08.4	03.0	4 37.9	44.9	1 57.9	46.3	Betelgeuse	271 28.1	N 7 24.1
23	201 49.3	159 57.1	31.1	171 09.1	03.6	19 40.5	45.0	17 00.5	46.4			
29 00	216 51.8	174 56.5	N15 32.1	186 09.7	N12 04.3	34 43.2	N 0 45.1	32 03.1	N 0 46.4	Canopus	264 07.3	S52 41.5
01	231 54.3	189 56.0	33.1	201 10.4	05.0	49 45.9	45.2	47 05.7	46.5	Capella	281 11.1	N45 58.8
02	246 56.7	204 55.4	34.1	216 11.1	05.6	64 48.5	45.2	62 08.3	46.5	Deneb	49 48.2	N45 12.5
03	261 59.2	219 54.8	·· 35.1	231 11.8	·· 06.3	79 51.2	·· 45.3	77 10.9	·· 46.6	Denebola	182 58.4	N14 40.6
04	277 01.7	234 54.3	36.1	246 12.4	07.0	94 53.8	45.4	92 13.5	46.6	Diphda	349 20.8	S18 05.5
05	292 04.1	249 53.7	37.1	261 13.1	07.6	109 56.5	45.5	107 16.1	46.7			
06	307 06.6	264 53.1	N15 38.1	276 13.8	N12 08.3	124 59.1	N 0 45.5	122 18.7	N 0 46.7	Dubhe	194 21.3	N61 51.4
07	322 09.1	279 52.6	39.1	291 14.5	08.9	140 01.8	45.6	137 21.3	46.8	Elnath	278 43.9	N28 35.5
08	337 11.5	294 52.0	40.1	306 15.1	09.6	155 04.5	45.7	152 23.9	46.8	Eltanin	90 57.2	N51 29.3
09	352 14.0	309 51.4	·· 41.1	321 15.8	·· 10.3	170 07.1	·· 45.8	167 26.5	·· 46.9	Enif	34 11.3	N 9 47.1
10	7 16.4	324 50.8	42.1	336 16.5	10.9	185 09.8	45.8	182 29.1	46.9	Fomalhaut	15 51.2	S29 43.3
11	22 18.9	339 50.3	43.1	351 17.2	11.6	200 12.4	45.9	197 31.7	47.0			
12	37 21.4	354 49.7	N15 44.1	6 17.9	N12 12.3	215 15.1	N 0 46.0	212 34.3	N 0 47.0	Gacrux	172 27.8	S57 00.6
13	52 23.8	9 49.1	45.1	21 18.5	12.9	230 17.7	46.1	227 36.9	47.1	Gienah	176 17.3	S17 26.4
14	67 26.3	24 48.6	46.1	36 19.2	13.6	245 20.4	46.1	242 39.5	47.1	Hadar	149 22.1	S60 17.0
15	82 28.8	39 48.0	·· 47.0	51 19.9	·· 14.2	260 23.0	·· 46.2	257 42.1	·· 47.2	Hamal	328 28.8	N23 22.2
16	97 31.2	54 47.4	48.0	66 20.6	14.9	275 25.7	46.3	272 44.7	47.2	Kaus Aust.	84 16.1	S34 23.5
17	112 33.7	69 46.8	49.0	81 21.2	15.6	290 28.3	46.4	287 47.2	47.3			
18	127 36.2	84 46.3	N15 50.0	96 21.9	N12 16.2	305 31.0	N 0 46.4	302 49.8	N 0 47.3	Kochab	137 17.8	N74 14.0
19	142 38.6	99 45.7	51.0	111 22.6	16.9	320 33.6	46.5	317 52.4	47.4	Markab	14 03.0	N15 06.0
20	157 41.1	114 45.1	52.0	126 23.3	17.5	335 36.3	46.6	332 55.0	47.4	Menkar	314 41.0	N 4 00.8
21	172 43.5	129 44.5	·· 53.0	141 23.9	·· 18.2	350 38.9	·· 46.7	347 57.6	·· 47.5	Menkent	148 36.2	S36 16.7
22	187 46.0	144 44.0	54.0	156 24.6	18.9	5 41.6	46.7	3 00.2	47.5	Miaplacidus	221 44.7	S69 38.7
23	202 48.5	159 43.4	54.9	171 25.3	19.5	20 44.2	46.8	18 02.8	47.5			
30 00	217 50.9	174 42.8	N15 55.9	186 26.0	N12 20.2	35 46.9	N 0 46.9	33 05.4	N 0 47.6	Mirfak	309 16.0	N49 47.6
01	232 53.4	189 42.2	56.9	201 26.6	20.8	50 49.5	46.9	48 08.0	47.7	Nunki	76 28.5	S26 19.2
02	247 55.9	204 41.7	57.9	216 27.3	21.5	65 52.2	47.0	63 10.6	47.7	Peacock	53 57.7	S56 47.5
03	262 58.3	219 41.1	·· 58.9	231 28.0	·· 22.1	80 54.9	·· 47.1	78 13.2	·· 47.8	Pollux	243 57.8	N28 04.4
04	278 00.8	234 40.5	15 59.8	246 28.7	22.8	95 57.5	47.2	93 15.8	47.8	Procyon	245 25.5	N 5 16.3
05	293 03.3	249 39.9	16 00.8	261 29.3	23.5	111 00.2	47.2	108 18.4	47.9			
06	308 05.7	264 39.3	N16 01.8	276 30.0	N12 24.1	126 02.8	N 0 47.3	123 21.0	N 0 47.9	Rasalhague	96 29.0	N12 34.3
07	323 08.2	279 38.8	02.8	291 30.7	24.8	141 05.5	47.4	138 23.6	48.0	Regulus	208 09.5	N12 03.5
08	338 10.7	294 38.2	03.8	306 31.4	25.4	156 08.1	47.4	153 26.2	48.0	Rigel	281 35.9	S 8 13.6
09	353 13.1	309 37.6	·· 04.7	321 32.0	·· 26.1	171 10.7	·· 47.5	168 28.8	·· 48.1	Rigil Kent.	140 24.6	S60 45.4
10	8 15.6	324 37.0	05.7	336 32.7	26.7	186 13.4	47.6	183 31.3	48.1	Sabik	102 40.4	S15 42.1
11	23 18.0	339 36.4	06.7	351 33.4	27.4	201 16.0	47.7	198 33.9	48.2			
12	38 20.5	354 35.8	N16 07.7	6 34.1	N12 28.1	216 18.7	N 0 47.7	213 36.5	N 0 48.2	Schedar	350 09.0	N56 25.8
13	53 23.0	9 35.3	08.6	21 34.7	28.7	231 21.3	47.8	228 39.1	48.3	Shaula	96 54.9	S37 05.3
14	68 25.4	24 34.7	09.6	36 35.4	29.4	246 24.0	47.9	243 41.7	48.3	Sirius	258 55.5	S16 41.7
15	83 27.9	39 34.1	·· 10.6	51 36.1	·· 30.0	261 26.6	·· 47.9	258 44.3	·· 48.4	Spica	158 56.8	S11 03.9
16	98 30.4	54 33.5	11.6	66 36.8	30.7	276 29.3	48.0	273 46.9	48.4	Suhail	223 10.4	S43 21.7
17	113 32.8	69 32.9	12.5	81 37.4	31.3	291 31.9	48.1	288 49.5	48.5			
18	128 35.3	84 32.3	N16 13.5	96 38.1	N12 32.0	306 34.6	N 0 48.2	303 52.1	N 0 48.5	Vega	80 55.3	N38 45.8
19	143 37.8	99 31.8	14.5	111 38.8	32.6	321 37.2	48.2	318 54.7	48.6	Zuben'ubi	137 32.3	S15 57.9
20	158 40.2	114 31.2	15.4	126 39.4	33.3	336 39.9	48.3	333 57.3	48.6		S.H.A.	Mer. Pass.
21	173 42.7	129 30.6	·· 16.4	141 40.1	·· 33.9	351 42.5	·· 48.4	348 59.9	·· 48.7			h m
22	188 45.2	144 30.0	17.4	156 40.8	34.6	6 45.2	48.4	4 02.5	48.7	Venus	318 04.7	12 21
23	203 47.6	159 29.4	18.3	171 41.5	35.2	21 47.8	48.5	19 05.0	48.8	Mars	329 17.9	11 35
	h m									Jupiter	177 51.4	21 37
Mer. Pass.	9 31.0	v −0.6	d 1.0	v 0.7	d 0.7	v 2.7	d 0.1	v 2.6	d 0.1	Saturn	175 11.3	21 48

G.M.T.	SUN G.H.A.	Dec.	MOON G.H.A.	v	Dec.	d	H.P.
	° '	° '	° '	'	° '	'	'
28 00	180 37.1	N14 03.1	258 42.0	9.9	S17 11.5	6.8	57.1
01	195 37.2	03.9	273 10.9	9.8	17 04.7	7.0	57.1
02	210 37.3	04.7	287 39.7	9.9	16 57.7	7.1	57.2
03	225 37.4	.. 05.5	302 08.6	9.9	16 50.6	7.1	57.2
04	240 37.5	06.3	316 37.5	9.9	16 43.5	7.3	57.3
05	255 37.6	07.1	331 06.4	9.8	16 36.2	7.3	57.3
06	270 37.7	N14 07.9	345 35.2	9.9	S16 28.9	7.5	57.3
07	285 37.8	08.7	0 04.1	9.8	16 21.4	7.6	57.4
08	300 37.9	09.4	14 32.9	9.9	16 13.8	7.6	57.4
09	315 38.0	.. 10.2	29 01.8	9.9	16 06.2	7.8	57.4
10	330 38.1	11.0	43 30.7	9.8	15 58.4	7.8	57.5
11	345 38.2	11.8	57 59.5	9.9	15 50.6	8.0	57.5
12	0 38.3	N14 12.6	72 28.4	9.8	S15 42.6	8.0	57.6
13	15 38.3	13.4	86 57.2	9.9	15 34.6	8.2	57.6
14	30 38.4	14.1	101 26.1	9.8	15 26.4	8.2	57.6
15	45 38.5	.. 14.9	115 54.9	9.9	15 18.2	8.3	57.7
16	60 38.6	15.7	130 23.8	9.8	15 09.9	8.5	57.7
17	75 38.7	16.5	144 52.6	9.8	15 01.4	8.5	57.8
18	90 38.8	N14 17.3	159 21.4	9.9	S14 52.9	8.6	57.8
19	105 38.9	18.1	173 50.3	9.8	14 44.3	8.7	57.8
20	120 39.0	18.8	188 19.1	9.9	14 35.6	8.8	57.9
21	135 39.1	.. 19.6	202 48.0	9.8	14 26.8	8.9	57.9
22	150 39.2	20.4	217 16.8	9.8	14 17.9	9.0	57.9
23	165 39.2	21.2	231 45.6	9.9	14 08.9	9.1	58.0
29 00	180 39.3	N14 22.0	246 14.5	9.8	S13 59.8	9.2	58.0
01	195 39.4	22.7	260 43.3	9.8	13 50.6	9.2	58.1
02	210 39.5	23.5	275 12.1	9.8	13 41.4	9.4	58.1
03	225 39.6	.. 24.3	289 40.9	9.8	13 32.0	9.4	58.1
04	240 39.7	25.1	304 09.7	9.9	13 22.6	9.5	58.2
05	255 39.8	25.9	318 38.6	9.8	13 13.1	9.6	58.2
06	270 39.9	N14 26.6	333 07.4	9.8	S13 03.5	9.7	58.3
07	285 40.0	27.4	347 36.2	9.8	12 53.8	9.8	58.3
08	300 40.0	28.2	2 05.0	9.8	12 44.0	9.9	58.3
09	315 40.1	.. 29.0	16 33.8	9.8	12 34.1	9.9	58.4
10	330 40.2	29.7	31 02.6	9.8	12 24.2	10.0	58.4
11	345 40.3	30.5	45 31.4	9.8	12 14.2	10.2	58.5
12	0 40.4	N14 31.3	60 00.2	9.7	S12 04.0	10.2	58.5
13	15 40.5	32.1	74 28.9	9.8	11 53.8	10.2	58.5
14	30 40.6	32.8	88 57.7	9.8	11 43.6	10.4	58.6
15	45 40.6	.. 33.6	103 26.5	9.7	11 33.2	10.4	58.6
16	60 40.7	34.4	117 55.2	9.8	11 22.8	10.6	58.7
17	75 40.8	35.2	132 24.0	9.8	11 12.2	10.6	58.7
18	90 40.9	N14 35.9	146 52.8	9.7	S11 01.6	10.6	58.7
19	105 41.0	36.7	161 21.5	9.7	10 51.0	10.8	58.8
20	120 41.1	37.5	175 50.2	9.8	10 40.2	10.8	58.8
21	135 41.1	.. 38.2	190 19.0	9.7	10 29.4	10.9	58.9
22	150 41.2	39.0	204 47.7	9.7	10 18.5	11.0	58.9
23	165 41.3	39.8	219 16.4	9.7	10 07.5	11.0	58.9
30 00	180 41.4	N14 40.6	233 45.1	9.7	S 9 56.5	11.1	59.0
01	195 41.5	41.3	248 13.8	9.7	9 45.4	11.2	59.0
02	210 41.6	42.1	262 42.5	9.7	9 34.2	11.3	59.0
03	225 41.6	.. 42.9	277 11.2	9.7	9 22.9	11.3	59.1
04	240 41.7	43.6	291 39.9	9.6	9 11.6	11.4	59.1
05	255 41.8	44.4	306 08.5	9.7	9 00.2	11.5	59.2
06	270 41.9	N14 45.2	320 37.2	9.6	S 8 48.7	11.5	59.2
07	285 42.0	45.9	335 05.8	9.6	8 37.2	11.6	59.2
08	300 42.1	46.7	349 34.4	9.6	8 25.6	11.7	59.3
09	315 42.1	.. 47.5	4 03.0	9.6	8 13.9	11.7	59.3
10	330 42.2	48.2	18 31.6	9.6	8 02.2	11.8	59.4
11	345 42.3	49.0	33 00.2	9.6	7 50.4	11.8	59.4
12	0 42.4	N14 49.8	47 28.8	9.6	S 7 38.6	11.9	59.4
13	15 42.5	50.5	61 57.4	9.5	7 26.7	12.0	59.5
14	30 42.5	51.3	76 25.9	9.5	7 14.7	12.0	59.5
15	45 42.6	.. 52.1	90 54.4	9.6	7 02.7	12.1	59.5
16	60 42.7	52.8	105 23.0	9.5	6 50.6	12.2	59.6
17	75 42.8	53.6	119 51.5	9.4·	6 38.4	12.1	59.6
18	90 42.9	N14 54.3	134 19.9	9.5	S 6 26.3	12.3	59.7
19	105 42.9	55.1	148 48.4	9.5	6 14.0	12.3	59.7
20	120 43.0	55.9	163 16.9	9.4	6 01.7	12.3	59.7
21	135 43.2	.. 56.6	177 45.3	9.4	5 49.4	12.4	59.8
22	150 43.2	57.4	192 13.7	9.4	5 37.0	12.5	59.8
23	165 43.3	58.1	206 42.1	9.4	5 24.5	12.5	59.8
	S.D. 15.9 d 0.8		S.D. 15.7		15.9		16.2

Day of week indicators: 28 TUESDAY, 29 WEDNESDAY, 30 THURSDAY

Lat.	Twilight Naut.	Twilight Civil	Sunrise	Moonrise 28	29	30	1
°	h m	h m	h m	h m	h m	h m	h m
N 72	////	////	02 09	05 25	04 53	04 35	04 20
N 70	////	////	02 43	04 39	04 29	04 21	04 14
68	////	01 28	03 07	04 08	04 09	04 10	04 09
66	////	02 08	03 26	03 45	03 54	04 00	04 05
64	////	02 35	03 41	03 27	03 41	03 52	04 01
62	01 18	02 55	03 53	03 12	03 31	03 45	03 58
60	01 54	03 12	04 04	02 59	03 21	03 39	03 55
N 58	02 19	03 26	04 13	02 48	03 13	03 34	03 53
56	02 38	03 37	04 21	02 39	03 06	03 30	03 51
54	02 54	03 47	04 28	02 30	03 00	03 25	03 49
52	03 07	03 56	04 35	02 23	02 54	03 21	03 47
50	03 18	04 04	04 40	02 16	02 49	03 18	03 45
45	03 41	04 21	04 53	02 01	02 37	03 10	03 42
N 40	03 58	04 34	05 03	01 49	02 28	03 04	03 39
35	04 12	04 45	05 12	01 39	02 20	02 59	03 36
30	04 24	04 54	05 19	01 30	02 13	02 54	03 34
20	04 42	05 09	05 32	01 14	02 00	02 45	03 30
N 10	04 56	05 22	05 43	01 00	01 49	02 38	03 26
0	05 08	05 33	05 54	00 47	01 39	02 31	03 23
S 10	05 18	05 45	06 04	00 34	01 29	02 24	03 20
20	05 26	05 53	06 15	00 21	01 18	02 16	03 16
30	05 35	06 03	06 28	00 05	01 05	02 08	03 12
35	05 39	06 08	06 35	24 58	00 58	02 03	03 10
40	05 43	06 15	06 43	24 50	00 50	01 57	03 07
45	05 47	06 21	06 52	24 40	00 40	01 51	03 04
S 50	05 51	06 29	07 03	24 28	00 28	01 43	03 01
52	05 53	06 33	07 09	24 23	00 23	01 39	02 59
54	05 55	06 37	07 14	24 17	00 17	01 35	02 57
56	05 57	06 41	07 21	24 10	00 10	01 31	02 55
58	05 59	06 46	07 28	24 02	00 02	01 26	02 53
S 60	06 01	06 51	07 36	23 54	25 20	01 20	02 51

Lat.	Sunset	Twilight Civil	Twilight Naut.	Moonset 28	29	30	1
°	h m	h m	h m	h m	h m	h m	h m
N 72	21 51	////	////	08 48	11 09	13 16	15 22
N 70	21 16	////	////	09 34	11 32	13 28	15 25
68	20 51	22 35	////	10 04	11 50	13 38	15 28
66	20 31	21 51	////	10 26	12 04	13 45	15 30
64	20 16	21 23	////	10 43	12 15	13 52	15 31
62	20 03	21 02	22 44	11 00	12 25	13 57	15 33
60	19 53	20 45	22 05	11 10	12 34	14 02	15 34
N 58	19 43	20 31	21 39	11 20	12 41	14 06	15 35
56	19 35	20 19	21 19	11 29	12 47	14 10	15 36
54	19 28	20 09	21 03	11 37	12 53	14 14	15 37
52	19 21	20 00	20 50	11 44	12 58	14 17	15 38
50	19 15	19 52	20 38	11 50	13 03	14 19	15 39
45	19 03	19 35	20 15	12 04	13 13	14 25	15 40
N 40	18 52	19 22	19 57	12 15	13 22	14 30	15 42
35	18 44	19 11	19 43	12 25	13 29	14 35	15 43
30	18 36	19 01	19 31	12 33	13 35	14 38	15 44
20	18 23	18 46	19 13	12 48	13 46	14 45	15 45
N 10	18 11	18 33	18 59	13 00	13 55	14 50	15 47
0	18 01	18 22	18 47	13 12	14 04	14 56	15 48
S 10	17 50	18 12	18 37	13 24	14 12	15 01	15 49
20	17 39	18 02	18 28	13 36	14 22	15 06	15 51
30	17 27	17 51	18 20	13 50	14 32	15 12	15 52
35	17 20	17 46	18 16	13 58	14 38	15 16	15 53
40	17 11	17 40	18 11	14 07	14 44	15 20	15 54
45	17 02	17 33	18 07	14 18	14 52	15 24	15 55
S 50	16 51	17 25	18 03	14 31	15 02	15 30	15 57
52	16 45	17 21	18 01	14 37	15 06	15 32	15 57
54	16 40	17 17	17 59	14 43	15 11	15 35	15 58
56	16 33	17 13	17 57	14 51	15 16	15 38	15 59
58	16 26	17 08	17 55	14 59	15 22	15 41	15 59
S 60	16 18	17 03	17 52	15 08	15 28	15 45	16 00

Day	SUN Eqn. of Time 00h	12h	Mer. Pass.	MOON Mer. Pass. Upper	Lower	Age	Phase
	m s	m s	h m	h m	h m	d	
28	02 28	02 33	11 57	07 00	19 26	24	
29	02 37	02 41	11 57	07 51	20 17	25	
30	02 45	02 49	11 57	08 43	21 09	26	

G.M.T.	ARIES G.H.A.	VENUS −3.4 G.H.A.	Dec.	MARS +1.5 G.H.A.	Dec.	JUPITER −1.9 G.H.A.	Dec.	SATURN +0.9 G.H.A.	Dec.	STARS Name	S.H.A.	Dec.
1 00	218 50.1	174 28.8	N16 19.3	186 42.1	N12 35.9	36 50.5	N 0 48.6	34 07.6	N 0 48.8	Acamar	315 37.4	S40 23.0
01	233 52.5	189 28.2	20.3	201 42.8	36.6	51 53.1	48.7	49 10.2	48.9	Achernar	335 45.5	S57 20.0
02	248 55.0	204 27.6	21.2	216 43.5	37.2	66 55.7	48.7	64 12.8	48.9	Acrux	173 36.2	S62 59.9
03	263 57.5	219 27.1	·· 22.2	231 44.2	·· 37.9	81 58.4	·· 48.8	79 15.4	·· 49.0	Adhara	255 32.0	S28 57.0
04	278 59.9	234 26.5	23.2	246 44.8	38.5	97 01.0	48.9	94 18.0	49.0	Aldebaran	291 17.9	N16 28.2
05	294 02.4	249 25.9	24.1	261 45.5	39.2	112 03.7	48.9	109 20.6	49.1			
06	309 04.9	264 25.3	N16 25.1	276 46.2	N12 39.8	127 06.3	N 0 49.0	124 23.2	N 0 49.1	Alioth	166 41.7	N56 03.9
07	324 07.3	279 24.7	26.1	291 46.9	40.5	142 09.0	49.1	139 25.8	49.2	Alkaid	153 17.7	N49 24.5
08	339 09.8	294 24.1	27.0	306 47.5	41.1	157 11.6	49.1	154 28.4	49.2	Al Na'ir	28 14.6	S47 03.0
F 09	354 12.3	309 23.5	·· 28.0	321 48.2	·· 41.8	172 14.3	·· 49.2	169 31.0	·· 49.2	Alnilam	276 11.5	S 1 13.0
R 10	9 14.7	324 22.9	28.9	336 48.9	42.4	187 16.9	49.3	184 33.6	49.3	Alphard	218 20.1	S 8 34.8
I 11	24 17.2	339 22.3	29.9	351 49.5	43.1	202 19.5	49.3	199 36.1	49.3			
D 12	39 19.6	354 21.7	N16 30.8	6 50.2	N12 43.7	217 22.2	N 0 49.4	214 38.7	N 0 49.4	Alphecca	126 31.4	N26 46.6
A 13	54 22.1	9 21.1	31.8	21 50.9	44.4	232 24.8	49.5	229 41.3	49.4	Alpheratz	358 09.2	N28 58.9
Y 14	69 24.6	24 20.5	32.8	36 51.6	45.0	247 27.5	49.5	244 43.9	49.5	Altair	62 32.0	N 8 49.0
15	84 27.0	39 19.9	·· 33.7	51 52.2	·· 45.7	262 30.1	·· 49.6	259 46.5	·· 49.5	Ankaa	353 40.2	S42 24.5
16	99 29.5	54 19.3	34.7	66 52.9	46.3	277 32.7	49.7	274 49.1	49.6	Antares	112 56.0	S26 23.4
17	114 32.0	69 18.7	35.6	81 53.6	47.0	292 35.4	49.8	289 51.7	49.6			
18	129 34.4	84 18.1	N16 36.6	96 54.3	N12 47.6	307 38.0	N 0 49.9	304 54.3	N 0 49.7	Arcturus	146 17.8	N19 16.8
19	144 36.9	99 17.6	37.5	111 54.9	48.3	322 40.7	49.9	319 56.9	49.7	Atria	108 19.5	S68 59.5
20	159 39.4	114 17.0	38.5	126 55.6	48.9	337 43.3	50.0	334 59.4	49.8	Avior	234 28.1	S59 27.3
21	174 41.8	129 16.4	·· 39.4	141 56.3	·· 49.6	352 45.9	·· 50.0	350 02.0	·· 49.8	Bellatrix	278 58.6	N 6 19.8
22	189 44.3	144 15.8	40.4	156 56.9	50.2	7 48.6	50.1	5 04.6	49.9	Betelgeuse	271 28.1	N 7 24.1
23	204 46.8	159 15.2	41.3	171 57.6	50.9	22 51.2	50.2	20 07.2	49.9			
2 00	219 49.2	174 14.6	N16 42.3	186 58.3	N12 51.5	37 53.9	N 0 50.2	35 09.8	N 0 50.0	Canopus	264 07.4	S52 41.4
01	234 51.7	189 14.0	43.2	201 59.0	52.1	52 56.5	50.3	50 12.4	50.0	Capella	281 11.1	N45 58.8
02	249 54.1	204 13.4	44.2	216 59.6	52.8	67 59.1	50.4	65 15.0	50.1	Deneb	49 48.2	N45 12.5
03	264 56.6	219 12.8	·· 45.1	232 00.3	·· 53.4	83 01.8	·· 50.4	80 17.6	·· 50.1	Denebola	182 58.4	N14 40.6
04	279 59.1	234 12.2	46.1	247 01.0	54.1	98 04.4	50.5	95 20.2	50.1	Diphda	349 20.8	S18 05.5
05	295 01.5	249 11.5	47.0	262 01.6	54.7	113 07.1	50.6	110 22.7	50.2			
06	310 04.0	264 10.9	N16 48.0	277 02.3	N12 55.4	128 09.7	N 0 50.6	125 25.3	N 0 50.2	Dubhe	194 21.3	N61 51.4
07	325 06.5	279 10.3	48.9	292 03.0	56.0	143 12.3	50.7	140 27.9	50.3	Elnath	278 43.9	N28 35.5
S 08	340 08.9	294 09.7	49.8	307 03.7	56.7	158 15.0	50.8	155 30.5	50.3	Eltanin	90 57.2	N51 29.3
A 09	355 11.4	309 09.1	·· 50.8	322 04.3	·· 57.3	173 17.6	·· 50.8	170 33.1	·· 50.4	Enif	34 11.3	N 9 47.1
T 10	10 13.9	324 08.5	51.7	337 05.0	58.0	188 20.2	50.9	185 35.7	50.4	Fomalhaut	15 51.2	S29 43.3
U 11	25 16.3	339 07.9	52.7	352 05.7	58.6	203 22.9	51.0	200 38.3	50.5			
R 12	40 18.8	354 07.3	N16 53.6	7 06.3	N12 59.2	218 25.5	N 0 51.0	215 40.9	N 0 50.5	Gacrux	172 27.8	S57 00.6
D 13	55 21.3	9 06.7	54.5	22 07.0	12 59.9	233 28.2	51.1	230 43.4	50.6	Gienah	176 17.3	S17 26.4
A 14	70 23.7	24 06.1	55.5	37 07.7	13 00.5	248 30.8	51.2	245 46.0	50.6	Hadar	149 22.1	S60 17.0
Y 15	85 26.2	39 05.5	·· 56.4	52 08.4	·· 01.2	263 33.4	·· 51.2	260 48.6	·· 50.7	Hamal	328 28.8	N23 22.2
16	100 28.6	54 04.9	57.4	67 09.0	01.8	278 36.1	51.3	275 51.2	50.7	Kaus Aust.	84 16.1	S34 23.5
17	115 31.1	69 04.3	58.3	82 09.7	02.5	293 38.7	51.4	290 53.8	50.8			
18	130 33.6	84 03.7	N16 59.2	97 10.4	N13 03.1	308 41.3	N 0 51.4	305 56.4	N 0 50.8	Kochab	137 17.8	N74 14.0
19	145 36.0	99 03.1	17 00.2	112 11.0	03.8	323 44.0	51.5	320 59.0	50.8	Markab	14 02.9	N15 06.0
20	160 38.5	114 02.5	01.1	127 11.7	04.4	338 46.6	51.5	336 01.6	50.9	Menkar	314 41.0	N 4 00.8
21	175 41.0	129 01.9	·· 02.0	142 12.4	·· 05.0	353 49.2	·· 51.6	351 04.1	·· 50.9	Menkent	148 36.2	S36 16.7
22	190 43.4	144 01.2	03.0	157 13.1	05.7	8 51.9	51.7	6 06.7	51.0	Miaplacidus	221 44.8	S69 38.7
23	205 45.9	159 00.6	03.9	172 13.7	06.3	23 54.5	51.7	21 09.3	51.0			
3 00	220 48.4	174 00.0	N17 04.8	187 14.4	N13 07.0	38 57.1	N 0 51.8	36 11.9	N 0 51.1	Mirfak	309 16.0	N49 47.6
01	235 50.8	188 59.4	05.8	202 15.1	07.6	53 59.8	51.9	51 14.5	51.1	Nunki	76 28.5	S26 19.2
02	250 53.3	203 58.8	06.7	217 15.7	08.2	69 02.4	51.9	66 17.1	51.2	Peacock	53 57.7	S56 47.5
03	265 55.7	218 58.2	·· 07.6	232 16.4	·· 08.9	84 05.0	·· 52.0	81 19.7	·· 51.2	Pollux	243 57.8	N28 04.4
04	280 58.2	233 57.6	08.5	247 17.1	09.5	99 07.7	52.1	96 22.2	51.3	Procyon	245 25.5	N 5 16.3
05	296 00.7	248 57.0	09.5	262 17.7	10.2	114 10.3	52.1	111 24.8	51.3			
06	311 03.1	263 56.3	N17 10.4	277 18.4	N13 10.8	129 12.9	N 0 52.2	126 27.4	N 0 51.3	Rasalhague	96 29.0	N12 34.3
07	326 05.6	278 55.7	11.3	292 19.1	11.4	144 15.6	52.3	141 30.0	51.4	Regulus	208 09.5	N12 03.5
08	341 08.1	293 55.1	12.2	307 19.8	12.1	159 18.2	52.3	156 32.6	51.4	Rigel	281 35.9	S 8 13.6
S 09	356 10.5	308 54.5	·· 13.2	322 20.4	·· 12.7	174 20.8	·· 52.4	171 35.2	·· 51.5	Rigil Kent.	140 24.6	S60 45.4
U 10	11 13.0	323 53.9	14.1	337 21.1	13.4	189 23.5	52.4	186 37.7	51.5	Sabik	102 40.4	S15 42.1
N 11	26 15.5	338 53.3	15.0	352 21.8	14.0	204 26.1	52.5	201 40.3	51.6			
D 12	41 17.9	353 52.6	N17 15.9	7 22.4	N13 14.6	219 28.7	N 0 52.6	216 42.9	N 0 51.6	Schedar	350 09.0	N56 25.8
A 13	56 20.4	8 52.0	16.9	22 23.1	15.3	234 31.4	52.6	231 45.5	51.7	Shaula	96 54.9	S37 05.3
Y 14	71 22.9	23 51.4	17.8	37 23.8	15.9	249 34.0	52.7	246 48.1	51.7	Sirius	258 55.5	S16 41.7
15	86 25.3	38 50.8	·· 18.7	52 24.4	·· 16.6	264 36.6	·· 52.8	261 50.7	·· 51.7	Spica	158 56.8	S11 03.9
16	101 27.8	53 50.2	19.6	67 25.1	17.2	279 39.2	52.8	276 53.3	51.8	Suhail	223 10.5	S43 21.7
17	116 30.2	68 49.6	20.5	82 25.8	17.8	294 41.9	52.9	291 55.8	51.8			
18	131 32.7	83 48.9	N17 21.4	97 26.4	N13 18.5	309 44.5	N 0 52.9	306 58.4	N 0 51.9	Vega	80 55.3	N38 45.8
19	146 35.2	98 48.3	22.4	112 27.1	19.1	324 47.1	53.0	322 01.0	51.9	Zuben'ubi	137 32.3	S15 57.9
20	161 37.6	113 47.7	23.3	127 27.8	19.7	339 49.8	53.1	337 03.6	52.0		S.H.A.	Mer. Pass.
21	176 40.1	128 47.1	·· 24.2	142 28.5	·· 20.4	354 52.4	·· 53.1	352 06.2	·· 52.0	Venus	314 25.3	12 24
22	191 42.6	143 46.5	25.1	157 29.1	21.0	9 55.0	53.2	7 08.8	52.1	Mars	327 09.1	11 32
23	206 45.0	158 45.8	26.0	172 29.8	21.7	24 57.6	53.3	22 11.3	52.1	Jupiter	178 04.6	21 25
Mer. Pass.	9 19.2	v −0.6	d 0.9	v 0.7	d 0.6	v 2.6	d 0.1	v 2.6	d 0.0	Saturn	175 20.6	21 36

G.M.T.	SUN G.H.A.	Dec.	MOON G.H.A.	v	Dec.	d	H.P.
d h	° ′	° ′	° ′	′	° ′	′	′
1 00	180 43.3	N14 58.9	221 10.5	9.3	S 5 12.0	12.5	59.9
01	195 43.4	14 59.7	235 38.8	9.4	4 59.5	12.6	59.9
02	210 43.5	15 00.4	250 07.2	9.3	4 46.9	12.7	59.9
03	225 43.6	·· 01.2	264 35.5	9.3	4 34.2	12.6	60.0
04	240 43.6	01.9	279 03.8	9.2	4 21.6	12.8	60.0
05	255 43.7	02.7	293 32.0	9.3	4 08.8	12.7	60.0
06	270 43.8	N15 03.5	308 00.3	9.2	S 3 56.1	12.8	60.1
07	285 43.9	04.2	322 28.5	9.2	3 43.3	12.8	60.1
08	300 43.9	05.0	336 56.7	9.2	3 30.5	12.9	60.1
F 09	315 44.0	·· 05.7	351 24.9	9.1	3 17.6	12.9	60.2
R 10	330 44.1	06.5	5 53.0	9.2	3 04.7	13.0	60.2
I 11	345 44.2	07.2	20 21.2	9.1	2 51.7	12.9	60.2
D 12	0 44.2	N15 08.0	34 49.3	9.0	S 2 38.8	13.0	60.3
A 13	15 44.3	08.7	49 17.3	9.1	2 25.8	13.1	60.3
Y 14	30 44.4	09.5	63 45.4	9.0	2 12.7	13.0	60.3
15	45 44.5	·· 10.3	78 13.4	9.0	1 59.7	13.1	60.4
16	60 44.5	11.0	92 41.4	8.9	1 46.6	13.1	60.4
17	75 44.6	11.8	107 09.3	9.0	1 33.5	13.2	60.4
18	90 44.7	N15 12.5	121 37.3	8.9	S 1 20.3	13.1	60.5
19	105 44.8	13.3	136 05.2	8.8	1 07.2	13.2	60.5
20	120 44.8	14.0	150 33.0	8.9	0 54.0	13.2	60.5
21	135 44.9	·· 14.8	165 00.9	8.8	0 40.8	13.2	60.5
22	150 45.0	15.5	179 28.7	8.7	0 27.6	13.3	60.6
23	165 45.1	16.3	193 56.4	8.8	0 14.3	13.2	60.6
2 00	180 45.1	N15 17.0	208 24.2	8.7	S 0 01.1	13.3	60.6
01	195 45.2	17.8	222 51.9	8.6	N 0 12.2	13.2	60.7
02	210 45.3	18.5	237 19.5	8.7	0 25.4	13.3	60.7
03	225 45.3	·· 19.3	251 47.2	8.6	0 38.7	13.3	60.7
04	240 45.4	20.0	266 14.8	8.5	0 52.0	13.3	60.7
05	255 45.5	20.8	280 42.3	8.6	1 05.3	13.3	60.8
06	270 45.6	N15 21.5	295 09.9	8.5	N 1 18.6	13.3	60.8
07	285 45.6	22.2	309 37.4	8.4	1 31.9	13.3	60.8
S 08	300 45.7	23.0	324 04.8	8.4	1 45.2	13.4	60.8
A 09	315 45.8	·· 23.7	338 32.2	8.4	1 58.6	13.3	60.9
T 10	330 45.8	24.5	352 59.6	8.3	2 11.9	13.3	60.9
U 11	345 45.9	25.2	7 26.9	8.3	2 25.2	13.3	60.9
R 12	0 46.0	N15 26.0	21 54.2	8.3	N 2 38.5	13.3	60.9
D 13	15 46.0	26.7	36 21.5	8.2	2 51.8	13.3	61.0
A 14	30 46.1	27.5	50 48.7	8.2	3 05.1	13.3	61.0
Y 15	45 46.2	·· 28.2	65 15.9	8.1	3 18.4	13.2	61.0
16	60 46.2	28.9	79 43.0	8.1	3 31.6	13.2	61.0
17	75 46.3	29.7	94 10.1	8.0	3 44.9	13.2	61.0
18	90 46.4	N15 30.4	108 37.1	8.1	N 3 58.1	13.3	61.1
19	105 46.4	31.2	123 04.2	7.9	4 11.4	13.2	61.1
20	120 46.5	31.9	137 31.1	7.9	4 24.6	13.2	61.1
21	135 46.6	·· 32.6	151 58.0	7.9	4 37.8	13.1	61.1
22	150 46.6	33.4	166 24.9	7.8	4 50.9	13.2	61.1
23	165 46.7	34.1	180 51.7	7.8	5 04.1	13.1	61.2
3 00	180 46.8	N15 34.9	195 18.5	7.8	N 5 17.2	13.1	61.2
01	195 46.8	35.6	209 45.3	7.6	5 30.3	13.1	61.2
02	210 46.9	36.3	224 11.9	7.7	5 43.4	13.0	61.2
03	225 47.0	·· 37.1	238 38.6	7.6	5 56.4	13.1	61.2
04	240 47.0	37.8	253 05.2	7.5	6 09.5	12.9	61.2
05	255 47.1	38.6	267 31.7	7.5	6 22.4	13.0	61.3
06	270 47.2	N15 39.3	281 58.2	7.5	N 6 35.4	12.9	61.3
07	285 47.2	40.0	296 24.7	7.4	6 48.3	12.9	61.3
08	300 47.3	40.8	310 51.1	7.4	7 01.2	12.8	61.3
S 09	315 47.4	·· 41.5	325 17.5	7.3	7 14.0	12.8	61.3
U 10	330 47.4	42.2	339 43.8	7.2	7 26.8	12.7	61.3
N 11	345 47.5	43.0	354 10.0	7.2	7 39.5	12.7	61.3
D 12	0 47.6	N15 43.7	8 36.2	7.2	N 7 52.2	12.7	61.3
A 13	15 47.6	44.4	23 02.4	7.1	8 04.9	12.6	61.3
Y 14	30 47.7	45.2	37 28.5	7.1	8 17.5	12.5	61.4
15	45 47.7	·· 45.9	51 54.6	7.0	8 30.0	12.5	61.4
16	60 47.8	46.6	66 20.6	7.0	8 42.5	12.3	61.4
17	75 47.9	47.4	80 46.6	6.9	8 55.0	12.3	61.4
18	90 47.9	N15 48.1	95 12.5	6.8	N 9 07.3	12.4	61.4
19	105 48.0	48.8	109 38.3	6.9	9 19.7	12.3	61.4
20	120 48.1	49.5	124 04.2	6.7	9 32.0	12.2	61.4
21	135 48.1	·· 50.3	138 29.9	6.7	9 44.2	12.1	61.4
22	150 48.2	51.0	152 55.6	6.7	9 56.3	12.1	61.4
23	165 48.2	51.7	167 21.3	6.6	10 08.4	12.0	61.4
	S.D. 15.9	d 0.7	S.D. 16.4		16.6		16.7

Lat.	Twilight Naut.	Twilight Civil	Sunrise	Moonrise 1	Moonrise 2	Moonrise 3	Moonrise 4
°	h m	h m	h m	h m	h m	h m	h m
N 72	////	////	01 45	04 20	04 06	03 53	03 36
N 70	////	////	02 26	04 14	04 07	04 01	03 54
68	////	00 57	02 53	04 09	04 08	04 08	04 08
66	////	01 50	03 14	04 05	04 09	04 13	04 19
64	////	02 21	03 31	04 01	04 10	04 18	04 29
62	00 50	02 44	03 44	03 58	04 10	04 23	04 37
60	01 38	03 02	03 56	03 55	04 10	04 26	04 45
N 58	02 06	03 17	04 06	03 53	04 11	04 30	04 51
56	02 28	03 29	04 14	03 51	04 11	04 33	04 57
54	02 45	03 40	04 22	03 49	04 12	04 35	05 02
52	02 59	03 50	04 29	03 47	04 12	04 38	05 06
50	03 11	03 58	04 35	03 45	04 12	04 40	05 11
45	03 35	04 16	04 48	03 42	04 13	04 45	05 20
N 40	03 54	04 30	04 59	03 39	04 13	04 49	05 27
35	04 09	04 41	05 08	03 36	04 14	04 53	05 34
30	04 21	04 51	05 16	03 34	04 14	04 56	05 40
20	04 40	05 07	05 30	03 30	04 15	05 01	05 50
N 10	04 55	05 20	05 42	03 26	04 16	05 06	05 59
0	05 07	05 32	05 54	03 23	04 16	05 11	06 08
S 10	05 18	05 43	06 05	03 20	04 17	05 16	06 16
20	05 27	05 53	06 16	03 16	04 18	05 21	06 26
30	05 36	06 05	06 29	03 12	04 19	05 27	06 36
35	05 41	06 11	06 37	03 10	04 19	05 30	06 42
40	05 45	06 17	06 46	03 07	04 20	05 34	06 50
45	05 50	06 25	06 56	03 04	04 20	05 39	06 58
S 50	05 55	06 34	07 08	03 01	04 21	05 44	07 08
52	05 57	06 37	07 13	02 59	04 22	05 47	07 12
54	06 00	06 42	07 20	02 57	04 22	05 49	07 18
56	06 02	06 46	07 26	02 55	04 23	05 52	07 23
58	06 04	06 51	07 34	02 53	04 23	05 56	07 30
S 60	06 07	06 57	07 43	02 51	04 24	06 00	07 37

Lat.	Sunset	Twilight Civil	Twilight Naut.	Moonset 1	Moonset 2	Moonset 3	Moonset 4
°	h m	h m	h m	h m	h m	h m	h m
N 72	22 17	////	////	15 22	17 30	19 44	22 10
N 70	21 33	////	////	15 25	17 25	19 29	21 39
68	21 04	23 10	////	15 28	17 20	19 17	21 16
66	20 43	22 09	////	15 30	17 17	19 07	20 58
64	20 26	21 36	////	15 31	17 14	18 58	20 44
62	20 12	21 13	23 16	15 33	17 11	18 51	20 32
60	20 00	20 54	22 21	15 34	17 09	18 45	20 22
N 58	19 50	20 39	21 51	15 35	17 06	18 40	20 13
56	19 41	20 26	21 29	15 36	17 05	18 35	20 06
54	19 33	20 15	21 11	15 37	17 03	18 31	19 59
52	19 26	20 05	20 57	15 38	17 02	18 27	19 53
50	19 20	19 57	20 44	15 39	17 00	18 23	19 47
45	19 07	19 39	20 20	15 40	16 57	18 16	19 35
N 40	18 55	19 25	20 01	15 42	16 55	18 10	19 25
35	18 46	19 13	19 46	15 43	16 53	18 04	19 17
30	18 38	19 03	19 34	15 44	16 51	18 00	19 09
20	18 24	18 47	19 14	15 45	16 48	17 51	18 57
N 10	18 12	18 34	18 59	15 47	16 45	17 44	18 46
0	18 00	18 22	18 47	15 48	16 42	17 38	18 35
S 10	17 49	18 11	18 36	15 49	16 39	17 31	18 25
20	17 37	18 00	18 26	15 51	16 36	17 24	18 14
30	17 24	17 49	18 17	15 52	16 33	17 16	18 01
35	17 16	17 43	18 13	15 53	16 31	17 11	17 54
40	17 08	17 36	18 08	15 54	16 29	17 06	17 46
45	16 58	17 28	18 03	15 55	16 27	17 00	17 36
S 50	16 45	17 20	17 58	15 57	16 24	16 52	17 25
52	16 40	17 16	17 56	15 57	16 22	16 49	17 20
54	16 34	17 11	17 54	15 58	16 21	16 46	17 14
56	16 27	17 07	17 51	15 59	16 19	16 41	17 07
58	16 19	17 02	17 48	15 59	16 17	16 37	17 00
S 60	16 10	16 56	17 46	16 00	16 15	16 32	16 52

Day	SUN Eqn. of Time 00ʰ	SUN Eqn. of Time 12ʰ	SUN Mer. Pass.	MOON Mer. Pass. Upper	MOON Mer. Pass. Lower	Age	Phase
	m s	m s	h m	h m	h m	d	
1	02 53	02 57	11 57	09 36	22 02	27	
2	03 00	03 04	11 57	10 29	22 56	28	
3	03 07	03 10	11 57	11 24	23 53	29	●

G.M.T.	ARIES G.H.A.	VENUS −3.4 G.H.A.	Dec.	MARS +1.5 G.H.A.	Dec.	JUPITER −1.9 G.H.A.	Dec.	SATURN +0.9 G.H.A.	Dec.	STARS Name	S.H.A.	Dec.
4 00	221 47.5	173 45.2	N17 26.9	187 30.5	N13 22.3	40 00.3	N 0 53.3	37 13.9	N 0 52.1	Acamar	315 37.4	S40 22.9
01	236 50.0	188 44.6	27.8	202 31.1	22.9	55 02.9	53.4	52 16.5	52.2	Achernar	335 45.5	S57 19.9
02	251 52.4	203 44.0	28.8	217 31.8	23.6	70 05.5	53.4	67 19.1	52.2	Acrux	173 36.2	S62 59.9
03	266 54.9	218 43.3	·· 29.7	232 32.5	·· 24.2	85 08.1	·· 53.5	82 21.7	·· 52.3	Adhara	255 32.0	S28 57.0
04	281 57.4	233 42.7	30.6	247 33.1	24.8	100 10.8	53.6	97 24.2	52.3	Aldebaran	291 17.9	N16 28.2
05	296 59.8	248 42.1	31.5	262 33.8	25.5	115 13.4	53.6	112 26.8	52.4			
06	312 02.3	263 41.5	N17 32.4	277 34.5	N13 26.1	130 16.0	N 0 53.7	127 29.4	N 0 52.4	Alioth	166 41.7	N56 03.9
07	327 04.7	278 40.8	33.3	292 35.1	26.7	145 18.6	53.7	142 32.0	52.5	Alkaid	153 17.7	N49 24.5
M 08	342 07.2	293 40.2	34.2	307 35.8	27.4	160 21.3	53.8	157 34.6	52.5	Al Na'ir	28 14.6	S47 03.0
O 09	357 09.7	308 39.6	·· 35.1	322 36.5	·· 28.0	175 23.9	·· 53.9	172 37.2	·· 52.5	Alnilam	276 11.5	S 1 13.0
N 10	12 12.1	323 39.0	36.0	337 37.1	28.6	190 26.5	53.9	187 39.7	52.6	Alphard	218 20.1	S 8 34.8
D 11	27 14.6	338 38.3	36.9	352 37.8	29.3	205 29.1	54.0	202 42.3	52.6			
A 12	42 17.1	353 37.7	N17 37.8	7 38.5	N13 29.9	220 31.8	N 0 54.1	217 44.9	N 0 52.7	Alphecca	126 31.4	N26 46.6
Y 13	57 19.5	8 37.1	38.7	22 39.1	30.5	235 34.4	54.1	232 47.5	52.7	Alpheratz	358 09.2	N28 58.9
14	72 22.0	23 36.4	39.6	37 39.8	31.2	250 37.0	54.2	247 50.1	52.8	Altair	62 32.0	N 8 49.0
15	87 24.5	38 35.8	·· 40.5	52 40.5	·· 31.8	265 39.6	·· 54.2	262 52.6	·· 52.8	Ankaa	353 40.2	S42 24.5
16	102 26.9	53 35.2	41.4	67 41.1	32.4	280 42.3	54.3	277 55.2	52.8	Antares	112 56.0	S26 23.4
17	117 29.4	68 34.5	42.3	82 41.8	33.1	295 44.9	54.4	292 57.8	52.9			
18	132 31.8	83 33.9	N17 43.2	97 42.5	N13 33.7	310 47.5	N 0 54.4	308 00.4	N 0 52.9	Arcturus	146 17.8	N19 16.8
19	147 34.3	98 33.3	44.1	112 43.2	34.3	325 50.1	54.5	323 03.0	53.0	Atria	108 19.4	S68 59.5
20	162 36.8	113 32.6	45.0	127 43.8	35.0	340 52.8	54.5	338 05.5	53.0	Avior	234 28.2	S59 27.3
21	177 39.2	128 32.0	·· 45.9	142 44.5	·· 35.6	355 55.4	·· 54.6	353 08.1	·· 53.1	Bellatrix	278 58.6	N 6 19.8
22	192 41.7	143 31.4	46.8	157 45.2	36.2	10 58.0	54.6	8 10.7	53.1	Betelgeuse	271 28.1	N 7 24.1
23	207 44.2	158 30.7	47.7	172 45.8	36.8	26 00.6	54.7	23 13.3	53.1			
5 00	222 46.6	173 30.1	N17 48.6	187 46.5	N13 37.5	41 03.2	N 0 54.8	38 15.9	N 0 53.2	Canopus	264 07.4	S52 41.4
01	237 49.1	188 29.5	49.5	202 47.2	38.1	56 05.9	54.8	53 18.4	53.2	Capella	281 11.1	N45 58.8
02	252 51.6	203 28.8	50.4	217 47.8	38.7	71 08.5	54.9	68 21.0	53.3	Deneb	49 48.1	N45 12.5
03	267 54.0	218 28.2	·· 51.3	232 48.5	·· 39.4	86 11.1	·· 54.9	83 23.6	·· 53.3	Denebola	182 58.4	N14 40.7
04	282 56.5	233 27.6	52.2	247 49.2	40.0	101 13.7	55.0	98 26.2	53.4	Diphda	349 20.7	S18 05.5
05	297 59.0	248 26.9	53.0	262 49.8	40.6	116 16.3	55.1	113 28.8	53.4			
06	313 01.4	263 26.3	N17 53.9	277 50.5	N13 41.2	131 19.0	N 0 55.1	128 31.3	N 0 53.4	Dubhe	194 21.3	N61 51.4
07	328 03.9	278 25.7	54.8	292 51.2	41.9	146 21.6	55.2	143 33.9	53.5	Elnath	278 43.9	N28 35.5
T 08	343 06.3	293 25.0	55.7	307 51.8	42.5	161 24.2	55.2	158 36.5	53.5	Eltanin	90 57.2	N51 29.3
U 09	358 08.8	308 24.4	·· 56.6	322 52.5	·· 43.1	176 26.8	·· 55.3	173 39.1	·· 53.6	Enif	34 11.2	N 9 47.2
E 10	13 11.3	323 23.7	57.5	337 53.1	43.8	191 29.4	55.3	188 41.7	53.6	Fomalhaut	15 51.1	S29 43.3
S 11	28 13.7	338 23.1	58.4	352 53.8	44.4	206 32.1	55.4	203 44.2	53.7			
D 12	43 16.2	353 22.5	N17 59.2	7 54.5	N13 45.0	221 34.7	N 0 55.5	218 46.8	N 0 53.7	Gacrux	172 27.8	S57 00.6
A 13	58 18.7	8 21.8	18 00.1	22 55.1	45.6	236 37.3	55.5	233 49.4	53.7	Gienah	176 17.3	S17 26.4
Y 14	73 21.1	23 21.2	01.0	37 55.8	46.3	251 39.9	55.6	248 52.0	53.8	Hadar	149 22.1	S60 17.0
15	88 23.6	38 20.5	·· 01.9	52 56.5	·· 46.9	266 42.5	·· 55.6	263 54.5	·· 53.8	Hamal	328 28.8	N23 22.2
16	103 26.1	53 19.9	02.8	67 57.1	47.5	281 45.1	55.7	278 57.1	53.9	Kaus Aust.	84 16.1	S34 23.5
17	118 28.5	68 19.3	03.6	82 57.8	48.1	296 47.8	55.7	293 59.7	53.9			
18	133 31.0	83 18.6	N18 04.5	97 58.5	N13 48.8	311 50.4	N 0 55.8	309 02.3	N 0 53.9	Kochab	137 17.8	N74 14.0
19	148 33.5	98 18.0	05.4	112 59.1	49.4	326 53.0	55.9	324 04.9	54.0	Markab	14 02.9	N15 06.0
20	163 35.9	113 17.3	06.3	127 59.8	50.0	341 55.6	55.9	339 07.4	54.0	Menkar	314 41.0	N 4 00.8
21	178 38.4	128 16.7	·· 07.2	143 00.5	·· 50.6	356 58.2	·· 56.0	354 10.0	·· 54.1	Menkent	148 36.1	S36 16.7
22	193 40.8	143 16.0	08.0	158 01.1	51.3	12 00.8	56.0	9 12.6	54.1	Miaplacidus	221 44.8	S69 38.7
23	208 43.3	158 15.4	08.9	173 01.8	51.9	27 03.5	56.1	24 15.2	54.2			
6 00	223 45.8	173 14.7	N18 09.8	188 02.5	N13 52.5	42 06.1	N 0 56.1	39 17.7	N 0 54.2	Mirfak	309 16.0	N49 47.6
01	238 48.2	188 14.1	10.7	203 03.1	53.1	57 08.7	56.2	54 20.3	54.2	Nunki	76 28.5	S26 19.2
02	253 50.7	203 13.4	11.5	218 03.8	53.8	72 11.3	56.3	69 22.9	54.3	Peacock	53 57.6	S56 47.5
03	268 53.2	218 12.8	·· 12.4	233 04.5	·· 54.4	87 13.9	·· 56.3	84 25.5	·· 54.3	Pollux	243 57.8	N28 04.4
04	283 55.6	233 12.2	13.3	248 05.1	55.0	102 16.5	56.4	99 28.1	54.4	Procyon	245 25.5	N 5 16.3
05	298 58.1	248 11.5	14.1	263 05.8	55.6	117 19.1	56.4	114 30.6	54.4			
06	314 00.6	263 10.9	N18 15.0	278 06.5	N13 56.3	132 21.8	N 0 56.5	129 33.2	N 0 54.5	Rasalhague	96 28.9	N12 34.3
07	329 03.0	278 10.2	15.9	293 07.1	56.9	147 24.4	56.5	144 35.8	54.5	Regulus	208 09.5	N12 03.6
W 08	344 05.5	293 09.6	16.7	308 07.8	57.5	162 27.0	56.6	159 38.4	54.5	Rigel	281 35.9	S 8 13.6
E 09	359 07.9	308 08.9	·· 17.6	323 08.4	·· 58.1	177 29.6	·· 56.6	174 40.9	·· 54.6	Rigil Kent.	140 24.6	S60 45.4
D 10	14 10.4	323 08.3	18.5	338 09.1	58.7	192 32.2	56.7	189 43.5	54.6	Sabik	102 40.4	S15 42.1
N 11	29 12.9	338 07.6	19.3	353 09.8	13 59.4	207 34.8	56.8	204 46.1	54.6			
E 12	44 15.3	353 07.0	N18 20.2	8 10.4	N14 00.0	222 37.4	N 0 56.8	219 48.7	N 0 54.7	Schedar	350 09.0	N56 25.8
S 13	59 17.8	8 06.3	21.1	23 11.1	00.6	237 40.0	56.9	234 51.2	54.7	Shaula	96 54.9	S37 05.3
D 14	74 20.3	23 05.6	21.9	38 11.8	01.2	252 42.7	56.9	249 53.8	54.8	Sirius	258 55.6	S16 41.7
A 15	89 22.7	38 05.0	·· 22.8	53 12.4	·· 01.8	267 45.3	·· 57.0	264 56.4	·· 54.8	Spica	158 56.8	S11 03.9
Y 16	104 25.2	53 04.3	23.6	68 13.1	02.5	282 47.9	57.0	279 59.0	54.8	Suhail	223 10.5	S43 21.7
17	119 27.7	68 03.7	24.5	83 13.8	03.1	297 50.5	57.1	295 01.5	54.9			
18	134 30.1	83 03.0	N18 25.4	98 14.4	N14 03.7	312 53.1	N 0 57.1	310 04.1	N 0 54.9	Vega	80 55.3	N38 45.8
19	149 32.6	98 02.4	26.2	113 15.1	04.3	327 55.7	57.2	325 06.7	55.0	Zuben'ubi	137 32.3	S15 57.9
20	164 35.1	113 01.7	27.1	128 15.8	04.9	342 58.3	57.2	340 09.3	55.0			
21	179 37.5	128 01.1	·· 27.9	143 16.4	·· 05.6	358 00.9	·· 57.3	355 11.8	·· 55.0		S.H.A.	Mer. Pass.
22	194 40.0	143 00.4	28.8	158 17.1	06.2	13 03.5	57.3	10 14.4	55.1	Venus	310 43.5	12 27
23	209 42.4	157 59.8	29.6	173 17.7	06.8	28 06.1	57.4	25 17.0	55.1	Mars	324 59.9	11 28
Mer. Pass.	9 07.4	v −0.6	d 0.9	v 0.7	d 0.6	v 2.6	d 0.1	v 2.6	d 0.0	Jupiter	178 16.6	21 12
										Saturn	175 29.2	21 23

G.M.T.	SUN G.H.A.	SUN Dec.	MOON G.H.A.	v	MOON Dec.	d	H.P.	Lat.	Twilight Naut.	Twilight Civil	Sunrise	Moonrise 4	Moonrise 5	Moonrise 6	Moonrise 7
	° '	° '	° '	'	° '	'	'	°	h m	h m	h m	h m	h m	h m	h m
4 00	180 48.3	N15 52.5	181 46.9	6.6	N10 20.4	12.0	61.4	N 72	////	////	01 15	03 36	03 12	▭	▭
01	195 48.4	53.2	196 12.5	6.5	10 32.4	11.8	61.4	N 70	////	////	02 07	03 54	03 45	03 32	▭
02	210 48.4	53.9	210 38.0	6.4	10 44.2	11.8	61.4	68	////	////	02 39	04 08	04 09	04 15	04 30
03	225 48.5	·· 54.6	225 03.4	6.4	10 56.0	11.8	61.4	66	////	01 29	03 02	04 19	04 28	04 44	05 12
04	240 48.5	55.4	239 28.8	6.4	11 07.8	11.6	61.4	64	////	02 07	03 20	04 29	04 44	05 05	05 40
05	255 48.6	56.1	253 54.2	6.3	11 19.4	11.6	61.4	62	////	02 32	03 35	04 37	04 56	05 23	06 02
06	270 48.7	N15 56.8	268 19.5	6.3	N11 31.0	11.5	61.4	60	01 19	02 52	03 48	04 45	05 07	05 38	06 20
07	285 48.7	57.5	282 44.8	6.2	11 42.5	11.4	61.4	N 58	01 53	03 08	03 58	04 51	05 17	05 51	06 35
08	300 48.8	58.3	297 10.0	6.1	11 53.9	11.4	61.4	56	02 17	03 22	04 08	04 57	05 25	06 01	06 47
M 09	315 48.8	·· 59.0	311 35.1	6.2	12 05.3	11.2	61.4	54	02 36	03 33	04 16	05 02	05 33	06 11	06 59
O 10	330 48.9	15 59.7	326 00.3	6.0	12 16.5	11.2	61.4	52	02 51	03 44	04 23	05 06	05 40	06 20	07 08
N 11	345 49.0	16 00.4	340 25.3	6.0	12 27.7	11.1	61.4	50	03 04	03 52	04 30	05 11	05 46	06 27	07 17
D 12	0 49.0	N16 01.2	354 50.3	6.0	N12 38.8	11.0	61.4	45	03 30	04 11	04 44	05 20	05 59	06 44	07 36
A 13	15 49.1	01.9	9 15.3	5.9	12 49.8	10.9	61.4	N 40	03 50	04 26	04 55	05 27	06 10	06 58	07 51
Y 14	30 49.1	02.6	23 40.2	5.9	13 00.7	10.8	61.4	35	04 05	04 38	05 05	05 34	06 19	07 09	08 04
15	45 49.2	·· 03.3	38 05.1	5.8	13 11.5	10.7	61.4	30	04 18	04 48	05 14	05 40	06 28	07 19	08 15
16	60 49.2	04.0	52 29.9	5.8	13 22.2	10.7	61.4	20	04 38	05 05	05 29	05 50	06 42	07 37	08 35
17	75 49.3	04.7	66 54.7	5.7	13 32.9	10.5	61.4	N 10	04 54	05 19	05 41	05 59	06 55	07 52	08 52
18	90 49.3	N16 05.5	81 19.4	5.7	N13 43.4	10.4	61.4	0	05 07	05 32	05 53	06 08	07 07	08 07	09 07
19	105 49.4	06.2	95 44.1	5.6	13 53.8	10.3	61.4	S 10	05 18	05 43	06 05	06 16	07 19	08 21	09 23
20	120 49.5	06.9	110 08.7	5.6	14 04.1	10.3	61.4	20	05 28	05 54	06 17	06 26	07 31	08 37	09 40
21	135 49.5	·· 07.6	124 33.3	5.6	14 14.4	10.1	61.3	30	05 38	06 06	06 31	06 36	07 46	08 55	10 00
22	150 49.6	08.4	138 57.9	5.5	14 24.5	10.0	61.3	35	05 43	06 13	06 39	06 42	07 55	09 05	10 12
23	165 49.6	09.1	153 22.4	5.4	14 34.5	10.0	61.3	40	05 48	06 20	06 49	06 50	08 05	09 18	10 25
5 00	180 49.7	N16 09.8	167 46.8	5.5	N14 44.5	9.8	61.3	45	05 53	06 28	06 59	06 58	08 16	09 32	10 40
01	195 49.7	10.5	182 11.3	5.3	14 54.3	9.7	61.3	S 50	05 59	06 38	07 12	07 08	08 31	09 49	11 00
02	210 49.8	11.2	196 35.6	5.4	15 04.0	9.6	61.3	52	06 01	06 42	07 18	07 12	08 37	09 58	11 09
03	225 49.8	·· 11.9	211 00.0	5.3	15 13.6	9.4	61.3	54	06 04	06 47	07 25	07 18	08 45	10 07	11 19
04	240 49.9	12.7	225 24.3	5.2	15 23.0	9.4	61.3	56	06 07	06 52	07 32	07 23	08 53	10 17	11 31
05	255 50.0	13.4	239 48.5	5.3	15 32.4	9.3	61.2	58	06 10	06 57	07 41	07 30	09 02	10 29	11 44
06	270 50.0	N16 14.1	254 12.8	5.1	N15 41.7	9.1	61.2	S 60	06 13	07 03	07 50	07 37	09 13	10 43	12 00

Lat.	Sunset	Twilight Civil	Twilight Naut.	Moonset 4	Moonset 5	Moonset 6	Moonset 7
07	285 50.1	14.8	268 36.9	5.2	15 50.8	9.0	61.2								

(continued)

G.M.T.	SUN G.H.A.	SUN Dec.	MOON G.H.A.	v	MOON Dec.	d	H.P.	Lat.	Sunset	Twilight Civil	Twilight Naut.	Moonset 4	Moonset 5	Moonset 6	Moonset 7
								°	h m	h m	h m	h m	h m	h m	h m
07	285 50.1	14.8	268 36.9	5.2	15 50.8	9.0	61.2	N 72	22 49	////	////	22 10	▭	▭	▭
08	300 50.1	15.5	283 01.1	5.1	15 59.8	8.9	61.2	N 70	21 51	////	////	21 39	23 58	▭	▭
T 09	315 50.2	·· 16.2	297 25.2	5.1	16 08.7	8.8	61.2	68	21 18	////	////	21 16	23 16	25 08	01 08
U 10	330 50.2	16.9	311 49.3	5.0	16 17.5	8.7	61.2	66	20 54	22 31	////	20 58	22 48	24 27	00 27
E 11	345 50.3	17.6	326 13.3	5.0	16 26.2	8.6	61.2	64	20 35	21 51	////	20 44	22 27	23 59	25 10
S 12	0 50.3	N16 18.4	340 37.3	5.0	N16 34.8	8.4	61.1	62	20 20	21 24	////	20 32	22 10	23 37	24 46
D 13	15 50.4	19.1	355 01.3	4.9	16 43.2	8.3	61.1	60	20 07	21 04	22 40	20 22	21 56	23 20	24 28
A 14	30 50.4	19.8	9 25.2	4.9	16 51.5	8.2	61.1	N 58	19 57	20 47	22 04	20 13	21 43	23 05	24 12
Y 15	45 50.5	·· 20.5	23 49.1	4.9	16 59.7	8.0	61.1	56	19 47	20 33	21 39	20 06	21 33	22 52	23 59
16	60 50.5	21.2	38 13.0	4.8	17 07.7	7.9	61.1	54	19 39	20 21	21 20	19 59	21 24	22 42	23 48
17	75 50.6	21.9	52 36.8	4.9	17 15.6	7.8	61.0	52	19 31	20 11	21 04	19 53	21 16	22 32	23 38
18	90 50.6	N16 22.6	67 00.7	4.8	N17 23.4	7.7	61.0	50	19 25	20 02	20 51	19 47	21 08	22 23	23 29
19	105 50.7	23.3	81 24.5	4.7	17 31.1	7.5	61.0	45	19 10	19 43	20 24	19 35	20 53	22 05	23 09
20	120 50.7	24.0	95 48.2	4.8	17 38.6	7.4	61.0	N 40	18 58	19 28	20 05	19 25	20 40	21 50	22 54
21	135 50.8	·· 24.7	110 12.0	4.7	17 46.0	7.3	60.9	35	18 48	19 16	19 49	19 17	20 29	21 37	22 41
22	150 50.8	25.4	124 35.7	4.7	17 53.3	7.1	60.9	30	18 40	19 05	19 36	19 09	20 19	21 26	22 29
23	165 50.9	26.1	138 59.4	4.7	18 00.4	6.9	60.9	20	18 25	18 48	19 16	18 57	20 03	21 08	22 09
6 00	180 50.9	N16 26.9	153 23.1	4.7	N18 07.4	6.9	60.9	N 10	18 12	18 34	19 00	18 46	19 48	20 51	21 52
01	195 51.0	27.6	167 46.8	4.6	18 14.3	6.7	60.9	0	18 00	18 22	18 47	18 35	19 35	20 36	21 36
02	210 51.0	28.3	182 10.4	4.7	18 21.0	6.6	60.8	S 10	17 48	18 10	18 35	18 25	19 22	20 20	21 20
03	225 51.1	·· 29.0	196 34.0	4.7	18 27.6	6.5	60.8	20	17 36	17 59	18 25	18 14	19 07	20 04	21 03
04	240 51.1	29.7	210 57.7	4.6	18 34.1	6.3	60.8	30	17 22	17 47	18 15	18 01	18 51	19 45	20 43
05	255 51.2	30.4	225 21.3	4.5	18 40.4	6.2	60.8	35	17 13	17 40	18 10	17 54	18 42	19 34	20 31
06	270 51.2	N16 31.1	254 08.4	4.6	N18 46.6	6.1	60.7	40	17 04	17 33	18 05	17 46	18 31	19 22	20 18
07	285 51.3	31.8	254 08.4	4.6	18 52.7	5.9	60.7	45	16 53	17 25	18 00	17 36	18 18	19 07	20 02
W 08	300 51.3	32.5	268 32.0	4.5	18 58.6	5.7	60.7	S 50	16 40	17 15	17 54	17 25	18 03	18 49	19 43
E 09	315 51.4	·· 33.2	282 55.5	4.6	19 04.3	5.6	60.7	52	16 34	17 11	17 51	17 20	17 56	18 40	19 33
D 10	330 51.4	33.9	297 19.1	4.6	19 09.9	5.5	60.6	54	16 28	17 06	17 48	17 14	17 48	18 31	19 23
N 11	345 51.4	34.6	311 42.6	4.6	19 15.4	5.4	60.6	56	16 20	17 01	17 46	17 07	17 39	18 20	19 12
E 12	0 51.5	N16 35.3	326 06.2	4.5	N19 20.8	5.2	60.6	58	16 12	16 55	17 43	17 00	17 29	18 08	18 58
S 13	15 51.5	36.0	340 29.7	4.6	19 26.0	5.1	60.5	S 60	16 02	16 49	17 39	16 52	17 18	17 54	18 42
D 14	30 51.6	36.7	354 53.3	4.5	19 31.0	4.9	60.5								
A 15	45 51.6	·· 37.4	9 16.8	4.5	19 35.9	4.8	60.5								
Y 16	60 51.7	38.1	23 40.3	4.6	19 40.7	4.6	60.5								
17	75 51.7	38.8	38 03.9	4.5	19 45.3	4.5	60.4								
18	90 51.8	N16 39.5	52 27.4	4.6	N19 49.8	4.3	60.4								
19	105 51.8	40.2	66 51.0	4.6	19 54.1	4.2	60.4								
20	120 51.9	40.9	81 14.6	4.5	19 58.3	4.1	60.3								
21	135 51.9	·· 41.6	95 38.1	4.6	20 02.4	3.9	60.3								
22	150 51.9	42.3	110 01.7	4.6	20 06.3	3.7	60.3								
23	165 52.0	43.0	124 25.3	4.6	20 10.0	3.6	60.2								

Day	SUN Eqn. of Time 00ʰ	SUN Eqn. of Time 12ʰ	SUN Mer. Pass.	MOON Mer. Pass. Upper	MOON Mer. Pass. Lower	Age	Phase
	m s	m s	h m	h m	h m	d	
4	03 13	03 16	11 57	12 21	24 51	00	
5	03 19	03 21	11 57	13 21	00 51	01	
6	03 24	03 26	11 57	14 21	01 51	02	●

	S.D. 15.9	d 0.7	S.D. 16.7		16.7		16.5

1981 MAY 7, 8, 9 (THURS., FRI., SAT.)

G.M.T.	ARIES G.H.A.	VENUS −3.4 G.H.A.	Dec.	MARS +1.5 G.H.A.	Dec.	JUPITER −1.9 G.H.A.	Dec.	SATURN +0.9 G.H.A.	Dec.	STARS Name	S.H.A.	Dec.
7 00	224 44.9	172 59.1	N18 30.5	188 18.4	N14 07.4	43 08.8	N 0 57.5	40 19.5	N 0 55.2	Acamar	315 37.4	S40 22.9
01	239 47.4	187 58.4	31.4	203 19.1	08.0	58 11.4	57.5	55 22.1	55.2	Achernar	335 45.5	S57 19.9
02	254 49.8	202 57.8	32.2	218 19.7	08.6	73 14.0	57.6	70 24.7	55.2	Acrux	173 36.2	S62 59.9
03	269 52.3	217 57.1	·· 33.1	233 20.4	·· 09.3	88 16.6	·· 57.6	85 27.3	·· 55.3	Adhara	255 32.0	S28 57.0
04	284 54.8	232 56.5	33.9	248 21.1	09.9	103 19.2	57.7	100 29.8	55.3	Aldebaran	291 17.9	N16 28.2
05	299 57.2	247 55.8	34.8	263 21.7	10.5	118 21.8	57.7	115 32.4	55.4	.		
06	314 59.7	262 55.1	N18 35.6	278 22.4	N14 11.1	133 24.4	N 0 57.8	130 35.0	N 0 55.4	Alioth	166 41.7	N56 03.9
07	330 02.2	277 54.5	36.5	293 23.0	11.7	148 27.0	57.8	145 37.6	55.4	Alkaid	153 17.7	N49 24.5
T 08	345 04.6	292 53.8	37.3	308 23.7	12.3	163 29.6	57.9	160 40.1	55.5	Al Na'ir	28 14.5	S47 03.0
H 09	0 07.1	307 53.2	·· 38.1	323 24.4	·· 13.0	178 32.2	·· 57.9	175 42.7	·· 55.5	Alnilam	276 11.5	S 1 13.0
U 10	15 09.6	322 52.5	39.0	338 25.0	13.6	193 34.8	58.0	190 45.3	55.6	Alphard	218 20.2	S 8 34.8
R 11	30 12.0	337 51.8	39.8	353 25.7	14.2	208 37.4	58.0	205 47.8	55.6			
S 12	45 14.5	352 51.2	N18 40.7	8 26.4	N14 14.8	223 40.0	N 0 58.1	220 50.4	N 0 55.6	Alphecca	126 31.4	N26 46.7
D 13	60 16.9	7 50.5	41.5	23 27.0	15.4	238 42.6	58.1	235 53.0	55.7	Alpheratz	358 09.1	N28 59.0
A 14	75 19.4	22 49.8	42.4	38 27.7	16.0	253 45.2	58.2	250 55.6	55.7	Altair	62 32.0	N 8 49.0
Y 15	90 21.9	37 49.2	·· 43.2	53 28.3	·· 16.6	268 47.9	·· 58.2	265 58.1	·· 55.7	Ankaa	353 40.2	S42 24.5
16	105 24.3	52 48.5	44.0	68 29.0	17.3	283 50.5	58.3	281 00.7	55.8	Antares	112 56.0	S26 23.4
17	120 26.8	67 47.8	44.9	83 29.7	17.9	298 53.1	58.3	296 03.3	55.8			
18	135 29.3	82 47.2	N18 45.7	98 30.3	N14 18.5	313 55.7	N 0 58.4	311 05.9	N 0 55.9	Arcturus	146 17.8	N19 16.8
19	150 31.7	97 46.5	46.6	113 31.0	19.1	328 58.3	58.4	326 08.4	55.9	Atria	108 19.4	S68 59.5
20	165 34.2	112 45.8	47.4	128 31.7	19.7	344 00.9	58.5	341 11.0	55.9	Avior	234 28.2	S59 27.3
21	180 36.7	127 45.2	·· 48.2	143 32.3	·· 20.3	359 03.5	·· 58.5	356 13.6	·· 56.0	Bellatrix	278 58.6	N 6 19.8
22	195 39.1	142 44.5	49.1	158 33.0	20.9	14 06.1	58.6	11 16.1	56.0	Betelgeuse	271 28.1	N 7 24.1
23	210 41.6	157 43.8	49.9	173 33.6	21.6	29 08.7	58.6	26 18.7	56.1			
8 00	225 44.0	172 43.2	N18 50.7	188 34.3	N14 22.2	44 11.3	N 0 58.7	41 21.3	N 0 56.1	Canopus	264 07.4	S52 41.4
01	240 46.5	187 42.5	51.6	203 35.0	22.8	59 13.9	58.7	56 23.8	56.1	Capella	281 11.1	N45 58.8
02	255 49.0	202 41.8	52.4	218 35.6	23.4	74 16.5	58.8	71 26.4	56.2	Deneb	49 48.1	N45 12.5
03	270 51.4	217 41.2	·· 53.2	233 36.3	·· 24.0	89 19.1	·· 58.8	86 29.0	·· 56.2	Denebola	182 58.4	N14 40.7
04	285 53.9	232 40.5	54.1	248 36.9	24.6	104 21.7	58.9	101 31.6	56.2	Diphda	349 20.7	S18 05.5
05	300 56.4	247 39.8	54.9	263 37.6	25.2	119 24.3	58.9	116 34.1	56.3			
06	315 58.8	262 39.1	N18 55.7	278 38.3	N14 25.8	134 26.9	N 0 59.0	131 36.7	N 0 56.3	Dubhe	194 21.3	N61 51.4
07	331 01.3	277 38.5	56.5	293 38.9	26.4	149 29.5	59.0	146 39.3	56.4	Elnath	278 43.9	N28 35.5
08	346 03.8	292 37.8	57.4	308 39.6	27.0	164 32.1	59.1	161 41.8	56.4	Eltanin	90 57.1	N51 29.3
F 09	1 06.2	307 37.1	·· 58.2	323 40.3	·· 27.7	179 34.7	·· 59.1	176 44.4	·· 56.4	Enif	34 11.2	N 9 47.2
R 10	16 08.7	322 36.4	59.0	338 40.9	28.3	194 37.3	59.2	191 47.0	56.5	Fomalhaut	15 51.1	S29 43.3
I 11	31 11.2	337 35.8	18 59.8	353 41.6	28.9	209 39.9	59.2	206 49.5	56.5			
D 12	46 13.6	352 35.1	N19 00.7	8 42.2	N14 29.5	224 42.5	N 0 59.3	221 52.1	N 0 56.5	Gacrux	172 27.8	S57 00.7
A 13	61 16.1	7 34.4	01.5	23 42.9	30.1	239 45.1	59.3	236 54.7	56.6	Gienah	176 17.3	S17 26.4
Y 14	76 18.5	22 33.7	02.3	38 43.6	30.7	254 47.7	59.4	251 57.2	56.6	Hadar	149 22.1	S60 17.0
15	91 21.0	37 33.1	·· 03.1	53 44.2	·· 31.3	269 50.3	·· 59.4	266 59.8	·· 56.7	Hamal	328 28.8	N23 22.2
16	106 23.5	52 32.4	03.9	68 44.9	31.9	284 52.9	59.5	282 02.4	56.7	Kaus Aust.	84 16.0	S34 23.5
17	121 25.9	67 31.7	04.8	83 45.5	32.5	299 55.5	59.5	297 05.0	56.7			
18	136 28.4	82 31.0	N19 05.6	98 46.2	N14 33.1	314 58.1	N 0 59.6	312 07.5	N 0 56.8	Kochab	137 17.9	N74 14.1
19	151 30.9	97 30.4	06.4	113 46.9	33.7	330 00.7	59.6	327 10.1	56.8	Markab	14 02.9	N15 06.0
20	166 33.3	112 29.7	07.2	128 47.5	34.3	345 03.3	59.7	342 12.7	56.8	Menkar	314 41.0	N 4 00.8
21	181 35.8	127 29.0	·· 08.0	143 48.2	·· 34.9	0 05.9	·· 59.7	357 15.2	·· 56.9	Menkent	148 36.1	S36 16.7
22	196 38.3	142 28.3	08.8	158 48.8	35.6	15 08.5	59.8	12 17.8	56.9	Miaplacidus	221 44.9	S69 38.7
23	211 40.7	157 27.6	09.7	173 49.5	36.2	30 11.1	59.8	27 20.4	57.0			
9 00	226 43.2	172 27.0	N19 10.5	188 50.2	N14 36.8	45 13.7	N 0 59.9	42 22.9	N 0 57.0	Mirfak	309 16.0	N49 47.6
01	241 45.7	187 26.3	11.3	203 50.8	37.4	60 16.2	0 59.9	57 25.5	57.0	Nunki	76 28.4	S26 19.2
02	256 48.1	202 25.6	12.1	218 51.5	38.0	75 18.8	1 00.0	72 28.1	57.1	Peacock	53 57.6	S56 47.5
03	271 50.6	217 24.9	·· 12.9	233 52.1	·· 38.6	90 21.4	·· 00.0	87 30.6	·· 57.1	Pollux	243 57.8	N28 04.4
04	286 53.0	232 24.2	13.7	248 52.8	39.2	105 24.0	00.1	102 33.2	57.1	Procyon	245 25.5	N 5 16.3
05	301 55.5	247 23.5	14.5	263 53.5	39.8	120 26.6	00.1	117 35.8	57.2			
06	316 58.0	262 22.9	N19 15.3	278 54.1	N14 40.4	135 29.2	N 1 00.1	132 38.3	N 0 57.2	Rasalhague	96 28.9	N12 34.3
07	332 00.4	277 22.2	16.1	293 54.8	41.0	150 31.8	00.2	147 40.9	57.2	Regulus	208 09.5	N12 03.6
S 08	347 02.9	292 21.5	16.9	308 55.4	41.6	165 34.4	00.2	162 43.5	57.3	Rigel	281 35.9	S 8 13.6
A 09	2 05.4	307 20.8	·· 17.7	323 56.1	·· 42.2	180 37.0	·· 00.3	177 46.0	·· 57.3	Rigil Kent.	140 24.6	S60 45.4
T 10	17 07.8	322 20.1	18.5	338 56.7	42.8	195 39.6	00.3	192 48.6	57.4	Sabik	102 40.4	S15 42.1
U 11	32 10.3	337 19.4	19.3	353 57.4	43.4	210 42.2	00.4	207 51.2	57.4			
R 12	47 12.8	352 18.7	N19 20.1	8 58.1	N14 44.0	225 44.8	N 1 00.4	222 53.7	N 0 57.4	Schedar	350 09.0	N56 25.8
D 13	62 15.2	7 18.1	20.9	23 58.7	44.6	240 47.4	00.5	237 56.3	57.5	Shaula	96 54.9	S37 05.3
A 14	77 17.7	22 17.4	21.7	38 59.4	45.2	255 50.0	00.5	252 58.9	57.5	Sirius	258 55.6	S16 41.7
Y 15	92 20.1	37 16.7	·· 22.5	54 00.0	·· 45.8	270 52.6	·· 00.6	268 01.4	·· 57.5	Spica	158 56.8	S11 03.9
16	107 22.6	52 16.0	23.3	69 00.7	46.4	285 55.1	00.6	283 04.0	57.6	Suhail	223 10.5	S43 21.7
17	122 25.1	67 15.3	24.1	84 01.4	47.0	300 57.7	00.6	298 06.5	57.6			
18	137 27.5	82 14.6	N19 24.9	99 02.0	N14 47.6	316 00.3	N 1 00.7	313 09.1	N 0 57.6	Vega	80 55.3	N38 45.8
19	152 30.0	97 13.9	25.7	114 02.7	48.2	331 02.9	00.7	328 11.7	57.7	Zuben'ubi	137 32.2	S15 57.9
20	167 32.5	112 13.2	26.5	129 03.3	48.8	346 05.5	00.8	343 14.2	57.7			
21	182 34.9	127 12.5	·· 27.3	144 04.0	·· 49.4	1 08.1	·· 00.8	358 16.8	·· 57.7			
22	197 37.4	142 11.9	28.1	159 04.7	50.0	16 10.7	00.9	13 19.4	57.8			
23	212 39.9	157 11.2	28.9	174 05.3	50.6	31 13.3	00.9	28 21.9	57.8			
Mer. Pass.	8 55.6	v −0.7	d 0.8	v 0.7	d 0.6	v 2.6	d 0.0	v 2.6	d 0.0			

	S.H.A.	Mer. Pass.
	° ′	h m
Venus	306 59.1	12 30
Mars	322 50.3	11 25
Jupiter	178 27.2	21 00
Saturn	175 37.2	21 11

G.M.T.	SUN G.H.A.	SUN Dec.	MOON G.H.A.	v	MOON Dec.	d	H.P.
7 00	180 52.0	N16 43.6	138 48.9	4.6	N20 13.6	3.5	60.2
01	195 52.1	44.3	153 12.5	4.7	20 17.1	3.3	60.2
02	210 52.1	45.0	167 36.2	4.6	20 20.4	3.1	60.1
03	225 52.2	·· 45.7	181 59.8	4.7	20 23.5	3.1	60.1
04	240 52.2	46.4	196 23.5	4.7	20 26.6	2.8	60.1
05	255 52.2	47.1	210 47.2	4.8	20 29.4	2.8	60.0
06	270 52.3	N16 47.8	225 11.0	4.7	N20 32.2	2.5	60.0
07	285 52.3	48.5	239 34.7	4.8	20 34.7	2.5	60.0
T 08	300 52.4	49.2	253 58.5	4.8	20 37.2	2.3	59.9
H 09	315 52.4	·· 49.9	268 22.3	4.8	20 39.5	2.1	59.9
U 10	330 52.4	50.6	282 46.1	4.9	20 41.6	2.0	59.9
R 11	345 52.5	51.2	297 10.0	4.9	20 43.6	1.9	59.8
S 12	0 52.5	N16 51.9	311 33.9	4.9	N20 45.5	1.7	59.8
D 13	15 52.6	52.6	325 57.8	5.0	20 47.2	1.5	59.8
A 14	30 52.6	53.3	340 21.8	5.0	20 48.7	1.4	59.7
Y 15	45 52.6	·· 54.0	354 45.8	5.0	20 50.1	1.3	59.7
16	60 52.7	54.7	9 09.8	5.1	20 51.4	1.1	59.6
17	75 52.7	55.4	23 33.9	5.1	20 52.5	1.0	59.6
18	90 52.8	N16 56.1	37 58.0	5.2	N20 53.5	0.9	59.6
19	105 52.8	56.7	52 22.2	5.2	20 54.4	0.7	59.5
20	120 52.8	57.4	66 46.4	5.3	20 55.1	0.5	59.5
21	135 52.9	·· 58.1	81 10.7	5.3	20 55.6	0.4	59.5
22	150 52.9	58.8	95 35.0	5.3	20 56.0	0.3	59.4
23	165 52.9	16 59.5	109 59.3	5.4	20 56.3	0.1	59.4
8 00	180 53.0	N17 00.2	124 23.7	5.5	N20 56.4	0.0	59.4
01	195 53.0	00.8	138 48.2	5.5	20 56.4	0.1	59.3
02	210 53.1	01.5	153 12.7	5.5	20 56.3	0.3	59.3
03	225 53.1	·· 02.2	167 37.2	5.6	20 56.0	0.4	59.2
04	240 53.1	02.9	182 01.8	5.7	20 55.6	0.6	59.2
05	255 53.2	03.6	196 26.5	5.7	20 55.0	0.7	59.2
06	270 53.2	N17 04.2	210 51.2	5.8	N20 54.3	0.8	59.1
07	285 53.2	04.9	225 16.0	5.9	20 53.5	1.0	59.1
08	300 53.3	05.6	239 40.9	5.9	20 52.5	1.1	59.0
F 09	315 53.3	·· 06.3	254 05.8	5.9	20 51.4	1.3	59.0
R 10	330 53.3	07.0	268 30.7	6.0	20 50.1	1.3	59.0
I 11	345 53.3	07.6	282 55.7	6.1	20 48.8	1.5	58.9
D 12	0 53.4	N17 08.3	297 20.8	6.2	N20 47.3	1.7	58.9
A 13	15 53.5	09.0	311 46.0	6.2	20 45.6	1.8	58.8
Y 14	30 53.5	09.7	326 11.2	6.3	20 43.8	1.9	58.8
15	45 53.5	·· 10.3	340 36.5	6.4	20 41.9	2.0	58.8
16	60 53.6	11.0	355 01.9	6.4	20 39.9	2.2	58.7
17	75 53.6	11.7	9 27.3	6.5	20 37.7	2.3	58.7
18	90 53.6	N17 12.4	23 52.8	6.5	N20 35.4	2.4	58.7
19	105 53.7	13.0	38 18.3	6.7	20 33.0	2.5	58.6
20	120 53.7	13.7	52 44.0	6.7	20 30.5	2.7	58.6
21	135 53.7	·· 14.4	67 09.7	6.8	20 27.8	2.8	58.5
22	150 53.7	15.0	81 35.5	6.8	20 25.0	2.9	58.5
23	165 53.8	15.7	96 01.3	7.0	20 22.1	3.0	58.5
9 00	180 53.8	N17 16.4	110 27.3	7.0	N20 19.1	3.2	58.4
01	195 53.8	17.1	124 53.3	7.1	20 15.9	3.3	58.4
02	210 53.9	17.7	139 19.4	7.1	20 12.6	3.4	58.3
03	225 53.9	·· 18.4	153 45.5	7.3	20 09.2	3.5	58.3
04	240 53.9	19.1	168 11.8	7.3	20 05.7	3.6	58.3
05	255 54.0	19.7	182 38.1	7.4	20 02.1	3.8	58.2
06	270 54.0	N17 20.4	197 04.5	7.5	N19 58.3	3.9	58.2
07	285 54.0	21.1	211 31.0	7.5	19 54.4	3.9	58.1
S 08	300 54.1	21.7	225 57.5	7.7	19 50.5	4.1	58.1
A 09	315 54.1	·· 22.4	240 24.2	7.7	19 46.4	4.3	58.1
T 10	330 54.1	23.1	254 50.9	7.8	19 42.1	4.3	58.0
U 11	345 54.1	23.7	269 17.7	7.9	19 37.8	4.4	58.0
R 12	0 54.2	N17 24.4	283 44.6	7.9	N19 33.4	4.6	57.9
D 13	15 54.2	25.1	298 11.5	8.1	19 28.8	4.6	57.9
A 14	30 54.2	25.7	312 38.6	8.1	19 24.2	4.8	57.9
Y 15	45 54.3	·· 26.4	327 05.7	8.2	19 19.4	4.8	57.8
16	60 54.3	27.0	341 32.9	8.3	19 14.6	5.0	57.8
17	75 54.3	27.7	356 00.2	8.4	19 09.6	5.1	57.7
18	90 54.3	N17 28.4	10 27.6	8.5	N19 04.5	5.2	57.7
19	105 54.4	29.0	24 55.1	8.5	18 59.3	5.2	57.7
20	120 54.4	29.7	39 22.6	8.7	18 54.1	5.4	57.6
21	135 54.4	·· 30.3	53 50.3	8.7	18 48.7	5.5	57.6
22	150 54.4	31.0	68 18.0	8.8	18 43.2	5.6	57.5
23	165 54.5	31.7	82 45.8	8.9	18 37.6	5.7	57.5
	S.D. 15.9 d 0.7		S.D. 16.3	16.0			15.8

Twilight / Moonrise

Lat.	Naut.	Civil	Sunrise	Moonrise 7	8	9	10
N 72	////	////	00 28	☐	☐		06 23
N 70	////	////	01 47	☐	☐	05 16	07 44
68	////	////	02 24	04 30	05 16	06 42	08 23
66	////	01 05	02 50	05 12	06 03	07 20	08 49
64	////	01 51	03 10	05 40	06 34	07 47	09 10
62	////	02 21	03 26	06 02	06 57	08 07	09 26
60	00 57	02 42	03 40	06 20	07 16	08 24	09 40
N 58	01 40	03 00	03 51	06 35	07 31	08 38	09 52
56	02 07	03 14	04 01	06 47	07 44	08 50	10 02
54	02 27	03 27	04 10	06 59	07 56	09 01	10 11
52	02 44	03 37	04 18	07 08	08 06	09 10	10 19
50	02 58	03 47	04 25	07 17	08 15	09 19	10 26
45	03 25	04 07	04 40	07 36	08 34	09 37	10 41
N 40	03 45	04 22	04 52	07 51	08 50	09 51	10 54
35	04 02	04 35	05 02	08 04	09 03	10 03	11 04
30	04 15	04 46	05 12	08 15	09 14	10 14	11 14
20	04 36	05 04	05 27	08 35	09 34	10 33	11 30
N 10	04 53	05 18	05 40	08 52	09 51	10 49	11 44
0	05 06	05 31	05 53	09 07	10 07	11 04	11 57
S 10	05 18	05 43	06 05	09 23	10 23	11 18	12 10
20	05 29	05 55	06 18	09 40	10 40	11 34	12 24
30	05 40	06 08	06 33	10 00	11 00	11 53	12 39
35	05 45	06 15	06 42	10 12	11 11	12 03	12 49
40	05 50	06 23	06 52	10 25	11 24	12 16	12 59
45	05 56	06 32	07 03	10 40	11 40	12 30	13 11
S 50	06 03	06 42	07 17	11 00	11 59	12 48	13 26
52	06 06	06 46	07 23	11 09	12 08	12 56	13 33
54	06 09	06 51	07 30	11 19	12 19	13 05	13 41
56	06 12	06 57	07 38	11 31	12 30	13 15	13 49
58	06 15	07 03	07 47	11 44	12 43	13 27	13 59
S 60	06 19	07 10	07 57	12 00	12 59	13 41	14 10

Twilight / Moonset

Lat.	Sunset	Civil	Naut.	Moonset 7	8	9	10
N 72	☐	☐	☐	☐	☐	☐	05 15
N 70	22 12	////	////	☐	☐	04 28	03 53
68	21 32	////	////	01 08	02 28	03 02	03 14
66	21 05	22 57	////	00 27	01 40	02 24	02 46
64	20 45	22 06	////	25 10	01 10	01 57	02 25
62	20 28	21 36	////	24 46	00 46	01 36	02 08
60	20 15	21 13	23 04	24 28	00 28	01 18	01 54
N 58	20 03	20 55	22 17	24 12	00 12	01 04	01 42
56	19 53	20 40	21 49	23 59	24 52	00 52	01 31
54	19 44	20 28	21 28	23 48	24 41	00 41	01 22
52	19 36	20 17	21 11	23 38	24 31	00 31	01 14
50	19 29	20 07	20 57	23 29	24 23	00 23	01 06
45	19 14	19 47	20 29	23 09	24 04	00 04	00 50
N 40	19 01	19 31	20 08	22 54	23 49	24 37	00 37
35	18 51	19 19	19 52	22 41	23 37	24 25	00 25
30	18 42	19 08	19 38	22 29	23 26	24 16	00 16
20	18 26	18 49	19 17	22 09	23 07	23 58	24 45
N 10	18 12	18 35	19 00	21 52	22 50	23 44	24 33
0	18 00	18 22	18 47	21 36	22 34	23 29	24 21
S 10	17 47	18 09	18 35	21 20	22 19	23 15	24 09
20	17 34	17 57	18 24	21 03	22 02	23 00	23 56
30	17 19	17 44	18 13	20 43	21 43	22 43	23 42
35	17 11	17 37	18 08	20 31	21 31	22 33	23 33
40	17 01	17 30	18 02	20 18	21 18	22 21	23 24
45	16 50	17 21	17 56	20 02	21 03	22 07	23 12
S 50	16 36	17 11	17 49	19 43	20 44	21 50	22 58
52	16 29	17 06	17 47	19 33	20 35	21 42	22 52
54	16 22	17 01	17 44	19 23	20 25	21 33	22 44
56	16 14	16 55	17 40	19 12	20 14	21 23	22 36
58	16 05	16 49	17 37	18 58	20 01	21 12	22 27
S 60	15 55	16 42	17 33	18 42	19 45	20 59	22 17

SUN / MOON

Day	SUN Eqn. of Time 00h	12h	Mer. Pass.	MOON Mer. Pass. Upper	Lower	Age	Phase
	m s	m s	h m	h m	h m	d	
7	03 28	03 30	11 56	15 22	02 52	03	
8	03 32	03 34	11 56	16 21	03 52	04	◑
9	03 35	03 37	11 56	17 17	04 49	05	

1981 MAY 10, 11, 12 (SUN., MON., TUES.)

G.M.T.	ARIES G.H.A.	VENUS −3.4 G.H.A.	Dec.	MARS +1.5 G.H.A.	Dec.	JUPITER −1.9 G.H.A.	Dec.	SATURN +0.9 G.H.A.	Dec.	STARS Name	S.H.A.	Dec.
10 00	227 42.3	172 10.5 N19 29.7		189 06.0 N14 51.2		46 15.9 N 1 01.0		43 24.5 N 0 57.9		Acamar	315 37.4	S40 22.9
01	242 44.8	187 09.8	30.5	204 06.6	51.8	61 18.5	01.0	58 27.1	57.9	Achernar	335 45.5	S57 19.9
02	257 47.3	202 09.1	31.3	219 07.3	52.4	76 21.0	01.0	73 29.6	57.9	Acrux	173 36.2	S62 59.9
03	272 49.7	217 08.4 ··	32.1	234 07.9 ··	53.0	91 23.6 ··	01.1	88 32.2 ··	58.0	Adhara	255 32.0	S28 57.0
04	287 52.2	232 07.7	32.8	249 08.6	53.6	106 26.2	01.1	103 34.8	58.0	Aldebaran	291 17.8	N16 28.2
05	302 54.6	247 07.0	33.6	264 09.3	54.2	121 28.8	01.2	118 37.3	58.0			
06	317 57.1	262 06.3 N19 34.4		279 09.9 N14 54.8		136 31.4 N 1 01.2		133 39.9 N 0 58.1		Alioth	166 41.7	N56 03.9
07	332 59.6	277 05.6	35.2	294 10.6	55.4	151 34.0	01.3	148 42.4	58.1	Alkaid	153 17.7	N49 24.5
08	348 02.0	292 04.9	36.0	309 11.2	56.0	166 36.6	01.3	163 45.0	58.1	Al Na'ir	28 14.5	S47 03.0
S 09	3 04.5	307 04.2 ··	36.8	324 11.9 ··	56.6	181 39.2 ··	01.4	178 47.6 ··	58.2	Alnilam	276 11.5	S 1 13.0
U 10	18 07.0	322 03.5	37.5	339 12.5	57.2	196 41.7	01.4	193 50.1	58.2	Alphard	218 20.2	S 8 34.7
N 11	33 09.4	337 02.8	38.3	354 13.2	57.8	211 44.3	01.4	208 52.7	58.2			
D 12	48 11.9	352 02.1 N19 39.1		9 13.9 N14 58.4		226 46.9 N 1 01.5		223 55.3 N 0 58.3		Alphecca	126 31.4	N26 46.7
A 13	63 14.4	7 01.4	39.9	24 14.5	59.0	241 49.5	01.5	238 57.8	58.3	Alpheratz	358 09.1	N28 59.0
Y 14	78 16.8	22 00.7	40.7	39 15.2	14 59.6	256 52.1	01.6	254 00.4	58.3	Altair	62 32.0	N 8 49.0
15	93 19.3	37 00.0 ··	41.4	54 15.8	15 00.2	271 54.7 ··	01.6	269 02.9 ··	58.4	Ankaa	353 40.1	S42 24.4
16	108 21.8	51 59.3	42.2	69 16.5	00.8	286 57.3	01.7	284 05.5	58.4	Antares	112 56.0	S26 23.4
17	123 24.2	66 58.6	43.0	84 17.1	01.4	301 59.8	01.7	299 08.1	58.4			
18	138 26.7	81 57.9 N19 43.8		99 17.8 N15 02.0		317 02.4 N 1 01.7		314 10.6 N 0 58.5		Arcturus	146 17.8	N19 16.8
19	153 29.1	96 57.2	44.5	114 18.5	02.6	332 05.0	01.8	329 13.2	58.5	Atria	108 19.3	S68 59.5
20	168 31.6	111 56.5	45.3	129 19.1	03.1	347 07.6	01.8	344 15.7	58.5	Avior	234 28.2	S59 27.3
21	183 34.1	126 55.8 ··	46.1	144 19.8 ··	03.7	2 10.2 ··	01.9	359 18.3 ··	58.6	Bellatrix	278 58.6	N 6 19.9
22	198 36.5	141 55.1	46.9	159 20.4	04.3	17 12.8	01.9	14 20.9	58.6	Betelgeuse	271 28.1	N 7 24.1
23	213 39.0	156 54.4	47.6	174 21.1	04.9	32 15.3	01.9	29 23.4	58.6			
11 00	228 41.5	171 53.7 N19 48.4		189 21.7 N15 05.5		47 17.9 N 1 02.0		44 26.0 N 0 58.7		Canopus	264 07.4	S52 41.4
01	243 43.9	186 53.0	49.2	204 22.4	06.1	62 20.5	02.0	59 28.6	58.7	Capella	281 11.1	N45 58.8
02	258 46.4	201 52.3	49.9	219 23.0	06.7	77 23.1	02.1	74 31.1	58.7	Deneb	49 48.1	N45 12.5
03	273 48.9	216 51.6 ··	50.7	234 23.7 ··	07.3	92 25.7 ··	02.1	89 33.7 ··	58.8	Denebola	182 58.4	N14 40.7
04	288 51.3	231 50.9	51.5	249 24.4	07.9	107 28.3	02.2	104 36.2	58.8	Diphda	349 20.7	S18 05.5
05	303 53.8	246 50.2	52.2	264 25.0	08.5	122 30.8	02.2	119 38.8	58.8			
06	318 56.2	261 49.5 N19 53.0		279 25.7 N15 09.1		137 33.4 N 1 02.2		134 41.4 N 0 58.9		Dubhe	194 21.4	N61 51.4
07	333 58.7	276 48.8	53.7	294 26.3	09.7	152 36.0	02.3	149 43.9	58.9	Elnath	278 43.9	N28 35.5
08	349 01.2	291 48.1	54.5	309 27.0	10.2	167 38.6	02.3	164 46.5	58.9	Eltanin	90 57.1	N51 29.3
M 09	4 03.6	306 47.4 ··	55.3	324 27.6 ··	10.8	182 41.2 ··	02.4	179 49.0 ··	59.0	Enif	34 11.2	N 9 47.2
O 10	19 06.1	321 46.6	56.0	339 28.3	11.4	197 43.7	02.4	194 51.6	59.0	Fomalhaut	15 51.1	S29 43.3
N 11	34 08.6	336 45.9	56.8	354 28.9	12.0	212 46.3	02.4	209 54.1	59.0			
D 12	49 11.0	351 45.2 N19 57.5		9 29.6 N15 12.6		227 48.9 N 1 02.5		224 56.7 N 0 59.1		Gacrux	172 27.8	S57 00.7
A 13	64 13.5	6 44.5	58.3	24 30.3	13.2	242 51.5	02.5	239 59.3	59.1	Gienah	176 17.3	S17 26.4
Y 14	79 16.0	21 43.8	59.1	39 30.9	13.8	257 54.1	02.6	255 01.8	59.1	Hadar	149 22.1	S60 17.0
15	94 18.4	36 43.1	19 59.8	54 31.6 ··	14.4	272 56.6 ··	02.6	270 04.4 ··	59.2	Hamal	328 28.8	N23 22.2
16	109 20.9	51 42.4	20 00.6	69 32.2	15.0	287 59.2	02.6	285 06.9	59.2	Kaus Aust.	84 16.0	S34 23.5
17	124 23.4	66 41.7	01.3	84 32.9	15.6	303 01.8	02.7	300 09.5	59.2			
18	139 25.8	81 41.0 N20 02.1		99 33.5 N15 16.1		318 04.4 N 1 02.7		315 12.1 N 0 59.3		Kochab	137 17.9	N74 14.1
19	154 28.3	96 40.2	02.8	114 34.2	16.7	333 07.0	02.8	330 14.6	59.3	Markab	14 02.9	N15 06.0
20	169 30.7	111 39.5	03.6	129 34.8	17.3	348 09.5	02.8	345 17.2	59.3	Menkar	314 41.0	N 4 00.8
21	184 33.2	126 38.8 ··	04.3	144 35.5 ··	17.9	3 12.1 ··	02.8	0 19.7 ··	59.4	Menkent	148 36.1	S36 16.7
22	199 35.7	141 38.1	05.1	159 36.1	18.5	18 14.7	02.9	15 22.3	59.4	Miaplacidus	221 44.9	S69 38.7
23	214 38.1	156 37.4	05.8	174 36.8	19.1	33 17.3	02.9	30 24.8	59.4			
12 00	229 40.6	171 36.7 N20 06.6		189 37.5 N15 19.7		48 19.8 N 1 02.9		45 27.4 N 0 59.5		Mirfak	309 16.0	N49 47.6
01	244 43.1	186 36.0	07.3	204 38.1	20.2	63 22.4	03.0	60 30.0	59.5	Nunki	76 28.4	S26 19.2
02	259 45.5	201 35.2	08.0	219 38.8	20.8	78 25.0	03.0	75 32.5	59.5	Peacock	53 57.6	S56 47.5
03	274 48.0	216 34.5 ··	08.8	234 39.4 ··	21.4	93 27.6 ··	03.1	90 35.1 ··	59.6	Pollux	243 57.8	N28 04.4
04	289 50.5	231 33.8	09.5	249 40.1	22.0	108 30.1	03.1	105 37.6	59.6	Procyon	245 25.5	N 5 16.3
05	304 52.9	246 33.1	10.3	264 40.7	22.6	123 32.7	03.1	120 40.2	59.6			
06	319 55.4	261 32.4 N20 11.0		279 41.4 N15 23.2		138 35.3 N 1 03.2		135 42.7 N 0 59.6		Rasalhague	96 28.9	N12 34.3
07	334 57.9	276 31.7	11.8	294 42.0	23.8	153 37.9	03.2	150 45.3	59.7	Regulus	208 09.5	N12 03.6
08	350 00.3	291 30.9	12.5	309 42.7	24.3	168 40.4	03.3	165 47.9	59.7	Rigel	281 35.9	S 8 13.6
T 09	5 02.8	306 30.2 ··	13.2	324 43.3 ··	24.9	183 43.0 ··	03.3	180 50.4 ··	59.7	Rigil Kent.	140 24.6	S60 45.5
U 10	20 05.2	321 29.5	14.0	339 44.0	25.5	198 45.6	03.3	195 53.0	59.8	Sabik	102 40.3	S15 42.1
E 11	35 07.7	336 28.8	14.7	354 44.6	26.1	213 48.2	03.4	210 55.5	59.8			
S 12	50 10.2	351 28.1 N20 15.4		9 45.3 N15 26.7		228 50.7 N 1 03.4		225 58.1 N 0 59.8		Schedar	350 08.9	N56 25.8
D 13	65 12.6	6 27.3	16.2	24 46.0	27.3	243 53.3	03.4	241 00.6	59.9	Shaula	96 54.8	S37 05.4
A 14	80 15.1	21 26.6	16.9	39 46.6	27.8	258 55.9	03.5	256 03.2	59.9	Sirius	258 55.6	S16 41.6
Y 15	95 17.6	36 25.9 ··	17.6	54 47.3 ··	28.4	273 58.4 ··	03.5	271 05.7	0 59.9	Spica	158 56.8	S11 03.9
16	110 20.0	51 25.2	18.4	69 47.9	29.0	289 01.0	03.5	286 08.3	1 00.0	Suhail	223 10.5	S43 21.7
17	125 22.5	66 24.4	19.1	84 48.6	29.6	304 03.6	03.6	301 10.9	00.0			
18	140 25.0	81 23.7 N20 19.8		99 49.2 N15 30.2		319 06.2 N 1 03.6		316 13.4 N 1 00.0		Vega	80 55.3	N38 45.8
19	155 27.4	96 23.0	20.6	114 49.9	30.7	334 08.7	03.7	331 16.0	00.1	Zuben'ubi	137 32.2	S15 57.9
20	170 29.9	111 22.3	21.3	129 50.5	31.3	349 11.3	03.7	346 18.5	00.1		S.H.A.	Mer. Pass.
21	185 32.4	126 21.5 ··	22.0	144 51.2 ··	31.9	4 13.9 ··	03.7	1 21.1 ··	00.1	Venus	303 12.2	12 33
22	200 34.8	141 20.8	22.7	159 51.8	32.5	19 16.4	03.8	16 23.6	00.1	Mars	320 40.3	11 22
23	215 37.3	156 20.1	23.5	174 52.5	33.1	34 19.0	03.8	31 26.2	00.2	Jupiter	178 36.5	20 47
Mer. Pass.	h m 8 43.8	v −0.7 d 0.8		v 0.7 d 0.6		v 2.6 d 0.0		v 2.6 d 0.0		Saturn	175 44.5	20 59

SUN / MOON

G.M.T.	SUN G.H.A.	Dec.	MOON G.H.A.	v	Dec.	d	H.P.
10 00	180 54.5	N17 32.3	97 13.7	9.0	N18 31.9	5.7	57.5
01	195 54.5	33.0	111 41.7	9.0	18 26.2	5.9	57.4
02	210 54.5	33.6	126 09.7	9.2	18 20.3	6.0	57.4
03	225 54.6	·· 34.3	140 37.9	9.2	18 14.3	6.0	57.4
04	240 54.6	35.0	155 06.1	9.3	18 08.3	6.2	57.3
05	255 54.6	35.6	169 34.4	9.4	18 02.1	6.2	57.3
06	270 54.6	N17 36.3	184 02.8	9.5	N17 55.9	6.3	57.3
07	285 54.7	36.9	198 31.3	9.6	17 49.6	6.5	57.2
08	300 54.7	37.6	212 59.9	9.6	17 43.1	6.5	57.2
S 09	315 54.7	·· 38.2	227 28.5	9.8	17 36.6	6.6	57.1
U 10	330 54.7	38.9	241 57.3	9.8	17 30.0	6.7	57.1
N 11	345 54.8	39.5	256 26.1	9.9	17 23.3	6.7	57.1
D 12	0 54.8	N17 40.2	270 55.0	10.0	N17 16.6	6.9	57.0
A 13	15 54.8	40.8	285 24.0	10.1	17 09.7	6.9	57.0
Y 14	30 54.8	41.5	299 53.1	10.2	17 02.8	7.0	57.0
15	45 54.9	·· 42.1	314 22.3	10.2	16 55.8	7.1	56.9
16	60 54.9	42.8	328 51.5	10.3	16 48.7	7.2	56.9
17	75 54.9	43.4	343 20.8	10.5	16 41.5	7.2	56.9
18	90 54.9	N17 44.1	357 50.3	10.5	N16 34.3	7.4	56.8
19	105 54.9	44.7	12 19.8	10.5	16 26.9	7.4	56.8
20	120 55.0	45.4	26 49.3	10.7	16 19.5	7.5	56.7
21	135 55.0	·· 46.0	41 19.0	10.7	16 12.0	7.5	56.7
22	150 55.0	46.7	55 48.7	10.9	16 04.5	7.7	56.7
23	165 55.0	47.3	70 18.6	10.9	15 56.8	7.7	56.6
11 00	180 55.0	N17 48.0	84 48.5	11.0	N15 49.1	7.7	56.6
01	195 55.1	48.6	99 18.5	11.0	15 41.4	7.9	56.6
02	210 55.1	49.3	113 48.5	11.2	15 33.5	7.9	56.5
03	225 55.1	·· 49.9	128 18.7	11.2	15 25.6	8.0	56.5
04	240 55.1	50.5	142 48.9	11.3	15 17.6	8.0	56.5
05	255 55.1	51.2	157 19.2	11.4	15 09.6	8.1	56.4
06	270 55.2	N17 51.8	171 49.6	11.5	N15 01.5	8.2	56.4
07	285 55.2	52.5	186 20.1	11.5	14 53.3	8.3	56.4
08	300 55.2	53.1	200 50.6	11.6	14 45.0	8.3	56.3
M 09	315 55.2	·· 53.8	215 21.2	11.7	14 36.7	8.4	56.3
O 10	330 55.2	54.4	229 51.9	11.8	14 28.3	8.4	56.3
N 11	345 55.2	55.0	244 22.7	11.8	14 19.9	8.5	56.2
D 12	0 55.3	N17 55.6	258 53.5	11.9	N14 11.4	8.5	56.2
A 13	15 55.3	56.3	273 24.4	12.0	14 02.9	8.7	56.2
Y 14	30 55.3	57.0	287 55.4	12.1	13 54.2	8.6	56.1
15	45 55.3	·· 57.6	302 26.5	12.1	13 45.6	8.7	56.1
16	60 55.3	58.2	316 57.6	12.2	13 36.9	8.8	56.1
17	75 55.3	58.9	331 28.8	12.3	13 28.1	8.9	56.1
18	90 55.4	N17 59.5	346 00.1	12.4	N13 19.2	8.9	56.0
19	105 55.4	18 00.1	0 31.5	12.4	13 10.3	8.9	56.0
20	120 55.4	00.8	15 02.9	12.5	13 01.4	9.0	56.0
21	135 55.4	·· 01.4	29 34.4	12.6	12 52.4	9.0	55.9
22	150 55.4	02.1	44 06.0	12.6	12 43.4	9.1	55.9
23	165 55.4	02.7	58 37.6	12.7	12 34.3	9.2	55.9
12 00	180 55.4	N18 03.3	73 09.3	12.8	N12 25.1	9.2	55.8
01	195 55.5	04.0	87 41.1	12.8	12 15.9	9.2	55.8
02	210 55.5	04.6	102 12.9	12.9	12 06.7	9.3	55.8
03	225 55.5	·· 05.2	116 44.8	13.0	11 57.4	9.4	55.8
04	240 55.5	05.8	131 16.8	13.0	11 48.0	9.3	55.7
05	255 55.5	06.5	145 48.8	13.1	11 38.7	9.5	55.7
06	270 55.5	N18 07.1	160 20.9	13.2	N11 29.2	9.4	55.7
07	285 55.5	07.7	174 53.1	13.2	11 19.8	9.5	55.6
08	300 55.5	08.4	189 25.3	13.3	11 10.3	9.6	55.6
T 09	315 55.6	·· 09.0	203 57.6	13.3	11 00.7	9.6	55.6
U 10	330 55.6	09.6	218 29.9	13.4	10 51.1	9.6	55.5
E 11	345 55.6	10.3	233 02.3	13.5	10 41.5	9.7	55.5
S 12	0 55.6	N18 10.9	247 34.8	13.5	N10 31.8	9.7	55.5
D 13	15 55.6	11.5	262 07.3	13.6	10 22.1	9.8	55.5
A 14	30 55.6	12.1	276 39.9	13.6	10 12.3	9.8	55.4
Y 15	45 55.6	·· 12.8	291 12.5	13.7	10 02.6	9.9	55.4
16	60 55.6	13.4	305 45.2	13.7	9 52.7	9.8	55.4
17	75 55.6	14.0	320 17.9	13.8	9 42.9	9.9	55.4
18	90 55.7	N18 14.6	334 50.7	13.9	N 9 33.0	9.9	55.4
19	105 55.7	15.3	349 23.6	13.9	9 23.1	10.0	55.3
20	120 55.7	15.9	3 56.5	13.9	9 13.1	10.0	55.3
21	135 55.7	·· 16.5	18 29.4	14.1	9 03.1	10.0	55.3
22	150 55.7	17.1	33 02.5	14.0	8 53.1	10.0	55.2
23	165 55.7	17.7	47 35.5	14.1	8 43.1	10.1	55.2
	S.D. 15.9	d 0.6	S.D. 15.5		15.3		15.1

Twilight / Moonrise

Lat.	Naut.	Civil	Sunrise	Moonrise 10	11	12	13
N 72	☐	☐	☐	06 23	09 08	11 08	12 56
N 70	////	////	01 24	07 44	09 40	11 26	13 05
68	////	////	02 09	08 23	10 04	11 40	13 13
66	////	00 27	02 39	08 49	10 22	11 52	13 19
64	////	01 35	03 00	09 10	10 36	12 01	13 24
62	////	02 08	03 18	09 26	10 48	12 09	13 29
60	00 24	02 33	03 32	09 40	10 58	12 16	13 33
N 58	01 25	02 51	03 45	09 52	11 07	12 22	13 36
56	01 56	03 07	03 55	10 02	11 15	12 28	13 39
54	02 18	03 20	04 04	10 11	11 22	12 33	13 42
52	02 36	03 32	04 13	10 19	11 28	12 37	13 44
50	02 51	03 42	04 20	10 26	11 34	12 41	13 47
45	03 20	04 02	04 36	10 41	11 46	12 50	13 52
N 40	03 41	04 19	04 49	10 54	11 56	12 57	13 56
35	03 58	04 32	05 00	11 04	12 04	13 03	13 59
30	04 12	04 43	05 09	11 14	12 12	13 08	14 02
20	04 34	05 02	05 26	11 30	12 25	13 17	14 08
N 10	04 52	05 18	05 40	11 44	12 36	13 25	14 13
0	05 06	05 31	05 53	11 57	12 46	13 33	14 17
S 10	05 18	05 44	06 06	12 10	12 57	13 41	14 22
20	05 30	05 56	06 20	12 24	13 08	13 49	14 26
30	05 41	06 10	06 35	12 39	13 21	13 58	14 32
35	05 47	06 17	06 44	12 49	13 28	14 03	14 35
40	05 53	06 26	06 54	12 59	13 36	14 09	14 38
45	05 59	06 35	07 06	13 11	13 46	14 16	14 42
S 50	06 06	06 46	07 21	13 26	13 58	14 24	14 47
52	06 10	06 51	07 28	13 33	14 03	14 28	14 49
54	06 13	06 56	07 35	13 41	14 09	14 32	14 52
56	06 16	07 02	07 44	13 49	14 16	14 37	14 54
58	06 20	07 08	07 53	13 59	14 23	14 42	14 57
S 60	06 24	07 16	08 04	14 10	14 31	14 47	15 01

Sunset / Twilight / Moonset

Lat.	Sunset	Civil	Naut.	Moonset 10	11	12	13
N 72	☐	☐	☐	05 15	04 15	03 53	03 38
N 70	22 36	////	////	03 53	03 42	03 34	03 27
68	21 48	////	////	03 14	03 17	03 18	03 17
66	21 17	////	////	02 46	02 58	03 05	03 10
64	20 55	22 23	////	02 25	02 43	02 55	03 03
62	20 37	21 48	////	02 08	02 30	02 46	02 58
60	20 22	21 23	////	01 54	02 19	02 38	02 53
N 58	20 10	21 03	22 32	01 42	02 10	02 31	02 48
56	19 59	20 47	22 00	01 31	02 01	02 25	02 44
54	19 49	20 34	21 37	01 22	01 54	02 19	02 41
52	19 41	20 22	21 18	01 14	01 47	02 14	02 37
50	19 33	20 12	21 03	01 06	01 41	02 10	02 35
45	19 17	19 51	20 34	00 50	01 28	02 00	02 28
N 40	19 04	19 35	20 12	00 37	01 17	01 52	02 23
35	18 53	19 21	19 55	00 25	01 08	01 45	02 18
30	18 44	19 10	19 41	00 16	01 00	01 39	02 14
20	18 27	18 51	19 18	24 45	00 45	01 28	02 07
N 10	18 13	18 35	19 01	24 33	00 33	01 18	02 00
0	18 00	18 22	18 47	24 21	00 21	01 09	01 54
S 10	17 47	18 09	18 34	24 09	00 09	01 00	01 48
20	17 33	17 56	18 23	23 56	24 50	00 50	01 42
30	17 17	17 42	18 11	23 42	24 39	00 39	01 34
35	17 08	17 35	18 05	23 33	24 33	00 33	01 30
40	16 57	17 27	17 59	23 24	24 25	00 25	01 25
45	16 46	17 17	17 53	23 12	24 17	00 17	01 20
S 50	16 31	17 06	17 46	22 58	24 06	00 06	01 13
52	16 24	17 01	17 42	22 52	24 01	00 01	01 09
54	16 17	16 56	17 39	22 44	23 56	25 06	01 06
56	16 08	16 50	17 36	22 36	23 50	25 02	01 02
58	15 59	16 44	17 32	22 27	23 43	24 58	00 58
S 60	15 48	16 36	17 28	22 17	23 35	24 53	00 53

SUN / MOON

Day	Eqn. of Time 00ʰ	12ʰ	Mer. Pass.	Mer. Pass. Upper	Lower	Age	Phase
10	03 38	03 39	11 56	18 09	05 43	06	
11	03 40	03 41	11 56	18 58	06 34	07	
12	03 42	03 42	11 56	19 44	07 21	08	◗

1981 MAY 13, 14, 15 (WED., THURS., FRI.)

G.M.T.	ARIES G.H.A.	VENUS −3.4 G.H.A. / Dec.	MARS +1.5 G.H.A. / Dec.	JUPITER −1.8 G.H.A. / Dec.	SATURN +1.0 G.H.A. / Dec.	STARS Name / S.H.A. / Dec.
13 00	230 39.7	171 19.4 N20 24.2	189 53.1 N15 33.6	49 21.6 N 1 03.8	46 28.7 N 1 00.2	Acamar 315 37.3 S40 22.9
01	245 42.2	186 18.6 24.9	204 53.8 34.2	64 24.1 03.9	61 31.3 00.2	Achernar 335 45.5 S57 19.9
02	260 44.7	201 17.9 25.6	219 54.4 34.8	79 26.7 03.9	76 33.8 00.3	Acrux 173 36.3 S62 59.9
03	275 47.1	216 17.2 ·· 26.3	234 55.1 ·· 35.4	94 29.3 ·· 03.9	91 36.4 ·· 00.3	Adhara 255 32.0 S28 57.0
04	290 49.6	231 16.5 27.1	249 55.7 36.0	109 31.9 04.0	106 39.0 00.3	Aldebaran 291 17.9 N16 28.2
05	305 52.1	246 15.7 27.8	264 56.4 36.6	124 34.4 04.0	121 41.5 00.4	
W 06	320 54.5	261 15.0 N20 28.5	279 57.0 N15 37.1	139 37.0 N 1 04.0	136 44.1 N 1 00.4	Alioth 166 41.7 N56 03.9
E 07	335 57.0	276 14.3 29.2	294 57.7 37.7	154 39.6 04.1	151 46.6 00.4	Alkaid 153 17.7 N49 24.6
D 08	350 59.5	291 13.5 29.9	309 58.3 38.3	169 42.1 04.1	166 49.2 00.4	Al Na'ir 28 14.5 S47 03.0
N 09	6 01.9	306 12.8 ·· 30.7	324 59.0 ·· 38.9	184 44.7 ·· 04.1	181 51.7 ·· 00.5	Alnilam 276 11.5 S 1 13.0
E 10	21 04.4	321 12.1 31.4	339 59.6 39.4	199 47.3 04.2	196 54.3 00.5	Alphard 218 20.2 S 8 34.7
S 11	36 06.8	336 11.4 32.1	355 00.3 40.0	214 49.8 04.2	211 56.8 00.5	
D 12	51 09.3	351 10.6 N20 32.8	10 01.0 N15 40.6	229 52.4 N 1 04.2	226 59.4 N 1 00.6	Alphecca 126 31.4 N26 46.7
A 13	66 11.8	6 09.9 33.5	25 01.6 41.2	244 55.0 04.3	242 01.9 00.6	Alpheratz 358 09.1 N28 59.0
Y 14	81 14.2	21 09.2 34.2	40 02.3 41.7	259 57.5 04.3	257 04.5 00.6	Altair 62 32.0 N 8 49.0
15	96 16.7	36 08.4 ·· 34.9	55 02.9 ·· 42.3	275 00.1 ·· 04.3	272 07.0 ·· 00.7	Ankaa 353 40.1 S42 24.4
16	111 19.2	51 07.7 35.6	70 03.6 42.9	290 02.6 04.4	287 09.6 00.7	Antares 112 56.0 S26 23.4
17	126 21.6	66 07.0 36.3	85 04.2 43.5	305 05.2 04.4	302 12.1 00.7	
18	141 24.1	81 06.2 N20 37.0	100 04.9 N15 44.0	320 07.8 N 1 04.4	317 14.7 N 1 00.7	Arcturus 146 17.8 N19 16.8
19	156 26.6	96 05.5 37.7	115 05.5 44.6	335 10.3 04.5	332 17.2 00.8	Atria 108 19.3 S68 59.5
20	171 29.0	111 04.7 38.4	130 06.2 45.2	350 12.9 04.5	347 19.8 00.8	Avior 234 28.2 S59 27.3
21	186 31.5	126 04.0 ·· 39.2	145 06.8 ·· 45.8	5 15.5 ·· 04.5	2 22.3 ·· 00.8	Bellatrix 278 58.6 N 6 19.9
22	201 34.0	141 03.3 39.9	160 07.5 46.3	20 18.0 04.6	17 24.9 00.9	Betelgeuse 271 28.1 N 7 24.1
23	216 36.4	156 02.5 40.6	175 08.1 46.9	35 20.6 04.6	32 27.4 00.9	
14 00	231 38.9	171 01.8 N20 41.3	190 08.8 N15 47.5	50 23.2 N 1 04.6	47 30.0 N 1 00.9	Canopus 264 07.4 S52 41.4
01	246 41.3	186 01.1 42.0	205 09.4 48.0	65 25.7 04.7	62 32.5 00.9	Capella 281 11.1 N45 58.8
02	261 43.8	201 00.3 42.7	220 10.1 48.6	80 28.3 04.7	77 35.1 01.0	Deneb 49 48.0 N45 12.5
03	276 46.3	215 59.6 ·· 43.3	235 10.7 ·· 49.2	95 30.8 ·· 04.7	92 37.6 ·· 01.0	Denebola 182 58.4 N14 40.7
04	291 48.7	230 58.8 44.0	250 11.4 49.8	110 33.4 04.8	107 40.2 01.0	Diphda 349 20.7 S18 05.4
05	306 51.2	245 58.1 44.7	265 12.0 50.3	125 36.0 04.8	122 42.7 01.1	
T 06	321 53.7	260 57.4 N20 45.4	280 12.7 N15 50.9	140 38.5 N 1 04.8	137 45.3 N 1 01.1	Dubhe 194 21.4 N61 51.4
H 07	336 56.1	275 56.6 46.1	295 13.3 51.5	155 41.1 04.9	152 47.8 01.1	Elnath 278 43.9 N28 35.5
U 08	351 58.6	290 55.9 46.8	310 14.0 52.0	170 43.7 04.9	167 50.4 01.1	Eltanin 90 57.1 N51 29.3
R 09	7 01.1	305 55.1 ·· 47.5	325 14.6 ·· 52.6	185 46.2 ·· 04.9	182 52.9 ·· 01.2	Enif 34 11.2 N 9 47.2
S 10	22 03.5	320 54.4 48.2	340 15.3 53.2	200 48.8 05.0	197 55.5 01.2	Fomalhaut 15 51.1 S29 43.3
D 11	37 06.0	335 53.7 48.9	355 15.9 53.8	215 51.3 05.0	212 58.0 01.2	
A 12	52 08.5	350 52.9 N20 49.6	10 16.6 N15 54.3	230 53.9 N 1 05.0	228 00.6 N 1 01.3	Gacrux 172 27.9 S57 00.7
Y 13	67 10.9	5 52.2 50.3	25 17.2 54.9	245 56.4 05.1	243 03.1 01.3	Gienah 176 17.3 S17 26.4
14	82 13.4	20 51.4 51.0	40 17.9 55.5	260 59.0 05.1	258 05.7 01.3	Hadar 149 22.1 S60 17.1
15	97 15.8	35 50.7 ·· 51.6	55 18.5 ·· 56.0	276 01.6 ·· 05.1	273 08.2 ·· 01.3	Hamal 328 28.8 N23 22.2
16	112 18.3	50 49.9 52.3	70 19.2 56.6	291 04.1 05.1	288 10.8 01.4	Kaus Aust. 84 16.0 S34 23.5
17	127 20.8	65 49.2 53.0	85 19.8 57.2	306 06.7 05.1	303 13.3 01.4	
18	142 23.2	80 48.4 N20 53.7	100 20.5 N15 57.7	321 09.2 N 1 05.2	318 15.9 N 1 01.4	Kochab 137 17.9 N74 14.1
19	157 25.7	95 47.7 54.4	115 21.1 58.3	336 11.8 05.2	333 18.4 01.4	Markab 14 02.9 N15 06.1
20	172 28.2	110 47.0 55.0	130 21.8 58.9	351 14.4 05.3	348 21.0 01.5	Menkar 314 41.0 N 4 00.8
21	187 30.6	125 46.2 ·· 55.7	145 22.4 15 59.4	6 16.9 ·· 05.3	3 23.5 ·· 01.5	Menkent 148 36.1 S36 16.7
22	202 33.1	140 45.5 56.4	160 23.0 16 00.0	21 19.5 05.3	18 26.1 01.5	Miaplacidus 221 45.0 S69 38.7
23	217 35.6	155 44.7 57.1	175 23.7 00.6	36 22.0 05.4	33 28.6 01.6	
15 00	232 38.0	170 44.0 N20 57.8	190 24.3 N16 01.1	51 24.6 N 1 05.4	48 31.2 N 1 01.6	Mirfak 309 16.0 N49 47.5
01	247 40.5	185 43.2 58.4	205 25.0 01.7	66 27.1 05.4	63 33.7 01.6	Nunki 76 28.4 S26 19.2
02	262 42.9	200 42.5 59.1	220 25.6 02.3	81 29.7 05.4	78 36.2 01.6	Peacock 53 57.5 S56 47.5
03	277 45.4	215 41.7 20 59.8	235 26.3 ·· 02.8	96 32.2 ·· 05.5	93 38.8 ·· 01.7	Pollux 243 57.8 N28 04.4
04	292 47.9	230 41.0 21 00.5	250 26.9 03.4	111 34.8 05.5	108 41.3 01.7	Procyon 245 25.5 N 5 16.3
05	307 50.3	245 40.2 01.1	265 27.6 04.0	126 37.4 05.5	123 43.9 01.7	
F 06	322 52.8	260 39.5 N21 01.8	280 28.2 N16 04.5	141 39.9 N 1 05.6	138 46.4 N 1 01.7	Rasalhague 96 28.9 N12 34.4
R 07	337 55.3	275 38.7 02.5	295 28.9 05.1	156 42.5 05.6	153 49.0 01.8	Regulus 208 09.5 N12 03.6
I 08	352 57.7	290 38.0 03.1	310 29.5 05.7	171 45.0 05.6	168 51.5 01.8	Rigel 281 35.9 S 8 13.5
D 09	8 00.2	305 37.2 ·· 03.8	325 30.2 ·· 06.2	186 47.6 ·· 05.6	183 54.1 ·· 01.8	Rigil Kent. 140 24.6 S60 45.5
A 10	23 02.7	320 36.5 04.5	340 30.8 06.8	201 50.1 05.7	198 56.6 01.8	Sabik 102 40.3 S15 42.1
Y 11	38 05.1	335 35.7 05.1	355 31.5 07.3	216 52.7 05.7	213 59.2 01.9	
12	53 07.6	350 35.0 N21 05.8	10 32.1 N16 07.9	231 55.2 N 1 05.7	229 01.7 N 1 01.9	Schedar 350 08.9 N56 25.8
13	68 10.1	5 34.2 06.5	25 32.8 08.5	246 57.8 05.8	244 04.3 01.9	Shaula 96 54.8 S37 05.4
14	83 12.5	20 33.4 07.1	40 33.4 09.0	262 00.3 05.8	259 06.8 02.0	Sirius 258 55.6 S16 41.6
15	98 15.0	35 32.7 ·· 07.8	55 34.1 ·· 09.6	277 02.9 ·· 05.8	274 09.3 ·· 02.0	Spica 158 56.8 S11 03.9
16	113 17.4	50 31.9 08.4	70 34.7 10.2	292 05.4 05.8	289 11.9 02.0	Suhail 223 10.5 S43 21.7
17	128 19.9	65 31.2 09.1	85 35.4 10.7	307 08.0 05.9	304 14.4 02.0	
18	143 22.4	80 30.4 N21 09.8	100 36.0 N16 11.3	322 10.5 N 1 05.9	319 17.0 N 1 02.1	Vega 80 55.2 N38 45.8
19	158 24.8	95 29.7 10.4	115 36.7 11.8	337 13.1 05.9	334 19.5 02.1	Zuben'ubi 137 32.2 S15 57.9
20	173 27.3	110 28.9 11.1	130 37.3 12.4	352 15.6 05.9	349 22.1 02.1	
21	188 29.8	125 28.1 ·· 11.7	145 37.9 ·· 13.0	7 18.2 ·· 06.0	4 24.6 ·· 02.1	
22	203 32.2	140 27.4 12.4	160 38.6 13.5	22 20.7 06.0	19 27.2 02.2	
23	218 34.7	155 26.6 13.0	175 39.2 14.1	37 23.3 06.0	34 29.7 02.2	

		S.H.A.	Mer. Pass.
Venus		299 22.9	12 37
Mars		318 29.9	11 19
Jupiter		178 44.3	20 35
Saturn		175 51.1	20 46

Mer. Pass.	8 32.0	v −0.7 d 0.7	v 0.6 d 0.6	v 2.6 d 0.0	v 2.5 d 0.0	

G.M.T.	SUN G.H.A.	Dec.	MOON G.H.A.	v	Dec.	d	H.P.
13 00	180 55.7	N18 18.4	62 08.6	14.2	N 8 33.0	10.1	55.2
01	195 55.7	19.0	76 41.8	14.2	8 22.9	10.2	55.2
02	210 55.7	19.6	91 15.0	14.3	8 12.7	10.1	55.2
03	225 55.7 ..	20.2	105 48.3	14.3	8 02.6	10.2	55.1
04	240 55.7	20.8	120 21.6	14.3	7 52.4	10.2	55.1
05	255 55.7	21.5	134 54.9	14.4	7 42.2	10.3	55.1
06	270 55.8	N18 22.1	149 28.3	14.4	N 7 31.9	10.3	55.1
W 07	285 55.8	22.7	164 01.7	14.5	7 21.6	10.2	55.1
E 08	300 55.8	23.3	178 35.2	14.6	7 11.4	10.4	55.0
D 09	315 55.8 ..	23.9	193 08.8	14.5	7 01.0	10.3	55.0
N 10	330 55.8	24.5	207 42.3	14.6	6 50.7	10.4	55.0
E 11	345 55.8	25.2	222 15.9	14.7	6 40.3	10.3	55.0
S 12	0 55.8	N18 25.8	236 49.6	14.7	N 6 30.0	10.4	54.9
D 13	15 55.8	26.4	251 23.3	14.7	6 19.6	10.4	54.9
A 14	30 55.8	27.0	265 57.0	14.8	6 09.2	10.5	54.9
Y 15	45 55.8 ..	27.6	280 30.8	14.8	5 58.7	10.4	54.9
16	60 55.8	28.2	295 04.6	14.8	5 48.3	10.5	54.9
17	75 55.8	28.8	309 38.4	14.9	5 37.8	10.5	54.8
18	90 55.8	N18 29.4	324 12.3	14.9	N 5 27.3	10.5	54.8
19	105 55.8	30.1	338 46.2	14.9	5 16.8	10.5	54.8
20	120 55.8	30.7	353 20.1	15.0	5 06.3	10.6	54.8
21	135 55.8 ..	31.3	7 54.1	15.0	4 55.7	10.6	54.8
22	150 55.8	31.9	22 28.1	15.1	4 45.2	10.6	54.8
23	165 55.8	32.5	37 02.2	15.0	4 34.6	10.6	54.7
14 00	180 55.8	N18 33.1	51 36.2	15.1	N 4 24.0	10.5	54.7
01	195 55.8	33.7	66 10.3	15.2	4 13.5	10.6	54.7
02	210 55.8	34.3	80 44.5	15.1	4 02.9	10.7	54.7
03	225 55.8 ..	34.9	95 18.6	15.2	3 52.2	10.6	54.7
04	240 55.8	35.5	109 52.8	15.2	3 41.6	10.6	54.6
05	255 55.8	36.1	124 27.0	15.2	3 31.0	10.6	54.6
06	270 55.8	N18 36.7	139 01.2	15.3	N 3 20.4	10.7	54.6
T 07	285 55.8	37.3	153 35.5	15.3	3 09.7	10.6	54.6
H 08	300 55.8	37.9	168 09.8	15.3	2 59.1	10.7	54.6
U 09	315 55.8 ..	38.5	182 44.1	15.3	2 48.4	10.7	54.6
R 10	330 55.8	39.1	197 18.4	15.4	2 37.7	10.6	54.5
S 11	345 55.8	39.7	211 52.8	15.4	2 27.1	10.7	54.5
D 12	0 55.8	N18 40.3	226 27.2	15.4	N 2 16.4	10.7	54.5
A 13	15 55.8	40.9	241 01.6	15.4	2 05.7	10.7	54.5
Y 14	30 55.8	41.5	255 36.0	15.4	1 55.0	10.7	54.5
15	45 55.8 ..	42.1	270 10.4	15.5	1 44.3	10.7	54.5
16	60 55.8	42.7	284 44.9	15.4	1 33.6	10.7	54.5
17	75 55.8	43.3	299 19.3	15.5	1 22.9	10.7	54.4
18	90 55.8	N18 43.9	313 53.8	15.5	N 1 12.2	10.7	54.4
19	105 55.8	44.5	328 28.3	15.5	1 01.5	10.7	54.4
20	120 55.8	45.1	343 02.8	15.6	0 50.8	10.6	54.4
21	135 55.8 ..	45.7	357 37.4	15.5	0 40.2	10.7	54.4
22	150 55.8	46.3	12 11.9	15.6	0 29.5	10.7	54.4
23	165 55.8	46.9	26 46.5	15.5	0 18.8	10.7	54.4
15 00	180 55.8	N18 47.5	41 21.0	15.6	N 0 08.1	10.7	54.4
01	195 55.8	48.1	55 55.6	15.6	S 0 02.6	10.7	54.3
02	210 55.8	48.7	70 30.2	15.6	0 13.3	10.7	54.3
03	225 55.8 ..	49.3	85 04.8	15.6	0 24.0	10.6	54.3
04	240 55.8	49.9	99 39.4	15.6	0 34.6	10.7	54.3
05	255 55.8	50.5	114 14.0	15.6	0 45.3	10.7	54.3
06	270 55.8	N18 51.1	128 48.6	15.7	S 0 56.0	10.6	54.3
07	285 55.8	51.7	143 23.3	15.6	1 06.6	10.7	54.3
08	300 55.8	52.3	157 57.9	15.7	1 17.3	10.6	54.3
F 09	315 55.8 ..	52.8	172 32.6	15.6	1 27.9	10.6	54.2
R 10	330 55.8	53.4	187 07.2	15.7	1 38.5	10.7	54.2
I 11	345 55.8	54.0	201 41.8	15.7	1 49.1	10.7	54.2
D 12	0 55.8	N18 54.6	216 16.5	15.6	S 1 59.8	10.6	54.2
A 13	15 55.8	55.2	230 51.1	15.7	2 10.4	10.5	54.2
Y 14	30 55.8	55.8	245 25.8	15.7	2 20.9	10.6	54.2
15	45 55.7 ..	56.4	260 00.5	15.6	2 31.5	10.6	54.2
16	60 55.7	57.0	274 35.1	15.7	2 42.1	10.5	54.2
17	75 55.7	57.5	289 09.8	15.6	2 52.6	10.6	54.2
18	90 55.7	N18 58.1	303 44.4	15.7	S 3 03.2	10.5	54.2
19	105 55.7	58.7	318 19.1	15.6	3 13.7	10.5	54.1
20	120 55.7	59.3	332 53.7	15.7	3 24.2	10.5	54.1
21	135 55.7	18 59.9	347 28.4	15.6	3 34.7	10.5	54.1
22	150 55.7	19 00.5	2 03.0	15.6	3 45.2	10.4	54.1
23	165 55.7	01.0	16 37.6	15.7	3 55.6	10.5	54.1
	S.D. 15.8	d 0.6	S.D. 15.0		14.9		14.8

Lat.	Twilight Naut.	Twilight Civil	Sunrise	Moonrise 13	14	15	16
°	h m	h m	h m	h m	h m	h m	h m
N 72	▢	▢	▢	12 56	14 38	16 17	17 58
N 70	////	////	00 55	13 05	14 40	16 13	17 47
68	////	////	01 53	13 13	14 42	16 10	17 38
66	////	////	02 27	13 19	14 44	16 07	17 31
64	////	01 16	02 51	13 24	14 45	16 05	17 25
62	////	01 56	03 10	13 29	14 46	16 03	17 19
60	////	02 23	03 25	13 33	14 47	16 01	17 15
N 58	01 08	02 43	03 38	13 36	14 48	16 00	17 11
56	01 45	03 00	03 49	13 39	14 49	15 58	17 07
54	02 10	03 14	03 59	13 42	14 50	15 57	17 04
52	02 29	03 26	04 08	13 44	14 51	15 57	17 01
50	02 45	03 37	04 16	13 47	14 51	15 55	16 58
45	03 15	03 58	04 32	13 52	14 53	15 53	16 52
N 40	03 38	04 15	04 46	13 56	14 54	15 51	16 48
35	03 55	04 29	04 57	13 59	14 55	15 49	16 44
30	04 10	04 41	05 07	14 02	14 56	15 48	16 40
20	04 33	05 01	05 24	14 08	14 57	15 46	16 34
N 10	04 51	05 17	05 39	14 13	14 58	15 43	16 28
0	05 06	05 31	05 53	14 17	15 00	15 41	16 23
S 10	05 19	05 44	06 06	14 22	15 01	15 40	16 18
20	05 31	05 57	06 21	14 26	15 02	15 38	16 13
30	05 43	06 12	06 37	14 32	15 04	15 35	16 07
35	05 49	06 20	06 46	14 35	15 05	15 34	16 04
40	05 55	06 28	06 57	14 38	15 06	15 33	16 00
45	06 02	06 38	07 10	14 42	15 07	15 31	15 55
S 50	06 10	06 49	07 25	14 47	15 08	15 29	15 50
52	06 13	06 55	07 32	14 49	15 09	15 28	15 47
54	06 17	07 00	07 40	14 52	15 10	15 27	15 45
56	06 21	07 07	07 49	14 54	15 10	15 26	15 42
58	06 25	07 14	07 59	14 57	15 11	15 25	15 39
S 60	06 30	07 21	08 11	15 01	15 12	15 23	15 35

Lat.	Sunset	Twilight Civil	Twilight Naut.	Moonset 13	14	15	16
°	h m	h m	h m	h m	h m	h m	h m
N 72	▢	▢	▢	03 38	03 25	03 13	03 01
N 70	23 10	////	////	03 27	03 20	03 14	03 08
68	22 04	////	////	03 17	03 16	03 15	03 13
66	21 29	////	////	03 10	03 13	03 15	03 18
64	21 04	22 43	////	03 03	03 10	03 16	03 21
62	20 45	22 00	////	02 58	03 07	03 16	03 25
60	20 29	21 32	////	02 53	03 05	03 16	03 28
N 58	20 16	21 11	22 50	02 48	03 03	03 17	03 30
56	20 05	20 54	22 11	02 44	03 01	03 17	03 32
54	19 55	20 40	21 45	02 41	02 59	03 17	03 35
52	19 46	20 28	21 26	02 38	02 58	03 17	03 36
50	19 38	20 17	21 09	02 35	02 57	03 17	03 38
45	19 21	19 55	20 38	02 28	02 54	03 18	03 42
N 40	19 07	19 38	20 16	02 23	02 51	03 18	03 45
35	18 56	19 24	19 58	02 18	02 49	03 18	03 48
30	18 46	19 12	19 43	02 14	02 47	03 19	03 50
20	18 28	18 52	19 20	02 07	02 44	03 19	03 54
N 10	18 14	18 36	19 02	02 00	02 41	03 20	03 58
0	18 00	18 22	18 47	01 54	02 38	03 20	04 02
S 10	17 46	18 08	18 34	01 48	02 35	03 20	04 05
20	17 32	17 55	18 22	01 42	02 32	03 21	04 09
30	17 15	17 41	18 10	01 34	02 28	03 21	04 13
35	17 06	17 33	18 03	01 30	02 26	03 21	04 16
40	16 55	17 24	17 57	01 25	02 24	03 21	04 18
45	16 42	17 14	17 50	01 20	02 21	03 22	04 22
S 50	16 25	17 03	17 42	01 13	02 18	03 22	04 25
52	16 20	16 57	17 39	01 09	02 16	03 22	04 27
54	16 12	16 52	17 35	01 06	02 15	03 22	04 29
56	16 04	16 45	17 31	01 02	02 13	03 22	04 31
58	15 53	16 38	17 27	00 58	02 11	03 23	04 34
S 60	15 41	16 30	17 22	00 53	02 09	03 23	04 36

Day	SUN Eqn. of Time 00h	SUN Eqn. of Time 12h	Mer. Pass.	MOON Mer. Pass. Upper	MOON Mer. Pass. Lower	Age	Phase
	m s	m s	h m	h m	h m	d	
13	03 43	03 43	11 56	20 27	08 06	09	
14	03 43	03 43	11 56	21 10	08 49	10	◖
15	03 43	03 43	11 56	21 52	09 31	11	

G.M.T.	ARIES G.H.A.	VENUS −3.4 G.H.A.	Dec.	MARS +1.5 G.H.A.	Dec.	JUPITER −1.8 G.H.A.	Dec.	SATURN +1.0 G.H.A.	Dec.	STARS Name	S.H.A.	Dec.
d h	° ′	° ′	° ′	° ′	° ′	° ′	° ′	° ′	° ′		° ′	° ′
16 00	233 37.2	170 25.9 N21 13.7		190 39.9 N16 14.6		52 25.8 N 1 06.1		49 32.2 N 1 02.2		Acamar	315 37.3	S40 22.9
01	248 39.6	185 25.1	14.3	205 40.5	15.2	67 28.4	06.1	64 34.8	02.2	Achernar	335 45.5	S57 19.9
02	263 42.1	200 24.4	15.0	220 41.2	15.8	82 30.9	06.1	79 37.3	02.3	Acrux	173 36.3	S62 59.9
03	278 44.6	215 23.6 ··	15.6	235 41.8 ··	16.3	97 33.5 ··	06.1	94 39.9 ··	02.3	Adhara	255 32.0	S28 57.0
04	293 47.0	230 22.8	16.3	250 42.5	16.9	112 36.0	06.2	109 42.4	02.3	Aldebaran	291 17.9	N16 28.2
05	308 49.5	245 22.1	16.9	265 43.1	17.4	127 38.6	06.2	124 45.0	02.3			
06	323 51.9	260 21.3 N21 17.6		280 43.8 N16 18.0		142 41.1 N 1 06.2		139 47.5 N 1 02.4		Alioth	166 41.7	N56 03.9
07	338 54.4	275 20.5	18.2	295 44.4	18.5	157 43.7	06.2	154 50.0	02.4	Alkaid	153 17.7	N49 24.6
S 08	353 56.9	290 19.8	18.9	310 45.1	19.1	172 46.2	06.3	169 52.6	02.4	Al Na'ir	28 14.4	S47 03.0
A 09	8 59.3	305 19.0 ··	19.5	325 45.7 ··	19.7	187 48.8 ··	06.3	184 55.1 ··	02.4	Alnilam	276 11.5	S 1 13.0
T 10	24 01.8	320 18.3	20.2	340 46.3	20.2	202 51.3	06.3	199 57.7	02.5	Alphard	218 20.2	S 8 34.7
U 11	39 04.3	335 17.5	20.8	355 47.0	20.8	217 53.9	06.3	215 00.2	02.5			
R 12	54 06.7	350 16.7 N21 21.4		10 47.6 N16 21.3		232 56.4 N 1 06.4		230 02.7 N 1 02.5		Alphecca	126 31.4	N26 46.7
D 13	69 09.2	5 16.0	22.1	25 48.3	21.9	247 59.0	06.4	245 05.3	02.5	Alpheratz	358 09.1	N28 59.0
A 14	84 11.7	20 15.2	22.7	40 48.9	22.4	263 01.5	06.4	260 07.8	02.6	Altair	62 31.9	N 8 49.0
Y 15	99 14.1	35 14.4 ··	23.3	55 49.6 ··	23.0	278 04.0 ··	06.4	275 10.4 ··	02.6	Ankaa	353 40.1	S42 24.4
16	114 16.6	50 13.7	24.0	70 50.2	23.6	293 06.6	06.5	290 12.9	02.6	Antares	112 56.0	S26 23.4
17	129 19.0	65 12.9	24.6	85 50.9	24.1	308 09.1	06.5	305 15.5	02.6			
18	144 21.5	80 12.1 N21 25.2		100 51.5 N16 24.7		323 11.7 N 1 06.5		320 18.0 N 1 02.7		Arcturus	146 17.8	N19 16.8
19	159 24.0	95 11.4	25.9	115 52.2	25.2	338 14.2	06.5	335 20.5	02.7	Atria	108 19.3	S68 59.6
20	174 26.4	110 10.6	26.5	130 52.8	25.8	353 16.8	06.6	350 23.1	02.7	Avior	234 28.3	S59 27.3
21	189 28.9	125 09.8 ··	27.1	145 53.4 ··	26.3	8 19.3 ··	06.6	5 25.6 ··	02.7	Bellatrix	278 58.6	N 6 19.9
22	204 31.4	140 09.1	27.8	160 54.1	26.9	23 21.9	06.6	20 28.2	02.8	Betelgeuse	271 28.1	N 7 24.1
23	219 33.8	155 08.3	28.4	175 54.7	27.4	38 24.4	06.6	35 30.7	02.8			
17 00	234 36.3	170 07.5 N21 29.0		190 55.4 N16 28.0		53 26.9 N 1 06.6		50 33.2 N 1 02.8		Canopus	264 07.4	S52 41.4
01	249 38.8	185 06.8	29.7	205 56.0	28.5	68 29.5	06.7	65 35.8	02.8	Capella	281 11.1	N45 58.7
02	264 41.2	200 06.0	30.3	220 56.7	29.1	83 32.0	06.7	80 38.3	02.8	Deneb	49 48.0	N45 12.5
03	279 43.7	215 05.2 ··	30.9	235 57.3 ··	29.6	98 34.6 ··	06.7	95 40.9 ··	02.9	Denebola	182 58.5	N14 40.7
04	294 46.2	230 04.4	31.5	250 58.0	30.2	113 37.1	06.7	110 43.4	02.9	Diphda	349 20.7	S18 05.4
05	309 48.6	245 03.7	32.1	265 58.6	30.7	128 39.6	06.8	125 45.9	02.9			
06	324 51.1	260 02.9 N21 32.8		280 59.2 N16 31.3		143 42.2 N 1 06.8		140 48.5 N 1 02.9		Dubhe	194 21.4	N61 51.4
07	339 53.5	275 02.1	33.4	295 59.9	31.8	158 44.7	06.8	155 51.0	03.0	Elnath	278 43.9	N28 35.5
08	354 56.0	290 01.4	34.0	311 00.5	32.4	173 47.3	06.8	170 53.6	03.0	Eltanin	90 57.1	N51 29.4
S 09	9 58.5	305 00.6 ··	34.6	326 01.2 ··	32.9	188 49.8 ··	06.9	185 56.1 ··	03.0	Enif	34 11.1	N 9 47.2
U 10	25 00.9	319 59.8	35.2	341 01.8	33.5	203 52.3	06.9	200 58.6	03.0	Fomalhaut	15 51.1	S29 43.3
N 11	40 03.4	334 59.0	35.9	356 02.5	34.0	218 54.9	06.9	216 01.2	03.1			
D 12	55 05.9	349 58.3 N21 36.5		11 03.1 N16 34.6		233 57.4 N 1 06.9		231 03.7 N 1 03.1		Gacrux	172 27.9	S57 00.7
A 13	70 08.3	4 57.5	37.1	26 03.8	35.1	249 00.0	06.9	246 06.2	03.1	Gienah	176 17.3	S17 26.4
Y 14	85 10.8	19 56.7	37.7	41 04.4	35.7	264 02.5	07.0	261 08.8	03.1	Hadar	149 22.1	S60 17.1
15	100 13.3	34 55.9 ··	38.3	56 05.0 ··	36.2	279 05.0 ··	07.0	276 11.3 ··	03.2	Hamal	328 28.8	N23 22.2
16	115 15.7	49 55.2	38.9	71 05.7	36.8	294 07.6	07.0	291 13.9	03.2	Kaus Aust.	84 16.0	S34 23.5
17	130 18.2	64 54.4	39.5	86 06.3	37.3	309 10.1	07.0	306 16.4	03.2			
18	145 20.7	79 53.6 N21 40.1		101 07.0 N16 37.9		324 12.6 N 1 07.0		321 18.9 N 1 03.2		Kochab	137 17.9	N74 14.1
19	160 23.1	94 52.8	40.8	116 07.6	38.4	339 15.2	07.1	336 21.5	03.2	Markab	14 02.8	N15 06.1
20	175 25.6	109 52.0	41.4	131 08.3	39.0	354 17.7	07.1	351 24.0	03.3	Menkar	314 41.0	N 4 00.8
21	190 28.0	124 51.3 ··	42.0	146 08.9 ··	39.5	9 20.3 ··	07.1	6 26.5 ··	03.3	Menkent	148 36.1	S36 16.8
22	205 30.5	139 50.5	42.6	161 09.5	40.1	24 22.8	07.1	21 29.1	03.3	Miaplacidus	221 45.0	S69 38.7
23	220 33.0	154 49.7	43.2	176 10.2	40.6	39 25.3	07.2	36 31.6	03.3			
18 00	235 35.4	169 48.9 N21 43.8		191 10.8 N16 41.1		54 27.9 N 1 07.2		51 34.2 N 1 03.4		Mirfak	309 16.0	N49 47.5
01	250 37.9	184 48.2	44.4	206 11.5	41.7	69 30.4	07.2	66 36.7	03.4	Nunki	76 28.4	S26 19.2
02	265 40.4	199 47.4	45.0	221 12.1	42.2	84 32.9	07.2	81 39.2	03.4	Peacock	53 57.5	S56 47.5
03	280 42.8	214 46.6 ··	45.6	236 12.8 ··	42.8	99 35.5 ··	07.2	96 41.8 ··	03.4	Pollux	243 57.9	N28 04.4
04	295 45.3	229 45.8	46.2	251 13.4	43.3	114 38.0	07.3	111 44.3	03.4	Procyon	245 25.5	N 5 16.3
05	310 47.8	244 45.0	46.8	266 14.0	43.9	129 40.5	07.3	126 46.8	03.5			
06	325 50.2	259 44.2 N21 47.4		281 14.7 N16 44.4		144 43.1 N 1 07.3		141 49.4 N 1 03.5		Rasalhague	96 28.9	N12 34.4
07	340 52.7	274 43.5	48.0	296 15.3	45.0	159 45.6	07.3	156 51.9	03.5	Regulus	208 09.5	N12 03.6
08	355 55.1	289 42.7	48.6	311 16.0	45.5	174 48.1	07.3	171 54.4	03.5	Rigel	281 35.9	S 8 13.5
M 09	10 57.6	304 41.9 ··	49.1	326 16.6 ··	46.0	189 50.7 ··	07.4	186 57.0 ··	03.5	Rigil Kent.	140 24.6	S60 45.5
O 10	26 00.1	319 41.1	49.7	341 17.2	46.6	204 53.2	07.4	201 59.5	03.6	Sabik	102 40.3	S15 42.1
N 11	41 02.5	334 40.3	50.3	356 17.9	47.1	219 55.7	07.4	217 02.0	03.6			
D 12	56 05.0	349 39.5 N21 50.9		11 18.5 N16 47.7		234 58.3 N 1 07.4		232 04.6 N 1 03.6		Schedar	350 08.9	N56 25.8
A 13	71 07.5	4 38.8	51.5	26 19.2	48.2	250 00.8	07.4	247 07.1	03.6	Shaula	96 54.8	S37 05.4
Y 14	86 09.9	19 38.0	52.1	41 19.8	48.8	265 03.3	07.5	262 09.6	03.7	Sirius	258 55.6	S16 41.6
15	101 12.4	34 37.2 ··	52.7	56 20.5 ··	49.3	280 05.9 ··	07.5	277 12.2 ··	03.7	Spica	158 56.8	S11 03.9
16	116 14.9	49 36.4	53.3	71 21.1	49.8	295 08.4	07.5	292 14.7	03.7	Suhail	223 10.6	S43 21.7
17	131 17.3	64 35.6	53.9	86 21.7	50.4	310 10.9	07.5	307 17.2	03.7			
18	146 19.8	79 34.8 N21 54.4		101 22.4 N16 50.9		325 13.5 N 1 07.5		322 19.8 N 1 03.7		Vega	80 55.2	N38 45.8
19	161 22.3	94 34.0	55.0	116 23.0	51.5	340 16.0	07.5	337 22.3	03.8	Zuben'ubi	137 32.2	S15 57.9
20	176 24.7	109 33.2	55.6	131 23.7	52.0	355 18.5	07.6	352 24.8	03.8			
21	191 27.2	124 32.5 ··	56.2	146 24.3 ··	52.5	10 21.0 ··	07.6	7 27.4 ··	03.8		S.H.A.	Mer. Pass.
22	206 29.6	139 31.7	56.8	161 24.9	53.1	25 23.6	07.6	22 29.9	03.8	Venus	° ′ 295 31.2	h m 12 40
23	221 32.1	154 30.9	57.3	176 25.6	53.6	40 26.1	07.6	37 32.4	03.8	Mars	316 19.1	11 16
Mer. Pass.	h m 8 20.2	v −0.8	d 0.6	v 0.6	d 0.5	v 2.5	d 0.0	v 2.5	d 0.0	Jupiter Saturn	178 50.6 175 56.9	20 23 20 34

G.M.T.	SUN G.H.A.	Dec.	MOON G.H.A.	v	Dec.	d	H.P.
16 00	180 55.7	N19 01.6	31 12.3	15.6	S 4 06.1	10.4	54.1
01	195 55.7	02.2	45 46.9	15.6	4 16.5	10.4	54.1
02	210 55.7	02.8	60 21.5	15.6	4 26.9	10.4	54.1
03	225 55.6 ··	03.4	74 56.1	15.6	4 37.3	10.4	54.1
04	240 55.6	03.9	89 30.7	15.6	4 47.7	10.3	54.1
05	255 55.6	04.5	104 05.3	15.6	4 58.0	10.3	54.1
06	270 55.6	N19 05.1	118 39.9	15.5	S 5 08.3	10.3	54.1
07	285 55.6	05.7	133 14.4	15.6	5 18.6	10.3	54.1
S 08	300 55.6	06.3	147 49.0	15.5	5 28.9	10.3	54.1
A 09	315 55.6 ··	06.8	162 23.5	15.6	5 39.2	10.2	54.1
T 10	330 55.6	07.4	176 58.1	15.5	5 49.4	10.2	54.0
U 11	345 55.6	08.0	191 32.6	15.5	5 59.6	10.2	54.0
R 12	0 55.5	N19 08.6	206 07.1	15.5	S 6 09.8	10.2	54.0
D 13	15 55.5	09.1	220 41.6	15.5	6 20.0	10.1	54.0
A 14	30 55.5	09.7	235 16.1	15.4	6 30.1	10.1	54.0
Y 15	45 55.5 ··	10.3	249 50.5	15.5	6 40.2	10.1	54.0
16	60 55.5	10.8	264 25.0	15.4	6 50.3	10.1	54.0
17	75 55.5	11.4	278 59.4	15.4	7 00.4	10.0	54.0
18	90 55.5	N19 12.0	293 33.8	15.4	S 7 10.4	10.0	54.0
19	105 55.5	12.6	308 08.2	15.4	7 20.4	10.0	54.0
20	120 55.4	13.1	322 42.6	15.3	7 30.4	9.9	54.0
21	135 55.4 ··	13.7	337 16.9	15.4	7 40.3	9.9	54.0
22	150 55.4	14.3	351 51.3	15.3	7 50.2	9.9	54.0
23	165 55.4	14.8	6 25.6	15.3	8 00.1	9.8	54.0
17 00	180 55.4	N19 15.4	20 59.9	15.3	S 8 09.9	9.8	54.0
01	195 55.4	16.0	35 34.2	15.2	8 19.7	9.8	54.0
02	210 55.4	16.5	50 08.4	15.3	8 29.5	9.8	54.0
03	225 55.3 ··	17.1	64 42.7	15.2	8 39.3	9.7	54.0
04	240 55.3	17.7	79 16.9	15.1	8 49.0	9.6	54.0
05	255 55.3	18.2	93 51.0	15.2	8 58.6	9.7	54.0
06	270 55.3	N19 18.8	108 25.2	15.1	S 9 08.3	9.6	54.0
07	285 55.3	19.4	122 59.3	15.1	9 17.9	9.6	54.0
08	300 55.3	19.9	137 33.4	15.1	9 27.5	9.5	54.0
S 09	315 55.2 ··	20.5	152 07.5	15.1	9 37.0	9.5	54.0
U 10	330 55.2	21.1	166 41.6	15.0	9 46.5	9.4	54.0
N 11	345 55.2	21.6	181 15.6	15.0	9 55.9	9.4	54.0
D 12	0 55.2	N19 22.2	195 49.6	15.0	S10 05.3	9.4	54.0
A 13	15 55.2	22.7	210 23.6	14.9	10 14.7	9.3	54.0
Y 14	30 55.2	23.3	224 57.5	15.0	10 24.0	9.3	54.0
15	45 55.1 ··	23.9	239 31.5	14.8	10 33.3	9.3	54.0
16	60 55.1	24.4	254 05.3	14.9	10 42.6	9.2	54.0
17	75 55.1	25.0	268 39.2	14.8	10 51.8	9.1	54.0
18	90 55.1	N19 25.5	283 13.0	14.8	S11 00.9	9.2	54.0
19	105 55.1	26.1	297 46.8	14.8	11 10.1	9.0	54.0
20	120 55.0	26.6	312 20.6	14.7	11 19.1	9.1	54.0
21	135 55.0 ··	27.2	326 54.3	14.7	11 28.2	8.9	54.0
22	150 55.0	27.8	341 28.0	14.7	11 37.1	9.0	54.0
23	165 55.0	28.3	356 01.7	14.7	11 46.1	8.9	54.0
18 00	180 55.0	N19 28.9	10 35.4	14.6	S11 55.0	8.8	54.0
01	195 54.9	29.4	25 09.0	14.5	12 03.8	8.8	54.0
02	210 54.9	30.0	39 42.5	14.6	12 12.6	8.7	54.0
03	225 54.9 ··	30.5	54 16.1	14.5	12 21.3	8.7	54.0
04	240 54.9	31.1	68 49.6	14.4	12 30.0	8.7	54.0
05	255 54.9	31.6	83 23.0	14.5	12 38.7	8.5	54.0
06	270 54.8	N19 32.2	97 56.5	14.4	S12 47.2	8.6	54.0
07	285 54.8	32.7	112 29.9	14.3	12 55.8	8.5	54.0
08	300 54.8	33.3	127 03.2	14.3	13 04.3	8.4	54.0
M 09	315 54.8 ··	33.8	141 36.6	14.3	13 12.7	8.4	54.0
O 10	330 54.7	34.4	156 09.9	14.2	13 21.1	8.3	54.0
N 11	345 54.7	34.9	170 43.1	14.2	13 29.4	8.3	54.0
D 12	0 54.7	N19 35.5	185 16.3	14.2	S13 37.7	8.2	54.0
A 13	15 54.7	36.0	199 49.5	14.1	13 45.9	8.1	54.0
Y 14	30 54.6	36.6	214 22.6	14.1	13 54.0	8.1	54.0
15	45 54.6 ··	37.1	228 55.7	14.1	14 02.1	8.1	54.0
16	60 54.6	37.6	243 28.8	14.0	14 10.2	8.0	54.0
17	75 54.6	38.2	258 01.8	14.0	14 18.2	7.9	54.0
18	90 54.5	N19 38.7	272 34.8	14.0	S14 26.1	7.9	54.0
19	105 54.5	39.3	287 07.8	13.9	14 34.0	7.8	54.0
20	120 54.5	39.8	301 40.7	13.8	14 41.8	7.7	54.0
21	135 54.5 ··	40.4	316 13.5	13.9	14 49.5	7.7	54.0
22	150 54.4	40.9	330 46.4	13.8	14 57.2	7.6	54.0
23	165 54.4	41.4	345 19.2	13.7	15 04.8	7.6	54.0
	S.D. 15.8	d 0.6	S.D. 14.7		14.7		14.7

Lat.	Twilight Naut.	Civil	Sunrise	Moonrise 16	17	18	19
°	h m	h m	h m	h m	h m	h m	h m
N 72	□	□	□	17 58	19 43	21 38	■
N 70	□	□	□	17 47	19 23	21 03	22 52
68	////	////	01 36	17 38	19 07	20 39	22 12
66	////	////	02 15	17 31	18 55	20 20	21 45
64	////	00 53	02 41	17 25	18 44	20 05	21 24
62	////	01 43	03 02	17 19	18 36	19 52	21 07
60	////	02 13	03 18	17 15	18 28	19 41	20 53
N 58	00 48	02 35	03 32	17 11	18 21	19 32	20 41
56	01 33	02 53	03 44	17 07	18 16	19 24	20 31
54	02 01	03 08	03 54	17 04	18 10	19 17	20 22
52	02 22	03 21	04 03	17 01	18 06	19 10	20 14
50	02 39	03 32	04 12	16 58	18 01	19 04	20 07
45	03 11	03 55	04 29	16 52	17 52	18 52	19 51
N 40	03 34	04 12	04 43	16 48	17 45	18 42	19 38
35	03 53	04 27	04 55	16 44	17 38	18 33	19 28
30	04 08	04 39	05 05	16 40	17 32	18 25	19 18
20	04 31	05 00	05 23	16 34	17 23	18 12	19 02
N 10	04 50	05 16	05 39	16 28	17 14	18 00	18 48
0	05 05	05 31	05 53	16 23	17 06	17 50	18 35
S 10	05 19	05 45	06 07	16 18	16 58	17 39	18 22
20	05 32	05 59	06 22	16 13	16 49	17 28	18 08
30	05 44	06 13	06 39	16 07	16 40	17 15	17 53
35	05 51	06 22	06 49	16 04	16 34	17 07	17 43
40	05 58	06 31	07 00	16 00	16 28	16 59	17 33
45	06 05	06 41	07 13	15 55	16 21	16 49	17 21
S 50	06 14	06 53	07 29	15 50	16 12	16 37	17 06
52	06 17	06 59	07 37	15 47	16 08	16 32	16 59
54	06 21	07 05	07 45	15 45	16 04	16 26	16 52
56	06 25	07 11	07 54	15 42	15 59	16 19	16 43
58	06 30	07 19	08 05	15 39	15 54	16 12	16 34
S 60	06 35	07 27	08 17	15 35	15 48	16 03	16 23

Lat.	Sunset	Twilight Civil	Naut.	Moonset 16	17	18	19
°	h m	h m	h m	h m	h m	h m	h m
N 72	□	□	□	03 01	02 48	02 32	02 08
N 70	□	□	□	03 08	03 01	02 54	02 44
68	22 22	////	////	03 13	03 12	03 10	03 10
66	21 41	////	////	03 18	03 20	03 24	03 30
64	21 14	23 08	////	03 21	03 28	03 35	03 46
62	20 53	22 13	////	03 25	03 34	03 45	03 59
60	20 36	21 42	////	03 28	03 40	03 54	04 11
N 58	20 22	21 19	23 13	03 30	03 45	04 01	04 20
56	20 10	21 01	22 23	03 32	03 49	04 07	04 29
54	20 00	20 46	21 54	03 35	03 53	04 13	04 37
52	19 50	20 33	21 33	03 36	03 56	04 18	04 44
50	19 42	20 22	21 16	03 38	04 00	04 23	04 50
45	19 24	19 59	20 43	03 42	04 07	04 34	05 03
N 40	19 10	19 41	20 19	03 45	04 13	04 42	05 14
35	18 58	19 26	20 01	03 48	04 18	04 50	05 24
30	18 48	19 14	19 45	03 50	04 22	04 56	05 32
20	18 30	18 53	19 21	03 54	04 30	05 08	05 47
N 10	18 14	18 37	19 03	03 58	04 37	05 18	06 00
0	18 00	18 22	18 47	04 02	04 44	05 27	06 11
S 10	17 46	18 08	18 34	04 05	04 50	05 36	06 23
20	17 31	17 54	18 21	04 09	04 57	05 46	06 36
30	17 14	17 39	18 08	04 13	05 05	05 58	06 51
35	17 04	17 31	18 01	04 16	05 10	06 05	06 59
40	16 52	17 22	17 54	04 18	05 15	06 12	07 09
45	16 39	17 11	17 47	04 22	05 21	06 21	07 21
S 50	16 23	16 59	17 39	04 25	05 29	06 32	07 34
52	16 15	16 53	17 35	04 27	05 32	06 37	07 41
54	16 07	16 47	17 31	04 29	05 36	06 42	07 48
56	15 58	16 41	17 27	04 31	05 40	06 48	07 56
58	15 47	16 33	17 22	04 34	05 45	06 55	08 05
S 60	15 35	16 25	17 17	04 36	05 50	07 03	08 16

Day	SUN Eqn. of Time 00h	12h	Mer. Pass.	MOON Mer. Pass. Upper	Lower	Age	Phase
	m s	m s	h m	h m	h m	d	
16	03 43	03 42	11 56	22 34	10 12	12	
17	03 42	03 41	11 56	23 16	10 55	13	◯
18	03 40	03 39	11 56	24 01	11 38	14	

G.M.T.	ARIES G.H.A.	VENUS −3.4 G.H.A.	VENUS Dec.	MARS +1.6 G.H.A.	MARS Dec.	JUPITER −1.8 G.H.A.	JUPITER Dec.	SATURN +1.0 G.H.A.	SATURN Dec.	STARS Name	S.H.A.	Dec.
19 00	236 34.6	169 30.1	N21 57.9	191 26.2	N16 54.2	55 28.6	N 1 07.6	52 35.0	N 1 03.9	Acamar	315 37.3	S40 22.9
01	251 37.0	184 29.3	58.5	206 26.9	54.7	70 31.2	07.6	67 37.5	03.9	Achernar	335 45.5	S57 19.9
02	266 39.5	199 28.5	59.1	221 27.5	55.2	85 33.7	07.7	82 40.0	03.9	Acrux	173 36.3	S62 59.9
03	281 42.0	214 27.7	21 59.6	236 28.1	.. 55.8	100 36.2	.. 07.7	97 42.6	.. 03.9	Adhara	255 32.0	S28 57.0
04	296 44.4	229 26.9	22 00.2	251 28.8	56.3	115 38.7	07.7	112 45.1	03.9	Aldebaran	291 17.8	N16 28.2
05	311 46.9	244 26.1	00.8	266 29.4	56.8	130 41.3	07.7	127 47.6	04.0			
06	326 49.4	259 25.3	N22 01.4	281 30.1	N16 57.4	145 43.8	N 1 07.7	142 50.2	N 1 04.0	Alioth	166 41.7	N56 03.9
07	341 51.8	274 24.6	01.9	296 30.7	57.9	160 46.3	07.7	157 52.7	04.0	Alkaid	153 17.8	N49 24.6
T 08	356 54.3	289 23.8	02.5	311 31.4	58.4	175 48.9	07.8	172 55.2	04.0	Al Na'ir	28 14.4	S47 03.0
U 09	11 56.8	304 23.0	.. 03.1	326 32.0	.. 59.0	190 51.4	.. 07.8	187 57.8	.. 04.0	Alnilam	276 11.5	S 1 12.9
E 10	26 59.2	319 22.2	03.6	341 32.6	16 59.5	205 53.9	07.8	203 00.3	04.1	Alphard	218 20.2	S 8 34.7
S 11	42 01.7	334 21.4	04.2	356 33.3	17 00.1	220 56.4	07.8	218 02.8	04.1			
D 12	57 04.1	349 20.6	N22 04.8	11 33.9	N17 00.6	235 59.0	N 1 07.8	233 05.4	N 1 04.1	Alphecca	126 31.4	N26 46.7
A 13	72 06.6	4 19.8	05.3	26 34.6	01.1	251 01.5	07.8	248 07.9	04.1	Alpheratz	358 09.1	N28 59.0
Y 14	87 09.1	19 19.0	05.9	41 35.2	01.7	266 04.0	07.8	263 10.4	04.1	Altair	62 31.9	N 8 49.0
15	102 11.5	34 18.2	.. 06.4	56 35.8	.. 02.2	281 06.5	.. 07.9	278 13.0	.. 04.2	Ankaa	353 40.1	S42 24.4
16	117 14.0	49 17.4	07.0	71 36.5	02.7	296 09.1	07.9	293 15.5	04.2	Antares	112 56.0	S26 23.4
17	132 16.5	64 16.6	07.6	86 37.1	03.3	311 11.6	07.9	308 18.0	04.2			
18	147 18.9	79 15.8	N22 08.1	101 37.7	N17 03.8	326 14.1	N 1 07.9	323 20.5	N 1 04.2	Arcturus	146 17.8	N19 16.9
19	162 21.4	94 15.0	08.7	116 38.4	04.3	341 16.6	07.9	338 23.1	04.2	Atria	108 19.3	S68 59.6
20	177 23.9	109 14.2	09.2	131 39.0	04.9	356 19.1	07.9	353 25.6	04.3	Avior	234 28.3	S59 27.3
21	192 26.3	124 13.4	.. 09.8	146 39.7	.. 05.4	11 21.7	.. 08.0	8 28.1	.. 04.3	Bellatrix	278 58.6	N 6 19.9
22	207 28.8	139 12.6	10.3	161 40.3	05.9	26 24.2	08.0	23 30.7	04.3	Betelgeuse	271 28.1	N 7 24.1
23	222 31.2	154 11.8	10.9	176 40.9	06.4	41 26.7	08.0	38 33.2	04.3			
20 00	237 33.7	169 11.0	N22 11.4	191 41.6	N17 07.0	56 29.2	N 1 08.0	53 35.7	N 1 04.3	Canopus	264 07.5	S52 41.4
01	252 36.2	184 10.2	12.0	206 42.2	07.5	71 31.8	08.0	68 38.2	04.4	Capella	281 11.1	N45 58.7
02	267 38.6	199 09.4	12.5	221 42.9	08.0	86 34.3	08.0	83 40.8	04.4	Deneb	49 48.0	N45 12.5
03	282 41.1	214 08.6	.. 13.1	236 43.5	.. 08.6	101 36.8	.. 08.0	98 43.3	.. 04.4	Denebola	182 58.5	N14 40.7
04	297 43.6	229 07.8	13.6	251 44.1	09.1	116 39.3	08.1	113 45.8	04.4	Diphda	349 20.7	S18 05.4
05	312 46.0	244 07.0	14.2	266 44.8	09.6	131 41.8	08.1	128 48.4	04.4			
06	327 48.5	259 06.2	N22 14.7	281 45.4	N17 10.2	146 44.4	N 1 08.1	143 50.9	N 1 04.4	Dubhe	194 21.4	N61 51.4
07	342 51.0	274 05.4	15.3	296 46.1	10.7	161 46.9	08.1	158 53.4	04.5	Elnath	278 43.9	N28 35.5
W 08	357 53.4	289 04.6	15.8	311 46.7	11.2	176 49.4	08.1	173 55.9	04.5	Eltanin	90 57.1	N51 29.4
E 09	12 55.9	304 03.8	.. 16.3	326 47.3	.. 11.7	191 51.9	.. 08.1	188 58.5	.. 04.5	Enif	34 11.1	N 9 47.2
D 10	27 58.4	319 03.0	16.9	341 48.0	12.3	206 54.4	08.1	204 01.0	04.5	Fomalhaut	15 51.0	S29 43.2
N 11	43 00.8	334 02.2	17.4	356 48.6	12.8	221 57.0	08.1	219 03.5	04.5			
E 12	58 03.3	349 01.4	N22 18.0	11 49.2	N17 13.3	236 59.5	N 1 08.2	234 06.1	N 1 04.6	Gacrux	172 27.9	S57 00.7
S 13	73 05.7	4 00.6	18.5	26 49.9	13.9	252 02.0	08.2	249 08.6	04.6	Gienah	176 17.3	S17 26.4
D 14	88 08.2	18 59.8	19.0	41 50.5	14.4	267 04.5	08.2	264 11.1	04.6	Hadar	149 22.1	S60 17.1
A 15	103 10.7	33 59.0	.. 19.6	56 51.2	.. 14.9	282 07.0	.. 08.2	279 13.6	.. 04.6	Hamal	328 28.7	N23 22.2
Y 16	118 13.1	48 58.2	20.1	71 51.8	15.4	297 09.5	08.2	294 16.2	04.6	Kaus Aust.	84 15.9	S34 23.5
17	133 15.6	63 57.4	20.6	86 52.4	16.0	312 12.1	08.2	309 18.7	04.6			
18	148 18.1	78 56.6	N22 21.2	101 53.1	N17 16.5	327 14.6	N 1 08.2	324 21.2	N 1 04.7	Kochab	137 17.9	N74 14.1
19	163 20.5	93 55.8	21.7	116 53.7	17.0	342 17.1	08.2	339 23.7	04.7	Markab	14 02.8	N15 06.1
20	178 23.0	108 55.0	22.2	131 54.3	17.5	357 19.6	08.2	354 26.3	04.7	Menkar	314 41.0	N 4 00.8
21	193 25.5	123 54.1	.. 22.8	146 55.0	.. 18.1	12 22.1	.. 08.3	9 28.8	.. 04.7	Menkent	148 36.1	S36 16.8
22	208 27.9	138 53.3	23.3	161 55.6	18.6	27 24.6	08.3	24 31.3	04.7	Miaplacidus	221 45.0	S69 38.7
23	223 30.4	153 52.5	23.8	176 56.3	19.1	42 27.2	08.3	39 33.8	04.7			
21 00	238 32.9	168 51.7	N22 24.3	191 56.9	N17 19.6	57 29.7	N 1 08.3	54 36.4	N 1 04.8	Mirfak	309 16.0	N49 47.5
01	253 35.3	183 50.9	24.9	206 57.5	20.2	72 32.2	08.3	69 38.9	04.8	Nunki	76 28.4	S26 19.2
02	268 37.8	198 50.1	25.4	221 58.2	20.7	87 34.7	08.3	84 41.4	04.8	Peacock	53 57.5	S56 47.5
03	283 40.2	213 49.3	.. 25.9	236 58.8	.. 21.2	102 37.2	.. 08.3	99 43.9	.. 04.8	Pollux	243 57.9	N28 04.4
04	298 42.7	228 48.5	26.4	251 59.4	21.7	117 39.7	08.3	114 46.5	04.8	Procyon	245 25.5	N 5 16.3
05	313 45.2	243 47.7	26.9	267 00.1	22.3	132 42.2	08.4	129 49.0	04.9			
06	328 47.6	258 46.9	N22 27.5	282 00.7	N17 22.8	147 44.8	N 1 08.4	144 51.5	N 1 04.9	Rasalhague	96 28.9	N12 34.4
07	343 50.1	273 46.1	28.0	297 01.3	23.3	162 47.3	08.4	159 54.0	04.9	Regulus	208 09.5	N12 03.6
T 08	358 52.6	288 45.2	28.5	312 02.0	23.8	177 49.8	08.4	174 56.6	04.9	Rigel	281 35.9	S 8 13.5
H 09	13 55.0	303 44.4	.. 29.0	327 02.6	.. 24.3	192 52.3	.. 08.4	189 59.1	.. 04.9	Rigil Kent.	140 24.6	S60 45.5
U 10	28 57.5	318 43.6	29.5	342 03.3	24.9	207 54.8	08.4	205 01.6	04.9	Sabik	102 40.3	S15 42.1
R 11	44 00.0	333 42.8	30.0	357 03.9	25.4	222 57.3	08.4	220 04.1	04.9			
S 12	59 02.4	348 42.0	N22 30.5	12 04.5	N17 25.9	237 59.8	N 1 08.4	235 06.7	N 1 05.0	Schedar	350 08.9	N56 25.8
D 13	74 04.9	3 41.2	31.1	27 05.2	26.4	253 02.3	08.4	250 09.2	05.0	Shaula	96 54.8	S37 05.4
A 14	89 07.3	18 40.4	31.6	42 05.8	26.9	268 04.9	08.4	265 11.7	05.0	Sirius	258 55.6	S16 41.6
Y 15	104 09.8	33 39.5	.. 32.1	57 06.4	.. 27.5	283 07.4	.. 08.5	280 14.2	.. 05.0	Spica	158 56.8	S11 03.9
16	119 12.3	48 38.7	32.6	72 07.1	28.0	298 09.9	08.5	295 16.8	05.0	Suhail	223 10.6	S43 21.7
17	134 14.7	63 37.9	33.1	87 07.7	28.5	313 12.4	08.5	310 19.3	05.0			
18	149 17.2	78 37.1	N22 33.6	102 08.3	N17 29.0	328 14.9	N 1 08.5	325 21.8	N 1 05.1	Vega	80 55.2	N38 45.8
19	164 19.7	93 36.3	34.1	117 09.0	29.5	343 17.4	08.5	340 24.3	05.1	Zuben'ubi	137 32.2	S15 57.9
20	179 22.1	108 35.5	34.6	132 09.6	30.1	358 19.9	08.5	355 26.8	05.1		S.H.A.	Mer. Pass.
21	194 24.6	123 34.7	.. 35.1	147 10.2	.. 30.6	13 22.4	.. 08.5	10 29.4	.. 05.1	Venus	291 37.3	12 44
22	209 27.1	138 33.8	35.6	162 10.9	31.1	28 24.9	08.5	25 31.9	05.1	Mars	314 07.9	11 13
23	224 29.5	153 33.0	36.1	177 11.5	31.6	43 27.4	08.5	40 34.4	05.1	Jupiter	178 55.5	20 11
Mer. Pass.	8ʰ 08.4ᵐ	v −0.8	d 0.5	v 0.6	d 0.5	v 2.5	d 0.0	v 2.5	d 0.0	Saturn	176 02.0	20 22

G.M.T.	SUN G.H.A.	SUN Dec.	MOON G.H.A.	v	Dec.	d	H.P.
19 00	180 54.4	N19 42.0	359 51.9	13.7	S15 12.4	7.5	54.0
01	195 54.4	42.5	14 24.6	13.7	15 19.9	7.4	54.0
02	210 54.3	43.1	28 57.3	13.6	15 27.3	7.4	54.0
03	225 54.3 ..	43.6	43 29.9	13.6	15 34.7	7.3	54.0
04	240 54.3	44.1	58 02.5	13.5	15 42.0	7.2	54.0
05	255 54.3	44.7	72 35.0	13.5	15 49.2	7.2	54.1
06	270 54.2	N19 45.2	87 07.5	13.5	S15 56.4	7.1	54.1
07	285 54.2	45.7	101 40.0	13.4	16 03.5	7.0	54.1
T 08	300 54.2	46.3	116 12.4	13.4	16 10.5	7.0	54.1
U 09	315 54.1 ..	46.8	130 44.8	13.3	16 17.5	6.9	54.1
E 10	330 54.1	47.4	145 17.1	13.3	16 24.4	6.8	54.1
S 11	345 54.1	47.9	159 49.4	13.3	16 31.2	6.7	54.1
D 12	0 54.1	N19 48.4	174 21.7	13.2	S16 37.9	6.7	54.1
A 13	15 54.0	49.0	188 53.9	13.2	16 44.6	6.6	54.1
Y 14	30 54.0	49.5	203 26.1	13.1	16 51.2	6.6	54.1
15	45 54.0 ..	50.0	217 58.2	13.1	16 57.8	6.5	54.1
16	60 53.9	50.5	232 30.3	13.0	17 04.3	6.3	54.1
17	75 53.9	51.1	247 02.3	13.0	17 10.6	6.4	54.1
18	90 53.9	N19 51.6	261 34.3	13.0	S17 17.0	6.2	54.1
19	105 53.8	52.1	276 06.3	12.9	17 23.2	6.2	54.1
20	120 53.8	52.7	290 38.2	12.9	17 29.4	6.1	54.2
21	135 53.8 ..	53.2	305 10.1	12.8	17 35.5	6.0	54.2
22	150 53.8	53.7	319 41.9	12.8	17 41.5	5.9	54.2
23	165 53.7	54.2	334 13.7	12.8	17 47.4	5.9	54.2
20 00	180 53.7	N19 54.8	348 45.5	12.7	S17 53.3	5.8	54.2
01	195 53.6	55.3	3 17.2	12.6	17 59.1	5.7	54.2
02	210 53.6	55.8	17 48.8	12.7	18 04.8	5.6	54.2
03	225 53.6 ..	56.3	32 20.5	12.5	18 10.4	5.6	54.2
04	240 53.6	56.9	46 52.0	12.6	18 16.0	5.4	54.2
05	255 53.5	57.4	61 23.6	12.5	18 21.4	5.4	54.2
06	270 53.5	N19 57.9	75 55.1	12.4	S18 26.8	5.3	54.2
W 07	285 53.5	58.4	90 26.5	12.4	18 32.1	5.2	54.2
E 08	300 53.4	59.0	104 57.9	12.4	18 37.3	5.2	54.3
D 09	315 53.4	19 59.5	119 29.3	12.4	18 42.5	5.0	54.3
N 10	330 53.4	20 00.0	134 00.7	12.2	18 47.5	5.0	54.3
E 11	345 53.3	00.5	148 31.9	12.3	18 52.5	4.9	54.3
S 12	0 53.3	N20 01.0	163 03.2	12.2	S18 57.4	4.8	54.3
D 13	15 53.3	01.6	177 34.4	12.2	19 02.2	4.7	54.3
A 14	30 53.2	02.1	192 05.6	12.1	19 06.9	4.6	54.3
Y 15	45 53.2 ..	02.6	206 36.7	12.1	19 11.5	4.5	54.3
16	60 53.2	03.1	221 07.8	12.1	19 16.0	4.5	54.3
17	75 53.1	03.6	235 38.9	12.0	19 20.5	4.4	54.3
18	90 53.1	N20 04.1	250 09.9	12.0	S19 24.9	4.2	54.4
19	105 53.0	04.7	264 40.9	11.9	19 29.1	4.2	54.4
20	120 53.0	05.2	279 11.8	11.9	19 33.3	4.1	54.4
21	135 53.0 ..	05.7	293 42.7	11.9	19 37.4	4.0	54.4
22	150 52.9	06.2	308 13.6	11.8	19 41.4	3.9	54.4
23	165 52.9	06.7	322 44.4	11.8	19 45.3	3.9	54.4
21 00	180 52.9	N20 07.2	337 15.2	11.7	S19 49.2	3.7	54.4
01	195 52.8	07.7	351 45.9	11.7	19 52.9	3.7	54.4
02	210 52.8	08.2	6 16.6	11.7	19 56.6	3.5	54.4
03	225 52.7 ..	08.8	20 47.3	11.6	20 00.1	3.5	54.5
04	240 52.7	09.3	35 17.9	11.6	20 03.6	3.3	54.5
05	255 52.7	09.8	49 48.5	11.6	20 06.9	3.3	54.5
06	270 52.6	N20 10.3	64 19.1	11.5	S20 10.2	3.2	54.5
07	285 52.6	10.8	78 49.6	11.5	20 13.4	3.1	54.5
T 08	300 52.5	11.3	93 20.1	11.5	20 16.5	2.9	54.5
H 09	315 52.5 ..	11.8	107 50.6	11.4	20 19.4	2.9	54.5
U 10	330 52.5	12.3	122 21.0	11.4	20 22.3	2.8	54.5
R 11	345 52.4	12.8	136 51.4	11.4	20 25.1	2.7	54.6
S 12	0 52.4	N20 13.3	151 21.8	11.3	S20 27.8	2.6	54.6
D 13	15 52.3	13.8	165 52.1	11.3	20 30.4	2.5	54.6
A 14	30 52.3	14.3	180 22.4	11.3	20 32.9	2.4	54.6
Y 15	45 52.3 ..	14.8	194 52.7	11.2	20 35.3	2.4	54.6
16	60 52.2	15.3	209 22.9	11.3	20 37.7	2.2	54.6
17	75 52.2	15.8	223 53.2	11.2	20 39.9	2.1	54.6
18	90 52.1	N20 16.3	238 23.3	11.2	S20 42.0	2.0	54.7
19	105 52.1	16.8	252 53.5	11.1	20 44.0	1.9	54.7
20	120 52.1	17.3	267 24.6	11.1	20 45.9	1.8	54.7
21	135 52.0 ..	17.8	281 53.7	11.1	20 47.7	1.7	54.7
22	150 52.0	18.3	296 23.8	11.0	20 49.4	1.6	54.7
23	165 51.9	18.8	310 53.8	11.0	20 51.0	1.6	54.7
	S.D. 15.8	d 0.5	S.D. 14.7		14.8		14.9

Lat.	Twilight Naut.	Civil	Sunrise	Moonrise 19	20	21	22
N 72	□	□	□	■	■	■	■
N 70	□	□	□	22 52	■	■	■
68	////	////	01 17	22 12	23 45	25 08	01 08
66	////	////	02 03	21 45	23 06	24 17	00 17
64	////	00 16	02 32	21 24	22 39	23 45	24 37
62	////	01 30	02 54	21 07	22 18	23 22	24 13
60	////	02 03	03 11	20 53	22 01	23 03	23 54
N 58	00 14	02 28	03 26	20 41	21 47	22 47	23 39
56	01 21	02 47	03 39	20 31	21 35	22 34	23 25
54	01 52	03 02	03 50	20 22	21 24	22 22	23 14
52	02 15	03 16	03 59	20 14	21 15	22 12	23 03
50	02 33	03 27	04 08	20 07	21 07	22 03	22 54
45	03 06	03 51	04 26	19 51	20 49	21 44	22 35
N 40	03 31	04 10	04 41	19 38	20 34	21 28	22 19
35	03 50	04 25	04 53	19 28	20 22	21 15	22 06
30	04 06	04 37	05 04	19 18	20 11	21 04	21 54
20	04 30	04 58	05 22	19 02	19 53	20 44	21 35
N 10	04 49	05 16	05 38	18 48	19 37	20 27	21 17
0	05 05	05 31	05 53	18 35	19 22	20 11	21 01
S 10	05 19	05 45	06 08	18 22	19 08	19 55	20 45
20	05 33	06 00	06 23	18 08	18 52	19 38	20 28
30	05 46	06 15	06 41	17 53	18 34	19 19	20 08
35	05 53	06 24	06 51	17 43	18 23	19 08	19 57
40	06 00	06 33	07 03	17 33	18 11	18 55	19 44
45	06 08	06 44	07 16	17 21	17 57	18 39	19 28
S 50	06 17	06 57	07 33	17 06	17 40	18 21	19 09
52	06 21	07 03	07 41	16 59	17 32	18 12	19 00
54	06 25	07 09	07 50	16 52	17 23	18 02	18 49
56	06 29	07 16	07 59	16 43	17 13	17 51	18 38
58	06 34	07 24	08 11	16 34	17 02	17 38	18 25
S 60	06 40	07 33	08 24	16 23	16 48	17 23	18 09

Lat.	Sunset	Twilight Civil	Naut.	Moonset 19	20	21	22
N 72	□	□	□	02 08	■	■	■
N 70	□	□	□	02 44	02 31	■	■
68	22 42	////	////	03 10	03 12	03 17	03 36
66	21 54	////	////	03 30	03 40	03 57	04 28
64	21 24	////	////	03 46	04 01	04 24	05 00
62	21 01	22 28	////	03 59	04 18	04 45	05 23
60	20 43	21 52	////	04 11	04 33	05 02	05 42
N 58	20 28	21 27	////	04 20	04 45	05 17	05 58
56	20 15	21 08	22 36	04 29	04 56	05 29	06 11
54	20 04	20 52	22 03	04 37	05 05	05 40	06 23
52	19 55	20 38	21 40	04 44	05 14	05 50	06 33
50	19 46	20 27	21 22	04 50	05 21	05 58	06 42
45	19 28	20 03	20 47	05 03	05 37	06 16	07 02
N 40	19 13	19 44	20 23	05 14	05 51	06 31	07 17
35	19 00	19 29	20 03	05 24	06 02	06 44	07 31
30	18 49	19 16	19 48	05 32	06 12	06 55	07 42
20	18 31	18 55	19 23	05 47	06 29	07 14	08 02
N 10	18 15	18 37	19 04	06 00	06 44	07 30	08 19
0	18 00	18 22	18 48	06 11	06 58	07 46	08 35
S 10	17 45	18 08	18 33	06 23	07 12	08 01	08 51
20	17 30	17 53	18 20	06 36	07 27	08 18	09 08
30	17 12	17 38	18 07	06 51	07 44	08 37	09 28
35	17 01	17 29	18 00	06 59	07 54	08 48	09 40
40	16 50	17 19	17 52	07 09	08 06	09 01	09 53
45	16 36	17 08	17 44	07 21	08 19	09 16	10 09
S 50	16 19	16 56	17 36	07 34	08 36	09 34	10 28
52	16 12	16 50	17 32	07 41	08 43	09 43	10 37
54	16 03	16 43	17 27	07 48	08 52	09 52	10 47
56	15 53	16 36	17 23	07 56	09 02	10 03	10 59
58	15 42	16 29	17 18	08 05	09 13	10 16	11 12
S 60	15 29	16 17	17 13	08 16	09 26	10 31	11 27

Day	SUN Eqn. of Time 00h	12h	Mer. Pass.	MOON Mer. Pass. Upper	Lower	Age	Phase
	m s	m s	h m	h m	h m	d	
19	03 38	03 36	11 56	00 01	12 23	15	
20	03 35	03 33	11 56	00 46	13 10	16	
21	03 31	03 30	11 57	01 34	13 58	17	○

G.M.T.	ARIES G.H.A.	VENUS −3.4 G.H.A.	Dec.	MARS +1.6 G.H.A.	Dec.	JUPITER −1.8 G.H.A.	Dec.	SATURN +1.0 G.H.A.	Dec.	STARS Name	S.H.A.	Dec.
22 00	239 32.0	168 32.2 N22 36.6		192 12.1 N17 32.1		58 29.9 N 1 08.5		55 36.9 N 1 05.2		Acamar	315 37.3	S40 22.8
01	254 34.5	183 31.4 37.1		207 12.8 32.6		73 32.5 08.5		70 39.5 05.2		Achernar	335 45.4	S57 19.8
02	269 36.9	198 30.6 37.6		222 13.4 33.2		88 35.0 08.5		85 42.0 05.2		Acrux	173 36.3	S62 59.9
03	284 39.4	213 29.7 ·· 38.1		237 14.1 ·· 33.7		103 37.5 ·· 08.6		100 44.5 ·· 05.2		Adhara	255 32.1	S28 57.0
04	299 41.8	228 28.9 38.6		252 14.7 34.2		118 40.0 08.6		115 47.0 05.2		Aldebaran	291 17.8	N16 28.2
05	314 44.3	243 28.1 39.1		267 15.3 34.7		133 42.5 08.6		130 49.5 05.2				
06	329 46.8	258 27.3 N22 39.6		282 16.0 N17 35.2		148 45.0 N 1 08.6		145 52.1 N 1 05.2		Alioth	166 41.8	N56 03.9
07	344 49.2	273 26.5 40.1		297 16.6 35.7		163 47.5 08.6		160 54.6 05.3		Alkaid	153 17.8	N49 24.6
08	359 51.7	288 25.6 40.5		312 17.2 36.2		178 50.0 08.6		175 57.1 05.3		Al Na'ir	28 14.4	S47 02.9
F 09	14 54.2	303 24.8 ·· 41.0		327 17.9 ·· 36.8		193 52.5 ·· 08.6		190 59.6 ·· 05.3		Alnilam	276 11.5	S 1 12.9
R 10	29 56.6	318 24.0 41.5		342 18.5 37.3		208 55.0 08.6		206 02.1 05.3		Alphard	218 20.2	S 8 34.7
I 11	44 59.1	333 23.2 42.0		357 19.1 37.8		223 57.5 08.6		221 04.7 05.3				
D 12	60 01.6	348 22.4 N22 42.5		12 19.8 N17 38.3		239 00.0 N 1 08.6		236 07.2 N 1 05.3		Alphecca	126 31.4	N26 46.7
A 13	75 04.0	3 21.5 43.0		27 20.4 38.8		254 02.5 08.6		251 09.7 05.4		Alpheratz	358 09.0	N28 59.0
Y 14	90 06.5	18 20.7 43.5		42 21.0 39.3		269 05.0 08.6		266 12.2 05.4		Altair	62 31.9	N 8 49.0
15	105 09.0	33 19.9 ·· 43.9		57 21.7 ·· 39.8		284 07.5 ·· 08.6		281 14.7 ·· 05.4		Ankaa	353 40.1	S42 24.4
16	120 11.4	48 19.1 44.4		72 22.3 40.3		299 10.0 08.6		296 17.3 05.4		Antares	112 55.9	S26 23.4
17	135 13.9	63 18.2 44.9		87 22.9 40.9		314 12.5 08.6		311 19.8 05.4				
18	150 16.3	78 17.4 N22 45.4		102 23.6 N17 41.4		329 15.0 N 1 08.7		326 22.3 N 1 05.4		Arcturus	146 17.8	N19 16.9
19	165 18.8	93 16.6 45.9		117 24.2 41.9		344 17.5 08.7		341 24.8 05.4		Atria	108 19.2	S68 59.6
20	180 21.3	108 15.8 46.3		132 24.8 42.4		359 20.0 08.7		356 27.3 05.5		Avior	234 28.3	S59 27.3
21	195 23.7	123 14.9 ·· 46.8		147 25.5 ·· 42.9		14 22.6 ·· 08.7		11 29.9 ·· 05.5		Bellatrix	278 58.6	N 6 19.9
22	210 26.2	138 14.1 47.3		162 26.1 43.4		29 25.1 08.7		26 32.4 05.5		Betelgeuse	271 28.1	N 7 24.1
23	225 28.7	153 13.3 47.8		177 26.7 43.9		44 27.6 08.7		41 34.9 05.5				
23 00	240 31.1	168 12.5 N22 48.2		192 27.4 N17 44.4		59 30.1 N 1 08.7		56 37.4 N 1 05.5		Canopus	264 07.5	S52 41.4
01	255 33.6	183 11.6 48.7		207 28.0 44.9		74 32.6 08.7		71 39.9 05.5		Capella	281 11.1	N45 58.7
02	270 36.1	198 10.8 49.2		222 28.6 45.4		89 35.1 08.7		86 42.4 05.5		Deneb	49 48.0	N45 12.5
03	285 38.5	213 10.0 ·· 49.6		237 29.3 ·· 46.0		104 37.6 ·· 08.7		101 45.0 ·· 05.5		Denebola	182 58.5	N14 40.7
04	300 41.0	228 09.2 50.1		252 29.9 46.5		119 40.1 08.7		116 47.5 05.6		Diphda	349 20.6	S18 05.4
05	315 43.4	243 08.3 50.6		267 30.5 47.0		134 42.6 08.7		131 50.0 05.6				
06	330 45.9	258 07.5 N22 51.0		282 31.2 N17 47.5		149 45.1 N 1 08.7		146 52.5 N 1 05.6		Dubhe	194 21.5	N61 51.4
07	345 48.4	273 06.7 51.5		297 31.8 48.0		164 47.6 08.7		161 55.0 05.6		Elnath	278 43.9	N28 35.5
S 08	0 50.8	288 05.8 52.0		312 32.4 48.5		179 50.1 08.7		176 57.6 05.6		Eltanin	90 57.0	N51 29.4
A 09	15 53.3	303 05.0 ·· 52.4		327 33.1 ·· 49.0		194 52.6 ·· 08.7		192 00.1 ·· 05.6		Enif	34 11.1	N 9 47.2
T 10	30 55.8	318 04.2 52.9		342 33.7 49.5		209 55.1 08.7		207 02.6 05.6		Fomalhaut	15 51.0	S29 43.2
U 11	45 58.2	333 03.4 53.3		357 34.3 50.0		224 57.5 08.7		222 05.1 05.7				
R 12	61 00.7	348 02.5 N22 53.8		12 35.0 N17 50.5		240 00.0 N 1 08.7		237 07.6 N 1 05.7		Gacrux	172 27.9	S57 00.7
D 13	76 03.2	3 01.7 54.2		27 35.6 51.0		255 02.5 08.7		252 10.1 05.7		Gienah	176 17.3	S17 26.4
A 14	91 05.6	18 00.9 54.7		42 36.2 51.5		270 05.0 08.7		267 12.6 05.7		Hadar	149 22.1	S60 17.1
Y 15	106 08.1	33 00.0 ·· 55.2		57 36.8 ·· 52.0		285 07.5 ·· 08.7		282 15.2 ·· 05.7		Hamal	328 28.7	N23 22.2
16	121 10.6	47 59.2 55.6		72 37.5 52.5		300 10.0 08.7		297 17.7 05.7		Kaus Aust.	84 15.9	S34 23.6
17	136 13.0	62 58.4 56.1		87 38.1 53.0		315 12.5 08.7		312 20.2 05.7				
18	151 15.5	77 57.5 N22 56.5		102 38.7 N17 53.5		330 15.0 N 1 08.8		327 22.7 N 1 05.7		Kochab	137 17.9	N74 14.1
19	166 17.9	92 56.7 57.0		117 39.4 54.0		345 17.5 08.8		342 25.2 05.8		Markab	14 02.8	N15 06.1
20	181 20.4	107 55.9 57.4		132 40.0 54.6		0 20.0 08.8		357 27.7 05.8		Menkar	314 41.0	N 4 00.8
21	196 22.9	122 55.0 ·· 57.9		147 40.6 ·· 55.1		15 22.5 ·· 08.8		12 30.3 ·· 05.8		Menkent	148 36.1	S36 16.8
22	211 25.3	137 54.2 58.3		162 41.3 55.6		30 25.0 08.8		27 32.8 05.8		Miaplacidus	221 45.1	S69 38.7
23	226 27.8	152 53.4 58.8		177 41.9 56.1		45 27.5 08.8		42 35.3 05.8				
24 00	241 30.3	167 52.5 N22 59.2		192 42.5 N17 56.6		60 30.0 N 1 08.8		57 37.8 N 1 05.8		Mirfak	309 16.0	N49 47.5
01	256 32.7	182 51.7 22 59.6		207 43.2 57.1		75 32.5 08.8		72 40.3 05.8		Nunki	76 28.3	S26 19.2
02	271 35.2	197 50.9 23 00.1		222 43.8 57.6		90 35.0 08.8		87 42.8 05.8		Peacock	53 57.4	S56 47.5
03	286 37.7	212 50.0 ·· 00.5		237 44.4 ·· 58.1		105 37.5 ·· 08.8		102 45.3 ·· 05.9		Pollux	243 57.9	N28 04.4
04	301 40.1	227 49.2 01.0		252 45.1 58.6		120 40.0 08.8		117 47.9 05.9		Procyon	245 25.5	N 5 16.3
05	316 42.6	242 48.4 01.4		267 45.7 59.1		135 42.5 08.8		132 50.4 05.9				
06	331 45.1	257 47.5 N23 01.8		282 46.3 N17 59.6		150 45.0 N 1 08.8		147 52.9 N 1 05.9		Rasalhague	96 28.9	N12 34.4
07	346 47.5	272 46.7 02.3		297 46.9 18 00.1		165 47.4 08.8		162 55.4 05.9		Regulus	208 09.6	N12 03.6
08	1 50.0	287 45.9 02.7		312 47.6 00.6		180 49.9 08.8		177 57.9 05.9		Rigel	281 35.9	S 8 13.5
S 09	16 52.4	302 45.0 ·· 03.1		327 48.2 ·· 01.1		195 52.4 ·· 08.8		193 00.4 ·· 05.9		Rigil Kent.	140 24.6	S60 45.5
U 10	31 54.9	317 44.2 03.6		342 48.8 01.6		210 54.9 08.8		208 02.9 05.9		Sabik	102 40.3	S15 42.1
N 11	46 57.4	332 43.3 04.0		357 49.5 02.1		225 57.4 08.8		223 05.4 05.9				
D 12	61 59.8	347 42.5 N23 04.4		12 50.1 N18 02.6		240 59.9 N 1 08.8		238 08.0 N 1 06.0		Schedar	350 08.8	N56 25.8
A 13	77 02.3	2 41.7 04.9		27 50.7 03.1		256 02.4 08.8		253 10.5 06.0		Shaula	96 54.8	S37 05.4
Y 14	92 04.8	17 40.8 05.3		42 51.4 03.6		271 04.9 08.8		268 13.0 06.0		Sirius	258 55.6	S16 41.6
15	107 07.2	32 40.0 ·· 05.7		57 52.0 ·· 04.0		286 07.4 ·· 08.8		283 15.5 ·· 06.0		Spica	158 56.8	S11 03.9
16	122 09.7	47 39.1 06.1		72 52.6 04.5		301 09.9 08.8		298 18.0 06.0		Suhail	223 10.6	S43 21.7
17	137 12.2	62 38.3 06.6		87 53.2 05.0		316 12.4 08.8		313 20.5 06.0				
18	152 14.6	77 37.5 N23 07.0		102 53.9 N18 05.5		331 14.8 N 1 08.8		328 23.0 N 1 06.0		Vega	80 55.2	N38 45.8
19	167 17.1	92 36.6 07.4		117 54.5 06.0		346 17.3 08.8		343 25.5 06.0		Zuben'ubi	137 32.2	S15 57.9
20	182 19.5	107 35.8 07.8		132 55.1 06.5		1 19.8 08.8		358 28.1 06.0			S.H.A.	Mer. Pass.
21	197 22.0	122 34.9 ·· 08.3		147 55.8 ·· 07.0		16 22.3 ·· 08.8		13 30.6 ·· 06.1		Venus	287 41.3	12 48
22	212 24.5	137 34.1 08.7		162 56.4 07.5		31 24.8 08.8		28 33.1 06.1		Mars	311 56.2	11 10
23	227 26.9	152 33.3 09.1		177 57.0 08.0		46 27.3 08.8		43 35.6 06.1		Jupiter	178 58.9	19 59
Mer. Pass.	7 56.6	v −0.8 d 0.5		v 0.6 d 0.5		v 2.5 d 0.0		v 2.5 d 0.0		Saturn	176 06.3	20 10

G.M.T.	SUN G.H.A.	Dec..	MOON G.H.A.	v	Dec.	d	H.P.
d h	° '	° '	° '	'	° '	'	'
22 00	180 51.9	N20 19.3	325 23.8	11.0	S20 52.6	1.4	54.8
01	195 51.8	19.8	339 53.8	10.9	20 54.0	1.3	54.8
02	210 51.8	20.3	354 23.7	11.0	20 55.3	1.2	54.8
03	225 51.8 ··	20.8	8 53.7	10.9	20 56.5	1.1	54.8
04	240 51.7	21.3	23 23.6	10.8	20 57.6	1.0	54.8
05	255 51.7	21.8	37 53.4	10.9	20 58.6	0.9	54.8
06	270 51.6	N20 22.3	52 23.3	10.8	S20 59.5	0.8	54.9
07	285 51.6	22.8	66 53.1	10.8	21 00.3	0.7	54.9
08	300 51.5	23.3	81 22.9	10.8	21 01.0	0.6	54.9
F 09	315 51.5 ··	23.8	95 52.7	10.9	21 01.6	0.5	54.9
R 10	330 51.4	24.3	110 22.5	10.7	21 02.1	0.4	54.9
I 11	345 51.4	24.8	124 52.2	10.8	21 02.5	0.3	54.9
D 12	0 51.3	N20 25.2	139 22.0	10.7	S21 02.8	0.1	55.0
A 13	15 51.3	25.7	153 51.7	10.7	21 02.9	0.1	55.0
Y 14	30 51.3	26.2	168 21.4	10.6	21 03.0	0.0	55.0
15	45 51.2 ··	26.7	182 51.0	10.7	21 03.0	0.2	55.0
16	60 51.2	27.2	197 20.7	10.6	21 02.8	0.2	55.0
17	75 51.1	27.7	211 50.3	10.6	21 02.6	0.3	55.0
18	90 51.1	N20 28.2	226 19.9	10.6	S21 02.3	0.5	55.1
19	105 51.0	28.7	240 49.5	10.6	21 01.8	0.5	55.1
20	120 51.0	29.1	255 19.1	10.5	21 01.2	0.6	55.1
21	135 50.9 ··	29.6	269 48.6	10.6	21 00.6	0.8	55.1
22	150 50.9	30.1	284 18.2	10.5	20 59.8	0.9	55.1
23	165 50.8	30.6	298 47.7	10.5	20 58.9	0.9	55.2
23 00	180 50.8	N20 31.1	313 17.2	10.6	S20 58.0	1.1	55.2
01	195 50.7	31.6	327 46.8	10.4	20 56.9	1.2	55.2
02	210 50.7	32.0	342 16.2	10.5	20 55.7	1.3	55.2
03	225 50.6 ··	32.5	356 45.7	10.5	20 54.4	1.4	55.2
04	240 50.6	33.0	11 15.2	10.5	20 53.0	1.5	55.3
05	255 50.5	33.5	25 44.7	10.4	20 51.5	1.6	55.3
06	270 50.5	N20 34.0	40 14.1	10.5	S20 49.9	1.7	55.3
07	285 50.4	34.4	54 43.6	10.4	20 48.2	1.9	55.3
S 08	300 50.4	34.9	69 13.0	10.4	20 46.3	1.9	55.3
A 09	315 50.3 ··	35.4	83 42.4	10.4	20 44.4	2.0	55.4
T 10	330 50.3	35.9	98 11.8	10.4	20 42.4	2.2	55.4
U 11	345 50.2	36.3	112 41.2	10.4	20 40.2	2.2	55.4
R 12	0 50.2	N20 36.8	127 10.6	10.4	S20 38.0	2.4	55.4
D 13	15 50.1	37.3	141 40.0	10.4	20 35.6	2.5	55.4
A 14	30 50.1	37.8	156 09.4	10.4	20 33.1	2.5	55.5
Y 15	45 50.0 ··	38.2	170 38.8	10.4	20 30.6	2.7	55.5
16	60 50.0	38.7	185 08.2	10.3	20 27.9	2.8	55.5
17	75 49.9	39.2	199 37.5	10.4	20 25.1	2.9	55.5
18	90 49.9	N20 39.7	214 06.9	10.4	S20 22.2	3.0	55.6
19	105 49.8	40.1	228 36.3	10.3	20 19.2	3.1	55.6
20	120 49.8	40.6	243 05.6	10.4	20 16.1	3.2	55.6
21	135 49.7 ··	41.1	257 35.0	10.3	20 12.9	3.3	55.6
22	150 49.6	41.5	272 04.3	10.4	20 09.6	3.4	55.7
23	165 49.6	42.0	286 33.7	10.3	20 06.2	3.5	55.7
24 00	180 49.5	N20 42.5	301 03.0	10.4	S20 02.7	3.7	55.7
01	195 49.5	43.0	315 32.4	10.3	19 59.0	3.7	55.7
02	210 49.4	43.4	330 01.7	10.4	19 55.3	3.8	55.7
03	225 49.4 ··	43.9	344 31.1	10.3	19 51.5	4.0	55.8
04	240 49.3	44.3	359 00.4	10.4	19 47.5	4.0	55.8
05	255 49.3	44.8	13 29.8	10.4	19 43.5	4.2	55.8
06	270 49.2	N20 45.3	27 59.2	10.3	S19 39.3	4.2	55.8
07	285 49.2	45.7	42 28.5	10.4	19 35.1	4.4	55.9
08	300 49.1	46.2	56 57.9	10.3	19 30.7	4.5	55.9
S 09	315 49.0 ··	46.7	71 27.2	10.4	19 26.2	4.5	55.9
U 10	330 49.0	47.1	85 56.6	10.3	19 21.7	4.7	55.9
N 11	345 48.9	47.6	100 26.0	10.3	19 17.0	4.8	56.0
D 12	0 48.9	N20 48.1	114 55.3	10.4	S19 12.2	4.9	56.0
A 13	15 48.8	48.5	129 24.7	10.4	19 07.3	4.9	56.0
Y 14	30 48.8	49.0	143 54.1	10.4	19 02.4	5.1	56.0
15	45 48.7 ··	49.4	158 23.5	10.4	18 57.3	5.2	56.1
16	60 48.6	49.9	172 52.9	10.4	18 52.1	5.3	56.1
17	75 48.6	50.3	187 22.3	10.4	18 46.8	5.4	56.1
18	90 48.5	N20 50.8	201 51.7	10.4	S18 41.4	5.5	56.2
19	105 48.5	51.3	216 21.1	10.4	18 35.9	5.6	56.2
20	120 48.4	51.7	230 50.5	10.4	18 30.3	5.7	56.2
21	135 48.4 ··	52.2	245 19.9	10.4	18 24.6	5.8	56.2
22	150 48.3	52.6	259 49.3	10.4	18 18.8	5.8	56.3
23	165 48.2	53.1	274 18.7	10.5	18 13.0	6.0	56.3
	S.D. 15.8	d 0.5	S.D. 15.0		15.1		15.3

Lat.	Twilight Naut.	Civil	Sunrise	Moonrise 22	23	24	25
°	h m	h m	h m	h m	h m	h m	h m
N 72	☐	☐	☐	■	■		04 17
N 70	☐	☐	☐	■	■	03 42	03 02
68	////	////	00 55	01 08	01 59	02 18	02 24
66	////	////	01 50	00 17	01 08	01 40	01 57
64	////	////	02 23	24 37	00 37	01 13	01 36
62	////	01 15	02 46	24 13	00 13	00 52	01 19
60	////	01 54	03 05	23 54	24 35	00 35	01 05
N 58	////	02 20	03 21	23 39	24 20	00 20	00 53
56	01 08	02 40	03 34	23 25	24 08	00 08	00 43
54	01 44	02 57	03 45	23 14	23 57	24 34	00 34
52	02 08	03 11	03 55	23 03	23 48	24 25	00 25
50	02 27	03 23	04 04	22 54	23 39	24 18	00 18
45	03 03	03 48	04 23	22 35	23 21	24 02	00 02
N 40	03 28	04 07	04 38	22 19	23 06	23 49	24 28
35	03 48	04 23	04 51	22 06	22 54	23 38	24 19
30	04 04	04 36	05 02	21 54	22 43	23 28	24 11
20	04 29	04 57	05 21	21 35	22 24	23 11	23 57
N 10	04 49	05 15	05 38	21 17	22 07	22 56	23 45
0	05 05	05 31	05 53	21 01	21 52	22 43	23 33
S 10	05 20	05 46	06 08	20 45	21 37	22 29	23 22
20	05 34	06 01	06 24	20 28	21 20	22 14	23 09
30	05 48	06 17	06 42	20 08	21 01	21 57	22 55
35	05 55	06 26	06 53	19 57	20 50	21 47	22 47
40	06 02	06 36	07 05	19 44	20 37	21 36	22 38
45	06 11	06 47	07 19	19 28	20 22	21 23	22 27
S 50	06 20	07 00	07 37	19 09	20 04	21 06	22 14
52	06 24	07 06	07 45	19 00	19 55	20 59	22 07
54	06 29	07 13	07 54	18 49	19 46	20 50	22 01
56	06 33	07 20	08 04	18 38	19 35	20 40	21 53
58	06 38	07 28	08 16	18 25	19 22	20 30	21 44
S 60	06 44	07 38	08 30	18 09	19 08	20 17	21 34

Lat.	Sunset	Twilight Civil	Naut.	Moonset 22	23	24	25
°	h m	h m	h m	h m	h m	h m	h m
N 72	☐	☐	☐	■	■		05 45
N 70	☐	☐	☐	■	■	04 33	06 59
68	23 07	////	////	03 36	04 30	05 57	07 36
66	22 07	////	////	04 28	05 20	06 35	08 03
64	21 33	////	////	05 00	05 52	07 01	08 23
62	21 09	22 43	////	05 23	06 16	07 22	08 39
60	20 50	22 02	////	05 42	06 34	07 39	08 52
N 58	20 34	21 35	////	05 58	06 50	07 53	09 04
56	20 21	21 14	22 50	06 11	07 03	08 05	09 14
54	20 09	20 58	22 12	06 23	07 15	08 15	09 23
52	19 59	20 43	21 47	06 33	07 25	08 24	09 31
50	19 50	20 31	21 28	06 42	07 34	08 33	09 38
45	19 31	20 06	20 52	07 02	07 53	08 50	09 53
N 40	19 15	19 47	20 26	07 17	08 09	09 05	10 05
35	19 02	19 31	20 06	07 31	08 22	09 17	10 16
30	18 51	19 18	19 50	07 42	08 33	09 28	10 25
20	18 32	18 56	19 24	08 02	08 53	09 46	10 40
N 10	18 16	18 38	19 05	08 19	09 10	10 02	10 54
0	18 00	18 22	18 48	08 35	09 26	10 16	11 07
S 10	17 45	18 07	18 33	08 51	09 41	10 31	11 20
20	17 29	17 52	18 19	09 08	09 58	10 47	11 33
30	17 11	17 36	18 06	09 28	10 18	11 04	11 48
35	17 00	17 27	17 58	09 40	10 29	11 15	11 57
40	16 48	17 17	17 51	09 53	10 42	11 27	12 07
45	16 34	17 06	17 42	10 09	10 57	11 41	12 19
S 50	16 16	16 53	17 33	10 28	11 16	11 58	12 33
52	16 08	16 47	17 29	10 37	11 25	12 05	12 42
54	15 59	16 40	17 24	10 47	11 35	12 14	12 47
56	15 48	16 33	17 19	10 59	11 46	12 24	12 56
58	15 37	16 24	17 14	11 12	11 58	12 36	13 05
S 60	15 23	16 15	17 09	11 27	12 13	12 49	13 15

Day	SUN Eqn. of Time 00ʰ	12ʰ	Mer. Pass.	MOON Mer. Pass. Upper	Lower	Age	Phase
	m s	m s	h m	h m	h m	d	
22	03 28	03 25	11 57	02 23	14 48	18	
23	03 23	03 21	11 57	03 13	15 39	19	◐
24	03 18	03 16	11 57	04 04	16 29	20	

G.M.T.	ARIES G.H.A.	VENUS −3.4 G.H.A.	Dec.	MARS +1.6 G.H.A.	Dec.	JUPITER −1.8 G.H.A.	Dec.	SATURN +1.0 G.H.A.	Dec.	STARS Name	S.H.A.	Dec.
25 00	242 29.4	167 32.4	N23 09.5	192 57.7	N18 08.5	61 29.8	N 1 08.8	58 38.1	N 1 06.1	Acamar	315 37.3	S40 22.8
01	257 31.9	182 31.6	09.9	207 58.3	09.0	76 32.3	08.8	73 40.6	06.1	Achernar	335 45.4	S57 19.8
02	272 34.3	197 30.7	10.3	222 58.9	09.5	91 34.7	08.8	88 43.1	06.1	Acrux	173 36.3	S62 59.9
03	287 36.8	212 29.9	·· 10.8	237 59.5	·· 10.0	106 37.2	·· 08.8	103 45.6	·· 06.1	Adhara	255 32.1	S28 57.0
04	302 39.3	227 29.0	11.2	253 00.2	10.5	121 39.7	08.8	118 48.1	06.1	Aldebaran	291 17.8	N16 28.2
05	317 41.7	242 28.2	11.6	268 00.8	11.0	136 42.2	08.8	133 50.6	06.1			
06	332 44.2	257 27.4	N23 12.0	283 01.4	N18 11.5	151 44.7	N 1 08.8	148 53.2	N 1 06.1	Alioth	166 41.8	N56 03.9
07	347 46.7	272 26.5	12.4	298 02.1	12.0	166 47.2	08.8	163 55.7	06.2	Alkaid	153 17.8	N49 24.6
08	2 49.1	287 25.7	12.8	313 02.7	12.5	181 49.7	08.8	178 58.2	06.2	Al Na'ir	28 14.3	S47 02.9
M 09	17 51.6	302 24.8	·· 13.2	328 03.3	·· 12.9	196 52.1	·· 08.8	194 00.7	·· 06.2	Alnilam	276 11.5	S 1 12.9
O 10	32 54.0	317 24.0	13.6	343 03.9	13.4	211 54.6	08.8	209 03.2	06.2	Alphard	218 20.2	S 8 34.7
N 11	47 56.5	332 23.1	14.0	358 04.6	13.9	226 57.1	08.8	224 05.7	06.2			
D 12	62 59.0	347 22.3	N23 14.4	13 05.2	N18 14.4	241 59.6	N 1 08.8	239 08.2	N 1 06.2	Alphecca	126 31.4	N26 46.7
A 13	78 01.4	2 21.4	14.8	28 05.8	14.9	257 02.1	08.7	254 10.7	06.2	Alpheratz	358 09.0	N28 59.0
Y 14	93 03.9	17 20.6	15.2	43 06.5	15.4	272 04.6	08.7	269 13.2	06.2	Altair	62 31.9	N 8 49.0
15	108 06.4	32 19.7	·· 15.6	58 07.1	·· 15.9	287 07.0	·· 08.7	284 15.7	·· 06.2	Ankaa	353 40.0	S42 24.4
16	123 08.8	47 18.9	16.0	73 07.7	16.4	302 09.5	08.7	299 18.2	06.2	Antares	112 55.9	S26 23.4
17	138 11.3	62 18.0	16.4	88 08.3	16.9	317 12.0	08.7	314 20.8	06.2			
18	153 13.8	77 17.2	N23 16.8	103 09.0	N18 17.4	332 14.5	N 1 08.7	329 23.3	N 1 06.3	Arcturus	146 17.8	N19 16.9
19	168 16.2	92 16.4	17.2	118 09.6	17.8	347 17.0	08.7	344 25.8	06.3	Atria	108 19.2	S68 59.6
20	183 18.7	107 15.5	17.6	133 10.2	18.3	2 19.5	08.7	359 28.3	06.3	Avior	234 28.3	S59 27.3
21	198 21.2	122 14.7	·· 18.0	148 10.8	·· 18.8	17 21.9	·· 08.7	14 30.8	·· 06.3	Bellatrix	278 58.6	N 6 19.9
22	213 23.6	137 13.8	18.4	163 11.5	19.3	32 24.4	08.7	29 33.3	06.3	Betelgeuse	271 28.1	N 7 24.1
23	228 26.1	152 13.0	18.8	178 12.1	19.8	47 26.9	08.7	44 35.8	06.3			
26 00	243 28.5	167 12.1	N23 19.2	193 12.7	N18 20.3	62 29.4	N 1 08.7	59 38.3	N 1 06.3	Canopus	264 07.5	S52 41.4
01	258 31.0	182 11.3	19.5	208 13.4	20.8	77 31.9	08.7	74 40.8	06.3	Capella	281 11.1	N45 58.7
02	273 33.5	197 10.4	19.9	223 14.0	21.2	92 34.3	08.7	89 43.3	06.3	Deneb	49 47.9	N45 12.6
03	288 35.9	212 09.6	·· 20.3	238 14.6	·· 21.7	107 36.8	·· 08.7	104 45.8	·· 06.3	Denebola	182 58.5	N14 40.7
04	303 38.4	227 08.7	20.7	253 15.2	22.2	122 39.3	08.7	119 48.3	06.3	Diphda	349 20.6	S18 05.4
05	318 40.9	242 07.9	21.1	268 15.9	22.7	137 41.8	08.7	134 50.8	06.4			
06	333 43.3	257 07.0	N23 21.5	283 16.5	N18 23.2	152 44.3	N 1 08.7	149 53.3	N 1 06.4	Dubhe	194 21.5	N61 51.4
07	348 45.8	272 06.2	21.9	298 17.1	23.7	167 46.7	08.7	164 55.8	06.4	Elnath	278 43.9	N28 35.5
08	3 48.3	287 05.3	22.2	313 17.7	24.2	182 49.2	08.7	179 58.4	06.4	Eltanin	90 57.0	N51 29.4
T 09	18 50.7	302 04.4	·· 22.6	328 18.4	·· 24.6	197 51.7	·· 08.7	195 00.9	·· 06.4	Enif	34 11.1	N 9 47.2
U 10	33 53.2	317 03.6	23.0	343 19.0	25.1	212 54.2	08.7	210 03.4	06.4	Fomalhaut	15 51.0	S29 43.2
E 11	48 55.6	332 02.7	23.4	358 19.6	25.6	227 56.6	08.7	225 05.9	06.4			
S 12	63 58.1	347 01.9	N23 23.7	13 20.2	N18 26.1	242 59.1	N 1 08.7	240 08.4	N 1 06.4	Gacrux	172 27.9	S57 00.7
D 13	79 00.6	2 01.0	24.1	28 20.9	26.6	258 01.6	08.6	255 10.9	06.4	Gienah	176 17.3	S17 26.4
A 14	94 03.0	17 00.2	24.5	43 21.5	27.1	273 04.1	08.6	270 13.4	06.4	Hadar	149 22.1	S60 17.1
Y 15	109 05.5	31 59.3	·· 24.9	58 22.1	·· 27.5	288 06.6	·· 08.6	285 15.9	·· 06.4	Hamal	328 28.7	N23 22.2
16	124 08.0	46 58.5	25.2	73 22.8	28.0	303 09.0	08.6	300 18.4	06.4	Kaus Aust.	84 15.9	S34 23.6
17	139 10.4	61 57.6	25.6	88 23.4	28.5	318 11.5	08.6	315 20.9	06.4			
18	154 12.9	76 56.8	N23 26.0	103 24.0	N18 29.0	333 14.0	N 1 08.6	330 23.4	N 1 06.5	Kochab	137 17.9	N74 14.1
19	169 15.4	91 55.9	26.3	118 24.6	29.5	348 16.5	08.6	345 25.9	06.5	Markab	14 02.8	N15 06.1
20	184 17.8	106 55.1	26.7	133 25.3	29.9	3 18.9	08.6	0 28.4	06.5	Menkar	314 41.0	N 4 00.8
21	199 20.3	121 54.2	·· 27.1	148 25.9	·· 30.4	18 21.4	·· 08.6	15 30.9	·· 06.5	Menkent	148 36.1	S36 16.8
22	214 22.8	136 53.3	27.4	163 26.5	30.9	33 23.9	08.6	30 33.4	06.5	Miaplacidus	221 45.1	S69 38.7
23	229 25.2	151 52.5	27.8	178 27.1	31.4	48 26.3	08.6	45 35.9	06.5			
27 00	244 27.7	166 51.6	N23 28.1	193 27.8	N18 31.9	63 28.8	N 1 08.6	60 38.4	N 1 06.5	Mirfak	309 15.9	N49 47.5
01	259 30.1	181 50.8	28.5	208 28.4	32.3	78 31.3	08.6	75 40.9	06.5	Nunki	76 28.3	S26 19.2
02	274 32.6	196 49.9	28.9	223 29.0	32.8	93 33.8	08.6	90 43.4	06.5	Peacock	53 57.4	S56 47.5
03	289 35.1	211 49.1	·· 29.2	238 29.6	·· 33.3	108 36.2	·· 08.6	105 45.9	·· 06.5	Pollux	243 57.9	N28 04.4
04	304 37.5	226 48.2	29.6	253 30.3	33.8	123 38.7	08.5	120 48.4	06.5	Procyon	245 25.5	N 5 16.3
05	319 40.0	241 47.3	29.9	268 30.9	34.3	138 41.2	08.5	135 50.9	06.5			
06	334 42.5	256 46.5	N23 30.3	283 31.5	N18 34.7	153 43.7	N 1 08.5	150 53.4	N 1 06.5	Rasalhague	96 28.8	N12 34.4
07	349 44.9	271 45.6	30.6	298 32.1	35.2	168 46.1	08.5	165 55.9	06.5	Regulus	208 09.6	N12 03.6
W 08	4 47.4	286 44.8	31.0	313 32.8	35.7	183 48.6	08.5	180 58.4	06.5	Rigel	281 35.9	S 8 13.5
E 09	19 49.9	301 43.9	·· 31.3	328 33.4	·· 36.2	198 51.1	·· 08.5	196 00.9	·· 06.6	Rigil Kent.	140 24.6	S60 45.5
D 10	34 52.3	316 43.0	31.7	343 34.0	36.6	213 53.5	08.5	211 03.4	06.6	Sabik	102 40.3	S15 42.1
N 11	49 54.8	331 42.2	32.0	358 34.6	37.1	228 56.0	08.5	226 05.9	06.6			
E 12	64 57.3	346 41.3	N23 32.4	13 35.3	N18 37.6	243 58.5	N 1 08.5	241 08.4	N 1 06.6	Schedar	350 08.8	N56 25.8
S 13	79 59.7	1 40.5	32.7	28 35.9	38.1	259 01.0	08.5	256 10.9	06.6	Shaula	96 54.7	S37 05.4
D 14	95 02.2	16 39.6	33.1	43 36.5	38.5	274 03.4	08.5	271 13.4	06.6	Sirius	258 55.6	S16 41.6
A 15	110 04.6	31 38.7	·· 33.4	58 37.1	·· 39.0	289 05.9	·· 08.5	286 15.9	·· 06.6	Spica	158 56.8	S11 03.9
Y 16	125 07.1	46 37.9	33.7	73 37.8	39.5	304 08.4	08.4	301 18.4	06.6	Suhail	223 16.5	S43 21.7
17	140 09.6	61 37.0	34.1	88 38.4	40.0	319 10.8	08.4	316 20.9	06.6			
18	155 12.0	76 36.2	N23 34.4	103 39.0	N18 40.4	334 13.3	N 1 08.4	331 23.4	N 1 06.6	Vega	80 55.2	N38 45.9
19	170 14.5	91 35.3	34.8	118 39.6	40.9	349 15.8	08.4	346 25.9	06.6	Zuben'ubi	137 32.2	S15 57.9
20	185 17.0	106 34.4	35.1	133 40.2	41.4	4 18.2	08.4	1 28.4	06.6		S.H.A.	Mer. Pass.
21	200 19.4	121 33.6	·· 35.4	148 40.9	·· 41.8	19 20.7	·· 08.4	16 30.9	·· 06.6	Venus	283 43.6	12 52
22	215 21.9	136 32.7	35.8	163 41.5	42.3	34 23.2	08.4	31 33.4	06.6	Mars	309 44.2	11 07
23	230 24.4	151 31.9	36.1	178 42.1	42.8	49 25.6	08.4	46 35.9	06.6	Jupiter	179 00.8	19 47
Mer. Pass.	7 44.8	v −0.9	d 0.4	v 0.6	d 0.5	v 2.5	d 0.0	v 2.5	d 0.0	Saturn	176 09.8	19 58

G.M.T.	SUN GHA	Dec.	MOON G.H.A.	v	Dec.	d	H.P.
25 00	180 48.2	N20 53.5	288 48.2	10.4	S18 07.0	6.1	56.3
01	195 48.1	54.0	303 17.6	10.5	18 00.9	6.2	56.3
02	210 48.1	54.4	317 47.1	10.4	17 54.7	6.3	56.4
03	225 48.0	·· 54.9	332 16.5	10.5	17 48.4	6.4	56.4
04	240 47.9	55.3	346 46.0	10.5	17 42.0	6.5	56.4
05	255 47.9	55.8	1 15.5	10.5	17 35.5	6.6	56.5
06	270 47.8	N20 56.2	15 45.0	10.4	S17 28.9	6.6	56.5
07	285 47.7	56.7	30 14.4	10.5	17 22.3	6.8	56.5
08	300 47.7	57.1	44 43.9	10.6	17 15.5	6.9	56.5
M 09	315 47.6	·· 57.6	59 13.4	10.6	17 08.6	6.9	56.6
O 10	330 47.6	58.0	73 43.0	10.5	17 01.7	7.1	56.6
N 11	345 47.5	58.5	88 12.5	10.5	16 54.6	7.2	56.6
D 12	0 47.4	N20 58.9	102 42.0	10.5	S16 47.4	7.2	56.7
A 13	15 47.4	59.4	117 11.5	10.6	16 40.2	7.4	56.7
Y 14	30 47.3	20 59.8	131 41.1	10.6	16 32.8	7.4	56.7
15	45 47.3	21 00.3	146 10.7	10.6	16 25.4	7.5	56.8
16	60 47.2	00.7	160 40.2	10.6	16 17.9	7.6	56.8
17	75 47.1	01.1	175 09.8	10.6	16 10.3	7.8	56.8
18	90 47.1	N21 01.6	189 39.4	10.6	S16 02.5	7.8	56.8
19	105 47.0	02.0	204 09.0	10.6	15 54.7	7.9	56.9
20	120 46.9	02.5	218 38.6	10.6	15 46.8	8.0	56.9
21	135 46.9	·· 02.9	233 08.2	10.6	15 38.8	8.0	56.9
22	150 46.8	03.3	247 37.8	10.6	15 30.8	8.2	57.0
23	165 46.7	03.8	262 07.4	10.6	15 22.6	8.3	57.0
26 00	180 46.7	N21 04.2	276 37.0	10.7	S15 14.3	8.3	57.0
01	195 46.6	04.7	291 06.7	10.6	15 06.0	8.4	57.1
02	210 46.5	05.1	305 36.3	10.7	14 57.6	8.6	57.1
03	225 46.5	·· 05.5	320 06.0	10.6	14 49.0	8.6	57.1
04	240 46.4	06.0	334 35.6	10.7	14 40.4	8.7	57.2
05	255 46.3	06.4	349 05.3	10.7	14 31.7	8.7	57.2
06	270 46.3	N21 06.8	3 35.0	10.6	S14 23.0	8.9	57.2
07	285 46.2	07.3	18 04.6	10.7	14 14.1	9.0	57.3
T 08	300 46.1	07.7	32 34.3	10.7	14 05.1	9.0	57.3
U 09	315 46.1	·· 08.1	47 04.0	10.7	13 56.1	9.1	57.3
E 10	330 46.0	08.6	61 33.7	10.7	13 47.0	9.2	57.4
S 11	345 45.9	09.0	76 03.4	10.7	13 37.8	9.3	57.4
D 12	0 45.9	N21 09.4	90 33.1	10.7	S13 28.5	9.3	57.4
A 13	15 45.8	09.9	105 02.8	10.8	13 19.2	9.5	57.5
Y 14	30 45.7	10.3	119 32.6	10.7	13 09.7	9.5	57.5
15	45 45.7	·· 10.7	134 02.3	10.7	13 00.2	9.6	57.5
16	60 45.6	11.1	148 32.0	10.8	12 50.6	9.7	57.6
17	75 45.5	11.6	163 01.8	10.7	12 40.9	9.7	57.6
18	90 45.5	N21 12.0	177 31.5	10.7	S12 31.2	9.9	57.6
19	105 45.4	12.4	192 01.2	10.8	12 21.3	9.9	57.7
20	120 45.3	12.9	206 31.0	10.7	12 11.4	10.0	57.7
21	135 45.3	·· 13.3	221 00.7	10.8	12 01.4	10.0	57.7
22	150 45.2	13.7	235 30.5	10.7	11 51.4	10.2	57.7
23	165 45.1	14.1	250 00.2	10.8	11 41.2	10.2	57.8
27 00	180 45.1	N21 14.5	264 30.0	10.8	S11 31.0	10.3	57.8
01	195 45.0	15.0	278 59.7	10.8	11 20.7	10.3	57.9
02	210 44.9	15.4	293 29.5	10.7	11 10.4	10.5	57.9
03	225 44.8	·· 15.8	307 59.2	10.8	10 59.9	10.5	57.9
04	240 44.8	16.2	322 29.0	10.7	10 49.4	10.5	58.0
05	255 44.7	16.6	336 58.7	10.8	10 38.9	10.7	58.0
06	270 44.6	N21 17.1	351 28.5	10.7	S10 28.2	10.7	58.1
07	285 44.6	17.5	5 58.2	10.8	10 17.5	10.8	58.1
W 08	300 44.5	17.9	20 28.0	10.7	10 06.7	10.8	58.1
E 09	315 44.4	·· 18.3	34 57.7	10.8	9 55.9	10.9	58.1
D 10	330 44.3	18.7	49 27.5	10.7	9 45.0	11.0	58.2
N 11	345 44.3	19.2	63 57.2	10.7	9 34.0	11.0	58.2
E 12	0 44.2	N21 19.6	78 26.9	10.8	S 9 23.0	11.1	58.2
S 13	15 44.1	20.0	92 56.7	10.7	9 11.9	11.2	58.3
D 14	30 44.0	20.4	107 26.4	10.7	9 00.7	11.2	58.3
A 15	45 44.0	·· 20.8	121 56.1	10.7	8 49.5	11.3	58.3
Y 16	60 43.9	21.2	136 25.8	10.7	8 38.2	11.3	58.4
17	75 43.8	21.6	150 55.5	10.7	8 26.9	11.4	58.4
18	90 43.8	N21 22.1	165 25.2	10.7	S 8 15.5	11.5	58.5
19	105 43.7	22.5	179 54.9	10.7	8 04.0	11.5	58.5
20	120 43.6	22.9	194 24.6	10.6	7 52.5	11.6	58.5
21	135 43.5	·· 23.3	208 54.2	10.7	7 40.9	11.6	58.6
22	150 43.5	23.7	223 23.9	10.7	7 29.3	11.7	58.6
23	165 43.4	24.1	237 53.6	10.6	7 17.6	11.8	58.6
	S.D. 15.8	d 0.4	S.D. 15.4		15.6		15.9

Lat.	Twilight Naut.	Civil	Sunrise	Moonrise 25	26	27	28
N 72	□	□	□	04 17	03 20	02 57	02 41
N 70	□	□	□	03 02	02 48	02 39	02 32
68	////	////	00 19	02 24	02 25	02 25	02 24
66	////	////	01 38	01 57	02 07	02 13	02 17
64	////	////	02 14	01 36	01 52	02 03	02 12
62	////	00 59	02 40	01 19	01 39	01 54	02 07
60	////	01 44	02 59	01 05	01 29	01 47	02 03
N 58	////	02 13	03 16	00 53	01 19	01 41	01 59
56	00 53	02 35	03 29	00 43	01 11	01 35	01 56
54	01 35	02 52	03 41	00 34	01 04	01 30	01 53
52	02 02	03 07	03 52	00 25	00 57	01 25	01 50
50	02 22	03 20	04 01	00 18	00 51	01 21	01 47
45	02 59	03 45	04 21	00 02	00 38	01 11	01 42
N 40	03 25	04 05	04 36	24 28	00 28	01 04	01 37
35	03 46	04 21	04 50	24 19	00 19	00 57	01 33
30	04 02	04 34	05 01	24 11	00 11	00 51	01 30
20	04 28	04 57	05 21	23 57	24 41	00 41	01 24
N 10	04 48	05 15	05 38	23 45	24 32	00 32	01 19
0	05 05	05 31	05 53	23 33	24 23	00 23	01 14
S 10	05 20	05 46	06 09	23 22	24 15	00 15	01 08
20	05 35	06 02	06 25	23 09	24 06	00 06	01 03
30	05 49	06 18	06 44	22 55	23 55	24 57	00 57
35	05 57	06 28	06 56	22 47	23 49	24 53	00 53
40	06 04	06 38	07 08	22 38	23 43	24 49	00 49
45	06 13	06 50	07 22	22 27	23 35	24 45	00 45
S 50	06 23	07 03	07 40	22 14	23 25	24 39	00 39
52	06 27	07 10	07 49	22 07	23 21	24 37	00 37
54	06 32	07 17	07 58	22 01	23 16	24 34	00 34
56	06 37	07 24	08 09	21 53	23 10	24 31	00 31
58	06 42	07 33	08 21	21 44	23 04	24 27	00 27
S 60	06 49	07 43	08 36	21 34	22 57	24 23	00 23

Lat.	Sunset	Twilight Civil	Naut.	Moonset 25	26	27	28
N 72	□	□	□	05 45	08 27	10 35	12 37
N 70	□	□	□	06 59	08 58	10 51	12 44
68	□	□	□	07 36	09 20	11 04	12 50
66	22 20	////	////	08 03	09 37	11 15	12 54
64	21 42	////	////	08 23	09 51	11 23	12 58
62	21 16	23 00	////	08 39	10 03	11 31	13 02
60	20 56	22 12	////	08 52	10 13	11 37	13 05
N 58	20 39	21 43	////	09 04	10 21	11 43	13 07
56	20 25	21 21	23 06	09 14	10 29	11 48	13 10
54	20 13	21 03	22 21	09 23	10 36	11 52	13 12
52	20 03	20 48	21 54	09 31	10 42	11 56	13 14
50	19 54	20 35	21 33	09 38	10 47	12 00	13 15
45	19 34	20 10	20 56	09 53	10 59	12 08	13 19
N 40	19 18	19 50	20 29	10 05	11 08	12 14	13 22
35	19 05	19 33	20 09	10 16	11 17	12 20	13 25
30	18 53	19 20	19 52	10 25	11 24	12 25	13 27
20	18 33	18 57	19 26	10 40	11 36	12 33	13 31
N 10	18 16	18 39	19 06	10 54	11 47	12 40	13 34
0	18 01	18 23	18 49	11 07	11 57	12 47	13 38
S 10	17 45	18 07	18 33	11 20	12 07	12 54	13 41
20	17 28	17 52	18 19	11 33	12 18	13 01	13 44
30	17 09	17 35	18 05	11 48	12 30	13 09	13 48
35	16 58	17 26	17 57	11 57	12 37	13 14	13 50
40	16 46	17 16	17 49	12 07	12 45	13 19	13 52
45	16 31	17 04	17 40	12 19	12 54	13 25	13 55
S 50	16 13	16 50	17 30	12 33	13 05	13 32	13 58
52	16 05	16 44	17 26	12 40	13 10	13 36	14 00
54	15 55	16 37	17 21	12 47	13 15	13 39	14 01
56	15 44	16 29	17 16	12 56	13 21	13 43	14 03
58	15 32	16 20	17 11	13 05	13 28	13 48	14 05
S 60	15 18	16 11	17 05	13 15	13 36	13 53	14 07

Day	SUN Eqn. of Time 00h	12h	Mer. Pass.	MOON Mer. Pass. Upper	Lower	Age	Phase
	m s	m s	h m	h m	h m	d	
25	03 13	03 10	11 57	04 55	17 20	21	
26	03 07	03 04	11 57	05 45	18 10	22	◖
27	03 00	02 57	11 57	06 35	19 00	23	

1981 MAY 28, 29, 30 (THURS., FRI., SAT.)

G.M.T.	ARIES G.H.A.	VENUS −3.4 G.H.A.	Dec.	MARS +1.6 G.H.A.	Dec.	JUPITER −1.8 G.H.A.	Dec.	SATURN +1.1 G.H.A.	Dec.	STARS Name	S.H.A.	Dec.
28 00	245 26.8	166 31.0 N23	36.4	193 42.7 N18	43.3	64 28.1 N 1	08.4	61 38.4 N 1	06.6	Acamar	315 37.3	S40 22:8
01	260 29.3	181 30.1	36.8	208 43.4	43.7	79 30.6	08.4	76 40.9	06.6	Achernar	335 45.4	S57 19.8
02	275 31.7	196 29.3	37.1	223 44.0	44.2	94 33.0	08.3	91 43.4	06.7	Acrux	173 36.4	S63 00.0
03	290 34.2	211 28.4 ··	37.4	238 44.6 ··	44.7	109 35.5 ··	08.3	106 45.9 ··	06.7	Adhara	255 32.1	S28 57.0
04	305 36.7	226 27.5	37.8	253 45.2	45.1	124 38.0	08.3	121 48.4	06.7	Aldebaran	291 17.8	N16 28.2
05	320 39.1	241 26.7	38.1	268 45.9	45.6	139 40.4	08.3	136 50.9	06.7			
06	335 41.6	256 25.8 N23	38.4	283 46.5 N18	46.1	154 42.9 N 1	08.3	151 53.4 N 1	06.7	Alioth	166 41.8	N56 04.0
07	350 44.1	271 24.9	38.7	298 47.1	46.6	169 45.4	08.3	166 55.9	06.7	Alkaid	153 17.8	N49 24.6
T 08	5 46.5	286 24.1	39.1	313 47.7	47.0	184 47.8	08.3	181 58.4	06.7	Al Na'ir	28 14.3	S47 02.9
H 09	20 49.0	301 23.2 ··	39.4	328 48.3 ··	47.5	199 50.3 ··	08.3	197 00.9 ··	06.7	Alnilam	276 11.5	S 1 12.9
U 10	35 51.5	316 22.3	39.7	343 49.0	48.0	214 52.7	08.3	212 03.4	06.7	Alphard	218 20.2	S 8 34.7
R 11	50 53.9	331 21.5	40.0	358 49.6	48.4	229 55.2	08.2	227 05.9	06.7			
S 12	65 56.4	346 20.6 N23	40.3	13 50.2 N18	48.9	244 57.7 N 1	08.2	242 08.4 N 1	06.7	Alphecca	126 31.4	N26 46.7
D 13	80 58.9	1 19.7	40.6	28 50.8	49.4	260 00.1	08.2	257 10.9	06.7	Alpheratz	358 09.0	N28 59.0
A 14	96 01.3	16 18.9	41.0	43 51.5	49.8	275 02.6	08.2	272 13.4	06.7	Altair	62 31.9	N 8 49.1
Y 15	111 03.8	31 18.0 ··	41.3	58 52.1 ··	50.3	290 05.1 ··	08.2	287 15.9 ··	06.7	Ankaa	353 40.0	S42 24.4
16	126 06.2	46 17.1	41.6	73 52.7	50.8	305 07.5	08.2	302 18.4	06.7	Antares	112 55.9	S26 23.4
17	141 08.7	61 16.3	41.9	88 53.3	51.2	320 10.0	08.2	317 20.9	06.7			
18	156 11.2	76 15.4 N23	42.2	103 54.0 N18	51.7	335 12.4 N 1	08.2	332 23.4 N 1	06.7	Arcturus	146 17.8	N19 16.9
19	171 13.6	91 14.5	42.5	118 54.6	52.2	350 14.9	08.1	347 25.9	06.7	Atria	108 19.2	S68 59.6
20	186 16.1	106 13.7	42.8	133 55.2	52.6	5 17.4	08.1	2 28.4	06.7	Avior	234 28.4	S59 27.2
21	201 18.6	121 12.8 ··	43.1	148 55.8 ··	53.1	20 19.8 ··	08.1	17 30.9 ··	06.7	Bellatrix	278 58.6	N 6 19.9
22	216 21.0	136 11.9	43.4	163 56.4	53.6	35 22.3	08.1	32 33.4	06.7	Betelgeuse	271 28.1	N 7 24.1
23	231 23.5	151 11.1	43.8	178 57.1	54.0	50 24.7	08.1	47 35.9	06.7			
29 00	246 26.0	166 10.2 N23	44.1	193 57.7 N18	54.5	65 27.2 N 1	08.1	62 38.4 N 1	06.7	Canopus	264 07.5	S52 41.3
01	261 28.4	181 09.3	44.4	208 58.3	54.9	80 29.7	08.1	77 40.9	06.7	Capella	281 11.1	N45 58.7
02	276 30.9	196 08.5	44.7	223 58.9	55.4	95 32.1	08.1	92 43.4	06.8	Deneb	49 47.9	N45 12.6
03	291 33.4	211 07.6 ··	45.0	238 59.5 ··	55.9	110 34.6 ··	08.0	107 45.9 ··	06.8	Denebola	182 58.5	N14 40.7
04	306 35.8	226 06.7	45.3	254 00.2	56.3	125 37.0	08.0	122 48.4	06.8	Diphda	349 20.6	S18 05.4
05	321 38.3	241 05.9	45.6	269 00.8	56.8	140 39.5	08.0	137 50.9	06.8			
06	336 40.7	256 05.0 N23	45.9	284 01.4 N18	57.3	155 42.0 N 1	08.0	152 53.3 N 1	06.8	Dubhe	194 21.5	N61 51.4
07	351 43.2	271 04.1	46.1	299 02.0	57.7	170 44.4	08.0	167 55.8	06.8	Elnath	278 43.9	N28 35.5
08	6 45.7	286 03.2	46.4	314 02.7	58.2	185 46.9	08.0	182 58.3	06.8	Eltanin	90 57.0	N51 29.4
F 09	21 48.1	301 02.4 ··	46.7	329 03.3 ··	58.6	200 49.3 ··	08.0	198 00.8 ··	06.8	Enif	34 11.1	N 9 47.2
R 10	36 50.6	316 01.5	47.0	344 03.9	59.1	215 51.8	07.9	213 03.3	06.8	Fomalhaut	15 50.9	S29 43.2
I 11	51 53.1	331 00.6	47.3	359 04.5 18	59.6	230 54.2	07.9	228 05.8	06.8			
D 12	66 55.5	345 59.8 N23	47.6	14 05.1 N19	00.0	245 56.7 N 1	07.9	243 08.3 N 1	06.8	Gacrux	172 27.9	S57 00.7
A 13	81 58.0	0 58.9	47.9	29 05.8	00.5	260 59.2	07.9	258 10.8	06.8	Gienah	176 17.4	S17 26.4
Y 14	97 00.5	15 58.0	48.2	44 06.4	00.9	276 01.6	07.9	273 13.3	06.8	Hadar	149 22.2	S60 17.1
15	112 02.9	30 57.1 ··	48.5	59 07.0 ··	01.4	291 04.1 ··	07.9	288 15.8 ··	06.8	Hamal	328 28.7	N23 22.2
16	127 05.4	45 56.3	48.7	74 07.6	01.9	306 06.5	07.9	303 18.3	06.8	Kaus Aust.	84 15.9	S34 23.6
17	142 07.8	60 55.4	49.0	89 08.2	02.3	321 09.0	07.8	318 20.8	06.8			
18	157 10.3	75 54.5 N23	49.3	104 08.9 N19	02.8	336 11.4 N 1	07.8	333 23.3 N 1	06.8	Kochab	137 17.9	N74 14.2
19	172 12.8	90 53.7	49.6	119 09.5	03.2	351 13.9	07.8	348 25.8	06.8	Markab	14 02.8	N15 06.1
20	187 15.2	105 52.8	49.9	134 10.1	03.7	6 16.3	07.8	3 28.3	06.8	Menkar	314 41.0	N 4 00.9
21	202 17.7	120 51.9 ··	50.2	149 10.7 ··	04.1	21 18.8 ··	07.8	18 30.7 ··	06.8	Menkent	148 36.1	S36 16.8
22	217 20.2	135 51.0	50.4	164 11.3	04.6	36 21.2	07.8	33 33.2	06.8	Miaplacidus	221 45.2	S69 38.7
23	232 22.6	150 50.2	50.7	179 12.0	05.1	51 23.7	07.7	48 35.7	06.8			
30 00	247 25.1	165 49.3 N23	51.0	194 12.6 N19	05.5	66 26.2 N 1	07.7	63 38.2 N 1	06.8	Mirfak	309 15.9	N49 47.5
01	262 27.6	180 48.4	51.3	209 13.2	06.0	81 28.6	07.7	78 40.7	06.8	Nunki	76 28.3	S26 19.2
02	277 30.0	195 47.5	51.5	224 13.8	06.4	96 31.1	07.7	93 43.2	06.8	Peacock	53 57.3	S56 47.5
03	292 32.5	210 46.7 ··	51.8	239 14.4 ··	06.9	111 33.5 ··	07.7	108 45.7 ··	06.8	Pollux	243 57.9	N28 04.4
04	307 35.0	225 45.8	52.1	254 15.1	07.3	126 36.0	07.7	123 48.2	06.8	Procyon	245 25.6	N 5 16.3
05	322 37.4	240 44.9	52.3	269 15.7	07.8	141 38.4	07.6	138 50.7	06.8			
06	337 39.9	255 44.0 N23	52.6	284 16.3 N19	08.2	156 40.9 N 1	07.6	153 53.2 N 1	06.8	Rasalhague	96 28.8	N12 34.4
07	352 42.3	270 43.2	52.9	299 16.9	08.7	171 43.3	07.6	168 55.7	06.8	Regulus	208 09.6	N12 03.6
S 08	7 44.8	285 42.3	53.1	314 17.5	09.1	186 45.8	07.6	183 58.1	06.8	Rigel	281 35.9	S 8 13.5
A 09	22 47.3	300 41.4 ··	53.4	329 18.2 ··	09.6	201 48.2 ··	07.6	199 00.6 ··	06.8	Rigil Kent.	140 24.6	S60 45.5
T 10	37 49.7	315 40.5	53.7	344 18.8	10.0	216 50.7	07.6	214 03.1	06.8	Sabik	102 40.3	S15 42.1
U 11	52 52.2	330 39.7	53.9	359 19.4	10.5	231 53.1	07.5	229 05.6	06.8			
R 12	67 54.7	345 38.8 N23	54.2	14 20.0 N19	10.9	246 55.6 N 1	07.5	244 08.1 N 1	06.8	Schedar	350 08.8	N56 25.8
D 13	82 57.1	0 37.9	54.4	29 20.6	11.4	261 58.0	07.5	259 10.6	06.8	Shaula	96 54.7	S37 05.4
A 14	97 59.6	15 37.0	54.6	44 21.2	11.9	277 00.5	07.5	274 13.1	06.8	Sirius	258 55.6	S16 41.6
Y 15	113 02.1	30 36.1 ··	55.0	59 21.9 ··	12.3	292 02.9 ··	07.5	289 15.6 ··	06.8	Spica	158 56.8	S11 03.8
16	128 04.5	45 35.3	55.2	74 22.5	12.8	307 05.4	07.4	304 18.1	06.8	Suhail	223 10.6	S43 21.7
17	143 07.0	60 34.4	55.5	89 23.1	13.2	322 07.8	07.4	319 20.5	06.8			
18	158 09.5	75 33.5 N23	55.7	104 23.7 N19	13.7	337 10.3 N 1	07.4	334 23.0 N 1	06.8	Vega	80 55.2	N38 45.9
19	173 11.9	90 32.6	56.0	119 24.3	14.1	352 12.7	07.4	349 25.5	06.8	Zuben'ubi	137 32.2	S15 57.9
20	188 14.4	105 31.8	56.2	134 25.0	14.6	7 15.1	07.4	4 28.0	06.8		S.H.A.	Mer. Pass.
21	203 16.8	120 30.9 ··	56.5	149 25.6 ··	15.0	22 17.6 ··	07.4	19 30.5 ··	06.8			h m
22	218 19.3	135 30.0	56.7	164 26.2	15.4	37 20.0	07.3	34 33.0	06.8	Venus	279 44.2	12 56
23	233 21.8	150 29.1	57.0	179 26.8	15.9	52 22.5	07.3	49 35.5	06.8	Mars	307 31.7	11 04
Mer. Pass.	7 33.0	v −0.9 d 0.3		v 0.6 d 0.5		v 2.5 d 0.0		v 2.5 d 0.0		Jupiter	179 01.2	19 35
										Saturn	176 12.4	19 46

G.M.T.	SUN G.H.A.	SUN Dec.	MOON G.H.A.	MOON v	MOON Dec.	MOON d	MOON H.P.
d h	° '	° '	° '	'	° '	'	'
28 00	180 43.3	N21 24.5	252 23.2	10.6	S 7 05.8	11.8	58.7
01	195 43.2	24.9	266 52.8	10.6	6 54.0	11.8	58.7
02	210 43.2	25.3	281 22.4	10.6	6 42.2	11.9	58.7
03	225 43.1 ··	25.7	295 52.0	10.6	6 30.3	12.0	58.8
04	240 43.0	26.1	310 21.6	10.6	6 18.3	12.0	58.8
05	255 42.9	26.5	324 51.2	10.5	6 06.3	12.0	58.8
06	270 42.8	N21 26.9	339 20.7	10.6	S 5 54.3	12.1	58.9
07	285 42.8	27.3	353 50.3	10.5	5 42.2	12.1	58.9
T 08	300 42.7	27.7	8 19.8	10.5	5 30.1	12.2	58.9
H 09	315 42.6 ··	28.1	22 49.3	10.5	5 17.9	12.3	59.0
U 10	330 42.5	28.5	37 18.8	10.4	5 05.6	12.2	59.0
R 11	345 42.5	28.9	51 48.2	10.5	4 53.4	12.3	59.0
S 12	0 42.4	N21 29.3	66 17.7	10.4	S 4 41.1	12.4	59.1
D 13	15 42.3	29.7	80 47.1	10.4	4 28.7	12.4	59.1
A 14	30 42.2	30.1	95 16.5	10.4	4 16.3	12.4	59.1
Y 15	45 42.1 ··	30.5	109 45.9	10.3	4 03.9	12.5	59.2
16	60 42.1	30.9	124 15.2	10.4	3 51.4	12.5	59.2
17	75 42.0	31.3	138 44.6	10.3	3 38.9	12.5	59.2
18	90 41.9	N21 31.7	153 13.9	10.3	S 3 26.4	12.6	59.3
19	105 41.8	32.1	167 43.2	10.3	3 13.8	12.6	59.3
20	120 41.8	32.5	182 12.4	10.3	3 01.2	12.7	59.3
21	135 41.7 ··	32.9	196 41.7	10.2	2 48.5	12.6	59.4
22	150 41.6	33.3	211 10.9	10.2	2 35.9	12.7	59.4
23	165 41.5	33.7	225 40.1	10.1	2 23.2	12.8	59.4
29 00	180 41.4	N21 34.1	240 09.2	10.1	S 2 10.4	12.7	59.5
01	195 41.4	34.5	254 38.3	10.1	1 57.7	12.8	59.5
02	210 41.3	34.9	269 07.4	10.1	1 44.9	12.8	59.5
03	225 41.2 ··	35.3	283 36.5	10.0	1 32.1	12.9	59.6
04	240 41.1	35.7	298 05.5	10.0	1 19.2	12.8	59.6
05	255 41.0	36.0	312 34.5	10.0	1 06.4	12.9	59.6
06	270 40.9	N21 36.4	327 03.5	9.9	S 0 53.5	12.9	59.7
07	285 40.9	36.8	341 32.4	9.9	0 40.6	12.9	59.7
08	300 40.8	37.2	356 01.3	9.8	0 27.7	12.9	59.7
F 09	315 40.7 ··	37.6	10 30.1	9.9	0 14.8	12.9	59.7
R 10	330 40.6	38.0	24 59.0	9.7	S 0 01.8	12.9	59.8
I 11	345 40.5	38.4	39 27.7	9.8	N 0 11.1	13.0	59.8
D 12	0 40.5	N21 38.8	53 56.5	9.7	N 0 24.1	13.0	59.9
A 13	15 40.4	39.1	68 25.2	9.7	0 37.1	13.0	59.9
Y 14	30 40.3	39.5	82 53.9	9.6	0 50.1	13.0	59.9
15	45 40.2 ··	39.9	97 22.5	9.6	1 03.1	13.0	60.0
16	60 40.1	40.3	111 51.1	9.5	1 16.1	13.1	60.0
17	75 40.0	40.7	126 19.6	9.5	1 29.2	13.0	60.0
18	90 40.0	N21 41.0	140 48.1	9.5	N 1 42.2	13.0	60.0
19	105 39.9	41.4	155 16.6	9.4	1 55.2	13.1	60.1
20	120 39.8	41.8	169 45.0	9.4	2 08.3	13.0	60.1
21	135 39.7 ··	42.2	184 13.4	9.3	2 21.3	13.0	60.1
22	150 39.6	42.6	198 41.7	9.3	2 34.3	13.1	60.2
23	165 39.5	42.9	213 10.0	9.2	2 47.4	13.0	60.2
30 00	180 39.4	N21 43.3	227 38.2	9.2	N 3 00.4	13.0	60.2
01	195 39.4	43.7	242 06.4	9.1	3 13.4	13.0	60.2
02	210 39.3	44.1	256 34.5	9.1	3 26.4	13.0	60.3
03	225 39.2 ··	44.4	271 02.6	9.1	3 39.4	13.0	60.3
04	240 39.1	44.8	285 30.7	9.0	3 52.4	13.0	60.3
05	255 39.0	45.2	299 58.7	8.9	4 05.4	13.0	60.4
06	270 38.9	N21 45.6	314 26.6	8.9	N 4 18.4	13.0	60.4
07	285 38.8	45.9	328 54.5	8.8	4 31.4	12.9	60.4
S 08	300 38.8	46.3	343 22.3	8.8	4 44.3	13.0	60.4
A 09	315 38.7 ··	46.7	357 50.1	8.7	4 57.3	12.9	60.5
T 10	330 38.6	47.0	12 17.8	8.7	5 10.2	12.9	60.5
U 11	345 38.5	47.4	26 45.5	8.6	5 23.1	12.8	60.5
R 12	0 38.4	N21 47.8	41 13.1	8.6	N 5 35.9	12.9	60.5
D 13	15 38.3	48.1	55 40.7	8.5	5 48.8	12.8	60.6
A 14	30 38.2	48.5	70 08.2	8.4	6 01.6	12.8	60.6
Y 15	45 38.2 ··	48.9	84 35.6	8.4	6 14.4	12.8	60.6
16	60 38.1	49.2	99 03.0	8.4	6 27.2	12.7	60.6
17	75 38.0	49.6	113 30.4	8.2	6 39.9	12.8	60.6
18	90 37.9	N21 50.0	127 57.6	8.3	N 6 52.7	12.6	60.7
19	105 37.8	50.3	142 24.9	8.1	7 05.3	12.7	60.7
20	120 37.7	50.7	156 52.0	8.1	7 18.0	12.6	60.7
21	135 37.6 ··	51.1	171 19.1	8.1	7 30.6	12.6	60.7
22	150 37.5	51.4	185 46.2	7.9	7 43.2	12.5	60.7
23	165 37.4	51.8	200 13.1	8.0	7 55.7	12.5	60.8
S.D. 15.8	d 0.4		S.D. 16.1		16.3		16.5

Lat.	Twilight Naut.	Twilight Civil	Sunrise	Moonrise 28	Moonrise 29	Moonrise 30	Moonrise 31
°	h m	h m	h m	h m	h m	h m	h m
N 72	▢	▢	▢	02 41	02 27	02 13	01 58
N 70	▢	▢	▢	02 32	02 24	02 18	02 10
68	▢	▢	▢	02 24	02 22	02 21	02 20
66	////	////	01 26	02 17	02 21	02 24	02 29
64	////	////	02 06	02 12	02 19	02 27	02 36
62	////	00 40	02 33	02 07	02 18	02 29	02 42
60	////	01 35	02 54	02 03	02 17	02 31	02 47
N 58	////	02 06	03 11	01 59	02 16	02 33	02 52
56	00 36	02 29	03 26	01 56	02 15	02 35	02 56
54	01 27	02 48	03 38	01 53	02 14	02 36	03 00
52	01 56	03 03	03 49	01 50	02 14	02 38	03 04
50	02 17	03 16	03 58	01 47	02 13	02 39	03 07
45	02 56	03 42	04 18	01 42	02 12	02 42	03 14
N 40	03 23	04 03	04 35	01 37	02 10	02 44	03 20
35	03 44	04 19	04 48	01 33	02 09	02 46	03 25
30	04 01	04 33	05 00	01 30	02 08	02 48	03 29
20	04 27	04 56	05 20	01 24	02 07	02 51	03 37
N 10	04 48	05 15	05 38	01 19	02 06	02 54	03 44
0	05 06	05 31	05 54	01 14	02 04	02 56	03 51
S 10	05 21	05 47	06 10	01 08	02 03	02 59	03 57
20	05 36	06 03	06 27	01 03	02 02	03 02	04 04
30	05 50	06 20	06 46	00 57	02 00	03 05	04 12
35	05 58	06 29	06 57	00 53	01 59	03 07	04 17
40	06 07	06 40	07 10	00 49	01 58	03 09	04 23
45	06 16	06 52	07 25	00 45	01 57	03 12	04 29
S 50	06 26	07 06	07 44	00 39	01 56	03 15	04 37
52	06 30	07 13	07 53	00 37	01 55	03 17	04 40
54	06 35	07 20	08 02	00 34	01 55	03 18	04 44
56	06 40	07 28	08 13	00 31	01 54	03 20	04 48
58	06 46	07 37	08 26	00 27	01 53	03 22	04 53
S 60	06 53	07 47	08 41	00 23	01 52	03 24	04 59

Lat.	Sunset	Twilight Civil	Twilight Naut.	Moonset 28	Moonset 29	Moonset 30	Moonset 31
°	h m	h m	h m	h m	h m	h m	h m
N 72	▢	▢	▢	12 37	14 40	16 47	19 03
N 70	▢	▢	▢	12 44	14 39	16 37	18 42
68	▢	▢	▢	12 50	14 38	16 29	18 25
66	22 33	////	////	12 54	14 37	16 23	18 12
64	21 51	////	////	12 58	14 36	16 17	18 01
62	21 23	23 23	////	13 02	14 36	16 12	17 52
60	21 02	22 22	////	13 05	14 35	16 08	17 44
N 58	20 45	21 50	////	13 07	14 35	16 04	17 37
56	20 30	21 27	23 26	13 10	14 34	16 01	17 30
54	20 18	21 08	22 30	13 12	14 34	15 58	17 25
52	20 07	20 53	22 01	13 14	14 33	15 56	17 20
50	19 57	20 39	21 39	13 15	14 33	15 53	17 16
45	19 37	20 13	21 00	13 19	14 32	15 48	17 06
N 40	19 20	19 52	20 32	13 22	14 32	15 44	16 58
35	19 07	19 36	20 11	13 25	14 31	15 40	16 51
30	18 55	19 22	19 54	13 27	14 31	15 37	16 45
20	18 34	18 59	19 27	13 31	14 30	15 31	16 35
N 10	18 17	18 40	19 07	13 34	14 29	15 26	16 25
0	18 01	18 23	18 49	13 38	14 29	15 22	16 17
S 10	17 45	18 07	18 33	13 41	14 28	15 17	16 09
20	17 28	17 52	18 19	13 44	14 27	15 12	16 00
30	17 09	17 34	18 04	13 48	14 26	15 07	15 49
35	16 57	17 25	17 56	13 50	14 26	15 03	15 44
40	16 44	17 14	17 48	13 52	14 25	15 00	15 37
45	16 29	17 02	17 39	13 55	14 25	14 55	15 29
S 50	16 11	16 48	17 28	13 58	14 24	14 50	15 20
52	16 02	16 41	17 24	14 00	14 23	14 48	15 16
54	15 52	16 34	17 19	14 01	14 23	14 46	15 11
56	15 41	16 26	17 14	14 03	14 23	14 43	15 06
58	15 28	16 17	17 08	14 05	14 22	14 40	15 00
S 60	15 13	16 07	17 02	14 07	14 22	14 36	14 53

Day	SUN Eqn. of Time 00ʰ	SUN Eqn. of Time 12ʰ	SUN Mer. Pass.	MOON Mer. Pass. Upper	MOON Mer. Pass. Lower	Age	Phase
	m s	m s	h m	h m	h m	d	
28	02 53	02 50	11 57	07 26	19 51	24	
29	02 46	02 42	11 57	08 16	20 42	25	
30	02 38	02 34	11 57	09 09	21 36	26	◖

G.M.T.	ARIES G.H.A.	VENUS −3.3 G.H.A.	Dec.	MARS +1.6 G.H.A.	Dec.	JUPITER −1.7 G.H.A.	Dec.	SATURN +1.1 G.H.A.	Dec.	STARS Name	S.H.A.	Dec.
31 00	248 24.2	165 28.2	N23 57.2	194 27.4	N19 16.3	67 24.9	N 1 07.3	64 38.0	N 1 06.8	Acamar	315 37.3	S40 22.8
01	263 26.7	180 27.4	57.5	209 28.1	16.8	82 27.4	07.3	79 40.5	06.8	Achernar	335 45.4	S57 19.8
02	278 29.2	195 26.5	57.7	224 28.7	17.2	97 29.8	07.3	94 42.9	06.8	Acrux	173 36.4	S63 00.0
03	293 31.6	210 25.6 ··	57.9	239 29.3 ··	17.7	112 32.3 ··	07.2	109 45.4 ··	06.8	Adhara	255 32.1	S28 57.0
04	308 34.1	225 24.7	58.2	254 29.9	18.1	127 34.7	07.2	124 47.9	06.8	Aldebaran	291 17.8	N16 28.2
05	323 36.6	240 23.8	58.4	269 30.5	18.6	142 37.2	07.2	139 50.4	06.8			
06	338 39.0	255 23.0	N23 58.7	284 31.1	N19 19.0	157 39.6	N 1 07.2	154 52.9	N 1 06.8	Alioth	166 41.8	N56 04.0
07	353 41.5	270 22.1	58.9	299 31.8	19.5	172 42.0	07.2	169 55.4	06.8	Alkaid	153 17.8	N49 24.6
08	8 43.9	285 21.2	59.1	314 32.4	19.9	187 44.5	07.1	184 57.9	06.8	Al Na'ir	28 14.3	S47 02.9
S 09	23 46.4	300 20.3 ··	59.4	329 33.0 ··	20.4	202 46.9 ··	07.1	200 00.3 ··	06.8	Alnilam	276 11.5	S 1 12.9
U 10	38 48.9	315 19.4	59.6	344 33.6	20.8	217 49.4	07.1	215 02.8	06.8	Alphard	218 20.2	S 8 34.7
N 11	53 51.3	330 18.6	23 59.8	359 34.2	21.2	232 51.8	07.1	230 05.3	06.8			
D 12	68 53.8	345 17.7	N24 00.1	14 34.8	N19 21.7	247 54.3	N 1 07.0	245 07.8	N 1 06.8	Alphecca	126 31.4	N26 46.7
A 13	83 56.3	0 16.8	00.3	29 35.5	22.1	262 56.7	07.0	260 10.3	06.8	Alpheratz	358 09.0	N28 59.0
Y 14	98 58.7	15 15.9	00.5	44 36.1	22.6	277 59.1	07.0	275 12.8	06.8	Altair	62 31.8	N 8 49.1
15	114 01.2	30 15.0 ··	00.7	59 36.7 ··	23.0	293 01.6 ··	07.0	290 15.3 ··	06.8	Ankaa	353 40.0	S42 24.3
16	129 03.7	45 14.2	01.0	74 37.3	23.5	308 04.0	07.0	305 17.7	06.8	Antares	112 55.9	S26 23.4
17	144 06.1	60 13.3	01.2	89 37.9	23.9	323 06.5	07.0	320 20.2	06.8			
18	159 08.6	75 12.4	N24 01.4	104 38.5	N19 24.3	338 08.9	N 1 06.9	335 22.7	N 1 06.8	Arcturus	146 17.8	N19 16.9
19	174 11.1	90 11.5	01.6	119 39.2	24.8	353 11.3	06.9	350 25.2	06.8	Atria	108 19.2	S68 59.6
20	189 13.5	105 10.6	01.9	134 39.8	25.2	8 13.8	06.9	5 27.7	06.8	Avior	234 28.4	S59 27.2
21	204 16.0	120 09.7 ··	02.1	149 40.4 ··	25.7	23 16.2 ··	06.9	20 30.2 ··	06.8	Bellatrix	278 58.6	N 6 19.9
22	219 18.4	135 08.9	02.3	164 41.0	26.1	38 18.7	06.8	35 32.7	06.8	Betelgeuse	271 28.1	N 7 24.1
23	234 20.9	150 08.0	02.5	179 41.6	26.6	53 21.1	06.8	50 35.1	06.8			
1 00	249 23.4	165 07.1	N24 02.7	194 42.2	N19 27.0	68 23.5	N 1 06.8	65 37.6	N 1 06.8	Canopus	264 07.5	S52 41.3
01	264 25.8	180 06.2	03.0	209 42.9	27.4	83 26.0	06.8	80 40.1	06.8	Capella	281 11.1	N45 58.7
02	279 28.3	195 05.3	03.2	224 43.5	27.9	98 28.4	06.8	95 42.6	06.8	Deneb	49 47.9	N45 12.6
03	294 30.8	210 04.4 ··	03.4	239 44.1 ··	28.3	113 30.9 ··	06.7	110 45.1 ··	06.8	Denebola	182 58.5	N14 40.7
04	309 33.2	225 03.6	03.6	254 44.7	28.7	128 33.3	06.7	125 47.6	06.8	Diphda	349 20.6	S18 05.4
05	324 35.7	240 02.7	03.8	269 45.3	29.2	143 35.7	06.7	140 50.0	06.8			
06	339 38.2	255 01.8	N24 04.0	284 45.9	N19 29.6	158 38.2	N 1 06.7	155 52.5	N 1 06.8	Dubhe	194 21.6	N61 51.4
07	354 40.6	270 00.9	04.2	299 46.6	30.1	173 40.6	06.6	170 55.0	06.8	Elnath	278 43.9	N28 35.5
08	9 43.1	285 00.0	04.4	314 47.2	30.5	188 43.0	06.6	185 57.5	06.8	Eltanin	90 57.0	N51 29.4
M 09	24 45.6	299 59.1 ··	04.6	329 47.8 ··	30.9	203 45.5 ··	06.6	201 00.0 ··	06.8	Enif	34 11.0	N 9 47.2
O 10	39 48.0	314 58.3	04.8	344 48.4	31.4	218 47.9	06.6	216 02.5	06.8	Fomalhaut	15 50.9	S29 43.2
N 11	54 50.5	329 57.4	05.0	359 49.0	31.8	233 50.4	06.5	231 04.9	06.8			
D 12	69 52.9	344 56.5	N24 05.2	14 49.6	N19 32.2	248 52.8	N 1 06.5	246 07.4	N 1 06.8	Gacrux	172 27.9	S57 00.7
A 13	84 55.4	359 55.6	05.4	29 50.3	32.7	263 55.2	06.5	261 09.9	06.8	Gienah	176 17.4	S17 26.4
Y 14	99 57.9	14 54.7	05.6	44 50.9	33.1	278 57.7	06.5	276 12.4	06.8	Hadar	149 22.2	S60 17.1
15	115 00.3	29 53.8 ··	05.8	59 51.5 ··	33.5	294 00.1 ··	06.5	291 14.9 ··	06.8	Hamal	328 28.7	N23 22.2
16	130 02.8	44 52.9	06.0	74 52.1	34.0	309 02.5	06.4	306 17.3	06.8	Kaus Aust.	84 15.9	S34 23.6
17	145 05.3	59 52.1	06.2	89 52.7	34.4	324 05.0	06.4	321 19.8	06.8			
18	160 07.7	74 51.2	N24 06.4	104 53.3	N19 34.9	339 07.4	N 1 06.4	336 22.3	N 1 06.8	Kochab	137 18.0	N74 14.2
19	175 10.2	89 50.3	06.6	119 53.9	35.3	354 09.8	06.4	351 24.8	06.8	Markab	14 02.7	N15 06.1
20	190 12.7	104 49.4	06.8	134 54.6	35.7	9 12.3	06.3	6 27.3	06.8	Menkar	314 41.0	N 4 00.9
21	205 15.1	119 48.5 ··	07.0	149 55.2 ··	36.2	24 14.7 ··	06.3	21 29.7 ··	06.8	Menkent	148 36.2	S36 16.8
22	220 17.6	134 47.6	07.2	164 55.8	36.6	39 17.1	06.3	36 32.2	06.7	Miaplacidus	221 45.2	S69 38.7
23	235 20.0	149 46.7	07.4	179 56.4	37.0	54 19.6	06.3	51 34.7	06.7			
2 00	250 22.5	164 45.9	N24 07.6	194 57.0	N19 37.4	69 22.0	N 1 06.2	66 37.2	N 1 06.7	Mirfak	309 15.9	N49 47.5
01	265 25.0	179 45.0	07.7	209 57.6	37.9	84 24.4	06.2	81 39.7	06.7	Nunki	76 28.3	S26 19.1
02	280 27.4	194 44.1	07.9	224 58.2	38.3	99 26.9	06.2	96 42.1	06.7	Peacock	53 57.3	S56 47.5
03	295 29.9	209 43.2 ··	08.1	239 58.7 ··	38.7	114 29.3 ··	06.2	111 44.6 ··	06.7	Pollux	243 57.9	N28 04.4
04	310 32.4	224 42.3	08.3	254 59.5	39.2	129 31.7	06.1	126 47.1	06.7	Procyon	245 25.6	N 5 16.3
05	325 34.8	239 41.4	08.5	270 00.1	39.6	144 34.2	06.1	141 49.6	06.7			
06	340 37.3	254 40.5	N24 08.7	285 00.7	N19 40.0	159 36.6	N 1 06.1	156 52.1	N 1 06.7	Rasalhague	96 28.8	N12 34.4
07	355 39.8	269 39.6	08.8	300 01.3	40.5	174 39.0	06.0	171 54.5	06.7	Regulus	208 09.6	N12 03.6
08	10 42.2	284 38.8	09.0	315 01.9	40.9	189 41.4	06.0	186 57.0	06.7	Rigel	281 35.9	S 8 13.5
T 09	25 44.7	299 37.9 ··	09.2	330 02.5 ··	41.3	204 43.9 ··	06.0	201 59.5 ··	06.7	Rigil Kent.	140 24.6	S60 45.5
U 10	40 47.2	314 37.0	09.4	345 03.2	41.7	219 46.3	06.0	217 02.0	06.7	Sabik	102 40.3	S15 42.1
E 11	55 49.6	329 36.1	09.5	0 03.8	42.2	234 48.7	05.9	232 04.5	06.7			
S 12	70 52.1	344 35.2	N24 09.7	15 04.4	N19 42.6	249 51.2	N 1 05.9	247 06.9	N 1 06.7	Schedar	350 08.7	N56 25.8
D 13	85 54.5	359 34.3	09.9	30 05.0	43.0	264 53.6	05.9	262 09.4	06.7	Shaula	96 54.7	S37 05.4
A 14	100 57.0	14 33.4	10.0	45 05.6	43.5	279 56.0	05.9	277 11.9	06.7	Sirius	258 55.6	S16 41.6
Y 15	115 59.5	29 32.5 ··	10.2	60 06.2 ··	43.9	294 58.4 ··	05.8	292 14.4 ··	06.7	Spica	158 56.8	S11 03.8
16	131 01.9	44 31.7	10.4	75 06.8	44.3	310 00.9	05.8	307 16.8	06.7	Suhail	223 10.6	S43 21.7
17	146 04.4	59 30.8	10.6	90 07.5	44.7	325 03.3	05.8	322 19.3	06.7			
18	161 06.9	74 29.9	N24 10.7	105 08.1	N19 45.2	340 05.7	N 1 05.7	337 21.8	N 1 06.7	Vega	80 55.1	N38 45.9
19	176 09.3	89 29.0	10.9	120 08.7	45.6	355 08.2	05.7	352 24.3	06.7	Zuben'ubi	137 32.2	S15 57.9
20	191 11.8	104 28.1	11.0	135 09.3	46.0	10 10.6	05.7	7 26.8	06.7			
21	206 14.3	119 27.2 ··	11.2	150 09.9 ··	46.4	25 13.0 ··	05.7	22 29.2 ··	06.7		S.H.A.	Mer. Pass.
22	221 16.7	134 26.3	11.4	165 10.5	46.9	40 15.4	05.6	37 31.7	06.6	Venus	275 43.7	13 00
23	236 19.2	149 25.4	11.5	180 11.1	47.3	55 17.9	05.6	52 34.2	06.6	Mars	305 18.9	11 01
Mer. Pass.	7 21.2	v −0.9	d 0.2	v 0.6	d 0.4	v 2.4	d 0.0	v 2.5	d 0.0	Jupiter	179 00.2	19 23
										Saturn	176 14.2	19 34

SUN and MOON

G.M.T.	SUN G.H.A.	Dec.	MOON G.H.A.	v	Dec.	d	H.P.
31 00	180 37.4	N21 52.2	214 40.1	7.8	N 8 08.2	12.4	60.8
01	195 37.3	52.5	229 06.9	7.8	8 20.6	12.4	60.8
02	210 37.2	52.9	243 33.7	7.7	8 33.0	12.4	60.8
03	225 37.1	·· 53.2	258 00.4	7.7	8 45.4	12.3	60.8
04	240 37.0	53.6	272 27.1	7.6	8 57.7	12.3	60.9
05	255 36.9	53.9	286 53.7	7.6	9 10.0	12.2	60.9
06	270 36.8	N21 54.3	301 20.3	7.4	N 9 22.2	12.1	60.9
07	285 36.7	54.7	315 46.7	7.5	9 34.3	12.1	60.9
08	300 36.6	55.0	330 13.2	7.3	9 46.4	12.1	60.9
S 09	315 36.5	·· 55.4	344 39.5	7.3	9 58.5	12.0	60.9
U 10	330 36.4	55.7	359 05.8	7.2	10 10.5	11.9	61.0
N 11	345 36.4	56.1	13 32.0	7.2	10 22.4	11.9	61.0
D 12	0 36.3	N21 56.4	27 58.2	7.1	N10 34.3	11.8	61.0
A 13	15 36.2	56.8	42 24.3	7.0	10 46.1	11.7	61.0
Y 14	30 36.1	57.1	56 50.3	7.0	10 57.8	11.7	61.0
15	45 36.0	·· 57.5	71 16.3	6.8	11 09.5	11.6	61.0
16	60 35.9	57.8	85 42.1	6.9	11 21.1	11.5	61.0
17	75 35.8	58.2	100 08.0	6.7	11 32.6	11.5	61.0
18	90 35.7	N21 58.5	114 33.7	6.7	N11 44.1	11.4	61.1
19	105 35.6	58.9	128 59.4	6.7	11 55.5	11.3	61.1
20	120 35.5	59.2	143 25.1	6.6	12 06.8	11.2	61.1
21	135 35.4	·· 59.6	157 50.7	6.5	12 18.0	11.2	61.1
22	150 35.3	21 59.9	172 16.2	6.4	12 29.2	11.1	61.1
23	165 35.2	22 00.3	186 41.6	6.4	12 40.3	11.0	61.1
1 00	180 35.1	N22 00.6	201 07.0	6.3	N12 51.3	10.9	61.1
01	195 35.0	01.0	215 32.3	6.2	13 02.2	10.8	61.1
02	210 35.0	01.3	229 57.5	6.2	13 13.0	10.8	61.1
03	225 34.9	·· 01.6	244 22.7	6.1	13 23.8	10.6	61.1
04	240 34.8	02.0	258 47.8	6.1	13 34.4	10.6	61.1
05	255 34.7	02.3	273 12.9	6.0	13 45.0	10.4	61.1
06	270 34.6	N22 02.7	287 37.9	5.9	N13 55.4	10.4	61.2
07	285 34.5	03.0	302 02.8	5.8	14 05.8	10.3	61.2
08	300 34.4	03.4	316 27.6	5.8	14 16.1	10.2	61.2
M 09	315 34.3	·· 03.7	330 52.4	5.8	14 26.3	10.1	61.2
O 10	330 34.2	04.0	345 17.2	5.6	14 36.4	10.0	61.2
N 11	345 34.1	04.4	359 41.8	5.7	14 46.4	9.9	61.2
D 12	0 34.0	N22 04.7	14 06.5	5.5	N14 56.3	9.8	61.2
A 13	15 33.9	05.0	28 31.0	5.5	15 06.1	9.6	61.2
Y 14	30 33.8	05.4	42 55.5	5.4	15 15.7	9.6	61.2
15	45 33.7	·· 05.7	57 19.9	5.4	15 25.3	9.5	61.2
16	60 33.6	06.0	71 44.3	5.3	15 34.8	9.4	61.2
17	75 33.5	06.4	86 08.6	5.3	15 44.2	9.2	61.2
18	90 33.4	N22 06.7	100 32.9	5.2	N15 53.4	9.1	61.2
19	105 33.3	07.0	114 57.1	5.1	16 02.5	9.1	61.2
20	120 33.2	07.4	129 21.2	5.1	16 11.6	8.9	61.2
21	135 33.1	·· 07.7	143 45.3	5.1	16 20.5	8.8	61.2
22	150 33.0	08.0	158 09.4	5.0	16 29.3	8.6	61.2
23	165 32.9	08.4	172 33.4	4.9	16 37.9	8.6	61.1
2 00	180 32.8	N22 08.7	186 57.3	4.9	N16 46.5	8.4	61.1
01	195 32.7	09.0	201 21.2	4.8	16 54.9	8.3	61.1
02	210 32.6	09.3	215 45.0	4.8	17 03.2	8.2	61.1
03	225 32.5	·· 09.7	230 08.8	4.7	17 11.4	8.1	61.1
04	240 32.4	10.0	244 32.5	4.7	17 19.5	7.9	61.1
05	255 32.3	10.3	258 56.2	4.7	17 27.4	7.9	61.1
06	270 32.2	N22 10.7	273 19.9	4.6	N17 35.3	7.6	61.1
07	285 32.1	11.0	287 43.5	4.5	17 42.9	7.6	61.1
08	300 32.0	11.3	302 07.0	4.5	17 50.5	7.4	61.1
T 09	315 31.9	·· 11.6	316 30.5	4.5	17 57.9	7.3	61.1
U 10	330 31.8	11.9	330 54.0	4.4	18 05.2	7.2	61.1
E 11	345 31.7	12.3	345 17.4	4.4	18 12.4	7.0	61.1
S 12	0 31.6	N22 12.6	359 40.8	4.4	N18 19.4	6.9	61.0
D 13	15 31.5	12.9	14 04.2	4.3	18 26.3	6.7	61.0
A 14	30 31.4	13.2	28 27.5	4.3	18 33.0	6.7	61.0
Y 15	45 31.3	·· 13.5	42 50.8	4.2	18 39.7	6.4	61.0
16	60 31.2	13.9	57 14.0	4.2	18 46.1	6.4	61.0
17	75 31.1	14.2	71 37.2	4.2	18 52.5	6.2	61.0
18	90 31.0	N22 14.5	86 00.4	4.2	N18 58.7	6.0	61.0
19	105 30.9	14.8	100 23.6	4.1	19 04.7	6.0	60.9
20	120 30.8	15.1	114 46.7	4.1	19 10.7	5.7	60.9
21	135 30.7	·· 15.4	129 09.8	4.1	19 16.4	5.7	60.9
22	150 30.6	15.8	143 32.9	4.1	19 22.1	5.5	60.9
23	165 30.5	16.1	157 56.0	4.0	19 27.6	5.3	60.9
	S.D. 15.8	d 0.3	S.D. 16.6		16.7		16.6

Twilight, Sunrise, Moonrise

Lat.	Naut.	Civil	Sunrise	Moonrise 31	1	2	3
N 72	□	□	□	01 58	01 39	01 03	□
N 70	□	□	□	02 10	02 02	01 51	01 28
68	□	□	□	02 20	02 20	02 22	02 30
66	////	////	01 13	02 29	02 35	02 46	03 05
64	////	////	01 58	02 42	02 47	03 04	03 31
62	////	////	02 27	02 42	02 58	03 19	03 51
60	////	01 26	02 49	02 47	03 07	03 32	04 08
N 58	////	02 00	03 07	02 52	03 15	03 43	04 21
56	////	02 25	03 22	02 56	03 22	03 53	04 33
54	01 19	02 44	03 35	03 00	03 28	04 02	04 44
52	01 50	03 00	03 46	03 04	03 33	04 09	04 53
50	02 13	03 13	03 56	03 07	03 39	04 16	05 02
45	02 53	03 40	04 17	03 14	03 50	04 31	05 20
N 40	03 21	04 01	04 33	03 20	03 59	04 44	05 34
35	03 42	04 18	04 47	03 25	04 07	04 54	05 47
30	04 00	04 32	04 59	03 29	04 14	05 03	05 58
20	04 27	04 56	05 20	03 37	04 26	05 19	06 16
N 10	04 48	05 15	05 38	03 44	04 37	05 34	06 33
0	05 06	05 32	05 54	03 51	04 47	05 47	06 48
S 10	05 22	05 48	06 10	03 57	04 58	06 00	07 04
20	05 37	06 04	06 28	04 04	05 09	06 15	07 20
30	05 52	06 21	06 48	04 12	05 21	06 31	07 39
35	06 00	06 31	06 59	04 17	05 29	06 41	07 51
40	06 08	06 42	07 12	04 23	05 37	06 52	08 03
45	06 18	06 55	07 28	04 29	05 47	07 05	08 19
S 50	06 28	07 09	07 47	04 37	05 59	07 21	08 37
52	06 33	07 16	07 56	04 40	06 05	07 28	08 46
54	06 38	07 24	08 06	04 44	06 11	07 37	08 56
56	06 44	07 32	08 17	04 48	06 18	07 46	09 07
58	06 50	07 41	08 31	04 53	06 26	07 57	09 20
S 60	06 56	07 51	08 46	04 59	06 35	08 09	09 35

Sunset, Twilight, Moonset

Lat.	Sunset	Civil	Naut.	Moonset 31	1	2	3
N 72	□	□	□	19 03	21 42	□	□
N 70	□	□	□	18 42	20 56	23 27	□
68	□	□	□	18 25	20 26	22 26	24 10
66	22 47	////	////	18 12	20 03	21 51	23 22
64	22 00	////	////	18 01	19 46	21 26	22 51
62	21 30	////	////	17 52	19 31	21 06	22 28
60	21 07	22 32	////	17 44	19 19	20 50	22 09
N 58	20 49	21 57	////	17 37	19 09	20 37	21 54
56	20 34	21 32	////	17 30	19 00	20 25	21 40
54	20 21	21 13	22 39	17 25	18 52	20 14	21 29
52	20 10	20 57	22 07	17 20	18 44	20 06	21 19
50	20 00	20 43	21 44	17 16	18 38	19 57	21 10
45	19 39	20 16	21 03	17 06	18 24	19 40	20 51
N 40	19 23	19 55	20 35	16 58	18 13	19 26	20 35
35	19 09	19 38	20 14	16 51	18 03	19 14	20 22
30	18 56	19 23	19 56	16 45	17 55	19 04	20 10
20	18 36	19 00	19 29	16 35	17 40	18 46	19 51
N 10	18 18	18 41	19 07	16 26	17 27	18 30	19 34
0	18 01	18 24	18 50	16 17	17 15	18 16	19 18
S 10	17 45	18 08	18 34	16 09	17 03	18 01	19 02
20	17 28	17 51	18 19	16 00	16 51	17 46	18 45
30	17 08	17 34	18 03	15 49	16 36	17 28	18 25
35	16 56	17 24	17 55	15 44	16 28	17 18	18 13
40	16 43	17 13	17 47	15 39	16 19	17 06	18 00
45	16 27	17 01	17 37	15 29	16 07	16 52	17 45
S 50	16 08	16 46	17 27	15 20	15 54	16 35	17 25
52	15 59	16 39	17 22	15 16	15 48	16 27	17 16
54	15 49	16 32	17 17	15 11	15 41	16 19	17 06
56	15 38	16 23	17 11	15 06	15 33	16 09	16 55
58	15 24	16 14	17 05	15 00	15 25	15 58	16 42
S 60	15 09	16 04	16 59	14 53	15 15	15 45	16 26

SUN / MOON

Day	SUN Eqn. of Time 00h	12h	Mer. Pass.	MOON Mer. Pass. Upper	Lower	Age	Phase
31	02 30	02 25	11 58	10 04	22 32	27	
1	02 21	02 16	11 58	11 01	23 31	28	
2	02 12	02 07	11 58	12 01	24 32	00	●

G.M.T.	ARIES G.H.A.	VENUS −3.3 G.H.A.	Dec.	MARS +1.6 G.H.A.	Dec.	JUPITER −1.7 G.H.A.	Dec.	SATURN +1.1 G.H.A.	Dec.	STARS Name	S.H.A.	Dec.
3 00	251 21.7	164 24.5	N24 11.7	195 11.7	N19 47.7	70 20.3	N 1 05.6	67 36.7	N 1 06.6	Acamar	315 37.3	S40 22.8
01	266 24.1	179 23.6	11.8	210 12.4	48.1	85 22.7	05.6	82 39.1	06.6	Achernar	335 45.3	S57 19.8
02	281 26.6	194 22.8	12.0	225 13.0	48.6	100 25.1	05.5	97 41.6	06.6	Acrux	173 36.4	S63 00.0
03	296 29.0	209 21.9	·· 12.1	240 13.6	·· 49.0	115 27.6	·· 05.5	112 44.1	·· 06.6	Adhara	255 32.1	S28 56.9
04	311 31.5	224 21.0	12.3	255 14.2	49.4	130 30.0	05.5	127 46.6	06.6	Aldebaran	291 17.8	N16 28.2
05	326 34.0	239 20.1	12.4	270 14.8	49.8	145 32.4	05.4	142 49.0	06.6			
W 06	341 36.4	254 19.2	N24 12.6	285 15.4	N19 50.2	160 34.8	N 1 05.4	157 51.5	N 1 06.6	Alioth	166 41.8	N56 04.0
E 07	356 38.9	269 18.3	12.7	300 16.0	50.7	175 37.3	05.4	172 54.0	06.6	Alkaid	153 17.8	N49 24.6
D 08	11 41.4	284 17.4	12.9	315 16.7	51.1	190 39.7	05.4	187 56.5	06.6	Al Na'ir	28 14.2	S47 02.9
N 09	26 43.8	299 16.5	·· 13.0	330 17.3	·· 51.5	205 42.1	·· 05.3	202 58.9	·· 06.6	Alnilam	276 11.5	S 1 12.9
E 10	41 46.3	314 15.6	13.2	345 17.9	51.9	220 44.5	05.3	218 01.4	06.6	Alphard	218 20.2	S 8 34.7
S 11	56 48.8	329 14.7	13.3	0 18.5	52.3	235 46.9	05.3	233 03.9	06.6			
D 12	71 51.2	344 13.9	N24 13.5	15 19.1	N19 52.8	250 49.4	N 1 05.2	248 06.4	N 1 06.6	Alphecca	126 31.4	N26 46.8
A 13	86 53.7	359 13.0	13.6	30 19.7	53.2	265 51.8	05.2	263 08.8	06.6	Alpheratz	358 08.9	N28 59.0
Y 14	101 56.2	14 12.1	13.8	45 20.3	53.6	280 54.2	05.2	278 11.3	06.6	Altair	62 31.8	N 8 49.1
15	116 58.6	29 11.2	·· 13.9	60 20.9	·· 54.0	295 56.6	·· 05.1	293 13.8	·· 06.6	Ankaa	353 40.0	S42 24.3
16	132 01.1	44 10.3	14.0	75 21.5	54.4	310 59.0	05.1	308 16.3	06.5	Antares	112 55.9	S26 23.4
17	147 03.5	59 09.4	14.2	90 22.2	54.9	326 01.5	05.1	323 18.7	06.5			
18	162 06.0	74 08.5	N24 14.3	105 22.8	N19 55.3	341 03.9	N 1 05.1	338 21.2	N 1 06.5	Arcturus	146 17.8	N19 16.9
19	177 08.5	89 07.6	14.4	120 23.4	55.7	356 06.3	05.0	353 23.7	06.5	Atria	108 19.1	S68 59.6
20	192 10.9	104 06.7	14.6	135 24.0	56.1	11 08.7	05.0	8 26.1	06.5	Avior	234 28.4	S59 27.2
21	207 13.4	119 05.8	·· 14.7	150 24.6	·· 56.5	26 11.1	·· 05.0	23 28.6	·· 06.5	Bellatrix	278 58.6	N 6 19.9
22	222 15.9	134 04.9	14.8	165 25.2	56.9	41 13.6	04.9	38 31.1	06.5	Betelgeuse	271 28.1	N 7 24.2
23	237 18.3	149 04.0	15.0	180 25.8	57.4	56 16.0	04.9	53 33.6	06.5			
4 00	252 20.8	164 03.2	N24 15.1	195 26.4	N19 57.8	71 18.4	N 1 04.9	68 36.0	N 1 06.5	Canopus	264 07.5	S52 41.3
01	267 23.3	179 02.3	15.2	210 27.1	58.2	86 20.8	04.8	83 38.5	06.5	Capella	281 11.1	N45 58.7
02	282 25.7	194 01.4	15.3	225 27.7	58.6	101 23.2	04.8	98 41.0	06.5	Deneb	49 47.9	N45 12.6
03	297 28.2	209 00.5	·· 15.5	240 28.3	·· 59.0	116 25.7	·· 04.8	113 43.5	·· 06.5	Denebola	182 58.5	N14 40.7
04	312 30.6	223 59.6	15.6	255 28.9	59.4	131 28.1	04.7	128 45.9	06.5	Diphda	349 20.6	S18 05.4
05	327 33.1	238 58.7	15.7	270 29.5	19 59.8	146 30.5	04.7	143 48.4	06.5			
06	342 35.6	253 57.8	N24 15.8	285 30.1	N20 00.3	161 32.9	N 1 04.7	158 50.9	N 1 06.5	Dubhe	194 21.6	N61 51.4
07	357 38.0	268 56.9	15.9	300 30.7	00.7	176 35.3	04.7	173 53.3	06.4	Elnath	278 43.9	N28 35.4
T 08	12 40.5	283 56.0	16.1	315 31.3	01.1	191 37.7	04.6	188 55.8	06.4	Eltanin	90 57.0	N51 29.4
H 09	27 43.0	298 55.1	·· 16.2	330 31.9	·· 01.5	206 40.2	·· 04.6	203 58.3	·· 06.4	Enif	34 11.0	N 9 47.2
U 10	42 45.4	313 54.2	16.3	345 32.6	01.9	221 42.6	04.6	219 00.8	06.4	Fomalhaut	15 50.9	S29 43.2
R 11	57 47.9	328 53.3	16.4	0 33.2	02.3	236 45.0	04.5	234 03.2	06.4			
S 12	72 50.4	343 52.4	N24 16.5	15 33.8	N20 02.7	251 47.4	N 1 04.5	249 05.7	N 1 06.4	Gacrux	172 28.0	S57 00.7
D 13	87 52.8	358 51.6	16.6	30 34.4	03.1	266 49.8	04.5	264 08.2	06.4	Gienah	176 17.4	S17 26.4
A 14	102 55.3	13 50.7	16.7	45 35.0	03.6	281 52.2	04.4	279 10.6	06.4	Hadar	149 22.2	S60 17.1
Y 15	117 57.8	28 49.8	·· 16.9	60 35.6	·· 04.0	296 54.6	·· 04.4	294 13.1	·· 06.4	Hamal	328 28.7	N23 22.2
16	133 00.2	43 48.9	17.0	75 36.2	04.4	311 57.1	04.4	309 15.6	06.4	Kaus Aust.	84 15.8	S34 23.6
17	148 02.7	58 48.0	17.1	90 36.8	04.8	326 59.5	04.3	324 18.0	06.4			
18	163 05.1	73 47.1	N24 17.2	105 37.4	N20 05.2	342 01.9	N 1 04.3	339 20.5	N 1 06.4	Kochab	137 18.0	N74 14.2
19	178 07.6	88 46.2	17.3	120 38.0	05.6	357 04.3	04.3	354 23.0	06.4	Markab	14 02.7	N15 06.1
20	193 10.1	103 45.3	17.4	135 38.7	06.0	12 06.7	04.2	9 25.5	06.3	Menkar	314 40.9	N 4 00.9
21	208 12.5	118 44.4	·· 17.5	150 39.3	·· 06.4	27 09.1	·· 04.2	24 27.9	·· 06.3	Menkent	148 36.1	S36 16.8
22	223 15.0	133 43.5	17.6	165 39.9	· 06.8	42 11.5	04.2	39 30.4	06.3	Miaplacidus	221 45.2	S69 38.7
23	238 17.5	148 42.6	17.7	180 40.5	07.2	57 14.0	04.1	54 32.9	06.3			
5 00	253 19.9	163 41.7	N24 17.8	195 41.1	N20 07.6	72 16.4	N 1 04.1	69 35.3	N 1 06.3	Mirfak	309 15.9	N49 47.5
01	268 22.4	178 40.8	17.9	210 41.7	08.1	87 18.8	04.1	84 37.8	06.3	Nunki	76 28.3	S26 19.1
02	283 24.9	193 39.9	18.0	225 42.3	08.5	102 21.2	04.0	99 40.3	06.3	Peacock	53 57.3	S56 47.5
03	298 27.3	208 39.0	·· 18.1	240 42.9	·· 08.9	117 23.6	·· 04.0	114 42.7	·· 06.3	Pollux	243 57.9	N28 04.4
04	313 29.8	223 38.2	18.2	255 43.5	09.3	132 26.0	04.0	129 45.2	06.3	Procyon	245 25.6	N 5 16.3
05	328 32.3	238 37.3	18.2	270 44.1	09.7	147 28.4	03.9	144 47.7	06.3			
06	343 34.7	253 36.4	N24 18.3	285 44.8	N20 10.1	162 30.8	N 1 03.9	159 50.1	N 1 06.3	Rasalhague	96 28.8	N12 34.4
07	358 37.2	268 35.5	18.4	300 45.4	10.5	177 33.2	03.8	174 52.6	06.2	Regulus	208 09.6	N12 03.6
08	13 39.6	283 34.6	18.5	315 46.0	10.9	192 35.6	03.8	189 55.1	06.2	Rigel	281 35.9	S 8 13.5
F 09	28 42.1	298 33.7	·· 18.6	330 46.6	·· 11.3	207 38.1	·· 03.8	204 57.5	·· 06.2	Rigil Kent.	140 24.6	S60 45.5
R 10	43 44.6	313 32.8	18.7	345 47.2	11.7	222 40.5	03.7	220 00.0	06.2	Sabik	102 40.2	S15 42.1
I 11	58 47.0	328 31.9	18.8	0 47.8	12.1	237 42.9	03.7	235 02.5	06.2			
D 12	73 49.5	343 31.0	N24 18.9	15 48.4	N20 12.5	252 45.3	N 1 03.7	250 04.9	N 1 06.2	Schedar	350 08.7	N56 25.8
A 13	88 52.0	358 30.1	18.9	30 49.0	12.9	267 47.7	03.6	265 07.4	06.2	Shaula	96 54.7	S37 05.4
Y 14	103 54.4	13 29.2	19.0	45 49.6	13.3	282 50.1	03.6	280 09.9	06.2	Sirius	258 55.6	S16 41.6
15	118 56.9	28 28.3	·· 19.1	60 50.2	·· 13.7	297 52.5	·· 03.6	295 12.3	·· 06.2	Spica	158 56.8	S11 03.8
16	133 59.4	43 27.4	19.2	75 50.9	14.1	312 54.9	03.5	310 14.8	06.2	Suhail	223 10.6	S43 21.6
17	149 01.8	58 26.5	19.3	90 51.5	14.5	327 57.3	03.5	325 17.3	06.2			
18	164 04.3	73 25.6	N24 19.3	105 52.1	N20 14.9	342 59.7	N 1 03.5	340 19.7	N 1 06.1	Vega	80 55.1	N38 45.9
19	179 06.7	88 24.7	19.4	120 52.7	15.3	358 02.1	03.4	355 22.2	06.1	Zuben'ubi	137 32.2	S15 57.9
20	194 09.2	103 23.8	19.5	135 53.3	15.7	13 04.5	03.4	10 24.7	06.1		S.H.A.	Mer. Pass.
21	209 11.7	118 23.0	·· 19.5	150 53.9	·· 16.1	28 06.9	·· 03.3	25 27.1	·· 06.1		° ′	h m
22	224 14.1	133 22.1	19.6	165 54.5	16.5	43 09.4	03.3	40 29.6	06.1	Venus	271 42.4	13 05
23	239 16.6	148 21.2	19.7	180 55.1	16.9	58 11.8	03.3	55 32.1	06.1	Mars	303 05.7	10 58
Mer. Pass.	h m 7 09.4	v −0.9	d 0.1	v 0.6	d 0.4	v 2.4	d 0.0	v 2.5	d 0.0	Jupiter	178 57.6	19 12
										Saturn	176 15.2	19 22

SUN / MOON

G.M.T. d h	SUN G.H.A.	SUN Dec.	MOON G.H.A.	v	MOON Dec.	d	H.P.
3 00	180 30.4	N22 16.4	172 19.0	4.0	N19 32.9	5.2	60.9
01	195 30.3	16.7	186 42.0	4.0	19 38.1	5.1	60.8
02	210 30.2	17.0	201 05.0	4.0	19 43.2	4.9	60.8
03	225 30.1 ··	17.3	215 28.0	4.0	19 48.1	4.7	60.8
04	240 30.0	17.6	229 51.0	4.0	19 52.8	4.6	60.8
05	255 29.9	17.9	244 14.0	3.9	19 57.4	4.5	60.8
W 06	270 29.8	N22 18.2	258 36.9	4.0	N20 01.9	4.3	60.7
07	285 29.7	18.6	272 59.9	3.9	20 06.2	4.2	60.7
E 08	300 29.6	18.9	287 22.8	3.9	20 10.4	4.0	60.7
D 09	315 29.5 ··	19.2	301 45.7	4.0	20 14.4	3.9	60.7
N 10	330 29.4	19.5	316 08.7	3.9	20 18.3	3.7	60.7
E 11	345 29.3	19.8	330 31.6	3.9	20 22.0	3.5	60.6
S 12	0 29.2	N22 20.1	344 54.5	4.0	N20 25.5	3.4	60.6
D 13	15 29.1	20.4	359 17.5	3.9	20 28.9	3.3	60.6
A 14	30 29.0	20.7	13 40.4	3.9	20 32.2	3.1	60.6
Y 15	45 28.9 ··	21.0	28 03.3	4.0	20 35.3	3.0	60.5
16	60 28.8	21.3	42 26.3	4.0	20 38.3	2.8	60.5
17	75 28.7	21.6	56 49.3	3.9	20 41.1	2.6	60.5
18	90 28.6	N22 21.9	71 12.2	4.0	N20 43.7	2.5	60.5
19	105 28.4	22.2	85 35.2	4.0	20 46.2	2.4	60.4
20	120 28.3	22.5	99 58.2	4.0	20 48.6	2.2	60.4
21	135 28.2 ··	22.8	114 21.2	4.1	20 50.8	2.0	60.4
22	150 28.1	23.1	128 44.3	4.0	20 52.8	1.9	60.4
23	165 28.0	23.4	143 07.3	4.1	20 54.7	1.7	60.3
4 00	180 27.9	N22 23.7	157 30.4	4.1	N20 56.4	1.6	60.3
01	195 27.8	24.0	171 53.5	4.1	20 58.0	1.5	60.3
02	210 27.7	24.3	186 16.6	4.2	20 59.5	1.2	60.2
03	225 27.6 ··	24.6	200 39.8	4.2	21 00.7	1.2	60.2
04	240 27.5	24.9	215 03.0	4.2	21 01.9	1.0	60.2
05	255 27.4	25.2	229 26.2	4.3	21 02.9	0.8	60.1
06	270 27.3	N22 25.5	243 49.5	4.3	N21 03.7	0.7	60.1
07	285 27.2	25.7	258 12.8	4.3	21 04.4	0.5	60.1
T 08	300 27.1	26.0	272 36.1	4.4	21 04.9	0.4	60.1
H 09	315 27.0 ··	26.3	286 59.5	4.4	21 05.3	0.2	60.0
U 10	330 26.8	26.6	301 22.9	4.4	21 05.5	0.1	60.0
R 11	345 26.7	26.9	315 46.3	4.5	21 05.6	0.1	60.0
S 12	0 26.6	N22 27.2	330 09.8	4.6	N21 05.5	0.2	59.9
D 13	15 26.5	27.5	344 33.4	4.5	21 05.3	0.3	59.9
A 14	30 26.4	27.8	358 56.9	4.7	21 05.0	0.5	59.9
Y 15	45 26.3 ··	28.1	13 20.6	4.7	21 04.5	0.7	59.8
16	60 26.2	28.3	27 44.3	4.7	21 03.8	0.8	59.8
17	75 26.1	28.6	42 08.0	4.8	21 03.0	0.9	59.8
18	90 26.0	N22 28.9	56 31.8	4.9	N21 02.1	1.1	59.7
19	105 25.9	29.2	70 55.7	4.9	21 01.0	1.2	59.7
20	120 25.8	29.5	85 19.6	4.9	20 59.8	1.4	59.7
21	135 25.7 ··	29.8	99 43.5	5.1	20 58.4	1.5	59.6
22	150 25.5	30.0	114 07.6	5.0	20 56.9	1.7	59.6
23	165 25.4	30.3	128 31.6	5.2	20 55.2	1.8	59.5
5 00	180 25.3	N22 30.6	142 55.8	5.2	N20 53.4	1.9	59.5
01	195 25.2	30.9	157 20.0	5.3	20 51.5	2.1	59.5
02	210 25.1	31.2	171 44.3	5.4	20 49.4	2.2	59.4
03	225 25.0 ··	31.4	186 08.7	5.4	20 47.2	2.3	59.4
04	240 24.9	31.7	200 33.1	5.5	20 44.9	2.5	59.4
05	255 24.8	32.0	214 57.6	5.5	20 42.4	2.6	59.3
06	270 24.7	N22 32.3	229 22.1	5.6	N20 39.8	2.8	59.3
07	285 24.6	32.5	243 46.7	5.8	20 37.0	2.9	59.3
08	300 24.4	32.8	258 11.5	5.7	20 34.1	3.0	59.2
F 09	315 24.3 ··	33.1	272 36.2	5.9	20 31.1	3.1	59.2
R 10	330 24.2	33.4	287 01.1	5.9	20 28.0	3.3	59.1
I 11	345 24.1	33.6	301 26.0	6.0	20 24.7	3.4	59.1
D 12	0 24.0	N22 33.9	315 51.0	6.1	N20 21.3	3.6	59.1
A 13	15 23.9	34.2	330 16.1	6.2	20 17.7	3.6	59.0
Y 14	30 23.8	34.5	344 41.3	6.2	20 14.1	3.8	59.0
15	45 23.7 ··	34.7	359 06.5	6.4	20 10.3	3.9	59.0
16	60 23.6	35.0	13 31.9	6.4	20 06.4	4.0	58.9
17	75 23.4	35.3	27 57.3	6.5	20 02.4	4.2	58.9
18	90 23.3	N22 35.5	42 22.8	6.6	N19 58.2	4.3	58.8
19	105 23.2	35.8	56 48.4	6.6	19 53.9	4.4	58.8
20	120 23.0	36.1	71 14.0	6.8	19 49.5	4.5	58.8
21	135 23.0 ··	36.3	85 39.8	6.8	19 45.0	4.6	58.7
22	150 22.9	36.6	100 05.6	6.9	19 40.4	4.8	58.7
23	165 22.8	36.9	114 31.5	7.1	19 35.6	4.8	58.6
S.D.	15.8	d 0.3	S.D. 16.5		16.3		16.1

Twilight — Sunrise — Moonrise

Lat.	Naut.	Civil	Sunrise	Moonrise 3	4	5	6
N 72	□	□	□	□	□	□	04 53
N 70	□	□	□	01 28	□	□	05 46
68	□	□	□	02 30	02 55	04 04	06 19
66	////	////	00 59	03 05	03 44	04 50	06 43
64	////	////	01 51	03 31	04 15	05 20	07 01
62	////	////	02 22	03 51	04 38	05 43	07 09
60	////	01 18	02 45	04 08	04 57	06 01	07 17
N 58	////	01 55	03 04	04 21	05 12	06 16	07 30
56	////	02 20	03 19	04 33	05 26	06 29	07 41
54	01 11	02 40	03 32	04 44	05 37	06 41	07 51
52	01 45	02 57	03 44	04 53	05 47	06 51	08 00
50	02 09	03 11	03 54	05 02	05 57	06 59	08 08
45	02 50	03 39	04 15	05 20	06 16	07 18	08 24
N 40	03 19	04 00	04 32	05 34	06 32	07 34	08 38
35	03 41	04 17	04 46	05 47	06 45	07 47	08 50
30	03 59	04 32	04 59	05 58	06 56	07 58	09 00
20	04 26	04 55	05 20	06 16	07 16	08 17	09 17
N 10	04 48	05 15	05 38	06 33	07 34	08 34	09 32
0	05 06	05 32	05 55	06 48	07 50	08 50	09 47
S 10	05 22	05 49	06 11	07 04	08 06	09 06	10 01
20	05 38	06 05	06 29	07 20	08 24	09 22	10 16
30	05 53	06 23	06 49	07 39	08 44	09 42	10 33
35	06 01	06 33	07 01	07 51	08 55	09 53	10 43
40	06 10	06 44	07 14	08 03	09 09	10 06	10 55
45	06 20	06 57	07 30	08 19	09 25	10 21	11 08
S 50	06 31	07 12	07 50	08 37	09 54	10 40	11 24
52	06 36	07 19	07 59	08 46	10 04	10 49	11 32
54	06 41	07 26	08 09	08 56	10 16	10 59	11 40
56	06 47	07 35	08 21	09 07	10 28	11 10	11 50
58	06 53	07 44	08 35	09 20	10 35	11 23	12 01
S 60	07 00	07 55	08 51	09 35	10 46	11 38	12 13

Sunset — Twilight — Moonset

Lat.	Sunset	Civil	Naut.	Moonset 3	4	5	6
N 72	□	□	□	□	□	□	02 21
N 70	□	□	□	24 10	00 10	01 08	01 27
68	□	□	□	23 22	24 22	00 22	00 53
66	23 01	////	////	22 51	23 24	24 29	00 20
64	22 07	////	////	22 28	23 29	24 10	00 19
62	21 36	////	////	22 09	23 10	23 54	24 24
60	21 12	22 41	////	22 01	23 02	23 47	24 18
N 58	20 54	22 03	////	21 54	22 55	23 40	24 13
56	20 38	21 37	////	21 40	22 42	23 29	24 04
54	20 25	21 17	22 48	21 29	22 30	23 19	23 55
52	20 13	21 00	22 13	21 19	22 20	23 09	23 48
50	20 03	20 46	21 48	21 10	22 11	23 01	23 41
45	19 42	20 18	21 07	20 51	21 52	22 44	23 26
N 40	19 25	19 57	20 38	20 35	21 37	22 30	23 14
35	19 10	19 40	20 16	20 22	21 23	22 17	23 04
30	18 58	19 25	19 58	20 10	21 12	22 07	22 55
20	18 37	19 01	19 30	19 51	20 52	21 48	22 39
N 10	18 19	18 42	19 08	19 34	20 35	21 32	22 25
0	18 02	18 24	18 50	19 18	20 19	21 17	22 12
S 10	17 45	18 08	18 34	19 02	20 03	21 02	21 59
20	17 27	17 51	18 19	18 45	19 45	20 46	21 45
30	17 07	17 33	18 03	18 25	19 25	20 27	21 29
35	16 55	17 23	17 55	18 13	19 14	20 16	21 20
40	16 42	17 12	17 46	18 00	19 00	20 04	21 09
45	16 26	16 59	17 36	17 45	18 44	19 49	20 56
S 50	16 07	16 44	17 25	17 25	18 25	19 31	20 41
52	15 57	16 37	17 20	17 16	18 15	19 22	20 33
54	15 47	16 30	17 15	17 06	18 05	19 13	20 25
56	15 35	16 21	17 10	16 55	17 53	19 02	20 16
58	15 21	16 12	17 03	16 42	17 39	18 49	20 06
S 60	15 05	16 01	16 56	16 26	17 23	18 35	19 54

SUN / MOON

Day	Eqn. of Time 00h	12h	Mer. Pass.	Mer. Pass. Upper	Lower	Age	Phase
	m s	m s	h m	h m	h m	d	
3	02 02	01 57	11 58	13 03	00 32	01	●
4	01 52	01 47	11 58	14 04	01 34	02	
5	01 42	01 36	11 58	15 04	02 34	03	

G.M.T.	ARIES G.H.A.	VENUS −3.3 G.H.A.	Dec.	MARS +1.6 G.H.A.	Dec.	JUPITER −1.7 G.H.A.	Dec.	SATURN +1.1 G.H.A.	Dec.	STARS Name	S.H.A.	Dec.
6 00	254 19.1	163 20.3 N24	19.8	195 55.7 N20	17.3	73 14.2 N 1	03.2	70 34.5 N 1	06.1	Acamar	315 37.3	S40 22.8
01	269 21.5	178 19.4	19.8	210 56.3	17.7	88 16.6	03.2	85 37.0	06.1	Achernar	335 45.3	S57 19.8
02	284 24.0	193 18.5	19.9	225 56.9	18.1	103 19.0	03.2	100 39.4	06.1	Acrux	173 36.4	S63 00.0
03	299 26.5	208 17.6 ··	20.0	240 57.5 ··	18.5	118 21.4 ··	03.1	115 41.9 ··	06.1	Adhara	255 32.1	S28 56.9
04	314 28.9	223 16.7	20.0	255 58.2	18.9	133 23.8	03.1	130 44.4	06.0	Aldebaran	291 17.8	N16 28.2
05	329 31.4	238 15.8	20.1	270 58.8	19.3	148 26.2	03.1	145 46.8	06.0			
06	344 33.9	253 14.9 N24	20.1	285 59.4 N20	19.7	163 28.6 N 1	03.0	160 49.3 N 1	06.0	Alioth	166 41.8	N56 04.0
07	359 36.3	268 14.0	20.2	301 00.0	20.1	178 31.0	03.0	175 51.8	06.0	Alkaid	153 17.8	N49 24.6
S 08	14 38.8	283 13.1	20.3	316 00.6	20.5	193 33.4	02.9	190 54.2	06.0	Al Na'ir	28 14.2	S47 02.9
A 09	29 41.2	298 12.2 ··	20.3	331 01.2 ··	20.9	208 35.8 ··	02.9	205 56.7 ··	06.0	Alnilam	276 11.5	S 1 12.9
T 10	44 43.7	313 11.3	20.4	346 01.8	21.3	223 38.2	02.9	220 59.2	06.0	Alphard	218 20.2	S 8 34.7
U 11	59 46.2	328 10.4	20.4	1 02.4	21.7	238 40.6	02.8	236 01.6	06.0			
R 12	74 48.6	343 09.5 N24	20.5	16 03.0 N20	22.1	253 43.0 N 1	02.8	251 04.1 N 1	06.0	Alphecca	126 31.4	N26 46.8
D 13	89 51.1	358 08.6	20.5	31 03.6	22.5	268 45.4	02.7	266 06.5	05.9	Alpheratz	358 08.9	N28 59.0
A 14	104 53.6	13 07.7	20.6	46 04.2	22.9	283 47.8	02.7	281 09.0	05.9	Altair	62 31.8	N 8 49.1
Y 15	119 56.0	28 06.9 ··	20.6	61 04.8 ··	23.3	298 50.2 ··	02.7	296 11.5 ··	05.9	Ankaa	353 39.9	S42 24.3
16	134 58.5	43 06.0	20.7	76 05.4	23.7	313 52.6	02.6	311 13.9	05.9	Antares	112 55.9	S26 23.4
17	150 01.0	58 05.1	20.7	91 06.1	24.1	328 55.0	02.6	326 16.4	05.9			
18	165 03.4	73 04.2 N24	20.8	106 06.7 N20	24.4	343 57.4 N 1	02.6	341 18.9 N 1	05.9	Arcturus	146 17.8	N19 16.9
19	180 05.9	88 03.3	20.8	121 07.3	24.8	358 59.8	02.5	356 21.3	05.9	Atria	108 19.1	S68 59.6
20	195 08.4	103 02.4	20.9	136 07.9	25.2	14 02.2	02.5	11 23.8	05.9	Avior	234 28.4	S59 27.2
21	210 10.8	118 01.5 ··	20.9	151 08.5 ··	25.6	29 04.6 ··	02.4	26 26.2 ··	05.8	Bellatrix	278 58.6	N 6 19.9
22	225 13.3	133 00.6	20.9	166 09.1	26.0	44 07.0	02.4	41 28.7	05.8	Betelgeuse	271 28.1	N 7 24.2
23	240 15.7	147 59.7	21.0	181 09.7	26.4	59 09.4	02.4	56 31.2	05.8			
7 00	255 18.2	162 58.8 N24	21.0	196 10.3 N20	26.8	74 11.8 N 1	02.3	71 33.6 N 1	05.8	Canopus	264 07.5	S52 41.3
01	270 20.7	177 57.9	21.1	211 10.9	27.2	89 14.2	02.3	86 36.1	05.8	Capella	281 11.1	N45 58.7
02	285 23.1	192 57.0	21.1	226 11.5	27.6	104 16.6	02.2	101 38.5	05.8	Deneb	49 47.8	N45 12.6
03	300 25.6	207 56.1 ··	21.1	241 12.1 ··	28.0	119 19.0 ··	02.2	116 41.0 ··	05.8	Denebola	182 58.5	N14 40.7
04	315 28.1	222 55.2	21.2	256 12.7	28.4	134 21.4	02.2	131 43.5	05.8	Diphda	349 20.5	S18 05.3
05	330 30.5	237 54.3	21.2	271 13.3	28.7	149 23.8	02.1	146 45.9	05.8			
06	345 33.0	252 53.4 N24	21.2	286 13.9 N20	29.1	164 26.2 N 1	02.1	161 48.4 N 1	05.7	Dubhe	194 21.6	N61 51.4
07	0 35.5	267 52.5	21.2	301 14.6	29.5	179 28.6	02.0	176 50.8	05.7	Elnath	278 43.9	N28 35.4
08	15 37.9	282 51.6	21.3	316 15.2	29.9	194 31.0	02.0	191 53.3	05.7	Eltanin	90 57.0	N51 29.5
S 09	30 40.4	297 50.7 ··	21.3	331 15.8 ··	30.3	209 33.4 ··	02.0	206 55.8 ··	05.7	Enif	34 11.0	N 9 47.3
U 10	45 42.8	312 49.9	21.3	346 16.4	30.7	224 35.8	01.9	221 58.2	05.7	Fomalhaut	15 50.9	S29 43.2
N 11	60 45.3	327 49.0	21.4	1 17.0	31.1	239 38.2	01.9	237 00.7	05.7			
D 12	75 47.8	342 48.1 N24	21.4	16 17.6 N20	31.5	254 40.6 N 1	01.8	252 03.1 N 1	05.7	Gacrux	172 28.0	S57 00.7
A 13	90 50.2	357 47.2	21.4	31 18.2	31.8	269 42.9	01.8	267 05.6	05.7	Gienah	176 17.4	S17 26.4
Y 14	105 52.7	12 46.3	21.4	46 18.8	32.2	284 45.3	01.7	282 08.1	05.6	Hadar	149 22.2	S60 17.1
15	120 55.2	27 45.4 ··	21.4	61 19.4 ··	32.6	299 47.7 ··	01.7	297 10.5 ··	05.6	Hamal	328 28.6	N23 22.3
16	135 57.6	42 44.5	21.5	76 20.0	33.0	314 50.1	01.7	312 13.0	05.6	Kaus Aust.	84 15.8	S34 23.6
17	151 00.1	57 43.6	21.5	91 20.6	33.4	329 52.5	01.6	327 15.4	05.6			
18	166 02.6	72 42.7 N24	21.5	106 21.2 N20	33.8	344 54.9 N 1	01.6	342 17.9 N 1	05.6	Kochab	137 18.0	N74 14.2
19	181 05.0	87 41.8	21.5	121 21.8	34.2	359 57.3	01.5	357 20.3	05.6	Markab	14 02.7	N15 06.1
20	196 07.5	102 40.9	21.5	136 22.4	34.5	14 59.7	01.5	12 22.8	05.6	Menkar	314 40.9	N 4 00.9
21	211 10.0	117 40.0 ··	21.5	151 23.0 ··	34.9	30 02.1 ··	01.5	27 25.3 ··	05.5	Menkent	148 36.2	S36 16.8
22	226 12.4	132 39.1	21.5	166 23.7	35.3	45 04.5	01.4	42 27.7	05.5	Miaplacidus	221 45.3	S69 38.7
23	241 14.9	147 38.2	21.5	181 24.3	35.7	60 06.9	01.4	57 30.2	05.5			
8 00	256 17.3	162 37.3 N24	21.6	196 24.9 N20	36.1	75 09.3 N 1	01.3	72 32.6 N 1	05.5	Mirfak	309 15.9	N49 47.5
01	271 19.8	177 36.4	21.6	211 25.5	36.5	90 11.7	01.3	87 35.1	05.5	Nunki	76 28.2	S26 19.1
02	286 22.3	192 35.5	21.6	226 26.1	36.8	105 14.1	01.2	102 37.5	05.5	Peacock	53 57.2	S56 47.5
03	301 24.7	207 34.6 ··	21.6	241 26.7 ··	37.2	120 16.4 ··	01.2	117 40.0 ··	05.5	Pollux	243 57.9	N28 04.4
04	316 27.2	222 33.8	21.6	256 27.3	37.6	135 18.8	01.2	132 42.5	05.5	Procyon	245 25.6	N 5 16.4
05	331 29.7	237 32.9	21.6	271 27.9	38.0	150 21.2	01.1	147 44.9	05.4			
06	346 32.1	252 32.0 N24	21.6	286 28.5 N20	38.4	165 23.6 N 1	01.1	162 47.4 N 1	05.4	Rasalhague	96 28.8	N12 34.4
07	1 34.6	267 31.1	21.6	301 29.1	38.7	180 26.0	01.0	177 49.8	05.4	Regulus	208 09.6	N12 03.6
08	16 37.1	282 30.2	21.6	316 29.7	39.1	195 28.4	01.0	192 52.3	05.4	Rigel	281 35.9	S 8 13.5
M 09	31 39.5	297 29.3 ··	21.6	331 30.3 ··	39.5	210 30.8 ··	00.9	207 54.7 ··	05.4	Rigil Kent.	140 24.6	S60 45.6
O 10	46 42.0	312 28.4	21.6	346 30.9	39.9	225 33.2	00.9	222 57.2	05.4	Sabik	102 40.2	S15 42.1
N 11	61 44.5	327 27.5	21.6	1 31.5	40.3	240 35.6	00.9	237 59.6	05.3			
D 12	76 46.9	342 26.6 N24	21.6	16 32.1 N20	40.6	255 37.9 N 1	00.8	253 02.1 N 1	05.3	Schedar	350 08.7	N56 25.8
A 13	91 49.4	357 25.7	21.5	31 32.7	41.0	270 40.3	00.8	268 04.6	05.3	Shaula	96 54.7	S37 05.4
Y 14	106 51.8	12 24.8	21.5	46 33.3	41.4	285 42.7	00.7	283 07.0	05.3	Sirius	258 55.6	S16 41.6
15	121 54.3	27 23.9 ··	21.5	61 33.9 ··	41.8	300 45.1 ··	00.7	298 09.5 ··	05.3	Spica	158 56.8	S11 03.8
16	136 56.8	42 23.0	21.5	76 34.5	42.1	315 47.5	00.6	313 11.9	05.3	Suhail	223 10.7	S43 21.6
17	151 59.2	57 22.1	21.5	91 35.2	42.5	330 49.9	00.6	328 14.4	05.3			
18	167 01.7	72 21.2 N24	21.5	106 35.8 N20	42.9	345 52.3 N 1	00.5	343 16.8 N 1	05.2	Vega	80 55.1	N38 45.9
19	182 04.2	87 20.3	21.5	121 36.4	43.3	0 54.7	00.5	358 19.3	05.2	Zuben'ubi	137 32.2	S15 57.9
20	197 06.6	102 19.4	21.5	136 37.0	43.6	15 57.0	00.4	13 21.7	05.2			
21	212 09.1	117 18.6 ··	21.4	151 37.6 ··	44.0	30 59.4 ··	00.4	28 24.2 ··	05.2		S.H.A.	Mer. Pass.
22	227 11.6	132 17.7	21.4	166 38.2	44.4	46 01.8	00.4	43 26.6	05.2	Venus	267 40.6	13 09
23	242 14.0	147 16.8	21.4	181 38.8	44.8	61 04.2	00.3	58 29.1	05.2	Mars	300 52.1	10 55
Mer. Pass.	6 57.6	v −0.9 d 0.0		v 0.6 d 0.4		v 2.4 d 0.0		v 2.5 d 0.0		Jupiter	178 53.6	19 00
										Saturn	176 15.4	19 11

G.M.T.	SUN G.H.A.	Dec.	MOON G.H.A.	v	Dec.	d	H.P.
d h	° ′	° ′	° ′	′	° ′	′	′
6 00	180 22.7	N22 37.1	128 57.6	7.1	N19 30.8	5.0	58.6
01	195 22.5	37.4	143 23.7	7.1	19 25.8	5.1	58.6
02	210 22.4	37.7	157 49.8	7.3	19 20.7	5.2	58.5
03	225 22.3 ··	37.9	172 16.1	7.4	19 15.5	5.3	58.5
04	240 22.2	38.2	186 42.5	7.5	19 10.2	5.5	58.4
05	255 22.1	38.4	201 09.0	7.5	19 04.7	5.5	58.4
06	270 22.0	N22 38.7	215 35.5	7.7	N18 59.2	5.6	58.4
07	285 21.9	39.0	230 02.2	7.7	18 53.6	5.8	58.3
S 08	300 21.7	39.2	244 28.9	7.8	18 47.8	5.8	58.3
A 09	315 21.6 ··	39.5	258 55.7	7.9	18 42.0	6.0	58.2
T 10	330 21.5	39.7	273 22.6	8.0	18 36.0	6.0	58.2
U 11	345 21.4	40.0	287 49.6	8.1	18 30.0	6.2	58.2
R 12	0 21.3	N22 40.2	302 16.7	8.2	N18 23.8	6.3	58.1
D 13	15 21.2	40.5	316 43.9	8.3	18 17.5	6.3	58.1
A 14	30 21.1	40.7	331 11.2	8.4	18 11.2	6.5	58.1
Y 15	45 20.9 ··	41.0	345 38.6	8.5	18 04.7	6.5	58.0
16	60 20.8	41.3	0 06.1	8.6	17 58.2	6.7	58.0
17	75 20.7	41.5	14 33.7	8.6	17 51.5	6.7	57.9
18	90 20.6	N22 41.8	29 01.3	8.8	N17 44.8	6.8	57.9
19	105 20.5	42.0	43 29.1	8.8	17 38.0	6.9	57.9
20	120 20.4	42.3	57 56.9	9.0	17 31.1	7.0	57.8
21	135 20.3 ··	42.5	72 24.9	9.0	17 24.1	7.1	57.8
22	150 20.1	42.8	86 52.9	9.2	17 17.0	7.2	57.7
23	165 20.0	43.0	101 21.1	9.2	17 09.8	7.3	57.7
7 00	180 19.9	N22 43.3	115 49.3	9.3	N17 02.5	7.3	57.7
01	195 19.8	43.5	130 17.6	9.4	16 55.2	7.5	57.6
02	210 19.7	43.7	144 46.0	9.5	16 47.7	7.5	57.6
03	225 19.6 ··	44.0	159 14.5	9.6	16 40.2	7.6	57.5
04	240 19.4	44.2	173 43.1	9.7	16 32.6	7.7	57.5
05	255 19.3	44.5	188 11.8	9.8	16 24.9	7.7	57.5
06	270 19.2	N22 44.7	202 40.6	9.9	N16 17.2	7.9	57.4
07	285 19.1	45.0	217 09.5	9.9	16 09.3	7.9	57.4
S 08	300 19.0	45.2	231 38.4	10.1	16 01.4	8.0	57.3
U 09	315 18.9 ··	45.4	246 07.5	10.1	15 53.4	8.0	57.3
N 10	330 18.7	45.7	260 36.6	10.3	15 45.4	8.2	57.3
11	345 18.6	45.9	275 05.9	10.3	15 37.2	8.2	57.2
D 12	0 18.5	N22 46.2	289 35.2	10.4	N15 29.0	8.3	57.2
A 13	15 18.4	46.4	304 04.6	10.5	15 20.7	8.3	57.2
Y 14	30 18.3	46.6	318 34.1	10.6	15 12.4	8.4	57.1
15	45 18.2 ··	46.9	333 03.7	10.7	15 04.0	8.5	57.1
16	60 18.0	47.1	347 33.4	10.8	14 55.5	8.6	57.0
17	75 17.9	47.3	2 03.2	10.9	14 46.9	8.6	57.0
18	90 17.8	N22 47.6	16 33.1	10.9	N14 38.3	8.6	57.0
19	105 17.7	47.8	31 03.0	11.0	14 29.7	8.8	56.9
20	120 17.6	48.1	45 33.0	11.2	14 20.9	8.8	56.9
21	135 17.4 ··	48.3	60 03.2	11.2	14 12.1	8.8	56.9
22	150 17.3	48.5	74 33.4	11.3	14 03.3	9.0	56.8
23	165 17.2	48.7	89 03.7	11.3	13 54.3	9.1	56.8
8 00	180 17.1	N22 49.0	103 34.0	11.5	N13 45.4	9.1	56.7
01	195 17.0	49.2	118 04.5	11.5	13 36.3	9.0	56.7
02	210 16.8	49.4	132 35.0	11.7	13 27.3	9.2	56.7
03	225 16.7 ··	49.7	147 05.7	11.7	13 18.1	9.2	56.6
04	240 16.6	49.9	161 36.4	11.8	13 08.9	9.2	56.6
05	255 16.5	50.1	176 07.2	11.8	12 59.7	9.3	56.6
06	270 16.4	N22 50.3	190 38.0	12.0	N12 50.4	9.4	56.5
07	285 16.3	50.6	205 09.0	12.0	12 41.0	9.4	56.5
08	300 16.1	50.8	219 40.0	12.1	12 31.6	9.4	56.5
M 09	315 16.0 ··	51.0	234 11.1	12.2	12 22.2	9.5	56.4
O 10	330 15.9	51.2	248 42.3	12.2	12 12.7	9.5	56.4
N 11	345 15.8	51.5	263 13.5	12.4	12 03.1	9.6	56.4
D 12	0 15.7	N22 51.7	277 44.9	12.4	N11 53.5	9.6	56.3
A 13	15 15.5	51.9	292 16.3	12.5	11 43.9	9.7	56.3
Y 14	30 15.4	52.1	306 47.8	12.5	11 34.2	9.7	56.3
15	45 15.3 ··	52.4	321 19.3	12.6	11 24.5	9.8	56.2
16	60 15.2	52.6	335 50.9	12.7	11 14.7	9.8	56.2
17	75 15.1	52.8	350 22.6	12.8	11 04.9	9.8	56.2
18	90 14.9	N22 53.0	4 54.4	12.9	N10 55.1	9.9	56.1
19	105 14.8	53.2	19 26.3	12.9	10 45.2	9.9	56.1
20	120 14.7	53.4	33 58.2	13.0	10 35.3	10.0	56.1
21	135 14.6 ··	53.7	48 30.2	13.0	10 25.3	10.0	56.1
22	150 14.4	53.9	63 02.2	13.1	10 15.3	10.0	56.0
23	165 14.3	54.1	77 34.3	13.2	10 05.3	10.1	56.0
S.D.	15.8	d 0.2	S.D. 15.8		15.6		15.3

Lat.	Twilight Naut.	Civil	Sunrise	Moonrise 6	7	8	9
°	h m	h m	h m	h m	h m	h m	h m
N 72	□	□	□	□	06 19	08 34	10 28
N 70	□	□	□	04 53	07 03	08 57	10 40
68	□	□	□	05 46	07 32	09 14	10 50
66	////	////	00 45	06 19	07 54	09 28	10 59
64	////	////	01 45	06 43	08 11	09 40	11 06
62	////	////	02 18	07 01	08 25	09 50	11 12
60	////	01 10	02 42	07 17	08 37	09 58	11 17
N 58	////	01 50	03 01	07 30	08 48	10 05	11 21
56	////	02 17	03 17	07 41	08 57	10 12	11 25
54	01 04	02 37	03 30	07 51	09 04	10 18	11 29
52	01 41	02 54	03 42	08 00	09 12	10 23	11 32
50	02 06	03 09	03 52	08 08	09 18	10 27	11 35
45	02 49	03 37	04 14	08 24	09 32	10 38	11 42
N 40	03 18	03 59	04 31	08 38	09 43	10 46	11 47
35	03 40	04 16	04 46	08 50	09 52	10 53	11 51
30	03 58	04 31	04 58	09 00	10 01	10 59	11 56
20	04 26	04 55	05 20	09 17	10 15	11 10	12 03
N 10	04 48	05 15	05 38	09 32	10 28	11 20	12 09
0	05 07	05 33	05 55	09 47	10 39	11 28	12 14
S 10	05 23	05 49	06 12	10 01	10 51	11 37	12 20
20	05 39	06 06	06 30	10 16	11 04	11 47	12 26
30	05 55	06 24	06 50	10 33	11 18	11 57	12 33
35	06 03	06 34	07 02	10 43	11 26	12 04	12 37
40	06 12	06 46	07 16	10 55	11 35	12 11	12 42
45	06 22	06 59	07 32	11 08	11 46	12 19	12 47
S 50	06 33	07 14	07 52	11 24	12 00	12 28	12 53
52	06 38	07 21	08 02	11 32	12 06	12 33	12 56
54	06 43	07 29	08 12	11 40	12 13	12 38	12 59
56	06 49	07 38	08 24	11 50	12 20	12 43	13 02
58	06 56	07 48	08 38	12 01	12 28	12 49	13 06
S 60	07 03	07 59	08 55	12 13	12 38	12 56	13 10

Lat.	Sunset	Twilight Civil	Naut.	Moonset 6	7	8	9
°	h m	h m	h m	h m	h m	h m	h m
N 72	□	□	□	□	02 48	02 17	01 59
N 70	□	□	□	02 21	02 02	01 52	01 44
68	□	□	□	01 27	01 32	01 33	01 33
66	23 17	////	////	00 53	01 09	01 18	01 23
64	22 15	////	////	00 29	00 51	01 05	01 15
62	21 41	////	////	00 10	00 37	00 55	01 08
60	21 17	22 50	////	24 24	00 24	00 46	01 02
N 58	20 57	22 09	////	24 13	00 13	00 38	00 56
56	20 41	21 42	////	24 04	00 04	00 30	00 52
54	20 28	21 21	22 56	23 55	24 24	00 24	00 47
52	20 16	21 04	22 18	23 48	24 18	00 18	00 43
50	20 03	20 49	21 53	23 41	24 13	00 13	00 40
45	19 44	20 21	21 10	23 26	24 02	00 02	00 32
N 40	19 26	19 59	20 40	23 14	23 52	24 25	00 25
35	19 12	19 41	20 18	23 04	23 44	24 20	00 20
30	18 59	19 27	20 00	22 55	23 37	24 15	00 15
20	18 38	19 02	19 31	22 39	23 25	24 06	00 06
N 10	18 19	18 42	19 09	22 25	23 14	23 58	24 40
0	18 02	18 25	18 51	22 12	23 03	23 51	24 36
S 10	17 45	18 08	18 34	21 59	22 53	23 43	24 31
20	17 28	17 51	18 19	21 45	22 42	23 36	24 27
30	17 07	17 33	18 03	21 29	22 29	23 27	24 22
35	16 55	17 23	17 54	21 20	22 22	23 21	24 19
40	16 41	17 12	17 45	21 09	22 13	23 15	24 16
45	16 25	16 59	17 36	20 56	22 03	23 08	24 12
S 50	16 05	16 43	17 24	20 41	21 51	23 00	24 07
52	15 56	16 36	17 19	20 33	21 45	22 56	24 05
54	15 45	16 28	17 14	20 25	21 39	22 52	24 02
56	15 33	16 19	17 08	20 16	21 32	22 47	24 00
58	15 19	16 10	17 02	20 06	21 24	22 42	23 57
S 60	15 02	15 59	16 55	19 54	21 15	22 36	23 54

Day	SUN Eqn. of Time 00ʰ	12ʰ	Mer. Pass.	MOON Mer. Pass. Upper	Lower	Age	Phase
	m s	m s	h m	h m	h m	d	
6	01 31	01 25	11 59	16 00	03 32	04	
7	01 20	01 14	11 59	16 51	04 26	05	
8	01 09	01 03	11 59	17 40	05 16	06	◗

G.M.T.	ARIES G.H.A.	VENUS −3.3 G.H.A.	Dec.	MARS +1.6 G.H.A.	Dec.	JUPITER −1.7 G.H.A.	Dec.	SATURN +1.1 G.H.A.	Dec.	STARS Name	S.H.A.	Dec.
9 00	257 16.5	162 15.9 N24 21.4		196 39.4 N20 45.1		76 06.6 N 1 00.3		73 31.5 N 1 05.2		Acamar	315 37.2	S40 22.7
01	272 18.9	177 15.0 21.4		211 40.0 45.5		91 09.0 00.2		88 34.0 05.1		Achernar	335 45.3	S57 19.7
02	287 21.4	192 14.1 21.3		226 40.6 45.9		106 11.4 00.2		103 36.4 05.1		Acrux	173 36.5	S63 00.0
03	302 23.9	207 13.2 ·· 21.3		241 41.2 ·· 46.3		121 13.7 ·· 00.1		118 38.9 ·· 05.1		Adhara	255 32.1	S28 56.9
04	317 26.3	222 12.3 21.3		256 41.8 46.6		136 16.1 00.1		133 41.4 05.1		Aldebaran	291 17.8	N16 28.2
05	332 28.8	237 11.4 21.2		271 42.4 47.0		151 18.5 00.0		148 43.8 05.1				
06	347 31.3	252 10.5 N24 21.2		286 43.0 N20 47.4		166 20.9 N 1 00.0		163 46.3 N 1 05.1		Alioth	166 41.9	N56 04.0
07	2 33.7	267 09.6 21.2		301 43.6 47.8		181 23.3 0 59.9		178 48.7 05.0		Alkaid	153 17.8	N49 24.7
T 08	17 36.2	282 08.7 21.2		316 44.2 48.1		196 25.7 59.9		193 51.2 05.0		Al Na'ir	28 14.2	S47 02.9
U 09	32 38.7	297 07.8 ·· 21.1		331 44.8 ·· 48.5		211 28.0 ·· 59.8		208 53.6 ·· 05.0		Alnilam	276 11.5	S 1 12.9
E 10	47 41.1	312 06.9 21.1		346 45.4 48.9		226 30.4 59.8		223 56.1 05.0		Alphard	218 20.3	S 8 34.7
S 11	62 43.6	327 06.0 21.1		1 46.0 49.2		241 32.8 59.8		238 58.5 05.0				
D 12	77 46.1	342 05.2 N24 21.0		16 46.6 N20 49.6		256 35.2 N 0 59.7		254 01.0 N 1 05.0		Alphecca	126 31.4	N26 46.8
A 13	92 48.5	357 04.3 21.0		31 47.2 50.0		271 37.6 59.7		269 03.4 04.9		Alpheratz	358 08.9	N28 59.0
Y 14	107 51.0	12 03.4 20.9		46 47.8 50.3		286 39.9 59.6		284 05.9 04.9		Altair	62 31.8	N 8 49.1
15	122 53.4	27 02.5 ·· 20.9		61 48.4 ·· 50.7		301 42.3 ·· 59.6		299 08.3 ·· 04.9		Ankaa	353 39.9	S42 24.3
16	137 55.9	42 01.6 20.9		76 49.1 51.1		316 44.7 59.5		314 10.8 04.9		Antares	112 55.9	S26 23.4
17	152 58.4	57 00.7 20.8		91 49.7 51.4		331 47.1 59.5		329 13.2 04.9				
18	168 00.8	71 59.8 N24 20.8		106 50.3 N20 51.8		346 49.5 N 0 59.4		344 15.7 N 1 04.9		Arcturus	146 17.8	N19 16.9
19	183 03.3	86 58.9 20.7		121 50.9 52.2		1 51.8 59.4		359 18.1 04.8		Atria	108 19.1	S68 59.7
20	198 05.8	101 58.0 20.7		136 51.5 52.6		16 54.2 59.3		14 20.6 04.8		Avior	234 28.5	S59 27.2
21	213 08.2	116 57.1 ·· 20.6		151 52.1 ·· 52.9		31 56.6 ·· 59.3		29 23.0 ·· 04.8		Bellatrix	278 58.6	N 6 19.9
22	228 10.7	131 56.2 20.6		166 52.7 53.3		46 59.0 59.2		44 25.5 04.8		Betelgeuse	271 28.1	N 7 24.2
23	243 13.2	146 55.3 20.5		181 53.3 53.6		62 01.4 59.2		59 27.9 04.8				
10 00	258 15.6	161 54.5 N24 20.5		196 53.9 N20 54.0		77 03.7 N 0 59.1		74 30.4 N 1 04.8		Canopus	264 07.5	S52 41.3
01	273 18.1	176 53.6 20.4		211 54.5 54.4		92 06.1 59.1		89 32.8 04.7		Capella	281 11.1	N45 58.7
02	288 20.6	191 52.7 20.4		226 55.1 54.7		107 08.5 59.0		104 35.3 04.7		Deneb	49 47.8	N45 12.6
03	303 23.0	206 51.8 ·· 20.3		241 55.7 ·· 55.1		122 10.9 ·· 59.0		119 37.7 ·· 04.7		Denebola	182 58.5	N14 40.7
04	318 25.5	221 50.9 20.3		256 56.3 55.5		137 13.2 58.9		134 40.2 04.7		Diphda	349 20.5	S18 05.3
05	333 27.9	236 50.0 20.2		271 56.9 55.8		152 15.6 58.9		149 42.6 04.7				
06	348 30.4	251 49.1 N24 20.1		286 57.5 N20 56.2		167 18.0 N 0 58.8		164 45.1 N 1 04.7		Dubhe	194 21.6	N61 51.4
07	3 32.9	266 48.2 20.1		301 58.1 56.6		182 20.4 58.8		179 47.5 04.6		Elnath	278 43.9	N28 35.4
W 08	18 35.3	281 47.3 20.0		316 58.7 56.9		197 22.8 58.7		194 49.9 04.6		Eltanin	90 57.0	N51 29.5
E 09	33 37.8	296 46.4 ·· 20.0		331 59.3 ·· 57.3		212 25.1 ·· 58.7		209 52.4 ·· 04.6		Enif	34 11.0	N 9 47.3
D 10	48 40.3	311 45.5 19.9		346 59.9 57.7		227 27.5 58.6		224 54.8 04.6		Fomalhaut	15 50.8	S29 43.2
N 11	63 42.7	326 44.7 19.8		2 00.5 58.0		242 29.9 58.6		239 57.3 04.6				
E 12	78 45.2	341 43.8 N24 19.8		17 01.1 N20 58.4		257 32.3 N 0 58.5		254 59.7 N 1 04.6		Gacrux	172 28.0	S57 00.7
S 13	93 47.7	356 42.9 19.7		32 01.7 58.7		272 34.6 58.5		270 02.2 04.5		Gienah	176 17.4	S17 26.4
D 14	108 50.1	11 42.0 19.6		47 02.3 59.1		287 37.0 58.4		285 04.6 04.5		Hadar	149 22.2	S60 17.1
A 15	123 52.6	26 41.1 ·· 19.6		62 02.9 ·· 59.5		302 39.4 ·· 58.4		300 07.1 ·· 04.5		Hamal	328 28.6	N23 22.3
Y 16	138 55.0	41 40.2 19.5		77 03.5 20 59.8		317 41.8 58.3		315 09.5 04.5		Kaus Aust.	84 15.8	S34 23.6
17	153 57.5	56 39.3 19.4		92 04.1 21 00.2		332 44.1 58.3		330 12.0 04.5				
18	169 00.0	71 38.4 N24 19.3		107 04.7 N21 00.5		347 46.5 N 0 58.2		345 14.4 N 1 04.4		Kochab	137 18.1	N74 14.2
19	184 02.4	86 37.5 19.3		122 05.3 00.9		2 48.9 58.2		0 16.9 04.4		Markab	14 02.7	N15 06.1
20	199 04.9	101 36.6 19.2		137 05.9 01.3		17 51.2 58.1		15 19.3 04.4		Menkar	314 40.9	N 4 00.9
21	214 07.4	116 35.8 ·· 19.1		152 06.5 ·· 01.6		32 53.6 ·· 58.1		30 21.8 ·· 04.4		Menkent	148 36.2	S36 16.8
22	229 09.8	131 34.9 19.0		167 07.1 02.0		47 56.0 58.0		45 24.2 04.4		Miaplacidus	221 45.3	S69 38.7
23	244 12.3	146 34.0 18.9		182 07.7 02.3		62 58.4 58.0		60 26.6 04.3				
11 00	259 14.8	161 33.1 N24 18.9		197 08.3 N21 02.7		78 00.7 N 0 57.9		75 29.1 N 1 04.3		Mirfak	309 15.9	N49 47.5
01	274 17.2	176 32.2 18.8		212 08.9 03.0		93 03.1 57.9		90 31.5 04.3		Nunki	76 28.2	S26 19.1
02	289 19.7	191 31.3 18.7		227 09.6 03.4		108 05.5 57.8		105 34.0 04.3		Peacock	53 57.2	S56 47.5
03	304 22.2	206 30.4 ·· 18.6		242 10.2 ·· 03.8		123 07.8 ·· 57.8		120 36.4 ·· 04.3		Pollux	243 57.9	N28 04.4
04	319 24.6	221 29.5 18.5		257 10.8 04.1		138 10.2 57.7		135 38.9 04.3		Procyon	245 25.6	N 5 16.4
05	334 27.1	236 28.6 18.4		272 11.4 04.5		153 12.6 57.7		150 41.3 04.2				
06	349 29.5	251 27.7 N24 18.3		287 12.0 N21 04.8		168 15.0 N 0 57.6		165 43.8 N 1 04.2		Rasalhague	96 28.8	N12 34.4
07	4 32.0	266 26.9 18.3		302 12.6 05.2		183 17.3 57.6		180 46.2 04.2		Regulus	208 09.6	N12 03.6
T 08	19 34.5	281 26.0 18.2		317 13.2 05.5		198 19.7 57.5		195 48.6 04.2		Rigel	281 35.9	S 8 13.5
H 09	34 36.9	296 25.1 ·· 18.1		332 13.8 ·· 05.9		213 22.1 ·· 57.5		210 51.1 ·· 04.2		Rigil Kent.	140 24.6	S60 45.6
U 10	49 39.4	311 24.2 18.0		347 14.4 06.2		228 24.4 57.4		225 53.5 04.1		Sabik	102 40.2	S15 42.1
R 11	64 41.9	326 23.3 17.9		2 15.0 06.6		243 26.8 57.4		240 56.0 04.1				
S 12	79 44.3	341 22.4 N24 17.8		17 15.6 N21 06.9		258 29.2 N 0 57.3		255 58.4 N 1 04.1		Schedar	350 08.6	N56 25.8
D 13	94 46.8	356 21.5 17.7		32 16.2 07.3		273 31.5 57.3		271 00.9 04.1		Shaula	96 54.7	S37 05.4
A 14	109 49.3	11 20.6 17.6		47 16.8 07.6		288 33.9 57.2		286 03.3 04.1		Sirius	258 55.6	S16 41.6
Y 15	124 51.7	26 19.8 ·· 17.5		62 17.4 ·· 08.0		303 36.3 ·· 57.2		301 05.8 ·· 04.0		Spica	158 56.9	S11 03.8
16	139 54.2	41 18.9 17.4		77 18.0 08.3		318 38.6 57.1		316 08.2 04.0		Suhail	223 10.7	S43 21.6
17	154 56.7	56 18.0 17.3		92 18.6 08.7		333 41.0 57.0		331 10.6 04.0				
18	169 59.1	71 17.1 N24 17.2		107 19.2 N21 09.1		348 43.4 N 0 57.0		346 13.1 N 1 04.0		Vega	80 55.1	N38 45.9
19	185 01.6	86 16.2 17.1		122 19.8 09.4		3 45.7 56.9		1 15.5 04.0		Zuben'ubi	137 32.2	S15 57.9
20	200 04.0	101 15.3 17.0		137 20.4 09.8		18 48.1 56.9		16 18.0 03.9			S.H.A.	Mer. Pass.
21	215 06.5	116 14.4 ·· 16.9		152 21.0 ·· 10.1		33 50.5 ·· 56.8		31 20.4 ·· 03.9		Venus	263 38.8	13 13
22	230 09.0	131 13.6 16.8		167 21.6 10.4		48 52.8 56.8		46 22.8 03.9		Mars	298 38.3	10 52
23	245 11.4	146 12.7 16.6		182 22.2 10.8		63 55.2 56.7		61 25.3 03.9		Jupiter	178 48.1	18 49
Mer. Pass.	h m 6 45.8	v −0.9 d 0.1		v 0.6 d 0.4		v 2.4 d 0.0		v 2.4 d 0.0		Saturn	176 14.7	18 59

G.M.T.	SUN G.H.A.	Dec.	MOON G.H.A.	v	Dec.	d	H.P.
d h	° '	° '	° '	'	° '	'	'
9 00	180 14.2	N22 54.3	92 06.5	13.3	N 9 55.2	10.1	55.9
01	195 14.1	54.5	106 38.8	13.3	9 45.1	10.1	55.9
02	210 14.0	54.7	121 11.1	13.3	9 35.0	10.2	55.9
03	225 13.8	.. 54.9	135 43.4	13.5	9 24.8	10.2	55.8
04	240 13.7	55.2	150 15.9	13.5	9 14.6	10.2	55.8
05	255 13.6	55.4	164 48.4	13.6	9 04.4	10.3	55.8
06	270 13.5	N22 55.6	179 21.0	13.6	N 8 54.1	10.3	55.7
07	285 13.4	55.8	193 53.6	13.7	8 43.8	10.3	55.7
T 08	300 13.2	56.0	208 26.3	13.7	8 33.5	10.3	55.7
U 09	315 13.1	.. 56.2	222 59.0	13.8	8 23.2	10.4	55.7
E 10	330 13.0	56.4	237 31.8	13.9	8 12.8	10.4	55.6
S 11	345 12.9	56.6	252 04.7	13.9	8 02.4	10.4	55.6
D 12	0 12.7	N22 56.8	266 37.6	13.9	N 7 52.0	10.4	55.6
A 13	15 12.6	57.0	281 10.5	14.1	7 41.6	10.5	55.5
Y 14	30 12.5	57.2	295 43.6	14.0	7 31.1	10.5	55.5
15	45 12.4	.. 57.4	310 16.6	14.2	7 20.7	10.6	55.5
16	60 12.3	57.6	324 49.8	14.1	7 10.1	10.5	55.5
17	75 12.1	57.8	339 22.9	14.3	6 59.6	10.5	55.4
18	90 12.0	N22 58.0	353 56.2	14.2	N 6 49.1	10.6	55.4
19	105 11.9	58.2	8 29.4	14.4	6 38.5	10.6	55.4
20	120 11.8	58.4	23 02.8	14.3	6 27.9	10.6	55.3
21	135 11.6	.. 58.6	37 36.1	14.5	6 17.3	10.6	55.3
22	150 11.5	58.8	52 09.6	14.4	6 06.7	10.6	55.3
23	165 11.4	59.0	66 43.0	14.5	5 56.1	10.7	55.3
10 00	180 11.3	N22 59.2	81 16.5	14.6	N 5 45.4	10.6	55.2
01	195 11.1	59.4	95 50.1	14.6	5 34.8	10.7	55.2
02	210 11.0	59.6	110 23.7	14.6	5 24.1	10.7	55.2
03	225 10.9	22 59.8	124 57.3	14.7	5 13.4	10.7	55.2
04	240 10.8	23 00.0	139 31.0	14.8	5 02.7	10.7	55.1
05	255 10.7	00.2	154 04.8	14.7	4 52.0	10.7	55.1
06	270 10.5	N23 00.4	168 38.5	14.8	N 4 41.3	10.8	55.1
W 07	285 10.4	00.6	183 12.3	14.9	4 30.5	10.7	55.1
E 08	300 10.3	00.8	197 46.2	14.8	4 19.8	10.8	55.0
D 09	315 10.2	.. 01.0	212 20.0	15.0	4 09.0	10.7	55.0
N 10	330 10.0	01.2	226 54.0	14.9	3 58.3	10.8	55.0
E 11	345 09.9	01.3	241 27.9	15.0	3 47.5	10.8	55.0
S 12	0 09.8	N23 01.5	256 01.9	15.0	N 3 36.7	10.8	55.0
D 13	15 09.7	01.7	270 35.9	15.1	3 25.9	10.8	54.9
A 14	30 09.5	01.9	285 10.0	15.0	3 15.1	10.8	54.9
Y 15	45 09.4	.. 02.1	299 44.0	15.2	3 04.3	10.8	54.9
16	60 09.3	02.3	314 18.2	15.1	2 53.5	10.8	54.9
17	75 09.2	02.5	328 52.3	15.2	2 42.7	10.8	54.9
18	90 09.0	N23 02.7	343 26.5	15.2	N 2 31.9	10.8	54.8
19	105 08.9	02.8	358 00.7	15.2	2 21.1	10.8	54.8
20	120 08.8	03.0	12 34.9	15.2	2 10.3	10.8	54.8
21	135 08.7	.. 03.2	27 09.1	15.3	1 59.5	10.8	54.8
22	150 08.5	03.4	41 43.4	15.3	1 48.7	10.8	54.8
23	165 08.4	03.6	56 17.7	15.3	1 37.9	10.9	54.7
11 00	180 08.3	N23 03.7	70 52.0	15.4	N 1 27.0	10.8	54.7
01	195 08.2	03.9	85 26.4	15.4	1 16.2	10.8	54.7
02	210 08.0	04.1	100 00.8	15.3	1 05.4	10.8	54.7
03	225 07.9	.. 04.3	114 35.1	15.5	0 54.6	10.8	54.7
04	240 07.8	04.5	129 09.6	15.4	0 43.8	10.8	54.6
05	255 07.7	04.6	143 44.0	15.4	0 33.0	10.8	54.6
06	270 07.5	N23 04.8	158 18.4	15.5	N 0 22.2	10.8	54.6
07	285 07.4	05.0	172 52.9	15.5	0 11.4	10.8	54.6
T 08	300 07.3	05.2	187 27.4	15.5	N 0 00.6	10.8	54.6
H 09	315 07.1	.. 05.3	202 01.9	15.5	S 0 10.2	10.7	54.5
U 10	330 07.0	05.5	216 36.4	15.5	0 20.9	10.8	54.5
R 11	345 06.9	05.7	231 10.9	15.5	0 31.7	10.8	54.5
S 12	0 06.8	N23 05.9	245 45.4	15.6	S 0 42.5	10.7	54.5
D 13	15 06.6	06.0	260 20.0	15.6	0 53.2	10.8	54.5
A 14	30 06.5	06.2	274 54.6	15.5	1 04.0	10.7	54.5
Y 15	45 06.4	.. 06.4	289 29.1	15.6	1 14.7	10.7	54.5
16	60 06.3	06.5	304 03.7	15.6	1 25.4	10.8	54.4
17	75 06.1	06.7	318 38.3	15.6	1 36.2	10.7	54.4
18	90 06.0	N23 06.9	333 12.9	15.6	S 1 46.9	10.7	54.4
19	105 05.9	07.0	347 47.5	15.6	1 57.6	10.6	54.4
20	120 05.8	07.2	2 22.1	15.6	2 08.2	10.7	54.4
21	135 05.6	.. 07.4	16 56.7	15.6	2 18.9	10.7	54.4
22	150 05.5	07.5	31 31.3	15.7	2 29.6	10.6	54.4
23	165 05.4	07.7	46 06.0	15.6	2 40.2	10.7	54.4
	S.D. 15.8	d 0.2	S.D. 15.1		15.0		14.9

Lat.	Twilight Naut.	Civil	Sunrise	Moonrise 9	10	11	12
°	h m	h m	h m	h m	h m	h m	h m
N 72	□	□	□	10 28	12 13	13 54	15 35
N 70	□	□	□	10 40	12 18	13 53	15 26
68	□	□	□	10 50	12 22	13 51	15 20
66	////	////	00 29	10 59	12 26	13 50	15 14
64	////	////	01 39	11 06	12 29	13 49	15 09
62	////	////	02 14	11 12	12 31	13 49	15 05
60	////	01 03	02 39	11 17	12 33	13 48	15 02
N 58	////	01 46	02 59	11 21	12 35	13 47	14 59
56	////	02 14	03 15	11 25	12 37	13 47	14 56
54	00 57	02 35	03 29	11 29	12 38	13 46	14 53
52	01 37	02 53	03 41	11 32	12 40	13 46	14 51
50	02 03	03 07	03 51	11 35	12 41	13 45	14 49
45	02 47	03 36	04 13	11 42	12 44	13 45	14 45
N 40	03 17	03 58	04 31	11 47	12 46	13 44	14 41
35	03 39	04 16	04 45	11 51	12 48	13 43	14 38
30	03 58	04 31	04 58	11 56	12 50	13 43	14 35
20	04 26	04 55	05 20	12 03	12 53	13 42	14 30
N 10	04 48	05 15	05 38	12 09	12 55	13 41	14 26
0	05 07	05 33	05 56	12 14	12 58	13 40	14 22
S 10	05 24	05 50	06 13	12 20	13 00	13 39	14 18
20	05 40	06 07	06 31	12 26	13 03	13 39	14 14
30	05 56	06 25	06 52	12 33	13 06	13 38	14 09
35	06 04	06 36	07 04	12 37	13 08	13 37	14 07
40	06 13	06 47	07 18	12 42	13 10	13 37	14 04
45	06 23	07 01	07 34	12 47	13 12	13 36	14 00
S 50	06 35	07 16	07 54	12 53	13 15	13 36	13 54
52	06 40	07 23	08 04	12 56	13 16	13 35	13 54
54	06 45	07 31	08 15	12 59	13 17	13 35	13 52
56	06 51	07 40	08 27	13 02	13 19	13 34	13 50
58	06 58	07 50	08 41	13 06	13 21	13 34	13 47
S 60	07 05	08 02	08 58	13 10	13 22	13 34	13 45

Lat.	Sunset	Twilight Civil	Naut.	Moonset 9	10	11	12
°	h m	h m	h m	h m	h m	h m	h m
N 72	□	□	□	01 59	01 45	01 32	01 20
N 70	□	□	□	01 44	01 38	01 31	01 24
68	□	□	□	01 33	01 31	01 30	01 28
66	23 37	////	////	01 23	01 26	01 29	01 31
64	22 21	////	////	01 15	01 22	01 28	01 33
62	21 46	////	////	01 08	01 18	01 27	01 36
60	21 20	22 58	////	01 02	01 15	01 26	01 38
N 58	21 01	22 14	////	00 56	01 12	01 26	01 39
56	20 44	21 46	////	00 52	01 09	01 25	01 41
54	20 31	21 24	23 04	00 47	01 07	01 25	01 42
52	20 19	21 07	22 22	00 43	01 05	01 24	01 43
50	20 08	20 52	21 56	00 40	01 03	01 24	01 45
45	19 46	20 23	21 12	00 32	00 58	01 23	01 47
N 40	19 28	20 01	20 42	00 25	00 55	01 22	01 49
35	19 13	19 43	20 19	00 20	00 52	01 22	01 51
30	19 01	19 28	20 01	00 15	00 49	01 21	01 53
20	18 39	19 03	19 33	00 06	00 44	01 20	01 56
N 10	18 20	18 43	19 10	24 40	00 40	01 19	01 58
0	18 03	18 25	18 52	24 36	00 36	01 18	02 00
S 10	17 46	18 09	18 35	24 31	00 31	01 17	02 03
20	17 28	17 52	18 19	24 27	00 27	01 17	02 05
30	17 07	17 33	18 03	24 22	00 22	01 15	02 08
35	16 55	17 23	17 54	24 19	00 19	01 15	02 10
40	16 41	17 11	17 45	24 16	00 16	01 14	02 11
45	16 24	16 58	17 35	24 12	00 12	01 13	02 14
S 50	16 04	16 42	17 24	24 07	00 07	01 12	02 16
52	15 54	16 35	17 19	24 05	00 05	01 12	02 17
54	15 44	16 27	17 13	24 02	00 02	01 11	02 19
56	15 31	16 18	17 07	24 00	00 00	01 10	02 20
58	15 17	16 08	17 00	23 57	25 10	01 10	02 22
S 60	15 00	15 57	16 53	23 54	25 09	01 09	02 23

Day	SUN Eqn. of Time 00h	12h	Mer. Pass.	MOON Mer. Pass. Upper	Lower	Age	Phase
	m s	m s	h m	h m	h m	d	
9	00 57	00 51	11 59	18 25	06 03	07	
10	00 45	00 39	11 59	19 08	06 47	08	◗
11	00 33	00 27	12 00	19 50	07 29	09	

1981 JUNE 12, 13, 14 (FRI., SAT., SUN.)

G.M.T.	ARIES G.H.A.	VENUS −3.3 G.H.A.	Dec.	MARS +1.7 G.H.A.	Dec.	JUPITER −1.7 G.H.A.	Dec.	SATURN +1.1 G.H.A.	Dec.	STARS Name	S.H.A.	Dec.
12 00	260 13.9	161 11.8 N24	16.5	197 22.8 N21	11.1	78 57.6 N 0	56.7	76 27.7 N 1	03.9	Acamar	315 37.2	S40 22.7
01	275 16.4	176 10.9	16.4	212 23.4	11.5	93 59.9	56.6	91 30.2	03.8	Achernar	335 45.2	S57 19.7
02	290 18.8	191 10.0	16.3	227 24.0	11.8	109 02.3	56.6	106 32.6	03.8	Acrux	173 36.5	S63 00.0
03	305 21.3	206 09.1 ··	16.2	242 24.6 ··	12.2	124 04.7 ··	56.5	121 35.1 ··	03.8	Adhara	255 32.1	S28 56.9
04	320 23.8	221 08.2	16.1	257 25.2	12.5	139 07.0	56.5	136 37.5	03.8	Aldebaran	291 17.8	N16 28.2
05	335 26.2	236 07.3	16.0	272 25.8	12.9	154 09.4	56.4	151 39.9	03.8			
06	350 28.7	251 06.5 N24	15.8	287 26.4 N21	13.2	169 11.8 N 0	56.3	166 42.4 N 1	03.7	Alioth	166 41.9	N56 04.0
07	5 31.1	266 05.6	15.7	302 27.0	13.6	184 14.1	56.3	181 44.8	03.7	Alkaid	153 17.8	N49 24.7
08	20 33.6	281 04.7	15.6	317 27.6	13.9	199 16.5	56.2	196 47.3	03.7	Al Na'ir	28 14.2	S47 02.9
F 09	35 36.1	296 03.8 ··	15.5	332 28.2 ··	14.3	214 18.8 ··	56.2	211 49.7 ··	03.7	Alnilam	276 11.5	S 1 12.9
R 10	50 38.5	311 02.9	15.3	347 28.8	14.6	229 21.2	56.1	226 52.1	03.7	Alphard	218 20.3	S 8 34.7
I 11	65 41.0	326 02.0	15.2	2 29.4	15.0	244 23.6	56.1	241 54.6	03.6			
D 12	80 43.5	341 01.2 N24	15.1	17 30.0 N21	15.3	259 25.9 N 0	56.0	256 57.0 N 1	03.6	Alphecca	126 31.4	N26 46.8
A 13	95 45.9	356 00.3	15.0	32 30.6	15.6	274 28.3	56.0	271 59.5	03.6	Alpheratz	358 08.9	N28 59.0
Y 14	110 48.4	10 59.4	14.8	47 31.2	16.0	289 30.7	55.9	287 01.9	03.6	Altair	62 31.8	N 8 49.1
15	125 50.9	25 58.5 ··	14.7	62 31.8 ··	16.3	304 33.0 ··	55.8	302 04.3 ··	03.5	Ankaa	353 39.9	S42 24.3
16	140 53.3	40 57.6	14.6	77 32.4	16.7	319 35.4	55.8	317 06.8	03.5	Antares	112 55.9	S26 23.4
17	155 55.8	55 56.7	14.4	92 33.0	17.0	334 37.7	55.7	332 09.2	03.5			
18	170 58.3	70 55.9 N24	14.3	107 33.6 N21	17.4	349 40.1 N 0	55.7	347 11.6 N 1	03.5	Arcturus	146 17.8	N19 16.9
19	186 00.7	85 55.0	14.2	122 34.2	17.7	4 42.5	55.6	2 14.1	03.5	Atria	108 19.1	S68 59.7
20	201 03.2	100 54.1	14.0	137 34.8	18.0	19 44.8	55.6	17 16.5	03.4	Avior	234 28.5	S59 27.2
21	216 05.6	115 53.2 ··	13.9	152 35.4 ··	18.4	34 47.2 ··	55.5	32 19.0 ··	03.4	Bellatrix	278 58.6	N 6 19.9
22	231 08.1	130 52.3	13.8	167 36.0	18.7	49 49.5	55.5	47 21.4	03.4	Betelgeuse	271 28.1	N 7 24.2
23	246 10.6	145 51.4	13.6	182 36.6	19.1	64 51.9	55.4	62 23.8	03.4			
13 00	261 13.0	160 50.6 N24	13.5	197 37.2 N21	19.4	79 54.3 N 0	55.3	77 26.3 N 1	03.3	Canopus	264 07.5	S52 41.3
01	276 15.5	175 49.7	13.3	212 37.8	19.7	94 56.6	55.3	92 28.7	03.3	Capella	281 11.1	N45 58.7
02	291 18.0	190 48.8	13.2	227 38.4	20.1	109 59.0	55.2	107 31.1	03.3	Deneb	49 47.8	N45 12.6
03	306 20.4	205 47.9 ··	13.1	242 39.0 ··	20.4	125 01.3 ··	55.2	122 33.6 ··	03.3	Denebola	182 58.5	N14 40.7
04	321 22.9	220 47.0	12.9	257 39.6	20.8	140 03.7	55.1	137 36.0	03.3	Diphda	349 20.5	S18 05.3
05	336 25.4	235 46.1	12.8	272 40.2	21.1	155 06.0	55.1	152 38.5	03.2			
06	351 27.8	250 45.3 N24	12.6	287 40.8 N21	21.4	170 08.4 N 0	55.0	167 40.9 N 1	03.2	Dubhe	194 21.6	N61 51.4
07	6 30.3	265 44.4	12.5	302 41.4	21.8	185 10.8	54.9	182 43.3	03.2	Elnath	278 43.9	N28 35.4
S 08	21 32.8	280 43.5	12.3	317 42.0	22.1	200 13.1	54.9	197 45.8	03.2	Eltanin	90 57.0	N51 29.5
A 09	36 35.2	295 42.6 ··	12.2	332 42.6 ··	22.5	215 15.5 ··	54.8	212 48.2 ··	03.1	Enif	34 10.9	N 9 47.3
T 10	51 37.7	310 41.7	12.0	347 43.2	22.8	230 17.8	54.8	227 50.6	03.1	Fomalhaut	15 50.8	S29 43.2
U 11	66 40.1	325 40.9	11.8	2 43.8	23.1	245 20.2	54.7	242 53.1	03.1			
R 12	81 42.6	340 40.0 N24	11.7	17 44.4 N21	23.5	260 22.5 N 0	54.7	257 55.5 N 1	03.1	Gacrux	172 28.0	S57 00.7
D 13	96 45.1	355 39.1	11.5	32 45.0	23.8	275 24.9	54.6	272 57.9	03.1	Gienah	176 17.4	S17 26.4
A 14	111 47.5	10 38.2	11.4	47 45.6	24.1	290 27.2	54.5	288 00.4	03.0	Hadar	149 22.2	S60 17.2
Y 15	126 50.0	25 37.3 ··	11.2	62 46.2 ··	24.5	305 29.6 ··	54.5	303 02.8 ··	03.0	Hamal	328 28.6	N23 22.3
16	141 52.5	40 36.5	11.1	77 46.8	24.8	320 32.0	54.4	318 05.2	03.0	Kaus Aust.	84 15.8	S34 23.6
17	156 54.9	55 35.6	10.9	92 47.4	25.1	335 34.3	54.4	333 07.7	03.0			
18	171 57.4	70 34.7 N24	10.7	107 48.0 N21	25.5	350 36.7 N 0	54.3	348 10.1 N 1	02.9	Kochab	137 18.1	N74 14.2
19	186 59.9	85 33.8	10.6	122 48.6	25.8	5 39.0	54.2	3 12.6	02.9	Markab	14 02.6	N15 06.1
20	202 02.3	100 32.9	10.4	137 49.2	26.1	20 41.4	54.2	18 15.0	02.9	Menkar	314 40.9	N 4 00.9
21	217 04.8	115 32.1 ··	10.2	152 49.8 ··	26.5	35 43.7 ··	54.1	33 17.4 ··	02.9	Menkent	148 36.2	S36 16.8
22	232 07.2	130 31.2	10.1	167 50.4	26.8	50 46.1	54.1	48 19.9	02.8	Miaplacidus	221 45.4	S69 38.7
23	247 09.7	145 30.3	09.9	182 51.0	27.1	65 48.4	54.0	63 22.3	02.8			
14 00	262 12.2	160 29.4 N24	09.7	197 51.6 N21	27.5	80 50.8 N 0	53.9	78 24.7 N 1	02.8	Mirfak	309 15.8	N49 47.5
01	277 14.6	175 28.5	09.6	212 52.2	27.8	95 53.1	53.9	93 27.2	02.8	Nunki	76 28.2	S26 19.1
02	292 17.1	190 27.7	09.4	227 52.8	28.1	110 55.5	53.8	108 29.6	02.7	Peacock	53 57.2	S56 47.5
03	307 19.6	205 26.8 ··	09.2	242 53.4 ··	28.5	125 57.8 ··	53.8	123 32.0 ··	02.7	Pollux	243 57.9	N28 04.4
04	322 22.0	220 25.9	09.0	257 54.0	28.8	141 00.2	53.7	138 34.5	02.7	Procyon	245 25.6	N 5 16.4
05	337 24.5	235 25.0	08.9	272 54.6	29.1	156 02.5	53.6	153 36.9	02.7			
06	352 27.0	250 24.2 N24	08.7	287 55.2 N21	29.4	171 04.9 N 0	53.6	168 39.3 N 1	02.7	Rasalhague	96 28.8	N12 34.4
07	7 29.4	265 23.3	08.5	302 55.8	29.8	186 07.2	53.5	183 41.8	02.6	Regulus	208 09.6	N12 03.6
08	22 31.9	280 22.4	08.3	317 56.4	30.1	201 09.6	53.5	198 44.2	02.6	Rigel	281 35.9	S 8 13.5
S 09	37 34.4	295 21.5 ··	08.1	332 57.0 ··	30.4	216 11.9 ··	53.4	213 46.6 ··	02.6	Rigil Kent.	140 24.7	S60 45.6
U 10	52 36.8	310 20.7	07.9	347 57.6	30.8	231 14.3	53.3	228 49.1	02.6	Sabik	102 40.2	S15 42.1
N 11	67 39.3	325 19.8	07.8	2 58.2	31.1	246 16.6	53.3	243 51.5	02.5			
D 12	82 41.7	340 18.9 N24	07.6	17 58.8 N21	31.4	261 19.0 N 0	53.2	258 53.9 N 1	02.5	Schedar	350 08.6	N56 25.8
A 13	97 44.2	355 18.0	07.4	32 59.4	31.7	276 21.3	53.2	273 56.3	02.5	Shaula	96 54.7	S37 05.4
Y 14	112 46.7	10 17.1	07.2	48 00.0	32.1	291 23.7	53.1	288 58.8	02.5	Sirius	258 55.6	S16 41.5
15	127 49.1	25 16.3 ··	07.0	63 00.6 ··	32.4	306 26.0 ··	53.0	304 01.2 ··	02.4	Spica	158 56.9	S11 03.8
16	142 51.6	40 15.4	06.8	78 01.2	32.7	321 28.4	53.0	319 03.6	02.4	Suhail	223 10.7	S43 21.6
17	157 54.1	55 14.5	06.6	93 01.8	33.0	336 30.7	52.9	334 06.1	02.4			
18	172 56.5	70 13.6 N24	06.4	108 02.4 N21	33.4	351 33.1 N 0	52.9	349 08.5 N 1	02.4	Vega	80 55.1	N38 45.9
19	187 59.0	85 12.8	06.2	123 03.0	33.7	6 35.4	52.8	4 10.9	02.3	Zuben'ubi	137 32.2	S15 57.9
20	203 01.5	100 11.9	06.0	138 03.6	34.0	21 37.8	52.7	19 13.4	02.3		S.H.A.	Mer. Pass.
21	218 03.9	115 11.0 ··	05.8	153 04.2 ··	34.3	36 40.1 ··	52.7	34 15.8 ··	02.3	Venus	259 37.5	13 17
22	233 06.4	130 10.2	05.7	168 04.8	34.7	51 42.5	52.6	49 18.2	02.3	Mars	296 24.2	10 49
23	248 08.9	145 09.3	05.5	183 05.4	35.0	66 44.8	52.5	64 20.7	02.2	Jupiter	178 41.2	18 37
Mer. Pass. 6 34.1		v −0.9 d 0.2		v 0.6 d 0.3		v 2.4 d 0.1		v 2.4 d 0.0		Saturn	176 13.2	18 47

G.M.T.	SUN G.H.A.	SUN Dec.	MOON G.H.A.	v	MOON Dec.	d	H.P.
12 00	180 05.2	N23 07.9	60 40.6	15.6	S 2 50.8	10.6	54.3
01	195 05.1	08.0	75 15.2	15.7	3 01.4	10.6	54.3
02	210 05.0	08.2	89 49.9	15.6	3 12.0	10.6	54.3
03	225 04.9	.. 08.3	104 24.5	15.6	3 22.6	10.6	54.3
04	240 04.7	08.5	118 59.1	15.7	3 33.2	10.5	54.3
05	255 04.6	08.7	133 33.8	15.6	3 43.7	10.5	54.3
06	270 04.5	N23 08.8	148 08.4	15.6	S 3 54.2	10.6	54.3
07	285 04.4	09.0	162 43.0	15.6	4 04.8	10.4	54.3
08	300 04.2	09.1	177 17.6	15.7	4 15.2	10.5	54.2
F 09	315 04.1	.. 09.3	191 52.3	15.6	4 25.7	10.5	54.2
R 10	330 04.0	09.5	206 26.9	15.6	4 36.2	10.4	54.2
I 11	345 03.8	09.6	221 01.5	15.6	4 46.6	10.4	54.2
D 12	0 03.7	N23 09.8	235 36.1	15.6	S 4 57.0	10.4	54.2
A 13	15 03.6	09.9	250 10.7	15.6	5 07.4	10.3	54.2
Y 14	30 03.5	10.1	264 45.3	15.5	5 17.7	10.4	54.2
15	45 03.3	.. 10.2	279 19.8	15.6	5 28.1	10.3	54.2
16	60 03.2	10.4	293 54.4	15.6	5 38.4	10.3	54.2
17	75 03.1	10.5	308 29.0	15.5	5 48.7	10.3	54.2
18	90 02.9	N23 10.7	323 03.5	15.5	S 5 59.0	10.2	54.2
19	105 02.8	10.8	337 38.0	15.6	6 09.2	10.2	54.2
20	120 02.7	11.0	352 12.6	15.5	6 19.4	10.2	54.1
21	135 02.6	.. 11.1	6 47.1	15.5	6 29.6	10.2	54.1
22	150 02.4	11.3	21 21.6	15.4	6 39.8	10.1	54.1
23	165 02.3	11.4	35 56.0	15.5	6 49.9	10.1	54.1
13 00	180 02.2	N23 11.6	50 30.5	15.5	S 7 00.0	10.0	54.1
01	195 02.0	11.7	65 05.0	15.4	7 10.1	10.1	54.1
02	210 01.9	11.9	79 39.4	15.4	7 20.1	10.0	54.1
03	225 01.8	.. 12.0	94 13.8	15.4	7 30.1	10.0	54.1
04	240 01.7	12.1	108 48.2	15.4	7 40.1	10.0	54.1
05	255 01.5	12.3	123 22.6	15.3	7 50.1	9.9	54.1
06	270 01.4	N23 12.4	137 56.9	15.4	S 8 00.0	9.9	54.1
07	285 01.3	12.6	152 31.3	15.3	8 09.9	9.9	54.1
S 08	300 01.1	12.7	167 05.6	15.3	8 19.8	9.8	54.1
A 09	315 01.0	.. 12.8	181 39.9	15.3	8 29.6	9.8	54.1
T 10	330 00.9	13.0	196 14.2	15.2	8 39.4	9.7	54.1
U 11	345 00.8	13.1	210 48.4	15.2	8 49.1	9.7	54.1
R 12	0 00.6	N23 13.3	225 22.6	15.2	S 8 58.8	9.7	54.1
D 13	15 00.5	13.4	239 56.8	15.2	9 08.5	9.7	54.1
A 14	30 00.4	13.5	254 31.0	15.2	9 18.2	9.6	54.1
Y 15	45 00.2	.. 13.7	269 05.2	15.1	9 27.8	9.6	54.1
16	60 00.1	13.8	283 39.3	15.1	9 37.4	9.5	54.0
17	75 00.0	13.9	298 13.4	15.1	9 46.9	9.5	54.0
18	89 59.8	N23 14.1	312 47.5	15.0	S 9 56.4	9.4	54.0
19	104 59.7	14.2	327 21.5	15.0	10 05.8	9.3	54.0
20	119 59.6	14.3	341 55.5	15.0	10 15.3	9.3	54.0
21	134 59.5	.. 14.5	356 29.5	15.0	10 24.6	9.4	54.0
22	149 59.3	14.6	11 03.5	14.9	10 34.0	9.3	54.0
23	164 59.2	14.7	25 37.4	14.9	10 43.3	9.2	54.0
14 00	179 59.1	N23 14.9	40 11.3	14.9	S10 52.5	9.2	54.0
01	194 58.9	15.0	54 45.2	14.8	11 01.7	9.2	54.0
02	209 58.8	15.1	69 19.0	14.8	11 10.9	9.1	54.0
03	224 58.7	.. 15.2	83 52.8	14.8	11 20.0	9.1	54.0
04	239 58.5	15.4	98 26.6	14.7	11 29.1	9.0	54.0
05	254 58.4	15.5	113 00.3	14.7	11 38.1	9.0	54.0
06	269 58.3	N23 15.6	127 34.0	14.7	S11 47.1	8.9	54.0
07	284 58.1	15.7	142 07.7	14.6	11 56.0	8.9	54.0
08	299 58.0	15.9	156 41.3	14.6	12 04.9	8.8	54.0
S 09	314 57.9	.. 16.0	171 14.9	14.6	12 13.7	8.8	54.0
U 10	329 57.8	16.1	185 48.5	14.5	12 22.5	8.8	54.0
N 11	344 57.6	16.2	200 22.0	14.5	12 31.3	8.7	54.0
D 12	359 57.5	N23 16.3	214 55.5	14.4	S12 40.0	8.6	54.1
A 13	14 57.4	16.5	229 28.9	14.5	12 48.6	8.6	54.1
Y 14	29 57.2	16.6	244 02.4	14.3	12 57.2	8.5	54.1
15	44 57.1	.. 16.7	258 35.7	14.4	13 05.7	8.5	54.1
16	59 57.0	16.8	273 09.1	14.3	13 14.2	8.4	54.1
17	74 56.8	16.9	287 42.4	14.2	13 22.6	8.4	54.1
18	89 56.7	N23 17.1	302 15.6	14.3	S13 31.0	8.3	54.1
19	104 56.6	17.2	316 48.9	14.1	13 39.3	8.3	54.1
20	119 56.4	17.3	331 22.0	14.2	13 47.6	8.2	54.1
21	134 56.3	.. 17.4	345 55.2	14.1	13 55.8	8.1	54.1
22	149 56.2	17.5	0 28.3	14.0	14 03.9	8.1	54.1
23	164 56.1	17.6	15 01.3	14.0	14 12.0	8.1	54.1
	S.D. 15.8	d 0.1	S.D. 14.8		14.7		14.7

Moonrise

Lat.	Twilight Naut.	Twilight Civil	Sunrise	12	13	14	15
N 72	□	□	□	15 35	17 18	19 09	21 23
N 70	□	□	□	15 26	17 01	18 40	20 26
68	□	□	□	15 20	16 49	18 19	19 53
66	□	□	□	15 14	16 38	18 03	19 29
64	////	////	01 35	15 09	16 29	17 49	19 10
62	////	////	02 11	15 05	16 22	17 38	18 54
60	////	00 56	02 37	15 02	16 15	17 29	18 42
N 58	////	01 43	02 57	14 59	16 10	17 20	18 31
56	////	02 12	03 14	14 56	16 04	17 13	18 21
54	00 52	02 34	03 28	14 53	16 00	17 07	18 13
52	01 35	02 51	03 40	14 51	15 56	17 01	18 05
50	02 01	03 06	03 50	14 49	15 52	16 55	17 58
45	02 46	03 35	04 13	14 45	15 44	16 44	17 44
N 40	03 16	03 58	04 30	14 41	15 38	16 35	17 32
35	03 39	04 16	04 45	14 38	15 32	16 27	17 22
30	03 58	04 31	04 58	14 35	15 27	16 20	17 13
20	04 26	04 56	05 20	14 30	15 19	16 08	16 58
N 10	04 49	05 16	05 39	14 26	15 11	15 57	16 45
0	05 08	05 34	05 56	14 22	15 04	15 47	16 32
S 10	05 24	05 51	06 14	14 18	14 57	15 38	16 20
20	05 40	06 08	06 32	14 14	14 50	15 27	16 07
30	05 57	06 27	06 53	14 09	14 42	15 16	15 52
35	06 05	06 37	07 05	14 07	14 37	15 09	15 44
40	06 15	06 49	07 19	14 04	14 31	15 01	15 34
45	06 25	07 02	07 36	14 00	14 25	14 52	15 22
S 50	06 37	07 18	07 56	13 56	14 18	14 42	15 09
52	06 42	07 25	08 06	13 54	14 14	14 37	15 02
54	06 47	07 33	08 17	13 52	14 11	14 31	14 55
56	06 53	07 42	08 30	13 50	14 06	14 25	14 47
58	07 00	07 52	08 44	13 47	14 02	14 18	14 39
S 60	07 07	08 04	09 01	13 45	13 57	14 11	14 28

Moonset

Lat.	Sunset	Twilight Civil	Twilight Naut.	12	13	14	15
N 72	□	□	□	01 20	01 07	00 52	{ 00 32 / 23 51 }
N 70	□	□	□	01 24	01 18	01 10	01 01
68	□	□	□	01 28	01 26	01 24	01 23
66	□	□	□	01 31	01 33	01 36	01 41
64	22 26	////	////	01 33	01 39	01 46	01 55
62	21 49	////	////	01 36	01 44	01 55	02 07
60	21 23	23 05	////	01 38	01 49	02 02	02 17
N 58	21 03	22 18	////	01 39	01 53	02 08	02 26
56	20 47	21 49	////	01 41	01 57	02 14	02 34
54	20 33	21 27	23 10	01 42	02 00	02 19	02 41
52	20 21	21 09	22 26	01 43	02 03	02 24	02 48
50	20 11	20 54	21 59	01 45	02 06	02 28	02 53
45	19 47	20 25	21 14	01 47	02 11	02 37	03 06
N 40	19 30	20 02	20 44	01 49	02 16	02 45	03 16
35	19 15	19 44	20 21	01 51	02 21	02 52	03 25
30	19 02	19 29	20 02	01 53	02 24	02 57	03 33
20	18 40	19 04	19 34	01 56	02 31	03 08	03 46
N 10	18 21	18 44	19 11	01 58	02 37	03 16	03 58
0	18 04	18 26	18 52	02 00	02 42	03 25	04 09
S 10	17 46	18 09	18 35	02 03	02 48	03 33	04 20
20	17 28	17 52	18 19	02 05	02 53	03 42	04 32
30	17 07	17 33	18 03	02 08	03 00	03 52	04 45
35	16 55	17 23	17 54	02 10	03 04	03 58	04 53
40	16 41	17 11	17 45	02 11	03 08	04 05	05 02
45	16 24	16 58	17 35	02 14	03 13	04 13	05 13
S 50	16 03	16 42	17 23	02 16	03 19	04 23	05 26
52	15 54	16 34	17 18	02 17	03 22	04 27	05 32
54	15 43	16 26	17 12	02 19	03 25	04 32	05 38
56	15 30	16 17	17 06	02 20	03 29	04 37	05 46
58	15 15	16 07	17 00	02 22	03 33	04 43	05 54
S 60	14 58	15 56	16 52	02 23	03 37	04 50	06 03

Day	SUN Eqn. of Time 00h	SUN Eqn. of Time 12h	SUN Mer. Pass.	MOON Mer. Pass. Upper	MOON Mer. Pass. Lower	Age	Phase
	m s	m s	h m	h m	h m	d	
12	00 21	00 15	12 00	20 32	08 11	10	
13	00 09	00 03	12 00	21 14	08 53	11	
14	00 03	00 10	12 00	21 58	09 36	12	◑

G.M.T.	ARIES G.H.A.	VENUS −3.3 G.H.A.	Dec.	MARS +1.7 G.H.A.	Dec.	JUPITER −1.6 G.H.A.	Dec.	SATURN +1.1 G.H.A.	Dec.	STARS Name	S.H.A.	Dec.
15 00	263 11.3	160 08.4	N24 05.3	198 06.0	N21 35.3	81 47.1	N 0 52.5	79 23.1	N 1 02.2	Acamar	315 37.2	S40 22.7
01	273 13.8	175 07.5	05.1	213 06.6	35.6	96 49.5	52.4	94 25.5	02.2	Achernar	335 45.2	S57 19.7
02	293 16.2	190 06.7	04.8	228 07.2	35.9	111 51.8	52.4	109 27.9	02.2	Acrux	173 36.5	S63 00.0
03	308 18.7	205 05.8 ··	04.6	243 07.8 ··	36.3	126 54.2 ··	52.3	124 30.4 ··	02.1	Adhara	255 32.1	S28 56.9
04	323 21.2	220 04.9	04.4	258 08.4	36.6	141 56.5	52.2	139 32.8	02.1	Aldebaran	291 17.8	N16 28.2
05	338 23.6	235 04.0	04.2	273 09.0	36.9	156 58.9	52.2	154 35.2	02.1			
06	353 26.1	250 03.2	N24 04.0	288 09.6	N21 37.2	172 01.2	N 0 52.1	169 37.7	N 1 02.0	Alioth	166 41.9	N56 04.0
M 07	8 28.6	265 02.3	03.8	303 10.2	37.6	187 03.6	52.0	184 40.1	02.0	Alkaid	153 17.9	N49 24.7
O 08	23 31.0	280 01.4	03.6	318 10.7	37.9	202 05.9	52.0	199 42.5	02.0	Al Na'ir	28 14.1	S47 02.9
N 09	38 33.5	295 00.6 ··	03.4	333 11.3 ··	38.2	217 08.2 ··	51.9	214 44.9 ··	02.0	Alnilam	276 11.5	S 1 12.9
D 10	53 36.0	309 59.7	03.2	348 11.9	38.5	232 10.6	51.9	229 47.4	01.9	Alphard	218 20.3	S 8 34.7
A 11	68 38.4	324 58.8	03.0	3 12.5	38.8	247 12.9	51.8	244 49.8	01.9			
Y 12	83 40.9	339 57.9	N24 02.8	18 13.1	N21 39.1	262 15.3	N 0 51.7	259 52.2	N 1 01.9	Alphecca	126 31.4	N26 46.8
13	98 43.4	354 57.1	02.5	33 13.7	39.5	277 17.6	51.7	274 54.7	01.9	Alpheratz	358 08.8	N28 59.0
14	113 45.8	9 56.2	02.3	48 14.3	39.8	292 20.0	51.6	289 57.1	01.8	Altair	62 31.8	N 8 49.1
15	128 48.3	24 55.3 ··	02.1	63 14.9 ··	40.1	307 22.3 ··	51.5	304 59.5 ··	01.8	Ankaa	353 39.8	S42 24.3
16	143 50.7	39 54.5	01.9	78 15.5	40.4	322 24.6	51.5	320 01.9	01.8	Antares	112 55.9	S26 23.4
17	158 53.2	54 53.6	01.7	93 16.1	40.7	337 27.0	51.4	335 04.4	01.8			
18	173 55.7	69 52.7	N24 01.4	108 16.7	N21 41.1	352 29.3	N 0 51.3	350 06.8	N 1 01.7	Arcturus	146 17.8	N19 16.9
19	188 58.1	84 51.9	01.2	123 17.3	41.4	7 31.7	51.3	5 09.2	01.7	Atria	108 19.1	S68 59.7
20	204 00.6	99 51.0	01.0	138 17.9	41.7	22 34.0	51.2	20 11.6	01.7	Avior	234 28.5	S59 27.2
21	219 03.1	114 50.1 ··	00.8	153 18.5 ··	42.0	37 36.3 ··	51.1	35 14.1 ··	01.7	Bellatrix	278 58.6	N 6 19.9
22	234 05.5	129 49.2	00.5	168 19.1	42.3	52 38.7	51.1	50 16.5	01.6	Betelgeuse	271 28.1	N 7 24.2
23	249 08.0	144 48.4	00.3	183 19.7	42.6	67 41.0	51.0	65 18.9	01.6			
16 00	264 10.5	159 47.5	N24 00.1	198 20.3	N21 42.9	82 43.4	N 0 51.0	80 21.3	N 1 01.6	Canopus	264 07.5	S52 41.2
01	279 12.9	174 46.6	23 59.8	213 20.9	43.3	97 45.7	50.9	95 23.8	01.5	Capella	281 11.0	N45 58.7
02	294 15.4	189 45.8	59.6	228 21.5	43.6	112 48.0	50.8	110 26.2	01.5	Deneb	49 47.8	N45 12.6
03	309 17.8	204 44.9 ··	59.4	243 22.1 ··	43.9	127 50.4 ··	50.8	125 28.6 ··	01.5	Denebola	182 58.5	N14 40.7
04	324 20.3	219 44.0	59.1	258 22.7	44.2	142 52.7	50.7	140 31.1	01.5	Diphda	349 20.5	S18 05.3
05	339 22.8	234 43.2	58.9	273 23.3	44.5	157 55.1	50.6	155 33.5	01.4			
06	354 25.2	249 42.3	N23 58.7	288 23.9	N21 44.8	172 57.4	N 0 50.6	170 35.9	N 1 01.4	Dubhe	194 21.7	N61 51.4
T 07	9 27.7	264 41.4	58.4	303 24.5	45.1	187 59.7	50.5	185 38.3	01.4	Elnath	278 43.9	N28 35.4
U 08	24 30.2	279 40.6	58.2	318 25.1	45.4	203 02.1	50.4	200 40.8	01.4	Eltanin	90 57.0	N51 29.5
E 09	39 32.6	294 39.7 ··	57.9	333 25.7 ··	45.8	218 04.4 ··	50.4	215 43.2 ··	01.3	Enif	34 10.9	N 9 47.3
S 10	54 35.1	309 38.8	57.7	348 26.3	46.1	233 06.7	50.3	230 45.6	01.3	Fomalhaut	15 50.8	S29 43.2
D 11	69 37.6	324 38.0	57.5	3 26.9	46.4	248 09.1	50.2	245 48.0	01.3			
A 12	84 40.0	339 37.1	N23 57.2	18 27.5	N21 46.7	263 11.4	N 0 50.2	260 50.4	N 1 01.2	Gacrux	172 28.0	S57 00.7
Y 13	99 42.5	354 36.2	57.0	33 28.1	47.0	278 13.8	50.1	275 52.9	01.2	Gienah	176 17.4	S17 26.3
14	114 45.0	9 35.4	56.7	48 28.7	47.3	293 16.1	50.0	290 55.3	01.2	Hadar	149 22.2	S60 17.2
15	129 47.4	24 34.5 ··	56.5	63 29.3 ··	47.6	308 18.4 ··	50.0	305 57.7 ··	01.2	Hamal	328 28.6	N23 22.3
16	144 49.9	39 33.7	56.2	78 29.9	47.9	323 20.8	49.9	321 00.1	01.1	Kaus Aust.	84 15.8	S34 23.6
17	159 52.3	54 32.8	56.0	93 30.5	48.2	338 23.1	49.8	336 02.6	01.1			
18	174 54.8	69 31.9	N23 55.7	108 31.1	N21 48.5	353 25.4	N 0 49.8	351 05.0	N 1 01.1	Kochab	137 18.1	N74 14.2
19	189 57.3	84 31.1	55.5	123 31.7	48.8	8 27.8	49.7	6 07.4	01.0	Markab	14 02.6	N15 06.1
20	204 59.7	99 30.2	55.2	138 32.3	49.1	23 30.1	49.6	21 09.8	01.0	Menkar	314 40.9	N 4 00.9
21	220 02.2	114 29.3 ··	55.0	153 32.9 ··	49.5	38 32.4 ··	49.6	36 12.3 ··	01.0	Menkent	148 36.2	S36 16.8
22	235 04.7	129 28.5	54.7	168 33.5	49.8	53 34.8	49.5	51 14.7	01.0	Miaplacidus	221 45.4	S69 38.7
23	250 07.1	144 27.6	54.4	183 34.0	50.1	68 37.1	49.4	66 17.1	00.9			
17 00	265 09.6	159 26.8	N23 54.2	198 34.6	N21 50.4	83 39.4	N 0 49.4	81 19.5	N 1 00.9	Mirfak	309 15.8	N49 47.5
01	280 12.1	174 25.9	53.9	213 35.2	50.7	98 41.8	49.3	96 21.9	00.9	Nunki	76 28.2	S26 19.1
02	295 14.5	189 25.0	53.7	228 35.8	51.0	113 44.1	49.2	111 24.4	00.8	Peacock	53 57.1	S56 47.5
03	310 17.0	204 24.2 ··	53.4	243 36.4 ··	51.3	128 46.4 ··	49.2	126 26.8 ··	00.8	Pollux	243 57.9	N28 04.3
04	325 19.5	219 23.3	53.1	258 37.0	51.6	143 48.8	49.1	141 29.2	00.8	Procyon	245 25.6	N 5 16.4
05	340 21.9	234 22.4	52.9	273 37.6	51.9	158 51.1	49.0	156 31.6	00.8			
06	355 24.4	249 21.6	N23 52.6	288 38.2	N21 52.2	173 53.4	N 0 48.9	171 34.1	N 1 00.7	Rasalhague	96 28.8	N12 34.5
W 07	10 26.8	264 20.7	52.3	303 38.8	52.5	188 55.8	48.9	186 36.5	00.7	Regulus	208 09.6	N12 03.6
E 08	25 29.3	279 19.9	52.1	318 39.4	52.8	203 58.1	48.8	201 38.9	00.7	Rigel	281 35.9	S 8 13.5
D 09	40 31.7	294 19.0 ··	51.8	333 40.0 ··	53.1	219 00.4 ··	48.7	216 41.3 ··	00.6	Rigil Kent.	140 24.7	S60 45.6
N 10	55 34.2	309 18.1	51.5	348 40.6	53.4	234 02.7	48.7	231 43.7	00.6	Sabik	102 40.2	S15 42.1
E 11	70 36.7	324 17.3	51.3	3 41.2	53.7	249 05.1	48.6	246 46.2	00.6			
S 12	85 39.2	339 16.4	N23 51.0	18 41.8	N21 54.0	264 07.4	N 0 48.5	261 48.6	N 1 00.5	Schedar	350 08.6	N56 25.8
D 13	100 41.6	354 15.6	50.7	33 42.4	54.3	279 09.7	48.5	276 51.0	00.5	Shaula	96 54.7	S37 05.4
A 14	115 44.1	9 14.7	50.4	48 43.0	54.6	294 12.1	48.4	291 53.4	00.5	Sirius	258 55.6	S16 41.5
Y 15	130 46.6	24 13.9 ··	50.2	63 43.6 ··	54.9	309 14.4 ··	48.3	306 55.8 ··	00.5	Spica	158 56.9	S11 03.8
16	145 49.0	39 13.0	49.9	78 44.2	55.2	324 16.7	48.3	321 58.3	00.4	Suhail	223 10.7	S43 21.6
17	160 51.5	54 12.1	49.6	93 44.8	55.5	339 19.0	48.2	337 00.7	00.4			
18	175 53.9	69 11.3	N23 49.3	108 45.4	N21 55.8	354 21.4	N 0 48.1	352 03.1	N 1 00.4	Vega	80 55.1	N38 46.0
19	190 56.4	84 10.4	49.0	123 46.0	56.1	9 23.7	48.0	7 05.5	00.3	Zuben'ubi	137 32.2	S15 57.9
20	205 58.9	99 09.6	48.8	138 46.6	56.4	24 26.0	48.0	22 07.9	00.3			
21	221 01.3	114 08.7 ··	48.5	153 47.2 ··	56.7	39 28.4 ··	47.9	37 10.4 ··	00.3		S.H.A.	Mer. Pass.
22	236 03.8	129 07.9	48.2	168 47.8	57.0	54 30.7	47.8	52 12.8	00.3	Venus	255 37.1	13 22
23	251 06.3	144 07.0	47.9	183 48.4	57.3	69 33.0	47.7	67 15.2	00.2	Mars	294 09.9	10 46
Mer. Pass. 6 22.3		v −0.9 d 0.2		v 0.6 d 0.3		v 2.3 d 0.1		v 2.4 d 0.0		Jupiter	178 32.9	18 26
										Saturn	176 10.9	18 36

G.M.T.	SUN G.H.A.	Dec.	MOON G.H.A.	v	Dec.	d	H.P.
15 00	179 55.9	N23 17.7	29 34.3	14.0	S14 20.1	8.0	54.1
01	194 55.8	17.8	44 07.3	14.0	14 28.1	7.9	54.1
02	209 55.7	18.0	58 40.3	13.8	14 36.0	7.8	54.1
03	224 55.5 ··	18.1	73 13.1	13.9	14 43.8	7.8	54.1
04	239 55.4	18.2	87 46.0	13.8	14 51.6	7.8	54.1
05	254 55.3	18.3	102 18.8	13.8	14 59.4	7.6	54.1
06	269 55.1	N23 18.4	116 51.6	13.7	S15 07.0	7.7	54.1
07	284 55.0	18.5	131 24.3	13.6	15 14.7	7.5	54.1
08	299 54.9	18.6	145 56.9	13.7	15 22.2	7.5	54.1
M 09	314 54.7 ··	18.7	160 29.6	13.6	15 29.7	7.4	54.1
O 10	329 54.6	18.8	175 02.2	13.5	15 37.1	7.4	54.1
N 11	344 54.5	18.9	189 34.7	13.5	15 44.5	7.3	54.1
D 12	359 54.3	N23 19.0	204 07.2	13.4	S15 51.8	7.2	54.1
A 13	14 54.2	19.1	218 39.6	13.5	15 59.0	7.2	54.2
Y 14	29 54.1	19.2	233 12.1	13.3	16 06.2	7.0	54.2
15	44 53.9 ··	19.3	247 44.4	13.3	16 13.2	7.1	54.2
16	59 53.8	19.4	262 16.7	13.3	16 20.3	6.9	54.2
17	74 53.7	19.5	276 49.0	13.2	16 27.2	6.9	54.2
18	89 53.5	N23 19.6	291 21.2	13.2	S16 34.1	6.8	54.2
19	104 53.4	19.7	305 53.4	13.1	16 40.9	6.8	54.2
20	119 53.3	19.8	320 25.5	13.1	16 47.7	6.6	54.2
21	134 53.1 ··	19.9	334 57.6	13.1	16 54.3	6.6	54.2
22	149 53.0	20.0	349 29.7	13.0	17 00.9	6.6	54.2
23	164 52.9	20.1	4 01.7	12.9	17 07.5	6.4	54.2
16 00	179 52.8	N23 20.2	18 33.6	12.9	S17 13.9	6.4	54.2
01	194 52.6	20.3	33 05.5	12.9	17 20.3	6.3	54.2
02	209 52.5	20.4	47 37.4	12.8	17 26.6	6.2	54.3
03	224 52.4 ··	20.5	62 09.2	12.7	17 32.8	6.2	54.3
04	239 52.2	20.6	76 40.9	12.7	17 39.0	6.0	54.3
05	254 52.1	20.7	91 12.6	12.7	17 45.0	6.0	54.3
06	269 52.0	N23 20.8	105 44.3	12.6	S17 51.0	6.0	54.3
07	284 51.8	20.8	120 15.9	12.6	17 57.0	5.8	54.3
08	299 51.7	20.9	134 47.5	12.5	18 02.8	5.8	54.3
T 09	314 51.6 ··	21.0	149 19.0	12.5	18 08.6	5.6	54.3
U 10	329 51.4	21.1	163 50.5	12.5	18 14.2	5.6	54.3
E 11	344 51.3	21.2	178 22.0	12.4	18 19.8	5.6	54.3
S 12	359 51.2	N23 21.3	192 53.4	12.3	S18 25.4	5.4	54.3
D 13	14 51.0	21.4	207 24.7	12.3	18 30.8	5.4	54.4
A 14	29 50.9	21.5	221 56.0	12.3	18 36.2	5.2	54.4
Y 15	44 50.8 ··	21.5	236 27.3	12.2	18 41.4	5.2	54.4
16	59 50.6	21.6	250 58.5	12.1	18 46.6	5.1	54.4
17	74 50.5	21.7	265 29.6	12.2	18 51.7	5.0	54.4
18	89 50.4	N23 21.8	280 00.8	12.0	S18 56.7	5.0	54.4
19	104 50.2	21.9	294 31.8	12.1	19 01.7	4.8	54.4
20	119 50.1	21.9	309 02.9	12.0	19 06.5	4.8	54.4
21	134 50.0 ··	22.0	323 33.9	11.9	19 11.3	4.7	54.4
22	149 49.8	22.1	338 04.8	11.9	19 16.0	4.5	54.5
23	164 49.7	22.2	352 35.7	11.9	19 20.5	4.5	54.5
17 00	179 49.6	N23 22.3	7 06.6	11.8	S19 25.0	4.5	54.5
01	194 49.4	22.3	21 37.4	11.7	19 29.5	4.3	54.5
02	209 49.3	22.4	36 08.1	11.8	19 33.8	4.2	54.5
03	224 49.2 ··	22.5	50 38.9	11.7	19 38.0	4.1	54.5
04	239 49.0	22.6	65 09.6	11.6	19 42.1	4.1	54.5
05	254 48.9	22.6	79 40.2	11.6	19 46.2	3.9	54.5
06	269 48.8	N23 22.7	94 10.8	11.6	S19 50.1	3.9	54.6
07	284 48.6	22.8	108 41.4	11.5	19 54.0	3.8	54.6
W 08	299 48.5	22.9	123 11.9	11.5	19 57.8	3.7	54.6
E 09	314 48.4 ··	22.9	137 42.4	11.4	20 01.5	3.5	54.6
D 10	329 48.2	23.0	152 12.8	11.4	20 05.0	3.5	54.6
N 11	344 48.1	23.1	166 43.2	11.3	20 08.5	3.4	54.6
E 12	359 48.0	N23 23.1	181 13.5	11.4	S20 11.9	3.3	54.6
S 13	14 47.8	23.2	195 43.9	11.3	20 15.2	3.2	54.6
D 14	29 47.7	23.3	210 14.2	11.2	20 18.4	3.1	54.7
A 15	44 47.5 ··	23.3	224 44.4	11.2	20 21.5	3.0	54.7
Y 16	59 47.4	23.4	239 14.6	11.2	20 24.5	3.0	54.7
17	74 47.3	23.5	253 44.8	11.1	20 27.5	2.8	54.7
18	89 47.1	N23 23.5	268 14.9	11.1	S20 30.3	2.7	54.7
19	104 47.0	23.6	282 45.0	11.1	20 33.0	2.6	54.7
20	119 46.9	23.7	297 15.1	11.0	20 35.6	2.5	54.7
21	134 46.7 ··	23.7	311 45.1	11.0	20 38.1	2.4	54.8
22	149 46.6	23.8	326 15.1	10.9	20 40.5	2.4	54.8
23	164 46.5	23.8	340 45.0	11.0	20 42.9	2.2	54.8
	S.D. 15.8 d 0.1		S.D. 14.8		14.8		14.9

Twilight / Sunrise / Moonrise

Lat.	Naut.	Civil	Sunrise	15	16	17	18
N 72	□	□	□	21 23	■	■	■
N 70	□	□	□	20 26	22 30	■	■
68	□	□	□	19 53	21 27	22 58	24 04
66	□	□	□	19 29	20 53	22 09	23 09
64	////	////	01 32	19 10	20 28	21 38	22 36
62	////	////	02 10	18 54	20 08	21 15	22 12
60	////	00 52	02 36	18 42	19 52	20 57	21 53
N 58	////	01 41	02 56	18 31	19 38	20 41	21 37
56	////	02 11	03 13	18 21	19 27	20 28	21 23
54	00 47	02 33	03 27	18 13	19 17	20 17	21 11
52	01 33	02 51	03 39	18 05	19 08	20 07	21 01
50	02 00	03 06	03 50	17 58	19 00	19 58	20 52
45	02 46	03 35	04 13	17 44	18 42	19 39	20 32
N 40	03 16	03 58	04 30	17 32	18 29	19 24	20 16
35	03 39	04 16	04 45	17 22	18 17	19 11	20 03
30	03 58	04 31	04 58	17 13	18 06	18 59	19 51
20	04 27	04 56	05 20	16 58	17 49	18 40	19 31
N 10	04 49	05 16	05 39	16 45	17 33	18 23	19 14
0	05 08	05 34	05 57	16 32	17 19	18 08	18 58
S 10	05 25	05 51	06 14	16 20	17 05	17 52	18 42
20	05 41	06 09	06 33	16 07	16 50	17 35	18 24
30	05 58	06 28	06 54	15 52	16 32	17 16	18 05
35	06 06	06 38	07 06	15 44	16 22	17 05	17 53
40	06 16	06 50	07 20	15 34	16 11	16 52	17 40
45	06 26	07 03	07 37	15 22	15 57	16 37	17 24
S 50	06 38	07 19	07 58	15 09	15 41	16 19	17 05
52	06 43	07 27	08 08	15 02	15 33	16 10	16 56
54	06 49	07 35	08 19	14 55	15 24	16 01	16 45
56	06 55	07 44	08 31	14 47	15 15	15 50	16 34
58	07 02	07 54	08 46	14 39	15 04	15 37	16 20
S 60	07 09	08 06	09 03	14 28	14 52	15 23	16 05

Sunset / Twilight / Moonset

Lat.	Sunset	Civil	Naut.	15	16	17	18
N 72	□	□	□	00 32 / 23 51	■	■	■
N 70	□	□	□	01 01	00 49	00 24	■
68	□	□	□	01 23	01 24	01 27	01 38
66	□	□	□	01 41	01 49	02 02	02 27
64	22 30	////	////	01 55	02 08	02 27	02 58
62	21 52	////	////	02 07	02 24	02 47	03 21
60	21 26	23 11	////	02 17	02 37	03 04	03 40
N 58	21 05	22 21	////	02 26	02 49	03 18	03 55
56	20 49	21 51	////	02 34	02 59	03 30	04 09
54	20 34	21 29	23 15	02 41	03 08	03 40	04 22
52	20 22	21 11	22 29	02 48	03 16	03 49	04 30
50	20 11	20 56	22 01	02 53	03 23	03 58	04 39
45	19 49	20 26	21 16	03 06	03 38	04 15	04 59
N 40	19 31	20 04	20 45	03 16	03 51	04 30	05 14
35	19 16	19 45	20 22	03 25	04 01	04 42	05 27
30	19 03	19 30	20 04	03 33	04 11	04 53	05 39
20	18 41	19 05	19 35	03 46	04 27	05 11	05 59
N 10	18 22	18 45	19 12	03 58	04 41	05 27	06 16
0	18 04	18 27	18 53	04 09	04 54	05 42	06 32
S 10	17 47	18 10	18 36	04 20	05 08	05 57	06 48
20	17 28	17 52	18 20	04 32	05 22	06 13	07 05
30	17 07	17 34	18 03	04 45	05 39	06 32	07 25
35	16 55	17 23	17 55	04 53	05 48	06 43	07 36
40	16 41	17 11	17 45	05 02	05 59	06 55	07 49
45	16 24	16 58	17 35	05 13	06 12	07 10	08 05
S 50	16 03	16 42	17 23	05 26	06 28	07 28	08 24
52	15 53	16 34	17 18	05 32	06 35	07 36	08 33
54	15 42	16 26	17 12	05 38	06 43	07 46	08 43
56	15 30	16 17	17 06	05 46	06 53	07 57	08 55
58	15 15	16 07	16 59	05 54	07 03	08 09	09 08
S 60	14 58	15 55	16 52	06 03	07 15	08 23	09 24

SUN / MOON

Day	SUN Eqn. of Time 00h	12h	Mer. Pass.	MOON Mer. Pass. Upper	Lower	Age	Phase
	m s	m s	h m	h m	h m	d	
15	00 16	00 22	12 00	22 43	10 20	13	
16	00 29	00 35	12 01	23 31	11 07	14	◯
17	00 42	00 48	12 01	24 20	11 55	15	

1981 JUNE 18, 19, 20 (THURS., FRI., SAT.)

G.M.T.	ARIES G.H.A.	VENUS −3.3 G.H.A.	Dec.	MARS +1.7 G.H.A.	Dec.	JUPITER −1.6 G.H.A.	Dec.	SATURN +1.2 G.H.A.	Dec.	STARS Name	S.H.A.	Dec.
18 00	266 08.7	159 06.1 N23 47.6		198 49.0 N21 57.6		84 35.3 N 0 47.7		82 17.6 N 1 00.2		Acamar	315 37.2	S40 22.7
01	281 11.2	174 05.3	47.3	213 49.6	57.9	99 37.7	47.6	97 20.0	00.2	Achernar	335 45.2	S57 19.7
02	296 13.7	189 04.4	47.0	228 50.1	58.2	114 40.0	47.6	112 22.4	00.1	Acrux	173 36.5	S63 00.0
03	311 16.1	204 03.6 ··	46.7	243 50.7 ··	58.5	129 42.3 ··	47.5	127 24.9 ··	00.1	Adhara	255 32.1	S28 56.9
04	326 18.6	219 02.7	46.4	258 51.3	58.8	144 44.6	47.4	142 27.3	00.1	Aldebaran	291 17.8	N16 28.2
05	341 21.1	234 01.9	46.1	273 51.9	59.1	159 47.0	47.3	157 29.7	00.0			
06	356 23.5	249 01.0 N23 45.9		288 52.5 N21 59.4		174 49.3 N 0 47.3		172 32.1 N 1 00.0		Alioth	166 41.9	N56 04.0
07	11 26.0	264 00.2	45.6	303 53.1 21 59.7		189 51.6	47.2	187 34.5 1 00.0		Alkaid	153 17.9	N49 24.7
T 08	26 28.4	278 59.3	45.3	318 53.7 22 00.0		204 53.9	47.1	202 36.9 0 59.9		Al Na'ir	28 14.1	S47 02.9
H 09	41 30.9	293 58.5 ··	45.0	333 54.3 ··	00.2	219 56.3 ··	47.1	217 39.4 ··	59.9	Alnilam	276 11.5	S 1 12.9
U 10	56 33.4	308 57.6	44.7	348 54.9	00.5	234 58.6	47.0	232 41.8	59.9	Alphard	218 20.3	S 8 34.7
R 11	71 35.8	323 56.8	44.4	3 55.5	00.8	250 00.9	46.9	247 44.2	59.9			
S 12	86 38.3	338 55.9 N23 44.1		18 56.1 N22 01.1		265 03.2 N 0 46.8		262 46.6 N 0 59.8		Alphecca	126 31.4	N26 46.8
D 13	101 40.8	353 55.0	43.7	33 56.7	01.4	280 05.6	46.8	277 49.0	59.8	Alpheratz	358 08.8	N28 59.0
A 14	116 43.2	8 54.2	43.4	48 57.3	01.7	295 07.9	46.7	292 51.4	59.8	Altair	62 31.7	N 8 49.1
Y 15	131 45.7	23 53.3 ··	43.1	63 57.9 ··	02.0	310 10.2 ··	46.6	307 53.9 ··	59.7	Ankaa	353 39.8	S42 24.3
16	146 48.2	38 52.5	42.8	78 58.5	02.3	325 12.5	46.6	322 56.3	59.7	Antares	112 55.9	S26 23.4
17	161 50.6	53 51.6	42.5	93 59.1	02.6	340 14.9	46.5	337 58.7	59.7			
18	176 53.1	68 50.8 N23 42.2		108 59.7 N22 02.9		355 17.2 N 0 46.4		353 01.1 N 0 59.6		Arcturus	146 17.8	N19 16.9
19	191 55.6	83 49.9	41.9	124 00.3	03.2	10 19.5	46.3	8 03.5	59.6	Atria	108 19.1	S68 59.7
20	206 58.0	98 49.1	41.6	139 00.9	03.4	25 21.8	46.3	23 05.9	59.6	Avior	234 28.5	S59 27.2
21	222 00.5	113 48.2 ··	41.3	154 01.5 ··	03.7	40 24.1 ··	46.2	38 08.4 ··	59.5	Bellatrix	278 58.5	N 6 19.9
22	237 02.9	128 47.4	41.0	169 02.1	04.0	55 26.5	46.1	53 10.8	59.5	Betelgeuse	271 28.1	N 7 24.2
23	252 05.4	143 46.5	40.6	184 02.7	04.3	70 28.8	46.0	68 13.2	59.5			
19 00	267 07.9	158 45.7 N23 40.3		199 03.3 N22 04.6		85 31.1 N 0 46.0		83 15.6 N 0 59.4		Canopus	264 07.5	S52 41.2
01	282 10.3	173 44.9	40.0	214 03.8	04.9	100 33.4	45.9	98 18.0	59.4	Capella	281 11.0	N45 58.7
02	297 12.8	188 44.0	39.7	229 04.4	05.2	115 35.7	45.8	113 20.4	59.4	Deneb	49 47.8	N45 12.7
03	312 15.3	203 43.2 ··	39.4	244 05.0 ··	05.5	130 38.1 ··	45.8	128 22.8 ··	59.3	Denebola	182 58.5	N14 40.7
04	327 17.7	218 42.3	39.0	259 05.6	05.7	145 40.4	45.7	143 25.3	59.3	Diphda	349 20.4	S18 05.3
05	342 20.2	233 41.5	38.7	274 06.2	06.0	160 42.7	45.6	158 27.7	59.3			
06	357 22.7	248 40.6 N23 38.4		289 06.8 N22 06.3		175 45.0 N 0 45.5		173 30.1 N 0 59.2		Dubhe	194 21.7	N61 51.4
07	12 25.1	263 39.8	38.1	304 07.4	06.6	190 47.3	45.5	188 32.5	59.2	Elnath	278 43.9	N28 35.4
08	27 27.6	278 38.9	37.7	319 08.0	06.9	205 49.7	45.4	203 34.9	59.2	Eltanin	90 57.0	N51 29.5
F 09	42 30.0	293 38.1 ··	37.4	334 08.6 ··	07.2	220 52.0 ··	45.3	218 37.3 ··	59.2	Enif	34 10.9	N 9 47.3
R 10	57 32.5	308 37.2	37.1	349 09.2	07.5	235 54.3	45.2	233 39.7	59.1	Fomalhaut	15 50.8	S29 43.2
I 11	72 35.0	323 36.4	36.8	4 09.8	07.7	250 56.6	45.2	248 42.1	59.1			
D 12	87 37.4	338 35.5 N23 36.4		19 10.4 N22 08.0		265 58.9 N 0 45.1		263 44.6 N 0 59.1		Gacrux	172 28.1	S57 00.7
A 13	102 39.9	353 34.7	36.1	34 11.0	08.3	281 01.3	45.0	278 47.0	59.0	Gienah	176 17.4	S17 26.3
Y 14	117 42.4	8 33.9	35.8	49 11.6	08.6	296 03.6	44.9	293 49.4	59.0	Hadar	149 22.2	S60 17.2
15	132 44.8	23 33.0 ··	35.4	64 12.2 ··	08.9	311 05.9 ··	44.9	308 51.8 ··	59.0	Hamal	328 28.5	N23 22.3
16	147 47.3	38 32.2	35.1	79 12.8	09.2	326 08.2	44.8	323 54.2	58.9	Kaus Aust.	84 15.8	S34 23.6
17	162 49.8	53 31.3	34.8	94 13.4	09.4	341 10.5	44.7	338 56.6	58.9			
18	177 52.2	68 30.5 N23 34.4		109 14.0 N22 09.7		356 12.8 N 0 44.6		353 59.0 N 0 58.9		Kochab	137 18.2	N74 14.2
19	192 54.7	83 29.6	34.1	124 14.6	10.0	11 15.2	44.6	9 01.4	58.8	Markab	14 02.6	N15 06.2
20	207 57.2	98 28.8	33.7	139 15.1	10.3	26 17.5	44.5	24 03.9	58.8	Menkar	314 40.9	N 4 00.9
21	222 59.6	113 28.0 ··	33.4	154 15.7 ··	10.6	41 19.8 ··	44.4	39 06.3 ··	58.8	Menkent	148 36.2	S36 16.8
22	238 02.1	128 27.1	33.0	169 16.3	10.8	56 22.1	44.3	54 08.7	58.7	Miaplacidus	221 45.4	S69 38.7
23	253 04.5	143 26.3	32.7	184 16.9	11.1	71 24.4	44.3	69 11.1	58.7			
20 00	268 07.0	158 25.4 N23 32.4		199 17.5 N22 11.4		86 26.7 N 0 44.2		84 13.5 N 0 58.7		Mirfak	309 15.8	N49 47.5
01	283 09.5	173 24.6	32.0	214 18.1	11.7	101 29.0	44.1	99 15.9	58.6	Nunki	76 28.2	S26 19.1
02	298 11.9	188 23.7	31.7	229 18.7	12.0	116 31.4	44.0	114 18.3	58.6	Peacock	53 57.1	S56 47.5
03	313 14.4	203 22.9 ··	31.3	244 19.3 ··	12.2	131 33.7 ··	44.0	129 20.7 ··	58.6	Pollux	243 57.9	N28 04.3
04	328 16.9	218 22.1	31.0	259 19.9	12.5	146 36.0	43.9	144 23.1	58.5	Procyon	245 25.6	N 5 16.4
05	343 19.3	233 21.2	30.6	274 20.5	12.8	161 38.3	43.8	159 25.6	58.5			
06	358 21.8	248 20.4 N23 30.3		289 21.1 N22 13.1		176 40.6 N 0 43.7		174 28.0 N 0 58.5		Rasalhague	96 28.8	N12 34.5
07	13 24.3	263 19.6	29.9	304 21.7	13.3	191 42.9	43.7	189 30.4	58.4	Regulus	208 09.6	N12 03.6
S 08	28 26.7	278 18.7	29.5	319 22.3	13.6	206 45.2	43.6	204 32.8	58.4	Rigel	281 35.9	S 8 13.4
A 09	43 29.2	293 17.9 ··	29.2	334 22.9 ··	13.9	221 47.5 ··	43.5	219 35.2 ··	58.3	Rigil Kent.	140 24.7	S60 45.6
T 10	58 31.7	308 17.0	28.8	349 23.5	14.2	236 49.9	43.4	234 37.6	58.3	Sabik	102 40.2	S15 42.1
U 11	73 34.1	323 16.2	28.5	4 24.1	14.4	251 52.2	43.3	249 40.0	58.3			
R 12	88 36.6	338 15.4 N23 28.1		19 24.7 N22 14.7		266 54.5 N 0 43.3		264 42.4 N 0 58.2		Schedar	350 08.5	N56 25.8
D 13	103 39.0	353 14.5	27.8	34 25.3	15.0	281 56.8	43.2	279 44.8	58.2	Shaula	96 54.6	S37 05.4
A 14	118 41.5	8 13.7	27.4	49 25.9	15.3	296 59.1	43.1	294 47.2	58.2	Sirius	258 55.6	S16 41.5
Y 15	133 44.0	23 12.9 ··	27.0	64 26.4 ··	15.5	312 01.4 ··	43.0	309 49.6 ··	58.1	Spica	158 56.9	S11 03.8
16	148 46.4	38 12.0	26.7	79 27.0	15.8	327 03.7	43.0	324 52.1	58.1	Suhail	223 10.7	S43 21.6
17	163 48.9	53 11.2	26.3	94 27.6	16.1	342 06.0	42.9	339 54.5	58.1			
18	178 51.4	68 10.3 N23 25.9		109 28.2 N22 16.4		357 08.3 N 0 42.8		354 56.9 N 0 58.0		Vega	80 55.1	N38 46.0
19	193 53.8	83 09.5	25.6	124 28.8	16.6	12 10.7	42.7	9 59.3	58.0	Zuben'ubi	137 32.2	S15 57.9
20	208 56.3	98 08.7	25.2	139 29.4	16.9	27 13.0	42.6	25 01.7	58.0			
21	223 58.8	113 07.8 ··	24.8	154 30.0 ··	17.2	42 15.3 ··	42.6	40 04.1 ··	57.9		S.H.A.	Mer. Pass.
22	239 01.2	128 07.0	24.5	169 30.6	17.4	57 17.6	42.5	55 06.5	57.9	Venus	251 37.8	13 26
23	254 03.7	143 06.2	24.1	184 31.2	17.7	72 19.9	42.4	70 08.9	57.9	Mars	291 55.4	10 43
Mer. Pass.	6 10.5	v −0.8 d 0.3		v 0.6 d 0.3		v 2.3 d 0.1		v 2.4 d 0.0		Jupiter	178 23.2	18 15
										Saturn	176 07.7	18 24

SUN and MOON

G.M.T.	SUN G.H.A.	Dec.	MOON G.H.A.	v	Dec.	d	H.P.
18 00	179 46.3	N23 23.9	355 15.0	10.9	S20 45.1	2.1	54.8
01	194 46.2	24.0	9 44.9	10.8	20 47.2	2.0	54.8
02	209 46.1	24.0	24 14.7	10.9	20 49.2	1.9	54.8
03	224 45.9	·· 24.1	38 44.6	10.8	20 51.1	1.9	54.8
04	239 45.8	24.1	53 14.4	10.7	20 53.0	1.7	54.9
05	254 45.7	24.2	67 44.1	10.8	20 54.7	1.6	54.9
06	269 45.5	N23 24.3	82 13.9	10.7	S20 56.3	1.5	54.9
07	284 45.4	24.3	96 43.6	10.7	20 57.8	1.4	54.9
T 08	299 45.3	24.4	111 13.3	10.6	20 59.2	1.3	54.9
H 09	314 45.1	·· 24.4	125 42.9	10.6	21 00.5	1.2	54.9
U 10	329 45.0	24.5	140 12.5	10.6	21 01.7	1.1	55.0
R 11	344 44.9	24.5	154 42.1	10.6	21 02.8	1.0	55.0
S 12	359 44.7	N23 24.6	169 11.7	10.6	S21 03.8	0.8	55.0
D 13	14 44.6	24.6	183 41.3	10.5	21 04.6	0.8	55.0
A 14	29 44.5	24.7	198 10.8	10.5	21 05.4	0.7	55.0
Y 15	44 44.3	·· 24.7	212 40.3	10.5	21 06.1	0.6	55.0
16	59 44.2	24.8	227 09.8	10.4	21 06.7	0.4	55.1
17	74 44.1	24.8	241 39.2	10.5	21 07.1	0.4	55.1
18	89 43.9	N23 24.9	256 08.7	10.4	S21 07.5	0.2	55.1
19	104 43.8	24.9	270 38.1	10.4	21 07.7	0.2	55.1
20	119 43.6	25.0	285 07.5	10.3	21 07.9	0.0	55.1
21	134 43.5	·· 25.0	299 36.8	10.4	21 07.9	0.1	55.1
22	149 43.4	25.0	314 06.2	10.3	21 07.8	0.2	55.2
23	164 43.2	25.1	328 35.5	10.4	21 07.6	0.3	55.2
19 00	179 43.1	N23 25.1	343 04.9	10.3	S21 07.3	0.3	55.2
01	194 43.0	25.2	357 34.2	10.2	21 07.0	0.6	55.2
02	209 42.8	25.2	12 03.4	10.3	21 06.4	0.6	55.2
03	224 42.7	·· 25.3	26 32.7	10.3	21 05.8	0.7	55.2
04	239 42.6	25.3	41 02.0	10.2	21 05.1	0.8	55.3
05	254 42.4	25.3	55 31.2	10.3	21 04.3	0.9	55.3
06	269 42.3	N23 25.4	70 00.5	10.2	S21 03.4	1.1	55.3
07	284 42.2	25.4	84 29.7	10.2	21 02.3	1.1	55.3
08	299 42.0	·· 25.5	98 58.9	10.2	21 01.2	1.3	55.3
F 09	314 41.9	·· 25.5	113 28.1	10.2	20 59.9	1.4	55.3
R 10	329 41.8	25.5	127 57.3	10.1	20 58.5	1.4	55.4
I 11	344 41.6	25.6	142 26.4	10.2	20 57.1	1.6	55.4
D 12	359 41.5	N23 25.6	156 55.6	10.2	S20 55.5	1.7	55.4
A 13	14 41.4	25.6	171 24.8	10.1	20 53.8	1.8	55.4
Y 14	29 41.2	25.7	185 53.9	10.2	20 52.0	1.9	55.4
15	44 41.1	·· 25.7	200 23.1	10.1	20 50.1	2.0	55.5
16	59 40.9	25.7	214 52.2	10.1	20 48.1	2.2	55.5
17	74 40.8	25.8	229 21.3	10.2	20 45.9	2.2	55.5
18	89 40.7	N23 25.8	243 50.5	10.1	S20 43.7	2.3	55.5
19	104 40.5	25.8	258 19.6	10.1	20 41.4	2.5	55.5
20	119 40.4	25.8	272 48.7	10.1	20 38.9	2.5	55.5
21	134 40.3	·· 25.9	287 17.8	10.1	20 36.4	2.7	55.6
22	149 40.1	25.9	301 46.9	10.2	20 33.7	2.8	55.6
23	164 40.0	25.9	316 16.1	10.1	20 30.9	2.9	55.6
20 00	179 39.9	N23 25.9	330 45.2	10.1	S20 28.0	2.9	55.6
01	194 39.7	26.0	345 14.3	10.1	20 25.1	3.1	55.6
02	209 39.6	26.0	359 43.4	10.1	20 22.0	3.2	55.7
03	224 39.5	·· 26.0	14 12.5	10.1	20 18.8	3.4	55.7
04	239 39.3	26.0	28 41.6	10.2	20 15.4	3.4	55.7
05	254 39.2	26.1	43 10.8	10.1	20 12.0	3.5	55.7
06	269 39.1	N23 26.1	57 39.9	10.2	S20 08.5	3.6	55.7
07	284 38.9	26.1	72 09.0	10.2	20 04.9	3.8	55.8
S 08	299 38.8	26.1	86 38.2	10.1	20 01.1	3.8	55.8
A 09	314 38.6	·· 26.1	101 07.3	10.1	19 57.3	4.0	55.8
T 10	329 38.5	26.2	115 36.4	10.2	19 53.3	4.0	55.8
U 11	344 38.4	26.2	130 05.6	10.2	19 49.3	4.2	55.8
R 12	359 38.2	N23 26.2	144 34.8	10.1	S19 45.1	4.2	55.9
D 13	14 38.1	26.2	159 03.9	10.2	19 40.9	4.4	55.9
A 14	29 38.0	26.2	173 33.1	10.2	19 36.5	4.5	55.9
Y 15	44 37.8	·· 26.2	188 02.3	10.2	19 32.0	4.6	55.9
16	59 37.7	26.3	202 31.5	10.2	19 27.4	4.6	55.9
17	74 37.6	26.3	217 00.7	10.2	19 22.8	4.8	56.0
18	89 37.4	N23 26.3	231 29.9	10.2	S19 18.0	4.9	56.0
19	104 37.3	26.3	245 59.1	10.2	19 13.1	5.0	56.0
20	119 37.2	26.3	260 28.3	10.3	19 08.1	5.1	56.0
21	134 37.0	·· 26.3	274 57.6	10.2	19 03.0	5.2	56.0
22	149 36.9	26.3	289 26.8	10.3	18 57.8	5.3	56.1
23	164 36.7	26.3	303 56.1	10.3	18 52.5	5.4	56.1
	S.D. 15.8	d 0.0	S.D. 15.0		15.1		15.2

Twilight, Sunrise and Moonrise

Lat.	Twilight Naut.	Civil	Sunrise	Moonrise 18	19	20	21
N 72	□	□	□	■	■	■	■
N 70	□	□	□	■	■	■	01 25
68	□	□	□	24 04	00 04	00 30	00 38
66	□	□	□	23 09	23 47	24 07	00 07
64	////	////	01 31	22 36	23 17	23 44	24 02
62	////	////	02 09	22 12	22 55	23 26	23 48
60	////	00 49	02 35	21 53	22 37	23 11	23 36
N 58	////	01 40	02 56	21 37	22 22	22 58	23 26
56	////	02 10	03 13	21 23	22 09	22 47	23 17
54	00 45	02 32	03 27	21 11	21 58	22 37	23 09
52	01 32	02 50	03 39	21 01	21 48	22 28	23 02
50	02 00	03 06	03 50	20 52	21 39	22 20	22 55
45	02 46	03 35	04 13	20 32	21 20	22 03	22 41
N 40	03 16	03 58	04 31	20 16	21 05	21 50	22 30
35	03 39	04 16	04 46	20 03	20 52	21 38	22 20
30	03 58	04 31	04 59	19 51	20 41	21 28	22 11
20	04 27	04 56	05 21	19 31	20 21	21 10	21 56
N 10	04 50	05 17	05 40	19 14	20 05	20 54	21 43
0	05 09	05 35	05 58	18 58	19 49	20 40	21 31
S 10	05 26	05 52	06 15	18 42	19 33	20 25	21 18
20	05 42	06 10	06 34	18 24	19 16	20 10	21 05
30	05 59	06 28	06 55	18 05	18 57	19 52	20 50
35	06 07	06 39	07 07	17 53	18 45	19 42	20 41
40	06 17	06 51	07 21	17 40	18 32	19 30	20 31
45	06 27	07 04	07 38	17 24	18 17	19 16	20 19
S 50	06 39	07 20	07 59	17 05	17 58	18 59	20 05
52	06 44	07 28	08 09	16 56	17 49	18 51	19 58
54	06 50	07 36	08 20	16 45	17 39	18 41	19 50
56	06 56	07 45	08 33	16 34	17 28	18 31	19 42
58	07 03	07 56	08 47	16 20	17 15	18 20	19 32
S 60	07 10	08 07	09 05	16 05	17 00	18 06	19 22

Sunset, Twilight and Moonset

Lat.	Sunset	Twilight Civil	Naut.	Moonset 18	19	20	21
N 72	□	□	□	■	■	■	■
N 70	□	□	□	■	■	■	04 29
68	□	□	□	01 38	02 17	03 37	05 15
66	□	□	□	02 27	03 12	04 20	05 45
64	22 32	////	////	02 58	03 45	04 49	06 08
62	21 54	////	////	03 21	04 09	05 11	06 26
60	21 27	23 14	////	03 40	04 28	05 29	06 40
N 58	21 07	22 23	////	03 55	04 44	05 44	06 53
56	20 50	21 53	////	04 09	04 58	05 56	07 04
54	20 36	21 30	23 18	04 20	05 09	06 07	07 13
52	20 23	21 12	22 31	04 30	05 20	06 17	07 22
50	20 12	20 57	22 03	04 39	05 29	06 26	07 29
45	19 50	20 27	21 17	04 59	05 48	06 44	07 45
N 40	19 32	20 05	20 46	05 14	06 04	06 59	07 59
35	19 17	19 46	20 23	05 27	06 17	07 12	08 10
30	19 04	19 31	20 04	05 39	06 29	07 23	08 20
20	18 42	19 06	19 35	05 59	06 49	07 42	08 36
N 10	18 23	18 46	19 13	06 16	07 06	07 58	08 51
0	18 05	18 27	18 54	06 32	07 22	08 13	09 04
S 10	17 47	18 10	18 37	06 48	07 38	08 29	09 18
20	17 29	17 53	18 20	07 05	07 56	08 45	09 32
30	17 08	17 34	18 04	07 25	08 15	09 03	09 49
35	16 55	17 23	17 55	07 36	08 27	09 14	09 58
40	16 41	17 12	17 46	07 49	08 40	09 27	10 09
45	16 24	16 58	17 35	08 05	08 56	09 41	10 21
S 50	16 03	16 42	17 24	08 24	09 15	09 59	10 37
52	15 54	16 35	17 18	08 33	09 24	10 07	10 44
54	15 42	16 26	17 13	08 43	09 34	10 17	10 52
56	15 30	16 17	17 06	08 55	09 45	10 27	11 01
58	15 15	16 07	17 00	09 08	09 58	10 39	11 11
S 60	14 57	15 55	16 52	09 24	10 14	10 53	11 22

SUN and MOON

Day	SUN Eqn. of Time 00h	12h	Mer. Pass.	MOON Mer. Pass. Upper	Lower	Age	Phase
	m s	m s	h m	h m	h m	d	
18	00 54	01 01	12 01	00 20	12 45	16	
19	01 07	01 14	12 01	01 10	13 36	17	
20	01 20	01 27	12 01	02 01	14 27	18	○

G.M.T.	ARIES G.H.A.	VENUS −3.3 G.H.A.	Dec.	MARS +1.7 G.H.A.	Dec.	JUPITER −1.6 G.H.A.	Dec.	SATURN +1.2 G.H.A.	Dec.	STARS Name	S.H.A.	Dec.
21 00	269 06.1	158 05.3	N23 23.7	199 31.8	N22 18.0	87 22.2	N 0 42.3	85 11.3	N 0 57.8	Acamar	315 37.2	S40 22.7
01	284 08.6	173 04.5	23.3	214 32.4	18.3	102 24.5	42.3	100 13.7	57.8	Achernar	335 45.1	S57 19.7
02	299 11.1	188 03.7	23.0	229 33.0	18.5	117 26.8	42.2	115 16.1	57.8	Acrux	173 36.6	S63 00.0
03	314 13.5	203 02.8 ..	22.6	244 33.6 ..	18.8	132 29.1 ..	42.1	130 18.5 ..	57.7	Adhara	255 32.1	S28 56.9
04	329 16.0	218 02.0	22.2	259 34.2	19.1	147 31.4	42.0	145 20.9	57.7	Aldebaran	291 17.7	N16 28.2
05	344 18.5	233 01.2	21.8	274 34.8	19.3	162 33.7	41.9	160 23.3	57.7			
06	359 20.9	248 00.4	N23 21.4	289 35.4	N22 19.6	177 36.0	N 0 41.9	175 25.8	N 0 57.6	Alioth	166 41.9	N56 04.0
07	14 23.4	262 59.5	21.1	304 35.9	19.9	192 38.3	41.8	190 28.2	57.6	Alkaid	153 17.9	N49 24.7
08	29 25.9	277 58.7	20.7	319 36.5	20.1	207 40.7	41.7	205 30.6	57.5	Al Na'ir	28 14.1	S47 02.9
S 09	44 28.3	292 57.9 ..	20.3	334 37.1 ..	20.4	222 43.0 ..	41.6	220 33.0 ..	57.5	Alnilam	276 11.5	S 1 12.9
U 10	59 30.8	307 57.0	19.9	349 37.7	20.7	237 45.3	41.5	235 35.4	57.5	Alphard	218 20.3	S 8 34.7
N 11	74 33.3	322 56.2	19.5	4 38.3	20.9	252 47.6	41.5	250 37.8	57.4			
D 12	89 35.7	337 55.4	N23 19.1	19 38.9	N22 21.2	267 49.9	N 0 41.4	265 40.2	N 0 57.4	Alphecca	126 31.4	N26 46.8
A 13	104 38.2	352 54.5	18.7	34 39.5	21.5	282 52.2	41.3	280 42.6	57.4	Alpheratz	358 08.8	N28 59.0
Y 14	119 40.6	7 53.7	18.3	49 40.1	21.7	297 54.5	41.2	295 45.0	57.3	Altair	62 31.7	N 8 49.1
15	134 43.1	22 52.9 ..	17.9	64 40.7 ..	22.0	312 56.8 ..	41.1	310 47.4 ..	57.3	Ankaa	353 39.8	S42 24.3
16	149 45.6	37 52.1	17.6	79 41.3	22.3	327 59.1	41.1	325 49.8	57.3	Antares	112 55.9	S26 23.5
17	164 48.0	52 51.2	17.2	94 41.9	22.5	343 01.4	41.0	340 52.2	57.2			
18	179 50.5	67 50.4	N23 16.8	109 42.5	N22 22.8	358 03.7	N 0 40.9	355 54.6	N 0 57.2	Arcturus	146 17.8	N19 16.9
19	194 53.0	82 49.6	16.4	124 43.1	23.1	13 06.0	40.8	10 57.0	57.2	Atria	108 19.1	S68 59.7
20	209 55.4	97 48.8	16.0	139 43.7	23.3	28 08.3	40.7	25 59.4	57.1	Avior	234 28.5	S59 27.2
21	224 57.9	112 47.9 ..	15.6	154 44.3 ..	23.6	43 10.6 ..	40.7	41 01.8 ..	57.1	Bellatrix	278 58.5	N 6 19.9
22	240 00.4	127 47.1	15.2	169 44.9	23.8	58 12.9	40.6	56 04.2	57.0	Betelgeuse	271 28.1	N 7 24.2
23	255 02.8	142 46.3	14.8	184 45.4	24.1	73 15.2	40.5	71 06.6	57.0			
22 00	270 05.3	157 45.5	N23 14.4	199 46.0	N22 24.4	88 17.5	N 0 40.4	86 09.0	N 0 57.0	Canopus	264 07.5	S52 41.2
01	285 07.8	172 44.6	14.0	214 46.6	24.6	103 19.8	40.3	101 11.4	56.9	Capella	281 11.0	N45 58.7
02	300 10.2	187 43.8	13.6	229 47.2	24.9	118 22.1	40.3	116 13.8	56.9	Deneb	49 47.7	N45 12.7
03	315 12.7	202 43.0 ..	13.2	244 47.8 ..	25.1	133 24.4 ..	40.2	131 16.2 ..	56.9	Denebola	182 58.6	N14 40.7
04	330 15.1	217 42.2	12.7	259 48.4	25.4	148 26.7	40.1	146 18.6	56.8	Diphda	349 20.4	S18 05.3
05	345 17.6	232 41.3	12.3	274 49.0	25.7	163 29.0	40.0	161 21.0	56.8			
06	0 20.1	247 40.5	N23 11.9	289 49.6	N22 25.9	178 31.3	N 0 39.9	176 23.4	N 0 56.7	Dubhe	194 21.7	N61 51.4
07	15 22.5	262 39.7	11.5	304 50.2	26.2	193 33.6	39.9	191 25.9	56.7	Elnath	278 43.9	N28 35.4
08	30 25.0	277 38.9	11.1	319 50.8	26.4	208 35.9	39.8	206 28.3	56.7	Eltanin	90 56.9	N51 29.5
M 09	45 27.5	292 38.1 ..	10.7	334 51.4 ..	26.7	223 38.2 ..	39.7	221 30.7 ..	56.6	Enif	34 10.9	N 9 47.3
O 10	60 29.9	307 37.2	10.3	349 52.0	27.0	238 40.5	39.6	236 33.1	56.6	Fomalhaut	15 50.7	S29 43.1
N 11	75 32.4	322 36.4	09.9	4 52.6	27.2	253 42.8	39.5	251 35.5	56.6			
D 12	90 34.9	337 35.6	N23 09.4	19 53.2	N22 27.5	268 45.1	N 0 39.4	266 37.9	N 0 56.5	Gacrux	172 28.1	S57 00.7
A 13	105 37.3	352 34.8	09.0	34 53.8	27.7	283 47.4	39.4	281 40.3	56.5	Gienah	176 17.4	S17 26.3
Y 14	120 39.8	7 34.0	08.6	49 54.3	28.0	298 49.7	39.3	296 42.7	56.4	Hadar	149 22.3	S60 17.2
15	135 42.2	22 33.1 ..	08.2	64 54.9 ..	28.2	313 52.0 ..	39.2	311 45.1 ..	56.4	Hamal	328 28.5	N23 22.3
16	150 44.7	37 32.3	07.8	79 55.5	28.5	328 54.3	39.1	326 47.5	56.4	Kaus Aust.	84 15.8	S34 23.6
17	165 47.2	52 31.5	07.3	94 56.1	28.7	343 56.6	39.0	341 49.9	56.3			
18	180 49.6	67 30.7	N23 06.9	109 56.7	N22 29.0	358 58.9	N 0 38.9	356 52.3	N 0 56.3	Kochab	137 18.2	N74 14.2
19	195 52.1	82 29.9	06.5	124 57.3	29.3	14 01.2	38.9	11 54.7	56.3	Markab	14 02.6	N15 06.2
20	210 54.6	97 29.1	06.1	139 57.9	29.5	29 03.5	38.8	26 57.1	56.2	Menkar	314 40.8	N 4 00.9
21	225 57.0	112 28.2 ..	05.6	154 58.5 ..	29.8	44 05.8 ..	38.7	41 59.5 ..	56.2	Menkent	148 36.2	S36 16.8
22	240 59.5	127 27.4	05.2	169 59.1	30.0	59 08.1	38.6	57 01.9	56.1	Miaplacidus	221 45.5	S69 38.7
23	256 02.0	142 26.6	04.8	184 59.7	30.3	74 10.4	38.5	72 04.3	56.1			
23 00	271 04.4	157 25.8	N23 04.4	200 00.3	N22 30.5	89 12.7	N 0 38.4	87 06.7	N 0 56.1	Mirfak	309 15.8	N49 47.5
01	286 06.9	172 25.0	03.9	215 00.9	30.8	104 15.0	38.4	102 09.1	56.0	Nunki	76 28.2	S26 19.1
02	301 09.4	187 24.2	03.5	230 01.5	31.0	119 17.3	38.3	117 11.5	56.0	Peacock	53 57.1	S56 47.6
03	316 11.8	202 23.3 ..	03.1	245 02.1 ..	31.3	134 19.6 ..	38.2	132 13.9 ..	56.0	Pollux	243 57.9	N28 04.3
04	331 14.3	217 22.5	02.6	260 02.6	31.5	149 21.9	38.1	147 16.3	55.9	Procyon	245 25.6	N 5 16.4
05	346 16.7	232 21.7	02.2	275 03.2	31.8	164 24.2	38.0	162 18.7	55.9			
06	1 19.2	247 20.9	N23 01.8	290 03.8	N22 32.0	179 26.5	N 0 37.9	177 21.1	N 0 55.8	Rasalhague	96 28.8	N12 34.5
07	16 21.7	262 20.1	01.3	305 04.4	32.3	194 28.8	37.9	192 23.5	55.8	Regulus	208 09.6	N12 03.6
08	31 24.1	277 19.3	00.9	320 05.0	32.5	209 31.1	37.8	207 25.9	55.8	Rigel	281 35.9	S 8 13.4
T 09	46 26.6	292 18.5 ..	00.4	335 05.6 ..	32.8	224 33.4 ..	37.7	222 28.3 ..	55.7	Rigil Kent.	140 24.7	S60 45.6
U 10	61 29.1	307 17.7	23 00.0	350 06.2	33.0	239 35.7	37.6	237 30.7	55.7	Sabik	102 40.2	S15 42.1
E 11	76 31.5	322 16.8	22 59.6	5 06.8	33.3	254 37.9	37.5	252 33.0	55.6			
S 12	91 34.0	337 16.0	N22 59.1	20 07.4	N22 33.5	269 40.2	N 0 37.4	267 35.4	N 0 55.6	Schedar	350 08.5	N56 25.8
D 13	106 36.5	352 15.2	58.7	35 08.0	33.8	284 42.5	37.4	282 37.8	55.6	Shaula	96 54.6	S37 05.4
A 14	121 38.9	7 14.4	58.2	50 08.6	34.0	299 44.8	37.3	297 40.2	55.5	Sirius	258 55.6	S16 41.5
Y 15	136 41.4	22 13.6 ..	57.8	65 09.2 ..	34.3	314 47.1 ..	37.2	312 42.6 ..	55.5	Spica	158 56.9	S11 03.8
16	151 43.9	37 12.8	57.3	80 09.8	34.5	329 49.4	37.1	327 45.0	55.4	Suhail	223 10.7	S43 21.6
17	166 46.3	52 12.0	56.9	95 10.3	34.8	344 51.7	37.0	342 47.4	55.4			
18	181 48.8	67 11.2	N22 56.4	110 10.9	N22 35.0	359 54.0	N 0 36.9	357 49.8	N 0 55.4	Vega	80 55.1	N38 46.0
19	196 51.2	82 10.4	56.0	125 11.5	35.3	14 56.3	36.8	12 52.2	55.3	Zuben'ubi	137 32.2	S15 57.9
20	211 53.7	97 09.6	55.5	140 12.1	35.5	29 58.6	36.8	27 54.6	55.3		S.H.A.	Mer. Pass.
21	226 56.2	112 08.8 ..	55.1	155 12.7 ..	35.7	45 00.9 ..	36.7	42 57.0 ..	55.2		° ′	h m
22	241 58.6	127 08.0	54.6	170 13.3	36.0	60 03.2	36.6	57 59.4	55.2	Venus	247 40.2	13 30
23	257 01.1	142 07.2	54.1	185 13.9	36.2	75 05.5	36.5	73 01.8	55.2	Mars	289 40.8	10 41
Mer. Pass.	5 58.7	v −0.8	d 0.4	v 0.6	d 0.3	v 2.3	d 0.1	v 2.4	d 0.0	Jupiter	178 12.2	18 04
										Saturn	176 03.7	18 12

G.M.T.	SUN G.H.A.	SUN Dec.	MOON G.H.A.	v	Dec.	d	H.P.
d h	° ′	° ′	° ′	′	° ′	′	′
21 00	179 36.6	N23 26.4	318 25.4	10.3	S18 47.1	5.5	56.1
01	194 36.5	26.4	332 54.7	10.3	18 41.6	5.6	56.1
02	209 36.3	26.4	347 24.0	10.3	18 36.0	5.7	56.2
03	224 36.2 ··	26.4	1 53.3	10.3	18 30.3	5.8	56.2
04	239 36.1	26.4	16 22.6	10.4	18 24.5	5.9	56.2
05	254 35.9	26.4	30 52.0	10.3	18 18.6	6.0	56.2
06	269 35.8	N23 26.4	45 21.3	10.4	S18 12.6	6.1	56.2
07	284 35.7	26.4	59 50.7	10.4	18 06.5	6.2	56.3
08	299 35.5	26.4	74 20.1	10.4	18 00.3	6.3	56.3
S 09	314 35.4 ··	26.4	88 49.5	10.4	17 54.0	6.4	56.3
U 10	329 35.3	26.4	103 18.9	10.5	17 47.6	6.5	56.3
N 11	344 35.1	26.4	117 48.4	10.4	17 41.1	6.6	56.4
D 12	359 35.0	N23 26.4	132 17.8	10.5	S17 34.5	6.7	56.4
A 13	14 34.8	26.4	146 47.3	10.5	17 27.8	6.8	56.4
Y 14	29 34.7	26.4	161 16.8	10.5	17 21.0	6.9	56.4
15	44 34.6 ··	26.4	175 46.3	10.5	17 14.1	6.9	56.4
16	59 34.4	26.4	190 15.8	10.6	17 07.2	7.1	56.5
17	74 34.3	26.4	204 45.4	10.5	17 00.1	7.1	56.5
18	89 34.2	N23 26.4	219 14.9	10.6	S16 53.0	7.3	56.5
19	104 34.0	26.4	233 44.5	10.6	16 45.7	7.3	56.5
20	119 33.9	26.4	248 14.1	10.6	16 38.4	7.5	56.6
21	134 33.8 ··	26.4	262 43.7	10.6	16 30.9	7.5	56.6
22	149 33.6	26.4	277 13.3	10.7	16 23.4	7.6	56.6
23	164 33.5	26.4	291 43.0	10.7	16 15.8	7.7	56.6
22 00	179 33.4	N23 26.3	306 12.7	10.7	S16 08.1	7.8	56.7
01	194 33.2	26.3	320 42.4	10.7	16 00.3	7.9	56.7
02	209 33.1	26.3	335 12.1	10.7	15 52.4	7.9	56.7
03	224 33.0 ··	26.3	349 41.8	10.7	15 44.5	8.1	56.7
04	239 32.8	26.3	4 11.5	10.8	15 36.4	8.1	56.7
05	254 32.7	26.3	18 41.3	10.7	15 28.3	8.3	56.8
06	269 32.5	N23 26.3	33 11.0	10.8	S15 20.0	8.3	56.8
07	284 32.4	26.3	47 40.8	10.8	15 11.7	8.4	56.8
08	299 32.3	26.2	62 10.6	10.9	15 03.3	8.4	56.8
M 09	314 32.1 ··	26.2	76 40.5	10.8	14 54.9	8.6	56.9
O 10	329 32.0	26.2	91 10.3	10.9	14 46.3	8.7	56.9
N 11	344 31.9	26.2	105 40.2	10.9	14 37.6	8.7	56.9
D 12	359 31.7	N23 26.2	120 10.1	10.9	S14 28.9	8.8	56.9
A 13	14 31.6	26.2	134 40.0	10.9	14 20.1	8.9	57.0
Y 14	29 31.5	26.1	149 09.9	10.9	14 11.2	9.0	57.0
15	44 31.3 ··	26.1	163 39.8	10.9	14 02.2	9.0	57.0
16	59 31.2	26.1	178 09.8	10.9	13 53.2	9.2	57.0
17	74 31.1	26.1	192 39.7	11.0	13 44.0	9.2	57.1
18	89 30.9	N23 26.1	207 09.7	11.0	S13 34.8	9.3	57.1
19	104 30.8	26.0	221 39.7	11.0	13 25.5	9.3	57.1
20	119 30.7	26.0	236 09.7	11.1	13 16.2	9.5	57.1
21	134 30.5 ··	26.0	250 39.8	11.0	13 06.7	9.5	57.2
22	149 30.4	26.0	265 09.8	11.1	12 57.2	9.6	57.2
23	164 30.3	25.9	279 39.9	11.0	12 47.6	9.6	57.2
23 00	179 30.1	N23 25.9	294 09.9	11.1	S12 38.0	9.8	57.2
01	194 30.0	25.9	308 40.0	11.2	12 28.2	9.8	57.3
02	209 29.8	25.9	323 10.1	11.2	12 18.4	9.8	57.3
03	224 29.7 ··	25.8	337 40.3	11.1	12 08.6	10.0	57.3
04	239 29.6	25.8	352 10.4	11.1	11 58.6	10.0	57.4
05	254 29.4	25.8	6 40.5	11.2	11 48.6	10.1	57.4
06	269 29.3	N23 25.8	21 10.7	11.2	S11 38.5	10.2	57.4
07	284 29.2	25.7	35 40.9	11.1	11 28.3	10.2	57.4
08	299 29.0	25.7	50 11.0	11.2	11 18.1	10.3	57.5
T 09	314 28.9 ··	25.7	64 41.2	11.2	11 07.8	10.3	57.5
U 10	329 28.8	25.6	79 11.4	11.3	10 57.5	10.4	57.5
E 11	344 28.6	25.6	93 41.7	11.2	10 47.1	10.5	57.5
S 12	359 28.5	N23 25.6	108 11.9	11.2	S10 36.6	10.6	57.5
D 13	14 28.4	25.5	122 42.1	11.3	10 26.0	10.6	57.6
A 14	29 28.2	25.5	137 12.4	11.2	10 15.4	10.7	57.6
Y 15	44 28.1 ··	25.5	151 42.6	11.3	10 04.7	10.7	57.6
16	59 28.0	25.4	166 12.9	11.2	9 54.0	10.8	57.6
17	74 27.8	25.4	180 43.1	11.3	9 43.2	10.9	57.7
18	89 27.7	N23 25.3	195 13.4	11.3	S 9 32.3	10.9	57.7
19	104 27.6	25.3	209 43.7	11.3	9 21.4	10.9	57.7
20	119 27.4	25.3	224 14.0	11.3	9 10.5	11.1	57.8
21	134 27.3 ··	25.2	238 44.3	11.3	8 59.4	11.1	57.8
22	149 27.2	25.2	253 14.6	11.3	8 48.3	11.1	57.8
23	164 27.0	25.1	267 44.9	11.3	8 37.2	11.2	57.8
S.D. 15.8	d 0.0		S.D. 15.4		15.5		15.7

Lat.	Twilight Naut.	Twilight Civil	Sunrise	Moonrise 21	Moonrise 22	Moonrise 23	Moonrise 24
°	h m	h m	h m	h m	h m	h m	h m
N 72	▯	▯	▯	■	01 47	01 19	01 01
N 70	▯	▯	▯	01 25	01 08	00 57	00 49
68	▯	▯	▯	00 38	00 40	00 40	00 39
66	▯	▯	▯	00 07	00 19	00 26	00 30
64	////	////	01 31	24 02	00 02	00 14	00 23
62	////	////	02 09	23 48	24 04	00 04	00 17
60	////	00 49	02 36	23 36	23 56	24 12	00 12
N 58	////	01 40	02 56	23 26	23 48	24 07	00 07
56	////	02 10	03 13	23 17	23 42	24 03	00 03
54	00 45	02 33	03 27	23 09	23 36	23 59	24 20
52	01 32	02 51	03 40	23 02	23 30	23 56	24 19
50	02 00	03 06	03 51	22 55	23 25	23 52	24 18
45	02 46	03 36	04 13	22 41	23 15	23 46	24 15
N 40	03 17	03 58	04 31	22 30	23 06	23 40	24 12
35	03 40	04 17	04 46	22 20	22 59	23 35	24 10
30	03 59	04 32	04 59	22 11	22 52	23 31	24 08
20	04 28	04 57	05 22	21 56	22 40	23 23	24 05
N 10	04 50	05 18	05 41	21 43	22 30	23 16	24 02
0	05 09	05 36	05 58	21 31	22 21	23 10	23 59
S 10	05 26	05 53	06 16	21 18	22 11	23 04	23 56
20	05 43	06 10	06 34	21 05	22 01	22 57	23 53
30	05 59	06 29	06 55	20 50	21 49	22 49	23 50
35	06 08	06 40	07 08	20 41	21 42	22 45	23 48
40	06 17	06 52	07 22	20 31	21 34	22 40	23 46
45	06 28	07 05	07 39	20 19	21 25	22 34	23 44
S 50	06 40	07 21	08 00	20 05	21 14	22 27	23 41
52	06 45	07 29	08 10	19 58	21 09	22 23	23 39
54	06 51	07 37	08 21	19 50	21 04	22 20	23 38
56	06 57	07 46	08 33	19 42	20 57	22 16	23 36
58	07 04	07 56	08 48	19 32	20 50	22 11	23 34
S 60	07 11	08 08	09 06	19 22	20 42	22 06	23 32

Lat.	Sunset	Twilight Civil	Twilight Naut.	Moonset 21	Moonset 22	Moonset 23	Moonset 24
°	h m	h m	h m	h m	h m	h m	h m
N 72	▯	▯	▯	■	05 53	08 06	10 07
N 70	▯	▯	▯	04 29	06 32	08 26	10 17
68	▯	▯	▯	05 15	06 58	08 42	10 25
66	▯	▯	▯	05 45	07 18	08 55	10 32
64	22 33	////	////	06 08	07 35	09 05	10 38
62	21 54	////	////	06 26	07 48	09 14	10 42
60	21 28	23 14	////	06 40	07 59	09 22	10 47
N 58	21 07	22 23	////	06 53	08 09	09 28	10 50
56	20 51	21 53	////	07 04	08 17	09 34	10 54
54	20 36	21 31	23 18	07 13	08 25	09 39	10 57
52	20 24	21 13	22 31	07 22	08 31	09 44	10 59
50	20 13	20 58	22 03	07 29	08 37	09 48	11 02
45	19 50	20 28	21 18	07 45	08 50	09 58	11 07
N 40	19 32	20 05	20 47	07 59	09 01	10 05	11 11
35	19 17	19 47	20 24	08 10	09 10	10 12	11 15
30	19 04	19 32	20 05	08 20	09 18	10 18	11 18
20	18 42	19 07	19 36	08 36	09 32	10 28	11 24
N 10	18 23	18 46	19 13	08 51	09 44	10 36	11 29
0	18 06	18 28	18 54	09 04	09 55	10 44	11 33
S 10	17 48	18 11	18 37	09 18	10 06	10 52	11 38
20	17 30	17 54	18 21	09 32	10 17	11 01	11 43
30	17 08	17 35	18 05	09 49	10 31	11 10	11 48
35	16 56	17 24	17 56	09 58	10 38	11 16	11 51
40	16 42	17 12	17 46	10 09	10 47	11 22	11 55
45	16 25	16 59	17 37	10 21	10 57	11 29	11 59
S 50	16 04	16 43	17 24	10 37	11 09	11 38	12 03
52	15 54	16 35	17 19	10 44	11 15	11 41	12 06
54	15 43	16 27	17 13	10 52	11 21	11 46	12 08
56	15 30	16 18	17 07	11 01	11 28	11 51	12 11
58	15 16	16 08	17 00	11 11	11 36	11 56	12 13
S 60	14 58	15 56	16 53	11 22	11 44	12 02	12 17

Day	SUN Eqn. of Time 00h	SUN Eqn. of Time 12h	SUN Mer. Pass.	MOON Mer. Pass. Upper	MOON Mer. Pass. Lower	Age	Phase
	m s	m s	h m	h m	h m	d	
21	01 33	01 40	12 02	02 52	15 18	19	
22	01 46	01 53	12 02	03 43	16 08	20	◐
23	01 59	02 06	12 02	04 32	16 57	21	

G.M.T.	ARIES G.H.A.	VENUS −3.3 G.H.A.	Dec.	MARS +1.7 G.H.A.	Dec.	JUPITER −1.6 G.H.A.	Dec.	SATURN +1.2 G.H.A.	Dec.	STARS Name	S.H.A.	Dec.
24 00	272 03.6	157 06.3	N22 53.7	200 14.5	N22 36.5	90 07.7	N 0 36.4	88 04.2	N 0 55.1	Acamar	315 37.1	S40 22.7
01	287 06.0	172 05.5	53.2	215 15.1	36.7	105 10.0	36.3	103 06.6	55.1	Achernar	335 45.1	S57 19.7
02	302 08.5	187 04.7	52.8	230 15.7	37.0	120 12.3	36.2	118 09.0	55.1	Acrux	173 36.6	S63 00.0
03	317 11.0	202 03.9 ··	52.3	245 16.3 ··	37.2	135 14.6 ··	36.2	133 11.4 ··	55.0	Adhara	255 32.1	S28 56.9
04	332 13.4	217 03.1	51.8	260 16.9	37.4	150 16.9	36.1	148 13.8	55.0	Aldebaran	291 17.7	N16 28.2
05	347 15.9	232 02.3	51.4	275 17.5	37.7	165 19.2	36.0	163 16.2	54.9			
06	2 18.3	247 01.5	N22 50.9	290 18.1	N22 37.9	180 21.5	N 0 35.9	178 18.6	N 0 54.9	Alioth	166 42.0	N56 04.0
W 07	17 20.8	262 00.7	50.4	305 18.6	38.2	195 23.8	35.8	193 21.0	54.9	Alkaid	153 17.9	N49 24.7
E 08	32 23.3	276 59.9	50.0	320 19.2	38.4	210 26.1	35.7	208 23.4	54.8	Al Na'ir	28 14.0	S47 02.9
D 09	47 25.7	291 59.1 ··	49.5	335 19.8 ··	38.7	225 28.3 ··	35.6	223 25.8 ··	54.8	Alnilam	276 11.5	S 1 12.9
N 10	62 28.2	306 58.3	49.0	350 20.4	38.9	240 30.6	35.5	238 28.2	54.7	Alphard	218 20.3	S 8 34.7
E 11	77 30.7	321 57.5	48.6	5 21.0	39.1	255 32.9	35.5	253 30.5	54.7			
S 12	92 33.1	336 56.7	N22 48.1	20 21.6	N22 39.4	270 35.2	N 0 35.4	268 32.9	N 0 54.6	Alphecca	126 31.4	N26 46.8
D 13	107 35.6	351 55.9	47.6	35 22.2	39.6	285 37.5	35.3	283 35.3	54.6	Alpheratz	358 08.8	N28 59.0
A 14	122 38.1	6 55.1	47.2	50 22.8	39.8	300 39.8	35.2	298 37.7	54.6	Altair	62 31.7	N 8 49.1
Y 15	137 40.5	21 54.3 ··	46.7	65 23.4 ··	40.1	315 42.1 ··	35.1	313 40.1 ··	54.5	Ankaa	353 39.8	S42 24.3
16	152 43.0	36 53.5	46.2	80 24.0	40.3	330 44.4	35.0	328 42.5	54.5	Antares	112 55.9	S26 23.5
17	167 45.5	51 52.7	45.7	95 24.6	40.6	345 46.6	34.9	343 44.9	54.4			
18	182 47.9	66 51.9	N22 45.2	110 25.2	N22 40.8	0 48.9	N 0 34.8	358 47.3	N 0 54.4	Arcturus	146 17.8	N19 16.9
19	197 50.4	81 51.1	44.8	125 25.7	41.0	15 51.2	34.8	13 49.7	54.4	Atria	108 19.1	S68 59.7
20	212 52.8	96 50.3	44.3	140 26.3	41.3	30 53.5	34.7	28 52.1	54.3	Avior	234 28.5	S59 27.1
21	227 55.3	111 49.5 ··	43.8	155 26.9 ··	41.5	45 55.8 ··	34.6	43 54.5 ··	54.3	Bellatrix	278 58.5	N 6 19.9
22	242 57.8	126 48.7	43.3	170 27.5	41.7	60 58.1	34.5	58 56.9	54.2	Betelgeuse	271 28.1	N 7 24.2
23	258 00.2	141 47.9	42.8	185 28.1	42.0	76 00.4	34.4	73 59.3	54.2			
25 00	273 02.7	156 47.2	N22 42.3	200 28.7	N22 42.2	91 02.6	N 0 34.3	89 01.7	N 0 54.1	Canopus	264 07.5	S52 41.2
01	288 05.2	171 46.4	41.9	215 29.3	42.4	106 04.9	34.2	104 04.1	54.1	Capella	281 11.0	N45 58.7
02	303 07.6	186 45.6	41.4	230 29.9	42.7	121 07.2	34.1	119 06.4	54.1	Deneb	49 47.7	N45 12.7
03	318 10.1	201 44.8 ··	40.9	245 30.5 ··	42.9	136 09.5 ··	34.1	134 08.8 ··	54.0	Denebola	182 58.6	N14 40.7
04	333 12.6	216 44.0	40.4	260 31.1	43.1	151 11.8	34.0	149 11.2	54.0	Diphda	349 20.4	S18 05.3
05	348 15.0	231 43.2	39.9	275 31.7	43.4	166 14.1	33.9	164 13.6	53.9			
06	3 17.5	246 42.4	N22 39.4	290 32.3	N22 43.6	181 16.3	N 0 33.8	179 16.0	N 0 53.9	Dubhe	194 21.7	N61 51.4
07	18 20.0	261 41.6	38.9	305 32.9	43.8	196 18.6	33.7	194 18.4	53.9	Elnath	278 43.9	N28 35.4
T 08	33 22.4	276 40.8	38.4	320 33.5	44.1	211 20.9	33.6	209 20.8	53.8	Eltanin	90 56.9	N51 29.6
H 09	48 24.9	291 40.0 ··	37.9	335 34.1 ··	44.3	226 23.2 ··	33.5	224 23.2 ··	53.8	Enif	34 10.9	N 9 47.3
U 10	63 27.3	306 39.2	37.4	350 34.6	44.5	241 25.5	33.4	239 25.6	53.7	Fomalhaut	15 50.7	S29 43.1
R 11	78 29.8	321 38.4	36.9	5 35.2	44.8	256 27.8	33.3	254 28.0	53.7			
S 12	93 32.3	336 37.6	N22 36.4	20 35.8	N22 45.0	271 30.0	N 0 33.3	269 30.4	N 0 53.6	Gacrux	172 28.1	S57 00.7
D 13	108 34.7	351 36.8	35.9	35 36.4	45.2	286 32.3	33.2	284 32.7	53.6	Gienah	176 17.4	S17 26.3
A 14	123 37.2	6 36.0	35.4	50 37.0	45.5	301 34.6	33.1	299 35.1	53.6	Hadar	149 22.3	S60 17.2
Y 15	138 39.7	21 35.3 ··	34.9	65 37.6 ··	45.7	316 36.9 ··	33.0	314 37.5 ··	53.5	Hamal	328 28.5	N23 22.3
16	153 42.1	36 34.5	34.4	80 38.2	45.9	331 39.2	32.9	329 39.9	53.5	Kaus Aust.	84 15.7	S34 23.6
17	168 44.6	51 33.7	33.9	95 38.8	46.1	346 41.4	32.8	344 42.3	53.4			
18	183 47.1	66 32.9	N22 33.4	110 39.4	N22 46.4	1 43.7	N 0 32.7	359 44.7	N 0 53.4	Kochab	137 18.3	N74 14.3
19	198 49.5	81 32.1	32.9	125 40.0	46.6	16 46.0	32.6	14 47.1	53.3	Markab	14 02.5	N15 06.2
20	213 52.0	96 31.3	32.4	140 40.6	46.8	31 48.3	32.5	29 49.5	53.3	Menkar	314 40.8	N 4 00.9
21	228 54.4	111 30.5 ··	31.9	155 41.2 ··	47.1	46 50.6 ··	32.4	44 51.9 ··	53.3	Menkent	148 36.2	S36 16.8
22	243 56.9	126 29.7	31.4	170 41.7	47.3	61 52.8	32.3	59 54.3	53.2	Miaplacidus	221 45.5	S69 38.7
23	258 59.4	141 29.0	30.9	185 42.3	47.5	76 55.1	32.3	74 56.6	53.2			
26 00	274 01.8	156 28.2	N22 30.4	200 42.9	N22 47.7	91 57.4	N 0 32.2	89 59.0	N 0 53.1	Mirfak	309 15.7	N49 47.5
01	289 04.3	171 27.4	29.9	215 43.5	48.0	106 59.7	32.1	105 01.4	53.1	Nunki	76 28.2	S26 19.1
02	304 06.8	186 26.6	29.4	230 44.1	48.2	122 02.0	32.0	120 03.8	53.0	Peacock	53 57.1	S56 47.6
03	319 09.2	201 25.8 ··	28.8	245 44.7 ··	48.4	137 04.2 ··	31.9	135 06.2 ··	53.0	Pollux	243 57.9	N28 04.3
04	334 11.7	216 25.0	28.3	260 45.3	48.6	152 06.5	31.8	150 08.6	53.0	Procyon	245 25.6	N 5 16.4
05	349 14.2	231 24.2	27.8	275 45.9	48.9	167 08.8	31.7	165 11.0	52.9			
06	4 16.6	246 23.5	N22 27.3	290 46.5	N22 49.1	182 11.1	N 0 31.6	180 13.4	N 0 52.9	Rasalhague	96 28.8	N12 34.5
07	19 19.1	261 22.7	26.8	305 47.1	49.3	197 13.3	31.5	195 15.7	52.8	Regulus	208 09.6	N12 03.6
08	34 21.6	276 21.9	26.2	320 47.7	49.5	212 15.6	31.4	210 18.1	52.8	Rigel	281 35.8	S 8 13.4
F 09	49 24.0	291 21.1 ··	25.7	335 48.3 ··	49.8	227 17.9 ··	31.3	225 20.5 ··	52.7	Rigil Kent.	140 24.7	S60 45.6
R 10	64 26.5	306 20.3	25.2	350 48.9	50.0	242 20.2	31.3	240 22.9	52.7	Sabik	102 40.2	S15 42.1
I 11	79 28.9	321 19.6	24.7	5 49.4	50.2	257 22.4	31.2	255 25.3	52.7			
D 12	94 31.4	336 18.8	N22 24.1	20 50.0	N22 50.4	272 24.7	N 0 31.1	270 27.7	N 0 52.6	Schedar	350 08.5	N56 25.8
A 13	109 33.9	351 18.0	23.6	35 50.6	50.6	287 27.0	31.0	285 30.1	52.6	Shaula	96 54.6	S37 05.4
Y 14	124 36.3	6 17.2	23.1	50 51.2	50.9	302 29.3	30.9	300 32.5	52.5	Sirius	258 55.6	S16 41.5
15	139 38.8	21 16.4 ··	22.6	65 51.8 ··	51.1	317 31.5 ··	30.8	315 34.8 ··	52.5	Spica	158 56.9	S11 03.8
16	154 41.3	36 15.7	22.0	80 52.4	51.3	332 33.8	30.7	330 37.2	52.4	Suhail	223 10.7	S43 21.6
17	169 43.7	51 14.9	21.5	95 53.0	51.5	347 36.1	30.6	345 39.6	52.4			
18	184 46.2	66 14.1	N22 21.0	110 53.6	N22 51.7	2 38.4	N 0 30.5	0 42.0	N 0 52.3	Vega	80 55.0	N38 46.0
19	199 48.7	81 13.3	20.4	125 54.2	52.0	17 40.6	30.4	15 44.4	52.3	Zuben'ubi	137 32.2	S15 57.9
20	214 51.1	96 12.6	19.9	140 54.8	52.2	32 42.9	30.3	30 46.8	52.3		S.H.A.	Mer. Pass.
21	229 53.6	111 11.8 ··	19.4	155 55.4 ··	52.4	47 45.2 ··	30.2	45 49.2 ··	52.2	Venus	243 44.5	13 34
22	244 56.1	126 11.0	18.8	170 56.0	52.6	62 47.5	30.1	60 51.5	52.2	Mars	287 26.0	10 38
23	259 58.5	141 10.2	18.3	185 56.5	52.8	77 49.7	30.0	75 53.9	52.1	Jupiter	177 59.9	17 53
Mer. Pass. 5 46.9		v −0.8 d 0.5		v 0.6 d 0.2		v 2.3 d 0.1		v 2.4 d 0.0		Saturn	175 59.0	18 01

SUN and MOON

G.M.T.	SUN G.H.A.	Dec.	MOON G.H.A.	v	Dec.	d	H.P.
24 00	179 26.9	N23 25.1	282 15.2	11.3	S 8 26.0	11.2	57.9
01	194 26.8	25.1	296 45.5	11.3	8 14.8	11.3	57.9
02	209 26.6	25.0	311 15.8	11.3	8 03.5	11.4	57.9
03	224 26.5	.. 25.0	325 46.1	11.3	7 52.1	11.4	57.9
04	239 26.4	24.9	340 16.4	11.3	7 40.7	11.4	58.0
05	254 26.2	24.9	354 46.7	11.3	7 29.3	11.5	58.0
06	269 26.1	N23 24.8	9 17.0	11.4	S 7 17.8	11.6	58.0
07	284 26.0	24.8	23 47.4	11.3	7 06.2	11.6	58.0
08	299 25.8	24.7	38 17.7	11.3	6 54.6	11.6	58.1
09	314 25.7	.. 24.7	52 48.0	11.3	6 43.0	11.7	58.1
10	329 25.6	24.6	67 18.3	11.3	6 31.3	11.8	58.1
11	344 25.4	24.6	81 48.6	11.3	6 19.5	11.7	58.1
12	359 25.3	N23 24.5	96 18.9	11.3	S 6 07.8	11.8	58.2
13	14 25.2	24.5	110 49.2	11.3	5 56.0	11.9	58.2
14	29 25.0	24.4	125 19.5	11.2	5 44.1	11.9	58.2
15	44 24.9	.. 24.4	139 49.7	11.3	5 32.2	11.9	58.3
16	59 24.8	24.3	154 20.0	11.3	5 20.3	12.0	58.3
17	74 24.6	24.3	168 50.3	11.2	5 08.3	12.0	58.3
18	89 24.5	N23 24.2	183 20.5	11.3	S 4 56.3	12.1	58.3
19	104 24.4	24.2	197 50.8	11.2	4 44.2	12.1	58.4
20	119 24.2	24.1	212 21.0	11.2	4 32.1	12.1	58.4
21	134 24.1	.. 24.0	226 51.2	11.3	4 20.0	12.2	58.4
22	149 24.0	24.0	241 21.5	11.2	4 07.8	12.1	58.4
23	164 23.9	23.9	255 51.7	11.1	3 55.7	12.3	58.5
25 00	179 23.7	N23 23.9	270 21.8	11.2	S 3 43.4	12.2	58.5
01	194 23.6	23.8	284 52.0	11.2	3 31.2	12.3	58.5
02	209 23.5	23.7	299 22.2	11.1	3 18.9	12.3	58.5
03	224 23.3	.. 23.7	313 52.3	11.1	3 06.6	12.4	58.6
04	239 23.2	23.6	328 22.4	11.2	2 54.2	12.3	58.6
05	254 23.0	23.5	342 52.6	11.0	2 41.9	12.4	58.6
06	269 22.9	N23 23.5	357 22.6	11.1	S 2 29.5	12.4	58.7
07	284 22.8	23.4	11 52.7	11.1	2 17.1	12.5	58.7
08	299 22.6	23.3	26 22.8	11.0	2 04.6	12.4	58.7
09	314 22.5	.. 23.3	40 52.8	11.0	1 52.2	12.5	58.7
10	329 22.4	23.2	55 22.8	11.0	1 39.7	12.5	58.8
11	344 22.2	23.1	69 52.8	10.9	1 27.2	12.5	58.8
12	359 22.1	N23 23.1	84 22.7	11.0	S 1 14.7	12.6	58.8
13	14 22.0	23.0	98 52.7	10.9	1 02.1	12.5	58.8
14	29 21.8	22.9	113 22.6	10.9	0 49.6	12.6	58.9
15	44 21.7	.. 22.9	127 52.5	10.8	0 37.0	12.6	58.9
16	59 21.6	22.8	142 22.3	10.9	0 24.4	12.6	58.9
17	74 21.4	22.7	156 52.2	10.8	S 0 11.8	12.6	58.9
18	89 21.3	N23 22.7	171 22.0	10.8	N 0 00.8	12.6	59.0
19	104 21.2	22.6	185 51.8	10.7	0 13.4	12.6	59.0
20	119 21.0	22.5	200 21.5	10.7	0 26.0	12.7	59.0
21	134 20.9	.. 22.4	214 51.2	10.7	0 38.7	12.6	59.0
22	149 20.8	22.4	229 20.9	10.7	0 51.3	12.7	59.1
23	164 20.6	22.3	243 50.6	10.6	1 04.0	12.7	59.1
26 00	179 20.5	N23 22.2	258 20.2	10.6	N 1 16.7	12.6	59.1
01	194 20.4	22.1	272 49.8	10.5	1 29.3	12.7	59.1
02	209 20.3	22.1	287 19.3	10.5	1 42.0	12.7	59.2
03	224 20.1	.. 22.0	301 48.8	10.5	1 54.7	12.6	59.2
04	239 20.0	21.9	316 18.3	10.4	2 07.3	12.7	59.2
05	254 19.9	21.8	330 47.7	10.4	2 20.0	12.7	59.2
06	269 19.7	N23 21.7	345 17.1	10.4	N 2 32.7	12.6	59.3
07	284 19.6	21.6	359 46.5	10.3	2 45.3	12.7	59.3
08	299 19.5	21.6	14 15.8	10.3	2 58.0	12.7	59.3
09	314 19.3	.. 21.5	28 45.1	10.2	3 10.7	12.6	59.3
10	329 19.2	21.4	43 14.3	10.2	3 23.3	12.6	59.4
11	344 19.1	21.3	57 43.5	10.1	3 35.9	12.7	59.4
12	359 18.9	N23 21.2	72 12.6	10.1	N 3 48.6	12.6	59.4
13	14 18.8	21.1	86 41.7	10.1	4 01.2	12.6	59.4
14	29 18.7	21.1	101 10.8	10.0	4 13.8	12.6	59.5
15	44 18.5	.. 21.0	115 39.8	10.0	4 26.4	12.6	59.5
16	59 18.4	20.9	130 08.8	9.9	4 39.0	12.5	59.5
17	74 18.3	20.8	144 37.7	9.9	4 51.5	12.6	59.5
18	89 18.1	N23 20.7	159 06.6	9.8	N 5 04.1	12.5	59.6
19	104 18.0	20.6	173 35.4	9.8	5 16.6	12.5	59.6
20	119 17.9	20.5	188 04.2	9.7	5 29.1	12.5	59.6
21	134 17.8	.. 20.4	202 32.9	9.7	5 41.6	12.5	59.6
22	149 17.6	20.3	217 01.6	9.6	5 54.1	12.4	59.6
23	164 17.5	20.2	231 30.2	9.5	6 06.5	12.4	59.7
	S.D. 15.8	d 0.1	S.D. 15.9		16.0		16.2

Day labels: 24 = WEDNESDAY; 25 = THURSDAY; 26 = FRIDAY.

Twilight / Sunrise / Moonrise

Lat.	Naut.	Civil	Sunrise	Moonrise 24	25	26	27
N 72	□	□	□	01 01	00 46	00 33	00 18
N 70	□	□	□	00 49	00 41	00 34	00 27
68	□	□	□	00 39	00 37	00 36	00 34
66	□	□	□	00 30	00 34	00 37	00 40
64	////	////	01 33	00 23	00 31	00 38	00 45
62	////	////	02 11	00 17	00 28	00 39	00 50
60	////	00 51	02 37	00 12	00 26	00 39	00 54
N 58	////	01 42	02 57	00 07	00 24	00 40	00 57
56	////	02 12	03 14	00 03	00 22	00 41	01 00
54	00 47	02 34	03 28	24 20	00 20	00 41	01 03
52	01 34	02 52	03 41	24 19	00 19	00 42	01 06
50	02 02	03 07	03 52	24 18	00 18	00 42	01 08
45	02 47	03 37	04 14	24 15	00 15	00 43	01 13
N 40	03 18	03 59	04 32	24 12	00 12	00 44	01 17
35	03 41	04 18	04 47	24 10	00 10	00 45	01 21
30	03 59	04 33	05 00	24 08	00 08	00 46	01 24
20	04 29	04 58	05 22	24 05	00 05	00 47	01 30
N 10	04 51	05 18	05 41	24 02	00 02	00 48	01 35
0	05 10	05 36	05 59	23 59	24 49	00 49	01 40
S 10	05 27	05 53	06 16	23 56	24 50	00 50	01 45
20	05 43	06 11	06 35	23 53	24 51	00 51	01 50
30	06 00	06 30	06 56	23 50	24 53	00 53	01 56
35	06 09	06 40	07 08	23 48	24 53	00 53	02 00
40	06 18	06 52	07 23	23 46	24 54	00 54	02 04
45	06 28	07 05	07 39	23 44	24 55	00 55	02 09
S 50	06 40	07 22	08 00	23 41	24 57	00 57	02 14
52	06 45	07 29	08 10	23 39	24 57	00 57	02 17
54	06 51	07 37	08 21	23 38	24 58	00 58	02 20
56	06 57	07 46	08 34	23 36	24 59	00 59	02 23
58	07 04	07 57	08 48	23 34	24 59	00 59	02 27
S 60	07 11	08 08	09 06	23 32	25 00	01 00	02 31

Sunset / Twilight / Moonset

Lat.	Sunset	Civil	Naut.	Moonset 24	25	26	27
N 72	□	□	□	10 07	12 06	14 06	16 14
N 70	□	□	□	10 17	12 08	14 00	15 58
68	□	□	□	10 25	12 09	13 55	15 46
66	□	□	□	10 32	12 11	13 55	15 36
64	22 32	////	////	10 38	12 12	13 48	15 27
62	21 54	////	////	10 42	12 13	13 45	15 20
60	21 28	23 13	////	10 47	12 13	13 42	15 14
N 58	21 07	22 23	////	10 50	12 14	13 40	15 08
56	20 51	21 53	////	10 54	12 15	13 38	15 03
54	20 36	21 31	23 17	10 57	12 15	13 36	14 59
52	20 23	21 13	22 31	10 59	12 16	13 35	14 55
50	20 13	20 58	22 03	11 02	12 16	13 33	14 52
45	19 51	20 28	21 18	11 07	12 18	13 30	14 44
N 40	19 33	20 06	20 47	11 11	12 18	13 27	14 38
35	19 18	19 47	20 24	11 15	12 19	13 25	14 32
30	19 05	19 32	20 06	11 18	12 20	13 23	14 28
20	18 43	19 07	19 36	11 24	12 21	13 19	14 19
N 10	18 24	18 47	19 14	11 29	12 22	13 16	14 12
0	18 06	18 29	18 55	11 33	12 23	13 13	14 05
S 10	17 49	18 12	18 38	11 38	12 23	13 10	13 59
20	17 30	17 54	18 22	11 43	12 24	13 07	13 51
30	17 09	17 35	18 05	11 48	12 25	13 03	13 43
35	16 57	17 25	17 57	11 51	12 26	13 01	13 39
40	16 43	17 13	17 47	11 55	12 26	12 59	13 33
45	16 26	17 00	17 37	11 59	12 27	12 56	13 27
S 50	16 05	16 44	17 25	12 03	12 28	12 53	13 20
52	15 55	16 36	17 20	12 06	12 28	12 51	13 16
54	15 44	16 28	17 14	12 08	12 29	12 50	13 13
56	15 31	16 19	17 08	12 11	12 29	12 48	13 09
58	15 17	16 09	17 01	12 13	12 30	12 46	13 04
S 60	14 59	15 57	16 54	12 17	12 30	12 44	12 59

SUN / MOON

Day	SUN Eqn. of Time 00h	12h	Mer. Pass.	MOON Mer. Pass. Upper	Lower	Age	Phase
	m s	m s	h m	h m	h m	d	
24	02 12	02 19	12 02	05 22	17 46	22	
25	02 25	02 31	12 03	06 11	18 36	23	
26	02 38	02 44	12 03	07 01	19 27	24	◖

G.M.T.	ARIES G.H.A.	VENUS −3.3 G.H.A.	Dec.	MARS +1.7 G.H.A.	Dec.	JUPITER −1.6 G.H.A.	Dec.	SATURN +1.2 G.H.A.	Dec.	STARS Name	S.H.A.	Dec.
27 00	275 01.0	156 09.5	N22 17.8	200 57.1	N22 53.0	92 52.0	N 0 30.0	90 56.3	N 0 52.1	Acamar	315 37.1	S40 22.7
01	290 03.4	171 08.7	17.2	215 57.7	53.3	107 54.3	29.9	105 58.7	52.0	Achernar	335 45.1	S57 19.7
02	305 05.9	186 07.9	16.7	230 58.3	53.5	122 56.6	29.8	121 01.1	52.0	Acrux	173 36.6	S63 00.0
03	320 08.4	201 07.1	·· 16.1	245 58.9	·· 53.7	137 58.8	·· 29.7	136 03.5	·· 51.9	Adhara	255 32.1	S28 56.8
04	335 10.8	216 06.4	15.6	260 59.5	53.9	153 01.1	29.6	151 05.8	51.9	Aldebaran	291 17.7	N16 28.2
05	350 13.3	231 05.6	15.0	276 00.1	54.1	168 03.4	29.5	166 08.2	51.9			
06	5 15.8	246 04.8	N22 14.5	291 00.7	N22 54.3	183 05.6	N 0 29.4	181 10.6	N 0 51.8	Alioth	166 42.0	N56 04.0
07	20 18.2	261 04.0	14.0	306 01.3	54.6	198 07.9	29.3	196 13.0	51.8	Alkaid	153 17.9	N49 24.7
S 08	35 20.7	276 03.3	13.4	321 01.9	54.8	213 10.2	29.2	211 15.4	51.7	Al Na'ir	28 14.0	S47 02.9
A 09	50 23.2	291 02.5	·· 12.9	336 02.5	·· 55.0	228 12.5	·· 29.1	226 17.8	·· 51.7	Alnilam	276 11.5	S 1 12.9
T 10	65 25.6	306 01.7	12.3	351 03.1	55.2	243 14.7	29.0	241 20.1	51.6	Alphard	218 20.3	S 8 34.7
U 11	80 28.1	321 01.0	11.8	6 03.7	55.4	258 17.0	28.9	256 22.5	51.6			
R 12	95 30.5	336 00.2	N22 11.2	21 04.2	N22 55.6	273 19.3	N 0 28.8	271 24.9	N 0 51.5	Alphecca	126 31.4	N26 46.8
D 13	110 33.0	350 59.4	10.7	36 04.8	55.8	288 21.5	28.7	286 27.3	51.5	Alpheratz	358 08.7	N28 59.0
A 14	125 35.5	5 58.7	10.1	51 05.4	56.0	303 23.8	28.6	301 29.7	51.5	Altair	62 31.7	N 8 49.2
Y 15	140 37.9	20 57.9	·· 09.5	66 06.0	·· 56.3	318 26.1	·· 28.5	316 32.1	·· 51.4	Ankaa	353 39.7	S42 24.3
16	155 40.4	35 57.1	09.0	81 06.6	56.5	333 28.3	28.4	331 34.4	51.4	Antares	112 55.9	S26 23.5
17	170 42.9	50 56.4	08.4	96 07.2	56.7	348 30.6	28.4	346 36.8	51.3			
18	185 45.3	65 55.6	N22 07.9	111 07.8	N22 56.9	3 32.9	N 0 28.3	1 39.2	N 0 51.3	Arcturus	146 17.8	N19 16.9
19	200 47.8	80 54.8	07.3	126 08.4	57.1	18 35.1	28.2	16 41.6	51.2	Atria	108 19.1	S68 59.7
20	215 50.3	95 54.1	06.8	141 09.0	57.3	33 37.4	28.1	31 44.0	51.2	Avior	234 28.6	S59 27.1
21	230 52.7	110 53.3	·· 06.2	156 09.6	·· 57.5	48 39.7	·· 28.0	46 46.4	·· 51.1	Bellatrix	278 58.5	N 6 19.9
22	245 55.2	125 52.5	05.6	171 10.2	57.7	63 42.0	27.9	61 48.7	51.1	Betelgeuse	271 28.0	N 7 24.2
23	260 57.7	140 51.8	05.1	186 10.8	57.9	78 44.2	27.8	76 51.1	51.0			
28 00	276 00.1	155 51.0	N22 04.5	201 11.4	N22 58.1	93 46.5	N 0 27.7	91 53.5	N 0 51.0	Canopus	264 07.5	S52 41.2
01	291 02.6	170 50.2	03.9	216 11.9	58.4	108 48.8	27.6	106 55.9	50.9	Capella	281 11.0	N45 58.7
02	306 05.0	185 49.5	03.4	231 12.5	58.6	123 51.0	27.5	121 58.3	50.9	Deneb	49 47.7	N45 12.7
03	321 07.5	200 48.7	·· 02.8	246 13.1	·· 58.8	138 53.3	·· 27.4	137 00.6	·· 50.9	Denebola	182 58.6	N14 40.7
04	336 10.0	215 48.0	02.2	261 13.7	59.0	153 55.6	27.3	152 03.0	50.8	Diphda	349 20.4	S18 05.3
05	351 12.4	230 47.2	01.7	276 14.3	59.2	168 57.8	27.2	167 05.4	50.8			
06	6 14.9	245 46.4	N22 01.1	291 14.9	N22 59.4	184 00.1	N 0 27.1	182 07.8	N 0 50.7	Dubhe	194 21.8	N61 51.4
07	21 17.4	260 45.7	22 00.5	306 15.5	59.6	199 02.3	27.0	197 10.2	50.7	Elnath	278 43.8	N28 35.4
08	36 19.8	275 44.9	21 59.9	321 16.1	22 59.8	214 04.6	26.9	212 12.5	50.6	Eltanin	90 56.9	N51 29.6
S 09	51 22.3	290 44.2	·· 59.4	336 16.7	23 00.0	229 06.9	·· 26.8	227 14.9	·· 50.6	Enif	34 10.8	N 9 47.3
U 10	66 24.8	305 43.4	58.8	351 17.3	00.2	244 09.1	26.7	242 17.3	50.5	Fomalhaut	15 50.7	S29 43.1
N 11	81 27.2	320 42.6	58.2	6 17.9	00.4	259 11.4	26.6	257 19.7	50.5			
D 12	96 29.7	335 41.9	N21 57.6	21 18.5	N23 00.6	274 13.7	N 0 26.5	272 22.1	N 0 50.4	Gacrux	172 28.1	S57 00.7
A 13	111 32.2	350 41.1	57.1	36 19.1	00.8	289 15.9	26.4	287 24.4	50.4	Gienah	176 17.4	S17 26.3
Y 14	126 34.6	5 40.4	56.5	51 19.6	01.0	304 18.2	26.3	302 26.8	50.3	Hadar	149 22.3	S60 17.2
15	141 37.1	20 39.6	·· 55.9	66 20.2	·· 01.2	319 20.5	·· 26.2	317 29.2	·· 50.3	Hamal	328 28.5	N23 22.3
16	156 39.5	35 38.9	55.3	81 20.8	01.4	334 22.7	26.1	332 31.6	50.2	Kaus Aust.	84 15.7	S34 23.6
17	171 42.0	50 38.1	54.7	96 21.4	01.6	349 25.0	26.0	347 34.0	50.2			
18	186 44.5	65 37.3	N21 54.1	111 22.0	N23 01.8	4 27.2	N 0 25.9	2 36.3	N 0 50.2	Kochab	137 18.3	N74 14.3
19	201 46.9	80 36.6	53.6	126 22.6	02.0	19 29.5	25.8	17 38.7	50.1	Markab	14 02.5	N15 06.2
20	216 49.4	95 35.8	53.0	141 23.2	02.2	34 31.8	25.7	32 41.1	50.1	Menkar	314 40.8	N 4 00.9
21	231 51.9	110 35.1	·· 52.4	156 23.8	·· 02.4	49 34.0	·· 25.6	47 43.5	·· 50.0	Menkent	148 36.2	S36 16.8
22	246 54.3	125 34.3	51.8	171 24.4	02.6	64 36.3	25.6	62 45.8	50.0	Miaplacidus	221 45.5	S69 38.6
23	261 56.8	140 33.6	51.2	186 25.0	02.8	79 38.6	25.5	77 48.2	49.9			
29 00	276 59.3	155 32.8	N21 50.6	201 25.6	N23 03.0	94 40.8	N 0 25.4	92 50.6	N 0 49.9	Mirfak	309 15.7	N49 47.5
01	292 01.7	170 32.1	50.0	216 26.2	03.2	109 43.1	25.3	107 53.0	49.8	Nunki	76 28.1	S26 19.1
02	307 04.2	185 31.3	49.4	231 26.7	03.4	124 45.3	25.2	122 55.4	49.8	Peacock	53 57.0	S56 47.6
03	322 06.6	200 30.6	·· 48.8	246 27.3	·· 03.6	139 47.6	·· 25.1	137 57.7	·· 49.7	Pollux	243 57.9	N28 04.3
04	337 09.1	215 29.8	48.2	261 27.9	03.8	154 49.9	25.0	153 00.1	49.7	Procyon	245 25.6	N 5 16.4
05	352 11.6	230 29.1	47.6	276 28.5	04.0	169 52.1	24.9	168 02.5	49.6			
06	7 14.0	245 28.3	N21 47.0	291 29.1	N23 04.2	184 54.4	N 0 24.8	183 04.9	N 0 49.6	Rasalhague	96 28.8	N12 34.5
07	22 16.5	260 27.6	46.4	306 29.7	04.4	199 56.6	24.7	198 07.2	49.5	Regulus	208 09.6	N12 03.6
08	37 19.0	275 26.8	45.8	321 30.3	04.6	214 58.9	24.6	213 09.6	49.5	Rigel	281 35.8	S 8 13.4
M 09	52 21.4	290 26.1	·· 45.2	336 30.9	·· 04.8	230 01.2	·· 24.5	228 12.0	·· 49.4	Rigil Kent.	140 24.7	S60 45.6
O 10	67 23.9	305 25.3	44.6	351 31.5	05.0	245 03.4	24.4	243 14.4	49.4	Sabik	102 40.2	S15 42.1
N 11	82 26.4	320 24.6	44.0	6 32.1	05.2	260 05.7	24.3	258 16.7	49.3			
D 12	97 28.8	335 23.8	N21 43.4	21 32.7	N23 05.4	275 07.9	N 0 24.2	273 19.1	N 0 49.3	Schedar	350 08.4	N56 25.8
A 13	112 31.3	350 23.1	42.8	36 33.3	05.6	290 10.2	24.1	288 21.5	49.2	Shaula	96 54.6	S37 05.4
Y 14	127 33.8	5 22.4	42.2	51 33.9	05.8	305 12.5	24.0	303 23.9	49.2	Sirius	258 55.6	S16 41.5
15	142 36.2	20 21.6	·· 41.6	66 34.4	·· 06.0	320 14.7	·· 23.9	318 26.2	·· 49.1	Spica	158 56.9	S11 03.8
16	157 38.7	35 20.9	41.0	81 35.0	06.2	335 17.0	23.8	333 28.6	49.1	Suhail	223 10.7	S43 21.6
17	172 41.1	50 20.1	40.4	96 35.6	06.4	350 19.2	23.7	348 31.0	49.0			
18	187 43.6	65 19.4	N21 39.8	111 36.2	N23 06.5	5 21.5	N 0 23.6	3 33.4	N 0 49.0	Vega	80 55.0	N38 46.0
19	202 46.1	80 18.6	39.2	126 36.8	06.7	20 23.7	23.5	18 35.7	49.0	Zuben'ubi	137 32.2	S15 57.9
20	217 48.5	95 17.9	38.6	141 37.4	06.9	35 26.0	23.4	33 38.1	48.9		S.H.A.	Mer. Pass.
21	232 51.0	110 17.2	·· 38.0	156 38.0	·· 07.1	50 28.2	·· 23.3	48 40.5	·· 48.9	Venus	239 50.9	13 37
22	247 53.5	125 16.4	37.3	171 38.6	07.3	65 30.5	23.2	63 42.9	48.8	Mars	285 11.2	10 35
23	262 55.9	140 15.7	36.7	186 39.2	07.5	80 32.8	23.1	78 45.2	48.8	Jupiter	177 46.4	17 42
Mer. Pass.	5 35.1	v −0.8	d 0.6	v 0.6	d 0.2	v 2.3	d 0.1	v 2.4	d 0.0	Saturn	175 53.4	17 50

SUN / MOON

G.M.T.	SUN G.H.A.	SUN Dec.	MOON G.H.A.	v	MOON Dec.	d	H.P.
27 00	179 17.4	N23 20.1	245 58.7	9.5	N 6 18.9	12.4	59.7
01	194 17.2	20.1	260 27.2	9.5	6 31.3	12.4	59.7
02	209 17.1	20.0	274 55.7	9.4	6 43.7	12.3	59.7
03	224 17.0	·· 19.9	289 24.1	9.3	6 56.0	12.3	59.8
04	239 16.8	19.8	303 52.4	9.3	7 08.3	12.3	59.8
05	254 16.7	19.7	318 20.7	9.3	7 20.6	12.2	59.8
06	269 16.6	N23 19.6	332 49.0	9.1	N 7 32.8	12.2	59.8
07	284 16.5	19.5	347 17.1	9.1	7 45.0	12.2	59.8
S 08	299 16.3	19.4	1 45.2	9.1	7 57.2	12.1	59.9
A 09	314 16.2	·· 19.3	16 13.3	9.0	8 09.3	12.1	59.9
T 10	329 16.1	19.2	30 41.3	8.9	8 21.4	12.0	59.9
U 11	344 15.9	19.1	45 09.2	8.9	8 33.4	12.0	59.9
R 12	359 15.8	N23 19.0	59 37.1	8.8	N 8 45.4	12.0	59.9
D 13	14 15.7	18.9	74 04.9	8.8	8 57.4	11.9	60.0
A 14	29 15.5	18.8	88 32.7	8.7	9 09.3	11.9	60.0
Y 15	44 15.4	·· 18.6	103 00.4	8.6	9 21.2	11.8	60.0
16	59 15.3	18.5	117 28.0	8.5	9 33.0	11.7	60.0
17	74 15.2	18.4	131 55.5	8.5	9 44.7	11.8	60.0
18	89 15.0	N23 18.3	146 23.0	8.5	N 9 56.5	11.6	60.1
19	104 14.9	18.2	160 50.5	8.3	10 08.1	11.6	60.1
20	119 14.8	18.1	175 17.8	8.3	10 19.7	11.6	60.1
21	134 14.6	·· 18.0	189 45.1	8.3	10 31.3	11.5	60.1
22	149 14.5	17.9	204 12.4	8.1	10 42.8	11.4	60.1
23	164 14.4	17.8	218 39.5	8.1	10 54.2	11.4	60.1
28 00	179 14.2	N23 17.7	233 06.6	8.1	N11 05.6	11.3	60.2
01	194 14.1	17.6	247 33.7	8.0	11 16.9	11.2	60.2
02	209 14.0	17.4	262 00.7	7.9	11 28.1	11.2	60.2
03	224 13.9	·· 17.3	276 27.6	7.8	11 39.3	11.2	60.2
04	239 13.7	17.2	290 54.4	7.8	11 50.5	11.0	60.2
05	254 13.6	17.1	305 21.2	7.6	12 01.5	11.0	60.2
06	269 13.5	N23 17.0	319 47.8	7.7	N12 12.5	10.9	60.2
07	284 13.3	16.9	334 14.5	7.5	12 23.4	10.8	60.3
08	299 13.2	16.8	348 41.0	7.5	12 34.2	10.8	60.3
S 09	314 13.1	·· 16.6	3 07.5	7.4	12 45.0	10.7	60.3
U 10	329 13.0	16.5	17 33.9	7.4	12 55.7	10.6	60.3
N 11	344 12.8	16.4	32 00.3	7.3	13 06.3	10.5	60.3
D 12	359 12.7	N23 16.3	46 26.6	7.2	N13 16.8	10.5	60.3
A 13	14 12.6	16.2	60 52.8	7.1	13 27.3	10.3	60.3
Y 14	29 12.5	16.0	75 18.9	7.1	13 37.6	10.3	60.3
15	44 12.3	·· 15.9	89 45.0	7.0	13 47.9	10.2	60.4
16	59 12.2	15.8	104 11.0	7.0	13 58.1	10.1	60.4
17	74 12.1	15.7	118 37.0	6.8	14 08.2	10.1	60.4
18	89 11.9	N23 15.5	133 02.8	6.8	N14 18.3	9.9	60.4
19	104 11.8	15.4	147 28.6	6.8	14 28.2	9.9	60.4
20	119 11.7	15.3	161 54.4	6.6	14 38.1	9.7	60.4
21	134 11.6	·· 15.2	176 20.0	6.6	14 47.8	9.7	60.4
22	149 11.4	15.0	190 45.6	6.5	14 57.5	9.5	60.4
23	164 11.3	14.9	205 11.1	6.5	15 07.0	9.5	60.4
29 00	179 11.2	N23 14.8	219 36.6	6.4	N15 16.5	9.4	60.4
01	194 11.1	14.7	234 02.0	6.3	15 25.9	9.3	60.5
02	209 10.9	14.5	248 27.3	6.3	15 35.2	9.1	60.5
03	224 10.8	·· 14.4	262 52.6	6.2	15 44.3	9.1	60.5
04	239 10.7	14.3	277 17.8	6.1	15 53.4	9.0	60.5
05	254 10.5	14.1	291 42.9	6.0	16 02.4	8.8	60.5
06	269 10.4	N23 14.0	306 07.9	6.0	N16 11.2	8.8	60.5
07	284 10.3	13.9	320 32.9	6.0	16 20.0	8.6	60.5
08	299 10.2	13.7	334 57.9	5.8	16 28.6	8.5	60.5
M 09	314 10.0	·· 13.6	349 22.7	5.8	16 37.1	8.5	60.5
O 10	329 09.9	13.5	3 47.5	5.8	16 45.6	8.3	60.5
N 11	344 09.8	13.3	18 12.3	5.7	16 53.9	8.2	60.5
D 12	359 09.7	N23 13.2	32 37.0	5.6	N17 02.1	8.1	60.5
A 13	14 09.5	13.0	47 01.6	5.5	17 10.2	7.9	60.5
Y 14	29 09.4	12.9	61 26.1	5.5	17 18.1	7.9	60.5
15	44 09.3	·· 12.8	75 50.6	5.5	17 26.0	7.7	60.5
16	59 09.2	12.6	90 15.1	5.4	17 33.7	7.6	60.5
17	74 09.0	12.5	104 39.5	5.3	17 41.3	7.5	60.5
18	89 08.9	N23 12.3	119 03.8	5.3	N17 48.8	7.4	60.5
19	104 08.8	12.2	133 28.1	5.2	17 56.2	7.2	60.5
20	119 08.7	12.1	147 52.3	5.1	18 03.4	7.1	60.5
21	134 08.5	·· 11.9	162 16.4	5.2	18 10.5	7.0	60.5
22	149 08.4	11.8	176 40.6	5.0	18 17.5	6.9	60.5
23	164 08.3	11.6	191 04.6	5.0	18 24.4	6.7	60.5
	S.D. 15.8	d 0.1	S.D. 16.3		16.4		16.5

Twilight / Sunrise / Moonrise

Lat.	Twilight Naut.	Twilight Civil	Sunrise	Moonrise 27	28	29	30
N 72	□	□	□	00 18	{00 02 / 23 37}	□	□
N 70	□	□	□	00 27	00 19	{00 06 / 23 55}	□
68	□	□	□	00 34	00 33	00 34	00 38
66	□	□	□	00 40	00 45	00 53	01 06
64	////	////	01 36	00 45	00 55	01 08	01 28
62	////	////	02 13	00 50	01 03	01 21	01 46
60	////	00 56	02 39	00 54	01 10	01 32	02 01
N 58	////	01 44	02 59	00 57	01 17	01 41	02 13
56	////	02 14	03 16	01 00	01 23	01 50	02 24
54	00 52	02 36	03 30	01 03	01 28	01 57	02 34
52	01 36	02 54	03 42	01 06	01 32	02 04	02 42
50	02 03	03 09	03 53	01 08	01 37	02 10	02 50
45	02 49	03 38	04 15	01 13	01 46	02 23	03 07
N 40	03 19	04 01	04 33	01 17	01 53	02 34	03 20
35	03 42	04 19	04 48	01 21	02 00	02 43	03 32
30	04 03	04 34	05 01	01 24	02 06	02 52	03 42
20	04 29	04 59	05 23	01 30	02 16	03 06	04 00
N 10	04 52	05 19	05 42	01 35	02 25	03 18	04 15
0	05 11	05 37	05 59	01 40	02 34	03 30	04 30
S 10	05 28	05 54	06 17	01 45	02 42	03 42	04 44
20	05 44	06 11	06 35	01 50	02 52	03 55	05 00
30	06 00	06 30	06 56	01 56	03 02	04 10	05 18
35	06 09	06 40	07 09	02 00	03 09	04 19	05 28
40	06 18	06 52	07 23	02 04	03 16	04 28	05 40
45	06 28	07 06	07 39	02 09	03 24	04 40	05 55
S 50	06 40	07 22	08 00	02 14	03 34	04 54	06 12
52	06 45	07 29	08 10	02 17	03 39	05 01	06 20
54	06 51	07 37	08 21	02 20	03 44	05 08	06 30
56	06 57	07 46	08 33	02 23	03 49	05 16	06 40
58	07 04	07 56	08 48	02 27	03 56	05 26	06 52
S 60	07 11	08 08	09 05	02 31	04 03	05 36	07 06

Sunset / Twilight / Moonset

Lat.	Sunset	Twilight Civil	Twilight Naut.	Moonset 27	28	29	30
N 72	□	□	□	16 14	18 34	□	□
N 70	□	□	□	15 58	18 03	20 20	□
68	□	□	□	15 46	17 41	19 39	21 33
66	□	□	□	15 36	17 23	19 11	20 51
64	22 29	////	////	15 27	17 09	18 50	20 23
62	21 53	////	////	15 20	16 57	18 33	20 01
60	21 27	23 09	////	15 14	16 47	18 18	19 43
N 58	21 07	22 21	////	15 08	16 38	18 06	19 28
56	20 50	21 52	////	15 03	16 30	17 56	19 16
54	20 36	21 30	23 13	14 59	16 23	17 47	19 05
52	20 24	21 12	22 29	14 55	16 17	17 39	18 55
50	20 13	20 57	22 02	14 52	16 12	17 31	18 46
45	19 51	20 28	21 17	14 44	16 00	17 15	18 28
N 40	19 33	20 06	20 47	14 38	15 50	17 03	18 13
35	19 18	19 48	20 24	14 32	15 42	16 52	18 00
30	19 05	19 32	20 06	14 28	15 34	16 42	17 49
20	18 43	19 08	19 37	14 21	15 22	16 26	17 30
N 10	18 24	18 47	19 14	14 12	15 11	16 12	17 14
0	18 07	18 29	18 56	14 05	15 00	15 58	16 59
S 10	17 50	18 12	18 39	13 59	14 50	15 45	16 43
20	17 31	17 55	18 23	13 51	14 39	15 31	16 27
30	17 10	17 36	18 06	13 43	14 27	15 15	16 08
35	16 58	17 26	17 58	13 39	14 19	15 05	15 57
40	16 44	17 14	17 48	13 33	14 11	14 54	15 44
45	16 27	17 01	17 38	13 27	14 02	14 42	15 29
S 50	16 06	16 45	17 26	13 20	13 50	14 27	15 11
52	15 57	16 37	17 21	13 16	13 45	14 20	15 03
54	15 46	16 29	17 15	13 13	13 39	14 12	14 53
56	15 33	16 20	17 09	13 09	13 33	14 03	14 42
58	15 19	16 10	17 03	13 04	13 25	13 53	14 30
S 60	15 01	15 59	16 55	12 59	13 17	13 42	14 16

SUN / MOON

Day	SUN Eqn. of Time 00h	SUN Eqn. of Time 12h	Mer. Pass.	MOON Mer. Pass. Upper	MOON Mer. Pass. Lower	Age	Phase
	m s	m s	h m	h m	h m	d	
27	02 50	02 57	12 03	07 53	20 20	25	
28	03 03	03 09	12 03	08 47	21 15	26	
29	03 15	03 21	12 03	09 44	22 14	27	◑

G.M.T.	ARIES G.H.A.	VENUS −3.3 G.H.A.	Dec.	MARS +1.7 G.H.A.	Dec.	JUPITER −1.5 G.H.A.	Dec.	SATURN +1.2 G.H.A.	Dec.	STARS Name	S.H.A.	Dec.
30 00	277 58.4	155 14.9 N21	36.1	201 39.8 N23	07.7	95 35.0 N 0	23.0	93 47.6 N 0	48.7	Acamar	315 37.1	S40 22.6
01	293 00.9	170 14.2	35.5	216 40.4	07.9	110 37.3	22.9	108 50.0	48.7	Achernar	335 45.0	S57 19.7
02	308 03.3	185 13.4	34.9	231 41.0	08.1	125 39.5	22.8	123 52.4	48.6	Acrux	173 36.6	S63 00.0
03	323 05.8	200 12.7 ··	34.3	246 41.6 ··	08.3	140 41.8 ··	22.7	138 54.7 ··	48.6	Adhara	255 32.1	S28 56.8
04	338 08.3	215 12.0	33.6	261 42.1	08.4	155 44.0	22.6	153 57.1	48.5	Aldebaran	291 17.7	N16 28.2
05	353 10.7	230 11.2	33.0	276 42.7	08.6	170 46.3	22.5	168 59.5	48.5			
06	8 13.2	245 10.5 N21	32.4	291 43.3 N23	08.8	185 48.5 N 0	22.4	184 01.9 N 0	48.4	Alioth	166 42.0	N56 04.0
07	23 15.6	260 09.8	31.8	306 43.9	09.0	200 50.8	22.3	199 04.2	48.4	Alkaid	153 17.9	N49 24.7
T 08	38 18.1	275 09.0	31.1	321 44.5	09.2	215 53.1	22.2	214 06.6	48.3	Al Na'ir	28 14.0	S47 02.9
U 09	53 20.6	290 08.3 ··	30.5	336 45.1 ··	09.4	230 55.3 ··	22.1	229 09.0 ··	48.3	Alnilam	276 11.4	S 1 12.8
E 10	68 23.0	305 07.6	29.9	351 45.7	09.6	245 57.6	22.0	244 11.3	48.2	Alphard	218 20.3	S 8 34.7
S 11	83 25.5	320 06.8	29.3	6 46.3	09.8	260 59.8	21.9	259 13.7	48.2			
D 12	98 28.0	335 06.1 N21	28.6	21 46.9 N23	09.9	276 02.1 N 0	21.8	274 16.1 N 0	48.1	Alphecca	126 31.4	N26 46.8
A 13	113 30.4	350 05.4	28.0	36 47.5	10.1	291 04.3	21.7	289 18.5	48.1	Alpheratz	358 08.7	N28 59.1
Y 14	128 32.9	5 04.6	27.4	51 48.1	10.3	306 06.6	21.5	304 20.8	48.0	Altair	62 31.7	N 8 49.2
15	143 35.4	20 03.9 ··	26.7	66 48.7 ··	10.5	321 08.8 ··	21.4	319 23.2 ··	48.0	Ankaa	353 39.7	S42 24.2
16	158 37.8	35 03.2	26.1	81 49.3	10.7	336 11.1	21.3	334 25.6	47.9	Antares	112 55.9	S26 23.5
17	173 40.3	50 02.4	25.5	96 49.9	10.9	351 13.3	21.2	349 27.9	47.9			
18	188 42.7	65 01.7 N21	24.8	111 50.4 N23	11.1	6 15.6 N 0	21.1	4 30.3 N 0	47.8	Arcturus	146 17.8	N19 16.9
19	203 45.2	80 01.0	24.2	126 51.0	11.2	21 17.8	21.0	19 32.7	47.8	Atria	108 19.1	S68 59.7
20	218 47.7	95 00.2	23.6	141 51.6	11.4	36 20.1	20.9	34 35.1	47.7	Avior	234 28.6	S59 27.1
21	233 50.1	109 59.5 ··	22.9	156 52.2 ··	11.6	51 22.3 ··	20.8	49 37.4 ··	47.7	Bellatrix	278 58.5	N 6 19.9
22	248 52.6	124 58.8	22.3	171 52.8	11.8	66 24.6	20.7	64 39.8	47.6	Betelgeuse	271 28.0	N 7 24.2
23	263 55.1	139 58.0	21.6	186 53.4	12.0	81 26.8	20.6	79 42.2	47.6			
1 00	278 57.5	154 57.3 N21	21.0	201 54.0 N23	12.1	96 29.1 N 0	20.5	94 44.5 N 0	47.5	Canopus	264 07.5	S52 41.2
01	294 00.0	169 56.6	20.4	216 54.6	12.3	111 31.3	20.4	109 46.9	47.5	Capella	281 11.0	N45 58.7
02	309 02.5	184 55.9	19.7	231 55.2	12.5	126 33.6	20.3	124 49.3	47.4	Deneb	49 47.7	N45 12.7
03	324 04.9	199 55.1 ··	19.1	246 55.8 ··	12.7	141 35.8 ··	20.2	139 51.6 ··	47.4	Denebola	182 58.6	N14 40.7
04	339 07.4	214 54.4	18.4	261 56.4	12.9	156 38.1	20.1	154 54.0	47.3	Diphda	349 20.3	S18 05.3
05	354 09.9	229 53.7	17.8	276 57.0	13.0	171 40.3	20.0	169 56.4	47.3			
06	9 12.3	244 53.0 N21	17.1	291 57.6 N23	13.2	186 42.6 N 0	19.9	184 58.8 N 0	47.2	Dubhe	194 21.8	N61 51.4
W 07	24 14.8	259 52.2	16.5	306 58.2	13.4	201 44.8	19.8	200 01.1	47.2	Elnath	278 43.8	N28 35.4
E 08	39 17.2	274 51.5	15.8	321 58.7	13.6	216 47.1	19.7	215 03.5	47.1	Eltanin	90 56.9	N51 29.6
D 09	54 19.7	289 50.8 ··	15.2	336 59.3 ··	13.8	231 49.3 ··	19.6	230 05.9 ··	47.0	Enif	34 10.8	N 9 47.3
N 10	69 22.2	304 50.1	14.5	351 59.9	13.9	246 51.6	19.5	245 08.2	47.0	Fomalhaut	15 50.7	S29 43.1
E 11	84 24.6	319 49.3	13.9	7 00.5	14.1	261 53.8	19.4	260 10.6	46.9			
S 12	99 27.1	334 48.6 N21	13.2	22 01.1 N23	14.3	276 56.1 N 0	19.3	275 13.0 N 0	46.9	Gacrux	172 28.1	S57 00.7
D 13	114 29.6	349 47.9	12.6	37 01.7	14.5	291 58.3	19.2	290 15.3	46.8	Gienah	176 17.4	S17 26.3
A 14	129 32.0	4 47.2	11.9	52 02.3	14.6	307 00.6	19.1	305 17.7	46.8	Hadar	149 22.3	S60 17.2
Y 15	144 34.5	19 46.5 ··	11.2	67 02.9 ··	14.8	322 02.8 ··	19.0	320 20.1 ··	46.7	Hamal	328 28.5	N23 22.3
16	159 37.0	34 45.7	10.6	82 03.5	15.0	337 05.0	18.9	335 22.4	46.7	Kaus Aust.	84 15.7	S34 23.6
17	174 39.4	49 45.0	09.9	97 04.1	15.2	352 07.3	18.8	350 24.8	46.6			
18	189 41.9	64 44.3 N21	09.3	112 04.7 N23	15.3	7 09.5 N 0	18.7	5 27.2 N 0	46.6	Kochab	137 18.4	N74 14.3
19	204 44.4	79 43.6	08.6	127 05.3	15.5	22 11.8	18.5	20 29.5	46.5	Markab	14 02.5	N15 06.2
20	219 46.8	94 42.9	07.9	142 05.9	15.7	37 14.0	18.4	35 31.9	46.5	Menkar	314 40.8	N 4 00.9
21	234 49.3	109 42.1 ··	07.3	157 06.5 ··	15.9	52 16.3 ··	18.3	50 34.3 ··	46.4	Menkent	148 36.2	S36 16.8
22	249 51.7	124 41.4	06.6	172 07.0	16.0	67 18.5	18.2	65 36.6	46.4	Miaplacidus	221 45.6	S69 38.6
23	264 54.2	139 40.7	05.9	187 07.6	16.2	82 20.8	18.1	80 39.0	46.3			
2 00	279 56.7	154 40.0 N21	05.3	202 08.2 N23	16.4	97 23.0 N 0	18.0	95 41.4 N 0	46.3	Mirfak	309 15.7	N49 47.5
01	294 59.1	169 39.3	04.6	217 08.8	16.6	112 25.3	17.9	110 43.7	46.2	Nunki	76 28.1	S26 19.1
02	310 01.6	184 38.6	03.9	232 09.4	16.7	127 27.5	17.8	125 46.1	46.2	Peacock	53 57.0	S56 47.6
03	325 04.1	199 37.8 ··	03.3	247 10.0 ··	16.9	142 29.7 ··	17.7	140 48.5 ··	46.1	Pollux	243 57.9	N28 04.3
04	340 06.5	214 37.1	02.6	262 10.6	17.1	157 32.0	17.6	155 50.8	46.1	Procyon	245 25.6	N 5 16.4
05	355 09.0	229 36.4	01.9	277 11.2	17.2	172 34.2	17.5	170 53.2	46.0			
06	10 11.5	244 35.7 N21	01.3	292 11.8 N23	17.4	187 36.5 N 0	17.4	185 55.6 N 0	46.0	Rasalhague	96 28.8	N12 34.5
07	25 13.9	259 35.0 21	00.6	307 12.4	17.6	202 38.7	17.3	200 57.9	45.9	Regulus	208 09.6	N12 03.6
T 08	40 16.4	274 34.3 20	59.9	322 13.0	17.7	217 41.0	17.2	216 00.3	45.9	Rigel	281 35.8	S 8 13.4
H 09	55 18.8	289 33.6 ··	59.2	337 13.6 ··	17.9	232 43.2 ··	17.1	231 02.7 ··	45.8	Rigil Kent.	140 24.7	S60 45.6
U 10	70 21.3	304 32.9	58.6	352 14.2	18.1	247 45.4	17.0	246 05.0	45.7	Sabik	102 40.2	S15 42.1
R 11	85 23.8	319 32.1	57.9	7 14.8	18.3	262 47.7	16.9	261 07.4	45.7			
S 12	100 26.2	334 31.4 N20	57.2	22 15.4 N23	18.4	277 49.9 N 0	16.8	276 09.8 N 0	45.6	Schedar	350 08.4	N56 25.8
D 13	115 28.7	349 30.7	56.5	37 15.9	18.6	292 52.2	16.6	291 12.1	45.6	Shaula	96 54.6	S37 05.4
A 14	130 31.2	4 30.0	55.8	52 16.5	18.8	307 54.4	16.5	306 14.5	45.5	Sirius	258 55.6	S16 41.5
Y 15	145 33.6	19 29.3 ··	55.2	67 17.1 ··	18.9	322 56.6 ··	16.4	321 16.9 ··	45.5	Spica	158 56.9	S11 03.8
16	160 36.1	34 28.6	54.5	82 17.7	19.1	337 58.9	16.3	336 19.2	45.4	Suhail	223 10.7	S43 21.6
17	175 38.6	49 27.9	53.8	97 18.3	19.3	353 01.1	16.2	351 21.6	45.4			
18	190 41.0	64 27.2 N20	53.1	112 18.9 N23	19.4	8 03.4 N 0	16.1	6 24.0 N 0	45.3	Vega	80 55.0	N38 46.0
19	205 43.5	79 26.5	52.4	127 19.6	19.6	23 05.6	16.0	21 26.3	45.3	Zuben'ubi	137 32.2	S15 57.9
20	220 46.0	94 25.8	51.7	142 20.1	19.7	38 07.8	15.9	36 28.7	45.2			
21	235 48.4	109 25.1 ··	51.1	157 20.7 ··	19.9	53 10.1 ··	15.8	51 31.0 ··	45.2			
22	250 50.9	124 24.4	50.4	172 21.3	20.1	68 12.3	15.7	66 33.4	45.1			
23	265 53.3	139 23.7	49.7	187 21.9	20.2	83 14.6	15.6	81 35.8	45.1			

										Name	S.H.A.	Mer. Pass.
										Venus	235 59.8	13 41
Mer. Pass. 5 23.3		v −0.7	d 0.7	v 0.6	d 0.2	v 2.2	d 0.1	v 2.4	d 0.1	Mars	282 56.5	10 32
										Jupiter	177 31.5	17 31
										Saturn	175 47.0	17 38

SUN and MOON

G.M.T.	SUN G.H.A.	SUN Dec.	MOON G.H.A.	v	MOON Dec.	d	H.P.
30 00	179 08.2	N23 11.5	205 28.6	5.0	N18 31.1	6.6	60.5
01	194 08.0	11.3	219 52.6	4.9	18 37.7	6.5	60.5
02	209 07.9	11.2	234 16.5	4.9	18 44.2	6.3	60.5
03	224 07.8	·· 11.0	248 40.4	4.8	18 50.5	6.2	60.5
04	239 07.7	10.9	263 04.2	4.8	18 56.7	6.1	60.5
05	254 07.5	10.7	277 28.0	4.7	19 02.8	5.9	60.5
06	269 07.4	N23 10.6	291 51.7	4.7	N19 08.7	5.8	60.5
07	284 07.3	10.4	306 15.4	4.6	19 14.5	5.7	60.5
08	299 07.2	10.3	320 39.0	4.6	19 20.2	5.5	60.5
09	314 07.0	·· 10.1	335 02.6	4.6	19 25.7	5.4	60.5
10	329 06.9	10.0	349 26.2	4.6	19 31.1	5.3	60.5
11	344 06.8	09.8	3 49.8	4.5	19 36.4	5.1	60.5
12	359 06.7	N23 09.7	18 13.3	4.4	N19 41.5	4.9	60.5
13	14 06.5	09.5	32 36.7	4.5	19 46.4	4.9	60.4
14	29 06.4	09.4	47 00.2	4.4	19 51.3	4.7	60.4
15	44 06.3	·· 09.2	61 23.6	4.4	19 56.0	4.5	60.4
16	59 06.2	09.1	75 47.0	4.3	20 00.5	4.4	60.4
17	74 06.0	08.9	90 10.3	4.4	20 04.9	4.3	60.4
18	89 05.9	N23 08.7	104 33.7	4.3	N20 09.2	4.1	60.4
19	104 05.8	08.6	118 57.0	4.3	20 13.3	3.9	60.4
20	119 05.7	08.4	133 20.3	4.2	20 17.2	3.8	60.4
21	134 05.6	·· 08.3	147 43.5	4.3	20 21.0	3.7	60.4
22	149 05.4	08.1	162 06.8	4.2	20 24.7	3.5	60.4
23	164 05.3	07.9	176 30.0	4.2	20 28.2	3.4	60.3
1 00	179 05.2	N23 07.8	190 53.2	4.2	N20 31.6	3.2	60.3
01	194 05.1	07.6	205 16.4	4.2	20 34.8	3.1	60.3
02	209 04.9	07.5	219 39.6	4.2	20 37.9	2.9	60.3
03	224 04.8	·· 07.3	234 02.8	4.2	20 40.8	2.8	60.3
04	239 04.7	07.1	248 26.0	4.2	20 43.6	2.6	60.3
05	254 04.6	07.0	262 49.2	4.1	20 46.2	2.5	60.3
06	269 04.4	N23 06.8	277 12.3	4.2	N20 48.7	2.3	60.2
07	284 04.3	06.6	291 35.5	4.2	20 51.0	2.2	60.2
08	299 04.2	06.5	305 58.7	4.2	20 53.2	2.0	60.2
09	314 04.1	·· 06.3	320 21.9	4.1	20 55.2	1.9	60.2
10	329 04.0	06.1	334 45.0	4.2	20 57.1	1.7	60.2
11	344 03.8	06.0	349 08.2	4.2	20 58.8	1.6	60.2
12	359 03.7	N23 05.8	3 31.4	4.2	N21 00.4	1.4	60.1
13	14 03.6	05.6	17 54.6	4.2	21 01.8	1.3	60.1
14	29 03.5	05.4	32 17.8	4.2	21 03.1	1.1	60.1
15	44 03.4	·· 05.3	46 41.0	4.3	21 04.2	1.0	60.1
16	59 03.2	05.1	61 04.3	4.2	21 05.2	0.8	60.1
17	74 03.1	04.9	75 27.5	4.3	21 06.0	0.7	60.1
18	89 03.0	N23 04.7	89 50.8	4.3	N21 06.7	0.5	60.0
19	104 02.9	04.6	104 14.1	4.3	21 07.2	0.4	60.0
20	119 02.7	04.4	118 37.4	4.4	21 07.6	0.2	60.0
21	134 02.6	·· 04.2	133 00.8	4.3	21 07.8	0.1	60.0
22	149 02.5	04.0	147 24.1	4.4	21 07.9	0.1	60.0
23	164 02.4	03.9	161 47.5	4.5	21 07.8	0.2	59.9
2 00	179 02.3	N23 03.7	176 11.0	4.4	N21 07.6	0.4	59.9
01	194 02.1	03.5	190 34.4	4.5	21 07.2	0.5	59.9
02	209 02.0	03.3	204 57.9	4.6	21 06.7	0.7	59.9
03	224 01.9	·· 03.1	219 21.5	4.5	21 06.0	0.8	59.9
04	239 01.8	03.0	233 45.0	4.6	21 05.2	1.0	59.8
05	254 01.7	02.8	248 08.6	4.7	21 04.2	1.1	59.8
06	269 01.5	N23 02.6	262 32.3	4.7	N21 03.1	1.2	59.8
07	284 01.4	02.4	276 56.0	4.7	21 01.9	1.4	59.7
08	299 01.3	02.2	291 19.7	4.8	21 00.5	1.6	59.7
09	314 01.2	·· 02.0	305 43.5	4.8	20 58.9	1.7	59.7
10	329 01.1	01.8	320 07.3	4.9	20 57.2	1.8	59.7
11	344 01.0	01.7	334 31.2	4.9	20 55.4	2.0	59.6
12	359 00.8	N23 01.5	348 55.1	5.0	N20 53.4	2.1	59.6
13	14 00.7	01.3	3 19.1	5.1	20 51.3	2.3	59.6
14	29 00.6	01.1	17 43.2	5.1	20 49.0	2.4	59.6
15	44 00.5	·· 00.9	32 07.3	5.1	20 46.6	2.5	59.5
16	59 00.4	00.7	46 31.4	5.2	20 44.1	2.7	59.5
17	74 00.2	00.5	60 55.6	5.3	20 41.4	2.8	59.5
18	89 00.1	N23 00.3	75 19.9	5.3	N20 38.6	2.9	59.4
19	104 00.0	23 00.1	89 44.2	5.4	20 35.7	3.1	59.4
20	118 59.9	22 59.9	104 08.6	5.5	20 32.6	3.2	59.4
21	133 59.8	·· 59.8	118 33.1	5.5	20 29.4	3.4	59.4
22	148 59.7	59.6	132 57.6	5.6	20 26.0	3.5	59.3
23	163 59.5	59.4	147 22.2	5.7	20 22.5	3.6	59.3
	S.D. 15.8	d 0.2	S.D. 16.5		16.4		16.2

(Left day labels: **TUESDAY** = 30, **WEDNESDAY** = 1, **THURSDAY** = 2)

Twilight, Sunrise, Moonrise

Lat.	Twilight Naut.	Twilight Civil	Sunrise	Moonrise 30	1	2	3
N 72	□	□	□	□	□	□	□
N 70	□	□	□	□	□	□	□
68	□	□	□	00 38	00 50	01 33	03 04
66	////	////	00 17	01 06	01 33	02 24	03 44
64	////	////	01 41	01 28	02 02	02 56	04 11
62	////	////	02 16	01 46	02 24	03 19	04 32
60	////	01 03	02 42	02 01	02 42	03 38	04 50
N 58	////	01 48	03 02	02 13	02 57	03 54	05 04
56	////	02 17	03 18	02 24	03 10	04 07	05 16
54	00 58	02 38	03 32	02 34	03 21	04 19	05 27
52	01 40	02 56	03 44	02 42	03 31	04 29	05 37
50	02 06	03 11	03 55	02 50	03 40	04 38	05 45
45	02 50	03 40	04 17	03 07	03 58	04 58	06 03
N 40	03 20	04 02	04 35	03 20	04 14	05 13	06 18
35	03 43	04 20	04 49	03 32	04 27	05 27	06 30
30	04 02	04 35	05 02	03 42	04 38	05 38	06 41
20	04 30	05 00	05 24	04 00	04 58	05 58	07 00
N 10	04 53	05 20	05 43	04 15	05 15	06 16	07 16
0	05 11	05 38	06 00	04 30	05 31	06 32	07 31
S 10	05 28	05 54	06 17	04 44	05 47	06 48	07 46
20	05 44	06 12	06 36	05 00	06 04	07 05	08 02
30	06 00	06 30	06 56	05 18	06 24	07 25	08 21
35	06 09	06 41	07 09	05 28	06 35	07 37	08 32
40	06 18	06 52	07 23	05 40	06 49	07 50	08 44
45	06 28	07 05	07 39	05 55	07 04	08 06	08 59
S 50	06 40	07 21	07 59	06 12	07 24	08 26	09 16
52	06 45	07 29	08 09	06 20	07 33	08 35	09 25
54	06 51	07 37	08 20	06 30	07 43	08 45	09 34
56	06 57	07 45	08 32	06 40	07 55	08 57	09 44
58	07 03	07 55	08 47	06 52	08 09	09 11	09 56
S 60	07 10	08 07	09 04	07 06	08 25	09 26	10 10

Sunset, Twilight, Moonset

Lat.	Sunset	Twilight Civil	Twilight Naut.	Moonset 30	1	2	3
N 72	□	□	□	□	□	□	□
N 70	□	□	□	□	□	□	□
68	□	□	□	21 33	22 59	23 34	23 44
66	23 41	////	////	20 51	22 08	22 54	23 16
64	22 25	////	////	20 23	21 37	22 26	22 55
62	21 50	////	////	20 01	21 13	22 04	22 38
60	21 25	23 03	////	19 43	20 54	21 47	22 24
N 58	21 05	22 18	////	19 28	20 38	21 32	22 12
56	20 49	21 50	////	19 16	20 25	21 20	22 01
54	20 35	21 29	23 08	19 05	20 13	21 09	21 51
52	20 23	21 11	22 27	18 55	20 03	20 59	21 43
50	20 12	20 57	22 01	18 46	19 54	20 50	21 36
45	19 50	20 27	21 17	18 28	19 34	20 32	21 19
N 40	19 33	20 05	20 47	18 13	19 19	20 16	21 06
35	19 18	19 47	20 24	18 00	19 05	20 04	20 55
30	19 05	19 32	20 06	17 49	18 54	19 52	20 45
20	18 43	19 08	19 37	17 30	18 34	19 33	20 27
N 10	18 25	18 48	19 15	17 14	18 16	19 16	20 12
0	18 07	18 30	18 56	16 59	18 00	19 00	19 58
S 10	17 50	18 13	18 39	16 43	17 44	18 45	19 44
20	17 32	17 56	18 23	16 27	17 26	18 28	19 29
30	17 11	17 37	18 07	16 08	17 06	18 08	19 11
35	16 59	17 27	17 59	15 57	16 54	17 57	19 01
40	16 45	17 15	17 49	15 44	16 41	17 43	18 49
45	16 29	17 02	17 39	15 29	16 25	17 28	18 35
S 50	16 08	16 46	17 28	15 11	16 05	17 09	18 18
52	15 58	16 39	17 23	15 03	15 56	16 59	18 10
54	15 48	16 31	17 17	14 53	15 46	16 49	18 01
56	15 35	16 22	17 11	14 42	15 34	16 38	17 51
58	15 21	16 12	17 05	14 30	15 20	16 24	17 39
S 60	15 04	16 01	16 57	14 16	15 04	16 09	17 26

SUN and MOON

Day	SUN Eqn. of Time 00h	SUN Eqn. of Time 12h	SUN Mer. Pass.	MOON Mer. Pass. Upper	MOON Mer. Pass. Lower	Age	Phase
30	03 27	03 33	12 04	10 44	23 15	28	
1	03 39	03 45	12 04	11 45	24 16	29	
2	03 51	03 56	12 04	12 46	00 16	01	●

G.M.T.	ARIES G.H.A.	VENUS −3.3 G.H.A.	Dec.	MARS +1.7 G.H.A.	Dec.	JUPITER −1.5 G.H.A.	Dec.	SATURN +1.2 G.H.A.	Dec.	STARS Name	S.H.A.	Dec.
3 00	280 55.8	154 23.0	N20 49.0	202 22.5	N23 20.4	98 16.8	N 0 15.5	96 38.1	N 0 45.0	Acamar	315 37.1	S40 22.6
01	295 58.3	169 22.3	48.3	217 23.1	20.6	113 19.0	15.4	111 40.5	44.9	Achernar	335 45.0	S57 19.7
02	311 00.7	184 21.6	47.6	232 23.7	20.7	128 21.3	15.3	126 42.9	44.9	Acrux	173 36.7	S63 00.0
03	326 03.2	199 20.9	·· 46.9	247 24.3	·· 20.9	143 23.5	·· 15.1	141 45.2	·· 44.8	Adhara	255 32.1	S28 56.8
04	341 05.7	214 20.2	46.2	262 24.8	21.1	158 25.8	15.0	156 47.6	44.8	Aldebaran	291 17.7	N16 28.2
05	356 08.1	229 19.5	45.5	277 25.4	21.2	173 28.0	14.9	171 49.9	44.7			
06	11 10.6	244 18.8	N20 44.8	292 26.0	N23 21.4	188 30.2	N 0 14.8	186 52.3	N 0 44.7	Alioth	166 42.0	N56 04.0
07	26 13.1	259 18.1	44.1	307 26.6	21.5	203 32.5	14.7	201 54.7	44.6	Alkaid	153 17.9	N49 24.7
08	41 15.5	274 17.4	43.4	322 27.2	21.7	218 34.7	14.6	216 57.0	44.6	Al Na'ir	28 13.9	S47 02.9
F 09	56 18.0	289 16.7	·· 42.7	337 27.8	·· 21.9	233 36.9	·· 14.5	231 59.4	·· 44.5	Alnilam	276 11.4	S 1 12.8
R 10	71 20.5	304 16.0	42.0	352 28.4	22.0	248 39.2	14.4	247 01.8	44.5	Alphard	218 20.3	S 8 34.7
I 11	86 22.9	319 15.3	41.3	7 29.0	22.2	263 41.4	14.3	262 04.1	44.4			
D 12	101 25.4	334 14.6	N20 40.6	22 29.6	N23 22.3	278 43.6	N 0 14.2	277 06.5	N 0 44.4	Alphecca	126 31.4	N26 46.8
A 13	116 27.8	349 13.9	39.9	37 30.2	22.5	293 45.9	14.1	292 08.8	44.3	Alpheratz	358 08.7	N28 59.1
Y 14	131 30.3	4 13.2	39.2	52 30.8	22.7	308 48.1	13.9	307 11.2	44.2	Altair	62 31.7	N 8 49.2
15	146 32.8	19 12.5	·· 38.5	67 31.4	·· 22.8	323 50.4	·· 13.8	322 13.6	·· 44.2	Ankaa	353 39.7	S42 24.2
16	161 35.2	34 11.8	37.8	82 32.0	23.0	338 52.6	13.7	337 15.9	44.1	Antares	112 55.9	S26 23.5
17	176 37.7	49 11.1	37.1	97 32.6	23.1	353 54.8	13.6	352 18.3	44.1			
18	191 40.2	64 10.4	N20 36.4	112 33.2	N23 23.3	8 57.1	N 0 13.5	7 20.6	N 0 44.0	Arcturus	146 17.8	N19 17.0
19	206 42.6	79 09.7	35.7	127 33.8	23.4	23 59.3	13.4	22 23.0	44.0	Atria	108 19.1	S68 59.8
20	221 45.1	94 09.0	35.0	142 34.4	23.6	39 01.5	13.3	37 25.4	43.9	Avior	234 28.6	S59 27.1
21	236 47.6	109 08.3	·· 34.2	157 34.9	·· 23.7	54 03.8	·· 13.2	52 27.7	·· 43.9	Bellatrix	278 58.5	N 6 19.9
22	251 50.0	124 07.6	33.5	172 35.5	23.9	69 06.0	13.1	67 30.1	43.8	Betelgeuse	271 28.0	N 7 24.2
23	266 52.5	139 06.9	32.8	187 36.1	24.1	84 08.2	13.0	82 32.4	43.8			
4 00	281 54.9	154 06.2	N20 32.1	202 36.7	N23 24.2	99 10.5	N 0 12.9	97 34.8	N 0 43.7	Canopus	264 07.5	S52 41.1
01	296 57.4	169 05.5	31.4	217 37.3	24.4	114 12.7	12.7	112 37.2	43.6	Capella	281 10.9	N45 58.7
02	311 59.9	184 04.9	30.7	232 37.9	24.5	129 14.9	12.6	127 39.5	43.6	Deneb	49 47.7	N45 12.7
03	327 02.3	199 04.2	·· 30.0	247 38.5	·· 24.7	144 17.2	·· 12.5	142 41.9	·· 43.5	Denebola	182 58.6	N14 40.7
04	342 04.8	214 03.5	29.2	262 39.1	24.8	159 19.4	12.4	157 44.2	43.5	Diphda	349 20.3	S18 05.3
05	357 07.3	229 02.8	28.5	277 39.7	25.0	174 21.6	12.3	172 46.6	43.4			
06	12 09.7	244 02.1	N20 27.8	292 40.3	N23 25.1	189 23.9	N 0 12.2	187 49.0	N 0 43.4	Dubhe	194 21.8	N61 51.4
07	27 12.2	259 01.4	27.1	307 40.9	25.3	204 26.1	12.1	202 51.3	43.3	Elnath	278 43.8	N28 35.4
S 08	42 14.7	274 00.7	26.4	322 41.5	25.4	219 28.3	12.0	217 53.7	43.3	Eltanin	90 56.9	N51 29.6
A 09	57 17.1	289 00.0	·· 25.6	337 42.1	·· 25.6	234 30.6	·· 11.9	232 56.0	·· 43.2	Enif	34 10.8	N 9 47.3
T 10	72 19.6	303 59.4	24.9	352 42.7	25.7	249 32.8	11.8	247 58.4	43.1	Fomalhaut	15 50.6	S29 43.1
U 11	87 22.1	318 58.7	24.2	7 43.3	25.9	264 35.0	11.6	263 00.8	43.1			
R 12	102 24.5	333 58.0	N20 23.5	22 43.9	N23 26.0	279 37.2	N 0 11.5	278 03.1	N 0 43.0	Gacrux	172 28.2	S57 00.7
D 13	117 27.0	348 57.3	22.7	37 44.5	26.2	294 39.5	11.4	293 05.5	43.0	Gienah	176 17.5	S17 26.3
A 14	132 29.4	3 56.6	22.0	52 45.1	26.3	309 41.7	11.3	308 07.8	42.9	Hadar	149 22.3	S60 17.2
Y 15	147 31.9	18 55.9	·· 21.3	67 45.7	·· 26.5	324 43.9	·· 11.2	323 10.2	·· 42.9	Hamal	328 28.4	N23 22.3
16	162 34.4	33 55.3	20.5	82 46.2	26.6	339 46.2	11.1	338 12.5	42.8	Kaus Aust.	84 15.7	S34 23.6
17	177 36.8	48 54.6	19.8	97 46.8	26.8	354 48.4	11.0	353 14.9	42.8			
18	192 39.3	63 53.9	N20 19.1	112 47.4	N23 26.9	9 50.6	N 0 10.9	8 17.3	N 0 42.7	Kochab	137 18.4	N74 14.3
19	207 41.8	78 53.2	18.3	127 48.0	27.1	24 52.9	10.7	23 19.6	42.6	Markab	14 02.5	N15 06.2
20	222 44.2	93 52.5	17.6	142 48.6	27.2	39 55.1	10.6	38 22.0	42.6	Menkar	314 40.7	N 4 01.0
21	237 46.7	108 51.9	·· 16.9	157 49.2	·· 27.4	54 57.3	·· 10.5	53 24.3	·· 42.5	Menkent	148 36.2	S36 16.8
22	252 49.2	123 51.2	16.1	172 49.8	27.5	69 59.5	10.4	68 26.7	42.5	Miaplacidus	221 45.6	S69 38.6
23	267 51.6	138 50.5	15.4	187 50.4	27.7	85 01.8	10.3	83 29.0	42.4			
5 00	282 54.1	153 49.8	N20 14.7	202 51.0	N23 27.8	100 04.0	N 0 10.2	98 31.4	N 0 42.4	Mirfak	309 15.6	N49 47.5
01	297 56.6	168 49.2	13.9	217 51.6	28.0	115 06.2	10.1	113 33.7	42.3	Nunki	76 28.1	S26 19.1
02	312 59.0	183 48.5	13.2	232 52.2	28.1	130 08.5	10.0	128 36.1	42.2	Peacock	53 57.0	S56 47.6
03	328 01.5	198 47.8	·· 12.4	247 52.8	·· 28.2	145 10.7	·· 09.9	143 38.5	·· 42.2	Pollux	243 57.9	N28 04.3
04	343 03.9	213 47.1	11.7	262 53.4	28.4	160 12.9	09.7	158 40.8	42.1	Procyon	245 25.5	N 5 16.4
05	358 06.4	228 46.4	11.0	277 54.0	28.5	175 15.1	09.6	173 43.2	42.1			
06	13 08.9	243 45.8	N20 10.2	292 54.6	N23 28.7	190 17.4	N 0 09.5	188 45.5	N 0 42.0	Rasalhague	96 28.7	N12 34.5
07	28 11.3	258 45.1	09.5	307 55.2	28.8	205 19.6	09.4	203 47.9	42.0	Regulus	208 09.6	N12 03.6
08	43 13.8	273 44.4	08.7	322 55.8	29.0	220 21.8	09.3	218 50.2	41.9	Rigel	281 35.8	S 8 13.4
S 09	58 16.3	288 43.8	·· 08.0	337 56.4	·· 29.1	235 24.0	·· 09.2	233 52.6	·· 41.8	Rigil Kent.	140 24.7	S60 45.6
U 10	73 18.7	303 43.1	07.2	352 57.0	29.2	250 26.3	09.1	248 54.9	41.8	Sabik	102 40.2	S15 42.1
N 11	88 21.2	318 42.4	06.5	7 57.6	29.4	265 28.5	09.0	263 57.3	41.7			
D 12	103 23.7	333 41.7	N20 05.7	22 58.2	N23 29.5	280 30.7	N 0 08.8	278 59.7	N 0 41.7	Schedar	350 08.3	N56 25.8
A 13	118 26.1	348 41.1	05.0	37 58.8	29.7	295 32.9	08.7	294 02.0	41.6	Shaula	96 54.6	S37 05.4
Y 14	133 28.6	3 40.4	04.2	52 59.3	29.8	310 35.2	08.6	309 04.4	41.6	Sirius	258 55.6	S16 41.5
15	148 31.0	18 39.7	·· 03.5	67 59.9	·· 29.9	325 37.4	·· 08.5	324 06.7	·· 41.5	Spica	158 56.9	S11 03.8
16	163 33.5	33 39.1	02.7	83 00.5	30.1	340 39.6	08.4	339 09.1	41.4	Suhail	223 10.8	S43 21.6
17	178 36.0	48 38.4	02.0	98 01.1	30.2	355 41.8	08.3	354 11.4	41.4			
18	193 38.4	63 37.7	N20 01.2	113 01.7	N23 30.4	10 44.1	N 0 08.2	9 13.8	N 0 41.3	Vega	80 55.0	N38 46.1
19	208 40.9	78 37.1	20 00.5	128 02.3	30.5	25 46.3	08.0	24 16.1	41.3	Zuben'ubi	137 32.3	S15 57.9
20	223 43.4	93 36.4	19 59.7	143 02.9	30.6	40 48.5	07.9	39 18.5	41.2		S.H.A.	Mer. Pass.
21	238 45.8	108 35.7	·· 59.0	158 03.5	·· 30.8	55 50.7	·· 07.8	54 20.8	·· 41.2		° '	h m
22	253 48.3	123 35.1	58.2	173 04.1	30.9	70 53.0	07.7	69 23.2	41.1	Venus	232 12.3	13 44
23	268 50.8	138 34.4	57.4	188 04.7	31.0	85 55.2	07.6	84 25.5	41.0	Mars	280 41.8	10 29
	h m									Jupiter	177 15.5	17 21
Mer. Pass.	5 11.5	*v* −0.7	*d* 0.7	*v* 0.6	*d* 0.1	*v* 2.2	*d* 0.1	*v* 2.4	*d* 0.1	Saturn	175 39.9	17 27

SUN / MOON

G.M.T. (d h)	SUN G.H.A.	Dec.	MOON G.H.A.	v	Dec.	d	H.P.
3 00	178 59.4	N22 59.2	161 46.9	5.7	N20 18.9	3.7	59.3
01	193 59.3	59.0	176 11.6	5.8	20 15.2	3.9	59.2
02	208 59.1	58.8	190 36.4	5.9	20 11.3	4.0	59.2
03	223 59.1	.. 58.6	205 01.3	5.9	20 07.3	4.2	59.2
04	238 59.0	58.4	219 26.2	6.0	20 03.1	4.2	59.1
05	253 58.8	58.2	233 51.2	6.1	19 58.9	4.4	59.1
06	268 58.7	N22 58.0	248 16.3	6.2	N19 54.5	4.5	59.1
07	283 58.6	57.8	262 41.5	6.3	19 50.0	4.7	59.1
08	298 58.5	57.6	277 06.8	6.3	19 45.3	4.7	59.0
F 09	313 58.4	.. 57.4	291 32.1	6.4	19 40.6	4.9	59.0
R 10	328 58.3	57.2	305 57.5	6.5	19 35.7	5.0	59.0
I 11	343 58.1	57.0	320 23.0	6.6	19 30.7	5.2	58.9
D 12	358 58.0	N22 56.8	334 48.6	6.6	N19 25.5	5.2	58.9
A 13	13 57.9	56.6	349 14.2	6.8	19 20.3	5.4	58.9
Y 14	28 57.8	56.4	3 40.0	6.8	19 14.9	5.4	58.8
15	43 57.7	.. 56.1	18 05.8	6.9	19 09.5	5.6	58.8
16	58 57.6	55.9	32 31.7	7.0	19 03.9	5.7	58.8
17	73 57.4	55.7	46 57.7	7.0	18 58.2	5.8	58.7
18	88 57.3	N22 55.5	61 23.7	7.2	N18 52.4	5.9	58.7
19	103 57.2	55.3	75 49.9	7.2	18 46.5	6.1	58.7
20	118 57.1	55.1	90 16.1	7.4	18 40.4	6.1	58.6
21	133 57.0	.. 54.9	104 42.5	7.4	18 34.3	6.2	58.6
22	148 56.9	54.7	119 08.9	7.5	18 28.1	6.4	58.6
23	163 56.8	54.5	133 35.4	7.6	18 21.7	6.4	58.5
4 00	178 56.6	N22 54.3	148 02.0	7.7	N18 15.3	6.6	58.5
01	193 56.5	54.0	162 28.7	7.8	18 08.7	6.7	58.5
02	208 56.4	53.8	176 55.5	7.9	18 02.0	6.7	58.4
03	223 56.3	.. 53.6	191 22.4	7.9	17 55.3	6.9	58.4
04	238 56.2	53.4	205 49.3	8.1	17 48.4	6.9	58.3
05	253 56.1	53.2	220 16.4	8.1	17 41.5	7.1	58.3
06	268 56.0	N22 53.0	234 43.5	8.3	N17 34.4	7.1	58.3
07	283 55.8	52.8	249 10.8	8.3	17 27.3	7.3	58.2
S 08	298 55.7	52.5	263 38.1	8.4	17 20.0	7.3	58.2
A 09	313 55.6	.. 52.3	278 05.5	8.5	17 12.7	7.4	58.2
T 10	328 55.5	52.1	292 33.0	8.6	17 05.3	7.5	58.1
U 11	343 55.4	51.9	307 00.6	8.7	16 57.8	7.6	58.1
R 12	358 55.3	N22 51.7	321 28.3	8.8	N16 50.2	7.7	58.1
D 13	13 55.2	51.4	335 56.1	8.9	16 42.5	7.8	58.0
A 14	28 55.1	51.2	350 24.0	8.9	16 34.7	7.8	58.0
Y 15	43 54.9	.. 51.0	4 51.9	9.1	16 26.9	8.0	58.0
16	58 54.8	50.8	19 20.0	9.1	16 18.9	8.0	57.9
17	73 54.7	50.5	33 48.1	9.3	16 10.9	8.1	57.9
18	88 54.6	N22 50.3	48 16.4	9.3	N16 02.8	8.2	57.8
19	103 54.5	50.1	62 44.7	9.4	15 54.6	8.3	57.8
20	118 54.4	49.9	77 13.1	9.6	15 46.3	8.3	57.8
21	133 54.3	.. 49.6	91 41.7	9.6	15 38.0	8.4	57.7
22	148 54.2	49.4	106 10.3	9.7	15 29.6	8.5	57.7
23	163 54.1	49.2	120 39.0	9.8	15 21.1	8.6	57.7
5 00	178 53.9	N22 49.0	135 07.8	9.8	N15 12.5	8.6	57.6
01	193 53.8	48.7	149 36.6	10.0	15 03.9	8.7	57.6
02	208 53.7	48.5	164 05.6	10.1	14 55.2	8.8	57.6
03	223 53.6	.. 48.3	178 34.7	10.1	14 46.4	8.8	57.5
04	238 53.5	48.0	193 03.8	10.3	14 37.6	8.9	57.5
05	253 53.4	47.8	207 33.1	10.3	14 28.7	9.0	57.5
06	268 53.3	N22 47.6	222 02.4	10.4	N14 19.7	9.0	57.4
07	283 53.2	47.3	236 31.8	10.5	14 10.7	9.1	57.4
08	298 53.1	47.1	251 01.3	10.6	14 01.6	9.2	57.3
S 09	313 53.0	.. 46.9	265 30.9	10.7	13 52.4	9.2	57.3
U 10	328 52.8	46.7	280 00.6	10.8	13 43.2	9.3	57.3
N 11	343 52.7	46.4	294 30.4	10.8	13 33.9	9.3	57.2
D 12	358 52.6	N22 46.2	309 00.2	11.0	N13 24.6	9.4	57.2
A 13	13 52.5	45.9	323 30.2	11.0	13 15.2	9.5	57.1
Y 14	28 52.4	45.7	338 00.2	11.1	13 05.7	9.5	57.1
15	43 52.3	.. 45.4	352 30.3	11.2	12 56.2	9.6	57.1
16	58 52.2	45.2	7 00.5	11.3	12 46.6	9.6	57.1
17	73 52.1	45.0	21 30.8	11.3	12 37.0	9.6	57.0
18	88 52.0	N22 44.7	36 01.1	11.4	N12 27.4	9.8	57.0
19	103 51.9	44.5	50 31.5	11.6	12 17.6	9.7	57.0
20	118 51.8	44.2	65 02.1	11.6	12 07.9	9.8	56.9
21	133 51.7	.. 44.0	79 32.7	11.6	11 58.1	9.9	56.9
22	148 51.5	43.7	94 03.3	11.8	11 48.2	9.9	56.8
23	163 51.4	43.5	108 34.1	11.9	11 38.3	9.9	56.8
S.D.	15.8	d 0.2	S.D. 16.0		15.8		15.6

Twilight / Sunrise / Moonrise

Lat.	Naut.	Civil	Sunrise	3	4	5	6
N 72	□	□	□	□	02 50	05 46	07 51
N 70	□	□	□		04 14	06 17	08 08
68	□	□	00 40	03 04	04 52	06 40	08 21
66	////	////	00 40	03 44	05 19	06 57	08 32
64	////	////	01 47	04 11	05 40	07 11	08 41
62	////	////	02 21	04 32	05 56	07 23	08 48
60	////	01 10	02 45	04 50	06 10	07 33	08 55
N 58	////	01 53	03 05	05 04	06 22	07 42	09 01
56	////	02 20	03 21	05 16	06 32	07 49	09 06
54	01 05	02 41	03 34	05 27	06 41	07 56	09 10
52	01 44	02 58	03 46	05 37	06 49	08 02	09 15
50	02 09	03 13	03 57	05 45	06 56	08 08	09 18
45	02 53	03 42	04 19	06 03	07 11	08 20	09 26
N 40	03 22	04 04	04 36	06 18	07 24	08 29	09 33
35	03 45	04 21	04 51	06 30	07 35	08 38	09 39
30	04 03	04 36	05 04	06 41	07 44	08 45	09 44
20	04 31	05 01	05 25	07 00	08 00	08 58	09 53
N 10	04 54	05 21	05 44	07 16	08 14	09 09	10 00
0	05 12	05 38	06 01	07 31	08 27	09 19	10 08
S 10	05 29	05 55	06 18	07 46	08 40	09 29	10 15
20	05 44	06 12	06 36	08 02	08 54	09 40	10 22
30	06 00	06 30	06 56	08 21	09 10	09 53	10 31
35	06 09	06 40	07 08	08 32	09 19	10 00	10 36
40	06 18	06 52	07 22	08 44	09 30	10 08	10 42
45	06 28	07 05	07 38	08 59	09 42	10 18	10 48
S 50	06 39	07 20	07 59	09 16	09 57	10 29	10 56
52	06 44	07 28	08 08	09 25	10 04	10 34	11 00
54	06 50	07 36	08 19	09 34	10 11	10 40	11 03
56	06 56	07 44	08 31	09 44	10 20	10 47	11 08
58	07 02	07 54	08 45	09 56	10 30	10 54	11 13
S 60	07 09	08 05	09 02	10 10	10 41	11 02	11 18

Sunset / Twilight / Moonset

Lat.	Sunset	Civil	Naut.	3	4	5	6
N 72	□	□	□	□	01 49	00 43	00 20
N 70	□	□	□		00 23	00 10	{00 01 / 23 54}
68	23 23	////	////	23 44	23 47	23 47	23 46
66	23 23	////	////	23 16	23 28	23 35	23 39
64	22 20	////	////	22 55	23 13	23 25	23 33
62	21 47	////	////	22 38	23 00	23 16	23 28
60	21 22	22 56	////	22 24	22 50	23 08	23 23
N 58	21 03	22 15	////	22 12	22 40	23 02	23 19
56	20 47	21 47	////	22 01	22 32	22 56	23 15
54	20 34	21 27	23 02	21 51	22 24	22 51	23 12
52	20 22	21 10	22 24	21 43	22 18	22 46	23 09
50	20 11	20 55	21 58	21 36	22 12	22 41	23 07
45	19 50	20 27	21 15	21 19	21 59	22 32	23 01
N 40	19 32	20 05	20 46	21 06	21 48	22 24	22 56
35	19 18	19 47	20 23	20 55	21 39	22 17	22 51
30	19 05	19 32	20 05	20 45	21 31	22 11	22 48
20	18 44	19 08	19 37	20 27	21 17	22 01	22 41
N 10	18 25	18 48	19 15	20 12	21 04	21 51	22 35
0	18 08	18 30	18 57	19 58	20 52	21 43	22 30
S 10	17 51	18 14	18 40	19 44	20 41	21 34	22 24
20	17 33	17 57	18 24	19 29	20 28	21 24	22 18
30	17 12	17 39	18 08	19 11	20 13	21 14	22 11
35	17 00	17 28	18 00	19 01	20 05	21 07	22 07
40	16 47	17 17	17 51	18 49	19 55	21 00	22 03
45	16 30	17 04	17 41	18 35	19 44	20 52	21 57
S 50	16 10	16 48	17 30	18 18	19 30	20 42	21 51
52	16 01	16 41	17 25	18 10	19 24	20 37	21 48
54	15 50	16 33	17 19	18 01	19 16	20 32	21 45
56	15 38	16 25	17 13	17 51	19 08	20 26	21 41
58	15 24	16 15	17 07	17 39	18 59	20 19	21 37
S 60	15 07	16 03	17 00	17 26	18 49	20 12	21 33

SUN / MOON

Day	Eqn. of Time 00h	Eqn. of Time 12h	Mer. Pass.	Mer. Pass. Upper	Mer. Pass. Lower	Age	Phase
3	04 02	04 08	12 04	13 45	01 16	02	
4	04 13	04 19	12 04	14 40	02 13	03	
5	04 24	04 29	12 04	15 31	03 06	04	◐

G.M.T.	ARIES G.H.A.	VENUS −3.3 G.H.A.	Dec.	MARS +1.7 G.H.A.	Dec.	JUPITER −1.5 G.H.A.	Dec.	SATURN +1.2 G.H.A.	Dec.	STARS Name	S.H.A.	Dec.
6 00	283 53.2	153 33.7	N19 56.7	203 05.3	N23 31.2	100 57.4	N 0 07.5	99 27.9	N 0 41.0	Acamar	315 37.0	S40 22.6
01	298 55.7	168 33.1	55.9	218 05.9	31.3	115 59.6	07.4	114 30.3	40.9	Achernar	335 45.0	S57 19.6
02	313 58.2	183 32.4	55.1	233 06.5	31.5	131 01.8	07.2	129 32.6	40.9	Acrux	173 36.7	S63 00.0
03	329 00.6	198 31.7	·· 54.4	248 07.1	·· 31.6	146 04.1	·· 07.1	144 35.0	·· 40.8	Adhara	255 32.1	S28 56.8
04	344 03.1	213 31.1	53.6	263 07.7	31.7	161 06.3	07.0	159 37.3	40.7	Aldebaran	291 17.7	N16 28.2
05	359 05.5	228 30.4	52.9	278 08.3	31.9	176 08.5	06.9	174 39.7	40.7			
06	14 08.0	243 29.8	N19 52.1	293 08.9	N23 32.0	191 10.7	N 0 06.8	189 42.0	N 0 40.6	Alioth	166 42.0	N56 04.0
07	29 10.5	258 29.1	51.3	308 09.5	32.1	206 13.0	06.7	204 44.4	40.6	Alkaid	153 18.0	N49 24.7
08	44 12.9	273 28.4	50.6	323 10.1	32.3	221 15.2	06.6	219 46.7	40.5	Al Na'ir	28 13.9	S47 02.9
M 09	59 15.4	288 27.8	·· 49.8	338 10.7	·· 32.4	236 17.4	·· 06.4	234 49.1	·· 40.5	Alnilam	276 11.4	S 1 12.8
O 10	74 17.9	303 27.1	49.0	353 11.3	32.5	251 19.6	06.3	249 51.4	40.4	Alphard	218 20.3	S 8 34.7
N 11	89 20.3	318 26.5	48.2	8 11.9	32.7	266 21.8	06.2	264 53.8	40.3			
D 12	104 22.8	333 25.8	N19 47.5	23 12.5	N23 32.8	281 24.1	N 0 06.1	279 56.1	N 0 40.3	Alphecca	126 31.4	N26 46.9
A 13	119 25.3	348 25.1	46.7	38 13.1	32.9	296 26.3	06.0	294 58.5	40.2	Alpheratz	358 08.7	N28 59.1
Y 14	134 27.7	3 24.5	45.9	53 13.7	33.1	311 28.5	05.9	310 00.8	40.2	Altair	62 31.7	N 8 49.2
15	149 30.2	18 23.8	·· 45.1	68 14.3	·· 33.2	326 30.7	·· 05.7	325 03.2	·· 40.1	Ankaa	353 39.6	S42 24.2
16	164 32.7	33 23.2	44.4	83 14.9	33.3	341 32.9	05.6	340 05.5	40.0	Antares	112 55.9	S26 23.5
17	179 35.1	48 22.5	43.6	98 15.5	33.4	356 35.2	05.5	355 07.9	40.0			
18	194 37.6	63 21.9	N19 42.8	113 16.0	N23 33.6	11 37.4	N 0 05.4	10 10.2	N 0 39.9	Arcturus	146 17.9	N19 17.0
19	209 40.0	78 21.2	42.0	128 16.6	33.7	26 39.6	05.3	25 12.6	39.9	Atria	108 19.1	S68 59.8
20	224 42.5	93 20.6	41.3	143 17.2	33.8	41 41.8	05.2	40 14.9	39.8	Avior	234 28.6	S59 27.1
21	239 45.0	108 19.9	·· 40.5	158 17.8	·· 34.0	56 44.0	·· 05.0	55 17.3	·· 39.7	Bellatrix	278 58.5	N 6 20.0
22	254 47.4	123 19.3	39.7	173 18.4	34.1	71 46.3	04.9	70 19.6	39.7	Betelgeuse	271 28.0	N 7 24.2
23	269 49.9	138 18.6	38.9	188 19.0	34.2	86 48.5	04.8	85 22.0	39.6			
7 00	284 52.4	153 18.0	N19 38.1	203 19.6	N23 34.3	101 50.7	N 0 04.7	100 24.3	N 0 39.6	Canopus	264 07.5	S52 41.1
01	299 54.8	168 17.3	37.3	218 20.2	34.5	116 52.9	04.6	115 26.7	39.5	Capella	281 10.9	N45 58.7
02	314 57.3	183 16.7	36.6	233 20.8	34.6	131 55.1	04.5	130 29.0	39.4	Deneb	49 47.7	N45 12.8
03	329 59.8	198 16.0	·· 35.8	248 21.4	·· 34.7	146 57.3	·· 04.3	145 31.4	·· 39.4	Denebola	182 58.6	N14 40.7
04	345 02.2	213 15.4	35.0	263 22.0	34.9	161 59.6	04.2	160 33.7	39.3	Diphda	349 20.3	S18 05.2
05	0 04.7	228 14.7	34.2	278 22.6	35.0	177 01.8	04.1	175 36.1	39.3			
06	15 07.2	243 14.1	N19 33.4	293 23.2	N23 35.1	192 04.0	N 0 04.0	190 38.4	N 0 39.2	Dubhe	194 21.8	N61 51.4
07	30 09.6	258 13.4	32.6	308 23.8	35.2	207 06.2	03.9	205 40.8	39.2	Elnath	278 43.8	N28 35.4
08	45 12.1	273 12.8	31.8	323 24.4	35.4	222 08.4	03.8	220 43.1	39.1	Eltanin	90 57.0	N51 29.6
T 09	60 14.5	288 12.1	·· 31.0	338 25.0	·· 35.5	237 10.6	·· 03.6	235 45.5	·· 39.0	Enif	34 10.8	N 9 47.4
U 10	75 17.0	303 11.5	30.2	353 25.6	35.6	252 12.8	03.5	250 47.8	39.0	Fomalhaut	15 50.6	S29 43.1
E 11	90 19.5	318 10.8	29.5	8 26.2	35.7	267 15.1	03.4	265 50.1	38.9			
S 12	105 21.9	333 10.2	N19 28.7	23 26.8	N23 35.8	282 17.3	N 0 03.3	280 52.5	N 0 38.9	Gacrux	172 28.2	S57 00.7
D 13	120 24.4	348 09.5	27.9	38 27.4	36.0	297 19.5	03.2	295 54.8	38.8	Gienah	176 17.5	S17 26.3
A 14	135 26.9	3 08.9	27.1	53 28.0	36.1	312 21.7	03.1	310 57.2	38.7	Hadar	149 22.4	S60 17.2
Y 15	150 29.3	18 08.3	·· 26.3	68 28.6	·· 36.2	327 23.9	·· 02.9	325 59.5	·· 38.7	Hamal	328 28.4	N23 22.3
16	165 31.8	33 07.6	25.5	83 29.2	36.3	342 26.1	02.8	341 01.9	38.6	Kaus Aust.	84 15.7	S34 23.6
17	180 34.3	48 07.0	24.7	98 29.8	36.5	357 28.3	02.7	356 04.2	38.5			
18	195 36.7	63 06.3	N19 23.9	113 30.4	N23 36.6	12 30.6	N 0 02.6	11 06.6	N 0 38.5	Kochab	137 18.5	N74 14.3
19	210 39.2	78 05.7	23.1	128 31.0	36.7	27 32.8	02.5	26 08.9	38.4	Markab	14 02.4	N15 06.2
20	225 41.6	93 05.1	22.3	143 31.6	36.8	42 35.0	02.4	41 11.3	38.4	Menkar	314 40.7	N 4 01.0
21	240 44.1	108 04.4	·· 21.5	158 32.2	·· 36.9	57 37.2	·· 02.2	56 13.6	·· 38.3	Menkent	148 36.2	S36 16.8
22	255 46.6	123 03.8	20.7	173 32.8	37.1	72 39.4	02.1	71 16.0	38.2	Miaplacidus	221 45.6	S69 38.6
23	270 49.0	138 03.1	19.9	188 33.4	37.2	87 41.6	02.0	86 18.3	38.2			
8 00	285 51.5	153 02.5	N19 19.1	203 34.0	N23 37.3	102 43.8	N 0 01.9	101 20.7	N 0 38.1	Mirfak	309 15.6	N49 47.5
01	300 54.0	168 01.9	18.2	218 34.6	37.4	117 46.1	01.8	116 23.0	38.1	Nunki	76 28.1	S26 19.2
02	315 56.4	183 01.2	17.4	233 35.2	37.5	132 48.3	01.6	131 25.3	38.0	Peacock	53 56.9	S56 47.6
03	330 58.9	198 00.6	·· 16.6	248 35.8	·· 37.6	147 50.5	·· 01.5	146 27.7	·· 37.9	Pollux	243 57.9	N28 04.3
04	346 01.4	213 00.0	15.8	263 36.4	37.8	162 52.7	01.4	161 30.0	37.9	Procyon	245 25.5	N 5 16.4
05	1 03.8	227 59.3	15.0	278 37.0	37.9	177 54.9	01.3	176 32.4	37.8			
06	16 06.3	242 58.7	N19 14.2	293 37.6	N23 38.0	192 57.1	N 0 01.2	191 34.7	N 0 37.8	Rasalhague	96 28.8	N12 34.5
W 07	31 08.8	257 58.1	13.4	308 38.2	38.1	207 59.3	01.0	206 37.1	37.7	Regulus	208 09.7	N12 03.6
E 08	46 11.2	272 57.4	12.6	323 38.8	38.2	223 01.5	00.9	221 39.4	37.6	Rigel	281 35.8	S 8 13.4
D 09	61 13.7	287 56.8	·· 11.8	338 39.4	·· 38.3	238 03.7	·· 00.8	236 41.8	·· 37.6	Rigil Kent.	140 24.8	S60 45.6
N 10	76 16.1	302 56.2	11.0	353 40.0	38.5	253 06.0	00.7	251 44.1	37.5	Sabik	102 40.2	S15 42.1
E 11	91 18.6	317 55.5	10.1	8 40.6	38.6	268 08.2	00.6	266 46.5	37.5			
S 12	106 21.1	332 54.9	N19 09.3	23 41.2	N23 38.7	283 10.4	N 0 00.4	281 48.8	N 0 37.4	Schedar	350 08.3	N56 25.8
D 13	121 23.5	347 54.3	08.5	38 41.8	38.8	298 12.6	00.3	296 51.1	37.3	Shaula	96 54.6	S37 05.4
A 14	136 26.0	2 53.6	07.7	53 42.4	38.9	313 14.8	00.2	311 53.5	37.3	Sirius	258 55.6	S16 41.5
Y 15	151 28.5	17 53.0	·· 06.9	68 43.0	·· 39.0	328 17.0	N 0 00.1	326 55.8	·· 37.2	Spica	158 56.9	S11 03.8
16	166 30.9	32 52.4	06.0	83 43.6	39.1	343 19.2	0 00.0	341 58.2	37.1	Suhail	223 10.8	S43 21.5
17	181 33.4	47 51.8	05.2	98 44.2	39.3	358 21.4	S 0 00.2	357 00.5	37.1			
18	196 35.9	62 51.1	N19 04.4	113 44.8	N23 39.4	13 23.6	S 0 00.3	12 02.9	N 0 37.0	Vega	80 55.0	N38 46.1
19	211 38.3	77 50.5	03.6	128 45.4	39.5	28 25.8	00.4	27 05.2	37.0	Zuben'ubi	137 32.3	S15 57.9
20	226 40.8	92 49.9	02.8	143 46.0	39.6	43 28.0	00.5	42 07.5	36.9		S.H.A.	Mer. Pass.
21	241 43.3	107 49.3	·· 01.9	158 46.6	·· 39.7	58 30.2	·· 00.6	57 09.9	·· 36.8			
22	256 45.7	122 48.6	01.1	173 47.2	39.8	73 32.5	00.8	72 12.2	36.8	Venus	228 25.6	13 47
23	271 48.2	137 48.0	00.3	188 47.8	39.9	88 34.7	00.9	87 14.6	36.7	Mars	278 27.3	10 26
Mer. Pass.	4 59.7	v −0.6	d 0.8	v 0.6	d 0.1	v 2.2	d 0.1	v 2.3	d 0.1	Jupiter	176 58.3	17 10
										Saturn	175 32.0	17 16

G.M.T.	SUN G.H.A.	SUN Dec.	MOON G.H.A.	v	MOON Dec.	d	H.P.
d h	° '	° '	° '	'	° '	'	'
6 00	178 51.3	N22 43.3	123 05.0	11.9	N11 28.4	10.0	56.8
01	193 51.2	43.0	137 35.9	12.0	11 18.4	10.1	56.7
02	208 51.1	42.8	152 06.9	12.0	11 08.3	10.0	56.7
03	223 51.0 ··	42.5	166 37.9	12.2	10 58.3	10.2	56.7
04	238 50.9	42.3	181 09.1	12.2	10 48.1	10.1	56.6
05	253 50.8	42.0	195 40.3	12.3	10 38.0	10.2	56.6
06	268 50.7	N22 41.8	210 11.6	12.4	N10 27.8	10.3	56.6
07	283 50.6	41.5	224 43.0	12.4	10 17.5	10.2	56.5
08	298 50.5	41.3	239 14.4	12.5	10 07.3	10.3	56.5
M 09	313 50.4 ··	41.0	253 45.9	12.6	9 57.0	10.3	56.5
O 10	328 50.3	40.8	268 17.5	12.7	9 46.6	10.3	56.4
N 11	343 50.2	40.5	282 49.2	12.7	9 36.3	10.4	56.4
D 12	358 50.1	N22 40.3	297 20.9	12.8	N 9 25.9	10.5	56.4
A 13	13 50.0	40.0	311 52.7	12.9	9 15.4	10.4	56.3
Y 14	28 49.9	39.7	326 24.6	12.9	9 05.0	10.5	56.3
15	43 49.8 ··	39.5	340 56.5	13.0	8 54.5	10.6	56.3
16	58 49.6	39.2	355 28.5	13.1	8 43.9	10.5	56.2
17	73 49.5	39.0	10 00.6	13.1	8 33.4	10.6	56.2
18	88 49.4	N22 38.7	24 32.7	13.2	N 8 22.8	10.6	56.2
19	103 49.3	38.5	39 04.9	13.2	8 12.2	10.6	56.1
20	118 49.2	38.2	53 37.1	13.4	8 01.6	10.7	56.1
21	133 49.1 ··	37.9	68 09.5	13.3	7 50.9	10.6	56.1
22	148 49.0	37.7	82 41.8	13.5	7 40.3	10.7	56.0
23	163 48.9	37.4	97 14.3	13.5	7 29.6	10.8	56.0
7 00	178 48.8	N22 37.2	111 46.8	13.5	N 7 18.8	10.7	56.0
01	193 48.7	36.9	126 19.3	13.7	7 08.1	10.8	56.0
02	208 48.6	36.6	140 52.0	13.6	6 57.3	10.7	55.9
03	223 48.5 ··	36.4	155 24.6	13.8	6 46.6	10.8	55.9
04	238 48.4	36.1	169 57.4	13.7	6 35.8	10.8	55.9
05	253 48.3	35.8	184 30.1	13.9	6 25.0	10.9	55.8
06	268 48.2	N22 35.6	199 03.0	13.9	N 6 14.1	10.8	55.8
07	283 48.1	35.3	213 35.9	13.9	6 03.3	10.9	55.8
08	298 48.0	35.0	228 08.8	14.0	5 52.4	10.8	55.7
T 09	313 47.9 ··	34.8	242 41.8	14.1	5 41.6	10.9	55.7
U 10	328 47.8	34.5	257 14.9	14.1	5 30.7	10.9	55.7
E 11	343 47.7	34.2	271 48.0	14.1	5 19.8	10.9	55.7
S 12	358 47.6	N22 34.0	286 21.1	14.2	N 5 08.9	11.0	55.6
D 13	13 47.5	33.7	300 54.3	14.2	4 57.9	10.9	55.6
A 14	28 47.4	33.4	315 27.5	14.3	4 47.0	10.9	55.6
Y 15	43 47.3 ··	33.1	330 00.8	14.4	4 36.1	11.0	55.5
16	58 47.2	32.9	344 34.2	14.3	4 25.1	10.9	55.5
17	73 47.1	32.6	359 07.5	14.5	4 14.2	11.0	55.5
18	88 47.0	N22 32.3	13 41.0	14.4	N 4 03.2	10.9	55.5
19	103 46.9	32.1	28 14.4	14.5	3 52.3	11.0	55.4
20	118 46.8	31.8	42 47.9	14.6	3 41.3	11.0	55.4
21	133 46.7 ··	31.5	57 21.5	14.6	3 30.3	11.0	55.4
22	148 46.6	31.2	71 55.1	14.6	3 19.3	11.0	55.4
23	163 46.5	30.9	86 28.7	14.6	3 08.3	11.0	55.3
8 00	178 46.4	N22 30.7	101 02.3	14.7	N 2 57.3	10.9	55.3
01	193 46.3	30.4	115 36.0	14.8	2 46.4	11.0	55.3
02	208 46.2	30.1	130 09.8	14.7	2 35.4	11.0	55.3
03	223 46.1 ··	29.8	144 43.5	14.8	2 24.4	11.0	55.2
04	238 46.0	29.6	159 17.3	14.9	2 13.4	11.0	55.2
05	253 45.9	29.3	173 51.2	14.8	2 02.4	11.0	55.2
06	268 45.8	N22 29.0	188 25.0	14.9	N 1 51.4	11.0	55.2
07	283 45.7	28.7	202 58.9	14.9	1 40.4	11.0	55.1
W 08	298 45.6	28.4	217 32.9	14.9	1 29.4	10.9	55.1
E 09	313 45.5 ··	28.1	232 06.8	15.0	1 18.5	11.0	55.1
D 10	328 45.4	27.9	246 40.8	15.0	1 07.5	11.0	55.1
N 11	343 45.3	27.6	261 14.8	15.1	0 56.5	11.0	55.0
E 12	358 45.2	N22 27.3	275 48.9	15.1	N 0 45.5	10.9	55.0
S 13	13 45.1	27.0	290 23.0	15.0	0 34.6	11.0	55.0
D 14	28 45.0	26.7	304 57.0	15.2	0 23.6	10.9	55.0
A 15	43 44.9 ··	26.4	319 31.2	15.1	0 12.7	11.0	55.0
Y 16	58 44.8	26.1	334 05.3	15.2	N 0 01.7	10.9	54.9
17	73 44.8	25.8	348 39.5	15.1	S 0 09.2	10.9	54.9
18	88 44.7	N22 25.5	3 13.6	15.3	S 0 20.1	10.9	54.9
19	103 44.6	25.3	17 47.9	15.0	0 31.0	10.9	54.9
20	118 44.5	25.0	32 22.1	15.2	0 41.9	10.9	54.9
21	133 44.4 ··	24.7	46 56.3	15.3	0 52.8	10.9	54.8
22	148 44.3	24.4	61 30.6	15.3	1 03.7	10.9	54.8
23	163 44.2	24.1	76 04.9	15.2	1 14.6	10.8	54.8
	S.D. 15.8	d 0.3	S.D. 15.4		15.2		15.0

Lat.	Twilight Naut.	Twilight Civil	Sunrise	Moonrise 6	Moonrise 7	Moonrise 8	Moonrise 9
°	h m	h m	h m	h m	h m	h m	h m
N 72	▢	▢	▢	07 51	09 42	11 26	13 08
N 70	▢	▢	▢	08 08	09 50	11 28	13 02
68	▢	▢	▢	08 21	09 57	11 28	12 58
66	////	////	00 57	08 32	10 02	11 29	12 54
64	////	////	01 53	08 41	10 07	11 30	12 51
62	////	////	02 26	08 48	10 11	11 30	12 48
60	////	01 19	02 49	08 55	10 14	11 31	12 46
N 58	////	01 58	03 08	09 01	10 17	11 31	12 44
56	////	02 24	03 24	09 06	10 20	11 32	12 42
54	01 13	02 45	03 37	09 10	10 22	11 32	12 40
52	01 49	03 02	03 49	09 15	10 24	11 32	12 39
50	02 13	03 16	03 59	09 18	10 26	11 33	12 37
45	02 56	03 44	04 21	09 26	10 31	11 33	12 34
N 40	03 25	04 06	04 38	09 33	10 34	11 34	12 32
35	03 47	04 23	04 52	09 39	10 37	11 34	12 29
30	04 05	04 38	05 05	09 44	10 40	11 35	12 28
20	04 33	05 02	05 26	09 53	10 45	11 35	12 24
N 10	04 54	05 21	05 44	10 00	10 49	11 36	12 21
0	05 13	05 39	06 01	10 08	10 53	11 36	12 19
S 10	05 29	05 55	06 18	10 15	10 57	11 37	12 16
20	05 45	06 12	06 36	10 22	11 01	11 38	12 13
30	06 00	06 30	06 56	10 31	11 06	11 38	12 10
35	06 09	06 40	07 08	10 36	11 08	11 39	12 09
40	06 17	06 51	07 22	10 42	11 12	11 39	12 06
45	06 27	07 04	07 38	10 48	11 15	11 40	12 04
S 50	06 38	07 19	07 57	10 56	11 19	11 41	12 01
52	06 43	07 26	08 07	11 00	11 21	11 41	12 00
54	06 48	07 34	08 17	11 03	11 23	11 41	11 59
56	06 54	07 43	08 29	11 08	11 26	11 42	11 57
58	07 01	07 52	08 43	11 13	11 28	11 42	11 56
S 60	07 07	08 03	08 59	11 18	11 31	11 43	11 54

Lat.	Sunset	Twilight Civil	Twilight Naut.	Moonset 6	Moonset 7	Moonset 8	Moonset 9
°	h m	h m	h m	h m	h m	h m	h m
N 72	▢	▢	▢	00 20	{ 00 04 / 23 51 }	23 39	23 26
N 70	▢	▢	▢	{ 00 01 / 23 54 }	23 47	23 41	23 34
68	▢	▢	▢	23 46	23 44	23 42	23 40
66	23 08	////	////	23 39	23 41	23 44	23 46
64	22 14	////	////	23 33	23 39	23 45	23 50
62	21 43	////	////	23 28	23 37	23 46	23 54
60	21 19	22 48	////	23 23	23 35	23 47	23 58
N 58	21 00	22 10	////	23 19	23 34	23 47	24 01
56	20 45	21 44	////	23 15	23 32	23 48	24 04
54	20 32	21 24	22 55	23 12	23 31	23 49	24 06
52	20 20	21 07	22 20	23 09	23 30	23 49	24 09
50	20 10	20 53	21 55	23 07	23 29	23 50	24 11
45	19 49	20 25	21 13	23 01	23 27	23 51	24 15
N 40	19 31	20 04	20 45	22 56	23 25	23 52	24 19
35	19 17	19 46	20 23	22 51	23 23	23 53	24 22
30	19 05	19 32	20 05	22 48	23 21	23 54	24 25
20	18 44	19 08	19 37	22 41	23 19	23 55	24 30
N 10	18 25	18 48	19 15	22 35	23 16	23 56	24 35
0	18 08	18 31	18 57	22 30	23 14	23 57	24 39
S 10	17 52	18 14	18 41	22 24	23 12	23 58	24 43
20	17 34	17 58	18 25	22 18	23 09	23 59	24 48
30	17 14	17 40	18 10	22 11	23 07	24 00	00 00
35	17 02	17 30	18 01	22 07	23 05	24 01	00 01
40	16 48	17 19	17 52	22 03	23 03	24 02	00 02
45	16 32	17 06	17 43	21 57	23 01	24 03	00 03
S 50	16 13	16 51	17 32	21 51	22 58	24 04	00 04
52	16 03	16 44	17 27	21 48	22 57	24 04	00 04
54	15 53	16 36	17 21	21 45	22 56	24 05	00 05
56	15 41	16 27	17 16	21 41	22 54	24 05	00 05
58	15 27	16 18	17 09	21 37	22 53	24 06	00 06
S 60	15 11	16 07	17 02	21 33	22 51	24 07	00 07

	SUN			MOON			
Day	Eqn. of Time 00ʰ	Eqn. of Time 12ʰ	Mer. Pass.	Mer. Pass. Upper	Mer. Pass. Lower	Age	Phase
	m s	m s	h m	h m	h m	d	
6	04 34	04 40	12 05	16 19	03 55	05	
7	04 45	04 49	12 05	17 04	04 41	06	
8	04 54	04 59	12 05	17 47	05 25	07	◖

G.M.T.	ARIES G.H.A.	VENUS −3.3 G.H.A.	Dec.	MARS +1.7 G.H.A.	Dec.	JUPITER −1.5 G.H.A.	Dec.	SATURN +1.2 G.H.A.	Dec.	STARS Name	S.H.A.	Dec.
9 00	286 50.6	152 47.4	N18 59.5	203 48.4	N23 40.0	103 36.9	S 0 01.0	102 16.9	N 0 36.6	Acamar	315 37.0	S40 22.6
01	301 53.1	167 46.8	58.6	218 49.0	40.1	118 39.1	01.1	117 19.3	36.6	Achernar	335 44.9	S57 19.6
02	316 55.6	182 46.1	57.8	233 49.6	40.2	133 41.3	01.2	132 21.6	36.5	Acrux	173 36.5	S63 00.0
03	331 58.0	197 45.5 ··	57.0	248 50.2 ··	40.4	148 43.5 ··	01.4	147 23.9 ··	36.5	Adhara	255 32.1	S28 56.8
04	347 00.5	212 44.9	56.1	263 50.8	40.5	163 45.7	01.5	162 26.3	36.4	Aldebaran	291 17.6	N16 28.3
05	2 03.0	227 44.3	55.3	278 51.4	40.6	178 47.9	01.6	177 28.6	36.3			
06	17 05.4	242 43.7	N18 54.5	293 52.0	N23 40.7	193 50.1	S 0 01.7	192 31.0	N 0 36.3	Alioth	166 42.1	N56 04.0
07	32 07.9	257 43.0	53.6	308 52.6	40.8	208 52.3	01.8	207 33.3	36.2	Alkaid	153 18.0	N49 24.7
T 08	47 10.4	272 42.4	52.8	323 53.2	40.9	223 54.5	02.0	222 35.6	36.1	Al Na'ir	28 13.9	S47 02.9
H 09	62 12.8	287 41.8 ··	52.0	338 53.8 ··	41.0	238 56.7 ··	02.1	237 38.0 ··	36.1	Alnilam	276 11.4	S 1 12.8
U 10	77 15.3	302 41.2	51.1	353 54.4	41.1	253 58.9	02.2	252 40.3	36.0	Alphard	218 20.3	S 8 34.6
R 11	92 17.7	317 40.6	50.3	8 55.0	41.2	269 01.1	02.3	267 42.7	36.0			
S 12	107 20.2	332 39.9	N18 49.5	23 55.6	N23 41.3	284 03.3	S 0 02.5	282 45.0	N 0 35.9	Alphecca	126 31.4	N26 46.9
D 13	122 22.7	347 39.3	48.6	38 56.2	41.4	299 05.5	02.6	297 47.4	35.8	Alpheratz	358 08.6	N28 59.1
A 14	137 25.1	2 38.7	47.8	53 56.8	41.5	314 07.7	02.7	312 49.7	35.8	Altair	62 31.7	N 8 49.2
Y 15	152 27.6	17 38.1 ··	46.9	68 57.4 ··	41.6	329 10.0 ··	02.8	327 52.0 ··	35.7	Ankaa	353 39.6	S42 24.2
16	167 30.1	32 37.5	46.1	83 58.0	41.7	344 12.2	02.9	342 54.4	35.6	Antares	112 55.9	S26 23.5
17	182 32.5	47 36.9	45.3	98 58.6	41.8	359 14.4	03.1	357 56.7	35.6			
18	197 35.0	62 36.3	N18 44.4	113 59.2	N23 41.9	14 16.6	S 0 03.2	12 59.1	N 0 35.5	Arcturus	146 17.9	N19 17.0
19	212 37.5	77 35.7	43.6	128 59.8	42.0	29 18.8	03.3	28 01.4	35.5	Atria	108 19.1	S68 59.8
20	227 39.9	92 35.0	42.7	144 00.4	42.1	44 21.0	03.4	43 03.7	35.4	Avior	234 28.6	S59 27.1
21	242 42.4	107 34.4 ··	41.9	159 01.0 ··	42.2	59 23.2 ··	03.6	58 06.1 ··	35.3	Bellatrix	278 58.5	N 6 20.0
22	257 44.9	122 33.8	41.0	174 01.6	42.3	74 25.4	03.7	73 08.4	35.3	Betelgeuse	271 28.0	N 7 24.2
23	272 47.3	137 33.2	40.2	189 02.2	42.4	89 27.6	03.8	88 10.8	35.2			
10 00	287 49.8	152 32.6	N18 39.3	204 02.8	N23 42.5	104 29.8	S 0 03.9	103 13.1	N 0 35.1	Canopus	264 07.5	S52 41.1
01	302 52.2	167 32.0	38.5	219 03.4	42.6	119 32.0	04.0	118 15.4	35.1	Capella	281 10.9	N45 58.6
02	317 54.7	182 31.4	37.6	234 04.0	42.7	134 34.2	04.2	133 17.8	35.0	Deneb	49 47.6	N45 12.8
03	332 57.2	197 30.8 ··	36.8	249 04.6 ··	42.8	149 36.4 ··	04.3	148 20.1 ··	34.9	Denebola	182 58.6	N14 40.7
04	347 59.6	212 30.2	35.9	264 05.2	42.9	164 38.6	04.4	163 22.4	34.9	Diphda	349 20.3	S18 05.2
05	3 02.1	227 29.6	35.1	279 05.8	43.0	179 40.8	04.5	178 24.8	34.8			
06	18 04.6	242 28.9	N18 34.2	294 06.4	N23 43.1	194 43.0	S 0 04.7	193 27.1	N 0 34.8	Dubhe	194 21.8	N61 51.4
07	33 07.0	257 28.3	33.4	309 07.0	43.2	209 45.2	04.8	208 29.5	34.7	Elnath	278 43.8	N28 35.4
08	48 09.5	272 27.7	32.5	324 07.6	43.3	224 47.4	04.9	223 31.8	34.6	Eltanin	90 57.0	N51 29.6
F 09	63 12.0	287 27.1 ··	31.7	339 08.2 ··	43.4	239 49.6 ··	05.0	238 34.1 ··	34.6	Enif	34 10.8	N 9 47.4
R 10	78 14.4	302 26.5	30.8	354 08.8	43.5	254 51.8	05.2	253 36.5	34.5	Fomalhaut	15 50.6	S29 43.1
I 11	93 16.9	317 25.9	30.0	9 09.4	43.6	269 54.0	05.3	268 38.8	34.4			
D 12	108 19.4	332 25.3	N18 29.1	24 10.0	N23 43.7	284 56.2	S 0 05.4	283 41.1	N 0 34.4	Gacrux	172 28.2	S57 00.7
A 13	123 21.8	347 24.7	28.2	39 10.6	43.8	299 58.4	05.5	298 43.5	34.3	Gienah	176 17.5	S17 26.3
Y 14	138 24.3	2 24.1	27.4	54 11.2	43.9	315 00.6	05.7	313 45.8	34.2	Hadar	149 22.4	S60 17.2
15	153 26.7	17 23.5 ··	26.5	69 11.8 ··	44.0	330 02.8 ··	05.8	328 48.2 ··	34.2	Hamal	328 28.4	N23 22.3
16	168 29.2	32 22.9	25.7	84 12.4	44.1	345 05.0	05.9	343 50.5	34.1	Kaus Aust.	84 15.7	S34 23.6
17	183 31.7	47 22.3	24.8	99 13.0	44.2	0 07.2	06.0	358 52.8	34.0			
18	198 34.1	62 21.7	N18 23.9	114 13.6	N23 44.3	15 09.4	S 0 06.2	13 55.2	N 0 34.0	Kochab	137 18.5	N74 14.3
19	213 36.6	77 21.1	23.1	129 14.2	44.4	30 11.6	06.3	28 57.5	33.9	Markab	14 02.4	N15 06.2
20	228 39.1	92 20.5	22.2	144 14.8	44.5	45 13.8	06.4	43 59.8	33.8	Menkar	314 40.7	N 4 01.0
21	243 41.5	107 19.9 ··	21.3	159 15.4 ··	44.6	60 16.0 ··	06.5	59 02.2 ··	33.8	Menkent	148 36.2	S36 16.8
22	258 44.0	122 19.3	20.5	174 16.0	44.7	75 18.2	06.7	74 04.5	33.7	Miaplacidus	221 45.6	S69 38.6
23	273 46.5	137 18.7	19.6	189 16.6	44.8	90 20.4	06.8	89 06.9	33.7			
11 00	288 48.9	152 18.1	N18 18.7	204 17.2	N23 44.9	105 22.6	S 0 06.9	104 09.2	N 0 33.6	Mirfak	309 15.6	N49 47.5
01	303 51.4	167 17.5	17.9	219 17.8	44.9	120 24.8	07.0	119 11.5	33.5	Nunki	76 28.1	S26 19.2
02	318 53.8	182 16.9	17.0	234 18.4	45.0	135 27.0	07.2	134 13.9	33.5	Peacock	53 56.9	S56 47.6
03	333 56.3	197 16.4 ··	16.1	249 19.0 ··	45.1	150 29.2 ··	07.3	149 16.2 ··	33.4	Pollux	243 57.9	N28 04.3
04	348 58.8	212 15.8	15.3	264 19.6	45.2	165 31.3	07.4	164 18.5	33.3	Procyon	245 25.5	N 5 16.4
05	4 01.2	227 15.2	14.4	279 20.2	45.3	180 33.5	07.5	179 20.9	33.3			
06	19 03.7	242 14.6	N18 13.5	294 20.8	N23 45.4	195 35.7	S 0 07.7	194 23.2	N 0 33.2	Rasalhague	96 28.8	N12 34.5
07	34 06.2	257 14.0	12.6	309 21.4	45.5	210 37.9	07.8	209 25.5	33.1	Regulus	208 09.7	N12 03.6
S 08	49 08.6	272 13.4	11.8	324 22.0	45.6	225 40.1	07.9	224 27.9	33.1	Rigel	281 35.8	S 8 13.4
A 09	64 11.1	287 12.8 ··	10.9	339 22.6 ··	45.7	240 42.3 ··	08.0	239 30.2 ··	33.0	Rigil Kent.	140 24.8	S60 45.6
T 10	79 13.6	302 12.2	10.0	354 23.2	45.7	255 44.5	08.2	254 32.5	32.9	Sabik	102 40.2	S15 42.1
U 11	94 16.0	317 11.6	09.1	9 23.8	45.8	270 46.7	08.3	269 34.9	32.9			
R 12	109 18.5	332 11.0	N18 08.2	24 24.4	N23 45.9	285 48.9	S 0 08.4	284 37.2	N 0 32.8	Schedar	350 08.3	N56 25.8
D 13	124 21.0	347 10.4	07.4	39 25.0	46.0	300 51.1	08.5	299 39.5	32.7	Shaula	96 54.6	S37 05.4
A 14	139 23.4	2 09.9	06.5	54 25.6	46.1	315 53.3	08.7	314 41.9	32.7	Sirius	258 55.6	S16 41.5
Y 15	154 25.9	17 09.3 ··	05.6	69 26.3 ··	46.2	330 55.5 ··	08.8	329 44.2 ··	32.6	Spica	158 56.9	S11 03.8
16	169 28.3	32 08.7	04.7	84 26.9	46.3	345 57.7	08.9	344 46.5	32.5	Suhail	223 10.8	S43 21.5
17	184 30.8	47 08.1	03.8	99 27.5	46.4	0 59.9	09.0	359 48.9	32.5			
18	199 33.3	62 07.5	N18 03.0	114 28.1	N23 46.4	16 02.1	S 0 09.2	14 51.2	N 0 32.4	Vega	80 55.0	N38 46.1
19	214 35.7	77 06.9	02.1	129 28.7	46.5	31 04.3	09.3	29 53.5	32.3	Zuben'ubi	137 32.3	S15 57.9
20	229 38.2	92 06.3	01.2	144 29.3	46.6	46 06.5	09.4	44 55.9	32.3			
21	244 40.7	107 05.8	18 00.3	159 29.9 ··	46.7	61 08.7 ··	09.5	59 58.2 ··	32.2	Venus	224 42.8	13 50
22	259 43.1	122 05.2	17 59.4	174 30.5	46.8	76 10.8	09.7	75 00.5	32.1	Mars	276 13.0	10 23
23	274 45.6	137 04.6	58.5	189 31.1	46.9	91 13.0	09.8	90 02.9	32.1	Jupiter	176 40.0	17 00
Mer. Pass. h m 4 47.9		*v* −0.6	*d* 0.9	*v* 0.6	*d* 0.1	*v* 2.2	*d* 0.1	*v* 2.3	*d* 0.1	Saturn	175 23.3	17 04

Note: for the STARS block the last three rows (Venus, Mars, Jupiter, Saturn) show S.H.A. and Mer. Pass. (h m):
- Venus 224 42.8 — 13 50
- Mars 276 13.0 — 10 23
- Jupiter 176 40.0 — 17 00
- Saturn 175 23.3 — 17 04

SUN / MOON

G.M.T.	SUN G.H.A.	Dec.	MOON G.H.A.	v	Dec.	d	H.P.
9 00	178 44.1	N22 23.8	90 39.1	15.4	S 1 25.4	10.9	54.8
01	193 44.0	23.5	105 13.5	15.3	1 36.3	10.8	54.8
02	208 43.9	23.2	119 47.8	15.3	1 47.1	10.8	54.7
03	223 43.8	·· 22.9	134 22.1	15.4	1 57.9	10.8	54.7
04	238 43.7	22.6	148 56.5	15.3	2 08.7	10.8	54.7
05	253 43.6	22.3	163 30.8	15.4	2 19.5	10.7	54.7
06	268 43.5	N22 22.0	178 05.2	15.4	S 2 30.2	10.8	54.7
07	283 43.4	21.7	192 39.6	15.4	2 41.0	10.7	54.7
T 08	298 43.3	21.4	207 14.0	15.4	2 51.7	10.7	54.6
H 09	313 43.2	·· 21.1	221 48.4	15.4	3 02.4	10.7	54.6
U 10	328 43.2	20.8	236 22.8	15.4	3 13.1	10.7	54.6
R 11	343 43.1	20.5	250 57.2	15.4	3 23.8	10.7	54.6
S 12	358 43.0	N22 20.2	265 31.6	15.4	S 3 34.5	10.6	54.6
D 13	13 42.9	19.9	280 06.0	15.4	3 45.1	10.6	54.6
A 14	28 42.8	19.6	294 40.4	15.5	3 55.7	10.6	54.5
Y 15	43 42.7	·· 19.3	309 14.9	15.4	4 06.3	10.6	54.5
16	58 42.6	19.0	323 49.3	15.4	4 16.9	10.6	54.5
17	73 42.5	18.7	338 23.7	15.4	4 27.5	10.5	54.5
18	88 42.4	N22 18.4	352 58.1	15.5	S 4 38.0	10.5	54.5
19	103 42.3	18.1	7 32.6	15.4	4 48.5	10.5	54.5
20	118 42.2	17.8	22 07.0	15.4	4 59.0	10.4	54.5
21	133 42.2	·· 17.5	36 41.4	15.5	5 09.4	10.5	54.4
22	148 42.1	17.2	51 15.9	15.4	5 19.9	10.4	54.4
23	163 42.0	16.8	65 50.3	15.4	5 30.3	10.3	54.4
10 00	178 41.9	N22 16.5	80 24.7	15.4	S 5 40.6	10.4	54.4
01	193 41.8	16.2	94 59.1	15.4	5 51.0	10.3	54.4
02	208 41.7	15.9	109 33.5	15.4	6 01.3	10.3	54.4
03	223 41.6	·· 15.6	124 07.9	15.4	6 11.6	10.3	54.4
04	238 41.5	15.3	138 42.3	15.4	6 21.9	10.2	54.4
05	253 41.4	15.0	153 16.7	15.3	6 32.1	10.2	54.4
06	268 41.4	N22 14.7	167 51.0	15.4	S 6 42.3	10.2	54.3
07	283 41.3	14.3	182 25.4	15.3	6 52.5	10.2	54.3
08	298 41.2	14.0	196 59.7	15.4	7 02.7	10.1	54.3
F 09	313 41.1	·· 13.7	211 34.1	15.3	7 12.8	10.1	54.3
R 10	328 41.0	13.4	226 08.4	15.3	7 22.9	10.0	54.3
I 11	343 40.9	13.1	240 42.7	15.3	7 32.9	10.1	54.3
D 12	358 40.9	N22 12.8	255 17.0	15.3	S 7 43.0	10.0	54.3
A 13	13 40.7	12.4	269 51.3	15.3	7 53.0	9.9	54.3
Y 14	28 40.6	12.1	284 25.6	15.2	8 02.9	9.9	54.3
15	43 40.6	·· 11.8	298 59.8	15.2	8 12.8	9.9	54.3
16	58 40.5	11.5	313 34.0	15.3	8 22.7	9.9	54.3
17	73 40.4	11.2	328 08.3	15.2	8 32.6	9.8	54.2
18	88 40.3	N22 10.8	342 42.5	15.1	S 8 42.4	9.8	54.2
19	103 40.2	10.5	357 16.6	15.2	8 52.2	9.7	54.2
20	118 40.1	10.2	11 50.8	15.1	9 01.9	9.7	54.2
21	133 40.0	·· 09.9	26 24.9	15.2	9 11.6	9.7	54.2
22	148 40.0	09.5	40 59.1	15.1	9 21.3	9.6	54.2
23	163 39.9	09.2	55 33.2	15.0	9 30.9	9.6	54.2
11 00	178 39.8	N22 08.9	70 07.2	15.1	S 9 40.5	9.5	54.2
01	193 39.7	08.6	84 41.3	15.0	9 50.0	9.5	54.2
02	208 39.6	08.2	99 15.3	15.0	9 59.5	9.5	54.2
03	223 39.5	·· 07.9	113 49.3	15.0	10 09.0	9.4	54.2
04	238 39.5	07.6	128 23.3	14.9	10 18.4	9.4	54.2
05	253 39.4	07.2	142 57.2	14.9	10 27.8	9.3	54.2
06	268 39.3	N22 06.9	157 31.1	14.9	S10 37.1	9.3	54.2
07	283 39.2	06.6	172 05.0	14.9	10 46.4	9.3	54.2
S 08	298 39.1	06.3	186 38.9	14.8	10 55.7	9.2	54.2
A 09	313 39.0	·· 05.9	201 12.7	14.8	11 04.9	9.1	54.2
T 10	328 39.0	05.6	215 46.5	14.8	11 14.0	9.2	54.2
U 11	343 38.9	05.3	230 20.3	14.8	11 23.2	9.0	54.2
R 12	358 38.8	N22 04.9	244 54.1	14.7	S11 32.2	9.1	54.2
D 13	13 38.7	04.6	259 27.8	14.7	11 41.3	8.9	54.2
A 14	28 38.6	04.3	274 01.5	14.6	11 50.2	8.9	54.2
Y 15	43 38.5	·· 03.9	288 35.1	14.6	11 59.2	8.8	54.2
16	58 38.5	03.6	303 08.7	14.6	12 08.0	8.9	54.2
17	73 38.4	03.2	317 42.3	14.6	12 16.9	8.7	54.2
18	88 38.3	N22 02.9	332 15.9	14.5	S12 25.6	8.8	54.2
19	103 38.2	02.6	346 49.4	14.5	12 34.4	8.6	54.2
20	118 38.1	02.2	1 22.9	14.4	12 43.0	8.7	54.2
21	133 38.1	·· 01.9	15 56.3	14.4	12 51.7	8.5	54.2
22	148 38.0	01.5	30 29.7	14.4	13 00.2	8.6	54.2
23	163 37.9	01.2	45 03.1	14.3	13 08.8	8.4	54.2
	S.D. 15.8	d 0.3	S.D. 14.9		14.8		14.8

Moonrise

Lat.	Twilight Naut.	Twilight Civil	Sunrise	Moonrise 9	10	11	12
N 72	□	□	□	13 08	14 50	16 37	18 38
N 70	□	□	□	13 02	14 37	16 15	17 57
68	□	□	□	12 58	14 27	15 57	17 29
66	////	////	01 12	12 54	14 18	15 43	17 08
64	////	////	02 01	12 51	14 11	15 31	16 52
62	////	////	02 31	12 48	14 05	15 22	16 38
60	////	01 28	02 54	12 46	14 00	15 13	16 27
N 58	////	02 04	03 12	12 44	13 55	15 06	16 17
56	////	02 29	03 28	12 42	13 51	15 00	16 08
54	01 21	02 49	03 41	12 40	13 47	14 54	16 00
52	01 54	03 05	03 52	12 39	13 44	14 49	15 53
50	02 18	03 19	04 02	12 37	13 41	14 44	15 47
45	02 59	03 47	04 23	12 34	13 34	14 34	15 34
N 40	03 27	04 08	04 40	12 32	13 29	14 26	15 23
35	03 49	04 25	04 54	12 29	13 24	14 19	15 14
30	04 06	04 39	05 06	12 28	13 20	14 13	15 06
20	04 34	05 03	05 27	12 24	13 13	14 02	14 52
N 10	04 55	05 22	05 45	12 21	13 07	13 53	14 39
0	05 13	05 39	06 02	12 19	13 01	13 44	14 28
S 10	05 29	05 55	06 18	12 16	12 55	13 35	14 17
20	05 45	06 12	06 36	12 13	12 49	13 26	14 05
30	06 00	06 30	06 56	12 10	12 42	13 16	13 51
35	06 08	06 39	07 07	12 09	12 38	13 09	13 43
40	06 17	06 50	07 21	12 06	12 34	13 03	13 34
45	06 26	07 03	07 36	12 04	12 29	12 55	13 24
S 50	06 37	07 18	07 56	12 01	12 23	12 45	13 11
52	06 42	07 25	08 05	12 00	12 20	12 41	13 05
54	06 47	07 32	08 15	11 59	12 17	12 36	12 59
56	06 52	07 41	08 26	11 57	12 13	12 31	12 52
58	06 59	07 50	08 40	11 56	12 10	12 25	12 44
S 60	07 05	08 01	08 56	11 54	12 05	12 19	12 35

Moonset

Lat.	Sunset	Twilight Civil	Twilight Naut.	Moonset 9	10	11	12
N 72	□	□	□	23 26	23 12	22 54	22 26
N 70	□	□	□	23 34	23 27	23 19	23 08
68	□	□	□	23 40	23 39	23 37	23 37
66	22 55	////	////	23 46	23 48	23 52	23 59
64	22 08	////	////	23 50	23 57	24 05	00 05
62	21 38	////	////	23 54	24 04	00 04	00 15
60	21 15	22 40	////	23 58	24 10	00 10	00 24
N 58	20 57	22 05	////	24 01	00 01	00 16	00 32
56	20 41	21 40	////	24 04	00 04	00 21	00 39
54	20 29	21 21	22 47	24 06	00 06	00 25	00 46
52	20 18	21 05	22 15	24 09	00 09	00 29	00 51
50	20 08	20 51	21 52	24 11	00 11	00 33	00 57
45	19 47	20 24	21 11	24 15	00 15	00 40	01 08
N 40	19 30	20 02	20 43	24 19	00 19	00 47	01 17
35	19 16	19 45	20 21	24 22	00 22	00 53	01 25
30	19 04	19 31	20 04	24 25	00 25	00 58	01 32
20	18 43	19 08	19 36	24 30	00 30	01 07	01 44
N 10	18 25	18 48	19 15	24 35	00 35	01 14	01 55
0	18 09	18 31	18 57	24 39	00 39	01 22	02 05
S 10	17 52	18 15	18 41	24 43	00 43	01 29	02 15
20	17 35	17 59	18 26	24 48	00 48	01 37	02 26
30	17 15	17 41	18 11	00 00	00 53	01 45	02 38
35	17 04	17 31	18 03	00 01	00 56	01 51	02 45
40	16 50	17 20	17 54	00 02	00 59	01 56	02 53
45	16 35	17 08	17 45	00 03	01 03	02 03	03 03
S 50	16 15	16 53	17 34	00 04	01 08	02 11	03 15
52	16 06	16 46	17 29	00 04	01 10	02 15	03 20
54	15 56	16 39	17 24	00 05	01 12	02 19	03 26
56	15 44	16 30	17 18	00 05	01 15	02 24	03 32
58	15 31	16 21	17 12	00 06	01 18	02 29	03 40
S 60	15 15	16 06	17 06	00 07	01 21	02 35	03 48

Day	SUN Eqn. of Time 00h	12h	Mer. Pass.	MOON Mer. Pass. Upper	Lower	Age	Phase
	m s	m s	h m	h m	h m	d	
9	05 03	05 08	12 05	18 29	06 08	08	
10	05 12	05 17	12 05	19 11	06 50	09	
11	05 21	05 25	12 05	19 54	07 33	10	

G.M.T.	ARIES G.H.A.	VENUS −3.3 G.H.A.	Dec.	MARS +1.7 G.H.A.	Dec.	JUPITER −1.5 G.H.A.	Dec.	SATURN +1.2 G.H.A.	Dec.	STARS Name	S.H.A.	Dec.
12 00	289 48.1	152 04.0 N17 57.6		204 31.7 N23 46.9		106 15.2 S 0 09.9		105 05.2 N 0 32.0		Acamar	315 37.0	S40 22.6
01	304 50.5	167 03.4 56.7		219 32.3 47.0		121 17.4 10.1		120 07.5 31.9		Achernar	335 44.9	S57 19.6
02	319 53.0	182 02.8 55.9		234 32.9 47.1		136 19.6 10.2		135 09.9 31.9		Acrux	173 36.7	S63 00.0
03	334 55.5	197 02.3 ·· 55.0		249 33.5 ·· 47.2		151 21.8 ·· 10.3		150 12.2 ·· 31.8		Adhara	255 32.1	S28 56.8
04	349 57.9	212 01.7 54.1		264 34.1 47.3		166 24.0 10.4		165 14.5 31.7		Aldebaran	291 17.6	N16 28.3
05	5 00.4	227 01.1 53.2		279 34.7 47.4		181 26.2 10.6		180 16.9 31.7				
06	20 02.8	242 00.5 N17 52.3		294 35.3 N23 47.4		196 28.4 S 0 10.7		195 19.2 N 0 31.6		Alioth	166 42.1	N56 04.0
07	35 05.3	256 59.9 51.4		309 35.9 47.5		211 30.6 10.8		210 21.5 31.5		Alkaid	153 18.0	N49 24.7
08	50 07.8	271 59.4 50.5		324 36.5 47.6		226 32.8 10.9		225 23.9 31.5		Al Na'ir	28 13.9	S47 02.9
S 09	65 10.2	286 58.8 ·· 49.6		339 37.1 ·· 47.7		241 34.9 ·· 11.1		240 26.2 ·· 31.4		Alnilam	276 11.4	S 1 12.8
U 10	80 12.7	301 58.2 48.7		354 37.7 47.8		256 37.1 11.2		255 28.5 31.3		Alphard	218 20.3	S 8 34.6
N 11	95 15.2	316 57.6 47.8		9 38.3 47.8		271 39.3 11.3		270 30.9 31.3				
D 12	110 17.6	331 57.1 N17 46.9		24 38.9 N23 47.9		286 41.5 S 0 11.5		285 33.2 N 0 31.2		Alphecca	126 31.4	N26 46.9
A 13	125 20.1	346 56.5 46.0		39 39.5 48.0		301 43.7 11.6		300 35.5 31.1		Alpheratz	358 08.6	N28 59.1
Y 14	140 22.6	1 55.9 45.1		54 40.1 48.1		316 45.9 11.7		315 37.8 31.1		Altair	62 31.6	N 8 49.2
15	155 25.0	16 55.3 ·· 44.2		69 40.8 ·· 48.1		331 48.1 ·· 11.8		330 40.2 ·· 31.0		Ankaa	353 39.6	S42 24.2
16	170 27.5	31 54.8 43.3		84 41.4 48.2		346 50.3 12.0		345 42.5 30.9		Antares	112 55.9	S26 23.5
17	185 29.9	46 54.2 42.4		99 42.0 48.3		1 52.5 12.1		0 44.8 30.9				
18	200 32.4	61 53.6 N17 41.5		114 42.6 N23 48.4		16 54.7 S 0 12.2		15 47.2 N 0 30.8		Arcturus	146 17.9	N19 17.0
19	215 34.9	76 53.1 40.6		129 43.2 48.4		31 56.8 12.4		30 49.5 30.7		Atria	108 19.2	S68 59.8
20	230 37.3	91 52.5 39.7		144 43.8 48.5		46 59.0 12.5		45 51.8 30.7		Avior	234 28.6	S59 27.1
21	245 39.8	106 51.9 ·· 38.8		159 44.4 ·· 48.6		62 01.2 ·· 12.6		60 54.2 ·· 30.6		Bellatrix	278 58.4	N 6 20.0
22	260 42.3	121 51.3 37.9		174 45.0 48.7		77 03.4 12.7		75 56.5 30.5		Betelgeuse	271 28.0	N 7 24.2
23	275 44.7	136 50.8 37.0		189 45.6 48.7		92 05.6 12.9		90 58.8 30.5				
13 00	290 47.2	151 50.2 N17 36.1		204 46.2 N23 48.8		107 07.8 S 0 13.0		106 01.1 N 0 30.4		Canopus	264 07.5	S52 41.1
01	305 49.7	166 49.6 35.1		219 46.8 48.9		122 10.0 13.1		121 03.5 30.3		Capella	281 10.9	N45 58.6
02	320 52.1	181 49.1 34.2		234 47.4 49.0		137 12.2 13.3		136 05.8 30.3		Deneb	49 47.6	N45 12.8
03	335 54.6	196 48.5 ·· 33.3		249 48.0 ·· 49.0		152 14.3 ·· 13.4		151 08.1 ·· 30.2		Denebola	182 58.6	N14 40.7
04	350 57.1	211 47.9 32.4		264 48.6 49.1		167 16.5 13.5		166 10.5 30.1		Diphda	349 20.3	S18 05.2
05	5 59.5	226 47.4 31.5		279 49.2 49.2		182 18.7 13.6		181 12.8 30.1				
06	21 02.0	241 46.8 N17 30.6		294 49.8 N23 49.3		197 20.9 S 0 13.8		196 15.1 N 0 30.0		Dubhe	194 21.9	N61 51.4
07	36 04.4	256 46.2 29.7		309 50.4 49.3		212 23.1 13.9		211 17.4 29.9		Elnath	278 43.8	N28 35.4
08	51 06.9	271 45.7 28.8		324 51.0 49.4		227 25.3 14.0		226 19.8 29.9		Eltanin	90 57.0	N51 29.7
M 09	66 09.4	286 45.1 ·· 27.8		339 51.6 ·· 49.5		242 27.5 ·· 14.2		241 22.1 ·· 29.8		Enif	34 10.8	N 9 47.4
O 10	81 11.8	301 44.6 26.9		354 52.3 49.5		257 29.6 14.3		256 24.4 29.7		Fomalhaut	15 50.6	S29 43.1
N 11	96 14.3	316 44.0 26.0		9 52.9 49.6		272 31.8 14.4		271 26.8 29.7				
D 12	111 16.8	331 43.4 N17 25.1		24 53.5 N23 49.7		287 34.0 S 0 14.6		286 29.1 N 0 29.6		Gacrux	172 28.2	S57 00.7
A 13	126 19.2	346 42.9 24.2		39 54.1 49.8		302 36.2 14.7		301 31.4 29.5		Gienah	176 17.5	S17 26.3
Y 14	141 21.7	1 42.3 23.3		54 54.7 49.8		317 38.4 14.8		316 33.7 29.4		Hadar	149 22.4	S60 17.2
15	156 24.2	16 41.8 ·· 22.3		69 55.3 ·· 49.9		332 40.6 ·· 14.9		331 36.1 ·· 29.4		Hamal	328 28.4	N23 22.3
16	171 26.6	31 41.2 21.4		84 55.9 50.0		347 42.7 15.1		346 38.4 29.3		Kaus Aust.	84 15.7	S34 23.6
17	186 29.1	46 40.6 20.5		99 56.5 50.0		2 44.9 15.2		1 40.7 29.2				
18	201 31.6	61 40.1 N17 19.6		114 57.1 N23 50.1		17 47.1 S 0 15.3		16 43.0 N 0 29.2		Kochab	137 18.6	N74 14.3
19	216 34.0	76 39.5 18.6		129 57.7 50.2		32 49.3 15.5		31 45.4 29.1		Markab	14 02.4	N15 06.2
20	231 36.5	91 39.0 17.7		144 58.3 50.2		47 51.5 15.6		46 47.7 29.0		Menkar	314 40.7	N 4 01.0
21	246 38.9	106 38.4 ·· 16.8		159 58.9 ·· 50.3		62 53.7 ·· 15.7		61 50.0 ·· 29.0		Menkent	148 36.3	S36 16.8
22	261 41.4	121 37.9 15.9		174 59.5 50.4		77 55.8 15.9		76 52.4 28.9		Miaplacidus	221 45.7	S69 38.6
23	276 43.9	136 37.3 14.9		190 00.1 50.4		92 58.0 16.0		91 54.7 28.8				
14 00	291 46.3	151 36.7 N17 14.0		205 00.7 N23 50.5		108 00.2 S 0 16.1		106 57.0 N 0 28.8		Mirfak	309 15.6	N49 47.5
01	306 48.8	166 36.2 13.1		220 01.4 50.6		123 02.4 16.3		121 59.3 28.7		Nunki	76 28.1	S26 19.2
02	321 51.3	181 35.6 12.2		235 02.0 50.6		138 04.6 16.4		137 01.7 28.6		Peacock	53 56.9	S56 47.6
03	336 53.7	196 35.1 ·· 11.2		250 02.6 ·· 50.7		153 06.8 ·· 16.5		152 04.0 ·· 28.6		Pollux	243 57.9	N28 04.3
04	351 56.2	211 34.5 10.3		265 03.2 50.7		168 08.9 16.6		167 06.3 28.5		Procyon	245 25.5	N 5 16.4
05	6 58.7	226 34.0 09.4		280 03.8 50.8		183 11.1 16.8		182 08.6 28.4				
06	22 01.1	241 33.4 N17 08.4		295 04.4 N23 50.9		198 13.3 S 0 16.9		197 11.0 N 0 28.3		Rasalhague	96 28.8	N12 34.5
07	37 03.6	256 32.9 07.5		310 05.0 50.9		213 15.5 17.0		212 13.3 28.3		Regulus	208 09.7	N12 03.6
08	52 06.0	271 32.3 06.6		325 05.6 51.0		228 17.7 17.2		227 15.6 28.2		Rigel	281 35.8	S 8 13.4
T 09	67 08.5	286 31.8 ·· 05.6		340 06.2 ·· 51.1		243 19.8 ·· 17.3		242 17.9 ·· 28.1		Rigil Kent.	140 24.8	S60 45.6
U 10	82 11.0	301 31.2 04.7		355 06.8 51.1		258 22.0 17.4		257 20.3 28.1		Sabik	102 40.2	S15 42.1
E 11	97 13.4	316 30.7 03.8		10 07.4 51.2		273 24.2 17.6		272 22.6 28.0				
S 12	112 15.9	331 30.1 N17 02.8		25 08.0 N23 51.2		288 26.4 S 0 17.7		287 24.9 N 0 27.9		Schedar	350 08.3	N56 25.8
D 13	127 18.4	346 29.6 01.9		40 08.6 51.3		303 28.6 17.8		302 27.2 27.9		Shaula	96 54.6	S37 05.4
A 14	142 20.8	1 29.0 00.9		55 09.3 51.4		318 30.7 18.0		317 29.6 27.8		Sirius	258 55.6	S16 41.4
Y 15	157 23.3	16 28.5 17 00.0		70 09.9 ·· 51.4		333 32.9 ·· 18.1		332 31.9 ·· 27.7		Spica	158 56.9	S11 03.8
16	172 25.8	31 27.9 16 59.1		85 10.5 51.5		348 35.1 18.2		347 34.2 27.6		Suhail	223 10.8	S43 21.5
17	187 28.2	46 27.4 58.1		100 11.1 51.5		3 37.3 18.4		2 36.5 27.6				
18	202 30.7	61 26.9 N16 57.2		115 11.7 N23 51.6		18 39.5 S 0 18.5		17 38.8 N 0 27.5		Vega	80 55.0	N38 46.1
19	217 33.2	76 26.3 56.2		130 12.3 51.7		33 41.6 18.6		32 41.2 27.4		Zuben'ubi	137 32.3	S15 57.9
20	232 35.6	91 25.8 55.3		145 12.9 51.7		48 43.8 18.8		47 43.5 27.4				
21	247 38.1	106 25.2 ·· 54.4		160 13.5 ·· 51.8		63 46.0 ·· 18.9		62 45.8 ·· 27.3			S.H.A.	Mer. Pass.
22	262 40.5	121 24.7 53.4		175 14.1 51.8		78 48.2 19.0		77 48.1 27.2		Venus	221 03.0	13 53
23	277 43.0	136 24.1 52.5		190 14.7 51.9		93 50.3 19.2		92 50.5 27.2		Mars	273 59.0	10 21
Mer. Pass.	h m 4 36.1	v −0.6 d 0.9		v 0.6 d 0.1		v 2.2 d 0.1		v 2.3 d 0.1		Jupiter Saturn	176 20.6 175 13.9	16 49 16 53

SUN / MOON

G.M.T.	SUN G.H.A.	SUN Dec.	MOON G.H.A.	v	MOON Dec.	d	H.P.
12 00	178 37.8	N22 00.9	59 36.4	14.3	S13 17.2	8.4	54.2
01	193 37.7	00.5	74 09.7	14.3	13 25.6	8.4	54.2
02	208 37.7	22 00.2	88 43.0	14.2	13 34.0	8.3	54.2
03	223 37.6	21 59.8	103 16.2	14.2	13 42.3	8.2	54.2
04	238 37.5	59.5	117 49.4	14.1	13 50.5	8.2	54.2
05	253 37.4	59.1	132 22.5	14.1	13 58.7	8.2	54.2
S 06	268 37.3	N21 58.8	146 55.6	14.1	S14 06.9	8.0	54.2
U 07	283 37.3	58.4	161 28.7	14.0	14 14.9	8.1	54.2
N 08	298 37.2	58.1	176 01.7	14.0	14 23.0	7.9	54.2
D 09	313 37.1	·· 57.8	190 34.7	13.9	14 30.9	7.9	54.2
A 10	328 37.0	57.4	205 07.6	13.9	14 38.8	7.9	54.2
Y 11	343 36.9	57.1	219 40.5	13.9	14 46.7	7.7	54.2
12	358 36.9	N21 56.7	234 13.4	13.8	S14 54.4	7.7	54.2
13	13 36.8	56.4	248 46.2	13.7	15 02.1	7.7	54.2
14	28 36.7	56.0	263 18.9	13.8	15 09.8	7.6	54.2
15	43 36.6	·· 55.7	277 51.7	13.6	15 17.4	7.5	54.2
16	58 36.6	55.3	292 24.3	13.7	15 24.9	7.5	54.2
17	73 36.5	54.9	306 57.0	13.6	15 32.4	7.4	54.2
18	88 36.4	N21 54.6	321 29.6	13.5	S15 39.8	7.3	54.2
19	103 36.3	54.2	336 02.1	13.5	15 47.1	7.3	54.2
20	118 36.3	53.9	350 34.6	13.5	15 54.4	7.2	54.3
21	133 36.2	·· 53.5	5 07.1	13.4	16 01.6	7.1	54.3
22	148 36.1	53.2	19 39.5	13.3	16 08.7	7.1	54.3
23	163 36.0	52.8	34 11.8	13.3	16 15.8	7.0	54.3
13 00	178 36.0	N21 52.5	48 44.1	13.3	S16 22.8	6.9	54.3
01	193 35.9	52.1	63 16.4	13.2	16 29.7	6.9	54.3
02	208 35.8	51.7	77 48.6	13.2	16 36.6	6.8	54.3
03	223 35.7	·· 51.4	92 20.8	13.1	16 43.4	6.7	54.3
04	238 35.7	51.0	106 52.9	13.1	16 50.1	6.6	54.3
05	253 35.6	50.7	121 25.0	13.0	16 56.7	6.6	54.3
M 06	268 35.5	N21 50.3	135 57.0	13.0	S17 03.3	6.5	54.3
O 07	283 35.4	49.9	150 29.0	12.9	17 09.8	6.4	54.3
N 08	298 35.4	49.6	165 00.9	12.9	17 16.2	6.4	54.3
D 09	313 35.3	·· 49.2	179 32.8	12.8	17 22.6	6.3	54.4
A 10	328 35.2	48.8	194 04.6	12.8	17 28.9	6.2	54.4
Y 11	343 35.1	48.5	208 36.4	12.7	17 35.1	6.1	54.4
12	358 35.1	N21 48.1	223 08.1	12.7	S17 41.2	6.0	54.4
13	13 35.0	47.7	237 39.8	12.7	17 47.2	6.0	54.4
14	28 34.9	47.4	252 11.5	12.6	17 53.2	5.9	54.4
15	43 34.9	·· 47.0	266 43.1	12.5	17 59.1	5.8	54.4
16	58 34.8	46.6	281 14.6	12.5	18 04.9	5.7	54.4
17	73 34.7	46.3	295 46.1	12.4	18 10.6	5.7	54.4
18	88 34.6	N21 45.9	310 17.5	12.4	S18 16.3	5.6	54.5
19	103 34.6	45.5	324 48.9	12.4	18 21.9	5.5	54.5
20	118 34.5	45.2	339 20.3	12.3	18 27.4	5.4	54.5
21	133 34.4	·· 44.8	353 51.6	12.2	18 32.8	5.3	54.5
22	148 34.4	44.4	8 22.8	12.2	18 38.1	5.3	54.5
23	163 34.3	44.1	22 54.0	12.2	18 43.4	5.1	54.5
14 00	178 34.2	N21 43.7	37 25.2	12.1	S18 48.5	5.1	54.5
01	193 34.2	43.3	51 56.3	12.0	18 53.6	5.0	54.5
02	208 34.1	42.9	66 27.3	12.0	18 58.6	4.9	54.6
03	223 34.0	·· 42.6	80 58.3	12.0	19 03.5	4.8	54.6
04	238 33.9	42.2	95 29.3	11.9	19 08.3	4.8	54.6
05	253 33.9	41.8	110 00.2	11.9	19 13.1	4.6	54.6
T 06	268 33.8	N21 41.4	124 31.1	11.8	S19 17.7	4.6	54.6
U 07	283 33.7	41.0	139 01.9	11.7	19 22.3	4.4	54.6
E 08	298 33.7	40.7	153 32.6	11.8	19 26.7	4.4	54.6
S 09	313 33.6	·· 40.3	168 03.4	11.6	19 31.1	4.3	54.6
D 10	328 33.5	39.9	182 34.0	11.7	19 35.4	4.2	54.7
A 11	343 33.5	39.5	197 04.7	11.5	19 39.6	4.1	54.7
Y 12	358 33.4	N21 39.1	211 35.2	11.6	S19 43.7	4.0	54.7
13	13 33.3	38.8	226 05.8	11.4	19 47.7	4.0	54.7
14	28 33.3	38.4	240 36.2	11.5	19 51.7	3.8	54.7
15	43 33.2	·· 38.0	255 06.7	11.4	19 55.5	3.8	54.7
16	58 33.1	37.6	269 37.1	11.3	19 59.3	3.6	54.7
17	73 33.1	37.2	284 07.4	11.3	20 02.9	3.6	54.8
18	88 33.0	N21 36.9	298 37.7	11.3	S20 06.5	3.4	54.8
19	103 32.9	36.5	313 08.0	11.2	20 09.9	3.4	54.8
20	118 32.9	36.1	327 38.2	11.2	20 13.3	3.2	54.8
21	133 32.8	·· 35.7	342 08.4	11.1	20 16.5	3.2	54.8
22	148 32.7	35.3	356 38.5	11.1	20 19.7	3.1	54.8
23	163 32.7	34.9	11 08.6	11.0	20 22.8	3.0	54.9
	S.D. 15.8	d 0.4	S.D. 14.8		14.8		14.9

Twilight / Moonrise

Lat.	Naut.	Civil	Sunrise	Moonrise 12	13	14	15
N 72	□	□	□	18 38	■	■	■
N 70	□	□	□	17 57	19 51	■	■
68	□	□	□	17 29	19 04	20 37	21 57
66	////	////	01 25	17 08	18 34	19 54	21 02
64	////	////	02 09	16 52	18 11	19 25	20 29
62	////	00 29	02 38	16 38	17 53	19 04	20 05
60	////	01 38	02 59	16 27	17 38	18 46	19 46
N 58	////	02 11	03 17	16 17	17 26	18 31	19 30
56	00 27	02 35	03 32	16 08	17 15	18 19	19 17
54	01 30	02 53	03 44	16 00	17 05	18 08	19 05
52	02 00	03 09	03 55	15 53	16 57	17 58	18 55
50	02 23	03 22	04 05	15 47	16 49	17 49	18 45
45	03 02	03 49	04 26	15 34	16 33	17 31	18 26
N 40	03 30	04 10	04 42	15 23	16 20	17 16	18 10
35	03 51	04 27	04 56	15 14	16 09	17 03	17 57
30	04 08	04 41	05 08	15 05	15 59	16 52	17 45
20	04 35	05 04	05 28	14 52	15 42	16 34	17 25
N 10	04 56	05 23	05 46	14 39	15 28	16 17	17 08
0	05 14	05 40	06 02	14 28	15 14	16 02	16 52
S 10	05 30	05 56	06 18	14 17	15 00	15 47	16 36
20	05 44	06 12	06 35	14 05	14 46	15 31	16 19
30	05 59	06 29	06 55	13 51	14 30	15 12	15 59
35	06 07	06 39	07 06	13 43	14 20	15 01	15 48
40	06 16	06 49	07 19	13 34	14 09	14 49	15 34
45	06 25	07 02	07 35	13 24	13 56	14 34	15 19
S 50	06 35	07 16	07 53	13 11	13 41	14 17	15 00
52	06 40	07 23	08 02	13 05	13 34	14 08	14 51
54	06 45	07 30	08 12	12 59	13 26	13 59	14 41
56	06 50	07 38	08 23	12 52	13 17	13 49	14 29
58	06 56	07 47	08 36	12 44	13 07	13 37	14 16
S 60	07 03	07 57	08 52	12 35	12 55	13 23	14 01

Sunset / Twilight / Moonset

Lat.	Sunset	Civil	Naut.	Moonset 12	13	14	15
N 72	□	□	□	22 26	■	■	■
N 70	□	□	□	23 08	22 51	■	■
68	□	□	□	23 37	23 38	23 46	24 11
66	22 42	////	////	23 59	24 09	00 09	00 29
64	22 00	////	////	00 05	00 16	00 32	00 58
62	21 32	23 32	////	00 15	00 30	00 47	01 20
60	21 11	22 31	////	00 24	00 42	01 06	01 38
N 58	20 53	21 59	////	00 32	00 53	01 19	01 53
56	20 39	21 35	23 35	00 39	01 02	01 30	02 06
54	20 26	21 17	22 39	00 46	01 10	01 40	02 17
52	20 15	21 01	22 09	00 51	01 17	01 49	02 27
50	20 06	20 48	21 47	00 57	01 24	01 57	02 36
45	19 45	20 21	21 08	01 08	01 38	02 13	02 54
N 40	19 29	20 01	20 41	01 17	01 50	02 27	03 10
35	19 15	19 44	20 20	01 25	02 00	02 39	03 23
30	19 03	19 30	20 03	01 32	02 09	02 49	03 34
20	18 43	19 07	19 36	01 44	02 24	03 07	03 53
N 10	18 25	18 48	19 15	01 55	02 37	03 22	04 10
0	18 09	18 32	18 57	02 05	02 50	03 37	04 26
S 10	17 53	18 16	18 42	02 15	03 02	03 51	04 42
20	17 36	18 00	18 27	02 26	03 16	04 07	04 58
30	17 17	17 43	18 12	02 38	03 31	04 25	05 18
35	17 05	17 33	18 04	02 45	03 40	04 35	05 29
40	16 52	17 22	17 56	02 53	03 50	04 47	05 42
45	16 37	17 10	17 47	03 03	04 02	05 01	05 57
S 50	16 18	16 56	17 36	03 15	04 17	05 18	06 16
52	16 09	16 49	17 32	03 20	04 24	05 26	06 25
54	15 59	16 42	17 27	03 26	04 32	05 35	06 35
56	15 48	16 34	17 21	03 32	04 40	05 46	06 47
58	15 35	16 25	17 16	03 40	04 50	05 57	07 00
S 60	15 20	16 14	17 09	03 48	05 01	06 11	07 15

SUN / MOON

Day	SUN Eqn. of Time 00h	12h	Mer. Pass.	MOON Mer. Pass. Upper	Lower	Age	Phase
	m s	m s	h m	h m	h m	d	
12	05 29	05 32	12 06	20 39	08 16	11	
13	05 36	05 40	12 06	21 25	09 02	12	◖
14	05 43	05 46	12 06	22 14	09 49	13	

G.M.T.	ARIES G.H.A.	VENUS −3.3 G.H.A.	Dec.	MARS +1.7 G.H.A.	Dec.	JUPITER −1.5 G.H.A.	Dec.	SATURN +1.2 G.H.A.	Dec.	STARS Name	S.H.A.	Dec.
15 00	292 45.5	151 23.6	N16 51.5	205 15.3	N23 51.9	108 52.5	S 0 19.3	107 52.8	N 0 27.1	Acamar	315 37.0	S40 22.6
01	307 47.9	166 23.1	.. 50.6	220 15.9	52.0	123 54.7	19.4	122 55.1	27.0	Achernar	335 44.9	S57 19.6
02	322 50.4	181 22.5	49.6	235 16.6	52.1	138 56.9	19.6	137 57.4	26.9	Acrux	173 36.8	S63 00.0
03	337 52.9	196 22.0	.. 48.7	250 17.2	.. 52.1	153 59.1	.. 19.7	152 59.8	.. 26.9	Adhara	255 32.0	S28 56.8
04	352 55.3	211 21.4	47.7	265 17.8	52.2	169 01.2	19.8	168 02.1	26.8	Aldebaran	291 17.6	N16 28.3
05	7 57.8	226 20.9	46.8	280 18.4	52.2	184 03.4	20.0	183 04.4	26.7			
06	23 00.3	241 20.4	N16 45.8	295 19.0	N23 52.3	199 05.6	S 0 20.1	198 06.7	N 0 26.7	Alioth	166 42.1	N56 04.0
W 07	38 02.7	256 19.8	44.9	310 19.6	52.3	214 07.8	20.2	213 09.0	26.6	Alkaid	153 18.0	N49 24.7
E 08	53 05.2	271 19.3	43.9	325 20.2	52.4	229 09.9	20.4	228 11.4	26.5	Al Na'ir	28 13.8	S47 02.9
D 09	68 07.7	286 18.8	.. 43.0	340 20.8	.. 52.4	244 12.1	.. 20.5	243 13.7	.. 26.5	Alnilam	276 11.4	S 1 12.8
N 10	83 10.1	301 18.2	42.0	355 21.4	52.5	259 14.3	20.6	258 16.0	26.4	Alphard	218 20.3	S 8 34.6
E 11	98 12.6	316 17.7	41.1	10 22.0	52.5	274 16.5	20.8	273 18.3	26.3			
S 12	113 15.0	331 17.2	N16 40.1	25 22.6	N23 52.6	289 18.6	S 0 20.9	288 20.7	N 0 26.2	Alphecca	126 31.4	N26 46.9
D 13	128 17.5	346 16.6	39.1	40 23.3	52.6	304 20.8	21.0	303 23.0	26.2	Alpheratz	358 08.6	N28 59.1
A 14	143 20.0	1 16.1	38.2	55 23.9	52.7	319 23.0	21.2	318 25.3	26.1	Altair	62 31.6	N 8 49.2
Y 15	158 22.4	16 15.6	.. 37.2	70 24.5	.. 52.7	334 25.2	.. 21.3	333 27.6	.. 26.0	Ankaa	353 39.6	S42 24.2
16	173 24.9	31 15.0	36.3	85 25.1	52.8	349 27.3	21.4	348 29.9	26.0	Antares	112 55.9	S26 23.5
17	188 27.4	46 14.5	35.3	100 25.7	52.8	4 29.5	21.6	3 32.3	25.9			
18	203 29.8	61 14.0	N16 34.4	115 26.3	N23 52.9	19 31.7	S 0 21.7	18 34.6	N 0 25.8	Arcturus	146 17.9	N19 17.0
19	218 32.3	76 13.4	33.4	130 26.9	52.9	34 33.9	21.8	33 36.9	25.7	Atria	108 19.2	S68 59.8
20	233 34.8	91 12.9	32.4	145 27.5	53.0	49 36.0	22.0	48 39.2	25.7	Avior	234 28.6	S59 27.0
21	248 37.2	106 12.4	.. 31.5	160 28.1	.. 53.0	64 38.2	.. 22.1	63 41.5	.. 25.6	Bellatrix	278 58.4	N 6 20.0
22	263 39.7	121 11.8	30.5	175 28.7	53.1	79 40.4	22.2	78 43.9	25.5	Betelgeuse	271 28.0	N 7 24.2
23	278 42.1	136 11.3	29.5	190 29.4	53.1	94 42.6	22.4	93 46.2	25.5			
16 00	293 44.6	151 10.8	N16 28.6	205 30.0	N23 53.2	109 44.7	S 0 22.5	108 48.5	N 0 25.4	Canopus	264 07.5	S52 41.1
01	308 47.1	166 10.3	27.6	220 30.6	53.2	124 46.9	22.6	123 50.8	25.3	Capella	281 10.9	N45 58.6
02	323 49.5	181 09.7	26.6	235 31.2	53.3	139 49.1	22.8	138 53.1	25.2	Deneb	49 47.6	N45 12.8
03	338 52.0	196 09.2	.. 25.7	250 31.8	.. 53.3	154 51.2	.. 22.9	153 55.5	.. 25.2	Denebola	182 58.6	N14 40.7
04	353 54.5	211 08.7	24.7	265 32.4	53.4	169 53.4	23.1	168 57.8	25.1	Diphda	349 20.2	S18 05.2
05	8 56.9	226 08.2	23.7	280 33.0	53.4	184 55.6	23.2	184 00.1	25.0			
06	23 59.4	241 07.6	N16 22.8	295 33.6	N23 53.5	199 57.8	S 0 23.3	199 02.4	N 0 25.0	Dubhe	194 21.9	N61 51.4
07	39 01.9	256 07.1	21.8	310 34.2	53.5	214 59.9	23.5	214 04.7	24.9	Elnath	278 43.7	N28 35.4
T 08	54 04.3	271 06.6	20.8	325 34.9	53.6	230 02.1	23.6	229 07.0	24.8	Eltanin	90 57.0	N51 29.7
H 09	69 06.8	286 06.1	.. 19.9	340 35.5	.. 53.6	245 04.3	.. 23.7	244 09.4	.. 24.7	Enif	34 10.7	N 9 47.4
U 10	84 09.3	301 05.5	18.9	355 36.1	53.6	260 06.4	23.9	259 11.7	24.7	Fomalhaut	15 50.5	S29 43.1
R 11	99 11.7	316 05.0	17.9	10 36.7	53.7	275 08.6	24.0	274 14.0	24.6			
S 12	114 14.2	331 04.5	N16 16.9	25 37.3	N23 53.7	290 10.8	S 0 24.1	289 16.3	N 0 24.5	Gacrux	172 28.2	S57 00.7
D 13	129 16.6	346 04.0	16.0	40 37.9	53.8	305 13.0	24.3	304 18.6	24.4	Gienah	176 17.5	S17 26.3
A 14	144 19.1	1 03.5	15.0	55 38.5	53.8	320 15.1	24.4	319 21.0	24.4	Hadar	149 22.4	S60 17.2
Y 15	159 21.6	16 02.9	.. 14.0	70 39.1	.. 53.9	335 17.3	.. 24.5	334 23.3	.. 24.3	Hamal	328 28.3	N23 22.3
16	174 24.0	31 02.4	13.0	85 39.7	53.9	350 19.5	24.7	349 25.6	24.2	Kaus Aust.	84 15.7	S34 23.6
17	189 26.5	46 01.9	12.1	100 40.4	53.9	5 21.6	24.8	4 27.9	24.2			
18	204 29.0	61 01.4	N16 11.1	115 41.0	N23 54.0	20 23.8	S 0 25.0	19 30.2	N 0 24.1	Kochab	137 18.6	N74 14.3
19	219 31.4	76 00.9	10.1	130 41.6	54.0	35 26.0	25.1	34 32.5	24.0	Markab	14 02.4	N15 06.3
20	234 33.9	91 00.4	09.1	145 42.2	54.1	50 28.1	25.2	49 34.9	23.9	Menkar	314 40.7	N 4 01.0
21	249 36.4	105 59.8	.. 08.1	160 42.8	.. 54.1	65 30.3	.. 25.4	64 37.2	.. 23.9	Menkent	148 36.3	S36 16.8
22	264 38.8	120 59.3	07.2	175 43.4	54.1	80 32.5	25.5	79 39.5	23.8	Miaplacidus	221 45.7	S69 38.6
23	279 41.3	135 58.8	06.2	190 44.0	54.2	95 34.7	25.6	94 41.8	23.7			
17 00	294 43.8	150 58.3	N16 05.2	205 44.6	N23 54.2	110 36.8	S 0 25.8	109 44.1	N 0 23.7	Mirfak	309 15.5	N49 47.5
01	309 46.2	165 57.8	04.2	220 45.3	54.3	125 39.0	25.9	124 46.4	23.6	Nunki	76 28.1	S26 19.2
02	324 48.7	180 57.3	03.2	235 45.9	54.3	140 41.2	26.0	139 48.8	23.5	Peacock	53 56.9	S56 47.6
03	339 51.1	195 56.8	.. 02.3	250 46.5	.. 54.3	155 43.3	.. 26.2	154 51.1	.. 23.4	Pollux	243 57.9	N28 04.3
04	354 53.6	210 56.2	01.3	265 47.1	54.4	170 45.5	26.3	169 53.4	23.4	Procyon	245 25.5	N 5 16.4
05	9 56.1	225 55.7	16 00.3	280 47.7	54.4	185 47.7	26.5	184 55.7	23.3			
06	24 58.5	240 55.2	N15 59.3	295 48.3	N23 54.4	200 49.8	S 0 26.6	199 58.0	N 0 23.2	Rasalhague	96 28.8	N12 34.5
07	40 01.0	255 54.7	58.3	310 48.9	54.5	215 52.0	26.7	215 00.3	23.1	Regulus	208 09.7	N12 03.6
08	55 03.5	270 54.2	57.3	325 49.5	54.5	230 54.2	26.9	230 02.7	23.1	Rigel	281 35.7	S 8 13.4
F 09	70 05.9	285 53.7	.. 56.3	340 50.2	.. 54.6	245 56.3	.. 27.0	245 05.0	.. 23.0	Rigil Kent.	140 24.8	S60 45.6
R 10	85 08.4	300 53.2	55.3	355 50.8	54.6	260 58.5	27.1	260 07.3	22.9	Sabik	102 40.2	S15 42.1
I 11	100 10.9	315 52.7	54.3	10 51.4	54.6	276 00.7	27.3	275 09.6	22.8			
D 12	115 13.3	330 52.2	N15 53.4	25 52.0	N23 54.7	291 02.8	S 0 27.4	290 11.9	N 0 22.8	Schedar	350 08.2	N56 25.8
A 13	130 15.8	345 51.7	52.4	40 52.6	54.7	306 05.0	27.6	305 14.2	22.7	Shaula	96 54.6	S37 05.4
Y 14	145 18.2	0 51.2	51.4	55 53.2	54.7	321 07.2	27.7	320 16.5	22.6	Sirius	258 55.5	S16 41.4
15	160 20.7	15 50.6	.. 50.4	70 53.8	.. 54.8	336 09.3	.. 27.8	335 18.9	.. 22.6	Spica	158 56.9	S11 03.8
16	175 23.2	30 50.1	49.4	85 54.5	54.8	351 11.5	28.0	350 21.2	22.5	Suhail	223 10.8	S43 21.5
17	190 25.6	45 49.6	48.4	100 55.1	54.8	6 13.6	28.1	5 23.5	22.4			
18	205 28.1	60 49.1	N15 47.4	115 55.7	N23 54.9	21 15.8	S 0 28.3	20 25.8	N 0 22.3	Vega	80 55.0	N38 46.1
19	220 30.6	75 48.6	46.4	130 56.3	54.9	36 18.0	28.4	35 28.1	22.3	Zuben'ubi	137 32.3	S15 57.9
20	235 33.0	90 48.1	45.4	145 56.9	54.9	51 20.1	28.5	50 30.4	22.2		S.H.A.	Mer. Pass.
21	250 35.5	105 47.6	.. 44.4	160 57.5	.. 54.9	66 22.3	.. 28.7	65 32.7	.. 22.1			
22	265 38.0	120 47.1	43.4	175 58.1	55.0	81 24.5	28.8	80 35.1	22.0	Venus	217 26.2	13 56
23	280 40.4	135 46.6	42.4	190 58.8	55.0	96 26.6	28.9	95 37.4	22.0	Mars	271 45.4	10 18
Mer. Pass.	h m 4 24.3	v −0.5 d 1.0		v 0.6 d 0.0		v 2.2 d 0.1		v 2.3 d 0.1		Jupiter	176 00.1	16 39
										Saturn	175 03.9	16 42

G.M.T.	SUN G.H.A.	SUN Dec.	MOON G.H.A.	v	Dec.	d	H.P.
15 00	178 32.6	N21 34.5	25 38.6	11.0	S20 25.8	2.8	54.9
01	193 32.5	34.1	40 08.6	11.0	20 28.6	2.8	54.9
02	208 32.5	33.7	54 38.6	10.9	20 31.4	2.7	54.9
03	223 32.4	·· 33.4	69 08.5	10.9	20 34.1	2.6	54.9
04	238 32.4	33.0	83 38.4	10.8	20 36.7	2.4	54.9
05	253 32.3	32.6	98 08.2	10.8	20 39.1	2.4	55.0
06	268 32.2	N21 32.2	112 38.0	10.8	S20 41.5	2.3	55.0
07	283 32.2	31.8	127 07.8	10.7	20 43.8	2.2	55.0
W 08	298 32.1	31.4	141 37.5	10.7	20 46.0	2.0	55.0
E 09	313 32.0	·· 31.0	156 07.2	10.6	20 48.0	2.0	55.0
D 10	328 32.0	30.6	170 36.8	10.6	20 50.0	1.9	55.0
N 11	343 31.9	30.2	185 06.4	10.6	20 51.9	1.8	55.1
E 12	358 31.8	N21 29.8	199 36.0	10.6	S20 53.7	1.6	55.1
S 13	13 31.8	29.4	214 05.6	10.5	20 55.3	1.6	55.1
D 14	28 31.7	29.0	228 35.1	10.4	20 56.9	1.4	55.1
A 15	43 31.7	·· 28.6	243 04.5	10.5	20 58.3	1.4	55.1
Y 16	58 31.6	28.2	257 34.0	10.4	20 59.7	1.2	55.2
17	73 31.5	27.8	272 03.4	10.3	21 00.9	1.1	55.2
18	88 31.5	N21 27.4	286 32.7	10.4	S21 02.0	1.1	55.2
19	103 31.4	27.0	301 02.1	10.3	21 03.1	0.9	55.2
20	118 31.4	26.6	315 31.4	10.3	21 04.0	0.8	55.2
21	133 31.3	·· 26.2	330 00.7	10.2	21 04.8	0.7	55.2
22	148 31.2	25.8	344 29.9	10.2	21 05.5	0.6	55.3
23	163 31.2	25.4	358 59.1	10.2	21 06.1	0.5	55.3
16 00	178 31.1	N21 25.0	13 28.3	10.2	S21 06.6	0.4	55.3
01	193 31.1	24.6	27 57.5	10.1	21 07.0	0.3	55.3
02	208 31.0	24.2	42 26.6	10.1	21 07.3	0.2	55.3
03	223 30.9	·· 23.8	56 55.7	10.1	21 07.5	0.0	55.4
04	238 30.9	23.4	71 24.8	10.1	21 07.5	0.2	55.4
05	253 30.8	23.0	85 53.9	10.0	21 07.5	0.2	55.4
06	268 30.8	N21 22.6	100 22.9	10.0	S21 07.3	0.4	55.4
07	283 30.7	22.2	114 51.9	10.0	21 07.1	0.4	55.4
T 08	298 30.7	21.8	129 20.9	10.0	21 06.7	0.5	55.5
H 09	313 30.6	·· 21.3	143 49.9	9.9	21 06.2	0.6	55.5
U 10	328 30.5	20.9	158 18.8	9.9	21 05.6	0.7	55.5
R 11	343 30.5	20.5	172 47.7	10.0	21 04.9	0.8	55.5
S 12	358 30.4	N21 20.1	187 16.7	9.8	S21 04.1	0.9	55.5
D 13	13 30.4	19.7	201 45.5	9.9	21 03.2	1.1	55.6
A 14	28 30.3	19.3	216 14.4	9.9	21 02.1	1.1	55.6
Y 15	43 30.3	·· 18.9	230 43.3	9.8	21 01.0	1.3	55.6
16	58 30.2	18.5	245 12.1	9.8	20 59.7	1.3	55.6
17	73 30.1	18.0	259 40.9	9.9	20 58.4	1.5	55.6
18	88 30.1	N21 17.6	274 09.8	9.8	S20 56.9	1.6	55.7
19	103 30.0	17.2	288 38.6	9.7	20 55.3	1.7	55.7
20	118 30.0	16.8	303 07.3	9.8	20 53.6	1.8	55.7
21	133 29.9	·· 16.4	317 36.1	9.8	20 51.8	2.0	55.7
22	148 29.9	16.0	332 04.9	9.7	20 49.8	2.0	55.7
23	163 29.8	15.5	346 33.6	9.8	20 47.8	2.1	55.8
17 00	178 29.8	N21 15.1	1 02.4	9.7	S20 45.7	2.3	55.8
01	193 29.7	14.7	15 31.1	9.7	20 43.4	2.4	55.8
02	208 29.7	14.3	29 59.8	9.7	20 41.0	2.4	55.8
03	223 29.6	·· 13.9	44 28.5	9.8	20 38.6	2.6	55.8
04	238 29.5	13.4	58 57.3	9.7	20 36.0	2.7	55.9
05	253 29.5	13.0	73 26.0	9.7	20 33.3	2.9	55.9
06	268 29.4	N21 12.6	87 54.7	9.7	S20 30.4	2.9	55.9
07	283 29.4	12.2	102 23.4	9.7	20 27.5	3.0	55.9
F 08	298 29.3	11.8	116 52.1	9.6	20 24.5	3.2	55.9
R 09	313 29.3	·· 11.3	131 20.7	9.7	20 21.3	3.2	56.0
I 10	328 29.2	10.9	145 49.4	9.7	20 18.1	3.4	56.0
11	343 29.2	10.5	160 18.1	9.7	20 14.7	3.5	56.0
D 12	358 29.1	N21 10.0	174 46.8	9.7	S20 11.2	3.6	56.0
A 13	13 29.1	09.6	189 15.5	9.7	20 07.6	3.6	56.0
Y 14	28 29.0	09.2	203 44.2	9.7	20 04.0	3.9	56.1
15	43 29.0	·· 08.8	218 12.9	9.7	20 00.1	3.9	56.1
16	58 28.9	08.3	232 41.6	9.7	19 56.2	4.0	56.1
17	73 28.9	07.9	247 10.3	9.7	19 52.2	4.1	56.1
18	88 28.8	N21 07.5	261 39.0	9.7	S19 48.1	4.3	56.2
19	103 28.8	07.0	276 07.7	9.7	19 43.8	4.3	56.2
20	118 28.7	06.6	290 36.4	9.7	19 39.5	4.5	56.2
21	133 28.7	·· 06.2	305 05.1	9.7	19 35.0	4.6	56.2
22	148 28.6	05.8	319 33.8	9.8	19 30.4	4.6	56.2
23	163 28.6	05.3	334 02.6	9.7	19 25.8	4.8	56.3
	S.D. 15.8	d 0.4	S.D. 15.0		15.1		15.3

Lat.	Twilight Naut.	Twilight Civil	Sunrise	Moonrise 15	Moonrise 16	Moonrise 17	Moonrise 18
N 72	□	□	□	■	■	■	■
N 70	□	□	□	■	■	23 51	23 26
68	□	□	□	21 57	22 37	22 50	22 53
66	////	////	01 39	21 02	21 48	22 15	22 29
64	////	////	02 18	20 29	21 17	21 50	22 10
62	////	00 56	02 44	20 05	20 54	21 30	21 55
60	////	01 47	03 05	19 46	20 35	21 13	21 42
N 58	////	02 18	03 22	19 30	20 21	21 00	21 31
56	00 51	02 40	03 36	19 17	20 07	20 48	21 21
54	01 39	02 58	03 48	19 05	19 55	20 37	21 12
52	02 07	03 13	03 59	18 55	19 45	20 28	21 04
50	02 28	03 26	04 08	18 45	19 36	20 20	20 57
45	03 06	03 52	04 28	18 26	19 17	20 02	20 42
N 40	03 33	04 12	04 44	18 10	19 01	19 48	20 30
35	03 53	04 29	04 58	17 57	18 48	19 35	20 19
30	04 10	04 43	05 09	17 45	18 36	19 25	20 10
20	04 37	05 05	05 29	17 25	18 16	19 06	19 54
N 10	04 57	05 24	05 46	17 08	17 59	18 50	19 40
0	05 14	05 40	06 02	16 52	17 43	18 35	19 27
S 10	05 30	05 56	06 18	16 36	17 27	18 20	19 14
20	05 44	06 11	06 35	16 19	17 10	18 04	19 00
30	05 59	06 28	06 54	15 59	16 50	17 45	18 43
35	06 06	06 37	07 05	15 48	16 39	17 35	18 34
40	06 14	06 48	07 18	15 34	16 26	17 22	18 23
45	06 23	07 00	07 33	15 19	16 10	17 08	18 10
S 50	06 33	07 14	07 51	15 00	15 51	16 50	17 55
52	06 38	07 20	07 59	14 51	15 42	16 41	17 48
54	06 42	07 27	08 09	14 41	15 32	16 32	17 40
56	06 48	07 35	08 20	14 29	15 20	16 21	17 31
58	06 53	07 44	08 32	14 16	15 07	16 09	17 20
S 60	06 59	07 54	08 47	14 01	14 51	15 55	17 08

Lat.	Sunset	Twilight Civil	Twilight Naut.	Moonset 15	Moonset 16	Moonset 17	Moonset 18
N 72	□	□	□	■	■	■	■
N 70	□	□	□	■	■	■	01 53
68	□	□	□	24 11	00 11	01 17	02 53
66	22 29	////	////	00 29	01 05	02 06	03 28
64	21 52	////	////	00 58	01 38	02 37	03 52
62	21 26	23 10	////	01 20	02 03	03 00	04 12
60	21 06	22 22	////	01 38	02 22	03 19	04 28
N 58	20 49	21 52	////	01 53	02 38	03 34	04 41
56	20 35	21 30	23 15	02 06	02 51	03 47	04 53
54	20 23	21 12	22 31	02 17	03 03	03 59	05 03
52	20 12	20 58	22 04	02 27	03 13	04 09	05 12
50	20 03	20 45	21 43	02 36	03 23	04 18	05 20
45	19 43	20 19	21 05	02 54	03 42	04 37	05 37
N 40	19 27	19 59	20 39	03 10	03 58	04 52	05 51
35	19 14	19 43	20 18	03 23	04 11	05 05	06 03
30	19 02	19 29	20 01	03 34	04 23	05 16	06 13
20	18 42	19 07	19 35	03 53	04 43	05 36	06 30
N 10	18 25	18 48	19 15	04 10	05 00	05 52	06 46
0	18 10	18 32	18 58	04 26	05 17	06 08	07 00
S 10	17 54	18 16	18 42	04 42	05 33	06 24	07 14
20	17 37	18 01	18 28	04 58	05 50	06 40	07 29
30	17 18	17 44	18 13	05 18	06 10	07 00	07 47
35	17 07	17 35	18 06	05 29	06 21	07 11	07 57
40	16 55	17 24	17 58	05 42	06 35	07 23	08 08
45	16 40	17 13	17 49	05 57	06 50	07 39	08 21
S 50	16 21	16 59	17 39	06 16	07 10	07 57	08 38
52	16 13	16 52	17 35	06 25	07 19	08 06	08 45
54	16 03	16 45	17 30	06 35	07 29	08 15	08 54
56	15 52	16 37	17 25	06 47	07 41	08 26	09 03
58	15 40	16 29	17 19	07 00	07 54	08 39	09 14
S 60	15 25	16 19	17 13	07 15	08 10	08 53	09 26

Day	SUN Eqn. of Time 00h	SUN Eqn. of Time 12h	SUN Mer. Pass.	MOON Mer. Pass. Upper	MOON Mer. Pass. Lower	Age	Phase
	m s	m s	h m	h m	h m	d	
15	05 49	05 52	12 06	23 04	10 39	14	
16	05 55	05 58	12 06	23 56	11 30	15	◯
17	06 01	06 03	12 06	24 48	12 22	16	

G.M.T.	ARIES G.H.A.	VENUS −3.3 G.H.A.	Dec.	MARS +1.8 G.H.A.	Dec.	JUPITER −1.4 G.H.A.	Dec.	SATURN +1.2 G.H.A.	Dec.	STARS Name	S.H.A.	Dec.
d h	° ′	° ′	° ′	° ′	° ′	° ′	° ′	° ′	° ′		° ′	° ′
18 00	295 42.9	150 46.1	N15 41.4	205 59.4	N23 55.0	111 28.8	S 0 29.1	110 39.7	N 0 21.9	Acamar	315 36.9	S40 22.6
01	310 45.4	165 45.6	40.4	221 00.0	55.1	126 31.0	29.2	125 42.0	21.8	Achernar	335 44.8	S57 19.6
02	325 47.8	180 45.1	39.4	236 00.6	55.1	141 33.1	29.4	140 44.3	21.7	Acrux	173 36.8	S63 00.0
03	340 50.3	195 44.6 ··	38.4	251 01.2 ··	55.1	156 35.3 ··	29.5	155 46.6 ··	21.7	Adhara	255 32.0	S28 56.8
04	355 52.7	210 44.1	37.4	266 01.8	55.2	171 37.5	29.6	170 48.9	21.6	Aldebaran	291 17.6	N16 28.3
05	10 55.2	225 43.6	36.4	281 02.4	55.2	186 39.6	29.8	185 51.2	21.5			
06	25 57.7	240 43.1	N15 35.4	296 03.1	N23 55.2	201 41.8	S 0 29.9	200 53.6	N 0 21.4	Alioth	166 42.1	N56 04.0
07	41 00.1	255 42.6	34.4	311 03.7	55.3	216 43.9	30.1	215 55.9	21.4	Alkaid	153 18.0	N49 24.7
S 08	56 02.6	270 42.1	33.4	326 04.3	55.3	231 46.1	30.2	230 58.2	21.3	Al Na'ir	28 13.8	S47 02.9
A 09	71 05.1	285 41.6 ··	32.4	341 04.9 ··	55.3	246 48.3 ··	30.3	246 00.5 ··	21.2	Alnilam	276 11.4	S 1 12.8
T 10	86 07.5	300 41.1	31.4	356 05.5	55.3	261 50.4	30.5	261 02.8	21.1	Alphard	218 20.3	S 8 34.6
U 11	101 10.0	315 40.6	30.4	11 06.1	55.3	276 52.6	30.6	276 05.1	21.1			
R 12	116 12.5	330 40.2	N15 29.4	26 06.7	N23 55.4	291 54.7	S 0 30.8	291 07.4	N 0 21.0	Alphecca	126 31.4	N26 46.9
D 13	131 14.9	345 39.7	28.4	41 07.4	55.4	306 56.9	30.9	306 09.7	20.9	Alpheratz	358 08.6	N28 59.1
A 14	146 17.4	0 39.2	27.3	56 08.0	55.4	321 59.1	31.0	321 12.1	20.8	Altair	62 31.6	N 8 49.2
Y 15	161 19.9	15 38.7 ··	26.3	71 08.6 ··	55.4	337 01.2 ··	31.2	336 14.4 ··	20.8	Ankaa	353 39.5	S42 24.2
16	176 22.3	30 38.2	25.3	86 09.2	55.5	352 03.4	31.3	351 16.7	20.7	Antares	112 55.9	S26 23.5
17	191 24.8	45 37.7	24.3	101 09.8	55.5	7 05.5	31.5	6 19.0	20.6			
18	206 27.2	60 37.2	N15 23.3	116 10.4	N23 55.5	22 07.7	S 0 31.6	21 21.3	N 0 20.5	Arcturus	146 17.9	N19 17.0
19	221 29.7	75 36.7	22.3	131 11.1	55.5	37 09.9	31.7	36 23.6	20.5	Atria	108 19.2	S68 59.8
20	236 32.2	90 36.2	21.3	146 11.7	55.6	52 12.0	31.9	51 25.9	20.4	Avior	234 28.6	S59 27.0
21	251 34.6	105 35.7 ··	20.3	161 12.3 ··	55.6	67 14.2 ··	32.0	66 28.2 ··	20.3	Bellatrix	278 58.4	N 6 20.0
22	266 37.1	120 35.2	19.2	176 12.9	55.6	82 16.3	32.2	81 30.5	20.2	Betelgeuse	271 27.9	N 7 24.2
23	281 39.6	135 34.8	18.2	191 13.5	55.6	97 18.5	32.3	96 32.9	20.2			
19 00	296 42.0	150 34.3	N15 17.2	206 14.1	N23 55.7	112 20.7	S 0 32.4	111 35.2	N 0 20.1	Canopus	264 07.5	S52 41.1
01	311 44.5	165 33.8	16.2	221 14.8	55.7	127 22.8	32.6	126 37.5	20.0	Capella	281 10.8	N45 58.6
02	326 47.0	180 33.3	15.2	236 15.4	55.7	142 25.0	32.7	141 39.8	19.9	Deneb	49 47.6	N45 12.8
03	341 49.4	195 32.8 ··	14.2	251 16.0 ··	55.7	157 27.1 ··	32.9	156 42.1 ··	19.9	Denebola	182 58.6	N14 40.7
04	356 51.9	210 32.3	13.1	266 16.6	55.7	172 29.3	33.0	171 44.4	19.8	Diphda	349 20.2	S18 05.2
05	11 54.3	225 31.8	12.1	281 17.2	55.8	187 31.5	33.1	186 46.7	19.7			
06	26 56.8	240 31.3	N15 11.1	296 17.8	N23 55.8	202 33.6	S 0 33.3	201 49.0	N 0 19.6	Dubhe	194 21.9	N61 51.4
07	41 59.3	255 30.9	10.1	311 18.5	55.8	217 35.8	33.4	216 51.3	19.6	Elnath	278 43.7	N28 35.4
08	57 01.7	270 30.4	09.1	326 19.1	55.8	232 37.9	33.6	231 53.6	19.5	Eltanin	90 57.0	N51 29.7
S 09	72 04.2	285 29.9 ··	08.0	341 19.7 ··	55.8	247 40.1 ··	33.7	246 55.9 ··	19.4	Enif	34 10.7	N 9 47.4
U 10	87 06.7	300 29.4	07.0	356 20.3	55.8	262 42.2	33.8	261 58.3	19.3	Fomalhaut	15 50.5	S29 43.1
N 11	102 09.1	315 28.9	06.0	11 20.9	55.9	277 44.4	34.0	277 00.6	19.3			
D 12	117 11.6	330 28.4	N15 05.0	26 21.5	N23 55.9	292 46.6	S 0 34.1	292 02.9	N 0 19.2	Gacrux	172 28.3	S57 00.7
A 13	132 14.1	345 28.0	03.9	41 22.2	55.9	307 48.7	34.3	307 05.2	19.1	Gienah	176 17.5	S17 26.3
Y 14	147 16.5	0 27.5	02.9	56 22.8	55.9	322 50.9	34.4	322 07.5	19.0	Hadar	149 22.4	S60 17.2
15	162 19.0	15 27.0 ··	01.9	71 23.4 ··	55.9	337 53.0 ··	34.6	337 09.8 ··	19.0	Hamal	328 28.3	N23 22.3
16	177 21.5	30 26.5	15 00.9	86 24.0	55.9	352 55.2	34.7	352 12.1	18.9	Kaus Aust.	84 15.7	S34 23.6
17	192 23.9	45 26.1	14 59.8	101 24.6	56.0	7 57.3	34.8	7 14.4	18.8			
18	207 26.4	60 25.6	N14 58.8	116 25.2	N23 56.0	22 59.5	S 0 35.0	22 16.7	N 0 18.7	Kochab	137 18.7	N74 14.3
19	222 28.8	75 25.1	57.8	131 25.9	56.0	38 01.7	35.1	37 19.0	18.7	Markab	14 02.4	N15 06.3
20	237 31.3	90 24.6	56.7	146 26.5	56.0	53 03.8	35.3	52 21.3	18.6	Menkar	314 40.6	N 4 01.0
21	252 33.8	105 24.1 ··	55.7	161 27.1 ··	56.0	68 06.0 ··	35.4	67 23.6 ··	18.5	Menkent	148 36.3	S36 16.8
22	267 36.2	120 23.7	54.7	176 27.7	56.0	83 08.1	35.5	82 26.0	18.4	Miaplacidus	221 45.7	S69 38.6
23	282 38.7	135 23.2	53.6	191 28.3	56.0	98 10.3	35.7	97 28.3	18.3			
20 00	297 41.2	150 22.7	N14 52.6	206 29.0	N23 56.1	113 12.4	S 0 35.8	112 30.6	N 0 18.3	Mirfak	309 15.5	N49 47.5
01	312 43.6	165 22.2	51.6	221 29.6	56.1	128 14.6	36.0	127 32.9	18.2	Nunki	76 28.1	S26 19.2
02	327 46.1	180 21.8	50.5	236 30.2	56.1	143 16.7	36.1	142 35.2	18.1	Peacock	53 56.9	S56 47.6
03	342 48.6	195 21.3 ··	49.5	251 30.8 ··	56.1	158 18.9 ··	36.3	157 37.5 ··	18.0	Pollux	243 57.8	N28 04.3
04	357 51.0	210 20.8	48.5	266 31.4	56.1	173 21.0	36.4	172 39.8	18.0	Procyon	245 25.5	N 5 16.4
05	12 53.5	225 20.3	47.4	281 32.0	56.1	188 23.2	36.5	187 42.1	17.9			
06	27 56.0	240 19.9	N14 46.4	296 32.7	N23 56.1	203 25.3	S 0 36.7	202 44.4	N 0 17.8	Rasalhague	96 28.8	N12 34.5
07	42 58.4	255 19.4	45.4	311 33.3	56.1	218 27.5	36.8	217 46.7	17.7	Regulus	208 09.7	N12 03.6
08	58 00.9	270 18.9	44.3	326 33.9	56.1	233 29.7	37.0	232 49.0	17.7	Rigel	281 35.7	S 8 13.3
M 09	73 03.3	285 18.5 ··	43.3	341 34.5 ··	56.2	248 31.8 ··	37.1	247 51.3 ··	17.6	Rigil Kent.	140 24.9	S60 45.7
O 10	88 05.8	300 18.0	42.3	356 35.1	56.2	263 34.0	37.3	262 53.6	17.5	Sabik	102 40.2	S15 42.1
N 11	103 08.3	315 17.5	41.2	11 35.8	56.2	278 36.1	37.4	277 55.9	17.4			
D 12	118 10.7	330 17.1	N14 40.2	26 36.4	N23 56.2	293 38.3	S 0 37.5	292 58.2	N 0 17.3	Schedar	350 08.2	N56 25.8
A 13	133 13.2	345 16.6	39.1	41 37.0	56.2	308 40.4	37.7	308 00.6	17.3	Shaula	96 54.6	S37 05.5
Y 14	148 15.7	0 16.1	38.1	56 37.6	56.2	323 42.6	37.8	323 02.9	17.2	Sirius	258 55.6	S16 41.4
15	163 18.1	15 15.7 ··	37.0	71 38.2 ··	56.2	338 44.7 ··	38.0	338 05.2 ··	17.1	Spica	158 57.0	S11 03.8
16	178 20.6	30 15.2	36.0	86 38.9	56.2	353 46.9	38.1	353 07.5	17.0	Suhail	223 10.8	S43 21.5
17	193 23.1	45 14.7	35.0	101 39.5	56.2	8 49.0	38.3	8 09.8	17.0			
18	208 25.5	60 14.3	N14 33.9	116 40.1	N23 56.2	23 51.2	S 0 38.4	23 12.1	N 0 16.9	Vega	80 55.0	N38 46.1
19	223 28.0	75 13.8	32.9	131 40.7	56.2	38 53.3	38.6	38 14.4	16.8	Zuben'ubi	137 32.3	S15 57.9
20	238 30.4	90 13.3	31.8	146 41.3	56.2	53 55.5	38.7	53 16.7	16.7		S.H.A.	Mer. Pass.
21	253 32.9	105 12.9 ··	30.8	161 42.0 ··	56.2	68 57.6 ··	38.8	68 19.0 ··	16.6		° ′	h m
22	268 35.4	120 12.4	29.7	176 42.6	56.2	83 59.8	39.0	83 21.3	16.6	Venus	213 52.2	13 58
23	283 38.7	135 11.9	28.7	191 43.2	56.2	99 01.9	39.1	98 23.6	16.5	Mars	269 32.1	10 15
	h m									Jupiter	175 38.6	16 28
Mer. Pass.	4 12.5	v −0.5	d 1.0	v 0.6	d 0.0	v 2.2	d 0.1	v 2.3	d 0.1	Saturn	174 53.1	16 31

G.M.T.	SUN G.H.A.	Dec.	MOON G.H.A.	v	Dec.	d	H.P.
d h	° ′	° ′	° ′	′	° ′	′	′
18 00	178 28.5	N21 04.9	348 31.3	9.8	S19 21.0	4.9	56.3
01	193 28.5	04.4	3 00.1	9.7	19 16.1	5.0	56.3
02	208 28.4	04.0	17 28.8	9.8	19 11.1	5.1	56.3
03	223 28.4	·· 03.6	31 57.6	9.8	19 06.0	5.2	56.3
04	238 28.3	03.1	46 26.4	9.8	19 00.8	5.3	56.4
05	253 28.3	02.7	60 55.2	9.8	18 55.5	5.4	56.4
06	268 28.2	N21 02.3	75 24.0	9.8	S18 50.1	5.6	56.4
07	283 28.2	01.8	89 52.8	9.8	18 44.5	5.6	56.4
S 08	298 28.1	01.4	104 21.6	9.8	18 38.9	5.7	56.5
A 09	313 28.1	·· 00.9	118 50.4	9.9	18 33.2	5.9	56.5
T 10	328 28.1	00.5	133 19.3	9.9	18 27.3	5.9	56.5
U 11	343 28.0	21 00.1	147 48.2	9.8	18 21.4	6.0	56.5
R 12	358 28.0	N20 59.6	162 17.0	9.9	S18 15.4	6.2	56.5
D 13	13 27.9	59.2	176 45.9	9.9	18 09.2	6.2	56.6
A 14	28 27.9	58.7	191 14.8	10.0	18 03.0	6.4	56.6
Y 15	43 27.8	·· 58.3	205 43.8	9.9	17 56.6	6.4	56.6
16	58 27.8	57.9	220 12.7	10.0	17 50.2	6.5	56.6
17	73 27.7	57.4	234 41.7	10.0	17 43.7	6.7	56.6
18	88 27.7	N20 57.0	249 10.7	10.0	S17 37.0	6.7	56.7
19	103 27.6	56.5	263 39.7	10.0	17 30.3	6.9	56.7
20	118 27.6	56.1	278 08.7	10.0	17 23.4	6.9	56.7
21	133 27.6	·· 55.6	292 37.7	10.1	17 16.5	7.0	56.7
22	148 27.5	55.2	307 06.8	10.1	17 09.5	7.2	56.7
23	163 27.5	54.7	321 35.9	10.0	17 02.3	7.2	56.8
19 00	178 27.4	N20 54.3	336 04.9	10.2	S16 55.1	7.3	56.8
01	193 27.4	53.8	350 34.1	10.1	16 47.8	7.4	56.8
02	208 27.3	53.4	5 03.2	10.1	16 40.4	7.5	56.8
03	223 27.3	·· 52.9	19 32.3	10.2	16 32.9	7.6	56.9
04	238 27.3	52.5	34 01.5	10.2	16 25.3	7.7	56.9
05	253 27.2	52.0	48 30.7	10.2	16 17.6	7.8	56.9
06	268 27.2	N20 51.6	62 59.9	10.3	S16 09.8	7.9	56.9
07	283 27.1	51.1	77 29.2	10.2	16 01.9	8.0	56.9
08	298 27.1	50.7	91 58.4	10.3	15 53.9	8.0	57.0
S 09	313 27.0	·· 50.2	106 27.7	10.3	15 45.9	8.2	57.0
U 10	328 27.0	49.8	120 57.0	10.3	15 37.7	8.2	57.0
N 11	343 27.0	49.3	135 26.3	10.4	15 29.5	8.3	57.0
D 12	358 26.9	N20 48.8	149 55.7	10.4	S15 21.2	8.4	57.0
A 13	13 26.9	48.4	164 25.1	10.3	15 12.8	8.5	57.1
Y 14	28 26.8	47.9	178 54.4	10.5	15 04.3	8.6	57.1
15	43 26.8	·· 47.5	193 23.9	10.4	14 55.7	8.7	57.1
16	58 26.8	47.0	207 53.3	10.5	14 47.0	8.7	57.1
17	73 26.7	46.6	222 22.8	10.4	14 38.3	8.9	57.1
18	88 26.7	N20 46.1	236 52.2	10.5	S14 29.4	8.9	57.2
19	103 26.7	45.6	251 21.7	10.6	14 20.5	9.0	57.2
20	118 26.6	45.2	265 51.3	10.5	14 11.5	9.1	57.2
21	133 26.6	·· 44.7	280 20.8	10.6	14 02.4	9.1	57.2
22	148 26.5	44.3	294 50.4	10.6	13 53.3	9.3	57.3
23	163 26.5	43.8	309 20.0	10.6	13 44.0	9.3	57.3
20 00	178 26.5	N20 43.3	323 49.6	10.6	S13 34.7	9.4	57.3
01	193 26.4	42.9	338 19.2	10.7	13 25.3	9.5	57.3
02	208 26.4	42.4	352 48.9	10.7	13 15.8	9.5	57.3
03	223 26.3	·· 41.9	7 18.6	10.7	13 06.3	9.6	57.4
04	238 26.3	41.5	21 48.3	10.7	12 56.7	9.7	57.4
05	253 26.3	41.0	36 18.0	10.7	12 47.0	9.8	57.4
06	268 26.2	N20 40.5	50 47.7	10.8	S12 37.2	9.8	57.4
07	283 26.2	40.1	65 17.5	10.8	12 27.4	9.9	57.4
08	298 26.2	39.6	79 47.3	10.8	12 17.5	10.0	57.5
M 09	313 26.1	·· 39.1	94 17.1	10.8	12 07.5	10.1	57.5
O 10	328 26.1	38.7	108 46.9	10.9	11 57.4	10.1	57.5
N 11	343 26.1	38.2	123 16.8	10.8	11 47.3	10.2	57.5
D 12	358 26.0	N20 37.7	137 46.6	10.9	S11 37.1	10.3	57.5
A 13	13 26.0	37.2	152 16.5	10.9	11 26.8	10.3	57.6
Y 14	28 26.0	36.8	166 46.4	10.9	11 16.5	10.4	57.6
15	43 25.9	·· 36.3	181 16.3	11.0	11 06.1	10.4	57.6
16	58 25.9	35.8	195 46.3	10.9	10 55.7	10.6	57.6
17	73 25.9	35.4	210 16.2	11.0	10 45.1	10.5	57.6
18	88 25.8	N20 34.9	224 46.2	11.0	S10 34.6	10.7	57.7
19	103 25.8	34.4	239 16.2	11.0	10 23.9	10.7	57.7
20	118 25.8	33.9	253 46.2	11.1	10 13.2	10.7	57.7
21	133 25.7	·· 33.5	268 16.3	11.0	10 02.5	10.9	57.7
22	148 25.7	33.0	282 46.3	11.1	9 51.6	10.9	57.7
23	163 25.7	32.5	297 16.4	11.1	9 40.7	10.9	57.8
	S.D. 15.8	d 0.5	S.D. 15.4		15.5		15.7

Lat.	Twilight Naut.	Civil	Sunrise	Moonrise 18	19	20	21
°	h m	h m	h m	h m	h m	h m	h m
N 72	□	□	□	■	{00 17 / 23 40}	23 19	23 04
N 70	□	□	□	23 26	23 13	23 04	22 57
68	////	////	00 44	22 53	22 53	22 52	22 51
66	////	////	01 52	22 29	22 37	22 42	22 46
64	////	////	02 27	22 10	22 24	22 34	22 42
62	////	01 14	02 52	21 55	22 13	22 27	22 38
60	////	01 57	03 11	21 42	22 03	22 20	22 35
N 58	////	02 25	03 27	21 31	21 55	22 15	22 32
56	01 08	02 46	03 41	21 21	21 47	22 10	22 29
54	01 47	03 03	03 52	21 12	21 41	22 05	22 27
52	02 13	03 18	04 03	21 04	21 35	22 01	22 25
50	02 33	03 30	04 12	20 57	21 29	21 58	22 23
45	03 10	03 56	04 31	20 42	21 18	21 50	22 19
N 40	03 36	04 15	04 47	20 30	21 08	21 43	22 15
35	03 56	04 31	05 00	20 19	21 00	21 37	22 12
30	04 12	04 44	05 11	20 10	20 52	21 32	22 10
20	04 38	05 06	05 30	19 54	20 39	21 23	22 05
N 10	04 58	05 25	05 47	19 40	20 28	21 15	22 01
0	05 15	05 40	06 03	19 27	20 18	21 08	21 57
S 10	05 30	05 56	06 18	19 14	20 07	21 00	21 53
20	05 44	06 11	06 34	19 00	19 56	20 52	21 49
30	05 58	06 27	06 53	18 43	19 43	20 43	21 44
35	06 05	06 36	07 04	18 34	19 35	20 38	21 42
40	06 13	06 46	07 16	18 23	19 27	20 32	21 39
45	06 21	06 58	07 30	18 10	19 17	20 25	21 35
S 50	06 31	07 11	07 48	17 55	19 05	20 17	21 31
52	06 35	07 17	07 56	17 48	18 59	20 13	21 29
54	06 40	07 24	08 06	17 40	18 53	20 09	21 27
56	06 45	07 32	08 16	17 31	18 46	20 04	21 24
58	06 50	07 40	08 28	17 20	18 38	19 59	21 22
S 60	06 56	07 50	08 42	17 08	18 29	19 53	21 19

Lat.	Sunset	Twilight Civil	Naut.	Moonset 18	19	20	21
°	h m	h m	h m	h m	h m	h m	h m
N 72	□	□	□	■	03 15	05 38	07 43
N 70	□	□	□	01 53	04 05	06 03	07 56
68	23 18	////	////	02 53	04 37	06 22	08 06
66	22 17	////	////	03 28	05 00	06 37	08 15
64	21 43	////	////	03 52	05 18	06 49	08 22
62	21 19	22 53	////	04 12	05 33	06 59	08 28
60	21 00	22 12	////	04 28	05 46	07 08	08 33
N 58	20 44	21 45	////	04 41	05 56	07 16	08 38
56	20 31	21 25	23 00	04 53	06 05	07 23	08 42
54	20 19	21 08	22 22	05 03	06 14	07 29	08 46
52	20 09	20 53	21 57	05 12	06 21	07 34	08 49
50	20 00	20 41	21 38	05 20	06 28	07 39	08 52
45	19 41	20 16	21 02	05 37	06 42	07 49	08 58
N 40	19 25	19 57	20 36	05 51	06 53	07 58	09 04
35	19 12	19 41	20 16	06 03	07 03	08 05	09 08
30	19 01	19 28	20 00	06 13	07 12	08 12	09 13
20	18 42	19 06	19 34	06 30	07 26	08 23	09 20
N 10	18 25	18 48	19 14	06 46	07 39	08 33	09 26
0	18 10	18 32	18 58	07 00	07 51	08 42	09 31
S 10	17 55	18 17	18 43	07 14	08 03	08 51	09 37
20	17 38	18 02	18 29	07 29	08 16	09 00	09 43
30	17 20	17 46	18 15	07 47	08 30	09 11	09 50
35	17 09	17 37	18 08	07 57	08 39	09 17	09 53
40	16 57	17 27	18 00	08 08	08 48	09 24	09 58
45	16 42	17 15	17 51	08 21	08 59	09 32	10 03
S 50	16 25	17 02	17 42	08 38	09 12	09 42	10 09
52	16 17	16 55	17 38	08 45	09 18	09 47	10 12
54	16 07	16 49	17 33	08 54	09 25	09 52	10 15
56	15 57	16 41	17 28	09 03	09 33	09 57	10 18
58	15 45	16 33	17 23	09 14	09 41	10 03	10 21
S 60	15 31	16 23	17 17	09 26	09 51	10 10	10 26

Day	SUN Eqn. of Time 00ʰ	12ʰ	Mer. Pass.	MOON Mer. Pass. Upper	Lower	Age	Phase
	m s	m s	h m	h m	h m	d	
18	06 06	06 08	12 06	00 48	13 13	17	
19	06 10	06 12	12 06	01 39	14 05	18	○
20	06 14	06 16	12 06	02 30	14 55	19	

G.M.T.	ARIES G.H.A.	VENUS −3.3 G.H.A.	Dec.	MARS +1.8 G.H.A.	Dec.	JUPITER −1.4 G.H.A.	Dec.	SATURN +1.2 G.H.A.	Dec.	STARS Name	S.H.A.	Dec.
d h	° '	° ' ° '		° ' ° '		° ' ° '		° ' ° '			° '	° '
21 00	298 40.3	150 11.5 N14 27.6		206 43.8 N23 56.3		114 04.1 S 0 39.3		113 25.9 N 0 16.4		Acamar	315 36.9	S40 22.6
01	313 42.8	165 11.0	26.6	221 44.4	56.3	129 06.2	39.4	128 28.2	16.3	Achernar	335 44.8	S57 19.6
02	328 45.2	180 10.5	25.5	236 45.1	56.3	144 08.4	39.6	143 30.5	16.3	Acrux	173 36.8	S63 00.0
03	343 47.7	195 10.1 ··	24.5	251 45.7 ··	56.3	159 10.5 ··	39.7	158 32.8 ··	16.2	Adhara	255 32.0	S28 56.7
04	358 50.2	210 09.6	23.4	266 46.3	56.3	174 12.7	39.9	173 35.1	16.1	Aldebaran	291 17.6	N16 28.3
05	13 52.6	225 09.2	22.4	281 46.9	56.3	189 14.8	40.0	188 37.4	16.0			
06	28 55.1	240 08.7 N14 21.3		296 47.5 N23 56.3		204 17.0 S 0 40.1		203 39.7 N 0 15.9		Alioth	166 42.1	N56 04.0
07	43 57.6	255 08.2	20.3	311 48.2	56.3	219 19.1	40.3	218 42.0	15.9	Alkaid	153 18.1	N49 24.7
T 08	59 00.0	270 07.8	19.2	326 48.8	56.3	234 21.3	40.4	233 44.3	15.8	Al Na'ir	28 13.8	S47 02.9
U 09	74 02.5	285 07.3 ··	18.2	341 49.4 ··	56.3	249 23.4 ··	40.6	248 46.6 ··	15.7	Alnilam	276 11.3	S 1 12.8
E 10	89 04.9	300 06.9	17.1	356 50.0	56.3	264 25.6	40.7	263 48.9	15.6	Alphard	218 20.3	S 8 34.6
S 11	104 07.4	315 06.4	16.1	11 50.7	56.3	279 27.7	40.9	278 51.2	15.6			
D 12	119 09.9	330 06.0 N14 15.0		26 51.3 N23 56.3		294 29.9 S 0 41.0		293 53.5 N 0 15.5		Alphecca	126 31.5	N26 46.9
A 13	134 12.3	345 05.5	13.9	41 51.9	56.3	309 32.0	41.2	308 55.8	15.4	Alpheratz	358 08.5	N28 59.1
Y 14	149 14.8	0 05.1	12.9	56 52.5	56.3	324 34.2	41.3	323 58.1	15.3	Altair	62 31.6	N 8 49.2
15	164 17.3	15 04.6 ··	11.8	71 53.1 ··	56.3	339 36.3 ··	41.4	339 00.5 ··	15.2	Ankaa	353 39.5	S42 24.2
16	179 19.7	30 04.1	10.8	86 53.8	56.3	354 38.5	41.6	354 02.8	15.2	Antares	112 55.9	S26 23.5
17	194 22.2	45 03.7	09.7	101 54.4	56.3	9 40.6	41.7	9 05.1	15.1			
18	209 24.7	60 03.2 N14 08.7		116 55.0 N23 56.3		24 42.7 S 0 41.9		24 07.4 N 0 15.0		Arcturus	146 17.9	N19 17.0
19	224 27.1	75 02.8	07.6	131 55.6	56.3	39 44.9	42.0	39 09.7	14.9	Atria	108 19.2	S68 59.8
20	239 29.6	90 02.3	06.5	146 56.3	56.3	54 47.0	42.2	54 12.0	14.8	Avior	234 28.6	S59 27.0
21	254 32.1	105 01.9 ··	05.5	161 56.9 ··	56.3	69 49.2 ··	42.3	69 14.3 ··	14.8	Bellatrix	278 58.4	N 6 20.0
22	269 34.5	120 01.4	04.4	176 57.5	56.3	84 51.3	42.5	84 16.6	14.7	Betelgeuse	271 27.9	N 7 24.2
23	284 37.0	135 01.0	03.3	191 58.1	56.2	99 53.5	42.6	99 18.9	14.6			
22 00	299 39.4	150 00.5 N14 02.3		206 58.7 N23 56.2		114 55.6 S 0 42.8		114 21.2 N 0 14.5		Canopus	264 07.5	S52 41.0
01	314 41.9	165 00.1	01.2	221 59.4	56.2	129 57.8	42.9	129 23.5	14.5	Capella	281 10.8	N45 58.6
02	329 44.4	179 59.6 14 00.2		237 00.0	56.2	144 59.9	43.1	144 25.8	14.4	Deneb	49 47.6	N45 12.8
03	344 46.8	194 59.2 13 59.1		252 00.6 ··	56.2	160 02.1 ··	43.2	159 28.1 ··	14.3	Denebola	182 58.6	N14 40.7
04	359 49.3	209 58.7	58.0	267 01.2	56.2	175 04.2	43.3	174 30.4	14.2	Diphda	349 20.2	S18 05.2
05	14 51.8	224 58.3	57.0	282 01.9	56.2	190 06.3	43.5	189 32.7	14.1			
06	29 54.2	239 57.8 N13 55.9		297 02.5 N23 56.2		205 08.5 S 0 43.6		204 35.0 N 0 14.1		Dubhe	194 21.9	N61 51.4
07	44 56.7	254 57.4	54.8	312 03.1	56.2	220 10.6	43.8	219 37.3	14.0	Elnath	278 43.7	N28 35.4
W 08	59 59.2	269 56.9	53.8	327 03.7	56.2	235 12.8	43.9	234 39.6	13.9	Eltanin	90 57.0	N51 29.7
E 09	75 01.6	284 56.5 ··	52.7	342 04.4 ··	56.2	250 14.9 ··	44.1	249 41.9 ··	13.8	Enif	34 10.7	N 9 47.4
D 10	90 04.1	299 56.1	51.6	357 05.0	56.2	265 17.1	44.2	264 44.2	13.7	Fomalhaut	15 50.5	S29 43.1
N 11	105 06.5	314 55.6	50.5	12 05.6	56.2	280 19.2	44.4	279 46.5	13.7			
E 12	120 09.0	329 55.2 N13 49.5		27 06.2 N23 56.2		295 21.4 S 0 44.5		294 48.8 N 0 13.6		Gacrux	172 28.3	S57 00.7
S 13	135 11.5	344 54.7	48.4	42 06.9	56.2	310 23.5	44.7	309 51.1	13.5	Gienah	176 17.5	S17 26.3
D 14	150 13.9	359 54.3	47.3	57 07.5	56.1	325 25.6	44.8	324 53.4	13.4	Hadar	149 22.5	S60 17.2
A 15	165 16.4	14 53.8 ··	46.3	72 08.1 ··	56.1	340 27.8 ··	45.0	339 55.7 ··	13.3	Hamal	328 28.3	N23 22.4
Y 16	180 18.9	29 53.4	45.2	87 08.7	56.1	355 29.9	45.1	354 58.0	13.3	Kaus Aust.	84 15.7	S34 23.6
17	195 21.3	44 53.0	44.1	102 09.3	56.1	10 32.1	45.3	10 00.3	13.2			
18	210 23.8	59 52.5 N13 43.0		117 10.0 N23 56.1		25 34.2 S 0 45.4		25 02.6 N 0 13.1		Kochab	137 18.7	N74 14.3
19	225 26.3	74 52.1	42.0	132 10.6	56.1	40 36.4	45.5	40 04.9	13.0	Markab	14 02.4	N15 06.3
20	240 28.7	89 51.6	40.9	147 11.2	56.1	55 38.5	45.7	55 07.2	12.9	Menkar	314 40.6	N 4 01.0
21	255 31.2	104 51.2 ··	39.8	162 11.8 ··	56.1	70 40.6 ··	45.8	70 09.5 ··	12.9	Menkent	148 36.3	S36 16.8
22	270 33.7	119 50.8	38.7	177 12.5	56.1	85 42.8	46.0	85 11.8	12.8	Miaplacidus	221 45.7	S69 38.5
23	285 36.1	134 50.3	37.7	192 13.1	56.0	100 44.9	46.1	100 14.1	12.7			
23 00	300 38.6	149 49.9 N13 36.6		207 13.7 N23 56.0		115 47.1 S 0 46.3		115 16.4 N 0 12.6		Mirfak	309 15.5	N49 47.5
01	315 41.0	164 49.4	35.5	222 14.3	56.0	130 49.2	46.4	130 18.7	12.5	Nunki	76 28.1	S26 19.2
02	330 43.5	179 49.0	34.4	237 15.0	56.0	145 51.3	46.6	145 21.0	12.5	Peacock	53 56.9	S56 47.6
03	345 46.0	194 48.6 ··	33.3	252 15.6 ··	56.0	160 53.5 ··	46.7	160 23.3 ··	12.4	Pollux	243 57.8	N28 04.3
04	0 48.4	209 48.1	32.3	267 16.2	56.0	175 55.6	46.9	175 25.6	12.3	Procyon	245 25.5	N 5 16.4
05	15 50.9	224 47.7	31.2	282 16.9	56.0	190 57.8	47.0	190 27.8	12.2			
06	30 53.4	239 47.3 N13 30.1		297 17.5 N23 55.9		205 59.9 S 0 47.2		205 30.1 N 0 12.1		Rasalhague	96 28.8	N12 34.6
07	45 55.8	254 46.8	29.0	312 18.1	55.9	221 02.1	47.3	220 32.4	12.1	Regulus	208 09.7	N12 03.6
T 08	60 58.3	269 46.4	27.9	327 18.7	55.9	236 04.2	47.5	235 34.7	12.0	Rigel	281 35.7	S 8 13.3
H 09	76 00.8	284 46.0 ··	26.8	342 19.4 ··	55.9	251 06.3 ··	47.6	250 37.0 ··	11.9	Rigil Kent.	140 24.9	S60 45.7
U 10	91 03.2	299 45.5	25.8	357 20.0	55.9	266 08.5	47.8	265 39.3	11.8	Sabik	102 40.2	S15 42.1
R 11	106 05.7	314 45.1	24.7	12 20.6	55.9	281 10.6	47.9	280 41.6	11.7			
S 12	121 08.2	329 44.7 N13 23.6		27 21.2 N23 55.8		296 12.7 S 0 48.1		295 43.9 N 0 11.7		Schedar	350 08.2	N56 25.9
D 13	136 10.6	344 44.2	22.5	42 21.9	55.8	311 14.9	48.2	310 46.2	11.6	Shaula	96 54.6	S37 05.5
A 14	151 13.1	359 43.8	21.4	57 22.5	55.8	326 17.0	48.4	325 48.5	11.5	Sirius	258 55.5	S16 41.4
Y 15	166 15.5	14 43.4 ··	20.3	72 23.1 ··	55.8	341 19.2 ··	48.5	340 50.8 ··	11.4	Spica	158 57.0	S11 03.8
16	181 18.0	29 42.9	19.2	87 23.7	55.8	356 21.3	48.7	355 53.1	11.3	Suhail	223 10.8	S43 21.5
17	196 20.5	44 42.5	18.2	102 24.4	55.7	11 23.4	48.8	10 55.4	11.3			
18	211 22.9	59 42.1 N13 17.1		117 25.0 N23 55.7		26 25.6 S 0 49.0		25 57.7 N 0 11.2		Vega	80 55.0	N38 46.1
19	226 25.4	74 41.7	16.0	132 25.6	55.7	41 27.7	49.1	41 00.0	11.1	Zuben'ubi	137 32.3	S15 57.9
20	241 27.9	89 41.2	14.9	147 26.3	55.7	56 29.9	49.3	56 02.3	11.0			
21	256 30.3	104 40.8 ··	13.8	162 26.9 ··	55.7	71 32.0 ··	49.4	71 04.6 ··	10.9		S.H.A.	Mer. Pass.
22	271 32.8	119 40.4	12.7	177 27.5	55.6	86 34.1	49.6	86 06.9	10.8	Venus	210 21.1	14 00
23	286 35.3	134 39.9	11.6	192 28.1	55.6	101 36.3	49.7	101 09.2	10.8	Mars	267 19.3	10 12
	h m									Jupiter	175 16.2	16 18
Mer. Pass.	4 00.7	v −0.4 d 1.1		v 0.6 d 0.0		v 2.1 d 0.1		v 2.3 d 0.1		Saturn	174 41.7	16 20

G.M.T.	SUN G.H.A.	SUN Dec.	MOON G.H.A.	v	Dec.	d	H.P.
21 00	178 25.6	N20 32.0	311 46.5	11.1	S 9 29.8	11.0	57.8
01	193 25.6	31.5	326 16.6	11.1	9 18.8	11.0	57.8
02	208 25.6	31.1	340 46.7	11.1	9 07.8	11.1	57.8
03	223 25.5	·· 30.6	355 16.8	11.1	8 56.7	11.2	57.8
04	238 25.5	30.1	9 46.9	11.2	8 45.5	11.2	57.8
05	253 25.5	29.6	24 17.1	11.1	8 34.3	11.3	57.9
06	268 25.4	N20 29.1	38 47.2	11.2	S 8 23.0	11.3	57.9
07	283 25.4	28.7	53 17.4	11.2	8 11.7	11.3	57.9
08	298 25.4	28.2	67 47.6	11.2	8 00.4	11.5	57.9
T 09	313 25.3	·· 27.7	82 17.8	11.2	7 48.9	11.4	57.9
U 10	328 25.3	27.2	96 48.0	11.2	7 37.5	11.5	58.0
E 11	343 25.3	26.7	111 18.2	11.3	7 26.0	11.6	58.0
S 12	358 25.3	N20 26.2	125 48.5	11.2	S 7 14.4	11.6	58.0
D 13	13 25.2	25.8	140 18.7	11.2	7 02.8	11.6	58.0
A 14	28 25.2	25.3	154 48.9	11.3	6 51.2	11.7	58.0
Y 15	43 25.2	·· 24.8	169 19.2	11.2	6 39.5	11.7	58.1
16	58 25.1	24.3	183 49.4	11.3	6 27.8	11.8	58.1
17	73 25.1	23.8	198 19.7	11.3	6 16.0	11.8	58.1
18	88 25.1	N20 23.3	212 50.0	11.3	S 6 04.2	11.8	58.1
19	103 25.1	22.8	227 20.3	11.3	5 52.4	11.9	58.1
20	118 25.0	22.3	241 50.6	11.2	5 40.5	11.9	58.2
21	133 25.0	·· 21.8	256 20.8	11.3	5 28.6	11.9	58.2
22	148 25.0	21.4	270 51.1	11.3	5 16.7	12.0	58.2
23	163 25.0	20.9	285 21.4	11.3	5 04.7	12.0	58.2
22 00	178 24.9	N20 20.4	299 51.7	11.3	S 4 52.7	12.1	58.2
01	193 24.9	19.9	314 22.0	11.3	4 40.6	12.1	58.2
02	208 24.9	19.4	328 52.3	11.3	4 28.5	12.1	58.3
03	223 24.8	·· 18.9	343 22.6	11.3	4 16.4	12.1	58.3
04	238 24.8	18.4	357 52.9	11.3	4 04.3	12.2	58.3
05	253 24.8	17.9	12 23.2	11.3	3 52.1	12.2	58.3
06	268 24.8	N20 17.4	26 53.5	11.3	S 3 39.9	12.2	58.3
W 07	283 24.7	16.9	41 23.8	11.3	3 27.7	12.2	58.4
E 08	298 24.7	16.4	55 54.0	11.3	3 15.5	12.3	58.4
D 09	313 24.7	·· 15.9	70 24.3	11.3	3 03.2	12.3	58.4
N 10	328 24.7	15.4	84 54.6	11.3	2 50.9	12.3	58.4
E 11	343 24.7	14.9	99 24.9	11.2	2 38.6	12.3	58.4
S 12	358 24.6	N20 14.4	113 55.1	11.3	S 2 26.3	12.4	58.4
D 13	13 24.6	13.9	128 25.4	11.2	2 13.9	12.4	58.5
A 14	28 24.6	13.4	142 55.6	11.3	2 01.5	12.4	58.5
Y 15	43 24.6	·· 12.9	157 25.9	11.2	1 49.2	12.5	58.5
16	58 24.5	12.4	171 56.1	11.2	1 36.7	12.4	58.5
17	73 24.5	11.9	186 26.3	11.2	1 24.3	12.4	58.5
18	88 24.5	N20 11.4	200 56.5	11.2	S 1 11.9	12.5	58.5
19	103 24.5	10.9	215 26.7	11.2	0 59.4	12.4	58.6
20	118 24.4	10.4	229 56.9	11.1	0 47.0	12.5	58.6
21	133 24.4	·· 09.9	244 27.0	11.1	0 34.5	12.5	58.6
22	148 24.4	09.4	258 57.2	11.1	0 22.0	12.5	58.6
23	163 24.4	08.9	273 27.3	11.1	S 0 09.5	12.4	58.6
23 00	178 24.4	N20 08.4	287 57.4	11.1	N 0 02.9	12.5	58.6
01	193 24.3	07.9	302 27.5	11.1	0 15.4	12.6	58.7
02	208 24.3	07.4	316 57.6	11.1	0 28.0	12.5	58.7
03	223 24.3	·· 06.9	331 27.7	11.0	0 40.5	12.5	58.7
04	238 24.3	06.4	345 57.7	11.1	0 53.0	12.5	58.7
05	253 24.3	05.8	0 27.8	11.0	1 05.5	12.5	58.7
06	268 24.2	N20 05.3	14 57.8	10.9	N 1 18.0	12.5	58.7
T 07	283 24.2	04.8	29 27.7	11.0	1 30.5	12.5	58.8
H 08	298 24.2	04.3	43 57.7	10.9	1 43.0	12.5	58.8
U 09	313 24.2	·· 03.8	58 27.6	10.9	1 55.5	12.6	58.8
R 10	328 24.2	03.3	72 57.5	10.9	2 08.1	12.5	58.8
S 11	343 24.2	02.8	87 27.4	10.9	2 20.6	12.5	58.8
D 12	358 24.1	N20 02.3	101 57.3	10.8	N 2 33.1	12.4	58.8
A 13	13 24.1	01.7	116 27.1	10.8	2 45.5	12.5	58.9
Y 14	28 24.1	01.2	130 56.9	10.8	2 58.0	12.5	58.9
15	43 24.1	·· 00.7	145 26.7	10.7	3 10.5	12.4	58.9
16	58 24.1	20 00.2	159 56.4	10.7	3 22.9	12.5	58.9
17	73 24.1	19 59.7	174 26.1	10.7	3 35.4	12.4	58.9
18	88 24.0	N19 59.2	188 55.8	10.7	N 3 47.8	12.4	58.9
19	103 24.0	58.7	203 25.5	10.6	4 00.2	12.5	58.9
20	118 24.0	58.1	217 55.1	10.6	4 12.7	12.3	59.0
21	133 24.0	·· 57.6	232 24.7	10.5	4 25.0	12.4	59.0
22	148 24.0	57.1	246 54.2	10.5	4 37.4	12.4	59.0
23	163 24.0	56.6	261 23.7	10.5	4 49.8	12.3	59.0
S.D. 15.8	*d* 0.5		S.D. 15.8		15.9		16.0

Lat.	Twilight Naut.	Twilight Civil	Sunrise	Moonrise 21	22	23	24
N 72	□	□	□	23 04	22 50	22 36	22 21
N 70	□	□	□	22 57	22 50	22 43	22 35
68	////	////	01 13	22 51	22 49	22 48	22 47
66	////	////	02 05	22 46	22 49	22 52	22 56
64	////	////	02 36	22 42	22 49	22 56	23 04
62	////	01 30	02 59	22 38	22 49	22 59	23 11
60	////	02 07	03 17	22 35	22 48	23 02	23 17
N 58	////	02 33	03 33	22 32	22 48	23 05	23 23
56	01 22	02 53	03 46	22 29	22 48	23 07	23 27
54	01 56	03 09	03 57	22 27	22 48	23 09	23 32
52	02 20	03 23	04 07	22 25	22 48	23 11	23 36
50	02 39	03 35	04 15	22 23	22 48	23 12	23 39
45	03 14	03 59	04 34	22 19	22 47	23 16	23 47
N 40	03 39	04 18	04 49	22 15	22 47	23 19	23 53
35	03 58	04 33	05 02	22 12	22 47	23 22	23 59
30	04 14	04 46	05 13	22 10	22 47	23 25	24 04
20	04 39	05 08	05 32	22 05	22 47	23 29	24 13
N 10	04 59	05 25	05 48	22 01	22 46	23 33	24 20
0	05 15	05 41	06 03	21 57	22 46	23 36	24 28
S 10	05 30	05 55	06 18	21 53	22 46	23 40	24 35
20	05 43	06 10	06 33	21 49	22 46	23 44	24 43
30	05 57	06 26	06 51	21 44	22 46	23 48	24 52
35	06 04	06 35	07 02	21 42	22 46	23 51	24 57
40	06 11	06 44	07 14	21 39	22 46	23 54	25 03
45	06 19	06 55	07 28	21 35	22 46	23 57	25 10
S 50	06 28	07 08	07 45	21 31	22 46	24 02	00 02
52	06 32	07 14	07 53	21 29	22 46	24 04	00 04
54	06 37	07 21	08 02	21 27	22 46	24 06	00 06
56	06 41	07 28	08 12	21 24	22 45	24 08	00 08
58	06 46	07 36	08 23	21 22	22 45	24 11	00 11
S 60	06 52	07 45	08 36	21 19	22 45	24 14	00 14

Lat.	Sunset	Twilight Civil	Twilight Naut.	Moonset 21	22	23	24
N 72	□	□	□	07 43	09 42	11 40	13 42
N 70	□	□	□	07 56	09 46	11 37	13 30
68	22 53	////	////	08 06	09 50	11 34	13 21
66	22 05	////	////	08 15	09 53	11 32	13 13
64	21 34	////	////	08 22	09 55	11 30	13 06
62	21 12	22 38	////	08 28	09 58	11 28	13 00
60	20 54	22 03	////	08 33	09 59	11 27	12 56
N 58	20 39	21 38	////	08 38	10 01	11 25	12 51
56	20 26	21 18	22 47	08 42	10 03	11 24	12 47
54	20 15	21 02	22 14	08 46	10 04	11 23	12 44
52	20 05	20 49	21 51	08 49	10 05	11 22	12 41
50	19 56	20 37	21 32	08 52	10 06	11 22	12 38
45	19 38	20 13	20 58	08 58	10 09	11 20	12 32
N 40	19 23	19 54	20 33	09 04	10 11	11 18	12 27
35	19 11	19 39	20 14	09 08	10 12	11 17	12 22
30	19 00	19 26	19 58	09 13	10 14	11 16	12 19
20	18 41	19 05	19 33	09 20	10 16	11 13	12 12
N 10	18 25	18 47	19 14	09 26	10 18	11 12	12 06
0	18 10	18 32	18 58	09 31	10 20	11 10	12 00
S 10	17 55	18 17	18 43	09 37	10 22	11 08	11 55
20	17 39	18 03	18 30	09 43	10 25	11 06	11 49
30	17 22	17 47	18 16	09 50	10 27	11 04	11 43
35	17 11	17 38	18 09	09 53	10 28	11 03	11 39
40	16 59	17 29	18 02	09 58	10 30	11 02	11 34
45	16 45	17 18	17 54	10 03	10 32	11 00	11 29
S 50	16 28	17 05	17 45	10 09	10 34	10 58	11 24
52	16 20	16 59	17 41	10 12	10 35	10 57	11 21
54	16 12	16 52	17 37	10 15	10 36	10 56	11 18
56	16 02	16 45	17 32	10 18	10 37	10 55	11 15
58	15 50	16 38	17 27	10 21	10 38	10 54	11 11
S 60	15 37	16 28	17 22	10 26	10 39	10 53	11 07

Day	SUN Eqn. of Time 00h	SUN Eqn. of Time 12h	SUN Mer. Pass.	MOON Mer. Pass. Upper	MOON Mer. Pass. Lower	Age	Phase
	m s	m s	h m	h m	h m	d	
21	06 17	06 19	12 06	03 20	15 44	20	
22	06 20	06 21	12 06	04 09	16 33	21	◖
23	06 22	06 23	12 06	04 58	17 23	22	

G.M.T.	ARIES G.H.A.	VENUS −3.4 G.H.A.	Dec.	MARS +1.8 G.H.A.	Dec.	JUPITER −1.4 G.H.A.	Dec.	SATURN +1.2 G.H.A.	Dec.
24 00	301 37.7	149 39.5 N13	10.5	207 28.8 N23	55.6	116 38.4 S 0	49.9	116 11.5 N 0	10.7
01	316 40.2	164 39.1	09.4	222 29.4	55.6	131 40.5	50.0	131 13.8	10.6
02	331 42.6	179 38.7	08.3	237 30.0	55.6	146 42.7	50.2	146 16.1	10.5
03	346 45.1	194 38.2 ··	07.2	252 30.6 ··	55.5	161 44.8 ··	50.3	161 18.4 ··	10.4
04	1 47.6	209 37.8	06.1	267 31.3	55.5	176 47.0	50.5	176 20.7	10.4
05	16 50.0	224 37.4	05.0	282 31.9	55.5	191 49.1	50.6	191 23.0	10.3
06	31 52.5	239 37.0 N13	04.0	297 32.5 N23	55.4	206 51.2 S 0	50.8	206 25.3 N 0	10.2
07	46 55.0	254 36.6	02.9	312 33.2	55.4	221 53.4	50.9	221 27.5	10.1
08	61 57.4	269 36.1	01.8	327 33.8	55.4	236 55.5	51.1	236 29.8	10.0
F 09	76 59.9	284 35.7 13	00.7	342 34.4 ··	55.4	251 57.6 ··	51.2	251 32.1 ··	10.0
R 10	92 02.4	299 35.3 12	59.6	357 35.0	55.4	266 59.8	51.4	266 34.4	09.9
I 11	107 04.8	314 34.9	58.5	12 35.7	55.3	282 01.9	51.5	281 36.7	09.8
D 12	122 07.3	329 34.4 N12	57.4	27 36.3 N23	55.3	297 04.0 S 0	51.7	296 39.0 N 0	09.7
A 13	137 09.8	344 34.0	56.3	42 36.9	55.3	312 06.2	51.8	311 41.3	09.6
Y 14	152 12.2	359 33.6	55.2	57 37.6	55.3	327 08.3	52.0	326 43.6	09.5
15	167 14.7	14 33.2 ··	54.1	72 38.2 ··	55.2	342 10.4 ··	52.1	341 45.9 ··	09.5
16	182 17.1	29 32.8	53.0	87 38.8	55.2	357 12.6	52.3	356 48.2	09.4
17	197 19.6	44 32.4	51.9	102 39.5	55.2	12 14.7	52.4	11 50.5	09.3
18	212 22.1	59 31.9 N12	50.8	117 40.1 N23	55.2	27 16.8 S 0	52.6	26 52.8 N 0	09.2
19	227 24.5	74 31.5	49.7	132 40.7	55.1	42 19.0	52.7	41 55.1	09.1
20	242 27.0	89 31.1	48.5	147 41.3	55.1	57 21.1	52.9	56 57.4	09.0
21	257 29.5	104 30.7 ··	47.4	162 42.0 ··	55.1	72 23.2 ··	53.0	71 59.7 ··	09.0
22	272 31.9	119 30.3	46.3	177 42.6	55.0	87 25.4	53.2	87 01.9	08.9
23	287 34.4	134 29.9	45.2	192 43.2	55.0	102 27.5	53.3	102 04.2	08.8
25 00	302 36.9	149 29.4 N12	44.1	207 43.9 N23	55.0	117 29.6 S 0	53.5	117 06.5 N 0	08.7
01	317 39.3	164 29.0	43.0	222 44.5	54.9	132 31.8	53.6	132 08.8	08.6
02	332 41.8	179 28.6	41.9	237 45.1	54.9	147 33.9	53.8	147 11.1	08.6
03	347 44.3	194 28.2 ··	40.8	252 45.8 ··	54.9	162 36.0 ··	53.9	162 13.4 ··	08.5
04	2 46.7	209 27.8	39.7	267 46.4	54.9	177 38.2	54.1	177 15.7	08.4
05	17 49.2	224 27.4	38.6	282 47.0	54.8	192 40.3	54.2	192 18.0	08.3
06	32 51.6	239 27.0 N12	37.5	297 47.6 N23	54.8	207 42.4 S 0	54.4	207 20.3 N 0	08.2
07	47 54.1	254 26.6	36.4	312 48.3	54.7	222 44.6	54.5	222 22.6	08.1
S 08	62 56.6	269 26.2	35.3	327 48.9	54.7	237 46.7	54.7	237 24.9	08.1
A 09	77 59.0	284 25.7 ··	34.1	342 49.5 ··	54.7	252 48.8 ··	54.8	252 27.2 ··	08.0
T 10	93 01.5	299 25.3	33.0	357 50.2	54.7	267 51.0	55.0	267 29.5	07.9
U 11	108 04.0	314 24.9	31.9	12 50.8	54.6	282 53.1	55.1	282 31.7	07.8
R 12	123 06.4	329 24.5 N12	30.8	27 51.4 N23	54.6	297 55.2 S 0	55.3	297 34.0 N 0	07.7
D 13	138 08.9	344 24.1	29.7	42 52.1	54.6	312 57.4	55.4	312 36.3	07.6
A 14	153 11.4	359 23.7	28.6	57 52.7	54.5	327 59.5	55.6	327 38.6	07.6
Y 15	168 13.8	14 23.3 ··	27.5	72 53.3 ··	54.5	343 01.6 ··	55.7	342 40.9 ··	07.5
16	183 16.3	29 22.9	26.4	87 54.0	54.4	358 03.7	55.9	357 43.2	07.4
17	198 18.7	44 22.5	25.2	102 54.6	54.4	13 05.9	56.0	12 45.5	07.3
18	213 21.2	59 22.1 N12	24.1	117 55.2 N23	54.4	28 08.0 S 0	56.2	27 47.8 N 0	07.2
19	228 23.7	74 21.7	23.0	132 55.9	54.3	43 10.1	56.3	42 50.1	07.1
20	243 26.1	89 21.3	21.9	147 56.5	54.3	58 12.3	56.5	57 52.4	07.1
21	258 28.6	104 20.9 ··	20.8	162 57.1 ··	54.3	73 14.4 ··	56.7	72 54.6 ··	07.0
22	273 31.1	119 20.5	19.7	177 57.8	54.2	88 16.5	56.8	87 56.9	06.9
23	288 33.5	134 20.1	18.5	192 58.4	54.2	103 18.7	57.0	102 59.2	06.8
26 00	303 36.0	149 19.7 N12	17.4	207 59.0 N23	54.2	118 20.8 S 0	57.1	118 01.5 N 0	06.7
01	318 38.5	164 19.2	16.3	222 59.7	54.1	133 22.9	57.3	133 03.8	06.6
02	333 40.9	179 18.8	15.2	238 00.3	54.1	148 25.0	57.4	148 06.1	06.6
03	348 43.4	194 18.4 ··	14.1	253 00.9 ··	54.0	163 27.2 ··	57.6	163 08.4 ··	06.5
04	3 45.9	209 18.0	12.9	268 01.6	54.0	178 29.3	57.7	178 10.7	06.4
05	18 48.3	224 17.6	11.8	283 02.2	54.0	193 31.4	57.9	193 13.0	06.3
06	33 50.8	239 17.2 N12	10.7	298 02.8 N23	53.9	208 33.5 S 0	58.0	208 15.2 N 0	06.2
07	48 53.2	254 16.8	09.6	313 03.5	53.9	223 35.7	58.2	223 17.5	06.1
08	63 55.7	269 16.4	08.4	328 04.1	53.8	238 37.8	58.3	238 19.8	06.1
S 09	78 58.2	284 16.0 ··	07.3	343 04.7 ··	53.8	253 39.9 ··	58.5	253 22.1 ··	06.0
U 10	94 00.6	299 15.6	06.2	358 05.4	53.7	268 42.1	58.6	268 24.4	05.9
N 11	109 03.1	314 15.3	05.1	13 06.0	53.7	283 44.2	58.8	283 26.7	05.8
D 12	124 05.6	329 14.9 N12	03.9	28 06.6 N23	53.7	298 46.3 S 0	59.0	298 29.0 N 0	05.7
A 13	139 08.0	344 14.5	02.8	43 07.3	53.6	313 48.4	59.1	313 31.3	05.6
Y 14	154 10.5	359 14.1	01.7	58 07.9	53.6	328 50.6	59.3	328 33.6	05.6
15	169 13.0	14 13.7 12	00.6	73 08.5 ··	53.5	343 52.7 ··	59.4	343 35.8 ··	05.5
16	184 15.4	29 13.3 11	59.4	88 09.2	53.5	358 54.8	59.6	358 38.1	05.4
17	199 17.9	44 12.9	58.3	103 09.8	53.4	13 56.9	59.7	13 40.4	05.3
18	214 20.4	59 12.5 N11	57.2	118 10.4 N23	53.4	28 59.1 S 0	59.9	28 42.7 N 0	05.2
19	229 22.8	74 12.1	56.0	133 11.1	53.4	44 01.2 1	00.0	43 45.0	05.1
20	244 25.3	89 11.7	54.9	148 11.7	53.3	59 03.3	00.2	58 47.3	05.0
21	259 27.7	104 11.3 ··	53.8	163 12.3 ··	53.3	74 05.4 ··	00.3	73 49.6 ··	05.0
22	274 30.2	119 10.9	52.6	178 13.0	53.2	89 07.6	00.5	88 51.9	04.9
23	289 32.7	134 10.5	51.5	193 13.6	53.2	104 09.7	00.6	103 54.1	04.8
Mer. Pass.	h m 3 48.9	v −0.4 d 1.1		v 0.6 d 0.0		v 2.1 d 0.2		v 2.3 d 0.1	

STARS

Name	S.H.A.	Dec.
Acamar	315 36.9	S40 22.5
Achernar	335 44.8	S57 19.6
Acrux	173 36.9	S63 00.0
Adhara	255 32.0	S28 56.7
Aldebaran	291 17.5	N16 28.3
Alioth	166 42.2	N56 04.0
Alkaid	153 18.1	N49 24.7
Al Na'ir	28 13.8	S47 02.9
Alnilam	276 11.3	S 1 12.8
Alphard	218 20.3	S 8 34.6
Alphecca	126 31.5	N26 46.9
Alpheratz	358 08.5	N28 59.2
Altair	62 31.6	N 8 49.2
Ankaa	353 39.5	S42 24.2
Antares	112 55.9	S26 23.5
Arcturus	146 17.9	N19 17.0
Atria	108 19.2	S68 59.8
Avior	234 28.6	S59 27.0
Bellatrix	278 58.4	N 6 20.0
Betelgeuse	271 27.9	N 7 24.2
Canopus	264 07.4	S52 41.0
Capella	281 10.8	N45 58.6
Deneb	49 47.6	N45 12.9
Denebola	182 58.6	N14 40.7
Diphda	349 20.2	S18 05.2
Dubhe	194 21.9	N61 51.4
Elnath	278 43.7	N28 35.4
Eltanin	90 57.0	N51 29.7
Enif	34 10.7	N 9 47.4
Fomalhaut	15 50.5	S29 43.1
Gacrux	172 28.3	S57 00.7
Gienah	176 17.5	S17 26.3
Hadar	149 22.5	S60 17.2
Hamal	328 28.3	N23 22.4
Kaus Aust.	84 15.7	S34 23.6
Kochab	137 18.8	N74 14.3
Markab	14 02.3	N15 06.3
Menkar	314 40.6	N 4 01.0
Menkent	148 36.3	S36 16.8
Miaplacidus	221 45.7	S69 38.5
Mirfak	309 15.4	N49 47.5
Nunki	76 28.1	S26 19.2
Peacock	53 56.9	S56 47.6
Pollux	243 57.8	N28 04.3
Procyon	245 25.5	N 5 16.4
Rasalhague	96 28.8	N12 34.6
Regulus	208 09.7	N12 03.6
Rigel	281 35.7	S 8 13.3
Rigil Kent.	140 24.9	S60 45.7
Sabik	102 40.2	S15 42.1
Schedar	350 08.1	N56 25.9
Shaula	96 54.6	S37 05.5
Sirius	258 55.5	S16 41.4
Spica	158 57.0	S11 03.8
Suhail	223 10.8	S43 21.5
Vega	80 55.0	N38 46.2
Zuben'ubi	137 32.3	S15 57.8

	S.H.A.	Mer. Pass.
	° '	h m
Venus	206 52.6	14 02
Mars	265 07.0	10 09
Jupiter	174 52.8	16 08
Saturn	174 29.7	16 09

G.M.T.	SUN G.H.A.	Dec.	MOON G.H.A.	v	Dec.	d	H.P.
24 00	178 23.9	N19 56.1	275 53.2	10.5	N 5 02.1	12.3	59.0
01	193 23.9	55.5	290 22.7	10.4	5 14.4	12.3	59.0
02	208 23.9	55.0	304 52.1	10.3	5 26.7	12.2	59.0
03	223 23.9 ··	54.5	319 21.4	10.4	5 38.9	12.3	59.1
04	238 23.9	54.0	333 50.8	10.3	5 51.2	12.2	59.1
05	253 23.9	53.4	348 20.1	10.2	6 03.4	12.1	59.1
06	268 23.9	N19 52.9	2 49.3	10.2	N 6 15.5	12.2	59.1
07	283 23.8	52.4	17 18.5	10.2	6 27.7	12.1	59.1
08	298 23.8	51.9	31 47.7	10.1	6 39.8	12.1	59.1
F 09	313 23.8 ··	51.3	46 16.8	10.1	6 51.9	12.1	59.1
R 10	328 23.8	50.8	60 45.9	10.0	7 04.0	12.0	59.2
I 11	343 23.8	50.3	75 14.9	10.0	7 16.0	12.0	59.2
D 12	358 23.8	N19 49.8	89 43.9	9.9	N 7 28.0	11.9	59.2
A 13	13 23.8	49.2	104 12.8	9.9	7 39.9	11.9	59.2
Y 14	28 23.8	48.7	118 41.7	9.9	7 51.8	11.9	59.2
15	43 23.8 ··	48.2	133 10.6	9.8	8 03.7	11.8	59.2
16	58 23.7	47.7	147 39.4	9.7	8 15.5	11.8	59.2
17	73 23.7	47.1	162 08.1	9.7	8 27.3	11.8	59.3
18	88 23.7	N19 46.6	176 36.8	9.7	N 8 39.1	11.7	59.3
19	103 23.7	46.1	191 05.5	9.6	8 50.8	11.6	59.3
20	118 23.7	45.5	205 34.1	9.6	9 02.4	11.6	59.3
21	133 23.7 ··	45.0	220 02.7	9.5	9 14.0	11.6	59.3
22	148 23.7	44.5	234 31.2	9.4	9 25.6	11.5	59.3
23	163 23.7	43.9	248 59.6	9.4	9 37.1	11.5	59.3
25 00	178 23.7	N19 43.4	263 28.0	9.4	N 9 48.6	11.4	59.3
01	193 23.7	42.9	277 56.4	9.2	10 00.0	11.3	59.3
02	208 23.6	42.3	292 24.6	9.3	10 11.3	11.3	59.4
03	223 23.6 ··	41.8	306 52.9	9.2	10 22.6	11.3	59.4
04	238 23.6	41.3	321 21.1	9.1	10 33.9	11.2	59.4
05	253 23.6	40.7	335 49.2	9.1	10 45.1	11.1	59.4
06	268 23.6	N19 40.2	350 17.3	9.0	N10 56.2	11.1	59.4
07	283 23.6	39.6	4 45.3	8.9	11 07.3	11.0	59.4
S 08	298 23.6	39.1	19 13.2	8.9	11 18.3	10.9	59.4
A 09	313 23.6 ··	38.6	33 41.1	8.9	11 29.2	10.9	59.4
T 10	328 23.6	38.0	48 09.0	8.8	11 40.1	10.8	59.4
U 11	343 23.6	37.5	62 36.8	8.7	11 50.9	10.8	59.5
R 12	358 23.6	N19 36.9	77 04.5	8.6	N12 01.7	10.6	59.5
D 13	13 23.6	36.4	91 32.1	8.7	12 12.3	10.7	59.5
A 14	28 23.6	35.9	105 59.8	8.5	12 23.0	10.5	59.5
Y 15	43 23.6 ··	35.3	120 27.3	8.5	12 33.5	10.5	59.5
16	58 23.6	34.8	134 54.8	8.4	12 44.0	10.4	59.5
17	73 23.6	34.2	149 22.2	8.4	12 54.4	10.3	59.5
18	88 23.5	N19 33.7	163 49.6	8.3	N13 04.7	10.2	59.5
19	103 23.5	33.1	178 16.9	8.2	13 14.9	10.2	59.5
20	118 23.5	32.6	192 44.1	8.2	13 25.1	10.1	59.5
21	133 23.5 ··	32.1	207 11.3	8.1	13 35.2	10.0	59.5
22	148 23.5	31.5	221 38.4	8.1	13 45.2	9.9	59.6
23	163 23.5	31.0	236 05.5	8.0	13 55.1	9.9	59.6
26 00	178 23.5	N19 30.4	250 32.5	7.9	N14 05.0	9.8	59.6
01	193 23.5	29.9	264 59.4	7.9	14 14.8	9.6	59.6
02	208 23.5	29.3	279 26.3	7.8	14 24.4	9.6	59.6
03	223 23.5 ··	28.8	293 53.1	7.8	14 34.0	9.6	59.6
04	238 23.5	28.2	308 19.9	7.7	14 43.6	9.4	59.6
05	253 23.5	27.7	322 46.6	7.6	14 53.0	9.3	59.6
06	268 23.5	N19 27.1	337 13.2	7.6	N15 02.3	9.2	59.6
07	283 23.5	26.6	351 39.8	7.5	15 11.5	9.2	59.6
08	298 23.5	26.0	6 06.3	7.4	15 20.7	9.0	59.6
S 09	313 23.5 ··	25.5	20 32.7	7.4	15 29.7	9.0	59.6
U 10	328 23.5	24.9	34 59.1	7.3	15 38.7	8.9	59.6
N 11	343 23.5	24.3	49 25.4	7.3	15 47.6	8.7	59.6
D 12	358 23.5	N19 23.8	63 51.7	7.2	N15 56.3	8.7	59.6
A 13	13 23.5	23.2	78 17.9	7.1	16 05.0	8.5	59.7
Y 14	28 23.5	22.7	92 44.0	7.1	16 13.5	8.5	59.7
15	43 23.5 ··	22.1	107 10.1	7.0	16 22.0	8.4	59.7
16	58 23.5	21.6	121 36.1	7.0	16 30.4	8.2	59.7
17	73 23.5	21.0	136 02.1	6.9	16 38.6	8.2	59.7
18	88 23.5	N19 20.5	150 28.0	6.8	N16 46.8	8.0	59.7
19	103 23.5	19.9	164 53.8	6.8	16 54.8	8.0	59.7
20	118 23.5	19.3	179 19.6	6.8	17 02.8	7.8	59.7
21	133 23.5 ··	18.8	193 45.4	6.6	17 10.6	7.7	59.7
22	148 23.5	18.2	208 11.0	6.6	17 18.3	7.6	59.7
23	163 23.5	17.7	222 36.6	6.6	17 25.9	7.5	59.7
	S.D. 15.8	d 0.5	S.D. 16.1		16.2		16.3

Lat.	Twilight Naut.	Twilight Civil	Sunrise	Moonrise 24	25	26	27
N 72	▭	▭	▭	22 21	22 01	21 22	▭
N 70	▭	▭	▭	22 35	22 27	22 15	21 49
68	////	////	01 34	22 47	22 46	22 48	22 56
66	////	////	02 17	22 56	23 02	23 13	23 32
64	////	00 42	02 45	23 04	23 15	23 32	23 58
62	////	01 44	03 07	23 11	23 26	23 47	24 18
60	////	02 17	03 24	23 17	23 36	24 01	00 01
N 58	00 38	02 40	03 38	23 23	23 44	24 12	00 12
56	01 35	02 59	03 51	23 27	23 52	24 22	00 22
54	02 05	03 15	04 01	23 32	23 58	24 31	00 31
52	02 27	03 28	04 11	23 36	24 04	00 04	00 38
50	02 45	03 39	04 19	23 39	24 10	00 10	00 46
45	03 18	04 02	04 37	23 47	24 21	00 21	01 01
N 40	03 42	04 21	04 52	23 53	24 31	00 31	01 13
35	04 01	04 36	05 04	23 59	24 39	00 39	01 24
30	04 16	04 48	05 15	24 04	00 04	00 47	01 34
20	04 41	05 09	05 33	24 13	00 13	01 00	01 50
N 10	05 00	05 26	05 48	24 20	00 20	01 11	02 04
0	05 15	05 41	06 03	24 28	00 28	01 21	02 18
S 10	05 29	05 55	06 17	24 35	00 35	01 32	02 31
20	05 42	06 09	06 33	24 43	00 43	01 44	02 46
30	05 55	06 24	06 50	24 52	00 52	01 57	03 03
35	06 02	06 33	07 00	24 57	00 57	02 05	03 13
40	06 09	06 42	07 11	25 03	01 03	02 14	03 24
45	06 17	06 53	07 25	25 10	01 10	02 24	03 37
S 50	06 25	07 05	07 41	00 02	01 19	02 36	03 53
52	06 29	07 11	07 49	00 04	01 23	02 42	04 01
54	06 33	07 17	07 57	00 06	01 27	02 49	04 09
56	06 37	07 24	08 07	00 08	01 32	02 56	04 19
58	06 42	07 31	08 18	00 11	01 37	03 04	04 30
S 60	06 47	07 40	08 30	00 14	01 43	03 14	04 42

Lat.	Sunset	Twilight Civil	Twilight Naut.	Moonset 24	25	26	27
N 72	▭	▭	▭	13 42	15 53	18 28	▭
N 70	▭	▭	▭	13 30	15 29	17 36	20 04
68	22 33	////	////	13 21	15 11	17 04	18 58
66	21 53	////	////	13 13	14 56	16 41	18 23
64	21 25	23 20	////	13 06	14 44	16 23	17 57
62	21 04	22 25	////	13 00	14 34	16 08	17 37
60	20 47	21 53	////	12 56	14 26	15 55	17 21
N 58	20 33	21 30	23 25	12 51	14 18	15 45	17 07
56	20 21	21 12	22 34	12 47	14 11	15 35	16 56
54	20 10	20 57	22 05	12 44	14 06	15 27	16 45
52	20 01	20 44	21 44	12 41	14 00	15 20	16 36
50	19 53	20 33	21 26	12 38	13 55	15 13	16 28
45	19 35	20 10	20 54	12 32	13 45	14 59	16 10
N 40	19 21	19 52	20 30	12 27	13 37	14 47	15 56
35	19 08	19 37	20 11	12 22	13 29	14 37	15 44
30	18 58	19 24	19 56	12 19	13 23	14 28	15 34
N 10	18 40	19 04	19 32	12 12	13 12	14 13	15 16
0	18 24	18 47	19 13	12 06	13 02	14 00	15 00
S 10	17 56	18 18	18 44	11 55	12 44	13 36	14 31
20	17 40	18 04	18 31	11 49	12 34	13 23	14 15
30	17 23	17 49	18 18	11 43	12 23	13 08	13 57
35	17 13	17 40	18 11	11 39	12 17	12 59	13 47
40	17 02	17 31	18 04	11 34	12 10	12 50	13 35
45	16 48	17 21	17 57	11 29	12 02	12 38	13 21
S 50	16 32	17 08	17 48	11 24	11 52	12 24	13 04
52	16 25	17 03	17 44	11 21	11 47	12 18	12 56
54	16 16	16 56	17 40	11 18	11 42	12 11	12 47
56	16 07	16 50	17 36	11 15	11 36	12 03	12 37
58	15 56	16 42	17 31	11 11	11 30	11 54	12 26
S 60	15 43	16 34	17 26	11 07	11 23	11 44	12 13

Day	SUN Eqn. of Time 00h	12h	Mer. Pass.	MOON Mer. Pass. Upper	Lower	Age	Phase
	m s	m s	h m	h m	h m	d	
24	06 24	06 25	12 06	05 48	18 14	23	
25	06 25	06 26	12 06	06 40	19 07	24	
26	06 26	06 26	12 06	07 35	20 03	25	◑

G.M.T.	ARIES G.H.A.	VENUS −3.4 G.H.A.	Dec.	MARS +1.8 G.H.A.	Dec.	JUPITER −1.4 G.H.A.	Dec.	SATURN +1.2 G.H.A.	Dec.	STARS Name	S.H.A.	Dec.
27 00	304 35.1	149 10.1 N11	50.4	208 14.3 N23	53.1	119 11.8 S 1	00.8	118 56.4 N 0	04.7	Acamar	315 36.9	S40 22.5
01	319 37.6	164 09.7	49.3	223 14.9	53.1	134 13.9	01.0	133 58.7	04.6	Achernar	335 44.7	S57 19.6
02	334 40.1	179 09.3	48.1	238 15.5	53.0	149 16.1	01.1	149 01.0	04.5	Acrux	173 36.9	S63 00.0
03	349 42.5	194 09.0 ··	47.0	253 16.2 ··	53.0	164 18.2 ··	01.3	164 03.3 ··	04.5	Adhara	255 32.0	S28 56.7
04	4 45.0	209 08.6	45.9	268 16.8	52.9	179 20.3	01.4	179 05.6	04.4	Aldebaran	291 17.5	N16 28.3
05	19 47.5	224 08.2	44.7	283 17.4	52.9	194 22.4	01.6	194 07.9	04.3			
06	34 49.9	239 07.8 N11	43.6	298 18.1 N23	52.8	209 24.6 S 1	01.7	209 10.1 N 0	04.2	Alioth	166 42.2	N56 04.0
07	49 52.4	254 07.4	42.4	313 18.7	52.8	224 26.7	01.9	224 12.4	04.1	Alkaid	153 18.1	N49 24.7
08	64 54.9	269 07.0	41.3	328 19.3	52.7	239 28.8	02.0	239 14.7	04.0	Al Na'ir	28 13.8	S47 02.9
M 09	79 57.3	284 06.6 ··	40.2	343 20.0 ··	52.7	254 30.9 ··	02.2	254 17.0 ··	03.9	Alnilam	276 11.3	S 1 12.8
O 10	94 59.8	299 06.2	39.0	358 20.6	52.6	269 33.1	02.3	269 19.3	03.9	Alphard	218 20.3	S 8 34.6
N 11	110 02.2	314 05.8	37.9	13 21.3	52.6	284 35.2	02.5	284 21.6	03.8			
D 12	125 04.7	329 05.5 N11	36.8	28 21.9 N23	52.5	299 37.3 S 1	02.7	299 23.9 N 0	03.7	Alphecca	126 31.5	N26 46.9
A 13	140 07.2	344 05.1	35.6	43 22.5	52.5	314 39.4	02.8	314 26.1	03.6	Alpheratz	358 08.5	N28 59.2
Y 14	155 09.6	359 04.7	34.5	58 23.2	52.4	329 41.5	03.0	329 28.4	03.5	Altair	62 31.6	N 8 49.2
15	170 12.1	14 04.3 ··	33.3	73 23.8 ··	52.4	344 43.7 ··	03.1	344 30.7 ··	03.4	Ankaa	353 39.4	S42 24.2
16	185 14.6	29 03.9	32.2	88 24.4	52.3	359 45.8	03.3	359 33.0	03.3	Antares	112 55.9	S26 23.5
17	200 17.0	44 03.5	31.1	103 25.1	52.3	14 47.9	03.4	14 35.3	03.3			
18	215 19.5	59 03.2 N11	29.9	118 25.7 N23	52.2	29 50.0 S 1	03.6	29 37.6 N 0	03.2	Arcturus	146 17.9	N19 17.0
19	230 22.0	74 02.8	28.8	133 26.4	52.2	44 52.2	03.7	44 39.9	03.1	Atria	108 19.3	S68 59.8
20	245 24.4	89 02.4	27.6	148 27.0	52.1	59 54.3	03.9	59 42.1	03.0	Avior	234 28.6	S59 27.0
21	260 26.9	104 02.0 ··	26.5	163 27.6 ··	52.1	74 56.4 ··	04.1	74 44.4 ··	02.9	Bellatrix	278 58.4	N 6 20.0
22	275 29.3	119 01.6	25.3	178 28.3	52.0	89 58.5	04.2	89 46.7	02.8	Betelgeuse	271 27.9	N 7 24.2
23	290 31.8	134 01.2	24.2	193 28.9	51.9	105 00.6	04.4	104 49.0	02.7			
28 00	305 34.3	149 00.9 N11	23.1	208 29.6 N23	51.9	120 02.8 S 1	04.5	119 51.3 N 0	02.7	Canopus	264 07.4	S52 41.0
01	320 36.7	164 00.5	21.9	223 30.2	51.8	135 04.9	04.7	134 53.6	02.6	Capella	281 10.8	N45 58.6
02	335 39.2	179 00.1	20.8	238 30.8	51.8	150 07.0	04.8	149 55.8	02.5	Deneb	49 47.6	N45 12.9
03	350 41.7	193 59.7 ··	19.6	253 31.5 ··	51.7	165 09.1 ··	05.0	164 58.1 ··	02.4	Denebola	182 58.6	N14 40.7
04	5 44.1	208 59.3	18.5	268 32.1	51.7	180 11.2	05.2	180 00.4	02.3	Diphda	349 20.1	S18 05.2
05	20 46.6	223 59.0	17.3	283 32.8	51.6	195 13.4	05.3	195 02.7	02.2			
06	35 49.1	238 58.6 N11	16.2	298 33.4 N23	51.6	210 15.5 S 1	05.5	210 05.0 N 0	02.1	Dubhe	194 21.9	N61 51.3
07	50 51.5	253 58.2	15.0	313 34.0	51.5	225 17.6	05.6	225 07.3	02.1	Elnath	278 43.7	N28 35.4
08	65 54.0	268 57.8	13.9	328 34.7	51.4	240 19.7	05.8	240 09.5	02.0	Eltanin	90 57.0	N51 29.7
T 09	80 56.5	283 57.5 ··	12.7	343 35.3 ··	51.4	255 21.8 ··	05.9	255 11.8 ··	01.9	Enif	34 10.7	N 9 47.4
U 10	95 58.9	298 57.1	11.6	358 36.0	51.3	270 24.0	06.1	270 14.1	01.8	Fomalhaut	15 50.5	S29 43.1
E 11	111 01.4	313 56.7	10.4	13 36.6	51.3	285 26.1	06.2	285 16.4	01.7			
S 12	126 03.8	328 56.3 N11	09.3	28 37.2 N23	51.2	300 28.2 S 1	06.4	300 18.7 N 0	01.6	Gacrux	172 28.3	S57 00.7
D 13	141 06.3	343 56.0	08.1	43 37.9	51.1	315 30.3	06.6	315 21.0	01.5	Gienah	176 17.5	S17 26.3
A 14	156 08.8	358 55.6	07.0	58 38.5	51.1	330 32.4	06.7	330 23.2	01.5	Hadar	149 22.5	S60 17.2
Y 15	171 11.2	13 55.2 ··	05.8	73 39.2 ··	51.0	345 34.5 ··	06.9	345 25.5 ··	01.4	Hamal	328 28.2	N23 22.4
16	186 13.7	28 54.8	04.7	88 39.8	51.0	0 36.7	07.0	0 27.8	01.3	Kaus Aust.	84 15.7	S34 23.6
17	201 16.2	43 54.5	03.5	103 40.4	50.9	15 38.8	07.2	15 30.1	01.2			
18	216 18.6	58 54.1 N11	02.4	118 41.1 N23	50.8	30 40.9 S 1	07.3	30 32.4 N 0	01.1	Kochab	137 18.8	N74 14.3
19	231 21.1	73 53.7	01.2	133 41.7	50.8	45 43.0	07.5	45 34.6	01.0	Markab	14 02.3	N15 06.3
20	246 23.6	88 53.3 11	00.1	148 42.4	50.7	60 45.1	07.7	60 36.9	00.9	Menkar	314 40.6	N 4 01.0
21	261 26.0	103 53.0 10	58.9	163 43.0 ··	50.6	75 47.3 ··	07.8	75 39.2 ··	00.9	Menkent	148 36.3	S36 16.8
22	276 28.5	118 52.6	57.8	178 43.6	50.6	90 49.4	08.0	90 41.5	00.8	Miaplacidus	221 45.7	S69 38.5
23	291 31.0	133 52.2	56.6	193 44.3	50.5	105 51.5	08.1	105 43.8	00.7			
29 00	306 33.4	148 51.9 N10	55.4	208 44.9 N23	50.5	120 53.6 S 1	08.3	120 46.1 N 0	00.6	Mirfak	309 15.4	N49 47.5
01	321 35.9	163 51.5	54.3	223 45.6	50.4	135 55.7	08.5	135 48.3	00.5	Nunki	76 28.1	S26 19.2
02	336 38.3	178 51.1	53.1	238 46.2	50.3	150 57.8	08.6	150 50.6	00.4	Peacock	53 56.8	S56 47.6
03	351 40.8	193 50.8 ··	52.0	253 46.9 ··	50.3	165 59.9 ··	08.8	165 52.9 ··	00.3	Pollux	243 57.8	N28 04.3
04	6 43.3	208 50.4	50.8	268 47.5	50.2	181 02.1	08.9	180 55.2	00.2	Procyon	245 25.5	N 5 16.4
05	21 45.7	223 50.0	49.7	283 48.1	50.1	196 04.2	09.1	195 57.5	00.2			
06	36 48.2	238 49.7 N10	48.5	298 48.8 N23	50.1	211 06.3 S 1	09.2	210 59.7 N 0	00.1	Rasalhague	96 28.8	N12 34.6
07	51 50.7	253 49.3	47.3	313 49.4	50.0	226 08.4	09.4	226 02.0 0	00.0	Regulus	208 09.7	N12 03.6
08	66 53.1	268 48.9	46.2	328 50.1	49.9	241 10.5	09.6	241 04.3 S 0	00.1	Rigel	281 35.7	S 8 13.3
W 09	81 55.6	283 48.6 ··	45.0	343 50.7 ··	49.9	256 12.6 ··	09.7	256 06.6 ··	00.2	Rigil Kent.	140 24.9	S60 45.7
E 10	96 58.1	298 48.2	43.9	358 51.4	49.8	271 14.8	09.9	271 08.9	00.3	Sabik	102 40.2	S15 42.1
D 11	112 00.5	313 47.8	42.7	13 52.0	49.8	286 16.9	10.0	286 11.1	00.4			
N 12	127 03.0	328 47.5 N10	41.5	28 52.6 N23	49.7	301 19.0 S 1	10.2	301 13.4 S 0	00.5	Schedar	350 08.1	N56 25.9
E 13	142 05.4	343 47.1	40.4	43 53.3	49.6	316 21.1	10.3	316 15.7	00.5	Shaula	96 54.6	S37 05.5
S 14	157 07.9	358 46.7	39.2	58 53.9	49.5	331 23.2	10.5	331 18.0	00.6	Sirius	258 55.5	S16 41.4
D 15	172 10.4	13 46.4 ··	38.1	73 54.6 ··	49.5	346 25.3 ··	10.7	346 20.3 ··	00.7	Spica	158 57.0	S11 03.8
A 16	187 12.8	28 46.0	36.9	88 55.2	49.4	1 27.4	10.8	1 22.5	00.8	Suhail	223 10.8	S43 21.4
Y 17	202 15.3	43 45.6	35.7	103 55.9	49.3	16 29.6	11.0	16 24.8	00.9			
18	217 17.8	58 45.3 N10	34.6	118 56.5 N23	49.3	31 31.7 S 1	11.1	31 27.1 S 0	01.0	Vega	80 55.0	N38 46.2
19	232 20.2	73 44.9	33.4	133 57.1	49.2	46 33.8	11.3	46 29.4	01.1	Zuben'ubi	137 32.3	S15 57.8
20	247 22.7	88 44.6	32.2	148 57.8	49.1	61 35.9	11.5	61 31.7	01.2			
21	262 25.2	103 44.2 ··	31.1	163 58.4 ··	49.0	76 38.0 ··	11.6	76 33.9 ··	01.2		S.H.A.	Mer. Pass.
22	277 27.6	118 43.8	29.9	178 59.1	49.0	91 40.1	11.8	91 36.2	01.3	Venus	203 26.6	14 04
23	292 30.1	133 43.5	28.7	193 59.7	48.9	106 42.2	11.9	106 38.5	01.4	Mars	262 55.3	10 06
										Jupiter	174 28.5	15 58
Mer. Pass. 3 37.1		v −0.4 d 1.2		v 0.6 d 0.1		v 2.1 d 0.2		v 2.3 d 0.1		Saturn	174 17.0	15 58

G.M.T.	SUN G.H.A.	Dec.	MOON G.H.A.	v	Dec.	d	H.P.
27 00	178 23.5	N19 17.1	237 02.2	6.5	N17 33.4	7.4	59.7
01	193 23.5	16.5	251 27.7	6.4	17 40.8	7.3	59.7
02	208 23.5	16.0	265 53.1	6.4	17 48.1	7.1	59.7
03	223 23.5 ··	15.4	280 18.5	6.3	17 55.2	7.1	59.7
04	238 23.6	14.8	294 43.8	6.3	18 02.3	6.9	59.7
05	253 23.6	14.3	309 09.1	6.3	18 09.2	6.8	59.7
06	268 23.6	N19 13.7	323 34.4	6.1	N18 16.0	6.7	59.7
07	283 23.6	13.2	337 59.5	6.2	18 22.7	6.5	59.7
08	298 23.6	12.6	352 24.7	6.0	18 29.2	6.5	59.7
M 09	313 23.6 ··	12.0	6 49.7	6.1	18 35.7	6.3	59.7
O 10	328 23.6	11.5	21 14.8	5.9	18 42.0	6.2	59.7
N 11	343 23.6	10.9	35 39.7	6.0	18 48.2	6.1	59.7
D 12	358 23.6	N19 10.3	50 04.7	5.8	N18 54.3	5.9	59.7
A 13	13 23.6	09.8	64 29.5	5.9	19 00.2	5.8	59.7
Y 14	28 23.6	09.2	78 54.4	5.8	19 06.0	5.7	59.7
15	43 23.6 ··	08.6	93 19.2	5.7	19 11.7	5.6	59.7
16	58 23.6	08.0	107 43.9	5.7	19 17.3	5.4	59.7
17	73 23.6	07.5	122 08.6	5.7	19 22.7	5.3	59.7
18	88 23.6	N19 06.9	136 33.3	5.6	N19 28.0	5.2	59.7
19	103 23.6	06.3	150 57.9	5.6	19 33.2	5.0	59.7
20	118 23.7	05.8	165 22.5	5.5	19 38.2	4.9	59.7
21	133 23.7 ··	05.2	179 47.0	5.6	19 43.1	4.8	59.7
22	148 23.7	04.6	194 11.6	5.4	19 47.9	4.6	59.7
23	163 23.7	04.0	208 36.0	5.5	19 52.5	4.6	59.7
28 00	178 23.7	N19 03.5	223 00.5	5.4	N19 57.1	4.3	59.7
01	193 23.7	02.9	237 24.9	5.4	20 01.4	4.3	59.7
02	208 23.7	02.3	251 49.3	5.3	20 05.7	4.1	59.7
03	223 23.7 ··	01.7	266 13.6	5.3	20 09.8	3.9	59.7
04	238 23.7	01.2	280 37.9	5.3	20 13.7	3.8	59.7
05	253 23.7	00.6	295 02.2	5.3	20 17.5	3.7	59.7
06	268 23.8	N19 00.0	309 26.5	5.2	N20 21.2	3.6	59.6
07	283 23.8	18 59.4	323 50.7	5.2	20 24.8	3.4	59.6
08	298 23.8	58.9	338 14.9	5.2	20 28.2	3.3	59.6
T 09	313 23.8 ··	58.3	352 39.1	5.2	20 31.5	3.1	59.6
U 10	328 23.8	57.7	7 03.3	5.1	20 34.6	3.0	59.6
E 11	343 23.8	57.1	21 27.4	5.1	20 37.6	2.8	59.6
S 12	358 23.8	N18 56.5	35 51.5	5.2	N20 40.4	2.7	59.6
D 13	13 23.8	56.0	50 15.7	5.1	20 43.1	2.6	59.6
A 14	28 23.9	55.4	64 39.8	5.0	20 45.7	2.4	59.6
Y 15	43 23.9 ··	54.8	79 03.8	5.1	20 48.1	2.3	59.6
16	58 23.9	54.2	93 27.9	5.1	20 50.4	2.1	59.6
17	73 23.9	53.6	107 52.0	5.0	20 52.5	2.0	59.6
18	88 23.9	N18 53.0	122 16.0	5.1	N20 54.5	1.8	59.6
19	103 23.9	52.5	136 40.1	5.0	20 56.3	1.7	59.5
20	118 23.9	51.9	151 04.1	5.1	20 58.0	1.6	59.5
21	133 23.9 ··	51.3	165 28.2	5.0	20 59.6	1.4	59.5
22	148 24.0	50.7	179 52.2	5.1	21 01.0	1.3	59.5
23	163 24.0	50.1	194 16.3	5.1	21 02.3	1.1	59.5
29 00	178 24.0	N18 49.5	208 40.3	5.0	N21 03.4	1.0	59.5
01	193 24.0	48.9	223 04.3	5.1	21 04.4	0.8	59.5
02	208 24.0	48.3	237 28.4	5.1	21 05.2	0.7	59.5
03	223 24.0 ··	47.8	251 52.5	5.0	21 05.9	0.5	59.5
04	238 24.1	47.2	266 16.5	5.1	21 06.4	0.4	59.4
05	253 24.1	46.6	280 40.6	5.1	21 06.8	0.3	59.4
06	268 24.1	N18 46.0	295 04.7	5.1	N21 07.1	0.1	59.4
07	283 24.1	45.4	309 28.8	5.1	21 07.2	0.0	59.4
W 08	298 24.1	44.8	323 52.9	5.1	21 07.2	0.0	59.4
E 09	313 24.1 ··	44.2	338 17.0	5.2	21 07.0	0.3	59.4
D 10	328 24.2	43.6	352 41.2	5.1	21 06.7	0.5	59.4
N 11	343 24.2	43.0	7 05.3	5.2	21 06.2	0.7	59.4
E 12	358 24.2	N18 42.4	21 29.5	5.2	N21 05.6	0.7	59.3
S 13	13 24.2	41.8	35 53.7	5.2	21 04.9	0.9	59.3
D 14	28 24.2	41.2	50 17.9	5.3	21 04.0	1.0	59.3
A 15	43 24.3 ··	40.7	64 42.2	5.3	21 03.0	1.2	59.3
Y 16	58 24.3	40.1	79 06.5	5.3	21 01.8	1.3	59.3
17	73 24.3	39.5	93 30.8	5.4	21 00.5	1.5	59.3
18	88 24.3	N18 38.9	107 55.2	5.3	N20 59.0	1.6	59.2
19	103 24.3	38.3	122 19.5	5.5	20 57.4	1.7	59.2
20	118 24.4	37.7	136 43.9	5.5	20 55.7	1.9	59.2
21	133 24.4 ··	37.1	151 08.4	5.5	20 53.8	2.0	59.2
22	148 24.4	36.5	165 32.9	5.5	20 51.8	2.1	59.2
23	163 24.4	35.9	179 57.4	5.6	20 49.7	2.3	59.2
	S.D. 15.8 d 0.6		S.D. 16.3	16.2			16.2

Moonrise

Lat.	Twilight Naut.	Civil	Sunrise	27	28	29	30
N 72	□	□	□	□	□	□	□
N 70	////	////	00 32	21 49	□	□	□
68	////	////	01 52	22 56	23 20	24 29	00 29
66	////	////	02 29	23 32	24 09	00 09	01 15
64	////	01 11	02 55	23 58	24 41	00 41	01 46
62	////	01 58	03 15	24 18	00 18	01 04	02 08
60	////	02 27	03 31	00 01	00 35	01 23	02 27
N 58	01 05	02 48	03 44	00 12	00 49	01 38	02 42
56	01 47	03 06	03 56	00 22	01 01	01 52	02 55
54	02 14	03 20	04 06	00 31	01 12	02 03	03 06
52	02 34	03 33	04 15	00 38	01 21	02 14	03 16
50	02 51	03 44	04 23	00 46	01 29	02 23	03 25
45	03 22	04 06	04 40	01 01	01 47	02 42	03 44
N 40	03 46	04 24	04 54	01 13	02 02	02 58	03 59
35	04 04	04 38	05 06	01 24	02 15	03 11	04 12
30	04 19	04 50	05 16	01 34	02 26	03 23	04 24
20	04 42	05 10	05 34	01 50	02 45	03 43	04 43
N 10	05 00	05 27	05 49	02 04	03 01	04 00	05 00
0	05 16	05 41	06 03	02 18	03 16	04 16	05 16
S 10	05 29	05 55	06 17	02 31	03 32	04 32	05 31
20	05 41	06 08	06 31	02 46	03 49	04 50	05 48
30	05 54	06 23	06 48	03 03	04 08	05 10	06 08
35	06 00	06 31	06 58	03 13	04 19	05 22	06 19
40	06 07	06 40	07 09	03 24	04 32	05 35	06 32
45	06 14	06 50	07 22	03 37	04 47	05 51	06 47
S 50	06 22	07 02	07 37	03 53	05 06	06 11	07 06
52	06 26	07 07	07 45	04 01	05 15	06 20	07 15
54	06 29	07 13	07 53	04 09	05 25	06 31	07 25
56	06 33	07 19	08 02	04 19	05 36	06 43	07 36
58	06 38	07 26	08 12	04 30	05 49	06 56	07 49
S 60	06 42	07 34	08 24	04 42	06 04	07 12	08 04

Moonset

Lat.	Sunset	Twilight Civil	Naut.	27	28	29	30
N 72	□	□	□	□	□	□	□
N 70	23 23	////	////	20 04	□	□	22 47
68	22 16	////	////	18 58	20 39	21 35	21 53
66	21 41	////	////	18 23	19 50	20 48	21 53
64	21 16	22 55	////	17 57	19 18	20 18	20 55
62	20 56	22 12	////	17 37	18 55	19 55	20 36
60	20 40	21 44	////	17 21	18 37	19 36	20 20
N 58	20 27	21 22	23 02	17 07	18 21	19 21	20 06
56	20 16	21 05	22 22	16 56	18 08	19 08	19 55
54	20 05	20 51	21 56	16 45	17 54	18 57	19 45
52	19 57	20 39	21 37	16 36	17 46	18 46	19 35
50	19 49	20 28	21 20	16 28	17 37	18 37	19 27
45	19 32	20 06	20 49	16 10	17 18	18 18	19 10
N 40	19 18	19 49	20 20	15 56	17 02	18 03	18 56
35	19 06	19 34	20 08	15 44	16 49	17 49	18 43
30	18 56	19 22	19 54	15 34	16 38	17 38	18 33
20	18 39	19 02	19 30	15 16	16 18	17 18	18 14
N 10	18 24	18 46	19 12	15 00	16 01	17 01	17 58
0	18 10	18 32	18 57	14 45	15 45	16 45	17 43
S 10	17 56	18 18	18 44	14 31	15 29	16 28	17 28
20	17 42	18 05	18 32	14 15	15 12	16 11	17 12
30	17 25	17 50	18 19	13 57	14 52	15 51	16 53
35	17 15	17 42	18 13	13 47	14 40	15 39	16 42
40	17 04	17 34	18 06	13 35	14 27	15 26	16 30
45	16 52	17 24	17 59	13 21	14 12	15 10	16 15
S 50	16 36	17 12	17 51	13 04	13 52	14 50	15 57
52	16 29	17 06	17 48	12 56	13 43	14 41	15 48
54	16 21	17 01	17 44	12 47	13 33	14 31	15 38
56	16 12	16 54	17 40	12 37	13 22	14 19	15 27
58	16 01	16 47	17 36	12 26	13 09	14 05	15 15
S 60	15 50	16 39	17 31	12 13	12 53	13 49	15 00

SUN / MOON

Day	SUN Eqn. of Time 00h	12h	Mer. Pass.	MOON Mer. Pass. Upper	Lower	Age	Phase
	m s	m s	h m	h m	h m	d	
27	06 26	06 26	12 06	08 32	21 01	26	
28	06 25	06 25	12 06	09 31	22 01	27	
29	06 24	06 23	12 06	10 30	23 00	28	

G.M.T.	ARIES G.H.A.	VENUS −3.4 G.H.A.	Dec.	MARS +1.8 G.H.A.	Dec.	JUPITER −1.4 G.H.A.	Dec.	SATURN +1.2 G.H.A.	Dec.	STARS Name	S.H.A.	Dec.
30 00	307 32.6	148 43.1	N10 27.6	209 00.4	N23 48.8	121 44.3	S 1 12.1	121 40.8	S 0 01.5	Acamar	315 36.8	S40 22.5
01	322 35.0	163 42.8	26.4	224 01.0	48.8	136 46.5	12.3	136 43.0	01.6	Achernar	335 44.7	S57 19.6
02	337 37.5	178 42.4	25.2	239 01.7	48.7	151 48.6	12.4	151 45.3	01.7	Acrux	173 36.9	S63 00.0
03	352 39.9	193 42.0	·· 24.1	254 02.3	·· 48.6	166 50.7	·· 12.6	166 47.6	·· 01.8	Adhara	255 32.0	S28 56.7
04	7 42.4	208 41.7	22.9	269 03.0	48.5	181 52.8	12.7	181 49.9	01.9	Aldebaran	291 17.5	N16 28.3
05	22 44.9	223 41.3	21.7	284 03.6	48.5	196 54.9	12.9	196 52.2	01.9			
06	37 47.3	238 41.0	N10 20.5	299 04.2	N23 48.4	211 57.0	S 1 13.1	211 54.4	S 0 02.0	Alioth	166 42.2	N56 04.0
07	52 49.8	253 40.6	19.4	314 04.9	48.3	226 59.1	13.2	226 56.7	02.1	Alkaid	153 18.1	N49 24.7
T 08	67 52.3	268 40.3	18.2	329 05.5	48.2	242 01.2	13.4	241 59.0	02.2	Al Na'ir	28 13.7	S47 02.9
H 09	82 54.7	283 39.9	·· 17.0	344 06.2	·· 48.2	257 03.4	·· 13.5	257 01.3	·· 02.3	Alnilam	276 11.3	S 1 12.8
U 10	97 57.2	298 39.5	15.9	359 06.8	48.1	272 05.5	13.7	272 03.5	02.4	Alphard	218 20.3	S 8 34.6
R 11	112 59.7	313 39.2	14.7	14 07.5	48.0	287 07.6	13.9	287 05.8	02.5			
S 12	128 02.1	328 38.8	N10 13.5	29 08.1	N23 47.9	302 09.7	S 1 14.0	302 08.1	S 0 02.6	Alphecca	126 31.5	N26 46.9
D 13	143 04.6	343 38.5	12.3	44 08.8	47.9	317 11.8	14.2	317 10.4	02.7	Alpheratz	358 08.5	N28 59.2
A 14	158 07.1	358 38.1	11.2	59 09.4	47.8	332 13.9	14.3	332 12.7	02.7	Altair	62 31.6	N 8 49.3
Y 15	173 09.5	13 37.8	·· 10.0	74 10.1	·· 47.7	347 16.0	·· 14.5	347 14.9	·· 02.8	Ankaa	353 39.4	S42 24.2
16	188 12.0	28 37.4	08.8	89 10.7	47.6	2 18.1	14.7	2 17.2	02.9	Antares	112 55.9	S26 23.5
17	203 14.4	43 37.1	07.7	104 11.4	47.6	17 20.2	14.8	17 19.5	03.0			
18	218 16.9	58 36.7	N10 06.5	119 12.0	N23 47.5	32 22.3	S 1 15.0	32 21.8	S 0 03.1	Arcturus	146 17.9	N19 17.0
19	233 19.4	73 36.4	05.3	134 12.7	47.4	47 24.5	15.1	47 24.0	03.2	Atria	108 19.3	S68 59.9
20	248 21.8	88 36.0	04.1	149 13.3	47.3	62 26.6	15.3	62 26.3	03.3	Avior	234 28.6	S59 27.0
21	263 24.3	103 35.7	·· 02.9	164 13.9	·· 47.2	77 28.7	·· 15.5	77 28.6	·· 03.4	Bellatrix	278 58.3	N 6 20.0
22	278 26.8	118 35.3	01.8	179 14.6	47.2	92 30.8	15.6	92 30.9	03.5	Betelgeuse	271 27.9	N 7 24.3
23	293 29.2	133 35.0	10 00.6	194 15.2	47.1	107 32.9	15.8	107 33.1	03.5			
31 00	308 31.7	148 34.6	N 9 59.4	209 15.9	N23 47.0	122 35.0	S 1 15.9	122 35.4	S 0 03.6	Canopus	264 07.4	S52 41.0
01	323 34.2	163 34.3	58.2	224 16.5	46.9	137 37.1	16.1	137 37.7	03.7	Capella	281 10.7	N45 58.6
02	338 36.6	178 33.9	57.1	239 17.2	46.8	152 39.2	16.3	152 40.0	03.8	Deneb	49 47.6	N45 12.9
03	353 39.1	193 33.6	·· 55.9	254 17.8	·· 46.8	167 41.3	·· 16.4	167 42.2	·· 03.9	Denebola	182 58.6	N14 40.7
04	8 41.5	208 33.2	54.7	269 18.5	46.7	182 43.4	16.6	182 44.5	04.0	Diphda	349 20.1	S18 05.2
05	23 44.0	223 32.9	53.5	284 19.1	46.6	197 45.5	16.7	197 46.8	04.1			
06	38 46.5	238 32.5	N 9 52.3	299 19.8	N23 46.5	212 47.7	S 1 16.9	212 49.1	S 0 04.2	Dubhe	194 21.9	N61 51.3
07	53 48.9	253 32.2	51.2	314 20.4	46.4	227 49.8	17.1	227 51.3	04.3	Elnath	278 43.6	N28 35.4
08	68 51.4	268 31.8	50.0	329 21.1	46.3	242 51.9	17.2	242 53.6	04.3	Eltanin	90 57.0	N51 29.7
F 09	83 53.9	283 31.5	·· 48.8	344 21.7	·· 46.3	257 54.0	·· 17.4	257 55.9	·· 04.4	Enif	34 10.7	N 9 47.4
R 10	98 56.3	298 31.1	47.6	359 22.4	46.2	272 56.1	17.5	272 58.2	04.5	Fomalhaut	15 50.4	S29 43.1
I 11	113 58.8	313 30.8	46.4	14 23.0	46.1	287 58.2	17.7	288 00.4	04.6			
D 12	129 01.3	328 30.5	N 9 45.2	29 23.7	N23 46.0	303 00.3	S 1 17.9	303 02.7	S 0 04.7	Gacrux	172 28.4	S57 00.7
A 13	144 03.7	343 30.1	44.1	44 24.3	45.9	318 02.4	18.0	318 05.0	04.8	Gienah	176 17.5	S17 26.3
Y 14	159 06.2	358 29.8	42.9	59 25.0	45.8	333 04.5	18.2	333 07.3	04.9	Hadar	149 22.5	S60 17.2
15	174 08.7	13 29.4	·· 41.7	74 25.6	·· 45.8	348 06.6	·· 18.4	348 09.5	·· 05.0	Hamal	328 28.2	N23 22.4
16	189 11.1	28 29.1	40.5	89 26.3	45.7	3 08.7	18.5	3 11.8	05.1	Kaus Aust.	84 15.7	S34 23.6
17	204 13.6	43 28.7	39.3	104 26.9	45.6	18 10.8	18.7	18 14.1	05.1			
18	219 16.0	58 28.4	N 9 38.1	119 27.6	N23 45.5	33 12.9	S 1 18.8	33 16.4	S 0 05.2	Kochab	137 18.9	N74 14.3
19	234 18.5	73 28.1	36.9	134 28.2	45.4	48 15.0	19.0	48 18.6	05.3	Markab	14 02.3	N15 06.3
20	249 21.0	88 27.7	35.8	149 28.9	45.3	63 17.1	19.2	63 20.9	05.4	Menkar	314 40.5	N 4 01.0
21	264 23.4	103 27.4	·· 34.6	164 29.5	·· 45.2	78 19.2	·· 19.3	78 23.2	·· 05.5	Menkent	148 36.3	S36 16.8
22	279 25.9	118 27.0	33.4	179 30.2	45.2	93 21.4	19.5	93 25.5	05.6	Miaplacidus	221 45.7	S69 38.5
23	294 28.4	133 26.7	32.2	194 30.8	45.1	108 23.5	19.7	108 27.7	05.7			
1 00	309 30.8	148 26.3	N 9 31.0	209 31.5	N23 45.0	123 25.6	S 1 19.8	123 30.0	S 0 05.8	Mirfak	309 15.4	N49 47.5
01	324 33.3	163 26.0	29.8	224 32.1	44.9	138 27.7	20.0	138 32.3	05.9	Nunki	76 28.1	S26 19.2
02	339 35.8	178 25.7	28.6	239 32.8	44.8	153 29.8	20.1	153 34.6	06.0	Peacock	53 56.8	S56 47.7
03	354 38.2	193 25.3	·· 27.4	254 33.5	·· 44.7	168 31.9	·· 20.3	168 36.8	·· 06.0	Pollux	243 57.8	N28 04.3
04	9 40.7	208 25.0	26.3	269 34.1	44.6	183 34.0	20.5	183 39.1	06.1	Procyon	245 25.5	N 5 16.4
05	24 43.2	223 24.7	25.1	284 34.8	44.5	198 36.1	20.6	198 41.4	06.2			
06	39 45.6	238 24.3	N 9 23.9	299 35.4	N23 44.4	213 38.2	S 1 20.8	213 43.6	S 0 06.3	Rasalhague	96 28.8	N12 34.6
07	54 48.1	253 24.0	22.7	314 36.1	44.4	228 40.3	21.0	228 45.9	06.4	Regulus	208 09.7	N12 03.6
S 08	69 50.5	268 23.6	21.5	329 36.7	44.3	243 42.4	21.1	243 48.2	06.5	Rigel	281 35.7	S 8 13.3
A 09	84 53.0	283 23.3	·· 20.3	344 37.4	·· 44.2	258 44.5	·· 21.3	258 50.5	·· 06.6	Rigil Kent.	140 25.0	S60 45.7
T 10	99 55.5	298 23.0	19.1	359 38.0	44.1	273 46.6	21.4	273 52.7	06.7	Sabik	102 40.2	S15 42.1
U 11	114 57.9	313 22.6	17.9	14 38.7	44.0	288 48.7	21.6	288 55.0	06.8			
R 12	130 00.4	328 22.3	N 9 16.7	29 39.3	N23 43.9	303 50.8	S 1 21.8	303 57.3	S 0 06.9	Schedar	350 08.0	N56 25.9
D 13	145 02.9	343 22.0	15.5	44 40.0	43.8	318 52.9	21.9	318 59.5	06.9	Shaula	96 54.6	S37 05.5
A 14	160 05.3	358 21.6	14.3	59 40.6	43.7	333 55.0	22.1	334 01.8	07.0	Sirius	258 55.5	S16 41.4
Y 15	175 07.8	13 21.3	·· 13.1	74 41.3	·· 43.6	348 57.1	·· 22.3	349 04.1	·· 07.1	Spica	158 57.0	S11 03.8
16	190 10.3	28 21.0	11.9	89 41.9	43.5	3 59.2	22.4	4 06.4	07.2	Suhail	223 10.8	S43 21.4
17	205 12.7	43 20.6	10.8	104 42.6	43.4	19 01.3	22.6	19 08.6	07.3			
18	220 15.2	58 20.3	N 9 09.6	119 43.2	N23 43.3	34 03.4	S 1 22.7	34 10.9	S 0 07.4	Vega	80 55.0	N38 46.2
19	235 17.6	73 20.0	08.4	134 43.9	43.2	49 05.5	22.9	49 13.2	07.5	Zuben'ubi	137 32.3	S15 57.8
20	250 20.1	88 19.6	07.2	149 44.6	43.1	64 07.6	23.1	64 15.4	07.6		S.H.A.	Mer. Pass.
21	265 22.6	103 19.3	·· 06.0	164 45.2	·· 43.0	79 09.7	·· 23.2	79 17.7	·· 07.7	Venus	200 02.9	14 06
22	280 25.0	118 19.0	04.8	179 45.9	43.0	94 11.8	23.4	94 20.0	07.8	Mars	260 44.2	10 03
23	295 27.5	133 18.6	03.6	194 46.5	42.9	109 13.9	23.6	109 22.3	07.9	Jupiter	174 03.3	15 47
Mer. Pass.	3 25.3	v −0.3	d 1.2	v 0.7	d 0.1	v 2.1	d 0.2	v 2.3	d 0.1	Saturn	174 03.7	15 47

SUN and MOON

G.M.T.	SUN G.H.A.	SUN Dec.	MOON G.H.A.	v	MOON Dec.	d	H.P.
30 00	178 24.4	N18 35.3	194 22.0	5.6	N20 47.4	2.5	59.1
01	193 24.5	34.7	208 46.6	5.6	20 44.9	2.5	59.1
02	208 24.5	34.1	223 11.2	5.7	20 42.4	2.7	59.1
03	223 24.5	.. 33.5	237 35.9	5.8	20 39.7	2.9	59.1
04	238 24.5	32.9	252 00.7	5.7	20 36.8	2.9	59.1
05	253 24.6	32.3	266 25.4	5.9	20 33.9	3.1	59.0
06	268 24.6	N18 31.7	280 50.3	5.9	N20 30.8	3.3	59.0
T 07	283 24.6	31.1	295 15.2	5.9	20 27.5	3.3	59.0
H 08	298 24.6	30.5	309 40.1	6.0	20 24.2	3.5	59.0
U 09	313 24.7	.. 29.8	324 05.1	6.0	20 20.7	3.7	59.0
R 10	328 24.7	29.2	338 30.1	6.1	20 17.0	3.7	58.9
S 11	343 24.7	28.6	352 55.2	6.2	20 13.3	3.9	58.9
D 12	358 24.7	N18 28.0	7 20.4	6.2	N20 09.4	4.0	58.9
A 13	13 24.8	27.4	21 45.6	6.3	20 05.4	4.2	58.9
Y 14	28 24.8	26.8	36 10.9	6.3	20 01.2	4.2	58.9
15	43 24.8	.. 26.2	50 36.2	6.4	19 57.0	4.4	58.8
16	58 24.8	25.6	65 01.6	6.4	19 52.6	4.6	58.8
17	73 24.9	25.0	79 27.0	6.6	19 48.0	4.6	58.8
18	88 24.9	N18 24.4	93 52.6	6.5	N19 43.4	4.8	58.8
19	103 24.9	23.8	108 18.1	6.7	19 38.6	4.9	58.8
20	118 24.9	23.2	122 43.8	6.7	19 33.7	5.0	58.7
21	133 25.0	.. 22.5	137 09.5	6.8	19 28.7	5.1	58.7
22	148 25.0	21.9	151 35.3	6.8	19 23.6	5.2	58.7
23	163 25.0	21.3	166 01.1	6.9	19 18.4	5.4	58.7
31 00	178 25.1	N18 20.7					
01	193 25.1	20.1					
02	208 25.1	19.5					
03	223 25.1	.. 18.9					
04	238 25.2	18.3					
05	253 25.2	17.6					
06	268 25.2	N18 17.0	267 04.0	7.4	N18 38.4	6.1	58.5
07	283 25.3	16.4	281 30.4	7.5	18 32.3	6.3	58.5
08	298 25.3	15.8	295 56.9	7.6	18 26.0	6.3	58.4
F 09	313 25.3	.. 15.2	310 23.5	7.7	18 19.7	6.5	58.4
R 10	328 25.3	14.6	324 50.2	7.7	18 13.2	6.6	58.4
I 11	343 25.4	13.9	339 16.9	7.8	18 06.6	6.7	58.4
D 12	358 25.4	N18 13.3	353 43.7	7.9	N17 59.9	6.8	58.3
A 13	13 25.4	12.7	8 10.6	7.9	17 53.1	6.9	58.3
Y 14	28 25.5	12.1	22 37.5	8.1	17 46.2	6.9	58.3
15	43 25.5	.. 11.5	37 04.6	8.1	17 39.3	7.1	58.3
16	58 25.5	10.8	51 31.7	8.2	17 32.2	7.2	58.2
17	73 25.6	10.2	65 58.9	8.3	17 25.0	7.3	58.2
18	88 25.6	N18 09.6	80 26.2	8.3	N17 17.7	7.4	58.2
19	103 25.6	09.0	94 53.5	8.5	17 10.3	7.4	58.1
20	118 25.7	08.4	109 21.0	8.5	17 02.9	7.6	58.1
21	133 25.7	.. 07.7	123 48.5	8.6	16 55.3	7.6	58.1
22	148 25.7	07.1	138 16.1	8.7	16 47.7	7.8	58.1
23	163 25.8	06.5	152 43.8	8.8	16 39.9	7.8	58.0
1 00	178 25.8	N18 05.9	167 11.6	8.8	N16 32.1	7.9	58.0
01	193 25.8	05.2	181 39.4	8.9	16 24.2	8.0	58.0
02	208 25.9	04.6	196 07.3	9.0	16 16.2	8.1	57.9
03	223 25.9	.. 04.0	210 35.3	9.1	16 08.1	8.2	57.9
04	238 25.9	03.3	225 03.4	9.2	15 59.9	8.2	57.9
05	253 26.0	02.7	239 31.6	9.3	15 51.7	8.4	57.9
06	268 26.0	N18 02.1	253 59.9	9.3	N15 43.3	8.4	57.8
07	283 26.1	01.5	268 28.2	9.4	15 34.9	8.5	57.8
S 08	298 26.1	00.8	282 56.6	9.6	15 26.4	8.5	57.8
A 09	313 26.1	N18 00.2	297 25.2	9.5	15 17.9	8.7	57.7
T 10	328 26.2	17 59.6	311 53.7	9.7	15 09.2	8.7	57.7
U 11	343 26.2	58.9	326 22.4	9.8	15 00.5	8.8	57.7
R 12	358 26.2	N17 58.3	340 51.2	9.8	N14 51.7	8.9	57.7
D 13	13 26.3	57.7	355 20.0	9.9	14 42.8	8.9	57.6
A 14	28 26.3	57.1	9 48.9	10.0	14 33.9	9.0	57.6
Y 15	43 26.4	.. 56.4	24 17.9	10.1	14 24.9	9.1	57.6
16	58 26.4	55.8	38 47.0	10.2	14 15.8	9.1	57.5
17	73 26.4	55.1	53 16.2	10.1	14 06.7	9.2	57.5
18	88 26.5	N17 54.5	67 45.4	10.3	N13 57.5	9.3	57.5
19	103 26.5	53.9	82 14.7	10.4	13 48.2	9.4	57.4
20	118 26.6	53.2	96 44.1	10.5	13 38.8	9.4	57.4
21	133 26.6	.. 52.6	111 13.6	10.6	13 29.4	9.4	57.4
22	148 26.6	52.0	125 43.2	10.6	13 20.0	9.5	57.4
23	163 26.7	51.3	140 12.8	10.7	13 10.5	9.6	57.3
	S.D. 15.8	d 0.6	S.D. 16.1		15.9		15.7

For 31 00–05 (MOON columns): *A Total Eclipse of the Sun occurs on this date. See page 5.*

Twilight · Sunrise · Moonrise

Lat.	Twilight Naut.	Twilight Civil	Sunrise	Moonrise 30	31	1	2
N 72	□	□	□	□	□	02 49	05 07
N 70	////	////	01 15	□	01 19	03 32	05 29
68	////	////	02 09	00 29	02 12	04 01	05 46
66	////	////	02 41	01 15	02 45	04 23	06 00
64	////	01 32	03 04	01 46	03 09	04 40	06 11
62	////	02 10	03 23	02 08	03 27	04 54	06 21
60	////	02 36	03 38	02 27	03 43	05 06	06 29
N 58	01 24	02 56	03 51	02 42	03 56	05 16	06 36
56	01 58	03 13	04 02	02 55	04 07	05 25	06 43
54	02 23	03 26	04 11	03 06	04 17	05 32	06 48
52	02 41	03 38	04 20	03 16	04 26	05 40	06 53
50	02 57	03 49	04 27	03 25	04 34	05 46	06 58
45	03 27	04 10	04 44	03 44	04 51	05 59	07 08
N 40	03 49	04 27	04 57	03 59	05 04	06 11	07 16
35	04 07	04 40	05 08	04 12	05 16	06 20	07 23
30	04 21	04 52	05 18	04 24	05 26	06 28	07 29
20	04 44	05 11	05 35	04 43	05 44	06 43	07 40
N 10	05 01	05 27	05 49	05 00	05 59	06 55	07 49
0	05 16	05 41	06 03	05 16	06 13	07 07	07 58
S 10	05 29	05 54	06 16	05 31	06 27	07 19	08 06
20	05 40	06 07	06 30	05 48	06 42	07 31	08 15
30	05 52	06 21	06 46	06 08	06 59	07 45	08 26
35	05 58	06 29	06 55	06 19	07 09	07 53	08 32
40	06 04	06 37	07 06	06 32	07 21	08 03	08 39
45	06 11	06 47	07 18	06 47	07 34	08 14	08 47
S 50	06 18	06 58	07 33	07 06	07 51	08 27	08 56
52	06 22	07 03	07 40	07 15	07 58	08 33	09 01
54	06 25	07 08	07 48	07 25	08 07	08 39	09 05
56	06 29	07 14	07 56	07 36	08 16	08 47	09 11
58	06 33	07 21	08 06	07 49	08 27	08 55	09 17
S 60	06 37	07 29	08 17	08 04	08 40	09 05	09 23

Sunset · Twilight · Moonset

Lat.	Sunset	Twilight Civil	Twilight Naut.	Moonset 30	31	1	2
N 72	□	□	□	□	23 12	22 41	22 23
N 70	22 49	////	////	22 47	22 28	22 17	22 10
68	21 59	////	////	21 53	21 58	21 59	21 58
66	21 29	////	////	21 20	21 36	21 44	21 49
64	21 06	22 35	////	20 55	21 18	21 32	21 41
62	20 48	21 59	////	20 36	21 03	21 21	21 35
60	20 33	21 34	////	20 20	20 50	21 12	21 29
N 58	20 21	21 14	22 44	20 06	20 40	21 04	21 24
56	20 10	20 58	22 11	19 55	20 30	20 57	21 19
54	20 00	20 45	21 48	19 45	20 22	20 51	21 15
52	19 52	20 33	21 29	19 35	20 14	20 45	21 11
50	19 45	20 23	21 14	19 27	20 08	20 40	21 08
45	19 28	20 02	20 45	19 10	19 53	20 29	21 00
N 40	19 15	19 45	20 23	18 56	19 41	20 20	20 54
35	19 04	19 32	20 05	18 43	19 31	20 12	20 48
30	18 54	19 20	19 51	18 33	19 22	20 05	20 44
20	18 37	19 01	19 29	18 14	19 06	19 53	20 35
N 10	18 23	18 45	19 11	17 58	18 52	19 42	20 28
0	18 10	18 32	18 57	17 43	18 39	19 32	20 21
S 10	17 57	18 19	18 44	17 28	18 26	19 21	20 14
20	17 43	18 06	18 32	17 12	18 12	19 10	20 06
30	17 27	17 52	18 21	16 53	17 56	18 58	19 57
35	17 17	17 44	18 15	16 42	17 47	18 50	19 52
40	17 07	17 36	18 09	16 30	17 36	18 42	19 46
45	16 55	17 27	18 02	16 15	17 23	18 32	19 40
S 50	16 40	17 15	17 55	15 57	17 08	18 20	19 32
52	16 33	17 10	17 52	15 48	17 00	18 15	19 28
54	16 25	17 05	17 48	15 38	16 52	18 08	19 24
56	16 17	16 59	17 44	15 27	16 43	18 02	19 19
58	16 07	16 52	17 41	15 15	16 33	17 54	19 14
S 60	15 56	16 45	17 36	15 00	16 21	17 45	19 08

Day	SUN Eqn. of Time 00h	SUN Eqn. of Time 12h	SUN Mer. Pass.	MOON Mer. Pass. Upper	MOON Mer. Pass. Lower	Age	Phase
30	06 22	06 21	12 06	11 29	23 58	29	
31	06 20	06 18	12 06	12 26	24 53	00	
1	06 17	06 15	12 06	13 19	00 53	01	●

G.M.T.	ARIES G.H.A.	VENUS −3.4 G.H.A.	Dec.	MARS +1.8 G.H.A.	Dec.	JUPITER −1.4 G.H.A.	Dec.	SATURN +1.2 G.H.A.	Dec.	STARS Name	S.H.A.	Dec.
2 00	310 30.0	148 18.3 N 9	02.4	209 47.2 N23	42.8	124 16.0 S 1	23.7	124 24.5 S 0	07.9	Acamar	315 36.8	S40 22.5
01	325 32.4	163 18.0	01.2	224 47.8	42.7	139 18.1	23.9	139 26.8	08.0	Achernar	335 44.7	S57 19.6
02	340 34.9	178 17.7 9	00.0	239 48.5	42.6	154 20.2	24.1	154 29.1	08.1	Acrux	173 36.9	S62 59.9
03	355 37.4	193 17.3 8	58.8	254 49.1 ..	42.5	169 22.3 ..	24.2	169 31.3 ..	08.2	Adhara	255 32.0	S28 56.7
04	10 39.8	208 17.0	57.6	269 49.8	42.4	184 24.4	24.4	184 33.6	08.3	Aldebaran	291 17.5	N16 28.3
05	25 42.3	223 16.7	56.4	284 50.5	42.3	199 26.5	24.5	199 35.9	08.4			
06	40 44.8	238 16.3 N 8	55.2	299 51.1 N23	42.2	214 28.6 S 1	24.7	214 38.1 S 0	08.5	Alioth	166 42.2	N56 04.0
07	55 47.2	253 16.0	54.0	314 51.8	42.1	229 30.7	24.9	229 40.4	08.6	Alkaid	153 18.1	N49 24.7
08	70 49.7	268 15.7	52.8	329 52.4	42.0	244 32.8	25.0	244 42.7	08.7	Al Na'ir	28 13.7	S47 02.9
S 09	85 52.1	283 15.4 ..	51.6	344 53.1 ..	41.9	259 34.9 ..	25.2	259 45.0 ..	08.8	Alnilam	276 11.3	S 1 12.8
U 10	100 54.6	298 15.0	50.4	359 53.7	41.8	274 37.0	25.4	274 47.2	08.9	Alphard	218 20.3	S 8 34.6
N 11	115 57.1	313 14.7	49.2	14 54.4	41.7	289 39.1	25.5	289 49.5	09.0			
D 12	130 59.5	328 14.4 N 8	48.0	29 55.1 N23	41.6	304 41.2 S 1	25.7	304 51.8 S 0	09.0	Alphecca	126 31.5	N26 46.9
A 13	146 02.0	343 14.1	46.8	44 55.7	41.5	319 43.3	25.9	319 54.0	09.1	Alpheratz	358 08.5	N28 59.2
Y 14	161 04.5	358 13.7	45.6	59 56.4	41.4	334 45.4	26.0	334 56.3	09.2	Altair	62 31.6	N 8 49.3
15	176 06.9	13 13.4 ..	44.4	74 57.0 ..	41.3	349 47.5 ..	26.2	349 58.6 ..	09.3	Ankaa	353 39.4	S42 24.2
16	191 09.4	28 13.1	43.2	89 57.7	41.2	4 49.6	26.4	5 00.8	09.4	Antares	112 55.9	S26 23.5
17	206 11.9	43 12.8	41.9	104 58.3	41.1	19 51.7	26.5	20 03.1	09.5			
18	221 14.3	58 12.4 N 8	40.7	119 59.0 N23	41.0	34 53.8 S 1	26.7	35 05.4 S 0	09.6	Arcturus	146 17.9	N19 17.0
19	236 16.8	73 12.1	39.5	134 59.7	40.9	49 55.9	26.9	50 07.6	09.7	Atria	108 19.3	S68 59.9
20	251 19.3	88 11.8	38.3	150 00.3	40.8	64 58.0	27.0	65 09.9	09.8	Avior	234 28.6	S59 26.9
21	266 21.7	103 11.5 ..	37.1	165 01.0 ..	40.7	80 00.1 ..	27.2	80 12.2 ..	09.9	Bellatrix	278 58.3	N 6 20.0
22	281 24.2	118 11.1	35.9	180 01.6	40.6	95 02.2	27.3	95 14.5	10.0	Betelgeuse	271 27.9	N 7 24.3
23	296 26.6	133 10.8	34.7	195 02.3	40.5	110 04.3	27.5	110 16.7	10.1			
3 00	311 29.1	148 10.5 N 8	33.5	210 02.9 N23	40.3	125 06.4 S 1	27.7	125 19.0 S 0	10.1	Canopus	264 07.4	S52 41.0
01	326 31.6	163 10.2	32.3	225 03.6	40.2	140 08.5	27.8	140 21.3	10.2	Capella	281 10.7	N45 58.6
02	341 34.0	178 09.9	31.1	240 04.3	40.1	155 10.6	28.0	155 23.5	10.3	Deneb	49 47.6	N45 12.9
03	356 36.5	193 09.5 ..	29.9	255 04.9 ..	40.0	170 12.7 ..	28.2	170 25.8 ..	10.4	Denebola	182 58.6	N14 40.7
04	11 39.0	208 09.2	28.7	270 05.6	39.9	185 14.8	28.3	185 28.1	10.5	Diphda	349 20.1	S18 05.2
05	26 41.4	223 08.9	27.5	285 06.2	39.8	200 16.9	28.5	200 30.3	10.6			
06	41 43.9	238 08.6 N 8	26.3	300 06.9 N23	39.7	215 19.0 S 1	28.7	215 32.6 S 0	10.7	Dubhe	194 21.9	N61 51.3
07	56 46.4	253 08.3	25.0	315 07.6	39.6	230 21.1	28.8	230 34.9	10.8	Elnath	278 43.6	N28 35.5
08	71 48.8	268 07.9	23.8	330 08.2	39.5	245 23.2	29.0	245 37.1	10.9	Eltanin	90 57.0	N51 29.7
M 09	86 51.3	283 07.6 ..	22.6	345 08.9 ..	39.4	260 25.3 ..	29.2	260 39.4 ..	11.0	Enif	34 10.7	N 9 47.4
O 10	101 53.7	298 07.3	21.4	0 09.5	39.3	275 27.4	29.3	275 41.7	11.1	Fomalhaut	15 50.4	S29 43.1
N 11	116 56.2	313 07.0	20.2	15 10.2	39.2	290 29.5	29.5	290 43.9	11.2			
D 12	131 58.7	328 06.7 N 8	19.0	30 10.9 N23	39.1	305 31.6 S 1	29.7	305 46.2 S 0	11.3	Gacrux	172 28.4	S57 00.7
A 13	147 01.1	343 06.4	17.8	45 11.5	39.0	320 33.7	29.8	320 48.5	11.3	Gienah	176 17.5	S17 26.3
Y 14	162 03.6	358 06.0	16.6	60 12.2	38.9	335 35.8	30.0	335 50.7	11.4	Hadar	149 22.6	S60 17.2
15	177 06.1	13 05.7 ..	15.4	75 12.8 ..	38.7	350 37.9 ..	30.2	350 53.0 ..	11.5	Hamal	328 28.2	N23 22.4
16	192 08.5	28 05.4	14.1	90 13.5	38.6	5 40.0	30.3	5 55.3	11.6	Kaus Aust.	84 15.7	S34 23.6
17	207 11.0	43 05.1	12.9	105 14.2	38.5	20 42.0	30.5	20 57.5	11.7			
18	222 13.5	58 04.8 N 8	11.7	120 14.8 N23	38.4	35 44.1 S 1	30.7	35 59.8 S 0	11.8	Kochab	137 18.9	N74 14.3
19	237 15.9	73 04.5	10.5	135 15.5	38.3	50 46.2	30.8	51 02.1	11.9	Markab	14 02.3	N15 06.3
20	252 18.4	88 04.2	09.3	150 16.1	38.2	65 48.3	31.0	66 04.3	12.0	Menkar	314 40.5	N 4 01.0
21	267 20.9	103 03.8 ..	08.1	165 16.8 ..	38.1	80 50.4 ..	31.2	81 06.6 ..	12.1	Menkent	148 36.3	S36 16.8
22	282 23.3	118 03.5	06.9	180 17.5	38.0	95 52.5	31.3	96 08.9	12.2	Miaplacidus	221 45.7	S69 38.5
23	297 25.8	133 03.2	05.6	195 18.1	37.9	110 54.6	31.5	111 11.1	12.3			
4 00	312 28.2	148 02.9 N 8	04.4	210 18.8 N23	37.7	125 56.7 S 1	31.7	126 13.4 S 0	12.4	Mirfak	309 15.3	N49 47.5
01	327 30.7	163 02.6	03.2	225 19.5	37.6	140 58.8	31.8	141 15.7	12.5	Nunki	76 28.1	S26 19.2
02	342 33.2	178 02.3	02.0	240 20.1	37.5	156 00.9	32.0	156 17.9	12.5	Peacock	53 56.8	S56 47.7
03	357 35.6	193 02.0 8	00.8	255 20.8 ..	37.4	171 03.0 ..	32.2	171 20.2 ..	12.6	Pollux	243 57.8	N28 04.3
04	12 38.1	208 01.7 7	59.6	270 21.4	37.3	186 05.1	32.3	186 22.4	12.7	Procyon	245 25.5	N 5 16.4
05	27 40.6	223 01.4	58.3	285 22.1	37.2	201 07.2	32.5	201 24.7	12.8			
06	42 43.0	238 01.0 N 7	57.1	300 22.8 N23	37.1	216 09.3 S 1	32.7	216 27.0 S 0	12.9	Rasalhague	96 28.8	N12 34.6
07	57 45.5	253 00.7	55.9	315 23.4	37.0	231 11.4	32.8	231 29.2	13.0	Regulus	208 09.7	N12 03.6
08	72 48.0	268 00.4	54.7	330 24.1	36.8	246 13.4	33.0	246 31.5	13.1	Rigel	281 35.6	S 8 13.3
T 09	87 50.4	283 00.1 ..	53.5	345 24.8 ..	36.7	261 15.5 ..	33.2	261 33.8 ..	13.2	Rigil Kent.	140 25.0	S60 45.7
U 10	102 52.9	297 59.8	52.2	0 25.4	36.6	276 17.6	33.3	276 36.0	13.3	Sabik	102 40.2	S15 42.1
E 11	117 55.4	312 59.5	51.0	15 26.1	36.5	291 19.7	33.5	291 38.3	13.4			
S 12	132 57.8	327 59.2 N 7	49.8	30 26.8 N23	36.4	306 21.8 S 1	33.7	306 40.6 S 0	13.5	Schedar	350 08.0	N56 25.9
D 13	148 00.3	342 58.9	48.6	45 27.4	36.3	321 23.9	33.8	321 42.8	13.6	Shaula	96 54.6	S37 05.5
A 14	163 02.7	357 58.6	47.4	60 28.1	36.1	336 26.0	34.0	336 45.1	13.7	Sirius	258 55.5	S16 41.4
Y 15	178 05.2	12 58.3 ..	46.1	75 28.7 ..	36.0	351 28.1 ..	34.2	351 47.4 ..	13.8	Spica	158 57.0	S11 03.8
16	193 07.7	27 58.0	44.9	90 29.4	35.9	6 30.2	34.3	6 49.6	13.9	Suhail	223 10.8	S43 21.4
17	208 10.1	42 57.7	43.7	105 30.1	35.8	21 32.3	34.5	21 51.9	13.9			
18	223 12.6	57 57.3 N 7	42.5	120 30.7 N23	35.7	36 34.4 S 1	34.7	36 54.1 S 0	14.0	Vega	80 55.1	N38 46.2
19	238 15.1	72 57.0	41.3	135 31.4	35.5	51 36.5	34.8	51 56.4	14.1	Zuben'ubi	137 32.3	S15 57.8
20	253 17.5	87 56.7	40.0	150 32.1	35.4	66 38.5	35.0	66 58.7	14.2		S.H.A.	Mer. Pass.
21	268 20.0	102 56.4 ..	38.8	165 32.7 ..	35.3	81 40.6 ..	35.2	82 00.9 ..	14.3	Venus	196 41.4	14 08
22	283 22.5	117 56.1	37.6	180 33.4	35.2	96 42.7	35.3	97 03.2	14.4	Mars	258 33.8	9 59
23	298 24.9	132 55.8	36.4	195 34.1	35.1	111 44.8	35.5	112 05.5	14.5	Jupiter	173 37.3	15 37
Mer. Pass.	3 13.5	v −0.3 d 1.2		v 0.7 d 0.1		v 2.1 d 0.2		v 2.3 d 0.1		Saturn	173 49.9	15 36

G.M.T.	SUN G.H.A.	SUN Dec.	MOON G.H.A.	MOON v	MOON Dec.	MOON d	MOON H.P.
d h	° ′	° ′	° ′	′	° ′	′	′
2 00	178 26.7	N17 50.7	154 42.5	10.8	N13 00.9	9.7	57.3
01	193 26.8	50.1	169 12.3	10.9	12 51.2	9.7	57.3
02	208 26.8	49.4	183 42.2	11.0	12 41.5	9.7	57.2
03	223 26.8	·· 48.8	198 12.2	11.0	12 31.8	9.8	57.2
04	238 26.9	48.1	212 42.2	11.1	12 22.0	9.9	57.2
05	253 26.9	47.5	227 12.3	11.2	12 12.1	9.9	57.1
06	268 27.0	N17 46.9	241 42.5	11.3	N12 02.2	9.9	57.1
07	283 27.0	46.2	256 12.8	11.3	11 52.3	10.1	57.1
08	298 27.1	45.6	270 43.1	11.4	11 42.2	10.0	57.0
S 09	313 27.1	·· 44.9	285 13.5	11.5	11 32.2	10.1	57.0
U 10	328 27.1	44.3	299 44.0	11.6	11 22.1	10.2	57.0
N 11	343 27.2	43.7	314 14.6	11.6	11 11.9	10.2	57.0
D 12	358 27.2	N17 43.0	328 45.2	11.7	N11 01.7	10.2	56.9
A 13	13 27.3	42.4	343 15.9	11.8	10 51.5	10.3	56.9
Y 14	28 27.3	41.7	357 46.7	11.9	10 41.2	10.3	56.9
15	43 27.4	·· 41.1	12 17.6	11.9	10 30.9	10.4	56.8
16	58 27.4	40.4	26 48.5	12.0	10 20.5	10.4	56.8
17	73 27.5	39.8	41 19.5	12.1	10 10.1	10.4	56.8
18	88 27.5	N17 39.1	55 50.6	12.1	N 9 59.7	10.5	56.7
19	103 27.5	38.5	70 21.7	12.2	9 49.2	10.5	56.7
20	118 27.6	37.9	84 52.9	12.3	9 38.7	10.5	56.7
21	133 27.6	·· 37.2	99 24.2	12.3	9 28.2	10.6	56.7
22	148 27.7	36.6	113 55.5	12.4	9 17.6	10.6	56.6
23	163 27.7	35.9	128 26.9	12.5	9 07.0	10.7	56.6
3 00	178 27.8	N17 35.3	142 58.4	12.6	N 8 56.3	10.7	56.6
01	193 27.8	34.6	157 30.0	12.6	8 45.6	10.7	56.5
02	208 27.9	34.0	172 01.6	12.6	8 34.9	10.7	56.5
03	223 27.9	·· 33.3	186 33.2	12.8	8 24.2	10.8	56.5
04	238 28.0	32.7	201 05.0	12.8	8 13.4	10.8	56.4
05	253 28.0	32.0	215 36.8	12.8	8 02.6	10.8	56.4
06	268 28.1	N17 31.4	230 08.6	12.9	N 7 51.8	10.8	56.4
07	283 28.1	30.7	244 40.5	13.0	7 41.0	10.9	56.4
08	298 28.2	30.0	259 12.5	13.0	7 30.1	10.9	56.3
M 09	313 28.2	·· 29.4	273 44.5	13.1	7 19.2	10.9	56.3
O 10	328 28.3	28.7	288 16.6	13.2	7 08.3	10.9	56.3
N 11	343 28.3	28.1	302 48.8	13.2	6 57.4	11.0	56.2
D 12	358 28.4	N17 27.4	317 21.0	13.3	N 6 46.4	10.9	56.2
A 13	13 28.4	26.8	331 53.3	13.3	6 35.5	11.0	56.2
Y 14	28 28.5	26.1	346 25.6	13.4	6 24.5	11.0	56.2
15	43 28.5	·· 25.5	0 58.0	13.4	6 13.5	11.0	56.1
16	58 28.6	24.8	15 30.4	13.5	6 02.5	11.1	56.1
17	73 28.6	24.1	30 02.9	13.5	5 51.4	11.0	56.1
18	88 28.7	N17 23.5	44 35.4	13.6	N 5 40.4	11.1	56.0
19	103 28.7	22.8	59 08.0	13.7	5 29.3	11.1	56.0
20	118 28.8	22.2	73 40.7	13.7	5 18.2	11.1	56.0
21	133 28.8	·· 21.5	88 13.4	13.7	5 07.2	11.1	56.0
22	148 28.9	20.9	102 46.1	13.8	4 56.1	11.1	55.9
23	163 28.9	20.2	117 18.9	13.8	4 45.0	11.2	55.9
4 00	178 29.0	N17 19.5	131 51.7	13.9	N 4 33.8	11.1	55.9
01	193 29.1	18.9	146 24.6	13.9	4 22.7	11.1	55.8
02	208 29.1	18.2	160 57.5	14.0	4 11.6	11.2	55.8
03	223 29.2	·· 17.5	175 30.5	14.0	4 00.4	11.1	55.8
04	238 29.2	16.9	190 03.5	14.1	3 49.3	11.2	55.8
05	253 29.3	16.2	204 36.6	14.1	3 38.1	11.1	55.7
06	268 29.3	N17 15.6	219 09.7	14.2	N 3 27.0	11.2	55.7
07	283 29.4	14.9	233 42.9	14.1	3 15.8	11.1	55.7
08	298 29.4	14.2	248 16.0	14.3	3 04.7	11.2	55.7
T 09	313 29.5	·· 13.6	262 49.3	14.2	2 53.5	11.2	55.6
U 10	328 29.6	12.9	277 22.5	14.3	2 42.3	11.1	55.6
E 11	343 29.6	12.2	291 55.8	14.4	2 31.2	11.2	55.6
S 12	358 29.7	N17 11.6	306 29.2	14.4	N 2 20.0	11.2	55.5
D 13	13 29.7	10.9	321 02.6	14.4	2 08.8	11.1	55.5
A 14	28 29.8	10.2	335 36.0	14.4	1 57.7	11.2	55.5
Y 15	43 29.8	·· 09.6	350 09.4	14.5	1 46.5	11.1	55.5
16	58 29.9	08.9	4 42.9	14.5	1 35.4	11.2	55.4
17	73 30.0	08.2	19 16.4	14.6	1 24.2	11.1	55.4
18	88 30.0	N17 07.5	33 50.0	14.6	N 1 13.1	11.2	55.4
19	103 30.1	06.9	48 23.6	14.6	1 01.9	11.1	55.4
20	118 30.1	06.2	62 57.2	14.6	0 50.8	11.2	55.4
21	133 30.2	·· 05.5	77 30.8	14.7	0 39.6	11.1	55.3
22	148 30.2	04.9	92 04.5	14.7	0 28.5	11.1	55.3
23	163 30.3	04.2	106 38.2	14.7	0 17.4	11.1	55.3
	S.D. 15.8	d 0.7	S.D. 15.5		15.3		15.1

Lat.	Twilight Naut.	Twilight Civil	Sunrise	Moonrise 2	3	4	5
°	h m	h m	h m	h m	h m	h m	h m
N 72	□	□	□	05 07	07 05	08 54	10 38
N 70	////	////	01 42	05 29	07 17	08 58	10 35
68	////	////	02 24	05 46	07 26	09 01	10 33
66	////	00 51	02 52	06 00	07 34	09 04	10 31
64	////	01 50	03 14	06 11	07 41	09 06	10 29
62	////	02 22	03 31	06 21	07 46	09 08	10 28
60	00 46	02 46	03 45	06 29	07 51	09 10	10 27
N 58	01 39	03 04	03 57	06 36	07 55	09 12	10 26
56	02 09	03 19	04 07	06 43	07 59	09 13	10 25
54	02 31	03 32	04 16	06 48	08 02	09 14	10 24
52	02 49	03 44	04 24	06 53	08 05	09 15	10 23
50	03 03	03 53	04 32	06 58	08 08	09 16	10 23
45	03 32	04 14	04 47	07 08	08 14	09 19	10 21
N 40	03 53	04 30	05 00	07 16	08 19	09 20	10 20
35	04 09	04 43	05 11	07 23	08 24	09 22	10 19
30	04 23	04 54	05 20	07 29	08 27	09 23	10 18
20	04 45	05 13	05 36	07 40	08 34	09 26	10 16
N 10	05 02	05 28	05 50	07 49	08 40	09 28	10 15
0	05 16	05 41	06 03	07 58	08 45	09 30	10 13
S 10	05 28	05 53	06 15	08 06	08 50	09 32	10 12
20	05 39	06 06	06 29	08 15	08 56	09 34	10 11
30	05 50	06 20	06 44	08 26	09 03	09 37	10 09
35	05 56	06 26	06 53	08 32	09 06	09 38	10 08
40	06 02	06 34	07 03	08 39	09 11	09 40	10 07
45	06 08	06 43	07 14	08 47	09 16	09 42	10 06
S 50	06 15	06 54	07 29	08 56	09 21	09 44	10 05
52	06 18	06 58	07 35	09 01	09 24	09 45	10 04
54	06 21	07 04	07 42	09 05	09 27	09 46	10 04
56	06 24	07 09	07 51	09 11	09 30	09 47	10 03
58	06 28	07 15	08 00	09 17	09 34	09 49	10 02
S 60	06 32	07 23	08 10	09 23	09 38	09 50	10 01

Lat.	Sunset	Twilight Civil	Twilight Naut.	Moonset 2	3	4	5
°	h m	h m	h m	h m	h m	h m	h m
N 72	□	□	□	22 33	22 09	21 56	21 44
N 70	22 24	////	////	22 10	22 02	21 56	21 49
68	21 44	////	////	21 58	21 57	21 55	21 53
66	21 17	23 10	////	21 49	21 53	21 55	21 57
64	20 56	22 18	////	21 41	21 49	21 55	22 00
62	20 39	21 47	////	21 35	21 45	21 54	22 03
60	20 26	21 24	23 16	21 29	21 42	21 54	22 05
N 58	20 14	21 06	22 29	21 24	21 40	21 54	22 08
56	20 04	20 51	22 00	21 19	21 37	21 54	22 10
54	19 55	20 38	21 39	21 15	21 35	21 54	22 11
52	19 47	20 27	21 22	21 11	21 33	21 53	22 13
50	19 40	20 18	21 07	21 08	21 31	21 53	22 14
45	19 24	19 58	20 40	21 00	21 28	21 53	22 17
N 40	19 12	19 42	20 19	20 54	21 24	21 53	22 20
35	19 01	19 29	20 02	20 48	21 21	21 52	22 22
30	18 52	19 18	19 49	20 44	21 19	21 52	22 24
20	18 36	18 59	19 27	20 35	21 14	21 52	22 28
N 10	18 22	18 44	19 10	20 28	21 11	21 51	22 31
0	18 10	18 31	18 56	20 21	21 07	21 51	22 34
S 10	17 57	18 19	18 44	20 14	21 03	21 51	22 37
20	17 44	18 07	18 33	20 06	20 59	21 50	22 40
30	17 28	17 54	18 22	19 57	20 55	21 50	22 44
35	17 20	17 46	18 17	19 52	20 52	21 49	22 46
40	17 10	17 39	18 11	19 46	20 49	21 49	22 48
45	16 58	17 30	18 05	19 40	20 45	21 49	22 51
S 50	16 44	17 19	17 58	19 32	20 41	21 48	22 54
52	16 38	17 15	17 55	19 28	20 39	21 48	22 55
54	16 30	17 09	17 52	19 24	20 37	21 48	22 57
56	16 22	17 04	17 49	19 19	20 35	21 48	22 59
58	16 13	16 57	17 45	19 14	20 32	21 47	23 01
S 60	16 03	16 51	17 42	19 08	20 29	21 47	23 03

Day	SUN Eqn. of Time 00h	SUN Eqn. of Time 12h	SUN Mer. Pass.	MOON Mer. Pass. Upper	MOON Mer. Pass. Lower	Age	Phase
	m s	m s	h m	h m	h m	d	
2	06 13	06 11	12 06	14 09	01 45	02	
3	06 09	06 07	12 06	14 56	02 33	03	◑
4	06 04	06 01	12 06	15 41	03 19	04	

G.M.T.	ARIES G.H.A.	VENUS −3.4 G.H.A.	Dec.	MARS +1.8 G.H.A.	Dec.	JUPITER −1.4 G.H.A.	Dec.	SATURN +1.2 G.H.A.	Dec.	STARS Name	S.H.A.	Dec.
5 00	313 27.4	147 55.5 N 7	35.1	210 34.7 N23	35.0	126 46.9 S 1	35.7	127 07.7 S 0	14.6	Acamar	315 36.8	S40 22.5
01	328 29.8	162 55.2	33.9	225 35.4	34.8	141 49.0	35.8	142 10.0	14.7	Achernar	335 44.6	S57 19.6
02	343 32.3	177 54.9	32.7	240 36.1	34.7	156 51.1	36.0	157 12.2	14.8	Acrux	173 37.0	S62 59.9
03	358 34.8	192 54.6 ··	31.5	255 36.7 ··	34.6	171 53.2 ··	36.2	172 14.5 ··	14.9	Adhara	255 32.0	S28 56.7
04	13 37.2	207 54.3	30.2	270 37.4	34.5	186 55.3	36.3	187 16.8	15.0	Aldebaran	291 17.4	N16 28.3
05	28 39.7	222 54.0	29.0	285 38.1	34.3	201 57.4	36.5	202 19.0	15.1			
W 06	43 42.2	237 53.7 N 7	27.8	300 38.7 N23	34.2	216 59.4 S 1	36.7	217 21.3 S 0	15.2	Alioth	166 42.2	N56 04.0
E 07	58 44.6	252 53.4	26.6	315 39.4	34.1	232 01.5	36.9	232 23.6	15.3	Alkaid	153 18.1	N49 24.7
D 08	73 47.1	267 53.1	25.3	330 40.1	34.0	247 03.6	37.0	247 25.8	15.4	Al Na'ir	28 13.7	S47 02.9
N 09	88 49.6	282 52.8 ··	24.1	345 40.7 ··	33.9	262 05.7 ··	37.2	262 28.1 ··	15.5	Alnilam	276 11.3	S 1 12.8
E 10	103 52.0	297 52.5	22.9	0 41.4	33.7	277 07.8	37.4	277 30.3	15.5	Alphard	218 20.3	S 8 34.6
S 11	118 54.5	312 52.2	21.7	15 42.1	33.6	292 09.9	37.5	292 32.6	15.6			
D 12	133 57.0	327 51.9 N 7	20.4	30 42.7 N23	33.5	307 12.0 S 1	37.7	307 34.9 S 0	15.7	Alphecca	126 31.5	N26 46.9
A 13	148 59.4	342 51.6	19.2	45 43.4	33.4	322 14.1	37.9	322 37.1	15.8	Alpheratz	358 08.4	N28 59.2
Y 14	164 01.9	357 51.3	18.0	60 44.1	33.2	337 16.2	38.0	337 39.4	15.9	Altair	62 31.6	N 8 49.3
15	179 04.3	12 51.0 ··	16.7	75 44.7 ··	33.1	352 18.2 ··	38.2	352 41.7 ··	16.0	Ankaa	353 39.4	S42 24.2
16	194 06.8	27 50.7	15.5	90 45.4	33.0	7 20.3	38.4	7 43.9	16.1	Antares	112 55.9	S26 23.5
17	209 09.3	42 50.4	14.3	105 46.1	32.9	22 22.4	38.5	22 46.2	16.2			
18	224 11.7	57 50.1 N 7	13.1	120 46.7 N23	32.7	37 24.5 S 1	38.7	37 48.4 S 0	16.3	Arcturus	146 18.0	N19 17.0
19	239 14.2	72 49.8	11.8	135 47.4	32.6	52 26.6	38.9	52 50.7	16.4	Atria	108 19.3	S68 59.9
20	254 16.7	87 49.5	10.6	150 48.1	32.5	67 28.7	39.0	67 53.0	16.5	Avior	234 28.6	S59 26.9
21	269 19.1	102 49.2 ··	09.4	165 48.8 ··	32.4	82 30.8 ··	39.2	82 55.2 ··	16.6	Bellatrix	278 58.3	N 6 20.0
22	284 21.6	117 48.9	08.1	180 49.4	32.2	97 32.9	39.4	97 57.5	16.7	Betelgeuse	271 27.9	N 7 24.3
23	299 24.1	132 48.6	06.9	195 50.1	32.1	112 34.9	39.6	112 59.7	16.8			
6 00	314 26.5	147 48.3 N 7	05.7	210 50.8 N23	32.0	127 37.0 S 1	39.7	128 02.0 S 0	16.9	Canopus	264 07.4	S52 41.0
01	329 29.0	162 48.0	04.4	225 51.4	31.8	142 39.1	39.9	143 04.3	17.0	Capella	281 10.7	N45 58.6
02	344 31.5	177 47.7	03.2	240 52.1	31.7	157 41.2	40.1	158 06.5	17.1	Deneb	49 47.6	N45 12.9
03	359 33.9	192 47.4 ··	02.0	255 52.8 ··	31.6	172 43.3 ··	40.2	173 08.8 ··	17.2	Denebola	182 58.7	N14 40.7
04	14 36.4	207 47.2 7	00.7	270 53.4	31.5	187 45.4	40.4	188 11.0	17.3	Diphda	349 20.1	S18 05.2
05	29 38.8	222 46.9 6	59.5	285 54.1	31.3	202 47.5	40.6	203 13.3	17.3			
T 06	44 41.3	237 46.6 N 6	58.3	300 54.8 N23	31.2	217 49.5 S 1	40.7	218 15.6 S 0	17.4	Dubhe	194 21.9	N61 51.3
H 07	59 43.8	252 46.3	57.0	315 55.5	31.1	232 51.6	40.9	233 17.8	17.5	Elnath	278 43.6	N28 35.5
U 08	74 46.2	267 46.0	55.8	330 56.1	30.9	247 53.7	41.1	248 20.1	17.6	Eltanin	90 57.1	N51 29.8
R 09	89 48.7	282 45.7 ··	54.6	345 56.8 ··	30.8	262 55.8 ··	41.3	263 22.3 ··	17.7	Enif	34 10.7	N 9 47.5
S 10	104 51.2	297 45.4	53.3	0 57.5	30.7	277 57.9	41.4	278 24.6	17.8	Fomalhaut	15 50.4	S29 43.1
D 11	119 53.6	312 45.1	52.1	15 58.1	30.5	293 00.0	41.6	293 26.9	17.9			
A 12	134 56.1	327 44.8 N 6	50.9	30 58.8 N23	30.4	308 02.1 S 1	41.8	308 29.1 S 0	18.0	Gacrux	172 28.4	S57 00.7
Y 13	149 58.6	342 44.5	49.6	45 59.5	30.3	323 04.1	41.9	323 31.4	18.1	Gienah	176 17.5	S17 26.3
14	165 01.0	357 44.2	48.4	61 00.2	30.1	338 06.2	42.1	338 33.6	18.2	Hadar	149 22.6	S60 17.2
15	180 03.5	12 43.9 ··	47.1	76 00.8 ··	30.0	353 08.3 ··	42.3	353 35.9 ··	18.3	Hamal	328 28.2	N23 22.4
16	195 06.0	27 43.6	45.9	91 01.5	29.9	8 10.4	42.4	8 38.2	18.4	Kaus Aust.	84 15.7	S34 23.6
17	210 08.4	42 43.4	44.7	106 02.2	29.7	23 12.5	42.6	23 40.4	18.5			
18	225 10.9	57 43.1 N 6	43.4	121 02.8 N23	29.6	38 14.6 S 1	42.8	38 42.7 S 0	18.6	Kochab	137 19.0	N74 14.3
19	240 13.3	72 42.8	42.2	136 03.5	29.5	53 16.6	43.0	53 44.9	18.7	Markab	14 02.3	N15 06.3
20	255 15.8	87 42.5	41.0	151 04.2	29.3	68 18.7	43.1	68 47.2	18.8	Menkar	314 40.5	N 4 01.0
21	270 18.3	102 42.2 ··	39.7	166 04.9 ··	29.2	83 20.8 ··	43.3	83 49.4 ··	18.9	Menkent	148 36.4	S36 16.8
22	285 20.7	117 41.9	38.5	181 05.5	29.1	98 22.9	43.5	98 51.7	19.0	Miaplacidus	221 45.7	S69 38.5
23	300 23.2	132 41.6	37.2	196 06.2	28.9	113 25.0	43.6	113 54.0	19.1			
7 00	315 25.7	147 41.3 N 6	36.0	211 06.9 N23	28.8	128 27.1 S 1	43.8	128 56.2 S 0	19.2	Mirfak	309 15.3	N49 47.5
01	330 28.1	162 41.0	34.8	226 07.6	28.7	143 29.1	44.0	143 58.5	19.3	Nunki	76 28.1	S26 19.2
02	345 30.6	177 40.8	33.5	241 08.2	28.5	158 31.2	44.1	159 00.7	19.3	Peacock	53 56.8	S56 47.7
03	0 33.1	192 40.5 ··	32.3	256 08.9 ··	28.4	173 33.3 ··	44.3	174 03.0 ··	19.4	Pollux	243 57.8	N28 04.3
04	15 35.5	207 40.2	31.0	271 09.6	28.3	188 35.4	44.5	189 05.2	19.5	Procyon	245 25.5	N 5 16.4
05	30 38.0	222 39.9	29.8	286 10.3	28.1	203 37.5	44.7	204 07.5	19.6			
F 06	45 40.4	237 39.6 N 6	28.6	301 10.9 N23	28.0	218 39.6 S 1	44.8	219 09.8 S 0	19.7	Rasalhague	96 28.8	N12 34.6
R 07	60 42.9	252 39.3	27.3	316 11.6	27.8	233 41.6	45.0	234 12.0	19.8	Regulus	208 09.7	N12 03.6
I 08	75 45.4	267 39.0	26.1	331 12.3	27.7	248 43.7	45.2	249 14.3	19.9	Rigel	281 35.6	S 8 13.3
09	90 47.8	282 38.8 ··	24.8	346 13.0 ··	27.6	263 45.8 ··	45.3	264 16.5 ··	20.0	Rigil Kent.	140 25.0	S60 45.7
10	105 50.3	297 38.5	23.6	1 13.6	27.4	278 47.9	45.5	279 18.8	20.1	Sabik	102 40.2	S15 42.1
11	120 52.8	312 38.2	22.4	16 14.3	27.3	293 50.0	45.7	294 21.0	20.2			
D 12	135 55.2	327 37.9 N 6	21.1	31 15.0 N23	27.1	308 52.0 S 1	45.9	309 23.3 S 0	20.3	Schedar	350 08.0	N56 25.9
A 13	150 57.7	342 37.6	19.9	46 15.7	27.0	323 54.1	46.0	324 25.6	20.4	Shaula	96 54.7	S37 05.5
Y 14	166 00.2	357 37.3	18.6	61 16.3	26.9	338 56.2	46.2	339 27.8	20.5	Sirius	258 55.5	S16 41.4
15	181 02.6	12 37.1 ··	17.4	76 17.0 ··	26.7	353 58.3 ··	46.4	354 30.1 ··	20.6	Spica	158 57.0	S11 03.8
16	196 05.1	27 36.8	16.1	91 17.7	26.6	9 00.4	46.5	9 32.3	20.7	Suhail	223 10.8	S43 21.4
17	211 07.6	42 36.5	14.9	106 18.4	26.4	24 02.4	46.7	24 34.6	20.8			
18	226 10.0	57 36.2 N 6	13.7	121 19.0 N23	26.3	39 04.5 S 1	46.9	39 36.8 S 0	20.9	Vega	80 55.1	N38 46.2
19	241 12.5	72 35.9	12.4	136 19.7	26.2	54 06.6	47.1	54 39.1	21.0	Zuben'ubi	137 32.4	S15 57.8
20	256 14.9	87 35.6	11.2	151 20.4	26.0	69 08.7	47.2	69 41.4	21.1		S.H.A.	Mer. Pass.
21	271 17.4	102 35.4 ··	09.9	166 21.1 ··	25.9	84 10.8 ··	47.4	84 43.6 ··	21.2	Venus	193 21.8	14 09
22	286 19.9	117 35.1	08.7	181 21.7	25.7	99 12.9	47.6	99 45.9	21.3	Mars	256 24.2	9 56
23	301 22.3	132 34.8	07.4	196 22.4	25.6	114 14.9	47.7	114 48.1	21.4	Jupiter	173 10.5	15 27
Mer. Pass.	3 01.7	v −0.3	d 1.2	v 0.7	d 0.1	v 2.1	d 0.2	v 2.3	d 0.1	Saturn	173 35.5	15 26

G.M.T.	SUN G.H.A.	SUN Dec.	MOON G.H.A.	v	Dec.	d	H.P.
d h	° ′	° ′	° ′	′	° ′	′	′
5 00	178 30.4	N17 03.5	121 11.9	14.8	N 0 06.3	11.1	55.3
01	193 30.4	02.8	135 45.7	14.8	S 0 04.8	11.1	55.2
02	208 30.5	02.2	150 19.5	14.8	0 15.9	11.1	55.2
03	223 30.6	·· 01.5	164 53.3	14.8	0 27.0	11.1	55.2
04	238 30.6	00.8	179 27.1	14.9	0 38.0	11.1	55.2
05	253 30.7	17 00.1	194 01.0	14.8	0 49.1	11.0	55.1
06	268 30.7	N16 59.5	208 34.8	14.9	S 1 00.1	11.0	55.1
W 07	283 30.8	58.8	223 08.7	14.9	1 11.1	11.0	55.1
E 08	298 30.9	58.1	237 42.6	15.0	1 22.1	11.0	55.1
D 09	313 30.9	·· 57.4	252 16.6	14.9	1 33.1	11.0	55.1
N 10	328 31.0	56.8	266 50.5	15.0	1 44.1	11.0	55.1
E 11	343 31.0	56.1	281 24.5	15.0	1 55.1	10.9	55.0
S 12	358 31.1	N16 55.4	295 58.5	15.0	S 2 06.0	10.9	55.0
D 13	13 31.2	54.7	310 32.5	15.0	2 16.9	11.0	55.0
A 14	28 31.2	54.1	325 06.5	15.1	2 27.9	10.9	55.0
Y 15	43 31.3	·· 53.4	339 40.6	15.0	2 38.8	10.8	54.9
16	58 31.4	52.7	354 14.6	15.1	2 49.6	10.9	54.9
17	73 31.4	52.0	8 48.7	15.0	3 00.5	10.8	54.9
18	88 31.5	N16 51.3	23 22.7	15.1	S 3 11.3	10.8	54.9
19	103 31.6	50.6	37 56.8	15.1	3 22.1	10.8	54.9
20	118 31.6	50.0	52 30.9	15.1	3 32.9	10.8	54.8
21	133 31.7	·· 49.3	67 05.0	15.2	3 43.7	10.7	54.8
22	148 31.8	48.6	81 39.2	15.1	3 54.4	10.7	54.8
23	163 31.8	47.9	96 13.3	15.1	4 05.1	10.7	54.8
6 00	178 31.9	N16 47.2	110 47.4	15.1	S 4 15.8	10.7	54.8
01	193 32.0	46.5	125 21.5	15.2	4 26.5	10.7	54.8
02	208 32.0	45.9	139 55.7	15.1	4 37.2	10.6	54.7
03	223 32.1	·· 45.2	154 29.8	15.2	4 47.8	10.6	54.7
04	238 32.2	44.5	169 04.0	15.1	4 58.4	10.5	54.7
05	253 32.2	43.8	183 38.1	15.2	5 08.9	10.6	54.7
06	268 32.3	N16 43.1	198 12.3	15.1	S 5 19.5	10.5	54.7
07	283 32.4	42.4	212 46.4	15.2	5 30.0	10.5	54.7
T 08	298 32.4	41.7	227 20.6	15.1	5 40.5	10.4	54.6
H 09	313 32.5	·· 41.1	241 54.8	15.1	5 50.9	10.5	54.6
U 10	328 32.6	40.4	256 28.9	15.2	6 01.4	10.4	54.6
R 11	343 32.6	39.7	271 03.1	15.1	6 11.8	10.3	54.6
S 12	358 32.7	N16 39.0	285 37.2	15.2	S 6 22.1	10.4	54.6
D 13	13 32.8	38.3	300 11.4	15.1	6 32.5	10.3	54.6
A 14	28 32.9	37.6	314 45.5	15.2	6 42.8	10.2	54.6
Y 15	43 32.9	·· 36.9	329 19.7	15.1	6 53.0	10.3	54.5
16	58 33.0	36.2	343 53.8	15.1	7 03.3	10.2	54.5
17	73 33.1	35.5	358 27.9	15.1	7 13.5	10.1	54.5
18	88 33.1	N16 34.8	13 02.0	15.2	S 7 23.6	10.2	54.5
19	103 33.2	34.1	27 36.2	15.1	7 33.8	10.1	54.5
20	118 33.3	33.5	42 10.3	15.1	7 43.9	10.0	54.5
21	133 33.4	·· 32.8	56 44.4	15.0	7 53.9	10.0	54.5
22	148 33.4	32.1	71 18.4	15.1	8 03.9	10.0	54.5
23	163 33.5	31.4	85 52.5	15.1	8 13.9	10.0	54.4
7 00	178 33.6	N16 30.7	100 26.6	15.0	S 8 23.9	9.9	54.4
01	193 33.6	30.0	115 00.6	15.1	8 33.8	9.9	54.4
02	208 33.7	29.3	129 34.7	15.0	8 43.7	9.8	54.4
03	223 33.8	·· 28.6	144 08.7	15.0	8 53.5	9.8	54.4
04	238 33.9	27.9	158 42.7	15.0	9 03.3	9.8	54.4
05	253 33.9	27.2	173 16.7	15.0	9 13.1	9.7	54.4
06	268 34.0	N16 26.5	187 50.7	14.9	S 9 22.8	9.6	54.4
07	283 34.1	25.8	202 24.6	15.0	9 32.4	9.7	54.4
08	298 34.2	25.1	216 58.6	14.9	9 42.1	9.6	54.4
F 09	313 34.2	·· 24.4	231 32.5	14.9	9 51.7	9.5	54.4
R 10	328 34.3	23.7	246 06.4	14.9	10 01.2	9.5	54.3
I 11	343 34.4	23.0	260 40.3	14.8	10 10.7	9.5	54.3
D 12	358 34.5	N16 22.3	275 14.1	14.9	S10 20.2	9.4	54.3
A 13	13 34.5	21.6	289 48.0	14.8	10 29.6	9.4	54.3
Y 14	28 34.6	20.9	304 21.8	14.8	10 39.0	9.3	54.3
15	43 34.7	·· 20.2	318 55.6	14.8	10 48.3	9.3	54.3
16	58 34.8	19.5	333 29.4	14.7	10 57.6	9.2	54.3
17	73 34.9	18.8	348 03.1	14.8	11 06.8	9.2	54.3
18	88 34.9	N16 18.1	2 36.9	14.7	S11 16.0	9.1	54.3
19	103 35.0	17.4	17 10.6	14.7	11 25.1	9.1	54.3
20	118 35.1	16.7	31 44.3	14.6	11 34.2	9.0	54.3
21	133 35.2	·· 16.0	46 17.9	14.6	11 43.2	9.0	54.3
22	148 35.2	15.3	60 51.5	14.6	11 52.2	9.0	54.3
23	163 35.3	14.6	75 25.1	14.6	12 01.2	8.8	54.3
	S.D. 15.8	d 0.7	S.D. 15.0		14.9		14.8

Lat.	Twilight Naut.	Twilight Civil	Sunrise	Moonrise 5	6	7	8
°	h m	h m	h m	h m	h m	h m	h m
N 72	////	////	00 55	10 38	12 21	14 06	16 00
N 70	////	////	02 03	10 35	12 11	13 47	15 28
68	////	////	02 39	10 33	12 03	13 33	15 05
66	////	01 22	03 04	10 31	11 56	13 21	14 47
64	////	02 06	03 23	10 29	11 51	13 12	14 32
62	////	02 34	03 39	10 28	11 46	13 03	14 20
60	01 14	02 55	03 52	10 27	11 42	12 56	14 10
N 58	01 53	03 12	04 03	10 26	11 38	12 50	14 01
56	02 19	03 26	04 13	10 25	11 35	12 45	13 53
54	02 39	03 38	04 22	10 24	11 32	12 40	13 46
52	02 56	03 49	04 29	10 23	11 30	12 35	13 40
50	03 09	03 58	04 36	10 23	11 27	12 31	13 34
45	03 36	04 18	04 51	10 21	11 22	12 23	13 22
N 40	03 56	04 33	05 03	10 20	11 18	12 15	13 13
35	04 12	04 45	05 13	10 19	11 14	12 09	13 04
30	04 25	04 56	05 22	10 18	11 11	12 04	12 57
20	04 46	05 14	05 37	10 16	11 05	11 55	12 44
N 10	05 02	05 28	05 50	10 15	11 01	11 46	12 33
0	05 16	05 41	06 02	10 13	10 56	11 39	12 22
S 10	05 27	05 53	06 14	10 12	10 52	11 31	12 12
20	05 38	06 04	06 27	10 11	10 47	11 23	12 01
30	05 48	06 17	06 42	10 09	10 41	11 14	11 49
35	05 53	06 24	06 50	10 08	10 38	11 09	11 42
40	05 59	06 31	07 00	10 07	10 35	11 03	11 33
45	06 04	06 39	07 11	10 06	10 31	10 56	11 24
S 50	06 10	06 49	07 24	10 05	10 26	10 48	11 13
52	06 13	06 54	07 30	10 04	10 24	10 45	11 07
54	06 16	06 58	07 37	10 04	10 22	10 40	11 02
56	06 19	07 04	07 45	10 03	10 19	10 36	10 55
58	06 22	07 10	07 53	10 02	10 16	10 31	10 48
S 60	06 26	07 16	08 03	10 01	10 13	10 25	10 40

Lat.	Sunset	Twilight Civil	Twilight Naut.	Moonset 5	6	7	8
°	h m	h m	h m	h m	h m	h m	h m
N 72	23 02	////	////	21 44	21 30	21 14	20 52
N 70	22 03	////	////	21 49	21 42	21 34	21 25
68	21 29	////	////	21 53	21 52	21 50	21 49
66	21 05	22 42	////	21 57	22 00	22 03	22 08
64	20 46	22 02	////	22 00	22 06	22 14	22 23
62	20 31	21 35	////	22 03	22 12	22 23	22 36
60	20 18	21 14	22 51	22 05	22 17	22 31	22 47
N 58	20 07	20 58	22 14	22 08	22 22	22 38	22 56
56	19 57	20 44	21 49	22 10	22 26	22 44	23 05
54	19 49	20 32	21 30	22 11	22 30	22 49	23 12
52	19 41	20 21	21 14	22 13	22 33	22 54	23 19
50	19 35	20 12	21 01	22 14	22 36	22 59	23 25
45	19 20	19 53	20 34	22 17	22 42	23 09	23 38
N 40	19 08	19 38	20 15	22 20	22 48	23 17	23 49
35	18 58	19 26	19 59	22 22	22 53	23 24	23 58
30	18 49	19 15	19 46	22 24	22 57	23 30	24 06
20	18 34	18 58	19 25	22 28	23 04	23 41	24 20
N 10	18 21	18 43	19 09	22 31	23 11	23 51	24 32
0	18 09	18 31	18 56	22 34	23 17	24 00	00 00
S 10	17 57	18 19	18 44	22 37	23 23	24 09	00 09
20	17 45	18 08	18 34	22 40	23 29	24 18	00 18
30	17 30	17 55	18 24	22 44	23 37	24 29	00 29
35	17 22	17 49	18 19	22 46	23 41	24 36	00 36
40	17 13	17 41	18 13	22 48	23 46	24 43	00 43
45	17 02	17 33	18 08	22 51	23 51	24 51	00 51
S 50	16 48	17 23	18 02	22 54	23 58	25 02	01 02
52	16 42	17 19	17 59	22 55	24 01	00 01	01 06
54	16 35	17 14	17 56	22 57	24 05	00 05	01 12
56	16 28	17 09	17 54	22 59	24 08	00 08	01 17
58	16 19	17 03	17 50	23 01	24 13	00 13	01 24
S 60	16 09	16 56	17 47	23 03	24 18	00 18	01 31

Day	SUN Eqn. of Time 00h	12h	Mer. Pass.	MOON Mer. Pass. Upper	Lower	Age	Phase
	m s	m s	h m	h m	h m	d	
5	05 59	05 56	12 06	16 24	04 02	05	
6	05 53	05 49	12 06	17 06	04 45	06	
7	05 46	05 42	12 06	17 49	05 28	07	◖

G.M.T.	ARIES G.H.A.	VENUS −3.4 G.H.A.	Dec.	MARS +1.8 G.H.A.	Dec.	JUPITER −1.3 G.H.A.	Dec.	SATURN +1.2 G.H.A.	Dec.	STARS Name	S.H.A.	Dec.
8 00	316 24.8	147 34.5 N 6	06.2	211 23.1 N23	25.4	129 17.0 S 1	47.9	129 50.4 S 0	21.5	Acamar	315 36.8	S40 22.5
01	331 27.3	162 34.2	04.9	226 23.8	25.3	144 19.1	48.1	144 52.6	21.6	Achernar	335 44.6	S57 19.6
02	346 29.7	177 34.0	03.7	241 24.5	25.2	159 21.2	48.3	159 54.9	21.7	Acrux	173 37.0	S62 59.9
03	1 32.2	192 33.7 ··	02.4	256 25.1 ··	25.0	174 23.2 ··	48.4	174 57.1 ··	21.8	Adhara	255 31.9	S28 56.7
04	16 34.7	207 33.4 6	01.2	271 25.8	24.9	189 25.3	48.6	189 59.4	21.9	Aldebaran	291 17.4	N16 28.3
05	31 37.1	222 33.1 5	59.9	286 26.5	24.7	204 27.4	48.8	205 01.7	22.0			
06	46 39.6	237 32.8 N 5	58.7	301 27.2 N23	24.6	219 29.5 S 1	49.0	220 03.9 S 0	22.0	Alioth	166 42.3	N56 04.0
07	61 42.1	252 32.6	57.5	316 27.8	24.4	234 31.6	49.1	235 06.2	22.1	Alkaid	153 18.2	N49 24.7
S 08	76 44.5	267 32.3	56.2	331 28.5	24.3	249 33.6	49.3	250 08.4	22.2	Al Na'ir	28 13.7	S47 02.9
A 09	91 47.0	282 32.0 ··	55.0	346 29.2 ··	24.1	264 35.7 ··	49.5	265 10.7 ··	22.3	Alnilam	276 11.2	S 1 12.7
T 10	106 49.4	297 31.7	53.7	1 29.9	24.0	279 37.8	49.6	280 12.9	22.4	Alphard	218 20.3	S 8 34.6
U 11	121 51.9	312 31.5	52.5	16 30.6	23.8	294 39.9	49.8	295 15.2	22.5			
R 12	136 54.4	327 31.2 N 5	51.2	31 31.2 N23	23.7	309 42.0 S 1	50.0	310 17.4 S 0	22.6	Alphecca	126 31.5	N26 46.9
D 13	151 56.8	342 30.9	50.0	46 31.9	23.5	324 44.0	50.2	325 19.7	22.7	Alpheratz	358 08.4	N28 59.2
A 14	166 59.3	357 30.6	48.7	61 32.6	23.4	339 46.1	50.3	340 21.9	22.8	Altair	62 31.6	N 8 49.3
Y 15	182 01.8	12 30.3 ··	47.5	76 33.3 ··	23.2	354 48.2 ··	50.5	355 24.2 ··	22.9	Ankaa	353 39.3	S42 24.2
16	197 04.2	27 30.1	46.2	91 34.0	23.1	9 50.3	50.7	10 26.5	23.0	Antares	112 56.0	S26 23.5
17	212 06.7	42 29.8	45.0	106 34.6	22.9	24 52.3	50.9	25 28.7	23.1			
18	227 09.2	57 29.5 N 5	43.7	121 35.3 N23	22.8	39 54.4 S 1	51.0	40 31.0 S 0	23.2	Arcturus	146 18.0	N19 17.0
19	242 11.6	72 29.2	42.5	136 36.0	22.7	54 56.5	51.2	55 33.2	23.3	Atria	108 19.4	S68 59.9
20	257 14.1	87 29.0	41.2	151 36.7	22.5	69 58.6	51.4	70 35.5	23.4	Avior	234 28.6	S59 26.9
21	272 16.5	102 28.7 ··	40.0	166 37.4 ··	22.4	85 00.6 ··	51.5	85 37.7 ··	23.5	Bellatrix	278 58.3	N 6 20.0
22	287 19.0	117 28.4	38.7	181 38.0	22.2	100 02.7	51.7	100 40.0	23.6	Betelgeuse	271 27.8	N 7 24.3
23	302 21.5	132 28.1	37.4	196 38.7	22.0	115 04.8	51.9	115 42.2	23.7			
9 00	317 23.9	147 27.9 N 5	36.2	211 39.4 N23	21.9	130 06.9 S 1	52.1	130 44.5 S 0	23.8	Canopus	264 07.3	S52 41.0
01	332 26.4	162 27.6	34.9	226 40.1	21.7	145 09.0	52.2	145 46.7	23.9	Capella	281 10.6	N45 58.6
02	347 28.9	177 27.3	33.7	241 40.8	21.6	160 11.0	52.4	160 49.0	24.0	Deneb	49 47.6	N45 12.9
03	2 31.3	192 27.1 ··	32.4	256 41.5 ··	21.4	175 13.1 ··	52.6	175 51.2 ··	24.1	Denebola	182 58.7	N14 40.7
04	17 33.8	207 26.8	31.2	271 42.1	21.3	190 15.2	52.8	190 53.5	24.2	Diphda	349 20.1	S18 05.2
05	32 36.3	222 26.5	29.9	286 42.8	21.1	205 17.3	52.9	205 55.7	24.3			
06	47 38.7	237 26.2 N 5	28.7	301 43.5 N23	21.0	220 19.3 S 1	53.1	220 58.0 S 0	24.4	Dubhe	194 22.0	N61 51.3
07	62 41.2	252 26.0	27.4	316 44.2	20.8	235 21.4	53.3	236 00.2	24.5	Elnath	278 43.6	N28 35.5
08	77 43.7	267 25.7	26.2	331 44.9	20.7	250 23.5	53.5	251 02.5	24.6	Eltanin	90 57.1	N51 29.8
S 09	92 46.1	282 25.4 ··	24.9	346 45.5 ··	20.5	265 25.6 ··	53.6	266 04.8 ··	24.7	Enif	34 10.6	N 9 47.5
U 10	107 48.6	297 25.2	23.7	1 46.2	20.4	280 27.6	53.8	281 07.0	24.8	Fomalhaut	15 50.4	S29 43.1
N 11	122 51.0	312 24.9	22.4	16 46.9	20.2	295 29.7	54.0	296 09.3	24.9			
D 12	137 53.5	327 24.6 N 5	21.2	31 47.6 N23	20.1	310 31.8 S 1	54.2	311 11.5 S 0	25.0	Gacrux	172 28.4	S57 00.7
A 13	152 56.0	342 24.3	19.9	46 48.3	19.9	325 33.9	54.3	326 13.8	25.1	Gienah	176 17.6	S17 26.3
Y 14	167 58.4	357 24.1	18.6	61 49.0	19.7	340 35.9	54.5	341 16.0	25.2	Hadar	149 22.6	S60 17.2
15	183 00.9	12 23.8 ··	17.4	76 49.7 ··	19.6	355 38.0 ··	54.7	356 18.3 ··	25.3	Hamal	328 28.1	N23 22.4
16	198 03.4	27 23.5	16.1	91 50.3	19.4	10 40.1	54.8	11 20.5	25.4	Kaus Aust.	84 15.7	S34 23.6
17	213 05.8	42 23.3	14.9	106 51.0	19.3	25 42.2	55.0	26 22.8	25.5			
18	228 08.3	57 23.0 N 5	13.6	121 51.7 N23	19.1	40 44.2 S 1	55.2	41 25.0 S 0	25.6	Kochab	137 19.1	N74 14.3
19	243 10.8	72 22.7	12.4	136 52.4	19.0	55 46.3	55.4	56 27.3	25.7	Markab	14 02.3	N15 06.3
20	258 13.2	87 22.5	11.1	151 53.1	18.8	70 48.4	55.5	71 29.5	25.8	Menkar	314 40.5	N 4 01.1
21	273 15.7	102 22.2 ··	09.8	166 53.8 ··	18.6	85 50.4 ··	55.7	86 31.8 ··	25.9	Menkent	148 36.4	S36 16.8
22	288 18.2	117 21.9	08.6	181 54.4	18.5	100 52.5	55.9	101 34.0	26.0	Miaplacidus	221 45.7	S69 38.4
23	303 20.6	132 21.7	07.3	196 55.1	18.3	115 54.6	56.1	116 36.3	26.1			
10 00	318 23.1	147 21.4 N 5	06.1	211 55.8 N23	18.2	130 56.7 S 1	56.2	131 38.5 S 0	26.1	Mirfak	309 15.3	N49 47.5
01	333 25.5	162 21.1	04.8	226 56.5	18.0	145 58.7	56.4	146 40.8	26.2	Nunki	76 28.1	S26 19.2
02	348 28.0	177 20.9	03.6	241 57.2	17.9	161 00.8	56.6	161 43.0	26.3	Peacock	53 56.8	S56 47.7
03	3 30.5	192 20.6 ··	02.3	256 57.9 ··	17.7	176 02.9 ··	56.8	176 45.3 ··	26.4	Pollux	243 57.8	N28 04.3
04	18 32.9	207 20.3 5	01.0	271 58.6	17.5	191 05.0	56.9	191 47.5	26.5	Procyon	245 25.4	N 5 16.4
05	33 35.4	222 20.1 4	59.8	286 59.2	17.4	206 07.0	57.1	206 49.8	26.6			
06	48 37.9	237 19.8 N 4	58.5	301 59.9 N23	17.2	221 09.1 S 1	57.3	221 52.0 S 0	26.7	Rasalhague	96 28.8	N12 34.6
07	63 40.3	252 19.5	57.3	317 00.6	17.1	236 11.2	57.5	236 54.3	26.8	Regulus	208 09.7	N12 03.6
08	78 42.8	267 19.3	56.0	332 01.3	16.9	251 13.2	57.6	251 56.5	26.9	Rigel	281 35.6	S 8 13.3
M 09	93 45.3	282 19.0 ··	54.7	347 02.0 ··	16.7	266 15.3 ··	57.8	266 58.8 ··	27.0	Rigil Kent.	140 25.1	S60 45.7
O 10	108 47.7	297 18.7	53.5	2 02.7	16.6	281 17.4	58.0	282 01.0	27.1	Sabik	102 40.2	S15 42.1
N 11	123 50.2	312 18.5	52.2	17 03.4	16.4	296 19.5	58.2	297 03.3	27.2			
D 12	138 52.6	327 18.2 N 4	51.0	32 04.1 N23	16.2	311 21.5 S 1	58.3	312 05.5 S 0	27.3	Schedar	350 08.0	N56 25.9
A 13	153 55.1	342 18.0	49.7	47 04.7	16.1	326 23.6	58.5	327 07.8	27.4	Shaula	96 54.7	S37 05.5
Y 14	168 57.6	357 17.7	48.4	62 05.4	15.9	341 25.7	58.7	342 10.0	27.5	Sirius	258 55.4	S16 41.4
15	184 00.0	12 17.4 ··	47.2	77 06.1 ··	15.8	356 27.7 ··	58.9	357 12.3 ··	27.6	Spica	158 57.0	S11 03.8
16	199 02.5	27 17.2	45.9	92 06.8	15.6	11 29.8	59.0	12 14.5	27.7	Suhail	223 10.8	S43 21.4
17	214 05.0	42 16.9	44.6	107 07.5	15.4	26 31.9	59.2	27 16.8	27.8			
18	229 07.4	57 16.6 N 4	43.4	122 08.2 N23	15.3	41 34.0 S 1	59.4	42 19.0 S 0	27.9	Vega	80 55.1	N38 46.2
19	244 09.9	72 16.4	42.1	137 08.9	15.1	56 36.0	59.6	57 21.3	28.0	Zuben'ubi	137 32.4	S15 57.8
20	259 12.4	87 16.1	40.9	152 09.6	14.9	71 38.1	59.7	72 23.5	28.1		S.H.A.	Mer. Pass.
21	274 14.8	102 15.9 ··	39.6	167 10.2 ··	14.8	86 40.2 2	00.1	87 25.8 ··	28.2			
22	289 17.3	117 15.6	38.3	182 10.9	14.6	101 42.2	00.1	102 28.0	28.3	Venus	190 03.9	14 10
23	304 19.8	132 15.3	37.1	197 11.6	14.4	116 44.3	00.3	117 30.3	28.4	Mars	254 15.5	9 53
Mer. Pass.	h m 2 49.9	*v* −0.3 *d* 1.3		*v* 0.7 *d* 0.2		*v* 2.1 *d* 0.2		*v* 2.3 *d* 0.1		Jupiter	172 42.9	15 17
										Saturn	173 20.5	15 15

G.M.T.	SUN G.H.A.	Dec.	MOON G.H.A.	v	Dec.	d	H.P.
d h	° '	° '	° '	'	° '	'	'
8 00	178 35.4	N16 13.9	89 58.7	14.6	S12 10.0	8.9	54.3
01	193 35.5	13.2	104 32.3	14.5	12 18.9	8.8	54.3
02	208 35.6	12.4	119 05.8	14.4	12 27.7	8.7	54.3
03	223 35.6 ··	11.7	133 39.2	14.5	12 36.4	8.7	54.3
04	238 35.7	11.0	148 12.7	14.4	12 45.1	8.6	54.3
05	253 35.8	10.3	162 46.1	14.4	12 53.7	8.6	54.3
06	268 35.9	N16 09.6	177 19.5	14.4	S13 02.3	8.5	54.2
07	283 36.0	08.9	191 52.9	14.3	13 10.8	8.5	54.2
S 08	298 36.0	08.2	206 26.2	14.3	13 19.3	8.4	54.2
A 09	313 36.1 ··	07.5	220 59.5	14.2	13 27.7	8.3	54.2
T 10	328 36.2	06.8	235 32.7	14.3	13 36.0	8.3	54.2
U 11	343 36.3	06.1	250 06.0	14.2	13 44.3	8.2	54.2
R 12	358 36.4	N16 05.3	264 39.2	14.1	S13 52.5	8.2	54.2
D 13	13 36.5	04.6	279 12.3	14.1	14 00.7	8.1	54.2
A 14	28 36.5	03.9	293 45.4	14.1	14 08.8	8.1	54.2
Y 15	43 36.6 ··	03.2	308 18.5	14.1	14 16.9	8.0	54.2
16	58 36.7	02.5	322 51.6	14.0	14 24.9	7.9	54.2
17	73 36.8	01.8	337 24.6	13.9	14 32.8	7.9	54.2
18	88 36.9	N16 01.1	351 57.5	14.0	S14 40.7	7.8	54.3
19	103 37.0	16 00.4	6 30.5	13.9	14 48.5	7.8	54.3
20	118 37.0	15 59.6	21 03.4	13.8	14 56.3	7.7	54.3
21	133 37.1 ··	58.9	35 36.2	13.8	15 04.0	7.6	54.3
22	148 37.2	58.2	50 09.0	13.8	15 11.6	7.6	54.3
23	163 37.3	57.5	64 41.8	13.7	15 19.2	7.5	54.3
9 00	178 37.4	N15 56.8	79 14.5	13.7	S15 26.7	7.4	54.3
01	193 37.5	56.1	93 47.2	13.7	15 34.1	7.4	54.3
02	208 37.6	55.3	108 19.9	13.6	15 41.5	7.3	54.3
03	223 37.6 ··	54.6	122 52.5	13.6	15 48.8	7.3	54.3
04	238 37.7	53.9	137 25.1	13.5	15 56.1	7.1	54.3
05	253 37.8	53.2	151 57.6	13.5	16 03.2	7.1	54.3
06	268 37.9	N15 52.5	166 30.1	13.4	S16 10.3	7.1	54.3
07	283 38.0	51.7	181 02.5	13.4	16 17.4	7.0	54.3
S 08	298 38.1	51.0	195 34.9	13.3	16 24.4	6.9	54.3
U 09	313 38.2 ··	50.3	210 07.2	13.4	16 31.3	6.8	54.3
N 10	328 38.2	49.6	224 39.6	13.2	16 38.1	6.7	54.3
11	343 38.3	48.9	239 11.8	13.2	16 44.8	6.7	54.3
D 12	358 38.4	N15 48.1	253 44.0	13.2	S16 51.5	6.6	54.3
A 13	13 38.5	47.4	268 16.2	13.1	16 58.1	6.6	54.3
Y 14	28 38.6	46.7	282 48.3	13.1	17 04.7	6.5	54.3
15	43 38.7 ··	46.0	297 20.4	13.1	17 11.2	6.4	54.4
16	58 38.8	45.2	311 52.5	12.9	17 17.6	6.3	54.4
17	73 38.9	44.5	326 24.4	13.0	17 23.9	6.2	54.4
18	88 39.0	N15 43.8	340 56.4	12.9	S17 30.1	6.2	54.4
19	103 39.1	43.1	355 28.3	12.8	17 36.3	6.1	54.4
20	118 39.1	42.3	10 00.1	12.8	17 42.4	6.0	54.4
21	133 39.2 ··	41.6	24 31.9	12.8	17 48.4	5.9	54.4
22	148 39.3	40.9	39 03.7	12.7	17 54.3	5.9	54.4
23	163 39.4	40.2	53 35.4	12.7	18 00.2	5.8	54.4
10 00	178 39.5	N15 39.4	68 07.1	12.6	S18 06.0	5.7	54.4
01	193 39.6	38.7	82 38.7	12.5	18 11.7	5.6	54.5
02	208 39.7	38.0	97 10.2	12.6	18 17.3	5.6	54.5
03	223 39.8 ··	37.3	111 41.8	12.4	18 22.9	5.4	54.5
04	238 39.9	36.5	126 13.2	12.5	18 28.3	5.4	54.5
05	253 40.0	35.8	140 44.7	12.3	18 33.7	5.3	54.5
06	268 40.1	N15 35.1	155 16.0	12.4	S18 39.0	5.2	54.5
07	283 40.2	34.3	169 47.4	12.2	18 44.2	5.2	54.5
08	298 40.3	33.6	184 18.6	12.3	18 49.4	5.0	54.5
M 09	313 40.3 ··	32.9	198 49.9	12.2	18 54.4	5.0	54.5
O 10	328 40.4	32.1	213 21.1	12.1	18 59.4	4.9	54.6
N 11	343 40.5	31.4	227 52.2	12.1	19 04.3	4.8	54.6
D 12	358 40.6	N15 30.7	242 23.3	12.0	S19 09.1	4.7	54.6
A 13	13 40.7	29.9	256 54.3	12.0	19 13.8	4.6	54.6
Y 14	28 40.8	29.2	271 25.3	12.0	19 18.4	4.5	54.6
15	43 40.9 ··	28.5	285 56.3	11.9	19 22.9	4.5	54.6
16	58 41.0	27.7	300 27.2	11.8	19 27.4	4.3	54.6
17	73 41.1	27.0	314 58.0	11.8	19 31.7	4.3	54.7
18	88 41.2	N15 26.3	329 28.8	11.8	S19 36.0	4.2	54.7
19	103 41.3	25.5	343 59.6	11.7	19 40.2	4.1	54.7
20	118 41.4	24.8	358 30.3	11.6	19 44.3	4.0	54.7
21	133 41.5 ··	24.1	13 00.9	11.6	19 48.3	3.9	54.7
22	148 41.6	23.3	27 31.5	11.6	19 52.2	3.8	54.7
23	163 41.7	22.6	42 02.1	11.5	19 56.0	3.7	54.7
	S.D. 15.8 d 0.7		S.D. 14.8		14.8		14.9

Lat.	Twilight Naut.	Civil	Sunrise	Moonrise 8	9	10	11
°	h m	h m	h m	h m	h m	h m	h m
N 72	////	////	01 33	16 00	18 30	■	■
N 70	////	////	02 22	15 28	17 15	19 31	■
68	////	00 23	02 53	15 05	16 38	18 12	19 40
66	////	01 45	03 15	14 47	16 12	17 35	18 49
64	////	02 20	03 33	14 32	15 52	17 09	18 17
62	00 21	02 45	03 47	14 20	15 36	16 48	17 54
60	01 34	03 04	03 59	14 10	15 22	16 32	17 35
N 58	02 06	03 20	04 10	14 01	15 11	16 18	17 19
56	02 29	03 33	04 19	13 53	15 01	16 06	17 06
54	02 48	03 45	04 27	13 46	14 52	15 55	16 54
52	03 03	03 54	04 34	13 40	14 44	15 46	16 44
50	03 15	04 03	04 40	13 34	14 37	15 38	16 35
45	03 41	04 21	04 54	13 22	14 22	15 20	16 16
N 40	04 00	04 36	05 06	13 13	14 09	15 06	16 01
35	04 15	04 48	05 15	13 04	13 59	14 54	15 47
30	04 28	04 58	05 24	12 57	13 50	14 43	15 36
20	04 48	05 15	05 38	12 44	13 34	14 25	15 16
N 10	05 03	05 29	05 50	12 33	13 20	14 09	14 59
0	05 16	05 41	06 02	12 22	13 08	13 55	14 44
S 10	05 26	05 52	06 13	12 12	12 55	13 40	14 28
20	05 36	06 03	06 26	12 01	12 41	13 24	14 11
30	05 46	06 14	06 39	11 49	12 26	13 07	13 52
35	05 51	06 21	06 47	11 42	12 17	12 56	13 40
40	05 55	06 28	06 56	11 33	12 07	12 44	13 27
45	06 01	06 35	07 06	11 24	11 55	12 31	13 12
S 50	06 06	06 45	07 19	11 13	11 41	12 14	12 53
52	06 08	06 49	07 25	11 07	11 34	12 06	12 45
54	06 11	06 53	07 31	11 02	11 27	11 57	12 35
56	06 13	06 58	07 38	10 55	11 18	11 47	12 24
58	06 16	07 03	07 46	10 48	11 09	11 36	12 11
S 60	06 19	07 09	07 55	10 40	10 58	11 23	11 56

Lat.	Sunset	Twilight Civil	Naut.	Moonset 8	9	10	11
°	h m	h m	h m	h m	h m	h m	h m
N 72	22 29	////	////	20 52	19 56	■	■
N 70	21 44	////	////	21 25	21 11	20 34	■
68	21 15	23 24	////	21 49	21 50	21 54	22 09
66	20 53	22 21	////	22 08	22 16	22 32	23 00
64	20 36	21 47	////	22 23	22 37	22 58	23 32
62	20 22	21 23	23 29	22 36	22 54	23 19	23 56
60	20 10	21 04	22 32	22 47	23 08	23 36	24 14
N 58	20 00	20 49	22 01	22 56	23 20	23 50	24 30
56	19 51	20 36	21 39	23 05	23 30	24 02	00 02
54	19 43	20 25	21 21	23 12	23 39	24 13	00 13
52	19 36	20 15	21 06	23 19	23 48	24 23	00 23
50	19 29	20 06	20 54	23 25	23 55	24 31	00 31
45	19 16	19 48	20 29	23 38	24 11	00 11	00 49
N 40	19 05	19 34	20 10	23 49	24 24	00 24	01 04
35	18 55	19 22	19 55	23 58	24 35	00 35	01 17
30	18 47	19 12	19 43	24 06	00 06	00 45	01 27
20	18 33	18 56	19 23	24 20	00 20	01 02	01 46
N 10	18 20	18 42	19 08	24 32	00 32	01 16	02 03
0	18 09	18 30	18 55	00 00	00 44	01 30	02 18
S 10	17 58	18 19	18 44	00 09	00 56	01 44	02 33
20	17 46	18 08	18 35	00 18	01 08	01 58	02 50
30	17 32	17 57	18 25	00 29	01 22	02 15	03 09
35	17 24	17 51	18 21	00 36	01 30	02 25	03 20
40	17 15	17 44	18 16	00 43	01 40	02 37	03 32
45	17 05	17 36	18 11	00 51	01 51	02 50	03 47
S 50	16 53	17 27	18 05	01 02	02 04	03 06	04 05
52	16 47	17 23	18 03	01 06	02 11	03 14	04 14
54	16 40	17 19	18 01	01 12	02 18	03 22	04 24
56	16 33	17 14	17 58	01 17	02 26	03 32	04 35
58	16 25	17 08	17 56	01 24	02 34	03 43	04 47
S 60	16 16	17 03	17 53	01 31	02 44	03 55	05 02

Day	SUN Eqn. of Time 00h	12h	Mer. Pass.	MOON Mer. Pass. Upper	Lower	Age	Phase
	m s	m s	h m	h m	h m	d	
8	05 39	05 35	12 06	18 33	06 11	08	
9	05 31	05 26	12 05	19 19	06 56	09	◖
10	05 22	05 18	12 05	20 06	07 42	10	

G.M.T.	ARIES G.H.A.	VENUS −3.4 G.H.A.	Dec.	MARS +1.8 G.H.A.	Dec.	JUPITER −1.3 G.H.A.	Dec.	SATURN +1.2 G.H.A.	Dec.	STARS Name	S.H.A.	Dec.
11 00	319 22.2	147 15.1 N 4	35.8	212 12.3 N23	14.3	131 46.4 S 2	00.4	132 32.5 S 0	28.5	Acamar	315 36.7	S40 22.5
01	334 24.7	162 14.8	34.5	227 13.0	14.1	146 48.4	00.6	147 34.8	28.6	Achernar	335 44.6	S57 19.6
02	349 27.1	177 14.6	33.3	242 13.7	13.9	161 50.5	00.8	162 37.0	28.7	Acrux	173 37.0	S62 59.9
03	4 29.6	192 14.3 ··	32.0	257 14.4 ··	13.8	176 52.6 ··	01.0	177 39.3 ··	28.8	Adhara	255 31.9	S28 56.7
04	19 32.1	207 14.0	30.8	272 15.1	13.6	191 54.6	01.2	192 41.5	28.9	Aldebaran	291 17.4	N16 28.3
05	34 34.5	222 13.8	29.5	287 15.8	13.4	206 56.7	01.3	207 43.8	29.0			
06	49 37.0	237 13.5 N 4	28.2	302 16.5 N23	13.3	221 58.8 S 2	01.5	222 46.0 S 0	29.1	Alioth	166 42.3	N56 04.0
07	64 39.5	252 13.3	27.0	317 17.1	13.1	237 00.9	01.7	237 48.3	29.2	Alkaid	153 18.2	N49 24.7
T 08	79 41.9	267 13.0	25.7	332 17.8	12.9	252 02.9	01.9	252 50.5	29.3	Al Na'ir	28 13.7	S47 03.0
U 09	94 44.4	282 12.7 ··	24.4	347 18.5 ··	12.8	267 05.0 ··	02.0	267 52.7 ··	29.4	Alnilam	276 11.2	S 1 12.7
E 10	109 46.9	297 12.5	23.2	2 19.2	12.6	282 07.1	02.2	282 55.0	29.5	Alphard	218 20.3	S 8 34.6
S 11	124 49.3	312 12.2	21.9	17 19.9	12.4	297 09.1	02.4	297 57.2	29.6			
D 12	139 51.8	327 12.0 N 4	20.6	32 20.6 N23	12.2	312 11.2 S 2	02.6	312 59.5 S 0	29.7	Alphecca	126 31.5	N26 46.9
A 13	154 54.3	342 11.7	19.4	47 21.3	12.1	327 13.3	02.7	328 01.7	29.8	Alpheratz	358 08.4	N28 59.2
Y 14	169 56.7	357 11.5	18.1	62 22.0	11.9	342 15.3	02.9	343 04.0	29.9	Altair	62 31.6	N 8 49.3
15	184 59.2	12 11.2 ··	16.8	77 22.7 ··	11.7	357 17.4 ··	03.1	358 06.2 ··	30.0	Ankaa	353 39.3	S42 24.2
16	200 01.6	27 10.9	15.6	92 23.4	11.6	12 19.5	03.3	13 08.5	30.1	Antares	112 56.0	S26 23.5
17	215 04.1	42 10.7	14.3	107 24.1	11.4	27 21.5	03.4	28 10.7	30.2			
18	230 06.6	57 10.4 N 4	13.0	122 24.8 N23	11.2	42 23.6 S 2	03.6	43 13.0 S 0	30.3	Arcturus	146 18.0	N19 17.0
19	245 09.0	72 10.2	11.8	137 25.5	11.0	57 25.7	03.8	58 15.2	30.4	Atria	108 19.4	S68 59.9
20	260 11.5	87 09.9	10.5	152 26.1	10.9	72 27.7	04.0	73 17.5	30.5	Avior	234 28.6	S59 26.9
21	275 14.0	102 09.7 ··	09.2	167 26.8 ··	10.7	87 29.8 ··	04.2	88 19.7 ··	30.6	Bellatrix	278 58.3	N 6 20.0
22	290 16.4	117 09.4	08.0	182 27.5	10.5	102 31.9	04.3	103 22.0	30.7	Betelgeuse	271 27.8	N 7 24.3
23	305 18.9	132 09.2	06.7	197 28.2	10.4	117 33.9	04.5	118 24.2	30.8			
12 00	320 21.4	147 08.9 N 4	05.4	212 28.9 N23	10.2	132 36.0 S 2	04.7	133 26.5 S 0	30.9	Canopus	264 07.3	S52 40.9
01	335 23.8	162 08.6	04.2	227 29.6	10.0	147 38.1	04.9	148 28.7	31.0	Capella	281 10.6	N45 58.6
02	350 26.3	177 08.4	02.9	242 30.3	09.8	162 40.1	05.0	163 30.9	31.1	Deneb	49 47.6	N45 13.0
03	5 28.7	192 08.1 ··	01.6	257 31.0 ··	09.7	177 42.2 ··	05.2	178 33.2 ··	31.2	Denebola	182 58.7	N14 40.7
04	20 31.2	207 07.9 4	00.3	272 31.7	09.5	192 44.3	05.4	193 35.4	31.3	Diphda	349 20.0	S18 05.2
05	35 33.7	222 07.6 3	59.1	287 32.4	09.3	207 46.3	05.6	208 37.7	31.4			
06	50 36.1	237 07.4 N 3	57.8	302 33.1 N23	09.1	222 48.4 S 2	05.7	223 39.9 S 0	31.5	Dubhe	194 22.0	N61 51.3
07	65 38.6	252 07.1	56.5	317 33.8	09.0	237 50.5	05.9	238 42.2	31.6	Elnath	278 43.5	N28 35.5
W 08	80 41.1	267 06.9	55.3	332 34.5	08.8	252 52.5	06.1	253 44.4	31.7	Eltanin	90 57.1	N51 29.8
E 09	95 43.5	282 06.6 ··	54.0	347 35.2 ··	08.6	267 54.6 ··	06.3	268 46.7 ··	31.8	Enif	34 10.6	N 9 47.5
D 10	110 46.0	297 06.4	52.7	2 35.9	08.4	282 56.7	06.5	283 48.9	31.9	Fomalhaut	15 50.4	S29 43.1
N 11	125 48.5	312 06.1	51.5	17 36.6	08.2	297 58.7	06.6	298 51.2	32.0			
E 12	140 50.9	327 05.9 N 3	50.2	32 37.3 N23	08.1	313 00.8 S 2	06.8	313 53.4 S 0	32.1	Gacrux	172 28.4	S57 00.7
S 13	155 53.4	342 05.6	48.9	47 38.0	07.9	328 02.8	07.0	328 55.6	32.2	Gienah	176 17.6	S17 26.3
D 14	170 55.9	357 05.4	47.6	62 38.6	07.7	343 04.9	07.2	343 57.9	32.3	Hadar	149 22.6	S60 17.2
A 15	185 58.3	12 05.1 ··	46.4	77 39.3 ··	07.5	358 07.0 ··	07.3	359 00.1 ··	32.4	Hamal	328 28.1	N23 22.4
Y 16	201 00.8	27 04.9	45.1	92 40.0	07.4	13 09.0	07.5	14 02.4	32.5	Kaus Aust.	84 15.7	S34 23.6
17	216 03.2	42 04.6	43.8	107 40.7	07.2	28 11.1	07.7	29 04.6	32.6			
18	231 05.7	57 04.4 N 3	42.6	122 41.4 N23	07.0	43 13.2 S 2	07.9	44 06.9 S 0	32.7	Kochab	137 19.1	N74 14.3
19	246 08.2	72 04.1	41.3	137 42.1	06.8	58 15.2	08.1	59 09.1	32.8	Markab	14 02.2	N15 06.4
20	261 10.6	87 03.9	40.0	152 42.8	06.6	73 17.3	08.2	74 11.4	32.9	Menkar	314 40.5	N 4 01.1
21	276 13.1	102 03.6 ··	38.7	167 43.5 ··	06.5	88 19.4 ··	08.4	89 13.6 ··	33.0	Menkent	148 36.4	S36 16.8
22	291 15.6	117 03.4	37.5	182 44.2	06.3	103 21.4	08.6	104 15.8	33.1	Miaplacidus	221 45.7	S69 38.4
23	306 18.0	132 03.1	36.2	197 44.9	06.1	118 23.5	08.8	119 18.1	33.2			
13 00	321 20.5	147 02.9 N 3	34.9	212 45.6 N23	05.9	133 25.5 S 2	08.9	134 20.3 S 0	33.3	Mirfak	309 15.2	N49 47.5
01	336 23.0	162 02.6	33.7	227 46.3	05.7	148 27.6	09.1	149 22.6	33.4	Nunki	76 28.1	S26 19.2
02	351 25.4	177 02.4	32.4	242 47.0	05.5	163 29.7	09.3	164 24.8	~33.5	Peacock	53 56.8	S56 47.7
03	6 27.9	192 02.1 ··	31.1	257 47.7 ··	05.4	178 31.7 ··	09.5	179 27.1 ··	33.6	Pollux	243 57.7	N28 04.3
04	21 30.4	207 01.9	29.8	272 48.4	05.2	193 33.8	09.7	194 29.3	33.7	Procyon	245 25.4	N 5 16.4
05	36 32.8	222 01.6	28.6	287 49.1	05.0	208 35.9	09.8	209 31.6	33.8			
06	51 35.3	237 01.4 N 3	27.3	302 49.8 N23	04.8	223 37.9 S 2	10.0	224 33.8 S 0	33.9	Rasalhague	96 28.8	N12 34.6
07	66 37.7	252 01.1	26.0	317 50.5	04.6	238 40.0	10.2	239 36.0	34.0	Regulus	208 09.7	N12 03.6
T 08	81 40.2	267 00.9	24.7	332 51.2	04.5	253 42.0	10.4	254 38.3	34.1	Rigel	281 35.6	S 8 13.3
H 09	96 42.7	282 00.6 ··	23.5	347 51.9 ··	04.3	268 44.1 ··	10.6	269 40.5 ··	34.2	Rigil Kent.	140 25.1	S60 45.7
U 10	111 45.1	297 00.0	22.2	2 52.6	04.1	283 46.2	10.7	284 42.8	34.3	Sabik	102 40.2	S15 42.1
R 11	126 47.6	312 00.1	20.9	17 53.3	03.9	298 48.2	10.9	299 45.0	34.4			
S 12	141 50.1	326 59.9 N 3	19.6	32 54.0 N23	03.7	313 50.3 S 2	11.1	314 47.3 S 0	34.5	Schedar	350 07.9	N56 25.9
D 13	156 52.5	341 59.6	18.4	47 54.7	03.5	328 52.4	11.3	329 49.5	34.6	Shaula	96 54.7	S37 05.5
A 14	171 55.0	356 59.4	17.1	62 55.4	03.3	343 54.4	11.4	344 51.7	34.7	Sirius	258 55.4	S16 41.3
Y 15	186 57.5	11 59.1 ··	15.8	77 56.1 ··	03.2	358 56.5 ··	11.6	359 54.0 ··	34.8	Spica	158 57.0	S11 03.8
16	201 59.9	26 58.9	14.5	92 56.8	03.0	13 58.5	11.8	14 56.2	34.9	Suhail	223 10.8	S43 21.4
17	217 02.4	41 58.7	13.3	107 57.5	02.8	29 00.6	12.0	29 58.5	35.0			
18	232 04.8	56 58.4 N 3	12.0	122 58.2 N23	02.6	44 02.7 S 2	12.2	45 00.7 S 0	35.1	Vega	80 55.1	N38 46.2
19	247 07.3	71 58.2	10.7	137 58.9	02.4	59 04.7	12.3	60 03.0	35.2	Zuben'ubi	137 32.4	S15 57.8
20	262 09.8	86 57.9	09.4	152 59.6	02.2	74 06.8	12.5	75 05.2	35.4			
21	277 12.2	101 57.7 ··	08.2	168 00.3 ··	02.0	89 08.8 ··	12.7	90 07.4 ··	35.5			
22	292 14.7	116 57.4	06.9	183 01.0	01.8	104 10.9	12.9	105 09.7	35.6	Venus	186 47.5	14 12
23	307 17.2	131 57.2	05.6	198 01.7	01.7	119 13.0	13.1	120 11.9	35.7	Mars	252 07.6	9 50
Mer. Pass.	2 38.1	v −0.3	d 1.3	v 0.7	d 0.2	v 2.1	d 0.2	v 2.2	d 0.1	Jupiter	172 14.6	15 08
										Saturn	173 05.1	15 04

Bottom-right panel:

	S.H.A.	Mer. Pass.
Venus	186 47.5	14 12
Mars	252 07.6	9 50
Jupiter	172 14.6	15 08
Saturn	173 05.1	15 04

SUN and MOON

G.M.T.	SUN G.H.A.	Dec.	MOON G.H.A.	v	Dec.	d	H.P.
11 00	178 41.8	N15 21.8	56 32.6	11.5	S19 59.7	3.7	54.8
01	193 41.9	21.1	71 03.1	11.4	20 03.4	3.5	54.8
02	208 42.0	20.4	85 33.5	11.4	20 06.9	3.4	54.8
03	223 42.1	·· 19.6	100 03.9	11.3	20 10.3	3.4	54.8
04	238 42.2	18.9	114 34.2	11.3	20 13.7	3.2	54.8
05	253 42.3	18.2	129 04.5	11.2	20 16.9	3.2	54.8
06	268 42.4	N15 17.4	143 34.7	11.2	S20 20.1	3.1	54.9
07	283 42.5	16.7	158 04.9	11.2	20 23.2	2.9	54.9
08	298 42.6	15.9	172 35.1	11.1	20 26.1	2.9	54.9
09	313 42.7	·· 15.2	187 05.2	11.1	20 29.0	2.8	54.9
10	328 42.8	14.4	201 35.3	11.0	20 31.8	2.6	54.9
11	343 42.9	13.7	216 05.3	11.0	20 34.4	2.6	55.0
12	358 43.0	N15 13.0	230 35.3	10.9	S20 37.0	2.5	55.0
13	13 43.1	12.2	245 05.2	10.9	20 39.5	2.3	55.0
14	28 43.2	11.5	259 35.1	10.8	20 41.8	2.3	55.0
15	43 43.3	·· 10.7	274 04.9	10.8	20 44.1	2.2	55.0
16	58 43.4	10.0	288 34.7	10.8	20 46.3	2.0	55.1
17	73 43.5	09.2	303 04.5	10.7	20 48.3	2.0	55.1
18	88 43.6	N15 08.5	317 34.2	10.7	S20 50.3	1.9	55.1
19	103 43.7	07.8	332 03.9	10.6	20 52.2	1.7	55.1
20	118 43.8	07.0	346 33.5	10.6	20 53.9	1.7	55.1
21	133 43.9	·· 06.3	1 03.1	10.6	20 55.6	1.5	55.2
22	148 44.0	05.5	15 32.7	10.5	20 57.1	1.5	55.2
23	163 44.1	04.8	30 02.2	10.5	20 58.6	1.3	55.2
12 00	178 44.2	N15 04.0	44 31.7	10.5	S20 59.9	1.3	55.2
01	193 44.3	03.3	59 01.2	10.4	21 01.2	1.1	55.2
02	208 44.4	02.5	73 30.6	10.4	21 02.3	1.0	55.3
03	223 44.5	·· 01.8	88 00.0	10.3	21 03.3	1.0	55.3
04	238 44.6	01.0	102 29.3	10.3	21 04.3	0.8	55.3
05	253 44.7	15 00.3	116 58.6	10.3	21 05.1	0.7	55.3
06	268 44.8	N14 59.5	131 27.9	10.2	S21 05.8	0.6	55.3
07	283 44.9	58.8	145 57.1	10.2	21 06.4	0.5	55.4
08	298 45.0	58.0	160 26.3	10.2	21 06.9	0.4	55.4
09	313 45.2	·· 57.3	174 55.5	10.1	21 07.3	0.3	55.4
10	328 45.3	56.5	189 24.6	10.1	21 07.6	0.1	55.4
11	343 45.4	55.8	203 53.7	10.1	21 07.7	0.1	55.5
12	358 45.5	N14 55.0	218 22.8	10.0	S21 07.8	0.1	55.5
13	13 45.6	54.3	232 51.8	10.1	21 07.7	0.1	55.5
14	28 45.7	53.5	247 20.9	9.9	21 07.6	0.3	55.5
15	43 45.8	·· 52.7	261 49.8	10.0	21 07.3	0.4	55.6
16	58 45.9	52.0	276 18.8	9.9	21 06.9	0.6	55.6
17	73 46.0	51.2	290 47.7	9.9	21 06.4	0.6	55.6
18	88 46.1	N14 50.5	305 16.6	9.9	S21 05.8	0.7	55.6
19	103 46.2	49.7	319 45.5	9.8	21 05.1	0.8	55.6
20	118 46.3	49.0	334 14.3	9.9	21 04.3	0.9	55.7
21	133 46.4	·· 48.2	348 43.2	9.8	21 03.4	1.1	55.7
22	148 46.5	47.5	3 12.0	9.7	21 02.3	1.1	55.7
23	163 46.7	46.7	17 40.7	9.7	21 01.2	1.3	55.7
13 00	178 46.8	N14 45.9	32 09.5	9.7	S20 59.9	1.4	55.8
01	193 46.9	45.2	46 38.2	9.7	20 58.5	1.5	55.8
02	208 47.0	44.4	61 06.9	9.7	20 57.0	1.6	55.8
03	223 47.1	·· 43.7	75 35.6	9.7	20 55.4	1.7	55.8
04	238 47.2	42.9	90 04.3	9.6	20 53.7	1.8	55.9
05	253 47.3	42.1	104 32.9	9.7	20 51.9	1.9	55.9
06	268 47.4	N14 41.4	119 01.6	9.6	S20 50.0	2.1	55.9
07	283 47.5	40.6	133 30.2	9.6	20 47.9	2.2	55.9
08	298 47.7	39.9	147 58.8	9.6	20 45.7	2.2	56.0
09	313 47.8	·· 39.1	162 27.4	9.5	20 43.5	2.4	56.0
10	328 47.9	38.3	176 55.9	9.6	20 41.1	2.5	56.0
11	343 48.0	37.6	191 24.5	9.5	20 38.6	2.7	56.0
12	358 48.1	N14 36.8	205 53.0	9.5	S20 35.9	2.7	56.1
13	13 48.2	36.1	220 21.5	9.6	20 33.2	2.8	56.1
14	28 48.3	35.3	234 50.1	9.5	20 30.4	3.0	56.1
15	43 48.4	·· 34.5	249 18.6	9.4	20 27.4	3.1	56.1
16	58 48.6	33.8	263 47.0	9.5	20 24.3	3.2	56.2
17	73 48.7	33.0	278 15.5	9.4	20 21.1	3.3	56.2
18	88 48.8	N14 32.2	292 44.0	9.5	S20 17.8	3.4	56.2
19	103 48.9	31.5	307 12.5	9.4	20 14.4	3.5	56.3
20	118 49.0	30.7	321 40.9	9.4	20 10.9	3.6	56.3
21	133 49.1	·· 29.9	336 09.3	9.4	20 07.3	3.8	56.3
22	148 49.2	29.2	350 37.8	9.4	20 03.5	3.8	56.3
23	163 49.4	28.4	5 06.2	9.4	19 59.7	4.0	56.4
	S.D. 15.8 d 0.8		S.D. 15.0		15.1		15.3

Left margin day labels: TUESDAY (11), WEDNESDAY (12), THURSDAY (13)

Moonrise

Lat.	Twilight Naut.	Twilight Civil	Sunrise	Moonrise 11	12	13	14
N 72	////	////	02 00	■	■	■	23 21
N 70	////	////	02 39				21 45
68	////	01 14	03 06	19 40	20 38	20 59	21 05
66	////	02 03	03 26	18 49	19 45	20 18	20 37
64	////	02 33	03 42	18 17	19 12	19 50	20 15
62	01 06	02 56	03 55	17 54	18 48	19 29	19 58
60	01 50	03 13	04 06	17 35	18 29	19 12	19 44
N 58	02 18	03 28	04 16	17 19	18 13	18 57	19 31
56	02 39	03 40	04 25	17 06	17 59	18 44	19 21
54	02 56	03 51	04 32	16 54	17 48	18 33	19 11
52	03 09	04 00	04 39	16 44	17 37	18 24	19 03
50	03 21	04 08	04 45	16 35	17 28	18 15	18 55
45	03 45	04 25	04 58	16 16	17 09	17 57	18 39
N 40	04 03	04 39	05 08	16 01	16 53	17 41	18 26
35	04 18	04 50	05 17	15 47	16 39	17 29	18 15
30	04 30	05 00	05 25	15 36	16 28	17 18	18 05
20	04 49	05 16	05 39	15 16	16 08	16 58	17 48
N 10	05 03	05 29	05 51	14 59	15 51	16 42	17 33
0	05 15	05 40	06 02	14 44	15 34	16 26	17 19
S 10	05 26	05 51	06 12	14 28	15 18	16 11	17 05
20	05 35	06 01	06 24	14 11	15 01	15 54	16 50
30	05 43	06 12	06 37	13 52	14 41	15 35	16 32
35	05 48	06 18	06 44	13 40	14 29	15 24	16 22
40	05 52	06 24	06 52	13 27	14 16	15 11	16 11
45	05 57	06 31	07 02	13 12	14 00	14 56	15 57
S 50	06 01	06 40	07 14	12 53	13 41	14 37	15 41
52	06 03	06 43	07 19	12 45	13 32	14 28	15 33
54	06 06	06 47	07 25	12 35	13 22	14 18	15 24
56	06 08	06 52	07 32	12 24	13 10	14 07	15 14
58	06 10	06 57	07 39	12 11	12 57	13 55	15 03
S 60	06 13	07 02	07 48	11 56	12 41	13 40	14 50

Moonset

Lat.	Sunset	Twilight Civil	Twilight Naut.	Moonset 11	12	13	14
N 72	22 03	////	////	■	■	■	23 54
N 70	21 26	////	////				■
68	21 01	22 46	////	22 09	22 57	24 25	00 25
66	20 41	22 02	////	23 00	23 50	25 05	01 05
64	20 26	21 33	////	23 32	24 23	00 23	01 33
62	20 13	21 12	22 55	23 56	24 47	00 47	01 54
60	20 02	20 54	22 15	24 14	00 14	01 06	02 11
N 58	19 52	20 40	21 49	24 30	00 30	01 22	02 25
56	19 44	20 28	21 29	00 02	00 44	01 35	02 38
54	19 37	20 18	21 12	00 13	00 55	01 47	02 48
52	19 30	20 09	20 59	00 23	01 05	01 57	02 58
50	19 24	20 01	20 47	00 31	01 15	02 06	03 06
45	19 11	19 44	20 24	00 49	01 34	02 26	03 24
N 40	19 01	19 30	20 06	01 04	01 50	02 41	03 39
35	18 52	19 19	19 51	01 17	02 03	02 55	03 51
30	18 44	19 09	19 40	01 27	02 15	03 06	04 02
20	18 29	18 54	19 21	01 46	02 34	03 26	04 20
N 10	18 19	18 41	19 06	02 03	02 52	03 43	04 36
0	18 08	18 30	18 55	02 18	03 08	03 59	04 51
S 10	17 58	18 19	18 44	02 33	03 24	04 15	05 06
20	17 46	18 09	18 35	02 50	03 41	04 32	05 22
30	17 34	17 58	18 27	03 09	04 01	04 52	05 40
35	17 26	17 53	18 23	03 20	04 13	05 03	05 51
40	17 17	17 46	18 18	03 32	04 26	05 16	06 03
45	17 08	17 39	18 14	03 47	04 41	05 32	06 17
S 50	16 57	17 31	18 09	04 05	05 01	05 51	06 34
52	16 51	17 27	18 07	04 14	05 10	06 00	06 42
54	16 46	17 23	18 05	04 24	05 20	06 10	06 51
56	16 39	17 19	18 03	04 35	05 32	06 21	07 01
58	16 32	17 14	18 01	04 47	05 45	06 34	07 13
S 60	16 23	17 09	17 58	05 02	06 01	06 49	07 26

SUN and MOON (summary)

Day	SUN Eqn. of Time 00h	12h	Mer. Pass.	MOON Mer. Pass. Upper	Lower	Age	Phase
11	05 13	05 08	12 05	20 56	08 31	11	
12	05 03	04 58	12 05	21 47	09 21	12	
13	04 53	04 48	12 05	22 39	10 13	13	◐

G.M.T.	ARIES G.H.A.	VENUS −3.4 G.H.A. / Dec.	MARS +1.8 G.H.A. / Dec.	JUPITER −1.3 G.H.A. / Dec.	SATURN +1.2 G.H.A. / Dec.	STARS Name / S.H.A. / Dec.
14 00	322 19.6	146 56.9 N 3 04.3	213 02.4 N23 01.5	134 15.0 S 2 13.2	135 14.2 S 0 35.8	Acamar 315 36.7 S40 22.5
01	337 22.1	161 56.7 03.1	228 03.1 01.3	149 17.1 13.4	150 16.4 35.9	Achernar 335 44.5 S57 19.6
02	352 24.6	176 56.5 01.8	243 03.8 01.1	164 19.1 13.6	165 18.6 36.0	Acrux 173 37.0 S62 59.9
03	7 27.0	191 56.2 3 00.5	258 04.5 ·· 00.9	179 21.2 ·· 13.8	180 20.9 ·· 36.1	Adhara 255 31.9 S28 56.6
04	22 29.5	206 56.0 2 59.2	273 05.2 00.7	194 23.3 14.0	195 23.1 36.2	Aldebaran 291 17.4 N16 28.3
05	37 32.0	221 55.7 57.9	288 05.9 00.5	209 25.3 14.1	210 25.4 36.3	
06	52 34.4	236 55.5 N 2 56.7	303 06.6 N23 00.3	224 27.4 S 2 14.3	225 27.6 S 0 36.4	Alioth 166 42.3 N56 03.9
07	67 36.9	251 55.2 55.4	318 07.3 23 00.1	239 29.4 14.5	240 29.9 36.5	Alkaid 153 18.2 N49 24.7
08	82 39.3	266 55.0 54.1	333 08.0 22 59.9	254 31.5 14.7	255 32.1 36.6	Al Na'ir 28 13.7 S47 03.0
F 09	97 41.8	281 54.8 ·· 52.8	348 08.8 ·· 59.8	269 33.6 ·· 14.9	270 34.3 ·· 36.7	Alnilam 276 11.2 S 1 12.7
R 10	112 44.3	296 54.5 51.6	3 09.5 59.6	284 35.6 15.0	285 36.6 36.8	Alphard 218 20.3 S 8 34.6
I 11	127 46.7	311 54.3 50.3	18 10.2 59.4	299 37.7 15.2	300 38.8 36.9	
D 12	142 49.2	326 54.0 N 2 49.0	33 10.9 N22 59.2	314 39.7 S 2 15.4	315 41.1 S 0 37.0	Alphecca 126 31.6 N26 46.9
A 13	157 51.7	341 53.8 47.7	48 11.6 59.0	329 41.8 15.6	330 43.3 37.1	Alpheratz 358 08.4 N28 59.2
Y 14	172 54.1	356 53.5 46.4	63 12.3 58.8	344 43.8 15.8	345 45.5 37.2	Altair 62 31.6 N 8 49.3
15	187 56.6	11 53.3 ·· 45.2	78 13.0 ·· 58.6	359 45.9 ·· 15.9	0 47.8 ·· 37.3	Ankaa 353 39.3 S42 24.2
16	202 59.1	26 53.1 43.9	93 13.7 58.4	14 48.0 16.1	15 50.0 37.4	Antares 112 56.0 S26 23.5
17	218 01.5	41 52.8 42.6	108 14.4 58.2	29 50.0 16.3	30 52.3 37.5	
18	233 04.0	56 52.6 N 2 41.3	123 15.1 N22 58.0	44 52.1 S 2 16.5	45 54.5 S 0 37.6	Arcturus 146 18.0 N19 17.0
19	248 06.5	71 52.3 40.0	138 15.8 57.8	59 54.1 16.7	60 56.7 37.7	Atria 108 19.4 S68 59.9
20	263 08.9	86 52.1 38.8	153 16.5 57.6	74 56.2 16.8	75 59.0 37.8	Avior 234 28.6 S59 26.9
21	278 11.4	101 51.9 ·· 37.5	168 17.2 ·· 57.4	89 58.2 ·· 17.0	91 01.2 ·· 37.9	Bellatrix 278 58.2 N 6 20.0
22	293 13.8	116 51.6 36.2	183 17.9 57.2	105 00.3 17.2	106 03.5 38.0	Betelgeuse 271 27.8 N 7 24.3
23	308 16.3	131 51.4 34.9	198 18.6 57.0	120 02.4 17.4	121 05.7 38.1	
15 00	323 18.8	146 51.1 N 2 33.6	213 19.3 N22 56.9	135 04.4 S 2 17.6	136 07.9 S 0 38.2	Canopus 264 07.3 S52 40.9
01	338 21.2	161 50.9 32.4	228 20.0 56.7	150 06.5 17.7	151 10.2 38.3	Capella 281 10.6 N45 58.6
02	353 23.7	176 50.7 31.1	243 20.7 56.5	165 08.5 17.9	166 12.4 38.4	Deneb 49 47.6 N45 13.0
03	8 26.2	191 50.4 ·· 29.8	258 21.4 ·· 56.3	180 10.6 ·· 18.1	181 14.7 ·· 38.5	Denebola 182 58.7 N14 40.7
04	23 28.6	206 50.2 28.5	273 22.2 56.1	195 12.6 18.3	196 16.9 38.6	Diphda 349 20.0 S18 05.2
05	38 31.1	221 49.9 27.2	288 22.9 55.9	210 14.7 18.5	211 19.1 38.7	
06	53 33.6	236 49.7 N 2 26.0	303 23.6 N22 55.7	225 16.8 S 2 18.6	226 21.4 S 0 38.8	Dubhe 194 22.0 N61 51.3
07	68 36.0	251 49.5 24.7	318 24.3 55.5	240 18.8 18.8	241 23.6 38.9	Elnath 278 43.5 N28 35.5
S 08	83 38.5	266 49.2 23.4	333 25.0 55.3	255 20.9 19.0	256 25.9 39.0	Eltanin 90 57.1 N51 29.8
A 09	98 40.9	281 49.0 ·· 22.1	348 25.7 ·· 55.1	270 22.9 ·· 19.2	271 28.1 ·· 39.1	Enif 34 10.6 N 9 47.5
T 10	113 43.4	296 48.8 20.8	3 26.4 54.9	285 25.0 19.4	286 30.3 39.2	Fomalhaut 15 50.4 S29 43.1
U 11	128 45.9	311 48.5 19.6	18 27.1 54.7	300 27.0 19.6	301 32.6 39.3	
R 12	143 48.3	326 48.3 N 2 18.3	33 27.8 N22 54.5	315 29.1 S 2 19.7	316 34.8 S 0 39.4	Gacrux 172 28.4 S57 00.7
D 13	158 50.8	341 48.0 17.0	48 28.5 54.3	330 31.1 19.9	331 37.0 39.5	Gienah 176 17.6 S17 26.3
A 14	173 53.3	356 47.8 15.7	63 29.2 54.1	345 33.2 20.1	346 39.3 39.7	Hadar 149 22.7 S60 17.2
Y 15	188 55.7	11 47.6 ·· 14.4	78 29.9 ·· 53.9	0 35.3 ·· 20.3	1 41.5 ·· 39.8	Hamal 328 28.1 N23 22.4
16	203 58.2	26 47.3 13.1	93 30.7 53.7	15 37.3 20.5	16 43.8 39.9	Kaus Aust. 84 15.7 S34 23.6
17	219 00.7	41 47.1 11.9	108 31.4 53.5	30 39.4 20.6	31 46.0 40.0	
18	234 03.1	56 46.9 N 2 10.6	123 32.1 N22 53.3	45 41.4 S 2 20.8	46 48.2 S 0 40.1	Kochab 137 19.2 N74 14.3
19	249 05.6	71 46.6 09.3	138 32.8 53.1	60 43.5 21.0	61 50.5 40.2	Markab 14 02.2 N15 06.4
20	264 08.1	86 46.4 08.0	153 33.5 52.9	75 45.5 21.2	76 52.7 40.3	Menkar 314 40.4 N 4 01.1
21	279 10.5	101 46.2 ·· 06.7	168 34.2 ·· 52.7	90 47.6 ·· 21.4	91 54.9 ·· 40.4	Menkent 148 36.4 S36 16.8
22	294 13.0	116 45.9 05.4	183 34.9 52.5	105 49.6 21.5	106 57.2 40.5	Miaplacidus 221 45.7 S69 38.4
23	309 15.4	131 45.7 04.2	198 35.6 52.3	120 51.7 21.7	121 59.4 40.6	
16 00	324 17.9	146 45.4 N 2 02.9	213 36.3 N22 52.1	135 53.7 S 2 21.9	137 01.7 S 0 40.7	Mirfak 309 15.2 N49 47.5
01	339 20.4	161 45.2 01.6	228 37.0 51.9	150 55.8 22.1	152 03.9 40.8	Nunki 76 28.1 S26 19.2
02	354 22.8	176 45.0 2 00.3	243 37.8 51.7	165 57.9 22.3	167 06.1 40.9	Peacock 53 56.8 S56 47.7
03	9 25.3	191 44.7 1 59.0	258 38.5 ·· 51.4	180 59.9 ·· 22.5	182 08.4 ·· 41.0	Pollux 243 57.7 N28 04.3
04	24 27.8	206 44.5 57.7	273 39.2 51.2	196 02.0 22.6	197 10.6 41.1	Procyon 245 25.4 N 5 16.4
05	39 30.2	221 44.3 56.5	288 39.9 51.0	211 04.0 22.8	212 12.8 41.2	
06	54 32.7	236 44.0 N 1 55.2	303 40.6 N22 50.8	226 06.1 S 2 23.0	227 15.1 S 0 41.3	Rasalhague 96 28.8 N12 34.6
07	69 35.2	251 43.8 53.9	318 41.3 50.6	241 08.1 23.2	242 17.3 41.4	Regulus 208 09.7 N12 03.6
08	84 37.6	266 43.6 52.6	333 42.0 50.4	256 10.2 23.4	257 19.6 41.5	Rigel 281 35.6 S 8 13.3
S 09	99 40.1	281 43.3 ·· 51.3	348 42.7 ·· 50.2	271 12.2 ·· 23.5	272 21.8 ·· 41.6	Rigil Kent. 140 25.1 S60 45.6
U 10	114 42.6	296 43.1 50.0	3 43.5 50.0	286 14.3 23.7	287 24.0 41.7	Sabik 102 40.3 S15 42.1
N 11	129 45.0	311 42.9 48.8	18 44.2 49.8	301 16.3 23.9	302 26.3 41.8	
D 12	144 47.5	326 42.6 N 1 47.5	33 44.9 N22 49.6	316 18.4 S 2 24.1	317 28.5 S 0 41.9	Schedar 350 07.9 N56 26.0
A 13	159 49.9	341 42.4 46.2	48 45.6 49.4	331 20.4 24.3	332 30.7 42.0	Shaula 96 54.7 S37 05.5
Y 14	174 52.4	356 42.2 44.9	63 46.3 49.2	346 22.5 24.5	347 33.0 42.1	Sirius 258 55.4 S16 41.3
15	189 54.9	11 41.9 ·· 43.6	78 47.0 ·· 49.0	1 24.5 ·· 24.6	2 35.2 ·· 42.2	Spica 158 57.0 S11 03.8
16	204 57.3	26 41.7 42.3	93 47.7 48.8	16 26.6 24.8	17 37.5 42.3	Suhail 223 10.8 S43 21.4
17	219 59.8	41 41.5 41.0	108 48.4 48.6	31 28.6 25.0	32 39.7 42.4	
18	235 02.3	56 41.2 N 1 39.8	123 49.2 N22 48.4	46 30.7 S 2 25.2	47 41.9 S 0 42.5	Vega 80 55.1 N38 46.2
19	250 04.7	71 41.0 38.5	138 49.9 48.1	61 32.7 25.4	62 44.2 42.6	Zuben'ubi 137 32.4 S15 57.8
20	265 07.2	86 40.8 37.2	153 50.6 47.9	76 34.8 25.6	77 46.4 42.7	
21	280 09.7	101 40.5 ·· 35.9	168 51.3 ·· 47.7	91 36.8 ·· 25.7	92 48.6 ·· 42.9	
22	295 12.1	116 40.3 34.6	183 52.0 47.5	106 38.9 25.9	107 50.9 43.0	
23	310 14.6	131 40.1 33.3	198 52.7 47.3	121 40.9 26.1	122 53.1 43.1	
Mer. Pass.	h m 2 26.3	v −0.2 d 1.3	v 0.7 d 0.2	v 2.1 d 0.2	v 2.2 d 0.1	

	S.H.A.	Mer. Pass.
	° '	h m
Venus	183 32.4	14 13
Mars	250 00.6	9 46
Jupiter	171 45.6	14 58
Saturn	172 49.2	14 53

G.M.T.	SUN G.H.A.	SUN Dec.	MOON G.H.A.	v	Dec.	d	H.P.
	° ′	° ′	° ′	′	° ′	′	′
14 00	178 49.5	N14 27.6	19 34.6	9.5	S19 55.7	4.1	56.4
01	193 49.6	26.9	34 03.1	9.4	19 51.6	4.2	56.4
02	208 49.7	26.1	48 31.5	9.4	19 47.4	4.3	56.4
03	223 49.8	·· 25.3	62 59.9	9.4	19 43.1	4.4	56.5
04	238 49.9	24.6	77 28.3	9.4	19 38.7	4.5	56.5
05	253 50.1	23.8	91 56.7	9.4	19 34.2	4.7	56.5
06	268 50.2	N14 23.0	106 25.1	9.5	S19 29.5	4.7	56.5
07	283 50.3	22.2	120 53.6	9.4	19 24.8	4.9	56.6
08	298 50.4	21.5	135 22.0	9.4	19 19.9	5.0	56.6
F 09	313 50.5	·· 20.7	149 50.4	9.4	19 14.9	5.1	56.6
R 10	328 50.6	19.9	164 18.8	9.4	19 09.8	5.2	56.6
I 11	343 50.8	19.2	178 47.2	9.4	19 04.6	5.3	56.7
D 12	358 50.9	N14 18.4	193 15.6	9.5	S18 59.3	5.4	56.7
A 13	13 51.0	17.6	207 44.1	9.4	18 53.9	5.5	56.7
Y 14	28 51.1	16.8	222 12.5	9.4	18 48.4	5.6	56.7
15	43 51.2	·· 16.1	236 40.9	9.5	18 42.8	5.8	56.8
16	58 51.3	15.3	251 09.4	9.4	18 37.0	5.8	56.8
17	73 51.5	14.5	265 37.8	9.5	18 31.2	5.9	56.8
18	88 51.6	N14 13.7	280 06.3	9.4	S18 25.3	6.1	56.9
19	103 51.7	13.0	294 34.7	9.5	18 19.2	6.2	56.9
20	118 51.8	12.2	309 03.2	9.5	18 13.0	6.2	56.9
21	133 51.9	·· 11.4	323 31.7	9.5	18 06.8	6.4	56.9
22	148 52.1	10.6	338 00.2	9.5	18 00.4	6.5	57.0
23	163 52.2	09.9	352 28.7	9.5	17 53.9	6.6	57.0
15 00	178 52.3	N14 09.1	6 57.2	9.5	S17 47.3	6.7	57.0
01	193 52.4	08.3	21 25.7	9.5	17 40.6	6.8	57.0
02	208 52.6	07.5	35 54.2	9.5	17 33.8	6.9	57.1
03	223 52.7	·· 06.8	50 22.7	9.6	17 26.9	7.0	57.1
04	238 52.8	06.0	64 51.3	9.6	17 19.9	7.1	57.1
05	253 52.9	05.2	79 19.9	9.5	17 12.8	7.2	57.1
06	268 53.0	N14 04.4	93 48.4	9.6	S17 05.6	7.3	57.2
07	283 53.2	03.6	108 17.0	9.6	16 58.3	7.4	57.2
S 08	298 53.3	02.9	122 45.6	9.6	16 50.9	7.5	57.2
A 09	313 53.4	·· 02.1	137 14.2	9.7	16 43.4	7.5	57.2
T 10	328 53.5	01.3	151 42.9	9.6	16 35.9	7.7	57.3
U 11	343 53.7	14 00.5	166 11.5	9.7	16 28.2	7.8	57.3
R 12	358 53.8	N13 59.7	180 40.2	9.7	S16 20.4	7.9	57.3
D 13	13 53.9	59.0	195 08.9	9.7	16 12.5	8.0	57.3
A 14	28 54.0	58.2	209 37.6	9.7	16 04.5	8.1	57.4
Y 15	43 54.2	·· 57.4	224 06.3	9.7	15 56.4	8.2	57.4
16	58 54.3	56.6	238 35.0	9.7	15 48.2	8.2	57.4
17	73 54.4	55.8	253 03.7	9.8	15 40.0	8.4	57.4
18	88 54.5	N13 55.0	267 32.5	9.8	S15 31.6	8.5	57.5
19	103 54.7	54.3	282 01.3	9.8	15 23.1	8.5	57.5
20	118 54.8	53.5	296 30.1	9.8	15 14.6	8.7	57.5
21	133 54.9	·· 52.7	310 58.9	9.8	15 05.9	8.7	57.5
22	148 55.0	51.9	325 27.7	9.8	14 57.2	8.8	57.6
23	163 55.2	51.1	339 56.5	9.9	14 48.4	8.9	57.6
16 00	178 55.3	N13 50.3	354 25.4	9.9	S14 39.5	9.0	57.6
01	193 55.4	49.5	8 54.3	9.9	14 30.5	9.1	57.6
02	208 55.5	48.8	23 23.2	9.9	14 21.4	9.2	57.7
03	223 55.7	·· 48.0	37 52.1	9.9	14 12.2	9.2	57.7
04	238 55.8	47.2	52 21.0	10.0	14 03.0	9.4	57.7
05	253 55.9	46.4	66 50.0	10.0	13 53.6	9.4	57.7
06	268 56.0	N13 45.6	81 19.0	10.0	S13 44.2	9.5	57.8
07	283 56.2	44.8	95 48.0	10.0	13 34.7	9.6	57.8
08	298 56.3	44.0	110 17.0	10.0	13 25.1	9.6	57.8
S 09	313 56.4	·· 43.2	124 46.0	10.1	13 15.5	9.8	57.8
U 10	328 56.5	42.4	139 15.1	10.0	13 05.7	9.8	57.9
N 11	343 56.7	41.7	153 44.1	10.1	12 55.9	9.9	57.9
D 12	358 56.8	N13 40.9	168 13.2	10.1	S12 46.0	10.0	57.9
A 13	13 56.9	40.1	182 42.3	10.2	12 36.0	10.1	57.9
Y 14	28 57.1	39.3	197 11.5	10.1	12 25.9	10.1	57.9
15	43 57.2	·· 38.5	211 40.6	10.2	12 15.8	10.2	58.0
16	58 57.3	37.7	226 09.8	10.1	12 05.6	10.3	58.0
17	73 57.4	36.9	240 38.9	10.2	11 55.3	10.3	58.0
18	88 57.6	N13 36.1	255 08.1	10.3	S11 45.0	10.5	58.0
19	103 57.7	35.3	269 37.4	10.2	11 34.5	10.5	58.0
20	118 57.9	34.5	284 06.6	10.3	11 24.0	10.5	58.1
21	133 58.0	·· 33.7	298 35.9	10.2	11 13.5	10.7	58.1
22	148 58.1	32.9	313 05.1	10.3	11 02.8	10.7	58.1
23	163 58.3	32.1	327 34.4	10.3	10 52.1	10.8	58.1
	S.D. 15.8	d 0.8	S.D. 15.4		15.6		15.8

Twilight / Sunrise / Moonrise

Lat.	Naut.	Civil	Sunrise	Moonrise 14	15	16	17
°	h m	h m	h m	h m	h m	h m	h m
N 72	////	////	02 23	23 21	22 02	21 38	21 21
N 70	////	////	02 55	21 45	21 30	21 20	21 11
68	////	01 42	03 19	21 05	21 06	21 05	21 04
66	////	02 20	03 37	20 37	20 47	20 53	20 57
64	////	02 46	03 51	20 15	20 32	20 43	20 51
62	01 31	03 06	04 03	19 58	20 19	20 34	20 47
60	02 05	03 22	04 14	19 44	20 08	20 27	20 42
N 58	02 29	03 35	04 23	19 31	19 59	20 20	20 39
56	02 50	03 47	04 30	19 21	19 50	20 14	20 35
54	03 03	03 57	04 37	19 11	19 43	20 09	20 32
52	03 16	04 05	04 44	19 03	19 36	20 04	20 29
50	03 28	04 13	04 49	18 55	19 30	20 00	20 21
45	03 50	04 29	05 01	18 39	19 17	19 51	20 21
N 40	04 07	04 42	05 11	18 26	19 06	19 43	20 17
35	04 21	04 53	05 20	18 15	18 57	19 36	20 13
30	04 32	05 02	05 27	18 05	18 49	19 30	20 09
20	04 50	05 17	05 40	17 48	18 35	19 20	20 03
N 10	05 04	05 29	05 51	17 33	18 22	19 11	19 58
0	05 15	05 40	06 01	17 19	18 11	19 02	19 53
S 10	05 25	05 50	06 11	17 05	17 59	18 54	19 48
20	05 33	05 59	06 22	16 50	17 47	18 44	19 42
30	05 41	06 09	06 34	16 32	17 32	18 34	19 36
35	05 45	06 15	06 41	16 21	17 24	18 28	19 33
40	05 49	06 20	06 48	16 11	17 15	18 21	19 29
45	05 52	06 27	06 57	15 57	17 04	18 13	19 24
S 50	05 57	06 35	07 08	15 41	16 50	18 03	19 18
52	05 58	06 38	07 13	15 33	16 44	17 59	19 16
54	06 00	06 42	07 19	15 24	16 37	17 54	19 13
56	06 02	06 46	07 25	15 14	16 29	17 48	19 09
58	06 04	06 50	07 32	15 03	16 20	17 42	19 06
S 60	06 06	06 55	07 40	14 50	16 10	17 35	19 02

Sunset / Twilight / Moonset

Lat.	Sunset	Civil	Naut.	Moonset 14	15	16	17
°	h m	h m	h m	h m	h m	h m	h m
N 72	21 40	////	////	23 54	27 01	03 01	05 13
N 70	21 09	23 35	////	■	01 29	03 33	05 29
68	20 47	22 20	////	00 25	02 08	03 55	05 42
66	20 30	21 44	////	01 05	02 35	04 13	05 53
64	20 15	21 19	23 39	01 33	02 56	04 27	06 02
62	20 04	21 00	22 32	01 54	03 13	04 39	06 09
60	19 53	20 45	22 00	02 11	03 27	04 49	06 16
N 58	19 45	20 31	21 37	02 25	03 38	04 58	06 21
56	19 37	20 20	21 18	02 38	03 49	05 06	06 26
54	19 30	20 11	21 03	02 48	03 58	05 13	06 31
52	19 24	20 02	20 51	02 58	04 06	05 19	06 35
50	19 19	19 54	20 40	03 06	04 13	05 24	06 39
45	19 07	19 39	20 18	03 24	04 28	05 36	06 46
N 40	18 57	19 26	20 01	03 39	04 41	05 46	06 53
35	18 49	19 15	19 47	03 51	04 52	05 54	06 59
30	18 41	19 06	19 36	04 02	05 01	06 02	07 04
20	18 27	18 52	19 19	04 24	05 17	06 14	07 12
N 10	18 18	18 40	19 05	04 36	05 31	06 25	07 19
0	18 08	18 29	18 54	04 51	05 44	06 35	07 26
S 10	17 58	18 19	18 44	05 06	05 57	06 46	07 33
20	17 47	18 10	18 36	05 22	06 10	06 56	07 40
30	17 35	18 00	18 28	05 40	06 26	07 08	07 49
35	17 29	17 55	18 25	05 51	06 35	07 15	07 53
40	17 21	17 49	18 21	06 03	06 45	07 23	07 59
45	17 12	17 42	18 17	06 17	06 57	07 33	08 05
S 50	17 01	17 35	18 13	06 34	07 12	07 44	08 12
52	16 56	17 32	18 11	06 42	07 18	07 49	08 15
54	16 51	17 28	18 10	06 51	07 26	07 54	08 19
56	16 45	17 24	18 08	07 01	07 34	08 01	08 23
58	16 38	17 20	18 06	07 13	07 43	08 08	08 28
S 60	16 30	17 15	18 04	07 26	07 54	08 15	08 33

SUN / MOON

Day	SUN Eqn. of Time 00ʰ	12ʰ	Mer. Pass.	MOON Mer. Pass. Upper	Lower	Age	Phase
	m s	m s	h m	h m	h m	d	
14	04 42	04 37	12 05	23 31	11 05	14	◯
15	04 31	04 25	12 04	24 23	11 57	15	
16	04 19	04 13	12 04	00 23	12 49	16	

G.M.T.	ARIES G.H.A.	VENUS −3.4 G.H.A.	Dec.	MARS +1.8 G.H.A.	Dec.	JUPITER −1.3 G.H.A.	Dec.	SATURN +1.2 G.H.A.	Dec.	STARS Name	S.H.A.	Dec.
17 00	325 17.0	146 39.9 N 1	32.0	213 53.5 N22	47.1	136 43.0 S 2	26.3	137 55.3 S 0	43.2	Acamar	315 36.7	S40 22.5
01	340 19.5	161 39.6	30.8	228 54.2	46.9	151 45.0	26.5	152 57.6	43.3	Achernar	335 44.5	S57 19.6
02	355 22.0	176 39.4	29.5	243 54.9	46.7	166 47.1	26.6	167 59.8	43.4	Acrux	173 37.0	S62 59.9
03	10 24.4	191 39.2 ··	28.2	258 55.6 ··	46.5	181 49.2 ··	26.8	183 02.0 ··	43.5	Adhara	255 31.9	S28 56.6
04	25 26.9	206 38.9	26.9	273 56.3	46.3	196 51.2	27.0	198 04.3	43.6	Aldebaran	291 17.4	N16 28.3
05	40 29.4	221 38.7	25.6	288 57.0	46.0	211 53.3	27.2	213 06.5	43.7			
06	55 31.8	236 38.5 N 1	24.3	303 57.7 N22	45.8	226 55.3 S 2	27.4	228 08.7 S 0	43.8	Alioth	166 42.3	N56 03.9
07	70 34.3	251 38.2	23.0	318 58.5	45.6	241 57.4	27.6	243 11.0	43.9	Alkaid	153 18.2	N49 24.7
08	85 36.8	266 38.0	21.8	333 59.2	45.4	256 59.4	27.7	258 13.2	44.0	Al Na'ir	28 13.7	S47 03.0
M 09	100 39.2	281 37.8 ··	20.5	348 59.9 ··	45.2	272 01.4 ··	27.9	273 15.5 ··	44.1	Alnilam	276 11.2	S 1 12.7
O 10	115 41.7	296 37.5	19.2	4 00.6	45.0	287 03.5	28.1	288 17.7	44.2	Alphard	218 20.3	S 8 34.6
N 11	130 44.2	311 37.3	17.9	19 01.3	44.8	302 05.5	28.3	303 19.9	44.3			
D 12	145 46.6	326 37.1 N 1	16.6	34 02.0 N22	44.6	317 07.6 S 2	28.5	318 22.2 S 0	44.4	Alphecca	126 31.6	N26 46.9
A 13	160 49.1	341 36.9	15.3	49 02.8	44.3	332 09.6	28.7	333 24.4	44.5	Alpheratz	358 08.4	N28 59.3
Y 14	175 51.5	356 36.6	14.0	64 03.5	44.1	347 11.7	28.8	348 26.6	44.6	Altair	62 31.6	N 8 49.3
15	190 54.0	11 36.4 ··	12.8	79 04.2 ··	43.9	2 13.7 ··	29.0	3 28.9 ··	44.7	Ankaa	353 39.3	S42 24.2
16	205 56.5	26 36.2	11.5	94 04.9	43.7	17 15.8	29.2	18 31.1	44.8	Antares	112 56.0	S26 23.5
17	220 58.9	41 35.9	10.2	109 05.6	43.5	32 17.8	29.4	33 33.3	44.9			
18	236 01.4	56 35.7 N 1	08.9	124 06.4 N22	43.3	47 19.9 S 2	29.6	48 35.6 S 0	45.0	Arcturus	146 18.0	N19 17.0
19	251 03.9	71 35.5	07.6	139 07.1	43.0	62 21.9	29.8	63 37.8	45.2	Atria	108 19.5	S68 59.9
20	266 06.3	86 35.3	06.3	154 07.8	42.8	77 24.0	29.9	78 40.0	45.3	Avior	234 28.5	S59 26.9
21	281 08.8	101 35.0 ··	05.0	169 08.5 ··	42.6	92 26.0 ··	30.1	93 42.3 ··	45.4	Bellatrix	278 58.2	N 6 20.0
22	296 11.3	116 34.8	03.7	184 09.2	42.4	107 28.1	30.3	108 44.5	45.5	Betelgeuse	271 27.8	N 7 24.3
23	311 13.7	131 34.6	02.5	199 10.0	42.2	122 30.1	30.5	123 46.7	45.6			
18 00	326 16.2	146 34.3 N 1	01.2	214 10.7 N22	42.0	137 32.2 S 2	30.7	138 49.0 S 0	45.7	Canopus	264 07.3	S52 40.9
01	341 18.7	161 34.1	0 59.9	229 11.4	41.7	152 34.2	30.9	153 51.2	45.8	Capella	281 10.6	N45 58.6
02	356 21.1	176 33.9	58.6	244 12.1	41.5	167 36.3	31.1	168 53.4	45.9	Deneb	49 47.6	N45 13.0
03	11 23.6	191 33.7 ··	57.3	259 12.8 ··	41.3	182 38.3 ··	31.2	183 55.7 ··	46.0	Denebola	182 58.7	N14 40.7
04	26 26.0	206 33.4	56.0	274 13.6	41.1	197 40.4	31.4	198 57.9	46.1	Diphda	349 20.0	S18 05.2
05	41 28.5	221 33.2	54.7	289 14.3	40.9	212 42.4	31.6	214 00.1	46.2			
06	56 31.0	236 33.0 N 0	53.4	304 15.0 N22	40.7	227 44.5 S 2	31.8	229 02.4 S 0	46.3	Dubhe	194 22.0	N61 51.3
07	71 33.4	251 32.7	52.1	319 15.7	40.4	242 46.5	32.0	244 04.6	46.4	Elnath	278 43.5	N28 35.5
08	86 35.9	266 32.5	50.9	334 16.4	40.2	257 48.6	32.2	259 06.8	46.5	Eltanin	90 57.1	N51 29.8
T 09	101 38.4	281 32.3 ··	49.6	349 17.2 ··	40.0	272 50.6 ··	32.3	274 09.1 ··	46.6	Enif	34 10.6	N 9 47.5
U 10	116 40.8	296 32.1	48.3	4 17.9	39.8	287 52.7	32.5	289 11.3	46.7	Fomalhaut	15 50.4	S29 43.1
E 11	131 43.3	311 31.8	47.0	19 18.6	39.6	302 54.7	32.7	304 13.5	46.8			
S 12	146 45.8	326 31.6 N 0	45.7	34 19.3 N22	39.3	317 56.7 S 2	32.9	319 15.8 S 0	46.9	Gacrux	172 28.5	S57 00.7
D 13	161 48.2	341 31.4	44.4	49 20.0	39.1	332 58.8	33.1	334 18.0	47.0	Gienah	176 17.6	S17 26.3
A 14	176 50.7	356 31.2	43.1	64 20.8	38.9	348 00.8	33.3	349 20.2	47.1	Hadar	149 22.7	S60 17.2
Y 15	191 53.1	11 30.9 ··	41.8	79 21.5 ··	38.7	3 02.9 ··	33.4	4 22.5 ··	47.3	Hamal	328 28.1	N23 22.4
16	206 55.6	26 30.7	40.5	94 22.2	38.5	18 04.9	33.6	19 24.7	47.4	Kaus Aust.	84 15.7	S34 23.7
17	221 58.1	41 30.5	39.3	109 22.9	38.2	33 07.0	33.8	34 26.9	47.5			
18	237 00.5	56 30.3 N 0	38.0	124 23.7 N22	38.0	48 09.0 S 2	34.0	49 29.1 S 0	47.6	Kochab	137 19.2	N74 14.3
19	252 03.0	71 30.0	36.7	139 24.4	37.8	63 11.1	34.2	64 31.4	47.7	Markab	14 02.2	N15 06.4
20	267 05.5	86 29.8	35.4	154 25.1	37.6	78 13.1	34.4	79 33.6	47.8	Menkar	314 40.4	N 4 01.1
21	282 07.9	101 29.6 ··	34.1	169 25.8 ··	37.3	93 15.2 ··	34.6	94 35.8 ··	47.9	Menkent	148 36.4	S36 16.8
22	297 10.4	116 29.4	32.8	184 26.5	37.1	108 17.2	34.7	109 38.1	48.0	Miaplacidus	221 45.7	S69 38.4
23	312 12.9	131 29.1	31.5	199 27.3	36.9	123 19.2	34.9	124 40.3	48.1			
19 00	327 15.3	146 28.9 N 0	30.2	214 28.0 N22	36.7	138 21.3 S 2	35.1	139 42.5 S 0	48.2	Mirfak	309 15.2	N49 47.5
01	342 17.8	161 28.7	28.9	229 28.7	36.4	153 23.3	35.3	154 44.8	48.3	Nunki	76 28.1	S26 19.2
02	357 20.3	176 28.5	27.7	244 29.4	36.2	168 25.4	35.5	169 47.0	48.4	Peacock	53 56.8	S56 47.7
03	12 22.7	191 28.2 ··	26.4	259 30.2 ··	36.0	183 27.4 ··	35.7	184 49.2 ··	48.5	Pollux	243 57.7	N28 04.3
04	27 25.2	206 28.0	25.1	274 30.9	35.8	198 29.5	35.8	199 51.5	48.6	Procyon	245 25.4	N 5 16.4
05	42 27.6	221 27.8	23.8	289 31.6	35.5	213 31.5	36.0	214 53.7	48.7			
06	57 30.1	236 27.6 N 0	22.5	304 32.3 N22	35.3	228 33.6 S 2	36.2	229 55.9 S 0	48.8	Rasalhague	96 28.8	N12 34.6
07	72 32.6	251 27.3	21.2	319 33.1	35.1	243 35.6	36.4	244 58.2	48.9	Regulus	208 09.7	N12 03.6
W 08	87 35.0	266 27.1	19.9	334 33.8	34.9	258 37.6	36.6	260 00.4	49.0	Rigel	281 35.5	S 8 13.3
E 09	102 37.5	281 26.9 ··	18.6	349 34.5 ··	34.6	273 39.7 ··	36.8	275 02.6 ··	49.2	Rigil Kent.	140 25.1	S60 45.6
D 10	117 40.0	296 26.7	17.3	4 35.2	34.4	288 41.7	37.0	290 04.8	49.3	Sabik	102 40.3	S15 42.1
N 11	132 42.4	311 26.4	16.0	19 36.0	34.2	303 43.8	37.1	305 07.1	49.4			
E 12	147 44.9	326 26.2 N 0	14.8	34 36.7 N22	34.0	318 45.8 S 2	37.3	320 09.3 S 0	49.5	Schedar	350 07.9	N56 26.0
S 13	162 47.4	341 26.0	13.5	49 37.4	33.7	333 47.9	37.5	335 11.5	49.6	Shaula	96 54.7	S37 05.5
D 14	177 49.8	356 25.8	12.2	64 38.2	33.5	348 49.9	37.7	350 13.8	49.7	Sirius	258 55.4	S16 41.3
A 15	192 52.3	11 25.5 ··	10.9	79 38.9 ··	33.3	3 52.0 ··	37.9	5 16.0 ··	49.8	Spica	158 57.0	S11 03.8
Y 16	207 54.8	26 25.3	09.6	94 39.6	33.0	18 54.0	38.1	20 18.2	49.9	Suhail	223 10.8	S43 21.3
17	222 57.2	41 25.1	08.3	109 40.3	32.8	33 56.0	38.3	35 20.5	50.0			
18	237 59.7	56 24.9 N 0	07.0	124 41.1 N22	32.6	48 58.1 S 2	38.4	50 22.7 S 0	50.1	Vega	80 55.1	N38 46.2
19	253 02.1	71 24.6	05.7	139 41.8	32.4	64 00.1	38.6	65 24.9	50.2	Zuben'ubi	137 32.4	S15 57.8
20	268 04.6	86 24.4	04.4	154 42.5	32.1	79 02.2	38.8	80 27.1	50.3		S.H.A.	Mer. Pass.
21	283 07.1	101 24.2 ··	03.1	169 43.2 ··	31.9	94 04.2 ··	39.0	95 29.4 ··	50.4	Venus	180 18.2	14 14
22	298 09.5	116 24.0	01.9	184 44.0	31.7	109 06.3	39.2	110 31.6	50.5	Mars	247 54.5	9 43
23	313 12.0	131 23.8	00.6	199 44.7	31.4	124 08.3	39.4	125 33.8	50.6	Jupiter	171 16.0	14 48
Mer. Pass.	2 14.6	v −0.2	d 1.3	v 0.7	d 0.2	v 2.0	d 0.2	v 2.2	d 0.1	Saturn	172 32.8	14 43

SUN and MOON

G.M.T.	SUN G.H.A.	SUN Dec.	MOON G.H.A.	v	MOON Dec.	d	H.P.
17 00	178 58.4	N13 31.3	342 03.7	10.3	S10 41.3	10.8	58.1
01	193 58.5	30.5	356 33.0	10.4	10 30.5	10.9	58.2
02	208 58.6	29.7	11 02.4	10.3	10 19.6	11.0	58.2
03	223 58.8 ··	29.0	25 31.7	10.4	10 08.6	11.0	58.2
04	238 58.9	28.2	40 01.1	10.4	9 57.6	11.1	58.2
05	253 59.0	27.4	54 30.5	10.4	9 46.5	11.1	58.2
06	268 59.2	N13 26.6	68 59.9	10.4	S 9 35.4	11.2	58.3
07	283 59.3	25.8	83 29.3	10.5	9 24.2	11.3	58.3
08	298 59.4	25.0	97 58.8	10.4	9 12.9	11.3	58.3
M 09	313 59.6 ··	24.2	112 28.2	10.5	9 01.6	11.4	58.3
O 10	328 59.7	23.4	126 57.7	10.5	8 50.2	11.4	58.3
N 11	343 59.8	22.6	141 27.2	10.5	8 38.8	11.5	58.4
D 12	359 00.0	N13 21.8	155 56.7	10.5	S 8 27.3	11.6	58.4
A 13	14 00.1	21.0	170 26.2	10.5	8 15.7	11.6	58.4
Y 14	29 00.3	20.2	184 55.7	10.5	8 04.1	11.6	58.4
15	44 00.4 ··	19.4	199 25.2	10.6	7 52.5	11.7	58.4
16	59 00.5	18.6	213 54.8	10.6	7 40.8	11.7	58.5
17	74 00.7	17.8	228 24.4	10.5	7 29.1	11.8	58.5
18	89 00.8	N13 17.0	242 53.9	10.6	S 7 17.3	11.9	58.5
19	104 00.9	16.2	257 23.5	10.6	7 05.4	11.9	58.5
20	119 01.1	15.4	271 53.1	10.6	6 53.5	11.9	58.5
21	134 01.2 ··	14.6	286 22.7	10.6	6 41.6	11.9	58.5
22	149 01.3	13.7	300 52.3	10.6	6 29.7	12.1	58.6
23	164 01.5	12.9	315 21.9	10.7	6 17.6	12.0	58.6
18 00	179 01.6	N13 12.1	329 51.6	10.6	S 6 05.6	12.1	58.6
01	194 01.8	11.3	344 21.2	10.7	5 53.5	12.1	58.6
02	209 01.9	10.5	358 50.9	10.6	5 41.4	12.2	58.6
03	224 02.0 ··	09.7	13 20.5	10.7	5 29.2	12.2	58.6
04	239 02.2	08.9	27 50.2	10.7	5 17.0	12.2	58.7
05	254 02.3	08.1	42 19.8	10.7	5 04.8	12.3	58.7
06	269 02.4	N13 07.3	56 49.5	10.7	S 4 52.5	12.3	58.7
07	284 02.6	06.5	71 19.2	10.7	4 40.2	12.3	58.7
08	299 02.7	05.7	85 48.9	10.7	4 27.9	12.4	58.7
T 09	314 02.9 ··	04.9	100 18.6	10.7	4 15.5	12.4	58.7
U 10	329 03.0	04.1	114 48.3	10.7	4 03.1	12.4	58.7
E 11	344 03.1	03.3	129 18.0	10.7	3 50.7	12.4	58.8
S 12	359 03.3	N13 02.5	143 47.7	10.7	S 3 38.3	12.5	58.8
D 13	14 03.4	01.7	158 17.4	10.7	3 25.8	12.5	58.8
A 14	29 03.6	00.8	172 47.1	10.7	3 13.3	12.5	58.8
Y 15	44 03.7	13 00.0	187 16.8	10.7	3 00.8	12.5	58.8
16	59 03.8	12 59.2	201 46.5	10.6	2 48.3	12.6	58.8
17	74 04.0	58.4	216 16.1	10.7	2 35.7	12.6	58.8
18	89 04.1	N12 57.6	230 45.8	10.7	S 2 23.1	12.6	58.9
19	104 04.3	56.8	245 15.5	10.7	2 10.5	12.6	58.9
20	119 04.4	56.0	259 45.2	10.7	1 57.9	12.6	58.9
21	134 04.5 ··	55.2	274 14.9	10.7	1 45.3	12.6	58.9
22	149 04.7	54.4	288 44.6	10.7	1 32.7	12.7	58.9
23	164 04.8	53.5	303 14.3	10.7	1 20.0	12.6	58.9
19 00	179 05.0	N12 52.7	317 44.0	10.6	S 1 07.4	12.7	58.9
01	194 05.1	51.9	332 13.6	10.7	0 54.7	12.7	58.9
02	209 05.3	51.1	346 43.3	10.6	0 42.0	12.7	59.0
03	224 05.4 ··	50.3	1 12.9	10.7	0 29.3	12.7	59.0
04	239 05.5	49.5	15 42.6	10.6	0 16.6	12.7	59.0
05	254 05.7	48.7	30 12.2	10.7	S 0 03.9	12.7	59.0
06	269 05.8	N12 47.8	44 41.9	10.6	N 0 08.8	12.7	59.0
07	284 06.0	47.0	59 11.5	10.6	0 21.5	12.7	59.0
W 08	299 06.1	46.2	73 41.1	10.6	0 34.2	12.7	59.0
E 09	314 06.3 ··	45.4	88 10.7	10.6	0 46.9	12.8	59.0
D 10	329 06.4	44.6	102 40.3	10.5	0 59.7	12.7	59.0
N 11	344 06.5	43.8	117 09.8	10.6	1 12.4	12.7	59.0
E 12	359 06.7	N12 42.9	131 39.4	10.5	N 1 25.1	12.7	59.1
S 13	14 06.8	42.1	146 08.9	10.6	1 37.8	12.7	59.1
D 14	29 07.0	41.3	160 38.5	10.5	1 50.5	12.7	59.1
A 15	44 07.1 ··	40.5	175 08.0	10.5	2 03.2	12.6	59.1
Y 16	59 07.3	39.7	189 37.5	10.5	2 15.8	12.7	59.1
17	74 07.4	38.9	204 07.0	10.4	2 28.5	12.7	59.1
18	89 07.6	N12 38.0	218 36.4	10.5	N 2 41.2	12.6	59.1
19	104 07.7	37.2	233 05.9	10.4	2 53.8	12.7	59.1
20	119 07.9	36.4	247 35.3	10.4	3 06.5	12.6	59.1
21	134 08.0 ··	35.6	262 04.7	10.4	3 19.1	12.6	59.1
22	149 08.1	34.8	276 34.1	10.3	3 31.7	12.6	59.1
23	164 08.3	33.9	291 03.4	10.4	3 44.3	12.5	59.2
	S.D. 15.8	d 0.8	S.D. 15.9		16.0		16.1

Twilight, Sunrise, Moonrise

Lat.	Twilight Naut.	Twilight Civil	Sunrise	Moonrise 17	18	19	20
N 72	////	////	02 43	21 21	21 07	20 53	20 38
N 70	////	01 11	03 11	21 11	21 04	20 57	20 49
68	////	02 04	03 31	21 04	21 02	21 00	20 59
66	////	02 35	03 47	20 57	21 00	21 03	21 07
64	01 02	02 58	04 00	20 51	20 59	21 06	21 14
62	01 50	03 16	04 11	20 47	20 57	21 08	21 19
60	02 18	03 31	04 21	20 42	20 56	21 10	21 25
N 58	02 40	03 43	04 29	20 39	20 55	21 12	21 29
56	02 57	03 54	04 36	20 35	20 54	21 13	21 33
54	03 11	04 03	04 43	20 32	20 54	21 15	21 37
52	03 23	04 11	04 48	20 29	20 53	21 16	21 40
50	03 33	04 18	04 54	20 27	20 52	21 17	21 43
45	03 54	04 33	05 05	20 21	20 51	21 20	21 50
N 40	04 11	04 45	05 14	20 17	20 49	21 22	21 55
35	04 23	04 55	05 22	20 13	20 48	21 24	22 00
30	04 34	05 04	05 29	20 09	20 47	21 25	22 04
20	04 51	05 18	05 41	20 03	20 46	21 28	22 12
N 10	05 04	05 29	05 51	19 58	20 44	21 31	22 18
0	05 15	05 39	06 00	19 53	20 43	21 33	22 25
S 10	05 23	05 48	06 10	19 48	20 42	21 36	22 31
20	05 31	05 57	06 20	19 42	20 40	21 39	22 38
30	05 38	06 06	06 31	19 36	20 39	21 42	22 46
35	05 41	06 11	06 37	19 33	20 38	21 44	22 50
40	05 45	06 17	06 44	19 29	20 37	21 46	22 55
45	05 48	06 22	06 53	19 24	20 36	21 48	23 01
S 50	05 51	06 29	07 03	19 18	20 34	21 51	23 08
52	05 53	06 32	07 07	19 16	20 34	21 52	23 12
54	05 54	06 36	07 12	19 13	20 33	21 54	23 15
56	05 56	06 39	07 18	19 09	20 32	21 56	23 20
58	05 57	06 43	07 24	19 06	20 31	21 57	23 24
S 60	05 59	06 47	07 31	19 02	20 30	21 59	23 29

Sunset, Twilight, Moonset

Lat.	Sunset	Twilight Civil	Naut.	Moonset 17	18	19	20
N 72	21 19	////	////	05 13	07 16	09 16	11 18
N 70	20 53	22 46	////	05 29	07 23	09 15	11 09
68	20 33	21 58	////	05 42	07 28	09 14	11 01
66	20 18	21 28	////	05 53	07 33	09 14	10 55
64	20 05	21 06	22 55	06 02	07 37	09 13	10 50
62	19 54	20 49	22 13	06 09	07 41	09 13	10 46
60	19 45	20 35	21 45	06 16	07 44	09 12	10 42
N 58	19 37	20 23	21 25	06 21	07 46	09 12	10 38
56	19 30	20 12	21 08	06 26	07 48	09 11	10 35
54	19 24	20 03	20 55	06 31	07 51	09 11	10 32
52	19 18	19 55	20 43	06 35	07 52	09 11	10 30
50	19 13	19 48	20 33	06 39	07 54	09 11	10 28
45	19 02	19 33	20 12	06 46	07 58	09 10	10 23
N 40	18 53	19 21	19 56	06 53	08 01	09 10	10 19
35	18 45	19 12	19 43	06 59	08 04	09 09	10 15
30	18 38	19 03	19 33	07 04	08 06	09 09	10 12
20	18 27	18 49	19 16	07 12	08 10	09 08	10 07
N 10	18 17	18 38	19 03	07 19	08 13	09 08	10 02
0	18 07	18 28	18 53	07 26	08 17	09 07	09 58
S 10	17 58	18 19	18 44	07 33	08 20	09 06	09 53
20	17 48	18 11	18 37	07 40	08 23	09 06	09 49
30	17 37	18 02	18 30	07 49	08 27	09 05	09 43
35	17 31	17 57	18 27	07 53	08 29	09 04	09 37
40	17 24	17 52	18 23	07 59	08 32	09 04	09 37
45	17 15	17 46	18 20	08 05	08 35	09 03	09 33
S 50	17 06	17 39	18 17	08 12	08 38	09 03	09 28
52	17 01	17 36	18 16	08 15	08 39	09 02	09 26
54	16 56	17 33	18 14	08 19	08 41	09 02	09 23
56	16 50	17 29	18 13	08 23	08 43	09 02	09 21
58	16 44	17 25	18 12	08 28	08 45	09 01	09 18
S 60	16 37	17 21	18 10	08 33	08 47	09 01	09 15

SUN / MOON

Day	Eqn. of Time 00h	12h	Mer. Pass.	Mer. Pass. Upper	Lower	Age	Phase
17	04 07	04 00	12 04	01 14	13 40	17	
18	03 54	03 47	12 04	02 05	14 30	18	
19	03 40	03 34	12 04	02 55	15 20	19	◐

G.M.T.	ARIES G.H.A.	VENUS −3.4 G.H.A.	Dec.	MARS +1.8 G.H.A.	Dec.	JUPITER −1.3 G.H.A.	Dec.	SATURN +1.2 G.H.A.	Dec.	STARS Name	S.H.A.	Dec.
20 00	328 14.5	146 23.5 S 0	00.7	214 45.4 N22	31.2	139 10.3 S 2	39.6	140 36.1 S 0	50.7	Acamar	315 36.7	S40 22.5
01	343 16.9	161 23.3	02.0	229 46.2	31.0	154 12.4	39.7	155 38.3	50.8	Achernar	335 44.5	S57 19.6
02	358 19.4	176 23.1	03.3	244 46.9	30.7	169 14.4	39.9	170 40.5	51.0	Acrux	173 37.1	S62 59.9
03	13 21.9	191 22.9 ··	04.6	259 47.6 ··	30.5	184 16.5 ··	40.1	185 42.8 ··	51.1	Adhara	255 31.9	S28 56.6
04	28 24.3	206 22.6	05.9	274 48.3	30.3	199 18.5	40.3	200 45.0	51.2	Aldebaran	291 17.3	N16 28.3
05	43 26.8	221 22.4	07.2	289 49.1	30.0	214 20.5	40.5	215 47.2	51.3			
06	58 29.2	236 22.2 S 0	08.5	304 49.8 N22	29.8	229 22.6 S 2	40.7	230 49.4 S 0	51.4	Alioth	166 42.3	N56 03.9
07	73 31.7	251 22.0	09.8	319 50.5	29.6	244 24.6	40.9	245 51.7	51.5	Alkaid	153 18.2	N49 24.7
T 08	88 34.2	266 21.8	11.1	334 51.3	29.3	259 26.7	41.0	260 53.9	51.6	Al Na'ir	28 13.7	S47 03.0
H 09	103 36.6	281 21.5 ··	12.3	349 52.0 ··	29.1	274 28.7 ··	41.2	275 56.1 ··	51.7	Alnilam	276 11.2	S 1 12.7
U 10	118 39.1	296 21.3	13.6	4 52.7	28.9	289 30.7	41.4	290 58.4	51.8	Alphard	218 20.3	S 8 34.6
R 11	133 41.6	311 21.1	14.9	19 53.5	28.6	304 32.8	41.6	306 00.6	51.9			
S 12	148 44.0	326 20.9 S 0	16.2	34 54.2 N22	28.4	319 34.8 S 2	41.8	321 02.8 S 0	52.0	Alphecca	126 31.6	N26 46.9
D 13	163 46.5	341 20.6	17.5	49 54.9	28.2	334 36.9	42.0	336 05.0	52.1	Alpheratz	358 08.4	N28 59.3
A 14	178 49.0	356 20.4	18.8	64 55.7	27.9	349 38.9	42.2	351 07.3	52.2	Altair	62 31.6	N 8 49.3
Y 15	193 51.4	11 20.2 ··	20.1	79 56.4 ··	27.7	4 41.0 ··	42.4	6 09.5 ··	52.3	Ankaa	353 39.3	S42 24.2
16	208 53.9	26 20.0	21.4	94 57.1	27.5	19 43.0	42.5	21 11.7	52.4	Antares	112 56.0	S26 23.5
17	223 56.4	41 19.8	22.7	109 57.8	27.2	34 45.0	42.7	36 14.0	52.6			
18	238 58.8	56 19.5 S 0	24.0	124 58.6 N22	27.0	49 47.1 S 2	42.9	51 16.2 S 0	52.7	Arcturus	146 18.0	N19 17.0
19	254 01.3	71 19.3	25.3	139 59.3	26.8	64 49.1	43.1	66 18.4	52.8	Atria	108 19.5	S68 59.9
20	269 03.7	86 19.1	26.5	155 00.0	26.5	79 51.2	43.3	81 20.6	52.9	Avior	234 28.5	S59 26.9
21	284 06.2	101 18.9 ··	27.8	170 00.8 ··	26.3	94 53.2 ··	43.5	96 22.9 ··	53.0	Bellatrix	278 58.2	N 6 20.0
22	299 08.7	116 18.7	29.1	185 01.5	26.0	109 55.2	43.7	111 25.1	53.1	Betelgeuse	271 27.8	N 7 24.3
23	314 11.1	131 18.4	30.4	200 02.2	25.8	124 57.3	43.8	126 27.3	53.2			
21 00	329 13.6	146 18.2 S 0	31.7	215 03.0 N22	25.6	139 59.3 S 2	44.0	141 29.6 S 0	53.3	Canopus	264 07.3	S52 40.9
01	344 16.1	161 18.0	33.0	230 03.7	25.3	155 01.3	44.2	156 31.8	53.4	Capella	281 10.5	N45 58.6
02	359 18.5	176 17.8	34.3	245 04.4	25.1	170 03.4	44.4	171 34.0	53.5	Deneb	49 47.6	N45 13.0
03	14 21.0	191 17.6 ··	35.6	260 05.2 ··	24.9	185 05.4 ··	44.6	186 36.2 ··	53.6	Denebola	182 58.7	N14 40.7
04	29 23.5	206 17.3	36.9	275 05.9	24.6	200 07.5	44.8	201 38.5	53.7	Diphda	349 20.0	S18 05.2
05	44 25.9	221 17.1	38.2	290 06.6	24.4	215 09.5	45.0	216 40.7	53.8			
06	59 28.4	236 16.9 S 0	39.5	305 07.4 N22	24.1	230 11.5 S 2	45.2	231 42.9 S 0	53.9	Dubhe	194 22.0	N61 51.2
07	74 30.9	251 16.7	40.7	320 08.1	23.9	245 13.6	45.3	246 45.1	54.0	Elnath	278 43.5	N28 35.5
08	89 33.3	266 16.5	42.0	335 08.8	23.7	260 15.6	45.5	261 47.4	54.2	Eltanin	90 57.2	N51 29.8
F 09	104 35.8	281 16.2 ··	43.3	350 09.6 ··	23.4	275 17.7 ··	45.7	276 49.6 ··	54.3	Enif	34 10.6	N 9 47.5
R 10	119 38.2	296 16.0	44.6	5 10.3	23.2	290 19.7	45.9	291 51.8	54.4	Fomalhaut	15 50.3	S29 43.1
I 11	134 40.7	311 15.8	45.9	20 11.1	22.9	305 21.7	46.1	306 54.0	54.5			
D 12	149 43.2	326 15.6 S 0	47.2	35 11.8 N22	22.7	320 23.8 S 2	46.3	321 56.3 S 0	54.6	Gacrux	172 28.5	S57 00.6
A 13	164 45.6	341 15.4	48.5	50 12.5	22.4	335 25.8	46.5	336 58.5	54.7	Gienah	176 17.6	S17 26.3
Y 14	179 48.1	356 15.1	49.8	65 13.3	22.2	350 27.8	46.7	352 00.7	54.8	Hadar	149 22.5	S60 17.2
15	194 50.6	11 14.9 ··	51.1	80 14.0 ··	22.0	5 29.9 ··	46.8	7 03.0 ··	54.9	Hamal	328 28.1	N23 22.4
16	209 53.0	26 14.7	52.4	95 14.7	21.7	20 31.9	47.0	22 05.2	55.0	Kaus Aust.	84 15.7	S34 23.7
17	224 55.5	41 14.5	53.7	110 15.5	21.5	35 34.0	47.2	37 07.4	55.1			
18	239 58.0	56 14.3 S 0	55.0	125 16.2 N22	21.2	50 36.0 S 2	47.4	52 09.6 S 0	55.2	Kochab	137 19.3	N74 14.3
19	255 00.4	71 14.0	56.2	140 16.9	21.0	65 38.0	47.6	67 11.9	55.3	Markab	14 02.2	N15 06.4
20	270 02.9	86 13.8	57.5	155 17.7	20.8	80 40.1	47.8	82 14.1	55.4	Menkar	314 40.4	N 4 01.1
21	285 05.3	101 13.6 0	58.8	170 18.4 ··	20.5	95 42.1 ··	48.0	97 16.3 ··	55.5	Menkent	148 36.4	S36 16.8
22	300 07.8	116 13.4 1	00.1	185 19.2	20.3	110 44.1	48.2	112 18.5	55.7	Miaplacidus	221 45.7	S69 38.4
23	315 10.3	131 13.2	01.4	200 19.9	20.0	125 46.2	48.3	127 20.8	55.8			
22 00	330 12.7	146 12.9 S 1	02.7	215 20.6 N22	19.8	140 48.2 S 2	48.5	142 23.0 S 0	55.9	Mirfak	309 15.1	N49 47.5
01	345 15.2	161 12.7	04.0	230 21.4	19.5	155 50.3	48.7	157 25.2	56.0	Nunki	76 28.1	S26 19.2
02	0 17.7	176 12.5	05.3	245 22.1	19.3	170 52.3	48.9	172 27.4	56.1	Peacock	53 56.8	S56 47.7
03	15 20.1	191 12.3 ··	06.6	260 22.8 ··	19.0	185 54.3 ··	49.1	187 29.7 ··	56.2	Pollux	243 57.7	N28 04.3
04	30 22.6	206 12.1	07.9	275 23.6	18.8	200 56.4	49.3	202 31.9	56.3	Procyon	245 25.4	N 5 16.4
05	45 25.1	221 11.9	09.2	290 24.3	18.5	215 58.4	49.5	217 34.1	56.4			
06	60 27.5	236 11.6 S 1	10.5	305 25.1 N22	18.3	231 00.4 S 2	49.7	232 36.3 S 0	56.5	Rasalhague	96 28.8	N12 34.6
07	75 30.0	251 11.4	11.7	320 25.8	18.1	246 02.5	49.8	247 38.6	56.6	Regulus	208 09.7	N12 03.6
S 08	90 32.5	266 11.2	13.0	335 26.5	17.8	261 04.5	50.0	262 40.8	56.7	Rigel	281 35.5	S 8 13.3
A 09	105 34.9	281 11.0 ··	14.3	350 27.3 ··	17.6	276 06.5 ··	50.2	277 43.0 ··	56.8	Rigil Kent.	140 25.2	S60 45.6
T 10	120 37.4	296 10.8	15.6	5 28.0	17.3	291 08.6	50.4	292 45.2	56.9	Sabik	102 40.3	S15 42.1
U 11	135 39.8	311 10.5	16.9	20 28.8	17.1	306 10.6	50.6	307 47.5	57.1			
R 12	150 42.3	326 10.3 S 1	18.2	35 29.5 N22	16.8	321 12.6 S 2	50.8	322 49.7 S 0	57.2	Schedar	350 07.9	N56 26.0
D 13	165 44.8	341 10.1	19.5	50 30.2	16.6	336 14.7	51.0	337 51.9	57.3	Shaula	96 54.7	S37 05.5
A 14	180 47.2	356 09.9	20.8	65 31.0	16.3	351 16.7	51.2	352 54.1	57.4	Sirius	258 55.4	S16 41.3
Y 15	195 49.7	11 09.7 ··	22.1	80 31.7 ··	16.1	6 18.8 ··	51.3	7 56.4 ··	57.5	Spica	158 57.1	S11 03.8
16	210 52.2	26 09.5	23.4	95 32.5	15.8	21 20.8	51.5	22 58.6	57.6	Suhail	223 10.8	S43 21.3
17	225 54.6	41 09.2	24.7	110 33.2	15.6	36 22.8	51.7	38 00.8	57.7			
18	240 57.1	56 09.0 S 1	26.0	125 33.9 N22	15.3	51 24.9 S 2	51.9	53 03.0 S 0	57.8	Vega	80 55.1	N38 46.2
19	255 59.6	71 08.8	27.2	140 34.7	15.1	66 26.9	52.1	68 05.3	57.9	Zuben'ubi	137 32.4	S15 57.8
20	271 02.0	86 08.6	28.5	155 35.4	14.8	81 28.9	52.3	83 07.5	58.0		S.H.A.	Mer. Pass.
21	286 04.5	101 08.4 ··	29.8	170 36.2 ··	14.6	96 31.0 ··	52.5	98 09.7 ··	58.1	Venus	177 04.6	14 15
22	301 07.0	116 08.1	31.1	185 36.9	14.3	111 33.0	52.7	113 11.9	58.2	Mars	245 49.4	9 39
23	316 09.4	131 07.9	32.4	200 37.6	14.1	126 35.0	52.9	128 14.2	58.4	Jupiter	170 45.7	14 38
Mer. Pass.	2 02.8	v −0.2 d 1.3		v 0.7 d 0.2		v 2.0 d 0.2		v 2.2 d 0.1		Saturn	172 15.9	14 32

G.M.T.	SUN G.H.A.	SUN Dec.	MOON G.H.A.	MOON v	MOON Dec.	MOON d	MOON H.P.
d h	° ′	° ′	° ′	′	° ′	′	′
20 00	179 08.4	N12 33.1	305 32.8	10.3	N 3 56.8	12.6	59.2
01	194 08.6	32.3	320 02.1	10.3	4 09.4	12.5	59.2
02	209 08.7	31.5	334 31.4	10.3	4 21.9	12.5	59.2
03	224 08.9	·· 30.7	349 00.7	10.2	4 34.4	12.5	59.2
04	239 09.0	29.8	3 29.9	10.2	4 46.9	12.5	59.2
05	254 09.2	29.0	17 59.1	10.2	4 59.4	12.4	59.2
06	269 09.3	N12 28.2	32 28.3	10.2	N 5 11.8	12.4	59.2
07	284 09.5	27.4	46 57.5	10.1	5 24.2	12.4	59.2
T 08	299 09.6	26.5	61 26.6	10.1	5 36.6	12.3	59.2
H 09	314 09.8	·· 25.7	75 55.7	10.1	5 48.9	12.4	59.2
U 10	329 09.9	24.9	90 24.8	10.1	6 01.3	12.2	59.2
R 11	344 10.1	24.1	104 53.9	10.0	6 13.5	12.3	59.2
S 12	359 10.2	N12 23.2	119 22.9	10.0	N 6 25.8	12.2	59.2
D 13	14 10.4	22.4	133 51.9	9.9	6 38.0	12.2	59.2
A 14	29 10.5	21.6	148 20.8	10.0	6 50.2	12.1	59.2
Y 15	44 10.7	·· 20.8	162 49.8	9.9	7 02.3	12.2	59.2
16	59 10.8	19.9	177 18.7	9.8	7 14.5	12.0	59.3
17	74 11.0	19.1	191 47.5	9.9	7 26.5	12.0	59.3
18	89 11.1	N12 18.3	206 16.4	9.8	N 7 38.5	12.0	59.3
19	104 11.3	17.4	220 45.2	9.7	7 50.5	12.0	59.3
20	119 11.4	16.6	235 13.9	9.7	8 02.5	11.9	59.3
21	134 11.6	·· 15.8	249 42.6	9.7	8 14.4	11.8	59.3
22	149 11.7	15.0	264 11.3	9.7	8 26.2	11.8	59.3
23	164 11.9	14.1	278 40.0	9.6	8 38.0	11.8	59.3
21 00	179 12.0	N12 13.3	293 08.6	9.6	N 8 49.8	11.7	59.3
01	194 12.2	12.5	307 37.2	9.5	9 01.5	11.6	59.3
02	209 12.3	11.6	322 05.7	9.5	9 13.1	11.6	59.3
03	224 12.5	·· 10.8	336 34.2	9.5	9 24.7	11.6	59.3
04	239 12.6	10.0	351 02.7	9.4	9 36.3	11.4	59.3
05	254 12.8	09.2	5 31.1	9.4	9 47.7	11.5	59.3
06	269 12.9	N12 08.3	19 59.5	9.3	N 9 59.2	11.4	59.3
07	284 13.1	07.5	34 27.8	9.3	10 10.6	11.3	59.3
08	299 13.3	06.7	48 56.1	9.3	10 21.9	11.2	59.3
F 09	314 13.4	·· 05.8	63 24.4	9.2	10 33.1	11.2	59.3
R 10	329 13.6	05.0	77 52.6	9.1	10 44.3	11.2	59.3
I 11	344 13.7	04.2	92 20.7	9.2	10 55.5	11.0	59.3
D 12	359 13.9	N12 03.3	106 48.9	9.0	N11 06.5	11.0	59.3
A 13	14 14.0	02.5	121 16.9	9.1	11 17.5	11.0	59.3
Y 14	29 14.2	01.7	135 45.0	9.0	11 28.5	10.9	59.3
15	44 14.3	·· 00.8	150 13.0	8.9	11 39.4	10.8	59.3
16	59 14.5	12 00.0	164 40.9	8.9	11 50.2	10.7	59.3
17	74 14.6	11 59.2	179 08.8	8.9	12 00.9	10.7	59.3
18	89 14.8	N11 58.3	193 36.7	8.8	N12 11.6	10.6	59.3
19	104 15.0	57.5	208 04.5	8.8	12 22.2	10.5	59.3
20	119 15.1	56.6	222 32.3	8.7	12 32.7	10.5	59.3
21	134 15.3	·· 55.8	237 00.0	8.7	12 43.1	10.4	59.3
22	149 15.4	55.0	251 27.7	8.6	12 53.5	10.3	59.3
23	164 15.6	54.1	265 55.3	8.6	13 03.8	10.2	59.3
22 00	179 15.7	N11 53.3	280 22.9	8.5	N13 14.0	10.1	59.3
01	194 15.9	52.5	294 50.4	8.5	13 24.1	10.1	59.3
02	209 16.0	51.6	309 17.9	8.4	13 34.2	10.0	59.3
03	224 16.2	·· 50.8	323 45.3	8.4	13 44.2	9.9	59.3
04	239 16.4	49.9	338 12.7	8.4	13 54.1	9.8	59.3
05	254 16.5	49.1	352 40.1	8.3	14 03.9	9.7	59.3
06	269 16.7	N11 48.3	7 07.4	8.2	N14 13.6	9.6	59.3
07	284 16.8	47.4	21 34.6	8.2	14 23.2	9.6	59.3
S 08	299 17.0	46.6	36 01.8	8.1	14 32.8	9.4	59.3
A 09	314 17.2	·· 45.7	50 28.9	8.1	14 42.2	9.4	59.3
T 10	329 17.3	44.9	64 56.0	8.1	14 51.6	9.3	59.3
U 11	344 17.5	44.1	79 23.1	8.0	15 00.9	9.1	59.3
R 12	359 17.6	N11 43.2	93 50.1	8.0	N15 10.0	9.1	59.3
D 13	14 17.8	42.4	108 17.1	7.9	15 19.1	9.0	59.3
A 14	29 17.9	41.5	122 44.0	7.8	15 28.1	8.9	59.3
Y 15	44 18.1	·· 40.7	137 10.8	7.8	15 37.0	8.8	59.3
16	59 18.3	39.9	151 37.6	7.8	15 45.8	8.8	59.3
17	74 18.4	39.0	166 04.4	7.7	15 54.6	8.6	59.3
18	89 18.6	N11 38.2	180 31.1	7.7	N16 03.2	8.5	59.3
19	104 18.7	37.3	194 57.8	7.6	16 11.7	8.4	59.3
20	119 18.9	36.5	209 24.4	7.6	16 20.1	8.3	59.3
21	134 19.1	·· 35.6	223 51.0	7.5	16 28.4	8.2	59.3
22	149 19.2	34.8	238 17.5	7.5	16 36.6	8.1	59.3
23	164 19.4	33.9	252 44.0	7.4	16 44.7	8.0	59.3
	S.D. 15.8	d 0.8	S.D. 16.1		16.2		16.2

Lat.	Twilight Naut.	Twilight Civil	Sunrise	Moonrise 20	Moonrise 21	Moonrise 22	Moonrise 23
°	h m	h m	h m	h m	h m	h m	h m
N 72	////	////	03 01	20 38	20 19	19 50	▢
N 70	////	01 43	03 25	20 49	20 41	20 31	20 12
68	////	02 23	03 43	20 59	20 58	20 59	21 03
66	////	02 50	03 58	21 07	21 12	21 20	21 35
64	01 30	03 10	04 09	21 14	21 24	21 38	21 59
62	02 06	03 26	04 20	21 19	21 33	21 52	22 18
60	02 31	03 39	04 28	21 25	21 42	22 04	22 34
N 58	02 50	03 51	04 36	21 29	21 49	22 14	22 47
56	03 05	04 00	04 42	21 33	21 56	22 24	22 59
54	03 18	04 09	04 48	21 37	22 02	22 32	23 09
52	03 29	04 16	04 53	21 40	22 07	22 39	23 18
50	03 39	04 23	04 58	21 43	22 12	22 46	23 26
45	03 59	04 37	05 08	21 50	22 23	23 00	23 43
N 40	04 14	04 48	05 17	21 55	22 32	23 12	23 57
35	04 26	04 58	05 24	22 00	22 39	23 22	24 10
30	04 36	05 06	05 31	22 04	22 46	23 31	24 20
20	04 52	05 19	05 42	22 12	22 58	23 46	24 38
N 10	05 04	05 29	05 51	22 18	23 08	24 00	00 00
0	05 14	05 39	06 00	22 25	23 18	24 12	00 12
S 10	05 22	05 47	06 08	22 31	23 27	24 25	00 25
20	05 29	05 55	06 17	22 38	23 38	24 39	00 39
30	05 35	06 03	06 28	22 46	23 50	24 55	00 55
35	05 38	06 08	06 34	22 50	23 57	25 04	01 04
40	05 41	06 13	06 40	22 55	24 05	00 05	01 15
45	05 44	06 18	06 48	23 01	24 14	00 14	01 27
S 50	05 46	06 24	06 57	23 08	24 26	00 26	01 42
52	05 47	06 26	07 01	23 12	24 31	00 31	01 49
54	05 48	06 29	07 06	23 15	24 37	00 37	01 57
56	05 49	06 32	07 11	23 20	24 44	00 44	02 06
58	05 50	06 36	07 17	23 24	24 51	00 51	02 16
S 60	05 51	06 40	07 23	23 29	24 59	00 59	02 28

Lat.	Sunset	Twilight Civil	Twilight Naut.	Moonset 20	Moonset 21	Moonset 22	Moonset 23
°	h m	h m	h m	h m	h m	h m	h m
N 72	21 00	23 38	////	11 18	13 26	15 50	▢
N 70	20 37	22 15	////	11 09	13 06	15 10	17 26
68	20 20	21 38	////	11 01	12 51	14 43	16 36
66	20 06	21 13	23 41	10 55	12 38	14 22	16 04
64	19 55	20 53	22 29	10 50	12 28	14 06	15 41
62	19 45	20 38	21 56	10 46	12 19	13 52	15 22
60	19 36	20 25	21 32	10 42	12 12	13 41	15 07
N 58	19 29	20 14	21 14	10 38	12 05	13 31	14 54
56	19 23	20 04	20 59	10 35	11 59	13 23	14 43
54	19 17	19 56	20 46	10 32	11 54	13 15	14 33
52	19 12	19 49	20 35	10 30	11 49	13 08	14 25
50	19 07	19 42	20 26	10 28	11 45	13 02	14 17
45	18 57	19 28	20 06	10 23	11 36	12 49	14 00
N 40	18 48	19 17	19 51	10 19	11 28	12 38	13 47
35	18 41	19 08	19 39	10 15	11 22	12 29	13 35
30	18 35	19 00	19 29	10 12	11 16	12 21	13 25
20	18 24	18 47	19 14	10 07	11 06	12 07	13 08
N 10	18 15	18 37	19 02	10 02	10 58	11 55	12 53
0	18 06	18 28	18 52	09 58	10 50	11 43	12 39
S 10	17 58	18 19	18 44	09 53	10 42	11 32	12 25
20	17 49	18 11	18 37	09 49	10 33	11 20	12 10
30	17 39	18 03	18 31	09 43	10 23	11 06	11 53
35	17 33	17 59	18 29	09 40	10 18	10 58	11 43
40	17 27	17 54	18 26	09 37	10 11	10 49	11 32
45	17 19	17 49	18 23	09 33	10 04	10 39	11 19
S 50	17 10	17 43	18 21	09 28	09 55	10 26	11 03
52	17 06	17 41	18 20	09 26	09 51	10 20	10 55
54	17 01	17 38	18 19	09 23	09 47	10 14	10 47
56	16 56	17 35	18 18	09 21	09 42	10 07	10 37
58	16 50	17 31	18 17	09 18	09 36	09 58	10 27
S 60	16 44	17 28	18 16	09 15	09 30	09 49	10 15

	SUN Eqn. of Time 00ʰ	SUN Eqn. of Time 12ʰ	SUN Mer. Pass.	MOON Mer. Pass. Upper	MOON Mer. Pass. Lower	Age	Phase
Day	m s	m s	h m	h m	h m	d	
20	03 27	03 19	12 03	03 46	16 11	20	
21	03 12	03 05	12 03	04 37	17 04	21	◑
22	02 57	02 50	12 03	05 30	17 58	22	

1981 AUGUST 23, 24, 25 (SUN., MON., TUES.)

G.M.T.	ARIES G.H.A.	VENUS −3.4 G.H.A.	VENUS Dec.	MARS +1.8 G.H.A.	MARS Dec.	JUPITER −1.3 G.H.A.	JUPITER Dec.	SATURN +1.2 G.H.A.	SATURN Dec.	STARS Name	S.H.A.	Dec.
23 00	331 11.9	146 07.7	S 1 33.7	215 38.4	N22 13.8	141 37.1	S 2 53.0	143 16.4	S 0 58.5	Acamar	315 36.6	S40 22.5
01	346 14.3	161 07.5	35.0	230 39.1	13.6	156 39.1	53.2	158 18.6	58.6	Achernar	335 44.4	S57 19.6
02	1 16.8	176 07.3	36.3	245 39.9	13.3	171 41.1	53.4	173 20.8	58.7	Acrux	173 37.1	S62 59.9
03	16 19.3	191 07.1	·· 37.6	260 40.6	·· 13.1	186 43.2	·· 53.6	188 23.0	·· 58.8	Adhara	255 31.9	S28 56.6
04	31 21.7	206 06.8	38.9	275 41.4	12.8	201 45.2	53.8	203 25.3	58.9	Aldebaran	291 17.3	N16 28.3
05	46 24.2	221 06.6	40.2	290 42.1	12.6	216 47.2	54.0	218 27.5	59.0			
06	61 26.7	236 06.4	S 1 41.4	305 42.9	N22 12.3	231 49.3	S 2 54.2	233 29.7	S 0 59.1	Alioth	166 42.3	N56 03.9
07	76 29.1	251 06.2	42.7	320 43.6	12.1	246 51.3	54.4	248 31.9	59.2	Alkaid	153 18.2	N49 24.7
08	91 31.6	266 06.0	44.0	335 44.3	11.8	261 53.3	54.6	263 34.2	59.3	Al Na'ir	28 13.6	S47 03.0
S 09	106 34.1	281 05.8	·· 45.3	350 45.1	·· 11.5	276 55.4	·· 54.7	278 36.4	·· 59.4	Alnilam	276 11.1	S 1 12.7
U 10	121 36.5	296 05.5	46.6	5 45.8	11.3	291 57.4	54.9	293 38.6	59.5	Alphard	218 20.3	S 8 34.6
N 11	136 39.0	311 05.3	47.9	20 46.6	11.0	306 59.4	55.1	308 40.8	59.7			
D 12	151 41.5	326 05.1	S 1 49.2	35 47.3	N22 10.8	322 01.5	S 2 55.3	323 43.1	S 0 59.8	Alphecca	126 31.6	N26 46.9
A 13	166 43.9	341 04.9	50.5	50 48.1	10.5	337 03.5	55.5	338 45.3	59.9	Alpheratz	358 08.3	N28 59.3
Y 14	181 46.4	356 04.7	51.8	65 48.8	10.3	352 05.5	55.7	353 47.5	1 00.0	Altair	62 31.6	N 8 49.3
15	196 48.8	11 04.4	·· 53.1	80 49.6	·· 10.0	7 07.6	·· 55.9	8 49.7	·· 00.1	Ankaa	353 39.2	S42 24.2
16	211 51.3	26 04.2	54.4	95 50.3	09.8	22 09.6	56.1	23 51.9	00.2	Antares	112 56.0	S26 23.5
17	226 53.8	41 04.0	55.6	110 51.0	09.5	37 11.6	56.3	38 54.2	00.3			
18	241 56.2	56 03.8	S 1 56.9	125 51.8	N22 09.2	52 13.7	S 2 56.5	53 56.4	S 1 00.4	Arcturus	146 18.0	N19 17.0
19	256 58.7	71 03.6	58.2	140 52.5	09.0	67 15.7	56.6	68 58.6	00.5	Atria	108 19.5	S68 59.9
20	272 01.2	86 03.4	1 59.5	155 53.3	08.7	82 17.7	56.8	84 00.8	00.6	Avior	234 28.5	S59 26.8
21	287 03.6	101 03.1	2 00.8	170 54.0	·· 08.5	97 19.7	·· 57.0	99 03.1	·· 00.7	Bellatrix	278 58.2	N 6 20.0
22	302 06.1	116 02.9	02.1	185 54.8	08.2	112 21.8	57.2	114 05.3	00.8	Betelgeuse	271 27.7	N 7 24.3
23	317 08.6	131 02.7	03.4	200 55.5	08.0	127 23.8	57.4	129 07.5	01.0			
24 00	332 11.0	146 02.5	S 2 04.7	215 56.3	N22 07.7	142 25.8	S 2 57.6	144 09.7	S 1 01.1	Canopus	264 07.2	S52 40.9
01	347 13.5	161 02.3	06.0	230 57.0	07.4	157 27.9	57.8	159 11.9	01.2	Capella	281 10.5	N45 58.6
02	2 15.9	176 02.1	07.3	245 57.8	07.2	172 29.9	58.0	174 14.2	01.3	Deneb	49 47.6	N45 13.0
03	17 18.4	191 01.8	·· 08.6	260 58.5	·· 06.9	187 31.9	·· 58.2	189 16.4	·· 01.4	Denebola	182 58.7	N14 40.7
04	32 20.9	206 01.6	09.8	275 59.3	06.7	202 34.0	58.3	204 18.6	01.5	Diphda	349 20.0	S18 05.2
05	47 23.3	221 01.4	11.1	291 00.0	06.4	217 36.0	58.5	219 20.8	01.6			
06	62 25.8	236 01.2	S 2 12.4	306 00.8	N22 06.2	232 38.0	S 2 58.7	234 23.1	S 1 01.7	Dubhe	194 22.0	N61 51.2
07	77 28.3	251 01.0	13.7	321 01.5	05.9	247 40.1	58.9	249 25.3	01.8	Elnath	278 43.5	N28 35.5
08	92 30.7	266 00.8	15.0	336 02.3	05.6	262 42.1	59.1	264 27.5	01.9	Eltanin	90 57.2	N51 29.8
M 09	107 33.2	281 00.5	·· 16.3	351 03.0	·· 05.4	277 44.1	·· 59.3	279 29.7	·· 02.0	Enif	34 10.6	N 9 47.5
O 10	122 35.7	296 00.3	17.6	6 03.8	05.1	292 46.1	59.5	294 31.9	02.2	Fomalhaut	15 50.3	S29 43.1
N 11	137 38.1	311 00.1	18.9	21 04.5	04.9	307 48.2	59.7	309 34.2	02.3			
D 12	152 40.6	325 59.9	S 2 20.2	36 05.2	N22 04.6	322 50.2	S 2 59.9	324 36.4	S 1 02.4	Gacrux	172 28.5	S57 00.6
A 13	167 43.1	340 59.7	21.5	51 06.0	04.3	337 52.2	3 00.1	339 38.6	02.5	Gienah	176 17.6	S17 26.2
Y 14	182 45.5	355 59.5	22.7	66 06.7	04.1	352 54.3	00.2	354 40.8	02.6	Hadar	149 22.7	S60 17.2
15	197 48.0	10 59.2	·· 24.0	81 07.5	·· 03.8	7 56.3	·· 00.4	9 43.0	·· 02.7	Hamal	328 28.0	N23 22.5
16	212 50.4	25 59.0	25.3	96 08.3	03.5	22 58.3	00.6	24 45.3	02.8	Kaus Aust.	84 15.8	S34 23.7
17	227 52.9	40 58.8	26.6	111 09.0	03.3	38 00.4	00.8	39 47.5	02.9			
18	242 55.4	55 58.6	S 2 27.9	126 09.8	N22 03.0	53 02.4	S 3 01.0	54 49.7	S 1 03.0	Kochab	137 19.3	N74 14.3
19	257 57.8	70 58.4	29.2	141 10.5	02.8	68 04.4	01.2	69 51.9	03.1	Markab	14 02.2	N15 06.4
20	273 00.3	85 58.2	30.5	156 11.3	02.5	83 06.4	01.4	84 54.1	03.2	Menkar	314 40.4	N 4 01.1
21	288 02.8	100 57.9	·· 31.8	171 12.0	·· 02.2	98 08.5	·· 01.6	99 56.4	·· 03.4	Menkent	148 36.4	S36 16.8
22	303 05.2	115 57.7	33.1	186 12.8	02.0	113 10.5	01.8	114 58.6	03.5	Miaplacidus	221 45.7	S69 38.4
23	318 07.7	130 57.5	34.3	201 13.5	01.7	128 12.5	02.0	130 00.8	03.6			
25 00	333 10.2	145 57.3	S 2 35.6	216 14.3	N22 01.4	143 14.6	S 3 02.2	145 03.0	S 1 03.7	Mirfak	309 15.1	N49 47.5
01	348 12.6	160 57.1	36.9	231 15.0	01.1	158 16.6	02.3	160 05.2	03.8	Nunki	76 28.1	S26 19.2
02	3 15.1	175 56.9	38.2	246 15.8	00.9	173 18.6	02.5	175 07.5	03.9	Peacock	53 56.8	S56 47.7
03	18 17.6	190 56.6	·· 39.5	261 16.5	·· 00.6	188 20.6	·· 02.7	190 09.7	·· 04.0	Pollux	243 57.7	N28 04.3
04	33 20.0	205 56.4	40.8	276 17.3	00.4	203 22.7	02.9	205 11.9	04.1	Procyon	245 25.4	N 5 16.5
05	48 22.5	220 56.2	42.1	291 18.0	22 00.1	218 24.7	03.1	220 14.1	04.2			
06	63 24.9	235 56.0	S 2 43.4	306 18.8	N21 59.8	233 26.7	S 3 03.3	235 16.3	S 1 04.3	Rasalhague	96 28.9	N12 34.6
07	78 27.4	250 55.8	44.7	321 19.5	59.6	248 28.8	03.5	250 18.6	04.4	Regulus	208 09.6	N12 03.6
08	93 29.9	265 55.6	46.0	336 20.3	59.3	263 30.8	03.7	265 20.8	04.6	Rigel	281 35.5	S 8 13.2
T 09	108 32.3	280 55.4	·· 47.2	351 21.0	·· 59.0	278 32.8	·· 03.9	280 23.0	·· 04.7	Rigil Kent.	140 25.2	S60 45.6
U 10	123 34.8	295 55.1	48.5	6 21.8	58.8	293 34.8	04.1	295 25.2	04.8	Sabik	102 40.3	S15 42.1
E 11	138 37.3	310 54.9	49.8	21 22.5	58.5	308 36.9	04.2	310 27.4	04.9			
S D 12	153 39.7	325 54.7	S 2 51.1	36 23.3	N21 58.2	323 38.9	S 3 04.4	325 29.7	S 1 05.0	Schedar	350 07.8	N56 26.0
A 13	168 42.2	340 54.5	52.4	51 24.1	58.0	338 40.9	04.6	340 31.9	05.1	Shaula	96 54.7	S37 05.5
Y 14	183 44.7	355 54.3	53.7	66 24.8	57.7	353 42.9	04.8	355 34.1	05.2	Sirius	258 55.4	S16 41.3
15	198 47.1	10 54.1	·· 55.0	81 25.6	·· 57.4	8 45.0	·· 05.0	10 36.3	·· 05.3	Spica	158 57.1	S11 03.8
16	213 49.6	25 53.8	56.3	96 26.3	57.2	23 47.0	05.2	25 38.5	05.4	Suhail	223 10.7	S43 21.3
17	228 52.0	40 53.6	57.5	111 27.1	56.9	38 49.0	05.4	40 40.8	05.5			
18	243 54.5	55 53.4	S 2 58.8	126 27.8	N21 56.6	53 51.1	S 3 05.6	55 43.0	S 1 05.7	Vega	80 55.1	N38 46.3
19	258 57.0	70 53.2	3 00.1	141 28.6	56.4	68 53.1	05.8	70 45.2	05.8	Zuben'ubi	137 32.4	S15 57.8
20	273 59.4	85 53.0	01.4	156 29.3	56.1	83 55.1	06.0	85 47.4	05.9		S.H.A.	Mer. Pass.
21	289 01.9	100 52.8	·· 02.7	171 30.1	·· 55.8	98 57.1	·· 06.2	100 49.6	·· 06.0			h m
22	304 04.4	115 52.5	04.0	186 30.9	55.6	113 59.2	06.4	115 51.9	06.1	Venus	173 51.5	14 16
23	319 06.8	130 52.3	05.3	201 31.6	55.3	129 01.2	06.5	130 54.1	06.2	Mars	243 45.2	9 36
Mer. Pass.	1 51.0	v −0.2	d 1.3	v 0.7	d 0.3	v 2.0	d 0.2	v 2.2	d 0.1	Jupiter	170 14.8	14 28
										Saturn	171 58.7	14 21

SUN / MOON

G.M.T. (d h)	SUN G.H.A.	Dec.	MOON G.H.A.	v	Dec.	d	H.P.
23 00	179 19.5	N11 33.1	267 10.4	7.4	N16 52.7	7.9	59.3
01	194 19.7	32.3	281 36.8	7.3	17 00.6	7.8	59.3
02	209 19.9	31.4	296 03.1	7.3	17 08.4	7.6	59.3
03	224 20.0 ··	30.6	310 29.4	7.3	17 16.0	7.6	59.3
04	239 20.2	29.7	324 55.7	7.2	17 23.6	7.4	59.2
05	254 20.4	28.9	339 21.9	7.1	17 31.0	7.4	59.2
06	269 20.5	N11 28.0	353 48.0	7.2	N17 38.4	7.2	59.2
07	284 20.7	27.2	8 14.2	7.0	17 45.6	7.1	59.2
S 08	299 20.8	26.3	22 40.2	7.1	17 52.7	7.0	59.2
U 09	314 21.0 ··	25.5	37 06.3	6.9	17 59.7	6.9	59.2
N 10	329 21.2	24.6	51 32.2	7.0	18 06.6	6.8	59.2
11	344 21.3	23.8	65 58.2	6.9	18 13.4	6.7	59.2
D 12	359 21.5	N11 22.9	80 24.1	6.8	N18 20.1	6.5	59.2
A 13	14 21.7	22.1	94 49.9	6.9	18 26.6	6.4	59.2
Y 14	29 21.8	21.2	109 15.8	6.8	18 33.0	6.3	59.2
15	44 22.0 ··	20.4	123 41.6	6.7	18 39.3	6.2	59.2
16	59 22.1	19.5	138 07.3	6.7	18 45.5	6.1	59.2
17	74 22.3	18.7	152 33.0	6.7	18 51.6	5.9	59.2
18	89 22.5	N11 17.8	166 58.7	6.6	N18 57.5	5.8	59.2
19	104 22.6	17.0	181 24.3	6.6	19 03.3	5.7	59.2
20	119 22.8	16.1	195 49.9	6.6	19 09.0	5.6	59.2
21	134 23.0 ··	15.2	210 15.5	6.5	19 14.6	5.5	59.2
22	149 23.1	14.4	224 41.0	6.5	19 20.1	5.3	59.1
23	164 23.3	13.6	239 06.5	6.4	19 25.4	5.2	59.1
24 00	179 23.5	N11 12.7	253 31.9	6.5	N19 30.6	5.1	59.1
01	194 23.6	11.9	267 57.4	6.4	19 35.7	4.9	59.1
02	209 23.8	11.0	282 22.8	6.3	19 40.6	4.8	59.1
03	224 24.0 ··	10.2	296 48.1	6.4	19 45.4	4.7	59.1
04	239 24.1	09.3	311 13.5	6.3	19 50.1	4.6	59.1
05	254 24.3	08.5	325 38.8	6.3	19 54.7	4.4	59.1
06	269 24.5	N11 07.6	340 04.1	6.2	N19 59.1	4.3	59.1
07	284 24.6	06.7	354 29.3	6.3	20 03.4	4.2	59.1
08	299 24.8	05.9	8 54.6	6.2	20 07.6	4.0	59.1
M 09	314 25.0 ··	05.0	23 19.8	6.1	20 11.6	3.9	59.1
O 10	329 25.1	04.2	37 44.9	6.2	20 15.5	3.8	59.1
N 11	344 25.3	03.3	52 10.1	6.2	20 19.3	3.6	59.0
D 12	359 25.5	N11 02.5	66 35.3	6.1	N20 22.9	3.5	59.0
A 13	14 25.6	01.6	81 00.4	6.1	20 26.4	3.4	59.0
Y 14	29 25.8	11 00.8	95 25.5	6.1	20 29.8	3.2	59.0
15	44 26.0	10 59.9	109 50.6	6.0	20 33.0	3.1	59.0
16	59 26.1	59.0	124 15.6	6.1	20 36.1	3.0	59.0
17	74 26.3	58.2	138 40.7	6.0	20 39.1	2.8	59.0
18	89 26.5	N10 57.3	153 05.7	6.1	N20 41.9	2.7	59.0
19	104 26.6	56.5	167 30.8	6.0	20 44.6	2.6	59.0
20	119 26.8	55.6	181 55.8	6.0	20 47.2	2.4	59.0
21	134 27.0 ··	54.7	196 20.8	6.0	20 49.6	2.3	58.9
22	149 27.2	53.9	210 45.8	6.0	20 51.9	2.1	58.9
23	164 27.3	53.0	225 10.8	6.0	20 54.0	2.1	58.9
25 00	179 27.5	N10 52.2	239 35.8	5.9	N20 56.1	1.8	58.9
01	194 27.7	51.3	254 00.7	6.0	20 57.9	1.8	58.9
02	209 27.8	50.4	268 25.7	6.0	20 59.7	1.6	58.9
03	224 28.0 ··	49.6	282 50.7	6.0	21 01.3	1.4	58.9
04	239 28.2	48.7	297 15.7	5.9	21 02.7	1.4	58.9
05	254 28.3	47.9	311 40.6	6.0	21 04.1	1.2	58.9
06	269 28.5	N10 47.0	326 05.6	6.0	N21 05.3	1.0	58.9
07	284 28.7	46.1	340 30.6	5.9	21 06.3	0.9	58.8
08	299 28.9	45.3	354 55.5	6.0	21 07.2	0.8	58.8
T 09	314 29.0 ··	44.4	9 20.5	6.0	21 08.0	0.6	58.8
U 10	329 29.2	43.5	23 45.5	6.0	21 08.6	0.5	58.8
E 11	344 29.4	42.7	38 10.5	6.0	21 09.1	0.4	58.8
S 12	359 29.5	N10 41.8	52 35.5	6.0	N21 09.5	0.2	58.8
D 13	14 29.7	41.0	67 00.5	6.1	21 09.7	0.1	58.8
A 14	29 29.9	40.1	81 25.6	6.0	21 09.8	0.0	58.8
Y 15	44 30.1 ··	39.2	95 50.6	6.1	21 09.8	0.2	58.7
16	59 30.2	38.4	110 15.7	6.0	21 09.6	0.3	58.7
17	74 30.4	37.6	124 40.7	6.1	21 09.3	0.5	58.7
18	89 30.6	N10 36.6	139 05.8	6.1	N21 08.8	0.6	58.7
19	104 30.7	35.8	153 30.9	6.2	21 08.2	0.7	58.7
20	119 30.9	34.9	167 56.1	6.1	21 07.5	0.9	58.7
21	134 31.1 ··	34.0	182 21.2	6.2	21 06.6	1.0	58.7
22	149 31.3	33.2	196 46.4	6.2	21 05.6	1.1	58.7
23	164 31.4	32.3	211 11.6	6.2	21 04.5	1.3	58.6
	S.D. 15.8	d 0.9	S.D. 16.1		16.1		16.0

Moonrise

Lat.	Twilight Naut.	Civil	Sunrise	Moonrise 23	24	25	26
N 72	////	01 12	03 19	□	□	□	□
N 70	////	02 08	03 39	20 12	□	□	22 16
68	////	02 40	03 55	21 03	21 19	22 08	23 40
66	01 03	03 03	04 08	21 35	22 05	22 58	24 19
64	01 51	03 21	04 18	21 59	22 35	23 30	24 45
62	02 21	03 35	04 28	22 18	22 58	23 54	25 06
60	02 42	03 48	04 35	22 34	23 16	24 12	00 12
N 58	03 00	03 58	04 42	22 47	23 31	24 28	00 28
56	03 14	04 07	04 48	22 59	23 44	24 41	00 41
54	03 26	04 15	04 53	23 09	23 56	24 53	00 53
52	03 36	04 22	04 58	23 18	24 06	00 06	01 03
50	03 45	04 28	05 03	23 26	24 15	00 15	01 12
45	04 03	04 41	05 12	23 43	24 34	00 34	01 32
N 40	04 17	04 52	05 20	23 57	24 49	00 49	01 47
35	04 29	05 00	05 27	24 10	00 10	01 03	02 01
30	04 38	05 08	05 32	24 20	00 20	01 14	02 12
20	04 53	05 20	05 42	24 38	00 38	01 34	02 32
N 10	05 04	05 30	05 51	00 00	00 54	01 51	02 49
0	05 13	05 38	05 59	00 12	01 09	02 07	03 05
S 10	05 21	05 46	06 07	00 25	01 24	02 23	03 21
20	05 27	05 53	06 15	00 39	01 40	02 41	03 39
30	05 32	06 00	06 24	00 55	01 59	03 01	03 59
35	05 35	06 04	06 30	01 04	02 10	03 12	04 10
40	05 37	06 08	06 36	01 15	02 22	03 26	04 23
45	05 39	06 13	06 43	01 27	02 37	03 42	04 39
S 50	05 41	06 18	06 51	01 42	02 55	04 01	04 58
52	05 41	06 20	06 55	01 49	03 04	04 11	05 08
54	05 42	06 23	06 59	01 57	03 13	04 21	05 18
56	05 42	06 26	07 04	02 06	03 24	04 33	05 29
58	05 43	06 28	07 09	02 16	03 36	04 46	05 43
S 60	05 43	06 32	07 15	02 28	03 51	05 03	05 58

Moonset

Lat.	Sunset	Twilight Civil	Naut.	Moonset 23	24	25	26
N 72	20 42	22 40	////	□	□	□	□
N 70	20 22	21 51	////	17 26	□	□	21 27
68	20 07	21 20	////	16 36	18 21	19 34	20 01
66	19 54	20 58	22 51	16 04	17 36	18 43	19 22
64	19 44	20 41	22 08	15 41	17 06	18 12	18 55
62	19 35	20 27	21 40	15 22	16 43	17 48	18 34
60	19 28	20 15	21 19	15 07	16 25	17 29	18 17
N 58	19 21	20 05	21 03	14 54	16 10	17 13	18 03
56	19 15	19 56	20 49	14 43	15 57	17 00	17 50
54	19 10	19 48	20 37	14 33	15 46	16 48	17 39
52	19 05	19 42	20 27	14 25	15 36	16 38	17 30
50	19 01	19 35	20 18	14 17	15 27	16 29	17 21
45	18 52	19 23	20 00	14 00	15 08	16 09	17 03
N 40	18 44	19 12	19 46	13 47	14 53	15 54	16 48
35	18 38	19 04	19 35	13 35	14 40	15 40	16 35
30	18 32	18 56	19 26	13 25	14 29	15 29	16 24
20	18 22	18 45	19 11	13 08	14 09	15 09	16 05
N 10	18 14	18 35	19 00	12 53	13 52	14 51	15 48
0	18 06	18 27	18 51	12 39	13 37	14 35	15 33
S 10	17 58	18 19	18 44	12 25	13 21	14 19	15 17
20	17 50	18 12	18 38	12 10	13 04	14 01	15 00
30	17 41	18 05	18 33	11 53	12 45	13 41	14 41
35	17 35	18 01	18 31	11 43	12 34	13 29	14 29
40	17 29	17 57	18 28	11 32	12 21	13 16	14 16
45	17 22	17 52	18 27	11 19	12 06	13 00	14 01
S 50	17 14	17 47	18 25	11 03	11 47	12 40	13 42
52	17 10	17 45	18 24	10 55	11 38	12 31	13 33
54	17 06	17 43	18 24	10 47	11 28	12 20	13 23
56	17 02	17 40	18 23	10 37	11 17	12 09	13 11
58	16 57	17 37	18 23	10 27	11 05	11 55	12 58
S 60	16 51	17 34	18 23	10 15	10 50	11 39	12 43

SUN / MOON

Day	SUN Eqn. of Time 00ʰ	12ʰ	Mer. Pass.	MOON Mer. Pass. Upper	Lower	Age	Phase
	m s	m s	h m	h m	h m	d	
23	02 42	02 34	12 03	06 26	18 54	23	
24	02 26	02 18	12 02	07 23	19 52	24	◐
25	02 10	02 02	12 02	08 21	20 50	25	

G.M.T.	ARIES G.H.A.	VENUS −3.5 G.H.A.	Dec.	MARS +1.8 G.H.A.	Dec.	JUPITER −1.3 G.H.A.	Dec.	SATURN +1.2 G.H.A.	Dec.	STARS Name	S.H.A.	Dec.
26 00	334 09.3	145 52.1 S 3 06.6		216 32.4 N21 55.0		144 03.2 S 3 06.7		145 56.3 S 1 06.3		Acamar	315 36.6	S40 22.5
01	349 11.8	160 51.9	07.9	231 33.1	54.7	159 05.2	06.9	160 58.5	06.4	Achernar	335 44.4	S57 19.6
02	4 14.2	175 51.7	09.1	246 33.9	54.5	174 07.3	07.1	176 00.7	06.5	Acrux	173 37.1	S62 59.9
03	19 16.7	190 51.5 ··	10.4	261 34.6 ··	54.2	189 09.3 ··	07.3	191 02.9 ··	06.6	Adhara	255 31.8	S28 56.6
04	34 19.2	205 51.2	11.7	276 35.4	53.9	204 11.3	07.5	206 05.2	06.8	Aldebaran	291 17.3	N16 28.3
05	49 21.6	220 51.0	13.0	291 36.2	53.7	219 13.3	07.7	221 07.4	06.9			
06	64 24.1	235 50.8 S 3 14.3		306 36.9 N21 53.4		234 15.4 S 3 07.9		236 09.6 S 1 07.0		Alioth	166 42.3	N56 03.9
W 07	79 26.5	250 50.6	15.6	321 37.7	53.1	249 17.4	08.1	251 11.8	07.1	Alkaid	153 18.3	N49 24.7
E 08	94 29.0	265 50.4	16.9	336 38.4	52.8	264 19.4	08.3	266 14.0	07.2	Al Na'ir	28 13.6	S47 03.0
D 09	109 31.5	280 50.2 ··	18.2	351 39.2 ··	52.6	279 21.4 ··	08.5	281 16.3 ··	07.3	Alnilam	276 11.1	S 1 12.7
N 10	124 33.9	295 49.9	19.4	6 39.9	52.3	294 23.5	08.7	296 18.5	07.4	Alphard	218 20.2	S 8 34.6
E 11	139 36.4	310 49.7	20.7	21 40.7	52.0	309 25.5	08.8	311 20.7	07.5			
S 12	154 38.9	325 49.5 S 3 22.0		36 41.5 N21 51.7		324 27.5 S 3 09.0		326 22.9 S 1 07.6		Alphecca	126 31.6	N26 46.9
D 13	169 41.3	340 49.3	23.3	51 42.2	51.5	339 29.5	09.2	341 25.1	07.7	Alpheratz	358 08.3	N28 59.3
A 14	184 43.8	355 49.1	24.6	66 43.0	51.2	354 31.6	09.4	356 27.3	07.9	Altair	62 31.6	N 8 49.3
Y 15	199 46.3	10 48.9 ··	25.9	81 43.7 ··	50.9	9 33.6 ··	09.6	11 29.6 ··	08.0	Ankaa	353 39.2	S42 24.2
16	214 48.7	25 48.6	27.2	96 44.5	50.6	24 35.6	09.8	26 31.8	08.1	Antares	112 56.0	S26 23.5
17	229 51.2	40 48.4	28.4	111 45.3	50.4	39 37.6	10.0	41 34.0	08.2			
18	244 53.7	55 48.2 S 3 29.7		126 46.0 N21 50.1		54 39.7 S 3 10.2		56 36.2 S 1 08.3		Arcturus	146 18.0	N19 17.0
19	259 56.1	70 48.0	31.0	141 46.8	49.8	69 41.7	10.4	71 38.4	08.4	Atria	108 19.6	S68 59.9
20	274 58.6	85 47.8	32.3	156 47.5	49.5	84 43.7	10.6	86 40.6	08.5	Avior	234 28.5	S59 26.8
21	290 01.0	100 47.6 ··	33.6	171 48.3 ··	49.3	99 45.7 ··	10.8	101 42.9 ··	08.6	Bellatrix	278 58.1	N 6 20.0
22	305 03.5	115 47.3	34.9	186 49.1	49.0	114 47.8	11.0	116 45.1	08.7	Betelgeuse	271 27.7	N 7 24.3
23	320 06.0	130 47.1	36.2	201 49.8	48.7	129 49.8	11.1	131 47.3	08.9			
27 00	335 08.4	145 46.9 S 3 37.4		216 50.6 N21 48.4		144 51.8 S 3 11.3		146 49.5 S 1 09.0		Canopus	264 07.2	S52 40.9
01	350 10.9	160 46.7	38.7	231 51.4	48.2	159 53.8	11.5	161 51.7	09.1	Capella	281 10.5	N45 58.6
02	5 13.4	175 46.5	40.0	246 52.1	47.9	174 55.9	11.7	176 53.9	09.2	Deneb	49 47.6	N45 13.0
03	20 15.8	190 46.3 ··	41.3	261 52.9 ··	47.6	189 57.9 ··	11.9	191 56.2 ··	09.3	Denebola	182 58.7	N14 40.7
04	35 18.3	205 46.0	42.6	276 53.6	47.3	204 59.9	12.1	206 58.4	09.4	Diphda	349 19.9	S18 05.2
05	50 20.8	220 45.8	43.9	291 54.4	47.0	220 01.9	12.3	222 00.6	09.5			
06	65 23.2	235 45.6 S 3 45.2		306 55.2 N21 46.8		235 03.9 S 3 12.5		237 02.8 S 1 09.6		Dubhe	194 22.0	N61 51.2
07	80 25.7	250 45.4	46.4	321 55.9	46.5	250 06.0	12.7	252 05.0	09.7	Elnath	278 43.4	N28 35.5
T 08	95 28.1	265 45.2	47.7	336 56.7	46.2	265 08.0	12.9	267 07.2	09.8	Eltanin	90 57.2	N51 29.8
H 09	110 30.6	280 45.0 ··	49.0	351 57.5 ··	45.9	280 10.0 ··	13.1	282 09.5 ··	10.0	Enif	34 10.6	N 9 47.5
U 10	125 33.1	295 44.7	50.3	6 58.2	45.6	295 12.0	13.3	297 11.7	10.1	Fomalhaut	15 50.3	S29 43.1
R 11	140 35.5	310 44.5	51.6	21 59.0	45.4	310 14.1	13.5	312 13.9	10.2			
S 12	155 38.0	325 44.3 S 3 52.9		36 59.7 N21 45.1		325 16.1 S 3 13.6		327 16.1 S 1 10.3		Gacrux	172 28.5	S57 00.6
D 13	170 40.5	340 44.1	54.1	52 00.5	44.8	340 18.1	13.8	342 18.3	10.4	Gienah	176 17.6	S17 26.2
A 14	185 42.9	355 43.9	55.4	67 01.3	44.5	355 20.1	14.0	357 20.5	10.5	Hadar	149 22.8	S60 17.2
Y 15	200 45.4	10 43.7 ··	56.7	82 02.0 ··	44.2	10 22.1 ··	14.2	12 22.8 ··	10.6	Hamal	328 28.0	N23 22.5
16	215 47.9	25 43.4	58.0	97 02.8	44.0	25 24.2	14.4	27 25.0	10.7	Kaus Aust.	84 15.8	S34 23.7
17	230 50.3	40 43.2	3 59.3	112 03.6	43.7	40 26.2	14.6	42 27.2	10.8			
18	245 52.8	55 43.0 S 4 00.6		127 04.3 N21 43.4		55 28.2 S 3 14.8		57 29.4 S 1 11.0		Kochab	137 19.4	N74 14.3
19	260 55.3	70 42.8	01.9	142 05.1	43.1	70 30.2	15.0	72 31.6	11.1	Markab	14 02.2	N15 06.4
20	275 57.7	85 42.6	03.1	157 05.9	42.8	85 32.3	15.2	87 33.8	11.2	Menkar	314 40.4	N 4 01.1
21	291 00.2	100 42.4 ··	04.4	172 06.6 ··	42.6	100 34.3 ··	15.4	102 36.0 ··	11.3	Menkent	148 36.5	S36 16.8
22	306 02.6	115 42.1	05.7	187 07.4	42.3	115 36.3	15.6	117 38.3	11.4	Miaplacidus	221 45.7	S69 38.4
23	321 05.1	130 41.9	07.0	202 08.2	42.0	130 38.3	15.8	132 40.5	11.5			
28 00	336 07.6	145 41.7 S 4 08.3		217 08.9 N21 41.7		145 40.3 S 3 16.0		147 42.7 S 1 11.6		Mirfak	309 15.1	N49 47.5
01	351 10.0	160 41.5	09.6	232 09.7	41.4	160 42.4	16.2	162 44.9	11.7	Nunki	76 28.1	S26 19.2
02	6 12.5	175 41.3	10.8	247 10.5	41.1	175 44.4	16.3	177 47.1	11.8	Peacock	53 56.8	S56 47.8
03	21 15.0	190 41.0 ··	12.1	262 11.2 ··	40.9	190 46.4 ··	16.5	192 49.3 ··	12.0	Pollux	243 57.7	N28 04.3
04	36 17.4	205 40.8	13.4	277 12.0	40.6	205 48.4	16.7	207 51.6	12.1	Procyon	245 25.4	N 5 16.5
05	51 19.9	220 40.6	14.7	292 12.8	40.3	220 50.4	16.9	222 53.8	12.2			
06	66 22.4	235 40.4 S 4 16.0		307 13.5 N21 40.0		235 52.5 S 3 17.1		237 56.0 S 1 12.3		Rasalhague	96 28.9	N12 34.6
07	81 24.8	250 40.2	17.2	322 14.3	39.7	250 54.5	17.3	252 58.2	12.4	Regulus	208 09.6	N12 03.6
08	96 27.3	265 40.0	18.5	337 15.1	39.4	265 56.5	17.5	268 00.4	12.5	Rigel	281 35.5	S 8 13.2
F 09	111 29.8	280 39.7 ··	19.8	352 15.8 ··	39.1	280 58.5 ··	17.7	283 02.6 ··	12.6	Rigil Kent.	140 25.2	S60 45.6
R 10	126 32.2	295 39.5	21.1	7 16.6	38.9	296 00.5	17.9	298 04.8	12.7	Sabik	102 40.3	S15 42.1
I 11	141 34.7	310 39.3	22.4	22 17.4	38.6	311 02.6	18.1	313 07.1	12.8			
D 12	156 37.1	325 39.1 S 4 23.7		37 18.1 N21 38.3		326 04.6 S 3 18.3		328 09.3 S 1 13.0		Schedar	350 07.8	N56 26.0
A 13	171 39.6	340 38.9	24.9	52 18.9	38.0	341 06.6	18.5	343 11.5	13.1	Shaula	96 54.7	S37 05.5
Y 14	186 42.1	355 38.6	26.2	67 19.7	37.7	356 08.6	18.7	358 13.7	13.2	Sirius	258 55.3	S16 41.3
15	201 44.5	10 38.4 ··	27.5	82 20.5 ··	37.4	11 10.6 ··	18.9	13 15.9 ··	13.3	Spica	158 57.1	S11 03.8
16	216 47.0	25 38.2	28.8	97 21.2	37.1	26 12.7	19.1	28 18.1	13.4	Suhail	223 10.7	S43 21.3
17	231 49.5	40 38.0	30.1	112 22.0	36.8	41 14.7	19.2	43 20.3	13.5			
18	246 51.9	55 37.8 S 4 31.3		127 22.8 N21 36.6		56 16.7 S 3 19.4		58 22.6 S 1 13.6		Vega	80 55.1	N38 46.3
19	261 54.4	70 37.6	32.6	142 23.5	36.3	71 18.7	19.6	73 24.8	13.7	Zuben'ubi	137 32.4	S15 57.8
20	276 56.9	85 37.3	33.9	157 24.3	36.0	86 20.7	19.8	88 27.0	13.9		S.H.A.	Mer. Pass.
21	291 59.3	100 37.1 ··	35.2	172 25.1 ··	35.7	101 22.8 ··	20.0	103 29.2 ··	14.0	Venus	170 38.5	14 17
22	307 01.8	115 36.9	36.5	187 25.8	35.4	116 24.8	20.2	118 31.4	14.1	Mars	241 42.2	9 32
23	322 04.2	130 36.7	37.7	202 26.6	35.1	131 26.8	20.4	133 33.6	14.2	Jupiter	169 43.4	14 19
Mer. Pass.	1 39.2	v −0.2 d 1.3		v 0.8 d 0.3		v 2.0 d 0.2		v 2.2 d 0.1		Saturn	171 41.1	14 11

G.M.T.	SUN G.H.A.	Dec.	MOON G.H.A.	v	Dec.	d	H.P.
26 00	179 31.6	N10 31.4	225 36.8	6.2	N21 03.2	1.4	58.6
01	194 31.8	30.6	240 02.0	6.3	21 01.8	1.6	58.6
02	209 32.0	29.7	254 27.3	6.3	21 00.2	1.6	58.6
03	224 32.1	·· 28.8	268 52.6	6.4	20 58.6	1.9	58.6
04	239 32.3	28.0	283 18.0	6.3	20 56.7	1.9	58.6
05	254 32.5	27.1	297 43.3	6.4	20 54.8	2.1	58.6
06	269 32.7	N10 26.2	312 08.7	6.4	N20 52.7	2.2	58.5
W 07	284 32.8	25.4	326 34.1	6.5	20 50.5	2.3	58.5
E 08	299 33.0	24.5	340 59.6	6.5	20 48.2	2.5	58.5
D 09	314 33.2	·· 23.6	355 25.1	6.6	20 45.7	2.6	58.5
N 10	329 33.4	22.7	9 50.7	6.6	20 43.1	2.7	58.5
E 11	344 33.5	21.9	24 16.2	6.6	20 40.4	2.9	58.5
S 12	359 33.7	N10 21.0	38 41.8	6.7	N20 37.5	3.0	58.4
D 13	14 33.9	20.1	53 07.5	6.7	20 34.5	3.1	58.4
A 14	29 34.1	19.3	67 33.2	6.8	20 31.4	3.3	58.4
Y 15	44 34.2	·· 18.4	81 59.0	6.7	20 28.1	3.3	58.4
16	59 34.4	17.5	96 24.7	6.9	20 24.8	3.5	58.4
17	74 34.6	16.6	110 50.6	6.9	20 21.3	3.7	58.4
18	89 34.8	N10 15.8	125 16.5	6.9	N20 17.6	3.7	58.3
19	104 34.9	14.9	139 42.4	7.0	20 13.9	3.9	58.3
20	119 35.1	14.0	154 08.4	7.0	20 10.0	4.0	58.3
21	134 35.3	·· 13.2	168 34.4	7.1	20 06.0	4.1	58.3
22	149 35.5	12.3	183 00.5	7.1	20 01.9	4.3	58.3
23	164 35.7	11.4	197 26.6	7.2	19 57.6	4.3	58.3
27 00	179 35.8	N10 10.5	211 52.8	7.2	N19 53.3	4.5	58.2
01	194 36.0	09.7	226 19.0	7.3	19 48.8	4.6	58.2
02	209 36.2	08.8	240 45.3	7.3	19 44.2	4.7	58.2
03	224 36.4	·· 07.9	255 11.6	7.4	19 39.5	4.9	58.2
04	239 36.5	07.0	269 38.0	7.5	19 34.6	4.9	58.2
05	254 36.7	06.2	284 04.5	7.5	19 29.7	5.1	58.2
06	269 36.9	N10 05.3	298 31.0	7.5	N19 24.6	5.2	58.1
07	284 37.1	04.4	312 57.5	7.7	19 19.4	5.3	58.1
T 08	299 37.3	03.5	327 24.2	7.7	19 14.1	5.4	58.1
H 09	314 37.4	·· 02.7	341 50.9	7.7	19 08.7	5.5	58.1
U 10	329 37.6	01.8	356 17.6	7.8	19 03.2	5.7	58.1
R 11	344 37.8	00.9	10 44.4	7.9	18 57.5	5.7	58.1
S 12	359 38.0	N10 00.0	25 11.3	7.9	N18 51.8	5.9	58.0
D 13	14 38.2	9 59.1	39 38.2	8.0	18 45.9	5.9	58.0
A 14	29 38.3	58.3	54 05.2	8.1	18 40.0	6.1	58.0
Y 15	44 38.5	·· 57.4	68 32.3	8.1	18 33.9	6.2	58.0
16	59 38.7	56.5	82 59.4	8.2	18 27.7	6.3	57.9
17	74 38.9	55.6	97 26.6	8.2	18 21.4	6.4	57.9
18	89 39.1	N 9 54.8	111 53.8	8.4	N18 15.0	6.5	57.9
19	104 39.2	53.9	126 21.2	8.4	18 08.5	6.6	57.9
20	119 39.4	53.0	140 48.6	8.4	18 01.9	6.7	57.9
21	134 39.6	·· 52.1	155 16.0	8.5	17 55.2	6.8	57.8
22	149 39.8	51.2	169 43.5	8.6	17 48.4	6.8	57.8
23	164 40.0	50.4	184 11.1	8.7	17 41.6	7.0	57.8
28 00	179 40.1	N 9 49.5	198 38.8	8.7	N17 34.6	7.1	57.8
01	194 40.3	48.6	213 06.5	8.8	17 27.5	7.2	57.8
02	209 40.5	47.7	227 34.3	8.8	17 20.3	7.3	57.7
03	224 40.7	·· 46.8	242 02.1	9.0	17 13.0	7.4	57.7
04	239 40.9	46.0	256 30.1	9.0	17 05.6	7.4	57.7
05	254 41.1	45.1	270 58.1	9.0	16 58.2	7.6	57.7
06	269 41.2	N 9 44.2	285 26.1	9.2	N16 50.6	7.6	57.7
07	284 41.4	43.3	299 54.3	9.2	16 43.0	7.8	57.6
08	299 41.6	42.4	314 22.5	9.3	16 35.2	7.8	57.6
F 09	314 41.8	·· 41.5	328 50.8	9.3	16 27.4	7.9	57.6
R 10	329 42.0	40.7	343 19.1	9.5	16 19.5	8.0	57.6
I 11	344 42.1	39.8	357 47.6	9.5	16 11.5	8.1	57.5
D 12	359 42.3	N 9 38.9	12 16.1	9.5	N16 03.4	8.2	57.5
A 13	14 42.5	38.0	26 44.6	9.7	15 55.2	8.2	57.5
Y 14	29 42.7	37.1	41 13.3	9.7	15 47.0	8.3	57.5
15	44 42.9	·· 36.2	55 42.0	9.7	15 38.7	8.4	57.5
16	59 43.1	35.3	70 10.7	9.9	15 30.3	8.5	57.4
17	74 43.3	34.5	84 39.6	9.9	15 21.8	8.6	57.4
18	89 43.4	N 9 33.6	99 08.5	10.0	N15 13.2	8.6	57.4
19	104 43.6	32.7	113 37.5	10.1	15 04.6	8.7	57.4
20	119 43.8	31.8	128 06.6	10.1	14 55.9	8.8	57.3
21	134 44.0	·· 30.9	142 35.7	10.2	14 47.1	8.9	57.3
22	149 44.2	30.0	157 04.9	10.3	14 38.2	8.9	57.3
23	164 44.4	29.1	171 34.2	10.3	14 29.3	9.0	57.3
	S.D. 15.9 *d* 0.9		S.D. 15.9		15.8		15.7

Lat.	Twilight Naut.	Civil	Sunrise	Moonrise 26	27	28	29
N 72	////	01 48	03 35	▭	23 42	26 23	02 23
N 70	////	02 28	03 53	22 16	24 51	00 51	02 52
68	////	02 55	04 07	23 40	25 27	01 27	03 14
66	01 33	03 16	04 18	24 19	00 19	01 53	03 30
64	02 09	03 32	04 27	24 45	00 45	02 13	03 44
62	02 34	03 45	04 35	25 06	01 06	02 29	03 55
60	02 53	03 56	04 42	00 12	01 23	02 42	04 05
N 58	03 09	04 05	04 49	00 28	01 37	02 54	04 14
56	03 22	04 13	04 54	00 41	01 49	03 04	04 21
54	03 33	04 21	04 59	00 53	02 00	03 13	04 28
52	03 42	04 27	05 03	01 03	02 09	03 20	04 34
50	03 50	04 33	05 07	01 12	02 18	03 27	04 39
45	04 08	04 45	05 16	01 32	02 35	03 42	04 50
N 40	04 21	04 55	05 23	01 47	02 50	03 55	05 00
35	04 32	05 03	05 29	02 01	03 02	04 05	05 08
30	04 40	05 09	05 34	02 12	03 13	04 14	05 15
20	04 54	05 21	05 43	02 32	03 31	04 30	05 27
N 10	05 05	05 30	05 51	02 49	03 47	04 44	05 38
0	05 13	05 37	05 58	03 05	04 02	04 57	05 48
S 10	05 19	05 44	06 05	03 21	04 17	05 09	05 58
20	05 25	05 50	06 13	03 39	04 33	05 23	06 09
30	05 29	05 57	06 21	03 59	04 51	05 39	06 21
35	05 31	06 00	06 26	04 10	05 02	05 48	06 28
40	05 33	06 04	06 31	04 23	05 14	05 58	06 36
45	05 34	06 08	06 38	04 39	05 28	06 10	06 45
S 50	05 35	06 12	06 45	04 58	05 46	06 24	06 56
52	05 35	06 14	06 48	05 08	05 54	06 31	07 01
54	05 35	06 16	06 52	05 18	06 03	06 39	07 07
56	05 35	06 18	06 56	05 29	06 13	06 47	07 13
58	05 35	06 21	07 01	05 43	06 25	06 56	07 20
S 60	05 35	06 23	07 06	05 58	06 39	07 07	07 28

Lat.	Sunset	Twilight Civil	Naut.	Moonset 26	27	28	29
N 72	20 24	22 07	////	▭	21 56	21 04	20 42
N 70	20 07	21 29	////	21 27	20 46	20 33	20 25
68	19 54	21 04	23 33	20 01	20 09	20 11	20 11
66	19 43	20 44	22 23	19 22	19 42	19 53	19 59
64	19 33	20 29	21 49	18 55	19 22	19 39	19 49
62	19 26	20 16	21 25	18 34	19 05	19 26	19 41
60	19 19	20 05	21 07	18 17	18 51	19 16	19 34
N 58	19 13	19 56	20 52	18 03	18 39	19 07	19 28
56	19 08	19 48	20 39	17 50	18 29	18 59	19 22
54	19 03	19 41	20 28	17 39	18 20	18 51	19 17
52	18 59	19 35	20 19	17 30	18 12	18 45	19 12
50	18 55	19 29	20 11	17 21	18 04	18 39	19 08
45	18 46	19 17	19 54	17 03	17 48	18 26	18 59
N 40	18 40	19 08	19 41	16 48	17 35	18 16	18 51
35	18 34	19 00	19 31	16 35	17 24	18 07	18 45
30	18 28	18 53	19 22	16 24	17 14	17 59	18 39
20	18 20	18 42	19 08	16 05	16 57	17 45	18 29
N 10	18 12	18 33	18 58	15 48	16 42	17 33	18 20
0	18 05	18 26	18 50	15 33	16 29	17 22	18 12
S 10	17 58	18 19	18 44	15 17	16 15	17 10	18 03
20	17 50	18 13	18 38	15 00	15 59	16 58	17 54
30	17 42	18 06	18 34	14 41	15 42	16 44	17 44
35	17 37	18 03	18 33	14 29	15 32	16 35	17 38
40	17 32	18 00	18 31	14 16	15 20	16 26	17 31
45	17 26	17 56	18 30	14 01	15 07	16 15	17 23
S 50	17 19	17 51	18 29	13 42	14 50	16 01	17 13
52	17 15	17 50	18 29	13 33	14 42	15 55	17 08
54	17 12	17 48	18 29	13 23	14 33	15 48	17 03
56	17 08	17 45	18 29	13 11	14 23	15 40	16 58
58	17 03	17 41	18 29	12 58	14 11	15 31	16 51
S 60	16 58	17 41	18 29	12 43	13 59	15 21	16 44

Day	SUN Eqn. of Time 00h	12h	Mer. Pass.	MOON Mer. Pass. Upper	Lower	Age	Phase
	m s	m s	h m	h m	h m	d	
26	01 54	01 46	12 02	09 19	21 47	26	
27	01 37	01 28	12 01	10 15	22 43	27	●
28	01 20	01 11	12 01	11 09	23 35	28	

G.M.T.	ARIES G.H.A.	VENUS −3.5 G.H.A.	Dec.	MARS +1.8 G.H.A.	Dec.	JUPITER −1.3 G.H.A.	Dec.	SATURN +1.2 G.H.A.	Dec.	STARS Name	S.H.A.	Dec.
29 00	337 06.7	145 36.5 S 4	39.0	217 27.4 N21	34.8	146 28.8 S 3	20.6	148 35.8 S 1	14.3	Acamar	315 36.6	S40 22.5
01	352 09.2	160 36.2	40.3	232 28.2	34.5	161 30.8	20.8	163 38.0	14.4	Achernar	335 44.4	S57 19.6
02	7 11.6	175 36.0	41.6	247 28.9	34.2	176 32.9	21.0	178 40.3	14.5	Acrux	173 37.1	S62 59.8
03	22 14.1	190 35.8 ··	42.9	262 29.7 ··	34.0	191 34.9 ··	21.2	193 42.5 ··	14.6	Adhara	255 31.8	S28 56.6
04	37 16.6	205 35.6	44.1	277 30.5	33.7	206 36.9	21.4	208 44.7	14.7	Aldebaran	291 17.3	N16 28.3
05	52 19.0	220 35.4	45.4	292 31.3	33.4	221 38.9	21.6	223 46.9	14.9			
06	67 21.5	235 35.2 S 4	46.7	307 32.0 N21	33.1	236 40.9 S 3	21.8	238 49.1 S 1	15.0	Alioth	166 42.4	N56 03.9
07	82 24.0	250 34.9	48.0	322 32.8	32.8	251 42.9	22.0	253 51.3	15.1	Alkaid	153 18.3	N49 24.7
S 08	97 26.4	265 34.7	49.3	337 33.6	32.5	266 45.0	22.2	268 53.5	15.2	Al Na'ir	28 13.6	S47 03.0
A 09	112 28.9	280 34.5 ··	50.5	352 34.3 ··	32.2	281 47.0 ··	22.4	283 55.8 ··	15.3	Alnilam	276 11.1	S 1 12.7
T 10	127 31.4	295 34.3	51.8	7 35.1	31.9	296 49.0	22.5	298 58.0	15.4	Alphard	218 20.2	S 8 34.6
U 11	142 33.8	310 34.1	53.1	22 35.9	31.6	311 51.0	22.7	314 00.2	15.5			
R 12	157 36.3	325 33.8 S 4	54.4	37 36.7 N21	31.3	326 53.0 S 3	22.9	329 02.4 S 1	15.6	Alphecca	126 31.6	N26 46.9
D 13	172 38.7	340 33.6	55.7	52 37.4	31.0	341 55.1	23.1	344 04.6	15.8	Alpheratz	358 08.3	N28 59.3
A 14	187 41.2	355 33.4	56.9	67 38.2	30.7	356 57.1	23.3	359 06.8	15.9	Altair	62 31.6	N 8 49.3
Y 15	202 43.7	10 33.2 ··	58.2	82 39.0 ··	30.4	11 59.1 ··	23.5	14 09.0 ··	16.0	Ankaa	353 39.2	S42 24.2
16	217 46.1	25 33.0 4	59.5	97 39.8	30.2	27 01.1	23.7	29 11.2	16.1	Antares	112 56.0	S26 23.5
17	232 48.6	40 32.7 5	00.8	112 40.5	29.9	42 03.1	23.9	44 13.5	16.2			
18	247 51.1	55 32.5 S 5	02.0	127 41.3 N21	29.6	57 05.1 S 3	24.1	59 15.7 S 1	16.3	Arcturus	146 18.0	N19 17.0
19	262 53.5	70 32.3	03.3	142 42.1	29.3	72 07.2	24.3	74 17.9	16.4	Atria	108 19.6	S68 59.9
20	277 56.0	85 32.1	04.6	157 42.9	29.0	87 09.2	24.5	89 20.1	16.5	Avior	234 28.5	S59 26.8
21	292 58.5	100 31.9 ··	05.9	172 43.6 ··	28.7	102 11.2 ··	24.7	104 22.3 ··	16.6	Bellatrix	278 58.1	N 6 20.1
22	308 00.9	115 31.6	07.2	187 44.4	28.4	117 13.2	24.9	119 24.5	16.8	Betelgeuse	271 27.7	N 7 24.3
23	323 03.4	130 31.4	08.4	202 45.2	28.1	132 15.2	25.1	134 26.7	16.9			
30 00	338 05.9	145 31.2 S 5	09.7	217 46.0 N21	27.8	147 17.2 S 3	25.3	149 28.9 S 1	17.0	Canopus	264 07.2	S52 40.9
01	353 08.3	160 31.0	11.0	232 46.7	27.5	162 19.3	25.5	164 31.1	17.1	Capella	281 10.4	N45 58.6
02	8 10.8	175 30.8	12.3	247 47.5	27.2	177 21.3	25.7	179 33.4	17.2	Deneb	49 47.6	N45 13.0
03	23 13.2	190 30.5 ··	13.5	262 48.3 ··	26.9	192 23.3 ··	25.9	194 35.6 ··	17.3	Denebola	182 58.7	N14 40.7
04	38 15.7	205 30.3	14.8	277 49.1	26.6	207 25.3	26.0	209 37.8	17.4	Diphda	349 19.9	S18 05.2
05	53 18.2	220 30.1	16.1	292 49.9	26.3	222 27.3	26.2	224 40.0	17.5			
06	68 20.6	235 29.9 S 5	17.4	307 50.6 N21	26.0	237 29.3 S 3	26.4	239 42.2 S 1	17.7	Dubhe	194 22.0	N61 51.2
07	83 23.1	250 29.7	18.6	322 51.4	25.7	252 31.3	26.6	254 44.4	17.8	Elnath	278 43.4	N28 35.5
08	98 25.6	265 29.4	19.9	337 52.2	25.4	267 33.4	26.8	269 46.6	17.9	Eltanin	90 57.2	N51 29.8
S 09	113 28.0	280 29.2 ··	21.2	352 53.0 ··	25.1	282 35.4 ··	27.0	284 48.8 ··	18.0	Enif	34 10.6	N 9 47.5
U 10	128 30.5	295 29.0	22.5	7 53.7	24.8	297 37.4	27.2	299 51.0	18.1	Fomalhaut	15 50.3	S29 43.1
N 11	143 33.0	310 28.8	23.7	22 54.5	24.5	312 39.4	27.4	314 53.3	18.2			
D 12	158 35.4	325 28.6 S 5	25.0	37 55.3 N21	24.2	327 41.4 S 3	27.6	329 55.5 S 1	18.3	Gacrux	172 28.5	S57 00.6
A 13	173 37.9	340 28.3	26.3	52 56.1	23.9	342 43.4	27.8	344 57.7	18.4	Gienah	176 17.6	S17 26.2
Y 14	188 40.3	355 28.1	27.6	67 56.9	23.6	357 45.5	28.0	359 59.9	18.6	Hadar	149 22.8	S60 17.2
15	203 42.8	10 27.9 ··	28.8	82 57.6 ··	23.3	12 47.5 ··	28.2	15 02.1 ··	18.7	Hamal	328 28.0	N23 22.5
16	218 45.3	25 27.7	30.1	97 58.4	23.0	27 49.5	28.4	30 04.3	18.8	Kaus Aust.	84 15.8	S34 23.7
17	233 47.7	40 27.4	31.4	112 59.2	22.7	42 51.5	28.6	45 06.5	18.9			
18	248 50.2	55 27.2 S 5	32.7	128 00.0 N21	22.4	57 53.5 S 3	28.8	60 08.7 S 1	19.0	Kochab	137 19.4	N74 14.3
19	263 52.7	70 27.0	33.9	143 00.8	22.1	72 55.5	29.0	75 10.9	19.1	Markab	14 02.2	N15 06.4
20	278 55.1	85 26.8	35.2	158 01.5	21.8	87 57.5	29.2	90 13.2	19.2	Menkar	314 40.3	N 4 01.1
21	293 57.6	100 26.6 ··	36.5	173 02.3 ··	21.5	102 59.6 ··	29.4	105 15.4 ··	19.3	Menkent	148 36.5	S36 16.8
22	309 00.1	115 26.3	37.7	188 03.1	21.2	118 01.6	29.6	120 17.6	19.5	Miaplacidus	221 45.7	S69 38.3
23	324 02.5	130 26.1	39.0	203 03.9	20.9	133 03.6	29.8	135 19.8	19.6			
31 00	339 05.0	145 25.9 S 5	40.3	218 04.7 N21	20.6	148 05.6 S 3	29.9	150 22.0 S 1	19.7	Mirfak	309 15.0	N49 47.6
01	354 07.5	160 25.7	41.6	233 05.5	20.3	163 07.6	30.1	165 24.2	19.8	Nunki	76 28.1	S26 19.2
02	9 09.9	175 25.4	42.8	248 06.2	20.0	178 09.6	30.3	180 26.4	19.9	Peacock	53 56.8	S56 47.8
03	24 12.4	190 25.2 ··	44.1	263 07.0 ··	19.7	193 11.6 ··	30.5	195 28.6 ··	20.0	Pollux	243 57.6	N28 04.3
04	39 14.8	205 25.0	45.4	278 07.8	19.4	208 13.7	30.7	210 30.8	20.1	Procyon	245 25.3	N 5 16.5
05	54 17.3	220 24.8	46.7	293 08.6	19.1	223 15.7	30.9	225 33.0	20.2			
06	69 19.8	235 24.6 S 5	47.9	308 09.4 N21	18.8	238 17.7 S 3	31.1	240 35.3 S 1	20.4	Rasalhague	96 28.9	N12 34.6
07	84 22.2	250 24.3	49.2	323 10.2	18.5	253 19.7	31.3	255 37.5	20.5	Regulus	208 09.6	N12 03.6
08	99 24.7	265 24.1	50.5	338 10.9	18.2	268 21.7	31.5	270 39.7	20.6	Rigel	281 35.5	S 8 13.2
M 09	114 27.2	280 23.9 ··	51.7	353 11.7 ··	17.9	283 23.7 ··	31.7	285 41.9 ··	20.7	Rigil Kent.	140 25.2	S60 45.6
O 10	129 29.6	295 23.7	53.0	8 12.5	17.6	298 25.7	31.9	300 44.1	20.8	Sabik	102 40.3	S15 42.1
N 11	144 32.1	310 23.4	54.3	23 13.3	17.3	313 27.7	32.1	315 46.3	20.9			
D 12	159 34.6	325 23.2 S 5	55.6	38 14.1 N21	17.0	328 29.8 S 3	32.3	330 48.5 S 1	21.0	Schedar	350 07.8	N56 26.0
A 13	174 37.0	340 23.0	56.8	53 14.9	16.7	343 31.8	32.5	345 50.7	21.2	Shaula	96 54.7	S37 05.5
Y 14	189 39.5	355 22.8	58.1	68 15.6	16.4	358 33.8	32.7	0 52.9	21.3	Sirius	258 55.3	S16 41.3
15	204 42.0	10 22.6 5	59.4	83 16.4 ··	16.1	13 35.8 ··	32.9	15 55.1 ··	21.4	Spica	158 57.1	S11 03.8
16	219 44.4	25 22.3 6	00.6	98 17.2	15.8	28 37.8	33.1	30 57.4	21.5	Suhail	223 10.7	S43 21.3
17	234 46.9	40 22.1	01.9	113 18.0	15.5	43 39.8	33.3	45 59.6	21.6			
18	249 49.3	55 21.9 S 6	03.2	128 18.8 N21	15.2	58 41.8 S 3	33.5	61 01.8 S 1	21.7	Vega	80 55.2	N38 46.3
19	264 51.8	70 21.7	04.4	143 19.6	14.8	73 43.8	33.7	76 04.0	21.8	Zuben'ubi	137 32.4	S15 57.8
20	279 54.3	85 21.4	05.7	158 20.4	14.5	88 45.9	33.9	91 06.2	21.9			
21	294 56.7	100 21.2 ··	07.0	173 21.1 ··	14.2	103 47.9 ··	34.1	106 08.4 ··	22.1	Venus	167 25.3	14 18
22	309 59.2	115 21.0	08.2	188 21.9	13.9	118 49.9	34.3	121 10.6	22.2	Mars	239 40.1	9 28
23	325 01.7	130 20.8	09.5	203 22.7	13.6	133 51.9	34.4	136 12.8	22.3	Jupiter	169 11.4	14 09
Mer. Pass.	1 27.4	v −0.2	d 1.3	v 0.8	d 0.3	v 2.0	d 0.2	v 2.2	d 0.1	Saturn	171 23.1	14 00

S.H.A. Mer. Pass. (bottom-right block):
Venus 167 25.3   14 18
Mars 239 40.1   9 28
Jupiter 169 11.4   14 09
Saturn 171 23.1   14 00

SUN / MOON

G.M.T.	SUN G.H.A.	SUN Dec.	MOON G.H.A.	v	MOON Dec.	d	H.P.
29 00	179 44.5	N 9 28.3	186 03.5	10.4	N14 20.3	9.1	57.3
01	194 44.7	27.4	200 32.9	10.5	14 11.2	9.1	57.2
02	209 44.9	26.5	215 02.4	10.6	14 02.1	9.3	57.2
03	224 45.1 ··	25.6	229 32.0	10.6	13 52.8	9.2	57.2
04	239 45.3	24.7	244 01.6	10.7	13 43.6	9.4	57.2
05	254 45.5	23.8	258 31.3	10.8	13 34.2	9.4	57.1
06	269 45.7	N 9 22.9	273 01.1	10.8	N13 24.8	9.4	57.1
07	284 45.8	22.0	287 30.9	10.9	13 15.4	9.6	57.1
S 08	299 46.0	21.2	302 00.8	11.0	13 05.8	9.6	57.1
A 09	314 46.2 ··	20.3	316 30.8	11.0	12 56.2	9.6	57.0
T 10	329 46.4	19.4	331 00.8	11.1	12 46.6	9.7	57.0
U 11	344 46.6	18.5	345 30.9	11.2	12 36.9	9.8	57.0
R 12	359 46.8	N 9 17.6	0 01.1	11.3	N12 27.1	9.8	57.0
D 13	14 47.0	16.7	14 31.4	11.3	12 17.3	9.9	57.0
A 14	29 47.2	15.8	29 01.7	11.4	12 07.4	9.9	56.9
Y 15	44 47.3 ··	14.9	43 32.1	11.4	11 57.5	10.0	56.9
16	59 47.5	14.0	58 02.5	11.5	11 47.5	10.0	56.9
17	74 47.7	13.1	72 33.0	11.6	11 37.5	10.1	56.9
18	89 47.9	N 9 12.2	87 03.6	11.6	N11 27.4	10.1	56.8
19	104 48.1	11.4	101 34.2	11.8	11 17.3	10.2	56.8
20	119 48.3	10.5	116 05.0	11.7	11 07.1	10.2	56.8
21	134 48.5 ··	09.6	130 35.7	11.9	10 56.9	10.3	56.8
22	149 48.7	08.7	145 06.6	11.9	10 46.6	10.3	56.7
23	164 48.8	07.8	159 37.5	11.9	10 36.3	10.4	56.7
30 00	179 49.0	N 9 06.9	174 08.4	12.1	N10 25.9	10.4	56.7
01	194 49.2	06.0	188 39.5	12.0	10 15.5	10.4	56.7
02	209 49.4	05.1	203 10.5	12.2	10 05.1	10.5	56.6
03	224 49.6 ··	04.2	217 41.7	12.2	9 54.6	10.5	56.6
04	239 49.8	03.3	232 12.9	12.3	9 44.1	10.6	56.6
05	254 50.0	02.4	246 44.2	12.3	9 33.5	10.6	56.6
06	269 50.2	N 9 01.5	261 15.5	12.4	N 9 22.9	10.6	56.5
07	284 50.4	9 00.6	275 46.9	12.5	9 12.3	10.7	56.5
S 08	299 50.5	8 59.7	290 18.4	12.5	9 01.6	10.7	56.5
U 09	314 50.7 ··	58.8	304 49.9	12.5	8 50.9	10.7	56.5
N 10	329 50.9	57.9	319 21.4	12.7	8 40.2	10.8	56.4
D 11	344 51.1	57.1	333 53.1	12.6	8 29.4	10.8	56.4
A 12	359 51.3	N 8 56.2	348 24.7	12.8	N 8 18.6	10.8	56.4
Y 13	14 51.5	55.3	2 56.5	12.8	8 07.8	10.9	56.4
14	29 51.7	54.4	17 28.3	12.8	7 56.9	10.9	56.3
15	44 51.9 ··	53.5	32 00.1	12.9	7 46.0	10.9	56.3
16	59 52.1	52.6	46 32.0	13.0	7 35.1	10.9	56.3
17	74 52.3	51.7	61 04.0	13.0	7 24.2	11.0	56.3
18	89 52.5	N 8 50.8	75 36.0	13.0	N 7 13.2	11.0	56.2
19	104 52.6	49.9	90 08.0	13.1	7 02.2	11.0	56.2
20	119 52.8	49.0	104 40.1	13.2	6 51.2	11.0	56.2
21	134 53.0 ··	48.1	119 12.3	13.2	6 40.2	11.1	56.2
22	149 53.2	47.2	133 44.5	13.3	6 29.1	11.1	56.1
23	164 53.4	46.3	148 16.8	13.3	6 18.1	11.1	56.1
31 00	179 53.6	N 8 45.4	162 49.1	13.3	N 6 07.0	11.1	56.1
01	194 53.8	44.5	177 21.4	13.4	5 55.9	11.2	56.1
02	209 54.0	43.6	191 53.8	13.5	5 44.7	11.1	56.1
03	224 54.2 ··	42.7	206 26.3	13.5	5 33.6	11.2	56.0
04	239 54.4	41.8	220 58.8	13.5	5 22.4	11.1	56.0
05	254 54.6	40.9	235 31.3	13.6	5 11.3	11.2	56.0
06	269 54.8	N 8 40.0	250 03.9	13.7	N 5 00.1	11.2	56.0
07	284 55.0	39.1	264 36.6	13.6	4 48.9	11.2	55.9
08	299 55.1	38.2	279 09.2	13.8	4 37.7	11.3	55.9
M 09	314 55.3 ··	37.3	293 42.0	13.7	4 26.4	11.2	55.9
O 10	329 55.5	36.4	308 14.7	13.8	4 15.2	11.2	55.9
N 11	344 55.7	35.5	322 47.5	13.9	4 04.0	11.3	55.8
D 12	359 55.9	N 8 34.6	337 20.4	13.8	N 3 52.7	11.2	55.8
A 13	14 56.1	33.7	351 53.2	14.0	3 41.5	11.3	55.8
Y 14	29 56.3	32.8	6 26.2	13.9	3 30.2	11.3	55.8
15	44 56.5 ··	31.9	20 59.1	14.0	3 18.9	11.3	55.7
16	59 56.7	31.0	35 32.1	14.1	3 07.6	11.2	55.7
17	74 56.9	30.1	50 05.2	14.0	2 56.4	11.3	55.7
18	89 57.1	N 8 29.2	64 38.2	14.1	N 2 45.1	11.3	55.7
19	104 57.3	28.2	79 11.3	14.2	2 33.8	11.3	55.6
20	119 57.5	27.3	93 44.5	14.2	2 22.5	11.3	55.6
21	134 57.7 ··	26.4	108 17.7	14.2	2 11.2	11.2	55.6
22	149 57.9	25.5	122 50.9	14.2	2 00.0	11.3	55.6
23	164 58.1	24.6	137 24.1	14.3	1 48.7	11.3	55.5
	S.D. 15.9	d 0.9	S.D. 15.5		15.4		15.2

Twilight / Sunrise / Moonrise

Lat.	Naut.	Civil	Sunrise	Moonrise 29	30	31	1
N 72	////	02 14	03 50	02 23	04 28	06 20	08 07
N 70	////	02 47	04 06	02 52	04 43	06 27	08 07
68	01 07	03 10	04 18	03 14	04 56	06 33	08 07
66	01 56	03 28	04 28	03 30	05 06	06 38	08 07
64	02 25	03 42	04 36	03 44	05 14	06 42	08 07
62	02 47	03 54	04 43	03 55	05 21	06 45	08 07
60	03 04	04 04	04 50	04 05	05 28	06 48	08 07
N 58	03 18	04 13	04 55	04 14	05 33	06 51	08 07
56	03 29	04 20	05 00	04 21	05 38	06 53	08 07
54	03 40	04 27	05 04	04 28	05 42	06 55	08 07
52	03 48	04 32	05 08	04 34	05 46	06 57	08 07
50	03 56	04 38	05 12	04 39	05 50	06 59	08 07
45	04 12	04 49	05 19	04 50	05 58	07 03	08 07
N 40	04 24	04 58	05 26	05 00	06 04	07 06	08 07
35	04 34	05 05	05 31	05 08	06 09	07 09	08 07
30	04 42	05 11	05 36	05 15	06 14	07 11	08 07
20	04 55	05 21	05 44	05 27	06 23	07 16	08 07
N 10	05 05	05 30	05 51	05 38	06 30	07 19	08 07
0	05 12	05 36	05 57	05 48	06 37	07 23	08 07
S 10	05 18	05 42	06 04	05 58	06 43	07 26	08 07
20	05 22	05 48	06 10	06 09	06 51	07 30	08 07
30	05 26	05 54	06 18	06 21	06 59	07 34	08 07
35	05 27	05 57	06 22	06 28	07 04	07 36	08 07
40	05 28	06 00	06 27	06 36	07 09	07 39	08 07
45	05 29	06 03	06 32	06 45	07 15	07 42	08 08
S 50	05 29	06 06	06 39	06 56	07 23	07 46	08 08
52	05 29	06 08	06 42	07 01	07 26	07 48	08 08
54	05 29	06 09	06 45	07 07	07 30	07 50	08 08
56	05 28	06 11	06 49	07 13	07 34	07 52	08 08
58	05 28	06 13	06 53	07 20	07 38	07 54	08 08
S 60	05 27	06 15	06 57	07 28	07 43	07 56	08 08

Sunset / Twilight / Moonset

Lat.	Sunset	Civil	Naut.	Moonset 29	30	31	1
N 72	20 07	21 40	////	20 42	20 26	20 13	20 00
N 70	19 52	21 10	////	20 25	20 17	20 09	20 03
68	19 41	20 47	22 43	20 11	20 09	20 07	20 05
66	19 31	20 30	22 00	19 59	20 03	20 05	20 07
64	19 23	20 16	21 32	19 49	19 57	20 04	20 09
62	19 16	20 05	21 11	19 41	19 53	20 02	20 11
60	19 10	19 55	20 55	19 34	19 48	20 01	20 12
N 58	19 05	19 47	20 41	19 28	19 45	19 59	20 13
56	19 00	19 40	20 30	19 22	19 41	19 58	20 14
54	18 56	19 33	20 20	19 17	19 38	19 57	20 15
52	18 52	19 27	20 11	19 12	19 36	19 56	20 16
50	18 49	19 22	20 04	19 08	19 33	19 56	20 17
45	18 41	19 12	19 48	18 59	19 28	19 54	20 19
N 40	18 35	19 03	19 36	18 51	19 23	19 52	20 20
35	18 30	18 56	19 26	18 45	19 19	19 51	20 21
30	18 25	18 49	19 18	18 39	19 16	19 50	20 23
20	18 17	18 39	19 06	18 29	19 10	19 48	20 25
N 10	18 10	18 31	18 56	18 20	19 04	19 46	20 26
0	18 04	18 25	18 49	18 12	18 59	19 44	20 28
S 10	17 58	18 19	18 43	18 03	18 54	19 42	20 29
20	17 51	18 13	18 39	17 54	18 48	19 40	20 31
30	17 44	18 08	18 36	17 44	18 42	19 38	20 33
35	17 40	18 05	18 35	17 38	18 38	19 37	20 34
40	17 35	18 02	18 34	17 31	18 34	19 36	20 35
45	17 29	17 59	18 33	17 23	18 29	19 34	20 37
S 50	17 23	17 56	18 33	17 13	18 23	19 32	20 39
52	17 20	17 54	18 33	17 08	18 20	19 31	20 39
54	17 17	17 53	18 34	17 03	18 17	19 30	20 40
56	17 13	17 51	18 34	16 58	18 14	19 29	20 41
58	17 09	17 49	18 35	16 51	18 10	19 27	20 42
S 60	17 05	17 47	18 35	16 44	18 06	19 26	20 43

SUN / MOON

Day	Eqn. of Time 00h	12h	Mer. Pass.	Mer. Pass. Upper	Lower	Age	Phase
	m s	m s	h m	h m	h m	d	
29	01 02	00 53	12 01	12 00	24 24	29	
30	00 44	00 35	12 01	12 48	00 24	01	●
31	00 26	00 17	12 00	13 33	01 11	02	

G.M.T.	ARIES G.H.A.	VENUS −3.5 G.H.A.	Dec.	MARS +1.8 G.H.A.	Dec.	JUPITER −1.3 G.H.A.	Dec.	SATURN +1.2 G.H.A.	Dec.	STARS Name	S.H.A.	Dec.
1 00	340 04.1	145 20.5 S 6 10.8		218 23.5 N21 13.3		148 53.9 S 3 34.6		151 15.0 S 1 22.4		Acamar	315 36.6	S40 22.5
01	355 06.6	160 20.3	12.0	233 24.3	13.0	163 55.9	34.8	166 17.2	22.5	Achernar	335 44.3	S57 19.6
02	10 09.1	175 20.1	13.3	248 25.1	12.7	178 57.9	35.0	181 19.4	22.6	Acrux	173 37.1	S62 59.8
03	25 11.5	190 19.9 ··	14.6	263 25.9 ··	12.4	193 59.9 ··	35.2	196 21.7 ··	22.7	Adhara	255 31.8	S28 56.6
04	40 14.0	205 19.6	15.9	278 26.6	12.1	209 02.0	35.4	211 23.9	22.8	Aldebaran	291 17.2	N16 28.3
05	55 16.4	220 19.4	17.1	293 27.4	11.8	224 04.0	35.6	226 26.1	23.0			
06	70 18.9	235 19.2 S 6 18.4		308 28.2 N21 11.5		239 06.0 S 3 35.8		241 28.3 S 1 23.1		Alioth	166 42.4	N56 03.9
07	85 21.4	250 19.0	19.7	323 29.0	11.2	254 08.0	36.0	256 30.5	23.2	Alkaid	153 18.3	N49 24.6
08	100 23.8	265 18.7	20.9	338 29.8	10.8	269 10.0	36.2	271 32.7	23.3	Al Na'ir	28 13.6	S47 03.0
T 09	115 26.3	280 18.5 ··	22.2	353 30.6 ··	10.5	284 12.0 ··	36.4	286 34.9 ··	23.4	Alnilam	276 11.1	S 1 12.7
U 10	130 28.8	295 18.3	23.5	8 31.4	10.2	299 14.0	36.6	301 37.1	23.5	Alphard	218 20.2	S 8 34.5
E 11	145 31.2	310 18.1	24.7	23 32.2	09.9	314 16.0	36.8	316 39.3	23.6			
S 12	160 33.7	325 17.8 S 6 26.0		38 33.0 N21 09.6		329 18.0 S 3 37.0		331 41.5 S 1 23.8		Alphecca	126 31.6	N26 46.9
D 13	175 36.2	340 17.6	27.2	53 33.7	09.3	344 20.1	37.2	346 43.7	23.9	Alpheratz	358 08.3	N28 59.3
A 14	190 38.6	355 17.4	28.5	68 34.5	09.0	359 22.1	37.4	1 45.9	24.0	Altair	62 31.6	N 8 49.3
Y 15	205 41.1	10 17.2 ··	29.8	83 35.3 ··	08.7	14 24.1 ··	37.6	16 48.2 ··	24.1	Ankaa	353 39.2	S42 24.2
16	220 43.6	25 16.9	31.0	98 36.1	08.4	29 26.1	37.8	31 50.4	24.2	Antares	112 56.1	S26 23.5
17	235 46.0	40 16.7	32.3	113 36.9	08.0	44 28.1	38.0	46 52.6	24.3			
18	250 48.5	55 16.5 S 6 33.6		128 37.7 N21 07.7		59 30.1 S 3 38.2		61 54.8 S 1 24.4		Arcturus	146 18.1	N19 17.0
19	265 50.9	70 16.3	34.8	143 38.5	07.4	74 32.1	38.4	76 57.0	24.5	Atria	108 19.7	S68 59.9
20	280 53.4	85 16.0	36.1	158 39.3	07.1	89 34.1	38.6	91 59.2	24.7	Avior	234 28.5	S59 26.8
21	295 55.9	100 15.8 ··	37.4	173 40.1 ··	06.8	104 36.1 ··	38.8	107 01.4 ··	24.8	Bellatrix	278 58.1	N 6 20.1
22	310 58.3	115 15.6	38.6	188 40.9	06.5	119 38.1	39.0	122 03.6	24.9	Betelgeuse	271 27.7	N 7 24.3
23	326 00.8	130 15.3	39.9	203 41.7	06.2	134 40.2	39.2	137 05.8	25.0			
2 00	341 03.3	145 15.1 S 6 41.2		218 42.4 N21 05.9		149 42.3 S 3 39.4		152 08.0 S 1 25.1		Canopus	264 07.2	S52 40.9
01	356 05.7	160 14.9	42.4	233 43.2	05.5	164 44.2	39.6	167 10.2	25.2	Capella	281 10.4	N45 58.6
02	11 08.2	175 14.7	43.7	248 44.0	05.2	179 46.2	39.7	182 12.4	25.3	Deneb	49 47.6	N45 13.0
03	26 10.7	190 14.4 ··	44.9	263 44.8 ··	04.9	194 48.2 ··	39.9	197 14.6 ··	25.5	Denebola	182 58.7	N14 40.7
04	41 13.1	205 14.2	46.2	278 45.6	04.6	209 50.2	40.1	212 16.8	25.6	Diphda	349 19.9	S18 05.2
05	56 15.6	220 14.0	47.5	293 46.4	04.3	224 52.2	40.3	227 19.1	25.7			
06	71 18.1	235 13.8 S 6 48.7		308 47.2 N21 04.0		239 54.2 S 3 40.5		242 21.3 S 1 25.8		Dubhe	194 22.0	N61 51.2
07	86 20.5	250 13.5	50.0	323 48.0	03.7	254 56.2	40.7	257 23.5	25.9	Elnath	278 43.4	N28 35.5
W 08	101 23.0	265 13.3	51.3	338 48.8	03.3	269 58.2	40.9	272 25.7	26.0	Eltanin	90 57.2	N51 29.8
E 09	116 25.4	280 13.1 ··	52.5	353 49.6 ··	03.0	285 00.2 ··	41.1	287 27.9 ··	26.1	Enif	34 10.6	N 9 47.5
D 10	131 27.9	295 12.8	53.8	8 50.4	02.7	300 02.3	41.3	302 30.1	26.3	Fomalhaut	15 50.3	S29 43.1
N 11	146 30.4	310 12.6	55.0	23 51.2	02.4	315 04.3	41.5	317 32.3	26.4			
E 12	161 32.8	325 12.4 S 6 56.3		38 52.0 N21 02.1		330 06.3 S 3 41.7		332 34.5 S 1 26.5		Gacrux	172 28.5	S57 00.6
S 13	176 35.3	340 12.2	57.6	53 52.8	01.8	345 08.3	41.9	347 36.7	26.6	Gienah	176 17.6	S17 26.2
D 14	191 37.8	355 11.9 6 58.8		68 53.6	01.4	0 10.3	42.1	2 38.9	26.7	Hadar	149 22.8	S60 17.1
A 15	206 40.2	10 11.7 7 00.1		83 54.4 ··	01.1	15 12.3 ··	42.3	17 41.1 ··	26.8	Hamal	328 28.0	N23 22.5
Y 16	221 42.7	25 11.5	01.3	98 55.1	00.8	30 14.3	42.5	32 43.3	26.9	Kaus Aust.	84 15.8	S34 23.7
17	236 45.2	40 11.2	02.6	113 55.9	00.5	45 16.3	42.7	47 45.5	27.1			
18	251 47.6	55 11.0 S 7 03.9		128 56.7 N21 00.2		60 18.3 S 3 42.9		62 47.7 S 1 27.2		Kochab	137 19.5	N74 14.2
19	266 50.1	70 10.8	05.1	143 57.5	20 59.9	75 20.3	43.1	77 49.9	27.3	Markab	14 02.2	N15 06.4
20	281 52.5	85 10.6	06.4	158 58.3	59.5	90 22.3	43.3	92 52.2	27.4	Menkar	314 40.3	N 4 01.1
21	296 55.0	100 10.3 ··	07.6	173 59.1 ··	59.2	105 24.3 ··	43.5	107 54.4 ··	27.5	Menkent	148 36.5	S36 16.8
22	311 57.5	115 10.1	08.9	188 59.8	58.9	120 26.3	43.7	122 56.6	27.6	Miaplacidus	221 45.7	S69 38.3
23	326 59.9	130 09.9	10.1	204 00.7	58.6	135 28.4	43.9	137 58.8	27.7			
3 00	342 02.4	145 09.6 S 7 11.4		219 01.5 N20 58.3		150 30.4 S 3 44.1		153 01.0 S 1 27.9		Mirfak	309 15.0	N49 47.6
01	357 04.9	160 09.4	12.7	234 02.3	57.9	165 32.4	44.3	168 03.2	28.0	Nunki	76 28.2	S26 19.2
02	12 07.3	175 09.2	13.9	249 03.1	57.6	180 34.4	44.5	183 05.4	28.1	Peacock	53 56.8	S56 47.8
03	27 09.8	190 08.9 ··	15.2	264 03.9 ··	57.3	195 36.4 ··	44.7	198 07.6 ··	28.2	Pollux	243 57.6	N28 04.3
04	42 12.3	205 08.7	16.4	279 04.7	57.0	210 38.4	44.9	213 09.8	28.3	Procyon	245 25.3	N 5 16.5
05	57 14.7	220 08.5	17.7	294 05.5	56.7	225 40.4	45.1	228 12.0	28.4			
06	72 17.2	235 08.3 S 7 18.9		309 06.3 N20 56.3		240 42.4 S 3 45.3		243 14.2 S 1 28.5		Rasalhague	96 28.9	N12 34.6
07	87 19.7	250 08.0	20.2	324 07.1	56.0	255 44.4	45.5	258 16.4	28.7	Regulus	208 09.6	N12 03.6
T 08	102 22.1	265 07.8	21.5	339 07.9	55.7	270 46.4	45.7	273 18.6	28.8	Rigel	281 35.4	S 8 13.2
H 09	117 24.6	280 07.6 ··	22.7	354 08.7 ··	55.4	285 48.4 ··	45.9	288 20.8 ··	28.9	Rigil Kent.	140 25.3	S60 45.6
U 10	132 27.0	295 07.3	24.0	9 09.5	55.1	300 50.4	46.1	303 23.0	29.0	Sabik	102 40.3	S15 42.1
R 11	147 29.5	310 07.1	25.2	24 10.3	54.7	315 52.4	46.3	318 25.2	29.1			
S 12	162 32.0	325 06.9 S 7 26.5		39 11.1 N20 54.4		330 54.4 S 3 46.5		333 27.4 S 1 29.2		Schedar	350 07.8	N56 26.1
D 13	177 34.4	340 06.6	27.7	54 11.9	54.1	345 56.5	46.7	348 29.6	29.3	Shaula	96 54.8	S37 05.5
A 14	192 36.9	355 06.4	29.0	69 12.7	53.8	0 58.5	46.9	3 31.9	29.5	Sirius	258 55.3	S16 41.3
Y 15	207 39.4	10 06.2 ··	30.2	84 13.5 ··	53.4	16 00.5 ··	47.0	18 34.1 ··	29.6	Spica	158 57.1	S11 03.8
16	222 41.8	25 05.9	31.5	99 14.3	53.1	31 02.5	47.2	33 36.3	29.7	Suhail	223 10.7	S43 21.3
17	237 44.3	40 05.7	32.8	114 15.1	52.8	46 04.5	47.4	48 38.5	29.8			
18	252 46.8	55 05.5 S 7 34.0		129 15.9 N20 52.5		61 06.5 S 3 47.6		63 40.7 S 1 29.9		Vega	80 55.2	N38 46.3
19	267 49.2	70 05.2	35.3	144 16.7	52.2	76 08.5	47.8	78 42.9	30.0	Zuben'ubi	137 32.5	S15 57.8
20	282 51.7	85 05.0	36.5	159 17.5	51.8	91 10.5	48.0	93 45.1	30.1			
21	297 54.2	100 04.8 ··	37.8	174 18.3 ··	51.5	106 12.5 ··	48.2	108 47.3 ··	30.3		S.H.A.	Mer. Pass.
22	312 56.6	115 04.5	39.0	189 19.1	51.2	121 14.5	48.4	123 49.5	30.4	Venus	164 11.9	14 19
23	327 59.1	130 04.3	40.3	204 19.9	50.9	136 16.5	48.6	138 51.7	30.5	Mars	237 39.2	9 25
										Jupiter	168 38.9	13 59
Mer. Pass.	1 15.6	v −0.2 d 1.3		v 0.8 d 0.3		v 2.0 d 0.2		v 2.2 d 0.1		Saturn	171 04.8	13 49

G.M.T.	SUN G.H.A.	Dec.	MOON G.H.A.	v	Dec.	d	H.P.
1 00	179 58.3	N 8 23.7	151 57.4	14.3	N 1 37.4	11.3	55.5
01	194 58.5	22.8	166 30.7	14.3	1 26.1	11.3	55.5
02	209 58.6	21.9	181 04.0	14.4	1 14.8	11.2	55.5
03	224 58.8	·· 21.0	195 37.4	14.4	1 03.6	11.3	55.5
04	239 59.0	20.1	210 10.8	14.4	0 52.3	11.3	55.4
05	254 59.2	19.2	224 44.2	14.5	0 41.0	11.2	55.4
06	269 59.4	N 8 18.3	239 17.7	14.4	N 0 29.8	11.3	55.4
07	284 59.6	17.4	253 51.1	14.6	0 18.5	11.2	55.4
T 08	299 59.8	16.5	268 24.7	14.5	N 0 07.3	11.2	55.4
U 09	315 00.0	·· 15.6	282 58.2	14.5	S 0 03.9	11.3	55.3
E 10	330 00.2	14.7	297 31.7	14.6	0 15.2	11.2	55.3
S 11	345 00.4	13.8	312 05.3	14.6	0 26.4	11.2	55.3
D 12	0 00.6	N 8 12.9	326 38.9	14.6	S 0 37.6	11.1	55.3
A 13	15 00.8	11.9	341 12.5	14.7	0 48.7	11.2	55.3
Y 14	30 01.0	11.0	355 46.2	14.6	0 59.9	11.2	55.2
15	45 01.2	·· 10.1	10 19.8	14.7	1 11.1	11.1	55.2
16	60 01.4	09.2	24 53.5	14.7	1 22.2	11.2	55.2
17	75 01.6	08.3	39 27.2	14.7	1 33.4	11.1	55.2
18	90 01.8	N 8 07.4	54 00.9	14.8	S 1 44.5	11.1	55.2
19	105 02.0	06.5	68 34.7	14.7	1 55.6	11.1	55.1
20	120 02.2	05.6	83 08.4	14.8	2 06.7	11.0	55.1
21	135 02.4	·· 04.7	97 42.2	14.8	2 17.7	11.1	55.1
22	150 02.6	03.8	112 16.0	14.8	2 28.8	11.0	55.1
23	165 02.8	02.9	126 49.8	14.8	2 39.8	11.0	55.1
2 00	180 03.0	N 8 01.9	141 23.6	14.8	S 2 50.8	11.0	55.0
01	195 03.2	01.0	155 57.4	14.9	3 01.8	11.0	55.0
02	210 03.4	8 00.1	170 31.3	14.8	3 12.8	10.9	55.0
03	225 03.6	7 59.2	185 05.1	14.9	3 23.7	10.9	55.0
04	240 03.8	58.3	199 39.0	14.9	3 34.6	11.0	55.0
05	255 04.0	57.4	214 12.9	14.9	3 45.6	10.8	54.9
06	270 04.2	N 7 56.5	228 46.8	14.9	S 3 56.4	10.9	54.9
07	285 04.4	55.6	243 20.7	14.9	4 07.3	10.8	54.9
W 08	300 04.6	54.6	257 54.6	14.9	4 18.1	10.8	54.9
E 09	315 04.8	·· 53.7	272 28.5	14.9	4 28.9	10.8	54.9
D 10	330 05.0	52.8	287 02.4	14.9	4 39.7	10.7	54.9
N 11	345 05.2	51.9	301 36.3	14.9	4 50.4	10.8	54.8
E 12	0 05.4	N 7 51.0	316 10.2	15.0	S 5 01.2	10.7	54.8
S 13	15 05.6	50.1	330 44.2	14.9	5 11.9	10.6	54.8
D 14	30 05.8	49.2	345 18.1	14.9	5 22.5	10.7	54.8
A 15	45 06.0	·· 48.3	359 52.0	15.0	5 33.2	10.6	54.8
Y 16	60 06.2	47.3	14 26.0	14.9	5 43.8	10.6	54.8
17	75 06.4	46.4	28 59.9	15.0	5 54.4	10.5	54.7
18	90 06.6	N 7 45.5	43 33.9	14.9	S 6 04.9	10.5	54.7
19	105 06.8	44.6	58 07.8	15.0	6 15.4	10.5	54.7
20	120 07.0	43.7	72 41.8	14.9	6 25.9	10.5	54.7
21	135 07.2	·· 42.8	87 15.7	14.9	6 36.4	10.4	54.7
22	150 07.4	41.9	101 49.6	15.0	6 46.8	10.4	54.7
23	165 07.6	40.9	116 23.6	14.9	6 57.2	10.3	54.6
3 00	180 07.8	N 7 40.0	130 57.5	14.9	S 7 07.5	10.3	54.6
01	195 08.0	39.1	145 31.4	15.0	7 17.8	10.3	54.6
02	210 08.2	38.2	160 05.4	14.9	7 28.1	10.2	54.6
03	225 08.4	·· 37.3	174 39.3	14.9	7 38.3	10.2	54.6
04	240 08.6	36.4	189 13.2	14.9	7 48.5	10.2	54.6
05	255 08.8	35.4	203 47.1	14.9	7 58.7	10.1	54.6
06	270 09.0	N 7 34.5	218 21.0	14.9	S 8 08.8	10.1	54.5
07	285 09.2	33.6	232 54.9	14.9	8 18.9	10.1	54.5
T 08	300 09.4	32.7	247 28.8	14.9	8 29.0	10.0	54.5
H 09	315 09.6	·· 31.8	262 02.7	14.8	8 39.0	9.9	54.5
U 10	330 09.8	30.9	276 36.5	14.9	8 48.9	10.0	54.5
R 11	345 10.0	29.9	291 10.4	14.8	8 58.9	9.9	54.5
S 12	0 10.2	N 7 29.0	305 44.2	14.9	S 9 08.8	9.8	54.5
D 13	15 10.4	28.1	320 18.1	14.8	9 18.6	9.8	54.5
A 14	30 10.6	27.2	334 51.9	14.8	9 28.4	9.8	54.4
Y 15	45 10.8	·· 26.3	349 25.7	14.8	9 38.2	9.7	54.4
16	60 11.0	25.3	3 59.5	14.8	9 47.9	9.6	54.4
17	75 11.2	24.4	18 33.3	14.7	9 57.5	9.7	54.4
18	90 11.4	N 7 23.5	33 07.0	14.8	S10 07.2	9.5	54.4
19	105 11.6	22.6	47 40.8	14.7	10 16.7	9.6	54.4
20	120 11.8	21.7	62 14.5	14.7	10 26.3	9.5	54.4
21	135 12.0	·· 20.7	76 48.2	14.7	10 35.8	9.4	54.4
22	150 12.3	19.8	91 21.9	14.7	10 45.2	9.4	54.4
23	165 12.5	18.9	105 55.6	14.7	10 54.6	9.3	54.4
	S.D. 15.9	d 0.9	S.D. 15.1		14.9		14.8

Sunrise / Moonrise

Lat.	Naut.	Civil	Sunrise	Moonrise 1	2	3	4
N 72	////	02 37	04 05	08 07	09 51	11 36	13 26
N 70	////	03 04	04 19	08 07	09 44	11 21	13 00
68	01 39	03 24	04 29	08 07	09 38	11 09	12 41
66	02 15	03 40	04 38	08 07	09 34	10 59	12 25
64	02 40	03 52	04 45	08 07	09 30	10 51	12 13
62	02 58	04 03	04 51	08 07	09 26	10 45	12 02
60	03 14	04 12	04 57	08 07	09 23	10 39	11 53
N 58	03 26	04 20	05 02	08 07	09 21	10 33	11 45
56	03 37	04 26	05 06	08 07	09 18	10 29	11 38
54	03 46	04 32	05 10	08 07	09 16	10 25	11 32
52	03 54	04 38	05 13	08 07	09 14	10 21	11 26
50	04 01	04 42	05 16	08 07	09 13	10 18	11 21
45	04 16	04 53	05 23	08 07	09 09	10 10	11 11
N 40	04 28	05 01	05 28	08 07	09 06	10 04	11 02
35	04 37	05 07	05 33	08 07	09 03	09 59	10 54
30	04 44	05 13	05 37	08 07	09 01	09 54	10 47
20	04 56	05 22	05 44	08 07	08 57	09 46	10 36
N 10	05 05	05 29	05 51	08 07	08 53	09 40	10 26
0	05 11	05 35	05 56	08 07	08 50	09 33	10 17
S 10	05 16	05 41	06 02	08 07	08 47	09 27	10 07
20	05 20	05 46	06 08	08 07	08 44	09 20	09 57
30	05 22	05 50	06 14	08 07	08 40	09 12	09 46
35	05 23	05 53	06 18	08 07	08 38	09 08	09 40
40	05 24	05 55	06 22	08 07	08 35	09 03	09 32
45	05 24	05 57	06 27	08 08	08 32	08 57	09 24
S 50	05 23	06 00	06 33	08 08	08 29	08 51	09 14
52	05 22	06 01	06 35	08 08	08 27	08 47	09 09
54	05 22	06 03	06 38	08 08	08 26	08 44	09 04
56	05 21	06 04	06 41	08 08	08 24	08 40	08 58
58	05 20	06 05	06 45	08 08	08 22	08 36	08 52
S 60	05 19	06 07	06 49	08 08	08 19	08 31	08 45

Sunset / Moonset

Lat.	Sunset	Civil	Naut.	Moonset 1	2	3	4
N 72	19 50	21 17	////	20 00	19 47	19 32	19 12
N 70	19 38	20 51	23 18	20 03	19 56	19 48	19 39
68	19 28	20 32	22 13	20 05	20 03	20 01	20 00
66	19 19	20 17	21 40	20 07	20 10	20 12	20 16
64	19 12	20 05	21 16	20 09	20 15	20 21	20 30
62	19 06	19 54	20 58	20 11	20 20	20 29	20 41
60	19 01	19 46	20 43	20 12	20 24	20 36	20 51
N 58	18 56	19 38	20 31	20 13	20 27	20 42	20 59
56	18 52	19 31	20 20	20 14	20 30	20 48	21 07
54	18 49	19 26	20 11	20 15	20 33	20 52	21 14
52	18 45	19 20	20 03	20 16	20 36	20 57	21 20
50	18 42	19 16	19 56	20 17	20 38	21 01	21 25
45	18 36	19 06	19 42	20 19	20 44	21 09	21 37
N 40	18 30	18 58	19 31	20 20	20 48	21 16	21 47
35	18 26	18 51	19 22	20 21	20 52	21 23	21 55
30	18 21	18 46	19 14	20 23	20 55	21 28	22 03
20	18 15	18 37	19 03	20 25	21 01	21 38	22 16
N 10	18 08	18 30	18 54	20 26	21 06	21 46	22 27
0	18 03	18 24	18 48	20 28	21 11	21 54	22 38
S 10	17 57	18 19	18 43	20 29	21 16	22 02	22 49
20	17 52	18 14	18 40	20 31	21 21	22 10	23 00
30	17 45	18 09	18 37	20 33	21 27	22 20	23 13
35	17 42	18 07	18 37	20 34	21 30	22 26	23 21
40	17 38	18 05	18 36	20 35	21 34	22 32	23 29
45	17 33	18 03	18 37	20 37	21 39	22 39	23 39
S 50	17 27	18 00	18 37	20 39	21 44	22 48	23 52
52	17 25	17 59	18 38	20 39	21 46	22 52	23 57
54	17 22	17 58	18 39	20 40	21 49	22 57	24 04
56	17 19	17 57	18 40	20 41	21 52	23 02	24 11
58	17 16	17 55	18 41	20 42	21 56	23 08	24 19
S 60	17 12	17 54	18 42	20 43	21 59	23 14	24 28

SUN / MOON

Day	Eqn. of Time 00h	12h	Mer. Pass.	Mer. Pass. Upper	Lower	Age	Phase
1	00 07	00 02	12 00	14 17	01 56	03	
2	00 12	00 21	12 00	15 01	02 39	04	
3	00 31	00 40	11 59	15 44	03 22	05	

1981 SEPTEMBER 4, 5, 6 (FRI., SAT., SUN.)

G.M.T.	ARIES G.H.A.	VENUS −3.5 G.H.A.	Dec.	MARS +1.8 G.H.A.	Dec.	JUPITER −1.2 G.H.A.	Dec.	SATURN +1.1 G.H.A.	Dec.	STARS Name	S.H.A.	Dec.
d h	° '	° '	° '	° '	° '	° '	° '	° '	° '		° '	° '
4 00	343 01.5	145 04.1	S 7 41.5	219 20.7	N20 50.5	151 18.5	S 3 48.8	153 53.9	S 1 30.6	Acamar	315 36.5	S40 22.5
01	358 04.0	160 03.8	42.8	234 21.5	50.2	166 20.5	49.0	168 56.1	30.7	Achernar	335 44.3	S57 19.6
02	13 06.5	175 03.6	44.0	249 22.3	49.9	181 22.5	49.2	183 58.3	30.8	Acrux	173 37.1	S62 59.8
03	28 08.9	190 03.4 ··	45.3	264 23.1 ··	49.6	196 24.5 ··	49.4	199 00.5 ··	30.9	Adhara	255 31.8	S28 56.6
04	43 11.4	205 03.1	46.5	279 23.9	49.2	211 26.5	49.6	214 02.7	31.1	Aldebaran	291 17.2	N16 28.3
05	58 13.9	220 02.9	47.8	294 24.7	48.9	226 28.5	49.8	229 04.9	31.2			
06	73 16.3	235 02.7	S 7 49.0	309 25.5	N20 48.6	241 30.5	S 3 50.0	244 07.1	S 1 31.3	Alioth	166 42.4	N56 03.9
07	88 18.8	250 02.4	50.3	324 26.3	48.3	256 32.5	50.2	259 09.3	31.4	Alkaid	153 18.3	N49 24.6
08	103 21.3	265 02.2	51.5	339 27.1	47.9	271 34.6	50.4	274 11.5	31.5	Al Na'ir	28 13.6	S47 03.0
F 09	118 23.7	280 02.0 ··	52.8	354 28.0 ··	47.6	286 36.6 ··	50.6	289 13.7 ··	31.6	Alnilam	276 11.1	S 1 12.7
R 10	133 26.2	295 01.7	54.0	9 28.8	47.3	301 38.6	50.8	304 15.9	31.7	Alphard	218 20.2	S 8 34.5
I 11	148 28.6	310 01.5	55.3	24 29.6	46.9	316 40.6	51.0	319 18.1	31.9			
D 12	163 31.1	325 01.3	S 7 56.5	39 30.4	N20 46.6	331 42.6	S 3 51.2	334 20.3	S 1 32.0	Alphecca	126 31.7	N26 46.9
A 13	178 33.6	340 01.0	57.8	54 31.2	46.3	346 44.6	51.4	349 22.6	32.1	Alpheratz	358 08.3	N28 59.3
Y 14	193 36.0	355 00.8	7 59.0	69 32.0	46.0	1 46.6	51.6	4 24.8	32.2	Altair	62 31.7	N 8 49.3
15	208 38.5	10 00.6	8 00.3	84 32.8 ··	45.6	16 48.6 ··	51.8	19 27.0 ··	32.3	Ankaa	353 39.2	S42 24.2
16	223 41.0	25 00.3	01.5	99 33.6	45.3	31 50.6	52.0	34 29.2	32.4	Antares	112 56.1	S26 23.5
17	238 43.4	40 00.1	02.8	114 34.4	45.0	46 52.6	52.2	49 31.4	32.5			
18	253 45.9	54 59.9	S 8 04.0	129 35.2	N20 44.6	61 54.6	S 3 52.4	64 33.6	S 1 32.7	Arcturus	146 18.1	N19 17.0
19	268 48.4	69 59.6	05.3	144 36.0	44.3	76 56.6	52.6	79 35.8	32.8	Atria	108 19.7	S68 59.9
20	283 50.8	84 59.4	06.5	159 36.8	44.0	91 58.6	52.8	94 38.0	32.9	Avior	234 28.4	S59 26.8
21	298 53.3	99 59.1 ··	07.8	174 37.6 ··	43.7	107 00.6 ··	53.0	109 40.2 ··	33.0	Bellatrix	278 58.1	N 6 20.1
22	313 55.8	114 58.9	09.0	189 38.4	43.3	122 02.6	53.2	124 42.4	33.1	Betelgeuse	271 27.7	N 7 24.3
23	328 58.2	129 58.7	10.2	204 39.2	43.0	137 04.6	53.4	139 44.6	33.2			
5 00	344 00.7	144 58.4	S 8 11.5	219 40.0	N20 42.7	152 06.6	S 3 53.6	154 46.8	S 1 33.3	Canopus	264 07.1	S52 40.9
01	359 03.1	159 58.2	12.7	234 40.9	42.3	167 08.6	53.8	169 49.0	33.5	Capella	281 10.4	N45 58.6
02	14 05.6	174 58.0	14.0	249 41.7	42.0	182 10.6	54.0	184 51.2	33.6	Deneb	49 47.6	N45 13.1
03	29 08.1	189 57.7 ··	15.2	264 42.5 ··	41.7	197 12.6 ··	54.2	199 53.4 ··	33.7	Denebola	182 58.7	N14 40.7
04	44 10.5	204 57.5	16.5	279 43.3	41.3	212 14.6	54.4	214 55.6	33.8	Diphda	349 19.9	S18 05.2
05	59 13.0	219 57.3	17.7	294 44.1	41.0	227 16.6	54.6	229 57.8	33.9			
06	74 15.5	234 57.0	S 8 19.0	309 44.9	N20 40.7	242 18.6	S 3 54.8	245 00.0	S 1 34.0	Dubhe	194 22.0	N61 51.2
07	89 17.9	249 56.8	20.2	324 45.7	40.3	257 20.6	55.0	260 02.2	34.2	Elnath	278 43.4	N28 35.5
S 08	104 20.4	264 56.5	21.4	339 46.5	40.0	272 22.6	55.2	275 04.4	34.3	Eltanin	90 57.3	N51 29.8
A 09	119 22.9	279 56.3 ··	22.7	354 47.3 ··	39.7	287 24.6 ··	55.4	290 06.6 ··	34.4	Enif	34 10.6	N 9 47.5
T 10	134 25.3	294 56.1	23.9	9 48.1	39.3	302 26.6	55.6	305 08.8	34.5	Fomalhaut	15 50.3	S29 43.1
U 11	149 27.8	309 55.8	25.2	24 48.9	39.0	317 28.6	55.8	320 11.0	34.6			
R 12	164 30.3	324 55.6	S 8 26.4	39 49.8	N20 38.7	332 30.6	S 3 56.0	335 13.2	S 1 34.7	Gacrux	172 28.5	S57 00.6
D 13	179 32.7	339 55.3	27.7	54 50.6	38.3	347 32.6	56.2	350 15.4	34.8	Gienah	176 17.6	S17 26.2
A 14	194 35.2	354 55.1	28.9	69 51.4	38.0	2 34.6	56.4	5 17.6	35.0	Hadar	149 22.8	S60 17.1
Y 15	209 37.6	9 54.9 ··	30.1	84 52.2 ··	37.7	17 36.7 ··	56.6	20 19.8 ··	35.1	Hamal	328 28.0	N23 22.5
16	224 40.1	24 54.6	31.4	99 53.0	37.3	32 38.7	56.8	35 22.0	35.2	Kaus Aust.	84 15.8	S34 23.7
17	239 42.6	39 54.4	32.6	114 53.8	37.0	47 40.7	57.0	50 24.2	35.3			
18	254 45.0	54 54.1	S 8 33.9	129 54.6	N20 36.7	62 42.7	S 3 57.2	65 26.4	S 1 35.4	Kochab	137 19.6	N74 14.2
19	269 47.5	69 53.9	35.1	144 55.4	36.3	77 44.7	57.4	80 28.6	35.5	Markab	14 02.2	N15 06.4
20	284 50.0	84 53.7	36.3	159 56.2	36.0	92 46.7	57.6	95 30.8	35.7	Menkar	314 40.3	N 4 01.1
21	299 52.4	99 53.4 ··	37.6	174 57.1 ··	35.7	107 48.7 ··	57.8	110 33.0 ··	35.8	Menkent	148 36.5	S36 16.7
22	314 54.9	114 53.2	38.8	189 57.9	35.3	122 50.7	58.0	125 35.2	35.9	Miaplacidus	221 45.7	S69 38.3
23	329 57.4	129 52.9	40.1	204 58.7	35.0	137 52.7	58.2	140 37.4	36.0			
6 00	344 59.8	144 52.7	S 8 41.3	219 59.5	N20 34.7	152 54.7	S 3 58.4	155 39.6	S 1 36.1	Mirfak	309 15.0	N49 47.6
01	0 02.3	159 52.5	42.5	235 00.3	34.3	167 56.7	58.6	170 41.8	36.2	Nunki	76 28.2	S26 19.2
02	15 04.7	174 52.2	43.8	250 01.1	34.0	182 58.7	58.8	185 44.1	36.3	Peacock	53 56.9	S56 47.8
03	30 07.2	189 52.0 ··	45.0	265 01.9 ··	33.7	198 00.7 ··	59.0	200 46.3 ··	36.5	Pollux	243 57.6	N28 04.3
04	45 09.7	204 51.7	46.3	280 02.8	33.3	213 02.7	59.2	215 48.5	36.6	Procyon	245 25.3	N 5 16.5
05	60 12.1	219 51.5	47.5	295 03.6	33.0	228 04.7	59.4	230 50.7	36.7			
06	75 14.6	234 51.3	S 8 48.7	310 04.4	N20 32.6	243 06.7	S 3 59.6	245 52.9	S 1 36.8	Rasalhague	96 28.9	N12 34.6
07	90 17.1	249 51.0	50.0	325 05.2	32.3	258 08.7	3 59.8	260 55.1	36.9	Regulus	208 09.4	N12 03.6
08	105 19.5	264 50.8	51.2	340 06.0	32.0	273 10.7	4 00.0	275 57.3	37.0	Rigel	281 35.4	S 8 13.2
S 09	120 22.0	279 50.5 ··	52.4	355 06.8 ··	31.6	288 12.7 ··	00.2	290 59.5 ··	37.2	Rigil Kent.	140 25.3	S60 45.6
U 10	135 24.5	294 50.3	53.7	10 07.6	31.3	303 14.7	00.4	306 01.7	37.3	Sabik	102 40.3	S15 42.1
N 11	150 26.9	309 50.0	54.9	25 08.5	31.0	318 16.7	00.6	321 03.9	37.4			
D 12	165 29.4	324 49.8	S 8 56.1	40 09.3	N20 30.6	333 18.7	S 4 00.8	336 06.1	S 1 37.5	Schedar	350 07.8	N56 26.1
A 13	180 31.9	339 49.6	57.4	55 10.1	30.3	348 20.7	01.0	351 08.3	37.6	Shaula	96 54.8	S37 05.5
Y 14	195 34.3	354 49.3	58.6	70 10.9	29.9	3 22.7	01.2	6 10.5	37.7	Sirius	258 55.5	S16 41.3
15	210 36.8	9 49.1	8 59.9	85 11.7 ··	29.6	18 24.7 ··	01.4	21 12.7 ··	37.8	Spica	158 57.1	S11 03.8
16	225 39.2	24 48.8	9 01.1	100 12.5	29.3	33 26.7	01.6	36 14.9	38.0	Suhail	223 10.7	S43 21.3
17	240 41.7	39 48.6	02.3	115 13.4	28.9	48 28.7	01.8	51 17.1	38.1			
18	255 44.2	54 48.3	S 9 03.6	130 14.2	N20 28.6	63 30.7	S 4 02.0	66 19.3	S 1 38.2	Vega	80 55.2	N38 46.3
19	270 46.6	69 48.1	04.8	145 15.0	28.2	78 32.7	02.2	81 21.5	38.3	Zuben'ubi	137 32.5	S15 57.8
20	285 49.1	84 47.9	06.0	160 15.8	27.9	93 34.7	02.4	96 23.7	38.4		S.H.A.	Mer. Pass.
21	300 51.6	99 47.6 ··	07.3	175 16.6 ··	27.6	108 36.7 ··	02.6	111 25.9 ··	38.5		° '	h m
22	315 54.0	114 47.4	08.5	190 17.4	27.2	123 38.7	02.8	126 28.1	38.7	Venus	160 57.8	14 20
23	330 56.5	129 47.1	09.7	205 18.3	26.9	138 40.7	03.0	141 30.3	38.8	Mars	235 39.4	9 21
Mer. Pass.	h m 1 03.8	v −0.2	d 1.2	v 0.8	d 0.3	v 2.0	d 0.2	v 2.2	d 0.1	Jupiter	168 05.9	13 50
										Saturn	170 46.1	13 39

G.M.T	SUN G.H.A.	SUN Dec.	MOON G.H.A.	v	Dec.	d	H.P.
d h	° ′	° ′	° ′	′	° ′	′	′
4 00	180 12.7	N 7 18.0	120 29.3	14.6	S11 03.9	9.3	54.3
01	195 12.9	17.1	135 02.9	14.6	11 13.2	9.3	54.3
02	210 13.1	16.1	149 36.5	14.6	11 22.5	9.2	54.3
03	225 13.3	·· 15.2	164 10.1	14.6	11 31.7	9.1	54.3
04	240 13.5	14.3	178 43.7	14.5	11 40.8	9.1	54.3
05	255 13.7	13.4	193 17.2	14.6	11 49.9	9.0	54.3
06	270 13.9	N 7 12.5	207 50.8	14.5	S11 58.9	9.0	54.3
07	285 14.1	11.5	222 24.3	14.5	12 07.9	9.0	54.3
08	300 14.3	10.6	236 57.8	14.4	12 16.9	8.8	54.3
F 09	315 14.5	·· 09.7	251 31.2	14.5	12 25.7	8.9	54.3
R 10	330 14.7	08.8	266 04.7	14.4	12 34.6	8.7	54.3
I 11	345 14.9	07.8	280 38.1	14.4	12 43.3	8.8	54.3
D 12	0 15.1	N 7 06.9	295 11.5	14.4	S12 52.1	8.6	54.3
A 13	15 15.3	06.0	309 44.9	14.3	13 00.7	8.6	54.3
Y 14	30 15.5	05.1	324 18.2	14.3	13 09.3	8.6	54.3
15	45 15.7	·· 04.1	338 51.5	14.3	13 17.9	8.5	54.3
16	60 15.9	03.2	353 24.8	14.2	13 26.4	8.4	54.2
17	75 16.2	02.3	7 58.0	14.3	13 34.8	8.4	54.2
18	90 16.4	N 7 01.4	22 31.3	14.2	S13 43.2	8.3	54.2
19	105 16.6	7 00.5	37 04.5	14.1	13 51.5	8.2	54.2
20	120 16.8	6 59.5	51 37.6	14.2	13 59.7	8.2	54.2
21	135 17.0	·· 58.6	66 10.8	14.1	14 07.9	8.2	54.2
22	150 17.2	57.7	80 43.9	14.0	14 16.1	8.1	54.2
23	165 17.4	56.8	95 16.9	14.1	14 24.2	8.0	54.2
5 00	180 17.6	N 6 55.8	109 50.0	14.0	S14 32.2	7.9	54.2
01	195 17.8	54.9	124 23.0	14.0	14 40.1	7.9	54.2
02	210 18.0	54.0	138 56.0	13.9	14 48.0	7.8	54.2
03	225 18.2	·· 53.0	153 28.9	13.9	14 55.8	7.8	54.2
04	240 18.4	52.1	168 01.8	13.9	15 03.6	7.7	54.2
05	255 18.6	51.2	182 34.7	13.9	15 11.3	7.6	54.2
06	270 18.8	N 6 50.3	197 07.6	13.8	S15 18.9	7.6	54.2
07	285 19.1	49.3	211 40.4	13.8	15 26.5	7.5	54.2
S 08	300 19.3	48.4	226 13.2	13.7	15 34.0	7.4	54.2
A 09	315 19.5	·· 47.5	240 45.9	13.7	15 41.4	7.4	54.2
T 10	330 19.7	46.6	255 18.6	13.7	15 48.8	7.3	54.2
U 11	345 19.9	45.6	269 51.3	13.6	15 56.1	7.3	54.2
R 12	0 20.1	N 6 44.7	284 23.9	13.6	S16 03.4	7.1	54.2
D 13	15 20.3	43.8	298 56.5	13.6	16 10.5	7.1	54.2
A 14	30 20.5	42.8	313 29.1	13.5	16 17.6	7.0	54.2
Y 15	45 20.7	·· 41.9	328 01.6	13.5	16 24.6	7.0	54.2
16	60 20.9	41.0	342 34.1	13.4	16 31.6	6.9	54.2
17	75 21.1	40.1	357 06.5	13.4	16 38.5	6.8	54.2
18	90 21.3	N 6 39.1	11 38.9	13.4	S16 45.3	6.7	54.2
19	105 21.6	38.2	26 11.3	13.3	16 52.0	6.7	54.2
20	120 21.8	37.3	40 43.6	13.3	16 58.7	6.6	54.2
21	135 22.0	·· 36.3	55 15.9	13.3	17 05.3	6.5	54.2
22	150 22.2	35.4	69 48.2	13.2	17 11.8	6.5	54.3
23	165 22.4	34.5	84 20.4	13.1	17 18.3	6.3	54.3
6 00	180 22.6	N 6 33.6	98 52.5	13.2	S17 24.6	6.3	54.3
01	195 22.8	32.6	113 24.7	13.1	17 30.9	6.3	54.3
02	210 23.0	31.7	127 56.8	13.0	17 37.2	6.1	54.3
03	225 23.2	·· 30.8	142 28.8	13.0	17 43.3	6.1	54.3
04	240 23.4	29.8	157 00.8	13.0	17 49.4	6.0	54.3
05	255 23.6	28.9	171 32.8	12.9	17 55.4	5.9	54.3
06	270 23.9	N 6 28.0	186 04.7	12.9	S18 01.3	5.8	54.3
07	285 24.1	27.0	200 36.6	12.8	18 07.1	5.8	54.3
08	300 24.3	26.1	215 08.4	12.9	18 12.9	5.7	54.3
S 09	315 24.5	·· 25.2	229 40.3	12.7	18 18.6	5.6	54.3
U 10	330 24.7	24.2	244 12.0	12.7	18 24.2	5.5	54.3
N 11	345 24.9	23.3	258 43.7	12.7	18 29.7	5.4	54.3
D 12	0 25.1	N 6 22.4	273 15.4	12.6	S18 35.1	5.4	54.3
A 13	15 25.3	21.4	287 47.0	12.6	18 40.5	5.2	54.4
Y 14	30 25.5	20.5	302 18.6	12.6	18 45.7	5.2	54.4
15	45 25.8	·· 19.6	316 50.2	12.5	18 50.9	5.1	54.4
16	60 26.0	18.6	331 21.7	12.4	18 56.0	5.1	54.4
17	75 26.2	17.7	345 53.1	12.4	19 01.1	4.9	54.4
18	90 26.4	N 6 16.8	0 24.5	12.4	S19 06.0	4.9	54.4
19	105 26.6	15.8	14 55.9	12.4	19 10.9	4.7	54.4
20	120 26.8	14.9	29 27.3	12.2	19 15.6	4.7	54.4
21	135 27.0	·· 14.0	43 58.5	12.3	19 20.3	4.6	54.4
22	150 27.2	13.0	58 29.8	12.2	19 24.9	4.5	54.4
23	165 27.4	12.1	73 01.0	12.2	19 29.4	4.4	54.5
	S.D. 15.9 d 0.9		S.D. 14.8		14.8		14.8

Twilight / Sunrise / Moonrise

Lat.	Naut.	Civil	Sunrise	Moonrise 4	5	6	7
°	h m	h m	h m	h m	h m	h m	h m
N 72	////	02 57	04 20	13 26	15 34	■	■
N 70	01 15	03 20	04 31	13 00	14 45	16 44	■
68	02 02	03 37	04 40	12 41	14 14	15 48	17 21
66	02 31	03 51	04 47	12 25	13 51	15 15	16 34
64	02 53	04 02	04 54	12 13	13 33	14 51	16 03
62	03 10	04 12	04 59	12 02	13 18	14 32	15 41
60	03 23	04 20	05 04	11 53	13 06	14 17	15 22
N 58	03 35	04 27	05 08	11 45	12 55	14 04	15 07
56	03 44	04 33	05 12	11 38	12 46	13 52	14 54
54	03 53	04 38	05 15	11 32	12 38	13 42	14 43
52	04 00	04 43	05 18	11 26	12 31	13 33	14 33
50	04 07	04 47	05 21	11 21	12 24	13 26	14 24
45	04 20	04 56	05 26	11 11	12 10	13 09	14 05
N 40	04 31	05 04	05 31	11 02	11 59	12 55	13 50
35	04 39	05 10	05 35	10 54	11 49	12 44	13 37
30	04 46	05 15	05 39	10 47	11 40	12 33	13 26
20	04 57	05 23	05 45	10 36	11 26	12 16	13 07
N 10	05 05	05 29	05 50	10 26	11 13	12 01	12 50
0	05 10	05 35	05 55	10 17	11 01	11 47	12 35
S 10	05 15	05 39	06 00	10 07	10 49	11 33	12 19
20	05 17	05 43	06 05	09 57	10 36	11 18	12 03
30	05 19	05 47	06 11	09 46	10 22	11 01	11 44
35	05 19	05 49	06 14	09 40	10 14	10 51	11 33
40	05 19	05 50	06 17	09 32	10 04	10 40	11 20
45	05 18	05 52	06 21	09 24	09 53	10 27	11 05
S 50	05 17	05 54	06 26	09 14	09 40	10 11	10 47
52	05 16	05 55	06 29	09 09	09 34	10 03	10 39
54	05 15	05 56	06 31	09 04	09 27	09 55	10 29
56	05 13	05 56	06 34	08 58	09 20	09 45	10 18
58	05 12	05 57	06 36	08 52	09 11	09 35	10 06
S 60	05 10	05 58	06 40	08 45	09 01	09 23	09 52

Twilight / Sunset / Moonset

Lat.	Sunset	Civil	Naut.	Moonset 4	5	6	7
°	h m	h m	h m	h m	h m	h m	h m
N 72	19 34	20 55	////	19 12	18 37	■	■
N 70	19 24	20 34	22 32	19 39	19 27	19 05	■
68	19 15	20 17	21 49	20 00	19 59	20 01	20 08
66	19 08	20 04	21 22	20 16	20 23	20 34	20 55
64	19 02	19 53	21 01	20 30	20 41	20 59	21 26
62	18 56	19 44	20 45	20 41	20 57	21 18	21 49
60	18 52	19 36	20 32	20 51	21 09	21 34	22 07
N 58	18 48	19 29	20 21	20 59	21 21	21 48	22 23
56	18 44	19 23	20 11	21 07	21 30	21 59	22 36
54	18 41	19 18	20 03	21 14	21 39	22 09	22 47
52	18 38	19 13	19 56	21 20	21 46	22 18	22 57
50	18 36	19 09	19 49	21 25	21 53	22 27	23 06
45	18 30	19 01	19 36	21 37	22 08	22 44	23 26
N 40	18 25	18 53	19 26	21 47	22 21	22 58	23 41
35	18 21	18 47	19 17	21 55	22 31	23 10	23 54
30	18 18	18 42	19 11	22 03	22 40	23 21	24 06
20	18 12	18 34	19 00	22 16	22 56	23 39	24 25
N 10	18 07	18 28	18 52	22 27	23 10	23 55	24 42
0	18 02	18 23	18 47	22 38	23 23	24 10	00 10
S 10	17 57	18 18	18 43	22 49	23 36	24 25	00 25
20	17 52	18 15	18 40	23 00	23 50	24 41	00 41
30	17 47	18 11	18 39	23 13	24 06	00 06	00 59
35	17 44	18 09	18 39	23 21	24 15	00 15	01 09
40	17 41	18 08	18 39	23 29	24 26	00 26	01 22
45	17 37	18 06	18 40	23 39	24 39	00 39	01 36
S 50	17 32	18 04	18 42	23 52	24 54	00 54	01 54
52	17 30	18 04	18 43	23 57	25 01	01 01	02 02
54	17 27	18 03	18 44	24 04	00 04	01 09	02 12
56	17 25	18 02	18 45	24 11	00 11	01 18	02 22
58	17 22	18 01	18 47	24 19	00 19	01 28	02 34
S 60	17 19	18 01	18 49	24 28	00 28	01 40	02 48

Day	SUN Eqn. of Time 00ʰ	SUN Eqn. of Time 12ʰ	Mer. Pass.	MOON Mer. Pass. Upper	MOON Mer. Pass. Lower	Age	Phase
	m s	m s	h m	h m	h m	d	
4	00 50	01 00	11 59	16 27	04 05	06	
5	01 10	01 20	11 59	17 12	04 49	07	
6	01 30	01 40	11 58	17 58	05 35	08	◖

G.M.T.	ARIES G.H.A.	VENUS −3.5 G.H.A.	Dec.	MARS +1.8 G.H.A.	Dec.	JUPITER −1.2 G.H.A.	Dec.	SATURN +1.1 G.H.A.	Dec.	STARS Name	S.H.A.	Dec.
7 00	345 59.0	144 46.9	S 9 10.9	220 19.1	N20 26.5	153 42.7	S 4 03.2	156 32.5	S 1 38.9	Acamar	315 36.5	S40 22.5
01	1 01.4	159 46.6	12.2	235 19.9	26.2	168 44.7	03.4	171 34.7	39.0	Achernar	335 44.3	S57 19.6
02	16 03.9	174 46.4	13.4	250 20.7	25.9	183 46.7	03.6	186 36.9	39.1	Acrux	173 37.1	S62 59.8
03	31 06.4	189 46.1	·· 14.6	265 21.5	·· 25.5	198 48.7	·· 03.8	201 39.1	·· 39.2	Adhara	255 31.8	S28 56.6
04	46 08.8	204 45.9	15.9	280 22.4	25.2	213 50.7	04.0	216 41.3	39.3	Aldebaran	291 17.2	N16 28.3
05	61 11.3	219 45.6	17.1	295 23.2	24.8	228 52.7	04.2	231 43.5	39.5			
06	76 13.7	234 45.4	S 9 18.3	310 24.0	N20 24.5	243 54.7	S 4 04.4	246 45.7	S 1 39.6	Alioth	166 42.4	N56 03.8
07	91 16.2	249 45.2	19.6	325 24.8	24.1	258 56.7	04.6	261 47.9	39.7	Alkaid	153 18.3	N49 24.6
08	106 18.7	264 44.9	20.8	340 25.6	23.8	273 58.7	04.8	276 50.1	39.8	Al Na'ir	28 13.6	S47 03.0
M 09	121 21.1	279 44.7	·· 22.0	355 26.5	·· 23.5	289 00.7	·· 05.0	291 52.3	·· 39.9	Alnilam	276 11.0	S 1 12.7
O 10	136 23.6	294 44.4	23.2	10 27.3	23.1	304 02.7	05.2	306 54.5	40.0	Alphard	218 20.2	S 8 34.5
N 11	151 26.1	309 44.2	24.5	25 28.1	22.8	319 04.7	05.4	321 56.7	40.2			
D 12	166 28.5	324 43.9	S 9 25.7	40 28.9	N20 22.4	334 06.7	S 4 05.6	336 58.9	S 1 40.3	Alphecca	126 31.7	N26 46.9
A 13	181 31.0	339 43.7	26.9	55 29.7	22.1	349 08.6	05.8	352 01.1	40.4	Alpheratz	358 08.3	N28 59.3
Y 14	196 33.5	354 43.4	28.2	70 30.6	21.7	4 10.6	06.0	7 03.3	40.5	Altair	62 31.7	N 8 49.3
15	211 35.9	9 43.2	·· 29.4	85 31.4	·· 21.4	19 12.6	·· 06.2	22 05.5	·· 40.6	Ankaa	353 39.2	S42 24.3
16	226 38.4	24 42.9	30.6	100 32.2	21.0	34 14.6	06.4	37 07.7	40.7	Antares	112 56.1	S26 23.5
17	241 40.9	39 42.7	31.8	115 33.0	20.7	49 16.6	06.6	52 09.9	40.9			
18	256 43.3	54 42.4	S 9 33.1	130 33.8	N20 20.4	64 18.6	S 4 06.8	67 12.1	S 1 41.0	Arcturus	146 18.1	N19 17.0
19	271 45.8	69 42.2	34.3	145 34.7	20.0	79 20.6	07.0	82 14.3	41.1	Atria	108 19.7	S68 59.9
20	286 48.2	84 41.9	35.5	160 35.5	19.7	94 22.6	07.2	97 16.5	41.2	Avior	234 28.4	S59 26.8
21	301 50.7	99 41.7	·· 36.7	175 36.3	·· 19.3	109 24.6	·· 07.4	112 18.7	·· 41.3	Bellatrix	278 58.1	N 6 20.1
22	316 53.2	114 41.4	38.0	190 37.1	19.0	124 26.6	07.6	127 20.9	41.4	Betelgeuse	271 27.6	N 7 24.3
23	331 55.6	129 41.2	39.2	205 38.0	18.6	139 28.6	07.8	142 23.1	41.6			
8 00	346 58.1	144 40.9	S 9 40.4	220 38.8	N20 18.3	154 30.6	S 4 08.0	157 25.3	S 1 41.7	Canopus	264 07.1	S52 40.9
01	2 00.6	159 40.7	41.6	235 39.6	17.9	169 32.6	08.2	172 27.5	41.8	Capella	281 10.3	N45 58.6
02	17 03.0	174 40.4	42.9	250 40.4	17.6	184 34.6	08.4	187 29.7	41.9	Deneb	49 47.6	N45 13.1
03	32 05.5	189 40.2	·· 44.1	265 41.3	·· 17.2	199 36.6	·· 08.6	202 31.9	·· 42.0	Denebola	182 58.7	N14 40.7
04	47 08.0	204 39.9	45.3	280 42.1	16.9	214 38.6	08.8	217 34.1	42.1	Diphda	349 19.9	S18 05.2
05	62 10.4	219 39.7	46.5	295 42.9	16.5	229 40.6	09.0	232 36.3	42.2			
06	77 12.9	234 39.4	S 9 47.7	310 43.7	N20 16.2	244 42.6	S 4 09.2	247 38.5	S 1 42.4	Dubhe	194 22.0	N61 51.1
07	92 15.3	249 39.2	49.0	325 44.6	15.8	259 44.6	09.4	262 40.7	42.5	Elnath	278 43.3	N28 35.5
08	107 17.8	264 38.9	50.2	340 45.4	15.5	274 46.6	09.6	277 42.9	42.6	Eltanin	90 57.3	N51 29.8
T 09	122 20.3	279 38.7	·· 51.4	355 46.2	·· 15.1	289 48.6	·· 09.8	292 45.1	·· 42.7	Enif	34 10.6	N 9 47.5
U 10	137 22.7	294 38.4	52.6	10 47.0	14.8	304 50.6	10.0	307 47.3	42.8	Fomalhaut	15 50.3	S29 43.1
E 11	152 25.2	309 38.2	53.9	25 47.9	14.4	319 52.6	10.2	322 49.5	42.9			
S 12	167 27.7	324 37.9	S 9 55.1	40 48.7	N20 14.1	334 54.6	S 4 10.4	337 51.7	S 1 43.1	Gacrux	172 28.5	S57 00.6
D 13	182 30.1	339 37.7	56.3	55 49.5	13.7	349 56.6	10.6	352 53.9	43.2	Gienah	176 17.6	S17 26.2
A 14	197 32.6	354 37.4	57.5	70 50.3	13.4	4 58.6	10.8	7 56.1	43.3	Hadar	149 22.9	S60 17.1
Y 15	212 35.1	9 37.2	·· 58.7	85 51.2	·· 13.0	20 00.6	·· 11.0	22 58.3	·· 43.4	Hamal	328 27.9	N23 22.5
16	227 37.5	24 36.9	9 59.9	100 52.0	12.7	35 02.6	11.2	38 00.5	43.5	Kaus Aust.	84 15.8	S34 23.7
17	242 40.0	39 36.7	10 01.2	115 52.8	12.3	50 04.6	11.4	53 02.7	43.6			
18	257 42.5	54 36.4	S10 02.4	130 53.7	N20 12.0	65 06.6	S 4 11.6	68 04.9	S 1 43.8	Kochab	137 19.6	N74 14.2
19	272 44.9	69 36.2	03.6	145 54.5	11.6	80 08.6	11.8	83 07.0	43.9	Markab	14 02.2	N15 06.4
20	287 47.4	84 35.9	04.8	160 55.3	11.3	95 10.6	12.0	98 09.2	44.0	Menkar	314 40.3	N 4 01.1
21	302 49.8	99 35.7	·· 06.0	175 56.1	·· 10.9	110 12.5	·· 12.2	113 11.4	·· 44.1	Menkent	148 36.5	S36 16.7
22	317 52.3	114 35.4	07.3	190 57.0	10.6	125 14.5	12.4	128 13.6	44.2	Miaplacidus	221 45.6	S69 38.3
23	332 54.8	129 35.1	08.5	205 57.8	10.2	140 16.5	12.6	143 15.8	44.3			
9 00	347 57.2	144 34.9	S10 09.7	220 58.6	N20 09.9	155 18.5	S 4 12.8	158 18.0	S 1 44.5	Mirfak	309 14.9	N49 47.6
01	2 59.7	159 34.6	10.9	235 59.5	09.5	170 20.5	13.0	173 20.2	44.6	Nunki	76 28.2	S26 19.2
02	18 02.2	174 34.4	12.1	251 00.3	09.2	185 22.5	13.2	188 22.4	44.7	Peacock	53 56.9	S56 47.8
03	33 04.6	189 34.1	·· 13.3	266 01.1	·· 08.8	200 24.5	·· 13.4	203 24.6	·· 44.8	Pollux	243 57.6	N28 04.3
04	48 07.1	204 33.9	14.5	281 01.9	08.5	215 26.5	13.6	218 26.8	44.9	Procyon	245 25.3	N 5 16.5
05	63 09.6	219 33.6	15.8	296 02.8	08.1	230 28.5	13.8	233 29.0	45.0			
06	78 12.0	234 33.4	S10 17.0	311 03.6	N20 07.8	245 30.5	S 4 14.0	248 31.2	S 1 45.2	Rasalhague	96 28.9	N12 34.6
07	93 14.5	249 33.1	18.2	326 04.4	07.4	260 32.5	14.2	263 33.4	45.3	Regulus	208 09.6	N12 03.6
08	108 17.0	264 32.8	19.4	341 05.3	07.1	275 34.5	14.4	278 35.6	45.4	Rigel	281 35.4	S 8 13.2
W 09	123 19.4	279 32.6	·· 20.6	356 06.1	·· 06.7	290 36.5	·· 14.6	293 37.8	·· 45.5	Rigil Kent.	140 25.3	S60 45.6
E 10	138 21.9	294 32.3	21.8	11 06.9	06.4	305 38.5	14.8	308 40.0	45.6	Sabik	102 40.4	S15 42.1
D 11	153 24.3	309 32.1	23.0	26 07.8	06.0	320 40.5	15.0	323 42.2	45.7			
N 12	168 26.8	324 31.8	S10 24.2	41 08.6	N20 05.7	335 42.5	S 4 15.2	338 44.4	S 1 45.9	Schedar	350 07.7	N56 26.1
E 13	183 29.3	339 31.6	25.5	56 09.4	05.3	350 44.5	15.4	353 46.6	46.0	Shaula	96 54.8	S37 05.5
S 14	198 31.7	354 31.3	26.7	71 10.3	04.9	5 46.5	15.6	8 48.8	46.1	Sirius	258 55.3	S16 41.3
D 15	213 34.2	9 31.1	·· 27.9	86 11.1	·· 04.6	20 48.5	·· 15.8	23 51.0	·· 46.2	Spica	158 57.1	S11 03.8
A 16	228 36.7	24 30.8	29.1	101 11.9	04.2	35 50.4	16.0	38 53.2	46.3	Suhail	223 10.7	S43 21.3
Y 17	243 39.1	39 30.5	30.3	116 12.8	03.9	50 52.4	16.2	53 55.4	46.4			
18	258 41.6	54 30.3	S10 31.5	131 13.6	N20 03.6	65 54.4	S 4 16.4	68 57.6	S 1 46.5	Vega	80 55.2	N38 46.3
19	273 44.1	69 30.0	32.7	146 14.4	03.2	80 56.4	16.6	83 59.8	46.7	Zuben'ubi	137 32.5	S15 57.8
20	288 46.5	84 29.8	33.9	161 15.3	02.8	95 58.4	16.8	99 02.0	46.8		S.H.A.	Mer. Pass.
21	303 49.0	99 29.5	·· 35.1	176 16.1	·· 02.5	111 00.4	·· 17.0	114 04.2	·· 46.9	Venus	157 42.8	14 22
22	318 51.4	114 29.2	36.3	191 16.9	02.1	126 02.4	17.2	129 06.4	47.0	Mars	233 40.7	9 17
23	333 53.9	129 29.0	37.5	206 17.8	01.7	141 04.4	17.4	144 08.6	47.1	Jupiter	167 32.5	13 40
Mer. Pass.	0 52.0	v −0.3	d 1.2	v 0.8	d 0.3	v 2.0	d 0.2	v 2.2	d 0.1	Saturn	170 27.2	13 28

G.M.T.	SUN G.H.A.	Dec.	MOON G.H.A.	v	Dec.	d	H.P.
7 00	180 27.7	N 6 11.2	87 32.2	12.1	S19 33.8	4.4	54.5
01	195 27.9	10.2	102 03.3	12.0	19 38.2	4.2	54.5
02	210 28.1	09.3	116 34.3	12.1	19 42.4	4.2	54.5
03	225 28.3 ··	08.4	131 05.4	12.0	19 46.6	4.0	54.5
04	240 28.5	07.4	145 36.4	11.9	19 50.6	4.0	54.5
05	255 28.7	06.5	160 07.3	11.9	19 54.6	3.9	54.5
06	270 28.9 N 6 05.6		174 38.2	11.9	S19 58.5	3.8	54.6
07	285 29.1	04.6	189 09.1	11.8	20 02.3	3.7	54.6
08	300 29.4	03.7	203 39.9	11.8	20 06.0	3.6	54.6
M 09	315 29.6 ··	02.8	218 10.7	11.7	20 09.6	3.5	54.6
O 10	330 29.8	01.8	232 41.4	11.7	20 13.1	3.4	54.6
N 11	345 30.0	6 00.9	247 12.1	11.6	20 16.5	3.4	54.6
D 12	0 30.2 N 5 59.9		261 42.7	11.6	S20 19.9	3.2	54.6
A 13	15 30.4	59.0	276 13.3	11.6	20 23.1	3.1	54.7
Y 14	30 30.6	58.1	290 43.9	11.5	20 26.2	3.1	54.7
15	45 30.8 ··	57.1	305 14.4	11.5	20 29.3	2.9	54.7
→16	60 31.1	56.2	319 44.9	11.4	20 32.2	2.9	54.7
→17	75 31.3	55.3	334 15.3	11.4	20 35.1	2.8	54.7
18	90 31.5 N 5 54.3		348 45.7	11.4	S20 37.9	2.6	54.7
19	105 31.7	53.4	3 16.1	11.3	20 40.5	2.6	54.8
20	120 31.9	52.5	17 46.4	11.3	20 43.1	2.4	54.8
21	135 32.1 ··	51.5	32 16.7	11.2	20 45.5	2.4	54.8
22	150 32.3	50.6	46 46.9	11.2	20 47.9	2.3	54.8
23	165 32.6	49.6	61 17.1	11.1	20 50.2	2.2	54.8
8 00	180 32.8 N 5 48.7		75 47.2	11.2	S20 52.4	2.0	54.9
01	195 33.0	47.8	90 17.4	11.0	20 54.4	2.0	54.9
02	210 33.2	46.8	104 47.4	11.1	20 56.4	1.9	54.9
03	225 33.4 ··	45.9	119 17.5	11.0	20 58.3	1.7	54.9
04	240 33.6	44.9	133 47.5	10.9	21 00.0	1.7	54.9
05	255 33.8	44.0	148 17.4	11.0	21 01.7	1.6	55.0
06	270 34.1 N 5 43.1		162 47.4	10.8	S21 03.3	1.4	55.0
07	285 34.3	42.1	177 17.2	10.9	21 04.7	1.4	55.0
08	300 34.5	41.2	191 47.1	10.8	21 06.1	1.2	55.0
T 09	315 34.7 ··	40.2	206 16.9	10.8	21 07.3	1.2	55.0
U 10	330 34.9	39.3	220 46.7	10.7	21 08.5	1.0	55.1
E 11	345 35.1	38.4	235 16.4	10.7	21 09.5	1.0	55.1
S 12	0 35.3 N 5 37.4		249 46.1	10.7	S21 10.5	0.8	55.1
D 13	15 35.6	36.5	264 15.8	10.6	21 11.3	0.8	55.1
A 14	30 35.8	35.5	278 45.4	10.6	21 12.1	0.6	55.1
Y 15	45 36.0 ··	34.6	293 15.0	10.6	21 12.7	0.5	55.2
16	60 36.2	33.7	307 44.6	10.5	21 13.2	0.4	55.2
17	75 36.4	32.7	322 14.1	10.5	21 13.6	0.4	55.2
18	90 36.6 N 5 31.8		336 43.6	10.5	S21 14.0	0.2	55.2
19	105 36.9	30.8	351 13.1	10.4	21 14.2	0.1	55.3
20	120 37.1	29.9	5 42.5	10.4	21 14.3	0.0	55.3
21	135 37.3 ··	28.9	20 11.9	10.4	21 14.3	0.2	55.3
22	150 37.5	28.0	34 41.3	10.4	21 14.1	0.2	55.3
23	165 37.7	27.1	49 10.7	10.3	21 13.9	0.3	55.4
9 00	180 37.9 N 5 26.1		63 40.0	10.3	S21 13.6	0.5	55.4
01	195 38.1	25.2	78 09.3	10.2	21 13.1	0.5	55.4
02	210 38.4	24.2	92 38.5	10.2	21 12.6	0.7	55.4
03	225 38.6 ··	23.3	107 07.7	10.2	21 11.9	0.7	55.5
04	240 38.8	22.4	121 36.9	10.2	21 11.2	0.9	55.5
05	255 39.0	21.4	136 06.1	10.2	21 10.3	1.0	55.5
06	270 39.2 N 5 20.5		150 35.3	10.1	S21 09.3	1.1	55.5
07	285 39.4	19.5	165 04.4	10.1	21 08.2	1.2	55.6
W 08	300 39.7	18.6	179 33.5	10.0	21 07.0	1.3	55.6
E 09	315 39.9 ··	17.6	194 02.5	10.1	21 05.7	1.5	55.6
D 10	330 40.1	16.7	208 31.6	10.0	21 04.2	1.5	55.7
N 11	345 40.3	15.7	223 00.6	10.0	21 02.7	1.6	55.7
E 12	0 40.5 N 5 14.8		237 29.6	10.0	S21 01.1	1.8	55.7
S 13	15 40.7	13.9	251 58.6	9.9	20 59.3	1.9	55.7
D 14	30 41.0	12.9	266 27.5	9.9	20 57.4	2.0	55.8
A 15	45 41.2 ··	12.0	280 56.4	9.9	20 55.4	2.1	55.8
Y 16	60 41.4	11.0	295 25.3	9.9	20 53.3	2.2	55.8
17	75 41.6	10.1	309 54.2	9.7	20 51.1	2.3	55.8
18	90 41.8 N 5 09.1		324 23.1	9.8	S20 48.8	2.4	55.9
19	105 42.0	08.2	338 51.9	9.9	20 46.4	2.6	55.9
20	120 42.3	07.2	353 20.8	9.8	20 43.8	2.6	55.9
21	135 42.5 ··	06.3	7 49.6	9.8	20 41.2	2.8	56.0
22	150 42.7	05.3	22 18.4	9.7	20 38.4	2.9	56.0
23	165 42.9	04.4	36 47.1	9.8	20 35.5	3.0	56.0
	S.D. 15.9	d 0.9	S.D. 14.9		15.0		15.2

Lat.	Naut.	Civil	Sunrise	Moonrise 7	8	9	10
N 72	00 32	03 15	04 34	■	■	■	■
N 70	01 47	03 35	04 43	■	■	■	20 12
68	02 22	03 50	04 51	17 21	18 35	19 08	19 16
66	02 47	04 02	04 57	16 34	17 38	18 20	18 43
64	03 05	04 12	05 02	16 03	17 04	17 49	18 18
62	03 20	04 20	05 07	15 41	16 39	17 26	17 59
60	03 32	04 27	05 11	15 22	16 20	17 07	17 43
N 58	03 43	04 34	05 14	15 07	16 04	16 52	17 30
56	03 52	04 39	05 17	14 54	15 50	16 38	17 18
54	03 59	04 44	05 20	14 43	15 38	16 27	17 08
52	04 06	04 48	05 23	14 33	15 28	16 17	16 59
50	04 12	04 52	05 25	14 24	15 19	16 08	16 50
45	04 24	05 00	05 30	14 05	14 59	15 48	16 33
N 40	04 34	05 07	05 34	13 50	14 43	15 33	16 19
35	04 42	05 12	05 38	13 37	14 30	15 20	16 07
30	04 48	05 16	05 41	13 26	14 18	15 08	15 56
20	04 58	05 24	05 46	13 07	13 58	14 48	15 38
N 10	05 05	05 29	05 50	12 50	13 40	14 31	15 22
0	05 10	05 34	05 54	12 35	13 24	14 15	15 07
S 10	05 13	05 37	05 58	12 19	13 08	13 59	14 52
20	05 15	05 40	06 03	12 03	12 51	13 42	14 36
30	05 15	05 43	06 07	11 44	12 31	13 22	14 18
35	05 15	05 44	06 10	11 33	12 19	13 11	14 07
40	05 14	05 46	06 13	11 20	12 06	12 58	13 55
45	05 13	05 47	06 16	11 05	11 50	12 42	13 40
S 50	05 10	05 48	06 20	10 47	11 31	12 23	13 23
52	05 09	05 48	06 22	10 39	11 22	12 14	13 14
54	05 08	05 48	06 24	10 29	11 11	12 03	13 05
56	05 06	05 49	06 26	10 18	11 00	11 52	12 54
58	05 04	05 49	06 28	10 06	10 46	11 39	12 42
S 60	05 01	05 49	06 31	09 52	10 31	11 23	12 28

Lat.	Sunset	Civil	Naut.	Moonset 7	8	9	10
N 72	19 18	20 35	23 01	■	■	■	■
N 70	19 09	20 17	22 01	■	■	■	22 36
68	19 02	20 02	21 28	20 08	20 37	21 51	23 31
66	18 56	19 51	21 05	20 55	21 35	22 39	24 04
64	18 51	19 41	20 47	21 26	22 09	23 10	24 28
62	18 47	19 33	20 32	21 49	22 33	23 33	24 47
60	18 43	19 26	20 21	22 07	22 53	23 51	25 03
N 58	18 40	19 20	20 10	22 23	23 09	24 07	00 07
56	18 37	19 15	20 02	22 36	23 22	24 20	00 20
54	18 34	19 10	19 54	22 47	23 34	24 31	00 31
52	18 31	19 06	19 48	22 57	23 45	24 41	00 41
50	18 29	19 02	19 42	23 06	23 54	24 50	00 50
45	18 25	18 54	19 30	23 26	24 14	00 14	01 09
N 40	18 21	18 48	19 20	23 41	24 30	00 30	01 24
35	18 17	18 43	19 13	23 54	24 43	00 43	01 37
30	18 14	18 38	19 07	24 06	00 06	00 55	01 48
20	18 09	18 31	18 57	24 25	00 25	01 15	02 08
N 10	18 05	18 26	18 51	24 42	00 42	01 32	02 24
0	18 01	18 22	18 46	00 10	00 58	01 49	02 40
S 10	17 57	18 18	18 43	00 25	01 14	02 05	02 56
20	17 53	18 15	18 41	00 41	01 31	02 22	03 12
30	17 49	18 13	18 40	00 59	01 51	02 42	03 31
35	17 46	18 11	18 41	01 09	02 03	02 54	03 42
40	17 43	18 10	18 42	01 22	02 16	03 07	03 55
45	17 40	18 09	18 43	01 36	02 31	03 23	04 10
S 50	17 36	18 09	18 46	01 54	02 50	03 42	04 28
52	17 35	18 08	18 47	02 02	03 00	03 51	04 37
54	17 33	18 08	18 49	02 12	03 10	04 02	04 46
56	17 31	18 08	18 51	02 22	03 21	04 13	04 57
58	17 28	18 07	18 53	02 34	03 34	04 27	05 09
S 60	17 26	18 07	18 56	02 48	03 50	04 42	05 24

	SUN			MOON			
Day	Eqn. of Time 00h	12h	Mer. Pass.	Mer. Pass. Upper	Lower	Age	Phase
	m s	m s	h m	h m	h m	d	
7	01 50	02 00	11 58	18 46	06 22	09	
8	02 11	02 21	11 58	19 36	07 11	10	
9	02 31	02 42	11 57	20 28	08 02	11	◖

G.M.T.	ARIES G.H.A.	VENUS −3.5 G.H.A.	Dec.	MARS +1.8 G.H.A.	Dec.	JUPITER −1.2 G.H.A.	Dec.	SATURN +1.1 G.H.A.	Dec.	STARS Name	S.H.A.	Dec.
d h	° ′	° ′	° ′	° ′	° ′	° ′	° ′	° ′	° ′		° ′	° ′
10 00	348 56.4	144 28.7 S10 38.7		221 18.6 N20 01.4		156 06.4 S 4 17.6		159 10.8 S 1 47.3		Acamar	315 36.5	S40 22.5
01	3 58.8	159 28.5	40.0	236 19.4	01.0	171 08.4	17.8	174 13.0	47.4	Achernar	335 44.3	S57 19.7
02	19 01.3	174 28.2	41.2	251 20.3	00.7	186 10.4	18.0	189 15.2	47.5	Acrux	173 37.2	S62 59.8
03	34 03.8	189 27.9 ··	42.4	266 21.1 20 00.3		201 12.4 ··	18.2	204 17.4 ··	47.6	Adhara	255 31.7	S28 56.6
04	49 06.2	204 27.7	43.6	281 21.9 19 59.9		216 14.4	18.4	219 19.6	47.7	Aldebaran	291 17.2	N16 28.4
05	64 08.7	219 27.4	44.8	296 22.8	59.6	231 16.4	18.6	234 21.8	47.8			
06	79 11.2	234 27.2 S10 46.0		311 23.6 N19 59.2		246 18.4 S 4 18.8		249 24.0 S 1 48.0		Alioth	166 42.4	N56 03.8
07	94 13.6	249 26.9	47.2	326 24.4	58.9	261 20.3	19.0	264 26.2	48.1	Alkaid	153 18.3	N49 24.6
T 08	109 16.1	264 26.6	48.4	341 25.3	58.5	276 22.3	19.2	279 28.4	48.2	Al Na'ir	28 13.6	S47 03.0
H 09	124 18.6	279 26.4 ··	49.6	356 26.1 ··	58.2	291 24.3 ··	19.4	294 30.5 ··	48.3	Alnilam	276 11.0	S 1 12.7
U 10	139 21.0	294 26.1	50.8	11 26.9	57.8	306 26.3	19.6	309 32.7	48.4	Alphard	218 20.2	S 8 34.5
R 11	154 23.5	309 25.9	52.0	26 27.8	57.4	321 28.3	19.8	324 34.9	48.5			
S 12	169 25.9	324 25.6 S10 53.2		41 28.6 N19 57.1		336 30.3 S 4 20.0		339 37.1 S 1 48.7		Alphecca	126 31.7	N26 46.9
D 13	184 28.4	339 25.3	54.4	56 29.5	56.7	351 32.3	20.2	354 39.3	48.8	Alpheratz	358 08.3	N28 59.3
A 14	199 30.9	354 25.1	55.6	71 30.3	56.4	6 34.3	20.4	9 41.5	48.9	Altair	62 31.7	N 8 49.3
Y 15	214 33.3	9 24.8 ··	56.8	86 31.1 ··	56.0	21 36.3 ··	20.6	24 43.7 ··	49.0	Ankaa	353 39.2	S42 24.3
16	229 35.8	24 24.5	58.0	101 32.0	55.6	36 38.3	20.8	39 45.9	49.1	Antares	112 56.1	S26 23.5
17	244 38.3	39 24.3 10 59.2		116 32.8	55.3	51 40.3	21.0	54 48.1	49.2			
18	259 40.7	54 24.0 S11 00.4		131 33.6 N19 54.9		66 42.3 S 4 21.2		69 50.3 S 1 49.4		Arcturus	146 18.1	N19 17.0
19	274 43.2	69 23.8	01.6	146 34.5	54.6	81 44.3	21.4	84 52.5	49.5	Atria	108 19.8	S68 59.9
20	289 45.7	84 23.5	02.8	161 35.3	54.2	96 46.3	21.6	99 54.7	49.6	Avior	234 28.4	S59 26.8
21	304 48.1	99 23.2 ··	04.0	176 36.2 ··	53.8	111 48.2 ··	21.8	114 56.9 ··	49.7	Bellatrix	278 58.0	N 6 20.1
22	319 50.6	114 23.0	05.2	191 37.0	53.5	126 50.2	22.0	129 59.1	49.8	Betelgeuse	271 27.6	N 7 24.3
23	334 53.1	129 22.7	06.4	206 37.8	53.1	141 52.2	22.2	145 01.3	49.9			
11 00	349 55.5	144 22.4 S11 07.6		221 38.7 N19 52.7		156 54.2 S 4 22.4		160 03.5 S 1 50.1		Canopus	264 07.1	S52 40.9
01	4 58.0	159 22.2	08.8	236 39.5	52.4	171 56.2	22.6	175 05.7	50.2	Capella	281 10.3	N45 58.6
02	20 00.4	174 21.9	10.0	251 40.4	52.0	186 58.2	22.8	190 07.9	50.3	Deneb	49 47.7	N45 13.1
03	35 02.9	189 21.6 ··	11.2	266 41.2 ··	51.7	202 00.2 ··	23.0	205 10.1 ··	50.4	Denebola	182 58.7	N14 40.7
04	50 05.4	204 21.4	12.4	281 42.0	51.3	217 02.2	23.2	220 12.3	50.5	Diphda	349 19.9	S18 05.2
05	65 07.8	219 21.1	13.6	296 42.9	50.9	232 04.2	23.4	235 14.5	50.6			
06	80 10.3	234 20.8 S11 14.8		311 43.7 N19 50.6		247 06.2 S 4 23.6		250 16.7 S 1 50.8		Dubhe	194 21.9	N61 51.1
07	95 12.8	249 20.6	16.0	326 44.6	50.2	262 08.2	23.8	265 18.9	50.9	Elnath	278 43.3	N28 35.5
08	110 15.2	264 20.3	17.2	341 45.4	49.8	277 10.1	24.0	280 21.1	51.0	Eltanin	90 57.3	N51 29.8
F 09	125 17.7	279 20.0 ··	18.4	356 46.2 ··	49.5	292 12.1 ··	24.2	295 23.3 ··	51.1	Enif	34 10.6	N 9 47.5
R 10	140 20.2	294 19.8	19.6	11 47.1	49.1	307 14.1	24.5	310 25.4	51.2	Fomalhaut	15 50.3	S29 43.1
I 11	155 22.6	309 19.5	20.7	26 47.9	48.8	322 16.1	24.7	325 27.6	51.3			
D 12	170 25.1	324 19.2 S11 21.9		41 48.8 N19 48.4		337 18.1 S 4 24.9		340 29.8 S 1 51.5		Gacrux	172 28.6	S57 00.6
A 13	185 27.5	339 19.0	23.1	56 49.6	48.0	352 20.1	25.1	355 32.0	51.6	Gienah	176 17.6	S17 26.2
Y 14	200 30.0	354 18.7	24.3	71 50.5	47.7	7 22.1	25.3	10 34.2	51.7	Hadar	149 22.9	S60 17.1
15	215 32.5	9 18.4 ··	25.5	86 51.3 ··	47.3	22 24.1 ··	25.5	25 36.4 ··	51.8	Hamal	328 27.9	N23 22.5
16	230 34.9	24 18.2	26.7	101 52.1	46.9	37 26.1	25.7	40 38.6	51.9	Kaus Aust.	84 15.8	S34 23.7
17	245 37.4	39 17.9	27.9	116 53.0	46.6	52 28.1	25.9	55 40.8	52.1			
18	260 39.9	54 17.6 S11 29.1		131 53.8 N19 46.2		67 30.1 S 4 26.1		70 43.0 S 1 52.2		Kochab	137 19.7	N74 14.2
19	275 42.3	69 17.3	30.3	146 54.7	45.8	82 32.0	26.3	85 45.2	52.3	Markab	14 02.2	N15 06.4
20	290 44.8	84 17.1	31.5	161 55.5	45.5	97 34.0	26.5	100 47.4	52.4	Menkar	314 40.3	N 4 01.1
21	305 47.3	99 16.8 ··	32.7	176 56.4 ··	45.1	112 36.0 ··	26.7	115 49.6 ··	52.5	Menkent	148 36.5	S36 16.7
22	320 49.7	114 16.5	33.8	191 57.2	44.7	127 38.0	26.9	130 51.8	52.6	Miaplacidus	221 45.6	S69 38.3
23	335 52.2	129 16.3	35.0	206 58.1	44.4	142 40.0	27.1	145 54.0	52.8			
12 00	350 54.7	144 16.0 S11 36.2		221 58.9 N19 44.0		157 42.0 S 4 27.3		160 56.2 S 1 52.9		Mirfak	309 14.9	N49 47.6
01	5 57.1	159 15.7	37.4	236 59.7	43.6	172 44.0	27.5	175 58.4	53.0	Nunki	76 28.2	S26 19.2
02	20 59.6	174 15.5	38.6	252 00.6	43.3	187 46.0	27.7	191 00.6	53.1	Peacock	53 56.9	S56 47.8
03	36 02.0	189 15.2 ··	39.8	267 01.4 ··	42.9	202 48.0 ··	27.9	206 02.8 ··	53.2	Pollux	243 57.6	N28 04.3
04	51 04.5	204 14.9	41.0	282 02.3	42.5	217 50.0	28.1	221 05.0	53.3	Procyon	245 25.3	N 5 16.5
05	66 07.0	219 14.6	42.2	297 03.1	42.2	232 51.9	28.3	236 07.1	53.5			
06	81 09.4	234 14.4 S11 43.3		312 04.0 N19 41.8		247 53.9 S 4 28.5		251 09.3 S 1 53.6		Rasalhague	96 28.9	N12 34.6
07	96 11.9	249 14.1	44.5	327 04.8	41.4	262 55.9	28.7	266 11.5	53.7	Regulus	208 09.6	N12 03.6
S 08	111 14.4	264 13.8	45.7	342 05.7	41.1	277 57.9	28.9	281 13.7	53.8	Rigel	281 35.4	S 8 13.2
A 09	126 16.8	279 13.5 ··	46.9	357 06.5 ··	40.7	292 59.9 ··	29.1	296 15.9 ··	53.9	Rigil Kent.	140 25.3	S60 45.6
T 10	141 19.3	294 13.3	48.1	12 07.4	40.3	308 01.9	29.3	311 18.1	54.0	Sabik	102 40.4	S15 42.1
U 11	156 21.8	309 13.0	49.3	27 08.2	39.9	323 03.9	29.5	326 20.3	54.2			
R 12	171 24.2	324 12.7 S11 50.4		42 09.1 N19 39.6		338 05.9 S 4 29.7		341 22.5 S 1 54.3		Schedar	350 07.7	N56 26.1
D 13	186 26.7	339 12.5	51.6	57 09.9	39.2	353 07.9	29.9	356 24.7	54.4	Shaula	96 54.8	S37 05.5
A 14	201 29.2	354 12.2	52.8	72 10.8	38.8	8 09.8	30.1	11 26.9	54.5	Sirius	258 55.2	S16 41.3
Y 15	216 31.6	9 11.9 ··	54.0	87 11.6 ··	38.5	23 11.8 ··	30.3	26 29.1 ··	54.6	Spica	158 57.1	S11 03.8
16	231 34.1	24 11.6	55.2	102 12.4	38.1	38 13.8	30.5	41 31.3	54.7	Suhail	223 10.7	S43 21.3
17	246 36.5	39 11.4	56.4	117 13.3	37.7	53 15.8	30.7	56 33.5	54.9			
18	261 39.0	54 11.1 S11 57.5		132 14.1 N19 37.4		68 17.8 S 4 30.9		71 35.7 S 1 55.0		Vega	80 55.2	N38 46.3
19	276 41.5	69 10.8	58.7	147 15.0	37.0	83 19.8	31.1	86 37.9	55.1	Zuben'ubi	137 32.5	S15 57.8
20	291 43.9	84 10.5 11 59.9		162 15.8	36.6	98 21.8	31.3	101 40.1	55.2			
21	306 46.4	99 10.3 12 01.1		177 16.7 ··	36.2	113 23.8 ··	31.5	116 42.3 ··	55.3		S.H.A.	Mer. Pass.
22	321 48.9	114 10.0	02.3	192 17.5	35.9	128 25.8	31.7	131 44.4	55.5		° ′	h m
23	336 51.3	129 09.7	03.4	207 18.4	35.5	143 27.7	31.9	146 46.6	55.6	Venus	154 26.9	14 23
										Mars	231 43.2	9 13
Mer. Pass.	h m 0 40.2	v −0.3 d 1.2		v 0.8 d 0.4		v 2.0 d 0.2		v 2.2 d 0.1		Jupiter	166 58.7	13 31
										Saturn	170 08.0	13 18

G.M.T.	SUN G.H.A.	Dec.	MOON G.H.A.	v	Dec.	d	H.P.
	° ′	° ′	° ′	′	° ′	′	′
10 00	180 43.1	N 5 03.5	51 15.9	9.7	S20 32.5	3.1	56.1
01	195 43.4	02.5	65 44.6	9.8	20 29.4	3.2	56.1
02	210 43.6	01.6	80 13.4	9.7	20 26.2	3.3	56.1
03	225 43.8	5 00.6	94 42.1	9.7	20 22.9	3.5	56.1
04	240 44.0	4 59.7	109 10.8	9.6	20 19.4	3.5	56.2
05	255 44.2	58.7	123 39.4	9.7	20 15.9	3.7	56.2
06	270 44.4	N 4 57.8	138 08.1	9.7	S20 12.2	3.8	56.2
07	285 44.7	56.8	152 36.8	9.6	20 08.4	3.8	56.3
T 08	300 44.9	55.9	167 05.4	9.6	20 04.6	4.1	56.3
H 09	315 45.1 ..	54.9	181 34.0	9.7	20 00.5	4.1	56.3
U 10	330 45.3	54.0	196 02.7	9.6	19 56.4	4.2	56.4
R 11	345 45.5	53.0	210 31.3	9.6	19 52.2	4.3	56.4
S 12	0 45.8	N 4 52.1	224 59.9	9.6	S19 47.9	4.5	56.4
D 13	15 46.0	51.1	239 28.5	9.6	19 43.4	4.5	56.4
A 14	30 46.2	50.2	253 57.1	9.5	19 38.9	4.7	56.5
Y 15	45 46.4 ..	49.2	268 25.6	9.6	19 34.2	4.8	56.5
16	60 46.6	48.3	282 54.2	9.6	19 29.4	4.9	56.5
17	75 46.8	47.3	297 22.8	9.5	19 24.5	5.0	56.6
18	90 47.1	N 4 46.4	311 51.3	9.6	S19 19.5	5.1	56.6
19	105 47.3	45.5	326 19.9	9.5	19 14.4	5.3	56.6
20	120 47.5	44.5	340 48.4	9.6	19 09.1	5.3	56.7
21	135 47.7 ..	43.6	355 17.0	9.5	19 03.8	5.4	56.7
22	150 47.9	42.6	9 45.5	9.6	18 58.4	5.6	56.7
23	165 48.2	41.7	24 14.0	9.6	18 52.8	5.7	56.8
11 00	180 48.4	N 4 40.7	38 42.6	9.5	S18 47.1	5.8	56.8
01	195 48.6	39.8	53 11.1	9.5	18 41.3	5.8	56.8
02	210 48.8	38.8	67 39.6	9.5	18 35.5	6.0	56.9
03	225 49.0 ..	37.9	82 08.2	9.5	18 29.5	6.1	56.9
04	240 49.3	36.9	96 36.7	9.5	18 23.4	6.3	56.9
05	255 49.5	36.0	111 05.2	9.5	18 17.1	6.3	57.0
06	270 49.7	N 4 35.0	125 33.7	9.5	S18 10.8	6.4	57.0
07	285 49.9	34.1	140 02.2	9.6	18 04.4	6.5	57.0
08	300 50.1	33.1	154 30.8	9.5	17 57.9	6.7	57.1
F 09	315 50.4 ..	32.2	168 59.3	9.5	17 51.2	6.7	57.1
R 10	330 50.6	31.2	183 27.8	9.5	17 44.5	6.9	57.1
I 11	345 50.8	30.3	197 56.3	9.6	17 37.6	6.9	57.2
D 12	0 51.0	N 4 29.3	212 24.9	9.5	S17 30.7	7.1	57.2
A 13	15 51.2	28.3	226 53.4	9.5	17 23.6	7.2	57.2
Y 14	30 51.5	27.4	241 21.9	9.5	17 16.4	7.2	57.3
15	45 51.7 ..	26.4	255 50.5	9.5	17 09.2	7.4	57.3
16	60 51.9	25.5	270 19.0	9.6	17 01.8	7.5	57.3
17	75 52.1	24.5	284 47.6	9.5	16 54.3	7.6	57.4
18	90 52.3	N 4 23.6	299 16.1	9.6	S16 46.7	7.7	57.4
19	105 52.6	22.6	313 44.7	9.5	16 39.0	7.7	57.4
20	120 52.8	21.7	328 13.2	9.6	16 31.3	7.9	57.5
21	135 53.0 ..	20.7	342 41.8	9.5	16 23.4	8.0	57.5
22	150 53.2	19.8	357 10.3	9.6	16 15.4	8.1	57.5
23	165 53.4	18.8	11 38.9	9.6	16 07.3	8.2	57.5
12 00	180 53.7	N 4 17.9	26 07.5	9.6	S15 59.1	8.3	57.6
01	195 53.9	16.9	40 36.1	9.6	15 50.8	8.4	57.6
02	210 54.1	16.0	55 04.7	9.6	15 42.4	8.4	57.6
03	225 54.3 ..	15.0	69 33.3	9.6	15 34.0	8.6	57.7
04	240 54.5	14.1	84 01.9	9.6	15 25.4	8.7	57.7
05	255 54.8	13.1	98 30.5	9.6	15 16.7	8.7	57.7
06	270 55.0	N 4 12.2	112 59.1	9.7	S15 08.0	8.9	57.8
07	285 55.2	11.2	127 27.8	9.6	14 59.1	9.0	57.8
S 08	300 55.4	10.2	141 56.4	9.6	14 50.1	9.0	57.8
A 09	315 55.6 ..	09.3	156 25.0	9.7	14 41.1	9.1	57.9
T 10	330 55.9	08.3	170 53.7	9.7	14 32.0	9.3	57.9
U 11	345 56.1	07.4	185 22.4	9.6	14 22.7	9.3	57.9
R 12	0 56.3	N 4 06.4	199 51.0	9.7	S14 13.4	9.4	58.0
D 13	15 56.5	05.5	214 19.7	9.7	14 04.0	9.5	58.0
A 14	30 56.8	04.5	228 48.4	9.7	13 54.5	9.6	58.0
Y 15	45 57.0 ..	03.6	243 17.1	9.7	13 44.9	9.7	58.1
16	60 57.2	02.6	257 45.8	9.7	13 35.2	9.7	58.1
17	75 57.4	01.7	272 14.5	9.7	13 25.5	9.9	58.1
18	90 57.6	N 4 00.7	286 43.2	9.7	S13 15.6	9.9	58.2
19	105 57.9	3 59.7	301 11.9	9.8	13 05.7	10.0	58.2
20	120 58.1	58.8	315 40.7	9.7	12 55.7	10.1	58.2
21	135 58.3 ..	57.8	330 09.4	9.8	12 45.6	10.2	58.2
22	150 58.5	56.9	344 38.2	9.8	12 35.4	10.3	58.3
23	165 58.7	55.9	359 07.0	9.7	12 25.1	10.3	58.3
	S.D. 15.9	d 1.0	S.D. 15.4		15.6		15.8

Lat.	Twilight Naut.	Civil	Sunrise	Moonrise 10	11	12	13
°	h m	h m	h m	h m	h m	h m	h m
N 72	01 26	03 33	04 48	■	20 34	20 00	19 40
N 70	02 11	03 49	04 56	20 12	19 48	19 36	19 27
68	02 40	04 02	05 02	19 16	19 18	19 18	19 16
66	03 01	04 13	05 07	18 43	18 56	19 03	19 07
64	03 17	04 21	05 11	18 18	18 38	18 51	19 00
62	03 30	04 29	05 15	17 59	18 23	18 40	18 54
60	03 41	04 35	05 17	17 43	18 10	18 31	18 48
N 58	03 51	04 40	05 21	17 30	17 59	18 23	18 43
56	03 59	04 45	05 23	17 18	17 50	18 16	18 39
54	04 06	04 49	05 26	17 08	17 42	18 10	18 35
52	04 12	04 53	05 28	16 59	17 34	18 04	18 31
50	04 17	04 57	05 30	16 50	17 27	17 59	18 28
45	04 28	05 04	05 34	16 31	17 13	17 48	18 20
N 40	04 37	05 10	05 37	16 19	17 01	17 39	18 14
35	04 44	05 14	05 40	16 07	16 50	17 31	18 09
30	04 50	05 18	05 42	15 56	16 41	17 24	18 05
20	04 59	05 24	05 46	15 38	16 26	17 12	17 57
N 10	05 04	05 29	05 50	15 22	16 12	17 01	17 50
0	05 09	05 33	05 53	15 07	15 59	16 51	17 43
S 10	05 11	05 36	05 57	14 52	15 46	16 41	17 36
20	05 12	05 38	06 00	14 36	15 33	16 31	17 29
30	05 12	05 40	06 03	14 18	15 17	16 18	17 21
35	05 11	05 40	06 05	14 07	15 08	16 11	17 17
40	05 09	05 41	06 08	13 55	14 57	16 03	17 11
45	05 07	05 41	06 10	13 40	14 45	15 54	17 05
S 50	05 04	05 41	06 13	13 23	14 30	15 42	16 58
52	05 02	05 41	06 15	13 14	14 23	15 37	16 54
54	05 00	05 41	06 16	13 05	14 15	15 31	16 50
56	04 58	05 41	06 18	12 54	14 06	15 24	16 46
58	04 55	05 41	06 20	12 42	13 56	15 17	16 41
S 60	04 52	05 40	06 22	12 28	13 45	15 08	16 36

Lat.	Sunset	Twilight Civil	Naut.	Moonset 10	11	12	13
°	h m	h m	h m	h m	h m	h m	h m
N 72	19 02	20 17	22 17	■	■	00 05	02 28
N 70	18 55	20 01	21 36	22 36	24 49	00 49	02 50
68	18 49	19 48	21 09	23 31	25 18	01 18	03 07
66	18 45	19 38	20 49	24 04	00 04	01 40	03 21
64	18 40	19 30	20 33	24 28	00 28	01 57	03 32
62	18 37	19 23	20 20	24 47	00 47	02 11	03 41
60	18 34	19 17	20 10	25 03	01 03	02 23	03 49
N 58	18 31	19 11	20 01	00 07	01 16	02 33	03 56
56	18 29	19 07	19 53	00 20	01 27	02 42	04 02
54	18 26	19 02	19 46	00 31	01 37	02 50	04 08
52	18 25	18 59	19 40	00 41	01 46	02 57	04 13
50	18 23	18 55	19 35	00 50	01 54	03 03	04 18
45	18 19	18 48	19 24	01 09	02 10	03 17	04 27
N 40	18 16	18 43	19 15	01 24	02 24	03 28	04 35
35	18 13	18 38	19 08	01 37	02 36	03 38	04 42
30	18 11	18 35	19 03	01 48	02 46	03 46	04 48
20	18 06	18 29	18 54	02 08	03 03	04 00	04 59
N 10	18 03	18 24	18 49	02 24	03 18	04 13	05 08
0	18 00	18 21	18 45	02 40	03 32	04 24	05 16
S 10	17 57	18 18	18 42	02 56	03 46	04 36	05 24
20	17 54	18 16	18 41	03 12	04 01	04 48	05 33
30	17 50	18 14	18 42	03 31	04 18	05 02	05 43
35	17 48	18 14	18 43	03 42	04 28	05 10	05 49
40	17 46	18 13	18 45	03 55	04 39	05 19	05 55
45	17 44	18 13	18 47	04 10	04 52	05 29	06 03
S 50	17 41	18 13	18 50	04 28	05 08	05 42	06 12
52	17 39	18 13	18 52	04 37	05 15	05 48	06 16
54	17 38	18 13	18 54	04 47	05 23	05 54	06 21
56	17 36	18 13	18 57	04 57	05 33	06 02	06 26
58	17 35	18 14	18 59	05 09	05 43	06 10	06 31
S 60	17 33	18 14	19 03	05 24	05 55	06 19	06 37

Day	SUN Eqn. of Time 00h	12h	Mer. Pass.	MOON Mer. Pass. Upper	Lower	Age	Phase
	m s	m s	h m	h m	h m	d	
10	02 52	03 03	11 57	21 20	08 54	12	
11	03 13	03 24	11 57	22 12	09 46	13	
12	03 34	03 45	11 56	23 04	10 38	14	◖

G.M.T.	ARIES G.H.A.	VENUS −3.6 G.H.A.	Dec.	MARS +1.8 G.H.A.	Dec.	JUPITER −1.2 G.H.A.	Dec.	SATURN +1.1 G.H.A.	Dec.	STARS Name	S.H.A.	Dec.
13 00	351 53.8	144 09.4	S12 04.6	222 19.2	N19 35.1	158 29.7	S 4 32.1	161 48.8	S 1 55.7	Acamar	315 36.5	S40 22.5
01	6 56.3	159 09.1	05.8	237 20.1	34.8	173 31.7	32.3	176 51.0	55.8	Achernar	335 44.2	S57 19.7
02	21 58.7	174 08.9	07.0	252 20.9	34.4	188 33.7	32.5	191 53.2	55.9	Acrux	173 37.2	S62 59.8
03	37 01.2	189 08.6	·· 08.1	267 21.8	·· 34.0	203 35.7	·· 32.7	206 55.4	·· 56.0	Adhara	255 31.7	S28 56.6
04	52 03.6	204 08.3	09.3	282 22.6	33.6	218 37.7	33.0	221 57.6	56.2	Aldebaran	291 17.2	N16 28.4
05	67 06.1	219 08.0	10.5	297 23.5	33.3	233 39.7	33.2	236 59.8	56.3			
06	82 08.6	234 07.8	S12 11.7	312 24.4	N19 32.9	248 41.7	S 4 33.4	252 02.0	S 1 56.4	Alioth	166 42.4	N56 03.8
07	97 11.0	249 07.5	12.8	327 25.2	32.5	263 43.6	33.6	267 04.2	56.5	Alkaid	153 18.3	N49 24.6
08	112 13.5	264 07.2	14.0	342 26.1	32.1	278 45.6	33.8	282 06.4	56.6	Al Na'ir	28 13.6	S47 03.1
S 09	127 16.0	279 06.9	·· 15.2	357 26.9	·· 31.8	293 47.6	·· 34.0	297 08.6	·· 56.7	Alnilam	276 11.0	S 1 12.7
U 10	142 18.4	294 06.6	16.4	12 27.8	31.4	308 49.6	34.2	312 10.8	56.9	Alphard	218 20.2	S 8 34.5
N 11	157 20.9	309 06.4	17.5	27 28.6	31.0	323 51.6	34.4	327 13.0	57.0			
D 12	172 23.4	324 06.1	S12 18.7	42 29.5	N19 30.6	338 53.6	S 4 34.6	342 15.2	S 1 57.1	Alphecca	126 31.7	N26 46.9
A 13	187 25.8	339 05.8	19.9	57 30.3	30.3	353 55.6	34.8	357 17.4	57.2	Alpheratz	358 08.3	N28 59.4
Y 14	202 28.3	354 05.5	21.1	72 31.2	29.9	8 57.6	35.0	12 19.5	57.3	Altair	62 31.7	N 8 49.3
15	217 30.8	9 05.2	·· 22.2	87 32.0	·· 29.5	23 59.5	·· 35.2	27 21.7	·· 57.5	Ankaa	353 39.1	S42 24.3
16	232 33.2	24 05.0	23.4	102 32.9	29.1	39 01.5	35.4	42 23.9	57.6	Antares	112 56.1	S26 23.5
17	247 35.7	39 04.7	24.6	117 33.7	28.8	54 03.5	35.6	57 26.1	57.7			
18	262 38.1	54 04.4	S12 25.7	132 34.6	N19 28.4	69 05.5	S 4 35.8	72 28.3	S 1 57.8	Arcturus	146 18.1	N19 16.9
19	277 40.6	69 04.1	26.9	147 35.4	28.0	84 07.5	36.0	87 30.5	57.9	Atria	108 19.8	S68 59.9
20	292 43.1	84 03.8	28.1	162 36.3	27.6	99 09.5	36.2	102 32.7	58.0	Avior	234 28.4	S59 26.8
21	307 45.5	99 03.6	·· 29.2	177 37.2	·· 27.3	114 11.5	·· 36.4	117 34.9	·· 58.2	Bellatrix	278 58.0	N 6 20.1
22	322 48.0	114 03.3	30.4	192 38.0	26.9	129 13.5	36.6	132 37.1	58.3	Betelgeuse	271 27.6	N 7 24.3
23	337 50.5	129 03.0	31.6	207 38.9	26.5	144 15.4	36.8	147 39.3	58.4			
14 00	352 52.9	144 02.7	S12 32.7	222 39.7	N19 26.1	159 17.4	S 4 37.0	162 41.5	S 1 58.5	Canopus	264 07.0	S52 40.8
01	7 55.4	159 02.4	33.9	237 40.6	25.8	174 19.4	37.2	177 43.7	58.6	Capella	281 10.3	N45 58.6
02	22 57.9	174 02.1	35.1	252 41.4	25.4	189 21.4	37.4	192 45.9	58.8	Deneb	49 47.7	N45 13.1
03	38 00.3	189 01.9	·· 36.2	267 42.3	·· 25.0	204 23.4	·· 37.6	207 48.0	·· 58.9	Denebola	182 58.7	N14 40.7
04	53 02.8	204 01.6	37.4	282 43.1	24.6	219 25.4	37.8	222 50.2	59.0	Diphda	349 19.9	S18 05.2
05	68 05.3	219 01.3	38.6	297 44.0	24.2	234 27.4	38.0	237 52.4	59.1			
06	83 07.7	234 01.0	S12 39.7	312 44.9	N19 23.9	249 29.3	S 4 38.2	252 54.6	S 1 59.2	Dubhe	194 21.9	N61 51.1
07	98 10.2	249 00.7	40.9	327 45.7	23.5	264 31.3	38.4	267 56.8	59.3	Elnath	278 43.3	N28 35.5
08	113 12.6	264 00.4	42.1	342 46.6	23.1	279 33.3	38.6	282 59.0	59.5	Eltanin	90 57.3	N51 29.8
M 09	128 15.1	279 00.1	·· 43.2	357 47.4	·· 22.7	294 35.3	·· 38.8	298 01.2	·· 59.6	Enif	34 10.6	N 9 47.5
O 10	143 17.6	293 59.9	44.4	12 48.3	22.4	309 37.3	39.0	313 03.4	59.7	Fomalhaut	15 50.3	S29 43.2
N 11	158 20.0	308 59.6	45.6	27 49.1	22.0	324 39.3	39.2	328 05.6	59.8			
D 12	173 22.5	323 59.3	S12 46.7	42 50.0	N19 21.6	339 41.3	S 4 39.4	343 07.8	S 1 59.9	Gacrux	172 28.6	S57 00.5
A 13	188 25.0	338 59.0	47.9	57 50.9	21.2	354 43.2	39.6	358 10.0	2 00.0	Gienah	176 17.6	S17 26.2
Y 14	203 27.4	353 58.7	49.0	72 51.7	20.8	9 45.2	39.9	13 12.2	00.2	Hadar	149 22.9	S60 17.1
15	218 29.9	8 58.4	·· 50.2	87 52.6	·· 20.5	24 47.2	·· 40.1	28 14.4	·· 00.3	Hamal	328 27.9	N23 22.5
16	233 32.4	23 58.1	51.4	102 53.4	20.1	39 49.2	40.3	43 16.5	00.4	Kaus Aust.	84 15.8	S34 23.7
17	248 34.8	38 57.8	52.5	117 54.3	19.7	54 51.2	40.5	58 18.7	00.5			
18	263 37.3	53 57.6	S12 53.7	132 55.2	N19 19.3	69 53.2	S 4 40.7	73 20.9	S 2 00.6	Kochab	137 19.7	N74 14.2
19	278 39.8	68 57.3	54.8	147 56.0	18.9	84 55.2	40.9	88 23.1	00.8	Markab	14 02.2	N15 06.5
20	293 42.2	83 57.0	56.0	162 56.9	18.6	99 57.1	41.1	103 25.3	00.9	Menkar	314 40.2	N 4 01.1
21	308 44.7	98 56.7	·· 57.2	177 57.7	·· 18.2	114 59.1	·· 41.3	118 27.5	·· 01.0	Menkent	148 36.5	S36 16.7
22	323 47.1	113 56.4	58.3	192 58.6	17.8	130 01.1	41.5	133 29.7	01.1	Miaplacidus	221 45.6	S69 38.3
23	338 49.6	128 56.1	12 59.5	207 59.5	17.4	145 03.1	41.7	148 31.9	01.2			
15 00	353 52.1	143 55.8	S13 00.6	223 00.3	N19 17.0	160 05.1	S 4 41.9	163 34.1	S 2 01.3	Mirfak	309 14.9	N49 47.6
01	8 54.5	158 55.5	01.8	238 01.2	16.7	175 07.1	42.1	178 36.3	01.5	Nunki	76 28.2	S26 19.2
02	23 57.0	173 55.2	02.9	253 02.0	16.3	190 09.1	42.3	193 38.5	01.6	Peacock	53 56.9	S56 47.8
03	38 59.5	188 55.0	·· 04.1	268 02.9	·· 15.9	205 11.0	·· 42.5	208 40.7	·· 01.7	Pollux	243 57.5	N28 04.3
04	54 01.9	203 54.7	05.2	283 03.8	15.5	220 13.0	42.7	223 42.8	01.8	Procyon	245 25.3	N 5 16.5
05	69 04.4	218 54.4	06.4	298 04.6	15.1	235 15.0	42.9	238 45.0	01.9			
06	84 06.9	233 54.1	S13 07.6	313 05.5	N19 14.7	250 17.0	S 4 43.1	253 47.2	S 2 02.1	Rasalhague	96 28.9	N12 34.6
07	99 09.3	248 53.8	08.7	328 06.4	14.4	265 19.0	43.3	268 49.4	02.2	Regulus	208 09.6	N12 03.6
08	114 11.8	263 53.5	09.9	343 07.2	14.0	280 21.0	43.5	283 51.6	02.3	Rigel	281 35.3	S 8 13.2
T 09	129 14.2	278 53.2	·· 11.0	358 08.1	·· 13.6	295 22.9	·· 43.7	298 53.8	·· 02.4	Rigil Kent.	140 25.4	S60 45.6
U 10	144 16.7	293 52.9	12.2	13 08.9	13.2	310 24.9	43.9	313 56.0	02.5	Sabik	102 40.4	S15 42.1
E 11	159 19.2	308 52.6	13.3	28 09.8	12.8	325 26.9	44.1	328 58.2	02.6			
S 12	174 21.6	323 52.3	S13 14.5	43 10.7	N19 12.4	340 28.9	S 4 44.3	344 00.4	S 2 02.8	Schedar	350 07.7	N56 26.1
D 13	189 24.1	338 52.0	15.6	58 11.5	12.1	355 30.9	44.5	359 02.6	02.9	Shaula	96 54.8	S37 05.5
A 14	204 26.6	353 51.7	16.8	73 12.4	11.7	10 32.9	44.7	14 04.8	03.0	Sirius	258 55.2	S16 41.3
Y 15	219 29.0	8 51.5	·· 17.9	88 13.3	·· 11.3	25 34.9	·· 44.9	29 07.0	·· 03.1	Spica	158 57.1	S11 03.8
16	234 31.5	23 51.2	19.1	103 14.1	10.9	40 36.8	45.1	44 09.1	03.2	Suhail	223 10.7	S43 21.2
17	249 34.0	38 50.9	20.2	118 15.0	10.5	55 38.8	45.3	59 11.3	03.4			
18	264 36.4	53 50.6	S13 21.4	133 15.9	N19 10.1	70 40.8	S 4 45.6	74 13.5	S 2 03.5	Vega	80 55.3	N38 46.3
19	279 38.9	68 50.3	22.5	148 16.7	09.8	85 42.8	45.8	89 15.7	03.6	Zuben'ubi	137 32.5	S15 57.8
20	294 41.4	83 50.0	23.6	163 17.6	09.4	100 44.8	46.0	104 17.9	03.7			
21	309 43.8	98 49.7	·· 24.8	178 18.4	·· 09.0	115 46.8	·· 46.2	119 20.1	·· 03.8		S.H.A.	Mer. Pass.
22	324 46.3	113 49.4	25.9	193 19.3	08.6	130 48.7	46.4	134 22.3	03.9	Venus	151 09.8	14 24
23	339 48.7	128 49.1	27.1	208 20.2	08.2	145 50.7	46.6	149 24.5	04.1	Mars	229 46.8	9 09
Mer. Pass.	0 28.4	v −0.3	d 1.2	v 0.9	d 0.4	v 2.0	d 0.2	v 2.2	d 0.1	Jupiter	166 24.5	13 21
										Saturn	169 48.5	13 07

G.M.T.	SUN G.H.A.	Dec.	MOON G.H.A.	v	Dec.	d	H.P.
d h	° '	° '	° '	'	° '	'	'
13 00	180 59.0	N 3 55.0	13 35.7	9.8	S12 14.8	10.5	58.3
01	195 59.2	54.0	28 04.5	9.8	12 04.3	10.5	58.4
02	210 59.4	53.1	42 33.3	9.8	11 53.8	10.6	58.4
03	225 59.6	·· 52.1	57 02.1	9.8	11 43.2	10.6	58.4
04	240 59.9	51.1	71 30.9	9.8	11 32.6	10.8	58.5
05	256 00.1	50.2	85 59.7	9.8	11 21.8	10.8	58.5
06	271 00.3	N 3 49.2	100 28.5	9.9	S11 11.0	10.9	58.5
07	286 00.5	48.3	114 57.4	9.8	11 00.1	10.9	58.5
08	301 00.7	47.3	129 26.2	9.9	10 49.2	11.0	58.6
S 09	316 01.0	·· 46.4	143 55.1	9.8	10 38.2	11.1	58.6
U 10	331 01.2	45.4	158 23.9	9.9	10 27.1	11.2	58.6
N 11	346 01.4	44.4	172 52.8	9.8	10 15.9	11.3	58.7
D 12	1 01.6	N 3 43.5	187 21.6	9.9	S10 04.6	11.3	58.7
A 13	16 01.8	42.5	201 50.5	9.9	9 53.3	11.3	58.7
Y 14	31 02.1	41.6	216 19.4	9.9	9 42.0	11.5	58.7
15	46 02.3	·· 40.6	230 48.3	9.9	9 30.5	11.5	58.8
16	61 02.5	39.7	245 17.2	9.9	9 19.0	11.6	58.8
17	76 02.7	38.7	259 46.1	9.9	9 07.4	11.6	58.8
18	91 03.0	N 3 37.7	274 15.0	9.9	S 8 55.8	11.7	58.8
19	106 03.2	36.8	288 43.9	9.9	8 44.1	11.7	58.9
20	121 03.4	35.8	303 12.8	9.9	8 32.4	11.8	58.9
21	136 03.6	·· 34.9	317 41.7	10.0	8 20.6	11.9	58.9
22	151 03.8	33.9	332 10.7	9.9	8 08.7	11.9	58.9
23	166 04.1	33.0	346 39.6	9.9	7 56.8	12.0	59.0
14 00	181 04.3	N 3 32.0	1 08.5	10.0	S 7 44.8	12.0	59.0
01	196 04.5	31.0	15 37.5	9.9	7 32.8	12.1	59.0
02	211 04.7	30.1	30 06.4	10.0	7 20.7	12.2	59.0
03	226 05.0	·· 29.1	44 35.4	9.9	7 08.5	12.2	59.1
04	241 05.2	28.2	59 04.3	9.9	6 56.3	12.2	59.1
05	256 05.4	27.2	73 33.2	10.0	6 44.1	12.3	59.1
06	271 05.6	N 3 26.2	88 02.2	10.0	S 6 31.8	12.3	59.1
07	286 05.9	25.3	102 31.2	9.9	6 19.5	12.4	59.2
08	301 06.1	24.3	117 00.1	10.0	6 07.1	12.4	59.2
M 09	316 06.3	·· 23.4	131 29.1	9.9	5 54.7	12.5	59.2
O 10	331 06.5	22.4	145 58.0	10.0	5 42.2	12.5	59.2
N 11	346 06.7	21.4	160 27.0	9.9	5 29.7	12.6	59.3
D 12	1 07.0	N 3 20.5	174 55.9	10.0	S 5 17.1	12.6	59.3
A 13	16 07.2	19.5	189 24.9	9.9	5 04.6	12.7	59.3
Y 14	31 07.4	18.6	203 53.8	10.0	4 51.9	12.6	59.3
15	46 07.6	·· 17.6	218 22.8	9.9	4 39.3	12.7	59.3
16	61 07.9	16.6	232 51.7	10.0	4 26.6	12.8	59.4
17	76 08.1	15.7	247 20.7	9.9	4 13.8	12.7	59.4
18	91 08.3	N 3 14.7	261 49.6	9.9	S 4 01.1	12.8	59.4
19	106 08.5	13.8	276 18.5	10.0	3 48.3	12.8	59.4
20	121 08.7	12.8	290 47.5	9.9	3 35.5	12.9	59.4
21	136 09.0	·· 11.8	305 16.4	9.9	3 22.6	12.9	59.5
22	151 09.2	10.9	319 45.3	9.9	3 09.7	12.9	59.5
23	166 09.4	09.9	334 14.2	9.9	2 56.8	12.9	59.5
15 00	181 09.6	N 3 09.0	348 43.1	10.0	S 2 43.9	13.0	59.5
01	196 09.9	08.0	3 12.1	9.8	2 30.9	13.0	59.5
02	211 10.1	07.0	17 40.9	9.9	2 17.9	13.0	59.5
03	226 10.3	·· 06.1	32 09.8	9.9	2 04.9	13.0	59.6
04	241 10.5	05.1	46 38.7	9.9	1 51.9	13.0	59.6
05	256 10.8	04.2	61 07.6	9.8	1 38.9	13.1	59.6
06	271 11.0	N 3 03.2	75 36.4	9.9	S 1 25.8	13.0	59.6
07	286 11.2	02.2	90 05.3	9.8	1 12.8	13.1	59.6
08	301 11.4	01.3	104 34.1	9.9	0 59.7	13.1	59.6
T 09	316 11.6	3 00.3	119 03.0	9.8	0 46.6	13.1	59.7
U 10	331 11.9	2 59.3	133 31.8	9.8	0 33.5	13.1	59.7
E 11	346 12.1	58.4	148 00.6	9.8	0 20.4	13.1	59.7
S 12	1 12.3	N 2 57.4	162 29.4	9.8	S 0 07.3	13.2	59.7
D 13	16 12.5	56.5	176 58.2	9.7	N 0 05.9	13.1	59.7
A 14	31 12.8	55.5	191 26.9	9.8	0 19.0	13.1	59.7
Y 15	46 13.0	·· 54.5	205 55.7	9.7	0 32.1	13.2	59.7
16	61 13.2	53.6	220 24.4	9.7	0 45.3	13.1	59.8
17	76 13.4	52.6	234 53.1	9.7	0 58.4	13.2	59.8
18	91 13.7	N 2 51.6	249 21.8	9.7	N 1 11.6	13.1	59.8
19	106 13.9	50.7	263 50.5	9.7	1 24.7	13.1	59.8
20	121 14.1	49.7	278 19.2	9.6	1 37.8	13.1	59.8
21	136 14.3	·· 48.8	292 47.8	9.7	1 50.9	13.2	59.8
22	151 14.5	47.8	307 16.5	9.6	2 04.1	13.1	59.8
23	166 14.8	46.8	321 45.1	9.6	2 17.2	13.1	59.8
	S.D. 15.9	d 1.0	S.D. 16.0		16.2		16.3

Lat.	Twilight Naut.	Civil	Sunrise	Moonrise 13	14	15	16
°	h m	h m	h m	h m	h m	h m	h m
N 72	01 57	03 49	05 02	19 40	19 24	19 09	18 54
N 70	02 32	04 03	05 08	19 27	19 19	19 11	19 03
68	02 56	04 14	05 12	19 16	19 14	19 12	19 10
66	03 14	04 23	05 16	19 07	19 11	19 14	19 17
64	03 28	04 31	05 20	19 00	19 08	19 15	19 22
62	03 40	04 37	05 22	18 54	19 05	19 15	19 27
60	03 50	04 42	05 25	18 48	19 02	19 16	19 31
N 58	03 58	04 47	05 27	18 43	19 00	19 17	19 34
56	04 06	04 51	05 29	18 39	18 58	19 18	19 37
54	04 12	04 55	05 31	18 35	18 57	19 18	19 40
52	04 17	04 58	05 33	18 31	18 55	19 19	19 43
50	04 22	05 01	05 34	18 28	18 54	19 19	19 45
45	04 32	05 08	05 37	18 20	18 51	19 20	19 51
N 40	04 40	05 12	05 40	18 14	18 48	19 21	19 55
35	04 47	05 16	05 42	18 09	18 46	19 22	19 59
30	04 52	05 20	05 44	18 05	18 44	19 23	20 02
20	04 59	05 25	05 47	17 57	18 40	19 24	20 08
N 10	05 04	05 29	05 50	17 50	18 37	19 25	20 14
0	05 08	05 32	05 52	17 43	18 35	19 26	20 19
S 10	05 09	05 34	05 55	17 36	18 32	19 27	20 24
20	05 10	05 35	05 57	17 29	18 29	19 29	20 29
30	05 08	05 36	06 00	17 21	18 25	19 30	20 35
35	05 07	05 36	06 01	17 17	18 23	19 31	20 39
40	05 05	05 36	06 03	17 11	18 21	19 32	20 43
45	05 01	05 35	06 05	17 05	18 18	19 33	20 48
S 50	04 57	05 35	06 07	16 58	18 15	19 34	20 54
52	04 55	05 34	06 08	16 54	18 14	19 35	20 57
54	04 53	05 34	06 09	16 50	18 12	19 35	20 59
56	04 50	05 33	06 10	16 46	18 10	19 36	21 03
58	04 47	05 32	06 11	16 41	18 09	19 37	21 06
S 60	04 43	05 31	06 13	16 36	18 06	19 38	21 11

Lat.	Sunset	Twilight Civil	Naut.	Moonset 13	14	15	16
°	h m	h m	h m	h m	h m	h m	h m
N 72	18 47	19 59	21 46	02 28	04 37	06 41	08 46
N 70	18 41	19 45	21 14	02 50	04 47	06 43	08 40
68	18 37	19 34	20 51	03 07	04 56	06 45	08 35
66	18 33	19 26	20 34	03 21	05 03	06 46	08 31
64	18 30	19 20	20 20	03 32	05 09	06 47	08 27
62	18 27	19 12	20 09	03 41	05 14	06 48	08 24
60	18 25	19 07	19 59	03 49	05 18	06 49	08 21
N 58	18 23	19 02	19 51	03 56	05 22	06 50	08 19
56	18 21	18 58	19 44	04 02	05 26	06 51	08 17
54	18 19	18 55	19 38	04 08	05 29	06 51	08 15
52	18 18	18 52	19 32	04 13	05 32	06 52	08 13
50	18 16	18 49	19 28	04 18	05 34	06 53	08 12
45	18 13	18 43	19 18	04 27	05 40	06 54	08 08
N 40	18 11	18 38	19 10	04 35	05 44	06 55	08 06
35	18 09	18 34	19 04	04 42	05 48	06 55	08 03
30	18 07	18 31	18 59	04 48	05 52	06 56	08 01
20	18 04	18 26	18 51	04 59	05 58	06 57	07 57
N 10	18 01	18 22	18 47	05 08	06 03	06 58	07 54
0	17 59	18 19	18 44	05 16	06 08	06 59	07 51
S 10	17 57	18 18	18 42	05 24	06 12	07 00	07 48
20	17 54	18 16	18 42	05 33	06 17	07 01	07 45
30	17 52	18 16	18 43	05 43	06 23	07 02	07 41
35	17 50	18 16	18 45	05 49	06 26	07 02	07 39
40	17 49	18 16	18 47	05 55	06 30	07 03	07 36
45	17 47	18 16	18 51	06 03	06 34	07 04	07 33
S 50	17 45	18 17	18 55	06 12	06 39	07 05	07 30
52	17 44	18 18	18 57	06 16	06 41	07 05	07 29
54	17 43	18 18	19 00	06 21	06 44	07 05	07 27
56	17 42	18 19	19 03	06 26	06 46	07 06	07 25
58	17 41	18 20	19 06	06 31	06 50	07 06	07 23
S 60	17 40	18 21	19 10	06 37	06 53	07 07	07 21

Day	SUN Eqn. of Time 00h	12h	Mer. Pass.	MOON Mer. Pass. Upper	Lower	Age	Phase
	m s	m s	h m	h m	h m	d	
13	03 55	04 06	11 56	23 55	11 30	15	
14	04 17	04 27	11 56	24 47	12 21	16	◯
15	04 38	04 49	11 55	00 47	13 13	17	

G.M.T.	ARIES G.H.A.	VENUS −3.6 G.H.A.	Dec.	MARS +1.8 G.H.A.	Dec.	JUPITER −1.2 G.H.A.	Dec.	SATURN +1.1 G.H.A.	Dec.	Name	S.H.A.	Dec.
16 00	354 51.2	143 48.8	S13 28.2	223 21.0	N19 07.8	160 52.7	S 4 46.8	164 26.7	S 2 04.2	Acamar	315 36.4	S40 22.5
01	9 53.7	158 48.5	29.4	238 21.9	07.4	175 54.7	47.0	179 28.9	04.3	Achernar	335 44.2	S57 19.7
02	24 56.1	173 48.2	30.5	253 22.8	07.0	190 56.7	47.2	194 31.1	04.4	Acrux	173 37.2	S62 59.8
03	39 58.6	188 47.9	·· 31.7	268 23.6	·· 06.7	205 58.7	·· 47.4	209 33.2	·· 04.5	Adhara	255 31.7	S28 56.6
04	55 01.1	203 47.6	32.8	283 24.5	06.3	221 00.6	47.6	224 35.4	04.7	Aldebaran	291 17.1	N16 28.4
05	70 03.5	218 47.3	33.9	298 25.4	05.9	236 02.6	47.8	239 37.6	04.8			
06	85 06.0	233 47.0	S13 35.1	313 26.2	N19 05.5	251 04.6	S 4 48.0	254 39.8	S 2 04.9	Alioth	166 42.4	N56 03.8
W 07	100 08.5	248 46.7	36.2	328 27.1	05.1	266 06.6	48.2	269 42.0	05.0	Alkaid	153 18.4	N49 24.6
E 08	115 10.9	263 46.4	37.4	343 28.0	04.7	281 08.6	48.4	284 44.2	05.1	Al Na'ir	28 13.6	S47 03.1
D 09	130 13.4	278 46.1	·· 38.5	358 28.8	·· 04.3	296 10.6	·· 48.6	299 46.4	·· 05.2	Alnilam	276 11.0	S 1 12.7
N 10	145 15.9	293 45.8	39.6	13 29.7	04.0	311 12.5	48.8	314 48.6	05.4	Alphard	218 20.2	S 8 34.5
E 11	160 18.3	308 45.5	40.8	28 30.6	03.6	326 14.5	49.0	329 50.8	05.5			
S 12	175 20.8	323 45.2	S13 41.9	43 31.5	N19 03.2	341 16.5	S 4 49.2	344 53.0	S 2 05.6	Alphecca	126 31.7	N26 46.9
D 13	190 23.2	338 44.9	43.1	58 32.3	02.8	356 18.5	49.4	359 55.1	05.7	Alpheratz	358 08.3	N28 59.4
A 14	205 25.7	353 44.6	44.2	73 33.2	02.4	11 20.5	49.6	14 57.3	05.8	Altair	62 31.7	N 8 49.3
Y 15	220 28.2	8 44.3	·· 45.3	88 34.1	·· 02.0	26 22.4	·· 49.8	29 59.5	·· 06.0	Ankaa	353 39.1	S42 24.3
16	235 30.6	23 44.0	46.5	103 34.9	01.6	41 24.4	50.0	45 01.7	06.1	Antares	112 56.1	S26 23.5
17	250 33.1	38 43.7	47.6	118 35.8	01.2	56 26.4	50.2	60 03.9	06.2			
18	265 35.6	53 43.4	S13 48.7	133 36.7	N19 00.8	71 28.4	S 4 50.4	75 06.1	S 2 06.3	Arcturus	146 18.1	N19 16.9
19	280 38.0	68 43.1	49.9	148 37.5	00.5	86 30.4	50.6	90 08.3	06.4	Atria	108 19.9	S68 59.9
20	295 40.5	83 42.8	51.0	163 38.4	19 00.1	101 32.4	50.9	105 10.5	06.5	Avior	234 28.3	S59 26.7
21	310 43.0	98 42.5	·· 52.2	178 39.3	18 59.7	116 34.3	·· 51.1	120 12.7	·· 06.7	Bellatrix	278 58.0	N 6 20.1
22	325 45.4	113 42.2	53.3	193 40.2	59.3	131 36.3	51.3	135 14.9	06.8	Betelgeuse	271 27.6	N 7 24.3
23	340 47.9	128 41.9	54.4	208 41.0	58.9	146 38.3	51.5	150 17.0	06.9			
17 00	355 50.3	143 41.6	S13 55.6	223 41.9	N18 58.5	161 40.3	S 4 51.7	165 19.2	S 2 07.0	Canopus	264 07.0	S52 40.8
01	10 52.8	158 41.3	56.7	238 42.8	58.1	176 42.3	51.9	180 21.4	07.1	Capella	281 10.3	N45 58.6
02	25 55.3	173 41.0	57.8	253 43.6	57.7	191 44.2	52.1	195 23.6	07.3	Deneb	49 47.7	N45 13.1
03	40 57.7	188 40.7	13 58.9	268 44.5	·· 57.3	206 46.2	·· 52.3	210 25.8	·· 07.4	Denebola	182 58.7	N14 40.7
04	56 00.2	203 40.4	14 00.1	283 45.4	56.9	221 48.2	52.5	225 28.0	07.5	Diphda	349 19.9	S18 05.2
05	71 02.7	218 40.1	01.2	298 46.3	56.5	236 50.2	52.7	240 30.2	07.6			
06	86 05.1	233 39.8	S14 02.3	313 47.1	N18 56.2	251 52.2	S 4 52.9	255 32.4	S 2 07.7	Dubhe	194 21.9	N61 51.1
T 07	101 07.6	248 39.5	03.5	328 48.0	55.8	266 54.2	53.1	270 34.6	07.9	Elnath	278 43.3	N28 35.5
H 08	116 10.1	263 39.1	04.6	343 48.9	55.4	281 56.1	53.3	285 36.8	08.0	Eltanin	90 57.4	N51 29.8
U 09	131 12.5	278 38.8	·· 05.7	358 49.7	·· 55.0	296 58.1	·· 53.5	300 38.9	·· 08.1	Enif	34 10.6	N 9 47.5
R 10	146 15.0	293 38.5	06.8	13 50.6	54.6	312 00.1	53.7	315 41.1	08.2	Fomalhaut	15 50.3	S29 43.2
S 11	161 17.5	308 38.2	08.0	28 51.5	54.2	327 02.1	53.9	330 43.3	08.3			
D 12	176 19.9	323 37.9	S14 09.1	43 52.4	N18 53.8	342 04.1	S 4 54.1	345 45.5	S 2 08.4	Gacrux	172 28.6	S57 00.5
A 13	191 22.4	338 37.6	10.2	58 53.2	53.4	357 06.0	54.3	0 47.7	08.6	Gienah	176 17.6	S17 26.2
Y 14	206 24.8	353 37.3	11.4	73 54.1	53.0	12 08.0	54.5	15 49.9	08.7	Hadar	149 22.9	S60 17.1
15	221 27.3	8 37.0	·· 12.5	88 55.0	·· 52.6	27 10.0	·· 54.7	30 52.1	·· 08.8	Hamal	328 27.9	N23 22.5
16	236 29.8	23 36.7	13.6	103 55.9	52.2	42 12.0	54.9	45 54.3	08.9	Kaus Aust.	84 15.9	S34 23.7
17	251 32.2	38 36.4	14.7	118 56.7	51.8	57 14.0	55.1	60 56.5	09.0			
18	266 34.7	53 36.1	S14 15.8	133 57.6	N18 51.4	72 15.9	S 4 55.3	75 58.7	S 2 09.2	Kochab	137 19.8	N74 14.2
19	281 37.2	68 35.8	17.0	148 58.5	51.0	87 17.9	55.5	91 00.8	09.3	Markab	14 02.2	N15 06.5
20	296 39.6	83 35.5	18.1	163 59.4	50.6	102 19.9	55.8	106 03.0	09.4	Menkar	314 40.2	N 4 01.1
21	311 42.1	98 35.1	·· 19.2	179 00.2	·· 50.3	117 21.9	·· 56.0	121 05.2	·· 09.5	Menkent	148 36.5	S36 16.7
22	326 44.6	113 34.8	20.3	194 01.1	49.9	132 23.9	56.2	136 07.4	09.6	Miaplacidus	221 45.6	S69 38.3
23	341 47.0	128 34.5	21.5	209 02.0	49.5	147 25.8	56.4	151 09.6	09.7			
18 00	356 49.5	143 34.2	S14 22.6	224 02.9	N18 49.1	162 27.8	S 4 56.6	166 11.8	S 2 09.9	Mirfak	309 14.9	N49 47.6
01	11 52.0	158 33.9	23.7	239 03.7	48.7	177 29.8	56.8	181 14.0	10.0	Nunki	76 28.2	S26 19.2
02	26 54.4	173 33.6	24.8	254 04.6	48.3	192 31.8	57.0	196 16.2	10.1	Peacock	53 56.9	S56 47.8
03	41 56.9	188 33.3	·· 25.9	269 05.5	·· 47.9	207 33.8	·· 57.2	211 18.4	·· 10.2	Pollux	243 57.5	N28 04.3
04	56 59.3	203 33.0	27.0	284 06.4	47.5	222 35.7	57.4	226 20.5	10.3	Procyon	245 25.2	N 5 16.5
05	72 01.8	218 32.7	28.2	299 07.3	47.1	237 37.7	57.6	241 22.7 ·	10.5			
06	87 04.3	233 32.3	S14 29.3	314 08.1	N18 46.7	252 39.7	S 4 57.8	256 24.9	S 2 10.6	Rasalhague	96 29.0	N12 34.6
F 07	102 06.7	248 32.0	30.4	329 09.0	46.3	267 41.7	58.0	271 27.1	10.7	Regulus	208 09.6	N12 03.6
R 08	117 09.2	263 31.7	31.5	344 09.9	45.9	282 43.7	58.2	286 29.3	10.8	Rigel	281 35.3	S 8 13.2
I 09	132 11.7	278 31.4	·· 32.6	359 10.8	·· 45.5	297 45.6	·· 58.4	301 31.5	·· 10.9	Rigil Kent.	140 25.4	S60 45.6
10	147 14.1	293 31.1	33.7	14 11.6	45.1	312 47.6	58.6	316 33.7	11.1	Sabik	102 40.4	S15 42.1
11	162 16.6	308 30.8	34.9	29 12.5	44.7	327 49.6	58.8	331 35.9	11.2			
D 12	177 19.1	323 30.5	S14 36.0	44 13.4	N18 44.3	342 51.6	S 4 59.0	346 38.1	S 2 11.3	Schedar	350 07.7	N56 26.1
A 13	192 21.5	338 30.1	37.1	59 14.3	43.9	357 53.5	59.2	1 40.2	11.4	Shaula	96 54.8	S37 05.5
Y 14	207 24.0	353 29.8	38.2	74 15.2	43.5	12 55.5	59.4	16 42.4	11.5	Sirius	258 55.2	S16 41.3
15	222 26.4	8 29.5	·· 39.3	89 16.0	·· 43.1	27 57.5	·· 59.6	31 44.6	·· 11.6	Spica	158 57.1	S11 03.7
16	237 28.9	23 29.2	40.4	104 16.9	42.7	42 59.5	4 59.8	46 46.8	11.8	Suhail	223 10.6	S43 21.2
17	252 31.4	38 28.9	41.5	119 17.8	42.3	58 01.5	5 00.0	61 49.0	11.9			
18	267 33.8	53 28.6	S14 42.6	134 18.7	N18 41.9	73 03.5	S 5 00.3	76 51.2	S 2 12.0	Vega	80 55.3	N38 46.3
19	282 36.3	68 28.2	43.8	149 19.6	41.5	88 05.4	00.5	91 53.4	12.1	Zuben'ubi	137 32.5	S15 57.8
20	297 38.8	83 27.9	44.9	164 20.4	41.1	103 07.4	00.7	106 55.6	12.2		S.H.A.	Mer. Pass.
21	312 41.2	98 27.6	·· 46.0	179 21.3	·· 40.7	118 09.4	·· 00.9	121 57.7	·· 12.4	Venus	147 51.2	14 26
22	327 43.7	113 27.3	47.1	194 22.2	40.3	133 11.4	01.1	136 59.9	12.5	Mars	227 51.5	9 05
23	342 46.2	128 27.0	48.2	209 23.1	39.9	148 13.4	01.3	152 02.1	12.6	Jupiter	165 49.9	13 12
Mer. Pass.	0 16.6	v −0.3	d 1.1	v 0.9	d 0.4	v 2.0	d 0.2	v 2.2	d 0.1	Saturn	169 28.9	12 57

G.M.T.	SUN G.H.A.	SUN Dec.	MOON G.H.A.	v	Dec.	d	H.P.
	° '	° '	° '	'	° '	'	'
16 00	181 15.0	N 2 45.9	336 13.7	9.6	N 2 30.3	13.1	59.8
01	196 15.2	44.9	350 42.3	9.5	2 43.4	13.1	59.8
02	211 15.4	43.9	5 10.8	9.5	2 56.5	13.0	59.9
03	226 15.7 ··	43.0	19 39.3	9.6	3 09.5	13.1	59.9
04	241 15.9	42.0	34 07.9	9.4	3 22.6	13.0	59.9
05	256 16.1	41.0	48 36.3	9.5	3 35.6	13.0	59.9
06	271 16.3	N 2 40.1	63 04.8	9.5	N 3 48.6	13.0	59.9
W 07	286 16.6	39.1	77 33.3	9.4	4 01.6	13.0	59.9
E 08	301 16.8	38.2	92 01.7	9.4	4 14.6	13.0	59.9
D 09	316 17.0 ··	37.2	106 30.1	9.3	4 27.6	12.9	59.9
N 10	331 17.2	36.2	120 58.4	9.4	4 40.5	12.9	59.9
E 11	346 17.4	35.3	135 26.8	9.3	4 53.4	12.9	59.9
S 12	1 17.7	N 2 34.3	149 55.1	9.3	N 5 06.3	12.8	59.9
D 13	16 17.9	33.3	164 23.4	9.3	5 19.1	12.8	59.9
A 14	31 18.1	32.4	178 51.7	9.2	5 31.9	12.8	59.9
Y 15	46 18.3 ··	31.4	193 19.9	9.2	5 44.7	12.8	59.9
16	61 18.6	30.4	207 48.1	9.2	5 57.5	12.7	59.9
17	76 18.8	29.5	222 16.3	9.1	6 10.2	12.7	60.0
18	91 19.0	N 2 28.5	236 44.4	9.1	N 6 22.9	12.6	60.0
19	106 19.2	27.5	251 12.5	9.1	6 35.5	12.6	60.0
20	121 19.5	26.6	265 40.6	9.1	6 48.1	12.6	60.0
21	136 19.7 ··	25.6	280 08.7	9.0	7 00.7	12.5	60.0
22	151 19.9	24.6	294 36.7	9.0	7 13.2	12.5	60.0
23	166 20.1	23.7	309 04.7	9.0	7 25.7	12.5	60.0
17 00	181 20.3	N 2 22.7	323 32.7	8.9	N 7 38.2	12.4	60.0
01	196 20.6	21.7	338 00.6	8.9	7 50.6	12.3	60.0
02	211 20.8	20.8	352 28.5	8.9	8 02.9	12.3	60.0
03	226 21.0 ··	19.8	6 56.4	8.8	8 15.2	12.3	60.0
04	241 21.2	18.9	21 24.2	8.8	8 27.5	12.2	60.0
05	256 21.5	17.9	35 52.0	8.8	8 39.7	12.1	60.0
06	271 21.7	N 2 16.9	50 19.8	8.7	N 8 51.8	12.1	60.0
07	286 21.9	16.0	64 47.5	8.7	9 03.9	12.0	60.0
T 08	301 22.1	15.0	79 15.2	8.7	9 15.9	12.0	60.0
H 09	316 22.4 ··	14.0	93 42.9	8.6	9 27.9	11.9	60.0
U 10	331 22.6	13.1	108 10.5	8.6	9 39.8	11.9	60.0
R 11	346 22.8	12.1	122 38.1	8.5	9 51.7	11.8	60.0
S 12	1 23.0	N 2 11.1	137 05.6	8.5	N10 03.5	11.7	60.0
D 13	16 23.2	10.2	151 33.1	8.5	10 15.2	11.7	60.0
A 14	31 23.5	09.2	166 00.6	8.4	10 26.9	11.6	60.0
Y 15	46 23.7 ··	08.2	180 28.0	8.4	10 38.5	11.6	60.0
16	61 23.9	07.3	194 55.4	8.4	10 50.1	11.4	59.9
17	76 24.1	06.3	209 22.8	8.3	11 01.5	11.4	59.9
18	91 24.4	N 2 05.3	223 50.1	8.3	N11 12.9	11.4	59.9
19	106 24.6	04.4	238 17.4	8.3	11 24.3	11.2	59.9
20	121 24.8	03.4	252 44.7	8.2	11 35.5	11.2	59.9
21	136 25.0 ··	02.4	267 11.9	8.1	11 46.7	11.1	59.9
22	151 25.3	01.5	281 39.0	8.2	11 57.8	11.1	59.9
23	166 25.5	2 00.5	296 06.2	8.1	12 08.9	10.9	59.9
18 00	181 25.7	N 1 59.5	310 33.3	8.0	N12 19.8	10.9	59.9
01	196 25.9	58.5	325 00.3	8.0	12 30.7	10.8	59.9
02	211 26.1	57.6	339 27.3	8.0	12 41.5	10.7	59.9
03	226 26.4 ··	56.6	353 54.3	7.9	12 52.2	10.7	59.9
04	241 26.6	55.6	8 21.2	7.9	13 02.9	10.5	59.9
05	256 26.8	54.7	22 48.1	7.9	13 13.4	10.5	59.9
06	271 27.0	N 1 53.7	37 15.0	7.8	N13 23.9	10.4	59.9
07	286 27.3	52.7	51 41.8	7.8	13 34.3	10.3	59.9
08	301 27.5	51.8	66 08.6	7.7	13 44.6	10.2	59.9
F 09	316 27.7 ··	50.8	80 35.3	7.7	13 54.8	10.1	59.8
R 10	331 27.9	49.8	95 02.0	7.6	14 04.9	10.0	59.8
I 11	346 28.2	48.9	109 28.6	7.7	14 14.9	9.9	59.8
D 12	1 28.4	N 1 47.9	123 55.3	7.5	N14 24.8	9.9	59.8
A 13	16 28.6	46.9	138 21.8	7.6	14 34.7	9.7	59.8
Y 14	31 28.8	46.0	152 48.4	7.5	14 44.4	9.6	59.8
15	46 29.0 ··	45.0	167 14.9	7.4	14 54.0	9.6	59.8
16	61 29.3	44.0	181 41.3	7.4	15 03.6	9.4	59.8
17	76 29.5	43.1	196 07.7	7.4	15 13.0	9.4	59.8
18	91 29.7	N 1 42.1	210 34.1	7.3	N15 22.4	9.2	59.8
19	106 29.9	41.1	225 00.4	7.4	15 31.6	9.2	59.7
20	121 30.2	40.2	239 26.8	7.2	15 40.8	9.0	59.7
21	136 30.4 ··	39.2	253 53.0	7.2	15 49.8	9.0	59.7
22	151 30.6	38.2	268 19.2	7.2	15 58.8	8.8	59.7
23	166 30.8	37.2	282 45.4	7.2	16 07.6	8.7	59.7
	S.D. 15.9	d 1.0	S.D. 16.3		16.3		16.3

Lat.	Twilight Naut.	Twilight Civil	Sunrise	Moonrise 16	17	18	19
°	h m	h m	h m	h m	h m	h m	h m
N 72	02 22	04 04	05 15	18 54	18 36	18 10	☐
N 70	02 50	04 16	05 19	19 03	18 55	18 44	18 27
68	03 11	04 26	05 23	19 10	19 09	19 09	19 11
66	03 26	04 33	05 26	19 17	19 21	19 28	19 40
64	03 39	04 40	05 28	19 22	19 31	19 43	20 02
62	03 49	04 45	05 30	19 27	19 40	19 56	20 20
60	03 58	04 50	05 32	19 31	19 47	20 07	20 35
N 58	04 06	04 54	05 34	19 34	19 54	20 17	20 47
56	04 12	04 57	05 35	19 37	19 59	20 26	20 59
54	04 18	05 01	05 36	19 40	20 05	20 33	21 08
52	04 23	05 03	05 37	19 43	20 09	20 40	21 17
50	04 27	05 06	05 38	19 45	20 14	20 46	21 25
45	04 36	05 11	05 41	19 51	20 23	21 00	21 41
N 40	04 43	05 15	05 43	19 55	20 31	21 11	21 55
35	04 49	05 19	05 44	19 59	20 38	21 20	22 07
30	04 53	05 21	05 45	20 02	20 44	21 28	22 17
20	05 00	05 26	05 48	20 08	20 54	21 43	22 35
N 10	05 04	05 29	05 50	20 14	21 04	21 56	22 50
0	05 07	05 31	05 51	20 19	21 12	22 08	23 05
S 10	05 07	05 32	05 53	20 24	21 21	22 20	23 19
20	05 07	05 32	05 54	20 29	21 31	22 33	23 35
30	05 04	05 32	05 56	20 35	21 41	22 48	23 53
35	05 02	05 32	05 57	20 39	21 48	22 56	24 03
40	05 00	05 31	05 58	20 43	21 55	23 06	24 16
45	04 56	05 30	05 59	20 48	22 03	23 18	24 30
S 50	04 51	05 28	06 00	20 54	22 14	23 32	24 47
52	04 48	05 27	06 01	20 57	22 18	23 39	24 56
54	04 45	05 26	06 01	20 59	22 24	23 46	25 05
56	04 42	05 25	06 02	21 03	22 30	23 55	25 16
58	04 38	05 24	06 03	21 06	22 36	24 04	00 04
S 60	04 34	05 22	06 04	21 11	22 44	24 15	00 15

Lat.	Sunset	Twilight Civil	Twilight Naut.	Moonset 16	17	18	19
°	h m	h m	h m	h m	h m	h m	h m
N 72	18 31	19 41	21 20	08 46	10 56	13 17	☐
N 70	18 27	19 30	20 54	08 40	10 40	12 45	15 00
68	18 24	19 21	20 35	08 35	10 27	12 22	14 18
66	18 21	19 13	20 20	08 31	10 17	12 04	13 49
64	18 19	19 07	20 07	08 27	10 08	11 49	13 28
62	18 17	19 02	19 57	08 24	10 01	11 37	13 10
60	18 16	18 57	19 49	08 21	09 54	11 27	12 56
N 58	18 14	18 54	19 41	08 19	09 49	11 18	12 44
56	18 13	18 50	19 35	08 17	09 44	11 10	12 33
54	18 12	18 47	19 30	08 15	09 39	11 03	12 24
52	18 10	18 44	19 25	08 13	09 35	10 57	12 16
50	18 10	18 42	19 20	08 12	09 32	10 51	12 08
45	18 07	18 37	19 12	08 08	09 24	10 39	11 52
N 40	18 06	18 33	19 05	08 06	09 17	10 29	11 39
35	18 04	18 30	18 59	08 03	09 12	10 20	11 28
30	18 03	18 27	18 55	08 01	09 07	10 13	11 19
20	18 01	18 23	18 49	07 57	08 58	10 00	11 02
N 10	17 59	18 20	18 45	07 54	08 51	09 49	10 48
0	17 58	18 18	18 42	07 51	08 44	09 38	10 35
S 10	17 56	18 17	18 42	07 48	08 37	09 28	10 21
20	17 55	18 17	18 42	07 45	08 30	09 17	10 07
30	17 53	18 17	18 45	07 41	08 21	09 04	09 51
35	17 53	18 18	18 47	07 39	08 16	08 57	09 41
40	17 52	18 19	18 50	07 36	08 11	08 48	09 30
45	17 51	18 20	18 54	07 33	08 05	08 39	09 18
S 50	17 50	18 22	19 00	07 30	07 57	08 27	09 02
52	17 49	18 23	19 02	07 29	07 54	08 22	08 55
54	17 49	18 24	19 05	07 27	07 50	08 16	08 47
56	17 48	18 25	19 09	07 25	07 46	08 09	08 38
58	17 47	18 26	19 13	07 23	07 41	08 02	08 28
S 60	17 47	18 28	19 17	07 21	07 36	07 54	08 17

Day	SUN Eqn. of Time 00h	SUN Eqn. of Time 12h	SUN Mer. Pass.	MOON Mer. Pass. Upper	MOON Mer. Pass. Lower	Age	Phase
	m s	m s	h m	h m	h m	d	
16	05 00	05 10	11 55	01 39	14 05	18	
17	05 21	05 32	11 54	02 31	14 58	19	◗
18	05 42	05 53	11 54	03 25	15 53	20	

G.M.T.	ARIES G.H.A.	VENUS −3.6 G.H.A.	Dec.	MARS +1.8 G.H.A.	Dec.	JUPITER −1.2 G.H.A.	Dec.	SATURN +1.1 G.H.A.	Dec.	STARS Name	S.H.A.	Dec.
19 00	357 48.6	143 26.7	S14 49.3	224 24.0	N18 39.5	163 15.3	S 5 01.5	167 04.3	S 2 12.7	Acamar	315 36.4	S40 22.5
01	12 51.1	158 26.3	50.4	239 24.9	39.1	178 17.3	01.7	182 06.5	12.8	Achernar	335 44.2	S57 19.7
02	27 53.6	173 26.0	51.5	254 25.7	38.7	193 19.3	01.9	197 08.7	13.0	Acrux	173 37.2	S62 59.8
03	42 56.0	188 25.7	·· 52.6	269 26.6	·· 38.3	208 21.3	·· 02.1	212 10.9	·· 13.1	Adhara	255 31.7	S28 56.6
04	57 58.5	203 25.4	53.7	284 27.5	37.9	223 23.3	02.3	227 13.1	13.2	Aldebaran	291 17.1	N16 28.4
05	73 00.9	218 25.1	54.8	299 28.4	37.5	238 25.2	02.5	242 15.3	13.3			
06	88 03.4	233 24.7	S14 55.9	314 29.3	N18 37.1	253 27.2	S 5 02.7	257 17.4	S 2 13.4	Alioth	166 42.4	N56 03.8
07	103 05.9	248 24.4	57.0	329 30.2	36.7	268 29.2	02.9	272 19.6	13.5	Alkaid	153 18.4	N49 24.6
S 08	118 08.3	263 24.1	58.1	344 31.0	36.3	283 31.2	03.1	287 21.8	13.7	Al Na'ir	28 13.6	S47 03.1
A 09	133 10.8	278 23.8	14 59.2	359 31.9	·· 35.9	298 33.1	·· 03.3	302 24.0	·· 13.8	Alnilam	276 10.9	S 1 12.7
T 10	148 13.3	293 23.5	15 00.3	14 32.8	35.5	313 35.1	03.5	317 26.2	13.9	Alphard	218 20.2	S 8 34.5
U 11	163 15.7	308 23.1	01.4	29 33.7	35.1	328 37.1	03.7	332 28.4	14.0			
R 12	178 18.2	323 22.8	S15 02.5	44 34.6	N18 34.7	343 39.1	S 5 03.9	347 30.6	S 2 14.1	Alphecca	126 31.7	N26 46.9
D 13	193 20.7	338 22.5	03.6	59 35.5	34.3	358 41.1	04.1	2 32.8	14.3	Alpheratz	358 08.3	N28 59.4
A 14	208 23.1	353 22.2	04.7	74 36.3	33.9	13 43.0	04.3	17 34.9	14.4	Altair	62 31.7	N 8 49.3
Y 15	223 25.6	8 21.8	·· 05.8	89 37.2	·· 33.5	28 45.0	·· 04.5	32 37.1	·· 14.5	Ankaa	353 39.1	S42 24.3
16	238 28.1	23 21.5	06.9	104 38.1	33.1	43 47.0	04.8	47 39.3	14.6	Antares	112 56.1	S26 23.5
17	253 30.5	38 21.2	08.0	119 39.0	32.7	58 49.0	05.0	62 41.5	14.7			
18	268 33.0	53 20.9	S15 09.1	134 39.9	N18 32.3	73 50.9	S 5 05.2	77 43.7	S 2 14.9	Arcturus	146 18.1	N19 16.9
19	283 35.4	68 20.5	10.2	149 40.8	31.9	88 52.9	05.4	92 45.9	15.0	Atria	108 19.9	S68 59.9
20	298 37.9	83 20.2	11.3	164 41.7	31.5	103 54.9	05.6	107 48.1	15.1	Avior	234 28.3	S59 26.7
21	313 40.4	98 19.9	·· 12.4	179 42.5	·· 31.1	118 56.9	·· 05.8	122 50.3	·· 15.2	Bellatrix	278 58.0	N 6 20.1
22	328 42.8	113 19.6	13.5	194 43.4	30.7	133 58.9	06.0	137 52.4	15.3	Betelgeuse	271 27.5	N 7 24.3
23	343 45.3	128 19.2	14.6	209 44.3	30.3	149 00.8	06.2	152 54.6	15.4			
20 00	358 47.8	143 18.9	S15 15.7	224 45.2	N18 29.9	164 02.8	S 5 06.4	167 56.8	S 2 15.6	Canopus	264 07.0	S52 40.8
01	13 50.2	158 18.6	16.8	239 46.1	29.5	179 04.8	06.6	182 59.0	15.7	Capella	281 10.2	N45 58.6
02	28 52.7	173 18.3	17.9	254 47.0	29.1	194 06.8	06.8	198 01.2	15.8	Deneb	49 47.7	N45 13.1
03	43 55.2	188 17.9	·· 19.0	269 47.9	·· 28.7	209 08.7	·· 07.0	213 03.4	·· 15.9	Denebola	182 58.7	N14 40.7
04	58 57.6	203 17.6	20.1	284 48.7	28.3	224 10.7	07.2	228 05.6	16.0	Diphda	349 19.9	S18 05.2
05	74 00.1	218 17.3	21.2	299 49.6	27.9	239 12.7	07.4	243 07.8	16.2			
06	89 02.5	233 16.9	S15 22.2	314 50.5	N18 27.5	254 14.7	S 5 07.6	258 09.9	S 2 16.3	Dubhe	194 21.9	N61 51.1
07	104 05.0	248 16.6	23.3	329 51.4	27.1	269 16.7	07.8	273 12.1	16.4	Elnath	278 43.2	N28 35.5
08	119 07.5	263 16.3	24.4	344 52.3	26.7	284 18.6	08.0	288 14.3	16.5	Eltanin	90 57.4	N51 29.8
S 09	134 09.9	278 16.0	·· 25.5	359 53.2	·· 26.3	299 20.6	·· 08.2	303 16.5	·· 16.6	Enif	34 10.6	N 9 47.6
U 10	149 12.4	293 15.6	26.6	14 54.1	25.8	314 22.6	08.4	318 18.7	16.8	Fomalhaut	15 50.3	S29 43.2
N 11	164 14.9	308 15.3	27.7	29 55.0	25.4	329 24.6	08.6	333 20.9	16.9			
D 12	179 17.3	323 15.0	S15 28.8	44 55.9	N18 25.0	344 26.5	S 5 08.9	348 23.1	S 2 17.0	Gacrux	172 28.6	S57 00.5
A 13	194 19.8	338 14.6	29.9	59 56.7	24.6	359 28.5	09.1	3 25.3	17.1	Gienah	176 17.6	S17 26.2
Y 14	209 22.3	353 14.3	30.9	74 57.6	24.2	14 30.5	09.3	18 27.4	17.2	Hadar	149 22.9	S60 17.1
15	224 24.7	8 14.0	·· 32.0	89 58.5	·· 23.8	29 32.5	·· 09.5	33 29.6	·· 17.3	Hamal	328 27.9	N23 22.5
16	239 27.2	23 13.6	33.1	104 59.4	23.4	44 34.4	09.7	48 31.8	17.5	Kaus Aust.	84 15.9	S34 23.7
17	254 29.7	38 13.3	34.2	120 00.3	23.0	59 36.4	09.9	63 34.0	17.6			
18	269 32.1	53 13.0	S15 35.3	135 01.2	N18 22.6	74 38.4	S 5 10.1	78 36.2	S 2 17.7	Kochab	137 19.8	N74 14.2
19	284 34.6	68 12.6	36.4	150 02.1	22.2	89 40.4	10.3	93 38.4	17.8	Markab	14 02.2	N15 06.5
20	299 37.0	83 12.3	37.4	165 03.0	21.8	104 42.3	10.5	108 40.6	17.9	Menkar	314 40.2	N 4 01.1
21	314 39.5	98 12.0	·· 38.5	180 03.9	·· 21.4	119 44.3	·· 10.7	123 42.7	·· 18.1	Menkent	148 36.5	S36 16.7
22	329 42.0	113 11.6	39.6	195 04.8	21.0	134 46.3	10.9	138 44.9	18.2	Miaplacidus	221 45.5	S69 38.2
23	344 44.4	128 11.3	40.7	210 05.7	20.6	149 48.3	11.1	153 47.1	18.3			
21 00	359 46.9	143 11.0	S15 41.8	225 06.6	N18 20.2	164 50.3	S 5 11.3	168 49.3	S 2 18.4	Mirfak	309 14.8	N49 47.6
01	14 49.4	158 10.6	42.8	240 07.4	19.7	179 52.2	11.5	183 51.5	18.5	Nunki	76 28.2	S26 19.2
02	29 51.8	173 10.3	43.9	255 08.3	19.3	194 54.2	11.7	198 53.7	18.7	Peacock	53 56.9	S56 47.8
03	44 54.3	188 10.0	·· 45.0	270 09.2	·· 18.9	209 56.2	·· 11.9	213 55.9	·· 18.8	Pollux	243 57.5	N28 04.3
04	59 56.8	203 09.6	46.1	285 10.1	18.5	224 58.2	12.1	228 58.1	18.9	Procyon	245 25.2	N 5 16.5
05	74 59.2	218 09.3	47.2	300 11.0	18.1	240 00.1	12.3	244 00.2	19.0			
06	90 01.7	233 09.0	S15 48.2	315 11.9	N18 17.7	255 02.1	S 5 12.5	259 02.4	S 2 19.1	Rasalhague	96 29.0	N12 34.6
07	105 04.2	248 08.6	49.3	330 12.8	17.3	270 04.1	12.8	274 04.6	19.3	Regulus	208 09.6	N12 03.6
08	120 06.6	263 08.3	50.4	345 13.7	16.9	285 06.1	13.0	289 06.8	19.4	Rigel	281 35.3	S 8 13.2
M 09	135 09.1	278 08.0	·· 51.5	0 14.6	·· 16.5	300 08.0	·· 13.2	304 09.0	·· 19.5	Rigil Kent.	140 25.4	S60 45.6
O 10	150 11.5	293 07.6	52.5	15 15.5	16.1	315 10.0	13.4	319 11.2	19.6	Sabik	102 40.4	S15 42.1
N 11	165 14.0	308 07.3	53.6	30 16.4	15.7	330 12.0	13.6	334 13.4	19.7			
D 12	180 16.5	323 06.9	S15 54.7	45 17.3	N18 15.2	345 14.0	S 5 13.8	349 15.5	S 2 19.8	Schedar	350 07.7	N56 26.1
A 13	195 18.9	338 06.6	55.7	60 18.2	14.8	0 15.9	14.0	4 17.7	20.0	Shaula	96 54.9	S37 05.5
Y 14	210 21.4	353 06.3	56.8	75 19.1	14.4	15 17.9	14.2	19 19.9	20.1	Sirius	258 55.2	S16 41.3
15	225 23.9	8 05.9	·· 57.9	90 20.0	·· 14.0	30 19.9	·· 14.4	34 22.1	·· 20.2	Spica	158 57.1	S11 03.7
16	240 26.3	23 05.6	15 59.0	105 20.9	13.6	45 21.9	14.6	49 24.3	20.3	Suhail	223 10.6	S43 21.2
17	255 28.8	38 05.2	16 00.0	120 21.8	13.2	60 23.8	14.8	64 26.5	20.4			
18	270 31.3	53 04.9	S16 01.1	135 22.6	N18 12.8	75 25.8	S 5 15.0	79 28.7	S 2 20.6	Vega	80 55.3	N38 46.3
19	285 33.7	68 04.6	02.2	150 23.5	12.4	90 27.8	15.2	94 30.9	20.7	Zuben'ubi	137 32.5	S15 57.8
20	300 36.2	83 04.3	03.2	165 24.4	12.0	105 29.8	15.4	109 33.0	20.8		S.H.A.	Mer. Pass.
21	315 38.6	98 03.9	·· 04.3	180 25.3	·· 11.5	120 31.7	·· 15.6	124 35.2	·· 20.9	Venus	144 31.1	14 27
22	330 41.1	113 03.5	05.4	195 26.2	11.1	135 33.7	15.8	139 37.4	21.0	Mars	225 57.4	9 00
23	345 43.6	128 03.2	06.4	210 27.1	10.7	150 35.7	16.0	154 39.6	21.2	Jupiter	165 15.0	13 02
Mer. Pass.	0 04.8	*v* −0.3	*d* 1.1	*v* 0.9	*d* 0.4	*v* 2.0	*d* 0.2	*v* 2.2	*d* 0.1	Saturn	169 09.1	12 46

G.M.T.	SUN G.H.A.	Dec.	MOON G.H.A.	v	Dec.	d	H.P.
19 00	181 31.0	N 1 36.3	297 11.6	7.1	N16 16.3	8.7	59.7
01	196 31.3	35.3	311 37.7	7.1	16 25.0	8.5	59.7
02	211 31.5	34.3	326 03.8	7.0	16 33.5	8.4	59.7
03	226 31.7	·· 33.4	340 29.8	7.0	16 41.9	8.3	59.7
04	241 31.9	32.4	354 55.8	7.0	16 50.2	8.2	59.6
05	256 32.2	31.4	9 21.8	6.9	16 58.4	8.0	59.6
06	271 32.4	N 1 30.5	23 47.7	6.9	N17 06.4	8.0	59.6
07	286 32.6	29.5	38 13.6	6.9	17 14.4	7.8	59.6
S 08	301 32.8	28.5	52 39.5	6.8	17 22.2	7.8	59.6
A 09	316 33.0	·· 27.6	67 05.3	6.8	17 30.0	7.6	59.6
T 10	331 33.3	26.6	81 31.1	6.8	17 37.6	7.5	59.6
U 11	346 33.5	25.6	95 56.9	6.7	17 45.1	7.4	59.5
R 12	1 33.7	N 1 24.6	110 22.6	6.7	N17 52.5	7.2	59.5
D 13	16 33.9	23.7	124 48.3	6.7	17 59.7	7.2	59.5
A 14	31 34.2	22.7	139 14.0	6.6	18 06.9	7.0	59.5
Y 15	46 34.4	·· 21.7	153 39.6	6.6	18 13.9	6.9	59.5
16	61 34.6	20.8	168 05.2	6.6	18 20.8	6.8	59.5
17	76 34.8	19.8	182 30.8	6.6	18 27.6	6.6	59.5
18	91 35.0	N 1 18.8	196 56.4	6.5	N18 34.2	6.6	59.4
19	106 35.3	17.9	211 21.9	6.5	18 40.8	6.4	59.4
20	121 35.5	16.9	225 47.4	6.5	18 47.2	6.3	59.4
21	136 35.7	·· 15.9	240 12.9	6.4	18 53.5	6.1	59.4
22	151 35.9	14.9	254 38.3	6.5	18 59.6	6.1	59.4
23	166 36.2	14.0	269 03.8	6.4	19 05.7	5.9	59.4
20 00	181 36.4	N 1 13.0	283 29.2	6.3	N19 11.6	5.7	59.3
01	196 36.6	12.0	297 54.5	6.4	19 17.3	5.7	59.3
02	211 36.8	11.1	312 19.9	6.3	19 23.0	5.5	59.3
03	226 37.0	·· 10.1	326 45.2	6.3	19 28.5	5.4	59.3
04	241 37.3	09.1	341 10.5	6.3	19 33.9	5.3	59.3
05	256 37.5	08.1	355 35.8	6.3	19 39.2	5.1	59.3
06	271 37.7	N 1 07.2	10 01.1	6.3	N19 44.3	5.0	59.3
07	286 37.9	06.2	24 26.4	6.2	19 49.3	4.9	59.2
08	301 38.2	05.2	38 51.6	6.3	19 54.2	4.7	59.2
S 09	316 38.4	·· 04.3	53 16.9	6.2	19 58.9	4.6	59.2
U 10	331 38.6	03.3	67 42.1	6.2	20 03.5	4.5	59.2
N 11	346 38.8	02.3	82 07.3	6.2	20 08.0	4.4	59.2
D 12	1 39.0	N 1 01.4	96 32.5	6.1	N20 12.4	4.2	59.1
A 13	16 39.3	1 00.4	110 57.6	6.2	20 16.6	4.0	59.1
Y 14	31 39.5	0 59.4	125 22.8	6.2	20 20.6	4.0	59.1
15	46 39.7	·· 58.4	139 48.0	6.1	20 24.6	3.8	59.1
16	61 39.9	57.5	154 13.1	6.1	20 28.4	3.6	59.1
17	76 40.1	56.5	168 38.2	6.2	20 32.0	3.6	59.1
18	91 40.4	N 0 55.5	183 03.4	6.1	N20 35.6	3.4	59.0
19	106 40.6	54.6	197 28.5	6.1	20 39.0	3.2	59.0
20	121 40.8	53.6	211 53.6	6.2	20 42.2	3.2	59.0
21	136 41.0	·· 52.6	226 18.8	6.1	20 45.4	3.0	59.0
22	151 41.2	51.6	240 43.9	6.1	20 48.4	2.8	59.0
23	166 41.5	50.7	255 09.0	6.1	20 51.2	2.7	58.9
21 00	181 41.7	N 0 49.7	269 34.1	6.1	N20 53.9	2.6	58.9
01	196 41.9	48.7	283 59.2	6.2	20 56.5	2.5	58.9
02	211 42.1	47.8	298 24.4	6.1	20 59.0	2.3	58.9
03	226 42.4	·· 46.8	312 49.5	6.2	21 01.3	2.1	58.9
04	241 42.6	45.8	327 14.6	6.2	21 03.4	2.1	58.9
05	256 42.8	44.8	341 39.8	6.1	21 05.5	1.9	58.8
06	271 43.0	N 0 43.9	356 04.9	6.2	N21 07.4	1.7	58.8
07	286 43.2	42.9	10 30.1	6.1	21 09.1	1.6	58.8
08	301 43.5	41.9	24 55.2	6.2	21 10.7	1.5	58.8
M 09	316 43.7	·· 40.9	39 20.4	6.2	21 12.2	1.4	58.8
O 10	331 43.9	40.0	53 45.6	6.2	21 13.6	1.2	58.7
N 11	346 44.1	39.0	68 10.8	6.2	21 14.8	1.0	58.7
D 12	1 44.3	N 0 38.0	82 36.0	6.2	N21 15.8	1.0	58.7
A 13	16 44.6	37.1	97 01.2	6.3	21 16.8	0.8	58.7
Y 14	31 44.8	36.1	111 26.5	6.2	21 17.6	0.6	58.7
15	46 45.0	·· 35.1	125 51.7	6.3	21 18.2	0.6	58.6
16	61 45.2	34.1	140 17.0	6.3	21 18.8	0.3	58.6
17	76 45.4	33.2	154 42.3	6.3	21 19.1	0.3	58.6
18	91 45.7	N 0 32.2	169 07.6	6.4	N21 19.4	0.1	58.6
19	106 45.9	31.2	183 33.0	6.4	21 19.5	0.0	58.6
20	121 46.1	30.3	197 58.4	6.4	21 19.5	0.2	58.5
21	136 46.3	·· 29.3	212 23.8	6.4	21 19.3	0.3	58.5
22	151 46.5	28.3	226 49.2	6.4	21 19.0	0.4	58.5
23	166 46.8	27.3	241 14.6	6.5	21 18.6	0.5	58.5
	S.D. 16.0	d 1.0	S.D. 16.2		16.1		16.0

Twilight / Sunrise / Moonrise

Lat.	Naut.	Civil	Sunrise	Moonrise 19	20	21	22
N 72	02 44	04 19	05 29	□	□	□	□
N 70	03 07	04 29	05 31	18 27	□	□	□
68	03 25	04 37	05 33	19 11	19 19	19 54	21 16
66	03 38	04 43	05 35	19 40	20 03	20 48	22 01
64	03 49	04 49	05 37	20 02	20 32	21 21	22 30
62	03 59	04 53	05 38	20 20	20 55	21 45	22 52
60	04 06	04 57	05 39	20 35	21 13	22 04	23 10
N 58	04 13	05 01	05 40	20 47	21 28	22 20	23 25
56	04 19	05 04	05 41	20 59	21 41	22 34	23 38
54	04 24	05 06	05 42	21 08	21 52	22 46	23 49
52	04 28	05 08	05 42	21 17	22 02	22 56	23 59
50	04 32	05 11	05 43	21 25	22 11	23 06	24 08
45	04 40	05 15	05 44	21 41	22 30	23 25	24 26
N 40	04 47	05 18	05 45	21 55	22 45	23 41	24 42
35	04 51	05 21	05 46	22 07	22 58	23 55	24 54
30	04 55	05 23	05 47	22 17	23 10	24 06	00 06
20	05 01	05 26	05 48	22 35	23 29	24 26	00 26
N 10	05 04	05 28	05 49	22 50	23 46	24 44	00 44
0	05 05	05 29	05 50	23 05	24 02	00 02	01 00
S 10	05 06	05 30	05 51	23 19	24 19	00 19	01 17
20	05 04	05 30	05 52	23 35	24 36	00 36	01 34
30	05 01	05 28	05 52	23 53	24 56	00 56	01 54
35	04 58	05 27	05 53	24 03	00 03	01 07	02 06
40	04 54	05 26	05 53	24 16	00 16	01 21	02 20
45	04 50	05 24	05 53	24 30	00 30	01 37	02 36
S 50	04 44	05 22	05 54	24 47	00 47	01 56	02 56
52	04 41	05 20	05 54	24 56	00 56	02 05	03 05
54	04 37	05 19	05 54	25 05	01 05	02 16	03 16
56	04 33	05 17	05 54	25 16	01 16	02 28	03 27
58	04 29	05 15	05 54	00 04	01 28	02 41	03 41
S 60	04 24	05 13	05 55	00 15	01 41	02 57	03 57

Sunset / Twilight / Moonset

Lat.	Sunset	Civil	Naut.	Moonset 19	20	21	22
N 72	18 15	19 24	20 58	□	□	□	□
N 70	18 13	19 15	20 36	15 00	□	□	□
68	18 11	19 08	20 19	14 18	16 10	17 37	18 13
66	18 10	19 01	20 06	13 49	15 26	16 42	17 28
64	18 09	18 56	19 55	13 28	14 57	16 09	16 59
62	18 07	18 52	19 46	13 10	14 35	15 45	16 36
60	18 06	18 48	19 38	12 56	14 18	15 26	16 18
N 58	18 06	18 45	19 32	12 44	14 03	15 10	16 03
56	18 05	18 42	19 26	12 33	13 50	14 56	15 50
54	18 04	18 39	19 22	12 24	13 39	14 45	15 38
52	18 03	18 37	19 17	12 16	13 29	14 34	15 28
50	18 03	18 35	19 13	12 08	13 20	14 25	15 19
45	18 02	18 31	19 06	11 52	13 02	14 05	15 00
N 40	18 01	18 28	18 59	11 39	12 47	13 49	14 45
35	18 00	18 25	18 55	11 28	12 34	13 36	14 32
30	17 59	18 23	18 51	11 19	12 23	13 24	14 20
20	17 58	18 20	18 46	11 02	12 04	13 04	14 01
N 10	17 57	18 18	18 43	10 48	11 48	12 47	13 44
0	17 57	18 17	18 41	10 35	11 32	12 30	13 27
S 10	17 56	18 17	18 41	10 21	11 17	12 14	13 11
20	17 56	18 18	18 43	10 07	11 00	11 56	12 54
30	17 55	18 19	18 47	09 51	10 41	11 36	12 34
35	17 55	18 20	18 49	09 41	10 30	11 24	12 22
40	17 55	18 22	18 53	09 30	10 18	11 11	12 09
45	17 54	18 24	18 58	09 18	10 03	10 55	11 53
S 50	17 54	18 26	19 04	09 02	09 44	10 35	11 34
52	17 54	18 27	19 07	08 55	09 36	10 25	11 24
54	17 54	18 29	19 11	08 47	09 26	10 15	11 14
56	17 54	18 31	19 15	08 38	09 15	10 03	11 02
58	17 54	18 33	19 19	08 28	09 03	09 49	10 48
S 60	17 54	18 35	19 25	08 17	08 49	09 33	10 32

SUN / MOON

Day	Eqn. of Time 00ʰ	12ʰ	Mer. Pass.	Mer. Pass. Upper	Lower	Age	Phase
	m s	m s	h m	h m	h m	d	
19	06 04	06 14	11 54	04 21	16 50	21	
20	06 25	06 36	11 53	05 18	17 47	22	◑
21	06 46	06 57	11 53	06 16	18 45	23	

G.M.T.	ARIES G.H.A.	VENUS −3.6 G.H.A.	Dec.	MARS +1.8 G.H.A.	Dec.	JUPITER −1.2 G.H.A.	Dec.	SATURN +1.1 G.H.A.	Dec.	STARS Name	S.H.A.	Dec.
22 00	0 46.0	143 02.8	S16 07.5	225 28.0	N18 10.3	165 37.7	S 5 16.2	169 41.8	S 2 21.3	Acamar	315 36.4	S40 22.5
01	15 48.5	158 02.5	08.6	240 28.9	09.9	180 39.6	16.4	184 44.0	21.4	Achernar	335 44.2	S57 19.7
02	30 51.0	173 02.2	09.6	255 29.8	09.5	195 41.6	16.7	199 46.2	21.5	Acrux	173 37.2	S62 59.7
03	45 53.4	188 01.8	·· 10.7	270 30.7	·· 09.1	210 43.6	·· 16.9	214 48.3	·· 21.6	Adhara	255 31.7	S28 56.6
04	60 55.9	203 01.5	11.8	285 31.6	08.7	225 45.6	17.1	229 50.5	21.8	Aldebaran	291 17.1	N16 28.4
05	75 58.4	218 01.1	12.8	300 32.5	08.3	240 47.5	17.3	244 52.7	21.9			
06	91 00.8	233 00.8	S16 13.9	315 33.4	N18 07.8	255 49.5	S 5 17.5	259 54.9	S 2 22.0	Alioth	166 42.4	N56 03.8
07	106 03.3	248 00.4	14.9	330 34.3	07.4	270 51.5	17.7	274 57.1	22.1	Alkaid	153 18.4	N49 24.6
08	121 05.8	263 00.1	16.0	345 35.2	07.0	285 53.5	17.9	289 59.3	22.2	Al Na'ir	28 13.6	S47 03.1
T 09	136 08.2	277 59.8	·· 17.1	0 36.1	·· 06.6	300 55.4	·· 18.1	305 01.5	·· 22.3	Alnilam	276 10.9	S 1 12.7
U 10	151 10.7	292 59.4	18.1	15 37.0	06.2	315 57.4	18.3	320 03.6	22.5	Alphard	218 20.1	S 8 34.5
E 11	166 13.1	307 59.1	19.2	30 37.9	05.8	330 59.4	18.5	335 05.8	22.6			
S 12	181 15.6	322 58.7	S16 20.2	45 38.8	N18 05.4	346 01.4	S 5 18.7	350 08.0	S 2 22.7	Alphecca	126 31.7	N26 46.9
D 13	196 18.1	337 58.4	21.3	60 39.7	04.9	1 03.3	18.9	5 10.2	22.8	Alpheratz	358 08.3	N28 59.4
A 14	211 20.5	352 58.0	22.3	75 40.6	04.5	16 05.3	19.1	20 12.4	22.9	Altair	62 31.7	N 8 49.3
Y 15	226 23.0	7 57.7	·· 23.4	90 41.5	·· 04.1	31 07.3	·· 19.3	35 14.6	·· 23.1	Ankaa	353 39.1	S42 24.3
16	241 25.5	22 57.3	24.5	105 42.4	03.7	46 09.3	19.5	50 16.8	23.2	Antares	112 56.2	S26 23.5
17	256 27.9	37 57.0	25.5	120 43.3	03.3	61 11.2	19.7	65 18.9	23.3			
18	271 30.4	52 56.6	S16 26.6	135 44.2	N18 02.9	76 13.2	S 5 19.9	80 21.1	S 2 23.4	Arcturus	146 18.1	N19 16.9
19	286 32.9	67 56.3	27.6	150 45.1	02.5	91 15.2	20.1	95 23.3	23.5	Atria	108 19.9	S68 59.9
20	301 35.3	82 55.9	28.7	165 46.0	02.0	106 17.1	20.4	110 25.5	23.7	Avior	234 28.3	S59 26.7
21	316 37.8	97 55.6	·· 29.7	180 46.9	·· 01.6	121 19.1	·· 20.6	125 27.7	·· 23.8	Bellatrix	278 58.0	N 6 20.1
22	331 40.3	112 55.2	30.8	195 47.8	01.2	136 21.1	20.8	140 29.9	23.9	Betelgeuse	271 27.5	N 7 24.3
23	346 42.7	127 54.9	31.8	210 48.7	00.8	151 23.1	21.0	155 32.1	24.0			
23 00	1 45.2	142 54.5	S16 32.9	225 49.6	N18 00.4	166 25.0	S 5 21.2	170 34.2	S 2 24.1	Canopus	264 06.9	S52 40.8
01	16 47.6	157 54.2	33.9	240 50.5	18 00.0	181 27.0	21.4	185 36.4	24.3	Capella	281 10.2	N45 58.6
02	31 50.1	172 53.8	35.0	255 51.4	17 59.5	196 29.0	21.6	200 38.6	24.4	Deneb	49 47.7	N45 13.1
03	46 52.6	187 53.5	·· 36.0	270 52.3	·· 59.1	211 31.0	·· 21.8	215 40.8	·· 24.5	Denebola	182 58.7	N14 40.7
04	61 55.0	202 53.1	37.1	285 53.2	58.7	226 32.9	22.0	230 43.0	24.6	Diphda	349 19.8	S18 05.2
05	76 57.5	217 52.8	38.1	300 54.1	58.3	241 34.9	22.2	245 45.2	24.7			
06	92 00.0	232 52.4	S16 39.2	315 55.1	N17 57.9	256 36.9	S 5 22.4	260 47.3	S 2 24.9	Dubhe	194 21.9	N61 51.1
W 07	107 02.4	247 52.1	40.2	330 56.0	57.5	271 38.9	22.6	275 49.5	25.0	Elnath	278 43.2	N28 35.5
E 08	122 04.9	262 51.7	41.3	345 56.9	57.0	286 40.8	22.8	290 51.7	25.1	Eltanin	90 57.4	N51 29.8
D 09	137 07.4	277 51.3	·· 42.3	0 57.8	·· 56.6	301 42.8	·· 23.0	305 53.9	·· 25.2	Enif	34 10.6	N 9 47.6
N 10	152 09.8	292 51.0	43.3	15 58.7	56.2	316 44.8	23.2	320 56.1	25.3	Fomalhaut	15 50.3	S29 43.2
E 11	167 12.3	307 50.6	44.4	30 59.6	55.8	331 46.7	23.4	335 58.3	25.4			
S 12	182 14.7	322 50.3	S16 45.4	46 00.5	N17 55.4	346 48.7	S 5 23.6	351 00.5	S 2 25.6	Gacrux	172 28.6	S57 00.5
D 13	197 17.2	337 49.9	46.5	61 01.4	55.0	1 50.7	23.8	6 02.6	25.7	Gienah	176 17.6	S17 26.2
A 14	212 19.7	352 49.6	47.5	76 02.3	54.5	16 52.7	24.1	21 04.8	25.8	Hadar	149 22.9	S60 17.1
Y 15	227 22.1	7 49.2	·· 48.6	91 03.2	·· 54.1	31 54.6	·· 24.3	36 07.0	·· 25.9	Hamal	328 27.9	N23 22.5
16	242 24.6	22 48.9	49.6	106 04.1	53.7	46 56.6	24.5	51 09.2	26.0	Kaus Aust.	84 15.9	S34 23.7
17	257 27.1	37 48.5	50.6	121 05.0	53.3	61 58.6	24.7	66 11.4	26.2			
18	272 29.5	52 48.1	S16 51.7	136 05.9	N17 52.9	77 00.6	S 5 24.9	81 13.6	S 2 26.3	Kochab	137 19.8	N74 14.2
19	287 32.0	67 47.8	52.7	151 06.8	52.4	92 02.5	25.1	96 15.8	26.4	Markab	14 02.2	N15 06.5
20	302 34.5	82 47.4	53.7	166 07.7	52.0	107 04.5	25.3	111 17.9	26.5	Menkar	314 40.2	N 4 01.1
21	317 36.9	97 47.1	·· 54.8	181 08.6	·· 51.6	122 06.5	·· 25.5	126 20.1	·· 26.6	Menkent	148 36.5	S36 16.7
22	332 39.4	112 46.7	55.8	196 09.5	51.2	137 08.4	25.7	141 22.3	26.8	Miaplacidus	221 45.5	S69 38.2
23	347 41.9	127 46.4	56.9	211 10.5	50.8	152 10.4	25.9	156 24.5	26.9			
24 00	2 44.3	142 46.0	S16 57.9	226 11.4	N17 50.3	167 12.4	S 5 26.1	171 26.7	S 2 27.0	Mirfak	309 14.8	N49 47.6
01	17 46.8	157 45.6	16 58.9	241 12.3	49.9	182 14.4	26.3	186 28.9	27.1	Nunki	76 28.2	S26 19.2
02	32 49.2	172 45.3	17 00.0	256 13.2	49.5	197 16.3	26.5	201 31.0	27.2	Peacock	53 56.9	S56 47.8
03	47 51.7	187 44.9	·· 01.0	271 14.1	·· 49.1	212 18.3	·· 26.7	216 33.2	·· 27.4	Pollux	243 57.5	N28 04.3
04	62 54.2	202 44.6	02.0	286 15.0	48.7	227 20.3	26.9	231 35.4	27.5	Procyon	245 25.2	N 5 16.5
05	77 56.6	217 44.2	03.1	301 15.9	48.2	242 22.2	27.1	246 37.6	27.6			
06	92 59.1	232 43.8	S17 04.1	316 16.8	N17 47.8	257 24.2	S 5 27.3	261 39.8	S 2 27.7	Rasalhague	96 29.0	N12 34.6
07	108 01.6	247 43.5	05.1	331 17.7	47.4	272 26.2	27.5	276 42.0	27.8	Regulus	208 09.5	N12 03.6
T 08	123 04.0	262 43.1	06.1	346 18.6	47.0	287 28.2	27.8	291 44.2	28.0	Rigel	281 35.3	S 8 13.2
H 09	138 06.5	277 42.7	·· 07.2	1 19.5	·· 46.6	302 30.1	·· 28.0	306 46.3	·· 28.1	Rigil Kent.	140 25.4	S60 45.6
U 10	153 09.0	292 42.4	08.2	16 20.5	46.1	317 32.1	28.2	321 48.5	28.2	Sabik	102 40.4	S15 42.1
R 11	168 11.4	307 42.0	09.2	31 21.4	45.7	332 34.1	28.4	336 50.7	28.3			
S 12	183 13.9	322 41.7	S17 10.3	46 22.3	N17 45.3	347 36.1	S 5 28.6	351 52.9	S 2 28.4	Schedar	350 07.7	N56 26.2
D 13	198 16.4	337 41.3	11.3	61 23.2	44.9	2 38.0	28.8	6 55.1	28.5	Shaula	96 54.9	S37 05.5
A 14	213 18.8	352 40.9	12.3	76 24.1	44.5	17 40.0	29.0	21 57.3	28.7	Sirius	258 55.2	S16 41.3
Y 15	228 21.3	7 40.6	·· 13.3	91 25.0	·· 44.0	32 42.0	·· 29.2	36 59.4	·· 28.8	Spica	158 57.1	S11 03.7
16	243 23.7	22 40.2	14.4	106 25.9	43.6	47 43.9	29.4	52 01.6	28.9	Suhail	223 10.6	S43 21.2
17	258 26.2	37 39.8	15.4	121 26.8	43.2	62 45.9	29.6	67 03.8	29.0			
18	273 28.7	52 39.5	S17 16.4	136 27.7	N17 42.8	77 47.9	S 5 29.8	82 06.0	S 2 29.1	Vega	80 55.3	N38 46.3
19	288 31.1	67 39.1	17.4	151 28.7	42.3	92 49.9	30.0	97 08.2	29.3	Zuben'ubi	137 32.5	S15 57.8
20	303 33.6	82 38.7	18.5	166 29.6	41.9	107 51.8	30.2	112 10.4	29.4		S.H.A.	Mer. Pass.
21	318 36.1	97 38.4	·· 19.5	181 30.5	·· 41.5	122 53.8	·· 30.4	127 12.6	·· 29.5	Venus	141 09.3	14 29
22	333 38.5	112 38.0	20.5	196 31.4	41.1	137 55.8	30.6	142 14.7	29.6	Mars	224 04.5	8 56
23	348 41.0	127 37.6	21.5	211 32.3	40.6	152 57.7	30.8	157 16.9	29.7	Jupiter	164 39.9	12 53
Mer. Pass. 23 49.1		v −0.4	d 1.0	v 0.9	d 0.4	v 2.0	d 0.2	v 2.2	d 0.1	Saturn	168 49.1	12 36

G.M.T.	SUN G.H.A.	Dec.	MOON G.H.A.	v	Dec.	d	H.P.
d h	° ′	° ′	° ′	′	° ′	′	′
22 00	181 47.0	N 0 26.4	255 40.1	6.5	N21 18.1	0.7	58.5
01	196 47.2	25.4	270 05.6	6.5	21 17.4	0.9	58.4
02	211 47.4	24.4	284 31.1	6.6	21 16.5	0.9	58.4
03	226 47.6	·· 23.4	298 56.7	6.6	21 15.6	1.1	58.4
04	241 47.9	22.5	313 22.3	6.6	21 14.5	1.3	58.4
05	256 48.1	21.5	327 47.9	6.7	21 13.2	1.3	58.4
06	271 48.3	N 0 20.5	342 13.6	6.7	N21 11.9	1.5	58.3
07	286 48.5	19.6	356 39.3	6.8	21 10.4	1.6	58.3
08	301 48.7	18.6	11 05.1	6.7	21 08.8	1.8	58.3
09	316 49.0	·· 17.6	25 30.8	6.9	21 07.0	1.9	58.3
10	331 49.2	16.6	39 56.7	6.8	21 05.1	2.0	58.3
11	346 49.4	15.7	54 22.5	6.9	21 03.1	2.1	58.2
12	1 49.6	N 0 14.7	68 48.4	7.0	N21 01.0	2.3	58.2
13	16 49.8	13.7	83 14.4	6.9	20 58.7	2.4	58.2
14	31 50.0	12.7	97 40.3	7.1	20 56.3	2.5	58.2
15	46 50.3	·· 11.8	112 06.4	7.0	20 53.8	2.7	58.2
16	61 50.5	10.8	126 32.4	7.2	20 51.1	2.8	58.1
17	76 50.7	09.8	140 58.6	7.1	20 48.3	2.9	58.1
18	91 50.9	N 0 08.8	155 24.7	7.2	N20 45.4	3.0	58.1
19	106 51.1	07.9	169 50.9	7.3	20 42.4	3.2	58.1
20	121 51.4	06.9	184 17.2	7.3	20 39.2	3.3	58.1
21	136 51.6	·· 05.9	198 43.5	7.4	20 35.9	3.4	58.0
22	151 51.8	05.0	213 09.9	7.4	20 32.5	3.5	58.0
23	166 52.0	04.0	227 36.3	7.4	20 29.0	3.6	58.0
23 00	181 52.2	N 0 03.0	242 02.7	7.5	N20 25.4	3.8	58.0
01	196 52.5	02.0	256 29.2	7.6	20 21.6	3.9	57.9
02	211 52.7	01.1	270 55.8	7.6	20 17.7	4.0	57.9
03	226 52.9	N 0 00.1	285 22.4	7.7	20 13.7	4.1	57.9
04	241 53.1	S 0 00.9	299 49.1	7.7	20 09.6	4.3	57.9
05	256 53.3	01.9	314 15.8	7.8	20 05.3	4.3	57.9
06	271 53.5	S 0 02.8	328 42.6	7.9	N20 01.0	4.5	57.8
07	286 53.8	03.8	343 09.5	7.9	19 56.5	4.6	57.8
08	301 54.0	04.8	357 36.4	7.9	19 51.9	4.7	57.8
09	316 54.2	·· 05.8	12 03.3	8.0	19 47.2	4.9	57.8
10	331 54.4	06.7	26 30.3	8.1	19 42.3	4.9	57.8
11	346 54.6	07.7	40 57.4	8.2	19 37.4	5.0	57.7
12	1 54.8	S 0 08.7	55 24.6	8.2	N19 32.4	5.2	57.7
13	16 55.1	09.7	69 51.8	8.2	19 27.2	5.3	57.7
14	31 55.3	10.6	84 19.0	8.3	19 21.9	5.3	57.7
15	46 55.5	·· 11.6	98 46.3	8.4	19 16.6	5.5	57.7
16	61 55.7	12.6	113 13.7	8.5	19 11.1	5.6	57.6
17	76 55.9	13.5	127 41.2	8.5	19 05.5	5.7	57.6
18	91 56.2	S 0 14.5	142 08.7	8.5	N18 59.8	5.8	57.6
19	106 56.4	15.5	156 36.2	8.7	18 54.0	5.9	57.6
20	121 56.6	16.5	171 03.9	8.7	18 48.1	6.1	57.6
21	136 56.8	·· 17.4	185 31.6	8.7	18 42.0	6.1	57.5
22	151 57.0	18.4	199 59.3	8.8	18 35.9	6.2	57.5
23	166 57.2	19.4	214 27.1	8.9	18 29.7	6.3	57.5
24 00	181 57.5	S 0 20.4	228 55.0	9.0	N18 23.4	6.4	57.5
01	196 57.7	21.3	243 23.0	9.0	18 17.0	6.6	57.4
02	211 57.9	22.3	257 51.0	9.1	18 10.4	6.6	57.4
03	226 58.1	·· 23.3	272 19.1	9.1	18 03.8	6.7	57.4
04	241 58.3	24.3	286 47.2	9.3	17 57.1	6.8	57.4
05	256 58.5	25.2	301 15.5	9.3	17 50.3	6.9	57.4
06	271 58.8	S 0 26.2	315 43.8	9.3	N17 43.4	7.0	57.3
07	286 59.0	27.2	330 12.1	9.4	17 36.4	7.1	57.3
08	301 59.2	28.2	344 40.5	9.5	17 29.3	7.2	57.3
09	316 59.4	·· 29.1	359 09.0	9.6	17 22.1	7.3	57.3
10	331 59.6	30.1	13 37.6	9.6	17 14.8	7.3	57.3
11	346 59.8	31.1	28 06.2	9.7	17 07.5	7.5	57.2
12	2 00.1	S 0 32.1	42 34.9	9.7	N17 00.0	7.5	57.2
13	17 00.3	33.0	57 03.6	9.8	16 52.5	7.7	57.2
14	32 00.5	34.0	71 32.4	9.9	16 44.8	7.7	57.2
15	47 00.7	·· 35.0	86 01.3	10.0	16 37.1	7.8	57.2
16	62 00.9	36.0	100 30.3	10.0	16 29.3	7.9	57.1
17	77 01.1	36.9	114 59.3	10.1	16 21.4	7.9	57.1
18	92 01.3	S 0 37.9	129 28.4	10.1	N16 13.5	8.1	57.1
19	107 01.6	38.9	143 57.5	10.3	16 05.4	8.1	57.1
20	122 01.8	39.8	158 26.8	10.3	15 57.3	8.2	57.0
21	137 02.0	·· 40.8	172 56.1	10.3	15 49.1	8.3	57.0
22	152 02.2	41.8	187 25.4	10.4	15 40.8	8.4	57.0
23	167 02.4	42.8	201 54.8	10.5	15 32.4	8.4	57.0
	S.D. 16.0	d 1.0	S.D. 15.9		15.7		15.6

Left margin day labels: TUESDAY (22), WEDNESDAY (23), THURSDAY (24)

Lat.	Naut.	Civil	Sunrise	Moonrise 22	23	24	25
°	h m	h m	h m	h m	h m	h m	h m
N 72	03 03	04 34	05 42	☐	☐	23 44	25 55
N 70	03 23	04 42	05 43	☐	22 15	24 22	00 22
68	03 38	04 48	05 44	21 16	23 01	24 48	00 48
66	03 50	04 53	05 45	22 01	23 31	25 07	01 07
64	03 59	04 58	05 45	22 30	23 54	25 23	01 23
62	04 07	05 01	05 46	22 52	24 12	00 12	01 36
60	04 14	05 04	05 46	23 10	24 26	00 26	01 47
N 58	04 20	05 07	05 46	23 25	24 39	00 39	01 57
56	04 25	05 10	05 47	23 38	24 50	00 50	02 05
54	04 30	05 12	05 47	23 49	24 59	00 59	02 13
52	04 34	05 14	05 47	23 59	25 08	01 08	02 19
50	04 37	05 15	05 47	24 08	00 08	01 15	02 25
45	04 44	05 19	05 48	24 26	00 26	01 32	02 38
N 40	04 50	05 21	05 48	24 42	00 42	01 45	02 49
35	04 54	05 23	05 48	24 54	00 54	01 56	02 58
30	04 57	05 25	05 49	00 06	01 05	02 06	03 06
20	05 01	05 27	05 49	00 26	01 25	02 23	03 19
N 10	05 04	05 28	05 49	00 44	01 41	02 37	03 31
0	05 04	05 28	05 49	01 00	01 57	02 51	03 42
S 10	05 04	05 28	05 49	01 17	02 12	03 05	03 53
20	05 01	05 27	05 49	01 34	02 29	03 19	04 05
30	04 57	05 25	05 48	01 54	02 48	03 36	04 19
35	04 54	05 23	05 48	02 06	02 59	03 46	04 27
40	04 49	05 21	05 48	02 20	03 12	03 57	04 35
45	04 44	05 18	05 48	02 36	03 27	04 10	04 46
S 50	04 37	05 15	05 47	02 56	03 45	04 25	04 58
52	04 33	05 13	05 47	03 05	03 54	04 33	05 04
54	04 29	05 11	05 47	03 16	04 03	04 41	05 10
56	04 25	05 09	05 46	03 27	04 14	04 50	05 17
58	04 20	05 07	05 46	03 41	04 27	05 00	05 25
S 60	04 14	05 04	05 45	03 57	04 41	05 12	05 34

Lat.	Sunset	Civil	Naut.	Moonset 22	23	24	25
°	h m	h m	h m	h m	h m	h m	h m
N 72	18 00	19 08	20 37	☐	☐	19 30	19 02
N 70	17 59	19 00	20 18	☐	19 09	18 51	18 41
68	17 59	18 54	20 04	18 13	18 22	18 24	18 24
66	17 58	18 49	19 52	17 28	17 52	18 04	18 10
64	17 58	18 45	19 43	16 59	17 29	17 47	17 59
62	17 58	18 42	19 35	16 36	17 10	17 33	17 49
60	17 57	18 39	19 29	16 18	16 55	17 21	17 41
N 58	17 57	18 36	19 23	16 03	16 42	17 11	17 33
56	17 57	18 34	19 18	15 50	16 31	17 02	17 27
54	17 57	18 32	19 14	15 38	16 21	16 54	17 21
52	17 56	18 30	19 10	15 28	16 12	16 47	17 16
50	17 56	18 28	19 06	15 19	16 04	16 41	17 11
45	17 56	18 25	19 00	15 00	15 47	16 27	17 00
N 40	17 56	18 23	18 54	14 45	15 33	16 15	16 52
35	17 56	18 21	18 50	14 32	15 22	16 05	16 44
30	17 56	18 19	18 47	14 20	15 11	15 57	16 37
20	17 55	18 17	18 43	14 01	14 53	15 42	16 26
N 10	17 55	18 16	18 41	13 44	14 38	15 28	16 16
0	17 56	18 16	18 40	13 27	14 23	15 16	16 06
S 10	17 56	18 17	18 41	13 11	14 08	15 03	15 56
20	17 56	18 18	18 44	12 54	13 52	14 50	15 46
30	17 57	18 21	18 48	12 34	13 34	14 35	15 34
35	17 57	18 22	18 52	12 22	13 24	14 26	15 27
40	17 57	18 24	18 56	12 09	13 11	14 15	15 19
45	17 58	18 27	19 02	11 53	12 57	14 03	15 10
S 50	17 59	18 31	19 09	11 34	12 39	13 48	14 59
52	17 59	18 33	19 13	11 24	12 31	13 41	14 54
54	17 59	18 35	19 17	11 14	12 21	13 34	14 48
56	18 00	18 37	19 21	11 02	12 11	13 25	14 41
58	18 00	18 39	19 26	10 48	11 59	13 15	14 34
S 60	18 01	18 42	19 33	10 32	11 44	13 04	14 26

Day	SUN Eqn. of Time 00ʰ	12ʰ	Mer. Pass.	MOON Mer. Pass. Upper	Lower	Age	Phase
	m s	m s	h m	h m	h m	d	
22	07 07	07 18	11 53	07 14	19 42	24	
23	07 28	07 39	11 52	08 10	20 37	25	◐
24	07 49	08 00	11 52	09 04	21 29	26	

G.M.T.	ARIES G.H.A.	VENUS −3.6 G.H.A.	Dec.	MARS +1.8 G.H.A.	Dec.	JUPITER −1.2 G.H.A.	Dec.	SATURN +1.0 G.H.A.	Dec.	STARS Name	S.H.A.	Dec.
25 00	3 43.5	142 37.3	S17 22.5	226 33.2	N17 40.2	167 59.7	S 5 31.0	172 19.1	S 2 29.9	Acamar	315 36.4	S40 22.5
01	18 45.9	157 36.9	23.6	241 34.1	39.8	183 01.7	31.3	187 21.3	30.0	Achernar	335 44.2	S57 19.7
02	33 48.4	172 36.5	24.6	256 35.1	39.4	198 03.6	31.5	202 23.5	30.1	Acrux	173 37.2	S62 59.7
03	48 50.8	187 36.2	·· 25.6	271 36.0	·· 39.0	213 05.6	·· 31.7	217 25.7	·· 30.2	Adhara	255 31.6	S28 56.6
04	63 53.3	202 35.8	26.6	286 36.9	38.5	228 07.6	31.9	232 27.8	30.3	Aldebaran	291 17.1	N16 28.4
05	78 55.8	217 35.4	27.6	301 37.8	38.1	243 09.6	32.1	247 30.0	30.5			
06	93 58.2	232 35.0	S17 28.6	316 38.7	N17 37.7	258 11.5	S 5 32.3	262 32.2	S 2 30.6	Alioth	166 42.4	N56 03.8
07	109 00.7	247 34.7	29.6	331 39.6	37.3	273 13.5	32.5	277 34.4	30.7	Alkaid	153 18.4	N49 24.5
08	124 03.2	262 34.3	30.7	346 40.5	36.8	288 15.5	32.7	292 36.6	30.8	Al Na'ir	28 13.7	S47 03.1
F 09	139 05.6	277 33.9	·· 31.7	1 41.5	·· 36.4	303 17.4	·· 32.9	307 38.8	·· 30.9	Alnilam	276 10.9	S 1 12.7
R 10	154 08.1	292 33.6	32.7	16 42.4	36.0	318 19.4	33.1	322 40.9	31.1	Alphard	218 20.1	S 8 34.5
I 11	169 10.6	307 33.2	33.7	31 43.3	35.6	333 21.4	33.3	337 43.1	31.2			
D 12	184 13.0	322 32.8	S17 34.7	46 44.2	N17 35.1	348 23.4	S 5 33.5	352 45.3	S 2 31.3	Alphecca	126 31.7	N26 46.9
A 13	199 15.5	337 32.4	35.7	61 45.1	34.7	3 25.3	33.7	7 47.5	31.4	Alpheratz	358 08.2	N28 59.4
Y 14	214 18.0	352 32.1	36.7	76 46.0	34.3	18 27.3	33.9	22 49.7	31.5	Altair	62 31.7	N 8 49.3
15	229 20.4	7 31.7	·· 37.7	91 47.0	·· 33.8	33 29.3	·· 34.1	37 51.9	·· 31.6	Ankaa	353 39.1	S42 24.3
16	244 22.9	22 31.3	38.7	106 47.9	33.4	48 31.2	34.3	52 54.0	31.8	Antares	112 56.2	S26 23.5
17	259 25.3	37 30.9	39.8	121 48.8	33.0	63 33.2	34.5	67 56.2	31.9			
18	274 27.8	52 30.6	S17 40.8	136 49.7	N17 32.6	78 35.2	S 5 34.8	82 58.4	S 2 32.0	Arcturus	146 18.1	N19 16.9
19	289 30.3	67 30.2	41.8	151 50.6	32.1	93 37.1	35.0	98 00.6	32.1	Atria	108 20.0	S68 59.9
20	304 32.7	82 29.8	42.8	166 51.5	31.7	108 39.1	35.2	113 02.8	32.2	Avior	234 28.3	S59 26.7
21	319 35.2	97 29.4	·· 43.8	181 52.5	·· 31.3	123 41.1	·· 35.4	128 05.0	·· 32.4	Bellatrix	278 57.9	N 6 20.1
22	334 37.7	112 29.1	44.8	196 53.4	30.9	138 43.1	35.6	143 07.2	32.5	Betelgeuse	271 27.5	N 7 24.3
23	349 40.1	127 28.7	45.8	211 54.3	30.4	153 45.0	35.8	158 09.3	32.6			
26 00	4 42.6	142 28.3	S17 46.8	226 55.2	N17 30.0	168 47.0	S 5 36.0	173 11.5	S 2 32.7	Canopus	264 06.9	S52 40.8
01	19 45.1	157 27.9	47.8	241 56.1	29.6	183 49.0	36.2	188 13.7	32.8	Capella	281 10.2	N45 58.6
02	34 47.5	172 27.6	48.8	256 57.1	29.2	198 50.9	36.4	203 15.9	33.0	Deneb	49 47.7	N45 13.1
03	49 50.0	187 27.2	·· 49.8	271 58.0	·· 28.7	213 52.9	·· 36.6	218 18.1	·· 33.1	Denebola	182 58.7	N14 40.7
04	64 52.5	202 26.8	50.8	286 58.9	28.3	228 54.9	36.8	233 20.3	33.2	Diphda	349 19.8	S18 05.2
05	79 54.9	217 26.4	51.8	301 59.8	27.9	243 56.8	37.0	248 22.4	33.3			
06	94 57.4	232 26.0	S17 52.8	317 00.7	N17 27.4	258 58.8	S 5 37.2	263 24.6	S 2 33.4	Dubhe	194 21.9	N61 51.0
07	109 59.8	247 25.7	53.8	332 01.7	27.0	274 00.8	37.4	278 26.8	33.6	Elnath	278 43.2	N28 35.5
S 08	125 02.3	262 25.3	54.8	347 02.6	26.6	289 02.8	37.6	293 29.0	33.7	Eltanin	90 57.5	N51 29.8
A 09	140 04.8	277 24.9	·· 55.8	2 03.5	·· 26.2	304 04.7	·· 37.8	308 31.2	·· 33.8	Enif	34 10.7	N 9 47.6
T 10	155 07.2	292 24.5	56.8	17 04.4	25.7	319 06.7	38.0	323 33.4	33.9	Fomalhaut	15 50.3	S29 43.2
U 11	170 09.7	307 24.1	57.8	32 05.3	25.3	334 08.7	38.3	338 35.5	34.0			
R 12	185 12.2	322 23.8	S17 58.8	47 06.3	N17 24.9	349 10.6	S 5 38.5	353 37.7	S 2 34.2	Gacrux	172 28.6	S57 00.5
D 13	200 14.6	337 23.4	17 59.8	62 07.2	24.4	4 12.6	38.7	8 39.9	34.3	Gienah	176 17.6	S17 26.2
A 14	215 17.1	352 23.0	18 00.8	77 08.1	24.0	19 14.6	38.9	23 42.1	34.4	Hadar	149 23.0	S60 17.1
Y 15	230 19.6	7 22.6	·· 01.8	92 09.0	·· 23.6	34 16.5	·· 39.1	38 44.3	·· 34.5	Hamal	328 27.8	N23 22.5
16	245 22.0	22 22.2	02.7	107 10.0	23.1	49 18.5	39.3	53 46.5	34.6	Kaus Aust.	84 15.9	S34 23.7
17	260 24.5	37 21.9	03.7	122 10.9	22.7	64 20.5	39.5	68 48.6	34.7			
18	275 27.0	52 21.5	S18 04.7	137 11.8	N17 22.3	79 22.4	S 5 39.7	83 50.8	S 2 34.9	Kochab	137 19.9	N74 14.2
19	290 29.4	67 21.1	05.7	152 12.7	21.9	94 24.4	39.9	98 53.0	35.0	Markab	14 02.2	N15 06.5
20	305 31.9	82 20.7	06.7	167 13.6	21.4	109 26.4	40.1	113 55.2	35.1	Menkar	314 40.2	N 4 01.1
21	320 34.3	97 20.3	·· 07.7	182 14.6	·· 21.0	124 28.4	·· 40.3	128 57.4	·· 35.2	Menkent	148 36.6	S36 16.7
22	335 36.8	112 19.9	08.7	197 15.5	20.6	139 30.3	40.5	143 59.6	35.3	Miaplacidus	221 45.5	S69 38.2
23	350 39.3	127 19.5	09.7	212 16.4	20.1	154 32.3	40.7	159 01.7	35.5			
27 00	5 41.7	142 19.2	S18 10.7	227 17.3	N17 19.7	169 34.3	S 5 40.9	174 03.9	S 2 35.6	Mirfak	309 14.8	N49 47.6
01	20 44.2	157 18.8	11.6	242 18.3	19.3	184 36.2	41.1	189 06.1	35.7	Nunki	76 28.2	S26 19.2
02	35 46.7	172 18.4	12.6	257 19.2	18.8	199 38.2	41.3	204 08.3	35.8	Peacock	53 57.0	S56 47.8
03	50 49.1	187 18.0	·· 13.6	272 20.1	·· 18.4	214 40.2	·· 41.6	219 10.5	·· 35.9	Pollux	243 57.4	N28 04.2
04	65 51.6	202 17.6	14.6	287 21.0	18.0	229 42.1	41.8	234 12.7	36.1	Procyon	245 25.2	N 5 16.5
05	80 54.1	217 17.2	15.6	302 22.0	17.5	244 44.1	42.0	249 14.8	36.2			
06	95 56.5	232 16.8	S18 16.6	317 22.9	N17 17.1	259 46.1	S 5 42.2	264 17.0	S 2 36.3	Rasalhague	96 29.0	N12 34.6
07	110 59.0	247 16.5	17.5	332 23.8	16.7	274 48.0	42.4	279 19.2	36.4	Regulus	208 09.5	N12 03.6
08	126 01.4	262 16.1	18.5	347 24.7	16.3	289 50.0	42.6	294 21.4	36.5	Rigel	281 35.3	S 8 13.2
S 09	141 03.9	277 15.7	·· 19.5	2 25.7	·· 15.8	304 52.0	·· 42.8	309 23.6	·· 36.7	Rigil Kent.	140 25.4	S60 45.5
U 10	156 06.4	292 15.3	20.5	17 26.6	15.4	319 53.9	43.0	324 25.8	36.8	Sabik	102 40.4	S15 42.1
N 11	171 08.8	307 14.9	21.5	32 27.5	15.0	334 55.9	43.2	339 27.9	36.9			
D 12	186 11.3	322 14.5	S18 22.4	47 28.4	N17 14.5	349 57.9	S 5 43.4	354 30.1	S 2 37.0	Schedar	350 07.7	N56 26.2
A 13	201 13.8	337 14.1	23.4	62 29.4	14.1	4 59.8	43.6	9 32.3	37.1	Shaula	96 54.9	S37 05.5
Y 14	216 16.2	352 13.7	24.4	77 30.3	13.7	20 01.8	43.8	24 34.5	37.3	Sirius	258 55.1	S16 41.3
15	231 18.7	7 13.3	·· 25.4	92 31.2	·· 13.2	35 03.8	·· 44.0	39 36.7	·· 37.4	Spica	158 57.1	S11 03.7
16	246 21.2	22 12.9	26.3	107 32.2	12.8	50 05.8	44.2	54 38.8	37.5	Suhail	223 10.6	S43 21.2
17	261 23.6	37 12.5	27.3	122 33.1	12.4	65 07.7	44.4	69 41.0	37.6			
18	276 26.1	52 12.2	S18 28.3	137 34.0	N17 11.9	80 09.7	S 5 44.6	84 43.2	S 2 37.7	Vega	80 55.3	N38 46.3
19	291 28.6	67 11.8	29.3	152 34.9	11.5	95 11.7	44.8	99 45.4	37.9	Zuben'ubi	137 32.5	S15 57.8
20	306 31.0	82 11.4	30.2	167 35.9	11.1	110 13.6	45.1	114 47.6	38.0		S.H.A.	Mer. Pass.
21	321 33.5	97 11.0	·· 31.2	182 36.8	·· 10.6	125 15.6	·· 45.3	129 49.8	·· 38.1	Venus	137 45.7	14 30
22	336 35.9	112 10.6	32.2	197 37.7	10.2	140 17.6	45.5	144 51.9	38.2	Mars	222 12.6	8 52
23	351 38.4	127 10.2	33.1	212 38.7	09.7	155 19.5	45.7	159 54.1	38.3	Jupiter	164 04.4	12 43
Mer. Pass.	23 37.3	v −0.4	d 1.0	v 0.9	d 0.4	v 2.0	d 0.2	v 2.2	d 0.1	Saturn	168 28.9	12 25

SUN / MOON

G.M.T.	SUN G.H.A.	SUN Dec.	MOON G.H.A.	v	MOON Dec.	d	H.P.
25 00	182 02.6	S 0 43.7	216 24.3	10.6	N15 24.0	8.5	57.0
01	197 02.9	44.7	230 53.9	10.6	15 15.5	8.6	56.9
02	212 03.1	45.7	245 23.5	10.7	15 06.9	8.7	56.9
03	227 03.3	·· 46.7	259 53.2	10.8	14 58.2	8.7	56.9
04	242 03.5	47.6	274 23.0	10.8	14 49.5	8.8	56.9
05	257 03.7	48.6	288 52.8	10.9	14 40.7	8.9	56.9
06	272 03.9	S 0 49.6	303 22.7	10.9	N14 31.8	9.0	56.8
07	287 04.1	50.6	317 52.6	11.0	14 22.8	9.0	56.8
08	302 04.4	51.5	332 22.6	11.1	14 13.8	9.1	56.8
F 09	317 04.6	·· 52.5	346 52.7	11.2	14 04.7	9.1	56.8
R 10	332 04.8	53.5	1 22.9	11.2	13 55.6	9.2	56.8
I 11	347 05.0	54.5	15 53.1	11.3	13 46.4	9.3	56.7
D 12	2 05.2	S 0 55.4	30 23.4	11.3	N13 37.1	9.4	56.7
A 13	17 05.4	56.4	44 53.7	11.4	13 27.7	9.4	56.7
Y 14	32 05.6	57.4	59 24.1	11.5	13 18.3	9.4	56.7
15	47 05.9	·· 58.4	73 54.6	11.5	13 08.9	9.6	56.7
16	62 06.1	0 59.3	88 25.1	11.6	12 59.3	9.5	56.6
17	77 06.3	1 00.3	102 55.7	11.6	12 49.8	9.7	56.6
18	92 06.5	S 1 01.3	117 26.3	11.7	N12 40.1	9.7	56.6
19	107 06.7	02.3	131 57.0	11.8	12 30.4	9.7	56.6
20	122 06.9	03.2	146 27.8	11.9	12 20.7	9.8	56.5
21	137 07.1	·· 04.2	160 58.7	11.9	12 10.9	9.9	56.5
22	152 07.4	05.2	175 29.6	11.9	12 01.0	9.9	56.5
23	167 07.6	06.2	190 00.5	12.0	11 51.1	10.0	56.5
26 00	182 07.8	S 1 07.1	204 31.5	12.1	N11 41.1	10.0	56.5
01	197 08.0	08.1	219 02.6	12.1	11 31.1	10.1	56.4
02	212 08.2	09.1	233 33.7	12.2	11 21.0	10.1	56.4
03	227 08.4	·· 10.1	248 04.9	12.3	11 10.9	10.2	56.4
04	242 08.6	11.0	262 36.2	12.3	11 00.7	10.2	56.4
05	257 08.8	12.0	277 07.5	12.3	10 50.5	10.2	56.4
06	272 09.1	S 1 13.0	291 38.8	12.5	N10 40.3	10.3	56.3
07	287 09.3	14.0	306 10.3	12.4	10 30.0	10.4	56.3
S 08	302 09.5	14.9	320 41.7	12.6	10 19.6	10.4	56.3
A 09	317 09.7	·· 15.9	335 13.3	12.6	10 09.2	10.4	56.3
T 10	332 09.9	16.9	349 44.9	12.6	9 58.8	10.5	56.3
U 11	347 10.1	17.8	4 16.5	12.7	9 48.3	10.5	56.2
R 12	2 10.3	S 1 18.8	18 48.2	12.7	N 9 37.8	10.5	56.2
D 13	17 10.5	19.8	33 19.9	12.8	9 27.3	10.6	56.2
A 14	32 10.8	20.8	47 51.7	12.9	9 16.7	10.6	56.2
Y 15	47 11.0	·· 21.7	62 23.6	12.9	9 06.1	10.7	56.2
16	62 11.2	22.7	76 55.5	12.9	8 55.4	10.7	56.1
17	77 11.4	23.7	91 27.4	13.0	8 44.7	10.7	56.1
18	92 11.6	S 1 24.7	105 59.4	13.1	N 8 34.0	10.8	56.1
19	107 11.8	25.6	120 31.5	13.1	8 23.3	10.8	56.1
20	122 12.0	26.6	135 03.6	13.1	8 12.5	10.9	56.1
21	137 12.2	·· 27.6	149 35.7	13.2	8 01.6	10.8	56.0
22	152 12.5	28.6	164 07.9	13.3	7 50.8	10.9	56.0
23	167 12.7	29.5	178 40.2	13.2	7 39.9	10.9	56.0
27 00	182 12.9	S 1 30.5	193 12.4	13.4	N 7 29.0	10.9	56.0
01	197 13.1	31.5	207 44.8	13.4	7 18.1	11.0	56.0
02	212 13.3	32.5	222 17.2	13.4	7 07.1	11.0	55.9
03	227 13.5	·· 33.4	236 49.6	13.5	6 56.1	11.0	55.9
04	242 13.7	34.4	251 22.1	13.5	6 45.1	11.0	55.9
05	257 13.9	35.4	265 54.6	13.5	6 34.1	11.1	55.9
06	272 14.1	S 1 36.4	280 27.1	13.6	N 6 23.0	11.0	55.9
07	287 14.4	37.3	294 59.7	13.7	6 12.0	11.1	55.8
08	302 14.6	38.3	309 32.4	13.6	6 00.9	11.2	55.8
S 09	317 14.8	·· 39.3	324 05.0	13.8	5 49.7	11.1	55.8
U 10	332 15.0	40.3	338 37.8	13.7	5 38.6	11.2	55.8
N 11	347 15.2	41.2	353 10.5	13.8	5 27.4	11.1	55.8
D 12	2 15.4	S 1 42.2	7 43.3	13.9	N 5 16.3	11.2	55.7
A 13	17 15.6	43.2	22 16.2	13.8	5 05.1	11.2	55.7
Y 14	32 15.8	44.1	36 49.0	13.9	4 53.9	11.2	55.7
15	47 16.0	·· 45.1	51 21.9	14.0	4 42.7	11.3	55.7
16	62 16.2	46.1	65 54.9	14.0	4 31.4	11.2	55.7
17	77 16.5	47.1	80 27.9	14.0	4 20.2	11.3	55.6
18	92 16.7	S 1 48.0	95 00.9	14.0	N 4 08.9	11.2	55.6
19	107 16.9	49.0	109 33.9	14.1	3 57.7	11.3	55.6
20	122 17.1	50.0	124 07.0	14.1	3 46.4	11.3	55.6
21	137 17.3	·· 51.0	138 40.1	14.2	3 35.1	11.3	55.6
22	152 17.5	51.9	153 13.3	14.2	3 23.8	11.3	55.5
23	167 17.7	52.9	167 46.5	14.2	3 12.5	11.3	55.5
	S.D. 16.0	d 1.0	S.D. 15.5		15.3		15.2

Twilight / Sunrise / Moonrise

Lat.	Naut.	Civil	Sunrise	Moonrise 25	26	27	28
N 72	03 21	04 48	05 56	25 55	01 55	03 50	05 38
N 70	03 38	04 54	05 55	00 22	02 15	04 00	05 41
68	03 50	04 59	05 55	00 48	02 30	04 08	05 43
66	04 01	05 03	05 54	01 07	02 42	04 15	05 45
64	04 09	05 06	05 54	01 23	02 53	04 21	05 46
62	04 16	05 09	05 53	01 36	03 02	04 25	05 47
60	04 22	05 12	05 53	01 47	03 09	04 30	05 49
N 58	04 27	05 14	05 53	01 57	03 16	04 33	05 50
56	04 32	05 16	05 53	02 05	03 21	04 37	05 50
54	04 36	05 17	05 52	02 13	03 27	04 40	05 51
52	04 39	05 19	05 52	02 19	03 31	04 42	05 52
50	04 42	05 20	05 52	02 25	03 36	04 45	05 53
45	04 48	05 22	05 52	02 38	03 45	04 50	05 54
N 40	04 53	05 24	05 51	02 49	03 52	04 55	05 55
35	04 56	05 25	05 51	02 58	03 59	04 58	05 56
30	04 59	05 26	05 50	03 06	04 05	05 02	05 57
20	05 02	05 28	05 50	03 19	04 14	05 07	05 59
N 10	05 04	05 28	05 49	03 31	04 23	05 13	06 00
0	05 03	05 27	05 48	03 42	04 31	05 17	06 02
S 10	05 02	05 26	05 47	03 53	04 39	05 22	06 03
20	04 58	05 24	05 46	04 05	04 48	05 27	06 05
30	04 53	05 21	05 45	04 19	04 57	05 33	06 06
35	04 49	05 19	05 44	04 27	05 03	05 36	06 07
40	04 44	05 16	05 43	04 35	05 09	05 40	06 08
45	04 38	05 13	05 42	04 46	05 17	05 44	06 10
S 50	04 30	05 08	05 40	04 58	05 25	05 49	06 11
52	04 26	05 06	05 40	05 04	05 30	05 52	06 12
54	04 22	05 04	05 39	05 10	05 34	05 54	06 13
56	04 16	05 01	05 38	05 17	05 39	05 57	06 13
58	04 11	04 58	05 37	05 25	05 44	06 00	06 14
S 60	04 04	04 55	05 36	05 34	05 51	06 04	06 15

Sunset / Twilight / Moonset

Lat.	Sunset	Civil	Naut.	Moonset 25	26	27	28
N 72	17 45	18 52	20 17	19 02	18 44	18 30	18 16
N 70	17 46	18 46	20 02	18 41	18 32	18 25	18 17
68	17 46	18 42	19 49	18 24	18 22	18 20	18 18
66	17 47	18 38	19 39	18 10	18 14	18 16	18 18
64	17 47	18 34	19 31	17 59	18 07	18 13	18 19
62	17 48	18 32	19 25	17 49	18 01	18 10	18 19
60	17 48	18 29	19 19	17 41	17 56	18 08	18 19
N 58	17 49	18 28	19 14	17 33	17 51	18 06	18 20
56	17 49	18 26	19 09	17 27	17 47	18 04	18 20
54	17 49	18 24	19 06	17 21	17 43	18 02	18 20
52	17 49	18 23	19 02	17 16	17 39	18 01	18 20
50	17 50	18 22	19 00	17 11	17 36	17 59	18 21
45	17 50	18 20	18 54	17 00	17 29	17 56	18 21
N 40	17 51	18 18	18 49	16 52	17 24	17 53	18 21
35	17 51	18 17	18 46	16 44	17 19	17 51	18 21
30	17 52	18 15	18 43	16 37	17 14	17 49	18 22
20	17 53	18 15	18 40	16 26	17 07	17 45	18 22
N 10	17 54	18 15	18 39	16 16	17 00	17 42	18 22
0	17 55	18 15	18 39	16 06	16 54	17 39	18 23
S 10	17 56	18 17	18 41	15 56	16 47	17 36	18 23
20	17 57	18 19	18 44	15 46	16 40	17 32	18 23
30	17 58	18 22	18 50	15 34	16 32	17 29	18 24
35	17 59	18 25	18 54	15 27	16 28	17 26	18 24
40	18 00	18 27	18 59	15 19	16 22	17 24	18 24
45	18 02	18 31	19 06	15 10	16 16	17 21	18 24
S 50	18 03	18 36	19 14	14 59	16 09	17 18	18 25
52	18 04	18 38	19 18	14 54	16 05	17 16	18 25
54	18 05	18 40	19 23	14 48	16 02	17 14	18 25
56	18 06	18 43	19 28	14 41	15 57	17 12	18 25
58	18 07	18 46	19 34	14 34	15 53	17 10	18 25
S 60	18 08	18 50	19 41	14 26	15 48	17 07	18 26

SUN / MOON

Day	SUN Eqn. of Time 00h	12h	Mer. Pass.	MOON Mer. Pass. Upper	Lower	Age	Phase
	m s	m s	h m	h m	h m	d	
25	08 10	08 20	11 52	09 54	22 19	27	
26	08 31	08 41	11 51	10 42	23 05	28	●
27	08 51	09 01	11 51	11 28	23 50	29	

G.M.T.	ARIES G.H.A.	VENUS −3.7 G.H.A.	Dec.	MARS +1.7 G.H.A.	Dec.	JUPITER −1.2 G.H.A.	Dec.	SATURN +1.0 G.H.A.	Dec.	STARS Name	S.H.A.	Dec.
28 00	6 40.9	142 09.8	S18 34.1	227 39.6	N17 09.3	170 21.5	S 5 45.9	174 56.3	S 2 38.4	Acamar	315 36.4	S40 22.5
01	21 43.3	157 09.4	35.1	242 40.5	08.9	185 23.5	46.1	189 58.5	38.6	Achernar	335 44.2	S57 19.7
02	36 45.8	172 09.0	36.0	257 41.5	08.4	200 25.4	46.3	205 00.7	38.7	Acrux	173 37.2	S62 59.7
03	51 48.3	187 08.6	·· 37.0	272 42.4	·· 08.0	215 27.4	·· 46.5	220 02.9	·· 38.8	Adhara	255 31.6	S28 56.6
04	66 50.7	202 08.2	38.0	287 43.3	07.6	230 29.4	46.7	235 05.0	38.9	Aldebaran	291 17.0	N16 28.4
05	81 53.2	217 07.8	38.9	302 44.2	07.1	245 31.3	46.9	250 07.2	39.0			
06	96 55.7	232 07.4	S18 39.9	317 45.2	N17 06.7	260 33.3	S 5 47.1	265 09.4	S 2 39.2	Alioth	166 42.4	N56 03.7
07	111 58.1	247 07.0	40.9	332 46.1	06.3	275 35.3	47.3	280 11.6	39.3	Alkaid	153 18.4	N49 24.5
08	127 00.6	262 06.6	41.8	347 47.0	05.8	290 37.2	47.5	295 13.8	39.4	Al Na'ir	28 13.7	S47 03.1
M 09	142 03.1	277 06.2	·· 42.8	2 48.0	·· 05.4	305 39.2	·· 47.7	310 16.0	·· 39.5	Alnilam	276 10.9	S 1 12.7
O 10	157 05.5	292 05.8	43.8	17 48.9	05.0	320 41.2	47.9	325 18.1	39.6	Alphard	218 20.1	S 8 34.5
N 11	172 08.0	307 05.4	44.7	32 49.8	04.5	335 43.1	48.1	340 20.3	39.8			
D 12	187 10.4	322 05.0	S18 45.7	47 50.8	N17 04.1	350 45.1	S 5 48.4	355 22.5	S 2 39.9	Alphecca	126 31.8	N26 46.9
A 13	202 12.9	337 04.6	46.6	62 51.7	03.7	5 47.1	48.6	10 24.7	40.0	Alpheratz	358 08.2	N28 59.4
Y 14	217 15.4	352 04.2	47.6	77 52.6	03.2	20 49.0	48.8	25 26.9	40.1	Altair	62 31.7	N 8 49.3
15	232 17.8	7 03.8	·· 48.6	92 53.6	·· 02.8	35 51.0	·· 49.0	40 29.0	·· 40.2	Ankaa	353 39.1	S42 24.3
16	247 20.3	22 03.4	49.5	107 54.5	02.3	50 53.0	49.2	55 31.2	40.4	Antares	112 56.2	S26 23.5
17	262 22.8	37 03.0	50.5	122 55.4	01.9	65 54.9	49.4	70 33.4	40.5			
18	277 25.2	52 02.6	S18 51.4	137 56.4	N17 01.5	80 56.9	S 5 49.6	85 35.6	S 2 40.6	Arcturus	146 18.1	N19 16.9
19	292 27.7	67 02.2	52.4	152 57.3	01.0	95 58.9	49.8	100 37.8	40.7	Atria	108 20.0	S68 59.9
20	307 30.2	82 01.8	53.3	167 58.2	00.6	111 00.8	50.0	115 40.0	40.8	Avior	234 28.2	S59 26.7
21	322 32.6	97 01.4	·· 54.3	182 59.2	17 00.2	126 02.8	·· 50.2	130 42.1	·· 41.0	Bellatrix	278 57.9	N 6 20.1
22	337 35.1	112 01.0	55.2	198 00.1	16 59.7	141 04.8	50.4	145 44.3	41.1	Betelgeuse	271 27.5	N 7 24.3
23	352 37.5	127 00.6	56.2	213 01.0	59.3	156 06.7	50.6	160 46.5	41.2			
29 00	7 40.0	142 00.2	S18 57.1	228 02.0	N16 58.8	171 08.7	S 5 50.8	175 48.7	S 2 41.3	Canopus	264 06.9	S52 40.8
01	22 42.5	156 59.8	58.1	243 02.9	58.4	186 10.7	51.0	190 50.9	41.4	Capella	281 10.1	N45 58.6
02	37 44.9	171 59.4	18 59.0	258 03.9	58.0	201 12.6	51.2	205 53.1	41.5	Deneb	49 47.8	N45 13.1
03	52 47.4	186 59.0	19 00.0	273 04.8	·· 57.5	216 14.6	·· 51.4	220 55.2	·· 41.7	Denebola	182 58.7	N14 40.7
04	67 49.9	201 58.6	00.9	288 05.7	57.1	231 16.6	51.7	235 57.4	41.8	Diphda	349 19.8	S18 05.2
05	82 52.3	216 58.2	01.9	303 06.7	56.6	246 18.5	51.9	250 59.6	41.9			
06	97 54.8	231 57.8	S19 02.8	318 07.6	N16 56.2	261 20.5	S 5 52.1	266 01.8	S 2 42.0	Dubhe	194 21.9	N61 51.0
07	112 57.3	246 57.4	03.8	333 08.5	55.8	276 22.5	52.3	281 04.0	42.1	Elnath	278 43.2	N28 35.5
08	127 59.7	261 57.0	04.7	348 09.5	55.3	291 24.4	52.5	296 06.1	42.3	Eltanin	90 57.5	N51 29.8
T 09	143 02.2	276 56.6	·· 05.7	3 10.4	·· 54.9	306 26.4	·· 52.7	311 08.3	·· 42.4	Enif	34 10.7	N 9 47.6
U 10	158 04.7	291 56.2	06.6	18 11.3	54.5	321 28.4	52.9	326 10.5	42.5	Fomalhaut	15 50.3	S29 43.2
E 11	173 07.1	306 55.8	07.6	33 12.3	54.0	336 30.3	53.1	341 12.7	42.6			
S 12	188 09.6	321 55.4	S19 08.5	48 13.2	N16 53.6	351 32.3	S 5 53.3	356 14.9	S 2 42.7	Gacrux	172 28.6	S57 00.5
D 13	203 12.0	336 55.0	09.4	63 14.2	53.1	6 34.3	53.5	11 17.1	42.9	Gienah	176 17.6	S17 26.2
A 14	218 14.5	351 54.5	10.4	78 15.1	52.7	21 36.2	53.7	26 19.2	43.0	Hadar	149 23.0	S60 17.1
Y 15	233 17.0	6 54.1	·· 11.3	93 16.0	·· 52.3	36 38.2	·· 53.9	41 21.4	·· 43.1	Hamal	328 27.8	N23 22.6
16	248 19.4	21 53.7	12.3	108 17.0	51.8	51 40.2	54.1	56 23.6	43.2	Kaus Aust.	84 15.9	S34 23.7
17	263 21.9	36 53.3	13.2	123 17.9	51.4	66 42.1	54.3	71 25.8	43.3			
18	278 24.4	51 52.9	S19 14.1	138 18.9	N16 50.9	81 44.1	S 5 54.5	86 28.0	S 2 43.5	Kochab	137 19.9	N74 14.1
19	293 26.8	66 52.5	15.1	153 19.8	50.5	96 46.1	54.7	101 30.1	43.6	Markab	14 02.2	N15 06.5
20	308 29.3	81 52.1	16.0	168 20.7	50.0	111 48.0	54.9	116 32.3	43.7	Menkar	314 40.2	N 4 01.1
21	323 31.8	96 51.7	·· 17.0	183 21.7	·· 49.6	126 50.0	·· 55.2	131 34.5	·· 43.8	Menkent	148 36.6	S36 16.7
22	338 34.2	111 51.3	17.9	198 22.6	49.2	141 52.0	55.4	146 36.7	43.9	Miaplacidus	221 45.4	S69 38.2
23	353 36.7	126 50.9	18.8	213 23.6	48.7	156 53.9	55.6	161 38.9	44.0			
30 00	8 39.2	141 50.4	S19 19.8	228 24.5	N16 48.3	171 55.9	S 5 55.8	176 41.1	S 2 44.2	Mirfak	309 14.8	N49 47.6
01	23 41.6	156 50.0	20.7	243 25.4	47.8	186 57.9	56.0	191 43.2	44.3	Nunki	76 28.3	S26 19.2
02	38 44.1	171 49.6	21.6	258 26.4	47.4	201 59.8	56.2	206 45.4	44.4	Peacock	53 57.0	S56 47.9
03	53 46.5	186 49.2	·· 22.6	273 27.3	·· 47.0	217 01.8	·· 56.4	221 47.6	·· 44.5	Pollux	243 57.4	N28 04.2
04	68 49.0	201 48.8	23.5	288 28.3	46.5	232 03.8	56.6	236 49.8	44.6	Procyon	245 25.2	N 5 16.5
05	83 51.5	216 48.4	24.4	303 29.2	46.1	247 05.7	56.8	251 52.0	44.8			
06	98 53.9	231 48.0	S19 25.3	318 30.1	N16 45.6	262 07.7	S 5 57.0	266 54.1	S 2 44.9	Rasalhague	96 29.0	N12 34.6
07	113 56.4	246 47.6	26.3	333 31.1	45.2	277 09.7	57.2	281 56.3	45.0	Regulus	208 09.5	N12 03.6
08	128 58.9	261 47.1	27.2	348 32.0	44.7	292 11.6	57.4	296 58.5	45.1	Rigel	281 35.2	S 8 13.2
W 09	144 01.3	276 46.7	·· 28.1	3 33.0	·· 44.3	307 13.6	·· 57.6	312 00.7	·· 45.2	Rigil Kent.	140 25.5	S60 45.5
E 10	159 03.8	291 46.3	29.0	18 33.9	43.9	322 15.6	57.8	327 02.9	45.4	Sabik	102 40.4	S15 42.1
D 11	174 06.3	306 45.9	30.0	33 34.9	43.4	337 17.5	58.0	342 05.1	45.5			
N 12	189 08.7	321 45.5	S19 30.9	48 35.8	N16 43.0	352 19.5	S 5 58.2	357 07.2	S 2 45.6	Schedar	350 07.7	N56 26.2
E 13	204 11.2	336 45.1	31.8	63 36.8	42.5	7 21.4	58.5	12 09.4	45.7	Shaula	96 54.9	S37 05.5
S 14	219 13.6	351 44.7	32.7	78 37.7	42.1	22 23.4	58.7	27 11.6	45.8	Sirius	258 55.1	S16 41.3
D 15	234 16.1	6 44.2	·· 33.7	93 38.6	·· 41.6	37 25.4	·· 58.9	42 13.8	·· 46.0	Spica	158 57.1	S11 03.7
A 16	249 18.6	21 43.8	34.6	108 39.6	41.2	52 27.3	59.1	57 16.0	46.1	Suhail	223 10.6	S43 21.2
Y 17	264 21.0	36 43.4	35.5	123 40.5	40.8	67 29.3	59.3	72 18.1	46.2			
18	279 23.5	51 43.0	S19 36.4	138 41.5	N16 40.3	82 31.3	S 5 59.5	87 20.3	S 2 46.3	Vega	80 55.4	N38 46.3
19	294 26.0	66 42.6	37.3	153 42.4	39.9	97 33.2	59.7	102 22.5	46.4	Zuben'ubi	137 32.5	S15 57.8
20	309 28.4	81 42.1	38.3	168 43.4	39.4	112 35.2	5 59.9	117 24.7	46.6			
21	324 30.9	96 41.7	·· 39.2	183 44.3	·· 39.0	127 37.2	6 00.1	132 26.9	·· 46.7		S.H.A.	Mer. Pass.
22	339 33.4	111 41.3	40.1	198 45.3	38.5	142 39.1	00.3	147 29.1	46.8	Venus	134 20.2	14 32
23	354 35.8	126 40.9	41.0	213 46.2	38.1	157 41.1	00.5	162 31.2	46.9	Mars	220 22.0	8 47
										Jupiter	163 28.7	12 34
Mer. Pass. 23 25.5		v −0.4	d 0.9	v 0.9	d 0.4	v 2.0	d 0.2	v 2.2	d 0.1	Saturn	168 08.7	12 15

G.M.T.	SUN G.H.A.	Dec.	MOON G.H.A.	v	Dec.	d	H.P.
28 00	182 17.9	S 1 53.9	182 19.7	14.2	N 3 01.2	11.3	55.5
01	197 18.1	54.9	196 52.9	14.3	2 49.9	11.3	55.5
02	212 18.3	55.8	211 26.2	14.3	2 38.6	11.3	55.5
03	227 18.6	.. 56.8	225 59.5	14.3	2 27.3	11.4	55.4
04	242 18.8	57.8	240 32.8	14.4	2 15.9	11.3	55.4
05	257 19.0	58.8	255 06.2	14.4	2 04.6	11.3	55.4
06	272 19.2	S 1 59.7	269 39.6	14.4	N 1 53.3	11.4	55.4
07	287 19.4	2 00.7	284 13.0	14.4	1 41.9	11.3	55.4
M 08	302 19.6	01.7	298 46.4	14.5	1 30.6	11.3	55.3
O 09	317 19.8	.. 02.7	313 19.9	14.5	1 19.3	11.3	55.3
N 10	332 20.0	03.6	327 53.4	14.5	1 08.0	11.4	55.3
D 11	347 20.2	04.6	342 26.9	14.5	0 56.6	11.3	55.3
A 12	2 20.4	S 2 05.6	357 00.4	14.6	N 0 45.3	11.3	55.3
Y 13	17 20.6	06.5	11 34.0	14.5	0 34.0	11.3	55.3
14	32 20.8	07.5	26 07.5	14.6	0 22.7	11.3	55.2
15	47 21.1	.. 08.5	40 41.1	14.7	0 11.4	11.3	55.2
16	62 21.3	09.5	55 14.8	14.6	N 0 00.1	11.3	55.2
17	77 21.5	10.4	69 48.4	14.6	S 0 11.2	11.3	55.2
18	92 21.7	S 2 11.4	84 22.0	14.7	S 0 22.5	11.3	55.2
19	107 21.9	12.4	98 55.7	14.7	0 33.8	11.3	55.1
20	122 22.1	13.4	113 29.4	14.7	0 45.1	11.2	55.1
21	137 22.3	.. 14.3	128 03.1	14.7	0 56.3	11.3	55.1
22	152 22.5	15.3	142 36.8	14.8	1 07.6	11.2	55.1
23	167 22.7	16.3	157 10.6	14.7	1 18.8	11.2	55.1
29 00	182 22.9	S 2 17.2	171 44.3	14.8	S 1 30.0	11.2	55.1
01	197 23.1	18.2	186 18.1	14.8	1 41.2	11.2	55.0
02	212 23.3	19.2	200 51.9	14.8	1 52.4	11.2	55.0
03	227 23.5	.. 20.2	215 25.7	14.8	2 03.6	11.2	55.0
04	242 23.7	21.1	229 59.5	14.8	2 14.8	11.1	55.0
05	257 24.0	22.1	244 33.3	14.8	2 25.9	11.1	55.0
06	272 24.2	S 2 23.1	259 07.1	14.8	S 2 37.0	11.2	55.0
07	287 24.4	24.1	273 40.9	14.9	2 48.2	11.1	54.9
T 08	302 24.6	25.0	288 14.8	14.9	2 59.3	11.0	54.9
U 09	317 24.8	.. 26.0	302 48.7	14.8	3 10.3	11.1	54.9
E 10	332 25.0	27.0	317 22.5	14.9	3 21.4	11.0	54.9
S 11	347 25.2	28.0	331 56.4	14.9	3 32.4	11.0	54.9
D 12	2 25.4	S 2 28.9	346 30.3	14.8	S 3 43.4	11.0	54.9
A 13	17 25.6	29.9	1 04.1	14.9	3 54.4	11.0	54.8
Y 14	32 25.8	30.9	15 38.0	14.9	4 05.4	11.0	54.8
15	47 26.0	.. 31.8	30 11.9	14.9	4 16.4	10.9	54.8
16	62 26.2	32.8	44 45.8	14.9	4 27.3	10.9	54.8
17	77 26.4	33.8	59 19.7	14.9	4 38.2	10.9	54.8
18	92 26.6	S 2 34.8	73 53.6	14.9	S 4 49.1	10.8	54.8
19	107 26.8	35.7	88 27.5	14.9	4 59.9	10.8	54.8
20	122 27.0	36.7	103 01.4	15.0	5 10.7	10.8	54.7
21	137 27.2	.. 37.7	117 35.4	14.9	5 21.5	10.8	54.7
22	152 27.4	38.6	132 09.3	14.9	5 32.3	10.7	54.7
23	167 27.7	39.6	146 43.2	14.9	5 43.0	10.7	54.7
30 00	182 27.9	S 2 40.6	161 17.1	14.9	S 5 53.7	10.7	54.7
01	197 28.1	41.6	175 51.0	14.9	6 04.4	10.6	54.7
02	212 28.3	42.5	190 24.9	14.9	6 15.0	10.7	54.6
03	227 28.5	.. 43.5	204 58.8	14.9	6 25.7	10.5	54.6
04	242 28.7	44.5	219 32.7	14.9	6 36.2	10.6	54.6
05	257 28.9	45.5	234 06.6	14.9	6 46.8	10.5	54.6
06	272 29.1	S 2 46.4	248 40.5	14.9	S 6 57.3	10.5	54.6
W 07	287 29.3	47.4	263 14.4	14.9	7 07.8	10.4	54.6
E 08	302 29.5	48.4	277 48.3	14.8	7 18.2	10.5	54.6
D 09	317 29.7	.. 49.3	292 22.1	14.9	7 28.7	10.3	54.6
N 10	332 29.9	50.3	306 56.0	14.9	7 39.0	10.4	54.5
E 11	347 30.1	51.3	321 29.9	14.8	7 49.4	10.3	54.5
S 12	2 30.3	S 2 52.3	336 03.7	14.9	S 7 59.7	10.2	54.5
D 13	17 30.5	53.2	350 37.6	14.8	8 09.9	10.3	54.5
A 14	32 30.7	54.2	5 11.4	14.8	8 20.2	10.1	54.5
Y 15	47 30.9	.. 55.2	19 45.2	14.8	8 30.3	10.2	54.5
16	62 31.1	56.1	34 19.0	14.8	8 40.5	10.1	54.5
17	77 31.3	57.1	48 52.8	14.8	8 50.6	10.1	54.5
18	92 31.5	S 2 58.1	63 26.6	14.8	S 9 00.7	10.0	54.4
19	107 31.7	2 59.1	78 00.4	14.8	9 10.7	10.0	54.4
20	122 31.9	3 00.0	92 34.2	14.7	9 20.7	9.9	54.4
21	137 32.1	.. 01.0	107 07.9	14.8	9 30.6	9.9	54.4
22	152 32.3	02.0	121 41.7	14.7	9 40.5	9.8	54.4
23	167 32.5	02.9	136 15.4	14.7	9 50.3	9.8	54.4
	S.D. 16.0	d 1.0	S.D. 15.1		14.9		14.9

Lat.	Twilight Naut.	Civil	Sunrise	Moonrise 28	29	30	1
N 72	03 38	05 02	06 09	05 38	07 23	09 08	10 57
N 70	03 52	05 06	06 07	05 41	07 19	08 56	10 35
68	04 02	05 10	06 05	05 43	07 15	08 47	10 19
66	04 11	05 13	06 04	05 45	07 12	08 39	10 05
64	04 19	05 15	06 02	05 46	07 10	08 32	09 54
62	04 25	05 17	06 01	05 47	07 08	08 27	09 45
60	04 30	05 19	06 00	05 49	07 06	08 22	09 37
N 58	04 34	05 20	05 59	05 50	07 04	08 18	09 30
56	04 38	05 22	05 59	05 50	07 03	08 14	09 24
54	04 41	05 23	05 58	05 51	07 01	08 11	09 19
52	04 44	05 24	05 57	05 52	07 00	08 08	09 14
50	04 47	05 24	05 57	05 53	06 59	08 05	09 09
45	04 52	05 26	05 55	05 54	06 57	07 59	09 00
N 40	04 56	05 27	05 54	05 55	06 55	07 54	08 52
35	04 58	05 28	05 53	05 56	06 53	07 49	08 45
30	05 00	05 28	05 52	05 57	06 52	07 46	08 39
20	05 03	05 28	05 50	05 59	06 49	07 39	08 29
N 10	05 03	05 28	05 49	06 00	06 47	07 34	08 20
0	05 02	05 26	05 47	06 02	06 45	07 28	08 11
S 10	05 00	05 24	05 45	06 03	06 43	07 23	08 03
20	04 56	05 21	05 43	06 05	06 41	07 17	07 54
30	04 49	05 17	05 41	06 06	06 39	07 11	07 44
35	04 45	05 14	05 40	06 07	06 37	07 08	07 39
40	04 39	05 11	05 38	06 08	06 36	07 04	07 32
45	04 32	05 07	05 36	06 10	06 34	06 59	07 25
S 50	04 23	05 01	05 34	06 11	06 32	06 53	07 16
52	04 18	04 59	05 33	06 12	06 31	06 51	07 12
54	04 13	04 56	05 32	06 13	06 30	06 48	07 07
56	04 08	04 53	05 30	06 13	06 29	06 45	07 02
58	04 01	04 49	05 29	06 14	06 28	06 41	06 56
S 60	03 54	04 45	05 27	06 15	06 26	06 38	06 50

Lat.	Sunset	Twilight Civil	Naut.	Moonset 28	29	30	1
N 72	17 29	18 36	19 59	18 16	18 03	17 48	17 30
N 70	17 32	18 32	19 46	18 17	18 10	18 02	17 53
68	17 34	18 29	19 35	18 18	18 15	18 13	18 10
66	17 35	18 26	19 27	18 18	18 20	18 22	18 25
64	17 37	18 24	19 20	18 19	18 24	18 30	18 37
62	17 38	18 22	19 14	18 19	18 27	18 36	18 47
60	17 39	18 20	19 09	18 19	18 30	18 42	18 55
N 58	17 40	18 19	19 05	18 20	18 33	18 47	19 03
56	17 41	18 18	19 01	18 20	18 35	18 52	19 10
54	17 42	18 17	18 58	18 20	18 38	18 56	19 16
52	17 42	18 16	18 55	18 20	18 40	19 00	19 21
50	17 43	18 15	18 53	18 20	18 41	19 03	19 26
45	17 45	18 14	18 48	18 21	18 45	19 10	19 37
N 40	17 46	18 13	18 44	18 21	18 49	19 17	19 46
35	17 47	18 12	18 42	18 21	18 51	19 22	19 54
30	17 48	18 12	18 40	18 22	18 54	19 27	20 01
20	17 50	18 12	18 38	18 22	18 58	19 35	20 13
N 10	17 52	18 13	18 37	18 22	19 02	19 42	20 23
0	17 54	18 14	18 38	18 23	19 06	19 49	20 33
S 10	17 56	18 16	18 41	18 23	19 10	19 56	20 42
20	17 58	18 20	18 45	18 23	19 13	20 03	20 53
30	18 00	18 24	18 52	18 24	19 16	20 11	21 05
35	18 02	18 27	18 57	18 24	19 20	20 16	21 12
40	18 03	18 30	19 02	18 24	19 23	20 22	21 20
45	18 05	18 35	19 10	18 24	19 27	20 28	21 29
S 50	18 08	18 40	19 19	18 25	19 31	20 36	21 40
52	18 09	18 43	19 24	18 25	19 33	20 39	21 45
54	18 10	18 46	19 29	18 25	19 35	20 43	21 51
56	18 12	18 49	19 35	18 25	19 37	20 48	21 57
58	18 13	18 53	19 41	18 26	19 40	20 53	22 05
S 60	18 15	18 57	19 49	18 26	19 42	20 58	22 13

Day	SUN Eqn. of Time 00h	12h	Mer. Pass.	MOON Mer. Pass. Upper	Lower	Age	Phase
28	09 11	09 21	11 51	12 12	24 34	00	
29	09 31	09 41	11 50	12 56	00 34	01	●
30	09 51	10 01	11 50	13 39	01 17	02	

1981 OCTOBER 1, 2, 3 (THURS., FRI., SAT.)

G.M.T.	ARIES G.H.A.	VENUS −3.7 G.H.A.	Dec.	MARS +1.7 G.H.A.	Dec.	JUPITER −1.2 G.H.A.	Dec.	SATURN +1.0 G.H.A.	Dec.	STARS Name	S.H.A.	Dec.
d h												
1 00	9 38.3	141 40.5	S19 41.9	228 47.1	N16 37.6	172 43.1	S 6 00.7	177 33.4	S 2 47.0	Acamar	315 36.4	S40 22.5
01	24 40.8	156 40.0	42.8	243 48.1	37.2	187 45.0	00.9	192 35.6	47.1	Achernar	335 44.2	S57 19.7
02	39 43.2	171 39.6	43.8	258 49.0	36.8	202 47.0	01.1	207 37.8	47.3	Acrux	173 37.2	S62 59.7
03	54 45.7	186 39.2	·· 44.7	273 50.0	·· 36.3	217 49.0	·· 01.3	222 40.0	·· 47.4	Adhara	255 31.6	S28 56.6
04	69 48.1	201 38.8	45.6	288 50.9	35.9	232 50.9	01.5	237 42.1	47.5	Aldebaran	291 17.0	N16 28.4
05	84 50.6	216 38.4	46.5	303 51.9	35.4	247 52.9	01.8	252 44.3	47.6			
06	99 53.1	231 37.9	S19 47.4	318 52.8	N16 35.0	262 54.8	S 6 02.0	267 46.5	S 2 47.7	Alioth	166 42.4	N56 03.7
07	114 55.5	246 37.5	48.3	333 53.8	34.5	277 56.8	02.2	282 48.7	47.9	Alkaid	153 18.4	N49 24.5
T 08	129 58.0	261 37.1	49.2	348 54.7	34.1	292 58.8	02.4	297 50.9	48.0	Al Na'ir	28 13.7	S47 03.1
H 09	145 00.5	276 36.7	·· 50.1	3 55.7	·· 33.6	308 00.7	·· 02.6	312 53.0	·· 48.1	Alnilam	276 10.9	S 1 12.7
U 10	160 02.9	291 36.3	51.0	18 56.6	33.2	323 02.7	02.8	327 55.2	48.2	Alphard	218 20.1	S 8 34.5
R 11	175 05.4	306 35.8	51.9	33 57.6	32.7	338 04.7	03.0	342 57.4	48.3			
S 12	190 07.9	321 35.4	S19 52.8	48 58.5	N16 32.3	353 06.6	S 6 03.2	357 59.6	S 2 48.5	Alphecca	126 31.8	N26 46.9
D 13	205 10.3	336 35.0	53.8	63 59.5	31.9	8 08.6	03.4	13 01.8	48.6	Alpheratz	358 08.2	N28 59.4
A 14	220 12.8	351 34.6	54.7	79 00.4	31.4	23 10.6	03.6	28 04.0	48.7	Altair	62 31.8	N 8 49.3
Y 15	235 15.3	6 34.1	·· 55.6	94 01.4	·· 31.0	38 12.5	·· 03.8	43 06.1	·· 48.8	Ankaa	353 39.1	S42 24.3
16	250 17.7	21 33.7	56.5	109 02.3	30.5	53 14.5	04.0	58 08.3	48.9	Antares	112 56.2	S26 23.4
17	265 20.2	36 33.3	57.4	124 03.3	30.1	68 16.5	04.2	73 10.5	49.1			
18	280 22.6	51 32.9	S19 58.3	139 04.2	N16 29.6	83 18.4	S 6 04.4	88 12.7	S 2 49.2	Arcturus	146 18.1	N19 16.9
19	295 25.1	66 32.4	19 59.2	154 05.2	29.2	98 20.4	04.6	103 14.9	49.3	Atria	108 20.1	S68 59.9
20	310 27.6	81 32.0	20 00.1	169 06.1	28.7	113 22.3	04.8	118 17.0	49.4	Avior	234 28.2	S59 26.7
21	325 30.0	96 31.6	·· 01.0	184 07.1	·· 28.3	128 24.3	·· 05.1	133 19.2	·· 49.5	Bellatrix	278 57.9	N 6 20.1
22	340 32.5	111 31.1	01.9	199 08.0	27.8	143 26.3	05.3	148 21.4	49.6	Betelgeuse	271 27.5	N 7 24.3
23	355 35.0	126 30.7	02.8	214 09.0	27.4	158 28.2	05.5	163 23.6	49.8			
2 00	10 37.4	141 30.3	S20 03.7	229 09.9	N16 26.9	173 30.2	S 6 05.7	178 25.8	S 2 49.9	Canopus	264 06.9	S52 40.8
01	25 39.9	156 29.9	04.5	244 10.9	26.5	188 32.2	05.9	193 28.0	50.0	Capella	281 10.1	N45 58.7
02	40 42.4	171 29.4	05.4	259 11.8	26.0	203 34.1	06.1	208 30.1	50.1	Deneb	49 47.8	N45 13.1
03	55 44.8	186 29.0	·· 06.3	274 12.8	·· 25.6	218 36.1	·· 06.3	223 32.3	·· 50.2	Denebola	182 58.6	N14 40.7
04	70 47.3	201 28.6	07.2	289 13.7	25.1	233 38.1	06.5	238 34.5	50.4	Diphda	349 19.8	S18 05.2
05	85 49.7	216 28.1	08.1	304 14.7	24.7	248 40.0	06.7	253 36.7	50.5			
06	100 52.2	231 27.7	S20 09.0	319 15.6	N16 24.2	263 42.0	S 6 06.9	268 38.9	S 2 50.6	Dubhe	194 21.8	N61 51.0
07	115 54.7	246 27.3	09.9	334 16.6	23.8	278 43.9	07.1	283 41.0	50.7	Elnath	278 43.1	N28 35.5
08	130 57.1	261 26.9	10.8	349 17.5	23.3	293 45.9	07.3	298 43.2	50.8	Eltanin	90 57.5	N51 29.8
F 09	145 59.6	276 26.4	·· 11.7	4 18.5	·· 22.9	308 47.9	·· 07.5	313 45.4	·· 51.0	Enif	34 10.7	N 9 47.6
R 10	161 02.1	291 26.0	12.6	19 19.4	22.4	323 49.8	07.7	328 47.6	51.1	Fomalhaut	15 50.3	S29 43.2
I 11	176 04.5	306 25.6	13.5	34 20.4	22.0	338 51.8	07.9	343 49.8	51.2			
D 12	191 07.0	321 25.1	S20 14.3	49 21.4	N16 21.5	353 53.8	S 6 08.1	358 51.9	S 2 51.3	Gacrux	172 28.6	S57 00.5
A 13	206 09.5	336 24.7	15.2	64 22.3	21.1	8 55.7	08.4	13 54.1	51.4	Gienah	176 17.6	S17 26.2
Y 14	221 11.9	351 24.3	16.1	79 23.3	20.6	23 57.7	08.6	28 56.3	51.5	Hadar	149 23.0	S60 17.0
15	236 14.4	6 23.8	·· 17.0	94 24.2	·· 20.2	38 59.7	·· 08.8	43 58.5	·· 51.7	Hamal	328 27.8	N23 22.6
16	251 16.9	21 23.4	17.9	109 25.2	19.7	54 01.6	09.0	59 00.7	51.8	Kaus Aust.	84 15.9	S34 23.7
17	266 19.3	36 23.0	18.8	124 26.1	19.3	69 03.6	09.2	74 02.8	51.9			
18	281 21.8	51 22.5	S20 19.6	139 27.1	N16 18.8	84 05.5	S 6 09.4	89 05.0	S 2 52.0	Kochab	137 20.0	N74 14.1
19	296 24.2	66 22.1	20.5	154 28.0	18.4	99 07.5	09.6	104 07.2	52.1	Markab	14 02.2	N15 06.5
20	311 26.7	81 21.7	21.4	169 29.0	17.9	114 09.5	09.8	119 09.4	52.3	Menkar	314 40.1	N 4 01.1
21	326 29.2	96 21.2	·· 22.3	184 29.9	·· 17.5	129 11.4	·· 10.0	134 11.6	·· 52.4	Menkent	148 36.6	S36 16.7
22	341 31.6	111 20.8	23.2	199 30.9	17.0	144 13.4	10.2	149 13.8	52.5	Miaplacidus	221 45.4	S69 38.2
23	356 34.1	126 20.4	24.0	214 31.9	16.6	159 15.4	10.4	164 15.9	52.6			
3 00	11 36.6	141 19.9	S20 24.9	229 32.8	N16 16.1	174 17.3	S 6 10.6	179 18.1	S 2 52.8	Mirfak	309 14.7	N49 47.7
01	26 39.0	156 19.5	25.8	244 33.8	15.7	189 19.3	10.8	194 20.3	52.9	Nunki	76 28.3	S26 19.2
02	41 41.5	171 19.0	26.7	259 34.7	15.2	204 21.2	11.0	209 22.5	53.0	Peacock	53 57.0	S56 47.9
03	56 44.0	186 18.6	·· 27.5	274 35.7	·· 14.8	219 23.2	·· 11.2	224 24.7	·· 53.1	Pollux	243 57.4	N28 04.2
04	71 46.4	201 18.2	28.4	289 36.6	14.3	234 25.2	11.5	239 26.8	53.2	Procyon	245 25.1	N 5 16.5
05	86 48.9	216 17.7	29.3	304 37.6	13.9	249 27.1	11.7	254 29.0	53.4			
06	101 51.4	231 17.3	S20 30.1	319 38.6	N16 13.4	264 29.1	S 6 11.9	269 31.2	S 2 53.5	Rasalhague	96 29.0	N12 34.6
07	116 53.8	246 16.9	31.0	334 39.5	13.0	279 31.1	12.1	284 33.4	53.6	Regulus	208 09.5	N12 03.6
S 08	131 56.3	261 16.4	31.9	349 40.5	12.5	294 33.0	12.3	299 35.6	53.7	Rigel	281 35.2	S 8 13.2
A 09	146 58.7	276 16.0	·· 32.8	4 41.4	·· 12.1	309 35.0	·· 12.5	314 37.7	·· 53.8	Rigil Kent.	140 25.5	S60 45.5
T 10	162 01.2	291 15.5	33.6	19 42.4	11.6	324 37.0	12.7	329 39.9	53.9	Sabik	102 40.5	S15 42.1
U 11	177 03.7	306 15.1	34.5	34 43.4	11.2	339 38.9	12.9	344 42.1	54.1			
R 12	192 06.1	321 14.7	S20 35.4	49 44.3	N16 10.7	354 40.9	S 6 13.1	359 44.3	S 2 54.2	Schedar	350 07.7	N56 26.2
D 13	207 08.6	336 14.2	36.2	64 45.3	10.3	9 42.8	13.3	14 46.5	54.3	Shaula	96 54.9	S37 05.5
A 14	222 11.1	351 13.8	37.1	79 46.2	09.8	24 44.8	13.5	29 48.7	54.4	Sirius	258 55.1	S16 41.3
Y 15	237 13.5	6 13.3	·· 38.0	94 47.2	·· 09.4	39 46.8	·· 13.7	44 50.8	·· 54.5	Spica	158 57.1	S11 03.7
16	252 16.0	21 12.9	38.8	109 48.2	08.9	54 48.7	13.9	59 53.0	54.7	Suhail	223 10.5	S43 21.2
17	267 18.5	36 12.4	39.7	124 49.1	08.5	69 50.7	14.1	74 55.2	54.8			
18	282 20.9	51 12.0	S20 40.5	139 50.1	N16 08.0	84 52.7	S 6 14.3	89 57.4	S 2 54.9	Vega	80 55.4	N38 46.3
19	297 23.4	66 11.6	41.4	154 51.0	07.6	99 54.6	14.5	104 59.6	55.0	Zuben'ubi	137 32.5	S15 57.8
20	312 25.8	81 11.1	42.3	169 52.0	07.1	114 56.6	14.7	120 01.7	55.1		S.H.A.	Mer. Pass.
21	327 28.3	96 10.7	·· 43.1	184 53.0	·· 06.6	129 58.5	·· 15.0	135 03.9	·· 55.3		° '	h m
22	342 30.8	111 10.2	44.0	199 53.9	06.2	145 00.5	15.2	150 06.1	55.4	Venus	130 52.9	14 34
23	357 33.2	126 09.8	44.8	214 54.9	05.7	160 02.5	15.4	165 08.3	55.5	Mars	218 32.5	8 43
Mer. Pass. 23 13.7	v −0.4 d 0.9	v 1.0	d 0.4	v 2.0	d 0.2	v 2.2	d 0.1			Jupiter	162 52.8	12 24
										Saturn	167 48.3	12 05

G.M.T.	SUN G.H.A.	Dec.	MOON G.H.A.	v	Dec.	d	H.P.
d h	° ′	° ′	° ′	′	° ′	′	′
1 00	182 32.7	S 3 03.9	150 49.1	14.7	S10 00.1	9.8	54.4
01	197 32.9	04.9	165 22.8	14.7	10 09.9	9.7	54.4
02	212 33.1	05.8	179 56.5	14.7	10 19.6	9.7	54.4
03	227 33.3	·· 06.8	194 30.2	14.6	10 29.3	9.6	54.3
04	242 33.5	07.8	209 03.8	14.7	10 38.9	9.6	54.3
05	257 33.7	08.8	223 37.5	14.6	10 48.5	9.5	54.3
06	272 33.9	S 3 09.7	238 11.1	14.6	S10 58.0	9.5	54.3
07	287 34.1	10.7	252 44.7	14.5	11 07.5	9.4	54.3
T 08	302 34.3	11.7	267 18.2	14.6	11 16.9	9.4	54.3
H 09	317 34.5	·· 12.6	281 51.8	14.5	11 26.3	9.3	54.3
U 10	332 34.7	13.6	296 25.3	14.6	11 35.6	9.3	54.3
R 11	347 34.9	14.6	310 58.9	14.5	11 44.9	9.2	54.3
S 12	2 35.1	S 3 15.6	325 32.4	14.4	S11 54.1	9.2	54.3
D 13	17 35.3	16.5	340 05.8	14.5	12 03.3	9.1	54.3
A 14	32 35.5	17.5	354 39.3	14.4	12 12.4	9.0	54.2
Y 15	47 35.7	·· 18.5	9 12.7	14.4	12 21.4	9.0	54.2
16	62 35.9	19.4	23 46.1	14.4	12 30.4	9.0	54.2
17	77 36.1	20.4	38 19.5	14.4	12 39.4	8.9	54.2
18	92 36.3	S 3 21.4	52 52.9	14.3	S12 48.3	8.8	54.2
19	107 36.5	22.3	67 26.2	14.4	12 57.1	8.8	54.2
20	122 36.7	23.3	81 59.6	14.3	13 05.9	8.7	54.2
21	137 36.9	·· 24.3	96 32.9	14.2	13 14.6	8.7	54.2
22	152 37.1	25.2	111 06.1	14.3	13 23.3	8.6	54.2
23	167 37.3	26.2	125 39.4	14.2	13 31.9	8.5	54.2
2 00	182 37.5	S 3 27.2	140 12.6	14.2	S13 40.4	8.5	54.2
01	197 37.7	28.2	154 45.8	14.1	13 48.9	8.5	54.2
02	212 37.9	29.1	169 18.9	14.2	13 57.4	8.3	54.2
03	227 38.1	·· 30.1	183 52.1	14.1	14 05.7	8.3	54.2
04	242 38.3	31.1	198 25.2	14.1	14 14.0	8.3	54.1
05	257 38.5	32.0	212 58.3	14.0	14 22.3	8.2	54.1
06	272 38.7	S 3 33.0	227 31.3	14.1	S14 30.5	8.1	54.1
07	287 38.9	34.0	242 04.4	14.0	14 38.6	8.1	54.1
08	302 39.1	34.9	256 37.4	13.9	14 46.7	8.0	54.1
F 09	317 39.3	·· 35.9	271 10.3	14.0	14 54.7	7.9	54.1
R 10	332 39.5	36.9	285 43.3	13.9	15 02.6	7.8	54.1
I 11	347 39.7	37.8	300 16.2	13.9	15 10.4	7.8	54.1
D 12	2 39.9	S 3 38.8	314 49.1	13.8	S15 18.2	7.8	54.1
A 13	17 40.1	39.8	329 21.9	13.8	15 26.0	7.6	54.1
Y 14	32 40.3	40.7	343 54.7	13.8	15 33.6	7.6	54.1
15	47 40.5	·· 41.7	358 27.5	13.8	15 41.2	7.6	54.1
16	62 40.7	42.7	13 00.3	13.7	15 48.8	7.4	54.1
17	77 40.9	43.7	27 33.0	13.7	15 56.2	7.4	54.1
18	92 41.1	S 3 44.6	42 05.7	13.7	S16 03.6	7.3	54.1
19	107 41.3	45.6	56 38.4	13.6	16 10.9	7.3	54.1
20	122 41.5	46.6	71 11.0	13.6	16 18.2	7.2	54.1
21	137 41.7	·· 47.5	85 43.6	13.6	16 25.4	7.1	54.1
22	152 41.9	48.5	100 16.2	13.5	16 32.5	7.0	54.1
23	167 42.0	49.5	114 48.7	13.5	16 39.5	7.0	54.1
3 00	182 42.2	S 3 50.4	129 21.2	13.4	S16 46.5	6.9	54.1
01	197 42.4	51.4	143 53.6	13.5	16 53.4	6.8	54.1
02	212 42.6	52.3	158 26.1	13.4	17 00.2	6.8	54.1
03	227 42.8	·· 53.3	172 58.5	13.3	17 07.0	6.6	54.1
04	242 43.0	54.3	187 30.8	13.4	17 13.6	6.6	54.1
05	257 43.2	55.3	202 03.2	13.3	17 20.2	6.6	54.1
06	272 43.4	S 3 56.2	216 35.5	13.2	S17 26.8	6.4	54.1
07	287 43.6	57.2	231 07.7	13.2	17 33.2	6.4	54.1
S 08	302 43.8	58.2	245 39.9	13.2	17 39.6	6.3	54.1
A 09	317 44.0	3 59.1	260 12.1	13.2	17 45.9	6.2	54.1
T 10	332 44.2	4 00.1	274 44.3	13.1	17 52.1	6.1	54.1
U 11	347 44.4	01.1	289 16.4	13.1	17 58.2	6.1	54.1
R 12	2 44.6	S 4 02.0	303 48.5	13.0	S18 04.3	6.0	54.1
D 13	17 44.8	03.0	318 20.5	13.1	18 10.3	5.9	54.1
A 14	32 45.0	04.0	332 52.6	12.9	18 16.2	5.8	54.1
Y 15	47 45.2	·· 04.9	347 24.5	13.0	18 22.0	5.8	54.1
16	62 45.4	05.9	1 56.5	12.9	18 27.8	5.6	54.1
17	77 45.6	06.9	16 28.4	12.8	18 33.4	5.6	54.1
18	92 45.8	S 4 07.8	31 00.2	12.9	S18 39.0	5.5	54.1
19	107 46.0	08.8	45 32.1	12.8	18 44.5	5.4	54.1
20	122 46.1	09.8	60 03.9	12.7	18 49.9	5.3	54.1
21	137 46.3	·· 10.7	74 35.6	12.8	18 55.2	5.3	54.1
22	152 46.5	11.7	89 07.4	12.7	19 00.5	5.2	54.2
23	167 46.7	12.7	103 39.1	12.6	19 05.7	5.0	54.2
S.D. 16.0	d 1.0		S.D. 14.8		14.7		14.7

Lat.	Twilight Naut.	Civil	Sunrise	Moonrise 1	2	3	4
°	h m	h m	h m	h m	h m	h m	h m
N 72	03 53	05 15	06 23	10 57	12 57	■	■
N 70	04 05	05 18	06 19	10 35	12 19	14 13	■
68	04 14	05 20	06 16	10 19	11 52	13 27	15 03
66	04 22	05 22	06 13	10 05	11 32	12 58	14 20
64	04 28	05 24	06 11	09 54	11 16	12 36	13 51
62	04 33	05 25	06 09	09 45	11 03	12 18	13 29
60	04 37	05 26	06 07	09 37	10 51	12 04	13 11
N 58	04 41	05 27	06 06	09 30	10 42	11 51	12 57
56	04 44	05 28	06 05	09 24	10 33	11 40	12 44
54	04 47	05 28	06 03	09 19	10 26	11 31	12 33
52	04 49	05 29	06 02	09 14	10 19	11 23	12 23
50	04 51	05 29	06 01	09 09	10 13	11 15	12 15
45	04 56	05 30	05 59	09 00	10 00	10 59	11 56
N 40	04 59	05 30	05 57	08 52	09 49	10 46	11 41
35	05 01	05 30	05 55	08 45	09 40	10 35	11 29
30	05 02	05 30	05 54	08 39	09 32	10 25	11 18
20	05 03	05 29	05 51	08 29	09 19	10 09	10 59
N 10	05 03	05 28	05 49	08 20	09 07	09 54	10 43
0	05 01	05 25	05 46	08 11	08 56	09 41	10 28
S 10	04 58	05 22	05 44	08 03	08 44	09 27	10 12
20	04 53	05 19	05 41	07 54	08 33	09 13	09 56
30	04 45	05 13	05 37	07 44	08 19	08 57	09 38
35	04 40	05 10	05 35	07 39	08 12	08 47	09 27
40	04 34	05 06	05 33	07 32	08 03	08 37	09 15
45	04 26	05 01	05 31	07 25	07 53	08 24	09 00
S 50	04 16	04 55	05 27	07 16	07 40	08 09	08 43
52	04 11	04 52	05 26	07 12	07 35	08 02	08 34
54	04 05	04 48	05 24	07 07	07 29	07 54	08 25
56	03 59	04 45	05 22	07 02	07 22	07 45	08 15
58	03 52	04 40	05 20	06 56	07 14	07 35	08 03
S 60	03 43	04 36	05 18	06 50	07 05	07 24	07 49

Lat.	Sunset	Twilight Civil	Naut.	Moonset 1	2	3	4
°	h m	h m	h m	h m	h m	h m	h m
N 72	17 14	18 21	19 42	17 30	17 01	■	■
N 70	17 18	18 18	19 31	17 53	17 41	17 22	■
68	17 21	18 16	19 22	18 10	18 08	18 08	18 09
66	17 24	18 15	19 15	18 25	18 29	18 38	18 53
64	17 26	18 13	19 09	18 37	18 46	19 00	19 22
62	17 28	18 12	19 04	18 47	19 04	19 18	19 45
60	17 30	18 11	19 00	18 55	19 12	19 34	20 02
N 58	17 32	18 11	18 56	19 03	19 22	19 46	20 17
56	17 33	18 10	18 53	19 10	19 31	19 57	20 30
54	17 34	18 09	18 51	19 16	19 39	20 07	20 42
52	17 36	18 09	18 48	19 21	19 46	20 16	20 51
50	17 37	18 09	18 46	19 26	19 53	20 24	21 00
45	17 39	18 08	18 42	19 37	20 07	20 40	21 19
N 40	17 41	18 08	18 39	19 46	20 18	20 54	21 34
35	17 43	18 08	18 37	19 54	20 28	21 06	21 47
30	17 44	18 08	18 36	20 01	20 37	21 16	21 59
20	17 47	18 09	18 35	20 13	20 52	21 34	22 18
N 10	17 50	18 11	18 35	20 23	21 05	21 49	22 35
0	17 53	18 13	18 37	20 33	21 17	22 03	22 51
S 10	17 55	18 16	18 41	20 42	21 30	22 18	23 07
20	17 58	18 20	18 46	20 53	21 44	22 33	23 23
30	18 02	18 26	18 54	21 05	21 58	22 51	23 43
35	18 04	18 29	18 59	21 12	22 07	23 01	23 54
40	18 06	18 33	19 06	21 20	22 17	23 13	24 07
45	18 09	18 39	19 14	21 29	22 29	23 27	24 23
S 50	18 12	18 45	19 24	21 40	22 43	23 44	24 42
52	18 14	18 48	19 29	21 45	22 50	23 52	24 51
54	18 16	18 52	19 35	21 51	22 57	24 01	00 01
56	18 18	18 55	19 41	21 57	23 06	24 11	00 11
58	18 20	19 00	19 49	22 05	23 15	24 23	00 23
S 60	18 22	19 05	19 58	22 13	23 26	24 36	00 36

Day	SUN Eqn. of Time 00ʰ	12ʰ	Mer. Pass.	MOON Mer. Pass. Upper	Lower	Age	Phase
	m s	m s	h m	h m	h m	d	
1	10 11	10 20	11 50	14 22	02 00	03	
2	10 30	10 39	11 49	15 06	02 44	04	
3	10 49	10 58	11 49	15 52	03 29	05	◑

G.M.T.	ARIES G.H.A.	VENUS −3.7 G.H.A. Dec.	MARS +1.7 G.H.A. Dec.	JUPITER −1.2 G.H.A. Dec.	SATURN +1.0 G.H.A. Dec.	STARS Name	S.H.A.	Dec.
4 00	12 35.7	141 09.3 S20 45.7	229 55.9 N16 05.3	175 04.4 S 6 15.6	180 10.5 S 2 55.6	Acamar	315 36.3	S40 22.6
01	27 38.2	156 08.9 46.5	244 56.8 04.8	190 06.4 15.8	195 12.6 55.7	Achernar	335 44.1	S57 19.7
02	42 40.6	171 08.5 47.4	259 57.8 04.4	205 08.4 16.0	210 14.8 55.8	Acrux	173 37.2	S62 59.7
03	57 43.1	186 08.0 ·· 48.3	274 58.7 ·· 03.9	220 10.3 ·· 16.2	225 17.0 ·· 56.0	Adhara	255 31.6	S28 56.6
04	72 45.6	201 07.6 49.1	289 59.7 03.5	235 12.3 16.4	240 19.2 56.1	Aldebaran	291 17.0	N16 28.4
05	87 48.0	216 07.1 50.0	305 00.7 03.0	250 14.2 16.6	255 21.4 56.2			
06	102 50.5	231 06.7 S20 50.8	320 01.6 N16 02.6	265 16.2 S 6 16.8	270 23.5 S 2 56.3	Alioth	166 42.4	N56 03.7
07	117 53.0	246 06.2 51.7	335 02.6 02.1	280 18.2 17.0	285 25.7 56.4	Alkaid	153 18.4	N49 24.5
08	132 55.4	261 05.8 52.5	350 03.6 01.6	295 20.1 17.2	300 27.9 56.6	Al Na'ir	28 13.7	S47 03.1
S 09	147 57.9	276 05.3 ·· 53.4	5 04.5 ·· 01.2	310 22.1 ·· 17.4	315 30.1 ·· 56.7	Alnilam	276 10.8	S 1 12.7
U 10	163 00.3	291 04.9 54.2	20 05.5 00.7	325 24.1 17.6	330 32.3 56.8	Alphard	218 20.1	S 8 34.5
N 11	178 02.8	306 04.4 55.1	35 06.5 16 00.3	340 26.0 17.8	345 34.4 56.9			
D 12	193 05.3	321 04.0 S20 55.9	50 07.4 N15 59.8	355 28.0 S 6 18.0	0 36.6 S 2 57.0	Alphecca	126 31.8	N26 46.9
A 13	208 07.7	336 03.5 56.7	65 08.4 59.4	10 29.9 18.2	15 38.8 57.1	Alpheratz	358 08.2	N28 59.4
Y 14	223 10.2	351 03.1 57.6	80 09.3 58.9	25 31.9 18.5	30 41.0 57.3	Altair	62 31.8	N 8 49.3
15	238 12.7	6 02.6 ·· 58.4	95 10.3 ·· 58.5	40 33.9 ·· 18.7	45 43.2 ·· 57.4	Ankaa	353 39.1	S42 24.3
16	253 15.1	21 02.2 20 59.3	110 11.3 58.0	55 35.8 18.9	60 45.4 57.5	Antares	112 56.2	S26 23.4
17	268 17.6	36 01.7 21 00.1	125 12.2 57.6	70 37.8 19.1	75 47.5 57.6			
18	283 20.1	51 01.3 S21 01.0	140 13.2 N15 57.1	85 39.7 S 6 19.3	90 49.7 S 2 57.7	Arcturus	146 18.1	N19 16.9
19	298 22.5	66 00.8 01.8	155 14.2 56.6	100 41.7 19.5	105 51.9 57.9	Atria	108 20.1	S68 59.9
20	313 25.0	81 00.4 02.6	170 15.1 56.2	115 43.7 19.7	120 54.1 58.0	Avior	234 28.2	S59 26.7
21	328 27.5	95 59.9 ·· 03.5	185 16.1 ·· 55.7	130 45.6 ·· 19.9	135 56.3 ·· 58.1	Bellatrix	278 57.9	N 6 20.1
22	343 29.9	110 59.5 04.3	200 17.1 55.3	145 47.6 20.1	150 58.4 58.2	Betelgeuse	271 27.4	N 7 24.3
23	358 32.4	125 59.0 05.1	215 18.0 54.8	160 49.6 20.3	166 00.6 58.3			
5 00	13 34.8	140 58.6 S21 06.0	230 19.0 N15 54.4	175 51.5 S 6 20.5	181 02.8 S 2 58.5	Canopus	264 06.8	S52 40.8
01	28 37.3	155 58.1 06.8	245 20.0 53.9	190 53.5 20.7	196 05.0 58.6	Capella	281 10.1	N45 58.7
02	43 39.8	170 57.7 07.7	260 20.9 53.4	205 55.4 20.9	211 07.2 58.7	Deneb	49 47.8	N45 13.2
03	58 42.2	185 57.2 ·· 08.5	275 21.9 ·· 53.0	220 57.4 ·· 21.1	226 09.3 ·· 58.8	Denebola	182 58.6	N14 40.7
04	73 44.7	200 56.8 09.3	290 22.9 52.5	235 59.4 21.3	241 11.5 58.9	Diphda	349 19.8	S18 05.2
05	88 47.2	215 56.3 10.2	305 23.9 52.1	251 01.3 21.5	256 13.7 59.0			
06	103 49.6	230 55.9 S21 11.0	320 24.8 N15 51.6	266 03.3 S 6 21.7	271 15.9 S 2 59.2	Dubhe	194 21.8	N61 51.0
07	118 52.1	245 55.4 11.8	335 25.8 51.2	281 05.3 22.0	286 18.1 59.3	Elnath	278 43.1	N28 35.5
08	133 54.6	260 54.9 12.6	350 26.8 50.7	296 07.2 22.2	301 20.2 59.4	Eltanin	90 57.5	N51 29.8
M 09	148 57.0	275 54.5 ·· 13.5	5 27.7 ·· 50.2	311 09.2 ·· 22.4	316 22.4 ·· 59.5	Enif	34 10.7	N 9 47.6
O 10	163 59.5	290 54.0 14.3	20 28.7 49.8	326 11.1 22.6	331 24.6 59.6	Fomalhaut	15 50.3	S29 43.2
N 11	179 01.9	305 53.6 15.1	35 29.7 49.3	341 13.1 22.8	346 26.8 59.8			
D 12	194 04.4	320 53.1 S21 16.0	50 30.6 N15 48.9	356 15.1 S 6 23.0	1 29.0 S 2 59.9	Gacrux	172 28.6	S57 00.5
A 13	209 06.9	335 52.7 16.8	65 31.6 48.4	11 17.0 23.2	16 31.1 3 00.0	Gienah	176 17.6	S17 26.2
Y 14	224 09.3	350 52.2 17.6	80 32.6 47.9	26 19.0 23.4	31 33.3 00.1	Hadar	149 23.0	S60 17.0
15	239 11.8	5 51.7 ·· 18.4	95 33.6 ·· 47.5	41 20.9 ·· 23.6	46 35.5 ·· 00.2	Hamal	328 27.8	N23 22.6
16	254 14.3	20 51.3 19.2	110 34.5 47.0	56 22.9 23.8	61 37.7 00.3	Kaus Aust.	84 16.0	S34 23.7
17	269 16.7	35 50.8 20.1	125 35.5 46.6	71 24.9 24.0	76 39.9 00.5			
18	284 19.2	50 50.4 S21 20.9	140 36.5 N15 46.1	86 26.8 S 6 24.2	91 42.0 S 3 00.6	Kochab	137 20.0	N74 14.1
19	299 21.7	65 49.9 21.7	155 37.4 45.7	101 28.8 24.4	106 44.2 00.7	Markab	14 02.2	N15 06.5
20	314 24.1	80 49.5 22.5	170 38.4 45.2	116 30.7 24.6	121 46.4 00.8	Menkar	314 40.1	N 4 01.1
21	329 26.6	95 49.0 ·· 23.3	185 39.4 ·· 44.7	131 32.7 ·· 24.8	136 48.6 ·· 00.9	Menkent	148 36.6	S36 16.7
22	344 29.1	110 48.5 24.2	200 40.4 44.3	146 34.7 25.0	151 50.8 01.1	Miaplacidus	221 45.3	S69 38.2
23	359 31.5	125 48.1 25.0	215 41.3 43.8	161 36.6 25.2	166 53.0 01.2			
6 00	14 34.0	140 47.6 S21 25.8	230 42.3 N15 43.4	176 38.6 S 6 25.5	181 55.1 S 3 01.3	Mirfak	309 14.7	N49 47.7
01	29 36.4	155 47.2 26.6	245 43.3 42.9	191 40.6 25.7	196 57.3 01.4	Nunki	76 28.3	S26 19.2
02	44 38.9	170 46.7 27.4	260 44.2 42.4	206 42.5 25.9	211 59.5 01.5	Peacock	53 57.0	S56 47.9
03	59 41.4	185 46.2 ·· 28.2	275 45.2 ·· 42.0	221 44.5 ·· 26.1	227 01.7 ·· 01.6	Pollux	243 57.4	N28 04.2
04	74 43.8	200 45.8 29.0	290 46.2 41.5	236 46.4 26.3	242 03.9 01.8	Procyon	245 25.1	N 5 16.4
05	89 46.3	215 45.3 29.9	305 47.2 41.1	251 48.4 26.5	257 06.0 01.9			
06	104 48.8	230 44.9 S21 30.7	320 48.1 N15 40.6	266 50.4 S 6 26.7	272 08.2 S 3 02.0	Rasalhague	96 29.0	N12 34.6
07	119 51.2	245 44.4 31.5	335 49.1 40.1	281 52.3 26.9	287 10.4 02.1	Regulus	208 09.5	N12 03.6
08	134 53.7	260 43.9 32.3	350 50.1 39.7	296 54.3 27.1	302 12.6 02.2	Rigel	281 35.2	S 8 13.2
T 09	149 56.2	275 43.5 ·· 33.1	5 51.1 ·· 39.2	311 56.2 ·· 27.3	317 14.8 ·· 02.4	Rigil Kent.	140 25.5	S60 45.5
U 10	164 58.6	290 43.0 33.9	20 52.0 38.8	326 58.2 27.5	332 16.9 02.5	Sabik	102 40.5	S15 42.1
E 11	180 01.1	305 42.5 34.7	35 53.0 38.3	342 00.2 27.7	347 19.1 02.6			
S 12	195 03.6	320 42.1 S21 35.5	50 54.0 N15 37.8	357 02.1 S 6 27.9	2 21.3 S 3 02.7	Schedar	350 07.7	N56 26.2
D 13	210 06.0	335 41.6 36.3	65 55.0 37.3	12 04.1 28.1	17 23.5 02.8	Shaula	96 54.9	S37 05.5
A 14	225 08.5	350 41.1 37.1	80 55.9 36.9	27 06.0 28.3	32 25.7 03.0	Sirius	258 55.1	S16 41.3
Y 15	240 10.9	5 40.7 ·· 37.9	95 56.9 ·· 36.5	42 08.0 ·· 28.5	47 27.8 ·· 03.1	Spica	158 57.1	S11 03.7
16	255 13.4	20 40.2 38.7	110 57.9 36.0	57 10.0 28.7	62 30.0 03.2	Suhail	223 10.5	S43 21.2
17	270 15.9	35 39.8 39.5	125 58.9 35.5	72 11.9 28.9	77 32.2 03.3			
18	285 18.3	50 39.3 S21 40.3	140 59.9 N15 35.1	87 13.9 S 6 29.2	92 34.4 S 3 03.4	Vega	80 55.4	N38 46.3
19	300 20.8	65 38.8 41.1	156 00.8 34.6	102 15.8 29.4	107 36.6 03.5	Zuben'ubi	137 32.6	S15 57.8
20	315 23.3	80 38.4 41.9	171 01.8 34.1	117 17.8 29.6	122 38.7 03.7			
21	330 25.7	95 37.9 ·· 42.7	186 02.8 ·· 33.7	132 19.8 ·· 29.8	137 40.9 ·· 03.8		S.H.A.	Mer. Pass.
22	345 28.2	110 37.4 43.5	201 03.8 33.2	147 21.7 30.0	152 43.1 03.9	Venus	127 23.7	14 37
23	0 30.7	125 37.0 44.3	216 04.7 32.8	162 23.7 30.2	167 45.3 04.0	Mars	216 44.2	8 38
Mer. Pass.	23 01.9	v −0.5 d 0.8	v 1.0 d 0.5	v 2.0 d 0.2	v 2.2 d 0.1	Jupiter	162 16.7	12 15
						Saturn	167 28.0	11 54

SUN and MOON

G.M.T.	SUN G.H.A.	Dec.	MOON G.H.A.	v	Dec.	d	H.P.
d h	° ′	° ′	° ′	′	° ′	′	′
4 00	182 46.9	S 4 13.6	118 10.7	12.6	S19 10.7	5.0	54.2
01	197 47.1	14.6	132 42.3	12.6	19 15.7	5.0	54.2
02	212 47.3	15.6	147 13.9	12.5	19 20.7	4.8	54.2
03	227 47.5 ··	16.5	161 45.4	12.6	19 25.5	4.7	54.2
04	242 47.7	17.5	176 17.0	12.4	19 30.2	4.7	54.2
05	257 47.9	18.5	190 48.4	12.5	19 34.9	4.5	54.2
06	272 48.1	S 4 19.4	205 19.9	12.4	S19 39.4	4.5	54.2
07	287 48.3	20.4	219 51.3	12.3	19 43.9	4.4	54.2
S 08	302 48.5	21.4	234 22.6	12.4	19 48.3	4.3	54.2
U 09	317 48.6 ··	22.3	248 54.0	12.2	19 52.6	4.2	54.2
N 10	332 48.8	23.3	263 25.2	12.3	19 56.8	4.1	54.2
D 11	347 49.0	24.2	277 56.5	12.2	20 00.9	4.1	54.2
A 12	2 49.2	S 4 25.2	292 27.7	12.2	S20 05.0	3.9	54.3
Y 13	17 49.4	26.2	306 58.9	12.1	20 08.9	3.9	54.3
14	32 49.6	27.1	321 30.0	12.2	20 12.8	3.7	54.3
15	47 49.8 ··	28.1	336 01.2	12.0	20 16.5	3.7	54.3
16	62 50.0	29.1	350 32.2	12.1	20 20.2	3.6	54.3
17	77 50.2	30.0	5 03.3	12.0	20 23.8	3.5	54.3
18	92 50.4	S 4 31.0	19 34.3	12.0	S20 27.3	3.4	54.3
19	107 50.5	32.0	34 05.3	11.9	20 30.7	3.3	54.3
20	122 50.7	32.9	48 36.2	11.9	20 34.0	3.2	54.3
21	137 50.9 ··	33.9	63 07.1	11.9	20 37.2	3.1	54.4
22	152 51.1	34.9	77 38.0	11.8	20 40.3	3.0	54.4
23	167 51.3	35.8	92 08.8	11.8	20 43.3	2.9	54.4
5 00	182 51.5	S 4 36.8	106 39.6	11.8	S20 46.2	2.8	54.4
01	197 51.7	37.7	121 10.4	11.7	20 49.0	2.8	54.4
02	212 51.9	38.7	135 41.1	11.7	20 51.8	2.6	54.4
03	227 52.1 ··	39.7	150 11.8	11.7	20 54.4	2.5	54.4
04	242 52.2	40.6	164 42.5	11.6	20 56.9	2.5	54.4
05	257 52.4	41.6	179 13.1	11.6	20 59.4	2.3	54.5
06	272 52.6	S 4 42.6	193 43.7	11.6	S21 01.7	2.1	54.5
07	287 52.8	43.5	208 14.3	11.5	21 04.0	2.1	54.5
08	302 53.0	44.5	222 44.8	11.5	21 06.1	2.1	54.5
M 09	317 53.2 ··	45.4	237 15.3	11.5	21 08.2	1.9	54.5
O 10	332 53.4	46.4	251 45.8	11.4	21 10.1	1.8	54.5
N 11	347 53.5	47.4	266 16.2	11.4	21 11.9	1.8	54.6
D 12	2 53.7	S 4 48.3	280 46.6	11.4	S21 13.7	1.6	54.6
A 13	17 53.9	49.3	295 17.0	11.3	21 15.3	1.6	54.6
Y 14	32 54.1	50.3	309 47.3	11.3	21 16.9	1.4	54.6
15	47 54.3 ··	51.2	324 17.6	11.3	21 18.3	1.4	54.6
16	62 54.5	52.2	338 47.9	11.3	21 19.7	1.2	54.6
17	77 54.7	53.1	353 18.2	11.2	21 20.9	1.2	54.7
18	92 54.9	S 4 54.1	7 48.4	11.2	S21 22.1	1.0	54.7
19	107 55.0	55.1	22 18.6	11.2	21 23.1	1.0	54.7
20	122 55.2	56.0	36 48.8	11.1	21 24.1	0.8	54.7
21	137 55.4 ··	57.0	51 18.9	11.1	21 24.9	0.7	54.7
22	152 55.6	57.9	65 49.0	11.1	21 25.6	0.7	54.8
23	167 55.8	58.9	80 19.1	11.1	21 26.3	0.5	54.8
6 00	182 56.0	S 4 59.9	94 49.2	11.0	S21 26.8	0.4	54.8
01	197 56.1	5 00.8	109 19.2	11.0	21 27.2	0.4	54.8
02	212 56.3	01.8	123 49.2	11.0	21 27.6	0.2	54.8
03	227 56.5 ··	02.7	138 19.2	10.9	21 27.8	0.1	54.9
04	242 56.7	03.7	152 49.1	11.0	21 27.9	0.0	54.9
05	257 56.9	04.7	167 19.1	10.9	21 27.9	0.1	54.9
06	272 57.1	S 5 05.6	181 49.0	10.8	S21 27.8	0.2	54.9
07	287 57.2	06.6	196 18.8	10.9	21 27.6	0.3	54.9
T 08	302 57.4	07.5	210 48.7	10.8	21 27.3	0.4	55.0
U 09	317 57.6 ··	08.5	225 18.5	10.8	21 26.9	0.5	55.0
E 10	332 57.8	09.5	239 48.3	10.8	21 26.4	0.7	55.0
S 11	347 58.0	10.4	254 18.1	10.8	21 25.7	0.7	55.0
D 12	2 58.2	S 5 11.4	268 47.9	10.7	S21 25.0	0.8	55.1
A 13	17 58.3	12.3	283 17.6	10.7	21 24.2	1.0	55.1
Y 14	32 58.5	13.3	297 47.3	10.7	21 23.2	1.0	55.1
15	47 58.7 ··	14.3	312 17.0	10.7	21 22.2	1.2	55.1
16	62 58.9	15.2	326 46.7	10.6	21 21.0	1.3	55.1
17	77 59.1	16.2	341 16.3	10.7	21 19.7	1.3	55.2
18	92 59.3	S 5 17.1	355 46.0	10.6	S21 18.4	1.5	55.2
19	107 59.4	18.1	10 15.6	10.6	21 16.9	1.6	55.2
20	122 59.6	19.1	24 45.2	10.6	21 15.3	1.7	55.2
21	137 59.8 ··	20.0	39 14.8	10.5	21 13.6	1.8	55.3
22	153 00.0	21.0	53 44.3	10.5	21 11.8	1.9	55.3
23	168 00.2	21.9	68 13.8	10.6	21 09.9	2.0	55.3
	S.D. 16.0	d 1.0	S.D. 14.8		14.9		15.0

Twilight, Sunrise and Moonrise

Lat.	Naut.	Civil	Sunrise	4	5	6	7
°	h m	h m	h m	h m	h m	h m	h m
N 72	04 08	05 29	06 36	■	■	■	■
N 70	04 18	05 30	06 31	■	■		
68	04 26	05 31	06 27	15 03	16 31	17 20	17 32
66	04 32	05 32	06 23	14 20	15 31	16 21	16 50
64	04 37	05 32	06 20	13 51	14 57	15 47	16 22
62	04 41	05 33	06 17	13 29	14 32	15 22	16 00
60	04 45	05 33	06 15	13 11	14 12	15 03	15 42
N 58	04 48	05 33	06 12	12 57	13 56	14 47	15 28
56	04 50	05 33	06 11	12 44	13 42	14 33	15 15
54	04 53	05 34	06 09	12 33	13 30	14 21	15 04
52	04 54	05 34	06 07	12 23	13 20	14 10	14 54
50	04 56	05 34	06 06	12 15	13 10	14 01	14 45
45	04 59	05 33	06 03	11 56	12 51	13 41	14 27
N 40	05 02	05 33	06 00	11 41	12 35	13 25	14 12
35	05 03	05 32	05 58	11 29	12 21	13 11	13 59
30	05 04	05 32	05 56	11 18	12 10	13 00	13 48
20	05 04	05 30	05 52	10 59	11 49	12 39	13 28
N 10	05 03	05 27	05 48	10 43	11 32	12 22	13 12
0	05 00	05 24	05 45	10 28	11 16	12 05	12 56
S 10	04 56	05 21	05 42	10 12	11 00	11 49	12 40
20	04 50	05 16	05 38	09 56	10 42	11 31	12 23
30	04 42	05 10	05 34	09 38	10 22	11 11	12 04
35	04 36	05 06	05 31	09 27	10 11	11 00	11 53
40	04 29	05 01	05 28	09 15	09 58	10 46	11 40
45	04 20	04 55	05 25	09 00	09 42	10 30	11 25
S 50	04 09	04 48	05 21	08 43	09 23	10 10	11 06
52	04 03	04 45	05 19	08 34	09 14	10 01	10 57
54	03 57	04 41	05 17	08 25	09 03	09 50	10 47
56	03 50	04 36	05 14	08 15	08 52	09 39	10 36
58	03 42	04 32	05 12	08 03	08 38	09 25	10 23
S 60	03 33	04 26	05 09	07 49	08 23	09 09	10 08

Sunset, Twilight and Moonset

Lat.	Sunset	Civil	Naut.	4	5	6	7
°	h m	h m	h m	h m	h m	h m	h m
N 72	16 59	18 06	19 25	■	■	■	■
N 70	17 04	18 05	19 16	■	■	■	■
68	17 09	18 04	19 09	18 09	18 22	19 17	20 51
66	17 12	18 03	19 03	18 53	19 23	20 16	21 32
64	17 16	18 03	18 58	19 22	19 57	20 50	22 00
62	17 19	18 03	18 54	19 45	20 22	21 14	22 22
60	17 21	18 02	18 51	20 02	20 42	21 34	22 39
N 58	17 23	18 02	18 48	20 17	20 58	21 50	22 53
56	17 25	18 02	18 45	20 30	21 12	22 04	23 06
54	17 27	18 02	18 43	20 42	21 24	22 16	23 17
52	17 29	18 02	18 41	20 51	21 35	22 26	23 26
50	17 30	18 02	18 40	21 00	21 44	22 35	23 35
45	17 33	18 03	18 37	21 19	22 04	22 55	23 53
N 40	17 36	18 03	18 35	21 34	22 20	23 11	24 08
35	17 39	18 04	18 33	21 47	22 33	23 24	24 20
30	17 41	18 05	18 32	21 59	22 45	23 36	24 31
20	17 45	18 07	18 32	22 18	23 06	23 56	24 49
N 10	17 48	18 09	18 34	22 35	23 23	24 13	00 13
0	17 52	18 12	18 37	22 51	23 40	24 30	00 30
S 10	17 55	18 16	18 41	23 07	23 56	24 46	00 46
20	17 59	18 21	18 47	23 23	24 14	00 14	01 03
30	18 04	18 28	18 56	23 43	24 34	00 34	01 23
35	18 06	18 32	19 02	23 54	24 46	00 46	01 34
40	18 09	18 37	19 09	24 07	00 07	00 59	01 48
45	18 13	18 43	19 18	24 23	00 23	01 15	02 03
S 50	18 17	18 50	19 30	24 42	00 42	01 35	02 22
52	18 19	18 53	19 35	24 51	00 51	01 44	02 31
54	18 21	18 57	19 41	00 01	01 01	01 55	02 43
56	18 24	19 02	19 49	00 11	01 12	02 07	02 53
58	18 26	19 07	19 57	00 23	01 25	02 20	03 06
S 60	18 29	19 12	20 06	00 36	01 41	02 36	03 21

SUN and MOON

Day	SUN Eqn. of Time 00ʰ	12ʰ	Mer. Pass.	MOON Mer. Pass. Upper	Lower	Age	Phase
	m s	m s	h m	h m	h m	d	
4	11 07	11 16	11 49	16 39	04 15	06	
5	11 26	11 35	11 48	17 28	05 03	07	
6	11 43	11 52	11 48	18 18	05 52	08	◑

G.M.T.	ARIES G.H.A.	VENUS −3.7 G.H.A.	VENUS Dec.	MARS +1.7 G.H.A.	MARS Dec.	JUPITER −1.2 G.H.A.	JUPITER Dec.	SATURN +1.0 G.H.A.	SATURN Dec.	STARS Name	S.H.A.	Dec.
7 00	15 33.1	140 36.5	S21 45.1	231 05.7	N15 32.3	177 25.7	S 6 30.4	182 47.5	S 3 04.1	Acamar	315 36.3	S40 22.6
01	30 35.6	155 36.0	45.9	246 06.7	31.8	192 27.6	30.6	197 49.6	04.3	Achernar	335 44.1	S57 19.8
02	45 38.0	170 35.5	46.7	261 07.7	31.4	207 29.6	30.8	212 51.8	04.4	Acrux	173 37.1	S62 59.7
03	60 40.5	185 35.1	·· 47.5	276 08.7	·· 30.9	222 31.5	·· 31.0	227 54.0	·· 04.5	Adhara	255 31.5	S28 56.6
04	75 43.0	200 34.6	48.3	291 09.6	30.4	237 33.5	31.2	242 56.2	04.6	Aldebaran	291 17.0	N16 28.4
05	90 45.4	215 34.1	49.0	306 10.6	30.0	252 35.5	31.4	257 58.4	04.7			
W 06	105 47.9	230 33.7	S21 49.8	321 11.6	N15 29.5	267 37.4	S 6 31.6	273 00.5	S 3 04.8	Alioth	166 42.4	N56 03.7
E 07	120 50.4	245 33.2	50.6	336 12.6	29.1	282 39.4	31.8	288 02.7	05.0	Alkaid	153 18.4	N49 24.5
D 08	135 52.8	260 32.7	51.4	351 13.6	28.6	297 41.3	32.0	303 04.9	05.1	Al Na'ir	28 13.7	S47 03.1
N 09	150 55.3	275 32.3	·· 52.2	6 14.5	·· 28.1	312 43.3	·· 32.2	318 07.1	·· 05.2	Alnilam	276 10.8	S 1 12.7
E 10	165 57.8	290 31.8	53.0	21 15.5	27.7	327 45.3	32.4	333 09.3	05.3	Alphard	218 20.1	S 8 34.5
S 11	181 00.2	305 31.3	53.8	36 16.5	27.2	342 47.2	32.7	348 11.5	05.4			
D 12	196 02.7	320 30.9	S21 54.6	51 17.5	N15 26.7	357 49.2	S 6 32.9	3 13.6	S 3 05.6	Alphecca	126 31.8	N26 46.8
A 13	211 05.2	335 30.4	55.3	66 18.5	26.3	12 51.1	33.1	18 15.8	05.7	Alpheratz	358 08.2	N28 59.4
Y 14	226 07.6	350 29.9	56.1	81 19.4	25.8	27 53.1	33.3	33 18.0	05.8	Altair	62 31.8	N 8 49.3
15	241 10.1	5 29.4	·· 56.9	96 20.4	·· 25.3	42 55.1	·· 33.5	48 20.2	·· 05.9	Ankaa	353 39.1	S42 24.4
16	256 12.5	20 29.0	57.7	111 21.4	24.9	57 57.0	33.7	63 22.4	06.0	Antares	112 56.2	S26 23.4
17	271 15.0	35 28.5	58.5	126 22.4	24.4	72 59.0	33.9	78 24.5	06.1			
18	286 17.5	50 28.0	S21 59.2	141 23.4	N15 24.0	88 00.9	S 6 34.1	93 26.7	S 3 06.3	Arcturus	146 18.1	N19 16.9
19	301 19.9	65 27.6	22 00.0	156 24.3	23.5	103 02.9	34.3	108 28.9	06.4	Atria	108 20.1	S68 59.9
20	316 22.4	80 27.1	00.8	171 25.3	23.0	118 04.9	34.5	123 31.1	06.5	Avior	234 28.1	S59 26.7
21	331 24.9	95 26.6	·· 01.6	186 26.3	·· 22.6	133 06.8	·· 34.7	138 33.3	·· 06.6	Bellatrix	278 57.8	N 6 20.1
22	346 27.3	110 26.1	02.3	201 27.3	22.1	148 08.8	34.9	153 35.4	06.7	Betelgeuse	271 27.4	N 7 24.3
23	1 29.8	125 25.7	03.1	216 28.3	21.6	163 10.7	35.1	168 37.6	06.9			
8 00	16 32.3	140 25.2	S22 03.9	231 29.3	N15 21.2	178 12.7	S 6 35.3	183 39.8	S 3 07.0	Canopus	264 06.8	S52 40.8
01	31 34.7	155 24.7	04.7	246 30.2	20.7	193 14.7	35.5	198 42.0	07.1	Capella	281 10.0	N45 58.7
02	46 37.2	170 24.2	05.4	261 31.2	20.2	208 16.6	35.7	213 44.2	07.2	Deneb	49 47.8	N45 13.2
03	61 39.7	185 23.8	·· 06.2	276 32.2	·· 19.8	223 18.6	·· 35.9	228 46.3	·· 07.3	Denebola	182 58.6	N14 40.6
04	76 42.1	200 23.3	07.0	291 33.2	19.3	238 20.5	36.1	243 48.5	07.4	Diphda	349 19.8	S18 05.2
05	91 44.6	215 22.8	07.7	306 34.2	18.8	253 22.5	36.3	258 50.7	07.6			
06	106 47.0	230 22.3	S22 08.5	321 35.2	N15 18.4	268 24.5	S 6 36.6	273 52.9	S 3 07.7	Dubhe	194 21.8	N61 51.0
07	121 49.5	245 21.9	09.3	336 36.2	17.9	283 26.4	36.8	288 55.1	07.8	Elnath	278 43.1	N28 35.5
T 08	136 52.0	260 21.4	10.0	351 37.1	17.4	298 28.4	37.0	303 57.2	07.9	Eltanin	90 57.6	N51 29.8
H 09	151 54.4	275 20.9	·· 10.8	6 38.1	·· 17.0	313 30.3	·· 37.2	318 59.4	·· 08.0	Enif	34 10.7	N 9 47.6
U 10	166 56.9	290 20.4	11.6	21 39.1	16.5	328 32.3	37.4	334 01.6	08.1	Fomalhaut	15 50.3	S29 43.2
R 11	181 59.4	305 19.9	12.3	36 40.1	16.0	343 34.2	37.6	349 03.8	08.3			
S 12	197 01.8	320 19.5	S22 13.1	51 41.1	N15 15.6	358 36.2	S 6 37.8	4 06.0	S 3 08.4	Gacrux	172 28.5	S57 00.4
D 13	212 04.3	335 19.0	13.8	66 42.1	15.1	13 38.2	38.0	19 08.1	08.5	Gienah	176 17.6	S17 26.2
A 14	227 06.8	350 18.5	14.6	81 43.1	14.6	28 40.1	38.2	34 10.3	08.6	Hadar	149 23.0	S60 17.0
Y 15	242 09.2	5 18.0	·· 15.4	96 44.0	·· 14.2	43 42.1	·· 38.4	49 12.5	·· 08.7	Hamal	328 27.8	N23 22.6
16	257 11.7	20 17.6	16.1	111 45.0	13.7	58 44.0	38.6	64 14.7	08.9	Kaus Aust.	84 16.0	S34 23.7
17	272 14.2	35 17.1	16.9	126 46.0	13.2	73 46.0	38.8	79 16.9	09.0			
18	287 16.6	50 16.6	S22 17.6	141 47.0	N15 12.8	88 48.0	S 6 39.0	94 19.0	S 3 09.1	Kochab	137 20.0	N74 14.1
19	302 19.1	65 16.1	18.4	156 48.0	12.3	103 49.9	39.2	109 21.2	09.2	Markab	14 02.2	N15 06.5
20	317 21.5	80 15.6	19.1	171 49.0	11.8	118 51.9	39.4	124 23.4	09.3	Menkar	314 40.1	N 4 01.1
21	332 24.0	95 15.2	·· 19.9	186 50.0	·· 11.4	133 53.8	·· 39.6	139 25.6	·· 09.4	Menkent	148 36.6	S36 16.7
22	347 26.5	110 14.7	20.6	201 51.0	10.9	148 55.8	39.8	154 27.8	09.6	Miaplacidus	221 45.3	S69 38.2
23	2 28.9	125 14.2	21.4	216 52.0	10.4	163 57.8	40.0	169 29.9	09.7			
9 00	17 31.4	140 13.7	S22 22.1	231 52.9	N15 10.0	178 59.7	S 6 40.3	184 32.1	S 3 09.8	Mirfak	309 14.7	N49 47.7
01	32 33.9	155 13.2	22.9	246 53.9	09.5	194 01.7	40.5	199 34.3	09.9	Nunki	76 28.3	S26 19.2
02	47 36.3	170 12.7	23.6	261 54.9	09.0	209 03.6	40.7	214 36.5	10.0	Peacock	53 57.1	S56 47.9
03	62 38.8	185 12.3	·· 24.4	276 55.9	·· 08.6	224 05.6	·· 40.9	229 38.7	·· 10.2	Pollux	243 57.4	N28 04.2
04	77 41.3	200 11.8	25.1	291 56.9	08.1	239 07.6	41.1	244 40.9	10.3	Procyon	245 25.1	N 5 16.4
05	92 43.7	215 11.3	25.9	306 57.9	07.6	254 09.5	41.3	259 43.0	10.4			
06	107 46.2	230 10.8	S22 26.6	321 58.9	N15 07.2	269 11.5	S 6 41.5	274 45.2	S 3 10.5	Rasalhague	96 29.1	N12 34.6
07	122 48.6	245 10.3	27.4	336 59.9	06.7	284 13.4	41.7	289 47.4	10.6	Regulus	208 09.5	N12 03.6
08	137 51.1	260 09.9	28.1	352 00.9	06.2	299 15.4	41.9	304 49.6	10.7	Rigel	281 35.2	S 8 13.2
F 09	152 53.6	275 09.4	·· 28.9	7 01.9	·· 05.8	314 17.4	·· 42.1	319 51.8	·· 10.9	Rigil Kent.	140 25.5	S60 45.5
R 10	167 56.0	290 08.9	29.6	22 02.8	05.3	329 19.3	42.3	334 53.9	11.0	Sabik	102 40.5	S15 42.1
I 11	182 58.5	305 08.4	30.3	37 03.8	04.8	344 21.3	42.5	349 56.1	11.1			
D 12	198 01.0	320 07.9	S22 31.1	52 04.8	N15 04.4	359 23.2	S 6 42.7	4 58.3	S 3 11.2	Schedar	350 07.7	N56 26.2
A 13	213 03.4	335 07.4	31.8	67 05.8	03.9	14 25.2	42.9	20 00.5	11.3	Shaula	96 55.0	S37 05.5
Y 14	228 05.9	350 06.9	32.5	82 06.8	03.4	29 27.1	43.1	35 02.7	11.5	Sirius	258 55.0	S16 41.3
15	243 08.4	5 06.5	·· 33.3	97 07.8	·· 02.9	44 29.1	·· 43.3	50 04.8	·· 11.6	Spica	158 57.1	S11 03.7
16	258 10.8	20 06.0	34.0	112 08.8	02.5	59 31.1	43.5	65 07.0	11.7	Suhail	223 10.5	S43 21.2
17	273 13.3	35 05.5	34.8	127 09.8	02.0	74 33.0	43.7	80 09.2	11.8			
18	288 15.8	50 05.0	S22 35.5	142 10.8	N15 01.5	89 35.0	S 6 43.9	95 11.4	S 3 11.9	Vega	80 55.4	N38 46.3
19	303 18.2	65 04.5	36.2	157 11.8	01.1	104 36.9	44.2	110 13.6	12.0	Zuben'ubi	137 32.6	S15 57.8
20	318 20.7	80 04.0	37.0	172 12.8	00.6	119 38.9	44.4	125 15.7	12.2		S.H.A.	Mer. Pass.
21	333 23.1	95 03.5	·· 37.7	187 13.8	15 00.1	134 40.9	·· 44.6	140 17.9	·· 12.3		° ′	h m
22	348 25.6	110 03.1	38.4	202 14.8	14 59.7	149 42.8	44.8	155 20.1	12.4	Venus	123 52.9	14 39
23	3 28.1	125 02.6	39.1	217 15.7	59.2	164 44.8	45.0	170 22.3	12.5	Mars	214 57.0	8 33
	h m									Jupiter	161 40.4	12 06
Mer. Pass. 22 50.1	v −0.5	d 0.8	v 1.0	d 0.5	v 2.0	d 0.2	v 2.2	d 0.1	Saturn	167 07.5	11 44

G.M.T.	SUN G.H.A.	Dec.	MOON G.H.A.	v	Dec.	d	H.P.
d h	° ′	° ′	° ′	′	° ′	′	′
7 00	183 00.3	S 5 22.9	82 43.4	10.5	S21 07.9	2.2	55.4
01	198 00.5	23.8	97 12.9	10.5	21 05.7	2.2	55.4
02	213 00.7	24.8	111 42.4	10.4	21 03.5	2.3	55.4
03	228 00.9	·· 25.8	126 11.8	10.5	21 01.2	2.5	55.4
04	243 01.1	26.7	140 41.3	10.4	20 58.7	2.6	55.5
05	258 01.2	27.7	155 10.7	10.4	20 56.1	2.6	55.5
06	273 01.4	S 5 28.6	169 40.1	10.4	S20 53.5	2.8	55.5
W 07	288 01.6	29.6	184 09.5	10.4	20 50.7	2.9	55.5
E 08	303 01.8	30.5	198 38.9	10.4	20 47.8	3.0	55.6
D 09	318 02.0	·· 31.5	213 08.3	10.4	20 44.8	3.1	55.6
N 10	333 02.1	32.5	227 37.7	10.3	20 41.7	3.2	55.6
E 11	348 02.3	33.4	242 07.0	10.4	20 38.5	3.4	55.7
S 12	3 02.5	S 5 34.4	256 36.4	10.3	S20 35.1	3.4	55.7
D 13	18 02.7	35.3	271 05.7	10.3	20 31.7	3.5	55.7
A 14	33 02.8	36.3	285 35.0	10.3	20 28.2	3.7	55.8
Y 15	48 03.0	·· 37.2	300 04.3	10.3	20 24.5	3.8	55.8
16	63 03.2	38.2	314 33.6	10.3	20 20.7	3.8	55.8
17	78 03.4	39.1	329 02.9	10.3	20 16.9	4.0	55.8
18	93 03.6	S 5 40.1	343 32.2	10.2	S20 12.9	4.1	55.9
19	108 03.7	41.1	358 01.4	10.3	20 08.8	4.2	55.9
20	123 03.9	42.0	12 30.7	10.2	20 04.6	4.3	55.9
21	138 04.1	·· 43.0	26 59.9	10.3	20 00.3	4.4	56.0
22	153 04.3	43.9	41 29.2	10.2	19 55.9	4.5	56.0
23	168 04.4	44.9	55 58.4	10.2	19 51.4	4.7	56.0
8 00	183 04.6	S 5 45.8	70 27.6	10.2	S19 46.7	4.7	56.1
01	198 04.8	46.8	84 56.8	10.2	19 42.0	4.8	56.1
02	213 05.0	47.7	99 26.0	10.2	19 37.2	5.0	56.1
03	228 05.1	·· 48.7	113 55.2	10.2	19 32.2	5.1	56.2
04	243 05.3	49.7	128 24.4	10.2	19 27.1	5.1	56.2
05	258 05.5	50.6	142 53.6	10.2	19 22.0	5.3	56.2
06	273 05.7	S 5 51.6	157 22.8	10.1	S19 16.7	5.4	56.3
07	288 05.9	52.5	171 51.9	10.2	19 11.3	5.5	56.3
T 08	303 06.0	53.5	186 21.1	10.2	19 05.8	5.6	56.3
H 09	318 06.2	·· 54.4	200 50.3	10.1	19 00.2	5.7	56.4
U 10	333 06.4	55.4	215 19.4	10.2	18 54.5	5.8	56.4
R 11	348 06.6	56.3	229 48.6	10.1	18 48.7	5.9	56.4
S 12	3 06.7	S 5 57.3	244 17.7	10.2	S18 42.8	6.0	56.5
D 13	18 06.9	58.2	258 46.9	10.1	18 36.8	6.2	56.5
A 14	33 07.1	5 59.2	273 16.0	10.1	18 30.6	6.2	56.5
Y 15	48 07.2	6 00.1	287 45.1	10.2	18 24.4	6.4	56.6
16	63 07.4	01.1	302 14.3	10.1	18 18.0	6.4	56.6
17	78 07.6	02.0	316 43.4	10.1	18 11.6	6.5	56.6
18	93 07.8	S 6 03.0	331 12.5	10.1	S18 05.1	6.7	56.7
19	108 07.9	03.9	345 41.6	10.1	17 58.4	6.8	56.7
20	123 08.1	04.9	0 10.8	10.1	17 51.6	6.8	56.8
21	138 08.3	·· 05.9	14 39.9	10.1	17 44.8	7.0	56.8
22	153 08.5	06.8	29 09.0	10.1	17 37.8	7.1	56.8
23	168 08.6	07.8	43 38.1	10.1	17 30.7	7.1	56.9
9 00	183 08.8	S 6 08.7	58 07.2	10.2	S17 23.6	7.3	56.9
01	198 09.0	09.7	72 36.4	10.1	17 16.3	7.4	56.9
02	213 09.1	10.6	87 05.5	10.1	17 08.9	7.5	57.0
03	228 09.3	·· 11.6	101 34.6	10.1	17 01.4	7.5	57.0
04	243 09.5	12.5	116 03.7	10.1	16 53.9	7.7	57.1
05	258 09.7	13.5	130 32.8	10.1	16 46.2	7.8	57.1
06	273 09.8	S 6 14.4	145 01.9	10.1	S16 38.4	7.9	57.1
07	288 10.0	15.4	159 31.0	10.1	16 30.5	8.0	57.2
08	303 10.2	16.3	174 00.1	10.1	16 22.5	8.0	57.2
F 09	318 10.3	·· 17.3	188 29.2	10.1	16 14.5	8.2	57.2
R 10	333 10.5	18.2	202 58.3	10.1	16 06.3	8.3	57.3
I 11	348 10.7	19.2	217 27.4	10.2	15 58.0	8.4	57.3
D 12	3 10.9	S 6 20.1	231 56.6	10.1	S15 49.6	8.4	57.4
A 13	18 11.0	21.1	246 25.7	10.1	15 41.2	8.6	57.4
Y 14	33 11.2	22.0	260 54.8	10.1	15 32.6	8.7	57.4
15	48 11.4	·· 23.0	275 23.9	10.1	15 23.9	8.7	57.5
16	63 11.5	23.9	289 53.0	10.1	15 15.2	8.9	57.5
17	78 11.7	24.9	304 22.1	10.1	15 06.3	8.9	57.5
18	93 11.9	S 6 25.8	318 51.2	10.1	S14 57.4	9.1	57.6
19	108 12.0	26.8	333 20.3	10.1	14 48.3	9.1	57.6
20	123 12.2	27.7	347 49.4	10.1	14 39.2	9.2	57.7
21	138 12.4	·· 28.6	2 18.5	10.1	14 30.0	9.3	57.7
22	153 12.6	29.6	16 47.6	10.1	14 20.7	9.4	57.7
23	168 12.7	30.5	31 16.7	10.1	14 11.3	9.5	57.8
	S.D. 16.0	d 1.0	S.D. 15.2		15.4		15.6

Twilight / Moonrise

Lat.	Naut.	Civil	Sunrise	7	8	9	10
°	h m	h m	h m	h m	h m	h m	h m
N 72	04 23	05 42	06 50	■	20 02	18 28	18 02
N 70	04 31	05 42	06 43	■	18 13	17 56	17 44
68	04 37	05 42	06 37	17 32	17 33	17 32	17 30
66	04 42	05 41	06 33	16 50	17 05	17 14	17 18
64	04 46	05 41	06 28	16 22	16 44	16 58	17 09
62	04 49	05 41	06 25	16 00	16 27	16 46	17 00
60	04 52	05 40	06 22	15 42	16 12	16 35	16 53
N 58	04 54	05 40	06 19	15 28	16 00	16 25	16 46
56	04 56	05 39	06 17	15 15	15 49	16 17	16 41
54	04 58	05 39	06 14	15 04	15 40	16 10	16 35
52	05 00	05 39	06 12	14 54	15 31	16 03	16 31
50	05 01	05 38	06 10	14 45	15 24	15 57	16 26
45	05 03	05 37	06 06	14 27	15 08	15 44	16 17
N 40	05 05	05 36	06 03	14 12	14 54	15 33	16 10
35	05 05	05 35	06 00	13 59	14 43	15 24	16 03
30	05 06	05 33	05 57	13 48	14 33	15 16	15 57
20	05 05	05 31	05 53	13 28	14 16	15 02	15 47
N 10	05 03	05 27	05 48	13 12	14 01	14 50	15 38
0	04 59	05 24	05 44	12 56	13 47	14 38	15 29
S 10	04 54	05 19	05 40	12 40	13 33	14 27	15 21
20	04 47	05 13	05 36	12 23	13 18	14 14	15 12
30	04 38	05 06	05 30	12 04	13 01	14 00	15 02
35	04 31	05 02	05 27	11 53	12 51	13 52	14 56
40	04 24	04 56	05 24	11 40	12 39	13 42	14 49
45	04 14	04 50	05 19	11 25	12 25	13 31	14 41
S 50	04 02	04 41	05 14	11 06	12 09	13 18	14 31
52	03 55	04 37	05 12	10 57	12 01	13 12	14 27
54	03 49	04 33	05 09	10 47	11 52	13 05	14 22
56	03 41	04 28	05 07	10 36	11 42	12 57	14 16
58	03 32	04 23	05 04	10 23	11 31	12 48	14 10
S 60	03 22	04 17	05 00	10 08	11 18	12 38	14 03

Twilight / Moonset

Lat.	Sunset	Civil	Naut.	7	8	9	10
°	h m	h m	h m	h m	h m	h m	h m
N 72	16 43	17 51	19 09	■	20 18	23 30	25 44
N 70	16 50	17 51	19 02	■	21 57	24 01	00 01
68	16 56	17 52	18 56	20 51	22 36	24 24	00 24
66	17 01	17 52	18 51	21 32	23 03	24 41	00 41
64	17 05	17 53	18 48	22 00	23 24	24 56	00 56
62	17 09	17 53	18 44	22 22	23 41	25 07	01 07
60	17 12	17 54	18 42	22 39	23 55	25 17	01 17
N 58	17 15	17 54	18 39	22 53	24 06	00 06	01 26
56	17 17	17 55	18 37	23 06	24 17	00 17	01 34
54	17 20	17 55	18 36	23 17	24 26	00 26	01 41
52	17 22	17 56	18 35	23 26	24 34	00 34	01 47
50	17 24	17 56	18 33	23 35	24 41	00 41	01 52
45	17 28	17 57	18 31	23 53	24 56	00 56	02 04
N 40	17 31	17 59	18 30	24 08	00 08	01 09	02 14
35	17 35	18 00	18 29	24 20	00 20	01 19	02 22
30	17 37	18 01	18 29	24 31	00 31	01 29	02 29
20	17 42	18 04	18 30	24 49	00 49	01 45	02 42
N 10	17 47	18 08	18 32	00 13	01 05	01 59	02 53
0	17 51	18 12	18 36	00 30	01 20	02 12	03 03
S 10	17 55	18 16	18 41	00 46	01 35	02 24	03 13
20	18 00	18 22	18 48	01 03	01 51	02 38	03 23
30	18 05	18 30	18 58	01 23	02 09	02 54	03 35
35	18 09	18 34	19 04	01 34	02 20	03 03	03 42
40	18 12	18 40	19 12	01 48	02 32	03 13	03 50
45	18 17	18 47	19 22	02 03	02 46	03 25	03 59
S 50	18 22	18 55	19 35	02 22	03 04	03 39	04 10
52	18 24	18 59	19 41	02 31	03 12	03 46	04 15
54	18 27	19 03	19 48	02 41	03 21	03 54	04 21
56	18 30	19 08	19 56	02 53	03 31	04 02	04 27
58	18 33	19 14	20 05	03 06	03 43	04 13	04 34
S 60	18 37	19 20	20 16	03 21	03 56	04 22	04 42

SUN / MOON

Day	SUN Eqn. of Time 00h	12h	Mer. Pass.	MOON Mer. Pass. Upper	Lower	Age	Phase
	m s	m s	h m	h m	h m	d	
7	12 01	12 10	11 48	19 08	06 43	09	
8	12 18	12 27	11 48	19 59	07 34	10	◗
9	12 35	12 43	11 47	20 50	08 25	11	

G.M.T.	ARIES G.H.A.	VENUS −3.8 G.H.A.	Dec.	MARS +1.7 G.H.A.	Dec.	JUPITER −1.2 G.H.A.	Dec.	SATURN +1.0 G.H.A.	Dec.	STARS Name	S.H.A.	Dec.
10 00	18 30.5	140 02.1	S22 39.9	232 16.7	N14 58.7	179 46.7	S 6 45.2	185 24.5	S 3 12.6	Acamar	315 36.3	S40 22.6
01	33 33.0	155 01.6	40.6	247 17.7	58.2	194 48.7	45.4	200 26.6	12.7	Achernar	335 44.1	S57 19.8
02	48 35.5	170 01.1	41.3	262 18.7	57.8	209 50.7	45.6	215 28.8	12.9	Acrux	173 37.1	S62 59.7
03	63 37.9	185 00.6	·· 42.0	277 19.7	·· 57.3	224 52.6	·· 45.8	230 31.0	·· 13.0	Adhara	255 31.5	S28 56.6
04	78 40.4	200 00.1	42.8	292 20.7	56.8	239 54.6	46.0	245 33.2	13.1	Aldebaran	291 17.0	N16 28.4
05	93 42.9	214 59.6	43.5	307 21.7	56.4	254 56.5	46.2	260 35.4	13.2			
06	108 45.3	229 59.2	S22 44.2	322 22.7	N14 55.9	269 58.5	S 6 46.4	275 37.5	S 3 13.3	Alioth	166 42.4	N56 03.7
07	123 47.8	244 58.7	44.9	337 23.7	55.4	285 00.5	46.6	290 39.7	13.5	Alkaid	153 18.4	N49 24.5
S 08	138 50.3	259 58.2	45.7	352 24.7	55.0	300 02.4	46.8	305 41.9	13.6	Al Na'ir	28 13.7	S47 03.1
A 09	153 52.7	274 57.7	·· 46.4	7 25.7	·· 54.5	315 04.4	·· 47.0	320 44.1	·· 13.7	Alnilam	276 10.8	S 1 12.7
T 10	168 55.2	289 57.2	47.1	22 26.7	54.0	330 06.3	47.2	335 46.3	13.8	Alphard	218 20.0	S 8 34.5
U 11	183 57.6	304 56.7	47.8	37 27.7	53.5	345 08.3	47.4	350 48.5	13.9			
R 12	199 00.1	319 56.2	S22 48.5	52 28.7	N14 53.1	0 10.2	S 6 47.6	5 50.6	S 3 14.0	Alphecca	126 31.8	N26 46.8
D 13	214 02.6	334 55.7	49.2	67 29.7	52.6	15 12.2	47.8	20 52.8	14.2	Alpheratz	358 08.2	N28 59.4
A 14	229 05.0	349 55.2	50.0	82 30.7	52.1	30 14.2	48.0	35 55.0	14.3	Altair	62 31.8	N 8 49.3
Y 15	244 07.5	4 54.7	·· 50.7	97 31.7	·· 51.7	45 16.1	·· 48.3	50 57.2	·· 14.4	Ankaa	353 39.1	S42 24.4
16	259 10.0	19 54.3	51.4	112 32.7	51.2	60 18.1	48.5	65 59.4	14.5	Antares	112 56.2	S26 23.4
17	274 12.4	34 53.8	52.1	127 33.7	50.7	75 20.0	48.7	81 01.5	14.6			
18	289 14.9	49 53.3	S22 52.8	142 34.7	N14 50.2	90 22.0	S 6 48.9	96 03.7	S 3 14.7	Arcturus	146 18.1	N19 16.9
19	304 17.4	64 52.8	53.5	157 35.7	49.8	105 24.0	49.1	111 05.9	14.9	Atria	108 20.1	S68 59.9
20	319 19.8	79 52.3	54.2	172 36.7	49.3	120 25.9	49.3	126 08.1	15.0	Avior	234 28.1	S59 26.7
21	334 22.3	94 51.8	·· 54.9	187 37.7	·· 48.8	135 27.9	·· 49.5	141 10.3	·· 15.1	Bellatrix	278 57.8	N 6 20.1
22	349 24.7	109 51.3	55.6	202 38.7	48.4	150 29.8	49.7	156 12.4	15.2	Betelgeuse	271 27.4	N 7 24.3
23	4 27.2	124 50.8	56.3	217 39.7	47.9	165 31.8	49.9	171 14.6	15.3			
11 00	19 29.7	139 50.3	S22 57.1	232 40.7	N14 47.4	180 33.7	S 6 50.1	186 16.8	S 3 15.4	Canopus	264 06.8	S52 40.8
01	34 32.1	154 49.8	57.8	247 41.7	46.9	195 35.7	50.3	201 19.0	15.6	Capella	281 10.0	N45 58.7
02	49 34.6	169 49.3	58.5	262 42.7	46.5	210 37.7	50.5	216 21.2	15.7	Deneb	49 47.8	N45 13.2
03	64 37.1	184 48.8	·· 59.2	277 43.7	·· 46.0	225 39.6	·· 50.7	231 23.3	·· 15.8	Denebola	182 58.6	N14 40.6
04	79 39.5	199 48.3	22 59.9	292 44.7	45.5	240 41.6	50.9	246 25.5	15.9	Diphda	349 19.8	S18 05.2
05	94 42.0	214 47.8	23 00.6	307 45.7	45.0	255 43.5	51.1	261 27.7	16.0			
06	109 44.5	229 47.3	S23 01.3	322 46.7	N14 44.6	270 45.5	S 6 51.3	276 29.9	S 3 16.2	Dubhe	194 21.8	N61 51.0
07	124 46.9	244 46.9	02.0	337 47.7	44.1	285 47.5	51.5	291 32.1	16.3	Elnath	278 43.1	N28 35.5
08	139 49.4	259 46.4	02.7	352 48.7	43.6	300 49.4	51.7	306 34.2	16.4	Eltanin	90 57.6	N51 29.8
S 09	154 51.9	274 45.9	·· 03.4	7 49.7	·· 43.1	315 51.4	·· 51.9	321 36.4	·· 16.5	Enif	34 10.7	N 9 47.6
U 10	169 54.3	289 45.4	04.0	22 50.7	42.7	330 53.3	52.1	336 38.6	16.6	Fomalhaut	15 50.3	S29 43.2
N 11	184 56.8	304 44.9	04.7	37 51.7	42.2	345 55.3	52.3	351 40.8	16.7			
D 12	199 59.2	319 44.4	S23 05.4	52 52.7	N14 41.7	0 57.2	S 6 52.6	6 43.0	S 3 16.9	Gacrux	172 28.5	S57 00.4
A 13	215 01.7	334 43.9	06.1	67 53.7	41.3	15 59.2	52.8	21 45.1	17.0	Gienah	176 17.6	S17 26.2
Y 14	230 04.2	349 43.4	06.8	82 54.7	40.8	31 01.2	53.0	36 47.3	17.1	Hadar	149 23.0	S60 17.0
15	245 06.6	4 42.9	·· 07.5	97 55.7	·· 40.3	46 03.1	·· 53.2	51 49.5	·· 17.2	Hamal	328 27.8	N23 22.6
16	260 09.1	19 42.4	08.2	112 56.7	39.8	61 05.1	53.4	66 51.7	17.3	Kaus Aust.	84 16.0	S34 23.7
17	275 11.6	34 41.9	08.9	127 57.7	39.4	76 07.0	53.6	81 53.9	17.4			
18	290 14.0	49 41.4	S23 09.6	142 58.7	N14 38.9	91 09.0	S 6 53.8	96 56.1	S 3 17.6	Kochab	137 20.1	N74 14.1
19	305 16.5	64 40.9	10.3	157 59.7	38.4	106 11.0	54.0	111 58.2	17.7	Markab	14 02.2	N15 06.5
20	320 19.0	79 40.4	10.9	173 00.7	37.9	121 12.9	54.2	127 00.4	17.8	Menkar	314 40.1	N 4 01.1
21	335 21.4	94 39.9	·· 11.6	188 01.7	·· 37.5	136 14.9	·· 54.4	142 02.6	·· 17.9	Menkent	148 36.6	S36 16.7
22	350 23.9	109 39.4	12.3	203 02.7	37.0	151 16.8	54.6	157 04.8	18.0	Miaplacidus	221 45.3	S69 38.2
23	5 26.4	124 38.9	13.0	218 03.7	36.5	166 18.8	54.8	172 07.0	18.1			
12 00	20 28.8	139 38.4	S23 13.7	233 04.7	N14 36.0	181 20.7	S 6 55.0	187 09.1	S 3 18.3	Mirfak	309 14.7	N49 47.7
01	35 31.3	154 37.9	14.4	248 05.7	35.6	196 22.7	55.2	202 11.3	18.4	Nunki	76 28.3	S26 19.2
02	50 33.7	169 37.4	15.0	263 06.7	35.1	211 24.7	55.4	217 13.5	18.5	Peacock	53 57.1	S56 47.9
03	65 36.2	184 36.9	·· 15.7	278 07.7	·· 34.6	226 26.6	·· 55.6	232 15.7	·· 18.6	Pollux	243 57.3	N28 04.2
04	80 38.7	199 36.4	16.4	293 08.8	34.1	241 28.6	55.8	247 17.9	18.7	Procyon	245 25.1	N 5 16.4
05	95 41.1	214 35.9	17.1	308 09.8	33.7	256 30.5	56.0	262 20.0	18.9			
06	110 43.6	229 35.4	S23 17.8	323 10.8	N14 33.2	271 32.5	S 6 56.2	277 22.2	S 3 19.0	Rasalhague	96 29.1	N12 34.6
07	125 46.1	244 34.9	18.4	338 11.8	32.7	286 34.4	56.4	292 24.4	19.1	Regulus	208 09.5	N12 03.5
08	140 48.5	259 34.4	19.1	353 12.8	32.2	301 36.4	56.6	307 26.6	19.2	Rigel	281 35.2	S 8 13.2
M 09	155 51.0	274 33.9	·· 19.8	8 13.8	·· 31.8	316 38.4	·· 56.9	322 28.8	·· 19.3	Rigil Kent.	140 25.5	S60 45.5
O 10	170 53.5	289 33.4	20.4	23 14.8	31.3	331 40.3	57.1	337 30.9	19.4	Sabik	102 40.5	S15 42.1
N 11	185 55.9	304 32.9	21.1	38 15.8	30.8	346 42.3	57.3	352 33.1	19.6			
D 12	200 58.4	319 32.4	S23 21.8	53 16.8	N14 30.3	1 44.2	S 6 57.5	7 35.3	S 3 19.7	Schedar	350 07.7	N56 26.3
A 13	216 00.8	334 31.9	22.5	68 17.8	29.9	16 46.2	57.7	22 37.5	19.8	Shaula	96 55.0	S37 05.5
Y 14	231 03.3	349 31.4	23.1	83 18.8	29.4	31 48.1	57.9	37 39.7	19.9	Sirius	258 55.0	S16 41.3
15	246 05.8	4 30.9	·· 23.8	98 19.8	·· 28.9	46 50.1	·· 58.1	52 41.9	·· 20.0	Spica	158 57.1	S11 03.7
16	261 08.2	19 30.4	24.5	113 20.8	28.4	61 52.1	58.3	67 44.0	20.1	Suhail	223 10.5	S43 21.2
17	276 10.7	34 29.9	25.1	128 21.8	28.0	76 54.0	58.5	82 46.2	20.3			
18	291 13.2	49 29.4	S23 25.8	143 22.9	N14 27.5	91 56.0	S 6 58.7	97 48.4	S 3 20.4	Vega	80 55.4	N38 46.3
19	306 15.6	64 28.9	26.4	158 23.9	27.0	106 57.9	58.9	112 50.6	20.5	Zuben'ubi	137 32.6	S15 57.8
20	321 18.1	79 28.4	27.1	173 24.9	26.5	121 59.9	59.1	127 52.8	20.6			
21	336 20.6	94 27.9	·· 27.8	188 25.9	·· 26.0	137 01.9	·· 59.3	142 54.9	·· 20.7		S.H.A.	Mer. Pass.
22	351 23.0	109 27.4	28.4	203 26.9	25.6	152 03.8	59.5	157 57.1	20.8	Venus	120 20.6	14 41
23	6 25.5	124 26.9	29.1	218 27.9	25.1	167 05.8	59.7	172 59.3	21.0	Mars	213 11.0	8 29
Mer. Pass. 22 38.3		v −0.5	d 0.7	v 1.0	d 0.5	v 2.0	d 0.2	v 2.2	d 0.1	Jupiter	161 04.1	11 56
										Saturn	166 47.1	11 33

G.M.T.	SUN G.H.A.	SUN Dec.	MOON G.H.A.	MOON v	MOON Dec.	MOON d	MOON H.P.
	° '	° '	° '	'	° '	'	'
10 00	183 12.9	S 6 31.5	45 45.8	10.1	S14 01.8	9.6	57.8
01	198 13.1	32.4	60 14.9	10.1	13 52.2	9.7	57.8
02	213 13.2	33.4	74 44.0	10.1	13 42.5	9.8	57.9
03	228 13.4	·· 34.3	89 13.1	10.1	13 32.7	9.8	57.9
04	243 13.6	35.3	103 42.2	10.1	13 22.9	10.0	58.0
05	258 13.7	36.2	118 11.3	10.1	13 12.9	10.0	58.0
06	273 13.9	S 6 37.2	132 40.4	10.1	S13 02.9	10.1	58.0
07	288 14.1	38.1	147 09.5	10.1	12 52.8	10.2	58.1
S 08	303 14.2	39.1	161 38.6	10.1	12 42.6	10.3	58.1
A 09	318 14.4	·· 40.0	176 07.7	10.1	12 32.3	10.4	58.2
T 10	333 14.6	41.0	190 36.8	10.1	12 21.9	10.4	58.2
U 11	348 14.7	41.9	205 05.9	10.1	12 11.5	10.5	58.2
R 12	3 14.9	S 6 42.9	219 35.0	10.1	S12 01.0	10.6	58.3
D 13	18 15.1	43.8	234 04.1	10.1	11 50.4	10.7	58.3
A 14	33 15.2	44.7	248 33.2	10.1	11 39.7	10.8	58.3
Y 15	48 15.4	·· 45.7	263 02.3	10.0	11 28.9	10.8	58.4
16	63 15.6	46.6	277 31.3	10.1	11 18.1	11.0	58.4
17	78 15.7	47.6	292 00.4	10.1	11 07.1	11.0	58.5
18	93 15.9	S 6 48.5	306 29.5	10.1	S10 56.1	11.1	58.5
19	108 16.0	49.5	320 58.6	10.0	10 45.0	11.1	58.5
20	123 16.2	50.4	335 27.6	10.1	10 33.9	11.2	58.6
21	138 16.4	·· 51.4	349 56.7	10.1	10 22.7	11.3	58.6
22	153 16.5	52.3	4 25.8	10.0	10 11.4	11.4	58.6
23	168 16.7	53.3	18 54.8	10.0	10 00.0	11.4	58.7
11 00	183 16.9	S 6 54.2	33 23.8	10.1	S 9 48.6	11.6	58.7
01	198 17.0	55.1	47 52.9	10.0	9 37.0	11.5	58.8
02	213 17.2	56.1	62 21.9	10.1	9 25.5	11.7	58.8
03	228 17.4	·· 57.0	76 51.0	10.0	9 13.8	11.7	58.8
04	243 17.5	58.0	91 20.0	10.0	9 02.1	11.8	58.9
05	258 17.7	58.9	105 49.0	10.0	8 50.3	11.8	58.9
06	273 17.8	S 6 59.9	120 18.0	10.0	S 8 38.5	12.0	58.9
07	288 18.0	7 00.8	134 47.0	10.0	8 26.5	11.9	59.0
08	303 18.2	01.7	149 16.0	10.0	8 14.6	12.1	59.0
S 09	318 18.3	·· 02.7	163 45.0	9.9	8 02.5	12.1	59.0
U 10	333 18.5	03.6	178 13.9	10.0	7 50.4	12.1	59.1
N 11	348 18.6	04.6	192 42.9	10.0	7 38.3	12.2	59.1
D 12	3 18.8	S 7 05.5	207 11.9	9.9	S 7 26.1	12.3	59.1
A 13	18 19.0	06.5	221 40.8	9.9	7 13.8	12.3	59.2
Y 14	33 19.1	07.4	236 09.7	10.0	7 01.5	12.4	59.2
15	48 19.3	·· 08.3	250 38.7	9.9	6 49.1	12.5	59.3
16	63 19.5	09.3	265 07.6	9.9	6 36.6	12.5	59.3
17	78 19.6	10.2	279 36.5	9.9	6 24.1	12.5	59.3
18	93 19.8	S 7 11.2	294 05.4	9.8	S 6 11.6	12.6	59.4
19	108 19.9	12.1	308 34.2	9.9	5 59.0	12.6	59.4
20	123 20.1	13.0	323 03.1	9.8	5 46.4	12.7	59.4
21	138 20.2	·· 14.0	337 31.9	9.9	5 33.7	12.8	59.5
22	153 20.4	14.9	352 00.8	9.8	5 20.9	12.8	59.5
23	168 20.6	15.9	6 29.6	9.8	5 08.1	12.8	59.5
12 00	183 20.7	S 7 16.8	20 58.4	9.8	S 4 55.3	12.9	59.5
01	198 20.9	17.7	35 27.2	9.8	4 42.4	12.9	59.6
02	213 21.0	18.7	49 56.0	9.7	4 29.5	12.9	59.6
03	228 21.2	·· 19.6	64 24.7	9.7	4 16.6	13.0	59.6
04	243 21.4	20.6	78 53.4	9.8	4 03.6	13.0	59.7
05	258 21.5	21.5	93 22.2	9.7	3 50.6	13.1	59.7
06	273 21.7	S 7 22.4	107 50.9	9.6	S 3 37.5	13.1	59.7
07	288 21.8	23.4	122 19.5	9.7	3 24.4	13.1	59.8
08	303 22.0	24.3	136 48.2	9.6	3 11.3	13.2	59.8
M 09	318 22.1	·· 25.2	151 16.8	9.7	2 58.1	13.2	59.8
O 10	333 22.3	26.2	165 45.5	9.6	2 44.9	13.2	59.9
N 11	348 22.5	27.1	180 14.1	9.5	2 31.7	13.3	59.9
D 12	3 22.6	S 7 28.1	194 42.6	9.6	S 2 18.4	13.3	59.9
A 13	18 22.8	29.0	209 11.2	9.5	2 05.1	13.3	59.9
Y 14	33 22.9	29.9	223 39.7	9.5	1 51.8	13.3	60.0
15	48 23.1	·· 30.9	238 08.2	9.5	1 38.5	13.4	60.0
16	63 23.2	31.8	252 36.7	9.5	1 25.1	13.3	60.0
17	78 23.4	32.8	267 05.2	9.4	1 11.8	13.4	60.0
18	93 23.5	S 7 33.7	281 33.6	9.4	S 0 58.4	13.5	60.1
19	108 23.7	34.6	296 02.0	9.4	0 44.9	13.4	60.1
20	123 23.8	35.6	310 30.4	9.3	0 31.5	13.4	60.1
21	138 24.0	·· 36.5	324 58.7	9.4	0 18.1	13.5	60.1
22	153 24.2	37.4	339 27.1	9.3	S 0 04.6	13.5	60.2
23	168 24.3	38.4	353 55.4	9.2	N 0 08.9	13.4	60.2
	S.D. 16.0	d 0.9	S.D. 15.9		16.1		16.3

Lat.	Twilight Naut.	Twilight Civil	Sunrise	Moonrise 10	Moonrise 11	Moonrise 12	Moonrise 13
°	h m	h m	h m	h m	h m	h m	h m
N 72	04 37	05 55	07 04	18 02	17 44	17 28	17 13
N 70	04 43	05 54	06 55	17 44	17 35	17 27	17 18
68	04 47	05 52	06 48	17 30	17 28	17 25	17 23
66	04 51	05 51	06 42	17 18	17 22	17 24	17 27
64	04 54	05 49	06 37	17 09	17 16	17 23	17 30
62	04 57	05 48	06 33	17 00	17 12	17 22	17 33
60	04 59	05 47	06 29	16 53	17 08	17 21	17 35
N 58	05 01	05 46	06 26	16 46	17 04	17 21	17 37
56	05 02	05 45	06 23	16 41	17 01	17 20	17 39
54	05 04	05 44	06 20	16 35	16 58	17 20	17 41
52	05 05	05 44	06 17	16 31	16 56	17 19	17 43
50	05 05	05 43	06 15	16 26	16 53	17 19	17 45
45	05 07	05 41	06 10	16 17	16 48	17 18	17 48
N 40	05 08	05 39	06 06	16 10	16 44	17 17	17 51
35	05 08	05 37	06 02	16 03	16 40	17 16	17 53
30	05 07	05 35	05 59	15 57	16 37	17 16	17 55
20	05 06	05 31	05 53	15 47	16 31	17 15	17 59
N 10	05 03	05 27	05 48	15 38	16 26	17 14	18 03
0	04 58	05 23	05 43	15 29	16 21	17 13	18 06
S 10	04 53	05 17	05 38	15 21	16 16	17 12	18 09
20	04 45	05 11	05 33	15 12	16 11	17 11	18 13
30	04 34	05 02	05 27	15 02	16 05	17 10	18 17
35	04 27	04 57	05 23	14 56	16 02	17 10	18 19
40	04 18	04 51	05 19	14 49	15 58	17 09	18 22
45	04 08	04 44	05 14	14 41	15 53	17 08	18 25
S 50	03 54	04 35	05 08	14 31	15 48	17 07	18 29
52	03 48	04 30	05 05	14 27	15 46	17 07	18 30
54	03 40	04 25	05 02	14 22	15 43	17 07	18 32
56	03 32	04 20	04 59	14 16	15 40	17 06	18 34
58	03 22	04 14	04 55	14 10	15 37	17 06	18 37
S 60	03 11	04 07	04 51	14 03	15 33	17 05	18 39

Lat.	Sunset	Twilight Civil	Twilight Naut.	Moonset 10	Moonset 11	Moonset 12	Moonset 13
°	h m	h m	h m	h m	h m	h m	h m
N 72	16 27	17 36	18 54	25 44	01 44	03 51	05 58
N 70	16 36	17 38	18 48	00 01	02 00	03 57	05 56
68	16 44	17 40	18 44	00 24	02 13	04 02	05 54
66	16 50	17 41	18 40	00 41	02 23	04 07	05 52
64	16 55	17 43	18 37	00 56	02 32	04 10	05 51
62	16 59	17 44	18 35	01 07	02 39	04 13	05 50
60	17 03	17 45	18 33	01 17	02 45	04 16	05 49
N 58	17 07	17 46	18 31	01 26	02 51	04 18	05 48
56	17 10	17 47	18 30	01 34	02 55	04 20	05 47
54	17 13	17 48	18 29	01 41	03 00	04 22	05 47
52	17 15	17 49	18 28	01 47	03 04	04 24	05 46
50	17 17	17 50	18 27	01 52	03 07	04 25	05 46
45	17 23	17 52	18 26	02 04	03 15	04 29	05 44
N 40	17 27	17 54	18 25	02 14	03 21	04 31	05 43
35	17 31	17 56	18 25	02 22	03 27	04 34	05 42
30	17 34	17 58	18 26	02 29	03 32	04 36	05 42
20	17 40	18 02	18 27	02 42	03 40	04 39	05 40
N 10	17 45	18 06	18 31	02 53	03 47	04 43	05 39
0	17 50	18 11	18 35	03 03	03 54	04 45	05 38
S 10	17 55	18 16	18 41	03 13	04 01	04 48	05 36
20	18 01	18 23	18 49	03 23	04 08	04 51	05 35
30	18 07	18 32	19 00	03 35	04 15	04 55	05 34
35	18 11	18 37	19 07	03 42	04 20	04 56	05 33
40	18 15	18 43	19 16	03 50	04 25	04 59	05 32
45	18 20	18 51	19 27	03 59	04 31	05 01	05 31
S 50	18 27	19 00	19 41	04 10	04 38	05 04	05 29
52	18 29	19 04	19 47	04 15	04 41	05 05	05 29
54	18 33	19 09	19 55	04 21	04 45	05 07	05 28
56	18 36	19 15	20 04	04 27	04 49	05 08	05 27
58	18 40	19 21	20 14	04 34	04 53	05 10	05 26
S 60	18 44	19 28	20 25	04 42	04 58	05 12	05 26

Day	SUN Eqn. of Time 00h	SUN Eqn. of Time 12h	SUN Mer. Pass.	MOON Mer. Pass. Upper	MOON Mer. Pass. Lower	Age	Phase
	m s	m s	h m	h m	h m	d	
10	12 51	12 59	11 47	21 42	09 16	12	
11	13 07	13 15	11 47	22 33	10 07	13	◯
12	13 23	13 30	11 47	23 25	10 59	14	

G.M.T.	ARIES G.H.A.	VENUS −3.8 G.H.A.	Dec.	MARS +1.7 G.H.A.	Dec.	JUPITER −1.2 G.H.A.	Dec.	SATURN +1.0 G.H.A.	Dec.	STARS Name	S.H.A.	Dec.
13 00	21 28.0	139 26.3 S23	29.8	233 28.9 N14	24.6	182 07.7 S 6	59.9	188 01.5 S 3	21.1	Acamar	315 36.3	S40 22.6
01	36 30.4	154 25.8	30.4	248 29.9	24.1	197 09.7 7	00.1	203 03.7	21.2	Achernar	335 44.1	S57 19.8
02	51 32.9	169 25.3	31.1	263 30.9	23.7	212 11.6	00.3	218 05.8	21.3	Acrux	173 37.1	S62 59.6
03	66 35.3	184 24.8 ··	31.7	278 31.9 ··	23.2	227 13.6 ··	00.5	233 08.0 ··	21.4	Adhara	255 31.5	S28 56.6
04	81 37.8	199 24.3	32.4	293 33.0	22.7	242 15.6	00.7	248 10.2	21.5	Aldebaran	291 17.0	N16 28.4
05	96 40.3	214 23.8	33.0	308 34.0	22.2	257 17.5	00.9	263 12.4	21.7			
06	111 42.7	229 23.3 S23	33.7	323 35.0 N14	21.7	272 19.5 S 7	01.1	278 14.6 S 3	21.8	Alioth	166 42.4	N56 03.7
07	126 45.2	244 22.8	34.3	338 36.0	21.3	287 21.4	01.3	293 16.7	21.9	Alkaid	153 18.4	N49 24.5
T 08	141 47.7	259 22.3	35.0	353 37.0	20.8	302 23.4	01.6	308 18.9	22.0	Al Na'ir	28 13.7	S47 03.2
U 09	156 50.1	274 21.8 ··	35.6	8 38.0 ··	20.3	317 25.3 ··	01.8	323 21.1 ··	22.1	Alnilam	276 10.8	S 1 12.7
E 10	171 52.6	289 21.3	36.3	23 39.0	19.8	332 27.3	02.0	338 23.3	22.2	Alphard	218 20.0	S 8 34.5
S 11	186 55.1	304 20.8	36.9	38 40.0	19.4	347 29.3	02.2	353 25.5	22.4			
D 12	201 57.5	319 20.3 S23	37.6	53 41.0 N14	18.9	2 31.2 S 7	02.4	8 27.7 S 3	22.5	Alphecca	126 31.8	N26 46.8
A 13	217 00.0	334 19.8	38.2	68 42.1	18.4	17 33.2	02.6	23 29.8	22.6	Alpheratz	358 08.2	N28 59.5
Y 14	232 02.5	349 19.3	38.9	83 43.1	17.9	32 35.1	02.8	38 32.0	22.7	Altair	62 31.8	N 8 49.3
15	247 04.9	4 18.8 ··	39.5	98 44.1 ··	17.4	47 37.1 ··	03.0	53 34.2 ··	22.8	Ankaa	353 39.1	S42 24.4
16	262 07.4	19 18.3	40.1	113 45.1	17.0	62 39.0	03.2	68 36.4	22.9	Antares	112 56.2	S26 23.4
17	277 09.8	34 17.7	40.8	128 46.1	16.5	77 41.0	03.4	83 38.6	23.1			
18	292 12.3	49 17.2 S23	41.4	143 47.1 N14	16.0	92 43.0 S 7	03.6	98 40.7 S 3	23.2	Arcturus	146 18.1	N19 16.9
19	307 14.8	64 16.7	42.1	158 48.1	15.5	107 44.9	03.8	113 42.9	23.3	Atria	108 20.2	S68 59.8
20	322 17.2	79 16.2	42.7	173 49.2	15.1	122 46.9	04.0	128 45.1	23.4	Avior	234 28.1	S59 26.7
21	337 19.7	94 15.7 ··	43.3	188 50.2 ··	14.6	137 48.8 ··	04.2	143 47.3 ··	23.5	Bellatrix	278 57.8	N 6 20.1
22	352 22.2	109 15.2	44.0	203 51.2	14.1	152 50.8	04.4	158 49.5	23.6	Betelgeuse	271 27.4	N 7 24.3
23	7 24.6	124 14.7	44.6	218 52.2	13.6	167 52.7	04.6	173 51.6	23.8			
14 00	22 27.1	139 14.2 S23	45.3	233 53.2 N14	13.1	182 54.7 S 7	04.8	188 53.8 S 3	23.9	Canopus	264 06.7	S52 40.9
01	37 29.6	154 13.7	45.9	248 54.2	12.7	197 56.7	05.0	203 56.0	24.0	Capella	281 10.0	N45 58.7
02	52 32.0	169 13.2	46.5	263 55.2	12.2	212 58.6	05.2	218 58.2	24.1	Deneb	49 47.9	N45 13.2
03	67 34.5	184 12.7 ··	47.1	278 56.3 ··	11.7	228 00.6 ··	05.4	234 00.4 ··	24.2	Denebola	182 58.6	N14 40.6
04	82 37.0	199 12.1	47.8	293 57.3	11.2	243 02.5	05.6	249 02.6	24.3	Diphda	349 19.8	S18 05.2
05	97 39.4	214 11.6	48.4	308 58.3	10.7	258 04.5	05.8	264 04.7	24.5			
06	112 41.9	229 11.1 S23	49.0	323 59.3 N14	10.3	273 06.4 S 7	06.0	279 06.9 S 3	24.6	Dubhe	194 21.8	N61 51.0
W 07	127 44.3	244 10.6	49.7	339 00.3	09.8	288 08.4	06.2	294 09.1	24.7	Elnath	278 43.0	N28 35.5
E 08	142 46.8	259 10.1	50.3	354 01.3	09.3	303 10.4	06.5	309 11.3	24.8	Eltanin	90 57.6	N51 29.8
D 09	157 49.3	274 09.6 ··	50.9	9 02.4 ··	08.8	318 12.3 ··	06.7	324 13.5 ··	24.9	Enif	34 10.7	N 9 47.6
N 10	172 51.7	289 09.1	51.5	24 03.4	08.3	333 14.3	06.9	339 15.6	25.0	Fomalhaut	15 50.3	S29 43.2
E 11	187 54.2	304 08.6	52.2	39 04.4	07.9	348 16.2	07.1	354 17.8	25.2			
S 12	202 56.7	319 08.1 S23	52.8	54 05.4 N14	07.4	3 18.2 S 7	07.3	9 20.0 S 3	25.3	Gacrux	172 28.5	S57 00.4
D 13	217 59.1	334 07.5	53.4	69 06.4	06.9	18 20.1	07.5	24 22.2	25.4	Gienah	176 17.6	S17 26.2
A 14	233 01.6	349 07.0	54.0	84 07.4	06.4	33 22.1	07.7	39 24.4	25.5	Hadar	149 23.0	S60 17.0
Y 15	248 04.1	4 06.5 ··	54.6	99 08.5 ··	05.9	48 24.1 ··	07.9	54 26.5 ··	25.6	Hamal	328 27.8	N23 22.6
16	263 06.5	19 06.0	55.3	114 09.5	05.5	63 26.0	08.1	69 28.7	25.7	Kaus Aust.	84 16.0	S34 23.7
17	278 09.0	34 05.5	55.9	129 10.5	05.0	78 28.0	08.3	84 30.9	25.9			
18	293 11.4	49 05.0 S23	56.5	144 11.5 N14	04.5	93 29.9 S 7	08.5	99 33.1 S 3	26.0	Kochab	137 20.1	N74 14.1
19	308 13.9	64 04.5	57.1	159 12.5	04.0	108 31.9	08.7	114 35.3	26.1	Markab	14 02.2	N15 06.5
20	323 16.4	79 04.0	57.7	174 13.6	03.5	123 33.8	08.9	129 37.5	26.2	Menkar	314 40.1	N 4 01.1
21	338 18.8	94 03.4 ··	58.3	189 14.6 ··	03.1	138 35.8 ··	09.1	144 39.6 ··	26.3	Menkent	148 36.6	S36 16.7
22	353 21.3	109 02.9	59.0	204 15.6	02.6	153 37.8	09.3	159 41.8	26.4	Miaplacidus	221 45.2	S69 38.2
23	8 23.8	124 02.4 23	59.6	219 16.6	02.1	168 39.7	09.5	174 44.0	26.6			
15 00	23 26.2	139 01.9 S24	00.2	234 17.6 N14	01.6	183 41.7 S 7	09.7	189 46.2 S 3	26.7	Mirfak	309 14.7	N49 47.7
01	38 28.7	154 01.4	00.8	249 18.7	01.1	198 43.6	09.9	204 48.4	26.8	Nunki	76 28.3	S26 19.2
02	53 31.2	169 00.9	01.4	264 19.7	00.7	213 45.6	10.1	219 50.5	26.9	Peacock	53 57.1	S56 47.9
03	68 33.6	184 00.4 ··	02.0	279 20.7 14	00.2	228 47.5 ··	10.3	234 52.7 ··	27.0	Pollux	243 57.3	N28 04.2
04	83 36.1	198 59.8	02.6	294 21.7 13	59.7	243 49.5	10.5	249 54.9	27.1	Procyon	245 25.1	N 5 16.4
05	98 38.6	213 59.3	03.2	309 22.7	59.2	258 51.5	10.7	264 57.1	27.3			
06	113 41.0	228 58.8 S24	03.8	324 23.8 N13	58.7	273 53.4 S 7	10.9	279 59.3 S 3	27.4	Rasalhague	96 29.1	N12 34.6
07	128 43.5	243 58.3	04.4	339 24.8	58.2	288 55.4	11.1	295 01.5	27.5	Regulus	208 09.4	N12 03.5
T 08	143 45.9	258 57.8	05.0	354 25.8	57.8	303 57.3	11.3	310 03.6	27.6	Rigel	281 35.1	S 8 13.2
H 09	158 48.4	273 57.3 ··	05.6	9 26.8 ··	57.3	318 59.3 ··	11.5	325 05.8 ··	27.7	Rigil Kent.	140 25.5	S60 45.5
U 10	173 50.9	288 56.8	06.2	24 27.9	56.8	334 01.2	11.8	340 08.0	27.8	Sabik	102 40.5	S15 42.1
R 11	188 53.3	303 56.2	06.8	39 28.9	56.3	349 03.2	12.0	355 10.2	28.0			
S 12	203 55.8	318 55.7 S24	07.4	54 29.9 N13	55.8	4 05.2 S 7	12.2	10 12.4 S 3	28.1	Schedar	350 07.7	N56 26.3
D 13	218 58.3	333 55.2	08.0	69 30.9	55.4	19 07.1	12.4	25 14.5	28.2	Shaula	96 55.0	S37 05.5
A 14	234 00.7	348 54.7	08.6	84 31.9	54.9	34 09.1	12.6	40 16.7	28.3	Sirius	258 55.0	S16 41.3
Y 15	249 03.2	3 54.2 ··	09.2	99 33.0 ··	54.4	49 11.0 ··	12.8	55 18.9 ··	28.4	Spica	158 57.1	S11 03.7
16	264 05.7	18 53.7	09.8	114 34.0	53.9	64 13.0	13.0	70 21.1	28.5	Suhail	223 10.4	S43 21.2
17	279 08.1	33 53.1	10.4	129 35.0	53.4	79 14.9	13.2	85 23.3	28.6			
18	294 10.6	48 52.6 S24	11.0	144 36.0 N13	52.9	94 16.9 S 7	13.4	100 25.4 S 3	28.8	Vega	80 55.5	N38 46.3
19	309 13.1	63 52.1	11.6	159 37.1	52.5	109 18.9	13.6	115 27.6	28.9	Zuben'ubi	137 32.6	S15 57.8
20	324 15.5	78 51.6	12.2	174 38.1	52.0	124 20.8	13.8	130 29.8	29.0		S.H.A.	Mer. Pass.
21	339 18.0	93 51.1 ··	12.8	189 39.1 ··	51.5	139 22.8 ··	14.0	145 32.0 ··	29.1		° '	h m
22	354 20.4	108 50.6	13.3	204 40.1	51.0	154 24.7	14.2	160 34.2	29.2	Venus	116 47.1	14 44
23	9 22.9	123 50.0	13.9	219 41.2	50.5	169 26.7	14.4	175 36.4	29.3	Mars	211 26.1	8 24
	h m									Jupiter	160 27.6	11 47
Mer. Pass. 22 26.5	v −0.5 d 0.6	v 1.0 d 0.5		v 2.0 d 0.2		v 2.2 d 0.1				Saturn	166 26.7	11 23

SUN and MOON

G.M.T.	SUN G.H.A.	SUN Dec.	MOON G.H.A.	v	MOON Dec.	d	H.P.
13 00	183 24.5	S 7 39.3	8 23.6	9.3	N 0 22.3	13.5	60.2
01	198 24.6	40.2	22 51.9	9.2	0 35.8	13.5	60.2
02	213 24.8	41.2	37 20.1	9.2	0 49.3	13.5	60.3
03	228 24.9	·· 42.1	51 48.3	9.1	1 02.8	13.5	60.3
04	243 25.1	43.1	66 16.4	9.2	1 16.3	13.6	60.3
05	258 25.2	44.0	80 44.6	9.0	1 29.9	13.5	60.3
06	273 25.4	S 7 44.9	95 12.6	9.1	N 1 43.4	13.5	60.4
07	288 25.5	45.9	109 40.7	9.0	1 56.9	13.5	60.4
T 08	303 25.7	46.8	124 08.7	9.0	2 10.4	13.5	60.4
U 09	318 25.8	·· 47.7	138 36.7	9.0	2 23.9	13.5	60.4
E 10	333 26.0	48.7	153 04.7	8.9	2 37.4	13.5	60.4
S 11	348 26.1	49.6	167 32.6	8.9	2 50.9	13.5	60.5
D 12	3 26.3	S 7 50.5	182 00.5	8.8	N 3 04.4	13.5	60.5
A 13	18 26.4	51.5	196 28.3	8.9	3 17.9	13.4	60.5
Y 14	33 26.6	52.4	210 56.2	8.7	3 31.3	13.5	60.5
15	48 26.7	·· 53.3	225 23.9	8.8	3 44.8	13.4	60.5
16	63 26.9	54.3	239 51.7	8.7	3 58.2	13.4	60.5
17	78 27.0	55.2	254 19.4	8.6	4 11.6	13.4	60.6
18	93 27.2	S 7 56.1	268 47.0	8.7	N 4 25.0	13.4	60.6
19	108 27.3	57.1	283 14.7	8.6	4 38.4	13.4	60.6
20	123 27.5	58.0	297 42.3	8.5	4 51.8	13.3	60.6
21	138 27.6	·· 58.9	312 09.8	8.5	5 05.1	13.3	60.6
22	153 27.8	7 59.9	326 37.3	8.5	5 18.4	13.3	60.6
23	168 27.9	8 00.8	341 04.8	8.4	5 31.7	13.3	60.6
14 00	183 28.1	S 8 01.7	355 32.2	8.4	N 5 45.0	13.2	60.7
01	198 28.2	02.7	9 59.6	8.4	5 58.2	13.2	60.7
02	213 28.4	03.6	24 27.0	8.3	6 11.4	13.2	60.7
03	228 28.5	·· 04.5	38 54.3	8.2	6 24.6	13.1	60.7
04	243 28.7	05.4	53 21.5	8.2	6 37.7	13.1	60.7
05	258 28.8	06.4	67 48.7	8.2	6 50.8	13.0	60.7
06	273 29.0	S 8 07.3	82 15.9	8.1	N 7 03.8	13.0	60.7
W 07	288 29.1	08.2	96 43.0	8.1	7 16.8	13.0	60.7
E 08	303 29.2	09.2	111 10.1	8.1	7 29.8	12.9	60.7
D 09	318 29.4	·· 10.1	125 37.2	8.0	7 42.7	12.9	60.8
N 10	333 29.5	11.0	140 04.2	7.9	7 55.6	12.9	60.8
E 11	348 29.7	12.0	154 31.1	7.9	8 08.5	12.8	60.8
S 12	3 29.8	S 8 12.9	168 58.0	7.9	N 8 21.3	12.7	60.8
D 13	18 30.0	13.8	183 24.9	7.8	8 34.0	12.7	60.8
A 14	33 30.1	14.7	197 51.7	7.8	8 46.7	12.6	60.8
Y 15	48 30.3	·· 15.7	212 18.5	7.7	8 59.3	12.6	60.8
16	63 30.4	16.6	226 45.2	7.7	9 11.9	12.5	60.8
17	78 30.5	17.5	241 11.9	7.6	9 24.4	12.5	60.8
18	93 30.7	S 8 18.5	255 38.5	7.6	N 9 36.9	12.4	60.8
19	108 30.8	19.4	270 05.1	7.5	9 49.3	12.3	60.8
20	123 31.0	20.3	284 31.6	7.5	10 01.6	12.3	60.8
21	138 31.1	·· 21.2	298 58.1	7.5	10 13.9	12.2	60.8
22	153 31.3	22.2	313 24.6	7.4	10 26.1	12.2	60.8
23	168 31.4	23.1	327 51.0	7.3	10 38.3	12.0	60.8
15 00	183 31.5	S 8 24.0	342 17.3	7.3	N10 50.3	12.0	60.8
01	198 31.7	24.9	356 43.6	7.3	11 02.3	12.0	60.8
02	213 31.8	25.9	11 09.7	7.2	11 14.3	11.8	60.8
03	228 32.0	·· 26.8	25 36.1	7.1	11 26.1	11.8	60.8
04	243 32.1	27.7	40 02.2	7.1	11 37.9	11.7	60.8
05	258 32.3	28.6	54 28.3	7.1	11 49.6	11.7	60.8
06	273 32.4	S 8 29.6	68 54.4	7.0	N12 01.3	11.5	60.8
07	288 32.5	30.5	83 20.4	7.0	12 12.8	11.5	60.8
T 08	303 32.7	31.4	97 46.4	6.9	12 24.3	11.4	60.8
H 09	318 32.8	·· 32.3	112 12.3	6.8	12 35.7	11.3	60.8
U 10	333 33.0	33.2	126 38.1	6.9	12 47.0	11.2	60.8
R 11	348 33.1	34.2	141 04.0	6.7	12 58.2	11.2	60.8
S 12	3 33.2	S 8 35.1	155 29.7	6.8	N13 09.4	11.0	60.8
D 13	18 33.4	36.0	169 55.5	6.6	13 20.4	11.0	60.8
A 14	33 33.5	37.0	184 21.1	6.7	13 31.4	10.8	60.8
Y 15	48 33.6	·· 37.9	198 46.8	6.5	13 42.2	10.8	60.8
16	63 33.8	38.8	213 12.3	6.6	13 53.0	10.7	60.8
17	78 33.9	39.7	227 37.9	6.5	14 03.7	10.5	60.8
18	93 34.1	S 8 40.7	242 03.4	6.4	N14 14.2	10.5	60.8
19	108 34.2	41.6	256 28.8	6.4	14 24.7	10.4	60.8
20	123 34.3	42.5	270 54.2	6.4	14 35.1	10.3	60.8
21	138 34.5	·· 43.4	285 19.6	6.3	14 45.4	10.2	60.7
22	153 34.6	44.4	299 44.9	6.3	14 55.6	10.0	60.7
23	168 34.7	45.3	314 10.2	6.2	15 05.6	10.0	60.7
	S.D. 16.1	d 0.9	S.D. 16.5		16.6		16.6

Twilight / Moonrise

Lat.	Naut.	Civil	Sunrise	Moonrise 13	14	15	16
N 72	04 50	06 08	07 19	17 13	16 55	16 32	15 41
N 70	04 55	06 05	07 08	17 18	17 09	16 58	16 42
68	04 58	06 02	06 59	17 23	17 20	17 19	17 18
66	05 01	06 00	06 52	17 27	17 30	17 35	17 44
64	05 03	05 58	06 46	17 30	17 38	17 48	18 04
62	05 05	05 56	06 41	17 33	17 45	17 59	18 20
60	05 06	05 54	06 36	17 35	17 51	18 09	18 34
N 58	05 07	05 53	06 32	17 37	17 56	18 18	18 46
56	05 08	05 51	06 29	17 39	18 01	18 25	18 56
54	05 09	05 50	06 26	17 41	18 05	18 32	19 05
52	05 10	05 49	06 23	17 43	18 09	18 38	19 13
50	05 10	05 47	06 20	17 45	18 12	18 44	19 20
45	05 11	05 45	06 14	17 48	18 20	18 55	19 36
N 40	05 11	05 42	06 09	17 51	18 26	19 05	19 49
35	05 10	05 39	06 05	17 53	18 32	19 14	20 00
30	05 09	05 37	06 01	17 55	18 37	19 21	20 10
20	05 07	05 32	05 54	17 59	18 45	19 35	20 27
N 10	05 03	05 27	05 48	18 03	18 53	19 46	20 42
0	04 58	05 22	05 43	18 06	19 00	19 57	20 55
S 10	04 51	05 16	05 37	18 09	19 08	20 08	21 09
20	04 42	05 08	05 31	18 13	19 16	20 20	21 24
30	04 30	04 59	05 23	18 17	19 25	20 33	21 42
35	04 23	04 53	05 19	18 19	19 30	20 41	21 52
40	04 13	04 46	05 14	18 22	19 36	20 50	22 03
45	04 02	04 38	05 09	18 25	19 43	21 01	22 17
S 50	03 47	04 28	05 02	18 29	19 51	21 14	22 34
52	03 40	04 23	04 58	18 30	19 55	21 20	22 42
54	03 32	04 18	04 55	18 32	19 59	21 26	22 51
56	03 23	04 12	04 51	18 34	20 04	21 34	23 00
58	03 12	04 05	04 47	18 37	20 10	21 42	23 12
S 60	02 59	03 57	04 42	18 39	20 16	21 52	23 25

Twilight / Moonset

Lat.	Sunset	Civil	Naut.	Moonset 13	14	15	16
N 72	16 12	17 21	18 39	05 58	08 09	10 30	13 23
N 70	16 22	17 25	18 35	05 56	07 58	10 06	12 23
68	16 31	17 28	18 32	05 54	07 49	09 47	11 48
66	16 38	17 30	18 29	05 52	07 41	09 32	11 24
64	16 44	17 33	18 27	05 51	07 35	09 20	11 04
62	16 50	17 35	18 26	05 50	07 29	09 10	10 49
60	16 54	17 36	18 24	05 49	07 24	09 01	10 36
N 58	16 59	17 38	18 23	05 48	07 20	08 53	10 25
56	17 02	17 40	18 23	05 47	07 17	08 46	10 15
54	17 06	17 41	18 22	05 47	07 13	08 40	10 06
52	17 09	17 42	18 21	05 46	07 10	08 35	09 59
50	17 11	17 44	18 21	05 46	07 07	08 30	09 52
45	17 17	17 47	18 21	05 44	07 02	08 20	09 37
N 40	17 22	17 49	18 21	05 43	06 57	08 11	09 25
35	17 27	17 52	18 21	05 42	06 52	08 04	09 15
30	17 31	17 55	18 22	05 42	06 49	07 57	09 06
20	17 37	18 00	18 25	05 40	06 42	07 46	08 51
N 10	17 43	18 05	18 29	05 39	06 37	07 36	08 37
0	17 49	18 10	18 34	05 38	06 31	07 27	08 25
S 10	17 55	18 17	18 41	05 36	06 26	07 18	08 12
20	18 02	18 24	18 50	05 35	06 21	07 08	07 59
30	18 09	18 34	19 02	05 34	06 14	06 57	07 43
35	18 14	18 39	19 10	05 33	06 10	06 51	07 35
40	18 19	18 46	19 20	05 32	06 06	06 43	07 25
45	18 24	18 55	19 31	05 31	06 02	06 35	07 13
S 50	18 31	19 05	19 46	05 29	05 56	06 25	06 59
52	18 35	19 10	19 54	05 29	05 53	06 20	06 52
54	18 38	19 16	20 02	05 28	05 50	06 15	06 45
56	18 42	19 22	20 11	05 27	05 47	06 10	06 37
58	18 47	19 29	20 23	05 26	05 44	06 03	06 28
S 60	18 52	19 37	20 36	05 26	05 40	05 56	06 17

SUN / MOON

Day	SUN Eqn. of Time 00h	12h	Mer. Pass.	MOON Mer. Pass. Upper	Lower	Age	Phase
13	13 38	13 45	11 46	24 19	11 52	15	
14	13 52	13 59	11 46	00 19	12 46	16	
15	14 06	14 13	11 46	01 14	13 42	17	○

G.M.T.	ARIES G.H.A.	VENUS −3.8 G.H.A.	Dec.	MARS +1.7 G.H.A.	Dec.	JUPITER −1.2 G.H.A.	Dec.	SATURN +1.0 G.H.A.	Dec.	STARS Name	S.H.A.	Dec.
16 00	24 25.4	138 49.5	S24 14.5	234 42.2	N13 50.0	184 28.6	S 7 14.6	190 38.5	S 3 29.5	Acamar	315 36.3	S40 22.6
01	39 27.8	153 49.0	15.1	249 43.2	49.6	199 30.6	14.8	205 40.7	29.6	Achernar	335 44.1	S57 19.8
02	54 30.3	168 48.5	15.7	264 44.2	49.1	214 32.6	15.0	220 42.9	29.7	Acrux	173 37.1	S62 59.6
03	69 32.8	183 48.0	·· 16.3	279 45.3	·· 48.6	229 34.5	·· 15.2	235 45.1	·· 29.8	Adhara	255 31.5	S28 56.6
04	84 35.2	198 47.5	16.8	294 46.3	48.1	244 36.5	15.4	250 47.3	29.9	Aldebaran	291 16.9	N16 28.4
05	99 37.7	213 46.9	17.4	309 47.3	47.6	259 38.4	15.6	265 49.4	30.0			
06	114 40.2	228 46.4	S24 18.0	324 48.3	N13 47.1	274 40.4	S 7 15.8	280 51.6	S 3 30.2	Alioth	166 42.4	N56 03.6
07	129 42.6	243 45.9	18.6	339 49.4	46.7	289 42.3	16.0	295 53.8	30.3	Alkaid	153 18.4	N49 24.4
08	144 45.1	258 45.4	19.2	354 50.4	46.2	304 44.3	16.2	310 56.0	30.4	Al Na'ir	28 13.7	S47 03.2
F 09	159 47.5	273 44.9	·· 19.7	9 51.4	·· 45.7	319 46.2	·· 16.4	325 58.2	·· 30.5	Alnilam	276 10.8	S 1 12.7
R 10	174 50.0	288 44.3	20.3	24 52.5	45.2	334 48.2	16.6	341 00.4	30.6	Alphard	218 20.0	S 8 34.5
I 11	189 52.5	303 43.8	20.9	39 53.5	44.7	349 50.2	16.8	356 02.5	30.7			
D 12	204 54.9	318 43.3	S24 21.5	54 54.5	N13 44.2	4 52.1	S 7 17.0	11 04.7	S 3 30.9	Alphecca	126 31.8	N26 46.8
A 13	219 57.4	333 42.8	22.0	69 55.5	43.8	19 54.1	17.2	26 06.9	31.0	Alpheratz	358 08.2	N28 59.5
Y 14	234 59.9	348 42.3	22.6	84 56.6	43.3	34 56.0	17.4	41 09.1	31.1	Altair	62 31.8	N 8 49.3
15	250 02.3	3 41.7	·· 23.2	99 57.6	·· 42.8	49 58.0	·· 17.6	56 11.3	·· 31.2	Ankaa	353 39.1	S42 24.4
16	265 04.8	18 41.2	23.7	114 58.6	42.3	64 59.9	17.9	71 13.4	31.3	Antares	112 56.2	S26 23.4
17	280 07.3	33 40.7	24.3	129 59.7	41.8	80 01.9	18.1	86 15.6	31.4			
18	295 09.7	48 40.2	S24 24.9	145 00.7	N13 41.3	95 03.9	S 7 18.3	101 17.8	S 3 31.5	Arcturus	146 18.1	N19 16.9
19	310 12.2	63 39.7	25.4	160 01.7	40.8	110 05.8	18.5	116 20.0	31.7	Atria	108 20.2	S68 59.8
20	325 14.7	78 39.1	26.0	175 02.7	40.4	125 07.8	18.7	131 22.2	31.8	Avior	234 28.0	S59 26.7
21	340 17.1	93 38.6	·· 26.6	190 03.8	·· 39.9	140 09.7	·· 18.9	146 24.4	·· 31.9	Bellatrix	278 57.8	N 6 20.1
22	355 19.6	108 38.1	27.1	205 04.8	39.4	155 11.7	19.1	161 26.5	32.0	Betelgeuse	271 27.3	N 7 24.3
23	10 22.0	123 37.6	27.7	220 05.8	38.9	170 13.6	19.3	176 28.7	32.1			
17 00	25 24.5	138 37.1	S24 28.3	235 06.9	N13 38.4	185 15.6	S 7 19.5	191 30.9	S 3 32.2	Canopus	264 06.7	S52 40.9
01	40 27.0	153 36.5	28.8	250 07.9	37.9	200 17.6	19.7	206 33.1	32.4	Capella	281 10.0	N45 58.7
02	55 29.4	168 36.0	29.4	265 08.9	37.5	215 19.5	19.9	221 35.3	32.5	Deneb	49 47.9	N45 13.2
03	70 31.9	183 35.5	·· 29.9	280 10.0	·· 37.0	230 21.5	·· 20.1	236 37.5	·· 32.6	Denebola	182 58.6	N14 40.6
04	85 34.4	198 35.0	30.5	295 11.0	36.5	245 23.4	20.3	251 39.6	32.7	Diphda	349 19.8	S18 05.2
05	100 36.8	213 34.4	31.0	310 12.0	36.0	260 25.4	20.5	266 41.8	32.8			
06	115 39.3	228 33.9	S24 31.6	325 13.0	N13 35.5	275 27.3	S 7 20.7	281 44.0	S 3 32.9	Dubhe	194 21.7	N61 50.9
07	130 41.8	243 33.4	32.2	340 14.1	35.0	290 29.3	20.9	296 46.2	33.0	Elnath	278 43.0	N28 35.5
S 08	145 44.2	258 32.9	32.7	355 15.1	34.5	305 31.3	21.1	311 48.4	33.2	Eltanin	90 57.6	N51 29.8
A 09	160 46.7	273 32.4	·· 33.3	10 16.1	·· 34.1	320 33.2	·· 21.3	326 50.5	·· 33.3	Enif	34 10.7	N 9 47.6
T 10	175 49.2	288 31.8	33.8	25 17.2	33.6	335 35.2	21.5	341 52.7	33.4	Fomalhaut	15 50.3	S29 43.2
U 11	190 51.6	303 31.3	34.4	40 18.2	33.1	350 37.1	21.7	356 54.9	33.5			
R 12	205 54.1	318 30.8	S24 34.9	55 19.2	N13 32.6	5 39.1	S 7 21.9	11 57.1	S 3 33.6	Gacrux	172 28.5	S57 00.4
D 13	220 56.5	333 30.3	35.5	70 20.3	32.1	20 41.0	22.1	26 59.3	33.7	Gienah	176 17.5	S17 26.2
A 14	235 59.0	348 29.7	36.0	85 21.3	31.6	35 43.0	22.3	42 01.5	33.9	Hadar	149 23.0	S60 17.0
Y 15	251 01.5	3 29.2	·· 36.5	100 22.3	·· 31.1	50 44.9	·· 22.5	57 03.6	·· 34.0	Hamal	328 27.8	N23 22.6
16	266 03.9	18 28.7	37.1	115 23.4	30.7	65 46.9	22.7	72 05.8	34.1	Kaus Aust.	84 16.0	S34 23.7
17	281 06.4	33 28.2	37.6	130 24.4	30.2	80 48.9	22.9	87 08.0	34.2			
18	296 08.9	48 27.7	S24 38.2	145 25.4	N13 29.7	95 50.8	S 7 23.1	102 10.2	S 3 34.3	Kochab	137 20.1	N74 14.0
19	311 11.3	63 27.1	38.7	160 26.5	29.2	110 52.8	23.3	117 12.4	34.4	Markab	14 02.2	N15 06.5
20	326 13.8	78 26.6	39.3	175 27.5	28.7	125 54.7	23.5	132 14.6	34.5	Menkar	314 40.1	N 4 01.1
21	341 16.3	93 26.1	·· 39.8	190 28.5	·· 28.2	140 56.7	·· 23.7	147 16.7	·· 34.7	Menkent	148 36.6	S36 16.6
22	356 18.7	108 25.6	40.3	205 29.6	27.7	155 58.6	23.9	162 18.9	34.8	Miaplacidus	221 45.2	S69 38.2
23	11 21.2	123 25.0	40.9	220 30.6	27.2	171 00.6	24.1	177 21.1	34.9			
18 00	26 23.6	138 24.5	S24 41.4	235 31.7	N13 26.8	186 02.6	S 7 24.3	192 23.3	S 3 35.0	Mirfak	309 14.6	N49 47.7
01	41 26.1	153 24.0	41.9	250 32.7	26.3	201 04.5	24.5	207 25.5	35.1	Nunki	76 28.4	S26 19.2
02	56 28.6	168 23.5	42.5	265 33.7	25.8	216 06.5	24.8	222 27.6	35.2	Peacock	53 57.5	S56 47.9
03	71 31.0	183 22.9	·· 43.0	280 34.8	·· 25.3	231 08.4	·· 25.0	237 29.8	·· 35.4	Pollux	243 57.3	N28 04.2
04	86 33.5	198 22.4	43.5	295 35.8	24.8	246 10.4	25.2	252 32.0	35.5	Procyon	245 25.0	N 5 16.4
05	101 36.0	213 21.9	44.1	310 36.8	24.3	261 12.3	25.4	267 34.2	35.6			
06	116 38.4	228 21.4	S24 44.6	325 37.9	N13 23.8	276 14.3	S 7 25.6	282 36.4	S 3 35.7	Rasalhague	96 29.1	N12 34.6
07	131 40.9	243 20.8	45.1	340 38.9	23.3	291 16.3	25.8	297 38.6	35.8	Regulus	208 09.4	N12 03.5
08	146 43.4	258 20.3	45.7	355 39.9	22.9	306 18.2	26.0	312 40.7	35.9	Rigel	281 35.1	S 8 13.2
S 09	161 45.8	273 19.8	·· 46.2	10 41.0	·· 22.4	321 20.2	·· 26.2	327 42.9	·· 36.0	Rigil Kent.	140 25.5	S60 45.5
U 10	176 48.3	288 19.3	46.7	25 42.0	21.9	336 22.1	26.4	342 45.1	36.2	Sabik	102 40.5	S15 42.1
N 11	191 50.8	303 18.7	47.2	40 43.1	21.4	351 24.1	26.6	357 47.3	36.3			
D 12	206 53.2	318 18.2	S24 47.8	55 44.1	N13 20.9	6 26.0	S 7 26.8	12 49.5	S 3 36.4	Schedar	350 07.7	N56 26.3
A 13	221 55.7	333 17.7	48.3	70 45.1	20.4	21 28.0	27.0	27 51.7	36.5	Shaula	96 55.0	S37 05.5
Y 14	236 58.1	348 17.2	48.8	85 46.2	19.9	36 29.9	27.2	42 53.8	36.6	Sirius	258 55.0	S16 41.3
15	252 00.6	3 16.6	·· 49.3	100 47.2	·· 19.4	51 31.9	·· 27.4	57 56.0	·· 36.7	Spica	158 57.1	S11 03.7
16	267 03.1	18 16.1	49.8	115 48.2	19.0	66 33.9	27.6	72 58.2	36.9	Suhail	223 10.4	S43 21.2
17	282 05.5	33 15.6	50.4	130 49.3	18.5	81 35.8	27.8	88 00.4	37.0			
18	297 08.0	48 15.1	S24 50.9	145 50.3	N13 18.0	96 37.8	S 7 28.0	103 02.6	S 3 37.1	Vega	80 55.5	N38 46.3
19	312 10.5	63 14.5	51.4	160 51.4	17.5	111 39.7	28.2	118 04.8	37.2	Zuben'ubi	137 32.6	S15 57.8
20	327 12.9	78 14.0	51.9	175 52.4	17.0	126 41.7	28.4	133 06.9	37.3			
21	342 15.4	93 13.5	·· 52.4	190 53.4	·· 16.5	141 43.6	·· 28.6	148 09.1	·· 37.4		S.H.A.	Mer. Pass.
22	357 17.9	108 13.0	52.9	205 54.4	16.0	156 45.6	28.8	163 11.3	37.5	Venus	113 12.5	14 46
23	12 20.3	123 12.4	53.4	220 55.5	15.5	171 47.6	29.0	178 13.5	37.7	Mars	209 42.3	8 19
										Jupiter	159 51.1	11 37
Mer. Pass. 22 14.7		v −0.5	d 0.5	v 1.0	d 0.5	v 2.0	d 0.2	v 2.2	d 0.1	Saturn	166 06.4	11 12

G.M.T.	SUN G.H.A.	SUN Dec.	MOON G.H.A.	v	Dec.	d	H.P.
16 00	183 34.9	S 8 46.2	328 35.4	6.2	N15 15.6	9.9	60.7
01	198 35.0	47.1	343 00.6	6.1	15 25.5	9.7	60.7
02	213 35.2	48.0	357 25.7	6.1	15 35.2	9.7	60.7
03	228 35.3 ··	49.0	11 50.8	6.0	15 44.9	9.5	60.7
04	243 35.4	49.9	26 15.8	6.1	15 54.4	9.4	60.7
05	258 35.6	50.8	40 40.9	5.9	16 03.8	9.3	60.7
06	273 35.7	S 8 51.7	55 05.8	6.0	N16 13.1	9.2	60.6
07	288 35.8	52.6	69 30.8	5.8	16 22.3	9.1	60.6
08	303 36.0	53.6	83 55.6	5.9	16 31.4	9.0	60.6
F 09	318 36.1 ··	54.5	98 20.5	5.8	16 40.4	8.8	60.6
R 10	333 36.2	55.4	112 45.3	5.8	16 49.2	8.8	60.6
I 11	348 36.4	56.3	127 10.1	5.7	16 58.0	8.6	60.6
D 12	3 36.5	S 8 57.2	141 34.8	5.7	N17 06.6	8.5	60.6
A 13	18 36.6	58.2	155 59.5	5.7	17 15.1	8.3	60.5
Y 14	33 36.8	8 59.1	170 24.2	5.6	17 23.4	8.3	60.5
15	48 36.9	9 00.0	184 48.8	5.6	17 31.7	8.1	60.5
16	63 37.0	00.9	199 13.4	5.6	17 39.8	8.0	60.5
17	78 37.2	01.8	213 38.0	5.5	17 47.8	7.9	60.5
18	93 37.3	S 9 02.8	228 02.5	5.5	N17 55.7	7.7	60.5
19	108 37.4	03.7	242 27.0	5.5	18 03.4	7.6	60.4
20	123 37.5	04.6	256 51.5	5.4	18 11.0	7.5	60.4
21	138 37.7 ··	05.5	271 15.9	5.5	18 18.5	7.3	60.4
22	153 37.8	06.4	285 40.4	5.4	18 25.8	7.3	60.4
23	168 37.9	07.3	300 04.8	5.3	18 33.1	7.1	60.4
17 00	183 38.1	S 9 08.3	314 29.1	5.4	N18 40.2	6.9	60.4
01	198 38.2	09.2	328 53.5	5.3	18 47.1	6.8	60.3
02	213 38.3	10.1	343 17.8	5.3	18 53.9	6.7	60.3
03	228 38.5 ··	11.0	357 42.1	5.2	19 00.6	6.6	60.3
04	243 38.6	11.9	12 06.3	5.3	19 07.2	6.4	60.3
05	258 38.7	12.8	26 30.6	5.2	19 13.6	6.3	60.2
06	273 38.8	S 9 13.7	40 54.8	5.2	N19 19.9	6.1	60.2
07	288 39.0	14.7	55 19.0	5.2	19 26.0	6.0	60.2
S 08	303 39.1	15.6	69 43.2	5.2	19 32.0	5.9	60.2
A 09	318 39.2 ··	16.5	84 07.4	5.1	19 37.9	5.7	60.2
T 10	333 39.3	17.4	98 31.5	5.2	19 43.6	5.6	60.1
U 11	348 39.5	18.3	112 55.7	5.1	19 49.2	5.4	60.1
R 12	3 39.6	S 9 19.2	127 19.8	5.1	N19 54.6	5.3	60.1
D 13	18 39.7	20.1	141 43.9	5.1	19 59.9	5.2	60.1
A 14	33 39.9	21.1	156 08.0	5.2	20 05.1	5.0	60.0
Y 15	48 40.0 ··	22.0	170 32.2	5.0	20 10.1	4.9	60.0
16	63 40.1	22.9	184 56.2	5.1	20 15.0	4.7	60.0
17	78 40.2	23.8	199 20.3	5.1	20 19.7	4.6	60.0
18	93 40.4	S 9 24.7	213 44.4	5.1	N20 24.3	4.5	60.0
19	108 40.5	25.6	228 08.5	5.1	20 28.8	4.3	59.9
20	123 40.6	26.5	242 32.6	5.1	20 33.1	4.1	59.9
21	138 40.7 ··	27.4	256 56.7	5.0	20 37.2	4.1	59.9
22	153 40.8	28.4	271 20.7	5.1	20 41.3	3.8	59.9
23	168 41.0	29.3	285 44.8	5.1	20 45.1	3.8	59.8
18 00	183 41.1	S 9 30.2	300 08.9	5.1	N20 48.9	3.5	59.8
01	198 41.2	31.1	314 33.0	5.1	20 52.4	3.5	59.8
02	213 41.3	32.0	328 57.1	5.1	20 55.9	3.3	59.7
03	228 41.5 ··	32.9	343 21.2	5.1	20 59.2	3.1	59.7
04	243 41.6	33.8	357 45.3	5.1	21 02.3	3.0	59.7
05	258 41.7	34.7	12 09.4	5.2	21 05.3	2.8	59.7
06	273 41.8	S 9 35.6	26 33.6	5.1	N21 08.1	2.7	59.6
07	288 42.0	36.6	40 57.7	5.2	21 10.8	2.6	59.6
08	303 42.1	37.5	55 21.9	5.1	21 13.4	2.4	59.6
S 09	318 42.2 ··	38.4	69 46.0	5.2	21 15.8	2.3	59.6
U 10	333 42.3	39.3	84 10.2	5.2	21 18.1	2.1	59.5
N 11	348 42.4	40.2	98 34.4	5.3	21 20.2	2.0	59.5
D 12	3 42.6	S 9 41.1	112 58.7	5.2	N21 22.2	1.8	59.5
A 13	18 42.7	42.0	127 22.9	5.3	21 24.0	1.7	59.4
Y 14	33 42.8	42.9	141 47.2	5.3	21 25.7	1.5	59.4
15	48 42.9 ··	43.8	156 11.5	5.3	21 27.2	1.4	59.4
16	63 43.0	44.7	170 35.8	5.4	21 28.6	1.2	59.4
17	78 43.2	45.6	185 00.2	5.3	21 29.8	1.1	59.3
18	93 43.3	S 9 46.5	199 24.5	5.5	N21 30.9	1.0	59.3
19	108 43.4	47.4	213 49.0	5.4	21 31.9	0.8	59.3
20	123 43.5	48.4	228 13.4	5.5	21 32.7	0.7	59.2
21	138 43.6 ··	49.3	242 37.9	5.5	21 33.4	0.5	59.2
22	153 43.7	50.2	257 02.4	5.5	21 33.9	0.4	59.2
23	168 43.9	51.1	271 26.9	5.6	21 34.3	0.2	59.2
	S.D. 16.1	d 0.9	S.D. 16.5		16.4		16.2

Twilight / Sunrise / Moonrise

Lat.	Naut.	Civil	Sunrise	Moonrise 16	17	18	19
N 72	05 03	06 22	07 33	15 41	☐	☐	☐
N 70	05 06	06 17	07 21	16 42	☐	☐	☐
68	05 08	06 13	07 11	17 18	17 21	17 40	18 51
66	05 10	06 09	07 02	17 44	18 01	18 38	19 44
64	05 11	06 06	06 55	18 04	18 29	19 12	20 16
62	05 12	06 04	06 49	18 20	18 51	19 37	20 40
60	05 13	06 01	06 44	18 34	19 08	19 56	20 59
N 58	05 14	05 59	06 39	18 46	19 23	20 12	21 15
56	05 14	05 57	06 35	18 56	19 35	20 26	21 28
54	05 14	05 55	06 31	19 05	19 47	20 38	21 40
52	05 15	05 54	06 28	19 13	19 56	20 49	21 50
50	05 15	05 52	06 25	19 20	20 05	20 59	21 59
45	05 14	05 48	06 18	19 36	20 24	21 18	22 19
N 40	05 14	05 45	06 12	19 49	20 39	21 34	22 35
35	05 12	05 42	06 07	20 00	20 52	21 48	22 48
30	05 11	05 39	06 03	20 10	21 03	22 00	22 59
20	05 07	05 33	05 55	20 27	21 22	22 20	23 19
N 10	05 03	05 27	05 49	20 42	21 39	22 38	23 37
0	04 57	05 21	05 42	20 55	21 55	22 55	23 53
S 10	04 49	05 14	05 35	21 09	22 11	23 11	24 09
20	04 40	05 06	05 28	21 24	22 28	23 29	24 26
30	04 27	04 56	05 20	21 42	22 48	23 50	24 46
35	04 18	04 49	05 15	21 52	22 59	24 02	00 02
40	04 08	04 42	05 10	22 03	23 13	24 16	00 16
45	03 56	04 33	05 03	22 17	23 28	24 32	00 32
S 50	03 40	04 22	04 55	22 34	23 48	24 52	00 52
52	03 32	04 16	04 52	22 42	23 57	25 02	01 02
54	03 23	04 10	04 48	22 51	24 07	00 07	01 13
56	03 13	04 04	04 44	23 00	24 19	00 19	01 25
58	03 01	03 56	04 39	23 12	24 33	00 33	01 39
S 60	02 47	03 48	04 33	23 25	24 48	00 48	01 56

Sunset / Twilight / Moonset

Lat.	Sunset	Civil	Naut.	Moonset 16	17	18	19
N 72	15 56	17 07	18 25	13 23	☐	☐	☐
N 70	16 08	17 12	18 22	12 23	☐	☐	☐
68	16 19	17 16	18 20	11 48	13 50	15 36	16 28
66	16 27	17 20	18 19	11 24	13 10	14 39	15 35
64	16 34	17 23	18 18	11 04	12 43	14 05	15 02
62	16 40	17 26	18 17	10 49	12 22	13 40	14 38
60	16 46	17 28	18 16	10 36	12 05	13 21	14 19
N 58	16 50	17 30	18 16	10 25	11 50	13 04	14 03
56	16 55	17 32	18 15	10 15	11 38	12 51	13 50
54	16 59	17 34	18 15	10 06	11 27	12 39	13 38
52	17 02	17 36	18 15	09 59	11 18	12 28	13 27
50	17 05	17 38	18 15	09 52	11 09	12 19	13 18
45	17 12	17 42	18 16	09 37	10 51	11 59	12 58
N 40	17 18	17 45	18 17	09 25	10 37	11 43	12 42
35	17 23	17 48	18 18	09 15	10 24	11 30	12 29
30	17 27	17 51	18 19	09 06	10 13	11 18	12 17
20	17 35	17 57	18 23	08 51	09 55	10 58	11 57
N 10	17 42	18 03	18 28	08 37	09 39	10 40	11 39
0	17 49	18 10	18 34	08 25	09 24	10 24	11 23
S 10	17 55	18 17	18 42	08 12	09 09	10 07	11 06
20	18 03	18 25	18 51	07 59	08 53	09 50	10 48
30	18 11	18 36	19 05	07 43	08 34	09 29	10 28
35	18 16	18 42	19 13	07 35	08 24	09 17	10 16
40	18 22	18 50	19 23	07 25	08 11	09 04	10 02
45	18 28	18 59	19 36	07 13	07 57	08 48	09 46
S 50	18 36	19 10	19 52	06 59	07 39	08 28	09 26
52	18 40	19 16	20 00	06 52	07 31	08 19	09 16
54	18 44	19 22	20 09	06 45	07 22	08 08	09 05
56	18 49	19 29	20 20	06 37	07 11	07 56	08 53
58	18 54	19 36	20 32	06 28	07 00	07 43	08 39
S 60	18 59	19 45	20 46	06 17	06 46	07 27	08 22

Day	SUN Eqn. of Time 00h	12h	Mer. Pass.	MOON Mer. Pass. Upper	Lower	Age	Phase
	m s	m s	h m	h m	h m	d	
16	14 19	14 26	11 46	02 11	14 40	18	
17	14 32	14 38	11 45	03 10	15 39	19	◖
18	14 44	14 50	11 45	04 09	16 39	20	

G.M.T.	ARIES G.H.A.	VENUS −3.8 G.H.A.	Dec.	MARS +1.7 G.H.A.	Dec.	JUPITER −1.2 G.H.A.	Dec.	SATURN +1.0 G.H.A.	Dec.	STARS Name	S.H.A.	Dec.
19 00	27 22.8	138 11.9 S24 53.9		235 56.6 N13 15.1		186 49.5 S 7 29.2		193 15.7 S 3 37.8		Acamar	315 36.3	S40 22.6
01	42 25.3	153 11.4 ..	54.5	250 57.6	14.6	201 51.5	29.4	208 17.9 ..	37.9	Achernar	335 44.1	S57 19.8
02	57 27.7	168 10.9	55.0	265 58.6	14.1	216 53.4	29.6	223 20.0	38.0	Acrux	173 37.1	S62 59.6
03	72 30.2	183 10.3 ..	55.5	280 59.7 ..	13.6	231 55.4 ..	29.8	238 22.2 ..	38.1	Adhara	255 31.4	S28 56.6
04	87 32.6	198 09.8	56.0	296 00.7	13.1	246 57.3	30.0	253 24.4	38.2	Aldebaran	291 16.9	N16 28.4
05	102 35.1	213 09.3	56.5	311 01.8	12.6	261 59.3	30.2	268 26.6	38.3			
06	117 37.6	228 08.7 S24 57.0		326 02.8 N13 12.1		277 01.2 S 7 30.4		283 28.8 S 3 38.5		Alioth	166 42.4	N56 03.6
07	132 40.0	243 08.2	57.5	341 03.9	11.6	292 03.2	30.6	298 31.0	38.6	Alkaid	153 18.4	N49 24.4
08	147 42.5	258 07.7	58.0	356 04.9	11.1	307 05.2	30.8	313 33.1	38.7	Al Na'ir	28 13.7	S47 03.2
M 09	162 45.0	273 07.2 ..	58.5	11 05.9 ..	10.7	322 07.1 ..	31.0	328 35.3 ..	38.8	Alnilam	276 10.7	S 1 12.7
O 10	177 47.4	288 06.6	59.0	26 07.0	10.2	337 09.1	31.2	343 37.5	38.9	Alphard	218 20.0	S 8 34.5
N 11	192 49.9	303 06.1 24 59.5		41 08.0	09.7	352 11.0	31.4	358 39.7	39.0			
D 12	207 52.4	318 05.6 S25 00.0		56 09.1 N13 09.2		7 13.0 S 7 31.6		13 41.9 S 3 39.1		Alphecca	126 31.8	N26 46.8
A 13	222 54.8	333 05.1	00.5	71 10.1	08.7	22 14.9	31.8	28 44.0	39.3	Alpheratz	358 08.2	N28 59.5
Y 14	237 57.3	348 04.5	01.0	86 11.2	08.2	37 16.9	32.0	43 46.2	39.4	Altair	62 31.8	N 8 49.3
15	252 59.7	3 04.0 ..	01.5	101 12.2 ..	07.7	52 18.9 ..	32.2	58 48.4 ..	39.5	Ankaa	353 39.1	S42 24.4
16	268 02.2	18 03.5	02.0	116 13.2	07.2	67 20.8	32.4	73 50.6	39.6	Antares	112 56.2	S26 23.4
17	283 04.7	33 02.9	02.5	131 14.3	06.7	82 22.8	32.6	88 52.8	39.7			
18	298 07.1	48 02.4 S25 03.0		146 15.3 N13 06.2		97 24.7 S 7 32.8		103 55.0 S 3 39.8		Arcturus	146 18.1	N19 16.9
19	313 09.6	63 01.9	03.4	161 16.4	05.8	112 26.7	33.0	118 57.1	40.0	Atria	108 20.2	S68 59.8
20	328 12.1	78 01.4	03.9	176 17.4	05.3	127 28.6	33.2	133 59.3	40.1	Avior	234 28.0	S59 26.7
21	343 14.5	93 00.8 ..	04.4	191 18.5 ..	04.8	142 30.6 ..	33.4	149 01.5 ..	40.2	Bellatrix	278 57.8	N 6 20.1
22	358 17.0	108 00.3	04.9	206 19.5	04.3	157 32.6	33.7	164 03.7	40.3	Betelgeuse	271 27.3	N 7 24.3
23	13 19.5	122 59.8	05.4	221 20.6	03.8	172 34.5	33.9	179 05.9	40.4			
20 00	28 21.9	137 59.3 S25 05.9		236 21.6 N13 03.3		187 36.5 S 7 34.1		194 08.1 S 3 40.5		Canopus	264 06.7	S52 40.9
01	43 24.4	152 58.7	06.4	251 22.6	02.8	202 38.4	34.3	209 10.2	40.6	Capella	281 09.9	N45 58.7
02	58 26.9	167 58.2	06.8	266 23.7	02.3	217 40.4	34.5	224 12.4	40.8	Deneb	49 47.9	N45 13.2
03	73 29.3	182 57.7 ..	07.3	281 24.7 ..	01.8	232 42.3 ..	34.7	239 14.6 ..	40.9	Denebola	182 58.6	N14 40.6
04	88 31.8	197 57.1	07.8	296 25.8	01.3	247 44.3	34.9	254 16.8	41.0	Diphda	349 19.8	S18 05.2
05	103 34.2	212 56.6	08.3	311 26.8	00.9	262 46.2	35.1	269 19.0	41.1			
06	118 36.7	227 56.1 S25 08.8		326 27.9 N13 00.4		277 48.2 S 7 35.3		284 21.2 S 3 41.2		Dubhe	194 21.7	N61 50.9
07	133 39.2	242 55.6	09.2	341 28.9 12 59.9		292 50.2	35.5	299 23.4	41.3	Elnath	278 43.0	N28 35.5
08	148 41.6	257 55.0	09.7	356 30.0	59.4	307 52.1	35.7	314 25.5	41.4	Eltanin	90 57.7	N51 29.8
T 09	163 44.1	272 54.5 ..	10.2	11 31.0 ..	58.9	322 54.1 ..	35.9	329 27.7 ..	41.6	Enif	34 10.7	N 9 47.6
U 10	178 46.6	287 54.0	10.7	26 32.1	58.4	337 56.0	36.1	344 29.9	41.7	Fomalhaut	15 50.3	S29 43.2
E 11	193 49.0	302 53.4	11.1	41 33.1	57.9	352 58.0	36.3	359 32.1	41.8			
S 12	208 51.5	317 52.9 S25 11.6		56 34.2 N12 57.4		7 59.9 S 7 36.5		14 34.3 S 3 41.9		Gacrux	172 28.5	S57 00.4
D 13	223 54.0	332 52.4	12.1	71 35.2	56.9	23 01.9	36.7	29 36.5	42.0	Gienah	176 17.5	S17 26.2
A 14	238 56.4	347 51.9	12.6	86 36.3	56.4	38 03.9	36.9	44 38.6	42.1	Hadar	149 23.0	S60 17.0
Y 15	253 58.9	2 51.3 ..	13.0	101 37.3 ..	56.0	53 05.8 ..	37.1	59 40.8 ..	42.2	Hamal	328 27.8	N23 22.6
16	269 01.4	17 50.8	13.5	116 38.4	55.5	68 07.8	37.3	74 43.0	42.4	Kaus Aust.	84 16.0	S34 23.7
17	284 03.8	32 50.3	14.0	131 39.4	55.0	83 09.7	37.5	89 45.2	42.5			
18	299 06.3	47 49.7 S25 14.4		146 40.5 N12 54.5		98 11.7 S 7 37.7		104 47.4 S 3 42.6		Kochab	137 20.1	N74 14.0
19	314 08.7	62 49.2	14.9	161 41.5	54.0	113 13.6	37.9	119 49.6	42.7	Markab	14 02.2	N15 06.5
20	329 11.2	77 48.7	15.4	176 42.6	53.5	128 15.6	38.1	134 51.7	42.8	Menkar	314 40.1	N 4 01.1
21	344 13.7	92 48.2 ..	15.8	191 43.6 ..	53.0	143 17.5 ..	38.3	149 53.9 ..	42.9	Menkent	148 36.6	S36 16.6
22	359 16.1	107 47.6	16.3	206 44.7	52.5	158 19.5	38.5	164 56.1	43.0	Miaplacidus	221 45.1	S69 38.2
23	14 18.6	122 47.1	16.7	221 45.7	52.0	173 21.5	38.7	179 58.3	43.2			
21 00	29 21.1	137 46.6 S25 17.2		236 46.8 N12 51.5		188 23.4 S 7 38.9		195 00.5 S 3 43.3		Mirfak	309 14.6	N49 47.7
01	44 23.5	152 46.0	17.7	251 47.8	51.0	203 25.4	39.1	210 02.7	43.4	Nunki	76 28.4	S26 19.2
02	59 26.0	167 45.5	18.1	266 48.9	50.5	218 27.3	39.3	225 04.8	43.5	Peacock	53 57.2	S56 47.9
03	74 28.5	182 45.0 ..	18.6	281 49.9 ..	50.1	233 29.3 ..	39.5	240 07.0 ..	43.6	Pollux	243 57.3	N28 04.2
04	89 30.9	197 44.5	19.0	296 51.0	49.6	248 31.2	39.7	255 09.2	43.7	Procyon	245 25.0	N 5 16.4
05	104 33.4	212 43.9	19.5	311 52.0	49.1	263 33.2	39.9	270 11.4	43.8			
06	119 35.8	227 43.4 S25 19.9		326 53.1 N12 48.6		278 35.2 S 7 40.1		285 13.6 S 3 44.0		Rasalhague	96 29.1	N12 34.6
W 07	134 38.3	242 42.9	20.4	341 54.1	48.1	293 37.1	40.3	300 15.8	44.1	Regulus	208 09.4	N12 03.5
E 08	149 40.8	257 42.3	20.8	356 55.2	47.6	308 39.1	40.5	315 17.9	44.2	Rigel	281 35.1	S 8 13.2
D 09	164 43.2	272 41.8 ..	21.3	11 56.2 ..	47.1	323 41.0 ..	40.7	330 20.1 ..	44.3	Rigil Kent.	140 25.5	S60 45.5
N 10	179 45.7	287 41.3	21.7	26 57.3	46.6	338 43.0	40.9	345 22.3	44.4	Sabik	102 40.5	S15 42.1
E 11	194 48.2	302 40.7	22.2	41 58.3	46.1	353 44.9	41.1	0 24.5	44.5			
S 12	209 50.6	317 40.2 S25 22.6		56 59.4 N12 45.6		8 46.9 S 7 41.3		15 26.7 S 3 44.6		Schedar	350 07.7	N56 26.3
D 13	224 53.1	332 39.7	23.1	72 00.4	45.1	23 48.8	41.5	30 28.9	44.7	Shaula	96 55.0	S37 05.5
A 14	239 55.6	347 39.2	23.5	87 01.5	44.6	38 50.8	41.7	45 31.1	44.9	Sirius	258 55.0	S16 41.3
Y 15	254 58.0	2 38.6 ..	24.0	102 02.5 ..	44.1	53 52.8 ..	41.9	60 33.2 ..	45.0	Spica	158 57.1	S11 03.7
16	270 00.5	17 38.1	24.4	117 03.6	43.7	68 54.7	42.1	75 35.4	45.1	Suhail	223 10.4	S43 21.2
17	285 03.0	32 37.6	24.8	132 04.7	43.2	83 56.7	42.3	90 37.6	45.2			
18	300 05.4	47 37.0 S25 25.3		147 05.7 N12 42.7		98 58.6 S 7 42.5		105 39.8 S 3 45.3		Vega	80 55.5	N38 46.3
19	315 07.9	62 36.5	25.7	162 06.8	42.2	114 00.6	42.7	120 42.0	45.4	Zuben'ubi	137 32.6	S15 57.8
20	330 10.3	77 36.0	26.2	177 07.8	41.7	129 02.5	42.9	135 44.2	45.5		S.H.A.	Mer. Pass.
21	345 12.8	92 35.4 ..	26.6	192 08.9 ..	41.2	144 04.5 ..	43.1	150 46.3 ..	45.7		° '	h m
22	0 15.3	107 34.9	27.0	207 09.9	40.7	159 06.5	43.3	165 48.5	45.8	Venus	109 37.3	14 49
23	15 17.7	122 34.4	27.5	222 11.0	40.2	174 08.4	43.5	180 50.7	45.9	Mars	207 59.7	8 14
										Jupiter	159 14.5	11 28
Mer. Pass. 22 02.9		v −0.5 d 0.5		v 1.0 d 0.5		v 2.0 d 0.2		v 2.2 d 0.1		Saturn	165 46.1	11 02

G.M.T.	SUN G.H.A.	SUN Dec.	MOON G.H.A.	v	Dec.	d	H.P.
19 d h	o '	o '	o '	'	o '	'	'
00	183 44.0	S 9 52.0	285 51.5	5.6	N21 34.5	0.1	59.1
01	198 44.1	52.9	300 16.1	5.7	21 34.6	0.1	59.1
02	213 44.2	53.8	314 40.8	5.7	21 34.5	0.1	59.0
03	228 44.3	·· 54.7	329 05.5	5.7	21 34.4	0.4	59.0
04	243 44.4	55.6	343 30.2	5.8	21 34.0	0.5	59.0
05	258 44.6	56.5	357 55.0	5.8	21 33.5	0.6	59.0
06	273 44.7	S 9 57.4	12 19.8	5.9	N21 32.9	0.7	59.0
07	288 44.8	58.3	26 44.7	5.9	21 32.2	0.9	58.9
08	303 44.9	9 59.2	41 09.6	5.9	21 31.3	1.0	58.9
M 09	318 45.0	10 00.1	55 34.5	6.0	21 30.3	1.2	58.9
O 10	333 45.1	01.0	69 59.5	6.1	21 29.1	1.3	58.8
N 11	348 45.2	01.9	84 24.6	6.1	21 27.8	1.5	58.8
D 12	3 45.4	S10 02.8	98 49.7	6.2	N21 26.3	1.5	58.8
A 13	18 45.5	03.7	113 14.9	6.2	21 24.8	1.8	58.7
Y 14	33 45.6	04.6	127 40.1	6.3	21 23.0	1.8	58.7
15	48 45.7	·· 05.5	142 05.4	6.3	21 21.2	2.0	58.7
16	63 45.8	06.4	156 30.7	6.4	21 19.2	2.1	58.7
17	78 45.9	07.3	170 56.1	6.4	21 17.1	2.3	58.6
18	93 46.0	S10 08.2	185 21.5	6.5	N21 14.8	2.4	58.6
19	108 46.1	09.1	199 47.0	6.6	21 12.4	2.5	58.6
20	123 46.2	10.0	214 12.6	6.6	21 09.9	2.6	58.5
21	138 46.4	·· 10.9	228 38.2	6.6	21 07.3	2.8	58.5
22	153 46.5	11.8	243 03.8	6.8	21 04.5	2.9	58.5
23	168 46.6	12.7	257 29.6	6.8	21 01.6	3.0	58.4
20 00	183 46.7	S10 13.6	271 55.4	6.8	N20 58.6	3.2	58.4
01	198 46.8	14.5	286 21.2	7.0	20 55.4	3.3	58.4
02	213 46.9	15.4	300 47.2	7.0	20 52.1	3.4	58.4
03	228 47.0	·· 16.3	315 13.2	7.0	20 48.7	3.5	58.3
04	243 47.1	17.2	329 39.2	7.1	20 45.2	3.7	58.3
05	258 47.2	18.1	344 05.3	7.2	20 41.5	3.8	58.3
06	273 47.3	S10 19.0	358 31.5	7.3	N20 37.7	3.9	58.2
07	288 47.4	19.9	12 57.8	7.3	20 33.8	4.0	58.2
08	303 47.6	20.8	27 24.1	7.4	20 29.8	4.1	58.2
T 09	318 47.7	·· 21.7	41 50.5	7.5	20 25.7	4.3	58.1
U 10	333 47.8	22.6	56 17.0	7.5	20 21.4	4.4	58.1
E 11	348 47.9	23.5	70 43.5	7.6	20 17.0	4.5	58.1
S 12	3 48.0	S10 24.4	85 10.1	7.7	N20 12.5	4.6	58.1
D 13	18 48.1	25.3	99 36.8	7.8	20 07.9	4.7	58.0
A 14	33 48.2	26.2	114 03.6	7.8	20 03.2	4.9	58.0
Y 15	48 48.3	·· 27.1	128 30.4	7.9	19 58.3	4.9	58.0
16	63 48.4	28.0	142 57.3	8.0	19 53.4	5.1	57.9
17	78 48.5	28.9	157 24.3	8.0	19 48.3	5.2	57.9
18	93 48.6	S10 29.8	171 51.3	8.1	N19 43.1	5.3	57.9
19	108 48.7	30.7	186 18.4	8.2	19 37.8	5.4	57.8
20	123 48.8	31.6	200 45.6	8.3	19 32.4	5.5	57.8
21	138 48.9	·· 32.4	215 12.9	8.3	19 26.9	5.6	57.8
22	153 49.0	33.3	229 40.2	8.4	19 21.3	5.7	57.8
23	168 49.1	34.2	244 07.6	8.5	19 15.6	5.9	57.7
21 00	183 49.2	S10 35.1	258 35.1	8.6	N19 09.7	5.9	57.7
01	198 49.3	36.0	273 02.7	8.7	19 03.8	6.1	57.7
02	213 49.4	36.9	287 30.4	8.7	18 57.7	6.1	57.6
03	228 49.5	·· 37.8	301 58.1	8.8	18 51.6	6.2	57.6
04	243 49.6	38.7	316 25.9	8.9	18 45.4	6.4	57.6
05	258 49.7	39.6	330 53.8	8.9	18 39.0	6.4	57.5
06	273 49.8	S10 40.5	345 21.7	9.1	N18 32.6	6.6	57.5
W 07	288 49.9	41.4	359 49.8	9.1	18 26.0	6.6	57.5
E 08	303 50.0	42.3	14 17.9	9.1	18 19.4	6.7	57.5
D 09	318 50.1	·· 43.1	28 46.0	9.3	18 12.7	6.9	57.4
N 10	333 50.2	44.0	43 14.3	9.3	18 05.8	6.9	57.4
E 11	348 50.3	44.9	57 42.6	9.5	17 58.9	7.0	57.4
S 12	3 50.4	S10 45.8	72 11.1	9.5	N17 51.9	7.1	57.3
D 13	18 50.5	46.7	86 39.6	9.5	17 44.8	7.2	57.3
A 14	33 50.6	47.6	101 08.1	9.7	17 37.6	7.3	57.3
Y 15	48 50.7	··· 48.5	115 36.8	9.7	17 30.3	7.4	57.3
16	63 50.8	49.4	130 05.5	9.8	17 22.9	7.4	57.2
17	78 50.9	50.3	144 34.3	9.9	17 15.5	7.6	57.2
18	93 51.0	S10 51.1	159 03.2	9.9	N17 07.9	7.6	57.2
19	108 51.1	52.0	173 32.1	10.1	17 00.3	7.7	57.2
20	123 51.2	52.9	188 01.2	10.1	16 52.6	7.8	57.1
21	138 51.3	·· 53.8	202 30.3	10.2	16 44.8	7.9	57.1
22	153 51.4	54.7	216 59.5	10.2	16 36.9	8.0	57.1
23	168 51.5	55.6	231 28.7	10.4	16 28.9	8.0	57.0
	S.D. 16.1	d 0.9	S.D. 16.0		15.8		15.6

Lat.	Twilight Naut.	Civil	Sunrise	Moonrise 19	20	21	22
o	h m	h m	h m	h m	h m	h m	h m
N 72	05 16	06 35	07 49	□	□	21 03	23 26
N 70	05 18	06 29	07 34	□	19 32	21 54	23 51
68	05 19	06 23	07 22	18 51	20 37	22 25	24 09
66	05 19	06 19	07 13	19 44	21 12	22 48	24 24
64	05 20	06 15	07 04	20 16	21 38	23 07	24 36
62	05 20	06 12	06 57	20 40	21 57	23 21	24 46
60	05 20	06 08	06 51	20 59	22 14	23 34	24 55
N 58	05 20	06 06	06 46	21 15	22 27	23 44	25 03
56	05 20	06 03	06 41	21 28	22 39	23 54	25 10
54	05 20	06 01	06 37	21 40	22 49	24 02	00 02
52	05 19	05 59	06 33	21 50	22 58	24 09	00 09
50	05 19	05 57	06 30	21 59	23 06	24 16	00 16
45	05 18	05 52	06 22	22 19	23 24	24 30	00 30
N 40	05 17	05 48	06 16	22 35	23 38	24 42	00 42
35	05 15	05 44	06 10	22 48	23 50	24 51	00 51
30	05 13	05 41	06 05	22 59	24 00	00 00	01 00
20	05 08	05 34	05 56	23 19	24 18	00 18	01 15
N 10	05 03	05 27	05 49	23 37	24 33	00 33	01 28
0	04 56	05 20	05 41	23 53	24 48	00 48	01 40
S 10	04 48	05 13	05 34	24 09	00 09	01 02	01 52
20	04 37	05 04	05 26	24 26	00 26	01 18	02 05
30	04 23	04 52	05 17	24 46	00 46	01 36	02 20
35	04 14	04 45	05 11	00 02	00 57	01 46	02 28
40	04 03	04 37	05 05	00 16	01 11	01 58	02 38
45	03 50	04 27	04 58	00 32	01 26	02 12	02 49
S 50	03 33	04 15	04 49	00 52	01 46	02 28	03 03
52	03 24	04 09	04 45	01 02	01 55	02 36	03 09
54	03 15	04 03	04 41	01 13	02 05	02 45	03 16
56	03 04	03 56	04 36	01 25	02 16	02 55	03 24
58	02 51	03 47	04 31	01 39	02 30	03 06	03 33
S 60	02 35	03 38	04 24	01 56	02 45	03 19	03 43

Lat.	Sunset	Twilight Civil	Naut.	Moonset 19	20	21	22
o	h m	h m	h m	h m	h m	h m	h m
N 72	15 39	16 53	18 11	□	□	18 05	17 25
N 70	15 54	16 59	18 10	□	17 45	17 13	16 59
68	16 06	17 05	18 09	16 28	16 39	16 41	16 39
66	16 16	17 09	18 09	15 35	16 03	16 17	16 23
64	16 24	17 13	18 08	15 02	15 37	15 58	16 10
62	16 31	17 17	18 08	14 38	15 17	15 42	15 59
60	16 37	17 20	18 08	14 19	15 01	15 29	15 50
N 58	16 43	17 23	18 08	14 03	14 47	15 18	15 41
56	16 47	17 25	18 09	13 50	14 34	15 08	15 34
54	16 52	17 28	18 09	13 38	14 24	14 59	15 27
52	16 56	17 30	18 09	13 28	14 15	14 52	15 21
50	16 59	17 32	18 10	13 18	14 06	14 45	15 16
45	17 07	17 37	18 11	12 58	13 48	14 30	15 04
N 40	17 14	17 41	18 12	12 42	13 33	14 17	14 54
35	17 19	17 45	18 14	12 29	13 21	14 06	14 46
30	17 24	17 48	18 16	12 17	13 10	13 57	14 39
20	17 33	17 55	18 21	11 57	12 51	13 41	14 26
N 10	17 41	18 02	18 27	11 39	12 35	13 27	14 15
0	17 48	18 09	18 34	11 23	12 19	13 13	14 04
S 10	17 56	18 17	18 42	11 06	12 04	13 00	13 53
20	18 04	18 26	18 53	10 48	11 47	12 45	13 42
30	18 13	18 38	19 07	10 28	11 28	12 29	13 28
35	18 19	18 45	19 16	10 16	11 17	12 19	13 21
40	18 25	18 53	19 27	10 02	11 04	12 08	13 12
45	18 32	19 03	19 41	09 46	10 49	11 55	13 02
S 50	18 41	19 16	19 58	09 26	10 30	11 39	12 49
52	18 45	19 22	20 07	09 16	10 21	11 31	12 43
54	18 50	19 28	20 17	09 05	10 11	11 23	12 37
56	18 55	19 36	20 28	08 53	10 00	11 14	12 30
58	19 01	19 44	20 41	08 39	09 47	11 03	12 21
S 60	19 07	19 54	20 57	08 22	09 32	10 51	12 12

Day	SUN Eqn. of Time 00h	12h	Mer. Pass.	MOON Mer. Pass. Upper	Lower	Age	Phase
	m s	m s	h m	h m	h m	d	
19	14 56	15 01	11 45	05 09	17 38	21	
20	15 07	15 12	11 45	06 06	18 34	22	◑
21	15 17	15 22	11 45	07 01	19 27	23	

G.M.T.	ARIES G.H.A.	VENUS −3.9 G.H.A.	Dec.	MARS +1.6 G.H.A.	Dec.	JUPITER −1.2 G.H.A.	Dec.	SATURN +1.0 G.H.A.	Dec.	STARS Name	S.H.A.	Dec.
22 00	30 20.2	137 33.9 S25 27.9		237 12.0 N12 39.7		189 10.4 S 7 43.7		195 52.9 S 3 46.0		Acamar	315 36.3	S40 22.6
01	45 22.7	152 33.3	28.3	252 12.3	39.2	204 12.3	43.9	210 55.1	46.1	Achernar	335 44.1	S57 19.8
02	60 25.1	167 32.8	28.8	267 14.2	38.7	219 14.3	44.1	225 57.3	46.2	Acrux	173 37.1	S62 59.6
03	75 27.6	182 32.3 ··	29.2	282 15.2 ··	38.2	234 16.2 ··	44.3	240 59.4 ··	46.3	Adhara	255 31.4	S28 56.6
04	90 30.1	197 31.7	29.6	297 16.3	37.7	249 18.2	44.5	256 01.6	46.5	Aldebaran	291 16.9	N16 28.4
05	105 32.5	212 31.2	30.0	312 17.3	37.2	264 20.2	44.7	271 03.8	46.6			
06	120 35.0	227 30.7 S25 30.5		327 18.4 N12 36.8		279 22.1 S 7 44.9		286 06.0 S 3 46.7		Alioth	166 42.4	N56 03.6
07	135 37.5	242 30.2	30.9	342 19.4	36.3	294 24.1	45.1	301 08.2	46.8	Alkaid	153 18.4	N49 24.4
T 08	150 39.9	257 29.6	31.3	357 20.5	35.8	309 26.0	45.3	316 10.4	46.9	Al Na'ir	28 13.8	S47 03.2
H 09	165 42.4	272 29.1 ··	31.7	12 21.6 ··	35.3	324 28.0 ··	45.5	331 12.6 ··	47.0	Alnilam	276 10.7	S 1 12.7
U 10	180 44.8	287 28.6	32.2	27 22.6	34.8	339 29.9	45.7	346 14.7	47.1	Alphard	218 20.0	S 8 34.5
R 11	195 47.3	302 28.0	32.6	42 23.7	34.3	354 31.9	45.9	1 16.9	47.2			
S 12	210 49.8	317 27.5 S25 33.0		57 24.7 N12 33.8		9 33.8 S 7 46.1		16 19.1 S 3 47.4		Alphecca	126 31.8	N26 46.8
D 13	225 52.2	332 27.0	33.4	72 25.8	33.3	24 35.8	46.3	31 21.3	47.5	Alpheratz	358 08.2	N28 59.5
A 14	240 54.7	347 26.4	33.8	87 26.8	32.8	39 37.8	46.5	46 23.5	47.6	Altair	62 31.8	N 8 49.3
Y 15	255 57.2	2 25.9 ··	34.3	102 27.9 ··	32.3	54 39.7 ··	46.7	61 25.7 ··	47.7	Ankaa	353 39.1	S42 24.4
16	270 59.6	17 25.4	34.7	117 29.0	31.8	69 41.7	46.9	76 27.9	47.8	Antares	112 56.3	S26 23.4
17	286 02.1	32 24.9	35.1	132 30.0	31.3	84 43.6	47.1	91 30.0	47.9			
18	301 04.6	47 24.3 S25 35.5		147 31.1 N12 30.8		99 45.6 S 7 47.3		106 32.2 S 3 48.0		Arcturus	146 18.1	N19 16.8
19	316 07.0	62 23.8	35.9	162 32.1	30.3	114 47.5	47.5	121 34.4	48.2	Atria	108 20.2	S68 59.8
20	331 09.5	77 23.3	36.3	177 33.2	29.8	129 49.5	47.7	136 36.6	48.3	Avior	234 27.9	S59 26.7
21	346 11.9	92 22.7 ··	36.7	192 34.3 ··	29.3	144 51.5 ··	47.9	151 38.8 ··	48.4	Bellatrix	278 57.7	N 6 20.1
22	1 14.4	107 22.2	37.1	207 35.3	28.9	159 53.4	48.1	166 41.0	48.5	Betelgeuse	271 27.3	N 7 24.3
23	16 16.9	122 21.7	37.6	222 36.4	28.4	174 55.4	48.3	181 43.1	48.6			
23 00	31 19.3	137 21.2 S25 38.0		237 37.4 N12 27.9		189 57.3 S 7 48.5		196 45.3 S 3 48.7		Canopus	264 06.6	S52 40.9
01	46 21.8	152 20.6	38.4	252 38.5	27.4	204 59.3	48.7	211 47.5	48.8	Capella	281 09.9	N45 58.7
02	61 24.3	167 20.1	38.8	267 39.6	26.9	220 01.2	48.9	226 49.7	48.9	Deneb	49 47.9	N45 13.2
03	76 26.7	182 19.6 ··	39.2	282 40.6 ··	26.4	235 03.2 ··	49.1	241 51.9 ··	49.1	Denebola	182 58.6	N14 40.6
04	91 29.2	197 19.0	39.6	297 41.7	25.9	250 05.2	49.3	256 54.1	49.2	Diphda	349 19.8	S18 05.2
05	106 31.7	212 18.5	40.0	312 42.8	25.4	265 07.1	49.5	271 56.3	49.3			
06	121 34.1	227 18.0 S25 40.4		327 43.8 N12 24.9		280 09.1 S 7 49.7		286 58.4 S 3 49.4		Dubhe	194 21.7	N61 50.9
07	136 36.6	242 17.4	40.8	342 44.9	24.4	295 11.0	49.9	302 00.6	49.5	Elnath	278 43.0	N28 35.5
08	151 39.1	257 16.9	41.2	357 45.9	23.9	310 13.0	50.1	317 02.8	49.6	Eltanin	90 57.7	N51 29.8
F 09	166 41.5	272 16.4 ··	41.6	12 47.0 ··	23.4	325 14.9 ··	50.3	332 05.0 ··	49.7	Enif	34 10.7	N 9 47.6
R 10	181 44.0	287 15.9	42.0	27 48.1	22.9	340 16.9	50.5	347 07.2	49.8	Fomalhaut	15 50.3	S29 43.2
I 11	196 46.4	302 15.3	42.4	42 49.1	22.4	355 18.8	50.7	2 09.4	50.0			
D 12	211 48.9	317 14.8 S25 42.8		57 50.2 N12 21.9		10 20.8 S 7 50.9		17 11.6 S 3 50.1		Gacrux	172 28.5	S57 00.4
A 13	226 51.4	332 14.3	43.2	72 51.3	21.4	25 22.8	51.1	32 13.7	50.2	Gienah	176 17.5	S17 26.2
Y 14	241 53.8	347 13.7	43.5	87 52.3	20.9	40 24.7	51.3	47 15.9	50.3	Hadar	149 23.0	S60 17.0
15	256 56.3	2 13.2 ··	43.9	102 53.4 ··	20.4	55 26.7 ··	51.5	62 18.1 ··	50.4	Hamal	328 27.7	N23 22.6
16	271 58.8	17 12.7	44.3	117 54.5	19.9	70 28.6	51.7	77 20.3	50.5	Kaus Aust.	84 16.0	S34 23.7
17	287 01.2	32 12.2	44.7	132 55.5	19.5	85 30.6	51.9	92 22.5	50.6			
18	302 03.7	47 11.6 S25 45.1		147 56.6 N12 19.0		100 32.5 S 7 52.1		107 24.7 S 3 50.8		Kochab	137 20.2	N74 14.0
19	317 06.2	62 11.1	45.5	162 57.7	18.5	115 34.5	52.3	122 26.9	50.9	Markab	14 02.2	N15 06.5
20	332 08.6	77 10.6	45.9	177 58.7	18.0	130 36.5	52.5	137 29.0	51.0	Menkar	314 40.1	N 4 01.1
21	347 11.1	92 10.0 ··	46.3	192 59.8 ··	17.5	145 38.4 ··	52.7	152 31.2 ··	51.1	Menkent	148 36.6	S36 16.6
22	2 13.6	107 09.5	46.6	208 00.8	17.0	160 40.4	52.9	167 33.4	51.2	Miaplacidus	221 45.1	S69 38.2
23	17 16.0	122 09.0	47.0	223 01.9	16.5	175 42.3	53.1	182 35.6	51.3			
24 00	32 18.5	137 08.5 S25 47.4		238 03.0 N12 16.0		190 44.3 S 7 53.3		197 37.8 S 3 51.4		Mirfak	309 14.6	N49 47.7
01	47 20.9	152 07.9	47.8	253 04.0	15.5	205 46.2	53.5	212 40.0	51.5	Nunki	76 28.4	S26 19.2
02	62 23.4	167 07.4	48.2	268 05.1	15.0	220 48.2	53.7	227 42.2	51.7	Peacock	53 57.2	S56 47.9
03	77 25.9	182 06.9 ··	48.5	283 06.2 ··	14.5	235 50.2 ··	53.9	242 44.3 ··	51.8	Pollux	243 57.2	N28 04.2
04	92 28.3	197 06.3	48.9	298 07.2	14.0	250 52.1	54.1	257 46.5	51.9	Procyon	245 25.0	N 5 16.4
05	107 30.8	212 05.8	49.3	313 08.3	13.5	265 54.1	54.3	272 48.7	52.0			
06	122 33.3	227 05.3 S25 49.7		328 09.4 N12 13.0		280 56.0 S 7 54.5		287 50.9 S 3 52.1		Rasalhague	96 29.1	N12 34.6
07	137 35.7	242 04.8	50.0	343 10.4	12.5	295 58.0	54.7	302 53.1	52.2	Regulus	208 09.4	N12 03.5
S 08	152 38.2	257 04.2	50.4	358 11.5	12.0	310 59.9	54.9	317 55.3	52.3	Rigel	281 35.1	S 8 13.2
A 09	167 40.7	272 03.7 ··	50.8	13 12.6 ··	11.5	326 01.9 ··	55.1	332 57.5 ··	52.4	Rigil Kent.	140 25.5	S60 45.4
T 10	182 43.1	287 03.2	51.2	28 13.7	11.0	341 03.9	55.3	347 59.6	52.6	Sabik	102 40.5	S15 42.1
U 11	197 45.6	302 02.6	51.5	43 14.7	10.5	356 05.8	55.5	3 01.8	52.7			
R 12	212 48.1	317 02.1 S25 51.9		58 15.8 N12 10.0		11 07.8 S 7 55.7		18 04.0 S 3 52.8		Schedar	350 07.7	N56 26.3
D 13	227 50.5	332 01.6	52.3	73 16.9	09.5	26 09.7	55.9	33 06.2	52.9	Shaula	96 55.0	S37 05.5
A 14	242 53.0	347 01.1	52.6	88 17.9	09.0	41 11.7	56.1	48 08.4	53.0	Sirius	258 54.9	S16 41.3
Y 15	257 55.4	2 00.5 ··	53.0	103 19.0 ··	08.5	56 13.6 ··	56.3	63 10.6 ··	53.1	Spica	158 57.1	S11 03.8
16	272 57.9	17 00.0	53.3	118 20.1	08.0	71 15.6	56.5	78 12.8	53.2	Suhail	223 10.4	S43 21.2
17	288 00.4	31 59.5	53.7	133 21.1	07.5	86 17.5	56.7	93 14.9	53.3			
18	303 02.8	46 59.0 S25 54.1		148 22.2 N12 07.1		101 19.5 S 7 56.9		108 17.1 S 3 53.5		Vega	80 55.5	N38 46.3
19	318 05.3	61 58.4	54.4	163 23.3	06.6	116 21.5	57.1	123 19.3	53.6	Zuben'ubi	137 32.6	S15 57.8
20	333 07.8	76 57.9	54.8	178 24.3	06.1	131 23.4	57.3	138 21.5	53.7			
21	348 10.2	91 57.4 ··	55.1	193 25.4 ··	05.6	146 25.4 ··	57.5	153 23.7 ··	53.8		S.H.A.	Mer. Pass.
22	3 12.7	106 56.8	55.5	208 26.5	05.1	161 27.3	57.7	168 25.9	53.9	Venus	106 01.8	14 51
23	18 15.2	121 56.3	55.9	223 27.6	04.6	176 29.3	57.9	183 28.1	54.0	Mars	206 18.1	8 09
										Jupiter	158 38.0	11 19
Mer. Pass. 21 51.1		v −0.5 d 0.4		v 1.1 d 0.5		v 2.0 d 0.2		v 2.2 d 0.1		Saturn	165 26.0	10 51

G.M.T.	SUN G.H.A.	SUN Dec.	MOON G.H.A.	MOON v	MOON Dec.	MOON d	MOON H.P.
d h	o '	o '	o '	'	o '	'	'
22 00	183 51.6	S10 56.5	245 58.1	10.4	N16 20.9	8.1	57.0
01	198 51.7	57.4	260 27.5	10.5	16 12.8	8.2	57.0
02	213 51.8	58.2	274 57.0	10.5	16 04.6	8.3	57.0
03	228 51.9	10 59.1	289 26.5	10.7	15 56.3	8.4	56.9
04	243 52.0	11 00.0	303 56.2	10.7	15 47.9	8.4	56.9
05	258 52.1	00.9	318 25.9	10.7	15 39.5	8.5	56.9
06	273 52.2	S11 01.8	332 55.6	10.9	N15 31.0	8.6	56.9
07	288 52.3	02.7	347 25.5	10.9	15 22.4	8.6	56.8
T 08	303 52.4	03.5	1 55.4	11.0	15 13.8	8.7	56.8
H 09	318 52.5 ··	04.4	16 25.4	11.1	15 05.1	8.8	56.8
U 10	333 52.5	05.3	30 55.5	11.2	14 56.3	8.9	56.7
R 11	348 52.6	06.2	45 25.7	11.2	14 47.4	8.9	56.7
S 12	3 52.7	S11 07.1	59 55.9	11.3	N14 38.5	9.0	56.7
D 13	18 52.8	08.0	74 26.2	11.3	14 29.5	9.1	56.7
A 14	33 52.9	08.8	88 56.5	11.5	14 20.4	9.1	56.6
Y 15	48 53.0 ··	09.7	103 27.0	11.5	14 11.3	9.2	56.6
16	63 53.1	10.6	117 57.5	11.5	14 02.1	9.2	56.6
17	78 53.2	11.5	132 28.0	11.7	13 52.9	9.3	56.6
18	93 53.3	S11 12.4	146 58.7	11.7	N13 43.6	9.4	56.5
19	108 53.4	13.3	161 29.4	11.7	13 34.2	9.4	56.5
20	123 53.5	14.1	176 00.1	11.9	13 24.8	9.5	56.5
21	138 53.5 ··	15.0	190 31.0	11.9	13 15.3	9.5	56.5
22	153 53.6	15.9	205 01.9	12.0	13 05.8	9.6	56.4
23	168 53.7	16.8	219 32.9	12.0	12 56.2	9.7	56.4
23 00	183 53.8	S11 17.7	234 03.9	12.1	N12 46.5	9.7	56.4
01	198 53.9	18.5	248 35.0	12.2	12 36.8	9.8	56.4
02	213 54.0	19.4	263 06.2	12.2	12 27.0	9.8	56.3
03	228 54.1 ··	20.3	277 37.4	12.3	12 17.2	9.8	56.3
04	243 54.2	21.2	292 08.7	12.4	12 07.4	10.0	56.3
05	258 54.3	22.0	306 40.1	12.4	11 57.4	9.9	56.3
06	273 54.3	S11 22.9	321 11.5	12.5	N11 47.5	10.0	56.3
07	288 54.4	23.8	335 43.0	12.5	11 37.5	10.1	56.2
08	303 54.5	24.7	350 14.5	12.6	11 27.4	10.1	56.2
F 09	318 54.6 ··	25.6	4 46.1	12.7	11 17.3	10.2	56.2
R 10	333 54.7	26.4	19 17.8	12.7	11 07.1	10.2	56.2
I 11	348 54.8	27.3	33 49.5	12.8	10 56.9	10.2	56.1
D 12	3 54.9	S11 28.2	48 21.3	12.8	N10 46.7	10.3	56.1
A 13	18 54.9	29.1	62 53.1	12.9	10 36.4	10.3	56.1
Y 14	33 55.0	29.9	77 25.0	12.9	10 26.1	10.4	56.1
15	48 55.1 ··	30.8	91 56.9	13.0	10 15.7	10.4	56.0
16	63 55.2	31.7	106 28.9	13.1	10 05.3	10.5	56.0
17	78 55.3	32.6	121 01.0	13.1	9 54.8	10.4	56.0
18	93 55.4	S11 33.4	135 33.1	13.2	N 9 44.4	10.6	56.0
19	108 55.4	34.3	150 05.3	13.2	9 33.8	10.5	56.0
20	123 55.5	35.2	164 37.5	13.3	9 23.3	10.6	55.9
21	138 55.6 ··	36.0	179 09.8	13.3	9 12.7	10.5	55.9
22	153 55.7	36.9	193 42.1	13.4	9 02.0	10.6	55.9
23	168 55.8	37.8	208 14.5	13.4	8 51.4	10.7	55.9
24 00	183 55.8	S11 38.7	222 46.9	13.5	N 8 40.7	10.7	55.8
01	198 55.9	39.5	237 19.4	13.5	8 30.0	10.8	55.8
02	213 56.0	40.4	251 51.9	13.6	8 19.2	10.8	55.8
03	228 56.1 ··	41.3	266 24.5	13.6	8 08.4	10.8	55.8
04	243 56.2	42.1	280 57.1	13.6	7 57.6	10.9	55.8
05	258 56.2	43.0	295 29.7	13.8	7 46.7	10.9	55.7
06	273 56.3	S11 43.9	310 02.5	13.7	N 7 35.8	10.9	55.7
07	288 56.4	44.8	324 35.2	13.8	7 24.9	10.9	55.7
S 08	303 56.5	45.6	339 08.0	13.8	7 14.0	10.9	55.7
A 09	318 56.6 ··	46.5	353 40.8	13.9	7 03.1	11.0	55.7
T 10	333 56.6	47.4	8 13.7	14.0	6 52.1	11.0	55.6
U 11	348 56.7	48.2	22 46.7	13.9	6 41.1	11.1	55.6
R 12	3 56.8	S11 49.1	37 19.6	14.0	N 6 30.0	11.0	55.6
D 13	18 56.9	50.0	51 52.6	14.1	6 19.0	11.1	55.6
A 14	33 56.9	50.8	66 25.7	14.1	6 07.9	11.1	55.6
Y 15	48 57.0 ··	51.7	80 58.8	14.1	5 56.8	11.1	55.5
16	63 57.1	52.6	95 31.9	14.2	5 45.7	11.1	55.5
17	78 57.2	53.4	110 05.1	14.2	5 34.6	11.1	55.5
18	93 57.3	S11 54.3	124 38.3	14.2	N 5 23.5	11.2	55.5
19	108 57.3	55.2	139 11.5	14.3	5 12.3	11.2	55.5
20	123 57.4	56.0	153 44.8	14.3	5 01.1	11.2	55.4
21	138 57.5 ··	56.9	168 18.1	14.3	4 49.9	11.2	55.4
22	153 57.5	57.8	182 51.4	14.4	4 38.7	11.2	55.4
23	168 57.6	58.6	197 24.8	14.4	4 27.5	11.2	55.4
	S.D. 16.1 d 0.9		S.D. 15.4	15.3			15.1

Lat.	Twilight Naut.	Civil	Sunrise	Moonrise 22	23	24	25
o	h m	h m	h m	h m	h m	h m	h m
N 72	05 29	06 48	08 04	23 26	25 25	01 25	03 14
N 70	05 29	06 40	07 47	23 51	25 38	01 38	03 19
68	05 29	06 34	07 34	24 09	00 09	01 48	03 23
66	05 28	06 28	07 23	24 24	00 24	01 57	03 27
64	05 28	06 23	07 14	24 36	00 36	02 04	03 29
62	05 28	06 19	07 06	24 46	00 46	02 10	03 32
60	05 27	06 16	06 59	24 55	00 55	02 16	03 34
N 58	05 26	06 12	06 53	25 03	01 03	02 20	03 36
56	05 26	06 09	06 48	25 10	01 10	02 24	03 38
54	05 25	06 06	06 43	00 02	01 16	02 28	03 40
52	05 24	06 04	06 38	00 09	01 21	02 32	03 41
50	05 24	06 01	06 35	00 16	01 26	02 35	03 42
45	05 22	05 56	06 26	00 30	01 36	02 41	03 45
N 40	05 20	05 51	06 19	00 42	01 45	02 47	03 47
35	05 17	05 47	06 13	00 51	01 52	02 52	03 49
30	05 15	05 43	06 07	01 00	01 59	02 56	03 51
20	05 09	05 35	05 58	01 15	02 10	03 03	03 54
N 10	05 03	05 28	05 49	01 28	02 20	03 09	03 57
0	04 55	05 20	05 41	01 40	02 29	03 15	04 00
S 10	04 46	05 11	05 33	01 52	02 38	03 21	04 02
20	04 35	05 01	05 24	02 05	02 48	03 27	04 05
30	04 20	04 49	05 14	02 20	02 59	03 35	04 08
35	04 10	04 42	05 08	02 28	03 05	03 39	04 10
40	03 59	04 33	05 01	02 38	03 13	03 43	04 12
45	03 44	04 22	04 53	02 49	03 21	03 49	04 14
S 50	03 26	04 09	04 43	03 03	03 31	03 55	04 17
52	03 17	04 02	04 39	03 09	03 36	03 58	04 18
54	03 06	03 55	04 34	03 16	03 41	04 01	04 20
56	02 54	03 47	04 29	03 24	03 46	04 05	04 21
58	02 40	03 38	04 23	03 33	03 53	04 09	04 23
S 60	02 23	03 28	04 16	03 43	04 00	04 13	04 25

Lat.	Sunset	Twilight Civil	Naut.	Moonset 22	23	24	25
o	h m	h m	h m	h m	h m	h m	h m
N 72	15 23	16 39	17 57	17 25	17 04	16 48	16 34
N 70	15 40	16 47	17 58	16 59	16 49	16 41	16 33
68	15 53	16 53	17 58	16 39	16 37	16 34	16 32
66	16 05	16 59	17 59	16 23	16 27	16 29	16 31
64	16 14	17 04	17 59	16 10	16 19	16 25	16 30
62	16 22	17 08	18 00	15 59	16 11	16 21	16 29
60	16 29	17 12	18 00	15 50	16 05	16 17	16 28
N 58	16 35	17 15	18 01	15 41	15 59	16 14	16 28
56	16 40	17 19	18 02	15 34	15 54	16 12	16 27
54	16 45	17 21	18 03	15 27	15 50	16 09	16 27
52	16 49	17 24	18 03	15 21	15 46	16 07	16 26
50	16 53	17 27	18 04	15 16	15 42	16 05	16 26
45	17 02	17 32	18 06	15 04	15 34	16 00	16 25
N 40	17 09	17 37	18 09	14 54	15 27	15 57	16 24
35	17 16	17 41	18 11	14 46	15 21	15 53	16 24
30	17 21	17 45	18 13	14 39	15 16	15 51	16 23
20	17 31	17 53	18 19	14 26	15 07	15 45	16 22
N 10	17 40	18 01	18 26	14 15	14 59	15 41	16 21
0	17 48	18 09	18 33	14 04	14 51	15 37	16 20
S 10	17 56	18 18	18 43	13 53	14 44	15 32	16 20
20	18 05	18 28	18 54	13 42	14 36	15 28	16 19
30	18 15	18 40	19 10	13 28	14 26	15 23	16 17
35	18 21	18 48	19 19	13 21	14 21	15 20	16 17
40	18 28	18 57	19 31	13 12	14 15	15 16	16 16
45	18 36	19 08	19 46	13 02	14 08	15 12	16 15
S 50	18 46	19 21	20 05	12 49	13 59	15 07	16 14
52	18 51	19 28	20 14	12 43	13 55	15 05	16 14
54	18 56	19 35	20 24	12 37	13 50	15 02	16 13
56	19 01	19 43	20 37	12 30	13 45	15 00	16 13
58	19 08	19 52	20 52	12 21	13 40	14 57	16 12
S 60	19 15	20 03	21 09	12 12	13 34	14 53	16 11

Day	SUN Eqn. of Time 00h	12h	Mer. Pass.	MOON Mer. Pass. Upper	Lower	Age	Phase
	m s	m s	h m	h m	h m	d	
22	15 26	15 31	11 44	07 52	20 17	24	
23	15 35	15 39	11 44	08 40	21 03	25	
24	15 43	15 47	11 44	09 26	21 48	26	◑

G.M.T.	ARIES G.H.A.	VENUS −3.9 G.H.A.	Dec.	MARS +1.6 G.H.A.	Dec.	JUPITER −1.2 G.H.A.	Dec.	SATURN +1.0 G.H.A.	Dec.	STARS Name	S.H.A.	Dec.
25 00	33 17.6	136 55.8 S25 56.2		238 28.6 N12 04.1		191 31.2 S 7 58.1		198 30.2 S 3 54.1		Acamar	315 36.2	S40 22.6
01	48 20.1	151 55.3	56.6	253 29.7	03.6	206 33.2	58.3	213 32.4	54.2	Achernar	335 44.1	S57 19.8
02	63 22.5	166 54.7	56.9	268 30.8	03.1	221 35.2	58.5	228 34.6	54.4	Acrux	173 37.1	S62 59.6
03	78 25.0	181 54.2 ··	57.3	283 31.9 ··	02.6	236 37.1 ··	58.7	243 36.8 ··	54.5	Adhara	255 31.4	S28 56.6
04	93 27.5	196 53.7	57.6	298 32.9	02.1	251 39.1	58.9	258 39.0	54.6	Aldebaran	291 16.9	N16 28.4
05	108 29.9	211 53.2	58.0	313 34.0	01.6	266 41.0	59.1	273 41.2	54.7			
06	123 32.4	226 52.6 S25 58.3		328 35.1 N12 01.1		281 43.0 S 7 59.3		288 43.4 S 3 54.8		Alioth	166 42.4	N56 03.6
07	138 34.9	241 52.1	58.7	343 36.1	00.6	296 44.9	59.5	303 45.6	54.9	Alkaid	153 18.4	N49 24.4
08	153 37.3	256 51.6	59.0	358 37.2	12 00.1	311 46.9	59.7	318 47.7	55.0	Al Na'ir	28 13.8	S47 03.2
S 09	168 39.8	271 51.1 ··	59.3	13 38.3	11 59.6	326 48.9	7 59.9	333 49.9 ··	55.1	Alnilam	276 10.7	S 1 12.7
U 10	183 42.3	286 50.5	25 59.7	28 39.4	59.1	341 50.8	8 00.1	348 52.1	55.2	Alphard	218 19.9	S 8 34.6
N 11	198 44.7	301 50.0	26 00.0	43 40.4	58.6	356 52.8	00.3	3 54.3	55.4			
D 12	213 47.2	316 49.5 S26 00.4		58 41.5 N11 58.1		11 54.7 S 8 00.5		18 56.5 S 3 55.5		Alphecca	126 31.8	N26 46.8
A 13	228 49.7	331 49.0	00.7	73 42.6	57.6	26 56.7	00.7	33 58.7	55.6	Alpheratz	358 08.3	N28 59.5
Y 14	243 52.1	346 48.4	01.1	88 43.7	57.1	41 58.6	00.9	49 00.9	55.7	Altair	62 31.9	N 8 49.3
15	258 54.6	1 47.9 ··	01.4	103 44.7 ··	56.6	57 00.6 ··	01.1	64 03.0 ··	55.8	Ankaa	353 39.1	S42 24.4
16	273 57.0	16 47.4	01.7	118 45.8	56.1	72 02.6	01.3	79 05.2	55.9	Antares	112 56.3	S26 23.4
17	288 59.5	31 46.9	02.1	133 46.9	55.6	87 04.5	01.5	94 07.4	56.0			
18	304 02.0	46 46.3 S26 02.4		148 48.0 N11 55.1		102 06.5 S 8 01.7		109 09.6 S 3 56.1		Arcturus	146 18.1	N19 16.8
19	319 04.4	61 45.8	02.7	163 49.0	54.6	117 08.4	01.9	124 11.8	56.3	Atria	108 20.3	S68 59.8
20	334 06.9	76 45.3	03.1	178 50.1	54.1	132 10.4	02.1	139 14.0	56.4	Avior	234 27.9	S59 26.7
21	349 09.4	91 44.8 ··	03.4	193 51.2 ··	53.6	147 12.3 ··	02.3	154 16.2 ··	56.5	Bellatrix	278 57.7	N 6 20.1
22	4 11.8	106 44.2	03.7	208 52.3	53.1	162 14.3	02.5	169 18.4	56.6	Betelgeuse	271 27.3	N 7 24.3
23	19 14.3	121 43.7	04.1	223 53.3	52.6	177 16.3	02.7	184 20.5	56.7			
26 00	34 16.8	136 43.2 S26 04.4		238 54.4 N11 52.1		192 18.2 S 8 02.9		199 22.7 S 3 56.8		Canopus	264 06.6	S52 40.9
01	49 19.2	151 42.7	04.7	253 55.5	51.6	207 20.2	03.1	214 24.9	56.9	Capella	281 09.9	N45 58.7
02	64 21.7	166 42.1	05.0	268 56.6	51.1	222 22.1	03.3	229 27.1	57.0	Deneb	49 47.9	N45 13.2
03	79 24.2	181 41.6 ··	05.4	283 57.6 ··	50.6	237 24.1 ··	03.5	244 29.3 ··	57.1	Denebola	182 58.6	N14 40.6
04	94 26.6	196 41.1	05.7	298 58.7	50.1	252 26.0	03.7	259 31.5	57.3	Diphda	349 19.8	S18 05.2
05	109 29.1	211 40.6	06.0	313 59.8	49.6	267 28.0	03.9	274 33.7	57.4			
06	124 31.5	226 40.0 S26 06.3		329 00.9 N11 49.1		282 30.0 S 8 04.1		289 35.9 S 3 57.5		Dubhe	194 21.6	N61 50.9
07	139 34.0	241 39.5	06.6	344 02.0	48.7	297 31.9	04.3	304 38.0	57.6	Elnath	278 42.9	N28 35.5
08	154 36.5	256 39.0	07.0	359 03.0	48.2	312 33.9	04.5	319 40.2	57.7	Eltanin	90 57.7	N51 29.8
M 09	169 38.9	271 38.5 ··	07.3	14 04.1 ··	47.7	327 35.8 ··	04.7	334 42.4 ··	57.8	Enif	34 10.7	N 9 47.6
O 10	184 41.4	286 38.0	07.6	29 05.2	47.2	342 37.8	04.9	349 44.6	57.9	Fomalhaut	15 50.4	S29 43.3
N 11	199 43.9	301 37.4	07.9	44 06.3	46.7	357 39.7	05.1	4 46.8	58.0			
D 12	214 46.3	316 36.9 S26 08.2		59 07.4 N11 46.2		12 41.7 S 8 05.3		19 49.0 S 3 58.1		Gacrux	172 28.5	S57 00.4
A 13	229 48.8	331 36.4	08.5	74 08.4	45.7	27 43.7	05.5	34 51.2	58.3	Gienah	176 17.5	S17 26.2
Y 14	244 51.3	346 35.9	08.8	89 09.5	45.2	42 45.6	05.7	49 53.4	58.4	Hadar	149 23.0	S60 16.9
15	259 53.7	1 35.3 ··	09.2	104 10.6 ··	44.7	57 47.6 ··	05.9	64 55.5 ··	58.5	Hamal	328 27.7	N23 22.6
16	274 56.2	16 34.8	09.5	119 11.7	44.2	72 49.5	06.1	79 57.7	58.6	Kaus Aust.	84 16.1	S34 23.7
17	289 58.6	31 34.3	09.8	134 12.8	43.7	87 51.5	06.3	94 59.9	58.7			
18	305 01.1	46 33.8 S26 10.1		149 13.8 N11 43.2		102 53.4 S 8 06.5		110 02.1 S 3 58.8		Kochab	137 20.2	N74 14.0
19	320 03.6	61 33.3	10.4	164 14.9	42.7	117 55.4	06.7	125 04.3	58.9	Markab	14 02.2	N15 06.5
20	335 06.0	76 32.7	10.7	179 16.0	42.2	132 57.4	06.9	140 06.5	59.0	Menkar	314 40.0	N 4 01.1
21	350 08.5	91 32.2 ··	11.0	194 17.1 ··	41.7	147 59.3 ··	07.1	155 08.7 ··	59.1	Menkent	148 36.6	S36 16.6
22	5 11.0	106 31.7	11.3	209 18.2	41.2	163 01.3	07.3	170 10.9	59.3	Miaplacidus	221 45.0	S69 38.2
23	20 13.4	121 31.2	11.6	224 19.2	40.7	178 03.2	07.5	185 13.0	59.4			
27 00	35 15.9	136 30.7 S26 11.9		239 20.3 N11 40.2		193 05.2 S 8 07.7		200 15.2 S 3 59.5		Mirfak	309 14.6	N49 47.7
01	50 18.4	151 30.1	12.2	254 21.4	39.7	208 07.2	07.9	215 17.4	59.6	Nunki	76 28.4	S26 19.2
02	65 20.8	166 29.6	12.5	269 22.5	39.2	223 09.1	08.1	230 19.6	59.7	Peacock	53 57.2	S56 47.9
03	80 23.3	181 29.1 ··	12.8	284 23.6 ··	38.7	238 11.1 ··	08.3	245 21.8 ··	59.8	Pollux	243 57.2	N28 04.2
04	95 25.8	196 28.6	13.1	299 24.7	38.2	253 13.0	08.5	260 24.0	3 59.9	Procyon	245 25.0	N 5 16.4
05	110 28.2	211 28.1	13.4	314 25.7	37.7	268 15.0	08.7	275 26.2	4 00.0			
06	125 30.7	226 27.5 S26 13.7		329 26.8 N11 37.2		283 16.9 S 8 08.9		290 28.4 S 4 00.1		Rasalhague	96 29.1	N12 34.6
07	140 33.1	241 27.0	14.0	344 27.9	36.7	298 18.9	09.1	305 30.6	00.3	Regulus	208 09.4	N12 03.5
08	155 35.6	256 26.5	14.3	359 29.0	36.2	313 20.9	09.3	320 32.7	00.4	Rigel	281 35.1	S 8 13.2
T 09	170 38.1	271 26.0 ··	14.6	14 30.1 ··	35.7	328 22.8 ··	09.5	335 34.9 ··	00.5	Rigil Kent.	140 25.5	S60 45.4
U 10	185 40.5	286 25.5	14.9	29 31.2	35.2	343 24.8	09.7	350 37.1	00.6	Sabik	102 40.5	S15 42.1
E 11	200 43.0	301 24.9	15.1	44 32.2	34.7	358 26.7	09.8	5 39.3	00.7			
S 12	215 45.5	316 24.4 S26 15.4		59 33.3 N11 34.2		13 28.7 S 8 10.0		20 41.5 S 4 00.8		Schedar	350 07.7	N56 26.3
D 13	230 47.9	331 23.9	15.7	74 34.4	33.7	28 30.6	10.2	35 43.7	00.9	Shaula	96 55.0	S37 05.5
A 14	245 50.4	346 23.4	16.0	89 35.5	33.2	43 32.6	10.4	50 45.9	01.0	Sirius	258 54.9	S16 41.3
Y 15	260 52.9	1 22.9 ··	16.3	104 36.6 ··	32.7	58 34.6 ··	10.6	65 48.1 ··	01.1	Spica	158 57.1	S11 03.8
16	275 55.3	16 22.3	16.6	119 37.7	32.2	73 36.5	10.8	80 50.2	01.3	Suhail	223 10.3	S43 21.2
17	290 57.8	31 21.8	16.9	134 38.8	31.7	88 38.5	11.0	95 52.4	01.4			
18	306 00.3	46 21.3 S26 17.1		149 39.8 N11 31.2		103 40.4 S 8 11.2		110 54.6 S 4 01.5		Vega	80 55.5	N38 46.3
19	321 02.7	61 20.8	17.4	164 40.9	30.7	118 42.4	11.4	125 56.8	01.6	Zuben'ubi	137 32.6	S15 57.8
20	336 05.2	76 20.3	17.7	179 42.0	30.2	133 44.3	11.6	140 59.0	01.7		S.H.A.	Mer. Pass.
21	351 07.6	91 19.8 ··	18.0	194 43.1 ··	29.7	148 46.3 ··	11.8	156 01.2 ··	01.8	Venus	102 26.4	14 54
22	6 10.1	106 19.2	18.2	209 44.2	29.2	163 48.3	12.0	171 03.4	01.9	Mars	204 37.7	8 04
23	21 12.6	121 18.7	18.5	224 45.3	28.7	178 50.2	12.2	186 05.6	02.0	Jupiter	158 01.5	11 09
Mer. Pass. 21 39.3		v −0.5 d 0.3		v 1.1 d 0.5		v 2.0 d 0.2		v 2.2 d 0.1		Saturn	165 06.0	10 41

G.M.T.	SUN G.H.A.	SUN Dec.	MOON G.H.A.	v	Dec.	d	H.P.
d h	° '	° '	° '	'	° '	'	'
25 00	183 57.7	S11 59.5	211 58.2	14.4	N 4 16.3	11.3	55.4
01	198 57.8	12 00.4	226 31.6	14.5	4 05.0	11.2	55.3
02	213 57.8	01.2	241 05.1	14.5	3 53.8	11.3	55.3
03	228 57.9	·· 02.1	255 38.6	14.5	3 42.5	11.2	55.3
04	243 58.0	03.0	270 12.1	14.6	3 31.3	11.3	55.3
05	258 58.1	03.8	284 45.7	14.6	3 20.0	11.3	55.3
06	273 58.1	S12 04.7	299 19.3	14.6	N 3 08.7	11.3	55.2
07	288 58.2	05.5	313 52.9	14.6	2 57.4	11.3	55.2
08	303 58.3	06.4	328 26.5	14.7	2 46.1	11.3	55.2
S 09	318 58.3	·· 07.3	343 00.2	14.7	2 34.8	11.4	55.2
U 10	333 58.4	08.1	357 33.9	14.7	2 23.4	11.3	55.2
N 11	348 58.5	09.0	12 07.6	14.7	2 12.1	11.3	55.2
D 12	3 58.6	S12 09.8	26 41.3	14.8	N 2 00.8	11.3	55.1
A 13	18 58.6	10.7	41 15.1	14.8	1 49.5	11.3	55.1
Y 14	33 58.7	11.6	55 48.9	14.8	1 38.2	11.4	55.1
15	48 58.8	·· 12.4	70 22.7	14.8	1 26.8	11.3	55.1
16	63 58.8	13.3	84 56.5	14.9	1 15.5	11.3	55.1
17	78 58.9	14.1	99 30.4	14.8	1 04.2	11.3	55.1
18	93 59.0	S12 15.0	114 04.2	14.9	N 0 52.9	11.4	55.0
19	108 59.0	15.9	128 38.1	14.9	0 41.5	11.3	55.0
20	123 59.1	16.7	143 12.0	14.9	0 30.2	11.3	55.0
21	138 59.2	·· 17.6	157 45.9	14.9	0 18.9	11.3	55.0
22	153 59.2	18.4	172 19.9	14.9	N 0 07.6	11.3	55.0
23	168 59.3	19.3	186 53.8	15.0	S 0 03.7	11.3	55.0
26 00	183 59.4	S12 20.2	201 27.8	15.0	S 0 15.0	11.3	54.9
01	198 59.4	21.0	216 01.8	14.9	0 26.3	11.3	54.9
02	213 59.5	21.9	230 35.7	15.0	0 37.6	11.3	54.9
03	228 59.6	·· 22.7	245 09.7	15.1	0 48.9	11.3	54.9
04	243 59.6	23.6	259 43.8	15.0	1 00.2	11.2	54.9
05	258 59.7	24.4	274 17.8	15.1	1 11.4	11.3	54.9
06	273 59.8	S12 25.3	288 51.8	15.1	S 1 22.7	11.2	54.9
07	288 59.8	26.1	303 25.9	15.0	1 33.9	11.3	54.8
08	303 59.9	27.0	317 59.9	15.1	1 45.2	11.2	54.8
M 09	319 00.0	·· 27.8	332 34.0	15.1	1 56.4	11.2	54.8
O 10	334 00.0	28.7	347 08.1	15.1	2 07.6	11.2	54.8
N 11	349 00.1	29.6	1 42.2	15.1	2 18.8	11.1	54.8
D 12	4 00.1	S12 30.4	16 16.3	15.0	S 2 29.9	11.2	54.8
A 13	19 00.2	31.3	30 50.3	15.1	2 41.1	11.1	54.7
Y 14	34 00.3	32.1	45 24.4	15.1	2 52.2	11.2	54.7
15	49 00.3	·· 33.0	59 58.5	15.2	3 03.4	11.1	54.7
16	64 00.4	33.8	74 32.7	15.1	3 14.5	11.1	54.7
17	79 00.4	34.7	89 06.8	15.1	3 25.6	11.0	54.7
18	94 00.5	S12 35.5	103 40.9	15.1	S 3 36.6	11.1	54.7
19	109 00.6	36.4	118 15.0	15.1	3 47.7	11.0	54.7
20	124 00.6	37.2	132 49.1	15.1	3 58.7	11.1	54.6
21	139 00.7	·· 38.1	147 23.2	15.2	4 09.8	10.9	54.6
22	154 00.7	38.9	161 57.4	15.1	4 20.7	11.0	54.6
23	169 00.8	39.8	176 31.5	15.1	4 31.7	11.0	54.6
27 00	184 00.9	S12 40.6	191 05.6	15.1	S 4 42.7	10.9	54.6
01	199 00.9	41.5	205 39.7	15.1	4 53.6	10.9	54.6
02	214 01.0	42.3	220 13.8	15.1	5 04.5	10.9	54.6
03	229 01.0	·· 43.2	234 47.9	15.1	5 15.4	10.8	54.6
04	244 01.1	44.0	249 22.0	15.1	5 26.2	10.8	54.5
05	259 01.1	44.9	263 56.1	15.1	5 37.0	10.8	54.5
06	274 01.2	S12 45.7	278 30.2	15.1	S 5 47.8	10.8	54.5
07	289 01.3	46.5	293 04.3	15.1	5 58.6	10.7	54.5
08	304 01.3	47.4	307 38.4	15.1	6 09.3	10.7	54.5
T 09	319 01.4	·· 48.2	322 12.5	15.0	6 20.0	10.7	54.5
U 10	334 01.4	49.1	336 46.5	15.1	6 30.7	10.7	54.5
E 11	349 01.5	49.9	351 20.6	15.1	6 41.4	10.6	54.5
S 12	4 01.5	S12 50.8	5 54.7	15.0	S 6 52.0	10.6	54.4
D 13	19 01.6	51.6	20 28.7	15.0	7 02.6	10.5	54.4
A 14	34 01.6	52.5	35 02.7	15.1	7 13.1	10.5	54.4
Y 15	49 01.7	·· 53.3	49 36.8	15.0	7 23.6	10.5	54.4
16	64 01.8	54.1	64 10.8	15.0	7 34.1	10.5	54.4
17	79 01.8	55.0	78 44.8	15.0	7 44.6	10.4	54.4
18	94 01.9	S12 55.8	93 18.8	14.9	S 7 55.0	10.4	54.4
19	109 01.9	56.7	107 52.7	15.0	8 05.4	10.3	54.4
20	124 02.0	57.5	122 26.7	15.0	8 15.7	10.3	54.4
21	139 02.0	58.4	137 00.7	14.9	8 26.0	10.3	54.3
22	154 02.1	12 59.2	151 34.6	14.9	8 36.3	10.2	54.3
23	169 02.1	13 00.0	166 08.5	14.9	8 46.5	10.2	54.3
	S.D. 16.1	d 0.9	S.D. 15.0		14.9		14.8

Lat.	Twilight Naut.	Civil	Sunrise	Moonrise 25	26	27	28
°	h m	h m	h m	h m	h m	h m	h m
N 72	05 41	07 02	08 21	03 14	04 59	06 43	08 30
N 70	05 40	06 52	08 01	03 19	04 57	06 34	08 13
68	05 39	06 44	07 46	03 23	04 55	06 27	07 59
66	05 37	06 38	07 33	03 27	04 54	06 21	07 48
64	05 36	06 32	07 23	03 29	04 53	06 16	07 38
62	05 35	06 27	07 14	03 32	04 52	06 11	07 30
60	05 34	06 23	07 07	03 34	04 51	06 08	07 23
N 58	05 33	06 19	07 00	03 36	04 51	06 04	07 17
56	05 32	06 15	06 54	03 38	04 50	06 01	07 12
54	05 30	06 12	06 49	03 40	04 50	05 59	07 07
52	05 29	06 09	06 44	03 41	04 49	05 56	07 03
50	05 28	06 06	06 39	03 42	04 49	05 54	06 59
45	05 25	06 00	06 30	03 45	04 48	05 49	06 51
N 40	05 23	05 54	06 22	03 47	04 47	05 45	06 44
35	05 20	05 49	06 15	03 49	04 46	05 42	06 38
30	05 17	05 45	06 09	03 51	04 45	05 39	06 32
20	05 10	05 36	05 59	03 54	04 44	05 34	06 23
N 10	05 03	05 28	05 49	03 57	04 44	05 30	06 16
0	04 55	05 19	05 41	04 00	04 43	05 25	06 08
S 10	04 45	05 10	05 32	04 02	04 42	05 21	06 01
20	04 33	04 59	05 22	04 05	04 41	05 17	05 53
30	04 16	04 46	05 11	04 08	04 40	05 12	05 44
35	04 06	04 38	05 04	04 10	04 40	05 09	05 39
40	03 54	04 28	04 57	04 12	04 39	05 06	05 34
45	03 39	04 17	04 48	04 14	04 38	05 02	05 27
S 50	03 19	04 03	04 38	04 17	04 37	04 58	05 19
52	03 09	03 56	04 33	04 18	04 37	04 56	05 16
54	02 58	03 48	04 27	04 20	04 37	04 54	05 12
56	02 44	03 39	04 21	04 21	04 36	04 51	05 07
58	02 29	03 30	04 15	04 23	04 36	04 49	05 03
S 60	02 09	03 18	04 07	04 25	04 35	04 46	04 57

Lat.	Sunset	Twilight Civil	Naut.	Moonset 25	26	27	28
°	h m	h m	h m	h m	h m	h m	h m
N 72	15 06	16 25	17 44	16 34	16 20	16 05	15 48
N 70	15 25	16 34	17 46	16 33	16 25	16 16	16 07
68	15 41	16 42	17 48	16 32	16 28	16 25	16 22
66	15 53	16 49	17 49	16 31	16 32	16 33	16 35
64	16 04	16 55	17 50	16 30	16 34	16 39	16 45
62	16 13	17 00	17 52	16 29	16 37	16 45	16 54
60	16 20	17 04	17 53	16 28	16 39	16 50	17 02
N 58	16 27	17 08	17 54	16 28	16 41	16 54	17 09
56	16 33	17 12	17 55	16 27	16 42	16 58	17 15
54	16 39	17 15	17 57	16 27	16 44	17 01	17 20
52	16 43	17 18	17 58	16 26	16 45	17 04	17 25
50	16 48	17 21	17 59	16 26	16 46	17 07	17 30
45	16 57	17 28	18 02	16 25	16 49	17 13	17 39
N 40	17 05	17 33	18 05	16 24	16 51	17 19	17 47
35	17 12	17 38	18 08	16 24	16 53	17 23	17 54
30	17 18	17 43	18 11	16 23	16 55	17 27	18 00
20	17 29	17 51	18 17	16 22	16 58	17 34	18 11
N 10	17 38	18 00	18 25	16 21	17 01	17 40	18 20
0	17 47	18 09	18 33	16 20	17 03	17 46	18 29
S 10	17 56	18 18	18 43	16 20	17 06	17 52	18 38
20	18 06	18 29	18 56	16 19	17 08	17 58	18 47
30	18 18	18 43	19 12	16 17	17 11	18 05	18 58
35	18 24	18 51	19 22	16 17	17 13	18 09	19 05
40	18 32	19 00	19 35	16 16	17 15	18 14	19 12
45	18 41	19 12	19 51	16 15	17 17	18 19	19 20
S 50	18 51	19 27	20 11	16 14	17 20	18 25	19 30
52	18 56	19 34	20 21	16 14	17 21	18 28	19 35
54	19 02	19 41	20 32	16 13	17 22	18 32	19 40
56	19 08	19 50	20 46	16 13	17 24	18 35	19 46
58	19 15	20 00	21 02	16 12	17 26	18 39	19 52
S 60	19 23	20 12	21 22	16 11	17 28	18 44	19 59

Day	SUN Eqn. of Time 00h	12h	Mer. Pass.	MOON Mer. Pass. Upper	Lower	Age	Phase
	m s	m s	h m	h m	h m	d	
25	15 51	15 54	11 44	10 10	22 32	27	
26	15 57	16 00	11 44	10 53	23 14	28	●
27	16 03	16 06	11 44	11 36	23 57	29	

G.M.T.	ARIES G.H.A.	VENUS −3.9 G.H.A.	Dec.	MARS +1.6 G.H.A.	Dec.	JUPITER −1.2 G.H.A.	Dec.	SATURN +1.0 G.H.A.	Dec.	STARS Name	S.H.A.	Dec.
28 00	36 15.0	136 18.2 S26 18.8		239 46.4 N11 28.2		193 52.2 S 8 12.4		201 07.8 S 4 02.1		Acamar	315 36.2	S40 22.6
01	51 17.5	151 17.7	19.1	254 47.4	27.7	208 54.1	12.6	216 09.9	02.3	Achernar	335 44.1	S57 19.9
02	66 20.0	166 17.2	19.3	269 48.5	27.2	223 56.1	12.8	231 12.1	02.4	Acrux	173 37.0	S62 59.6
03	81 22.4	181 16.7 ··	19.6	284 49.6 ··	26.7	238 58.1 ··	13.0	246 14.3 ··	02.5	Adhara	255 31.4	S28 56.6
04	96 24.9	196 16.2	19.9	299 50.7	26.2	254 00.0	13.2	261 16.5	02.6	Aldebaran	291 16.9	N16 28.4
05	111 27.4	211 15.6	20.1	314 51.8	25.7	269 02.0	13.4	276 18.7	02.7			
06	126 29.8	226 15.1 S26 20.4		329 52.9 N11 25.2		284 03.9 S 8 13.6		291 20.9 S 4 02.8		Alioth	166 42.4	N56 03.6
07	141 32.3	241 14.6	20.7	344 54.0	24.7	299 05.9	13.8	306 23.1	02.9	Alkaid	153 18.4	N49 24.4
W 08	156 34.7	256 14.1	20.9	359 55.1	24.2	314 07.8	14.0	321 25.3	03.0	Al Na'ir	28 13.8	S47 03.2
E 09	171 37.2	271 13.6 ··	21.2	14 56.2 ··	23.7	329 09.8 ··	14.2	336 27.5 ··	03.1	Alnilam	276 10.7	S 1 12.7
D 10	186 39.7	286 13.1	21.5	29 57.2	23.2	344 11.8	14.4	351 29.6	03.2	Alphard	218 19.9	S 8 34.6
N 11	201 42.1	301 12.5	21.7	44 58.3	22.7	359 13.7	14.6	6 31.8	03.4			
E 12	216 44.6	316 12.0 S26 22.0		59 59.4 N11 22.2		14 15.7 S 8 14.8		21 34.0 S 4 03.5		Alphecca	126 31.8	N26 46.8
S 13	231 47.1	331 11.5	22.3	75 00.5	21.7	29 17.6	15.0	36 36.2	03.6	Alpheratz	358 08.3	N28 59.5
D 14	246 49.5	346 11.0	22.5	90 01.6	21.2	44 19.6	15.2	51 38.4	03.7	Altair	62 31.9	N 8 49.3
A 15	261 52.0	1 10.5 ··	22.8	105 02.7 ··	20.7	59 21.5 ··	15.4	66 40.6 ··	03.8	Ankaa	353 39.1	S42 24.4
Y 16	276 54.5	16 10.0	23.0	120 03.8	20.2	74 23.5	15.6	81 42.8	03.9	Antares	112 56.3	S26 23.4
17	291 56.9	31 09.5	23.3	135 04.9	19.7	89 25.5	15.8	96 45.0	04.0			
18	306 59.4	46 09.0 S26 23.5		150 06.0 N11 19.2		104 27.4 S 8 16.0		111 47.2 S 4 04.1		Arcturus	146 18.1	N19 16.8
19	322 01.9	61 08.4	23.8	165 07.1	18.7	119 29.4	16.2	126 49.4	04.2	Atria	108 20.3	S68 59.8
20	337 04.3	76 07.9	24.0	180 08.1	18.2	134 31.3	16.4	141 51.5	04.3	Avior	234 27.9	S59 26.7
21	352 06.8	91 07.4 ··	24.3	195 09.2 ··	17.7	149 33.3 ··	16.6	156 53.7 ··	04.5	Bellatrix	278 57.7	N 6 20.1
22	7 09.2	106 06.9	24.5	210 10.3	17.2	164 35.3	16.8	171 55.9	04.6	Betelgeuse	271 27.3	N 7 24.3
23	22 11.7	121 06.4	24.8	225 11.4	16.7	179 37.2	17.0	186 58.1	04.7			
29 00	37 14.2	136 05.9 S26 25.0		240 12.5 N11 16.2		194 39.2 S 8 17.2		202 00.3 S 4 04.8		Canopus	264 06.6	S52 40.9
01	52 16.6	151 05.4	25.3	255 13.6	15.7	209 41.1	17.4	217 02.5	04.9	Capella	281 09.9	N45 58.7
02	67 19.1	166 04.9	25.5	270 14.7	15.2	224 43.1	17.5	232 04.7	05.0	Deneb	49 48.0	N45 13.2
03	82 21.6	181 04.4 ··	25.8	285 15.8 ··	14.7	239 45.0 ··	17.7	247 06.9 ··	05.1	Denebola	182 58.5	N14 40.6
04	97 24.0	196 03.8	26.0	300 16.9	14.2	254 47.0	17.9	262 09.1	05.2	Diphda	349 19.8	S18 05.2
05	112 26.5	211 03.3	26.3	315 18.0	13.7	269 49.0	18.1	277 11.2	05.3			
06	127 29.0	226 02.8 S26 26.5		330 19.1 N11 13.2		284 50.9 S 8 18.3		292 13.4 S 4 05.4		Dubhe	194 21.6	N61 50.9
07	142 31.4	241 02.3	26.7	345 20.2	12.7	299 52.9	18.5	307 15.6	05.6	Elnath	278 42.9	N28 35.5
T 08	157 33.9	256 01.8	27.0	0 21.3	12.2	314 54.8	18.7	322 17.8	05.7	Eltanin	90 57.7	N51 29.8
H 09	172 36.4	271 01.3 ··	27.2	15 22.4 ··	11.7	329 56.8 ··	18.9	337 20.0 ··	05.8	Enif	34 10.8	N 9 47.6
U 10	187 38.8	286 00.8	27.4	30 23.5	11.2	344 58.8	19.1	352 22.2	05.9	Fomalhaut	15 50.4	S29 43.3
R 11	202 41.3	301 00.3	27.7	45 24.6	10.7	0 00.7	19.3	7 24.4	06.0			
S 12	217 43.7	315 59.8 S26 27.9		60 25.6 N11 10.2		15 02.7 S 8 19.5		22 26.6 S 4 06.1		Gacrux	172 28.5	S57 00.4
D 13	232 46.2	330 59.3	28.1	75 26.7	09.7	30 04.6	19.7	37 28.8	06.2	Gienah	176 17.5	S17 26.2
A 14	247 48.7	345 58.8	28.4	90 27.8	09.2	45 06.6	19.9	52 31.0	06.3	Hadar	149 23.0	S60 16.9
Y 15	262 51.1	0 58.3 ··	28.6	105 28.9 ··	08.7	60 08.5 ··	20.1	67 33.1 ··	06.4	Hamal	328 27.7	N23 22.6
16	277 53.6	15 57.8	28.8	120 30.0	08.2	75 10.5	20.3	82 35.3	06.5	Kaus Aust.	84 16.1	S34 23.7
17	292 56.1	30 57.2	29.1	135 31.1	07.7	90 12.5	20.5	97 37.5	06.7			
18	307 58.5	45 56.7 S26 29.3		150 32.2 N11 07.2		105 14.4 S 8 20.7		112 39.7 S 4 06.8		Kochab	137 20.2	N74 14.0
19	323 01.0	60 56.2	29.5	165 33.3	06.7	120 16.4	20.9	127 41.9	06.9	Markab	14 02.2	N15 06.5
20	338 03.5	75 55.7	29.7	180 34.4	06.2	135 18.3	21.1	142 44.1	07.0	Menkar	314 40.0	N 4 01.1
21	353 05.9	90 55.2 ··	30.0	195 35.5 ··	05.7	150 20.3 ··	21.3	157 46.3 ··	07.1	Menkent	148 36.6	S36 16.6
22	8 08.4	105 54.7	30.2	210 36.6	05.2	165 22.3	21.5	172 48.5	07.2	Miaplacidus	221 45.0	S69 38.2
23	23 10.8	120 54.2	30.4	225 37.7	04.7	180 24.2	21.7	187 50.7	07.3			
30 00	38 13.3	135 53.7 S26 30.6		240 38.8 N11 04.2		195 26.2 S 8 21.9		202 52.9 S 4 07.4		Mirfak	309 14.6	N49 47.8
01	53 15.8	150 53.2	30.9	255 39.9	03.7	210 28.1	22.1	217 55.1	07.5	Nunki	76 28.4	S26 19.2
02	68 18.2	165 52.7	31.1	270 41.0	03.2	225 30.1	22.3	232 57.2	07.6	Peacock	53 57.2	S56 47.9
03	83 20.7	180 52.2 ··	31.3	285 42.1 ··	02.7	240 32.1 ··	22.5	247 59.4 ··	07.7	Pollux	243 57.2	N28 04.2
04	98 23.2	195 51.7	31.5	300 43.2	02.2	255 34.0	22.7	263 01.6	07.9	Procyon	245 24.9	N 5 16.4
05	113 25.6	210 51.2	31.7	315 44.3	01.7	270 36.0	22.9	278 03.8	08.0			
06	128 28.1	225 50.7 S26 31.9		330 45.4 N11 01.2		285 37.9 S 8 23.0		293 06.0 S 4 08.1		Rasalhague	96 29.1	N12 34.6
07	143 30.6	240 50.2	32.1	345 46.5	00.7	300 39.9	23.2	308 08.2	08.2	Regulus	208 09.3	N12 03.5
08	158 33.0	255 49.7	32.4	0 47.6	11 00.2	315 41.8	23.4	323 10.4	08.3	Rigel	281 35.1	S 8 13.3
F 09	173 35.5	270 49.2 ··	32.6	15 48.7	10 59.7	330 43.8 ··	23.6	338 12.6 ··	08.4	Rigil Kent.	140 25.5	S60 45.4
R 10	188 38.0	285 48.7	32.8	30 49.8	59.2	345 45.8	23.8	353 14.8	08.5	Sabik	102 40.5	S15 42.1
I 11	203 40.4	300 48.2	33.0	45 50.9	58.7	0 47.7	24.0	8 17.0	08.6			
D 12	218 42.9	315 47.7 S26 33.2		60 52.0 N10 58.1		15 49.7 S 8 24.2		23 19.2 S 4 08.7		Schedar	350 07.7	N56 26.3
A 13	233 45.3	330 47.2	33.4	75 53.1	57.6	30 51.6	24.4	38 21.3	08.8	Shaula	96 55.0	S37 05.5
Y 14	248 47.8	345 46.7	33.6	90 54.2	57.1	45 53.6	24.6	53 23.5	08.9	Sirius	258 54.9	S16 41.3
15	263 50.3	0 46.2 ··	33.8	105 55.3 ··	56.6	60 55.6 ··	24.8	68 25.7 ··	09.1	Spica	158 57.1	S11 03.8
16	278 52.7	15 45.7	34.0	120 56.4	56.1	75 57.5	25.0	83 27.9	09.2	Suhail	223 10.3	S43 21.2
17	293 55.2	30 45.2	34.2	135 57.5	55.6	90 59.5	25.2	98 30.1	09.3			
18	308 57.7	45 44.7 S26 34.4		150 58.6 N10 55.1		106 01.4 S 8 25.4		113 32.3 S 4 09.4		Vega	80 55.5	N38 46.3
19	324 00.1	60 44.2	34.6	165 59.7	54.6	121 03.4	25.6	128 34.5	09.5	Zuben'ubi	137 32.6	S15 57.8
20	339 02.6	75 43.7	34.8	181 00.8	54.1	136 05.4	25.8	143 36.7	09.6			
21	354 05.1	90 43.2 ··	35.0	196 01.9 ··	53.6	151 07.3 ··	26.0	158 38.9 ··	09.7		S.H.A.	Mer. Pass.
22	9 07.5	105 42.7	35.2	211 03.0	53.1	166 09.3	26.2	173 41.1	09.8	Venus	98 51.7	14 56
23	24 10.0	120 42.2	35.4	226 04.1	52.6	181 11.2	26.4	188 43.3	09.9	Mars	202 58.3	7 59
										Jupiter	157 25.0	11 00
Mer. Pass. 21 27.5		v −0.5 d 0.2		v 1.1 d 0.5		v 2.0 d 0.2		v 2.2 d 0.1		Saturn	164 46.1	10 30

G.M.T.	SUN G.H.A.	SUN Dec.	MOON G.H.A.	v	MOON Dec.	d	H.P.
28 00	184 02.2	S13 00.9	180 42.4	14.9	S 8 56.7	10.2	54.3
01	199 02.2	01.7	195 16.3	14.9	9 06.9	10.1	54.3
02	214 02.3	02.6	209 50.2	14.8	9 17.0	10.0	54.3
03	229 02.3 ..	03.4	224 24.0	14.9	9 27.0	10.1	54.3
04	244 02.4	04.2	238 57.9	14.8	9 37.1	10.0	54.3
05	259 02.4	05.1	253 31.7	14.8	9 47.1	9.9	54.3
06	274 02.5	S13 05.9	268 05.5	14.8	S 9 57.0	9.9	54.3
07	289 02.5	06.8	282 39.3	14.8	10 06.9	9.8	54.2
W 08	304 02.6	07.6	297 13.1	14.7	10 16.7	9.9	54.2
E 09	319 02.6 ..	08.4	311 46.8	14.7	10 26.6	9.7	54.2
D 10	334 02.7	09.3	326 20.5	14.8	10 36.3	9.7	54.2
N 11	349 02.7	10.1	340 54.3	14.6	10 46.0	9.7	54.2
E 12	4 02.8	S13 10.9	355 27.9	14.7	S10 55.7	9.6	54.2
S 13	19 02.8	11.8	10 01.6	14.7	11 05.3	9.6	54.2
D 14	34 02.8	12.6	24 35.3	14.6	11 14.9	9.5	54.2
A 15	49 02.9 ..	13.4	39 08.9	14.6	11 24.4	9.5	54.2
Y 16	64 02.9	14.3	53 42.5	14.6	11 33.9	9.4	54.2
17	79 03.0	15.1	68 16.1	14.5	11 43.3	9.4	54.2
18	94 03.0	S13 15.9	82 49.6	14.5	S11 52.7	9.3	54.2
19	109 03.1	16.8	97 23.1	14.5	12 02.0	9.3	54.1
20	124 03.1	17.6	111 56.6	14.5	12 11.3	9.2	54.1
21	139 03.2 ..	18.4	126 30.1	14.5	12 20.5	9.2	54.1
22	154 03.2	19.3	141 03.6	14.4	12 29.7	9.1	54.1
23	169 03.2	20.1	155 37.0	14.4	12 38.8	9.0	54.1
29 00	184 03.3	S13 20.9	170 10.4	14.4	S12 47.8	9.0	54.1
01	199 03.3	21.8	184 43.8	14.3	12 56.8	8.9	54.1
02	214 03.4	22.6	199 17.1	14.4	13 05.8	8.9	54.1
03	229 03.4 ..	23.4	213 50.5	14.3	13 14.7	8.8	54.1
04	244 03.5	24.3	228 23.8	14.2	13 23.5	8.8	54.1
05	259 03.5	25.1	242 57.0	14.3	13 32.3	8.7	54.1
06	274 03.5	S13 25.9	257 30.3	14.2	S13 41.0	8.6	54.1
07	289 03.6	26.8	272 03.5	14.2	13 49.6	8.6	54.1
T 08	304 03.6	27.6	286 36.7	14.1	13 58.2	8.6	54.1
H 09	319 03.7 ..	28.4	301 09.8	14.2	14 06.8	8.4	54.1
U 10	334 03.7	29.2	315 43.0	14.1	14 15.2	8.5	54.1
R 11	349 03.7	30.1	330 16.1	14.0	14 23.7	8.3	54.0
S 12	4 03.8	S13 30.9	344 49.1	14.1	S14 32.0	8.3	54.0
D 13	19 03.8	31.7	359 22.2	14.0	14 40.3	8.2	54.0
A 14	34 03.9	32.6	13 55.2	14.0	14 48.5	8.2	54.0
Y 15	49 03.9 ..	33.4	28 28.2	13.9	14 56.7	8.1	54.0
16	64 03.9	34.2	43 01.1	13.9	15 04.8	8.0	54.0
17	79 04.0	35.0	57 34.0	13.9	15 12.8	8.0	54.0
18	94 04.0	S13 35.9	72 06.9	13.9	S15 20.8	7.9	54.0
19	109 04.0	36.7	86 39.8	13.8	15 28.7	7.8	54.0
20	124 04.1	37.5	101 12.6	13.8	15 36.5	7.8	54.0
21	139 04.1 ..	38.3	115 45.4	13.7	15 44.3	7.7	54.0
22	154 04.1	39.2	130 18.1	13.8	15 52.0	7.6	54.0
23	169 04.2	40.0	144 50.9	13.7	15 59.6	7.6	54.0
30 00	184 04.2	S13 40.8	159 23.6	13.6	S16 07.2	7.4	54.0
01	199 04.3	41.6	173 56.2	13.7	16 14.6	7.5	54.0
02	214 04.3	42.5	188 28.9	13.6	16 22.1	7.3	54.0
03	229 04.3 ..	43.3	203 01.5	13.5	16 29.4	7.3	54.0
04	244 04.4	44.1	217 34.0	13.6	16 36.7	7.2	54.0
05	259 04.4	44.9	232 06.6	13.5	16 43.9	7.1	54.0
06	274 04.4	S13 45.7	246 39.1	13.4	S16 51.0	7.1	54.0
07	289 04.5	46.5	261 11.5	13.5	16 58.1	7.0	54.0
08	304 04.5	47.4	275 44.0	13.4	17 05.1	6.9	54.0
F 09	319 04.5 ..	48.2	290 16.4	13.3	17 12.0	6.8	54.0
R 10	334 04.6	49.0	304 48.7	13.4	17 18.8	6.8	54.0
I 11	349 04.6	49.8	319 21.1	13.3	17 25.6	6.7	54.0
D 12	4 04.6	S13 50.6	333 53.4	13.2	S17 32.3	6.6	54.0
A 13	19 04.7	51.5	348 25.6	13.3	17 38.9	6.5	54.0
Y 14	34 04.7	52.3	2 57.9	13.2	17 45.4	6.5	54.0
15	49 04.7 ..	53.1	17 30.1	13.1	17 51.9	6.3	54.0
16	64 04.7	53.9	32 02.2	13.2	17 58.2	6.3	54.0
17	79 04.8	54.7	46 34.4	13.1	18 04.5	6.3	54.0
18	94 04.8	S13 55.5	61 06.5	13.0	S18 10.8	6.1	54.0
19	109 04.8	56.4	75 38.5	13.1	18 16.9	6.1	54.0
20	124 04.9	57.2	90 10.6	13.0	18 23.0	5.9	54.0
21	139 04.9 ..	58.0	104 42.6	12.9	18 28.9	5.9	54.0
22	154 04.9	58.8	119 14.5	13.0	18 34.8	5.8	54.0
23	169 04.9	59.6	133 46.5	12.9	18 40.6	5.8	54.0
	S.D. 16.1	d 0.8	S.D. 14.8		14.7		14.7

Lat.	Twilight Naut.	Twilight Civil	Sunrise	Moonrise 28	29	30	31
N 72	05 54	07 15	08 38	08 30	10 27	13 07	■
N 70	05 51	07 04	08 15	08 13	09 55	11 47	■
68	05 48	06 55	07 58	07 59	09 33	11 09	12 47
66	05 46	06 47	07 44	07 48	09 15	10 42	12 07
64	05 44	06 40	07 32	07 38	09 00	10 22	11 40
62	05 42	06 35	07 23	07 30	08 49	10 06	11 19
60	05 41	06 30	07 14	07 23	08 38	09 52	11 02
N 58	05 39	06 25	07 07	07 17	08 30	09 40	10 48
56	05 37	06 21	07 00	07 12	08 22	09 30	10 36
54	05 36	06 17	06 54	07 07	08 15	09 21	10 25
52	05 34	06 14	06 49	07 03	08 09	09 13	10 16
50	05 33	06 11	06 44	06 59	08 03	09 06	10 07
45	05 29	06 04	06 34	06 51	07 51	08 51	09 49
N 40	05 26	05 58	06 25	06 44	07 42	08 39	09 35
35	05 22	05 52	06 18	06 38	07 33	08 28	09 23
30	05 19	05 47	06 11	06 32	07 26	08 19	09 12
20	05 11	05 37	06 00	06 23	07 13	08 03	08 54
N 10	05 03	05 28	05 50	06 16	07 02	07 50	08 38
0	04 54	05 19	05 40	06 08	06 52	07 37	08 23
S 10	04 44	05 09	05 31	06 01	06 42	07 24	08 08
20	04 31	04 57	05 20	05 53	06 31	07 10	07 52
30	04 13	04 43	05 08	05 44	06 19	06 55	07 34
35	04 02	04 34	05 01	05 39	06 11	06 46	07 24
40	03 49	04 24	04 53	05 34	06 03	06 36	07 12
45	03 33	04 12	04 44	05 27	05 54	06 24	06 58
S 50	03 12	03 56	04 32	05 19	05 43	06 10	06 41
52	03 01	03 49	04 27	05 16	05 38	06 03	06 33
54	02 49	03 41	04 21	05 12	05 32	05 55	06 24
56	02 35	03 32	04 14	05 07	05 26	05 47	06 14
58	02 17	03 21	04 07	05 03	05 19	05 38	06 02
S 60	01 56	03 08	03 59	04 57	05 11	05 27	05 49

Lat.	Sunset	Twilight Civil	Twilight Naut.	Moonset 28	29	30	31
N 72	14 48	16 11	17 32	15 48	15 23	14 17	■
N 70	15 11	16 22	17 37	16 07	15 55	15 38	■
68	15 28	16 31	17 37	16 22	16 19	16 17	16 15
66	15 42	16 39	17 40	16 35	16 38	16 44	16 55
64	15 54	16 46	17 42	16 45	16 53	17 05	17 22
62	16 04	16 52	17 44	16 54	17 06	17 22	17 44
60	16 12	16 57	17 46	17 02	17 17	17 36	18 01
N 58	16 20	17 01	17 48	17 09	17 26	17 48	18 16
56	16 26	17 06	17 49	17 15	17 34	17 58	18 28
54	16 32	17 09	17 51	17 20	17 42	18 08	18 39
52	16 38	17 13	17 52	17 25	17 48	18 16	18 49
50	16 42	17 16	17 54	17 30	17 54	18 23	18 57
45	16 53	17 23	17 58	17 39	18 07	18 39	19 16
N 40	17 02	17 29	18 01	17 47	18 18	18 52	19 31
35	17 09	17 35	18 05	17 54	18 27	19 04	19 43
30	17 16	17 40	18 08	18 00	18 36	19 13	19 55
20	17 27	17 50	18 16	18 11	18 50	19 30	20 14
N 10	17 37	17 59	18 24	18 20	19 02	19 45	20 30
0	17 47	18 08	18 33	18 29	19 13	19 59	20 46
S 10	17 57	18 19	18 44	18 38	19 25	20 13	21 01
20	18 08	18 30	18 57	18 47	19 37	20 28	21 18
30	18 20	18 45	19 15	18 58	19 52	20 45	21 37
35	18 27	18 54	19 26	19 05	20 00	20 55	21 48
40	18 35	19 04	19 39	19 12	20 09	21 06	22 01
45	18 45	19 17	19 56	19 20	20 20	21 19	22 16
S 50	18 56	19 32	20 18	19 30	20 34	21 36	22 35
52	19 02	19 40	20 28	19 35	20 40	21 44	22 44
54	19 08	19 48	20 41	19 40	20 47	21 52	22 54
56	19 15	19 58	20 55	19 46	20 55	22 02	23 05
58	19 22	20 09	21 13	19 52	21 04	22 13	23 18
S 60	19 31	20 21	21 36	19 59	21 14	22 26	23 33

Day	SUN Eqn. of Time 00h	12h	Mer. Pass.	MOON Mer. Pass. Upper	Lower	Age	Phase
	m s	m s	h m	h m	h m	d	
28	16 09	16 11	11 44	12 19	24 41	01	
29	16 13	16 15	11 44	13 03	00 41	02	●
30	16 17	16 18	11 44	13 48	01 25	03	

G.M.T.	ARIES G.H.A.	VENUS −4.0 G.H.A.	Dec.	MARS +1.6 G.H.A.	Dec.	JUPITER −1.2 G.H.A.	Dec.	SATURN +1.0 G.H.A.	Dec.	STARS Name	S.H.A.	Dec.
31 00	39 12.5	135 41.7	S26 35.6	241 05.2	N10 52.1	196 13.2	S 8 26.6	203 45.4	S 4 10.0	Acamar	315 36.2	S40 22.7
01	54 14.9	150 41.2	35.8	256 06.3	51.6	211 15.2	26.8	218 47.6	10.1	Achernar	335 44.1	S57 19.9
02	69 17.4	165 40.7	36.0	271 07.4	51.1	226 17.1	27.0	233 49.8	10.3	Acrux	173 37.0	S62 59.6
03	84 19.8	180 40.2 ··	36.2	286 08.5 ··	50.6	241 19.1 ··	27.2	248 52.0 ··	10.4	Adhara	255 31.4	S28 56.6
04	99 22.3	195 39.7	36.3	301 09.6	50.1	256 21.0	27.4	263 54.2	10.5	Aldebaran	291 16.8	N16 28.4
05	114 24.8	210 39.2	36.5	316 10.7	49.6	271 23.0	27.6	278 56.4	10.6			
06	129 27.2	225 38.7	S26 36.7	331 11.8	N10 49.1	286 24.9	S 8 27.7	293 58.6	S 4 10.7	Alioth	166 42.3	N56 03.5
07	144 29.7	240 38.2	36.9	346 12.9	48.6	301 26.9	27.9	309 00.8	10.8	Alkaid	153 18.4	N49 24.4
S 08	159 32.2	255 37.7	37.1	1 14.1	48.1	316 28.9	28.1	324 03.0	10.9	Al Na'ir	28 13.8	S47 03.2
A 09	174 34.6	270 37.2 ··	37.3	16 15.2 ··	47.6	331 30.8 ··	28.3	339 05.2 ··	11.0	Alnilam	276 10.7	S 1 12.7
T 10	189 37.1	285 36.7	37.5	31 16.3	47.1	346 32.8	28.5	354 07.4	11.1	Alphard	218 19.9	S 8 34.6
U 11	204 39.6	300 36.2	37.6	46 17.4	46.6	1 34.7	28.7	9 09.6	11.2			
R 12	219 42.0	315 35.7	S26 37.8	61 18.5	N10 46.1	16 36.7	S 8 28.9	24 11.7	S 4 11.3	Alphecca	126 31.8	N26 46.8
D 13	234 44.5	330 35.3	38.0	76 19.6	45.6	31 38.7	29.1	39 13.9	11.4	Alpheratz	358 08.3	N28 59.5
A 14	249 46.9	345 34.8	38.2	91 20.7	45.1	46 40.6	29.3	54 16.1	11.6	Altair	62 31.9	N 8 49.3
Y 15	264 49.4	0 34.3 ··	38.3	106 21.8 ··	44.6	61 42.6 ··	29.5	69 18.3 ··	11.7	Ankaa	353 39.1	S42 24.4
16	279 51.9	15 33.8	38.5	121 22.9	44.1	76 44.5	29.7	84 20.5	11.8	Antares	112 56.3	S26 23.4
17	294 54.3	30 33.3	38.7	136 24.0	43.6	91 46.5	29.9	99 22.7	11.9			
18	309 56.8	45 32.8	S26 38.9	151 25.1	N10 43.1	106 48.5	S 8 30.1	114 24.9	S 4 12.0	Arcturus	146 18.1	N19 16.8
19	324 59.3	60 32.3	39.0	166 26.2	42.6	121 50.4	30.3	129 27.1	12.1	Atria	108 20.3	S68 59.8
20	340 01.7	75 31.8	39.2	181 27.3	42.1	136 52.4	30.5	144 29.3	12.2	Avior	234 27.8	S59 26.7
21	355 04.2	90 31.3 ··	39.4	196 28.4 ··	41.6	151 54.3 ··	30.7	159 31.5 ··	12.3	Bellatrix	278 57.7	N 6 20.0
22	10 06.7	105 30.8	39.6	211 29.5	41.1	166 56.3	30.9	174 33.7	12.4	Betelgeuse	271 27.2	N 7 24.3
23	25 09.1	120 30.3	39.7	226 30.6	40.6	181 58.3	31.1	189 35.9	12.5			
1 00	40 11.6	135 29.9	S26 39.9	241 31.8	N10 40.1	197 00.2	S 8 31.3	204 38.1	S 4 12.6	Canopus	264 06.6	S52 40.9
01	55 14.1	150 29.4	40.1	256 32.9	39.6	212 02.2	31.5	219 40.2	12.7	Capella	281 09.8	N45 58.7
02	70 16.5	165 28.9	40.2	271 34.0	39.1	227 04.1	31.7	234 42.4	12.9	Deneb	49 48.0	N45 13.2
03	85 19.0	180 28.4 ··	40.4	286 35.1 ··	38.6	242 06.1 ··	31.8	249 44.6 ··	13.0	Denebola	182 58.5	N14 40.6
04	100 21.4	195 27.9	40.5	301 36.2	38.1	257 08.1	32.0	264 46.8	13.1	Diphda	349 19.8	S18 05.2
05	115 23.9	210 27.4	40.7	316 37.3	37.6	272 10.0	32.2	279 49.0	13.2			
06	130 26.4	225 26.9	S26 40.9	331 38.4	N10 37.1	287 12.0	S 8 32.4	294 51.2	S 4 13.3	Dubhe	194 21.6	N61 50.9
07	145 28.8	240 26.4	41.0	346 39.5	36.6	302 13.9	32.6	309 53.4	13.4	Elnath	278 42.9	N28 35.5
08	160 31.3	255 26.0	41.2	1 40.6	36.1	317 15.9	32.8	324 55.6	13.5	Eltanin	90 57.7	N51 29.8
S 09	175 33.8	270 25.5 ··	41.3	16 41.7 ··	35.6	332 17.9 ··	33.0	339 57.8 ··	13.6	Enif	34 10.8	N 9 47.6
U 10	190 36.2	285 25.0	41.5	31 42.9	35.1	347 19.8	33.2	355 00.0	13.7	Fomalhaut	15 50.4	S29 43.3
N 11	205 38.7	300 24.5	41.6	46 44.0	34.5	2 21.8	33.4	10 02.2	13.8			
D 12	220 41.2	315 24.0	S26 41.8	61 45.1	N10 34.0	17 23.7	S 8 33.6	25 04.4	S 4 13.9	Gacrux	172 28.4	S57 00.4
A 13	235 43.6	330 23.5	42.0	76 46.2	33.5	32 25.7	33.8	40 06.6	14.0	Gienah	176 17.5	S17 26.2
Y 14	250 46.1	345 23.1	42.1	91 47.3	33.0	47 27.7	34.0	55 08.8	14.1	Hadar	149 23.0	S60 16.9
15	265 48.6	0 22.6 ··	42.3	106 48.4 ··	32.5	62 29.6 ··	34.2	70 10.9 ··	14.3	Hamal	328 27.7	N23 22.6
16	280 51.0	15 22.1	42.4	121 49.5	32.0	77 31.6	34.4	85 13.1	14.4	Kaus Aust.	84 16.1	S34 23.7
17	295 53.5	30 21.6	42.5	136 50.6	31.5	92 33.5	34.6	100 15.3	14.5			
18	310 55.9	45 21.1	S26 42.7	151 51.7	N10 31.0	107 35.5	S 8 34.8	115 17.5	S 4 14.6	Kochab	137 20.2	N74 13.9
19	325 58.4	60 20.6	42.8	166 52.9	30.5	122 37.5	35.0	130 19.7	14.7	Markab	14 02.2	N15 06.5
20	341 00.9	75 20.2	43.0	181 54.0	30.0	137 39.4	35.2	145 21.9	14.8	Menkar	314 40.0	N 4 01.1
21	356 03.3	90 19.7 ··	43.1	196 55.1 ··	29.5	152 41.4 ··	35.3	160 24.1 ··	14.9	Menkent	148 36.5	S36 16.6
22	11 05.8	105 19.2	43.3	211 56.2	29.0	167 43.3	35.5	175 26.3	15.0	Miaplacidus	221 44.9	S69 38.2
23	26 08.3	120 18.7	43.4	226 57.3	28.5	182 45.3	35.7	190 28.5	15.1			
2 00	41 10.7	135 18.2	S26 43.5	241 58.4	N10 28.0	197 47.3	S 8 35.9	205 30.7	S 4 15.2	Mirfak	309 14.5	N49 47.8
01	56 13.2	150 17.8	43.7	256 59.5	27.5	212 49.2	36.1	220 32.9	15.3	Nunki	76 28.4	S26 19.2
02	71 15.7	165 17.3	43.8	272 00.7	27.0	227 51.2	36.3	235 35.1	15.4	Peacock	53 57.3	S56 47.9
03	86 18.1	180 16.8 ··	44.0	287 01.8 ··	26.5	242 53.1 ··	36.5	250 37.3 ··	15.5	Pollux	243 57.2	N28 04.2
04	101 20.6	195 16.3	44.1	302 02.9	26.0	257 55.1	36.7	265 39.5	15.7	Procyon	245 24.9	N 5 16.4
05	116 23.1	210 15.8	44.2	317 04.0	25.5	272 57.1	36.9	280 41.7	15.8			
06	131 25.5	225 15.4	S26 44.4	332 05.1	N10 25.0	287 59.0	S 8 37.1	295 43.9	S 4 15.9	Rasalhague	96 29.1	N12 34.6
07	146 28.0	240 14.9	44.5	347 06.2	24.5	303 01.0	37.3	310 46.0	16.0	Regulus	208 09.3	N12 03.5
08	161 30.4	255 14.4	44.6	2 07.3	24.0	318 02.9	37.5	325 48.2	16.1	Rigel	281 35.0	S 8 13.3
M 09	176 32.9	270 13.9 ··	44.8	17 08.5 ··	23.5	333 04.9 ··	37.7	340 50.4 ··	16.2	Rigil Kent.	140 25.5	S60 45.4
O 10	191 35.4	285 13.5	44.9	32 09.6	23.0	348 06.9	37.9	355 52.6	16.3	Sabik	102 40.6	S15 42.1
N 11	206 37.8	300 13.0	45.0	47 10.7	22.5	3 08.8	38.1	10 54.8	16.4			
D 12	221 40.3	315 12.5	S26 45.1	62 11.8	N10 22.0	18 10.8	S 8 38.3	25 57.0	S 4 16.5	Schedar	350 07.7	N56 26.4
A 13	236 42.8	330 12.0	45.3	77 12.9	21.5	33 12.8	38.5	40 59.2	16.6	Shaula	96 55.1	S37 05.5
Y 14	251 45.2	345 11.6	45.4	92 14.0	21.0	48 14.7	38.6	56 01.4	16.7	Sirius	258 54.9	S16 41.3
15	266 47.7	0 11.1 ··	45.5	107 15.2 ··	20.5	63 16.7 ··	38.8	71 03.6 ··	16.8	Spica	158 57.1	S11 03.8
16	281 50.2	15 10.6	45.6	122 16.3	20.0	78 18.6	39.0	86 05.8	16.9	Suhail	223 10.3	S43 21.2
17	296 52.6	30 10.2	45.8	137 17.4	19.5	93 20.6	39.2	101 08.0	17.0			
18	311 55.1	45 09.7	S26 45.9	152 18.5	N10 19.0	108 22.6	S 8 39.4	116 10.2	S 4 17.1	Vega	80 55.6	N38 46.3
19	326 57.5	60 09.2	46.0	167 19.6	18.5	123 24.5	39.6	131 12.4	17.2	Zuben'ubi	137 32.6	S15 57.8
20	342 00.0	75 08.7	46.1	182 20.7	17.9	138 26.5	39.8	146 14.6	17.4		S.H.A.	Mer. Pass.
21	357 02.5	90 08.3 ··	46.2	197 21.9 ··	17.4	153 28.4 ··	40.0	161 16.8 ··	17.5		° ′	h m
22	12 04.9	105 07.8	46.3	212 23.0	16.9	168 30.4	40.2	176 19.0	17.6	Venus	95 18.3	14 58
23	27 07.4	120 07.3	46.5	227 24.1	16.4	183 32.4	40.4	191 21.2	17.7	Mars	201 20.2	7 53
	h m									Jupiter	156 48.6	10 51
Mer. Pass. 21 15.7		v −0.5	d 0.2	v 1.1	d 0.5	v 2.0	d 0.2	v 2.2	d 0.1	Saturn	164 26.5	10 20

SUN / MOON

G.M.T.	SUN G.H.A.	Dec.	MOON G.H.A.	v	Dec.	d	H.P.
31 00	184 05.0	S14 00.4	148 18.4	12.8	S18 46.4	5.6	54.0
01	199 05.0	01.2	162 50.2	12.9	18 52.0	5.6	54.0
02	214 05.0	02.1	177 22.1	12.7	18 57.6	5.5	54.0
03	229 05.0 ··	02.9	191 53.8	12.8	19 03.1	5.4	54.0
04	244 05.1	03.7	206 25.6	12.7	19 08.5	5.3	54.0
05	259 05.1	04.5	220 57.3	12.7	19 13.8	5.2	54.0
06	274 05.1	S14 05.3	235 29.0	12.7	S19 19.0	5.2	54.0
07	289 05.1	·06.1	250 00.7	12.6	19 24.2	5.0	54.0
S 08	304 05.2	06.9	264 32.3	12.6	19 29.2	5.0	54.0
A 09	319 05.2 ··	07.7	279 03.9	12.6	19 34.2	4.9	54.0
T 10	334 05.2	08.5	293 35.5	12.5	19 39.1	4.8	54.0
U 11	349 05.2	09.4	308 07.0	12.5	19 43.9	4.7	54.0
R 12	4 05.3	S14 10.2	322 38.5	12.5	S19 48.6	4.6	54.0
D 13	19 05.3	11.0	337 10.0	12.4	19 53.2	4.5	54.0
A 14	34 05.3	11.8	351 41.4	12.4	19 57.7	4.5	54.0
Y 15	49 05.3 ··	12.6	6 12.8	12.4	20 02.2	4.3	54.0
16	64 05.3	13.4	20 44.2	12.4	20 06.5	4.3	54.0
17	79 05.4	14.2	35 15.6	12.3	20 10.8	4.2	54.0
18	94 05.4	S14 15.0	49 46.9	12.2	S20 15.0	4.1	54.0
19	109 05.4	15.8	64 18.1	12.3	20 19.1	3.9	54.0
20	124 05.4	16.6	78 49.4	12.2	20 23.0	3.9	54.0
21	139 05.5 ··	17.4	93 20.6	12.2	20 26.9	3.8	54.1
22	154 05.5	18.2	107 51.8	12.2	20 30.7	3.8	54.1
23	169 05.5	19.0	122 23.0	12.1	20 34.5	3.6	54.1
1 00	184 05.5	S14 19.8	136 54.1	12.1	S20 38.1	3.5	54.1
01	199 05.5	20.6	151 25.2	12.1	20 41.6	3.4	54.1
02	214 05.5	21.5	165 56.3	12.0	20 45.0	3.4	54.1
03	229 05.6 ··	22.3	180 27.3	12.0	20 48.4	3.2	54.1
04	244 05.6	23.1	194 58.3	12.0	20 51.6	3.2	54.1
05	259 05.6	23.9	209 29.3	11.9	20 54.8	3.0	54.1
06	274 05.6	S14 24.7	224 00.2	12.0	S20 57.8	3.0	54.1
07	289 05.6	25.5	238 31.2	11.9	21 00.8	2.8	54.1
08	304 05.7	26.3	253 02.1	11.8	21 03.6	2.8	54.1
S 09	319 05.7 ··	27.1	267 32.9	11.9	21 06.4	2.7	54.1
U 10	334 05.7	27.9	282 03.8	11.8	21 09.1	2.6	54.2
N 11	349 05.7	28.7	296 34.6	11.8	21 11.7	2.4	54.2
D 12	4 05.7	S14 29.5	311 05.4	11.8	S21 14.1	2.4	54.2
A 13	19 05.7	30.3	325 36.2	11.7	21 16.5	2.3	54.2
Y 14	34 05.7	31.1	340 06.9	11.7	21 18.8	2.2	54.2
15	49 05.8 ··	31.9	354 37.6	11.7	21 21.0	2.1	54.2
16	64 05.8	32.7	9 08.3	11.7	21 23.1	1.9	54.2
17	79 05.8	33.5	23 39.0	11.6	21 25.0	1.9	54.2
18	94 05.8	S14 34.3	38 09.6	11.7	S21 26.9	1.8	54.2
19	109 05.8	35.0	52 40.3	11.6	21 28.7	1.7	54.2
20	124 05.8	35.8	67 10.9	11.5	21 30.4	1.6	54.3
21	139 05.8 ··	36.6	81 41.4	11.6	21 32.0	1.5	54.3
22	154 05.9	37.4	96 12.0	11.5	21 33.5	1.4	54.3
23	169 05.9	38.2	110 42.5	11.5	21 34.9	1.2	54.3
2 00	184 05.9	S14 39.0	125 13.0	11.5	S21 36.1	1.2	54.3
01	199 05.9	39.8	139 43.5	11.5	21 37.3	1.1	54.3
02	214 05.9	40.6	154 14.0	11.4	21 38.4	1.0	54.3
03	229 05.9 ··	41.4	168 44.4	11.4	21 39.4	0.9	54.3
04	244 05.9	42.2	183 14.8	11.4	21 40.3	0.7	54.4
05	259 05.9	43.0	197 45.2	11.4	21 41.0	0.7	54.4
06	274 05.9	S14 43.8	212 15.6	11.4	S21 41.7	0.6	54.4
07	289 05.9	44.6	226 46.0	11.3	21 42.3	0.5	54.4
08	304 05.9	45.4	241 16.3	11.4	21 42.8	0.3	54.4
M 09	319 05.9 ··	46.2	255 46.7	11.3	21 43.1	0.3	54.4
O 10	334 06.0	46.9	270 17.0	11.3	21 43.4	0.1	54.4
N 11	349 06.0	47.7	284 47.3	11.3	21 43.5	0.1	54.5
D 12	4 06.0	S14 48.5	299 17.6	11.2	S21 43.6	0.0	54.5
A 13	19 06.0	49.3	313 47.8	11.3	21 43.6	0.2	54.5
Y 14	34 06.0	50.1	328 18.1	11.2	21 43.4	0.2	54.5
15	49 06.0 ··	50.9	342 48.3	11.2	21 43.2	0.4	54.5
16	64 06.0	51.7	357 18.5	11.2	21 42.8	0.5	54.5
17	79 06.0	52.5	11 48.7	11.2	21 42.3	0.5	54.6
18	94 06.0	S14 53.3	26 18.9	11.2	S21 41.8	0.7	54.6
19	109 06.0	54.0	40 49.1	11.1	21 41.1	0.8	54.6
20	124 06.0	54.8	55 19.2	11.2	21 40.3	0.8	54.6
21	139 06.0 ··	55.6	69 49.4	11.1	21 39.5	1.0	54.6
22	154 06.0	56.4	84 19.5	11.2	21 38.5	1.1	54.6
23	169 06.0	57.2	98 49.7	11.1	21 37.4	1.2	54.7
S.D.	16.1	d 0.8	S.D. 14.7		14.8		14.8

Twilight / Sunrise / Moonrise

Lat.	Naut.	Civil	Sunrise	Moonrise 31	1	2	3
N 72	06 06	07 29	08 56	■■	■■	■■	■■
N 70	06 02	07 16	08 30	■■	■■	■■	■■
68	05 58	07 05	08 10	12 47	14 25	15 38	15 52
66	05 55	06 56	07 55	12 07	13 25	14 24	14 59
64	05 52	06 49	07 42	11 40	12 51	13 47	14 27
62	05 50	06 42	07 31	11 19	12 26	13 21	14 03
60	05 47	06 37	07 22	11 02	12 06	13 01	13 44
N 58	05 45	06 32	07 14	10 48	11 50	12 44	13 28
56	05 43	06 27	07 07	10 36	11 36	12 30	13 14
54	05 41	06 23	07 00	10 25	11 24	12 17	13 03
52	05 39	06 19	06 55	10 16	11 14	12 06	12 52
50	05 37	06 15	06 49	10 07	11 05	11 57	12 43
45	05 33	06 08	06 38	09 49	10 45	11 37	12 23
N 40	05 29	06 01	06 29	09 35	10 29	11 20	12 08
35	05 25	05 55	06 21	09 23	10 16	11 06	11 54
30	05 21	05 49	06 14	09 12	10 04	10 54	11 42
20	05 13	05 39	06 01	08 54	09 44	10 34	11 22
N 10	05 04	05 29	05 51	08 38	09 27	10 16	11 05
0	04 54	05 19	05 40	08 23	09 11	09 59	10 49
S 10	04 43	05 08	05 30	08 08	08 54	09 43	10 32
20	04 29	04 56	05 18	07 52	08 37	09 25	10 15
30	04 10	04 40	05 06	07 34	08 17	09 04	09 55
35	03 59	04 31	04 58	07 24	08 06	08 52	09 43
40	03 45	04 20	04 49	07 12	07 53	08 39	09 30
45	03 27	04 07	04 39	06 58	07 37	08 22	09 14
S 50	03 05	03 51	04 27	06 41	07 18	08 02	08 54
52	02 53	03 43	04 21	06 33	07 09	07 53	08 45
54	02 40	03 34	04 15	06 24	06 59	07 42	08 34
56	02 25	03 24	04 08	06 14	06 48	07 30	08 23
58	02 05	03 12	04 00	06 02	06 34	07 16	08 09
S 60	01 41	02 59	03 50	05 49	06 19	07 00	07 53

Sunset / Twilight / Moonset

Lat.	Sunset	Civil	Naut.	Moonset 31	1	2	3
N 72	14 30	15 57	17 20	■■	■■	■■	■■
N 70	14 56	16 10	17 24	■■	■■	■■	■■
68	15 16	16 21	17 28	16 15	16 16	16 45	18 15
66	15 31	16 30	17 31	16 55	17 17	17 59	19 07
64	15 44	16 37	17 34	17 22	17 51	18 36	19 39
62	15 55	16 44	17 36	17 44	18 16	19 02	20 03
60	16 04	16 50	17 39	18 01	18 36	19 22	20 21
N 58	16 13	16 55	17 41	18 16	18 52	19 39	20 37
56	16 20	16 59	17 43	18 28	19 06	19 53	20 50
54	16 26	17 04	17 45	18 39	19 18	20 05	21 02
52	16 32	17 07	17 47	18 49	19 28	20 16	21 12
50	16 37	17 11	17 49	18 57	19 38	20 26	21 21
45	16 48	17 19	17 54	19 16	19 58	20 46	21 40
N 40	16 58	17 26	17 58	19 31	20 14	21 02	21 56
35	17 06	17 32	18 02	19 43	20 28	21 16	22 09
30	17 13	17 38	18 06	19 55	20 39	21 28	22 20
20	17 26	17 48	18 14	20 14	21 00	21 49	22 40
N 10	17 37	17 58	18 23	20 30	21 17	22 06	22 57
0	17 47	18 08	18 33	20 46	21 34	22 23	23 13
S 10	17 58	18 18	18 45	21 01	21 50	22 40	23 28
20	18 09	18 32	18 59	21 18	22 08	22 57	23 45
30	18 22	18 47	19 18	21 37	22 28	23 18	24 04
35	18 30	18 57	19 29	21 48	22 40	23 30	24 16
40	18 39	19 08	19 43	22 01	22 54	23 43	24 28
45	18 49	19 21	20 01	22 16	23 10	23 59	24 44
S 50	19 02	19 38	20 24	22 35	23 30	24 19	00 19
52	19 07	19 46	20 36	22 44	23 39	24 29	00 29
54	19 14	19 55	20 49	22 54	23 50	24 39	00 39
56	19 21	20 05	21 05	23 05	24 02	00 02	00 51
58	19 29	20 17	21 25	23 18	24 16	00 16	01 05
S 60	19 39	20 31	21 51	23 33	24 32	00 32	01 21

SUN / MOON

Day	Eqn. of Time 00ʰ	12ʰ	Mer. Pass.	Mer. Pass. Upper	Lower	Age	Phase
	m s	m s	h m	h m	h m	d	
31	16 20	16 21	11 44	14 34	02 11	04	
1	16 22	16 23	11 44	15 22	02 58	05	
2	16 23	16 24	11 44	16 11	03 47	06	◑

G.M.T.	ARIES G.H.A.	VENUS −4.0 G.H.A.	Dec.	MARS +1.6 G.H.A.	Dec.	JUPITER −1.2 G.H.A.	Dec.	SATURN +1.0 G.H.A.	Dec.	STARS Name	S.H.A.	Dec.
3 00	42 09.9	135 06.9	S26 46.6	242 25.2	N10 15.9	198 34.3	S 8 40.6	206 23.3	S 4 17.8	Acamar	315 36.2	S40 22.7
01	57 12.3	150 06.4	46.7	257 26.3	15.4	213 36.3	40.8	221 25.5	17.9	Achernar	335 44.1	S57 19.9
02	72 14.8	165 05.9	46.8	272 27.5	14.9	228 38.2	41.0	236 27.7	18.0	Acrux	173 37.0	S62 59.6
03	87 17.3	180 05.5	·· 46.9	287 28.6	·· 14.4	243 40.2	·· 41.2	251 29.9	·· 18.1	Adhara	255 31.3	S28 56.6
04	102 19.7	195 05.0	47.0	302 29.7	13.9	258 42.2	41.4	266 32.1	18.2	Aldebaran	291 16.8	N16 28.4
05	117 22.2	210 04.5	47.1	317 30.8	13.4	273 44.1	41.5	281 34.3	18.3			
06	132 24.7	225 04.1	S26 47.2	332 31.9	N10 12.9	288 46.1	S 8 41.7	296 36.5	S 4 18.4	Alioth	166 42.3	N56 03.5
07	147 27.1	240 03.6	47.3	347 33.1	12.4	303 48.1	41.9	311 38.7	18.5	Alkaid	153 18.4	N49 24.3
T 08	162 29.6	255 03.1	47.4	2 34.2	11.9	318 50.0	42.1	326 40.9	18.6	Al Na'ir	28 13.8	S47 03.2
U 09	177 32.0	270 02.7	·· 47.5	17 35.3	·· 11.4	333 52.0	·· 42.3	341 43.1	·· 18.7	Alnilam	276 10.6	S 1 12.7
E 10	192 34.5	285 02.2	47.6	32 36.4	10.9	348 53.9	42.5	356 45.3	18.9	Alphard	218 19.9	S 8 34.6
S 11	207 37.0	300 01.7	47.7	47 37.5	10.4	3 55.9	42.7	11 47.5	19.0			
D 12	222 39.4	315 01.3	S26 47.8	62 38.7	N10 09.9	18 57.9	S 8 42.9	26 49.7	S 4 19.1	Alphecca	126 31.8	N26 46.7
A 13	237 41.9	330 00.8	47.9	77 39.8	09.4	33 59.8	43.1	41 51.9	19.2	Alpheratz	358 08.3	N28 59.5
Y 14	252 44.4	345 00.3	48.0	92 40.9	08.9	49 01.8	43.3	56 54.1	19.3	Altair	62 31.9	N 8 49.3
15	267 46.8	359 59.9	·· 48.1	107 42.0	·· 08.4	64 03.7	·· 43.5	71 56.3	·· 19.4	Ankaa	353 39.1	S42 24.5
16	282 49.3	14 59.4	48.2	122 43.1	07.9	79 05.7	43.7	86 58.5	19.5	Antares	112 56.3	S26 23.4
17	297 51.8	29 59.0	48.3	137 44.3	07.4	94 07.7	43.9	102 00.7	19.6			
18	312 54.2	44 58.5	S26 48.4	152 45.4	N10 06.9	109 09.6	S 8 44.1	117 02.9	S 4 19.7	Arcturus	146 18.1	N19 16.8
19	327 56.7	59 58.0	48.5	167 46.5	06.4	124 11.6	44.3	132 05.1	19.8	Atria	108 20.3	S68 59.8
20	342 59.2	74 57.6	48.6	182 47.6	05.9	139 13.6	44.4	147 07.3	19.9	Avior	234 27.8	S59 26.7
21	358 01.6	89 57.1	·· 48.7	197 48.8	·· 05.4	154 15.5	·· 44.6	162 09.4	·· 20.0	Bellatrix	278 57.7	N 6 20.0
22	13 04.1	104 56.7	48.8	212 49.9	04.9	169 17.5	44.8	177 11.6	20.1	Betelgeuse	271 27.2	N 7 24.3
23	28 06.5	119 56.2	48.8	227 51.0	04.4	184 19.4	45.0	192 13.8	20.2			
4 00	43 09.0	134 55.7	S26 48.9	242 52.1	N10 03.9	199 21.4	S 8 45.2	207 16.0	S 4 20.3	Canopus	264 06.5	S52 40.9
01	58 11.5	149 55.3	49.0	257 53.3	03.4	214 23.4	45.4	222 18.2	20.4	Capella	281 09.8	N45 58.7
02	73 13.9	164 54.8	49.1	272 54.4	02.8	229 25.3	45.6	237 20.4	20.6	Deneb	49 48.0	N45 13.2
03	88 16.4	179 54.4	·· 49.2	287 55.5	·· 02.3	244 27.3	·· 45.8	252 22.6	·· 20.7	Denebola	182 58.5	N14 40.6
04	103 18.9	194 53.9	49.3	302 56.6	01.8	259 29.2	46.0	267 24.8	20.8	Diphda	349 19.8	S18 05.3
05	118 21.3	209 53.5	49.3	317 57.8	01.3	274 31.2	46.2	282 27.0	20.9			
06	133 23.8	224 53.0	S26 49.4	332 58.9	N10 00.8	289 33.2	S 8 46.4	297 29.2	S 4 21.0	Dubhe	194 21.5	N61 50.8
07	148 26.3	239 52.6	49.5	348 00.0	10 00.3	304 35.1	46.6	312 31.4	21.1	Elnath	278 42.9	N28 35.5
W 08	163 28.7	254 52.1	49.6	3 01.1	9 59.8	319 37.1	46.8	327 33.6	21.2	Eltanin	90 57.8	N51 29.7
E 09	178 31.2	269 51.7	·· 49.7	18 02.3	·· 59.3	334 39.1	·· 46.9	342 35.8	·· 21.3	Enif	34 10.8	N 9 47.6
D 10	193 33.6	284 51.2	49.7	33 03.4	58.8	349 41.0	47.1	357 38.0	21.4	Fomalhaut	15 50.4	S29 43.3
N 11	208 36.1	299 50.7	49.8	48 04.5	58.3	4 43.0	47.3	12 40.2	21.5			
E 12	223 38.6	314 50.3	S26 49.9	63 05.6	N 9 57.8	19 44.9	S 8 47.5	27 42.4	S 4 21.6	Gacrux	172 28.4	S57 00.4
S 13	238 41.0	329 49.8	49.9	78 06.8	57.3	34 46.9	47.7	42 44.6	21.7	Gienah	176 17.5	S17 26.2
D 14	253 43.5	344 49.4	50.0	93 07.9	56.8	49 48.9	47.9	57 46.8	21.8	Hadar	149 22.9	S60 16.9
A 15	268 46.0	359 48.9	·· 50.1	108 09.0	·· 56.3	64 50.8	·· 48.1	72 49.0	·· 21.9	Hamal	328 27.7	N23 22.6
Y 16	283 48.4	14 48.5	50.2	123 10.1	55.8	79 52.8	48.3	87 51.2	22.0	Kaus Aust.	84 16.1	S34 23.7
17	298 50.9	29 48.0	50.2	138 11.3	55.3	94 54.8	48.5	102 53.4	22.1			
18	313 53.4	44 47.6	S26 50.3	153 12.4	N 9 54.8	109 56.7	S 8 48.7	117 55.6	S 4 22.2	Kochab	137 20.2	N74 13.9
19	328 55.8	59 47.2	50.4	168 13.5	54.3	124 58.7	48.9	132 57.8	22.4	Markab	14 02.2	N15 06.5
20	343 58.3	74 46.7	50.4	183 14.7	53.8	140 00.6	49.1	148 00.0	22.5	Menkar	314 40.0	N 4 01.1
21	359 00.8	89 46.3	·· 50.5	198 15.8	·· 53.3	155 02.6	·· 49.3	163 02.2	·· 22.6	Menkent	148 36.5	S36 16.6
22	14 03.2	104 45.8	50.5	213 16.9	52.8	170 04.6	49.4	178 04.4	22.7	Miaplacidus	221 44.9	S69 38.2
23	29 05.7	119 45.4	50.6	228 18.0	52.3	185 06.5	49.6	193 06.6	22.8			
5 00	44 08.1	134 44.9	S26 50.7	243 19.2	N 9 51.8	200 08.5	S 8 49.8	208 08.7	S 4 22.9	Mirfak	309 14.5	N49 47.8
01	59 10.6	149 44.5	50.7	258 20.3	51.3	215 10.5	50.0	223 10.9	23.0	Nunki	76 28.4	S26 19.2
02	74 13.1	164 44.0	50.8	273 21.4	50.8	230 12.4	50.2	238 13.1	23.1	Peacock	53 57.3	S56 47.9
03	89 15.5	179 43.6	·· 50.8	288 22.6	·· 50.3	245 14.4	·· 50.4	253 15.3	·· 23.2	Pollux	243 57.1	N28 04.2
04	104 18.0	194 43.2	50.9	303 23.7	49.8	260 16.3	50.6	268 17.5	23.3	Procyon	245 24.9	N 5 16.4
05	119 20.5	209 42.7	50.9	318 24.8	49.2	275 18.3	50.8	283 19.7	23.4			
06	134 22.9	224 42.3	S26 51.0	333 26.0	N 9 48.7	290 20.3	S 8 51.0	298 21.9	S 4 23.5	Rasalhague	96 29.1	N12 34.6
07	149 25.4	239 41.8	51.0	348 27.1	48.2	305 22.2	51.2	313 24.1	23.6	Regulus	208 09.3	N12 03.5
T 08	164 27.9	254 41.4	51.1	3 28.2	47.7	320 24.2	51.4	328 26.3	23.7	Rigel	281 35.0	S 8 13.3
H 09	179 30.3	269 40.9	·· 51.1	18 29.3	·· 47.2	335 26.2	·· 51.6	343 28.5	·· 23.8	Rigil Kent.	140 25.5	S60 45.4
U 10	194 32.8	284 40.5	51.2	33 30.5	46.7	350 28.1	51.7	358 30.7	23.9	Sabik	102 40.6	S15 42.1
R 11	209 35.3	299 40.1	51.2	48 31.6	46.2	5 30.1	51.9	13 32.9	24.0			
S 12	224 37.7	314 39.6	S26 51.3	63 32.7	N 9 45.7	20 32.0	S 8 52.1	28 35.1	S 4 24.1	Schedar	350 07.7	N56 26.4
D 13	239 40.2	329 39.2	51.3	78 33.9	45.2	35 34.0	52.3	43 37.3	24.2	Shaula	96 55.1	S37 05.5
A 14	254 42.6	344 38.8	51.4	93 35.0	44.7	50 36.0	52.5	58 39.5	24.4	Sirius	258 54.9	S16 41.3
Y 15	269 45.1	359 38.3	·· 51.4	108 36.1	·· 44.2	65 37.9	·· 52.7	73 41.7	·· 24.5	Spica	158 57.1	S11 03.8
16	284 47.6	14 37.9	51.5	123 37.3	43.7	80 39.9	52.9	88 43.9	24.6	Suhail	223 10.3	S43 21.2
17	299 50.0	29 37.5	51.5	138 38.4	43.2	95 41.9	53.1	103 46.1	24.7			
18	314 52.5	44 37.0	S26 51.5	153 39.5	N 9 42.7	110 43.8	S 8 53.3	118 48.3	S 4 24.8	Vega	80 55.6	N38 46.3
19	329 55.0	59 36.6	51.6	168 40.7	42.2	125 45.8	53.5	133 50.5	24.9	Zuben'ubi	137 32.5	S15 57.8
20	344 57.4	74 36.1	51.6	183 41.8	41.7	140 47.8	53.7	148 52.7	25.0			
21	359 59.9	89 35.7	·· 51.7	198 42.9	·· 41.2	155 49.7	·· 53.9	163 54.9	·· 25.1			
22	15 02.4	104 35.3	51.7	213 44.1	40.7	170 51.7	54.0	178 57.1	25.2			
23	30 04.8	119 34.9	51.7	228 45.2	40.2	185 53.6	54.2	193 59.3	25.3			

											S.H.A.	Mer. Pass.
										Venus	91 46.7	15 01
										Mars	199 43.1	7 48
Mer. Pass. 21 03.9		v −0.5 d 0.1		v 1.1 d 0.5		v 2.0 d 0.2		v 2.2 d 0.1		Jupiter	156 12.4	10 41
										Saturn	164 07.0	10 09

G.M.T.	SUN G.H.A.	SUN Dec.	MOON G.H.A.	v	Dec.	d	H.P.
3 00	184 06.0	S14 58.0	113 19.8	11.1	S21 36.2	1.3	54.7
01	199 06.0	58.8	127 49.9	11.1	21 34.9	1.4	54.7
02	214 06.0	14 59.5	142 20.0	11.0	21 33.5	1.5	54.7
03	229 06.0	15 00.3	156 50.0	11.1	21 32.0	1.6	54.7
04	244 06.0	01.1	171 20.1	11.1	21 30.4	1.7	54.8
05	259 06.0	01.9	185 50.2	11.1	21 28.7	1.9	54.8
06	274 06.0	S15 02.7	200 20.3	11.1	S21 26.8	2.0	54.8
07	289 06.0	03.4	214 50.3	11.0	21 24.9	2.0	54.8
08	304 06.0	04.2	229 20.3	11.0	21 22.9	2.2	54.8
09	319 06.0	·· 05.0	243 50.3	11.1	21 20.7	2.2	54.9
10	334 06.0	05.8	258 20.4	11.0	21 18.5	2.4	54.9
11	349 06.0	06.6	272 50.4	11.0	21 16.1	2.4	54.9
12	4 06.0	S15 07.3	287 20.4	11.0	S21 13.7	2.6	54.9
13	19 06.0	08.1	301 50.4	11.0	21 11.1	2.6	55.0
14	34 06.0	08.9	316 20.4	11.0	21 08.5	2.8	55.0
15	49 06.0	·· 09.7	330 50.4	10.9	21 05.7	2.9	55.0
16	64 06.0	10.5	345 20.3	11.0	21 02.8	3.0	55.0
17	79 06.0	11.2	359 50.3	11.0	20 59.8	3.0	55.0
18	94 06.0	S15 12.0	14 20.3	11.0	S20 56.8	3.2	55.1
19	109 06.0	12.8	28 50.3	10.9	20 53.6	3.3	55.1
20	124 06.0	13.6	43 20.2	11.0	20 50.3	3.4	55.1
21	139 06.0	·· 14.3	57 50.2	10.9	20 46.9	3.5	55.1
22	154 06.0	15.1	72 20.1	11.0	20 43.4	3.6	55.2
23	169 06.0	15.9	86 50.1	11.0	20 39.8	3.8	55.2
4 00	184 06.0	S15 16.7	101 20.1	10.9	S20 36.0	3.8	55.2
01	199 06.0	17.4	115 50.0	11.0	20 32.2	3.9	55.2
02	214 06.0	18.2	130 20.0	11.0	20 28.3	4.0	55.3
03	229 06.0	·· 19.0	144 49.9	11.0	20 24.3	4.2	55.3
04	244 06.0	19.8	159 19.9	10.9	20 20.1	4.2	55.3
05	259 05.9	20.5	173 49.8	11.0	20 15.9	4.3	55.4
06	274 05.9	S15 21.3	188 19.8	10.9	S20 11.6	4.5	55.4
07	289 05.9	22.1	202 49.7	10.9	20 07.1	4.5	55.4
08	304 05.9	22.8	217 19.6	11.0	20 02.6	4.7	55.4
09	319 05.9	·· 23.6	231 49.6	10.9	19 57.9	4.7	55.5
10	334 05.9	24.4	246 19.5	11.0	19 53.2	4.9	55.5
11	349 05.9	25.2	260 49.5	10.9	19 48.3	4.9	55.5
12	4 05.9	S15 25.9	275 19.4	11.0	S19 43.4	5.1	55.5
13	19 05.9	26.7	289 49.4	10.9	19 38.3	5.2	55.6
14	34 05.9	27.5	304 19.3	11.0	19 33.1	5.2	55.6
15	49 05.9	·· 28.2	318 49.3	10.9	19 27.9	5.4	55.6
16	64 05.8	29.0	333 19.2	11.0	19 22.5	5.5	55.7
17	79 05.8	29.8	347 49.2	11.0	19 17.0	5.5	55.7
18	94 05.8	S15 30.5	2 19.2	10.9	S19 11.5	5.7	55.7
19	109 05.8	31.3	16 49.1	11.0	19 05.8	5.8	55.8
20	124 05.8	32.1	31 19.1	10.9	19 00.0	5.9	55.8
21	139 05.8	·· 32.8	45 49.0	11.0	18 54.1	5.9	55.8
22	154 05.8	33.6	60 19.0	11.0	18 48.2	6.1	55.8
23	169 05.8	34.4	74 49.0	10.9	18 42.1	6.2	55.9
5 00	184 05.7	S15 35.1	89 18.9	11.0	S18 35.9	6.3	55.9
01	199 05.7	35.9	103 48.9	11.0	18 29.6	6.3	55.9
02	214 05.7	36.6	118 18.9	11.0	18 23.3	6.5	56.0
03	229 05.7	·· 37.4	132 48.9	11.0	18 16.8	6.6	56.0
04	244 05.7	38.2	147 18.9	11.0	18 10.2	6.7	56.0
05	259 05.7	38.9	161 48.8	11.0	18 03.5	6.7	56.1
06	274 05.6	S15 39.7	176 18.8	11.0	S17 56.8	6.9	56.1
07	289 05.6	40.4	190 48.8	11.0	17 49.9	7.0	56.1
08	304 05.6	41.2	205 18.8	11.0	17 42.9	7.0	56.2
09	319 05.6	·· 42.0	219 48.8	11.0	17 35.9	7.2	56.2
10	334 05.6	42.7	234 18.8	11.0	17 28.7	7.3	56.2
11	349 05.6	43.5	248 48.8	11.0	17 21.4	7.3	56.3
12	4 05.5	S15 44.2	263 18.8	11.1	S17 14.1	7.5	56.3
13	19 05.5	45.0	277 48.9	11.0	17 06.6	7.5	56.3
14	34 05.5	45.8	292 18.9	11.0	16 59.1	7.7	56.4
15	49 05.5	·· 46.5	306 48.9	11.0	16 51.4	7.7	56.4
16	64 05.5	47.3	321 18.9	11.0	16 43.7	7.8	56.4
17	79 05.4	48.0	335 48.9	11.1	16 35.9	7.9	56.5
18	94 05.4	S15 48.8	350 19.0	11.0	S16 28.0	8.1	56.5
19	109 05.4	49.5	4 49.0	11.0	16 19.9	8.1	56.6
20	124 05.4	50.3	19 19.0	11.1	16 11.8	8.2	56.6
21	139 05.4	·· 51.0	33 49.1	11.0	16 03.6	8.3	56.6
22	154 05.3	51.8	48 19.1	11.0	15 55.3	8.4	56.7
23	169 05.3	52.6	62 49.1	11.1	15 46.9	8.4	56.7
	S.D. 16.2	d 0.8	S.D. 15.0		15.1		15.3

Days marked: TUESDAY (rows 3 00–23), WEDNESDAY (rows 4 00–23), THURSDAY (rows 5 00–23).

Moonrise

Lat.	Twilight Naut.	Civil	Sunrise	Moonrise 3	4	5	6
N 72	06 18	07 42	09 16	■	■	17 07	16 29
N 70	06 12	07 28	08 45	■	16 50	16 20	16 05
68	06 08	07 16	08 23	15 52	15 51	15 49	15 46
66	06 03	07 06	08 06	14 59	15 17	15 26	15 31
64	06 00	06 57	07 51	14 27	14 52	15 08	15 19
62	05 57	06 50	07 40	14 03	14 32	14 53	15 08
60	05 54	06 44	07 30	13 44	14 16	14 40	14 59
N 58	05 51	06 38	07 21	13 28	14 02	14 29	14 51
56	05 49	06 33	07 13	13 14	13 51	14 20	14 44
54	05 46	06 28	07 06	13 03	13 40	14 11	14 37
52	05 44	06 24	07 00	12 52	13 31	14 04	14 32
50	05 42	06 20	06 54	12 43	13 23	13 57	14 27
45	05 37	06 11	06 42	12 23	13 05	13 42	14 15
N 40	05 32	06 04	06 32	12 08	12 51	13 30	14 06
35	05 27	05 57	06 24	11 54	12 39	13 20	13 58
30	05 23	05 51	06 16	11 42	12 28	13 11	13 51
20	05 14	05 40	06 03	11 22	12 09	12 55	13 39
N 10	05 05	05 29	05 51	11 05	11 53	12 41	13 28
0	04 54	05 19	05 40	10 49	11 38	12 28	13 18
S 10	04 42	05 07	05 29	10 32	11 23	12 15	13 08
20	04 27	04 54	05 17	10 15	11 07	12 01	12 57
30	04 07	04 38	05 03	09 55	10 49	11 45	12 44
35	03 55	04 28	04 55	09 43	10 38	11 36	12 37
40	03 41	04 16	04 46	09 30	10 26	11 26	12 29
45	03 22	04 02	04 35	09 14	10 11	11 13	12 19
S 50	02 58	03 45	04 22	08 54	09 53	10 58	12 08
52	02 46	03 36	04 15	08 45	09 45	10 51	12 02
54	02 31	03 27	04 09	08 34	09 35	10 43	11 56
56	02 14	03 16	04 01	08 23	09 24	10 34	11 50
58	01 53	03 04	03 52	08 09	09 12	10 24	11 42
S 60	01 24	02 49	03 42	07 53	08 58	10 12	11 33

Moonset

Lat.	Sunset	Twilight Civil	Naut.	Moonset 3	4	5	6
N 72	14 10	15 43	17 08	■	■	20 28	22 50
N 70	14 41	15 58	17 13	■	19 00	21 14	23 13
68	15 03	16 10	17 18	18 15	19 58	21 44	23 30
66	15 20	16 20	17 22	19 07	20 32	22 06	23 44
64	15 35	16 29	17 26	19 39	20 57	22 23	23 55
62	15 47	16 36	17 29	20 03	21 16	22 38	24 05
60	15 57	16 43	17 32	20 21	21 32	22 50	24 13
N 58	16 06	16 48	17 35	20 37	21 45	23 00	24 20
56	16 13	16 53	17 38	20 50	21 56	23 09	24 27
54	16 20	16 58	17 40	21 02	22 06	23 17	24 32
52	16 26	17 02	17 43	21 12	22 15	23 24	24 37
50	16 32	17 06	17 45	21 21	22 23	23 31	24 42
45	16 44	17 15	17 50	21 40	22 40	23 44	24 52
N 40	16 54	17 23	17 55	21 56	22 54	23 56	25 00
35	17 03	17 29	17 59	22 09	23 06	24 05	00 05
30	17 11	17 36	18 04	22 20	23 16	24 13	00 13
20	17 24	17 47	18 13	22 40	23 33	24 28	00 28
N 10	17 36	17 58	18 23	22 57	23 48	24 40	00 40
0	17 47	18 09	18 33	23 13	24 02	00 02	00 52
S 10	17 58	18 20	18 46	23 28	24 16	00 16	01 04
20	18 11	18 34	19 01	23 45	24 31	00 31	01 16
30	18 25	18 50	19 20	24 04	00 04	00 48	01 30
35	18 33	19 00	19 33	24 16	00 16	00 58	01 38
40	18 42	19 12	19 48	24 28	00 28	01 10	01 47
45	18 53	19 26	20 06	24 44	00 44	01 23	01 58
S 50	19 07	19 44	20 31	00 19	01 02	01 39	02 10
52	19 13	19 52	20 43	00 29	01 11	01 46	02 16
54	19 20	20 02	20 58	00 39	01 20	01 55	02 23
56	19 28	20 13	21 16	00 50	01 31	02 04	02 30
58	19 37	20 26	21 38	01 05	01 44	02 15	02 38
S 60	19 47	20 41	22 08	01 21	01 59	02 27	02 48

Day	SUN Eqn. of Time 00h	12h	Mer. Pass.	MOON Mer. Pass. Upper	Lower	Age	Phase
3	16 24	16 24	11 44	17 01	04 36	07	
4	16 24	16 24	11 44	17 50	05 26	08	
5	16 23	16 22	11 44	18 40	06 15	09	◑

G.M.T.	ARIES G.H.A.	VENUS −4.0 G.H.A.	Dec.	MARS +1.5 G.H.A.	Dec.	JUPITER −1.2 G.H.A.	Dec.	SATURN +1.0 G.H.A.	Dec.	STARS Name	S.H.A.	Dec.
6 00	45 07.3	134 34.4	S26 51.8	243 46.3	N 9 39.7	200 55.6	S 8 54.4	209 01.5	S 4 25.4	Acamar	315 36.2	S40 22.7
01	60 09.7	149 34.0	51.8	258 47.5	39.2	215 57.6	54.6	224 03.7	25.5	Achernar	335 44.1	S57 19.9
02	75 12.2	164 33.6	51.8	273 48.6	38.7	230 59.5	54.8	239 05.9	25.6	Acrux	173 36.9	S62 59.6
03	90 14.7	179 33.1	·· 51.8	288 49.7	·· 38.2	246 01.5	·· 55.0	254 08.1	·· 25.7	Adhara	255 31.3	S28 56.6
04	105 17.1	194 32.7	51.9	303 50.9	37.7	261 03.5	55.2	269 10.3	25.8	Aldebaran	291 16.8	N16 28.4
05	120 19.6	209 32.3	51.9	318 52.0	37.2	276 05.4	55.4	284 12.5	25.9			
06	135 22.1	224 31.8	S26 51.9	333 53.2	N 9 36.6	291 07.4	S 8 55.6	299 14.7	S 4 26.0	Alioth	166 42.3	N56 03.5
07	150 24.5	239 31.4	52.0	348 54.3	36.1	306 09.4	55.8	314 16.9	26.1	Alkaid	153 18.4	N49 24.3
08	165 27.0	254 31.0	52.0	3 55.4	35.6	321 11.3	56.0	329 19.1	26.2	Al Na'ir	28 13.8	S47 03.2
F 09	180 29.5	269 30.6	·· 52.0	18 56.6	·· 35.1	336 13.3	·· 56.1	344 21.3	·· 26.3	Alnilam	276 10.6	S 1 12.7
R 10	195 31.9	284 30.1	52.0	33 57.7	34.6	351 15.2	56.3	359 23.5	26.4	Alphard	218 19.8	S 8 34.6
I 11	210 34.4	299 29.7	52.0	48 58.8	34.1	6 17.2	56.5	14 25.7	26.5			
D 12	225 36.9	314 29.3	S26 52.1	64 00.0	N 9 33.6	21 19.2	S 8 56.7	29 27.9	S 4 26.7	Alphecca	126 31.8	N26 46.7
A 13	240 39.3	329 28.9	52.1	79 01.1	33.1	36 21.1	56.9	44 30.1	26.8	Alpheratz	358 08.3	N28 59.5
Y 14	255 41.8	344 28.5	52.1	94 02.2	32.6	51 23.1	57.1	59 32.3	26.9	Altair	62 31.9	N 8 49.3
15	270 44.2	359 28.0	·· 52.1	109 03.4	·· 32.1	66 25.1	·· 57.3	74 34.5	·· 27.0	Ankaa	353 39.1	S42 24.5
16	285 46.7	14 27.6	52.1	124 04.5	31.6	81 27.0	57.5	89 36.7	27.1	Antares	112 56.3	S26 23.4
17	300 49.2	29 27.2	52.1	139 05.7	31.1	96 29.0	57.7	104 38.9	27.2			
18	315 51.6	44 26.8	S26 52.2	154 06.8	N 9 30.6	111 31.0	S 8 57.9	119 41.1	S 4 27.3	Arcturus	146 18.1	N19 16.8
19	330 54.1	59 26.4	52.2	169 07.9	30.1	126 32.9	58.1	134 43.3	27.4	Atria	108 20.3	S68 59.8
20	345 56.6	74 25.9	52.2	184 09.1	29.6	141 34.9	58.2	149 45.5	27.5	Avior	234 27.8	S59 26.7
21	0 59.0	89 25.5	·· 52.2	199 10.2	·· 29.1	156 36.8	·· 58.4	164 47.7	·· 27.6	Bellatrix	278 57.7	N 6 20.0
22	16 01.5	104 25.1	52.2	214 11.4	28.6	171 38.8	58.6	179 49.9	27.7	Betelgeuse	271 27.2	N 7 24.3
23	31 04.0	119 24.7	52.2	229 12.5	28.1	186 40.8	58.8	194 52.1	27.8			
7 00	46 06.4	134 24.3	S26 52.2	244 13.6	N 9 27.6	201 42.7	S 8 59.0	209 54.3	S 4 27.9	Canopus	264 06.5	S52 40.9
01	61 08.9	149 23.8	52.2	259 14.8	27.1	216 44.7	59.2	224 56.5	28.0	Capella	281 09.8	N45 58.7
02	76 11.4	164 23.4	52.2	274 15.9	26.6	231 46.7	59.4	239 58.7	28.1	Deneb	49 48.0	N45 13.2
03	91 13.8	179 22.9	·· 52.2	289 17.1	·· 26.1	246 48.6	·· 59.6	255 00.9	·· 28.2	Denebola	182 58.5	N14 40.5
04	106 16.3	194 22.6	52.2	304 18.2	25.6	261 50.6	8 59.8	270 03.1	28.3	Diphda	349 19.8	S18 05.3
05	121 18.7	209 22.2	52.2	319 19.3	25.1	276 52.6	9 00.0	285 05.3	28.4			
06	136 21.2	224 21.8	S26 52.2	334 20.5	N 9 24.6	291 54.5	S 9 00.1	300 07.5	S 4 28.5	Dubhe	194 21.5	N61 50.8
07	151 23.7	239 21.4	52.2	349 21.6	24.1	306 56.5	00.3	315 09.7	28.6	Elnath	278 42.9	N28 35.5
S 08	166 26.1	254 21.0	52.2	4 22.8	23.5	321 58.5	00.5	330 11.9	28.7	Eltanin	90 57.8	N51 29.7
A 09	181 28.6	269 20.5	·· 52.2	19 23.9	·· 23.0	337 00.4	·· 00.7	345 14.1	·· 28.8	Enif	34 10.8	N 9 47.6
T 10	196 31.1	284 20.1	52.2	34 25.0	22.5	352 02.4	00.9	0 16.3	28.9	Fomalhaut	15 50.4	S29 43.3
U 11	211 33.5	299 19.7	52.2	49 26.2	22.0	7 04.4	01.1	15 18.5	29.0			
R 12	226 36.0	314 19.3	S26 52.2	64 27.3	N 9 21.5	22 06.3	S 9 01.3	30 20.7	S 4 29.1	Gacrux	172 28.4	S57 00.4
D 13	241 38.5	329 18.9	52.2	79 28.5	21.0	37 08.3	01.5	45 22.9	29.2	Gienah	176 17.4	S17 26.2
A 14	256 40.9	344 18.5	52.2	94 29.6	20.5	52 10.2	01.7	60 25.1	29.4	Hadar	149 22.9	S60 16.9
Y 15	271 43.4	359 18.1	·· 52.2	109 30.8	·· 20.0	67 12.2	·· 01.9	75 27.3	·· 29.5	Hamal	328 27.7	N23 22.6
16	286 45.9	14 17.7	52.2	124 31.9	19.5	82 14.2	02.0	90 29.5	29.6	Kaus Aust.	84 16.1	S34 23.7
17	301 48.3	29 17.3	52.2	139 33.0	19.0	97 16.1	02.2	105 31.7	29.7			
18	316 50.8	44 16.9	S26 52.1	154 34.2	N 9 18.5	112 18.1	S 9 02.4	120 33.9	S 4 29.8	Kochab	137 20.2	N74 13.9
19	331 53.2	59 16.5	52.1	169 35.3	18.0	127 20.1	02.6	135 36.1	29.9	Markab	14 02.3	N15 06.5
20	346 55.7	74 16.1	52.1	184 36.5	17.5	142 22.0	02.8	150 38.3	30.0	Menkar	314 40.0	N 4 01.1
21	1 58.2	89 15.7	·· 52.1	199 37.6	·· 17.0	157 24.0	·· 03.0	165 40.5	·· 30.1	Menkent	148 36.5	S36 16.6
22	17 00.6	104 15.3	52.1	214 38.8	16.5	172 26.0	03.2	180 42.7	30.2	Miaplacidus	221 44.8	S69 38.2
23	32 03.1	119 14.9	52.1	229 39.9	16.0	187 27.9	03.4	195 44.9	30.3			
8 00	47 05.6	134 14.5	S26 52.0	244 41.0	N 9 15.5	202 29.9	S 9 03.6	210 47.1	S 4 30.4	Mirfak	309 14.5	N49 47.8
01	62 08.0	149 14.1	52.0	259 42.2	15.0	217 31.9	03.7	225 49.3	30.5	Nunki	76 28.4	S26 19.2
02	77 10.5	164 13.7	52.0	274 43.3	14.5	232 33.8	03.9	240 51.5	30.6	Peacock	53 57.3	S56 47.9
03	92 13.0	179 13.3	·· 51.9	289 44.5	·· 14.0	247 35.8	·· 04.1	255 53.7	·· 30.7	Pollux	243 57.1	N28 04.2
04	107 15.4	194 12.9	51.9	304 45.6	13.5	262 37.8	04.3	270 55.9	30.8	Procyon	245 24.9	N 5 16.4
05	122 17.9	209 12.5	51.9	319 46.8	13.0	277 39.7	04.5	285 58.1	30.9			
06	137 20.3	224 12.1	S26 51.9	334 47.9	N 9 12.5	292 41.7	S 9 04.7	301 00.3	S 4 31.0	Rasalhague	96 29.2	N12 34.6
07	152 22.8	239 11.7	51.9	349 49.1	12.0	307 43.7	04.9	316 02.5	31.1	Regulus	208 09.3	N12 03.5
S 08	167 25.3	254 11.3	51.8	4 50.2	11.5	322 45.6	05.1	331 04.7	31.2	Rigel	281 35.0	S 8 13.3
U 09	182 27.7	269 10.9	·· 51.8	19 51.4	·· 11.0	337 47.6	·· 05.3	346 06.9	·· 31.3	Rigil Kent.	140 25.5	S60 45.4
N 10	197 30.2	284 10.5	51.8	34 52.5	10.4	352 49.6	05.5	1 09.1	31.4	Sabik·	102 40.6	S15 42.1
D 11	212 32.7	299 10.1	51.7	49 53.7	09.9	7 51.5	05.6	16 11.3	31.5			
A 12	227 35.1	314 09.7	S26 51.7	64 54.8	N 9 09.4	22 53.5	S 9 05.8	31 13.5	S 4 31.6	Schedar	350 07.7	N56 26.4
Y 13	242 37.6	329 09.3	51.7	79 55.9	08.9	37 55.5	06.0	46 15.7	31.7	Shaula	96 55.1	S37 05.5
14	257 40.1	344 09.0	51.6	94 57.1	08.4	52 57.4	06.2	61 17.9	31.8	Sirius	258 54.8	S16 41.3
15	272 42.5	359 08.6	·· 51.6	109 58.2	·· 07.9	67 59.4	·· 06.4	76 20.1	·· 31.9	Spica	158 57.0	S11 03.8
16	287 45.0	14 08.2	51.6	124 59.4	07.4	83 01.3	06.6	91 22.3	32.0	Suhail	223 10.2	S43 21.2
17	302 47.5	29 07.8	51.5	140 00.5	06.9	98 03.3	06.8	106 24.5	32.1			
18	317 49.9	44 07.4	S26 51.5	155 01.7	N 9 06.4	113 05.3	S 9 07.0	121 26.7	S 4 32.2	Vega	80 55.6	N38 46.2
19	332 52.4	59 07.0	51.5	170 02.8	05.9	128 07.2	07.2	136 28.9	32.3	Zuben'ubi	137 32.5	S15 57.8
20	347 54.8	74 06.6	51.4	185 04.0	05.4	143 09.2	07.3	151 31.1	32.4		S.H.A.	Mer. Pass.
21	2 57.3	89 06.2	·· 51.4	200 05.1	·· 04.9	158 11.2	·· 07.5	166 33.3	·· 32.5		° ′	h m
22	17 59.8	104 05.9	51.3	215 06.3	04.4	173 13.1	07.7	181 35.5	32.6	Venus	88 17.8	15 03
23	33 02.2	119 05.5	51.3	230 07.4	03.9	188 15.1	07.9	196 37.7	32.7	Mars	198 07.2	7 43
	h m									Jupiter	155 36.3	10 32
Mer. Pass.	20 52.1	*v* −0.4	*d* 0.0	*v* 1.1	*d* 0.5	*v* 2.0	*d* 0.2	*v* 2.2	*d* 0.1	Saturn	163 47.8	9 59

G.M.T.	SUN G.H.A.	SUN Dec.	MOON G.H.A.	MOON v	MOON Dec.	MOON d	MOON H.P.	Lat.	Twilight Naut.	Twilight Civil	Sunrise	Moonrise 6	Moonrise 7	Moonrise 8	Moonrise 9
d h	° '	° '	° '	'	° '	'	'	°	h m	h m	h m	h m	h m	h m	h m
6 00	184 05.3	S15 53.3	77 19.2	11.0	S15 38.5	8.6	56.7	N 72	06 29	07 56	09 37	16 29	16 07	15 50	15 34
01	199 05.3	54.1	91 49.2	11.1	15 29.9	8.7	56.8	N 70	06 22	07 40	09 01	16 05	15 54	15 44	15 35
02	214 05.2	54.8	106 19.3	11.0	15 21.2	8.7	56.8	68	06 17	07 26	08 36	15 46	15 43	15 40	15 37
03	229 05.2	·· 55.6	120 49.3	11.1	15 12.5	8.9	56.8	66	06 12	07 15	08 17	15 31	15 34	15 36	15 38
04	244 05.2	56.3	135 19.4	11.0	15 03.6	8.9	56.9	64	06 08	07 06	08 01	15 19	15 26	15 33	15 39
05	259 05.2	57.1	149 49.4	11.1	14 54.7	9.0	56.9	62	06 04	06 58	07 48	15 08	15 20	15 30	15 40
06	274 05.2	S15 57.8	164 19.5	11.0	S14 45.7	9.1	57.0	60	06 00	06 51	07 37	14 59	15 14	15 27	15 40
07	289 05.1	58.6	178 49.5	11.1	14 36.6	9.2	57.0	N 58	05 57	06 44	07 28	14 51	15 09	15 25	15 41
08	304 05.1	15 59.3	193 19.6	11.0	14 27.4	9.3	57.0	56	05 54	06 39	07 19	14 44	15 04	15 23	15 41
F 09	319 05.1	16 00.1	207 49.6	11.1	14 18.1	9.3	57.1	54	05 51	06 34	07 12	14 37	15 00	15 21	15 42
R 10	334 05.1	00.8	222 19.7	11.0	14 08.8	9.5	57.1	52	05 49	06 29	07 05	14 32	14 57	15 20	15 42
I 11	349 05.0	01.6	236 49.7	11.1	13 59.3	9.5	57.1	50	05 46	06 25	06 59	14 27	14 53	15 18	15 43
D 12	4 05.0	S16 02.3	251 19.8	11.0	S13 49.8	9.6	57.2	45	05 40	06 15	06 46	14 15	14 46	15 15	15 44
A 13	19 05.0	03.0	265 49.8	11.1	13 40.2	9.7	57.2	N 40	05 35	06 07	06 36	14 06	14 40	15 12	15 45
Y 14	34 04.9	03.8	280 19.9	11.0	13 30.5	9.8	57.3	35	05 30	06 00	06 27	13 58	14 34	15 10	15 45
15	49 04.9	·· 04.5	294 49.9	11.1	13 20.7	9.9	57.3	30	05 25	05 53	06 18	13 51	14 30	15 08	15 46
16	64 04.9	05.3	309 20.0	11.0	13 10.8	10.0	57.3	20	05 15	05 41	06 04	13 39	14 21	15 04	15 47
17	79 04.9	06.0	323 50.0	11.1	13 00.8	10.0	57.4	N 10	05 05	05 30	05 52	13 28	14 14	15 01	15 48
18	94 04.8	S16 06.8	338 20.1	11.0	S12 50.8	10.1	57.4	0	04 54	05 19	05 40	13 18	14 08	14 58	15 49
19	109 04.8	07.5	352 50.1	11.0	12 40.7	10.2	57.5	S 10	04 41	05 06	05 28	13 08	14 01	14 55	15 50
20	124 04.8	08.3	7 20.1	11.1	12 30.5	10.3	57.5	20	04 25	04 52	05 16	12 57	13 53	14 52	15 51
21	139 04.7	·· 09.0	21 50.2	11.0	12 20.2	10.3	57.5	30	04 05	04 35	05 01	12 44	13 45	14 48	15 53
22	154 04.7	09.7	36 20.2	11.0	12 09.9	10.4	57.6	35	03 52	04 25	04 52	12 37	13 40	14 46	15 53
23	169 04.7	10.5	50 50.2	11.0	11 59.5	10.6	57.6	40	03 36	04 13	04 42	12 29	13 35	14 43	15 54
7 00	184 04.6	S16 11.2	65 20.2	11.0	S11 48.9	10.5	57.7	45	03 17	03 58	04 31	12 19	13 29	14 41	15 55
01	199 04.6	12.0	79 50.2	11.0	11 38.4	10.7	57.7	S 50	02 51	03 39	04 17	12 08	13 21	14 37	15 57
02	214 04.6	12.7	94 20.2	11.0	11 27.7	10.7	57.7	52	02 38	03 30	04 10	12 02	13 17	14 36	15 57
03	229 04.6	·· 13.5	108 50.2	11.0	11 17.0	10.9	57.8	54	02 23	03 20	04 03	11 56	13 14	14 34	15 58
04	244 04.5	14.2	123 20.2	11.0	11 06.1	10.8	57.8	56	02 04	03 09	03 54	11 50	13 09	14 32	15 59
05	259 04.5	14.9	137 50.2	11.0	10 55.3	11.0	57.9	58	01 40	02 55	03 45	11 42	13 04	14 30	15 59
06	274 04.5	S16 15.7	152 20.2	10.9	S10 44.3	11.0	57.9	S 60	01 06	02 39	03 34	11 33	12 59	14 28	16 00
07	289 04.4	16.4	166 50.1	11.0	10 33.3	11.1	57.9								

G.M.T.	SUN G.H.A.	SUN Dec.	MOON G.H.A.	MOON v	MOON Dec.	MOON d	MOON H.P.	Lat.	Sunset	Twilight Civil	Twilight Naut.	Moonset 6	Moonset 7	Moonset 8	Moonset 9
S 08	304 04.4	17.1	181 20.1	10.9	10 22.2	11.2	58.0	°	h m	h m	h m	h m	h m	h m	h m
A 09	319 04.3	·· 17.9	195 50.0	11.0	10 11.0	11.3	58.0								
T 10	334 04.3	18.6	210 20.0	10.9	9 59.7	11.3	58.1	N 72	13 49	15 30	16 57	22 50	24 57	00 57	03 02
U 11	349 04.3	19.4	224 49.9	10.9	9 48.4	11.4	58.1	N 70	14 25	15 47	17 03	23 13	25 08	01 08	03 04
R 12	4 04.2	S16 20.1	239 19.8	10.9	S 9 37.0	11.4	58.1	68	14 50	16 00	17 09	23 30	25 17	01 17	03 06
D 13	19 04.2	20.8	253 49.7	10.9	9 25.6	11.5	58.2	66	15 10	16 11	17 14	23 44	25 24	01 24	03 07
A 14	34 04.2	21.6	268 19.6	10.9	9 14.1	11.6	58.2	64	15 25	16 21	17 19	23 55	25 31	01 31	03 09
Y 15	49 04.1	·· 22.3	282 49.5	10.9	9 02.5	11.7	58.3	62	15 38	16 29	17 23	24 05	00 05	01 36	03 10
16	64 04.1	23.0	297 19.4	10.8	8 50.8	11.7	58.3	60	15 49	16 36	17 26	24 13	00 13	01 40	03 11
17	79 04.1	23.8	311 49.2	10.9	8 39.1	11.7	58.4	N 58	15 59	16 42	17 29	24 20	00 20	01 45	03 12
18	94 04.0	S16 24.5	326 19.1	10.8	S 8 27.4	11.9	58.4	56	16 07	16 48	17 33	24 27	00 27	01 48	03 13
19	109 04.0	25.2	340 48.9	10.8	8 15.5	11.9	58.4	54	16 15	16 53	17 35	24 32	00 32	01 51	03 13
20	124 03.9	26.0	355 18.7	10.8	8 03.6	12.0	58.5	52	16 21	16 58	17 38	24 37	00 37	01 54	03 14
21	139 03.9	·· 26.7	9 48.5	10.8	7 51.6	12.0	58.5	50	16 27	17 02	17 41	24 42	00 42	01 57	03 15
22	154 03.9	27.4	24 18.3	10.8	7 39.6	12.1	58.6	45	16 40	17 11	17 47	24 52	00 52	02 03	03 16
23	169 03.8	28.2	38 48.1	10.7	7 27.5	12.1	58.6	N 40	16 51	17 20	17 52	25 00	01 00	02 07	03 17
8 00	184 03.8	S16 28.9	53 17.8	10.7	S 7 15.4	12.2	58.6	35	17 00	17 27	17 57	00 05	01 07	02 11	03 18
01	199 03.7	29.6	67 47.5	10.7	7 03.2	12.2	58.7	30	17 09	17 34	18 02	00 13	01 13	02 15	03 19
02	214 03.7	30.3	82 17.2	10.7	6 51.0	12.4	58.7	20	17 23	17 46	18 12	00 28	01 24	02 21	03 20
03	229 03.7	·· 31.1	96 46.9	10.7	6 38.6	12.3	58.8	N 10	17 35	17 57	18 22	00 40	01 33	02 26	03 21
04	244 03.6	31.8	111 16.6	10.6	6 26.3	12.4	58.8	0	17 47	18 09	18 34	00 52	01 41	02 31	03 22
05	259 03.6	32.5	125 46.2	10.7	6 13.9	12.5	58.9	S 10	17 59	18 21	18 47	01 04	01 50	02 36	03 23
06	274 03.5	S16 33.3	140 15.9	10.6	S 6 01.4	12.5	58.9	20	18 12	18 35	19 03	01 16	01 59	02 41	03 24
07	289 03.5	34.0	154 45.5	10.6	5 48.9	12.6	58.9	30	18 27	18 53	19 23	01 30	02 09	02 47	03 25
08	304 03.5	34.7	169 15.1	10.5	5 36.3	12.6	59.0	35	18 36	19 04	19 36	01 38	02 15	02 51	03 26
S 09	319 03.4	·· 35.4	183 44.6	10.5	5 23.7	12.7	59.0	40	18 46	19 15	19 52	01 47	02 22	02 54	03 27
U 10	334 03.4	36.2	198 14.1	10.5	5 11.0	12.7	59.0	45	18 57	19 30	20 12	01 58	02 29	02 59	03 27
N 11	349 03.3	36.9	212 43.6	10.5	4 58.3	12.7	59.1	S 50	19 12	19 49	20 38	02 10	02 38	03 04	03 28
D 12	4 03.3	S16 37.6	227 13.1	10.5	S 4 45.6	12.8	59.1	52	19 19	19 58	20 51	02 16	02 43	03 06	03 29
A 13	19 03.2	38.3	241 42.6	10.4	4 32.8	12.9	59.2	54	19 26	20 09	21 07	02 23	02 47	03 09	03 29
Y 14	34 03.2	39.1	256 12.0	10.4	4 19.9	12.9	59.2	56	19 34	20 21	21 26	02 30	02 52	03 12	03 30
15	49 03.1	·· 39.8	270 41.4	10.4	4 07.0	12.9	59.2	58	19 44	20 34	21 51	02 38	02 58	03 15	03 31
16	64 03.1	40.5	285 10.8	10.3	3 54.1	13.0	59.3	S 60	19 55	20 51	22 28	02 48	03 04	03 18	03 31
17	79 03.1	41.2	299 40.1	10.3	3 41.1	13.0	59.3								
18	94 03.0	S16 41.9	314 09.4	10.3	S 3 28.1	13.0	59.4								
19	109 03.0	42.7	328 38.7	10.3	3 15.1	13.1	59.4								
20	124 02.9	43.4	343 08.0	10.2	3 02.0	13.1	59.4								
21	139 02.9	·· 44.1	357 37.2	10.2	2 48.9	13.2	59.5								
22	154 02.8	44.8	12 06.4	10.1	2 35.7	13.2	59.5								
23	169 02.8	45.5	26 35.5	10.1	2 22.5	13.2	59.6								

Day	SUN Eqn. of Time 00h	SUN Eqn. of Time 12h	SUN Mer. Pass.	MOON Mer. Pass. Upper	MOON Mer. Pass. Lower	Age	Phase
	m s	m s	h m	h m	h m	d	
6	16 21	16 20	11 44	19 30	07 05	10	
7	16 19	16 17	11 44	20 19	07 54	11	
8	16 15	16 13	11 44	21 10	08 44	12	◐

	SUN		MOON		
S.D. 16.2	d 0.7	S.D. 15.6	15.8	16.1	

G.M.T.	ARIES G.H.A.	VENUS −4.1 G.H.A.	Dec.	MARS +1.5 G.H.A.	Dec.	JUPITER −1.2 G.H.A.	Dec.	SATURN +1.0 G.H.A.	Dec.	STARS Name	S.H.A.	Dec.
9 00	48 04.7	134 05.1	S26 51.2	245 08.6	N 9 03.4	203 17.1	S 9 08.1	211 39.9	S 4 32.8	Acamar	315 36.2	S40 22.7
01	63 07.2	149 04.7	51.2	260 09.7	02.9	218 19.0	08.3	226 42.1	33.0	Achernar	335 44.1	S57 19.9
02	78 09.6	164 04.3	51.1	275 10.9	02.4	233 21.0	08.5	241 44.3	33.1	Acrux	173 36.9	S62 59.6
03	93 12.1	179 03.9	·· 51.1	290 12.0	·· 01.9	248 23.0	·· 08.7	256 46.5	·· 33.2	Adhara	255 31.3	S28 56.6
04	108 14.6	194 03.6	51.0	305 13.2	01.4	263 24.9	08.9	271 48.7	33.3	Aldebaran	291 16.8	N16 28.4
05	123 17.0	209 03.2	51.0	320 14.3	00.9	278 26.9	09.0	286 50.9	33.4			
06	138 19.5	224 02.8	S26 50.9	335 15.5	N 9 00.4	293 28.9	S 9 09.2	301 53.1	S 4 33.5	Alioth	166 42.3	N56 03.5
07	153 22.0	239 02.4	50.9	350 16.6	8 59.9	308 30.8	09.4	316 55.3	33.6	Alkaid	153 18.3	N49 24.3
08	168 24.4	254 02.1	50.8	5 17.8	59.4	323 32.8	09.6	331 57.5	33.7	Al Na'ir	28 13.9	S47 03.2
M 09	183 26.9	269 01.7	·· 50.8	20 18.9	·· 58.9	338 34.8	·· 09.8	346 59.7	·· 33.8	Alnilam	276 10.6	S 1 12.7
O 10	198 29.3	284 01.3	50.7	35 20.1	58.4	353 36.7	10.0	2 01.9	33.9	Alphard	218 19.8	S 8 34.6
N 11	213 31.8	299 00.9	50.7	50 21.3	57.9	8 38.7	10.2	17 04.1	34.0			
D 12	228 34.3	314 00.6	S26 50.6	65 22.4	N 8 57.4	23 40.7	S 9 10.4	32 06.3	S 4 34.1	Alphecca	126 31.8	N26 46.7
A 13	243 36.7	329 00.2	50.5	80 23.6	56.8	38 42.6	10.5	47 08.5	34.2	Alpheratz	358 08.3	N28 59.5
Y 14	258 39.2	343 59.8	50.5	95 24.7	56.3	53 44.6	10.7	62 10.7	34.3	Altair	62 31.9	N 8 49.3
15	273 41.7	358 59.4	·· 50.4	110 25.9	·· 55.8	68 46.6	·· 10.9	77 12.9	·· 34.4	Ankaa	353 39.2	S42 24.5
16	288 44.1	13 59.1	50.4	125 27.0	55.3	83 48.5	11.1	92 15.2	34.5	Antares	112 56.3	S26 23.4
17	303 46.6	28 58.7	50.3	140 28.2	54.8	98 50.5	11.3	107 17.4	34.6			
18	318 49.1	43 58.3	S26 50.2	155 29.3	N 8 54.3	113 52.5	S 9 11.5	122 19.6	S 4 34.7	Arcturus	146 18.1	N19 16.8
19	333 51.5	58 58.0	50.2	170 30.5	53.8	128 54.4	11.7	137 21.8	34.8	Atria	108 20.4	S68 59.7
20	348 54.0	73 57.6	50.1	185 31.6	53.3	143 56.4	11.9	152 24.0	34.9	Avior	234 27.7	S59 26.7
21	3 56.4	88 57.2	·· 50.0	200 32.8	·· 52.8	158 58.4	·· 12.0	167 26.2	·· 35.0	Bellatrix	278 57.6	N 6 20.0
22	18 58.9	103 56.9	50.0	215 33.9	52.3	174 00.3	12.2	182 28.4	35.1	Betelgeuse	271 27.2	N 7 24.3
23	34 01.4	118 56.5	49.9	230 35.1	51.8	189 02.3	12.4	197 30.6	35.2			
10 00	49 03.8	133 56.1	S26 49.8	245 36.3	N 8 51.3	204 04.3	S 9 12.6	212 32.8	S 4 35.3	Canopus	264 06.5	S52 40.9
01	64 06.3	148 55.8	49.7	260 37.4	50.8	219 06.3	12.8	227 35.0	35.4	Capella	281 09.8	N45 58.7
02	79 08.8	163 55.4	49.7	275 38.6	50.3	234 08.2	13.0	242 37.2	35.5	Deneb	49 48.0	N45 13.2
03	94 11.2	178 55.0	·· 49.6	290 39.7	·· 49.8	249 10.2	·· 13.2	257 39.4	·· 35.6	Denebola	182 58.5	N14 40.5
04	109 13.7	193 54.7	49.5	305 40.9	49.3	264 12.2	13.4	272 41.6	35.7	Diphda	349 19.8	S18 05.3
05	124 16.2	208 54.3	49.4	320 42.0	48.8	279 14.1	13.5	287 43.8	35.8			
06	139 18.6	223 54.0	S26 49.4	335 43.2	N 8 48.3	294 16.1	S 9 13.7	302 46.0	S 4 35.9	Dubhe	194 21.5	N61 50.8
07	154 21.1	238 53.6	49.3	350 44.3	47.8	309 18.1	13.9	317 48.2	36.0	Elnath	278 42.8	N28 35.5
08	169 23.6	253 53.2	49.2	5 45.5	47.3	324 20.0	14.1	332 50.4	36.1	Eltanin	90 57.8	N51 29.7
T 09	184 26.0	268 52.9	·· 49.1	20 46.7	·· 46.8	339 22.0	·· 14.3	347 52.6	·· 36.2	Enif	34 10.8	N 9 47.6
U 10	199 28.5	283 52.5	49.0	35 47.8	46.3	354 24.0	14.5	2 54.8	36.3	Fomalhaut	15 50.4	S29 43.3
E 11	214 30.9	298 52.2	49.0	50 49.0	45.8	9 25.9	14.7	17 57.0	36.4			
S 12	229 33.4	313 51.8	S26 48.9	65 50.1	N 8 45.3	24 27.9	S 9 14.9	32 59.2	S 4 36.5	Gacrux	172 28.4	S57 00.3
D 13	244 35.9	328 51.5	48.8	80 51.3	44.8	39 29.9	15.0	48 01.4	36.6	Gienah	176 17.4	S17 26.2
A 14	259 38.3	343 51.1	48.7	95 52.4	44.3	54 31.8	15.2	63 03.6	36.7	Hadar	149 22.9	S60 16.9
Y 15	274 40.8	358 50.8	·· 48.6	110 53.6	·· 43.8	69 33.8	·· 15.4	78 05.8	·· 36.8	Hamal	328 27.7	N23 22.6
16	289 43.3	13 50.4	48.5	125 54.8	43.3	84 35.8	15.6	93 08.0	36.9	Kaus Aust.	84 16.1	S34 23.7
17	304 45.7	28 50.1	48.4	140 55.9	42.8	99 37.7	15.8	108 10.2	37.0			
18	319 48.2	43 49.7	S26 48.3	155 57.1	N 8 42.2	114 39.7	S 9 16.0	123 12.5	S 4 37.1	Kochab	137 20.2	N74 13.9
19	334 50.7	58 49.4	48.3	170 58.2	41.7	129 41.7	16.2	138 14.7	37.2	Markab	14 02.3	N15 06.5
20	349 53.1	73 49.0	48.2	185 59.4	41.2	144 43.6	16.4	153 16.9	37.3	Menkar	314 40.0	N 4 01.1
21	4 55.6	88 48.7	·· 48.1	201 00.6	·· 40.7	159 45.6	·· 16.5	168 19.1	·· 37.4	Menkent	148 36.5	S36 16.6
22	19 58.1	103 48.3	48.0	216 01.7	40.2	174 47.6	16.7	183 21.3	37.5	Miaplacidus	221 44.8	S69 38.2
23	35 00.5	118 48.0	47.9	231 02.9	39.7	189 49.5	16.9	198 23.5	37.6			
11 00	50 03.0	133 47.6	S26 47.8	246 04.0	N 8 39.2	204 51.5	S 9 17.1	213 25.7	S 4 37.7	Mirfak	309 14.5	N49 47.8
01	65 05.4	148 47.3	47.7	261 05.2	38.7	219 53.5	17.3	228 27.9	37.8	Nunki	76 28.4	S26 19.2
02	80 07.9	163 46.9	47.5	276 06.4	38.2	234 55.5	17.5	243 30.1	37.9	Peacock	53 57.3	S56 47.9
03	95 10.4	178 46.6	·· 47.5	291 07.5	·· 37.7	249 57.4	·· 17.7	258 32.3	·· 38.0	Pollux	243 57.1	N28 04.2
04	110 12.8	193 46.3	47.4	306 08.7	37.2	264 59.4	17.9	273 34.5	38.1	Procyon	245 24.8	N 5 16.4
05	125 15.3	208 45.9	47.3	321 09.8	36.7	280 01.4	18.0	288 36.7	38.2			
06	140 17.8	223 45.6	S26 47.2	336 11.0	N 8 36.2	295 03.3	S 9 18.2	303 38.9	S 4 38.3	Rasalhague	96 29.2	N12 34.6
07	155 20.2	238 45.2	47.1	351 12.2	35.7	310 05.3	18.4	318 41.1	38.4	Regulus	208 09.3	N12 03.5
W 08	170 22.7	253 44.9	47.0	6 13.3	35.2	325 07.3	18.6	333 43.3	38.5	Rigel	281 35.0	S 8 13.3
E 09	185 25.2	268 44.6	·· 46.9	21 14.5	·· 34.7	340 09.2	·· 18.8	348 45.5	·· 38.6	Rigil Kent.	140 25.5	S60 45.4
D 10	200 27.6	283 44.2	46.8	36 15.7	34.2	355 11.2	19.0	3 47.7	38.7	Sabik	102 40.6	S15 42.1
N 11	215 30.1	298 43.9	46.6	51 16.8	33.7	10 13.2	19.2	18 49.9	38.8			
E 12	230 32.5	313 43.6	S26 46.5	66 18.0	N 8 33.2	25 15.1	S 9 19.3	33 52.1	S 4 38.9	Schedar	350 07.7	N56 26.4
S 13	245 35.0	328 43.2	46.4	81 19.1	32.7	40 17.1	19.5	48 54.4	39.0	Shaula	96 55.1	S37 05.5
D 14	260 37.5	343 42.9	46.3	96 20.3	32.2	55 19.1	19.7	63 56.6	39.1	Sirius	258 54.8	S16 41.3
A 15	275 39.9	358 42.6	·· 46.2	111 21.5	·· 31.7	70 21.0	·· 19.9	78 58.8	·· 39.2	Spica	158 57.0	S11 03.8
Y 16	290 42.4	13 42.2	46.1	126 22.6	31.2	85 23.0	20.1	94 01.0	39.3	Suhail	223 10.2	S43 21.2
17	305 44.9	28 41.9	46.0	141 23.8	30.7	100 25.0	20.3	109 03.2	39.4			
18	320 47.3	43 41.6	S26 45.9	156 25.0	N 8 30.2	115 27.0	S 9 20.5	124 05.4	S 4 39.5	Vega	80 55.6	N38 46.2
19	335 49.8	58 41.2	45.7	171 26.1	29.7	130 28.9	20.6	139 07.6	39.6	Zuben'ubi	137 32.5	S15 57.8
20	350 52.3	73 40.9	45.6	186 27.3	29.2	145 30.9	20.8	154 09.8	39.7			
21	5 54.7	88 40.6	·· 45.5	201 28.5	·· 28.7	160 32.9	·· 21.0	169 12.0	·· 39.8		S.H.A.	Mer. Pass.
22	20 57.2	103 40.3	45.4	216 29.6	28.2	175 34.8	21.2	184 14.2	39.9	Venus	84 52.3	15 05
23	35 59.7	118 39.9	45.3	231 30.8	27.7	190 36.8	21.4	199 16.4	40.0	Mars	196 32.4	7 37
Mer. Pass. 20 40.3	v −0.4 d 0.1	v 1.2	d 0.5	v 2.0	d 0.2	v 2.2	d 0.1			Jupiter	155 00.4	10 22
										Saturn	163 28.9	9 48

SUN and MOON

G.M.T.	SUN G.H.A.	SUN Dec.	MOON G.H.A.	v	MOON Dec.	d	H.P.
9 00	184 02.7	S16 46.3	41 04.6	10.1	S 2 09.3	13.3	59.6
01	199 02.7	47.0	55 33.7	10.0	1 56.0	13.2	59.6
02	214 02.6	47.7	70 02.7	10.1	1 42.8	13.3	59.7
03	229 02.6	.. 48.4	84 31.8	9.9	1 29.5	13.4	59.7
04	244 02.5	49.1	99 00.7	10.0	1 16.1	13.3	59.7
05	259 02.5	49.9	113 29.7	9.8	1 02.8	13.4	59.8
06	274 02.4	S16 50.6	127 58.5	9.9	S 0 49.4	13.4	59.8
07	289 02.4	51.3	142 27.4	9.8	0 36.0	13.4	59.9
08	304 02.3	52.0	156 56.2	9.8	0 22.6	13.5	59.9
M 09	319 02.3	.. 52.7	171 25.0	9.7	S 0 09.1	13.4	59.9
O 10	334 02.2	53.4	185 53.7	9.7	N 0 04.3	13.5	60.0
N 11	349 02.2	54.1	200 22.4	9.7	0 17.8	13.5	60.0
D 12	4 02.1	S16 54.8	214 51.1	9.6	N 0 31.3	13.5	60.0
A 13	19 02.1	55.6	229 19.7	9.5	0 44.8	13.5	60.1
Y 14	34 02.0	56.3	243 48.2	9.5	0 58.3	13.6	60.1
15	49 02.0	.. 57.0	258 16.7	9.5	1 11.9	13.5	60.1
16	64 01.9	57.7	272 45.2	9.4	1 25.4	13.6	60.2
17	79 01.8	58.4	287 13.6	9.4	1 39.0	13.6	60.2
18	94 01.8	S16 59.1	301 42.0	9.3	N 1 52.5	13.6	60.2
19	109 01.7	16 59.8	316 10.3	9.3	2 06.1	13.5	60.3
20	124 01.7	17 00.5	330 38.6	9.2	2 19.6	13.6	60.3
21	139 01.6	.. 01.2	345 06.8	9.2	2 33.2	13.6	60.3
22	154 01.6	01.9	359 35.0	9.1	2 46.8	13.5	60.4
23	169 01.5	02.7	14 03.1	9.1	3 00.3	13.6	60.4
10 00	184 01.4	S17 03.4	28 31.2	9.0	N 3 13.9	13.5	60.4
01	199 01.4	04.1	42 59.2	8.9	3 27.4	13.5	60.5
02	214 01.3	04.8	57 27.1	9.0	3 41.0	13.5	60.5
03	229 01.3	.. 05.5	71 55.1	8.8	3 54.5	13.6	60.5
04	244 01.2	06.2	86 22.9	8.8	4 08.1	13.5	60.5
05	259 01.2	06.9	100 50.7	8.8	4 21.6	13.5	60.6
06	274 01.1	S17 07.6	115 18.5	8.7	N 4 35.1	13.5	60.6
07	289 01.0	08.3	129 46.2	8.6	4 48.6	13.5	60.6
08	304 01.0	09.0	144 13.8	8.6	5 02.1	13.4	60.7
T 09	319 00.9	.. 09.7	158 41.4	8.5	5 15.5	13.5	60.7
U 10	334 00.9	10.4	173 08.9	8.4	5 29.0	13.4	60.7
E 11	349 00.8	11.1	187 36.3	8.4	5 42.4	13.4	60.7
S 12	4 00.7	S17 11.8	202 03.7	8.4	N 5 55.8	13.4	60.8
D 13	19 00.7	12.5	216 31.1	8.3	6 09.2	13.3	60.8
A 14	34 00.6	13.2	230 58.4	8.2	6 22.5	13.4	60.8
Y 15	49 00.5	.. 13.9	245 25.6	8.1	6 35.9	13.3	60.8
16	64 00.5	14.6	259 52.7	8.1	6 49.2	13.2	60.9
17	79 00.4	15.3	274 19.8	8.1	7 02.4	13.2	60.9
18	94 00.4	S17 16.0	288 46.9	7.9	N 7 15.6	13.2	60.9
19	109 00.3	16.7	303 13.8	7.9	7 28.8	13.2	60.9
20	124 00.2	17.4	317 40.7	7.9	7 42.0	13.1	61.0
21	139 00.2	.. 18.1	332 07.6	7.8	7 55.1	13.1	61.0
22	154 00.1	18.8	346 34.4	7.7	8 08.2	13.0	61.0
23	169 00.0	19.5	1 01.1	7.6	8 21.2	13.0	61.0
11 00	184 00.0	S17 20.2	15 27.7	7.6	N 8 34.2	13.0	61.0
01	198 59.9	20.9	29 54.3	7.5	8 47.2	12.9	61.1
02	213 59.8	21.5	44 20.8	7.5	9 00.1	12.8	61.1
03	228 59.8	.. 22.2	58 47.3	7.4	9 12.9	12.8	61.1
04	243 59.7	22.9	73 13.7	7.3	9 25.7	12.8	61.1
05	258 59.6	23.6	87 40.0	7.3	9 38.5	12.6	61.1
06	273 59.6	S17 24.3	102 06.3	7.1	N 9 51.1	12.7	61.2
07	288 59.5	25.0	116 32.4	7.2	10 03.8	12.5	61.2
W 08	303 59.4	25.7	130 58.6	7.0	10 16.3	12.6	61.2
E 09	318 59.3	.. 26.4	145 24.6	7.0	10 28.9	12.4	61.2
D 10	333 59.3	27.1	159 50.6	6.9	10 41.3	12.4	61.2
N 11	348 59.2	27.8	174 16.5	6.9	10 53.7	12.3	61.2
E 12	3 59.1	S17 28.5	188 42.4	6.7	N11 06.0	12.3	61.3
S 13	18 59.1	29.1	203 08.1	6.7	11 18.3	12.2	61.3
D 14	33 59.0	29.8	217 33.8	6.7	11 30.5	12.1	61.3
A 15	48 58.9	.. 30.5	231 59.5	6.6	11 42.6	12.0	61.3
Y 16	63 58.8	31.2	246 25.1	6.5	11 54.6	12.0	61.3
17	78 58.8	31.9	260 50.6	6.4	12 06.6	11.9	61.3
18	93 58.7	S17 32.6	275 16.0	6.4	N12 18.5	11.8	61.3
19	108 58.6	33.3	289 41.4	6.3	12 30.3	11.7	61.3
20	123 58.6	33.9	304 06.7	6.2	12 42.0	11.6	61.3
21	138 58.5	.. 34.6	318 31.9	6.2	12 53.6	11.6	61.3
22	153 58.4	35.3	332 57.1	6.1	13 05.2	11.5	61.4
23	168 58.3	36.0	347 22.2	6.0	13 16.7	11.4	61.4
	S.D. 16.2	d 0.7	S.D. 16.4		16.6		16.7

Moonrise

Lat.	Twilight Naut.	Twilight Civil	Sunrise	Moonrise 9	10	11	12
N 72	06 41	08 10	10 02	15 34	15 17	14 57	14 24
N 70	06 33	07 51	09 18	15 35	15 26	15 16	15 02
68	06 26	07 36	08 49	15 37	15 34	15 31	15 28
66	06 20	07 24	08 28	15 38	15 40	15 43	15 49
64	06 15	07 14	08 11	15 39	15 45	15 54	16 06
62	06 11	07 05	07 57	15 40	15 50	16 03	16 20
60	06 07	06 57	07 45	15 40	15 54	16 10	16 31
N 58	06 03	06 51	07 35	15 41	15 58	16 17	16 42
56	05 59	06 45	07 26	15 41	16 01	16 23	16 51
54	05 56	06 39	07 18	15 42	16 04	16 29	16 59
52	05 53	06 34	07 11	15 42	16 07	16 34	17 06
50	05 51	06 29	07 04	15 43	16 09	16 38	17 12
45	05 44	06 19	06 51	15 44	16 14	16 48	17 26
N 40	05 38	06 11	06 39	15 45	16 19	16 56	17 38
35	05 32	06 03	06 29	15 45	16 23	17 03	17 48
30	05 27	05 56	06 21	15 46	16 26	17 09	17 57
20	05 16	05 43	06 06	15 47	16 32	17 20	18 12
N 10	05 06	05 31	05 53	15 48	16 38	17 30	18 25
0	04 54	05 19	05 40	15 49	16 43	17 39	18 38
S 10	04 40	05 06	05 28	15 50	16 48	17 48	18 50
20	04 24	04 51	05 14	15 51	16 53	17 58	19 04
30	04 02	04 33	04 59	15 53	17 00	18 09	19 20
35	03 49	04 22	04 50	15 53	17 04	18 16	19 29
40	03 33	04 09	04 39	15 54	17 08	18 23	19 39
45	03 12	03 54	04 27	15 55	17 13	18 32	19 52
S 50	02 45	03 34	04 12	15 57	17 19	18 43	20 07
52	02 31	03 25	04 05	15 57	17 21	18 48	20 14
54	02 14	03 14	03 57	15 58	17 24	18 53	20 22
56	01 53	03 01	03 48	15 59	17 28	18 59	20 31
58	01 26	02 47	03 38	15 59	17 32	19 06	20 41
S 60	00 43	02 29	03 27	16 00	17 36	19 14	20 53

Moonset

Lat.	Sunset	Twilight Civil	Twilight Naut.	Moonset 9	10	11	12
N 72	13 25	15 16	16 46	03 02	05 09	07 26	10 01
N 70	14 09	15 35	16 54	03 04	05 03	07 09	09 25
68	14 37	15 50	17 01	03 06	04 58	06 56	08 59
66	14 59	16 03	17 07	03 07	04 54	06 45	08 40
64	15 16	16 13	17 12	03 09	04 50	06 36	08 24
62	15 30	16 22	17 16	03 10	04 47	06 28	08 11
60	15 42	16 30	17 20	03 11	04 45	06 21	08 00
N 58	15 52	16 36	17 24	03 12	04 42	06 16	07 51
56	16 01	16 43	17 28	03 13	04 40	06 11	07 42
54	16 09	16 48	17 31	03 13	04 38	06 06	07 35
52	16 16	16 53	17 34	03 14	04 37	06 02	07 28
50	16 23	16 58	17 37	03 15	04 35	05 58	07 22
45	16 37	17 08	17 43	03 16	04 32	05 50	07 10
N 40	16 48	17 17	17 49	03 17	04 29	05 43	06 59
35	16 58	17 25	17 55	03 18	04 26	05 38	06 50
30	17 07	17 32	18 00	03 19	04 24	05 33	06 43
20	17 22	17 45	18 11	03 20	04 21	05 24	06 29
N 10	17 35	17 57	18 22	03 21	04 17	05 16	06 17
0	17 47	18 09	18 34	03 22	04 14	05 09	06 06
S 10	18 00	18 22	18 48	03 23	04 11	05 02	05 56
20	18 14	18 37	19 05	03 24	04 08	04 54	05 44
30	18 29	18 55	19 26	03 25	04 04	04 46	05 31
35	18 39	19 06	19 40	03 26	04 02	04 41	05 23
40	18 49	19 19	19 56	03 27	04 00	04 35	05 14
45	19 02	19 35	20 17	03 27	03 57	04 28	05 04
S 50	19 17	19 55	20 45	03 28	03 54	04 21	04 52
52	19 24	20 05	20 59	03 29	03 52	04 17	04 46
54	19 32	20 16	21 16	03 29	03 50	04 13	04 40
56	19 41	20 28	21 37	03 30	03 49	04 09	04 33
58	19 51	20 43	22 06	03 31	03 47	04 04	04 25
S 60	20 03	21 01	22 54	03 31	03 44	03 59	04 17

SUN and MOON

Day	SUN Eqn. of Time 00h	SUN Eqn. of Time 12h	Mer. Pass.	MOON Mer. Pass. Upper	MOON Mer. Pass. Lower	Age	Phase
	m s	m s	h m	h m	h m	d	
9	16 11	16 09	11 44	22 02	09 36	13	
10	16 06	16 03	11 44	22 56	10 28	14	○
11	16 00	15 57	11 44	23 53	11 24	15	

G.M.T.	ARIES G.H.A.	VENUS −4.1 G.H.A.	Dec.	MARS +1.5 G.H.A.	Dec.	JUPITER −1.2 G.H.A.	Dec.	SATURN +1.0 G.H.A.	Dec.	STARS Name	S.H.A.	Dec.
12 00	51 02.1	133 39.6	S26 45.1	246 32.0	N 8 27.2	205 38.8	S 9 21.6	214 18.6	S 4 40.1	Acamar	315 36.2	S40 22.7
01	66 04.6	148 39.3	45.0	261 33.1	26.7	220 40.7	21.8	229 20.8	40.2	Achernar	335 44.1	S57 19.9
02	81 07.0	163 39.0	44.9	276 34.3	26.2	235 42.7	21.9	244 23.0	40.3	Acrux	173 36.9	S62 59.6
03	96 09.5	178 38.6	·· 44.8	291 35.5	·· 25.6	250 44.7	·· 22.1	259 25.2	·· 40.4	Adhara	255 31.3	S28 56.6
04	111 12.0	193 38.3	44.6	306 36.6	25.1	265 46.7	22.3	274 27.4	40.5	Aldebaran	291 16.8	N16 28.4
05	126 14.4	208 38.0	44.5	321 37.8	24.6	280 48.6	22.5	289 29.7	40.6			
06	141 16.9	223 37.7	S26 44.4	336 39.0	N 8 24.1	295 50.6	S 9 22.7	304 31.9	S 4 40.7	Alioth	166 42.3	N56 03.5
T 07	156 19.4	238 37.4	44.2	351 40.1	23.6	310 52.6	22.9	319 34.1	40.8	Alkaid	153 18.3	N49 24.3
H 08	171 21.8	253 37.0	44.1	6 41.3	23.1	325 54.5	23.1	334 36.3	40.9	Al Na'ir	28 13.9	S47 03.2
U 09	186 24.3	268 36.7	·· 44.0	21 42.5	·· 22.6	340 56.5	·· 23.2	349 38.5	·· 41.0	Alnilam	276 10.6	S 1 12.7
R 10	201 26.8	283 36.4	43.9	36 43.6	22.1	355 58.5	23.4	4 40.7	41.1	Alphard	218 19.8	S 8 34.6
S 11	216 29.2	298 36.1	43.7	51 44.8	21.6	11 00.4	23.6	19 42.9	41.2			
D 12	231 31.7	313 35.8	S26 43.6	66 46.0	N 8 21.1	26 02.4	S 9 23.8	34 45.1	S 4 41.3	Alphecca	126 31.8	N26 46.7
A 13	246 34.2	328 35.5	43.4	81 47.1	20.6	41 04.4	24.0	49 47.3	41.4	Alpheratz	358 08.3	N28 59.5
Y 14	261 36.6	343 35.2	43.3	96 48.3	20.1	56 06.4	24.2	64 49.5	41.5	Altair	62 31.9	N 8 49.3
15	276 39.1	358 34.8	·· 43.2	111 49.5	·· 19.6	71 08.3	·· 24.4	79 51.7	·· 41.6	Ankaa	353 39.2	S42 24.5
16	291 41.5	13 34.5	43.0	126 50.6	19.1	86 10.3	24.5	94 53.9	41.7	Antares	112 56.3	S26 23.4
17	306 44.0	28 34.2	42.9	141 51.8	18.6	101 12.3	24.7	109 56.1	41.8			
18	321 46.5	43 33.9	S26 42.8	156 53.0	N 8 18.1	116 14.2	S 9 24.9	124 58.4	S 4 41.9	Arcturus	146 18.1	N19 16.8
19	336 48.9	58 33.6	42.6	171 54.1	17.6	131 16.2	25.1	140 00.6	42.0	Atria	108 20.4	S68 59.7
20	351 51.4	73 33.3	42.5	186 55.3	17.1	146 18.2	25.3	155 02.8	42.1	Avior	234 27.7	S59 26.7
21	6 53.9	88 33.0	·· 42.3	201 56.5	·· 16.6	161 20.1	·· 25.5	170 05.0	·· 42.2	Bellatrix	278 57.6	N 6 20.0
22	21 56.3	103 32.7	42.2	216 57.6	16.1	176 22.1	25.7	185 07.2	42.3	Betelgeuse	271 27.2	N 7 24.3
23	36 58.8	118 32.4	42.0	231 58.8	15.6	191 24.1	25.8	200 09.4	42.4			
13 00	52 01.3	133 32.1	S26 41.9	247 00.0	N 8 15.1	206 26.1	S 9 26.0	215 11.6	S 4 42.5	Canopus	264 06.5	S52 40.9
01	67 03.7	148 31.8	41.7	262 01.2	14.6	221 28.0	26.2	230 13.8	42.6	Capella	281 09.7	N45 58.7
02	82 06.2	163 31.5	41.6	277 02.3	14.1	236 30.0	26.4	245 16.0	42.7	Deneb	49 48.1	N45 13.2
03	97 08.6	178 31.2	·· 41.4	292 03.5	·· 13.6	251 32.0	·· 26.6	260 18.2	·· 42.8	Denebola	182 58.5	N14 40.5
04	112 11.1	193 30.9	41.3	307 04.7	13.1	266 33.9	26.8	275 20.4	42.9	Diphda	349 19.8	S18 05.3
05	127 13.6	208 30.6	41.1	322 05.8	12.6	281 35.9	26.9	290 22.6	43.0			
06	142 16.0	223 30.3	S26 41.0	337 07.0	N 8 12.1	296 37.9	S 9 27.1	305 24.8	S 4 43.1	Dubhe	194 21.4	N61 50.8
07	157 18.5	238 30.0	40.8	352 08.2	11.6	311 39.9	27.3	320 27.1	43.2	Elnath	278 42.8	N28 35.5
08	172 21.0	253 29.7	40.7	7 09.4	11.1	326 41.8	27.5	335 29.3	43.3	Eltanin	90 57.8	N51 29.7
F 09	187 23.4	268 29.4	·· 40.5	22 10.5	·· 10.6	341 43.8	·· 27.7	350 31.5	·· 43.4	Enif	34 10.8	N 9 47.6
R 10	202 25.9	283 29.1	40.4	37 11.7	10.1	356 45.8	27.9	5 33.7	43.5	Fomalhaut	15 50.4	S29 43.3
I 11	217 28.4	298 28.8	40.2	52 12.9	09.6	11 47.7	28.1	20 35.9	43.6			
D 12	232 30.8	313 28.5	S26 40.0	67 14.1	N 8 09.1	26 49.7	S 9 28.2	35 38.1	S 4 43.7	Gacrux	172 28.3	S57 00.3
A 13	247 33.3	328 28.2	39.9	82 15.2	08.6	41 51.7	28.4	50 40.3	43.8	Gienah	176 17.4	S17 26.2
Y 14	262 35.8	343 27.9	39.7	97 16.4	08.1	56 53.7	28.6	65 42.5	43.9	Hadar	149 22.9	S60 16.9
15	277 38.2	358 27.6	·· 39.6	112 17.6	·· 07.6	71 55.6	·· 28.8	80 44.7	·· 44.0	Hamal	328 27.7	N23 22.6
16	292 40.7	13 27.4	39.4	127 18.8	07.1	86 57.6	29.0	95 46.9	44.1	Kaus Aust.	84 16.1	S34 23.7
17	307 43.1	28 27.1	39.2	142 19.9	06.6	101 59.6	29.2	110 49.1	44.2			
18	322 45.6	43 26.8	S26 39.1	157 21.1	N 8 06.1	117 01.5	S 9 29.3	125 51.4	S 4 44.3	Kochab	137 20.2	N74 13.9
19	337 48.1	58 26.5	38.9	172 22.3	05.6	132 03.5	29.5	140 53.6	44.4	Markab	14 02.3	N15 06.5
20	352 50.5	73 26.2	38.7	187 23.5	05.1	147 05.5	29.7	155 55.8	44.5	Menkar	314 40.0	N 4 01.1
21	7 53.0	88 25.9	·· 38.6	202 24.6	·· 04.6	162 07.5	·· 29.9	170 58.0	·· 44.6	Menkent	148 36.5	S36 16.6
22	22 55.5	103 25.7	38.4	217 25.8	04.1	177 09.4	30.1	186 00.2	44.7	Miaplacidus	221 44.7	S69 38.2
23	37 57.9	118 25.4	38.2	232 27.0	03.6	192 11.4	30.3	201 02.4	44.8			
14 00	53 00.4	133 25.1	S26 38.0	247 28.2	N 8 03.0	207 13.4	S 9 30.4	216 04.6	S 4 44.9	Mirfak	309 14.5	N49 47.8
01	68 02.9	148 24.8	37.9	262 29.3	02.5	222 15.4	30.6	231 06.8	45.0	Nunki	76 28.5	S26 19.2
02	83 05.3	163 24.5	37.7	277 30.5	02.0	237 17.3	30.8	246 09.0	45.1	Peacock	53 57.3	S56 47.9
03	98 07.8	178 24.3	·· 37.5	292 31.7	·· 01.5	252 19.3	·· 31.0	261 11.2	·· 45.2	Pollux	243 57.1	N28 04.2
04	113 10.3	193 24.0	37.4	307 32.9	01.0	267 21.3	31.2	276 13.5	45.3	Procyon	245 24.8	N 5 16.4
05	128 12.7	208 23.7	37.2	322 34.0	00.5	282 23.2	31.4	291 15.7	45.4			
06	143 15.2	223 23.4	S26 37.0	337 35.2	N 8 00.0	297 25.2	S 9 31.6	306 17.9	S 4 45.5	Rasalhague	96 29.2	N12 34.5
07	158 17.6	238 23.2	36.8	352 36.4	7 59.5	312 27.2	31.7	321 20.1	45.6	Regulus	208 09.2	N12 03.5
S 08	173 20.1	253 22.9	36.6	7 37.6	59.0	327 29.2	31.9	336 22.3	45.7	Rigel	281 35.0	S 8 13.3
A 09	188 22.6	268 22.6	·· 36.5	22 38.7	·· 58.5	342 31.1	·· 32.1	351 24.5	·· 45.8	Rigil Kent.	140 25.5	S60 45.4
T 10	203 25.0	283 22.4	36.3	37 39.9	58.0	357 33.1	32.3	6 26.7	45.9	Sabik	102 40.6	S15 42.1
U 11	218 27.5	298 22.1	36.1	52 41.1	57.5	12 35.1	32.5	21 28.9	46.0			
R 12	233 30.0	313 21.8	S26 35.9	67 42.3	N 7 57.0	27 37.0	S 9 32.7	36 31.1	S 4 46.1	Schedar	350 07.7	N56 26.4
D 13	248 32.4	328 21.6	35.7	82 43.5	56.5	42 39.0	32.8	51 33.3	46.2	Shaula	96 55.1	S37 05.5
A 14	263 34.9	343 21.3	35.5	97 44.6	56.0	57 41.0	33.0	66 35.6	46.3	Sirius	258 54.8	S16 41.4
Y 15	278 37.4	358 21.0	·· 35.3	112 45.8	·· 55.5	72 43.0	·· 33.2	81 37.8	·· 46.3	Spica	158 57.0	S11 03.8
16	293 39.8	13 20.8	35.2	127 47.0	55.0	87 44.9	33.4	96 40.0	46.4	Suhail	223 10.2	S43 21.2
17	308 42.3	28 20.5	35.0	142 48.2	54.5	102 46.9	33.6	111 42.2	46.5			
18	323 44.8	43 20.2	S26 34.8	157 49.4	N 7 54.0	117 48.9	S 9 33.8	126 44.4	S 4 46.6	Vega	80 55.6	N38 46.2
19	338 47.2	58 20.0	34.6	172 50.5	53.5	132 50.9	33.9	141 46.6	46.7	Zuben'ubi	137 32.5	S15 57.8
20	353 49.7	73 19.7	34.4	187 51.7	53.0	147 52.8	34.1	156 48.8	46.8			
21	8 52.1	88 19.5	·· 34.2	202 52.9	·· 52.5	162 54.8	·· 34.3	171 51.0	·· 46.9		S.H.A.	Mer. Pass.
22	23 54.6	103 19.2	34.0	217 54.1	52.0	177 56.8	34.5	186 53.2	47.0	Venus	81 30.8	15 06
23	38 57.1	118 18.9	33.8	232 55.3	51.5	192 58.8	34.7	201 55.5	47.1	Mars	194 58.7	7 31
Mer. Pass. 20 28.6		v −0.3	d 0.2	v 1.2	d 0.5	v 2.0	d 0.2	v 2.2	d 0.1	Jupiter	154 24.8	10 13
										Saturn	163 10.3	9 38

G.M.T.	SUN G.H.A.	Dec.	MOON G.H.A.	v	Dec.	d	H.P.
12 00	183 58.3	S17 36.7	1 47.2	6.0	N13 28.1	11.3	61.4
01	198 58.2	37.3	16 12.2	5.9	13 39.4	11.2	61.4
02	213 58.1	38.0	30 37.1	5.8	13 50.6	11.1	61.4
03	228 58.0	·· 38.7	45 01.9	5.8	14 01.7	11.0	61.4
04	243 58.0	39.4	59 26.7	5.7	14 12.7	10.9	61.4
05	258 57.9	40.1	73 51.4	5.6	14 23.6	10.8	61.4
06	273 57.8	S17 40.7	88 16.0	5.6	N14 34.4	10.8	61.4
07	288 57.7	41.4	102 40.6	5.5	14 45.2	10.6	61.4
T 08	303 57.6	42.1	117 05.1	5.4	14 55.8	10.5	61.4
H 09	318 57.6	·· 42.8	131 29.5	5.4	15 06.3	10.4	61.4
U 10	333 57.5	43.5	145 53.9	5.3	15 16.7	10.3	61.4
R 11	348 57.4	44.1	160 18.2	5.3	15 27.0	10.2	61.4
S 12	3 57.3	S17 44.8	174 42.5	5.2	N15 37.2	10.1	61.4
D 13	18 57.2	45.5	189 06.7	5.1	15 47.3	10.0	61.4
A 14	33 57.2	46.2	203 30.8	5.1	15 57.3	9.8	61.4
Y 15	48 57.1	·· 46.8	217 54.9	5.0	16 07.1	9.8	61.4
16	63 57.0	47.5	232 18.9	4.9	16 16.9	9.6	61.4
17	78 56.9	48.2	246 42.8	4.9	16 26.5	9.5	61.4
18	93 56.8	S17 48.8	261 06.7	4.9	N16 36.0	9.4	61.4
19	108 56.8	49.5	275 30.6	4.8	16 45.4	9.3	61.4
20	123 56.7	50.2	289 54.4	4.7	16 54.7	9.1	61.4
21	138 56.6	·· 50.9	304 18.1	4.7	17 03.8	9.1	61.4
22	153 56.5	51.5	318 41.8	4.6	17 12.9	8.9	61.4
23	168 56.4	52.2	333 05.4	4.5	17 21.8	8.7	61.4
13 00	183 56.3	S17 52.9	347 28.9	4.6	N17 30.5	8.7	61.4
01	198 56.3	53.5	1 52.5	4.4	17 39.2	8.5	61.3
02	213 56.2	54.2	16 15.9	4.4	17 47.7	8.4	61.3
03	228 56.1	·· 54.9	30 39.3	4.4	17 56.1	8.2	61.3
04	243 56.0	55.5	45 02.7	4.3	18 04.3	8.1	61.3
05	258 55.9	56.2	59 26.0	4.3	18 12.4	8.0	61.3
06	273 55.8	S17 56.9	73 49.3	4.2	N18 20.4	7.8	61.3
07	288 55.7	57.5	88 12.5	4.2	18 28.2	7.7	61.3
08	303 55.7	58.2	102 35.7	4.2	18 35.9	7.6	61.3
F 09	318 55.6	·· 58.9	116 58.9	4.1	18 43.5	7.4	61.3
R 10	333 55.5	17 59.5	131 22.0	4.1	18 50.9	7.3	61.3
I 11	348 55.4	18 00.2	145 45.1	4.0	18 58.2	7.2	61.2
D 12	3 55.3	S18 00.9	160 08.1	4.0	N19 05.4	7.0	61.2
A 13	18 55.2	01.5	174 31.1	3.9	19 12.4	6.8	61.2
Y 14	33 55.1	02.2	188 54.0	4.0	19 19.2	6.7	61.2
15	48 55.0	·· 02.8	203 17.0	3.9	19 25.9	6.6	61.2
16	63 54.9	03.5	217 39.9	3.8	19 32.5	6.4	61.2
17	78 54.9	04.2	232 02.7	3.9	19 38.9	6.3	61.1
18	93 54.8	S18 04.8	246 25.6	3.8	N19 45.2	6.1	61.1
19	108 54.7	05.5	260 48.4	3.8	19 51.3	6.0	61.1
20	123 54.6	06.1	275 11.2	3.7	19 57.3	5.8	61.1
21	138 54.5	·· 06.8	289 33.9	3.8	20 03.1	5.7	61.1
22	153 54.4	07.4	303 56.7	3.7	20 08.8	5.5	61.1
23	168 54.3	08.1	318 19.4	3.7	20 14.3	5.3	61.0
14 00	183 54.2	S18 08.8	332 42.1	3.7	N20 19.6	5.3	61.0
01	198 54.1	09.4	347 04.8	3.7	20 24.9	5.0	61.0
02	213 54.0	10.1	1 27.5	3.6	20 29.9	4.9	61.0
03	228 53.9	·· 10.7	15 50.1	3.7	20 34.8	4.8	61.0
04	243 53.8	11.4	30 12.8	3.6	20 39.6	4.6	60.9
05	258 53.7	12.0	44 35.4	3.7	20 44.2	4.4	60.9
06	273 53.7	S18 12.7	58 58.1	3.6	N20 48.6	4.3	60.9
07	288 53.6	13.3	73 20.7	3.6	20 52.9	4.1	60.9
S 08	303 53.5	14.0	87 43.3	3.7	20 57.0	4.0	60.8
A 09	318 53.4	·· 14.6	102 06.0	3.6	21 01.0	3.8	60.8
T 10	333 53.3	15.3	116 28.6	3.6	21 04.8	3.6	60.8
U 11	348 53.2	15.9	130 51.2	3.6	21 08.4	3.5	60.8
R 12	3 53.1	S18 16.6	145 13.8	3.7	N21 11.9	3.3	60.7
D 13	18 53.0	17.2	159 36.5	3.6	21 15.2	3.2	60.7
A 14	33 52.9	17.9	173 59.1	3.7	21 18.4	3.0	60.7
Y 15	48 52.8	·· 18.5	188 21.8	3.6	21 21.4	2.9	60.7
16	63 52.7	19.2	202 44.4	3.7	21 24.3	2.7	60.6
17	78 52.6	19.8	217 07.1	3.7	21 27.0	2.5	60.6
18	93 52.5	S18 20.5	231 29.8	3.7	N21 29.5	2.4	60.6
19	108 52.4	21.1	245 52.5	3.7	21 31.9	2.2	60.6
20	123 52.3	21.8	260 15.2	3.8	21 34.1	2.1	60.5
21	138 52.2	·· 22.4	274 38.0	3.7	21 36.2	1.9	60.5
22	153 52.1	23.0	289 00.7	3.8	21 38.1	1.8	60.5
23	168 52.0	23.7	303 23.5	3.9	21 39.9	1.5	60.4
	S.D. 16.2 d 0.7		S.D. 16.7		16.7		16.6

Lat.	Twilight Naut.	Civil	Sunrise	Moonrise 12	13	14	15
N 72	06 52	08 24	10 32	14 24	□	□	□
N 70	06 43	08 03	09 36	15 02	14 33	□	□
68	06 35	07 47	09 03	15 28	15 28	15 32	16 15
66	06 28	07 33	08 39	15 49	16 01	16 27	17 21
64	06 22	07 22	08 21	16 06	16 25	17 00	17 57
62	06 17	07 13	08 05	16 20	16 45	17 24	18 22
60	06 13	07 04	07 53	16 31	17 01	17 43	18 42
N 58	06 09	06 57	07 42	16 42	17 15	18 00	18 59
56	06 05	06 50	07 32	16 51	17 26	18 13	19 13
54	06 01	06 44	07 24	16 59	17 37	18 25	19 25
52	05 58	06 39	07 16	17 06	17 46	18 36	19 36
50	05 55	06 34	07 09	17 12	17 54	18 45	19 45
45	05 48	06 23	06 55	17 26	18 12	19 05	20 06
N 40	05 41	06 14	06 43	17 38	18 26	19 21	20 22
35	05 35	06 06	06 32	17 48	18 38	19 35	20 36
30	05 29	05 58	06 23	17 57	18 49	19 47	20 48
20	05 18	05 44	06 08	18 12	19 08	20 07	21 08
N 10	05 06	05 32	05 54	18 25	19 24	20 25	21 26
0	04 54	05 19	05 41	18 38	19 39	20 41	21 43
S 10	04 39	05 05	05 28	18 50	19 54	20 58	21 59
20	04 22	04 50	05 13	19 04	20 11	21 16	22 17
30	04 00	04 31	04 57	19 20	20 30	21 37	22 38
35	03 46	04 20	04 47	19 29	20 41	21 49	22 50
40	03 29	04 06	04 36	19 39	20 54	22 03	23 04
45	03 07	03 50	04 23	19 52	21 09	22 19	23 20
S 50	02 38	03 29	04 08	20 07	21 28	22 40	23 40
52	02 23	03 19	04 00	20 14	21 36	22 50	23 50
54	02 05	03 08	03 52	20 22	21 46	23 00	24 01
56	01 43	02 54	03 42	20 31	21 57	23 13	24 13
58	01 11	02 39	03 32	20 41	22 10	23 27	24 27
S 60	00 05	02 19	03 19	20 53	22 25	23 44	24 43

Lat.	Sunset	Twilight Civil	Naut.	Moonset 12	13	14	15
N 72	12 56	15 03	16 35	10 01	□	□	□
N 70	13 52	15 24	16 45	09 25	12 01	□	□
68	14 25	15 41	16 53	08 59	11 07	13 13	14 40
66	14 48	15 54	16 59	08 40	10 34	12 19	13 34
64	15 07	16 06	17 05	08 24	10 11	11 46	12 58
62	15 22	16 15	17 10	08 11	09 52	11 22	12 33
60	15 35	16 24	17 15	08 00	09 36	11 03	12 12
N 58	15 46	16 31	17 19	07 51	09 23	10 47	11 56
56	15 56	16 38	17 23	07 42	09 12	10 34	11 42
54	16 04	16 44	17 27	07 35	09 02	10 22	11 29
52	16 12	16 49	17 30	07 28	08 53	10 12	11 19
50	16 19	16 54	17 33	07 22	08 45	10 02	11 09
45	16 33	17 05	17 40	07 10	08 29	09 43	10 49
N 40	16 46	17 14	17 47	06 59	08 15	09 27	10 32
35	16 56	17 23	17 53	06 50	08 03	09 14	10 19
30	17 05	17 30	17 59	06 43	07 53	09 02	10 06
20	17 21	17 44	18 11	06 29	07 36	08 42	09 46
N 10	17 35	17 57	18 22	06 17	07 21	08 25	09 28
0	17 48	18 10	18 35	06 06	07 07	08 09	09 11
S 10	18 01	18 23	18 49	05 56	06 53	07 53	08 54
20	18 15	18 39	19 07	05 44	06 38	07 35	08 36
30	18 32	18 58	19 29	05 31	06 20	07 15	08 15
35	18 42	19 09	19 43	05 23	06 10	07 04	08 03
40	18 53	19 23	20 01	05 14	05 59	06 51	07 49
45	19 06	19 40	20 22	05 04	05 46	06 35	07 32
S 50	19 22	20 01	20 52	04 52	05 30	06 16	07 12
52	19 30	20 11	21 07	04 46	05 22	06 07	07 02
54	19 38	20 23	21 26	04 40	05 14	05 56	06 51
56	19 48	20 36	21 49	04 33	05 04	05 45	06 38
58	19 58	20 52	22 22	04 25	04 53	05 32	06 24
S 60	20 11	21 12	////	04 17	04 41	05 16	06 07

Day	SUN Eqn. of Time 00h	12h	Mer. Pass.	MOON Mer. Pass. Upper	Lower	Age	Phase
12	15 53	15 49	11 44	24 52	12 22	16	
13	15 46	15 41	11 44	00 52	13 23	17	○
14	15 37	15 32	11 44	01 54	14 25	18	

G.M.T.	ARIES G.H.A.	VENUS −4.1 G.H.A.	Dec.	MARS +1.5 G.H.A.	Dec.	JUPITER −1.2 G.H.A.	Dec.	SATURN +1.0 G.H.A.	Dec.	STARS Name	S.H.A.	Dec.
15 00	53 59.5	133 18.7	S26 33.6	247 56.4	N 7 51.0	208 00.7	S 9 34.8	216 57.7	S 4 47.2	Acamar	315 36.2	S40 22.7
01	69 02.0	148 18.4	33.4	262 57.6	50.5	223 02.7	35.0	231 59.9	47.3	Achernar	335 44.1	S57 19.9
02	84 04.5	163 18.2	33.2	277 58.8	50.0	238 04.7	35.2	247 02.1	47.4	Acrux	173 36.8	S62 59.5
03	99 06.9	178 17.9	·· 33.0	293 00.0	·· 49.5	253 06.6	·· 35.4	262 04.3	·· 47.5	Adhara	255 31.2	S28 56.7
04	114 09.4	193 17.7	32.8	308 01.2	49.0	268 08.6	35.6	277 06.5	47.6	Aldebaran	291 16.8	N16 28.4
05	129 11.9	208 17.4	32.6	323 02.4	48.5	283 10.6	35.8	292 08.7	47.7			
06	144 14.3	223 17.2	S26 32.4	338 03.5	N 7 48.0	298 12.6	S 9 35.9	307 10.9	S 4 47.8	Alioth	166 42.2	N56 03.5
07	159 16.8	238 16.9	32.2	353 04.7	47.5	313 14.5	36.1	322 13.1	47.9	Alkaid	153 18.3	N49 24.3
08	174 19.2	253 16.7	32.0	8 05.9	47.0	328 16.5	36.3	337 15.4	48.0	Al Na'ir	28 13.9	S47 03.2
S 09	189 21.7	268 16.4	·· 31.8	23 07.1	·· 46.5	343 18.5	·· 36.5	352 17.6	·· 48.1	Alnilam	276 10.6	S 1 12.8
U 10	204 24.2	283 16.2	31.6	38 08.3	46.0	358 20.5	36.7	7 19.8	48.2	Alphard	218 19.8	S 8 34.6
N 11	219 26.6	298 15.9	31.4	53 09.5	45.5	13 22.4	36.9	22 22.0	48.3			
D 12	234 29.1	313 15.7	S26 31.2	68 10.6	N 7 45.0	28 24.4	S 9 37.0	37 24.2	S 4 48.4	Alphecca	126 31.8	N26 46.7
A 13	249 31.6	328 15.4	31.0	83 11.8	44.5	43 26.4	37.2	52 26.4	48.5	Alpheratz	358 08.3	N28 59.5
Y 14	264 34.0	343 15.2	30.8	98 13.0	44.0	58 28.4	37.4	67 28.6	48.6	Altair	62 31.9	N 8 49.3
15	279 36.5	358 15.0	·· 30.6	113 14.2	·· 43.5	73 30.3	·· 37.6	82 30.8	·· 48.7	Ankaa	353 39.2	S42 24.5
16	294 39.0	13 14.7	30.4	128 15.4	43.0	88 32.3	37.8	97 33.1	48.8	Antares	112 56.3	S26 23.4
17	309 41.4	28 14.5	30.1	143 16.6	42.5	103 34.3	38.0	112 35.3	48.9			
18	324 43.9	43 14.2	S26 29.9	158 17.7	N 7 42.0	118 36.3	S 9 38.1	127 37.5	S 4 49.0	Arcturus	146 18.1	N19 16.7
19	339 46.4	58 14.0	29.7	173 18.9	41.5	133 38.2	38.3	142 39.7	49.1	Atria	108 20.3	S68 59.7
20	354 48.8	73 13.8	29.5	188 20.1	41.0	148 40.2	38.5	157 41.9	49.2	Avior	234 27.7	S59 26.7
21	9 51.3	88 13.5	·· 29.3	203 21.3	·· 40.5	163 42.2	·· 38.7	172 44.1	·· 49.3	Bellatrix	278 57.6	N 6 20.0
22	24 53.7	103 13.3	29.1	218 22.5	40.0	178 44.2	38.9	187 46.3	49.4	Betelgeuse	271 27.1	N 7 24.3
23	39 56.2	118 13.1	28.8	233 23.7	39.5	193 46.1	39.0	202 48.5	49.5			
16 00	54 58.7	133 12.8	S26 28.6	248 24.9	N 7 39.0	208 48.1	S 9 39.2	217 50.8	S 4 49.5	Canopus	264 06.4	S52 41.0
01	70 01.1	148 12.6	28.4	263 26.0	38.5	223 50.1	39.4	232 53.0	49.6	Capella	281 09.7	N45 58.7
02	85 03.6	163 12.4	28.2	278 27.2	38.0	238 52.1	39.6	247 55.2	49.7	Deneb	49 48.1	N45 13.2
03	100 06.1	178 12.2	·· 28.0	293 28.4	·· 37.5	253 54.0	·· 39.8	262 57.4	·· 49.8	Denebola	182 58.4	N14 40.5
04	115 08.5	193 11.9	27.7	308 29.6	37.0	268 56.0	40.0	277 59.6	49.9	Diphda	349 19.8	S18 05.3
05	130 11.0	208 11.7	27.5	323 30.8	36.5	283 58.0	40.1	293 01.8	50.0			
06	145 13.5	223 11.5	S26 27.3	338 32.0	N 7 36.0	299 00.0	S 9 40.3	308 04.0	S 4 50.1	Dubhe	194 21.4	N61 50.8
07	160 15.9	238 11.3	27.1	353 33.2	35.5	314 01.9	40.5	323 06.3	50.2	Elnath	278 42.8	N28 35.5
08	175 18.4	253 11.0	26.8	8 34.4	35.0	329 03.9	40.7	338 08.5	50.3	Eltanin	90 57.8	N51 29.7
M 09	190 20.9	268 10.8	·· 26.6	23 35.5	·· 34.5	344 05.9	·· 40.9	353 10.7	·· 50.4	Enif	34 10.8	N 9 47.6
O 10	205 23.3	283 10.6	26.4	38 36.7	34.0	359 07.9	41.0	8 12.9	50.5	Fomalhaut	15 50.4	S29 43.3
N 11	220 25.8	298 10.4	26.1	53 37.9	33.5	14 09.8	41.2	23 15.1	50.6			
D 12	235 28.2	313 10.2	S26 25.9	68 39.1	N 7 33.0	29 11.8	S 9 41.4	38 17.3	S 4 50.7	Gacrux	172 28.3	S57 00.3
A 13	250 30.7	328 09.9	25.7	83 40.3	32.5	44 13.8	41.6	53 19.5	50.8	Gienah	176 17.4	S17 26.2
Y 14	265 33.2	343 09.7	25.4	98 41.5	32.0	59 15.8	41.8	68 21.8	50.9	Hadar	149 22.9	S60 16.9
15	280 35.6	358 09.5	·· 25.2	113 42.7	·· 31.5	74 17.7	·· 42.0	83 24.0	·· 51.0	Hamal	328 27.7	N23 22.6
16	295 38.1	13 09.3	25.0	128 43.9	31.0	89 19.7	42.1	98 26.2	51.1	Kaus Aust.	84 16.1	S34 23.7
17	310 40.6	28 09.1	24.7	143 45.1	30.5	104 21.7	42.3	113 28.4	51.2			
18	325 43.0	43 08.9	S26 24.5	158 46.3	N 7 30.0	119 23.7	S 9 42.5	128 30.6	S 4 51.3	Kochab	137 20.2	N74 13.8
19	340 45.5	58 08.7	24.3	173 47.4	29.5	134 25.6	42.7	143 32.8	51.4	Markab	14 02.3	N15 06.5
20	355 48.0	73 08.5	24.0	188 48.6	29.0	149 27.6	42.9	158 35.0	51.5	Menkar	314 40.0	N 4 01.1
21	10 50.4	88 08.2	·· 23.8	203 49.8	·· 28.5	164 29.6	·· 43.0	173 37.3	·· 51.6	Menkent	148 36.5	S36 16.6
22	25 52.9	103 08.0	23.5	218 51.0	28.0	179 31.6	43.2	188 39.5	51.7	Miaplacidus	221 44.7	S69 38.2
23	40 55.3	118 07.8	23.3	233 52.2	27.5	194 33.5	43.4	203 41.7	51.8			
17 00	55 57.8	133 07.6	S26 23.1	248 53.4	N 7 27.0	209 35.5	S 9 43.6	218 43.9	S 4 51.8	Mirfak	309 14.5	N49 47.8
01	71 00.3	148 07.4	22.8	263 54.6	26.5	224 37.5	43.8	233 46.1	51.9	Nunki	76 28.5	S26 19.2
02	86 02.7	163 07.2	22.6	278 55.8	26.0	239 39.5	43.9	248 48.3	52.0	Peacock	53 57.4	S56 47.9
03	101 05.2	178 07.0	·· 22.3	293 57.0	·· 25.5	254 41.5	·· 44.1	263 50.5	·· 52.1	Pollux	243 57.0	N28 04.2
04	116 07.7	193 06.8	22.1	308 58.2	25.0	269 43.4	44.3	278 52.8	52.2	Procyon	245 24.8	N 5 16.4
05	131 10.1	208 06.6	21.8	323 59.4	24.5	284 45.4	44.5	293 55.0	52.3			
06	146 12.6	223 06.4	S26 21.6	339 00.6	N 7 24.0	299 47.4	S 9 44.7	308 57.2	S 4 52.4	Rasalhague	96 29.2	N12 34.5
07	161 15.1	238 06.2	21.3	354 01.8	23.5	314 49.4	44.8	323 59.4	52.5	Regulus	208 09.2	N12 03.4
08	176 17.5	253 06.0	21.1	9 02.9	23.0	329 51.3	45.0	339 01.6	52.6	Rigel	281 35.0	S 8 13.3
T 09	191 20.0	268 05.8	·· 20.8	24 04.1	·· 22.5	344 53.3	·· 45.2	354 03.8	·· 52.7	Rigil Kent.	140 25.4	S60 45.4
U 10	206 22.5	283 05.6	20.6	39 05.3	22.0	359 55.3	45.4	9 06.0	52.8	Sabik	102 40.6	S15 42.1
E 11	221 24.9	298 05.4	20.3	54 06.5	21.5	14 57.3	45.6	24 08.3	52.9			
S 12	236 27.4	313 05.3	S26 20.1	69 07.7	N 7 21.0	29 59.2	S 9 45.7	39 10.5	S 4 53.0	Schedar	350 07.7	N56 26.4
D 13	251 29.8	328 05.1	19.8	84 08.9	20.5	45 01.2	45.9	54 12.7	53.1	Shaula	96 55.1	S37 05.4
A 14	266 32.3	343 04.9	19.5	99 10.1	20.0	60 03.2	46.1	69 14.9	53.2	Sirius	258 54.8	S16 41.4
Y 15	281 34.8	358 04.7	·· 19.3	114 11.3	·· 19.5	75 05.2	·· 46.3	84 17.1	·· 53.3	Spica	158 57.0	S11 03.8
16	296 37.2	13 04.5	19.0	129 12.5	19.0	90 07.2	46.5	99 19.3	53.4	Suhail	223 10.1	S43 21.2
17	311 39.7	28 04.3	18.8	144 13.7	18.5	105 09.1	46.6	114 21.6	53.5			
18	326 42.2	43 04.1	S26 18.5	159 14.9	N 7 18.0	120 11.1	S 9 46.8	129 23.8	S 4 53.6	Vega	80 55.6	N38 46.2
19	341 44.6	58 03.9	18.2	174 16.1	17.5	135 13.1	47.0	144 26.0	53.7	Zuben'ubi	137 32.5	S15 57.8
20	356 47.1	73 03.8	18.0	189 17.3	17.0	150 15.1	47.2	159 28.2	53.7		S.H.A.	Mer. Pass.
21	11 49.6	88 03.6	·· 17.7	204 18.5	·· 16.5	165 17.0	·· 47.4	174 30.4	·· 53.8			h m
22	26 52.0	103 03.4	17.5	219 19.7	16.0	180 19.0	47.5	189 32.6	53.9	Venus	78 14.2	15 07
23	41 54.5	118 03.2	17.2	234 20.9	15.5	195 21.0	47.7	204 34.9	54.0	Mars	193 26.2	7 26
Mer. Pass.	h m 20 16.8	v −0.2	d 0.2	v 1.2	d 0.5	v 2.0	d 0.2	v 2.2	d 0.1	Jupiter	153 49.4	10 03
										Saturn	162 52.1	9 27

G.M.T.	SUN G.H.A.	SUN Dec.	MOON G.H.A.	v	MOON Dec.	d	H.P.
	° ′	° ′	° ′	′	° ′	′	′
15 00	183 51.9	S18 24.3	317 46.4	3.8	N21 41.4	1.5	60.4
01	198 51.8	25.0	332 09.2	3.9	21 42.9	1.2	60.4
02	213 51.7	25.6	346 32.1	3.9	21 44.1	1.2	60.3
03	228 51.6	.. 26.3	0 55.0	3.9	21 45.3	0.9	60.3
04	243 51.5	26.9	15 17.9	4.0	21 46.2	0.8	60.3
05	258 51.4	27.5	29 40.9	4.0	21 47.0	0.7	60.3
06	273 51.3	S18 28.2	44 03.9	4.1	N21 47.7	0.4	60.2
07	288 51.1	28.8	58 27.0	4.1	21 48.1	0.4	60.2
08	303 51.0	29.4	72 50.1	4.2	21 48.5	0.1	60.2
S 09	318 50.9	.. 30.1	87 13.3	4.1	21 48.6	0.1	60.1
U 10	333 50.8	30.7	101 36.4	4.3	21 48.7	0.2	60.1
N 11	348 50.7	31.4	115 59.7	4.3	21 48.5	0.3	60.1
D 12	3 50.6	S18 32.0	130 23.0	4.3	N21 48.2	0.4	60.0
A 13	18 50.5	32.6	144 46.3	4.4	21 47.8	0.6	60.0
Y 14	33 50.4	33.3	159 09.7	4.4	21 47.2	0.7	60.0
15	48 50.3	.. 33.9	173 33.1	4.5	21 46.5	0.9	59.9
16	63 50.2	34.5	187 56.6	4.6	21 45.6	1.1	59.9
17	78 50.1	35.2	202 20.2	4.6	21 44.5	1.2	59.9
18	93 50.0	S18 35.8	216 43.8	4.6	N21 43.3	1.3	59.8
19	108 49.9	36.4	231 07.4	4.7	21 42.0	1.5	59.8
20	123 49.8	37.1	245 31.1	4.8	21 40.5	1.6	59.8
21	138 49.6	.. 37.7	259 54.9	4.9	21 38.9	1.8	59.7
22	153 49.5	38.3	274 18.8	4.9	21 37.1	2.0	59.7
23	168 49.4	38.9	288 42.7	5.0	21 35.1	2.0	59.6
16 00	183 49.3	S18 39.6	303 06.7	5.0	N21 33.1	2.3	59.6
01	198 49.2	40.2	317 30.7	5.2	21 30.8	2.3	59.6
02	213 49.1	40.8	331 54.9	5.2	21 28.5	2.5	59.5
03	228 49.0	.. 41.5	346 19.1	5.2	21 26.0	2.7	59.5
04	243 48.9	42.1	0 43.3	5.4	21 23.3	2.8	59.5
05	258 48.8	42.7	15 07.7	5.4	21 20.5	2.9	59.4
06	273 48.6	S18 43.3	29 32.1	5.5	N21 17.6	3.1	59.4
07	288 48.5	44.0	43 56.6	5.5	21 14.5	3.2	59.4
08	303 48.4	44.6	58 21.1	5.7	21 11.3	3.3	59.3
M 09	318 48.3	.. 45.2	72 45.8	5.7	21 08.0	3.5	59.3
O 10	333 48.2	45.8	87 10.5	5.8	21 04.5	3.6	59.2
N 11	348 48.1	46.5	101 35.3	5.8	21 00.9	3.7	59.2
D 12	3 48.0	S18 47.1	116 00.1	6.0	N20 57.2	3.9	59.1
A 13	18 47.8	47.7	130 25.1	6.1	20 53.3	4.0	59.1
Y 14	33 47.7	48.3	144 50.2	6.1	20 49.3	4.1	59.1
15	48 47.6	.. 48.9	159 15.3	6.2	20 45.2	4.3	59.1
16	63 47.5	49.6	173 40.5	6.3	20 40.9	4.4	59.0
·17	78 47.4	50.2	188 05.8	6.4	20 36.5	4.5	59.0
18	93 47.3	S18 50.8	202 31.2	6.4	N20 32.0	4.6	58.9
19	108 47.1	51.4	216 56.6	6.6	20 27.4	4.8	58.9
20	123 47.0	52.0	231 22.2	6.6	20 22.6	4.9	58.9
21	138 46.9	.. 52.7	245 47.8	6.8	20 17.7	5.0	58.8
22	153 46.8	53.3	260 13.6	6.8	20 12.7	5.1	58.8
23	168 46.7	53.9	274 39.4	6.9	20 07.6	5.2	58.8
17 00	183 46.5	S18 54.5	289 05.3	7.0	N20 02.4	5.4	58.7
01	198 46.4	55.1	303 31.3	7.1	19 57.0	5.5	58.7
02	213 46.3	55.7	317 57.4	7.2	19 51.5	5.6	58.6
03	228 46.2	.. 56.3	332 23.6	7.2	19 45.9	5.7	58.6
04	243 46.1	57.0	346 49.8	7.4	19 40.2	5.8	58.6
05	258 46.0	57.6	1 16.2	7.5	19 34.4	5.9	58.5
06	273 45.8	S18 58.2	·15 42.7	7.5	N19 28.5	6.1	58.5
07	288 45.7	58.8	30 09.2	7.7	19 22.4	6.1	58.5
08	303 45.6	18 59.4	44 35.9	7.7	19 16.3	6.3	58.4
T 09	318 45.5	19 00.0	59 02.6	7.8	19 10.0	6.3	58.4
U 10	333 45.3	00.6	73 29.4	7.9	19 03.7	6.5	58.3
E 11	348 45.2	01.2	87 56.3	8.1	18 57.2	6.6	58.3
S 12	3 45.1	S19 01.8	102 23.4	8.1	N18 50.6	6.7	58.3
D 13	18 45.0	02.4	116 50.5	8.2	18 43.9	6.7	58.2
A 14	33 44.8	03.0	131 17.7	8.3	18 37.2	6.9	58.2
Y 15	48 44.7	.. 03.7	145 45.0	8.4	18 30.3	7.0	58.1
16	63 44.6	04.3	160 12.4	8.5	18 23.3	7.1	58.1
17	78 44.5	04.9	174 39.9	8.5	18 16.2	7.1	58.1
18	93 44.3	S19 05.5	189 07.4	8.7	N18 09.1	7.3	58.0
19	108 44.2	06.1	203 35.1	8.8	18 01.8	7.3	58.0
20	123 44.1	06.7	218 02.9	8.8	17 54.5	7.5	58.0
21	138 43.9	.. 07.3	232 30.7	9.0	17 47.0	7.5	57.9
22	153 43.8	07.9	246 58.7	9.1	17 39.5	7.7	57.9
23	168 43.7	08.5	261 26.8	9.1	17 31.8	7.7	57.8
	S.D. 16.2	d 0.6	S.D. 16.4		16.1		15.9

Twilight / Sunrise / Moonrise

Lat.	Naut.	Civil	Sunrise	15	16	17	18
°	h m	h m	h m	h m	h m	h m	h m
N 72	07 03	08 39	11 26	□	□		20 53
N 70	06 52	08 15	09 55			19 17	21 24
68	06 43	07 57	09 17	16 15	18 03	19 58	21 47
66	06 36	07 42	08 51	17 21	18 47	20 25	22 04
64	06 30	07 30	08 30	17 57	19 16	20 46	22 19
62	06 24	07 20	08 14	18 22	19 38	21 03	22 30
60	06 19	07 11	08 00	18 42	19 56	21 17	22 41
N 58	06 14	07 03	07 48	18 59	20 11	21 29	22 49
56	06 10	06 56	07 38	19 13	20 23	21 40	22 57
54	06 06	06 50	07 29	19 25	20 34	21 49	23 04
52	06 02	06 44	07 21	19 36	20 44	21 57	23 10
50	05 59	06 38	07 14	19 45	20 53	22 04	23 15
45	05 51	06 27	06 59	20 06	21 11	22 20	23 27
N 40	05 44	06 17	06 46	20 22	21 27	22 32	23 37
35	05 38	06 08	06 35	20 36	21 39	22 43	23 46
30	05 31	06 00	06 26	20 48	21 50	22 53	23 53
20	05 19	05 46	06 09	21 08	22 09	23 09	24 06
N 10	05 07	05 33	05 55	21 26	22 26	23 23	24 17
0	04 54	05 19	05 41	21 43	22 41	23 36	24 27
S 10	04 39	05 05	05 27	21 59	22 57	23 49	24 37
20	04 21	04 49	05 13	22 17	23 13	24 03	00 03
30	03 58	04 29	04 55	22 38	23 32	24 19	00 19
35	03 43	04 17	04 45	22 50	23 43	24 29	00 29
40	03 26	04 03	04 34	23 04	23 56	24 39	00 39
45	03 03	03 46	04 20	23 20	24 10	00 10	00 52
S 50	02 32	03 24	04 04	23 40	24 29	00 29	01 07
52	02 16	03 14	03 56	23 50	24 37	00 37	01 14
54	01 57	03 02	03 47	24 01	00 01	00 47	01 21
56	01 31	02 47	03 37	24 13	00 13	00 57	01 30
58	00 54	02 31	03 26	24 27	00 27	01 10	01 40
S 60	////	02 10	03 12	24 43	00 43	01 24	01 51

Sunset / Twilight / Moonset

Lat.	Sunset	Civil	Naut.	15	16	17	18
°	h m	h m	h m	h m	h m	h m	h m
N 72	12 02	14 50	16 26	□	□		15 53
N 70	13 33	15 13	16 36			15 39	15 20
68	14 12	15 32	16 45	14 40	14 57	14 58	14 56
66	14 38	15 46	16 53	13 34	14 13	14 30	14 37
64	15 00	15 59	16 59	12 58	13 43	14 08	14 22
62	15 15	16 09	17 05	12 33	13 20	13 50	14 10
60	15 29	16 18	17 10	12 12	13 02	13 36	13 59
N 58	15 40	16 26	17 15	11 56	12 47	13 23	13 49
56	15 51	16 33	17 19	11 42	12 34	13 12	13 41
54	16 00	16 39	17 23	11 29	12 23	13 03	13 33
52	16 08	16 45	17 27	11 19	12 13	12 54	13 27
50	16 15	16 51	17 30	11 09	12 04	12 47	13 21
45	16 30	17 02	17 38	10 49	11 45	12 30	13 08
N 40	16 43	17 12	17 45	10 32	11 29	12 17	12 57
35	16 54	17 21	17 52	10 19	11 16	12 05	12 48
30	17 04	17 29	17 58	10 06	11 04	11 55	12 39
20	17 20	17 43	18 10	09 46	10 45	11 38	12 25
N 10	17 35	17 57	18 22	09 28	10 27	11 22	12 13
0	17 48	18 10	18 36	09 11	10 11	11 08	12 01
S 10	18 02	18 25	18 51	08 54	09 55	10 54	11 49
20	18 17	18 41	19 09	08 36	09 37	10 38	11 36
30	18 34	19 01	19 32	08 15	09 17	10 20	11 22
35	18 45	19 13	19 47	08 03	09 06	10 10	11 13
40	18 56	19 27	20 05	07 49	08 52	09 58	11 03
45	19 10	19 44	20 28	07 32	08 36	09 44	10 52
S 50	19 27	20 06	20 59	07 12	08 16	09 26	10 38
52	19 35	20 17	21 15	07 02	08 07	09 18	10 31
54	19 44	20 30	21 35	06 51	07 56	09 09	10 24
56	19 54	20 44	22 02	06 38	07 44	08 58	10 16
58	20 06	21 01	22 42	06 24	07 30	08 47	10 07
S 60	20 19	21 23	////	06 07	07 14	08 33	09 56

Day	SUN Eqn. of Time 00ʰ	12ʰ	Mer. Pass.	MOON Mer. Pass. Upper	Lower	Age	Phase
	m s	m s	h m	h m	h m	d	
15	15 28	15 23	11 45	02 56	15 27	19	
16	15 17	15 12	11 45	03 57	16 26	20	◐
17	15 06	15 01	11 45	04 55	17 22	21	

G.M.T.	ARIES G.H.A.	VENUS −4.2 G.H.A.	Dec.	MARS +1.4 G.H.A.	Dec.	JUPITER −1.3 G.H.A.	Dec.	SATURN +1.0 G.H.A.	Dec.	STARS Name	S.H.A.	Dec.
18 00	56 57.0	133 03.1	S26 16.9	249 22.1	N 7 15.0	210 23.0	S 9 47.9	219 37.1	S 4 54.1	Acamar	315 36.2	S40 22.7
01	71 59.4	148 02.9	16.7	264 23.3	14.5	225 25.0	48.1	234 39.3	54.2	Achernar	335 44.2	S57 20.0
02	87 01.9	163 02.7	16.4	279 24.5	14.0	240 26.9	48.3	249 41.5	54.3	Acrux	173 36.8	S62 59.5
03	102 04.3	178 02.5	·· 16.1	294 25.7	·· 13.5	255 28.9	·· 48.4	264 43.7	·· 54.4	Adhara	255 31.2	S28 56.7
04	117 06.8	193 02.4	15.9	309 26.9	13.0	270 30.9	48.6	279 45.9	54.5	Aldebaran	291 16.8	N16 28.4
05	132 09.3	208 02.2	15.6	324 28.1	12.5	285 32.9	48.8	294 48.2	54.6			
06	147 11.7	223 02.0	S26 15.3	339 29.3	N 7 12.0	300 34.8	S 9 49.0	309 50.4	S 4 54.7	Alioth	166 42.2	N56 03.4
07	162 14.2	238 01.8	15.0	354 30.5	11.5	315 36.8	49.2	324 52.6	54.8	Alkaid	153 18.3	N49 24.2
W 08	177 16.7	253 01.7	14.8	9 31.7	11.0	330 38.8	49.3	339 54.8	54.9	Al Na'ir	28 13.9	S47 03.2
E 09	192 19.1	268 01.5	·· 14.5	24 32.9	·· 10.5	345 40.8	·· 49.5	354 57.0	·· 55.0	Alnilam	276 10.6	S 1 12.8
D 10	207 21.6	283 01.3	14.2	39 34.1	10.0	0 42.8	49.7	9 59.2	55.1	Alphard	218 19.7	S 8 34.6
N 11	222 24.1	298 01.2	13.9	54 35.3	09.5	15 44.7	49.9	25 01.5	55.2			
E 12	237 26.5	313 01.0	S26 13.7	69 36.5	N 7 09.0	30 46.7	S 9 50.1	40 03.7	S 4 55.3	Alphecca	126 31.8	N26 46.7
S 13	252 29.0	328 00.9	13.4	84 37.7	08.5	45 48.7	50.2	55 05.9	55.4	Alpheratz	358 08.3	N28 59.5
D 14	267 31.4	343 00.7	13.1	99 38.9	08.1	60 50.7	50.4	70 08.1	55.4	Altair	62 31.9	N 8 49.3
A 15	282 33.9	358 00.5	·· 12.8	114 40.1	·· 07.6	75 52.7	·· 50.6	85 10.3	·· 55.5	Ankaa	353 39.2	S42 24.5
Y 16	297 36.4	13 00.4	12.5	129 41.3	07.1	90 54.6	50.8	100 12.5	55.6	Antares	112 56.3	S26 23.4
17	312 38.8	28 00.2	12.3	144 42.5	06.6	105 56.6	51.0	115 14.8	55.7			
18	327 41.3	43 00.1	S26 12.0	159 43.7	N 7 06.1	120 58.6	S 9 51.1	130 17.0	S 4 55.8	Arcturus	146 18.1	N19 16.7
19	342 43.8	57 59.9	11.7	174 44.9	05.6	136 00.6	51.3	145 19.2	55.9	Atria	108 20.3	S68 59.7
20	357 46.2	72 59.7	11.4	189 46.1	05.1	151 02.6	51.5	160 21.4	56.0	Avior	234 27.6	S59 26.7
21	12 48.7	87 59.6	·· 11.1	204 47.3	·· 04.6	166 04.5	·· 51.7	175 23.6	·· 56.1	Bellatrix	278 57.6	N 6 20.0
22	27 51.2	102 59.4	10.8	219 48.5	04.1	181 06.5	51.9	190 25.9	56.2	Betelgeuse	271 27.1	N 7 24.3
23	42 53.6	117 59.3	10.5	234 49.7	03.6	196 08.5	52.0	205 28.1	56.3			
19 00	57 56.1	132 59.1	S26 10.3	249 50.9	N 7 03.1	211 10.5	S 9 52.2	220 30.3	S 4 56.4	Canopus	264 06.4	S52 41.0
01	72 58.6	147 59.0	10.0	264 52.1	02.6	226 12.4	52.4	235 32.5	56.5	Capella	281 09.7	N45 58.7
02	88 01.0	162 58.9	09.7	279 53.3	02.1	241 14.4	52.6	250 34.7	56.6	Deneb	49 48.1	N45 13.2
03	103 03.5	177 58.7	·· 09.4	294 54.5	·· 01.6	256 16.4	·· 52.7	265 36.9	·· 56.7	Denebola	182 58.4	N14 40.5
04	118 05.9	192 58.6	09.1	309 55.7	01.1	271 18.4	52.9	280 39.2	56.8	Diphda	349 19.8	S18 05.3
05	133 08.4	207 58.4	08.8	324 56.9	00.6	286 20.4	53.1	295 41.4	56.9			
06	148 10.9	222 58.3	S26 08.5	339 58.1	N 7 00.1	301 22.3	S 9 53.3	310 43.6	S 4 56.9	Dubhe	194 21.3	N61 50.8
07	163 13.3	237 58.1	08.2	354 59.3	6 59.6	316 24.3	53.5	325 45.8	57.0	Elnath	278 42.8	N28 35.5
T 08	178 15.8	252 58.0	07.9	10 00.5	59.1	331 26.3	53.6	340 48.0	57.1	Eltanin	90 57.8	N51 29.7
H 09	193 18.3	267 57.9	·· 07.6	25 01.7	·· 58.6	346 28.3	·· 53.8	355 50.3	·· 57.2	Enif	34 10.8	N 9 47.6
U 10	208 20.7	282 57.7	07.3	40 02.9	58.1	1 30.3	54.0	10 52.5	57.3	Fomalhaut	15 50.4	S29 43.3
R 11	223 23.2	297 57.6	07.0	55 04.1	57.6	16 32.2	54.2	25 54.7	57.4			
S 12	238 25.7	312 57.5	S26 06.7	70 05.3	N 6 57.1	31 34.2	S 9 54.4	40 56.9	S 4 57.5	Gacrux	172 28.3	S57 00.3
D 13	253 28.1	327 57.3	06.4	85 06.5	56.6	46 36.2	54.5	55 59.1	57.6	Gienah	176 17.4	S17 26.2
A 14	268 30.6	342 57.2	06.1	100 07.7	56.1	61 38.2	54.7	71 01.4	57.7	Hadar	149 22.8	S60 16.9
Y 15	283 33.1	357 57.1	·· 05.8	115 08.9	·· 55.6	76 40.2	·· 54.9	86 03.6	·· 57.8	Hamal	328 27.7	N23 22.6
16	298 35.5	12 56.9	05.5	130 10.1	55.1	91 42.2	55.1	101 05.8	57.9	Kaus Aust.	84 16.1	S34 23.7
17	313 38.0	27 56.8	05.2	145 11.4	54.6	106 44.1	55.2	116 08.0	58.0			
18	328 40.4	42 56.7	S26 04.9	160 12.6	N 6 54.1	121 46.1	S 9 55.4	131 10.2	S 4 58.1	Kochab	137 20.2	N74 13.8
19	343 42.9	57 56.5	04.6	175 13.8	53.6	136 48.1	55.6	146 12.5	58.2	Markab	14 02.3	N15 06.5
20	358 45.4	72 56.4	04.3	190 15.0	53.1	151 50.1	55.8	161 14.7	58.2	Menkar	314 40.0	N 4 01.1
21	13 47.8	87 56.3	·· 04.0	205 16.2	·· 52.6	166 52.1	·· 56.0	176 16.9	·· 58.3	Menkent	148 36.5	S36 16.6
22	28 50.3	102 56.2	03.7	220 17.4	52.1	181 54.0	56.1	191 19.1	58.4	Miaplacidus	221 44.6	S69 38.2
23	43 52.8	117 56.1	03.4	235 18.6	51.6	196 56.0	56.3	206 21.3	58.5			
20 00	58 55.2	132 55.9	S26 03.0	250 19.8	N 6 51.1	211 58.0	S 9 56.5	221 23.6	S 4 58.6	Mirfak	309 14.5	N49 47.8
01	73 57.7	147 55.8	02.7	265 21.0	50.6	227 00.0	56.7	236 25.8	58.7	Nunki	76 28.5	S26 19.2
02	89 00.2	162 55.7	02.4	280 22.2	50.2	242 02.0	56.8	251 28.0	58.8	Peacock	53 57.4	S56 47.9
03	104 02.6	177 55.6	·· 02.1	295 23.4	·· 49.7	257 03.9	·· 57.0	266 30.2	·· 58.9	Pollux	243 57.0	N28 04.2
04	119 05.1	192 55.5	01.8	310 24.6	49.2	272 05.9	57.2	281 32.4	59.0	Procyon	245 24.8	N 5 16.4
05	134 07.5	207 55.4	01.5	325 25.8	48.7	287 07.9	57.4	296 34.7	59.1			
06	149 10.0	222 55.3	S26 01.2	340 27.1	N 6 48.2	302 09.9	S 9 57.5	311 36.9	S 4 59.2	Rasalhague	96 29.2	N12 34.5
07	164 12.5	237 55.1	00.8	355 28.3	47.7	317 11.9	57.7	326 39.1	59.3	Regulus	208 09.2	N12 03.4
08	179 14.9	252 55.0	00.5	10 29.5	47.2	332 13.8	57.9	341 41.3	59.4	Rigel	281 34.9	S 8 13.3
F 09	194 17.4	267 54.9	26 00.2	25 30.7	·· 46.7	347 15.8	·· 58.1	356 43.5	·· 59.4	Rigil Kent.	140 25.4	S60 45.3
R 10	209 19.9	282 54.8	25 59.9	40 31.9	46.2	2 17.8	58.3	11 45.8	59.5	Sabik	102 40.6	S15 42.1
I 11	224 22.3	297 54.7	59.6	55 33.1	45.7	17 19.8	58.4	26 48.0	59.6			
D 12	239 24.8	312 54.6	S25 59.2	70 34.3	N 6 45.2	32 21.8	S 9 58.6	41 50.2	S 4 59.7	Schedar	350 07.7	N56 26.4
A 13	254 27.3	327 54.5	58.9	85 35.5	44.7	47 23.8	58.8	56 52.4	59.8	Shaula	96 55.1	S37 05.4
Y 14	269 29.7	342 54.4	58.6	100 36.7	44.2	62 25.7	59.0	71 54.6	59.9	Sirius	258 54.8	S16 41.4
15	284 32.2	357 54.3	·· 58.3	115 38.0	·· 43.7	77 27.7	·· 59.1	86 56.9	5 00.0	Spica	158 57.0	S11 03.8
16	299 34.7	12 54.2	57.9	130 39.2	43.2	92 29.7	59.3	101 59.1	00.1	Suhail	223 10.1	S43 21.2
17	314 37.1	27 54.1	57.6	145 40.4	42.7	107 31.7	59.5	117 01.3	00.2			
18	329 39.6	42 54.0	S25 57.3	160 41.6	N 6 42.2	122 33.7	S 9 59.7	132 03.5	S 5 00.3	Vega	80 55.6	N38 46.2
19	344 42.0	57 53.9	57.0	175 42.8	41.7	137 35.7	9 59.9	147 05.8	00.4	Zuben'ubi	137 32.5	S15 57.8
20	359 44.5	72 53.8	56.6	190 44.0	41.2	152 37.6	10 00.0	162 08.0	00.5			
21	14 47.0	87 53.7	·· 56.3	205 45.2	·· 40.7	167 39.6	·· 00.2	177 10.2	·· 00.6		S.H.A.	Mer. Pass.
22	29 49.4	102 53.6	56.0	220 46.4	40.2	182 41.6	00.4	192 12.4	00.6	Venus	75 03.1	15 08
23	44 51.9	117 53.6	55.6	235 47.7	39.7	197 43.6	00.6	207 14.6	00.7	Mars	191 54.8	7 20
										Jupiter	153 14.4	9 54
Mer. Pass. 20 05.0		v −0.1	d 0.3	v 1.2	d 0.5	v 2.0	d 0.2	v 2.2	d 0.1	Saturn	162 34.2	9 17

G.M.T.	SUN G.H.A.	Dec.	MOON G.H.A.	v	Dec.	d	H.P.
d h	° ′	° ′	° ′	′	° ′	′	′
18 00	183 43.6	S19 09.1	275 54.9	9.2	N17 24.1	7.8	57.8
01	198 43.4	09.7	290 23.1	9.4	17 16.3	7.9	57.8
02	213 43.3	10.3	304 51.5	9.4	17 08.4	8.0	57.7
03	228 43.2 ··	10.9	319 19.9	9.5	17 00.4	8.0	57.7
04	243 43.0	11.5	333 48.4	9.6	16 52.4	8.2	57.7
05	258 42.9	12.1	348 17.0	9.7	16 44.2	8.2	57.6
06	273 42.8	S19 12.7	2 45.7	9.8	N16 36.0	8.3	57.6
W 07	288 42.7	13.3	17 14.5	9.9	16 27.7	8.4	57.6
E 08	303 42.5	13.9	31 43.4	10.0	16 19.3	8.4	57.5
D 09	318 42.4 ··	14.5	46 12.4	10.0	16 10.9	8.6	57.5
N 10	333 42.3	15.1	60 41.4	10.2	16 02.3	8.6	57.4
E 11	348 42.1	15.7	75 10.6	10.2	15 53.7	8.7	57.4
S 12	3 42.0	S19 16.2	89 39.8	10.3	N15 45.0	8.7	57.4
D 13	18 41.9	16.8	104 09.1	10.5	15 36.3	8.8	57.3
A 14	33 41.7	17.4	118 38.6	10.5	15 27.5	8.9	57.3
Y 15	48 41.6 ··	18.0	133 08.1	10.6	15 18.6	9.0	57.3
16	63 41.5	18.6	147 37.7	10.6	15 09.6	9.0	57.2
17	78 41.3	19.2	162 07.3	10.8	15 00.6	9.1	57.2
18	93 41.2	S19 19.8	176 37.1	10.9	N14 51.5	9.2	57.2
19	108 41.1	20.4	191 07.0	10.9	14 42.3	9.3	57.1
20	123 40.9	21.0	205 36.9	11.0	14 33.0	9.2	57.1
21	138 40.8 ··	21.6	220 06.9	11.1	14 23.8	9.4	57.1
22	153 40.6	22.1	234 37.0	11.2	14 14.4	9.4	57.0
23	168 40.5	22.7	249 07.2	11.3	14 05.0	9.5	57.0
19 00	183 40.4	S19 23.3	263 37.5	11.4	N13 55.5	9.6	57.0
01	198 40.2	23.9	278 07.9	11.4	13 45.9	9.5	56.9
02	213 40.1	24.5	292 38.3	11.5	13 36.4	9.7	56.9
03	228 40.0 ··	25.1	307 08.8	11.6	13 26.7	9.7	56.9
04	243 39.8	25.7	321 39.4	11.7	13 17.0	9.8	56.8
05	258 39.7	26.2	336 10.1	11.8	13 07.2	9.8	56.8
06	273 39.5	S19 26.8	350 40.9	11.8	N12 57.4	9.9	56.8
07	288 39.4	27.4	5 11.7	11.9	12 47.5	9.9	56.7
T 08	303 39.3	28.0	19 42.6	12.0	12 37.6	10.0	56.7
H 09	318 39.1 ··	28.6	34 13.6	12.1	12 27.6	10.0	56.7
U 10	333 39.0	29.2	48 44.7	12.1	12 17.6	10.1	56.6
R 11	348 38.8	29.7	63 15.8	12.2	12 07.5	10.1	56.6
S 12	3 38.7	S19 30.3	77 47.0	12.3	N11 57.4	10.1	56.6
D 13	18 38.6	30.9	92 18.3	12.4	11 47.3	10.3	56.5
A 14	33 38.4	31.5	106 49.7	12.4	11 37.0	10.2	56.5
Y 15	48 38.3 ··	32.0	121 21.1	12.5	11 26.8	10.3	56.5
16	63 38.1	32.6	135 52.6	12.6	11 16.5	10.4	56.4
17	78 38.0	33.2	150 24.2	12.6	11 06.1	10.3	56.4
18	93 37.8	S19 33.8	164 55.8	12.7	N10 55.8	10.5	56.4
19	108 37.7	34.3	179 27.5	12.8	10 45.3	10.4	56.3
20	123 37.5	34.9	193 59.3	12.8	10 34.9	10.5	56.3
21	138 37.4 ··	35.5	208 31.1	12.9	10 24.4	10.6	56.3
22	153 37.3	36.1	223 03.0	13.0	10 13.8	10.6	56.3
23	168 37.1	36.6	237 35.0	13.0	10 03.3	10.6	56.2
20 00	183 37.0	S19 37.2	252 07.0	13.2	N 9 52.7	10.7	56.2
01	198 36.8	37.8	266 39.2	13.1	9 42.0	10.7	56.2
02	213 36.7	38.4	281 11.3	13.2	9 31.3	10.7	56.1
03	228 36.5 ··	38.9	295 43.5	13.3	9 20.6	10.7	56.1
04	243 36.4	39.5	310 15.8	13.4	9 09.9	10.8	56.1
05	258 36.2	40.1	324 48.2	13.4	8 59.1	10.8	56.1
06	273 36.1	S19 40.6	339 20.6	13.5	N 8 48.3	10.8	56.0
07	288 35.9	41.2	353 53.1	13.5	8 37.5	10.9	56.0
08	303 35.8	41.8	8 25.6	13.6	8 26.6	10.9	56.0
F 09	318 35.6 ··	42.3	22 58.2	13.6	8 15.7	10.9	55.9
R 10	333 35.5	42.9	37 30.8	13.7	8 04.8	11.0	55.9
I 11	348 35.3	43.5	52 03.5	13.7	7 53.8	10.9	55.9
D 12	3 35.2	S19 44.0	66 36.2	13.8	N 7 42.9	11.0	55.8
A 13	18 35.0	44.6	81 09.0	13.9	7 31.9	11.0	55.8
Y 14	33 34.9	45.2	95 41.9	13.9	7 20.9	11.1	55.8
15	48 34.7 ··	45.7	110 14.8	13.9	7 09.8	11.0	55.8
16	63 34.6	46.3	124 47.7	14.0	6 58.8	11.1	55.7
17	78 34.4	46.8	139 20.7	14.1	6 47.7	11.1	55.7
18	93 34.3	S19 47.4	153 53.8	14.0	N 6 36.6	11.1	55.7
19	108 34.1	48.0	168 26.8	14.2	6 25.5	11.2	55.7
20	123 33.9	48.5	183 00.0	14.2	6 14.3	11.1	55.6
21	138 33.8 ··	49.1	197 33.2	14.2	6 03.2	11.2	55.6
22	153 33.7	49.6	212 06.4	14.3	5 52.0	11.2	55.6
23	168 33.5	50.2	226 39.7	14.3	5 40.8	11.2	55.6
	S.D. 16.2 d 0.6		S.D. 15.6		15.4		15.2

Lat.	Twilight Naut.	Civil	Sunrise	Moonrise 18	19	20	21
°	h m	h m	h m	h m	h m	h m	h m
N 72	07 13	08 53	■	20 53	22 59	24 51	00 51
N 70	07 01	08 27	10 17	21 24	23 16	24 59	00 59
68	06 52	08 07	09 32	21 47	23 29	25 05	01 05
66	06 44	07 51	09 02	22 04	23 39	25 10	01 10
64	06 36	07 38	08 40	22 19	23 48	25 15	01 15
62	06 30	07 27	08 22	22 30	23 56	25 19	01 19
60	06 25	07 17	08 08	22 41	24 02	00 02	01 22
N 58	06 20	07 09	07 55	22 49	24 08	00 08	01 25
56	06 15	07 01	07 44	22 57	24 13	00 13	01 27
54	06 11	06 55	07 35	23 04	24 18	00 18	01 30
52	06 07	06 49	07 27	23 10	24 22	00 22	01 32
50	06 03	06 43	07 19	23 15	24 26	00 26	01 34
45	05 55	06 31	07 03	23 27	24 34	00 34	01 38
N 40	05 47	06 20	06 50	23 37	24 40	00 40	01 41
35	05 40	06 11	06 38	23 46	24 46	00 46	01 44
30	05 34	06 03	06 28	23 53	24 51	00 51	01 47
20	05 21	05 48	06 11	24 06	00 06	01 00	01 51
N 10	05 08	05 34	05 56	24 17	00 17	01 07	01 55
0	04 54	05 19	05 42	24 27	00 27	01 14	01 59
S 10	04 39	05 05	05 27	24 37	00 37	01 21	02 03
20	04 20	04 48	05 12	00 03	00 48	01 29	02 07
30	03 56	04 28	04 54	00 19	01 01	01 37	02 11
35	03 41	04 15	04 44	00 29	01 08	01 42	02 14
40	03 23	04 01	04 32	00 39	01 16	01 48	02 17
45	02 59	03 43	04 17	00 52	01 25	01 54	02 20
S 50	02 26	03 20	04 00	01 07	01 37	02 02	02 24
52	02 09	03 09	03 52	01 14	01 42	02 06	02 26
54	01 48	02 56	03 42	01 21	01 48	02 10	02 28
56	01 20	02 41	03 32	01 30	01 54	02 14	02 30
58	00 32	02 23	03 20	01 40	02 02	02 19	02 33
S 60	////	02 00	03 06	01 51	02 10	02 24	02 36

Lat.	Sunset	Twilight Civil	Naut.	Moonset 18	19	20	21
°	h m	h m	h m	h m	h m	h m	h m
N 72	■	14 37	16 16	15 53	15 26	15 08	14 53
N 70	13 12	15 03	16 28	15 20	15 08	14 58	14 50
68	13 58	15 23	16 38	14 56	14 53	14 50	14 47
66	14 28	15 39	16 46	14 37	14 41	14 43	14 45
64	14 50	15 52	16 53	14 22	14 31	14 38	14 42
62	15 08	16 03	17 00	14 10	14 23	14 33	14 41
60	15 23	16 13	17 05	13 59	14 15	14 28	14 39
N 58	15 35	16 21	17 10	13 49	14 09	14 24	14 38
56	15 46	16 29	17 15	13 41	14 03	14 21	14 36
54	15 55	16 36	17 19	13 33	13 58	14 18	14 35
52	16 04	16 42	17 23	13 27	13 53	14 15	14 34
50	16 11	16 47	17 27	13 21	13 48	14 12	14 33
45	16 28	17 00	17 36	13 08	13 39	14 06	14 31
N 40	16 41	17 10	17 43	12 57	13 31	14 02	14 29
35	16 52	17 19	17 50	12 48	13 24	13 57	14 28
30	17 02	17 28	17 57	12 39	13 18	13 54	14 26
20	17 20	17 43	18 10	12 25	13 08	13 47	14 24
N 10	17 35	17 57	18 23	12 13	12 59	13 41	14 22
0	17 49	18 11	18 36	12 01	12 50	13 36	14 20
S 10	18 03	18 26	18 52	11 49	12 41	13 31	14 18
20	18 19	18 43	19 11	11 36	12 32	13 25	14 16
30	18 37	19 03	19 35	11 22	12 21	13 18	14 13
35	18 48	19 16	19 50	11 13	12 15	13 14	14 12
40	19 00	19 31	20 09	11 03	12 08	13 10	14 10
45	19 14	19 49	20 33	10 52	11 59	13 05	14 08
S 50	19 32	20 12	21 06	10 38	11 49	12 58	14 06
52	19 40	20 23	21 24	10 31	11 44	12 55	14 05
54	19 50	20 36	21 45	10 24	11 39	12 52	14 03
56	20 00	20 52	22 15	10 16	11 33	12 49	14 02
58	20 13	21 10	23 08	10 07	11 27	12 45	14 01
S 60	20 27	21 33	////	09 56	11 20	12 41	13 59

Day	SUN Eqn. of Time 00h	12h	Mer. Pass.	MOON Mer. Pass. Upper	Lower	Age	Phase
	m s	m s	h m	h m	h m	d	
18	14 55	14 48	11 45	05 49	18 14	22	
19	14 42	14 35	11 45	06 39	19 02	23	
20	14 28	14 21	11 46	07 25	19 48	24	◖

G.M.T.	ARIES G.H.A.	VENUS −4.2 G.H.A.	Dec.	MARS +1.4 G.H.A.	Dec.	JUPITER −1.3 G.H.A.	Dec.	SATURN +1.0 G.H.A.	Dec.	STARS Name	S.H.A.	Dec.
21 00	59 54.4	132 53.5	S25 55.3	250 48.9	N 6 39.2	212 45.6	S10 00.7	222 16.9	S 5 00.8	Acamar	315 36.2	S40 22.8
01	74 56.8	147 53.4	55.0	265 50.1	38.7	227 47.5	00.9	237 19.1	00.9	Achernar	335 44.2	S57 20.0
02	89 59.3	162 53.3	54.6	280 51.3	38.3	242 49.5	01.1	252 21.3	01.0	Acrux	173 36.8	S62 59.5
03	105 01.8	177 53.2	·· 54.3	295 52.5	·· 37.8	257 51.5	·· 01.3	267 23.5	·· 01.1	Adhara	255 31.2	S28 56.7
04	120 04.2	192 53.1	54.0	310 53.7	37.3	272 53.5	01.4	282 25.8	01.2	Aldebaran	291 16.7	N16 28.4
05	135 06.7	207 53.0	53.6	325 54.9	36.8	287 55.5	01.6	297 28.0	01.3			
06	150 09.2	222 53.0	S25 53.3	340 56.2	N 6 36.3	302 57.5	S10 01.8	312 30.2	S 5 01.4	Alioth	166 42.2	N56 03.4
07	165 11.6	237 52.9	53.0	355 57.4	35.8	317 59.4	02.0	327 32.4	01.5	Alkaid	153 18.3	N49 24.2
S 08	180 14.1	252 52.8	52.6	10 58.6	35.3	333 01.4	02.1	342 34.6	01.6	Al Na'ir	28 13.9	S47 03.2
A 09	195 16.5	267 52.7	·· 52.3	25 59.8	·· 34.8	348 03.4	·· 02.3	357 36.9	·· 01.7	Alnilam	276 10.5	S 1 12.8
T 10	210 19.0	282 52.7	51.9	41 01.0	34.3	3 05.4	02.5	12 39.1	01.7	Alphard	218 19.7	S 8 34.6
U 11	225 21.5	297 52.6	51.6	56 02.2	33.8	18 07.4	02.7	27 41.3	01.8			
R 12	240 23.9	312 52.5	S25 51.3	71 03.5	N 6 33.3	33 09.4	S10 02.8	42 43.5	S 5 01.9	Alphecca	126 31.8	N26 46.7
D 13	255 26.4	327 52.4	50.9	86 04.7	32.8	48 11.3	03.0	57 45.8	02.0	Alpheratz	358 08.3	N28 59.5
A 14	270 28.9	342 52.4	50.6	101 05.9	32.3	63 13.3	03.2	72 48.0	02.1	Altair	62 32.0	N 8 49.3
Y 15	285 31.3	357 52.3	·· 50.2	116 07.1	·· 31.8	78 15.3	·· 03.4	87 50.2	·· 02.2	Ankaa	353 39.2	S42 24.5
16	300 33.8	12 52.2	49.9	131 08.3	31.3	93 17.3	03.6	102 52.4	02.3	Antares	112 56.3	S26 23.4
17	315 36.3	27 52.2	49.5	146 09.5	30.8	108 19.3	03.7	117 54.7	02.4			
18	330 38.7	42 52.1	S25 49.2	161 10.8	N 6 30.3	123 21.3	S10 03.9	132 56.9	S 5 02.5	Arcturus	146 18.1	N19 16.7
19	345 41.2	57 52.0	48.8	176 12.0	29.8	138 23.3	04.1	147 59.1	02.6	Atria	108 20.4	S68 59.7
20	0 43.6	72 52.0	48.5	191 13.2	29.3	153 25.2	04.3	163 01.3	02.7	Avior	234 27.6	S59 26.8
21	15 46.1	87 51.9	·· 48.1	206 14.4	·· 28.9	168 27.2	·· 04.4	178 03.6	·· 02.7	Bellatrix	278 57.6	N 6 20.0
22	30 48.6	102 51.9	47.8	221 15.6	28.4	183 29.2	04.6	193 05.8	02.8	Betelgeuse	271 27.1	N 7 24.3
23	45 51.0	117 51.8	47.4	236 16.8	27.9	198 31.2	04.8	208 08.0	02.9			
22 00	60 53.5	132 51.7	S25 47.1	251 18.1	N 6 27.4	213 33.2	S10 05.0	223 10.2	S 5 03.0	Canopus	264 06.4	S52 41.0
01	75 56.0	147 51.7	46.7	266 19.3	26.9	228 35.2	05.1	238 12.5	03.1	Capella	281 09.7	N45 58.7
02	90 58.4	162 51.6	46.4	281 20.5	26.4	243 37.1	05.3	253 14.7	03.2	Deneb	49 48.1	N45 13.2
03	106 00.9	177 51.6	·· 46.0	296 21.7	·· 25.9	258 39.1	·· 05.5	268 16.9	·· 03.3	Denebola	182 58.4	N14 40.5
04	121 03.4	192 51.5	45.6	311 22.9	25.4	273 41.1	05.7	283 19.1	03.4	Diphda	349 19.9	S18 05.3
05	136 05.8	207 51.5	45.3	326 24.2	24.9	288 43.1	05.8	298 21.3	03.5			
06	151 08.3	222 51.4	S25 44.9	341 25.4	N 6 24.4	303 45.1	S10 06.0	313 23.6	S 5 03.6	Dubhe	194 21.3	N61 50.8
07	166 10.8	237 51.4	44.6	356 26.6	23.9	318 47.1	06.2	328 25.8	03.6	Elnath	278 42.8	N28 35.5
08	181 13.2	252 51.3	44.2	11 27.8	23.4	333 49.1	06.4	343 28.0	03.7	Eltanin	90 57.8	N51 29.7
S 09	196 15.7	267 51.3	·· 43.9	26 29.0	·· 22.9	348 51.0	·· 06.5	358 30.2	·· 03.8	Enif	34 10.8	N 9 47.6
U 10	211 18.1	282 51.3	43.5	41 30.3	22.4	3 53.0	06.7	13 32.5	03.9	Fomalhaut	15 50.5	S29 43.3
N 11	226 20.6	297 51.2	43.1	56 31.5	21.9	18 55.0	06.9	28 34.7	04.0			
D 12	241 23.1	312 51.2	S25 42.8	71 32.7	N 6 21.4	33 57.0	S10 07.1	43 36.9	S 5 04.1	Gacrux	172 28.2	S57 00.3
A 13	256 25.5	327 51.1	42.4	86 33.9	21.0	48 59.0	07.2	58 39.1	04.2	Gienah	176 17.3	S17 26.2
Y 14	271 28.0	342 51.1	42.0	101 35.2	20.5	64 01.0	07.4	73 41.4	04.3	Hadar	149 22.8	S60 16.9
15	286 30.5	357 51.1	·· 41.7	116 36.4	·· 20.0	79 03.0	·· 07.6	88 43.6	·· 04.4	Hamal	328 27.7	N23 22.6
16	301 32.9	12 51.0	41.3	131 37.6	19.5	94 04.9	07.8	103 45.8	04.5	Kaus Aust.	84 16.1	S34 23.7
17	316 35.4	27 51.0	40.9	146 38.8	19.0	109 06.9	07.9	118 48.0	04.5			
18	331 37.9	42 51.0	S25 40.6	161 40.1	N 6 18.5	124 08.9	S10 08.1	133 50.3	S 5 04.6	Kochab	137 20.2	N74 13.8
19	346 40.3	57 50.9	40.2	176 41.3	18.0	139 10.9	08.3	148 52.5	04.7	Markab	14 02.3	N15 06.5
20	1 42.8	72 50.9	39.8	191 42.5	17.5	154 12.9	08.5	163 54.7	04.8	Menkar	314 40.0	N 4 01.1
21	16 45.3	87 50.9	·· 39.4	206 43.7	·· 17.0	169 14.9	·· 08.6	178 57.0	·· 04.9	Menkent	148 36.4	S36 16.6
22	31 47.7	102 50.9	39.1	221 44.9	16.5	184 16.9	08.8	193 59.2	05.0	Miaplacidus	221 44.6	S69 38.2
23	46 50.2	117 50.8	38.7	236 46.2	16.0	199 18.8	09.0	209 01.4	05.1			
23 00	61 52.6	132 50.8	S25 38.3	251 47.4	N 6 15.5	214 20.8	S10 09.2	224 03.6	S 5 05.2	Mirfak	309 14.5	N49 47.8
01	76 55.1	147 50.8	38.0	266 48.6	15.0	229 22.8	09.3	239 05.9	05.3	Nunki	76 28.5	S26 19.2
02	91 57.6	162 50.8	37.6	281 49.8	14.5	244 24.8	09.5	254 08.1	05.4	Peacock	53 57.4	S56 47.9
03	107 00.0	177 50.7	·· 37.2	296 51.1	·· 14.1	259 26.8	·· 09.7	269 10.3	·· 05.4	Pollux	243 57.0	N28 04.2
04	122 02.5	192 50.7	36.8	311 52.3	13.6	274 28.8	09.8	284 12.5	05.5	Procyon	245 24.8	N 5 16.4
05	137 05.0	207 50.7	36.4	326 53.5	13.1	289 30.8	10.0	299 14.8	05.6			
06	152 07.4	222 50.7	S25 35.9	341 54.8	N 6 12.6	304 32.7	S10 10.2	314 17.0	S 5 05.7	Rasalhague	96 29.2	N12 34.5
07	167 09.9	237 50.7	35.7	356 56.0	12.1	319 34.7	10.4	329 19.2	05.8	Regulus	208 09.2	N12 03.4
08	182 12.4	252 50.7	35.3	11 57.2	11.6	334 36.7	10.5	344 21.4	05.9	Rigel	281 34.9	S 8 13.3
M 09	197 14.8	267 50.7	·· 34.9	26 58.4	·· 11.1	349 38.7	·· 10.7	359 23.7	·· 06.0	Rigil Kent.	140 25.4	S60 45.3
O 10	212 17.3	282 50.7	34.5	41 59.7	10.6	4 40.7	10.9	14 25.9	06.1	Sabik	102 40.6	S15 42.1
N 11	227 19.8	297 50.7	34.2	57 00.9	10.1	19 42.7	11.1	29 28.1	06.2			
D 12	242 22.2	312 50.6	S25 33.8	72 02.1	N 6 09.6	34 44.7	S10 11.2	44 30.4	S 5 06.2	Schedar	350 07.8	N56 26.4
A 13	257 24.7	327 50.6	33.4	87 03.3	09.1	49 46.7	11.4	59 32.6	06.3	Shaula	96 55.1	S37 05.4
Y 14	272 27.1	342 50.6	33.0	102 04.6	08.6	64 48.6	11.6	74 34.8	06.4	Sirius	258 54.7	S16 41.4
15	287 29.6	357 50.6	·· 32.6	117 05.8	·· 08.2	79 50.6	·· 11.8	89 37.0	·· 06.5	Spica	158 57.0	S11 03.8
16	302 32.1	12 50.6	32.2	132 07.0	07.7	94 52.6	11.9	104 39.3	06.6	Suhail	223 10.1	S43 21.2
17	317 34.5	27 50.6	31.8	147 08.3	07.2	109 54.6	12.1	119 41.5	06.7			
18	332 37.0	42 50.6	S25 31.5	162 09.5	N 6 06.7	124 56.6	S10 12.3	134 43.7	S 5 06.8	Vega	80 55.6	N38 46.2
19	347 39.5	57 50.6	31.1	177 10.7	06.2	139 58.6	12.5	149 45.9	06.9	Zuben'ubi	137 32.5	S15 57.8
20	2 41.9	72 50.7	30.7	192 11.9	05.7	155 00.6	12.6	164 48.2	07.0			
21	17 44.4	87 50.7	·· 30.3	207 13.2	·· 05.2	170 02.6	·· 12.8	179 50.4	·· 07.0		S.H.A.	Mer. Pass.
22	32 46.9	102 50.7	29.9	222 14.4	04.7	185 04.6	13.0	194 52.6	07.1	Venus	71 58.2	15 09
23	47 49.3	117 50.7	29.5	237 15.6	04.2	200 06.5	13.1	209 54.9	07.2	Mars	190 24.6	7 14
Mer. Pass. 19 53.2		v 0.0	d 0.4	v 1.2	d 0.5	v 2.0	d 0.2	v 2.2	d 0.1	Jupiter	152 39.7	9 44
										Saturn	162 16.7	9 06

SUN and MOON

G.M.T.	SUN G.H.A.	Dec.	MOON G.H.A.	v	Dec.	d	H.P.
21 00	183 33.4	S19 50.7	241 13.0	14.4	N 5 29.6	11.2	55.5
01	198 33.2	51.3	255 46.4	14.4	5 18.4	11.3	55.5
02	213 33.0	51.9	270 19.8	14.4	5 07.1	11.2	55.5
03	228 32.9	·· 52.4	284 53.2	14.5	4 55.9	11.3	55.5
04	243 32.7	53.0	299 26.7	14.5	4 44.6	11.2	55.4
05	258 32.6	53.5	314 00.2	14.6	4 33.4	11.3	55.4
06	273 32.4	S19 54.1	328 33.8	14.6	N 4 22.1	11.3	55.4
07	288 32.3	54.6	343 07.4	14.6	4 10.8	11.3	55.4
S 08	303 32.1	55.2	357 41.0	14.6	3 59.5	11.3	55.3
A 09	318 32.0	·· 55.7	12 14.6	14.7	3 48.2	11.3	55.3
T 10	333 31.8	56.3	26 48.3	14.8	3 36.9	11.4	55.3
U 11	348 31.6	56.8	41 22.1	14.7	3 25.5	11.3	55.3
R 12	3 31.5	S19 57.4	55 55.8	14.8	N 3 14.2	11.3	55.3
D 13	18 31.3	57.9	70 29.6	14.9	3 02.9	11.4	55.2
A 14	33 31.2	58.5	85 03.5	14.8	2 51.5	11.3	55.2
Y 15	48 31.0	·· 59.0	99 37.3	14.9	2 40.2	11.4	55.2
16	63 30.8	19 59.6	114 11.2	14.9	2 28.8	11.3	55.2
17	78 30.7	20 00.1	128 45.1	15.0	2 17.5	11.4	55.1
18	93 30.5	S20 00.7	143 19.1	14.9	N 2 06.1	11.3	55.1
19	108 30.4	01.2	157 53.0	15.0	1 54.8	11.4	55.1
20	123 30.2	01.8	172 27.0	15.0	1 43.4	11.3	55.1
21	138 30.0	·· 02.3	187 01.0	15.1	1 32.1	11.4	55.1
22	153 29.9	02.8	201 35.1	15.0	1 20.7	11.3	55.0
23	168 29.7	03.4	216 09.1	15.1	1 09.4	11.4	55.0
22 00	183 29.5	S20 03.9	230 43.2	15.1	N 0 58.0	11.3	55.0
01	198 29.4	04.5	245 17.3	15.2	0 46.7	11.4	55.0
02	213 29.2	05.0	259 51.5	15.1	0 35.3	11.3	55.0
03	228 29.1	·· 05.5	274 25.6	15.2	0 24.0	11.3	54.9
04	243 28.9	06.1	288 59.8	15.2	0 12.7	11.4	54.9
05	258 28.7	06.6	303 34.0	15.1	N 0 01.3	11.3	54.9
06	273 28.6	S20 07.2	318 08.1	15.3	S 0 10.0	11.3	54.9
07	288 28.4	07.7	332 42.4	15.2	0 21.3	11.3	54.9
08	303 28.2	08.2	347 16.6	15.2	0 32.6	11.3	54.9
S 09	318 28.1	·· 08.8	1 50.8	15.3	0 43.9	11.3	54.8
U 10	333 27.9	09.3	16 25.1	15.3	0 55.2	11.3	54.8
N 11	348 27.7	09.8	30 59.4	15.3	1 06.5	11.2	54.8
D 12	3 27.6	S20 10.4	45 33.7	15.2	S 1 17.7	11.3	54.8
A 13	18 27.4	10.9	60 07.9	15.4	1 29.0	11.2	54.8
Y 14	33 27.2	11.4	74 42.3	15.3	1 40.2	11.3	54.7
15	48 27.1	·· 12.0	89 16.6	15.3	1 51.5	11.2	54.7
16	63 26.9	12.5	103 50.9	15.3	2 02.7	11.2	54.7
17	78 26.7	13.0	118 25.2	15.4	2 13.9	11.2	54.7
18	93 26.5	S20 13.6	132 59.6	15.3	S 2 25.1	11.2	54.7
19	108 26.4	14.1	147 33.9	15.4	2 36.3	11.1	54.7
20	123 26.2	14.6	162 08.3	15.3	2 47.4	11.2	54.6
21	138 26.0	·· 15.2	176 42.6	15.4	2 58.6	11.1	54.6
22	153 25.9	15.7	191 17.0	15.3	3 09.7	11.1	54.6
23	168 25.7	16.2	205 51.3	15.4	3 20.8	11.1	54.6
23 00	183 25.5	S20 16.7	220 25.7	15.4	S 3 31.9	11.1	54.6
01	198 25.4	17.3	235 00.1	15.3	3 43.0	11.0	54.6
02	213 25.2	17.8	249 34.4	15.4	3 54.0	11.1	54.6
03	228 25.0	·· 18.3	264 08.8	15.4	4 05.1	11.0	54.5
04	243 24.8	18.8	278 43.2	15.3	4 16.1	11.0	54.5
05	258 24.7	19.4	293 17.5	15.4	4 27.1	11.0	54.5
06	273 24.5	S20 19.9	307 51.9	15.4	S 4 38.1	10.9	54.5
07	288 24.3	20.4	322 26.3	15.3	4 49.0	10.9	54.5
08	303 24.1	20.9	337 00.6	15.4	4 59.9	10.9	54.5
M 09	318 24.0	·· 21.4	351 35.0	15.3	5 10.8	10.9	54.5
O 10	333 23.8	22.0	6 09.3	15.4	5 21.7	10.8	54.4
N 11	348 23.6	22.5	20 43.7	15.3	5 32.5	10.9	54.4
D 12	3 23.4	S20 23.0	35 18.0	15.3	S 5 43.4	10.8	54.4
A 13	18 23.3	23.5	49 52.3	15.4	5 54.2	10.7	54.4
Y 14	33 23.1	24.0	64 26.7	15.3	6 04.9	10.8	54.4
15	48 22.9	·· 24.5	79 01.0	15.3	6 15.7	10.7	54.4
16	63 22.7	25.1	93 35.3	15.3	6 26.4	10.7	54.4
17	78 22.6	25.6	108 09.6	15.3	6 37.1	10.6	54.4
18	93 22.4	S20 26.1	122 43.9	15.3	S 6 47.7	10.6	54.3
19	108 22.2	26.6	137 18.2	15.2	6 58.3	10.6	54.3
20	123 22.0	27.1	151 52.4	15.3	7 08.9	10.6	54.3
21	138 21.8	·· 27.6	166 26.7	15.2	7 19.5	10.5	54.3
22	153 21.7	28.1	181 00.9	15.2	7 30.0	10.5	54.3
23	168 21.5	28.7	195 35.1	15.2	7 40.5	10.5	54.3
	S.D. 16.2 d 0.5		S.D. 15.1		14.9		14.8

Twilight, Sunrise and Moonrise

Lat.	Twilight Naut.	Twilight Civil	Sunrise	Moonrise 21	22	23	24
N 72	07 23	09 07	■	00 51	02 37	04 21	06 07
N 70	07 10	08 38	10 44	00 59	02 38	04 15	05 52
68	07 00	08 17	09 47	01 05	02 38	04 09	05 41
66	06 51	08 00	09 13	01 10	02 38	04 05	05 31
64	06 43	07 46	08 49	01 15	02 39	04 01	05 23
62	06 36	07 34	08 30	01 19	02 39	03 58	05 17
60	06 30	07 23	08 15	01 22	02 39	03 55	05 11
N 58	06 25	07 15	08 02	01 25	02 39	03 53	05 06
56	06 20	07 07	07 50	01 27	02 40	03 51	05 01
54	06 15	07 00	07 40	01 30	02 40	03 49	04 57
52	06 11	06 53	07 32	01 32	02 40	03 47	04 54
50	06 07	06 47	07 24	01 34	02 40	03 45	04 50
45	05 58	06 34	07 07	01 38	02 40	03 42	04 43
N 40	05 50	06 23	06 53	01 41	02 41	03 39	04 37
35	05 43	06 14	06 41	01 44	02 41	03 37	04 32
30	05 36	06 05	06 31	01 47	02 41	03 35	04 28
20	05 23	05 49	06 13	01 51	02 42	03 31	04 20
N 10	05 09	05 35	05 57	01 55	02 42	03 28	04 13
0	04 55	05 21	05 43	01 59	02 42	03 24	04 07
S 10	04 39	05 05	05 28	02 03	02 43	03 21	04 01
20	04 19	04 48	05 12	02 07	02 43	03 18	03 54
30	03 55	04 27	04 53	02 11	02 43	03 15	03 46
35	03 39	04 14	04 42	02 14	02 44	03 13	03 42
40	03 20	03 58	04 30	02 17	02 44	03 10	03 37
45	02 55	03 40	04 15	02 20	02 44	03 08	03 32
S 50	02 21	03 16	03 56	02 24	02 45	03 05	03 25
52	02 03	03 04	03 48	02 26	02 45	03 03	03 22
54	01 40	02 51	03 38	02 28	02 45	03 02	03 19
56	01 07	02 35	03 27	02 30	02 45	03 00	03 15
58	////	02 15	03 14	02 33	02 45	02 58	03 11
S 60	////	01 51	02 59	02 36	02 46	02 56	03 06

Sunset, Twilight and Moonset

Lat.	Sunset	Twilight Civil	Twilight Naut.	Moonset 21	22	23	24
N 72	■	14 24	16 08	14 53	14 39	14 24	14 07
N 70	12 47	14 53	16 21	14 50	14 41	14 33	14 23
68	13 45	15 15	16 32	14 47	14 43	14 40	14 36
66	14 18	15 32	16 41	14 45	14 45	14 46	14 47
64	14 42	15 46	16 48	14 42	14 47	14 51	14 56
62	15 01	15 58	16 55	14 41	14 48	14 55	15 04
60	15 17	16 08	17 01	14 39	14 49	14 59	15 11
N 58	15 30	16 17	17 07	14 38	14 50	15 03	15 16
56	15 41	16 25	17 12	14 36	14 51	15 06	15 22
54	15 51	16 32	17 16	14 35	14 52	15 09	15 27
52	16 00	16 39	17 21	14 34	14 53	15 11	15 31
50	16 08	16 45	17 25	14 33	14 53	15 13	15 35
45	16 25	16 58	17 34	14 31	14 55	15 19	15 43
N 40	16 39	17 09	17 42	14 29	14 56	15 23	15 50
35	16 51	17 19	17 49	14 28	14 57	15 26	15 57
30	17 01	17 27	17 56	14 26	14 58	15 30	16 02
20	17 19	17 43	18 10	14 24	15 00	15 35	16 11
N 10	17 35	17 57	18 23	14 22	15 01	15 40	16 20
0	17 50	18 12	18 37	14 20	15 03	15 45	16 27
S 10	18 05	18 27	18 54	14 18	15 04	15 50	16 35
20	18 21	18 45	19 13	14 16	15 05	15 54	16 44
30	18 40	19 06	19 38	14 13	15 07	16 00	16 53
35	18 51	19 19	19 54	14 12	15 08	16 03	16 59
40	19 03	19 34	20 13	14 10	15 09	16 07	17 05
45	19 18	19 53	20 38	14 08	15 10	16 12	17 12
S 50	19 37	20 17	21 13	14 06	15 12	16 17	17 21
52	19 45	20 29	21 32	14 05	15 12	16 19	17 25
54	19 55	20 43	21 55	14 03	15 13	16 22	17 30
56	20 07	20 59	22 29	14 02	15 14	16 25	17 35
58	20 19	21 19	////	14 01	15 15	16 28	17 41
S 60	20 35	21 44	////	13 59	15 16	16 32	17 47

SUN and MOON

Day	SUN Eqn. of Time 00h	12h	Mer. Pass.	MOON Mer. Pass. Upper	Lower	Age	Phase
	m s	m s	h m	h m	h m	d	
21	14 14	14 06	11 46	08 10	20 31	25	
22	13 58	13 51	11 46	08 52	21 14	26	◐
23	13 42	13 34	11 46	09 35	21 56	27	

G.M.T.	ARIES G.H.A.	VENUS −4.2 G.H.A.	Dec.	MARS +1.4 G.H.A.	Dec.	JUPITER −1.3 G.H.A.	Dec.	SATURN +1.0 G.H.A.	Dec.	STARS Name	S.H.A.	Dec.
24 00	62 51.8	132 50.7	S25 29.1	252 16.9	N 6 03.7	215 08.5	S10 13.3	224 57.1	S 5 07.3	Acamar	315 36.2	S40 22.8
01	77 54.2	147 50.7	28.7	267 18.1	03.2	230 10.5	13.5	239 59.3	07.4	Achernar	335 44.2	S57 20.0
02	92 56.7	162 50.7	28.3	282 19.3	02.7	245 12.5	13.7	255 01.5	07.5	Acrux	173 36.7	S62 59.5
03	107 59.2	177 50.7 ··	27.9	297 20.6 ··	02.3	260 14.5 ··	13.8	270 03.8 ··	07.6	Adhara	255 31.2	S28 56.7
04	123 01.6	192 50.8	27.5	312 21.8	01.8	275 16.5	14.0	285 06.0	07.7	Aldebaran	291 16.7	N16 28.4
05	138 04.1	207 50.8	27.1	327 23.0	01.3	290 18.5	14.2	300 08.2	07.8			
06	153 06.6	222 50.8	S25 26.7	342 24.3	N 6 00.8	305 20.5	S10 14.4	315 10.5	S 5 07.8	Alioth	166 42.2	N56 03.4
07	168 09.0	237 50.8	26.3	357 25.5	6 00.3	320 22.4	14.5	330 12.7	07.9	Alkaid	153 18.3	N49 24.2
T 08	183 11.5	252 50.8	25.9	12 26.7	5 59.8	335 24.4	14.7	345 14.9	08.0	Al Na'ir	28 14.0	S47 03.2
U 09	198 14.0	267 50.9 ··	25.5	27 28.0 ··	59.3	350 26.4 ··	14.9	0 17.1 ··	08.1	Alnilam	276 10.5	S 1 12.8
E 10	213 16.4	282 50.9	25.1	42 29.2	58.8	5 28.4	15.0	15 19.4	08.2	Alphard	218 19.7	S 8 34.6
S 11	228 18.9	297 50.9	24.7	57 30.4	58.3	20 30.4	15.2	30 21.6	08.3			
D 12	243 21.4	312 50.9	S25 24.3	72 31.7	N 5 57.8	35 32.4	S10 15.4	45 23.8	S 5 08.4	Alphecca	126 31.8	N26 46.6
A 13	258 23.8	327 51.0	23.9	87 32.9	57.3	50 34.4	15.6	60 26.1	08.5	Alpheratz	358 08.3	N28 59.5
Y 14	273 26.3	342 51.0	23.5	102 34.1	56.9	65 36.4	15.7	75 28.3	08.5	Altair	62 32.0	N 8 49.3
15	288 28.7	357 51.0 ··	23.1	117 35.4 ··	56.4	80 38.4 ··	15.9	90 30.5 ··	08.6	Ankaa	353 39.2	S42 24.5
16	303 31.2	12 51.1	22.7	132 36.6	55.9	95 40.4	16.1	105 32.7	08.7	Antares	112 56.3	S26 23.4
17	318 33.7	27 51.1	22.3	147 37.8	55.4	110 42.3	16.3	120 35.0	08.8			
18	333 36.1	42 51.2	S25 21.9	162 39.1	N 5 54.9	125 44.3	S10 16.4	135 37.2	S 5 08.9	Arcturus	146 18.0	N19 16.7
19	348 38.6	57 51.2	21.5	177 40.3	54.4	140 46.3	16.6	150 39.4	09.0	Atria	108 20.4	S68 59.7
20	3 41.1	72 51.2	21.1	192 41.5	53.9	155 48.3	16.8	165 41.7	09.1	Avior	234 27.6	S59 26.8
21	18 43.5	87 51.3 ··	20.6	207 42.8 ··	53.4	170 50.3 ··	16.9	180 43.9 ··	09.2	Bellatrix	278 57.6	N 6 20.0
22	33 46.0	102 51.3	20.2	222 44.0	52.9	185 52.3	17.1	195 46.1	09.3	Betelgeuse	271 27.1	N 7 24.3
23	48 48.5	117 51.4	19.8	237 45.2	52.4	200 54.3	17.3	210 48.4	09.3			
25 00	63 50.9	132 51.4	S25 19.4	252 46.5	N 5 52.0	215 56.3	S10 17.5	225 50.6	S 5 09.4	Canopus	264 06.4	S52 41.0
01	78 53.4	147 51.5	19.0	267 47.7	51.5	230 58.3	17.6	240 52.8	09.5	Capella	281 09.7	N45 58.8
02	93 55.9	162 51.5 -	18.6	282 48.9 \	51.0	246 00.3	17.8	255 55.0	09.6	Deneb	49 48.1	N45 13.2
03	108 58.3	177 51.6 ··	18.2	297 50.2 ··	50.5	261 02.2 ··	18.0	270 57.3 ··	09.7	Denebola	182 58.4	N14 40.5
04	124 00.8	192 51.6	17.7	312 51.4	50.0	276 04.2	18.1	285 59.5	09.8	Diphda	349 19.9	S18 05.3
05	139 03.2	207 51.7	17.3	327 52.7	49.5	291 06.2	18.3	301 01.7	09.9			
06	154 05.7	222 51.7	S25 16.9	342 53.9	N 5 49.0	306 08.2	S10 18.5	316 04.0	S 5 09.9	Dubhe	194 21.3	N61 50.8
W 07	169 08.2	237 51.8	16.5	357 55.1	48.5	321 10.2	18.7	331 06.2	10.0	Elnath	278 42.8	N28 35.5
E 08	184 10.6	252 51.9	16.1	12 56.4	48.0	336 12.2	18.8	346 08.4	10.1	Eltanin	90 57.9	N51 29.7
D 09	199 13.1	267 51.9 ··	15.6	27 57.6 ··	47.6	351 14.2 ··	19.0	1 10.7 ··	10.2	Enif	34 10.9	N 9 47.6
N 10	214 15.6	282 52.0	15.2	42 58.8	47.1	6 16.2	19.2	16 12.9	10.3	Fomalhaut	15 50.5	S29 43.3
E 11	229 18.0	297 52.1	14.8	58 00.1	46.6	21 18.2	19.3	31 15.1	10.4			
S 12	244 20.5	312 52.1	S25 14.4	73 01.3	N 5 46.1	36 20.2	S10 19.5	46 17.4	S 5 10.5	Gacrux	172 28.2	S57 00.3
D 13	259 23.0	327 52.2	14.0	88 02.6	45.6	51 22.2	19.7	61 19.6	10.6	Gienah	176 17.3	S17 26.2
A 14	274 25.4	342 52.3	13.5	103 03.8	45.1	66 24.1	19.9	76 21.8	10.6	Hadar	149 22.8	S60 16.8
Y 15	289 27.9	357 52.3 ··	13.1	118 05.0 ··	44.6	81 26.1 ··	20.0	91 24.1 ··	10.7	Hamal	328 27.7	N23 22.6
16	304 30.3	12 52.4	12.7	133 06.3	44.1	96 28.1	20.2	106 26.3	10.8	Kaus Aust.	84 16.1	S34 23.7
17	319 32.8	27 52.5	12.3	148 07.5	43.6	111 30.1	20.4	121 28.5	10.9			
18	334 35.3	42 52.6	S25 11.8	163 08.8	N 5 43.2	126 32.1	S10 20.5	136 30.7	S 5 11.0	Kochab	137 20.2	N74 13.8
19	349 37.7	57 52.6	11.4	178 10.0	42.7	141 34.1	20.7	151 33.0	11.1	Markab	14 02.3	N15 06.5
20	4 40.2	72 52.7	11.0	193 11.2	42.2	156 36.1	20.9	166 35.2	11.2	Menkar	314 40.0	N 4 01.1
21	19 42.7	87 52.8 ··	10.5	208 12.5 ··	41.7	171 38.1 ··	21.1	181 37.4 ··	11.3	Menkent	148 36.4	S36 16.6
22	34 45.1	102 52.9	10.1	223 13.7	41.2	186 40.1	21.2	196 39.7	11.3	Miaplacidus	221 44.5	S69 38.2
23	49 47.6	117 53.0	09.7	238 15.0	40.7	201 42.1	21.4	211 41.9	11.4			
26 00	64 50.1	132 53.0	S25 09.2	253 16.2	N 5 40.2	216 44.1	S10 21.6	226 44.1	S 5 11.5	Mirfak	309 14.5	N49 47.8
01	79 52.5	147 53.1	08.8	268 17.5	39.7	231 46.1	21.7	241 46.4	11.6	Nunki	76 28.5	S26 19.2
02	94 55.0	162 53.2	08.4	283 18.7	39.2	246 48.0	21.9	256 48.6	11.7	Peacock	53 57.4	S56 47.9
03	109 57.5	177 53.3 ··	07.9	298 19.9 ··	38.8	261 50.0 ··	22.1	271 50.8 ··	11.8	Pollux	243 57.0	N28 04.2
04	124 59.9	192 53.4	07.5	313 21.2	38.3	276 52.0	22.2	286 53.1	11.9	Procyon	245 24.7	N 5 16.4
05	140 02.4	207 53.5	07.1	328 22.4	37.8	291 54.0	22.4	301 55.3	11.9			
06	155 04.8	222 53.6	S25 06.6	343 23.7	N 5 37.3	306 56.0	S10 22.6	316 57.5	S 5 12.0	Rasalhague	96 29.2	N12 34.5
07	170 07.3	237 53.7	06.2	358 24.9	36.8	321 58.0	22.8	331 59.8	12.1	Regulus	208 09.1	N12 03.4
T 08	185 09.8	252 53.8	05.8	13 26.2	36.3	337 00.0	22.9	347 02.0	12.2	Rigel	281 34.9	S 8 13.3
H 09	200 12.2	267 53.9 ··	05.3	28 27.4 ··	35.8	352 02.0 ··	23.1	2 04.2 ··	12.3	Rigil Kent.	140 25.4	S60 45.3
U 10	215 14.7	282 54.0	04.9	43 28.6	35.3	7 04.0	23.3	17 06.5	12.4	Sabik	102 40.6	S15 42.1
R 11	230 17.2	297 54.1	04.4	58 29.9	34.9	22 06.0	23.4	32 08.7	12.5			
S 12	245 19.6	312 54.2	S25 04.0	73 31.1	N 5 34.4	37 08.0	S10 23.6	47 10.9	S 5 12.5	Schedar	350 07.8	N56 26.4
D 13	260 22.1	327 54.3	03.6	88 32.4	33.9	52 10.0	23.8	62 13.2	12.6	Shaula	96 55.1	S37 05.4
A 14	275 24.6	342 54.4	03.1	103 33.6	33.4	67 12.0	23.9	77 15.4	12.7	Sirius	258 54.7	S16 41.4
Y 15	290 27.0	357 54.5 ··	02.7	118 34.9 ··	32.9	82 14.0 ··	24.1	92 17.6 ··	12.8	Spica	158 57.0	S11 03.8
16	305 29.5	12 54.6	02.2	133 36.1	32.4	97 15.9	24.3	107 19.9	12.9	Suhail	223 10.1	S43 21.2
17	320 32.0	27 54.7	01.8	148 37.4	31.9	112 17.9	24.5	122 22.1	13.0			
18	335 34.4	42 54.8	S25 01.3	163 38.6	N 5 31.4	127 19.9	S10 24.6	137 24.3	S 5 13.1	Vega	80 55.7	N38 46.2
19	350 36.9	57 55.0	00.9	178 39.9	31.0	142 21.9	24.8	152 26.6	13.1	Zuben'ubi	137 32.5	S15 57.8
20	5 39.3	72 55.1	00.4	193 41.1	30.5	157 23.9	25.0	167 28.8	13.2		S.H.A.	Mer. Pass.
21	20 41.8	87 55.2	25 00.0	208 42.4 ··	30.0	172 25.9 ··	25.1	182 31.0 ··	13.3	Venus	69 00.5	15 09
22	35 44.3	102 55.3	24 59.5	223 43.6	29.5	187 27.9	25.3	197 33.3	13.4	Mars	188 55.5	7 08
23	50 46.7	117 55.4	59.1	238 44.9	29.0	202 29.9	25.5	212 35.5	13.5	Jupiter	152 05.3	9 35
Mer. Pass. 19 41.4	v 0.1 d 0.4	v 1.2 d 0.5		v 2.0 d 0.2		v 2.2 d 0.1				Saturn	161 59.7	8 55

G.M.T.	SUN G.H.A.	Dec.	MOON G.H.A.	v	Dec.	d	H.P.
d h	° '	° '	° '	'	° '	'	'
24 00	183 21.3	S20 29.2	210 09.3	15.2	S 7 51.0	10.4	54.3
01	198 21.1	29.7	224 43.5	15.2	8 01.4	10.4	54.3
02	213 21.0	30.2	239 17.7	15.2	8 11.8	10.4	54.3
03	228 20.8 ..	30.7	253 51.9	15.1	8 22.2	10.3	54.2
04	243 20.6	31.2	268 26.0	15.2	8 32.5	10.3	54.2
05	258 20.4	31.7	283 00.2	15.1	8 42.8	10.2	54.2
06	273 20.2	S20 32.2	297 34.3	15.1	S 8 53.0	10.2	54.2
07	288 20.0	32.7	312 08.4	15.1	9 03.2	10.2	54.2
T 08	303 19.9	33.2	326 42.5	15.0	9 13.4	10.1	54.2
U 09	318 19.7 ..	33.7	341 16.5	15.1	9 23.5	10.1	54.2
E 10	333 19.5	34.2	355 50.6	15.0	9 33.6	10.0	54.2
S 11	348 19.3	34.7	10 24.6	15.0	9 43.6	10.0	54.2
D 12	3 19.1	S20 35.2	24 58.6	15.0	S 9 53.6	10.0	54.2
A 13	18 18.9	35.7	39 32.6	14.9	10 03.6	9.9	54.2
Y 14	33 18.8	36.2	54 06.5	14.9	10 13.5	9.9	54.1
15	48 18.6 ..	36.7	68 40.5	14.9	10 23.4	9.8	54.1
16	63 18.4	37.2	83 14.4	14.9	10 33.2	9.8	54.1
17	78 18.2	37.7	97 48.3	14.8	10 43.0	9.8	54.1
18	93 18.0	S20 38.2	112 22.1	14.9	S10 52.8	9.7	54.1
19	108 17.8	38.7	126 56.0	14.8	11 02.5	9.6	54.1
20	123 17.7	39.2	141 29.8	14.7	11 12.1	9.6	54.1
21	138 17.5 ..	39.7	156 03.5	14.8	11 21.7	9.6	54.1
22	153 17.3	40.2	170 37.3	14.7	11 31.3	9.5	54.1
23	168 17.1	40.7	185 11.0	14.7	11 40.8	9.4	54.1
25 00	183 16.9	S20 41.2	199 44.7	14.7	S11 50.2	9.4	54.1
01	198 16.7	41.7	214 18.4	14.7	11 59.6	9.4	54.1
02	213 16.5	42.2	228 52.1	14.6	12 09.0	9.3	54.1
03	228 16.3 ..	42.7	243 25.7	14.6	12 18.3	9.3	54.1
04	243 16.1	43.2	257 59.3	14.6	12 27.6	9.2	54.0
05	258 16.0	43.7	272 32.9	14.5	12 36.8	9.1	54.0
06	273 15.8	S20 44.2	287 06.4	14.5	S12 45.9	9.1	54.0
W 07	288 15.6	44.7	301 39.9	14.5	12 55.0	9.0	54.0
E 08	303 15.4	45.2	316 13.4	14.4	13 04.0	9.0	54.0
D 09	318 15.2 ..	45.6	330 46.8	14.4	13 13.0	9.0	54.0
N 10	333 15.0	46.1	345 20.2	14.4	13 22.0	8.8	54.0
E 11	348 14.8	46.6	359 53.6	14.4	13 30.8	8.8	54.0
S 12	3 14.6	S20 47.1	14 27.0	14.3	S13 39.6	8.8	54.0
D 13	18 14.4	47.6	29 00.3	14.3	13 48.4	8.7	54.0
A 14	33 14.2	48.1	43 33.6	14.2	13 57.1	8.6	54.0
Y 15	48 14.1 ..	48.6	58 06.8	14.3	14 05.7	8.6	54.0
16	63 13.9	49.0	72 40.1	14.1	14 14.3	8.6	54.0
17	78 13.7	49.5	87 13.2	14.2	14 22.9	8.4	54.0
18	93 13.5	S20 50.0	101 46.4	14.1	S14 31.3	8.4	54.0
19	108 13.3	50.5	116 19.5	14.1	14 39.7	8.4	54.0
20	123 13.1	51.0	130 52.6	14.1	14 48.1	8.2	54.0
21	138 12.9 ..	51.5	145 25.7	14.0	14 56.3	8.2	54.0
22	153 12.7	51.9	159 58.7	14.0	15 04.5	8.2	54.0
23	168 12.5	52.4	174 31.7	13.9	15 12.7	8.1	54.0
26 00	183 12.3	S20 52.9	189 04.6	13.9	S15 20.8	8.0	54.0
01	198 12.1	53.4	203 37.5	13.9	15 28.8	8.0	54.0
02	213 11.9	53.9	218 10.4	13.8	15 36.8	7.9	53.9
03	228 11.7 ..	54.3	232 43.2	13.9	15 44.6	7.9	53.9
04	243 11.5	54.8	247 16.1	13.7	15 52.5	7.7	53.9
05	258 11.3	55.3	261 48.8	13.8	16 00.2	7.7	53.9
06	273 11.1	S20 55.8	276 21.6	13.7	S16 07.9	7.6	53.9
07	288 10.9	56.2	290 54.3	13.6	16 15.5	7.6	53.9
T 08	303 10.7	56.7	305 26.9	13.6	16 23.1	7.4	53.9
H 09	318 10.5 ..	57.2	319 59.5	13.6	16 30.5	7.4	53.9
U 10	333 10.3	57.6	334 32.1	13.6	16 37.9	7.4	53.9
R 11	348 10.1	58.1	349 04.7	13.5	16 45.3	7.2	53.9
S 12	3 09.9	S20 58.6	3 37.2	13.5	S16 52.5	7.2	53.9
D 13	18 09.7	59.1	18 09.7	13.4	16 59.7	7.1	53.9
A 14	33 09.5	20 59.5	32 42.1	13.4	17 06.8	7.1	53.9
Y 15	48 09.3	21 00.0	47 14.5	13.4	17 13.9	7.0	53.9
16	63 09.1	00.5	61 46.9	13.3	17 20.9	6.8	53.9
17	78 08.9	00.9	76 19.2	13.3	17 27.7	6.9	53.9
18	93 08.7	S21 01.4	90 51.5	13.3	S17 34.6	6.7	53.9
19	108 08.5	01.9	105 23.8	13.2	17 41.3	6.7	53.9
20	123 08.3	02.3	119 56.0	13.2	17 48.0	6.6	53.9
21	138 08.1 ..	02.8	134 28.2	13.1	17 54.6	6.5	53.9
22	153 07.9	03.3	149 00.3	13.1	18 01.1	6.4	53.9
23	168 07.7	03.7	163 32.4	13.1	18 07.5	6.4	53.9
	S.D. 16.2 d 0.5		S.D. 14.8		14.7		14.7

Lat.	Twilight Naut.	Civil	Sunrise	Moonrise 24	25	26	27
°	h m	h m	h m	h m	h m	h m	h m
N 72	07 33	09 21	■	06 07	07 59	10 14	■
N 70	07 19	08 49	11 30	05 52	07 33	09 22	11 33
68	07 07	08 26	10 02	05 41	07 14	08 50	10 29
66	06 58	08 08	09 25	05 31	06 58	08 26	09 54
64	06 49	07 53	08 59	05 23	06 46	08 08	09 28
62	06 42	07 40	08 38	05 17	06 35	07 53	09 09
60	06 36	07 29	08 22	05 11	06 26	07 41	08 53
N 58	06 30	07 20	08 08	05 06	06 18	07 30	08 39
56	06 25	07 12	07 56	05 01	06 11	07 21	08 28
54	06 20	07 04	07 46	04 57	06 05	07 12	08 18
52	06 15	06 58	07 36	04 54	06 00	07 05	08 08
50	06 11	06 51	07 28	04 50	05 55	06 58	08 00
45	06 02	06 38	07 11	04 43	05 44	06 44	07 43
N 40	05 53	06 27	06 56	04 37	05 35	06 32	07 29
35	05 45	06 17	06 44	04 32	05 27	06 23	07 17
30	05 38	06 07	06 33	04 28	05 21	06 14	07 07
20	05 24	05 51	06 15	04 20	05 09	05 59	06 50
N 10	05 10	05 36	05 59	04 13	04 59	05 46	06 34
0	04 56	05 21	05 43	04 07	04 50	05 34	06 20
S 10	04 39	05 05	05 28	04 01	04 41	05 22	06 06
20	04 19	04 47	05 11	03 54	04 31	05 09	05 51
30	03 53	04 26	04 52	03 46	04 20	04 55	05 33
35	03 37	04 12	04 41	03 42	04 13	04 47	05 23
40	03 17	03 57	04 28	03 37	04 06	04 37	05 12
45	02 52	03 37	04 13	03 32	03 57	04 26	04 58
S 50	02 16	03 12	03 53	03 25	03 47	04 13	04 42
52	01 56	03 00	03 44	03 22	03 43	04 06	04 34
54	01 31	02 46	03 34	03 19	03 38	03 59	04 26
56	00 54	02 29	03 23	03 15	03 32	03 52	04 16
58	////	02 08	03 09	03 11	03 26	03 43	04 05
S 60	////	01 41	02 54	03 06	03 18	03 33	03 53

Lat.	Sunset	Twilight Civil	Naut.	Moonset 24	25	26	27
°	h m	h m	h m	h m	h m	h m	h m
N 72	■	14 12	16 00	14 07	13 45	13 03	■
N 70	12 04	14 44	16 14	14 23	14 12	13 56	13 21
68	13 31	15 07	16 26	14 36	14 33	14 29	14 25
66	14 09	15 26	16 35	14 47	14 49	14 53	15 01
64	14 35	15 41	16 44	14 56	15 03	15 12	15 27
62	14 55	15 53	16 51	15 04	15 14	15 28	15 47
60	15 12	16 04	16 58	15 11	15 24	15 41	16 03
N 58	15 26	16 13	17 04	15 16	15 32	15 52	16 17
56	15 37	16 22	17 09	15 22	15 40	16 02	16 29
54	15 48	16 29	17 14	15 27	15 47	16 11	16 40
52	15 57	16 36	17 18	15 31	15 53	16 18	16 49
50	16 06	16 42	17 22	15 35	15 58	16 25	16 57
45	16 23	16 56	17 32	15 43	16 10	16 40	17 15
N 40	16 38	17 07	17 40	15 50	16 20	16 53	17 30
35	16 50	17 17	17 48	15 57	16 29	17 03	17 42
30	17 01	17 26	17 56	16 02	16 36	17 13	17 53
20	17 19	17 43	18 10	16 11	16 49	17 29	18 11
N 10	17 35	17 58	18 24	16 20	17 00	17 43	18 27
0	17 51	18 13	18 39	16 27	17 11	17 56	18 43
S 10	18 06	18 29	18 55	16 35	17 22	18 09	18 58
20	18 23	18 47	19 15	16 44	17 33	18 23	19 14
30	18 42	19 09	19 41	16 53	17 46	18 40	19 33
35	18 53	19 22	19 57	16 59	17 54	18 49	19 44
40	19 07	19 38	20 17	17 05	18 03	19 00	19 56
45	19 22	19 58	20 43	17 12	18 13	19 13	20 11
S 50	19 41	20 23	21 20	17 21	18 25	19 28	20 29
52	19 50	20 35	21 40	17 25	18 31	19 36	20 38
54	20 01	20 50	22 05	17 30	18 37	19 44	20 47
56	20 12	21 07	22 45	17 35	18 45	19 53	20 58
58	20 26	21 28	////	17 41	18 53	20 03	21 11
S 60	20 42	21 56	////	17 47	19 02	20 15	21 25

Day	SUN Eqn. of Time 00h	12h	Mer. Pass.	MOON Mer. Pass. Upper	Lower	Age	Phase
	m s	m s	h m	h m	h m	d	
24	13 26	13 17	11 47	10 17	22 39	28	
25	13 08	12 59	11 47	11 00	23 23	29	
26	12 50	12 40	11 47	11 45	24 08	30	●

G.M.T.	ARIES G.H.A.	VENUS −4.3 G.H.A.	Dec.	MARS +1.4 G.H.A.	Dec.	JUPITER −1.3 G.H.A.	Dec.	SATURN +1.0 G.H.A.	Dec.	STARS Name	S.H.A.	Dec.
27 00	65 49.2	132 55.6 S24	58.6	253 46.1 N 5	28.5	217 31.9 S10	25.6	227 37.7 S 5	13.6	Acamar	315 36.2	S40 22.8
01	80 51.7	147 55.7	58.2	268 47.3	28.0	232 33.9	25.8	242 44.0	13.7	Achernar	335 44.2	S57 20.0
02	95 54.1	162 55.8	57.7	283 48.6	27.6	247 35.9	26.0	257 42.2	13.7	Acrux	173 36.7	S62 59.5
03	110 56.6	177 56.0 ··	57.3	298 49.8 ··	27.1	262 37.9 ··	26.1	272 44.5 ··	13.8	Adhara	255 31.2	S28 56.7
04	125 59.1	192 56.1	56.8	313 51.1	26.6	277 39.9	26.3	287 46.7	13.9	Aldebaran	291 16.7	N16 28.4
05	141 01.5	207 56.2	56.4	328 52.3	26.1	292 41.9	26.5	302 48.9	14.0			
06	156 04.0	222 56.3 S24	55.9	343 53.6 N 5	25.6	307 43.9 S10	26.7	317 51.2 S 5	14.1	Alioth	166 42.1	N56 03.4
07	171 06.5	237 56.5	55.5	358 54.8	25.1	322 45.9	26.8	332 53.4	14.2	Alkaid	153 18.2	N49 24.2
08	186 08.9	252 56.6	55.0	13 56.1	24.6	337 47.9	27.0	347 55.6	14.3	Al Na'ir	28 14.0	S47 03.2
F 09	201 11.4	267 56.8 ··	54.6	28 57.3 ··	24.2	352 49.9 ··	27.2	2 57.9 ··	14.3	Alnilam	276 10.5	S 1 12.8
R 10	216 13.8	282 56.9	54.1	43 58.6	23.7	7 51.8	27.3	18 00.1	14.4	Alphard	218 19.7	S 8 34.6
I 11	231 16.3	297 57.0	53.6	58 59.8	23.2	22 53.8	27.5	33 02.3	14.5			
D 12	246 18.8	312 57.2 S24	53.2	74 01.1 N 5	22.7	37 55.8 S10	27.7	48 04.6 S 5	14.6	Alphecca	126 31.8	N26 46.6
A 13	261 21.2	327 57.3	52.7	89 02.3	22.2	52 57.8	27.8	63 06.8	14.7	Alpheratz	358 08.3	N28 59.5
Y 14	276 23.7	342 57.5	52.3	104 03.6	21.7	67 59.8	28.0	78 09.0	14.8	Altair	62 32.0	N 8 49.3
15	291 26.2	357 57.6 ··	51.8	119 04.8 ··	21.2	83 01.8 ··	28.2	93 11.3 ··	14.8	Ankaa	353 39.2	S42 24.5
16	306 28.6	12 57.8	51.3	134 06.1	20.8	98 03.8	28.3	108 13.5	14.9	Antares	112 56.3	S26 23.4
17	321 31.1	27 57.9	50.9	149 07.4	20.3	113 05.8	28.5	123 15.8	15.0			
18	336 33.6	42 58.1 S24	50.4	164 08.6 N 5	19.8	128 07.8 S10	28.7	138 18.0 S 5	15.1	Arcturus	146 18.0	N19 16.7
19	351 36.0	57 58.2	50.0	179 09.9	19.3	143 09.8	28.9	153 20.2	15.2	Atria	108 20.3	S68 59.7
20	6 38.5	72 58.4	49.5	194 11.1	18.8	158 11.8	29.0	168 22.5	15.3	Avior	234 27.5	S59 26.8
21	21 40.9	87 58.6 ··	49.0	209 12.4 ··	18.3	173 13.8 ··	29.2	183 24.7 ··	15.4	Bellatrix	278 57.6	N 6 20.0
22	36 43.4	102 58.7	48.6	224 13.6	17.8	188 15.8	29.4	198 26.9	15.4	Betelgeuse	271 27.1	N 7 24.2
23	51 45.9	117 58.9	48.1	239 14.9	17.4	203 17.8	29.5	213 29.2	15.5			
28 00	66 48.3	132 59.0 S24	47.6	254 16.1 N 5	16.9	218 19.8 S10	29.7	228 31.4 S 5	15.6	Canopus	264 06.4	S52 41.0
01	81 50.8	147 59.2	47.2	269 17.4	16.4	233 21.8	29.9	243 33.6	15.7	Capella	281 09.6	N45 58.8
02	96 53.3	162 59.4	46.7	284 18.6	15.9	248 23.8	30.0	258 35.9	15.8	Deneb	49 48.1	N45 13.1
03	111 55.7	177 59.6 ··	46.2	299 19.9 ··	15.4	263 25.8 ··	30.2	273 38.1 ··	15.9	Denebola	182 58.3	N14 40.5
04	126 58.2	192 59.7	45.7	314 21.1	14.9	278 27.8	30.4	288 40.4	15.9	Diphda	349 19.9	S18 05.3
05	142 00.7	207 59.9	45.3	329 22.4	14.5	293 29.8	30.5	303 42.6	16.0			
06	157 03.1	223 00.1 S24	44.8	344 23.7 N 5	14.0	308 31.8 S10	30.7	318 44.8 S 5	16.1	Dubhe	194 21.2	N61 50.8
07	172 05.6	238 00.2	44.3	359 24.9	13.5	323 33.8	30.9	333 47.1	16.2	Elnath	278 42.7	N28 35.5
S 08	187 08.1	253 00.4	43.9	14 26.2	13.0	338 35.8	31.0	348 49.3	16.3	Eltanin	90 57.9	N51 29.6
A 09	202 10.5	268 00.6 ··	43.4	29 27.4 ··	12.5	353 37.8 ··	31.2	3 51.5 ··	16.4	Enif	34 10.9	N 9 47.6
T 10	217 13.0	283 00.8	42.9	44 28.7	12.0	8 39.8	31.4	18 53.8	16.4	Fomalhaut	15 50.5	S29 43.3
U 11	232 15.4	298 01.0	42.4	59 29.9	11.6	23 41.8	31.5	33 56.0	16.5			
R 12	247 17.9	313 01.2 S24	42.0	74 31.2 N 5	11.1	38 43.8 S10	31.7	48 58.3 S 5	16.6	Gacrux	172 28.2	S57 00.3
D 13	262 20.4	328 01.3	41.5	89 32.5	10.6	53 45.8	31.9	64 00.5	16.7	Gienah	176 17.3	S17 26.2
A 14	277 22.8	343 01.5	41.0	104 33.7	10.1	68 47.8	32.0	79 02.7	16.8	Hadar	149 22.8	S60 16.8
Y 15	292 25.3	358 01.7 ··	40.5	119 35.0 ··	09.6	83 49.7 ··	32.2	94 05.0 ··	16.9	Hamal	328 27.7	N23 22.6
16	307 27.8	13 01.9	40.0	134 36.2	09.1	98 51.7	32.4	109 07.2	17.0	Kaus Aust.	84 16.1	S34 23.6
17	322 30.2	28 02.1	39.6	149 37.5	08.6	113 53.7	32.5	124 09.5	17.0			
18	337 32.7	43 02.3 S24	39.1	164 38.7 N 5	08.2	128 55.7 S10	32.7	139 11.7 S 5	17.1	Kochab	137 20.1	N74 13.8
19	352 35.2	58 02.5	38.6	179 40.0	07.7	143 57.7	32.9	154 13.9	17.2	Markab	14 02.3	N15 06.5
20	7 37.6	73 02.7	38.1	194 41.3	07.2	158 59.7	33.0	169 16.2	17.3	Menkar	314 40.0	N 4 01.1
21	22 40.1	88 02.9 ··	37.6	209 42.5 ··	06.7	174 01.7 ··	33.2	184 18.4 ··	17.4	Menkent	148 36.4	S36 16.6
22	37 42.6	103 03.1	37.1	224 43.8	06.2	189 03.7	33.4	199 20.6	17.5	Miaplacidus	221 44.5	S69 38.2
23	52 45.0	118 03.3	36.7	239 45.0	05.8	204 05.7	33.5	214 22.9	17.5			
29 00	67 47.5	133 03.5 S24	36.2	254 46.3 N 5	05.3	219 07.7 S10	33.7	229 25.1 S 5	17.6	Mirfak	309 14.5	N49 47.9
01	82 49.9	148 03.7	35.7	269 47.6	04.8	234 09.7	33.9	244 27.4	17.7	Nunki	76 28.5	S26 19.2
02	97 52.4	163 03.9	35.2	284 48.8	04.3	249 11.7	34.0	259 29.6	17.8	Peacock	53 57.4	S56 47.9
03	112 54.9	178 04.1 ··	34.7	299 50.1 ··	03.8	264 13.7 ··	34.2	274 31.8 ··	17.9	Pollux	243 56.9	N28 04.2
04	127 57.3	193 04.4	34.2	314 51.3	03.3	279 15.7	34.4	289 34.1	17.9	Procyon	245 24.7	N 5 16.3
05	142 59.8	208 04.6	33.7	329 52.6	02.9	294 17.7	34.5	304 36.3	18.0			
06	158 02.3	223 04.8 S24	33.3	344 53.9 N 5	02.4	309 19.7 S10	34.7	319 38.6 S 5	18.1	Rasalhague	96 29.2	N12 34.5
07	173 04.7	238 05.0	32.8	359 55.1	01.9	324 21.7	34.9	334 40.8	18.2	Regulus	208 09.1	N12 03.4
08	188 07.2	253 05.2	32.3	14 56.4	01.4	339 23.7	35.0	349 43.0	18.3	Rigel	281 34.9	S 8 13.3
S 09	203 09.7	268 05.4 ··	31.8	29 57.6 ··	00.9	354 25.7 ··	35.2	4 45.3 ··	18.4	Rigil Kent.	140 25.4	S60 45.3
U 10	218 12.1	283 05.7	31.3	44 58.9	00.4	9 27.7	35.4	19 47.5	18.4	Sabik	102 40.6	S15 42.1
N 11	233 14.6	298 05.9	30.8	60 00.2	5 00.0	24 29.7	35.5	34 49.8	18.5			
D 12	248 17.0	313 06.1 S24	30.3	75 01.4 N 4	59.5	39 31.7 S10	35.7	49 52.0 S 5	18.6	Schedar	350 07.8	N56 26.4
A 13	263 19.5	328 06.4	29.8	90 02.7	59.0	54 33.7	35.9	64 54.2	18.7	Shaula	96 55.1	S37 05.4
Y 14	278 22.0	343 06.6	29.3	105 04.0	58.5	69 35.7	36.0	79 56.5	18.8	Sirius	258 54.7	S16 41.4
15	293 24.4	358 06.8 ··	28.8	120 05.2 ··	58.0	84 37.7 ··	36.2	94 58.7 ··	18.9	Spica	158 56.9	S11 03.8
16	308 26.9	13 07.1	28.3	135 06.5	57.6	99 39.7	36.4	110 01.0	18.9	Suhail	223 10.0	S43 21.3
17	323 29.4	28 07.3	27.8	150 07.8	57.1	114 41.7	36.5	125 03.2	19.0			
18	338 31.8	43 07.5 S24	27.3	165 09.0 N 4	56.6	129 43.7 S10	36.7	140 05.4 S 5	19.1	Vega	80 55.7	N38 46.2
19	353 34.3	58 07.8	26.8	180 10.3	56.1	144 45.7	36.9	155 07.7	19.2	Zuben'ubi	137 32.5	S15 57.8
20	8 36.8	73 08.0	26.3	195 11.5	55.6	159 47.7	37.0	170 09.9	19.3		S.H.A.	Mer. Pass.
21	23 39.2	88 08.3 ··	25.8	210 12.8 ··	55.1	174 49.7 ··	37.2	185 12.2 ··	19.4	Venus	66 10.7	15 08
22	38 41.7	103 08.5	25.3	225 14.1	54.7	189 51.7	37.4	200 14.4	19.4	Mars	187 27.8	7 02
23	53 44.2	118 08.7	24.8	240 15.3	54.2	204 53.7	37.5	215 16.7	19.5	Jupiter	151 31.5	9 25
Mer. Pass. 19 29.6		v 0.2	d 0.5	v 1.3	d 0.5	v 2.0	d 0.2	v 2.2	d 0.1	Saturn	161 43.1	8 45

G.M.T.	SUN G.H.A.	SUN Dec.	MOON G.H.A.	MOON v	MOON Dec.	MOON d	MOON H.P.
d h	° '	° '	° '	'	° '	'	'
27 00	183 07.5	S21 04.2	178 04.5	13.0	S18 13.9	6.2	53.9
01	198 07.3	04.6	192 36.5	13.0	18 20.1	6.2	53.9
02	213 07.1	05.1	207 08.5	13.0	18 26.3	6.1	53.9
03	228 06.9	·· 05.6	221 40.5	12.9	18 32.4	6.1	53.9
04	243 06.7	06.0	236 12.4	12.9	18 38.5	5.9	53.9
05	258 06.5	06.5	250 44.3	12.9	18 44.4	5.9	53.9
06	273 06.3	S21 06.9	265 16.2	12.8	S18 50.3	5.8	53.9
07	288 06.1	07.4	279 48.0	12.8	18 56.1	5.7	53.9
08	303 05.9	07.9	294 19.8	12.7	19 01.8	5.6	53.9
F 09	318 05.7	·· 08.3	308 51.5	12.7	19 07.4	5.5	53.9
R 10	333 05.5	08.8	323 23.2	12.7	19 12.9	5.5	53.9
I 11	348 05.3	09.2	337 54.9	12.6	19 18.4	5.3	53.9
D 12	3 05.1	S21 09.7	352 26.5	12.6	S19 23.7	5.3	53.9
A 13	18 04.9	10.1	6 58.1	12.6	19 29.0	5.2	53.9
Y 14	33 04.6	10.6	21 29.7	12.5	19 34.2	5.1	53.9
15	48 04.4	·· 11.0	36 01.2	12.5	19 39.3	5.0	53.9
16	63 04.2	11.5	50 32.7	12.5	19 44.3	4.9	54.0
17	78 04.0	11.9	65 04.2	12.4	19 49.2	4.9	54.0
18	93 03.8	S21 12.4	79 35.6	12.4	S19 54.1	4.7	54.0
19	108 03.6	12.8	94 07.0	12.4	19 58.8	4.7	54.0
20	123 03.4	13.3	108 38.4	12.3	20 03.5	4.6	54.0
21	138 03.2	·· 13.7	123 09.7	12.3	20 08.1	4.4	54.0
22	153 03.0	14.2	137 41.0	12.3	20 12.5	4.4	54.0
23	168 02.8	14.6	152 12.3	12.2	20 16.9	4.3	54.0
28 00	183 02.6	S21 15.1	166 43.5	12.2	S20 21.2	4.2	54.0
01	198 02.3	15.5	181 14.7	12.2	20 25.4	4.1	54.0
02	213 02.1	16.0	195 45.9	12.1	20 29.5	4.1	54.0
03	228 01.9	·· 16.4	210 17.0	12.1	20 33.6	3.9	54.0
04	243 01.7	16.8	224 48.1	12.1	20 37.5	3.8	54.0
05	258 01.5	17.3	239 19.2	12.0	20 41.3	3.8	54.0
06	273 01.3	S21 17.7	253 50.2	12.0	S20 45.1	3.6	54.0
07	288 01.1	18.2	268 21.2	12.0	20 48.7	3.6	54.0
S 08	303 00.9	18.6	282 52.2	12.0	20 52.3	3.4	54.0
A 09	318 00.6	·· 19.0	297 23.2	11.9	20 55.7	3.4	54.0
T 10	333 00.4	19.5	311 54.1	11.9	20 59.1	3.2	54.0
U 11	348 00.2	19.9	326 25.0	11.9	21 02.3	3.2	54.0
R 12	3 00.0	S21 20.4	340 55.9	11.8	S21 05.5	3.1	54.0
D 13	17 59.8	20.8	355 26.7	11.8	21 08.6	2.9	54.0
A 14	32 59.6	21.2	9 57.5	11.8	21 11.5	2.9	54.1
Y 15	47 59.4	·· 21.7	24 28.3	11.8	21 14.4	2.8	54.1
16	62 59.1	22.1	38 59.1	11.7	21 17.2	2.7	54.1
17	77 58.9	22.5	53 29.8	11.7	21 19.9	2.6	54.1
18	92 58.7	S21 23.0	68 00.5	11.7	S21 22.5	2.4	54.1
19	107 58.5	23.4	82 31.2	11.7	21 24.9	2.4	54.1
20	122 58.3	23.8	97 01.9	11.6	21 27.3	2.3	54.1
21	137 58.1	·· 24.3	111 32.5	11.7	21 29.6	2.2	54.1
22	152 57.8	24.7	126 03.2	11.6	21 31.8	2.1	54.1
23	167 57.6	25.1	140 33.8	11.5	21 33.9	2.0	54.1
29 00	182 57.4	S21 25.5	155 04.3	11.6	S21 35.9	1.8	54.1
01	197 57.2	26.0	169 34.9	11.5	21 37.7	1.8	54.1
02	212 57.0	26.4	184 05.4	11.5	21 39.5	1.7	54.1
03	227 56.8	·· 26.8	198 35.9	11.5	21 41.2	1.6	54.2
04	242 56.5	27.3	213 06.4	11.5	21 42.8	1.5	54.2
05	257 56.3	27.7	227 36.9	11.5	21 44.3	1.4	54.2
06	272 56.1	S21 28.1	242 07.4	11.4	S21 45.7	1.2	54.2
07	287 55.9	28.5	256 37.8	11.4	21 46.9	1.2	54.2
08	302 55.7	29.0	271 08.2	11.4	21 48.1	1.1	54.2
S 09	317 55.4	·· 29.4	285 38.6	11.4	21 49.2	0.9	54.2
U 10	332 55.2	29.8	300 09.0	11.4	21 50.1	0.9	54.2
N 11	347 55.0	30.2	314 39.4	11.3	21 51.0	0.8	54.2
D 12	2 54.8	S21 30.6	329 09.7	11.4	S21 51.8	0.6	54.2
A 13	17 54.6	31.1	343 40.1	11.3	21 52.4	0.6	54.2
Y 14	32 54.3	31.5	358 10.4	11.3	21 53.0	0.4	54.3
15	47 54.1	·· 31.9	12 40.7	11.3	21 53.4	0.4	54.3
16	62 53.9	32.3	27 11.0	11.3	21 53.8	0.2	54.3
17	77 53.7	32.7	41 41.3	11.3	21 54.0	0.2	54.3
18	92 53.4	S21 33.1	56 11.6	11.2	S21 54.2	0.0	54.3
19	107 53.2	33.6	70 41.8	11.3	21 54.2	0.1	54.3
20	122 53.0	34.0	85 12.1	11.2	21 54.1	0.1	54.3
21	137 52.8	·· 34.4	99 42.3	11.3	21 54.0	0.3	54.3
22	152 52.5	34.8	114 12.6	11.2	21 53.7	0.4	54.3
23	167 52.3	35.2	128 42.8	11.2	21 53.3	0.5	54.4
	S.D. 16.2	d 0.4	S.D. 14.7	14.7			14.8

Lat.	Twilight Naut.	Twilight Civil	Sunrise	Moonrise 27	Moonrise 28	Moonrise 29	Moonrise 30
°	h m	h m	h m	h m	h m	h m	h m
N 72	07 42	09 36	■	■	■	■	■
N 70	07 27	09 00	■	11 33	■	■	■
68	07 15	08 35	10 18	10 29	12 11	13 55	14 14
66	07 04	08 16	09 36	09 54	11 16	12 24	13 07
64	06 55	08 00	09 07	09 28	10 43	11 46	12 31
62	06 48	07 47	08 46	09 09	10 19	11 19	12 06
60	06 41	07 35	08 28	08 53	10 00	10 58	11 45
N 58	06 35	07 25	08 14	08 39	09 44	10 41	11 29
56	06 29	07 17	08 02	08 28	09 31	10 27	11 15
54	06 24	07 09	07 51	08 18	09 19	10 15	11 03
52	06 19	07 02	07 41	08 08	09 09	10 04	10 52
50	06 15	06 55	07 32	08 00	09 00	09 54	10 42
45	06 05	06 41	07 14	07 43	08 40	09 34	10 22
N 40	05 56	06 30	06 59	07 29	08 25	09 17	10 06
35	05 48	06 19	06 47	07 17	08 11	09 03	09 52
30	05 40	06 10	06 36	07 07	08 00	08 51	09 40
20	05 26	05 53	06 17	06 50	07 40	08 30	09 19
N 10	05 12	05 38	06 00	06 34	07 23	08 12	09 02
0	04 56	05 22	05 44	06 20	07 07	07 56	08 45
S 10	04 39	05 06	05 28	06 06	06 51	07 39	08 28
20	04 19	04 47	05 11	05 51	06 34	07 21	08 10
30	03 52	04 25	04 52	05 33	06 15	07 01	07 50
35	03 36	04 11	04 40	05 23	06 04	06 49	07 38
40	03 15	03 55	04 27	05 12	05 51	06 35	07 24
45	02 49	03 35	04 11	04 58	05 36	06 19	07 08
S 50	02 11	03 09	03 51	04 42	05 17	05 59	06 48
52	01 50	02 56	03 42	04 34	05 08	05 49	06 38
54	01 23	02 41	03 31	04 26	04 58	05 38	06 27
56	00 39	02 24	03 19	04 16	04 47	05 26	06 15
58	////	02 05	03 05	04 05	04 34	05 12	06 01
S 60	////	01 32	02 48	03 53	04 19	04 56	05 44

Lat.	Sunset	Twilight Civil	Twilight Naut.	Moonset 27	Moonset 28	Moonset 29	Moonset 30
°	h m	h m	h m	h m	h m	h m	h m
N 72	■	13 59	15 53	■	■	■	■
N 70	■	14 35	16 08	13 21	■	■	■
68	13 17	15 00	16 21	14 25	14 22	14 19	15 43
66	14 00	15 20	16 31	15 01	15 17	15 51	16 50
64	14 28	15 36	16 40	15 27	15 50	16 29	17 25
62	14 50	15 49	16 48	15 47	16 15	16 55	17 51
60	15 07	16 00	16 55	16 03	16 34	17 16	18 11
N 58	15 22	16 10	17 01	16 17	16 50	17 33	18 27
56	15 34	16 19	17 06	16 29	17 04	17 48	18 41
54	15 45	16 27	17 11	16 40	17 16	18 00	18 53
52	15 55	16 34	17 16	16 49	17 26	18 11	19 04
50	16 03	16 40	17 21	16 57	17 35	18 21	19 13
45	16 21	16 54	17 31	17 15	17 55	18 41	19 33
N 40	16 36	17 06	17 40	17 30	18 11	18 58	19 49
35	16 49	17 17	17 48	17 42	18 25	19 12	20 03
30	17 00	17 26	17 55	17 53	18 36	19 24	20 15
20	17 19	17 43	18 10	18 11	18 57	19 45	20 35
N 10	17 36	17 58	18 24	18 27	19 14	20 03	20 52
0	17 52	18 14	18 40	18 43	19 31	20 19	21 09
S 10	18 08	18 30	18 57	18 58	19 47	20 36	21 25
20	18 25	18 49	19 17	19 14	20 05	20 54	21 42
30	18 45	19 11	19 44	19 33	20 25	21 15	22 02
35	18 56	19 25	20 01	19 44	20 37	21 27	22 14
40	19 10	19 42	20 21	19 56	20 50	21 41	22 27
45	19 26	20 02	20 48	20 11	21 06	21 57	22 43
S 50	19 46	20 28	21 26	20 29	21 26	22 17	23 02
52	19 55	20 41	21 47	20 38	21 35	22 27	23 12
54	20 06	20 56	22 16	20 47	21 46	22 38	23 22
56	20 18	21 14	23 03	20 58	21 58	22 50	23 33
58	20 32	21 36	////	21 11	22 12	23 04	23 47
S 60	20 49	22 07	////	21 25	22 28	23 21	24 02

Day	SUN Eqn. of Time 00h	SUN Eqn. of Time 12h	SUN Mer. Pass.	MOON Mer. Pass. Upper	MOON Mer. Pass. Lower	Age	Phase
	m s	m s	h m	h m	h m	d	
27	12 30	12 21	11 48	12 31	00 08	01	
28	12 11	12 00	11 48	13 19	00 55	02	
29	11 50	11 40	11 48	14 08	01 43	03	●

G.M.T.	ARIES G.H.A.	VENUS −4.3 G.H.A.	VENUS Dec.	MARS +1.3 G.H.A.	MARS Dec.	JUPITER −1.3 G.H.A.	JUPITER Dec.	SATURN +1.0 G.H.A.	SATURN Dec.	STARS Name	S.H.A.	Dec.
30 00	68 46.6	133 09.0	S24 24.3	255 16.6	N 4 53.7	219 55.7	S10 37.7	230 18.9	S 5 19.6	Acamar	315 36.2	S40 22.8
01	83 49.1	148 09.2	23.8	270 17.9	53.2	234 57.7	37.9	245 21.1	19.7	Achernar	335 44.2	S57 20.0
02	98 51.5	163 09.5	23.3	285 19.1	52.7	249 59.7	38.0	260 23.4	19.8	Acrux	173 36.7	S62 59.5
03	113 54.0	178 09.8	·· 22.8	300 20.4	·· 52.3	265 01.7	·· 38.2	275 25.6	·· 19.8	Adhara	255 31.1	S28 56.7
04	128 56.5	193 10.0	22.3	315 21.7	51.8	280 03.7	38.4	290 27.9	19.9	Aldebaran	291 16.7	N16 28.4
05	143 58.9	208 10.3	21.8	330 22.9	51.3	295 05.7	38.5	305 30.1	20.0			
06	159 01.4	223 10.5	S24 21.3	345 24.2	N 4 50.8	310 07.7	S10 38.7	320 32.3	S 5 20.1	Alioth	166 42.1	N56 03.4
07	174 03.9	238 10.8	20.8	0 25.5	50.3	325 09.7	38.9	335 34.6	20.2	Alkaid	153 18.2	N49 24.2
08	189 06.3	253 11.1	20.3	15 26.7	49.9	340 11.7	39.0	350 36.8	20.3	Al Na'ir	28 14.0	S47 03.2
M 09	204 08.8	268 11.3	·· 19.8	30 28.0	·· 49.4	355 13.7	·· 39.2	5 39.1	·· 20.3	Alnilam	276 10.5	S 1 12.8
O 10	219 11.3	283 11.6	19.3	45 29.3	48.9	10 15.7	39.3	20 41.3	20.4	Alphard	218 19.7	S 8 34.6
N 11	234 13.7	298 11.9	18.8	60 30.6	48.4	25 17.7	39.5	35 43.6	20.5			
D 12	249 16.2	313 12.1	S24 18.3	75 31.8	N 4 47.9	40 19.7	S10 39.7	50 45.8	S 5 20.6	Alphecca	126 31.8	N26 46.6
A 13	264 18.7	328 12.4	17.8	90 33.1	47.5	55 21.8	39.8	65 48.0	20.7	Alpheratz	358 08.3	N28 59.5
Y 14	279 21.1	343 12.7	17.3	105 34.4	47.0	70 23.8	40.0	80 50.3	20.7	Altair	62 32.0	N 8 49.3
15	294 23.6	358 13.0	·· 16.8	120 35.6	·· 46.5	85 25.8	·· 40.2	95 52.5	·· 20.8	Ankaa	353 39.2	S42 24.5
16	309 26.0	13 13.2	16.2	135 36.9	46.0	100 27.8	40.3	110 54.8	20.9	Antares	112 56.2	S26 23.4
17	324 28.5	28 13.5	15.7	150 38.2	45.5	115 29.8	40.5	125 57.0	21.0			
18	339 31.0	43 13.8	S24 15.2	165 39.4	N 4 45.1	130 31.8	S10 40.7	140 59.3	S 5 21.1	Arcturus	146 18.0	N19 16.7
19	354 33.4	58 14.1	14.7	180 40.7	44.6	145 33.8	40.8	156 01.5	21.1	Atria	108 20.3	S68 59.7
20	9 35.9	73 14.4	14.2	195 42.0	44.1	160 35.8	41.0	171 03.7	21.2	Avior	234 27.5	S59 26.8
21	24 38.4	88 14.7	·· 13.7	210 43.3	·· 43.6	175 37.8	·· 41.2	186 06.0	·· 21.3	Bellatrix	278 57.5	N 6 20.0
22	39 40.8	103 14.9	13.2	225 44.5	43.1	190 39.8	41.3	201 08.2	21.4	Betelgeuse	271 27.1	N 7 24.2
23	54 43.3	118 15.2	12.6	240 45.8	42.7	205 41.8	41.5	216 10.5	21.5			
1 00	69 45.8	133 15.5	S24 12.1	255 47.1	N 4 42.2	220 43.8	S10 41.7	231 12.7	S 5 21.6	Canopus	264 06.3	S52 41.0
01	84 48.2	148 15.8	11.6	270 48.3	41.7	235 45.8	41.8	246 15.0	21.6	Capella	281 09.6	N45 58.8
02	99 50.7	163 16.1	11.1	285 49.6	41.2	250 47.8	42.0	261 17.2	21.7	Deneb	49 48.2	N45 13.1
03	114 53.1	178 16.4	·· 10.6	300 50.9	·· 40.8	265 49.8	·· 42.1	276 19.5	·· 21.8	Denebola	182 58.3	N14 40.5
04	129 55.6	193 16.7	10.1	315 52.2	40.3	280 51.8	42.3	291 21.7	21.9	Diphda	349 19.9	S18 05.3
05	144 58.1	208 17.0	09.5	330 53.4	39.8	295 53.8	42.5	306 23.9	22.0			
06	160 00.5	223 17.3	S24 09.0	345 54.7	N 4 39.3	310 55.8	S10 42.6	321 26.2	S 5 22.0	Dubhe	194 21.2	N61 50.7
07	175 03.0	238 17.6	08.5	0 56.0	38.8	325 57.8	42.8	336 28.4	22.1	Elnath	278 42.7	N28 35.5
T 08	190 05.5	253 18.0	08.0	15 57.3	38.4	340 59.8	43.0	351 30.7	22.2	Eltanin	90 57.9	N51 29.6
U 09	205 07.9	268 18.3	·· 07.5	30 58.5	·· 37.9	356 01.8	·· 43.1	6 32.9	·· 22.3	Enif	34 10.9	N 9 47.5
E 10	220 10.4	283 18.6	06.9	45 59.8	37.4	11 03.8	43.3	21 35.2	22.4	Fomalhaut	15 50.5	S29 43.3
S 11	235 12.9	298 18.9	06.4	61 01.1	36.9	26 05.8	43.5	36 37.4	22.4			
D 12	250 15.3	313 19.2	S24 05.9	76 02.4	N 4 36.5	41 07.8	S10 43.6	51 39.7	S 5 22.5	Gacrux	172 28.1	S57 00.3
A 13	265 17.8	328 19.5	05.4	91 03.6	36.0	56 09.8	43.8	66 41.9	22.6	Gienah	176 17.3	S17 26.2
Y 14	280 20.3	343 19.9	04.8	106 04.9	35.5	71 11.8	43.9	81 44.1	22.7	Hadar	149 22.7	S60 16.8
15	295 22.7	358 20.2	·· 04.3	121 06.2	·· 35.0	86 13.8	·· 44.1	96 46.4	·· 22.8	Hamal	328 27.7	N23 22.6
16	310 25.2	13 20.5	03.8	136 07.5	34.5	101 15.8	44.3	111 48.6	22.8	Kaus Aust.	84 16.1	S34 23.6
17	325 27.6	28 20.8	03.3	151 08.7	34.1	116 17.9	44.4	126 50.9	22.9			
18	340 30.1	43 21.2	S24 02.7	166 10.0	N 4 33.6	131 19.9	S10 44.6	141 53.1	S 5 23.0	Kochab	137 20.1	N74 13.8
19	355 32.6	58 21.5	02.2	181 11.3	33.1	146 21.9	44.8	156 55.4	23.1	Markab	14 02.3	N15 06.5
20	10 35.0	73 21.8	01.7	196 12.6	32.6	161 23.9	44.9	171 57.6	23.2	Menkar	314 40.0	N 4 01.1
21	25 37.5	88 22.2	·· 01.1	211 13.8	·· 32.2	176 25.9	·· 45.1	186 59.9	·· 23.2	Menkent	148 36.4	S36 16.6
22	40 40.0	103 22.5	00.6	226 15.1	31.7	191 27.9	45.3	202 02.1	23.3	Miaplacidus	221 44.4	S69 38.2
23	55 42.4	118 22.8	24 00.1	241 16.4	31.2	206 29.9	45.4	217 04.4	23.4			
2 00	70 44.9	133 23.2	S23 59.6	256 17.7	N 4 30.7	221 31.9	S10 45.6	232 06.6	S 5 23.5	Mirfak	309 14.4	N49 47.9
01	85 47.4	148 23.5	59.0	271 19.0	30.3	236 33.9	45.7	247 08.9	23.6	Nunki	76 28.5	S26 19.2
02	100 49.8	163 23.9	58.5	286 20.2	29.8	251 35.9	45.9	262 11.1	23.6	Peacock	53 57.4	S56 47.9
03	115 52.3	178 24.2	·· 58.0	301 21.5	·· 29.3	266 37.9	·· 46.1	277 13.3	·· 23.7	Pollux	243 56.9	N28 04.2
04	130 54.8	193 24.6	57.4	316 22.8	28.8	281 39.9	46.2	292 15.6	23.8	Procyon	245 24.7	N 5 16.3
05	145 57.2	208 24.9	56.9	331 24.1	28.3	296 41.9	46.4	307 17.8	23.9			
06	160 59.7	223 25.3	S23 56.4	346 25.4	N 4 27.9	311 43.9	S10 46.6	322 20.1	S 5 24.0	Rasalhague	96 29.2	N12 34.5
W 07	176 02.1	238 25.6	55.8	1 26.6	27.4	326 45.9	46.7	337 22.3	24.0	Regulus	208 09.1	N12 03.4
E 08	191 04.6	253 26.0	55.3	16 27.9	26.9	341 47.9	46.9	352 24.6	24.1	Rigel	281 34.9	S 8 13.3
D 09	206 07.1	268 26.3	·· 54.7	31 29.2	·· 26.4	356 49.9	·· 47.0	7 26.8	·· 24.2	Rigil Kent.	140 25.3	S60 45.3
N 10	221 09.5	283 26.6	54.2	46 30.5	26.0	11 52.0	47.2	22 29.1	24.3	Sabik	102 40.6	S15 42.1
E 11	236 12.0	298 27.0	53.7	61 31.8	25.5	26 54.0	47.4	37 31.3	24.4			
S 12	251 14.5	313 27.4	S23 53.1	76 33.0	N 4 25.0	41 56.0	S10 47.5	52 33.6	S 5 24.4	Schedar	350 07.8	N56 26.5
D 13	266 16.9	328 27.8	52.6	91 34.3	24.5	56 58.0	47.7	67 35.8	24.5	Shaula	96 55.1	S37 05.4
A 14	281 19.4	343 28.1	52.1	106 35.6	24.1	72 00.0	47.9	82 38.1	24.6	Sirius	258 54.7	S16 41.4
Y 15	296 21.9	358 28.5	·· 51.5	121 36.9	·· 23.6	87 02.0	·· 48.0	97 40.3	·· 24.7	Spica	158 56.9	S11 03.8
16	311 24.3	13 28.9	51.0	136 38.2	23.1	102 04.0	48.2	112 42.6	24.7	Suhail	223 10.0	S43 21.3
17	326 26.8	28 29.3	50.4	151 39.5	22.6	117 06.0	48.4	127 44.8	24.8			
18	341 29.2	43 29.6	S23 49.9	166 40.7	N 4 22.2	132 08.0	S10 48.5	142 47.1	S 5 24.9	Vega	80 55.7	N38 46.2
19	356 31.7	58 30.0	49.4	181 42.0	21.7	147 10.0	48.7	157 49.3	25.0	Zuben'ubi	137 32.5	S15 57.8
20	11 34.2	73 30.4	48.8	196 43.3	21.2	162 12.0	48.8	172 51.6	25.1			
21	26 36.6	88 30.8	·· 48.2	211 44.6	·· 20.7	177 14.0	·· 49.0	187 53.8	·· 25.1			
22	41 39.1	103 31.2	47.7	226 45.9	20.3	192 16.0	49.1	202 56.1	25.2			
23	56 41.6	118 31.6	47.2	241 47.2	19.8	207 18.0	49.3	217 58.3	25.3			
Mer. Pass.	19 17.8	v 0.3	d 0.5	v 1.3	d 0.5	v 2.0	d 0.2	v 2.2	d 0.1			

	S.H.A.	Mer. Pass.
	° ′	h m
Venus	63 29.8	15 07
Mars	186 01.3	6 56
Jupiter	150 58.0	9 16
Saturn	161 27.0	8 34

SUN / MOON

G.M.T.	SUN G.H.A.	Dec.	MOON G.H.A.	v	Dec.	d	H.P.
30 00	182 52.1	S21 35.6	143 13.0	11.2	S21 52.8	0.6	54.4
01	197 51.9	36.0	157 43.2	11.2	21 52.2	0.7	54.4
02	212 51.6	36.5	172 13.4	11.2	21 51.5	0.8	54.4
03	227 51.4	.. 36.9	186 43.6	11.2	21 50.7	0.9	54.4
04	242 51.2	37.3	201 13.8	11.2	21 49.8	1.0	54.4
05	257 51.0	37.7	215 44.0	11.1	21 48.8	1.1	54.4
M 06	272 50.7	S21 38.1	230 14.1	11.2	S21 47.7	1.2	54.4
O 07	287 50.5	38.5	244 44.3	11.2	21 46.5	1.3	54.5
N 08	302 50.3	38.9	259 14.5	11.2	21 45.2	1.4	54.5
D 09	317 50.1	.. 39.3	273 44.7	11.1	21 43.8	1.6	54.5
A 10	332 49.8	39.7	288 14.8	11.2	21 42.2	1.6	54.5
Y 11	347 49.6	40.1	302 45.0	11.1	21 40.6	1.8	54.5
12	2 49.4	S21 40.5	317 15.1	11.2	S21 38.8	1.8	54.5
13	17 49.1	40.9	331 45.3	11.1	21 37.0	2.0	54.5
14	32 48.9	41.3	346 15.4	11.2	21 35.0	2.0	54.6
15	47 48.7	.. 41.7	0 45.6	11.2	21 33.0	2.2	54.6
16	62 48.5	42.1	15 15.8	11.1	21 30.8	2.2	54.6
17	77 48.2	42.5	29 45.9	11.2	21 28.6	2.4	54.6
18	92 48.0	S21 42.9	44 16.1	11.1	S21 26.2	2.5	54.6
19	107 47.8	43.3	58 46.2	11.2	21 23.7	2.6	54.6
20	122 47.5	43.7	73 16.4	11.2	21 21.1	2.6	54.7
21	137 47.3	.. 44.1	87 46.6	11.1	21 18.5	2.8	54.7
22	152 47.1	44.5	102 16.7	11.2	21 15.7	2.9	54.7
23	167 46.8	44.9	116 46.9	11.2	21 12.8	3.0	54.7
1 00	182 46.6	S21 45.3	131 17.1	11.2	S21 09.8	3.1	54.7
01	197 46.4	45.7	145 47.3	11.2	21 06.7	3.2	54.7
02	212 46.1	46.1	160 17.5	11.2	21 03.5	3.3	54.8
03	227 45.9	.. 46.5	174 47.7	11.2	21 00.2	3.4	54.8
04	242 45.7	46.9	189 17.9	11.2	20 56.8	3.5	54.8
05	257 45.5	47.3	203 48.1	11.2	20 53.3	3.6	54.8
T 06	272 45.2	S21 47.6	218 18.3	11.2	S20 49.7	3.7	54.8
U 07	287 45.0	48.0	232 48.5	11.2	20 46.0	3.8	54.9
E 08	302 44.8	48.4	247 18.7	11.3	20 42.2	4.0	54.9
S 09	317 44.5	.. 48.8	261 49.0	11.2	20 38.2	4.0	54.9
D 10	332 44.3	49.2	276 19.2	11.2	20 34.2	4.1	54.9
A 11	347 44.0	49.6	290 49.4	11.3	20 30.1	4.2	54.9
Y 12	2 43.8	S21 50.0	305 19.7	11.3	S20 25.9	4.3	54.9
13	17 43.6	50.4	319 50.0	11.3	20 21.6	4.5	55.0
14	32 43.3	50.7	334 20.3	11.3	20 17.1	4.5	55.0
15	47 43.1	.. 51.1	348 50.6	11.3	20 12.6	4.6	55.0
16	62 42.9	51.5	3 20.9	11.3	20 08.0	4.7	55.0
17	77 42.6	51.9	17 51.2	11.3	20 03.3	4.9	55.0
18	92 42.4	S21 52.3	32 21.5	11.3	S19 58.4	4.9	55.1
19	107 42.2	52.7	46 51.8	11.4	19 53.5	5.0	55.1
20	122 41.9	53.0	61 22.2	11.3	19 48.5	5.1	55.1
21	137 41.7	.. 53.4	75 52.5	11.4	19 43.4	5.3	55.1
22	152 41.4	53.8	90 22.9	11.4	19 38.1	5.3	55.2
23	167 41.2	54.1	104 53.3	11.4	19 32.8	5.4	55.2
2 00	182 41.0	S21 54.5	119 23.7	11.4	S19 27.4	5.5	55.2
01	197 40.7	54.9	133 54.1	11.4	19 21.9	5.6	55.2
02	212 40.5	55.3	148 24.5	11.4	19 16.3	5.7	55.2
03	227 40.3	.. 55.7	162 54.9	11.5	19 10.6	5.8	55.3
04	242 40.0	56.1	177 25.4	11.4	19 04.8	5.9	55.3
05	257 39.8	56.4	191 55.8	11.5	18 58.9	6.0	55.3
W 06	272 39.5	S21 56.8	206 26.3	11.5	S18 52.9	6.1	55.3
E 07	287 39.3	57.2	220 56.8	11.5	18 46.8	6.2	55.4
D 08	302 39.1	57.5	235 27.3	11.5	18 40.6	6.3	55.4
N 09	317 38.8	.. 57.9	249 57.8	11.5	18 34.3	6.4	55.4
E 10	332 38.6	58.3	264 28.3	11.5	18 27.9	6.5	55.4
S 11	347 38.3	58.6	278 58.8	11.6	18 21.4	6.5	55.5
D 12	2 38.1	S21 59.0	293 29.4	11.6	S18 14.9	6.7	55.5
A 13	17 37.9	59.4	308 00.0	11.5	18 08.2	6.8	55.5
Y 14	32 37.6	21 59.8	322 30.5	11.6	18 01.4	6.8	55.5
15	47 37.4	22 00.1	337 01.1	11.6	17 54.6	6.9	55.6
16	62 37.1	00.5	351 31.7	11.7	17 47.7	7.1	55.6
17	77 36.9	00.9	6 02.4	11.6	17 40.6	7.1	55.6
18	92 36.6	S22 01.2	20 33.0	11.6	S17 33.5	7.2	55.6
19	107 36.4	01.6	35 03.6	11.7	17 26.3	7.3	55.7
20	122 36.2	01.9	49 34.3	11.7	17 19.0	7.4	55.7
21	137 35.9	.. 02.3	64 05.0	11.7	17 11.6	7.5	55.7
22	152 35.7	02.7	78 35.7	11.7	17 04.1	7.6	55.7
23	167 35.4	03.0	93 06.4	11.7	16 56.5	7.6	55.8
	S.D. 16.2	d 0.4	S.D. 14.9		15.0		15.1

Moonrise

Lat.	Twilight Naut.	Civil	Sunrise	Moonrise 30	1	2	3
N 72	07 51	09 50	■	■	■	16 08	14 57
N 70	07 35	09 11	■	■	■	14 46	14 26
68	07 21	08 44	10 36	14 14	14 10	14 07	14 03
66	07 10	08 23	09 47	13 07	13 29	13 39	13 45
64	07 01	08 06	09 16	12 31	13 00	13 18	13 30
62	06 53	07 52	08 53	12 06	12 39	13 01	13 17
60	06 46	07 41	08 35	11 45	12 21	12 47	13 07
N 58	06 39	07 30	08 20	11 29	12 06	12 35	12 58
56	06 33	07 21	08 07	11 15	11 54	12 24	12 49
54	06 28	07 13	07 55	11 03	11 42	12 15	12 42
52	06 23	07 06	07 45	10 52	11 33	12 07	12 36
50	06 18	06 59	07 37	10 42	11 24	11 59	12 30
45	06 08	06 45	07 18	10 22	11 05	11 43	12 17
N 40	05 59	06 32	07 02	10 06	10 50	11 30	12 06
35	05 50	06 22	06 49	09 52	10 37	11 19	11 57
30	05 43	06 12	06 38	09 40	10 26	11 09	11 49
20	05 28	05 55	06 19	09 19	10 07	10 52	11 35
N 10	05 13	05 39	06 01	09 02	09 50	10 37	11 23
0	04 57	05 23	05 45	08 45	09 34	10 23	11 12
S 10	04 40	05 06	05 29	08 28	09 19	10 09	11 00
20	04 19	04 47	05 12	08 10	09 02	09 54	10 48
30	03 52	04 24	04 51	07 50	08 42	09 37	10 34
35	03 35	04 10	04 39	07 38	08 31	09 27	10 26
40	03 13	03 54	04 26	07 24	08 18	09 16	10 17
45	02 46	03 33	04 09	07 08	08 03	09 02	10 06
S 50	02 07	03 06	03 49	06 48	07 44	08 46	09 52
52	01 45	02 53	03 39	06 38	07 35	08 38	09 46
54	01 15	02 38	03 28	06 27	07 25	08 29	09 39
56	00 18	02 19	03 16	06 15	07 13	08 20	09 32
58	////	01 55	03 02	06 01	07 00	08 09	09 23
S 60	////	01 23	02 44	05 44	06 45	07 56	09 13

Moonset

Lat.	Sunset	Twilight Civil	Naut.	Moonset 30	1	2	3
N 72	■	13 48	15 47	■	■	17 16	20 07
N 70	■	14 27	16 03	■	■	18 37	20 37
68	13 02	14 54	16 16	15 43	17 29	19 15	20 59
66	13 51	15 15	16 27	16 50	18 10	19 41	21 16
64	14 22	15 31	16 37	17 25	18 38	20 02	21 30
62	14 45	15 45	16 45	17 51	19 00	20 18	21 41
60	15 03	15 57	16 52	18 11	19 17	20 31	21 51
N 58	15 18	16 07	16 58	18 27	19 31	20 43	22 00
56	15 31	16 16	17 04	18 41	19 44	20 53	22 07
54	15 42	16 25	17 10	18 53	19 55	21 02	22 14
52	15 52	16 32	17 15	19 04	20 04	21 10	22 20
50	16 01	16 39	17 19	19 13	20 13	21 17	22 25
45	16 20	16 53	17 30	19 33	20 31	21 32	22 37
N 40	16 35	17 05	17 39	19 49	20 45	21 45	22 47
35	16 48	17 16	17 47	20 03	20 58	21 55	22 55
30	17 00	17 26	17 55	20 15	21 09	22 04	23 02
20	17 19	17 43	18 10	20 35	21 27	22 20	23 14
N 10	17 37	17 59	18 25	20 52	21 43	22 34	23 25
0	17 53	18 15	18 41	21 09	21 58	22 47	23 35
S 10	18 09	18 32	18 58	21 25	22 13	22 59	23 45
20	18 27	18 51	19 20	21 42	22 29	23 13	23 55
30	18 47	19 14	19 47	22 02	22 47	23 28	24 07
35	18 59	19 28	20 04	22 14	22 57	23 37	24 14
40	19 13	19 45	20 25	22 27	23 09	23 47	24 22
45	19 29	20 06	20 53	22 43	23 24	23 59	24 31
S 50	19 50	20 33	21 33	23 02	23 41	24 13	00 13
52	20 00	20 46	21 55	23 12	23 49	24 20	00 20
54	20 11	21 02	22 26	23 22	23 58	24 27	00 27
56	20 24	21 21	23 31	23 33	24 08	00 08	00 36
58	20 38	21 45	////	23 47	24 20	00 20	00 45
S 60	20 56	22 13	////	24 02	00 02	00 33	00 55

SUN / MOON

Day	SUN Eqn. of Time 00h	12h	Mer. Pass.	MOON Mer. Pass. Upper	Lower	Age	Phase
	m s	m s	h m	h m	h m	d	
30	11 29	11 18	11 49	14 57	02 32	04	
1	11 07	10 56	11 49	15 46	03 22	05	
2	10 44	10 33	11 49	16 35	04 11	06	◑

G.M.T.	ARIES G.H.A.	VENUS −4.3 G.H.A.	Dec.	MARS +1.3 G.H.A.	Dec.	JUPITER −1.3 G.H.A.	Dec.	SATURN +1.0 G.H.A.	Dec.
3 00	71 44.0	133 31.9	S23 46.6	256 48.4	N 4 19.3	222 20.1	S10 49.5	233 00.5	S 5 25.4
01	86 46.5	148 32.3	46.1	271 49.7	18.8	237 22.1	49.6	248 02.8	25.5
02	101 49.0	163 32.7	45.5	286 51.0	18.4	252 24.1	49.8	263 05.0	25.5
03	116 51.4	178 33.1	·· 45.0	301 52.3	·· 17.9	267 26.1	·· 50.0	278 07.3	·· 25.6
04	131 53.9	193 33.5	44.4	316 53.6	17.4	282 28.1	50.1	293 09.5	25.7
05	146 56.4	208 33.9	43.9	331 54.9	16.9	297 30.1	50.3	308 11.8	25.8
06	161 58.8	223 34.3	S23 43.3	346 56.2	N 4 16.5	312 32.1	S10 50.4	323 14.0	S 5 25.8
07	177 01.3	238 34.7	42.8	1 57.4	16.0	327 34.1	50.6	338 16.3	25.9
T 08	192 03.7	253 35.1	42.3	16 58.7	15.5	342 36.1	50.8	353 18.5	26.0
H 09	207 06.2	268 35.5	·· 41.7	32 00.0	·· 15.1	357 38.1	·· 50.9	8 20.8	·· 26.1
U 10	222 08.7	283 35.9	41.2	47 01.3	14.6	12 40.1	51.1	23 23.0	26.2
R 11	237 11.1	298 36.4	40.6	62 02.6	14.1	27 42.2	51.2	38 25.3	26.2
S 12	252 13.6	313 36.8	S23 40.0	77 03.9	N 4 13.6	42 44.2	S10 51.4	53 27.5	S 5 26.3
D 13	267 16.1	328 37.2	39.5	92 05.2	13.2	57 46.2	51.6	68 29.8	26.4
A 14	282 18.5	343 37.6	38.9	107 06.5	12.7	72 48.2	51.7	83 32.0	26.5
Y 15	297 21.0	358 38.0	·· 38.4	122 07.7	·· 12.2	87 50.2	·· 51.9	98 34.3	·· 26.6
16	312 23.5	13 38.4	37.8	137 09.0	11.7	102 52.2	52.0	113 36.5	26.6
17	327 25.9	28 38.9	37.3	152 10.3	11.3	117 54.2	52.2	128 38.8	26.7
18	342 28.4	43 39.3	S23 36.7	167 11.6	N 4 10.8	132 56.2	S10 52.4	143 41.0	S 5 26.8
19	357 30.9	58 39.7	36.2	182 12.9	10.3	147 58.2	52.5	158 43.3	26.9
20	12 33.3	73 40.1	35.6	197 14.2	09.8	163 00.2	52.7	173 45.5	26.9
21	27 35.8	88 40.6	·· 35.1	212 15.5	·· 09.4	178 02.3	·· 52.8	188 47.8	·· 27.0
22	42 38.2	103 41.0	34.5	227 16.8	08.9	193 04.3	53.0	203 50.0	27.1
23	57 40.7	118 41.4	33.9	242 18.1	08.4	208 06.3	53.2	218 52.3	27.2
4 00	72 43.2	133 41.9	S23 33.4	257 19.3	N 4 08.0	223 08.3	S10 53.3	233 54.6	S 5 27.2
01	87 45.6	148 42.3	32.8	272 20.6	07.5	238 10.3	53.5	248 56.8	27.3
02	102 48.1	163 42.8	32.3	287 21.9	07.0	253 12.3	53.6	263 59.1	27.4
03	117 50.6	178 43.2	·· 31.7	302 23.2	·· 06.5	268 14.3	·· 53.8	279 01.3	·· 27.5
04	132 53.0	193 43.7	31.1	317 24.5	06.1	283 16.3	54.0	294 03.6	27.6
05	147 55.5	208 44.1	30.6	332 25.8	05.6	298 18.3	54.1	309 05.8	27.6
06	162 58.0	223 44.6	S23 30.0	347 27.1	N 4 05.1	313 20.3	S10 54.3	324 08.1	S 5 27.7
07	178 00.4	238 45.0	29.5	2 28.4	04.7	328 22.4	54.4	339 10.3	27.8
08	193 02.9	253 45.5	28.9	17 29.7	04.2	343 24.4	54.6	354 12.6	27.9
F 09	208 05.4	268 45.9	·· 28.3	32 31.0	·· 03.7	358 26.4	·· 54.8	9 14.8	·· 27.9
R 10	223 07.8	283 46.4	27.8	47 32.3	03.2	13 28.4	54.9	24 17.1	28.0
I 11	238 10.3	298 46.8	27.2	62 33.6	02.8	28 30.4	55.1	39 19.3	28.1
D 12	253 12.7	313 47.3	S23 26.6	77 34.9	N 4 02.3	43 32.4	S10 55.2	54 21.6	S 5 28.2
A 13	268 15.2	328 47.8	26.1	92 36.2	01.8	58 34.4	55.4	69 23.8	28.3
Y 14	283 17.7	343 48.2	25.5	107 37.4	01.4	73 36.4	55.6	84 26.1	28.3
15	298 20.1	358 48.7	·· 24.9	122 38.7	·· 00.9	88 38.5	·· 55.7	99 28.3	·· 28.4
16	313 22.6	13 49.2	24.4	137 40.0	4 00.4	103 40.5	55.9	114 30.6	28.5
17	328 25.1	28 49.7	23.8	152 41.3	3 59.9	118 42.5	56.0	129 32.8	28.6
18	343 27.5	43 50.1	S23 23.2	167 42.6	N 3 59.5	133 44.5	S10 56.2	144 35.1	S 5 28.6
19	358 30.0	58 50.6	22.7	182 43.9	59.0	148 46.5	56.4	159 37.3	28.7
20	13 32.5	73 51.1	22.1	197 45.2	58.5	163 48.5	56.5	174 39.6	28.8
21	28 34.9	88 51.6	·· 21.5	212 46.5	·· 58.1	178 50.5	·· 56.7	189 41.9	·· 28.9
22	43 37.4	103 52.1	21.0	227 47.8	57.6	193 52.5	56.8	204 44.1	28.9
23	58 39.8	118 52.6	20.4	242 49.1	57.1	208 54.6	57.0	219 46.4	29.0
5 00	73 42.3	133 53.0	S23 19.8	257 50.4	N 3 56.7	223 56.6	S10 57.2	234 48.6	S 5 29.1
01	88 44.8	148 53.5	19.3	272 51.7	56.2	238 58.6	57.3	249 50.9	29.2
02	103 47.2	163 54.0	18.7	287 53.0	55.7	254 00.6	57.5	264 53.1	29.2
03	118 49.7	178 54.5	·· 18.1	302 54.3	·· 55.2	269 02.6	·· 57.6	279 55.4	·· 29.3
04	133 52.2	193 55.0	17.5	317 55.6	54.8	284 04.6	57.8	294 57.6	29.4
05	148 54.6	208 55.5	17.0	332 56.9	54.3	299 06.6	57.9	309 59.9	29.5
06	163 57.1	223 56.0	S23 16.4	347 58.2	N 3 53.8	314 08.7	S10 58.1	325 02.1	S 5 29.5
07	178 59.6	238 56.5	15.8	2 59.5	53.4	329 10.7	58.3	340 04.4	29.6
S 08	194 02.0	253 57.0	15.2	18 00.8	52.9	344 12.7	58.4	355 06.6	29.7
A 09	209 04.5	268 57.6	·· 14.7	33 02.1	·· 52.4	359 14.7	·· 58.6	10 08.9	·· 29.8
T 10	224 07.0	283 58.1	14.1	48 03.4	52.0	14 16.7	58.7	25 11.2	29.8
U 11	239 09.4	298 58.6	13.5	63 04.7	51.5	29 18.7	58.9	40 13.4	29.9
R 12	254 11.9	313 59.1	S23 12.9	78 06.0	N 3 51.0	44 20.7	S10 59.1	55 15.7	S 5 30.0
D 13	269 14.3	328 59.6	12.4	93 07.3	50.6	59 22.8	59.2	70 17.9	30.1
A 14	284 16.8	344 00.1	11.8	108 08.6	50.1	74 24.8	59.4	85 20.2	30.2
Y 15	299 19.3	359 00.7	·· 11.2	123 09.9	·· 49.6	89 26.8	·· 59.5	100 22.4	·· 30.2
16	314 21.7	14 01.2	10.6	138 11.2	49.2	104 28.8	59.7	115 24.7	30.3
17	329 24.2	29 01.7	10.0	153 12.5	48.7	119 30.8	10 59.8	130 26.9	30.4
18	344 26.7	44 02.2	S23 09.5	168 13.8	N 3 48.2	134 32.8	S11 00.0	145 29.2	S 5 30.5
19	359 29.1	59 02.8	08.9	183 15.1	47.8	149 34.8	00.2	160 31.5	30.5
20	14 31.6	74 03.3	08.3	198 16.4	47.3	164 36.9	00.3	175 33.7	30.6
21	29 34.1	89 03.8	·· 07.7	213 17.7	·· 46.8	179 38.9	·· 00.5	190 36.0	·· 30.7
22	44 36.5	104 04.4	07.1	228 19.0	46.3	194 40.9	00.6	205 38.2	30.8
23	59 39.0	119 04.9	06.6	243 20.3	45.9	209 42.9	00.8	220 40.5	30.8
Mer. Pass.	19 06.0	v 0.5	d 0.6	v 1.3	d 0.5	v 2.0	d 0.2	v 2.3	d 0.1

STARS

Name	S.H.A.	Dec.
Acamar	315 36.2	S40 22.8
Achernar	335 44.2	S57 20.0
Acrux	173 36.6	S62 59.5
Adhara	255 31.1	S28 56.7
Aldebaran	291 16.7	N16 28.4
Alioth	166 42.1	N56 03.4
Alkaid	153 18.2	N49 24.2
Al Na'ir	28 14.0	S47 03.2
Alnilam	276 10.5	S 1 12.8
Alphard	218 19.6	S 8 34.7
Alphecca	126 31.8	N26 46.6
Alpheratz	358 08.4	N28 59.5
Altair	62 32.0	N 8 49.3
Ankaa	353 39.2	S42 24.5
Antares	112 56.2	S26 23.4
Arcturus	146 18.0	N19 16.7
Atria	108 20.3	S68 59.6
Avior	234 27.5	S59 26.8
Bellatrix	278 57.5	N 6 20.0
Betelgeuse	271 27.1	N 7 24.2
Canopus	264 06.3	S52 41.1
Capella	281 09.6	N45 58.8
Deneb	49 48.2	N45 13.1
Denebola	182 58.3	N14 40.4
Diphda	349 19.9	S18 05.3
Dubhe	194 21.1	N61 50.7
Elnath	278 42.7	N28 35.5
Eltanin	90 57.9	N51 29.6
Enif	34 10.9	N 9 47.5
Fomalhaut	15 50.5	S29 43.3
Gacrux	172 28.1	S57 00.3
Gienah	176 17.3	S17 26.2
Hadar	149 22.7	S60 16.8
Hamal	328 27.7	N23 22.6
Kaus Aust.	84 16.1	S34 23.6
Kochab	137 20.1	N74 13.7
Markab	14 02.3	N15 06.5
Menkar	314 40.0	N 4 01.1
Menkent	148 36.4	S36 16.6
Miaplacidus	221 44.4	S69 38.2
Mirfak	309 14.4	N49 47.9
Nunki	76 28.5	S26 19.2
Peacock	53 57.5	S56 47.9
Pollux	243 56.9	N28 04.2
Procyon	245 24.7	N 5 16.3
Rasalhague	96 29.2	N12 34.5
Regulus	208 09.1	N12 03.4
Rigel	281 34.9	S 8 13.3
Rigil Kent.	140 25.3	S60 45.3
Sabik	102 40.5	S15 42.1
Schedar	350 07.8	N56 26.5
Shaula	96 55.1	S37 05.4
Sirius	258 54.7	S16 41.4
Spica	158 56.9	S11 03.8
Suhail	223 10.0	S43 21.3
Vega	80 55.7	N38 46.1
Zuben'ubi	137 32.4	S15 57.8

	S.H.A.	Mer. Pass.
Venus	60 58.7	15 05
Mars	184 36.2	6 50
Jupiter	150 25.1	9 06
Saturn	161 11.4	8 23

SUN / MOON

G.M.T. (d h)	SUN G.H.A.	SUN Dec.	MOON G.H.A.	v	MOON Dec.	d	H.P.
3 00	182 35.2	S22 03.4	107 37.1	11.7	S16 48.9	7.8	55.8
01	197 34.9	03.7	122 07.8	11.8	16 41.1	7.8	55.8
02	212 34.7	04.1	136 38.6	11.7	16 33.3	7.9	55.9
03	227 34.4 ··	04.5	151 09.3	11.8	16 25.4	8.0	55.9
04	242 34.2	04.8	165 40.1	11.8	16 17.4	8.1	55.9
05	257 34.0	05.2	180 10.9	11.8	16 09.3	8.2	55.9
06	272 33.7	S22 05.5	194 41.7	11.8	S16 01.1	8.3	56.0
07	287 33.5	05.9	209 12.5	11.8	15 52.8	8.4	56.0
T 08	302 33.2	06.2	223 43.3	11.8	15 44.4	8.4	56.0
H 09	317 33.0 ··	06.6	238 14.1	11.9	15 36.0	8.5	56.1
U 10	332 32.7	06.9	252 45.0	11.8	15 27.5	8.6	56.1
R 11	347 32.5	07.3	267 15.8	11.9	15 18.9	8.7	56.1
S 12	2 32.2	S22 07.6	281 46.7	11.9	S15 10.2	8.8	56.2
D 13	17 32.0	08.0	296 17.6	11.8	15 01.4	8.8	56.2
A 14	32 31.7	08.3	310 48.4	11.9	14 52.6	9.0	56.2
Y 15	47 31.5 ··	08.7	325 19.3	11.9	14 43.6	9.0	56.2
16	62 31.2	09.0	339 50.2	12.0	14 34.6	9.1	56.3
17	77 31.0	09.4	354 21.2	11.9	14 25.5	9.2	56.3
18	92 30.7	S22 09.7	8 52.1	11.9	S14 16.3	9.2	56.3
19	107 30.5	10.1	23 23.0	11.9	14 07.1	9.3	56.4
20	122 30.2	10.4	37 53.9	12.0	13 57.8	9.5	56.4
21	137 30.0 ··	10.8	52 24.9	12.0	13 48.3	9.4	56.4
22	152 29.7	11.1	66 55.9	11.9	13 38.9	9.6	56.5
23	167 29.5	11.4	81 26.8	12.0	13 29.3	9.6	56.5
4 00	182 29.2	S22 11.8	95 57.8	12.0	S13 19.7	9.8	56.5
01	197 29.0	12.1	110 28.8	11.9	13 09.9	9.8	56.6
02	212 28.7	12.5	124 59.7	12.0	13 00.1	9.8	56.6
03	227 28.5 ··	12.8	139 30.7	12.0	12 50.3	10.0	56.6
04	242 28.2	13.1	154 01.7	12.0	12 40.3	10.1	56.7
05	257 28.0	13.5	168 32.7	12.0	12 30.3	10.1	56.7
06	272 27.7	S22 13.8	183 03.7	12.0	S12 20.2	10.1	56.7
07	287 27.5	14.2	197 34.7	12.0	12 10.1	10.2	56.8
F 08	302 27.2	14.5	212 05.7	12.0	11 59.9	10.3	56.8
R 09	317 27.0 ··	14.8	226 36.7	12.1	11 49.6	10.4	56.8
I 10	332 26.7	15.2	241 07.8	12.0	11 39.2	10.4	56.9
D 11	347 26.5	15.5	255 38.8	12.0	11 28.8	10.6	56.9
A 12	2 26.2	S22 15.8	270 09.8	12.0	S11 18.2	10.5	56.9
Y 13	17 26.0	16.2	284 40.8	12.0	11 07.7	10.7	57.0
14	32 25.7	16.5	299 11.8	12.0	10 57.0	10.7	57.0
15	47 25.5 ··	16.8	313 42.8	12.0	10 46.3	10.8	57.0
16	62 25.2	17.2	328 13.8	12.1	10 35.5	10.8	57.1
17	77 24.9	17.5	342 44.9	12.0	10 24.7	10.9	57.1
18	92 24.7	S22 17.8	357 15.9	12.0	S10 13.8	11.0	57.1
19	107 24.4	18.1	11 46.9	12.0	10 02.8	11.0	57.2
20	122 24.2	18.5	26 17.9	12.0	9 51.8	11.1	57.2
21	137 23.9 ··	18.8	40 48.9	11.9	9 40.7	11.2	57.3
22	152 23.7	19.1	55 19.8	12.0	9 29.5	11.2	57.3
23	167 23.4	19.4	69 50.8	12.0	9 18.3	11.3	57.3
5 00	182 23.2	S22 19.8	84 21.8	12.0	S 9 07.0	11.3	57.4
01	197 22.9	20.1	98 52.8	11.9	8 55.7	11.4	57.4
02	212 22.6	20.4	113 23.7	12.0	8 44.3	11.5	57.4
03	227 22.4 ··	20.7	127 54.7	11.9	8 32.8	11.5	57.5
04	242 22.1	21.1	142 25.6	12.0	8 21.3	11.5	57.5
05	257 21.9	21.4	156 56.6	11.9	8 09.8	11.7	57.5
06	272 21.6	S22 21.7	171 27.5	11.9	S 7 58.1	11.7	57.6
07	287 21.4	22.0	185 58.4	11.9	7 46.4	11.7	57.6
S 08	302 21.1	22.3	200 29.3	11.9	7 34.7	11.8	57.7
A 09	317 20.8 ··	22.6	215 00.2	11.9	7 22.9	11.8	57.7
T 10	332 20.6	23.0	229 31.1	11.8	7 11.1	11.9	57.7
U 11	347 20.3	23.3	244 01.9	11.9	6 59.2	12.0	57.8
R 12	2 20.1	S22 23.6	258 32.8	11.8	S 6 47.2	12.0	57.8
D 13	17 19.8	23.9	273 03.6	11.8	6 35.2	12.0	57.8
A 14	32 19.5	24.2	287 34.4	11.8	6 23.2	12.1	57.9
Y 15	47 19.3 ··	24.5	302 05.2	11.8	6 11.1	12.1	57.9
16	62 19.0	24.8	316 36.0	11.7	5 59.0	12.2	58.0
17	77 18.8	25.2	331 06.7	11.7	5 46.8	12.2	58.0
18	92 18.5	S22 25.5	345 37.4	11.7	S 5 34.5	12.2	58.0
19	107 18.2	25.8	0 08.1	11.7	5 22.3	12.4	58.1
20	122 18.0	26.1	14 38.8	11.7	5 09.9	12.3	58.1
21	137 17.7 ··	26.4	29 09.5	11.6	4 57.6	12.4	58.2
22	152 17.5	26.7	43 40.1	11.7	4 45.2	12.5	58.2
23	167 17.2	27.0	58 10.8	11.6	4 32.7	12.5	58.2
S.D.	16.3	d 0.3	S.D. 15.3		15.5		15.8

Twilight / Sunrise / Moonrise

Lat.	Naut.	Civil	Sunrise	Moonrise 3	4	5	6
N 72	07 59	10 04	■	14 57	14 31	14 12	13 56
N 70	07 41	09 20	■	14 26	14 13	14 03	13 54
68	07 28	08 51	10 55	14 03	13 59	13 56	13 52
66	07 16	08 30	09 57	13 45	13 48	13 49	13 51
64	07 06	08 12	09 24	13 30	13 38	13 44	13 49
62	06 58	07 58	09 00	13 17	13 30	13 39	13 48
60	06 50	07 46	08 41	13 07	13 22	13 35	13 47
N 58	06 43	07 35	08 25	12 58	13 16	13 32	13 47
56	06 37	07 26	08 11	12 49	13 10	13 29	13 46
54	06 32	07 17	08 00	12 42	13 05	13 26	13 45
52	06 27	07 10	07 50	12 36	13 00	13 23	13 45
50	06 22	07 03	07 40	12 30	12 56	13 21	13 44
45	06 11	06 48	07 21	12 17	12 47	13 15	13 43
N 40	06 02	06 35	07 05	12 06	12 40	13 11	13 42
35	05 53	06 24	06 52	11 57	12 33	13 07	13 41
30	05 45	06 14	06 40	11 49	12 27	13 04	13 40
20	05 29	05 57	06 21	11 35	12 17	12 58	13 39
N 10	05 14	05 40	06 03	11 23	12 08	12 53	13 38
0	04 58	05 24	05 47	11 12	12 00	12 48	13 37
S 10	04 40	05 07	05 30	11 00	11 51	12 43	13 36
20	04 19	04 48	05 12	10 48	11 43	12 38	13 35
30	03 51	04 24	04 51	10 34	11 32	12 32	13 33
35	03 34	04 10	04 39	10 26	11 26	12 29	13 33
40	03 12	03 53	04 25	10 17	11 20	12 25	13 32
45	02 44	03 32	04 08	10 06	11 12	12 20	13 31
S 50	02 03	03 04	03 47	09 52	11 02	12 15	13 30
52	01 40	02 50	03 37	09 46	10 58	12 12	13 29
54	01 07	02 34	03 26	09 39	10 53	12 10	13 29
56	////	02 15	03 13	09 32	10 48	12 06	13 28
58	////	01 50	02 58	09 23	10 42	12 03	13 27
S 60	////	01 15	02 40	09 13	10 35	11 59	13 27

Sunset / Twilight / Moonset

Lat.	Sunset	Civil	Naut.	Moonset 3	4	5	6
N 72	■	13 36	15 41	20 07	22 14	24 14	00 14
N 70	■	14 20	15 58	20 37	22 30	24 21	00 21
68	12 45	14 49	16 12	20 59	22 42	24 26	00 26
66	13 43	15 10	16 24	21 16	22 52	24 31	00 31
64	14 16	15 28	16 34	21 30	23 01	24 34	00 34
62	14 40	15 42	16 42	21 41	23 08	24 37	00 37
60	14 59	15 55	16 50	21 51	23 14	24 40	00 40
N 58	15 15	16 05	16 57	22 00	23 20	24 43	00 43
56	15 29	16 15	17 03	22 07	23 25	24 45	00 45
54	15 40	16 23	17 08	22 14	23 29	24 47	00 47
52	15 51	16 31	17 14	22 20	23 33	24 49	00 49
50	16 00	16 37	17 18	22 25	23 36	24 50	00 50
45	16 19	16 52	17 29	22 37	23 44	24 54	00 54
N 40	16 35	17 05	17 39	22 47	23 50	24 56	00 56
35	16 48	17 16	17 47	22 55	23 56	24 59	00 59
30	17 00	17 26	17 56	23 02	24 01	00 01	01 01
20	17 20	17 44	18 11	23 14	24 09	00 09	01 05
N 10	17 37	18 00	18 26	23 25	24 16	00 16	01 08
0	17 54	18 16	18 42	23 35	24 23	00 23	01 11
S 10	18 11	18 33	19 00	23 45	24 29	00 29	01 14
20	18 29	18 53	19 22	23 55	24 36	00 36	01 17
30	18 49	19 17	19 49	24 07	00 07	00 44	01 21
35	19 02	19 31	20 07	24 14	00 14	00 49	01 23
40	19 16	19 48	20 29	24 22	00 22	00 54	01 25
45	19 33	20 09	20 57	24 31	00 31	01 00	01 27
S 50	19 54	20 37	21 38	00 13	00 42	01 07	01 31
52	20 04	20 51	22 02	00 20	00 47	01 10	01 32
54	20 15	21 07	22 36	00 27	00 52	01 14	01 33
56	20 29	21 27	////	00 36	00 58	01 18	01 35
58	20 44	21 52	////	00 45	01 05	01 22	01 37
S 60	21 02	22 29	////	00 55	01 13	01 27	01 39

SUN / MOON

Day	Eqn. of Time 00ʰ	Eqn. of Time 12ʰ	Mer. Pass.	Mer. Pass. Upper	Mer. Pass. Lower	Age	Phase
	m s	m s	h m	h m	h m	d	
3	10 21	10 09	11 50	17 23	04 59	07	
4	09 57	09 45	11 50	18 11	05 47	08	
5	09 33	09 21	11 51	18 59	06 35	09	◗

G.M.T.	ARIES G.H.A.	VENUS −4.3 G.H.A.	Dec.	MARS +1.3 G.H.A.	Dec.	JUPITER −1.3 G.H.A.	Dec.	SATURN +1.0 G.H.A.	Dec.	STARS Name	S.H.A.	Dec.
6 00	74 41.5	134 05.5	S23 06.0	258 21.6	N 3 45.4	224 44.9	S11 00.9	235 42.7	S 5 30.9	Acamar	315 36.2	S40 22.8
01	89 43.9	149 06.0	05.4	273 22.9	44.9	239 46.9	01.1	250 45.0	31.0	Achernar	335 44.2	S57 20.0
02	104 46.4	164 06.6	04.8	288 24.2	44.5	254 49.0	01.3	265 47.3	31.1	Acrux	173 36.6	S62 59.5
03	119 48.8	179 07.1	·· 04.2	303 25.5	·· 44.0	269 51.0	·· 01.4	280 49.5	·· 31.1	Adhara	255 31.1	S28 56.7
04	134 51.3	194 07.7	03.6	318 26.8	43.5	284 53.0	01.6	295 51.8	31.2	Aldebaran	291 16.7	N16 28.4
05	149 53.8	209 08.2	03.1	333 28.1	43.1	299 55.0	01.7	310 54.0	31.3			
06	164 56.2	224 08.8	S23 02.5	348 29.5	N 3 42.6	314 57.0	S11 01.9	325 56.3	S 5 31.4	Alioth	166 42.0	N56 03.4
07	179 58.7	239 09.3	01.9	3 30.8	42.1	329 59.0	02.0	340 58.5	31.4	Alkaid	153 18.2	N49 24.1
08	195 01.2	254 09.9	01.3	18 32.1	41.7	345 01.1	02.2	356 00.8	31.5	Al Na'ir	28 14.0	S47 03.2
S 09	210 03.6	269 10.5	·· 00.7	33 33.4	·· 41.2	0 03.1	·· 02.4	11 03.1	·· 31.6	Alnilam	276 10.5	S 1 12.8
U 10	225 06.1	284 11.0	23 00.1	48 34.7	40.7	15 05.1	02.5	26 05.3	31.7	Alphard	218 19.6	S 8 34.7
N 11	240 08.6	299 11.6	22 59.5	63 36.0	40.3	30 07.1	02.7	41 07.6	31.7			
D 12	255 11.0	314 12.2	S22 58.9	78 37.3	N 3 39.8	45 09.1	S11 02.8	56 09.8	S 5 31.8	Alphecca	126 31.8	N26 46.6
A 13	270 13.5	329 12.7	58.4	93 38.6	39.4	60 11.1	03.0	71 12.1	31.9	Alpheratz	358 08.4	N28 59.5
Y 14	285 15.9	344 13.3	57.8	108 39.9	38.9	75 13.2	03.1	86 14.3	31.9	Altair	62 32.0	N 8 49.3
15	300 18.4	359 13.9	·· 57.2	123 41.2	·· 38.4	90 15.2	·· 03.3	101 16.6	·· 32.0	Ankaa	353 39.3	S42 24.6
16	315 20.9	14 14.5	56.6	138 42.5	38.0	105 17.2	03.5	116 18.9	32.1	Antares	112 56.2	S26 23.4
17	330 23.3	29 15.0	56.0	153 43.8	37.5	120 19.2	03.6	131 21.1	32.2			
18	345 25.8	44 15.6	S22 55.4	168 45.1	N 3 37.0	135 21.2	S11 03.8	146 23.4	S 5 32.2	Arcturus	146 18.0	N19 16.6
19	0 28.3	59 16.2	54.8	183 46.4	36.6	150 23.2	03.9	161 25.6	32.3	Atria	108 20.3	S68 59.6
20	15 30.7	74 16.8	54.2	198 47.8	36.1	165 25.3	04.1	176 27.9	32.4	Avior	234 27.4	S59 26.8
21	30 33.2	89 17.4	·· 53.6	213 49.1	·· 35.6	180 27.3	·· 04.2	191 30.2	·· 32.5	Bellatrix	278 57.5	N 6 20.0
22	45 35.7	104 18.0	53.0	228 50.4	35.2	195 29.3	04.4	206 32.4	32.5	Betelgeuse	271 27.0	N 7 24.2
23	60 38.1	119 18.6	52.4	243 51.7	34.7	210 31.3	04.5	221 34.7	32.6			
7 00	75 40.6	134 19.2	S22 51.9	258 53.0	N 3 34.2	225 33.3	S11 04.7	236 36.9	S 5 32.7	Canopus	264 06.3	S52 41.1
01	90 43.1	149 19.8	51.3	273 54.3	33.8	240 35.4	04.9	251 39.2	32.8	Capella	281 09.6	N45 58.8
02	105 45.5	164 20.4	50.7	288 55.6	33.3	255 37.4	05.0	266 41.4	32.8	Deneb	49 48.2	N45 13.1
03	120 48.0	179 21.0	·· 50.1	303 56.9	·· 32.8	270 39.4	·· 05.2	281 43.7	·· 32.9	Denebola	182 58.3	N14 40.4
04	135 50.4	194 21.6	49.5	318 58.2	32.4	285 41.4	05.3	296 46.0	33.0	Diphda	349 19.9	S18 05.3
05	150 52.9	209 22.2	48.9	333 59.5	31.9	300 43.4	05.5	311 48.2	33.1			
06	165 55.4	224 22.8	S22 48.3	349 00.9	N 3 31.4	315 45.5	S11 05.6	326 50.5	S 5 33.1	Dubhe	194 21.1	N61 50.7
07	180 57.8	239 23.4	47.7	4 02.2	31.0	330 47.5	05.8	341 52.7	33.2	Elnath	278 42.7	N28 35.5
08	196 00.3	254 24.0	47.1	19 03.5	30.5	345 49.5	05.9	356 55.0	33.3	Eltanin	90 57.9	N51 29.6
M 09	211 02.8	269 24.7	·· 46.5	34 04.8	·· 30.1	0 51.5	·· 06.1	11 57.3	·· 33.3	Enif	34 10.9	N 9 47.5
O 10	226 05.2	284 25.3	45.9	49 06.1	29.6	15 53.5	06.3	26 59.5	33.4	Fomalhaut	15 50.5	S29 43.3
N 11	241 07.7	299 25.9	45.3	64 07.4	29.1	30 55.5	06.4	42 01.8	33.5			
D 12	256 10.2	314 26.5	S22 44.7	79 08.7	N 3 28.7	45 57.6	S11 06.6	57 04.0	S 5 33.6	Gacrux	172 28.1	S57 00.3
A 13	271 12.6	329 27.2	44.1	94 10.0	28.2	60 59.6	06.7	72 06.3	33.6	Gienah	176 17.2	S17 26.3
Y 14	286 15.1	344 27.8	43.5	109 11.4	27.7	76 01.6	06.9	87 08.6	33.7	Hadar	149 22.7	S60 16.8
15	301 17.6	359 28.4	·· 42.9	124 12.7	·· 27.3	91 03.6	·· 07.0	102 10.8	·· 33.8	Hamal	328 27.7	N23 22.6
16	316 20.0	14 29.1	42.3	139 14.0	26.8	106 05.7	07.2	117 13.1	33.9	Kaus Aust.	84 16.1	S34 23.6
17	331 22.5	29 29.7	41.7	154 15.3	26.4	121 07.7	07.3	132 15.3	33.9			
18	346 24.9	44 30.3	S22 41.1	169 16.6	N 3 25.9	136 09.7	S11 07.5	147 17.6	S 5 34.0	Kochab	137 20.1	N74 13.7
19	1 27.4	59 31.0	40.5	184 17.9	25.4	151 11.7	07.7	162 19.9	34.1	Markab	14 02.3	N15 06.5
20	16 29.9	74 31.6	39.9	199 19.3	25.0	166 13.7	07.8	177 22.1	34.2	Menkar	314 40.0	N 4 01.1
21	31 32.3	89 32.3	·· 39.3	214 20.6	·· 24.5	181 15.8	·· 08.0	192 24.4	·· 34.2	Menkent	148 36.3	S36 16.6
22	46 34.8	104 32.9	38.7	229 21.9	24.0	196 17.8	08.1	207 26.7	34.3	Miaplacidus	221 44.3	S69 38.2
23	61 37.3	119 33.6	38.1	244 23.2	23.6	211 19.8	08.3	222 28.9	34.4			
8 00	76 39.7	134 34.2	S22 37.5	259 24.5	N 3 23.1	226 21.8	S11 08.4	237 31.2	S 5 34.4	Mirfak	309 14.4	N49 47.9
01	91 42.2	149 34.9	36.9	274 25.8	22.7	241 23.8	08.6	252 33.4	34.5	Nunki	76 28.5	S26 19.2
02	106 44.7	164 35.6	36.3	289 27.1	22.2	256 25.9	08.7	267 35.7	34.6	Peacock	53 57.5	S56 47.9
03	121 47.1	179 36.2	·· 35.7	304 28.5	·· 21.7	271 27.9	·· 08.9	282 38.0	·· 34.7	Pollux	243 56.9	N28 04.2
04	136 49.6	194 36.9	35.1	319 29.8	21.3	286 29.9	09.0	297 40.2	34.7	Procyon	245 24.7	N 5 16.3
05	151 52.0	209 37.5	34.5	334 31.1	20.8	301 31.9	09.2	312 42.5	34.8			
06	166 54.5	224 38.2	S22 33.8	349 32.4	N 3 20.3	316 33.9	S11 09.4	327 44.8	S 5 34.9	Rasalhague	96 29.2	N12 34.5
07	181 57.0	239 38.9	33.2	4 33.7	19.9	331 36.0	09.5	342 47.0	34.9	Regulus	208 09.0	N12 03.4
08	196 59.4	254 39.6	32.6	19 35.1	19.4	346 38.0	09.7	357 49.3	35.0	Rigel	281 34.9	S 8 13.4
T 09	212 01.9	269 40.2	·· 32.0	34 36.4	·· 19.0	1 40.0	·· 09.8	12 51.5	·· 35.1	Rigil Kent.	140 25.3	S60 45.3
U 10	227 04.4	284 40.9	31.4	49 37.7	18.5	16 42.0	10.0	27 53.8	35.2	Sabik	102 40.5	S15 42.1
E 11	242 06.8	299 41.6	30.8	64 39.0	18.0	31 44.1	10.1	42 56.1	35.2			
S D 12	257 09.3	314 42.3	S22 30.2	79 40.3	N 3 17.6	46 46.1	S11 10.3	57 58.3	S 5 35.3	Schedar	350 07.8	N56 26.5
A 13	272 11.8	329 43.0	29.6	94 41.7	17.1	61 48.1	10.4	73 00.6	35.4	Shaula	96 55.1	S37 05.4
Y 14	287 14.2	344 43.7	29.0	109 43.0	16.7	76 50.1	10.6	88 02.9	35.4	Sirius	258 54.7	S16 41.4
15	302 16.7	359 44.3	·· 28.4	124 44.3	·· 16.2	91 52.2	·· 10.7	103 05.1	·· 35.5	Spica	158 56.9	S11 03.8
16	317 19.2	14 45.0	27.8	139 45.6	15.7	106 54.2	10.9	118 07.4	35.6	Suhail	223 09.9	S43 21.3
17	332 21.6	29 45.7	27.2	154 46.9	15.3	121 56.2	11.0	133 09.6	35.7			
18	347 24.1	44 46.4	S22 26.5	169 48.3	N 3 14.8	136 58.2	S11 11.2	148 11.9	S 5 35.7	Vega	80 55.7	N38 46.1
19	2 26.5	59 47.1	25.9	184 49.6	14.4	152 00.2	11.4	163 14.2	35.8	Zuben'ubi	137 32.4	S15 57.8
20	17 29.0	74 47.8	25.3	199 50.9	13.9	167 02.3	11.5	178 16.4	35.9		S.H.A.	Mer. Pass.
21	32 31.5	89 48.5	·· 24.7	214 52.2	·· 13.4	182 04.3	·· 11.7	193 18.7	·· 36.0		° ′	h m
22	47 33.9	104 49.3	24.1	229 53.6	13.0	197 06.3	11.8	208 21.0	36.0	Venus	58 38.6	15 02
23	62 36.4	119 50.0	23.5	244 54.9	12.5	212 08.3	12.0	223 23.2	36.1	Mars	183 12.4	6 44
Mer. Pass. 18 54.2		v 0.6	d 0.6	v 1.3	d 0.5	v 2.0	d 0.2	v 2.3	d 0.1	Jupiter	149 52.7	8 57
										Saturn	160 56.3	8 12

G.M.T.	SUN G.H.A.	Dec.	MOON G.H.A.	v	Dec.	d	H.P.
6 00	182 16.9	S22 27.3	72 41.4	11.5	S 4 20.2	12.5	58.3
01	197 16.7	27.6	87 11.9	11.6	4 07.7	12.6	58.3
02	212 16.4	27.9	101 42.5	11.5	3 55.1	12.6	58.4
03	227 16.1	·· 28.2	116 13.0	11.5	3 42.5	12.6	58.4
04	242 15.9	28.5	130 43.5	11.4	3 29.9	12.7	58.4
05	257 15.6	28.8	145 13.9	11.4	3 17.2	12.7	58.5
06	272 15.4	S22 29.1	159 44.3	11.4	S 3 04.5	12.8	58.5
07	287 15.1	29.4	174 14.7	11.4	2 51.7	12.8	58.5
08	302 14.8	29.7	188 45.1	11.3	2 38.9	12.8	58.6
S 09	317 14.6	·· 30.0	203 15.4	11.3	2 26.1	12.8	58.6
U 10	332 14.3	30.3	217 45.7	11.2	2 13.3	12.9	58.7
N 11	347 14.0	30.6	232 15.9	11.3	2 00.4	12.9	58.7
D 12	2 13.8	S22 30.9	246 46.2	11.1	S 1 47.5	12.9	58.7
A 13	17 13.5	31.2	261 16.3	11.2	1 34.6	13.0	58.8
Y 14	32 13.2	31.5	275 46.5	11.1	1 21.6	13.0	58.8
15	47 13.0	·· 31.8	290 16.6	11.1	1 08.6	13.0	58.9
16	62 12.7	32.1	304 46.7	11.0	0 55.6	13.0	58.9
17	77 12.4	32.4	319 16.7	11.0	0 42.6	13.0	58.9
18	92 12.2	S22 32.7	333 46.7	10.9	S 0 29.6	13.1	59.0
19	107 11.9	33.0	348 16.6	10.9	0 16.5	13.1	59.0
20	122 11.6	33.3	2 46.5	10.9	S 0 03.4	13.1	59.0
21	137 11.4	·· 33.5	17 16.4	10.8	N 0 09.7	13.1	59.1
22	152 11.1	33.8	31 46.2	10.7	0 22.8	13.1	59.1
23	167 10.8	34.1	46 15.9	10.8	0 36.0	13.1	59.2
7 00	182 10.6	S22 34.4	60 45.7	10.6	N 0 49.1	13.2	59.2
01	197 10.3	34.7	75 15.3	10.6	1 02.3	13.2	59.2
02	212 10.0	35.0	89 44.9	10.6	1 15.5	13.2	59.3
03	227 09.8	·· 35.3	104 14.5	10.5	1 28.7	13.2	59.3
04	242 09.5	35.6	118 44.0	10.5	1 41.9	13.2	59.4
05	257 09.2	35.8	133 13.5	10.4	1 55.1	13.2	59.4
06	272 09.0	S22 36.1	147 42.9	10.4	N 2 08.3	13.2	59.4
07	287 08.7	36.4	162 12.3	10.3	2 21.5	13.3	59.5
08	302 08.4	36.7	176 41.6	10.2	2 34.8	13.2	59.5
M 09	317 08.2	·· 37.0	191 10.8	10.2	2 48.0	13.2	59.5
O 10	332 07.9	37.2	205 40.0	10.2	3 01.2	13.3	59.6
N 11	347 07.6	37.5	220 09.2	10.0	3 14.5	13.2	59.6
D 12	2 07.4	S22 37.8	234 38.2	10.1	N 3 27.7	13.0	59.7
A 13	17 07.1	38.1	249 07.3	9.9	3 40.9	13.2	59.7
Y 14	32 06.8	38.4	263 36.2	9.9	3 54.1	13.0	59.7
15	47 06.5	·· 38.6	278 05.1	9.8	4 07.4	13.2	59.8
16	62 06.3	38.9	292 33.9	9.8	4 20.6	13.2	59.8
17	77 06.0	39.2	307 02.7	9.7	4 33.8	13.2	59.8
18	92 05.7	S22 39.5	321 31.4	9.7	N 4 47.0	13.2	59.9
19	107 05.5	39.7	336 00.1	9.6	5 00.2	13.2	59.9
20	122 05.2	40.0	350 28.7	9.5	5 13.4	13.1	59.9
21	137 04.9	·· 40.3	4 57.2	9.4	5 26.5	13.2	60.0
22	152 04.7	40.5	19 25.6	9.4	5 39.7	13.1	60.0
23	167 04.4	40.8	33 54.0	9.3	5 52.8	13.1	60.0
8 00	182 04.1	S22 41.1	48 22.3	9.3	N 6 05.9	13.1	60.1
01	197 03.8	41.3	62 50.6	9.2	6 19.0	13.1	60.1
02	212 03.6	41.6	77 18.8	9.1	6 32.1	13.0	60.1
03	227 03.3	·· 41.9	91 46.9	9.0	6 45.1	13.0	60.2
04	242 03.0	42.1	106 14.9	9.0	6 58.1	13.0	60.2
05	257 02.7	42.4	120 42.9	8.8	7 11.1	13.0	60.2
06	272 02.5	S22 42.7	135 10.7	8.9	N 7 24.1	12.9	60.3
07	287 02.2	42.9	149 38.6	8.7	7 37.0	13.0	60.3
08	302 01.9	43.2	164 06.3	8.7	7 50.0	12.8	60.3
T 09	317 01.6	·· 43.5	178 34.0	8.6	8 02.8	12.9	60.4
U 10	332 01.4	43.7	193 01.6	8.5	8 15.7	12.8	60.4
E 11	347 01.1	44.0	207 29.1	8.4	8 28.5	12.7	60.4
S 12	2 00.8	S22 44.2	221 56.5	8.4	N 8 41.2	12.8	60.5
D 13	17 00.5	44.5	236 23.9	8.3	8 54.0	12.7	60.5
A 14	32 00.3	44.8	250 51.2	8.2	9 06.7	12.6	60.5
Y 15	47 00.0	·· 45.0	265 18.4	8.1	9 19.3	12.6	60.6
16	61 59.7	45.3	279 45.5	8.0	9 31.9	12.6	60.6
17	76 59.4	45.5	294 12.5	8.0	9 44.5	12.5	60.6
18	91 59.2	S22 45.8	308 39.5	7.9	N 9 57.0	12.4	60.6
19	106 58.9	46.0	323 06.4	7.8	10 09.4	12.4	60.7
20	121 58.6	46.3	337 33.2	7.7	10 21.8	12.4	60.7
21	136 58.3	·· 46.5	351 59.9	7.6	10 34.2	12.3	60.7
22	151 58.1	46.8	6 26.5	7.6	10 46.5	12.2	60.8
23	166 57.8	47.0	20 53.1	7.5	10 58.7	12.2	60.8
	S.D. 16.3 d 0.3		S.D. 16.0		16.3		16.5

Twilight / Sunrise / Moonrise

Lat.	Naut.	Civil	Sunrise	Moonrise 6	7	8	9
N 72	08 06	10 17	▬	13 56	13 39	13 21	12 57
N 70	07 48	09 29	▬	13 54	13 44	13 34	13 22
68	07 33	08 59	11 18	13 52	13 48	13 45	13 42
66	07 21	08 36	10 07	13 51	13 52	13 54	13 58
64	07 11	08 18	09 31	13 49	13 55	14 01	14 11
62	07 02	08 03	09 06	13 48	13 57	14 08	14 22
60	06 54	07 50	08 46	13 47	14 00	14 14	14 31
N 58	06 47	07 39	08 30	13 47	14 02	14 19	14 39
56	06 41	07 29	08 16	13 46	14 04	14 23	14 47
54	06 35	07 21	08 04	13 45	14 05	14 27	14 53
52	06 30	07 13	07 53	13 45	14 07	14 31	14 59
50	06 25	07 06	07 44	13 44	14 08	14 34	15 05
45	06 14	06 51	07 24	13 43	14 11	14 42	15 16
N 40	06 04	06 38	07 08	13 42	14 14	14 48	15 26
35	05 55	06 27	06 55	13 41	14 16	14 53	15 34
30	05 47	06 17	06 43	13 40	14 18	14 58	15 42
20	05 31	05 59	06 22	13 39	14 21	15 06	15 55
N 10	05 16	05 42	06 05	13 38	14 24	15 13	16 06
0	04 59	05 25	05 48	13 37	14 27	15 20	16 17
S 10	04 41	05 08	05 31	13 36	14 30	15 27	16 27
20	04 19	04 48	05 13	13 35	14 33	15 35	16 39
30	03 51	04 24	04 51	13 33	14 37	15 43	16 52
35	03 33	04 10	04 39	13 33	14 39	15 48	17 00
40	03 11	03 52	04 25	13 32	14 41	15 54	17 09
45	02 42	03 31	04 07	13 31	14 44	16 01	17 19
S 50	02 00	03 02	03 46	13 30	14 48	16 09	17 32
52	01 36	02 48	03 36	13 29	14 49	16 12	17 38
54	01 00	02 32	03 24	13 29	14 51	16 17	17 45
56	////	02 11	03 11	13 28	14 53	16 21	17 52
58	////	01 45	02 55	13 27	14 55	16 26	18 00
S 60	////	01 07	02 36	13 27	14 57	16 32	18 10

Sunset / Twilight / Moonset

Lat.	Sunset	Civil	Naut.	Moonset 6	7	8	9
N 72	▬	13 26	15 37	00 14	02 16	04 23	06 43
N 70	▬	14 13	15 55	00 21	02 14	04 12	06 20
68	12 24	14 44	16 09	00 26	02 13	04 04	06 02
66	13 36	15 07	16 21	00 31	02 12	03 57	05 47
64	14 12	15 25	16 32	00 34	02 11	03 51	05 36
62	14 37	15 40	16 41	00 37	02 10	03 46	05 26
60	14 57	15 53	16 48	00 40	02 09	03 41	05 17
N 58	15 13	16 04	16 55	00 43	02 08	03 38	05 10
56	15 27	16 13	17 02	00 45	02 08	03 34	05 03
54	15 39	16 22	17 08	00 47	02 07	03 31	04 58
52	15 49	16 30	17 13	00 49	02 07	03 28	04 52
50	15 59	16 37	17 18	00 50	02 06	03 26	04 48
45	16 19	16 52	17 29	00 54	02 05	03 20	04 38
N 40	16 35	17 05	17 39	00 56	02 05	03 16	04 29
35	16 48	17 16	17 48	00 59	02 04	03 12	04 22
30	17 00	17 26	17 56	01 01	02 03	03 08	04 16
20	17 21	17 44	18 12	01 05	02 02	03 02	04 05
N 10	17 38	18 01	18 27	01 08	02 01	02 57	03 55
0	17 55	18 18	18 44	01 11	02 00	02 52	03 46
S 10	18 12	18 35	19 02	01 14	01 59	02 47	03 38
20	18 30	18 55	19 24	01 17	01 58	02 42	03 28
30	18 52	19 19	19 52	01 21	01 57	02 36	03 17
35	19 04	19 34	20 10	01 23	01 57	02 32	03 11
40	19 19	19 51	20 32	01 25	01 56	02 28	03 04
45	19 36	20 13	21 01	01 27	01 55	02 24	02 56
S 50	19 58	20 41	21 44	01 31	01 54	02 19	02 46
52	20 08	20 55	22 09	01 32	01 53	02 16	02 42
54	20 20	21 12	22 45	01 33	01 53	02 14	02 37
56	20 33	21 33	////	01 35	01 52	02 11	02 32
58	20 49	21 59	////	01 37	01 52	02 07	02 26
S 60	21 08	22 39	////	01 39	01 51	02 04	02 19

SUN / MOON

Day	Eqn. of Time 00h	Eqn. of Time 12h	Mer. Pass.	Mer. Pass. Upper	Mer. Pass. Lower	Age	Phase
	m s	m s	h m	h m	h m	d	
6	09 08	08 56	11 51	19 49	07 24	10	
7	08 43	08 30	11 51	20 39	08 14	11	◖
8	08 17	08 04	11 52	21 33	09 06	12	

G.M.T.	ARIES G.H.A.	VENUS −4.4 G.H.A.	Dec.	MARS +1.2 G.H.A.	Dec.	JUPITER −1.3 G.H.A.	Dec.	SATURN +1.0 G.H.A.	Dec.	STARS Name	S.H.A.	Dec.
9 00	77 38.9	134 50.7	S22 22.9	259 56.2	N 3 12.1	227 10.4	S11 12.1	238 25.5	S 5 36.2	Acamar	315 36.2	S40 22.8
01	92 41.3	149 51.4	22.3	274 57.5	11.6	242 12.4	12.3	253 27.8	36.2	Achernar	335 44.3	S57 20.0
02	107 43.8	164 52.1	21.6	289 58.8	11.1	257 14.4	12.4	268 30.0	36.3	Acrux	173 36.5	S62 59.5
03	122 46.3	179 52.8	·· 21.0	305 00.2	·· 10.7	272 16.4	·· 12.6	283 32.3	·· 36.4	Adhara	255 31.1	S28 56.8
04	137 48.7	194 53.6	20.4	320 01.5	10.2	287 18.5	12.7	298 34.6	36.4	Aldebaran	291 16.7	N16 28.4
05	152 51.2	209 54.3	19.8	335 02.8	09.8	302 20.5	12.9	313 36.8	36.5			
06	167 53.7	224 55.0	S22 19.2	350 04.1	N 3 09.3	317 22.5	S11 13.0	328 39.1	S 5 36.6	Alioth	166 42.0	N56 03.3
W 07	182 56.1	239 55.7	18.6	5 05.5	08.8	332 24.5	13.2	343 41.4	36.7	Alkaid	153 18.2	N49 24.1
E 08	197 58.6	254 56.5	18.0	20 06.8	08.4	347 26.6	13.3	358 43.6	36.7	Al Na'ir	28 14.0	S47 03.2
D 09	213 01.0	269 57.2	·· 17.3	35 08.1	·· 07.9	2 28.6	·· 13.5	13 45.9	·· 36.8	Alnilam	276 10.5	S 1 12.8
N 10	228 03.5	284 58.0	16.7	50 09.4	07.5	17 30.6	13.6	28 48.1	36.9	Alphard	218 19.6	S 8 34.7
E 11	243 06.0	299 58.7	16.1	65 10.8	07.0	32 32.6	13.8	43 50.4	36.9			
S 12	258 08.4	314 59.4	S22 15.5	80 12.1	N 3 06.6	47 34.7	S11 13.9	58 52.7	S 5 37.0	Alphecca	126 31.7	N26 46.6
D 13	273 10.9	330 00.2	14.9	95 13.4	06.1	62 36.7	14.1	73 54.9	37.1	Alpheratz	358 08.4	N28 59.5
A 14	288 13.4	345 00.9	14.3	110 14.8	05.6	77 38.7	14.3	88 57.2	37.2	Altair	62 32.0	N 8 49.3
Y 15	303 15.8	0 01.7	·· 13.6	125 16.1	·· 05.2	92 40.7	·· 14.4	103 59.5	·· 37.2	Ankaa	353 39.3	S42 24.6
16	318 18.3	15 02.4	13.0	140 17.4	04.7	107 42.8	14.6	119 01.7	37.3	Antares	112 56.2	S26 23.4
17	333 20.8	30 03.2	12.4	155 18.7	04.3	122 44.8	14.7	134 04.0	37.4			
18	348 23.2	45 03.9	S22 11.8	170 20.1	N 3 03.8	137 46.8	S11 14.9	149 06.3	S 5 37.4	Arcturus	146 18.0	N19 16.6
19	3 25.7	60 04.7	11.2	185 21.4	03.4	152 48.9	15.0	164 08.5	37.5	Atria	108 20.3	S68 59.6
20	18 28.1	75 05.5	10.5	200 22.7	02.9	167 50.9	15.2	179 10.8	37.6	Avior	234 27.4	S59 26.8
21	33 30.6	90 06.2	·· 09.9	215 24.0	·· 02.4	182 52.9	·· 15.3	194 13.1	·· 37.6	Bellatrix	278 57.5	N 6 20.0
22	48 33.1	105 07.0	09.3	230 25.4	02.0	197 54.9	15.5	209 15.3	37.7	Betelgeuse	271 27.0	N 7 24.2
23	63 35.5	120 07.8	08.7	245 26.7	01.5	212 57.0	15.6	224 17.6	37.8			
10 00	78 38.0	135 08.6	S22 08.1	260 28.0	N 3 01.1	227 59.0	S11 15.8	239 19.9	S 5 37.9	Canopus	264 06.3	S52 41.1
01	93 40.5	150 09.3	07.4	275 29.4	00.6	243 01.0	15.9	254 22.1	37.9	Capella	281 09.6	N45 58.8
02	108 42.9	165 10.1	06.8	290 30.7	3 00.2	258 03.0	16.1	269 24.4	38.0	Deneb	49 48.2	N45 13.1
03	123 45.4	180 10.9	·· 06.2	305 32.0	2 59.7	273 05.1	·· 16.2	284 26.7	·· 38.1	Denebola	182 58.2	N14 40.4
04	138 47.9	195 11.7	05.6	320 33.4	59.2	288 07.1	16.4	299 29.0	38.1	Diphda	349 19.9	S18 05.3
05	153 50.3	210 12.5	04.9	335 34.7	58.8	303 09.1	16.5	314 31.2	38.2			
06	168 52.8	225 13.3	S22 04.3	350 36.0	N 2 58.3	318 11.2	S11 16.7	329 33.5	S 5 38.3	Dubhe	194 21.0	N61 50.7
07	183 55.3	240 14.0	03.7	5 37.4	57.9	333 13.2	16.8	344 35.8	38.3	Elnath	278 42.7	N28 35.5
T 08	198 57.7	255 14.8	03.1	20 38.7	57.4	348 15.2	17.0	359 38.0	38.4	Eltanin	90 57.9	N51 29.6
H 09	214 00.2	270 15.6	·· 02.4	35 40.0	·· 57.0	3 17.2	·· 17.1	14 40.3	·· 38.5	Enif	34 10.9	N 9 47.5
U 10	229 02.6	285 16.4	01.8	50 41.4	56.5	18 19.3	17.3	29 42.6	38.6	Fomalhaut	15 50.5	S29 43.3
R 11	244 05.1	300 17.2	01.2	65 42.7	56.1	33 21.3	17.4	44 44.8	38.6			
S 12	259 07.6	315 18.0	S22 00.6	80 44.0	N 2 55.6	48 23.3	S11 17.6	59 47.1	S 5 38.7	Gacrux	172 28.0	S57 00.3
D 13	274 10.0	330 18.9	21 59.9	95 45.4	55.2	63 25.4	17.7	74 49.4	38.8	Gienah	176 17.2	S17 26.3
A 14	289 12.5	345 19.7	59.3	110 46.7	54.7	78 27.4	17.9	89 51.6	38.8	Hadar	149 22.6	S60 16.8
Y 15	304 15.0	0 20.5	·· 58.7	125 48.0	·· 54.2	93 29.4	·· 18.0	104 53.9	·· 38.9	Hamal	328 27.7	N23 22.7
16	319 17.4	15 21.3	58.1	140 49.4	53.8	108 31.4	18.2	119 56.2	39.0	Kaus Aust.	84 16.1	S34 23.6
17	334 19.9	30 22.1	57.4	155 50.7	53.3	123 33.5	18.3	134 58.4	39.0			
18	349 22.4	45 22.9	S21 56.8	170 52.0	N 2 52.9	138 35.5	S11 18.5	150 00.7	S 5 39.1	Kochab	137 20.0	N74 13.7
19	4 24.8	60 23.7	56.2	185 53.4	52.4	153 37.5	18.6	165 03.0	39.2	Markab	14 02.4	N15 06.5
20	19 27.3	75 24.6	55.6	200 54.7	52.0	168 39.6	18.8	180 05.3	39.2	Menkar	314 40.0	N 4 01.1
21	34 29.8	90 25.4	·· 54.9	215 56.0	·· 51.5	183 41.6	·· 18.9	195 07.5	·· 39.3	Menkent	148 36.3	S36 16.6
22	49 32.2	105 26.2	54.3	230 57.4	51.1	198 43.6	19.1	210 09.8	39.4	Miaplacidus	221 44.3	S69 38.2
23	64 34.7	120 27.1	53.7	245 58.7	50.6	213 45.6	19.2	225 12.1	39.5			
11 00	79 37.1	135 27.9	S21 53.0	261 00.0	N 2 50.2	228 47.7	S11 19.4	240 14.3	S 5 39.5	Mirfak	309 14.4	N49 47.9
01	94 39.6	150 28.7	52.4	276 01.4	49.7	243 49.7	19.5	255 16.6	39.6	Nunki	76 28.5	S26 19.2
02	109 42.1	165 29.6	51.8	291 02.7	49.2	258 51.7	19.7	270 18.9	39.7	Peacock	53 57.5	S56 47.8
03	124 44.5	180 30.4	·· 51.2	306 04.1	·· 48.8	273 53.8	·· 19.8	285 21.1	·· 39.7	Pollux	243 56.8	N28 04.2
04	139 47.0	195 31.3	50.5	321 05.4	48.3	288 55.8	20.0	300 23.4	39.8	Procyon	245 24.6	N 5 16.3
05	154 49.5	210 32.1	49.9	336 06.7	47.9	303 57.8	20.1	315 25.7	39.9			
06	169 51.9	225 33.0	S21 49.3	351 08.1	N 2 47.4	318 59.9	S11 20.3	330 28.0	S 5 39.9	Rasalhague	96 29.2	N12 34.5
07	184 54.4	240 33.8	48.6	6 09.4	47.0	334 01.9	20.4	345 30.2	40.0	Regulus	208 09.0	N12 03.4
08	199 56.9	255 34.7	48.0	21 10.7	46.5	349 03.9	20.6	0 32.5	40.1	Rigel	281 34.9	S 8 13.4
F 09	214 59.3	270 35.6	·· 47.4	36 12.1	·· 46.1	4 06.0	·· 20.7	15 34.8	·· 40.1	Rigil Kent.	140 25.3	S60 45.3
R 10	230 01.8	285 36.4	46.7	51 13.4	45.6	19 08.0	20.9	30 37.0	40.2	Sabik	102 40.5	S15 42.1
I 11	245 04.3	300 37.3	46.1	66 14.8	45.2	34 10.0	21.0	45 39.3	40.3			
D 12	260 06.7	315 38.1	S21 45.5	81 16.1	N 2 44.7	49 12.0	S11 21.2	60 41.6	S 5 40.3	Schedar	350 07.9	N56 26.5
A 13	275 09.2	330 39.0	44.8	96 17.4	44.3	64 14.1	21.3	75 43.9	40.4	Shaula	96 55.1	S37 05.4
Y 14	290 11.6	345 39.9	44.2	111 18.8	43.8	79 16.1	21.5	90 46.1	40.5	Sirius	258 54.6	S16 41.5
15	305 14.1	0 40.8	·· 43.6	126 20.1	·· 43.4	94 18.1	·· 21.6	105 48.4	·· 40.5	Spica	158 56.8	S11 03.8
16	320 16.6	15 41.6	42.9	141 21.5	42.9	109 20.2	21.8	120 50.7	40.6	Suhail	223 09.9	S43 21.3
17	335 19.0	30 42.5	42.3	156 22.8	42.5	124 22.2	21.9	135 52.9	40.7			
18	350 21.5	45 43.4	S21 41.7	171 24.1	N 2 42.0	139 24.2	S11 22.1	150 55.2	S 5 40.7	Vega	80 55.7	N38 46.1
19	5 24.0	60 44.3	41.0	186 25.5	41.6	154 26.3	22.2	165 57.5	40.8	Zuben'ubi	137 32.4	S15 57.8
20	20 26.4	75 45.2	40.4	201 26.8	41.1	169 28.3	22.4	180 59.8	40.9		S.H.A.	Mer. Pass.
21	35 28.9	90 46.1	·· 39.8	216 28.2	·· 40.7	184 30.3	·· 22.5	196 02.0	·· 40.9	Venus	56 30.5	14 59
22	50 31.4	105 47.0	39.1	231 29.5	40.2	199 32.4	22.7	211 04.3	41.0	Mars	181 50.0	6 38
23	65 33.8	120 47.9	38.5	246 30.9	39.8	214 34.4	22.8	226 06.6	41.1	Jupiter	149 21.0	8 47
Mer. Pass. 18 42.4		*v* 0.8	*d* 0.6	*v* 1.3	*d* 0.5	*v* 2.0	*d* 0.2	*v* 2.3	*d* 0.1	Saturn	160 41.9	8 01

G.M.T.	SUN G.H.A.	Dec.	MOON G.H.A.	v	Dec.	d	H.P.
d h	° ′	° ′	° ′		° ′	′	′
9 00	181 57.5	S22 47.3	35 19.6	7.4	N11 10.9	12.1	60.8
01	196 57.2	47.5	49 46.0	7.3	11 23.0	12.1	60.8
02	211 57.0	47.8	64 12.3	7.2	11 35.1	11.9	60.9
03	226 56.7	·· 48.0	78 38.5	7.1	11 47.0	12.0	60.9
04	241 56.4	48.3	93 04.6	7.1	11 59.0	11.8	60.9
05	256 56.1	48.5	107 30.7	6.9	12 10.8	11.8	60.9
W 06	271 55.8	S22 48.8	121 56.6	6.9	N12 22.6	11.7	61.0
E 07	286 55.6	49.0	136 22.5	6.8	12 34.3	11.7	61.0
D 08	301 55.3	49.3	150 48.3	6.7	12 46.0	11.6	61.0
N 09	316 55.0	·· 49.5	165 14.0	6.7	12 57.6	11.4	61.0
E 10	331 54.7	49.8	179 39.7	6.5	13 09.0	11.5	61.0
S 11	346 54.5	50.0	194 05.2	6.5	13 20.5	11.3	61.1
D 12	1 54.2	S22 50.2	208 30.7	6.3	N13 31.8	11.2	61.1
A 13	16 53.9	50.5	222 56.0	6.3	13 43.0	11.2	61.1
Y 14	31 53.6	50.7	237 21.3	6.2	13 54.2	11.1	61.1
15	46 53.3	·· 51.0	251 46.5	6.1	14 05.3	11.0	61.1
16	61 53.1	51.2	266 11.6	6.1	14 16.3	10.9	61.2
17	76 52.8	51.4	280 36.7	5.9	14 27.2	10.8	61.2
18	91 52.5	S22 51.7	295 01.6	5.9	N14 38.0	10.7	61.2
19	106 52.2	51.9	309 26.5	5.8	14 48.7	10.6	61.2
20	121 51.9	52.1	323 51.3	5.7	14 59.3	10.6	61.2
21	136 51.7	·· 52.4	338 16.0	5.6	15 09.9	10.4	61.2
22	151 51.4	52.6	352 40.6	5.5	15 20.3	10.3	61.3
23	166 51.1	52.8	7 05.1	5.4	15 30.6	10.2	61.3
10 00	181 50.8	S22 53.1	21 29.5	5.4	N15 40.8	10.2	61.3
01	196 50.5	53.3	35 53.9	5.3	15 51.0	10.0	61.3
02	211 50.3	53.5	50 18.2	5.2	16 01.0	9.9	61.3
03	226 50.0	·· 53.8	64 42.4	5.1	16 10.9	9.8	61.3
04	241 49.7	54.0	79 06.5	5.0	16 20.7	9.7	61.3
05	256 49.4	54.2	93 30.5	5.0	16 30.4	9.5	61.4
06	271 49.1	S22 54.4	107 54.5	4.9	N16 39.9	9.5	61.4
07	286 48.8	54.7	122 18.4	4.8	16 49.4	9.3	61.4
T 08	301 48.6	54.9	136 42.2	4.7	16 58.7	9.3	61.4
H 09	316 48.3	·· 55.1	151 05.9	4.7	17 08.0	9.1	61.4
U 10	331 48.0	55.3	165 29.6	4.5	17 17.1	8.9	61.4
R 11	346 47.7	55.6	179 53.1	4.5	17 26.0	8.9	61.4
S 12	1 47.4	S22 55.8	194 16.6	4.5	N17 34.9	8.7	61.4
D 13	16 47.1	56.0	208 40.1	4.3	17 43.6	8.6	61.4
A 14	31 46.9	56.2	223 03.4	4.3	17 52.2	8.5	61.4
Y 15	46 46.6	·· 56.4	237 26.7	4.2	18 00.7	8.4	61.4
16	61 46.3	56.7	251 49.9	4.2	18 09.1	8.2	61.4
17	76 46.0	56.9	266 13.1	4.0	18 17.3	8.1	61.4
18	91 45.7	S22 57.1	280 36.1	4.0	N18 25.4	7.9	61.4
19	106 45.4	57.3	294 59.1	4.0	18 33.3	7.8	61.5
20	121 45.1	57.5	309 22.1	3.9	18 41.1	7.7	61.5
21	136 44.9	·· 57.7	323 45.0	3.8	18 48.8	7.6	61.5
22	151 44.6	58.0	338 07.8	3.7	18 56.4	7.4	61.5
23	166 44.3	58.2	352 30.5	3.7	19 03.8	7.2	61.5
11 00	181 44.0	S22 58.4	6 53.2	3.7	N19 11.0	7.1	61.5
01	196 43.7	58.6	21 15.9	3.5	19 18.1	7.0	61.5
02	211 43.4	58.8	35 38.4	3.6	19 25.1	6.8	61.5
03	226 43.2	·· 59.0	50 01.0	3.4	19 31.9	6.7	61.5
04	241 42.9	59.2	64 23.4	3.4	19 38.6	6.5	61.5
05	256 42.6	59.4	78 45.8	3.4	19 45.1	6.4	61.5
06	271 42.3	S22 59.6	93 08.2	3.3	N19 51.5	6.3	61.4
07	286 42.0	22 59.9	107 30.5	3.3	19 57.8	6.0	61.4
08	301 41.7	23 00.1	121 52.8	3.2	20 03.8	6.0	61.4
F 09	316 41.4	·· 00.3	136 15.0	3.2	20 09.8	5.7	61.4
R 10	331 41.1	00.5	150 37.2	3.2	20 15.5	5.7	61.4
I 11	346 40.9	00.7	164 59.4	3.1	20 21.2	5.4	61.4
D 12	1 40.6	S23 00.9	179 21.5	3.0	N20 26.6	5.3	61.4
A 13	16 40.3	01.1	193 43.5	3.1	20 31.9	5.2	61.4
Y 14	31 40.0	01.3	208 05.6	3.0	20 37.1	5.0	61.4
15	46 39.7	·· 01.5	222 27.6	2.9	20 42.1	4.8	61.4
16	61 39.4	01.7	236 49.5	3.0	20 46.9	4.7	61.4
17	76 39.1	01.9	251 11.5	2.9	20 51.6	4.5	61.4
18	91 38.8	S23 02.1	265 33.4	2.9	N20 56.1	4.4	61.4
19	106 38.6	02.3	279 55.3	2.8	21 00.5	4.2	61.4
20	121 38.3	02.5	294 17.1	2.9	21 04.7	4.0	61.3
21	136 38.0	·· 02.7	308 39.0	2.8	21 08.7	3.9	61.3
22	151 37.7	02.9	323 00.8	2.8	21 12.6	3.7	61.3
23	166 37.4	03.1	337 22.6	2.8	21 16.3	3.5	61.3
	S.D. 16.3	d 0.2	S.D. 16.6		16.7		16.7

Lat.	Twilight Naut.	Civil	Sunrise	Moonrise 9	10	11	12
°	h m	h m	h m	h m	h m	h m	h m
N 72	08 12	10 29	■	12 57	12 04	☐	☐
N 70	07 53	09 37	■	13 22	13 04	☐	☐
68	07 38	09 05	■	13 42	13 39	13 39	13 49
66	07 26	08 41	10 15	13 58	14 05	14 21	14 58
64	07 15	08 23	09 38	14 11	14 25	14 50	15 34
62	07 06	08 07	09 11	14 22	14 41	15 12	16 00
60	06 58	07 54	08 51	14 31	14 55	15 29	16 20
N 58	06 51	07 43	08 34	14 39	15 07	15 44	16 37
56	06 44	07 33	08 20	14 47	15 17	15 57	16 51
54	06 38	07 24	08 08	14 53	15 26	16 09	17 04
52	06 33	07 16	07 57	14 59	15 34	16 18	17 14
50	06 28	07 09	07 47	15 05	15 41	16 27	17 24
45	06 16	06 54	07 27	15 16	15 57	16 46	17 44
N 40	06 06	06 40	07 11	15 26	16 10	17 02	18 01
35	05 57	06 29	06 57	15 34	16 21	17 15	18 15
30	05 49	06 19	06 45	15 42	16 31	17 26	18 27
20	05 33	06 00	06 24	15 55	16 48	17 46	18 48
N 10	05 17	05 43	06 06	16 06	17 03	18 03	19 06
0	05 01	05 27	05 49	16 17	17 17	18 19	19 23
S 10	04 42	05 09	05 32	16 27	17 31	18 36	19 40
20	04 20	04 49	05 13	16 39	17 46	18 53	19 58
30	03 51	04 25	04 52	16 52	18 03	19 13	20 19
35	03 33	04 10	04 39	17 00	18 13	19 25	20 32
40	03 11	03 52	04 25	17 09	18 25	19 38	20 46
45	02 41	03 30	04 07	17 19	18 39	19 54	21 03
S 50	01 58	03 01	03 45	17 32	18 55	20 14	21 23
52	01 32	02 47	03 35	17 38	19 03	20 24	21 33
54	00 53	02 30	03 23	17 45	19 12	20 34	21 44
56	////	02 09	03 09	17 52	19 22	20 46	21 57
58	////	01 41	02 53	18 00	19 34	21 00	22 12
S 60	////	00 59	02 34	18 10	19 47	21 17	22 29

Lat.	Sunset	Twilight Civil	Naut.	Moonset 9	10	11	12
°	h m	h m	h m	h m	h m	h m	h m
N 72	■	13 16	15 33	06 43	09 40	☐	☐
N 70	■	14 08	15 52	06 20	08 41	☐	☐
68	■	14 40	16 07	06 02	08 07	10 18	12 22
66	13 30	15 04	16 20	05 47	07 43	09 37	11 13
64	14 08	15 23	16 30	05 36	07 24	09 08	10 37
62	14 34	15 38	16 39	05 26	07 08	08 47	10 11
60	14 55	15 51	16 47	05 17	06 55	08 29	09 51
N 58	15 11	16 03	16 55	05 10	06 44	08 15	09 34
56	15 26	16 12	17 01	05 03	06 34	08 02	09 20
54	15 38	16 21	17 07	04 58	06 26	07 51	09 08
52	15 49	16 29	17 13	04 52	06 18	07 42	08 57
50	15 58	16 36	17 18	04 48	06 11	07 33	08 48
45	16 18	16 52	17 29	04 38	05 57	07 15	08 27
N 40	16 35	17 05	17 39	04 29	05 45	07 00	08 11
35	16 49	17 17	17 48	04 22	05 35	06 47	07 57
30	17 01	17 27	17 57	04 16	05 26	06 36	07 45
20	17 21	17 45	18 13	04 05	05 10	06 18	07 24
N 10	17 39	18 02	18 29	03 55	04 57	06 01	07 06
0	17 57	18 19	18 45	03 46	04 45	05 46	06 50
S 10	18 14	18 37	19 04	03 38	04 32	05 31	06 33
20	18 32	18 57	19 26	03 28	04 19	05 15	06 15
30	18 54	19 21	19 54	03 17	04 04	04 56	05 54
35	19 07	19 36	20 13	03 11	03 55	04 45	05 42
40	19 21	19 54	20 35	03 04	03 45	04 33	05 28
45	19 39	20 16	21 05	02 56	03 34	04 18	05 12
S 50	20 01	20 45	21 49	02 46	03 20	04 00	04 52
52	20 11	20 59	22 15	02 42	03 13	03 52	04 42
54	20 23	21 17	22 54	02 37	03 06	03 43	04 31
56	20 37	21 38	////	02 32	02 58	03 32	04 19
58	20 53	22 06	////	02 26	02 49	03 20	04 05
S 60	21 13	22 49	////	02 19	02 38	03 07	03 48

Day	SUN Eqn. of Time 00h	12h	Mer. Pass.	MOON Mer. Pass. Upper	Lower	Age	Phase
	m s	m s	h m	h m	h m	d	
9	07 51	07 37	11 52	22 30	10 01	13	
10	07 24	07 10	11 53	23 31	11 00	14	◯
11	06 57	06 43	11 53	24 35	12 03	15	

G.M.T.	ARIES G.H.A.	VENUS −4.4 G.H.A.	Dec.	MARS +1.2 G.H.A.	Dec.	JUPITER −1.3 G.H.A.	Dec.	SATURN +1.0 G.H.A.	Dec.	STARS Name	S.H.A.	Dec.
12 00	80 36.3	135 48.8	S21 37.9	261 32.2	N 2 39.3	229 36.4	S11 23.0	241 08.9	S 5 41.1	Acamar	315 36.2	S40 22.8
01	95 38.7	150 49.7	37.2	276 33.6	38.9	244 38.5	23.1	256 11.1	41.2	Achernar	335 44.3	S57 20.0
02	110 41.2	165 50.6	36.6	291 34.9	38.4	259 40.5	23.3	271 13.4	41.3	Acrux	173 36.5	S62 59.5
03	125 43.7	180 51.5	·· 36.0	306 36.2	·· 38.0	274 42.5	·· 23.4	286 15.7	·· 41.4	Adhara	255 31.1	S28 56.8
04	140 46.1	195 52.4	35.3	321 37.6	37.5	289 44.6	23.6	301 17.9	41.4	Aldebaran	291 16.7	N16 28.4
05	155 48.6	210 53.3	34.7	336 38.9	37.1	304 46.6	23.7	316 20.2	41.5			
06	170 51.1	225 54.2	S21 34.0	351 40.3	N 2 36.6	319 48.6	S11 23.9	331 22.5	S 5 41.6	Alioth	166 42.0	N56 03.3
07	185 53.5	240 55.2	33.4	6 41.6	36.2	334 50.7	24.0	346 24.8	41.6	Alkaid	153 18.1	N49 24.1
S 08	200 56.0	255 56.1	32.8	21 43.0	35.7	349 52.7	24.1	1 27.0	41.7	Al Na'ir	28 14.0	S47 03.2
A 09	215 58.5	270 57.0	·· 32.1	36 44.3	·· 35.3	4 54.7	·· 24.3	16 29.3	·· 41.8	Alnilam	276 10.5	S 1 12.8
T 10	231 00.9	285 57.9	31.5	51 45.7	34.8	19 56.8	24.4	31 31.6	41.8	Alphard	218 19.6	S 8 34.7
U 11	246 03.4	300 58.9	30.8	66 47.0	34.4	34 58.8	24.6	46 33.9	41.9			
R 12	261 05.9	315 59.8	S21 30.2	81 48.4	N 2 33.9	50 00.9	S11 24.7	61 36.1	S 5 42.0	Alphecca	126 31.7	N26 46.6
D 13	276 08.3	331 00.7	29.6	96 49.7	33.5	65 02.9	24.9	76 38.4	42.0	Alpheratz	358 08.4	N28 59.5
A 14	291 10.8	346 01.7	28.9	111 51.0	33.0	80 04.9	25.0	91 40.7	42.1	Altair	62 32.0	N 8 49.3
Y 15	306 13.2	1 02.6	·· 28.3	126 52.4	·· 32.6	95 07.0	·· 25.2	106 43.0	·· 42.2	Ankaa	353 39.3	S42 24.6
16	321 15.7	16 03.6	27.7	141 53.7	32.1	110 09.0	25.3	121 45.2	42.2	Antares	112 56.2	S26 23.4
17	336 18.2	31 04.5	27.0	156 55.1	31.7	125 11.0	25.5	136 47.5	42.3			
18	351 20.6	46 05.5	S21 26.4	171 56.4	N 2 31.2	140 13.1	S11 25.6	151 49.8	S 5 42.4	Arcturus	146 17.9	N19 16.6
19	6 23.1	61 06.4	25.7	186 57.8	30.8	155 15.1	25.8	166 52.1	42.4	Atria	108 20.2	S68 59.6
20	21 25.6	76 07.4	25.1	201 59.1	30.3	170 17.1	25.9	181 54.3	42.5	Avior	234 27.4	S59 26.8
21	36 28.0	91 08.3	·· 24.5	217 00.5	·· 29.9	185 19.2	·· 26.1	196 56.6	·· 42.6	Bellatrix	278 57.5	N 6 20.0
22	51 30.5	106 09.3	23.8	232 01.8	29.4	200 21.2	26.2	211 58.9	42.6	Betelgeuse	271 27.0	N 7 24.2
23	66 33.0	121 10.2	23.2	247 03.2	29.0	215 23.2	26.4	227 01.2	42.7			
13 00	81 35.4	136 11.2	S21 22.5	262 04.5	N 2 28.5	230 25.3	S11 26.5	242 03.4	S 5 42.7	Canopus	264 06.3	S52 41.1
01	96 37.9	151 12.2	21.9	277 05.9	28.1	245 27.3	26.7	257 05.7	42.8	Capella	281 09.6	N45 58.8
02	111 40.4	166 13.2	21.2	292 07.2	27.6	260 29.4	26.8	272 08.0	42.9	Deneb	49 48.2	N45 13.1
03	126 42.8	181 14.1	·· 20.6	307 08.6	·· 27.2	275 31.4	·· 26.9	287 10.3	·· 42.9	Denebola	182 58.2	N14 40.4
04	141 45.3	196 15.1	20.0	322 09.9	26.8	290 33.4	27.1	302 12.5	43.0	Diphda	349 19.9	S18 05.3
05	156 47.7	211 16.1	19.3	337 11.3	26.3	305 35.5	27.2	317 14.8	43.1			
06	171 50.2	226 17.1	S21 18.7	352 12.6	N 2 25.9	320 37.5	S11 27.4	332 17.1	S 5 43.1	Dubhe	194 21.0	N61 50.7
07	186 52.7	241 18.1	18.0	7 14.0	25.4	335 39.5	27.5	347 19.4	43.2	Elnath	278 42.7	N28 35.5
08	201 55.1	256 19.1	17.4	22 15.4	25.0	350 41.6	27.7	2 21.6	43.3	Eltanin	90 57.9	N51 29.6
S 09	216 57.6	271 20.0	·· 16.7	37 16.7	·· 24.5	5 43.6	·· 27.8	17 23.9	·· 43.3	Enif	34 10.9	N 9 47.5
U 10	232 00.1	286 21.0	16.1	52 18.1	24.1	20 45.7	28.0	32 26.2	43.4	Fomalhaut	15 50.5	S29 43.3
N 11	247 02.5	301 22.0	15.5	67 19.4	23.6	35 47.7	28.1	47 28.5	43.5			
D 12	262 05.0	316 23.0	S21 14.8	82 20.8	N 2 23.2	50 49.7	S11 28.3	62 30.8	S 5 43.5	Gacrux	172 28.0	S57 00.3
A 13	277 07.5	331 24.0	14.2	97 22.1	22.7	65 51.8	28.4	77 33.0	43.6	Gienah	176 17.2	S17 26.3
Y 14	292 09.9	346 25.0	13.5	112 23.5	22.3	80 53.8	28.6	92 35.3	43.7	Hadar	149 22.6	S60 16.8
15	307 12.4	1 26.1	·· 12.9	127 24.8	·· 21.8	95 55.8	·· 28.7	107 37.6	·· 43.7	Hamal	328 27.7	N23 22.7
16	322 14.9	16 27.1	12.2	142 26.2	21.4	110 57.9	28.8	122 39.9	43.8	Kaus Aust.	84 16.1	S34 23.6
17	337 17.3	31 28.1	11.6	157 27.5	21.0	125 59.9	29.0	137 42.1	43.9			
18	352 19.8	46 29.1	S21 10.9	172 28.9	N 2 20.5	141 02.0	S11 29.1	152 44.4	S 5 43.9	Kochab	137 20.0	N74 13.7
19	7 22.2	61 30.1	10.3	187 30.3	20.1	156 04.0	29.3	167 46.7	44.0	Markab	14 02.4	N15 06.5
20	22 24.7	76 31.1	09.7	202 31.6	19.6	171 06.0	29.4	182 49.0	44.1	Menkar	314 40.0	N 4 01.3
21	37 27.2	91 32.2	·· 09.0	217 33.0	·· 19.2	186 08.1	·· 29.6	197 51.3	·· 44.1	Menkent	148 36.3	S36 16.6
22	52 29.6	106 33.2	08.4	232 34.3	18.7	201 10.1	29.7	212 53.5	44.2	Miaplacidus	221 44.2	S69 38.3
23	67 32.1	121 34.2	07.7	247 35.7	18.3	216 12.2	29.9	227 55.8	44.3			
14 00	82 34.6	136 35.3	S21 07.1	262 37.0	N 2 17.8	231 14.2	S11 30.0	242 58.1	S 5 44.3	Mirfak	309 14.4	N49 47.9
01	97 37.0	151 36.3	06.4	277 38.4	17.4	246 16.2	30.2	258 00.4	44.4	Nunki	76 28.5	S26 19.2
02	112 39.5	166 37.4	05.8	292 39.8	17.0	261 18.3	30.3	273 02.7	44.4	Peacock	53 57.5	S56 47.8
03	127 42.0	181 38.4	·· 05.1	307 41.1	·· 16.5	276 20.3	·· 30.4	288 04.9	·· 44.5	Pollux	243 56.8	N28 04.2
04	142 44.4	196 39.4	04.5	322 42.5	16.1	291 22.4	30.6	303 07.2	44.6	Procyon	245 24.6	N 5 16.3
05	157 46.9	211 40.5	03.8	337 43.8	15.6	306 24.4	30.7	318 09.5	44.6			
06	172 49.3	226 41.5	S21 03.2	352 45.2	N 2 15.2	321 26.4	S11 30.9	333 11.8	S 5 44.7	Rasalhague	96 29.2	N12 34.4
07	187 51.8	241 42.6	02.5	7 46.5	14.7	336 28.5	31.0	348 14.1	44.8	Regulus	208 09.0	N12 03.4
08	202 54.3	256 43.7	01.9	22 47.9	14.3	351 30.5	31.2	3 16.3	44.8	Rigel	281 34.9	S 8 13.4
M 09	217 56.7	271 44.7	·· 01.2	37 49.3	·· 13.9	6 32.6	·· 31.3	18 18.6	·· 44.9	Rigil Kent.	140 25.2	S60 45.3
O 10	232 59.2	286 45.8	21 00.6	52 50.6	13.4	21 34.6	31.5	33 20.9	45.0	Sabik	102 40.5	S15 42.1
N 11	248 01.7	301 46.9	20 59.9	67 52.0	13.0	36 36.6	31.6	48 23.2	45.0			
D 12	263 04.1	316 47.9	S20 59.3	82 53.4	N 2 12.5	51 38.7	S11 31.8	63 25.5	S 5 45.1	Schedar	350 07.9	N56 26.5
A 13	278 06.6	331 49.0	58.7	97 54.7	12.1	66 40.7	31.9	78 27.7	45.2	Shaula	96 55.0	S37 05.4
Y 14	293 09.1	346 50.1	58.0	112 56.1	11.6	81 42.8	32.0	93 30.0	45.2	Sirius	258 54.6	S16 41.5
15	308 11.5	1 51.2	·· 57.4	127 57.4	·· 11.2	96 44.8	·· 32.2	108 32.3	·· 45.3	Spica	158 56.8	S11 03.8
16	323 14.0	16 52.2	56.7	142 58.8	10.8	111 46.8	32.3	123 34.6	45.3	Suhail	223 09.9	S43 21.3
17	338 16.5	31 53.3	56.1	158 00.2	10.3	126 48.9	32.5	138 36.9	45.4			
18	353 18.9	46 54.4	S20 55.4	173 01.5	N 2 09.9	141 50.9	S11 32.6	153 39.1	S 5 45.5	Vega	80 55.7	N38 46.1
19	8 21.4	61 55.5	54.8	188 02.9	09.4	156 53.0	32.8	168 41.4	45.5	Zuben'ubi	137 32.4	S15 57.8
20	23 23.8	76 56.6	54.1	203 04.2	09.0	171 55.0	32.9	183 43.7	45.6		S.H.A.	Mer. Pass.
21	38 26.3	91 57.7	·· 53.5	218 05.6	·· 08.5	186 57.1	·· 33.0	198 46.0	·· 45.7	Venus	54 35.8	14 54
22	53 28.8	106 58.8	52.8	233 07.0	08.1	201 59.1	33.2	213 48.3	45.7	Mars	180 29.1	6 31
23	68 31.2	121 59.9	52.2	248 08.3	07.7	217 01.1	33.3	228 50.5	45.8	Jupiter	148 49.9	8 37
Mer. Pass. 18 30.6		v 1.0	d 0.6	v 1.4	d 0.4	v 2.0	d 0.1	v 2.3	d 0.1	Saturn	160 28.0	7 51

G.M.T.	SUN		MOON					Lat.	Twilight		Sunrise	Moonrise			
	G.H.A.	Dec.	G.H.A.	v	Dec.	d	H.P.		Naut.	Civil		12	13	14	15
	° ′	° ′	° ′	′	° ′	′	′	°	h m	h m	h m	h m	h m	h m	h m
12 00	181 37.1	S23 03.3	351 44.4	2.8	N21 19.8	3.4	61.3	N 72	08 17	10 40	■■	▢	▢	▢	17 59
01	196 36.8	03.4	6 06.2	2.7	21 23.2	3.2	61.3	N 70	07 58	09 44	■■	▢	▢	16 12	18 43
02	211 36.5	03.6	20 27.9	2.8	21 26.4	3.1	61.3	68	07 42	09 10	■■	13 49	15 12	17 15	19 12
03	226 36.2 ··	03.8	34 49.7	2.7	21 29.5	2.8	61.2	66	07 30	08 46	10 23	14 58	16 11	17 50	19 34
04	241 35.9	04.0	49 11.4	2.8	21 32.3	2.6	61.2	64	07 19	08 27	09 43	15 34	16 45	18 15	19 51
05	256 35.7	04.2	63 33.2	2.7	21 35.1	2.5	61.2	62	07 09	08 11	09 16	16 00	17 09	18 35	20 05
06	271 35.4	S23 04.4	77 54.9	2.8	N21 37.6	2.4	61.2	60	07 01	07 58	08 55	16 20	17 29	18 51	20 17
07	286 35.1	04.6	92 16.7	2.7	21 40.0	2.2	61.2	N 58	06 54	07 46	08 38	16 37	17 45	19 04	20 28
S 08	301 34.8	04.8	106 38.4	2.8	21 42.2	2.1	61.2	56	06 47	07 36	08 23	16 51	17 59	19 16	20 37
A 09	316 34.5 ··	05.0	121 00.2	2.8	21 44.3	1.8	61.1	54	06 41	07 27	08 11	17 04	18 11	19 26	20 44
T 10	331 34.2	05.1	135 22.0	2.8	21 46.1	1.7	61.1	52	06 36	07 19	08 00	17 14	18 21	19 35	20 51
U 11	346 33.9	05.3	149 43.8	2.8	21 47.8	1.6	61.1	50	06 30	07 12	07 50	17 24	18 31	19 43	20 58
R 12	1 33.6	S23 05.5	164 05.6	2.8	N21 49.4	1.4	61.1	45	06 19	06 56	07 30	17 44	18 50	20 01	21 11
D 13	16 33.3	05.7	178 27.4	2.8	21 50.8	1.2	61.1	N 40	06 09	06 43	07 13	18 01	19 06	20 15	21 23
A 14	31 33.0	05.9	192 49.2	2.8	21 52.0	1.0	61.0	35	05 59	06 31	06 59	18 15	19 20	20 26	21 32
Y 15	46 32.7 ··	06.1	207 11.0	2.9	21 53.0	0.9	61.0	30	05 51	06 21	06 47	18 27	19 32	20 37	21 41
16	61 32.5	06.2	221 32.9	2.9	21 53.9	0.7	61.0	20	05 35	06 02	06 26	18 48	19 52	20 55	21 55
17	76 32.2	06.4	235 54.8	2.9	21 54.6	0.6	61.0	N 10	05 19	05 45	06 08	19 06	20 09	21 10	22 07
18	91 31.9	S23 06.6	250 16.7	3.0	N21 55.2	0.4	60.9	0	05 02	05 28	05 50	19 23	20 26	21 25	22 19
19	106 31.6	06.8	264 38.7	3.0	21 55.6	0.2	60.9	S 10	04 43	05 10	05 33	19 40	20 42	21 39	22 31
20	121 31.3	07.0	279 00.7	3.0	21 55.8	0.0	60.9	20	04 21	04 50	05 14	19 58	20 59	21 54	22 43
21	136 31.0 ··	07.1	293 22.7	3.0	21 55.8	0.1	60.9	30	03 52	04 25	04 53	20 19	21 19	22 12	22 57
22	151 30.7	07.3	307 44.7	3.1	21 55.7	0.2	60.8	35	03 34	04 10	04 40	20 32	21 31	22 22	23 06
23	166 30.4	07.5	322 06.8	3.1	21 55.5	0.5	60.8	40	03 11	03 52	04 25	20 46	21 45	22 34	23 15
								45	02 41	03 30	04 07	21 03	22 00	22 48	23 26
13 00	181 30.1	S23 07.7	336 28.9	3.2	N21 55.0	0.6	60.8	S 50	01 56	03 01	03 45	21 23	22 20	23 04	23 39
01	196 29.8	07.8	350 51.1	3.2	21 54.4	0.7	60.8	52	01 30	02 46	03 34	21 33	22 29	23 12	23 45
02	211 29.5	08.0	5 13.3	3.3	21 53.7	1.0	60.7	54	00 48	02 28	03 22	21 44	22 40	23 21	23 52
03	226 29.2 ··	08.2	19 35.6	3.3	21 52.7	1.1	60.7	56	////	02 07	03 08	21 57	22 51	23 31	23 59
04	241 28.9	08.3	33 57.9	3.4	21 51.6	1.2	60.7	58	////	01 38	02 52	22 12	23 05	23 42	24 08
05	256 28.6	08.5	48 20.3	3.4	21 50.4	1.4	60.7	S 60	////	00 53	02 32	22 29	23 20	23 54	24 17
06	271 28.4	S23 08.7	62 42.7	3.5	N21 49.0	1.6	60.6								

Lat.	Sunset	Twilight		Moonset			
		Civil	Naut.	12	13	14	15

G.M.T.	SUN		MOON												
07	286 28.1	08.9	77 05.2	3.5	21 47.4	1.7	60.6	°	h m	h m	h m	h m	h m	h m	h m
08	301 27.8	09.0	91 27.7	3.6	21 45.7	1.9	60.6	N 72	■■	13 08	15 31	▢	▢	▢	14 28
S 09	316 27.5 ··	09.2	105 50.3	3.6	21 43.8	2.0	60.5	N 70	■■	14 04	15 50	▢	▢	14 18	13 43
U 10	331 27.2	09.4	120 12.9	3.7	21 41.8	2.2	60.5	68	■■	14 38	16 06	12 22	13 11	13 14	13 12
N 11	346 26.9	09.5	134 35.6	3.8	21 39.6	2.4	60.5	66	13 25	15 02	16 19	11 13	12 12	12 38	12 50
D 12	1 26.6	S23 09.7	148 58.4	3.8	N21 37.2	2.5	60.4	64	14 05	15 22	16 29	10 37	11 38	12 13	12 31
A 13	16 26.3	09.9	163 21.2	3.9	21 34.7	2.6	60.4	62	14 32	15 37	16 39	10 11	11 13	11 52	12 17
Y 14	31 26.0	10.0	177 44.1	4.0	21 32.1	2.8	60.4	60	14 53	15 51	16 47	09 51	10 53	11 36	12 04
15	46 25.7 ··	10.2	192 07.1	4.1	21 29.3	3.0	60.3	N 58	15 11	16 02	16 54	09 34	10 37	11 22	11 53
16	61 25.4	10.3	206 30.2	4.1	21 26.3	3.1	60.3	56	15 25	16 12	17 01	09 20	10 23	11 10	11 43
17	76 25.1	10.5	220 53.3	4.2	21 23.2	3.2	60.3	54	15 37	16 21	17 07	09 08	10 11	10 59	11 35
18	91 24.8	S23 10.7	235 16.5	4.2	N21 20.0	3.4	60.2	52	15 48	16 29	17 13	08 57	10 00	10 50	11 27
19	106 24.5	10.8	249 39.7	4.4	21 16.6	3.6	60.2	50	15 58	16 36	17 18	08 48	09 51	10 41	11 21
20	121 24.2	11.0	264 03.1	4.4	21 13.0	3.7	60.2	45	16 19	16 52	17 29	08 27	09 31	10 23	11 06
21	136 23.9 ··	11.1	278 26.5	4.5	21 09.3	3.8	60.1	N 40	16 35	17 06	17 40	08 11	09 14	10 08	10 54
22	151 23.6	11.3	292 50.0	4.6	21 05.5	4.0	60.1	35	16 49	17 17	17 49	07 57	09 01	09 56	10 43
23	166 23.3	11.5	307 13.6	4.7	21 01.5	4.1	60.1	30	17 01	17 28	17 58	07 45	08 49	09 45	10 34
14 00	181 23.0	S23 11.6	321 37.3	4.7	N20 57.4	4.3	60.0	20	17 22	17 46	18 14	07 24	08 28	09 26	10 18
01	196 22.7	11.8	336 01.0	4.9	20 53.1	4.4	60.0	N 10	17 41	18 03	18 30	07 06	08 10	09 10	10 04
02	211 22.4	11.9	350 24.9	4.9	20 48.7	4.5	60.0	0	17 58	18 20	18 47	06 50	07 53	08 54	09 51
03	226 22.1 ··	12.1	4 48.8	5.0	20 44.2	4.7	59.9	S 10	18 15	18 38	19 05	06 33	07 36	08 39	09 38
04	241 21.9	12.2	19 12.8	5.1	20 39.5	4.8	59.9	20	18 34	18 59	19 28	06 15	07 18	08 22	09 24
05	256 21.6	12.4	33 36.9	5.2	20 34.7	5.0	59.9	30	18 56	19 23	19 57	05 54	06 57	08 03	09 08
06	271 21.3	S23 12.5	48 01.1	5.3	N20 29.7	5.1	59.8	35	19 09	19 38	20 15	05 42	06 45	07 51	08 58
07	286 21.0	12.7	62 25.4	5.4	20 24.6	5.2	59.8	40	19 24	19 56	20 38	05 28	06 31	07 38	08 47
08	301 20.7	12.8	76 49.8	5.5	20 19.4	5.3	59.7	45	19 41	20 19	21 08	05 12	06 14	07 23	08 34
M 09	316 20.4 ··	13.0	91 14.3	5.6	20 14.1	5.5	59.7	S 50	20 04	20 48	21 53	04 52	05 54	07 04	08 18
O 10	331 20.1	13.1	105 38.9	5.6	20 08.6	5.6	59.7	52	20 14	21 03	22 20	04 42	05 44	06 55	08 11
N 11	346 19.8	13.3	120 03.5	5.8	20 03.0	5.7	59.6	54	20 27	21 21	23 03	04 31	05 33	06 45	08 03
D 12	1 19.5	S23 13.4	134 28.3	5.9	N19 57.3	5.8	59.6	56	20 41	21 42	////	04 19	05 20	06 34	07 54
A 13	16 19.2	13.6	148 53.2	5.9	19 51.5	6.0	59.6	58	20 57	22 11	////	04 05	05 06	06 20	07 43
Y 14	31 18.9	13.7	163 18.1	6.1	19 45.5	6.1	59.5	S 60	21 17	22 58	////	03 48	04 48	06 05	07 31
15	46 18.6 ··	13.8	177 43.2	6.2	19 39.4	6.2	59.5								
16	61 18.3	14.0	192 08.4	6.2	19 33.2	6.3	59.4								
17	76 18.0	14.1	206 33.6	6.4	19 26.9	6.5	59.4								

	SUN			MOON			
Day	Eqn. of Time		Mer.	Mer. Pass.		Age	Phase
	00ʰ	12ʰ	Pass.	Upper	Lower		
	m s	m s	h m	h m	h m	d	
18	91 17.7	S23 14.3	220 59.0	6.4	N19 20.4	6.5	59.3
19	106 17.4	14.4	235 24.4	6.6	19 13.9	6.7	59.3
20	121 17.1	14.5	249 50.0	6.7	19 07.2	6.8	59.3
21	136 16.8 ··	14.7	264 15.7	6.7	19 00.4	6.9	59.2
22	151 16.5	14.8	278 41.4	6.9	18 53.5	7.0	59.2
23	166 16.2	15.0	293 07.3	7.0	18 46.5	7.1	59.2

Day	Eqn. of Time 00ʰ	Eqn. of Time 12ʰ	Mer. Pass.	Mer. Pass. Upper	Mer. Pass. Lower	Age	Phase
	m s	m s	h m	h m	h m	d	
12	06 29	06 15	11 54	00 35	13 06	16	◯
13	06 01	05 47	11 54	01 38	14 09	17	
14	05 33	05 18	11 55	02 40	15 09	18	

S.D. 16.3	d 0.2	S.D. 16.6	16.5	16.2

G.M.T.	ARIES G.H.A.	VENUS −4.4 G.H.A.	Dec.	MARS +1.1 G.H.A.	Dec.	JUPITER −1.4 G.H.A.	Dec.	SATURN +1.0 G.H.A.	Dec.	STARS Name	S.H.A.	Dec.
15 00	83 33.7	137 01.0	S20 51.5	263 09.7 N 2	07.2	232 03.2 S11	33.5	243 52.8 S 5	45.9	Acamar	315 36.2	S40 22.9
01	98 36.2	152 02.1	50.9	278 11.1	06.8	247 05.2	33.6	258 55.1	45.9	Achernar	335 44.3	S57 20.1
02	113 38.6	167 03.2	50.2	293 12.4	06.3	262 07.3	33.8	273 57.4	46.0	Acrux	173 36.4	S62 59.5
03	128 41.1	182 04.3 ··	49.6	308 13.8 ··	05.9	277 09.3 ··	33.9	288 59.7 ··	46.0	Adhara	255 31.1	S28 56.8
04	143 43.6	197 05.4	48.9	323 15.2	05.5	292 11.4	34.1	304 02.0	46.1	Aldebaran	291 16.7	N16 28.4
05	158 46.0	212 06.6	48.3	338 16.5	05.0	307 13.4	34.2	319 04.2	46.2			
06	173 48.5	227 07.7	S20 47.6	353 17.9 N 2	04.6	322 15.4 S11	34.3	334 06.5 S 5	46.2	Alioth	166 41.9	N56 03.3
07	188 51.0	242 08.8	46.9	8 19.3	04.1	337 17.5	34.5	349 08.8	46.3	Alkaid	153 18.1	N49 24.1
T 08	203 53.4	257 09.9	46.3	23 20.6	03.7	352 19.5	34.6	4 11.1	46.4	Al Na'ir	28 14.0	S47 03.2
U 09	218 55.9	272 11.1 ··	45.6	38 22.0 ··	03.3	7 21.6 ··	34.8	19 13.4 ··	46.4	Alnilam	276 10.5	S 1 12.8
E 10	233 58.3	287 12.2	45.0	53 23.4	02.8	22 23.6	34.9	34 15.7	46.5	Alphard	218 19.5	S 8 34.7
S 11	249 00.8	302 13.4	44.3	68 24.7	02.4	37 25.7	35.1	49 17.9	46.5			
D 12	264 03.3	317 14.5	S20 43.7	83 26.1 N 2	01.9	52 27.7 S11	35.2	64 20.2 S 5	46.6	Alphecca	126 31.7	N26 46.5
A 13	279 05.7	332 15.6	43.0	98 27.5	01.5	67 29.8	35.3	79 22.5	46.7	Alpheratz	358 08.4	N28 59.5
Y 14	294 08.2	347 16.8	42.4	113 28.8	01.1	82 31.8	35.5	94 24.8	46.7	Altair	62 32.0	N 8 49.2
15	309 10.7	2 17.9 ··	41.7	128 30.2 ··	00.6	97 33.8 ··	35.6	109 27.1 ··	46.8	Ankaa	353 39.3	S42 24.6
16	324 13.1	17 19.1	41.1	143 31.6 2	00.2	112 35.9	35.8	124 29.4	46.9	Antares	112 56.2	S26 23.4
17	339 15.6	32 20.2	40.4	158 33.0 1	59.8	127 37.9	35.9	139 31.6	46.9			
18	354 18.1	47 21.4	S20 39.8	173 34.3 N 1	59.3	142 40.0 S11	36.1	154 33.9 S 5	47.0	Arcturus	146 17.9	N19 16.6
19	9 20.5	62 22.6	39.1	188 35.7	58.9	157 42.0	36.2	169 36.2	47.0	Atria	108 20.2	S68 59.6
20	24 23.0	77 23.7	38.5	203 37.1	58.4	172 44.1	36.3	184 38.5	47.1	Avior	234 27.3	S59 26.9
21	39 25.4	92 24.9 ··	37.8	218 38.4 ··	58.0	187 46.1 ··	36.5	199 40.8 ··	47.2	Bellatrix	278 57.5	N 6 20.0
22	54 27.9	107 26.1	37.2	233 39.8	57.6	202 48.2	36.6	214 43.1	47.2	Betelgeuse	271 27.0	N 7 24.2
23	69 30.4	122 27.3	36.5	248 41.2	57.1	217 50.2	36.8	229 45.3	47.3			
16 00	84 32.8	137 28.4	S20 35.9	263 42.5 N 1	56.7	232 52.3 S11	36.9	244 47.6 S 5	47.4	Canopus	264 06.3	S52 41.1
01	99 35.3	152 29.6	35.2	278 43.9	56.2	247 54.3	37.1	259 49.9	47.4	Capella	281 09.5	N45 58.8
02	114 37.8	167 30.8	34.6	293 45.3	55.8	262 56.3	37.2	274 52.2	47.5	Deneb	49 48.2	N45 13.1
03	129 40.2	182 32.0 ··	33.9	308 46.7 ··	55.4	277 58.4 ··	37.3	289 54.5 ··	47.5	Denebola	182 58.2	N14 40.4
04	144 42.7	197 33.2	33.2	323 48.0	54.9	293 00.4	37.5	304 56.8	47.6	Diphda	349 19.9	S18 05.3
05	159 45.2	212 34.4	32.6	338 49.4	54.5	308 02.5	37.6	319 59.1	47.7			
06	174 47.6	227 35.6	S20 31.9	353 50.8 N 1	54.1	323 04.5 S11	37.8	335 01.3 S 5	47.7	Dubhe	194 20.9	N61 50.7
W 07	189 50.1	242 36.8	31.3	8 52.2	53.6	338 06.6	37.9	350 03.6	47.8	Elnath	278 42.7	N28 35.5
E 08	204 52.6	257 38.0	30.6	23 53.5	53.2	353 08.6	38.0	5 05.9	47.8	Eltanin	90 57.9	N51 29.5
D 09	219 55.0	272 39.2 ··	30.0	38 54.9 ··	52.8	8 10.7 ··	38.2	20 08.2 ··	47.9	Enif	34 10.9	N 9 47.5
N 10	234 57.5	287 40.4	29.3	53 56.3	52.3	23 12.7	38.3	35 10.5	48.0	Fomalhaut	15 50.5	S29 43.3
E 11	249 59.9	302 41.6	28.7	68 57.7	51.9	38 14.8	38.5	50 12.8	48.0			
S 12	265 02.4	317 42.8	S20 28.0	83 59.0 N 1	51.4	53 16.8 S11	38.6	65 15.1 S 5	48.1	Gacrux	172 27.9	S57 00.3
D 13	280 04.9	332 44.0	27.4	99 00.4	51.0	68 18.9	38.7	80 17.3	48.2	Gienah	176 17.1	S17 26.3
A 14	295 07.3	347 45.2	26.7	114 01.8	50.6	83 20.9	38.9	95 19.6	48.2	Hadar	149 22.5	S60 16.8
Y 15	310 09.8	2 46.5 ··	26.0	129 03.2 ··	50.1	98 23.0 ··	39.0	110 21.9 ··	48.3	Hamal	328 27.7	N23 22.7
16	325 12.3	17 47.7	25.4	144 04.5	49.7	113 25.0	39.2	125 24.2	48.3	Kaus Aust.	84 16.1	S34 23.6
17	340 14.7	32 48.9	24.7	159 05.9	49.3	128 27.1	39.3	140 26.5	48.4			
18	355 17.2	47 50.2	S20 24.1	174 07.3 N 1	48.8	143 29.1 S11	39.5	155 28.8 S 5	48.5	Kochab	137 19.9	N74 13.7
19	10 19.7	62 51.4	23.4	189 08.7	48.4	158 31.2	39.6	170 31.1	48.5	Markab	14 02.4	N15 06.5
20	25 22.1	77 52.6	22.8	204 10.1	48.0	173 33.2	39.7	185 33.4	48.6	Menkar	314 40.0	N 4 01.1
21	40 24.6	92 53.9 ··	22.1	219 11.4 ··	47.5	188 35.3 ··	39.9	200 35.6 ··	48.6	Menkent	148 36.3	S36 16.6
22	55 27.1	107 55.1	21.5	234 12.8	47.1	203 37.3	40.0	215 37.9	48.7	Miaplacidus	221 44.2	S69 38.3
23	70 29.5	122 56.4	20.8	249 14.2	46.7	218 39.4	40.2	230 40.2	48.8			
17 00	85 32.0	137 57.6	S20 20.2	264 15.6 N 1	46.2	233 41.4 S11	40.3	245 42.5 S 5	48.8	Mirfak	309 14.4	N49 47.9
01	100 34.4	152 58.9	19.5	279 16.9	45.8	248 43.5	40.4	260 44.8	48.9	Nunki	76 28.5	S26 19.2
02	115 36.9	168 00.1	18.8	294 18.3	45.4	263 45.5	40.6	275 47.1	48.9	Peacock	53 57.5	S56 47.8
03	130 39.4	183 01.4 ··	18.2	309 19.7 ··	44.9	278 47.6 ··	40.7	290 49.4 ··	49.0	Pollux	243 56.8	N28 04.2
04	145 41.8	198 02.7	17.5	324 21.1	44.5	293 49.6	40.9	305 51.7	49.1	Procyon	245 24.6	N 5 16.3
05	160 44.3	213 03.9	16.9	339 22.5	44.1	308 51.7	41.0	320 53.9	49.1			
06	175 46.8	228 05.2	S20 16.2	354 23.9 N 1	43.6	323 53.7 S11	41.1	335 56.2 S 5	49.2	Rasalhague	96 29.1	N12 34.4
07	190 49.2	243 06.5	15.6	9 25.2	43.2	338 55.8	41.3	350 58.5	49.2	Regulus	208 09.0	N12 03.4
T 08	205 51.7	258 07.8	14.9	24 26.6	42.8	353 57.8	41.4	6 00.8	49.3	Rigel	281 34.8	S 8 13.4
H 09	220 54.2	273 09.0 ··	14.2	39 28.0 ··	42.3	8 59.9 ··	41.6	21 03.1 ··	49.4	Rigil Kent.	140 25.2	S60 45.3
U 10	235 56.6	288 10.3	13.6	54 29.4	41.9	24 01.9	41.7	36 05.4	49.4	Sabik	102 40.5	S15 42.1
R 11	250 59.1	303 11.6	12.9	69 30.8	41.5	39 04.0	41.8	51 07.7	49.5			
S 12	266 01.5	318 12.9	S20 12.3	84 32.1 N 1	41.0	54 06.0 S11	42.0	66 10.0 S 5	49.5	Schedar	350 07.9	N56 26.5
D 13	281 04.0	333 14.2	11.6	99 33.5	40.6	69 08.1	42.1	81 12.3	49.6	Shaula	96 55.0	S37 05.4
A 14	296 06.5	348 15.5	11.0	114 34.9	40.2	84 10.1	42.3	96 14.5	49.7	Sirius	258 54.6	S16 41.5
Y 15	311 08.9	3 16.8 ··	10.3	129 36.3 ··	39.7	99 12.2 ··	42.4	111 16.8 ··	49.7	Spica	158 56.8	S11 03.9
16	326 11.4	18 18.1	09.7	144 37.7	39.3	114 14.2	42.5	126 19.1	49.8	Suhail	223 09.9	S43 21.3
17	341 13.9	33 19.4	09.0	159 39.1	38.9	129 16.3	42.7	141 21.4	49.8			
18	356 16.3	48 20.7	S20 08.3	174 40.5 N 1	38.4	144 18.3 S11	42.8	156 23.7 S 5	49.9	Vega	80 55.7	N38 46.1
19	11 18.8	63 22.0	07.7	189 41.8	38.0	159 20.4	43.0	171 26.0	50.0	Zuben'ubi	137 32.4	S15 57.8
20	26 21.3	78 23.4	07.0	204 43.2	37.6	174 22.4	43.1	186 28.3	50.0		S.H.A.	Mer. Pass.
21	41 23.7	93 24.7 ··	06.4	219 44.6 ··	37.2	189 24.5 ··	43.2	201 30.6 ··	50.1		° ′	h m
22	56 26.2	108 26.0	05.7	234 46.0	36.7	204 26.5	43.4	216 32.9	50.1	Venus	52 55.6	14 49
23	71 28.7	123 27.3	05.1	249 47.4	36.3	219 28.6	43.5	231 35.2	50.2	Mars	179 09.7	6 25
Mer. Pass. 18 18.8		v 1.2 d 0.7		v 1.4 d 0.4		v 2.0 d 0.1		v 2.3 d 0.1		Jupiter	148 19.4	8 27
										Saturn	160 14.8	7 40

G.M.T.	SUN G.H.A.	SUN Dec.	MOON G.H.A.	v	MOON Dec.	d	H.P.
	° ′	° ′	° ′	′	° ′	′	′
15 00	181 15.9	S23 15.1	307 33.3	7.1	N18 39.4	7.2	59.1
01	196 15.6	15.2	321 59.4	7.1	18 32.2	7.4	59.1
02	211 15.3	15.4	336 25.5	7.3	18 24.8	7.4	59.0
03	226 15.0	·· 15.5	350 51.8	7.4	18 17.4	7.5	59.0
04	241 14.7	15.6	5 18.2	7.5	18 09.9	7.7	59.0
05	256 14.4	15.8	19 44.7	7.6	18 02.2	7.7	58.9
06	271 14.1	S23 15.9	34 11.3	7.7	N17 54.5	7.8	58.9
07	286 13.8	16.0	48 38.0	7.8	17 46.7	8.0	58.8
T 08	301 13.5	16.2	63 04.8	7.9	17 38.7	8.0	58.8
U 09	316 13.2	·· 16.3	77 31.7	8.1	17 30.7	8.1	58.8
E 10	331 12.9	16.4	91 58.8	8.1	17 22.6	8.2	58.7
S 11	346 12.6	16.5	106 25.9	8.2	17 14.4	8.3	58.7
D 12	1 12.3	S23 16.7	120 53.1	8.3	N17 06.1	8.4	58.6
A 13	16 12.0	16.8	135 20.4	8.5	16 57.7	8.5	58.6
Y 14	31 11.7	16.9	149 47.9	8.5	16 49.2	8.5	58.6
15	46 11.4	·· 17.0	164 15.4	8.7	16 40.7	8.7	58.5
16	61 11.1	17.2	178 43.1	8.7	16 32.0	8.7	58.5
17	76 10.8	17.3	193 10.8	8.9	16 23.3	8.8	58.4
18	91 10.5	S23 17.4	207 38.7	8.9	N16 14.5	8.9	58.4
19	106 10.2	17.5	222 06.6	9.1	16 05.6	8.9	58.3
20	121 09.9	17.6	236 34.7	9.1	15 56.7	9.1	58.3
21	136 09.6	·· 17.8	251 02.8	9.3	15 47.6	9.1	58.3
22	151 09.3	17.9	265 31.1	9.3	15 38.5	9.2	58.2
23	166 09.0	18.0	279 59.4	9.5	15 29.3	9.3	58.2
16 00	181 08.7	S23 18.1	294 27.9	9.6	N15 20.0	9.3	58.1
01	196 08.4	18.2	308 56.5	9.6	15 10.7	9.3	58.1
02	211 08.1	18.3	323 25.1	9.8	15 01.3	9.5	58.1
03	226 07.8	·· 18.5	337 53.9	9.9	14 51.8	9.5	58.0
04	241 07.5	18.6	352 22.8	9.9	14 42.3	9.6	58.0
05	256 07.2	18.7	6 51.7	10.1	14 32.7	9.7	57.9
06	271 06.9	S23 18.8	21 20.8	10.1	N14 23.0	9.8	57.9
W 07	286 06.5	18.9	35 49.9	10.3	14 13.2	9.8	57.9
E 08	301 06.2	19.0	50 19.2	10.3	14 03.4	9.8	57.8
D 09	316 05.9	·· 19.1	64 48.5	10.5	13 53.6	10.0	57.8
N 10	331 05.6	19.2	79 18.0	10.5	13 43.6	9.9	57.7
E 11	346 05.3	19.3	93 47.5	10.6	13 33.7	10.1	57.7
S 12	1 05.0	S23 19.4	108 17.1	10.8	N13 23.6	10.1	57.7
D 13	16 04.7	19.6	122 46.9	10.8	13 13.5	10.1	57.6
A 14	31 04.4	19.7	137 16.7	10.9	13 03.4	10.2	57.6
Y 15	46 04.1	·· 19.8	151 46.6	11.0	12 53.2	10.3	57.5
16	61 03.8	19.9	166 16.6	11.1	12 42.9	10.3	57.5
17	76 03.5	20.0	180 46.7	11.2	12 32.6	10.3	57.5
18	91 03.2	S23 20.1	195 16.9	11.2	N12 22.3	10.4	57.4
19	106 02.9	20.2	209 47.1	11.4	12 11.9	10.5	57.4
20	121 02.6	20.3	224 17.5	11.4	12 01.4	10.5	57.3
21	136 02.3	·· 20.4	238 47.9	11.6	11 50.9	10.5	57.3
22	151 02.0	20.5	253 18.5	11.6	11 40.4	10.6	57.3
23	166 01.7	20.6	267 49.1	11.7	11 29.8	10.6	57.2
17 00	181 01.4	S23 20.7	282 19.8	11.8	N11 19.2	10.7	57.2
01	196 01.1	20.8	296 50.6	11.8	11 08.5	10.7	57.1
02	211 00.8	20.9	311 21.4	12.0	10 57.8	10.7	57.1
03	226 00.5	·· 21.0	325 52.4	12.0	10 47.1	10.8	57.1
04	241 00.2	21.1	340 23.4	12.1	10 36.3	10.9	57.0
05	255 59.9	21.1	354 54.5	12.2	10 25.4	10.8	57.0
06	270 59.6	S23 21.2	9 25.7	12.3	N10 14.6	10.9	56.9
07	285 59.3	21.3	23 57.0	12.3	10 03.7	10.9	56.9
T 08	300 58.9	21.4	38 28.3	12.4	9 52.8	11.0	56.9
H 09	315 58.6	·· 21.5	52 59.7	12.5	9 41.8	11.0	56.8
U 10	330 58.3	21.6	67 31.2	12.6	9 30.8	11.0	56.8
R 11	345 58.0	21.7	82 02.8	12.6	9 19.8	11.1	56.8
S 12	0 57.7	S23 21.8	96 34.4	12.8	N 9 08.7	11.0	56.7
D 13	15 57.4	21.9	111 06.2	12.7	8 57.7	11.1	56.7
A 14	30 57.1	21.9	125 37.9	12.9	8 46.6	11.2	56.7
Y 15	45 56.8	·· 22.0	140 09.8	12.9	8 35.4	11.1	56.6
16	60 56.5	22.1	154 41.7	13.0	8 24.3	11.2	56.6
17	75 56.2	22.1	169 13.7	13.1	8 13.1	11.2	56.5
18	90 55.9	S23 22.3	183 45.8	13.1	N 8 01.9	11.3	56.5
19	105 55.6	22.4	198 17.9	13.2	7 50.6	11.2	56.5
20	120 55.3	22.4	212 50.1	13.3	7 39.4	11.3	56.4
21	135 55.0	·· 22.5	227 22.4	13.3	7 28.1	11.3	56.4
22	150 54.7	22.6	241 54.7	13.4	7 16.8	11.3	56.4
23	165 54.4	22.7	256 27.1	13.4	7 05.5	11.3	56.3
	S.D. 16.3 d 0.1		S.D. 16.0		15.7		15.5

Lat.	Twilight Naut.	Twilight Civil	Sunrise	Moonrise 15	16	17	18
°	h m	h m	h m	h m	h m	h m	h m
N 72	08 21	10 49	■	17 59	20 23	22 23	24 13
N 70	08 02	09 49	■	18 43	20 45	22 34	24 16
68	07 46	09 15	■	19 12	21 01	22 43	24 18
66	07 33	08 50	10 29	19 34	21 15	22 50	24 20
64	07 22	08 30	09 47	19 51	21 26	22 56	24 22
62	07 12	08 14	09 20	20 05	21 35	23 01	24 24
60	07 04	08 01	08 58	20 17	21 43	23 06	24 25
N 58	06 56	07 49	08 41	20 28	21 50	23 10	24 26
56	06 50	07 39	08 26	20 37	21 56	23 13	24 27
54	06 44	07 30	08 14	20 44	22 02	23 16	24 28
52	06 38	07 22	08 03	20 51	22 07	23 19	24 29
50	06 33	07 14	07 53	20 58	22 11	23 22	24 30
45	06 21	06 58	07 32	21 11	22 21	23 27	24 32
N 40	06 11	06 45	07 15	21 23	22 29	23 32	24 33
35	06 01	06 33	07 01	21 32	22 36	23 36	24 34
30	05 53	06 23	06 49	21 41	22 42	23 40	24 36
20	05 36	06 04	06 28	21 55	22 52	23 46	24 37
N 10	05 20	05 46	06 09	22 07	23 01	23 51	24 39
0	05 03	05 29	05 52	22 19	23 10	23 56	24 41
S 10	04 44	05 11	05 34	22 31	23 18	24 01	00 01
20	04 22	04 51	05 16	22 43	23 27	24 07	00 07
30	03 53	04 26	04 54	22 57	23 37	24 13	00 13
35	03 34	04 11	04 41	23 06	23 43	24 16	00 16
40	03 11	03 53	04 26	23 15	23 50	24 20	00 20
45	02 41	03 30	04 08	23 26	23 58	24 25	00 25
S 50	01 56	03 01	03 45	23 39	24 07	00 07	00 30
52	01 28	02 46	03 34	23 45	24 11	00 11	00 33
54	00 44	02 28	03 22	23 52	24 16	00 16	00 36
56	////	02 06	03 08	23 59	24 21	00 21	00 39
58	////	01 37	02 51	24 08	00 08	00 27	00 42
S 60	////	00 48	02 31	24 17	00 17	00 33	00 46

Lat.	Sunset	Twilight Civil	Twilight Naut.	Moonset 15	16	17	18
°	h m	h m	h m	h m	h m	h m	h m
N 72	■	13 02	15 30	14 28	13 51	13 30	13 13
N 70	■	14 02	15 50	13 43	13 27	13 17	13 07
68	■	14 37	16 05	13 12	13 09	13 06	13 03
66	13 22	15 02	16 18	12 50	12 55	12 57	12 59
64	14 04	15 21	16 29	12 31	12 43	12 50	12 55
62	14 32	15 37	16 39	12 17	12 32	12 43	12 52
60	14 53	15 51	16 47	12 04	12 23	12 38	12 49
N 58	15 10	16 02	16 55	11 53	12 16	12 33	12 47
56	15 25	16 12	17 01	11 43	12 09	12 28	12 45
54	15 38	16 21	17 08	11 35	12 02	12 24	12 43
52	15 49	16 30	17 13	11 27	11 57	12 21	12 41
50	15 59	16 37	17 19	11 21	11 52	12 17	12 40
45	16 19	16 53	17 30	11 06	11 41	12 10	12 36
N 40	16 36	17 06	17 41	10 54	11 32	12 04	12 33
35	16 50	17 18	17 50	10 43	11 24	11 59	12 31
30	17 02	17 29	17 59	10 34	11 17	11 54	12 29
20	17 24	17 48	18 15	10 16	11 05	11 46	12 25
N 10	17 42	18 05	18 31	10 04	10 54	11 39	12 21
0	17 59	18 22	18 48	09 51	10 44	11 32	12 18
S 10	18 17	18 40	19 07	09 38	10 34	11 26	12 15
20	18 36	19 00	19 30	09 24	10 23	11 18	12 11
30	18 58	19 25	19 59	09 08	10 10	11 10	12 07
35	19 11	19 40	20 17	08 58	10 03	11 05	12 04
40	19 26	19 59	20 40	08 47	09 55	10 59	12 02
45	19 44	20 21	21 11	08 34	09 45	10 53	11 59
S 50	20 06	20 51	21 56	08 18	09 33	10 45	11 55
52	20 17	21 06	22 24	08 11	09 27	10 42	11 53
54	20 29	21 24	23 09	08 03	09 21	10 38	11 51
56	20 43	21 46	////	07 54	09 14	10 33	11 49
58	21 00	22 15	////	07 43	09 07	10 28	11 47
S 60	21 21	23 05	////	07 31	08 58	10 23	11 44

Day	SUN Eqn. of Time 00h	SUN Eqn. of Time 12h	SUN Mer. Pass.	MOON Mer. Pass. Upper	MOON Mer. Pass. Lower	Age	Phase
	m s	m s	h m	h m	h m	d	
15	05 04	04 50	11 55	03 38	16 05	19	
16	04 35	04 21	11 56	04 32	16 57	20	
17	04 06	03 52	11 56	05 21	17 44	21	◑

1981 DECEMBER 18, 19, 20 (FRI., SAT., SUN.)

G.M.T.	ARIES G.H.A.	VENUS G.H.A.	Dec.	MARS G.H.A.	Dec.	JUPITER G.H.A.	Dec.	SATURN G.H.A.	Dec.	STARS Name	S.H.A.	Dec.
18 00	86 31.1	138 28.7	S20 04.4	264 48.8	N 1 35.9	234 30.6	S11 43.6	246 37.5	S 5 50.3	Acamar	315 36.2	S40 22.9
01	101 33.6	153 30.0	03.8	279 50.2	35.4	249 32.7	43.8	261 39.7	50.3	Achernar	335 44.3	S57 20.1
02	116 36.0	168 31.3	03.1	294 51.5	35.0	264 34.8	43.9	276 42.0	50.4	Acrux	173 36.4	S62 59.5
03	131 38.5	183 32.7	·· 02.4	309 52.9	·· 34.6	279 36.8	·· 44.1	291 44.3	·· 50.4	Adhara	255 31.1	S28 56.8
04	146 41.0	198 34.0	01.8	324 54.3	34.1	294 38.9	44.2	306 46.6	50.5	Aldebaran	291 16.7	N16 28.4
05	161 43.4	213 35.3	01.1	339 55.7	33.7	309 40.9	44.3	321 48.9	50.6			
06	176 45.9	228 36.7	S20 00.5	354 57.1	N 1 33.3	324 43.0	S11 44.5	336 51.2	S 5 50.6	Alioth	166 41.9	N56 03.3
07	191 48.4	243 38.0	19 59.8	9 58.5	32.9	339 45.0	44.6	351 53.5	50.7	Alkaid	153 18.1	N49 24.1
08	206 50.8	258 39.4	59.2	24 59.9	32.4	354 47.1	44.8	6 55.8	50.7	Al Na'ir	28 14.1	S47 03.2
F 09	221 53.3	273 40.8	·· 58.5	40 01.3	·· 32.0	9 49.1	·· 44.9	21 58.1	·· 50.8	Alnilam	276 10.4	S 1 12.8
R 10	236 55.8	288 42.1	57.8	55 02.7	31.6	24 51.2	45.0	37 00.4	50.9	Alphard	218 19.5	S 8 34.7
I 11	251 58.2	303 43.5	57.2	70 04.0	31.1	39 53.2	45.2	52 02.7	50.9			
D 12	267 00.7	318 44.9	S19 56.5	85 05.4	N 1 30.7	54 55.3	S11 45.3	67 05.0	S 5 51.0	Alphecca	126 31.7	N26 46.5
A 13	282 03.2	333 46.2	55.9	100 06.8	30.3	69 57.4	45.4	82 07.2	51.0	Alpheratz	358 08.4	N28 59.5
Y 14	297 05.6	348 47.6	55.2	115 08.2	29.9	84 59.4	45.6	97 09.5	51.1	Altair	62 32.0	N 8 49.2
15	312 08.1	3 49.0	·· 54.6	130 09.6	·· 29.4	100 01.5	·· 45.7	112 11.8	·· 51.1	Ankaa	353 39.3	S42 24.6
16	327 10.5	18 50.4	53.9	145 11.0	29.0	115 03.5	45.9	127 14.1	51.2	Antares	112 56.2	S26 23.4
17	342 13.0	33 51.7	53.2	160 12.4	28.6	130 05.6	46.0	142 16.4	51.3			
18	357 15.5	48 53.1	S19 52.6	175 13.8	N 1 28.1	145 07.6	S11 46.1	157 18.7	S 5 51.3	Arcturus	146 17.9	N19 16.6
19	12 17.9	63 54.5	51.9	190 15.2	27.7	160 09.7	46.3	172 21.0	51.4	Atria	108 20.2	S68 59.6
20	27 20.4	78 55.9	51.3	205 16.6	27.3	175 11.7	46.4	187 23.3	51.4	Avior	234 27.3	S59 26.9
21	42 22.9	93 57.3	·· 50.6	220 18.0	·· 26.9	190 13.8	·· 46.5	202 25.6	·· 51.5	Bellatrix	278 57.5	N 6 20.0
22	57 25.3	108 58.7	50.0	235 19.4	26.4	205 15.9	46.7	217 27.9	51.6	Betelgeuse	271 27.0	N 7 24.2
23	72 27.8	124 00.1	49.3	250 20.8	26.0	220 17.9	46.8	232 30.2	51.6			
19 00	87 30.3	139 01.5	S19 48.6	265 22.2	N 1 25.6	235 20.0	S11 47.0	247 32.5	S 5 51.7	Canopus	264 06.3	S52 41.1
01	102 32.7	154 03.0	48.0	280 23.5	25.2	250 22.0	47.1	262 34.8	51.7	Capella	281 09.5	N45 58.8
02	117 35.2	169 04.4	47.3	295 24.9	24.7	265 24.1	47.2	277 37.1	51.8	Deneb	49 48.2	N45 13.1
03	132 37.6	184 05.8	·· 46.7	310 26.3	·· 24.3	280 26.1	·· 47.4	292 39.4	·· 51.8	Denebola	182 58.2	N14 40.4
04	147 40.1	199 07.2	46.0	325 27.7	23.9	295 28.2	47.5	307 41.7	51.9	Diphda	349 19.9	S18 05.3
05	162 42.6	214 08.6	45.4	340 29.1	23.4	310 30.3	47.6	322 43.9	52.0			
06	177 45.0	229 10.1	S19 44.7	355 30.5	N 1 23.0	325 32.3	S11 47.8	337 46.2	S 5 52.0	Dubhe	194 20.9	N61 50.7
07	192 47.5	244 11.5	44.1	10 31.9	22.6	340 34.4	47.9	352 48.5	52.1	Elnath	278 42.7	N28 35.5
S 08	207 50.0	259 12.9	43.4	25 33.3	22.2	355 36.4	48.1	7 50.8	52.1	Eltanin	90 57.9	N51 29.5
A 09	222 52.4	274 14.4	·· 42.7	40 34.7	·· 21.7	10 38.5	·· 48.2	22 53.1	·· 52.2	Enif	34 10.9	N 9 47.5
T 10	237 54.9	289 15.8	42.1	55 36.1	21.3	25 40.5	48.3	37 55.4	52.2	Fomalhaut	15 50.5	S29 43.3
U 11	252 57.4	304 17.3	41.4	70 37.5	20.9	40 42.6	48.5	52 57.7	52.3			
R 12	267 59.8	319 18.7	S19 40.8	85 38.9	N 1 20.5	55 44.7	S11 48.6	68 00.0	S 5 52.4	Gacrux	172 27.9	S57 00.3
D 13	283 02.3	334 20.2	40.1	100 40.3	20.0	70 46.7	48.7	83 02.3	52.4	Gienah	176 17.1	S17 26.3
A 14	298 04.8	349 21.6	39.5	115 41.7	19.6	85 48.8	48.9	98 04.6	52.5	Hadar	149 22.5	S60 16.8
Y 15	313 07.2	4 23.1	·· 38.8	130 43.1	·· 19.2	100 50.8	·· 49.0	113 06.9	·· 52.5	Hamal	328 27.7	N23 22.7
16	328 09.7	19 24.5	38.1	145 44.5	18.8	115 52.9	49.1	128 09.2	52.6	Kaus Aust.	84 16.1	S34 23.6
17	343 12.1	34 26.0	37.5	160 45.9	18.3	130 55.0	49.3	143 11.5	52.6			
18	358 14.6	49 27.5	S19 36.8	175 47.3	N 1 17.9	145 57.0	S11 49.4	158 13.8	S 5 52.7	Kochab	137 19.9	N74 13.6
19	13 17.1	64 28.9	36.2	190 48.7	17.5	160 59.1	49.6	173 16.1	52.8	Markab	14 02.4	N15 06.5
20	28 19.5	79 30.4	35.5	205 50.1	17.1	176 01.1	49.7	188 18.4	52.8	Menkar	314 40.0	N 4 01.1
21	43 22.0	94 31.9	·· 34.9	220 51.5	·· 16.7	191 03.2	·· 49.8	203 20.7	·· 52.9	Menkent	148 36.2	S36 16.6
22	58 24.5	109 33.4	34.2	235 52.9	16.2	206 05.3	50.0	218 23.0	52.9	Miaplacidus	221 44.2	S69 38.3
23	73 26.9	124 34.9	33.6	250 54.3	15.8	221 07.3	50.1	233 25.3	53.0			
20 00	88 29.4	139 36.3	S19 32.9	265 55.7	N 1 15.4	236 09.4	S11 50.2	248 27.6	S 5 53.0	Mirfak	309 14.4	N49 47.9
01	103 31.9	154 37.8	32.2	280 57.1	15.0	251 11.4	50.4	263 29.9	53.1	Nunki	76 28.5	S26 19.2
02	118 34.3	169 39.3	31.6	295 58.5	14.5	266 13.5	50.5	278 32.2	53.1	Peacock	53 57.5	S56 47.8
03	133 36.8	184 40.8	·· 30.9	310 59.9	·· 14.1	281 15.6	·· 50.6	293 34.5	·· 53.2	Pollux	243 56.8	N28 04.2
04	148 39.3	199 42.3	30.3	326 01.3	13.7	296 17.6	50.8	308 36.8	53.3	Procyon	245 24.6	N 5 16.3
05	163 41.7	214 43.8	29.6	341 02.7	13.3	311 19.7	50.9	323 39.1	53.3			
06	178 44.2	229 45.4	S19 29.0	356 04.1	N 1 12.9	326 21.7	S11 51.0	338 41.4	S 5 53.4	Rasalhague	96 29.1	N12 34.4
07	193 46.6	244 46.9	28.3	11 05.5	12.4	341 23.8	51.2	353 43.7	53.4	Regulus	208 08.9	N12 03.4
08	208 49.1	259 48.4	27.7	26 07.0	12.0	356 25.9	51.3	8 46.0	53.5	Rigel	281 34.8	S 8 13.4
S 09	223 51.6	274 49.9	·· 27.0	41 08.4	·· 11.6	11 27.9	·· 51.4	23 48.3	·· 53.5	Rigil Kent.	140 25.2	S60 45.3
U 10	238 54.0	289 51.4	26.4	56 09.8	11.2	26 30.0	51.6	38 50.6	53.6	Sabik	102 40.5	S15 42.1
N 11	253 56.5	304 53.0	25.7	71 11.2	10.7	41 32.1	51.7	53 52.9	53.7			
D 12	268 59.0	319 54.5	S19 25.0	86 12.6	N 1 10.3	56 34.1	S11 51.9	68 55.2	S 5 53.7	Schedar	350 07.9	N56 26.5
A 13	284 01.4	334 56.0	24.4	101 14.0	09.9	71 36.2	52.0	83 57.5	53.8	Shaula	96 55.0	S37 05.4
Y 14	299 03.9	349 57.6	23.7	116 15.4	09.5	86 38.2	52.1	98 59.8	53.8	Sirius	258 54.6	S16 41.5
15	314 06.4	4 59.1	·· 23.1	131 16.8	·· 09.1	101 40.3	·· 52.3	114 02.1	·· 53.9	Spica	158 56.8	S11 03.9
16	329 08.8	20 00.7	22.4	146 18.2	08.6	116 42.4	52.4	129 04.4	53.9	Suhail	223 09.8	S43 21.3
17	344 11.3	35 02.2	21.8	161 19.6	08.2	131 44.4	52.5	144 06.7	54.0			
18	359 13.8	50 03.8	S19 21.1	176 21.0	N 1 07.8	146 46.5	S11 52.7	159 09.0	S 5 54.0	Vega	80 55.7	N38 46.1
19	14 16.2	65 05.3	20.5	191 22.4	07.4	161 48.6	52.8	174 11.3	54.1	Zuben'ubi	137 32.3	S15 57.9
20	29 18.7	80 06.9	19.8	206 23.8	07.0	176 50.6	52.9	189 13.6	54.2			
21	44 21.1	95 08.4	·· 19.2	221 25.3	·· 06.5	191 52.7	·· 53.1	204 15.9	·· 54.2			
22	59 23.6	110 10.0	18.5	236 26.7	06.1	206 54.7	53.2	219 18.2	54.3			
23	74 26.1	125 11.6	17.8	251 28.1	05.7	221 56.8	53.3	234 20.5	54.3			
Mer. Pass. 18 07.0		v 1.5	d 0.7	v 1.4	d 0.4	v 2.1	d 0.1	v -2.3	d 0.1			

Name	S.H.A.	Mer. Pass.
Venus	51 31.3	14 42
Mars	177 51.9	6 18
Jupiter	147 49.7	8 18
Saturn	160 02.2	7 29

G.M.T.	SUN G.H.A.	Dec.	MOON G.H.A.	v	Dec.	d	H.P.
18 00	180 54.1	S23 22.8	270 59.5	13.5	N 6 54.2	11.4	56.3
01	195 53.7	22.8	285 32.0	13.6	6 42.8	11.4	56.3
02	210 53.4	22.9	300 04.6	13.6	6 31.4	11.3	56.2
03	225 53.1	·· 23.0	314 37.2	13.7	6 20.1	11.4	56.2
04	240 52.8	23.1	329 09.9	13.8	6 08.7	11.4	56.2
05	255 52.5	23.1	343 42.7	13.8	5 57.3	11.5	56.1
06	270 52.2	S23 23.2	358 15.5	13.8	N 5 45.8	11.4	56.1
07	285 51.9	23.3	12 48.3	13.9	5 34.4	11.4	56.1
08	300 51.6	23.4	27 21.2	14.0	5 23.0	11.5	56.0
F 09	315 51.3	·· 23.4	41 54.2	14.0	5 11.5	11.5	56.0
R 10	330 51.0	23.5	56 27.2	14.1	5 00.0	11.5	56.0
I 11	345 50.7	23.6	71 00.3	14.1	4 48.6	11.5	55.9
D 12	0 50.4	S23 23.6	85 33.4	14.1	N 4 37.1	11.5	55.9
A 13	15 50.1	23.7	100 06.5	14.2	4 25.6	11.5	55.9
Y 14	30 49.7	23.8	114 39.7	14.3	4 14.1	11.5	55.8
15	45 49.4	·· 23.8	129 13.0	14.3	4 02.6	11.5	55.8
16	60 49.1	23.9	143 46.3	14.3	3 51.1	11.5	55.8
17	75 48.8	24.0	158 19.6	14.4	3 39.6	11.5	55.7
18	90 48.5	S23 24.0	172 53.0	14.4	N 3 28.1	11.6	55.7
19	105 48.2	24.1	187 26.4	14.5	3 16.5	11.5	55.7
20	120 47.9	24.1	201 59.9	14.5	3 05.0	11.5	55.7
21	135 47.6	·· 24.2	216 33.4	14.6	2 53.5	11.5	55.6
22	150 47.3	24.3	231 07.0	14.6	2 42.0	11.5	55.6
23	165 47.0	24.3	245 40.6	14.6	2 30.5	11.6	55.6
19 00	180 46.7	S23 24.4	260 14.2	14.6	N 2 18.9	11.5	55.5
01	195 46.4	24.5	274 47.8	14.7	2 07.4	11.5	55.5
02	210 46.1	24.5	289 21.5	14.8	1 55.9	11.5	55.5
03	225 45.7	·· 24.5	303 55.3	14.7	1 44.4	11.5	55.5
04	240 45.4	24.6	318 29.0	14.8	1 32.9	11.5	55.4
05	255 45.1	24.7	333 02.8	14.9	1 21.4	11.5	55.4
06	270 44.8	S23 24.7	347 36.7	14.8	N 1 09.9	11.5	55.4
07	285 44.5	24.8	2 10.5	14.9	0 58.4	11.5	55.4
S 08	300 44.2	24.8	16 44.4	14.9	0 46.9	11.5	55.3
A 09	315 43.9	·· 24.9	31 18.3	15.0	0 35.4	11.5	55.3
T 10	330 43.6	24.9	45 52.3	15.0	0 23.9	11.4	55.3
U 11	345 43.3	25.0	60 26.3	15.0	0 12.5	11.5	55.2
R 12	0 43.0	S23 25.0	75 00.3	15.0	N 0 01.0	11.5	55.2
D 13	15 42.7	25.1	89 34.3	15.0	S 0 10.4	11.5	55.2
A 14	30 42.3	25.1	104 08.3	15.1	0 21.9	11.4	55.2
Y 15	45 42.0	·· 25.2	118 42.4	15.1	0 33.3	11.4	55.1
16	60 41.7	25.2	133 16.5	15.1	0 44.7	11.4	55.1
17	75 41.4	25.2	147 50.6	15.2	0 56.1	11.4	55.1
18	90 41.1	S23 25.3	162 24.8	15.1	S 1 07.5	11.3	55.1
19	105 40.8	25.3	176 58.9	15.2	1 18.8	11.4	55.1
20	120 40.5	25.4	191 33.1	15.2	1 30.2	11.4	55.0
21	135 40.2	·· 25.4	206 07.3	15.2	1 41.5	11.4	55.0
22	150 39.9	25.5	220 41.5	15.2	1 52.9	11.3	55.0
23	165 39.6	25.5	235 15.7	15.2	2 04.2	11.3	55.0
20 00	180 39.2	S23 25.5	249 49.9	15.3	S 2 15.5	11.2	54.9
01	195 38.9	25.6	264 24.2	15.3	2 26.7	11.3	54.9
02	210 38.6	25.6	278 58.5	15.2	2 38.0	11.2	54.9
03	225 38.3	·· 25.6	293 32.7	15.3	2 49.2	11.3	54.9
04	240 38.0	25.7	308 07.0	15.3	3 00.5	11.2	54.8
05	255 37.7	25.7	322 41.3	15.3	3 11.7	11.1	54.8
06	270 37.4	S23 25.8	337 15.6	15.3	S 3 22.8	11.2	54.8
07	285 37.1	25.8	351 49.9	15.4	3 34.0	11.2	54.8
08	300 36.8	25.8	6 24.3	15.3	3 45.1	11.2	54.8
S 09	315 36.5	·· 25.8	20 58.6	15.3	3 56.3	11.0	54.7
U 10	330 36.1	25.9	35 32.9	15.4	4 07.3	11.1	54.7
N 11	345 35.8	25.9	50 07.3	15.3	4 18.4	11.1	54.7
D 12	0 35.5	S23 25.9	64 41.6	15.3	S 4 29.5	11.0	54.7
A 13	15 35.2	26.0	79 15.9	15.4	4 40.5	11.0	54.7
Y 14	30 34.9	26.0	93 50.3	15.3	4 51.5	10.9	54.7
15	45 34.6	·· 26.0	108 24.6	15.4	5 02.4	11.0	54.6
16	60 34.3	26.0	122 59.0	15.3	5 13.4	10.9	54.6
17	75 34.0	26.1	137 33.3	15.4	5 24.3	10.9	54.6
18	90 33.7	S23 26.1	152 07.7	15.3	S 5 35.2	10.8	54.6
19	105 33.4	26.1	166 42.0	15.4	5 46.0	10.9	54.6
20	120 33.0	26.1	181 16.4	15.3	5 56.9	10.8	54.5
21	135 32.7	·· 26.2	195 50.7	15.4	6 07.7	10.7	54.5
22	150 32.4	26.2	210 25.1	15.3	6 18.4	10.8	54.5
23	165 32.1	26.2	224 59.4	15.3	6 29.2	10.7	54.5
S.D. 16.3	d 0.0		S.D. 15.2		15.0		14.9

Lat.	Twilight Naut.	Twilight Civil	Sunrise	Moonrise 18	19	20	21
°	h m	h m	h m	h m	h m	h m	h m
N 72	08 24	10 56	■	24 13	00 13	01 58	03 43
N 70	08 04	09 53	■	24 16	00 16	01 54	03 31
68	07 48	09 18	■	24 18	00 18	01 51	03 22
66	07 35	08 52	10 33	24 20	00 20	01 48	03 15
64	07 24	08 33	09 51	24 22	00 22	01 46	03 08
62	07 15	08 17	09 22	24 24	00 24	01 44	03 03
60	07 06	08 03	09 01	24 25	00 25	01 42	02 58
N 58	06 59	07 51	08 43	24 26	00 26	01 41	02 54
56	06 52	07 41	08 28	24 27	00 27	01 39	02 50
54	06 46	07 32	08 16	24 28	00 28	01 38	02 47
52	06 40	07 24	08 05	24 29	00 29	01 37	02 44
50	06 35	07 16	07 55	24 30	00 30	01 36	02 41
45	06 23	07 00	07 34	24 32	00 32	01 34	02 35
N 40	06 13	06 47	07 17	24 33	00 33	01 32	02 31
35	06 03	06 35	07 03	24 34	00 34	01 31	02 26
30	05 54	06 24	06 51	24 36	00 36	01 30	02 23
20	05 38	06 05	06 29	24 37	00 37	01 27	02 16
N 10	05 22	05 48	06 11	24 39	00 39	01 25	02 11
0	05 05	05 31	05 53	24 41	00 41	01 23	02 06
S 10	04 46	05 13	05 36	00 01	00 42	01 22	02 01
20	04 23	04 52	05 17	00 07	00 44	01 20	01 55
30	03 54	04 27	04 55	00 13	00 46	01 18	01 49
35	03 35	04 12	04 42	00 17	00 47	01 16	01 46
40	03 12	03 54	04 27	00 20	00 48	01 15	01 42
45	02 41	03 31	04 09	00 25	00 50	01 13	01 37
S 50	01 56	03 01	03 46	00 30	00 51	01 11	01 32
52	01 28	02 46	03 35	00 33	00 52	01 11	01 29
54	00 41	02 28	03 23	00 36	00 53	01 10	01 26
56	////	02 06	03 09	00 39	00 54	01 09	01 23
58	////	01 36	02 52	00 42	00 55	01 08	01 20
S 60	////	00 46	02 31	00 46	00 56	01 06	01 16

Lat.	Sunset	Twilight Civil	Twilight Naut.	Moonset 18	19	20	21
°	h m	h m	h m	h m	h m	h m	h m
N 72	■	12 59	15 30	13 13	12 58	12 44	12 27
N 70	■	14 01	15 50	13 07	12 59	12 50	12 41
68	■	14 36	16 06	13 03	12 59	12 55	12 51
66	13 21	15 02	16 19	12 59	12 59	13 00	13 00
64	14 04	15 22	16 30	12 55	12 59	13 03	13 08
62	14 32	15 38	16 40	12 52	13 00	13 07	13 15
60	14 53	15 51	16 48	12 49	13 00	13 10	13 20
N 58	15 11	16 03	16 56	12 47	13 00	13 12	13 25
56	15 26	16 13	17 02	12 45	13 00	13 15	13 30
54	15 38	16 22	17 09	12 43	13 00	13 17	13 34
52	15 50	16 31	17 14	12 41	13 00	13 19	13 38
50	15 59	16 38	17 20	12 40	13 00	13 20	13 41
45	16 20	16 54	17 31	12 36	13 00	13 24	13 48
N 40	16 37	17 08	17 42	12 33	13 01	13 27	13 54
35	16 51	17 19	17 51	12 31	13 01	13 30	14 00
30	17 04	17 30	18 00	12 29	13 01	13 32	14 04
20	17 25	17 49	18 16	12 25	13 01	13 37	14 12
N 10	17 43	18 06	18 33	12 21	13 01	13 40	14 19
0	18 01	18 23	18 50	12 18	13 01	13 44	14 26
S 10	18 18	18 42	19 09	12 15	13 01	13 47	14 33
20	18 37	19 02	19 31	12 11	13 02	13 51	14 40
30	19 00	19 27	20 00	12 07	13 02	13 55	14 48
35	19 13	19 42	20 19	12 04	13 02	13 58	14 53
40	19 28	20 01	20 42	12 02	13 02	14 01	14 58
45	19 46	20 23	21 13	11 59	13 02	14 04	15 05
S 50	20 08	20 53	21 59	11 55	13 02	14 08	15 12
52	20 19	21 08	22 27	11 53	13 02	14 09	15 16
54	20 32	21 26	23 14	11 51	13 02	14 11	15 20
56	20 46	21 48	////	11 49	13 02	14 14	15 24
58	21 03	22 18	////	11 47	13 02	14 16	15 29
S 60	21 23	22 59	////	11 44	13 02	14 19	15 34

Day	SUN Eqn. of Time 00h	Eqn. of Time 12h	Mer. Pass.	MOON Mer. Pass. Upper	Mer. Pass. Lower	Age	Phase
	m s	m s	h m	h m	h m	d	
18	03 37	03 22	11 57	06 07	18 29	22	
19	03 07	02 52	11 57	06 51	19 12	23	◑
20	02 38	02 23	11 58	07 34	19 55	24	

G.M.T.	ARIES G.H.A.	VENUS −4.4 G.H.A.	Dec.	MARS +1.0 G.H.A.	Dec.	JUPITER −1.4 G.H.A.	Dec.	SATURN +1.0 G.H.A.	Dec.	STAR Name	S.H.A.	Dec.
21 00	89 28.5	140 13.1	S19 17.2	266 29.5	N 1 05.3	236 58.9	S11 53.5	249 22.8	S 5 54.4	Acamar	315 36.3	S40 22.9
01	104 31.0	155 14.7	16.5	281 30.9	04.9	252 00.9	53.6	264 25.1	54.4	Achernar	335 44.3	S57 20.1
02	119 33.5	170 16.3	15.9	296 32.3	04.4	267 03.0	53.7	279 27.4	54.5	Acrux	173 36.4	S62 59.5
03	134 35.9	185 17.9	·· 15.2	311 33.7	·· 04.0	282 05.1	·· 53.9	294 29.7	·· 54.5	Adhara	255 31.1	S28 56.8
04	149 38.4	200 19.5	14.6	326 35.1	03.6	297 07.1	54.0	309 32.0	54.6	Aldebaran	291 16.7	N16 28.4
05	164 40.9	215 21.1	13.9	341 36.5	03.2	312 09.2	54.1	324 34.3	54.6			
06	179 43.3	230 22.6	S19 13.3	356 38.0	N 1 02.8	327 11.3	S11 54.3	339 36.6	S 5 54.7	Alioth	166 41.9	N56 03.3
07	194 45.8	245 24.2	12.6	11 39.4	02.4	342 13.3	54.4	354 38.9	54.8	Alkaid	153 18.0	N49 24.1
08	209 48.2	260 25.8	12.0	26 40.8	01.9	357 15.4	54.5	9 41.2	54.8	Al Na'ir	28 14.1	S47 03.2
M 09	224 50.7	275 27.5	·· 11.3	41 42.2	·· 01.5	12 17.5	·· 54.7	24 43.5	·· 54.9	Alnilam	276 10.4	S 1 12.8
O 10	239 53.2	290 29.1	10.7	56 43.6	01.1	27 19.5	54.8	39 45.8	54.9	Alphard	218 19.5	S 8 34.7
N 11	254 55.6	305 30.7	10.0	71 45.0	00.7	42 21.6	54.9	54 48.1	55.0			
D 12	269 58.1	320 32.3	S19 09.4	86 46.4	N 1 00.3	57 23.7	S11 55.1	69 50.4	S 5 55.0	Alphecca	126 31.7	N26 46.5
A 13	285 00.6	335 33.9	08.7	101 47.9	0 59.8	72 25.7	55.2	84 52.7	55.1	Alpheratz	358 08.4	N28 59.5
Y 14	300 03.0	350 35.5	08.1	116 49.3	59.4	87 27.8	55.3	99 55.0	55.1	Altair	62 32.0	N 8 49.2
15	315 05.5	5 37.2	·· 07.4	131 50.7	·· 59.0	102 29.9	·· 55.5	114 57.3	·· 55.2	Ankaa	353 39.3	S42 24.6
16	330 08.0	20 38.8	06.8	146 52.1	58.6	117 31.9	55.6	129 59.6	55.2	Antares	112 56.1	S26 23.4
17	345 10.4	35 40.4	06.1	161 53.5	58.2	132 34.0	55.7	145 01.9	55.3			
18	0 12.9	50 42.1	S19 05.4	176 54.9	N 0 57.8	147 36.1	S11 55.9	160 04.2	S 5 55.4	Arcturus	146 17.9	N19 16.6
19	15 15.4	65 43.7	04.8	191 56.3	57.4	162 38.1	56.0	175 06.5	55.4	Atria	108 20.2	S68 59.6
20	30 17.8	80 45.3	04.1	206 57.8	56.9	177 40.2	56.1	190 08.8	55.5	Avior	234 27.3	S59 26.9
21	45 20.3	95 47.0	·· 03.5	221 59.2	·· 56.5	192 42.3	·· 56.3	205 11.1	·· 55.5	Bellatrix	278 57.5	N 6 20.0
22	60 22.7	110 48.6	02.8	237 00.6	56.1	207 44.3	56.4	220 13.4	55.6	Betelgeuse	271 27.0	N 7 24.2
23	75 25.2	125 50.3	02.2	252 02.0	55.7	222 46.4	56.5	235 15.7	55.6			
22 00	90 27.7	140 52.0	S19 01.5	267 03.4	N 0 55.3	237 48.5	S11 56.7	250 18.0	S 5 55.7	Canopus	264 06.3	S52 41.2
01	105 30.1	155 53.6	00.9	282 04.9	54.9	252 50.5	56.8	265 20.3	55.7	Capella	281 09.5	N45 58.8
02	120 32.6	170 55.3	19 00.2	297 06.3	54.4	267 52.6	56.9	280 22.6	55.8	Deneb	49 48.3	N45 13.1
03	135 35.1	185 57.0	18 59.6	312 07.7	·· 54.0	282 54.7	·· 57.0	295 24.9	·· 55.8	Denebola	182 58.1	N14 40.4
04	150 37.5	200 58.6	58.9	327 09.1	53.6	297 56.7	57.2	310 27.2	55.9	Diphda	349 19.9	S18 05.3
05	165 40.0	216 00.3	58.3	342 10.5	53.2	312 58.8	57.3	325 29.5	55.9			
06	180 42.5	231 02.0	S18 57.6	357 12.0	N 0 52.8	328 00.9	S11 57.4	340 31.8	S 5 56.0	Dubhe	194 20.9	N61 50.7
07	195 44.9	246 03.7	57.0	12 13.4	52.4	343 02.9	57.6	355 34.1	56.0	Elnath	278 42.7	N28 35.5
08	210 47.4	261 05.4	56.3	27 14.8	52.0	358 05.0	57.7	10 36.4	56.1	Eltanin	90 57.9	N51 29.5
T 09	225 49.9	276 07.1	·· 55.7	42 16.2	·· 51.5	13 07.1	·· 57.8	25 38.7	·· 56.2	Enif	34 10.9	N 9 47.5
U 10	240 52.3	291 08.7	55.0	57 17.6	51.1	28 09.2	58.0	40 41.1	56.2	Fomalhaut	15 50.6	S29 43.3
E 11	255 54.8	306 10.4	54.4	72 19.1	50.7	43 11.2	58.1	55 43.4	56.3			
S 12	270 57.2	321 12.1	S18 53.7	87 20.5	N 0 50.3	58 13.3	S11 58.2	70 45.7	S 5 56.3	Gacrux	172 27.9	S57 00.3
D 13	285 59.7	336 13.9	53.1	102 21.9	49.9	73 15.4	58.4	85 48.0	56.4	Gienah	176 17.1	S17 26.3
A 14	301 02.2	351 15.6	52.5	117 23.3	49.5	88 17.4	58.5	100 50.3	56.4	Hadar	149 22.5	S60 16.8
Y 15	316 04.6	6 17.3	·· 51.8	132 24.8	·· 49.1	103 19.5	·· 58.6	115 52.6	·· 56.5	Hamal	328 27.8	N23 22.7
16	331 07.1	21 19.0	51.2	147 26.2	48.7	118 21.6	58.8	130 54.9	56.5	Kaus Aust.	84 16.1	S34 23.6
17	346 09.6	36 20.7	50.5	162 27.6	48.2	133 23.6	58.9	145 57.2	56.6			
18	1 12.0	51 22.4	S18 49.9	177 29.0	N 0 47.8	148 25.7	S11 59.0	160 59.5	S 5 56.6	Kochab	137 19.9	N74 13.6
19	16 14.5	66 24.2	49.2	192 30.5	47.4	163 27.8	59.1	176 01.8	56.7	Markab	14 02.4	N15 06.5
20	31 17.0	81 25.9	48.6	207 31.9	47.0	178 29.9	59.3	191 04.1	56.7	Menkar	314 40.0	N 4 01.1
21	46 19.4	96 27.6	·· 47.9	222 33.3	·· 46.6	193 31.9	·· 59.4	206 06.4	·· 56.8	Menkent	148 36.2	S36 16.6
22	61 21.9	111 29.4	47.3	237 34.7	46.2	208 34.0	59.5	221 08.7	56.8	Miaplacidus	221 44.1	S69 38.3
23	76 24.3	126 31.1	46.6	252 36.2	45.8	223 36.1	59.7	236 11.0	56.9			
23 00	91 26.8	141 32.9	S18 46.0	267 37.6	N 0 45.4	238 38.1	S11 59.8	251 13.3	S 5 56.9	Mirfak	309 14.5	N49 47.9
01	106 29.3	156 34.6	45.3	282 39.0	45.0	253 40.2	11 59.9	266 15.7	57.0	Nunki	76 28.5	S26 19.2
02	121 31.7	171 36.4	44.7	297 40.5	44.5	268 42.3	12 00.1	281 18.0	57.0	Peacock	53 57.5	S56 47.8
03	136 34.2	186 38.1	·· 44.0	312 41.9	·· 44.1	283 44.4	·· 00.2	296 20.3	·· 57.1	Pollux	243 56.8	N28 04.2
04	151 36.7	201 39.9	43.4	327 43.3	43.7	298 46.4	00.3	311 22.6	57.1	Procyon	245 24.6	N 5 16.3
05	166 39.1	216 41.7	42.7	342 44.7	43.3	313 48.5	00.5	326 24.9	57.2			
06	181 41.6	231 43.4	S18 42.1	357 46.2	N 0 42.9	328 50.6	S12 00.6	341 27.2	S 5 57.3	Rasalhague	96 29.1	N12 34.4
07	196 44.1	246 45.2	41.5	12 47.6	42.5	343 52.6	00.7	356 29.5	57.3	Regulus	208 08.9	N12 03.3
08	211 46.5	261 47.0	40.8	27 49.0	42.1	358 54.7	00.8	11 31.8	57.4	Rigel	281 34.8	S 8 13.4
W 09	226 49.0	276 48.8	·· 40.2	42 50.5	·· 41.7	13 56.8	·· 01.0	26 34.1	·· 57.4	Rigil Kent.	140 25.1	S60 45.3
E 10	241 51.5	291 50.5	39.5	57 51.9	41.3	28 58.9	01.1	41 36.4	57.5	Sabik	102 40.5	S15 42.1
D 11	256 53.9	306 52.3	38.9	72 53.3	40.9	44 00.9	01.2	56 38.7	57.5			
N 12	271 56.4	321 54.1	S18 38.2	87 54.8	N 0 40.4	59 03.0	S12 01.4	71 41.0	S 5 57.6	Schedar	350 07.9	N56 26.5
E 13	286 58.8	336 55.9	37.6	102 56.2	40.0	74 05.1	01.5	86 43.4	57.6	Shaula	96 55.0	S37 05.4
S 14	302 01.3	351 57.7	36.9	117 57.6	39.6	89 07.2	01.6	101 45.7	57.7	Sirius	258 54.6	S16 41.5
D 15	317 03.8	6 59.5	·· 36.3	132 59.1	·· 39.2	104 09.2	·· 01.7	116 48.0	·· 57.7	Spica	158 56.8	S11 03.9
A 16	332 06.2	22 01.3	35.7	148 00.5	38.8	119 11.3	01.9	131 50.3	57.8	Suhail	223 09.8	S43 21.4
Y 17	347 08.7	37 03.1	35.0	163 01.9	38.4	134 13.4	02.0	146 52.6	57.8			
18	2 11.2	52 05.0	S18 34.4	178 03.4	N 0 38.0	149 15.5	S12 02.1	161 54.9	S 5 57.9	Vega	80 55.7	N38 46.1
19	17 13.6	67 06.8	33.7	193 04.8	37.6	164 17.5	02.3	176 57.2	57.9	Zuben'ubi	137 32.3	S15 57.9
20	32 16.1	82 08.6	33.1	208 06.2	37.2	179 19.6	02.4	191 59.5	58.0		S.H.A.	Mer. Pass.
21	47 18.6	97 10.4	·· 32.4	223 07.7	·· 36.8	194 21.7	·· 02.5	207 01.8	·· 58.0	Venus	50 24.3	14 35
22	62 21.0	112 12.3	31.8	238 09.1	36.4	209 23.8	02.7	222 04.1	58.1	Mars	176 35.8	6 11
23	77 23.5	127 14.1	31.2	253 10.5	36.0	224 25.8	02.8	237 06.4	58.1	Jupiter	147 20.8	8 08
Mer. Pass.	17 55.2	v 1.7	d 0.6	v 1.4	d 0.4	v 2.1	d 0.1	v 2.3	d 0.1	Saturn	159 50.3	7 18

G.M.T.	SUN G.H.A.	SUN Dec.	MOON G.H.A.	v	MOON Dec.	d	H.P.
21 00	180 31.8	S23 26.2	239 33.7	15.4	S 6 39.9	10.7	54.5
01	195 31.5	26.2	254 08.1	15.3	6 50.6	10.6	54.5
02	210 31.2	26.2	268 42.4	15.3	7 01.2	10.6	54.5
03	225 30.9	·· 26.3	283 16.7	15.3	7 11.8	10.6	54.4
04	240 30.6	26.3	297 51.0	15.3	7 22.4	10.5	54.4
05	255 30.2	26.3	312 25.3	15.2	7 32.9	10.6	54.4
06	270 29.9	S23 26.3	326 59.5	15.3	S 7 43.5	10.4	54.4
07	285 29.6	26.3	341 33.8	15.3	7 53.9	10.5	54.4
08	300 29.3	26.3	356 08.1	15.2	8 04.4	10.4	54.4
M 09	315 29.0	·· 26.3	10 42.3	15.2	8 14.8	10.3	54.4
O 10	330 28.7	26.4	25 16.5	15.3	8 25.1	10.4	54.3
N 11	345 28.4	26.4	39 50.8	15.2	8 35.5	10.2	54.3
D 12	0 28.1	S23 26.4	54 25.0	15.1	S 8 45.7	10.3	54.3
A 13	15 27.8	26.4	68 59.1	15.2	8 56.0	10.2	54.3
Y 14	30 27.4	26.4	83 33.3	15.2	9 06.2	10.2	54.3
15	45 27.1	·· 26.4	98 07.5	15.1	9 16.4	10.1	54.3
16	60 26.8	26.4	112 41.6	15.1	9 26.5	10.1	54.3
17	75 26.5	26.4	127 15.7	15.1	9 36.6	10.0	54.3
18	90 26.2	S23 26.4	141 49.8	15.1	S 9 46.6	10.1	54.2
19	105 25.9	26.4	156 23.9	15.1	9 56.7	9.9	54.2
20	120 25.6	26.4	170 58.0	15.0	10 06.6	9.9	54.2
21	135 25.3	·· 26.4	185 32.0	15.0	10 16.5	9.9	54.2
22	150 25.0	26.4	200 06.0	15.0	10 26.4	9.8	54.2
23	165 24.6	26.4	214 40.0	15.0	10 36.2	9.8	54.2
22 00	180 24.3	S23 26.4	229 14.0	14.9	S10 46.0	9.8	54.2
01	195 24.0	26.4	243 47.9	15.0	10 55.8	9.7	54.2
02	210 23.7	26.4	258 21.9	14.9	11 05.5	9.6	54.2
03	225 23.4	·· 26.4	272 55.8	14.9	11 15.1	9.6	54.2
04	240 23.1	26.4	287 29.7	14.8	11 24.7	9.5	54.1
05	255 22.8	26.4	302 03.5	14.8	11 34.2	9.5	54.1
06	270 22.5	S23 26.4	316 37.3	14.8	S11 43.7	9.5	54.1
07	285 22.1	26.4	331 11.1	14.8	11 53.2	9.4	54.1
08	300 21.8	26.4	345 44.9	14.7	12 02.6	9.4	54.1
T 09	315 21.5	·· 26.4	0 18.6	14.8	12 12.0	9.3	54.1
U 10	330 21.2	26.4	14 52.4	14.7	12 21.3	9.2	54.1
E 11	345 20.9	26.4	29 26.1	14.6	12 30.5	9.2	54.1
S 12	0 20.6	S23 26.4	43 59.7	14.6	S12 39.7	9.1	54.1
D 13	15 20.3	26.3	58 33.3	14.6	12 48.8	9.1	54.1
A 14	30 20.0	26.3	73 06.9	14.6	12 57.9	9.1	54.1
Y 15	45 19.7	·· 26.3	87 40.5	14.5	13 07.0	8.9	54.1
16	60 19.3	26.3	102 14.0	14.6	13 15.9	9.0	54.0
17	75 19.0	26.3	116 47.6	14.4	13 24.9	8.8	54.0
18	90 18.7	S23 26.3	131 21.0	14.5	S13 33.7	8.8	54.0
19	105 18.4	26.3	145 54.5	14.4	13 42.5	8.8	54.0
20	120 18.1	26.2	160 27.9	14.3	13 51.3	8.7	54.0
21	135 17.8	·· 26.2	175 01.2	14.4	14 00.0	8.6	54.0
22	150 17.5	26.2	189 34.6	14.3	14 08.6	8.6	54.0
23	165 17.2	26.2	204 07.9	14.3	14 17.2	8.5	54.0
23 00	180 16.8	S23 26.2	218 41.2	14.2	S14 25.7	8.5	54.0
01	195 16.5	26.1	233 14.4	14.2	14 34.2	8.4	54.0
02	210 16.2	26.1	247 47.6	14.2	14 42.6	8.3	54.0
03	225 15.9	·· 26.1	262 20.8	14.1	14 50.9	8.3	54.0
04	240 15.6	26.1	276 53.9	14.1	14 59.2	8.2	54.0
05	255 15.3	26.1	291 27.0	14.1	15 07.4	8.1	54.0
06	270 15.0	S23 26.0	306 00.1	14.0	S15 15.5	8.1	54.0
07	285 14.7	26.0	320 33.1	14.0	15 23.6	8.0	54.0
08	300 14.3	26.0	335 06.1	13.9	15 31.6	8.0	54.0
W 09	315 14.0	·· 25.9	349 39.0	13.9	15 39.6	7.9	54.0
E 10	330 13.7	25.9	4 11.9	13.9	15 47.5	7.8	54.0
D 11	345 13.4	25.9	18 44.8	13.8	15 55.3	7.8	54.0
N 12	0 13.1	S23 25.9	33 17.6	13.8	S16 03.1	7.6	54.0
E 13	15 12.8	25.8	47 50.4	13.8	16 10.7	7.7	54.0
S 14	30 12.5	25.8	62 23.2	13.7	16 18.4	7.5	54.0
D 15	45 12.2	·· 25.8	76 55.9	13.7	16 25.9	7.5	54.0
A 16	60 11.9	25.7	91 28.6	13.6	16 33.4	7.4	54.0
Y 17	75 11.5	25.7	106 01.2	13.6	16 40.8	7.3	54.0
18	90 11.2	S23 25.7	120 33.8	13.6	S16 48.1	7.3	54.0
19	105 10.9	25.6	135 06.4	13.5	16 55.4	7.2	54.0
20	120 10.6	25.6	149 38.9	13.4	17 02.6	7.1	54.0
21	135 10.3	·· 25.6	164 11.3	13.5	17 09.7	7.1	54.0
22	150 10.0	25.5	178 43.8	13.4	17 16.8	6.9	54.0
23	165 09.7	25.5	193 16.2	13.3	17 23.7	6.9	54.0
	S.D. 16.3	d 0.0	S.D. 14.8		14.7		14.7

Lat.	Twilight Naut.	Twilight Civil	Sunrise	Moonrise 21	22	23	24
°	h m	h m	h m	h m	h m	h m	h m
N 72	08 26	10 58	■	03 43	05 32	07 35	■
N 70	08 06	09 55	■	03 31	05 11	06 56	08 55
68	07 50	09 20	■	03 22	04 54	06 29	08 07
66	07 37	08 54	10 35	03 15	04 41	06 09	07 37
64	07 26	08 34	09 53	03 08	04 30	05 53	07 14
62	07 16	08 18	09 24	03 03	04 21	05 39	06 56
60	07 08	08 05	09 03	02 58	04 13	05 28	06 41
N 58	07 00	07 53	08 45	02 54	04 06	05 18	06 29
56	06 53	07 43	08 30	02 50	04 00	05 10	06 18
54	06 47	07 34	08 17	02 47	03 55	05 02	06 08
52	06 42	07 25	08 06	02 44	03 50	04 56	06 00
50	06 36	07 18	07 56	02 41	03 46	04 50	05 52
45	06 24	07 02	07 36	02 35	03 36	04 37	05 36
N 40	06 14	06 48	07 19	02 31	03 28	04 26	05 23
35	06 05	06 36	07 05	02 26	03 22	04 17	05 12
30	05 56	06 26	06 52	02 23	03 16	04 09	05 02
20	05 39	06 07	06 31	02 16	03 05	03 55	04 45
N 10	05 23	05 49	06 12	02 11	02 57	03 43	04 31
0	05 06	05 32	05 55	02 06	02 48	03 32	04 17
S 10	04 47	05 14	05 37	02 01	02 40	03 21	04 04
20	04 24	04 54	05 18	01 55	02 31	03 09	03 49
30	03 55	04 29	04 56	01 49	02 21	02 56	03 33
35	03 37	04 13	04 43	01 46	02 16	02 48	03 23
40	03 13	03 55	04 28	01 42	02 09	02 39	03 12
45	02 42	03 32	04 10	01 37	02 02	02 29	03 00
S 50	01 57	03 03	03 47	01 32	01 53	02 17	02 44
52	01 29	02 47	03 36	01 29	01 49	02 11	02 37
54	00 42	02 29	03 24	01 26	01 44	02 05	02 29
56	////	02 07	03 10	01 23	01 39	01 58	02 20
58	////	01 37	02 53	01 20	01 34	01 50	02 10
S 60	////	00 46	02 32	01 16	01 28	01 41	01 59

Lat.	Sunset	Twilight Civil	Twilight Naut.	Moonset 21	22	23	24
°	h m	h m	h m	h m	h m	h m	h m
N 72	■	12 59	15 31	12 27	12 07	11 36	■
N 70	■	14 02	15 51	12 41	12 30	12 16	11 51
68	■	14 38	16 07	12 51	12 48	12 44	12 40
66	13 22	15 03	16 20	13 00	13 02	13 05	13 11
64	14 05	15 23	16 31	13 08	13 14	13 22	13 34
62	14 33	15 39	16 41	13 15	13 24	13 36	13 52
60	14 55	15 53	16 49	13 20	13 32	13 48	14 08
N 58	15 12	16 04	16 57	13 25	13 40	13 58	14 21
56	15 27	16 15	17 04	13 30	13 47	14 07	14 32
54	15 40	16 24	17 10	13 34	13 53	14 15	14 42
52	15 51	16 32	17 16	13 38	13 58	14 22	14 51
50	16 01	16 39	17 21	13 41	14 03	14 29	14 59
45	16 22	16 55	17 33	13 48	14 14	14 43	15 16
N 40	16 38	17 09	17 43	13 54	14 23	14 54	15 29
35	16 53	17 21	17 53	14 00	14 31	15 04	15 41
30	17 05	17 31	18 01	14 04	14 37	15 13	15 52
20	17 26	17 50	18 18	14 12	14 49	15 28	16 09
N 10	17 45	18 08	18 34	14 19	14 59	15 41	16 25
0	18 02	18 25	18 51	14 26	15 09	15 54	16 39
S 10	18 20	18 43	19 10	14 33	15 19	16 06	16 54
20	18 39	19 04	19 33	14 40	15 29	16 19	17 10
30	19 01	19 29	20 02	14 48	15 41	16 34	17 28
35	19 14	19 44	20 22	14 53	15 48	16 43	17 38
40	19 29	20 02	20 44	14 58	15 56	16 53	17 50
45	19 47	20 25	21 15	15 05	16 05	17 05	18 04
S 50	20 10	20 55	22 00	15 12	16 16	17 20	18 22
52	20 21	21 10	22 28	15 16	16 22	17 27	18 30
54	20 33	21 28	23 16	15 20	16 27	17 34	18 39
56	20 47	21 50	////	15 24	16 34	17 43	18 49
58	21 04	22 20	////	15 29	16 41	17 52	19 01
S 60	21 25	23 11	////	15 34	16 49	18 03	19 15

Day	SUN Eqn. of Time 00ʰ	SUN Eqn. of Time 12ʰ	SUN Mer. Pass.	MOON Mer. Pass. Upper	MOON Mer. Pass. Lower	Age	Phase
	m s	m s	h m	h m	h m	d	
21	02 08	01 53	11 58	08 16	20 37	25	
22	01 38	01 23	11 59	08 59	21 21	26	
23	01 08	00 53	11 59	09 43	22 05	27	◗

G.M.T.	ARIES G.H.A.	VENUS −4.3 G.H.A.	Dec.	MARS +1.0 G.H.A.	Dec.	JUPITER −1.4 G.H.A.	Dec.	SATURN +0.9 G.H.A.	Dec.	STARS Name	S.H.A.	Dec.
24 00	92 26.0	142 15.9 S18 30.5		268 12.0 N 0 35.5		239 27.9 S12 02.9		252 08.8 S 5 58.2		Acamar	315 36.3	S40 22.9
01	107 28.4	157 17.8	29.9	283 13.4	35.1	254 30.0	03.0	267 11.1	58.2	Achernar	335 44.4	S57 20.1
02	122 30.9	172 19.6	29.2	298 14.8	34.7	269 32.1	03.2	282 13.4	58.3	Acrux	173 36.3	S62 59.6
03	137 33.3	187 21.5 ··	28.6	313 16.3 ··	34.3	284 34.1 ··	03.3	297 15.7 ··	58.3	Adhara	255 31.0	S28 56.8
04	152 35.8	202 23.3	28.0	328 17.7	33.9	299 36.2	03.4	312 18.0	58.4	Aldebaran	291 16.7	N16 28.4
05	167 38.3	217 25.2	27.3	343 19.1	33.5	314 38.3	03.5	327 20.3	58.4			
06	182 40.7	232 27.0 S18 26.7		358 20.6 N 0 33.1		329 40.4 S12 03.7		342 22.6 S 5 58.5		Alioth	166 41.8	N56 03.3
07	197 43.2	247 28.9	26.0	13 22.0	32.7	344 42.4	03.8	357 24.9	58.5	Alkaid	153 18.0	N49 24.1
T 08	212 45.7	262 30.8	25.4	28 23.5	32.3	359 44.5	03.9	12 27.2	58.6	Al Na'ir	28 14.1	S47 03.2
H 09	227 48.1	277 32.6 ··	24.8	43 24.9 ··	31.9	14 46.6 ··	04.1	27 29.6 ··	58.6	Alnilam	276 10.4	S 1 12.8
U 10	242 50.6	292 34.5	24.1	58 26.3	31.5	29 48.7	04.2	42 31.9	58.7	Alphard	218 19.5	S 8 34.7
R 11	257 53.1	307 36.4	23.5	73 27.8	31.1	44 50.8	04.3	57 34.2	58.7			
S 12	272 55.5	322 38.3 S18 22.8		88 29.2 N 0 30.7		59 52.8 S12 04.4		72 36.5 S 5 58.8		Alphecca	126 31.7	N26 46.5
D 13	287 58.0	337 40.2	22.2	103 30.7	30.3	74 54.9	04.6	87 38.8	58.8	Alpheratz	358 08.4	N28 59.5
A 14	303 00.4	352 42.1	21.6	118 32.1	29.9	89 57.0	04.7	102 41.1	58.9	Altair	62 32.0	N 8 49.2
Y 15	318 02.9	7 44.0 ··	20.9	133 33.5 ··	29.5	104 59.1 ··	04.8	117 43.4 ··	58.9	Ankaa	353 39.3	S42 24.6
16	333 05.4	22 45.9	20.3	148 35.0	29.1	120 01.1	05.0	132 45.7	59.0	Antares	112 56.1	S26 23.4
17	348 07.8	37 47.8	19.7	163 36.4	28.7	135 03.2	05.1	147 48.1	59.0			
18	3 10.3	52 49.7 S18 19.0		178 37.9 N 0 28.3		150 05.3 S12 05.2		162 50.4 S 5 59.1		Arcturus	146 17.9	N19 16.6
19	18 12.8	67 51.6	18.4	193 39.3	27.9	165 07.4	05.3	177 52.7	59.1	Atria	108 20.1	S68 59.6
20	33 15.2	82 53.5	17.7	208 40.8	27.4	180 09.5	05.5	192 55.0	59.2	Avior	234 27.3	S59 26.9
21	48 17.7	97 55.4 ··	17.1	223 42.2 ··	27.0	195 11.5 ··	05.6	207 57.3 ··	59.2	Bellatrix	278 57.5	N 6 20.0
22	63 20.2	112 57.3	16.5	238 43.6	26.6	210 13.6	05.7	222 59.6	59.3	Betelgeuse	271 27.0	N 7 24.2
23	78 22.6	127 59.3	15.8	253 45.1	26.2	225 15.7	05.8	238 01.9	59.3			
25 00	93 25.1	143 01.2 S18 15.2		268 46.5 N 0 25.8		240 17.8 S12 06.0		253 04.3 S 5 59.4		Canopus	264 06.3	S52 41.2
01	108 27.6	158 03.1	14.6	283 48.0	25.4	255 19.9	06.1	268 06.6	59.4	Capella	281 09.5	N45 58.8
02	123 30.0	173 05.1	13.9	298 49.4	25.0	270 21.9	06.2	283 08.9	59.5	Deneb	49 48.3	N45 13.1
03	138 32.5	188 07.0 ··	13.3	313 50.9 ··	24.6	285 24.0 ··	06.4	298 11.2 ··	59.5	Denebola	182 58.1	N14 40.4
04	153 34.9	203 08.9	12.7	328 52.3	24.2	300 26.1	06.5	313 13.5	59.6	Diphda	349 19.9	S18 05.4
05	168 37.4	218 10.9	12.0	343 53.8	23.8	315 28.2	06.6	328 15.8	59.6			
06	183 39.9	233 12.9 S18 11.4		358 55.2 N 0 23.4		330 30.3 S12 06.7		343 18.1 S 5 59.7		Dubhe	194 20.8	N61 50.7
07	198 42.3	248 14.8	10.8	13 56.7	23.0	345 32.3	06.9	358 20.5	59.7	Elnath	278 42.6	N28 35.5
08	213 44.8	263 16.8	10.1	28 58.1	22.6	0 34.4	07.0	13 22.8	59.8	Eltanin	90 57.9	N51 29.5
F 09	228 47.3	278 18.7 ··	09.5	43 59.6 ··	22.2	15 36.5 ··	07.1	28 25.1 ··	59.8	Enif	34 10.9	N 9 47.5
R 10	243 49.7	293 20.7	08.9	59 01.0	21.8	30 38.6	07.2	43 27.4	59.9	Fomalhaut	15 50.6	S29 43.3
I 11	258 52.2	308 22.7	08.2	74 02.5	21.4	45 40.7	07.4	58 29.7	5 59.9			
D 12	273 54.7	323 24.7 S18 07.6		89 03.9 N 0 21.0		60 42.8 S12 07.5		73 32.0 S 6 00.0		Gacrux	172 27.8	S57 00.3
A 13	288 57.1	338 26.6	07.0	104 05.4	20.6	75 44.8	07.6	88 34.3	00.0	Gienah	176 17.1	S17 26.3
Y 14	303 59.6	353 28.6	06.3	119 06.8	20.2	90 46.9	07.7	103 36.7	00.0	Hadar	149 22.4	S60 16.8
15	319 02.1	8 30.6 ··	05.7	134 08.3 ··	19.8	105 49.0 ··	07.9	118 39.0 ··	00.1	Hamal	328 27.8	N23 22.7
16	334 04.5	23 32.6	05.1	149 09.7	19.4	120 51.1	08.0	133 41.3	00.1	Kaus Aust.	84 16.1	S34 23.6
17	349 07.0	38 34.6	04.4	164 11.2	19.0	135 53.2	08.1	148 43.6	00.2			
18	4 09.4	53 36.6 S18 03.8		179 12.6 N 0 18.6		150 55.2 S12 08.2		163 45.9 S 6 00.2		Kochab	137 19.8	N74 13.6
19	19 11.9	68 38.6	03.2	194 14.1	18.2	165 57.3	08.4	178 48.2	00.3	Markab	14 02.4	N15 06.5
20	34 14.4	83 40.6	02.6	209 15.5	17.8	180 59.4	08.5	193 50.6	00.3	Menkar	314 40.0	N 4 01.1
21	49 16.8	98 42.6 ··	01.9	224 17.0 ··	17.4	196 01.5 ··	08.6	208 52.9 ··	00.4	Menkent	148 36.2	S36 16.6
22	64 19.3	113 44.7	01.3	239 18.4	17.0	211 03.6	08.7	223 55.2	00.4	Miaplacidus	221 44.1	S69 38.3
23	79 21.8	128 46.7	00.7	254 19.9	16.6	226 05.7	08.9	238 57.5	00.5			
26 00	94 24.2	143 48.7 S18 00.0		269 21.3 N 0 16.2		241 07.7 S12 09.0		253 59.8 S 6 00.5		Mirfak	309 14.5	N49 47.9
01	109 26.7	158 50.7 17 59.4		284 22.8	15.8	256 09.8	09.1	269 02.1	00.6	Nunki	76 28.5	S26 19.2
02	124 29.2	173 52.8	58.8	299 24.2	15.4	271 11.9	09.2	284 04.5	00.6	Peacock	53 57.5	S56 47.8
03	139 31.6	188 54.8 ··	58.2	314 25.7 ··	15.0	286 14.0 ··	09.4	299 06.8 ··	00.7	Pollux	243 56.7	N28 04.2
04	154 34.1	203 56.8	57.5	329 27.1	14.6	301 16.1	09.5	314 09.1	00.7	Procyon	245 24.6	N 5 16.3
05	169 36.6	218 58.9	56.9	344 28.6	14.2	316 18.2	09.6	329 11.4	00.8			
06	184 39.0	234 00.9 S17 56.3		359 30.1 N 0 13.8		331 20.3 S12 09.7		344 13.7 S 6 00.8		Rasalhague	96 29.1	N12 34.4
07	199 41.5	249 03.0	55.7	14 31.5	13.4	346 22.3	09.9	359 16.1	00.9	Regulus	208 08.9	N12 03.3
S 08	214 43.9	264 05.1	55.0	29 33.0	13.0	1 24.4	10.0	14 18.4	00.9	Rigel	281 34.8	S 8 13.4
A 09	229 46.4	279 07.1 ··	54.4	44 34.4 ··	12.7	16 26.5 ··	10.1	29 20.7 ··	01.0	Rigil Kent.	140 25.1	S60 45.3
T 10	244 48.9	294 09.2	53.8	59 35.9	12.3	31 28.6	10.2	44 23.0	01.0	Sabik	102 40.5	S15 42.1
U 11	259 51.3	309 11.3	53.2	74 37.3	11.9	46 30.7	10.4	59 25.3	01.0			
R 12	274 53.8	324 13.3 S17 52.5		89 38.8 N 0 11.5		61 32.8 S12 10.5		74 27.7 S 6 01.1		Schedar	350 08.0	N56 26.5
D 13	289 56.3	339 15.4	51.9	104 40.3	11.1	76 34.9	10.6	89 30.0	01.1	Shaula	96 55.0	S37 05.4
A 14	304 58.7	354 17.5	51.3	119 41.7	10.7	91 36.9	10.7	104 32.3	01.2	Sirius	258 54.6	S16 41.5
Y 15	320 01.2	9 19.6 ··	50.7	134 43.2 ··	10.3	106 39.0 ··	10.9	119 34.6 ··	01.2	Spica	158 56.7	S11 03.9
16	335 03.7	24 21.7	50.0	149 44.6	09.9	121 41.1	11.0	134 36.9	01.3	Suhail	223 09.8	S43 21.4
17	350 06.1	39 23.8	49.4	164 46.1	09.5	136 43.2	11.1	149 39.2	01.3			
18	5 08.6	54 25.9 S17 48.8		179 47.6 N 0 09.1		151 45.3 S12 11.2		164 41.6 S 6 01.4		Vega	80 55.7	N38 46.0
19	20 11.0	69 28.0	48.2	194 49.0	08.7	166 47.4	11.4	179 43.9	01.4	Zuben'ubi	137 32.3	S15 57.9
20	35 13.5	84 30.1	47.6	209 50.5	08.3	181 49.5	11.5	194 46.2	01.5			
21	50 16.0	99 32.2 ··	46.9	224 51.9 ··	07.9	196 51.6 ··	11.6	209 48.5 ··	01.5		S.H.A.	Mer. Pass.
22	65 18.4	114 34.3	46.3	239 53.4	07.5	211 53.6	11.7	224 50.9	01.6	Venus	49 36.1	14 26
23	80 20.9	129 36.4	45.7	254 54.9	07.1	226 55.7	11.8	239 53.2	01.6	Mars	175 21.4	6 04
Mer. Pass. 17 43.4		v 2.0 d 0.6		v 1.4 d 0.4		v 2.1 d 0.1		v 2.3 d 0.0		Jupiter	146 52.7	7 58
										Saturn	159 39.2	7 07

SUN / MOON

G.M.T.	SUN G.H.A.	Dec.	MOON G.H.A.	v	Dec.	d	H.P.
24 00	180 09.4	S23 25.4	207 48.5	13.4	S17 30.6	6.9	54.0
01	195 09.0	25.4	222 20.9	13.2	17 37.5	6.7	54.0
02	210 08.7	25.4	236 53.1	13.3	17 44.2	6.7	54.0
03	225 08.4 ··	25.3	251 25.4	13.2	17 50.9	6.6	54.0
04	240 08.1	25.3	265 57.6	13.1	17 57.5	6.5	54.0
05	255 07.8	25.2	280 29.7	13.1	18 04.0	6.4	54.0
06	270 07.5	S23 25.2	295 01.8	13.1	S18 10.4	6.4	54.0
07	285 07.2	25.1	309 33.9	13.0	18 16.8	6.3	54.0
T 08	300 06.9	25.1	324 05.9	13.0	18 23.1	6.2	54.0
H 09	315 06.6 ··	25.0	338 37.9	13.0	18 29.3	6.1	54.0
U 10	330 06.2	25.0	353 09.9	12.9	18 35.4	6.1	54.0
R 11	345 05.9	24.9	7 41.8	12.9	18 41.5	5.9	54.0
S 12	0 05.6	S23 24.9	22 13.7	12.8	S18 47.4	5.9	54.0
D 13	15 05.3	24.8	36 45.5	12.8	18 53.3	5.8	54.0
A 14	30 05.0	24.8	51 17.3	12.7	18 59.1	5.7	54.0
Y 15	45 04.7 ··	24.7	65 49.0	12.7	19 04.8	5.6	54.0
16	60 04.4	24.7	80 20.7	12.7	19 10.4	5.6	54.0
17	75 04.1	24.6	94 52.4	12.6	19 16.0	5.4	54.0
18	90 03.7	S23 24.6	109 24.0	12.6	S19 21.4	5.4	54.0
19	105 03.4	24.5	123 55.6	12.6	19 26.8	5.3	54.0
20	120 03.1	24.5	138 27.2	12.5	19 32.1	5.2	54.0
21	135 02.8 ··	24.4	152 58.7	12.5	19 37.3	5.1	54.0
22	150 02.5	24.4	167 30.2	12.4	19 42.4	5.0	54.0
23	165 02.2	24.3	182 01.6	12.4	19 47.4	5.0	54.0
25 00	180 01.9	S23 24.2	196 33.0	12.3	S19 52.4	4.8	54.0
01	195 01.6	24.2	211 04.3	12.4	19 57.2	4.8	54.0
02	210 01.3	24.1	225 35.7	12.2	20 02.0	4.7	54.0
03	225 00.9 ··	24.0	240 06.9	12.3	20 06.7	4.5	54.0
04	240 00.6	24.0	254 38.2	12.2	20 11.2	4.5	54.0
05	255 00.3	23.9	269 09.4	12.1	20 15.7	4.4	54.0
06	270 00.0	S23 23.9	283 40.5	12.2	S20 20.1	4.3	54.0
07	284 59.7	23.8	298 11.7	12.1	20 24.4	4.2	54.0
F 08	299 59.4	23.7	312 42.8	12.0	20 28.6	4.2	54.1
R 09	314 59.1 ··	23.7	327 13.8	12.1	20 32.8	4.0	54.1
I 10	329 58.8	23.6	341 44.9	11.9	20 36.8	3.9	54.1
D 11	344 58.5	23.5	356 15.8	12.0	20 40.7	3.9	54.1
A 12	359 58.1	S23 23.5	10 46.8	11.9	S20 44.6	3.7	54.1
Y 13	14 57.8	23.4	25 17.7	11.9	20 48.3	3.7	54.1
14	29 57.5	23.3	39 48.6	11.9	20 52.0	3.5	54.1
15	44 57.2 ··	23.2	54 19.5	11.8	20 55.5	3.5	54.1
16	59 56.9	23.2	68 50.3	11.8	20 59.0	3.3	54.1
17	74 56.6	23.1	83 21.1	11.7	21 02.3	3.3	54.1
18	89 56.3	S23 23.0	97 51.8	11.7	S21 05.6	3.2	54.1
19	104 56.0	22.9	112 22.5	11.7	21 08.8	3.1	54.1
20	119 55.7	22.9	126 53.2	11.7	21 11.9	2.9	54.1
21	134 55.3 ··	22.8	141 23.9	11.6	21 14.8	2.9	54.1
22	149 55.0	22.7	155 54.5	11.6	21 17.7	2.8	54.1
23	164 54.7	22.6	170 25.1	11.6	21 20.5	2.7	54.2
26 00	179 54.4	S23 22.6	184 55.7	11.5	S21 23.2	2.5	54.2
01	194 54.1	22.5	199 26.2	11.6	21 25.7	2.5	54.2
02	209 53.8	22.4	213 56.8	11.4	21 28.2	2.4	54.2
03	224 53.5 ··	22.3	228 27.2	11.5	21 30.6	2.3	54.2
04	239 53.2	22.2	242 57.7	11.4	21 32.9	2.1	54.2
05	254 52.9	22.2	257 28.1	11.4	21 35.0	2.1	54.2
06	269 52.5	S23 22.1	271 58.5	11.4	S21 37.1	2.0	54.2
07	284 52.2	22.0	286 28.9	11.4	21 39.1	1.9	54.2
S 08	299 51.9	21.9	300 59.3	11.3	21 41.0	1.7	54.2
A 09	314 51.6 ··	21.8	315 29.6	11.3	21 42.7	1.7	54.2
T 10	329 51.3	21.7	329 59.9	11.3	21 44.4	1.5	54.2
U 11	344 51.0	21.6	344 30.2	11.3	21 45.9	1.5	54.3
R 12	359 50.7	S23 21.6	359 00.5	11.2	S21 47.4	1.4	54.3
D 13	14 50.4	21.5	13 30.7	11.3	21 48.8	1.2	54.3
A 14	29 50.1	21.4	28 01.0	11.2	21 50.0	1.2	54.3
Y 15	44 49.8 ··	21.3	42 31.2	11.1	21 51.2	1.0	54.3
16	59 49.4	21.2	57 01.3	11.2	21 52.2	0.9	54.3
17	74 49.1	21.1	71 31.5	11.2	21 53.1	0.9	54.3
18	89 48.8	S23 21.0	86 01.7	11.1	S21 54.0	0.7	54.3
19	104 48.5	20.9	100 31.8	11.1	21 54.7	0.6	54.3
20	119 48.2	20.8	115 01.9	11.1	21 55.3	0.6	54.3
21	134 47.9 ··	20.7	129 32.0	11.1	21 55.9	0.4	54.3
22	149 47.6	20.6	144 02.1	11.0	21 56.3	0.3	54.4
23	164 47.3	20.5	158 32.1	11.1	21 56.6	0.2	54.4
	S.D. 16.3 d 0.1		S.D. 14.7		14.7		14.8

Twilight / Sunrise / Moonrise

Lat.	Naut.	Civil	Sunrise	Moonrise 24	25	26	27
N 72	08 27	10 57	■	■	■	■	■
N 70	08 07	09 55	■	08 55	■	■	■
68	07 51	09 20	■	08 07	09 49	11 37	12 34
66	07 38	08 55	10 35	07 37	09 02	10 17	11 10
64	07 27	08 35	09 53	07 14	08 32	09 40	10 32
62	07 17	08 19	09 25	06 56	08 09	09 14	10 06
60	07 09	08 06	09 03	06 41	07 51	08 53	09 45
N 58	07 01	07 54	08 46	06 29	07 36	08 36	09 28
56	06 55	07 44	08 31	06 18	07 23	08 22	09 13
54	06 49	07 35	08 19	06 08	07 12	08 10	09 01
52	06 43	07 27	08 08	06 00	07 02	07 59	08 50
50	06 38	07 19	07 58	05 52	06 53	07 49	08 40
45	06 26	07 03	07 37	05 36	06 34	07 29	08 20
N 40	06 15	06 50	07 20	05 23	06 19	07 13	08 03
35	06 06	06 38	07 06	05 12	06 06	06 59	07 49
30	05 57	06 27	06 54	05 02	05 55	06 47	07 37
20	05 41	06 08	06 32	04 45	05 36	06 27	07 17
N 10	05 25	05 51	06 14	04 31	05 19	06 09	06 58
0	05 08	05 34	05 56	04 17	05 04	05 52	06 42
S 10	04 49	05 16	05 39	04 04	04 48	05 36	06 25
20	04 26	04 55	05 20	03 49	04 32	05 18	06 07
30	03 57	04 30	04 58	03 33	04 13	04 58	05 46
35	03 38	04 15	04 45	03 23	04 02	04 46	05 34
40	03 15	03 57	04 30	03 12	03 50	04 32	05 20
45	02 44	03 34	04 12	03 00	03 35	04 16	05 04
S 50	01 59	03 04	03 49	02 44	03 17	03 56	04 43
52	01 31	02 49	03 38	02 37	03 09	03 47	04 34
54	00 44	02 31	03 26	02 29	02 59	03 37	04 23
56	////	02 09	03 12	02 20	02 49	03 25	04 10
58	////	01 39	02 55	02 10	02 36	03 11	03 56
S 60	////	00 49	02 34	01 59	02 22	02 55	03 39

Sunset / Twilight / Moonset

Lat.	Sunset	Civil	Naut.	Moonset 24	25	26	27
N 72	■	13 03	15 33	■	■	■	■
N 70	■	14 05	15 53	11 51	■	■	■
68	■	14 40	16 09	12 40	12 35	12 29	13 15
66	13 25	15 05	16 22	13 11	13 23	13 49	14 39
64	14 07	15 25	16 33	13 34	13 54	14 26	15 17
62	14 35	15 41	16 43	13 52	14 17	14 53	15 43
60	14 57	15 55	16 51	14 08	14 35	15 13	16 04
N 58	15 14	16 06	16 59	14 21	14 51	15 30	16 21
56	15 29	16 16	17 06	14 32	15 04	15 44	16 35
54	15 42	16 26	17 12	14 42	15 15	15 57	16 47
52	15 53	16 34	17 17	14 51	15 25	16 08	16 58
50	16 03	16 41	17 23	14 59	15 35	16 17	17 08
45	16 23	16 57	17 34	15 16	15 54	16 38	17 28
N 40	16 40	17 11	17 45	15 29	16 09	16 54	17 45
35	16 54	17 23	17 54	15 41	16 23	17 08	17 59
30	17 07	17 33	18 03	15 52	16 34	17 20	18 11
20	17 28	17 52	18 19	16 09	16 54	17 41	18 31
N 10	17 46	18 09	18 36	16 25	17 11	17 59	18 49
0	18 04	18 26	18 53	16 39	17 27	18 16	19 06
S 10	18 21	18 45	19 12	16 54	17 43	18 33	19 22
20	18 40	19 05	19 34	17 10	18 00	18 51	19 40
30	19 02	19 30	20 03	17 28	18 20	19 12	20 00
35	19 15	19 45	20 22	17 38	18 32	19 24	20 12
40	19 30	20 03	20 45	17 50	18 45	19 38	20 26
45	19 48	20 26	21 16	18 04	19 01	19 54	20 42
S 50	20 11	20 56	22 01	18 22	19 20	20 14	21 02
52	20 22	21 11	22 29	18 30	19 30	20 24	21 11
54	20 34	21 29	23 15	18 39	19 40	20 35	21 22
56	20 48	21 51	////	18 49	19 52	20 47	21 34
58	21 05	22 15	////	19 01	20 05	21 01	21 48
S 60	21 26	23 11	////	19 15	20 22	21 18	22 04

SUN / MOON

Day	Eqn. of Time 00h	12h	Mer. Pass.	Mer. Pass. Upper	Lower	Age	Phase
	m s	m s	h m	h m	h m	d	
24	00 38	00 23	12 00	10 28	22 52	28	
25	00 08	00 07	12 00	11 15	23 40	29	●
26	00 22	00 37	12 01	12 04	24 29	00	

G.M.T.	ARIES G.H.A.	VENUS −4.3 G.H.A.	Dec.	MARS +1.0 G.H.A.	Dec.	JUPITER −1.4 G.H.A.	Dec.	SATURN +0.9 G.H.A.	Dec.	STARS Name	S.H.A.	Dec.
27 00	95 23.4	144 38.5 S17	45.1	269 56.3 N 0	06.7	241 57.8 S12	12.0	254 55.5 S 6	01.7	Acamar	315 36.3	S40 22.9
01	110 25.8	159 40.7	44.5	284 57.8	06.3	256 59.9	12.1	269 57.8	01.7	Achernar	335 44.4	S57 20.1
02	125 28.3	174 42.8	43.8	299 59.3	05.9	272 02.0	12.2	285 00.1	01.7	Acrux	173 36.3	S62 59.6
03	140 30.8	189 44.9 ··	43.2	315 00.7 ··	05.5	287 04.1 ··	12.3	300 02.5 ··	01.8	Adhara	255 31.0	S28 56.8
04	155 33.2	204 47.1	42.6	330 02.2	05.2	302 06.2	12.5	315 04.8	01.8	Aldebaran	291 16.7	N16 28.4
05	170 35.7	219 49.2	42.0	345 03.6	04.8	317 08.3	12.6	330 07.1	01.9			
06	185 38.2	234 51.4 S17	41.4	0 05.1 N 0	04.4	332 10.3 S12	12.7	345 09.4 S 6	01.9	Alioth	166 41.8	N56 03.3
07	200 40.6	249 53.5	40.8	15 06.6	04.0	347 12.4	12.8	0 11.7	02.0	Alkaid	153 18.0	N49 24.0
08	215 43.1	264 55.7	40.1	30 08.0	03.6	2 14.5	13.0	15 14.1	02.0	Al Na'ir	28 14.1	S47 03.2
S 09	230 45.5	279 57.8 ··	39.5	45 09.5 ··	03.2	17 16.6 ··	13.1	30 16.4 ··	02.1	Alnilam	276 10.4	S 1 12.9
U 10	245 48.0	295 00.0	38.9	60 11.0	02.8	32 18.7	13.2	45 18.7	02.1	Alphard	218 19.5	S 8 34.7
N 11	260 50.5	310 02.2	38.3	75 12.4	02.4	47 20.8	13.3	60 21.0	02.2			
D 12	275 52.9	325 04.3 S17	37.7	90 13.9 N 0	02.0	62 22.9 S12	13.4	75 23.4 S 6	02.2	Alphecca	126 31.6	N26 46.5
A 13	290 55.4	340 06.5	37.1	105 15.4	01.6	77 25.0	13.6	90 25.7	02.2	Alpheratz	358 08.4	N28 59.5
Y 14	305 57.9	355 08.7	36.4	120 16.9	01.2	92 27.1	13.7	105 28.0	02.3	Altair	62 32.0	N 8 49.2
15	321 00.3	10 10.9 ··	35.8	135 18.3 ··	00.8	107 29.2 ··	13.8	120 30.3 ··	02.3	Ankaa	353 39.3	S42 24.6
16	336 02.8	25 13.1	35.2	150 19.8	00.4	122 31.2	13.9	135 32.6	02.4	Antares	112 56.1	S26 23.4
17	351 05.3	40 15.3	34.6	165 21.3 N 0	00.1	137 33.3	14.1	150 35.0	02.4			
18	6 07.7	55 17.5 S17	34.0	180 22.7 S 0	00.3	152 35.4 S12	14.2	165 37.3 S 6	02.5	Arcturus	146 17.8	N19 16.6
19	21 10.2	70 19.7	33.4	195 24.2	00.7	167 37.5	14.3	180 39.6	02.5	Atria	108 20.1	S68 59.6
20	36 12.7	85 21.9	32.8	210 25.7	01.1	182 39.6	14.4	195 41.9	02.6	Avior	234 27.3	S59 26.9
21	51 15.1	100 24.1 ··	32.2	225 27.1 ··	01.5	197 41.7 ··	14.5	210 44.3 ··	02.6	Bellatrix	278 57.5	N 6 20.0
22	66 17.6	115 26.3	31.5	240 28.6	01.9	212 43.8	14.7	225 46.6	02.7	Betelgeuse	271 27.0	N 7 24.2
23	81 20.0	130 28.5	30.9	255 30.1	02.3	227 45.9	14.8	240 48.9	02.7			
28 00	96 22.5	145 30.7 S17	30.3	270 31.6 S 0	02.7	242 48.0 S12	14.9	255 51.2 S 6	02.7	Canopus	264 06.2	S52 41.2
01	111 25.0	160 33.0	29.7	285 33.0	03.1	257 50.1	15.0	270 53.6	02.8	Capella	281 09.5	N45 58.8
02	126 27.4	175 35.2	29.1	300 34.5	03.4	272 52.2	15.1	285 55.9	02.8	Deneb	49 48.3	N45 13.0
03	141 29.9	190 37.4 ··	28.5	315 36.0 ··	03.8	287 54.3 ··	15.3	300 58.2 ··	02.9	Denebola	182 58.1	N14 40.4
04	156 32.4	205 39.7	27.9	330 37.5	04.2	302 56.4	15.4	316 00.5	02.9	Diphda	349 19.9	S18 05.4
05	171 34.8	220 41.9	27.3	345 38.9	04.6	317 58.4	15.5	331 02.9	03.0			
06	186 37.3	235 44.2 S17	26.7	0 40.4 S 0	05.0	333 00.5 S12	15.6	346 05.2 S 6	03.0	Dubhe	194 20.8	N61 50.7
07	201 39.8	250 46.4	26.1	15 41.9	05.4	348 02.6	15.8	1 07.5	03.0	Elnath	278 42.6	N28 35.5
08	216 42.2	265 48.7	25.5	30 43.4	05.8	3 04.7	15.9	16 09.8	03.1	Eltanin	90 57.9	N51 29.5
M 09	231 44.7	280 50.9 ··	24.9	45 44.8 ··	06.2	18 06.8 ··	16.0	31 12.2 ··	03.1	Enif	34 10.9	N 9 47.5
O 10	246 47.2	295 53.2	24.2	60 46.3	06.6	33 08.9	16.1	46 14.5	03.2	Fomalhaut	15 50.6	S29 43.3
N 11	261 49.6	310 55.5	23.6	75 47.8	06.9	48 11.0	16.2	61 16.8	03.2			
D 12	276 52.1	325 57.7 S17	23.0	90 49.3 S 0	07.3	63 13.1 S12	16.4	76 19.1 S 6	03.3	Gacrux	172 27.8	S57 00.4
A 13	291 54.5	341 00.0	22.4	105 50.7	07.7	78 15.2	16.5	91 21.5	03.3	Gienah	176 17.0	S17 26.3
Y 14	306 57.0	356 02.3	21.8	120 52.2	08.1	93 17.3	16.6	106 23.8	03.4	Hadar	149 22.4	S60 16.8
15	321 59.5	11 04.6 ··	21.2	135 53.7 ··	08.5	108 19.4 ··	16.7	121 26.1 ··	03.4	Hamal	328 27.8	N23 22.7
16	337 01.9	26 06.9	20.6	150 55.2	08.9	123 21.5	16.8	136 28.4	03.4	Kaus Aust.	84 16.1	S34 23.6
17	352 04.4	41 09.2	20.0	165 56.7	09.3	138 23.6	17.0	151 30.8	03.5			
18	7 06.9	56 11.5 S17	19.4	180 58.1 S 0	09.6	153 25.7 S12	17.1	166 33.1 S 6	03.5	Kochab	137 19.8	N74 13.6
19	22 09.3	71 13.8	18.8	195 59.6	10.0	168 27.8	17.2	181 35.4	03.6	Markab	14 02.4	N15 06.5
20	37 11.8	86 16.1	18.2	211 01.1	10.4	183 29.9	17.3	196 37.8	03.6	Menkar	314 40.0	N 4 01.1
21	52 14.3	101 18.4 ··	17.6	226 02.6 ··	10.8	198 32.0 ··	17.4	211 40.1 ··	03.7	Menkent	148 36.2	S36 16.6
22	67 16.7	116 20.7	17.0	241 04.1	11.2	213 34.1	17.6	226 42.4	03.7	Miaplacidus	221 44.0	S69 38.3
23	82 19.2	131 23.0	16.4	256 05.5	11.6	228 36.2	17.7	241 44.7	03.7			
29 00	97 21.6	146 25.4 S17	15.8	271 07.0 S 0	12.0	243 38.3 S12	17.8	256 47.1 S 6	03.8	Mirfak	309 14.5	N49 47.9
01	112 24.1	161 27.7	15.2	286 08.5	12.3	258 40.4	17.9	271 49.4	03.8	Nunki	76 28.5	S26 19.2
02	127 26.6	176 30.0	14.6	301 10.0	12.7	273 42.4	18.0	286 51.7	03.9	Peacock	53 57.5	S56 47.8
03	142 29.0	191 32.4 ··	14.0	316 11.5 ··	13.1	288 44.5 ··	18.2	301 54.0 ··	03.9	Pollux	243 56.7	N28 04.2
04	157 31.5	206 34.7	13.4	331 13.0	13.5	303 46.6	18.3	316 56.4	04.0	Procyon	245 24.5	N 5 16.3
05	172 34.0	221 37.0	12.8	346 14.4	13.9	318 48.7	18.4	331 58.7	04.0			
06	187 36.4	236 39.4 S17	12.2	1 15.9 S 0	14.3	333 50.8 S12	18.5	347 01.0 S 6	04.0	Rasalhague	96 29.1	N12 34.4
07	202 38.9	251 41.7	11.6	16 17.4	14.6	348 52.9	18.6	2 03.4	04.1	Regulus	208 08.9	N12 03.3
08	217 41.4	266 44.1	11.0	31 18.9	15.0	3 55.0	18.8	17 05.7	04.1	Rigel	281 34.8	S 8 13.4
T 09	232 43.8	281 46.5 ··	10.4	46 20.4 ··	15.4	18 57.1 ··	18.9	32 08.0 ··	04.2	Rigil Kent.	140 25.0	S60 45.3
U 10	247 46.3	296 48.8	09.8	61 21.9	15.8	33 59.2	19.0	47 10.4	04.2	Sabik	102 40.5	S15 42.1
E 11	262 48.8	311 51.2	09.2	76 23.3	16.2	49 01.3	19.1	62 12.7	04.3			
S 12	277 51.2	326 53.6 S17	08.7	91 24.8 S 0	16.6	64 03.4 S12	19.2	77 15.0 S 6	04.3	Schedar	350 08.0	N56 26.5
D 13	292 53.7	341 56.0	08.1	106 26.3	16.9	79 05.5	19.3	92 17.3	04.3	Shaula	96 55.0	S37 05.4
A 14	307 56.1	356 58.3	07.5	121 27.8	17.3	94 07.6	19.5	107 19.7	04.4	Sirius	258 54.6	S16 41.5
Y 15	322 58.6	12 00.7 ··	06.9	136 29.3 ··	17.7	109 09.7 ··	19.6	122 22.0 ··	04.4	Spica	158 56.7	S11 03.9
16	338 01.1	27 03.1	06.3	151 30.8	18.1	124 11.8	19.7	137 24.3	04.5	Suhail	223 09.8	S43 21.4
17	353 03.5	42 05.5	05.7	166 32.3	18.5	139 13.9	19.8	152 26.7	04.5			
18	8 06.0	57 07.9 S17	05.1	181 33.8 S 0	18.8	154 16.0 S12	19.9	167 29.0 S 6	04.6	Vega	80 55.7	N38 46.0
19	23 08.5	72 10.3	04.5	196 35.3	19.2	169 18.1	20.1	182 31.3	04.6	Zuben'ubi	137 32.3	S15 57.9
20	38 10.9	87 12.7	03.9	211 36.7	19.6	184 20.2	20.2	197 33.7	04.6		S.H.A.	Mer. Pass.
21	53 13.4	102 15.2 ··	03.3	226 38.2 ··	20.0	199 22.3 ··	20.3	212 36.0 ··	04.7	Venus	49 08.2	14 16
22	68 15.9	117 17.6	02.7	241 39.7	20.4	214 24.4	20.4	227 38.3	04.7	Mars	174 09.1	5 57
23	83 18.3	132 20.0	02.2	256 41.2	20.7	229 26.5	20.5	242 40.6	04.8	Jupiter	146 25.5	7 48
Mer. Pass. 17 31.6		v 2.3	d 0.6	v 1.5	d 0.4	v 2.1	d 0.1	v 2.3	d 0.0	Saturn	159 28.7	6 56

SUN / MOON

G.M.T.	SUN G.H.A.	SUN Dec.	MOON G.H.A.	v	MOON Dec.	d	H.P.
27 00	179 47.0	S23 20.4	173 02.2	11.0	S21 56.8	0.1	54.4
01	194 46.7	20.3	187 32.2	11.1	21 56.9	0.0	54.4
02	209 46.3	20.2	202 02.3	11.0	21 56.9	0.1	54.4
03	224 46.0 ··	20.1	216 32.3	11.0	21 56.8	0.3	54.4
04	239 45.7	20.0	231 02.3	11.0	21 56.5	0.3	54.4
05	254 45.4	19.9	245 32.3	11.0	21 56.2	0.4	54.4
06	269 45.1	S23 19.8	260 02.3	10.9	S21 55.8	0.6	54.5
07	284 44.8	19.7	274 32.2	11.0	21 55.2	0.6	54.5
08	299 44.5	19.6	289 02.2	10.9	21 54.6	0.8	54.5
S 09	314 44.2 ··	19.5	303 32.1	11.0	21 53.8	0.8	54.5
U 10	329 43.9	19.4	318 02.1	10.9	21 53.0	1.0	54.5
N 11	344 43.6	19.3	332 32.0	11.0	21 52.0	1.0	54.5
D 12	359 43.3	S23 19.2	347 02.0	10.9	S21 51.0	1.2	54.5
A 13	14 42.9	19.1	1 31.9	10.9	21 49.8	1.3	54.5
Y 14	29 42.6	19.0	16 01.8	11.0	21 48.5	1.4	54.5
15	44 42.3 ··	18.8	30 31.8	10.9	21 47.1	1.5	54.6
16	59 42.0	18.7	45 01.7	10.9	21 45.6	1.6	54.6
17	74 41.7	18.6	59 31.6	10.9	21 44.0	1.7	54.6
18	89 41.4	S23 18.5	74 01.5	11.0	S21 42.3	1.8	54.6
19	104 41.1	18.4	88 31.5	10.9	21 40.5	2.0	54.6
20	119 40.8	18.3	103 01.4	10.9	21 38.5	2.0	54.6
21	134 40.5 ··	18.2	117 31.3	10.9	21 36.5	2.1	54.6
22	149 40.2	18.0	132 01.2	10.9	21 34.4	2.3	54.6
23	164 39.9	17.9	146 31.1	11.0	21 32.1	2.3	54.7
28 00	179 39.6	S23 17.8	161 01.1	10.9	S21 29.8	2.5	54.7
01	194 39.3	17.7	175 31.0	11.0	21 27.3	2.5	54.7
02	209 38.9	17.6	190 00.9	11.0	21 24.8	2.7	54.7
03	224 38.6 ··	17.5	204 30.9	10.9	21 22.1	2.8	54.7
04	239 38.3	17.3	219 00.8	11.0	21 19.3	2.8	54.7
05	254 38.0	17.2	233 30.8	10.9	21 16.5	3.0	54.7
06	269 37.7	S23 17.1	248 00.7	11.0	S21 13.5	3.1	54.8
07	284 37.4	17.0	262 30.7	10.9	21 10.4	3.2	54.8
08	299 37.1	16.8	277 00.6	11.0	21 07.2	3.3	54.8
M 09	314 36.8 ··	16.7	291 30.6	11.0	21 03.9	3.4	54.8
O 10	329 36.5	16.6	306 00.6	11.0	21 00.5	3.5	54.8
N 11	344 36.2	16.5	320 30.6	11.0	20 57.0	3.6	54.8
D 12	359 35.9	S23 16.3	335 00.6	11.0	S20 53.4	3.7	54.8
A 13	14 35.6	16.2	349 30.6	11.1	20 49.7	3.8	54.9
Y 14	29 35.3	16.1	4 00.7	11.0	20 45.9	4.0	54.9
15	44 35.0 ··	15.9	18 30.7	11.0	20 41.9	4.0	54.9
16	59 34.6	15.8	33 00.7	11.1	20 37.9	4.1	54.9
17	74 34.3	15.7	47 30.8	11.1	20 33.8	4.2	54.9
18	89 34.0	S23 15.5	62 00.9	11.1	S20 29.6	4.4	54.9
19	104 33.7	15.4	76 31.0	11.1	20 25.2	4.4	55.0
20	119 33.4	15.3	91 01.1	11.1	20 20.8	4.5	55.0
21	134 33.1 ··	15.1	105 31.2	11.1	20 16.3	4.7	55.0
22	149 32.8	15.0	120 01.3	11.2	20 11.6	4.7	55.0
23	164 32.5	14.9	134 31.5	11.2	20 06.9	4.8	55.0
29 00	179 32.2	S23 14.7	149 01.7	11.1	S20 02.1	5.0	55.0
01	194 31.9	14.6	163 31.8	11.2	19 57.1	5.0	55.1
02	209 31.6	14.5	178 02.0	11.3	19 52.1	5.1	55.1
03	224 31.3 ··	14.3	192 32.3	11.2	19 47.0	5.3	55.1
04	239 31.0	14.2	207 02.5	11.2	19 41.7	5.3	55.1
05	254 30.7	14.0	221 32.7	11.3	19 36.4	5.4	55.1
06	269 30.4	S23 13.9	236 03.0	11.3	S19 31.0	5.6	55.1
07	284 30.1	13.8	250 33.3	11.3	19 25.4	5.6	55.2
08	299 29.8	13.6	265 03.6	11.3	19 19.8	5.7	55.2
T 09	314 29.4 ··	13.5	279 33.9	11.4	19 14.1	5.8	55.2
U 10	329 29.1	13.3	294 04.3	11.4	19 08.3	5.9	55.2
E 11	344 28.8	13.2	308 34.7	11.3	19 02.4	6.1	55.2
S 12	359 28.5	S23 13.0	323 05.0	11.4	S18 56.3	6.1	55.2
D 13	14 28.2	12.9	337 35.4	11.5	18 50.2	6.2	55.3
A 14	29 27.9	12.7	352 05.9	11.4	18 44.0	6.3	55.3
Y 15	44 27.6 ··	12.6	6 36.3	11.5	18 37.7	6.3	55.3
16	59 27.3	12.4	21 06.8	11.5	18 31.4	6.5	55.3
17	74 27.0	12.3	35 37.3	11.5	18 24.9	6.6	55.3
18	89 26.7	S23 12.1	50 07.8	11.5	S18 18.3	6.7	55.4
19	104 26.4	12.0	64 38.3	11.6	18 11.6	6.7	55.4
20	119 26.1	11.8	79 08.9	11.6	18 04.9	6.9	55.4
21	134 25.8 ··	11.7	93 39.5	11.6	17 58.0	6.9	55.4
22	149 25.5	11.5	108 10.1	11.6	17 51.1	7.1	55.4
23	164 25.2	11.4	122 40.7	11.6	17 44.0	7.1	55.5
S.D.	16.3	d 0.1	S.D. 14.9		14.9		15.1

Twilight / Sunrise / Moonrise

Lat.	Twilight Naut.	Civil	Sunrise	Moonrise 27	28	29	30
N 72	08 27	10 53	■	■	■	■	13 25
N 70	08 07	09 54	■	■	■	13 11	12 46
68	07 51	09 20	■	12 34	12 27	12 22	12 18
66	07 38	08 55	10 34	11 10	11 38	11 51	11 57
64	07 27	08 36	09 53	10 32	11 07	11 28	11 41
62	07 18	08 20	09 25	10 06	10 43	11 09	11 27
60	07 10	08 06	09 04	09 45	10 24	10 53	11 15
N 58	07 02	07 55	08 46	09 28	10 09	10 40	11 05
56	06 55	07 45	08 32	09 13	09 56	10 29	10 56
54	06 49	07 35	08 19	09 01	09 44	10 19	10 48
52	06 43	07 27	08 08	08 50	09 34	10 10	10 41
50	06 38	07 20	07 58	08 40	09 25	10 02	10 34
45	06 27	07 04	07 38	08 20	09 05	09 45	10 20
N 40	06 17	06 51	07 21	08 03	08 50	09 31	10 09
35	06 07	06 39	07 07	07 49	08 36	09 19	09 59
30	05 59	06 28	06 55	07 37	08 25	09 09	09 50
20	05 42	06 10	06 34	07 17	08 05	08 51	09 35
N 10	05 26	05 52	06 15	06 58	07 48	08 36	09 22
0	05 09	05 35	05 58	06 42	07 31	08 21	09 10
S 10	04 50	05 17	05 40	06 25	07 15	08 06	08 57
20	04 28	04 57	05 21	06 07	06 58	07 51	08 44
30	03 59	04 32	05 00	05 46	06 38	07 33	08 29
35	03 40	04 17	04 47	05 34	06 26	07 22	08 20
40	03 17	03 59	04 32	05 20	06 13	07 10	08 10
45	02 47	03 36	04 14	05 04	05 57	06 56	07 58
S 50	02 02	03 07	03 51	04 43	05 38	06 38	07 44
52	01 34	02 52	03 41	04 34	05 28	06 30	07 37
54	00 50	02 34	03 28	04 23	05 18	06 21	07 29
56	////	02 12	03 14	04 10	05 06	06 10	07 21
58	////	01 43	02 58	03 56	04 52	05 58	07 11
S 60	////	00 54	02 37	03 39	04 36	05 45	07 00

Sunset / Twilight / Moonset

Lat.	Sunset	Twilight Civil	Naut.	Moonset 27	28	29	30
N 72	■	13 10	15 37	■	■	■	17 33
N 70	■	14 09	15 56	■	■	16 05	18 11
68	■	14 44	16 12	13 15	15 06	16 53	18 38
66	13 30	15 08	16 25	14 39	15 55	17 24	18 58
64	14 11	15 28	16 36	15 17	16 26	17 47	19 13
62	14 38	15 44	16 45	15 43	16 49	18 05	19 27
60	15 00	15 57	16 54	16 04	17 07	18 20	19 38
N 58	15 17	16 09	17 01	16 21	17 22	18 32	19 47
56	15 32	16 19	17 08	16 35	17 35	18 43	19 56
54	15 44	16 28	17 14	16 47	17 47	18 53	20 03
52	15 55	16 36	17 20	16 58	17 57	19 01	20 10
50	16 05	16 43	17 25	17 08	18 06	19 09	20 16
45	16 25	16 59	17 36	17 28	18 24	19 25	20 29
N 40	16 42	17 13	17 47	17 45	18 40	19 38	20 39
35	16 56	17 24	17 56	17 59	18 53	19 50	20 48
30	17 09	17 35	18 05	18 11	19 04	19 59	20 56
20	17 30	17 54	18 21	18 31	19 23	20 16	21 10
N 10	17 48	18 11	18 37	18 49	19 40	20 31	21 22
0	18 05	18 28	18 54	19 06	19 55	20 44	21 33
S 10	18 23	18 46	19 13	19 22	20 11	20 58	21 44
20	18 42	19 06	19 35	19 40	20 27	21 12	21 55
30	19 04	19 31	20 04	20 00	20 46	21 29	22 08
35	19 16	19 46	20 23	20 12	20 57	21 38	22 16
40	19 31	20 04	20 46	20 26	21 10	21 49	22 25
45	19 49	20 27	21 16	20 42	21 25	22 02	22 35
S 50	20 12	20 56	22 01	21 02	21 43	22 17	22 47
52	20 22	21 11	22 28	21 11	21 51	22 24	22 52
54	20 35	21 29	23 12	21 22	22 01	22 32	22 58
56	20 49	21 51	////	21 34	22 11	22 41	23 05
58	21 05	22 20	////	21 48	22 24	22 51	23 13
S 60	21 25	23 07	////	22 04	22 38	23 03	23 21

SUN / MOON

Day	SUN Eqn. of Time 00h	12h	Mer. Pass.	MOON Mer. Pass. Upper	Lower	Age	Phase
27	00 52	01 06	12 01	12 54	00 29	01	●
28	01 21	01 36	12 02	13 43	01 19	02	
29	01 51	02 05	12 02	14 33	02 08	03	

1981 DEC. 30, 31, 1982 JAN. 1 (WED., THURS., FRI.)

G.M.T.	ARIES G.H.A.	VENUS −4.2 G.H.A.	Dec.	MARS +0.9 G.H.A.	Dec.	JUPITER −1.4 G.H.A.	Dec.	SATURN +0.9 G.H.A.	Dec.	STARS Name	S.H.A.	Dec.
30 00	98 20.8	147 22.4	S17 01.6	271 42.7	S 0 21.1	244 28.6	S12 20.6	257 43.0	S 6 04.8	Acamar	315 36.3	S40 22.9
01	113 23.3	162 24.9	01.0	286 44.2	21.5	259 30.7	20.8	272 45.3	04.8	Achernar	335 44.4	S57 20.1
02	128 25.7	177 27.3	17 00.4	301 45.7	21.9	274 32.8	20.9	287 47.6	04.9	Acrux	173 36.2	S62 59.6
03	143 28.2	192 29.7	16 59.8	316 47.2 ··	22.3	289 34.9 ··	21.0	302 50.0 ··	04.9	Adhara	255 31.0	S28 56.9
04	158 30.6	207 32.2	59.2	331 48.7	22.6	304 37.0	21.1	317 52.3	05.0	Aldebaran	291 16.7	N16 28.4
05	173 33.1	222 34.6	58.6	346 50.2	23.0	319 39.1	21.2	332 54.6	05.0			
06	188 35.6	237 37.1	S16 58.1	1 51.7	S 0 23.4	334 41.2	S12 21.3	347 57.0	S 6 05.1	Alioth	166 41.8	N56 03.3
W 07	203 38.0	252 39.6	57.5	16 53.2	23.8	349 43.3	21.5	2 59.3	05.1	Alkaid	153 17.9	N49 24.0
E 08	218 40.5	267 42.0	56.9	31 54.7	24.2	4 45.4	21.6	18 01.6	05.1	Al Na'ir	28 14.1	S47 03.2
D 09	233 43.0	282 44.5 ··	56.3	46 56.2 ··	24.5	19 47.5 ··	21.7	33 04.0 ··	05.2	Alnilam	276 10.4	S 1 12.9
N 10	248 45.4	297 47.0	55.7	61 57.7	24.9	34 49.6	21.8	48 06.3	05.2	Alphard	218 19.4	S 8 34.8
E 11	263 47.9	312 49.4	55.1	76 59.1	25.3	49 51.8	21.9	63 08.6	05.3			
S 12	278 50.4	327 51.9	S16 54.6	92 00.6	S 0 25.7	64 53.9	S12 22.0	78 11.0	S 6 05.3	Alphecca	126 31.6	N26 46.5
D 13	293 52.8	342 54.4	54.0	107 02.1	26.0	79 56.0	22.2	93 13.3	05.3	Alpheratz	358 08.4	N28 59.5
A 14	308 55.3	357 56.9	53.4	122 03.6	26.4	94 58.1	22.3	108 15.6	05.4	Altair	62 32.0	N 8 49.2
Y 15	323 57.7	12 59.4 ··	52.8	137 05.1 ··	26.8	110 00.2 ··	22.4	123 18.0 ··	05.4	Ankaa	353 39.4	S42 24.6
16	339 00.2	28 01.9	52.2	152 06.6	27.2	125 02.3	22.5	138 20.3	05.5	Antares	112 56.1	S26 23.4
17	354 02.7	43 04.4	51.7	167 08.1	27.6	140 04.4	22.6	153 22.6	05.5			
18	9 05.1	58 06.9	S16 51.1	182 09.6	S 0 27.9	155 06.5	S12 22.7	168 25.0	S 6 05.5	Arcturus	146 17.8	N19 16.5
19	24 07.6	73 09.4	50.5	197 11.1	28.3	170 08.6	22.9	183 27.3	05.6	Atria	108 20.1	S68 59.5
20	39 10.1	88 11.9	49.9	212 12.6	28.7	185 10.7	23.0	198 29.6	05.6	Avior	234 27.2	S59 27.0
21	54 12.5	103 14.4 ··	49.3	227 14.1 ··	29.1	200 12.8 ··	23.1	213 32.0 ··	05.7	Bellatrix	278 57.5	N 6 20.0
22	69 15.0	118 17.0	48.8	242 15.6	29.4	215 14.9	23.2	228 34.3	05.7	Betelgeuse	271 27.0	N 7 24.2
23	84 17.5	133 19.5	48.2	257 17.1	29.8	230 17.0	23.3	243 36.6	05.7			
31 00	99 19.9	148 22.0	S16 47.6	272 18.6	S 0 30.2	245 19.1	S12 23.4	258 39.0	S 6 05.8	Canopus	264 06.2	S52 41.2
01	114 22.4	163 24.6	47.0	287 20.1	30.6	260 21.2	23.6	273 41.3	05.8	Capella	281 09.5	N45 58.8
02	129 24.9	178 27.1	46.5	302 21.6	30.9	275 23.3	23.7	288 43.7	05.9	Deneb	49 48.3	N45 13.0
03	144 27.3	193 29.6 ··	45.9	317 23.2 ··	31.3	290 25.4 ··	23.8	303 46.0 ··	05.9	Denebola	182 58.1	N14 40.4
04	159 29.8	208 32.2	45.3	332 24.7	31.7	305 27.5	23.9	318 48.3	05.9	Diphda	349 20.0	S18 05.4
05	174 32.2	223 34.8	44.7	347 26.2	32.1	320 29.6	24.0	333 50.7	06.0			
06	189 34.7	238 37.3	S16 44.2	2 27.7	S 0 32.4	335 31.7	S12 24.1	348 53.0	S 6 06.0	Dubhe	194 20.7	N61 50.7
07	204 37.2	253 39.9	43.6	17 29.2	32.8	350 33.9	24.3	3 55.3	06.1	Elnath	278 42.6	N28 35.5
T 08	219 39.6	268 42.4	43.0	32 30.7	33.2	5 36.0	24.4	18 57.7	06.1	Eltanin	90 57.9	N51 29.4
H 09	234 42.1	283 45.0 ··	42.5	47 32.2 ··	33.6	20 38.1 ··	24.5	34 00.0 ··	06.1	Enif	34 10.9	N 9 47.5
U 10	249 44.6	298 47.6	41.9	62 33.7	33.9	35 40.2	24.6	49 02.3	06.2	Fomalhaut	15 50.6	S29 43.3
R 11	264 47.0	313 50.2	41.3	77 35.2	34.3	50 42.3	24.7	64 04.7	06.2			
S 12	279 49.5	328 52.8	S16 40.8	92 36.7	S 0 34.7	65 44.4	S12 24.8	79 07.0	S 6 06.3	Gacrux	172 27.8	S57 00.4
D 13	294 52.0	343 55.4	40.2	107 38.2	35.0	80 46.5	24.9	94 09.4	06.3	Gienah	176 17.0	S17 26.3
A 14	309 54.4	358 57.9	39.6	122 39.7	35.4	95 48.6	25.1	109 11.7	06.3	Hadar	149 22.4	S60 16.8
Y 15	324 56.9	14 00.5 ··	39.1	137 41.2 ··	35.8	110 50.7 ··	25.2	124 14.0 ··	06.4	Hamal	328 27.8	N23 22.7
16	339 59.4	29 03.2	38.5	152 42.7	36.2	125 52.8	25.3	139 16.4	06.4	Kaus Aust.	84 16.1	S34 23.6
17	355 01.8	44 05.8	37.9	167 44.2	36.5	140 54.9	25.4	154 18.7	06.5			
18	10 04.3	59 08.4	S16 37.4	182 45.7	S 0 36.9	155 57.0	S12 25.5	169 21.0	S 6 06.5	Kochab	137 19.7	N74 13.6
19	25 06.7	74 11.0	36.8	197 47.3	37.3	170 59.2	25.6	184 23.4	06.5	Markab	14 02.4	N15 06.5
20	40 09.2	89 13.6	36.2	212 48.8	37.6	186 01.3	25.7	199 25.7	06.6	Menkar	314 40.0	N 4 01.1
21	55 11.7	104 16.2 ··	35.7	227 50.3 ··	38.0	201 03.4 ··	25.9	214 28.1 ··	06.6	Menkent	148 36.1	S36 16.6
22	70 14.1	119 18.9	35.1	242 51.8	38.4	216 05.5	26.0	229 30.4	06.6	Miaplacidus	221 44.0	S69 38.3
23	85 16.6	134 21.5	34.5	257 53.3	38.8	231 07.6	26.1	244 32.7	06.7			
1 00	100 19.1	149 24.1	S16 34.0	272 54.8	S 0 39.1	246 09.7	S12 26.2	259 35.1	S 6 06.7	Mirfak	309 14.5	N49 48.0
01	115 21.5	164 26.8	33.4	287 56.3	39.5	261 11.8	26.3	274 37.4	06.8	Nunki	76 28.4	S26 19.2
02	130 24.0	179 29.4	32.9	302 57.8	39.9	276 13.9	26.4	289 39.7	06.8	Peacock	53 57.5	S56 47.8
03	145 26.5	194 32.1 ··	32.3	317 59.4 ··	40.2	291 16.0 ··	26.5	304 42.1 ··	06.8	Pollux	243 56.7	N28 04.2
04	160 28.9	209 34.7	31.7	333 00.9	40.6	306 18.1	26.7	319 44.4	06.9	Procyon	245 24.5	N 5 16.3
05	175 31.4	224 37.4	31.2	348 02.4	41.0	321 20.3	26.8	334 46.8	06.9			
06	190 33.8	239 40.1	S16 30.6	3 03.9	S 0 41.3	336 22.4	S12 26.9	349 49.1	S 6 07.0	Rasalhague	96 29.1	N12 34.4
07	205 36.3	254 42.7	30.1	18 05.4	41.7	351 24.5	27.0	4 51.4	07.0	Regulus	208 08.8	N12 03.3
08	220 38.8	269 45.4	29.5	33 06.9	42.1	6 26.6	27.1	19 53.8	07.0	Rigel	281 34.8	S 8 13.4
F 09	235 41.2	284 48.1 ··	29.0	48 08.4 ··	42.4	21 28.7 ··	27.2	34 56.1 ··	07.1	Rigil Kent.	140 25.0	S60 45.3
R 10	250 43.7	299 50.8	28.4	63 10.0	42.8	36 30.8	27.3	49 58.5	07.1	Sabik	102 40.4	S15 42.1
I 11	265 46.2	314 53.5	27.9	78 11.5	43.2	51 32.9	27.4	65 00.8	07.1			
D 12	280 48.6	329 56.2	S16 27.3	93 13.0	S 0 43.6	66 35.0	S12 27.6	80 03.1	S 6 07.2	Schedar	350 08.0	N56 26.5
A 13	295 51.1	344 58.9	26.7	108 14.5	43.9	81 37.2	27.7	95 05.5	07.2	Shaula	96 55.0	S37 05.4
Y 14	310 53.6	0 01.6	26.2	123 16.0	44.3	96 39.3	27.8	110 07.8	07.3	Sirius	258 54.6	S16 41.5
15	325 56.0	15 04.3 ··	25.6	138 17.5 ··	44.7	111 41.4 ··	27.9	125 10.2 ··	07.3	Spica	158 56.7	S11 03.9
16	340 58.5	30 07.0	25.1	153 19.1	45.0	126 43.5	28.0	140 12.5	07.3	Suhail	223 09.8	S43 21.4
17	356 01.0	45 09.7	24.5	168 20.6	45.4	141 45.6	28.1	155 14.8	07.4			
18	11 03.4	60 12.4	S16 24.0	183 22.1	S 0 45.8	156 47.7	S12 28.2	170 17.2	S 6 07.4	Vega	80 55.7	N38 46.0
19	26 05.9	75 15.1	23.4	198 23.6	46.1	171 49.8	28.3	185 19.5	07.4	Zuben'ubi	137 32.3	S15 57.9
20	41 08.3	90 17.9	22.9	213 25.1	46.5	186 51.9	28.5	200 21.9	07.5		S.H.A.	Mer. Pass.
21	56 10.8	105 20.6 ··	22.3	228 26.7 ··	46.9	201 54.1 ··	28.6	215 24.2 ··	07.5	Venus	49 02.1	14 04
22	71 13.3	120 23.3	21.8	243 28.2	47.2	216 56.2	28.7	230 26.6	07.6	Mars	172 58.7	5 50
23	86 15.7	135 26.1	21.2	258 29.7	47.6	231 58.3	28.8	245 28.9	07.6	Jupiter	145 59.2	7 38
Mer. Pass. 17 19.8		v 2.6	d 0.6	v 1.5	d 0.4	v 2.1	d 0.1	v 2.3	d 0.0	Saturn	159 19.1	6 44

	G.M.T. d h	SUN G.H.A. ° ′	SUN Dec. ° ′	MOON G.H.A. ° ′	MOON v ′	MOON Dec. ° ′	MOON d ′	MOON H.P. ′
	30 00	179 24.9	S23 11.2	137 11.3	11.7	S17 36.9	7.2	55.5
	01	194 24.6	11.0	151 42.0	11.7	17 29.7	7.3	55.5
	02	209 24.3	10.9	166 12.7	11.7	17 22.4	7.4	55.5
	03	224 24.0	·· 10.7	180 43.4	11.7	17 15.0	7.4	55.5
	04	239 23.7	10.6	195 14.1	11.8	17 07.6	7.6	55.6
	05	254 23.4	10.4	209 44.9	11.8	17 00.0	7.7	55.6
	06	269 23.1	S23 10.2	224 15.7	11.8	S16 52.3	7.7	55.6
W	07	284 22.8	10.1	238 46.5	11.8	16 44.6	7.8	55.6
E	08	299 22.5	09.9	253 17.3	11.8	16 36.8	7.9	55.6
D	09	314 22.2	·· 09.7	267 48.1	11.9	16 28.9	8.0	55.7
N	10	329 21.9	09.6	282 19.0	11.9	16 20.9	8.1	55.7
E	11	344 21.6	09.4	296 49.9	11.9	16 12.8	8.1	55.7
S	12	359 21.3	S23 09.3	311 20.8	11.9	S16 04.7	8.3	55.7
D	13	14 21.0	09.1	325 51.7	12.0	15 56.4	8.3	55.7
A	14	29 20.6	08.9	340 22.7	12.0	15 48.1	8.4	55.8
Y	15	44 20.3	·· 08.7	354 53.7	12.0	15 39.7	8.5	55.8
	16	59 20.0	08.6	9 24.7	12.0	15 31.2	8.5	55.8
	17	74 19.7	08.4	23 55.7	12.0	15 22.7	8.7	55.8
	18	89 19.4	S23 08.2	38 26.7	12.1	S15 14.0	8.7	55.9
	19	104 19.1	08.1	52 57.8	12.1	15 05.3	8.8	55.9
	20	119 18.8	07.9	67 28.9	12.1	14 56.5	8.9	55.9
	21	134 18.5	·· 07.7	82 00.0	12.1	14 47.6	8.9	55.9
	22	149 18.2	07.5	96 31.1	12.1	14 38.7	9.1	55.9
	23	164 17.9	07.4	111 02.2	12.2	14 29.6	9.1	56.0
	31 00	179 17.6	S23 07.2	125 33.4	12.2	S14 20.5	9.1	56.0
	01	194 17.3	07.0	140 04.6	12.2	14 11.4	9.3	56.0
	02	209 17.0	06.8	154 35.8	12.2	14 02.1	9.3	56.0
	03	224 16.7	·· 06.7	169 07.0	12.2	13 52.8	9.4	56.1
	04	239 16.4	06.5	183 38.2	12.3	13 43.4	9.5	56.1
	05	254 16.1	06.3	198 09.5	12.3	13 33.9	9.5	56.1
	06	269 15.8	S23 06.1	212 40.8	12.3	S13 24.4	9.7	56.1
	07	284 15.5	05.9	227 12.1	12.3	13 14.7	9.7	56.2
T	08	299 15.2	05.8	241 43.4	12.3	13 05.0	9.7	56.2
H	09	314 14.9	·· 05.6	256 14.7	12.3	12 55.3	9.8	56.2
U	10	329 14.6	05.4	270 46.0	12.4	12 45.5	9.9	56.2
R	11	344 14.3	05.2	285 17.4	12.4	12 35.6	10.0	56.3
S	12	359 14.0	S23 05.0	299 48.8	12.4	S12 25.6	10.0	56.3
D	13	14 13.7	04.8	314 20.2	12.4	12 15.6	10.1	56.3
A	14	29 13.4	04.6	328 51.6	12.4	12 05.5	10.2	56.3
Y	15	44 13.1	·· 04.5	343 23.0	12.4	11 55.3	10.2	56.3
	16	59 12.8	04.3	357 54.4	12.5	11 45.1	10.3	56.4
	17	74 12.5	04.1	12 25.9	12.4	11 34.8	10.3	56.4
	18	89 12.2	S23 03.9	26 57.3	12.5	S11 24.5	10.5	56.4
	19	104 12.0	03.7	41 28.8	12.5	11 14.0	10.4	56.5
	20	119 11.7	03.5	56 00.3	12.5	11 03.6	10.6	56.5
	21	134 11.4	·· 03.3	70 31.8	12.5	10 53.0	10.6	56.5
	22	149 11.1	03.1	85 03.3	12.5	10 42.4	10.6	56.5
	23	164 10.8	02.9	99 34.8	12.5	10 31.8	10.8	56.6
	1 00	179 10.5	S23 02.7	114 06.3	12.5	S10 21.0	10.7	56.6
	01	194 10.2	02.5	128 37.8	12.6	10 10.3	10.9	56.6
	02	209 09.9	02.3	143 09.4	12.5	9 59.4	10.9	56.6
	03	224 09.6	·· 02.1	157 40.9	12.6	9 48.5	10.9	56.7
	04	239 09.3	01.9	172 12.5	12.5	9 37.6	11.0	56.7
	05	254 09.0	01.7	186 44.0	12.6	9 26.6	11.1	56.7
	06	269 08.7	S23 01.5	201 15.6	12.6	S 9 15.5	11.1	56.7
	07	284 08.4	01.3	215 47.2	12.5	9 04.4	11.1	56.8
	08	299 08.1	01.1	230 18.7	12.6	8 53.3	11.3	56.8
F	09	314 07.8	·· 00.9	244 50.3	12.6	8 42.0	11.2	56.8
R	10	329 07.5	00.7	259 21.9	12.6	8 30.8	11.3	56.8
I	11	344 07.2	00.5	273 53.5	12.6	8 19.5	11.4	56.9
D	12	359 06.9	S23 00.3	288 25.1	12.5	S 8 08.1	11.4	56.9
A	13	14 06.6	23 00.1	302 56.6	12.6	7 56.7	11.5	56.9
Y	14	29 06.3	22 59.9	317 28.2	12.6	7 45.2	11.5	57.0
	15	44 06.0	·· 59.7	331 59.8	12.6	7 33.7	11.6	57.0
	16	59 05.7	59.5	346 31.4	12.6	7 22.1	11.6	57.0
	17	74 05.4	59.3	1 03.0	12.5	7 10.5	11.6	57.0
	18	89 05.1	S22 59.1	15 34.5	12.6	S 6 58.9	11.7	57.1
	19	104 04.8	58.9	30 06.1	12.6	6 47.2	11.8	57.1
	20	119 04.5	58.6	44 37.7	12.6	6 35.4	11.8	57.1
	21	134 04.3	·· 58.4	59 09.3	12.5	6 23.6	11.8	57.2
	22	149 04.0	58.2	73 40.8	12.6	6 11.8	11.9	57.2
	23	164 03.7	58.0	88 12.4	12.5	5 59.9	11.9	57.2
		S.D. 16.3	d 0.2	S.D. 15.2		15.3		15.5

Lat. °	Twilight Naut. h m	Twilight Civil h m	Sunrise h m	Moonrise 30 h m	Moonrise 31 h m	Moonrise 1 h m	Moonrise 2 h m
N 72	08 25	10 46	■	13 25	12 53	12 32	12 15
N 70	08 06	09 51	■	12 46	12 31	12 20	12 11
68	07 50	09 18	■	12 18	12 14	12 11	12 07
66	07 38	08 54	10 30	11 57	12 01	12 03	12 04
64	07 27	08 35	09 51	11 41	11 49	11 56	12 01
62	07 18	08 19	09 24	11 27	11 40	11 50	11 58
60	07 10	08 06	09 03	11 15	11 31	11 45	11 56
N 58	07 02	07 55	08 46	11 05	11 24	11 40	11 54
56	06 56	07 45	08 32	10 56	11 17	11 36	11 53
54	06 50	07 36	08 19	10 48	11 11	11 32	11 51
52	06 44	07 28	08 08	10 41	11 06	11 29	11 50
50	06 39	07 20	07 59	10 34	11 01	11 26	11 49
45	06 27	07 05	07 38	10 20	10 51	11 19	11 46
N 40	06 17	06 51	07 22	10 09	10 42	11 14	11 44
35	06 08	06 40	07 08	09 59	10 35	11 09	11 42
30	06 00	06 29	06 56	09 50	10 28	11 05	11 40
20	05 43	06 11	06 35	09 35	10 17	10 57	11 37
N 10	05 27	05 54	06 17	09 22	10 07	10 51	11 34
0	05 11	05 37	05 59	09 10	09 57	10 44	11 32
S 10	04 52	05 19	05 42	08 57	09 48	10 38	11 29
20	04 30	04 59	05 23	08 44	09 38	10 32	11 26
30	04 01	04 34	05 02	08 29	09 26	10 24	11 23
35	03 43	04 19	04 49	08 20	09 19	10 20	11 21
40	03 20	04 01	04 34	08 10	09 12	10 15	11 19
45	02 50	03 39	04 16	07 58	09 03	10 09	11 17
S 50	02 05	03 10	03 54	07 44	08 52	10 02	11 14
52	01 39	02 55	03 43	07 37	08 47	09 59	11 13
54	00 57	02 38	03 31	07 29	08 41	09 56	11 12
56	////	02 16	03 17	07 21	08 35	09 52	11 10
58	////	01 47	03 01	07 11	08 28	09 47	11 08
S 60	////	01 02	02 41	07 00	08 20	09 43	11 07

Lat. °	Sunset h m	Twilight Civil h m	Twilight Naut. h m	Moonset 30 h m	Moonset 31 h m	Moonset 1 h m	Moonset 2 h m
N 72	■	13 20	15 41	17 33	19 45	21 44	23 41
N 70	■	14 15	16 01	18 11	20 05	21 54	23 42
68	■	14 48	16 16	18 38	20 20	22 02	23 44
66	13 36	15 13	16 29	18 58	20 33	22 08	23 45
64	14 16	15 32	16 39	19 13	20 43	22 13	23 46
62	14 43	15 47	16 49	19 27	20 52	22 18	23 46
60	15 03	16 00	16 57	19 38	20 59	22 22	23 47
N 58	15 20	16 12	17 04	19 47	21 06	22 26	23 48
56	15 35	16 22	17 11	19 56	21 11	22 29	23 48
54	15 47	16 31	17 17	20 03	21 16	22 32	23 49
52	15 58	16 39	17 22	20 10	21 21	22 34	23 49
50	16 08	16 46	17 27	20 16	21 25	22 36	23 49
45	16 28	17 02	17 39	20 29	21 34	22 41	23 50
N 40	16 44	17 15	17 49	20 39	21 42	22 46	23 51
35	16 58	17 26	17 58	20 48	21 48	22 49	23 51
30	17 11	17 37	18 07	20 56	21 54	22 52	23 52
20	17 31	17 55	18 23	21 10	22 04	22 58	23 53
N 10	17 50	18 12	18 39	21 22	22 12	23 02	23 54
0	18 07	18 29	18 55	21 33	22 20	23 07	23 54
S 10	18 24	18 47	19 14	21 44	22 28	23 11	23 55
20	18 43	19 07	19 36	21 55	22 36	23 16	23 55
30	19 04	19 32	20 05	22 08	22 45	23 21	23 56
35	19 17	19 47	20 23	22 16	22 51	23 24	23 57
40	19 32	20 05	20 46	22 25	22 57	23 27	23 57
45	19 50	20 27	21 16	22 35	23 04	23 31	23 58
S 50	20 12	20 56	22 00	22 47	23 12	23 36	23 58
52	20 22	21 11	22 26	22 52	23 16	23 38	23 58
54	20 34	21 28	23 07	22 58	23 20	23 40	23 59
56	20 48	21 49	////	23 05	23 25	23 43	23 59
58	21 04	22 17	////	23 13	23 30	23 45	23 59
S 60	21 24	23 02	////	23 21	23 36	23 48	24 00

Day	SUN Eqn. of Time 00^h m s	SUN Eqn. of Time 12^h m s	SUN Mer. Pass. h m	MOON Mer. Pass. Upper h m	MOON Mer. Pass. Lower h m	MOON Age d	MOON Phase
30	02 20	02 34	12 03	15 21	02 57	04	
31	02 49	03 03	12 03	16 09	03 45	05	◐
1	03 18	03 32	12 04	16 56	04 32	06	

EXPLANATION

PRINCIPLE AND ARRANGEMENT

1. *Object.* The object of this Almanac is to provide, in a convenient form, the data required for the practice of astronomical navigation at sea.

2. *Principle.* The main contents of the Almanac consist of data from which the *Greenwich Hour Angle* (G.H.A.) and the *Declination* (Dec.) of all the bodies used for navigation can be obtained for any instant of *Greenwich Mean Time* (G.M.T.). The *Local Hour Angle* (L.H.A.) can then be obtained by means of the formula:

$$\text{L.H.A.} = \text{G.H.A.} \; {- \text{ west} \atop + \text{ east}} \; \text{longitude}$$

The remaining data consist of: times of rising and setting of the Sun and Moon, and times of twilight; miscellaneous calendarial and planning data and auxiliary tables, including a list of Standard Times; corrections to be applied to observed altitude.

For the Sun, Moon, and planets the G.H.A. and Dec. are tabulated directly for each hour of G.M.T. throughout the year. For the stars the *Sidereal Hour Angle* (S.H.A.) is given, and the G.H.A. is obtained from:

$$\text{G.H.A. Star} = \text{G.H.A. Aries} + \text{S.H.A. Star}$$

The S.H.A. and Dec. of the stars change slowly and may be regarded as constant over periods of several days. G.H.A. Aries, or the Greenwich Hour Angle of the first point of Aries (the Vernal Equinox), is tabulated for each hour. Permanent tables give the appropriate increments and corrections to the tabulated hourly values of G.H.A. and Dec. for the minutes and seconds of G.M.T.

The six-volume series of *Sight Reduction Tables for Marine Navigation* (published in U.S.A. as Pub. No. 229 and in U.K. as N.P. 401) has been designed for the solution of the navigational triangle and is intended for use with *The Nautical Almanac*.

The tabular accuracy is 0'·1 throughout. The time argument on the daily pages of this Almanac is $12^h +$ the Greenwich Hour Angle of the mean sun and is here denoted by G.M.T., although it is also known as universal time (UT, or UT1). This scale may differ from the broadcast time signals (UTC) by an amount which, if ignored, will introduce an error of up to 0'·2 in longitude determined from astronomical observations. (The difference arises because the time argument depends on the variable rate of rotation of the Earth while the broadcast time signals are now based on an atomic time-scale.) Step adjustments of exactly one second are made to the time signals as required (normally at 24^h on December 31 and June 30) so that the difference between the time signals and G.M.T., as used in this Almanac, may not exceed $0^s\cdot9$. Those who require to reduce observations to a precision of better than 1^s must therefore obtain the correction to the time signals from coding in the signal, or from other sources. The correction may be applied to each of the times of observation; alternatively, the longitude, when determined from astronomical observations, may be corrected by the corresponding amount shown in the following table:

Correction to time signals	Correction to longitude
$-0^s\cdot9$ to $-0^s\cdot7$	0'·2 to east
$-0^s\cdot6$ to $-0^s\cdot3$	0'·1 to east
$-0^s\cdot2$ to $+0^s\cdot2$	no correction
$+0^s\cdot3$ to $+0^s\cdot6$	0'·1 to west
$+0^s\cdot7$ to $+0^s\cdot9$	0'·2 to west

3. *Lay-out.* The ephemeral data for three days are presented on an opening of two pages: the left-hand page contains the data for the planets and stars; the right-hand page contains the data for the Sun and Moon, together with times of twilight, sunrise, sunset, moonrise and moonset.

The remaining contents are arranged as follows: for ease of reference the altitude-correction tables are given on pages A2, A3, A4, xxxiv and xxxv; calendar, Moon's phases, eclipses, and planet notes (i.e. data of general interest) precede the main tabulations; the other data follow the main tabulations and are arranged, as far as possible, in order of importance or frequency of use backwards from page xxxv.

MAIN DATA

4. *Daily pages.* The daily pages give the G.H.A. of Aries, the G.H.A. and Dec. of the Sun, Moon, and the four navigational planets, for each hour of G.M.T. For the Moon, values of v and d are also tabulated for each hour to facilitate the correction of G.H.A. and Dec. to intermediate times; v and d for the Sun and planets change so slowly that they are given, at the foot of the appropriate columns, once only on the page; v is zero for Aries and negligible for the Sun, and is omitted. The S.H.A. and Dec. of the 57 selected stars, arranged in alphabetical order of proper name, are also given.

5. *Stars.* The S.H.A. and Dec. of 173 stars, including the 57 selected stars, are tabulated for each month on pages 268-273; no interpolation is required and the data can be used in precisely the same way as those for the selected stars on the daily pages. The stars are arranged in order of S.H.A.

The list of 173 includes all stars down to magnitude 3·0, together with a few fainter ones to fill the larger gaps. The 57 selected stars have been chosen from amongst these on account of brightness and distribution in the sky; they will suffice for the majority of observations.

The 57 selected stars are known by their proper names, but they are also numbered in descending order of S.H.A. In the list of 173 stars, the constellation names are always given on the left-hand page; on the facing page proper names are given where well-known names exist. Numbers for the selected stars are given in both columns.

An index to the selected stars, containing lists in both alphabetical and numerical order, is given on page xxxiii and is also reprinted on the bookmark.

6. *Increments and corrections.* These tables, printed on tinted paper (pages ii-xxxi) at the back of the Almanac, provide the increments and corrections for minutes and seconds to be applied to the hourly values of G.H.A. and Déc. They consist of sixty tables, one for each minute, separated into two parts: increments to G.H.A. for Sun and planets, Aries, and Moon for every minute and second; and, for each minute, corrections to be applied to G.H.A. and Dec. corresponding to the values of v and d given on the daily pages.

The increments are based on the following adopted hourly rates of increase of the G.H.A.: Sun and planets, $15°$ precisely; Aries, $15° 02'·46$; Moon, $14° 19'·0$. The values of v on the daily pages are the excesses of the actual hourly motions over the adopted values; they are generally positive, except for Venus. The tabulated hourly values of the Sun's G.H.A. have been adjusted to reduce to a minimum the error caused by treating v as negligible. The values of d on the daily pages are the hourly differences of the Dec. For the Moon, the true values of v and d are given for each hour; otherwise mean values are given for the three days on the page.

7. *Method of entry.* The G.M.T. of an observation is expressed as a day and hour, followed by a number of minutes and seconds. The tabular values of G.H.A. and Dec., and, where necessary, the corresponding values of v and d, are taken directly from the daily pages for the day and hour of G.M.T.; this hour is always *before* the time of observation. S.H.A. and Dec. of the selected stars are also taken from the daily pages.

The table of Increments and Corrections for the minute of G.M.T. is then selected. For the G.H.A., the increment for minutes and seconds is taken from the appropriate column opposite the seconds of G.M.T.; the v-correction is taken from the second part of the same table opposite the value of v as given on the daily pages. Both increment and v-correction are to be added to the G.H.A., except for Venus when v is prefixed by a minus sign and the v-correction is to be subtracted. For the Dec. there is no increment, but a d-correction is applied in the same way as the v-correction; d is given without sign on the daily pages and the sign of the correction is to be supplied by inspection of the Dec. column. In many cases the correction may be applied mentally.

8. *Examples.* (a) Sun and Moon. Required the G.H.A. and Dec. of the Sun and Moon on 1981 January 22 at G.M.T. $15^h 47^m 13^s$.

	SUN			MOON			
	G.H.A.	Dec.	d	G.H.A.	v	Dec.	d
	° ′	° ′	′	° ′	′	° ′	′
Daily page, Jan. $22^d 15^h$	42 04·7	S.19 35·9	0·6	193 38·8	11·8	N.12 57·4	8·8
Increments for $47^m 13^s$	11 48·3			11 16·0			
v or d corrections for 47^m		−0·5			+9·3	−7·0	
Sum for Jan. $22^d 15^h 47^m 13^s$	53 53·0	S.19 35·4		205 04·1		N.12 50·4	

(b) Planets. Required the L.H.A. and Dec. of (i) Venus on 1981 January 22 at G.M.T. $12^h 57^m 28^s$ in longitude W. 107° 12′; (ii) Jupiter on 1981 January 22 at G.M.T. $03^h 48^m 51^s$ in longitude E. 27° 45′.

	VENUS				JUPITER			
	G.H.A.	v	Dec.	d	G.H.A.	v	Dec.	d
	° ′	′	° ′	′	° ′	′	° ′	′
Daily page, Jan. 22^d (12^h)	16 30·1	−0·9	S.22 45·7	0·2	(03^h) 336 17·5	2·5	S.2 49·2	0·0
Increments (planets) $(57^m 28^s)$	14 22·0				$(48^m 51^s)$ 12 12·8			
v or d corrections (57^m)	−0·9		−0·2		(48^m) +2·0		0·0	
Sum = G.H.A. and Dec.	30 51·2		S.22 45·5		348 32·3		S.2 49·2	
Longitude (west)	−107 12·0				(east) + 27 45·0			
Multiples of 360°	+360				−360			
L.H.A. planet	283 39·2				16 17·3			

(c) Stars. Required the G.H.A. and Dec. of (i) *Aldebaran* on 1981 January 22 at G.M.T. $15^h 55^m 13^s$; (ii) *Vega* on 1981 January 22 at G.M.T. $16^h 02^m 45^s$.

		Aldebaran		Vega	
		G.H.A.	Dec.	G.H.A.	Dec.
		° ′	° ′	° ′	° ′
Daily page (S.H.A. and Dec.)		291 17·5	N.16 28·2	80 56·1	N.38 45·9
Daily page (G.H.A. Aries)	(15^h)	346 52·3		(16^h) 1 54·8	
Increments (Aries)	$(55^m 13^s)$	13 50·5		$(02^m 45^s)$ 0 41·4	
Sum = G.H.A. star		652 00·3		83 32·3	
Multiples of 360°		−360			
G.H.A. star		292 00·3		83 32·3	

9. *Polaris (Pole Star) tables.* The tables on pages 274-276 provide means by which the latitude can be deduced from an observed altitude of *Polaris*, and they also give its azimuth; their use is explained and illustrated on those pages. They are based on the following formula:

$$\text{Latitude} - Ho = -p \cos h + \tfrac{1}{2} p \sin p \sin^2 h \tan (\text{latitude})$$

where
Ho = Apparent altitude (corrected for refraction)
p = polar distance of *Polaris* = 90° − Dec.
h = local hour angle of *Polaris* = L.H.A. Aries + S.H.A.

a_0, which is a function of L.H.A. Aries only, is the value of both terms of the above formula calculated for mean values of the S.H.A. (326° 42′) and Dec. (N.89° 10′·8) of *Polaris*, for a mean latitude of 50°, and adjusted by the addition of a constant (58′·8). a_1, which is a function of

L.H.A. Aries and latitude, is the excess of the value of the second term over its mean value for latitude 50°, increased by a constant (0′·6) to make it always positive. a_2, which is a function of L.H.A. Aries and date, is the correction to the first term for the variation of *Polaris* from its adopted mean position; it is increased by a constant (0′·6) to make it positive. The sum of the added constants is 1°, so that:

$$\text{Latitude} = \text{Apparent altitude (corrected for refraction)} - 1° + a_0 + a_1 + a_2$$

RISING AND SETTING PHENOMENA

10. *General.*   On the right-hand daily pages are given the times of sunrise and sunset, of the beginning and end of civil and nautical twilights, and of moonrise and moonset for a range of latitudes from N. 72° to S. 60°. These times, which are given to the nearest minute, are strictly the G.M.T. of the phenomena on the Greenwich meridian; they are given for every day for moonrise and moonset, but only for the middle day of the three on each page for the solar phenomena.

They are approximately the Local Mean Times (L.M.T.) of the corresponding phenomena on other meridians; they can be formally interpolated if desired. The G.M.T. of a phenomenon is obtained from the L.M.T. by:

$$\text{G.M.T.} = \text{L.M.T.} \begin{array}{l} + \text{ west} \\ - \text{ east} \end{array} \text{longitude}$$

in which the longitude must first be converted to time by the table on page i or otherwise.

Interpolation for latitude can be done mentally or with the aid of Table I on page xxxii.

The following symbols are used to indicate the conditions under which, in high latitudes, some of the phenomena do not occur:

◻ Sun or Moon remains continuously above the horizon;

■ Sun or Moon remains continuously below the horizon;

//// twilight lasts all night.

Basis of the tabulations.   At sunrise and sunset 16′ is allowed for semi-diameter and 34′ for horizontal refraction, so that at the times given the Sun's upper limb is on the visible horizon; all times refer to phenomena as seen from sea level with a clear horizon.

At the times given for the beginning and end of twilight, the Sun's zenith distance is 96° for civil, and 102° for nautical twilight. The degree of illumination at the times given for civil twilight (in good conditions and in the absence of other illumination) is such that the brightest stars are visible and the horizon is clearly defined. At the times given for nautical twilight the horizon is in general not visible, and it is too dark for observation with a marine sextant.

Times corresponding to other depressions of the Sun may be obtained by interpolation or, for depressions of more than 12°, less reliably, by extrapolation; times so obtained will be subject to considerable uncertainty near extreme conditions.

At moonrise and moonset allowance is made for semi-diameter, parallax, and refraction (34′), so that at the times given the Moon's upper limb is on the visible horizon as seen from sea level.

11. *Sunrise, sunset, twilight.*   The tabulated times may be regarded, without serious error, as the L.M.T. of the phenomena on any of the three days on the page and in any longitude. Precise times may normally be obtained by interpolating the tabular values for latitude and to the correct day and longitude, the latter being expressed as a fraction of a day by dividing it by 360°, positive for west and negative for east longitudes. In the extreme conditions near ◻ , ■ or //// interpolation may not be possible in one direction, but accurate times are of little value in these circumstances.

Examples.   Required the G.M.T. of (a) the beginning of morning twilights and sunrise on 1981 January 22 for latitude S. 48° 55′, longitude E. 75° 18′; (b) sunset and the end of evening twilights on 1981 January 24 for latitude N. 67° 10′, longitude W. 168° 05′.

	(a)	Twilight Nautical	Civil	Sunrise	(b)	Sunset	Twilight Civil	Nautical
		d h m	d h m	d h m		d h m	d h m	d h m
From p. 25								
L.M.T. for								
Lat.	S.45°	22 03 25	22 04 09	22 04 44	N. 66°	24 14 57	24 16 08	24 17 15
Corr. to	S.48° 55′	−27	−20	−16	N. 67° 10′	−17	−9	−6
(p. xxxii, Table I)								
Long. (p. i)	E.75° 18′	−5 01	−5 01	−5 01	W.168° 05′	+11 12	+11 12	+11 12
G.M.T.		21 21 57	21 22 48	21 23 27		25 01 52	25 03 11	25 04 21

The L.M.T. are strictly for January 23 (middle date on page) and 0° longitude; for more precise times it is necessary to interpolate, but rounding errors may accumulate to about 2^m:

(a) to January 22^d − 75°/360° = Jan. 21^d·8, i.e. $\frac{1}{5}$ (1·2) = 0·4 backwards towards the data for the same latitude interpolated similarly from page 23; the corrections are −2^m to nautical twilight, −2^m to civil twilight and −2^m to sunrise.

(b) to January 24^d + 168°/360° = Jan. 24^d·5, i.e. $\frac{1}{5}$ (1·5) = 0·5 forwards towards the data for the same latitude interpolated similarly from page 27; the corrections are +8^m to sunset, +5^m to civil twilight, and +4^m to nautical twilight.

12. *Moonrise, moonset.* Precise times of moonrise and moonset are rarely needed; a glance at the tables will generally give sufficient indication of whether the Moon is available for observation and of the hours of rising and setting. If needed, precise times may be obtained as follows. Interpolate for latitude, using Table I on page xxxii, on the day wanted and also on the preceding day in east longitudes or the following day in west longitudes, take the difference between these times and interpolate for longitude by applying to the time for the day wanted the correction from Table II on page xxxii, so that the resulting time is between the two times used. In extreme conditions near □ or ■ interpolation for latitude or longitude may be possible only in one direction; accurate times are of little value in these circumstances.

To facilitate this interpolation the times of moonrise and moonset are given for four days on each page; where no phenomenon occurs during a particular day (as happens once a month) the time of the phenomenon on the following day, increased by 24^h, is given; extra care must be taken when interpolating between two values, when one of those values exceeds 24^h. In practice it suffices to use the daily difference between the times for the nearest tabular latitude, and generally, to enter Table II with the nearest tabular arguments as in the example below.

Examples. Required the G.M.T. of moonrise and moonset in latitude S.47° 10′, longitudes E.124° 00′ and W.78° 31′ on 1981 January 23.

	Longitude E.124° 00′ Moonrise	Moonset	Longitude W.78° 31′ Moonrise	Moonset
	d h m	d h m	d h m	d h m
L.M.T. for Lat. S.45°	23 21 37	23 07 55	23 21 37	23 07 55
Lat. correction (p. xxxii, Table I)	+02	−04	+02	−04
Long. correction (p. xxxii, Table II)	−10	−23	+07	+16
Correct L.M.T.	23 21 29	23 07 28	23 21 46	23 08 07
Longitude (p. i)	−8 16	−8 16	+5 14	+5 14
G.M.T.	23 13 13	22 23 12	24 03 00	23 13 21

ALTITUDE CORRECTION TABLES

13. *General.* In general two corrections are given for application to altitudes observed with a marine sextant; additional corrections are required for Venus and Mars and also for very low altitudes.

Tables of the correction for dip of the horizon, due to height of eye above sea level, are given on pages A2 and xxxiv. Strictly this correction should be applied first and subtracted from the sextant altitude to give apparent altitude, which is the correct argument for the other tables.

Separate tables are given of the second correction for the Sun, for stars and planets (on pages A2 and A3), and for the Moon (on pages xxxiv and xxxv). For the Sun, values are given for both lower and upper limbs, for two periods of the year. The star tables are used for the planets, but additional corrections (page A2) are required for Venus and Mars. The Moon tables are in two parts: the main correction is a function of apparent altitude only and is tabulated for the lower limb (30′ must be subtracted to obtain the correction for the upper limb); the other, which is given for both lower and upper limbs, depends also on the horizontal parallax, which has to be taken from the daily pages.

An additional correction, given on page A4, is required for the change in the refraction, due to variations of pressure and temperature from the adopted standard conditions; it may generally be ignored for altitudes greater than 10°, except possibly in extreme conditions. The correction tables for the Sun, stars, and planets are in two parts; only those for altitudes greater than 10° are reprinted on the bookmark.

14. *Critical tables.*   Some of the altitude correction tables are arranged as critical tables. In these an interval of apparent altitude (or height of eye) corresponds to a single value of the correction; no interpolation is required. At a "critical" entry the upper of the two possible values of the correction is to be taken. For example, in the table of dip, a correction of $-4′\cdot 1$ corresponds to all values of the height of eye from 5·3 to 5·5 metres (17·5 to 18·3 feet) inclusive.

15. *Examples.*   The following examples illustrate the use of the altitude correction tables; the sextant altitudes given are assumed to be taken on 1981 January 22 with a marine sextant at height 5·4 metres (18 feet), temperature $-3°C$. and pressure 982 mb., the Moon sights being taken at about 10^{h} G.M.T.

	SUN lower limb	SUN upper limb	MOON lower limb	MOON upper limb	VENUS	*Polaris*
Sextant altitude	21 19·7	3 20·2	33 27·6	26 06·7	4 32·6	49 36·5
Dip, height 5·4 metres (18 feet)	−4·1	−4·1	−4·1	−4·1	−4·1	−4·1
Main correction	+13·8	−29·6	+57·4	+60·5	−10·8	−0·8
−30′ for upper limb (Moon)	—	—	—	−30·0	—	—
L, U correction for Moon	—	—	+3·5	+2·8	—	—
Additional correction for Venus	—	—	—	—	+0·1	—
Additional refraction correction	−0·1	−0·3	0·0	−0·1	−0·3	0·0
Corrected sextant altitude	21 29·3	2 46·2	34 24·4	26 35·8	4 17·5	49 31·6

The main corrections have been taken out with apparent altitude (sextant altitude corrected for dip) as argument, interpolating where possible. These refinements are rarely necessary.

16. *Basis of the corrections.*   The table for the dip of the sea horizon is based on the formula:

$$\text{Correction for dip} = -1′\cdot 76\sqrt{\text{(height of eye in metres)}} = -0′\cdot 97\sqrt{\text{(height of eye in feet)}}$$

The mean refraction, given explicitly in the correction table for the stars and planets and incorporated into those for the Sun and Moon, is based on Garfinkel's theory and is for a temperature of 10°C. (50°F.) and a pressure of 1010 mb. (29·83 inches). The additional corrections for variations of temperature and pressure from these adopted means are also based on Garfinkel's theory; there is no significant difference between the various theories to the accuracy given.

The correction table for the Sun includes the effects of semi-diameter and parallax, as well as the mean refraction; no correction for irradiation is included.

The additional corrections for Venus and Mars allow for parallax and phase, and are given by $p \cos H - k \cos \theta$, where H is the altitude, θ the angle at the planet between the vertical and the Sun: p and k are, for Venus, for 1981:

	Jan. 1	Sept. 30	Nov. 21	Dec. 15	Dec. 30	Dec. 31
p	0·1	0·2	0·3	0·4	0·5	
k	0·0	0·1	0·2	0·3	0·4	

The corrections given on page A2, and on the bookmark, are mean values applicable, in the case of Venus, only when the Sun is below the horizon. For daylight observations of Venus the observed values of H and θ should be used to calculate the correction directly; the term $-k \cos \theta$ is positive when the Sun is lower than Venus, zero when they have the same altitude, and negative when the Sun is higher.

In the case of the Moon the correction table includes the effects of semi-diameter, parallax and augmentation as well as the mean refraction; no correction for irradiation is included.

17. *Bubble sextant observations.* When observing with a bubble sextant no correction is necessary for dip, semi-diameter, or augmentation. For the stars and planets the corrections given may be used unchanged, and they should also be used for the Sun; for the Moon it is easiest to take the mean of the corrections for lower and upper limbs and subtract 15′ from the altitude; the correction for dip must not be applied.

AUXILIARY AND PLANNING DATA

18. *Sun and Moon.* On the daily pages are given: the semi-diameters and the times of meridian passage of both Sun and Moon over the Greenwich meridian; the equation of time; the horizontal parallax and the age of the Moon, together with a symbol indicating the phase. For the Moon, the semi-diameters for each of the three days are given, in order, at the foot of the column; for the Sun a single value is sufficient. The equation of time is given, without sign, for 00^h and 12^h G.M.T. on each day. To obtain apparent time, apply the equation of time to mean time with a *positive* sign when G.H.A. Sun at 00^h G.M.T. *exceeds* 180°, or at 12^h *exceeds* 0°, corresponding to a meridian passage of the Sun *before* 12^h G.M.T.; *otherwise* apply with a *negative* sign.

The times of the phases of the Moon are given in G.M.T. on page 4.

19. *Planets.* The magnitudes of the planets are given immediately following their names in the headings on the daily pages; also given, for the middle day of the three on the page, are their S.H.A. at 00^h G.M.T. and their times of meridian passage.

The planet notes and diagram on pages 8 and 9 provide descriptive information as to the suitability of the planets for observation during the year, and of their positions and movements.

20. *Stars.* The time of meridian passage of the first point of Aries over the Greenwich meridian is given on the daily pages, for the middle day of the three on the page, to 0^m·1. The interval between successive meridian passages is 23^h 56^m·1 (24^h less 3^m·9) so that times for intermediate days and other meridians can readily be derived. If a precise time is required it may be obtained by finding the G.M.T. at which L.H.A. Aries is zero.

The meridian passage of a star occurs when its L.H.A. is zero, that is when L.H.A. Aries + S.H.A. = 360°. An approximate time can be obtained from the planet diagram on page 9.

The star charts on pages 266 and 267 are intended to assist identification. They show the relative positions of the stars in the sky as seen from the Earth and include all 173 stars used in the Almanac, together with a few others to complete the main constellation configurations. The local meridian at any time may be located on the chart by means of its S.H.A. which is 360° – L.H.A. Aries, or west longitude – G.H.A. Aries.

21. *Star globe.* To set a star globe on which is printed a scale of L.H.A. Aries, first set the globe for latitude and then rotate about the polar axis until the scale under the edge of the meridian circle reads L.H.A. Aries.

To mark the positions of the Sun, Moon, and planets on the star globe, take the difference G.H.A. Aries – G.H.A. body and use this along the L.H.A. Aries scale, in conjunction with the declination, to plot the position. G.H.A. Aries – G.H.A. body is most conveniently found by taking the difference when the G.H.A. of the body is small (less than 15°), which happens once a day.

22. *Calendar.* On page 4 are given lists of ecclesiastical festivals, and of the principal anniversaries and holidays in the United Kingdom and the United States of America. The calendar on page 5 includes the day of the year as well as the day of the week.

Brief particulars are given, at the foot of page 5, of the solar and lunar eclipses occurring during the year; the times given are in G.M.T. The principal features of the more important solar eclipses are shown on the maps on pages 6 and 7.

23. *Standard times.* The lists on pages 262–265 give the standard times used in most countries. In general no attempt is made to give details of the beginning and end of summer time, since they are liable to frequent changes at short notice.

The Date or Calendar Line is an arbitrary line, on either side of which the date differs by one day; when crossing this line on a westerly course, the date must be advanced one day; when crossing it on an easterly course, the date must be put back one day. The line is a modification of the line of the 180th meridian, and is drawn so as to include, as far as possible, islands of any one group, etc., on the same side of the line. It may be traced by starting at the South Pole and joining up to the following positions:

Lat.	S. 51°·0	S. 45°·0	S. 15°·0	S. 5°·0	N. 48°·0	N. 53°·0	N. 65°·5
Long.	180·0	W. 172·5	W. 172·5	180·0	180·0	E. 170·0	W. 169·0

thence through the middle of the Diomede Islands to Lat. N.68°·0, Long. W.169°·0, passing east of Ostrov Vrangelya (Wrangel Island) to Lat. N.75°·0, Long. 180°·0, and thence to the North Pole.

ACCURACY

24. *Main data.* The quantities tabulated in this Almanac are generally correct to the nearest 0′·1; the exception is the Sun's G.H.A. which is deliberately adjusted by up to 0′·15 to reduce the error due to ignoring the *v*-correction. The G.H.A. and Dec. at intermediate times cannot be obtained to this precision, since at least two quantities must be added; moreover, the *v*- and *d*-corrections are based on mean values of *v* and *d* and are taken from tables for the whole minute only. The largest error that can occur in the G.H.A. or Dec. of any body other than the Sun or Moon is less than 0′·2; it may reach 0′·25 for the G.H.A. of the Sun and 0′·3 for that of the Moon.

In practice it may be expected that only one third of the values of G.H.A. and Dec. taken out will have errors larger than 0′·05 and less than one-tenth will have errors larger than 0′·1.

25. *Altitude corrections.* The errors in the altitude corrections are nominally of the same order as those in G.H.A. and Dec., as they result from the addition of several quantities each correctly rounded off to 0′·1. But the actual values of the dip and of the refraction at low altitudes may, in extreme atmospheric conditions, differ considerably from the mean values used in the tables.

USE OF THIS ALMANAC IN 1982

This Almanac may be used for the Sun and stars in 1982 in the following manner.

For the Sun, take out the G.H.A. and Dec. for the same date but for a time 5^h 48^m 00^s *earlier* than the G.M.T. of observation; add 87° 00′ to the G.H.A. so obtained. The error, mainly due to planetary perturbations of the Earth, is unlikely to exceed 0′·4.

For the stars, calculate the G.H.A. and Dec. for the same date and the same time, but *subtract* 15′·1 from the G.H.A. so found. The error, due to incomplete correction for precession and nutation, is unlikely to exceed 0′·4. If preferred, the same result can be obtained by using a time 5^h 48^m 00^s earlier than the G.M.T. of observation (as for the Sun) and adding 86° 59′·2 to the G.H.A. (or adding 87° as for the Sun and subtracting 0′·8, for precession, from the S.H.A. of the star).

The Almanac cannot be so used for the Moon or planets.

LIST I—PLACES FAST ON G.M.T. (mainly those EAST OF GREENWICH)

The times given ⎱ *added* to G.M.T. to give Standard Time.
below should be ⎰ *subtracted* from Standard Time to give G.M.T.

	h	m		h	m
Admiralty Islands	10		Egypt (United Arab Republic) ...	02	
Afghanistan	04	30	Equatorial Guinea, Republic of ...	01	
Albania*	01		Estonia	03	
Algeria*	01		Ethiopia	03	
Amirante Islands	04				
Andaman Islands	05	30	Fernando Póo‡	01	
Angola	01		Fiji	12	
Annobon Island‡	01		Finland	02	
Arabian Emirates, Federation of ...	04		France*	01	
Australia			Friendly Islands	13	
Australian Capital Territory* ...	10				
New South Wales[1]*	10		Gabon	01	
Northern Territory	09	30	Germany, East	01	
Queensland	10		West[3]	01	
South Australia*	09	30	Gibraltar‡	01	
Tasmania*	10		Gilbert Islands	12	
Victoria*	10		Greece*	02	
Western Australia	08		Guam*	10	
Austria	01				
			Holland (The Netherlands)*	01	
Balearic Islands*	01		Hong Kong	08	
Bangladesh	06		Hungary...	01	
Belgium*	01				
Benin (Dahomey)	01		India	05	30
Botswana, Republic of	02		Indonesia, Republic of		
Brunei	08		Bali, Bangka, Billiton, Java,		
Bulgaria	02		Lombok, Madura, Sumatra ...	07	
Burma	06	30	Borneo, Celebes, Flores, Sumba,		
Burundi	02		Sumbawa, Timor	08	
			Aru, Kei, Moluccas, Tanimbar,		
Cambodia (Democratic Kampuchea) ...	07		Irian Jaya	09	
Cameroun Republic	01		Iran‡*	04	
Caroline Islands, east of long. E. 160°	12		Iraq	03	
west of long. E. 150°	10		Israel	02	
Truk, Ponape ...	11		Italy*	01	
Central African Empire	01				
Chad	01		Japan	09	
Chagos Archipelago‡	06		Jordan*	02	
Chatham Islands‡	12	45			
China[2]	08		Kamchatka Peninsula	12	
Christmas Island, Indian Ocean ...	07		Kenya	03	
Cocos Keeling Islands	06	30	Korea, North	09	
Comoro Islands (Comoros)	03		Republic of (South)	09	
Congo Republic	01		Kuril Islands	11	
Corsica‡*	01		Kuwait	03	
Crete*	02				
Cyprus, Ercan*	02		Laccadive Islands	05	30
Larnaca	02		Ladrone Islands	10	
Czechoslovakia	01		Laos	07	
			Latvia	03	
Denmark	01		Lebanon*	02	
Djibouti	03				

* Summer time may be kept in these countries.
‡ The legal time may differ from that given here.
[1] Except Broken Hill Area which keeps 09ʰ 30ᵐ.
[2] All the coast, but some areas may keep summer time.
[3] Including West Berlin.

	h	m			h	m
Lesotho	02		Schouten Islands	09	
Libya‡	02		Seychelles	04	
Liechtenstein	01		Sicily*	01	
Lord Howe Island	10		Singapore	07	30
Luxembourg*	01		Socotra	03	
			Solomon Islands	11	
			Somalia Republic	03	
Macao	08		South Africa, Republic of ...	02	
Madagascar, Democratic Republic of...	03		Southern Yemen	03	
Malawi	02		South West Africa (Namibia) ...	02	
Malaysia			Spain*	01	
Malaya	07	30	Spanish Morocco*	01	
Sabah, Sarawak	08		Spitsbergen (Svalbard)	01	
Maldives, Republic of The	05		Sri Lanka	05	30
Malta*	01		Sudan, Republic of	02	
Manchuria	09		Swaziland	02	
Mariana Islands	10		Sweden	01	
Marshall Islands[1]	12		Switzerland	01	
Mauritius	04		Syria* (Syrian Arab Republic) ...	02	
Monaco*	01				
Mozambique	02		Taiwan	08	
			Tanzania	03	
Namibia (South West Africa) ...	02		Thailand	07	
Nauru	11	30	Tonga Islands	13	
Netherlands, The*	01		Truk	11	
New Caledonia*	11		Tunisia	01	
New Hebrides	11		Turkey*	02	
New Zealand*	12		Tuvalu Islands...	12	
Nicobar Islands	05	30			
Niger	01		Uganda	03	
Nigeria, Republic of	01		Union of Soviet Socialist Republics[2]		
Norfolk Island	11	30	west of long. E. 40°... ...	03	
Norway	01		long. E. 40° to E. 52° 30′ ...	04	
Novaya Zemlya	05		long. E. 52° 30′ to E. 67° 30′	05	
			long. E. 67° 30′ to E. 82° 30′	06	
Ocean Island	11	30	long. E. 82° 30′ to E. 97° 30′	07	
Okinawa	09		long. E. 97° 30′ to E. 112° 30′	08	
Oman	04		long. E. 112° 30′ to E. 127° 30′	09	
			long. E. 127° 30′ to E. 142° 30′	10	
Pakistan	05		long. E. 142° 30′ to E. 157° 30′	11	
Papua New Guinea	10		long. E. 157° 30′ to E. 172° 30′	12	
Pescadores Islands	08		east of long. E. 172° 30′ ...	13	
Philippine Republic	08				
Poland*	01		Vietnam, Northern	07	
			Southern‡	07	
Réunion	04				
Rhodesia	02		Wrangell Island	13	
Romania	02				
Rwanda	02		Yugoslavia	01	
Ryukyu Islands	09				
			Zaire		
Sakhalin	11		Kinshasa, Mbandaka	01	
Santa Cruz Islands	11		Haut-Zaire, Kivu, Kasai, Shaba ...	02	
Sardinia*	01		Zambia, Republic of	02	
Saudi Arabia	03				

   * Summer time may be kept in these countries.
   ‡ The legal time may differ from that given here.
   [1] Except the islands of Kwajalein and Eniwetok which keep a time 24ʰ slow on that of the rest of the islands.
   [2] The boundaries between the zones are irregular; the longitudes given are approximate only.

LIST II—PLACES NORMALLY KEEPING G.M.T.

Ascension Island	Great Britain[1]	Irish Republic*	Morocco	Senegal
Canary Islands*	Guinea Bissau	Ivory Coast	Portugal*	Sierra Leone
Channel Islands[1]	Guinea Republic	Liberia	Principe	Tangier
Faeroes, The	Iceland	Madeira	Rio de Oro†	Togo Republic
Gambia	Ifni	Mali	St. Helena	Tristan da Cunha
Ghana	Ireland, Northern[1]	Mauritania (Dakhla)	São Tomé	Upper Volta

* Summer time may be kept in these countries.
‡ The legal time may differ from that given here.
[1] Summer time, one hour in advance of G.M.T., is kept from March 22[d] 02[h] to October 25[d] 02[h] G.M.T.

LIST III—PLACES SLOW ON G.M.T. (WEST OF GREENWICH)

The times given ⎱ subtracted from G.M.T. to give Standard Time.
below should be ⎰ added to Standard Time to give G.M.T.

	h	m		h	m
Argentina‡	03		Cape Verde Islands‡	01	
Austral Islands[1]	10		Cayman Islands	05	
Azores	01		Chile*	04	
			Christmas Island, Pacific Ocean ...	10	
Bahamas*	05		Colombia	05	
Barbados*	04		Cook Islands, except Niue	10	30
Belize	06		Costa Rica	06	
Bermuda*	04		Cuba*	05	
Bolivia	04		Curaçao Island...	04	
Brazil, eastern[2]...	03				
Territory of Acre	05		Dominican Republic‡	04	
western	04				
British Antarctic Territory[3]	03		Easter Island (I. de Pascua)* ...	07	
			Ecuador	05	
Canada					
Alberta*	07		Falkland Islands[4]	04	
British Columbia*	08		Fanning Island	10	
Labrador*	04		Fernando de Noronha Island... ...	02	
Manitoba*	06		French Guiana‡	03	
New Brunswick*	04				
Newfoundland*	03	30	Galápagos Islands	06	
Northwest Territories*			Greenland, Scoresby Sound[5] ...	02	
east of long. W. 68°	04		Angmagssalik and west coast ...	03	
long. W. 68° to W. 85° ...	05		Thule area	04	
long. W. 85° to W. 102° ...	06		Grenada	04	
west of long. W. 102° ...	07		Guadeloupe	04	
Nova Scotia*	04		Guatemala	06	
Ontario*, east of long. W. 90° ...	05		Guiana, French‡	03	
west of long. W. 90° ...	06		Guyana, Republic of‡	03	
Prince Edward Island* ...	04				
Quebec*, east of long. W. 63° ...	04		Haiti	05	
west of long. W. 63° ...	05		Honduras	06	
Saskatchewan*					
east of long. W. 106° ...	06		Jamaica*	05	
west of long. W. 106° ...	07		Jan Mayen Island	01	
Yukon	08		Johnston Island	10	

* Summer time may be kept in these countries.
‡ The legal time may differ from that given here.
[1] This is the legal standard time, but local mean time is generally used.
[2] Including all the coast and Brasilia.
[3] Except South Georgia which keeps 02[h].
[4] Except Port Stanley which keeps 03[h]‡.
[5] Scoresby Sound may keep 03[h] in summer.

				h	m
Juan Fernandez Islands	...	...	...	04	
Leeward Islands	...	...	...	04	
Low Archipelago	...	...	...	10	
Marquesas Islands[1]	...	...	...	09	30
Martinique	...	...	...	04	
Mexico‡*[2]	...	...	...	06	
Midway Islands	...	...	...	11	
Miquelon	...	...	...	03	
Nicaragua‡	...	...	...	06	
Niue Island	...	...	...	11	
Panama Canal Zone	...	...	...	05	
Panama, Republic of	...	...	...	05	
Paraguay*	...	...	...	04	
Peru	...	...	...	05	
Puerto Rico	...	...	...	04	
Rarotonga	...	...	...	10	30
St. Pierre and Miquelon*	...	...	04	
Salvador, El	...	...	...	06	
Samoa	...	...	...	11	
Society Islands[1]	...	...	...	10	
South Georgia	...	...	...	02	
Surinam	...	...	...	03	30
Tobago	...	...	...	04	
Trindade Island, South Atlantic	...	02	
Trinidad	...	...	...	04	
Tuamotu Archipelago[1]	...	...	10	
Tubuai Islands[1]	...	....	10	
Turks and Caicos Islands*	...	...	05	

United States of America

				h	m
Alabama[3]	...	...	...	06	
Alaska[3], east of long. W. 137°	...	08	
long. W. 137° to W. 141°	...	09	
long. W. 141° to W. 161°	...	10	
long. W. 161° to W. 172° 30'	...	11	
Aleutian Islands	...	...	11	
Arizona	...	...	...	07	
Arkansas[3]	...	...	...	06	
California[3]	...	...	...	08	
Colorado[3]	...	...	...	07	
Connecticut[3]	...	...	...	05	
Delaware[3]	...	...	...	05	
District of Columbia[3]	...	...	05	
Florida[3, 4]	...	...	...	05	

United States of America *(continued)*

				h
Georgia[3]	...	...	...	05
Hawaii	...	...	...	10
Idaho[3, 4]	...	...	...	07
Illinois[3]	...	...	...	06
Indiana[4]	...	...	...	05
Iowa[3]	...	...	...	06
Kansas[3, 4]	...	...	...	06
Kentucky[3, 4]	...	...	...	05
Louisiana[3]	...	...	...	06
Maine[3]	...	...	...	05
Maryland[3]	...	...	...	05
Massachusetts[3]	...	...	...	05
Michigan[3, 4]	...	...	...	05
Minnesota[3]	...	...	...	06
Mississippi[3]	...	...	...	06
Missouri[3]	...	...	...	06
Montana[3]	...	...	...	07
Nebraska[3, 4]	...	...	...	06
Nevada[3]	...	...	...	08
New Hampshire[3]	...	...	...	05
New Jersey[3]	...	...	...	05
New Mexico[3]	...	...	...	07
New York[3]	...	...	...	05
North Carolina[3]	...	...	...	05
North Dakota[3, 4]	...	...	...	06
Ohio[3]	...	...	...	05
Oklahoma[3]	...	...	...	06
Oregon[3, 4]	...	...	...	08
Pennsylvania[3]	...	...	...	05
Rhode Island[3]	...	...	...	05
South Carolina[3]	...	...	...	05
South Dakota[3], eastern part	...	06
western part	...	07
Tennessee[3, 4]	...	...	...	06
Texas[3, 4]	...	...	...	06
Utah[3]	...	...	...	07
Vermont[3]	...	...	...	05
Virginia[3]	...	...	...	05
Washington, D.C.[3]	...	...	...	05
Washington[3]	...	...	...	08
West Virginia[3]	...	...	...	05
Wisconsin[3]	...	...	...	06
Wyoming[3]	...	...	...	07
Uruguay	...	...	...	03
Venezuela‡	...	...	...	04
Virgin Islands	...	...	...	04
Windward Islands	...	...	...	04

---

* Summer time may be kept in these countries.
‡ The legal time may differ from that given here.
[1] This is the legal standard time, but local mean time is generally used.
[2] Except the states of Sonora, Sinaloa, Nayarit, and the Southern District of Lower California which keep 07[h], and the Northern District of Lower California which keeps 08[h].
[3] Summer (daylight-saving) time, one hour fast on the time given, is kept in these states from the last Sunday in April to the last Sunday in October, changing at 02[h] 00[m] local clock time.
[4] This applies to the greater portion of the state.

STAR CHARTS

NORTHERN STARS

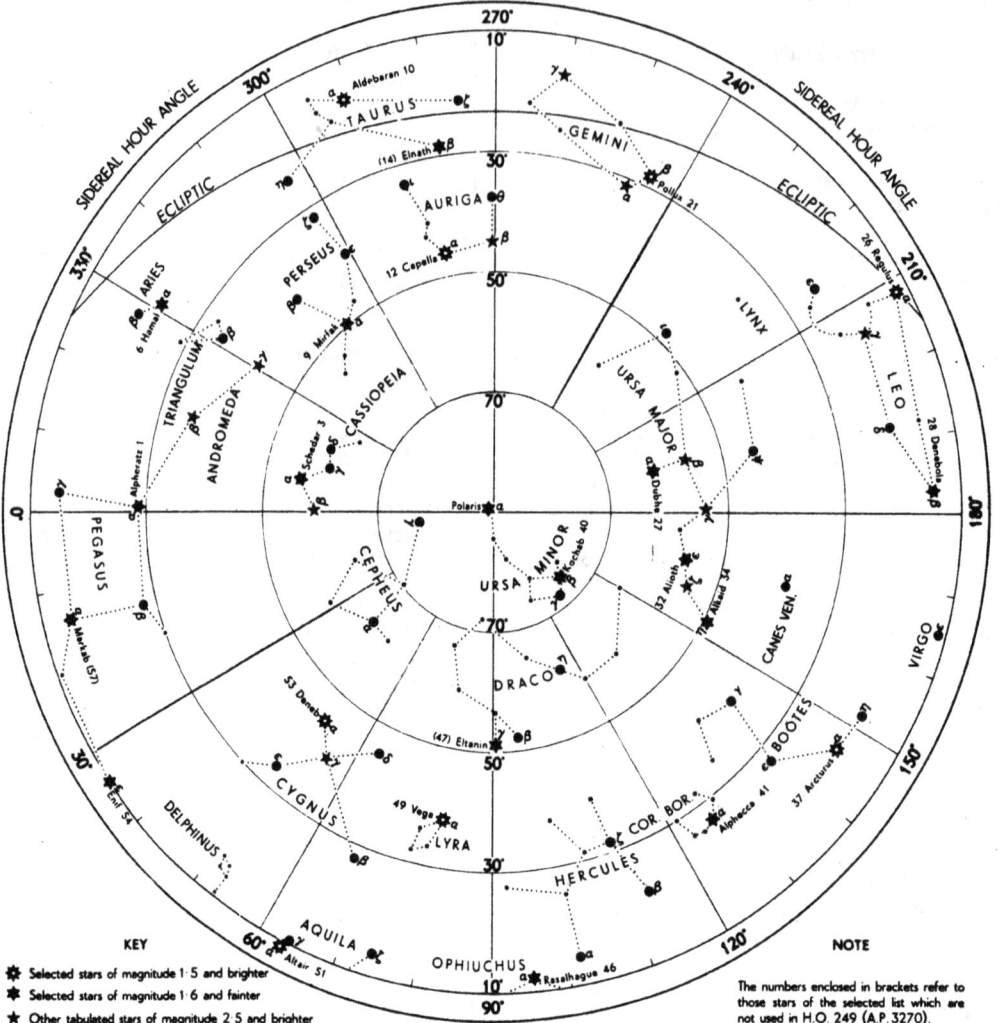

270°
10°
SIDEREAL HOUR ANGLE
300°
ECLIPTIC
330°
0°
30°
60°
90°
120°
150°
180°
210°
240°
SIDEREAL HOUR ANGLE
ECLIPTIC

Aldebaran 10
TAURUS
(14) Elnath
AURIGA
12 Capella
PERSEUS
α
9 Mirfak
ARIES
6 Hamal
β
TRIANGULUM
γ
ANDROMEDA
Schedar 3
CASSIOPEIA
β
γ
Alpheratz 1
PEGASUS
Markab (57)
53 Deneb
CYGNUS
Enif 54
DELPHINUS
49 Vega
LYRA
β
AQUILA
Altair 51
OPHIUCHUS
Rasalhague 46
GEMINI
Pollux 21
α
28 Regulus
LYNX
LEO
28 Denebola
β
δ
URSA MAJOR
Dubhe 27
32 Alioth
Alkaid 34
CANES VEN.
α
VIRGO
γ
BOOTES
Alphecca 41
37 Arcturus
ε
COR. BOR.
HERCULES
β
Polaris α
Kochab 40
URSA MINOR
DRACO
γ
(47) Eltanin
β

KEY

✸ Selected stars of magnitude 1·5 and brighter
✦ Selected stars of magnitude 1·6 and fainter
★ Other tabulated stars of magnitude 2·5 and brighter
● Other tabulated stars of magnitude 2·6 and fainter
· Untabulated stars

NOTE

The numbers enclosed in brackets refer to
those stars of the selected list which are
not used in H.O. 249 (A.P. 3270).

EQUATORIAL STARS (S.H.A. 0° to 180°)

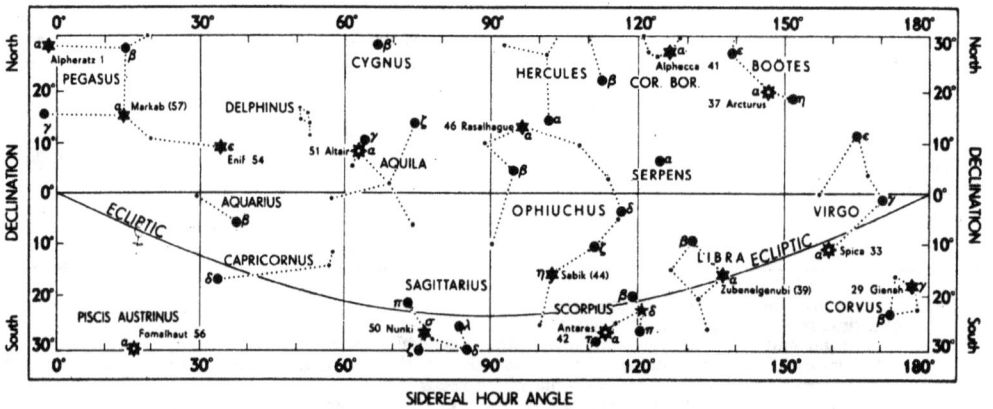

	0°	30°	60°	90°	120°	150°	180°	
North								North

α
Alpheratz 1
β
PEGASUS
Markab (57)
γ
DELPHINUS
Enif 54
51 Altair
AQUILA
AQUARIUS
β
ECLIPTIC
CAPRICORNUS
δ
PISCIS AUSTRINUS
Fomalhaut 56
SAGITTARIUS
50 Nunki
CYGNUS
β
HERCULES
β
COR. BOR.
Alphecca 41
BOOTES
37 Arcturus
46 Rasalhague
SERPENS
α
OPHIUCHUS
δ
VIRGO
γ
Spica 33
LIBRA
ECLIPTIC
Zubenelgenubi (39)
Sabik (44)
SCORPIUS
Antares 42
CORVUS
29 Gienah
δ
β

North
30° 20° 10° 0° 10° 20° 30°
DECLINATION
South

SIDEREAL HOUR ANGLE

SOUTHERN STARS

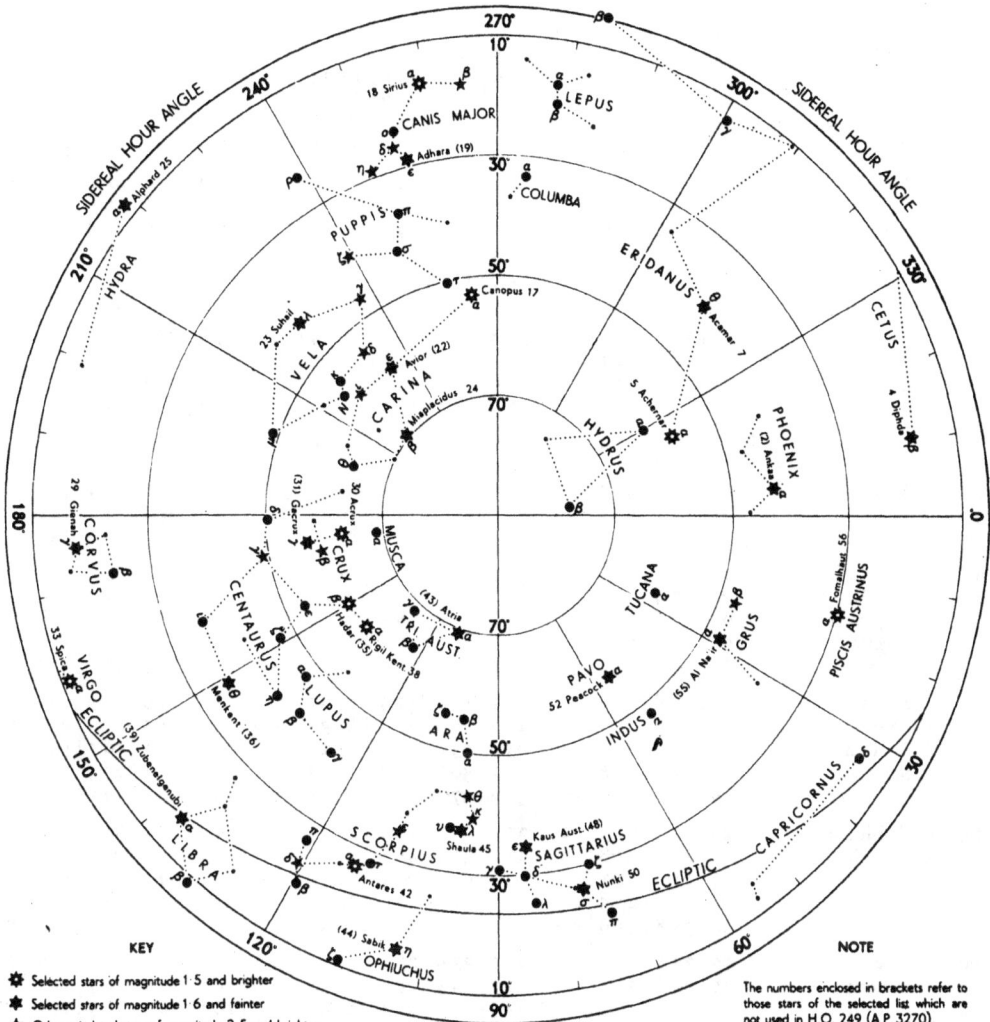

KEY

✷ Selected stars of magnitude 1·5 and brighter
★ Selected stars of magnitude 1·6 and fainter
★ Other tabulated stars of magnitude 2·5 and brighter
● Other tabulated stars of magnitude 2·6 and fainter
· Untabulated stars

NOTE

The numbers enclosed in brackets refer to those stars of the selected list which are not used in H.O. 249 (A.P. 3270).

EQUATORIAL STARS (S.H.A. 180° to 360°)

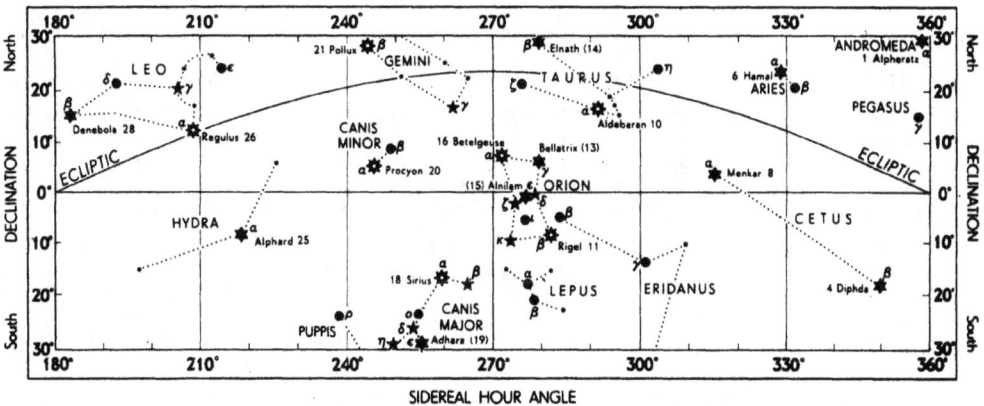

SIDEREAL HOUR ANGLE

Mag.	Name and Number		S.H.A. °	JAN.	FEB.	MAR.	APR.	MAY	JUNE	Dec.	JAN.	FEB.	MAR.	APR.	MAY	JUNE
3·4	γ Cephei		5	22·1	22·6	22·8	22·5	22·0	21·2	N. 77	31·8	31·7	31·5	31·4	31·3	31·3
2·6	α Pegasi	57	14	03·1	03·2	03·2	03·0	02·9	02·6	N. 15	06·1	06·1	06·0	06·0	06·1	06·1
2·6	β Pegasi		14	17·6	17·6	17·6	17·5	17·3	17·0	N. 27	58·8	58·7	58·6	58·6	58·6	58·7
1·3	α Piscis Aust.	56	15	51·4	51·5	51·4	51·3	51·1	50·8	S. 29	43·6	43·6	43·5	43·4	43·3	43·2
2·2	β Gruis		19	37·6	37·6	37·5	37·3	37·1	36·8	S. 46	59·3	59·2	59·1	59·0	58·8	58·8
2·9	α Tucanæ		25	42·7	42·7	42·6	42·4	42·0	41·6	S. 60	21·5	21·4	21·2	21·1	21·0	20·9
2·2	α Gruis	55	28	15·1	15·1	15·0	14·7	14·5	14·1	S. 47	03·4	03·3	03·2	03·1	03·0	02·9
3·0	δ Capricorni		33	30·6	30·6	30·5	30·3	30·1	29·8	S. 16	12·9	12·9	12·9	12·8	12·8	12·7
2·5	ε Pegasi	54	34	11·6	11·6	11·5	11·4	11·2	10·9	N. 9	47·2	47·2	47·1	47·1	47·2	47·3
3·1	β Aquarii		37	22·1	22·1	21·9	21·8	21·6	21·3	S. 5	39·4	39·4	39·4	39·4	39·3	39·2
2·6	α Cephei		40	28·7	28·7	28·6	28·3	27·9	27·5	N. 62	30·4	30·3	30·1	30·0	30·0	30·1
2·6	ε Cygni		48	38·8	38·8	38·7	38·4	38·2	38·0	N. 33	54·0	53·8	53·7	53·7	53·7	53·9
1·3	α Cygni	53	49	48·8	48·7	48·6	48·3	48·0	47·8	N. 45	12·8	12·6	12·5	12·5	12·5	12·6
3·2	α Indi		50	57·2	57·1	56·9	56·6	56·3	56·0	S. 47	21·6	21·5	21·4	21·3	21·3	21·3
2·1	α Pavonis	52	53	58·7	58·5	58·3	57·9	57·5	57·2	S. 56	47·9	47·8	47·7	47·6	47·5	47·5
2·3	γ Cygni		54	37·3	37·2	37·1	36·9	36·6	36·4	N. 40	11·8	11·6	11·5	11·5	11·5	11·7
0·9	α Aquilæ	51	62	32·7	32·5	32·4	32·2	32·0	31·8	N. 8	49·1	49·0	48·9	48·9	49·0	49·1
2·8	γ Aquilæ		63	40·1	40·0	39·9	39·7	39·5	39·3	N. 10	34·0	33·9	33·9	33·9	33·9	34·0
3·0	δ Cygni		63	54·8	54·7	54·5	54·3	54·0	53·8	N. 45	05·1	04·9	04·8	04·8	04·9	05·0
3·2	β Cygni		67	31·2	31·1	30·9	30·7	30·4	30·2	N. 27	55·2	55·0	55·0	55·0	55·0	55·2
3·0	π Sagittarii		72	51·1	50·9	50·7	50·5	50·2	50·0	S. 21	03·3	03·3	03·2	03·2	03·2	03·2
3·0	ζ Aquilæ		73	52·4	52·3	52·1	51·9	51·7	51·5	N. 13	50·1	50·0	49·9	49·9	50·0	50·1
2·7	ζ Sagittarii		74	39·6	39·4	39·2	38·9	38·7	38·5	S. 29	54·4	54·4	54·4	54·4	54·4	54·4
2·1	σ Sagittarii	50	76	29·3	29·1	28·9	28·6	28·4	28·2	S. 26	19·2	19·2	19·2	19·2	19·2	19·1
0·1	α Lyræ	49	80	56·1	55·9	55·7	55·5	55·2	55·1	N. 38	45·9	45·8	45·7	45·7	45·8	46·0
2·9	λ Sagittarii		83	18·6	18·4	18·2	17·9	17·7	17·5	S. 25	25·9	25·9	25·9	25·9	25·9	25·9
2·0	ε Sagittarii	48	84	16·9	16·7	16·5	16·2	16·0	15·8	S. 34	23·6	23·6	23·5	23·5	23·5	23·6
2·8	δ Sagittarii		85	03·9	03·7	03·5	03·2	03·0	02·8	S. 29	50·1	50·1	50·1	50·1	50·1	50·1
3·1	γ Sagittarii		88	51·8	51·6	51·3	51·1	50·8	50·7	S. 30	25·4	25·4	25·4	25·4	25·4	25·4
2·4	γ Draconis	47	90	58·1	57·9	57·6	57·3	57·1	57·0	N. 51	29·4	29·3	29·2	29·2	29·3	29·5
2·9	β Ophiuchi		94	22·5	22·3	22·1	21·9	21·7	21·6	N. 4	34·5	34·4	34·4	34·4	34·5	34·5
2·5	κ Scorpii		94	43·0	42·8	42·5	42·2	42·0	41·8	S. 39	01·1	01·1	01·1	01·1	01·2	01·2
2·0	θ Scorpii		96	01·3	01·1	00·8	00·5	00·3	00·1	S. 42	59·0	59·0	59·0	59·0	59·1	59·1
2·1	α Ophiuchi	46	96	29·7	29·5	29·3	29·1	28·9	28·8	N. 12	34·4	34·3	34·3	34·3	34·4	34·5
1·7	λ Scorpii	45	96	55·8	55·6	55·3	55·0	54·8	54·7	S. 37	05·3	05·3	05·3	05·3	05·4	05·4
3·0	α Aræ		97	25·1	24·8	24·5	24·2	23·9	23·7	S. 49	51·5	51·5	51·5	51·5	51·6	51·7
3·0	β Draconis		97	30·6	30·3	30·0	29·7	29·5	29·4	N. 52	18·8	18·7	18·7	18·7	18·8	19·0
2·8	υ Scorpii		97	38·5	38·3	38·0	37·7	37·5	37·4	S. 37	16·7	16·7	16·7	16·7	16·8	16·8
2·8	β Aræ		99	05·0	04·6	04·3	03·9	03·6	03·4	S. 55	30·6	30·5	30·5	30·6	30·7	30·7
Var.‡	α Herculis		101	33·7	33·5	33·3	33·1	32·9	32·9	N. 14	24·7	24·6	24·5	24·6	24·6	24·7
2·6	η Ophiuchi	44	102	41·2	40·9	40·7	40·5	40·3	40·2	S. 15	42·0	42·1	42·1	42·1	42·1	42·1
3·1	ζ Aræ		105	45·0	44·7	44·3	44·0	43·7	43·5	S. 55	57·4	57·4	57·4	57·5	57·6	57·7
2·4	ε Scorpii		107	46·5	46·3	46·0	45·8	45·6	45·5	S. 34	15·4	15·4	15·4	15·5	15·5	15·6
1·9	α Triang. Aust.	43	108	21·3	20·8	20·2	19·7	19·3	19·1	S. 68	59·4	59·3	59·4	59·4	59·5	59·7
3·0	ζ Herculis		109	51·9	51·7	51·4	51·2	51·1	51·0	N. 31	38·2	38·0	38·0	38·1	38·2	38·3
2·7	ζ Ophiuchi		110	58·8	58·5	58·3	58·1	58·0	57·9	S. 10	31·7	31·7	31·8	31·8	31·8	31·7
2·9	τ Scorpii		111	20·0	19·7	19·5	19·3	19·1	19·0	S. 28	10·5	10·5	10·5	10·6	10·6	10·6
2·8	β Herculis		112	39·4	39·2	38·9	38·7	38·6	38·5	N. 21	31·8	31·7	31·7	31·7	31·8	31·9
1·2	α Scorpii	42	112	56·8	56·6	56·4	56·1	56·0	55·9	S. 26	23·3	23·3	23·4	23·4	23·4	23·4
2·9	η Draconis		114	04·7	04·3	03·9	03·6	03·4	03·4	N. 61	33·3	33·2	33·2	33·3	33·4	33·6
3·0	δ Ophiuchi		116	40·2	39·9	39·7	39·5	39·4	39·3	S. 3	38·7	38·8	38·8	38·8	38·8	38·7
2·8	β Scorpii		118	55·4	55·2	55·0	54·8	54·6	54·6	S. 19	45·1	45·2	45·2	45·3	45·3	45·3
2·5	δ Scorpii		120	12·3	12·0	11·8	11·6	11·5	11·4	S. 22	33·9	34·0	34·0	34·1	34·1	34·1
3·0	π Scorpii		120	34·9	34·6	34·4	34·2	34·1	34·0	S. 26	03·4	03·5	03·5	03·6	03·6	03·6
3·0	β Trianguli Aust.		121	38·8	38·3	37·9	37·5	37·3	37·2	S. 63	22·1	22·1	22·1	22·2	22·4	22·5
2·8	α Serpentis		124	10·4	10·2	10·0	09·8	09·7	09·6	N. 6	29·1	29·0	29·0	29·0	29·1	29·1
2·3	α Coronæ Bor.	41	126	32·1	31·9	31·7	31·5	31·4	31·4	N. 26	46·6	46·5	46·5	46·6	46·7	46·8
3·0	γ Lupi		126	32·3	32·0	31·8	31·6	31·4	31·4	S. 41	06·0	06·0	06·1	06·2	06·2	06·3

‡3·0—3·7

Mag.	Name and Number		S.H.A.							Dec.					
			JULY	AUG.	SEPT.	OCT.	NOV.	DEC.		JULY	AUG.	SEPT.	OCT.	NOV.	DEC.
		°	′	′	′	′	′	′	°	′	′	′	′	′	′
3·4	γ Cephei	5	20·4	19·9	19·7	19·8	20·3	20·9	N. 77	31·4	31·5	31·7	31·9	32·1	32·1
2·6	Markab 57	14	02·4	02·2	02·2	02·2	02·3	02·4	N. 15	06·3	06·4	06·5	06·5	06·5	06·5
2·6	Scheat	14	16·8	16·6	16·6	16·6	16·7	16·8	N. 27	58·8	58·9	59·1	59·1	59·2	59·2
1·3	Fomalhaut 56	15	50·6	50·4	50·3	50·3	50·4	50·5	S. 29	43·1	43·1	43·2	43·2	43·3	43·3
2·2	β Gruis	19	36·5	36·3	36·2	36·3	36·4	36·6	S. 46	58·7	58·8	58·9	59·0	59·1	59·1
2·9	α Tucanæ	25	41·2	41·0	40·9	41·0	41·3	41·5	S. 60	21·0	21·0	21·2	21·3	21·3	21·3
2·2	Al Na'ir 55	28	13·9	13·7	13·6	13·7	13·9	14·0	S. 47	02·9	03·0	03·1	03·2	03·2	03·2
3·0	δ Capricorni	33	29·6	29·5	29·5	29·6	29·7	29·8	S. 16	12·6	12·6	12·6	12·6	12·7	12·7
2·5	Enif 54	34	10·7	10·6	10·6	10·7	10·8	10·9	N. 9	47·4	47·5	47·5	47·6	47·6	47·5
3·1	β Aquarii	37	21·1	21·0	21·0	21·1	21·2	21·3	S. 5	39·1	39·1	39·1	39·1	39·1	39·1
2·6	Alderamin	40	27·3	27·2	27·3	27·6	27·9	28·2	N. 62	30·3	30·5	30·6	30·8	30·8	30·8
2·6	ε Cygni	48	37·8	37·8	37·8	38·0	38·1	38·2	N. 33	54·0	54·2	54·3	54·3	54·3	54·3
1·3	Deneb 53	49	47·6	47·6	47·7	47·9	48·1	48·2	N. 45	12·8	13·0	13·1	13·2	13·2	13·1
3·2	α Indi	50	55·8	55·7	55·7	55·9	56·1	56·2	S. 47	21·3	21·4	21·5	21·5	21·5	21·5
2·1	Peacock 52	53	56·9	56·8	56·9	57·1	57·4	57·5	S. 56	47·6	47·7	47·8	47·9	47·9	47·8
2·3	γ Cygni	54	36·2	36·2	36·3	36·5	36·7	36·8	N. 40	11·8	12·0	12·1	12·2	12·1	12·1
0·9	Altair 51	62	31·6	31·6	31·7	31·8	31·9	32·0	N. 8	49·2	49·3	49·3	49·3	49·3	49·3
2·8	γ Aquilæ	63	39·1	39·1	39·2	39·3	39·4	39·5	N. 10	34·1	34·2	34·3	34·3	34·2	34·2
3·0	δ Cygni	63	53·7	53·7	53·8	54·0	54·2	54·4	N. 45	05·2	05·3	05·4	05·5	05·4	05·3
3·2	Albireo	67	30·1	30·1	30·3	30·4	30·6	30·6	N. 27	55·3	55·4	55·5	55·5	55·5	55·4
3·0	π Sagittarii	72	49·9	49·9	50·0	50·1	50·2	50·3	S. 21	03·1	03·2	03·2	03·2	03·2	03·2
3·0	ζ Aquilæ	73	51·4	51·4	51·6	51·7	51·8	51·8	N. 13	50·2	50·3	50·4	50·4	50·3	50·2
2·7	ζ Sagittarii	74	38·3	38·3	38·4	38·6	38·7	38·7	S. 29	54·4	54·4	54·4	54·5	54·5	54·4
2·1	Nunki 50	76	28·1	28·1	28·2	28·3	28·5	28·5	S. 26	19·2	19·2	19·2	19·2	19·2	19·2
0·1	Vega 49	80	55·0	55·1	55·3	55·5	55·6	55·7	N. 38	46·1	46·2	46·3	46·3	46·2	46·1
2·9	λ Sagittarii	83	17·5	17·5	17·6	17·7	17·8	17·8	S. 25	25·9	25·9	25·9	25·9	25·9	25·9
2·0	Kaus Australis 48	84	15·7	15·7	15·9	16·0	16·1	16·1	S. 34	23·6	23·6	23·7	23·7	23·7	23·6
2·8	δ Sagittarii	85	02·7	02·8	02·9	03·0	03·1	03·1	S. 29	50·2	50·2	50·2	50·2	50·2	50·2
3·1	γ Sagittarii	88	50·6	50·6	50·8	50·9	51·0	51·0	S. 30	25·5	25·5	25·5	25·5	25·5	25·5
2·4	Eltanin 47	90	57·0	57·1	57·4	57·6	57·8	57·9	N. 51	29·7	29·8	29·8	29·8	29·7	29·5
2·9	β Ophiuchi	94	21·5	21·6	21·7	21·8	21·9	21·9	N. 4	34·6	34·7	34·7	34·7	34·6	34·5
2·5	κ Scorpii	94	41·8	41·8	42·0	42·2	42·2	42·2	S. 39	01·3	01·3	01·3	01·3	01·3	01·2
2·0	θ Scorpii	96	00·0	00·1	00·3	00·5	00·5	00·5	S. 42	59·2	59·3	59·3	59·3	59·2	59·2
2·1	Rasalhague 46	96	28·8	28·8	28·9	29·1	29·2	29·1	N. 12	34·5	34·6	34·6	34·6	34·5	34·4
1·7	Shaula 45	96	54·6	54·7	54·8	55·0	55·1	55·0	S. 37	05·4	05·5	05·5	05·5	05·5	05·4
3·0	α Aræ	97	23·7	23·8	24·0	24·2	24·3	24·2	S. 49	51·8	51·8	51·9	51·8	51·8	51·7
3·0	β Draconis	97	29·4	29·6	29·9	30·1	30·3	30·3	N. 52	19·1	19·2	19·3	19·2	19·1	18·9
2·8	υ Scorpii	97	37·3	37·4	37·5	37·7	37·8	37·7	S. 37	16·9	16·9	17·0	16·9	16·9	16·9
2·8	β Aræ	99	03·4	03·5	03·7	04·0	04·1	04·0	S. 55	30·8	30·9	30·9	30·9	30·8	30·7
Var.‡	α Herculis	101	32·8	32·9	33·0	33·2	33·3	33·2	N. 14	24·8	24·9	24·9	24·9	24·8	24·7
2·6	Sabik 44	102	40·2	40·3	40·4	40·5	40·6	40·5	S. 15	42·1	42·1	42·1	42·1	42·1	42·1
3·1	ζ Aræ	105	43·5	43·7	43·9	44·1	44·2	44·1	S. 55	57·8	57·8	57·9	57·8	57·7	57·6
2·4	ε Scorpii	107	45·5	45·6	45·7	45·9	45·9	45·8	S. 34	15·6	15·6	15·6	15·6	15·6	15·5
1·9	Atria 43	108	19·2	19·7	20·1	20·2	20·4	20·2	S. 68	59·8	59·9	59·9	59·8	59·7	59·6
3·0	ζ Herculis	109	51·0	51·2	51·3	51·5	51·6	51·5	N. 31	38·4	38·5	38·5	38·4	38·3	38·2
2·7	ζ Ophiuchi	110	57·9	58·0	58·1	58·2	58·2	58·2	S. 10	31·7	31·7	31·7	31·7	31·7	31·6
2·9	τ Scorpii	111	19·0	19·1	19·2	19·4	19·4	19·3	S. 28	10·7	10·7	10·7	10·7	10·6	10·6
2·8	β Herculis	112	38·6	38·7	38·8	38·9	39·0	38·9	N. 21	32·0	32·0	32·1	32·0	31·9	31·8
1·2	Antares 42	112	55·9	56·0	56·1	56·2	56·3	56·2	S. 26	23·5	23·5	23·5	23·4	23·4	23·4
2·9	η Draconis	114	03·6	03·9	04·2	04·5	04·7	04·7	N. 61	33·7	33·8	33·8	33·7	33·5	33·3
3·0	δ Ophiuchi	116	39·4	39·4	39·6	39·7	39·7	39·6	S. 3	38·7	38·7	38·7	38·7	38·7	38·8
2·8	β Scorpii	118	54·6	54·7	54·8	54·9	54·9	54·8	S. 19	45·3	45·3	45·2	45·2	45·2	45·2
2·5	Dschubba	120	11·4	11·5	11·7	11·8	11·8	11·7	S. 22	34·1	34·1	34·1	34·1	34·1	34·1
3·0	π Scorpii	120	34·0	34·1	34·3	34·4	34·4	34·3	S. 26	03·7	03·7	03·6	03·6	03·6	03·6
3·0	β Trianguli Aust.	121	37·3	37·5	37·8	38·1	38·1	37·9	S. 63	22·6	22·6	22·6	22·5	22·4	22·3
2·8	α Serpentis	124	09·7	09·8	09·9	10·0	10·0	09·9	N. 6	29·2	29·2	29·2	29·2	29·1	29·0
2·3	Alphecca 41	126	31·4	31·6	31·7	31·8	31·8	31·7	N. 26	46·9	46·9	46·9	46·8	46·7	46·5
3·0	γ Lupi	126	31·4	31·6	31·7	31·8	31·8	31·7	S. 41	06·4	06·4	06·3	06·3	06·2	06·2

‡ 3·0—3·7

Mag.	Name and Number		S.H.A.						Dec.						
			JAN.	FEB.	MAR.	APR.	MAY	JUNE		JAN.	FEB.	MAR.	APR.	MAY	JUNE
		°	′	′	′	′	′	′	°	′	′	′	′	′	′
3·1	γ Ursæ Minoris 129		49·5	48·9	48·4	48·0	47·9	48·1	N. 71	53·9	53·9	53·9	54·0	54·2	54·3
3·1	γ Trianguli Aust. 130		43·8	43·2	42·7	42·3	42·1	42·1	S. 68	36·2	36·3	36·4	36·5	36·6	36·8
2·7	β Libræ 130		60·6	60·3	60·1	60·0	59·9	59·9	S. 9	18·7	18·8	18·8	18·9	18·8	18·8
2·8	β Lupi 135		41·1	40·8	40·5	40·3	40·2	40·2	S. 43	03·2	03·3	03·4	03·5	03·6	03·6
2·2	β Ursæ Minoris 40 137		19·5	18·8	18·3	17·9	17·9	18·1	N. 74	13·8	13·7	13·8	13·9	14·1	14·2
2·9	α Libræ 39 137		32·9	32·7	32·5	32·3	32·2	32·2	S. 15	57·7	57·7	57·8	57·8	57·9	57·9
2·6	ε Bootis 138		58·0	57·7	57·5	57·3	57·3	57·3	N. 27	09·1	09·1	09·1	09·1	09·2	09·3
2·9	α Lupi 139		50·4	50·1	49·8	49·6	49·5	49·5	S. 47	18·1	18·2	18·3	18·4	18·5	18·6
0·1	α Centauri 38 140		25·7	25·3	24·9	24·7	24·6	24·7	S. 60	45·0	45·1	45·2	45·3	45·5	45·6
2·6	η Centauri 141		25·8	25·5	25·3	25·1	25·0	25·1	S. 42	04·2	04·3	04·4	04·5	04·6	04·7
3·0	γ Bootis 142		10·6	10·3	10·1	10·0	09·9	10·0	N. 38	23·3	23·3	23·3	23·4	23·5	23·6
0·2	α Bootis 37 146		18·3	18·1	17·9	17·8	17·8	17·8	N. 19	16·8	16·7	16·7	16·8	16·8	16·9
2·3	θ Centauri 36 148		36·8	36·5	36·3	36·2	36·1	36·2	S. 36	16·4	16·5	16·6	16·7	16·7	16·8
0·9	β Centauri 35 149		23·1	22·7	22·4	22·2	22·1	22·2	S. 60	16·5	16·6	16·8	16·9	17·1	17·2
3·1	ζ Centauri 151		24·9	24·6	24·4	24·3	24·2	24·3	S. 47	11·4	11·5	11·6	11·8	11·9	11·9
2·8	η Bootis 151		33·5	33·3	33·1	33·0	33·0	33·0	N. 18	29·5	29·4	29·4	29·5	29·5	29·6
1·9	η Ursæ Majoris 34 153		18·4	18·1	17·8	17·7	17·7	17·8	N. 49	24·3	24·3	24·3	24·4	24·6	24·7
2·6	ε Centauri 155		20·0	19·6	19·4	19·2	19·2	19·3	S. 53	21·9	22·0	22·1	22·3	22·4	22·5
1·2	α Virginis 33 158		57·3	57·1	56·9	56·8	56·8	56·9	S. 11	03·6	03·7	03·8	03·8	03·9	03·8
2·2	ζ Ursæ Majoris 159		12·8	12·5	12·2	12·1	12·2	12·3	N. 55	01·2	01·2	01·3	01·4	01·6	01·7
2·9	ι Centauri 160		07·2	07·0	06·8	06·7	06·7	06·8	S. 36	36·5	36·6	36·7	36·8	36·9	37·0
3·0	ε Virginis 164		41·7	41·5	41·3	41·3	41·3	41·3	N. 11	03·6	03·6	03·5	03·6	03·6	03·7
2·9	α Canum Venat. 166		13·1	12·8	12·6	12·6	12·6	12·7	N. 38	25·1	25·1	25·1	25·2	25·3	25·4
1·7	ε Ursæ Majoris 32 166		42·3	41·9	41·7	41·6	41·7	41·9	N. 56	03·5	03·6	03·6	03·8	03·9	04·0
1·5	β Crucis 168		20·8	20·5	20·3	20·2	20·3	20·5	S. 59	34·8	34·9	35·0	35·2	35·3	35·4
2·9	γ Virginis 169		49·7	49·4	49·3	49·3	49·3	49·4	S. 1	20·7	20·8	20·8	20·8	20·8	20·8
2·4	γ Centauri 169		53·0	52·7	52·6	52·5	52·6	52·7	S. 48	51·0	51·2	51·3	51·5	51·6	51·6
2·9	α Muscæ 170		59·1	58·7	58·4	58·4	58·5	58·8	S. 69	01·5	01·6	01·8	02·0	02·1	02·2
2·8	β Corvi 171		39·2	39·0	38·9	38·9	38·9	39·0	S. 23	17·3	17·5	17·6	17·6	17·7	17·7
1·6	γ Crucis 31 172		28·3	28·0	27·8	27·8	27·9	28·0	S. 57	00·1	00·2	00·4	00·6	00·7	00·7
1·1	α Crucis 30 173		36·7	36·4	36·2	36·1	36·3	36·5	S. 62	59·3	59·4	59·6	59·8	59·9	60·0
2·8	γ Corvi 29 176		17·6	17·4	17·3	17·3	17·3	17·4	S. 17	26·1	26·2	26·3	26·3	26·4	26·4
2·9	δ Centauri 178		09·3	09·1	08·9	08·9	09·0	09·2	S. 50	36·7	36·9	37·0	37·2	37·3	37·3
2·5	γ Ursæ Majoris 181		47·5	47·2	47·1	47·1	47·2	47·4	N. 53	47·8	47·8	47·9	48·1	48·2	48·2
2·2	β Leonis 28 182		58·7	58·5	58·4	58·4	58·4	58·5	N. 14	40·6	40·6	40·6	40·6	40·7	40·7
2·6	δ Leonis 191		43·5	43·3	43·3	43·3	43·4	43·5	N. 20	37·6	37·5	37·6	37·6	37·7	37·7
3·2	ψ Ursæ Majoris 192		51·0	50·8	50·7	50·8	50·9	51·0	N. 44	35·9	36·0	36·0	36·1	36·2	36·3
2·0	α Ursæ Majoris 27 194		21·5	21·2	21·1	21·2	21·4	21·7	N. 61	51·0	51·1	51·2	51·3	51·4	51·4
2·4	β Ursæ Majoris 194		49·4	49·2	49·1	49·2	49·3	49·6	N. 56	28·9	28·9	29·0	29·0	29·2	29·3
2·8	μ Velorum 198		30·4	30·3	30·2	30·3	30·5	30·7	S. 49	19·0	19·2	19·3	19·4	19·5	19·5
3·0	θ Carinæ 199		25·2	25·0	25·0	25·2	25·5	25·8	S. 64	17·4	17·6	17·8	18·0	18·0	18·1
2·3	γ Leonis 205		16·0	15·9	15·9	15·9	16·0	16·1	N. 19	56·2	56·2	56·2	56·2	56·3	56·3
1·3	α Leonis 26 208		09·5	09·4	09·4	09·4	09·5	09·6	N. 12	03·5	03·5	03·5	03·5	03·6	03·6
3·1	ε Leonis 213		48·3	48·2	48·2	48·3	48·4	48·5	N. 23	51·6	51·6	51·6	51·7	51·7	51·7
3·0	N Velorum 217		19·8	19·7	19·8	20·0	20·3	20·5	S. 56	56·9	57·1	57·3	57·4	57·4	57·4
2·2	α Hydræ 25 218		20·0	20·0	20·0	20·1	20·2	20·3	S. 8	34·6	34·7	34·7	34·8	34·7	34·7
2·6	κ Velorum 219		36·6	36·5	36·6	36·8	37·1	37·3	S. 54	55·7	55·9	56·0	56·1	56·1	56·1
2·2	ι Carinæ 220		50·6	50·6	50·7	50·9	51·2	51·5	S. 59	11·6	11·8	12·0	12·1	12·1	12·1
1·8	β Carinæ 24 221		44·0	43·9	44·1	44·5	45·0	45·4	S. 69	38·2	38·4	38·6	38·7	38·7	38·7
2·2	λ Velorum 23 223		10·2	10·1	10·2	10·4	10·5	10·7	S. 43	21·3	21·5	21·6	21·7	21·7	21·6
3·1	ι Ursæ Majoris 225		31·1	31·0	31·1	31·3	31·4	31·6	N. 48	06·9	06·9	07·0	07·1	07·1	07·1
2·0	δ Velorum 228		56·7	56·7	56·9	57·1	57·4	57·6	S. 54	38·3	38·5	38·6	38·7	38·7	38·6
1·7	ε Carinæ 22 234		27·4	27·5	27·6	27·9	28·2	28·5	S. 59	26·9	27·1	27·2	27·3	27·3	27·2
1·9	γ Velorum 237		45·3	45·4	45·5	45·7	45·9	46·1	S. 47	16·9	17·0	17·1	17·2	17·2	17·1
2·9	ρ Puppis 238		18·7	18·7	18·8	18·9	19·1	19·2	S. 24	15·0	15·1	15·2	15·2	15·2	15·1
2·3	ζ Puppis 239		15·9	15·9	16·0	16·2	16·4	16·5	S. 39	57·0	57·2	57·3	57·3	57·3	57·2
1·2	β Geminorum 21 243		57·5	57·5	57·6	57·7	57·8	57·9	N. 28	04·3	04·3	04·3	04·4	04·4	04·3
0·5	α Canis Minoris 20 245		25·2	25·2	25·3	25·4	25·5	25·6	N. 5	16·3	16·3	16·3	16·3	16·3	16·4

Mag.	Name and Number		S.H.A. JULY	AUG.	SEPT.	OCT.	NOV.	DEC.	Dec.	JULY	AUG.	SEPT.	OCT.	NOV.	DEC.
			° ′	′	′	′	′	′	°	′	′	′	′	′	′
3·1	γ Ursæ Minoris		129 48·4	48·9	49·5	49·8	50·0	49·9	N. 71	54·4	54·4	54·4	54·2	54·0	53·8
3·1	γ Trianguli Aust.		130 42·3	42·6	43·0	43·3	43·3	43·0	S. 68	36·9	36·9	36·9	36·8	36·6	36·5
2·7	β Libræ		130 59·9	60·0	60·1	60·2	60·2	60·0	S. 9	18·8	18·8	18·8	18·8	18·8	18·9
2·8	β Lupi		135 40·3	40·4	40·6	40·7	40·7	40·5	S. 43	03·7	03·7	03·6	03·5	03·5	03·4
2·2	Kochab	40	137 18·6	19·2	19·7	20·1	20·2	20·0	N. 74	14·3	14·3	14·2	14·1	13·9	13·7
2·9	Zubenelgenubi	39	137 32·3	32·4	32·5	32·6	32·5	32·4	S. 15	57·9	57·8	57·8	57·8	57·8	57·8
2·6	ε Bootis		138 57·4	57·5	57·6	57·7	57·7	57·6	N. 27	09·4	09·4	09·4	09·3	09·2	09·0
2·9	α Lupi		139 49·6	49·8	50·0	50·1	50·0	49·8	S. 47	18·6	18·6	18·6	18·5	18·4	18·4
0·1	Rigil Kent.	38	140 24·9	25·1	25·4	25·5	25·5	25·2	S. 60	45·6	45·6	45·6	45·5	45·3	45·3
2·6	η Centauri		141 25·1	25·3	25·5	25·5	25·5	25·3	S. 42	04·7	04·7	04·6	04·5	04·5	04·5
3·0	γ Bootis		142 10·1	10·2	10·4	10·5	10·4	10·3	N. 38	23·7	23·7	23·6	23·5	23·4	23·2
0·2	Arcturus	37	146 17·9	18·0	18·1	18·1	18·1	17·9	N. 19	17·0	17·0	16·9	16·9	16·7	16·6
2·3	Menkent	36	148 36·3	36·4	36·5	36·6	36·5	36·3	S. 36	16·8	16·8	16·7	16·7	16·6	16·6
0·9	Hadar	35	149 22·4	22·7	22·9	23·0	22·9	22·6	S. 60	17·2	17·2	17·1	17·0	16·9	16·8
3·1	ζ Centauri		151 24·4	24·6	24·7	24·8	24·7	24·4	S. 47	12·0	11·9	11·9	11·8	11·7	11·7
2·8	η Bootis		151 33·1	33·2	33·3	33·3	33·3	33·1	N. 18	29·7	29·7	29·6	29·6	29·4	29·3
1·9	Alkaid	34	153 18·0	18·2	18·3	18·4	18·3	18·1	N. 49	24·7	24·7	24·6	24·5	24·3	24·1
2·6	ε Centauri		155 19·5	19·7	19·9	19·9	19·8	19·5	S. 53	22·5	22·5	22·4	22·3	22·2	22·1
1·2	Spica	33	158 56·9	57·0	57·1	57·1	57·0	56·8	S. 11	03·8	03·8	03·8	03·7	03·8	03·8
2·2	Mizar		159 12·5	12·7	12·9	12·9	12·8	12·6	N. 55	01·7	01·7	01·6	01·4	01·2	01·0
2·9	ι Centauri		160 06·9	07·0	07·1	07·1	07·0	06·7	S. 36	37·0	36·9	36·8	36·8	36·7	36·7
3·0	ε Virginis		164 41·4	41·5	41·6	41·5	41·4	41·2	N. 11	03·7	03·7	03·7	03·6	03·5	03·4
2·9	Cor Caroli		166 12·8	13·0	13·0	13·0	12·9	12·7	N. 38	25·4	25·4	25·3	25·2	25·0	24·9
1·7	Alioth	32	166 42·1	42·3	42·4	42·4	42·3	42·0	N. 56	04·0	03·9	03·8	03·7	03·5	03·3
1·5	Mimosa		168 20·7	20·9	21·1	21·1	20·9	20·5	S. 59	35·4	35·4	35·2	35·1	35·0	35·0
2·9	γ Virginis		169 49·4	49·5	49·6	49·5	49·4	49·2	S. 1	20·7	20·7	20·7	20·7	20·8	20·9
2·4	Muhlifain		169 52·9	53·0	53·1	53·1	52·9	52·6	S. 48	51·6	51·5	51·4	51·3	51·3	51·3
2·9	α Muscæ		170 59·2	59·5	59·8	59·7	59·4	59·0	S. 69	02·2	02·1	02·0	01·9	01·8	01·7
2·8	β Corvi		171 39·1	39·1	39·2	39·2	39·0	38·8	S. 23	17·7	17·6	17·5	17·5	17·5	17·6
1·6	Gacrux	31	172 28·2	28·4	28·6	28·5	28·3	28·0	S. 57	00·7	00·7	00·5	00·4	00·3	00·3
1·1	Acrux	30	173 36·8	37·0	37·2	37·1	36·9	36·5	S. 62	60·0	59·9	59·8	59·6	59·5	59·5
2·8	Gienah	29	176 17·5	17·6	17·6	17·6	17·4	17·2	S. 17	26·3	26·3	26·2	26·2	26·2	26·3
2·9	δ Centauri		178 09·3	09·5	09·6	09·5	09·3	09·0	S. 50	37·3	37·2	37·1	37·0	36·9	36·9
2·5	Phecda		181 47·6	47·7	47·8	47·7	47·4	47·1	N. 53	48·2	48·1	48·0	47·8	47·7	47·5
2·2	Denebola	28	182 58·6	58·7	58·7	58·6	58·4	58·2	N. 14	40·7	40·7	40·7	40·6	40·5	40·4
2·6	δ Leonis		191 43·5	43·6	43·6	43·5	43·3	43·0	N. 20	37·7	37·7	37·6	37·6	37·5	37·3
3·2	ψ Ursæ Majoris		192 51·1	51·2	51·2	51·1	50·8	50·5	N. 44	36·2	36·2	36·0	35·9	35·8	35·7
2·0	Dubhe	27	194 21·9	22·0	21·9	21·8	21·4	21·0	N. 61	51·4	51·3	51·1	50·9	50·8	50·7
2·4	Merak		194 49·7	49·8	49·8	49·6	49·3	48·9	N. 56	29·2	29·1	29·0	28·8	28·7	28·6
2·8	μ Velorum		198 30·8	30·9	30·9	30·8	30·5	30·2	S. 49	19·4	19·3	19·2	19·1	19·1	19·1
3·0	θ Carinæ		199 26·1	26·2	26·2	26·0	25·7	25·2	S. 64	18·0	17·9	17·7	17·6	17·5	17·6
2·3	Algeiba		205 16·2	16·2	16·1	16·0	15·7	15·5	N. 19	56·3	56·3	56·2	56·2	56·1	56·0
1·3	Regulus	26	208 09·7	09·7	09·6	09·4	09·2	09·0	N. 12	03·6	03·6	03·6	03·5	03·5	03·4
3·1	ε Leonis		213 48·5	48·5	48·4	48·2	48·0	47·7	N. 23	51·7	51·7	51·7	51·6	51·5	51·4
3·0	N Velorum		217 20·6	20·7	20·6	20·3	20·0	19·7	S. 56	57·3	57·1	57·0	56·9	56·9	57·0
2·2	Alphard	25	218 20·3	20·3	20·2	20·0	19·8	19·5	S. 8	34·6	34·6	34·5	34·5	34·6	34·7
2·6	κ Velorum		219 37·4	37·4	37·3	37·1	36·8	36·4	S. 54	56·0	55·8	55·7	55·6	55·6	55·7
2·2	ι Carinæ		220 51·6	51·7	51·6	51·3	50·9	50·6	S. 59	11·9	11·8	11·6	11·6	11·6	11·7
1·8	Miaplacidus	24	221 45·7	45·7	45·6	45·2	44·7	44·2	S. 69	38·6	38·4	38·3	38·2	38·2	38·3
2·2	Suhail	23	223 10·8	10·8	10·6	10·4	10·2	09·9	S. 43	21·5	21·4	21·2	21·2	21·2	21·3
3·1	ι Ursæ Majoris		225 31·6	31·5	31·3	31·1	30·7	30·4	N. 48	07·0	06·9	06·8	06·7	06·7	06·6
2·0	δ Velorum		228 57·7	57·7	57·5	57·2	56·9	56·6	S. 54	38·5	38·3	38·2	38·1	38·2	38·3
1·7	Avior	22	234 28·6	28·6	28·4	28·1	27·7	27·4	S. 59	27·1	26·9	26·7	26·7	26·7	26·9
1·9	γ Velorum		237 46·1	46·1	45·9	45·6	45·3	45·1	S. 47	16·9	16·8	16·7	16·6	16·7	16·8
2·9	ρ Puppis		238 19·2	19·1	18·9	18·7	18·5	18·3	S. 24	15·0	14·9	14·8	14·8	14·9	15·0
2·3	ζ Puppis		239 16·5	16·5	16·3	16·1	15·8	15·5	S. 39	57·1	56·9	56·8	56·8	56·8	57·0
1·2	Pollux	21	243 57·9	57·7	57·5	57·3	57·0	56·8	N. 28	04·3	04·3	04·3	04·2	04·2	04·2
0·5	Procyon	20	245 25·5	25·4	25·2	25·0	24·8	24·6	N. 5	16·4	16·4	16·5	16·4	16·4	16·3

Mag.	Name and Number		S.H.A.							Dec.						
			JAN.	FEB.	MAR.	APR.	MAY	JUNE		JAN.	FEB.	MAR.	APR.	MAY	JUNE
		°	′	′	′	′	′	′	°	′	′	′	′	′	′
1·6	α Geminorum	246	39·0	39·0	39·1	39·2	39·4	39·4	N. 31	55·7	55·8	55·8	55·9	55·9	55·8
3·3	σ Puppis	247	50·2	50·2	50·4	50·6	50·8	50·9	S. 43	15·9	16·0	16·1	16·1	16·1	16·0
3·1	β Canis Minoris	248	28·0	28·0	28·1	28·2	28·3	28·4	N. 8	19·6	19·6	19·5	19·6	19·6	19·6
2·4	η Canis Majoris	249	09·6	09·6	09·7	09·9	10·0	10·1	S. 29	16·1	16·2	16·3	16·3	16·2	16·1
2·7	π Puppis	250	52·6	52·6	52·8	53·0	53·1	53·2	S. 37	03·9	04·0	04·1	04·1	04·1	04·0
2·0	δ Canis Majoris	253	05·5	05·5	05·6	05·8	05·9	06·0	S. 26	21·9	22·0	22·1	22·1	22·0	21·9
3·1	o Canis Majoris	254	26·3	26·3	26·4	26·6	26·7	26·8	S. 23	48·4	48·6	48·6	48·6	48·6	48·5
1·6	ε Canis Majoris 19	255	31·6	31·6	31·7	31·9	32·0	32·1	S. 28	56·9	57·0	57·1	57·1	57·0	56·9
2·8	τ Puppis	257	37·6	37·7	37·9	38·1	38·4	38·5	S. 50	35·7	35·8	35·9	35·9	35·8	35·7
−1·6	α Canis Majoris 18	258	55·2	55·2	55·3	55·5	55·6	55·6	S. 16	41·6	41·7	41·7	41·7	41·6	41·5
1·9	γ Geminorum	260	50·6	50·7	50·8	50·9	51·0	51·0	N. 16	24·9	24·9	24·9	24·9	24·9	24·9
−0·9	α Carinæ 17	264	06·6	06·7	06·9	07·2	07·4	07·5	S. 52	41·3	41·4	41·5	41·5	41·4	41·3
2·0	β Canis Majoris	264	31·9	31·9	32·0	32·2	32·3	32·3	S. 17	56·9	57·0	57·1	57·0	57·0	56·9
2·7	θ Aurigæ	270	23·4	23·5	23·7	23·8	23·9	23·9	N. 37	12·7	12·7	12·7	12·7	12·7	12·7
2·1	β Aurigæ	270	27·8	27·9	28·0	28·2	28·3	28·3	N. 44	56·8	56·8	56·9	56·8	56·8	56·7
Var.‡	α Orionis 16	271	27·7	27·8	27·9	28·0	28·1	28·1	N. 7	24·1	24·1	24·1	24·1	24·1	24·2
2·2	κ Orionis	273	17·0	17·1	17·2	17·4	17·4	17·4	S. 9	40·7	40·8	40·8	40·8	40·7	40·6
1·9	ζ Orionis	275	02·9	02·9	03·1	03·2	03·3	03·2	S. 1	57·3	57·3	57·3	57·3	57·3	57·2
2·8	α Columbæ	275	15·4	15·5	15·6	15·8	15·9	15·9	S. 34	05·3	05·4	05·4	05·4	05·3	05·1
3·0	ζ Tauri	275	52·2	52·3	52·4	52·6	52·6	52·6	N. 21	07·8	07·8	07·8	07·8	07·8	07·8
1·8	ε Orionis 15	276	11·1	11·2	11·3	11·5	11·5	11·5	S. 1	13·0	13·0	13·0	13·0	13·0	12·9
2·9	ι Orionis	276	22·3	22·4	22·5	22·6	22·7	22·7	S. 5	55·5	55·5	55·5	55·5	55·5	55·4
2·7	α Leporis	277	01·5	01·6	01·7	01·8	01·9	01·9	S. 17	50·3	50·4	50·4	50·4	50·3	50·2
2·5	δ Orionis	277	14·4	14·4	14·5	14·7	14·7	14·7	S. 0	18·9	18·9	19·0	18·9	18·9	18·8
3·0	β Leporis	278	08·4	08·5	08·6	08·8	08·8	08·8	S. 20	46·7	46·7	46·8	46·7	46·6	46·5
1·8	β Tauri 14	278	43·5	43·6	43·7	43·9	43·9	43·9	N. 28	35·5	35·5	35·5	35·5	35·5	35·4
1·7	γ Orionis 13	278	58·2	58·3	58·4	58·5	58·6	58·6	N. 6	19·9	19·8	19·8	19·8	19·9	19·9
0·2	α Aurigæ 12	281	10·6	10·7	10·8	11·0	11·1	11·1	N. 45	58·8	58·8	58·8	58·8	58·8	58·7
0·3	β Orionis 11	281	35·5	35·6	35·7	35·9	35·9	35·9	S. 8	13·6	13·6	13·6	13·6	13·5	13·5
2·9	β Eridani	283	16·2	16·3	16·4	16·5	16·6	16·5	S. 5	06·8	06·8	06·9	06·8	06·8	06·7
2·9	ι Aurigæ	286	03·6	03·7	03·8	03·9	04·0	03·9	N. 33	08·2	08·2	08·2	08·2	08·1	08·1
1·1	α Tauri 10	291	17·5	17·6	17·7	17·8	17·9	17·8	N. 16	28·2	28·2	28·2	28·2	28·2	28·2
3·2	γ Eridani	300	42·8	42·9	43·1	43·2	43·2	43·1	S. 13	34·0	34·0	34·0	33·9	33·9	33·7
3·0	ε Persei	300	51·3	51·4	51·6	51·7	51·7	51·6	N. 39	57·4	57·4	57·4	57·3	57·3	57·2
2·9	ζ Persei	301	45·9	46·0	46·2	46·3	46·3	46·2	N. 31	49·7	49·7	49·6	49·6	49·6	49·5
3·0	η Tauri	303	24·7	24·8	24·9	25·0	25·0	24·9	N. 24	02·8	02·8	02·7	02·7	02·7	02·7
1·9	α Persei 9	309	15·5	15·7	15·9	16·0	16·0	15·8	N. 49	47·7	47·8	47·7	47·6	47·5	47·5
Var.§	β Persei	313	16·1	16·2	16·4	16·5	16·4	16·2	N. 40	53·0	53·0	53·0	52·9	52·9	52·8
2·8	α Ceti 8	314	40·8	40·9	41·0	41·0	41·0	40·9	N. 4	00·8	00·8	00·8	00·8	00·8	00·9
3·1	θ Eridani 7	315	36·9	37·1	37·3	37·4	37·3	37·2	S. 40	23·2	23·2	23·2	23·0	22·9	22·7
2·1	α Ursæ Minoris	326	42·6	53·3	61·9	66·2	63·7	56·1	N. 89	10·9	10·9	10·8	10·7	10·5	10·4
3·1	β Trianguli	327	53·9	54·1	54·2	54·2	54·1	53·9	N. 34	53·9	53·9	53·8	53·8	53·7	53·7
2·2	α Arietis 6	328	28·6	28·7	28·8	28·8	28·8	28·6	N. 23	22·4	22·3	22·3	22·2	22·2	22·3
2·2	γ Andromedæ	329	19·1	19·3	19·4	19·5	19·4	19·2	N. 42	14·4	14·4	14·3	14·2	14·2	14·2
3·0	α Hydri	330	27·6	27·9	28·1	28·2	28·2	27·9	S. 61	40·2	40·1	40·0	39·8	39·7	39·5
2·7	β Arietis	331	36·3	36·4	36·5	36·5	36·4	36·2	N. 20	42·9	42·9	42·8	42·8	42·8	42·8
0·6	α Eridani 5	335	45·1	45·4	45·5	45·6	45·5	45·2	S. 57	20·4	20·4	20·2	20·1	19·9	19·7
2·8	δ Cassiopeiæ	338	51·6	51·9	52·1	52·1	51·9	51·6	N. 60	08·4	08·3	08·2	08·1	08·0	08·0
2·4	β Andromedæ	342	50·2	50·3	50·4	50·4	50·3	50·0	N. 35	31·3	31·2	31·1	31·1	31·0	31·0
Var.‖	γ Cassiopeiæ	346	06·9	07·1	07·3	07·2	07·0	06·7	N. 60	37·0	37·0	36·8	36·7	36·6	36·6
2·2	β Ceti 4	349	20·7	20·8	20·9	20·8	20·7	20·5	S. 18	05·7	05·7	05·6	05·6	05·4	05·3
2·5	α Cassiopeiæ 3	350	08·9	09·1	09·2	09·1	08·9	08·6	N. 56	26·2	26·1	26·0	25·8	25·8	25·8
2·4	α Phœnicis 2	353	40·2	40·3	40·3	40·3	40·1	39·9	S. 42	24·9	24·8	24·7	24·6	24·4	24·3
2·9	β Hydri	353	49·4	50·0	50·2	50·1	49·7	48·9	S. 77	22·1	22·0	21·8	21·6	21·4	21·3
2·9	γ Pegasi	356	56·4	56·5	56·5	56·5	56·3	56·1	N. 15	04·6	04·6	04·5	04·5	04·6	04·6
2·4	β Cassiopeiæ	357	57·9	58·1	58·2	58·1	57·8	57·5	N. 59	02·9	02·8	02·6	02·5	02·4	02·5
2·2	α Andromedæ 1	358	09·2	09·3	09·3	09·3	09·1	08·9	N. 28	59·2	59·1	59·0	59·0	59·0	59·0

‡ 0·1—1·2   § 2·3—3·5   ‖ Irregular variable; 1978 mag. 2·7

Mag.	Name and Number		S.H.A. °	JULY	AUG.	SEPT.	OCT.	NOV.	DEC.	Dec. °	JULY	AUG.	SEPT.	OCT.	NOV.	DEC.
1·6	*Castor*		246	39·4	39·2	39·0	38·8	38·5	38·2	N. 31	55·8	55·8	55·7	55·7	55·7	55·6
3·3	σ Puppis		247	50·9	50·8	50·6	50·3	50·1	49·9	S. 43	15·8	15·7	15·6	15·5	15·6	15·8
3·1	β Canis Minoris		248	28·3	28·2	28·0	27·8	27·6	27·4	N. 8	19·7	19·7	19·7	19·7	19·6	19·6
2·4	η Canis Majoris		249	10·1	10·0	09·8	09·6	09·3	09·1	S. 29	16·0	15·9	15·8	15·8	15·8	16·0
2·7	π Puppis		250	53·2	53·1	52·9	52·7	52·4	52·2	S. 37	03·8	03·7	03·6	03·6	03·7	03·8
2·0	*Wezen*		253	05·9	05·8	05·6	05·4	05·2	05·0	S. 26	21·8	21·7	21·6	21·6	21·7	21·8
3·1	o Canis Majoris		254	26·7	26·6	26·4	26·2	26·0	25·8	S. 23	48·3	48·2	48·1	48·1	48·2	48·3
1·6	*Adhara*	19	255	32·0	31·9	31·7	31·5	31·3	31·1	S. 28	56·8	56·6	56·6	56·6	56·6	56·8
2·8	τ Puppis		257	38·4	38·3	38·0	37·8	37·5	37·3	S. 50	35·5	35·4	35·3	35·3	35·4	35·5
-1·6	*Sirius*	18	258	55·5	55·4	55·2	55·0	54·8	54·6	S. 16	41·4	41·3	41·3	41·3	41·4	41·5
1·9	*Alhena*		260	50·9	50·8	50·5	50·3	50·1	49·9	N. 16	24·9	24·9	25·0	24·9	24·9	24·9
-0·9	*Canopus*	17	264	07·5	07·3	07·0	06·7	06·4	06·3	S. 52	41·1	40·9	40·8	40·9	41·0	41·1
2·0	*Mirzam*		264	32·2	32·1	31·9	31·7	31·5	31·3	S. 17	56·8	56·7	56·6	56·6	56·7	56·8
2·7	θ Aurigæ		270	23·8	23·5	23·3	23·0	22·7	22·6	N. 37	12·6	12·6	12·6	12·6	12·6	12·7
2·1	*Menkalinan*		270	28·2	27·9	27·6	27·3	27·0	26·8	N. 44	56·7	56·6	56·6	56·6	56·7	56·7
Var.‡	*Betelgeuse*	16	271	28·0	27·8	27·6	27·4	27·2	27·0	N. 7	24·2	24·3	24·3	24·3	24·3	24·2
2·2	κ Orionis		273	17·3	17·1	16·9	16·7	16·5	16·4	S. 9	40·5	40·5	40·4	40·4	40·5	40·6
1·9	*Alnitak*		275	03·1	02·9	02·7	02·5	02·3	02·2	S. 1	57·1	57·1	57·0	57·0	57·1	57·1
2·8	*Phact*		275	15·8	15·6	15·4	15·2	15·0	14·9	S. 34	05·0	04·8	04·8	04·8	04·9	05·1
3·0	ζ Tauri		275	52·5	52·3	52·0	51·8	51·6	51·4	N. 21	07·8	07·9	07·9	07·9	07·9	07·9
1·8	*Alnilam*	15	276	11·4	11·2	11·0	10·8	10·6	10·5	S. 1	12·8	12·7	12·7	12·7	12·8	12·8
2·9	ι Orionis		276	22·6	22·4	22·2	22·0	21·8	21·7	S. 5	55·3	55·2	55·2	55·2	55·2	55·3
2·7	α Leporis		277	01·8	01·6	01·4	01·2	01·0	00·9	S. 17	50·1	50·0	49·9	49·9	50·0	50·1
2·5	δ Orionis		277	14·6	14·4	14·2	14·0	13·8	13·7	S. 0	18·8	18·7	18·6	18·6	18·7	18·8
3·0	β Leporis		278	08·7	08·5	08·3	08·1	07·9	07·8	S. 20	46·4	46·3	46·2	46·3	46·3	46·5
1·8	*Elnath*	14	278	43·7	43·5	43·3	43·0	42·8	42·7	N. 28	35·4	35·5	35·5	35·5	35·5	35·5
1·7	*Bellatrix*	13	278	58·4	58·2	58·0	57·8	57·6	57·5	N. 6	20·0	20·0	20·1	20·1	20·0	20·0
0·2	*Capella*	12	281	10·9	10·6	10·3	10·0	09·7	09·5	N. 45	58·6	58·6	58·6	58·7	58·7	58·8
0·3	*Rigel*	11	281	35·8	35·6	35·3	35·1	35·0	34·9	S. 8	13·4	13·3	13·2	13·2	13·3	13·4
2·9	β Eridani		283	16·4	16·2	16·0	15·8	15·6	15·5	S. 5	06·6	06·5	06·5	06·5	06·5	06·6
2·9	ι Aurigæ		286	03·8	03·5	03·2	03·0	02·8	02·7	N. 33	08·1	08·1	08·2	08·2	08·2	08·3
1·1	*Aldebaran*	10	291	17·6	17·4	17·2	16·9	16·8	16·7	N. 16	28·3	28·3	28·4	28·4	28·4	28·4
3·2	γ Eridani		300	42·9	42·7	42·5	42·3	42·2	42·1	S. 13	33·6	33·5	33·5	33·5	33·6	33·7
3·0	ε Persei		300	51·4	51·1	50·8	50·6	50·4	50·3	N. 39	57·2	57·3	57·3	57·4	57·5	57·5
2·9	ζ Persei		301	46·0	45·7	45·4	45·2	45·1	45·0	N. 31	49·6	49·6	49·7	49·7	49·8	49·8
3·0	*Alcyone*		303	24·7	24·4	24·2	24·0	23·9	23·8	N. 24	02·7	02·8	02·9	02·9	03·0	03·0
1·9	*Mirfak*	9	309	15·5	15·2	14·9	14·6	14·5	14·4	N. 49	47·5	47·5	47·6	47·7	47·8	47·9
Var.§	*Algol*		313	16·0	15·7	15·4	15·2	15·1	15·1	N. 40	52·8	52·9	53·0	53·1	53·2	53·2
2·8	*Menkar*	8	314	40·7	40·4	40·2	40·1	40·0	40·0	N. 4	01·0	01·1	01·1	01·1	01·1	01·1
3·1	*Acamar*	7	315	37·0	36·7	36·5	36·3	36·2	36·2	S. 40	22·6	22·5	22·5	22·6	22·7	22·8
2·1	*Polaris*		326	45·3	33·9	24·3	18·4	17·5	22·5	N. 89	10·4	10·4	10·6	10·7	10·9	11·1
3·1	β Trianguli		327	53·7	53·4	53·2	53·1	53·0	53·0	N. 34	53·8	53·9	54·0	54·1	54·1	54·2
2·2	*Hamal*	6	328	28·3	28·1	27·9	27·8	27·7	27·7	N. 23	22·3	22·4	22·5	22·6	22·6	22·7
2·2	*Almak*		329	18·9	18·6	18·4	18·2	18·1	18·2	N. 42	14·2	14·3	14·4	14·5	14·6	14·7
3·0	α Hydri		330	27·5	27·1	26·8	26·6	26·6	26·8	S. 61	39·4	39·3	39·4	39·5	39·7	39·8
2·7	*Sheratan*		331	36·0	35·8	35·6	35·5	35·4	35·4	N. 20	42·9	43·0	43·1	43·2	43·2	43·2
0·6	*Achernar*	5	335	44·9	44·5	44·2	44·1	44·1	44·3	S. 57	19·6	19·6	19·7	19·8	19·9	20·1
2·8	*Ruchbah*		338	51·2	50·8	50·5	50·4	50·4	50·5	N. 60	08·0	08·1	08·3	08·4	08·6	08·7
2·4	*Mirach*		342	49·7	49·5	49·3	49·2	49·2	49·3	N. 35	31·1	31·2	31·4	31·5	31·5	31·6
Var.‖	γ Cassiopeiæ		346	06·3	05·9	05·7	05·6	05·6	05·8	N. 60	36·6	36·8	36·9	37·1	37·2	37·3
2·2	*Diphda*	4	349	20·2	20·0	19·9	19·8	19·8	19·9	S. 18	05·2	05·2	05·2	05·2	05·3	05·3
2·5	*Schedar*	3	350	08·2	07·9	07·7	07·7	07·7	07·9	N. 56	25·8	26·0	26·1	26·3	26·4	26·5
2·4	*Ankaa*	2	353	39·6	39·3	39·1	39·1	39·2	39·3	S. 42	24·2	24·2	24·3	24·4	24·5	24·6
2·9	β Hydri		353	48·1	47·4	46·9	46·9	47·2	47·8	S. 77	21·3	21·3	21·4	21·6	21·7	21·8
2·9	*Algenib*		356	55·8	55·6	55·5	55·5	55·5	55·6	N. 15	04·7	04·8	04·9	05·0	05·0	05·0
2·4	*Caph*		357	57·1	56·8	56·6	56·6	56·7	56·9	N. 59	02·5	02·7	02·9	03·0	03·1	03·2
2·2	*Alpheratz*	1	358	08·6	08·4	08·3	08·2	08·3	08·4	N. 28	59·1	59·2	59·4	59·5	59·5	59·5

‡ 0·1—1·2   § 2·3—3·5   ‖ Irregular variable; 1978 mag. 2·7

POLARIS (POLE STAR) TABLES, 1981
FOR DETERMINING LATITUDE FROM SEXTANT ALTITUDE AND FOR AZIMUTH

L.H.A. ARIES	0°– 9°	10°– 19°	20°– 29°	30°– 39°	40°– 49°	50°– 59°	60°– 69°	70°– 79°	80°– 89°	90°– 99°	100°– 109°	110°– 119°
	a_0	a_0	a_0	a_0	a_0	a_0	a_0	a_0	a_0	a_0	a_0	a_0
°	° ′	° ′	° ′	° ′	° ′	° ′	° ′	° ′	° ′	° ′	° ′	° ′
0	0 17·8	0 13·7	0 10·9	0 09·7	0 09·9	0 11·7	0 14·9	0 19·5	0 25·3	0 32·1	0 39·7	0 47·9
1	17·3	13·3	10·7	09·6	10·1	12·0	15·3	20·0	25·9	32·8	40·5	48·7
2	16·9	13·0	10·6	09·6	10·2	12·2	15·7	20·6	26·6	33·5	41·3	49·6
3	16·4	12·7	10·4	09·6	10·3	12·5	16·2	21·1	27·2	34·3	42·1	50·4
4	16·0	12·4	10·3	09·6	10·5	12·8	16·6	21·7	27·9	35·0	42·9	51·3
5	0 15·6	0 12·1	0 10·1	0 09·6	0 10·6	0 13·1	0 17·1	0 22·3	0 28·6	0 35·8	0 43·7	0 52·1
6	15·2	11·9	10·0	09·7	10·8	13·5	17·5	22·8	29·3	36·6	44·6	53·0
7	14·8	11·6	09·9	09·7	11·0	13·8	18·0	23·4	29·9	37·3	45·4	53·8
8	14·4	11·4	09·8	09·8	11·2	14·2	18·5	24·0	30·6	38·1	46·2	54·7
9	14·0	11·2	09·7	09·8	11·5	14·5	19·0	24·7	31·4	38·9	47·0	55·5
10	0 13·7	0 10·9	0 09·7	0 09·9	0 11·7	0 14·9	0 19·5	0 25·3	0 32·1	0 39·7	0 47·9	0 56·4

Lat.	a_1	a_1	a_1	a_1	a_1	a_1	a_1	a_1	a_1	a_1	a_1	a_1
°	′	′	′	′	′	′	′	′	′	′	′	′
0	0·5	0·6	0·6	0·6	0·6	0·5	0·5	0·4	0·3	0·3	0·2	0·2
10	·5	·6	·6	·6	·6	·6	·5	·4	·4	·3	·3	·2
20	·5	·6	·6	·6	·6	·6	·5	·5	·4	·4	·3	·3
30	·6	·6	·6	·6	·6	·6	·5	·5	·5	·4	·4	·4
40	0·6	0·6	0·6	0·6	0·6	0·6	0·6	0·5	0·5	0·5	0·5	0·5
45	·6	·6	·6	·6	·6	·6	·6	·6	·6	·5	·5	·5
50	·6	·6	·6	·6	·6	·6	·6	·6	·6	·6	·6	·6
55	·6	·6	·6	·6	·6	·6	·6	·6	·7	·7	·7	·7
60	·6	·6	·6	·6	·6	·6	·7	·7	·7	·7	·8	·8
62	0·7	0·6	0·6	0·6	0·6	0·6	0·7	0·7	0·7	0·8	0·8	0·8
64	·7	·6	·6	·6	·6	·6	·7	·7	·8	·8	·9	0·9
66	·7	·6	·6	·6	·6	·7	·7	·8	·8	0·9	0·9	1·0
68	0·7	0·6	0·6	0·6	0·6	0·7	0·7	0·8	0·9	1·0	1·0	1·0

Month	a_2	a_2	a_2	a_2	a_2	a_2	a_2	a_2	a_2	a_2	a_2	a_2
	′	′	′	′	′	′	′	′	′	′	′	′
Jan.	0·7	0·7	0·7	0·7	0·7	0·7	0·7	0·7	0·7	0·6	0·6	0·6
Feb.	·6	·6	·7	·7	·7	·7	·8	·8	·8	·8	·8	·8
Mar.	·5	·5	·6	·6	·7	·7	·8	·8	·8	·9	·9	·9
Apr.	0·3	0·4	0·4	0·5	0·5	0·6	0·7	0·7	0·8	0·8	0·9	0·9
May	·2	·2	·3	·3	·4	·5	·5	·6	·7	·7	·8	·9
June	·2	·2	·2	·2	·3	·3	·4	·5	·5	·6	·7	·7
July	0·2	0·2	0·2	0·2	0·2	0·2	0·3	0·3	0·4	0·4	0·5	0·6
Aug.	·3	·3	·3	·2	·2	·2	·2	·3	·3	·3	·4	·4
Sept.	·5	·5	·4	·4	·3	·3	·3	·3	·3	·3	·3	·3
Oct.	0·7	0·6	0·6	0·5	0·5	0·4	0·4	0·3	0·3	0·3	0·3	0·3
Nov.	0·9	0·8	·8	·7	·6	·6	·5	·5	·4	·3	·3	·3
Dec.	1·0	1·0	0·9	0·9	0·8	0·8	0·7	0·6	0·6	0·5	0·4	0·4

Lat.						AZIMUTH						
°	°	°	°	°	°	°	°	°	°	°	°	°
0	0·4	0·3	0·1	0·0	359·8	359·7	359·6	359·5	359·4	359·3	359·2	359·2
20	0·4	0·3	0·1	0·0	359·8	359·7	359·5	359·4	359·3	359·2	359·2	359·1
40	0·5	0·3	0·2	0·0	359·8	359·6	359·4	359·3	359·2	359·1	359·0	358·9
50	0·6	0·4	0·2	0·0	359·7	359·5	359·3	359·1	359·0	358·9	358·8	358·7
55	0·7	0·5	0·2	0·0	359·7	359·5	359·2	359·0	358·9	358·7	358·6	358·6
60	0·8	0·5	0·2	0·0	359·7	359·4	359·1	358·9	358·7	358·5	358·4	358·4
65	0·9	0·6	0·3	359·9	359·6	359·3	359·0	358·7	358·4	358·3	358·1	358·1

Latitude = Apparent altitude (corrected for refraction) − 1° + a_0 + a_1 + a_2

The table is entered with L.H.A. Aries to determine the column to be used; each column refers to a range of 10°. a_0 is taken, with mental interpolation, from the upper table with the units of L.H.A. Aries in degrees as argument; a_1, a_2 are taken, without interpolation, from the second and third tables with arguments latitude and month respectively. a_0, a_1, a_2 are always positive. The final table gives the azimuth of *Polaris*.

L.H.A. ARIES	120°–129°	130°–139°	140°–149°	150°–159°	160°–169°	170°–179°	180°–189°	190°–199°	200°–209°	210°–219°	220°–229°	230°–239°
	a_0	a_0	a_0	a_0	a_0	a_0	a_0	a_0	a_0	a_0	a_0	a_0
	° ′	° ′	° ′	° ′	° ′	° ′	° ′	° ′	° ′	° ′	° ′	° ′
0	0 56·4	1 05·0	1 13·3	1 21·2	1 28·5	1 34·8	1 40·0	1 44·1	1 46·7	1 47·9	1 47·7	1 46·0
1	57·2	05·8	14·1	22·0	29·1	35·4	40·5	44·4	46·9	48·0	47·6	45·7
2	58·1	06·7	15·0	22·7	29·8	35·9	41·0	44·7	47·1	48·0	47·4	45·4
3	59·0	07·5	15·8	23·5	30·5	36·5	41·4	45·0	47·2	48·0	47·3	45·2
4	0 59·8	08·3	16·6	24·2	31·1	37·0	41·8	45·3	47·4	48·0	47·2	44·9
5	1 00·7	1 09·2	1 17·4	1 25·0	1 31·8	1 37·6	1 42·2	1 45·6	1 47·5	1 48·0	1 47·0	1 44·6
6	01·5	10·0	18·1	25·7	32·4	38·1	42·6	45·8	47·6	47·9	46·8	44·3
7	02·4	10·8	18·9	26·4	33·0	38·6	43·0	46·1	47·7	47·9	46·6	43·9
8	03·2	11·7	19·7	27·1	33·6	39·1	43·4	46·3	47·8	47·8	46·4	43·6
9	04·1	12·5	20·5	27·8	34·2	39·6	43·7	46·5	47·9	47·8	46·2	43·2
10	1 05·0	1 13·3	1 21·2	1 28·5	1 34·8	1 40·0	1 44·1	1 46·7	1 47·9	1 47·7	1 46·0	1 42·8

Lat.	a_1	a_1	a_1	a_1	a_1	a_1	a_1	a_1	a_1	a_1	a_1	a_1
°	′	′	′	′	′	′	′	′	′	′	′	′
0	0·2	0·2	0·2	0·3	0·4	0·4	0·5	0·6	0·6	0·6	0·6	0·5
10	·2	·3	·3	·3	·4	·5	·5	·6	·6	·6	·6	·6
20	·3	·3	·3	·4	·4	·5	·5	·6	·6	·6	·6	·6
30	·4	·4	·4	·4	·5	·5	·6	·6	·6	·6	·6	·6
40	0·5	0·5	0·5	0·5	0·5	0·6	0·6	0·6	0·6	0·6	0·6	0·6
45	·5	·5	·5	·6	·6	·6	·6	·6	·6	·6	·6	·6
50	·6	·6	·6	·6	·6	·6	·6	·6	·6	·6	·6	·6
55	·7	·7	·7	·7	·6	·6	·6	·6	·6	·6	·6	·6
60	·8	·8	·8	·7	·7	·7	·6	·6	·6	·6	·6	·6
62	0·8	0·8	0·8	0·8	0·7	0·7	0·7	0·6	0·6	0·6	0·6	0·6
64	0·9	0·9	·9	·8	·8	·7	·7	·6	·6	·6	·6	·6
66	1·0	1·0	0·9	·9	·8	·7	·7	·6	·6	·6	·6	·7
68	1·1	1·0	1·0	0·9	0·9	0·8	0·7	0·6	0·6	0·6	0·6	0·7

Month	a_2	a_2	a_2	a_2	a_2	a_2	a_2	a_2	a_2	a_2	a_2	a_2
	′	′	′	′	′	′	′	′	′	′	′	′
Jan.	0·6	0·6	0·6	0·6	0·5	0·5	0·5	0·5	0·5	0·5	0·5	0·5
Feb.	·8	·7	·7	·7	·7	·6	·6	·6	·5	·5	·5	·5
Mar.	·9	0·9	0·9	0·8	·8	·8	·7	·7	·6	·6	·5	·5
Apr.	0·9	1·0	1·0	1·0	0·9	0·9	0·9	0·8	0·8	0·7	0·7	0·6
May	·9	1·0	1·0	1·0	1·0	1·0	1·0	1·0	0·9	0·9	·8	·7
June	·8	0·9	0·9	1·0	1·0	1·0	1·0	1·0	1·0	1·0	0·9	0·9
July	0·7	0·7	0·8	0·9	0·9	0·9	1·0	1·0	1·0	1·0	1·0	1·0
Aug.	·5	·6	·6	·7	·7	·8	0·9	0·9	0·9	1·0	1·0	1·0
Sept.	·4	·4	·5	·5	·6	·6	·7	·7	·8	0·8	0·9	0·9
Oct.	0·3	0·3	0·3	0·3	0·4	0·4	0·5	0·6	0·6	0·7	0·7	0·8
Nov.	·2	·2	·2	·2	·3	·3	·3	·4	·4	·5	·6	·6
Dec.	0·3	0·3	0·2	0·2	0·2	0·2	0·2	0·2	0·3	0·3	0·4	0·4

Lat.	AZIMUTH											
°	°	°	°	°	°	°	°	°	°	°	°	°
0	359·2	359·2	359·2	359·3	359·4	359·5	359·6	359·7	359·9	0·0	0·2	0·3
20	359·1	359·1	359·2	359·3	359·4	359·5	359·6	359·7	359·9	0·0	0·2	0·3
40	358·9	359·0	359·0	359·1	359·2	359·3	359·5	359·7	359·8	0·0	0·2	0·4
50	358·7	358·8	358·8	358·9	359·1	359·2	359·4	359·6	359·8	0·0	0·3	0·5
55	358·6	358·6	358·7	358·8	358·9	359·1	359·3	359·6	359·8	0·0	0·3	0·5
60	358·4	358·4	358·5	358·6	358·8	359·0	359·2	359·5	359·8	0·0	0·3	0·6
65	358·1	358·1	358·2	358·4	358·6	358·8	359·1	359·4	359·7	0·1	0·4	0·7

								° ′
ILLUSTRATION		From the daily pages:	° ′		*Ho*		49 31·6
On 1981 April 21 at G.M.T.		G.H.A. Aries (23ʰ)	194 55·4		a_0 (argument 162° 26′)	–	1 30·1
23ʰ 18ᵐ 56ˢ in longitude		Increment (18ᵐ 56ˢ)	4 44·8		a_1 (lat. 50° approx.)		0·6
W. 37° 14′ the apparent altitude		Longitude (west)	−37 14		a_2 (April)		0·9
(corrected for refraction), *Ho*, of							
Polaris was 49° 31′·6.		L.H.A. Aries	162 26		Sum −1° = Lat. =		50 03·2

POLARIS (POLE STAR) TABLES, 1981
FOR DETERMINING LATITUDE FROM SEXTANT ALTITUDE AND FOR AZIMUTH

L.H.A. ARIES	240°–249°	250°–259°	260°–269°	270°–279°	280°–289°	290°–299°	300°–309°	310°–319°	320°–329°	330°–339°	340°–349°	350°–359°
	a_0	a_0	a_0	a_0	a_0	a_0	a_0	a_0	a_0	a_0	a_0	a_0
0	1 42·8	1 38·4	1 32·8	1 26·1	1 18·6	1 10·5	1 02·1	0 53·5	0·45·0	0 37·0	0 29·7	0 23·2
1	42·5	37·9	32·1	25·4	17·8	09·7	01·2	52·6	44·2	36·3	29·0	22·6
2	42·1	37·4	31·5	24·7	17·0	08·8	1 00·3	51·8	43·4	35·5	28·3	22·0
3	41·6	36·8	30·9	23·9	16·2	08·0	0 59·5	50·9	42·6	34·7	27·6	21·5
4	41·2	36·3	30·2	23·2	15·4	07·2	58·6	50·1	41·8	34·0	27·0	20·9
5	1 40·8	1 35·7	1 29·6	1 22·5	1 14·6	1 06·3	0 57·8	0 49·2	0 41·0	0 33·3	0 26·3	0 20·4
6	40·3	35·2	28·9	21·7	13·8	05·5	56·9	48·4	40·2	32·5	25·7	19·8
7	39·9	34·6	28·2	20·9	13·0	04·6	56·0	47·5	39·4	31·8	25·0	19·3
8	39·4	34·0	27·5	20·2	12·2	03·8	55·2	46·7	38·6	31·1	24·4	18·8
9	38·9	33·4	26·8	19·4	11·3	02·9	54·3	45·9	37·8	30·4	23·8	18·3
10	1 38·4	1 32·8	1 26·1	1 18·6	1 10·5	1 02·1	0 53·5	0 45·0	0 37·0	0 29·7	0 23·2	0 17·8

Lat.	a_1	a_1	a_1	a_1	a_1	a_1	a_1	a_1	a_1	a_1	a_1	a_1
0	0·5	0·4	0·3	0·3	0·2	0·2	0·2	0·2	0·2	0·3	0·4	0·4
10	·5	·4	·4	·3	·3	·2	·2	·3	·3	·3	·4	·5
20	·5	·5	·4	·4	·3	·3	·3	·3	·3	·4	·4	·5
30	·5	·5	·5	·4	·4	·4	·4	·4	·4	·4	·5	·5
40	0·6	0·5	0·5	0·5	0·5	0·5	0·5	0·5	0·5	0·5	0·5	0·6
45	·6	·6	·6	·5	·5	·5	·5	·5	·5	·6	·6	·6
50	·6	·6	·6	·6	·6	·6	·6	·6	·6	·6	·6	·6
55	·6	·6	·7	·7	·7	·7	·7	·7	·7	·7	·6	·6
60	·7	·7	·7	·7	·8	·8	·8	·8	·8	·7	·7	·7
62	0·7	0·7	0·7	0·8	0·8	0·8	0·8	0·8	0·8	0·8	0·7	0·7
64	·7	·7	·8	·8	·9	0·9	0·9	0·9	·9	·8	·8	·7
66	·7	·8	·8	0·9	0·9	1·0	1·0	1·0	0·9	·9	·8	·7
68	0·7	0·8	0·9	1·0	1·0	1·0	1·1	1·0	1·0	0·9	0·9	0·8

Month	a_2	a_2	a_2	a_2	a_2	a_2	a_2	a_2	a_2	a_2	a_2	a_2
Jan.	0·5	0·5	0·5	0·6	0·6	0·6	0·6	0·6	0·6	0·6	0·7	0·7
Feb.	·4	·4	·4	·4	·4	·4	·4	·5	·5	·5	·5	·6
Mar.	·4	·4	·4	·3	·3	·3	·3	·3	·3	·4	·4	·4
Apr.	0·5	0·5	0·4	0·4	0·3	0·3	0·3	0·2	0·2	0·2	0·3	0·3
May	·7	·6	·5	·5	·4	·3	·3	·2	·2	·2	·2	·2
June	·8	·7	·7	·6	·5	·5	·4	·3	·3	·2	·2	·2
July	0·9	0·9	0·8	0·8	0·7	0·6	0·5	0·5	0·4	0·3	0·3	0·3
Aug.	1·0	·9	·9	·9	·8	·8	·7	·6	·6	·5	·5	·4
Sept.	0·9	·9	·9	·9	·9	·9	·8	·8	·7	·7	·6	·6
Oct.	0·8	0·9	0·9	0·9	0·9	0·9	0·9	0·9	0·9	0·9	0·8	0·8
Nov.	·7	·7	·8	·9	·9	·9	1·0	1·0	1·0	1·0	0·9	0·9
Dec.	0·5	0·6	0·6	0·7	0·8	0·8	0·9	0·9	1·0	1·0	1·0	1·0

Lat.	AZIMUTH											
0	0·4	0·5	0·6	0·7	0·8	0·8	0·8	0·8	0·8	0·7	0·6	0·5
20	0·5	0·6	0·7	0·8	0·8	0·9	0·9	0·9	0·8	0·7	0·7	0·5
40	0·6	0·7	0·8	0·9	1·0	1·1	1·1	1·1	1·0	0·9	0·8	0·7
50	0·7	0·8	1·0	1·1	1·2	1·3	1·3	1·3	1·2	1·1	1·0	0·8
55	0·7	0·9	1·1	1·2	1·3	1·4	1·4	1·4	1·3	1·2	1·1	0·9
60	0·8	1·1	1·3	1·4	1·5	1·6	1·6	1·6	1·5	1·4	1·2	1·0
65	1·0	1·3	1·5	1·7	1·8	1·9	1·9	1·9	1·8	1·7	1·5	1·2

Latitude = Apparent altitude (corrected for refraction) $- 1° + a_0 + a_1 + a_2$

The table is entered with L.H.A. Aries to determine the column to be used; each column refers to a range of 10°. a_0 is taken, with mental interpolation, from the upper table with the units of L.H.A. Aries in degrees as argument; a_1, a_2 are taken, without interpolation, from the second and third tables with arguments latitude and month respectively. a_0, a_1, a_2 are always positive. The final table gives the azimuth of *Polaris*.

CONVERSION OF ARC TO TIME

0°–59°		60°–119°		120°–179°		180°–239°		240°–299°		300°–359°			0′.00	0′.25	0′.50	0′.75
°	h m	°	h m	°	h m	°	h m	°	h m	°	h m	′	m s	m s	m s	m s
0	0 00	60	4 00	120	8 00	180	12 00	240	16 00	300	20 00	0	0 00	0 01	0 02	0 03
1	0 04	61	4 04	121	8 04	181	12 04	241	16 04	301	20 04	1	0 04	0 05	0 06	0 07
2	0 08	62	4 08	122	8 08	182	12 08	242	16 08	302	20 08	2	0 08	0 09	0 10	0 11
3	0 12	63	4 12	123	8 12	183	12 12	243	16 12	303	20 12	3	0 12	0 13	0 14	0 15
4	0 16	64	4 16	124	8 16	184	12 16	244	16 16	304	20 16	4	0 16	0 17	0 18	0 19
5	0 20	65	4 20	125	8 20	185	12 20	245	16 20	305	20 20	5	0 20	0 21	0 22	0 23
6	0 24	66	4 24	126	8 24	186	12 24	246	16 24	306	20 24	6	0 24	0 25	0 26	0 27
7	0 28	67	4 28	127	8 28	187	12 28	247	16 28	307	20 28	7	0 28	0 29	0 30	0 31
8	0 32	68	4 32	128	8 32	188	12 32	248	16 32	308	20 32	8	0 32	0 33	0 34	0 35
9	0 36	69	4 36	129	8 36	189	12 36	249	16 36	309	20 36	9	0 36	0 37	0 38	0 39
10	0 40	70	4 40	130	8 40	190	12 40	250	16 40	310	20 40	10	0 40	0 41	0 42	0 43
11	0 44	71	4 44	131	8 44	191	12 44	251	16 44	311	20 44	11	0 44	0 45	0 46	0 47
12	0 48	72	4 48	132	8 48	192	12 48	252	16 48	312	20 48	12	0 48	0 49	0 50	0 51
13	0 52	73	4 52	133	8 52	193	12 52	253	16 52	313	20 52	13	0 52	0 53	0 54	0 55
14	0 56	74	4 56	134	8 56	194	12 56	254	16 56	314	20 56	14	0 56	0 57	0 58	0 59
15	1 00	75	5 00	135	9 00	195	13 00	255	17 00	315	21 00	15	1 00	1 01	1 02	1 03
16	1 04	76	5 04	136	9 04	196	13 04	256	17 04	316	21 04	16	1 04	1 05	1 06	1 07
17	1 08	77	5 08	137	9 08	197	13 08	257	17 08	317	21 08	17	1 08	1 09	1 10	1 11
18	1 12	78	5 12	138	9 12	198	13 12	258	17 12	318	21 12	18	1 12	1 13	1 14	1 15
19	1 16	79	5 16	139	9 16	199	13 16	259	17 16	319	21 16	19	1 16	1 17	1 18	1 19
20	1 20	80	5 20	140	9 20	200	13 20	260	17 20	320	21 20	20	1 20	1 21	1 22	1 23
21	1 24	81	5 24	141	9 24	201	13 24	261	17 24	321	21 24	21	1 24	1 25	1 26	1 27
22	1 28	82	5 28	142	9 28	202	13 28	262	17 28	322	21 28	22	1 28	1 29	1 30	1 31
23	1 32	83	5 32	143	9 32	203	13 32	263	17 32	323	21 32	23	1 32	1 33	1 34	1 35
24	1 36	84	5 36	144	9 36	204	13 36	264	17 36	324	21 36	24	1 36	1 37	1 38	1 39
25	1 40	85	5 40	145	9 40	205	13 40	265	17 40	325	21 40	25	1 40	1 41	1 42	1 43
26	1 44	86	5 44	146	9 44	206	13 44	266	17 44	326	21 44	26	1 44	1 45	1 46	1 47
27	1 48	87	5 48	147	9 48	207	13 48	267	17 48	327	21 48	27	1 48	1 49	1 50	1 51
28	1 52	88	5 52	148	9 52	208	13 52	268	17 52	328	21 52	28	1 52	1 53	1 54	1 55
29	1 56	89	5 56	149	9 56	209	13 56	269	17 56	329	21 56	29	1 56	1 57	1 58	1 59
30	2 00	90	6 00	150	10 00	210	14 00	270	18 00	330	22 00	30	2 00	2 01	2 02	2 03
31	2 04	91	6 04	151	10 04	211	14 04	271	18 04	331	22 04	31	2 04	2 05	2 06	2 07
32	2 08	92	6 08	152	10 08	212	14 08	272	18 08	332	22 08	32	2 08	2 09	2 10	2 11
33	2 12	93	6 12	153	10 12	213	14 12	273	18 12	333	22 12	33	2 12	2 13	2 14	2 15
34	2 16	94	6 16	154	10 16	214	14 16	274	18 16	334	22 16	34	2 16	2 17	2 18	2 19
35	2 20	95	6 20	155	10 20	215	14 20	275	18 20	335	22 20	35	2 20	2 21	2 22	2 23
36	2 24	96	6 24	156	10 24	216	14 24	276	18 24	336	22 24	36	2 24	2 25	2 26	2 27
37	2 28	97	6 28	157	10 28	217	14 28	277	18 28	337	22 28	37	2 28	2 29	2 30	2 31
38	2 32	98	6 32	158	10 32	218	14 32	278	18 32	338	22 32	38	2 32	2 33	2 34	2 35
39	2 36	99	6 36	159	10 36	219	14 36	279	18 36	339	22 36	39	2 36	2 37	2 38	2 39
40	2 40	100	6 40	160	10 40	220	14 40	280	18 40	340	22 40	40	2 40	2 41	2 42	2 43
41	2 44	101	6 44	161	10 44	221	14 44	281	18 44	341	22 44	41	2 44	2 45	2 46	2 47
42	2 48	102	6 48	162	10 48	222	14 48	282	18 48	342	22 48	42	2 48	2 49	2 50	2 51
43	2 52	103	6 52	163	10 52	223	14 52	283	18 52	343	22 52	43	2 52	2 53	2 54	2 55
44	2 56	104	6 56	164	10 56	224	14 56	284	18 56	344	22 56	44	2 56	2 57	2 58	2 59
45	3 00	105	7 00	165	11 00	225	15 00	285	19 00	345	23 00	45	3 00	3 01	3 02	3 03
46	3 04	106	7 04	166	11 04	226	15 04	286	19 04	346	23 04	46	3 04	3 05	3 06	3 07
47	3 08	107	7 08	167	11 08	227	15 08	287	19 08	347	23 08	47	3 08	3 09	3 10	3 11
48	3 12	108	7 12	168	11 12	228	15 12	288	19 12	348	23 12	48	3 12	3 13	3 14	3 15
49	3 16	109	7 16	169	11 16	229	15 16	289	19 16	349	23 16	49	3 16	3 17	3 18	3 19
50	3 20	110	7 20	170	11 20	230	15 20	290	19 20	350	23 20	50	3 20	3 21	3 22	3 23
51	3 24	111	7 24	171	11 24	231	15 24	291	19 24	351	23 24	51	3 24	3 25	3 26	3 27
52	3 28	112	7 28	172	11 28	232	15 28	292	19 28	352	23 28	52	3 28	3 29	3 30	3 31
53	3 32	113	7 32	173	11 32	233	15 32	293	19 32	353	23 32	53	3 32	3 33	3 34	3 35
54	3 36	114	7 36	174	11 36	234	15 36	294	19 36	354	23 36	54	3 36	3 37	3 38	3 39
55	3 40	115	7 40	175	11 40	235	15 40	295	19 40	355	23 40	55	3 40	3 41	3 42	3 43
56	3 44	116	7 44	176	11 44	236	15 44	296	19 44	356	23 44	56	3 44	3 45	3 46	3 47
57	3 48	117	7 48	177	11 48	237	15 48	297	19 48	357	23 48	57	3 48	3 49	3 50	3 51
58	3 52	118	7 52	178	11 52	238	15 52	298	19 52	358	23 52	58	3 52	3 53	3 54	3 55
59	3 56	119	7 56	179	11 56	239	15 56	299	19 56	359	23 56	59	3 56	3 57	3 58	3 59

The above table is for converting expressions in arc to their equivalent in time ; its main use in this Almanac is for the conversion of longitude for application to L.M.T. (*added* if *west*, *subtracted* if *east*) to give G.M.T. or vice versa, particularly in the case of sunrise, sunset, etc.

m 0 (s)	SUN PLANETS (° ′)	ARIES (° ′)	MOON (° ′)	v or Corrn d (′ ′)	v or Corrn d (′ ′)	v or Corrn d (′ ′)
00	0 00·0	0 00·0	0 00·0	0·0 0·0	6·0 0·1	12·0 0·1
01	0 00·3	0 00·3	0 00·2	0·1 0·0	6·1 0·1	12·1 0·1
02	0 00·5	0 00·5	0 00·5	0·2 0·0	6·2 0·1	12·2 0·1
03	0 00·8	0 00·8	0 00·7	0·3 0·0	6·3 0·1	12·3 0·1
04	0 01·0	0 01·0	0 01·0	0·4 0·0	6·4 0·1	12·4 0·1
05	0 01·3	0 01·3	0 01·2	0·5 0·0	6·5 0·1	12·5 0·1
06	0 01·5	0 01·5	0 01·4	0·6 0·0	6·6 0·1	12·6 0·1
07	0 01·8	0 01·8	0 01·7	0·7 0·0	6·7 0·1	12·7 0·1
08	0 02·0	0 02·0	0 01·9	0·8 0·0	6·8 0·1	12·8 0·1
09	0 02·3	0 02·3	0 02·1	0·9 0·0	6·9 0·1	12·9 0·1
10	0 02·5	0 02·5	0 02·4	1·0 0·0	7·0 0·1	13·0 0·1
11	0 02·8	0 02·8	0 02·6	1·1 0·0	7·1 0·1	13·1 0·1
12	0 03·0	0 03·0	0 02·9	1·2 0·0	7·2 0·1	13·2 0·1
13	0 03·3	0 03·3	0 03·1	1·3 0·0	7·3 0·1	13·3 0·1
14	0 03·5	0 03·5	0 03·3	1·4 0·0	7·4 0·1	13·4 0·1
15	0 03·8	0 03·8	0 03·6	1·5 0·0	7·5 0·1	13·5 0·1
16	0 04·0	0 04·0	0 03·8	1·6 0·0	7·6 0·1	13·6 0·1
17	0 04·3	0 04·3	0 04·1	1·7 0·0	7·7 0·1	13·7 0·1
18	0 04·5	0 04·5	0 04·3	1·8 0·0	7·8 0·1	13·8 0·1
19	0 04·8	0 04·8	0 04·5	1·9 0·0	7·9 0·1	13·9 0·1
20	0 05·0	0 05·0	0 04·8	2·0 0·0	8·0 0·1	14·0 0·1
21	0 05·3	0 05·3	0 05·0	2·1 0·0	8·1 0·1	14·1 0·1
22	0 05·5	0 05·5	0 05·2	2·2 0·0	8·2 0·1	14·2 0·1
23	0 05·8	0 05·8	0 05·5	2·3 0·0	8·3 0·1	14·3 0·1
24	0 06·0	0 06·0	0 05·7	2·4 0·0	8·4 0·1	14·4 0·1
25	0 06·3	0 06·3	0 06·0	2·5 0·0	8·5 0·1	14·5 0·1
26	0 06·5	0 06·5	0 06·2	2·6 0·0	8·6 0·1	14·6 0·1
27	0 06·8	0 06·8	0 06·4	2·7 0·0	8·7 0·1	14·7 0·1
28	0 07·0	0 07·0	0 06·7	2·8 0·0	8·8 0·1	14·8 0·1
29	0 07·3	0 07·3	0 06·9	2·9 0·0	8·9 0·1	14·9 0·1
30	0 07·5	0 07·5	0 07·2	3·0 0·0	9·0 0·1	15·0 0·1
31	0 07·8	0 07·8	0 07·4	3·1 0·0	9·1 0·1	15·1 0·1
32	0 08·0	0 08·0	0 07·6	3·2 0·0	9·2 0·1	15·2 0·1
33	0 08·3	0 08·3	0 07·9	3·3 0·0	9·3 0·1	15·3 0·1
34	0 08·5	0 08·5	0 08·1	3·4 0·0	9·4 0·1	15·4 0·1
35	0 08·8	0 08·8	0 08·4	3·5 0·0	9·5 0·1	15·5 0·1
36	0 09·0	0 09·0	0 08·6	3·6 0·0	9·6 0·1	15·6 0·1
37	0 09·3	0 09·3	0 08·8	3·7 0·0	9·7 0·1	15·7 0·1
38	0 09·5	0 09·5	0 09·1	3·8 0·0	9·8 0·1	15·8 0·1
39	0 09·8	0 09·8	0 09·3	3·9 0·0	9·9 0·1	15·9 0·1
40	0 10·0	0 10·0	0 09·5	4·0 0·0	10·0 0·1	16·0 0·1
41	0 10·3	0 10·3	0 09·8	4·1 0·0	10·1 0·1	16·1 0·1
42	0 10·5	0 10·5	0 10·0	4·2 0·0	10·2 0·1	16·2 0·1
43	0 10·8	0 10·8	0 10·3	4·3 0·0	10·3 0·1	16·3 0·1
44	0 11·0	0 11·0	0 10·5	4·4 0·0	10·4 0·1	16·4 0·1
45	0 11·3	0 11·3	0 10·7	4·5 0·0	10·5 0·1	16·5 0·1
46	0 11·5	0 11·5	0 11·0	4·6 0·0	10·6 0·1	16·6 0·1
47	0 11·8	0 11·8	0 11·2	4·7 0·0	10·7 0·1	16·7 0·1
48	0 12·0	0 12·0	0 11·5	4·8 0·0	10·8 0·1	16·8 0·1
49	0 12·3	0 12·3	0 11·7	4·9 0·0	10·9 0·1	16·9 0·1
50	0 12·5	0 12·5	0 11·9	5·0 0·0	11·0 0·1	17·0 0·1
51	0 12·8	0 12·8	0 12·2	5·1 0·0	11·1 0·1	17·1 0·1
52	0 13·0	0 13·0	0 12·4	5·2 0·0	11·2 0·1	17·2 0·1
53	0 13·3	0 13·3	0 12·6	5·3 0·0	11·3 0·1	17·3 0·1
54	0 13·5	0 13·5	0 12·9	5·4 0·0	11·4 0·1	17·4 0·1
55	0 13·8	0 13·8	0 13·1	5·5 0·0	11·5 0·1	17·5 0·1
56	0 14·0	0 14·0	0 13·4	5·6 0·0	11·6 0·1	17·6 0·1
57	0 14·3	0 14·3	0 13·6	5·7 0·0	11·7 0·1	17·7 0·1
58	0 14·5	0 14·5	0 13·8	5·8 0·0	11·8 0·1	17·8 0·1
59	0 14·8	0 14·8	0 14·1	5·9 0·0	11·9 0·1	17·9 0·1
60	0 15·0	0 15·0	0 14·3	6·0 0·1	12·0 0·1	18·0 0·2

m 1 (s)	SUN PLANETS (° ′)	ARIES (° ′)	MOON (° ′)	v or Corrn d (′ ′)	v or Corrn d (′ ′)	v or Corrn d (′ ′)
00	0 15·0	0 15·0	0 14·3	0·0 0·0	6·0 0·2	12·0 0·3
01	0 15·3	0 15·3	0 14·6	0·1 0·0	6·1 0·2	12·1 0·3
02	0 15·5	0 15·5	0 14·8	0·2 0·0	6·2 0·2	12·2 0·3
03	0 15·8	0 15·8	0 15·0	0·3 0·0	6·3 0·2	12·3 0·3
04	0 16·0	0 16·0	0 15·3	0·4 0·0	6·4 0·2	12·4 0·3
05	0 16·3	0 16·3	0 15·5	0·5 0·0	6·5 0·2	12·5 0·3
06	0 16·5	0 16·5	0 15·7	0·6 0·0	6·6 0·2	12·6 0·3
07	0 16·8	0 16·8	0 16·0	0·7 0·0	6·7 0·2	12·7 0·3
08	0 17·0	0 17·0	0 16·2	0·8 0·0	6·8 0·2	12·8 0·3
09	0 17·3	0 17·3	0 16·5	0·9 0·0	6·9 0·2	12·9 0·3
10	0 17·5	0 17·5	0 16·7	1·0 0·0	7·0 0·2	13·0 0·3
11	0 17·8	0 17·8	0 16·9	1·1 0·0	7·1 0·2	13·1 0·3
12	0 18·0	0 18·0	0 17·2	1·2 0·0	7·2 0·2	13·2 0·3
13	0 18·3	0 18·3	0 17·4	1·3 0·0	7·3 0·2	13·3 0·3
14	0 18·5	0 18·6	0 17·7	1·4 0·0	7·4 0·2	13·4 0·3
15	0 18·8	0 18·8	0 17·9	1·5 0·0	7·5 0·2	13·5 0·3
16	0 19·0	0 19·1	0 18·1	1·6 0·0	7·6 0·2	13·6 0·3
17	0 19·3	0 19·3	0 18·4	1·7 0·0	7·7 0·2	13·7 0·3
18	0 19·5	0 19·6	0 18·6	1·8 0·0	7·8 0·2	13·8 0·3
19	0 19·8	0 19·8	0 18·9	1·9 0·0	7·9 0·2	13·9 0·3
20	0 20·0	0 20·1	0 19·1	2·0 0·1	8·0 0·2	14·0 0·4
21	0 20·3	0 20·3	0 19·3	2·1 0·1	8·1 0·2	14·1 0·4
22	0 20·5	0 20·6	0 19·6	2·2 0·1	8·2 0·2	14·2 0·4
23	0 20·8	0 20·8	0 19·8	2·3 0·1	8·3 0·2	14·3 0·4
24	0 21·0	0 21·1	0 20·0	2·4 0·1	8·4 0·2	14·4 0·4
25	0 21·3	0 21·3	0 20·3	2·5 0·1	8·5 0·2	14·5 0·4
26	0 21·5	0 21·6	0 20·5	2·6 0·1	8·6 0·2	14·6 0·4
27	0 21·8	0 21·8	0 20·8	2·7 0·1	8·7 0·2	14·7 0·4
28	0 22·0	0 22·1	0 21·0	2·8 0·1	8·8 0·2	14·8 0·4
29	0 22·3	0 22·3	0 21·2	2·9 0·1	8·9 0·2	14·9 0·4
30	0 22·5	0 22·6	0 21·5	3·0 0·1	9·0 0·2	15·0 0·4
31	0 22·8	0 22·8	0 21·7	3·1 0·1	9·1 0·2	15·1 0·4
32	0 23·0	0 23·1	0 22·0	3·2 0·1	9·2 0·2	15·2 0·4
33	0 23·3	0 23·3	0 22·2	3·3 0·1	9·3 0·2	15·3 0·4
34	0 23·5	0 23·6	0 22·4	3·4 0·1	9·4 0·2	15·4 0·4
35	0 23·8	0 23·8	0 22·7	3·5 0·1	9·5 0·2	15·5 0·4
36	0 24·0	0 24·1	0 22·9	3·6 0·1	9·6 0·2	15·6 0·4
37	0 24·3	0 24·3	0 23·1	3·7 0·1	9·7 0·2	15·7 0·4
38	0 24·5	0 24·6	0 23·4	3·8 0·1	9·8 0·2	15·8 0·4
39	0 24·8	0 24·8	0 23·6	3·9 0·1	9·9 0·2	15·9 0·4
40	0 25·0	0 25·1	0 23·9	4·0 0·1	10·0 0·3	16·0 0·4
41	0 25·3	0 25·3	0 24·1	4·1 0·1	10·1 0·3	16·1 0·4
42	0 25·5	0 25·6	0 24·3	4·2 0·1	10·2 0·3	16·2 0·4
43	0 25·8	0 25·8	0 24·6	4·3 0·1	10·3 0·3	16·3 0·4
44	0 26·0	0 26·1	0 24·8	4·4 0·1	10·4 0·3	16·4 0·4
45	0 26·3	0 26·3	0 25·1	4·5 0·1	10·5 0·3	16·5 0·4
46	0 26·5	0 26·6	0 25·3	4·6 0·1	10·6 0·3	16·6 0·4
47	0 26·8	0 26·8	0 25·5	4·7 0·1	10·7 0·3	16·7 0·4
48	0 27·0	0 27·1	0 25·8	4·8 0·1	10·8 0·3	16·8 0·4
49	0 27·3	0 27·3	0 26·0	4·9 0·1	10·9 0·3	16·9 0·4
50	0 27·5	0 27·6	0 26·2	5·0 0·1	11·0 0·3	17·0 0·4
51	0 27·8	0 27·8	0 26·5	5·1 0·1	11·1 0·3	17·1 0·4
52	0 28·0	0 28·1	0 26·7	5·2 0·1	11·2 0·3	17·2 0·4
53	0 28·3	0 28·3	0 27·0	5·3 0·1	11·3 0·3	17·3 0·4
54	0 28·5	0 28·6	0 27·2	5·4 0·1	11·4 0·3	17·4 0·4
55	0 28·8	0 28·8	0 27·4	5·5 0·1	11·5 0·3	17·5 0·4
56	0 29·0	0 29·1	0 27·7	5·6 0·1	11·6 0·3	17·6 0·4
57	0 29·3	0 29·3	0 27·9	5·7 0·1	11·7 0·3	17·7 0·4
58	0 29·5	0 29·6	0 28·2	5·8 0·1	11·8 0·3	17·8 0·4
59	0 29·8	0 29·8	0 28·4	5·9 0·1	11·9 0·3	17·9 0·4
60	0 30·0	0 30·1	0 28·6	6·0 0·2	12·0 0·3	18·0 0·5

2^m	SUN PLANETS	ARIES	MOON	v or Corrⁿ d		v or Corrⁿ d		v or Corrⁿ d	
s	° ′	° ′	° ′	′	′	′	′	′	′
00	0 30·0	0 30·1	0 28·6	0·0	0·0	6·0	0·3	12·0	0·5
01	0 30·3	0 30·3	0 28·9	0·1	0·0	6·1	0·3	12·1	0·5
02	0 30·5	0 30·6	0 29·1	0·2	0·0	6·2	0·3	12·2	0·5
03	0 30·8	0 30·8	0 29·3	0·3	0·0	6·3	0·3	12·3	0·5
04	0 31·0	0 31·1	0 29·6	0·4	0·0	6·4	0·3	12·4	0·5
05	0 31·3	0 31·3	0 29·8	0·5	0·0	6·5	0·3	12·5	0·5
06	0 31·5	0 31·6	0 30·1	0·6	0·0	6·6	0·3	12·6	0·5
07	0 31·8	0 31·8	0 30·3	0·7	0·0	6·7	0·3	12·7	0·5
08	0 32·0	0 32·1	0 30·5	0·8	0·0	6·8	0·3	12·8	0·5
09	0 32·3	0 32·3	0 30·8	0·9	0·0	6·9	0·3	12·9	0·5
10	0 32·5	0 32·6	0 31·0	1·0	0·0	7·0	0·3	13·0	0·5
11	0 32·8	0 32·8	0 31·3	1·1	0·0	7·1	0·3	13·1	0·5
12	0 33·0	0 33·1	0 31·5	1·2	0·1	7·2	0·3	13·2	0·6
13	0 33·3	0 33·3	0 31·7	1·3	0·1	7·3	0·3	13·3	0·6
14	0 33·5	0 33·6	0 32·0	1·4	0·1	7·4	0·3	13·4	0·6
15	0 33·8	0 33·8	0 32·2	1·5	0·1	7·5	0·3	13·5	0·6
16	0 34·0	0 34·1	0 32·5	1·6	0·1	7·6	0·3	13·6	0·6
17	0 34·3	0 34·3	0 32·7	1·7	0·1	7·7	0·3	13·7	0·6
18	0 34·5	0 34·6	0 32·9	1·8	0·1	7·8	0·3	13·8	0·6
19	0 34·8	0 34·8	0 33·2	1·9	0·1	7·9	0·3	13·9	0·6
20	0 35·0	0 35·1	0 33·4	2·0	0·1	8·0	0·3	14·0	0·6
21	0 35·3	0 35·3	0 33·6	2·1	0·1	8·1	0·3	14·1	0·6
22	0 35·5	0 35·6	0 33·9	2·2	0·1	8·2	0·3	14·2	0·6
23	0 35·8	0 35·8	0 34·1	2·3	0·1	8·3	0·3	14·3	0·6
24	0 36·0	0 36·1	0 34·4	2·4	0·1	8·4	0·4	14·4	0·6
25	0 36·3	0 36·3	0 34·6	2·5	0·1	8·5	0·4	14·5	0·6
26	0 36·5	0 36·6	0 34·8	2·6	0·1	8·6	0·4	14·6	0·6
27	0 36·8	0 36·9	0 35·1	2·7	0·1	8·7	0·4	14·7	0·6
28	0 37·0	0 37·1	0 35·3	2·8	0·1	8·8	0·4	14·8	0·6
29	0 37·3	0 37·4	0 35·6	2·9	0·1	8·9	0·4	14·9	0·6
30	0 37·5	0 37·6	0 35·8	3·0	0·1	9·0	0·4	15·0	0·6
31	0 37·8	0 37·9	0 36·0	3·1	0·1	9·1	0·4	15·1	0·6
32	0 38·0	0 38·1	0 36·3	3·2	0·1	9·2	0·4	15·2	0·6
33	0 38·3	0 38·4	0 36·5	3·3	0·1	9·3	0·4	15·3	0·6
34	0 38·5	0 38·6	0 36·7	3·4	0·1	9·4	0·4	15·4	0·6
35	0 38·8	0 38·9	0 37·0	3·5	0·1	9·5	0·4	15·5	0·6
36	0 39·0	0 39·1	0 37·2	3·6	0·2	9·6	0·4	15·6	0·7
37	0 39·3	0 39·4	0 37·5	3·7	0·2	9·7	0·4	15·7	0·7
38	0 39·5	0 39·6	0 37·7	3·8	0·2	9·8	0·4	15·8	0·7
39	0 39·8	0 39·9	0 37·9	3·9	0·2	9·9	0·4	15·9	0·7
40	0 40·0	0 40·1	0 38·2	4·0	0·2	10·0	0·4	16·0	0·7
41	0 40·3	0 40·4	0 38·4	4·1	0·2	10·1	0·4	16·1	0·7
42	0 40·5	0 40·6	0 38·7	4·2	0·2	10·2	0·4	16·2	0·7
43	0 40·8	0 40·9	0 38·9	4·3	0·2	10·3	0·4	16·3	0·7
44	0 41·0	0 41·1	0 39·1	4·4	0·2	10·4	0·4	16·4	0·7
45	0 41·3	0 41·4	0 39·4	4·5	0·2	10·5	0·4	16·5	0·7
46	0 41·5	0 41·6	0 39·6	4·6	0·2	10·6	0·4	16·6	0·7
47	0 41·8	0 41·9	0 39·8	4·7	0·2	10·7	0·4	16·7	0·7
48	0 42·0	0 42·1	0 40·1	4·8	0·2	10·8	0·5	16·8	0·7
49	0 42·3	0 42·4	0 40·3	4·9	0·2	10·9	0·5	16·9	0·7
50	0 42·5	0 42·6	0 40·6	5·0	0·2	11·0	0·5	17·0	0·7
51	0 42·8	0 42·9	0 40·8	5·1	0·2	11·1	0·5	17·1	0·7
52	0 43·0	0 43·1	0 41·0	5·2	0·2	11·2	0·5	17·2	0·7
53	0 43·3	0 43·4	0 41·3	5·3	0·2	11·3	0·5	17·3	0·7
54	0 43·5	0 43·6	0 41·5	5·4	0·2	11·4	0·5	17·4	0·7
55	0 43·8	0 43·9	0 41·8	5·5	0·2	11·5	0·5	17·5	0·7
56	0 44·0	0 44·1	0 42·0	5·6	0·2	11·6	0·5	17·6	0·7
57	0 44·3	0 44·4	0 42·2	5·7	0·2	11·7	0·5	17·7	0·7
58	0 44·5	0 44·6	0 42·5	5·8	0·2	11·8	0·5	17·8	0·7
59	0 44·8	0 44·9	0 42·7	5·9	0·2	11·9	0·5	17·9	0·7
60	0 45·0	0 45·1	0 43·0	6·0	0·3	12·0	0·5	18·0	0·8

3^m	SUN PLANETS	ARIES	MOON	v or Corrⁿ d		v or Corrⁿ d		v or Corrⁿ d	
s	° ′	° ′	° ′	′	′	′	′	′	′
00	0 45·0	0 45·1	0 43·0	0·0	0·0	6·0	0·4	12·0	0·7
01	0 45·3	0 45·4	0 43·2	0·1	0·0	6·1	0·4	12·1	0·7
02	0 45·5	0 45·6	0 43·4	0·2	0·0	6·2	0·4	12·2	0·7
03	0 45·8	0 45·9	0 43·7	0·3	0·0	6·3	0·4	12·3	0·7
04	0 46·0	0 46·1	0 43·9	0·4	0·0	6·4	0·4	12·4	0·7
05	0 46·3	0 46·4	0 44·1	0·5	0·0	6·5	0·4	12·5	0·7
06	0 46·5	0 46·6	0 44·4	0·6	0·0	6·6	0·4	12·6	0·7
07	0 46·8	0 46·9	0 44·6	0·7	0·0	6·7	0·4	12·7	0·7
08	0 47·0	0 47·1	0 44·9	0·8	0·0	6·8	0·4	12·8	0·7
09	0 47·3	0 47·4	0 45·1	0·9	0·1	6·9	0·4	12·9	0·8
10	0 47·5	0 47·6	0 45·3	1·0	0·1	7·0	0·4	13·0	0·8
11	0 47·8	0 47·9	0 45·6	1·1	0·1	7·1	0·4	13·1	0·8
12	0 48·0	0 48·1	0 45·8	1·2	0·1	7·2	0·4	13·2	0·8
13	0 48·3	0 48·4	0 46·1	1·3	0·1	7·3	0·4	13·3	0·8
14	0 48·5	0 48·6	0 46·3	1·4	0·1	7·4	0·4	13·4	0·8
15	0 48·8	0 48·9	0 46·5	1·5	0·1	7·5	0·4	13·5	0·8
16	0 49·0	0 49·1	0 46·8	1·6	0·1	7·6	0·4	13·6	0·8
17	0 49·3	0 49·4	0 47·0	1·7	0·1	7·7	0·4	13·7	0·8
18	0 49·5	0 49·6	0 47·2	1·8	0·1	7·8	0·5	13·8	0·8
19	0 49·8	0 49·9	0 47·5	1·9	0·1	7·9	0·5	13·9	0·8
20	0 50·0	0 50·1	0 47·7	2·0	0·1	8·0	0·5	14·0	0·8
21	0 50·3	0 50·4	0 48·0	2·1	0·1	8·1	0·5	14·1	0·8
22	0 50·5	0 50·6	0 48·2	2·2	0·1	8·2	0·5	14·2	0·8
23	0 50·8	0 50·9	0 48·4	2·3	0·1	8·3	0·5	14·3	0·8
24	0 51·0	0 51·1	0 48·7	2·4	0·1	8·4	0·5	14·4	0·8
25	0 51·3	0 51·4	0 48·9	2·5	0·1	8·5	0·5	14·5	0·8
26	0 51·5	0 51·6	0 49·2	2·6	0·2	8·6	0·5	14·6	0·9
27	0 51·8	0 51·9	0 49·4	2·7	0·2	8·7	0·5	14·7	0·9
28	0 52·0	0 52·1	0 49·6	2·8	0·2	8·8	0·5	14·8	0·9
29	0 52·3	0 52·4	0 49·9	2·9	0·2	8·9	0·5	14·9	0·9
30	0 52·5	0 52·6	0 50·1	3·0	0·2	9·0	0·5	15·0	0·9
31	0 52·8	0 52·9	0 50·3	3·1	0·2	9·1	0·5	15·1	0·9
32	0 53·0	0 53·1	0 50·6	3·2	0·2	9·2	0·5	15·2	0·9
33	0 53·3	0 53·4	0 50·8	3·3	0·2	9·3	0·5	15·3	0·9
34	0 53·5	0 53·6	0 51·1	3·4	0·2	9·4	0·5	15·4	0·9
35	0 53·8	0 53·9	0 51·3	3·5	0·2	9·5	0·6	15·5	0·9
36	0 54·0	0 54·1	0 51·5	3·6	0·2	9·6	0·6	15·6	0·9
37	0 54·3	0 54·4	0 51·8	3·7	0·2	9·7	0·6	15·7	0·9
38	0 54·5	0 54·6	0 52·0	3·8	0·2	9·8	0·6	15·8	0·9
39	0 54·8	0 54·9	0 52·3	3·9	0·2	9·9	0·6	15·9	0·9
40	0 55·0	0 55·2	0 52·5	4·0	0·2	10·0	0·6	16·0	0·9
41	0 55·3	0 55·4	0 52·7	4·1	0·2	10·1	0·6	16·1	0·9
42	0 55·5	0 55·7	0 53·0	4·2	0·2	10·2	0·6	16·2	0·9
43	0 55·8	0 55·9	0 53·2	4·3	0·3	10·3	0·6	16·3	1·0
44	0 56·0	0 56·2	0 53·4	4·4	0·3	10·4	0·6	16·4	1·0
45	0 56·3	0 56·4	0 53·7	4·5	0·3	10·5	0·6	16·5	1·0
46	0 56·5	0 56·7	0 53·9	4·6	0·3	10·6	0·6	16·6	1·0
47	0 56·8	0 56·9	0 54·2	4·7	0·3	10·7	0·6	16·7	1·0
48	0 57·0	0 57·2	0 54·4	4·8	0·3	10·8	0·6	16·8	1·0
49	0 57·3	0 57·4	0 54·6	4·9	0·3	10·9	0·6	16·9	1·0
50	0 57·5	0 57·7	0 54·9	5·0	0·3	11·0	0·6	17·0	1·0
51	0 57·8	0 57·9	0 55·1	5·1	0·3	11·1	0·6	17·1	1·0
52	0 58·0	0 58·2	0 55·4	5·2	0·3	11·2	0·7	17·2	1·0
53	0 58·3	0 58·4	0 55·6	5·3	0·3	11·3	0·7	17·3	1·0
54	0 58·5	0 58·7	0 55·8	5·4	0·3	11·4	0·7	17·4	1·0
55	0 58·8	0 58·9	0 56·1	5·5	0·3	11·5	0·7	17·5	1·0
56	0 59·0	0 59·2	0 56·3	5·6	0·3	11·6	0·7	17·6	1·0
57	0 59·3	0 59·4	0 56·6	5·7	0·3	11·7	0·7	17·7	1·0
58	0 59·5	0 59·7	0 56·8	5·8	0·3	11·8	0·7	17·8	1·0
59	0 59·8	0 59·9	0 57·0	5·9	0·3	11·9	0·7	17·9	1·0
60	1 00·0	1 00·2	0 57·3	6·0	0·4	12·0	0·7	18·0	1·1

4	SUN PLANETS	ARIES	MOON	v or Corrn d		v or Corrn d		v or Corrn d	
s	° ′	° ′	° ′	′	′	′	′	′	′
00	1 00·0	1 00·2	0 57·3	0·0	0·0	6·0	0·5	12·0	0·9
01	1 00·3	1 00·4	0 57·5	0·1	0·0	6·1	0·5	12·1	0·9
02	1 00·5	1 00·7	0 57·7	0·2	0·0	6·2	0·5	12·2	0·9
03	1 00·8	1 00·9	0 58·0	0·3	0·0	6·3	0·5	12·3	0·9
04	1 01·0	1 01·2	0 58·2	0·4	0·0	6·4	0·5	12·4	0·9
05	1 01·3	1 01·4	0 58·5	0·5	0·0	6·5	0·5	12·5	0·9
06	1 01·5	1 01·7	0 58·7	0·6	0·0	6·6	0·5	12·6	0·9
07	1 01·8	1 01·9	0 58·9	0·7	0·1	6·7	0·5	12·7	1·0
08	1 02·0	1 02·2	0 59·2	0·8	0·1	6·8	0·5	12·8	1·0
09	1 02·3	1 02·4	0 59·4	0·9	0·1	6·9	0·5	12·9	1·0
10	1 02·5	1 02·7	0 59·7	1·0	0·1	7·0	0·5	13·0	1·0
11	1 02·8	1 02·9	0 59·9	1·1	0·1	7·1	0·5	13·1	1·0
12	1 03·0	1 03·2	1 00·1	1·2	0·1	7·2	0·5	13·2	1·0
13	1 03·3	1 03·4	1 00·4	1·3	0·1	7·3	0·5	13·3	1·0
14	1 03·5	1 03·7	1 00·6	1·4	0·1	7·4	0·6	13·4	1·0
15	1 03·8	1 03·9	1 00·8	1·5	0·1	7·5	0·6	13·5	1·0
16	1 04·0	1 04·2	1 01·1	1·6	0·1	7·6	0·6	13·6	1·0
17	1 04·3	1 04·4	1 01·3	1·7	0·1	7·7	0·6	13·7	1·0
18	1 04·5	1 04·7	1 01·6	1·8	0·1	7·8	0·6	13·8	1·0
19	1 04·8	1 04·9	1 01·8	1·9	0·1	7·9	0·6	13·9	1·0
20	1 05·0	1 05·2	1 02·0	2·0	0·2	8·0	0·6	14·0	1·1
21	1 05·3	1 05·4	1 02·3	2·1	0·2	8·1	0·6	14·1	1·1
22	1 05·5	1 05·7	1 02·5	2·2	0·2	8·2	0·6	14·2	1·1
23	1 05·8	1 05·9	1 02·8	2·3	0·2	8·3	0·6	14·3	1·1
24	1 06·0	1 06·2	1 03·0	2·4	0·2	8·4	0·6	14·4	1·1
25	1 06·3	1 06·4	1 03·2	2·5	0·2	8·5	0·6	14·5	1·1
26	1 06·5	1 06·7	1 03·5	2·6	0·2	8·6	0·6	14·6	1·1
27	1 06·8	1 06·9	1 03·7	2·7	0·2	8·7	0·7	14·7	1·1
28	1 07·0	1 07·2	1 03·9	2·8	0·2	8·8	0·7	14·8	1·1
29	1 07·3	1 07·4	1 04·2	2·9	0·2	8·9	0·7	14·9	1·1
30	1 07·5	1 07·7	1 04·4	3·0	0·2	9·0	0·7	15·0	1·1
31	1 07·8	1 07·9	1 04·7	3·1	0·2	9·1	0·7	15·1	1·1
32	1 08·0	1 08·2	1 04·9	3·2	0·2	9·2	0·7	15·2	1·1
33	1 08·3	1 08·4	1 05·1	3·3	0·2	9·3	0·7	15·3	1·1
34	1 08·5	1 08·7	1 05·4	3·4	0·3	9·4	0·7	15·4	1·2
35	1 08·8	1 08·9	1 05·6	3·5	0·3	9·5	0·7	15·5	1·2
36	1 09·0	1 09·2	1 05·9	3·6	0·3	9·6	0·7	15·6	1·2
37	1 09·3	1 09·4	1 06·1	3·7	0·3	9·7	0·7	15·7	1·2
38	1 09·5	1 09·7	1 06·3	3·8	0·3	9·8	0·7	15·8	1·2
39	1 09·8	1 09·9	1 06·6	3·9	0·3	9·9	0·7	15·9	1·2
40	1 10·0	1 10·2	1 06·8	4·0	0·3	10·0	0·8	16·0	1·2
41	1 10·3	1 10·4	1 07·0	4·1	0·3	10·1	0·8	16·1	1·2
42	1 10·5	1 10·7	1 07·3	4·2	0·3	10·2	0·8	16·2	1·2
43	1 10·8	1 10·9	1 07·5	4·3	0·3	10·3	0·8	16·3	1·2
44	1 11·0	1 11·2	1 07·8	4·4	0·3	10·4	0·8	16·4	1·2
45	1 11·3	1 11·4	1 08·0	4·5	0·3	10·5	0·8	16·5	1·2
46	1 11·5	1 11·7	1 08·2	4·6	0·3	10·6	0·8	16·6	1·2
47	1 11·8	1 11·9	1 08·5	4·7	0·4	10·7	0·8	16·7	1·3
48	1 12·0	1 12·2	1 08·7	4·8	0·4	10·8	0·8	16·8	1·3
49	1 12·3	1 12·4	1 09·0	4·9	0·4	10·9	0·8	16·9	1·3
50	1 12·5	1 12·7	1 09·2	5·0	0·4	11·0	0·8	17·0	1·3
51	1 12·8	1 12·9	1 09·4	5·1	0·4	11·1	0·8	17·1	1·3
52	1 13·0	1 13·2	1 09·7	5·2	0·4	11·2	0·8	17·2	1·3
53	1 13·3	1 13·5	1 09·9	5·3	0·4	11·3	0·8	17·3	1·3
54	1 13·5	1 13·7	1 10·2	5·4	0·4	11·4	0·9	17·4	1·3
55	1 13·8	1 14·0	1 10·4	5·5	0·4	11·5	0·9	17·5	1·3
56	1 14·0	1 14·2	1 10·6	5·6	0·4	11·6	0·9	17·6	1·3
57	1 14·3	1 14·5	1 10·9	5·7	0·4	11·7	0·9	17·7	1·3
58	1 14·5	1 14·7	1 11·1	5·8	0·4	11·8	0·9	17·8	1·3
59	1 14·8	1 15·0	1 11·3	5·9	0·4	11·9	0·9	17·9	1·3
60	1 15·0	1 15·2	1 11·6	6·0	0·5	12·0	0·9	18·0	1·4

5	SUN PLANETS	ARIES	MOON	v or Corrn d		v or Corrn d		v or Corrn d	
s	° ′	° ′	° ′	′	′	′	′	′	′
00	1 15·0	1 15·2	1 11·6	0·0	0·0	6·0	0·6	12·0	1·1
01	1 15·3	1 15·5	1 11·8	0·1	0·0	6·1	0·6	12·1	1·1
02	1 15·5	1 15·7	1 12·1	0·2	0·0	6·2	0·6	12·2	1·1
03	1 15·8	1 16·0	1 12·3	0·3	0·0	6·3	0·6	12·3	1·1
04	1 16·0	1 16·2	1 12·5	0·4	0·0	6·4	0·6	12·4	1·1
05	1 16·3	1 16·5	1 12·8	0·5	0·0	6·5	0·6	12·5	1·1
06	1 16·5	1 16·7	1 13·0	0·6	0·1	6·6	0·6	12·6	1·2
07	1 16·8	1 17·0	1 13·3	0·7	0·1	6·7	0·6	12·7	1·2
08	1 17·0	1 17·2	1 13·5	0·8	0·1	6·8	0·6	12·8	1·2
09	1 17·3	1 17·5	1 13·7	0·9	0·1	6·9	0·6	12·9	1·2
10	1 17·5	1 17·7	1 14·0	1·0	0·1	7·0	0·6	13·0	1·2
11	1 17·8	1 18·0	1 14·2	1·1	0·1	7·1	0·7	13·1	1·2
12	1 18·0	1 18·2	1 14·4	1·2	0·1	7·2	0·7	13·2	1·2
13	1 18·3	1 18·5	1 14·7	1·3	0·1	7·3	0·7	13·3	1·2
14	1 18·5	1 18·7	1 14·9	1·4	0·1	7·4	0·7	13·4	1·2
15	1 18·8	1 19·0	1 15·2	1·5	0·1	7·5	0·7	13·5	1·2
16	1 19·0	1 19·2	1 15·4	1·6	0·1	7·6	0·7	13·6	1·2
17	1 19·3	1 19·5	1 15·6	1·7	0·2	7·7	0·7	13·7	1·3
18	1 19·5	1 19·7	1 15·9	1·8	0·2	7·8	0·7	13·8	1·3
19	1 19·8	1 20·0	1 16·1	1·9	0·2	7·9	0·7	13·9	1·3
20	1 20·0	1 20·2	1 16·4	2·0	0·2	8·0	0·7	14·0	1·3
21	1 20·3	1 20·5	1 16·6	2·1	0·2	8·1	0·7	14·1	1·3
22	1 20·5	1 20·7	1 16·8	2·2	0·2	8·2	0·8	14·2	1·3
23	1 20·8	1 21·0	1 17·1	2·3	0·2	8·3	0·8	14·3	1·3
24	1 21·0	1 21·2	1 17·3	2·4	0·2	8·4	0·8	14·4	1·3
25	1 21·3	1 21·5	1 17·5	2·5	0·2	8·5	0·8	14·5	1·3
26	1 21·5	1 21·7	1 17·8	2·6	0·2	8·6	0·8	14·6	1·3
27	1 21·8	1 22·0	1 18·0	2·7	0·2	8·7	0·8	14·7	1·3
28	1 22·0	1 22·2	1 18·3	2·8	0·3	8·8	0·8	14·8	1·4
29	1 22·3	1 22·5	1 18·5	2·9	0·3	8·9	0·8	14·9	1·4
30	1 22·5	1 22·7	1 18·7	3·0	0·3	9·0	0·8	15·0	1·4
31	1 22·8	1 23·0	1 19·0	3·1	0·3	9·1	0·8	15·1	1·4
32	1 23·0	1 23·2	1 19·2	3·2	0·3	9·2	0·8	15·2	1·4
33	1 23·3	1 23·5	1 19·5	3·3	0·3	9·3	0·9	15·3	1·4
34	1 23·5	1 23·7	1 19·7	3·4	0·3	9·4	0·9	15·4	1·4
35	1 23·8	1 24·0	1 19·9	3·5	0·3	9·5	0·9	15·5	1·4
36	1 24·0	1 24·2	1 20·2	3·6	0·3	9·6	0·9	15·6	1·4
37	1 24·3	1 24·5	1 20·4	3·7	0·3	9·7	0·9	15·7	1·4
38	1 24·5	1 24·7	1 20·7	3·8	0·3	9·8	0·9	15·8	1·4
39	1 24·8	1 25·0	1 20·9	3·9	0·4	9·9	0·9	15·9	1·5
40	1 25·0	1 25·2	1 21·1	4·0	0·4	10·0	0·9	16·0	1·5
41	1 25·3	1 25·5	1 21·4	4·1	0·4	10·1	0·9	16·1	1·5
42	1 25·5	1 25·7	1 21·6	4·2	0·4	10·2	0·9	16·2	1·5
43	1 25·8	1 26·0	1 21·8	4·3	0·4	10·3	0·9	16·3	1·5
44	1 26·0	1 26·2	1 22·1	4·4	0·4	10·4	1·0	16·4	1·5
45	1 26·3	1 26·5	1 22·3	4·5	0·4	10·5	1·0	16·5	1·5
46	1 26·5	1 26·7	1 22·6	4·6	0·4	10·6	1·0	16·6	1·5
47	1 26·8	1 27·0	1 22·8	4·7	0·4	10·7	1·0	16·7	1·5
48	1 27·0	1 27·2	1 23·0	4·8	0·4	10·8	1·0	16·8	1·5
49	1 27·3	1 27·5	1 23·3	4·9	0·4	10·9	1·0	16·9	1·5
50	1 27·5	1 27·7	1 23·5	5·0	0·5	11·0	1·0	17·0	1·6
51	1 27·8	1 28·0	1 23·8	5·1	0·5	11·1	1·0	17·1	1·6
52	1 28·0	1 28·2	1 24·0	5·2	0·5	11·2	1·0	17·2	1·6
53	1 28·3	1 28·5	1 24·2	5·3	0·5	11·3	1·0	17·3	1·6
54	1 28·5	1 28·7	1 24·5	5·4	0·5	11·4	1·0	17·4	1·6
55	1 28·8	1 29·0	1 24·7	5·5	0·5	11·5	1·1	17·5	1·6
56	1 29·0	1 29·2	1 24·9	5·6	0·5	11·6	1·1	17·6	1·6
57	1 29·3	1 29·5	1 25·2	5·7	0·5	11·7	1·1	17·7	1·6
58	1 29·5	1 29·7	1 25·4	5·8	0·5	11·8	1·1	17·8	1·6
59	1 29·8	1 30·0	1 25·7	5·9	0·5	11·9	1·1	17·9	1·6
60	1 30·0	1 30·2	1 25·9	6·0	0·6	12·0	1·1	18·0	1·7

6ᵐ

6	SUN PLANETS	ARIES	MOON	v or Corrⁿ d	v or Corrⁿ d	v or Corrⁿ d
s	° ′	° ′	° ′	′ ′	′ ′	′ ′
00	1 30·0	1 30·2	1 25·9	0·0 0·0	6·0 0·7	12·0 1·3
01	1 30·3	1 30·5	1 26·1	0·1 0·0	6·1 0·7	12·1 1·3
02	1 30·5	1 30·7	1 26·4	0·2 0·0	6·2 0·7	12·2 1·3
03	1 30·8	1 31·0	1 26·6	0·3 0·0	6·3 0·7	12·3 1·3
04	1 31·0	1 31·2	1 26·9	0·4 0·0	6·4 0·7	12·4 1·3
05	1 31·3	1 31·5	1 27·1	0·5 0·1	6·5 0·7	12·5 1·4
06	1 31·5	1 31·8	1 27·3	0·6 0·1	6·6 0·7	12·6 1·4
07	1 31·8	1 32·0	1 27·6	0·7 0·1	6·7 0·7	12·7 1·4
08	1 32·0	1 32·3	1 27·8	0·8 0·1	6·8 0·7	12·8 1·4
09	1 32·3	1 32·5	1 28·0	0·9 0·1	6·9 0·7	12·9 1·4
10	1 32·5	1 32·8	1 28·3	1·0 0·1	7·0 0·8	13·0 1·4
11	1 32·8	1 33·0	1 28·5	1·1 0·1	7·1 0·8	13·1 1·4
12	1 33·0	1 33·3	1 28·8	1·2 0·1	7·2 0·8	13·2 1·4
13	1 33·3	1 33·5	1 29·0	1·3 0·1	7·3 0·8	13·3 1·4
14	1 33·5	1 33·8	1 29·2	1·4 0·2	7·4 0·8	13·4 1·5
15	1 33·8	1 34·0	1 29·5	1·5 0·2	7·5 0·8	13·5 1·5
16	1 34·0	1 34·3	1 29·7	1·6 0·2	7·6 0·8	13·6 1·5
17	1 34·3	1 34·5	1 30·0	1·7 0·2	7·7 0·8	13·7 1·5
18	1 34·5	1 34·8	1 30·2	1·8 0·2	7·8 0·8	13·8 1·5
19	1 34·8	1 35·0	1 30·4	1·9 0·2	7·9 0·9	13·9 1·5
20	1 35·0	1 35·3	1 30·7	2·0 0·2	8·0 0·9	14·0 1·5
21	1 35·3	1 35·5	1 30·9	2·1 0·2	8·1 0·9	14·1 1·5
22	1 35·5	1 35·8	1 31·1	2·2 0·2	8·2 0·9	14·2 1·5
23	1 35·8	1 36·0	1 31·4	2·3 0·2	8·3 0·9	14·3 1·5
24	1 36·0	1 36·3	1 31·6	2·4 0·3	8·4 0·9	14·4 1·6
25	1 36·3	1 36·5	1 31·9	2·5 0·3	8·5 0·9	14·5 1·6
26	1 36·5	1 36·8	1 32·1	2·6 0·3	8·6 0·9	14·6 1·6
27	1 36·8	1 37·0	1 32·3	2·7 0·3	8·7 0·9	14·7 1·6
28	1 37·0	1 37·3	1 32·6	2·8 0·3	8·8 1·0	14·8 1·6
29	1 37·3	1 37·5	1 32·8	2·9 0·3	8·9 1·0	14·9 1·6
30	1 37·5	1 37·8	1 33·1	3·0 0·3	9·0 1·0	15·0 1·6
31	1 37·8	1 38·0	1 33·3	3·1 0·3	9·1 1·0	15·1 1·6
32	1 38·0	1 38·3	1 33·5	3·2 0·3	9·2 1·0	15·2 1·6
33	1 38·3	1 38·5	1 33·8	3·3 0·4	9·3 1·0	15·3 1·7
34	1 38·5	1 38·8	1 34·0	3·4 0·4	9·4 1·0	15·4 1·7
35	1 38·8	1 39·0	1 34·3	3·5 0·4	9·5 1·0	15·5 1·7
36	1 39·0	1 39·3	1 34·5	3·6 0·4	9·6 1·0	15·6 1·7
37	1 39·3	1 39·5	1 34·7	3·7 0·4	9·7 1·1	15·7 1·7
38	1 39·5	1 39·8	1 35·0	3·8 0·4	9·8 1·1	15·8 1·7
39	1 39·8	1 40·0	1 35·2	3·9 0·4	9·9 1·1	15·9 1·7
40	1 40·0	1 40·3	1 35·4	4·0 0·4	10·0 1·1	16·0 1·7
41	1 40·3	1 40·5	1 35·7	4·1 0·4	10·1 1·1	16·1 1·7
42	1 40·5	1 40·8	1 35·9	4·2 0·5	10·2 1·1	16·2 1·8
43	1 40·8	1 41·0	1 36·2	4·3 0·5	10·3 1·1	16·3 1·8
44	1 41·0	1 41·3	1 36·4	4·4 0·5	10·4 1·1	16·4 1·8
45	1 41·3	1 41·5	1 36·6	4·5 0·5	10·5 1·1	16·5 1·8
46	1 41·5	1 41·8	1 36·9	4·6 0·5	10·6 1·1	16·6 1·8
47	1 41·8	1 42·0	1 37·1	4·7 0·5	10·7 1·2	16·7 1·8
48	1 42·0	1 42·3	1 37·4	4·8 0·5	10·8 1·2	16·8 1·8
49	1 42·3	1 42·5	1 37·6	4·9 0·5	10·9 1·2	16·9 1·8
50	1 42·5	1 42·8	1 37·8	5·0 0·5	11·0 1·2	17·0 1·8
51	1 42·8	1 43·0	1 38·1	5·1 0·6	11·1 1·2	17·1 1·9
52	1 43·0	1 43·3	1 38·3	5·2 0·6	11·2 1·2	17·2 1·9
53	1 43·3	1 43·5	1 38·5	5·3 0·6	11·3 1·2	17·3 1·9
54	1 43·5	1 43·8	1 38·8	5·4 0·6	11·4 1·2	17·4 1·9
55	1 43·8	1 44·0	1 39·0	5·5 0·6	11·5 1·2	17·5 1·9
56	1 44·0	1 44·3	1 39·3	5·6 0·6	11·6 1·3	17·6 1·9
57	1 44·3	1 44·5	1 39·5	5·7 0·6	11·7 1·3	17·7 1·9
58	1 44·5	1 44·8	1 39·7	5·8 0·6	11·8 1·3	17·8 1·9
59	1 44·8	1 45·0	1 40·0	5·9 0·6	11·9 1·3	17·9 1·9
60	1 45·0	1 45·3	1 40·2	6·0 0·7	12·0 1·3	18·0 2·0

7ᵐ

7	SUN PLANETS	ARIES	MOON	v or Corrⁿ d	v or Corrⁿ d	v or Corrⁿ d
s	° ′	° ′	° ′	′ ′	′ ′	′ ′
00	1 45·0	1 45·3	1 40·2	0·0 0·0	6·0 0·8	12·0 1·5
01	1 45·3	1 45·5	1 40·5	0·1 0·0	6·1 0·8	12·1 1·5
02	1 45·5	1 45·8	1 40·7	0·2 0·0	6·2 0·8	12·2 1·5
03	1 45·8	1 46·0	1 40·9	0·3 0·0	6·3 0·8	12·3 1·5
04	1 46·0	1 46·3	1 41·2	0·4 0·1	6·4 0·8	12·4 1·6
05	1 46·3	1 46·5	1 41·4	0·5 0·1	6·5 0·8	12·5 1·6
06	1 46·5	1 46·8	1 41·6	0·6 0·1	6·6 0·8	12·6 1·6
07	1 46·8	1 47·0	1 41·9	0·7 0·1	6·7 0·8	12·7 1·6
08	1 47·0	1 47·3	1 42·1	0·8 0·1	6·8 0·9	12·8 1·6
09	1 47·3	1 47·5	1 42·4	0·9 0·1	6·9 0·9	12·9 1·6
10	1 47·5	1 47·8	1 42·6	1·0 0·1	7·0 0·9	13·0 1·6
11	1 47·8	1 48·0	1 42·8	1·1 0·1	7·1 0·9	13·1 1·6
12	1 48·0	1 48·3	1 43·1	1·2 0·2	7·2 0·9	13·2 1·7
13	1 48·3	1 48·5	1 43·3	1·3 0·2	7·3 0·9	13·3 1·7
14	1 48·5	1 48·8	1 43·6	1·4 0·2	7·4 0·9	13·4 1·7
15	1 48·8	1 49·0	1 43·8	1·5 0·2	7·5 0·9	13·5 1·7
16	1 49·0	1 49·3	1 44·0	1·6 0·2	7·6 1·0	13·6 1·7
17	1 49·3	1 49·5	1 44·3	1·7 0·2	7·7 1·0	13·7 1·7
18	1 49·5	1 49·8	1 44·5	1·8 0·2	7·8 1·0	13·8 1·7
19	1 49·8	1 50·1	1 44·8	1·9 0·2	7·9 1·0	13·9 1·7
20	1 50·0	1 50·3	1 45·0	2·0 0·3	8·0 1·0	14·0 1·8
21	1 50·3	1 50·6	1 45·2	2·1 0·3	8·1 1·0	14·1 1·8
22	1 50·5	1 50·8	1 45·5	2·2 0·3	8·2 1·0	14·2 1·8
23	1 50·8	1 51·1	1 45·7	2·3 0·3	8·3 1·0	14·3 1·8
24	1 51·0	1 51·3	1 45·9	2·4 0·3	8·4 1·1	14·4 1·8
25	1 51·3	1 51·6	1 46·2	2·5 0·3	8·5 1·1	14·5 1·8
26	1 51·5	1 51·8	1 46·4	2·6 0·3	8·6 1·1	14·6 1·8
27	1 51·8	1 52·1	1 46·7	2·7 0·3	8·7 1·1	14·7 1·8
28	1 52·0	1 52·3	1 46·9	2·8 0·4	8·8 1·1	14·8 1·9
29	1 52·3	1 52·6	1 47·1	2·9 0·4	8·9 1·1	14·9 1·9
30	1 52·5	1 52·8	1 47·4	3·0 0·4	9·0 1·1	15·0 1·9
31	1 52·8	1 53·1	1 47·6	3·1 0·4	9·1 1·1	15·1 1·9
32	1 53·0	1 53·3	1 47·9	3·2 0·4	9·2 1·2	15·2 1·9
33	1 53·3	1 53·6	1 48·1	3·3 0·4	9·3 1·2	15·3 1·9
34	1 53·5	1 53·8	1 48·3	3·4 0·4	9·4 1·2	15·4 1·9
35	1 53·8	1 54·1	1 48·6	3·5 0·4	9·5 1·2	15·5 1·9
36	1 54·0	1 54·3	1 48·8	3·6 0·5	9·6 1·2	15·6 2·0
37	1 54·3	1 54·6	1 49·0	3·7 0·5	9·7 1·2	15·7 2·0
38	1 54·5	1 54·8	1 49·3	3·8 0·5	9·8 1·2	15·8 2·0
39	1 54·8	1 55·1	1 49·5	3·9 0·5	9·9 1·2	15·9 2·0
40	1 55·0	1 55·3	1 49·8	4·0 0·5	10·0 1·3	16·0 2·0
41	1 55·3	1 55·6	1 50·0	4·1 0·5	10·1 1·3	16·1 2·0
42	1 55·5	1 55·8	1 50·2	4·2 0·5	10·2 1·3	16·2 2·0
43	1 55·8	1 56·1	1 50·5	4·3 0·5	10·3 1·3	16·3 2·0
44	1 56·0	1 56·3	1 50·7	4·4 0·6	10·4 1·3	16·4 2·1
45	1 56·3	1 56·6	1 51·0	4·5 0·6	10·5 1·3	16·5 2·1
46	1 56·5	1 56·8	1 51·2	4·6 0·6	10·6 1·3	16·6 2·1
47	1 56·8	1 57·1	1 51·4	4·7 0·6	10·7 1·3	16·7 2·1
48	1 57·0	1 57·3	1 51·7	4·8 0·6	10·8 1·4	16·8 2·1
49	1 57·3	1 57·6	1 51·9	4·9 0·6	10·9 1·4	16·9 2·1
50	1 57·5	1 57·8	1 52·1	5·0 0·6	11·0 1·4	17·0 2·1
51	1 57·8	1 58·1	1 52·4	5·1 0·6	11·1 1·4	17·1 2·1
52	1 58·0	1 58·3	1 52·6	5·2 0·7	11·2 1·4	17·2 2·2
53	1 58·3	1 58·6	1 52·9	5·3 0·7	11·3 1·4	17·3 2·2
54	1 58·5	1 58·8	1 53·1	5·4 0·7	11·4 1·4	17·4 2·2
55	1 58·8	1 59·1	1 53·3	5·5 0·7	11·5 1·4	17·5 2·2
56	1 59·0	1 59·3	1 53·6	5·6 0·7	11·6 1·5	17·6 2·2
57	1 59·3	1 59·6	1 53·8	5·7 0·7	11·7 1·5	17·7 2·2
58	1 59·5	1 59·8	1 54·1	5·8 0·7	11·8 1·5	17·8 2·2
59	1 59·8	2 00·1	1 54·3	5·9 0·7	11·9 1·5	17·9 2·2
60	2 00·0	2 00·3	1 54·5	6·0 0·8	12·0 1·5	18·0 2·3

8 s	SUN PLANETS	ARIES	MOON	v or Corrⁿ d	v or Corrⁿ d	v or Corrⁿ d
00	2 00·0	2 00·3	1 54·5	0·0 0·0	6·0 0·9	12·0 1·7
01	2 00·3	2 00·6	1 54·8	0·1 0·0	6·1 0·9	12·1 1·7
02	2 00·5	2 00·8	1 55·0	0·2 0·0	6·2 0·9	12·2 1·7
03	2 00·8	2 01·1	1 55·2	0·3 0·0	6·3 0·9	12·3 1·7
04	2 01·0	2 01·3	1 55·5	0·4 0·1	6·4 0·9	12·4 1·8
05	2 01·3	2 01·6	1 55·7	0·5 0·1	6·5 0·9	12·5 1·8
06	2 01·5	2 01·8	1 56·0	0·6 0·1	6·6 0·9	12·6 1·8
07	2 01·8	2 02·1	1 56·2	0·7 0·1	6·7 0·9	12·7 1·8
08	2 02·0	2 02·3	1 56·4	0·8 0·1	6·8 1·0	12·8 1·8
09	2 02·3	2 02·6	1 56·7	0·9 0·1	6·9 1·0	12·9 1·8
10	2 02·5	2 02·8	1 56·9	1·0 0·1	7·0 1·0	13·0 1·8
11	2 02·8	2 03·1	1 57·2	1·1 0·2	7·1 1·0	13·1 1·9
12	2 03·0	2 03·3	1 57·4	1·2 0·2	7·2 1·0	13·2 1·9
13	2 03·3	2 03·6	1 57·6	1·3 0·2	7·3 1·0	13·3 1·9
14	2 03·5	2 03·8	1 57·9	1·4 0·2	7·4 1·0	13·4 1·9
15	2 03·8	2 04·1	1 58·1	1·5 0·2	7·5 1·1	13·5 1·9
16	2 04·0	2 04·3	1 58·4	1·6 0·2	7·6 1·1	13·6 1·9
17	2 04·3	2 04·6	1 58·6	1·7 0·2	7·7 1·1	13·7 1·9
18	2 04·5	2 04·8	1 58·8	1·8 0·3	7·8 1·1	13·8 2·0
19	2 04·8	2 05·1	1 59·1	1·9 0·3	7·9 1·1	13·9 2·0
20	2 05·0	2 05·3	1 59·3	2·0 0·3	8·0 1·1	14·0 2·0
21	2 05·3	2 05·6	1 59·5	2·1 0·3	8·1 1·1	14·1 2·0
22	2 05·5	2 05·8	1 59·8	2·2 0·3	8·2 1·2	14·2 2·0
23	2 05·8	2 06·1	2 00·0	2·3 0·3	8·3 1·2	14·3 2·0
24	2 06·0	2 06·3	2 00·3	2·4 0·3	8·4 1·2	14·4 2·0
25	2 06·3	2 06·6	2 00·5	2·5 0·4	8·5 1·2	14·5 2·1
26	2 06·5	2 06·8	2 00·7	2·6 0·4	8·6 1·2	14·6 2·1
27	2 06·8	2 07·1	2 01·0	2·7 0·4	8·7 1·2	14·7 2·1
28	2 07·0	2 07·3	2 01·2	2·8 0·4	8·8 1·2	14·8 2·1
29	2 07·3	2 07·6	2 01·5	2·9 0·4	8·9 1·3	14·9 2·1
30	2 07·5	2 07·8	2 01·7	3·0 0·4	9·0 1·3	15·0 2·1
31	2 07·8	2 08·1	2 01·9	3·1 0·4	9·1 1·3	15·1 2·1
32	2 08·0	2 08·4	2 02·2	3·2 0·5	9·2 1·3	15·2 2·2
33	2 08·3	2 08·6	2 02·4	3·3 0·5	9·3 1·3	15·3 2·2
34	2 08·5	2 08·9	2 02·6	3·4 0·5	9·4 1·3	15·4 2·2
35	2 08·8	2 09·1	2 02·9	3·5 0·5	9·5 1·3	15·5 2·2
36	2 09·0	2 09·4	2 03·1	3·6 0·5	9·6 1·4	15·6 2·2
37	2 09·3	2 09·6	2 03·4	3·7 0·5	9·7 1·4	15·7 2·2
38	2 09·5	2 09·9	2 03·6	3·8 0·5	9·8 1·4	15·8 2·2
39	2 09·8	2 10·1	2 03·8	3·9 0·6	9·9 1·4	15·9 2·3
40	2 10·0	2 10·4	2 04·1	4·0 0·6	10·0 1·4	16·0 2·3
41	2 10·3	2 10·6	2 04·3	4·1 0·6	10·1 1·4	16·1 2·3
42	2 10·5	2 10·9	2 04·6	4·2 0·6	10·2 1·4	16·2 2·3
43	2 10·8	2 11·1	2 04·8	4·3 0·6	10·3 1·5	16·3 2·3
44	2 11·0	2 11·4	2 05·0	4·4 0·6	10·4 1·5	16·4 2·3
45	2 11·3	2 11·6	2 05·3	4·5 0·6	10·5 1·5	16·5 2·3
46	2 11·5	2 11·9	2 05·5	4·6 0·7	10·6 1·5	16·6 2·4
47	2 11·8	2 12·1	2 05·7	4·7 0·7	10·7 1·5	16·7 2·4
48	2 12·0	2 12·4	2 06·0	4·8 0·7	10·8 1·5	16·8 2·4
49	2 12·3	2 12·6	2 06·2	4·9 0·7	10·9 1·5	16·9 2·4
50	2 12·5	2 12·9	2 06·5	5·0 0·7	11·0 1·6	17·0 2·4
51	2 12·8	2 13·1	2 06·7	5·1 0·7	11·1 1·6	17·1 2·4
52	2 13·0	2 13·4	2 06·9	5·2 0·7	11·2 1·6	17·2 2·4
53	2 13·3	2 13·6	2 07·2	5·3 0·8	11·3 1·6	17·3 2·5
54	2 13·5	2 13·9	2 07·4	5·4 0·8	11·4 1·6	17·4 2·5
55	2 13·8	2 14·1	2 07·7	5·5 0·8	11·5 1·6	17·5 2·5
56	2 14·0	2 14·4	2 07·9	5·6 0·8	11·6 1·6	17·6 2·5
57	2 14·3	2 14·6	2 08·1	5·7 0·8	11·7 1·7	17·7 2·5
58	2 14·5	2 14·9	2 08·4	5·8 0·8	11·8 1·7	17·8 2·5
59	2 14·8	2 15·1	2 08·6	5·9 0·8	11·9 1·7	17·9 2·5
60	2 15·0	2 15·4	2 08·9	6·0 0·9	12·0 1·7	18·0 2·6

9 s	SUN PLANETS	ARIES	MOON	v or Corrⁿ d	v or Corrⁿ d	v or Corrⁿ d
00	2 15·0	2 15·4	2 08·9	0·0 0·0	6·0 1·0	12·0 1·9
01	2 15·3	2 15·6	2 09·1	0·1 0·0	6·1 1·0	12·1 1·9
02	2 15·5	2 15·9	2 09·3	0·2 0·0	6·2 1·0	12·2 1·9
03	2 15·8	2 16·1	2 09·6	0·3 0·0	6·3 1·0	12·3 1·9
04	2 16·0	2 16·4	2 09·8	0·4 0·1	6·4 1·0	12·4 2·0
05	2 16·3	2 16·6	2 10·0	0·5 0·1	6·5 1·0	12·5 2·0
06	2 16·5	2 16·9	2 10·3	0·6 0·1	6·6 1·0	12·6 2·0
07	2 16·8	2 17·1	2 10·5	0·7 0·1	6·7 1·1	12·7 2·0
08	2 17·0	2 17·4	2 10·8	0·8 0·1	6·8 1·1	12·8 2·0
09	2 17·3	2 17·6	2 11·0	0·9 0·1	6·9 1·1	12·9 2·0
10	2 17·5	2 17·9	2 11·2	1·0 0·2	7·0 1·1	13·0 2·1
11	2 17·8	2 18·1	2 11·5	1·1 0·2	7·1 1·1	13·1 2·1
12	2 18·0	2 18·4	2 11·7	1·2 0·2	7·2 1·1	13·2 2·1
13	2 18·3	2 18·6	2 12·0	1·3 0·2	7·3 1·2	13·3 2·1
14	2 18·5	2 18·9	2 12·2	1·4 0·2	7·4 1·2	13·4 2·1
15	2 18·8	2 19·1	2 12·4	1·5 0·2	7·5 1·2	13·5 2·1
16	2 19·0	2 19·4	2 12·7	1·6 0·3	7·6 1·2	13·6 2·2
17	2 19·3	2 19·6	2 12·9	1·7 0·3	7·7 1·2	13·7 2·2
18	2 19·5	2 19·9	2 13·1	1·8 0·3	7·8 1·2	13·8 2·2
19	2 19·8	2 20·1	2 13·4	1·9 0·3	7·9 1·3	13·9 2·2
20	2 20·0	2 20·4	2 13·6	2·0 0·3	8·0 1·3	14·0 2·2
21	2 20·3	2 20·6	2 13·9	2·1 0·3	8·1 1·3	14·1 2·2
22	2 20·5	2 20·9	2 14·1	2·2 0·3	8·2 1·3	14·2 2·2
23	2 20·8	2 21·1	2 14·3	2·3 0·4	8·3 1·3	14·3 2·3
24	2 21·0	2 21·4	2 14·6	2·4 0·4	8·4 1·3	14·4 2·3
25	2 21·3	2 21·6	2 14·8	2·5 0·4	8·5 1·3	14·5 2·3
26	2 21·5	2 21·9	2 15·1	2·6 0·4	8·6 1·4	14·6 2·3
27	2 21·8	2 22·1	2 15·3	2·7 0·4	8·7 1·4	14·7 2·3
28	2 22·0	2 22·4	2 15·5	2·8 0·4	8·8 1·4	14·8 2·3
29	2 22·3	2 22·6	2 15·8	2·9 0·5	8·9 1·4	14·9 2·4
30	2 22·5	2 22·9	2 16·0	3·0 0·5	9·0 1·4	15·0 2·4
31	2 22·8	2 23·1	2 16·2	3·1 0·5	9·1 1·4	15·1 2·4
32	2 23·0	2 23·4	2 16·5	3·2 0·5	9·2 1·5	15·2 2·4
33	2 23·3	2 23·6	2 16·7	3·3 0·5	9·3 1·5	15·3 2·4
34	2 23·5	2 23·9	2 17·0	3·4 0·5	9·4 1·5	15·4 2·4
35	2 23·8	2 24·1	2 17·2	3·5 0·6	9·5 1·5	15·5 2·5
36	2 24·0	2 24·4	2 17·4	3·6 0·6	9·6 1·5	15·6 2·5
37	2 24·3	2 24·6	2 17·7	3·7 0·6	9·7 1·5	15·7 2·5
38	2 24·5	2 24·9	2 17·9	3·8 0·6	9·8 1·6	15·8 2·5
39	2 24·8	2 25·1	2 18·2	3·9 0·6	9·9 1·6	15·9 2·5
40	2 25·0	2 25·4	2 18·4	4·0 0·6	10·0 1·6	16·0 2·5
41	2 25·3	2 25·6	2 18·6	4·1 0·6	10·1 1·6	16·1 2·5
42	2 25·5	2 25·9	2 18·9	4·2 0·7	10·2 1·6	16·2 2·6
43	2 25·8	2 26·1	2 19·1	4·3 0·7	10·3 1·6	16·3 2·6
44	2 26·0	2 26·4	2 19·3	4·4 0·7	10·4 1·6	16·4 2·6
45	2 26·3	2 26·7	2 19·6	4·5 0·7	10·5 1·7	16·5 2·6
46	2 26·5	2 26·9	2 19·8	4·6 0·7	10·6 1·7	16·6 2·6
47	2 26·8	2 27·2	2 20·1	4·7 0·7	10·7 1·7	16·7 2·6
48	2 27·0	2 27·4	2 20·3	4·8 0·8	10·8 1·7	16·8 2·7
49	2 27·3	2 27·7	2 20·5	4·9 0·8	10·9 1·7	16·9 2·7
50	2 27·5	2 27·9	2 20·8	5·0 0·8	11·0 1·7	17·0 2·7
51	2 27·8	2 28·2	2 21·0	5·1 0·8	11·1 1·8	17·1 2·7
52	2 28·0	2 28·4	2 21·3	5·2 0·8	11·2 1·8	17·2 2·7
53	2 28·3	2 28·7	2 21·5	5·3 0·8	11·3 1·8	17·3 2·7
54	2 28·5	2 28·9	2 21·7	5·4 0·9	11·4 1·8	17·4 2·8
55	2 28·8	2 29·2	2 22·0	5·5 0·9	11·5 1·8	17·5 2·8
56	2 29·0	2 29·4	2 22·2	5·6 0·9	11·6 1·8	17·6 2·8
57	2 29·3	2 29·7	2 22·5	5·7 0·9	11·7 1·9	17·7 2·8
58	2 29·5	2 29·9	2 22·7	5·8 0·9	11·8 1·9	17·8 2·8
59	2 29·8	2 30·2	2 22·9	5·9 0·9	11·9 1·9	17·9 2·8
60	2 30·0	2 30·4	2 23·2	6·0 1·0	12·0 1·9	18·0 2·9

10	SUN PLANETS	ARIES	MOON	v or Corr^n d	v or Corr^n d	v or Corr^n d
s	° ′	° ′	° ′	′ ′	′ ′	′ ′
00	2 30·0	2 30·4	2 23·2	0·0 0·0	6·0 1·1	12·0 2·1
01	2 30·3	2 30·7	2 23·4	0·1 0·0	6·1 1·1	12·1 2·1
02	2 30·5	2 30·9	2 23·6	0·2 0·0	6·2 1·1	12·2 2·1
03	2 30·8	2 31·2	2 23·9	0·3 0·1	6·3 1·1	12·3 2·2
04	2 31·0	2 31·4	2 24·1	0·4 0·1	6·4 1·1	12·4 2·2
05	2 31·3	2 31·7	2 24·4	0·5 0·1	6·5 1·1	12·5 2·2
06	2 31·5	2 31·9	2 24·6	0·6 0·1	6·6 1·2	12·6 2·2
07	2 31·8	2 32·2	2 24·8	0·7 0·1	6·7 1·2	12·7 2·2
08	2 32·0	2 32·4	2 25·1	0·8 0·1	6·8 1·2	12·8 2·2
09	2 32·3	2 32·7	2 25·3	0·9 0·2	6·9 1·2	12·9 2·3
10	2 32·5	2 32·9	2 25·6	1·0 0·2	7·0 1·2	13·0 2·3
11	2 32·8	2 33·2	2 25·8	1·1 0·2	7·1 1·2	13·1 2·3
12	2 33·0	2 33·4	2 26·0	1·2 0·2	7·2 1·3	13·2 2·3
13	2 33·3	2 33·7	2 26·3	1·3 0·2	7·3 1·3	13·3 2·3
14	2 33·5	2 33·9	2 26·5	1·4 0·2	7·4 1·3	13·4 2·3
15	2 33·8	2 34·2	2 26·7	1·5 0·3	7·5 1·3	13·5 2·4
16	2 34·0	2 34·4	2 27·0	1·6 0·3	7·6 1·3	13·6 2·4
17	2 34·3	2 34·7	2 27·2	1·7 0·3	7·7 1·3	13·7 2·4
18	2 34·5	2 34·9	2 27·5	1·8 0·3	7·8 1·4	13·8 2·4
19	2 34·8	2 35·2	2 27·7	1·9 0·3	7·9 1·4	13·9 2·4
20	2 35·0	2 35·4	2 27·9	2·0 0·4	8·0 1·4	14·0 2·5
21	2 35·3	2 35·7	2 28·2	2·1 0·4	8·1 1·4	14·1 2·5
22	2 35·5	2 35·9	2 28·4	2·2 0·4	8·2 1·4	14·2 2·5
23	2 35·8	2 36·2	2 28·7	2·3 0·4	8·3 1·5	14·3 2·5
24	2 36·0	2 36·4	2 28·9	2·4 0·4	8·4 1·5	14·4 2·5
25	2 36·3	2 36·7	2 29·1	2·5 0·4	8·5 1·5	14·5 2·5
26	2 36·5	2 36·9	2 29·4	2·6 0·5	8·6 1·5	14·6 2·6
27	2 36·8	2 37·2	2 29·6	2·7 0·5	8·7 1·5	14·7 2·6
28	2 37·0	2 37·4	2 29·8	2·8 0·5	8·8 1·6	14·8 2·6
29	2 37·3	2 37·7	2 30·1	2·9 0·5	8·9 1·6	14·9 2·6
30	2 37·5	2 37·9	2 30·3	3·0 0·5	9·0 1·6	15·0 2·6
31	2 37·8	2 38·2	2 30·6	3·1 0·5	9·1 1·6	15·1 2·6
32	2 38·0	2 38·4	2 30·8	3·2 0·6	9·2 1·6	15·2 2·7
33	2 38·3	2 38·7	2 31·0	3·3 0·6	9·3 1·6	15·3 2·7
34	2 38·5	2 38·9	2 31·3	3·4 0·6	9·4 1·6	15·4 2·7
35	2 38·8	2 39·2	2 31·5	3·5 0·6	9·5 1·7	15·5 2·7
36	2 39·0	2 39·4	2 31·8	3·6 0·6	9·6 1·7	15·6 2·7
37	2 39·3	2 39·7	2 32·0	3·7 0·6	9·7 1·7	15·7 2·7
38	2 39·5	2 39·9	2 32·2	3·8 0·7	9·8 1·7	15·8 2·8
39	2 39·8	2 40·2	2 32·5	3·9 0·7	9·9 1·7	15·9 2·8
40	2 40·0	2 40·4	2 32·7	4·0 0·7	10·0 1·8	16·0 2·8
41	2 40·3	2 40·7	2 32·9	4·1 0·7	10·1 1·8	16·1 2·8
42	2 40·5	2 40·9	2 33·2	4·2 0·7	10·2 1·8	16·2 2·8
43	2 40·8	2 41·2	2 33·4	4·3 0·8	10·3 1·8	16·3 2·9
44	2 41·0	2 41·4	2 33·7	4·4 0·8	10·4 1·8	16·4 2·9
45	2 41·3	2 41·7	2 33·9	4·5 0·8	10·5 1·8	16·5 2·9
46	2 41·5	2 41·9	2 34·1	4·6 0·8	10·6 1·9	16·6 2·9
47	2 41·8	2 42·2	2 34·4	4·7 0·8	10·7 1·9	16·7 2·9
48	2 42·0	2 42·4	2 34·6	4·8 0·8	10·8 1·9	16·8 2·9
49	2 42·3	2 42·7	2 34·9	4·9 0·9	10·9 1·9	16·9 3·0
50	2 42·5	2 42·9	2 35·1	5·0 0·9	11·0 1·9	17·0 3·0
51	2 42·8	2 43·2	2 35·3	5·1 0·9	11·1 1·9	17·1 3·0
52	2 43·0	2 43·4	2 35·6	5·2 0·9	11·2 2·0	17·2 3·0
53	2 43·3	2 43·7	2 35·8	5·3 0·9	11·3 2·0	17·3 3·0
54	2 43·5	2 43·9	2 36·1	5·4 0·9	11·4 2·0	17·4 3·0
55	2 43·8	2 44·2	2 36·3	5·5 1·0	11·5 2·0	17·5 3·1
56	2 44·0	2 44·4	2 36·5	5·6 1·0	11·6 2·0	17·6 3·1
57	2 44·3	2 44·7	2 36·8	5·7 1·0	11·7 2·0	17·7 3·1
58	2 44·5	2 45·0	2 37·0	5·8 1·0	11·8 2·1	17·8 3·1
59	2 44·8	2 45·2	2 37·2	5·9 1·0	11·9 2·1	17·9 3·1
60	2 45·0	2 45·5	2 37·5	6·0 1·1	12·0 2·1	18·0 3·2

11	SUN PLANETS	ARIES	MOON	v or Corr^n d	v or Corr^n d	v or Corr^n d
s	° ′	° ′	° ′	′ ′	′ ′	′ ′
00	2 45·0	2 45·5	2 37·5	0·0 0·0	6·0 1·2	12·0 2·3
01	2 45·3	2 45·7	2 37·7	0·1 0·0	6·1 1·2	12·1 2·3
02	2 45·5	2 46·0	2 38·0	0·2 0·0	6·2 1·2	12·2 2·3
03	2 45·8	2 46·2	2 38·2	0·3 0·1	6·3 1·2	12·3 2·4
04	2 46·0	2 46·5	2 38·4	0·4 0·1	6·4 1·2	12·4 2·4
05	2 46·3	2 46·7	2 38·7	0·5 0·1	6·5 1·2	12·5 2·4
06	2 46·5	2 47·0	2 38·9	0·6 0·1	6·6 1·3	12·6 2·4
07	2 46·8	2 47·2	2 39·2	0·7 0·1	6·7 1·3	12·7 2·4
08	2 47·0	2 47·5	2 39·4	0·8 0·2	6·8 1·3	12·8 2·5
09	2 47·3	2 47·7	2 39·6	0·9 0·2	6·9 1·3	12·9 2·5
10	2 47·5	2 48·0	2 39·9	1·0 0·2	7·0 1·3	13·0 2·5
11	2 47·8	2 48·2	2 40·1	1·1 0·2	7·1 1·4	13·1 2·5
12	2 48·0	2 48·5	2 40·3	1·2 0·2	7·2 1·4	13·2 2·5
13	2 48·3	2 48·7	2 40·6	1·3 0·2	7·3 1·4	13·3 2·5
14	2 48·5	2 49·0	2 40·8	1·4 0·3	7·4 1·4	13·4 2·6
15	2 48·8	2 49·2	2 41·1	1·5 0·3	7·5 1·4	13·5 2·6
16	2 49·0	2 49·5	2 41·3	1·6 0·3	7·6 1·5	13·6 2·6
17	2 49·3	2 49·7	2 41·5	1·7 0·3	7·7 1·5	13·7 2·6
18	2 49·5	2 50·0	2 41·8	1·8 0·3	7·8 1·5	13·8 2·6
19	2 49·8	2 50·2	2 42·0	1·9 0·4	7·9 1·5	13·9 2·7
20	2 50·0	2 50·5	2 42·3	2·0 0·4	8·0 1·5	14·0 2·7
21	2 50·3	2 50·7	2 42·5	2·1 0·4	8·1 1·6	14·1 2·7
22	2 50·5	2 51·0	2 42·7	2·2 0·4	8·2 1·6	14·2 2·7
23	2 50·8	2 51·2	2 43·0	2·3 0·4	8·3 1·6	14·3 2·7
24	2 51·0	2 51·5	2 43·2	2·4 0·5	8·4 1·6	14·4 2·8
25	2 51·3	2 51·7	2 43·4	2·5 0·5	8·5 1·6	14·5 2·8
26	2 51·5	2 52·0	2 43·7	2·6 0·5	8·6 1·6	14·6 2·8
27	2 51·8	2 52·2	2 43·9	2·7 0·5	8·7 1·7	14·7 2·8
28	2 52·0	2 52·5	2 44·2	2·8 0·5	8·8 1·7	14·8 2·8
29	2 52·3	2 52·7	2 44·4	2·9 0·6	8·9 1·7	14·9 2·9
30	2 52·5	2 53·0	2 44·6	3·0 0·6	9·0 1·7	15·0 2·9
31	2 52·8	2 53·2	2 44·9	3·1 0·6	9·1 1·7	15·1 2·9
32	2 53·0	2 53·5	2 45·1	3·2 0·6	9·2 1·8	15·2 2·9
33	2 53·3	2 53·7	2 45·4	3·3 0·6	9·3 1·8	15·3 2·9
34	2 53·5	2 54·0	2 45·6	3·4 0·7	9·4 1·8	15·4 3·0
35	2 53·8	2 54·2	2 45·8	3·5 0·7	9·5 1·8	15·5 3·0
36	2 54·0	2 54·5	2 46·1	3·6 0·7	9·6 1·8	15·6 3·0
37	2 54·3	2 54·7	2 46·3	3·7 0·7	9·7 1·9	15·7 3·0
38	2 54·5	2 55·0	2 46·6	3·8 0·7	9·8 1·9	15·8 3·0
39	2 54·8	2 55·2	2 46·8	3·9 0·7	9·9 1·9	15·9 3·0
40	2 55·0	2 55·5	2 47·0	4·0 0·8	10·0 1·9	16·0 3·1
41	2 55·3	2 55·7	2 47·3	4·1 0·8	10·1 1·9	16·1 3·1
42	2 55·5	2 56·0	2 47·5	4·2 0·8	10·2 2·0	16·2 3·1
43	2 55·8	2 56·2	2 47·7	4·3 0·8	10·3 2·0	16·3 3·1
44	2 56·0	2 56·5	2 48·0	4·4 0·8	10·4 2·0	16·4 3·1
45	2 56·3	2 56·7	2 48·2	4·5 0·9	10·5 2·0	16·5 3·2
46	2 56·5	2 57·0	2 48·5	4·6 0·9	10·6 2·0	16·6 3·2
47	2 56·8	2 57·2	2 48·7	4·7 0·9	10·7 2·1	16·7 3·2
48	2 57·0	2 57·5	2 48·9	4·8 0·9	10·8 2·1	16·8 3·2
49	2 57·3	2 57·7	2 49·2	4·9 0·9	10·9 2·1	16·9 3·2
50	2 57·5	2 58·0	2 49·4	5·0 1·0	11·0 2·1	17·0 3·3
51	2 57·8	2 58·2	2 49·7	5·1 1·0	11·1 2·1	17·1 3·3
52	2 58·0	2 58·5	2 49·9	5·2 1·0	11·2 2·1	17·2 3·3
53	2 58·3	2 58·7	2 50·1	5·3 1·0	11·3 2·2	17·3 3·3
54	2 58·5	2 59·0	2 50·4	5·4 1·0	11·4 2·2	17·4 3·3
55	2 58·8	2 59·2	2 50·6	5·5 1·1	11·5 2·2	17·5 3·4
56	2 59·0	2 59·5	2 50·8	5·6 1·1	11·6 2·2	17·6 3·4
57	2 59·3	2 59·7	2 51·1	5·7 1·1	11·7 2·2	17·7 3·4
58	2 59·5	3 00·0	2 51·3	5·8 1·1	11·8 2·3	17·8 3·4
59	2 59·8	3 00·2	2 51·6	5·9 1·1	11·9 2·3	17·9 3·4
60	3 00·0	3 00·5	2 51·8	6·0 1·2	12·0 2·3	18·0 3·5

12	SUN PLANETS	ARIES	MOON	v or Corrn d	v or Corrn d	v or Corrn d
s	° ′	° ′	° ′	′ ′	′ ′	′ ′
00	3 00·0	3 00·5	2 51·8	0·0 0·0	6·0 1·3	12·0 2·5
01	3 00·3	3 00·7	2 52·0	0·1 0·0	6·1 1·3	12·1 2·5
02	3 00·5	3 01·0	2 52·3	0·2 0·0	6·2 1·3	12·2 2·5
03	3 00·8	3 01·2	2 52·5	0·3 0·1	6·3 1·3	12·3 2·6
04	3 01·0	3 01·5	2 52·8	0·4 0·1	6·4 1·3	12·4 2·6
05	3 01·3	3 01·7	2 53·0	0·5 0·1	6·5 1·4	12·5 2·6
06	3 01·5	3 02·0	2 53·2	0·6 0·1	6·6 1·4	12·6 2·6
07	3 01·8	3 02·2	2 53·5	0·7 0·1	6·7 1·4	12·7 2·6
08	3 02·0	3 02·5	2 53·7	0·8 0·2	6·8 1·4	12·8 2·7
09	3 02·3	3 02·7	2 53·9	0·9 0·2	6·9 1·4	12·9 2·7
10	3 02·5	3 03·0	2 54·2	1·0 0·2	7·0 1·5	13·0 2·7
11	3 02·8	3 03·3	2 54·4	1·1 0·2	7·1 1·5	13·1 2·7
12	3 03·0	3 03·5	2 54·7	1·2 0·3	7·2 1·5	13·2 2·8
13	3 03·3	3 03·8	2 54·9	1·3 0·3	7·3 1·5	13·3 2·8
14	3 03·5	3 04·0	2 55·1	1·4 0·3	7·4 1·5	13·4 2·8
15	3 03·8	3 04·3	2 55·4	1·5 0·3	7·5 1·6	13·5 2·8
16	3 04·0	3 04·5	2 55·6	1·6 0·3	7·6 1·6	13·6 2·8
17	3 04·3	3 04·8	2 55·9	1·7 0·4	7·7 1·6	13·7 2·9
18	3 04·5	3 05·0	2 56·1	1·8 0·4	7·8 1·6	13·8 2·9
19	3 04·8	3 05·3	2 56·3	1·9 0·4	7·9 1·6	13·9 2·9
20	3 05·0	3 05·5	2 56·6	2·0 0·4	8·0 1·7	14·0 2·9
21	3 05·3	3 05·8	2 56·8	2·1 0·4	8·1 1·7	14·1 2·9
22	3 05·5	3 06·0	2 57·0	2·2 0·5	8·2 1·7	14·2 3·0
23	3 05·8	3 06·3	2 57·3	2·3 0·5	8·3 1·7	14·3 3·0
24	3 06·0	3 06·5	2 57·5	2·4 0·5	8·4 1·8	14·4 3·0
25	3 06·3	3 06·8	2 57·8	2·5 0·5	8·5 1·8	14·5 3·0
26	3 06·5	3 07·0	2 58·0	2·6 0·5	8·6 1·8	14·6 3·0
27	3 06·8	3 07·3	2 58·2	2·7 0·6	8·7 1·8	14·7 3·1
28	3 07·0	3 07·5	2 58·5	2·8 0·6	8·8 1·8	14·8 3·1
29	3 07·3	3 07·8	2 58·7	2·9 0·6	8·9 1·9	14·9 3·1
30	3 07·5	3 08·0	2 59·0	3·0 0·6	9·0 1·9	15·0 3·1
31	3 07·8	3 08·3	2 59·2	3·1 0·6	9·1 1·9	15·1 3·1
32	3 08·0	3 08·5	2 59·4	3·2 0·7	9·2 1·9	15·2 3·2
33	3 08·3	3 08·8	2 59·7	3·3 0·7	9·3 1·9	15·3 3·2
34	3 08·5	3 09·0	2 59·9	3·4 0·7	9·4 2·0	15·4 3·2
35	3 08·8	3 09·3	3 00·2	3·5 0·7	9·5 2·0	15·5 3·2
36	3 09·0	3 09·5	3 00·4	3·6 0·8	9·6 2·0	15·6 3·3
37	3 09·3	3 09·8	3 00·6	3·7 0·8	9·7 2·0	15·7 3·3
38	3 09·5	3 10·0	3 00·9	3·8 0·8	9·8 2·0	15·8 3·3
39	3 09·8	3 10·3	3 01·1	3·9 0·8	9·9 2·1	15·9 3·3
40	3 10·0	3 10·5	3 01·3	4·0 0·8	10·0 2·1	16·0 3·3
41	3 10·3	3 10·8	3 01·6	4·1 0·9	10·1 2·1	16·1 3·4
42	3 10·5	3 11·0	3 01·8	4·2 0·9	10·2 2·1	16·2 3·4
43	3 10·8	3 11·3	3 02·1	4·3 0·9	10·3 2·1	16·3 3·4
44	3 11·0	3 11·5	3 02·3	4·4 0·9	10·4 2·2	16·4 3·4
45	3 11·3	3 11·8	3 02·5	4·5 0·9	10·5 2·2	16·5 3·4
46	3 11·5	3 12·0	3 02·8	4·6 1·0	10·6 2·2	16·6 3·5
47	3 11·8	3 12·3	3 03·0	4·7 1·0	10·7 2·2	16·7 3·5
48	3 12·0	3 12·5	3 03·3	4·8 1·0	10·8 2·3	16·8 3·5
49	3 12·3	3 12·8	3 03·5	4·9 1·0	10·9 2·3	16·9 3·5
50	3 12·5	3 13·0	3 03·7	5·0 1·0	11·0 2·3	17·0 3·5
51	3 12·8	3 13·3	3 04·0	5·1 1·1	11·1 2·3	17·1 3·6
52	3 13·0	3 13·5	3 04·2	5·2 1·1	11·2 2·3	17·2 3·6
53	3 13·3	3 13·8	3 04·4	5·3 1·1	11·3 2·4	17·3 3·6
54	3 13·5	3 14·0	3 04·7	5·4 1·1	11·4 2·4	17·4 3·6
55	3 13·8	3 14·3	3 04·9	5·5 1·1	11·5 2·4	17·5 3·6
56	3 14·0	3 14·5	3 05·2	5·6 1·2	11·6 2·4	17·6 3·7
57	3 14·3	3 14·8	3 05·4	5·7 1·2	11·7 2·4	17·7 3·7
58	3 14·5	3 15·0	3 05·6	5·8 1·2	11·8 2·5	17·8 3·7
59	3 14·8	3 15·3	3 05·9	5·9 1·2	11·9 2·5	17·9 3·7
60	3 15·0	3 15·5	3 06·1	6·0 1·3	12·0 2·5	18·0 3·8

13	SUN PLANETS	ARIES	MOON	v or Corrn d	v or Corrn d	v or Corrn d
s	° ′	° ′	° ′	′ ′	′ ′	′ ′
00	3 15·0	3 15·5	3 06·1	0·0 0·0	6·0 1·4	12·0 2·7
01	3 15·3	3 15·8	3 06·4	0·1 0·0	6·1 1·4	12·1 2·7
02	3 15·5	3 16·0	3 06·6	0·2 0·0	6·2 1·4	12·2 2·7
03	3 15·8	3 16·3	3 06·8	0·3 0·1	6·3 1·4	12·3 2·8
04	3 16·0	3 16·5	3 07·1	0·4 0·1	6·4 1·4	12·4 2·8
05	3 16·3	3 16·8	3 07·3	0·5 0·1	6·5 1·5	12·5 2·8
06	3 16·5	3 17·0	3 07·5	0·6 0·1	6·6 1·5	12·6 2·8
07	3 16·8	3 17·3	3 07·8	0·7 0·2	6·7 1·5	12·7 2·9
08	3 17·0	3 17·5	3 08·0	0·8 0·2	6·8 1·5	12·8 2·9
09	3 17·3	3 17·8	3 08·3	0·9 0·2	6·9 1·6	12·9 2·9
10	3 17·5	3 18·0	3 08·5	1·0 0·2	7·0 1·6	13·0 2·9
11	3 17·8	3 18·3	3 08·7	1·1 0·2	7·1 1·6	13·1 2·9
12	3 18·0	3 18·5	3 09·0	1·2 0·3	7·2 1·6	13·2 3·0
13	3 18·3	3 18·8	3 09·2	1·3 0·3	7·3 1·6	13·3 3·0
14	3 18·5	3 19·0	3 09·5	1·4 0·3	7·4 1·7	13·4 3·0
15	3 18·8	3 19·3	3 09·7	1·5 0·3	7·5 1·7	13·5 3·0
16	3 19·0	3 19·5	3 09·9	1·6 0·4	7·6 1·7	13·6 3·1
17	3 19·3	3 19·8	3 10·2	1·7 0·4	7·7 1·7	13·7 3·1
18	3 19·5	3 20·0	3 10·4	1·8 0·4	7·8 1·8	13·8 3·1
19	3 19·8	3 20·3	3 10·7	1·9 0·4	7·9 1·8	13·9 3·1
20	3 20·0	3 20·5	3 10·9	2·0 0·5	8·0 1·8	14·0 3·2
21	3 20·3	3 20·8	3 11·1	2·1 0·5	8·1 1·8	14·1 3·2
22	3 20·5	3 21·0	3 11·4	2·2 0·5	8·2 1·8	14·2 3·2
23	3 20·8	3 21·3	3 11·6	2·3 0·5	8·3 1·9	14·3 3·2
24	3 21·0	3 21·6	3 11·8	2·4 0·5	8·4 1·9	14·4 3·2
25	3 21·3	3 21·8	3 12·1	2·5 0·6	8·5 1·9	14·5 3·3
26	3 21·5	3 22·1	3 12·3	2·6 0·6	8·6 1·9	14·6 3·3
27	3 21·8	3 22·3	3 12·6	2·7 0·6	8·7 2·0	14·7 3·3
28	3 22·0	3 22·6	3 12·8	2·8 0·6	8·8 2·0	14·8 3·3
29	3 22·3	3 22·8	3 13·0	2·9 0·7	8·9 2·0	14·9 3·4
30	3 22·5	3 23·1	3 13·3	3·0 0·7	9·0 2·0	15·0 3·4
31	3 22·8	3 23·3	3 13·5	3·1 0·7	9·1 2·0	15·1 3·4
32	3 23·0	3 23·6	3 13·8	3·2 0·7	9·2 2·1	15·2 3·4
33	3 23·3	3 23·8	3 14·0	3·3 0·7	9·3 2·1	15·3 3·4
34	3 23·5	3 24·1	3 14·2	3·4 0·8	9·4 2·1	15·4 3·5
35	3 23·8	3 24·3	3 14·5	3·5 0·8	9·5 2·1	15·5 3·5
36	3 24·0	3 24·6	3 14·7	3·6 0·8	9·6 2·2	15·6 3·5
37	3 24·3	3 24·8	3 14·9	3·7 0·8	9·7 2·2	15·7 3·5
38	3 24·5	3 25·1	3 15·2	3·8 0·9	9·8 2·2	15·8 3·5
39	3 24·8	3 25·3	3 15·4	3·9 0·9	9·9 2·2	15·9 3·6
40	3 25·0	3 25·6	3 15·7	4·0 0·9	10·0 2·3	16·0 3·6
41	3 25·3	3 25·8	3 15·9	4·1 0·9	10·1 2·3	16·1 3·6
42	3 25·5	3 26·1	3 16·1	4·2 0·9	10·2 2·3	16·2 3·6
43	3 25·8	3 26·3	3 16·4	4·3 1·0	10·3 2·3	16·3 3·7
44	3 26·0	3 26·6	3 16·6	4·4 1·0	10·4 2·3	16·4 3·7
45	3 26·3	3 26·8	3 16·9	4·5 1·0	10·5 2·4	16·5 3·7
46	3 26·5	3 27·1	3 17·1	4·6 1·0	10·6 2·4	16·6 3·7
47	3 26·8	3 27·3	3 17·3	4·7 1·1	10·7 2·4	16·7 3·8
48	3 27·0	3 27·6	3 17·6	4·8 1·1	10·8 2·4	16·8 3·8
49	3 27·3	3 27·8	3 17·8	4·9 1·1	10·9 2·5	16·9 3·8
50	3 27·5	3 28·1	3 18·0	5·0 1·1	11·0 2·5	17·0 3·8
51	3 27·8	3 28·3	3 18·3	5·1 1·1	11·1 2·5	17·1 3·8
52	3 28·0	3 28·6	3 18·5	5·2 1·2	11·2 2·5	17·2 3·9
53	3 28·3	3 28·8	3 18·8	5·3 1·2	11·3 2·5	17·3 3·9
54	3 28·5	3 29·1	3 19·0	5·4 1·2	11·4 2·6	17·4 3·9
55	3 28·8	3 29·3	3 19·2	5·5 1·2	11·5 2·6	17·5 3·9
56	3 29·0	3 29·6	3 19·5	5·6 1·3	11·6 2·6	17·6 3·9
57	3 29·3	3 29·8	3 19·7	5·7 1·3	11·7 2·6	17·7 4·0
58	3 29·5	3 30·1	3 20·0	5·8 1·3	11·8 2·7	17·8 4·0
59	3 29·8	3 30·3	3 20·2	5·9 1·3	11·9 2·7	17·9 4·0
60	3 30·0	3 30·6	3 20·4	6·0 1·4	12·0 2·7	18·0 4·1

14ᵐ

14	SUN PLANETS	ARIES	MOON	v or Corrn d	v or Corrn d	v or Corrn d
s	° ′	° ′	° ′	′ ′	′ ′	′ ′
00	3 30·0	3 30·6	3 20·4	0·0 0·0	6·0 1·5	12·0 2·9
01	3 30·3	3 30·8	3 20·7	0·1 0·0	6·1 1·5	12·1 2·9
02	3 30·5	3 31·1	3 20·9	0·2 0·0	6·2 1·5	12·2 2·9
03	3 30·8	3 31·3	3 21·1	0·3 0·1	6·3 1·5	12·3 3·0
04	3 31·0	3 31·6	3 21·4	0·4 0·1	6·4 1·5	12·4 3·0
05	3 31·3	3 31·8	3 21·6	0·5 0·1	6·5 1·6	12·5 3·0
06	3 31·5	3 32·1	3 21·9	0·6 0·1	6·6 1·6	12·6 3·0
07	3 31·8	3 32·3	3 22·1	0·7 0·2	6·7 1·6	12·7 3·1
08	3 32·0	3 32·6	3 22·3	0·8 0·2	6·8 1·6	12·8 3·1
09	3 32·3	3 32·8	3 22·6	0·9 0·2	6·9 1·7	12·9 3·1
10	3 32·5	3 33·1	3 22·8	1·0 0·2	7·0 1·7	13·0 3·1
11	3 32·8	3 33·3	3 23·1	1·1 0·3	7·1 1·7	13·1 3·2
12	3 33·0	3 33·6	3 23·3	1·2 0·3	7·2 1·7	13·2 3·2
13	3 33·3	3 33·8	3 23·5	1·3 0·3	7·3 1·8	13·3 3·2
14	3 33·5	3 34·1	3 23·8	1·4 0·3	7·4 1·8	13·4 3·2
15	3 33·8	3 34·3	3 24·0	1·5 0·4	7·5 1·8	13·5 3·3
16	3 34·0	3 34·6	3 24·3	1·6 0·4	7·6 1·8	13·6 3·3
17	3 34·3	3 34·8	3 24·5	1·7 0·4	7·7 1·9	13·7 3·3
18	3 34·5	3 35·1	3 24·7	1·8 0·4	7·8 1·9	13·8 3·3
19	3 34·8	3 35·3	3 25·0	1·9 0·5	7·9 1·9	13·9 3·4
20	3 35·0	3 35·6	3 25·2	2·0 0·5	8·0 1·9	14·0 3·4
21	3 35·3	3 35·8	3 25·4	2·1 0·5	8·1 2·0	14·1 3·4
22	3 35·5	3 36·1	3 25·7	2·2 0·5	8·2 2·0	14·2 3·4
23	3 35·8	3 36·3	3 25·9	2·3 0·6	8·3 2·0	14·3 3·5
24	3 36·0	3 36·6	3 26·2	2·4 0·6	8·4 2·0	14·4 3·5
25	3 36·3	3 36·8	3 26·4	2·5 0·6	8·5 2·1	14·5 3·5
26	3 36·5	3 37·1	3 26·6	2·6 0·6	8·6 2·1	14·6 3·5
27	3 36·8	3 37·3	3 26·9	2·7 0·7	8·7 2·1	14·7 3·6
28	3 37·0	3 37·6	3 27·1	2·8 0·7	8·8 2·1	14·8 3·6
29	3 37·3	3 37·8	3 27·4	2·9 0·7	8·9 2·2	14·9 3·6
30	3 37·5	3 38·1	3 27·6	3·0 0·7	9·0 2·2	15·0 3·6
31	3 37·8	3 38·3	3 27·8	3·1 0·7	9·1 2·2	15·1 3·6
32	3 38·0	3 38·6	3 28·1	3·2 0·8	9·2 2·2	15·2 3·7
33	3 38·3	3 38·8	3 28·3	3·3 0·8	9·3 2·2	15·3 3·7
34	3 38·5	3 39·1	3 28·5	3·4 0·8	9·4 2·3	15·4 3·7
35	3 38·8	3 39·3	3 28·8	3·5 0·8	9·5 2·3	15·5 3·7
36	3 39·0	3 39·6	3 29·0	3·6 0·9	9·6 2·3	15·6 3·8
37	3 39·3	3 39·8	3 29·3	3·7 0·9	9·7 2·3	15·7 3·8
38	3 39·5	3 40·1	3 29·5	3·8 0·9	9·8 2·4	15·8 3·8
39	3 39·8	3 40·4	3 29·7	3·9 0·9	9·9 2·4	15·9 3·8
40	3 40·0	3 40·6	3 30·0	4·0 1·0	10·0 2·4	16·0 3·9
41	3 40·3	3 40·9	3 30·2	4·1 1·0	10·1 2·4	16·1 3·9
42	3 40·5	3 41·1	3 30·5	4·2 1·0	10·2 2·5	16·2 3·9
43	3 40·8	3 41·4	3 30·7	4·3 1·0	10·3 2·5	16·3 3·9
44	3 41·0	3 41·6	3 30·9	4·4 1·1	10·4 2·5	16·4 4·0
45	3 41·3	3 41·9	3 31·2	4·5 1·1	10·5 2·5	16·5 4·0
46	3 41·5	3 42·1	3 31·4	4·6 1·1	10·6 2·6	16·6 4·0
47	3 41·8	3 42·4	3 31·6	4·7 1·1	10·7 2·6	16·7 4·0
48	3 42·0	3 42·6	3 31·9	4·8 1·2	10·8 2·6	16·8 4·1
49	3 42·3	3 42·9	3 32·1	4·9 1·2	10·9 2·6	16·9 4·1
50	3 42·5	3 43·1	3 32·4	5·0 1·2	11·0 2·7	17·0 4·1
51	3 42·8	3 43·4	3 32·6	5·1 1·2	11·1 2·7	17·1 4·1
52	3 43·0	3 43·6	3 32·8	5·2 1·3	11·2 2·7	17·2 4·2
53	3 43·3	3 43·9	3 33·1	5·3 1·3	11·3 2·7	17·3 4·2
54	3 43·5	3 44·1	3 33·3	5·4 1·3	11·4 2·8	17·4 4·2
55	3 43·8	3 44·4	3 33·6	5·5 1·3	11·5 2·8	17·5 4·2
56	3 44·0	3 44·6	3 33·8	5·6 1·4	11·6 2·8	17·6 4·3
57	3 44·3	3 44·9	3 34·0	5·7 1·4	11·7 2·8	17·7 4·3
58	3 44·5	3 45·1	3 34·3	5·8 1·4	11·8 2·9	17·8 4·3
59	3 44·8	3 45·4	3 34·5	5·9 1·4	11·9 2·9	17·9 4·3
60	3 45·0	3 45·6	3 34·8	6·0 1·5	12·0 2·9	18·0 4·4

15ᵐ

15	SUN PLANETS	ARIES	MOON	v or Corrn d	v or Corrn d	v or Corrn d
s	° ′	° ′	° ′	′ ′	′ ′	′ ′
00	3 45·0	3 45·6	3 34·8	0·0 0·0	6·0 1·6	12·0 3·1
01	3 45·3	3 45·9	3 35·0	0·1 0·1	6·1 1·6	12·1 3·1
02	3 45·5	3 46·1	3 35·2	0·2 0·1	6·2 1·6	12·2 3·2
03	3 45·8	3 46·4	3 35·5	0·3 0·1	6·3 1·6	12·3 3·2
04	3 46·0	3 46·6	3 35·7	0·4 0·1	6·4 1·7	12·4 3·2
05	3 46·3	3 46·9	3 35·9	0·5 0·1	6·5 1·7	12·5 3·2
06	3 46·5	3 47·1	3 36·2	0·6 0·2	6·6 1·7	12·6 3·3
07	3 46·8	3 47·4	3 36·4	0·7 0·2	6·7 1·7	12·7 3·3
08	3 47·0	3 47·6	3 36·7	0·8 0·2	6·8 1·8	12·8 3·3
09	3 47·3	3 47·9	3 36·9	0·9 0·2	6·9 1·8	12·9 3·3
10	3 47·5	3 48·1	3 37·1	1·0 0·3	7·0 1·8	13·0 3·4
11	3 47·8	3 48·4	3 37·4	1·1 0·3	7·1 1·8	13·1 3·4
12	3 48·0	3 48·6	3 37·6	1·2 0·3	7·2 1·9	13·2 3·4
13	3 48·3	3 48·9	3 37·9	1·3 0·3	7·3 1·9	13·3 3·4
14	3 48·5	3 49·1	3 38·1	1·4 0·4	7·4 1·9	13·4 3·5
15	3 48·8	3 49·4	3 38·3	1·5 0·4	7·5 1·9	13·5 3·5
16	3 49·0	3 49·6	3 38·6	1·6 0·4	7·6 2·0	13·6 3·5
17	3 49·3	3 49·9	3 38·8	1·7 0·4	7·7 2·0	13·7 3·5
18	3 49·5	3 50·1	3 39·0	1·8 0·5	7·8 2·0	13·8 3·6
19	3 49·8	3 50·4	3 39·3	1·9 0·5	7·9 2·0	13·9 3·6
20	3 50·0	3 50·6	3 39·5	2·0 0·5	8·0 2·1	14·0 3·6
21	3 50·3	3 50·9	3 39·8	2·1 0·5	8·1 2·1	14·1 3·6
22	3 50·5	3 51·1	3 40·0	2·2 0·6	8·2 2·1	14·2 3·7
23	3 50·8	3 51·4	3 40·2	2·3 0·6	8·3 2·1	14·3 3·7
24	3 51·0	3 51·6	3 40·5	2·4 0·6	8·4 2·2	14·4 3·7
25	3 51·3	3 51·9	3 40·7	2·5 0·6	8·5 2·2	14·5 3·7
26	3 51·5	3 52·1	3 41·0	2·6 0·7	8·6 2·2	14·6 3·8
27	3 51·8	3 52·4	3 41·2	2·7 0·7	8·7 2·2	14·7 3·8
28	3 52·0	3 52·6	3 41·4	2·8 0·7	8·8 2·3	14·8 3·8
29	3 52·3	3 52·9	3 41·7	2·9 0·7	8·9 2·3	14·9 3·8
30	3 52·5	3 53·1	3 41·9	3·0 0·8	9·0 2·3	15·0 3·9
31	3 52·8	3 53·4	3 42·1	3·1 0·8	9·1 2·4	15·1 3·9
32	3 53·0	3 53·6	3 42·4	3·2 0·8	9·2 2·4	15·2 3·9
33	3 53·3	3 53·9	3 42·6	3·3 0·9	9·3 2·4	15·3 4·0
34	3 53·5	3 54·1	3 42·9	3·4 0·9	9·4 2·4	15·4 4·0
35	3 53·8	3 54·4	3 43·1	3·5 0·9	9·5 2·5	15·5 4·0
36	3 54·0	3 54·6	3 43·3	3·6 0·9	9·6 2·5	15·6 4·0
37	3 54·3	3 54·9	3 43·6	3·7 1·0	9·7 2·5	15·7 4·1
38	3 54·5	3 55·1	3 43·8	3·8 1·0	9·8 2·5	15·8 4·1
39	3 54·8	3 55·4	3 44·1	3·9 1·0	9·9 2·6	15·9 4·1
40	3 55·0	3 55·6	3 44·3	4·0 1·0	10·0 2·6	16·0 4·1
41	3 55·3	3 55·9	3 44·5	4·1 1·1	10·1 2·6	16·1 4·2
42	3 55·5	3 56·1	3 44·8	4·2 1·1	10·2 2·6	16·2 4·2
43	3 55·8	3 56·4	3 45·0	4·3 1·1	10·3 2·7	16·3 4·2
44	3 56·0	3 56·6	3 45·2	4·4 1·1	10·4 2·7	16·4 4·2
45	3 56·3	3 56·9	3 45·5	4·5 1·2	10·5 2·7	16·5 4·3
46	3 56·5	3 57·1	3 45·7	4·6 1·2	10·6 2·7	16·6 4·3
47	3 56·8	3 57·4	3 46·0	4·7 1·2	10·7 2·8	16·7 4·3
48	3 57·0	3 57·6	3 46·2	4·8 1·2	10·8 2·8	16·8 4·3
49	3 57·3	3 57·9	3 46·4	4·9 1·3	10·9 2·8	16·9 4·4
50	3 57·5	3 58·2	3 46·7	5·0 1·3	11·0 2·8	17·0 4·4
51	3 57·8	3 58·4	3 46·9	5·1 1·3	11·1 2·9	17·1 4·4
52	3 58·0	3 58·7	3 47·2	5·2 1·3	11·2 2·9	17·2 4·4
53	3 58·3	3 58·9	3 47·4	5·3 1·4	11·3 2·9	17·3 4·5
54	3 58·5	3 59·2	3 47·6	5·4 1·4	11·4 2·9	17·4 4·5
55	3 58·8	3 59·4	3 47·9	5·5 1·4	11·5 3·0	17·5 4·5
56	3 59·0	3 59·7	3 48·1	5·6 1·4	11·6 3·0	17·6 4·5
57	3 59·3	3 59·9	3 48·4	5·7 1·5	11·7 3·0	17·7 4·6
58	3 59·5	4 00·2	3 48·6	5·8 1·5	11·8 3·0	17·8 4·6
59	3 59·8	4 00·4	3 48·8	5·9 1·5	11·9 3·1	17·9 4·6
60	4 00·0	4 00·7	3 49·1	6·0 1·6	12·0 3·1	18·0 4·7

16ᵐ

16	SUN PLANETS	ARIES	MOON	v or Corrn d		v or Corrn d		v or Corrn d	
s	° ′	° ′	° ′	′	′	′	′	′	′
00	4 00·0	4 00·7	3 49·1	0·0	0·0	6·0	1·7	12·0	3·3
01	4 00·3	4 00·9	3 49·3	0·1	0·0	6·1	1·7	12·1	3·3
02	4 00·5	4 01·2	3 49·5	0·2	0·1	6·2	1·7	12·2	3·4
03	4 00·8	4 01·4	3 49·8	0·3	0·1	6·3	1·7	12·3	3·4
04	4 01·0	4 01·7	3 50·0	0·4	0·1	6·4	1·8	12·4	3·4
05	4 01·3	4 01·9	3 50·3	0·5	0·1	6·5	1·8	12·5	3·4
06	4 01·5	4 02·2	3 50·5	0·6	0·2	6·6	1·8	12·6	3·5
07	4 01·8	4 02·4	3 50·7	0·7	0·2	6·7	1·8	12·7	3·5
08	4 02·0	4 02·7	3 51·0	0·8	0·2	6·8	1·9	12·8	3·5
09	4 02·3	4 02·9	3 51·2	0·9	0·2	6·9	1·9	12·9	3·5
10	4 02·5	4 03·2	3 51·5	1·0	0·3	7·0	1·9	13·0	3·6
11	4 02·8	4 03·4	3 51·7	1·1	0·3	7·1	2·0	13·1	3·6
12	4 03·0	4 03·7	3 51·9	1·2	0·3	7·2	2·0	13·2	3·6
13	4 03·3	4 03·9	3 52·2	1·3	0·4	7·3	2·0	13·3	3·7
14	4 03·5	4 04·2	3 52·4	1·4	0·4	7·4	2·0	13·4	3·7
15	4 03·8	4 04·4	3 52·6	1·5	0·4	7·5	2·1	13·5	3·7
16	4 04·0	4 04·7	3 52·9	1·6	0·4	7·6	2·1	13·6	3·7
17	4 04·3	4 04·9	3 53·1	1·7	0·5	7·7	2·1	13·7	3·8
18	4 04·5	4 05·2	3 53·4	1·8	0·5	7·8	2·1	13·8	3·8
19	4 04·8	4 05·4	3 53·6	1·9	0·5	7·9	2·2	13·9	3·8
20	4 05·0	4 05·7	3 53·8	2·0	0·6	8·0	2·2	14·0	3·9
21	4 05·3	4 05·9	3 54·1	2·1	0·6	8·1	2·2	14·1	3·9
22	4 05·5	4 06·2	3 54·3	2·2	0·6	8·2	2·3	14·2	3·9
23	4 05·8	4 06·4	3 54·6	2·3	0·6	8·3	2·3	14·3	3·9
24	4 06·0	4 06·7	3 54·8	2·4	0·7	8·4	2·3	14·4	4·0
25	4 06·3	4 06·9	3 55·0	2·5	0·7	8·5	2·3	14·5	4·0
26	4 06·5	4 07·2	3 55·3	2·6	0·7	8·6	2·4	14·6	4·0
27	4 06·8	4 07·4	3 55·5	2·7	0·7	8·7	2·4	14·7	4·0
28	4 07·0	4 07·7	3 55·7	2·8	0·8	8·8	2·4	14·8	4·1
29	4 07·3	4 07·9	3 56·0	2·9	0·8	8·9	2·4	14·9	4·1
30	4 07·5	4 08·2	3 56·2	3·0	0·8	9·0	2·5	15·0	4·1
31	4 07·8	4 08·4	3 56·5	3·1	0·9	9·1	2·5	15·1	4·2
32	4 08·0	4 08·7	3 56·7	3·2	0·9	9·2	2·5	15·2	4·2
33	4 08·3	4 08·9	3 56·9	3·3	0·9	9·3	2·6	15·3	4·2
34	4 08·5	4 09·2	3 57·2	3·4	0·9	9·4	2·6	15·4	4·2
35	4 08·8	4 09·4	3 57·4	3·5	1·0	9·5	2·6	15·5	4·3
36	4 09·0	4 09·7	3 57·7	3·6	1·0	9·6	2·6	15·6	4·3
37	4 09·3	4 09·9	3 57·9	3·7	1·0	9·7	2·7	15·7	4·3
38	4 09·5	4 10·2	3 58·1	3·8	1·0	9·8	2·7	15·8	4·3
39	4 09·8	4 10·4	3 58·4	3·9	1·1	9·9	2·7	15·9	4·4
40	4 10·0	4 10·7	3 58·6	4·0	1·1	10·0	2·8	16·0	4·4
41	4 10·3	4 10·9	3 58·8	4·1	1·1	10·1	2·8	16·1	4·4
42	4 10·5	4 11·2	3 59·1	4·2	1·2	10·2	2·8	16·2	4·5
43	4 10·8	4 11·4	3 59·3	4·3	1·2	10·3	2·8	16·3	4·5
44	4 11·0	4 11·7	3 59·6	4·4	1·2	10·4	2·9	16·4	4·5
45	4 11·3	4 11·9	3 59·8	4·5	1·2	10·5	2·9	16·5	4·5
46	4 11·5	4 12·2	4 00·0	4·6	1·3	10·6	2·9	16·6	4·6
47	4 11·8	4 12·4	4 00·3	4·7	1·3	10·7	2·9	16·7	4·6
48	4 12·0	4 12·7	4 00·5	4·8	1·3	10·8	3·0	16·8	4·6
49	4 12·3	4 12·9	4 00·8	4·9	1·3	10·9	3·0	16·9	4·6
50	4 12·5	4 13·2	4 01·0	5·0	1·4	11·0	3·0	17·0	4·7
51	4 12·8	4 13·4	4 01·2	5·1	1·4	11·1	3·1	17·1	4·7
52	4 13·0	4 13·7	4 01·5	5·2	1·4	11·2	3·1	17·2	4·7
53	4 13·3	4 13·9	4 01·7	5·3	1·5	11·3	3·1	17·3	4·8
54	4 13·5	4 14·2	4 02·0	5·4	1·5	11·4	3·1	17·4	4·8
55	4 13·8	4 14·4	4 02·2	5·5	1·5	11·5	3·2	17·5	4·8
56	4 14·0	4 14·7	4 02·4	5·6	1·5	11·6	3·2	17·6	4·8
57	4 14·3	4 14·9	4 02·7	5·7	1·6	11·7	3·2	17·7	4·9
58	4 14·5	4 15·2	4 02·9	5·8	1·6	11·8	3·2	17·8	4·9
59	4 14·8	4 15·4	4 03·1	5·9	1·6	11·9	3·3	17·9	4·9
60	4 15·0	4 15·7	4 03·4	6·0	1·7	12·0	3·3	18·0	5·0

17ᵐ

17	SUN PLANETS	ARIES	MOON	v or Corrn d		v or Corrn d		v or Corrn d	
s	° ′	° ′	° ′	′	′	′	′	′	′
00	4 15·0	4 15·7	4 03·4	0·0	0·0	6·0	1·8	12·0	3·5
01	4 15·3	4 15·9	4 03·6	0·1	0·0	6·1	1·8	12·1	3·5
02	4 15·5	4 16·2	4 03·9	0·2	0·1	6·2	1·8	12·2	3·6
03	4 15·8	4 16·5	4 04·1	0·3	0·1	6·3	1·8	12·3	3·6
04	4 16·0	4 16·7	4 04·3	0·4	0·1	6·4	1·9	12·4	3·6
05	4 16·3	4 17·0	4 04·6	0·5	0·1	6·5	1·9	12·5	3·6
06	4 16·5	4 17·2	4 04·8	0·6	0·2	6·6	1·9	12·6	3·7
07	4 16·8	4 17·5	4 05·1	0·7	0·2	6·7	2·0	12·7	3·7
08	4 17·0	4 17·7	4 05·3	0·8	0·2	6·8	2·0	12·8	3·7
09	4 17·3	4 18·0	4 05·5	0·9	0·3	6·9	2·0	12·9	3·8
10	4 17·5	4 18·2	4 05·8	1·0	0·3	7·0	2·0	13·0	3·8
11	4 17·8	4 18·5	4 06·0	1·1	0·3	7·1	2·1	13·1	3·8
12	4 18·0	4 18·7	4 06·2	1·2	0·4	7·2	2·1	13·2	3·9
13	4 18·3	4 19·0	4 06·5	1·3	0·4	7·3	2·1	13·3	3·9
14	4 18·5	4 19·2	4 06·7	1·4	0·4	7·4	2·2	13·4	3·9
15	4 18·8	4 19·5	4 07·0	1·5	0·4	7·5	2·2	13·5	3·9
16	4 19·0	4 19·7	4 07·2	1·6	0·5	7·6	2·2	13·6	4·0
17	4 19·3	4 20·0	4 07·4	1·7	0·5	7·7	2·2	13·7	4·0
18	4 19·5	4 20·2	4 07·7	1·8	0·5	7·8	2·3	13·8	4·0
19	4 19·8	4 20·5	4 07·9	1·9	0·6	7·9	2·3	13·9	4·1
20	4 20·0	4 20·7	4 08·2	2·0	0·6	8·0	2·3	14·0	4·1
21	4 20·3	4 21·0	4 08·4	2·1	0·6	8·1	2·4	14·1	4·1
22	4 20·5	4 21·2	4 08·6	2·2	0·6	8·2	2·4	14·2	4·1
23	4 20·8	4 21·5	4 08·9	2·3	0·7	8·3	2·4	14·3	4·2
24	4 21·0	4 21·7	4 09·1	2·4	0·7	8·4	2·5	14·4	4·2
25	4 21·3	4 22·0	4 09·3	2·5	0·7	8·5	2·5	14·5	4·2
26	4 21·5	4 22·2	4 09·6	2·6	0·8	8·6	2·5	14·6	4·3
27	4 21·8	4 22·5	4 09·8	2·7	0·8	8·7	2·5	14·7	4·3
28	4 22·0	4 22·7	4 10·1	2·8	0·8	8·8	2·6	14·8	4·3
29	4 22·3	4 23·0	4 10·3	2·9	0·8	8·9	2·6	14·9	4·3
30	4 22·5	4 23·2	4 10·5	3·0	0·9	9·0	2·6	15·0	4·4
31	4 22·8	4 23·5	4 10·8	3·1	0·9	9·1	2·7	15·1	4·4
32	4 23·0	4 23·7	4 11·0	3·2	0·9	9·2	2·7	15·2	4·4
33	4 23·3	4 24·0	4 11·3	3·3	1·0	9·3	2·7	15·3	4·5
34	4 23·5	4 24·2	4 11·5	3·4	1·0	9·4	2·7	15·4	4·5
35	4 23·8	4 24·5	4 11·7	3·5	1·0	9·5	2·8	15·5	4·5
36	4 24·0	4 24·7	4 12·0	3·6	1·1	9·6	2·8	15·6	4·6
37	4 24·3	4 25·0	4 12·2	3·7	1·1	9·7	2·8	15·7	4·6
38	4 24·5	4 25·2	4 12·5	3·8	1·1	9·8	2·9	15·8	4·6
39	4 24·8	4 25·5	4 12·7	3·9	1·1	9·9	2·9	15·9	4·6
40	4 25·0	4 25·7	4 12·9	4·0	1·2	10·0	2·9	16·0	4·7
41	4 25·3	4 26·0	4 13·2	4·1	1·2	10·1	2·9	16·1	4·7
42	4 25·5	4 26·2	4 13·4	4·2	1·2	10·2	3·0	16·2	4·7
43	4 25·8	4 26·5	4 13·6	4·3	1·3	10·3	3·0	16·3	4·8
44	4 26·0	4 26·7	4 13·9	4·4	1·3	10·4	3·0	16·4	4·8
45	4 26·3	4 27·0	4 14·1	4·5	1·3	10·5	3·1	16·5	4·8
46	4 26·5	4 27·2	4 14·4	4·6	1·3	10·6	3·1	16·6	4·8
47	4 26·8	4 27·5	4 14·6	4·7	1·4	10·7	3·1	16·7	4·9
48	4 27·0	4 27·7	4 14·8	4·8	1·4	10·8	3·2	16·8	4·9
49	4 27·3	4 28·0	4 15·1	4·9	1·4	10·9	3·2	16·9	4·9
50	4 27·5	4 28·2	4 15·3	5·0	1·5	11·0	3·2	17·0	5·0
51	4 27·8	4 28·5	4 15·6	5·1	1·5	11·1	3·2	17·1	5·0
52	4 28·0	4 28·7	4 15·8	5·2	1·5	11·2	3·3	17·2	5·0
53	4 28·3	4 29·0	4 16·0	5·3	1·5	11·3	3·3	17·3	5·0
54	4 28·5	4 29·2	4 16·3	5·4	1·6	11·4	3·3	17·4	5·1
55	4 28·8	4 29·5	4 16·5	5·5	1·6	11·5	3·4	17·5	5·1
56	4 29·0	4 29·7	4 16·7	5·6	1·6	11·6	3·4	17·6	5·1
57	4 29·3	4 30·0	4 17·0	5·7	1·7	11·7	3·4	17·7	5·2
58	4 29·5	4 30·2	4 17·2	5·8	1·7	11·8	3·4	17·8	5·2
59	4 29·8	4 30·5	4 17·5	5·9	1·7	11·9	3·5	17·9	5·2
60	4 30·0	4 30·7	4 17·7	6·0	1·8	12·0	3·5	18·0	5·3

18	SUN PLANETS	ARIES	MOON	v or Corrⁿ d		v or Corrⁿ d		v or Corrⁿ d		19	SUN PLANETS	ARIES	MOON	v or Corrⁿ d		v or Corrⁿ d		v or Corrⁿ d	
s	° ′	° ′	° ′	′ ′		′ ′		′ ′		s	° ′	° ′	° ′	′ ′		′ ′		′ ′	
00	4 30·0	4 30·7	4 17·7	0·0	0·0	6·0	1·9	12·0	3·7	00	4 45·0	4 45·8	4 32·0	0·0	0·0	6·0	2·0	12·0	3·9
01	4 30·3	4 31·0	4 17·9	0·1	0·0	6·1	1·9	12·1	3·7	01	4 45·3	4 46·0	4 32·3	0·1	0·0	6·1	2·0	12·1	3·9
02	4 30·5	4 31·2	4 18·2	0·2	0·1	6·2	1·9	12·2	3·8	02	4 45·5	4 46·3	4 32·5	0·2	0·1	6·2	2·0	12·2	4·0
03	4 30·8	4 31·5	4 18·4	0·3	0·1	6·3	1·9	12·3	3·8	03	4 45·8	4 46·5	4 32·7	0·3	0·1	6·3	2·0	12·3	4·0
04	4 31·0	4 31·7	4 18·7	0·4	0·1	6·4	2·0	12·4	3·8	04	4 46·0	4 46·8	4 33·0	0·4	0·1	6·4	2·1	12·4	4·0
05	4 31·3	4 32·0	4 18·9	0·5	0·2	6·5	2·0	12·5	3·9	05	4 46·3	4 47·0	4 33·2	0·5	0·2	6·5	2·1	12·5	4·1
06	4 31·5	4 32·2	4 19·1	0·6	0·2	6·6	2·0	12·6	3·9	06	4 46·5	4 47·3	4 33·4	0·6	0·2	6·6	2·1	12·6	4·1
07	4 31·8	4 32·5	4 19·4	0·7	0·2	6·7	2·1	12·7	3·9	07	4 46·8	4 47·5	4 33·7	0·7	0·2	6·7	2·2	12·7	4·1
08	4 32·0	4 32·7	4 19·6	0·8	0·2	6·8	2·1	12·8	3·9	08	4 47·0	4 47·8	4 33·9	0·8	0·3	6·8	2·2	12·8	4·2
09	4 32·3	4 33·0	4 19·8	0·9	0·3	6·9	2·1	12·9	4·0	09	4 47·3	4 48·0	4 34·2	0·9	0·3	6·9	2·2	12·9	4·2
10	4 32·5	4 33·2	4 20·1	1·0	0·3	7·0	2·2	13·0	4·0	10	4 47·5	4 48·3	4 34·4	1·0	0·3	7·0	2·3	13·0	4·2
11	4 32·8	4 33·5	4 20·3	1·1	0·3	7·1	2·2	13·1	4·0	11	4 47·8	4 48·5	4 34·6	1·1	0·4	7·1	2·3	13·1	4·3
12	4 33·0	4 33·7	4 20·6	1·2	0·4	7·2	2·2	13·2	4·1	12	4 48·0	4 48·8	4 34·9	1·2	0·4	7·2	2·3	13·2	4·3
13	4 33·3	4 34·0	4 20·8	1·3	0·4	7·3	2·3	13·3	4·1	13	4 48·3	4 49·0	4 35·1	1·3	0·4	7·3	2·4	13·3	4·3
14	4 33·5	4 34·2	4 21·0	1·4	0·4	7·4	2·3	13·4	4·1	14	4 48·5	4 49·3	4 35·4	1·4	0·5	7·4	2·4	13·4	4·4
15	4 33·8	4 34·5	4 21·3	1·5	0·5	7·5	2·3	13·5	4·2	15	4 48·8	4 49·5	4 35·6	1·5	0·5	7·5	2·4	13·5	4·4
16	4 34·0	4 34·8	4 21·5	1·6	0·5	7·6	2·3	13·6	4·2	16	4 49·0	4 49·8	4 35·8	1·6	0·5	7·6	2·5	13·6	4·4
17	4 34·3	4 35·0	4 21·8	1·7	0·5	7·7	2·4	13·7	4·2	17	4 49·3	4 50·0	4 36·1	1·7	0·6	7·7	2·5	13·7	4·5
18	4 34·5	4 35·3	4 22·0	1·8	0·6	7·8	2·4	13·8	4·3	18	4 49·5	4 50·3	4 36·3	1·8	0·6	7·8	2·5	13·8	4·5
19	4 34·8	4 35·5	4 22·2	1·9	0·6	7·9	2·4	13·9	4·3	19	4 49·8	4 50·5	4 36·6	1·9	0·6	7·9	2·6	13·9	4·5
20	4 35·0	4 35·8	4 22·5	2·0	0·6	8·0	2·5	14·0	4·3	20	4 50·0	4 50·8	4 36·8	2·0	0·7	8·0	2·6	14·0	4·6
21	4 35·3	4 36·0	4 22·7	2·1	0·6	8·1	2·5	14·1	4·3	21	4 50·3	4 51·0	4 37·0	2·1	0·7	8·1	2·6	14·1	4·6
22	4 35·5	4 36·3	4 22·9	2·2	0·7	8·2	2·5	14·2	4·4	22	4 50·5	4 51·3	4 37·3	2·2	0·7	8·2	2·7	14·2	4·6
23	4 35·8	4 36·5	4 23·2	2·3	0·7	8·3	2·6	14·3	4·4	23	4 50·8	4 51·5	4 37·5	2·3	0·7	8·3	2·7	14·3	4·6
24	4 36·0	4 36·8	4 23·4	2·4	0·7	8·4	2·6	14·4	4·4	24	4 51·0	4 51·8	4 37·7	2·4	0·8	8·4	2·7	14·4	4·7
25	4 36·3	4 37·0	4 23·7	2·5	0·8	8·5	2·6	14·5	4·5	25	4 51·3	4 52·0	4 38·0	2·5	0·8	8·5	2·8	14·5	4·7
26	4 36·5	4 37·3	4 23·9	2·6	0·8	8·6	2·7	14·6	4·5	26	4 51·5	4 52·3	4 38·2	2·6	0·8	8·6	2·8	14·6	4·7
27	4 36·8	4 37·5	4 24·1	2·7	0·8	8·7	2·7	14·7	4·5	27	4 51·8	4 52·5	4 38·5	2·7	0·9	8·7	2·8	14·7	4·8
28	4 37·0	4 37·8	4 24·4	2·8	0·9	8·8	2·7	14·8	4·6	28	4 52·0	4 52·8	4 38·7	2·8	0·9	8·8	2·9	14·8	4·8
29	4 37·3	4 38·0	4 24·6	2·9	0·9	8·9	2·7	14·9	4·6	29	4 52·3	4 53·1	4 38·9	2·9	0·9	8·9	2·9	14·9	4·8
30	4 37·5	4 38·3	4 24·9	3·0	0·9	9·0	2·8	15·0	4·6	30	4 52·5	4 53·3	4 39·2	3·0	1·0	9·0	2·9	15·0	4·9
31	4 37·8	4 38·5	4 25·1	3·1	1·0	9·1	2·8	15·1	4·7	31	4 52·8	4 53·6	4 39·4	3·1	1·0	9·1	3·0	15·1	4·9
32	4 38·0	4 38·8	4 25·3	3·2	1·0	9·2	2·8	15·2	4·7	32	4 53·0	4 53·8	4 39·7	3·2	1·0	9·2	3·0	15·2	4·9
33	4 38·3	4 39·0	4 25·6	3·3	1·0	9·3	2·9	15·3	4·7	33	4 53·3	4 54·1	4 39·9	3·3	1·1	9·3	3·0	15·3	5·0
34	4 38·5	4 39·3	4 25·8	3·4	1·0	9·4	2·9	15·4	4·7	34	4 53·5	4 54·3	4 40·1	3·4	1·1	9·4	3·1	15·4	5·0
35	4 38·8	4 39·5	4 26·1	3·5	1·1	9·5	2·9	15·5	4·8	35	4 53·8	4 54·6	4 40·4	3·5	1·1	9·5	3·1	15·5	5·0
36	4 39·0	4 39·8	4 26·3	3·6	1·1	9·6	3·0	15·6	4·8	36	4 54·0	4 54·8	4 40·6	3·6	1·2	9·6	3·1	15·6	5·1
37	4 39·3	4 40·0	4 26·5	3·7	1·1	9·7	3·0	15·7	4·8	37	4 54·3	4 55·1	4 40·8	3·7	1·2	9·7	3·2	15·7	5·1
38	4 39·5	4 40·3	4 26·8	3·8	1·2	9·8	3·0	15·8	4·9	38	4 54·5	4 55·3	4 41·1	3·8	1·2	9·8	3·2	15·8	5·1
39	4 39·8	4 40·5	4 27·0	3·9	1·2	9·9	3·1	15·9	4·9	39	4 54·8	4 55·6	4 41·3	3·9	1·3	9·9	3·2	15·9	5·2
40	4 40·0	4 40·8	4 27·2	4·0	1·2	10·0	3·1	16·0	4·9	40	4 55·0	4 55·8	4 41·6	4·0	1·3	10·0	3·3	16·0	5·2
41	4 40·3	4 41·0	4 27·5	4·1	1·3	10·1	3·1	16·1	5·0	41	4 55·3	4 56·1	4 41·8	4·1	1·3	10·1	3·3	16·1	5·2
42	4 40·5	4 41·3	4 27·7	4·2	1·3	10·2	3·1	16·2	5·0	42	4 55·5	4 56·3	4 42·0	4·2	1·4	10·2	3·3	16·2	5·3
43	4 40·8	4 41·5	4 28·0	4·3	1·3	10·3	3·2	16·3	5·0	43	4 55·8	4 56·6	4 42·3	4·3	1·4	10·3	3·3	16·3	5·3
44	4 41·0	4 41·8	4 28·2	4·4	1·4	10·4	3·2	16·4	5·1	44	4 56·0	4 56·8	4 42·5	4·4	1·4	10·4	3·4	16·4	5·3
45	4 41·3	4 42·0	4 28·4	4·5	1·4	10·5	3·2	16·5	5·1	45	4 56·3	4 57·1	4 42·8	4·5	1·5	10·5	3·4	16·5	5·4
46	4 41·5	4 42·3	4 28·7	4·6	1·4	10·6	3·3	16·6	5·1	46	4 56·5	4 57·3	4 43·0	4·6	1·5	10·6	3·4	16·6	5·4
47	4 41·8	4 42·5	4 28·9	4·7	1·4	10·7	3·3	16·7	5·1	47	4 56·8	4 57·6	4 43·2	4·7	1·5	10·7	3·5	16·7	5·4
48	4 42·0	4 42·8	4 29·2	4·8	1·5	10·8	3·3	16·8	5·2	48	4 57·0	4 57·8	4 43·5	4·8	1·6	10·8	3·5	16·8	5·5
49	4 42·3	4 43·0	4 29·4	4·9	1·5	10·9	3·4	16·9	5·2	49	4 57·3	4 58·1	4 43·7	4·9	1·6	10·9	3·5	16·9	5·5
50	4 42·5	4 43·3	4 29·6	5·0	1·5	11·0	3·4	17·0	5·2	50	4 57·5	4 58·3	4 43·9	5·0	1·6	11·0	3·6	17·0	5·5
51	4 42·8	4 43·5	4 29·9	5·1	1·6	11·1	3·4	17·1	5·3	51	4 57·8	4 58·6	4 44·2	5·1	1·7	11·1	3·6	17·1	5·6
52	4 43·0	4 43·8	4 30·1	5·2	1·6	11·2	3·5	17·2	5·3	52	4 58·0	4 58·8	4 44·4	5·2	1·7	11·2	3·6	17·2	5·6
53	4 43·3	4 44·0	4 30·3	5·3	1·6	11·3	3·5	17·3	5·3	53	4 58·3	4 59·1	4 44·7	5·3	1·7	11·3	3·7	17·3	5·6
54	4 43·5	4 44·3	4 30·6	5·4	1·7	11·4	3·5	17·4	5·4	54	4 58·5	4 59·3	4 44·9	5·4	1·8	11·4	3·7	17·4	5·7
55	4 43·8	4 44·5	4 30·8	5·5	1·7	11·5	3·5	17·5	5·4	55	4 58·8	4 59·6	4 45·1	5·5	1·8	11·5	3·7	17·5	5·7
56	4 44·0	4 44·8	4 31·1	5·6	1·7	11·6	3·6	17·6	5·4	56	4 59·0	4 59·8	4 45·4	5·6	1·8	11·6	3·8	17·6	5·7
57	4 44·3	4 45·0	4 31·3	5·7	1·8	11·7	3·6	17·7	5·5	57	4 59·3	5 00·1	4 45·6	5·7	1·9	11·7	3·8	17·7	5·8
58	4 44·5	4 45·3	4 31·5	5·8	1·8	11·8	3·6	17·8	5·5	58	4 59·5	5 00·3	4 45·9	5·8	1·9	11·8	3·8	17·8	5·8
59	4 44·8	4 45·5	4 31·8	5·9	1·8	11·9	3·7	17·9	5·5	59	4 59·8	5 00·6	4 46·1	5·9	1·9	11·9	3·9	17·9	5·8
60	4 45·0	4 45·8	4 32·0	6·0	1·9	12·0	3·7	18·0	5·6	60	5 00·0	5 00·8	4 46·3	6·0	2·0	12·0	3·9	18·0	5·9

20ᵐ s	SUN PLANETS	ARIES	MOON	v or d Corrⁿ	v or d Corrⁿ	v or d Corrⁿ
00	5 00·0	5 00·8	4 46·3	0·0 0·0	6·0 2·1	12·0 4·1
01	5 00·3	5 01·1	4 46·6	0·1 0·0	6·1 2·1	12·1 4·1
02	5 00·5	5 01·3	4 46·8	0·2 0·1	6·2 2·1	12·2 4·2
03	5 00·8	5 01·6	4 47·0	0·3 0·1	6·3 2·2	12·3 4·2
04	5 01·0	5 01·8	4 47·3	0·4 0·1	6·4 2·2	12·4 4·2
05	5 01·3	5 02·1	4 47·5	0·5 0·2	6·5 2·2	12·5 4·3
06	5 01·5	5 02·3	4 47·8	0·6 0·2	6·6 2·3	12·6 4·3
07	5 01·8	5 02·6	4 48·0	0·7 0·2	6·7 2·3	12·7 4·3
08	5 02·0	5 02·8	4 48·2	0·8 0·3	6·8 2·3	12·8 4·4
09	5 02·3	5 03·1	4 48·5	0·9 0·3	6·9 2·4	12·9 4·4
10	5 02·5	5 03·3	4 48·7	1·0 0·3	7·0 2·4	13·0 4·4
11	5 02·8	5 03·6	4 49·0	1·1 0·4	7·1 2·4	13·1 4·5
12	5 03·0	5 03·8	4 49·2	1·2 0·4	7·2 2·5	13·2 4·5
13	5 03·3	5 04·1	4 49·4	1·3 0·4	7·3 2·5	13·3 4·5
14	5 03·5	5 04·3	4 49·7	1·4 0·5	7·4 2·5	13·4 4·6
15	5 03·8	5 04·6	4 49·9	1·5 0·5	7·5 2·6	13·5 4·6
16	5 04·0	5 04·8	4 50·2	1·6 0·5	7·6 2·6	13·6 4·6
17	5 04·3	5 05·1	4 50·4	1·7 0·6	7·7 2·6	13·7 4·7
18	5 04·5	5 05·3	4 50·6	1·8 0·6	7·8 2·7	13·8 4·7
19	5 04·8	5 05·6	4 50·9	1·9 0·6	7·9 2·7	13·9 4·7
20	5 05·0	5 05·8	4 51·1	2·0 0·7	8·0 2·7	14·0 4·8
21	5 05·3	5 06·1	4 51·3	2·1 0·7	8·1 2·8	14·1 4·8
22	5 05·5	5 06·3	4 51·6	2·2 0·8	8·2 2·8	14·2 4·9
23	5 05·8	5 06·6	4 51·8	2·3 0·8	8·3 2·8	14·3 4·9
24	5 06·0	5 06·8	4 52·1	2·4 0·8	8·4 2·9	14·4 4·9
25	5 06·3	5 07·1	4 52·3	2·5 0·9	8·5 2·9	14·5 5·0
26	5 06·5	5 07·3	4 52·5	2·6 0·9	8·6 2·9	14·6 5·0
27	5 06·8	5 07·6	4 52·8	2·7 0·9	8·7 3·0	14·7 5·0
28	5 07·0	5 07·8	4 53·0	2·8 1·0	8·8 3·0	14·8 5·1
29	5 07·3	5 08·1	4 53·3	2·9 1·0	8·9 3·0	14·9 5·1
30	5 07·5	5 08·3	4 53·5	3·0 1·0	9·0 3·1	15·0 5·1
31	5 07·8	5 08·6	4 53·7	3·1 1·1	9·1 3·1	15·1 5·2
32	5 08·0	5 08·8	4 54·0	3·2 1·1	9·2 3·1	15·2 5·2
33	5 08·3	5 09·1	4 54·2	3·3 1·1	9·3 3·2	15·3 5·2
34	5 08·5	5 09·3	4 54·4	3·4 1·2	9·4 3·2	15·4 5·3
35	5 08·8	5 09·6	4 54·7	3·5 1·2	9·5 3·2	15·5 5·3
36	5 09·0	5 09·8	4 54·9	3·6 1·2	9·6 3·3	15·6 5·3
37	5 09·3	5 10·1	4 55·2	3·7 1·3	9·7 3·3	15·7 5·4
38	5 09·5	5 10·3	4 55·4	3·8 1·3	9·8 3·3	15·8 5·4
39	5 09·8	5 10·6	4 55·6	3·9 1·3	9·9 3·4	15·9 5·4
40	5 10·0	5 10·8	4 55·9	4·0 1·4	10·0 3·4	16·0 5·5
41	5 10·3	5 11·1	4 56·1	4·1 1·4	10·1 3·5	16·1 5·5
42	5 10·5	5 11·4	4 56·4	4·2 1·4	10·2 3·5	16·2 5·5
43	5 10·8	5 11·6	4 56·6	4·3 1·5	10·3 3·5	16·3 5·6
44	5 11·0	5 11·9	4 56·8	4·4 1·5	10·4 3·6	16·4 5·6
45	5 11·3	5 12·1	4 57·1	4·5 1·5	10·5 3·6	16·5 5·6
46	5 11·5	5 12·4	4 57·3	4·6 1·6	10·6 3·6	16·6 5·7
47	5 11·8	5 12·6	4 57·5	4·7 1·6	10·7 3·7	16·7 5·7
48	5 12·0	5 12·9	4 57·8	4·8 1·6	10·8 3·7	16·8 5·7
49	5 12·3	5 13·1	4 58·0	4·9 1·7	10·9 3·7	16·9 5·8
50	5 12·5	5 13·4	4 58·3	5·0 1·7	11·0 3·8	17·0 5·8
51	5 12·8	5 13·6	4 58·5	5·1 1·7	11·1 3·8	17·1 5·8
52	5 13·0	5 13·9	4 58·7	5·2 1·8	11·2 3·8	17·2 5·9
53	5 13·3	5 14·1	4 59·0	5·3 1·8	11·3 3·9	17·3 5·9
54	5 13·5	5 14·4	4 59·2	5·4 1·8	11·4 3·9	17·4 5·9
55	5 13·8	5 14·6	4 59·5	5·5 1·9	11·5 3·9	17·5 6·0
56	5 14·0	5 14·9	4 59·7	5·6 1·9	11·6 4·0	17·6 6·0
57	5 14·3	5 15·1	4 59·9	5·7 1·9	11·7 4·0	17·7 6·0
58	5 14·5	5 15·4	5 00·2	5·8 2·0	11·8 4·0	17·8 6·1
59	5 14·8	5 15·6	5 00·4	5·9 2·0	11·9 4·1	17·9 6·1
60	5 15·0	5 15·9	5 00·7	6·0 2·1	12·0 4·1	18·0 6·2

21ᵐ s	SUN PLANETS	ARIES	MOON	v or d Corrⁿ	v or d Corrⁿ	v or d Corrⁿ
00	5 15·0	5 15·9	5 00·7	0·0 0·0	6·0 2·2	12·0 4·3
01	5 15·3	5 16·1	5 00·9	0·1 0·0	6·1 2·2	12·1 4·3
02	5 15·5	5 16·4	5 01·1	0·2 0·1	6·2 2·2	12·2 4·4
03	5 15·8	5 16·6	5 01·4	0·3 0·1	6·3 2·3	12·3 4·4
04	5 16·0	5 16·9	5 01·6	0·4 0·1	6·4 2·3	12·4 4·4
05	5 16·3	5 17·1	5 01·8	0·5 0·2	6·5 2·3	12·5 4·5
06	5 16·5	5 17·4	5 02·1	0·6 0·2	6·6 2·4	12·6 4·5
07	5 16·8	5 17·6	5 02·3	0·7 0·3	6·7 2·4	12·7 4·6
08	5 17·0	5 17·9	5 02·6	0·8 0·3	6·8 2·4	12·8 4·6
09	5 17·3	5 18·1	5 02·8	0·9 0·3	6·9 2·5	12·9 4·6
10	5 17·5	5 18·4	5 03·0	1·0 0·4	7·0 2·5	13·0 4·7
11	5 17·8	5 18·6	5 03·3	1·1 0·4	7·1 2·5	13·1 4·7
12	5 18·0	5 18·9	5 03·5	1·2 0·4	7·2 2·6	13·2 4·7
13	5 18·3	5 19·1	5 03·8	1·3 0·5	7·3 2·6	13·3 4·8
14	5 18·5	5 19·4	5 04·0	1·4 0·5	7·4 2·7	13·4 4·8
15	5 18·8	5 19·6	5 04·2	1·5 0·5	7·5 2·7	13·5 4·8
16	5 19·0	5 19·9	5 04·5	1·6 0·6	7·6 2·7	13·6 4·9
17	5 19·3	5 20·1	5 04·7	1·7 0·6	7·7 2·8	13·7 4·9
18	5 19·5	5 20·4	5 04·9	1·8 0·6	7·8 2·8	13·8 4·9
19	5 19·8	5 20·6	5 05·2	1·9 0·7	7·9 2·8	13·9 5·0
20	5 20·0	5 20·9	5 05·4	2·0 0·7	8·0 2·9	14·0 5·0
21	5 20·3	5 21·1	5 05·7	2·1 0·8	8·1 2·9	14·1 5·1
22	5 20·5	5 21·4	5 05·9	2·2 0·8	8·2 2·9	14·2 5·1
23	5 20·8	5 21·6	5 06·1	2·3 0·8	8·3 3·0	14·3 5·1
24	5 21·0	5 21·9	5 06·4	2·4 0·9	8·4 3·0	14·4 5·2
25	5 21·3	5 22·1	5 06·6	2·5 0·9	8·5 3·0	14·5 5·2
26	5 21·5	5 22·4	5 06·9	2·6 0·9	8·6 3·1	14·6 5·2
27	5 21·8	5 22·6	5 07·1	2·7 1·0	8·7 3·1	14·7 5·3
28	5 22·0	5 22·9	5 07·3	2·8 1·0	8·8 3·2	14·8 5·3
29	5 22·3	5 23·1	5 07·6	2·9 1·0	8·9 3·2	14·9 5·3
30	5 22·5	5 23·4	5 07·8	3·0 1·1	9·0 3·2	15·0 5·4
31	5 22·8	5 23·6	5 08·0	3·1 1·1	9·1 3·3	15·1 5·4
32	5 23·0	5 23·9	5 08·3	3·2 1·1	9·2 3·3	15·2 5·4
33	5 23·3	5 24·1	5 08·5	3·3 1·2	9·3 3·3	15·3 5·5
34	5 23·5	5 24·4	5 08·8	3·4 1·2	9·4 3·4	15·4 5·5
35	5 23·8	5 24·6	5 09·0	3·5 1·3	9·5 3·4	15·5 5·6
36	5 24·0	5 24·9	5 09·2	3·6 1·3	9·6 3·4	15·6 5·6
37	5 24·3	5 25·1	5 09·5	3·7 1·3	9·7 3·5	15·7 5·6
38	5 24·5	5 25·4	5 09·7	3·8 1·4	9·8 3·5	15·8 5·7
39	5 24·8	5 25·6	5 10·0	3·9 1·4	9·9 3·5	15·9 5·7
40	5 25·0	5 25·9	5 10·2	4·0 1·4	10·0 3·6	16·0 5·7
41	5 25·3	5 26·1	5 10·4	4·1 1·5	10·1 3·6	16·1 5·8
42	5 25·5	5 26·4	5 10·7	4·2 1·5	10·2 3·7	16·2 5·8
43	5 25·8	5 26·6	5 10·9	4·3 1·5	10·3 3·7	16·3 5·8
44	5 26·0	5 26·9	5 11·1	4·4 1·6	10·4 3·7	16·4 5·9
45	5 26·3	5 27·1	5 11·4	4·5 1·6	10·5 3·8	16·5 5·9
46	5 26·5	5 27·4	5 11·6	4·6 1·6	10·6 3·8	16·6 5·9
47	5 26·8	5 27·6	5 11·9	4·7 1·7	10·7 3·8	16·7 6·0
48	5 27·0	5 27·9	5 12·1	4·8 1·7	10·8 3·9	16·8 6·0
49	5 27·3	5 28·1	5 12·3	4·9 1·8	10·9 3·9	16·9 6·1
50	5 27·5	5 28·4	5 12·6	5·0 1·8	11·0 3·9	17·0 6·1
51	5 27·8	5 28·6	5 12·8	5·1 1·8	11·1 4·0	17·1 6·1
52	5 28·0	5 28·9	5 13·1	5·2 1·9	11·2 4·0	17·2 6·2
53	5 28·3	5 29·1	5 13·3	5·3 1·9	11·3 4·0	17·3 6·2
54	5 28·5	5 29·4	5 13·5	5·4 1·9	11·4 4·1	17·4 6·2
55	5 28·8	5 29·7	5 13·8	5·5 2·0	11·5 4·1	17·5 6·3
56	5 29·0	5 29·9	5 14·0	5·6 2·0	11·6 4·2	17·6 6·3
57	5 29·3	5 30·2	5 14·3	5·7 2·0	11·7 4·2	17·7 6·3
58	5 29·5	5 30·4	5 14·5	5·8 2·1	11·8 4·2	17·8 6·4
59	5 29·8	5 30·7	5 14·7	5·9 2·1	11·9 4·3	17·9 6·4
60	5 30·0	5 30·9	5 15·0	6·0 2·2	12·0 4·3	18·0 6·5

22ᵐ

22 ᵐ s	SUN PLANETS	ARIES	MOON	v or Corrⁿ d	v or Corrⁿ d	v or Corrⁿ d
00	5 30·0	5 30·9	5 15·0	0·0 0·0	6·0 2·3	12·0 4·5
01	5 30·3	5 31·2	5 15·2	0·1 0·0	6·1 2·3	12·1 4·5
02	5 30·5	5 31·4	5 15·4	0·2 0·1	6·2 2·3	12·2 4·6
03	5 30·8	5 31·7	5 15·7	0·3 0·1	6·3 2·4	12·3 4·6
04	5 31·0	5 31·9	5 15·9	0·4 0·2	6·4 2·4	12·4 4·7
05	5 31·3	5 32·2	5 16·2	0·5 0·2	6·5 2·4	12·5 4·7
06	5 31·5	5 32·4	5 16·4	0·6 0·2	6·6 2·5	12·6 4·7
07	5 31·8	5 32·7	5 16·6	0·7 0·3	6·7 2·5	12·7 4·8
08	5 32·0	5 32·9	5 16·9	0·8 0·3	6·8 2·6	12·8 4·8
09	5 32·3	5 33·2	5 17·1	0·9 0·3	6·9 2·6	12·9 4·8
10	5 32·5	5 33·4	5 17·4	1·0 0·4	7·0 2·6	13·0 4·9
11	5 32·8	5 33·7	5 17·6	1·1 0·4	7·1 2·7	13·1 4·9
12	5 33·0	5 33·9	5 17·8	1·2 0·5	7·2 2·7	13·2 5·0
13	5 33·3	5 34·2	5 18·1	1·3 0·5	7·3 2·7	13·3 5·0
14	5 33·5	5 34·4	5 18·3	1·4 0·5	7·4 2·8	13·4 5·0
15	5 33·8	5 34·7	5 18·5	1·5 0·6	7·5 2·8	13·5 5·1
16	5 34·0	5 34·9	5 18·8	1·6 0·6	7·6 2·9	13·6 5·1
17	5 34·3	5 35·2	5 19·0	1·7 0·6	7·7 2·9	13·7 5·1
18	5 34·5	5 35·4	5 19·3	1·8 0·7	7·8 2·9	13·8 5·2
19	5 34·8	5 35·7	5 19·5	1·9 0·7	7·9 3·0	13·9 5·2
20	5 35·0	5 35·9	5 19·7	2·0 0·8	8·0 3·0	14·0 5·3
21	5 35·3	5 36·2	5 20·0	2·1 0·8	8·1 3·0	14·1 5·3
22	5 35·5	5 36·4	5 20·2	2·2 0·8	8·2 3·1	14·2 5·3
23	5 35·8	5 36·7	5 20·5	2·3 0·9	8·3 3·1	14·3 5·4
24	5 36·0	5 36·9	5 20·7	2·4 0·9	8·4 3·2	14·4 5·4
25	5 36·3	5 37·2	5 20·9	2·5 0·9	8·5 3·2	14·5 5·4
26	5 36·5	5 37·4	5 21·2	2·6 1·0	8·6 3·2	14·6 5·5
27	5 36·8	5 37·7	5 21·4	2·7 1·0	8·7 3·3	14·7 5·5
28	5 37·0	5 37·9	5 21·6	2·8 1·1	8·8 3·3	14·8 5·6
29	5 37·3	5 38·2	5 21·9	2·9 1·1	8·9 3·3	14·9 5·6
30	5 37·5	5 38·4	5 22·1	3·0 1·1	9·0 3·4	15·0 5·6
31	5 37·8	5 38·7	5 22·4	3·1 1·2	9·1 3·4	15·1 5·7
32	5 38·0	5 38·9	5 22·6	3·2 1·2	9·2 3·5	15·2 5·7
33	5 38·3	5 39·2	5 22·8	3·3 1·2	9·3 3·5	15·3 5·7
34	5 38·5	5 39·4	5 23·1	3·4 1·3	9·4 3·5	15·4 5·8
35	5 38·8	5 39·7	5 23·3	3·5 1·3	9·5 3·6	15·5 5·8
36	5 39·0	5 39·9	5 23·6	3·6 1·4	9·6 3·6	15·6 5·9
37	5 39·3	5 40·2	5 23·8	3·7 1·4	9·7 3·6	15·7 5·9
38	5 39·5	5 40·4	5 24·0	3·8 1·4	9·8 3·7	15·8 5·9
39	5 39·8	5 40·7	5 24·3	3·9 1·5	9·9 3·7	15·9 6·0
40	5 40·0	5 40·9	5 24·5	4·0 1·5	10·0 3·8	16·0 6·0
41	5 40·3	5 41·2	5 24·7	4·1 1·5	10·1 3·8	16·1 6·0
42	5 40·5	5 41·4	5 25·0	4·2 1·6	10·2 3·8	16·2 6·1
43	5 40·8	5 41·7	5 25·2	4·3 1·6	10·3 3·9	16·3 6·1
44	5 41·0	5 41·9	5 25·5	4·4 1·7	10·4 3·9	16·4 6·2
45	5 41·3	5 42·2	5 25·7	4·5 1·7	10·5 3·9	16·5 6·2
46	5 41·5	5 42·4	5 25·9	4·6 1·7	10·6 4·0	16·6 6·2
47	5 41·8	5 42·7	5 26·2	4·7 1·8	10·7 4·0	16·7 6·3
48	5 42·0	5 42·9	5 26·4	4·8 1·8	10·8 4·1	16·8 6·3
49	5 42·3	5 43·2	5 26·7	4·9 1·8	10·9 4·1	16·9 6·3
50	5 42·5	5 43·4	5 26·9	5·0 1·9	11·0 4·1	17·0 6·4
51	5 42·8	5 43·7	5 27·1	5·1 1·9	11·1 4·2	17·1 6·4
52	5 43·0	5 43·9	5 27·4	5·2 2·0	11·2 4·2	17·2 6·5
53	5 43·3	5 44·2	5 27·6	5·3 2·0	11·3 4·2	17·3 6·5
54	5 43·5	5 44·4	5 27·9	5·4 2·0	11·4 4·3	17·4 6·5
55	5 43·8	5 44·7	5 28·1	5·5 2·1	11·5 4·3	17·5 6·6
56	5 44·0	5 44·9	5 28·3	5·6 2·1	11·6 4·4	17·6 6·6
57	5 44·3	5 45·2	5 28·6	5·7 2·1	11·7 4·4	17·7 6·6
58	5 44·5	5 45·4	5 28·8	5·8 2·2	11·8 4·4	17·8 6·7
59	5 44·8	5 45·7	5 29·0	5·9 2·2	11·9 4·5	17·9 6·7
60	5 45·0	5 45·9	5 29·3	6·0 2·3	12·0 4·5	18·0 6·8

23ᵐ

23 ᵐ s	SUN PLANETS	ARIES	MOON	v or Corrⁿ d	v or Corrⁿ d	v or Corrⁿ d
00	5 45·0	5 45·9	5 29·3	0·0 0·0	6·0 2·4	12·0 4·7
01	5 45·3	5 46·2	5 29·5	0·1 0·0	6·1 2·4	12·1 4·7
02	5 45·5	5 46·4	5 29·8	0·2 0·1	6·2 2·4	12·2 4·8
03	5 45·8	5 46·7	5 30·0	0·3 0·1	6·3 2·5	12·3 4·8
04	5 46·0	5 46·9	5 30·2	0·4 0·2	6·4 2·5	12·4 4·9
05	5 46·3	5 47·2	5 30·5	0·5 0·2	6·5 2·5	12·5 4·9
06	5 46·5	5 47·4	5 30·7	0·6 0·2	6·6 2·6	12·6 4·9
07	5 46·8	5 47·7	5 31·0	0·7 0·3	6·7 2·6	12·7 5·0
08	5 47·0	5 48·0	5 31·2	0·8 0·3	6·8 2·7	12·8 5·0
09	5 47·3	5 48·2	5 31·4	0·9 0·4	6·9 2·7	12·9 5·1
10	5 47·5	5 48·5	5 31·7	1·0 0·4	7·0 2·7	13·0 5·1
11	5 47·8	5 48·7	5 31·9	1·1 0·4	7·1 2·8	13·1 5·1
12	5 48·0	5 49·0	5 32·1	1·2 0·5	7·2 2·8	13·2 5·2
13	5 48·3	5 49·2	5 32·4	1·3 0·5	7·3 2·9	13·3 5·2
14	5 48·5	5 49·5	5 32·6	1·4 0·5	7·4 2·9	13·4 5·2
15	5 48·8	5 49·7	5 32·9	1·5 0·6	7·5 2·9	13·5 5·3
16	5 49·0	5 50·0	5 33·1	1·6 0·6	7·6 3·0	13·6 5·3
17	5 49·3	5 50·2	5 33·3	1·7 0·7	7·7 3·0	13·7 5·4
18	5 49·5	5 50·5	5 33·6	1·8 0·7	7·8 3·1	13·8 5·4
19	5 49·8	5 50·7	5 33·8	1·9 0·7	7·9 3·1	13·9 5·4
20	5 50·0	5 51·0	5 34·1	2·0 0·8	8·0 3·1	14·0 5·5
21	5 50·3	5 51·2	5 34·3	2·1 0·8	8·1 3·2	14·1 5·5
22	5 50·5	5 51·5	5 34·5	2·2 0·9	8·2 3·2	14·2 5·6
23	5 50·8	5 51·7	5 34·8	2·3 0·9	8·3 3·3	14·3 5·6
24	5 51·0	5 52·0	5 35·0	2·4 0·9	8·4 3·3	14·4 5·6
25	5 51·3	5 52·2	5 35·2	2·5 1·0	8·5 3·3	14·5 5·7
26	5 51·5	5 52·5	5 35·5	2·6 1·0	8·6 3·4	14·6 5·7
27	5 51·8	5 52·7	5 35·7	2·7 1·1	8·7 3·4	14·7 5·8
28	5 52·0	5 53·0	5 36·0	2·8 1·1	8·8 3·4	14·8 5·8
29	5 52·3	5 53·2	5 36·2	2·9 1·1	8·9 3·5	14·9 5·8
30	5 52·5	5 53·5	5 36·4	3·0 1·2	9·0 3·5	15·0 5·9
31	5 52·8	5 53·7	5 36·7	3·1 1·2	9·1 3·6	15·1 5·9
32	5 53·0	5 54·0	5 36·9	3·2 1·3	9·2 3·6	15·2 6·0
33	5 53·3	5 54·2	5 37·2	3·3 1·3	9·3 3·6	15·3 6·0
34	5 53·5	5 54·5	5 37·4	3·4 1·3	9·4 3·7	15·4 6·0
35	5 53·8	5 54·7	5 37·6	3·5 1·4	9·5 3·7	15·5 6·1
36	5 54·0	5 55·0	5 37·9	3·6 1·4	9·6 3·8	15·6 6·1
37	5 54·3	5 55·2	5 38·1	3·7 1·5	9·7 3·8	15·7 6·1
38	5 54·5	5 55·5	5 38·4	3·8 1·5	9·8 3·8	15·8 6·2
39	5 54·8	5 55·7	5 38·6	3·9 1·5	9·9 3·9	15·9 6·2
40	5 55·0	5 56·0	5 38·8	4·0 1·6	10·0 3·9	16·0 6·3
41	5 55·3	5 56·2	5 39·1	4·1 1·6	10·1 4·0	16·1 6·3
42	5 55·5	5 56·5	5 39·3	4·2 1·6	10·2 4·0	16·2 6·3
43	5 55·8	5 56·7	5 39·5	4·3 1·7	10·3 4·0	16·3 6·4
44	5 56·0	5 57·0	5 39·8	4·4 1·7	10·4 4·1	16·4 6·4
45	5 56·3	5 57·2	5 40·0	4·5 1·8	10·5 4·1	16·5 6·5
46	5 56·5	5 57·5	5 40·3	4·6 1·8	10·6 4·2	16·6 6·5
47	5 56·8	5 57·7	5 40·5	4·7 1·8	10·7 4·2	16·7 6·5
48	5 57·0	5 58·0	5 40·7	4·8 1·9	10·8 4·2	16·8 6·6
49	5 57·3	5 58·2	5 41·0	4·9 1·9	10·9 4·3	16·9 6·6
50	5 57·5	5 58·5	5 41·2	5·0 2·0	11·0 4·3	17·0 6·7
51	5 57·8	5 58·7	5 41·5	5·1 2·0	11·1 4·3	17·1 6·7
52	5 58·0	5 59·0	5 41·7	5·2 2·0	11·2 4·4	17·2 6·7
53	5 58·3	5 59·2	5 41·9	5·3 2·1	11·3 4·4	17·3 6·8
54	5 58·5	5 59·5	5 42·2	5·4 2·1	11·4 4·5	17·4 6·8
55	5 58·8	5 59·7	5 42·4	5·5 2·2	11·5 4·5	17·5 6·9
56	5 59·0	6 00·0	5 42·6	5·6 2·2	11·6 4·5	17·6 6·9
57	5 59·3	6 00·2	5 42·9	5·7 2·2	11·7 4·6	17·7 6·9
58	5 59·5	6 00·5	5 43·1	5·8 2·3	11·8 4·6	17·8 7·0
59	5 59·8	6 00·7	5 43·4	5·9 2·3	11·9 4·7	17·9 7·0
60	6 00·0	6 01·0	5 43·6	6·0 2·4	12·0 4·7	18·0 7·1

24ᵐ	SUN PLANETS	ARIES	MOON	v or Corrⁿ d		v or Corrⁿ d		v or Corrⁿ d		25ᵐ	SUN PLANETS	ARIES	MOON	v or Corrⁿ d		v or Corrⁿ d		v or Corrⁿ d	
s	° ′	° ′	° ′	′	′	′	′	′	′	s	° ′	° ′	° ′	′	′	′	′	′	′
00	6 00·0	6 01·0	5 43·6	0·0	0·0	6·0	2·5	12·0	4·9	00	6 15·0	6 16·0	5 57·9	0·0	0·0	6·0	2·6	12·0	5·1
01	6 00·3	6 01·2	5 43·8	0·1	0·0	6·1	2·5	12·1	4·9	01	6 15·3	6 16·3	5 58·2	0·1	0·0	6·1	2·6	12·1	5·1
02	6 00·5	6 01·5	5 44·1	0·2	0·1	6·2	2·5	12·2	5·0	02	6 15·5	6 16·5	5 58·4	0·2	0·1	6·2	2·6	12·2	5·2
03	6 00·8	6 01·7	5 44·3	0·3	0·1	6·3	2·6	12·3	5·0	03	6 15·8	6 16·8	5 58·6	0·3	0·1	6·3	2·7	12·3	5·2
04	6 01·0	6 02·0	5 44·6	0·4	0·2	6·4	2·6	12·4	5·1	04	6 16·0	6 17·0	5 58·9	0·4	0·2	6·4	2·7	12·4	5·3
05	6 01·3	6 02·2	5 44·8	0·5	0·2	6·5	2·7	12·5	5·1	05	6 16·3	6 17·3	5 59·1	0·5	0·2	6·5	2·8	12·5	5·3
06	6 01·5	6 02·5	5 45·0	0·6	0·2	6·6	2·7	12·6	5·1	06	6 16·5	6 17·5	5 59·3	0·6	0·3	6·6	2·8	12·6	5·4
07	6 01·8	6 02·7	5 45·3	0·7	0·3	6·7	2·7	12·7	5·2	07	6 16·8	6 17·8	5 59·6	0·7	0·3	6·7	2·8	12·7	5·4
08	6 02·0	6 03·0	5 45·5	0·8	0·3	6·8	2·8	12·8	5·2	08	6 17·0	6 18·0	5 59·8	0·8	0·3	6·8	2·9	12·8	5·4
09	6 02·3	6 03·2	5 45·7	0·9	0·4	6·9	2·8	12·9	5·3	09	6 17·3	6 18·3	6 00·1	0·9	0·4	6·9	2·9	12·9	5·5
10	6 02·5	6 03·5	5 46·0	1·0	0·4	7·0	2·9	13·0	5·3	10	6 17·5	6 18·5	6 00·3	1·0	0·4	7·0	3·0	13·0	5·5
11	6 02·8	6 03·7	5 46·2	1·1	0·4	7·1	2·9	13·1	5·3	11	6 17·8	6 18·8	6 00·5	1·1	0·5	7·1	3·0	13·1	5·6
12	6 03·0	6 04·0	5 46·5	1·2	0·5	7·2	2·9	13·2	5·4	12	6 18·0	6 19·0	6 00·8	1·2	0·5	7·2	3·1	13·2	5·6
13	6 03·3	6 04·2	5 46·7	1·3	0·5	7·3	3·0	13·3	5·4	13	6 18·3	6 19·3	6 01·0	1·3	0·6	7·3	3·1	13·3	5·7
14	6 03·5	6 04·5	5 46·9	1·4	0·6	7·4	3·0	13·4	5·5	14	6 18·5	6 19·5	6 01·3	1·4	0·6	7·4	3·1	13·4	5·7
15	6 03·8	6 04·7	5 47·2	1·5	0·6	7·5	3·1	13·5	5·5	15	6 18·8	6 19·8	6 01·5	1·5	0·6	7·5	3·2	13·5	5·7
16	6 04·0	6 05·0	5 47·4	1·6	0·7	7·6	3·1	13·6	5·6	16	6 19·0	6 20·0	6 01·7	1·6	0·7	7·6	3·2	13·6	5·8
17	6 04·3	6 05·2	5 47·7	1·7	0·7	7·7	3·1	13·7	5·6	17	6 19·3	6 20·3	6 02·0	1·7	0·7	7·7	3·3	13·7	5·8
18	6 04·5	6 05·5	5 47·9	1·8	0·7	7·8	3·2	13·8	5·6	18	6 19·5	6 20·5	6 02·2	1·8	0·8	7·8	3·3	13·8	5·9
19	6 04·8	6 05·7	5 48·1	1·9	0·8	7·9	3·2	13·9	5·7	19	6 19·8	6 20·8	6 02·5	1·9	0·8	7·9	3·4	13·9	5·9
20	6 05·0	6 06·0	5 48·4	2·0	0·8	8·0	3·3	14·0	5·7	20	6 20·0	6 21·0	6 02·7	2·0	0·9	8·0	3·4	14·0	6·0
21	6 05·3	6 06·3	5 48·6	2·1	0·9	8·1	3·3	14·1	5·8	21	6 20·3	6 21·3	6 02·9	2·1	0·9	8·1	3·4	14·1	6·0
22	6 05·5	6 06·5	5 48·8	2·2	0·9	8·2	3·3	14·2	5·8	22	6 20·5	6 21·5	6 03·2	2·2	0·9	8·2	3·5	14·2	6·0
23	6 05·8	6 06·8	5 49·1	2·3	0·9	8·3	3·4	14·3	5·8	23	6 20·8	6 21·8	6 03·4	2·3	1·0	8·3	3·5	14·3	6·1
24	6 06·0	6 07·0	5 49·3	2·4	1·0	8·4	3·4	14·4	5·9	24	6 21·0	6 22·0	6 03·6	2·4	1·0	8·4	3·6	14·4	6·1
25	6 06·3	6 07·3	5 49·6	2·5	1·0	8·5	3·5	14·5	5·9	25	6 21·3	6 22·3	6 03·9	2·5	1·1	8·5	3·6	14·5	6·2
26	6 06·5	6 07·5	5 49·8	2·6	1·1	8·6	3·5	14·6	6·0	26	6 21·5	6 22·5	6 04·1	2·6	1·1	8·6	3·7	14·6	6·2
27	6 06·8	6 07·8	5 50·0	2·7	1·1	8·7	3·6	14·7	6·0	27	6 21·8	6 22·8	6 04·4	2·7	1·1	8·7	3·7	14·7	6·2
28	6 07·0	6 08·0	5 50·3	2·8	1·1	8·8	3·6	14·8	6·0	28	6 22·0	6 23·0	6 04·6	2·8	1·2	8·8	3·7	14·8	6·3
29	6 07·3	6 08·3	5 50·5	2·9	1·2	8·9	3·6	14·9	6·1	29	6 22·3	6 23·3	6 04·8	2·9	1·2	8·9	3·8	14·9	6·3
30	6 07·5	6 08·5	5 50·8	3·0	1·2	9·0	3·7	15·0	6·1	30	6 22·5	6 23·5	6 05·1	3·0	1·3	9·0	3·8	15·0	6·4
31	6 07·8	6 08·8	5 51·0	3·1	1·3	9·1	3·7	15·1	6·2	31	6 22·8	6 23·8	6 05·3	3·1	1·3	9·1	3·9	15·1	6·4
32	6 08·0	6 09·0	5 51·2	3·2	1·3	9·2	3·8	15·2	6·2	32	6 23·0	6 24·0	6 05·6	3·2	1·4	9·2	3·9	15·2	6·5
33	6 08·3	6 09·3	5 51·5	3·3	1·3	9·3	3·8	15·3	6·2	33	6 23·3	6 24·3	6 05·8	3·3	1·4	9·3	4·0	15·3	6·5
34	6 08·5	6 09·5	5 51·7	3·4	1·4	9·4	3·8	15·4	6·3	34	6 23·5	6 24·5	6 06·0	3·4	1·4	9·4	4·0	15·4	6·5
35	6 08·8	6 09·8	5 52·0	3·5	1·4	9·5	3·9	15·5	6·3	35	6 23·8	6 24·8	6 06·3	3·5	1·5	9·5	4·0	15·5	6·6
36	6 09·0	6 10·0	5 52·2	3·6	1·5	9·6	3·9	15·6	6·4	36	6 24·0	6 25·1	6 06·5	3·6	1·5	9·6	4·1	15·6	6·6
37	6 09·3	6 10·3	5 52·4	3·7	1·5	9·7	4·0	15·7	6·4	37	6 24·3	6 25·3	6 06·7	3·7	1·6	9·7	4·1	15·7	6·7
38	6 09·5	6 10·5	5 52·7	3·8	1·6	9·8	4·0	15·8	6·5	38	6 24·5	6 25·6	6 07·0	3·8	1·6	9·8	4·2	15·8	6·7
39	6 09·8	6 10·8	5 52·9	3·9	1·6	9·9	4·0	15·9	6·5	39	6 24·8	6 25·8	6 07·2	3·9	1·7	9·9	4·2	15·9	6·8
40	6 10·0	6 11·0	5 53·1	4·0	1·6	10·0	4·1	16·0	6·5	40	6 25·0	6 26·1	6 07·5	4·0	1·7	10·0	4·3	16·0	6·8
41	6 10·3	6 11·3	5 53·4	4·1	1·7	10·1	4·1	16·1	6·6	41	6 25·3	6 26·3	6 07·7	4·1	1·7	10·1	4·3	16·1	6·8
42	6 10·5	6 11·5	5 53·6	4·2	1·7	10·2	4·2	16·2	6·6	42	6 25·5	6 26·6	6 07·9	4·2	1·8	10·2	4·3	16·2	6·9
43	6 10·8	6 11·8	5 53·9	4·3	1·8	10·3	4·2	16·3	6·7	43	6 25·8	6 26·8	6 08·2	4·3	1·8	10·3	4·4	16·3	6·9
44	6 11·0	6 12·0	5 54·1	4·4	1·8	10·4	4·2	16·4	6·7	44	6 26·0	6 27·1	6 08·4	4·4	1·9	10·4	4·4	16·4	7·0
45	6 11·3	6 12·3	5 54·3	4·5	1·8	10·5	4·3	16·5	6·7	45	6 26·3	6 27·3	6 08·7	4·5	1·9	10·5	4·5	16·5	7·0
46	6 11·5	6 12·5	5 54·6	4·6	1·9	10·6	4·3	16·6	6·8	46	6 26·5	6 27·6	6 08·9	4·6	2·0	10·6	4·5	16·6	7·1
47	6 11·8	6 12·8	5 54·8	4·7	1·9	10·7	4·4	16·7	6·8	47	6 26·8	6 27·8	6 09·1	4·7	2·0	10·7	4·5	16·7	7·1
48	6 12·0	6 13·0	5 55·1	4·8	2·0	10·8	4·4	16·8	6·9	48	6 27·0	6 28·1	6 09·4	4·8	2·0	10·8	4·6	16·8	7·1
49	6 12·3	6 13·3	5 55·3	4·9	2·0	10·9	4·5	16·9	6·9	49	6 27·3	6 28·3	6 09·6	4·9	2·1	10·9	4·6	16·9	7·2
50	6 12·5	6 13·5	5 55·5	5·0	2·0	11·0	4·5	17·0	6·9	50	6 27·5	6 28·6	6 09·8	5·0	2·1	11·0	4·7	17·0	7·2
51	6 12·8	6 13·8	5 55·8	5·1	2·1	11·1	4·5	17·1	7·0	51	6 27·8	6 28·8	6 10·1	5·1	2·2	11·1	4·7	17·1	7·3
52	6 13·0	6 14·0	5 56·0	5·2	2·1	11·2	4·6	17·2	7·0	52	6 28·0	6 29·1	6 10·3	5·2	2·2	11·2	4·8	17·2	7·3
53	6 13·3	6 14·3	5 56·2	5·3	2·2	11·3	4·6	17·3	7·1	53	6 28·3	6 29·3	6 10·6	5·3	2·3	11·3	4·8	17·3	7·4
54	6 13·5	6 14·5	5 56·5	5·4	2·2	11·4	4·7	17·4	7·1	54	6 28·5	6 29·6	6 10·8	5·4	2·3	11·4	4·8	17·4	7·4
55	6 13·8	6 14·8	5 56·7	5·5	2·2	11·5	4·7	17·5	7·1	55	6 28·8	6 29·8	6 11·0	5·5	2·3	11·5	4·9	17·5	7·5
56	6 14·0	6 15·0	5 57·0	5·6	2·3	11·6	4·7	17·6	7·2	56	6 29·0	6 30·1	6 11·3	5·6	2·4	11·6	4·9	17·6	7·5
57	6 14·3	6 15·3	5 57·2	5·7	2·3	11·7	4·8	17·7	7·2	57	6 29·3	6 30·3	6 11·5	5·7	2·4	11·7	5·0	17·7	7·5
58	6 14·5	6 15·5	5 57·4	5·8	2·4	11·8	4·8	17·8	7·3	58	6 29·5	6 30·6	6 11·8	5·8	2·5	11·8	5·0	17·8	7·6
59	6 14·8	6 15·8	5 57·7	5·9	2·4	11·9	4·9	17·9	7·3	59	6 29·8	6 30·8	6 12·0	5·9	2·5	11·9	5·1	17·9	7·6
60	6 15·0	6 16·0	5 57·9	6·0	2·5	12·0	4·9	18·0	7·4	60	6 30·0	6 31·1	6 12·2	6·0	2·6	12·0	5·1	18·0	7·7

26ᵐ

26ᵐ	SUN PLANETS	ARIES	MOON	v or Corrⁿ d	v or Corrⁿ d	v or Corrⁿ d
s	° ′	° ′	° ′	′ ′	′ ′	′ ′
00	6 30.0	6 31.1	6 12.2	0.0 0.0	6.0 2.7	12.0 5.3
01	6 30.3	6 31.3	6 12.5	0.1 0.0	6.1 2.7	12.1 5.3
02	6 30.5	6 31.6	6 12.7	0.2 0.1	6.2 2.7	12.2 5.4
03	6 30.8	6 31.8	6 12.9	0.3 0.1	6.3 2.8	12.3 5.4
04	6 31.0	6 32.1	6 13.2	0.4 0.2	6.4 2.8	12.4 5.5
05	6 31.3	6 32.3	6 13.4	0.5 0.2	6.5 2.9	12.5 5.5
06	6 31.5	6 32.6	6 13.7	0.6 0.3	6.6 2.9	12.6 5.6
07	6 31.8	6 32.8	6 13.9	0.7 0.3	6.7 3.0	12.7 5.6
08	6 32.0	6 33.1	6 14.1	0.8 0.4	6.8 3.0	12.8 5.7
09	6 32.3	6 33.3	6 14.4	0.9 0.4	6.9 3.0	12.9 5.7
10	6 32.5	6 33.6	6 14.6	1.0 0.4	7.0 3.1	13.0 5.7
11	6 32.8	6 33.8	6 14.8	1.1 0.5	7.1 3.1	13.1 5.8
12	6 33.0	6 34.1	6 15.1	1.2 0.5	7.2 3.2	13.2 5.8
13	6 33.3	6 34.3	6 15.3	1.3 0.6	7.3 3.2	13.3 5.9
14	6 33.5	6 34.6	6 15.6	1.4 0.6	7.4 3.3	13.4 5.9
15	6 33.8	6 34.8	6 15.8	1.5 0.7	7.5 3.3	13.5 6.0
16	6 34.0	6 35.1	6 16.1	1.6 0.7	7.6 3.4	13.6 6.0
17	6 34.3	6 35.3	6 16.3	1.7 0.8	7.7 3.4	13.7 6.1
18	6 34.5	6 35.6	6 16.5	1.8 0.8	7.8 3.4	13.8 6.1
19	6 34.8	6 35.8	6 16.8	1.9 0.8	7.9 3.5	13.9 6.1
20	6 35.0	6 36.1	6 17.0	2.0 0.9	8.0 3.5	14.0 6.2
21	6 35.3	6 36.3	6 17.2	2.1 0.9	8.1 3.6	14.1 6.2
22	6 35.5	6 36.6	6 17.5	2.2 1.0	8.2 3.6	14.2 6.3
23	6 35.8	6 36.8	6 17.7	2.3 1.0	8.3 3.7	14.3 6.3
24	6 36.0	6 37.1	6 18.0	2.4 1.1	8.4 3.7	14.4 6.4
25	6 36.3	6 37.3	6 18.2	2.5 1.1	8.5 3.8	14.5 6.4
26	6 36.5	6 37.6	6 18.4	2.6 1.1	8.6 3.8	14.6 6.4
27	6 36.8	6 37.8	6 18.7	2.7 1.2	8.7 3.8	14.7 6.5
28	6 37.0	6 38.1	6 18.9	2.8 1.2	8.8 3.9	14.8 6.5
29	6 37.3	6 38.3	6 19.2	2.9 1.3	8.9 3.9	14.9 6.6
30	6 37.5	6 38.6	6 19.4	3.0 1.3	9.0 4.0	15.0 6.6
31	6 37.8	6 38.8	6 19.6	3.1 1.4	9.1 4.0	15.1 6.7
32	6 38.0	6 39.1	6 19.9	3.2 1.4	9.2 4.1	15.2 6.7
33	6 38.3	6 39.3	6 20.1	3.3 1.5	9.3 4.1	15.3 6.8
34	6 38.5	6 39.6	6 20.3	3.4 1.5	9.4 4.2	15.4 6.8
35	6 38.8	6 39.8	6 20.6	3.5 1.5	9.5 4.2	15.5 6.8
36	6 39.0	6 40.1	6 20.8	3.6 1.6	9.6 4.2	15.6 6.9
37	6 39.3	6 40.3	6 21.1	3.7 1.6	9.7 4.3	15.7 6.9
38	6 39.5	6 40.6	6 21.3	3.8 1.7	9.8 4.3	15.8 7.0
39	6 39.8	6 40.8	6 21.5	3.9 1.7	9.9 4.4	15.9 7.0
40	6 40.0	6 41.1	6 21.8	4.0 1.8	10.0 4.4	16.0 7.1
41	6 40.3	6 41.3	6 22.0	4.1 1.8	10.1 4.5	16.1 7.1
42	6 40.5	6 41.6	6 22.3	4.2 1.9	10.2 4.5	16.2 7.2
43	6 40.8	6 41.8	6 22.5	4.3 1.9	10.3 4.5	16.3 7.2
44	6 41.0	6 42.1	6 22.7	4.4 1.9	10.4 4.6	16.4 7.2
45	6 41.3	6 42.3	6 23.0	4.5 2.0	10.5 4.6	16.5 7.3
46	6 41.5	6 42.6	6 23.2	4.6 2.0	10.6 4.7	16.6 7.3
47	6 41.8	6 42.8	6 23.4	4.7 2.1	10.7 4.7	16.7 7.4
48	6 42.0	6 43.1	6 23.7	4.8 2.1	10.8 4.8	16.8 7.4
49	6 42.3	6 43.4	6 23.9	4.9 2.2	10.9 4.8	16.9 7.5
50	6 42.5	6 43.6	6 24.2	5.0 2.2	11.0 4.9	17.0 7.5
51	6 42.8	6 43.9	6 24.4	5.1 2.3	11.1 4.9	17.1 7.6
52	6 43.0	6 44.1	6 24.6	5.2 2.3	11.2 4.9	17.2 7.6
53	6 43.3	6 44.4	6 24.9	5.3 2.3	11.3 5.0	17.3 7.6
54	6 43.5	6 44.6	6 25.1	5.4 2.4	11.4 5.0	17.4 7.7
55	6 43.8	6 44.9	6 25.4	5.5 2.4	11.5 5.1	17.5 7.7
56	6 44.0	6 45.1	6 25.6	5.6 2.5	11.6 5.1	17.6 7.8
57	6 44.3	6 45.4	6 25.8	5.7 2.5	11.7 5.2	17.7 7.8
58	6 44.5	6 45.6	6 26.1	5.8 2.6	11.8 5.2	17.8 7.9
59	6 44.8	6 45.9	6 26.3	5.9 2.6	11.9 5.3	17.9 7.9
60	6 45.0	6 46.1	6 26.6	6.0 2.7	12.0 5.3	18.0 8.0

27ᵐ

27ᵐ	SUN PLANETS	ARIES	MOON	v or Corrⁿ d	v or Corrⁿ d	v or Corrⁿ d
s	° ′	° ′	° ′	′ ′	′ ′	′ ′
00	6 45.0	6 46.1	6 26.6	0.0 0.0	6.0 2.8	12.0 5.5
01	6 45.3	6 46.4	6 26.8	0.1 0.0	6.1 2.8	12.1 5.5
02	6 45.5	6 46.6	6 27.0	0.2 0.1	6.2 2.8	12.2 5.6
03	6 45.8	6 46.9	6 27.3	0.3 0.1	6.3 2.9	12.3 5.6
04	6 46.0	6 47.1	6 27.5	0.4 0.2	6.4 2.9	12.4 5.7
05	6 46.3	6 47.4	6 27.7	0.5 0.2	6.5 3.0	12.5 5.7
06	6 46.5	6 47.6	6 28.0	0.6 0.3	6.6 3.0	12.6 5.8
07	6 46.8	6 47.9	6 28.2	0.7 0.3	6.7 3.1	12.7 5.8
08	6 47.0	6 48.1	6 28.5	0.8 0.4	6.8 3.1	12.8 5.9
09	6 47.3	6 48.4	6 28.7	0.9 0.4	6.9 3.2	12.9 5.9
10	6 47.5	6 48.6	6 29.0	1.0 0.5	7.0 3.2	13.0 6.0
11	6 47.8	6 48.9	6 29.2	1.1 0.5	7.1 3.3	13.1 6.0
12	6 48.0	6 49.1	6 29.4	1.2 0.6	7.2 3.3	13.2 6.1
13	6 48.3	6 49.4	6 29.7	1.3 0.6	7.3 3.3	13.3 6.1
14	6 48.5	6 49.6	6 29.9	1.4 0.6	7.4 3.4	13.4 6.1
15	6 48.8	6 49.9	6 30.1	1.5 0.7	7.5 3.4	13.5 6.2
16	6 49.0	6 50.1	6 30.4	1.6 0.7	7.6 3.5	13.6 6.2
17	6 49.3	6 50.4	6 30.6	1.7 0.8	7.7 3.5	13.7 6.3
18	6 49.5	6 50.6	6 30.8	1.8 0.8	7.8 3.6	13.8 6.3
19	6 49.8	6 50.9	6 31.1	1.9 0.9	7.9 3.6	13.9 6.4
20	6 50.0	6 51.1	6 31.3	2.0 0.9	8.0 3.7	14.0 6.4
21	6 50.3	6 51.4	6 31.6	2.1 1.0	8.1 3.7	14.1 6.5
22	6 50.5	6 51.6	6 31.8	2.2 1.0	8.2 3.8	14.2 6.5
23	6 50.8	6 51.9	6 32.0	2.3 1.1	8.3 3.8	14.3 6.6
24	6 51.0	6 52.1	6 32.3	2.4 1.1	8.4 3.9	14.4 6.6
25	6 51.3	6 52.4	6 32.5	2.5 1.1	8.5 3.9	14.5 6.6
26	6 51.5	6 52.6	6 32.8	2.6 1.2	8.6 3.9	14.6 6.7
27	6 51.8	6 52.9	6 33.0	2.7 1.2	8.7 4.0	14.7 6.7
28	6 52.0	6 53.1	6 33.2	2.8 1.3	8.8 4.0	14.8 6.8
29	6 52.3	6 53.4	6 33.5	2.9 1.3	8.9 4.1	14.9 6.8
30	6 52.5	6 53.6	6 33.7	3.0 1.4	9.0 4.1	15.0 6.9
31	6 52.8	6 53.9	6 33.9	3.1 1.4	9.1 4.2	15.1 6.9
32	6 53.0	6 54.1	6 34.2	3.2 1.5	9.2 4.2	15.2 7.0
33	6 53.3	6 54.4	6 34.4	3.3 1.5	9.3 4.3	15.3 7.0
34	6 53.5	6 54.6	6 34.7	3.4 1.6	9.4 4.3	15.4 7.1
35	6 53.8	6 54.9	6 34.9	3.5 1.6	9.5 4.4	15.5 7.1
36	6 54.0	6 55.1	6 35.1	3.6 1.7	9.6 4.4	15.6 7.2
37	6 54.3	6 55.4	6 35.4	3.7 1.7	9.7 4.4	15.7 7.2
38	6 54.5	6 55.6	6 35.6	3.8 1.7	9.8 4.5	15.8 7.2
39	6 54.8	6 55.9	6 35.9	3.9 1.8	9.9 4.5	15.9 7.3
40	6 55.0	6 56.1	6 36.1	4.0 1.8	10.0 4.6	16.0 7.3
41	6 55.3	6 56.4	6 36.3	4.1 1.9	10.1 4.6	16.1 7.4
42	6 55.5	6 56.6	6 36.6	4.2 1.9	10.2 4.7	16.2 7.4
43	6 55.8	6 56.9	6 36.8	4.3 2.0	10.3 4.7	16.3 7.5
44	6 56.0	6 57.1	6 37.0	4.4 2.0	10.4 4.8	16.4 7.5
45	6 56.3	6 57.4	6 37.3	4.5 2.1	10.5 4.8	16.5 7.6
46	6 56.5	6 57.6	6 37.5	4.6 2.1	10.6 4.9	16.6 7.6
47	6 56.8	6 57.9	6 37.8	4.7 2.2	10.7 4.9	16.7 7.7
48	6 57.0	6 58.1	6 38.0	4.8 2.2	10.8 5.0	16.8 7.7
49	6 57.3	6 58.4	6 38.2	4.9 2.2	10.9 5.0	16.9 7.7
50	6 57.5	6 58.6	6 38.5	5.0 2.3	11.0 5.0	17.0 7.8
51	6 57.8	6 58.9	6 38.7	5.1 2.3	11.1 5.1	17.1 7.8
52	6 58.0	6 59.1	6 39.0	5.2 2.4	11.2 5.1	17.2 7.9
53	6 58.3	6 59.4	6 39.2	5.3 2.4	11.3 5.2	17.3 7.9
54	6 58.5	6 59.6	6 39.4	5.4 2.5	11.4 5.2	17.4 8.0
55	6 58.8	6 59.9	6 39.7	5.5 2.5	11.5 5.3	17.5 8.0
56	6 59.0	7 00.1	6 39.9	5.6 2.6	11.6 5.3	17.6 8.1
57	6 59.3	7 00.4	6 40.2	5.7 2.6	11.7 5.4	17.7 8.1
58	6 59.5	7 00.6	6 40.4	5.8 2.7	11.8 5.4	17.8 8.2
59	6 59.8	7 00.9	6 40.6	5.9 2.7	11.9 5.5	17.9 8.2
60	7 00.0	7 01.1	6 40.9	6.0 2.8	12.0 5.5	18.0 8.3

28^m / 29^m (header with m superscripts)

28	SUN PLANETS	ARIES	MOON	v or Corrn d		v or Corrn d		v or Corrn d	
s	° ′	° ′	° ′	′	′	′	′	′	′
00	7 00·0	7 01·1	6 40·9	0·0	0·0	6·0	2·9	12·0	5·7
01	7 00·3	7 01·4	6 41·1	0·1	0·0	6·1	2·9	12·1	5·7
02	7 00·5	7 01·7	6 41·3	0·2	0·1	6·2	2·9	12·2	5·8
03	7 00·8	7 01·9	6 41·6	0·3	0·1	6·3	3·0	12·3	5·8
04	7 01·0	7 02·2	6 41·8	0·4	0·2	6·4	3·0	12·4	5·9
05	7 01·3	7 02·4	6 42·1	0·5	0·2	6·5	3·1	12·5	5·9
06	7 01·5	7 02·7	6 42·3	0·6	0·3	6·6	3·1	12·6	6·0
07	7 01·8	7 02·9	6 42·5	0·7	0·3	6·7	3·2	12·7	6·0
08	7 02·0	7 03·2	6 42·8	0·8	0·4	6·8	3·2	12·8	6·1
09	7 02·3	7 03·4	6 43·0	0·9	0·4	6·9	3·3	12·9	6·1
10	7 02·5	7 03·7	6 43·3	1·0	0·5	7·0	3·3	13·0	6·2
11	7 02·8	7 03·9	6 43·5	1·1	0·5	7·1	3·4	13·1	6·2
12	7 03·0	7 04·2	6 43·7	1·2	0·6	7·2	3·4	13·2	6·3
13	7 03·3	7 04·4	6 44·0	1·3	0·6	7·3	3·5	13·3	6·3
14	7 03·5	7 04·7	6 44·2	1·4	0·7	7·4	3·5	13·4	6·4
15	7 03·8	7 04·9	6 44·4	1·5	0·7	7·5	3·6	13·5	6·4
16	7 04·0	7 05·2	6 44·7	1·6	0·8	7·6	3·6	13·6	6·5
17	7 04·3	7 05·4	6 44·9	1·7	0·8	7·7	3·7	13·7	6·5
18	7 04·5	7 05·7	6 45·2	1·8	0·9	7·8	3·7	13·8	6·6
19	7 04·8	7 05·9	6 45·4	1·9	0·9	7·9	3·8	13·9	6·6
20	7 05·0	7 06·2	6 45·6	2·0	1·0	8·0	3·8	14·0	6·7
21	7 05·3	7 06·4	6 45·9	2·1	1·0	8·1	3·8	14·1	6·7
22	7 05·5	7 06·7	6 46·1	2·2	1·0	8·2	3·9	14·2	6·7
23	7 05·8	7 06·9	6 46·4	2·3	1·1	8·3	3·9	14·3	6·8
24	7 06·0	7 07·2	6 46·6	2·4	1·1	8·4	4·0	14·4	6·8
25	7 06·3	7 07·4	6 46·8	2·5	1·2	8·5	4·0	14·5	6·9
26	7 06·5	7 07·7	6 47·1	2·6	1·2	8·6	4·1	14·6	6·9
27	7 06·8	7 07·9	6 47·3	2·7	1·3	8·7	4·1	14·7	7·0
28	7 07·0	7 08·2	6 47·5	2·8	1·3	8·8	4·2	14·8	7·0
29	7 07·3	7 08·4	6 47·8	2·9	1·4	8·9	4·2	14·9	7·1
30	7 07·5	7 08·7	6 48·0	3·0	1·4	9·0	4·3	15·0	7·1
31	7 07·8	7 08·9	6 48·3	3·1	1·5	9·1	4·3	15·1	7·2
32	7 08·0	7 09·2	6 48·5	3·2	1·5	9·2	4·4	15·2	7·2
33	7 08·3	7 09·4	6 48·7	3·3	1·6	9·3	4·4	15·3	7·3
34	7 08·5	7 09·7	6 49·0	3·4	1·6	9·4	4·5	15·4	7·3
35	7 08·8	7 09·9	6 49·2	3·5	1·7	9·5	4·5	15·5	7·4
36	7 09·0	7 10·2	6 49·5	3·6	1·7	9·6	4·6	15·6	7·4
37	7 09·3	7 10·4	6 49·7	3·7	1·8	9·7	4·6	15·7	7·5
38	7 09·5	7 10·7	6 49·9	3·8	1·8	9·8	4·7	15·8	7·5
39	7 09·8	7 10·9	6 50·2	3·9	1·9	9·9	4·7	15·9	7·6
40	7 10·0	7 11·2	6 50·4	4·0	1·9	10·0	4·8	16·0	7·6
41	7 10·3	7 11·4	6 50·6	4·1	1·9	10·1	4·8	16·1	7·6
42	7 10·5	7 11·7	6 50·9	4·2	2·0	10·2	4·8	16·2	7·7
43	7 10·8	7 11·9	6 51·1	4·3	2·0	10·3	4·9	16·3	7·7
44	7 11·0	7 12·2	6 51·4	4·4	2·1	10·4	4·9	16·4	7·8
45	7 11·3	7 12·4	6 51·6	4·5	2·1	10·5	5·0	16·5	7·8
46	7 11·5	7 12·7	6 51·8	4·6	2·2	10·6	5·0	16·6	7·9
47	7 11·8	7 12·9	6 52·1	4·7	2·2	10·7	5·1	16·7	7·9
48	7 12·0	7 13·2	6 52·3	4·8	2·3	10·8	5·1	16·8	8·0
49	7 12·3	7 13·4	6 52·6	4·9	2·3	10·9	5·2	16·9	8·0
50	7 12·5	7 13·7	6 52·8	5·0	2·4	11·0	5·2	17·0	8·1
51	7 12·8	7 13·9	6 53·0	5·1	2·4	11·1	5·3	17·1	8·1
52	7 13·0	7 14·2	6 53·3	5·2	2·5	11·2	5·3	17·2	8·2
53	7 13·3	7 14·4	6 53·5	5·3	2·5	11·3	5·4	17·3	8·2
54	7 13·5	7 14·7	6 53·8	5·4	2·6	11·4	5·4	17·4	8·3
55	7 13·8	7 14·9	6 54·0	5·5	2·6	11·5	5·5	17·5	8·3
56	7 14·0	7 15·2	6 54·2	5·6	2·7	11·6	5·5	17·6	8·4
57	7 14·3	7 15·4	6 54·5	5·7	2·7	11·7	5·6	17·7	8·4
58	7 14·5	7 15·7	6 54·7	5·8	2·8	11·8	5·6	17·8	8·5
59	7 14·8	7 15·9	6 54·9	5·9	2·8	11·9	5·7	17·9	8·5
60	7 15·0	7 16·2	6 55·2	6·0	2·9	12·0	5·7	18·0	8·6

29	SUN PLANETS	ARIES	MOON	v or Corrn d		v or Corrn d		v or Corrn d	
s	° ′	° ′	° ′	′	′	′	′	′	′
00	7 15·0	7 16·2	6 55·2	0·0	0·0	6·0	3·0	12·0	5·9
01	7 15·3	7 16·4	6 55·4	0·1	0·0	6·1	3·0	12·1	5·9
02	7 15·5	7 16·7	6 55·7	0·2	0·1	6·2	3·0	12·2	6·0
03	7 15·8	7 16·9	6 55·9	0·3	0·1	6·3	3·1	12·3	6·0
04	7 16·0	7 17·2	6 56·1	0·4	0·2	6·4	3·1	12·4	6·1
05	7 16·3	7 17·4	6 56·4	0·5	0·2	6·5	3·2	12·5	6·1
06	7 16·5	7 17·7	6 56·6	0·6	0·3	6·6	3·2	12·6	6·2
07	7 16·8	7 17·9	6 56·9	0·7	0·3	6·7	3·3	12·7	6·2
08	7 17·0	7 18·2	6 57·1	0·8	0·4	6·8	3·3	12·8	6·3
09	7 17·3	7 18·4	6 57·3	0·9	0·4	6·9	3·4	12·9	6·3
10	7 17·5	7 18·7	6 57·6	1·0	0·5	7·0	3·4	13·0	6·4
11	7 17·8	7 18·9	6 57·8	1·1	0·5	7·1	3·5	13·1	6·4
12	7 18·0	7 19·2	6 58·0	1·2	0·6	7·2	3·5	13·2	6·5
13	7 18·3	7 19·4	6 58·3	1·3	0·6	7·3	3·6	13·3	6·5
14	7 18·5	7 19·7	6 58·5	1·4	0·7	7·4	3·6	13·4	6·6
15	7 18·8	7 20·0	6 58·8	1·5	0·7	7·5	3·7	13·5	6·6
16	7 19·0	7 20·2	6 59·0	1·6	0·8	7·6	3·7	13·6	6·7
17	7 19·3	7 20·5	6 59·2	1·7	0·8	7·7	3·8	13·7	6·7
18	7 19·5	7 20·7	6 59·5	1·8	0·9	7·8	3·8	13·8	6·8
19	7 19·8	7 21·0	6 59·7	1·9	0·9	7·9	3·9	13·9	6·8
20	7 20·0	7 21·2	7 00·0	2·0	1·0	8·0	3·9	14·0	6·9
21	7 20·3	7 21·5	7 00·2	2·1	1·0	8·1	4·0	14·1	6·9
22	7 20·5	7 21·7	7 00·4	2·2	1·1	8·2	4·0	14·2	7·0
23	7 20·8	7 22·0	7 00·7	2·3	1·1	8·3	4·1	14·3	7·0
24	7 21·0	7 22·2	7 00·9	2·4	1·2	8·4	4·1	14·4	7·1
25	7 21·3	7 22·5	7 01·1	2·5	1·2	8·5	4·2	14·5	7·1
26	7 21·5	7 22·7	7 01·4	2·6	1·3	8·6	4·2	14·6	7·2
27	7 21·8	7 23·0	7 01·6	2·7	1·3	8·7	4·3	14·7	7·2
28	7 22·0	7 23·2	7 01·9	2·8	1·4	8·8	4·3	14·8	7·3
29	7 22·3	7 23·5	7 02·1	2·9	1·4	8·9	4·4	14·9	7·3
30	7 22·5	7 23·7	7 02·3	3·0	1·5	9·0	4·4	15·0	7·4
31	7 22·8	7 24·0	7 02·6	3·1	1·5	9·1	4·5	15·1	7·4
32	7 23·0	7 24·2	7 02·8	3·2	1·6	9·2	4·5	15·2	7·5
33	7 23·3	7 24·5	7 03·1	3·3	1·6	9·3	4·6	15·3	7·5
34	7 23·5	7 24·7	7 03·3	3·4	1·7	9·4	4·6	15·4	7·6
35	7 23·8	7 25·0	7 03·5	3·5	1·7	9·5	4·7	15·5	7·6
36	7 24·0	7 25·2	7 03·8	3·6	1·8	9·6	4·7	15·6	7·7
37	7 24·3	7 25·5	7 04·0	3·7	1·8	9·7	4·8	15·7	7·7
38	7 24·5	7 25·7	7 04·3	3·8	1·9	9·8	4·8	15·8	7·8
39	7 24·8	7 26·0	7 04·5	3·9	1·9	9·9	4·9	15·9	7·8
40	7 25·0	7 26·2	7 04·7	4·0	2·0	10·0	4·9	16·0	7·9
41	7 25·3	7 26·5	7 05·0	4·1	2·0	10·1	5·0	16·1	7·9
42	7 25·5	7 26·7	7 05·2	4·2	2·1	10·2	5·0	16·2	8·0
43	7 25·8	7 27·0	7 05·4	4·3	2·1	10·3	5·1	16·3	8·0
44	7 26·0	7 27·2	7 05·7	4·4	2·2	10·4	5·1	16·4	8·1
45	7 26·3	7 27·5	7 05·9	4·5	2·2	10·5	5·2	16·5	8·1
46	7 26·5	7 27·7	7 06·2	4·6	2·3	10·6	5·2	16·6	8·2
47	7 26·8	7 28·0	7 06·4	4·7	2·3	10·7	5·3	16·7	8·2
48	7 27·0	7 28·2	7 06·6	4·8	2·4	10·8	5·3	16·8	8·3
49	7 27·3	7 28·5	7 06·9	4·9	2·4	10·9	5·4	16·9	8·3
50	7 27·5	7 28·7	7 07·1	5·0	2·5	11·0	5·4	17·0	8·4
51	7 27·8	7 29·0	7 07·4	5·1	2·5	11·1	5·5	17·1	8·4
52	7 28·0	7 29·2	7 07·6	5·2	2·6	11·2	5·5	17·2	8·5
53	7 28·3	7 29·5	7 07·8	5·3	2·6	11·3	5·6	17·3	8·5
54	7 28·5	7 29·7	7 08·1	5·4	2·7	11·4	5·6	17·4	8·6
55	7 28·8	7 30·0	7 08·3	5·5	2·7	11·5	5·7	17·5	8·6
56	7 29·0	7 30·2	7 08·5	5·6	2·8	11·6	5·7	17·6	8·7
57	7 29·3	7 30·5	7 08·8	5·7	2·8	11·7	5·8	17·7	8·7
58	7 29·5	7 30·7	7 09·0	5·8	2·9	11·8	5·8	17·8	8·8
59	7 29·8	7 31·0	7 09·3	5·9	2·9	11·9	5·9	17·9	8·8
60	7 30·0	7 31·2	7 09·5	6·0	3·0	12·0	5·9	18·0	8·9

30 s	SUN PLANETS	ARIES	MOON	v or Corrn d	v or Corrn d	v or Corrn d
	° ′	° ′	° ′	′ ′	′ ′	′ ′
00	7 30·0	7 31·2	7 09·5	0·0 0·0	6·0 3·1	12·0 6·1
01	7 30·3	7 31·5	7 09·7	0·1 0·1	6·1 3·1	12·1 6·2
02	7 30·5	7 31·7	7 10·0	0·2 0·1	6·2 3·2	12·2 6·2
03	7 30·8	7 32·0	7 10·2	0·3 0·2	6·3 3·2	12·3 6·3
04	7 31·0	7 32·2	7 10·5	0·4 0·2	6·4 3·3	12·4 6·3
05	7 31·3	7 32·5	7 10·7	0·5 0·3	6·5 3·3	12·5 6·4
06	7 31·5	7 32·7	7 10·9	0·6 0·3	6·6 3·4	12·6 6·4
07	7 31·8	7 33·0	7 11·2	0·7 0·4	6·7 3·4	12·7 6·5
08	7 32·0	7 33·2	7 11·4	0·8 0·4	6·8 3·5	12·8 6·5
09	7 32·3	7 33·5	7 11·6	0·9 0·5	6·9 3·5	12·9 6·6
10	7 32·5	7 33·7	7 11·9	1·0 0·5	7·0 3·6	13·0 6·6
11	7 32·8	7 34·0	7 12·1	1·1 0·6	7·1 3·6	13·1 6·7
12	7 33·0	7 34·2	7 12·4	1·2 0·6	7·2 3·7	13·2 6·7
13	7 33·3	7 34·5	7 12·6	1·3 0·7	7·3 3·7	13·3 6·8
14	7 33·5	7 34·7	7 12·8	1·4 0·7	7·4 3·8	13·4 6·8
15	7 33·8	7 35·0	7 13·1	1·5 0·8	7·5 3·8	13·5 6·9
16	7 34·0	7 35·2	7 13·3	1·6 0·8	7·6 3·9	13·6 6·9
17	7 34·3	7 35·5	7 13·6	1·7 0·9	7·7 3·9	13·7 7·0
18	7 34·5	7 35·7	7 13·8	1·8 0·9	7·8 4·0	13·8 7·0
19	7 34·8	7 36·0	7 14·0	1·9 1·0	7·9 4·0	13·9 7·1
20	7 35·0	7 36·2	7 14·3	2·0 1·0	8·0 4·1	14·0 7·1
21	7 35·3	7 36·5	7 14·5	2·1 1·1	8·1 4·1	14·1 7·2
22	7 35·5	7 36·7	7 14·7	2·2 1·1	8·2 4·2	14·2 7·2
23	7 35·8	7 37·0	7 15·0	2·3 1·2	8·3 4·2	14·3 7·3
24	7 36·0	7 37·2	7 15·2	2·4 1·2	8·4 4·3	14·4 7·3
25	7 36·3	7 37·5	7 15·5	2·5 1·3	8·5 4·3	14·5 7·4
26	7 36·5	7 37·7	7 15·7	2·6 1·3	8·6 4·4	14·6 7·4
27	7 36·8	7 38·0	7 15·9	2·7 1·4	8·7 4·4	14·7 7·5
28	7 37·0	7 38·3	7 16·2	2·8 1·4	8·8 4·5	14·8 7·5
29	7 37·3	7 38·5	7 16·4	2·9 1·5	8·9 4·5	14·9 7·6
30	7 37·5	7 38·8	7 16·7	3·0 1·5	9·0 4·6	15·0 7·6
31	7 37·8	7 39·0	7 16·9	3·1 1·6	9·1 4·6	15·1 7·7
32	7 38·0	7 39·3	7 17·1	3·2 1·6	9·2 4·7	15·2 7·7
33	7 38·3	7 39·5	7 17·4	3·3 1·7	9·3 4·7	15·3 7·8
34	7 38·5	7 39·8	7 17·6	3·4 1·7	9·4 4·8	15·4 7·8
35	7 38·8	7 40·0	7 17·9	3·5 1·8	9·5 4·8	15·5 7·9
36	7 39·0	7 40·3	7 18·1	3·6 1·8	9·6 4·9	15·6 7·9
37	7 39·3	7 40·5	7 18·3	3·7 1·9	9·7 4·9	15·7 8·0
38	7 39·5	7 40·8	7 18·6	3·8 1·9	9·8 5·0	15·8 8·0
39	7 39·8	7 41·0	7 18·8	3·9 2·0	9·9 5·0	15·9 8·1
40	7 40·0	7 41·3	7 19·0	4·0 2·0	10·0 5·1	16·0 8·1
41	7 40·3	7 41·5	7 19·3	4·1 2·1	10·1 5·1	16·1 8·2
42	7 40·5	7 41·8	7 19·5	4·2 2·1	10·2 5·2	16·2 8·2
43	7 40·8	7 42·0	7 19·8	4·3 2·2	10·3 5·2	16·3 8·3
44	7 41·0	7 42·3	7 20·0	4·4 2·2	10·4 5·3	16·4 8·3
45	7 41·3	7 42·5	7 20·2	4·5 2·3	10·5 5·3	16·5 8·4
46	7 41·5	7 42·8	7 20·5	4·6 2·3	10·6 5·4	16·6 8·4
47	7 41·8	7 43·0	7 20·7	4·7 2·4	10·7 5·4	16·7 8·5
48	7 42·0	7 43·3	7 21·0	4·8 2·4	10·8 5·5	16·8 8·5
49	7 42·3	7 43·5	7 21·2	4·9 2·5	10·9 5·5	16·9 8·6
50	7 42·5	7 43·8	7 21·4	5·0 2·5	11·0 5·6	17·0 8·6
51	7 42·8	7 44·0	7 21·7	5·1 2·6	11·1 5·6	17·1 8·7
52	7 43·0	7 44·3	7 21·9	5·2 2·6	11·2 5·7	17·2 8·7
53	7 43·3	7 44·5	7 22·1	5·3 2·7	11·3 5·7	17·3 8·8
54	7 43·5	7 44·8	7 22·4	5·4 2·7	11·4 5·8	17·4 8·8
55	7 43·8	7 45·0	7 22·6	5·5 2·8	11·5 5·8	17·5 8·9
56	7 44·0	7 45·3	7 22·9	5·6 2·8	11·6 5·9	17·6 8·9
57	7 44·3	7 45·5	7 23·1	5·7 2·9	11·7 5·9	17·7 9·0
58	7 44·5	7 45·8	7 23·3	5·8 2·9	11·8 6·0	17·8 9·0
59	7 44·8	7 46·0	7 23·6	5·9 3·0	11·9 6·0	17·9 9·1
60	7 45·0	7 46·3	7 23·8	6·0 3·1	12·0 6·1	18·0 9·2

31 s	SUN PLANETS	ARIES	MOON	v or Corrn d	v or Corrn d	v or Corrn d
	° ′	° ′	° ′	′ ′	′ ′	′ ′
00	7 45·0	7 46·3	7 23·8	0·0 0·0	6·0 3·2	12·0 6·3
01	7 45·3	7 46·5	7 24·1	0·1 0·1	6·1 3·2	12·1 6·4
02	7 45·5	7 46·8	7 24·3	0·2 0·1	6·2 3·3	12·2 6·4
03	7 45·8	7 47·0	7 24·5	0·3 0·2	6·3 3·3	12·3 6·5
04	7 46·0	7 47·3	7 24·8	0·4 0·2	6·4 3·4	12·4 6·5
05	7 46·3	7 47·5	7 25·0	0·5 0·3	6·5 3·4	12·5 6·6
06	7 46·5	7 47·8	7 25·2	0·6 0·3	6·6 3·5	12·6 6·6
07	7 46·8	7 48·0	7 25·5	0·7 0·4	6·7 3·5	12·7 6·7
08	7 47·0	7 48·3	7 25·7	0·8 0·4	6·8 3·6	12·8 6·7
09	7 47·3	7 48·5	7 26·0	0·9 0·5	6·9 3·6	12·9 6·8
10	7 47·5	7 48·8	7 26·2	1·0 0·5	7·0 3·7	13·0 6·8
11	7 47·8	7 49·0	7 26·4	1·1 0·6	7·1 3·7	13·1 6·9
12	7 48·0	7 49·3	7 26·7	1·2 0·6	7·2 3·8	13·2 6·9
13	7 48·3	7 49·5	7 26·9	1·3 0·7	7·3 3·8	13·3 7·0
14	7 48·5	7 49·8	7 27·2	1·4 0·7	7·4 3·9	13·4 7·0
15	7 48·8	7 50·0	7 27·4	1·5 0·8	7·5 3·9	13·5 7·1
16	7 49·0	7 50·3	7 27·6	1·6 0·8	7·6 4·0	13·6 7·1
17	7 49·3	7 50·5	7 27·9	1·7 0·9	7·7 4·0	13·7 7·2
18	7 49·5	7 50·8	7 28·1	1·8 0·9	7·8 4·1	13·8 7·2
19	7 49·8	7 51·0	7 28·4	1·9 1·0	7·9 4·1	13·9 7·3
20	7 50·0	7 51·3	7 28·6	2·0 1·1	8·0 4·2	14·0 7·4
21	7 50·3	7 51·5	7 28·8	2·1 1·1	8·1 4·3	14·1 7·4
22	7 50·5	7 51·8	7 29·1	2·2 1·2	8·2 4·3	14·2 7·5
23	7 50·8	7 52·0	7 29·3	2·3 1·2	8·3 4·4	14·3 7·5
24	7 51·0	7 52·3	7 29·5	2·4 1·3	8·4 4·4	14·4 7·6
25	7 51·3	7 52·5	7 29·8	2·5 1·3	8·5 4·5	14·5 7·6
26	7 51·5	7 52·8	7 30·0	2·6 1·4	8·6 4·5	14·6 7·7
27	7 51·8	7 53·0	7 30·3	2·7 1·4	8·7 4·6	14·7 7·7
28	7 52·0	7 53·3	7 30·5	2·8 1·5	8·8 4·6	14·8 7·8
29	7 52·3	7 53·5	7 30·7	2·9 1·5	8·9 4·7	14·9 7·8
30	7 52·5	7 53·8	7 31·0	3·0 1·6	9·0 4·7	15·0 7·9
31	7 52·8	7 54·0	7 31·2	3·1 1·6	9·1 4·8	15·1 7·9
32	7 53·0	7 54·3	7 31·5	3·2 1·7	9·2 4·8	15·2 8·0
33	7 53·3	7 54·5	7 31·7	3·3 1·7	9·3 4·9	15·3 8·0
34	7 53·5	7 54·8	7 31·9	3·4 1·8	9·4 4·9	15·4 8·1
35	7 53·8	7 55·0	7 32·2	3·5 1·8	9·5 5·0	15·5 8·1
36	7 54·0	7 55·3	7 32·4	3·6 1·9	9·6 5·0	15·6 8·2
37	7 54·3	7 55·5	7 32·6	3·7 1·9	9·7 5·1	15·7 8·2
38	7 54·5	7 55·8	7 32·9	3·8 2·0	9·8 5·1	15·8 8·3
39	7 54·8	7 56·0	7 33·1	3·9 2·0	9·9 5·2	15·9 8·3
40	7 55·0	7 56·3	7 33·4	4·0 2·1	10·0 5·3	16·0 8·4
41	7 55·3	7 56·6	7 33·6	4·1 2·2	10·1 5·3	16·1 8·5
42	7 55·5	7 56·8	7 33·8	4·2 2·2	10·2 5·4	16·2 8·5
43	7 55·8	7 57·1	7 34·1	4·3 2·3	10·3 5·4	16·3 8·6
44	7 56·0	7 57·3	7 34·3	4·4 2·3	10·4 5·5	16·4 8·6
45	7 56·3	7 57·6	7 34·6	4·5 2·4	10·5 5·5	16·5 8·7
46	7 56·5	7 57·8	7 34·8	4·6 2·4	10·6 5·6	16·6 8·7
47	7 56·8	7 58·1	7 35·0	4·7 2·5	10·7 5·6	16·7 8·8
48	7 57·0	7 58·3	7 35·3	4·8 2·5	10·8 5·7	16·8 8·8
49	7 57·3	7 58·6	7 35·5	4·9 2·6	10·9 5·7	16·9 8·9
50	7 57·5	7 58·8	7 35·7	5·0 2·6	11·0 5·8	17·0 8·9
51	7 57·8	7 59·1	7 36·0	5·1 2·7	11·1 5·8	17·1 9·0
52	7 58·0	7 59·3	7 36·2	5·2 2·7	11·2 5·9	17·2 9·0
53	7 58·3	7 59·6	7 36·5	5·3 2·8	11·3 5·9	17·3 9·1
54	7 58·5	7 59·8	7 36·7	5·4 2·8	11·4 6·0	17·4 9·1
55	7 58·8	8 00·1	7 36·9	5·5 2·9	11·5 6·0	17·5 9·2
56	7 59·0	8 00·3	7 37·2	5·6 2·9	11·6 6·1	17·6 9·2
57	7 59·3	8 00·6	7 37·4	5·7 3·0	11·7 6·1	17·7 9·3
58	7 59·5	8 00·8	7 37·7	5·8 3·0	11·8 6·2	17·8 9·3
59	7 59·8	8 01·1	7 37·9	5·9 3·1	11·9 6·2	17·9 9·4
60	8 00·0	8 01·3	7 38·1	6·0 3·2	12·0 6·3	18·0 9·5

32	SUN PLANETS	ARIES	MOON	v or Corrn d	v or Corrn d	v or Corrn d
s	° ′	° ′	° ′	′ ′	′ ′	′ ′
00	8 00·0	8 01·3	7 38·1	0·0 0·0	6·0 3·3	12·0 6·5
01	8 00·3	8 01·6	7 38·4	0·1 0·1	6·1 3·3	12·1 6·6
02	8 00·5	8 01·8	7 38·6	0·2 0·1	6·2 3·4	12·2 6·6
03	8 00·8	8 02·1	7 38·8	0·3 0·2	6·3 3·4	12·3 6·7
04	8 01·0	8 02·3	7 39·1	0·4 0·2	6·4 3·5	12·4 6·7
05	8 01·3	8 02·6	7 39·3	0·5 0·3	6·5 3·5	12·5 6·8
06	8 01·5	8 02·8	7 39·6	0·6 0·3	6·6 3·6	12·6 6·8
07	8 01·8	8 03·1	7 39·8	0·7 0·4	6·7 3·6	12·7 6·9
08	8 02·0	8 03·3	7 40·0	0·8 0·4	6·8 3·7	12·8 6·9
09	8 02·3	8 03·6	7 40·3	0·9 0·5	6·9 3·7	12·9 7·0
10	8 02·5	8 03·8	7 40·5	1·0 0·5	7·0 3·8	13·0 7·0
11	8 02·8	8 04·1	7 40·8	1·1 0·6	7·1 3·8	13·1 7·1
12	8 03·0	8 04·3	7 41·0	1·2 0·7	7·2 3·9	13·2 7·2
13	8 03·3	8 04·6	7 41·2	1·3 0·7	7·3 4·0	13·3 7·2
14	8 03·5	8 04·8	7 41·5	1·4 0·8	7·4 4·0	13·4 7·3
15	8 03·8	8 05·1	7 41·7	1·5 0·8	7·5 4·1	13·5 7·3
16	8 04·0	8 05·3	7 42·0	1·6 0·9	7·6 4·1	13·6 7·4
17	8 04·3	8 05·6	7 42·2	1·7 0·9	7·7 4·2	13·7 7·4
18	8 04·5	8 05·8	7 42·4	1·8 1·0	7·8 4·2	13·8 7·5
19	8 04·8	8 06·1	7 42·7	1·9 1·0	7·9 4·3	13·9 7·5
20	8 05·0	8 06·3	7 42·9	2·0 1·1	8·0 4·3	14·0 7·6
21	8 05·3	8 06·6	7 43·1	2·1 1·1	8·1 4·4	14·1 7·6
22	8 05·5	8 06·8	7 43·4	2·2 1·2	8·2 4·4	14·2 7·7
23	8 05·8	8 07·1	7 43·6	2·3 1·2	8·3 4·5	14·3 7·7
24	8 06·0	8 07·3	7 43·9	2·4 1·3	8·4 4·6	14·4 7·8
25	8 06·3	8 07·6	7 44·1	2·5 1·4	8·5 4·6	14·5 7·9
26	8 06·5	8 07·8	7 44·3	2·6 1·4	8·6 4·7	14·6 7·9
27	8 06·8	8 08·1	7 44·6	2·7 1·5	8·7 4·7	14·7 8·0
28	8 07·0	8 08·3	7 44·8	2·8 1·5	8·8 4·8	14·8 8·0
29	8 07·3	8 08·6	7 45·1	2·9 1·6	8·9 4·8	14·9 8·1
30	8 07·5	8 08·8	7 45·3	3·0 1·6	9·0 4·9	15·0 8·1
31	8 07·8	8 09·1	7 45·5	3·1 1·7	9·1 4·9	15·1 8·2
32	8 08·0	8 09·3	7 45·8	3·2 1·7	9·2 5·0	15·2 8·2
33	8 08·3	8 09·6	7 46·0	3·3 1·8	9·3 5·0	15·3 8·3
34	8 08·5	8 09·8	7 46·2	3·4 1·8	9·4 5·1	15·4 8·3
35	8 08·8	8 10·1	7 46·5	3·5 1·9	9·5 5·1	15·5 8·4
36	8 09·0	8 10·3	7 46·7	3·6 2·0	9·6 5·2	15·6 8·5
37	8 09·3	8 10·6	7 47·0	3·7 2·0	9·7 5·3	15·7 8·5
38	8 09·5	8 10·8	7 47·2	3·8 2·1	9·8 5·3	15·8 8·6
39	8 09·8	8 11·1	7 47·4	3·9 2·1	9·9 5·4	15·9 8·6
40	8 10·0	8 11·3	7 47·7	4·0 2·2	10·0 5·4	16·0 8·7
41	8 10·3	8 11·6	7 47·9	4·1 2·2	10·1 5·5	16·1 8·7
42	8 10·5	8 11·8	7 48·2	4·2 2·3	10·2 5·5	16·2 8·8
43	8 10·8	8 12·1	7 48·4	4·3 2·3	10·3 5·6	16·3 8·8
44	8 11·0	8 12·3	7 48·6	4·4 2·4	10·4 5·6	16·4 8·9
45	8 11·3	8 12·6	7 48·9	4·5 2·4	10·5 5·7	16·5 8·9
46	8 11·5	8 12·8	7 49·1	4·6 2·5	10·6 5·7	16·6 9·0
47	8 11·8	8 13·1	7 49·3	4·7 2·5	10·7 5·8	16·7 9·0
48	8 12·0	8 13·3	7 49·6	4·8 2·6	10·8 5·9	16·8 9·1
49	8 12·3	8 13·6	7 49·8	4·9 2·7	10·9 5·9	16·9 9·2
50	8 12·5	8 13·8	7 50·1	5·0 2·7	11·0 6·0	17·0 9·2
51	8 12·8	8 14·1	7 50·3	5·1 2·8	11·1 6·0	17·1 9·3
52	8 13·0	8 14·3	7 50·5	5·2 2·8	11·2 6·1	17·2 9·3
53	8 13·3	8 14·6	7 50·8	5·3 2·9	11·3 6·1	17·3 9·4
54	8 13·5	8 14·9	7 51·0	5·4 2·9	11·4 6·2	17·4 9·4
55	8 13·8	8 15·1	7 51·3	5·5 3·0	11·5 6·2	17·5 9·5
56	8 14·0	8 15·4	7 51·5	5·6 3·0	11·6 6·3	17·6 9·5
57	8 14·3	8 15·6	7 51·7	5·7 3·1	11·7 6·3	17·7 9·6
58	8 14·5	8 15·9	7 52·0	5·8 3·1	11·8 6·4	17·8 9·6
59	8 14·8	8 16·1	7 52·2	5·9 3·2	11·9 6·4	17·9 9·7
60	8 15·0	8 16·4	7 52·5	6·0 3·3	12·0 6·5	18·0 9·8

33	SUN PLANETS	ARIES	MOON	v or Corrn d	v or Corrn d	v or Corrn d
s	° ′	° ′	° ′	′ ′	′ ′	′ ′
00	8 15·0	8 16·4	7 52·5	0·0 0·0	6·0 3·4	12·0 6·7
01	8 15·3	8 16·6	7 52·7	0·1 0·1	6·1 3·4	12·1 6·8
02	8 15·5	8 16·9	7 52·9	0·2 0·1	6·2 3·5	12·2 6·8
03	8 15·8	8 17·1	7 53·2	0·3 0·2	6·3 3·5	12·3 6·9
04	8 16·0	8 17·4	7 53·4	0·4 0·2	6·4 3·6	12·4 6·9
05	8 16·3	8 17·6	7 53·6	0·5 0·3	6·5 3·6	12·5 7·0
06	8 16·5	8 17·9	7 53·9	0·6 0·3	6·6 3·7	12·6 7·0
07	8 16·8	8 18·1	7 54·1	0·7 0·4	6·7 3·7	12·7 7·1
08	8 17·0	8 18·4	7 54·4	0·8 0·4	6·8 3·8	12·8 7·1
09	8 17·3	8 18·6	7 54·6	0·9 0·5	6·9 3·9	12·9 7·2
10	8 17·5	8 18·9	7 54·8	1·0 0·6	7·0 3·9	13·0 7·3
11	8 17·8	8 19·1	7 55·1	1·1 0·6	7·1 4·0	13·1 7·3
12	8 18·0	8 19·4	7 55·3	1·2 0·7	7·2 4·0	13·2 7·4
13	8 18·3	8 19·6	7 55·6	1·3 0·7	7·3 4·1	13·3 7·4
14	8 18·5	8 19·9	7 55·8	1·4 0·8	7·4 4·1	13·4 7·5
15	8 18·8	8 20·1	7 56·0	1·5 0·8	7·5 4·2	13·5 7·5
16	8 19·0	8 20·4	7 56·3	1·6 0·9	7·6 4·2	13·6 7·6
17	8 19·3	8 20·6	7 56·5	1·7 0·9	7·7 4·3	13·7 7·6
18	8 19·5	8 20·9	7 56·7	1·8 1·0	7·8 4·4	13·8 7·7
19	8 19·8	8 21·1	7 57·0	1·9 1·1	7·9 4·4	13·9 7·8
20	8 20·0	8 21·4	7 57·2	2·0 1·1	8·0 4·5	14·0 7·8
21	8 20·3	8 21·6	7 57·5	2·1 1·2	8·1 4·5	14·1 7·9
22	8 20·5	8 21·9	7 57·7	2·2 1·2	8·2 4·6	14·2 7·9
23	8 20·8	8 22·1	7 57·9	2·3 1·3	8·3 4·6	14·3 8·0
24	8 21·0	8 22·4	7 58·2	2·4 1·3	8·4 4·7	14·4 8·0
25	8 21·3	8 22·6	7 58·4	2·5 1·4	8·5 4·7	14·5 8·1
26	8 21·5	8 22·9	7 58·7	2·6 1·5	8·6 4·8	14·6 8·2
27	8 21·8	8 23·1	7 58·9	2·7 1·5	8·7 4·9	14·7 8·2
28	8 22·0	8 23·4	7 59·1	2·8 1·6	8·8 4·9	14·8 8·3
29	8 22·3	8 23·6	7 59·4	2·9 1·6	8·9 5·0	14·9 8·3
30	8 22·5	8 23·9	7 59·6	3·0 1·7	9·0 5·0	15·0 8·4
31	8 22·8	8 24·1	7 59·8	3·1 1·7	9·1 5·1	15·1 8·4
32	8 23·0	8 24·4	8 00·1	3·2 1·8	9·2 5·1	15·2 8·5
33	8 23·3	8 24·6	8 00·3	3·3 1·8	9·3 5·2	15·3 8·5
34	8 23·5	8 24·9	8 00·6	3·4 1·9	9·4 5·2	15·4 8·6
35	8 23·8	8 25·1	8 00·8	3·5 2·0	9·5 5·3	15·5 8·7
36	8 24·0	8 25·4	8 01·0	3·6 2·0	9·6 5·4	15·6 8·7
37	8 24·3	8 25·6	8 01·3	3·7 2·1	9·7 5·4	15·7 8·8
38	8 24·5	8 25·9	8 01·5	3·8 2·1	9·8 5·5	15·8 8·8
39	8 24·8	8 26·1	8 01·8	3·9 2·2	9·9 5·5	15·9 8·9
40	8 25·0	8 26·4	8 02·0	4·0 2·2	10·0 5·6	16·0 8·9
41	8 25·3	8 26·6	8 02·2	4·1 2·3	10·1 5·6	16·1 9·0
42	8 25·5	8 26·9	8 02·5	4·2 2·3	10·2 5·7	16·2 9·0
43	8 25·8	8 27·1	8 02·7	4·3 2·4	10·3 5·8	16·3 9·1
44	8 26·0	8 27·4	8 02·9	4·4 2·5	10·4 5·8	16·4 9·2
45	8 26·3	8 27·6	8 03·2	4·5 2·5	10·5 5·9	16·5 9·2
46	8 26·5	8 27·9	8 03·4	4·6 2·6	10·6 5·9	16·6 9·3
47	8 26·8	8 28·1	8 03·7	4·7 2·6	10·7 6·0	16·7 9·3
48	8 27·0	8 28·4	8 03·9	4·8 2·7	10·8 6·0	16·8 9·4
49	8 27·3	8 28·6	8 04·1	4·9 2·7	10·9 6·1	16·9 9·4
50	8 27·5	8 28·9	8 04·4	5·0 2·8	11·0 6·1	17·0 9·5
51	8 27·8	8 29·1	8 04·6	5·1 2·8	11·1 6·2	17·1 9·5
52	8 28·0	8 29·4	8 04·9	5·2 2·9	11·2 6·3	17·2 9·6
53	8 28·3	8 29·6	8 05·1	5·3 3·0	11·3 6·3	17·3 9·7
54	8 28·5	8 29·9	8 05·3	5·4 3·0	11·4 6·4	17·4 9·7
55	8 28·8	8 30·1	8 05·6	5·5 3·1	11·5 6·4	17·5 9·8
56	8 29·0	8 30·4	8 05·8	5·6 3·1	11·6 6·5	17·6 9·8
57	8 29·3	8 30·6	8 06·1	5·7 3·2	11·7 6·5	17·7 9·9
58	8 29·5	8 30·9	8 06·3	5·8 3·2	11·8 6·6	17·8 9·9
59	8 29·8	8 31·1	8 06·5	5·9 3·3	11·9 6·6	17·9 10·0
60	8 30·0	8 31·4	8 06·8	6·0 3·4	12·0 6·7	18·0 10·1

34ᵐ	SUN PLANETS	ARIES	MOON	v or Corrⁿ d		v or Corrⁿ d		v or Corrⁿ d		35ᵐ	SUN PLANETS	ARIES	MOON	v or Corrⁿ d		v or Corrⁿ d		v or Corrⁿ d	
s	° ′	° ′	° ′	′	′	′	′	′	′	s	° ′	° ′	° ′	′	′	′	′	′	′
00	8 30·0	8 31·4	8 06·8	0·0	0·0	6·0	3·5	12·0	6·9	00	8 45·0	8 46·4	8 21·1	0·0	0·0	6·0	3·6	12·0	7·1
01	8 30·3	8 31·6	8 07·0	0·1	0·1	6·1	3·5	12·1	7·0	01	8 45·3	8 46·7	8 21·3	0·1	0·1	6·1	3·6	12·1	7·2
02	8 30·5	8 31·9	8 07·2	0·2	0·1	6·2	3·6	12·2	7·0	02	8 45·5	8 46·9	8 21·6	0·2	0·1	6·2	3·7	12·2	7·3
03	8 30·8	8 32·1	8 07·5	0·3	0·2	6·3	3·6	12·3	7·1	03	8 45·8	8 47·2	8 21·8	0·3	0·2	6·3	3·7	12·3	7·3
04	8 31·0	8 32·4	8 07·7	0·4	0·2	6·4	3·7	12·4	7·1	04	8 46·0	8 47·4	8 22·0	0·4	0·2	6·4	3·8	12·4	7·3
05	8 31·3	8 32·6	8 08·0	0·5	0·3	6·5	3·7	12·5	7·2	05	8 46·3	8 47·7	8 22·3	0·5	0·3	6·5	3·8	12·5	7·4
06	8 31·5	8 32·9	8 08·2	0·6	0·3	6·6	3·8	12·6	7·2	06	8 46·5	8 47·9	8 22·5	0·6	0·4	6·6	3·9	12·6	7·5
07	8 31·8	8 33·2	8 08·4	0·7	0·4	6·7	3·9	12·7	7·3	07	8 46·8	8 48·2	8 22·8	0·7	0·4	6·7	4·0	12·7	7·5
08	8 32·0	8 33·4	8 08·7	0·8	0·5	6·8	3·9	12·8	7·4	08	8 47·0	8 48·4	8 23·0	0·8	0·5	6·8	4·0	12·8	7·6
09	8 32·3	8 33·7	8 08·9	0·9	0·5	6·9	4·0	12·9	7·4	09	8 47·3	8 48·7	8 23·2	0·9	0·5	6·9	4·1	12·9	7·6
10	8 32·5	8 33·9	8 09·2	1·0	0·6	7·0	4·0	13·0	7·5	10	8 47·5	8 48·9	8 23·5	1·0	0·6	7·0	4·1	13·0	7·7
11	8 32·8	8 34·2	8 09·4	1·1	0·6	7·1	4·1	13·1	7·5	11	8 47·8	8 49·2	8 23·7	1·1	0·7	7·1	4·2	13·1	7·8
12	8 33·0	8 34·4	8 09·6	1·2	0·7	7·2	4·1	13·2	7·6	12	8 48·0	8 49·4	8 23·9	1·2	0·7	7·2	4·3	13·2	7·8
13	8 33·3	8 34·7	8 09·9	1·3	0·7	7·3	4·2	13·3	7·6	13	8 48·3	8 49·7	8 24·2	1·3	0·8	7·3	4·3	13·3	7·9
14	8 33·5	8 34·9	8 10·1	1·4	0·8	7·4	4·3	13·4	7·7	14	8 48·5	8 49·9	8 24·4	1·4	0·8	7·4	4·4	13·4	7·9
15	8 33·8	8 35·2	8 10·3	1·5	0·9	7·5	4·3	13·5	7·8	15	8 48·8	8 50·2	8 24·7	1·5	0·9	7·5	4·4	13·5	8·0
16	8 34·0	8 35·4	8 10·6	1·6	0·9	7·6	4·4	13·6	7·8	16	8 49·0	8 50·4	8 24·9	1·6	0·9	7·6	4·5	13·6	8·0
17	8 34·3	8 35·7	8 10·8	1·7	1·0	7·7	4·4	13·7	7·9	17	8 49·3	8 50·7	8 25·1	1·7	1·0	7·7	4·6	13·7	8·1
18	8 34·5	8 35·9	8 11·1	1·8	1·0	7·8	4·5	13·8	7·9	18	8 49·5	8 50·9	8 25·4	1·8	1·1	7·8	4·6	13·8	8·2
19	8 34·8	8 36·2	8 11·3	1·9	1·1	7·9	4·5	13·9	8·0	19	8 49·8	8 51·2	8 25·6	1·9	1·1	7·9	4·7	13·9	8·2
20	8 35·0	8 36·4	8 11·5	2·0	1·2	8·0	4·6	14·0	8·1	20	8 50·0	8 51·5	8 25·9	2·0	1·2	8·0	4·7	14·0	8·3
21	8 35·3	8 36·7	8 11·8	2·1	1·2	8·1	4·7	14·1	8·1	21	8 50·3	8 51·7	8 26·1	2·1	1·2	8·1	4·8	14·1	8·3
22	8 35·5	8 36·9	8 12·0	2·2	1·3	8·2	4·7	14·2	8·2	22	8 50·5	8 52·0	8 26·3	2·2	1·3	8·2	4·9	14·2	8·4
23	8 35·8	8 37·2	8 12·3	2·3	1·3	8·3	4·8	14·3	8·2	23	8 50·8	8 52·2	8 26·6	2·3	1·4	8·3	4·9	14·3	8·5
24	8 36·0	8 37·4	8 12·5	2·4	1·4	8·4	4·8	14·4	8·3	24	8 51·0	8 52·5	8 26·8	2·4	1·4	8·4	5·0	14·4	8·5
25	8 36·3	8 37·7	8 12·7	2·5	1·4	8·5	4·9	14·5	8·3	25	8 51·3	8 52·7	8 27·0	2·5	1·5	8·5	5·0	14·5	8·6
26	8 36·5	8 37·9	8 13·0	2·6	1·5	8·6	4·9	14·6	8·4	26	8 51·5	8 53·0	8 27·3	2·6	1·5	8·6	5·1	14·6	8·6
27	8 36·8	8 38·2	8 13·2	2·7	1·6	8·7	5·0	14·7	8·5	27	8 51·8	8 53·2	8 27·5	2·7	1·6	8·7	5·1	14·7	8·7
28	8 37·0	8 38·4	8 13·4	2·8	1·6	8·8	5·1	14·8	8·5	28	8 52·0	8 53·5	8 27·8	2·8	1·7	8·8	5·2	14·8	8·8
29	8 37·3	8 38·7	8 13·7	2·9	1·7	8·9	5·1	14·9	8·6	29	8 52·3	8 53·7	8 28·0	2·9	1·7	8·9	5·3	14·9	8·8
30	8 37·5	8 38·9	8 13·9	3·0	1·7	9·0	5·2	15·0	8·6	30	8 52·5	8 54·0	8 28·2	3·0	1·8	9·0	5·3	15·0	8·9
31	8 37·8	8 39·2	8 14·2	3·1	1·8	9·1	5·2	15·1	8·7	31	8 52·8	8 54·2	8 28·5	3·1	1·8	9·1	5·4	15·1	8·9
32	8 38·0	8 39·4	8 14·4	3·2	1·8	9·2	5·3	15·2	8·7	32	8 53·0	8 54·5	8 28·7	3·2	1·9	9·2	5·4	15·2	9·0
33	8 38·3	8 39·7	8 14·6	3·3	1·9	9·3	5·3	15·3	8·8	33	8 53·3	8 54·7	8 29·0	3·3	2·0	9·3	5·5	15·3	9·1
34	8 38·5	8 39·9	8 14·9	3·4	2·0	9·4	5·4	15·4	8·9	34	8 53·5	8 55·0	8 29·2	3·4	2·0	9·4	5·6	15·4	9·1
35	8 38·8	8 40·2	8 15·1	3·5	2·0	9·5	5·5	15·5	8·9	35	8 53·8	8 55·2	8 29·4	3·5	2·1	9·5	5·6	15·5	9·2
36	8 39·0	8 40·4	8 15·4	3·6	2·1	9·6	5·5	15·6	9·0	36	8 54·0	8 55·5	8 29·7	3·6	2·1	9·6	5·7	15·6	9·2
37	8 39·3	8 40·7	8 15·6	3·7	2·1	9·7	5·6	15·7	9·0	37	8 54·3	8 55·7	8 29·9	3·7	2·2	9·7	5·7	15·7	9·3
38	8 39·5	8 40·9	8 15·8	3·8	2·2	9·8	5·6	15·8	9·1	38	8 54·5	8 56·0	8 30·2	3·8	2·2	9·8	5·8	15·8	9·3
39	8 39·8	8 41·2	8 16·1	3·9	2·2	9·9	5·7	15·9	9·1	39	8 54·8	8 56·2	8 30·4	3·9	2·3	9·9	5·9	15·9	9·4
40	8 40·0	8 41·4	8 16·3	4·0	2·3	10·0	5·8	16·0	9·2	40	8 55·0	8 56·5	8 30·6	4·0	2·4	10·0	5·9	16·0	9·5
41	8 40·3	8 41·7	8 16·5	4·1	2·4	10·1	5·8	16·1	9·3	41	8 55·3	8 56·7	8 30·9	4·1	2·4	10·1	6·0	16·1	9·5
42	8 40·5	8 41·9	8 16·8	4·2	2·4	10·2	5·9	16·2	9·3	42	8 55·5	8 57·0	8 31·1	4·2	2·5	10·2	6·0	16·2	9·6
43	8 40·8	8 42·2	8 17·0	4·3	2·5	10·3	5·9	16·3	9·4	43	8 55·8	8 57·2	8 31·3	4·3	2·5	10·3	6·1	16·3	9·6
44	8 41·0	8 42·4	8 17·3	4·4	2·5	10·4	6·0	16·4	9·4	44	8 56·0	8 57·5	8 31·6	4·4	2·6	10·4	6·2	16·4	9·7
45	8 41·3	8 42·7	8 17·5	4·5	2·6	10·5	6·0	16·5	9·5	45	8 56·3	8 57·7	8 31·8	4·5	2·7	10·5	6·2	16·5	9·8
46	8 41·5	8 42·9	8 17·7	4·6	2·6	10·6	6·1	16·6	9·5	46	8 56·5	8 58·0	8 32·1	4·6	2·7	10·6	6·3	16·6	9·8
47	8 41·8	8 43·2	8 18·0	4·7	2·7	10·7	6·2	16·7	9·6	47	8 56·8	8 58·2	8 32·3	4·7	2·8	10·7	6·3	16·7	9·9
48	8 42·0	8 43·4	8 18·2	4·8	2·8	10·8	6·2	16·8	9·7	48	8 57·0	8 58·5	8 32·5	4·8	2·8	10·8	6·4	16·8	9·9
49	8 42·3	8 43·7	8 18·5	4·9	2·8	10·9	6·3	16·9	9·7	49	8 57·3	8 58·7	8 32·8	4·9	2·9	10·9	6·4	16·9	10·0
50	8 42·5	8 43·9	8 18·7	5·0	2·9	11·0	6·3	17·0	9·8	50	8 57·5	8 59·0	8 33·0	5·0	3·0	11·0	6·5	17·0	10·1
51	8 42·8	8 44·2	8 18·9	5·1	2·9	11·1	6·4	17·1	9·8	51	8 57·8	8 59·2	8 33·3	5·1	3·0	11·1	6·6	17·1	10·1
52	8 43·0	8 44·4	8 19·2	5·2	3·0	11·2	6·4	17·2	9·9	52	8 58·0	8 59·5	8 33·5	5·2	3·1	11·2	6·6	17·2	10·2
53	8 43·3	8 44·7	8 19·4	5·3	3·0	11·3	6·5	17·3	9·9	53	8 58·3	8 59·7	8 33·7	5·3	3·1	11·3	6·7	17·3	10·2
54	8 43·5	8 44·9	8 19·7	5·4	3·1	11·4	6·6	17·4	10·0	54	8 58·5	9 00·0	8 34·0	5·4	3·2	11·4	6·7	17·4	10·3
55	8 43·8	8 45·2	8 19·9	5·5	3·2	11·5	6·6	17·5	10·1	55	8 58·8	9 00·2	8 34·2	5·5	3·3	11·5	6·8	17·5	10·4
56	8 44·0	8 45·4	8 20·1	5·6	3·2	11·6	6·7	17·6	10·1	56	8 59·0	9 00·5	8 34·4	5·6	3·3	11·6	6·9	17·6	10·4
57	8 44·3	8 45·7	8 20·4	5·7	3·3	11·7	6·7	17·7	10·2	57	8 59·3	9 00·7	8 34·7	5·7	3·4	11·7	6·9	17·7	10·5
58	8 44·5	8 45·9	8 20·6	5·8	3·3	11·8	6·8	17·8	10·2	58	8 59·5	9 01·0	8 34·9	5·8	3·4	11·8	7·0	17·8	10·5
59	8 44·8	8 46·2	8 20·8	5·9	3·4	11·9	6·8	17·9	10·3	59	8 59·8	9 01·2	8 35·2	5·9	3·5	11·9	7·0	17·9	10·6
60	8 45·0	8 46·4	8 21·1	6·0	3·5	12·0	6·9	18·0	10·4	60	9 00·0	9 01·5	8 35·4	6·0	3·6	12·0	7·1	18·0	10·7

36ˢ	SUN PLANETS	ARIES	MOON	v or Corrⁿ d	v or Corrⁿ d	v or Corrⁿ d
s	° ′	° ′	° ′	′ ′	′ ′	′ ′
00	9 00·0	9 01·5	8 35·4	0·0 0·0	6·0 3·7	12·0 7·3
01	9 00·3	9 01·7	8 35·6	0·1 0·1	6·1 3·7	12·1 7·4
02	9 00·5	9 02·0	8 35·9	0·2 0·1	6·2 3·8	12·2 7·4
03	9 00·8	9 02·2	8 36·1	0·3 0·2	6·3 3·8	12·3 7·5
04	9 01·0	9 02·5	8 36·4	0·4 0·2	6·4 3·9	12·4 7·5
05	9 01·3	9 02·7	8 36·6	0·5 0·3	6·5 4·0	12·5 7·6
06	9 01·5	9 03·0	8 36·8	0·6 0·4	6·6 4·0	12·6 7·7
07	9 01·8	9 03·2	8 37·1	0·7 0·4	6·7 4·1	12·7 7·7
08	9 02·0	9 03·5	8 37·3	0·8 0·5	6·8 4·1	12·8 7·8
09	9 02·3	9 03·7	8 37·5	0·9 0·5	6·9 4·2	12·9 7·8
10	9 02·5	9 04·0	8 37·8	1·0 0·6	7·0 4·3	13·0 7·9
11	9 02·8	9 04·2	8 38·0	1·1 0·7	7·1 4·3	13·1 8·0
12	9 03·0	9 04·5	8 38·3	1·2 0·7	7·2 4·4	13·2 8·0
13	9 03·3	9 04·7	8 38·5	1·3 0·8	7·3 4·4	13·3 8·1
14	9 03·5	9 05·0	8 38·7	1·4 0·9	7·4 4·5	13·4 8·2
15	9 03·8	9 05·2	8 39·0	1·5 0·9	7·5 4·6	13·5 8·2
16	9 04·0	9 05·5	8 39·2	1·6 1·0	7·6 4·6	13·6 8·3
17	9 04·3	9 05·7	8 39·5	1·7 1·0	7·7 4·7	13·7 8·3
18	9 04·5	9 06·0	8 39·7	1·8 1·1	7·8 4·7	13·8 8·4
19	9 04·8	9 06·2	8 39·9	1·9 1·2	7·9 4·8	13·9 8·5
20	9 05·0	9 06·5	8 40·2	2·0 1·2	8·0 4·9	14·0 8·5
21	9 05·3	9 06·7	8 40·4	2·1 1·3	8·1 4·9	14·1 8·6
22	9 05·5	9 07·0	8 40·6	2·2 1·3	8·2 5·0	14·2 8·6
23	9 05·8	9 07·2	8 40·9	2·3 1·4	8·3 5·0	14·3 8·7
24	9 06·0	9 07·5	8 41·1	2·4 1·5	8·4 5·1	14·4 8·8
25	9 06·3	9 07·7	8 41·4	2·5 1·5	8·5 5·2	14·5 8·8
26	9 06·5	9 08·0	8 41·6	2·6 1·6	8·6 5·2	14·6 8·9
27	9 06·8	9 08·2	8 41·8	2·7 1·6	8·7 5·3	14·7 8·9
28	9 07·0	9 08·5	8 42·1	2·8 1·7	8·8 5·4	14·8 9·0
29	9 07·3	9 08·7	8 42·3	2·9 1·8	8·9 5·4	14·9 9·1
30	9 07·5	9 09·0	8 42·6	3·0 1·8	9·0 5·5	15·0 9·1
31	9 07·8	9 09·2	8 42·8	3·1 1·9	9·1 5·5	15·1 9·2
32	9 08·0	9 09·5	8 43·0	3·2 1·9	9·2 5·6	15·2 9·2
33	9 08·3	9 09·8	8 43·3	3·3 2·0	9·3 5·7	15·3 9·3
34	9 08·5	9 10·0	8 43·5	3·4 2·1	9·4 5·7	15·4 9·4
35	9 08·8	9 10·3	8 43·8	3·5 2·1	9·5 5·8	15·5 9·4
36	9 09·0	9 10·5	8 44·0	3·6 2·2	9·6 5·8	15·6 9·5
37	9 09·3	9 10·8	8 44·2	3·7 2·3	9·7 5·9	15·7 9·6
38	9 09·5	9 11·0	8 44·5	3·8 2·3	9·8 6·0	15·8 9·6
39	9 09·8	9 11·3	8 44·7	3·9 2·4	9·9 6·0	15·9 9·7
40	9 10·0	9 11·5	8 44·9	4·0 2·4	10·0 6·1	16·0 9·7
41	9 10·3	9 11·8	8 45·2	4·1 2·5	10·1 6·1	16·1 9·8
42	9 10·5	9 12·0	8 45·4	4·2 2·6	10·2 6·2	16·2 9·9
43	9 10·8	9 12·3	8 45·7	4·3 2·6	10·3 6·3	16·3 9·9
44	9 11·0	9 12·5	8 45·9	4·4 2·7	10·4 6·3	16·4 10·0
45	9 11·3	9 12·8	8 46·1	4·5 2·7	10·5 6·4	16·5 10·0
46	9 11·5	9 13·0	8 46·4	4·6 2·8	10·6 6·4	16·6 10·1
47	9 11·8	9 13·3	8 46·6	4·7 2·9	10·7 6·5	16·7 10·2
48	9 12·0	9 13·5	8 46·9	4·8 2·9	10·8 6·6	16·8 10·2
49	9 12·3	9 13·8	8 47·1	4·9 3·0	10·9 6·6	16·9 10·3
50	9 12·5	9 14·0	8 47·3	5·0 3·0	11·0 6·7	17·0 10·3
51	9 12·8	9 14·3	8 47·6	5·1 3·1	11·1 6·8	17·1 10·4
52	9 13·0	9 14·5	8 47·8	5·2 3·2	11·2 6·8	17·2 10·5
53	9 13·3	9 14·8	8 48·0	5·3 3·2	11·3 6·9	17·3 10·5
54	9 13·5	9 15·0	8 48·3	5·4 3·3	11·4 6·9	17·4 10·6
55	9 13·8	9 15·3	8 48·5	5·5 3·3	11·5 7·0	17·5 10·6
56	9 14·0	9 15·5	8 48·8	5·6 3·4	11·6 7·1	17·6 10·7
57	9 14·3	9 15·8	8 49·0	5·7 3·5	11·7 7·1	17·7 10·8
58	9 14·5	9 16·0	8 49·2	5·8 3·5	11·8 7·2	17·8 10·8
59	9 14·8	9 16·3	8 49·5	5·9 3·6	11·9 7·2	17·9 10·9
60	9 15·0	9 16·5	8 49·7	6·0 3·7	12·0 7·3	18·0 11·0

37ˢ	SUN PLANETS	ARIES	MOON	v or Corrⁿ d	v or Corrⁿ d	v or Corrⁿ d
s	° ′	° ′	° ′	′ ′	′ ′	′ ′
00	9 15·0	9 16·5	8 49·7	0·0 0·0	6·0 3·8	12·0 7·5
01	9 15·3	9 16·8	8 50·0	0·1 0·1	6·1 3·8	12·1 7·6
02	9 15·5	9 17·0	8 50·2	0·2 0·1	6·2 3·9	12·2 7·6
03	9 15·8	9 17·3	8 50·4	0·3 0·2	6·3 3·9	12·3 7·7
04	9 16·0	9 17·5	8 50·7	0·4 0·3	6·4 4·0	12·4 7·8
05	9 16·3	9 17·8	8 50·9	0·5 0·3	6·5 4·1	12·5 7·8
06	9 16·5	9 18·0	8 51·1	0·6 0·4	6·6 4·1	12·6 7·9
07	9 16·8	9 18·3	8 51·4	0·7 0·4	6·7 4·2	12·7 7·9
08	9 17·0	9 18·5	8 51·6	0·8 0·5	6·8 4·3	12·8 8·0
09	9 17·3	9 18·8	8 51·9	0·9 0·6	6·9 4·3	12·9 8·1
10	9 17·5	9 19·0	8 52·1	1·0 0·6	7·0 4·4	13·0 8·1
11	9 17·8	9 19·3	8 52·3	1·1 0·7	7·1 4·4	13·1 8·2
12	9 18·0	9 19·5	8 52·6	1·2 0·8	7·2 4·5	13·2 8·3
13	9 18·3	9 19·8	8 52·8	1·3 0·8	7·3 4·6	13·3 8·3
14	9 18·5	9 20·0	8 53·1	1·4 0·9	7·4 4·6	13·4 8·4
15	9 18·8	9 20·3	8 53·3	1·5 0·9	7·5 4·7	13·5 8·4
16	9 19·0	9 20·5	8 53·5	1·6 1·0	7·6 4·8	13·6 8·5
17	9 19·3	9 20·8	8 53·8	1·7 1·1	7·7 4·8	13·7 8·6
18	9 19·5	9 21·0	8 54·0	1·8 1·1	7·8 4·9	13·8 8·6
19	9 19·8	9 21·3	8 54·3	1·9 1·2	7·9 4·9	13·9 8·7
20	9 20·0	9 21·5	8 54·5	2·0 1·3	8·0 5·0	14·0 8·8
21	9 20·3	9 21·8	8 54·7	2·1 1·3	8·1 5·1	14·1 8·8
22	9 20·5	9 22·0	8 55·0	2·2 1·4	8·2 5·1	14·2 8·9
23	9 20·8	9 22·3	8 55·2	2·3 1·4	8·3 5·2	14·3 8·9
24	9 21·0	9 22·5	8 55·4	2·4 1·5	8·4 5·3	14·4 9·0
25	9 21·3	9 22·8	8 55·7	2·5 1·6	8·5 5·3	14·5 9·1
26	9 21·5	9 23·0	8 55·9	2·6 1·6	8·6 5·4	14·6 9·1
27	9 21·8	9 23·3	8 56·2	2·7 1·7	8·7 5·4	14·7 9·2
28	9 22·0	9 23·5	8 56·4	2·8 1·8	8·8 5·5	14·8 9·3
29	9 22·3	9 23·8	8 56·6	2·9 1·8	8·9 5·6	14·9 9·3
30	9 22·5	9 24·0	8 56·9	3·0 1·9	9·0 5·6	15·0 9·4
31	9 22·8	9 24·3	8 57·1	3·1 1·9	9·1 5·7	15·1 9·4
32	9 23·0	9 24·5	8 57·4	3·2 2·0	9·2 5·8	15·2 9·5
33	9 23·3	9 24·8	8 57·6	3·3 2·1	9·3 5·8	15·3 9·6
34	9 23·5	9 25·0	8 57·8	3·4 2·1	9·4 5·9	15·4 9·6
35	9 23·8	9 25·3	8 58·1	3·5 2·2	9·5 5·9	15·5 9·7
36	9 24·0	9 25·5	8 58·3	3·6 2·3	9·6 6·0	15·6 9·8
37	9 24·3	9 25·8	8 58·5	3·7 2·3	9·7 6·1	15·7 9·8
38	9 24·5	9 26·0	8 58·8	3·8 2·4	9·8 6·1	15·8 9·9
39	9 24·8	9 26·3	8 59·0	3·9 2·4	9·9 6·2	15·9 9·9
40	9 25·0	9 26·5	8 59·3	4·0 2·5	10·0 6·3	16·0 10·0
41	9 25·3	9 26·8	8 59·5	4·1 2·6	10·1 6·3	16·1 10·1
42	9 25·5	9 27·0	8 59·7	4·2 2·6	10·2 6·4	16·2 10·1
43	9 25·8	9 27·3	9 00·0	4·3 2·7	10·3 6·4	16·3 10·2
44	9 26·0	9 27·5	9 00·2	4·4 2·8	10·4 6·5	16·4 10·3
45	9 26·3	9 27·8	9 00·5	4·5 2·8	10·5 6·6	16·5 10·3
46	9 26·5	9 28·1	9 00·7	4·6 2·9	10·6 6·6	16·6 10·4
47	9 26·8	9 28·3	9 00·9	4·7 2·9	10·7 6·7	16·7 10·4
48	9 27·0	9 28·6	9 01·2	4·8 3·0	10·8 6·8	16·8 10·5
49	9 27·3	9 28·8	9 01·4	4·9 3·1	10·9 6·8	16·9 10·6
50	9 27·5	9 29·1	9 01·6	5·0 3·1	11·0 6·9	17·0 10·6
51	9 27·8	9 29·3	9 01·9	5·1 3·2	11·1 6·9	17·1 10·7
52	9 28·0	9 29·6	9 02·1	5·2 3·3	11·2 7·0	17·2 10·8
53	9 28·3	9 29·8	9 02·4	5·3 3·3	11·3 7·1	17·3 10·8
54	9 28·5	9 30·1	9 02·6	5·4 3·4	11·4 7·1	17·4 10·9
55	9 28·8	9 30·3	9 02·8	5·5 3·4	11·5 7·2	17·5 10·9
56	9 29·0	9 30·6	9 03·1	5·6 3·5	11·6 7·3	17·6 11·0
57	9 29·3	9 30·8	9 03·3	5·7 3·6	11·7 7·3	17·7 11·1
58	9 29·5	9 31·1	9 03·6	5·8 3·6	11·8 7·4	17·8 11·1
59	9 29·8	9 31·3	9 03·8	5·9 3·7	11·9 7·4	17·9 11·2
60	9 30·0	9 31·6	9 04·0	6·0 3·8	12·0 7·5	18·0 11·3

38ᵐ

38ᵐ s	SUN PLANETS	ARIES	MOON	v or d	Corrⁿ	v or d	Corrⁿ	v or d	Corrⁿ
00	9 30·0	9 31·6	9 04·0	0·0	0·0	6·0	3·9	12·0	7·7
01	9 30·3	9 31·8	9 04·3	0·1	0·1	6·1	3·9	12·1	7·8
02	9 30·5	9 32·1	9 04·5	0·2	0·1	6·2	4·0	12·2	7·8
03	9 30·8	9 32·3	9 04·7	0·3	0·2	6·3	4·0	12·3	7·9
04	9 31·0	9 32·6	9 05·0	0·4	0·3	6·4	4·1	12·4	8·0
05	9 31·3	9 32·8	9 05·2	0·5	0·3	6·5	4·2	12·5	8·0
06	9 31·5	9 33·1	9 05·5	0·6	0·4	6·6	4·2	12·6	8·1
07	9 31·8	9 33·3	9 05·7	0·7	0·4	6·7	4·3	12·7	8·1
08	9 32·0	9 33·6	9 05·9	0·8	0·5	6·8	4·4	12·8	8·2
09	9 32·3	9 33·8	9 06·2	0·9	0·6	6·9	4·4	12·9	8·3
10	9 32·5	9 34·1	9 06·4	1·0	0·6	7·0	4·5	13·0	8·3
11	9 32·8	9 34·3	9 06·7	1·1	0·7	7·1	4·6	13·1	8·4
12	9 33·0	9 34·6	9 06·9	1·2	0·8	7·2	4·6	13·2	8·5
13	9 33·3	9 34·8	9 07·1	1·3	0·8	7·3	4·7	13·3	8·5
14	9 33·5	9 35·1	9 07·4	1·4	0·9	7·4	4·7	13·4	8·6
15	9 33·8	9 35·3	9 07·6	1·5	1·0	7·5	4·8	13·5	8·7
16	9 34·0	9 35·6	9 07·9	1·6	1·0	7·6	4·9	13·6	8·7
17	9 34·3	9 35·8	9 08·1	1·7	1·1	7·7	4·9	13·7	8·8
18	9 34·5	9 36·1	9 08·3	1·8	1·2	7·8	5·0	13·8	8·9
19	9 34·8	9 36·3	9 08·6	1·9	1·2	7·9	5·1	13·9	8·9
20	9 35·0	9 36·6	9 08·8	2·0	1·3	8·0	5·1	14·0	9·0
21	9 35·3	9 36·8	9 09·0	2·1	1·3	8·1	5·2	14·1	9·0
22	9 35·5	9 37·1	9 09·3	2·2	1·4	8·2	5·3	14·2	9·1
23	9 35·8	9 37·3	9 09·5	2·3	1·5	8·3	5·3	14·3	9·2
24	9 36·0	9 37·6	9 09·8	2·4	1·5	8·4	5·4	14·4	9·2
25	9 36·3	9 37·8	9 10·0	2·5	1·6	8·5	5·5	14·5	9·3
26	9 36·5	9 38·1	9 10·2	2·6	1·7	8·6	5·5	14·6	9·4
27	9 36·8	9 38·3	9 10·5	2·7	1·7	8·7	5·6	14·7	9·4
28	9 37·0	9 38·6	9 10·7	2·8	1·8	8·8	5·6	14·8	9·5
29	9 37·3	9 38·8	9 11·0	2·9	1·9	8·9	5·7	14·9	9·6
30	9 37·5	9 39·1	9 11·2	3·0	1·9	9·0	5·8	15·0	9·6
31	9 37·8	9 39·3	9 11·4	3·1	2·0	9·1	5·8	15·1	9·7
32	9 38·0	9 39·6	9 11·7	3·2	2·1	9·2	5·9	15·2	9·8
33	9 38·3	9 39·8	9 11·9	3·3	2·1	9·3	6·0	15·3	9·8
34	9 38·5	9 40·1	9 12·1	3·4	2·2	9·4	6·0	15·4	9·9
35	9 38·8	9 40·3	9 12·4	3·5	2·2	9·5	6·1	15·5	9·9
36	9 39·0	9 40·6	9 12·6	3·6	2·3	9·6	6·2	15·6	10·0
37	9 39·3	9 40·8	9 12·9	3·7	2·4	9·7	6·2	15·7	10·1
38	9 39·5	9 41·1	9 13·1	3·8	2·4	9·8	6·3	15·8	10·1
39	9 39·8	9 41·3	9 13·3	3·9	2·5	9·9	6·4	15·9	10·2
40	9 40·0	9 41·6	9 13·6	4·0	2·6	10·0	6·4	16·0	10·3
41	9 40·3	9 41·8	9 13·8	4·1	2·6	10·1	6·5	16·1	10·3
42	9 40·5	9 42·1	9 14·1	4·2	2·7	10·2	6·5	16·2	10·4
43	9 40·8	9 42·3	9 14·3	4·3	2·8	10·3	6·6	16·3	10·5
44	9 41·0	9 42·6	9 14·5	4·4	2·8	10·4	6·7	16·4	10·5
45	9 41·3	9 42·8	9 14·8	4·5	2·9	10·5	6·7	16·5	10·6
46	9 41·5	9 43·1	9 15·0	4·6	3·0	10·6	6·8	16·6	10·7
47	9 41·8	9 43·3	9 15·2	4·7	3·0	10·7	6·9	16·7	10·7
48	9 42·0	9 43·6	9 15·5	4·8	3·1	10·8	6·9	16·8	10·8
49	9 42·3	9 43·8	9 15·7	4·9	3·1	10·9	7·0	16·9	10·8
50	9 42·5	9 44·1	9 16·0	5·0	3·2	11·0	7·1	17·0	10·9
51	9 42·8	9 44·3	9 16·2	5·1	3·3	11·1	7·1	17·1	11·0
52	9 43·0	9 44·6	9 16·4	5·2	3·3	11·2	7·2	17·2	11·0
53	9 43·3	9 44·8	9 16·7	5·3	3·4	11·3	7·3	17·3	11·1
54	9 43·5	9 45·1	9 16·9	5·4	3·5	11·4	7·3	17·4	11·2
55	9 43·8	9 45·3	9 17·2	5·5	3·5	11·5	7·4	17·5	11·2
56	9 44·0	9 45·6	9 17·4	5·6	3·6	11·6	7·4	17·6	11·3
57	9 44·3	9 45·8	9 17·6	5·7	3·7	11·7	7·5	17·7	11·4
58	9 44·5	9 46·1	9 17·9	5·8	3·7	11·8	7·6	17·8	11·4
59	9 44·8	9 46·4	9 18·1	5·9	3·8	11·9	7·6	17·9	11·5
60	9 45·0	9 46·6	9 18·4	6·0	3·9	12·0	7·7	18·0	11·6

39ᵐ

39ᵐ s	SUN PLANETS	ARIES	MOON	v or d	Corrⁿ	v or d	Corrⁿ	v or d	Corrⁿ
00	9 45·0	9 46·6	9 18·4	0·0	0·0	6·0	4·0	12·0	7·9
01	9 45·3	9 46·9	9 18·6	0·1	0·1	6·1	4·0	12·1	8·0
02	9 45·5	9 47·1	9 18·8	0·2	0·1	6·2	4·1	12·2	8·0
03	9 45·8	9 47·4	9 19·1	0·3	0·2	6·3	4·1	12·3	8·1
04	9 46·0	9 47·6	9 19·3	0·4	0·3	6·4	4·2	12·4	8·2
05	9 46·3	9 47·9	9 19·5	0·5	0·3	6·5	4·3	12·5	8·2
06	9 46·5	9 48·1	9 19·8	0·6	0·4	6·6	4·3	12·6	8·3
07	9 46·8	9 48·4	9 20·0	0·7	0·5	6·7	4·4	12·7	8·4
08	9 47·0	9 48·6	9 20·3	0·8	0·5	6·8	4·5	12·8	8·4
09	9 47·3	9 48·9	9 20·5	0·9	0·6	6·9	4·5	12·9	8·5
10	9 47·5	9 49·1	9 20·7	1·0	0·7	7·0	4·6	13·0	8·6
11	9 47·8	9 49·4	9 21·0	1·1	0·7	7·1	4·7	13·1	8·6
12	9 48·0	9 49·6	9 21·2	1·2	0·8	7·2	4·7	13·2	8·7
13	9 48·3	9 49·9	9 21·5	1·3	0·9	7·3	4·8	13·3	8·8
14	9 48·5	9 50·1	9 21·7	1·4	0·9	7·4	4·9	13·4	8·8
15	9 48·8	9 50·4	9 21·9	1·5	1·0	7·5	4·9	13·5	8·9
16	9 49·0	9 50·6	9 22·2	1·6	1·1	7·6	5·0	13·6	9·0
17	9 49·3	9 50·9	9 22·4	1·7	1·1	7·7	5·1	13·7	9·0
18	9 49·5	9 51·1	9 22·6	1·8	1·2	7·8	5·1	13·8	9·1
19	9 49·8	9 51·4	9 22·9	1·9	1·3	7·9	5·2	13·9	9·2
20	9 50·0	9 51·6	9 23·1	2·0	1·3	8·0	5·3	14·0	9·2
21	9 50·3	9 51·9	9 23·4	2·1	1·4	8·1	5·3	14·1	9·3
22	9 50·5	9 52·1	9 23·6	2·2	1·4	8·2	5·4	14·2	9·3
23	9 50·8	9 52·4	9 23·8	2·3	1·5	8·3	5·5	14·3	9·4
24	9 51·0	9 52·6	9 24·1	2·4	1·6	8·4	5·5	14·4	9·5
25	9 51·3	9 52·9	9 24·3	2·5	1·6	8·5	5·6	14·5	9·5
26	9 51·5	9 53·1	9 24·6	2·6	1·7	8·6	5·7	14·6	9·6
27	9 51·8	9 53·4	9 24·8	2·7	1·8	8·7	5·7	14·7	9·7
28	9 52·0	9 53·6	9 25·0	2·8	1·8	8·8	5·8	14·8	9·7
29	9 52·3	9 53·9	9 25·3	2·9	1·9	8·9	5·9	14·9	9·8
30	9 52·5	9 54·1	9 25·5	3·0	2·0	9·0	5·9	15·0	9·9
31	9 52·8	9 54·4	9 25·7	3·1	2·0	9·1	6·0	15·1	9·9
32	9 53·0	9 54·6	9 26·0	3·2	2·1	9·2	6·1	15·2	10·0
33	9 53·3	9 54·9	9 26·2	3·3	2·2	9·3	6·1	15·3	10·1
34	9 53·5	9 55·1	9 26·5	3·4	2·2	9·4	6·2	15·4	10·1
35	9 53·8	9 55·4	9 26·7	3·5	2·3	9·5	6·3	15·5	10·2
36	9 54·0	9 55·6	9 26·9	3·6	2·4	9·6	6·3	15·6	10·3
37	9 54·3	9 55·9	9 27·2	3·7	2·4	9·7	6·4	15·7	10·3
38	9 54·5	9 56·1	9 27·4	3·8	2·5	9·8	6·5	15·8	10·4
39	9 54·8	9 56·4	9 27·7	3·9	2·6	9·9	6·5	15·9	10·5
40	9 55·0	9 56·6	9 27·9	4·0	2·6	10·0	6·6	16·0	10·5
41	9 55·3	9 56·9	9 28·1	4·1	2·7	10·1	6·6	16·1	10·6
42	9 55·5	9 57·1	9 28·4	4·2	2·8	10·2	6·7	16·2	10·7
43	9 55·8	9 57·4	9 28·6	4·3	2·8	10·3	6·8	16·3	10·7
44	9 56·0	9 57·6	9 28·8	4·4	2·9	10·4	6·8	16·4	10·8
45	9 56·3	9 57·9	9 29·1	4·5	3·0	10·5	6·9	16·5	10·9
46	9 56·5	9 58·1	9 29·3	4·6	3·0	10·6	7·0	16·6	10·9
47	9 56·8	9 58·4	9 29·6	4·7	3·1	10·7	7·0	16·7	11·0
48	9 57·0	9 58·6	9 29·8	4·8	3·2	10·8	7·1	16·8	11·1
49	9 57·3	9 58·9	9 30·0	4·9	3·2	10·9	7·2	16·9	11·1
50	9 57·5	9 59·1	9 30·3	5·0	3·3	11·0	7·2	17·0	11·2
51	9 57·8	9 59·4	9 30·5	5·1	3·4	11·1	7·3	17·1	11·3
52	9 58·0	9 59·6	9 30·8	5·2	3·4	11·2	7·4	17·2	11·3
53	9 58·3	9 59·9	9 31·0	5·3	3·5	11·3	7·4	17·3	11·4
54	9 58·5	10 00·1	9 31·2	5·4	3·6	11·4	7·5	17·4	11·5
55	9 58·8	10 00·4	9 31·5	5·5	3·6	11·5	7·6	17·5	11·5
56	9 59·0	10 00·6	9 31·7	5·6	3·7	11·6	7·6	17·6	11·6
57	9 59·3	10 00·9	9 32·0	5·7	3·8	11·7	7·7	17·7	11·7
58	9 59·5	10 01·1	9 32·2	5·8	3·8	11·8	7·8	17·8	11·7
59	9 59·8	10 01·4	9 32·4	5·9	3·9	11·9	7·8	17·9	11·8
60	10 00·0	10 01·6	9 32·7	6·0	4·0	12·0	7·9	18·0	11·9

40ᵐ

s	SUN PLANETS	ARIES	MOON	v or Corrn d	v or Corrn d	v or Corrn d
00	10 00·0	10 01·6	9 32·7	0·0 0·0	6·0 4·1	12·0 8·1
01	10 00·3	10 01·9	9 32·9	0·1 0·1	6·1 4·1	12·1 8·2
02	10 00·5	10 02·1	9 33·1	0·2 0·1	6·2 4·2	12·2 8·2
03	10 00·8	10 02·4	9 33·4	0·3 0·2	6·3 4·3	12·3 8·3
04	10 01·0	10 02·6	9 33·6	0·4 0·3	6·4 4·3	12·4 8·4
05	10 01·3	10 02·9	9 33·9	0·5 0·3	6·5 4·4	12·5 8·4
06	10 01·5	10 03·1	9 34·1	0·6 0·4	6·6 4·5	12·6 8·5
07	10 01·8	10 03·4	9 34·3	0·7 0·5	6·7 4·5	12·7 8·6
08	10 02·0	10 03·6	9 34·6	0·8 0·5	6·8 4·6	12·8 8·6
09	10 02·3	10 03·9	9 34·8	0·9 0·6	6·9 4·7	12·9 8·7
10	10 02·5	10 04·1	9 35·1	1·0 0·7	7·0 4·7	13·0 8·8
11	10 02·8	10 04·4	9 35·3	1·1 0·7	7·1 4·8	13·1 8·8
12	10 03·0	10 04·7	9 35·5	1·2 0·8	7·2 4·9	13·2 8·9
13	10 03·3	10 04·9	9 35·8	1·3 0·9	7·3 4·9	13·3 9·0
14	10 03·5	10 05·2	9 36·0	1·4 0·9	7·4 5·0	13·4 9·0
15	10 03·8	10 05·4	9 36·2	1·5 1·0	7·5 5·1	13·5 9·1
16	10 04·0	10 05·7	9 36·5	1·6 1·1	7·6 5·1	13·6 9·2
17	10 04·3	10.05·9	9 36·7	1·7 1·1	7·7 5·2	13·7 9·2
18	10 04·5	10 06·2	9 37·0	1·8 1·2	7·8 5·3	13·8 9·3
19	10 04·8	10 06·4	9 37·2	1·9 1·3	7·9 5·3	13·9 9·4
20	10 05·0	10 06·7	9 37·4	2·0 1·4	8·0 5·4	14·0 9·5
21	10 05·3	10 06·9	9 37·7	2·1 1·4	8·1 5·5	14·1 9·5
22	10 05·5	10 07·2	9 37·9	2·2 1·5	8·2 5·5	14·2 9·6
23	10 05·8	10 07·4	9 38·2	2·3 1·6	8·3 5·6	14·3 9·7
24	10 06·0	10 07·7	9 38·4	2·4 1·6	8·4 5·7	14·4 9·7
25	10 06·3	10 07·9	9 38·6	2·5 1·7	8·5 5·7	14·5 9·8
26	10 06·5	10 08·2	9 38·9	2·6 1·8	8·6 5·8	14·6 9·9
27	10 06·8	10 08·4	9 39·1	2·7 1·8	8·7 5·9	14·7 9·9
28	10 07·0	10 08·7	9 39·3	2·8 1·9	8·8 5·9	14·8 10·0
29	10 07·3	10 08·9	9 39·6	2·9 2·0	8·9 6·0	14·9 10·1
30	10 07·5	10 09·2	9 39·8	3·0 2·0	9·0 6·1	15·0 10·1
31	10 07·8	10 09·4	9 40·1	3·1 2·1	9·1 6·1	15·1 10·2
32	10 08·0	10 09·7	9 40·3	3·2 2·2	9·2 6·2	15·2 10·3
33	10 08·3	10 09·9	9 40·5	3·3 2·2	9·3 6·3	15·3 10·3
34	10 08·5	10 10·2	9 40·8	3·4 2·3	9·4 6·3	15·4 10·4
35	10 08·8	10 10·4	9 41·0	3·5 2·4	9·5 6·4	15·5 10·5
36	10 09·0	10 10·7	9 41·3	3·6 2·4	9·6 6·5	15·6 10·5
37	10 09·3	10 10·9	9 41·5	3·7 2·5	9·7 6·5	15·7 10·6
38	10 09·5	10 11·2	9 41·7	3·8 2·6	9·8 6·6	15·8 10·7
39	10 09·8	10 11·4	9 42·0	3·9 2·6	9·9 6·7	15·9 10·7
40	10 10·0	10 11·7	9 42·2	4·0 2·7	10·0 6·8	16·0 10·8
41	10 10·3	10 11·9	9 42·4	4·1 2·8	10·1 6·8	16·1 10·9
42	10 10·5	10 12·2	9 42·7	4·2 2·8	10·2 6·9	16·2 10·9
43	10 10·8	10 12·4	9 42·9	4·3 2·9	10·3 7·0	16·3 11·0
44	10 11·0	10 12·7	9 43·2	4·4 3·0	10·4 7·0	16·4 11·1
45	10 11·3	10 12·9	9 43·4	4·5 3·0	10·5 7·1	16·5 11·1
46	10 11·5	10 13·2	9 43·6	4·6 3·1	10·6 7·2	16·6 11·2
47	10 11·8	10 13·4	9 43·9	4·7 3·2	10·7 7·2	16·7 11·3
48	10 12·0	10 13·7	9 44·1	4·8 3·2	10·8 7·3	16·8 11·3
49	10 12·3	10 13·9	9 44·4	4·9 3·3	10·9 7·4	16·9 11·4
50	10 12·5	10 14·2	9 44·6	5·0 3·4	11·0 7·4	17·0 11·5
51	10 12·8	10 14·4	9 44·8	5·1 3·4	11·1 7·5	17·1 11·5
52	10 13·0	10 14·7	9 45·1	5·2 3·5	11·2 7·6	17·2 11·6
53	10 13·3	10 14·9	9 45·3	5·3 3·6	11·3 7·6	17·3 11·7
54	10 13·5	10 15·2	9 45·6	5·4 3·6	11·4 7·7	17·4 11·7
55	10 13·8	10 15·4	9 45·8	5·5 3·7	11·5 7·8	17·5 11·8
56	10 14·0	10 15·7	9 46·0	5·6 3·8	11·6 7·8	17·6 11·9
57	10 14·3	10 15·9	9 46·3	5·7 3·8	11·7 7·9	17·7 11·9
58	10 14·5	10 16·2	9 46·5	5·8 3·9	11·8 8·0	17·8 12·0
59	10 14·8	10 16·4	9 46·7	5·9 4·0	11·9 8·0	17·9 12·1
60	10 15·0	10 16·7	9 47·0	6·0 4·1	12·0 8·1	18·0 12·2

41ᵐ

s	SUN PLANETS	ARIES	MOON	v or Corrn d	v or Corrn d	v or Corrn d
00	10 15·0	10 16·7	9 47·0	0·0 0·0	6·0 4·2	12·0 8·3
01	10 15·3	10 16·9	9 47·2	0·1 0·1	6·1 4·2	12·1 8·4
02	10 15·5	10 17·2	9 47·5	0·2 0·1	6·2 4·3	12·2 8·4
03	10 15·8	10 17·4	9 47·7	0·3 0·2	6·3 4·4	12·3 8·5
04	10 16·0	10 17·7	9 47·9	0·4 0·3	6·4 4·4	12·4 8·6
05	10 16·3	10 17·9	9 48·2	0·5 0·3	6·5 4·5	12·5 8·6
06	10 16·5	10 18·2	9 48·4	0·6 0·4	6·6 4·6	12·6 8·7
07	10 16·8	10 18·4	9 48·7	0·7 0·5	6·7 4·6	12·7 8·8
08	10 17·0	10 18·7	9 48·9	0·8 0·6	6·8 4·7	12·8 8·9
09	10 17·3	10 18·9	9 49·1	0·9 0·6	6·9 4·8	12·9 8·9
10	10 17·5	10 19·2	9 49·4	1·0 0·7	7·0 4·8	13·0 9·0
11	10 17·8	10 19·4	9 49·6	1·1 0·8	7·1 4·9	13·1 9·1
12	10 18·0	10 19·7	9 49·8	1·2 0·8	7·2 5·0	13·2 9·1
13	10 18·3	10 19·9	9 50·1	1·3 0·9	7·3 5·0	13·3 9·2
14	10 18·5	10 20·2	9 50·3	1·4 1·0	7·4 5·1	13·4 9·3
15	10 18·8	10 20·4	9 50·6	1·5 1·0	7·5 5·2	13·5 9·3
16	10 19·0	10 20·7	9 50·8	1·6 1·1	7·6 5·3	13·6 9·4
17	10 19·3	10 20·9	9 51·0	1·7 1·2	7·7 5·3	13·7 9·5
18	10 19·5	10 21·2	9 51·3	1·8 1·2	7·8 5·4	13·8 9·5
19	10 19·8	10 21·4	9 51·5	1·9 1·3	7·9 5·5	13·9 9·6
20	10 20·0	10 21·7	9 51·8	2·0 1·4	8·0 5·5	14·0 9·7
21	10 20·3	10 21·9	9 52·0	2·1 1·5	8·1 5·6	14·1 9·8
22	10 20·5	10 22·2	9 52·2	2·2 1·5	8·2 5·7	14·2 9·8
23	10 20·8	10 22·4	9 52·5	2·3 1·6	8·3 5·7	14·3 9·9
24	10 21·0	10 22·7	9 52·7	2·4 1·7	8·4 5·8	14·4 10·0
25	10 21·3	10 23·0	9 52·9	2·5 1·7	8·5 5·9	14·5 10·0
26	10 21·5	10 23·2	9 53·2	2·6 1·8	8·6 5·9	14·6 10·1
27	10 21·8	10 23·5	9 53·4	2·7 1·9	8·7 6·0	14·7 10·2
28	10 22·0	10 23·7	9 53·7	2·8 1·9	8·8 6·1	14·8 10·2
29	10 22·3	10 24·0	9 53·9	2·9 2·0	8·9 6·2	14·9 10·3
30	10 22·5	10 24·2	9 54·1	3·0 2·1	9·0 6·2	15·0 10·4
31	10 22·8	10 24·5	9 54·4	3·1 2·1	9·1 6·3	15·1 10·4
32	10 23·0	10 24·7	9 54·6	3·2 2·2	9·2 6·4	15·2 10·5
33	10 23·3	10 25·0	9 54·9	3·3 2·3	9·3 6·4	15·3 10·6
34	10 23·5	10 25·2	9 55·1	3·4 2·4	9·4 6·5	15·4 10·7
35	10 23·8	10 25·5	9 55·3	3·5 2·4	9·5 6·6	15·5 10·7
36	10 24·0	10 25·7	9 55·6	3·6 2·5	9·6 6·6	15·6 10·8
37	10 24·3	10 26·0	9 55·8	3·7 2·6	9·7 6·7	15·7 10·9
38	10 24·5	10 26·2	9 56·1	3·8 2·6	9·8 6·8	15·8 10·9
39	10 24·8	10 26·5	9 56·3	3·9 2·7	9·9 6·8	15·9 11·0
40	10 25·0	10 26·7	9 56·5	4·0 2·8	10·0 6·9	16·0 11·1
41	10 25·3	10 27·0	9 56·8	4·1 2·8	10·1 7·0	16·1 11·1
42	10 25·5	10 27·2	9 57·0	4·2 2·9	10·2 7·1	16·2 11·2
43	10 25·8	10 27·5	9 57·2	4·3 3·0	10·3 7·1	16·3 11·3
44	10 26·0	10 27·7	9 57·5	4·4 3·0	10·4 7·2	16·4 11·3
45	10 26·3	10 28·0	9 57·7	4·5 3·1	10·5 7·3	16·5 11·4
46	10 26·5	10 28·2	9 58·0	4·6 3·2	10·6 7·3	16·6 11·5
47	10 26·8	10 28·5	9 58·2	4·7 3·3	10·7 7·4	16·7 11·6
48	10 27·0	10 28·7	9 58·4	4·8 3·3	10·8 7·5	16·8 11·6
49	10 27·3	10 29·0	9 58·7	4·9 3·4	10·9 7·5	16·9 11·7
50	10 27·5	10 29·2	9 58·9	5·0 3·5	11·0 7·6	17·0 11·8
51	10 27·8	10 29·5	9 59·2	5·1 3·5	11·1 7·7	17·1 11·8
52	10 28·0	10 29·7	9 59·4	5·2 3·6	11·2 7·7	17·2 11·9
53	10 28·3	10 30·0	9 59·6	5·3 3·7	11·3 7·8	17·3 12·0
54	10 28·5	10 30·2	9 59·9	5·4 3·7	11·4 7·9	17·4 12·0
55	10 28·8	10 30·5	10 00·1	5·5 3·8	11·5 8·0	17·5 12·1
56	10 29·0	10 30·7	10 00·3	5·6 3·9	11·6 8·0	17·6 12·2
57	10 29·3	10 31·0	10 00·6	5·7 3·9	11·7 8·1	17·7 12·2
58	10 29·5	10 31·2	10 00·8	5·8 4·0	11·8 8·2	17·8 12·3
59	10 29·8	10 31·5	10 01·1	5·9 4·1	11·9 8·2	17·9 12·4
60	10 30·0	10 31·7	10 01·3	6·0 4·2	12·0 8·3	18·0 12·5

42ᵐ

42ᵐ	SUN PLANETS	ARIES	MOON	v or Corrⁿ d	v or Corrⁿ d	v or Corrⁿ d
s	° ′	° ′	° ′	′ ′	′ ′	′ ′
00	10 30.0	10 31.7	10 01.3	0.0 0.0	6.0 4.3	12.0 8.5
01	10 30.3	10 32.0	10 01.5	0.1 0.1	6.1 4.3	12.1 8.6
02	10 30.5	10 32.2	10 01.8	0.2 0.1	6.2 4.4	12.2 8.6
03	10 30.8	10 32.5	10 02.0	0.3 0.2	6.3 4.5	12.3 8.7
04	10 31.0	10 32.7	10 02.3	0.4 0.3	6.4 4.5	12.4 8.8
05	10 31.3	10 33.0	10 02.5	0.5 0.4	6.5 4.6	12.5 8.9
06	10 31.5	10 33.2	10 02.7	0.6 0.4	6.6 4.7	12.6 8.9
07	10 31.8	10 33.5	10 03.0	0.7 0.5	6.7 4.7	12.7 9.0
08	10 32.0	10 33.7	10 03.2	0.8 0.6	6.8 4.8	12.8 9.1
09	10 32.3	10 34.0	10 03.4	0.9 0.6	6.9 4.9	12.9 9.1
10	10 32.5	10 34.2	10 03.7	1.0 0.7	7.0 5.0	13.0 9.2
11	10 32.8	10 34.5	10 03.9	1.1 0.8	7.1 5.0	13.1 9.3
12	10 33.0	10 34.7	10 04.2	1.2 0.9	7.2 5.1	13.2 9.4
13	10 33.3	10 35.0	10 04.4	1.3 0.9	7.3 5.2	13.3 9.4
14	10 33.5	10 35.2	10 04.6	1.4 1.0	7.4 5.2	13.4 9.5
15	10 33.8	10 35.5	10 04.9	1.5 1.1	7.5 5.3	13.5 9.6
16	10 34.0	10 35.7	10 05.1	1.6 1.1	7.6 5.4	13.6 9.6
17	10 34.3	10 36.0	10 05.4	1.7 1.2	7.7 5.5	13.7 9.7
18	10 34.5	10 36.2	10 05.6	1.8 1.3	7.8 5.5	13.8 9.8
19	10 34.8	10 36.5	10 05.8	1.9 1.3	7.9 5.6	13.9 9.8
20	10 35.0	10 36.7	10 06.1	2.0 1.4	8.0 5.7	14.0 9.9
21	10 35.3	10 37.0	10 06.3	2.1 1.5	8.1 5.7	14.1 10.0
22	10 35.5	10 37.2	10 06.5	2.2 1.6	8.2 5.8	14.2 10.1
23	10 35.8	10 37.5	10 06.8	2.3 1.6	8.3 5.9	14.3 10.1
24	10 36.0	10 37.7	10 07.0	2.4 1.7	8.4 6.0	14.4 10.2
25	10 36.3	10 38.0	10 07.3	2.5 1.8	8.5 6.0	14.5 10.3
26	10 36.5	10 38.2	10 07.5	2.6 1.8	8.6 6.1	14.6 10.3
27	10 36.8	10 38.5	10 07.7	2.7 1.9	8.7 6.2	14.7 10.4
28	10 37.0	10 38.7	10 08.0	2.8 2.0	8.8 6.2	14.8 10.5
29	10 37.3	10 39.0	10 08.2	2.9 2.1	8.9 6.3	14.9 10.6
30	10 37.5	10 39.2	10 08.5	3.0 2.1	9.0 6.4	15.0 10.6
31	10 37.8	10 39.5	10 08.7	3.1 2.2	9.1 6.4	15.1 10.7
32	10 38.0	10 39.7	10 08.9	3.2 2.3	9.2 6.5	15.2 10.8
33	10 38.3	10 40.0	10 09.2	3.3 2.3	9.3 6.6	15.3 10.8
34	10 38.5	10 40.2	10 09.4	3.4 2.4	9.4 6.7	15.4 10.9
35	10 38.8	10 40.5	10 09.7	3.5 2.5	9.5 6.7	15.5 11.0
36	10 39.0	10 40.7	10 09.9	3.6 2.6	9.6 6.8	15.6 11.1
37	10 39.3	10 41.0	10 10.1	3.7 2.6	9.7 6.9	15.7 11.1
38	10 39.5	10 41.3	10 10.4	3.8 2.7	9.8 6.9	15.8 11.2
39	10 39.8	10 41.5	10 10.6	3.9 2.8	9.9 7.0	15.9 11.3
40	10 40.0	10 41.8	10 10.8	4.0 2.8	10.0 7.1	16.0 11.3
41	10 40.3	10 42.0	10 11.1	4.1 2.9	10.1 7.2	16.1 11.4
42	10 40.5	10 42.3	10 11.3	4.2 3.0	10.2 7.2	16.2 11.5
43	10 40.8	10 42.5	10 11.6	4.3 3.0	10.3 7.3	16.3 11.5
44	10 41.0	10 42.8	10 11.8	4.4 3.1	10.4 7.4	16.4 11.6
45	10 41.3	10 43.0	10 12.0	4.5 3.2	10.5 7.4	16.5 11.7
46	10 41.5	10 43.3	10 12.3	4.6 3.3	10.6 7.5	16.6 11.8
47	10 41.8	10 43.5	10 12.5	4.7 3.3	10.7 7.6	16.7 11.8
48	10 42.0	10 43.8	10 12.8	4.8 3.4	10.8 7.7	16.8 11.9
49	10 42.3	10 44.0	10 13.0	4.9 3.5	10.9 7.7	16.9 12.0
50	10 42.5	10 44.3	10 13.2	5.0 3.5	11.0 7.8	17.0 12.0
51	10 42.8	10 44.5	10 13.5	5.1 3.6	11.1 7.9	17.1 12.1
52	10 43.0	10 44.8	10 13.7	5.2 3.7	11.2 7.9	17.2 12.2
53	10 43.3	10 45.0	10 13.9	5.3 3.8	11.3 8.0	17.3 12.3
54	10 43.5	10 45.3	10 14.2	5.4 3.8	11.4 8.1	17.4 12.3
55	10 43.8	10 45.5	10 14.4	5.5 3.9	11.5 8.1	17.5 12.4
56	10 44.0	10 45.8	10 14.7	5.6 4.0	11.6 8.2	17.6 12.5
57	10 44.3	10 46.0	10 14.9	5.7 4.0	11.7 8.3	17.7 12.5
58	10 44.5	10 46.3	10 15.1	5.8 4.1	11.8 8.4	17.8 12.6
59	10 44.8	10 46.5	10 15.4	5.9 4.2	11.9 8.4	17.9 12.7
60	10 45.0	10 46.8	10 15.6	6.0 4.3	12.0 8.5	18.0 12.8

43ᵐ

43ᵐ	SUN PLANETS	ARIES	MOON	v or Corrⁿ d	v or Corrⁿ d	v or Corrⁿ d
s	° ′	° ′	° ′	′ ′	′ ′	′ ′
00	10 45.0	10 46.8	10 15.6	0.0 0.0	6.0 4.4	12.0 8.7
01	10 45.3	10 47.0	10 15.9	0.1 0.1	6.1 4.4	12.1 8.8
02	10 45.5	10 47.3	10 16.1	0.2 0.1	6.2 4.5	12.2 8.8
03	10 45.8	10 47.5	10 16.3	0.3 0.2	6.3 4.6	12.3 8.9
04	10 46.0	10 47.8	10 16.6	0.4 0.3	6.4 4.6	12.4 9.0
05	10 46.3	10 48.0	10 16.8	0.5 0.4	6.5 4.7	12.5 9.1
06	10 46.5	10 48.3	10 17.0	0.6 0.4	6.6 4.8	12.6 9.1
07	10 46.8	10 48.5	10 17.3	0.7 0.5	6.7 4.9	12.7 9.2
08	10 47.0	10 48.8	10 17.5	0.8 0.6	6.8 4.9	12.8 9.3
09	10 47.3	10 49.0	10 17.8	0.9 0.7	6.9 5.0	12.9 9.4
10	10 47.5	10 49.3	10 18.0	1.0 0.7	7.0 5.1	13.0 9.4
11	10 47.8	10 49.5	10 18.2	1.1 0.8	7.1 5.1	13.1 9.5
12	10 48.0	10 49.8	10 18.5	1.2 0.9	7.2 5.2	13.2 9.6
13	10 48.3	10 50.0	10 18.7	1.3 0.9	7.3 5.3	13.3 9.6
14	10 48.5	10 50.3	10 19.0	1.4 1.0	7.4 5.4	13.4 9.7
15	10 48.8	10 50.5	10 19.2	1.5 1.1	7.5 5.4	13.5 9.8
16	10 49.0	10 50.8	10 19.4	1.6 1.2	7.6 5.5	13.6 9.9
17	10 49.3	10 51.0	10 19.7	1.7 1.2	7.7 5.6	13.7 9.9
18	10 49.5	10 51.3	10 19.9	1.8 1.3	7.8 5.7	13.8 10.0
19	10 49.8	10 51.5	10 20.2	1.9 1.4	7.9 5.7	13.9 10.1
20	10 50.0	10 51.8	10 20.4	2.0 1.5	8.0 5.8	14.0 10.2
21	10 50.3	10 52.0	10 20.6	2.1 1.5	8.1 5.9	14.1 10.2
22	10 50.5	10 52.3	10 20.9	2.2 1.6	8.2 5.9	14.2 10.3
23	10 50.8	10 52.5	10 21.1	2.3 1.7	8.3 6.0	14.3 10.4
24	10 51.0	10 52.8	10 21.3	2.4 1.7	8.4 6.1	14.4 10.4
25	10 51.3	10 53.0	10 21.6	2.5 1.8	8.5 6.2	14.5 10.5
26	10 51.5	10 53.3	10 21.8	2.6 1.9	8.6 6.2	14.6 10.6
27	10 51.8	10 53.5	10 22.1	2.7 2.0	8.7 6.3	14.7 10.7
28	10 52.0	10 53.8	10 22.3	2.8 2.0	8.8 6.4	14.8 10.7
29	10 52.3	10 54.0	10 22.5	2.9 2.1	8.9 6.5	14.9 10.8
30	10 52.5	10 54.3	10 22.8	3.0 2.2	9.0 6.5	15.0 10.9
31	10 52.8	10 54.5	10 23.0	3.1 2.2	9.1 6.6	15.1 10.9
32	10 53.0	10 54.8	10 23.3	3.2 2.3	9.2 6.7	15.2 11.0
33	10 53.3	10 55.0	10 23.5	3.3 2.4	9.3 6.7	15.3 11.1
34	10 53.5	10 55.3	10 23.7	3.4 2.5	9.4 6.8	15.4 11.2
35	10 53.8	10 55.5	10 24.0	3.5 2.5	9.5 6.9	15.5 11.2
36	10 54.0	10 55.8	10 24.2	3.6 2.6	9.6 7.0	15.6 11.3
37	10 54.3	10 56.0	10 24.4	3.7 2.7	9.7 7.0	15.7 11.4
38	10 54.5	10 56.3	10 24.7	3.8 2.8	9.8 7.1	15.8 11.5
39	10 54.8	10 56.5	10 24.9	3.9 2.8	9.9 7.2	15.9 11.5
40	10 55.0	10 56.8	10 25.2	4.0 2.9	10.0 7.3	16.0 11.6
41	10 55.3	10 57.0	10 25.4	4.1 3.0	10.1 7.3	16.1 11.7
42	10 55.5	10 57.3	10 25.6	4.2 3.0	10.2 7.4	16.2 11.7
43	10 55.8	10 57.5	10 25.9	4.3 3.1	10.3 7.5	16.3 11.8
44	10 56.0	10 57.8	10 26.1	4.4 3.2	10.4 7.5	16.4 11.9
45	10 56.3	10 58.0	10 26.4	4.5 3.3	10.5 7.6	16.5 12.0
46	10 56.5	10 58.3	10 26.6	4.6 3.3	10.6 7.7	16.6 12.0
47	10 56.8	10 58.5	10 26.8	4.7 3.4	10.7 7.8	16.7 12.1
48	10 57.0	10 58.8	10 27.1	4.8 3.5	10.8 7.8	16.8 12.2
49	10 57.3	10 59.0	10 27.3	4.9 3.6	10.9 7.9	16.9 12.3
50	10 57.5	10 59.3	10 27.5	5.0 3.6	11.0 8.0	17.0 12.3
51	10 57.8	10 59.6	10 27.8	5.1 3.7	11.1 8.0	17.1 12.4
52	10 58.0	10 59.8	10 28.0	5.2 3.8	11.2 8.1	17.2 12.5
53	10 58.3	11 00.1	10 28.3	5.3 3.8	11.3 8.2	17.3 12.5
54	10 58.5	11 00.3	10 28.5	5.4 3.9	11.4 8.3	17.4 12.6
55	10 58.8	11 00.6	10 28.7	5.5 4.0	11.5 8.3	17.5 12.7
56	10 59.0	11 00.8	10 29.0	5.6 4.1	11.6 8.4	17.6 12.8
57	10 59.3	11 01.1	10 29.2	5.7 4.1	11.7 8.5	17.7 12.8
58	10 59.5	11 01.3	10 29.5	5.8 4.2	11.8 8.6	17.8 12.9
59	10 59.8	11 01.6	10 29.7	5.9 4.3	11.9 8.6	17.9 13.0
60	11 00.0	11 01.8	10 29.9	6.0 4.4	12.0 8.7	18.0 13.1

44ᵐ	SUN PLANETS	ARIES	MOON	v or Corrⁿ d	v or Corrⁿ d	v or Corrⁿ d
s	° ′	° ′	° ′	′ ′	′ ′	′ ′
00	11 00·0	11 01·8	10 29·9	0·0 0·0	6·0 4·5	12·0 8·9
01	11 00·3	11 02·1	10 30·2	0·1 0·1	6·1 4·5	12·1 9·0
02	11 00·5	11 02·3	10 30·4	0·2 0·1	6·2 4·6	12·2 9·0
03	11 00·8	11 02·6	10 30·6	0·3 0·2	6·3 4·7	12·3 9·1
04	11 01·0	11 02·8	10 30·9	0·4 0·3	6·4 4·7	12·4 9·2
05	11 01·3	11 03·1	10 31·1	0·5 0·4	6·5 4·8	12·5 9·3
06	11 01·5	11 03·3	10 31·4	0·6 0·4	6·6 4·9	12·6 9·3
07	11 01·8	11 03·6	10 31·6	0·7 0·5	6·7 5·0	12·7 9·4
08	11 02·0	11 03·8	10 31·8	0·8 0·6	6·8 5·0	12·8 9·5
09	11 02·3	11 04·1	10 32·1	0·9 0·7	6·9 5·1	12·9 9·6
10	11 02·5	11 04·3	10 32·3	1·0 0·7	7·0 5·2	13·0 9·6
11	11 02·8	11 04·6	10 32·6	1·1 0·8	7·1 5·3	13·1 9·7
12	11 03·0	11 04·8	10 32·8	1·2 0·9	7·2 5·3	13·2 9·8
13	11 03·3	11 05·1	10 33·0	1·3 1·0	7·3 5·4	13·3 9·9
14	11 03·5	11 05·3	10 33·3	1·4 1·0	7·4 5·5	13·4 9·9
15	11 03·8	11 05·6	10 33·5	1·5 1·1	7·5 5·6	13·5 10·0
16	11 04·0	11 05·8	10 33·8	1·6 1·2	7·6 5·6	13·6 10·1
17	11 04·3	11 06·1	10 34·0	1·7 1·3	7·7 5·7	13·7 10·2
18	11 04·5	11 06·3	10 34·2	1·8 1·3	7·8 5·8	13·8 10·2
19	11 04·8	11 06·6	10 34·5	1·9 1·4	7·9 5·9	13·9 10·3
20	11 05·0	11 06·8	10 34·7	2·0 1·5	8·0 5·9	14·0 10·4
21	11 05·3	11 07·1	10 34·9	2·1 1·6	8·1 6·0	14·1 10·5
22	11 05·5	11 07·3	10 35·2	2·2 1·6	8·2 6·1	14·2 10·5
23	11 05·8	11 07·6	10 35·4	2·3 1·7	8·3 6·2	14·3 10·6
24	11 06·0	11 07·8	10 35·7	2·4 1·8	8·4 6·2	14·4 10·7
25	11 06·3	11 08·1	10 35·9	2·5 1·9	8·5 6·3	14·5 10·8
26	11 06·5	11 08·3	10 36·1	2·6 1·9	8·6 6·4	14·6 10·8
27	11 06·8	11 08·6	10 36·4	2·7 2·0	8·7 6·5	14·7 10·9
28	11 07·0	11 08·8	10 36·6	2·8 2·1	8·8 6·5	14·8 11·0
29	11 07·3	11 09·1	10 36·9	2·9 2·2	8·9 6·6	14·9 11·1
30	11 07·5	11 09·3	10 37·1	3·0 2·2	9·0 6·7	15·0 11·1
31	11 07·8	11 09·6	10 37·3	3·1 2·3	9·1 6·7	15·1 11·2
32	11 08·0	11 09·8	10 37·6	3·2 2·4	9·2 6·8	15·2 11·3
33	11 08·3	11 10·1	10 37·8	3·3 2·4	9·3 6·9	15·3 11·3
34	11 08·5	11 10·3	10 38·0	3·4 2·5	9·4 7·0	15·4 11·4
35	11 08·8	11 10·6	10 38·3	3·5 2·6	9·5 7·0	15·5 11·5
36	11 09·0	11 10·8	10 38·5	3·6 2·7	9·6 7·1	15·6 11·6
37	11 09·3	11 11·1	10 38·8	3·7 2·7	9·7 7·2	15·7 11·6
38	11 09·5	11 11·3	10 39·0	3·8 2·8	9·8 7·3	15·8 11·7
39	11 09·8	11 11·6	10 39·2	3·9 2·9	9·9 7·3	15·9 11·8
40	11 10·0	11 11·8	10 39·5	4·0 3·0	10·0 7·4	16·0 11·9
41	11 10·3	11 12·1	10 39·7	4·1 3·0	10·1 7·5	16·1 11·9
42	11 10·5	11 12·3	10 40·0	4·2 3·1	10·2 7·6	16·2 12·0
43	11 10·8	11 12·6	10 40·2	4·3 3·2	10·3 7·6	16·3 12·1
44	11 11·0	11 12·8	10 40·4	4·4 3·3	10·4 7·7	16·4 12·2
45	11 11·3	11 13·1	10 40·7	4·5 3·3	10·5 7·8	16·5 12·2
46	11 11·5	11 13·3	10 40·9	4·6 3·4	10·6 7·9	16·6 12·3
47	11 11·8	11 13·6	10 41·1	4·7 3·5	10·7 7·9	16·7 12·4
48	11 12·0	11 13·8	10 41·4	4·8 3·6	10·8 8·0	16·8 12·5
49	11 12·3	11 14·1	10 41·6	4·9 3·6	10·9 8·1	16·9 12·5
50	11 12·5	11 14·3	10 41·9	5·0 3·7	11·0 8·2	17·0 12·6
51	11 12·8	11 14·6	10 42·1	5·1 3·8	11·1 8·2	17·1 12·7
52	11 13·0	11 14·8	10 42·3	5·2 3·9	11·2 8·3	17·2 12·8
53	11 13·3	11 15·1	10 42·6	5·3 3·9	11·3 8·4	17·3 12·8
54	11 13·5	11 15·3	10 42·8	5·4 4·0	11·4 8·5	17·4 12·9
55	11 13·8	11 15·6	10 43·1	5·5 4·1	11·5 8·5	17·5 13·0
56	11 14·0	11 15·8	10 43·3	5·6 4·2	11·6 8·6	17·6 13·1
57	11 14·3	11 16·1	10 43·5	5·7 4·2	11·7 8·7	17·7 13·1
58	11 14·5	11 16·3	10 43·8	5·8 4·3	11·8 8·8	17·8 13·2
59	11 14·8	11 16·6	10 44·0	5·9 4·4	11·9 8·8	17·9 13·3
60	11 15·0	11 16·8	10 44·3	6·0 4·5	12·0 8·9	18·0 13·4

45ᵐ	SUN PLANETS	ARIES	MOON	v or Corrⁿ d	v or Corrⁿ d	v or Corrⁿ d
s	° ′	° ′	° ′	′ ′	′ ′	′ ′
00	11 15·0	11 16·8	10 44·3	0·0 0·0	6·0 4·6	12·0 9·1
01	11 15·3	11 17·1	10 44·5	0·1 0·1	6·1 4·6	12·1 9·2
02	11 15·5	11 17·3	10 44·7	0·2 0·2	6·2 4·7	12·2 9·3
03	11 15·8	11 17·6	10 45·0	0·3 0·2	6·3 4·8	12·3 9·3
04	11 16·0	11 17·9	10 45·2	0·4 0·3	6·4 4·9	12·4 9·4
05	11 16·3	11 18·1	10 45·4	0·5 0·4	6·5 4·9	12·5 9·5
06	11 16·5	11 18·4	10 45·7	0·6 0·5	6·6 5·0	12·6 9·6
07	11 16·8	11 18·6	10 45·9	0·7 0·5	6·7 5·1	12·7 9·6
08	11 17·0	11 18·9	10 46·2	0·8 0·6	6·8 5·2	12·8 9·7
09	11 17·3	11 19·1	10 46·4	0·9 0·7	6·9 5·2	12·9 9·8
10	11 17·5	11 19·4	10 46·6	1·0 0·8	7·0 5·3	13·0 9·9
11	11 17·8	11 19·6	10 46·9	1·1 0·8	7·1 5·4	13·1 9·9
12	11 18·0	11 19·9	10 47·1	1·2 0·9	7·2 5·5	13·2 10·0
13	11 18·3	11 20·1	10 47·4	1·3 1·0	7·3 5·5	13·3 10·1
14	11 18·5	11 20·4	10 47·6	1·4 1·1	7·4 5·6	13·4 10·2
15	11 18·8	11 20·6	10 47·8	1·5 1·1	7·5 5·7	13·5 10·2
16	11 19·0	11 20·9	10 48·1	1·6 1·2	7·6 5·8	13·6 10·3
17	11 19·3	11 21·1	10 48·3	1·7 1·3	7·7 5·8	13·7 10·4
18	11 19·5	11 21·4	10 48·5	1·8 1·4	7·8 5·9	13·8 10·5
19	11 19·8	11 21·6	10 48·8	1·9 1·4	7·9 6·0	13·9 10·5
20	11 20·0	11 21·9	10 49·0	2·0 1·5	8·0 6·1	14·0 10·6
21	11 20·3	11 22·1	10 49·3	2·1 1·6	8·1 6·1	14·1 10·7
22	11 20·5	11 22·4	10 49·5	2·2 1·7	8·2 6·2	14·2 10·8
23	11 20·8	11 22·6	10 49·7	2·3 1·7	8·3 6·3	14·3 10·8
24	11 21·0	11 22·9	10 50·0	2·4 1·8	8·4 6·4	14·4 10·9
25	11 21·3	11 23·1	10 50·2	2·5 1·9	8·5 6·4	14·5 11·0
26	11 21·5	11 23·4	10 50·5	2·6 2·0	8·6 6·5	14·6 11·1
27	11 21·8	11 23·6	10 50·7	2·7 2·0	8·7 6·6	14·7 11·1
28	11 22·0	11 23·9	10 50·9	2·8 2·1	8·8 6·7	14·8 11·2
29	11 22·3	11 24·1	10 51·2	2·9 2·2	8·9 6·7	14·9 11·3
30	11 22·5	11 24·4	10 51·4	3·0 2·3	9·0 6·8	15·0 11·4
31	11 22·8	11 24·6	10 51·6	3·1 2·4	9·1 6·9	15·1 11·5
32	11 23·0	11 24·9	10 51·9	3·2 2·4	9·2 7·0	15·2 11·5
33	11 23·3	11 25·1	10 52·1	3·3 2·5	9·3 7·1	15·3 11·6
34	11 23·5	11 25·4	10 52·4	3·4 2·6	9·4 7·1	15·4 11·7
35	11 23·8	11 25·6	10 52·6	3·5 2·7	9·5 7·2	15·5 11·8
36	11 24·0	11 25·9	10 52·8	3·6 2·7	9·6 7·3	15·6 11·8
37	11 24·3	11 26·1	10 53·1	3·7 2·8	9·7 7·4	15·7 11·9
38	11 24·5	11 26·4	10 53·3	3·8 2·9	9·8 7·4	15·8 12·0
39	11 24·8	11 26·6	10 53·6	3·9 3·0	9·9 7·5	15·9 12·1
40	11 25·0	11 26·9	10 53·8	4·0 3·0	10·0 7·6	16·0 12·1
41	11 25·3	11 27·1	10 54·0	4·1 3·1	10·1 7·7	16·1 12·2
42	11 25·5	11 27·4	10 54·3	4·2 3·2	10·2 7·7	16·2 12·3
43	11 25·8	11 27·6	10 54·5	4·3 3·3	10·3 7·8	16·3 12·4
44	11 26·0	11 27·9	10 54·7	4·4 3·3	10·4 7·9	16·4 12·4
45	11 26·3	11 28·1	10 55·0	4·5 3·4	10·5 8·0	16·5 12·5
46	11 26·5	11 28·4	10 55·2	4·6 3·5	10·6 8·0	16·6 12·6
47	11 26·8	11 28·6	10 55·5	4·7 3·6	10·7 8·1	16·7 12·7
48	11 27·0	11 28·9	10 55·7	4·8 3·6	10·8 8·2	16·8 12·7
49	11 27·3	11 29·1	10 55·9	4·9 3·7	10·9 8·3	16·9 12·8
50	11 27·5	11 29·4	10 56·2	5·0 3·8	11·0 8·3	17·0 12·9
51	11 27·8	11 29·6	10 56·4	5·1 3·9	11·1 8·4	17·1 13·0
52	11 28·0	11 29·9	10 56·7	5·2 3·9	11·2 8·5	17·2 13·0
53	11 28·3	11 30·1	10 56·9	5·3 4·0	11·3 8·6	17·3 13·1
54	11 28·5	11 30·4	10 57·1	5·4 4·1	11·4 8·6	17·4 13·2
55	11 28·8	11 30·6	10 57·4	5·5 4·2	11·5 8·7	17·5 13·3
56	11 29·0	11 30·9	10 57·6	5·6 4·2	11·6 8·8	17·6 13·3
57	11 29·3	11 31·1	10 57·9	5·7 4·3	11·7 8·9	17·7 13·4
58	11 29·5	11 31·4	10 58·1	5·8 4·4	11·8 8·9	17·8 13·5
59	11 29·8	11 31·6	10 58·3	5·9 4·5	11·9 9·0	17·9 13·6
60	11 30·0	11 31·9	10 58·6	6·0 4·6	12·0 9·1	18·0 13·7

46ᵐ

46	SUN PLANETS	ARIES	MOON	v or Corrⁿ d	v or Corrⁿ d	v or Corrⁿ d
s	° ′	° ′	° ′	′ ′	′ ′	′ ′
00	11 30·0	11 31·9	10 58·6	0·0 0·0	6·0 4·7	12·0 9·3
01	11 30·3	11 32·1	10 58·8	0·1 0·1	6·1 4·7	12·1 9·4
02	11 30·5	11 32·4	10 59·0	0·2 0·2	6·2 4·8	12·2 9·5
03	11 30·8	11 32·6	10 59·3	0·3 0·2	6·3 4·9	12·3 9·5
04	11 31·0	11 32·9	10 59·5	0·4 0·3	6·4 5·0	12·4 9·6
05	11 31·3	11 33·1	10 59·8	0·5 0·4	6·5 5·0	12·5 9·7
06	11 31·5	11 33·4	11 00·0	0·6 0·5	6·6 5·1	12·6 9·8
07	11 31·8	11 33·6	11 00·2	0·7 0·5	6·7 5·2	12·7 9·8
08	11 32·0	11 33·9	11 00·5	0·8 0·6	6·8 5·3	12·8 9·9
09	11 32·3	11 34·1	11 00·7	0·9 0·7	6·9 5·3	12·9 10·0
10	11 32·5	11 34·4	11 01·0	1·0 0·8	7·0 5·4	13·0 10·1
11	11 32·8	11 34·6	11 01·2	1·1 0·9	7·1 5·5	13·1 10·2
12	11 33·0	11 34·9	11 01·4	1·2 0·9	7·2 5·6	13·2 10·2
13	11 33·3	11 35·1	11 01·7	1·3 1·0	7·3 5·7	13·3 10·3
14	11 33·5	11 35·4	11 01·9	1·4 1·1	7·4 5·7	13·4 10·4
15	11 33·8	11 35·6	11 02·1	1·5 1·2	7·5 5·8	13·5 10·5
16	11 34·0	11 35·9	11 02·4	1·6 1·2	7·6 5·9	13·6 10·5
17	11 34·3	11 36·2	11 02·6	1·7 1·3	7·7 6·0	13·7 10·6
18	11 34·5	11 36·4	11 02·9	1·8 1·4	7·8 6·0	13·8 10·7
19	11 34·8	11 36·7	11 03·1	1·9 1·5	7·9 6·1	13·9 10·8
20	11 35·0	11 36·9	11 03·3	2·0 1·6	8·0 6·2	14·0 10·9
21	11 35·3	11 37·2	11 03·6	2·1 1·6	8·1 6·3	14·1 10·9
22	11 35·5	11 37·4	11 03·8	2·2 1·7	8·2 6·4	14·2 11·0
23	11 35·8	11 37·7	11 04·1	2·3 1·8	8·3 6·4	14·3 11·1
24	11 36·0	11 37·9	11 04·3	2·4 1·9	8·4 6·5	14·4 11·2
25	11 36·3	11 38·2	11 04·5	2·5 1·9	8·5 6·6	14·5 11·2
26	11 36·5	11 38·4	11 04·8	2·6 2·0	8·6 6·7	14·6 11·3
27	11 36·8	11 38·7	11 05·0	2·7 2·1	8·7 6·7	14·7 11·4
28	11 37·0	11 38·9	11 05·2	2·8 2·2	8·8 6·8	14·8 11·5
29	11 37·3	11 39·2	11 05·5	2·9 2·2	8·9 6·9	14·9 11·5
30	11 37·5	11 39·4	11 05·7	3·0 2·3	9·0 7·0	15·0 11·6
31	11 37·8	11 39·7	11 06·0	3·1 2·4	9·1 7·1	15·1 11·7
32	11 38·0	11 39·9	11 06·2	3·2 2·5	9·2 7·1	15·2 11·8
33	11 38·3	11 40·2	11 06·4	3·3 2·6	9·3 7·2	15·3 11·9
34	11 38·5	11 40·4	11 06·7	3·4 2·6	9·4 7·3	15·4 11·9
35	11 38·8	11 40·7	11 06·9	3·5 2·7	9·5 7·4	15·5 12·0
36	11 39·0	11 40·9	11 07·2	3·6 2·8	9·6 7·4	15·6 12·1
37	11 39·3	11 41·2	11 07·4	3·7 2·9	9·7 7·5	15·7 12·2
38	11 39·5	11 41·4	11 07·6	3·8 2·9	9·8 7·6	15·8 12·2
39	11 39·8	11 41·7	11 07·9	3·9 3·0	9·9 7·7	15·9 12·3
40	11 40·0	11 41·9	11 08·1	4·0 3·1	10·0 7·8	16·0 12·4
41	11 40·3	11 42·2	11 08·3	4·1 3·2	10·1 7·8	16·1 12·5
42	11 40·5	11 42·4	11 08·6	4·2 3·3	10·2 7·9	16·2 12·6
43	11 40·8	11 42·7	11 08·8	4·3 3·3	10·3 8·0	16·3 12·6
44	11 41·0	11 42·9	11 09·1	4·4 3·4	10·4 8·1	16·4 12·7
45	11 41·3	11 43·2	11 09·3	4·5 3·5	10·5 8·1	16·5 12·8
46	11 41·5	11 43·4	11 09·5	4·6 3·6	10·6 8·2	16·6 12·9
47	11 41·8	11 43·7	11 09·8	4·7 3·6	10·7 8·3	16·7 12·9
48	11 42·0	11 43·9	11 10·0	4·8 3·7	10·8 8·4	16·8 13·0
49	11 42·3	11 44·2	11 10·3	4·9 3·8	10·9 8·4	16·9 13·1
50	11 42·5	11 44·4	11 10·5	5·0 3·9	11·0 8·5	17·0 13·2
51	11 42·8	11 44·7	11 10·7	5·1 4·0	11·1 8·6	17·1 13·3
52	11 43·0	11 44·9	11 11·0	5·2 4·0	11·2 8·7	17·2 13·3
53	11 43·3	11 45·2	11 11·2	5·3 4·1	11·3 8·8	17·3 13·4
54	11 43·5	11 45·4	11 11·5	5·4 4·2	11·4 8·8	17·4 13·5
55	11 43·8	11 45·7	11 11·7	5·5 4·3	11·5 8·9	17·5 13·6
56	11 44·0	11 45·9	11 11·9	5·6 4·3	11·6 9·0	17·6 13·6
57	11 44·3	11 46·2	11 12·2	5·7 4·4	11·7 9·1	17·7 13·7
58	11 44·5	11 46·4	11 12·4	5·8 4·5	11·8 9·1	17·8 13·8
59	11 44·8	11 46·7	11 12·6	5·9 4·6	11·9 9·2	17·9 13·9
60	11 45·0	11 46·9	11 12·9	6·0 4·7	12·0 9·3	18·0 14·0

47ᵐ

47	SUN PLANETS	ARIES	MOON	v or Corrⁿ d	v or Corrⁿ d	v or Corrⁿ d
s	° ′	° ′	° ′	′ ′	′ ′	′ ′
00	11 45·0	11 46·9	11 12·9	0·0 0·0	6·0 4·8	12·0 9·5
01	11 45·3	11 47·2	11 13·1	0·1 0·1	6·1 4·8	12·1 9·6
02	11 45·5	11 47·4	11 13·4	0·2 0·2	6·2 4·9	12·2 9·7
03	11 45·8	11 47·7	11 13·6	0·3 0·2	6·3 5·0	12·3 9·7
04	11 46·0	11 47·9	11 13·8	0·4 0·3	6·4 5·1	12·4 9·8
05	11 46·3	11 48·2	11 14·1	0·5 0·4	6·5 5·1	12·5 9·9
06	11 46·5	11 48·4	11 14·3	0·6 0·5	6·6 5·2	12·6 10·0
07	11 46·8	11 48·7	11 14·6	0·7 0·6	6·7 5·3	12·7 10·1
08	11 47·0	11 48·9	11 14·8	0·8 0·6	6·8 5·4	12·8 10·1
09	11 47·3	11 49·2	11 15·0	0·9 0·7	6·9 5·5	12·9 10·2
10	11 47·5	11 49·4	11 15·3	1·0 0·8	7·0 5·5	13·0 10·3
11	11 47·8	11 49·7	11 15·5	1·1 0·9	7·1 5·6	13·1 10·4
12	11 48·0	11 49·9	11 15·7	1·2 1·0	7·2 5·7	13·2 10·5
13	11 48·3	11 50·2	11 16·0	1·3 1·0	7·3 5·8	13·3 10·5
14	11 48·5	11 50·4	11 16·2	1·4 1·1	7·4 5·9	13·4 10·6
15	11 48·8	11 50·7	11 16·5	1·5 1·2	7·5 5·9	13·5 10·7
16	11 49·0	11 50·9	11 16·7	1·6 1·3	7·6 6·0	13·6 10·8
17	11 49·3	11 51·2	11 16·9	1·7 1·3	7·7 6·1	13·7 10·8
18	11 49·5	11 51·4	11 17·2	1·8 1·4	7·8 6·2	13·8 10·9
19	11 49·8	11 51·7	11 17·4	1·9 1·5	7·9 6·3	13·9 11·0
20	11 50·0	11 51·9	11 17·7	2·0 1·6	8·0 6·3	14·0 11·1
21	11 50·3	11 52·2	11 17·9	2·1 1·7	8·1 6·4	14·1 11·2
22	11 50·5	11 52·4	11 18·1	2·2 1·7	8·2 6·5	14·2 11·2
23	11 50·8	11 52·7	11 18·4	2·3 1·8	8·3 6·6	14·3 11·3
24	11 51·0	11 52·9	11 18·6	2·4 1·9	8·4 6·7	14·4 11·4
25	11 51·3	11 53·2	11 18·8	2·5 2·0	8·5 6·7	14·5 11·5
26	11 51·5	11 53·4	11 19·1	2·6 2·1	8·6 6·8	14·6 11·6
27	11 51·8	11 53·7	11 19·3	2·7 2·1	8·7 6·9	14·7 11·6
28	11 52·0	11 53·9	11 19·6	2·8 2·2	8·8 7·0	14·8 11·7
29	11 52·3	11 54·2	11 19·8	2·9 2·3	8·9 7·0	14·9 11·8
30	11 52·5	11 54·5	11 20·0	3·0 2·4	9·0 7·1	15·0 11·9
31	11 52·8	11 54·7	11 20·3	3·1 2·5	9·1 7·2	15·1 12·0
32	11 53·0	11 55·0	11 20·5	3·2 2·5	9·2 7·3	15·2 12·0
33	11 53·3	11 55·2	11 20·8	3·3 2·6	9·3 7·4	15·3 12·1
34	11 53·5	11 55·5	11 21·0	3·4 2·7	9·4 7·4	15·4 12·2
35	11 53·8	11 55·7	11 21·2	3·5 2·8	9·5 7·5	15·5 12·3
36	11 54·0	11 56·0	11 21·5	3·6 2·9	9·6 7·6	15·6 12·4
37	11 54·3	11 56·2	11 21·7	3·7 2·9	9·7 7·7	15·7 12·4
38	11 54·5	11 56·5	11 22·0	3·8 3·0	9·8 7·8	15·8 12·5
39	11 54·8	11 56·7	11 22·2	3·9 3·1	9·9 7·8	15·9 12·6
40	11 55·0	11 57·0	11 22·4	4·0 3·2	10·0 7·9	16·0 12·7
41	11 55·3	11 57·2	11 22·7	4·1 3·2	10·1 8·0	16·1 12·7
42	11 55·5	11 57·5	11 22·9	4·2 3·3	10·2 8·1	16·2 12·8
43	11 55·8	11 57·7	11 23·1	4·3 3·4	10·3 8·2	16·3 12·9
44	11 56·0	11 58·0	11 23·4	4·4 3·5	10·4 8·2	16·4 13·0
45	11 56·3	11 58·2	11 23·6	4·5 3·6	10·5 8·3	16·5 13·1
46	11 56·5	11 58·5	11 23·9	4·6 3·6	10·6 8·4	16·6 13·1
47	11 56·8	11 58·7	11 24·1	4·7 3·7	10·7 8·5	16·7 13·2
48	11 57·0	11 59·0	11 24·3	4·8 3·8	10·8 8·6	16·8 13·3
49	11 57·3	11 59·2	11 24·6	4·9 3·9	10·9 8·6	16·9 13·4
50	11 57·5	11 59·5	11 24·8	5·0 4·0	11·0 8·7	17·0 13·5
51	11 57·8	11 59·7	11 25·1	5·1 4·0	11·1 8·8	17·1 13·5
52	11 58·0	12 00·0	11 25·3	5·2 4·1	11·2 8·9	17·2 13·6
53	11 58·3	12 00·2	11 25·5	5·3 4·2	11·3 8·9	17·3 13·7
54	11 58·5	12 00·5	11 25·8	5·4 4·3	11·4 9·0	17·4 13·8
55	11 58·8	12 00·7	11 26·0	5·5 4·4	11·5 9·1	17·5 13·9
56	11 59·0	12 01·0	11 26·2	5·6 4·4	11·6 9·2	17·6 13·9
57	11 59·3	12 01·2	11 26·5	5·7 4·5	11·7 9·3	17·7 14·0
58	11 59·5	12 01·5	11 26·7	5·8 4·6	11·8 9·3	17·8 14·1
59	11 59·8	12 01·7	11 27·0	5·9 4·7	11·9 9·4	17·9 14·2
60	12 00·0	12 02·0	11 27·2	6·0 4·8	12·0 9·5	18·0 14·3

48ᵐ	SUN PLANETS	ARIES	MOON	v or Corrn d	v or Corrn d	v or Corrn d
s	° ′	° ′	° ′	′ ′	′ ′	′ ′
00	12 00·0	12 02·0	11 27·2	0·0 0·0	6·0 4·9	12·0 9·7
01	12 00·3	12 02·2	11 27·4	0·1 0·1	6·1 4·9	12·1 9·8
02	12 00·5	12 02·5	11 27·7	0·2 0·2	6·2 5·0	12·2 9·9
03	12 00·8	12 02·7	11 27·9	0·3 0·2	6·3 5·1	12·3 9·9
04	12 01·0	12 03·0	11 28·2	0·4 0·3	6·4 5·2	12·4 10·0
05	12 01·3	12 03·2	11 28·4	0·5 0·4	6·5 5·3	12·5 10·1
06	12 01·5	12 03·5	11 28·6	0·6 0·5	6·6 5·3	12·6 10·2
07	12 01·8	12 03·7	11 28·9	0·7 0·6	6·7 5·4	12·7 10·3
08	12 02·0	12 04·0	11 29·1	0·8 0·6	6·8 5·5	12·8 10·3
09	12 02·3	12 04·2	11 29·3	0·9 0·7	6·9 5·6	12·9 10·4
10	12 02·5	12 04·5	11 29·6	1·0 0·8	7·0 5·7	13·0 10·5
11	12 02·8	12 04·7	11 29·8	1·1 0·9	7·1 5·7	13·1 10·6
12	12 03·0	12 05·0	11 30·1	1·2 1·0	7·2 5·8	13·2 10·7
13	12 03·3	12 05·2	11 30·3	1·3 1·1	7·3 5·9	13·3 10·8
14	12 03·5	12 05·5	11 30·5	1·4 1·1	7·4 6·0	13·4 10·8
15	12 03·8	12 05·7	11 30·8	1·5 1·2	7·5 6·1	13·5 10·9
16	12 04·0	12 06·0	11 31·0	1·6 1·3	7·6 6·1	13·6 11·0
17	12 04·3	12 06·2	11 31·3	1·7 1·4	7·7 6·2	13·7 11·1
18	12 04·5	12 06·5	11 31·5	1·8 1·5	7·8 6·3	13·8 11·2
19	12 04·8	12 06·7	11 31·7	1·9 1·5	7·9 6·4	13·9 11·2
20	12 05·0	12 07·0	11 32·0	2·0 1·6	8·0 6·5	14·0 11·3
21	12 05·3	12 07·2	11 32·2	2·1 1·7	8·1 6·5	14·1 11·4
22	12 05·5	12 07·5	11 32·4	2·2 1·8	8·2 6·6	14·2 11·5
23	12 05·8	12 07·7	11 32·7	2·3 1·9	8·3 6·7	14·3 11·6
24	12 06·0	12 08·0	11 32·9	2·4 1·9	8·4 6·8	14·4 11·6
25	12 06·3	12 08·2	11 33·2	2·5 2·0	8·5 6·9	14·5 11·7
26	12 06·5	12 08·5	11 33·4	2·6 2·1	8·6 7·0	14·6 11·8
27	12 06·8	12 08·7	11 33·6	2·7 2·2	8·7 7·0	14·7 11·9
28	12 07·0	12 09·0	11 33·9	2·8 2·3	8·8 7·1	14·8 12·0
29	12 07·3	12 09·2	11 34·1	2·9 2·3	8·9 7·2	14·9 12·0
30	12 07·5	12 09·5	11 34·4	3·0 2·4	9·0 7·3	15·0 12·1
31	12 07·8	12 09·7	11 34·6	3·1 2·5	9·1 7·4	15·1 12·2
32	12 08·0	12 10·0	11 34·8	3·2 2·6	9·2 7·4	15·2 12·3
33	12 08·3	12 10·2	11 35·1	3·3 2·7	9·3 7·5	15·3 12·4
34	12 08·5	12 10·5	11 35·3	3·4 2·7	9·4 7·6	15·4 12·4
35	12 08·8	12 10·7	11 35·6	3·5 2·8	9·5 7·7	15·5 12·5
36	12 09·0	12 11·0	11 35·8	3·6 2·9	9·6 7·8	15·6 12·6
37	12 09·3	12 11·2	11 36·0	3·7 3·0	9·7 7·8	15·7 12·7
38	12 09·5	12 11·5	11 36·3	3·8 3·1	9·8 7·9	15·8 12·8
39	12 09·8	12 11·7	11 36·5	3·9 3·2	9·9 8·0	15·9 12·9
40	12 10·0	12 12·0	11 36·7	4·0 3·2	10·0 8·1	16·0 12·9
41	12 10·3	12 12·2	11 37·0	4·1 3·3	10·1 8·2	16·1 13·0
42	12 10·5	12 12·5	11 37·2	4·2 3·4	10·2 8·2	16·2 13·1
43	12 10·8	12 12·8	11 37·5	4·3 3·5	10·3 8·3	16·3 13·2
44	12 11·0	12 13·0	11 37·7	4·4 3·6	10·4 8·4	16·4 13·3
45	12 11·3	12 13·3	11 37·9	4·5 3·6	10·5 8·5	16·5 13·3
46	12 11·5	12 13·5	11 38·2	4·6 3·7	10·6 8·6	16·6 13·4
47	12 11·8	12 13·8	11 38·4	4·7 3·8	10·7 8·6	16·7 13·5
48	12 12·0	12 14·0	11 38·7	4·8 3·9	10·8 8·7	16·8 13·6
49	12 12·3	12 14·3	11 38·9	4·9 4·0	10·9 8·8	16·9 13·7
50	12 12·5	12 14·5	11 39·1	5·0 4·0	11·0 8·9	17·0 13·7
51	12 12·8	12 14·8	11 39·4	5·1 4·1	11·1 9·0	17·1 13·8
52	12 13·0	12 15·0	11 39·6	5·2 4·2	11·2 9·1	17·2 13·9
53	12 13·3	12 15·3	11 39·8	5·3 4·3	11·3 9·1	17·3 14·0
54	12 13·5	12 15·5	11 40·1	5·4 4·4	11·4 9·2	17·4 14·1
55	12 13·8	12 15·8	11 40·3	5·5 4·4	11·5 9·3	17·5 14·1
56	12 14·0	12 16·0	11 40·6	5·6 4·5	11·6 9·4	17·6 14·2
57	12 14·3	12 16·3	11 40·8	5·7 4·6	11·7 9·5	17·7 14·3
58	12 14·5	12 16·5	11 41·0	5·8 4·7	11·8 9·5	17·8 14·4
59	12 14·8	12 16·8	11 41·3	5·9 4·8	11·9 9·6	17·9 14·5
60	12 15·0	12 17·0	11 41·5	6·0 4·9	12·0 9·7	18·0 14·6

49ᵐ	SUN PLANETS	ARIES	MOON	v or Corrn d	v or Corrn d	v or Corrn d
s	° ′	° ′	° ′	′ ′	′ ′	′ ′
00	12 15·0	12 17·0	11 41·5	0·0 0·0	6·0 5·0	12·0 9·9
01	12 15·3	12 17·3	11 41·8	0·1 0·1	6·1 5·0	12·1 10·0
02	12 15·5	12 17·5	11 42·0	0·2 0·2	6·2 5·1	12·2 10·1
03	12 15·8	12 17·8	11 42·2	0·3 0·2	6·3 5·2	12·3 10·1
04	12 16·0	12 18·0	11 42·5	0·4 0·3	6·4 5·3	12·4 10·2
05	12 16·3	12 18·3	11 42·7	0·5 0·4	6·5 5·4	12·5 10·3
06	12 16·5	12 18·5	11 42·9	0·6 0·5	6·6 5·4	12·6 10·4
07	12 16·8	12 18·8	11 43·2	0·7 0·6	6·7 5·5	12·7 10·5
08	12 17·0	12 19·0	11 43·4	0·8 0·7	6·8 5·6	12·8 10·6
09	12 17·3	12 19·3	11 43·7	0·9 0·7	6·9 5·7	12·9 10·6
10	12 17·5	12 19·5	11 43·9	1·0 0·8	7·0 5·8	13·0 10·7
11	12 17·8	12 19·8	11 44·1	1·1 0·9	7·1 5·9	13·1 10·8
12	12 18·0	12 20·0	11 44·4	1·2 1·0	7·2 5·9	13·2 10·9
13	12 18·3	12 20·3	11 44·6	1·3 1·1	7·3 6·0	13·3 11·0
14	12 18·5	12 20·5	11 44·9	1·4 1·2	7·4 6·1	13·4 11·1
15	12 18·8	12 20·8	11 45·1	1·5 1·2	7·5 6·2	13·5 11·1
16	12 19·0	12 21·0	11 45·3	1·6 1·3	7·6 6·3	13·6 11·2
17	12 19·3	12 21·3	11 45·6	1·7 1·4	7·7 6·4	13·7 11·3
18	12 19·5	12 21·5	11 45·8	1·8 1·5	7·8 6·4	13·8 11·4
19	12 19·8	12 21·8	11 46·1	1·9 1·6	7·9 6·5	13·9 11·5
20	12 20·0	12 22·0	11 46·3	2·0 1·7	8·0 6·6	14·0 11·6
21	12 20·3	12 22·3	11 46·5	2·1 1·7	8·1 6·7	14·1 11·6
22	12 20·5	12 22·5	11 46·8	2·2 1·8	8·2 6·8	14·2 11·7
23	12 20·8	12 22·8	11 47·0	2·3 1·9	8·3 6·8	14·3 11·8
24	12 21·0	12 23·0	11 47·2	2·4 2·0	8·4 6·9	14·4 11·9
25	12 21·3	12 23·3	11 47·5	2·5 2·1	8·5 7·0	14·5 12·0
26	12 21·5	12 23·5	11 47·7	2·6 2·1	8·6 7·1	14·6 12·0
27	12 21·8	12 23·8	11 48·0	2·7 2·2	8·7 7·2	14·7 12·1
28	12 22·0	12 24·0	11 48·2	2·8 2·3	8·8 7·3	14·8 12·2
29	12 22·3	12 24·3	11 48·4	2·9 2·4	8·9 7·3	14·9 12·3
30	12 22·5	12 24·5	11 48·7	3·0 2·5	9·0 7·4	15·0 12·4
31	12 22·8	12 24·8	11 48·9	3·1 2·6	9·1 7·5	15·1 12·5
32	12 23·0	12 25·0	11 49·2	3·2 2·6	9·2 7·6	15·2 12·5
33	12 23·3	12 25·3	11 49·4	3·3 2·7	9·3 7·7	15·3 12·6
34	12 23·5	12 25·5	11 49·6	3·4 2·8	9·4 7·8	15·4 12·7
35	12 23·8	12 25·8	11 49·9	3·5 2·9	9·5 7·8	15·5 12·8
36	12 24·0	12 26·0	11 50·1	3·6 3·0	9·6 7·9	15·6 12·9
37	12 24·3	12 26·3	11 50·3	3·7 3·1	9·7 8·0	15·7 13·0
38	12 24·5	12 26·5	11 50·6	3·8 3·1	9·8 8·1	15·8 13·0
39	12 24·8	12 26·8	11 50·8	3·9 3·2	9·9 8·2	15·9 13·1
40	12 25·0	12 27·0	11 51·1	4·0 3·3	10·0 8·3	16·0 13·2
41	12 25·3	12 27·3	11 51·3	4·1 3·4	10·1 8·3	16·1 13·3
42	12 25·5	12 27·5	11 51·5	4·2 3·5	10·2 8·4	16·2 13·4
43	12 25·8	12 27·8	11 51·8	4·3 3·5	10·3 8·5	16·3 13·4
44	12 26·0	12 28·0	11 52·0	4·4 3·6	10·4 8·6	16·4 13·5
45	12 26·3	12 28·3	11 52·3	4·5 3·7	10·5 8·7	16·5 13·6
46	12 26·5	12 28·5	11 52·5	4·6 3·8	10·6 8·7	16·6 13·7
47	12 26·8	12 28·8	11 52·7	4·7 3·9	10·7 8·8	16·7 13·8
48	12 27·0	12 29·0	11 53·0	4·8 4·0	10·8 8·9	16·8 13·9
49	12 27·3	12 29·3	11 53·2	4·9 4·0	10·9 9·0	16·9 13·9
50	12 27·5	12 29·5	11 53·4	5·0 4·1	11·0 9·1	17·0 14·0
51	12 27·8	12 29·8	11 53·7	5·1 4·2	11·1 9·2	17·1 14·1
52	12 28·0	12 30·0	11 53·9	5·2 4·3	11·2 9·2	17·2 14·2
53	12 28·3	12 30·3	11 54·2	5·3 4·4	11·3 9·3	17·3 14·3
54	12 28·5	12 30·5	11 54·4	5·4 4·5	11·4 9·4	17·4 14·4
55	12 28·8	12 30·8	11 54·6	5·5 4·5	11·5 9·5	17·5 14·4
56	12 29·0	12 31·1	11 54·9	5·6 4·6	11·6 9·6	17·6 14·5
57	12 29·3	12 31·3	11 55·1	5·7 4·7	11·7 9·7	17·7 14·6
58	12 29·5	12 31·6	11 55·4	5·8 4·8	11·8 9·7	17·8 14·7
59	12 29·8	12 31·8	11 55·6	5·9 4·9	11·9 9·8	17·9 14·8
60	12 30·0	12 32·1	11 55·8	6·0 5·0	12·0 9·9	18·0 14·9

50ᵐ

50ᵐ (s)	SUN PLANETS	ARIES	MOON	v or Corrⁿ d	v or Corrⁿ d	v or Corrⁿ d
00	12 30·0	12 32·1	11 55·8	0·0 0·0	6·0 5·1	12·0 10·1
01	12 30·3	12 32·3	11 56·1	0·1 0·1	6·1 5·1	12·1 10·2
02	12 30·5	12 32·6	11 56·3	0·2 0·2	6·2 5·2	12·2 10·3
03	12 30·8	12 32·8	11 56·5	0·3 0·3	6·3 5·3	12·3 10·4
04	12 31·0	12 33·1	11 56·8	0·4 0·3	6·4 5·4	12·4 10·4
05	12 31·3	12 33·3	11 57·0	0·5 0·4	6·5 5·5	12·5 10·5
06	12 31·5	12 33·6	11 57·3	0·6 0·5	6·6 5·6	12·6 10·6
07	12 31·8	12 33·8	11 57·5	0·7 0·6	6·7 5·6	12·7 10·7
08	12 32·0	12 34·1	11 57·7	0·8 0·7	6·8 5·7	12·8 10·8
09	12 32·3	12 34·3	11 58·0	0·9 0·8	6·9 5·8	12·9 10·9
10	12 32·5	12 34·6	11 58·2	1·0 0·8	7·0 5·9	13·0 10·9
11	12 32·8	12 34·8	11 58·5	1·1 0·9	7·1 6·0	13·1 11·0
12	12 33·0	12 35·1	11 58·7	1·2 1·0	7·2 6·1	13·2 11·1
13	12 33·3	12 35·3	11 58·9	1·3 1·1	7·3 6·1	13·3 11·2
14	12 33·5	12 35·6	11 59·2	1·4 1·2	7·4 6·2	13·4 11·3
15	12 33·8	12 35·8	11 59·4	1·5 1·3	7·5 6·3	13·5 11·4
16	12 34·0	12 36·1	11 59·7	1·6 1·3	7·6 6·4	13·6 11·4
17	12 34·3	12 36·3	11 59·9	1·7 1·4	7·7 6·5	13·7 11·5
18	12 34·5	12 36·6	12 00·1	1·8 1·5	7·8 6·6	13·8 11·6
19	12 34·8	12 36·8	12 00·4	1·9 1·6	7·9 6·6	13·9 11·7
20	12 35·0	12 37·1	12 00·6	2·0 1·7	8·0 6·7	14·0 11·8
21	12 35·3	12 37·3	12 00·8	2·1 1·8	8·1 6·8	14·1 11·9
22	12 35·5	12 37·6	12 01·1	2·2 1·9	8·2 6·9	14·2 12·0
23	12 35·8	12 37·8	12 01·3	2·3 1·9	8·3 7·0	14·3 12·0
24	12 36·0	12 38·1	12 01·6	2·4 2·0	8·4 7·1	14·4 12·1
25	12 36·3	12 38·3	12 01·8	2·5 2·1	8·5 7·2	14·5 12·2
26	12 36·5	12 38·6	12 02·0	2·6 2·2	8·6 7·2	14·6 12·3
27	12 36·8	12 38·8	12 02·3	2·7 2·3	8·7 7·3	14·7 12·4
28	12 37·0	12 39·1	12 02·5	2·8 2·4	8·8 7·4	14·8 12·5
29	12 37·3	12 39·3	12 02·8	2·9 2·4	8·9 7·5	14·9 12·5
30	12 37·5	12 39·6	12 03·0	3·0 2·5	9·0 7·6	15·0 12·6
31	12 37·8	12 39·8	12 03·2	3·1 2·6	9·1 7·7	15·1 12·7
32	12 38·0	12 40·1	12 03·5	3·2 2·7	9·2 7·7	15·2 12·8
33	12 38·3	12 40·3	12 03·7	3·3 2·8	9·3 7·8	15·3 12·9
34	12 38·5	12 40·6	12 03·9	3·4 2·9	9·4 7·9	15·4 13·0
35	12 38·8	12 40·8	12 04·2	3·5 2·9	9·5 8·0	15·5 13·0
36	12 39·0	12 41·1	12 04·4	3·6 3·0	9·6 8·1	15·6 13·1
37	12 39·3	12 41·3	12 04·7	3·7 3·1	9·7 8·2	15·7 13·2
38	12 39·5	12 41·6	12 04·9	3·8 3·2	9·8 8·2	15·8 13·3
39	12 39·8	12 41·8	12 05·1	3·9 3·3	9·9 8·3	15·9 13·4
40	12 40·0	12 42·1	12 05·4	4·0 3·4	10·0 8·4	16·0 13·5
41	12 40·3	12 42·3	12 05·6	4·1 3·5	10·1 8·5	16·1 13·6
42	12 40·5	12 42·6	12 05·9	4·2 3·5	10·2 8·6	16·2 13·6
43	12 40·8	12 42·8	12 06·1	4·3 3·6	10·3 8·7	16·3 13·7
44	12 41·0	12 43·1	12 06·3	4·4 3·7	10·4 8·8	16·4 13·8
45	12 41·3	12 43·3	12 06·6	4·5 3·8	10·5 8·8	16·5 13·9
46	12 41·5	12 43·6	12 06·8	4·6 3·9	10·6 8·9	16·6 14·0
47	12 41·8	12 43·8	12 07·0	4·7 4·0	10·7 9·0	16·7 14·1
48	12 42·0	12 44·1	12 07·3	4·8 4·0	10·8 9·1	16·8 14·1
49	12 42·3	12 44·3	12 07·5	4·9 4·1	10·9 9·2	16·9 14·2
50	12 42·5	12 44·6	12 07·8	5·0 4·2	11·0 9·3	17·0 14·3
51	12 42·8	12 44·8	12 08·0	5·1 4·3	11·1 9·3	17·1 14·4
52	12 43·0	12 45·1	12 08·2	5·2 4·4	11·2 9·4	17·2 14·5
53	12 43·3	12 45·3	12 08·5	5·3 4·5	11·3 9·5	17·3 14·6
54	12 43·5	12 45·6	12 08·7	5·4 4·5	11·4 9·6	17·4 14·6
55	12 43·8	12 45·8	12 09·0	5·5 4·6	11·5 9·7	17·5 14·7
56	12 44·0	12 46·1	12 09·2	5·6 4·7	11·6 9·8	17·6 14·8
57	12 44·3	12 46·3	12 09·4	5·7 4·8	11·7 9·8	17·7 14·9
58	12 44·5	12 46·6	12 09·7	5·8 4·9	11·8 9·9	17·8 15·0
59	12 44·8	12 46·8	12 09·9	5·9 5·0	11·9 10·0	17·9 15·1
60	12 45·0	12 47·1	12 10·2	6·0 5·1	12·0 10·1	18·0 15·2

51ᵐ

51ᵐ (s)	SUN PLANETS	ARIES	MOON	v or Corrⁿ d	v or Corrⁿ d	v or Corrⁿ d
00	12 45·0	12 47·1	12 10·2	0·0 0·0	6·0 5·2	12·0 10·3
01	12 45·3	12 47·3	12 10·4	0·1 0·1	6·1 5·2	12·1 10·4
02	12 45·5	12 47·6	12 10·6	0·2 0·2	6·2 5·3	12·2 10·5
03	12 45·8	12 47·8	12 10·9	0·3 0·3	6·3 5·4	12·3 10·6
04	12 46·0	12 48·1	12 11·1	0·4 0·3	6·4 5·5	12·4 10·6
05	12 46·3	12 48·3	12 11·3	0·5 0·4	6·5 5·6	12·5 10·7
06	12 46·5	12 48·6	12 11·6	0·6 0·5	6·6 5·7	12·6 10·8
07	12 46·8	12 48·8	12 11·8	0·7 0·6	6·7 5·8	12·7 10·9
08	12 47·0	12 49·1	12 12·1	0·8 0·7	6·8 5·8	12·8 11·0
09	12 47·3	12 49·4	12 12·3	0·9 0·8	6·9 5·9	12·9 11·1
10	12 47·5	12 49·6	12 12·5	1·0 0·9	7·0 6·0	13·0 11·2
11	12 47·8	12 49·9	12 12·8	1·1 0·9	7·1 6·1	13·1 11·2
12	12 48·0	12 50·1	12 13·0	1·2 1·0	7·2 6·2	13·2 11·3
13	12 48·3	12 50·4	12 13·3	1·3 1·1	7·3 6·3	13·3 11·4
14	12 48·5	12 50·6	12 13·5	1·4 1·2	7·4 6·4	13·4 11·5
15	12 48·8	12 50·9	12 13·7	1·5 1·3	7·5 6·4	13·5 11·6
16	12 49·0	12 51·1	12 14·0	1·6 1·4	7·6 6·5	13·6 11·7
17	12 49·3	12 51·4	12 14·2	1·7 1·5	7·7 6·6	13·7 11·8
18	12 49·5	12 51·6	12 14·4	1·8 1·5	7·8 6·7	13·8 11·8
19	12 49·8	12 51·9	12 14·7	1·9 1·6	7·9 6·8	13·9 11·9
20	12 50·0	12 52·1	12 14·9	2·0 1·7	8·0 6·9	14·0 12·0
21	12 50·3	12 52·4	12 15·2	2·1 1·8	8·1 7·0	14·1 12·1
22	12 50·5	12 52·6	12 15·4	2·2 1·9	8·2 7·0	14·2 12·2
23	12 50·8	12 52·9	12 15·6	2·3 2·0	8·3 7·1	14·3 12·3
24	12 51·0	12 53·1	12 15·9	2·4 2·1	8·4 7·2	14·4 12·4
25	12 51·3	12 53·4	12 16·1	2·5 2·1	8·5 7·3	14·5 12·4
26	12 51·5	12 53·6	12 16·4	2·6 2·2	8·6 7·4	14·6 12·5
27	12 51·8	12 53·9	12 16·6	2·7 2·3	8·7 7·5	14·7 12·6
28	12 52·0	12 54·1	12 16·8	2·8 2·4	8·8 7·6	14·8 12·7
29	12 52·3	12 54·4	12 17·1	2·9 2·5	8·9 7·6	14·9 12·8
30	12 52·5	12 54·6	12 17·3	3·0 2·6	9·0 7·7	15·0 12·9
31	12 52·8	12 54·9	12 17·5	3·1 2·7	9·1 7·8	15·1 13·0
32	12 53·0	12 55·1	12 17·8	3·2 2·7	9·2 7·9	15·2 13·0
33	12 53·3	12 55·4	12 18·0	3·3 2·8	9·3 8·0	15·3 13·1
34	12 53·5	12 55·6	12 18·3	3·4 2·9	9·4 8·1	15·4 13·2
35	12 53·8	12 55·9	12 18·5	3·5 3·0	9·5 8·2	15·5 13·3
36	12 54·0	12 56·1	12 18·7	3·6 3·1	9·6 8·2	15·6 13·4
37	12 54·3	12 56·4	12 19·0	3·7 3·2	9·7 8·3	15·7 13·5
38	12 54·5	12 56·6	12 19·2	3·8 3·3	9·8 8·4	15·8 13·6
39	12 54·8	12 56·9	12 19·5	3·9 3·3	9·9 8·5	15·9 13·6
40	12 55·0	12 57·1	12 19·7	4·0 3·4	10·0 8·6	16·0 13·7
41	12 55·3	12 57·4	12 19·9	4·1 3·5	10·1 8·7	16·1 13·8
42	12 55·5	12 57·6	12 20·2	4·2 3·6	10·2 8·8	16·2 13·9
43	12 55·8	12 57·9	12 20·4	4·3 3·7	10·3 8·8	16·3 14·0
44	12 56·0	12 58·1	12 20·6	4·4 3·8	10·4 8·9	16·4 14·1
45	12 56·3	12 58·4	12 20·9	4·5 3·9	10·5 9·0	16·5 14·2
46	12 56·5	12 58·6	12 21·1	4·6 3·9	10·6 9·1	16·6 14·3
47	12 56·8	12 58·9	12 21·4	4·7 4·0	10·7 9·2	16·7 14·3
48	12 57·0	12 59·1	12 21·6	4·8 4·1	10·8 9·3	16·8 14·4
49	12 57·3	12 59·4	12 21·8	4·9 4·2	10·9 9·4	16·9 14·5
50	12 57·5	12 59·6	12 22·1	5·0 4·3	11·0 9·4	17·0 14·6
51	12 57·8	12 59·9	12 22·3	5·1 4·4	11·1 9·5	17·1 14·7
52	12 58·0	13 00·1	12 22·6	5·2 4·5	11·2 9·6	17·2 14·8
53	12 58·3	13 00·4	12 22·8	5·3 4·5	11·3 9·7	17·3 14·8
54	12 58·5	13 00·6	12 23·0	5·4 4·6	11·4 9·8	17·4 14·9
55	12 58·8	13 00·9	12 23·3	5·5 4·7	11·5 9·9	17·5 15·0
56	12 59·0	13 01·1	12 23·5	5·6 4·8	11·6 10·0	17·6 15·1
57	12 59·3	13 01·4	12 23·8	5·7 4·9	11·7 10·0	17·7 15·2
58	12 59·5	13 01·6	12 24·0	5·8 5·0	11·8 10·1	17·8 15·3
59	12 59·8	13 01·9	12 24·2	5·9 5·1	11·9 10·2	17·9 15·4
60	13 00·0	13 02·1	12 24·5	6·0 5·2	12·0 10·3	18·0 15·5

52ᵐ	SUN PLANETS	ARIES	MOON	v or d	Corrⁿ	v or d	Corrⁿ	v or d	Corrⁿ
s	° ′	° ′	° ′	′	′	′	′	′	′
00	13 00·0	13 02·1	12 24·5	0·0	0·0	6·0	5·3	12·0	10·5
01	13 00·3	13 02·4	12 24·7	0·1	0·1	6·1	5·3	12·1	10·6
02	13 00·5	13 02·6	12 24·9	0·2	0·2	6·2	5·4	12·2	10·7
03	13 00·8	13 02·9	12 25·2	0·3	0·3	6·3	5·5	12·3	10·8
04	13 01·0	13 03·1	12 25·4	0·4	0·4	6·4	5·6	12·4	10·9
05	13 01·3	13 03·4	12 25·7	0·5	0·4	6·5	5·7	12·5	10·9
06	13 01·5	13 03·6	12 25·9	0·6	0·5	6·6	5·8	12·6	11·0
07	13 01·8	13 03·9	12 26·1	0·7	0·6	6·7	5·9	12·7	11·1
08	13 02·0	13 04·1	12 26·4	0·8	0·7	6·8	6·0	12·8	11·2
09	13 02·3	13 04·4	12 26·6	0·9	0·8	6·9	6·0	12·9	11·3
10	13 02·5	13 04·6	12 26·9	1·0	0·9	7·0	6·1	13·0	11·4
11	13 02·8	13 04·9	12 27·1	1·1	1·0	7·1	6·2	13·1	11·5
12	13 03·0	13 05·1	12 27·3	1·2	1·1	7·2	6·3	13·2	11·6
13	13 03·3	13 05·4	12 27·6	1·3	1·1	7·3	6·4	13·3	11·6
14	13 03·5	13 05·6	12 27·8	1·4	1·2	7·4	6·5	13·4	11·7
15	13 03·8	13 05·9	12 28·0	1·5	1·3	7·5	6·6	13·5	11·8
16	13 04·0	13 06·1	12 28·3	1·6	1·4	7·6	6·7	13·6	11·9
17	13 04·3	13 06·4	12 28·5	1·7	1·5	7·7	6·7	13·7	12·0
18	13 04·5	13 06·6	12 28·8	1·8	1·6	7·8	6·8	13·8	12·1
19	13 04·8	13 06·9	12 29·0	1·9	1·7	7·9	6·9	13·9	12·2
20	13 05·0	13 07·1	12 29·2	2·0	1·8	8·0	7·0	14·0	12·3
21	13 05·3	13 07·4	12 29·5	2·1	1·8	8·1	7·1	14·1	12·3
22	13 05·5	13 07·7	12 29·7	2·2	1·9	8·2	7·2	14·2	12·4
23	13 05·8	13 07·9	12 30·0	2·3	2·0	8·3	7·3	14·3	12·5
24	13 06·0	13 08·2	12 30·2	2·4	2·1	8·4	7·4	14·4	12·6
25	13 06·3	13 08·4	12 30·4	2·5	2·2	8·5	7·4	14·5	12·7
26	13 06·5	13 08·7	12 30·7	2·6	2·3	8·6	7·5	14·6	12·8
27	13 06·8	13 08·9	12 30·9	2·7	2·4	8·7	7·6	14·7	12·9
28	13 07·0	13 09·2	12 31·1	2·8	2·5	8·8	7·7	14·8	13·0
29	13 07·3	13 09·4	12 31·4	2·9	2·5	8·9	7·8	14·9	13·0
30	13 07·5	13 09·7	12 31·6	3·0	2·6	9·0	7·9	15·0	13·1
31	13 07·8	13 09·9	12 31·9	3·1	2·7	9·1	8·0	15·1	13·2
32	13 08·0	13 10·2	12 32·1	3·2	2·8	9·2	8·1	15·2	13·3
33	13 08·3	13 10·4	12 32·3	3·3	2·9	9·3	8·1	15·3	13·4
34	13 08·5	13 10·7	12 32·6	3·4	3·0	9·4	8·2	15·4	13·5
35	13 08·8	13 10·9	12 32·8	3·5	3·1	9·5	8·3	15·5	13·6
36	13 09·0	13 11·2	12 33·1	3·6	3·2	9·6	8·4	15·6	13·7
37	13 09·3	13 11·4	12 33·3	3·7	3·2	9·7	8·5	15·7	13·7
38	13 09·5	13 11·7	12 33·5	3·8	3·3	9·8	8·6	15·8	13·8
39	13 09·8	13 11·9	12 33·8	3·9	3·4	9·9	8·7	15·9	13·9
40	13 10·0	13 12·2	12 34·0	4·0	3·5	10·0	8·8	16·0	14·0
41	13 10·3	13 12·4	12 34·2	4·1	3·6	10·1	8·8	16·1	14·1
42	13 10·5	13 12·7	12 34·5	4·2	3·7	10·2	8·9	16·2	14·2
43	13 10·8	13 12·9	12 34·7	4·3	3·8	10·3	9·0	16·3	14·3
44	13 11·0	13 13·2	12 35·0	4·4	3·9	10·4	9·1	16·4	14·4
45	13 11·3	13 13·4	12 35·2	4·5	3·9	10·5	9·2	16·5	14·4
46	13 11·5	13 13·7	12 35·4	4·6	4·0	10·6	9·3	16·6	14·5
47	13 11·8	13 13·9	12 35·7	4·7	4·1	10·7	9·4	16·7	14·6
48	13 12·0	13 14·2	12 35·9	4·8	4·2	10·8	9·5	16·8	14·7
49	13 12·3	13 14·4	12 36·2	4·9	4·3	10·9	9·5	16·9	14·8
50	13 12·5	13 14·7	12 36·4	5·0	4·4	11·0	9·6	17·0	14·9
51	13 12·8	13 14·9	12 36·6	5·1	4·5	11·1	9·7	17·1	15·0
52	13 13·0	13 15·2	12 36·9	5·2	4·6	11·2	9·8	17·2	15·1
53	13 13·3	13 15·4	12 37·1	5·3	4·6	11·3	9·9	17·3	15·1
54	13 13·5	13 15·7	12 37·4	5·4	4·7	11·4	10·0	17·4	15·2
55	13 13·8	13 15·9	12 37·6	5·5	4·8	11·5	10·1	17·5	15·3
56	13 14·0	13 16·2	12 37·8	5·6	4·9	11·6	10·2	17·6	15·4
57	13 14·3	13 16·4	12 38·1	5·7	5·0	11·7	10·2	17·7	15·5
58	13 14·5	13 16·7	12 38·3	5·8	5·1	11·8	10·3	17·8	15·6
59	13 14·8	13 16·9	12 38·5	5·9	5·2	11·9	10·4	17·9	15·7
60	13 15·0	13 17·2	12 38·8	6·0	5·3	12·0	10·5	18·0	15·8

53ᵐ	SUN PLANETS	ARIES	MOON	v or d	Corrⁿ	v or d	Corrⁿ	v or d	Corrⁿ
s	° ′	° ′	° ′	′	′	′	′	′	′
00	13 15·0	13 17·2	12 38·8	0·0	0·0	6·0	5·4	12·0	10·7
01	13 15·3	13 17·4	12 39·0	0·1	0·1	6·1	5·4	12·1	10·8
02	13 15·5	13 17·7	12 39·3	0·2	0·2	6·2	5·5	12·2	10·9
03	13 15·8	13 17·9	12 39·5	0·3	0·3	6·3	5·6	12·3	11·0
04	13 16·0	13 18·2	12 39·7	0·4	0·4	6·4	5·7	12·4	11·1
05	13 16·3	13 18·4	12 40·0	0·5	0·4	6·5	5·8	12·5	11·1
06	13 16·5	13 18·7	12 40·2	0·6	0·5	6·6	5·9	12·6	11·2
07	13 16·8	13 18·9	12 40·5	0·7	0·6	6·7	6·0	12·7	11·3
08	13 17·0	13 19·2	12 40·7	0·8	0·7	6·8	6·1	12·8	11·4
09	13 17·3	13 19·4	12 40·9	0·9	0·8	6·9	6·2	12·9	11·5
10	13 17·5	13 19·7	12 41·2	1·0	0·9	7·0	6·2	13·0	11·6
11	13 17·8	13 19·9	12 41·4	1·1	1·0	7·1	6·3	13·1	11·7
12	13 18·0	13 20·2	12 41·6	1·2	1·1	7·2	6·4	13·2	11·8
13	13 18·3	13 20·4	12 41·9	1·3	1·2	7·3	6·5	13·3	11·9
14	13 18·5	13 20·7	12 42·1	1·4	1·2	7·4	6·6	13·4	11·9
15	13 18·8	13 20·9	12 42·4	1·5	1·3	7·5	6·7	13·5	12·0
16	13 19·0	13 21·2	12 42·6	1·6	1·4	7·6	6·8	13·6	12·1
17	13 19·3	13 21·4	12 42·8	1·7	1·5	7·7	6·9	13·7	12·2
18	13 19·5	13 21·7	12 43·1	1·8	1·6	7·8	7·0	13·8	12·3
19	13 19·8	13 21·9	12 43·3	1·9	1·7	7·9	7·0	13·9	12·4
20	13 20·0	13 22·2	12 43·6	2·0	1·8	8·0	7·1	14·0	12·5
21	13 20·3	13 22·4	12 43·8	2·1	1·9	8·1	7·2	14·1	12·6
22	13 20·5	13 22·7	12 44·0	2·2	2·0	8·2	7·3	14·2	12·7
23	13 20·8	13 22·9	12 44·3	2·3	2·1	8·3	7·4	14·3	12·8
24	13 21·0	13 23·2	12 44·5	2·4	2·1	8·4	7·5	14·4	12·8
25	13 21·3	13 23·4	12 44·7	2·5	2·2	8·5	7·6	14·5	12·9
26	13 21·5	13 23·7	12 45·0	2·6	2·3	8·6	7·7	14·6	13·0
27	13 21·8	13 23·9	12 45·2	2·7	2·4	8·7	7·8	14·7	13·1
28	13 22·0	13 24·2	12 45·5	2·8	2·5	8·8	7·8	14·8	13·2
29	13 22·3	13 24·4	12 45·7	2·9	2·6	8·9	7·9	14·9	13·3
30	13 22·5	13 24·7	12 45·9	3·0	2·7	9·0	8·0	15·0	13·4
31	13 22·8	13 24·9	12 46·2	3·1	2·8	9·1	8·1	15·1	13·5
32	13 23·0	13 25·2	12 46·4	3·2	2·9	9·2	8·2	15·2	13·6
33	13 23·3	13 25·4	12 46·7	3·3	2·9	9·3	8·3	15·3	13·6
34	13 23·5	13 25·7	12 46·9	3·4	3·0	9·4	8·4	15·4	13·7
35	13 23·8	13 26·0	12 47·1	3·5	3·1	9·5	8·5	15·5	13·8
36	13 24·0	13 26·2	12 47·4	3·6	3·2	9·6	8·6	15·6	13·9
37	13 24·3	13 26·5	12 47·6	3·7	3·3	9·7	8·6	15·7	14·0
38	13 24·5	13 26·7	12 47·9	3·8	3·4	9·8	8·7	15·8	14·1
39	13 24·8	13 27·0	12 48·1	3·9	3·5	9·9	8·8	15·9	14·2
40	13 25·0	13 27·2	12 48·3	4·0	3·6	10·0	8·9	16·0	14·3
41	13 25·3	13 27·5	12 48·6	4·1	3·7	10·1	9·0	16·1	14·4
42	13 25·5	13 27·7	12 48·8	4·2	3·7	10·2	9·1	16·2	14·4
43	13 25·8	13 28·0	12 49·0	4·3	3·8	10·3	9·2	16·3	14·5
44	13 26·0	13 28·2	12 49·3	4·4	3·9	10·4	9·3	16·4	14·6
45	13 26·3	13 28·5	12 49·5	4·5	4·0	10·5	9·4	16·5	14·7
46	13 26·5	13 28·7	12 49·8	4·6	4·1	10·6	9·5	16·6	14·8
47	13 26·8	13 29·0	12 50·0	4·7	4·2	10·7	9·5	16·7	14·9
48	13 27·0	13 29·2	12 50·2	4·8	4·3	10·8	9·6	16·8	15·0
49	13 27·3	13 29·5	12 50·5	4·9	4·4	10·9	9·7	16·9	15·1
50	13 27·5	13 29·7	12 50·7	5·0	4·5	11·0	9·8	17·0	15·2
51	13 27·8	13 30·0	12 51·0	5·1	4·5	11·1	9·9	17·1	15·2
52	13 28·0	13 30·2	12 51·2	5·2	4·6	11·2	10·0	17·2	15·3
53	13 28·3	13 30·5	12 51·4	5·3	4·7	11·3	10·1	17·3	15·4
54	13 28·5	13 30·7	12 51·7	5·4	4·8	11·4	10·2	17·4	15·5
55	13 28·8	13 31·0	12 51·9	5·5	4·9	11·5	10·3	17·5	15·6
56	13 29·0	13 31·2	12 52·1	5·6	5·0	11·6	10·3	17·6	15·7
57	13 29·3	13 31·5	12 52·4	5·7	5·1	11·7	10·4	17·7	15·8
58	13 29·5	13 31·7	12 52·6	5·8	5·2	11·8	10·5	17·8	15·9
59	13 29·8	13 32·0	12 52·9	5·9	5·3	11·9	10·6	17·9	16·0
60	13 30·0	13 32·2	12 53·1	6·0	5·4	12·0	10·7	18·0	16·1

54ᵐ (s)	SUN PLANETS	ARIES	MOON	v or Corrⁿ d	v or Corrⁿ d	v or Corrⁿ d
00	13 30·0	13 32·2	12 53·1	0·0 0·0	6·0 5·5	12·0 10·9
01	13 30·3	13 32·5	12 53·3	0·1 0·1	6·1 5·5	12·1 11·0
02	13 30·5	13 32·7	12 53·6	0·2 0·2	6·2 5·6	12·2 11·1
03	13 30·8	13 33·0	12 53·8	0·3 0·3	6·3 5·7	12·3 11·2
04	13 31·0	13 33·2	12 54·1	0·4 0·4	6·4 5·8	12·4 11·3
05	13 31·3	13 33·5	12 54·3	0·5 0·5	6·5 5·9	12·5 11·4
06	13 31·5	13 33·7	12 54·5	0·6 0·5	6·6 6·0	12·6 11·4
07	13 31·8	13 34·0	12 54·8	0·7 0·6	6·7 6·1	12·7 11·5
08	13 32·0	13 34·2	12 55·0	0·8 0·7	6·8 6·2	12·8 11·6
09	13 32·3	13 34·5	12 55·2	0·9 0·8	6·9 6·3	12·9 11·7
10	13 32·5	13 34·7	12 55·5	1·0 0·9	7·0 6·4	13·0 11·8
11	13 32·8	13 35·0	12 55·7	1·1 1·0	7·1 6·4	13·1 11·9
12	13 33·0	13 35·2	12 56·0	1·2 1·1	7·2 6·5	13·2 12·0
13	13 33·3	13 35·5	12 56·2	1·3 1·2	7·3 6·6	13·3 12·1
14	13 33·5	13 35·7	12 56·4	1·4 1·3	7·4 6·7	13·4 12·2
15	13 33·8	13 36·0	12 56·7	1·5 1·4	7·5 6·8	13·5 12·3
16	13 34·0	13 36·2	12 56·9	1·6 1·5	7·6 6·9	13·6 12·4
17	13 34·3	13 36·5	12 57·2	1·7 1·5	7·7 7·0	13·7 12·4
18	13 34·5	13 36·7	12 57·4	1·8 1·6	7·8 7·1	13·8 12·5
19	13 34·8	13 37·0	12 57·6	1·9 1·7	7·9 7·2	13·9 12·6
20	13 35·0	13 37·2	12 57·9	2·0 1·8	8·0 7·3	14·0 12·7
21	13 35·3	13 37·5	12 58·1	2·1 1·9	8·1 7·4	14·1 12·8
22	13 35·5	13 37·7	12 58·3	2·2 2·0	8·2 7·4	14·2 12·9
23	13 35·8	13 38·0	12 58·6	2·3 2·1	8·3 7·5	14·3 13·0
24	13 36·0	13 38·2	12 58·8	2·4 2·2	8·4 7·6	14·4 13·1
25	13 36·3	13 38·5	12 59·1	2·5 2·3	8·5 7·7	14·5 13·2
26	13 36·5	13 38·7	12 59·3	2·6 2·4	8·6 7·8	14·6 13·3
27	13 36·8	13 39·0	12 59·5	2·7 2·5	8·7 7·9	14·7 13·4
28	13 37·0	13 39·2	12 59·8	2·8 2·5	8·8 8·0	14·8 13·4
29	13 37·3	13 39·5	13 00·0	2·9 2·6	8·9 8·1	14·9 13·5
30	13 37·5	13 39·7	13 00·3	3·0 2·7	9·0 8·2	15·0 13·6
31	13 37·8	13 40·0	13 00·5	3·1 2·8	9·1 8·3	15·1 13·7
32	13 38·0	13 40·2	13 00·7	3·2 2·9	9·2 8·4	15·2 13·8
33	13 38·3	13 40·5	13 01·0	3·3 3·0	9·3 8·4	15·3 13·9
34	13 38·5	13 40·7	13 01·2	3·4 3·1	9·4 8·5	15·4 14·0
35	13 38·8	13 41·0	13 01·5	3·5 3·2	9·5 8·6	15·5 14·1
36	13 39·0	13 41·2	13 01·7	3·6 3·3	9·6 8·7	15·6 14·2
37	13 39·3	13 41·5	13 02·0	3·7 3·4	9·7 8·8	15·7 14·3
38	13 39·5	13 41·7	13 02·2	3·8 3·5	9·8 8·9	15·8 14·4
39	13 39·8	13 42·0	13 02·4	3·9 3·5	9·9 9·0	15·9 14·4
40	13 40·0	13 42·2	13 02·6	4·0 3·6	10·0 9·1	16·0 14·5
41	13 40·3	13 42·5	13 02·9	4·1 3·7	10·1 9·2	16·1 14·6
42	13 40·5	13 42·7	13 03·1	4·2 3·8	10·2 9·3	16·2 14·7
43	13 40·8	13 43·0	13 03·4	4·3 3·9	10·3 9·4	16·3 14·8
44	13 41·0	13 43·2	13 03·6	4·4 4·0	10·4 9·4	16·4 14·9
45	13 41·3	13 43·5	13 03·8	4·5 4·1	10·5 9·5	16·5 15·0
46	13 41·5	13 43·7	13 04·1	4·6 4·2	10·6 9·6	16·6 15·1
47	13 41·8	13 44·0	13 04·3	4·7 4·3	10·7 9·7	16·7 15·2
48	13 42·0	13 44·3	13 04·6	4·8 4·4	10·8 9·8	16·8 15·3
49	13 42·3	13 44·5	13 04·8	4·9 4·5	10·9 9·9	16·9 15·4
50	13 42·5	13 44·8	13 05·0	5·0 4·5	11·0 10·0	17·0 15·4
51	13 42·8	13 45·0	13 05·3	5·1 4·6	11·1 10·1	17·1 15·5
52	13 43·0	13 45·3	13 05·5	5·2 4·7	11·2 10·2	17·2 15·6
53	13 43·3	13 45·5	13 05·7	5·3 4·8	11·3 10·3	17·3 15·7
54	13 43·5	13 45·8	13 06·0	5·4 4·9	11·4 10·4	17·4 15·8
55	13 43·8	13 46·0	13 06·2	5·5 5·0	11·5 10·4	17·5 15·9
56	13 44·0	13 46·3	13 06·5	5·6 5·1	11·6 10·5	17·6 16·0
57	13 44·3	13 46·5	13 06·7	5·7 5·2	11·7 10·6	17·7 16·1
58	13 44·5	13 46·8	13 06·9	5·8 5·3	11·8 10·7	17·8 16·2
59	13 44·8	13 47·0	13 07·2	5·9 5·4	11·9 10·8	17·9 16·3
60	13 45·0	13 47·3	13 07·4	6·0 5·5	12·0 10·9	18·0 16·4

55ᵐ (s)	SUN PLANETS	ARIES	MOON	v or Corrⁿ d	v or Corrⁿ d	v or Corrⁿ d
00	13 45·0	13 47·3	13 07·4	0·0 0·0	6·0 5·6	12·0 11·1
01	13 45·3	13 47·5	13 07·7	0·1 0·1	6·1 5·6	12·1 11·2
02	13 45·5	13 47·8	13 07·9	0·2 0·2	6·2 5·7	12·2 11·3
03	13 45·8	13 48·0	13 08·1	0·3 0·3	6·3 5·8	12·3 11·4
04	13 46·0	13 48·3	13 08·4	0·4 0·4	6·4 5·9	12·4 11·5
05	13 46·3	13 48·5	13 08·6	0·5 0·5	6·5 6·0	12·5 11·6
06	13 46·5	13 48·8	13 08·8	0·6 0·6	6·6 6·1	12·6 11·7
07	13 46·8	13 49·0	13 09·1	0·7 0·6	6·7 6·2	12·7 11·7
08	13 47·0	13 49·3	13 09·3	0·8 0·7	6·8 6·3	12·8 11·8
09	13 47·3	13 49·5	13 09·6	0·9 0·8	6·9 6·4	12·9 11·9
10	13 47·5	13 49·8	13 09·8	1·0 0·9	7·0 6·5	13·0 12·0
11	13 47·8	13 50·0	13 10·0	1·1 1·0	7·1 6·6	13·1 12·1
12	13 48·0	13 50·3	13 10·3	1·2 1·1	7·2 6·7	13·2 12·2
13	13 48·3	13 50·5	13 10·5	1·3 1·2	7·3 6·8	13·3 12·3
14	13 48·5	13 50·8	13 10·8	1·4 1·3	7·4 6·8	13·4 12·4
15	13 48·8	13 51·0	13 11·0	1·5 1·4	7·5 6·9	13·5 12·5
16	13 49·0	13 51·3	13 11·2	1·6 1·5	7·6 7·0	13·6 12·6
17	13 49·3	13 51·5	13 11·5	1·7 1·6	7·7 7·1	13·7 12·7
18	13 49·5	13 51·8	13 11·7	1·8 1·7	7·8 7·2	13·8 12·8
19	13 49·8	13 52·0	13 12·0	1·9 1·8	7·9 7·3	13·9 12·9
20	13 50·0	13 52·3	13 12·2	2·0 1·9	8·0 7·4	14·0 13·0
21	13 50·3	13 52·5	13 12·4	2·1 1·9	8·1 7·5	14·1 13·0
22	13 50·5	13 52·8	13 12·7	2·2 2·0	8·2 7·6	14·2 13·1
23	13 50·8	13 53·0	13 12·9	2·3 2·1	8·3 7·7	14·3 13·2
24	13 51·0	13 53·3	13 13·1	2·4 2·2	8·4 7·8	14·4 13·3
25	13 51·3	13 53·5	13 13·4	2·5 2·3	8·5 7·9	14·5 13·4
26	13 51·5	13 53·8	13 13·6	2·6 2·4	8·6 8·0	14·6 13·5
27	13 51·8	13 54·0	13 13·9	2·7 2·5	8·7 8·0	14·7 13·6
28	13 52·0	13 54·3	13 14·1	2·8 2·6	8·8 8·1	14·8 13·7
29	13 52·3	13 54·5	13 14·3	2·9 2·7	8·9 8·2	14·9 13·8
30	13 52·5	13 54·8	13 14·6	3·0 2·8	9·0 8·3	15·0 13·9
31	13 52·8	13 55·0	13 14·8	3·1 2·9	9·1 8·4	15·1 14·0
32	13 53·0	13 55·3	13 15·1	3·2 3·0	9·2 8·5	15·2 14·1
33	13 53·3	13 55·5	13 15·3	3·3 3·1	9·3 8·6	15·3 14·2
34	13 53·5	13 55·8	13 15·5	3·4 3·1	9·4 8·7	15·4 14·2
35	13 53·8	13 56·0	13 15·8	3·5 3·2	9·5 8·8	15·5 14·3
36	13 54·0	13 56·3	13 16·0	3·6 3·3	9·6 8·9	15·6 14·4
37	13 54·3	13 56·5	13 16·2	3·7 3·4	9·7 9·0	15·7 14·5
38	13 54·5	13 56·8	13 16·5	3·8 3·5	9·8 9·1	15·8 14·6
39	13 54·8	13 57·0	13 16·7	3·9 3·6	9·9 9·2	15·9 14·7
40	13 55·0	13 57·3	13 17·0	4·0 3·7	10·0 9·3	16·0 14·8
41	13 55·3	13 57·5	13 17·2	4·1 3·8	10·1 9·3	16·1 14·9
42	13 55·5	13 57·8	13 17·4	4·2 3·9	10·2 9·4	16·2 15·0
43	13 55·8	13 58·0	13 17·7	4·3 4·0	10·3 9·5	16·3 15·1
44	13 56·0	13 58·3	13 17·9	4·4 4·1	10·4 9·6	16·4 15·2
45	13 56·3	13 58·5	13 18·2	4·5 4·2	10·5 9·7	16·5 15·3
46	13 56·5	13 58·8	13 18·4	4·6 4·3	10·6 9·8	16·6 15·4
47	13 56·8	13 59·0	13 18·6	4·7 4·3	10·7 9·9	16·7 15·4
48	13 57·0	13 59·3	13 18·9	4·8 4·4	10·8 10·0	16·8 15·5
49	13 57·3	13 59·5	13 19·1	4·9 4·5	10·9 10·1	16·9 15·6
50	13 57·5	13 59·8	13 19·3	5·0 4·6	11·0 10·2	17·0 15·7
51	13 57·8	14 00·0	13 19·6	5·1 4·7	11·1 10·3	17·1 15·8
52	13 58·0	14 00·3	13 19·8	5·2 4·8	11·2 10·4	17·2 15·9
53	13 58·3	14 00·5	13 20·1	5·3 4·9	11·3 10·5	17·3 16·0
54	13 58·5	14 00·8	13 20·3	5·4 5·0	11·4 10·5	17·4 16·1
55	13 58·8	14 01·0	13 20·5	5·5 5·1	11·5 10·6	17·5 16·2
56	13 59·0	14 01·3	13 20·8	5·6 5·2	11·6 10·7	17·6 16·3
57	13 59·3	14 01·5	13 21·0	5·7 5·3	11·7 10·8	17·7 16·4
58	13 59·5	14 01·8	13 21·3	5·8 5·4	11·8 10·9	17·8 16·5
59	13 59·8	14 02·0	13 21·5	5·9 5·5	11·9 11·0	17·9 16·6
60	14 00·0	14 02·3	13 21·7	6·0 5·6	12·0 11·1	18·0 16·7

56ᵐ	SUN PLANETS	ARIES	MOON	v or Corrⁿ d	v or Corrⁿ d	v or Corrⁿ d
s	° ′	° ′	° ′	′ ′	′ ′	′ ′
00	14 00·0	14 02·3	13 21·7	0·0 0·0	6·0 5·7	12·0 11·3
01	14 00·3	14 02·6	13 22·0	0·1 0·1	6·1 5·7	12·1 11·4
02	14 00·5	14 02·8	13 22·2	0·2 0·2	6·2 5·8	12·2 11·5
03	14 00·8	14 03·1	13 22·4	0·3 0·3	6·3 5·9	12·3 11·6
04	14 01·0	14 03·3	13 22·7	0·4 0·4	6·4 6·0	12·4 11·7
05	14 01·3	14 03·6	13 22·9	0·5 0·5	6·5 6·1	12·5 11·8
06	14 01·5	14 03·8	13 23·2	0·6 0·6	6·6 6·2	12·6 11·9
07	14 01·8	14 04·1	13 23·4	0·7 0·7	6·7 6·3	12·7 12·0
08	14 02·0	14 04·3	13 23·6	0·8 0·8	6·8 6·4	12·8 12·1
09	14 02·3	14 04·6	13 23·9	0·9 0·8	6·9 6·5	12·9 12·1
10	14 02·5	14 04·8	13 24·1	1·0 0·9	7·0 6·6	13·0 12·2
11	14 02·8	14 05·1	13 24·4	1·1 1·0	7·1 6·7	13·1 12·3
12	14 03·0	14 05·3	13 24·6	1·2 1·1	7·2 6·8	13·2 12·4
13	14 03·3	14 05·6	13 24·8	1·3 1·2	7·3 6·9	13·3 12·5
14	14 03·5	14 05·8	13 25·1	1·4 1·3	7·4 7·0	13·4 12·6
15	14 03·8	14 06·1	13 25·3	1·5 1·4	7·5 7·1	13·5 12·7
16	14 04·0	14 06·3	13 25·6	1·6 1·5	7·6 7·2	13·6 12·8
17	14 04·3	14 06·6	13 25·8	1·7 1·6	7·7 7·3	13·7 12·9
18	14 04·5	14 06·8	13 26·0	1·8 1·7	7·8 7·3	13·8 13·0
19	14 04·8	14 07·1	13 26·3	1·9 1·8	7·9 7·4	13·9 13·1
20	14 05·0	14 07·3	13 26·5	2·0 1·9	8·0 7·5	14·0 13·2
21	14 05·3	14 07·6	13 26·7	2·1 2·0	8·1 7·6	14·1 13·3
22	14 05·5	14 07·8	13 27·0	2·2 2·1	8·2 7·7	14·2 13·4
23	14 05·8	14 08·1	13 27·2	2·3 2·2	8·3 7·8	14·3 13·5
24	14 06·0	14 08·3	13 27·5	2·4 2·3	8·4 7·9	14·4 13·6
25	14 06·3	14 08·6	13 27·7	2·5 2·4	8·5 8·0	14·5 13·7
26	14 06·5	14 08·8	13 27·9	2·6 2·4	8·6 8·1	14·6 13·7
27	14 06·8	14 09·1	13 28·2	2·7 2·5	8·7 8·2	14·7 13·8
28	14 07·0	14 09·3	13 28·4	2·8 2·6	8·8 8·3	14·8 13·9
29	14 07·3	14 09·6	13 28·7	2·9 2·7	8·9 8·4	14·9 14·0
30	14 07·5	14 09·8	13 28·9	3·0 2·8	9·0 8·5	15·0 14·1
31	14 07·8	14 10·1	13 29·1	3·1 2·9	9·1 8·6	15·1 14·2
32	14 08·0	14 10·3	13 29·4	3·2 3·0	9·2 8·7	15·2 14·3
33	14 08·3	14 10·6	13 29·6	3·3 3·1	9·3 8·8	15·3 14·4
34	14 08·5	14 10·8	13 29·8	3·4 3·2	9·4 8·9	15·4 14·5
35	14 08·8	14 11·1	13 30·1	3·5 3·3	9·5 8·9	15·5 14·6
36	14 09·0	14 11·3	13 30·3	3·6 3·4	9·6 9·0	15·6 14·7
37	14 09·3	14 11·6	13 30·6	3·7 3·5	9·7 9·1	15·7 14·8
38	14 09·5	14 11·8	13 30·8	3·8 3·6	9·8 9·2	15·8 14·9
39	14 09·8	14 12·1	13 31·0	3·9 3·7	9·9 9·3	15·9 15·0
40	14 10·0	14 12·3	13 31·3	4·0 3·8	10·0 9·4	16·0 15·1
41	14 10·3	14 12·6	13 31·5	4·1 3·9	10·1 9·5	16·1 15·2
42	14 10·5	14 12·8	13 31·8	4·2 4·0	10·2 9·6	16·2 15·3
43	14 10·8	14 13·1	13 32·0	4·3 4·0	10·3 9·7	16·3 15·3
44	14 11·0	14 13·3	13 32·2	4·4 4·1	10·4 9·8	16·4 15·4
45	14 11·3	14 13·6	13 32·5	4·5 4·2	10·5 9·9	16·5 15·5
46	14 11·5	14 13·8	13 32·7	4·6 4·3	10·6 10·0	16·6 15·6
47	14 11·8	14 14·1	13 32·9	4·7 4·4	10·7 10·1	16·7 15·7
48	14 12·0	14 14·3	13 33·2	4·8 4·5	10·8 10·2	16·8 15·8
49	14 12·3	14 14·6	13 33·4	4·9 4·6	10·9 10·3	16·9 15·9
50	14 12·5	14 14·8	13 33·7	5·0 4·7	11·0 10·4	17·0 16·0
51	14 12·8	14 15·1	13 33·9	5·1 4·8	11·1 10·5	17·1 16·1
52	14 13·0	14 15·3	13 34·1	5·2 4·9	11·2 10·5	17·2 16·2
53	14 13·3	14 15·6	13 34·4	5·3 5·0	11·3 10·6	17·3 16·3
54	14 13·5	14 15·8	13 34·6	5·4 5·1	11·4 10·7	17·4 16·4
55	14 13·8	14 16·1	13 34·9	5·5 5·2	11·5 10·8	17·5 16·5
56	14 14·0	14 16·3	13 35·1	5·6 5·3	11·6 10·9	17·6 16·6
57	14 14·3	14 16·6	13 35·3	5·7 5·4	11·7 11·0	17·7 16·7
58	14 14·5	14 16·8	13 35·6	5·8 5·5	11·8 11·1	17·8 16·8
59	14 14·8	14 17·1	13 35·8	5·9 5·6	11·9 11·2	17·9 16·9
60	14 15·0	14 17·3	13 36·1	6·0 5·7	12·0 11·3	18·0 17·0

57ᵐ	SUN PLANETS	ARIES	MOON	v or Corrⁿ d	v or Corrⁿ d	v or Corrⁿ d
s	° ′	° ′	° ′	′ ′	′ ′	′ ′
00	14 15·0	14 17·3	13 36·1	0·0 0·0	6·0 5·8	12·0 11·5
01	14 15·3	14 17·6	13 36·3	0·1 0·1	6·1 5·8	12·1 11·6
02	14 15·5	14 17·8	13 36·5	0·2 0·2	6·2 5·9	12·2 11·7
03	14 15·8	14 18·1	13 36·8	0·3 0·3	6·3 6·0	12·3 11·8
04	14 16·0	14 18·3	13 37·0	0·4 0·4	6·4 6·1	12·4 11·9
05	14 16·3	14 18·6	13 37·2	0·5 0·5	6·5 6·2	12·5 12·0
06	14 16·5	14 18·8	13 37·5	0·6 0·6	6·6 6·3	12·6 12·1
07	14 16·8	14 19·1	13 37·7	0·7 0·7	6·7 6·4	12·7 12·2
08	14 17·0	14 19·3	13 38·0	0·8 0·8	6·8 6·5	12·8 12·3
09	14 17·3	14 19·6	13 38·2	0·9 0·9	6·9 6·6	12·9 12·4
10	14 17·5	14 19·8	13 38·4	1·0 1·0	7·0 6·7	13·0 12·5
11	14 17·8	14 20·1	13 38·7	1·1 1·1	7·1 6·8	13·1 12·6
12	14 18·0	14 20·3	13 38·9	1·2 1·2	7·2 6·9	13·2 12·7
13	14 18·3	14 20·6	13 39·2	1·3 1·2	7·3 7·0	13·3 12·7
14	14 18·5	14 20·9	13 39·4	1·4 1·3	7·4 7·1	13·4 12·8
15	14 18·8	14 21·1	13 39·6	1·5 1·4	7·5 7·2	13·5 12·9
16	14 19·0	14 21·4	13 39·9	1·6 1·5	7·6 7·3	13·6 13·0
17	14 19·3	14 21·6	13 40·1	1·7 1·6	7·7 7·4	13·7 13·1
18	14 19·5	14 21·9	13 40·3	1·8 1·7	7·8 7·5	13·8 13·2
19	14 19·8	14 22·1	13 40·6	1·9 1·8	7·9 7·6	13·9 13·3
20	14 20·0	14 22·4	13 40·8	2·0 1·9	8·0 7·7	14·0 13·4
21	14 20·3	14 22·6	13 41·1	2·1 2·0	8·1 7·8	14·1 13·5
22	14 20·5	14 22·9	13 41·3	2·2 2·1	8·2 7·9	14·2 13·6
23	14 20·8	14 23·1	13 41·5	2·3 2·2	8·3 8·0	14·3 13·7
24	14 21·0	14 23·4	13 41·8	2·4 2·3	8·4 8·1	14·4 13·8
25	14 21·3	14 23·6	13 42·0	2·5 2·4	8·5 8·1	14·5 13·9
26	14 21·5	14 23·9	13 42·3	2·6 2·5	8·6 8·2	14·6 14·0
27	14 21·8	14 24·1	13 42·5	2·7 2·6	8·7 8·3	14·7 14·1
28	14 22·0	14 24·4	13 42·7	2·8 2·7	8·8 8·4	14·8 14·2
29	14 22·3	14 24·6	13 43·0	2·9 2·8	8·9 8·5	14·9 14·3
30	14 22·5	14 24·9	13 43·2	3·0 2·9	9·0 8·6	15·0 14·4
31	14 22·8	14 25·1	13 43·4	3·1 3·0	9·1 8·7	15·1 14·5
32	14 23·0	14 25·4	13 43·7	3·2 3·1	9·2 8·8	15·2 14·6
33	14 23·3	14 25·6	13 43·9	3·3 3·2	9·3 8·9	15·3 14·7
34	14 23·5	14 25·9	13 44·2	3·4 3·3	9·4 9·0	15·4 14·8
35	14 23·8	14 26·1	13 44·4	3·5 3·4	9·5 9·1	15·5 14·9
36	14 24·0	14 26·4	13 44·6	3·6 3·5	9·6 9·2	15·6 15·0
37	14 24·3	14 26·6	13 44·9	3·7 3·5	9·7 9·3	15·7 15·1
38	14 24·5	14 26·9	13 45·1	3·8 3·6	9·8 9·4	15·8 15·1
39	14 24·8	14 27·1	13 45·4	3·9 3·7	9·9 9·5	15·9 15·2
40	14 25·0	14 27·4	13 45·6	4·0 3·8	10·0 9·6	16·0 15·3
41	14 25·3	14 27·6	13 45·8	4·1 3·9	10·1 9·7	16·1 15·4
42	14 25·5	14 27·9	13 46·1	4·2 4·0	10·2 9·8	16·2 15·5
43	14 25·8	14 28·1	13 46·3	4·3 4·1	10·3 9·9	16·3 15·6
44	14 26·0	14 28·4	13 46·5	4·4 4·2	10·4 10·0	16·4 15·7
45	14 26·3	14 28·6	13 46·8	4·5 4·3	10·5 10·1	16·5 15·8
46	14 26·5	14 28·9	13 47·0	4·6 4·4	10·6 10·2	16·6 15·9
47	14 26·8	14 29·1	13 47·3	4·7 4·5	10·7 10·3	16·7 16·0
48	14 27·0	14 29·4	13 47·5	4·8 4·6	10·8 10·4	16·8 16·1
49	14 27·3	14 29·6	13 47·7	4·9 4·7	10·9 10·4	16·9 16·2
50	14 27·5	14 29·9	13 48·0	5·0 4·8	11·0 10·5	17·0 16·3
51	14 27·8	14 30·1	13 48·2	5·1 4·9	11·1 10·6	17·1 16·4
52	14 28·0	14 30·4	13 48·5	5·2 5·0	11·2 10·7	17·2 16·5
53	14 28·3	14 30·6	13 48·7	5·3 5·1	11·3 10·8	17·3 16·6
54	14 28·5	14 30·9	13 48·9	5·4 5·2	11·4 10·9	17·4 16·7
55	14 28·8	14 31·1	13 49·2	5·5 5·3	11·5 11·0	17·5 16·8
56	14 29·0	14 31·4	13 49·4	5·6 5·4	11·6 11·1	17·6 16·9
57	14 29·3	14 31·6	13 49·7	5·7 5·5	11·7 11·2	17·7 17·0
58	14 29·5	14 31·9	13 49·9	5·8 5·6	11·8 11·3	17·8 17·1
59	14 29·8	14 32·1	13 50·1	5·9 5·7	11·9 11·4	17·9 17·2
60	14 30·0	14 32·4	13 50·4	6·0 5·8	12·0 11·5	18·0 17·3

58^m	SUN PLANETS	ARIES	MOON	v or d / Corrn	v or d / Corrn	v or d / Corrn
s	° ′	° ′	° ′	′ ′	′ ′	′ ′
00	14 30·0	14 32·4	13 50·4	0·0 0·0	6·0 5·9	12·0 11·7
01	14 30·3	14 32·6	13 50·6	0·1 0·1	6·1 5·9	12·1 11·8
02	14 30·5	14 32·9	13 50·8	0·2 0·2	6·2 6·0	12·2 11·9
03	14 30·8	14 33·1	13 51·1	0·3 0·3	6·3 6·1	12·3 12·0
04	14 31·0	14 33·4	13 51·3	0·4 0·4	6·4 6·2	12·4 12·1
05	14 31·3	14 33·6	13 51·6	0·5 0·5	6·5 6·3	12·5 12·2
06	14 31·5	14 33·9	13 51·8	0·6 0·6	6·6 6·4	12·6 12·3
07	14 31·8	14 34·1	13 52·0	0·7 0·7	6·7 6·5	12·7 12·4
08	14 32·0	14 34·4	13 52·3	0·8 0·8	6·8 6·6	12·8 12·5
09	14 32·3	14 34·6	13 52·5	0·9 0·9	6·9 6·7	12·9 12·6
10	14 32·5	14 34·9	13 52·8	1·0 1·0	7·0 6·8	13·0 12·7
11	14 32·8	14 35·1	13 53·0	1·1 1·1	7·1 6·9	13·1 12·8
12	14 33·0	14 35·4	13 53·2	1·2 1·2	7·2 7·0	13·2 12·9
13	14 33·3	14 35·6	13 53·5	1·3 1·3	7·3 7·1	13·3 13·0
14	14 33·5	14 35·9	13 53·7	1·4 1·4	7·4 7·2	13·4 13·1
15	14 33·8	14 36·1	13 53·9	1·5 1·5	7·5 7·3	13·5 13·2
16	14 34·0	14 36·4	13 54·2	1·6 1·6	7·6 7·4	13·6 13·3
17	14 34·3	14 36·6	13 54·4	1·7 1·7	7·7 7·5	13·7 13·4
18	14 34·5	14 36·9	13 54·7	1·8 1·8	7·8 7·6	13·8 13·5
19	14 34·8	14 37·1	13 54·9	1·9 1·9	7·9 7·7	13·9 13·6
20	14 35·0	14 37·4	13 55·1	2·0 2·0	8·0 7·8	14·0 13·7
21	14 35·3	14 37·6	13 55·4	2·1 2·0	8·1 7·9	14·1 13·7
22	14 35·5	14 37·9	13 55·6	2·2 2·1	8·2 8·0	14·2 13·8
23	14 35·8	14 38·1	13 55·9	2·3 2·2	8·3 8·1	14·3 13·9
24	14 36·0	14 38·4	13 56·1	2·4 2·3	8·4 8·2	14·4 14·0
25	14 36·3	14 38·6	13 56·3	2·5 2·4	8·5 8·3	14·5 14·1
26	14 36·5	14 38·9	13 56·6	2·6 2·5	8·6 8·4	14·6 14·2
27	14 36·8	14 39·2	13 56·8	2·7 2·6	8·7 8·5	14·7 14·3
28	14 37·0	14 39·4	13 57·0	2·8 2·7	8·8 8·6	14·8 14·4
29	14 37·3	14 39·7	13 57·3	2·9 2·8	8·9 8·7	14·9 14·5
30	14 37·5	14 39·9	13 57·5	3·0 2·9	9·0 8·8	15·0 14·6
31	14 37·8	14 40·2	13 57·8	3·1 3·0	9·1 8·9	15·1 14·7
32	14 38·0	14 40·4	13 58·0	3·2 3·1	9·2 9·0	15·2 14·8
33	14 38·3	14 40·7	13 58·2	3·3 3·2	9·3 9·1	15·3 14·9
34	14 38·5	14 40·9	13 58·5	3·4 3·3	9·4 9·2	15·4 15·0
35	14 38·8	14 41·2	13 58·7	3·5 3·4	9·5 9·3	15·5 15·1
36	14 39·0	14 41·4	13 59·0	3·6 3·5	9·6 9·4	15·6 15·2
37	14 39·3	14 41·7	13 59·2	3·7 3·6	9·7 9·5	15·7 15·3
38	14 39·5	14 41·9	13 59·4	3·8 3·7	9·8 9·6	15·8 15·4
39	14 39·8	14 42·2	13 59·7	3·9 3·8	9·9 9·7	15·9 15·5
40	14 40·0	14 42·4	13 59·9	4·0 3·9	10·0 9·8	16·0 15·6
41	14 40·3	14 42·7	14 00·1	4·1 4·0	10·1 9·8	16·1 15·7
42	14 40·5	14 42·9	14 00·4	4·2 4·1	10·2 9·9	16·2 15·8
43	14 40·8	14 43·2	14 00·6	4·3 4·2	10·3 10·0	16·3 15·9
44	14 41·0	14 43·4	14 00·9	4·4 4·3	10·4 10·1	16·4 16·0
45	14 41·3	14 43·7	14 01·1	4·5 4·4	10·5 10·2	16·5 16·1
46	14 41·5	14 43·9	14 01·3	4·6 4·5	10·6 10·3	16·6 16·2
47	14 41·8	14 44·2	14 01·6	4·7 4·6	10·7 10·4	16·7 16·3
48	14 42·0	14 44·4	14 01·8	4·8 4·7	10·8 10·5	16·8 16·4
49	14 42·3	14 44·7	14 02·1	4·9 4·8	10·9 10·6	16·9 16·5
50	14 42·5	14 44·9	14 02·3	5·0 4·9	11·0 10·7	17·0 16·6
51	14 42·8	14 45·2	14 02·5	5·1 5·0	11·1 10·8	17·1 16·7
52	14 43·0	14 45·4	14 02·8	5·2 5·1	11·2 10·9	17·2 16·8
53	14 43·3	14 45·7	14 03·0	5·3 5·2	11·3 11·0	17·3 16·9
54	14 43·5	14 45·9	14 03·3	5·4 5·3	11·4 11·1	17·4 17·0
55	14 43·8	14 46·2	14 03·5	5·5 5·4	11·5 11·2	17·5 17·1
56	14 44·0	14 46·4	14 03·7	5·6 5·5	11·6 11·3	17·6 17·2
57	14 44·3	14 46·7	14 04·0	5·7 5·6	11·7 11·4	17·7 17·3
58	14 44·5	14 46·9	14 04·2	5·8 5·7	11·8 11·5	17·8 17·4
59	14 44·8	14 47·2	14 04·4	5·9 5·8	11·9 11·6	17·9 17·5
60	14 45·0	14 47·4	14 04·7	6·0 5·9	12·0 11·7	18·0 17·6

59^m	SUN PLANETS	ARIES	MOON	v or d / Corrn	v or d / Corrn	v or d / Corrn
s	° ′	° ′	° ′	′ ′	′ ′	′ ′
00	14 45·0	14 47·4	14 04·7	0·0 0·0	6·0 6·0	12·0 11·9
01	14 45·3	14 47·7	14 04·9	0·1 0·1	6·1 6·0	12·1 12·0
02	14 45·5	14 47·9	14 05·2	0·2 0·2	6·2 6·1	12·2 12·1
03	14 45·8	14 48·2	14 05·4	0·3 0·3	6·3 6·2	12·3 12·2
04	14 46·0	14 48·4	14 05·6	0·4 0·4	6·4 6·3	12·4 12·3
05	14 46·3	14 48·7	14 05·9	0·5 0·5	6·5 6·4	12·5 12·4
06	14 46·5	14 48·9	14 06·1	0·6 0·6	6·6 6·5	12·6 12·5
07	14 46·8	14 49·2	14 06·4	0·7 0·7	6·7 6·6	12·7 12·6
08	14 47·0	14 49·4	14 06·6	0·8 0·8	6·8 6·7	12·8 12·7
09	14 47·3	14 49·7	14 06·8	0·9 0·9	6·9 6·8	12·9 12·8
10	14 47·5	14 49·9	14 07·1	1·0 1·0	7·0 6·9	13·0 12·9
11	14 47·8	14 50·2	14 07·3	1·1 1·1	7·1 7·0	13·1 13·0
12	14 48·0	14 50·4	14 07·5	1·2 1·2	7·2 7·1	13·2 13·1
13	14 48·3	14 50·7	14 07·8	1·3 1·3	7·3 7·2	13·3 13·2
14	14 48·5	14 50·9	14 08·0	1·4 1·4	7·4 7·3	13·4 13·3
15	14 48·8	14 51·2	14 08·3	1·5 1·5	7·5 7·4	13·5 13·4
16	14 49·0	14 51·4	14 08·5	1·6 1·6	7·6 7·5	13·6 13·5
17	14 49·3	14 51·7	14 08·7	1·7 1·7	7·7 7·6	13·7 13·6
18	14 49·5	14 51·9	14 09·0	1·8 1·8	7·8 7·7	13·8 13·7
19	14 49·8	14 52·2	14 09·2	1·9 1·9	7·9 7·8	13·9 13·8
20	14 50·0	14 52·4	14 09·5	2·0 2·0	8·0 7·9	14·0 13·9
21	14 50·3	14 52·7	14 09·7	2·1 2·1	8·1 8·0	14·1 14·0
22	14 50·5	14 52·9	14 09·9	2·2 2·2	8·2 8·1	14·2 14·1
23	14 50·8	14 53·2	14 10·2	2·3 2·3	8·3 8·2	14·3 14·2
24	14 51·0	14 53·4	14 10·4	2·4 2·4	8·4 8·3	14·4 14·3
25	14 51·3	14 53·7	14 10·6	2·5 2·5	8·5 8·4	14·5 14·4
26	14 51·5	14 53·9	14 10·9	2·6 2·6	8·6 8·5	14·6 14·5
27	14 51·8	14 54·2	14 11·1	2·7 2·7	8·7 8·6	14·7 14·6
28	14 52·0	14 54·4	14 11·4	2·8 2·8	8·8 8·7	14·8 14·7
29	14 52·3	14 54·7	14 11·6	2·9 2·9	8·9 8·8	14·9 14·8
30	14 52·5	14 54·9	14 11·8	3·0 3·0	9·0 8·9	15·0 14·9
31	14 52·8	14 55·2	14 12·1	3·1 3·1	9·1 9·0	15·1 15·0
32	14 53·0	14 55·4	14 12·3	3·2 3·2	9·2 9·1	15·2 15·1
33	14 53·3	14 55·7	14 12·6	3·3 3·3	9·3 9·2	15·3 15·2
34	14 53·5	14 55·9	14 12·8	3·4 3·4	9·4 9·3	15·4 15·3
35	14 53·8	14 56·2	14 13·0	3·5 3·5	9·5 9·4	15·5 15·4
36	14 54·0	14 56·4	14 13·3	3·6 3·6	9·6 9·5	15·6 15·5
37	14 54·3	14 56·7	14 13·5	3·7 3·7	9·7 9·6	15·7 15·6
38	14 54·5	14 56·9	14 13·8	3·8 3·8	9·8 9·7	15·8 15·7
39	14 54·8	14 57·2	14 14·0	3·9 3·9	9·9 9·8	15·9 15·8
40	14 55·0	14 57·5	14 14·2	4·0 4·0	10·0 9·9	16·0 15·9
41	14 55·3	14 57·7	14 14·5	4·1 4·1	10·1 10·0	16·1 16·0
42	14 55·5	14 58·0	14 14·7	4·2 4·2	10·2 10·1	16·2 16·1
43	14 55·8	14 58·2	14 14·9	4·3 4·3	10·3 10·2	16·3 16·2
44	14 56·0	14 58·5	14 15·2	4·4 4·4	10·4 10·3	16·4 16·3
45	14 56·3	14 58·7	14 15·4	4·5 4·5	10·5 10·4	16·5 16·4
46	14 56·5	14 59·0	14 15·7	4·6 4·6	10·6 10·5	16·6 16·5
47	14 56·8	14 59·2	14 15·9	4·7 4·7	10·7 10·6	16·7 16·6
48	14 57·0	14 59·5	14 16·1	4·8 4·8	10·8 10·7	16·8 16·7
49	14 57·3	14 59·7	14 16·4	4·9 4·9	10·9 10·8	16·9 16·8
50	14 57·5	15 00·0	14 16·6	5·0 5·0	11·0 10·9	17·0 16·9
51	14 57·8	15 00·2	14 16·9	5·1 5·1	11·1 11·0	17·1 17·0
52	14 58·0	15 00·5	14 17·1	5·2 5·2	11·2 11·1	17·2 17·1
53	14 58·3	15 00·7	14 17·3	5·3 5·3	11·3 11·2	17·3 17·2
54	14 58·5	15 01·0	14 17·6	5·4 5·4	11·4 11·3	17·4 17·3
55	14 58·8	15 01·2	14 17·8	5·5 5·5	11·5 11·4	17·5 17·4
56	14 59·0	15 01·5	14 18·0	5·6 5·6	11·6 11·5	17·6 17·5
57	14 59·3	15 01·7	14 18·3	5·7 5·7	11·7 11·6	17·7 17·6
58	14 59·5	15 02·0	14 18·5	5·8 5·8	11·8 11·7	17·8 17·7
59	14 59·8	15 02·2	14 18·8	5·9 5·9	11·9 11·8	17·9 17·8
60	15 00·0	15 02·5	14 19·0	6·0 6·0	12·0 11·9	18·0 17·9

TABLES FOR INTERPOLATING SUNRISE, MOONRISE, ETC.

TABLE I—FOR LATITUDE

10° (Tab. Int.)	5°	2°	5^m	10^m	15^m	20^m	25^m	30^m	35^m	40^m	45^m	50^m	55^m	60^m	$1^h 05^m$	$1^h 10^m$	$1^h 15^m$	$1^h 20^m$
° ′	° ′	° ′	m	m	m	m	m	m	m	m	m	m	m	m	h m	h m	h m	h m
0 30	0 15	0 06	0	0	1	1	1	1	1	2	2	2	2	2	0 02	0 02	0 02	0 02
1 00	0 30	0 12	0	1	1	2	2	3	3	3	4	4	4	5	05	05	05	05
1 30	0 45	0 18	1	1	2	3	3	4	4	5	5	6	7	7	07	07	07	07
2 00	1 00	0 24	1	2	3	4	5	5	6	7	7	8	9	10	10	10	10	10
2 30	1 15	0 30	1	2	4	5	6	7	8	9	9	10	11	12	12	13	13	13
3 00	1 30	0 36	1	3	4	6	7	8	9	10	11	12	13	14	0 15	0 15	0 16	0 16
3 30	1 45	0 42	2	3	5	7	8	10	11	12	13	14	16	17	18	18	19	19
4 00	2 00	0 48	2	4	6	8	9	11	13	14	15	16	18	19	20	21	22	22
4 30	2 15	0 54	2	4	7	9	11	13	15	16	18	19	21	22	23	24	25	26
5 00	2 30	1 00	2	5	7	10	12	14	16	18	20	22	23	25	26	27	28	29
5 30	2 45	1 06	3	5	8	11	13	16	18	20	22	24	26	28	0 29	0 30	0 31	0 32
6 00	3 00	1 12	3	6	9	12	14	17	20	22	24	26	29	31	32	33	34	36
6 30	3 15	1 18	3	6	10	13	16	19	22	24	26	29	31	34	36	37	38	40
7 00	3 30	1 24	3	7	10	14	17	20	23	26	29	31	34	37	39	41	42	44
7 30	3 45	1 30	4	7	11	15	18	22	25	28	31	34	37	40	43	44	46	48
8 00	4 00	1 36	4	8	12	16	20	23	27	30	34	37	41	44	0 47	0 48	0 51	0 53
8 30	4 15	1 42	4	8	13	17	21	25	29	33	36	40	44	48	0 51	0 53	0 56	0 58
9 00	4 30	1 48	4	9	13	18	22	27	31	35	39	43	47	52	0 55	0 58	1 01	1 04
9 30	4 45	1 54	5	9	14	19	24	28	33	38	42	47	51	56	1 00	1 04	1 08	1 12
10 00	5 00	2 00	5	10	15	20	25	30	35	40	45	50	55	60	1 05	1 10	1 15	1 20

Table I is for interpolating the L.M.T. of sunrise, twilight, moonrise, etc., for latitude. It is to be entered, in the appropriate column on the left, with the difference between true latitude and the nearest tabular latitude which is *less* than the true latitude; and with the argument at the top which is the nearest value of the difference between the times for the tabular latitude and the next higher one; the correction so obtained is applied to the time for the tabular latitude; the sign of the correction can be seen by inspection. It is to be noted that the interpolation is not linear, so that when using this table it is essential to take out the tabular phenomenon for the latitude *less* than the true latitude.

TABLE II—FOR LONGITUDE

Long. East or West	10^m	20^m	30^m	40^m	50^m	60^m	1^h+ 10^m	20^m	30^m	1^h+ 40^m	50^m	60^m	$2^h 10^m$	$2^h 20^m$	$2^h 30^m$	$2^h 40^m$	$2^h 50^m$	$3^h 00^m$
°	m	m	m	m	m	m	m	m	m	m	m	m	h m	h m	h m	h m	h m	h m
0	0	0	0	0	0	0	0	0	0	0	0	0	0 00	0 00	0 00	0 00	0 00	0 00
10	0	1	1	1	1	2	2	2	2	3	3	3	04	04	04	04	05	05
20	1	1	2	2	3	3	4	4	5	6	6	7	07	08	08	09	09	10
30	1	2	2	3	4	5	6	7	7	8	9	10	11	12	12	13	14	15
40	1	2	3	4	6	7	8	9	10	11	12	13	14	16	17	18	19	20
50	1	3	4	6	7	8	10	11	12	14	15	17	0 18	0 19	0 21	0 22	0 24	0 25
60	2	3	5	7	8	10	12	13	15	17	18	20	22	23	25	27	28	30
70	2	4	6	8	10	12	14	16	17	19	21	23	25	27	29	31	33	35
80	2	4	7	9	11	13	16	18	20	22	24	27	29	31	33	36	38	40
90	2	5	7	10	12	15	17	20	22	25	27	30	32	35	37	40	42	45
100	3	6	8	11	14	17	19	22	25	28	31	33	0 36	0 39	0 42	0 44	0 47	0 50
110	3	6	9	12	15	18	21	24	27	31	34	37	40	43	46	49	0 52	0 55
120	3	7	10	13	17	20	23	27	30	33	37	40	43	47	50	53	0 57	1 00
130	4	7	11	14	18	22	25	29	32	36	40	43	47	51	54	0 58	1 01	1 05
140	4	8	12	16	19	23	27	31	35	39	43	47	51	54	0 58	1 02	1 06	1 10
150	4	8	13	17	21	25	29	33	38	42	46	50	0 54	0 58	1 03	1 07	1 11	1 15
160	4	9	13	18	22	27	31	36	40	44	49	53	0 58	1 02	1 07	1 11	1 16	1 20
170	5	9	14	19	24	28	33	38	42	47	52	57	1 01	1 06	1 11	1 16	1 20	1 25
180	5	10	15	20	25	30	35	40	45	50	55	60	1 05	1 10	1 15	1 20	1 25	1 30

Table II is for interpolating the L.M.T. of moonrise, moonset and the Moon's meridian passage for longitude. It is entered with longitude and with the difference between the times for the given date and for the preceding date (in east longitudes) or following date (in west longitudes). The correction is normally *added* for west longitudes and *subtracted* for east longitudes, but if, as occasionally happens, the times become earlier each day instead of later, the signs of the corrections must be reversed.

xxxii

U.S. GOVERNMENT PRINTING OFFICE : 1980 O—252-796

INDEX TO SELECTED STARS, 1981

Name	No.	Mag.	S.H.A.	Dec.
Acamar	7	3·1	316	S. 40
Achernar	5	0·6	336	S. 57
Acrux	30	1·1	174	S. 63
Adhara	19	1·6	256	S. 29
Aldebaran	10	1·1	291	N. 16
Alioth	32	1·7	167	N. 56
Alkaid	34	1·9	153	N. 49
Al Na'ir	55	2·2	28	S. 47
Alnilam	15	1·8	276	S. 1
Alphard	25	2·2	218	S. 9
Alphecca	41	2·3	127	N. 27
Alpheratz	1	2·2	358	N. 29
Altair	51	0·9	63	N. 9
Ankaa	2	2·4	354	S. 42
Antares	42	1·2	113	S. 26
Arcturus	37	0·2	146	N. 19
Atria	43	1·9	108	S. 69
Avior	22	1·7	234	S. 59
Bellatrix	13	1·7	279	N. 6
Betelgeuse	16	Var.*	271	N. 7
Canopus	17	-0·9	264	S. 53
Capella	12	0·2	281	N. 46
Deneb	53	1·3	50	N. 45
Denebola	28	2·2	183	N. 15
Diphda	4	2·2	349	S. 18
Dubhe	27	2·0	194	N. 62
Elnath	14	1·8	279	N. 29
Eltanin	47	2·4	91	N. 51
Enif	54	2·5	34	N. 10
Fomalhaut	56	1·3	16	S. 30
Gacrux	31	1·6	172	S. 57
Gienah	29	2·8	176	S. 17
Hadar	35	0·9	149	S. 60
Hamal	6	2·2	328	N. 23
Kaus Australis	48	2·0	84	S. 34
Kochab	40	2·2	137	N. 74
Markab	57	2·6	14	N. 15
Menkar	8	2·8	315	N. 4
Menkent	36	2·3	149	S. 36
Miaplacidus	24	1·8	222	S. 70
Mirfak	9	1·9	309	N. 50
Nunki	50	2·1	76	S. 26
Peacock	52	2·1	54	S. 57
Pollux	21	1·2	244	N. 28
Procyon	20	0·5	245	N. 5
Rasalhague	46	2·1	96	N. 13
Regulus	26	1·3	208	N. 12
Rigel	11	0·3	282	S. 8
Rigil Kentaurus	38	0·1	140	S. 61
Sabik	44	2·6	103	S. 16
Schedar	3	2·5	350	N. 56
Shaula	45	1·7	97	S. 37
Sirius	18	-1·6	259	S. 17
Spica	33	1·2	159	S. 11
Suhail	23	2·2	223	S. 43
Vega	49	0·1	81	N. 39
Zubenelgenubi	39	2·9	138	S. 16

No.	Name	Mag.	S.H.A.	Dec.
1	Alpheratz	2·2	358	N. 29
2	Ankaa	2·4	354	S. 42
3	Schedar	2·5	350	N. 56
4	Diphda	2·2	349	S. 18
5	Achernar	0·6	336	S. 57
6	Hamal	2·2	328	N. 23
7	Acamar	3·1	316	S. 40
8	Menkar	2·8	315	N. 4
9	Mirfak	1·9	309	N. 50
10	Aldebaran	1·1	291	N. 16
11	Rigel	0·3	282	S. 8
12	Capella	0·2	281	N. 46
13	Bellatrix	1·7	279	N. 6
14	Elnath	1·8	279	N. 29
15	Alnilam	1·8	276	S. 1
16	Betelgeuse	Var.*	271	N. 7
17	Canopus	-0·9	264	S. 53
18	Sirius	-1·6	259	S. 17
19	Adhara	1·6	256	S. 29
20	Procyon	0·5	245	N. 5
21	Pollux	1·2	244	N. 28
22	Avior	1·7	234	S. 59
23	Suhail	2·2	223	S. 43
24	Miaplacidus	1·8	222	S. 70
25	Alphard	2·2	218	S. 9
26	Regulus	1·3	208	N. 12
27	Dubhe	2·0	194	N. 62
28	Denebola	2·2	183	N. 15
29	Gienah	2·8	176	S. 17
30	Acrux	1·1	174	S. 63
31	Gacrux	1·6	172	S. 57
32	Alioth	1·7	167	N. 56
33	Spica	1·2	159	S. 11
34	Alkaid	1·9	153	N. 49
35	Hadar	0·9	149	S. 60
36	Menkent	2·3	149	S. 36
37	Arcturus	0·2	146	N. 19
38	Rigil Kentaurus	0·1	140	S. 61
39	Zubenelgenubi	2·9	138	S. 16
40	Kochab	2·2	137	N. 74
41	Alphecca	2·3	127	N. 27
42	Antares	1·2	113	S. 26
43	Atria	1·9	108	S. 69
44	Sabik	2·6	103	S. 16
45	Shaula	1·7	97	S. 37
46	Rasalhague	2·1	96	N. 13
47	Eltanin	2·4	91	N. 51
48	Kaus Australis	2·0	84	S. 34
49	Vega	0·1	81	N. 39
50	Nunki	2·1	76	S. 26
51	Altair	0·9	63	N. 9
52	Peacock	2·1	54	S. 57
53	Deneb	1·3	50	N. 45
54	Enif	2·5	34	N. 10
55	Al Na'ir	2·2	28	S. 47
56	Fomalhaut	1·3	16	S. 30
57	Markab	2·6	14	N. 15

* 0·1—1·2

ALTITUDE CORRECTION TABLES 0°–35°—MOON

App. Alt.	0°–4° Corrⁿ	5°–9° Corrⁿ	10°–14° Corrⁿ	15°–19° Corrⁿ	20°–24° Corrⁿ	25°–29° Corrⁿ	30°–34° Corrⁿ	App. Alt.
00	0° 33.8	5 58.2	10 62.1	15 62.8	20 62.2	25 60.8	30 58.9	00
10	35.9	58.5	62.2	62.8	62.1	60.8	58.8	10
20	37.8	58.7	62.2	62.8	62.1	60.7	58.8	20
30	39.6	58.9	62.3	62.8	62.1	60.7	58.7	30
40	41.2	59.1	62.3	62.8	62.0	60.6	58.6	40
50	42.6	59.3	62.4	62.7	62.0	60.6	58.5	50
00	1 44.0	6 59.5	11 62.4	16 62.7	21 62.0	26 60.5	31 58.5	00
10	45.2	59.7	62.4	62.7	61.9	60.4	58.4	10
20	46.3	59.9	62.5	62.7	61.9	60.4	58.3	20
30	47.3	60.0	62.5	62.7	61.9	60.3	58.2	30
40	48.3	60.2	62.5	62.7	61.8	60.3	58.2	40
50	49.2	60.3	62.6	62.7	61.8	60.2	58.1	50
00	2 50.0	7 60.5	12 62.6	17 62.7	22 61.7	27 60.1	32 58.0	00
10	50.8	60.6	62.6	62.6	61.7	60.1	57.9	10
20	51.4	60.7	62.6	62.6	61.6	60.0	57.8	20
30	52.1	60.9	62.7	62.6	61.6	59.9	57.8	30
40	52.7	61.0	62.7	62.6	61.5	59.9	57.7	40
50	53.3	61.1	62.7	62.6	61.5	59.8	57.6	50
00	3 53.8	8 61.2	13 62.7	18 62.5	23 61.5	28 59.7	33 57.5	00
10	54.3	61.3	62.7	62.5	61.4	59.7	57.4	10
20	54.8	61.4	62.7	62.5	61.4	59.6	57.4	20
30	55.2	61.5	62.8	62.5	61.3	59.6	57.3	30
40	55.6	61.6	62.8	62.4	61.3	59.5	57.2	40
50	56.0	61.6	62.8	62.4	61.2	59.4	57.1	50
00	4 56.4	9 61.7	14 62.8	19 62.4	24 61.2	29 59.3	34 57.0	00
10	56.7	61.8	62.8	62.3	61.1	59.3	56.9	10
20	57.1	61.9	62.8	62.3	61.1	59.2	56.9	20
30	57.4	61.9	62.8	62.3	61.0	59.1	56.8	30
40	57.7	62.0	62.8	62.2	60.9	59.1	56.7	40
50	57.9	62.1	62.8	62.2	60.9	59.0	56.6	50

H.P.	L	U	L	U	L	U	L	U	L	U	L	U	L	U	H.P.
54.0	0.3	0.9	0.3	0.9	0.4	1.0	0.5	1.1	0.6	1.2	0.7	1.3	0.9	1.5	54.0
54.3	0.7	1.1	0.7	1.2	0.7	1.2	0.8	1.3	0.9	1.4	1.1	1.5	1.2	1.7	54.3
54.6	1.1	1.4	1.1	1.4	1.1	1.4	1.2	1.5	1.3	1.6	1.4	1.7	1.5	1.8	54.6
54.9	1.4	1.6	1.5	1.6	1.5	1.6	1.6	1.7	1.6	1.8	1.8	1.9	1.9	2.0	54.9
55.2	1.8	1.8	1.8	1.8	1.9	1.9	1.9	1.9	2.0	2.0	2.1	2.1	2.2	2.2	55.2
55.5	2.2	2.0	2.2	2.0	2.3	2.1	2.3	2.1	2.4	2.2	2.4	2.3	2.5	2.4	55.5
55.8	2.6	2.2	2.6	2.2	2.6	2.3	2.7	2.3	2.7	2.4	2.8	2.4	2.9	2.5	55.8
56.1	3.0	2.4	3.0	2.5	3.0	2.5	3.0	2.5	3.1	2.6	3.1	2.6	3.2	2.7	56.1
56.4	3.4	2.7	3.4	2.7	3.4	2.7	3.4	2.7	3.4	2.8	3.5	2.8	3.5	2.9	56.4
56.7	3.7	2.9	3.7	2.9	3.8	2.9	3.8	2.9	3.8	3.0	3.8	3.0	3.9	3.0	56.7
57.0	4.1	3.1	4.1	3.1	4.1	3.1	4.1	3.1	4.2	3.1	4.2	3.2	4.2	3.2	57.0
57.3	4.5	3.3	4.5	3.3	4.5	3.3	4.5	3.3	4.5	3.3	4.5	3.4	4.6	3.4	57.3
57.6	4.9	3.5	4.9	3.5	4.9	3.5	4.9	3.5	4.9	3.5	4.9	3.5	4.9	3.6	57.6
57.9	5.3	3.8	5.3	3.8	5.2	3.8	5.2	3.7	5.2	3.7	5.2	3.7	5.2	3.7	57.9
58.2	5.6	4.0	5.6	4.0	5.6	4.0	5.6	4.0	5.6	3.9	5.6	3.9	5.6	3.9	58.2
58.5	6.0	4.2	6.0	4.2	6.0	4.2	6.0	4.2	6.0	4.1	5.9	4.1	5.9	4.1	58.5
58.8	6.4	4.4	6.4	4.4	6.4	4.4	6.3	4.4	6.3	4.3	6.3	4.3	6.2	4.2	58.8
59.1	6.8	4.6	6.8	4.6	6.7	4.6	6.7	4.6	6.7	4.5	6.6	4.5	6.6	4.4	59.1
59.4	7.2	4.8	7.1	4.8	7.1	4.8	7.1	4.8	7.0	4.7	7.0	4.7	6.9	4.6	59.4
59.7	7.5	5.1	7.5	5.0	7.5	5.0	7.5	5.0	7.4	4.9	7.3	4.8	7.2	4.7	59.7
60.0	7.9	5.3	7.9	5.3	7.9	5.2	7.8	5.2	7.8	5.1	7.7	5.0	7.6	4.9	60.0
60.3	8.3	5.5	8.3	5.5	8.2	5.4	8.2	5.4	8.1	5.3	8.0	5.2	7.9	5.1	60.3
60.6	8.7	5.7	8.7	5.7	8.6	5.7	8.6	5.6	8.5	5.5	8.4	5.4	8.2	5.3	60.6
60.9	9.1	5.9	9.0	5.9	9.0	5.9	8.9	5.8	8.8	5.7	8.7	5.6	8.6	5.4	60.9
61.2	9.5	6.2	9.4	6.1	9.4	6.1	9.3	6.0	9.2	5.9	9.1	5.8	8.9	5.6	61.2
61.5	9.8	6.4	9.8	6.3	9.7	6.3	9.7	6.2	9.5	6.1	9.4	5.9	9.2	5.8	61.5

DIP

Ht. of Eye	Corrⁿ	Ht. of Eye	Ht. of Eye	Corrⁿ	Ht. of Eye
m		ft.	m		ft.
2.4	−2.8	8.0	9.5	−5.5	31.5
2.6	−2.9	8.6	9.9	−5.6	32.7
2.8	−3.0	9.2	10.3	−5.7	33.9
3.0	−3.1	9.8	10.6	−5.8	35.1
3.2	−3.2	10.5	11.0	−5.9	36.3
3.4	−3.3	11.2	11.4	−6.0	37.6
3.6	−3.4	11.9	11.8	−6.1	38.9
3.8	−3.5	12.6	12.2	−6.2	40.1
4.0	−3.6	13.3	12.6	−6.3	41.5
4.3	−3.7	14.1	13.0	−6.4	42.8
4.5	−3.8	14.9	13.4	−6.5	44.2
4.7	−3.9	15.7	13.8	−6.6	45.5
5.0	−4.0	16.5	14.2	−6.7	46.9
5.2	−4.1	17.4	14.7	−6.8	48.4
5.5	−4.2	18.3	15.1	−6.9	49.8
5.8	−4.3	19.1	15.5	−7.0	51.3
6.1	−4.4	20.1	16.0	−7.1	52.8
6.3	−4.5	21.0	16.5	−7.2	54.3
6.6	−4.6	22.0	16.9	−7.3	55.8
6.9	−4.7	22.9	17.4	−7.4	57.4
7.2	−4.8	23.9	17.9	−7.5	58.9
7.5	−4.9	24.9	18.4	−7.6	60.5
7.9	−5.0	26.0	18.8	−7.7	62.1
8.2	−5.1	27.1	19.3	−7.8	63.8
8.5	−5.2	28.1	19.8	−7.9	65.4
8.8	−5.3	29.2	20.4	−8.0	67.1
9.2	−5.4	30.4	20.9	−8.1	68.8
9.5		31.5	21.4		70.5

MOON CORRECTION TABLE

The correction is in two parts; the first correction is taken from the upper part of the table with argument apparent altitude, and the second from the lower part, with argument H.P., in the same column as that from which the first correction was taken. Separate corrections are given in the lower part for lower (L) and upper (U) limbs. All corrections are to be **added** to apparent altitude, *but 30' is to be subtracted from the altitude of the upper limb.*

For corrections for pressure and temperature see page A4.

For bubble sextant observations ignore dip, take the mean of upper and lower limb corrections and subtract 15' from the altitude.

App. Alt. = Apparent altitude = Sextant altitude corrected for index error and dip.

ALTITUDE CORRECTION TABLES 35°–90°—MOON

App. Alt.	35°–39°	40°–44°	45°–49°	50°–54°	55°–59°	60°–64°	65°–69°	70°–74°	75°–79°	80°–84°	85°–89°	App. Alt.
	Corr^{n}	Corr^{n}	Corr^{n}	Corr^{n}	Corr^{n}	Corr^{n}	Corr^{n}	Corr^{n}	Corr^{n}	Corr^{n}	Corr^{n}	
00	35 56.5	40 53.7	45 50.5	50 46.9	55 43.1	60 38.9	65 34.6	70 30.1	75 25.3	80 20.5	85 15.6	00
10	56.4	53.6	50.4	46.8	42.9	38.8	34.4	29.9	25.2	20.4	15.5	10
20	56.3	53.5	50.2	46.7	42.8	38.7	34.3	29.7	25.0	20.2	15.3	20
30	56.2	53.4	50.1	46.5	42.7	38.5	34.1	29.6	24.7	20.0	15.1	30
40	56.2	53.3	50.0	46.4	42.5	38.4	34.0	29.4	24.7	19.9	15.0	40
50	56.1	53.2	49.9	46.3	42.4	38.2	33.8	29.3	24.5	19.7	14.8	50
00	36 56.0	41 53.1	46 49.8	51 46.2	56 42.3	61 38.1	66 33.7	71 29.1	76 24.4	81 19.6	86 14.6	00
10	55.9	53.0	49.7	46.0	42.1	37.9	33.5	29.0	24.2	19.4	14.5	10
20	55.8	52.8	49.5	45.9	42.0	37.8	33.4	28.8	24.1	19.2	14.3	20
30	55.7	52.7	49.4	45.8	41.8	37.7	33.2	28.7	23.9	19.1	14.1	30
40	55.6	52.6	49.3	45.7	41.7	37.5	33.1	28.5	23.8	18.9	14.0	40
50	55.5	52.5	49.2	45.5	41.6	37.4	32.9	28.3	23.6	18.7	13.8	50
00	37 55.4	42 52.4	47 49.1	52 45.4	57 41.4	62 37.2	67 32.8	72 28.2	77 23.4	82 18.6	87 13.7	00
10	55.3	52.3	49.0	45.3	41.3	37.1	32.6	28.0	23.3	18.4	13.5	10
20	55.2	52.2	48.8	45.2	41.2	36.9	32.5	27.9	23.1	18.2	13.3	20
30	55.1	52.1	48.7	45.0	41.0	36.8	32.3	27.7	22.9	18.1	13.2	30
40	55.0	52.0	48.6	44.9	40.9	36.6	32.2	27.6	22.8	17.9	13.0	40
50	55.0	51.9	48.5	44.8	40.8	36.5	32.0	27.4	22.6	17.8	12.8	50
00	38 54.9	43 51.8	48 48.4	53 44.6	58 40.6	63 36.4	68 31.9	73 27.2	78 22.5	83 17.6	88 12.7	00
10	54.8	51.7	48.2	44.5	40.5	36.2	31.7	27.1	22.3	17.4	12.5	10
20	54.7	51.6	48.1	44.4	40.3	36.1	31.6	26.9	22.1	17.3	12.3	20
30	54.6	51.5	48.0	44.2	40.2	35.9	31.4	26.8	22.0	17.1	12.2	30
40	54.5	51.4	47.9	44.1	40.1	35.8	31.3	26.6	21.8	16.9	12.0	40
50	54.4	51.2	47.8	44.0	39.9	35.6	31.1	26.5	21.7	16.8	11.8	50
00	39 54.3	44 51.1	49 47.6	54 43.9	59 39.8	64 35.5	69 31.0	74 26.3	79 21.5	84 16.6	89 11.7	00
10	54.2	51.0	47.5	43.7	39.6	35.3	30.8	26.1	21.3	16.5	11.5	10
20	54.1	50.9	47.4	43.6	39.5	35.2	30.7	26.0	21.2	16.3	11.4	20
30	54.0	50.8	47.3	43.5	39.4	35.0	30.5	25.8	21.0	16.1	11.2	30
40	53.9	50.7	47.2	43.3	39.2	34.9	30.4	25.7	20.9	16.0	11.0	40
50	53.8	50.6	47.0	43.2	39.1	34.7	30.2	25.5	20.7	15.8	10.9	50

H.P.	35°–39°	40°–44°	45°–49°	50°–54°	55°–59°	60°–64°	65°–69°	70°–74°	75°–79°	80°–84°	85°–89°	H.P.
	L U	L U	L U	L U	L U	L U	L U	L U	L U	L U	L U	
54.0	1.1 1.7	1.3 1.9	1.5 2.1	1.7 2.4	2.0 2.6	2.3 2.9	2.6 3.2	2.9 3.5	3.2 3.8	3.5 4.1	3.8 4.5	54.0
54.3	1.4 1.8	1.6 2.0	1.8 2.2	2.0 2.5	2.3 2.7	2.5 3.0	2.8 3.2	3.0 3.5	3.3 3.8	3.6 4.1	3.9 4.4	54.3
54.6	1.7 2.0	1.9 2.2	2.1 2.4	2.3 2.6	2.5 2.8	2.7 3.0	3.0 3.3	3.2 3.5	3.5 3.8	3.7 4.1	4.0 4.3	54.6
54.9	2.0 2.2	2.2 2.3	2.3 2.5	2.5 2.7	2.7 2.9	2.9 3.1	3.2 3.3	3.4 3.5	3.6 3.8	3.9 4.0	4.1 4.3	54.9
55.2	2.3 2.3	2.5 2.4	2.6 2.6	2.8 2.8	3.0 2.9	3.2 3.1	3.4 3.3	3.6 3.5	3.8 3.7	4.0 4.0	4.2 4.2	55.2
55.5	2.7 2.5	2.8 2.6	2.9 2.7	3.1 2.9	3.2 3.0	3.4 3.2	3.6 3.4	3.7 3.5	3.9 3.7	4.1 3.9	4.3 4.1	55.5
55.8	3.0 2.6	3.1 2.7	3.2 2.8	3.3 3.0	3.5 3.1	3.6 3.3	3.8 3.4	3.9 3.6	4.1 3.7	4.2 3.9	4.4 4.0	55.8
56.1	3.3 2.8	3.4 2.9	3.5 3.0	3.6 3.1	3.7 3.2	3.8 3.3	4.0 3.4	4.1 3.6	4.2 3.7	4.4 3.8	4.5 4.0	56.1
56.4	3.6 2.9	3.7 3.0	3.8 3.1	3.9 3.2	3.9 3.3	4.0 3.4	4.1 3.5	4.3 3.6	4.4 3.7	4.5 3.8	4.6 3.9	56.4
56.7	3.9 3.1	4.0 3.1	4.1 3.2	4.1 3.3	4.2 3.3	4.3 3.4	4.3 3.5	4.4 3.6	4.5 3.7	4.6 3.8	4.7 3.8	56.7
57.0	4.3 3.2	4.3 3.3	4.3 3.3	4.4 3.4	4.4 3.4	4.5 3.5	4.5 3.5	4.6 3.6	4.7 3.6	4.7 3.7	4.8 3.8	57.0
57.3	4.6 3.4	4.6 3.4	4.6 3.4	4.6 3.5	4.7 3.5	4.7 3.5	4.7 3.6	4.8 3.6	4.8 3.6	4.8 3.7	4.9 3.7	57.3
57.6	4.9 3.6	4.9 3.6	4.9 3.6	4.9 3.6	4.9 3.6	4.9 3.6	4.9 3.6	4.9 3.6	5.0 3.6	5.0 3.6	5.0 3.6	57.6
57.9	5.2 3.7	5.2 3.7	5.2 3.7	5.2 3.7	5.2 3.7	5.1 3.6	5.1 3.6	5.1 3.6	5.1 3.6	5.1 3.6	5.1 3.6	57.9
58.2	5.5 3.9	5.5 3.8	5.5 3.8	5.4 3.8	5.4 3.7	5.4 3.7	5.3 3.7	5.3 3.6	5.2 3.6	5.2 3.5	5.2 3.5	58.2
58.5	5.9 4.0	5.8 4.0	5.8 3.9	5.7 3.9	5.6 3.8	5.6 3.8	5.5 3.7	5.5 3.6	5.4 3.6	5.3 3.5	5.3 3.4	58.5
58.8	6.2 4.2	6.1 4.1	6.0 4.1	6.0 4.0	5.9 3.9	5.8 3.8	5.7 3.7	5.6 3.6	5.5 3.5	5.4 3.5	5.3 3.4	58.8
59.1	6.5 4.3	6.4 4.3	6.3 4.2	6.2 4.1	6.1 4.0	6.0 3.9	5.9 3.8	5.8 3.6	5.7 3.5	5.6 3.4	5.4 3.3	59.1
59.4	6.8 4.5	6.7 4.4	6.6 4.3	6.5 4.2	6.4 4.1	6.2 3.9	6.1 3.8	6.0 3.7	5.8 3.5	5.7 3.4	5.5 3.2	59.4
59.7	7.1 4.6	7.0 4.5	6.9 4.4	6.8 4.3	6.6 4.1	6.5 4.0	6.3 3.8	6.2 3.7	6.0 3.5	5.8 3.3	5.6 3.2	59.7
60.0	7.5 4.8	7.3 4.7	7.2 4.5	7.0 4.4	6.9 4.2	6.7 4.0	6.5 3.9	6.3 3.7	6.1 3.5	5.9 3.3	5.7 3.1	60.0
60.3	7.8 5.0	7.6 4.8	7.5 4.7	7.3 4.5	7.1 4.3	6.9 4.1	6.7 3.9	6.5 3.7	6.3 3.5	6.0 3.2	5.8 3.0	60.3
60.6	8.1 5.1	7.9 5.0	7.7 4.8	7.6 4.6	7.3 4.4	7.1 4.2	6.9 3.9	6.7 3.7	6.4 3.4	6.2 3.2	5.9 2.9	60.6
60.9	8.4 5.3	8.2 5.1	8.0 4.9	7.8 4.7	7.6 4.5	7.3 4.2	7.1 4.0	6.8 3.7	6.6 3.4	6.3 3.2	6.0 2.9	60.9
61.2	8.7 5.4	8.5 5.2	8.3 5.0	8.1 4.8	7.8 4.5	7.6 4.3	7.3 4.0	7.0 3.7	6.7 3.4	6.4 3.1	6.1 2.8	61.2
61.5	9.1 5.6	8.8 5.4	8.6 5.1	8.3 4.9	8.1 4.6	7.8 4.3	7.5 4.0	7.2 3.7	6.9 3.4	6.5 3.1	6.2 2.7	61.5